TWENTIETH-CENTURY ROMANCE AND HISTORICAL WRITERS

Twentieth-Century Writers Series

Twentieth-Century Children's Writers

Twentieth-Century Crime and Mystery Writers

Twentieth-Century Science-Fiction Writers

Twentieth-Century Romance and Historical Writers

Twentieth-Century Western Writers

Twentieth-Century Young Adult Writers

Forthcoming genre titles

St James Guide to Fantasy Writers

St James Guide to Horror, Ghost, and Gothic Writers

TWENTIETH-CENTURY ROMANCE AND HISTORICAL WRITERS

THIRD EDITION

PREFACE TO THE FIRST AND SECOND EDITIONS BY
KAY MUSSELL

PREFACE TO THE THIRD EDITION BY
ALISON LIGHT

EDITOR
ARUNA VASUDEVAN

CONSULTING EDITOR
LESLEY HENDERSON

St J

St James Press

London   Detroit   Washington DC

While every effort has been made to ensure the reliability of the information presented in this publication, St James Press does not guarantee the accuracy of the data contained herein. St James Press accepts no payment for listing; and inclusion in the publication of any organization, agency, institution, publication, service, or individual does not imply endorsement of the editors or publishere. Errors brought to the attention of the publisher and verified to the satisfaction of the publisher will be corrected in future editions.

Copyright © 1994 by Gale Research International Ltd.

All rights reserved including the right of reproduction in whole or in part in any form. For information, write:

Gale Research International Ltd.
PO Box 699
Cheriton House
North Way
Andover
Hants SP10 5YE
United Kingdom

or

Gale Research Inc.
835 Penobscot Bldg.
Detroit, MI 48226–4094
USA

ST JAMES PRESS is an imprint of Gale Research International Ltd.
An Affiliated Company of Gale Research Inc.

A CIP catalogue record for this book is available from the British Library.

ISBN 1–55862–180–6

First edition published 1982; second edition 1990

Typeset by Tradespools Ltd, Frome, England
Printed in the United States

Published simultaneously in the United Kingdom and the United States of America

The paper used in this publication meets the minimum requirements of American National Standard for Information Sciences — Permanence Paper for printed Library Materials, ANSI Z 39.48–1984.

The trade mark ITP is used under license

CONTENTS

PREFACE
revised from the second edition

The roots of both romance and historical fiction lie in the origins of the novel form itself. In the 18th and early-19th centuries the most prominent types of fiction—the seduction story and the gothic tale of terror—were the novelistic predecessors of today's romance and historical fiction; and for two centuries, writers on both sides of the Atlantic have written stories of romantic adventure, frequently set in the past, that appealed to a largely middle-class female audience.

In their popular manifestations—romance and historical fiction aimed at a mass audience—there is considerable overlap between the two genres. Many novels categorized as romances are set in the past and rely on the conventions of historical fiction. Many novels categorized as historical also employ romance conventions. The works of authors profiled in this volume might best be seen as forming a continuum of novels from straight romances (such as those published by Mills and Boon and Harlequin, with contemporary settings and a clear focus on a single romantic relationship) through historical novels (such as those by Mary Renault, Naomi Mitchison, or Gore Vidal, in which romance is less significant than the fictional reconstruction of historical events). In between lie many varieties of fiction that blend romance and historical elements. Historical fiction as a category is far more diverse than romance.

In the 18th and early-19th centuries many of the most important early novels were either romantic or gothic. The seduction story (Samuel Richardson's *Pamela* or *Clarissa Harlowe*, Susanna Rowson's *Charlotte Temple*) shared the qualities of today's straight romance, a tale that focused almost exclusively on the potential consequences, rewards, and risks of being a woman in love. The gothic novel (Ann Radcliffe's *The Castle of Otranto*) frequently included a romance but derived much of its appeal from exploitation of its setting in the mediaeval past, much as today's historical novels interpret the past for contemporary readers. As the novel matured as a genre and form, the sensational romance and gothic subject matter became the province of popular writers who continued to write such tales. Critics of early fiction often noted the high percentage of female readers for gothic and romance, in a period when most 'serious' novelists were men who usually assumed they were addressing themselves to an audience that was not sex-specific. Two early exceptions to male dominance of the writing and criticism of serious fiction (Jane Austen and Charlotte Brontë) both wrote novels that derived from romance conventions, and Brontë used gothic conventions as well. Popular romances, however, continued to flourish even in eclipse. Although these novels received little critical attention, publishers and readers kept them alive. The books were written, published, read, and enjoyed whether or not the literary establishment took notice of them and despite the disrepute into which they had fallen.

In the 20th century gothic and romance novels have had a steady popularity, although only a handful of authors before 1960 enjoyed significant public attention, usually through the repeated production of bestsellers or by writing a single blockbuster novel. Mary Roberts Rinehart, for example, who wrote both romantic mysteries and straight romances, was so prolific and so successful that she achieved considerable public prominence over a long period of time. Alternatively, the historical novelists Margaret Mitchell and Ross Lockridge, each the author of one exceptionally popular blockbuster novel, influenced scores of lesser writers who never earned an audience as large and devoted as theirs.

For the most part, however, writers of romance and historical novels have worked in relative obscurity. While gothics and romances have been categorized by critics and scholars as 'mere' love stories or as unrealistic emotional adventures unworthy of serious consideration, historical novels may be labeled 'sensation fiction' or 'potboilers'. Nevertheless, in the early 1980s two of the five best-selling authors in the world were Janet Dailey—an American author of straight romances—and Barbara Cartland—author of several hundred romantic adventure novels, many with settings in Regency England. More recently, writers such as Danielle Steel—whose books are contemporary romances with sensational overtones—and some authors who began as series romance writers—such as Janet Dailey, Nora Roberts, Sandra Brown, LaVyrle Spencer, and Jayne Ann Krentz—have written mainstream romances that have attracted a wide audience. In addition, many romance and historical novels that would previously have appeared only in paperback are now being published first in hardcover editions.

Romance and historical novels are closely related forms of fiction, although within the range of plot conventions there is significant variation in both form and quality. Like other narrative formulas, these books share a common set of interests and take place in predictable fictional worlds. Detective and mystery novels, for example, share a fascination with the mythology of crime. Horror novels and science fiction are always interested in the 'what-if', the speculation about alien conditions that might impinge upon the rational world. Westerns are concerned with the grand adventure of settling new territory and building a civilization in the wilderness. Spy stories involve the clash of nations and the dirty business of espionage. Romances, female gothics, and some historical novels take place in a world in which love and domesticity are central to the protagonist's value system and in which conventional conflicts are often centred around the family, however adventurous a novel's plot may be. Suspense may derive from the exciting historical adventure of living in an age of turmoil; it may come from the titillation of the outrageous and horrifying; or it may result from the exquisite conflict between potential lovers. But whatever the ingredients of the individual plot or formula, all romantic novels share a concern with the details of women's personal lives, of mate selection and family formation, of problems between lovers, and of the impact of events—both public and private—upon domestic affairs. Writers of gothics and romances delineate the effect of extreme situations upon women and men in the realm of their conventional domestic concerns; and these novels often—although not always—portray a woman at the centre of the action.

The impact of public and private events upon individuals is also a central concern of historical fiction. Historical novels are unified as a category by only one convention: the novels must be set in a period in the past that is demonstrably different in time from that of the reader. Thus Tolstoy's *War and Peace* is as much an historical novel as Georgette Heyer's *The Grand Sophy* or Belva Plain's *Evergreen*. In an historical novel, history is made accessible to modern readers through dramatizing the impact of public events on individuals, although the historical interpretation need not be 'accurate' as historians would judge it. Some historical novels take a position on a historical controversy involving people who actually lived (William Styron's *The Confessions of Nat Turner* or Thomas Keneally's *The Playmaker*). Others are 'fictional biographies' of real people (Robert Graves's *I, Claudius*, Gore Vidal's *Burr*, Irving Stone's *Lust for Life* and *The Agony and the Ecstasy*, Anya Seton's *Katherine*). Still others portray fictional characters involved in real historical events (Margaret Mitchell's *Gone with the Wind*, Baroness Orczy's *The Scarlet Pimpernel*, Kathleen Winsor's *Forever Amber*). All historical novels, however, derive at least a measure of their appeal for an audience through purporting to explain or show what life was like in an era far distant from the reader's own.

In general, historical novels are more overtly adventurous than romance novels; but romance authors portray the adventure that can be found within the framework of love relationships. The novels of the softcover romance series focus upon the private, intimate relationships between lovers, charting the course of the couple's developing feelings until they make a lifetime commitment to each other. These romances are usually relatively short and resemble each other to a remarkable degree. Even in series novels, however, there is variation in quality and inventiveness. In the more adventurous gothic romances and some historical romances, characters are threatened less by their personal difficulties than by forces from the world outside. In gothics, potential lovers are kept apart by the machinations of the villain; in historical romances, by the momentous events in the larger world.

Series romances aim at an audience that is almost totally female, and the adventure of such novels rarely transcends the conflicts of the love story; on the other hand, historical romances and family saga romances paint a picture on a wider canvas, with the family rather than an individual woman at the centre. The very essence of romance and gothic, however, remains personal and interior, concerned with motivation and action that brings a story to a kind of domestic stasis. The lovers may be separated or united, the family may be intact or disrupted, but the stories are always told against a domestic value system in which characters are rewarded or punished according to conventional moral norms.

Romance and historical fiction, then, intersect; categorizing some novels as one or the other may depend less on specific characteristics than on the marketing strategy of the publisher. Historical novels, however, are frequently taken more seriously by critics than are romances; they are, for example, reviewed far more often. Compared with many romances, historical novels may seem more substantial; they are usually longer, and they may appeal to a wider audience made up of men as well as women. Both readers and critics consider authors such as Mary Renault, Ford Madox Ford, John Steinbeck, Robert Graves, and John Fowles, to be mainstream writers who employ historical settings in writing serious fiction. The reputation of historical fiction also benefits from the apparent assumption that history as a subject is more significant than are stories about love.

Romance and historical formulas have both changed and merged in the past half-century. In the early 1960s the most popular type of fiction in the gothic/romance genre was the novel of romantic suspense, called conveniently by publishers 'gothic romance'. Most had 19th- or early 20th-century settings. British writers were most prominent, but their American colleagues were also active. The modern popularity of the gothic romance can probably be most accurately dated from the publication in 1960 of *Mistress of Mellyn* by Eleanor Burford Hibbert (writing as Victoria Holt). The novel showed its derivation from the Brontës and Daphne du Maurier on almost every page; but it captured the imaginations of readers and writers alike and sparked an upsurge in novels of domestic adventure with sprightly heroines who solved mysteries, protected families and children (not necessarily their own), and won the love of the hero by the final page. For most of that decade, the output of gothic romances remained high, led by Holt, Dorothy Eden, Mary Stewart, and Phyllis A. Whitney, who were imitated by a host of other writers. As the popularity of the gothic romance grew, other romance formulas also achieved wider distribution. Historical romances became more prevalent as publishers searched for new authors while also reprinting older works by such writers as Georgette Heyer and Barbara Cartland. In the latter part of the decade and throughout the 1970s Regency romances, inspired by Heyer, achieved great success.

Although the gothic and historical romance formulas were the best known, other related types of women's fiction continued to sell. Various series of romantic love stories with contemporary settings were popular in Britain, although their distribution in the United States was only a fraction of its current volume. The United States was more an audience for romances than a major producer until the first of the erotic romances (known as 'bodice-rippers') with historical settings by American authors, such as Kathleen E. Woodiwiss and Rosemary Rogers in the mid-1970s. The new American romance formula of the 1970s differed from its predecessors in several significant ways. The books were much more sexually explicit, featuring heroines whose sexual encounters (in or out of marriage) were described more graphically than in other romances. Before this change, premarital sex had always been a sign that a character was a 'fallen woman', similar to the heroine of Kathleen Winsor's *Forever Amber*, and therefore unworthy of a lasting marriage. The new romances also featured heroines who were more independent and assertive than the women in more traditional romances. Relationships between heroes and heroines, while still deriving from traditional cultural expectations about men and women, also became more egalitarian. At first, these changes were seen primarily in romances with historical settings; but by the middle of the decade, the emerging conventions of the erotic romance began to appear in romances with contemporary settings. When the publishers of the traditional series romances (including Mills & Boon/Harlequin) recognized the popularity of the new romances, they inaugurated similar changes in their own formulas.

In the late 1970s and early 1980s, the United States was the scene of intense competition among publishers of series romances. Sales and distribution of series romances increased rapidly as the alliance between Mills and Boon in Britain and Harlequin in Canada moved to dominance in the American market. Both those firms had exceptionally effective marketing strategies, selling books by mail order and subscription as well as in retail outlets. As American publishers recognized the success of the Mills and Boon/Harlequin strategy, competition ignited. Simon and Schuster, formerly Harlequin's American distributor, inaugurated the Silhouette Romance series in 1980 to compete for a share of the lucrative market. In the next two years, Silhouette Romances proliferated into four distinct series of romances, including a line for teenagers, a growing segment of the market. Silhouette also lured Mills and Boon authors with some success and began aggressively marketing abroad. After a few years of increasingly destructive competition, Harlequin and Silhouette merged.

In the same period other American paperback publishers (Dell, Berkley, Bantam) followed suit. Each of the new series emphasized the company's product through packaging, formula control enforced by author's 'tip-sheets', and advertizing to promote an image of the series' quality and diversity within a narrow range of predictable plots. The formula control of these romance publishers relies upon extensive market research aimed at discovering what women want to read so that editors can tailor the product to particular segments of the market. Such publisher control is relatively new in popular fiction. To be sure, series of novels were published in the 19th century, and certain publishing houses have long been known for issuing particular kinds of genre fiction; but the production and marketing of series romance novels represents a more complex development in popular entertainment, comparable to the way television programs are developed, packaged, and sold. In the past decade, some of the series publishers have marketed historical novels in similar ways, although with less success. Readers of historical fiction seem less interested in series packaging than do romance readers.

The romances and historical novels of the 1980s and early 1990s show the influence of changing roles for women. Although they are still dominated by a domestic value system, the novels frequently feature heroines who are far more assertive and competent than those of past decades, as well as heroes who are more nurturing and less domineering. Interestingly, these new character types may exist in both historical novels and those with contemporary settings. An additional sub-genre has also emerged, generally known as 'time-travel' romances. In these novels—perhaps best exemplified by Diana Gabaldon's *Outlander*—a heroine finds herself suddenly transported to a different time and place. (In *Outlander* and its sequels, the main character touches a magic rock in Scotland and wakes up in the 18th century.) The conflict between the modern heroine's values and those of the past becomes centred in a romantic relationship, although the novels derive much of their interest from the historical details of daily life.

Institutional support for romances has also increased. The Romance Writers of America was established to provide services to American authors similar to those offered British writers by the older Romantic Novelists Association. Newsletters for fans of romances proliferated, and conventions for romance readers and authors have been held. Romance is big business today, and the book establishment has had to take notice. The current popularity of romances, however, is probably an aberration, one of those historical moments when the gothic and romance formulas are particularly appealing to a wide audience. Over the past two centuries, these formulas have experienced intermittent waves of prominence that eventually receded, although their production has never entirely disappeared. The novels of especially popular authors remain in print for generations while the more ephemeral works are forgotten.

All kinds of popular fiction experience periods of high popularity followed by periods when sales, although steady, are lower. In the United States, the decade of the 1930s was particularly rich for historical novels, including *Gone with the Wind,* while the 1970s were especially fruitful for romance writers. Some scholars speculate that historical fiction was popular in the 1930s because the widespread social disruption of the era encouraged the reading public's interest in stories of the past. Such stories demonstrate that even under circumstances far more terrible than the readers' own, human beings could survive and prosper. Romances may have been especially interesting to women in the 1970s and 1980s, when the new and sometimes threatening social change fostered by the newly emerging women's movement seemed to call into question the value of traditional female roles.

Some commentators have speculated that popular genres of fiction, such as romances and historical novels, will fade away—romances because of changing women's roles and other popular genres because of the emergence of new and competing technologies for entertainment. Frequent alarms about the decline of literacy abound. These predictions may someday be true, but a visit to any suburban bookstore in either the USA or Britain will demonstrate that the popularity of these genres with the reading public has not yet measurably diminished.

—KAY MUSSELL

PREFACE
to the third edition

History and romance—nothing, it might seem, could be further apart. The one purporting to offer a purely factual record based on a knowable past, claiming truth and authenticity, an enlightened and a rational view of our doings grounded in substantive causes and material effects; the other suggesting a world of fancy and faery, inspired by an extravagant longing to go beyond what we have and what we know to be the case, to transform our workaday selves through the enhancements of adventure or the giddy metamorphoses of love, or simply by the power of wishing hard enough.

Yet novelists, and above all historical novelists, have long refused that polarization, insisting instead upon a twilight world between fact and feeling where the outlines of both are blurred. In fact a study of the authors in this volume might suggest that far from being spiritual and epistemological contraries, history and romance, like all opposites, are actually inseparable. For how can either lay claim to a territory of its own, without, as it were, defining the other, relegating (and thereby drawing attention) to what it is not? Perhaps it is because history and story have so much in common, because they are so close, rather than so alien to each other, that their differences have needed to be constantly, and sometimes anxiously, asserted.

For one of the most helpful ways of thinking about the rise of the novel as a literary form is to see it as a kind of history. This is easy for us when we find ourselves fascinated by the social detail of furnishing, mealtimes, or fashion in novels from earlier times. But it is harder to remember that it was this very emphasis upon recording the apparently humdrum, charting the daily lives of ordinary, unglamorous people, (people recognizably like the readers), that made the novel novel. Moving away from the well-worn tropes but also the social elevation of classical poetry, and the reliance upon the fantastic or the magical in older kinds of romance, the novel offered instead the history of a Tom Jones or a Moll Flanders: the *roman* was a fable of the everyday.

And novels went further in laying their stress upon human motivation and causation in the changes which they mapped. Though moral judgements would be made manifest in the outcomes of plots and the delineation of character, the readers of novels, as the 19th century progressed, came not to expect Providence to be too obvious in its workings, but to anticipate a subtle or sophisticated concentration upon human vicissitudes. That sense of life as a constantly changing process, subject to human laws and controls, would be increasingly attributed to the effects of larger social forces rather than supernatural intervention; the new forms of living and working which were demanded by, for example, industrialization, seem to set problems to be solved, in the first place, by the men and women at their centre. The novel played a crucial part in creating our modern and secular way of thinking historically, looking for the patterns and underlying motors of change inside the workings and actions of human society. Nor would change be any longer a matter of the gradual sweep of the centuries. A lifetime, or even a generation, might be enough to measure the utter transformation of social behaviour and expectations.

What was new about the novel, and central to the historical novel, as Kay Mussell has suggested in her essay for this volume, was the evoking of a relationship between private feeling and public event, the connections made between these larger social forces and the inner, psychic dramas of the individuals concerned: *War and Peace* is a family saga as well as an account of the Napoleonic wars. The novel, especially what critics call the domestic novel, took over from Romantic poetry the creation of a sense of self as an interior space which had its own history. To some extent, then, all novels are romantic histories—histories of feeling as well as records of the outer life, though novelists will place their emphasis differently. But always in the midst of the social processes which novels give us, is the question of the shaping of human desires and human subjectivity.

What we call 'the romantic' is not therefore 'outside' history but at its heart. Walter Scott, 'the Wizard of the North' and conventionally the founding father of the historical novel, understood this completely when he wrote *Waverley* (his first novel, published in 1814, an extraordinary bestseller), as an account of the Jacobite rebellion mediated through his foolish hero's sentimental education and the changes in outlook and attitude which we see him experiencing. Waverley, like many of Scott's Southern readers, can only see the Highlands romantically as the object of his 'intense curiosity and exalted imagination'. However, Scott is also clear that this romanticism, this idealizing capacity, which is frequently at a loss when confronted by the blood realities of the Jacobite struggle, is also a powerful agent for change. Though it may take Waverley out of his depth, it does propel him into new sympathies, new causes, and otherwise alien worlds. Wild dreams and utopias, reckless identifications, and overflowing imaginations—as historical novelists tell us over and over again—are also what fuel human beings. A history which is not also a history of motivation, of belief, of faith, of feeling, is not a history at all.

Writing in his Preface to *The American*, Henry James tried to find a definition of romance. Whereas the real represented for him, 'the things we cannot possibly *not* know, sooner or later, in one way or another', 'the romantic stands' he wrote, 'for the things that ... we never *can* directly know; the things that can reach us only through the beautiful circuit and subterfuge of our thought and our desire'. For James the only general definition of romance was not a matter of identifying particular settings or trappings—'of boats or caravans, or of tigers, or of 'historical characters', or of ghosts or of forgers, or of detectives, or of beautiful wicked women, or of pistols and knives' but of the kind of experience with which it deals: 'experience liberated ... exempt from the conditions that we usually know to attach to it'. Like the emancipation we experience in dreams (or the perverse freedom of nightmares which is mirrored in the Gothic) we can only gauge its meaning, dialectically, by knowing what the particular social conditions and pressures might be from which we wish to be set free. If we follow this way of thinking, it might be helpful to see romance and romance writing as history's unconscious, the dreams, fantasies, aspirations, hopes and fears which make up the socially impossible. Romance, to draw on the French historian, Michelet, is like love, history's protest, the place where writers and readers speak out against the actual and the legitimate, and offer visionary alternatives.

II

The intimate interrelationship between romantic and historical writing has set many problems for critics and scholars. One response—which this volume will help enlarge—has been the setting up of 'genre studies', which seek to isolate and identify the formal characteristics and narrative habits of different kinds of story. Such taxonomies take us back to the very beginnings of all storytelling, as the American critic, Northrop Frye has shown us in his analysis of myths and archetypes, or in the Russian formalistic critic, Vladimir Propp's study, *The Morphology of the Folk Tale*. More recent explorations of 20th-century popular fictions, like John G. Cawelti's *Adventure, Mystery and Romance*, often point to recurring narrative patterns and narrative elements across time: the quest in adventure fiction, for example, from the romances of the Holy Grail to *Raiders of the Lost Ark*, or the trials of the innocent hero, be he Parsifal or Crocodile Dundee. The ubiquity of these common elements can usefully call into question, among other things, the often obstructive division between high and low culture, and help erode the condescension toward 'low' cultural forms.

The strengths of a formalistic genre study are, however, also its limits: the emphasis upon what is shared tends toward a transhistorical, transcultural account both of the production of fiction and its appeal to the reader, as well as a universalizing of the readers themselves. It tends to isolate the deep structures of a work at the expense of understanding the particular appetites and tastes of the society which produced it. To place R.L. Stevenson's *Treasure Island* in a long line of adventure stories, linking it back perhaps to Homer's *Odyssey*, or further back still to ancient myths of the journey as a metaphor for life, and especially as the rite of passage into manhood, begs as many questions as it answers. We need to see too how the narrative elements and symbols are modified historically; How, for example, the particular image of the island takes on new meanings in Stevenson, whose provenance we might trace through Ballantyne and Defoe (and Shakespeare's *Tempest*) back to a very specific history of European colonial expansion and masculine mastery. (On this point, see Martin Green, *Dreams of Adventure, Deeds of Empire* and Graham Dawson, *Soldier Heroes*.) Purely formalistic studies of genre tend to look for continuities rather than disruptions. They might alert us to the elements of 'Cinderella', 'Beauty and the Beast', and 'Blue Beard' in *Jane Eyre*; it needs a different kind of account, however, to conjure up the precise social and sexual resonances of Daphne du Maurier's reworking of Brontë's novel for the English middle-classes in *Rebecca*, and why this should become a bestseller in 1938.

The 20th-century student would have to be hard-hearted indeed not to be moved by the idea that any study of popular fiction is tapping into a huge reservoir of human storytelling, going back to the mists of time. And to see how much of what we call 'popular' today still has plenty in common with the values and practices of folk and oral tradition. This is especially true of the crucial emphasis upon the pleasures of repetition and ritual, on a community of well-known stories, rehearsed as variations upon a theme. But they will want to ask local and specific questions, about why certain cultural forms and practices come to be deemed 'popular' in the first place, and how the meaning of 'the popular' changes over time. A definition of popular writing is inevitably, too, a definition of its opposite, of 'high' culture, and even a cursory historical glance will reveal that these definitions are constantly shifting. The novel is an obvious case in point. Once thought, 'like the polecat' to 'have a reputation for bad odour' (as a reviewer put it in 1874), the novel has been synonymous with a low, feminine taste and (thereby) associated with idleness and moral laxity. Nevertheless, it managed by the late 19th century to assume a moral seriousness and claim a cultural respectability. Within popular genres themselves, valencies can shift. Crime stories, for example, began as very low entertainment based on the reports of 'memoirs' of the criminals' exploits from prisons like London's notorious Newgate. They underwent an *embourgeoisement* along with their readers when the narrative shifted to spotlight and activities of the detective. Ranking exists within popular genres as well across all forms of cultural pleasure: though both crime and romance reading are seen as light reading, crime fiction has more social cachet.

The pecking order of genres, the cultural value attached to particular kinds of reading and not to others is clearly linked to the question of who does the reading. As different (and often overlapping) subordinated social groups have become literate, fears about the new autonomies which reading and writing might offer, proliferate. Outbursts against the effects of Gothic novels in the 1790s and products of the Minerva press were stimulated by the growth in female literacy and the very idea of the woman on the sofa having her own private thoughts and fantasies. The denigration of romance fiction in our own day carries with it a disparagement of feminine concerns, even of femininity itself. Recent feminist criticism has therefore proposed the idea of a sexual politics of reading: the notion that ideas about the proper role of women and ideological judgements about women inevitably colour literary judgements and are implicit in the canons of literary value. Take, for example, this apparently judicious statement from a recent Penguin paperback edition (the kind used by most British students), by the editor of Scott's *Waverley*, with its superbly masculine self confidence:

> Scott's triumph became a triumph for the form as he wrote it. The novel gained a new authority and prestige, and even more important perhaps a new masculinity. After Scott the novel was no longer in danger of becoming the preserve of the woman writer and the woman reader. Instead it became the appropriate form for writers' richest and deepest exploration of human experience.

What a wealth of social and sexual assumptions lies in that 'instead', and what a curiously warped view of the history of the novel.

The last 20 years or so has seen a burgeoning of feminist literary criticism especially alert to the outcast forms of romantic fiction (the lowest of the low) as offering a buried history of women's lives. Turning the tables on literary judgements like the one above, and championing exactly what has been previously scorned, the female culture of romance reading and writing has been reassessed. American critics like Janice Radway, in *Reading the Romance*, and Tania Modleski, in *Loving with a Vengeance*, have looked at how women use popular reading in their daily lives, and at the kinds of alternative space—often preciously guarded against the constant demands of being a wife and mother—that romance can offer. Other projects have tried to offer more specifically historical accounts of the appeal of particular authors or novels: Jean Radford's *The Progress of Romance*; Helen Taylor's *Scarlett's Women: 'Gone with the Wind' and its Female Fans*, which, like Radway's, draws on readership questionnaires, and my own study, *Forever England*, which offered an account of some of the pleasures of whodunits and of romances for women readers and writers between the wars. There is still much to be done on popular female reading, however, charting the popular romance and complementing the work on fiction for the working man, as Louise James's classic study dubbed it. We have no history of the historical novel which tries to map its course across the sexes and the classes, and its take-up by other subaltern social groups, in their attempts to write their own history. If the historical novel has been an unofficial people's history (which is not to say that it has been a radical one), its recent transformations in the hands of black and ethnic writers, especially in the USA, demonstrates its continuing fertility.

The study of popular fiction thus needs to work both diachronically and synchronically—that is, to look longitudinally across historical periods, but also to analyze the individual work in the immediacy of its own time and place. It needs to see the popular work always as part of a larger contemporary culture, rife with social divisions and assumptions, and it needs to understand not only how genres are gendered but how the meanings and values given to all forms of reading can never be divorced from the status of the reader. And—as though that weren't enough—it needs also to temper its literary critical and historical awareness with hard questions about the production of literature itself: the machinery of publications, of distribution, of the circulation of stories. These questions are as relevant to balladmongery, and to broadsheets, as they are to the selling of today's Harlequin romances or Mills and Boon. One of the great advantages of studying popular fiction is that you are put in touch with what Samuel Johnson in the 18th century (echoed by Virginia Woolf in the 20th) called 'the common reader'. But the critic and scholar will also come up against powerful authorities and controls. She will find it hard to avoid the social and political issues which more traditional literary criticism frequently eschews, questions whose answers can only be found by going beyond or outside the literary text. To some this will seem like a travesty, to others like myself, it seems not a narrowing of literature but an enlargement of it, the point at which literary study emerges from the chrysalis and takes off into the world outside.

III

The 20th century has, of course, an enormous expansion in the production of commercial fiction and the buying and selling of popular genre fiction. This expansion must be linked not only to the development of new technologies of printing and publishing but also to the growth in literacy: more people are reading than ever before. Since the late 19th century fears about the manipulation—social, emotional, or political—of these huge readerships by publishing companies inevitably bent upon profit and themselves increasingly part of national, and nowadays multinational conglomerates, have been reiterated by critics and educationalists. The 1920s and 1930s—the period which (as Joseph McAleer argues in *Popular Reading and Publishing in Britain*) saw a new and vital phase of the commodification of popular fiction, and the firm establishment of many of the genre categories with which we are familiar today, also witnessed virulent attacks upon the 'mass market'. (It is worth noting, as Raymond Williams has argued in *Culture and Society*, that the derogatory term 'mass market', always implies that the masses are other people, never oneself.) In Britain these assaults upon the corrupt forces of 'mass civilization' (to use F.R. Leavis's phrase) were often mingled with fears about Americanization, whether it lay in the influence of new advertising techniques and American methods of marketing, American 'hard-boiled' thrillers, American film, or the cultural cacophony (as some saw it) of jazz. In 1932 Q.D. Leavis's pioneering study, *Fiction and the Reading Public*, offered an almost entirely disparaging account of popular novels as debased 'kill-time interests' written in a modern suburban idiom, crude, puerile and clichéd. Social snobbery and condescension could inform the views of progressives like the feminist and novelist Rebecca West who sneeringly dismissed the 'lower animals' who read bestsellers. More sympathetic to working-class readers, but equally troubled by the ideological power of popular writing and the new mass media's capacity to propagandize, George Orwell saw a correspondence between the bully-worship of boys' comics and the growing appeal of fascism.

This rich vein of moral criticism and political interpretation, an urgent sense of the need to understand (or speculate about) the effects of reading upon readers, has run through much of what has now come to be called 'cultural studies' in Britain and the USA, where the studying of popular fiction and forms usually goes on. From the work of writers like Richard Hoggart in his *Uses of Literacy*, looking at women's magazines and youth culture in the 1950s, to arguments about the representation of race in works like *Uncle Tom's Cabin* or *Gone With the Wind*, the question of literary value has been intertwined with cultural and political judgement. When Germaine Greer attacked romance reading as 'dope for dopes' in *The Female Eunuch* in 1971, she was actually echoing one of the first feminists, Mary Wollstonecraft, whose *Vindication of the Rights of Woman* in 1792 also blamed 'a romantic twist of the mind' catered for by 'the stupid novelists' whose stale tales accustom women to the idea of female helplessness. As a feminist poster in the 1970s put it, 'you begin by sinking into his arms and end up with your arms in his sink'.

The danger with such accounts is that they can encourage a purely passive notion of the reader as 'consumer' and what can often be a conspiratorial sense of publishers and writers. Against this reductionism, others have wanted to emphasize the agency and self-consciousness of the reader, the consolatory and compensating pleasures of reading. Scott took this view as early as 1829 when he wrote of Mrs Radcliffe, whose *The Mysteries of Udolpho* (1794) had shivered the timbers of many a good citizen.

> If those who rail indiscriminately at this species of composition, were to consider the quantity of actual pleasure which it produces, and the much greater proportion of real sorrow and distress which it alleviates, their philanthropy ought to moderate their critical pride, or religious intolerance.

If, to adapt Karl Marx on religion, bestsellers are 'the opium of the people', they are also 'the heart of a heartless world', and tell us, in fact that much is wrong with that world. Why, after all, seek 'escapism', if the world does not need escaping from? Yet do not such fictions, in recasting the world for us, remind us as forcibly of its inadequacies when we lay our book aside, and feed those very discontents which we had hoped to pacify in our reading? Is that not part of the addictive quality of many popular genres? Or simply part of the tease, and the lure, of fiction itself?

In the end we can see that these are questions about all art and not only about what we call popular fictions. We are returned in guise to that role played in our daily lives by the imagined, the desired, the unreal. In the late 20th century these questions of discrimination—of the pleasure and power of the images which saturate our lives—have become especially complicated given not only the enormous reach of the so-called mass media, but also the influence which they exercise in the turn upon other cultural forms, like fiction, and upon the very quality of our consciousness. Cultural theorists and historians of the present day agree, for example, that we live in an age intensely self-conscious about the past, and marvellously inventive in producing versions of it. Perhaps the past has never been so familiar and never so frequently reproduced for fun as well as serious purposes. 'Retrochic', or vintage chic, heritage, period revivals in fashion or furniture, the expansion of museum culture, the theme-park, or 'themed' restaurant or decor: late 20th century people (as the historian Raphael Samuel has argued in *Theatres of Memory*) seem to spend most of their waking lives revisiting the past. Whilst it is true that many former generations learnt their history through historical novels, for us that sensibility has been vastly extended by costume dramas and films, by advertising, but magazines and newspapers, but shopping and collecting, by a whole wide world of consumerism (from the traditional granary loaf to the 'period' home) which has made the past our playground, as well as our learning-place, as never before.

Time was, perhaps, when historical novelists knew the limits of their craft. Anya Seton's preface to *Katherine* (1954) could thus confidently claim 'I have based my story on actual history and tried never to distort time, or place, or character to suit my convenience'. Though she felt compelled in all honesty to add, 'it has sometimes of course been necessary to bring my own interpretations', this compromise, however uneasy, between the given record and the novelist's poetic license, at least seemed acceptable. By contrast, many writers in the 1980s and 1990s are much more sophisticated and self-conscious about their work (though this does not necessarily make them better novelists). Hilary Mantel in the note to her award-winning novel of the French Revolution, *A Place of Greater Safety* (1992) appears to make the usual proviso when she says that her novel 'is closely tied to historical facts', but only, she continues, 'as far as those facts are agreed, which isn't really very far.' In the course of the novel Mantel has Robespierre say 'history is fiction': the gap between historian (as truthteller) and storyteller (as liar), always hard to maintain, now seems to have closed. 'Actual history', as Seton calls it, becomes for Mantel a matter of dispute between its actors; she uses the technique of the oral historian in her novel to give eyewitness accounts in the present tense, and to recreate history as an ongoing immediacy, a texture of profound certainty.

Once it is implied that the line to be drawn between an historical event—a fact—and its interpretation, is not just a thin, but an imaginary one, a vertiginous prospect opens up in which the meaning of history is 'only' in the eye of the beholder: it becomes nothing less, and nothing more, than the place of stories. This is one of the effects of a novel like Julian Barnes's *A History of the World in 10½ Chapters* or Adam Thorpe's *Ulverton* (to take two recent British examples). Thorpe's novel, which revolves around the life of an English village, offers us neither the point of view of a continuous character whose experiences secure our relation to the past nor even of a continuous historical period unfolding across the narrative. Instead we encounter brief soundbites taken at 30- or 50-year intervals, from Oliver Cromwell's defeat to the present day, and a range of characters (whose lives only briefly converge) speaking in a variety of historical and local dialects. At times the pastiche is so convincing, it is hard to to believe that we are reading actual historical documents. Ironically, Thorpe achieves this effect by limiting his narrative to the materials with which historians usually work: we move (in what is also a historical sequence of kinds of evidence) from folktale to a sermon, to diary, letters, to court depositions, to oral testimony, to photography, to archaeology, to radio, and finally a television script, until it comes to seem that history is only a series of representations. A unity is offered—the history of the village—but that is a unity precariously maintained in the face of so many changes.

Writers of popular fiction have always enjoyed playing with genre. A genre precisely allows you to know the rules in order to break them (as when Agatha Christie turned the whodunit on its head with *The Murder of Roger Ackroyd*), and this is part of their pleasure. And genre fiction has—in this century at least—always relied upon a strong, partisan loyalty from its readers who see themselves often as part of a particular following or cult—a tendency with recent lesbian romance or feminist detective fiction has exploited to the full. But many of today's writers go much further in transgressing the boundaries of genre expectations and forms, in suing pastiche and parody, and even plagiarism, deliberately blurring the distinctions between fiction and non-fiction types, and between the usual hierarchies of high or low art. A writer like the American, Kathy Acker, who reads her works at rock concerts between two bands, is aiming at a mixed-media experience: *Don Quixote* merrily recycles Cervantes, and lurches between (amongst other things) political satire, history lesson, the love stories of pulp fiction, and drama. Such writing destabilizes our critical judgements and terminologies. Just as publishing companies become more and more adept at packaging, styling and pricing their products so as to target increasingly differentiated readerships, so this endless proliferation of fractional groups threatens to overwhelm our capacity to understand the whole. Historical novelists or romance writers who know nothing of these developments and simply want to stick to the familiar formulae, are likely to find themselves newly earmarked as 'traditional'. This self-conscious interface between forms or representation, consumerism and an impulse to historicize, is one of the characteristic features of what has been called, by the French theorist, J-F. Lyorard and others, 'the postmodern condition'.

All this makes the job of this reference book much harder. This volume is a child of its times in wanting to lay down ever-more precise taxonomies in a culture, where, it could be argued, the forms of romance and historical writing are spiralling at such a dizzying rate as to defy any fixed or lasting definition. One of the great excitements of this late 20th century may well be this implosion of boundaries, the emergence of new forms from old, new fictional and cultural hybridizations. But this also makes for new anxieties, not least in asking us to reformulate our questions about the politics and pleasures of reading. Perhaps we can hope that one of the new hybrids may be emergence of more scholars and critics from the ranks of the common readers, since in the culture of the future, the meaning of popular fictions, and especially of the romance of history, is likely to become a more, not less urgent object of inquiry.

—ALISON LIGHT

EDITOR'S NOTE

The selection of writers in this book is based on the recommendations of the advisers listed on page xix.

The focus is on romance and historical literature; gothic writers have been excluded from this edition and will feature in a forthcoming St James Press title.

Each entry consists of a biography, a complete list of works, and a signed critical essay. In addition, living authors were invited to comment on their own work.

Original British and United States editions of all books have been listed; other editions are only listed if they are first editions, though an exception has been made to include publications of Harlequin Books (Toronto). Series characters/locations have been indicated for romance and historical publications. Entries include notations of collections, and critical studies. Other critical materials appear in the Reading List of secondary works on the genres at the back of the book.

For this edition the format has been adapted and expanded for greater clarity. A film adaptations section has been included where relevant. Furthermore, while the existing entries have been updated, some 100 new entries have been added.

ACKNOWLEDGEMENTS

I would like to thank the following people: all those who worked on the first two editions; all the new advisers and contributors for their advice and cooperation; the staff of the British Library, London; Lesley Henderson; Deirdre Clark; Barbara Archer; Tracy Chevalier; Mike Downey; Mrs R. Vasudevan; my colleagues and friends at St James Press and Gale Research; and my family.

ADVISERS

Rachel Anderson
Mary Cadogan
Barbara Cartland
Irene Collins
Bridget Fowler
Warren French
Rosemary Guiley
David Leon Higdon
Barbara E. Kemp
Alison Light
Kay Mussell

Victor Neuburg
Marina Oliver
David Powell
David Pringle
Elsa J. Radcliffe
Jean Radford
Janice Radway
Jean Saunders
Marcia L. Thomas
Carol Thurston
Frances Whitehead

CONTRIBUTORS

Patricia Altner
Rachel Anderson
Jane S. Bakerman
Michael Ballin
Earl F. Bargainnier
Linda S. Bergmann
Susan Quinn Berneis
E.F. Bleiler
Marylaine Block
Elizabeth P. Boykin
W.H. Bradley
Tracy Brain
Susan Branch
Jean Buchanan
Angela Bull
Dennis Butts
Mary Cadogan
Jane Campbell
Margaret Campbell
P. Campbell
Jennifer Cargill
Glen Cavaliero
Tessa Rose Chester
Pamela Cleaver
Scott Coombs
Edmund Cusick
Carol Klimick Cyganowski
Doreen D'Cruz
Peter Desy
Mike Downey
Warren French
Judith A. Gifford
Paul Gillen
Thomas S. Gladsky
Pat Gordon-Smith
Jane Gottschalk
John Gough
Elizabeth Grey
Albert Guerard
Janet V. Haedicke
Marion Hanscom
Marion Hatchard
Barrie Hayne
Joanne Harack Hayne
Michael Held
Allayne C. Heyduk
David Leon Higdon
Joan Hinkemeyer
Chris Hopkins

Lisa Hopkins
Ferelith Hordon
Louis James
Margaret Jensen
Heather Iris Jones
Richard Kelly
Barbara E. Kemp
Richard Kerridge
Rachel Kumar
Larry N. Landrum
Linda Lee
Lornie Leete-Hodge
Frank R. Levstick
Barry Lewis
Marilyn Lockhart
George C. Longest
Mary C. Lynn
Andrew Macdonald
Gina Macdonald
Radmila May
Alan J. McFarlane
Joan McGrath
P.R. Meldrum
Leonard R. Mendelsohn
J. Lawrence Mitchell
Christian H. Moe
Charmaine Moldrich
Arlene Moore
Thomas J. Morrisey
Marilynn Motteler
Alan Murphy
Kay Mussell
Necia A. Musser
Judie Newman
John O'Leary
Marina Oliver
Larry Olpin
Kim F. Paynter
Kathy Piehl
John Plowright
Nancy H. Pogel
David Powell
Joanna Price
Lyn Pykett
Naya Quin
L.M. Quinn
Janice Radway
Nancy Regan
Judith Rhodes

Karen Robertson
Lucy Rogers
Sara Corben de Romero
S.A. Rowland
Sobhana Rowland
Josephine A. Ruggiero
Geoffrey Sadler
Hana Sambrook
Andy Sawyer
Marion Shaw
Anne M. Shields
Alan R. Shucard
Andrea Lee Shuey
Roy S. Simmonds
Christopher N. Smith
David Waldron Smithers
Katherine Staples
Susannah Steel
Sanford Sternlicht
Nancy P. Stevenson
Jackie Stopyra
Judith Summers
Welford Dunaway Taylor

Marcia L. Thomas
Kate Thompson
Carol Thurston
Thomas R. Tietze
Felicity Trotman
Eleanor Ty
Peter Vansittart
W.M. von Zharen
Iris Wakulenko
George Walsh
Catherine S. Wearing
Marcia G. Welsh
Louise C. Weston
Kerry White
Ray Lewis White
Francis Whitehead
Dorothy Wood
Margaret Woodward
M. Jeanne Yardley
Peggy York
Alan R. Young

TWENTIETH-CENTURY ROMANCE AND HISTORICAL WRITERS

Names of authors who have a complete entry appear in bold. Pseudonyms appear in roman type.

Christine Abbey
Peter Ackroyd
Frances Adrian
Joan Aiken
Harriet Ainsworth
Patricia Ainsworth
Catherine Airlie
Madame Albanesi
James Albany
Donna Alexander
Kate Alexander
Paula Allardyce
Barbara Allen
Charlotte Vale Allen
Hervey Allen
Jennifer Ames
Valerie Anand
Lucilla Andrews
Barbara Annandale
Evelyn Anthony
Lisa Appignanesi
William Ard
Judith Arden
Leslie Arlen
Michael Arlen
Lindsay Armstrong
Tilly Armstrong
Caroline Arnett
Elizabeth von Arnim
Harriette Arnow
Helen Ashfield
Ellen Ashley
Sharon Ashton
Nan Asquith
Juliet Astley
Grace Murray Atkin
Mary Atkinson
Jean M. Auel
Lynn Avery
Jessica Ayre
Ruby M. Ayres

Irving Bacheller
H.C. Bailey
Faith Baldwin
Lydia Balmain
Mary Balogh
Noel Barber
Ann Barclay
Florence L. Barclay
Marguerite Barclay
Tessa Barclay
Countess Barcynska
Margaret Campbell Barnes
Pat Barr
Jocelyn Barry
John Barth
Jennie Bates
M.C. Beaton
Georgianna Bell
Henry Bellamann
Pamela Belle
Peter Benedict
Elizabeth Bennett
Pamela Bennetts
Jayne Bentley

Phyllis Bentley
Elisabeth Beresford
Thomas Berger
Anne Betteridge
Gloria Bevan
Jamunadevi Bhatia
June Bhatia
Maeve Binchy
Sheila Bishop
Laura Black
Veronica Black
Charity Blackstock
Lee Blackstock
Emma Blair
Iain Blair
Jennifer Blair
Kathryn Blair
Andrea Blake **Jennifer Blake**
Sally Blake
Stephanie Blake
Jennifer Bland
Diana Blayne
Ursula Bloom
Elizabeth Bolton
Mary Borden
Lesley Bourne
Jean Bowden
Marjorie Bowen
Harry Bowling
Edgar Box
James Boyd
Barbara Taylor Bradford
Melvyn Bragg
Rebecca Brandewyne
Sheila Brandon
Frank Brennan
Madeleine Brent
Rosalind Brett
Ann Bridge
Jane Brindle
P.A. Brisco
Patty Brisco
Jacqueline Briskin
Gwen Bristow
Louis Bromfield
Iris Bromige
Beth Brookes
D.K. Broster
Sandra Brown
Dixie Browning
Bryher
Anna Buchan
Elizabeth Buchan
John Buchan
Pearl S. Buck
Nancy Buckingham
Mary Burchell
Eleanor Burford
Lolah Burford
Anthony Burgess
Anita Burgh
G.B. Burgin
Sheila Burns
Shirlee Busbee
Michael Butterworth
A.S. Byatt

Donn Byrne

Robin Cade
Elizabeth Cadell
Hall Caine
Taylor Caldwell
Ann Cameron
Jolyon Carr
Philippa Carr
Roberta Carr
Robyn Carr
Netta Carstens
Ashley Carter
Elizabeth Eliot Carter
Barbara Cartland
Jayne Castle
Willa Cather
Nancy Cato
Isobel Chace
Catherine E. Chambers
Kate Chambers
Fay Chandos
Hester W. Chapman
Mollie Chappell
Judy Chard
Theresa Charles
Lowell Charters
Elaine Raco Chase
Lyndon Chase
Daniel Chaucer
Marion Chesney
Denise Chesterton
Berry Chetwynd
Philip Child
Alice Cholmondeley
Frederick H. Christian
Agatha Christie
Winston Churchill
Ellen Clare
Brenda Clarke
James Clavell
C. Guy Clayton
Brian Cleeve
Sophia Cleugh
John Cleveland
Sheila Coates
Marian Cockrell
Geoffrey Coffin
Peggie Coghlan
Marion Collin
Zandra Colt
Celine Conway
Jaelyn Conlee
Catherine Cookson
Ann Coombs
Nina Coombs
Jilly Cooper
Lettice Cooper
Barbara Corcoran
Alexander Cordell
Marie Corelli
Bernard Cornwell
Thomas B. Costain
Catherine Coulter
Caroline Courtney
Frances Cowen
Josephine Cox
William Coyle

Helen Crampton
Sara Craven
Robert Crawford
Lucilla Crichton
Caroline Crosby
Cecily Crowe
E.V. Cunningham
Katy Currie
Avon Curry
Philip Curtin
Peter Curtis
Lucia Curzon

Janet Dailey
Clemence Dane
Eva Dane
Max Daniels
Olga Daniels
Catherine Darby
Clare Darcy
Emma Darcy
Pamela D'Arcy
Eleanor Dark
Elizabeth Darrell
Julia Davis
Lindsey Davis
Robert Hart Davis
Edna Dawes
Shelley Dean
Celeste De Blasis
Charles de Crespigny
Warwick Deeping
Elizabeth de Guise
E.M. Delafield
Denis Delaney
Mazo de la Roche
R.F. Delderfield
Barbara Delinsky
Belinda Dell
Ethel M. Dell
Viña Delmar
Donna Teresa de Salvallo
Jude Deveraux
Jane de Vere
Raynard Devine
W.S. Dill
Maud Diver
Paige Dixon
Thomas Dixon
William Dobson
E.L. Doctorow
Robyn Donald
Jane Donnelly
Barbara Douglas
Lloyd C. Douglas
O. Douglas
Billie Douglass
Arthur Conan Doyle
John Doyle
Zoe Dozier
Bonnie Drake
Connie Drake
Shannon Drake
Eleanor Drew
John Drinkrow
Emma Drummond
Lennox Dryden
Pamela Dryden

Nancy Dudley
Anne Duffield
Alfred Duggan
Daphne du Maurier
Dorothy Dunnett
Allan Dwight
Alice Dwyer-Joyce
Juliet Dymoke

Evelyn Eaton
Suzanne Ebel
Dorothy Eden
Josephine Edgar
Walter D. Edmonds
June Edwards
Mary Elgin
Anne Eliot
Elizabeth
Rosemary Ellerbeck
Julie Ellis
John Elton
Walter Ericson
Audrey Erskine-Lindop
Susan Ertz
Mary Essex
John Esteven
Tabor Evans
Annette Eyre

Zabrina Faire
Ann Fairfax
Jeffrey Farnol
J.G. Farrell
M.J. Farrell
Howard Fast
Constance Fecher
Connie Feddersen
Jennie Felix
Catherine Fellows
Edna Ferber
Rachel Field
Carol Finch
Timothy Findley
Fiona Finlay
Sharon Fiske
Ellen Fitzgerald
Julia Fitzgerald
Valerie Fitzgerald
Thomas Flanagan
Caroline Fleming
Inglis Fletcher
Shelby Foote
Esther Forbes
Elbur Ford
Elizabeth Ford
Ford Madox Ford
C.S. Forester
Helen Forrester
Martha Fortina
John Fowles
Hugh Fowlis
Gilbert Frankau
Rose Franken
Christine Marion Fraser
George Macdonald Fraser
Jane Fraser
Cynthia Freeman
Ashley French

Ernest J. Gaines
Patricia Gallagher
Jennie Gallant
Robert Conington Galway
Ernest K. Gann
Charles Garvice
Marguerite Gascoigne
Catherine Gaskin
Catherine Gavin
Roberta Gellis
Mary Ann Gibbs
Charles Gibson
Anna Gilbert
Janice Holt Giles
Lucy Gillen
Maggie Gladstone
Ellen Glasgow
Amanda Glass
Judith Glover
Constance Gluyas
Elinor Glyn
Rumer Godden
William Golding
Suzanne Goodwin
Deborah Gordon
Diana Gordon
Ethel Edison Gordon
Elizabeth Goudge
Iris Gower
Heather Graham
Winston Graham
Peter Grange
Margaret Grant
Fern Gravel
Robert Graves
Caroline Gray
Ellington Gray
Harriet Gray
Richard Greaves
Peter Green
Philippa Gregory
Maysie Greig
Belinda Grey
Brenda Grey
Georgina Grey
Mabel Barnes Grundy

H. Rider Haggard
Fenil Haig
Pamela Haines
James Norman Hall
Radclyffe Hall
Dorothy Halliday
Gail Hamilton
Hervey Hamilton
Julia Hamilton
Mollie Hamilton
Priscilla Hamilton
Anne Hampson
J.D. Hardin
Mollie Hardwick
Laura Hardy
W.G. Hardy
Christina Harland
Elizabeth Harle
John Harley
Lavinia Harris
Marilyn Harris

Elizabeth Harrison
Sarah Harrison
Whit Harrison
Cynthia Harrod-Eagles
Caroline Hart
Caroline Harvey
Kathryn Harvey
Rachel Harvey
Alice Harwood
Brooke Hastings
Harrington Hastings
Phyllis Hastings
Vesta Hathaway
Zachary Hawkes
Arnold G. Haygood
Sharon Heath
Constance Heaven
Maurice Hewlett
Georgette Heyer
Robert Hichens
James Hill
Pamela Hill
Susan Hill
Margery Hilton
Jeanne Hines
Jane Aiken Hodge
Joan Hohl
Cecelia Holland
Kel Holland
Sheila Holland
Victoria Holt
Winifred Holtby
Brenda Honeyman
Kay Hooper
Anthony Hope
Lance Horner, Kyle Onstott, and Ashley Carter
R.B. Houston
Audrey Howard
Linda Howard
Linden Howard
Mary Howard
Susan Howatch
Elizabeth Hoy
Susan Hufford
E.M. Hull
Donna Hunt
Elizabeth Hunter
Hall Hunter
Fannie Hurst
Baroness von Hutten
Eleanor Hyde

Eva Ibbotson
Ion L. Idriess
Jean Innes
Margaret Irwin

Naomi Jacob
Leah Jacobs
Brenda Jagger
John Jakes
Margaret James
Norah James
Robin James
Sally James
Stephanie James
Storm Jameson
Rosemary Hawley Jarman

Veronica Jason
Gary Jennings
Sara Jennings
Ruth Prawer Jhabvala
Iris Johansen
Nancy John
Barbara Ferry Johnson
Susan Johnson
Mary Johnston
Norma Johnston
Velda Johnston
Laura Jordan
Penny Jordan
Marie Joseph

Julia Kane
MacKinlay Kantor
M.M. Kaye
Molly Keane
Joseph Kell
Kathleen Kellow
Susannah Kells
Sarah Kemp
Thomas Keneally
Margaret Kennedy
Alexander Kent
Charlotte Keppel
Frances Parkinson Keyes
Flora Kidd
Alexandra Kirk
Gilbert Knox
Jayne Ann Krentz
Mary Kuczkir
Susan Kyle

Christina Laffeaty
Rozella Lake
Rosalind Laker
Charlotte Lamb
William Lamb
Marianne Lamont
Dinah Lampitt
Sheila Lancaster
Leslie Lance
Jane Lane
Tania Langley
Anne Lattin
Elizabeth Law
Irene Lawrence
Rosamond Lehmann
Roberta Leigh
Annie Leith
C. Lenanton
Doris Leslie
Anne L'Estrange
Janet Lewis
Maynah Lewis
Marjorie Lewty
Alice Chetwynd Ley
Sophie Leyton
Laura Jean Libbey
Mary Lide
Jack Lindsay
Rachel Lindsay
Johanna Lindsey
Levanah Lloyd
Ross Lockridge
Norah Lofts

Jake Logan
Mark Logan
Mary Lomer
Laura London
Nancy London
William Stuart Long
Alison Lord
Jeffrey Lord
Amii Lorin
Emilie Loring
Peter Loring
Claire Lorrimer
Elizabeth Lowell
Marie Belloc Lowndes
Lester Lurgan
Mary Lutyens
David Lyall
Ann Lynton
Andrew Lytle

Rose Macaulay
Madge Macbeth
Mrs Patrick MacGill
Colin MacInnes
Lee Mackenzie
Pierce MacKenzie
Leila Mackinlay
Bridget Maclagan
Jean S. MacLeod
Duncan MacNeil
Anne MacNeill
Margaret Maddocks
E.B. Majors
Eric Malpass
Audrie Manley-Tucker
Deborah Mann
Alexandra Manners
Hilary Mantel
Catherine Marchant
Joanna Marcus
Susan Marino
Katherine Marlowe
Michael Marlowe
Jean Marsh
Joan Marsh
John Marsh
Edison Marshall
Joanne Marshall
Rosamond Marshall
Rhona Martin
Ruth Martin
Stella Martin
Julia Martines
Susan Marvin
A.E.W. Mason
F. Van Wyck Mason
Frank W. Mason
John Masters
Anne Mather
Patricia Matthews
A.E. Maxwell
Ann Maxwell
Patricia Maxwell
Vicky Maxwell
Wynne May
Anne Maybury
Julia Mayfield
Laurie McBain

Barbara McCorquodale
Colleen McCullough
Philip McCutchan
George Barr McCutcheon
Adeline McElfresh
Simon McKay
Lindsay McKenna
Judith McNaught
Susan Meadmore
Franken Meloney
Anne Melville
Christina Merlin
Barbara G. Mertz
Grace Metalious
Barbara Michaels
Fern Michaels
James A. Michener
Lady Miles
Linda Lael Miller
Margaret Mitchell
Naomi Mitchison
L.M. Montgomery
Doris Langley Moore
Gwyneth Moore
Toni Morrison
Carole Mortimer
Annette Motley
Edwin Mullins
Neil Munro
D.L. Murray
Fiona Murray
Frances Murray
Netta Muskett
Harriet Kathryn Myers

Susan Napier
Eileen Nauman
Hilary Neal
Betty Neels
Sarah Neilan
Margaret Newman
C.R. Nicholson
Christina Nicholson
Jane Nicholson
Robin Nicholson
Christopher Nicole
Frederick Niven
Frederick Nolan
Lisabet Norcross
Charles Nordhoff and James Norman Hall
Kathleen Norris
Bess Norton
Kate Norway
Robert Nye

Patrick O'Brian
Kate O'Brien
Julia O'Faolain
Elisabeth Ogilvie
Pamela Oldfield
Marina Oliver
Yvonne Oliver
David Olivieri
Carola Oman
Kyle Onstott
Baroness Orczy
Barbara Øvstedal

Diana Palmer
Mary Paradise
Edith Pargeter
Margaret Pargeter
C. Northcote Parkinson
Isabel M. Paterson
Maxine Patrick
Barbara Paul
Barbara Anne Pauley
Robert Paye
Alan Payne
Rachel Ann Payne
Lilian Peake
Jack Pearl
Diane Pearson
Margaret Pedler
Margaret Pemberton
Nan Pemberton
Sharon K. Penman
Elizabeth O. Peter
Elizabeth Peters
Ellis Peters
Maureen Peters
Natasha Peters
Rosamunde Pilcher
Erin Pizzey
Jean Plaidy
Belva Plain
Madeleine A. Polland
D.A. Ponsonby
Dudley Pope
Eleanor H. Porter
Gene Stratton Porter
Hal Porter
Margaret Potter
Nora Powers
Heather Graham Pozzessere
George Preedy
H.F.M. Prescott
Fayrene Preston
Ivy Preston
Richard Preston
Evadne Price
Lozania Prole
Nina Pykare

Erica Quest
Amanda Quick
Gabriel Quyth

Marguerite Radclyffe-Hall
Thomas Head Raddall
Hugh C. Rae
J. Rana
Rona Randall
Claire Rayner
John Redfern
Douglas Reeman
Max Reiner
Mary Renault
Elizabeth Renier
M.P. Revere
Elvi Rhodes
Jean Rhys
Barbara Rich
Susan Richard
Emilie Richards
Henry Handel Richardson

Grace Richmond
A.R. Riefe
Alan Riefe
Barbara Riefe
Mary Roberts Rinehart
Alexandra Ripley
Claire Ritchie
Francine Rivers
Kay Robbins
Adrian Robert
Elizabeth Madox Roberts
I.M. Roberts
Irene Roberts
Ivor Roberts
Kenneth Roberts
Nora Roberts
Paula Roberts
Willo Davis Roberts
Denise Robins
Gina Robins
Patricia Robins
Mary Linn Roby
Danielle Rockfern
Jan Roffman
Rosemary Rogers
Judith Rothman
Iris Rowland
Effie Rowlands
Brandon Roy
Rosamond Royal
Berta Ruck
Anne Rundle
Rachel Ryan
Doris Rybot

Rafael Sabatini
Erin St Claire
Mabel St John
Nicole St John
Carola Salisbury
Susan Sallis
Laura Goodman Salverson
Oliver Sandys
Helen Hooven Santmyer
Jean Saunders
Jeanne Saunders
Alan Savage
Elizabeth Savage
Petra Sawley
Isobel Saxe
Judith Saxton
Dallas Schulze
Jay Scotland
Evelyn Scott
Jane Scott
Janey Scott
Paul Scott
Margaret Sebastian
John Sedges
Kate Sedley
Maura Seger
Kathleen Gilles Seidel
Elizabeth Seifert
Alexandra Sellers
Anya Seton
Donald Severn
Irene Shaw
Virna Sheard

Joseph Shearing
Cecily Shelbourne
Samuel Shellabarger
Suzanne Sherrill
Valerie Sherwood
Kathleen A. Shoesmith
Nevil Shute
James Sinclair
Julian Sinclair
M.A. St C. Sinclair
Mary Sinclair
May Sinclair
Olga Sinclair
Rosemary Anne Sisson
Frank G. Slaughter
Sara Sloane
Bertrice Small
Doris E. Smith
Lady Eleanor Smith
Helen Zenna Smith
Joan Smith
Sylvie Sommerfield
Susan Sontag
Ernest Souza
Cathy Cash Spellman
LaVyrle Spencer
Elizabeth Sprigge
Sondra Stanford
Mary Jane Staples
Danielle Steel
Jessica Steele
Marcia Steele
Marguerite Steen
John Steinbeck
G.B. Stern
Stuart Stern
Blaine Stevens
Robert Tyler Stevens
Tricia Stevens
Anne Stevenson
D.E. Stevenson
Florence Stevenson
Mary Stewart
Jessica Stirling
Irving Stone
Virginia Storm
Josephine Story
Rebecca Stratton
Alex Stuart
Clay Stuart
Eleanor Stuart
V.A. Stuart
Vivian Stuart
Jean Stubbs
Alice Stuyvesant
William Styron
Essie Summers
Rowena Summers
Margaret Summerton
Annalise Sun
Rosemary Sutcliff
Annie S. Swan
Neil H. Swanson
Madge Swindells

Reay Tannahill
Allen Tate
Ellalice Tate

Janelle Taylor
Jayne Taylor
Jan Tempest
Sarah Tempest
C.V. Terry
Elswyth Thane
Rosie Thomas
E.V. Thompson
Bridget Thorn
Nicola Thorne
Kay Thorpe
Sylvia Thorpe
Marcella Thum
Ursula Torday
Regina Towers
Nigel Tranter
Betty Trask
Elizabeth Treahearne
Nye Tredgold
Henry Treece
Rose Tremain
Jennie Tremaine
Richard Tresillian
Joanna Trollope
Katherine Troy
Judy Turner

Mrs George de Horne Vaizey
Karen van der Zee
Peter Vansittart
Helen Van Slyke
Mona van Wieren
Patricia Veryan
Gore Vidal
Claire Vincent
Donna Vitek

Helen Waddell
Lucy Walker
Margaret Walker
Hugh Walpole
Sheila Walsh
Monica Ware
Rex Warner
Sylvia Townsend Warner
Mary Douglas Warre
Mary Douglas Warren
Robert Penn Warren
Margaret Way
Ai Gvhdi Waya
Anne Weale
Ward Weaver
Jean Webster
Elizabeth Welles
Hondo Wells
Eudora Welty
Sally Wentworth
Elizabeth Wesley
Mary Wesley
Jessamyn West
Jan Westcott
Mary Westmacott
Stanley Weyman
Edith Wharton
Sharon Whitby
Harriet White
Patrick White
Cilla Whitmore

Hallam Whitney
Phyllis A. Whitney
Harry Whittington
Philippa Wiat
Rudy Wiebe
T.I.G. Wigg
Thornton Wilder
Bronwyn Williams
Claudette Williams
C.N. and A.M. Williamson
Harcourt Williamson
Mary Wilson
John Winch
Laurel Winslow
Kathleen Winsor
Violet Winspear
Daoma Winston
Jeanette Winterson
Barbara Wood
Sara Wood

Emma Woodhouse
Sarah Woodhouse
Kathleen E. Woodiwiss
Richard Woodman
Sherryl Woods
Lilian Woodward
Victoria Woolf
Anne Worboys
Anne Eyre Worboys
P.C. Wren
Francesca Wright
Laura Wylie
Esther Wyndham

May Wynne
Frank Yerby
Alison York
Andrew York
Katherine Yorke
Stark Young

Writers not included in this volume who appear in previous editions.
(see listing within text for reference to appropriate edition.)

Alice Abbott
Jane Arbor
Charlotte Armstrong
Elizabeth Ashton

Susan Barrie
Betty Beaty
Helen Beauclerk
L. Adams Beck
Stephen Vincent Benét
Evelyn Berckman
John Berger
Eileen Bigland
Jane Blackmore
Marion Zimmer Bradley
Gillian Bradshaw
Katrina Britt
Rose Burghley
Gwendoline Butler

James Branch Cabell
Janet Caird
Sacha Carnegie
Angela Carter
David Case
Robert W. Chambers
Virginia Coffman
Juanita Coulson

Iris Danbury
Dorothy Daniels
Marcia Davenport
Dorothy Salisbury Davis
August Derleth
Joyce Dingwell

Mignon G. Eberhart
May Edginton
Anne Edwards
M. Barnard Eldershaw
Hebe Elsna

Clare Emsley
John Erskine

Eleanor Farnes
Glenna Finley
Ronald Fraser

David Garnett
Joan Grant
Hettie Grimstead

Rosemary Harris
Grace Livingston Hill
Naomi A. Hintze
Isabelle Holland

Susan Inglis

Shirley Jackson

Barbara Kevern
Katheryn Kimbrough
Russell Kirk
Alanna Knight
Arthur Koestler

Roumelia Lane
Jacqueline La Tourette
Elsie Lee
Morgan Llewelyn
Dorothy Mackie Low
Margaret Lynn

Dorothy Macardle
Charlotte MacLeod
John Masefield
Marjorie McEvoy
Margaret Millar
Marlys Millhiser
Alice Morgan

Sharan Newman

Joyce Carol Oates
Rohan O'Grady
Oliver Onions

Phyllis Taylor Pianka
Bentz Plagemann
John Cowper Powys

Florence Engel Randall
Henrietta Reid
Janet Louise Roberts

Margaret Rome

Sara Seale

Jill Tattersall

Jean Francis Webb
Gwen Westwood
T.H. White
Chelsea Quinn Yarbro
Dornford Yates

ABBEY, Christine. See **BUCKINGHAM, Nancy.**

ABBOTT, Alice. Pseudonym for Kathryn Borland (1916—) and Helen Ross Speicher (1915—). Americans. See 1st edition, 1982.

ACKROYD, Peter.
Nationality: British. **Born:** London, 5 October 1949. **Education:** St Benedict's, Ealing, 1960–67; Clare College, Cambridge, 1968–71; Yale University, New Haven, Connecticut (Mellon fellow), 1971–73. **Career:** literary editor, 1973–77, and joint managing editor, 1978–81, *The Spectator*, London. Since 1986, chief book reviewer, *The Times*, London. **Recipient:** Maugham award, 1984, for *The Last Testament of Oscar Wilde*; Whitbread award for biography, 1984, for *T.S. Eliot*, and for fiction, 1986, for *Hawksmoor*; Royal Society of Literature Heinemann award for non-fiction, 1985, for *T.S. Eliot*; *The Guardian* fiction prize, 1985, for *Hawksmoor*. Fellow, Royal Society of Literature, 1984. **Agent:** Anthony Sheil Associates, 43 Doughty Street, London WC1N 2LF, England.

ROMANCE AND HISTORICAL PUBLICATIONS

Novels

The Last Testament of Oscar Wilde. London, Hamish Hamilton, and New York, Harper, 1983.
Hawksmoor. London, Hamish Hamilton, 1985; New York, Harper, 1986.
Chatterton. London, Hamish Hamilton, 1985; New York, Grove Press, 1988.
Doctor Dee. London, Hamish Hamilton, 1993.

OTHER PUBLICATIONS

Novels

The Great Fire of London. London, Hamish Hamilton, 1982; Chicago, University of Chicago Press, 1988.
First Light. London, Hamish Hamilton, and New York, Grove Weidenfeld, 1989.
English Music. London, Hamish Hamilton, 1992.

Poetry

Ouch. London, The Curiously Strong, 1971.
London Lickpenny. London, Ferry Press, 1973.
Country Life. London, Ferry Press, 1978.
The Diversions of Purley and Other Poems. London, Hamish Hamilton, 1987.

Other

Notes for a New Culture: An Essay on Modernism. London, Vision Press, and New York, Barnes and Noble, 1976.
Dressing Up: Transvestism and Drag: The History of an Obsession. London, Thames and Hudson, and New York, Simon and Schuster, 1979.
Ezra Pound and His World. London, Thames and Hudson, and New York, Scribner, 1981.
T.S. Eliot (biography). London, Hamish Hamilton, and New York, Simon and Schuster, 1984.
Dickens (biography). London, Sinclair Stevenson, and New York, HarperCollins, 1990.

Introduction to Dickens. London, Sinclair Stevenson, 1991.

Editor, *PEN New Fiction*. London, Quartet, 1984.
Editor, *The Picture of Dorian Gray*, by Oscar Wilde. London, Penguin, 1985.
Editor, *Dickens' London: An Imaginative Vision*. London, Headline, 1987.

*   *   *

The past is paradigmatic, a living presence illuminating and explaining contemporary existence. In the novels of Peter Ackroyd the central search for a meaning for the self in time is placed in a structural and thematic relationship to events and characters from the past. The historical becomes not only the means of explaining the present, but is in fact an essential part of our present existence.

The title of *Hawksmoor*, and the very real presence of the seven London churches, mean that the historical figure of architect Nicholas Hawksmoor casts a shadow over events, despite Ackroyd's assertion that 'this version of history is my own invention'. The dual time-scheme places the events in early 18th-century London with the story of architect Nicholas Dyer, and the 20th-century murder enquiry, conducted by Chief Superintendent Hawksmoor. Ackroyd creates a vivid backdrop for Dyer's narrative.

At the beginning of the 18th century, London was a rapidly expanding metropolis in which, beneath the surface of middle-class mercantile respectability, the impoverished seethed in crowded alleys. Dyer recognizes this darker side; the dirt and the disease, and the asylum of Bedlam visited by Dyer and Wren, have a more tangible reality than the rarified atmosphere of the Royal Society. Ackroyd vividly brings this period to life with great narrative control: a childhood dominated by the plague and its concomitant suffering, and the purging effects of the Great Fire of 1666, houses tumbling, and people crying out amid the roar of the flames. These incidents are recollected by Dyer as an adult, exploring the genesis of his fascination with man's latent darkness, symbolized by the cryptic pattern of his churches.

The crucial debates raging in the Age of Reason are developed in the conflict between Dyer and his fellow architects Sir Christopher Wren and John Vanbrugh. Dyer attends one of Wren's lectures at the Royal Society but rejects the rational ideology of such men; his vision and understanding of man cannot be reconciled with such reasoned philosophy. Indeed the whole novel seems to be Ackroyd's testament to the post-modernist sense of questioning and the fragmentation of truth. During Dyer's final illness the time parameters of the novel are set with a vision of the 1715 Jacobite rebellion; the events become, indeed, inseparable from his own suffering. As so often with Ackroyd, the essentially poetic language expresses the anguish and the pain—and the humour, too—of human experience with great beauty and power.

These historical facts are underlined by a masterly control of pastiche, capturing the spelling, punctuation, and idiom of the time perfectly (a skill that Ackroyd also displays in *The Last Testament of Oscar Wilde*). Contemporary London, inhabited by vagrants and the poor, cohabits the fictional world, and is indeed dominated by the presence of the living past. This is an underworld of 18th-century mysticism and 20th-century alienation, a world in which Hawksmoor vainly tries to find the murderer whose victims are inextricably linked to Dyer's churches. It is a haunting story, all the more so for the inconclusive ending which leaves the murders unsolved.

This difficulty in distinguishing between reality and fiction is at the heart of *Chatterton*. Woven through three different time schemes, the dominant story concerns Charles Wychwood, a struggling poet who 'discovers' a painting and manuscripts that prove Thomas Chatterton did not in fact die young. Developed around this are the two 'real' events of Chatterton's death, and the painting by

Henry Wallis of 'Chatterton'—and the accompanying story of the estrangement of the poet George Meredith and his wife Mary—which add to the novel's layered pattern. Chatterton, creator of the mediaeval monk Thomas Rowley, dominates the novel, although he does not actually appear until Part Three. The questions of plagiarism and fiction, historical fact and assumption, reverberate throughout the novel; the wonderfully eccentric gin-sipping novelist Harriet Scrope suggests that history seems so unreal: 'It's the one thing we have to make up for ourselves'.

This time it is not so much the living presence of London that gives the novel its historical basis—although once again the city remains a potent symbol. Rather, it is Ackroyd's portrayal of the characters that captures us, as we see them caught up in something greater than any of them can understand. The act of the creation of the painting alters the lives of Wallis and the Merediths for ever. We experience George Meredith's struggle with his poetry, and the sense of the developing relationship between Wallis and Mary, who remains a distant and ethereal figure. All of this is imagined 'truth', challenged most daringly in the death of Thomas Chatterton. The last part of the novel stresses the poet's high spirits on that fateful day, and we are left not with the image of a despairing suicide, but instead with something less certain. The overdose of arsenic and opium is a mistake made while very drunk; but it also becomes a gateway to the visionary moment when Chatterton realizes the sense of immortality paradoxically achieved by his death. The Romantic image of the 'marvellous boy' has perhaps itself created a fiction surrounding the young poet's death.

The historical framework is a particularly suitable vehicle for Ackroyd's fiction. The past comes alive; the sense of time and place is remarkable, given an even greater reality by the historical figures that inhabit or define the novels. The living presence of the past and the synthesis of identity across time give his novels their power; Ackroyd challenges the whole relationship between history, fact, and historical fiction.

—Alan J. McFarlane

ADRIAN, Frances. See **POLLAND, Madelaine A.**

AIKEN, Joan (Delano).
Nationality: British. **Born:** Rye, Sussex, 4 September 1924. **Education:** Wychwood School, Oxford, 1936–40. **Relations:** married 1) Ronald George Brown in 1945 (died 1955), one son and one daughter; 2) Julius Goldstein in 1976. Daughter of the writer Conrad Aiken; sister of Jane Aiken Hodge, *q.v.* **Career:** worked for the BBC, 1942–43; information officer, then librarian, United Nations Information Centre, London, 1943–49; subeditor and features editor, *Argosy*, London, 1955–60; copywriter, J. Walter Thompson, London, 1960–61. **Recipient:** *The Guardian* award for children's literature, 1969; Lewis Carroll award, 1970; Mystery Writers of America Edgar Allan Poe award, 1972. **Agent:** A.M. Heath, 79 St Martin's Lane, London, WC2N 4AA, England; or, Brandt and Brandt, 1501 Broadway, New York, New York 10036, USA. **Address:** The Hermitage, East Street, Petworth, West Sussex GU28 0AB, England.

ROMANCE AND HISTORICAL PUBLICATIONS

Novels (series: Petworth)

The Silence of Herondale. New York, Doubleday, 1964; London, Gollancz, 1965.

The Fortune Hunters. New York, Doubleday, 1965.
Trouble with Product X. London, Gollancz, 1966; as *Beware of the Banquet*, New York, Doubleday, 1966.
Hate Begins at Home. London, Gollancz, 1967; as *Dark Interval*, New York, Doubleday, 1967.
The Ribs of Death. London, Gollancz, 1967; as *The Crystal Crow*, New York, Doubleday, 1968.
The Embroidered Sunset. London, Gollancz, and New York, Doubleday, 1970.
Died on a Rainy Sunday. London, Gollancz, and New York, Holt Rinehart, 1972.
The Butterfly Picnic. London, Gollancz, 1972; as *A Cluster of Separate Sparks*, New York, Doubleday, 1972.
Voices in an Empty House. London, Gollancz, and New York, Doubleday, 1975.
Castle Barebane. London, Gollancz, and New York, Viking Press, 1976.
Last Movement. London, Gollancz, and New York, Doubleday, 1977.
The Five-Minute Marriage. London, Gollancz, 1977; New York, Doubleday, 1978.
The Smile of the Stranger (Petworth). London, Gollancz, and New York, Doubleday, 1978.
The Lightning Tree (Petworth). London, Gollancz, 1980; as *The Weeping Ash*, New York, Doubleday, 1980.
The Young Lady from Paris. London, Gollancz, 1982; as *The Girl from Paris*, New York, Doubleday, 1982.
Foul Matter. London, Gollancz, and New York, Doubleday, 1983.
Mansfield Revisited. London, Gollancz, 1984; New York, Doubleday, 1985.
Deception. London, Gollancz, 1987; as *If I Were You*, New York, Doubleday, 1987.
Blackground. London, Gollancz, and New York, Doubleday, 1989.
Jane Fairfax (sequel to *Emma* by Jane Austen). London, Gollancz, and New York, St Martin's Press, 1990.
The Haunting of Lamb House. London, Cape, 1991; New York, St Martin's Press, 1993.
Morningquest. London, Gollancz, 1992.

OTHER PUBLICATIONS (for children)

Fiction

All You've Ever Wanted and Other Stories. London, Cape, 1953.
More Than You Bargained For and Other Stories. London, Cape, 1955; New York, Abelard Schuman, 1957.
The Kingdom and the Cave. London, Abelard Schuman, 1960; New York, Doubleday, 1974.
The Wolves of Willoughby Chase. London, Cape, 1962; New York, Doubleday, 1963.
Black Hearts in Battersea. New York, Doubleday, 1964; London, Cape, 1965.
Nightbirds on Nantucket. London, Cape, and New York, Doubleday, 1966.
The Whispering Mountain. London, Cape, 1968; New York, Doubleday, 1969.
A Necklace of Raindrops and Other Stories. London, Cape, and New York, Doubleday, 1968.
Armitage, Armitage, Fly Away Home. New York, Doubleday, 1968.
A Small Pinch of Weather and Other Stories. London, Cape, 1969.
The Windscreen Weepers and Other Tales of Horror and Suspense (for adults). London, Gollancz, 1969.
A Night Fall. London, Macmillan, 1969; New York, Holt Rinehart, 1971.
Smoke from Cromwell's Time and Other Stories. New York, Doubleday, 1970.

The Green Flash and Other Tales of Horror, Suspense, and Fantasy. New York, Holt Rinehart, 1971.
The Cuckoo Tree. London, Cape, and New York, Doubleday, 1971.
All and More. London, Cape, 1971.
A Harp of Fishbones and Other Stories. London, Cape, 1972.
The Escaped Black Mamba. London, BBC Publications, 1973; as *Arabel and the Escaped Black Mamba,* London, BBC Publications, 1984.
Tales of Arabel's Raven. London, BBC Publications, 1974; as *Arabel's Raven,* New York, Doubleday, 1974.
All But a Few. London, Penguin, 1974.
The Bread Bin. London, BBC Publications, 1974.
Midnight Is a Place. London, Cape, and New York, Viking Press, 1974.
Not What You Expected: A Collection of Short Stories. New York, Doubleday, 1974.
Mortimer's Tie. London, BBC Publications, 1976.
A Bundle of Nerves: Stories of Horror, Suspense, and Fantasy. London, Gollancz, 1976.
The Faithless Lollybird and Other Stories. London, Cape, 1977; New York, Doubleday, 1978.
The Far Forests: Tales of Romance, Fantasy, and Suspense. New York, Viking Press, 1977.
Go Saddle the Sea. New York, Doubleday, 1977; London, Cape, 1978.
Tale of a One-Way Street and Other Stories. London, Cape, 1978; New York, Doubleday, 1979.
Mice and Mendelson, music by John Sebastian Brown. London, Cape, 1978.
Mortimer and the Sword Excalibur. London, BBC Publications, 1979.
The Spiral Stair. London, BBC Publications, 1979.
A Touch of Chill: Stories of Horror, Suspense and Fantasy. London, Gollancz, 1979; New York, Delacorte Press, 1980.
Arabel and Mortimer (includes *Mortimer's Tie; The Spiral Stair; Mortimer and the Sword Excalibur*). London, Cape, 1980; New York, Doubleday, 1981.
The Shadow Guests. London, Cape, and New York, Delacorte Press, 1980.
Mortimer's Portrait on Glass. London, Hodder and Stoughton, 1981.
The Stolen Lake. London, Cape, and New York, Delacorte Press, 1981.
The Mystery of Mr Jones's Disappearing Taxi. London, Hodder and Stoughton, 1982.
A Whisper in the Night: Tales of Terror and Suspense. London, Gollancz, 1982; New York, Delacorte Press, 1983.
Mortimer's Cross. London, Cape, 1983; New York, Harper, 1984.
Bridle the Wind. London, Cape, and New York, Delacorte Press, 1983.
The Kitchen Warriors. London, BBC Publications, 1983.
Up the Chimney Down. London, Cape, and New York, Harper, 1984.
Fog Hounds, Wind Cat, Sea Mice. London, Macmillan, 1984.
Mortimer Says Nothing and Other Stories. London, Cape, 1985; New York, Harper, 1987.
The Last Slice of Rainbow and Other Stories. London, Cape, 1985; New York, Harper, 1988.
Dido and Pa. London, Cape, and New York, Delacorte Press, 1986.
Past Eight O'Clock: Goodnight Stories. London, Cape, 1986.
A Goose on Your Grave. London, Gollancz, 1987.
The Moon's Revenge, illustrated by Alan Lee. London, Cape, and New York, Knopf, 1987; New York, Red Fox, 1990.
The Teeth of the Gale. London, Cape, and New York, Harper, 1988.
The Erl King's Daughter. London, Heinemann, 1988; New York, Barron, 1989.

Voices. London, Hippo, 1988; as *Return to Harken House,* New York, Delacorte Press, 1989.
Give Yourself a Fright: Thirteen Tales of the Supernatural. New York, Delacorte Press, 1989.
A Fit of Shivers. London, Gollancz, 1990.
The Shoemaker's Boy. New York, Simon and Schuster, 1991.
A Foot in the Grave, illustrated by Jan Pienkowski. London, Cape, 1989; New York, Viking, 1991.
The Midnight Moropus. New York, Simon and Schuster, 1993.
Hatching Trouble. London, BBC Publications, 1993.
A Creepy Company. London, Gollancz, 1993.

Plays

Winterthing, music by John Sebastian Brown (produced Albany, New York, 1977). New York, Holt Rinehart, 1972; in *Winterthing, and The Mooncusser's Daughter,* 1973.
Winterthing, and The Mooncusser's Daughter, music by John Sebastian Brown. London, Cape, 1973; *The Mooncusser's Daughter* published separately, New York, Viking Press, 1974.
Street, music by John Sebastian Brown, (produced London, 1977). New York, Viking Press, 1978.
Moon Mill (produced London, 1982).

Television Plays: *The Dark Streets of Kimballs Green,* 1976; *The Apple of Trouble,* 1977; *Midnight Is a Place* (serial), from her own story, 1977; *The Rose of Puddle Fratrum,* 1978; *Armitage, Armitage, Fly Away Home,* from her own story, 1978.

Poetry

The Skin Spinners. New York, Viking Press, 1976.

Other

The Kingdom under the Sea and Other Stories (retellings). London, Cape, 1971.
The Way to Write for Children (for adults). London, Elm Tree, 1982; New York, St Martin's Press, 1983.

Translator, *The Angel Inn,* by Comtesse de Ségur. London, Cape, 1976; Owings Mills, Maryland, Stemmer House, 1978.

*

Film Adaptations: *Midnight Is a Place,* 1977; *Died on a Rainy Sunday,* 1986; *The Wolves of Willoughby Chase,* 1989.

Joan Aiken comments:
I first began reading romantic and gothic fiction professionally in the 1950s when I was working for an English publishing firm, Amalgamated Press, which in its various magazines (*Woman's Journal, Argosy, Suspense, Woman & Home*) used a number of writers such as Charlotte Armstrong, Dorothy Eden, Mary Stewart, Mignon G. Eberhart. I became interested in the gothic/suspense form and, encouraged by my agent, Jean LeRoy (who wrote a useful little manual *Sell Them a Story,* in which, among other things, she urged would-be gothic writers to study *Jane Eyre* as a model), I decided to try my hand at the genre. My first attempt, *House of Shadows,* never got finished (that title has been used several times since, though) but my next, *Hit and Run,* was used serially in *Suspense,* and several others appeared serially in *Everywoman.* At this time a children's book of mine had been sold to the American publishers, Doubleday, whose Crime Club editor, Isabelle Taylor, asked if I had any adult fiction. I showed her my serialized stories and she encouraged me to extend them into full-length novels, which were published as *Hate*

Begins at Home, *The Silence of Herondale*, etc. As the gothic market then began to be somewhat saturated I tried my hand at Regency romances, but I still prefer the classic gothic and wish it had not been so over-used. However as this is the case I propose to stick to domestic suspense for my next books.

*   *   *

The very fecundity of her ideas makes Joan Aiken's books difficult to summarize, or indeed to categorize. One of those authors who writes both contemporary gothics and historical romances, Aiken ornaments her conceits with more purely literary skill than many other romance writers. Yet at some point in almost all of her books she seems to skirt, or even fall over, the edge of absurdity. This willingness to take risks, if that is what it is to be called, is one of the most characteristic elements of the Aiken style. For instance, in *Last Movement* Mike Meiklejohn learns the terrible secret about her missing father: following a sex change operation, (s)he is now a prominent Irish soprano. This element of the fantastically improbable, as opposed to the merely unearthly fantastic (forebodings, dreams that foretell the future, haunted houses occur in Aiken's novels), makes Mike laugh when she first hears it; a purely nervous reaction, she claims. But may not the reader, too, laugh? Aiken's fantasies for children are full of this kind of improbability, which is what gives them their air of light-hearted charm. It does not always blend as successfully with the more serious, terrifying, and, sometimes, erotic matter of her adult books.

Aiken's technical virtuosity also shows in her unwillingness to be bound to a simple narrative formula. Several books—*Last Movement*, *The Lightning Tree*,—alternate chapters from different viewpoints. An encounter will be described, perhaps, in a third-person narrative focusing on one character's feelings; then a first-person account shows the episode from a different point of view. In *The Lightning Tree* the story goes back and forth between two sets of characters in different continents whose lives are connected as they gradually approach the moment when their paths will converge and the conflicts that exist among them will be settled. In *Voices in an Empty House*, which is possibly more a straight novel than a romance/gothic, this technique is overlaid with multiple flashbacks that explore the relationships between a man, his ex-wife, her dead first husband, and her son, as the man desperately tries to find his step-son to persuade him to undergo crucial heart surgery.

There is nothing unusual in one of Aiken's characters needing surgery: a strong element in her style is her intense interest in physical illness. From Lucy's heart condition in *The Embroidered Sunset* to Mrs Carteret's frailness and invalidism in *The Five-Minute Marriage*, there is always someone with a serious ailment. This is not mere soap opera. The conditions and consequences of disease play a significant role in the novels. More specifically, many of the ailments involve periods of amnesia. Thomas in *Voices in an Empty House*, Annette in *The Fortune Hunters*, and Caroline in *Hate Begins at Home* are all inconvenienced to some extent and even endangered by their frustrating bouts of amnesia. Scylla, in *The Lightning Tree*, is semi-conscious for long periods; her brother Cal has epilepsy; their cousin by marriage Fanny has spells that she cannot explain to her domineering and brutal husband.

Death itself is omnipresent in her most recent book, *Morningquest*. Pandora's mother dies in the first chapter; her glamorous adoptive family of two parents, two parental surrogates, and seven siblings sees four deaths by the time she has found her feet. *The Lightning Tree* is also an example of Aiken's use of recurrent characters. The benefactor of Fanny's husband is the same Juliana who escaped from the French Revolution by a daring balloon flight in *The Smile of the Stranger*. Juliana herself does not appear in the second book, but some of the other characters from *The Smile of the Stranger* do. Mike Meiklejohn's wooer in *Last Movement* is the ebullient Dr Adnan who had loved and lost Lucy in *The Embroidered Sunset*.

Children bring out a tenderness in Aiken; even a young infant in *Trouble with Product X* can win hearts. But she can also sacrifice them to the exigencies of her plot; two children die in *Hate Begins at Home*. So the threat to a young child and her infant brother keeps nerves taut in *Died on a Rainy Sunday*. Aside from young children, warm family relationships are almost nonexistent. Only peripheral characters are allowed normal families. The heroines are confined to mothers who are neglectful (*The Ribs of Death*), malignant (*The Smile of the Stranger*), or, at best, dead at an early age (*Died on a Rainy Sunday*). Siblings are usually equally hostile, although the twins Scylla and Cal in *The Lightning Tree* are a rare exception.

Another notable facet of Aiken's style is her sense of place: the isle of Dendros in *Last Movement*, the island of Manhattan in *Voices in an Empty House*, India in *The Lightning Tree* are all actual presences in the stories, seeming at times to come alive as characters in their own right.

Her recent book, *The Haunting of Lamb House*, shows Aiken turning to a more experimental mode. Her sense of the mystic is displayed in this tale of three generations (two of them famous) who lived in the same house, and the manuscript that ties them together.

Although Aiken has ambitions beyond the gothic, her own wayward imagination keeps the novels at genre level. Her spiky, independent heroines, capable in their careers, nonetheless fall helplessly in love with the wrong person and only free themselves after bizarre struggles, sometimes to find happiness, sometimes just to find the endurance to continue the struggle (*The Ribs of Death*, like *Morningquest*, has an inconclusive ending). Yet her gripping, sensitive style transcends formulas; her well-rounded characters and strong plots carry the reader with her.

—Susan Branch

AINSWORTH, Harriet.   See CADELL, Elizabeth.

AINSWORTH, Patricia.
Pseudonym for Patricia Nina Bigg. **Nationality:** Australian. **Born:** Adelaide, South Australia, 20 March 1932. **Education:** Technical High School, Adelaide. **Relations:** married Robert Bigg in 1955; two sons. **Career:** secretary, Commonwealth Trading Bank, 1948–51, and G.R. Wills and Company Ltd, 1952–55, both Adelaide. **Address:** 3/2 Lorraine Avenue, Mitcham, South Australia 5062, Australia.

Romance and Historical Publications

Novels (series: Seventeenth-Century England)

Seventeenth-Century England:
    The Flickering Candle. London, Hale, 1968.
    The Candle Rekindled. London, Hale, 1969.
    Steady Burns the Candle. London, Hale, 1970.
The Devil's Hole. London, Hale, 1971.
Portrait in Gold. London, Hale, 1971.
A String of Silver Beads. London, Hale, 1972.
The Bridal Lamp. London, Hale, 1975.
The Enchanted Cup. London, Hale, 1980.

*   *   *

The Australian writer Patricia Ainsworth writes meticulously researched and detailed historical novels set in both England and her native country. She has written eight books to date and is a popular writer with a substantial following of avid fans.

The Flickering Candle, The Candle Rekindled, and Steady Burns the Candle are set in 17th-century England, and feature many of the same characters. These books centre around the relationship between landowners, Frances Faraday and the Earl of Debenham, from the outbreak of Civil War to the reign of Charles II. Some of the characters appearing in this trilogy also feature in The Enchanted Cup, one of the author's later novels. Although the books contain considerable detail about England during this period, Ainsworth seems uncomfortable in her handling of her material. Her characterization is sometimes extremely weak, and plot strands are often left undeveloped. A String of Silver Beads and The Bridal Lamp are also set in England. The former book is set in late 15th-century England, at the time of the Spanish Armada, and focuses on the relationship between Crispin Wynwood and Felice Averil. The author returns to Charles II's reign for her novel The Bridal Lamp. This book is probably the most ambitious of all of Ainsworth's works. It introduces elements of mystery and suspense against a historical background, as the plot revolves around a wife's suspicion that her husband is trying to kill her. It is surprisingly successful and the reader is left wanting more.

Ainsworth's Australian novels are more successful than those with an English historical background. The Devil's Hole is set in Australia during the 1870s, and the author's love of her country is reflected in evocative description of her country's beautiful coast. Portrait in Gold is also set in Australia but this time during the gold rush in Victoria. The author creates a real sense of the fever and tension of the time, and the descriptions of Victoria during this period evoke the place and period well.

While it is obvious that Ainsworth's work is well researched and presented, she sometimes appears to have difficulty in believing her own characters which leads them to behave often in unconvincing ways. Consequently, some of her novels, particularly the earlier ones set in England, feature distressingly weak characters, with unrealistic dialogue—and themes that are not followed through properly.

—P. Campbell

———

AIRLIE, Catherine. See **MacLEOD, Jean S.**

———

ALBANESI, Madame (Effie Adelaide Maria Albanesi). Pseudonym for Effie Henderson. **Other Pseudonym:** Effie Rowlands. **Nationality:** British. **Born:** 1859. **Relations:** married Le Chevalier Carlo Albanesi (died 1926); one daughter. **Died:** 16 October 1936.

ROMANCE AND HISTORICAL PUBLICATIONS

Novels

Margery Daw (published anonymously). London, Stevens, and New York, Munro, 1886.
The Blunder of an Innocent. London, Sands, 1899.
Peter, A Parasite. London, Sands, 1901.
Brave Barbara. New York, Street and Smith, 1901.
Love and Louisa. London, Sands; and Philadelphia, Lippincott, 1902.
Susannah and One Elder. London, Methuen, 1903; as Susannah and One Other, Methuen, and New York, McClure, 1904.

Capricious Caroline. London, Methuen, 1904.
Marian Sax. London, Hurst and Blackett, 1905.
The Brown Eyes of Mary. London, Methuen, 1905.
Sweet William. London, Hodder and Stoughton, 1906.
I Know a Maiden. London, Methuen, 1906.
A Little Brown Mouse. London, Hodder and Stoughton, 1906.
A Young Man from the Country. London, Hurst and Blackett, 1906.
Love-in-a-Mist. London, Hodder and Stoughton, 1907.
The Strongest of All Things. London, Hurst and Blackett, 1907.
Simple Simon. London, Newnes, 1907.
Sister Anne. London, Hodder and Stoughton, 1908.
The Rose of Yesterday. London, Hodder and Stoughton, 1908.
Drusilla's Point of View. London, Hurst and Blackett, 1908.
Pretty Polly Pennington. London, Collins, 1908; as Sweet and Lovely, 1933.
The Forbidden Road. New York, Cupples and Leon, 1908.
The Laughter of Life. New York, Cupples and Leon, 1908.
The Invincible Amelia; or The Polite Adventuress. London, Methuen, 1909.
A Question of Quality. London, Hurst and Blackett, 1909.
Envious Eliza. London, Nash, 1909.
The Marriage of Margaret. London, Pearson, 1909.
The Glad Heart. London, Methuen, 1910.
For Love of Anne Lambert. London, Pearson, 1910.
Maisie's Romance. London, Pearson, 1910.
A Wonder of Love. London, Stanley Paul, 1911.
Poppies in the Corn. London, Hutchinson, 1911.
Heart of His Heart. London, Stanley Paul, 1911.
Olivia Mary. London, Methuen, 1912.
The Beloved Enemy. London, Methuen, 1913.
One of the Crowd. London, Chapman and Hall, 1913.
Cissy. London, Collins, 1913.
The Cap of Youth. London, Hutchinson, 1914.
The Sunlit Hills. London, Hutchinson, 1914.
Hearts and Sweethearts. London, Hutchinson, 1916.
When Michael Came to Town. London, Hutchinson, 1917.
Truant Happiness. London, Ward Lock, 1918.
Diana Falls in Love. London, Ward Lock, 1919.
Tony's Wife. London, Holden and Hardingham, 1919; as Punch and Judy, London, Hardingham, 1919.
Patricia and Life. London, Ward Lock, 1920.
The House That Jane Built. London, Ward Lock, 1921.
Roseanne. London, Collins, 1922.
Truth in a Circle. London, Collins, 1922.
A Bird in a Storm. London, Collins, 1924.
Sally in Her Alley. London, Collins, 1925.
The Shadow Wife. London, Stanley Paul, 1925.
Sally Gets Married. London, Collins, 1927.
The Green Country. London, Ward Lock, 1927.
The Moon Through Glass. London, Collins, 1928.
Claire and Circumstances. London, Collins, 1928; as In Love with Claire, 1932.
Gold in the Dust. London, Ward Lock, 1929.
A Heart for Sale. London, Ward Lock, 1929.
The Clear Stream. London, Ward Lock, 1930.
Loyalty. London, Collins, 1930.
The Courage of Love. London, Ward Lock, 1930.
White Flame. London, Ward Lock, 1930.
Coloured Lights. London, Ward Lock, 1931.
All's Well with the World. London, Ward Lock, 1932.
The Moon of Romance. London, Ward Lock, 1932.
Snow in Summer. London, Ward Lock, 1932.
A Star in the Dark. London, Ward Lock, 1933.
White Branches. London, Ward Lock, 1933.
Through the Mist. London, Ward Lock, 1934.
The Half Open Door. London, Ward Lock, 1934.

An Unframed Portrait. London, Nicholson and Watson, 1935.
As a Man Loves. London, Ward Lock, 1936.
The Hidden Gift. London, Nicholson and Watson, 1936.
A Leaf Turned Down. London, Ward Lock, 1936.
The Little Lady. London, Ward Lock, 1937.
The Love That Lives. London, Mellifont Press, 1937.
The One Who Counted. London, Ward Lock, 1937.

Novels as Effie Rowlands

The Spell of Ursula. Philadelphia, Lippincott, 1894.
The Woman Who Came Between. London, Pearson, 1895; New York, Street and Smith, n.d.
At Great Cost. New York, Bonner, 1895.
Little Kit. New York, Bonner, 1895.
A Faithful Traitor. London, Stevens, and Philadelphia, Lippincott, 1896.
The Fault of One. London, Kegan Paul, and Philadelphia, Lippincott, 1897.
The Kingdom of a Heart. London and New York, Routledge, 1899.
They Laugh That Win. London and New York, Routledge, 1899.
A Woman Scorned. New York, Street and Smith, 1899.
A King and a Coward. New York, Street and Smith, 1899; London, Hodder and Stoughton, 1912.
Little Lady Charles. New York, Street and Smith, 1899; London, Stanley Paul, 1910.
The Heart of Hetta. Chicago, Laird and Lee, 1900.
Husband and Foe. New York, Street and Smith, 1900; London, Hutchinson, 1911.
Beneath a Spell. New York, Street and Smith, 1900; London, Stanley Paul, 1910.
A Charity Girl. New York, Street and Smith, 1900; London, Stanley Paul, 1911.
The Man She Loved. New York, Street and Smith, 1900; London, Ward Lock, 1911.
One Man's Evil. New York, Street and Smith, 1900; London, Newnes, 1910.
For Ever True. New York, Street and Smith, 1904; London, Hodder and Stoughton, 1910.
A Love Almost Lost. London, Henderson, 1905.
Angel of Evil. New York, Street and Smith, 1905.
Her Husband and Her Love. New York, Street and Smith, 1905.
So Like a Man. New York, Street and Smith, 1905.
The Splendid Man. New York, Street and Smith, 1905.
The Wiles of a Siren. New York, Street and Smith, 1906.
The End Crowns All. New York, Street and Smith, 1906; London, Hutchinson, 1910.
A Shadowed Happiness. New York, Street and Smith, 1906; London, Newnes, 1910.
For Love of Sigrid. New York, Street and Smith, 1906.
Love's Greatest Gift. New York, Street and Smith, 1906; as *The White in the Black* (as Madame Albanesi), London, Collins, 1926.
My Lady of Dreadwood. New York, Street and Smith, 1906.
A Wife's Triumph. New York, Street and Smith, 1906.
Pretty Penelope. London, Cassell, 1907.
Her Punishment. London, Hurst and Blackett, 1910.
The Man She Married. London, Stanley Paul, 1910.
After Many Days. London, Newnes, 1910.
Contrary Mary. London, Hodder and Stoughton, 1910.
A Dangerous Woman. London, Ward Lock, 1910.
For Love of Speranza. London, Hodder and Stoughton, 1910.
The Game of Life. London, Ward Lock, 1910.
Her Heart's Longing. London, Hurst and Blackett, 1910.
Her Kingdom. London, Amalgamated Press, 1910.
John Galbraith's Wife. London, Hodder and Stoughton, 1910.
Love for Love. London, Hodder and Stoughton, 1910.

A Loyal Man's Love. London, Newnes, 1910.
The Master of Lynch Towers. London, Hodder and Stoughton, 1910.
The Mistress of the Farm. London, Newnes, 1910.
Bitter Sweet. London, Newnes, 1910.
A Splendid Destiny. London, Stanley Paul, 1910.
Barbara's Love Story. London, Hodder and Stoughton, 1911.
Brave Heart. London, Amalgamated Press, 1911.
Carlton's Wife. London, Ward Lock, 1911.
Dare and Do. London, Stanley Paul, 1911.
False Faith. London, Amalgamated Press, 1911.
For Ever and a Day. London, Amalgamated Press, 1911.
A Girl with a Heart. London, Ward Lock, 1911.
Her Mistake. London, Amalgamated Press, 1911.
Leila Vane's Burden. London, Amalgamated Press, 1911.
A Life's Love. London, Hodder and Stoughton, 1911.
Love's Harvest. London, Amalgamated Press, 1911.
The Madness of Love. London, Hodder and Stoughton, 1911.
The Man at the Gate. London, Amalgamated Press, 1911.
The One Woman. London, Hodder and Stoughton, 1911.
The Power of Love. London, Amalgamated Press, 1911.
Splendid Love. London, Amalgamated Press, 1911.
White Abbey. London, Stanley Paul, 1911.
A Wild Rose. London, Amalgamated Press, 1911.
A Woman Worth Winning. London, Amalgamated Press, 1911.
A Woman's Heart. London, Hodder and Stoughton, 1911.
The Young Wife. London, Hodder and Stoughton, 1911.
Love's Fire. London, Hutchinson, 1911.
The Triumph of Love. London, Pearson, 1911.
On the Wings of Fate. New York, Street and Smith, n.d.; London, Newnes, 1916.
Andrew Leicester's Love. New York, Street and Smith, n.d.
Carla. New York, Street and Smith, n.d.
Change of Heart. New York, Street and Smith, n.d.
False and True. New York, Street and Smith, n.d.
For Love and Honor. New York, Street and Smith, n.d.
The Girl's Kingdom. New York, Street and Smith, n.d.
Interloper. Chicago, Donohue, n.d.
Kinsman's Sin. New York, Street and Smith, n.d.
Love's Cruel Whim. New York, Street and Smith, n.d.
Selina's Love Story. New York, Street and Smith, n.d.
Siren's Heart. New York, Street and Smith, n.d.
Spurned Proposal. New York, Street and Smith, n.d.
Temptation of Mary Barr. New York, Street and Smith, n.d.
Tempted by Love. New York, Street and Smith, n.d.
With Heart So True. New York, Street and Smith, n.d.
Woman Against Her. New York, Street and Smith, n.d.
Woman Against Woman. New York, Street and Smith, n.d.
Woman Scorned. New York, Street and Smith, n.d.
A Golden Dawn. London, Hodder and Stoughton, 1912.
A Heart's Triumph. London, Hodder and Stoughton, 1912; New York, Street and Smith, n.d.
Hester Trefusis. London, Hurst and Blackett, 1912.
The House of Sunshine. London, Stanley Paul, 1912.
In Love's Land. London, Ward Lock, 1912.
A Love Match. London, Amalgamated Press, 1912.
The Love of His Life. London, Stanley Paul, 1912.
The Rose of Life. London, Ward Lock, 1912.
Temptation. London, Newnes, 1912.
To Love and to Cherish. London, Everett, 1912.
The Wooing of Rose. London, Stanley Paul, 1912.
His One Love. London, Hurst and Blackett, 1912.
Lavender's Love Story. London, Hurst and Blackett, 1912.
Love Wins. London, Hurst and Blackett, 1912.
A Modern Witch. London, Hurst and Blackett, 1912.
Beth Mason. London, Hodder and Stoughton, 1913.
Elsie Brant's Romance. London, Cassell, 1913.

Hearts at War. London, Hurst and Blackett, 1913.
The Joy of Life. London, Cassell, 1913.
Lady Patricia's Faith. London, Hodder, and Stoughton, 1913.
Love's Mask. London, Stanley Paul, 1913.
Margaret Dent. London, Cassell, 1913.
Ruth's Romance. London, Hodder and Stoughton, 1913.
Stranger Than Truth. London, Hodder and Stoughton, 1913.
The Surest Bond. London, Cassell, 1913.
Through Weal and Through Woe. London, Ward Lock, 1913.
In Daffodil Time. London, Pearson, 1913.
The Heart of a Woman. London, Pearson, 1913.
Judged by Fate. London, Hurst and Blackett, 1913.
The Hand of Fate. London, Hodder and Stoughton, 1914.
Her Husband. London, Chatto and Windus, 1914.
An Irish Lover. London, Hodder and Stoughton, 1914.
Money or Wife. London, Ward Lock, 1914.
On the High Road. London, Hurst and Blackett, 1914.
Two Waifs. London, Hodder and Stoughton, 1914.
At Her Mercy. London, Pearson, 1914.
The Price Paid. London, Chatto and Windus, 1914.
Prudence Langford's Ordeal. London, Pearson, 1914.
Love's Young Dream. London, Ward Lock, 1914.
Above All Things. London, Newnes, 1915.
Sunset and Dawn. London, Ward Lock, 1915.
The Woman's Fault. London, Hurst and Blackett, 1915.
The Girl Who Was Brave. London, Pearson, 1916.
The Splendid Friend. London, Hutchinson, 1917.
The Heart of Angela Brent. London, Pearson, 1917.
A Strange Love Story. London, Hurst and Blackett, 1919.
John Helsby's Wife. London, Hurst and Blackett, 1920.
Mary Dunbar's Love. London, Pearson, 1921.
Against the World. London, Pearson, 1923.
The Flame of Love. London, Ward Lock, 1923.
The Garland of Youth. London, Ward Lock, 1923.
Young Hearts. London, Ward Lock, 1924.
The Life Line. London, Hodder and Stoughton, 1924.
Real Gold. London, Hodder and Stoughton, 1924.
Out of a Clear Sky. London, Ward Lock, 1925.
The Way of Youth. London, Hodder and Stoughton, 1925.
Brave Love. London, Ward Lock, 1926.
A Bunch of Blue Ribbons. London, Ward Lock, 1926.
Lady Feo's Daughter. London, Hodder and Stoughton, 1926.
The Gates of Happiness. London, Ward Lock, 1927.
A Man from the West. London, Ward Lock, 1927.
Fateful Promise. New York, Street and Smith, n.d.
Her Golden Secret. New York, Street and Smith, n.d.
Hero for Love's Sake. New York, Street and Smith, n.d.
Unhappy Bargain. New York, Street and Smith, n.d.
Fine Feathers. London, Ward Lock, 1928.
Lights and Shadows. London, Ward Lock, 1928.
Spring in the Heart. London, Ward Lock, 1929.
While Faith Endures. London, Ward Lock, 1929.
Coulton's Wife. London, Ward Lock, 1930.
Dorinda's Lovers. London, Wright and Brown, 1930.
The Fighting Spirit. London, Ward Lock, 1930.
Sunlight Beyond. London, Ward Lock, 1930.
Wings of Chance. London, Ward Lock, 1931.
Princess Charming. London, Wright and Brown, 1931.
Green Valleys. London, Wright and Brown, 1932.
The Laughter of Life. London, Ward Lock, 1932; New York, Cupples and Leon, n.d.
A Loyal Defence. London, Ward Lock, 1932.
A Ministering Angel. London, Ward Lock, 1933.
Frances Fights for Herself. London, Ward Lock, 1934.
A School for Hearts. London, Ward Lock, 1934.
A World of Dreams. London, Ward Lock, 1935.

The One Who Paid. London, Ward Lock, 1935.
The Heart Line. London, Ward Lock, 1936.
The Lamp of Friendship. London, Ward Lock, 1936.
Her Father's Wish. London, Ward Lock, 1937.
The Top of the Tree. London, Ward Lock, 1937.

OTHER PUBLICATIONS

Other

Meggie Albanesi. London, Hodder and Stoughton, 1928.

*　　　*　　　*

The upper-class Edwardian's concern for physical comfort and material value is well illustrated by Madame Albanesi's *Temptation* (published under the name Effie Rowlands), in which a young orphaned girl, destitute and starving, is offered a life of ease if she succumbs to the temptation of impersonating a missing heiress, and thus eventually securing for herself marriage to the local squire. The moral, far from suggesting that love brings its own rewards, or that girls who sell their souls risk their lives for material gain will endure a fate worse than death, seems to be the reverse: that ill-gotten gains bring you 'all the luxury of appointment that is so necessary and so very ordinary to the very rich'.

Albanesi's style is marked by lavish use of the exclamation mark, and the repetition of key words: 'Alone in the world! Alone! With only seventeen years of life behind her! She, poor little soul, was alone! Quite-quite alone!' Heroes are sometimes 'stained with shame', a blot on their character which can only be lifted by the true love of a good lady (not woman). During her long career, Albanesi produced over 200 novels, all variations on true-love-with-complications, though none with any marked note of religious, political, or moral quest. There is more than a suggestion that the state of being in love brings in its wake not only mortal happiness but material good fortune too. If a girl's love is true, she will marry the right man, and continue to be rich and happy for the rest of her life. Although many of her titles contain 'Love' —*Love's Harvest, Love for Love, Brave Love, The Love of His Life, The Flame of Love, The Man She Loved*, and so on—there is surprisingly very little kissing. Some of her heroines avoid the kiss by fainting. Others faint anyway: 'She gave a low cry, and stretched out her hands. She reeled forward, struggled a little, and then, catching impotently at a chair as she fell, she sank huddled and unconscious.'

Albanesi would have shared with a publisher's reader of the time a thorough appreciation of the 'eternal importance of love in the financial and popular success of a novel'. However, occasionally she branched out from love. *The Clear Stream*, for example, is a family saga, about Marcella Dolamore and her many children; and *An Irish Lover*, although not strictly a hospital romance, contains some details about nurses in the home (circa 1914), and curious notes about home-nursing methods of those days. For instance, that one important item towards helping save the life of Henry is to keep the sound of passing traffic deadened by having straw placed on the street. The ensuing silence, combined with nurse Rachel's miraculous (though unexplained) nursing power, restores his health.

What is most astonishing about Albanesi is how she managed to produce over 200 novels during her career, at a time when the electric tape-recorder had not yet been invented.

—Rachel Anderson

———

ALBANY, James. See **STIRLING, Jessica.**

———

ALEXANDER, Donna. See **VITEK, Donna.**

ALEXANDER, Kate.
Pseudonym for Tania Armstrong. **Other Pseudonyms:** Tilly Armstrong; Tania Langley. **Nationality:** British. **Born:** Sutton, Surrey, 8 April 1927. **Education:** Sutton West Central School for Girls, Surrey, 1937–41; Wimbledon Commercial School, London, 1941–43. **Career:** secretary, World Health Organization, Geneva, 1956–59, Glenbow Foundation, Calgary, Alberta, 1959–61, British Steel Corporation, London, 1963–85. Chair, Romantic Novelists' Association, 1987–89. **Agent:** Felicity Bryan, 2A North Parade, Banbury Road, Oxford, England. **Address:** 23 Leslie Gardens, Sutton, Surrey SM2 6QU, England.

ROMANCE AND HISTORICAL PUBLICATIONS

Novels

Fields of Battle. London, Macdonald, and New York, St Martin's Press, 1981.
Friends and Enemies. London, Macdonald, 1981; St Martin's Press, 1982.
Paths of Peace. London, Macdonald, 1984.
Bright Tomorrows. London, Macdonald, 1985.
Songs of War. London, Macdonald, 1987.
Great Possessions. London, Century, 1989.
The Shining Country. London, Piatkus, 1991.
The House of Hope. London, Century, 1992.

Novels as Tilly Armstrong

Lightly Like a Flower. London, Collins, 1978.
Come Live with Me. London, Collins, 1979.
Joy Runs High. London, Collins, 1979; New York, Dell, 1980.
A Limited Engagement. London, New English Library, 1980.
Summer Tangle. London, Piatkus, 1983.
Small Town Girl. London, Piatkus, 1984.
Pretty Penny. London, Piatkus, 1985.

Novels as Tania Langley

Dawn, New York, Fawcett, 1980; as *Mademoiselle Madelaine.* London, Corgi, 1981.
London Linnet. London, Severn House, 1985.
Genevra. London, Grafton, 1987.

*

Kate Alexander comments:
My Tilly Armstrong novels are light romantic stories which have all been serialized in *Woman's Weekly.* The Tania Langley books are historical fiction, set in the 19th century. The Kate Alexander novels are longer and more dramatic. I particularly enjoy doing the research required for writing about the past.

* * *

The novels of Kate Alexander are set mainly in the early-20th century. Her 'sagas' are always produced concisely—they do not overwhelm the reader through their length, the enormous list of characters, or the complicated plot. Her books are, nevertheless, full of events and sympathetic characters.
Fields of Battle sets the pattern followed, to a great extent, by Alexander's later books. Set in 1939 Britain, dashing, selfish, aristo-cratic Barney Wainwright is posted to the Surrey village of Barbury where he meets Rilla Gray. He sweeps the innocent and shy Rilla off her feet, seduces her, and Rilla has to marry Barney when she finds out that she is pregnant. This is not an ideal reason to marry, and complications arise as Rilla is not from the same social class as her husband's family. Like other Alexander heroines, underneath her timid exterior Rilla is extremely resourceful and has enormous strength of character. She needs it to face the vicissitudes of her life which involve among other things: the birth and death of her son; her husband's posting to France and subsequent capture by the Nazis; his infidelities and their subsequent estrangement; and her own love for Enk, a Norwegian, and his death at sea.

Alexander does not confine her attention to the fortunes of her heroine. The reader follows Barney to France sharing his escapades; his involvement with other women—especially the glamorous Yvette; his work with the Resistance; and his gradual realization that his relationship with Rilla is the most important thing in his life.

Fields of Battle displays many of the characteristics that are prevalent in other Alexander novels, for example, the war setting, which also appears in *Friends and Enemies* and *Songs of War.* Other titles use the early years of the century for their historical context: *Bright Tomorrows* is set in the 1930s; *Great Possessions* opens in 1921; and *Paths of Peace* spans the 1950s.

The emergence of the heroine as a strong character able to make her own way, taking her own decisions, and very often involving herself in business ventures or social issues, is a common theme. In *Friends and Enemies,* Christine Brookfield, the sheltered daughter of a middle-class family falls in love with a German, Gunther. When war breaks out, Gunther joins the Luftwaffe and Christina becomes a radiographer in the WAAF. It seems as if fate has driven them apart, but during the war Christine revisits Germany and meets Gunther again. He is amazed by how much she has changed: when he first encountered her in England she was just 'pretty and very young'; in Germany, however, he is struck by her 'new seriousness, her shadowed eyes, [and] her air of cool authority'. Lonnie, in *Great Possessions,* is another heroine who comes from a glamorous background but who later establishes herself as something more than just a 'rich kid' when she sets up a housing-cooperative among her own tenants; and Nicola, in *Bright Tomorrows,* meets her future husband Ben when she is 'a slip of a girl . . . sweet, vulnerable and shy', but she ends the novel with a job, a baby, and a husband newly released from prison—not surprisingly 'she had a look of maturity she had never had before'.

Though Alexander's sympathies lie very clearly with her female characters, the men in her books are also interesting. Nearly all possess ambition and drive and are successful in their chosen fields—Guy (*Great Possessions*) is a talented, world famous musician; Nicholas (*The House of Hope*), is the founder of a successful auction house; Gunther (*Friends and Enemies*) is both a talented architect and an outstanding fighter-pilot. They come from mixed backgrounds—Jocelin (*Paths of Peace*) is the son of Sir Fred Tyndall, the owner of Wallenshares Steel Works; and Ben, in contrast, (*Bright Tomorrows*) comes from the backstreets of Jarrow. Alexander's heroes are also usually involved in unsuccessful relationships and are rarely faithful to their partners.

Frequently, Alexander introduces characters who act as a contrast or foil to her main protagonists and whose lives, loves, and relationships interweave with the main plot, adding an extra dimension to the story. Thus, Lucy—shy, retiring and empathetic—is the perfect foil to the extrovert 'gypsy' Lonnie (*Great Possessions*); dashing political Josie contrasts with Nicola (*Bright Tomorrows*); and the worldly but selfish Conrad highlights Luke's sympathetic character (*Songs of War*).

It is the relationship between her characters and the development of their lives that most interests Alexander. Consequently, little time is wasted on long, descriptive passages; the dialogue creates immediacy and relays information. Her readers' sympathies are quickly engaged by the material realism with which Alexander portrays her world. Background events, though providing opportunities for action or the setting for adventures, are not emphasized. The reader is not expected to wade through obtrusive details, though the sense of period is strong and is accurately portrayed.

It is her ability to create believable characters in believable situations that is Alexander's strongest talent, and readers return to her books with anticipation, secure in the knowledge that they will enjoy a satisfactory read—romance but with its feet firmly on the ground.

—Ferelith Hordon

ALLARDYCE, Paula.   See BLACKSTOCK, Charity.

ALLEN, Barbara.   See STUART, Vivian.

ALLEN, Charlotte Vale.
Pseudonyms: Katherine Marlowe, Claire Vincent. **Nationality:** Canadian. **Born:** Toronto, Ontario, 19 January 1941. **Education:** Harbord Collegiate and Northview Heights Collegiate, both Toronto. **Relations:** married 1) Walter Allen in 1970 (divorced 1976), one daughter; 2) Barrie Baldaro in 1980 (divorced 1982). **Career:** actress and singer, London, England, 1961–64, Toronto, 1964–66, and in USA, 1966–70. **Agent:** Harold Ober Associates Inc, 425 Madison Avenue, New York, New York 10017, USA; or, David Higham Associates Ltd, 5–8 Lower John Street, London W1R 4HA, England. **Address:** 144 Rowayton Woods Drive, Norwalk, Connecticut 06854, USA.

ROMANCE AND HISTORICAL PUBLICATIONS

Novels

Hidden Meanings. New York, Warner, 1976; London, New English Library, 1983.
Love Life. New York, Delacorte Press, 1976; London, New English Library, 1981.
Sweeter Music. New York, Warner, 1976.
Another Kind of Magic. New York, Warner, 1977.
Becoming. New York, Warner, 1977.
Gentle Stranger. New York, Warner, 1977; London, Severn House, 1990.
Mixed Emotions. New York, Warner, 1977; London, Severn House, 1991.
Running Away. New York, New American Library, 1977; London, Magnum, 1979.
Believing in Giants (as Claire Vincent). New York, New American Library, 1978; (as Charlotte Vale Allen) London, New English Library, 1983; as *Memories,* New York, Berkley, 1983.
Gifts of Love. New York, New American Library, 1978; London, Magnum, 1980.
Julia's Sister. New York, Warner, 1978; London, New English Library, 1985.
Meet Me in Time. New York, Warner, 1978; London, New English Library, 1980.
Acts of Kindness. New York, New American Library, 1979; London, New English Library, 1982.

Moments of Meaning. New York, New American Library, 1979; London, New English Library, 1982.
Times of Triumph. New York, New American Library, 1979; London, New English Library, 1980.
Promises. New York, Dutton, and London, Hutchinson, 1980.
The Marmalade Man. New York, Dutton, 1981; as *Destinies,* London, Hutchinson, 1981.
Perfect Fools. London, New English Library, and New York, New American Library, 1981.
Intimate Friends. New York, Dutton, and London, Hutchinson, 1983.
Pieces of Dreams. London, Hutchinson, 1984; Boston, Hall, 1985.
Matters of the Heart. London, Hutchinson, and New York, Berkley, 1985.
Time/Steps. New York, Atheneum, 1986; London, Weidenfeld and Nicolson, 1987.
Illusions. New York, Atheneum, and London, Weidenfeld and Nicolson, 1987.
Dream Train. New York, Atheneum, 1988; London, Weidenfeld and Nicolson, 1989.
Night Magic. New York, Atheneum, 1989; London, Severn House, 1991.
Painted Lives. New York, Atheneum, 1990; London, Severn House, 1992.
Leftover Dreams. London, Severn House, and New York, Doubleday, 1992.
Dreaming In Color. New York, Doubleday, and London, Secker and Warburg, 1993.

Novels as Katherine Marlowe

Heart's Desires. New York, Fine, 1991; London, Piatkus, 1992.
Secrets. London, Severn House, and New York, Fine, 1992.
Nightfall. London, Severn House, and New York, Tor, 1993.

OTHER PUBLICATIONS

Other

Daddy's Girl (autobiography). New York, Wyndham, 1980; London, New English Library, 1983.

*   *   *

Charlotte Vale Allen's stories are about women: women hard-done-by; women who rise above the odds to conquer all hardship, earn their dream, and find happiness. They are usually faced with far greater obstacles than they deserve, yet their guile, beauty, talent, and intelligence carry them to not only find happiness but through hardship to find themselves. Allen's women are not portrayed as cardboard-cut-out beauties, breathless and lithe, but as headstrong, thinking women who carve a niche for themselves. Romance, love, sex, and men are all central to Allen's books, however, the heroine's story is of more importance than the man with whom she cohabits.

Allen's women are not always good but their evil usually stems from isolation, a hard life, or a bad marriage. Children play a central part in her stories, they are woven into every woman's life and work. The protagonists are real heroines, who work, play, and struggle through careers, to be independent of their partners both financially and emotionally. The female characters are not necessarily feminists, there is too much traditional romance for this to be the case, however, neither are they easily swayed by men, despite their total commitment to their loved ones.

Allen is not reticent in presenting the horror of life. Her women are raped, victims of car accidents, abducted and held hostage; they may be alcoholics or may live through highly traumatic childhood experiences. The recurrent theme is that they conquer and win against all the odds. Allen's painful autobiography *Daddy's Girl* looks at her horrific childhood experience as the victim of her father's sexual abuse; this gives some insight into Allen's characterization of pain, hardship, and horror.

Leftover Dreams is a working-class saga that spans 20 years and covers the lives of three generations of women. Set in the working-class districts of Toronto, it revolves around Maggie Parker who is a hard-done-by woman. Pregnant at 18, she is the 20-year-old mother of two girls when her wayward but handsome husband, Johnny Parker, leaves her. Her response to the situation is to become bitter and work hard to provide for her children, giving them very little of herself. Maggie's mother, Ellen, becomes her granddaughters' confidante, while Maggie moves from one disaster to the next distancing herself through her fear of yet another rejection. Consequently her daughters grow up hating her and Maggie is isolated and rejected. She finds solace in selling her body to the highest bidder and prostitution meets her dual needs of money and sexual pleasure without commitment. This seems a very bitter ending for a heroine, but one which follows through with the psychology of the character. Ellen, Maggie's widowed mother, finds true happiness with her boss, Bob Welford. He is rich, handsome and successful and this forms a fitting and traditional ending for a true and kind romantic. Maggie's daughter, Faye, a kind, gentle, caring girl, dies after a botched abortion that she has after being raped. Louise, Maggie's fiery and rebellious daughter, finds comfort in the arms of her dark and handsome English teacher, Daniel Craven.

As much as *Leftover Dreams* is a saga that belongs to working-class women, *Illusions* is a story of upper-class women. Marietta, one of the main characters in *Illusions*, is a romantic novelist. Divorced from her rich English husband, she brings up her daughter, Stanleigh, in North America. Marietta is beautiful, successful, and held in awe by everyone around her. Although Stanleigh is beautiful, a talented writer, and an illustrator of children's books, she grows up in her mother's shadow and is terribly insecure. She finds true happiness with her husband and son but they are both killed in a car accident and she marries badly on the rebound, seduced not by her new husband but by his lonely son who later dies. She embarks on a journey to find her father while still grieving for her stepson and meets Daniel Goddard, a rich businessman who is getting over the suicide of his wife. They have an affair, which means very little to Stanleigh but means a lot to Daniel who is obsessed with her. He abducts her and holds her prisoner in the hope that she might fall in love with him. Stanleigh is saved by Daniel's loving daughter, Lane, who is a fan of her books. She forgives Daniel and he seeks help. Stanleigh 'finds' a daughter in Lane and love with her long suffering agent Miles who has always loved her.

Women keep battling against the odds but win in the end. This is the classic Cinderella story told with more horror and much more sexual detail. The heroes are not so important in Allen's stories, they, in fact, embroider the tale. In *Times of Triumph*, Leonie is left orphaned in Africa after her father's death. She is sent to England to her cousin, Augusta, and falls in love with Augusta's journalist husband, Gray. While he is on an assignment in France, Augusta, aware of her husband's liaison with Leonie, sends her to America. Leonie has a baby, and then sets up her own restaurant, which becomes a huge success. She opens a chain of restaurants and becomes the toast of New York, which is how Gray eventually finds her. Their love has not died but Gray remains in the background of Leonie's life. Leonie is the triumphant one, Gray the prop to her story.

This theme recurs in *Meet Me in Time*, another family saga. In this novel Lisette Burgess is the heroine and her happy marriage to Ray is inconsequential, providing a focus for her life and a father for her children. Lisette is the powerful one, it is her life that impacts on all those around. Her husband dies of grief after her tragic death (she

dies saving a child from a car collision) and her children career through their lives experimenting with sex, drugs, and alcohol. They overcome their addictions and find strength through their own talents, and through true love.

Allen is a true weaver of stories. She takes her personal experience as a woman and tells each tale from this point of view. Eventually all her heroines triumph over their hardships and find themselves, and love and success. Their success is what makes Allen's stories—the romance, the sex, and the men are peripheral to a much greater end.

—Charmaine Moldrich

ALLEN, Hervey.
Nationality: American. **Born:** William Hervey Allen Jr, Pittsburgh, Pennsylvania, 8 December 1889. **Education:** Shady Side Academy; United States Naval Academy, Annapolis, Maryland, 1910–11; University of Pittsburgh, B.Sc. 1915 (Phi Beta Kappa); Harvard University, Cambridge, Massachusetts, 1920–22. **Military Service:** served in the Pennsylvania National Guard, 1916, and in the United States infantry in France, 1917–18; served with the War Manpower Commission during World War II. **Relations:** married Ann Hyde Andrew in 1927; two daughters and one son. **Career:** worked for Bell Telephone Company, 1915; English teacher, Porter Military Academy, Charleston, South Carolina, 1920–21, and Charleston High School, 1922–24; lecturer, Columbia University, New York, 1924–25, Vassar College, Poughkeepsie, New York, 1926–27, and Bread Loaf School, Vermont, 1930–31. Staff member, *Saturday Review,* New York. Member of the Board of Governors, St John's College, Annapolis; trustee, University of Miami. **Recipient:** Litt.D.: University of Pittsburgh, 1934; Washington and Jefferson College, Washington, Pennsylvania, 1947. **Member:** American Academy, and Royal Society of Arts. **Died:** 28 December 1949.

ROMANCE AND HISTORICAL PUBLICATIONS

Novels

Anthony Adverse. New York, Farrar and Rinehart, 1933; London, Gollancz, 1934.
Action at Aquila. New York, Farrar and Rinehart, and London, Gollancz, 1938.
The City in the Dawn. New York, Rinehart, 1950.
　The Forest and the Fort. New York, Farrar and Rinehart, and London, Heinemann, 1943.
　Bedford Village. New York, Farrar and Rinehart, and London, Heinemann, 1944.
　Toward the Morning. New York, Rinehart, 1948.

Short Stories

It Was Like This: Two Stories of the Great War. New York, Farrar and Rinehart, 1940.

OTHER PUBLICATIONS

Poetry

Ballads of the Border. Privately printed, 1916.
Wampum and Old Gold. New Haven, Connecticut, Yale University Press, 1921.

Carolina Chansons: Legends of the Low Country, with DuBose Heyward. New York, Macmillan, 1922.
The Bride of Huitzil: An Aztec Legend. New York, Drake, 1922.
Christmas Epithalamium. Privately printed, 1923.
The Blindman: A Ballad of Nogant L'Aartaud. New Haven, Connecticut, Yale University Press, 1923.
Earth Moods and Other Poems. New York, Harper, 1925.
New Legends. New York, Farrar and Rinehart, 1929.
Sarah Simon, Character Atlantean. New York, Doubleday, 1929.
Songs for Annette. New York, Rudge, 1929.

Other

Israfel: The Life and Times of Edgar Allan Poe. New York, Doran, 1926; London, Gollancz, 1935.
Toward the Flame: A War Diary. New York, Doran, 1926; London, Gollancz, 1934.
DuBose Heyward: A Critical and Biographical Sketch. New York, Doran, 1927.

Editor, with others, *Year Book of the Poetry Society of South Carolina 1921–23.* Privately printed, 3 vols, 1921–23.
Editor, with Thomas Ollive Mabbott, *Poe's Brother: The Poems of William Henry Leonard Poe.* New York, Doran, 1926.
Editor, *The Works of Edgar Allan Poe.* New York, Black, 1927.
Editor, *The Best Known Works of Edgar Allan Poe.* New York, Blue Ribbon, 1931.

*

Manuscript Collection: Hillman Library, University of Pittsburgh, Pennsylvania.

*   *   *

Before the sprawling historical novel had become a bestselling commonplace, Hervey Allen's *Anthony Adverse* seemed a revolutionary creation. One huge work, it contained three volumes: each volume made up of three books, and, after all, an epilogue: it was of a breadth unheard of since the palmy days of the Victorian three-decker, and all to tell the story of a single adventurous life.

Allen was a storyteller who assumed the indulgence as well as the interest of a patient audience. He digressed to offer tendentious opinions, to discourse upon the scenery of Europe, Africa, and the New World, to say nothing of the open seas; to wax lyrical, toss in snippets of poems, epitaphs culled from tombstones, proverbs, and trivia of all sorts. The continuity of his story is tenuous at best, and the hero's character does not so much develop as alter with chameleon rapidity from one episode to the next. From the opening chapters in which Anthony's ill-starred parents Maria and Denis have their brief, glorious affair and provoke the undying vengeance of Maria's cuckolded husband Don Luis, to the end of the marathon story, Anthony careers from destitution to enormous wealth and back again. He has at least three great loves in his life, as well as numerous passing interludes; he becomes embroiled in several hideous tragedies, in the loathsome slave trade, in the Napoleonic campaigns, in financial dealings with the Rothschilds, in a lazar house-cum-prison, and in this fashion, practically ad infinitum, the story of the romantic foundling plunges and lurches along, from one unlikely coincidence to the next.

Into this one fictional lifetime are crammed enough events and exploits to furnish several novels of ordinary length with plot and to spare. There is a certain fascination in the long-drawn-out odyssey, but throughout the reader is uneasily conscious of prodigious stage management. If ever a novel demanded of its readers 'a willing suspension of disbelief', that novel was *Anthony Adverse*. Once com-

mitted to this niagara of improbability, one is swept into a world where no loose ends are ever left to dangle, where parted lovers always meet again, where revenge never falters or fails, and where nemesis stalks the hero as the crocodile stalked Captain Hook. There are a few very affecting scenes, as well as a great deal of material that is totally unnecessary; in that respect, at least, the novel closely resembles life.

Allen went on to write other novels, planning indeed to conjure up a panoramic picture of colonial America, but died before completing the gigantic task. His name was made by and will be remembered for his tremendously successful fictional offspring, Anthony, the nameless waif born under 'adverse conditions' to embody a life of epic adventure.

—Joan McGrath

———

AMES, Jennifer.   See **GREIG, Maysie.**

———

ANAND, Valerie.
Pseudonym for Fiona Buckley. **Nationality:** British. **Born:** London, 6 July 1937. **Education:** convents and local public school. **Relations:** married Dalip Singh Anand in 1970. **Career:** secretary, 1956–59; secretary, then sub-editor, *Quarry Managers' Journal,* London; assistant public relations officer, Institute of British Launderers, London, 1960–63; reporter on office equipment, *Accountancy,* London, 1963–66; reporter and feature writer, *Index to Office Equipment,* Croydon, Surrey, 1966–68; public relations officer, and feature writer, E.J. Poole Associates, London, 1968–71; assistant editor, 1971–72, then editor, 1972–75, Heale and Son Ltd, London. Since 1975, editor, Matthew Hall PLC, London. **Member:** British Association of Industrial Editors. **Address:** c/o Headline Book Publishing, Headline House, 79 Great Titchfield Street, London W1P 7FN, England.

ROMANCE AND HISTORICAL PUBLICATIONS

Novels (series: Bridges Over Time; Wessex Trilogy)

Wessex Trilogy:
    Gildenford. New York, Scribner, 1977; London, Chatto and Windus, 1978.
    The Norman Pretender. New York, Scribner, 1979; London, Chatto and Windus, 1982.
    The Disputed Crown. New York, Scribner, 1979; London, Chatto and Windus, 1982.
Crown of Roses. London, Headline, and New York, St Martin's Press, 1989.
King of the Wood. London, Headline, 1988; New York, St Martin's Press, 1989.
Women of Ashdon. London, Headline, 1992.
West of Sunset. London, Hodder and Stoughton, 1992.
Bridges Over Time:
    1. *The Proud Villeins.* London, Headline, 1990.
    2. *The Ruthless Yeoman.* London, Headline, 1991; New York, St Martin's Press, 1993.

OTHER PUBLICATIONS

Novel

To a Native Shore: A Novel of India. New York, Scribner, 1984; London, Piatkus, 1985.

*   *   *

Valerie Anand's substantial, well-researched historical novels present a convincing picture of Saxon, Norman, and Plantagenet England. The backgrounds of her novels may be more familiar to English than to American readers, but such aids as family trees, and lists of characters and their relationships provide welcome support to those with limited knowledge of the period.

The 'Wessex Trilogy' covers the period from the kingship of Cnut's son, Harold Harefoot, to the final triumph of William the Conqueror. Anand's methods of involving the reader in the life of the period include rapid cuts between historical fact, and the entrancing lives of fictional characters, who may interact, to a limited extent, with real actors on the historical stage. Starting with *Gildenford*, we follow house carle, later thane, then monk Brand Woodcutter to his peaceful retirement at Ely. Another way that Anand maintains reader interest is to start with a young character—Brand in *Gildenford*, Petronell in *Crown of Roses*.

Brand is one of Anand's most interesting characters, having the characteristics of a modern man. Brought as a youth into the household of Earl Godwin of Wessex, a place that would normally be far above his social station, Brand rises in stature because he is reliable, hardworking, honest, and above all, loyal. He is befriended by Godwin's nephew, Beorn, and Godwin's second son, Harold (later to be, for so short a time, King of England). However, Brand eventually finds himself in a modern dilemma—he realizes that he is in a position in which whatever he does, he must betray a trust. The person he chooses to betray is Godwin, who is also the person he most admires. This betrayal means he must leave for Normandy, where he becomes liegeman to William of Normandy. In *The Disputed Crown*, he must abandon his allegiance to William and fight with Anglo-Saxon rebels against the Normans, to make good his renewed promise to defend the rights of Godwin's family. Only towards the end of his life does he again acknowledge William, to prevent his illegitimate daughter, Wulfhild, from being dispossessed of the small holding she received from her Norman husband.

King of the Wood follows the fate of Wulfhild's family further, as her uncontrollable daughter, Sybil, marries Ralph, a follower and one-time lover of William Rufus. Ralph is torn by some of the same conflicts that touched Brand, but he never becomes as much a fully-realized character, much less the voice of compassion and common sense that Brand grows to be. Given the thaneship of a tiny village in the New Forest, Ralph feels he must support his people through the sad years of higher taxes and smaller harvests that precede the turn of the century. Both he and the villagers have been brought up in the Old Religion that preceded Christianity. It seems that as King of the Wood, he must offer himself as sacrifice to save his people. But—as William Rufus's scheming brother Henry points out—the troubles affect more than one village, they harm the whole country. Surely it is the King of England, not the King of the Wood, who should be the sacrifice. We watch as, above the level of peasants hungry for their daily bread, the nobles and William of Normandy's three sons play a game of power and greed. Despite his gratitude to William Rufus, Ralph finds his allegiance to Sybil and the villagers is stronger. And despite his betrayal of William Rufus, Henry is aware of their kinship.

In this world of force and conflict, women, like thralls and animals, are pawns—in theory. In practice, strong-minded women like Edith of Scotland, or William of Normandy's wife, Matilda, have roles of their own, based on the weapons of the weak—plots and poison. In the field of war and politics, men take priority, and Anand draws striking, distinctive male characters, both real and fictional. It is difficult to speak of the accuracy with which she recreates historical figures—the true nature of William Rufus or of Hereward the Wake can never be known with much assurance. But Anand's

William Rufus, the brave soldier who is afraid of the dark and of the finality of death, is in the end a touching and convincing character as he goes to a sacrificial death at the hands of a man he loved. His brother Henry, who can be kind in some ways, yet is willing to dispose of anyone who stands between him and the throne, is the eternal dispossessed younger brother. Richard III, in *Crown of Roses*, carries the weight of many theories about this controversial monarch. Anand presents him as noble but curiously short-sighted about his enemies. He is set off by the wily Bishop John Alcock, who serves the Crown and the York family in many ways. Ultimately, he realizes that he too has been trapped by the York loyalists who are plotting against the victorious Henry Tudor.

At home both in her descriptions of the English countryside, for which she clearly has considerable fondness, and the fields of Normandy and other parts of France, where some action is set, Anand excels in scenes of bloodshed and violence. Her artfulness lies in avoiding the two main downfalls of the historical novelist: creating characters who are really just 20th-century people in fancy dress, and creating characters who are totally alien to modern readers. Although she skirts the first danger when she makes her characters too aware of their own emotions (William Rufus looks to the priest who first molested him as the cause of his homosexuality), she is usually able to make even the most alien emotions acceptable without romanticizing the period. Petronell, in *Crown of Roses*, is married off at 14 to a sour and unattractive man of 50. It is her duty to obey, and she does, enduring his abusive lovemaking until he beats her for failing to produce an heir to his lands. Only then does she follow her own inclination and allow herself to be seduced by his young and attractive nephew. Wulfhild never looks for a love match, but accepts her Norman lord, Simon Inconnu, to protect the peasants who look to her for support.

The work of deromanticizing the historical novel continues in her new series, 'Bridges over Time', starting with *The Proud Villeins*. She returns to the massacre of Norman knights at Gildenford, the focus of her first novel, this time following one of the few Norman knights who survived the initial slaughter, only to be sold into thralldom. The efforts of this knight and his descendants to regain their freedom covers the period from before the Conquest to the granting of the Magna Carta. The second book, *The Ruthless Yeoman*, follows the fortunes of this family until 1399, following the Peasants' Revolt. Although each generation is not covered in detail, there is still not enough room for extended character development in the vignettes that describe the life of the thralls under the victorious Normans. The descendants of Ivon de Clairpont finally achieve yeoman status, although they must murder to do it, but life is still difficult and dangerous. It is not clear whether Anand can invest further social climbing in this series with the same interest that she has stimulated thus far.

The historical record lends focus to Anand's plotting, as actual coronations, battles, births, and deaths must be worked into the chronicle of the average Saxon, Dane, or Norman—people who will eventually become English. Important in the novels is the gradual change in at least some of the Normans as they realize their Saxon underlings are not the same as the oppressed Norman peasants. The slow, gradual civilizing influence progresses in both directions as the Normans bring their more sophisticated tastes and skills to bear on the fierce independence of the English, and the Normans realize that their underlings too understand freedom.

Anand has also written an excellent contemporary romance, *To a Native Shore*, in which Melanie, an English woman married to a Sikh doctor, tries to decide in which country her future really lies.

—Susan Branch

ANDREWS, Lucilla (Mathew).

Pseudonyms: Lucilla Crichton; Diana Gordon; Joanna Marcus.
Nationality: British. **Born:** Suez, Egypt. **Education:** trained as a
nurse at St Thomas's Hospital, London, during World War II.
Relations: married a doctor in 1947 (died 1954); one daughter.
Lives in Edinburgh. **Address:** c/o Heinemann, Michelin House, 81
Fulham Road, London SW3 6RB, England.

ROMANCE AND HISTORICAL PUBLICATIONS

Novels (series: St Martha's Hospital)

The Print Petticoat. London, Harrap, 1954.
The Secret Armour. London, Harrap, 1955.
The Quiet Wards. London, Harrap, 1956.
The First Year. London, Harrap, 1957.
A Hospital Summer. London, Harrap, 1958.
The Wife of the Red Haired Man. London, Transworld, 1959.
My Friend the Professor. London, Harrap, 1960.
Nurse Errant. London, Harrap, 1961.
The Young Doctors Downstairs. London, Harrap, 1963.
Flowers for the Doctor. London, Harrap, 1963.
The New Sister Theatre. London, Harrap, 1964.
The Light in the Ward. London, Harrap, 1965.
A House for Sister Mary. London, Harrap, 1966.
Hospital Circles. London, Harrap, 1967.
A Few Days in Endel (as Diana Gordon). London, Corgi, 1968.
Highland Interlude. London, Harrap, 1968.
The Healing Time. London, Harrap, 1969.
The Edinburgh Excursion. London, Harrap, 1970.
Ring o' Roses. London, Harrap, 1972.
Silent Song. London, Harrap, 1973.
In Storm and in Calm. London, Harrap, 1975.
Busmans Holiday. London, Corgi,1977.
The Crystal Gull. London, Harrap, 1978.
One Night in London (St Martha's). London, Heinemann, 1979.
Marsh Blood (as Joanna Marcus). London, Hutchinson, 1980.
A Weekend in the Garden (St Martha's). London, Heinemann, 1981.
In an Edinburgh Drawing Room (St Martha's). London, Heine-
    mann, 1983.
After a Famous Victory. London, Heinemann, 1984.
The Lights of London. London, Heinemann, 1985.
The Phoenix Syndrome. London, Heinemann, 1987.
Front Line. London, Heinemann, 1990.

OTHER PUBLICATIONS

Other

*No Time for Romance: An Autobiographical Account of a Few Mo-
    ments in British and Personal History.* London, Harrap, 1977.

*   *   *

Lucilla Andrews writes her hospital romances from a personal
knowledge of the medical profession and the protocol surrounding
hospital life during World War II and the post-war period. Her use
of technical jargon, and her familiarity with hospital procedure are
based on her own experiences as a nurse in London during World
War II. Her novels are seen through the eyes of a nurse, whether it be
from the angle of a qualified practitioner, or as a trainee.

Her war-time novels have a strong emotional impact on the
reader, especially the books set during the Blitz (the night-time

bombing of Britain by Germany, 1940–41). The *joie de vivre* and
camaraderie that are experienced by everyone, irrespective of class
or background, result from war-time experience and are described
by Andrews in minute detail. Time is a precious commodity, and life
is to be lived to the full. Death is no stranger to the characters in
these books, and is treated with resignation and with the typical, but
sometimes irritating, British 'stiff upper lip'. The anger and frustration at the maiming and unnecessary waste of life, especially youth,
is evident in most of the author's books (this is also seen in
Andrews's treatment of drink and drive accidents).

Relationships attain an urgency and honesty not felt in her post-
war books. In *One Night in London*, Carter, a first-year-student
nurse, and Jason, a junior doctor, cement an unspoken mutual attraction, after sharing a series of traumatic experiences which culminate
in the death of a colleague in a bombing raid. However, in most of
Andrews's books the ethical and moral dilemma of conducting a romance with a colleague is apparent. During Andrews's time as a
practitioner medical etiquette dictated that liaisons between hospital
staff, at any level, were prohibited. The struggle between doing ones
duty and following natural romantic inclinations, is mentioned time
and time again.

In *The Phoenix Syndrome*, a staff nurse falls in love with an
American journalist who is based in London. His job is to go to the
front line of the war zone. Tension is created and sustained because
neither lover knows whether the other will be alive at the end of the
day. Both characters have to carry on with their respective important
professions as though they are living under normal conditions.
Andrews's patriotism emerges most strongly in the resilience of her
characters. Both hero and heroine must do their bit for England to
the best of their abilities: romance is only a secondary consideration.
Love might only be a fleeting sensation which must be taken advantage of where ever possible.

Andrews's post-war novels are lighter in tone, often depicting the
fun lifestyle of a good looking, but hard working, nurse after the
war. The emphasis of these books is much more on romance, although the seriousness of the heroine's work is depicted, often in
shocking detail. Andrews often uses Scotland as a setting. Many of
her novels are set in Edinburgh, or on remote North Sea islands. One
such novel is *In Storm and in Calm* in which the heroine goes to a
small, but extremely well-equipped hospital in the Shetlands, and
falls in love.

Andrews has brought the hospital romance alive to a new audience. Her descriptive, well written novels make it easy for the lay
person to understand the day-to-day working of a hospital. Her obvious respect for her profession make her books extremely readable
and well loved by her fans.

—Naya Quin

––––––––

ANNANDALE, Barbara.   See BARCLAY, Tessa.

––––––––

ANTHONY, Evelyn.

Pseudonym for Evelyn Ward-Thomas. **Nationality:** British. **Born:**
Evelyn Bridget Patricia Stephens, London, 3 July 1928. **Education:**
Convent of the Sacred Heart, Roehampton, to 1944, and then privately educated. **Relations:** married Michael Ward-Thomas in
1955; two daughters and four sons. **Recipient:** *Yorkshire Post*
award, 1973. Freeman, City of London, 1987; Liveryman, Needle-
makers' Company, London, 1987. **Agent:** A.P. Watt Ltd, 20 John
Street, London WC1N 2DL, England. **Address:** Horham Hall,
Thaxted, Essex, England.

ROMANCE AND HISTORICAL PUBLICATIONS

Novels (series: Davina Graham)

Imperial Highness. London, Museum Press, 1953; as *Rebel Princess*, New York, Crowell, 1953.
Curse Not the King. London, Museum Press, 1954; as *Royal Intrigue*, New York, Crowell, 1954.
Far Flies the Eagle. New York, Crowell, 1955; as *Far Fly the Eagles*, London, Coronet Books, 1989.
Anne Boleyn. London, Museum Press, and New York, Crowell, 1957.
Victoria and Albert. London, Crowell, 1958; as *Victoria*, London, Museum Press, 1959.
Elizabeth. London, Museum Press, 1960: as *All the Queen's Men*, New York, Crowell, 1960.
Charles the King. London, Museum Press, and New York, Doubleday, 1961.
Clandara. London, Hurst and Blackett, and New York, Doubleday, 1963.
The Heiress. London, Hurst and Blackett; as *The French Bride*, New York, Doubleday, 1964; London, Arrow, 1966.
Valentina. London, Hurst and Blackett, and New York, Doubleday, 1966.
The Rendezvous. London, Hutchinson, 1967; New York, Coward McCann, 1968.
Anne of Austria. London, Hurst and Blackett, 1968; as *The Cardinal and the Queen*, New York, Coward McCann, 1968.
The Legend. London, Hutchinson, and New York, Coward McCann, 1969.
The Assassin. London, Hutchinson, and New York, Coward McCann, 1970.
The Tamarind Seed. London, Hutchinson, and New York, Coward McCann, 1971.
The Poellenberg Inheritance. London, Hutchinson, and New York, Coward McCann, 1972.
The Occupying Power. London, Hutchinson, 1973; as *Stranger at the Gates*, New York, Coward McCann, 1973.
The Malaspiga Exit. London, Hutchinson, 1974; as *Mission to Malaspiga*, New York, Coward McCann, 1974.
The Persian Ransom. London, Hutchinson, 1975; as *The Persian Price*, New York, Coward McCann, 1975.
The Silver Falcon. London, Hutchinson, and New York, Coward McCann, 1977.
The Return. London, Hutchinson, and New York, Coward McCann, 1978.
The Grave of Truth. London, Hutchinson; as *The Janus Imperative*, New York, Coward McCann, 1980.
The Defector (Graham). London, Hutchinson, 1980; New York, Coward McCann, 1981.
The Avenue of the Dead (Graham). London, Hutchinson, 1981; New York, Coward McCann, 1982.
Albatross (Graham). London, Hutchinson, 1982; New York, Putnam, 1983.
The Company of Saints (Graham). London, Hutchinson, 1983; New York, Putnam, 1984.
Voices on the Wind. London, Hutchinson, and New York, Putnam, 1985.
No Enemy But Time. London, Hutchinson, 1987; as *A Place to Hide*, New York, Putnam, 1987.
The House of Vandekar. London, Hutchinson, and New York, Putnam, 1988.
The Scarlet Thread. London, Century Hutchinson, 1989; New York, HarperCollins, 1990.
The Relic. London, Hutchinson, and New York, HarperCollins, 1991.
The Doll's House. London, Bantam, and New York, HarperCollins, 1992.
Exposure. London, Bantam Press, 1993.

*

Film Adaptation: *The Tamarind Seed*, 1974.

*   *   *

Evelyn Anthony's historical writing is stamped with an immaculate individuality which has won her awards and worldwide translation. Even in her thrillers the historical element is always strong, while a romantic theme significantly binds the plot.

History is rarely out of fashion but its presentation changes from one decade to the next, veering between biography, narrative, or social comment. There has, for example, been much argument about Elizabeth I's kindness to Mary Stuart. Anthony, in *Elizabeth*, makes a powerful case when justifying the Scottish queen's unwavering belief in her own right of succession to the English throne. In Catholic eyes Elizabeth was illegitimate and thus Mary had a moral right to the throne, filling Elizabeth with doubt about the legitimacy of her own claim to the sovereignty of England. Anthony enters both minds, displaying a remarkable gift for making her characters become real; they often appear as painfully human. We see them warts and all, and warts are ugly. She can also crystallize the perceptions of a period, a rare gift, startling the reader with its clarity.

In both *The Grave of Truth* and *The Tamarind Seed* we enter and shudder at the corrupt and violent times of Hitler. In *Imperial Highness*, Catherine the Great both attracts and repels—her evil son even more so as we see him through the eyes of himself and his peers. More topically in *No Enemy But Time* the author deals with the painful question of the Irish divide, leaving us shaking with frustration at the blindness of characters who cannot bridge the gap in their attitudes, a gap so obviously reconciliable to the onlooker.

When public taste for court drama waned Anthony began to specialize in thrillers. In these she examines the nature of decision-making, psychological reactions to danger and moral dilemmas posed by social and civil conflict, in conditioning of thought and the synthesizing and fracturing of attitudes. She is especially interested in World War II, the time of her own youth. In the 'Davina Graham' spy series she draws on her knowledge of a tortured USSR, sculpting a vivid image of the Cold War from various less well-known stances. Readers are invited to reassess their own attitudes—prejudices even—as she anatomizes minds under different influences and pressures: of people under siege; assassins; fanatics; rationalists; believers; victims of pogroms or unjust imprisonment; perpetrators of vile crimes; carers forced into invidious, inevitable choices; guardians of precious relics; power-brokers corrupted or faced with irreconcilable conflict; the guilty punished or fleeing scot free; the innocent destroyed or redeemed; and the long term psychological effect within the socio-historical context.

Swift and immaculate in execution, her plotting is complex and ingenious, sex and violence only occasionally explicit, never erotic or gratuitous. She appeals to the mind not the heart, demanding attention and intelligent response rather than laughter and tears. In spite of its vigour her writing brings to mind that of Addison both in elegance of style and in narrative stance. It was he who pointed out that the observer sees more of life than the participant. Anthony certainly views a vast panoply and reports it faithfully and accurately, even when alien or illogical to the reader.

A common element in her books is the use of a severe personality disorder to explain evil (the strange assassins in *The Company of Saints*, and poor mad, vindictive Boris in *The Relic* are examples). Often we have an exposition on how a fixation grew out of graphically described early experiences, as seen in Boris's early protegé,

Viktor, witnessing his mother's murder from inside a cupboard. Human relationships are seen as mobile—developing, clashing, resolving—as individuals make decisions in the face of social and moral demands. Her comprehension of the historic dimensions of Russian politics was underlined when she produced an alarmingly accurate and detailed foretelling of Gorbachev's instatement and fall, particularly in *The Relic*.

In *Voices on the Wind* she returns to a 1970s-type story and shows an acute awareness of her market by milking the Klaus Barbie case in a story of a Resistance incident re-examined. As so often in her work, the book contains real historical comment, bringing to the forefront the wider and longer-term aspects of, in this case, military and strategic decisions and the ethics and impact of making sacrifices for the greater good.

The House of Vandekar is the nearest that Anthony comes to a tearjerking story, but the grief lies in the situation development rather than in the emotions of the characters, more pathos than sorrow. Her recreation of life in a 30s 'great house' is vivid and controlled, as is its tragic conversion into a convalescence hospital which mirrors the painful adaptation of the characters to a more selfless existence demanding greater responsibility both socially and personally. As she does so often, Anthony uses a flashback from a contemporary situation to bring past generations alive. This can be seen again in *The Scarlet Thread* and *The Return*, which visit wartime Sicily and Russia. Yet again she brings the reader to within tiptoe proximity of the action, barely beyond danger of being sucked in. Wonderful plotting demonstrates her superb ability to make what is really a string of coincidences seem as if deliberate events were preordained by fate, within the historical 'presence' she creates. This is why Evelyn Anthony is highly credible in evoking the spirit of any period she chooses to present.

—Margaret Woodward

———

APPIGNANESI, Lisa.
Pseudonym: Jessica Ayre. **Nationality:** Canadian. **Born:** Poland, 4 January 1946. **Education:** McGill University, Montreal, B.A. 1966, M.A. 1967; Sussex University, Brighton, Ph.D. 1971. **Relations:** married Richard Appignanesi (divorced); current partner, John Forrester; two children. **Career:** staff writer, Community Research Centre, New York, 1970–71; lecturer, University of Essex, Colchester, 1971–73; assistant professor, New England College, Arundel, West Sussex, 1973–80; editor, Writers and Readers, London, 1975–81; director of talks, 1981–86, and deputy director, 1986–90, Institute of Contemporary Arts, London. Since 1986, independent television producer, Channel 4 and BBC; has also worked as a broadcaster and journalist. **Recipient:** Chevalier de l'Ordre des Arts et des Lettres, 1987; various university fellowships. **Agent:** Caradoc King, A.P. Watt Ltd, 20 John Street, London WC1N 2DL, England. **Address:** 69 Whitehall Park, London N19 3TW, England.

ROMANCE AND HISTORICAL PUBLICATIONS

Novel

Memory and Desire. London, HarperCollins, 1991; New York, New American Library, 1992.

Novels as Jessica Ayre

Not to Be Trusted. London, Mills and Boon, and Toronto, Harlequin, 1981.
One Man Woman. London, Mills and Boon, and Toronto, Harlequin, 1982.

Hard to Handle. London, Mills and Boon, and Toronto, Harlequin, 1983.
New Discovery. London, Mills and Boon, and Toronto, Harlequin, 1984.

OTHER PUBLICATIONS

Other

Language of Trust, with Douglas and Monica Holmes. London, Science House, 1972.
Feminity and the Creative Imagination: A Study of Henry James, Robert Musil, and Marcel Proust. London, Vision Press, and New York, Barnes and Noble, 1973.
The Cabaret. London, Studio Vista, 1975; New York, Universe, 1976; revised edition, as *Cabaret: First Hundred Years*, London, Methuen, and New York, Basic, 1985.
Brand New York. London, Namara Press, 1982.
Feminism for Beginners. London, Pantheon, 1983.
Simone de Beauvoir. London, Penguin, and New York, Viking, 1986.
Freud's Women, with John Forrester. London, Weidenfeld and Nicolson, 1992; New York, Basic, 1993.

Editor, *Desire*. London, Institute of Contemporary Arts, 1984.
Editor, *Ideas from France*. London, Institute of Contemporary Arts, 1985.
Editor, *Postmodernism*. London, Institute of Contemporary Arts, 1986.
Editor, with Stephen Rose, *Science and Beyond*. London, Blackwell, 1986.
Editor, with Hilary Lawson, *Dismantling Truth*. London, Weidenfeld and Nicolson, 1989.
Editor, with Sara Maitland, *The Rushdie File*. London, Rough Estate, and New York, Syracuse University Press, 1989.

Translator, *Little Girls: Social Conditioning and its Effects on the Stereotyped Role of Women During Infancy*, by Elena Gianini Belotti. London, Writers and Readers Publishing Cooperative, 1975.

*

Lisa Appignanesi comments:

I started writing fiction rather late in my professional life and was only brave enough to take it up full-time in 1990—after a varied career in the arts, media, and the Academy. My interest in writing fiction is to attempt to integrate serious concerns in a popular and compelling fictional forum—as the 19th-century novel used to do. *Memory and Desire*—whose hero is a psychoanalyst—explores the Freudian family romance, the psychology of love, as well as the ways in which people are shaped and defined by their history.

*   *   *

'We inflict the oedipal story on our children and attribute emotions and intentions to them which are more properly our own', says Thomas Sachs in *Memory and Desire*. Lisa Appignanesi has stated that *Memory and Desire* was intended as a Freudian family romance and that her aim in writing was to 'attempt to integrate serious concerns in a popular and compelling fictional form'.

The form chosen by Appignanesi in *Memory and Desire* is the 'glitz' novel. It is the story of Sylvie Kowalska with her 'face childlike in its innocence, yet rampantly seductive', and of how her deep despair, stemming from her childhood experiences of which she cannot bear to speak ('she had her secret places, this Sylvie'), let alone confront, wreaks havoc on all around her particularly her husband, Jacob Jardine, her daughter, Katherine, and Alexei Gismondi, Katherine's eventual lover. Sylvie's confused and ambivalent feelings about her parents, her subconscious conflicts which she is unable to resolve because she lacks the insight to know that they are there, lead her to ever wilder excesses which exacerbate her distress. But Katherine is more fortunate, although she has to pass through many trials and tribulations before she can find happiness. She does so, with the assistance of her father, her friend and mentor Thomas Sachs, and her father's friend and former lover Princess Mathilde (Katherine's 'good mother' as opposed to Sylvie, 'the bad mother ... cold, cruel, rejecting ... sexy'). In this context Katherine's dream re-enactment of her own birth is most significant. And when Katherine has learnt the truth about herself and Alexei, and the strange story of her birth, she is free to marry him and thus fulfil the oedipal dream which Sylvie so passionately desired and failed to achieve.

The novel follows the conventions of the genre. It is long, over 500 pages. It spans a period of 60 or so years and takes place in varied locales: Paris, Rome, New York et al, although the most-powerfully written chapter is set in Poland just after the end of World War II. The world described is that of the super-rich: for instance, Sachs provides the capital for Katherine to set up her own gallery with barely the flicker of an eyelid. There is a wide cast of characters and although most of the story is told from the point of view of the five main characters—Sylvie, Jardine, Mathilde, Katherine, and Alexei—we learn a great deal about many of the other characters, in spite of the fact that some of them appear only for a page or two and serve no real function in the story. However, that is irrelevant; unlike more economically-written novels, the big saga with a purpose, is the story of a life, or lives, in and out of which other people float as they do in real life. There are a number of explicit sex scenes which have a somewhat perfunctory feel to them rather than the 'black eroticism' promised by the dustjacket.

Although the psychological aspect of the novel is the most important, Appignanesi's other interests are evident. Sylvie, as a cover for her activities in the French Resistance in World War II, sings in cabaret/nightclubs. Katherine is deeply involved in the world of the fine arts. Sartre and de Beauvoir make a one-sentence appearance. Throughout the book as the decades roll by there are glimpses of important cultural influences of time: the artistic and literary bohemia of 1930s Paris, the drive towards domesticity of mid-50s USA, the beat scene of late 1950s New York, Swinging-Sixties London, and in the 1970s, Italian revolutionary politics and the arrival of feminism in England and America.

The writing is most notable for the adroit use of epigrams. The book begins with one, 'There is nothing quite like spying to feed the erotic imagination', and thereafter epigram succeeds epigram neatly encapsulating or pointing out whatever message Appignanesi wishes to convey. There is also, however, a tendency to cliché, for example, 'veritable magpie'; 'Princess Mathilde sped lightly'.

The four Mills and Boon novels, published as Jessica Ayre, show interesting parallels with the larger and later work. There is the connection with the arts: one heroine is an interior designer, another works as a make-up artist but is actually a talented artist. One hero is a photographer, and in the fourth novel the parents of the heroine are artists and the hero's son is a talented—and precocious—cartoonist. The use of vibrant colour, particularly in the heroines' clothes, is exciting. The psychological theme is important: in three of the novels the heroine has a significant dream revealing a hidden conflict which has to be resolved before happiness can be attained. The novels contain apt epigrams often making a feminist point: '"women's talk" ... seemed to be mostly about men ...' (Not to Be Trusted); 'men wouldn't pose for women. It reversed all suppositions about art and life. Drawing [the hero] she was actively possessing him, shaping

him while he had to remain at least momentarily passive' (One Man Woman). These are daring and subversive statements for a genre as conservative as category romance; one would like to know how they are received by readers. All four novels have international settings and the heroes are high achievers in their professions—architecture, scriptwriting, photography, publishing—but the milieux depicted are those of the prosperous and successful, not the 'glitzy' super-rich. Images recur: the comparison of New York to a mediaeval town at the beginning of Memory and Desire is an elaboration of a similar comparison in New Discovery.

The writing in these four novels is among the best on the publisher's list. There is a vividness, a spontaneity, even, once or twice a flash of humour, lacking in the longer work which sometimes seems to sink beneath the vastness of its theme, its time scale, its cast of characters, its complex narrative structure ... its sheer number of words. The characterization in the Jessica Ayre novels is particularly adept; most memorable perhaps is the sad, frightened, repressed Jennie in One Man Woman. The greater proportion of dialogue to text no doubt accounts for the impression of immediacy; although the various hostile exchanges between hero and heroine follow the course usual in books of this kind, they do demonstrate that action described is more dramatic than action recollected, and that conflict between characters (however banal) creates tension and stimulates reader interest.

In spite of the similarities between the Mills and Boon novels and Memory and Desire, they serve two very different purposes. The former are in a genre which has very tight constraints and is designed to be primarily escapist; any serious concern has to be incorporated with skill and delicacy. The latter is a much more ambitious project: if it does not altogether achieve its aim it must be remembered that its scope is very much wider.

—Radmila May

———

ARBOR, Jane. British. See 2nd edition, 1990.

———

ARD, William. See **JAKES, John.**

———

ARDEN, Judith. See **SAXTON, Judith.**

———

ARLEN, Leslie. See **NICOLE, Christopher.**

———

ARLEN, Michael.
Nationality: British. Emigrated to England, 1901; naturalized as Michael Arlen, 1922. **Born:** Dikran Kouyoumdjian, Rustchuk, Bulgaria, 16 November 1895. **Education:** Malvern College, Worcestershire; studied medicine at the University of Edinburgh, 1913. **Military Service:** served as Civil Defence public relations officer in the West Midlands, 1940–41. **Relations:** married Atalanta, daughter of Count Mercati, in 1928; one son and one daughter. **Career:** staff member, Ararat: A Searchlight on Armenia, London, 1916, and columnist, the Tatler, London, 1939–40; lived in Cannes, 1928–39, and in New York City after 1945. Friends with the writer D.H. Lawrence and satanist Philip Heseltine. **Died:** 23 June 1956.

ROMANCE AND HISTORICAL PUBLICATIONS

Novels

The London Venture. London, Heinemann, and New York, Dodd
Mead, 1920.
Piracy: A Romantic Chronicle of These Days. London, Collins,
1922; New York, Doran, 1923.
The Green Hat: A Romance for a Few People. London, Collins, and
New York, Doran, 1924.
Young Men in Love. London, Hutchinson, and New York, Doran,
1927.
Lily Christine. New York, Doubleday, 1928; London, Hutchinson,
1929.
Men Dislike Women: A Romance. London, Heinemann, and New
York, Doubleday, 1931.
Man's Mortality. London, Heinemann, and New York, Doubleday,
1933.
Hell! Said the Duchess: A Bed-Time Story. London, Heinemann,
and New York, Doubleday, 1934.
Flying Dutchman. London, Heinemann, and New York, Double-
day, 1939.

Short Stories

The Romantic Lady. London, Collins, and New York, Dodd Mead,
1921.
These Charming People. London, Collins, 1923; New York, Doran,
1924; selection, as *The Man with the Broken Nose and Other
Stories,* Collins, 1927.
*May Fair, in Which Are Told the Last Adventures of These Charm-
ing People.* London, Collins, and New York, Doran, 1925; selec-
tion, as *The Ace of Cads and Other Stories,* Collins, 1927.
Ghost Stories. London, Collins, 1927; New York, Arno Press, 1976.
Babes in the Wood. London, Hutchinson, and New York, Double-
day, 1929.
The Ancient Sin and Other Stories. London, Collins, 1930.
A Young Man Comes to London. Privately printed, 1931.
The Short Stories. London, Collins, 1933.
*The Crooked Coronet and Other Misrepresentations of the Real
Facts of Life.* London, Heinemann, and New York, Doubleday,
1937.

OTHER PUBLICATIONS

Plays

Dear Father (produced London, 1924; revised version, as *These
Charming People,* produced New York, 1925).
Why Shelmerdene Was Late for Dinner, adaptation of his story 'The
Real Reason Why Shelmerdene Was Late for Dinner' (produced
London, 1924).
The Green Hat, adaptation of his own novel (produced Detroit, Lon-
don, and New York, 1925). New York, Doran, 1925.
The Zoo, with Winchell Smith (produced Southsea and Pittsburgh,
1927). New York and London, French, 1927.
Good Losers, with Walter Hackett (produced London, 1931). Lon-
don, French, 1933.

Screenplay: *The Heavenly Body,* with others, 1943.

*

Film Adaptations: *The Green Hat,* 1934; *Golden Arrow,* 1936.

Critical Study: *Michael Arlen* by Harry Keyishian, Boston, Twayne,
1975.

*   *   *

'To be as improbable as life will be is as far beyond the honest
novelist's courage as it must be against the temper of his craft . . . '
Michael Arlen said this, but his own story reads like the most far-
fetched romance: unknown young Armenian with an unpronounce-
able name offers his first novel to a world-famous London publisher, and is accepted. Following his publisher's advice, he changes
his name to Michael Arlen, goes on to write *The Green Hat: A Romance for a Few People,* and takes the world by storm. (Literally,
for his heroine Iris Storm proved the truth of Oscar Wilde's contention that Nature copies Art. The world did its best to copy Iris.) The
impact of this single novel is now difficult to comprehend. In these
television-dominated days, it is impossible to recapture the atmosphere of a time before even radio had taken firm hold; a time when
everyone read, not just the few, and not only read but discussed the
latest releases as a matter of some significance.

World War I had recently rocked the firm foundation of the universe, and suddenly the unthinkable had become the possible. The
audience of *The Green Hat* had just come through the war to end all
wars, but which instead ended all peace. Old rules and beliefs were
crumbling. The young people fortunate enough to have escaped the
Holocaust were disillusioned and jaded. They were the Bright
Young Things; they frightened and disturbed the older generation
who did not, *could* not, understand them. These were the young
people who recognized, or thought they recognized, themselves as
the characters of Arlen's novels, and they made *The Green Hat* in
particular one of the greatest bestsellers of all time.

Today it is a period piece. Even in his lifetime, Arlen was left behind, while time and fashion remorselessly forged ahead, and he
could not. He was a writer who could do but one thing, and was fortunate enough to do it at exactly the propitious moment. Even his
quirky brand of idiosyncratic English was forgiven him then, as it
would not have been at another time. And what, after all, was the
furore about? *The Green Hat* is the muddled story of Iris, a troubled
young woman with a 'past' and a dissolute present. She wears two
wedding rings—for two husbands now dead: she carries a smouldering torch for the one true love of her life, her girlhood sweetheart,
from whom she was parted by his father's interference, and who is
but newly married to a fluttering ingenue named Venice.

Iris does a great deal of restless rushing to and fro in her huge yellow Hispano-Suiza, which to Arlen seemed to typify the spirit of the
entire era. She is regarded by all her acquaintance as a depraved
character, yet aside from her free-love life-style, she behaves
throughout with self-sacrificing nobility. Much evil is hinted at,
little is explicit, but it becomes plain as the action lumbers clumsily
along that there were dark doings at the time of Iris's tragic first marriage, and that her husband, idolized by everyone but his young
bride, was not the hero he seemed to be. The spectre of syphilis,
hitherto unmentionable, is raised; it was a daring stroke for a novelist of the 1920s. For young women, though not young men, were expected to behave with a certain decorum and restraint, which Iris did
not. The story ends with the great yellow Hispano-Suiza in flames,
and Iris's green hat, worn *pour le sport,* lying in the grass by the
roadside. One last time, the déclassé lady has sacrificed herself for
her true love.

Iris and her set represented for Arlen a distinct race of English that
he believed could not survive the crassness of the 20th century, belonging as they did to a time of different standards and ideals. 'They
of the superior nerves had failed, they died that slow white death
which is reserved for privilege in defeat.'

—Joan McGrath

ARMSTRONG, Charlotte. American. 1905–1969. See 2nd edition, 1990.

———

ARMSTRONG, Lindsay.
Born: South Africa. **Relations:** married; five children. **Career:** horse training; farming. Lives in Australia. **Address:** c/o Mills and Boon Ltd, Eton House, 18–24 Paradise Road, Richmond, Surrey, TW9 1SR, England.

ROMANCE AND HISTORICAL PUBLICATIONS

Novels

Spitfire. London, Mills and Boon, 1981.
My Dear Innocent. London, Mills and Boon, 1981; Toronto, Harlequin, 1982.
Enter My Jungle. London, Mills and Boon, 1982; Toronto, Harlequin, 1983.
Perhaps Love. London, Mills and Boon, and Toronto, Harlequin, 1983.
Melt a Frozen Heart. London, Mills and Boon, and Toronto, Harlequin, 1983.
Don't Call it Love. London, Mills and Boon, 1984.
Love Me Not. London, Mills and Boon, 1985.
Standing on the Outside. London, Mills and Boon, 1986.
An Elusive Mistress. London, Mills and Boon, 1986.
Some Say Love. London, Mills and Boon, 1986.
The Heart of the Matter. London, Mills and Boon, 1987.
Reluctant Wife. London, Mills and Boon, 1987.
In the Shadow of the Moonlight. London, Mills and Boon, 1987.
When the Night Grows Cold. London, Mills and Boon, 1987.
Heat of the Moment. London, Mills and Boon, 1988; Toronto, Harlequin, 1989.
The Marrying Game. London, Mills and Boon, 1989; Toronto, Harlequin, 1989.
A Love Affair. London, Mills and Boon, 1989.
One More Night. London, Mills and Boon, 1990.
Leave Love Alone. London, Mills and Boon, 1991.
Dark Captor. London, Mills and Boon, 1991.
The Director's Wife. London, Mills and Boon, 1991.
An Unusual Affair. London, Mills and Boon, 1992; Toronto, Harlequin, 1993.
The Seduction Stakes. London, Mills and Boon, 1992; Toronto, Harlequin, 1994.
Dangerous Lover. London, Mills and Boon, 1992; Toronto, Harlequin, 1993.
Difficult Man. London, Mills and Boon, 1993.

*   *   *

The romantic novelist Lindsay Armstrong has published over 20 novels since her first, *Spitfire*, appeared in 1981. Set in Australia (where Armstrong lives) her novels detail the trials, tribulations, and pitfalls of relationships, in what is undoubtedly classic romantic fiction. The principal strength of Armstrong's writing lies in her ability to create a broad range of characters, with different backgrounds, emotions, and preconceptions, battling in pursuit of the perfect relationship and often battling against their own natures. This leads Armstrong to reflect the full range of human emotion, behaviour and experience. Similarly, as none of her heroines resemble each other, the whole arena of 'female experience' is presented to the reader: wives, widows, academics, farmers, and lawyers, all are portrayed with equal vigour, candour and above all understanding, by this novelist.

Whatever their occupation, independence of mind and freedom of spirit head the list of female attributes in all of Armstrong's heroines. A strong wish not to be yoked to an unsuitable man, just for the sake of marriage, underlies their behaviour. Feminism and the emancipation of women solves many of their day-to-day problems, but often at the expense of their emotional lives and their sexual nature. The majority of Armstrong's heroines do not really know what it is they are missing, or searching for, and when they do become aware they try, albeit unsuccessfully, to ignore it.

In *The Seduction Stakes* Jane Mathieson, a lawyer, confronts the battle of the sexes frequently at her workplace. She describes one incident in which a client sacks his barrister: 'she's a woman, the barrister; he's a very macho male as well as being a farmer with absolutely no understanding of the mechanics of the law . . . women don't figure very highly in his estimation at the moment . . . his wife who persuaded him to retain her as his barrister . . . left him soon after'. This judgement, that men act on impulse (rather than through reason) is one that 'plain Jane' holds and is certain of. As the novel develops, the reader becomes aware that her lack of trust in men is a reflection on her past, and most particularly her childhood. Her father left home when Jane was very young, and as a result she has never trusted men. At the age of 24 she is still a virgin. Her father returns during the course of the novel and Jane becomes uncomfortably aware that it was her mother who was the manipulator of the truth, and was the reason that her father left home. This casts doubt on Jane's opinions and allows her to follow her instincts with regard to the hero Liam Benedict.

Jane mistrusts Liam. She believes him to be promiscuous (because he is good looking) and a layabout (she doesn't know how rich he is). Believing that '24 year old virgins can be laughed at or held up to ridicule' Jane, when drunk, attempts to seduce Liam. He does not respond (because she is drunk, is a virgin and he believes she will regret having had sex with him when she is sober). Jane does not understand and considers that Liam's rebuff must have something to do with her being a virgin: perhaps he finds her dull and boring? Eventually she realizes that he does have her best interests at heart, and that attributing motives to Liam's behaviour, without communicating her feelings, is a dangerous game to play when searching for the truth.

One of the outstanding characters in this novel is Laura, Jane's legal secretary, whose attitude towards life, men, and sex differs substantially from Jane's. Laura advises Jane both to make the most of her looks and of the opportunity she has with Liam and to affirm her feelings, not deny them.

When the Night Grows Cold depicts the developing relationship between Kate Wiley, a widow and impoverished farmer whom local rumour has 'eating the flies off the wall', and Grevil Robertson, a rich and successful farmer. Since her husband's death, Kate's estate, Kununnurra, has fallen into disrepair, not because Kate is incompetent or needs a man around but due to circumstances beyond her control—alternate drought and floods which have wiped out the value of her crops. Grevil Robertson, who was saved from the wreckage of a motoring accident by Kate's late husband, regenerates Kununnurra by leasing some land from Kate.

One of the most memorable characters in this novel is Mrs Robertson (Grevil's grandmother), a sprightly woman in her seventies, who gives her advice freely to all parties (whether they want it or not) and whose attitude and beliefs are set up in opposition to those of Kate. Mrs Robertson advises Kate to re-marry, 'I don't think it healthy or wise for any woman to live like a nun'. Kate suffered genuine grief with the death of her husband and has since devoted herself to raising her twins single-handedly. However, she needs to be awakened again, both emotionally and sexually. Armstrong handles this difficult subject with a deftness and sensitivity that is neither preachy nor too sentimental, and which, in the hands of a less assured novelist, could all too easily be overplayed.

Armstrong demonstrates her ability as a novelist and her flexible view of the romantic novel in *Dark Captor*, a novel which centres, like *The Director's Wife*, on a loveless marriage. The heroine of *Dark Captor* loved her husband once, but the manner of their marriage leads her to be repelled by him and contemptuous of the 'compulsory bedding you subject me to every couple of months'. Through a process of getting to know each other again, both Stephanie and her husband, Dominic, eventually realize that their feelings towards each other have not changed that much. Communication between the two of them allows them to identify each other's needs and hopes and thereby realize their mutual aspirations.

It is the lack of real communication between the partners that leads to a growing tension in their relationships in all of Armstrong's work. This is best illustrated in *An Unusual Affair*, in which the heroine, Rachel, is presumed by her admirer, Dr Mel Carlisle, to be an older man's kept mistress. Rachel, who initially despises the doctor, does not point out his error of judgement until the end of the novel. Dr Carlisle is both attracted to and repelled by his vision of Rachel's life and the tension between his morals and his desires makes him one of the most intriguing of all Armstrong's heroes. His dilemma also illustrates the point that you cannot necessarily choose who it is you fall in love with.

—Charmaine Moldrich

ARMSTRONG, Tilly.   See **ALEXANDER, Kate.**

ARNETT, Caroline.   See **ELIOT, Anne.**

ARNIM, Elizabeth von.
Pseudonym for Mary Annette, Countess von Arnim, later Countess Russell. **Other Pseudonym:** Alice Cholmondeley. **Nationality:** British. **Born:** Mary Annette Beauchamp, Sydney, New South Wales, Australia, 31 August 1866; grew up in Lausanne and London. **Education:** privately; Blythwood House, London; Miss Summerhayes's School, Ealing, London, 1881–84; Royal College of Music, London. **Relations:** married 1) Count Henning August von Arnim-Schlagenthin in 1891 (died 1910), four daughters and one son; 2) Francis Russell, Earl Russell in 1916 (separated 1919; died 1931). **Career:** writer. Lived in Germany, 1891–1908, then in England. **Died:** 9 February 1941.

ROMANCE AND HISTORICAL PUBLICATIONS

Novels

The Benefactress. London and New York, Macmillan, 1901.
The Ordeal of Elizabeth. New York, Taylor, 1901.
The Princess Priscilla's Fortnight. London, Smith Elder, and New York, Scribner, 1905.
Fräulein Schmidt and Mr Anstruther, Being the Letters of an Independent Woman. London, Smith Elder, and New York, Scribner, 1907.
The Caravaners. London, Smith Elder, and New York, Doubleday, 1909.
The Pastor's Wife. London, Smith Elder, and New York, Doubleday, 1914.
Christine (as Alice Cholmondeley). London and New York, Macmillan, 1917.

Christopher and Columbus. London, Macmillan, and New York, Doubleday, 1919.
In the Mountains (published anonymously). London, Macmillan, and New York, Doubleday, 1920.
Vera. London, Macmillan, and New York, Doubleday, 1921.
The Enchanted April. London, Macmillan, 1922; New York, Doubleday, 1923.
Love. London, Macmillan, and New York, Doubleday, 1925.
Introduction to Sally. London, Macmillan, and New York, Doubleday, 1926.
Expiation. London, Macmillan, and New York, Doubleday, 1929.
Father. London, Macmillan, and New York, Doubleday, 1931.
Jasmine Farm. London, Heinemann, and New York, Doubleday, 1934.
Mr Skeffington. London, Heinemann, and New York, Doubleday, 1940.

Short Stories

The Pious Pilgrimage. Boston, Badger, 1901.

OTHER PUBLICATIONS

Play

Priscilla Runs Away, adaptation of her novel *The Princess Priscilla's Fortnight* (produced London, 1910).

Other

Elizabeth and Her German Garden. London and New York, Macmillan, 1898; revised edition, 1900.
The Solitary Summer. London and New York, Macmillan, 1899.
The April Baby's Book of Tunes, with the Story of How They Came to Be Written (for children). London and New York, Macmillan, 1900.
The Adventures of Elizabeth in Rügen. London and New York, Macmillan, 1904.
All the Dogs of My Life. London, Heinemann, and New York, Doubleday, 1936.
One Thing in Common (omnibus). New York, Doubleday, 1941.

*

Film Adaptations: *Mr Skeffington*, 1944; *The Enchanted April*, 1991.

Manuscript Collection: Huntington Library, San Marino, California.

Critical Studies: *Elizabeth of the German Garden: A Biography* by Leslie de Charms, London, Heinemann, 1958; *Elizabeth: The Author of 'Elizabeth and Her German Garden'* by Karen Usborne, London, Bodley Head, 1986.

*   *   *

After reading Virginia Woolf's *To the Lighthouse*, Elizabeth wrote to a friend: 'it beats everything anyone else has done hollow. How strident, how vulgar, how coarse *my* stuff for instance seems (and is) after reading that' (quoted in Leslie de Charms's biography). Yet Elizabeth does herself an injustice. She was generally praised by serious critics throughout her long writing career (John Middleton Murry, the husband of her cousin Katherine Mansfield, referred to her novel *Vera* as 'a *Wuthering Heights* written by Jane

Austen'), and her intelligence and wit are as admirable now as they were when Elizabeth was an internationally known author.

Her first book—*Elizabeth and Her German Garden*, a huge success—was a short autobiographical account of the first year (spring to spring) spent in the country house near Stetten in north Germany of her husband, Count von Arnim. The charm and verbal facility on the surface of the account—of her April, May, and June babies, of the servants who don't know how to account for a (foreign) mistress who won't take regular meals and who prefers roses and hollyhocks to domestic routine, of her husband, the Man of Wrath, who doesn't understand her interest in the seemingly boring landscape, of the friends who fear her husband has exiled her away from the pleasures of Berlin—are undeniable, but we aren't surprised when the dark side of all the charm is revealed in her later books, after her first marriage (to von Arnim), and indeed her second (to Earl Russell), had broken down.

Many of the novels are light and charming, though almost all have a touch of irony about them. *The Benefactress* is an elaborate 'opening out' of several motifs of *Elizabeth and Her German Garden*. The socially sophisticated but emotionally naive Anna Estcourt, on inheriting a large estate in north Germany, decides to open the house to women of good family with no means of support. The society friends—both English and German—are given space to reveal themselves ('Trudi's new friends always did think her delightful; and she never has any old ones'); the local middle class is ineffably snobbish and blinkered (the parson 'puffing Christianity as though it were a quack medicine'). The Man of Wrath motif is transferred to almost all the men in the book (except her brother, who has become a philosopher and spends his time fishing): even the 20-year-old assistant vicar condescends to Anna, since she is a woman. The English-German theme is solidly used as the basis of the general misunderstandings that run through the book. The actual plot—a rather thin one—centres on her landowning neighbour who aids but disapproves of her charity: when she is finally able to comfort *him* (he is falsely imprisoned), she realizes she loves him. *The Princess Priscilla's Fortnight* and *The Caravaners* reverse the English-Lady-in-Germany theme by bringing a runaway German princess to a small Somerset village in the first, and a pompous German Baron and his party of holiday-makers to Kent in the second. (The German theme is more negatively presented in *Christine*, published during World War I under a pseudonym: what had been a subject of irony and fun in previous works becomes the basis of tragedy in this book.) Sally (*Introduction to Sally*) is a luscious grocer's daughter who marries a Cambridge undergraduate; his snobbish mother drives her away, but Sally's charm is such that a duke and his daughter rescue her, and facilitate a reconciliation. Snobbery figures again in *Jasmine Farm*, where Lady Terence has an affair with her mother's married secretary, Andrew. Since her mother had a rake for a husband, she is very moral; since Andrew's wife's mother is an ex-actress and a social climber, she is willing to compromise—so the two older ladies are able to resolve the dilemma.

Other novels deal with groups of women in differing relationships to each other. *The Enchanted April* shows the effect of the Mediterranean on four women, all of whom are troubled and react to the beauty of the setting in positive ways. *In the Mountains*, set in Switzerland, has a similar theme, though here the three ladies have a more complicated relationship. The narrator (the book is in diary form) is getting away from an intolerable personal situation (never explained), licking her wounds, and the other two are strangers, one ultra conventional, the other a charming, mindless beauty, Dolly, who had kept marrying Germans. The arrival of the narrator's uncle, a Dean ('relieved to find his niece . . . securely, as it were, embedded in widows') solves all problems, since he promptly falls in love with Dolly.

Expiation centres on a widow, Millie Bott, forced to live out her widowhood in 'correct' form surrounded by female Botts; her old

lover of ten years standing can't help her, though her mother-in-law, the only charming Bott, can.

If *Expiation* is a rather bleak look at love and marriage, several of Elizabeth's other novels are even more revealing. *Love*, which according to Elizabeth's biographer had an autobiographical basis, concerns a 47-year old widow courted by and possibly in love with a 25-year-old man. The climax comes when her priggish son-in-law forces her to marry the young man because they had been forced to stay overnight together. (The theme of the aging beauty is neatly and touchingly told in *Mr Skeffington*, possibly her best-known work, at least indirectly, since it was made into a movie starring Bette Davis.) But *Fräulein Schmidt and Mr Anstruther* and *Vera* are probably her bleakest books. The first consists of letters from Fräulein Rose-Marie Schmidt to Roger Anstruther, who had stayed for a year in the Schmidt's house in Jena where he was coached in German by Rose-Marie's father, Professor Schmidt. Reversing the usual progress from coolness to passion, the book begins with Rose-Marie utterly in love with Roger, based on a last-minute avowal before Roger returned to England, and moves haltingly through their break-up, his engagement to an English girl, that engagement's break-up in turn, and Roger's slowly revived interest in Rose-Marie, who by this time regards him only as a friend. Rose-Marie's sensitivity and charm, and her cooling passion, are beautifully revealed (we never read the other side of the correspondence). *Vera* is even more chilling—a convincing portrait of a pure egotist, Everard Wemyss, and a charming woman, Lucy Entwhistle, who becomes involved with him. Wemyss's egotism is revealed to the reader only as Lucy becomes aware of it—she marries him, finds out the ambiguous nature of his previous wife's suicide, and at the end of the book is caught in a position that can lead only to her complete submission to her husband or to an end like his first wife's.

Despite her sometimes bleak views (possibly reflecting her own marriages), what is remembered of Elizabeth's books is their wit and charm. We are often given the chance to see the bully bullied, the egotist defeated, the worm turning—and almost always with a lightness of touch and a verbal felicity that remind us of the numerous comparisons her contemporaries made to Jane Austen.

—George Walsh

ARNOW, Harriette.
Nationality: American. **Born:** Harriette Louisa Simpson, Wayne County, Kentucky, 7 July 1908. **Education:** St Helen's Academy; Stanton Academy; Burnside High School, graduated 1924; Berea College, Kentucky, 1924–26; University of Louisville, B.S. 1931. **Relations:** married Harold B. Arnow in 1939 (died 1985); one daughter and one son. **Career:** teacher in Pulaski County, Kentucky, 1926–28, 1931–34, and Louisville, 1934; waitress, Cincinnati, 1934–39. **Recipient:** Berea College Centennial award, 1955; Friends of American Writers award, 1955; American Association for State and Local History award, 1971; University of Louisville Outstanding Alumni award, 1979. D.Litt.: Albion College, Michigan, 1955; Transylvania University, Lexington, Kentucky, 1979; University of Kentucky, Lexington, 1981. **Died:** 22 March 1986.

ROMANCE AND HISTORICAL PUBLICATIONS

Novel

The Kentucky Trace: A Novel of the American Revolution. New York, Knopf, 1974.

OTHER PUBLICATIONS

Novels

Mountain Path. New York, Covici Friede, 1936.
Hunter's Horn. New York, Macmillan, 1949; London, Collins, 1950.
The Dollmaker. New York, Macmillan, 1954; London, Heinemann, 1955.
The Weedkiller's Daughter. New York, Knopf, 1970.

Other

Seedtime on the Cumberland. New York, Macmillan, 1960.
Flowering of the Cumberland. New York, Macmillan, 1963.
Some Musings on the Nature of History (lecture). Ann Arbor, Michigan, Historical Society of Michigan, 1968.
Old Burnside. Lexington, University Press of Kentucky, 1978.

*

Manuscript Collection: Margaret I. King Library, University of Kentucky, Lexington.

Critical Studies: by Joyce Carol Oates, in *Rediscoveries* edited by David Madden, New York, Crown, 1971; *Harriette Arnow* by Wilton Eckley, New York, Twayne, 1974.

*　　*　　*

Despite Harriette Arnow's proven skill as a writer, her contributions to American literature have been largely ignored by scholars. The pre-eminence of William Faulkner and the influence of the New Critics have overshadowed many figures who played important roles in the 'Southern Literary Renaissance'. Arnow's insightful and realistic portrayal of Kentucky rural life, and its ultimate disintegration in the face of industrialism, is a valuable achievement in American letters. Her natural skill at storytelling and rendering memorable characters combined with a unity of plot and theme to produce novels of high merit. Like that of many fine American novelists Arnow's work has a regional focus which transcends provincialism. Glenda Hobbs wrote that, 'Arnow alone has rendered Kentucky highlanders fully and fairly, her unique obstinate characters, even in the face of economic ruin and spiritual exhaustion, will endure and prevail.' Arnow's work falls into two distinct categories. The first is fiction, the bulk of which is contained in a trilogy exploring the mountain people and lifestyle she knew as a girl. It begins with *Mountain Path*, which was not a commercial success; however, *Hunter's Horn* and *The Dollmaker*, the other two books in the trilogy were both bestsellers. The second group of writing covers social history. Two later books, *Seedtime on the Cumberland* and *Flowering of the Cumberland*, integrate history with reminiscence and commentary further to document the world Arnow describes in her novels. 'I was aware that nothing had been written on the Southern migrants', she explained in 1976. Hers was an attempt to show 'what was actually happening to them and to their culture'.

Mountain Path is the most autobiographical of Arnow's works, concerning a young and naive schoolteacher who goes to a remote village in the Kentucky mountains. The plot itself is contrived, but the real strength of the book lies in the close attention to character and the everyday affairs of the region. This ability rescues her story from the usual melodrama and sentimentality which can plague similar fiction.

Arnow's second novel, *Hunter's Horn*, focuses on the family of Nunnelly Ballew, whose obsession for killing an elusive fox he calls 'King Devil' brings his family close to destruction. This novel addresses the individual's struggle to find meaning in a circumscribed environment. In many ways it is a conscious attempt at the heroic stature and epic sweep of Melville or Steinbeck. In one particularly powerful scene the townspeople bury Lureenie Cramer, who has starved while her husband is working in Detroit. Because of a recent religious revival they ignore her suffering, and now they hurry with the ceremony because leaving an open grave after sundown brings bad luck. Superstition increases the callousness initiated by their fundamentalism. In their impatience to get the coffin into the grave, the men tip it too far and there is a dull thud as Lureenie's body strikes the side. Later her husband makes a triumphant return wearing tailored clothes, toting a gilt-edged bible, and claiming he has 'seen the light'.

Arnow's most well-known work is *The Dollmaker*. It completes her portrait of Kentucky migrants, 'rescuing the literary stereotype of the lazy, suspicious, ignorant, maniacally violent hillbilly'. It also gives readers Arnow's most resilient and complex character—Gertie Nevels. When her husband is lured to Detroit by tales of wealth and luxury, Gertie sacrifices her own dreams of self-sufficiency to join him. With her she brings a huge block of cherry wood, which she tries to form into a figure of Christ. In the exploitative and vulgar conditions of Detroit slums her family disintegrates, and Gertie feels the corruption of religious intolerance, racism, and self-interest undermine her artistic integrity. The final scene shows Gertie relinquishing her precious, near-completed statue to a scrapwood dealer, where it will be used for cheap, mass-produced dolls.

Arnow's only historical novel, *The Kentucky Trace*, is set in the Kentucky mountains during the Revolutionary War. The novel traces the story of Leslie Collins, a surveyor who had been serving with the rebel colonists. After being captured by bandits and rescued by 'overmountain' men, Collins makes his way home only to discover that his farm is deserted and his family gone. In his subsequent search for his family down the Kentucky trace, he comes upon a camp of survivors, each one displaced by the ravages of war. Arnow provides a descriptive document of the daily life and customs of the people of Cumberland during the Revolutionary War. The hero's attempts at healing himself and the land around him of war wounds produces both a namesake and an adoptive son. Although the novel verges on the sentimental, Arnow offers a new and refreshing angle on the revolution focusing on the everyday struggles of families and individuals to stay united and to survive, rather than accounts of battles. Her meticulous research is carefully blended into her fiction giving a precise and detailed description of the time.

Although Arnow wrote only one historical novel, her dark view of history as presented in *The Kentucky Trace* is not untypical of her other work. She held a depressing vision of what history has done to the people who live through it, the people who populate her novels. In Arnow's eyes Americans themselves have ruined their country and must bear this guilt.

—Scott Coombs

ASHFIELD, Helen.　　See **BENNETTS, Pamela.**

ASHLEY, Ellen.　　See **SEIFERT, Elizabeth.**

ASHTON, Elizabeth.　　British. 1902—. See 2nd edition, 1990.

ASHTON, Sharon. See **VAN SLYKE, Helen.**

ASQUITH, Nan.
Pseudonym for Nancy Evelyn Pattinson. **Nationality:** British. **Born:** Barnsley, Yorkshire. **Education:** St Winifred's school, Broadstairs, Kent; Wintersthorpe, Birkdale, Lancashire. **Relations:** married to Denis F.C. Pattinson. **Career:** worked as an advertising copywriter. **Died:** November 1979.

ROMANCE AND HISTORICAL PUBLICATIONS

Novels

My Dream Is Yours. London, Mills and Boon, 1954; as *Doctor Robert Comes Around,* Toronto, Harlequin, 1965.
With All My Heart. London, Mills and Boon, 1954; Toronto, Harlequin, 1968.
Believe in To-morrow. London, Mills and Boon, 1955; Toronto, Harlequin, 1971.
Only My Heart to Give. London, Mills and Boon, 1955; Toronto, Harlequin, 1969.
The Certain Spring. London, Mills and Boon, 1956; Toronto, Harlequin, 1968.
Honey Island. London, Mills and Boon, 1957.
The House on Brinden Water. London, Mills and Boon, 1958; as *The Doctor Is Engaged,* Toronto, Harlequin, 1962.
The Time for Happiness. London, Mills and Boon, 1959.
Time May Change. London, Mills and Boon, 1961; Toronto, Harlequin, 1974.
The Way the Wind Blows. London, Mills and Boon, 1963.
The Quest. London, Mills and Boon, 1964.
The Summer at San Milo. London, Mills and Boon, 1965.
Dangerous Yesterday. London, Mills and Boon, 1967.
The Garden of Persephone. London, Mills and Boon, 1967; Toronto, Harlequin, 1978.
The Admiral's House. London, Mills and Boon, 1969.
Turn the Page. London, Mills and Boon, and Toronto, Harlequin, 1970.
Beyond the Mountain. London, Mills and Boon, 1970.
Carnival at San Cristobal. London, Mills and Boon, 1971.
Out of the Dark. London, Mills and Boon, 1972.
The Girl from Rome. London, Mills and Boon, and Toronto, Harlequin, 1973.
The Sun in the Morning. London, Mills and Boon, 1974.

* * *

Nan Asquith was one of the more traditional romance writers of the 1950s and 1960s. Ten of her novels appeared in the Harlequin Romances beginning in 1962 with the publication of *The House on Brinden Water.* Her charming stories and attractive heroines gained her a wide reading audience during this period. Although some of her novels were written 40 years ago, there is a dateless quality in her novels that makes her just as readable today as then.

Despite the fact that they are traditional in formula, there is nothing simplistic about her novels. Complexity of character and well-thought-out plots show Asquith's talent as a romance writer. In her novels she pays close attention to developing her heroines by showing their inner growth. Jane Roper in *The Girl from Rome* falls in love with a young Italian, Gino, only to realize that he has no intention of marrying her. She has just completed the tourist season in Rome as a tour guide and had planned on remaining there, expecting his proposal. Her own moral standards and the realization that she has placed herself in a difficult position eventually force her to leave.

Rowan Langham in *Time May Change* meets Blake Hobart again after several years. She had been engaged to him, but did not have the maturity to make her own decision; consequently, her family influenced her to break the engagement. Since then, Rowan's father has died and she has had to grow up and assume more responsibility. Because of her added maturity, she is able to see Blake and her love in a more adult perspective.

Asquith is able to show the heroines' dilemma in such a way that their actions are well motivated and logical given their background and personality. She provides sufficient depth of character to make them believable by permitting frequent bouts of indecision and 'might-have-been' regrets.

Her plots tend to be slower paced and less complicated than those in more recent novels. She makes use of foreign settings and romantic activities such as a Mediterranean cruise, but the focus of her stories remains on her characters.

In developing the personalities of her heroes, Asquith again tends to keep them low key and approachable. They are human with touching lapses of weakness that makes them more realistic. Vance Morley takes Jane with him as his fiancée because he had once been engaged to Anthea, his sister-in-law. He is not sure of his feelings toward her and feels the need of protection, so that his brother will not be upset. Blake Hobart pretends to continue his racing career in order to learn if Rowan really is willing to acknowledge their love regardless of his occupation, for she had originally wanted him to give it up and join her father's company.

Both men show sensitive needs to protect themselves and it adds a further dimension to their characters. They are portrayed as vulnerable people trying to cope with life just as others must. In a sense, it is their masculine outlook and an awareness of their responsibilities that cause them to act as they do. Blake must know that Rowan's sense of love and loyalty will withstand pressures of time and circumstances, a test she had failed once before. Vance, aware of his sister-in-law's tendency to see things only as she wishes to, tries to protect his brother the best way he can.

In a way, Asquith is a subtle writer. On the surface, her novels seem light and frothy. Yet hidden beneath the surface is a delicate blending of love and people. Her readers are constantly exposed to ideals that surround the relationships of men and women. Step by step, she lets her characters realize their own needs and the needs of their loved ones so that the ending is a satisfying blend of suspense and certainty, both for her characters and her readers alike.

—Arlene Moore

ASTLEY, Juliet. See **LOFTS, Norah.**

ATKIN, Grace Murray.
Nationality: Canadian. **Born:** 1891. **Died.**

ROMANCE AND HISTORICAL PUBLICATIONS

Novels

The New World. New York, Crowell, 1921.
The Captive Herd. Toronto, McClelland and Stewart, 1922; London, Nash, 1923.
That Which Is Passed. New York, Crowell, 1923.
A Shadow Falls. Toronto, Ryerson Press, and New York, Bouregy, 1954; London, Wright and Brown, 1956.

OTHER PUBLICATIONS

Poetry

Flowers of the Wind. New York, Kennerley, 1919.

*   *   *

Grace Murray Atkin is a modernist novelist whose historical sense includes the idea of personal, psychological history. On the dedication page of her novel *The New World* she notes: 'I am one of those for whom character exists much more forcibly than action'. Unfortunately, characterization is more frequently defeated than supported by the modernist aspects of her narrative style. Atkin portrays characters moving through events rather than reflecting on the meaning of those events. Often commentary is given to a third-person narrator and the reader loses the illusion of perceiving events from a character's point of view as well as the accompanying sense of understanding the characters that this identificatory illusion gives.

In her two earliest novels, *The New World* and *The Captive Herd*, Atkin explores differing ethnic experiences of the new world. In the former novel, the Italian community in Canada is represented through the adolescence and early manhood years of the main character, Dante Ricci. The novel is set in the period just before, during, and just after World War I and traces Dante's progression from his old world family past to his election to the House of Commons. In the latter novel, the Jewish community in Manhattan provides the context for the events of the story. Both novels are set in time periods contemporaneous with the author's own life. Nevertheless, because of the ethnic point of view, both novels have a strong sense of historical moment. But, even here, the evocation of character psychology is constrained by the problems of narration already noted. The reader does not get a sense of character growth but rather a history of the events the characters have passed through. The conflicting purposes in the text make otherwise well-constructed stories seem trite.

The last novel Atkin wrote for a period of some 30 years, *That Which Is Passed*, is an experiment in an increasingly spare style. The novel is set in Paris shortly after World War I. Atkin develops a complex plot in which youth and age are at once contrasted and reconciled and the opposites of purity and scandal are presented in order to examine the impact of events on personal history. The central character, Peter Magdalen, was a fighter pilot in the war. Magdalen is an Englishman who was raised in Brittany and is fluent in French; he is an outsider who does not feel 'outside'. The plot unravels the mystery of his parentage skilfully, yet too predictably. While this novel is not strictly historical or a romance, it imaginatively captures a flavour of Paris between the wars from a refreshing perspective, other than that of bohemia and the café scene.

A Shadow Falls is an uneven novel divided into three parts, the first part of which is the least effective in its attempt to develop a 'stream-of-consciousness' technique. Parts two and three are closer to conventional realist writing and are more successful. Against a backdrop of the Laurentian mountains and the nearby Canadian capital city, Ottawa, the conflict between Old and New World cultures is enacted. The failure of technique is due to its incompatibility with the treatment of a chronology of the events, rather than a psychological study of the personal history presented from the narrating character's point of view. However, the tension between realist and modernist technique serves to enhance the dramatic possibilities of the plot.

Atkin's work cannot be identified as historical realist fiction or modernist, stream-of-consciousness psychological writing, but rather a transitional state between realism and the quality of reflexive self-awareness that has become known as metafiction. Her work seems unsatisfying because it does not fit the expectations of readers who may be reading from one of these three points of view. Nevertheless, from a literary historical perspective, her novels are fascinating as they struggle with changing ideas about what writing should or could be.

—Heather Iris Jones

———

ATKINSON, Mary.   See HARDWICK, Mollie.

———

AUEL, Jean M(arie).
Nationality: American. **Born:** Jean Marie Untinen, Chicago, Illinois, 18 February 1936. **Education:** Portland State University, Oregon; University of Portland, Oregon, M.B.A. 1976. **Relations:** married Ray Auel in 1954; three daughters and two sons. **Career:** clerk, Tektronix Inc, Beaverton, Oregon, 1965–66; circuit board designer, 1966–73; technical writer, 1973–74; credit manager, 1974–76. **Agent:** Jean V. Naggar Literary Agency, 216 East 75th Street, New York, New York 10021, USA.

ROMANCE AND HISTORICAL PUBLICATIONS

Novels (series: Earth's Children in all books)

The Clan of the Cave Bear. New York, Crown, and London, Hodder and Stoughton, 1980.
The Valley of Horses. New York, Crown, 1982; London, Hodder and Stoughton, 1983.
The Mammoth Hunters. New York, Crown, and London, Hodder and Stoughton, 1985.
The Plains of Passage. New York, Crown, and London, Hodder and Stoughton, 1990.

*

Film Adaptations: *Valley of the Horses*, 1984; *The Clan of the Cave Bear*, 1986.

*   *   *

The novels in Jean M. Auel's 'Earth's Children' series can perhaps best be described as feminist prehistorical romances. Drawing on feminist theories of matriarchal prehistory and fertility-based religion as well as presenting a portrayal of the minutiae of daily cave life drawn from contemporary archaeology, Auel uses the conventions of historical romance to create prehistoric feminist utopias. Throughout the series Auel's sensual and intellectually vibrant characters try to understand and overcome major cultural differences.

The Clan of the Cave Bear, the first book in the series, is the story of the adoption of the orphaned girl Ayla, who is Homo Sapiens, into a Neanderthal clan. Raised by the clan's shaman and medicine woman, Ayla struggles to adapt to clan ways, but since the differences between her adopted 'clan' and the 'others' of her birth are based on physiology and rooted in history and culture, her struggles to adjust are doomed. Ayla violates rigid clan conventions, particularly of male dominance and rigid gender separation, by learning to hunt, by resisting rape, by hiding her mixed-breed child to prevent his being killed as deformed, and by eavesdropping on male rituals. Torn between her needs to belong and to follow her own destiny, Ayla grows into a sensitive and intelligent young woman despite the oppressive clan social order. However, because she is never sufficiently submissive to that order, she is ultimately banished.

The Valley of Horses juxtaposes the story of Ayla's solitary life after leaving the clan with the story of the journey of two brothers of her race, Jondalar and Thonolan of the Zelandonii, who are undertaking a sort of prehistoric Grand Tour. The happy but shallow Thonolan loses interest in life after his wife's death and is ultimately killed by a cave lion. The brooding Jondalar, searching for a deeper meaning to life, attracts many women, but cannot fall in love until he meets Ayla. Because of the dual plot, Auel's second novel offers less sustained emotional involvement than her first. The novel's main interest is in the well-told details of prehistoric life. The brothers' journey introduces a succession of Stone Age cultures—all female-centred, worshipping a divine 'Mother' in various guises—and their ingenious ways of providing themselves with the necessary food, shelter, clothing, and entertainment for a satisfying life. Ayla's story has a different focus; in addition to establishing a cave household, the isolated Ayla learns to tame a horse and a cave lion and to produce fire by striking iron pyrite onto flint. Naturally, Ayla's and Jondalar's paths cross, and the final part of the book details their gradual drawing together, surmounting the cultural obstacles to mutual understanding, and their ultimate ecstatic union. Auel's explicit depiction of sexuality, particularly female sexuality, has led to accusations of obscenity; certainly in Jondalar, Auel has provided her heroine with a mate who compensates for the sexual and emotional violation and deprivation of her earlier years.

The Mammoth Hunters sets the romance of Ayla and Jondalar in a social context. Auel recaptures the sexual tension of the previous novel by using the difficulty of communicating across different cultural assumptions to estrange the lovers. A tribe of Mamutoi adopts Ayla, who is considered valuable not only as a female of childbearing age, but also as the bearer of fire stones and of extraordinary knowledge of medicine and animals. The lovers' relationship barely survives this year, as Jondalar grows jealous of Ayla's position and ashamed of her upbringing by the 'flatheads'—Neanderthals—his culture despises. This novel is about race, on two levels. When Ayla is courted by a black Mamutoi, Auel shows how racial differences can be considered 'interesting' rather than crucial. However, in this culture differences between Neanderthals and Homo Sapiens *are* crucial, and Jondalar's fears about how first the Mamutoi and then his own people will accept a woman who has borne a mixed son estrange him from Ayla. Only when they face final separation do they gain the courage to risk ignoring the dictates of culture.

The Plains of Passage is a Stone Age 'road novel', recounting the return of Jondalar with Ayla to the Zelandonii, with stops along the way to visit and bid farewell to the tribes Jondalar met on his outward journey. Although there is a slight overall plot-tension about whether or not Ayla and Jondalar will manage to cross the glacier before the ice melts and about whether Jondalar and Ayla can conceive a baby, the narrative is, for the most part, episodic. It offers a reprise of previous settings and characters and repeats the questions raised in earlier novels about where babies come from and whether Neanderthals are human. Jondalar continues to worry about whether his people will accept Ayla. In the second half of the novel, Jondalar is captured by a tribe of man-hating women and rescued by Ayla and her tame wolf. Ayla sets the broken leg of a Neanderthal who has been besieged by rebellious adolescent Homo Sapiens, and begins the process of negotiating relations between the two groups. Although Ayla and Jondalar make it back safely to the Zelandoii, and the happily pregnant Ayla is accepted warmly by them, the lack of a clear plot tension makes the book less engaging than the previous three.

Throughout this series Ayla matures as she moves from the repressive, male-dominated society of the clan, to an isolation in which she makes her own meanings, and finally to acceptance and love among the 'others', her own kind. Auel has given Ayla heroic attributes, and there is pleasure in seeing a 'heroine' who is important in herself, rather than merely a reward for the hero at the end of

his quest. If Ayla and Jondalar seem too much the typical WASP romantic leads, and if the correspondence between contemporary feminism and Auel's conception of cave society seems too pat, these excesses are forgivable because of the larger strengths of the novels. For although this series is set in the Stone Age, it raises contemporary feminist concerns about gender roles, and is as much about our own time as about prehistory. Auel uses the Stone Age setting and the conventions of historical romance to suggest that if human equality were institutionalized by a culture and its social structures, then passionate love between men and women would not only exist, but flourish.

—Linda S. Bergmann

———

AVERY, Lynn. See **ELIOT, Anne.**

———

AYRE, Jessica. See **APPIGNANESI, Lisa.**

———

AYRES, Ruby M(ildred).
Nationality: British. **Born:** January 1883. **Relations:** married Reginald William Pocock in 1909. **Career:** regular contributor to the *Daily Chronicle* and *Daily Mirror*, both London. **Died:** 14 November 1955.

ROMANCE AND HISTORICAL PUBLICATIONS

Novels

Richard Chatterton, VC. London, Hodder and Stoughton, 1915; New York, Watt, 1919.
The Long Lane to Happiness. London, Hodder and Stoughton, 1915.
The Making of a Man. London, Newnes, 1915.
The Road That Bends. London, Hodder and Stoughton, 1916.
Paper Roses. London, Hodder and Stoughton, 1916.
A Man of His Word. London, Hodder and Stoughton, 1916.
The Year After. London, Newnes, 1916.
The Littl'st Lover. London, Hodder and Stoughton, 1917; New York, Doran, 1925.
The Black Sheep. London, Hodder and Stoughton, 1917.
The Winds of the World. London, Hodder and Stoughton, 1918; New York, Watt, 1921.
The Remembered Kiss. London, Hodder and Stoughton, 1918.
For Love. London, Hodder and Stoughton, 1918.
The Second Honeymoon. London, Hodder and Stoughton, 1918; New York, Watt, 1921.
Invalided Out. London, Hodder and Stoughton, 1918.
The Phantom Lover. London, Hodder and Stoughton, 1919; New York, Watt, 1921.
The Girl Next Door. London, Hodder and Stoughton, 1919.
The One Who Forgot. London, Hodder and Stoughton, 1919.
The Scar. London, Hodder and Stoughton, 1920; New York, Watt, 1921.
A Bachelor Husband. London, Hodder and Stoughton, and New York, Watt, 1920.
The Master Man. London, Hodder and Stoughton, 1920.
The Woman Hater. London, Hodder and Stoughton, 1920.
The Marriage of Barry Wicklow. London, Hodder and Stoughton, 1920; New York, Watt, 1921.

The Beggar Man. London, Hodder and Stoughton, 1920.
The Dancing Master. London, Hodder and Stoughton, 1920.
The Uphill Road. New York, Watt, 1921.
The Waif's Wedding. London, Hodder and Stoughton, 1921.
The Fortune Hunter. London, Hodder and Stoughton, 1921.
Her Way and His. London, Hodder and Stoughton, 1921.
The Highest Bidder. London, Hodder and Stoughton, 1921.
His Word of Honour. London, Hodder and Stoughton, 1921.
The Love of Robert Dennison. London, Hodder and Stoughton, 1921.
Brown Sugar. London, Hodder and Stoughton, 1921.
A Loveless Marriage. London, Hodder and Stoughton, 1921.
The Making of a Lover. London, Hodder and Stoughton, 1921.
The Man's Way. London, Hodder and Stoughton, 1921.
Nobody's Lovers. London, Hodder and Stoughton, 1921.
The One Unwanted. London, Hodder and Stoughton, 1921.
The Street Below. London, Hodder and Stoughton, 1922; New York, Doran, n.d.
A Gamble with Love. London, Hodder and Stoughton, 1922.
The Little Lady in Lodgings. London, Hodder and Stoughton, 1922.
The Lover Who Died. London, Hodder and Stoughton, 1922.
The Matherson Marriage. London, Hodder and Stoughton, 1922; New York, Doran, 1923.
The Romance of a Rogue. London, Hodder and Stoughton, and New York, Doran, 1923.
Love and a Lie. London, Hodder and Stoughton, 1923.
The Man Without a Heart. London, Hodder and Stoughton, 1923; New York, Doran, 1924.
The One Who Stood By. London, Hodder and Stoughton, 1923.
The Eager Search. London, Hodder and Stoughton, 1923.
Candle Light. London, Hodder and Stoughton, and New York, Doran, 1924.
Ribbons and Laces. London, Hodder and Stoughton, 1924.
Paul in Possession. London, Hodder and Stoughton, 1924.
The Man the Women Loved. London, Hodder and Stoughton, 1925; New York, Doran, 1926.
The Marriage Handicap. London, Hodder and Stoughton, 1925.
Overheard. London, Hodder and Stoughton, 1925; New York, Doran, 1926.
Charity's Chosen. London, Hodder and Stoughton, and New York, Doran, 1926.
Spoilt Music. London, Hodder and Stoughton, and New York, Doran, 1926.
The Faint Heart. London, Hodder and Stoughton, 1926.
The Planter and the Tree. London, Hodder and Stoughton, 1926; New York, Doran, 1927.
Wynne of Windwhistle. London, Hodder and Stoughton, 1926.
By the Gate of Pity. New York, Street and Smith, 1927.
The Luckiest Lady. London, Hodder and Stoughton, and New York, Doran, 1927.
Life Steps In. London, Hodder and Stoughton, 1928; New York, Doubleday, 1929.
The Family. London, Hodder and Stoughton, 1928.
Broken. London, Hodder and Stoughton, and New York, Doubleday, 1928.
Lovers. London, Hodder and Stoughton, and New York, Doubleday, 1929.
The Heartbreak Marriage. London, Hodder and Stoughton, 1929.
One Month at Sea, Together with George Who Believed in Allah. London, Hodder and Stoughton, 1929.
In the Day's March. London, Hodder and Stoughton, and New York, Doubleday, 1930.
Giving Him Up. London, Hodder and Stoughton, 1930.
My Old Love Came. London, Hodder and Stoughton, 1930.
One Summer. London, Hodder and Stoughton, and New York, Doubleday, 1930.

The Big Fellah. London, Hodder and Stoughton, and New York, Doubleday, 1931; as *Love Comes to Mary*, New York, Grosset and Dunlap, 1932.
Men Made the Town. London, Hodder and Stoughton, and New York, Doubleday, 1931.
The Little Man. London, Hodder and Stoughton, 1931; as *Winner Take All*, New York, Doubleday, 1937.
The Princess Passes. London, Hodder and Stoughton, 1931.
By the World Forgot. London, Hodder and Stoughton, 1932; New York, Doubleday, 1933.
So Many Miles. New York, Doubleday, 1932; London, Hodder and Stoughton, 1933.
Changing Pilots. London, Hodder and Stoughton, and New York, Doubleday, 1932.
Look to the Spring. London, Hodder and Stoughton, 1932; New York, Doubleday, 1933.
Always Tomorrow. London, Hodder and Stoughton, 1933; New York, Doubleday, 1934.
Come to My Wedding. London, Hodder and Stoughton, and New York, Doubleday, 1933.
Love Is So Blind. London, Hodder and Stoughton, 1933; New York, Doubleday, 1934.
All Over Again. New York, Doubleday, 1934; London, Hodder and Stoughton, 1935.
From This Day Forward. London, Hodder and Stoughton, and New York, Doubleday, 1934.
Much-Loved. London, Hodder and Stoughton, and New York, Doubleday, 1934.
Than This World Dreams Of. London, Hodder and Stoughton, 1934; New York, Doubleday, 1935.
Between You and Me. London, Hodder and Stoughton, 1935.
Feather. New York, Doubleday, 1935; London, Hodder and Stoughton, 1936.
The Man in Her Life. London, Hodder and Stoughton, and New York, Doubleday, 1935.
Some Day. London, Hodder and Stoughton, and New York, Doubleday, 1935.
The Sun and the Sea. London, Hodder and Stoughton, and New York, Doubleday, 1935.
Compromise. London, Hodder and Stoughton, and New York, Doubleday, 1936.
After-Glow. London, Hodder and Stoughton, and New York, Doubleday, 1936.
Follow the Shadow. London, Hodder and Stoughton, 1936; New York, Doubleday, 1937.
High Noon. London, Hodder and Stoughton, 1936; New York, Doubleday, 1937.
Somebody Else. New York, Doubleday, 1936; London, Hodder and Stoughton, 1937.
Too Much Together. London, Hodder and Stoughton, and New York, Doubleday, 1936.
Living Apart. New York, Doubleday, 1937; London, Hodder and Stoughton, 1938.
Owner Gone Abroad. London, Hodder and Stoughton, and New York, Doubleday, 1937.
Silver Wedding. London, Hodder and Stoughton, 1937.
Unofficial Wife. New York, Doubleday, 1937; London, Hodder and Stoughton, 1938.
The Tree Drops a Leaf. London, Hodder and Stoughton, and New York, Doubleday, 1938.
Return Journey. New York, Doubleday, 1938; London, Hodder and Stoughton, 1939.
And Still They Dream. New York, Doubleday, 1938; London, Hodder and Stoughton, 1939.
One to Live With. London, Hodder and Stoughton, and New York, Doubleday, 1938.

There Was Another. London, Hodder and Stoughton, and New York, Doubleday, 1938.

Big Ben. New York, Doubleday, 1939.

The Moon in the Water. New York, Doubleday, 1939.

The Thousandth Man. London, Hodder and Stoughton, and New York, Doubleday, 1939.

Week-End Woman. London, Hodder and Stoughton, and New York, Doubleday, 1939.

Little and Good. London, Hodder and Stoughton, and New York, Doubleday, 1940.

The Little Sinner. London, Hodder and Stoughton, and New York, Doubleday, 1940.

Wallflower. London, Hodder and Stoughton, and New York, Doubleday, 1940.

Sometimes Spring Is Late. London, Hodder and Stoughton, 1941.

Sunrise for Georgie. London, Hodder and Stoughton, 1941.

Still Waters. London, Hodder and Stoughton, and New York, Doubleday, 1941.

The Constant Heart. New York, Doubleday, 1941.

Rosemary—For Forgetting. London, Hodder and Stoughton, 1941.

Young Is My Love. New York, Doubleday, 1941; as *The Young at Heart*, London, Hodder and Stoughton, 1942.

Nothing Lovelier. London, Hodder and Stoughton, 1942.

Lost Property. New York, Doubleday, 1943.

Man Friday. London, Hodder and Stoughton, 1943.

Love Comes Unseen. New York, Doubleday, 1943; as *One Woman Too Many*, London, Hodder and Stoughton, 1952.

Starless Night. London, Hodder and Stoughton, 1943.

The Lady from London. London, Hodder and Stoughton, 1944.

The Dreamer Wakes. London, Hodder and Stoughton, 1945.

April's Day. London, Macdonald, 1945.

Where Are You Going? London, Hodder and Stoughton, 1946.

Salt of the Earth. London, Macdonald, 1946.

Young Shoulders. London, Hodder and Stoughton, 1947.

Missing the Tide. London, Hodder and Stoughton, 1948.

The Story of John Willie. London, Macdonald, 1948.

Steering by a Star. London, Hodder and Stoughton, 1949.

The Day Comes Round. London, Hodder and Stoughton, 1949; New York, Arcadia House, 1950.

The Man from Ceylon. London, Hodder and Stoughton, 1950.

The Man Who Lived Alone. London, Macdonald, 1950.

The Story of Fish and Chips. London, Macdonald, 1951; as *Bright Destiny*, New York, Arcadia House, 1952.

Twice a Boy. London, Hodder and Stoughton, 1951.

The Youngest Aunt. London, Hodder and Stoughton, 1952.

One Sees Stars. London, Hodder and Stoughton, 1952.

Love Without Wings. London, Hodder and Stoughton, 1953; New York, Arcadia House, 1954.

Dark Gentleman. London, Hodder and Stoughton, 1953.

Old-Fashioned Heart. New York, Arcadia House, 1953.

Short Stories

The Shadow Man and Other Stories. London, Hutchinson, 1919.

Our Avenue and Other Stories. London, Pearson, 1922; New York, Arcadia House, 1936.

Happy Endings. London, Jarrolds, 1935.

Autumn Fires: Two Love Stories. London, Hodder and Stoughton, 1951.

OTHER PUBLICATIONS

Other

Castles in Spain: The Chronicles of an April Month. London, Cassell, 1912.

*   *   *

Ruby M. Ayres's first novel (of some 150) was published in the 1910s. Most of them were made of a bland and jokey mixture which proved to be almost timeless. Consequently, many were still selling under the guise of new novels well into the 1960s and 1970s.

Publishers are naturally reluctant to relinquish a steady-selling commercial name. If, by misfortune, a publisher's bestselling author runs out of steam, dies, or cannot keep up with the insatiable appetite of her readers, demand for her works can be fulfilled by re-issuing the novels, just as they are, or as a new novel with an up-to-date dust jacket, or in a modified version. Ayres's novels were eminently suitable for this treatment. *Week-End Woman*, for example, made its first appearance in 1939. Some 30 years later it re-appeared with a newly designed jacket, but only minor alterations to the text. In 1939 Slane the shady suitor is, for example, said to be 'a man on leave from India'. In 1969 he has become 'a man on leave from the Middle East oil company in which he had a good job'. In 1939 Mariette, 'heroine with an angel's face', wears hats when she goes out to lunch. In the less constricting 1960s, she must lunch hatless. In 1939 her rich husband's imperious treatment of restaurant waiters is demanding and aggressive: 'Here waiter, keep this stuff hot till I come back', he orders. Then, 'Where's my dinner?' and 'Come and light the fire some of you fellows—don't just stand there gaping'. In the 1969 text the publisher's editor had realized that such treatment of minions is no longer socially acceptable. The stereotype of the ideal man however, remains quite unchanged. In both versions, he has 'grey eyes, dark brows, dark hair and a certain ruthlessness about the mouth and chin, good-looking in a manly, rather severe way'.

The slightly suggestive title and blurb might lead one to expect some titillation, or at least a hint of illicit sexual activity: 'Wealth alone could not compensate for the lack of any real affection. And so she turned to other men. One affair followed another in quick succession as she sought vainly for something real to cling to'. This blurb is misleading. Mariette's behaviour may seem plain daft, but is never adulterous, for, as she repeatedly wails to one of her admirers: 'I can't—I'm afraid. Yes, of course I love you—but I can't face it—I'm not made that way. I hate scandal—I'm afraid'. She has little to be afraid of. We read how the man 'ran his hands over her shoulders and slim body'. By 1969, even this innocuous move has been omitted, and he does not lay a finger on her. The book's principal concern, in both versions, is upholding the reputation of the heroine. As society became more permissive, Ayres's stories were re-created to seem more straitlaced.

Rosemary—For Forgetting, similarly, was a successful reissue. It is the tale of a rich girl who falls irrevocably in love with an 'unsuitable person'. The rich father has him sent away; the engagement is broken off. Rosemary spends the rest of the book trying to forget her childhood sweetheart until, on the penultimate page, her father now being dead, the lovers are reunited. Although first published in 1941, the novel is so totally lacking in topicality that it could be successfully re-issued in 1966 with only minor changes to the text. Indeed, the one careless point is the publishers' choice of illustration. Rosemary is said to live in a large country house a few hours from Paddington Station. She has 'fair hair, and her eyes were as blue as forget-me-nots; her tiny hands and feet were perfect, and when she laughed one corner of her mouth lifted itself a little higher than the other corner in an oddly fascinating manner'. In the 1966 jacket, although no doubt still oddly fascinating, she is shown as having raven-black hair, coal-dark eyes, and thick symmetrical lips. While being kissed on the ear by a man in a lime-green sports shirt, she is standing in front of what is clearly no wealthy Home Counties residence, but a North American log-chalet. This kind of carelessness in presentation can have done little to raise the prestige of romantic fiction, then at a low ebb.

The cheap re-issues of popular fiction have always been seen as a threat to the more serious novelist. E.H. Lacon Watson, a journalist lecturing in the 1930s, said that they were actually destroying the livelihood of the writers who sold less well. 'In recent years, every change that has been made in the world of publishing and bookselling has been in favour of the few big sellers and against the author with a small, if select, audience'. In fact, the readership of these two types of fiction was different. Ayres herself described, with a touch of self-mockery, the kind of girl who might be reading her own novels. There is 'a kind-eyed, sentimental under housemaid', in *The Master Man* 'who was young and romantic and devoured every novel she could get hold of'.

By 'every novel' Ayres clearly does not mean the highbrow heavy weights, but novels such as her own. Hers are fantasy-spinning, harmless escapism, jauntily written, with convoluted plots, and an excess of metaphors piled one on the other. If she had been out to expound some profound message, these many varied metaphors might well have obscured the meaning. But she was not. She was out to entertain. Just occasionally, there is a heroine, such as Marlene (*Where Are You Going?*) who not only starts out confused and upset, but ends up with second best too. 'She asked herself the question, "Where are you going?" and failed to find an answer'. Luckily, she ends up with a partner equally unsure where he is going, a tired-looking, discharged soldier 'with a slight limp'.

Ayres had her craft in perspective, and was quite aware of where *she* was going.

Do you believe really believe in the romance you've written so much about? Do you believe it lasts? I'm frequently asked the question by people who are kind enough to enjoy reading my books and I can imagine it would be very disillusioning if I were to reply—'No, I don't believe in it. I just write love stories because they sell'. That wouldn't be true either. I must certainly believe in romance and know that it can and does last providing it is mixed with two most important ingredients—tolerance and a sense of humour. ... I'm not pretending to be original when I say that more marriages have been ruined by a nagging wife than there can ever be by an atomic bomb. I firmly believe that romance can be lively even when the strawberry season is over and there is only bread and cheese in the larder and no matter whether you agree with me or not, I'll go on writing love stories with happy endings.

—Rachel Anderson

BACHELLER, Irving (Addison).
Nationality: American. **Born:** Piedmont, New York, 26 September 1859. **Education:** St. Lawrence University, Canton, New York, M.S. 1892, M.A. 1901; Middlebury College, Vermont, Ph.D. **Relations:** married 1) Anna Detmar Schultz in 1883 (died 1924); 2) Mary Elizabeth Sollace (died 1949). **Career:** editor, New York *World*, 1898–1900. **Recipient:** LL.D.: Rollins College, Winter Park, Florida, 1939. **Died:** 24 February 1950.

ROMANCE AND HISTORICAL PUBLICATIONS

Novels (series: Eben Holden)

The Master of Silence. New York, Webster, 1892.
The Still House of O'Darrow. London, Cassell, 1894.
The Story of a Passion. East Aurora, New York, Roycroft, 1899.
Eben Holden. Boston, Lothrop, and London, Richards, 1900.
D'Iri and I. Boston, Lothrop, and London, Richards, 1901.
Darrel of the Blessed Isles. Boston, Lothrop, and London, Watt, 1903.

Vergilius: A Tale of the Coming of Christ. New York, Harper, 1904.
Silas Strong: Emperor of the Woods. New York, Harper, and London, Fisher Unwin, 1906.
Eben Holden's Last Day a-Fishing. New York, Harper, 1907.
The Hand-Made Gentleman. New York, Harper, 1909; as *Cricket Heron*, London, Unwin, 1909.
The Master. New York, Doubleday, 1909.
Keeping Up with Lizzy. New York, Harper, 1911.
Charge It; or, Keeping Up with Harry. New York, Harper, 1912.
The Turning of Griggsby. New York, Harper, 1913.
Marryers. New York, Harper, 1914.
The Light in the Clearing. Indianapolis, Bobbs Merrill, 1917; London, Collins, 1918.
Keeping Up with William. Indianapolis, Bobbs Merrill, 1918.
A Man for the Ages. Indianapolis, Bobbs Merrill, 1919; London, Constable, 1920.
The Prodigal Village: A Christmas Tale. Indianapolis, Bobbs Merrill, 1920.
In the Days of Poor Richard. Indianapolis, Bobbs Merrill, 1922; London, Hutchinson, 1923.
The Scudders: A Story of Today. New York, Macmillan, 1923; London, Mills and Boon, 1924.
Father Abraham. Indianapolis, Bobbs Merrill, and London, Hutchinson, 1925.
Dawn: A Lost Romance of the Time of Christ. New York, Macmillan, 1927; as *The Trumpets of God*, London, Melrose, 1927.
The House of the Three Ganders. Indianapolis, Bobbs Merrill, 1928; London, Hutchinson, 1929.
A Candle in the Wilderness. Indianapolis, Bobbs Merrill, 1930.
Master of Chaos. Indianapolis, Bobbs Merrill, 1932.
Uncle Peel. New York, Grosset and Dunlap, 1933.
The Harvesting. New York, Stokes, 1934.
The Oxen of the Sun. New York, Stokes, 1935.
A Boy for the Ages. New York, Farrar and Rinehart, 1937.

OTHER PUBLICATIONS

Novel

The Winds of God (for children). New York, Farrar and Rinehart, 1941.

Poetry

In Various Moods. New York, Harper, 1910.

Other

Opinions of a Cheerful Yankee (autobiography). Indianapolis, Bobbs Merrill, 1926.
Coming Up the Road: Memories of a North Country Boyhood. Indianapolis, Bobbs Merrill, 1928.
Great Moments in the Life of Washington. New York, Grosset and Dunlap, 1932.
From Stores of Memory (memoirs). New York, Farrar and Rinehart, 1938.

Editor, *Best Things from American Literature.* New York, Christian Herald, 1899.

*   *   *

It is difficult to think of Irving Bacheller's literary output without concentrating on the region where he spent his formative years, upstate New York, and the historical romance. Bacheller's most effective creative works are ones which focus on his native state and chronicle the lives and adventures of fictional characters native to that area and nearby states. Written in first-person narrative, Bacheller's work generally is set in the 18th and early 19th centuries; his characters meet major figures in American history such as George Washington, Abraham Lincoln, or Benjamin Franklin.

By far Bacheller's most commercially successful work was *Eben Holden*, which is set in upstate New York and is an account of country life through the eyes of a homespun farmhand. During Bacheller's lifetime this novel sold nearly three-quarters of a million copies. The rural New York connection is pursued with *In the Days of Poor Richard*, which opens in the wilderness of northern New York and closes in Philadelphia. In keeping with Bacheller's dominant chronological emphasis, the reader progresses through the Revolutionary War meeting some of its leading figures and travelling to urban centres intimately associated with that era. Romance is provided as hardy Jack Irons falls in love with Margaret Hare, marries her, and proves himself valiant in peace and war. In *Master of Chaos* Bacheller presents another Revolutionary era romance between Colin Cabot, a Harvard educated supporter of the rebel cause, and Patience Fayer-weather, daughter of a strong Loyalist family. Not unlike Irons, Cabot joins the Continental Army serving as a secretary and later recruiting officer under George Washington. *The Light in the Clearing* covers the early portion of the 19th century in upstate New York and revolves around the life of Silas Wright, an early New York governor who befriends a boy named Barton Baynes. Baynes's early years with his Aunt Deel and Uncle Peabody provide a glimpse into the social life of those times.

Bacheller's penchant for characters moving across time and location is further exemplified in *A Man for the Ages*, which concentrates on the early manhood of Abraham Lincoln. The Traylors move from Vermont to New Salem, Illinois in the 1830s and there meet the young Abe Lincoln, become friends, and share in his growth in the frontier community to the point of his entering the United States House of Representatives. Another Lincoln portrait is preserved in *Father Abraham*, where the youthful northerner Randall Hope, inspired by the personality of 'Father Abraham' moves south to the home of a relative and engages in a predictable clash of ideas. Hope becomes involved in the Civil War and finds romance and adventure.

Perhaps the most dramatic geographical shift in Bacheller's writing comes in *Dawn: A Lost Romance of the Time of Christ* in which a young Greek woman, Doris of Colossae, falls in love with Apollos, a Christian Jew. Apollos, already married, leaves Doris. Doris converts to Christianity and comes into contact with a number of biblical characters and events. Bacheller's last novel, *The Winds of God*, tells the story of an Adirondack guide and timber cutter.

Bacheller wrote more than 30 novels, the majority of which are historical romance. His works emphasize strength of individual character, patriotism, and sturdy American ideals. Critically, the novels met with mixed success; his deification of figures in American history is now unfashionable. The strength of Bacheller's literary work centres on his recreation of the personal character of upstate New Yorkers and his action-filled plots.

—Frank R. Levstick

_____

BAILEY, H(enry) C(hristopher).
Nationality: British. **Born:** London, 1 February 1878. **Education:** City of London School; Corpus Christi College, Oxford (scholar), B.A. 1901. **Relations:** married Lydia Haden Janet Guest in 1908; two daughters. **Career:** drama critic, war correspondent, and leader writer, *Daily Telegraph*, London, 1901–46. **Died:** 24 March 1961.

ROMANCE AND HISTORICAL PUBLICATIONS

Novels

My Lady of Orange. London and New York, Longman, 1901.
Karl of Erbach. New York, Longman, 1902; London, Longman, 1903.
The Master of Gray. London and New York, Longman, 1903.
Beaujeu. London, Murray, 1905.
Under Castle Walls. New York, Appleton, 1906; as *Springtime*, London, Murray, 1907.
Raoul, Gentleman of Fortune. London, Hutchinson, 1907; as *A Gentleman of Fortune*, New York, Appleton, 1907.
The God of Clay. London, Hutchinson, and New York, Brentano's, 1908.
Colonel Stow. London, Hutchinson, 1908; as *Colonel Greatheart*, Indianapolis, Bobbs Merrill, 1908.
Storm and Treasure. London, Methuen, and New York, Brentano's, 1910.
The Lonely Queen. London, Methuen, and New York, Doran, 1911.
The Sea Captain. New York, Doran, 1913; London, Methuen, 1914.
The Gentleman Adventurer. London, Methuen, 1914; New York, Doran, 1915.
The Highwayman. London, Methuen, 1915; New York, Dutton, 1918.
The Gamesters. London, Methuen, 1916; New York, Dutton, 1919.
The Young Lovers. London, Methuen, 1917; New York, Dutton, 1929.
The Pillar of Fire. London, Methuen, 1918.
Barry Leroy. London, Methuen, 1919; New York, Dutton, 1920.
His Serene Highness. London, Methuen, 1920; New York, Dutton, 1922.
The Fool. London, Methuen, 1921; New York, Dutton, 1927.
The Plot. London, Methuen, 1922.
The Rebel. London, Methuen, 1923.
Knight at Arms. London, Methuen, 1924; New York, Dutton, 1925.
The Golden Fleece. London, Methuen, 1925.
The Merchant Prince. London, Methuen, 1926; New York, Dutton, 1929.
Bonaventure. London, Methuen, 1927.
Judy Bovenden. London, Methuen, 1928.
Mr Cardonnel. London, Ward Lock, 1931.
The Bottle Party. New York, Doubleday, 1940.

OTHER PUBLICATIONS

Novels

Rimingtons. London, Chapman and Hall, 1904.
The Suburban. London, Methuen, 1912.
Garstons. London, Methuen, 1930; as *The Garston Murder Case*, New York, Doubleday, 1930.
The Red Castle. London, Ward Lock, 1932; as *The Red Castle Mystery*, New York, Doubleday, 1932.
The Man in the Cape. London, Benn, 1933.
Shadow on the Wall. London, Gollancz, and New York, Doubleday, 1934.
The Sullen Sky Mystery. London, Gollancz, and New York, Doubleday, 1935.
Black Land, White Land. London, Gollancz, and New York, Doubleday, 1937.
Clunk's Claimant. London, Gollancz, 1937; as *The Twittering Bird Mystery*, New York, Doubleday, 1937.
The Great Game. London, Gollancz, and New York, Doubleday, 1939.

The Veron Mystery. London, Gollancz, 1939; as *Mr Clunk's Text*, New York, Doubleday, 1939.

The Bishop's Crime. London, Gollancz, 1940; New York, Doubleday, 1941.

The Little Captain. London, Gollancz, 1941; as *Orphan Ann*, New York, Doubleday, 1941.

Dead Man's Shoes. London, Gollancz, 1942; as *Nobody's Vineyard*, New York, Doubleday, 1942.

No Murder. London, Gollancz, 1942; as *The Apprehensive Dog*, New York, Doubleday, 1942.

Mr Fortune Finds a Pig. London, Gollancz, and New York, Doubleday, 1943.

Slippery Ann. London, Gollancz, 1944; as *The Queen of Spades*, New York, Doubleday, 1944.

The Cat's Whisker. New York, Doubleday, 1944; as *Dead Man's Effects*, London, Macdonald, 1945.

The Wrong Man. New York, Doubleday, 1945; London, Macdonald, 1946.

The Life Sentence. London, Macdonald, and New York, Doubleday, 1946.

Honour among Thieves. London, Macdonald, and New York, Doubleday, 1947.

Saving a Rope. London, Macdonald, 1948; as *Save a Rope*, New York, Doubleday, 1948.

Shrouded Death. London, Macdonald, 1950.

Short Stories

Call Mr Fortune. London, Methuen, 1920; New York, Dutton, 1921.

Mr Fortune's Practice. London, Methuen, 1923; New York, Dutton, 1924.

Mr Fortune's Trials. London, Methuen, 1925; New York, Dutton, 1926.

Mr Fortune, Please. London, Methuen, and New York, Dutton, 1928.

Mr Fortune Speaking. London, Ward Lock, 1930; New York, Dutton, 1931.

Mr Fortune Explains. London, Ward Lock, 1930; New York, Dutton, 1931.

Case for Mr Fortune. London, Ward Lock, and New York, Doubleday, 1932.

Mr Fortune Wonders. London, Ward Lock, and New York, Doubleday, 1933.

Mr Fortune Objects. London, Gollancz, and New York, Doubleday, 1935.

A Clue for Mr Fortune. London, Gollancz, and New York, Doubleday, 1936.

Mr Fortune's Case Book (omnibus). London, Methuen, 1936.

This Is Mr Fortune. London, Gollancz, and New York, Doubleday, 1938.

Mr Fortune Here. London, Gollancz, and New York, Doubleday, 1940.

Meet Mr Fortune (selection). New York, Doubleday, 1942.

The Best of Mr Fortune. New York, Pocket Books, 1943.

Play

The White Hawk, with David Kimball, adaptation of the novel *Beaujeu* by Bailey (produced London, 1909).

Other

Forty Years After: The Story of the Franco-German War, 1870. London, Hodder and Stoughton, 1914.

The Roman Eagles (for children). London, Gill, 1929.

*   *   *

A writer of healthy outdoor swashbucklers that are only passingly concerned with plausibility or characterization, H.C. Bailey does not specialize in time or place, but sets his novels indifferently in an England or Europe with some historical basis (the Peninsular War in *The Young Lovers*, Plantagenet England in *The Fool*) or in a fantasy of Renaissance Italy (*Under Castle Walls*). Real characters are introduced to some extent, but the emphasis is always on the creatures of Bailey's imagination.

Bailey usually imagined men—and the men who are his heroes are brave, quick-witted, and misunderstood. In some respects, they have the appeal of a jolly English public schoolboy. The noble Lionardo of *Under Castle Walls* is thought negligible by his court until he is motivated by the cruelties of a neighbouring lord to make war. John Newstead, the mercenary soldier who transfers his loyalty from the Duke of Alva to William the Silent in *My Lady of Orange* finds his motives misunderstood by the Dutch and even by his adored Gabrielle, until he proves to them all that he is driven by natural goodness as well as desire for riches. The *Knight at Arms*, Silvain St Lo, is a kind of Don Quixote, going through 15th-century France and Italy fighting for his honour, confounding again and again those who expect him to seek wealth, love, or political power. His encounters leave him worse off than before, despite his undoubted soldierly skills and his quick mind, because he will not seek advantage for himself or for his cynical squire Thibaut. Of course Bran, *The Fool*, who becomes a companion of Henry II, makes up for his low social status by his cleverness and instinctive understanding of the English people.

Similarly, Bailey's evil protagonists are villainous indeed: Castracane's vicious tortures in *Under Castle Walls* are as well not described since the one that bears description involves feeding his enemies to his wolf pack. We meet the unspeakable betrayals of John Lackland in *The Fool*, although other historical villains, including Roger Mortimer, are treated more gently. Minor henchmen, bullies and rogues, however, are pilloried. The villainous French mercenary Henri Vermeil, who tries to betray Newstead in *My Lady of Orange*, is dyed with darker colours than the Duke of Alva himself. *The Young Lovers*, with a stronger historical basis than most, includes at least one noble French enemy and even a likeable and idealistically motivated French spy.

The Young Lovers is unusual in that circumstances, and the protagonist Jack Lavington himself, are Jack's worst enemies. Showing a weakness in plotting that becomes almost comic, Lavington's whole family and some of his friends are remarkably susceptible to kidnapping: cousin David is twice kidnapped for reasons that have nothing to do with Jack, and Jack is twice blamed by David's father and society generally; Jack himself is abducted; Miss Amberly and the Portuguese girl she has befriended are also kidnapped by a French officer who refuses to believe Juana is serious about marrying David Lavington; and Jack's uncle was kidnapped years ago in Venice. Jack ends up a successful officer under Pakenham, heir to his uncle's large fortune, and engaged to the enchanting Mary Amberly—a happier end than many of Bailey's heroes have. While Bran finally retires to his adoptive daughter's home after Henry II's ignominious death in *The Fool*, Silvain St Lo, bereft of horses, allies and friends, ends *Knight at Arms* as he began, seeking honour on the field of battle.

The women that Bailey creates have much in common, too. They are beautiful, and they may be kind. The three heroines of *Under Castle Walls* are: the beautiful Lucrezia, who is more spirited, more fallible—and hence more human—than most; the beautiful and serene Beatrice, who almost loses her husband because of her placidity; and the lovely but pathetic waif Cecilia, the Marchioness of Frido, a cousin to the witch child Ia in *The Fool*. It would be easy to call these figures stereotypes, but they are not similar enough to any real people to be called that. They are more like archetypes, living in a sunny, Britannic Arcady. (None of Bailey's heroes are English, but if Englishmen are available, they are given heroic roles.)

Note should be made of the enticing descriptions of rural scenes with which Bailey enlivens his novels, well-written yet causing no more than a ripple in the smoothly flowing narratives. Although *The Fool* and *Knight at Arms* are both episodic in nature, Bailey contrives to keep the reader interested as event follows event.

While Bailey's novels deal mostly with the upper strata of society, his work is relatively free of the political and racial prejudices that mar other work of the period in which he was writing—largely because he seems to be uninterested in such mundane details. Bran is concerned with peasant and serf in *The Fool*, being himself of the lower orders, and Silvain is kind to the poor—it's the knightly thing to do.

Reading Bailey, one can relax in the conviction that no character the author allows one to become fond of will be killed or even injured (except those whose demise is historically well established—though Bran tries in vain to save Thomas à Becket) and that all will end well for the right people.

—Susan Branch

BALDWIN, Faith.
Nationality: American. **Born:** New Rochelle, New York, 1 October 1893. **Education:** Packer School; Miss Fuller School; Briarcliff School. **Relations:** married Hugh H. Cuthrell in 1920 (died 1953); two sons and two daughters. **Career:** freelance writer: faculty member, Famous Writers School, Westport, Connecticut. **Died:** 18 March 1978.

ROMANCE AND HISTORICAL PUBLICATIONS

Novels

Mavis of Green Hill. Boston, Small Maynard, and London, Hodder and Stoughton, 1921.
Laurel of Stonystream. Boston, Small Maynard, 1923; as *The Maid of Stonystream*, London, Sampson Low, 1924.
Magic and Mary Rose. Boston, Small Maynard, 1924.
Thresholds. Boston, Small Maynard, 1925; London, Sampson Low, 1926.
Those Difficult Years. Boston, Small Maynard, 1925; London, Sampson Low, 1926.
Three Women. New York, Dodd Mead, 1926; London, Sampson Low, 1927.
Departing Wings. New York, Dodd Mead, 1927; London, Sampson Low, 1928.
Rosalie's Career. New York, Clode, 1928.
Betty. New York, Clode, and London, Sampson Low, 1928.
Alimony. New York, Dodd Mead, 1928; London, Sampson Low, 1929.
The Incredible Year. New York, Dodd Mead, 1929; London, Sampson Low, 1930.
Garden Oats. New York, Dodd Mead, and London, Sampson Low, 1929.
Broadway Interlude, with Achmed Abdullah. New York, Payson and Clarke, 1929; London, Selwyn and Blount, 1930.
Make-Believe. New York, Dodd Mead, 1930; London, Sampson Low, 1931.
The Office Wife. New York, Dodd Mead, and London, Sampson Low, 1930.

Skyscraper. New York, Cosmopolitan, 1931; London, Sampson Low, 1932; as *Skyscraper Souls*, New York, Grosset and Dunlap, 1932.
Today's Virtue. New York, Dodd Mead, 1931.
Self-Made Woman. New York, Farrar and Rinehart, 1932; London, Sampson Low, 1933.
Week-End Marriage. New York, Farrar and Rinehart, and London, Sampson Low, 1932.
Girl on the Make, with Achmed Abdullah. New York, Long and Smith, and London, Selwyn and Blount, 1932.
District Nurse. New York, Farrar and Rinehart, 1932; London, Sampson Low, 1933.
White-Collar Girl. New York, Farrar and Rinehart, 1933; London, Sampson Low, 1934.
Beauty. New York, Farrar and Rinehart, and London, Sampson Low, 1933.
Love's a Puzzle. New York, Farrar and Rinehart, 1933; London, Sampson Low, 1934.
Innocent Bystander. New York, Farrar and Rinehart, 1934; London, Sampson Low, 1935.
Within a Year. New York, Farrar and Rinehart, and London, Sampson Low, 1934.
Honor Bound. New York, Farrar and Rinehart, 1934; London, Sampson Low, 1936.
American Family. New York, Farrar and Rinehart, 1935; as *Conflict*, London, Sampson Low, 1935.
The Puritan Strain. New York, Farrar and Rinehart, and London, Sampson Low, 1935.
The Moon's Our Home. New York, Farrar and Rinehart, 1936; London, Sampson Low, 1937.
Men Are Such Fools! New York, Farrar and Rinehart, 1936; London, Sampson Low, 1937.
Private Duty. New York, Farrar and Rinehart, 1936; London, Sampson Low, 1938.
That Man Is Mine! London, Sampson Low, 1936; New York, Farrar and Rinehart, 1937.
The Heart Has Wings. New York, Farrar and Rinehart, 1937; London, Sampson Low, 1938.
Twenty-Four Hours a Day. New York, Farrar and Rinehart, 1937; London, Sampson Low, 1939.
Manhattan Nights. New York, Farrar and Rinehart, 1937.
Hotel Hostess. New York, Farrar and Rinehart, 1938; London, Sampson Low, 1940.
Enchanted Oasis. New York, Farrar and Rinehart, 1938; London, Sampson Low, 1940.
Rich Girl, Poor Girl. New York, Farrar and Rinehart, 1938; London, Sampson Low, 1939.
White Magic. New York, Farrar and Rinehart, 1939; London, Sampson Low, 1945.
Station Wagon Set. New York, Farrar and Rinehart, 1939; London, Hale, 1945.
The High Road. New York, Farrar and Rinehart, 1939; London, Sampson Low, 1944.
Career by Proxy. New York, Farrar and Rinehart, 1939; London, Sampson Low, 1943.
Letty and the Law. New York, Farrar and Rinehart, 1940; London, Hale, 1946.
Medical Center. New York, Farrar and Rinehart, 1940; London, Hale, 1946.
Rehearsal for Love. New York, Farrar and Rinehart, 1940; London, Hale, 1946.
Something Special. New York, Farrar and Rinehart, 1940.
Temporary Address: Reno. New York, Farrar and Rinehart, 1941.
And New Stars Burn. New York, Farrar and Rinehart, 1941; London, Hale, 1948.
The Heart Remembers. New York, Farrar and Rinehart, 1941.

Blue Horizons. New York, Farrar and Rinehart, 1942; London, Hale, 1951.

Breath of Life. New York, Farrar and Rinehart, 1942; London, Hale, 1953.

The Rest of My Life with You. New York, Farrar and Rinehart, 1942; London, Hale, 1947.

You Can't Escape. New York, Farrar and Rinehart, 1943; London, Hale, 1952.

Washington, USA. New York, Farrar and Rinehart, 1943.

Change of Heart. New York, Farrar and Rinehart, 1944; London, Hale, 1949.

He Married a Doctor. New York, Farrar and Rinehart, 1944; London, Hale, 1953.

A Job for Jenny. New York, Farrar and Rinehart, 1945; as *Tell Me My Heart*, 1950.

Arizona Star. New York, Farrar and Rinehart, 1945; London, Hale, 1949.

No Private Heaven. New York, Farrar and Rinehart, 1946; London, Hale, 1954.

Woman on Her Own. New York, Rinehart, 1946; London, Hale, 1954.

Give Love the Air. New York, Rinehart, 1947; London, Hale, 1955.

Sleeping Beauty. New York, Rinehart, 1947; London, Hale, 1954.

Marry for Money. New York, Rinehart, 1948; London, Hale, 1955.

The Golden Shoestring. New York, Rinehart, 1949; London, Hale, 1956.

Look Out for Liza. New York, Rinehart, 1950; London, Hale, 1956.

The Whole Armor. New York, Rinehart, 1951; London, Hale, 1956.

The Juniper Tree. New York, Rinehart, 1952; London, Hale, 1957.

Three Faces of Love. New York, Rinehart, 1957; London, Hale, 1958.

Blaze of Sunlight. New York, Rinehart, 1959; London, Hale, 1960.

Testament of Trust. New York, Holt Rinehart, 1960.

Harvest of Hope. New York, Holt Rinehart, 1962.

The West Wind. New York, Holt Rinehart, 1962; London, Hale, 1963.

The Lonely Man. New York, Holt Rinehart, 1964; as *The Lonely Doctor*, London, Hale, 1964; as *Echoes of Another Spring*, New York, Dell, 1965.

There Is a Season. New York, Holt Rinehart, and London, Hale, 1966.

Evening Star. New York, Holt Rinehart, 1966.

The Velvet Hammer. New York, Holt Rinehart, and London, Hale, 1969.

Take What You Want. New York, Holt Rinehart, 1970; London, Hale, 1971.

Any Village. New York, Holt Rinehart, 1971; London, Hale, 1972.

One More Time. New York, Holt Rinehart, 1972; London, Hale, 1974.

No Bed of Roses. New York, Holt Rinehart, 1973; London, Hale, 1975.

Time and the Hour. New York, Holt Rinehart, 1974; London, Hale, 1975.

New Girl in Town. New York, Holt Rinehart, 1975.

Thursday's Child. New York, Holt Rinehart, 1976; London, Hale, 1977.

Hold On to Your Heart. London, Hale, 1976.

Adam's Eden. New York, Holt Rinehart, 1977; London, Hale, 1978.

Short Stories

Wife vs Secretary. New York, Grosset and Dunlap, 1934.

Five Woman (includes *Star on Her Shoulder, Detour, Let's Do the Town*). New York, Farrar and Rinehart, 1942; London, Hale, 1946.

They Who Love. New York, Rinehart, 1948.

OTHER PUBLICATIONS

Play

Screenplay: *Portia on Trial*, with Samuel Ornitz and E.E. Paramore, Jr, 1937.

Poetry

Sign Posts. Boston, Small Maynard, 1924.
Widow's Walk: Variations on a Theme. New York, Rinehart, 1954.

Other

Judy: A Story of Divine Corners (for children). New York, Dodd Mead, 1930.

Babs: A Story of Divine Corners (for children). New York, Dodd Mead, and London, Sampson Low, 1931.

Mary Lou: A Story of Divine Corners (for children). New York, Dodd Mead, 1931.

Myra: A Story of Divine Corners (for children). New York, Dodd Mead, 1932.

Face Toward the Spring. New York, Rinehart, 1956; London, Davies, 1957.

Many Windows: Seasons of the Heart. New York, Rinehart, 1958; London, Davies, 1959.

Living by Faith. New York, Holt Rinehart, 1964.

*

Film Adaptations: *Skyscraper Souls*, 1932, from the novel *Skyscraper*, 1931; *Beauty for Sale*, 1933, from the novel *Beauty*; *The Moon's our Home*; *Love Before Dinner*, 1936, from *Spinster Dinner*; *Wife Vs Secretary*, 1936; *Portia on Trial*, 1937; *Men are such Fools*, 1938.

*   *   *

Unlike most popular romances, Faith Baldwin's novels are neither predatory nor manipulative. In that sense, they are old-fashioned. Most contemporary romances prey on their readers' needs and insecurities, perhaps on their need for insecurity, their mostly unconscious desire to prolong adolescence, that uncertain, indeterminate state where—despite probability—one might indeed turn out to be beautiful, to be wildly loved. Baldwin's books appeal to the obverse of this romantic fantasy, to the need for stability, life-long sharing, patient familiarity. There is a bit of adolescence to them, particularly to her earlier books, but it is the cosy adolescent fantasy of proximity and protection, as when the young heroines of *The Heart Has Wings* and *Enchanted Oasis* are compelled by 'accidents' to spend innocent nights with the men of their dreams. Baldwin's novels are less romances than comedies: ripe, full of sunlight, crowded with people making do with each other. Comedies in the classical sense, her books are pledges of our willingness to live life with others no better than they might be and certainly no better than ourselves.

The folk who populate these novels are usually rich, solid (if sometimes troubled), and almost never dull. They are, fancifully, the burghers of Dutch painting come out of their dark counting houses into sunlit American suburbs. Ministers, country doctors, district nurses, lawyers (both urban and suburban), booksellers, aviators, real estate agents, and occasionally—earlier in Baldwin's half-century career—a movie star, the idle rich: this is the litany of

Baldwin's saints. Remarkably, she makes them come to life, and sometimes brilliantly. Baldwin seems able to do this out of her own generosity of spirit, her willingness to see characters as they are, not (in the unspoken imperative of romance fiction) as they should—but dare not—be. The aptly titled *Blaze of Sunlight*, to my mind Baldwin's richest novel, illustrates her tolerant generosity. Rose Holmes, the widowed heroine, ought to be an exemplar of romance fiction: passionately, almost single-mindedly devoted to her man, during his life and after his death. Yet Baldwin shows that this devotion has enriched Rose by impoverishing her children, and, by inference, the community around her, for it has deprived them of her gifts. This is the lesson Rose must learn. If, unlike classical comedy, *Blaze of Sunlight* does not end with a marriage, it does culminate in Rose's re-attachment: Rose walks out of the dark tunnel of her grief into the sunlit community where actions, even private emotions, have consequence.

Baldwin's tunnel metaphor suits both this character and her work as a whole. For, although her books are love stories, Baldwin is always stretching the radically tight focus of romance fiction and the tunnel-vision it imposes. Children and neighbours are frequent in her books and rarely serve as stage-props: rather they seem about to live busy lives of their own. In a multi-generation novel like *American Family* we get to see those lives intertwine. Moreover, Baldwin's protagonists—almost as often male as female, another departure from standard romance—have careers, again believably, not just as props. Like as not these careers encourage and express human connectedness—lawyers, doctors, teachers, ministers—and, equally likely, Baldwin's characters are immersed in the dailiness of their occupations, not in the moments of high drama each affords.

There are occasional false notes, of course. *Take What You Want*, a late novel, is tonally dissonant, sounding like a standard off-the-rack romance: girl swept off her feet by a rich older man and disapproved of by his family. Or, earlier, the falsely countrified speech of *Make-Believe* where Baldwin's gift for dialogue fails her. Yet Baldwin's is a remarkable 50-year, 60-plus novel career of comfort and progress. Her books are not quite real: there's no landedness to them, no root. Yet they are real as the mind is real, inhabiting problems; living, not without trouble, but with good humour and companionship.

—Nancy Regan

———

BALMAIN, Lydia.   See **SAXTON, Judith.**

———

BALOGH, Mary.
Nationality: Canadian/British. **Born:** Swansea, Wales, 24 March 1944. **Education:** University of Wales, Cardiff, B.A. 1965, Dip. Ed. 1967. **Relations:** married Robert Balogh in 1969; three children. **Career:** English teacher, Kipling High School, Saskatchewan, 1967–82; principal and English teacher, Windhurst High School, Saskatchewan, 1982–88. **Recipient:** *Romantic Times* lifetime achievement award, 1989. **Agent:** Maria Carvainis, 235 West End Avenue, New York, New York 10023, USA. **Address:** Box 571, Kipling, Saskatchewan, Canada, S0G 2S0.

ROMANCE AND HISTORICAL PUBLICATIONS

Novels

A Masked Deception. New York, New American Library, 1985.
The Double Wager. New York, New American Library, 1985.

A Chance Encounter. New York, New American Library, 1985.
Red Rose. New York, New American Library, 1986.
The Trysting Place. New York, New American Library, 1986.
The First Snowdrop. New York, New American Library, 1987.
The Wood Nymph. New York, New American Library, 1987.
The Constant Heart. New York, New American Library, 1987.
Gentle Conquest. New York, New American Library, 1987.
Secrets of the Heart. New York, New American Library, 1988.
The Ungrateful Governess. New York, New American Library, 1988.
An Unacceptable Offer. New York, New American Library, 1988.
Daring Masquerade. New York, New American Library, 1989.
A Gift of Daisies. New York, New American Library, 1989.
The Obedient Bride. New York, New American Library, 1989.
Lady with a Black Umbrella. New York, New American Lbirary, 1989.
The Gilded Web. New York, New American Library, 1989.
A Promise of Spring. New York, New American Library, 1990.
Web of Love. New York, New American Library, 1990.
The Incurable Matchmaker. New York, New American Library, 1990.
Devil's Web. New York, New American Library, 1990.
An Unlikely Duchess. New York, New American Library, 1990.
A Certain Magic. New York, New American Library, 1991.
Snow Angel. New York, New American Library, 1991.
The Secret Pearl. New York, New American Library, 1991.
The Ideal Wife. New York, New American Library, and London, Severn House, 1991.
Christmas Beau. New York, New American Library, 1991.
The Counterfeit Betrothal. New York, New American Library, 1992.
The Notorious Rake. New York, New American Library, 1992.
A Christmas Promise. New York, New American Library, 1992.
Beyond the Sunrise. New York, New American Library, 1992.
A Precious Jewel. New York, New American Library, 1993.
Deceived. New York, New American Library, 1993.
Courting Julia. New York, New American Library, 1993.
Dancing with Clara. New York, New American Library, and London, Severn House, 1994.

Short Stories

Full Moon Magic, with others. New York, New American Library, 1992.
Tokens of Love. New York, New American Library, 1993.
Rakes and Rogues. New York, New American Library, 1993.
Moonlight Lovers. New York, New American Library, 1993.

*

Mary Balogh comments:
Most of my books are Regency romances—that is, upper-class British comedies of manners set between 1811–20. In addition to the wit and formal style characteristic of Regencies generally, I have added the dimension of character-depth and passion. I like to show how a character's background affects his/her present life and his/her ability to form meaningful relationships. I like to show the distinctions between appearance and reality—the kind of masks all people like to wear to varying degrees, often unconsciously—and the way in which these masks have to be stripped away before the hero and heroine are free to love, and to commit their lives to each other.

More recently I have been writing historicals—two set in the Regency period: one in the 1850s, the other in the 1830s. I explore the same themes and use very much the same intense, passionate approach to life in the longer books. Hey—I'm Welsh! Need I say more?

* * *

In a world full of competent Regency writers, Mary Balogh is an important name. The author of over 30 novels Balogh is well known in the North American market as a writer and a creator of stylish lively books. Balogh admits that Georgette Heyer, Jane Austen, and Charlotte Brontë are among her favourite authors, and their influence can be seen in the plot development, characterization, and style of Balogh's writing.

Balogh's plots revolve around handsome, aristocratic, slightly disillusioned heroes, who have reached the age when they either need to, or are required to get married, and heroines who are ordinary but spirited young misses who exist in a world where marriage, spinsterhood, or prostitution are the only alternatives for a young woman. In *The Ungrateful Governess*, in typical Heyeresque style, a young governess, Jessica Moore, is propositioned in her employer's library by a jaded but attractive rake, the Earl of Rutherford. On losing her job, Jessica is propositioned by the earl again, but he shows that he is a gentleman by accepting her refusal gracefully and taking her to stay with his grandmother. This formidable lady takes Jessica Moore under her wing and Jessica is introduced to society under her auspices. Thus the chrysalis emerges as a butterfly prompting the rake, the Earl of Rutherford, to re-evaluate his life and to realize that his world is meaningless without Jessica: consequently he proposes—marriage. In *Gentle Conquest* the parents of the spirited Georgina Burton are desperate to get her married; they find an unlikely ally in the dowager Countess of Chartleigh, whose eldest son, Ralph is distressingly intellectual, and is seemingly uninterested in finding a wife. In bringing together this unlikely pair, Balogh shows humour and versatility in keeping the reader interested in both her characterization and her plot.

Balogh also introduces slightly unusual twists into her romances. In *Christmas Beau* a young widow returns to London with her two children and encounters the man whom she jilted years earlier. As they fall in love over again, the heroine is left to ponder whether her lover is interested in her in reality, or as part of some bitter kind of revenge. Similarly in *The Wood Nymph* the hero seduces a young naive daughter of a neighbour and then abandons her, only to renew his suit when he realizes that he is in love with her. He spends a good part of the book trying to win her trust all over again. Christopher Atwell also has to win the trust of his beloved, in *Deceived*, after being caught in the arms of another woman. Elizabeth, his wife, obtains a divorce, but on the eve of her marriage to another man, is abducted by Christopher. Suffering from amnesia after a carriage accident, Elizabeth forgets their divorce, and the couple are given a second chance until Elizabeth's memory returns. However, Christopher discovers that he has a child and is determined to regain his wife, daughter, and life. With the help of his sister and an old friend, he shows Elizabeth that someone framed him, and even tried to ruin his sibling. Thus the couple are given another chance.

Miles Ripley, Earl of Severn, conforms to the more stereotypical Regency hero. Described by a friend, in *The Ideal Wife*, as, 'thirty years old—in the very prime of life. And of course, you still have those looks, which have been throwing females into the flutters and the vapors for the past 10 years or so', Miles is looking for a wife. He eventually decides on Abigail, his cousin, and marries her because she is someone who will 'fade into the background of [his] life'. He is quickly proved wrong, and falls in love with Abigail.

In *Courting Julia*, the heroine Julia Maynard is used to suitors being drawn to her reputed inheritance. Unfortunately Julia is not attracted by the respectable ones, and remains heart free until she meets a rake, the Earl of Beaconswood. Julia meets her match in her hero.

What makes Balogh a successful writer is her attention to the minute details of the Regency period. She describes the clothing, customs, and social manners of the day in copious detail, a fact which makes her books all the more enjoyable. It is this accuracy, combined with interesting plots and exciting characters, that make Balogh such a popular writer with her North American audience.

—P. Campbell

BARBER, Noel (John Lysberg).
Nationality: British. **Born:** 9 September 1909. **Education:** erratic (interrupted at the age of 14 by case of lockjaw). **Military Service:** navigator, Royal Air Force, 1942–45. **Relations:** married 1) Helen Whichello in 1938; 2) Countess de Feo of Florence in 1954, one son, one daughter. **Career:** journalist, Yorkshire Post group, *Daily Express*, Manchester, 1930s; editor, *Malaya Tribune*, Singapore, 1937–38, *Overseas Daily Mail*, London, 1940; editor, and managing director, *Continental Daily Mail*, Paris, 1945–53; artist, exhibition, Salon d'Hiver, Paris, 1950–53; foreign correspondent, *Daily Mail*, 1953–65; expedition to the South Pole (first Briton to successfully reach the Pole since Captain Scott in 1957); presenter, *Assignment Unknown* (television documentary travelogue series) 1959–60; foreign manager, syndication manager, and director, Associated Newspapers Ltd, London, 1962–73. **Recipient:** Légion d'honneur, 1945; Ridder of Danneborg, Denmark, 1948; Jordanian Order of Merit, 1961. **Died:** 10 July 1988.

ROMANCE AND HISTORICAL PUBLICATIONS

Novels

Tanamera: A Novel of Singapore. London, Hodder and Stoughton, and New York, Macmillan, 1981.
A Farewell to France. London, Hodder and Stoughton, and New York, Macmillan, 1983.
A Woman of Cairo. London, Hodder and Stoughton, 1984.
The Other Side of Paradise. London, Hodder and Stoughton, 1986; New York, Macmillan, 1987.
The Weeping and the Laughter. London, Hodder and Stoughton, 1988.
The Daughters of the Prince (unfinished: completed by Alan Wykes). London, Hodder and Stoughton, 1989.

OTHER PUBLICATIONS

Fiction (for children)

Adventures at Both Poles. London, Heinemann, 1958.
Let's Visit the USA. London, Burke, 1960; New York, Day, 1968; revised edition, London, Burke, 1971.

Other

Newspaper Reporting: A Practical Guide for Young Journalists. London, Pitman, 1936.
How Strong is America? London, Harrap, 1942.
How Strong is Japan? London, Harrap, 1942.
Hitler's Last Hope, with Ernest Phillips. London, Harrap, 1942.
Trans-Siberian. London, Harrap, 1943.
Prisoner of War: The Story of British Prisoners of War Held by the Enemy. London, Harrap, 1944.
Cities, with Rupert Croft-Cooke. London, Wingate, 1946.
Fires of Spring (autobiography). London, Bles, 1952.
Strangers in the Sun (autobiography). London, Bles, 1952.

A Handful of Ashes. London, Wingate, 1957.
The White Desert. London, Hodder and Stoughton, 1958.
Distant Places. London, Wingate, 1959.
The Flight of the Dalai Lama. London, Hodder and Stoughton, 1960.
Life with Titina (autobiography). London, Hodder and Stoughton, 1961.
Conversations with Painters. London, Collins, 1964.
The Black Hole of Calcutta: A Reconstruction. London, Collins, 1965; Boston, Houghton Mifflin, 1966.
An Island to Oneself, with Tom Neale. London, Collins, 1966.
Sinister Twilight: The Fall and Rise of Singapore. London, Collins, and Boston, Houghton Mifflin, 1968.
From the Land of the Lost Continent: The Dalai Lama's Fight for Tibet. London, Collins, 1969; Boston, Houghton Mifflin, 1970.
The War of the Running Dogs: How Malaya Defeated the Communist Guerrillas, 1948–60. London, Collins, 1971; New York, Weybright and Talley, 1972.
Lords of the Golden Horn: From Suleiman the Magnificent to Kamal Ataturk. London, Macmillan, 1973; as *Sultans,* New York, Simon and Schuster, 1973.
Seven Days of Freedom: The Hungarian Uprising. London, Macmillan, and New York, Stern and Day, 1974.
The Week France Fell. London, Macmillan, and New York, Stern and Day, 1976.
The Natives Were Friendly, So We Stayed the Night (autobiography). London, Macmillan, 1977.
The Singapore Story: From Raffles to Lee Kuan Yew. London, Fontana, 1978.
The Fall of Shanghai. London, Macmillan, and New York, Coward McCann and Geoghegan, 1979.

*   *   *

If persistence is the hallmark of an earnest writer, Noel Barber, by any standard of assessment, well deserved a laudation. Undeterred by what many would regard as the ignominy of having no less than 19 full-length books rejected by publishers, Barber went on to successfully write another 20. His books deal with an array of subjects, particularly history and politics, and in the latter part of his life, fiction. A lifetime profession as a journalist, and a wealth of experience gained in his travels, held him in good stead, and his books clearly reflect this asset. He capitalized, in particular, on his intimate knowledge of World War II—he was a navigator for the RAF—and it is roughly this period that forms the backdrop for most of his fictional work.

Interestingly, Barber's five novels, *Tanamera, A Farewell to France, A Woman of Cairo, The Other Side of Paradise,* and *The Weeping and the Laughter,* are love stories whose characters are enmeshed in the throes of human passion. Yet, romance forms only a broader canvas for an expatiation of historical narrative. Thus, while his book *The Other Side of Paradise* is ostensibly the story of the love between Kit Masters, a doctor from London, and Aleena, the princess of a Polynesian island, the reader is exposed to a slice of life in Colonial times—the languid and fine life-styles of the British living abroad prior to the outbreak of war, the vulnerability of the islanders to the ravages of tropical diseases, superstitious beliefs, the natural elements, and the atom bomb. Similarly, in *The Weeping and the Laughter,* set in Europe before the war, Nicki Koralev, a Russian prince forced to flee revolutionary Russia, is drawn into a seemingly hopeless love affair with Natasha. Nicki and Natasha, believe, for most of the book, that they have an incestuous marriage. Similarly, Mark Holt and Serena Sirry, in *A Woman of Cairo,* are entangled in an extramarital affair that is to all appearances futile.

Possibly conditioned by the demands of his vocation, Barber strove to be accurate, and the depth of research that went into the writing of each book is evident. Be it the dynamics of a disease, or the route to Switzerland, his elaborate descriptions clearly indicate the hand of the well informed.

Real life persons—Benito Mussolini, Winston Churchill, and Gordon Selfridge, among others—appear in Barber's novels. They are not treated as distant characters but are made vital to the plot, and actively participate in the development of the story line. An occasional remark about some personal trait, or a deliberate attempt to highlight contemporaneous gossip further, adds a touch of realism.

The principal character in Barber's books is always a male, and his books were normally written from the protagonist's point of view. This helped to convey the immediacy of the situation to the reader. The settings for his novels are varied and exotic. *Tanamera* is set in Singapore, *A Woman of Cairo* in Egypt, *The Other Side of Paradise* in the Polynesian island of Koraloona, *The Weeping and the Laughter* and *A Farewell to France* in parts of France.

At the time of Barber's death in 1988, he was working on his last novel, *The Daughters of the Prince.* Published posthumously, with portions written by a close friend, this work does not evoke the sense of high drama evident in his earlier novels. Perhaps by following the same pattern set by the success of his earlier novels, the suspense of the outcome has been dulled by the predictability of the story.

Noel Barber did not pretend to be a stylist, and his works are easy to comprehend. His ability to bring together different elements of popular fiction—he mixes together the right quantity of romance, explicit passion, personal struggle, and wider historical events—resulted in several bestselling novels.

—Rachel Kumar

————

BARCLAY, Ann. See GREIG, Maysie.

————

BARCLAY, Florence L(ouisa).
Pseudonym: Brandon Roy. **Nationality:** British. **Born:** Florence Charlesworth, Limpsfield, Surrey, 2 December 1862. **Relations:** married Charles W. Barclay in 1881; two sons and six daughters. **Died:** 10 March 1921.

<small>ROMANCE AND HISTORICAL PUBLICATIONS</small>

Novels

Guy Mervyn (as Brandon Roy). London, Blackett, 3 vols, 1891; edition revised by one of her daughters, New York and London, Putnam, 1932.
A Notable Prisoner. London, Marshall, 1905.
The Wheels of Time. New York, Crowell, 1908; London, Putnam, 1910.
The Rosary. New York and London, Putnam, 1909.
The Mistress of Shenstone. New York and London, Putnam, 1910.
The Following of the Star. New York and London, Putnam, 1911.
Through the Postern Gate. New York and London, Putnam, 1912.
The Upas Tree. London and New York, Putnam, 1912.
The Broken Halo. London and New York, Putnam, 1913.
The Wall of Partition. London and New York, Putnam, 1914.
My Heart's Right There. London and New York, Putnam, 1914.
The White Ladies of Worcester. London and New York, Putnam, 1917.
Returned Empty. London and New York, Putnam, 1920.

OTHER PUBLICATIONS

Other

The Golden Censer. London, Hodder and Stoughton, and New York, Doran, 1914.
In Hoc + Vince: The Story of a Red Cross Flag. London and New York, Putnam, 1915.

*

Critical Study: *The Life of Florence L. Barclay: A Study in Personality* by One of Her Daughters, London and New York, Putnam, 1921.

*   *   *

Florence L. Barclay was not as prolific as most of her contemporaries in the field. She did not need to be. *The Rosary*, published in 1909, roughly halfway through her literary career, secured her an ample readership, for, as the *Publisher's Circular* had already pronounced: 'Of all forms of fiction, the semi-religious is the most popular'. Within nine months *The Rosary* sold 150,000 hardback copies; it was still a bestseller 20 years later, and in 1928 was serialized in *Woman's World*, 'the favourite paper of a Million Homes'. One admirer of her work assessed that, within two years of publication, *The Rosary* had been 'read and wept over by threequarters of the housemaids in Great Britain' (though this generous statistic must be tempered by another popular novelist's judgement that 'the tears of the uneducated are proverbially near their eyes').

The predominant theme of all her novels—as befits the work of a parson's wife—concerns the Christian conversion of one or other of the partners in love. Mortal love cannot be wholly real, wholly acceptable, until he, or she, has also found the love of God, this state of grace being described in a succession of metaphors: 'Come home to the Father's House', 'had his broken halo restored', 'until her heart beats in unison with the heart of the Virgin Mother in Bethlehem's starlit stable'. The revelation of true earthly love and of true heavenly love is often simultaneous, the one acting as a catalyst on the other.

A recurring subsidiary theme is of the younger man in love with the much older woman, which Barclay first, delicately, touched on in *Guy Mervyn*. This was her first novel, but it made little impact when it originally appeared, chiefly because the publishing firm went bankrupt and only a few copies were distributed. *The Rosary*, too, appeared originally in another form, as a short story or (as she herself preferred it to be known) a novella, under the title *Wheels of Fortune*. Unlike some romantic novelists who prided themselves in never changing a line once written, Barclay saw the need for rewriting, reworking, and polishing. No amount of rewriting would diminish her main message:

My aim is: Never to write a line which could introduce the taint of sin or the shadow of shame into any home. Never to draw a character which would tend to lower the ideals of those who, by means of my pen, make intimate acquaintance with a man or a woman of my own creating. There is enough sin in the world without an author's powers of imagination being used in order to add even fictitious sin to the amount. Too many bad, mean, morbid characters already, alas! walk this earth. Why should writers add to their numbers and risk introducing them into beautiful homes, where such people in actual life would never for one moment be tolerated? A great French writer and savant has said: 'The only excuse for fiction is that it should be more beautiful than fact'.

The result of writing only on subjects which are more beautiful than fact is that there can be no villains in her plots, and the denoue-ments must be brought about by some highly improbable act of fate or natural disaster. *The Rosary* has, probably, the silliest plot of all, its motive force, its suspense, being maintained by the 'masquerade device', a technique always popular with romantic novelists in which the heroine poses as maid/titled lady/nurse/secretary in order to be near the one she loves. However, only when her true identity is revealed can love flourish.

The religious atmosphere of the books, the tone of spiritual reverence, is conveyed by enthusiastic use of capital letters, both for the personal pronouns of the members of the trinity and for abstractions of anything which sounds remotely mystical—the Unseen, The Great Chance, Love, Life, The Little White Lady. There is a frequent repetition of emotive adverbs and adjectives—thrill, throb, tender, soul, gentle, and strange and sweet, this last one being a compound adjective, like sweet and sour, or his and hers. The religion is chiefly one of nostalgia, for reader as well as the characters. Christmas carols, well-known hymns, and long quotations from the better-known scriptures bring about strange emotional feelings in the players. Searing remembrances of lost childhood result in Christian conversion, and it is in shared emotional-cum-religious experiences that the lovers find their true unity, rather than in any explicit sexual activity. Whenever possible, the desire or opportunity for physical union is postponed, or made impossible by the intricacies of plot. Thus in *The Broken Halo* the elderly wife has a weak heart, and so her youthful husband must keep himself in a separate bedroom and endure an unconsummated marriage. On the night that he finally realizes his true, deep burning love for her, she dies of a heart attack, thus putting off till the Great Forever any possible consummation.

Similarly, in *The Following of the Star* the alliance between rich heiress and poor missionary is entirely a *mariage de convenance*, enabling her to give money for his excellent work in the typhoid-ridden swamps of Central Africa. Immediately after their marriage, he departs forever. Unknown to them, but abundantly clear to the reader, they are desperately in love. An impossible courtship, riddled with crossed letters and misunderstandings, ensues. When at last they are re-united, and a normal relationship for two healthy people would seem feasible, the author's religious imagination prevents them going about it in the normal way. Instead, they enjoy an unusual life-giving intercourse through the arms. The missionary (temporarily indisposed) lies in bed while the heiress kneels at his side in what she admits to be an exceedingly uncomfortable position, clutches his head against her breast and, it being Christmas Eve (note the novel's title), croons 'Hark the Herald Angels Sing' to him, knowing that this is the one thing which will save his life. 'Every moment of contact with your vital force is vitalizing him', announces a bystander to the scene. 'It is like pouring blood into empty veins, only a more subtle and mysterious process, and more wonderful in its result.' It was not physiological ignorance which caused Barclay to write so often about marital union in this way. (She herself was happily married, and produced eight children.) As one of her daughters wrote: 'She was out to supply her fellow men with joy, refreshment, inspiration. She was not out to make art for art's sake, or to perform a literary tour de force. [Her readers] ask merely to be pleased, rested, interested, amused, inspired to a more living faith in the beauty of human affection and the goodness of God.'

The mystical euphoria of her novels gave genuine spiritual comfort to many, for, as the novelist-hero in one of her books explains: 'The thing of first importance is to uplift your readers; to raise their ideals; to leave them with a sense of hopefulness, which shall arouse within them a brave optimism such as inspired Browning's oft-quoted noble lines.' Even today, there are readers who recall being moved and uplifted by *The Rosary*. A fellow novelist of the time paid Barclay this tribute: '*The Rosary* will probably live, because its power is very uncommon—as uncommon, on its lower plane, as the power of *Wuthering Heights* . . . Mrs Barclay . . . was undoubtedly a great writer on her plane—Shakespeare of the servants' hall. Her power is terrific—at any rate in *The Rosary*. I had infinitely rather have written *The Rosary* than *The Forsyte Saga*.'

—Rachel Anderson

BARCLAY, Marguerite. See **BARCYNSKA, Countess.**

BARCLAY, Tessa.

Pseudonym for Jean Bowden. **Other Pseudonyms:** Barbara Annandale; Jocelyn Barry; Jennifer Bland; Avon Curry; Belinda Dell; Lee Mackenzie; also writes as Jean Bowden. **Nationality:** British. **Born:** 1928. **Career:** editorial assistant, Panther Books, 1957–59, Four Square Books, 1959–61, and Armada Books, 1961–62; feature writer, *Woman's Mirror*, London, 1962–64; assistant fiction editor, *Woman's Own*, London, 1964–67. Editorial consultant, Mills and Boon Ltd, London. **Address:** Headline Book Publishing, Headline House, 79 Great Titchfield Street, London W1P 7FN, England.

ROMANCE AND HISTORICAL PUBLICATIONS

Novels (series: Craigallans; Wine Widow Trilogy; Corvill Weavers Trilogy)

A Sower Went Forth (Craigallans). London, W.H. Allen, 1980.
High Barbaree (as Barbara Annandale). New York, Ballantine, 1980.
Wendy Craig's Nanny (as Jean Bowden). London, Granada, 1981.
The Stony Places (Craigallans). London, W.H. Allen, 1981.
The Breadwinner. London, W.H. Allen, 1982.
Garland of War. London, W.H. Allen, 1983.
Harvest of Thorns (Craigallans). London, W.H. Allen, 1983.
The Good Ground (Craigallans). London, W.H. Allen, 1984.
Wine Widow Trilogy:
    The Wine Widow. London, W.H. Allen, 1984.
    The Champagne Girls. London, W.H. Allen, 1986.
    The Last Heiress. London, W.H. Allen, 1987.
Corvill Weavers Trilogy:
    A Web of Dreams. London, W.H. Allen, 1988.
    Broken Threads. London, W.H. Allen, 1989.
    The Final Pattern. London, W.H. Allen, 1990.
Gleam of Gold. London, Headline, 1992.
A Hidden Beauty. London, Headline, 1993.
A Professional Woman. London, Headline, 1993.

Novels as Belinda Dell

Lake of Silver. London, Mills and Boon, 1974.
Dancing on my Heart. London, Mills and Boon, 1974.
Stars over Sentosa. London, Mills and Boon, 1975.

OTHER PUBLICATIONS

Novels as Lee Mackenzie

The Brothers. London, Sphere, 1975.
Beryl's Lot, with Margaret Powell. London, Wingate, 1977.
Emmerdale Farm, the Legacy. London, Wingate, 1977.
A Sad and Happy Summer. London, Star, 1978.

Whispers of Scandal. London, Star, 1979.
Early Days at Emmerdale Farm. London, Star, 1979.
The Couple at Demdyke Row. London, Star, 1979.
Lucky for Some. London, Star, 1980.
Shadows from the Past. London, Star, 1980.
Face Value. Glasgow, Fontana, 1980.
Innocent Victim. London, Fontana, 1981.
False Witness. London, Fontana, 1981.
The Homecoming. London, Fontana, 1982.
Old Flames. Glasgow, Fontana, 1982.
Wedding Bells. London, Fontana, 1983.
Family Feuds. London, Fontana, 1984.
Young Passions. London, Severn House, 1985.
Another Door Opens. London, Fontana, 1986.

*   *   *

Tessa Barclay has written three multi-volume family sagas, each centred around a different industry or industries; the backgrounds are interesting and well researched, and are often enlivened by the presence of actual historical figures, ranging from assassins to royalty.

The 'Craigallans' saga, is the rags-to-riches story of Rob Craigallan who emigrates from Scotland to America in the 19th century. The first novel, *A Sower Went Forth*, has as its background wheat farming, then, as Rob marries the daughter of his wealthy landowning employer, moves into the world of dealing and finance. As is obligatory in a family saga, the focus changes from one generation to the next as the story develops, and in this case the background also changes. The second book, *The Stony Places*, moves into the world of politics, and Rob's son-in-law, Curtis Bracebridge, is aide to President McKinley; *Harvest of Thorns* is set at the time of World War I, and Curtis and Ellie-Rose (Rob's daughter) move in the diplomatic circles of English society, in the company of Nancy Astor and the Cliveden set. Among the other historical characters in the saga are Alexander Graham Bell, who teaches Rob Craigallan's deaf son, Cornelius, in *A Sower Went Forth*, and Emma Goldman and Sylvia Pankhurst, who make belligerent appearances in *The Stony Places* and *Harvest of Thorns* respectively. The background for much of the final book, *The Good Ground*, is Hollywood, a setting ripe for short appearances by famous people from Louella Parsons to Sergei Eisenstein, via Irving Thalberg and Upton Sinclair. This introduction of genuine historical figures into such novels is a device which must be handled with care, and all too often such characters obtrude—their presence is unreal and deflects attention from the fictional characters in the story. However, it must be said that in general Barclay introduces the real figures successfully, and it is only rarely that their presence jars.

The 'Wine Widow Trilogy' is a saga running from 1850 to the 1930s, and centres around the French champagne house of Tramont. The heroine of the first novel, *The Wine Widow*, and matriarch of the second, *The Champagne Girls*, is Nicole, a peasant girl (but a suitably cultured and educated one) who marries into the Tramont family. Widowed young, she assumes the running of the business; single-handed, this amazing woman apparently revitalizes the entire champagne industry with various innovations including the introduction of stronger glass from England and a technique for removing sediment. (In actual fact Dom Perignon introduced the former in the 17th century and la Veuve Clicquot invented the latter in 1805, but any reader in search of complete accuracy will probably not be turning to a historical romance.) A strong-willed woman, as are her descendants (throughout the trilogy it is almost invariably a woman who is at the head of the House—the men who marry them obligingly add the name Tramont to their own), Nicole finds time not only to run the business but also to have a couple of affairs, bear an illegitimate son (who is brought up as her nephew and who inconveniently but predictably falls in love with one of her legitimate daughters) and later to cope with the trials and tribulations of the Franco-Prussian war.

The Champagne Girls moves on to Nicole's granddaughters Nicolette (Netta) and Gabrielle (Gaby); Netta gradually (and again predictably) finds love in a marriage of convenience, while Gaby moves through affair after affair finding little lasting happiness. The historical backdrop to much of this novel is the Dreyfus affair (in the context of which Emile Zola has a walk-on part) followed by World War I, and the narration suffers from the breadth of this setting. Major characters die in rapid succession (not totally unreasonable in such troubled times) but we are given little chance to assess reaction to their demise from the survivors. The remaining protagonists seem to take the deaths completely in their stride, and they exhibit little or no emotion as events pursue their breathless course.

The heroine of *The Last Heiress* is Elinore (Nora), Netta's daughter and thus Nicole's great-granddaughter, and the time is the 1920s and 1930s. Nora, the heir to the House of Tramont, is brought up by Gaby, and like Gaby has a series of ultimately unfulfilling relationships, ending in a proxy wedding to a man whom she loves, but who is afflicted with leprosy. The sequence comes full circle with a widow once more running the House of Tramont, but not before we have witnessed a run of death and disaster to rival those of the earlier novels. However, the novels also contain much interesting detail about the champagne industry, about the political turmoil associated with the Dreyfus affair, and occasionally about fashion—the detailed description of clothes always being a useful device for setting the scene in periods of history.

The 'Corvill Weavers Trilogy', again with the background of a business and details of its development and innovations, this time has the same heroine throughout the saga. Jenny Corvill, daughter of an Edinburgh webster or weaver, manages to obtain a royal commission to produce a certain plaid (Queen Victoria and Prince Albert turn up like a sort of leitmotif throughout the trilogy, dispensing commissions like royal confetti). The business prospers and Jenny organizes a move to Galashiels in the border country. The remainder of the trilogy deals with the fortunes of the business with Jenny at its head, and with the loves and lives of her and her family. She is cursed with probably the most unlikeable sister-in-law to grace the pages of romance fiction: vain, grasping, manipulative, and scheming—and ultimately murderous, not a particularly credible character, but a suitable contrast to the worthy Jenny. This saga works rather better than the 'Wine Widow Trilogy'; as virtually the same set of characters occupies all three novels it is possible to achieve a far greater sense of involvement, and there is space in the context of each novel for all the major characters to evolve, and to react and interact.

Tessa Barclay has also written several novels which stand alone. *The Breadwinner* is an unusual and interesting story: Margaret Durley is a successful career woman with a powerful executive job and her husband Jack, a sculptor, works at home, keeps house, and looks after their three-year-old son. This role reversal, which was agreed by both parties and which works very successfully, is viewed dimly by Margaret's parents and, when she is made redundant, by her bank manager and by prospective employers. Margaret's failure to find new employment places intolerable stress on hers and Jack's relationship, and the novel deals efficiently yet sensitively with this issue, and with Margaret's loss of self-esteem.

Barclay's other single novels, by contrast, tend to deal with women as they create their careers. *Garland of War* traces the career of Linda Thackerley. As a provincial 17-year-old she auditions for a part with a new ballet company, and an improbably short five-and-a-half years later she is artistic director of her own company. During these years, as well as building an incredibly successful career for herself, she marries, loses her husband in World War II (although he later reappears, having merely been taken prisoner), divorces the

aforesaid husband, has an affair, bears a child, and loses her lover. In order to fulfil her ambition as a dancer Linda has to fight her parents and fiancé, and is obviously intended to be a courageous, strong-minded heroine. But alas!—she is a dull girl, and many of the elements of her story are somewhat well-worn, having been told in the hundreds of stories written for ballet-mad schoolgirls from the 1930s onwards. Madame Gadina, the autocratic, demanding, and emotional Russian owner of the ballet company, must be a familiar figure to thousands of ex-schoolgirls.

What a contrast to the uninspiring Linda is Christina Holt in *A Professional Woman*. Another 17-year-old rebelling against her parents in the early years of the 20th century, this time Christina wants to become a doctor. Here is a highly intelligent, very articulate young woman, who engages the reader's sympathy at every step from her lengthy, well-reasoned arguments with her domineering father, through her struggles with male students and teachers at university, to the various complex personal relationships which beset her as a successful doctor, specializing in child psychiatry. Especially well portrayed are her early years and the accounts of her conflicts with male authority; her later problems are a little more routine in this genre—an unhappy love affair, an illegitimate child, a lover lost for years in the aftermath of war—but Christina handles herself, her problems and those of her family and friends, with admirable common-sense. Similarly, in *Gleam of Gold* the background of Gwendolen Whitchurch's career as a cabinet-maker, the fascinating details of her work and then of her life as a young married woman in Japan, struggling with Japanese tradition and etiquette, make her later trials and tribulations fleeing from Japanese-occupied Singapore seem fairly run-of-the-mill; after all, the latter are encountered in many a romantic adventure story, but it is not every heroine who is a talented furniture-designer and cabinet-maker.

Barclay's historical sagas are competent, well-written examples of the genre, but it is in two of her single novels, *The Breadwinner* and *A Professional Woman*, that she demonstrates the wider range of her abilities, in the former building an interesting story round an unusual situation and in the latter creating in Christina Holt a memorable and admirable heroine. Barclay is obviously capable of far more individual work than she is able to produce within the limitations of her chosen field.

—Judith Rhodes

BARCYNSKA, Countess (Hélène).
Pseudonym for Marguerite Florence Jervice. **Other Pseudonyms:** Marguerite Barclay; Oliver Sandys. **Nationality:** British. **Born:** Henzada, Burma, in 1894; grew up in India. **Education:** schools in Herne Bay, Kent, Crouch End, London, and near Radlett, Hertfordshire; Academy of Dramatic Art, London. **Relations:** married 1) Armiger Barclay (Count Barcynsky); 2) Caradoc Evans in 1933 (died 1945), one son. **Career:** journalist, *Sievier's Monthly*, *World*, and *Answers*, all London; manager, Rogues and Vagabonds Repertory Players in Wales, and a theatre in Broadstairs, Kent. **Died:** 10 March 1964.

ROMANCE AND HISTORICAL PUBLICATIONS

Novels (series: Honey Pot)

The Honey Pot: A Story of the Stage. London, Hurst and Blackett, and New York, Dutton, 1916.
If Wishes Were Horses. London, Hurst and Blackett, and New York, Dutton, 1917.
Love Maggy. London, Hurst and Blackett, 1918.

Sanity Jane. London, Hurst and Blackett, 1919.
Love's Last Reward. London, Hurst and Blackett, 1920.
Pretty Dear: A Romance. London, Hurst and Blackett, 1920; as *Rose o' the Sea*, Boston, Houghton Mifflin, 1920.
Jackie. London, Hurst and Blackett, and Boston, Houghton Mifflin, 1921.
Ships Come Home. London, Hurst and Blackett, 1922.
Webs. London, Hurst and Blackett, 1922.
Tesha, A Plaything of Destiny. London, Hurst and Blackett, 1923.
We Women! London, Hurst and Blackett, 1923.
The Russet Jacket: A Story of the Turf. London, Hurst and Blackett, 1924.
Back to the Honey-Pot: A Story of the Stage. London, Hurst and Blackett, 1925.
Hand Painted. London, Hurst and Blackett, 1925.
Decameron Cocktails. London, Hurst and Blackett, 1926.
Mint Walk. London, Hurst and Blackett, 1927.
A Certified Bride. London, Hurst and Blackett, 1928.
Milly Comes to Town. London, Chapman and Hall, 1928.
He Married His Parlourmaid. London, Chapman and Hall, 1929.
Fantoccini. London, Chapman and Hall, 1930.
The Joy Shop. London, Chapman and Hall, 1931.
A Woman of Experience. London, Hurst and Blackett, 1931.
I Loved a Fairy. London, Hurst and Blackett, 1933.
Under the Big Top. London, Hurst and Blackett, 1933.
Exit Renee. London, Hurst and Blackett, 1934.
Publicity Baby. London, Hurst and Blackett, 1935.
Pick Up and Smile. London, Hutchinson, 1936.
God and Mr Aaronson. London, Hutchinson, 1937.
Keep Cheery. London, Hutchinson, 1937.
Hearts for Gold. London, Hutchinson, 1938.
Sweetbriar Lane. London, Hutchinson, 1938.
Writing Man. London, Hutchinson, 1939.
That Trouble Piece! London, Rich and Cowan, 1939.
Let the Storm Burst. London, Rich and Cowan, 1941.
Black-Out Symphony. London, Rich and Cowan, 1942.
The Wood Is My Pulpit. London, Rich and Cowan, 1942.
Joy Comes After. London, Rich and Cowan, 1943.
Love Never Dies. London, Rich and Cowan, 1943.
Astrologer. London, Rich and Cowan, 1944.
The Tears of Peace. London, Rich and Cowan, 1944.
Love Is a Lady. London, Rich and Cowan, 1945.
We Lost Our Way. London, Rich and Cowan, 1948.
Gorgeous Brute. London, Rich and Cowan, 1949.
Conjuror. London, Rich and Cowan, 1950.
Bubble over Thorn. London, Rich and Cowan, 1951.
Those Dominant Hills. London, Rich and Cowan, 1951.
Beloved Burden. London, Rich and Cowan, 1954.
Miss Venus of Aberdovey. London, Rich and Cowan, 1956.
Angel's Eyes. London, Hurst and Blackett, 1957.
The Jackpot. London, Hurst and Blackett, 1957.
Two Faces of Love. London, Hurst and Blackett, 1958.
Prince's Story. London, Hurst and Blackett, 1959.
Black Harvest. London, Hurst and Blackett, 1960.
These Changing Years. London, Hurst and Blackett, 1961.
I Was Shown Heaven. London, Hurst and Blackett, 1962.
Smile in the Mirror. London, Hurst and Blackett, 1963.

Novels as Oliver Sandys

The Woman in the Firelight. London, Long, 1911.
Chicane. London, Long, 1912.
The Garment of Gold. London, Hurst and Blackett, 1921.
Chappy—That's All. London, Hurst and Blackett, 1922.
The Green Caravan. London, Hurst and Blackett, 1922.
Old Roses. London, Hurst and Blackett, 1923.

The Pleasure Garden. London, Hurst and Blackett, 1923.
Sally Serene. London, Hurst and Blackett, 1924.
Tilly-Make-Haste. London, Hurst and Blackett, 1924.
Blinkeyes. London, Hurst and Blackett, 1925.
Mr Anthony. London, Hurst and Blackett, 1925.
The Curled Hands. London, Hurst and Blackett, 1926.
The Ginger-Jar. London, Hurst and Blackett, 1926.
The Crimson Ramblers. London, Hurst and Blackett, 1927.
The Sorcerers. London, Hurst and Blackett, 1927.
Mops. London, Hurst and Blackett, 1928.
Vista, The Dancer. London, Hurst and Blackett, 1928.
Cherry. London, Hurst and Blackett, 1929.
The Champagne Kiss. London, Hurst and Blackett, 1929.
Bad Lad. London, Hurst and Blackett, 1930.
Mr Scribbles. London, Hurst and Blackett, 1930.
Sally of Sloper's. London, Hurst and Blackett, 1930.
Jinks. London, Hurst and Blackett, 1931.
Misty Angel. London, Hurst and Blackett, 1931.
Butterflies. London, Hurst and Blackett, 1932.
Squire. London, Hurst and Blackett, 1932.
Just Lil. London, Hurst and Blackett, 1933.
Sir Boxer. London, Hurst and Blackett, 1933.
Happy Day. London, Hurst and Blackett, 1934.
Spangles. London, Hurst and Blackett, 1934.
Tiptoes. London, Hurst and Blackett, 1935.
The Curtain Will Go Up. London, Hutchinson, 1936.
The Show Must Go On. London, Hutchinson, 1936.
Angel's Kiss. London, Hutchinson, 1937.
The Happy Mummers. London, Hutchinson, 1937.
Prince Charming. London, Hutchinson, 1937.
Crinklenose. London, Hutchinson, 1938.
Love Is a Flower. London, Hurst and Blackett, 1938.
Mud on My Stockings. London, Hurst and Blackett, 1938.
Hollywood Honeymoon. London, Hurst and Blackett, 1939.
Old Hat. London, Hurst and Blackett, 1939.
Whatagirl. London, Hurst and Blackett, 1939.
Calm Waters. London, Hurst and Blackett, 1940.
Singing Uphill. London, Hurst and Blackett, 1940.
Jack Be Nimble. London, Hurst and Blackett, 1941.
Wellington Wendy. London, Hurst and Blackett, 1941.
Lame Daddy. London, Hurst and Blackett, 1942.
Meadowsweet. London, Hurst and Blackett, 1942.
Swell Fellows. London, Hurst and Blackett, 1942.
Merrily All the Way. London, Hurst and Blackett, 1943.
No Faint Heart. London, Hurst and Blackett, 1943.
Miss Paraffin. London, Hurst and Blackett, 1944.
Poppet & Co. London, Hurst and Blackett, 1944.
Deputy Pet. London, Hurst and Blackett, 1945.
Learn to Laugh Again. London, Hurst and Blackett, 1947.
The Constant Rabbit. London, Hurst and Blackett, 1949.
Dot on the Spot. London, Hurst and Blackett, 1949.
Shining Failure. London, Hurst and Blackett, 1950.
Bachelor's Tonic. London, Hurst and Blackett, 1951.
Kiss the Moon. London, Hurst and Blackett, 1951.
Let's All Be Happy. London, Hurst and Blackett, 1952.
Quaint Place. London, Hurst and Blackett, 1952.
Shine My Wings. London, Hurst and Blackett, 1954.
Suffer to Sing. London, Hurst and Blackett, 1955.
The Happiness Stone. London, Hurst and Blackett, 1956.
A New Day. London, Hurst and Blackett, 1957.
Dear Mr Dean. London, Hurst and Blackett, 1957.
Butterflies in the Rain. London, Hurst and Blackett, 1958.
Cherrystones. London, Hurst and Blackett, 1959.
The Tinsel and the Gold. London, Hurst and Blackett, 1959.
The Wise and the Steadfast. London, Hurst and Blackett, 1961.
The Golden Flame. London, Ward Lock, 1961.

The Poppy and the Rose. London, Hurst and Blackett, 1962.
The Happy Hearts. London, Ward Lock, 1962.
Laughter and Love Remain. London, Ward Lock, 1962.
Madame Adastra. London, Hurst and Blackett, 1964.

Novels as Marguerite Barclay

The Activities of Lavie Jutt, with Armiger Barclay. London, Stanley Paul, 1911.
Letters from Fleet Street, with Armiger Barclay. London, Palmer, 1912.
Where There Are Women, with Armiger Barclay. London, Unwin, 1915; revised edition, as *The Five-Hooded Cobra* (as Oliver Sandys), London, Hurst and Blackett, 1932.
Peter Day-by-Day, with Armiger Barclay. London, Simpkin Marshall, 1916.
Yesterday Is Tomorrow. London, Rich and Cowan, 1950.
Sunset Is Dawn. London, Rich and Cowan, 1953.
The Miracle Stone of Wales. London, Rider, 1957.

Short Stories

Twenty-One. London, Hurst and Blackett, 1924.
The Golden Snail and Other Stories. London, Hurst and Blackett, 1927.
S.O.S. Queenie and Other Stories (as Oliver Sandys). London, Hurst and Blackett, 1928.
Running Free and Other Stories. London, Chapman and Hall, 1929.

OTHER PUBLICATIONS

Other as Oliver Sandys

Full and Frank: The Private Life of a Woman Novelist. London, Hurst and Blackett, 1941.
Caradoc Evans. London, Hurst and Blackett, 1946.
Unbroken Thread: An Intimate Journal. London, Rider, 1948.

Editor (as Countess Barcynska), *The Little Mother Who Sits at Home.* London, Jack, and New York, Dutton, 1915.

*   *   *

Despite a prolific output of novels, published over a span of more than 50 years, Countess Barcynska nevertheless managed to maintain great popularity, beginning with her first full-length novel, *The Honey Pot*, through to her final works in the 1960s. This achievement was due to a high degree of ingenuity in characterization and plot, combined with the consistent ability to produce a gripping story.

The writer's use of two pseudonyms, Countess Barcynska and Oliver Sandys, was due more to the circumstances in which she found herself than to any real dichotomy in style or subject matter of the novels. Fortunately these vicissitudes of her life (described in her autobiography *Full and Frank*) seem to have provided her with a wealth of experience in life and love, enabling her to portray a wide variety of situations and relationships most convincingly.

The experience of running a repertory company herself led to a preoccupation with the theatre in many of her novels, e.g., *The Curtain Will Go Up* and *The Happy Mummers* as Oliver Sandys and *I Was Shown Heaven*, *Smile in the Mirror*, *The Honey Pot*, and *Back to the Honey-Pot*, as Countess Barcynska. In the 'honey-pot' novels, for example, the insecurity, frustrations, and glamour of the theatre are clearly witnessed through the story of Maggie Oliver—at first the leading light in her company but later returning under a false name to experience the life of a chorus girl.

Another feature common to many of the novels is the description of various 'spiritual experiences' felt by the characters. The schoolboy Peter, in *Joy Comes After*, 'sees' his dead mother in the attic, and Martin Leffley from *If Wishes Were Horses* is 'moved' in an unusual way while listening to a simple sermon in a country church to pray for forgiveness for the wrong he did his servant Ada. However, such experiences, where they occur, are not frightening to the characters concerned or to the reader, and indeed the writer took comfort from such experiences in her own life.

To find a weak man such as Martin Leffley in these novels is not unusual, for it was into developing her female characters that Countess Barcynska seems to have channelled most of her energies. When the detail of the plots has long faded, it is the women—the indomitable Aunt Polly in *If Wishes Were Horses*, the gypsy Molly Yetta in *Astrologer*, or the actress Phyllis Clun in *I Was Shown Heaven*—who remain strong in one's memory. Indeed it is in such characterization that the writer's strength lies, for one will look in vain for detailed scenic descriptions or great subtleties of plot. Many of the plots place great reliance on coincidence, as in *Black Harvest* where the two children of the heroine (one adopted, one not), fall in love and wish to marry, but in fact turn out to be half-brother and sister, an occurrence caused by an extremely unusual set of coincidences!

The 'happy-ever-after' ending is also a marked feature of these novels. However many tragedies happen in the course of the books, they always seem to end on a happy note. In *Writing Man*, for example, Dick's wife and baby have both died separately in tragic circumstances but the novel ends with him beginning to write another book, inspired by an awareness of his wife's 'presence'. Perhaps the authoress Daisy Bell, also in *Writing Man*, expresses Countess Barcynska's own feeling when she says 'It's very consoling to make one's characters happy at the end of one's books and it makes people who read them happy too—especially the ones who are sad.'

Countess Barcynska took great pains to show, through the fates of various characters, the inevitable consequences of wrong-doing. In her earlier novels the moralistic aphorisms can become rather tiresome. However, in later novels, the morals are less overt and are often centred around the problems of love and human relationships. The penalties of marrying for the wrong reasons came to Evan Evans in *Astrologer*, who married out of chivalry, and to Martin Leffley in *If Wishes Were Horses* for marrying his deceased landlady's daughter almost for convenience.

Despite showing some of the characteristics of an earlier age in her writings, Countess Barcynska was a writer of great ability who, as she said herself, knew how 'to make people laugh and smile and weep'. In all, her stories have a certain elusive combination which makes for very compelling reading.

—Kim F. Paynter

BARNES, Margaret Campbell.
Nationality: British. **Born:** Margaret Wood, London, 27 February 1891. **Education:** St Ronan's, Hedley Wood, Middlesex; Pension Collot, Paris, France. **Relations:** married George Alfred Campbell Barnes; two sons. **Career:** buyer of silent French and American films, and film-title translator for an English agency; travel writer. **Died:** 1963.

ROMANCE AND HISTORICAL PUBLICATIONS

Novels

Like Us They Lived. London, Macdonald, 1944; as *The Passionate Brood*, Philadelphia, McCrae-Smith, 1945; London, Macdonald, 1954.

My Lady of Cleves. London, Macdonald, and London, McCrae-
Smith, 1946.

Within the Hollow Crown. Philadelphia, McCrae-Smith, 1947; London, Macdonald, 1948.

Brief Gaudy Hour: A Novel of Anne Boleyn. London, Macdonald,
and Philadelphia, McCrae-Smith, 1949.

With All My Heart. London, Macdonald, and Philadelphia, McCrae-
Smith, 1951.

The Tudor Rose. London, Macdonald, and Philadelphia, McCrae-
Smith, 1953.

Mary of Carisbrooke. London, Macdonald, and Philadelphia,
McCrae-Smith, 1956.

Isabel the Fair. London, Macdonald, and Philadelphia, McCrae-
Smith, 1957.

Within the Hollow Crown. London, Macdonald, 1958.

King's Fool. London, Macdonald, and Philadelphia, McCrae-
Smith, 1959.

The King's Bed. London, Macdonald, 1961; Philadelphia, McCrae-
Smith, 1962.

Lady on the Coin (unfinished; completed by Hebe Elsna). London,
Macdonald, and Philadelphia, McCrae-Smith, 1963.

*   *   *

Those of Margaret Campbell Barnes's novels for which she was
able to find little or no written record, as in her 12th-century work
Like Us They Lived, and those in which she was dealing with meagre
documentation and much legend—*The King's Bed*, *King's Fool*,
and *Mary of Carisbrooke*—are described as *tales*. Her other novels,
well documented records of kings and queens of the later Plantagenet era, and the Houses of Lancaster, York, Tudor, and Stuart, are
called *stories*. The former are historically possible. The latter, as far
as her considerable ability as a novelist and her careful research can
make them, are historically correct.

Like Us They Lived, a turbulent tale of the quarrelsome Plantagenet family of Henry II and Eleanor of Aquitaine, is partly the love
story of Richard I and Berengaria of Navarre. However, Barnes's
portrayal of the mother, Eleanor, referred to in history as the most
accomplished woman of the Middle Ages, leaves her in the reader's
mind as the character to remember. It was Eleanor that kept the passionate brood turbulent in the constant maelstrom of her own ambition and discontent. The author's inclusion of 'Robin [Hood]
foster-brother' in this family is disappointing and unnecessary.

Isabel the Fair, the most dramatic of the novels, tells of the
French princess's tragic marriage to Edward II. The young bride,
confronted with her husband's flagrant homosexuality, grows bitter
and vengeful watching Edward's determination to enrich his favourites and amuse himself with various disagreeable intrigues. Isabel's life is treated compassionately by the author. With Edward,
Barnes is restrained, not delving deeply into the motives behind his
behaviour for 'he accepted the easy palliative of self-deception and
avoided discussion of anything that was unjustifiable in his past'.

The story of Richard II, last Plantagenet king, is told in *Within the
Hollow Crown*. Richard's love of peace and beauty, ridiculed by the
mediaeval world in which he lived, gives the author an outlet for her
free-flowing descriptions of settings, buildings, countryside, and
people as seen through his discerning eyes. For the tender love story
of Richard and Anne of Bohemia, Barnes pulls out all the romantic
stops. Against a background of ongoing civil war and clamorous relatives it is the love story which holds the reader. The scene of
Anne's death and the description of Richard's continuing sorrow are
outstanding.

The Tudor Rose is, above all else, a superb mystery novel. Elizabeth of York's marriage to Henry VII is secondary to the question of
what happened to her brothers, the princes in the Tower. The complex character of Richard III and the fascination Elizabeth felt for

him are particularly well written and neither Elizabeth of York nor
the readers ever come to a conclusion as to his guilt or innocence.

Brief Gaudy Hour and *My Lady of Cleves*, probably the best
known of Barnes's novels, are the stories of Anne Boleyn and Anne
of Cleves and their marriages to Henry VIII. Anne Boleyn is described as a bewitching, careless, carefree girl in a marriage which
quickly deteriorates from passion to petulance. The swiftly moving
narrative follows in the wake of her undoing as Henry, eventually
unable to stand the turmoil, accepts evidence brought before him by
her enemies and has her executed for adultery.

In keeping with the woman herself, the pace of *My Lady of Cleves*
is slower, more sedate. Henry found her unattractive, bland, boring.
However, Barnes's fine delineation of Anne's character leaves the
reader wondering if she is the wife he should have kept and, towards
the end of his life and after a renewed friendship with Anne, we see
Henry wondering as well.

In the two novels, *With All My Heart*, the love story of Charles II
and Catherine of Braganza, and *Lady on the Coin*, the story of Charles and his mistress, Frances Stuart, Barnes presents two sides of the
Merry Monarch and, with convincing narrative, makes both sides
plausible. A shrewd politician and a clever liar, Charles had a large
sexual appetite. He was charming, much loved by the people, stead-
fastly refused to divorce the childless wife he loved and had many
mistresses for whom he had no love but much enthusiasm. Frances
Stuart left him to become Duchess of Richmond and Lennox and is
best remembered as the model for the figure of Britannia on the old
English penny.

The King's Bed, a tale of Richard III's natural son, Dickon, *Mary
of Carisbrooke*, a tale of Charles I during his imprisonment on the
Isle of Wight, and *King's Fool*, the tale of Will Somers, court jester
to Henry VIII, all provide insightful glimpses of the major characters involved as described by those close to and serving them.

I can think of no other writer in whose novels history and romance
are better blended. Barnes provided us with a recreation of mediaeval England peopled by characters full of life and colour. Historian, researcher, story-teller—it is hard to place these facets of her
writing in their proper linear perspective. Throughout her novels
they braid in and back upon themselves in such a way the reader is
lost in the story-telling.

—Nancy P. Stevenson

BARR, Pat.
Nationality: British. **Born:** Patricia Miriam Copping, Norwich,
Norfolk, 25 April 1934. **Education:** Birmingham University, B.A.
(honours) in English 1956; University College, London, M.A. 1964.
Relations: married John Marshall Barr in 1956 (died). **Career:**
English teacher, Yokohama International School, Japan, 1959–61,
and University of Maryland overseas program, Japan, 1961–62; as-
sistant secretary, National Old People's Welfare Council, London,
1965–66. Since 1966, freelance writer and journalist. **Recipient:**
Churchill fellowship, for non-fiction, 1971. **Agent:** Murray
Pollinger, 222 Old Brompton Road, London SW5 0B2, England.
Address: 6 Mount Pleasant, Norwich, Norfolk NR2 2DG, England.

ROMANCE AND HISTORICAL PUBLICATIONS

Novels (series: Alice Greenwood)

Jade: A Novel of China (Greenwood). New York, St Martin's Press,
1982; London, Corgi, 1983.
Chinese Alice. London, Secker and Warburg, 1981.
Uncut Jade. London, Secker and Warburg, 1983.

Kenjiro. London, Secker and Warburg, 1985.
Coromandel. London, Hamish Hamilton, 1988.

OTHER PUBLICATIONS

Other

The Coming of the Barbarians. London, Macmillan, and New York, Dutton, 1967.
The Deer Cry Pavillion (sequel to *The Coming of the Barbarians*). London, Macmillan, 1968; New York, Harcourt Brace, 1969.
The Elderly: Handbook on Care and Services. London, National Council of Social Service, 1968.
A Curious Life for a Lady. London, Macmillan, and New York, Doubleday, 1970.
Foreign Devils: Westerners in the Far East. London, Penguin, 1970.
To China with Love. London, Secker and Warburg, 1972; New York, Doubleday, 1973.
The Memsahibs: The Women of Victorian India. London, Secker and Warburg, 1976.
Taming the Jungle. London, Secker and Warburg, 1977.
The Framing of the Female (for children). London, Kestrel, 1978.
Simla: A Hill Station in British India, with Ray Desmond. London, Scolar Press, and New York, Scribner, 1978.
Japan. London, Batsford, 1980.
The Dust in the Balance: British Women in India, 1905–1945. London, Hamish Hamilton, 1989.

Editor, *I Remember: An Arrangement for Many Voices*. London, Macmillan, 1970.

*   *   *

Pat Barr's novels are underpinned by personal experience and detailed research, and follow a substantial collection of nonfiction works on China, Japan and the Indian sub-continent. At their best, Barr's novels—like *Chinese Alice* and its sequel *Uncut Jade*—combine her interests and examine the impact and interaction of European and Asian cultures revealed through the eyes of a liberated heroine with definite opinions of her own.

Chinese Alice, the first and possibly the best of Barr's fictional works, introduces the most formidable, and likeable, of her heroines, Alice Greenwood. Daughter of missionary parents killed in anti-Western riots in Tientsin, Alice undergoes capture and concubinage in Hunan, and escapes only to find herself regarded as an outsider by the British family to whom she returns. Caught between two modes of life, British by birth but Chinese by upbringing and predilection, Alice undergoes endless journeyings from one city to another which mirror her own restless search for identity. Through her eyes, Barr shows us the China of the late-19th and early-20th centuries; an ancient civilization overrun by European merchants and missionaries, its traditions increasingly challenged by a growing reformist movement. No attempt is made to romanticize; Barr depicts the filth and squalor, the ignorance and cruelty, while at the same time retaining a genuine love for China and respect for its culture. With the redoubtable Alice the reader encounters the religious bigotry of the Western missionaries, the superficial refinement of Treaty Port society and the internecine warfare of the Chinese conservatives and reformers. A strong, resilient personality with remarkably modern sexual attitudes, Alice meets love and suffering on equal terms, emerging unbroken from rape and widowhood, surviving the Boxer siege of Peking in *Uncut Jade*, to bid a final farewell to the country that has been her home. Her adventures in these first two novels paint an unforgettable picture in the mind, while

Alice herself impresses as one of the most notable heroines of recent historical fiction.

Kenjiro is set in 19th-century Japan, and explores the mixed marriage of the samurai hero and an English woman against the background of the country's own struggle between tradition and reform. Interwoven with the central love story of Kenjiro and Elinor are other relationships, in particular the illicit affair of two British expatriates, and the courtship of Kenjiro's sister Ryo. Although this time Barr gives a male character the leading role, the women are far from being subordinates, and for the most part rebel against the stereotypical behaviour which is expected of them; Elinor condemns her brother's hypocrisy while Ryo takes up the cause of women's rights as a teacher of young girls. The novel reaches a tragic climax with the death of Kenjiro and Elinor's son at the siege of Port Arthur in 1895. A quieter, more diffuse work than the two previous novels, *Kenjiro* nevertheless holds the interest, and is thought-provoking. As always, the theme of women seeking identity in a man's world is subtly, but strongly, conveyed.

With *Coromandel*, Barr moves further afield, exploring the world of British exiles in Southern India during the 1830s. Her heroine, Amelia, arrives to join her husband—an official employed by the local native ruler—and is quickly drawn into the tangled network of relationships that comprise the uneasy alliance of East and West. Under the surface of a fixed—even tediously routine—universe, lie barely suppressed passions, whether the acquisitive lust of the East India Company for the Raja's land, or the desire of Amelia's husband for his youthful Indian mistress Rukmini. The Afghan War, fought 'offstage' and at a distance, serves as an omen of disasters to come. Barr once more provides a superb vision of a country on the verge of colonialism, contrasting the naive conservatism of the Raja with the greed of the Western merchants, and the more subtle prejudices of the anglicizing missionaries. A heroine less charismatic and more conventional than Chinese Alice, Amelia has the customary virtues of courage and independence. Barr has her survive the ordeal of her husband's death from cholera to make her own way in the world. Rejecting offers of marriage, Amelia uses her inheritance to establish a school for girls. The novel ends as she visualizes the future: 'In her imagination the room was already repeopled with little girls studying at those desks, learning ways to survive'.

—Geoffrey Sadler

BARRIE, Susan. British. See 2nd edition, 1990.

BARRY, Jocelyn. See **BARCLAY, Tessa.**

BARTH, John (Simmons).
Nationality: American. **Born:** Cambridge, Maryland, 27 May 1930. **Education:** Juilliard School of Music, New York; Johns Hopkins University, Baltimore, A.B. 1951, M.A. 1952. **Relations:** married 1) Anne Strickland in 1950 (divorced 1969), one daughter and two sons; 2) Shelly Rosenberg in 1970. **Career:** junior instructor in English, Johns Hopkins University, 1951–53; instructor 1953–56, assistant professor, 1957–60, and associate professor of English, 1960–65, Pennsylvania State University, University Park; professor of English, 1965–73, and Butler professor, 1971–73, State University of New York, Buffalo. Since 1973 Centennial professor of English and Creative Writing, now emeritus, Johns Hopkins University. **Recipient:** Brandeis University Creative Arts award, 1965; Rockefeller grant, 1965; American Academy grant, 1966; National

Book award, 1973. D.Litt.: University of Maryland, College Park, 1969. **Member:** American Academy, 1977, and American Academy of Arts and Sciences, 1977. **Agent:** Wylie Aitken and Stone, 250 West 57th Street, New York, New York 10107, USA. **Address:** c/o Writing Seminars, Johns Hopkins University, Baltimore, Maryland 21218, USA.

Romance and Historical Publications

Novel

The Sot-Weed Factor. New York, Doubleday, 1960; London, Secker and Warburg, 1961; revised edition, New York, Doubleday, 1967.

Other Publications

Novels

The Floating Opera. New York, Appleton Century Crofts, 1956; revised edition, New York, Doubleday, 1967; London, Secker and Warburg, 1968.
The End of the Road. New York, Doubleday, 1958; London, Secker and Warburg, 1962; revised edition, Doubleday, 1967.
Giles Goat-Boy; or, The Revised New Syllabus. New York, Doubleday, 1966; London, Secker and Warburg, 1967.
Letters. New York, Putnam, 1979; London, Secker and Warburg, 1980.
Sabbatical: A Romance. New York, Putnam, and London, Secker and Warburg, 1982.
The Tidewater Tales: A Novel (sequel to *Sabbatical*). New York, Putnam, 1987; London, Methuen, 1988.
The Last Voyage of Somebody the Sailor. New York, Little Brown, and London, Hodder and Stoughton, 1991.

Short Stories

Lost in the Funhouse: Fiction for Print, Tape, Live Voice. New York, Doubleday, 1968; London, Secker and Warburg, 1969.
Chimera (3 novellas). New York, Random House, 1972; London, Deutsch, 1974.
Todd Andrews to the Author. Northridge, California, Lord John Press, 1979.

Other

The Literature of Exhaustion, and The Literature of Replenishment (essays). Northridge, California, Lord John Press, 1982.
The Friday Book: Essays and Other Nonfiction. New York, Putnam, 1984.
Don't Count on It: A Note on the Number of the 1001 Nights. Northridge, California, Lord John Press, 1984.

*

Film Adaptation: *The End of the Road*, 1970.

Bibliography: *John Barth: A Descriptive Primary and Annotated Secondary Bibliography* by Joseph Weixlmann, New York, Garland, 1976; *John Barth: An Annotated Bibliography* by Richard Allan Vine, Metuchen, New Jersey, Scarecrow Press, 1977; *John Barth, Jerzy Kosinski, and Thomas Pynchon: A Reference Guide* by Thomas P. Walsh and Cameron Northouse, Boston, Hall, 1977.

Manuscript Collection: Library of Congress, Washington, DC.

Critical Studies: *John Barth* by Gerhard Joseph, Minneapolis, University of Minnesota Press, 1970; *John Barth: The Comic Sublimity of Paradox* by Jac Tharpe, Carbondale, Southern Illinois University Press, 1974; *The Literature of Exhaustion: Borges, Nabokov, and Barth* by John O. Stark, Durham, North Carolina, Duke University Press, 1974; *John Barth: An Introduction* by David Morrell, University Park, Pennsylvania State University Press, 1976; *Critical Essays on John Barth* edited by Joseph J. Waldmeir, Boston, Hall, 1980; *Passionate Virtuosity: The Fiction of John Barth* by Charles B. Harris, Urbana, University of Illinois Press, 1983; *John Barth* by Heide Ziegler, London, Methuen, 1987; *Understanding John Barth* by Stan Fogel and Gorden Slethaug, Columbia, University of South Carolina Press, 1990.

*   *   *

No 20th-century American novelist has had more influence on the shape and scope of recent fiction than has John Barth, who in practice and in theory has named and exemplified the 'literature of exhaustion'—literature written by men and women who have observed the ultimate futility of both living and writing and who must yet somehow write while they choose to live, whether or not their writings happen to be read. Barth, who began his publishing career with two seemingly realistic novels, *The Floating Opera*, a light-hearted debate over suicide; and *The End of the Road*, a satiric study of a triangular love relationship, conceived the idea of writing a third such 'nihilistic comedy'; the best result, however, was his third novel, *The Sot-Weed Factor*, a delightful picaresque historical work.

The student of Colonial American literature, after wading through acres of Puritan sermons, political and religious tracts, documentaries of exploration, devotional poetry, and precious little else, comes with delight upon a satiric poem by Ebenezer Cooke (c1667–c1732)—*The Sot-Weed Factor*, or *A Voyage to Maryland* (1708). Almost alone in early American literature this short verse satire, in direct imitation of Samuel Butler's Restoration-era *Hudibras*—that well-remembered satire of puritanism, heroism, and chivalry—brightens with its sharp English wit an otherwise grey American landscape. The young Barth was struck by his own discovery of Cooke's *Sot-Weed Factor* and its satires of life in the colony of Maryland. Immersing himself in the poem, in Cooke, in the annals of Maryland, and in colonial-era diaries and letters (especially the diaries of William Byrd), Barth in four years wrote and published his own *Sot-Weed Factor*, a very long novel which amazed readers with its wealth of invention as well as its apparent faithfulness to 17th-century American and English history, culture, and language. So well did Barth get right the smallest details of life and speech in his chosen historical era and locale that he could take the greatest liberties in the invention of his fantastic plot, which is expanded far beyond the skeleton story present in Cooke's poetic satire or the few facts actually known about the historical Ebenezer Cooke.

Drawing upon these few facts and upon his own close reading of the satiric picaresque novels by Henry Fielding, Barth presents in *The Sot-Weed Factor* (the title meaning a merchant of tobacco) the same virginal hero who must at the expense of his purse and his happiness protect his virtue in a lusty and materialistic world. Beset by men and women who would gladly take both his innocence and his inheritance, Ebenezer Cooke is bedeviled by all manner of people and events, tossed blithely upon a sea of mischance, mistaken identity, and mischief, so misused in his chosen profession of heroic poet of Maryland that he writes instead of his planned colonial epic, a bitter satire of that colony—the original poem *The Sot-Weed Factor*.

Although the misunderstandings, mistakings, disguises, and revelations in Barth's rich picaresque plot are interesting and exciting to read, his long novel of the innocent (and thus dangerous) tobacco merchant and poet is wonderfully enhanced with fixed debates on such topics as history, innocence, justice, and civility; elaborate literary dreams; bi-lingual swearing contests; catalogues of foods, customs, and proverbs; hitherto unknown diaries, one by Captain John Smith with entries on the epic deflowering of Pocahontas; and revisionist explorations of the sexual preferences of famous English dons, politicians, and scientists.

Yet the pure invention of plot, character, and language is the notable achievement of Barth in *The Sot-Weed Factor*, along with the invention of a would-be poet and his would-be (and, of course, actual) poem about 17th-century England and America. And it is in returning to the source of the English novel that *The Sot-Weed Factor* set the course of Barth's career, for in later novels he recreated and expanded other forms of the early English novel—the universal satire, *Giles Goat-Boy*; the epistolary novel, *Letters*; and the adventure-romance, *Sabbatical*. For an author who believes in and demonstrates the uselessness of the art of writing, Barth has certainly lived well and richly in his imaginative recreation of storytelling in English.

—Ray Lewis White

————

BATES, Jennie. See **SEGER, Maura.**

————

BEATON, M.C. See **CHESNEY, Marion.**

————

BEATY, Betty. British. See 2nd edition, 1990.

————

BEAUCLERK, Helen. British. 1892–1969. See 2nd edition, 1990.

————

BECK, L(ily) Adams. British. Died 1931. See 2nd edition, 1990.

————

BELL, Georgianna. See **MANNERS, Alexandra.**

————

BELLAMANN, Henry.
Pseudonym for Heinrich Hauer. **Nationality:** American. **Born:** Fulton, Missouri, 28 April 1882. **Education:** Westminster College, Missouri; University of Denver; studied in London, Paris, and New York, 1898–1900. **Relations:** married Katherine Jones in 1907. **Career:** dean, School of Fine Arts, Chicora College for Women, Columbia, South Carolina, 1907–24; chair of the Examining Board, Juilliard Musical Foundation, 1924–26, and Rockefeller Foundation, 1926–28; lecturer, Vassar College, Poughkeepsie, New York, 1928–29; Dean, Curtis Institute of Music, Philadelphia. **Recipient:** Chevalier, Légion d'honneur, 1931. **Died:** 16 June 1945.

ROMANCE AND HISTORICAL PUBLICATIONS

Novels

Petenera's Daughter. New York, Harcourt Brace, 1926; London, Cape, 1927.

Crescendo. New York, Harcourt Brace, 1928.
The Richest Woman in Town. New York, Century, 1932.
Kings Row. New York, Simon and Schuster, 1940; London, Cape, 1941.
Floods of Spring. New York, Simon and Schuster, 1942; London, Cape, 1943.
Victoria Grandolet. New York, Simon and Schuster, 1944; London, Cassell, 1945.
Parris Mitchell of Kings Row, with K.J. Bellamann. New York, Simon and Schuster, 1948; London, Cassell, 1949.

OTHER PUBLICATIONS

Novel

The Gray Man Walks. New York, Doubleday, 1936.

Poetry

A Music Teacher's Note Book. New York, Poetry Bookshop, 1920.
Cups of Illusion. Boston, Houghton Mifflin, 1923.
The Upward Pass. Boston, Houghton Mifflin, 1928.

*

Film Adaptation: *Kings Row*, 1941.

*   *   *

Henry Bellamann was a distinguished musician and music educator who aspired to be a poet. Praise for his novels most often focuses upon his lyrical evocation of pastoral scenes in the 19th-century Mississippi River valley. His early novels, which one reviewer described as 'atmosphere saturated', gave little hint of his eventual success and have virtually disappeared. He made his reputation overnight, when he was nearly 60, with *Kings Row*, a revelation of the psychic distresses of a small Missouri community at the turn of the century, which critics compared to Faulkner's work. The *New Yorker*'s taste-making and Faulkner-baiting Clifton Fadiman, in fact, described Bellamann's 'operatic concept of character' as less easy to 'laugh off' than Faulkner's work, though others found that he lacked the compelling power that distinguished Faulkner. Bellamann is best remembered for the first two-thirds of *Kings Row*, which describes the adolescent sexual awakening of Parris Mitchell, a boy isolated from the rest of the community by his intellectual interests and his love of music, whose first fumbling seduction of a country girl and tactful rejection of the homosexual advances of a classmate were daring subjects for the closeted 1940s. Bellamann provides, however, only fragmentary glimpses of the five years that Parris spends in Vienna studying the then fashionable new Freudian psychiatry; and after Dr Mitchell returns to Missouri to practice, the focus shifts to the account of the tragic accident that destroys another promising young man (played by Ronald Reagan in the highly successful film version).

Kings Row was originally planned as the first volume of a trilogy that would expose the town's secret life from 1890 to 1940, but Bellamann was diverted from his epic by two grandiose attempts to dip further back into the frontier past. *Floods of Spring*, set in rural Missouri in the middle of the 19th century, followed the career of a figure like Faulkner's Sutpen whose obsessive dedication to building an empire destroyed all his family and personal relationships, but reviewers complained that, although the frontier atmosphere was powerfully evoked, Bellamann never made clear what motivated his character's self-destructive pursuits. The evocation of the sultry atmosphere of plantation Louisiana during the same period in

Victoria Grandolet was even more highly praised, but again reviewers complained of Bellamann's failure adequately to animate and motivate his stereotyped characters in the conflict between a moody Yankee bride and her hidebound and highly traditional Southern in-laws.

Meanwhile Bellamann, during five years of furious activity following his first great success, had been making notes for a continuation of *Kings Row*, but he died before beginning to fill in the story outline that he had developed. His wife Katherine, also a poet, undertook to finish *Parris Mitchell of Kings Row*, which she explained was originally intended to have presented a psychoanalysis of the town as viewed and understood by Dr Mitchell, but which had turned into a personal history of his struggles to drag the backward community, which distrusted his controversial therapies for mental illness, into the 20th century. Ultimately, after being dismissed from his position at the local state hospital for the insane, he regains the respect of the community with his heroic efforts during the dreadful influenza epidemic after World War I and a happier future is unconvincingly predicted.

Bellamann enjoyed his greatest success for his effusive presentations of the frustrations of alienated adolescents in backward and suspicious communities. Although he exhibited great interest in Freudian psychiatry, he got out of his depth when he tried to imagine and articulate the complex psychological distresses of inhibited adults. Instead of the great gallery of grotesques that—influenced also by Sherwood Anderson's *Winesburg, Ohio*—Faulkner produced, Bellamann populated his lush settings with only conventional shadows.

—Warren French

BELLE, Pamela.
Nationality: British. **Born:** Ipswich, Suffolk, 16 June 1952. **Education:** Ipswich High School, 1964–69; Ipswich School of Art, 1969–70; Ipswich Civic College, 1970–71; University of Sussex, Brighton, 1972–75, B.A. (honours) in history 1975; Coventry College of Education, 1975–76, postgraduate certificate in education 1976. **Relations:** married Alan Fincher in 1976 (divorced 1983). **Career:** library assistant, Hemel Hempstead, Hertfordshire, 1976–77; primary school teacher, Hemel Hempstead, Tring and Berkhamsted, Hertfordshire, 1977–78, and Northchurch St Mary's School, Berkhamsted, 1978–85. **Agent:** Vivienne Schuster, John Farquharson Ltd, 162–168 Regent Street, London W1R 5TB. **Address:** 184 Melksham Lane, Broughton Gifford, Melksham, Wiltshire SN12 8LN, England.

ROMANCE AND HISTORICAL PUBLICATIONS

Novels (series: Goldhayes Trilogy (Heron Family); Wintercombe)

Goldhayes Trilogy:
    The Moon in the Water. London, Pan, 1983; New York, Berkley, 1984.
    The Chains of Fate. London, Pan, and New York, Berkley, 1984.
    Alathea. London, Pan, and New York, Berkley, 1985.
The Lodestar (Heron). London, Bodley Head, 1987.
Wintercombe:
    1. *Wintercombe*. London, Bodley Head, and New York, St Martin's Press, 1988.
    2. *Herald of Joy*. London, Bodley Head, 1989; New York, St Martin's Press, 1990.
    3. *A Falling Star*. London, Century, 1990.
    4. *Treason's Gift*. London, Century, 1992.

*

Pamela Belle comments:
    I take a great deal of trouble to make my books as historically accurate as possible. My characters seem so real to me that I must make the place and time in which they are set as vivid and convincing as I am able, and try to fit plot and characters into real events, rather than the other way about. All history fascinates me, especially the 17th century, and my particular interests always seem to surface in each book: children, animals (especially dogs, cats, and horses), music, poetry, architecture, warfare, and the minutiae of daily life in a country house, in the garden or on the farm.

*   *   *

Pamela Belle's novels are a combination of family saga and romance set against a background of well-researched history and can be confidently recommended to all who enjoy a romantic story, forceful characters and fast-moving action.

She draws characters well and handles large casts with aplomb. She is good at sinister villains like the treacherous, beautiful Meraud Trevelyan in the 'Goldhayes Trilogy', and the Drakelons both in the trilogy and *The Lodestar*.

For the 'Goldhayes Trilogy'(*The Moon in the Water*, *The Chains of Fate* and *Alathea*), Belle created the Herons, a family with several branches—Drakelons, Trevelyans, Grahams and their friends the Sewells. *The Lodestar* tells of 15th-century Herons and Drakelons. In all her books there are delightful children and endearing animals.

Her heroines are strong women like Thomazine Heron and her daughter Alathea in the 'Goldhayes Trilogy'. Silence St Barbe in *Wintercombe* and *Herald of Joy*, is quiet but has an inner strength and her flighty granddaughter, Louise, in *A Falling Star* and *Treason's Gift*, although prepared to defy convention, has an underlying sensibility. Only one book, *The Lodestar*, has a man, Christie Heron, as the main character but the girl he marries, Julian Bray, is another strong woman. Belle is good at creating believable children, especially Silence's offspring who play large parts and carry much of the plot in *Wintercombe* and *Herald of Joy*.

Her villains are splendidly bad like beautiful, amoral Meraut Trevelyan, the evil Puritan grandmother, Thomazine's first husband, Dominic Drakelon in the Goldhayes books, and savage Colonel Ridgely in *Wintercombe*. Perhaps her best villain is Charles, in *A Falling Star* and *Treason's Gift*, because his appalling traits are so subtly conveyed.

Belle has a strong affinity with place, describing scenery with feeling but her most loving descriptions are reserved for the houses her characters inhabit—Goldhayes in Suffolk, Ashcott in Oxfordshire, and Wintercombe, the beautiful house in Somerset, all of which feature as prominently as the people and are lovingly described.

Apart from *The Lodestar* which is set in the reign of Richard III and has an intriguing theory about the fate of the princes in the Tower, the 17th century is Belle's chosen period. Thomazine's love story in all its joys and disasters is the central subject of *The Moon in the Water* and its sequel *The Chains of Fate*, but the enterprises of her cousins and friends during the Civil War are interwoven in this Royalist tale. The Parliamentarian point of view is shown in *Wintercombe*. Silence St Barbe, Puritan by upbringing, is married to a stern, elderly Roundhead and faces many challenges when her household is disrupted, and is threatened by being taken over by a brutal Royalist garrison. Nevertheless, she falls in love with one of them, Captain Hellier, who marches away at the end of the book, without knowing that she is pregnant. In *Herald of Joy*, he returns to Wintercombe for sanctuary after the disastrous Battle of Worcester, and after adventures and mishaps, Silence and Nick Hellier achieve their happy ending.

Alathea (the name of the daughter of Thomazine Heron) is set after the Restoration. We see the fringes of court life and witness the Great Fire through Alathea's eyes. Alathea is a female artist who is threatened by her half-brother's incestuous love before she becomes the mistress of the notorious Earl of Rochester.

In *A Falling Star*, against the background of the romantic love story of Alexander St Barbe and the wayward Louise Chevalier, Silence's grandmother and nephews become involved in Monmouth's ill-fated rising. Louise and Alex's story continues in *Treason's Gift* (the fourth Wintercombe novel) set in 1686. Their marriage is coming apart and the villainous Charles is in possession of Wintercombe because Alex, working for William of Orange, is deemed a traitor until the Glorious Revolution provides a happy ending.

The love stories at the heart of these historical romances are warm and full of feeling. The complications the lovers suffer are devious and difficult, her plots are full of action and excitement, keeping the reader happily turning the pages. Her knowledge of 17th-century housekeeping and nursing is well integrated and the thoughts and attitudes of her characters always ring true to their time.

—Pamela Cleaver

* * *

BENEDICT, Peter. See **PARGETER, Edith.**

* * *

BENET, Stephen Vincent. American. 1898–1943. See 2nd edition, 1990.

* * *

BENNETT, Elizabeth. See **HARROD-EAGLES, Cynthia.**

* * *

BENNETTS, Pamela.
Pseudonyms: Helen Ashfield; Margaret James. **Nationality:** British. **Born:** Pamela James, Hampstead, London, 23 July 1922. **Education:** Emmanuel Church School, Hampstead; St Marylebone School for Girls, London. **Relations:** married William George Bennetts in 1942; one daughter. **Career:** staff member, London Diocesan Fund, 1938–80: retired as deputy secretary, 1980. **Died:** 11 December 1986.

ROMANCE AND HISTORICAL PUBLICATIONS

Novels (series: Royal Jewel)

The Borgia Prince. London, Hale, 1968; New York, St Martin's Press, 1975.
The Borgia Bull. London, Hale, 1968.
The Venetian. London, Hale, 1968.
The Suzerain. London, Hale, 1968.
The Adversaries. London, Hale, 1969.
The Black Plantagenet. London, Hale, 1969.
Envoy from Elizabeth. London, Hale, 1970; New York, St Martin's Press, 1973.
Richard and the Knights of God. London, Hale, 1970; New York, St Martin's Press, 1973.
The Tudor Ghosts. London, Hale, 1971.
Royal Sword at Agincourt. London, Hale, and New York, St Martin's Press, 1971.

A Crown for Normandy. London, Hale, 1971.
Bright Son of York. London, Hale, 1971.
The Third Richard. London, Hale, 1972.
The Angevin King. London, Hale, 1972.
The de Montfort Legacy. London, Hale, and New York, St Martin's Press, 1973.
The Lords of Lancaster. London, Hale, and New York, St Martin's Press, 1973.
The Barons of Runnymede. London, Hale, and New York, St Martin's Press, 1974.
A Dragon for Edward. London, Hale, and New York, St Martin's Press, 1975.
My Dear Lover England. London, Hale, and New York, St Martin's Press, 1975.
The She-Wolf. London, Hale, 1975; New York, St Martin's Press, 1976.
Death of the Red King. London, Hale, and New York, St Martin's Press, 1976.
Stephen and the Sleeping Saints. London, Hale, and New York, St Martin's Press, 1977.
The House in Candle Square. London, Hale, 1977; as *The Haunting of Sara Lessingham* (as Margaret James), New York, St Martin's Press, 1978.
Don Pedro's Captain. London, Hale, and New York, St Martin's Press, 1978.
Ring the Bell Softly. London, Hale, 1978; (as Margaret James) New York, St Martin's Press, 1978.
One Dark Night. London, Hale, 1978.
Footsteps in the Fog. London, Hale, 1979; (as Margaret James) New York, St Martin's Press, 1979.
Marionette. London, Hale, 1979; (as Margaret James) New York, St Martin's Press, 1979.
A Voice in the Darkness. London, Hale, 1979; (as Margaret James) New York, St Martin's Press, 1979.
Amberstone. London, Hale, 1980; (as Margaret James) New York, St Martin's Press, 1980.
The Quick and the Dead. London, Hale, 1980; (as Margaret James) New York, St Martin's Press, 1980.
Lucy's Cottage. London, Hale, 1981; (as Margaret James) New York, St Martin's Press, 1981.
Beau Barron's Lady. London, Hale, 1981.
The Marquis and Miss Jones. London, Hale, 1981; (as Helen Ashfield) New York, St Martin's Press, 1982.
Regency Rogue. London, Hale, 1982.
The Michaelmas Tree. London, Hale, 1982; New York, St Martin's Press, 1982.
Lady of the Masque. London, Hale, 1982.
The Slave Masters. London, Hale, 1983.
The Loving Highwayman. London, Hale, and New York, St Martin's Press, 1983.
Emerald (Royal Jewel). London, Hale, 1983; (as Helen Ashfield) New York, St Martin's Press, 1983.
Midsummer Morning. London, Hale, 1984; (as Helen Ashfield) New York, St Martin's Press, 1984.
Ruby (Royal Jewel). London, Hale, 1984; (as Helen Ashfield) New York, St Martin's Press, 1984.
Pearl (Royal Jewel). London, Hale, 1984; (as Helen Ashfield) New York, St Martin's Press, 1985.
Garnet (Royal Jewel). London, Hale, 1985; (as Helen Ashfield) New York, St Martin's Press, 1985.
Sapphire (Royal Jewel). London, Hale, 1985; (as Helen Ashfield) New York, St Martin's Press, 1985.
Opal (Royal Jewel). London, Hale, 1986; (as Helen Ashfield) New York, St Martin's Press, 1986.
Topaz (Royal Jewel). London, Hale, 1987; (as Helen Ashfield) New York, St Martin's Press, 1987.

Crystal (Royal Jewel). London, Hale, 1987.

*

Pamela Bennetts commented (1982):

I had always wanted to write, but kept telling myself that I hadn't got time, having a full-time job, plus a home to run. In 1966 I decided to try: now or never! My intention was, and still is, to entertain my readers. My books, whether historical romances, gothic thrillers, or Georgian romances, are intended as a means of escape from the trials and tribulations of everyday modern life. I want people who are kind enough to read them to enjoy them and forget the H-bomb and the kitchen sink. However, I am always extremely careful to do my research carefully, for I would never knowingly cheat my readers by including inaccurate facts. Being human, I'm sure I fail sometimes, but I do my very best. I hope I can go on writing for many years yet, as I'm only happy when I'm working on a work, and like a lost soul in between novels.

*   *   *

Pamela Bennetts's stories breathe life into characters from the turbulent past. In the Holy Land the Crusader king, Richard the Lionheart, fights the infidel Saladin (*Richard and the Knights of God*). Richard's brother King John reluctantly acknowledges the rights of his nobles in *The Barons of Runnymede*. After initial defeat Henry III and his son, the future Edward I, overcome the enigmatic Simon de Montfort (*The de Montfort Legacy*), and the glory of Edward's own reign is captured in the novel *A Dragon for Edward*. All of the stories are well researched and often contain a bibliography for any reader wishing to pursue the subject.

Although the major historical figures are convincingly portrayed in a Bennetts novel, it is the development of the minor characters that gives substance to the stories. Their private lives and loves thread through the plots and keep the novels from becoming mere fictionalized popular history. There is always a romance and it often centres on a love/hate relationship which keeps the lovers at odds until almost the very end.

Bennetts was a born storyteller with an appealing way of alternating historical narrative and dramatic scenarios. She conveys a vivid sense of what life was like in those distant times and lightly weaves descriptions of dress, manners, foods, and furnishings into the story.

Bennetts also wrote light romantic tales with a 19th-century setting (these appear in the USA under the pseudonym Helen Ashfield). Among these is the popular 'Royal Jewel' series in which each title is not only the name of a precious stone but the name of the heroine as well. In *Sapphire* the heroine is the daughter of a country parson who shares a childhood friendship with Ashton, the son of the Earl of Stonehurst. As adults that friendship turns to love but the difference in their social station as well as the intervention of the wicked Lyndon FitzMaurice prove difficult barriers to surmount. They do overcome these obstacles, of course, as does Opal (in the book of the same name), a music hall singer born in London's worst slums, and the man who loves her, handsome Edward Adare, Earl of Kynston. In these stories and others Bennetts is at her best when describing the difficult life of the poorer classes. This aspect is one often overlooked in romance novels which tend to focus on the upper strata of society.

Another group of novels are stories of frightening events which take over the lives of the innocent (these are published in the USA under the pseudonym Margaret James). Through vignettes of action, thought, or dialogue, in short mysteries teeming with characters, Bennetts creates a cast of suspicious rogues, any one of whom could be the perpetrator of some horror. As an example, in the novel *Footsteps in the Fog*, terror reigns in Victorian London. An axe-killer is on the loose, but nowhere is the fear more intense than in the house of prostitution where two women have been hideously murdered by decapitation. False clues and innuendo abound in these novels, teasing the reader and keeping her guessing all the way to the end. For the female protagonist there is usually a hint of romance as in *A Voice in the Darkness*. At one point young governess Harriet no longer doubts that her handsome employer (whom she secretly loves) is guilty of the murder and mayhem which beset the village. Of course, he is really innocent. Bennetts has an excellent ear for dialogue and her use of colloquial speech is superb. This British writer's mysteries have proven to be quite popular imports for readers in the United States.

—Patricia Altner

BENTLEY, Jayne.   See **KRENTZ, Jayne Ann.**

BENTLEY, Phyllis (Eleanor).
Nationality: British. **Born:** Halifax, Yorkshire, 19 November 1894. **Education:** Cheltenham Ladies' College, Gloucestershire; University of London, B.A. 1914. **Military Service:** clerk, Ministry of Munitions during World War I; worked in American division of the Ministry of Information during World War II. **Career:** teacher, boys' grammar school; librarian. Lectured in USA in 1930s. Friends with Winifred Holtby and Vera Brittain. **Recipient:** Fellow, Royal Society of Literature, 1958. D.Litt.: University of Leeds, 1949. OBE (Officer, Order of the British Empire), 1970. **Died:** 27 June 1977.

ROMANCE AND HISTORICAL PUBLICATIONS

Novels

Environment. London, Sidgwick and Jackson, 1922; New York, Hillman Curl, 1935.
Cat-in-the-Manger. London, Sidgwick and Jackson, 1923.
The Spinner of the Years. London, Unwin, 1928; New York, Henkle, 1929.
The Partnership. London, Benn, 1928; Boston, Little Brown, 1929.
Carr: The Biography of Philip Joseph Carr. London, Benn, 1929; New York, Macmillan, 1933.
Trio. London, Gollancz, 1930.
Inheritance. London, Gollancz, and New York, Macmillan, 1932.
A Modern Tragedy. London, Gollancz, and New York, Macmillan, 1934.
Freedom, Farewell!. London, Gollancz, and New York, Macmillan, 1936.
Sleep in Peace. London, Gollancz, and New York, Macmillan, 1938.
Take Courage. London, Gollancz, 1940; as *The Power and the Glory*, New York, Macmillan, 1940.
Manhold. London, Gollancz, and New York, Macmillan, 1941.
The Rise of Henry Morcar. London, Gollancz, and New York, Macmillan, 1946.
Life Story. London, Gollancz, and New York, Macmillan, 1948.
Quorum. London, Gollancz, 1950; New York, Macmillan, 1951.
The House of Moreys. London, Gollancz, and New York, Macmillan, 1953.
Noble in Reason. London, Gollancz, and New York, Macmillan, 1955.
Crescendo. London, Gollancz, and New York, Macmillan, 1958.
A Man of His Time. London, Gollancz, and New York, Macmillan, 1966.

Oath of Silence. New York, Doubleday, 1967.
Ring in the New. London, Gollancz, 1969.

Short Stories (series: West Riding)

The World's Bane and Other Stories. London, Unwin, 1918.
The Whole of the Short. London, Gollancz, 1935.
Panorama: Tales of the West Riding. London, Gollancz, and New York, Macmillan, 1952.
Love and Money: Seven Tales of the West Riding. London, Gollancz, and New York, Macmillan, 1957.
Kith and Kin: Nine Tales of Family Life. London, Gollancz, and New York, Macmillan, 1960.
More Tales of the West Riding, with John Ogden. London, Gollancz, 1974.

OTHER PUBLICATIONS

Fiction (for children)

The Young Brontës. London, Parrish, 1960; New York, Roy, 1961.
The Adventures of Tom Leigh. London, Macdonald, 1964; New York, Doubleday, 1966.
Ned Carver in Danger. London, Macdonald, 1967.
Gold Pieces. London, Macdonald, 1968; as *Forgery,* New York, Doubleday, 1968.
Sheep May Safely Graze. London, Gollancz, 1972.
The New Venturers. London, Gollancz, 1973.

Play (for children)

The New Apprentice. London, French, 1959.

Other

Pedagomania; or, The Gentle Art of Teaching. London, Unwin, 1918.
Here Is America. London, Gollancz, 1941.
The English Regional Novel. London, Allen and Unwin, 1941.
Some Observations on the Art of the Narrative. London, Home and Van Thal, 1946.
Colne Valley Cloth: From the Earliest Times to the Present Day. Huddersfield, Huddersfield and District Woollen Export Group, 1947.
The Brontës. London, Home and Van Thal, 1947; Denver, Swallow, 1948; revised edition, London, Barker, 1966.
The Brontë Sisters. London, Longman, 1950.
O Dreams, O Destinations (autobiography). London, Gollancz, and New York, Macmillan, 1962.
Committees. London, Collins, 1962.
Public Speaking. London, Collins, 1964.
Enjoy Books: Reading and Collecting. London, Gollancz, 1964.
The Brontës and Their World. London, Thames and Hudson, and New York, Viking Press, 1969.
Haworth of the Brontës. London, Dalton, 1977.

*   *   *

Phyllis Bentley was proud to call herself a regional novelist. Her region was the old West Riding of Yorkshire. Its landscape of rocky hillsides, heathery moors, tumbling streams, and bustling towns provides a constant backdrop to her stories; her characters—strong-willed, stubborn, passionate, and uncompromising—are seen as the natural products of their setting.

For Bentley, industrial and private life went hand in hand, as her historical sagas demonstrate. The upswings of the Industrial Re-

volution bring excitement and good fortune to the families in her stories. The downturns cause disaster and tragedy—as they did in Bentley's own life.

Families always fascinated her. Many novels centre on some archetypal Yorkshire mill-owning family, with its money-making and its intellectual branches, and its feuds over marriages, wills, and business affairs. She planted them in the imaginary Ire Valley, with its principal town, Annotsfield; and, as her novels and their sequels proliferated, she constructed whole networks of mingling Oldroyds and Armitages and Bamforths, to be unravelled by diligent readers.

Writing historical romances was not Bentley's first intention. She meant to be a 'serious' novelist, depicting life with unsparing realism; hoping that if she showed it 'as it really was' (to quote her autobiography), readers might begin to understand their own motives and actions better, and so learn to live more nobly and happily.

Such were the naively idealistic objectives of her early novels. In *The Partnership* her heroine, a plain, earnest girl, finds a vicarious fulfilment in promoting the robustly amorous career of her maid. *The Spinner of the Years* dissects a marriage between a high-minded girl and a down-to-earth millowner, entered upon with good will, but foundering on reefs of total incomprehension. They fit into the feminist novel tradition of the 1920s, without being particularly outstanding.

The novel which brought Bentley fame was *Inheritance*; 'my West Riding novel' as she called it, long before she had chosen the name. It is based on the theory that all actions, good or bad, pass as an inheritance from one generation to the next. The story begins with the Luddites of 1812, opposing the introduction of machinery at an Ire Valley mill, and murdering the millowner. It then follows the fortunes of the descendants of all the main characters in this tragedy, for more than a hundred years. The millowners prosper, while the heirs of the Luddites turn to other forms of opposition, industrial and intellectual. Finally, through a carefully designed series of marriages, the inheritance of them all is fused in one young man, who, at the genuinely historical point of the 1931 textile slump, draws inspiration from his ancestors to start afresh at the old mill where the murder was committed.

Bentley loved pattern in her novels, but *Inheritance* has more than careful construction. For the first time she really let herself go, in a sweeping saga of passion, aspiration, and tragedy. Bentley found that she could write colourfully about romantic love; and her earlier, earnest heroines change to lively women, matching, and sometimes mastering, their determined, hot-blooded men.

Earnestness was not banished for ever. Bentley felt keenly about the rise of the Fascist tyrannies, using political conflict as the background to a Civil War novel, *Take Courage,* and an ambitious, but not very successful, life of Julius Caesar in *Freedom, Farewell!,* her only non-Yorkshire novel. But she was at her best when she forgot political theorizing, and concentrated on the closely-woven complexities of family life, as in *Carr* and *Life Story,* based respectively on the lives of her father and mother. Even in her best-selling melodrama, *The House of Moreys,* the picture of an early 19th-century household lingers in the mind far longer than the gypsy plots and murders.

Bentley's imagination kindled most, in fact, to middle-class Victorian and Edwardian life, when the distinctions between rich and poor were clear, when women gossiped in their drawing rooms, and men dominated their mills. With a wealth of accurate detail—the legacy of her early passion for 'life as it was'—she fitted fiction to fact; and threw a romantic glow over a past when Yorkshire was the proudest county in England, and Yorkshiremen believed themselves to be the most exciting and dynamic people on earth.

—Angela Bull

BERCKMAN, Evelyn (Domenica). American. 1900–1978. See 2nd edition, 1990.

————

BERESFORD, Elisabeth.
Nationality: British. **Born:** Paris, France. **Education:** St Mary's Hall, Brighton; St Catherines, Bramley; Ditchling Dame School, Sussex; Brighton and Hove High School. **Military Service:** served as a radio operator in the Women's Royal Naval Service during World War II. **Relations:** married Max Robertson in 1949; one daughter and one son. **Career:** since 1948 freelance journalist. **Agent:** David Higham Associates Ltd, 5–8 Lower John Street, London W1R 4HA, England; or A.M. Heath, 79 St Martin's Lane, London WC2N 4AA, England. **Address:** 22 Little Street, Alderney, Channel Islands.

ROMANCE AND HISTORICAL PUBLICATIONS

Novels

Paradise Island. London, Hale, 1963.
Escape to Happiness. London, Hale, 1964; New York, Nordon, 1980.
Roses round the Door. London, Hale, and New York, Paperback Library, 1965.
Island of Shadows. London, Hale, 1966; New York, Dale, 1980.
Veronica. London, Hale, 1967; New York, Nordon, 1980.
A Tropical Affair. London, Hale, 1967; as *Tropical Affairs*, New York, Dell, 1978.
Saturday's Child. London, Hale, 1968; as *Echoes of Love*, New York, Dell, 1979.
Love Remembered. London, Hale, 1970; New York, Dale, 1978.
Love and the S.S. Beatrice. London, Hale, 1972; as *Thunder of Her Heart*, New York, Dale, 1978.
Pandora. London, Hale, 1974.
The Steadfast Lover. London, Hale, 1980.
The Silver Chain. London, Hale, 1980.
The Restless Heart. New York, Valueback, 1982.
Flight to Happiness. London, Hale, 1983.
A Passionate Adventure. London, Hale, 1983.

OTHER PUBLICATIONS

Fiction (for children)

The Television Mystery. London, Parrish, 1957.
The Flying Doctor Mystery. London, Parrish, 1958.
Trouble at Tullington Castle. London, Parrish, 1958.
Cocky and the Missing Castle. London, Constable, 1959.
Gappy Goes West. London, Parrish, 1959.
The Tullington Film-Makers. London, Parrish, 1960.
Two Gold Dolphins. London, Constable, 1961; Indianapolis, Bobbs Merrill, 1964.
Danger on the Old Pull'n Push. London, Parrish, 1962.
Strange Hiding Place. London, Parrish, 1962.
Diana in Television. London, Collins, 1963.
The Missing Formula Mystery. London, Parrish, 1963.
The Mulberry Street Team. Penshurst, Kent, Friday Press, 1963.
Awkward Magic. London, Hart Davis, 1964; as *The Magic World*, Indianapolis, Bobbs Merrill, 1965.
The Flying Doctor to the Rescue. London, Parrish, 1964.
Holiday for Slippy. Penshurst, Kent, Friday Press, 1964.
Game, Set, and Match. London, Parrish, 1965.

Knights of the Cardboard Castle. London, Methuen, 1965.
Travelling Magic. London, Hart Davis, 1965; as *The Vanishing Garden*, New York, Funk and Wagnalls, 1967.
The Hidden Mill. London, Benn, 1965; New York, Meredith Press, 1967.
Peter Climbs a Tree. London, Benn, 1966.
Fashion Girl. London, Collins, 1967.
The Black Mountain Mystery. London, Parrish, 1967.
Looking for a Friend. London, Benn, 1967.
The Island Bus. London, Methuen, 1968.
Sea-Green Magic. London, Hart Davis, 1968.
The Wombles. London, Benn, 1968; New York, Meredith Press, 1969.
David Goes Fishing. London, Benn, 1969.
Gordon's Go-Kart. London, Benn, 1970.
Stephen and the Shaggy Dog. London, Methuen, 1970.
Vanishing Magic. London, Hart Davis, 1970.
The Wandering Wombles. London, Benn, 1970.
Dangerous Magic. London, Hart Davis, 1972.
The Invisible Womble and Other Stories. London, Benn, 1973.
The Secret Railway. London, Methuen, 1973.
The Wombles in Danger. London, Benn, 1973.
The Wombles at Work. London, Benn, 1973.
Invisible Magic. London, Hart Davis, 1974.
The Wombles Go to the Seaside. London, World Distributors, 1974.
The Wombles Gift Book. London, Benn, 1975.
The Snow Womble. London, Benn, 1975.
Snuffle to the Rescue. London, Kestrel, 1975.
Tomsk and the Tired Tree. London, Benn, 1975.
Wellington and the Blue Balloon. London, Benn, 1975.
Orinoco Runs Away. London, Benn, 1975.
The Wombles Make a Clean Sweep. London, Benn, 1975.
The Wombles to the Rescue. London, Benn, 1975.
The MacWomble's Pipe Band. London, Benn, 1976.
Madame Cholet's Picnic Party. London, Benn, 1976.
Bungo Knows Best. London, Benn, 1976.
Tobermory's Big Surprise. London, Benn, 1976.
The Wombles Go Round the World. London, Benn, 1976.
The World of the Wombles. London, World Distributors, 1976.
Wombling Free. London, Benn, 1978.
Toby's Luck. London, Methuen, 1978.
Secret Magic. London, Hart Davis, 1978.
The Happy Ghost. London, Methuen, 1979.
The Treasure Hunters. London, Methuen, and New York, Elsevier Nelson, 1980.
Curious Magic. London, Granada, and New York, Elsevier Nelson, 1980.
The Four of Us. London, Hutchinson, 1981.
The Animals Nobody Wanted. London, Methuen, 1982.
The Tovers. London, Methuen, 1982.
The Adventures of Poon. London, Hutchinson, 1984.
The Mysterious Island. London, Methuen, 1984.
One of the Family. London, Hutchinson, 1985.
The Ghosts of Lupus Street School. London, Methuen, 1986.
Strange Magic. London, Methuen, 1986.
Emily and the Haunted Castle. London, Hutchinson, 1987.
Once upon a Time Stories. London, Methuen, 1987.
The Secret Room. London, Methuen, 1987.
The Armada Adventure. London, Methuen, 1988.
The Island Railway. London, Hamish Hamilton, 1988.
Rose. London, Hutchinson, 1989.
The Wooden Gun. London, Hutchinson, 1989.
Charlie's Ark. London, Methuen, 1989.
Tim the Trumpet. London, Blackie, 1992.
Jamie and the Rolla Pola Bear. London, Blackie, 1993.
Lizzy's War. London, Simon and Schuster, 1993.

Plays

The Wombles, adaptation of her own stories (produced London, 1974).
Road to Albutal, with Nick Renton (produced Edinburgh, 1976).
The Best of Friends (produced in the Channel Islands, 1982).

Screenplay: *The Wombles*, 1971.

Television Plays: 60 scripts for *The Wombles* series, from 1973.

Other

The Wombles Annual 1975–1978 (for children). London, World Distributors, 4 vols, 1974–77.
Move On, with Peter Spence. London, BBC Publications, 1978.
Jack and the Magic Stove (for children). London, Hutchinson, 1982.

*

Film Adaptation: *Wombling Free*, 1977.

Elisabeth Beresford comments:
In some of my romantic novels, I have based the plot on a mystery including crime and espionage. I try to give all my characters believable personalities, and there's always an occasional touch of humour.

*   *   *

Elisabeth Beresford is a prolific writer whose romances tend to focus on the modern career woman as the central figure. In most of her novels the heroine reaches a point where a tragedy in her personal life dictates the necessity for a complete and radical break from her present circumstances. This is exemplified in *Escape to Happiness* where the heroine, who has a successful career, is not so successful in her personal life and is jilted by her boyfriend in favour of an actress. In order to make a complete break from her past she acts on impulse and accepts a job working on a remote Australian sheep station. Although she initially feels a strong antipathy to both her employer and Australia, she eventually falls in love with both.

The contrast between wet, gloomy London (which is used to highlight the heroine's mood) and the burning, unrelenting heat and primitiveness of the Australian outback is vividly depicted by Beresford in order to heighten the reader's awareness of the heroine's struggle to adapt to both the changes in her physical and emotional environment. There is also a sub-plot detailing a romance between the hero's sister and a member of the minority Greek community. Beresford is not afraid to mention the racial tensions that arise when members of a different culture endeavour to assimilate into a small community, and the prejudices that result. The heroine manages to help the star-crossed lovers fight and win against the local prejudice, while at the same time achieving happiness herself.

The issue of racial intolerance and bigotry is delicately handled. The fears of the Australian community that the incoming Greek community would take away their jobs is expressed by one character in the book when she explains her antipathy to the Greeks by saying that 'they want to poison us all—that's what'. Conversely, the Greeks' desire for assimilation into the community is poignantly expressed by the matriarchal head of the Greek clan when she says, 'We do not expect happiness, only a place to live in peace'. Australian colloquialisms such as 'galah' to denote a fool, are carefully and convincingly sprinkled throughout the narrative by the author to give a flavour of the Australian way of life. Beresford also handles the minor characters well, breathing life into such characters as the sad, pathetic expatriate who cannot adjust to the Australian outback until she finds her sense of worth in coping with the injuries resulting from a bush fire.

The background to her novel *Veronica* is of a completely different nature. Beresford breaks away from a contemporary setting and sets the story in London at the turn of this century. The plot is based around the heroine's attempt to deal with the rigours of life on her own, facilitated by her own strong personality, and the period setting is well described. There is a further change of style in *Love Remembered* where she creates an atmosphere of menace in describing the events surrounding the main character, Achilles Vidal. Beresford appears here to be trying to extend the parameters of her own personal style of writing, but in a different way from *Veronica*.

In a later novel, *The Steadfast Lover*, Beresford mixes both the past and present by linking the lives of the broken-hearted heroine, Emma Smith, and that of her equally tragic predecessor, who is an imaginary childhood friend of the heroine's. The heroine here seeks solace from a disastrous love affair and ruined career by fleeing to her childhood home on a remote island. She finds comfort in comparing her situation with the tragic plight of her predecessor, who fell in love with a soldier who left her pregnant, and thus faced the highly disapproving social mores of the time. Emma realizes her own predicament is resolvable and finds the strength to overcome her own personal anguish. The strongest drawn characters in this story are in fact the women who each have to battle to resolve their individual crises. The wild scenery of the island is adeptly described in the story. In this, as in *Escape to Happiness*, Beresford seems to stress the importance of achieving emotional healing by breaking away from the heroine's familiar pattern of life and instead making a completely fresh start in new surroundings. Beresford compares the advantages of the simplicity of a country/rural lifestyle over that of a sophisticated city life in both *Escape to Happiness* and *The Steadfast Lover*. What is particularly interesting in these two novels is that although the respective heroines appear to be running away in what may appear to be a cowardly fashion from confronting their problems, nonetheless by doing so they come round full circle and achieve the perspective necessary to actually confront and defeat their personal demons, albeit in totally different circumstances.

Beresford's romantic novels thus explore the recurrent theme of personal transformation through suffering, and ultimately love, in an emotional Calvary experienced by the main character. Beresford's vision of life is therefore ultimately optimistic, albeit that she appears to espouse the Darwinian theory of 'survival of the fittest' when she posits her main characters in situations of adversity.

—Sobhana Rowland

BERGER, John (Peter).   British. 1926—. See 2nd edition, 1990.

BERGER, Thomas (Louis).
Nationality: American. **Born:** Cincinnati, Ohio, 20 July 1924.
Education: University of Cincinnati, B.A. 1948; postgraduate studies, Columbia University, New York, 1950–51. **Military Service:** served in the United States Army, 1943–46. **Relations:** married Jeanne Redpath in 1950. **Career:** librarian, Rand School of Social Science, New York, 1948–51; staff member, *New York Times Index*, 1951–52; associate editor, *Popular Science Monthly*, New York, 1952–54; film critic, *Esquire*, New York, 1972–73; writer-in-residence, University of Kansas, Lawrence, 1974; Distinguished Visiting Professor, Southampton College, New York, 1975–76; visiting lecturer, Yale University, New Haven, Connecticut, 1981, 1982; Regents' Lecturer, University of California, Davis, 1982.
Recipient: Dial fellowship, 1962; Western Heritage award, 1965; Rosenthal award, 1965. D.Litt.: Long Island University, Greenvale, New York, 1986. **Agent:** Don Congdon Associates, 156 Fifth Avenue, Suite 625, New York, New York 10010, USA.

ROMANCE AND HISTORICAL PUBLICATIONS

Novels

Little Big Man. New York, Dial Press, 1964; London, Eyre and
Spottiswoode, 1965.
Arthur Rex: A Legendary Novel. New York, Delacorte Press, 1978;
London, Methuen, 1979.

OTHER PUBLICATIONS

Novels

Crazy in Berlin. New York, Scribner, 1958; New York, Delacorte
Press, 1982.
Reinhart in Love. New York, Scribner, 1962; London, Eyre and
Spottiswoode, 1963.
Killing Time. New York, Dial Press, 1967; London, Eyre and Spot-
tiswoode, 1968.
Vital Parts. New York, Baron, 1970; London, Eyre and Spot-
tiswoode, 1971.
Regiment of Women. New York, Simon and Schuster, 1973; Lon-
don, Eyre Methuen, 1974.
Sneaky People. New York, Simon and Schuster, 1975; London,
Methuen, 1980.
Who Is Teddy Villanova? New York, Delacorte Press, and London,
Eyre Methuen, 1977.
Neighbors. New York, Delacorte Press, 1980; London, Methuen,
1981.
Reinhart's Women. New York, Delacorte Press, 1981; London,
Methuen, 1982.
The Feud. New York, Delacorte Press, 1983; London, Methuen,
1984.
Nowhere. New York, Delacorte Press, 1985; London, Methuen,
1986.
Being Invisible. Boston, Little Brown, 1987; London, Methuen,
1988.
The Houseguest. Boston, Little Brown, 1988; London, Weidenfeld
and Nicolson, 1989.
Changing the Past. Boston, Little Brown, 1989; London, Weiden-
feld and Nicolson, 1990.
Meeting Evil. Boston, Little Brown, 1992.

Short Story

Granted Wishes. Northridge, California, Lord John Press, 1984.

Play

Other People (produced Stockbridge, Massachusetts, 1970).
'The Burglars', *New Letters* (Kansas City, Missouri), Fall, 1988.

*

Film Adaptations: *Little Big Man*, 1970; *Neighbors*, 1981; *The
Feud*, 1990.

Bibliography: in Thomas Berger issue of *Studies in American Humor* (San Marcos, Texas), Spring and Fall,1983.

Critical Studies: *Thomas Berger* by Brooks Landon, Boston,
Twayne, 1989.

Manuscript Collection: Boston University Library.

*   *   *

Thomas Berger's fictional world is typically bawdy, a Rabelaisian exhibition of the strengths and weaknesses of humankind. *Little*

Big Man takes this perspective and applies it to the great American
myth of the Wild West. Its hero, the 111-year-old Jack Crabb, narrates his life history from an old folks' home; these reminiscences
make up the vast bulk of the voluminous text. His is the tallest story
ever told, and the 'Editorial Epilogue' admits the possibility that he
might be 'a liar of insane proportions'. He tells of his wild and troubled career as, variously, adopted Cheyenne Indian warrior, trader,
gold prospector, card sharp, buffalo hunter, mule driver, army scout,
and gunfighter; of his acquaintance with Wild Bill Hickok, General
Custer, and other legendary figures; of his being the sole survivor of
the Battle of the Little Bighorn. In outline his story seems absurd
and incredible, but Berger applies detailed research and a realist's
eye to his material, enchanting the reader with the story in the same
way Crabb enchants the priggish 'editor' of the text.

Jack Crabb is an American Odysseus, the trickster whose very
inobstrusiveness and instinct for survival allow him to adapt a new
identity at every crisis. First adopted by the Indians at the age of ten,
he grows up as a Cheyenne until recaptured by the United States
Cavalry; in a typical switch of identity he reveals himself as a white
captive when cornered by the troops. From this point on his adventures take him back and forth from white to Indian society, though
he never finds himself on the winning side. The character is a triumph for Berger, who has captured the bawdy, laconic style of the
American folktale in his presentation of Crabb, who is at once sceptical and sentimental, amoral and compassionate, a storyteller
whose wit matches, and masterfully understates, his sensational
subject.

Jack Crabb's lazy amorality is made all the more appealing by the
background against which his story is told. It is the era of 'manifest
destiny', the ugly ideology which the white man so successfully
used to justify the theft of Indian lands and the genocide which accompanied it. During the course of the narrative—which covers
only 24 years—the Cheyenne tribe who had adopted Crabb are reduced to a small, beaten group of renegades. At first the story emphasizes the complete otherness of the Indian, being dedicated to the
proposition that 'Indians are altogether different from anybody you
ever knew'. The opening scenes are masterpieces of absurd mis-
communication, exemplified by the fact that Jack's eccentric father
believes the Cheyenne talk Hebrew. But gradually, through the eyes
of the growing boy's initiation into the tribe, we begin to see the Indians in the context of their own beliefs and logic. After his recapture, in an episode strongly reminiscent of Huck Finn's rejection of
'civilization', the boy is brought back to be fostered by a preacher
and his wife. Typically of Berger, both this and the previous adventures are presented with an eye to the ridiculous, though for both the
Indian and white cultures the author maintains evident sympathy.
Like the boy's Indian foster-father, he respects the fact that both cultures have their patterns and reasons; but the easy tolerance exhibited here is hard to come by in the frontier.

Ultimately the Indians have their sole victory, defeating Custer at
Little Bighorn; and the narrative of Jack Crabb ends at this point, the
narrator finally succumbing to his incredible old age. The rest, as
they say, is history. At several points the novel refers to the mythology of the West, preserved on the rest-home television, only to ex-
plode these ballooning myths with their own incredibility.

A similar process is undergone in *Arthur Rex: A Legendary
Novel.* This time the target is Arthurian legend. As with the Old
West, the Dark Age is presented with its own historical squalor and
made to laugh uneasily. The deeds of the court are deflated simply
by the shabby details of reality, but the discarded detail of myth is
what engages the mind of Berger. T.H. White did something similar
with the Arthurian legend in *The Once and Future King*, scaling it
down from epic to comic proportions; but Berger's humour is
bleaker and less comfortable.

Berger invokes an altogether more indifferent world to that prevalent in our fondest folktales. He moulds a better fiction from their

resemblance to our own less excited response to the historical event, the ordinary face of the present. Only after the reader's acceptance of this illusion comes the suspicion, like that of *Little Big Man's* 'editor', that it is all a heroic farce. By this time all that matters is the story.

—Alan Murphy

————

BETTERIDGE, Anne.   See **MELVILLE, Anne.**

————

BEVAN, Gloria.

Pseudonym for Glory Isabel Bevan. **Other Pseudonym:** Fiona Murray. **Nationality:** New Zealander. **Born:** Kalgoorlie, Western Australia, 20 July 1911. **Relations:** married Thomas Henry Bevan in 1937 (died); three daughters. **Career:** typist, Watkin and Wallis, Auckland, 1926–36. **Address:** 1 Hoberia Road, Onehunga, Auckland, New Zealand.

ROMANCE AND HISTORICAL PUBLICATIONS

Novels

The Distant Trap. London, Mills and Boon, 1969; Toronto, Harlequin, 1970.
The Hills of Maketu. London, Mills and Boon, and Toronto, Harlequin, 1969.
Beyond the Ranges. London, Mills and Boon, 1970; Toronto, Harlequin, 1971.
Make Way for Tomorrow. London, Mills and Boon, and Toronto, Harlequin, 1971.
It Began in Te Rangi. London, Mills and Boon, 1971; Toronto, Harlequin, 1972.
Vineyard in a Valley. London, Mills and Boon, and Toronto, Harlequin, 1972.
Flame in Fiji. London, Mills and Boon, and Toronto, Harlequin, 1973.
The Frost and the Fire. London, Mills and Boon, and Toronto, Harlequin, 1973.
Connelly's Castle. London, Mills and Boon, and Toronto, Harlequin, 1974.
High-Country Wife. London, Mills and Boon, 1974; Toronto, Harlequin, 1975.
Always a Rainbow. London, Mills and Boon, and Toronto, Harlequin, 1975.
Dolphin Bay. London, Mills and Boon, and Toronto, Harlequin, 1976.
Bachelor Territory. London, Mills and Boon, and Toronto, Harlequin, 1977.
Plantation Moon. London, Mills and Boon, 1977; Toronto, Harlequin, 1978.
Fringe of Heaven. London, Mills and Boon, and Toronto, Harlequin, 1978.
Kowhai Country. London, Mills and Boon, 1979.
Half a World Away. London, Mills and Boon, 1980; Toronto, Harlequin, 1981.
Master of Mahia. London, Mills and Boon, and Toronto, Harlequin, 1981.
Emerald Cave. London, Mills and Boon, 1981; Toronto, Harlequin, 1982.
Greek Island Magic. London, Mills and Boon, 1983.
The Rouseabout Girl. London, Mills and Boon, and Toronto, Harlequin, 1983.
Southern Sunshine. London, Mills and Boon, 1985.
Golden Bay. London, Mills and Boon, 1987; Toronto, Harlequin, 1991.
Pacific Paradise. London, Mills and Boon, 1989.
Summer's Vintage. London, Mills and Boon, 1992.

OTHER PUBLICATIONS

Novels as Fiona Murray

Invitation to Danger. London, Hale, 1965.
Gold Coast Affair. Sydney, Horowitz, 1967.
A Nice Day for Murder. London, Hale, 1971.

*

Gloria Bevan comments:

I began my writing life as a mystery writer then changed to romance writing, and have been fascinated with it ever since. Writing for Mills and Boon and Harlequin has been a privilege and a pleasure.

Living in far away New Zealand I try to convey to overseas readers the air of freshness, the clarity of atmosphere, and the sparkling seas edged with flawless sandy beaches that I know so well. The climate is sub-tropical, hibiscus flowers bloom in suburban gardens and dense native bush clothes the neighbouring hillsides.

Often I write with a background of wide open spaces where an owner of a sheep station may control thousands of acres of green hills and paddocks.

Exciting holidays spent at the islands of Fiji and Rarotonga have sparked me to write of these beautiful islands that are our neighbours in the South Pacific ocean. I strive to convey the perfume of frangipani, the feeling of warm seas, and a relaxed way of life there. I hope I've succeeded.

*   *   *

Gloria Bevan began her writing career as a mystery writer under the pseudonym of Fiona Murray, however, luckily for her fans, she soon discovered her talents lay in producing formula romances. Bevan has produced over 25 novels, all published by the popular English publisher Mills and Boon. She is a successful novelist, if only because she pays considerable detail to creating credible and interesting characters. The exotic settings of her books also help to attract readers—and her characters may find themselves falling in love in Australia, Fiji, or the author's native New Zealand.

Bevan is obviously proud of New Zealand and most of her books reflect this love, whether it be through descriptions of the landscape or in her attention to the most minute detail of clothing or custom. Bevan allows the reader to gain some insight into the history of her country—through a background reference to the historical settlement of an ethnic group, or a Maori custom (for example, *Bachelor Territory* manages to mix romantic dialogue with Maori proverbs).

Bevan's heroes and heroines are the sort of people the reader might encounter in everyday life. Her heroine is usually a slim young woman with a spark of vitality which marks her out as different from the kind of women the hero is used to. She combines a naivety with a sense of adventure, and is willing to travel half way round the world to pursue a dream. Joanne, in *Pacific Paradise*, travels to the perfection of Rarotonga, to keep a rendezvous with a fiancé that she has not seen in two years—she ends up falling in love with handsome Craig Summers instead. Similarly, Christine, in *Fringe of Heaven*, travels from her native England to Te Wekai, New Zealand, to claim an inheritance; and Sarah, in *Summer's*

Vintage, also travels to New Zealand to claim a prosperous vineyard.

The hero is an attractive, confident man who is sure of who he is, and what he wants. David, the hero in *Flame in Fiji*, is sure that he wants Robyn Carlisle even though he despises her brother, and Craig Summers offers Joanne help after meeting her on a plane, in *Pacific Paradise*, so certain is he that her beloved fiancé will not keep their meeting. Bevan's hero normally has a manly job—sheep farmer, hotelier, vintner—and the heroine encounters him through an offer of employment, or through some connection with her family. Fleur, in *Southern Sunshine*, returns to her home to find her father ill and that Logan Page is now his partner. On their first meeting Fleur notices that with his tall, lithe frame and 'his deep mahogany tan, he just had to be a sheep farmer'. Joanne is offered a job as a chef by Craig Summers, the hero of *Pacific Paradise*, when her fiancé fails to materialize—inevitably she falls under the hero's spell.

Secondary characters include the glamorous 'other' woman who serves to make the heroine jealous, and the weak male character who shows the heroine how worthy the hero is, and how superior he is to other men.

In *Flame in Fiji*, architect David Kinnear meets and falls in love with Robyn when he agrees to help redesign her house. Robyn and her brother are extremely close, and Robyn seems to cling to him despite the fact that he isn't the most dependable of men. He thus serves the dual purpose of showing both the reader and the heroine how stable and strong the hero is. Despite disliking the brother, David has to resolve this issue to win his heroine. The storyline is set against the beautiful background of Fiji—the countryside of the island is described in detail and the reader can imagine the hero and heroine falling in love. Robyn also has an intensive course in island culture, experiencing, among other things, an island feast.

Joanne, the heroine of *Pacific Paradise*, spends the two years away from Rick, her fiancé, idolizing him. Joanne chose to take a job with the VSO, teaching in Zimbabwe, over sailing around the world with Rick. She, thus, shows the reader how worthy and interesting she is, but also that she sacrificed her love for a job, proving that she really can't have loved Rick that much. Joanne spends a lot of time waiting in hotel lobbies for her fiancé to turn up, fighting her growing attraction for the real hero, Craig. She, eventually, tracks Rick down with Craig's help, and the former shows how unworthy he is of her trust and affection by failing to keep their meeting, and by the fact that he has fallen in love and married someone else. Joanne, thus, has all the justification she needs for falling in love with her hero.

The plots of Bevan's books usually revolve around one specific point. In Joanne's case it is the search for her missing fiancé, and the reader doesn't know what has happened to him until the confrontation between Joanne and Rick. In other books, the storyline revolves around a misunderstanding or secret. In *Fringe of Heaven*, Christine inherits an estate in New Zealand from an uncle, Ben, only to discover on her arrival that Ben had died before keeping an appointment to change his will. Being a very worthy individual, Christine agrees to turn the estate back to Laurie, the man who should have inherited, on the condition that he keeps it a secret, particularly from his cousin, Kevin 'The King' Hawke. Kevin is the romantic interest and the encounters between the two protagonists hinge on the misunderstanding, resentment, and mutual attraction that exists between them. Similarly, Nick Jurovich mistakes Sarah for a casual labourer, when she comes to claim the vineyard left to her. Sarah goes along with this and comes to realize how much the estate means to Nick. It also gives Bevan the chance to describe her beautiful country. As time passes, Sarah finds it increasingly difficult to tell her hero that she has lied to him, and decides to leave instead.

Luckily—as is the way in old good formula romances—everything is resolved in the end.

—P. Campbell

BHATIA, Jamunadevi.   See FORRESTER, Helen.

BHATIA, June.   See FORRESTER, Helen.

BIGLAND, Eileen.   British. See 2nd edition, 1990.

BINCHY, Maeve.
Nationality: Irish. **Born:** Dublin, 28 May 1940. **Education:** Holy Child Convent, Killiney, County Dublin; University College, Dublin, B.A. in history; diploma in education. **Relations:** married Gordon Snell in 1977. **Career:** History and French teacher, Pembroke School, Dublin, 1961–68. Since 1968 columnist, *Irish Times*, Dublin. **Agent:** Christine Green, 2 Barbon Close, London WC1N 3JX, England. **Address:** Daekey, County Dublin, Ireland.

ROMANCE AND HISTORICAL PUBLICATIONS

Novels

Light a Penny Candle. London, Century, 1982; New York, Viking Press, 1983.
Echoes. London, Century, 1985; New York, Viking, 1986.
Firefly Summer. London, Century, 1987; New York, Delacorte Press, 1988.
Circle of Friends. London, Century, 1990; New York, Delacorte Press, 1991.
The Copper Beech. London, Orion, 1992.

Short Stories

Central Line: Stories of Big City Life. London, Quartet, 1978.
Victoria Line. London, Quartet, 1980.
Dublin 4. Dublin, Ward River Press, 1982; London, Century, 1983.
London Transports (includes *Central Line* and *Victoria Line*). London, Century, 1983.
The Lilac Bus. Dublin, Ward River Press, 1984; London, Century, 1986.
Silver Wedding. London, Century, 1988; New York, Delacorte Press, 1989.
The Storyteller. London, Longman, 1990.

OTHER PUBLICATIONS

Plays

End of Term (produced Dublin, 1978).
The Half Promised Land (produced Dublin, 1979).

Television Plays: *Deeply Regretted by—*, 1976; *Ireland of the Welcomes*, 1980; *Echoes*, from her own novel, 1988; *The Lilac Bus*, from her own story, 1991.

Other

Maeve's Diary. Dublin, Irish Times, 1979.

*

Maeve Binchy comments:

I write novels and stories set within my own experience of time and place, but they are not autobiographical. They mainly touch on the emotions of women and the aspirations and hopes of young Irishwomen growing up in the relatively closed society of Ireland in the 1950s and 1960s.

*   *   *

Maeve Binchy's novels all have two qualities in common: they are extremely readable, and they are very long, in other words, 'a good read'. She is indeed a born story-teller, not satisfied with just one person's story to tell, preferring a complex yarn with a number of strands, of people's lives meeting, touching, and perhaps parting again. This being so, inevitably perhaps there is a sameness in the structure of her novels: *Light a Penny Candle, Echoes, Firefly Summer, Circle of Friends*, all more or less begin with childhood and take their leading characters through to adulthood. In *Firefly Summer* it is only the threshold of adulthood, the first stirrings of love, the first disappointments experienced in the course of one fateful summer, while in *Light a Penny Candle*, in *Echoes*, and in *Circle of Friends* we watch children growing up, growing wiser perhaps and certainly unhappier, leaving the happiness of childhood behind.

In Binchy's novels childhood is a time of happiness, idealized, golden years, safe under the care of a wise, caring mother figure (Eileen O'Connor in *Light a Penny Candle*, Kate Ryan in *Firefly Summer*, Mother Francis in *Circle of Friends*), set against a loving recreated rural Ireland. It may be described in unrealistic terms, this golden age of childhood, but there is real pleasure for the readers in sharing this remembered happiness. There is of course all the greater shock in meeting adulthood, encountering tragedy, death, betrayal, violence, pain, disappointment. Interestingly in two of the novels the reader is warned in advance: *Light a Penny Candle* starts with an inquest on the violent death which brings the book to its close, and *Echoes* begins with the drowning of Gerry Doyle and ends with his funeral. The form of these two novels is circular, beginning and ending with the death that will mark the irrevocable end of any happiness of dreams. In *Firefly Summer* and *Circle of Friends* the action moves forward, promising the return of quiet happiness after pain and suffering.

It must be said that Binchy's heroines are spared nothing in the course of their adult lives: abortion, alcoholism, madness, a crippling accident, the betrayal of love, and of friendship. Disasters come thick and fast (as Johnny in *Light a Penny Candle* remarks so rightly of the two heroines, Elizabeth and Aisling, 'to think that both their husbands has more or less died from drink. The odds against that must be overwhelming'). The contrast with their childhood is so marked that it must surely be deliberate. Childhood, the time of innocence, is the time of bliss which cannot be recaptured in adulthood, except in the rare delight of a happy marriage (the O'Connors in *Light a Penny Candle*, the Ryans in *Firefly Summer*, and, perhaps, one day, Eve and Aidan in *Circle of Friends*). The teaching of the church comes across strongly here: married love set against the misery of sin. In this context it is useful to recall Binchy's short stories of the *London Transports* genre: the unhappiness and sheer messiness of women's lives in London are in stark contrast to the descriptions of happy times in her Irish novels.

Though her short stories make entertaining reading, Maeve Binchy is very much a novelist, needing the space to bring her narrative talent fully into play. At the same time, though, she prefers fragmentation to sustained narrative concentrating on one character.

Mention has been made of her predilection for a group of heroes and heroines whose lives she weaves into her story. In order to keep her readers abreast of all developments she resorts to brief descriptions, often no more than a paragraph in length, a confusing technique which often leaves the reader wishing ardently for even one tiny asterisk to indicate yet another switch in time and place. Indeed it is a triumph of her narrative skill that at the end of the novel there are no loose threads in the complex woven fabric. Instead the reader will find with pleasure a satisfactory completed pattern.

Something should be said here of her characters. Because the structure and basic themes of her novels are so similar, we might expect a similarity between her characters as well. There are some resemblances: the pretty, smartly turned out, watchful Nan in *Circle of Friends* does remind us of the pale, elegant, self-contained Elizabeth in *Light a Penny Candle*, especially as both encounter the disaster of an unwanted pregnancy. Yet the effect of such an event on both girls' lives, the manner in which they deal with it, point to the differences between them. Nan may be a stereotype of a ruthless gogetter, yet in the same novel we meet Benny Hogan, the big, jolly girl who learns not to play the clown to hide her shyness, and in doing so becomes a real, living convincing character, testifying to the author's skill in telling her stories with enjoyment and zest, and telling them well.

—Hana Sambrook

———

BISHOP, Sheila (Grencarn).
Nationality: British. **Born:** Stroud, Gloucestershire, in 1918. **Relations:** married Captain G.C.N. Bishop (died). **Career:** commercial artist, and writer. **Address:** Mills and Boon Ltd, Eton House, 18–24 Paradise Road, Richmond, Surrey, TW9 1SR, England.

ROMANCE AND HISTORICAL PUBLICATIONS

Novels

The Durable Fire: A Novel of Elizabethan England 1577–1584. London, Jarrolds, 1958; New York, Ace, 1972.
House with Two Faces. London, Hurst and Blackett, 1960; New York, Ace, 1971.
The Second Husband. London, Jarrolds, 1964; New York, Ace, 1972.
Impatient Griselda. London, Hurst and Blackett, 1965; as *Desperate Decision*, New York, Silhouette, 1972.
Sweet Nightingale. London, Hurst and Blackett, 1966; New York, Ace, 1972.
Penelope Deveraux. London, Hurst and Blackett, 1966; New York, Ace, 1972.
The Favourite Sister. London, Hurst and Blackett, 1967; as *The Favorite Sister*, New York, Ace, 1972.
Goldsmith's Row. London, Hurst and Blackett, 1969; New York, Ace, 1971.
The Onlooker. London, Hurst and Blackett, 1970; New York, Ace, 1971.
No Hint of Scandal. London, Hurst and Blackett, 1971; New York, Ace, 1971.
The Quick Brown Fox. London, Hurst and Blackett, 1972; New York, Ace, 1973.
That Night at the Villa. New York, Ace, 1972.
The Wilderness Walk. New York, Ace, 1973; Leicester, Ulverscroft, 1990.
The Phantom Garden. London, Hurst and Blackett, 1974; New York, Fawcett, 1977.

A London Season. London, Hurst and Blackett, 1975.
A Speaking Likeness. London, Hurst and Blackett, and New York, Fawcett, 1976.
Bath Assembly. New York, Ace, 1977.
Lucasta. New York, Fawcett, 1978.
Long Summer Shadows. London, Hurst and Blackett, 1978.
The Rules of Marriage. New York, Fawcett, 1978; London, Hurst and Blackett, 1979.
The Parson's Daughter. London, Hurst and Blackett, 1979.
The School in Belmont. London, Corgi, 1980.
Consequences. London, Corgi, and New York, Fawcett, 1981.
Rosalba. London, Hale, and New York, Fawcett, 1982.
True Lover's Knot. London, Mills and Boon, 1986.
A Well-Matched Pair. London, Mills and Boon, 1987.
A Marriage Made on Earth. New York, Fawcett, 1989; London, Mills and Boon, 1990.
Fair Game. London, Mills and Boon, 1992.

*   *   *

Unlike most other popular Regency writers Sheila Bishop's novels possess a streak of realism which allows the reader greater insight into the society and culture of the time. While detailing the sumptuous fashions, customs, and manners of the age, Bishop also permits us to see the prevalent hypocrisy of the time. Her heroines, especially those who appear in her earlier books, are spirited ladies who often encounter the disapproval of society for openly breaking the rules.

'It does seem unfair that ladies have to be married before they have lovers', declares the Honourable Charlotte Rivers in *The Rules of Marriage*. Brought up in a household in which her mother openly entertains both her lover and her husband, Charlotte thinks that affairs are the normal sophisticated way to behave in society. She very nearly loses her husband, the debonair Marquess of Brancaster, when she enters into an affair with one of his friends. Charlotte is also ostracized by society for behaving openly in the manner that she perceives others (for example, her mother) behave; it is this very hypocrisy that Bishop depicts so well. Bishop also gives us an insight into the political events of the time as Kit Brancaster is involved in fighting Adam Smith.

In *Rosalba* the eponymous heroine enters a loveless marriage to a weak and dishonest man who tries to extort money from Sir Augustus Rainham by locking Rainham and Rosalba in a bedroom together. The heroine is, of course, far too honest to help her husband and succeeds in losing her reputation and her husband (who leaves her). She is, subsequently, rescued by Rainham's cousin, Hugh, who sets her up as his mistress. Rosalba encounters a completely different world, full of ostracized gentlewomen who live on the edge of society. By making her heroine assume the character of the mistress/fallen woman Bishop gives attention to women who are most often seen in Regency novels as peripheral characters. Rosalba is a woman in love, but her life has been dictated by circumstance. She cannot marry Hugh until her husband dies—apparently in a drowning incident. Rosalba then finds out that she has entered a bigamous marriage as her first husband is still alive, and she has been misled by a friend who wants to marry her himself. However, love does win through in the end as Hugh still loves Rosalba.

Bishop's characters fall into the stereotypical Regency hero/heroine form. The female characters are attractive, gently reared young ladies, or young widows who find themselves forced to reconsider their futures, usually as a result of the death of a close relative. The heroes are dark, good-looking men who are strong, opinionated and, for the most part, wealthy—they are the reasonable alternative for the heroine. In this sense Bishop's novels vary from her peers as her heroines always appear to be slightly disillusioned at the start of her books, and marriage is seen as an option, though

not necessarily the most favoured one. In *A Marriage Made on Earth*, the young heroine Pamela is forced into marriage with Lord Blaise because her father's poor investments have left her future uncertain. Pamela, of course, comes to love the scarred Richard Blaise, but not before the reader has become aware of the reality of the girl's marrying, and being forced into intimacy, with a stranger: the fate of most women during that time.

Honora Clare is one of Bishop's more conventional heroines. When her father dies she goes to live with obnoxious relatives who perceive her as a potential nanny for their children. Honora, rather on a whim, decides to set up school, *The School in Belmont*, with the children's ex-governess, and by luck they find themselves running a small private school. The romantic interest comes in the form of the irate Marcus Colvin, the father of one of the girls at the school. Colvin initially thinks Honora is too inexperienced to run a school, but changes his mind when he gets to know her. He also rescues her from various precarious situations, and inevitably ends up falling in love with her.

Although Bishop is known and loved predominantly for her Regency romances, today published by Mills and Boon, her earlier novels are more weighty, satisfying books. *The Durable Fire* is set as its subtitle suggests in Elizabethan England, and tells the love story of Kate and her cousin Chepstow. The book is full of historical detail, and illustrates the customs, and fashions of the time. Similarly *Penelope Deveraux* is set in Tudor England. The heroine, Penelope Deveraux, is the daughter of Lady Essex who married Elizabeth I's favourite, Robert Dudley. Penelope is almost betrothed to the poet Philip Sidney at the beginning of the book, and Sidney is the real love of her life, although they both marry other people. The book is a consummate romance set against a beautifully detailed Elizabethan court. The characters are well crafted and the reader gains a real insight into life in 16th-century England.

Bishop has been writing historical romances for over 30 years, and during this time she has perfected her craft. Her characters are carefully created to stand as independent and interesting people. Her plots are well designed and tightly bound together, with succinct sub-plots and mini-intrigues, the well-used devices of the successful historical romance.

—P. Campbell

BLACK, Laura.
Nationality: British. **Born:** Edinburgh, Scotland. **Agent:** Curtis Brown Ltd, 162–168 Regent Street, London W1R 5TB, England.

ROMANCE AND HISTORICAL PUBLICATIONS

Novels

Glendraco. London, Hamish Hamilton, and New York, St Martin's Press, 1977.
Castle Raven. London, Hamish Hamilton, 1978; as *Ravenburn*, New York, St Martin's Press, 1978.
Wild Cat. London, Hamish Hamilton, and New York, St Martin's Press, 1979.
Strathgallant. London, Hamish Hamilton, and New York, St Martin's Press, 1981.
Albany. London, Hamish Hamilton, and New York, St Martin's Press, 1984.
Falls of Gard. London, Hamish Hamilton, and New York, St Martin's Press, 1986.

*

Laura Black comments:

My novels are set in West Perthshire in the 1860s. The area is one of breathtaking natural beauty, which I know well and in which I have ancient ancestral roots. The period is particularly attractive—remote enough to be a foreign country, near enough to have familiar patterns of speech and attitude. A few minor characters reappear, as do a few imaginary places, but the books do not form a series. The stories take place largely in the castles and palaces of the highest aristocracy, this being the setting of a way of life—for the very last time—of glamour and high excitement without the suffocating opulence and vulgarity of a generation later. My heroines are beautiful and high spirited, and readers have reportedly grown fond of them. The books are much borrowed from public libraries, and my impression is that readers have recommended them to one another. This is extremely gratifying to me.

*   *   *

Laura Black's novels are reminiscent of morality plays, with vice punished and virtue rewarded in the end. What comes before the expected conclusion is more like old-fashioned melodrama. The villain is unredeemably villainous, the heroine utterly pure, and the hero as perfect as the romantic imagination can construct him.

These novels read like pure froth, but they are threaded with a sophisticated good humour that parodies the very style that it copies. There seems to be no middle ground in Black's work. Her heroines are *impossibly* beautiful, *impossibly* spirited, and *impossibly* capable. At the same time, the characters are almost irresistible to the reader, perhaps because there is no common ground between any reader and these literary paragons. The heroes are alluring for much the same reason; they are superhuman creations endowed with every virtue and advantage. The villains are personifications of vice, and yet they manage to show remorse or to die with great style by the end of the books. This is not to say, however, that any of the characters are less than believable. Their greatest charm is their naturalness in the face of such positive and negative perfection.

The plots of Black's novels are difficult to characterize as they contain elements of the pure romance, the gothic, the historical romance, and the novel of romantic suspense. Each style seems to be represented by a sub-plot in each book. No single style takes constant precedence; all are blended into a surprisingly cohesive whole. What remains constant from book to book are the devices that create the romantic tension. The heroine must choose between suitors, one of whom may mean her harm. Likewise, a personality clash between the heroine and a male character virtually guarantees his eventual success in winning her hand. The books are more frankly sexual than most examples of the genres represented, save the historical romance. While not graphic, the sex goes beyond mere bodice-ripping; incest is a major theme in *Castle Raven*. The resolution of this sexual dilemma is not at all unexpected, for these novels are not meant to shock. Marriage is the goal for these men and women. There may be superbly able women here, but there is no feminism in these pages.

All of Black's work deals with the rather closed society of upper-class Victorian Scotland. The relative smallness of the social circle represented leads to one of the intriguing facets of the novels. The major characters from one book appear in succeeding books, sometimes as relatively important secondary characters and sometimes as figures in the background. This habit of Black's makes her works seem more of a social chronicle rather than individual novels. It is amusing to contemplate a society whose members lead such sequentially romantic and exciting lives. The cleverness and unpredictability of the plots render this milieu real, and at the same time keep each book from reading like a repeat of the previous one.

Black has a genuine ear for both dialogue and dialect. Many of the secondary characters speak Scots dialect, which she makes almost audible to the reader. She also manages to solve the problem of an unfamiliar dialect vocabulary by defining words in context without becoming didactic. The descriptive passages are worthy of note. They are highly detailed yet fluid, so that the reader feels that she knows the smallest facet of the lives and surroundings of the heroines.

Black's work could be called florid, but it is evocative of a florid world that no longer exists—if it ever did. She has created romantic fantasies with a tenuous base in reality, but spun so attractively that the reader can hardly refuse to be drawn within.

—Susan Quinn Berneis

BLACK, Veronica.   See **PETERS, Maureen.**

BLACKMORE, Jane.   British. See 2nd edition, 1990.

BLACKSTOCK, Charity.
Pseudonym for Ursula Torday. **Other Pseudonyms:** Paula Allardyce; Lee Blackstock; Charlotte Keppel. Also wrote as Ursula Torday. **Nationality:** British. **Born:** London. **Education:** Kensington High School, London; Lady Margaret Hall, Oxford, B.A. in English; London School of Economics, social science certificate. **Career:** worked as a typist at the National Central Library, London. **Recipient:** Romantic Novelists Association major award, 1961. **Agent:** Andrew Hewson, John Johnson Literary Agency, 45–47 Clerkenwell Road, London EC1R 0HT, England. **Address:** Balcombe Place, Balcombe, West Sussex RH17 6Q7, England.

ROMANCE AND HISTORICAL PUBLICATIONS

Novels

Dewey Death. London, Heinemann, 1956; with *The Foggy, Foggy Dew*, New York, British Book Centre, 1959.
Miss Fenny. London, Hodder and Stoughton, 1957; as *The Woman in the Woods* (as Lee Blackstock), New York, Doubleday, 1958.
The Foggy, Foggy Dew. London, Hodder and Stoughton, 1958; with *Dewey Death*, New York, British Book Centre, 1959.
All Men Are Murderers (as Lee Blackstock). New York, Doubleday, 1958; as *The Shadow of Murder* (as Charity Blackstock), London, Hodder and Stoughton, 1959.
The Bitter Conquest. London, Hodder and Stoughton, 1959; New York, Ballantine, 1964.
The Briar Patch. London, Hodder and Stoughton, 1960; as *Young Lucifer*, Philadelphia, Lippincott, 1960.
The Exorcism. London, Hodder and Stoughton, 1961; as *A House Possessed*, Philadelphia, Lippincott, 1962.
The Gallant. London, Hodder and Stoughton, 1962; New York, Ballantine, 1966.
Mr Christopoulos. London, Hodder and Stoughton, 1963; New York, British Book Centre, 1964.
The Factor's Wife. London, Hodder and Stoughton, 1964; as *The English Wife*, New York, Coward McCann, 1964.
When the Sun Goes Down. London, Hodder and Stoughton, 1965; as *Monkey on a Chain*, New York, Coward McCann, 1965.
The Knock at Midnight. London, Hodder and Stoughton, 1966; New York, Coward McCann, 1967.
Party in Dolly Creek. London, Hodder and Stoughton, 1967; as *The Widow*, New York, Coward McCann, 1967.

The Melon in the Cornfield. London, Hodder and Stoughton, 1969; as *The Lemmings*, New York, Coward McCann, 1969.
The Daughter, New York, Coward McCann, 1970; London, Hodder and Stoughton, 1971.
The Encounter. New York, Coward McCann, 1971; Loughton, Essex, Piatkus, 1981.
The Jungle. London, Hodder and Stoughton, and New York, Coward McCann, 1972.
The Lonely Strangers. New York, Coward McCann, 1972; London, Hodder and Stoughton, 1973.
People in Glass Houses. London, Hodder and Stoughton, and New York, Coward McCann, 1975.
Ghost Town. London, Hodder and Stoughton, and New York, Coward McCann, 1976.
I Met Murder on the Way. London, Hodder and Stoughton, 1977; as *The Shirt Front*, New York, Coward McCann, 1977.
Miss Charley. London, Hodder and Stoughton, 1979.
With Fondest Thoughts. London, Hodder and Stoughton, 1980.
Dream Towers. London, Hodder and Stoughton, 1981.

Novels as Ursula Torday

The Ballad-Maker of Paris. London, Allan, 1935.
No Peace for the Wicked. London, Nelson, 1937.
The Mirror of the Sun. London, Nelson, 1938.

Novels as Paula Allardyce

After the Lady. London, Ward Lock, 1954.
The Doctor's Daughter. London, Ward Lock, 1955.
A Game of Hazard. London, Ward Lock, 1955.
Adam and Evelina. London, Ward Lock, 1956.
The Man of Wrath. London, Ward Lock, 1956.
The Lady and the Pirate. London, Ward Lock, 1957.
Southarn Folly. London, Ward Lock, 1957.
Beloved Enemy. London, Ward Lock, 1958.
My Dear Miss Emma. London, Ward Lock, 1958; Chicago, Playboy Press, 1980.
Death, My Lover. London, Ward Lock, 1959.
A Marriage Has Been Arranged. London, Ward Lock, 1959.
Johnny Danger. London, Ward Lock, 1960; as *The Rebel Lover*, Chicago, Playboy Press, 1979.
Witches' Sabbath. London, Ward Lock, 1961; New York, Macmillan, 1962.
The Gentle Highwayman. London, Ward Lock, 1961.
Adam's Rib. London, Hodder and Stoughton, 1963; as *Legacy of Pride*, New York, Dell, 1975.
The Respectable Miss Parkington-Smith. London, Hodder and Stoughton, 1964; as *Paradise Row*, New York, Dell, 1976.
Octavia; or, The Trials of a Romantic Novelist. London, Hodder and Stoughton, 1965; New York, Dell, 1977.
The Moonlighters. London, Hodder and Stoughton, 1966; as *Gentleman Rogue*, New York, Dell, 1975.
Six Passengers for the 'Sweet Bird'. London, Hodder and Stoughton, 1967.
Waiting at the Church. London, Hodder and Stoughton, 1968; as *Emily*, New York, Dell, 1976.
The Ghost of Archie Gilroy. London, Hodder and Stoughton, 1970; as *Shadowed Love*, New York, Dell, 1977.
Miss Jonas's Boy. London, Hodder and Stoughton, 1972; as *Eliza*, New York, Dell, 1975.
The Gentle Sex. London, Hodder and Stoughton, 1974; as *The Carradine Affair*, New York, Pocket Books, 1976.
Miss Philadelphia Smith. London, Hodder and Stoughton, 1977.
Haunting Me. London, Hodder and Stoughton, 1978; New York, St Martin's Press, 1979.

The Rogue's Lady. Chicago, Playboy Press, 1979.
The Vixen's Revenge. Chicago, Playboy Press, 1980.

Novels as Charlotte Keppel

Madam, You Must Die. London, Hodder and Stoughton, 1975; as *Loving Sands, Deadly Sands*, New York, Delacorte Press, 1975.
My Name Is Clary Brown. New York, Random House, 1976; as *When I Say Goodbye, I'm Clary Brown*, London, Hodder and Stoughton, 1977.
I Could Be Good to You. London, Hutchinson, and New York, St Martin's Press, 1980.
The Villains. Loughton, Essex, Piatkus, 1980; New York, St Martin's Press, 1982.
The Ghosts of Fontenoy. Loughton, Essex, Piatkus, 1981.

OTHER PUBLICATIONS

Other

The Children. Boston, Little Brown, 1966; as *Wednesday's Children*, London, Hutchinson, 1967.

*   *   *

A wide-ranging and fertile imagination, tempered by common sense, is a rare quality in a writer of romantic fiction, yet this is a quality that Charity Blackstock possesses. From the beginning of her career her fiction has spanned countries and eras with confident skill.

Two early novels display this diversity and reveal literary techniques that can be observed to develop steadily. *The Bitter Conquest*, a historical novel set in the Scotland of 1750, has as its central character a somewhat reluctant hero, Adams. He is an English soldier bitterly disillusioned by futile bloodletting for a cause in which he has no conviction. The romantic element is introduced early, and develops in careful counterpoint to Adams's exploration of his own and his country's motives. There are gothic elements in the novel as well, including macabre descriptions of the bleak moors around Culloden—and even a severed head. By contrast, *The Briar Patch* is set in Paris four years after World War II, and the protagonists are two teenagers: Deirdre is Irish, attending a finishing school, and Max is a Jewish survivor of Nazi-occupied Poland. Though the portrayal of their developing intimacy is clouded by hopeless pessimism, the novel holds the reader's interest by its sensitive characterization and a plot packed with exciting incident.

Blackstock returned to a similar period in *The Knock at Midnight*, but switched to modern-day Australia for *Party in Dolly Creek*. This book introduces the theme of soul-searching that pervades many of Blackstock's subsequent novels.

Perhaps the least successful of Blackstock's works is *The Melon in the Cornfield*, mainly because the characters involved in this tale of racial conflict in a West London technical college never come to life. Blackstock, like many other romantic novelists, does not contrive to avoid a patronizing tone when dealing with a primarily political subject. *The Lonely Strangers*, however, shows Blackstock at full strength; in it she returns to the mid-18th century and to the people of Scotland, this time a group of exiles in Paris whose spirits are broken by defeat but whose characters are alive with emotion.

The majority of Blackstock's later works have a contemporary setting and rely for their interest and success upon a realistic presentation of modern-day crises. A good example is *Ghost Town* whose main character, Elizabeth Walters, is a former journalist, past middle age, with several unsuccessful relationships behind her. Her mental journey to self-realization is presented by flashbacks that juxtapose past and present experiences. Mrs Walters's own views on literature form another aspect of the novel. In *Dream Towers* Barbara Wyatt leaves her unfaithful husband to retreat to their country cottage. The working out of her true feelings towards Ben is linked metaphorically with her curiosity about the occupant of a mysterious mansion—and the laying of the village's 'ghost' enables Barbara to lay her own 'ghosts' to rest.

Blackstock's consistently realistic characters, whose reactions can be readily related to common experience, have contributed to her success in the field of romantic fiction. Hers is not remote, high-flown romanticism but has at its base 'heart and sincerity' without which, as Elizabeth Walters proposed in *Ghost Town*, writing is 'no use at all'.

—Anne M. Shields

BLACKSTOCK, Lee.   See **BLACKSTOCK, Charity.**

BLAIR, Emma.

Pseudonym for Iain Blair. **Nationality:** British. **Born:** Glasgow, 12 August 1942. **Education:** West Division High school, Milwaukee; Royal Scottish Academy of Music and Dramatic Art, Glasgow. **Relations:** married; two sons. **Career:** worked for insurance company, Glasgow; emigrated to Australia, 1959; proof reader, *Sydney Bulletin* (newspaper), Sydney, New South Wales; lifeguard, South Steyne Beach, Sydney, New South Wales; journalist, *The Sunday Post*, Glasgow. Actor, Royal Shakespeare Company, London; also playwright. Lives in Devon. **Address:** c/o Transworld Publishers Ltd, 61–63 Uxbridge Road, London W5 5SA, England.

ROMANCE AND HISTORICAL PUBLICATIONS

Novels

Where No Man Cries. London, Arrow, 1982.
Nellie Wildchild. London, Arrow, 1983.
Hester Dark. London, Severn House, 1984.
This Side of Heaven. London, Severn House, 1985.
Street Song. London, Joseph, 1986.
Jessie Gray. London, Severn House, 1986.
The Princess of Poor Street. London, Joseph, 1986.
When Dreams Come True. London, Joseph, 1987.
A Most Determined Woman. London, Joseph, 1988.
The Blackbird's Tale. London, Joseph, 1989.
Maggie Jordan. London, Bantam, 1990.
Scarlet Ribbons. London, Bantam, 1992.
The Water Meadows. London, Bantam, 1993.
The Sweetest Thing. London, Bantam, 1993.

OTHER PUBLICATIONS

Novels as Iain Blair (crime and mystery)

Bone. London, Sphere, 1977.
Duff. London, Sphere, 1977.
True. London, Sphere, 1977.
Hooligan's Rant. London, New English Library, 1979.

Play

The Love Songs of Martha Canary. N.d.

* * *

Emma Blair soon became a bestselling author, but it was only after a dozen or so novels, when *Scarlet Ribbons* was short listed for the Romantic Novelists' award in 1992, that it became generally known that Emma was in fact Iain. Previously Iain had written thrillers and a play under his own name, but when he began to write regional sagas about women he was asked to change his sex as well as his style. The attitude towards 'women's fiction' in the 1970s and 1980s persuaded his publishers that he could succeed only under a female pseudonym. It is interesting to speculate what might have happened otherwise!

The Emma Blair novels are rather more than regional sagas, although they are either set in or have a strong connection with Glasgow, usually in the grinding poverty of the 1920s slump. The theme is most often how women fight to escape their background. There are always tough, resilient heroines, capable of rising above despair, betrayal, and misfortune to survive triumphantly. The author gets into the minds and hearts of these gritty, determined women with immense skill.

A typical story is *Nellie Wildchild*, in which the heroine, a factory girl, is desperate to escape from the poverty and religious bigotry of Glasgow. She loves Frank, who is a Catholic, not her father's choice, Jim. Through initial happiness, then tribulations, Nellie remains strong.

Jessie Gray is a different kind of book in that it starts in 1947 with a heroine from the middle classes. Jessie, the minister's daughter, falls in love as a schoolgirl with Tommy McBride, a fighter. They meet again in the mid-1950s when Tommy has become the 'King of the Glasgow Teds', and Jessie rejects her family and becomes involved with rival gangs. She helps start a skiffle band, becoming its manager and in part its inspiration. Jessie flees when Tommy, persuaded that it is the only way to win a talent contest, betrays her, and goes to live in London. After they have both tried to rebuild their lives with other people they meet again, come together, and return to Glasgow.

Returning to Glasgow is a regular theme in Blair's books. The heroine of *Maggie Jordan* has a conventional life, she is orphaned, works in Glasgow, and she becomes engaged to Neville, and then her life is totally disrupted when Neville goes to fight in the Spanish Civil War. She goes to Spain, at first to be with him, but then is drawn into fighting alongside him. However, Neville has changed, and is jealous of her friendship with the American journalist Howard Taft. When Neville dies in Spain, she returns to Glasgow, marries and has a child. The child dies, and husband Andy, bereft, throws himself under a train. Then, Maggie marries Howard and goes to America with him.

In *Scarlet Ribbons* the heroine has a degenerative hip and is left at an orphanage when her mother, widowed and destitute, can no longer care for her. Her hip cured, she is sent to Canada, where she becomes a drudge, but meets and marries a rich young man. She learns to adapt to her new life with such conspicuous success that she becomes the mainstay of the family company.

Blair devises stories which are appealing in many ways. Although set largely in Glasgow, the often appalling conditions described are reminiscent of many big industrial cities, and most readers have experienced or have been told of similar situations. This nostalgia for the fairly recent past—although not the conditions that prevailed then—is currently very popular. Blair's novels, however, provide more than simply memories—they give hope and optimism. Heroines who fight against appalling odds and win will always be attractive. More than that, the heroines are very human in their faults, which occasionally help but sometimes hinder progress. In the later books such as *Maggie Jordan*, *Scarlet Ribbons*, and *The Water Meadows*, Blair moves the action away from Glasgow, widening the scope of the books and putting the characters on broader stages. This is a good development, permitting the inclusion of such events as the Spanish Civil War and World War II, and making use of the author's own experience of life in North America and Australia.

The well-deserved success of these novels is due to the storytelling ability of the author, who sweeps us along at a great pace and with a wealth of detail that shows meticulous research.

—Marina Oliver

———

BLAIR, Iain. See **BLAIR, Emma.**

———

BLAIR, Jennifer.   See **McELFRESH, Adeline.**

———

BLAIR, Kathryn.
Pseudonyms: Rosalind Brett; Celine Conway. **Nationality:** British. **Address:** c/o Mills and Boon Ltd, Eton House, 18–24 Paradise Road, Richmond, Surrey TW9 1SR, England.

ROMANCE AND HISTORICAL PUBLICATIONS

Novels

Bewildered Heart. London, Mills and Boon, 1950; Toronto, Harlequin, 1964.
The House at Tegwani. London, Mills and Boon, 1950; Toronto, Harlequin, 1963.
No Other Haven. London, Mills and Boon, 1950; Toronto, Harlequin, 1966.
Dearest Enemy. London, Mills and Boon, 1951; Toronto, Harlequin, 1967.
Flowering Wilderness. London, Mills and Boon, 1951; Toronto, Harlequin, 1967.
Mayenga Farm. London, Mills and Boon, 1951; Toronto, Harlequin, 1965.
The Enchanting Island. London, Mills and Boon, 1952; Toronto, Harlequin, 1963.
The Fair Invader. London, Mills and Boon, 1952; as *Plantation Doctor,* Toronto, Harlequin, 1962.
The White Oleander. London, Mills and Boon, 1953; as *Nurse Laurie,* Toronto, Harlequin, 1962.
Dear Adversary. London, Mills and Boon, 1953; Toronto, Harlequin, 1964.
Barbary Moon. London, Mills and Boon, 1954; Toronto, Harlequin, 1965.
Sweet Deceiver. London, Mills and Boon, 1955; Toronto, Harlequin, 1965.
Tamarisk Bay. London, Mills and Boon, 1956; Toronto, Harlequin, 1962.
Wild Crocus. London, Mills and Boon, 1956; Toronto, Harlequin, 1963.
Valley of Flowers. London, Mills and Boon, 1957.
The Tulip Tree. London, Mills and Boon, 1958; Toronto, Harlequin, 1966.
Love This Enemy. London, Mills and Boon, 1958; Toronto, Harlequin, 1964.
The Golden Rose. London, Mills and Boon, 1959; Toronto, Harlequin, 1962.
The Man at Mulera. London, Mills and Boon, 1959; Toronto, Harlequin, 1965.

A Summer at Barbazon. London, Mills and Boon, 1960; as *A Nurse at Barbazon,* Toronto, Harlequin, 1964.
The Primrose Bride. London, Mills and Boon, 1961; Toronto, Harlequin, 1966.
Children's Nurse. Toronto, Harlequin, 1961.
Battle of Love. London, Mills and Boon, 1961; Toronto, Harlequin, 1966.
The Affair in Tangier. London, Mills and Boon, 1962.
They Met in Zanzibar. London, Mills and Boon, 1962; Toronto, Harlequin, 1967.
The Surgeon's Marriage. London, Mills and Boon, 1963; Toronto, Harlequin, 1964.
The Dangerous Kind of Love. London, Mills and Boon, 1964.
This Kind of Love. Toronto, Harlequin, 1964.
Doctor Westland. Toronto, Harlequin, 1965.
Home Is the Sailor. New York, Silhouette, 1990.
Dancing in the Aisles. Toronto, Harlequin, 1990.

Novels as Rosalind Brett

Green Leaves. Hanley, Staffordshire, Locker, 1947.
Pagan Interlude. Hanley, Staffordshire, Locker, 1947.
Secret Marriage. Hanley, Staffordshire, Locker, 1947.
And No Regrets. London, Rich and Cowan, 1948; Toronto, Harlequin, 1974.
Winds of Enchantment. London, Rich and Cowan, 1949; Toronto, Harlequin, 1968.
They Came to Valeira. London, Rich and Cowan, 1950; Toronto, Harlequin, 1974.
Brittle Bondage. London, Rich and Cowan, 1951; Toronto, Harlequin, 1969.
Love This Stranger. London, Rich and Cowan, 1951; Toronto, Harlequin, 1974.
Stormy Haven. London, Mills and Boon, 1952; Toronto, Harlequin, 1962.
Fair Horizon. London, Mills and Boon, 1952; Toronto, Harlequin, 1963.
Towards the Sun. London, Mills and Boon, 1953; Toronto, Harlequin, 1962.
Whispering Palms. London, Mills and Boon, 1954; Toronto, Harlequin, 1963.
Winds in the Wilderness. London, Mills and Boon, 1954; Toronto, Harlequin, 1963.
Sweet Waters. London, Mills and Boon, 1955; Toronto, Harlequin, 1964.
A Cottage in Spain. London, Mills and Boon, 1955; Toronto, Harlequin, 1975.
Portrait of Susan. London, Mills and Boon, 1956; Toronto, Harlequin, 1963.
Quiet Holiday. London, Mills and Boon, 1957; as *Nurse on Holiday,* Toronto, Harlequin, 1963.
Tangle in Sunshine. London, Mills and Boon, 1957; Toronto, Harlequin, 1964.
Young Tracy. London, Mills and Boon, 1958; Toronto, Harlequin, 1964.
Too Young to Marry. London, Mills and Boon, 1958; Toronto, Harlequin, 1964.
The Reluctant Guest. London, Mills and Boon, 1959; Toronto, Harlequin, 1964.
Hotel Mirador. London, Mills and Boon, 1959; Toronto, Harlequin, 1966.
Dangerous Waters. London, Mills and Boon, 1960; Toronto, Harlequin, 1964.
The Bolambo Affair. London, Mills and Boon, 1961; Toronto, Harlequin, 1967.

Spring at the Villa. London, Mills and Boon, 1961; as *Elizabeth Browne, Children's Nurse,* Toronto, Harlequin, 1965.
The Girl at White Drift. London, Mills and Boon, 1962; Toronto, Harlequin, 1967.
For My Sins. London, Mills and Boon, 1966.

Novels as Celine Conway

Return of Simon. London, Mills and Boon, 1953; Toronto, Harlequin, 1965.
The Blue Caribbean. London, Mills and Boon, 1954; Toronto, Harlequin, 1964.
Flowers in the Wind. London, Mills and Boon, 1954; as *Doctor's Assistant,* Toronto, Harlequin, 1964.
Full Tide. London, Mills and Boon, 1954; Toronto, Harlequin, 1964.
Three Women. London, Mills and Boon, 1955; Toronto, Harlequin, 1966.
The Tall Pines. London, Mills and Boon, 1956; Toronto, Harlequin, 1963.
The Rustle of Bamboo. London, Mills and Boon, 1957.
Wide Pastures. London, Mills and Boon, 1957; Toronto, Harlequin, 1962.
At the Villa Massina. London, Mills and Boon, 1958; Toronto, Harlequin, 1965.
My Dear Cousin. London, Mills and Boon, 1959; Toronto, Harlequin, 1965.
Came a Stranger. London, Mills and Boon, 1960; Toronto, Harlequin, 1965.
Flower of the Morning. London, Mills and Boon, 1960; Toronto, Harlequin, 1966.
Perchance to Marry. London, Mills and Boon, 1961; Toronto, Harlequin, 1966.
White Doctor. Toronto, Harlequin, 1961.
The Rancher Needs a Wife. London, Mills and Boon, 1962; Toronto, Harlequin, 1963.
Ship's Surgeon. London, Mills and Boon, 1962; Toronto, Harlequin, 1963.

*   *   *

Kathryn Blair's writing began in the late 1940s and she published numerous novels through the 1960s. She is also a writer who preferred to use a pseudonym, and for years her novels appeared under the names of Rosalind Brett and Celine Conway. In fact, she wrote and published under all three names for some time during the 1950s and 1960s.

Her style of writing is surprising, however, for one does not find the usual limitations in plot or characters that seem to typify romances of those years. In fact, she is quite modern and could easily be mistaken for a contemporary writer. She uses strong characterization, emotional and dramatic involvement, and exotic backgrounds to tell her stories. Many take place in Africa and Europe. Underlying psychological difficulties also seem to play a part in her motivation, as characters fight circumstances and their own hidden fears and desires.

In *Young Tracy* (written as Rosalind Brett) the heroine, Maggie Tracy, finds herself left in charge of a supply store deep in the wilds of Africa while her parents return on a trip to England. Nick Heward arrives to set up a construction base for a projected bridge in the area. He seeks to establish the store as a base for supplies and encounters Maggie. Another complication in the novel is Don Caldwell and his mother. Don falls in love with Maggie, but she can only think of him as a friend. Gradually Nick and Maggie fall in love, but events constantly set them at odds, until Mrs Caldwell's growing psychological difficulties bring things to a head. Maggie's youthful-

ness, her unawareness, and, most of all, her stubborn idealistic need to help her parents all bring out the anger and frustration that Nick feels as he seeks to protect Maggie. The story line centres on several layers of conflict as the heroine and hero finally cut through the many elements of disagreement and confusion.

The Man at Mulera is no less complex as Lou Prentice arrives in Africa to take charge of her cousin's little boy, Keith. She is disturbed and later horrified to learn that the will making her a guardian of the child also stipulates that she and Ross Gilmore act as joint guardians, even to the extent that neither can marry without the other's permission. Lou finds herself forced to remain in Africa and slowly she becomes involved with Ross on questions of care and discipline for the boy. In this novel Blair makes full use of her creative ability as she draws numerous threads of conflict together in a seemingly impossible situation. Secondary characters such as Greg Allwyn, Ross Gilmore's new manager, and Paula Craddock, the District Commissioner's sister, add their strands to the various sub-plots and conflicts. Greg is a weak, spineless person who plays on Lou's sympathies. Paula is determined to become Ross's wife, regardless of his inclinations. Again Blair's use of psychological overtones raises the suspense and adds tremendously to character motivation.

One may not dismiss Blair as simply another romance writer. She shows unusual talent in developing complex characters and in letting them write their own stories. Her heroines are far from the simple peaches-and-cream caricatures that one thinks of in romances, neither are her heroes so predictable and stereotyped. A timeless quality in her writings makes her one of those rare writers who has something to say to any generation reading her, a fact that modern readers appreciate as they often re-read one of her well-written novels.

—Arlene Moore

———

BLAKE, Andrea.   See WEALE, Anne.

———

BLAKE, Jennifer.
Pseudonym for Patricia Maxwell. **Other Pseudonyms:** Maxine Patrick; Elizabeth Treahearne, with Carol Albritton. Also writes as Patricia Maxwell. **Nationality:** American. **Born:** Patricia Ponder, Winn Parish, Louisiana (or Goldonna, Louisiana), 9 March 1942. **Relations:** married J.R. Maxwell in 1957; two sons, two daughters. **Career:** writer. **Recipient:** Romance Writers of America, Golden Treasure award in 1987. **Address:** 5151 Beech Springs Road, Quitman, Louisiana 71268, USA.

ROMANCE AND HISTORICAL PUBLICATIONS

Novels

Storm at Midnight (as Elizabeth Treahearne). New York, Ace, 1973.
Haven of Fear (as Patricia Ponder). London, Manor Books, 1977.
Murder for Charity (as Patricia Ponder). London, Manor Books, 1977.
Love's Wild Desire. New York, Popular Library, 1977; London, Sphere, 1978.
Tender Betrayal. London, Sphere, and New York, Popular Library, 1979.
The Storm and the Splendor. London, Sphere, and New York, Fawcett, 1979.
Golden Fancy. New York, Fawcett, 1979; London, Sphere, 1980.

Louisiana Dawn. London, Piatkus, 1980; New York, Fawcett Columbine, 1987.
Embrace and Conquer. New York, Fawcett Columbine, 1981; London, Severn House 1992.
Royal Seduction. New York, Fawcett Columbine, 1981.
Surrender in Moonlight. New York, Fawcett Columbine, 1984.
Midnight Waltz. New York, Fawcett Columbine, 1985.
Fierce Eden. New York, Fawcett Columbine, 1985.
Royal Passion. New York, Fawcett Columbine, 1986; London, Severn House, 1993.
Prisoner of Desire. New York, Fawcett Columbine, 1986.
Southern Rapture. New York, Fawcett Columbine, 1987.
Perfume of Paradise. New York, Fawcett Columbine, 1987.
Love and Smoke. New York, Fawcett Columbine, 1989.
Spanish Serenade. New York, Fawcett Columbine, 1990.
Joy and Anger. New York, Fawcett Columbine, 1992.
Wildest Dreams. New York, Fawcett Columbine, 1992.
Arrow to the Heart. New York, Fawcett, Columbine, 1993.

Novels as Patricia Maxwell

The Secret of Mirror House. New York, Fawcett, 1970.
Stranger at Plantation Inn. New York, Fawcett, 1971.
Dark Masquerade. New York, Fawcett, 1974; (as Jennifer Blake) London, Severn House, 1990.
The Bewitching Grace. New York, Popular Library, 1974.
The Court of the Thorn Tree. New York, Popular Library, 1974.
Bride of a Stranger. New York, Fawcett, 1974; (as Jennifer Blake) London, Severn House, 1990.
The Notorious Angel. New York, Fawcett, 1977; (as Jennifer Blake) New York, Fawcett, 1983.
Sweet Piracy Fawcett. New York, Fawcett, 1978.
Night of the Candles. New York, Fawcett, 1978; (as Jennifer Blake) London, Severn House, 1991.

Novels as Maxine Patrick

The Abducted Heart. New York, Signet, 1978.
Bayou Bride. New York, Signet, 1979.
Snowbound Heart. New York, Signet, 1979.
Love at Sea. New York, Signet, 1980.
Captive Kisses. New York, Signet, 1980.
April of Enchantment. New York, Signet, 1981.

*

Critical Study: in *Love's Leading Ladies* edited by Kathryn Falk. New York, Pinnacle, 1982.

*   *   *

American author Jennifer Blake has been prolific for more than 20 years, 13 of her books have been published in Britain—unfortunately, far too many of them have suggestive cover illustrations designed to repel readers that give no indication whatever of the feast within.

As recipient of the Golden Treasure award for a 'lifetime achievement in the romance genre' she satisfies requirements on both sides of the Atlantic which have differing perceptions of the terminology. There is also a difference between romance and romantic fiction. Whereas a romance, particularly in Britain, is predominantly if not exclusively a love story, the latter category conforms more closely to the original mediaeval ideal, namely a tale of high adventure and challenge as well as human emotion. The scope is thrown open to permit history, suspense, espionage, even psychology and philosophy to play a major part alongside the love interest, which may be hot and steamy or delicately understated, though always significant. Blake commits herself unashamedly to stories with a highly emotional content, much of it erotic, increasing this as licence becomes freer. Love, however, nearly always has a dark side with which the heroine must come to terms, for she requires character resolution and progression in men too. Where sagas continue into further volumes, an idyllic ending in one book frequently turns sour in a subsequent tale.

The term 'romance' became degraded in the 18th century when tawdry translations of improbable French tales of dalliance and manners flooded Europe's popular markets. These were regarded as suitable reading only for feather-brained young ladies, infinitely more suitable for them than the bawdy English novels then available. Unfortunately this perception hangs on grimly. In most of Blake's books the French connection returns, but handled with a rumbustiousness that Sterne and Fielding would have envied. They throb with passion, thrill with excitement and race from one surprising incident to another. Plots twist and turn wildly, carrying the reader on a journey very like a roller-coaster. In *Love's Wild Desire*, for instance, she begins with an heiress sneaking into a quadroon ball, a seduction and an obligation on the seducer to marry his victim. By way of escape from the tired glory of the hero's old swamp farmhouse, abduction by a jealous, vicious past suitor, near drowning in the Mississippi, rescue and shelter by kindly Scottish water gypsies, mishandling by a preacher, escape to serve as maid in a bordello and much else the heroine is eventually returned to her husband, only to face renewed voodoo threats and a slave revolt. It is unashamed, exuberant escapism, rich and sensuous, full of magic and money, passion and politics bundled together with shining descriptions, soaked in period and location detail.

But it is far more. Blake is a historian with a thorough knowledge of her field, especially old New Orleans and the Deep South during the 18th and 19th centuries. In vivid, merciless prose she recreates the social mores and pretensions hedging in the upper classes who were rich and enviable and thoroughly spoiled. 'Society' was predominantly French with injections from other European lands. Class stratas were divided racially, though not yet completely segregated, with black slaves at the bottom, mulatto in the artisan divide and whites, rich and poor, forming a large, complex dominant group with fairly rigid subdivisions within it, these determined by country of origin, level of birth and wealth, inherited, earned or less honourably acquired. Movement within classes was tolerated more easily than between them. Cross racial progress was almost invariably downwards, and not forgiven. Such attitudes inevitably set into the immutable prejudices of the future, while all the more positive Creole aspects developed and flourished alongside. She explains and hints, teaching without overt social moralizing, relying on her tale to tell the truths she wishes to impart.

On a higher political plain *Dark Masquerade* (written as Patricia Maxwell) and its sequels also deal with the negotiations and undercover manipulations leading to the transfer of Louisiana from France to America against a Napoleonic backcloth. Some events take place in Europe, often with the hero dominating the action but as a rule Blake follows the convention of telling her story through female eyes. She sticks to other conventions too. The heroine is beautiful, of course, and the hero striking if not handsome, and probably arrogant, definitely rich or potentially so. Politics, business, gambling, and clubland are in the province of men, household management, child-rearing, and society intercourse of women. Independent or eccentric individuals may encroach on areas allotted to the other sex, or another class, provided they are prepared to risk unpleasant consequences, which are often realized. Stereotypical qualities are accorded, passion and style to the French, honour but unbending pride to the English. Characters are required to undergo the tempering of danger and despair before reaching happiness beyond, having resolved at least some of their personality defects on the way.

The main regret is the dearth of little things concerning the life of the lower classes: details of what actually happened on farms, in banks, on the river, how affairs were actually managed at the slave compound, in the gambling dens. Even the running of a household is barely mentioned except for touches of the unusual, i.e. how a society woman saved her hair combings in a special box to be made into a hairpiece for later life. The reader wants to know what they ate, how it was cooked, served, where it came from, what the markets were like, who did the buying or deciding. Mundane as they are, such facts might have added credibility to decidedly exotic, over-burdened plots. Or would they, on reflection, merely impede the escape into rolling romance and adventure?

—Margaret Woodward

—————

BLAKE, Sally.   See SAUNDERS, Jean.

—————

BLAKE, Stephanie.
Pseudonym for Jacques Bain Pearl. **Other Pseudonyms:** Jack Pearl; Tricia Stevens. **Nationality:** American. **Born:** Richmond Hill, New York, 12 September 1923. **Education:** Columbia University, New York, A.B. 1949, M.A. 1950. **Military Service:** US Army, World War II; served in Sicily, Africa, and Italy. **Relations:** married June Hewes in 1947, two daughters. **Career:** part-time advertising copywriter, 1947–50; editor, *Gangbusters* television programme, 1952–53; editor, MacFadden Publications, New York, 1953–60. Since 1961, freelance writer. **Address:** c/o Berkley Publishing Group, 200 Madison Avenue, New York, New York 10016, USA.

ROMANCE AND HISTORICAL PUBLICATIONS

Novels

Flowers of Fire. Chicago, Playboy Press, 1977; London, Hamlyn, 1978.
Daughter of Destiny. Chicago, Playboy Press, 1977; London, Hamlyn, 1978.
Blaze of Passion. Chicago, Playboy Press, 1978; London, Hamlyn, 1979.
So Wicked My Desire. Chicago, Playboy Press, and London, Hamlyn, 1979.
Secret Sins. Chicago, Playboy Press, 1980; London, Hamlyn, 1983.
Wicked Is My Flesh. Chicago, Playboy Press, 1980; London, Hamlyn, 1981.
Scarlet Kisses. Chicago, Playboy Press, 1981; London, Hamlyn, 1982.
Unholy Desires. Chicago, Playboy Press, 1981; London, Hamlyn, 1982.
Fires of the Heart. London, Hamlyn, 1983.
Bride of the Wind. New York, Berkley, 1984.
Texas Lily. New York, Ace, 1987.
The World Is Mine. New York, Berkley, 1988.
Devil in My Heart. New York, Jove, 1990.

OTHER PUBLICATIONS

Novels as Jack Pearl

Robin and the Seven Hoods (novelization). New York, Pocket Books, 1964.

The Yellow Rolls Royce (novelization). New York, Pocket Books, 1965.
Ambush Bay (novelization). New York, New American Library, 1966.
Garrison's Gorillas (novelization). New York, Dell, 1967.
Funny Girl (novelization). New York, Pocket Books, 1968.
A Time to Kill . . . A Time to Die. New York, Norton, 1971; London, Hale, 1974.
The Cops. New York, Pinnacle, 1972.
Victims. New York, Trident Press, 1972; London, Hale, 1976.
The Plot to Kill the President. New York, Pinnacle, 1972.
Callie Knight. New York, Saturday Review Press, 1974; (as Stephanie Blake) London, Hamlyn, 1983.
A Jury of His Peers. Englewood Cliffs, New Jersey, 1975.
Lepke (novelization). New York, Pocket Books, 1975.
Our Man Flint (novelization). New York, Pocket Books, 1975.

Other as Jack Pearl

Blood-and-Guts Patton: The Swashbuckling Life Story of America's Most Daring and Controversial General. New York, Monarch, 1961.
General Douglas. New York, Monarch, 1961.
Bruce Larkin, Air Force Cadet. Maplewood, New Jersey, Hammond, 1962.
Aerial Dogfights of World War II. New York, Monarch, 1962.
The Young Falcons. Maplewood, New Jersey, Hammond, 1962.
Admiral 'Bull' Halsey. New York, Monarch, 1962.
Great Air Battles of World War II. New York, Monarch, 1962.
Battlegrounds, World War I: The Exciting Saga of the AEF in France. New York, Monarch, 1964.
The Dangerous Assassins. New York, Monarch, 1964.
Stockade. Seattle, Washington, Trident Press, 1964.
The Crucifixion of Pete McCabe. Seattle, Washington, Trident Press, 1966.
The Space Eagle: Operation Doomsday, illustrated by Arnie Kohn. New York, Whitman Publishing, 1968.
Masque of Honor, with Nick Vasile. New York, Norton, 1969.
Pollution Solution Revolution. New York, Pyramid, 1972.
Hooker for a Day (as Tricia Stevens). New York, Pocket Books, 1975.
Bar Belles (as Tricia Stevens). New York, Pocket Books, 1976.
Sado Cop, with Nick Vasile. New York, Playboy Press, 1976.
The Affair of the Unhappy Hooker, with David Toma. New York, Dell, 1976.

*   *   *

Sin, passion, and alliteration mark the titles of Stephanie Blake's novels: *Scarlet Kisses, Flowers of Fire, Daughter of Destiny, Blaze of Passion, So Wicked My Desire, Secret Sins, Wicked Is My Flesh, Unholy Desires, Fires of the Heart, Bride of the Wind, Texas Lily, The World is Mine, Devil in My Heart*. In the most recent novels, Blake has shuttled between stories of incredible coincidence, lifted-from-the-textbook history, trite literary allusions and those of aggressive female sexuality, contemporary faddishness, and spoken vulgarity. However, her fast-moving stories hypnotize like flaming fires, and the passion-filled pages keep the reader's fingers yearning, burning, turning for more. It is easy to understand Blake's popularity.

Flowers of Fire spans the Irish Revolution, the American Civil War, the California Gold Rush, and the early West (with Custer's Last Stand, Chief Crazy Horse, and Butch Cassidy), as it follows Ravena Wilding, a stunningly beautiful woman torn between the twin O'Neil brothers: Roger, 'the treacherous, twisted brother who, through lies and deception, takes lovely Ravena for his own', and

Brian, 'the rogue, who said, "Hate me or love me, but never forget me", and captured Ravena's heart for all time'. Jefferson Davis and other historical figures appear as characters in the appropriate places, along with characters from other fictions: Scarlett O'Hara ('I tell you', Jefferson Davis tells Ravena, 'the last time I set eyes on a beauty such as yours was in Savannah, Georgia. Come to think of it, she was of Irish extraction, too. Scarlett O'Hara is her name. Lovely. Reminds me very much of you, Miss Ravena. Except for the eyes. And to tell the truth, she was a trifle skinny for my tastes'), as does Rhett Butler's new-found brother, Dan, who carries on a love affair with the insatiable Ravena. Ravena is given to quoting John Donne ('No man is an island . . . ') and Alfred Lord Tennyson ('Into the valley of death,/Rode the Six Hundred . . . ') at critical moments.

In *Daughter of Destiny*, the sweeping continuation of the O'Neil saga, Ravena's daughter, Sabrina, voyages from violent Ireland and England (where her mother has a meeting with Queen Victoria, who 'looked like a stouter version of *Whistler's Mother*') to violent India (and the cult of the 'Thuggee'), and back to Britain, where she rejects the advances of a rude Winston Churchill. Dan Butler reappears, and Colette, the casual amour of Glenn Blake, Sabrina's fiancé (and *not* the French author), sees him at a church wedding and speculates: 'Dan Butler . . . Hmmm . . . I'll bet he's good in bed'.

Hope Cox is the protagonist of *Bride of the Wind*. 'Could any man tame her wild, wanting heart?' teases the novel's paperback cover. It is, in fact, Hope herself who uses sex (or, more accurately, sexual teasing) to tame not only the jailer who can free her father Pap, the married minister who can get her the money to buy a small newspaper, indeed the whole Mafia-like Cheyenne Ring. Although Hope does not travel as far, geographically, as do Blake's other heroines—she moves from the Texas wastelands to the Powder River near Cheyenne—she travels incredibly far politically, from being the 16-year-old daughter of the drunken, lazy Pap to owning her own ranch, being named justice of the peace for the area, and finally being elected governor of the state of Wyoming. In the meantime, of course, she falls in love with the green-eyed Irishman, Timothy O'Callahan, who likewise adores her ('I could forget the Auld Sod sooner than I could forget you'). The novel ends with Tim in jail for his explosive contempt-of-court defence of his beloved's purity, and Hope being sworn in as governor:

> 'What is the first thing you are going to do in office, Governor Mason?' a reporter asked when the ceremony was over.
> 'My first action will be to order the Cheyenne Club closed down as a hazard to public health and safety', Hope said. 'After that, I'm going to . . . '
> Timothy lifted his handcuffed wrist and shook it, a comical expression of pleading on his face.
> '. . . And then I'm going to get married to a prisoner in the city jail', Hope finished, slanting her laughing turquoise eyes upward to meet Tim's ardent green gaze.

Blaze of Passion tracks another fiery woman from 19th-century England to a penal colony in Australia. *Secret Sins* details the adventures of three generations of Tate women 'from the watery wreckage of the Titanic to the bottomless maelstrom of the Bermuda Triangle'. *Wicked Is My Flesh* combines the eruption of Mauna Loa, the San Francisco Fire, and a Swiss avalanche. *Fires of the Heart* follows Dawn Price (who 'hides her passionate nature beneath a rough, tomboy exterior') from the backwoods of Michigan to the Far East. It ends with Dawn and her lumberjack husband Jack in their bed in a New York City hotel suite where they decide to return to Michigan.

Texas Lily follows cinnamon-haired Lily Dewar from her home in Titusville, Pennsylvannia, to Beaumont, Texas. The time is 1859, and people like old family friend Colonel Drake see Texas as:

> . . . The bowels of this great country. It is populated by barbarians and half-breeds, none of whom have the slightest idea of what civilized behaviour is all about. I tell you this—it is no place for a woman of your breeding and upbringing.

However, Lily has read about Texas, impressed with 'some of the people who've made their mark there'. She goes there, builds an oil empire 'beyond compare', but also sacrifices 'her innocence and true desire to the men who masked their greed in all-consuming love'.

In *This World Is Mine*, green-eyed beauty Holly Cavendish travels to America from the streets of London; becomes a reporter for the *San Francisco Herald*, gaining local prominence, and a job from Horace Greeley; she risks her life to expose corruption in New York City; campaigns for women's suffrage with Susan B. Anthony; and, of course, finds the all-consuming love for which her heart has longed.

Samantha West, also emerald-eyed, and daughter of Sir Robert West, chairman of the British East India Company, is sent to live with her brother, John, minister of the First Church in Salem, Massachusetts. She is tried for witchcraft and sentenced to hang, but is miraculously rescued by her lover, the handsome Raymond Grant, and his colourful acquaintance, Captain Kidd.

Under his other pseudonym, Jack Pearl, Jacques Bain Pearl has written a number of westerns, biographies, and general histories, and his interest in and wide knowledge of historical figures and events shines through in Stephanie Blake's fleshy and fiery historical romances.

—Marcia G. Welsh

BLAND, Jennifer.   See **BARCLAY, Tessa.**

BLAYNE, Diana.   See **PALMER, Diana.**

BLOOM, Ursula (Harvey).
Pseudonyms: Sheila Burns; Mary Essex; Rachel Harvey; Deborah Mann; Lozania Prole; Sara Sloane. **Nationality:** British. **Born:** Chelmsford, Essex, in 1893. **Relations:** married 1) Arthur Brownlow Denham-Cookes in 1916 (died 1918), one son; 2) Charles Gower Robinson in 1925 (died 1979). **Career:** crime reporter, *Empire News* and *Sunday Dispatch*, London; beauty editor, *Woman's Own*; staff member, *Sunday Pictorial*. **Recipient:** Fellow, Royal Historical Society. **Died:** 29 October 1984.

ROMANCE AND HISTORICAL PUBLICATIONS

Novels

The Great Beginning. London, Hutchinson, 1924.
Vagabond Harvest. London, Hutchinson, 1925.
The Driving of Destiny. London, Hutchinson, 1925.
Our Lady of Marble. London, Hutchinson, 1926.
The Judge of Jerusalem. London, Harrap, 1926.
Spilled Salt: The Story of a Spy. London, Hutchinson, 1927.
Candleshades: The Story of a Soul. London, Hutchinson, 1927; New York, Watt, 1928.
Base Metal: The Story of a Man. London, Hutchinson, 1928; as *Veneer*, New York, Watt, 1929.

An April After. London, Hutchinson, 1928.
To-morrow for Apricots. London, Hutchinson, 1929; as *The Eternal Tomorrow*, New York, Watt, 1929.
Tarnish. London, Hutchinson, 1929.
The Secret Lover. London, Hutchinson, 1930; New York, Dutton, 1931.
The Passionate Heart. London, Hutchinson, 1930; Canoga Park, California, Major, 1978.
The Gossamer Dream. London, Hutchinson, 1931.
Pack Mule. London, Hutchinson, 1931; New York, Dutton, 1932.
Trackless Way. London, Hurst and Blackett, 1931.
Fruit on the Bough: The Story of a Brother and Sister. London, Hutchinson, 1931; as *Flood of Passion*, New York, Dutton, 1932.
The Pilgrim Soul. London, Hutchinson, 1932.
Breadwinners. London, Hutchinson, 1932.
The Cypresses Grow Dark. London, Hutchinson, 1932.
Love's Playthings. London, Hutchinson, 1932.
The Log of a Naval Officer's Wife. London, Hurst and Blackett, 1932.
Rose Sweetman. London, Hutchinson, 1933.
Spread Wings. London, Hutchinson, 1933.
Better to Marry. New York, Dutton, 1933.
Wonder Cruise. London, Hutchinson, 1933; New York, Dutton, 1934.
Enchanted Journey. London, Hutchinson, 1933.
Love Is Everything. London, Hutchinson, 1933; as *Love, Old and New*, New York, Dutton, 1933.
Mediterranean Madness. London, Hutchinson, 1934.
The Questing Trout. London, Hutchinson, 1934.
Pastoral. London, Hutchinson, 1934.
Young Parent. London, Hutchinson, 1934.
This Is Marriage. London, Hutchinson, 1935.
Harvest of a House. London, Hutchinson, 1935.
The Gipsy Vans Come Through. London, Hutchinson, 1936.
The Laughing Lady. London, Collins, 1936.
Laughter in Cheyne Walk. London, Collins, 1936; Philadelphia, Lippincott, 1937.
Marriage of Pierrot. London, Cherry Tree, 1936.
Three Cedars. London, Collins, 1937.
Leaves Before the Storm. London, Rich and Cowan, 1937.
The Golden Venture. London, Rich and Cowan, 1938.
Lily-of-the-Valley. London, Rich and Cowan, 1938.
The Brittle Shadow. London, Readers Library, 1938.
Beloved Creditor. London, Cassell, 1939.
These Roots Go Deep. London, Cassell, 1939.
Trailing Glory. London, Hale, 1940.
The Woman Who Was To-morrow. London, Cassell, 1940.
The Flying Swans. London, Cassell, 1940.
Spring in September. London, Hale, 1941.
Silver Orchids. London, Hale, 1941.
The Virgin Thorn. London, Cassell, 1941.
Dinah's Husband. London, Cassell, 1941.
The Golden Flame. London, Hale, 1941.
Age Cannot Wither. London, Cassell, 1942.
Lovely Shadow. London, Cassell, 1942.
Marriage in Heaven. London, Hale, 1943.
A Robin in a Cage. London, Cassell, 1943.
Nightshade at Morning. London, Mellifont Press, 1944.
The Fourth Cedar. London, Cassell, 1944.
The Painted Lady. London, Macdonald, 1945.
The Faithless Dove. London, Cassell, 1945.
Three Sons. London, Macdonald, 1946.
A Garden for My Child. London, Gifford, 1946.
Adam's Daughters. London, Macdonald, 1947.
Alien Corn. London, Hamish Hamilton, 1947.
Facade. London, Macdonald, 1948.

Next Tuesday. London, Macdonald, 1949.
Gipsy Flower. London, Hale, 1949.
The King's Wife. London, Hutchinson, 1950; Canoga Park, California, Major, 1979.
Eleanor Jowitt, Antiques. London, Macdonald, 1950.
The Song of Philomel. London, Macdonald, 1950.
How Dark, My Lady! A Novel Concerning the Life of William Shakespeare. London, Hutchinson, 1951.
Pavilion. London, Hutchinson, 1951.
Nine Lives. London, Macdonald, 1951.
Orange Blossom for Sandra. London, Hale, 1951.
The Sentimental Family. London, Macdonald, 1951.
As Bends the Bough. London, Macdonald, 1952.
Twilight of a Tudor. London, Hutchinson, 1952; New York, White Lion, 1976.
Moon Song. London, Hale, 1953.
Sea Fret. London, Hutchinson, 1953.
Marriage of Leonora. London, Hale, 1953.
The First Elizabeth. London, Hutchinson, 1953.
Matthew, Mark, Luke, and John. London, Hutchinson, 1954.
Daughters of the Rectory. London, Hutchinson, 1955.
The Gracious Lady. London, Hutchinson, 1955.
The Girl Who Loved Crippen. London, Hutchinson, 1955.
The Silver Ring. London, Hutchinson, 1955.
The Tides of Spring Flow Fast. London, Hutchinson, 1956.
Brief Springtime. London, Hutchinson, 1957.
The Abiding City. London, Hutchinson, 1958.
Monkey Tree in a Flower Pot. London, Hutchinson, 1958.
Undarkening Green. London, Undarkening, 1959.
The Romance of Charles Dickens. London, Hale, 1960.
The Thieving Magpie. London, Hutchinson, 1960.
The Cactus Has Courage. London, Hutchinson, 1961.
Prelude to Yesterday. London, Hutchinson, 1961; Los Angeles, Pinnacle, 1978.
Harvest-Home Come Sunday. London, Hutchinson, 1962.
Ship in a Bottle. London, Hutchinson, 1962.
The Gated Road. London, Hutchinson, 1963.
The Ring Tree. London, Hutchinson, 1964.
The House That Died Alone. London, Hutchinson, 1964.
The Quiet Village. London, Hutchinson, 1965.
The Ugly Head. London, Hutchinson, 1965.
The Dandelion Clock. London, Hutchinson, 1966.
The Old Adam. London, Hutchinson, 1967.
Two Pools in a Field. London, Hutchinson, 1967.
Yesterday's Tomorrow. London, Hutchinson, 1968; Canoga Park, California, Major, 1978.
The Dragonfly. London, Hutchinson, 1968.
The Flight of the Falcon. London, Hutchinson, 1969.
The Hunter's Moon. London, Hutchinson, 1969.
The Tune of Time. London, Hutchinson, 1970.
Perchance to Dream. London, Hutchinson, 1971.
The Caravan of Chance. London, Hutchinson, 1971.
Edwardian Day-Dream. London, Hutchinson, 1972.
The Cheval Glass. London, Hutchinson, 1973.
The Old Rectory. London, Hutchinson, 1973.
Mirage on the Horizon. London, Hutchinson, 1974; Canoga Park, California, Major, 1979.
The Old Elm Tree. London, Hutchinson, 1974.
The Twisted Road. London, Hutchinson, 1975.
The Turn of Life's Tide. London, Hutchinson, 1976.
The House on the Hill. London, Hutchinson, 1977.
The Fire and the Rose. Canoga Park, California, Major, 1977.
The Woman Doctor. London, Hutchinson, 1978.
Bittersweet. Canoga Park, California, Major, 1978.
Born for Love. Canoga Park, California, Major, 1978.
Mirage of Love. Canoga Park, California, Major, 1978.

Sunday Love. Canoga Park, California, Major, 1978.
A Change of Heart. Canoga Park, California, Major, 1979.
Forever Autumn. Canoga Park, California, Major, 1979.
Gypsy Flame. Canoga Park, California, Major, 1979.
Honor's Price. Canoga Park, California, Major, 1979.
The Queen's Affair. Canoga Park, California, Major, 1979.
Sweet Spring of April. Canoga Park, California, Major, 1979.

Novels as Sheila Burns

The Passionate Adventure. London, Cassell, 1936.
Dream Awhile. London, Cassell, 1937.
Take a Chance. London, Cassell, 1937.
Honeymoon Island. London, Cassell, 1938.
Lady! This Is Love! London, Cassell, 1938.
Week-end Bride. London, Cassell, 1939.
Wonder Trip. London, Cassell, 1939.
Adventurous Heart. London, Cassell, 1940.
Meet Love on Holiday. London, Cassell, 1940.
Romance Is Mine. London, Cassell, 1941.
The Stronger Passion. London, Cassell, 1941.
Bridal Sweet. London, Cassell, 1942; as *Bride Alone*, New York,
    Arcadia House, 1943.
Thy Bride Am I. London, Cassell, 1942.
Romantic Fugitive. London, Cassell, 1943; New York, Arcadia
    House, 1944.
Romance of Jenny W.R.E.N. London, Cassell, 1944; as *Jenny
    W.R.E.N.*, New York, Arcadia House, 1945.
Vagrant Lover. London, Macdonald, 1945.
Hold Hard, My Heart. London, Macdonald, 1946.
Bride—Maybe. London, Macdonald, 1946.
Desire Is Not Dead. London, Macdonald, 1947.
The Chance Romance. London, Eldon Press, 1948.
Air Liner. London, Eldon Press, 1948.
To-morrow Is Eternal. London, Macdonald, 1948.
Faint with Pursuit. London, Eldon Press, 1949.
No Trespassers in Love. London, Macdonald, 1949.
The Cuckoo Never Weds. London, Eldon Press, 1950.
Primula and Hyacinth. New York, Arcadia House, 1950.
Not Free to Love. London, Eldon Press, 1950; as *Heaven Lies Ahead*
    (as Sara Sloane), New York, Arcadia House, 1951.
Hold Back the Heart. New York, Arcadia House, 1951.
Rosebud and Stardust. London, Eldon Press, 1951.
Live Happily—Love Song. London, Eldon Press, 1952.
Love Me To-morrow. London, Eldon Press, 1952.
Romantic Intruder. London, Hutchinson, 1952.
Tomorrow We Marry. London, Hutchinson, 1953.
Beloved and Unforgettable. London, Hutchinson, 1953.
Please Burn after Reading. London, Hutchinson, 1954.
How Dear Is My Delight! London, Hutchinson, 1955.
Adventure in Romance. London, Hutchinson, 1955.
Romantic Summer Sea. London, Hutchinson, 1956.
The Sweet Impulse. London, Hutchinson, 1956.
How Rich Is Love? London, Hurst and Blackett, 1957.
The Beloved Man. London, Hurst and Blackett, 1957.
This Dragon of Desire. London, Hurst and Blackett, 1958.
The Storm Bird. London, Hurst and Blackett, 1959.
The Lasting Lover. London, Hurst and Blackett, 1959.
Doctor Gregory's Partner. London, Hurst and Blackett, 1960.
Doctor to the Rescue. London, Hurst and Blackett, 1961.
The Disheartened Doctor. London, Hale, 1961.
Dr Irresistible, M.D. London, Hale, 1962.
The Eyes of Doctor Karl. London, Hale, 1962.
Heartbreak Surgeon. London, Hale, 1963.
Theatre Sister in Love. London, Hale, 1963.
When Doctors Love. London, Hale, 1964.

Doctor's Distress. London, Digit, 1964.
Doctor Delightful. London, Hale, 1964.
Doctor Called David. London, Hale, 1966.
Doctor Divine. London, Hale, 1966.
A Surgeon's Sweetheart. London, Hale, 1966.
The Beauty Surgeon. London, Hale, 1967.
The Flying Nurse. London, Hale, 1967.
Romantic Cottage Hospital. London, Hale, 1967.
The Dark-eyed Sister. London, Hale, 1968.
Casualty Ward. London, Hale, 1968.
Acting Sister. London, Hale, 1968.
Surgeon at Sea. London, Hale, 1969.
The Nurse Who Shocked the Matron. London, Hale, 1970.
Sister Loving Heart. London, Hale, 1971.
Cornish Rhapsody. London, Hale, 1972.
Romance and Nurse Margaret. London, Hale, 1972.
The Bells Still Ring. London, Hale, 1976.

Novels as Mary Essex

Haircut for Samson. London, Chapman and Hall, 1940.
Nesting Cats. London, Chapman and Hall, 1941.
Eve Didn't Care. London, Chapman and Hall, 1941.
Marry to Taste. London, Chapman and Hall, 1942.
Freddy for Fun. London, Chapman and Hall, 1943.
The Amorous Bicycle. London, Chapman and Hall, 1944.
Divorce? Of Course. London, Chapman and Hall, 1945.
Young Kangaroos Prefer Riding. London, Chapman and Hall, 1947.
Domestic Blister. London, Chapman and Hall, 1948.
Six Fools and a Fairy. London, Jenkins, 1948.
Full Fruit Flavour. London, Jenkins, 1949.
The Herring's Nest. London, Jenkins, 1949.
An Apple for the Doctor. London, Jenkins, 1950.
Tea Is So Intoxicating. London, Jenkins, 1950.
Dark Gentleman, Fair Lady. London, Jenkins, 1951.
A Gentleman Called James. London, Jenkins, 1951.
She Had What It Takes. London, Jenkins, 1952.
Forty Is Beginning. London, Jenkins, 1952.
Danielle, My Darling. London, Dakers, 1954.
The Passionate Springtime. London, Hale, 1956.
Forbidden Fiancé. London, Hale, 1957.
The Dark Lover. London, Hale, 1957.
A Nightingale Once Sang. London, Hale, 1958.
It's Spring, My Heart! London, Hale, 1958.
Romance of Summer. London, Hale, 1959.
This Man Is Not for Marrying. London, Hale, 1959.
The Fugitive Romantic. London, Hale, 1960.
The Love Story of Duke. London, Hale, 1960.
A Sailor's Love. London, Hale, 1961.
Doctor on Call. London, Hale, 1961.
Date with a Doctor. London, Hale, 1962.
Dr Guardian of the Gate. London, Hale, 1962.
Nurse from Killarney. London, Hale, 1963.
A Strange Patient for Sister Smith. London, Hale, 1963.
The Sangor Hospital Story. London, Hale, 1963.
The Hard-Hearted Doctor. London, Hale, 1964.
Doctor and Lover. London, Hale, 1964.
Dare-Devil Doctor. London, Hale, 1965.
Romantic Theatre Sister. London, Hale, 1965.
Hospital of the Heart. London, Hale, 1966.
The Little Nurse. London, Hale, 1967.
The Romance of Dr Dinah. London, Hale, 1967.
Assistant Matron. London, Hale, 1967.
The Adorable Doctor. London, Hale, 1968.
The Ghost of Fiddler's Hill. London, Hale, 1968.
The Sympathetic Surgeon. London, Hale, 1968.

Doctor on Duty Bound. London, Hale, 1969.
When a Woman Doctor Loves. London, Hale, 1969.
The Dangerous Doctor. London, Hale, 1970.
Heart Surgeon. London, Hale, 1971.
The Fascinating Doctor. London, Hale, 1972.
The Nurse Who Fell in Love. London, Hale, 1972.
A Nurse Called Liza. London, Hale, 1973.
The Dark Farm. London, Hale, 1974.
A Doctor's Love. London, Hale, 1974.

Novels as Lozania Prole

Our Dearest Emma. London, Museum Press, 1949; as *The Magnificent Courtesan*, New York, McBride, 1950; as *Emma Hart*, Toronto, Harlequin, 1951.
Pretty, Witty Nell! London, Hale, and New York, McGraw Hill, 1953; as *The Fabulous Nell Gwynne*, Toronto, Harlequin, 1954; as *Sweet Nell*, London, Corgi, 1965.
To-night, Josephine! London, Hale, and New York, McGraw Hill, 1954.
The King's Pleasure. London, Hale, and New York, McGraw Hill, 1954.
The Enchanting Courtesan. London, Hale, 1955; New York, Pocket Books, 1975.
My Wanton Tudor Rose: The Love Story of Lady Katheryn Howard. London, Hale, 1956.
The Little Victoria. London, Hale, 1957.
A Queen for England. London, Hale, 1957.
Harry's Last Love. London, Hale, 1958.
The Stuart Sisters. London, Hale, 1958.
Consort to the Queen. London, Hale, 1959.
The Little Wig-Maker of Bread Street. London, Hale, 1959.
For Love of the King. London, Hale, 1960.
The Tudor Boy. London, Hale, 1960.
The Queen's Midwife. London, Hale, 1961.
My Love! My Little Queen! London, Hale, 1961.
A King's Plaything. London, Hale, 1962.
Queen Guillotine. London, Hale, 1962.
The Ghost That Haunted a King. London, Hale, 1963.
The Wild Daughter. London, Hale, 1963.
Daughter of the Devil. London, Hale, 1963; New York, Pocket Books, 1974.
Henry's Golden Queen. London, Hale, 1964.
The Three Passionate Queens. London, Hale, 1964.
Marlborough's Unfair Lady. London, Hale, 1965.
The Haunted Headsman. London, Hale, 1965.
The Dangerous Husband. London, Hale, 1966.
Nelson's Love. London, Hale, 1966.
The Dark-Eyed Queen. London, Hale, 1967; New York, Pocket Books, 1976.
King Henry's Sweetheart. London, Hale, 1967.
The Queen Who Was a Nun. London, Hale, 1967.
The Greatest Nurse of Them All. London, Hale, 1968.
Prince Philanderer. London, Hale, 1968.
The Loves of a Virgin Princess. London, Hale, 1968.
Sweet Marie-Antoinette. London, Hale, 1969; New York, Pocket Books, 1973.
The Boutique of the Singing Clocks. London, Hale, 1969.
The Enchanting Princess. London, Hale, 1970.
The Last Tsarina. London, Hale, 1970.
Judas Iscariot—Traitor! London, Hale, 1971.
A Queen for the Regent. London, Hale, 1971.
The Two Queen Annes. London, Hale, 1971; New York, Pocket Books, 1973.
The Orange Girl. London, Hale, 1972.
The Ten-Day Queen. London, Hale, 1972.

Taj Mahal, Shrine of Desire. London, Hale, 1972.
The Queen's Daughters. London, Hale, 1973.
Albert the Beloved. London, Hale, 1974.
The Last Love of a King. London, Hale, 1974.
The Lass a King Loved. London, Hale, 1975.
The King's Daughter. London, Hale, 1975.
When Paris Fell. London, Hale, 1976.

Novels as Deborah Mann (series: Christ Trilogy)

The Woman Called Mary. London, Hale, 1960; as *A Woman Called Mary*, London, Corgi, 1966; (as Ursula Bloom) London, Severn House, 1978.
Christ Trilogy:
    Now Barabbas Was a Robber. London, Corgi, 1968; (as Ursula Bloom) London, Severn House, 1977.
    The Song of Salome. London, Corgi, 1969; (as Ursula Bloom) London Severn House, 1978.
    Pilate's Wife. London, Corgi, 1976; (as Ursula Bloom) London, Severn House, 1978.

Novels as Rachel Harvey

The Village Nurse. London, Hurst and Blackett, 1967.
Dearest Doctor. London, Hurst and Blackett, 1968.
Weep Not for Dreams. London, Hale, 1968.
The Little Matron of the Cottage Hospital. London, Hale, 1969.
Darling District Nurse. London, Hale, 1970.
Nurse on Bodmin Moor. London, Hale, 1970.
Doctor Called Harry. London, Hale, 1971.
Sister to a Stranger. London, Hale, 1971.
Love Has No Secrets. London, Hale, 1972.
The Gipsy Lover. London, Hale, 1973.
The Doctor Who Fell in Love. London, Hale, 1974.
The Love Story of Nurse Julie. London, Hale, 1975.

Short Stories

Tiger. Privately printed, 1903(?).
Winifred. Privately printed, 1903.
Girlie. Privately printed, 1904.
The Cherry Hat. Privately printed, 1904.
Crazy Quilt: A Volume of Stories. London, Hutchinson, 1933.
Wartime Beauty. London, Todd, 1943.

OTHER PUBLICATIONS

Plays

A Paymaster in Every Family. London, French, 1943.
One Wedding, Two Brides. London, French, 1943.
What's in a Name? A Nativity Play. London, French, 1947.
Displaced Person. London, French, 1948.

Radio Plays

Dog Collar series, 1961, 1963; *Way Through the Wilderness*, 1962; *The Mother*, 1964; *Jean Meadows, Vet* series, 1964; *Green Finger*, 1965; and others.

Other

A Lamp in the Darkness: A Series of Essays on Religion. London, Hutchinson, 1930; Los Angeles, Corwin, 1978.
Mistress of None (autobiography). London, Hutchinson, 1933.
Holiday Mood. London, Hutchinson, 1934.
Without Make-Up. London, Joseph, 1938.

The ABC of Authorship. London, Blackie, 1938; Philadelphia, Westminster, 1973.

A Cad's Guide to Cruising. London, Rich and Cowan, 1938.

Letters to My Son. London, Cassell, 1939.

The Log of No Lady, Being the Story of a London Woman Evacuated Before the Outbreak of War. London, Chapman and Hall, 1940.

The Housewife's Beauty Book. London, Hale, 1941.

Time, Tide and I. London, Chapman and Hall, 1942.

No Lady Buys a Cot. London, Chapman and Hall, 1943.

No Lady in Bed. London, Chapman and Hall, 1944.

Me—After the War: A Book for Girls Considering the Future. London, Gifford, 1944.

The Changed Village. London, Chapman and Hall, 1945.

The Little Fir Tree (for children). London, Hutchinson, 1945.

Rude Forefathers. London, Macdonald, 1945.

Questions Answered about Knitting [*Beauty*]. London, Jordan, 2 vols, 1945–46.

Ursula's Cook Book for the Woman Who Has No Time to Spare. London, Gifford, 1946.

You and Your Holiday [*Child, Home, Dog, Looks, Life, Fun, Needle*]. London, Gifford, 8 vols, 1946–50.

No Lady with a Pen. London, Chapman and Hall, 1947.

No Lady Meets No Gentleman. London, Low, 1947.

Pumpkin the Pup (for children). London, Hutchinson, 1947.

Smugglers Cave (for children). London, Riddle, 1947.

Caravan for Three (for children). London, University of London Press, 1947.

Cookery. London, Foyle, 1949.

No Lady in the Cart. London, Low, 1949.

Three Girls Come to Town (for children). London, Macdonald, 1950.

Mum's Girl Was No Lady. London, Convoy, 1951.

New World round the Corner. London, British Rubber Development Board, 1951.

For the Bride. London, Museum Press, 1952.

Trilogy (autobiography). London, Hutchinson, 1954.

No Lady on the Spree. London, Hutchinson, 1954.

Curtain Call for the Guv'nor: A Biography of George Edwardes. London, Hutchinson, 1954.

The Girls' Book of Popular Hobbies. London, Burke, 1954; New York, Roy, 1956.

Hitler's Eva. London, Hutchinson, 1954.

No Lady Has a Dog's Day A Casual Book of Reminiscences. London, Hutchinson, 1956.

Victorian Vinaigrette (autobiography). London, Hutchinson, 1956.

The Elegant Edwardians (autobiography). London, Hutchinson, 1957.

Down to the Sea in Ships (autobiography). London, Hutchinson, 1958.

He Lit the Lamp: A Biography of Professor A.M. Low. London, Burke, 1958.

Wanting to Write: A Complete Guide for Would-Be Writers. London, Stanley Paul, 1958.

The Inspired Needle. London, Hurst and Blackett, 1959.

Youth at the Gate (autobiography). London, Hutchinson, 1959.

Sixty Years of Home. London, Hurst and Blackett, 1960.

War Isn't Wonderful (autobiography). London, Hutchinson, 1961.

Mrs Bunthorpe's Respects: A Chronicle of Cooks. London, Hutchinson, 1963.

Parson Extraordinary. London, Hale, 1963.

The Rose of Norfolk. London, Hale, 1964.

Price Above Rubies. London, Hutchinson, 1965.

Rosemary for Stratford-on-Avon. London, Hale, 1966.

The Mightier Sword. London, Hale, 1966.

A Roof and Four Walls. London, Hale, 1967.

The House of Kent. London, Hale, 1969.

Rosemary for Frinton. London, Hale, 1970.

The Great Tomorrow. London, Hale, 1971; New York, Zebra, 1978.

Rosemary for Chelsea. London, Hale, 1971.

The Duke of Windsor. London, Hale, 1972.

Requesting the Pleasure. London, Hale, 1973.

Princesses in Love. London, Hale, 1973.

The Royal Baby. London, Hale, 1975.

Life Is No Fairy Tale (autobiography). London, Hale, 1976.

The Great Queen Consort. London, Hale, 1976.

Edward and Victoria. London, Hale, 1977.

Editor, *Woman's Annual 1951.* London, Elek, 1950.

*   *   *

Ursula Bloom was a woman of rare quality, a great professional, whose writing career spanned many decades. From childhood she wanted to write and began with a children's story, *Tiger*, privately printed when she was seven-years-old. Marie Corelli helped her, and one of her stories was given to Prince Edward and his sister, Princess Mary. Always keenly interested in people, she was a natural reporter, though women were frowned on in that profession in the years after World War I. She covered the Crippen murder story which was later used as part of one of her books, as was her coverage of the Ruth Ellis case.

One of the most prolific authors in the country, Bloom is credited in the *Guinness Book of Records* with 500 full-length titles by 1975. Her first novel, appropriately called *The Great Beginning*, and a bestseller, told of a young 'slip of a girl who passionately desired motherhood', but whose scheming mother married her to a man whose ancestry, filled with a dreaded disease, denied her children. But in true romantic fiction style she finds love and there is a happy ending. This success was followed with many romances with a simple boy meets girl theme. Bloom has drawn on her own experience for many of her characters and settings: time spent in hospitals, for instance, was used in her popular hospital tales.

Romantic novels with memorable titles (*An April After*—after what?) soon filled the shelves. She was proud of her family, especially her gypsy forebear (*The Rose of Norfolk*), and this gave her accurate background when writing about gypsies in stories such as *Gipsy Flower* and *The Caravan of Chance*.

Always an adventurous and energetic writer, Ursula Bloom would tackle any hurdle. She wrote stories, articles, beauty counselling, plays, biographies of her family, autobiographies, and works on the Royal Family. There were books of memory on places such as Stratford-on-Avon where much of her childhood was spent, and she always retained her knowledge and love of the works of Shakespeare. Chelsea took on a new look under her penmanship, and she wrote cookery books and others. Sheila Burns, Mary Essex, Deborah Mann were among the pseudonyms she used for her romances, Burns for the hospital stories, Essex for modern romances, and Mann for historical tales, though at first she used her own name for romances.

In all her books she wrote with a transparent honesty that shines through her lines, setting down life as she experienced it, without varnish. In many ways, her personal life was unusual, tinged with sadness, pain and suffering, grief and pleasure, and she could write with ease about all of those experiences. Maybe her upbringing in a vicarage had an effect, for her heroines were always chaste, though to be fair so were most heroines of the period. She was ever helpful to others—again her 'parish' caring background—and was an agony columnist and wrote much on religion, God, and death for a Sunday paper, collecting material from all over the country, indulging herself in reporting. Bloom could write movingly on conditions in the Welsh coal valleys where lack of work created social problems.

Her book *The Secret Lover* was a new departure, a diary telling of an old bachelor hermit who had been an old roué with a secret love in his imagination. The idea of the editor of the former *Sunday Dispatch* for her to write a historical novel, to be first serialized in the paper, was the forerunner of much success. It was decided that a book on Lady Hamilton would launch the series, and *Our Dearest Emma* was the result. It tells the story of one of the country's most notorious, most forgiven women, and Bloom's simple style of telling that tale without lurid details makes it a historical classic to this day. *Our Dearest Emma* was written under a new pseudonym, Lozania Prole, and began a long series of historical novels. She chose to write many biographical novels of famous women, Nell Gwynn, Florence Nightingale, Mrs Fitzherbert, Hitler's Eva, Ethel Le Neve; the French Revolution and Regency Brighton formed the background for many of these stirring, robust books.

A resourceful worker, Bloom devoted her life to keeping the wheels of authorship turning with hospital life, light romances, historical novels, and biographies of herself and others. When writing of her own life, her family, her mother (one of her most moving books, *Price Above Rubies*), she spared nothing, and the reader joined her when buying a house, living in the country or with the Edwardians. Essentially honest, she never held back from her readers, and they lived again with her the days of poverty, selling possessions, finding a bargain, and the problems of a struggling writer. She had a deep sense of awareness of religion. This is often hidden, as with so many children of the vicarage, though she wrote of religious characters, often unusual ones—Judas Iscariot, Barabbas—and a moving story of the Taj Mahal revealing a depth of sensitivity not often revealed in light romances.

—Lornie Leete-Hodge

BOLTON, Elizabeth. See **ST JOHN, Nicola.**

BORDEN, Mary.

Pseudonym: Bridget Maclagan. **Nationality:** American. Settled in England after her second marriage. **Born:** Chicago, Illinois, 15 May 1886. **Education:** Vassar College, Poughkeepsie, New York, B.A. 1907. **Relations:** married 1) George Douglas Turner; 2) Sir Edward Spears in 1918; two daughters and one son. **Career:** director of French field hospitals in both World Wars; resided in England after marriage; official hostess at British legations, Beirut and Damascus, 1942–44; script writer for *Saturday Night Theatre*, BBC Radio, London. **Awards:** Légion d'honneur; Croix de Guerre with bar and palm. **Died:** 2 December 1968.

ROMANCE AND HISTORICAL PUBLICATIONS

Novels

The Tortoise. New York, Knopf, 1921.
Jane—Our Stranger. London, Heinemann, and New York, Knopf, 1923.
The Technique of Marriage. London, Heinemann, 1924; New York, Doubleday Doran, 1933.
Three Pilgrims and a Tinker. London, Heinemann, and New York, Knopf, 1924.
Jericho Sands. London, Heinemann, 1925; New York, Knopf, 1926.
Flamingo; or, The American Tower. London, Heinemann, and New York, Doubleday Page, 1927.

Jehovah's Day. London, Heinemann, 1928; New York, Doubleday Doran, 1929.
A Woman with White Eyes. London, Heinemann, and Doubleday Doran, 1930.
Sarah Defiant. New York, Doubleday Doran, 1931.
Sarah Gay. London, Heinemann, 1931.
Mary of Nazareth. London, Heinemann, and Doubleday Doran, 1933.
The King of the Jews. London, Heinemann, 1935; as *King of the Jews*, New York, Little Brown, 1935.
Action for Slander. London, Heinemann, 1936; New York, Harper, 1937.
The Black Virgin. London, Heinemann, 1937; as *Strange Week-end*, New York, Harper, 1938.
Passport for a Girl. London, Heinemann, and New York, Harper, 1939.
No 2 Shovel Street. London, Heinemann, 1949.
For the Record. London, Heinemann, 1950; as *Catspaw*, New York, Longmans Green, 1950.
Martin Merriedew. London, Heinemann, 1952; as *You, The Jury*, New York, Longman, 1952.
Margin of Error. London, Heinemann, 1952; New York, Longman, 1954.
The Hungry Leopard. London, Heinemann, and New York, Longman, 1956.

Novels as Bridget Maclagan

The Mistress of Kingdoms or Smoking Wax. London, Duckworth, 1912.
Collision. London, Duckworth, 1913.
The Romantic Lady. London, Constable, 1916; (as Mary Borden) New York, Knopf, 1920; (as Mary Borden-Turner) London, Heinemann, 1924.

OTHER PUBLICATIONS

Short Stories

Four O'clock and Other Stories. London, Heinemann, 1926; New York, Doubleday Page, 1927.

Other

The Forbidden Zone (autobiography). London, Heinemann, 1929; New York, Doubleday Doran, 1930.
Man, Proud Man, with E.M. Delafield, and Susan Ertz. London, Hamilton, 1932.
Journey Down a Blind Alley (autobiographical). London, Hutchinson, 1946.

*

Film Adaptation: *Action for Slander*, 1937.

*   *   *

Mary Borden was an American who settled in England on her marriage to an English officer. Borden served in French field hospitals in both World Wars, and received commendations for her bravery. She used the experience and knowledge gained through her hospital work, and her knowledge of British political life as a background to several of her novels. Borden wrote in a tightly scripted style, every word carefully chosen to evoke the right feeling and atmosphere. Whether set in a courtroom (*Action for Slander*), or in

Vienna after the annexation of Austria (*Passport for a Girl*), her books have intricate backgrounds against which her characters can act out their parts.

Passport for a Girl is probably one of Borden's most interesting books. Set against World War II, it tells the love story of April, an English girl from an aristocratic and politically powerful family, and Hans Hartmann, an Austrian Jew. However, more importantly it gives a good insight into British attitudes to the rise of Nazism. The political background to the annexation of Austria and Britain's reaction to it is seen through the eyes of Hag Goodchild, a British diplomat who has 'hands-on' experience of the machinations of the government.

April, Hag's stepdaughter, goes to Vienna and falls in love with Hans, a journalist and a political dissident wanted by the Nazis. Borden contrasts the experiences of Hag and Christine, who don't believe that there will be a war, and Hans and April, experiencing the tension and danger firsthand. Written in 1939, *Passport for a Girl* is an extremely interesting book with copious detail about the politics and war of the time. The love of Hans and April defies boundaries, fascism, and war—and the reader knows if Hans dies in the concentration camp April would rather die than live without him.

Sarah Gay is a different kind of love story, dealing with an adulterous love. It begins in France in 1918, and the story revolves around the strong love between Sarah and John. While working for the French Red Cross (like Borden herself) Sarah meets and falls in love with John Gay, and gives up her marriage, her reputation, and her children for him. The couple live in Paris until she has to return to England when her child becomes ill. Circumstances prevent her from returning to Paris, and John begins an affair with someone else. Sarah tries to shoot his lover but the couple end up marrying at the end of the book. The male characters in *Sarah Gay* are unappealing: George is weak, boring, flaccid; John is charming, feckless, and unfaithful. Sarah comes out of this book well, but only after she has shown herself to have some moral fibre, staying in England because of her children, her nurse, and her husband.

For the time that she was writing in, Borden introduces seemingly risqué subjects—passion, affairs, and sexual relationships are discussed honestly and openly. She tackles a particularly sensitive subject in *Collision*, when, writing as Bridget Maclagan, she introduces the subject of interracial love and marriage. Imogen, a socialist, comes to India wanting to meet real Indian men and women, and ends up falling in love with a married English man. Their relationship ends when his wife falls ill, and Imogen realizes that she really wants Choula, an Indian doctor. Ironically, she offers herself to him as a workmate and life-partner, but Choula says: ' . . . intermarriage is revolting to my taste for the fitness of things . . . And you', he was saying, 'wanted to do it because it was, you thought, a brave and daring thing to do'.

Illicit love affairs are also featured in many of Borden's other books. In *Action for Slander*, the story revolves around a court case in which Major Daviot has been accused of cheating at cards—Daviot is actually having an affair with the wife of the man that accused him of cheating.

In addition to books set in the war and love stories, Borden also produced two very interesting and very ambitious books, *Mary of Nazareth* and *The King of the Jews*. The first book, *Mary of Nazareth* is based on the life of Jesus and his mother according to the four gospels. Borden also wrote a couple of autobiographical books about her life in France during the war, and an interesting sociological study on marriage.

—P. Campbell

BOURNE, Lesley.   See **MARSH, Jean.**

BOWDEN, Jean.   See **BARCLAY, Tessa.**

BOWEN, Marjorie.
Pseudonym for Gabrielle Margaret Vere Campbell. **Other Pseudonyms:** Robert Paye; George Preedy; Joseph Shearing; John Winch. **Nationality:** British. **Born:** Hayling Island, Hampshire, 29 October 1886. **Relations:** married 1) Zeffrino Emilio Costanzo in 1912 (died 1916), one son; 2) Arthur L. Long in 1917, two sons. **Died:** 23 December 1952.

<small>ROMANCE AND HISTORICAL PUBLICATIONS</small>

Novels (series: Renaissance Trilogy; William III Trilogy)

The Viper of Milan. London, Alston Rivers, and New York, McClure Phillips, 1906.
The Glen o' Weeping. London, Alston Rivers, 1907; as *The Master of Stair*, New York, McClure Phillips, 1907.
The Sword Decides! London, Alston Rivers, and New York, McClure, 1908.
Black Magic: A Tale of the Rise and Fall of Antichrist. London, Alston Rivers, 1909.
The Leopard and the Lily. New York, Doubleday, 1909; London, Methuen, 1920.
William III Trilogy:
    I Will Maintain. London, Methuen, 1910; New York, Dutton, 1911; revised edition, London, Penguin, 1943.
    Defender of the Faith. London, Methuen, and New York, Dutton, 1911.
    God and the King. London, Methuen, 1911; New York, Dutton, 1912.
Lovers' Knots. London, Everett, 1912.
The Quest of Glory. London, Methuen, and New York, Dutton, 1912.
The Rake's Progress. London, Rider, 1912.
The Soldier from Virginia. New York, Appleton, 1912; as *Mister Washington*, London, Methuen, 1915.
The Governor of England. London, Methuen, 1913; New York, Dutton, 1914.
A Knight of Spain. London, Methuen, 1913.
The Two Carnations. London, Cassell, and New York, Reynolds, 1913.
Prince and Heretic. London, Methuen, 1914; New York, Dutton, 1915.
Because of These Things ... . London, Methuen, 1915.
The Carnival of Florence. London, Methuen, and New York, Dutton, 1915.
William, By the Grace of God—. London, Methuen, 1916; New York, Dutton, 1917; abridged edition, Methuen, 1928.
The Third Estate. London, Methuen, 1917; New York, Dutton, 1918; revised edition, as *Eugénie*, London, Fontana, 1971.
The Burning Glass. London, Collins, 1918; New York, Dutton, 1919.
Kings-at-Arms. London, Methuen, 1918; New York, Dutton, 1919.
Mr Misfortunate. London, Collins, 1919.
The Cheats. London, Collins, 1920.
The Haunted Vintage. London, Odhams Press, 1921.
Rococo. London, Odhams Press, 1921.
The Jest. London, Odhams Press, 1922.
Affairs of Men (selections from novels). London, Cranton, 1922.

Stinging Nettles. London, Ward Lock, and Boston, Small Maynard, 1923.
The Presence and the Power. London, Ward Lock, 1924.
Five People. London, Ward Lock, 1925.
Boundless Water. London, Ward Lock, 1926.
Nell Gwyn: A Decoration. London, Hodder and Stoughton, 1926; as *Mistress Nell Gwyn*, New York, Appleton, 1926.
Five Winds. London, Hodder and Stoughton, 1927.
The Pagoda: Le Pagode de Chanteloup. London, Hodder and Stoughton, 1927.
The Countess Fanny. London, Hodder and Stoughton, 1928.
Renaissance Trilogy:
    The Golden Roof. London, Hodder and Stoughton, 1928.
    The Triumphant Beast. London, Lane, 1934.
    Trumpets at Rome. London, Hutchinson, 1936.
Dickon. London, Hodder and Stoughton, 1929.
The English Paragon. London, Hodder and Stoughton, 1930.
The Devil's Jig (as Robert Paye). London, Lane, 1930.
Brave Employments. London, Collins, 1931.
Withering Fires. London, Collins, 1931.
The Shadow on Mockways. London, Collins, 1932.
Dark Rosaleen. London, Collins, 1932; Boston, Houghton Mifflin, 1933.
Passion Flower. London, Collins, 1932; as *Beneath the Passion Flower* (as George Preedy), New York, McBride, 1932.
Idlers' Gate (as John Winch). London, Collins, and New York, Morrow, 1932.
Julia Roseingrave (as Robert Paye). London, Benn, 1933.
I Dwelt in High Places. London, Collins, 1933.
Set with Green Herbs. London, Benn, 1933.
The Stolen Bride. London, Lovat Dickson, 1933; abridged edition, London, Mellifont Press, 1946.
The Veil'd Delight. London, Odhams Press, 1933.
A Giant in Chains: Prelude to Revolution—France 1775–1791. London, Hutchinson, 1938.
Trilogy:
    God and the Wedding Dress. London, Hutchinson, 1938.
    Mr Tyler's Saints. London, Hutchinson, 1939.
    The Circle in the Water. London, Hutchinson, 1939.
Exchange Royal. London, Hutchinson, 1940.
Today Is Mine. London, Hutchinson, 1941.
The Man with the Scales. London, Hutchinson, 1954.

Novels as George Preedy

General Crack. London, Lane, and New York, Dodd Mead, 1928.
The Rocklitz. London, Lane, 1930; as *The Prince's Darling*, New York, Dodd Mead, 1930.
Tumult in the North. London, Lane, and New York, Dodd Mead, 1931.
The Pavilion of Honour. London, Lane, 1932.
Violante: Circe and Ermine. London, Cassell, 1932.
The Devil Snar'd. London, Benn, 1932.
Dr Chaos, and The Devil Snar'd. London, Cassell, 1933.
Double Dallilay. London, Cassell, 1933; as *Queen's Caprice*, New York, King, 1934.
The Autobiography of Cornelius Blake, 1773–1810, of Ditton See, Cambridgeshire. London, Cassell, 1934.
Laurell'd Captains. London, Hutchinson, 1935.
The Poisoners. London, Hutchinson, 1936.
My Tattered Loving. London, Jenkins, 1937; as *The King's Favourite* (as Marjorie Bowen), London, Fontana, 1971.
Painted Angel. London, Jenkins, 1938.
The Fair Young Widow. London, Jenkins, 1939.
Dove in the Mulberry Tree. London, Jenkins, 1939.
Primula. London, Hodder and Stoughton, 1940.

Black Man—White Maiden. London, Hodder and Stoughton, 1941.
Findernes' Flowers. London, Hodder and Stoughton, 1941.
Lyndley Waters. London, Hodder and Stoughton, 1942.
Lady in a Veil. London, Hodder and Stoughton, 1943.
The Fourth Chamber. London, Hodder and Stoughton, 1944.
Nightcap and Plume. London, Hodder and Stoughton, 1945.
No Way Home. London, Hodder and Stoughton, 1947.
The Sacked City. London, Hodder and Stoughton, 1949.
Julia Ballantyne. London, Hodder and Stoughton, 1952.

Novels as Joseph Shearing

Forget-Me-Not. London, Heinemann, 1932; as *Lucile Cléry*, New York, Harper, 1932; as *The Strange Case of Lucile Cléry*, Harper, 1941.
Album Leaf. London, Heinemann, 1933; as *The Spider in the Cup*, New York, Smith and Haas, 1934.
Moss Rose. London, Heinemann, 1934; New York, Smith and Haas, 1935.
The Golden Violet: The Story of a Lady Novelist. London, Heinemann, 1936; New York, Smith and Durrell, 1941; as *Night's Dark Secret* (as Margaret Campbell), New York, New American Library, 1975.
Blanche Fury; or, Fury's Ape. London, Heinemann, and New York, Harrison Hilton, 1939.
Aunt Beardie. London, Hutchinson, and New York, Harrison Hilton, 1940.
Laura Sarelle. London, Hutchinson, 1940; as *The Crime of Laura Sarelle*, New York, Smith and Durrell, 1941.
The Fetch. London, Hutchinson, 1942; as *The Spectral Bride*, New York, Smith and Durrell, 1942.
Airing in a Closed Carriage. London, Hutchinson, and New York, Harper, 1943.
The Abode of Love. London, Hutchinson, 1945.
For Her to See. London, Hutchinson, 1947; as *So Evil My Love*, New York, Harper, 1947.
Mignonette. New York, Harper, 1948; London, Heinemann, 1949.
Within the Bubble. London, Heinemann, 1950; as *The Heiress of Frascati*, New York, Berkley, 1966.
To Bed at Noon. London, Heinemann, 1951.

Short Stories

God's Playthings. London, Smith Elder, 1912; New York, Dutton, 1913.
Shadows of Yesterday: Stories from an Old Catalogue. London, Smith Elder, and New York, Dutton, 1916.
Curious Happenings. London, Mills and Boon, 1917.
Crimes of Old London. London, Odhams Press, 1919.
The Pleasant Husband and Other Stories. London, Hurst and Blackett, 1921.
Seeing Life! and Other Stories. London, Hurst and Blackett, 1923.
The Seven Deadly Sins. London, Hurst and Blackett, 1926.
Dark Ann and Other Stories. London, Lane, 1927.
The Gorgeous Lover and Other Tales. London, Lane, 1929.
Sheep's-Head and Babylon, and Other Stories of Yesterday and To-day. London, Lane, 1929.
Old Patch's Medley; or, A London Miscellany. London, Selwyn and Blount, 1930.
Bagatelle and Some Other Diversions (as George Preedy). London, Lane, 1930; New York, Dodd Mead, 1931.
Grace Latouche and the Warringtons: Some Nineteenth-Century Pieces, Mostly Victorian. London, Selwyn and Blount, 1931.
Fond Fancy and Other Stories. London, Selwyn and Blount, 1932.
The Last Bouquet: Some Twilight Tales. London, Lane, 1932.
The Knot Garden: Some Old Fancies Re-Set (as George Preedy). London, Lane, 1933.

Orange Blossoms (as Joseph Shearing). London, Heinemann, 1938.
The Bishop of Hell and Other Stories. London, Lane, 1949.
Kecksies and Other Twilight Tales. Sauk City, Wisconsin, Arkham House, 1976.

OTHER PUBLICATIONS

Plays as George Preedy

Captain Banner (produced London, 1929). London, Lane, 1930.
A Family Comedy, 1840 (as Marjorie Bowen). London, French, 1930.
The Question. London, French, 1931.
The Rocklitz (produced London, 1931).
Rose Giralda (produced London, 1933).
Court Cards (produced London, 1934).
Royal Command (produced Wimbledon, Surrey, 1952).

Screenplay: *The Black Tulip* (as Marjorie Bowen), 1921.

Other

Luctor et Emergo, Being an Historical Essay on the State of England at the Peace of Ryswyck. Newcastle upon Tyne, Northumberland Press, 1925.
The Netherlands Display'd; or, The Delights of the Low Countries. London, Lane, 1926; New York, Dodd Mead, 1927.
Holland, Being a General Survey of the Netherlands. London, Harrap, 1928; New York, Doubleday, 1929.
The Winged Trees (for children). Oxford, Blackwell, 1928.
The Story of the Temple and Its Associations. London, Griffin Press, 1928.
Sundry Great Gentlemen: Some Essays in Historical Biography. London, Lane, and New York, Dodd Mead, 1928.
William, Prince of Orange, Afterwards King of England, Being an Account of His Early Life. London, Lane, and New York, Dodd Mead, 1928.
The Lady's Prisoner (for children). Oxford, Blackwell, 1929.
Mademoiselle Maria Gloria (for children). Oxford, Blackwell, 1929.
The Third Mary Stuart, Being a Character Study with Memoirs and Letters of Queen Mary II of England 1662–1694. London, Lane, 1929.
Exits and Farewells, Being Some Account of the Last Days of Certain Historical Characters. London, Selwyn and Blount, 1930.
Mary, Queen of Scots, Daughter of Debate. London, Lane, 1934; New York, Putnam, 1935.
The Scandal of Sophie Dawes. London, Lane, 1934; New York, Appleton Century, 1935.
Patriotic Lady: A Study of Emma, Lady Hamilton, and the Neapolitan Revolution of 1799. London, Lane, 1935; New York, Appleton Century, 1936.
The Angel of Assassination: Marie-Charlotte de Corday d'Armont, Jean-Paul Marat, Jean-Adam Lux: Three Disciples of Rousseau (as Joseph Shearing). London, Heinemann, and New York, Smith and Haas, 1935.
Peter Porcupine: A Study of William Cobbett 1762–1835. London, Longman, 1935; New York, Longman, 1936.
William Hogarth, The Cockney's Mirror. London, Methuen, and New York, Appleton Century, 1936.
Crowns and Sceptres: The Romance and Pageantry of Coronations. London, Long, 1937.
The Lady and the Arsenic: The Life and Death of a Romantic, Marie Capelle, Madame Lafarge (as Joseph Shearing). London, Heinemann, 1937; New York, A.S. Barnes, 1944.

This Shining Woman: Mary Wollstonecraft Godwin 1759–1797 (as George Preedy). London, Collins, and New York, Appleton Century, 1937.
Wrestling Jacob: A Study of the Life of John Wesley and Some Members of His Family. London, Heinemann, 1937; abridged edition, London, Watts, 1948.
World's Wonder and Other Essays. London, Hutchinson, 1938.
The Trumpet and the Swan: An Adventure of the Civil War (for children). London, Pitman, 1938.
The Debate Continues, Being the Autobiography of Marjorie Bowen, by Margaret Campbell. London, Heinemann, 1939.
Ethics in Modern Art (lecture). London, Watts, 1939.
Child of Chequer'd Fortune: The Life, Loves, and Battles of Maurice de Saxe, Maréchal de France (as George Preedy). London, Jenkins, 1939.
Strangers to Freedom (for children). London, Dent, 1940.
The Life of John Knox (as George Preedy). London, Jenkins, 1940.
The Life of Rear-Admiral John Paul Jones 1747–1792 (as George Preedy). London, Jenkins, 1940.
The Courtly Charlatan: The Enigmatic Comte de St Germain (as George Preedy). London, Jenkins, 1942.
The Church and Social Progress: An Exposition of Rationalism and Reaction. London, Watts, 1945.
In the Steps of Mary, Queen of Scots. London, Rich and Cowan, 1952.

Editor, *Great Tales of Horror.* London, Lane, 1933.
Editor, *More Great Tales of Horror.* London, Lane, 1935.
Editor, *Some Famous Love Letters.* London, Jenkins, 1937.

*   *   *

Most of Margaret Campbell's books, under whichever pseudonym she wrote, are historical novels about real people or romances set in the past. Many of her crime novels either use period settings or are imaginative reconstructions of historical crimes. *My Tattered Loving (The King's Favourite)*, for instance, is a fictionalized account of the celebrated 17th-century Overbury murder.

Her historical novels as Marjorie Bowen are usually fictional biographies, and strongly partisan. She portrays Richard III in *Dickon* as a perfect mediaeval knight, *sans peur, sans reproche* (but let us not forget he was a contemporary of the Borgias). Her Richard could never have killed his brother Clarence, or Henry VI, much less the Princes in the Tower, although the book shys away from this last issue. Her Richard is physically attractive—no mention of a withered arm or hunchback here. In *The Governor of England* she portrays Cromwell as a compassionate private man who nevertheless believes that he has a divine mission and so reluctantly concludes that the king's death is necessary. Indeed Bowen seems to have held low opinions of all the Stuarts bar one. She draws a harsh portrait of James I slobbering and fawning in *The King's Favourite*, she refers to Charles II as a man who would but for his birth 'have spent his life as a tavern idler buying his indulgences with his quips', and James II she castigates as 'a pompous dull bigot—vain, sensuous and arrogant and to a curious degree cruel'. Her great hero is William II, one of our dullest kings, little loved by his English subjects, who had little liking for England. Even her partisan writing fails to hide the fact that William only accepted the English crown as a means of vanquishing Louis XIV. Her trilogy on William's life, *I Will Maintain, Defender of the Faith,* and *God and the King,* shows this clearly. The first book covers his early years up to the Dutch Revolution of 1672 when he became Stadtholder; the second relates how he reluctantly married his cousin, the English princess Mary, fought Louis, and drew Holland together. The third book is about his time as King of England and shows his frustrations dealing with the English who disliked him. Bowen is above all William's apologist—she even tries to absolve him of any guilt for the Massacre of Glencoe in *The Glen o' Weeping*, but hardly convinces this reader. So fond was she of William and of Holland that, besides several nonfiction books on the subject, she also wrote about William III's ancestor William the Silent in *Prince and Heretic* and *William by the Grace of God—*.

Bowen often featured revolution in her books. *A Giant in Chains* is about the causes of the French revolution of 1789; *Forget-Me-Not* (as Joseph Shearing) concerns France in 1848 in the last days of Louis Philippe. *Dark Rosaleen* tells of the ill-fated Irish uprising of 1798; in it she draws a sympathetic portrait of Edward Fitzgerald, the idealistic younger son of one of Ireland's most important families who, influenced by the French revolution, was anxious to set Ireland free from English oppression. Because he was too noble and selfless to see or expect treachery, he died—not untypically for a Bowen book, for she dearly loved a doom-laden plot—seldom for her the happy ending. In her romances she created unhappy people and loaded the dice against them. *The Viper of Milan*, her first and probably most famous book (written when she was 17), is set in her version of 14th-century Italy. The chief character (one can hardly call one so infamous 'hero') is the cruel, ruthless Visconti, ruler of Milan who kills or maims every member of his family, betrays his allies, and even kills his own true love. *Findernes' Flowers* (as George Preedy) and *The Rake's Progress* are typical of her light romances: both are set in the 18th century and tell of doomed families and star-crossed lovers; both have sad endings heavy with wasted lives.

Her historical backgrounds are full of well-researched details with rich descriptions of period clothes, but her style is too florid for today's taste and her dialogue is the most serious stumbling block for the modern reader, being full of 'fair sirs', beseeching 't'were', and 'wert'. Immensely popular in her own day, her books are rather neglected nowadays, for modern readers prefer faster moving stories and a lighter touch. Her characterization lacks depth, and the thoughts and motives attributed to her characters (especially in the romances) are a little superficial, although her historical judgments are usually sound when she is not gripped by bias.

—Pamela Cleaver

BOWLING, Harry.
Nationality: British. **Born:** Bermondsey, London. **Relations:** married. **Career:** joined the merchant navy. Various jobs. **Address:** c/o Headline Book Publishing, Headline House, 79 Great Titchfield Street, London W1P 7FN, England.

Romance and Historical Publications

Novels

Conner Street's War. London, Headline, 1987.
Ironmonger's Daughter. London, Headline, 1989.
Tuppence to Tooley Street. London, Headline, 1989.
Paragon Place. London, Headline, 1990.
Gaslight in Page Street. London, Headline, 1991.
The Girl from the Cotton Lane. London, Headline, 1992.
Backstreet Child. London, Headline, 1993.
Pedlar's Row. London, Headline, 1994.

*   *   *

Harry Bowling has made a powerful impact on the field of fiction, breaking several moulds while aiming squarely at the popular saga market. Firstly, he defied the notorious prejudice publishers have

against dialect. Perhaps because 'Eastenders' (the popular British soap) had created a national familiarity with London speech, overlaying an ever widening veneer of Estuary English on our language, Headline (his publishers) decided to take the risk. It paid off. The books are highly successful, in spite of the admitted slowing of the reading pace which printed dialect imposes. When faced with less familiar letter combinations the reader is obliged to subvocalize at least initially but with practice and persistence it soon becomes second nature.

The second sacred cow he kills is adherence to a single dominant theme, unless the overall story of a community counts. It should, because the result of Bowling's work is the unique distillation of the spirit of an urban village in which disparate groups, concurrently interdependent and aggressively interactive, cohere into a discrete, vibrant whole. The greater the threat to the cohesion the more vehemently the community fights for its life and its values. While he does have a romantic element in each novel, well aware that sagas are read mainly by women who, in turn, are purported by publishers to require romance, it is just one of many strands and by no means always the strongest or most dominant. Many threads are used, dark and light, strong and gentle, brittle or forever binding, interweaving with the complexity of real life. Touches of more distant colour are added, snatched from the tails of passing events, say in the big city markets, in the hopfields or hospitals, on the warfront, at sea, in Wales, Australia or any other place to which Bermondsey youth fled, determined to leave behind the poverty and struggle of their origins but mindful still of the folk they left behind.

He also defies convention by telling his tale from different points of view. As a result we pop in and out of almost every house or business in the street and become privy to the secret joys and anguish of every individual taking part in the action. We are treated to a double focus on events by having an inside motivation from the main protagonists as well as an overall external view— or views because everybody has an opinion. This is a difficult and dangerous technique, but magnificently handled, by accident or design. Bowling has the raconteur's gift of maintaining his listener's interest in every character he introduces and absorbing him in every tale he has to tell. He keeps his multifarious strands distinct and vivid. Each character is wholly credible and consistent, even when carried through more than one book, while nevertheless developing and changing as people do in reality as they react to aging and experience.

In one respect Bowling is gloriously typical of Cockneyland which possesses a very special brand of humour, rooted in banter and comic, kindly tormenting, frequently involving unfortunate misadventure adroitly managed, or mismanaged if you are on the receiving end of a prank. Ill-will is decried, despised, and distrusted. The ability to distil this quality into words and evoke outright laughter is rare and precious. He uses it with liberal Shakespearian judiciousness, leavening pathos and tragedy with fun. Different types of humour seem reserved for different groups of people. The young lads romp wickedly together but tease the girls with more care. The old biddies snipe slyly about any of their number who is absent, knowing their own turn will come. Old hands prepare all manner of gleeful pitfalls for the unsuspecting new boy. In fiction as in reality it is humour which carries these citizens through poverty, adversity and despair, even through the terrors and deprivations of war; the humour always hovers just beneath the surface, and is an essential ingredient in these most English of English people who are neither good nor bad but a thoroughly humane mixture of both. Without the humour, one feels, they would give up, so great is their burden.

The double focus in observation is found also in the overall impression the author leaves with us. A community is not static. It must change over the years, developing, maturing, deteriorating, progressing, in response to social and civic pressures. Perceptions modulate, values readjust, the old order changeth for better and for worse. From inside, the characters push and pull to have their own particular way with varying degrees of success. Interference from beyond stirs the pot into eddies unplanned or unforeseen, however the inhabitants or their external influences may try to manage matters. Bowling has created a precious record of his own community in the process of change during the past century, albeit while using fictional inhabitants. In doing so he is preserving in a most entertaining form knowledge gleaned from oral reservoirs, particularly vulnerable to loss. The results will surely be of permanent value as a social documentation of 20th-century community life in London's docklands.

—Margaret Woodward

———

BOX, Edgar.   See **VIDAL, Gore.**

———

BOYD, James.
Nationality: American. **Born:** Harrisburg, Pennsylvania, 2 July 1888. **Education:** Hill School, Pottstown, Pennsylvania, 1901–06; Princeton University, New Jersey 1906–10, B.A. 1910; Trinity College, Cambridge, 1910–12. **Military Service:** served in the New York Infantry, 1916, as a Red Cross volunteer, 1917, and in the United States Army Ambulance Service, in Italy and France, 1917–19: lieutenant. **Relations:** married Katharine Lamont in 1917; two sons and one daughter. **Career:** staff writer and cartoonist, Harrisburg *Patriot*, 1910; teacher of English and French, Harrisburg Academy, 1912–14; member of the editorial staff, *Country Life in America*, New York, 1916; settled on a farm in Southern Pines, North Carolina, 1919; owner and editor, Southern Pines *Pilot*, 1941–44. Founder and first National Chairman, Free Company of Players, 1941. **Recipient:** honorary degree: University of North Carolina, Chapel Hill, 1938. **Member:** American Academy, 1937; Society of American Historians, 1939. **Died:** 25 February 1944.

ROMANCE AND HISTORICAL PUBLICATIONS

Novels

Drums. New York, Scribner, 1925; London, Unwin, 1928.
Marching On. New York, Scribner, 1927; London, Heinemann, 1928.
Long Hunt. New York, Scribner, 1930; London, Jarrolds, 1931.
Roll River. New York, Scribner, 1935; London, Jarrolds, 1936.
Bitter Creek. New York, Scribner, 1939; London, Heinemann, 1940.

Short Stories

Old Pines and Other Stories. Chapel Hill, University of North Carolina Press, 1952.

OTHER PUBLICATIONS

Play

One More Free Man (broadcast 1941). Published in *The Free Company Presents*, edited by Boyd, New York, Dodd Mead, 1941.

Radio Play: *One More Free Man*, 1941.

Poetry

Eighteen Poems. New York, Scribner, 1944.

Other

Mr Hugh David MacWhirr Looks after His $1.00 Investment in the Pilot Newspaper (sketches). Southern Pines, North Carolina, The Pilot, 1943.

Editor, *The Free Company Presents: A Collection of Plays about the Meaning of America*. New York, Dodd Mead, 1941.

*

Critical Study: *James Boyd* by David E. Whisnant, New York, Twayne, 1972.

*   *   *

How significant is the central event to the success of a work of historical fiction? The American Civil War has provided the inspiration for several masterpieces, along with a list of books amounting to one a day since its battles ceased. By contrast, the American Revolution, for all its importance in world history, has failed to generate a single memorable work. James Boyd's endeavours with both of these monumental conflagrations provide a perspective not only on his own fiction, but also point up suggestions why a war largely confined to the southern United States shapes a global imagination, while the conflict which to a large effect served to separate Europe from the Americans remains a musty domain inhabited principally by historians and biographers.

Curiously, *Drums*, Boyd's treatment of, what is called by Americans, the War of Independence, is much better known than *Marching On*, which deals with the same family several generations later during the Civil War. *Marching On* still points up issues which were permanently to seize the mind of the young protagonist and which continue as passionate topics to the current day.

> James Fraser was listening now, fascinated and scandalized. These folks mixed up salvation, liquor, parsons and niggers in their talk—made a kind of joke of heaven, anyhow got fun out of talking about heaven—like it was any other place. No good would come of that.

Loosely paraphrased, themes of religion, race, utopia, leaders, and private passions first penetrate the mind through casual eavesdropping, expand into gossip, then take hold as ambition and livelihood, and sometimes embroil the fascinated in destructive conflicts in which the one-time entertained onlookers become the sacrificial pawns of maniacal designs.

Somehow the often meandering, sometimes unwieldy structures of Boyd's books place the reader in a situation similar to that of the cast of characters. Like the reader, the figures which appear from page to page seem swept along by circumstance. While it is true they retain a recognizable degree of self-determination, seldom sacrificing principle or surrendering quirks of personality, their principal function turns out to be spectators to grim, if sometime heroic events. Dr Clapton, who occupies a minor role in *Drums*, is a committed scholar and a promising author, one whose devotion to art and learning is unshakeable. Yet the war takes as its tithe not only his life, but also destroys the work dedicated to a posterity whose ranks have also been abbreviated by the ravages of sanctioned violence. John Fraser (presumably the great-uncle to James in *Marching On*) is ostensibly an active figure. He becomes a student of the classics, studies in England, takes a quiet but dangerous loyalist position in North Carolina, but ends up fighting the British alongside John Paul Jones on the *Bonhomme Richard*. He evades the permanent attachments of love in a way consistent with the sexually unconcerned heroes of American fiction—Ahab, Huck Finn, Natty Bumppo (and their descendants Dick Tracy, Li'l Abner and

Dagwood Bumstead), who are primarily walking philosophies rather than flesh and blood figures. John Fraser, for all his travels and involvements, remains that perpetual spectator, a feeling but detached extra on the set of a cinematic spectacular. James Fraser of *Marching On* is also an observer of grand if gory events, but there are signs that he wants to be the centre of his own story just as Scarlett O'Hara dominated *Gone with the Wind* and Henry Fleming, in *The Red Badge of Courage*, emerges as perhaps the quintessential character of all Civil War fiction. James is a fiddler, a type of wandering minstrel, even when he remains in one place. He is conscious of ghosts of times past, times he had experienced but was never part of. The girl who occupies his thoughts started out as a voice, not a face or a figure. Eventually, however, the novel concludes with an impending marriage. James is not really a finely drawn character, but there are hints that he could become one. Perhaps it is the ultimate legacy of Civil War figures to seek out the meaning of life in terms of themselves since regional and national ideals proved so devastatingly inhumane. And it is such inward looking self-determination that separates a novel from a treatise. The American Revolution, by contrast, generates the theories which subordinate private lives to epic ideals.

Boyd is more concerned with events and settings than with characters. There is enough in his fiction, however to stimulate the excited status of the onlooker. What he subtracts from his characters he gives in full measure to his readers.

—Leonard R. Mendelsohn

BRADFORD, Barbara Taylor.
Nationality: British. **Born:** Leeds, Yorkshire, 10 May 1933. **Relations:** married Bob Bradley in 1963. **Career:** reporter, 1949–51, and women's editor, 1951–53, *Yorkshire Evening Post*, Leeds; fashion editor, *Woman's Own*, London, 1953–54; columnist, London *Evening News*, 1955–57; freelance editor, London, 1959–62; features editor, *Woman*, London, 1962–64; editor, National Design Center, New York, 1964–65; syndicated columnist, *Newsday*, Long Island, New York, 1966. **Recipient:** honorary degree: Leeds University, 1990. **Address:** 450 Park Avenue South, New York, New York 10003, USA.

ROMANCE AND HISTORICAL PUBLICATIONS

Novels (series: Harte Family)

A Woman of Substance (Harte). New York, Doubleday, 1979; London, Granada, 1980; revised edition (includes new wartime chapter), London, Grafton, 1990.
Voice of the Heart. New York, Doubleday, and London, Granada, 1983.
Hold the Dream (Harte). New York, Doubleday, and London, Granada, 1985.
Act of Will. New York, Doubleday, and London, Grafton, 1986.
To Be the Best (Harte). New York, Doubleday, and London, Granada, 1988.
The Women in His life. London, Grafton, and New York, Random House, 1990.
Remember. London, HarperCollins, 1992.
Angel. London, HarperCollins, 1993.

OTHER PUBLICATIONS

Other

How to Be the Perfect Wife: Entertaining to Please Him [*Etiquette to Please Him, Fashions That Please Him*]. New York, Essandess, 3 vols, 1969–70.
Easy Steps to Successful Decorating. New York, Simon and Schuster, 1971.
How to Solve Your Decorating Problems. New York, Simon and Schuster, 1976.
Decorating Ideas for Casual Living. New York, Simon and Schuster, 1977.
Making Space Grow. New York, Simon and Schuster, 1979.
Luxury Designs for Apartment Living. New York, Doubleday, 1981.

Editor, *Children's Stories of the Bible from the Old Testament.* New York, Lion Press, 1966.
Editor, *Children's Stories of Jesus from the New Testament.* New York, Lion Press, 1966.
Editor, *The Dictionary of One Thousand Famous People*, by Samuel Nisenson. New York, Lion Press, 1966.
Editor, *A Garland of Children's Verse.* New York, Lion Press, 1968.
Editor, *The Complete Encyclopedia of Homemaking Ideas.* New York, Meredith Press, 1968.

*

Film Adaptations: *A Woman of Substance*, 1984; *Hold the Dream*, 1986; *Act of Will*, 1989; *Voice of the Heart*, 1989.

*   *   *

From the moment *A Woman of Substance* reached the shelves of libraries and bookstores, readers were aware that in Barbara Taylor Bradford they had discovered something special. The first of the trilogy of generational novels, it traces the rise of Emma Harte from a pregnant 15-year-old servant to shopkeeper, department store owner, and finally corporate mogul, among the world's richest women. Pain and disappointment temper her success as friends, enemies, and family offer their support, disruption, love and envy to attract the attention and stir the emotions of the reader.

The story continues as Emma seeks to ensure the future of her empire, leaving to granddaughter Paula Fairley her position as head of both the family and business, as well as the dream she worked so hard to establish. Emma's blessing does not guarantee Paula's success, and she must fight both corporate enemies and personal demons in her effort to find happiness and *Hold the Dream*.

The saga of Emma Harte's empire concludes as Paula O'Neill, Emma's protegée and heir, travels from Yorkshire to Australia, New York to Hong Kong battling on both the business and family fronts to maintain her legacy in *To Be the Best*.

In another generational novel, the settings of which move from the Yorkshire Dales to the glamour capitals of the world, Bradford follows the fortunes of Audra Kenton, nurse and mother, determined to ensure a better life for her daughter Christine, whose dreams of becoming an artist are altered by her own determination to repay her mother's sacrifices. When Audra's granddaughter Kyle refuses to have her life dictated by others, it appears that the family's hard-won success will be destroyed, but it is the *Act of Will* which closes the circle of the three women's love, duty, and devotion.

Handsome wealthy, and powerful Sir Maximilian West would seem to have it all, yet he realizes that some facet of his existence is wanting. Having narrowly escaped death, he turns his attention inward, reviewing a life that spans the period from the rise of Nazi Germany to the fall of the Berlin Wall, through a series of loving and tumultuous experiences with *The Women in His Life*.

In *Remember*, it is three years after the death of her fiancé, and television correspondent Nicky Wells seems to have come to terms with her grief and is pleasantly surprised to find her relationship with photographer Clee Donovan developing beyond the bounds of professional camaraderie. Unexpectedly, she then finds herself facing the possibility that her late fiancé, Charles Devereaux, is still alive and embroiled in mysterious operations that could devastate the lives of those who were close to him.

Bradford's novels allow her audience to glimpse the glamorous lives and enjoy the exotic playgrounds of the rich and famous while developing characters who engage the reader's interest and emotions.

—Judith A. Gifford

* * *

BRADLEY, Marion Zimmer. American. 1930—. See 2nd edition, 1990.

* * *

BRADSHAW, Gillian (Marusha). American. 1956—. See 2nd edition, 1990.

* * *

BRAGG, Melvyn.
Nationality: British. **Born:** Carlisle, Cumberland, 6 October 1939. **Education:** Nelson-Thomlinson Grammar School, Wigton, Cumberland, 1950–58; Wadham College, Oxford, 1958–61, M.A. (honours)in modern history, 1961. **Relations:** married 1) Marie-Elisabeth Roche, 1961 (died 1971), one daughter; 2) Catherine Mary Haste, 1973; one daughter, one son. **Career:** worked at BBC Television and Radio from 1961: general trainee, 1961–62; producer on *Monitor*, 1963; BBC2 editor on *New Release* (later *Review*, then *Arena*), *Writers World*, and *Take It or Leave It*, 1964–70; presenter, *In the Picture*, Tyne Tees Television, Newcastle-upon-Tyne, 1971, and *Second House*, 1973–77, and *Read All About It*, 1976–77, BBC, London. Since 1978 editor and presenter, *South Bank Show*, Head of Arts, 1982–90, and since 1990 Controller of Arts, London Weekend Television; since 1988, presenter, *Start the Week*, BBC Radio 4; chairman, Border Television, Carlisle. Since 1969, member, and chairman, 1977–80, Arts Council Literature Panel; President, Northern Arts, 1983–87, and National Campaign for the Arts since 1986. **Recipient:** Writers Guild award for screenplay, 1966; Rhys Memorial prize, 1968; Northern Arts Association prose award, 1970; Silver Pen award, 1970; Broadcasting Guild award, 1984; Ivor Novello award, for musical, 1985; BAFTA Dimbleby award, 1987; R.T.S. Gold medal (for outstanding contribution to television). D.Litt.: University of Liverpool, 1986; University of Lancaster, 1990; D.Univ.: Open University, Milton Keynes, Buckinghamshire, 1988; LL.D.: University of St Andrews, 1993. Fellow, Royal Society of Literature, 1970, and Royal Television Society; Honorary Fellow, Lancashire Polytechnic; Domus Fellow, St Catherine's College, Oxford, 1990. **Address:** 12 Hampstead Hill Gardens, London N.W.3., England.

ROMANCE AND HISTORICAL PUBLICATIONS

Novels (series: Cumbrian Trilogy)

The Cumbrian Trilogy. London, Coronet, 1984.
    The Hired Man. London, Secker and Warburg, 1969; New York, Knopf, 1970.
    A Place in England. London, Secker and Warburg, 1970; New York, Knopf, 1971.
    Kingdom Come. London, Secker and Warburg, 1980.

The Maid of Buttermere. London, Hodder and Stoughton, and New York, Putnam, 1987.
A Time to Dance. London, Hodder and Stoughton, 1990; Boston, Little Brown, 1991.

OTHER PUBLICATIONS

Novels

For Want of a Nail. London, Secker and Warburg, and New York, Knopf, 1965.
The Second Inheritance. London, Secker and Warburg, 1966; New York, Knopf, 1969.
Without a City Wall. London, Secker and Warburg, 1968; New York, Knopf, 1969.
The Nerve. London, Secker and Warburg, 1971.
The Hunt. London, Secker and Warburg, 1971.
Josh Lawton. London, Secker and Warburg, and New York, Knopf, 1972.
The Silken Net. London, Secker and Warburg, and New York, Knopf, 1974.
A Christmas Child (for children). London, Secker and Warburg, 1976.
Autumn Manoeuvres. London, Secker and Warburg, 1978.
Love and Glory. London, Secker and Warburg, 1983.
Crystal Rooms. London, Hodder and Stoughton, 1992.

Plays

Mardi Gras, music by Alan Blaikley and Ken Howard (produced London, 1976).
The Hired Man, adaptation of his own novel, music and lyrics by Howard Goodall (produced Southampton and London, 1984). London, French, 1986.
King Lear, adaptation of Shakespeare's play (produced New York, and Chichester, 1992).

Screenplays: *Play Dirty*, with Lotte Colin, 1968; *Isadora*, with Clive Exton and Margaret Drabble, 1969; *The Music Lovers*, 1970; *Jesus Christ Superstar*, with Norman Jewison, 1973; *A Time To Dance*, 1992.

Radio Play: *Robin Hood*, 1971.

Television Plays: *The Debussy File*, with Ken Russell, 1965; *Charity Begins at Home*, 1970; *Zinotchka*, 1972; *Orion*, music by Ken Howard and Alan Blaikley, 1977; *Clouds of Glory*, with Ken Russell, 1978.

Other

Speak for England: An Essay on England 1900–1975. London, Secker and Warburg, 1976; revised edition, London, Coronet, 1978; as *Speak for England: An Oral History of England 1900–1975*, New York, Knopf, 1977.
Land of the Lakes. London, Secker and Warburg, 1983; New York, Norton, 1984.
Laurence Olivier. London, Hutchinson, 1984; New York, St Martin's Press, 1985.
Abuses of Literacy? with Michael Holroyd. London, Folio Society, 1985.
Rich: The Life of Richard Burton. London, Hodder and Stoughton, 1988; as *Richard Burton: A Life*, Boston, Little Brown, 1989.
The Seventh Seal. London, BFI Film Publications, 1993.

Editor, *My Favourite Stories of Lakeland*. Guildford, Surrey, Littleworth Press, 1981.

Editor, *Cumbria in Verse*. London, Secker and Warburg, 1984.

*   *   *

Melvyn Bragg, a major personality in British television, made his name in a series of powerful serious novels that stand in the line of development from D.H. Lawrence which can perhaps best be categorized as poetic realism. Set in Bragg's native Cumbria for the most part, they tell of the stresses and strains of impoverished working-class life in the present century. *The Maid of Buttermere*, first published in 1987, is rather different in both character and manner.

As its title suggests, *The Maid of Buttermere* is set in that particularly beautiful part of the Lake District, where mountains and two extensive sheets of water combine to create a charming and secluded spot. Though quite well known, Buttermere is, in fact, still somewhat off the beaten tourist track. It seemed far more remote and idyllic, of course, at the beginning of the 19th century, the period when the action of the novel takes place. At that time, thanks partly to the growing fame of the Lake Poets, such as William Wordsworth and Samuel Taylor Coleridge, the region was becoming sufficiently well known to attract comfortably-off visitors who came to admire the picturesque views, but it had not yet been invaded by hordes of holidaymakers and back-packers.

At Buttermere stood an inn. Its name was The Fish, but because of the painting on its sign, it was often called The Char, after the fish that thrives only in the deepest lakes and which had become a delicacy much sought after by fashionable folk in London. It is tempting to see this as a symbol of Mary Robinson, the innkeeper's daughter, who was a noted rural beauty. Even in the capital people had heard about the 'Maid of Buttermere' whose good looks and kindly nature were taken by those who were touched by Sensibility and the early Romantic movement to be in some strange way a reflection of the idyllic surroundings in which it was her lot to live out her untroubled existence.

Complications arise for the Maid of Buttermere with the arrival of a mysterious stranger who turns out to be nothing other than a clever and plausible adventurer with no scruples. We first meet him, significantly enough, making a solitary crossing of the treacherous sands at Morecambe. He is escaping from some threat whose nature is not revealed at the time and which seems all the more menacing for that very reason, and we soon see him assuming an impressive false identity. He has with him a dressing case and a pair of pistols, and he takes the name and style of their former owner, Alexander Augustus Hope, M.P., brother of the wealthy Earl of Hopetoun. Instead of following his original impulse of trying to find a ship that will carry him to safety in America, he decides to seek out what fortune has in store for him in Cumbria, and with this air of distinction and apparently good prospects, he has little difficulty in turning heads.

Bragg, who generally has no difficulty in identifying with the underprivileged classes, reveals that he knows the social history of the Lake District in the first decade of the 19th century as well as its topography when he contrasts the smart world of Colonel Moore and his ward Miss D'Arcy in the town of Keswick with the simpler ways and more modest expectations of Mary in rural surroundings. There are always threats in the background for Hope, particularly from his sinister accomplice, Newton. It seems for a while that he will, however, be able to achieve his aims, but he cannot resist the temptation to over-reach, as indeed he does in picking an identity that was so conspicuous and also so easy to check up on. This was brought home to him when, after proposing to Miss D'Arcy, he was told that there could be no question of such an advantageous marriage until he had furnished adequate proofs of his wealth and family status. While temporizing, he set off to Buttermere, where he had already met Mary while passing through, and proposes to her too. He even harbours the delicious dream of having two wives, 'Miss D'Arcy abroad and Mary at home'.

After an episode at Morecambe involving Newton, Hope returns to the Lake District, making arrangements for his wedding at Keswick with Miss D'Arcy and marrying Mary by special licence in Lorton Church. The newly-weds set off, supposedly for Hopetoun, but scarcely have they crossed the border than Hope insists on returning to Buttermere. Mary begins to realize that her husband is a liar and a rogue, and Colonel Moore is provided with incontrovertible proof that Hope is an impostor. A warrant is issued for his arrest, and after some attempts at escape he is captured. For him the story ends on the gallows, while Mary makes friends with Miss D'Arcy and, after a time, marries a local farmer with whom she lives happily until her death.

The Maid of Buttermere has the scope and passion of the best romances, and the evocation of the period, especially of its social hierarchies and their importance in people's lives, is very satisfying. What is more striking still is the constant intertwining of attested fact and responsibly imagined fiction. At the end of the novel there is a list of 70-odd 'characters based on real people and of the historical figures' who appear in it. This is a work of imaginative fiction, but it is closely linked to real life at every stage. That makes it all the more enthralling, even if you are not already familiar with the story and situations which Bragg brings back to life in a novel written in a style that is striking and has a distinct period flavour.

—Christopher N. Smith

BRANDEWYNE, Rebecca.
Nationality: American. **Born:** Knoxville, Tennessee, 4 March 1955. **Education:** Wichita State University, Kansas, B.A. (cum laude) in journalism, 1975, M.A. in communications, 1979. **Relations:** married Gary D. Brock; one son. **Career:** worked as a secretary; freelance writer in public relations and advertising. **Address:** 2203 Winstead Circle, Wichita, Kansas 67226, USA.

ROMANCE AND HISTORICAL PUBLICATIONS

Novels (series: Chronicles of Tintagel; Highclyffe Hall)

No Gentle Love. New York, Warner, 1980.
Forever My Love. New York, Warner, 1982; London, Severn House, 1992.
Love, Cherish Me. New York, Warner, 1983; London, Panther, 1984.
Rose of Rapture. New York, Warner, and London, Panther, 1984.
And Gold Was Ours. New York, Warner, 1984; London, Grafton, 1986.
The Outlaw Hearts. New York, Warner, 1986; London, Grafton, 1987.
Desire in Disguise. New York, Warner, 1987.
Passion Moon Rising (Chronicles). New York, Pocket Books, 1988.
Upon a Moon-Dark Moor (Highclyffe Hall). New York, Warner, 1988; London, Severn House, 1989.
Across a Starlit Sea (Highclyffe Hall). New York, Warner, 1989; London, Severn House, 1991.
Heartland. New York, Warner, 1990.
Beyond the Starlit Forest (Chronicles). New York, Pocket Books, 1991.
Desperado. New York, Warner, 1992.
Rainbow's End. New York, Warner, and London, Severn House, 1992.

*

Critical Studies: in *Love's Leading Ladies*, by Kathryn Falk, New York, Pinnacle, 1982; *My First Real Romance* edited by Jerry Biederman and Tom Silberkleit, New York, Stein and Day, 1985.

*   *   *

The historical romances of Rebecca Brandewyne have proved extremely popular since the publication of her first novel *No Gentle Love*. This prolific author's poetic style, unique characters, and love of lavish detail provide her readers with many pleasurable hours. Of course the hero and heroine will find their love for each other in the end, but there are many barriers and misunderstandings to overcome. In *No Gentle Love*, the cousins Morgana and Rian are forced into a marriage plotted by their grandfather. Rian, a notorious womanizer, has trouble acknowledging that there can be only one woman in his life while Morgana consistently misreads the actions of her husband even when he does reach out to her. Not until almost the very last page do they discover what the reader has known all along, that yes, indeed, they do love one another. In *Upon a Moon-Dark Moor* the desperately unhappy Maggie and the brooding, half-gypsy hero Draco only gradually come to appreciate and care for one another. The sequel, *Across a Starlit Sea*, tells the story of Draco's niece Laura, who is betrothed to Jarrett but thinks she loves his brother, Nicholas, a spoiled young man who eventually proves himself unworthy of her.

The historical settings for Brandewyne's stories vary widely. *The Outlaw Hearts* takes place in Missouri where Jenny, a young woman with traumatic memories of the Civil War, falls in love with the handsome outlaw Luke Morgan. (A point worth noting is that this heroine is not beautiful but plain and walks with a noticeable limp; hardly standard fare in a romance novel.) In *Upon a Moon-Dark Moor* Maggie grows up a lonely privileged child, in early 19th-century Cornwall. Lady Isabella Ashley (*Rose of Rapture*) lives under the protection of the English king, Richard III. Mary Carmichael, in *Forever My Love*, meets her heart's desire in the highlands of 15th-century Scotland; and Aramita Winthrop, of *Desperado*, finds wild passion and romance in the arms of Mexican revolutionary Rigo de Castillo. *Rainbow's End* takes place in Central City, Colorado, during the late 19th century. In this tale of the wild west Josselyn O'Rourke must find out who caused her father's death. His former partner the roguishly handsome Durango is a prime suspect. When the author researches thoroughly she capably portrays historical events; however, it is painfully obvious when Brandewyne's research is incomplete. The African scenes of *No Gentle Love* have stereotypical natives marauding through the jungle. There is no pretence of trying to convey the horrifying effects of the slave trade on the African people. Thankfully this lapse seems to be the exception rather than the rule in her books.

Brandewyne has a fascination with 'other worldly' events which surfaces from time to time in her works. A ghost haunts the mansion in *No Gentle Love*. Aurora, the heroine of *And Gold Was Ours*, has haunting visions of a lover from a time three centuries before her own. It is, therefore, not surprising that Brandewyne is an author who has successfully combined two genres—romance and fantasy—as she did with the publication of 'The Chronicles of Tintagel'. In Book I, *Passion Moon Rising*, a universal, apocalyptic battle between forces of Light and Darkness has taken place, and the war continues on isolated planets like Tintagel. Here the Lady Ileana sin Ariel carries the power of Light and the hero Lord Cain holds both Light and Darkness within him. In Book II, *Beyond the Starlit Forest*, the war against Darkness continues with Lady Rhiannon and Lord Iskander using their powers to keep evil at bay. The elaborate writing style of these novels is often found in other works of fantasy; yet, it contrasts with the crisper style found in Brandewyne's other novels.

In all of her works this writer is especially good at constructing dialogue, making the conversation sound natural, even witty at times. The breathless prose associated with romance novels is saved for scenes of love and passion. Brandewyne's novels are suffused with energy, intelligence, and passion.

—Patricia Altner

————

BRANDON, Sheila.   See **RAYNER, Claire.**

————

BRENNAN, Frank.   See **DARCY, Emma.**

————

BRENT, Madeleine.
A pseudonym. **Recipient:** Romantic Novelists Association major award, 1978. **Address:** c/o Souvenir Press Ltd, 43 Great Russell Street, London WC1B 3PA, England.

ROMANCE AND HISTORICAL PUBLICATIONS

Novels

Tregaron's Daughter. London, Souvenir Press, and New York, Doubleday, 1971.
Moonraker's Bride. London, Souvenir Press, and New York, Doubleday, 1973.
Kirkby's Changeling. London, Souvenir Press, 1975; as *Stranger at Wildings*, New York, Doubleday, 1976.
Merlin's Keep. London, Souvenir Press, 1977; New York, Doubleday, 1978.
The Capricorn Stone. London, Souvenir Press, 1979; New York, Doubleday, 1980.
The Long Masquerade. London, Souvenir Press, 1981; New York, Doubleday, 1982.
A Heritage of Shadows. London, Souvenir Press, 1983; New York, Doubleday, 1984.
Stormswift. London, Souvenir Press, 1984; New York, Doubleday, 1985.
Golden Urchin. London, Souvenir Press, 1986; New York, Doubleday, 1987.

*   *   *

Madeleine Brent's exciting tales of adventure and travel do for young women what Robert Louis Stevenson's do for young men: provide intrigue and adventure in exotic lands, a dangerous underworld of gypsies, spies, smugglers, fortune hunters, thieves and murderers, and young people trapped, their character tested. Her novels divide into two contrasting sections: the first placing the heroine in an alien world (the London underworld; the circus; the Parisian artist's quarter; Italy; Kafiristan; China; the Caribbean; Hungary; the Dordogne; Tibet; the Australian Outback); the second moving her into proper British society, ending with the two worlds meeting or the first world as lessons providing the basis for social criticism, often gender related, and the means for survival in the second.

Brent's heroines, though modest and self-effacing, are role-models of feminine virtues: daring, determined, resourceful, and spirited but also patient, persistent, and enduring. They have left behind (or never had) the trappings of 'proper' upbringing, see the world with alien eyes, and in fact learn to look with humour on Victorian hypocrisies and proprieties, particularly pretences that ladies are not sexual creatures with hearts and minds. They are honest and warm-hearted, trading innocence and naiveté for the experienced wisdom of heartbreak. They patiently endure social restraints, but yield to their instinct for right: befriending servants and social outcasts, saving children from hunger, cold, abuse, and war. They speak honestly without forethought, but glare like alley cats when angered. Bridie Chance, of *The Capricorn Stone*, is typical. Shocked to learn of her proper Victorian father's lifetime of cat burglary, she suddenly has to fend for herself. Although despairing, she remains cool and competent, deals with lawyers, swallows her pride, and, with time, starts a new life as a comic in a London music hall. Although her new acquaintances would shock her old friends, she quickly adjusts. Her ingenuity helps her finance her talented sister's musical career and overcome her father's depraved partner in crime.

Brent focuses on young girls from pampered, overprotective homes cut off by circumstances from family and friends and plunged into an alien world of degradation, abuse, and hard physical labour. They must face harsh terrain, inclement weather, and barbaric treatment. In *Golden Urchin*, for example, Meg, raised from infancy by an aborigine Australian tribe, has learned to see with aborigine eyes and to survive the scorching desert as huntress. Where many would submit, Brent's heroines discover within themselves a deep-seated fortitude that allows them to bear daily burdens. They are survivors, learning a new culture, a new language, a new way of life, and pride in strength of body and mind. Though battered, they stand up to ruffians, warlords, and chieftains. They defy conventions, becoming social outcasts. When they can, they make their own choices and accept the consequences. When they can't, they do their best within imposed limits. The skills and fortitude developed of necessity later serve them well when returned to their own culture and class. Often this return is precipitated by a handsome but enigmatic man from their own culture, a puzzling mixture of hot and cold, heroic and ignoble, kind and cruel.

In *Moonraker's Bride*, Lucy Waring, for example, born of missionary parents and raised in China, is more Chinese than British in outlook. At a youthful age, she has been responsible for a group of orphans: stretching the rice, protecting the infants, serving as local midwife, and eventually begging and stealing to feed them. When she is arrested for theft, in danger of losing hand or head, a condemned English prisoner funds the bribes necessary to free her, on the condition that they wed, precipitating a move to England and unexpected new dangers. The heroine of *Kirkby's Changeling*, in turn, learns that, instead of heir to a family fortune, she is an unwanted changeling; she runs away with the circus, wins the hearts of a rough-and-ready circus family and learns to be a trapeze artist, who stands up to chauvinistic circus men and wins their respect. In *Stormswift*, Jemimah Lawley, the wealthy heiress of an English estate, sees her parents slaughtered by Afghan soldiers; sold to Hindu traders, then to a mad Kafiristan ruler, she becomes slave to a captured Italian doctor.

Brent's 19th-century heroines all come from a culture that denies their capabilities and their sexuality, that expects upper-class women to be delicate, mindless, and incapable, and that uses them as pawns in power struggles between members of the landed class. Therefore, returning to 'civilization', they find their manners, expectations and values at odds with those of their class and are more comfortable with those outside proper society. Bored by the useless, sedentary life of women of their class, they are disdained by staid conservatives but admired by experienced travellers. Lucy Waring, for example, shocks the family which takes her in when she misunderstands the father's intentions and thinks she is meant to be his concubine (as would be her fate in China), while Jani's trust in the High Lama's prophecies, her belief in reincarnation and demons,

and her communication with animals disturbs her English acquaintances as does Meg's ability to scent strangers and to use a boomerang and spear. Because of their blunt honesty, grim realism, and alien experiences, people dismiss them as liars, but the advice of older males proves invaluable. With time, their virtues are rewarded, their place in society confirmed. Jani, for instance, the heroine of *Merlin's Keep*, though raised as a half-caste orphan in Tibet, turns out to be a deposed Indian princess, whose parents were murdered for their fabled jewels, and other Brent heroines prove heiresses as well.

The romance segment of each story emphasizes deceptive appearances. On the one hand, the young ladies are often courted by handsome, seemingly kindly gentlemen really motivated by desire for an estate, a hidden fortune, an inheritance. On the other hand, these ladies are often assisted by cold, distant, surly gentlemen, with curt manners and questionable motives, who prove reliable when needed and genuinely in love. Emma Delaney, of *The Long Masquerade*, for example, accepts an arranged marriage to the most eligible bachelor in her social circle only to learn he is a malevolent brute; she finds sailing the Caribbean as the deckhand of a former servant a better life. Later a friend's aloof brother, seemingly a gambler and wastrel, proves honourable, protective, and loving. Brent's heroes are no prigs. Often the black sheep of their families, they are experienced men of the world, competent but not always proper. Their heroism sometimes consists of doing the dirty jobs no one else would do, like going native to collect vital military information or gambling professionally to repay a dead father's debts.

Brent's novels are fast-paced, moving from crisis to crisis, danger to danger, with cleverly contrived murder attempts, ambushes, attacks, and battles. Their mysteries grow out of character, with a focus on the deceptive nature of appearances and the mix of good and bad that makes people hard to read, so that in *Stormswift* the most popular, attractive female character, the seeming protector of the heroine, proves the most depraved and in *Moonraker's Bride* it is very difficult to tell which character is the hero and which the villain until the denouement. Like Helen McInnis's spy stories or M.M. Kaye's romances, Brent's novels are artfully drawn portraits of distant lands, which mix danger and intrigue with contrasting details of language, food, manners, and customs—details that grow naturally out of plot and circumstance.

—Gina Macdonald

BRETT, Rosalind. See **BLAIR, Kathryn.**

BRIDGE, Ann.
Pseudonym for Lady Mary Dolling O'Malley. **Nationality:** British. **Born:** Mary Dolling Sanders, in Shenley, Hertfordshire, 11 September 1889. **Education:** London School of Economics, diploma 1913. **Relations:** married Sir Owen St Clair O'Malley in 1913; two daughters and one son. **Career:** secretary, Charity Organization Society, London, 1911–13; British Red Cross representative in Hungary, 1940–41; worked with the Polish Red Cross, 1944–45, and relief worker in France after World War II. Fellow, Society of Antiquaries in Scotland. **Died:** 9 March 1974.

ROMANCE AND HISTORICAL PUBLICATIONS

Novels (series: Julia Probyn in *The Lighthearted Quest* and all books thereafter)

Peking Picnic. London, Chatto and Windus, and Boston, Little Brown, 1932.

The Ginger Griffin. London, Chatto and Windus, and Boston, Little Brown, 1934.

Illyrian Spring. London, Chatto and Windus, and Boston, Little Brown, 1935.

Enchanter's Nightshade. London, Chatto and Windus, and Boston, Little Brown, 1937.

Four-Part Setting. London, Chatto and Windus, and Boston, Little Brown, 1939.

Frontier Passage. London, Chatto and Windus, and Boston, Little Brown, 1942.

Singing Waters. London, Chatto and Windus, 1945; New York, Macmillan, 1946.

And Then You Came. London, Chatto and Windus, 1948; New York, Macmillan, 1949.

The Dark Moment. London, Chatto and Windus, 1951; New York, Macmillan, 1952.

A Place to Stand. London, Chatto and Windus, and New York, Macmillan, 1953.

The Lighthearted Quest. London, Chatto and Windus, and New York, Macmillan, 1956.

The Portuguese Escape. London, Chatto and Windus, and New York, Macmillan, 1958.

The Numbered Account, with Susan Lowndes. London, Chatto and Windus, and New York, McGraw Hill, 1960.

Julia Involved (omnibus). New York, McGraw Hill, 1962.

The Tightening String. London, Chatto and Windus, and New York, McGraw Hill, 1962.

The Dangerous Islands. New York, McGraw Hill, 1963; London, Chatto and Windus, 1964.

Emergency in the Pyrenees. London, Chatto and Windus, and New York, McGraw Hill, 1965.

The Episode at Toledo. New York, McGraw Hill, 1966; London, Chatto and Windus, 1967.

The Malady in Madeira. New York, McGraw Hill, 1969; London, Chatto and Windus, 1970.

Julia in Ireland. New York, McGraw Hill, 1973.

Short Stories

The Song in the House. London, Chatto and Windus, 1936.

OTHER PUBLICATIONS

Other

The Selective Traveller in Portugal, with Susan Lowndes. London, Evans, 1949; New York, Knopf, 1952; revised edition, London, Chatto and Windus, 1958, 1967; New York, McGraw Hill, 1961.

The House of Kilmartin (for children). London, Evans, 1951.

Portrait of My Mother. London, Chatto and Windus, 1955; as *A Family of Two Worlds*, New York, Macmillan, 1955.

Facts and Fictions: Some Literary Recollections. London, Chatto and Windus, and New York, McGraw Hill, 1968.

Moments of Knowing: Some Personal Experiences Beyond Normal Knowledge. London, Hodder and Stoughton, and New York, McGraw Hill, 1970.

Permission to Resign: Goings-On in the Corridors of Power. London, Sidgwick and Jackson, 1971.

*   *   *

In one of her novels Ann Bridge wrote, 'is there any human pleasure much keener than the return after absence to a well-loved place, a place long familiar, full of associations of happiness?' This is the key to her writing, because in each of her books, besides setting in

motion believable characters and exploring a human situation, she uses a place as the mainspring of her work. Her experiences as a diplomatic wife in China gave her the background for *Peking Picnic, The Ginger Griffin, Four-Part Setting* and her best short story 'The Buick Saloon'. Her experiences and the places she visited while *en poste* with her husband are used in *Frontier Passage*, a novel about the Spanish civil war, and *A Place to Stand* and *The Tightening String*, about Hungary in the 1940s. These three are semi-documentaries, blending historical and imaginary happenings. Another 'modern historical novel' is *The Dark Moment*, about the part played by women in Kemal Ataturk's revolution in Turkey. While she was in Turkey she researched it by talking to women who actually took part in the events. *Illyrian Spring*, a story set in former Yugoslavia, actually popularized tourism there, a fact she laughs at, caricaturing herself as Susan Glanfield, the author who achieved this in *Singing Waters*, a novel about Albania which is otherwise a dull, tiresome read with unsympathetic characters.

Usually her characterization is good. She mostly writes about well-bred, upper-class people with money and servants—apart from the occasional highland laird who is terribly poor but so well connected that it does not matter (Glasdeir's well-married daughter in *And Then You Came*, for instance, provides new cars and cattle gates with the wave of a fairy godmother's wand). In most of her books there is a charming middle-aged woman in whom the younger heroine can confide—the middle-aged lady is often the nicest character in the book, and is, one feels, probably based on herself. She usually has several aristocratic men about the place—either strong and silent or sensitive and articulate, and always very capable. Her plots centre on happy and unhappy love affairs set against marvellous descriptions of her beloved places. Her characters are not only concerned about marriage but about making the right sort of marriage, and there is a snobbish preoccupation with money and breeding, which was probably acceptable in the 1930s and 1940s when she wrote but which jars a little today.

Bridge's writing has a leisurely pace and a certain coolness. If occasionally she runs to a purple passage when her characters' emotions are aroused she soon brings them down to earth by sending them into the village to fetch the fish or down to the market to collect flowers to decorate their charming houses. Nothing really nasty ever happens in a Bridge book, although she often puts an illness into the story to give it tension and does not shy away from death but treats it rather sentimentally. Details of her research are sometimes used too fully with an almost teacherly eagerness, but her plots are well thought out and her characters well rounded.

Bridge's later books are a series of romantic thrillers using a basic cast of the same characters centred on her heroine, Julia Probyn (a cool, beautiful journalist who looks dumb but is not), and Julia's charming middle-aged godmother, Mrs Hathaway, who do amateur sleuthing in exotic places among delightful, well-connected people—the strain of snobbery is stronger than ever in this series. *The Lighthearted Quest* has Morocco for its setting and smuggling for its plot, *The Episode at Toledo* and *Emergency in the Pyrenees* are set in Spain and Portugal, *The Numbered Account* takes place in Switzerland and contrasts banking and diplomacy, and *The Dangerous Islands* (like her interesting fantasy book *And Then You Came*) uses the West Highlands of Scotland and archaeology.

All Bridge's books (with the exception of *Singing Waters*) have a great deal of charm, many acute observations on life and people, and are very satisfying to read.

—Pamela Cleaver

BRINDLE, Jane. See **COX, Josephine.**

BRISCO, P.A. See **MATTHEWS, Patricia.**

BRISCO, Patty. See **MATTHEWS, Patricia.**

BRISKIN, Jacqueline.
Nationality: American. **Born:** Jacqueline Orgell, London, England, 18 December 1927. **Educated:** University of California, Los Angeles, 1946–47. **Relations:** married Bert Briskin in 1948; two sons, one daughter. **Career:** writer. **Address:** c/o Delacorte Press, 666 Fifth Avenue, New York, New York 10103, USA.

ROMANCE AND HISTORICAL PUBLICATIONS

Novels

California Generation. London, Blond, and Philadelphia, Lippincott, 1970; as *Decade*, London, Granada, 1981.
Afterlove. New York, Bantam, 1973.
Rich Friends. New York, Delacorte, 1976; London, Granada, 1980.
Paloverde. New York, McGraw-Hill, 1978; London, Hart-Davis MacGibbon, 1979.
The Onyx. New York, Delacorte, and London, Granada, 1982.
Everything and More. New York, Putnam, and London, Granada, 1983.
Too Much, Too Soon. New York, Putnam, and London, Bantam, 1985.
Dreams Are Not Enough. London, Bantam, 1987; New York, Putnam, 1988.
The Naked Heart. London, Bantam, and New York, Delacorte, 1989.
The Other Side of Love. London, Bantam, and New York, Delacorte, 1991.

*　　*　　*

There is nothing subtle about Jacqueline Briskin's novels. In a style typical of many contemporary American authors of bestselling family sagas, heroes and heroines move boldly through their time and place in history. Along the way they collect lovers, riches, misfortune, and ultimately, happiness. Her characters are strongly delineated and plots move at an exciting pace. As a result, she is a very popular writer of commercial fiction. In fact, Briskin received an advance of one million dollars for her third bestseller, *Too Much, Too Soon*, making her one of America's highest paid authors. Gioia Diliberto in *People Weekly* wrote, 'Late bloomer she may be, but author Jacqueline Briskin clearly has played her cards right'.

Briskin writes her family sagas and historical romances according to the usual tried-and-true formula of the genre. Her novels deal with the rise and decline of families and groups of families as depicted in the interpersonal relationships of the characters. They span decades, if not many generations. Much of the action revolves around one or two, but occasionally three to five, characters in any one book. Given the span of years covered in any one novel, they are necessarily historical in nature.

If her books are so formulaic, what has propelled Briskin to predictable success? In short, she consistently delivers the goods. The larger-than-life characters, despite their grand scale, capture our sympathy or chill our hearts as they endure the joys and sorrows of life. Except for the occasional malicious villain, even her most har-

dened characters have all-too-human vulnerabilities. But it is not psychological drama that draws her readers. It is the external lives of her characters that fascinate. Many of them move from rags to riches by sheer determination, reinforced by good luck and innate survival skills. On the way to the top they tackle human obstacles: jealous siblings, vindictive ex-lovers, corrupt officials, vengeful children. Rape, blackmail, violence, and theft are but a sample of the weapons wielded against heroes and heroines. To further entice her readers, there is a lot of sexual energy among the inhabitants of Briskin's fiction. Interestingly, a special charge ignites flames between close blood relations. Marilyn, in *Everything and More*, falls in love with Linc, her husband's son by a former marriage and her own son's step-brother. Close friends are vulnerable to attractions to each other's spouse. Consequently, a number of illegitimate children are born. One of Briskin's favorite sub-plots is the baby given up for adoption by its mother to a closely related couple, as the glamorous movie-star Alyssia Del Mar does in *Dreams Are Not Enough*. Needless to say, there's plenty of racy though not very erotic sex in Briskin's novels—just enough detail to spice things up. She doesn't linger, simply delivers the facts about whatever sexual encounter is taking place, then moves on to more important action.

Although personal conflicts and relationships provide most of the narrative tension in Briskin's books, social conflict also moves along their high-powered pace. In *California Generation*, her first novel, characters' lives are intertwined with events that typify the deeply divided America of the late 1960s and early 1970s. Best friends at California High, class of 1960, are thrown into the turbulent decade whose dramatic events alter the course of their lives. One of these classmates, Clay Gillies, becomes a radical opponent of the Viet Nam Conflict and meets his death during a demonstration against the war. World War II is the setting for Briskin's most recent two novels, *The Naked Heart* and *The Other Side of Love*. She changes her usual background of America to Europe. Heroines are captured and abused by demonic Nazi soldiers; lovers are parted by war; members of families are lost in the violence.

If Briskin's plots are at times contrived, if characters are sometimes overdrawn, or if endings are unbelievably happy, it is Briskin's sure handle on her historical material that raises her writing above ordinary commercial writing. It is clear that her own English/American background gives her writing a cosmopolitan flare. Whether a scene is set in California, England, Africa, or the Middle East, whether placed a century or a decade ago, Briskin easily incorporates believable historical details. She conveys an impressive knowledge of both the broad historical picture and the subtle ambience of another culture. Her knowledge of the business world is equally impressive. Since so many of Briskin's protagonists are either born wealthy or attain riches, the ease with which she conveys the upper stratosphere of a society adds considerable credibility to her stories. This is particularly true of *Too Much, Too Soon*, in which three impoverished English sisters find shelter with their rich American uncle. The plot sounds ordinary, the sisters are 'types', the writing is short on literary quality, but the background of the book, much of it centred on the international oil scene of the 1970s, places *Too Much, Too Soon* several notches above many contemporary novels of this kind.

Not all of Briskin's books are equally successful at maintaining the reader's interest. *The Naked Heart*, for example, has some incredible plot twists. *The Other Side of Love* was criticized by Sybil Steinberg in *Publisher's Weekly* for having 'short chapters and subsections that give the plot a disjointed, bits-and-pieces feel' and 'predictable finale'. However, fans of contemporary romances, family sagas, and historical romances are likely to agree with the assessment of *Dreams Are Not Enough* in this review by Michele Leber in *Library Journal*, 'And, as is her style, Briskin . . . hooks the reader in the opening pages, making it near-impossible to stop reading. So if characters are sometimes less than well-rounded, dialogue less than dazzling, and style sometimes stiff, still the story is relentless. A bonbon of a book'.

—Marcia L. Thomas

BRISTOW, Gwen.
Nationality: American. **Born:** Marion, South Carolina, 16 September 1903. **Education:** Anderson College, South Carolina; Judson College, Marion, Alabama, A.B. 1924; Columbia University School of Journalism, New York, 1924–25. **Relations:** married Bruce Manning in 1929 (died). **Career:** Journalist, New Orleans *Times-Picayune*, 1925–34. **Died:** 16 August 1980.

ROMANCE AND HISTORICAL PUBLICATIONS

Novels (series: Plantation Trilogy)

Plantation Trilogy. New York, Crowell, 1962.
  Deep Summer. New York, Crowell, and London, Heinemann, 1937.
  The Handsome Road. New York, Crowell, and London, Heinemann, 1938.
  This Side of Glory. New York, Crowell, and London, Heinemann, 1940.
Tomorrow Is Forever. New York, Crowell, 1943; London, Heinemann, 1944.
Jubilee Trail. New York, Crowell, 1950; London, Eyre and Spottiswoode, 1953.
Celia Garth. New York, Crowell, 1959; London, Eyre and Spottiswoode, 1960.
Calico Palace. New York, Crowell, 1970; London, Eyre and Spottiswoode, 1971.

OTHER PUBLICATIONS

Novels with Bruce Manning

The Invisible Host. New York, Mystery League, 1930; as *The Ninth Guest*, New York, Popular Library, 1975.
The Gutenberg Murders. New York, Mystery League, 1931.
Two and Two Make Twenty-Two. New York, Mystery League, 1932.
The Mardi Gras Murders. New York, Mystery League, 1932.

Poetry

The Alien and Other Poems. Boston, Badger, 1926.

Other

Gwen Bristow: A Self Portrait. New York, Crowell, 1940.
Golden Dreams. New York, Lippincott and Crowell, 1980.

*   *   *

History takes precedence over romance in the novels of Gwen Bristow. Her plots are detailed and neatly resolved and her characters are sharply drawn, if with broad strokes; but she reserves her greatest skill for the unfolding of American history as displayed around the lives of the people who created it.

For the most part, Bristow's novels follow a central female character through a tumultuous period of America's development. Her

Plantation Trilogy (which includes *Deep Summer*, *The Handsome Road* and *This Side of Glory*) reads like a single volume with three heroines. They are united by the location of neighbouring plantations in Louisiana but separated in time from the 1700s to the 1920s. These three relatively short works form a unified whole about equal in length to the longer single novels like *Jubilee Trail* or *Calico Palace*. Each of the three sections of the trilogy stands alone quite effectively, but only when taken as a whole do they give the author's characteristic overview of history. *Tomorrow Is Forever*, a shorter work published at the height of America's involvement in World War II, is her only contemporary novel. Even so, it flashes back to World War I through the life of Elizabeth, the heroine. There is less emphasis upon the flow of history in this work and more upon the examination of war and its effect on men and nations. The overall effect is more that of propaganda piece than historical novel, and *Tomorrow Is Forever* as a whole seems atypical of Bristow's body of work.

If fault can be found with Bristow's plots it lies in the foreshadowing of pivotal events in the characters' lives, often through undue emphasis on minor details. For example, when Loren in *Calico Palace* warns a child not to sit on a dirty nail the unconscious focus on this minor transaction predicts Loren's death from an injury received from the same nail. At that point in the narrative Loren has served his purpose in the heroine's life and his departure seems ordained. On a larger scale, the true identity of Mr Kessler in *Tomorrow Is Forever* is predictable, based on the emphasis given to Elizabeth's special relationship with her first husband, Arthur. The tragedies and triumphs experienced by the characters follow relatively obvious patterns with few surprises for the reader. The stories are quite adequate, however, when played out against such exciting times and settings.

Bristow's characters suffer somewhat in comparison to the breadth of her historical knowledge and her skill at developing an era. The heroines of all the novels are nearly identical, being described as attractive rather than beautiful and wilful in a style out of keeping with their times. Additionally each is drawn as a loner who craves love and a sense of belonging. The secondary female characters are often 'bad girls' and Bristow lavishes more attention on them, sometimes to the detriment of the heroine. In *Calico Palace* she unexpectedly switches the point of view several times from the beleaguered heroine Kendra to the delightfully wicked Marny. The men, the putative makers of history, are divided between charming, weak connivers who appear early in the heroine's life and strong, capable men who form bonds with her after she has proven that she can take care of herself. In some works, these two types are represented by a single hero with both strong and weak traits. The most interesting aspect of the characters in all the novels is how they are changed by history even as they live it. In *Celia Garth* the Tories and the rebels trade social status and power with their fluctuating success in war. In the *Plantation Trilogy* some farmers become aristocrats and some become 'poor white trash' depending upon chance and personal choices.

The novelistic portions of these volumes are pleasant, palatable garments for the real focus: American history. While the reader is being entertained, there is also instruction. The periods that Bristow selects are exciting enough in themselves; her eye for just the right detail and her breakneck pace make history a living entity guaranteed to capture her audience.

—Susan Quinn Berneis

BRITT, Katrina. See 2nd edition, 1990.

BROMFIELD, Louis.

Nationality: American. **Born:** Mansfield, Ohio, 27 December 1896. **Education:** Cornell University Agricultural College, Ithaca, New York, 1914–15; Columbia University School of Journalism, New York, 1916, honorary war degree 1920. **Military Service:** served in the American Ambulance Corps, with the 34th and 168th divisions of the French Army, 1917–19: Croix de Guerre. **Relations:** married Mary Appleton Wood in 1921 (died 1952); three daughters. **Career:** reporter, City News Service and Associated Press, New York, 1920–22; editor and/or critic, *Musical America*, the *Bookman*, and *Time*; also worked as an assistant to a theatrical producer and as advertising manager of Putnam's, publishers, all New York, 1922–25; lived in Senlis, France, 1925–38; lived on a farm in Richland County, Ohio, 1939–56. President, Emergency Committee for the American Wounded in Spain, 1938; director, United States Chamber of Commerce. **Recipient:** Pulitzer prize, 1927. LL.D: Marshall College, Huntington, West Virginia; Parsons College, Fairfield, Iowa; D.Litt.: Ohio Northern University, Ada. Chevalier, Légion d'honneur, 1939. **Member:** American Academy. **Died:** 18 March 1956.

ROMANCE AND HISTORICAL PUBLICATIONS

Novels

The Green Bay Tree. New York, Stokes, and London, Unwin, 1924.
Possession. New York, Stokes, 1925; as *Lilli Barr*. London, Unwin, 1926.
Early Autumn. New York, Stokes, and London, Cape, 1926.
A Good Woman. New York, Stokes and London, Cape, 1927.
The Strange Case of Miss Annie Spragg. New York, Stokes, and London, Cape, 1928.
Twenty-Four Hours. New York, Stokes, and London, Cassell, 1930.
A Modern Hero. New York, Stokes, and London, Cassell, 1932.
The Farm. New York, Harper, and London, Cassell, 1933.
The Man Who Had Everything. New York, Harper, and London, Cassell, 1935.
It Had to Happen. London, Cassell, 1936.
The Rains Came: A Novel of Modern India. New York, Harper, and London, Cassell, 1937.
Night in Bombay. New York, Harper, and London, Cassell, 1940.
Wild Is the River. New York, Harper, 1941; London, Cassell, 1942.
Until the Day Break. New York, Harper, 1942; London, Cassell, 1943.
Mrs Parkington. New York, Harper, 1943; London, Cassell, 1944.
What Became of Anna Bolton. New York, Harper, 1944; London, Cassell, 1945.
Colorado. New York, Harper, 1947; London, Cassell, 1950.
The Wild Country. New York, Harper, 1948; London, Cassell, 1950.
Mr Smith. New York, Harper, 1951; London, Cassell, 1952.

Short Stories

Awake and Rehearse. New York, Stokes, and London, Cape, 1929.
Tabloid News. New York, Random House, 1930.
Here Today and Gone Tomorrow: Four Short Novels. New York, Harper, and London, Cassell, 1934.
It Takes All Kinds. New York, Harper, and London, Cassell, 1939; *Bitter Lotus* (published separately). Cleveland, World, 1944; selection as *Five Long Short Stories*. New York, Avon, 1945; *McLeod's Folly* published separately, Cleveland, World, 1948; selection as *You Get What You Give*. London, Cassell, 1951.
The World We Live In. New York, Harper, 1944; London, Cassell, 1946.
Kenny. New York, Harper, 1947; London, Cassell, 1949.

OTHER PUBLICATIONS

Plays

The House of Women, adaptation of his novel *The Green Bay Tree* (produced New York, 1927; London, 1928).
De Luxe, with John Gearon (produced New York, 1935).
Times Have Changed, adaptation of a play by Edouard Bourdet (produced New York, 1935).

Screenplays: *One Heavenly Night*, with Sidney Howard, 1930; *Brigham Young—Frontiersman*, with Lamar Trotti, 1940.

Other

The Work of Robert Nathan. Indianapolis, Bobbs Merrill, 1927.
England, A Dying Oligarchy. New York, Harper, 1939.
Pleasant Valley. New York, Harper, 1945; London, Cassell, 1946.
A Few Brass Tacks. New York, Harper, 1946.
Malabar Farm. New York, Harper, 1948; London, Cassell, 1949.
The Works (Malabar Edition). London, Cassell, 15 vols, 1949–54.
Out of the Earth. New York, Harper, 1950; London, Cassell, 1951.
The Wealth of the Soil. Detroit, Ferguson, 1952.
A New Pattern for a Tired World. New York, Harper, and London, Cassell, 1954.
From My Experience: The Pleasures and Miseries of Life on a Farm. New York, Harper, 1955; London, Cassell, 1956.
Animals and Other People. New York, Harper, 1955; London, Cassell, 1956.
Walt Disney's Vanishing Prairie. New York, Simon and Schuster, and London, Harrap, 1956.
Louis Bromfield at Malabar: Writings on Farming and Country Life, edited by Charles E. Little. Baltimore, Johns Hopkins University Press, 1988.

*

Film Adaptation: *The Rains Came*, 1939.

Critical Studies: *Louis Bromfield and His Books: An Evaluation* by Morrison Brown, London, Cassell, 1956, Fair Lawn, New Jersey, Essential, 1957; *The Heritage: A Daughter's Memories of Louis Bromfield* by Ellen Geld, New York, Harper, 1962; *Louis Bromfield* by David D. Anderson, New York, Twayne, 1964.

* * *

Louis Bromfield is a neglected author who in his own day was very popular and much respected—indeed, he won the Pulitzer Prize for literature with *Early Autumn*, the third book of an interrelated series in which he set out to present a pageant of the changing American scene in the early years of this century while at the same time exploring the idea of escape from convention. The first book of this saga was *The Green Bay Tree*, set in a small town in Ohio at the time when it was changing from a farming community to an industrial town. He shows us different aspects of the community's life by portraying several different families, but the main focus is Lily, a 'new woman'—very attractive to men with opportunities to marry, all of whom she rejects fearing to be tied down, preferring to have her child outside wedlock. *Possession* is the next book which runs parallel in time and place to the first, but shows us another set of families and glimpses of some of the people from the first book. A new woman is at the centre of this book too: she makes her bid for freedom by rejecting family life for the concert platform. *Early Autumn* is connected with the previous books when the daughter of the family at the centre of this book marries Lily's illegitimate son. This portrait of an old New England family is almost an American

Forsyte saga, for it has the same emphasis on money and property and it is the heroine's devotion to duty that triumphs over her longing to escape convention. The fourth book is *A Good Woman*, an ironic title, since the woman arranges her son's life to such a degree that she manoeuvres not only his call to the mission field but also his marriage, and in so doing she ruins three lives while thinking herself good and righteous. The good woman's daughter-in-law can only find escape through death.

Bromfield would have pleased his fans had he gone on with his richly plotted, intricate panoramas but he was ready for another format. *The Strange Case of Miss Annie Spragg* is a loosely connected set of short stories making up a novel. Each chapter tells the tale of one of the several witnesses to a miracle in Italy. The stories are skilfully told, cleverly meshed with superbly drawn characters. *Twenty-Four Hours* was another book of the same type: each of the people attending a dinner one night relates what happens to him or her between dinner and teatime the next day. The whole makes a surprisingly complete book.

The Rains Came is Bromfield's most famous book—perhaps because it became a much-acclaimed film, but also because it was an excellent book. He visited India in 1932 and it took him four years to digest the experience and process it into a novel. Ranchipur, where the story is set, is based on Baroda, one of the most up-to-date Indian states of the time. The destinies of a large number of people are worked out against the tension of the dry season and the bursting of the dam that comes with the monsoon. Bromfield symbolizes the decadence of Europe in the character of Ransome, America through Aunt Phoebe, and contrasts it with awakening India symbolized by the Maharajah. *Night in Bombay*. his other Indian novel, was not nearly as successful; nevertheless, the characters are interesting and the descriptions evocative of the sights, sounds, smells, and the feel of India.

Bromfield could write other kinds of books, too. *Wild Is the River* is a romantic historical novel about the American Civil War set against the background of the occupation of New Orleans by the Yankees; *Until the Day Break*, a melodramatic spy story, is set against occupied Paris in the 1940s. *Colorado* is a send-up of the Western, and *The Wild Country* is a strangely beautiful story of a boy growing up on his grandfather's farm observing the people round him.

In all Bromfield's books there is good solid characterization, strong plotting, lush romance, and the exploration of a socially significant theme against beautiful descriptions. It is high time some of his books were brought to the attention of a new generation to whom they would have a great deal to say.

—Pamela Cleaver

BROMIGE, Iris (Amy Edna).
Nationality: British. **Born:** London in 1910. **Education:** Clapham County Secondary School, London. **Relations:** married to Alan Frank Bromige. **Address:** c/o Hodder and Stoughton Ltd, Mill Road, Dunton Green, Sevenoaks, Kent TN13 2YA, England.

ROMANCE AND HISTORICAL PUBLICATIONS

Novels (series: Rainwood Family)

The Traceys. London, Longman, 1946; New York, Beagle, 1974.
Stay But till Tomorrow. London, Longman, 1946; New York, Ballantine, 1975.
Chequered Pattern. London, Longman, 1947; as *A Chance for Love*, New York, Ballantine, 1975.

Tangled Roots. London, Longman, 1948; New York, Ballantine, 1975.
Marchwood. London, Hodder and Stoughton, 1949; New York, Beagle, 1974.
The Golden Cage. London, Hodder and Stoughton, 1950; New York, Ballantine, 1974.
April Wooing. London, Hodder and Stoughton, 1951; New York, Beagle, 1973.
Laurian Vale. London, Hodder and Stoughton, 1952; New York, Ballantine, 1975.
The House of Conflict. London, Hodder and Stoughton, 1953; as *Shall Love Be Lost?*, New York, Beagle, 1974.
Gay Intruder. London, Hodder and Stoughton, 1954; New York, Ballantine, 1973.
Diana Comes Home. London, Hodder and Stoughton, 1955; New York, Beagle, 1974.
The New Owner. London, Hodder and Stoughton, 1956; New York, Ballantine, 1973.
The Enchanted Garden. London, Hodder and Stoughton, 1956; New York, Beagle, 1972.
A New Life for Joanna. London, Hodder and Stoughton, 1957; New York, Beagle, 1973.
Family Group. London, Hodder and Stoughton, 1958; New York, Ballantine, 1975.
The Conway Touch. London, Hodder and Stoughton, 1958; New York, Ballantine, 1974.
The Flowering Year. London, Hodder and Stoughton, 1959; New York, Beagle, 1973.
The Second Mrs Rivers. London, Hodder and Stoughton, 1960; New York, Beagle, 1973.
Fair Prisoner. London, Hodder and Stoughton, 1960; New York, Beagle, 1974.
Alex and the Raynhams. London, Hodder and Stoughton, 1961; New York, Pocket Books, 1972.
Come Love, Come Hope. London, Hodder and Stoughton, 1962; New York, Beagle, 1972.
Rosevean. London, Hodder and Stoughton, 1962; Philadelphia, Chilton, 1963.
The Family Web. London, Hodder and Stoughton, 1963; New York, Beagle, 1972.
A House Without Love. London, Hodder and Stoughton, 1964; New York, Beagle, 1973.
The Young Romantic. London, Hodder and Stoughton, 1964; New York, Ballantine, 1975.
The Challenge of Spring. London, Hodder and Stoughton, 1965; New York, Beagle, 1972.
The Lydian Inheritance. London, Hodder and Stoughton, 1966; New York, Beagle, 1972.
The Stepdaughter (Rainwood). London, Hodder and Stoughton, 1966.
The Quiet Hills (Rainwood). London, Hodder and Stoughton, 1967; New York, Beagle, 1974.
An April Girl (Rainwood). London, Hodder and Stoughton, 1967; New York, Beagle, 1971.
Only Our Love. London, Hodder and Stoughton, 1968; New York, Beagle, 1974.
The Master of Heronsbridge. London, Hodder and Stoughton, 1969; New York, Beagle, 1974.
The Tangled Wood (Rainwood). London, Hodder and Stoughton, 1969; New York, Beagle, 1971.
Encounter at Alpenrose. London, Hodder and Stoughton, 1970; New York, Beagle, 1973.
A Sheltering Tree. London, Hodder and Stoughton, 1970; New York, Beagle, 1973.
A Magic Place (Rainwood). London, Hodder and Stoughton, 1971; New York, Beagle, 1973.

Rough Weather. London, Hodder and Stoughton, 1972; New York, Pinnacle, 1981.
Golden Summer. London, Hodder and Stoughton, 1972; New York, Beagle, 1973.
The Broken Bough. London, Hodder and Stoughton, 1973.
The Night of the Party. London, Hodder and Stoughton, 1974.
The Bend in the River (Rainwood). London, Hodder and Stoughton, 1975.
A Haunted Landscape. London, Hodder and Stoughton, 1976.
A Distant Song. London, Hodder and Stoughton, 1977; New York, Pinnacle, 1980.
The Happy Fortress (Rainwood). London, Hodder and Stoughton, 1978.
The Paths of Summer. London, Hodder and Stoughton, 1979.
One Day, My Love (Rainwood). London, Hodder and Stoughton, 1980.
Old Love's Domain. London, Hodder and Stoughton, 1982.
A Slender Thread. London, Hodder and Stoughton, 1985.
Farewell to Winter. London, Hodder and Stoughton, 1986.
The Changing Tide. London, Hodder and Stoughton, 1987.
The Years Between. London, Hodder and Stoughton, 1991.

*   *   *

Iris Bromige's stories are pleasant, family oriented novels set in an England where late 20th-century realism rarely intrudes, and the reader who looks for references to inner city decay and the teenage drug-scene will search in vain. This is a timeless world where solid middle-class values are endorsed; a cosy, secure environment where virtues such as hard work, duty and family love win out over vices such as greed and idleness.

This does not mean that Bromige characters, particularly the hero and heroine, are removed from life's problems. On the contrary they suffer more than their fair share of disasters, and central to many Bromige stories is the realization that enduring happiness is often achieved only as a result of pain. As the hero's dying mother points out to the heroine in *A Sheltering Tree*, 'Because you have both known grief, you'll have greater understanding, and it will deepen your happiness together because you'll never take it for granted'.

A Bromige heroine has ideals. Although young—usually in her mid-twenties—she puts duty and conscience before everything. A recurring theme is her decision to make some kind of sacrifice for family reasons. Emma, in *Farewell to Winter*, has dreamt of becoming a journalist, but puts the needs of her invalid mother first, as does Sarah, in *Fair Prisoner*, who becomes a lowly paid drudge in her uncle's household in order to give her delicate mother a decent home. If a Bromige heroine has a full-time career of her own choosing it is usually in some branch of the arts—for example, Josephine, in *The Paths of Summer*, is secretary to a famous author. But generally her practical skills in organizing a household and her obvious affinity with children, animals, and sensitivity to those less fortunate than herself point to her true vocation: that of wife, mother, and support figure in the local community.

The Bromige hero is intelligent and a man of honour and integrity, who does not unbend easily. He is usually in his late twenties or early thirties, but his responsibilities often make him appear older. His aloofness can initially make him seem bleak and remote. This is usually due to the misfortunes he has suffered. Joel, in *A Sheltering Tree*, has to endure the loss of the woman he loved in an avalanche, a dying mother, an unruly young niece whose parents are abroad, and the problems of the family business to which he is a reluctant recruit. The Bromige hero learns to make the best of things, finding consolation in the knowledge that 'Life has a way of turning up unexpected compensations after she's clobbered you'. He takes pleasure in the arts and, often, a shared interest in music or poetry provides a bridge between him and the heroine as they enjoy a Chopin concert or exchange quotations from Wordsworth or Tennyson. A countryman, he enjoys the outdoor life and appreciates local tradition and the importance of maintaining it (often the reason behind his decision to try to make a go of a languishing business).He may even turn out to support the village cricket team. In the community he is universally respected.

His courtship of the heroine is slow and steady and not physically demonstrative. A sympathetic hand resting on hers is as far as he is likely to go before marriage. Although his feelings are deep and sincere, his proposal is often low-key, speaking of a future of contentment in shared interests rather than scaling impossible heights of passion. He does not express himself in flowery phrases, but here is a man who, once committed to marriage, will be a thoroughly reliable husband. For a heroine who is in need of comfort he is irresistible and much of his appeal lies in the competent way in which he takes over her life. Jennifer, in *A Sheltering Tree*, recognizes 'like a traveller lost and floundering in treacherous bogs, the granite rock of his assurance'.

The characters surrounding hero and heroine are lightly sketched, but are convincing. Often they are literary or artistic. Bromige excels at presenting pictures of happy family life and is also good at capturing small children (for example, four-year-old Emma, in *A Sheltering Tree*, is a wonderfully eccentric, but very believable child with an individual personality). Substitute mother figures are always present for the heroine, whether cheerful members of the lower orders or middle-class matrons. Most obvious in the latter category is, of course, Mirabel Rainwood, indomitable matriarch of the Rainwood clan whose members feature prominently in Bromige's stories. But often the heroine turns for advice to an older spinster, for example, the formidable Miss Brecon, the heroine's ex-headmistress, in *Farewell to Winter* or Hester Northbridge, the quirky writer of detective stories who appears in *The Paths of Summer*. Bromige's single women are always shown as strong, positive characters who do not need a man to make their lives complete. Less successful, perhaps, are attempts to portray the unattractive sides of human nature and these sometimes acquire a touch of melodrama, for example, the heroine's uncle in *Fair Prisoner*.

Apart from occasional forays abroad to the more conventional resorts of the South of France and Switzerland Bromige bases her stories mainly in the English countryside. The passing of time is often cleverly shown with reference to nature: the heroine will notice 'hawthorn berries showing red in the hedgerows' or 'the long grass dotted with vetch and clover'. The countryside is a place for spiritual refreshment for both hero and heroine. As Sarah, in *Fair Prisoner* notices, 'To see Spring come to the country after so many years in London made it impossible not to be happy'.

Bromige offers the romance reader a predictable blend of escapism and reassurance, but the mixture is competently crafted and has worked well over the years.

—Frances Whitehead

BROOKES, Beth.   See **McKENNA, Lyndsay.**

BROSTER, D(orothy) K(athleen).
Nationality: British. **Born:** 1877. **Education:** Cheltenham Ladies' College, Gloucestershire; St. Hilda's College, Oxford, M.A. **Died:** 7 February 1950.

ROMANCE AND HISTORICAL PUBLICATIONS

Novels (series: Jacobite Trilogy)

Chantemerle, with Gertrude Winifred Taylor. London, Murray, and New York, Brentano's, 1911.
The Vision Splendid, with Gertrude Winifred Taylor. London, Murray, 1913; New York, Brentano's, 1914.
Sir Isumbras at the Ford. London, Murray, 1918.
The Yellow Poppy. London, Duckworth, 1920; New York, McBride, 1922.
The Wounded Name. London, Murray, 1922; New York, Doubleday, 1923.
Mr Rowl. London, Heinemann, and New York, Doubleday, 1924.
A Jacobite Trilogy. London, Penguin, 1984.
   The Flight of the Heron. London, Heinemann, 1925; New York, Dodd Mead, 1926.
   The Gleam in the North. London, Heinemann, 1927; New York, Coward McCann, 1931.
   The Dark Mile. London, Heinemann, 1929; New York, Coward McCann, 1934.
Ships in the Bay! London, Heinemann, and New York, Coward McCann, 1931.
Almond, Wild Almond. London, Heinemann, 1933.
World under Snow, with G. Forester. London, Heinemann, 1935.
Child Royal. London, Heinemann, 1937.
The Sea Without a Haven. London, Heinemann, 1941.
The Captain's Lady. London, Heinemann, 1947.

Short Stories

A Fire of Driftwood. London, Heinemann, 1932.
Couching at the Door. London, Heinemann, 1942.

OTHER PUBLICATIONS

Poetry

The Short Voyage and Other Verses. Privately printed, 1950.

Other

The Happy Warrior. London, Cayme Press, 1926.

*   *   *

D.K. Broster's first two novels, *Chantemerle* and *The Vision Splendid*, were written in collaboration with Miss G.W. Taylor. Although they were not as polished as Broster's later work, they established a writing pattern: carefully constructed historical settings; intelligent presentation, with some consideration of historical ideas behind action; and clear characterizations. Romance per se is central in *Chantemerle*, but in general Broster's work is secondary to period political matters. All in all, the general model for Broster's work would seem to be Robert Louis Stevenson.

The author's most important work is usually considered to be *A Jacobite Trilogy* (*The Flight of the Heron, The Gleam in the North*, and *The Dark Mile*). Set in Scotland from 1745 to 1755, they are essentially concerned with the psychological concomitants and aftermaths of the uprising. In *The Flight of the Heron*, when Prince Charles is being hunted by English troops, the focus of the story is on the odd friendship that arises between Ewen Cameron, one of the prince's supporters, and Captain Windham, the leader of the English troops. *The Gleam in the North*, set several years later, centres around the historical capture and execution of Dr Archibald Cameron, an agent of Prince Charles's. The Scottish feeling that Cameron

was being treated harshly in being executed without trial (on the basis of an earlier judgment) is contrasted with the English feeling that Cameron was a dangerous agitator who had done much harm and would do more. The story is told via Ewen Cameron. *The Dark Mile*, set in the Highlands, examines the psychological damage done by the rebellion. Young lovers, one related to Ewen Cameron, discover that family loyalty is stronger than love. Olivia's father had commanded troops that killed Ian's brother in battle, and this can never be forgiven, even though it was only the fortune of war. (The obstacle to love is removed, unfortunately, by a device unworthy of the author). Moving in the background of the last two books is a fictional version of Pickle the spy. Broster follows Andrew Lang's identification of Pickle. All three volumes are well plotted and carry conviction.

Other historical novels include *Sir Isumbras at the Ford*, set in Scotland and France in the 1790s; *The Wounded Name*, France just before Napoleon's return from Elba; and *Ships in the Bay!*, Wales, 1796, with Irish rebels and French Revolutionaries.

Broster's best-known story is the short story 'Couching at the Door', from the collection of the same name. Often anthologized and highly regarded, it is based on the personalities of Oscar Wilde (mingled a little with Aleister Crowley) and Aubrey Beardsley. It describes a unique punishment for having attended a Black Mass.

—E.F. Bleiler

———

BROWN, Sandra.
Pseudonyms: Laura Jordan; Rachel Ryan; Erin St Claire. **Nationality:** American. **Born:** Waco, Texas, 12 March 1948. **Education:** Texas Christian University, Fort Worth; Oklahoma State University, Stillwater; University of Texas, Arlington, 1966–70. **Relations:** married Michael Brown in 1968; one daughter and one son. **Career:** manager, Merle Norman Cosmetics Studio, Tyler, Texas, 1971–73; weather reporter, KLTV-Television, Tyler, 1972–75, and WFAA-Television, Dallas, 1976–79; model, Dallas Apparel Mart, 1976–87. **Agent:** Maria Carvainis Agency, 235 West End Avenue, New York, New York 10023, USA. **Address:** 1000 North Bowen, Arlington, Texas 76012, USA.

ROMANCE AND HISTORICAL PUBLICATIONS

Novels (series: Alicia; Coleman and Langston)

Hidden Fires (as Laura Jordan). New York, Pocket Books, 1982.
The Silken Web (as Laura Jordan). New York, Pocket Books, 1982.
Breakfast in Bed (Alicia). New York, Bantam, 1983.
Heaven's Price. New York, Bantam, 1983.
Relentless Desire. New York, Berkley, 1983.
Tempest in Eden. New York, Berkley, 1983.
Temptation's Kiss. New York, Berkley, 1983.
Tomorrow's Promise. Toronto, Harlequin, 1983.
In a Class by Itself. New York, Bantam, 1984.
Send No Flowers (Alicia). New York, Bantam, 1984.
Sunset Embrace (Coleman and Langston). New York, Bantam, 1984.
Riley in the Morning. New York, Bantam, 1985.
Thursday's Child. New York, Bantam, 1985.
Another Dawn (Coleman and Langston). New York, Bantam, 1985.
22 Indigo Place. New York, Bantam, 1986.
The Rana Look. New York, Bantam, 1986.
Demon Rumm. New York, Bantam, 1987.
Fanta C. New York, Bantam, 1987.

Sunny Chandler's Return. New York, Bantam, 1987.
Tidings of Great Joy. New York, Bantam, 1987.
Adam's Fall. New York, Bantam, 1988.
Hawk O'Toole's Hostage. New York, Bantam, 1988.
Slow Heat in Heaven. New York, Warner, 1988; London, Severn House, 1990.
Long Time Coming. New York, Bantam, 1989.
Temperatures Rising. New York, Bantam, 1989.
Best Kept Secrets. New York, Warner, 1989; London, Severn House, 1990.
A Whole New Light. New York, Bantam, 1989.
Mirror Image. New York, Warner, and London, Mandarin, 1990.
Texas! Lucky. New York, Doubleday, 1990.
Texas! Chase. New York, Doubleday, 1990.
Breath of Scandal. New York, Warner, 1991.
French Silk. New York, Warner, and London, Heinemann, 1992.
Texas! Sage. New York, Bantam, 1992.
Where There's Smoke. New York, Warner, and London, Little Brown, 1993.
Tomorrow's Promise. Toronto, Harlequin, 1993.

Novels as Rachel Ryan

Love Beyond Reason. New York, Dell, 1981.
Love's Encore. New York, Dell, 1981.
Eloquent Silence. New York, Dell, 1982.
A Treasure Worth Seeking. New York, Dell, 1982.
Prime Time. New York, Dell, 1983.

Novels as Erin St Claire (series: Jennifer and Cage)

Not Even for Love. New York, Silhouette, 1982.
A Kiss Remembered. New York, Silhouette, 1983.
A Secret Splendor. New York, Silhouette, 1983.
Seduction by Design. New York, Silhouette, 1983.
Bittersweet Rain. New York, Silhouette, 1984.
Words of Silk. New York, Silhouette, 1984.
Led Astray (Jennifer and Cage). New York, Silhouette, 1985.
A Sweet Anger. New York, Silhouette, 1985.
Tiger Prince. New York, Silhouette, 1985.
Above and Beyond. New York, Silhouette, 1986.
Honor Bound. New York, Silhouette, 1986.
The Devil's Own (Jennifer and Cage). New York, Silhouette, 1987.
Two Alone. New York, Silhouette, 1987.
Thrill of Victory. New York, Silhouette, 1989.

*

Sandra Brown comments:

I write love stories about characters I would like to know, incorporating fantasy into realism.

*   *   *

Sandra Brown has the distinction of being one of the few writers to have had three books on *The New York Times* bestsellers list at the same time. After forging a solid career in category romances, she has broadened her scope to longer, more complex novels. In doing so, she has become one of the stars of romantic fiction.

Under her own name and the pseudonyms Rachel Ryan, Erin St Claire, and Laura Jordan, Brown writes mostly contemporary romances, but she has tried her hand at historical romances. In the shorter category romances she has focused on the emotions involved in a romantic relationship, skilfully bringing the reader into a lush romantic world by providing detailed descriptions of the physical environment and sensual descriptions of the emotions and actions of the lovers. Brown especially tugs at the reader's heart when she incorporates children or the desire for children into the story. *Above and Beyond*, as Erin St Claire, opens with Kyla Stroud giving birth to a child and almost immediately learning of her husband's death in a Cairo bombing. It is her son who helps her pull through the worst times. Arden Gentry's search for the child for whom she was a surrogate mother, the reasons behind her actions, and her subsequent marriage to Drew McCasslin, the child's father, are sensitively described in *A Secret Splendor*. Her decision to give her son up a second time when it seems she can only hurt him and her new husband is sure to move the reader to tears. Her ultimate reunion with her two loves is all the more joyous because of the pain she has suffered and her uncertainty of finding happiness. Avery Daniels (*Mirror Image*) is both selfless and tireless in her devotion to another woman's child. Avery's growing love for Mandy forms a strong secondary plot in the novel.

Brown is perhaps best known now for her longer novels of romantic suspense. The basic outline for these stories has passionate love, lust, and violence playing out against a background of unravelling secrets and skeletons jumping out of family closets. As Reede Lambert says in *Best Kept Secrets*, 'Everybody's got a secret. If you're lucky, the next guy's secret is juicier than yours. You use his secret to keep him quiet about yours.' Usually Brown sets the scene in the South, often in her native Texas or in neighbouring Louisiana. The steamy settings with a touch of decadence that she creates so effectively contribute greatly to a brooding, oppressive atmosphere. This, in turn, increases the underlying menace and tension surrounding the characters. Murder, sexual cruelty, rape, revenge, blackmail, and homosexuality are only some of the secrets and dangers confronting Brown's lovers as she weaves dark themes into her love stories.

Brown usually leaves at least one unexpected dramatic twist or disclosure until the very end of the story. The family secrets of *Mirror Image* reach back to the Korean War. Throughout the story, Brown focuses the reader's attention on tangled emotions and events in a contemporary political campaign, building tension over a planned assassination and the ramifications of a daring though improbable imposture. All the threads come together in a fast-paced climax when Brown reveals a revenge planned and carried out over more than 30 years. In *Best Kept Secrets*, a 25-year-old murder is the catalyst for contemporary murder, suicide and romance as old friendships are ripped apart and dirty family secrets are revealed. Again, Brown decoys the reader as the heroine pursues three suspects, only to have the real murderer step forward unexpectedly at the end. In *Where There's Smoke*, the disclosure of a politician's homosexuality, the sudden reappearance of the heroine's husband, who was long believed to be dead, and the revelation of the depths of his treachery come as rapid-fire discoveries at the end of the book. Even readers who have guessed at part of these disclosures are probably surprised by the extra twists provided by Brown. Sometimes, she leaves threads still dangling, as in *French Silk*, when the fate of the killer is not clearly defined. Brown has even broken the traditional happy ending formula in her historical romance, *Another Dawn*. Ross Coleman, a major character and the hero of *Sunset Embrace*, is brutally killed just as his daughter has found her happiness. The shock of the death of a man still deeply in love with his wife, leaving her totally bereft, as an end to a story is totally unexpected and very unusual in romantic fiction. It is a risk to have such a sombre ending, but Brown has the skill to bring it off.

Brown writes with skill and sensitivity. Her characters are vividly drawn, with even the secondary characters being fully developed. Her dialogue is sharp, and she keeps the reader guessing at plot twists until the end. However, her greatest key to success is probably that she invites her readers into a fantasy world of passion, intrigue, and danger. They too can face the moral and emotional dilemmas of the heroine, safe in the knowledge that justice and love will prevail.

—Barbara E. Kemp

* * *

BROWNING, Dixie (Burrus).
Pseudonyms: Zoe Dozier; Bronwyn Williams, with Mary Williams. **Nationality:** American. **Born:** Elizabeth City, North Carolina, 9 September 1930. Sister of the writer Mary Williams. **Education:** Mary Washington College, Fredericksburg, Virginia, 1946–47; Richmond Professional Institute (now Virginia Commonwealth University), 1947–48; City Memorial School of Nursing, Winston-Salem, North Carolina, 1948–49. **Relations:** married Leonard Larkin Browning, Jr, in 1950; one daughter and one son. **Career:** founder and co-director, Art Gallery Originals, Winston-Salem, 1968–73; co-director, Art V Gallery, Clemmons, North Carolina, 1974–75. Since 1984 president and co-owner, Browning Artworks, Frisco, North Carolina. President, Watercolor Society of North Carolina, 1972–73. **Recipient:** Romance Writers of America golden medallion, 1983; Maggie award, 1989, for *Dandelion*, and 1990, for *Stormwalker*. **Address:** 5316 Robinhood Road, Winston-Salem, North Carolina 27106, USA.

ROMANCE AND HISTORICAL PUBLICATIONS

Novels

Tumbled Wall. New York, Silhouette, 1980.
Unreasonable Summer. New York, Silhouette, 1980.
Chance Tomorrow. New York, Silhouette, 1981.
East of Today. New York, Silhouette, 1981.
Winter Blossom. New York, Silhouette, 1981; London, Hodder and Stoughton, 1982.
Wren of Paradise. New York, Silhouette, 1981.
Finders Keepers. New York, Silhouette, 1982.
Island on the Hill. New York, Silhouette, 1982.
Logic of the Heart. New York, Silhouette, 1982; London, Hodder and Stoughton, 1983.
The Loving Rescue. New York, Silhouette, 1982.
Renegade Player. New York, Silhouette, 1982.
Practical Dreamer. New York, Silhouette, and London, Hodder and Stoughton, 1983.
Reach Out to Cherish. New York, Silhouette, 1983.
A Secret Valentine. New York, Silhouette, 1983.
Shadow of Yesterday. New York, Silhouette, 1983.
First Things Last. New York, Silhouette, 1984.
The Hawk and the Honey. New York, Silhouette, 1984.
Image of Love. New York, Silhouette, 1984.
Journey to Quiet Waters. New York, Silhouette, 1984.
Just Desserts. New York, Silhouette, 1984.
Late Rising Moon. New York, Silhouette, 1984.
The Love Thing. New York, Silhouette, 1984.
Stormwatch. New York, Silhouette, 1984.
Time and Tide. New York, Silhouette, 1984.
Visible Heart. New York, Silhouette, 1984.
A Bird in Hand. New York, Silhouette, 1985.
By Any Other Name. New York, Silhouette, 1985.
Matchmaker's Moon. New York, Silhouette, 1985.
Something for Herself. New York, Silhouette, 1985.
The Tender Barbarian. New York, Silhouette, 1985.
Reluctant Dreamer. New York, Silhouette, 1986.
The Security Man. New York, Silhouette, 1986.
In the Palm of Her Hand. New York, Silhouette, 1986.

A Winter Woman. New York, Silhouette, 1986.
Belonging. New York, Silhouette, 1987.
Henry the Ninth. New York, Silhouette, 1987.
A Matter of Timing. New York, Silhouette, 1987.
There Once Was a Lover. New York, Silhouette, 1987.
Along Came Jones. New York, Silhouette, 1988.
Fate Takes a Holiday. New York, Silhouette, 1988.
Thin Ice. New York, Silhouette, 1989.
Ships in the Night. New York, Silhouette, 1990.
Beginner's Luck. New York, Silhouette, 1990.
Just Say Yes. New York, Silhouette, 1991.
Twice in a Blue Moon. New York, Silhouette, 1991.
Gus and the Nice Lady. New York, Silhouette, 1992.
Not a Marrying Man. New York, Silhouette, 1992.
Best Man for the Job. New York. Silhouette, 1992.
Hazards of the Heart. New York, Silhouette, 1993.
Kane's Way. New York, Silhouette, 1993.
Keegan's Hunt. New York, Silhouette, 1993.

Novels as Zoe Dozier

Home Again My Love. New York, Bouregy, 1977.
Warm Side of the Island. New York, Bouregy, 1977.

Novels as Bronwyn Williams (with Mary Williams)

White Witch. Toronto, Harlequin, 1988.
Dandelion. Toronto, Harlequin, 1989.
Stormwalker. Toronto, Harlequin, 1990.
Gideon's Fall. Toronto, Harlequin, 1991.
The Mariner's Bride. Toronto, Harlequin, 1991.
A Promise Kept. Toronto, Harlequin, 1992.

*

Manuscript Collection: University of North Carolina Library, Chapel Hill.

Dixie Browning comments:

Just as yesterday's vernacular work is hailed as today's classic, genre literature written today will need the perspective of time to be judged fairly. Romances have always been maligned by those who don't take the time to understand them. Writers of today's romances are merely retelling fables that are as old as language, fables that have enabled women to deal with their often unenviable relationships with men. The basic conflict is the diverse nature of men and women, and, set against a backdrop of today's world with its complex problems, the scope is enormous. Styles change, settings change, but the basic plot structure of the romance novel deals with an underlying truth that will never change. I write about the sort of men and women I know, dealing with problems I can understand. What's ordinary to one person is often exotic to another. Other writers deal with far more glamorous types, with settings I can only dream about, yet the underlying truth in any good romance enables a diverse audience to appreciate and to relate on an emotional level with at least one of the characters. That, I believe, is what ensures the genre a large and varied readership.

* * *

Most of Dixie Browning's 50 contemporary romances take place in or near to the author's native North Carolina. Browning is an artist as well as a writer, and her artist's eye for detail translates well onto the printed page. She uses her settings advantageously, often as backdrops for love scenes, as in *Thin Ice* when Maggie Duncan and Sam Canady make love in a duck blind. Weather phenomena such as thunderstorms, heat lightning, and high temperatures also enhance the encounters of hero and heroine.

Heroines are often involved in some aspect of the art world: art teacher, painter, gallery worker, wood carver among others. Heroes include an environmentalist, a power plant specialist, an investigator. Browning is skilful at endowing her characters with physical and other traits that individualize them and make them seem like real people. In *Just Say Yes*, Daisy Valentine has the long legs of a model. Gioia Murphy, in *Ships in the Night*, has large ears. On the other hand, the dialogue, comprised mostly of witty banter, could be interchangeable from book to book—an exception is Clement Barto's shy stammering in *Beginner's Luck*. The dialogue is, however, one of the strengths of Browning's writing.

Plots follow a definite formula. First, Browning creates a situation in which the hero and heroine must spend time in each other's company; sometimes, they must live under the same roof. In *Unreasonable Summer*, art teacher and painter Emily Fairchild rents a cottage for the summer, only to find that the owner has rented it to art critic George Brandon also. *Journey to Quiet Waters* has Ivy de Coursey employed as caretaker of Hunter Smith's estate. MacCasky Ford, in *Not a Marrying Man*, finds himself marooned on an island with Banner Keaton. Other situations in which the two lovers-to-be are thrown together include a Mexican vacation for Daisy Valentine and Gardiner Gentry in *Just Say Yes*, and a chase to find their eloping younger siblings for Rex Ryder and Carrie Lanier in *Best Man for the Job*.

Next, the author creates conflict between hero and heroine—but, nothing too serious. Earlier books, such as *Island on the Hill* and *Belonging*, use the beautiful 'other woman'. Either the hero or the heroine has had an unhappy past relationship that makes him/her reluctant to enter into another liaison. In *Gus and the Nice Lady*, Gus Galanos's divorce has made him bitter, and, therefore, he keeps himself aloof from heroine Phoebe Shaw. Sometimes the conflict arises from the fact that the protagonists only have a short time together and eventually return to their respective homes.

Browning creates an abundance of witty dialogue and verbal fencing and parrying as the characters get to know each other, or, as in some cases, to renew their acquaintance.

Almost every book has an occasion in which a physical injury allows the two to begin tentative, yet highly sensual, physical contact. In *Just Say Yes*, Gardiner Gentry ministers to Daisy Valentine's severe sunburn, and in *Thrice in a Blue Moon*, Tucker Owen comes to Hope Outlaw's aid when she injures her hand trying to open a stuck window.

Eventually, the characters fall in love and consummate their relationship, but, afterwards conflicts keep them apart. As the story draws to a close, the conflicts are easily solved by having one or the other character change his mind about what was bothering him. Even if they live great distances from each other, one of them seems to find no problem in relocating.

Secondary characters are kept to a minimum. Sometimes, they might initiate the action, only to be dropped as hero and heroine take over the story line. In *Beginner's Luck*, Hubert Odwell follows Martha Eberly, hoping to seize an alleged emerald she has found, but he disappears once she meets hero Clement Barto. A secondary character may also help to pad the story to the required number of pages, as in *Island on the Hill* when Frances and Cabel travel to a Caribbean island to meet his mother and her latest husband, people are not important to the main plot. Occasionally, minor characters perform more important functions, as does *Twice in a Blue Moon*'s Billy when he helps Tucker to realize Hope is a mature woman who can take care of herself.

Browning's strength as a genre writer lies in her ability to focus on the romantic relationship, to create clever dialogue, and to individualize her characters so that one does not so much notice her contrivances and her use of cliché in her plot.

Using the pseudonym Bronwyn Williams, Browning and her sister, writer Mary Williams, have written several Harlequin historical romances. Like Browning's contemporary novels, these are set in North Carolina and its environs. The historicals are rich in detail, and although romance is the focus, they have other strong plot elements, too. In *White Witch*, Kinnahauk must put aside his loyalty to the traditions of his Hatorask Indian heritage and take English woman Bridget Abbott as his wife. The clash of cultures theme continues in *Stormwalker*, the story of Kinnawauk and Bridget's son, Stormwalker, and his white wife, Laura Gray. *The Mariner's Bride* revolves around the often-used marriage of convenience, but at the same time delves into deeper issues as Kathleen Stevens learns self-esteem and independence. In *Gideon's Fall*, economic hardship forces twins Prudence and Pride Andros to disguise themselves as thieves and to steal from the pirates who had robbed their father.

The heroines of these historical novels endure great hardships and cruelty. When Prudence, disguised as a man, joins Gideon McNair's whaling crew, she works as hard as any of the others. Later, while taking her brother's place in a duel, she is shot in the back by the villain, who is also after her father's hidden treasure.

White Witch's Bridget Abbot is orphaned, imprisoned, shipwrecked, and kidnapped by evil Indians who turn her over to an equally evil white trader, all before finally ending up happily-ever-after with Kinnahauk. *Stormwalker*'s intended, Laura Gray, suffers an even worse fate. After her parents are killed by the evil Three Turtles, he rapes her. Pregnant, she is shunned by her own community and runs away to an island to have her baby. Later, Three Turtles returns and kidnaps the child.

These sometimes incredible experiences of the heroines seem more the focus of the novels than the love story; nevertheless, the Bronwyn Williams books do offer the reader plenty of historical detail and a complex, suspenseful plot.

—Linda Lee

BRYHER.

Pseudonym for Annie Winifred Ellerman. **Nationality:** British. **Born:** Margate, Kent, in 1894. **Education:** privately educated; Queenwood School, Eastbourne, Sussex. **Relations:** married 1) the writer Robert McAlmon in 1921 (marriage dissolved 1926); 2) Kenneth Macpherson in 1927 (marriage dissolved 1947); one adopted daughter. Began long relationship with the writer Hilda Doolittle ('H.D.') in 1919. **Career:** joint founder and editor, *Close Up* film journal, Territet, Switzerland, 1927–33. **Died:** 28 January 1983.

ROMANCE AND HISTORICAL PUBLICATIONS

Novels

The Fourteenth of October. New York, Pantheon, 1952; London, Collins, 1954.
The Player's Boy. New York, Pantheon, 1953; London, Collins, 1957.
Roman Wall. New York, Pantheon, 1954; London, Collins, 1955.
Gate to the Sea. New York, Pantheon, 1958; London, Collins, 1959.
Ruan. New York, Pantheon, 1960; London, Collins, 1961.
The Coin of Carthage. New York, Harcourt Brace, 1963; London, Collins, 1964.
This January Tale. New York, Harcourt Brace, 1966; London, Secker and Warburg, 1968.
The Colors of Vaud. New York, Harcourt Brace, 1969.

OTHER PUBLICATIONS

Novels

Development. London, Constable, and New York, Macmillan, 1920.
Two Selves. Paris, Contact, 1923(?); New York, Chaucer Head, 1927(?).
Civilians. Territet, Switzerland, Pool, 1927; London, Pool, 1930.
The Light-Hearted Student, with Trude Weiss. Dijon, Pool, 1930.
Beowulf. New York, Pantheon, 1956.
Visa for Avalon. New York, Harcourt Brace, 1965.

Poetry

Region of Lutany (as A.W. Ellerman). London, Chapman and Hall, 1914.
Arrow Music, with others. London, Bumpus, 1924.

Other

Amy Lowell: A Critical Appreciation. London, Eyre and Spottiswoode, 1918.
A Picture Geography for Little Children: Asia. London, Cape, 1925.
West (on the USA). London, Cape, 1925.
Film Problems of Soviet Russia. Territet, Switzerland, Pool, 1929.
Cinema Survey, with Robert Herring and Dallas Bower. London, Brendin, 1937.
The Heart to Artemis: A Writer's Memoirs. New York, Harcourt Brace, 1962; London, Collins, 1963.
The Days of Mars: A Memoir 1940–1946. New York, Harcourt Brace, and London, Calder and Boyars, 1972.

Translator, *The Lament for Adonis*, by Bion. London, Humphreys, 1918.

*   *   *

Bryher's historical novels cover a wide variety of settings, both in time and place, ranging from Paestum in the 4th century B.C. (*Gate to the Sea*) to late 18th-century Switzerland (*The Colors of Vaud*). *The Coin of Carthage* is set on the coasts of southern Italy and North Africa at the time of the Punic Wars, and *Roman Wall* takes place during the 3rd century A.D. in an outpost of the by now crumbling Empire close to the German border. *Ruan* is concerned with the world of Celtic Britain and Ireland in the middle of the 6th century, *The Fourteenth of October* and *This January Tale* with the events surrounding the Norman Conquest and its aftermath and *The Player's Boy* describes the life of a young actor in early 17th-century London. All of these books reveal Bryher's scholarly interest in the past, but if the background events which they describe are historically momentous, their immediate content is largely personal and domestic. The backgrounds themselves are designed to illustrate the particular qualities of certain periods when civilizations were in a state of transition; to this extent Bryher's historical novels are closely related to the period in which she wrote them. They are all by implication concerned with the political, personal, and social issues confronting Europe during the rise of the fascist dictatorships between the two world wars.

Bryher's novels are full of escapes and perilous journeys, and of people who have been ejected from their homes: several of them are poignant with a sense of exile. As she stresses repeatedly in her two books of memoirs, *The Heart to Artemis* and *The Days of Mars*, she clearly foresaw the inevitability of World War II, and her descriptions of the declining Roman Empire and of Anglo-Saxon England are critical portraits of enlightened civilizations which had grown complacent and effete and thus unprepared to defend themselves by fighting their aggressors.

The most well known, if in certain ways the most conventional, of Bryher's historical tales is the first of them, *The Fourteenth of October*. It is the story of a Yorkshire boy who is dispossessed of his family home by Danish raiders and carried overseas as the captive of a Norman baron. He escapes to Cornwall, where he finds love and security. But with the threat of a Norman invasion loyalty compels him to take part in a march across Southern England in support of the beleaguered King Harold, only to witness the aftermath of his defeat at Hastings. He returns to Cornwall, but faced with the prospect of living as a dependent of the hated Normans, he chooses freedom and becomes an exile.

All Bryher's leading themes and concerns are to be found in this novel: her sympathy with those ordinary working people who always have to bear the brunt of the contending ambitions of the powerful and greedy; an affection for the diurnal routines of life, for domesticity and daily work; a response to an atmosphere of mystery, exemplified here in the person of an old Cornish woman who embodies the beliefs and values of a bygone age; a hunger for personal liberty and a delight in the sea as an image of such freedom. This last named theme also features prominently in *Ruan*.

Other novels are more panoramic in technique and less personal in their focus. In *Roman Wall* the Germanic tribes are about to cross the Rhine and assault the slackly guarded borders of the Roman empire in Helvetia. Bryher portrays the onset of catastrophe with obvious reference to events in the Europe of her own day, and does so through a wide range of characters—the decadent Roman governor of the province, his aging mistress and his steward, a Greek trader with an eye to the main chance, soldiers, craftsmen, farmers, a family of loyal Roman settlers. She provides a picture of an entire community; their thoughts and fears and observations build up a mental world that makes the past come most convincingly alive. Bryher employs a similar technique, though on a smaller scale, in her account of life in post-Conquest Exeter, *This January Tale*, in which the plight of refugees is presented with understanding and compassionate restraint.

For all the research that went into their making, her novels are personal statements. This is particularly true of *The Fourteenth of October, The Player's Boy* and *Ruan;* in each of them the author impersonates an adolescent boy who grows painfully into manhood. All three are told in the first person; but perhaps because of this one is more aware of inhabiting a bygone environment than one is of inhabiting a bygone consciousness. The language and feelings inevitably are products of the 20th century in their literary style and sophisticated awareness. In *The Player's Boy*, which reflects Bryher's love for the work of the Jacobean dramatists, a vein of pessimism obtrudes. This novel stands apart from the others in its relatively static action and its meditative tone. It lacks the delight in travel that inspires the other novels, and which was a strong element in Bryher's character.

Of the books which deal with the Classical world, *Gate to the Sea* is little more than a novella; it describes the escape of a handful of Greek colonists from the conquered city of Paestum, and is a good example of the deft way in which Bryher can evoke suspense. *The Coin of Carthage* is more ambitious, portraying in episodic fashion the separate fortunes of two Greek traders at the time of Rome's wars with Carthage. In both novels the use of third-person narrative ensures a measure of detachment without any loss of physical immediacy, and *The Coin of Carthage* in particular gives one an insight into what life must actually have been like for working people living at the time. The book is also rich in accounts of plants and animals and ancient dwelling places, and conveys a powerful sense of the timelessness of daily life which is an underlying element in all the author's most successful work.

Bryher's novels are distinguished from most historical fiction in dispensing with the intricacies of plot and by their concentration on random happenings. The narrative approach is frequently cinematic; it moves easily from scene to scene, from consciousness to consciousness. A strong sense of fatality pervades the books; Bryher's vision is essentially a tragic one. Very much the products of a particular time, her novels are written in an informal style which in the later books becomes almost offhand, but which gives them at times a parabolic character. Their simplicity makes them readily accessible to younger readers, and indeed one of Bryher's favourite historical novelists was the children's author G.A. Henty. A strong vein of instruction is present in, for instance, *The Colors of Vaud*, which describes the attainment of independence from Bern of the Swiss canton in which Bryher had made her home; in this book characterization (never a strong point) is sacrificed to the making of historical points. But Bryher is usually more imaginative in her approach than here, and at her finest, as in *The Fourteenth of October*, *The Coin of Carthage*, and *Roman Wall*, her sense of human dignity and the austere and gracious cadence of her prose make these short, deeply felt novels resound with the force and suggestiveness of poetry.

—Glen Cavaliero

BUCHAN, Anna. See **DOUGLAS, O.**

BUCHAN, Elizabeth (Mary).
Nationality: British. **Born:** 21 May 1948. **Education:** Royal School, Bath; Rosemead School, Littlehampton, Sussex; University of Kent at Canterbury, B.A. (honours) in English and History. **Relations:** married Benjamin Buchan (the grandson of the writer John Buchan, *q.v.*) in 1974; two sons and one daughter. **Career:** cover editor, Penguin, London, 1971–89. Since 1989, senior fiction editor, Random House (publishers), London; regularly reviews books for *The Sunday Times*, London, and *Daily Telegraph*, London; committee member, Romantic Novelists Association, London, from 1992. **Agent:** Caroline Sheldon, 71 Hillgate Place, London W8 9SS, England. **Address:** c/o Macmillan Publishers (UK) Ltd, 4 Little Essex Street, London WC2R 3LF, England.

ROMANCE AND HISTORICAL PUBLICATIONS

Novels

Daughters of the Storm. London, Macmillan, 1988; New York, Bantam, 1990.
Light of the Moon. London, Macmillan, 1991.
Consider the Lily. London, Macmillan, and New York, Crown, 1993.

OTHER PUBLICATIONS

Other (for children)

Ice Dancer, with Tessa Strickland. London, Puffin, 1985.
Beatrice Potter: The Story of the Creator of Peter Rabbit. London, Hamish Hamilton, 1987.

Editor, *A Dashing Young Tiger Named Jack: A Collection of Silly Limericks*. London, Piccolo, 1987.

*

Elizabeth Buchan comments:

I aim always to entertain—but also to incorporate moral, social, and perhaps even spiritual considerations (without being sententious I hope). Each book is a journey, and so it should be, and I strive for high standards.

*   *   *

Elizabeth Buchan's novel, *Daughters of the Storm*, is set during the French Revolution and tells the story of three young women whose lives are irrevocably changed as a result of the political climate and subsequent revolution that swept through France in the last decade of the 18th century.

The three central characters, Sophie, an English girl visiting her cousins in France, Héloïse, Sophie's cousin, and Marie-Victoire, Héloïse's maid, are all caught up in events over which they have little or no control. Sophie is engaged to her cousin Ned, and Héloïse is betrothed and later married to a nobleman, the Count de Choissy. Neither are happy in these relationships and as the repressive society of the 18th century gradually breaks down, the clarion call of 'Liberté, egalité, fraternité' is applied as much to sexual mores as anything else. Héloïse takes as her lover a royalist named Louis, while Sophie, who has become politically as well as sexually awakened, falls for the American spy William. The arranged marriage of Sophie and the unhappy marriage of Héloïse break down.

The safety of the characters is jeopardized early in the novel and provides the revolutionary Jacques Maillard with all the excuses he needs to attempt to punish the ruling classes. He is guilty of raping Marie-Victoire and is punished by Héloïse with a beating. This single event inspires him with a desire for revenge which he enacts through the medium of revolution.

Maillard becomes a judge at the Revolutionary Tribunal set up in the spring of 1793 to 'judge without appeal the disturbers of the public peace!' He has Héloïse's father, the one time minister of supplies, arrested and executed, and explains to Héloïse that it was at her family home that he learnt his revolutionary zeal.

Buchan's great skill in this novel lies with her ability to relate to the reader the events of the revolution at a pace which suits the flow of the book and at the pace through which people lived through it. Although we, as 20th-century readers, know that the king will be executed and that the reign of terror will claim many lives, the characters at the time did not, and the historical passages of this novel, italicized and separate from the text, take us through the events of this time with a novelist's eye for a good story and a historian's desire for accuracy. The battle between King Louis and the French people, and the battle for supremacy within the revolutionary faction (the Feuillants, Girondins, and Jacobins) is superbly drawn and illustrates the tensions between the characters.

Of all the characters in this novel it is perhaps Sophie, the English girl, who deserves most attention. Her development, from girlhood to womanhood, can be seen as a symbol of the supposed regeneration of France through revolution. As she becomes interested in politics and becomes a pamphleteer, she sees her independence and embraces feminism: 'truly, I am increasingly of the opinion that the subject of our sex's position in society should be addressed'. It is no surprise to find that she falls in love with William, and returns to America with him.

The love and co-operation which exists between Sophie, as a revolutionary, and her cousin Héloïse, who is a royalist and traditionalist in political terms, again mirrors the revolution, but shows that co-operation can exist between two people with opposing political beliefs.

Buchan's *Light of the Moon* is again set against a background of political turmoil, although this time it is World War II and relates the story of Evelyn St John, a Special Operations Executive (SOE) and her growing love for a German army intelligence officer, Paul von

Hoch. The battle of love versus patriotism replaces the battle of the sexes and is a truly compelling read.

Buchan's meticulous research into the SOE pays dividends. The training that Evelyn receives is noted carefully and is based upon primary sources. The work she is to do, behind enemy lines in France, is portrayed convincingly and gives the reader as true a sense of the dangers as is possible. Interestingly the SOE operation which Evelyn heads concerns itself as much with others working for the liberation of France as it does with attacking the Germans. Communist inspired insurrections against the Nazis have to be defeated, or deterred to prevent the massacre of the innocent Frenchmen and women in retaliation. After one such operation Charles de Bourgrave, who is responsible for the circuit Evelyn works in, is killed. Evelyn returns to England and asks to head the circuit, and this is agreed by her superiors. The following passage illustrates the problems she faces and the sophistication of Buchan's prose and research:

> The death of Charles meant that the Merry-go-round circuit which he had started to build was leaderless. It was also blown. Without Charles' influence and authority, the attempt to unify the resistance forces in the area fizzled out and they splintered into factions: royalists, socialists, communists and those who supported General de Gaulle in Exile. It was a confusing situation to understand, even more difficult to work with.

As in *Daughters of the Storm*, Buchan leads the reader through the story in a very measured way. Events do not all happen at once and the characters' concerns for the future do not strike the 20th-century reader as foolish. Small touches, such as a recipe in *Good Housekeeping* for a sugarless Christmas pudding help to convey a vision of life in war. At one point Buchan reveals that the black marketeers in France, where they rate cuisine very highly, were known as 'bofs', which stands for 'beurre, oeufs, fromage'. These touches help to propel Buchan into a class of her own. Her fiction does not lend itself to categorization very easily, nor should it.

Buchan's latest novel, *Consider the Lily*, is a story of the regeneration of a garden, of marriage, and of coming to terms with loss. It has been described as 'one of the most poignant and beautiful novels of England between the wars you will ever read', and by Joanna Trollope as 'an excellent story ... strong imaginative power ... wonderful sense of atmosphere'. The praise is deserved.

—Kate Thompson

BUCHAN, John, 1st Baron Tweedsmuir of Elsfield.
Nationality: British. **Born:** Broughton Green, Peebles-shire, Scotland, 26 August 1875. Brother of the writer Anna Buchan (O Douglas, *q.v.*). **Education:** Hutchison Grammar School, Glasgow; University of Glasgow; Brasenose College, Oxford (scholar, 1895; Stanhope prize, 1897; Newdigate prize, 1898; President of the Union, 1899), B.A. (honours) 1899; Middle Temple, London, called to the Bar, 1901. **Military Service:** served on the Headquarters Staff of the British Army in France, as temporary Lieutenant Colonel, 1916–17; Director of Information under the Prime Minister, 1917–18. **Relations:** married Susan Charlotte Grosvenor in 1907; three sons and one daughter. **Career:** private secretary to the High Commissioner for South Africa, Lord Milner, 1901–03; director, Nelson, publishers, London, from 1903, and Reuters, London, 1919; Conservative Member of Parliament for the Scottish Universities, 1927–35; Lord High Commissioner, Church of Scotland, 1933, 1934; Governor-General of Canada, 1935–40; Privy Councillor, 1937. Curator, Oxford University Chest, 1924–30; President, Scottish History Society, 1929–33; bencher, Middle Temple, 1935;

Chancellor, University of Edinburgh, 1937–40; Justice of the Peace, Peebles-shire and Oxfordshire. **Recipient:** James Tait Black memorial prize, 1929. D.C.L.: Oxford University; LL.D.: University of Glasgow: University of St Andrews; University of Edinburgh; McGill University, Montreal; University of Toronto; University of Manitoba, Winnipeg; Harvard University, Cambridge, Massachusetts; Yale University, New Haven, Connecticut; D.Litt.: Columbia University, New York; University of British Columbia, Vancouver; McMaster University, Hamilton, Ontario. Honorary Fellow, Brasenose College, Oxford. Companion of Honour, 1932; created Baron Tweedsmuir, 1935; GCMG (Knight Grand Cross, Order of St Michael and St George), 1935; GCVO (Knight Grand Cross, Royal Victorian Order), 1939. **Died:** 11 February 1940.

ROMANCE AND HISTORICAL PUBLICATIONS

Novels

Sir Quixote of the Moors, Being Some Account of an Episode in the Life of the Sieur de Rohaine. London, Unwin, and New York, Holt, 1895.
John Burnet of Barns. London, Lane, and New York, Dodd Mead, 1898.
A Lost Lady of Old Years. London, Lane, 1899.
Salute to Adventurers. London, Nelson, and Boston, Houghton Mifflin, 1915.
Midwinter: Certain Travellers in Old England. London, Hodder and Stoughton, and New York, Doran, 1923.
Witch Wood. London, Hodder and Stoughton, and Boston, Houghton Mifflin, 1927.
The Blanket of the Dark. London, Hodder and Stoughton, and Boston, Houghton Mifflin, 1931.
The Free Fishers. London, Hodder and Stoughton, and Boston, Houghton Mifflin, 1934.
The Long Traverse. London, Hodder and Stoughton, 1941; as *Lake of Gold*, Boston, Houghton Mifflin, 1941.

Short Stories

The Moon Endureth: Tales and Fancies. Edinburgh, Blackwood, and New York, Sturgis, 1912.
The Path of the King. London, Hodder and Stoughton, and New York, Doran, 1921.

OTHER PUBLICATIONS

Novels

The Half-Hearted. London, Isbister, and Boston, Houghton Mifflin, 1900.
Prester John. London, Nelson, 1910; as *The Great Diamond Pipe*, New York, Dodd Mead, 1911.
The Thirty-Nine Steps. Edinburgh, Blackwood, 1915; New York, Doran, 1916.
The Power-House. Edinburgh, Blackwood, and New York, Doran, 1916.
Greenmantle. London, Hodder and Stoughton, and New York, Doran, 1916.
Mr Standfast. London, Hodder and Stoughton, and New York, Doran, 1919.
Huntingtower. London, Hodder and Stoughton, and New York, Doran, 1922.
The Three Hostages. London, Hodder and Stoughton, and Boston, Houghton Mifflin, 1924.

John Macnab. London, Hodder and Stoughton, and Boston, Houghton Mifflin, 1925.
The Dancing Floor. London, Hodder and Stoughton, and Boston, Houghton Mifflin, 1926.
The Courts of the Morning. London, Hodder and Stoughton, and Boston, Houghton Mifflin, 1929.
Castle Gay. London, Hodder and Stoughton, and Boston, Houghton Mifflin, 1929.
A Prince of the Captivity. London, Hodder and Stoughton, and Boston, Houghton Mifflin, 1933.
The House of the Four Winds. London, Hodder and Stoughton, and Boston, Houghton Mifflin, 1935.
The Island of Sheep. London, Hodder and Stoughton, 1936; as *The Man from the Norlands*, Boston, Houghton Mifflin, 1936.
Sick Heart River. London, Hodder and Stoughton, 1941; as *Mountain Meadow*, Boston, Houghton Mifflin, 1941.

Short Stories

Grey Weather: Moorland Tales of My Own People. London, Lane, 1899.
The Watcher by the Threshold and Other Tales. Edinburgh, Blackwood, 1902; augmented edition, New York, Doran, 1918.
Ordeal by Marriage: An Eclogue. London, R. Clay, 1915.
The Runagates Club. London, Hodder and Stoughton, and Boston, Houghton Mifflin, 1928.
The Gap in the Curtain. London, Hodder and Stoughton, and Boston, Houghton Mifflin, 1932.
The Best Short Stories of John Buchan, edited by David Daniell. London, Joseph, 2 vols, 1980–82.

Play

Screenplay: *The Battles of Coronel and Falkland Islands*, with Harry Engholm and Merritt Crawford, 1927.

Poetry

The Pilgrim Fathers. Oxford, Blackwell, 1898.
Poems, Scots and English. London, Jack, 1917; revised edition, London, Nelson, 1936.

Other

Scholar Gipsies. London, Lane, and New York, Macmillan, 1896.
Sir Walter Raleigh. Oxford, Blackwell, 1897.
Brasenose College. London, Robinson, 1898.
The African Colony: Studies in the Reconstruction. Edinburgh, Blackwell, 1903.
The Law Relating to the Taxation of Foreign Income. London, Stevens, 1905.
A Lodge in the Wilderness (published anonymously). Edinburgh, Blackwood, 1906.
Some Eighteenth Century Byways and Other Essays. Edinburgh, Blackwood, 1908.
Sir Walter Raleigh (for children). London, Nelson, and New York, Holt, 1911.
What the Home Rule Bill Means (speech). Peebles, Smythe, 1912.
The Marquis of Montrose. London, Nelson, and New York, Scribner, 1913.
Andrew Jameson, Lord Ardwall. Edinburgh, Blackwood, 1913.
Britain's War by Land. London, Oxford University Press, 1915.
Nelson's History of the War. London, Nelson, 24 vols, 1915–19; as *A History of the Great War*, Nelson, and Boston, Houghton Mifflin, 4 vols, 1921–22.
The Achievement of France. London, Methuen, 1915.

The Future of the War (speech). London, Boyle Son and Watchurst, 1916.
The Purpose of War (speech). London, Dent, 1916.
These for Remembrance. Privately printed, 1919.
The Island of Sheep, with Susan Buchan (as Cadmus and Harmonia). London, Hodder and Stoughton, 1919; Boston, Houghton Mifflin, 1920.
The Battle-Honours of Scotland 1914–1918. Glasgow, Outram, 1919.
The History of the South African Forces in France. London, Nelson, 1920.
Francis and Riversdale Grenfell: A Memoir. London, Nelson, 1920.
A Book of Escapes and Hurried Journeys. London, Nelson, 1922; Boston, Houghton Mifflin, 1923.
The Last Secrets: The Final Mysteries of Exploration. London, Nelson, 1923; Boston, Houghton Mifflin, 1924.
The Memoir of Sir Walter Scott (speech). Privately printed, 1923.
Days to Remember: The British Empire in the Great War, with Henry Newbolt. London, Nelson, 1923.
Some Notes on Sir Walter Scott (speech). London, Oxford University Press, 1924.
Lord Minto: A Memoir. London, Nelson, 1924.
The History of the Royal Scots Fusiliers (1678–1918). London, Nelson, 1925.
The Man and the Book: Sir Walter Raleigh. London, Nelson, 1925.
Two Ordeals of Democracy (lecture). Boston, Houghton Mifflin, 1925.
Homilies and Recreations. London, Nelson, and Boston, Houghton Mifflin, 1926.
To the Electors of the Scottish Universities (speech). Glasgow, Anderson, 1927.
The Fifteenth—Scottish—Division 1914–1919, with John Stewart. Edinburgh, Blackwood, 1926.
Montrose. London, Nelson, and Boston, Houghton Mifflin, 1928.
The Causal and the Casual in History (lecture). Cambridge, University Press, and New York, Macmillan, 1929.
What the Union of the Churches Means to Scotland. Edinburgh, McNivern and Wallace, 1929.
The Kirk in Scotland 1560–1929, with George Adam Smith. London, Hodder and Stoughton, 1930.
Montrose and Leadership (lecture). London, Oxford University Press, 1930.
The Revision of Dogmas (lecture). Ashridge, Wisconsin, Ashridge Journal, 1930.
Lord Rosebery 1847–1930. London, Oxford University Press, 1930.
The Novel and the Fairy Tale. London, Oxford University Press, 1931.
Sir Walter Scott. London, Cassell, and New York, Coward McCann, 1932.
The Magic Walking-Stick (for children). London, Hodder and Stoughton, and Boston, Houghton Mifflin, 1932.
Julius Caesar. London, Davies, and New York, Appleton, 1932.
The Massacre of Glencoe. London, Davies, and New York, Putnam, 1933.
Andrew Lang and the Border (lecture). London, Oxford University Press, 1933.
The Margins of Life (speech). London, Birkbeck College, 1933.
The Principles of Social Service (lecture). Glasgow, Glasgow Society of Social Service, 1934(?).
The Scottish Church and the Empire (speech). Glasgow, Church of Scotland Commission on Colonial Churches, 1934.
Gordon at Khartoum. London, Davies, 1934.
Oliver Cromwell. London, Hodder and Stoughton, and Boston, Houghton Mifflin, 1934.
Men and Deeds. London, Davies, 1935; Freeport, New York, Books for Libraries, 1969.

The King's Grace 1910–35 (on George V). London, Hodder and Stoughton, 1935; as *The People's King*, Boston, Houghton Mifflin, 1935.

An Address [The Western Mind]. Montreal, McGill University, 1935.

Address [A University's Bequest to Youth]. Toronto, Victoria University, 1936.

Augustus. London, Hodder and Stoughton, and Boston, Houghton Mifflin, 1937.

The Interpreter's House (speech). London, Hodder and Stoughton, 1938.

Presbyterianism Yesterday, Today, and Tomorrow. Edinburgh, Church of Scotland, 1938.

Memory Hold-the-Door. London, Hodder and Stoughton, 1940; as *Pilgrim's War: An Essay in Recollection*, Boston, Houghton Mifflin, 1940.

Comments and Characters, edited by W. Forbes Gray. London, Nelson, 1940; Freeport, New York, Books for Libraries, 1970.

Canadian Occasions (lectures). London, Hodder and Stoughton, 1940.

The Clearing House: A Survey of One Man's Mind, edited by Lady Tweedsmuir. London, Hodder and Stoughton, 1946.

Life's Adventure: Extracts from the Works of John Buchan, edited by Lady Tweedsmuir. London, Hodder and Stoughton, 1947.

Editor, *Essays and Apothegms*, by Francis Bacon. London, Scott, 1894.

Editor, *Musa Piscatrix*. London, Lane, and Chicago, McClurg, 1896.

Editor, *The Compleat Angler*, by Izaak Walton. London, Methuen, 1901.

Editor, *The Long Road to Victory*. London, Nelson, 1920.

Editor, *Great Hours in Sport*. London, Nelson, 1921.

Editor, *Miscellanies, Literary and Historical*, by Archibald Primrose, Earl of Rosebery. London, Hodder and Stoughton, 1921.

Editor, *A History of English Literature*. London, Nelson, 1923; New York, Ronald Press, 1938.

Editor, *The Nations of Today; A New History of the World*. London, Hodder and Stoughton, and Boston, Houghton Mifflin, 12 vols, 1923–24.

Editor, *The Northern Muse: An Anthology of Scots Vernacular Poetry*. London, Nelson, 1924.

Editor, *Modern Short Stories*. London, Nelson, 1926.

Editor, *Essays and Studies 12*. Oxford, Clarendon Press, 1926.

Editor, *South Africa*. London, British Empire Educational Press, 1928.

Editor, *The Teaching of History*. London, Nelson, 11 vols, 1928–30.

Editor, *The Poetry of Neil Munro*. Edinburgh, Blackwood, 1931.

*

Film Adaptations: *The Thirty-Nine Steps*, 1935, 1959, 1978.

Bibliography: *John Buchan: A Bibliography* by Archibald Hanna, Jr, Hamden, Connecticut, Shoe String Press, 1953; by J. Randolph Cox, in *English Literature in Transition* (Tempe, Arizona), 1966–67; *The First Editions of John Buchan: A Collector's Bibliography* by Robert G. Blanchard, Hamden, Connecticut, Archon, 1981.

Manuscript Collections: National Library of Scotland, Edinburgh; Edinburgh University Library; Douglas Library, Queen's University, Kingston, Ontario.

Critical Studies: *The Interpreter's House: A Critical Assessment of John Buchan* by David Daniell, London, Nelson, 1975; *John Buchan and His World* by Janet Adam Smith, London, Thames and Hudson, 1979; *John Buchan: A Memoir* by William Buchan, London, Buchan and Enright, 1982.

*   *   *

It is ironic that a writer of such high moral seriousness as John Buchan should be best known because of an inaccurate movie rendition of one of his novels. Yet everyone remembers *The Thirty-Nine Steps*, while his historical novels are left unread. Of course, it is also ironic that this scholar, attorney, soldier, and statesman should have chosen to express so much of his moral passion in the form of historical novels. Yet no matter how breathtaking the action, Buchan's real interest is the demonstration of what he regards as the truths of history and the truths of human psychology.

One of the truths that runs through his books is explicit when Nandy Lammas, that minister of the church and professor of philosophy thinks, 'It lay with him to prove that a scholar could also be a man'. From Nandy, who is called upon to save his former student from a designing woman and, with *The Free Fishers*, to protect England from Napoleon's spies, to another minister, David Semphill in *Witch Wood*, who must fight the ancient lures of witchcraft in his small parish while the forces of Montrose and the Covenanters fight for the allegiance and lives of the Scottish people, to—almost unbelievably—Samuel Johnson himself, the middle-aged tutor whose loyalty almost lands him on the bloody battlefield of Culloden in *Midwinter*, Buchan portrays the opposing lures of the life of the mind and the spirit and the physical life. Only Dr Johnson is ultimately unable to combine both. He must say goodbye to his Scottish friend Alistair McLean, who goes to a losing battle with his Prince, and return to London, to his wife, and to the life of the mind where he will be a victor. Yet even the losses others endure have something good in them. Nandy has served his country well and has had a glimpse of romance, although he knows that the beautiful, wronged Mrs Cranmer is not for an aging don. He is willing to reenter his scholarly world. But the brotherhood of the free fishers is still open to him, and he has renewed eternally the youth that makes the poet. Similarly, in *Witch Wood*, David exposes the chief of the coven who has made the ancient wood of Caledon heavy and oppressive. But Katrine, the love of his life, lies dead of the plague, and he finds the strictures of the covenant, which he had once gladly accepted, place an intolerable burden on him. He may still serve his God, but he will do it as a soldier of Montrose.

Of all British writers, Buchan may be the one who loves most and writes best about the United States. *Salute to Adventurers* is set in Virginia, and parts of *The Path of the King* in Kentucky, Indiana, and Illinois. *The Path of the King* is a daring experiment for Buchan, perhaps best described as touching and unsuccessful. Starting with the premise that no one knows what noble blood may run in the veins of someone of humble birth who rises to greatness, Buchan traces the fortunes of the descendants of a Viking lordling captured in a raid on the Norman coast. A golden ring passes from parent to child through generations, with the rumor that they are of royal blood. The descendants rise and fall with fortune, although perhaps they rise too much to be quite convincing as humble folk. Creditably for Buchan, the ring passes through the female line on a number of occasions (including a French noblewoman who befriends Joan of Arc). One ring holder is the regicide Lovel, and after the Restoration things go badly for his family, until the remnants move to the American colonies. When the last woman to own the ring learns, on her death bed, that it has been lost, she realizes that the purpose of the ring has been fulfilled; the son she has born to Thomas Linkhorn will be a saviour of his people. The description of Lincoln's last days is impressive both in scholarship and in emotion, but the message of the book as a whole is less convincing.

In one of his short stories, Buchan remarks 'Every man has a creed, but in his soul he knows that the creed has another side, possibly not less logical, which it does not suit him to produce'. This is true of Buchan himself, notably in his attitude toward the House of Stuart. Lovel, the regicide, is perhaps the most balanced, sanest of the portrayals in *The Path of the King;* the aged pretender Charles, Duke of Albany, is shown as a helpless sot in the short story 'The Company of Marjorlaine'. Yet McLain in *Midwinter* is not the only one devoted to His Majesty's cause, and the Covenanters in *Witch Wood* are clearly drunk with excess of authority. Buchan could compromise on everything except the need for balance. His political views as a whole are less simplistic than it is currently the fashion to believe, and in the historical novels particularly the important things are loyalty and courage, exercised in whatever cause.

The independent, quirky, and stubbornly idiosyncratic have a special place in Buchan's affections, overshadowing his more conventional heroes. *Midwinter*'s eponymous hero is a representative of Old England which Dr Johnson, another figure wildly out of place in the rigours of an adventure novel, rejects for the hive of London and which McLain also rejects because Scotland is his country, even if it must be a country of exile. John Burnet's serving man Nicol in *John Burnet of Barns* is an honourable eccentric, loyal and reluctant to be bound by routine. Eben Garnock and the other free fishers of that novel counterpoise the English horseman Sir Turnour Wyse as studies of the characteristics of their respective nations.

Buchan's style can be more sophisticated than the impetus of the plots would suggest. The use of music in *Midwinter*, for instance, is an effective unifying theme.

When all that can be said in praise of Buchan has been said—his supple prose, his soldier's grasp of terrain, his naturalist's feeling for the countryside, his depictions of desperate journeys taken against the constraints of time and weather—one must still ask if there is something for the modern reader in his books. The answer must be a qualified yes. Buchan, like his great forebear Scott, often starts his stories slowly and one must wait for the action to begin. There are passages of near-impenetrable dialect (certainly for the American reader). Sadly, one of the worst obstacles between Buchan and the modern reader is his assumption that the reader will recognize minor historical figures and events without undue explanation. Yet for all that, the sweep and magnificence of the history, the flashes of humour, the portrayals of the life of the ordinary Scottish people and the pious warmth of the humble folk, and above all the sheer excitement of the plot will always provide rewards for readers of Buchan.

—Susan Branch

BUCK, Pearl S(ydenstricker).
Pseudonym: John Sedges. **Nationality:** American. **Born:** Hillsboro, West Virginia, 26 June 1892; daughter of Presbyterian missionaries in China. **Education:** boarding school in Shanghai, 1907–09; Randolph-Macon Woman's College, Lynchburg, Virginia, B.A. 1914 (Phi Beta Kappa); Cornell University, Ithaca, New York, M.A. 1926. **Relations:** married 1) John Lossing Buck in 1917 (divorced 1935), one daughter; 2) Richard J. Walsh in 1935 (died 1960); eight adopted children. **Career:** Psychology teacher, Randolph-Macon Woman's College, 1914; English teacher, University of Nanking, 1921–31, Southeastern University, Nanking, 1925–27, and Chung Yang University, Nanking, 1928–30; returned to the United States, 1935; co-editor, *Asia* magazine, New York, 1941–46; founder and director, East and West Association, 1941–51; founder, Welcome House, an adoption agency, 1949, and Pearl S. Buck Foundation, 1964; member of the Board of Directors, Weather Engineering Corporation of America, Manchester, New Hampshire, 1966. **Recipient:** Pulitzer prize, 1932; American Academy Howells medal, 1935; Nobel prize for literature, 1938; National Conference of Christians and Jews Brotherhood award, 1955; President's Commission on Employment of the Physically Handicapped citation, 1958; Women's National Book Association Skinner award, 1960; ELA award, 1969. M.A.: Yale University, New Haven, Connecticut, 1933; D.Litt.: University of West Virginia, Morgantown, 1940; St Lawrence University, Canton, New York, 1942; Delaware Valley College, Doylestown, Pennsylvania, 1965; LL.D.: Howard University, Washington, D.C., 1942; Muhlenberg College, Allentown, Pennsylvania, 1966; L.H.D.: Lincoln University, Pennsylvania, 1953; Woman's Medical College of Philadelphia, 1954; University of Pittsburgh, 1960; Bethany College, West Virginia, 1963; Hahnemann Medical College, Philadelphia, 1966; Rutgers University, New Brunswick, New Jersey, 1969; D.Mus.: Combs College of Music, Philadelphia, 1962; H.H.D.: West Virginia State College, Institute, 1963. Member, American Academy. **Died:** 6 March 1973.

ROMANCE AND HISTORICAL PUBLICATIONS

Novels

East Wind: West Wind. New York, Day, 1930; London, Methuen, 1931.
House of Earth. New York, Reynal, 1935; London, Methuen, 1936.
    The Good Earth. New York, Day, and London, Methuen, 1931.
    Sons. New York, Day, and London, Methuen, 1932.
The Mother. New York, Day, and London, Methuen, 1934.
A House Divided. New York, Reynal, and London, Methuen, 1935.
China Sky. Philadelphia, Triangle, 1942.
China Flight. Philadelphia, Triangle, 1945.
The Townsman (as John Sedges). New York, Day, 1945; London, Methuen, 1946.
Portrait of a Marriage. New York, Day, 1945; London, Methuen, 1946.
Pavilion of Women. New York, Day, 1946; London, Methuen, 1947.
The Angry Wife (as John Sedges). New York, Day, 1947; London, Methuen, 1948.
Peony. New York, Day, 1948; as *The Bondmaid*, London, Methuen, 1949.
Kin Folk. New York, Day, 1949; London, Methuen, 1950.
God's Men. New York, Day, and London, Methuen, 1951.
The Hidden Flower. New York, Day, and London, Methuen, 1952.
Satan Never Sleeps. New York, Pocket Books, 1952.
Come, My Beloved. New York, Day, and London, Methuen, 1953.
Imperial Woman. New York, Day, and London, Methuen, 1956.
Letter from Peking. New York, Day, and London, Methuen, 1957.
The Living Reed. New York, Day, and London, Methuen, 1963.
Death in the Castle. New York, Day, and London, Methuen, 1966.
The Time Is Noon. New York, Day, and London, Methuen, 1967.
The New Year. New York, Day, and London, Methuen, 1968.
The Three Daughters of Madame Liang. New York, Day, and London, Methuen, 1969.
Mandala. New York, Day, 1970; London, Methuen, 1971.
The Goddess Abides. New York, Day, and London, Methuen, 1972.
All under Heaven. New York, Day, and London, Methuen, 1973.
The Rainbow. New York, Day, 1974; London, Eyre Methuen, 1976.

Short Stories

The First Wife and Other Stories. New York, Day, and London, Methuen, 1933.
Today and Forever: Stories of China. New York, Day, and London, Macmillan, 1941.

Twenty-Seven Stories. New York, Sun Dial Press, 1943.
Far and Near: Stories of Japan, China, and America. New York, Day, 1947; as *Far and Near: Stories of East and West*, London, Methuen, 1949.
Fourteen Stories. New York, Day, 1961; as *With a Delicate Air and Other Stories*, London, Methuen, 1962.
Hearts Come Home and Other Stories. New York, Pocket Books, 1962.
Stories of China (includes *The First Wife* and *Today and Forever*). New York, Day, 1964.
Escape at Midnight and Other Stories. New York, Dragonfly Books, 1964.
The Good Deed and Other Stories of Asia, Past and Present. New York, Day, 1969; London, Methuen, 1970.
Once upon a Christmas. New York, Day, 1972.
East and West: Stories. New York, Day, 1975; London, Prior, 1976.
Secrets of the Heart: Stories. New York, Day, 1976.
The Lovers and Other Stories. New York, Day, 1977; London, Eyre Methuen, 1978.
Mrs Stoner and the Sea and Other Stories. New York, Ace Books, 1978.
The Woman Who Was Changed and Other Stories. New York, Crowell, 1979.

OTHER PUBLICATIONS

Novels

This Proud Heart. New York, Reynal and Hitchcock, and London, Methuen, 1938.
The Patriot. New York, Day, 1939; London, Methuen, 1941.
Other Gods: An American Legend. New York, Day, and London, Macmillan, 1940.
Dragon Seed. New York, Day, and London, Macmillan, 1942.
The Story of Dragon Seed. New York, Day, 1944.
The Promise. New York, Day, 1943; London, Methuen, 1945.
Command the Morning. New York, Day, and London, Methuen, 1959.

Novels as John Sedges

American Triptych: Three 'John Sedges' Novels. New York, Day, 1958.
 The Long Love. New York, Day, 1949; London, Methuen, 1950.
 Bright Procession. New York, Day, and London, Methuen, 1952.
 Voices in the House. New York, Day, 1953; London, Methuen, 1954.

Plays

Flight into China (produced New York, 1939).
Sun Yat Sen: A Play, Preceded by a Lecture by Dr Hu-shih. New York, Universal Distributors, and London, China Campaign Committee, 1944(?).
China to America (radio play), in *Free World Theatre*, edited by Arch Oboler and Stephen Longstreet. New York, Random House, 1944.
Will This Earth Hold? (radio play), in *Radio Drama in Action*, edited by Erik Barnouw. New York, Farrar and Rinehart, 1945.
The First Wife (produced New York, 1945).
A Desert Incident (produced New York, 1959).
Christine, with Charles K. Peck, Jr, music by Sammy Fain, lyrics by Paul Francis Webster, adaptation of the novel *My Indian Family* by Hilda Wernher (produced New York, 1960).

The Guide, adaptation of the novel by R.K. Narayan (produced New York, 1965).

Screenplays (with Ted Danielewski): *The Big Wave*, 1962; *The Guide*, 1965.

Poetry

Words of Love. New York, Day, 1974.

Other (for children)

The Young Revolutionist. New York, Day, and London, Methuen, 1932.
Stories for Little Children. New York, Day, 1940.
When Fun Begins. London, Methuen, 1941.
The Chinese Children Next Door. New York, Day, 1942; London, Methuen, 1943.
The Water Buffalo Children. New York, Day, 1943; London, Methuen, 1945.
The Dragon Fish. New York, Day, 1944; (as John Sedges) London, Methuen, 1946.
Yu Lan: Flying Boy of China. New York, Day, 1945; London, Methuen, 1947.
The Big Wave. New York, Day, 1948; London, Methuen, 1956.
One Bright Day. New York, Day, 1950; as *One Bright Day and Other Stories for Children*, London, Methuen, 1952.
The Man Who Changed China: The Story of Sun Yat Sen. New York, Random House, 1953; London, Methuen, 1955.
The Beech Tree. New York, Day, 1954.
Johnny Jack and His Beginnings. New York, Day, 1954; London, Methuen, 1955.
Christmas Miniature. New York, Day, 1957; as *The Christmas Mouse*, London, Methuen, 1958.
The Christmas Ghost. New York, Day, 1960; London, Methuen, 1962.
Welcome Child. New York, Day, 1964.
The Big Fight. New York, Day, 1965.
The Little Fox in the Middle. New York, Collier, and London, Macmillan, 1966.
Matthew, Mark, Luke, and John. New York, Day, 1967.
The Chinese Storyteller. New York, Day, 1971.
A Gift for the Children. New York, Day, 1973.
Mrs Starling's Problem. New York, Day, 1973.

Other

Is There a Case for Foreign Missions? (pamphlet). New York, Day, 1932; London, Methuen, 1933.
East and West and the Novel: Sources of the Early Chinese Novel. Peking, College of Chinese Studies, 1932.
The Spirit and the Flesh. New York, Day, 1944.
 The Exile (biography). New York, Reynal, and London, Methuen, 1936.
 Fighting Angel: Portrait of a Soul (biography). New York, Reynal, 1936; London, Methuen, 1937.
The Chinese Novel (lecture). New York, Day, and London, Macmillan, 1939.
Of Men and Women. New York, Day, 1941; London, Methuen, 1942.
Freedom for All. New York, Post-War World Council, 1942(?).
American Unity and Asia. New York, Day, 1942; as *Asia and Democracy*, London, Methuen, 1943.
What America Means to Me. New York, Day, 1943; London, Methuen, 1944.

Talk about Russia, with Masha Scott. New York, Day, 1945.
Tell the People: Talks with James Yen about the Mass Education Movement. New York, Day, 1945.
Tell the People: Mass Education in China. Institute of Pacific Relations, 1945.
How It Happens: Talk about the German People 1914–1933, with Erna von Pustau. New York, Day, 1947.
American Argument, with Eslanda Goode Robeson. New York, Day, 1949; London, Methuen, 1950.
The Child Who Never Grew. New York, Day, 1950; London, Methuen, 1951.
My Several Worlds: A Personal Record (autobiography). New York, Day, 1954; London, Methuen, 1955.
Friend to Friend: A Candid Exchange between Pearl S. Buck and Carlos P.Romulo. New York, Day, 1958.
The Delights of Learning. Pittsburgh, University of Pittsburgh Press, 1960.
A Bridge for Passing (autobiography). New York, Day, 1962; London, Methuen, 1963.
The Joy of Children. New York, Day, 1964.
The Gifts They Bring: Our Debts to the Mentally Retarded, with Gweneth T. Zarfoss. New York, Day, 1965.
Children for Adoption. New York, Random House, 1965.
The People of Japan. New York, Simon and Schuster, 1966; London, Hale, 1968.
For Spacious Skies: Journey in Dialogue, with Theodore F. Harris. New York, Day, 1966.
My Mother's House, with others. Richwood, West Virginia, Appalachia Press, 1966.
To My Daughters, With Love. New York, Day, 1967.
The People of China. London, Hale, 1968.
The Kennedy Women: A Personal Appraisal. New York, Cowles-Day, and London, Methuen, 1970.
China as I See It, edited by Theodore F. Harris. New York, Day, 1970; London, Methuen, 1971.
The Story Bible. New York, Bartholomew House, 1971.
Pearl S. Buck's America. New York, Bartholomew House, 1971.
China Past and Present. New York, Day, 1972.
A Community Success Story: The Founding of the Pearl Buck Center. New York, Day, 1972.
Oriental Cookbook. New York, Simon and Schuster, 1972; London, Eyre Methuen, 1974.

Editor, *China in Black and White: An Album of Woodcuts by Contemporary Chinese Artists*. New York, Day, 1945.
Editor, *Fairy Tales of the Orient*. New York, Simon and Schuster, 1965.
Editor, *Pearl S. Buck's Book of Christmas*. New York, Simon and Schuster, 1974.

Translator, *All Men Are Brothers*, by Shui Hu Chan. New York, Day, and London, Methuen, 1933.

*

Film Adaptations: *The Good Earth*, 1937; *Dragon Seed*, 1944; *China Sky*, 1945; *The Devil Never Sleeps*, 1962.

Bibliography: by Lucille S. Zinn, in *Bulletin of Bibliography* 36 (Boston), 1979.

Critical Studies: *Pearl S. Buck* by Paul A. Doyle, New York, Twayne, 1965, revised edition, 1980; *Pearl S. Buck: A Biography* by Theodore F. Harris, New York, Day, 2 vols, 1969–71, London, Eyre Methuen, 2 vols, 1970–72; *Pearl S. Buck: A Woman in Conflict* by Nora Stirling, Piscataway, New Jersey, New Century, 1983.

*   *   *

In an astonishingly prolific career, during which she produced more than 70 major works, many of her novels with an American setting under the pseudonym John Sedges, Pearl S. Buck did more to bring the East and West closer together in empathy and understanding than had any previous writer. No Western reader who had come to care, intensely and personally, about the fate of a character in a work of fiction, is likely to pay more than passing attention to the race or creed of that character; what matters is a shared humanity. Through Buck's writings, millions cared, as they had never before been persuaded to do, about the men and women of China, Korea, Japan, and India.

Buck's lasting fame is chiefly that of the writer who made China a real place peopled by three-dimensional human beings; a concept quite revolutionary to readers accustomed to read, if at all, of cardboard figures either quaint, comic, or sinister, moving in a stilted, stylized fashion about an exotic and artificial stage not even intended to convince. *The Good Earth*, Buck's most successful and important novel, changed all that forever.

Buck's Chinese men, and perhaps even more so her women, were convincingly as real and true to life as were her readers; so too were her Koreans, Indians, Japanese, and Americans. Herself a 'missionary kid', Buck well understood the difficulties as well as the benefits of belonging simultaneously to two worlds. She understood too, through personal experience, the unique and fragile bridge between two cultures that can give the deepest joy, and inflict the most bitter pain: that of love between men and women of different races, bestowed in opposition to the hopes, even the demands, of family and community.

Interracial love, almost always star-crossed, rarely allowed to come to rewarding fulfilment, is the recurring theme of Buck's work. Madame Wu, in *Pavilion of Women*, discovers after years of correct and tepid marriage what love can mean, and that even the pain of such a love can be very sweet, through her firmly controlled and suppressed passion for the Italian Brother Andre. What Madame Wu has learned through this forbidden love gives her strength and understanding to help her son when in his turn he loses his heart to an impossible, non-Chinese love.

In *The Hidden Flower*, a traditional Japanese family is overset when the beloved and sheltered daughter, Josui, already betrothed in the correct manner to a worthy young Japanese man, is swept up into a most untraditional, ill-fated love match with Allen Kennedy, an American soldier with the army of occupation. Not even a love story, merely a casual interlude, the coming together of Soonya, a Korean girl, and Chris, an American soldier, has resulted in the birth of a son. In *The New Year*, the forgotten son reaches out to touch the life of his casual American parent, now married to a woman of his own people.

The love of Bettina, a former slave, and Tom, a southerner who fought for the army of the North, tears a proud old family to shreds in *The Angry Wife*. Livy MacArd of *Come My Beloved* is the daughter of a missionary in India, who preached the brotherhood of man, and of equality before God, but who cannot live up to his own professed faith when his daughter falls in love with a young Indian, Jatin.

Peony, a bondmaid in the house of Ezra ben Israel, loves her young master David, but his mother is determined that he shall have a Jewish bride. It is not to be: David does in time marry a Chinese girl, but not faithful Peony, who has helped him to win Kueilan, the rival who supplants her. She knows only too well that a Jewish wife would shut her out of David's life entirely, whereas a Chinese woman would allow their friendship to continue; and her love finds the sacrifice worthwhile.

No matter the setting, the pain is the same, and the outcome over and over again is a slow working-out over generations of the reverberations set astir by patterns broken; the patterns will mend, imperceptibly as a pond mends a shattered reflection; the disruptive rock remains, hidden beneath the calm surface.

Time has passed Buck's work by; in most of the world, the sanctions that caused her people such pain and grief have lost their power, and as the world grows ever smaller, insular attitudes become untenable. It is only fair to remember, however, that 'a journey of a thousand miles begins with a single step'. Not so very long ago, Buck first invited a great many people to make that all-important step into the future.

—Joan McGrath

_____

BUCKINGHAM, Nancy.
Pseudonym for John and Nancy Sawyer. **Other Pseudonyms:** Christina Abbey; Nancy John; Nancy London; Erica Quest. **SAWYER, John. Nationality:** British. **Born:** London, 4 October 1919. **Relations:** married Nancy Buckingham in 1949; one son and one daughter. **Career:** director of a London advertising firm. Full-time writer. **Died:** 1990. **SAWYER, Nancy. Nationality:** British. **Born:** Nancy Buckingham, in Bristol, 10 August 1924. **Career:** worked as medical social worker. Full-time writer. **Agent:** A.M. Heath, 79 St Martin's Lane, London WC2N 4AA, England; or, Brandt and Brandt, 1501 Broadway, New York, New York 10036, USA.

ROMANCE AND HISTORICAL PUBLICATIONS

Novels

Victim of Love. London, Hale, 1967; as *The Hour Before Moonrise*, New York, Ace, 1967.
Cloud over Malverton. New York, Ace, 1967; London, Hale, 1970.
Heart of Marble. London, Hale, 1967; as *Storm in the Mountains*, New York, Ace, 1967.
Romantic Journey. London, Hale, 1968; as *The Legend of Baverstock Manor*, New York, Ace, 1968.
The Dark Summer. London, Hale, and New York, Ace, 1968.
Call of Glengarron. London, Ace, 1968; New York, Hale, 1969.
Kiss of Hot Sun. London, Hale, 1969.
The Secret of the Ghostly Shroud. New York, Lancer, 1969; as *Shroud of Silence*, London, Hale, 1970.
The House Called Edenhythe. London, Hale, 1970; New York, Hawthorn, 1972.
Return to Vienna. New York, Dell, 1971; London, Hale, 1973.
Quest for Alexis. New York, Hawthorn, 1973; London, Hale, 1974.
Valley of the Ravens. New York, Hawthorn, 1973; London, Hale, 1975.
The Jade Dragon. New York, Hawthorn, 1974; London, Hale, 1976.
The Other Cathy. London, Eyre Methuen, 1978; South Yarmouth, Massachusetts, Curley, 1981.
Vienna Summer. London, Eyre Methuen, and New York, St Martin's Press, 1979.
Marianna. London, Eyre Methuen, 1981.

Novels as Erica Quest

The Silver Castle. New York, Doubleday, 1978; Long Preston, Yorkshire, Magna, 1988.
The October Cabaret. New York, Doubleday, 1979; London, Hale, 1986.

Design for Murder. New York, Doubleday, 1981.
Death Walk. New York, Doubleday, 1988; London, Piatkus, 1990.
Cold Coffin. London Piatkus, 1990.
Model Murder. London, Piatkus, 1991.
Deadly Deceit. London, Piatkus, 1992.

Novels as Nancy John

The Spanish House. New York, Pocket Books, and London, Hodder and Stoughton, 1981.
Tormenting Flame. New York, Pocket Books, and London, Hodder and Stoughton, 1981.
To Trust Tomorrow. New York, Pocket Books, and London, Hodder and Stoughton, 1981.
A Man for Always. New York, Pocket Books, 1981; London, Hodder and Stoughton, 1982.
Outback Summer. New York, Pocket Books, and London, Hodder and Stoughton, 1981.
So Many Tomorrows. New York, Pocket Books, and London, Hodder and Stoughton, 1982.
Web of Passion. New York, Pocket Books, 1982; London, Hodder and Stoughton, 1983.
Make-Believe Bride. New York, Pocket Books, and London, Hodder and Stoughton, 1982.
Window to Happiness. New York, Pocket Books, and London, Hodder and Stoughton, 1983.
Summer Rhapsody. New York, Pocket Books, and London, Hodder and Stoughton, 1983.
Never Too Late. New York, Pocket Books, and London, Hodder and Stoughton, 1983.
Dream of Yesterday. New York, Pocket Books, and London, Hodder and Stoughton, 1984.
Champagne Nights. New York, Pocket Books, and London, Hodder and Stoughton, 1984.
Night with a Stranger. New York, Silhouette, 1984.
Rendezvous. New York and London, Silhouette, 1985.
The Moongate Wish. New York and London, Silhouette, 1985.
Lookalike Love. New York and London, Silhouette, 1986.
Secret Love. New York and London, Silhouette, 1986.

*   *   *

Nancy Buckingham is one of the pseudonyms used by the highly successful writing team, Nancy and John Sawyer. While fans must lament the fact that John Sawyer died in 1990, they will no doubt hope that Nancy Sawyer will continue to produce well-written and enjoyable gothic/suspense-romances.

The early Buckingham books can be compared to Mary Stewart's mystery romances. They contain twisted plots, set in interesting locations with just that hint of romantic interest to sustain the romance-orientated reader. The heroine is usually young, independent but quite unsophisticated. Her hero is older, worldly-wise, and is practised at rescuing his lady from 'hairy situations'. Another man or woman is also introduced to make the hero or heroine jealous.

In *Shroud of Silence*, the heroine Kim Bennett, a speech therapist, comes to Milden Hall in her capacity to cure a little girl of her stammer. Kim finds herself drawn into the lives of the Mr Rochester-like Drew and his glamorous but seemingly unstable wife, Connie. The plot would not be complete without a demented older aunt, a suspicious accident which resulted in the death of Drew's cousin, and attempts on Kim's life. After many setbacks, Kim manages to help the child, fall in love with Drew, and discover that Connie had an affair with Brian (the cousin) and killed him in a fit of jealousy—she dies after trying to drown Kim in a lake.

Another young heroine finds herself involved in adventure—this time international art smuggling, nazism, and espionage in *Return to Vienna*. Jessica Varley loses her newly-wed husband in a car accident in Austria. She returns from leading a glamorous life in Vienna to relative poverty in London, only to be approached by Richard Wilson who claims that her husband was really an intelligence officer. She is also told, much to her horror, that Max was murdered. Jessica returns to Vienna, and meets Steve, an old friend who is in love with her. With his help she finds out that her husband led a double life—he was really a womanizer and was involved in smuggling art treasures out of communist countries for some resurgent Nazis. Steve saves her life and gets her out of an almost impossible situation in the end.

Kit (Catherine) Anderson also has some strange encounters while seeking out her long-lost relatives in England. Having spent three months in her firm's London office, American-born Kit goes to visit her family's ancestral home in Devonshire. She meets charming Eliot Webster, an artist and her aunt's protegé—and also encounters her aunt Emma's doctor, Ross Vernon. He informs her that an American Catherine Anderson already exists and has been in England for some time. Kit sets out to prove that this woman is an imposter, and in her investigations discovers some extremely old murals hidden in secret chambers beneath the house. Kit also finds love with Ross.

In *Marianna*, Buckingham sets her story in 19th-century Madeira and England. Marianna Dalby is a spoilt, wilful girl whose only saving graces are her charm, beauty, and her wish to help her childhood friend, Jacinto, an intelligent peasant boy. She is married at 16 to a wealthy landowner, 40 years older than her. Jacinto passionately declares his love for her but Marianna is too proud and too class-conscious to realize that she is in love with him. Years later Marianna encounters Jacinto again, this time as an educated, well-dressed man. Marianna and Jacinto embark on a passionate affair, and Jacinto kills her husband by accident and has to leave England. Years pass before the couple can be reunited and finally enjoy their lives together. This book is a departure from Buckingham's suspense-romances and is more in the vain of a Victoria Holt novel.

Buckingham also writes formula romances as Nancy John, and highly successful mysteries as Erica Quest. A prolific partnership, the Sawyers have produced some of the most enjoyable gothic/suspense romances around today.

—P. Campbell

BURCHELL, Mary.
Pseudonym for Ida Cook. **Nationality:** British. **Born:** Sunderland, County Durham. **Education:** Duchess' School, Alnwick, Northumberland. **Career:** writer; former president, Romantic Novelists Association. **Died:** 22 December 1986.

ROMANCE AND HISTORICAL PUBLICATIONS

Novels

Wife to Christopher. London, Mills and Boon, 1936.
Nobody Asked Me. London, Mills and Boon, 1937; Toronto, Harlequin, 1976.
Except My Love. London, Mills and Boon, 1937; Toronto, Harlequin, 1973.
Call—And I'll Come. London, Mills and Boon, 1937; Toronto, Harlequin, 1973.

But Not for Me. London, Mills and Boon, 1938; Toronto, Harlequin, 1971.
Other Lips Have Loved You. London, Mills and Boon, 1938; as *Two Loves Have I*, 1976.
With All My Worldly Goods. London, Mills and Boon, 1938; Toronto, Harlequin, 1961.
Yet Love Remains. London, Mills and Boon, 1938; Toronto, Harlequin, 1975.
After Office Hours. London, Mills and Boon, 1939.
Little Sister. London, Mills and Boon, 1939; New York, Arcadia House, 1947.
One of the Family. London, Mills and Boon, 1939.
Such Is Love. London, Mills and Boon, 1939; Toronto, Harlequin, 1975.
Yours with Love. London, Mills and Boon, 1940.
Pay Me Tomorrow. London, Mills and Boon, 1940; Toronto, Harlequin, 1974.
One Man's Heart. London, Mills and Boon, 1940; Toronto, Harlequin, 1972.
I'll Go With You. London, Mills and Boon, 1940.
Accompanied by His Wife. London, Mills and Boon, 1941; Toronto, Harlequin, 1974.
Always Yours. London, Mills and Boon, 1941.
Just a Nice Girl. London, Mills and Boon, 1941; Toronto, Harlequin, 1975.
Strangers May Marry. London, Mills and Boon, 1941; Toronto, Harlequin, 1974.
Where Shall I Wander? London, Mills and Boon, 1942.
Thine Is My Heart. London, Mills and Boon, 1942.
Love Made the Choice. London, Mills and Boon, 1942; Toronto, Harlequin, 1975.
Dare I Be Happy? London, Mills and Boon, 1943; Toronto, Harlequin, 1975.
My Old Love Came. London, Mills and Boon, 1943.
Thanks to Elizabeth. London, Mills and Boon, 1944.
Take Me with You. London, Mills and Boon, 1944; Toronto, Harlequin, 1965.
Dearly Beloved. London, Mills and Boon, 1944; Toronto, Harlequin, 1967.
Away Went Love. London, Mills and Boon, 1945; Toronto, Harlequin, 1964.
Cinderella after Midnight. London, Mills and Boon, 1945; Toronto, Harlequin, 1967.
Meant for Each Other. London, Mills and Boon, 1945; Toronto, Harlequin, 1966.
Wife by Arrangement. London, Mills and Boon, 1946; Toronto, Harlequin, 1960.
It's Rumoured in the Village. London, Mills and Boon, 1946; Toronto, Harlequin, 1973.
First Love—Last Love. London, Mills and Boon, 1946.
Find Out the Way. London, Mills and Boon, 1946.
Not Without You. London, Mills and Boon, 1947.
Under Joint Management. London, Mills and Boon, 1947.
Ward of Lucifer. London, Mills and Boon, 1947; Toronto, Harlequin, 1975.
The Brave in Heart. London, Mills and Boon, 1948; Toronto, Harlequin, 1975.
If You Care. London, Mills and Boon, 1948.
Then Come Kiss Me. London, Mills and Boon, 1948; Toronto, Harlequin, 1958.
Wish on the Moon. London, Mills and Boon, 1949.
If This Were All. London, Mills and Boon, 1949.
I Will Love You Still. London, Mills and Boon, 1949.
Choose Which You Will. London, Mills and Boon, 1949; Toronto, Harlequin, 1966.
At First Sight. London, Mills and Boon, 1950.

A Letter for Don. London, Mills and Boon, 1950.

Love Him or Leave Him. London, Mills and Boon, 1950; Toronto, Harlequin, 1961.

Tell Me My Fortune. London, Mills and Boon, 1951; Toronto, Harlequin, 1975.

Mine for a Day. London, Mills and Boon, 1951.

Here I Belong. London, Mills and Boon, 1951.

Over the Blue Mountains. London, Mills and Boon, 1952; Toronto, Harlequin, 1960.

Stolen Heart. London, Mills and Boon, 1952; Toronto, Harlequin, 1962.

Sweet Adventure. London, Mills and Boon, 1952; Toronto, Harlequin, 1968.

A Ring on Her Finger. London, Mills and Boon, 1953.

No Real Relation. London, Mills and Boon, 1953.

The Heart Must Choose. London, Mills and Boon, 1953.

The Heart Cannot Forget. London, Mills and Boon, 1953; Toronto, Harlequin, 1966.

Meet Me Again. London, Mills and Boon, 1954; as *Nurse Alison's Trust*, Toronto, Harlequin, 1964.

When Love's Beginning. London, Mills and Boon, 1954; Toronto, Harlequin, 1969.

Under the Stars of Paris. London, Mills and Boon, 1954; Toronto, Harlequin, 1976.

Yours to Command. London, Mills and Boon, 1955; Toronto, Harlequin, 1964.

The Prettiest Girl. London, Mills and Boon, 1955.

Hospital Corridors. London, Mills and Boon, 1955; Toronto, Harlequin, 1958.

For Ever and Ever. London, Mills and Boon, 1956; Toronto, Harlequin, 1959.

Loving Is Giving. London, Mills and Boon, 1956; Toronto, Harlequin, 1967.

On the Air. London, Mills and Boon, 1956; Toronto, Harlequin, 1960.

To Journey Together. London, Mills and Boon, 1956; Toronto, Harlequin, 1970.

Loyal in All. London, Mills and Boon, 1957; as *Nurse Marika, Loyal in All*, Toronto, Harlequin, 1963.

Love Is My Reason. London, Mills and Boon, 1957; Toronto, Harlequin, 1959.

Joanna at the Grange. London, Mills and Boon, 1957.

And Falsely Pledge My Love. London, Mills and Boon, 1957; Toronto, Harlequin, 1965.

Dear Sir. London, Mills and Boon, 1958; Toronto, Harlequin, 1961.

Dear Trustee. London, Mills and Boon, 1958; Toronto, Harlequin, 1959.

The Girl in the Blue Dress. London, Mills and Boon, 1958; Toronto, Harlequin, 1976.

Star Quality. London, Mills and Boon, 1959; as *Surgeon of Distinction*, Toronto, Harlequin, 1959.

Honey. London, Mills and Boon, 1959; Toronto, Harlequin, 1977.

Corner House. London, Mills and Boon, 1959.

Across the Counter. London, Mills and Boon, 1960; Toronto, Harlequin, 1961.

Choose the One You'll Marry. London, Mills and Boon, and Toronto, Harlequin, 1960.

Paris—And My Love. London, Mills and Boon, 1960; Toronto, Harlequin, 1961.

My Sister Celia. London, Mills and Boon, 1961; Toronto, Harlequin, 1971.

Reluctant Relation. London, Mills and Boon, 1961; Toronto, Harlequin, 1962.

The Wedding Dress. London, Mills and Boon, 1962; Toronto, Harlequin, 1964.

House of Conflict. London, Mills and Boon, 1962; Toronto, Harlequin, 1963.

Inherit My Heart. London, Mills and Boon, 1962; Toronto, Harlequin, 1963.

Dangerous Loving. London, Mills and Boon, 1963.

Sweet Meadows. London, Mills and Boon, 1963.

Do Not Go, My Love. London, Mills and Boon, 1964; Toronto, Harlequin, 1972.

The Strange Quest of Anne Weston. London, Mills and Boon, 1964; as *The Strange Quest of Nurse Anne*, Toronto, Harlequin, 1965.

Girl with a Challenge. London, Mills and Boon, 1965; Toronto, Harlequin, 1970.

Her Sister's Children. London, Mills and Boon, 1965.

A Song Begins. London, Mills and Boon, 1965; Toronto, Harlequin, 1966.

The Other Linding Girl. London, Mills and Boon, 1966; Toronto, Harlequin, 1970.

The Broken Wing. London, Mills and Boon, 1966; Toronto, Harlequin, 1967; as *Damaged Angel*, Mills and Boon, 1967.

When Love Is Blind. London, Mills and Boon, 1967; Toronto, Harlequin, 1968.

Though Worlds Apart. London, Mills and Boon, 1967; Toronto, Harlequin, 1969.

The Marshall Family. London, Mills and Boon, 1967; Toronto, Harlequin, 1968.

A Home for Joy. London, Mills and Boon, 1968; Toronto, Harlequin, 1969.

Missing from Home. London, Mills and Boon, 1968; Toronto, Harlequin, 1969.

The Curtain Rises. London, Mills and Boon, 1969; Toronto, Harlequin, 1970.

The Rosewood Box. London, Mills and Boon, 1970.

Child of Music. London, Mills and Boon, 1970; Toronto, Harlequin, 1971.

Second Marriage. London, Mills and Boon, 1971.

Music of the Heart. London, Mills and Boon, and Toronto, Harlequin, 1972.

Design for Loving. London, Mills and Boon, 1972.

Unbidden Melody. London, Mills and Boon, 1973; Toronto, Harlequin, 1974.

Song Cycle. London, Mills and Boon, and Toronto, Harlequin, 1974.

Remembered Serenade. London, Mills and Boon, and Toronto, Harlequin, 1975.

Elusive Harmony. London, Mills and Boon, 1976; Toronto, Harlequin, 1977.

Nightingales. London, Mills and Boon, and Toronto, Harlequin, 1980.

Masquerade with Music. London, Mills and Boon, 1982.

On Wings of Song. London, Mills and Boon, 1985.

OTHER PUBLICATIONS

Other as Ida Cook

We Followed Our Stars (on opera singers). London, Hamish Hamilton, and New York, Morrow, 1950.

My Life, with Tito Gobbi. London, Macdonald and Jane's, 1979.

*   *   *

Mary Burchell's favourite setting for her contemporary romances is the world of opera. An avid fan herself, Burchell realistically describes the hard work and discipline required from opera singers who must fiercely compete for prize roles at the same time that she lovingly portrays the excitement and glamour that result from the creation of beautiful music by talented, temperamental stars. Burchell's world of opera is a proverbial 'small world', for these romances either revolve around or at least mention the same cast of characters. In fact, a number of the romances have been grouped together as 'The Warrender Saga' after one of the main characters, Sir Oscar Warrender, a conductor. His romance with and marriage to a young girl whom he trains to be a singer are told in *A Song Begins*. He and his wife play an essential but supporting role in the other romances. Other musical characters who reappear include Conrad Schreiner, another teacher and conductor, and his mistress, Manora Venescu, a singer. Florian, a fashion designer, is also alluded to in several novels. Thus, once Burchell develops a character she is fond of, she carries him or her over into other novels. This is an interesting, effective technique for involving the reader.

Burchell experiments in other ways as well. For example, in one novel *Call—And I'll Come*, the first three chapters and the last chapter are written from the perspective of the hero while the middle of the novel is written from the heroine's perspective, an unusual arrangement for a formula romance. In other Burchell romances the reader is aware that she is being told a story by a narrator who occasionally draws back to make editorial comments on the characters and their behaviour, although the narrator is usually telling the story from the heroine's perspective.

Burchell is not a dramatic writer with a taste for flamboyant, impossible characters and fast-paced, violent action. Most of the characters in her romances, even the rival suitors, are nice but flawed human beings. There are very few arch villains. The heroines are quiet, serious, maternal young women who have sufficient flashes of humour and temper to make them intriguing to the heroes who are basically unromantic but loyal and thoughtful, vitally alive men who are dedicated to their work. Most of the 'action' consists of the heroes and heroines maturing. The heroines develop their occupational and social skills and become increasingly self-confident while the heroes are shaken from their rather oblivious confidence that they will get their way in all things. This growth takes place over weeks or even months, and much of that time is spent apart from each other. In the end, of course, they are united, both wiser than before.

Burchell was a romance writer whose approach to romance changed very little over the last 20 years. She did not dwell on passion; nor did she describe fiery love-making between the hero and heroine. These traits may make her romances seem rather tame for modern tastes but what they lack in passion they make up for in sincerity and a certain charm, particularly the novels that deal with opera.

—Margaret Jensen

BURFORD, Eleanor. See **PLAIDY, Jean.**

BURFORD, Lolah.
Nationality: American. **Born:** 1931. **Education:** Bryn Mawr College, Pennsylvania. **Address:** c/o Macmillan, 866 Third Avenue, New York, New York, 10022, USA.

ROMANCE AND HISTORICAL PUBLICATIONS

Novels

Vice Avenged: A Moral Tale. New York, Macmillan, and London, Macmillan, 1971.

The Vision of Stephen: An Elegy. New York, Macmillan, 1972; London, Cassell, 1973.
Edward, Edward. New York, Macmillan, 1973; London, Cassell, 1974.
MacLyon. New York, Macmillan, 1974; London, Weidenfeld and Nicolson, 1975.
Alyx. New York, Macmillan, 1977.
Seacage. New York, Macmillan, 1979.

*   *   *

Lolah Burford's novels are neither for the meek nor the militant, the little old lady or the strident feminist. Raw sex is the major element of each novel—sex of every variety, from rape to incest, sadism, and homosexuality. Though cloaked in velvet prose, Burford's 'polite pornography' is explicit and pervasive.

The typical Burford novel begins with an act of sexual violence. *Vice Avenged: A Moral Tale*, Burford's first novel, set in 18th-century London, opens with a round of cards; the winner must 'ravish' a 'virgin of good family' and return with the bloody proof of his deed. Young Marquis Bysshe Gore is the rakish victor in this cruel and dangerous game. Cressida, daughter of the Duke of Salisbury, is the innocent victim whom the players have chosen by lot. The rape occurs: Gore is violent and merciless; Cressida frightened and submissive, but (according to Burford) she gradually enjoys being taken and falls in love with Gore. *Alyx*, a more recent Burford effusion, set on an 18th-century Caribbean sugar plantation, begins with Smith, the 'plantation stud', taking by force an inexperienced young slave girl. Alyx, too, falls in love with the rapacious villain. But villain turns out to be hero when 'Smith' turns out to be Simon, the kidnapped Sixth Earl of Halford. As if to justify these fictional reactions, Burford quotes Alexander Pope: 'Ev'ry woman is at heart a rake'.

Diverging from her standard plot devices, Burford, in *The Vision of Stephen*, combines the 7th century with the 19th. Young Margery discovers behind her piano a grate through which 7th-century Stephen enters her world—the England of 1822. To establish validity for her deft contraposition of time sequences, Burford studied Bede's *Ecclesiastical History of the English Nation*. Rather pretentiously, Burford concludes her novel with Alfred's preface to the translation of *The Pastoral Care* (A.D. 894), in Old English—a bit difficult for those who are not mediaevalists.

Burford's plots are fast-paced, full of action and intrigue. The well-researched, historically correct settings are various: 18th-century London (*Vice Avenged*); the 7th-century Anglo-Saxon kingdom of Northumbria (*The Vision of Stephen*); the 19th-century pre-Regency unrest in England, Napoleonic Wars, and flowering of Vienna (*Edward, Edward*); the 18th-century Protestant Rebellion in Scotland (*MacLyon*); the 18th-century Caribbean sugar plantation (*Alyx*); and 'Another Time' in an unnamed land (*Seacage*). Burford's prose style is sophisticated, and consists mostly of dialogue, spoken with the formality and grandiloquence of times past, and few descriptive passages.

—Marcia G. Welsh

BURGESS, Anthony.
Pseudonym for John Anthony Burgess Wilson. **Other Pseudonym:** Joseph Kell. **Nationality:** British. **Born:** Manchester, 25 February 1917. **Education:** Xaverian College, Manchester; Manchester University, B.A. (honours) in English 1940. **Military Service:** British

Army Education Corps, 1940–46: sergeant-major. **Relations:** married 1) Llewela Isherwood Jones in 1942 (died 1968); 2) Liliana Macellari in 1968, one son. **Career:** lecturer, Extra-Mural Department, Birmingham University, 1946–48; education officer and lecturer, Central Advisory Council for Adult Education in the Forces, 1946–48; lecturer in phonetics, Ministry of Education, 1948–50; English master, Banbury Grammar School, Oxfordshire, 1950–54; senior lecturer in English, Malayan Teachers Training College, Khata Baru, 1954–57; English language specialist, Department of Education, Brunei, Borneo, 1958–59. Writer-in-residence, University of North Carolina, Chapel Hill, 1969–70; professor, Columbia University, New York, 1970–71; visiting fellow, Princeton University, New Jersey, 1970–71; distinguished professor, City University of New York, 1972–73; literary adviser, Guthrie Theatre, Minneapolis, 1972–75. Also composer. **Recipient:** National Arts Club award, 1973; Foreign book prize (France), 1981; *The Sunday Times* Mont Blanc award, 1987. D. Litt.: Manchester University, 1982; University of St Andrews, Scotland, 1991. Fellow, Royal Society of Literature, 1969; Commandeur de Mérite Culturel (Monaco), 1986; Commandeur des Arts et des Lettres (France), 1986. **Died:** 26 November 1993.

ROMANCE AND HISTORICAL PUBLICATIONS

Novels (series: Malayan Trilogy)

Malayan Trilogy. London, Penguin, 1972; as *The Long Day Wanes: A Malayan Trilogy*, London, Heinemann, 1984.
   Time for a Tiger. London, Heinemann, 1956.
   The Enemy in the Blanket. London, Heinemann, 1958.
   Beds in the East. London, Heinemann, 1959.
Devil of a State. London, Heinemann, 1961; New York, Norton, 1962.
Nothing Like the Sun: A Story of Shakespeare's Love-Life. London, Heinemann, and New York, Norton, 1964.
MF. London, Cape, and New York, Knopf, 1971.
Napoleon Symphony. London, Cape, and New York, Knopf, 1974.
Abba Abba. London, Faber, and Boston, Little Brown, 1977.
Man of Nazareth. New York, McGraw Hill, 1979; London, Magnum, 1980.
The End of the World News. London, Hutchinson, 1982; New York, McGraw Hill, 1983.
The Kingdom of the Wicked. London, Hutchinson, and New York, Arbor House, 1985.
Any Old Iron. London, Hutchinson, and New York, Random House, 1989.
Motzart and the Wolf Gang. London, Hutchinson, 1991.
A Dead Man in Deptford. London, Hutchinson, 1993.

Short Stories

The Devil's Mode and Other Short Stories. London, Hutchinson, and New York, Random House, 1989.

OTHER PUBLICATIONS

Novels

The Right to an Answer. London, Heinemann, 1960; New York, Norton, 1961.
The Doctor Is Sick. London, Heinemann, and New York, Norton, 1960.
The Worm and the Ring. London, Heinemann, 1961; revised edition, 1970.

One Hand Clapping (as Joseph Kell). London, Davies, 1961; (as Anthony Burgess) New York, New York, Knopf, 1972.
A Clockwork Orange. London, Heinemann, 1962; New York, Norton, 1963.
The Wanting Seed. London, Heinemann, 1962; New York, Norton, 1963.
Honey for the Bears. London, Heinemann, 1963; New York, Norton, 1964.
Inside Mr Enderby (as Joseph Kell). London, Heinemann, 1963.
The Eve of Saint Venus. London, Sidgwick and Jackson, 1964; New York, Norton, 1967.
A Vision of Battlements. London, Sidgwick and Jackson, 1965; New York, Norton, 1966.
Tremor of Intent. London, Heinemann, and New York, Norton, 1966.
Enderby Outside. London, Heinemann, 1968.
Enderby (includes *Inside Mr Enderby* and *Enderby Outside*). New York, Norton, 1968.
The Clockwork Testament; or, Enderby's End. London, Hart Davis MacGibbon, 1974; New York, Knopf, 1975.
Beard's Roman Women. New York, McGraw Hill, 1976; London, Hutchinson, 1977.
1985. London, Hutchinson, and New York, Simon and Schuster, 1980.
Earthly Powers. London, Hutchinson, and New York, Simon and Schuster, 1980.
Enderby (includes *Inside Mr Enderby, Enderby Outside, The Clockwork Testament*). London, Penguin, 1982.
Enderby's Dark Lady; or, No End to Enderby. London, Hutchinson, and New York, McGraw Hill, 1984.
The Pianoplayers. London, Hutchinson, and New York, Arbor House, 1986.

Short Story

Will and Testament: A Fragment of Biography. Verona, Italy, Plain Wrapper Press, 1977.

Plays

Cyrano de Bergerac, adaptation of the play by Rostand (produced Minneapolis, 1971). New York, Knopf, 1971; musical version, as *Cyrano*, music by Michael Lewis, lyrics by Burgess (produced New York, 1972).
Oedipus the King, adaptation of a play by Sophocles (produced Minneapolis, 1972; Southampton, Hampshire, 1979). Minneapolis, University of Minnesota Press, 1972; London, Oxford University Press, 1973.
The Cavalier of the Rose (story adaptation), in *Der Rosenkavalier*, libretto by Hofmannsthal, music by Richard Strauss. Boston, Little Brown, 1982; London, Joseph, 1983.
Cyrano de Bergerac (not same as 1971 version), adaptation of the play by Rostand (produced London, 1983). London, Hutchinson, 1985.
Blooms of Dublin, music by Burgess, adaptation of the novel *Ulysses* by Joyce (broadcast 1983). London, Hutchinson, 1986.
Oberon Old and New (includes original libretto by James Robinson Planché), music by Carl Maria von Weber. London, Hutchinson, 1985.
Carmen, adaptation of the libretto by Henri Meilhac and Ludovic Halévy, music by Georges Bizet (produced London, 1986). London, Hutchinson, 1986.
A Clockwork Orange, music by Burgess, adaptation of his own novel. London, Hutchinson, 1987.

Screenplay: special languages for *Quest for Fire*, 1981.

Radio Play: *Blooms of Dublin*, music by Burgess, 1983; *A Meeting in Valladolid*, 1991.

Television Plays: *Moses—The Lawgiver*, with others, 1975; *Jesus of Nazareth*, with Suso Cecchi d'Amico, 1977; *A Kind of Failure* (documentary; *Writers and Places* series), 1981; *The Childhood of Christ*, music by Berlioz, 1985; *A.D.*, 1985.

Poetry

Moses: A Narrative. London, Dempsey and Squires, and New York, Stonehill, 1976.
A Christmas Recipe. Verona, Italy, Plain Wrapper Press, 1977.

Other

English Literature: A Survey for Students (as John Burgess Wilson). London, Longman, 1958.
The Novel Today. London, Longman, 1963.
Language Made Plain (as John Burgess Wilson). London, English Universities Press, 1964; New York, Crowell, 1965; revised edition, London, Fontana, 1975.
Here Comes Everybody: An Introduction to James Joyce for the Ordinary Reader. London, Faber, 1965; revised edition, London, Hamlyn, 1982; as *Re Joyce*, New York, Norton, 1965.
The Novel Now: A Student's Guide to Contemporary Fiction. London, Faber, and New York, Norton, 1967; revised edition, Faber, 1971.
Urgent Copy: Literary Studies. London, Cape, and New York, Norton, 1968.
Shakespeare. London, Cape, and New York, Knopf, 1970.
Joysprick: An Introduction to the Language of James Joyce. London, Deutsch, 1973; New York, Harcourt Brace, 1975.
Obscenity and the Arts (lecture). Valletta, Malta Library Association, 1973.
A Long Trip to Teatime (for children). London, Dempsey and Squires, and New York, Stonehill, 1976.
New York, with the editors of Time-Life books. New York, Time-Life, 1976.
Ernest Hemingway and His World. London, Thames and Hudson, and New York, Scribner, 1978.
The Land Where Ice Cream Grows (for children). London, Benn, and New York, Doubleday, 1979.
On Going to Bed. London, Deutsch, and New York, Abbeville, 1982.
This Man and Music. London, Hutchinson, 1982; New York, McGraw Hill, 1983.
Ninety-Nine Novels: The Best in English since 1939: A Personal Choice. London, Allison and Busby, and New York, Summit, 1984.
Flame into Being: The Life and Work of D.H. Lawrence. London, Heinemann, and New York, Arbor House, 1985.
Homage to QWERT YUIOP: Selected Journalism 1978–1985. London, Hutchinson, 1986; as *But Do Blondes Prefer Gentlemen?*, New York, McGraw Hill, 1986.
Little Wilson and Big God, Being the First Part of the Confessions of Anthony Burgess. New York, Weidenfeld and Nicolson, 1986; London, Heinemann, 1987.
They Wrote in English. London, Hutchinson, 1988.
You've Had Your Time, Being the Second Part of the Confessions of Anthony Burgess. London, Heinemann, and New York, Grove Weidenfeld, 1991.
A Mouthful of Air: Language and Languages. London, Hutchinson, 1992.

Editor, *The Coaching Days of England 1750–1850*. London, Elek, and New York, Time-Life, 1966.

Editor, *A Journal of the Plague Year*, by Daniel Defoe. London, Penguin, 1966.
Editor, *A Shorter Finnegans Wake*, by James Joyce. London, Faber, and New York, Viking Press, 1966.
Editor, with Francis Haskell, *The Age of the Grand Tour*. London, Elek, and New York, Crown, 1967.
Editor, *Malaysian Stories*, by W. Somerset Maugham. Singapore, Heinemann, 1969.

Translator, with Llewela Burgess, *The New Aristocrats*, by Michel de Saint-Pierre. London, Gollancz, 1962; Boston, Houghton Mifflin, 1963.
Translator, with Llewela Burgess, *The Olive Trees of Justice*, by Jean Pelegri. London, Sidgwick and Jackson, 1962.
Translator, *The Man Who Robbed Poor Boxes*, by Jean Servin. London, Gollancz, 1965.
Translator, *Carmen: An Opera in Four Acts*, from the story by Prosper Mérimée. London, Hutchinson, 1986.

*

Film Adaptation: *A Clockwork Orange*, 1971.

Bibliography: *Anthony Burgess: A Bibliography* by Jeutonne Brewer, Metuchen, New Jersey, Scarecrow Press, 1980; *Anthony Burgess: An Annotated Bibliography and Reference Guide* by Paul Boytinck, New York, Garland, 1985.

Manuscript Collection: Mills Memorial Library, Hamilton, Ontario.

Critical Studies: in *The Red Hot Vacuum* by Theodore Solotaroff, New York, Atheneum, 1970; *Shakespeare's Lives* by Samuel Schoenbaum, Oxford, Clarendon Press, 1970; *Anthony Burgess* by Carol M. Dix, London, Longman, 1971; *The Consolations of Ambiguity: An Essay on the Novels of Anthony Burgess* by Robert K. Morris, Columbia, University of Missouri Press, 1971; *Anthony Burgess* by A. A. DeVitis, New York, Twayne, 1972; *The Clockwork Universe of Anthony Burgess* by Richard Mathews, San Bernardino, California, Borgo Press, 1978; *Anthony Burgess: The Artist as Novelist* by Geoffrey Aggeler, University, University of Alabama Press, 1979, and *Critical Essays on Anthony Burgess* edited by Aggeler, Boston, Hall 1986; *Anthony Burgess* by Samuel Coale, New York, Ungar, 1981; *Anthony Burgess: A Study in Character* by Martina Ghosh-Schellhorn, Frankfurt, Germany, Lang, 1986.

*   *   *

Anthony Burgess would seem to be at first glance a less focused, less committed, more sentimental George Orwell: he was a teacher and critic with socialist interests mixed with a dislike of colonialism and a cynicism about government hierarchies. Yet an inescapable Roman Catholic heritage affected his vision and produced its moral and philosophical ambiguities. He took an almost exhibitionist delight in metaphoric and linguistic by-play and almost always incorporates in his oeuvre rag-tags from various languages, both modern and classical. His style was to debunk, demythologize, and mock, while at the same time to sympathize and to revere; in other words, he tried to have it both ways: comic and serious, liberal and conservative, believer and sceptic, humanist and scientist, historian and fantasy writer. His two-volume autobiography, *Little Wilson and Big God*, and *You've Had Your Time*, render his historical works more understandable, for both are a kind of fiction, an exhibitionist confession, entertaining and lively and disconcertingly frank.

Burgess's historical fiction suggests there is no real factual record and that all is subject to interpretation, but he also postulates a need for values. It is scatological and melodramatic, with images of mindless violence, sexual ambiguity, double think, and evil with a capital 'E'. It usually denounces materialism and opts for the life of the mind, while at the same time demonstrating the hatred, divisiveness, and fanaticism of mankind, particularly man en masse, and the powerful sway of the physical, and most particularly the sexual, over the intellectual. It combines philosophic despair with slapstick, and suggests a cyclical view of history which Burgess saw as alternating between two negative extremes, the 'Pelagian' and the 'Augustinian': socialist and liberal humanism and idealism, and brutal, unregenerate tyranny. Its central characters are bumbling anti-heroes, at odds with authority, weak, well-meaning, powerless, and out-of-touch with themselves and with reality; rather than actively participate in life, they tend merely to look on as 'human beings squeaked and gibbered, and their passions and convictions buzzed like gnats'. Burgess was preoccupied with fate, with the role of the artist, with the decay of society paralleled in the decay of love, and with a quest for meaning amid alien cultures. In exploring these themes, he sacrificed verisimilitude and exactness for his personal reinterpretations of the past as indicative of the present and the future, all a mythological mix of truth and lie, just as in his literary criticism he sacrificed critical analysis for personal testimony (*Flames into Being* is as much about Burgess as about D.H. Lawrence).

Burgess's literary works grow out of his personal experiences and build on central characters that incorporate much of himself. A number of these figures are teachers, searching for knowledge and understanding, expecting the best, but somehow too often finding the worst, hence the vaguely cynical stance that dominates his canon. *The Malayan Trilogy*, with its realistic portraits of British Colonials in Malaya and events from the 1950s, reflects Burgess's lifetime interest in language, weaving in numerous words and phrases from Malay, Urdu, Arabic, Tamil, and Chinese, with a glossary at the end (as he later did in his innovative experimentation with a futuristic language in *A Clockwork Orange*). It depicts the dark side of Eastern civilization, the internecine strife, the bigotry, the corruption that continued to plague Malaya as it moved toward self-rule. *Devil of a State*, possibly based on Burgess's experience in Borneo, also treats of the transition from British colony to independent state.

Burgess's treatment of Shelley and Byron in Switzerland, James Joyce, Shakespeare, Keats, Moses, Jesus, and Napoleon mingle fact with fiction to project personal interpretations of great literary and historical figures. His novel, *Nothing Like the Sun*, gives a sense of the violent, lively, but unsanitary nature of Elizabethan England, while at the same time it reconstructs the unknowable, Shakespeare's love-life, to argue a totally personal thesis: that satyriasis was responsible for the literary productivity of Shakespeare (WS). In fact, WS scornfully dismisses spiritual pretensions by saying, 'There is the flesh and the flesh makes all. Literature is an epiphenomenon of the action of the flesh'. The novel was Burgess's final lecture to his Malaysian students, and, as such, attempts to transport them into 16th-century England, imitating its diction and peeking in on a young Shakespeare dreaming of his 'dark golden lady' who inspires his verse and his sexual exploits. Nevertheless, it suggests that pederasty forced him into an acting career, that the Earl of Southampton won his homosexual attentions, and that an East Indian was the dark lady who sexually enslaved him until her personal ambitions led to her affair with the bisexual Southampton. Shakespeare ends up a syphilitic—a disease Burgess found responsible for the flowering of genius in a number of individuals.

The Burgess pattern throughout his canon was to focus on the physical to try to bring the historical myth to the human level and to fuse his own concerns and identity with that of his historical figure so that Moses and Jesus, Saul and the martyred Stephen, Sha-

kespeare, and Napoleon all at some point voice the Burgess view. Overall, Burgess's women inspire, tease and damage, while his men are often frail posturers, seeking a tenuous salvation.

Napoleon Symphony builds most precisely on Beethoven's *Eroica* Symphony in four movements to trace the life of Napoleon Bonaparte from an overture to Josephine to his immortalization in the final coda. Burgess's Napoleon is the erotic lover, the farcical cuckold, the domineering and capable soldier with his ups and downs, the tyrant Colossus straddling a continent, the doomed Prometheus, bringer of the fire of a new order, and finally the mythical legend who remakes fact to create his own self-image, posthumously crowned for, to some degree, unifying Europe. He slides down the Alps, eats a new chicken dish on the battlefield, and faces Russian wastelands and Waterloo with equal gusto. The point of view shifts from Napoleon's own self-rationalizations to the more cynical perspectives of less romantic observers (Josephine, his foot soldiers, political observers), and the work itself is more about the creative process than about Napoleon *per se*.

Abba Abba, mainly a series of translated sonnets, introduces a literary mystery, the hypothetical meeting of John Keats and the Italian sonneteer Giuseppe Belli (noted for his blasphemous street diction) in Rome of the 1820s, just before Keats's death, and raises questions about hypothetical potential influences, each on each. It was followed by television specials on historical figures: Moses, Shakespeare, Michelangelo, Jesus of Nazareth, 'Vinegar Joe' Stillwell, and Cyrus the Great. (The Jesus production was based on *Man of Nazareth*, the story of Christ from the perspective of an accountant for a wine merchant.) *The End of the World News* provides a fictional biography of Sigmund Freud (the intellectual giant vs the failed husband and father), a musical based on Leon Trotsky's 1917 visit to New York (rhetorical spouting delivered with song and dance), and a projected cosmic disaster in 2000, with each in its own way bringing an end to history. *The Kingdom of the Wicked*, in turn, builds on *I, Claudius* and the movie *Caligula* to interpret the early years of Christianity set against the decline of a decadent, sadistic, ineffectual Rome. Burgess's Jesus is a burly hulk, a con man colossus who survived crucifixion and merely used the idea of resurrection to promote himself. The book proceeds in this vein with miracles explained away and the raising of Dorcas from the dead, for example, transformed into slapstick. His two-dimensional characters and trivial substance transform a complex historical situation into a superficial mockery, but one replete with convincing debates between disagreeing factions.

The Pianoplayers recreates working-class Manchester and Blackpool during the 1920s and corny music-hall routines as narrator Ellen Henshaw, the proprietress of a 'school of love' and a comedic cross between Fanny Hill and Mrs Malaprop, recalls her disreputable father's career as a piano player in silent movie houses, his confrontation with the talkies, and his fatal 30-day nonstop piano marathon to save his career. *Any Old Iron*, a serio-comic melange of fact and fiction, connects, in a driving narrative, the sinking of the *Titanic*, the Irish Rebellion, the Spanish Civil War, World War I and World War II, and terrorism and nationalism in Israel and Wales. It traces the passage of a lump of gold and a battered sword believed to be that of Attila the Hun and King Arthur, and the related adventures of a Welsh-Russian and a Jewish-French family as German loot becomes Russian and then Welsh. Amid violent confrontations (British Prisoners of War killed escaping, Russian Prisoners of War repatriated and doomed, Welsh nationalists engaging in futile skirmishes), Burgess's characters gesticulate passionately about the disorders of modern life and find respite from danger in love that rarely satisfies. *The Devil's Mode*, a series of historical tales, flaunts Burgess's erudition at the expense of character, plot, and authenticity. It includes a new Sherlock Holmes tale narrated by a pompous Dr Watson, a new version of *Der Rosenkavalier*, the story of Attila the Hun's Roman conquests with fears about the judgments of posterity interspersed between the killing and pillaging, and a meeting at a Spanish peace council between an embittered Cervantes and a queasy Shakespeare. One critic calls this the 'slap and tickle' school of history.

Burgess always incorporated long Greek and Latinate terms (phrases like 'an octopudium of hoofs'), and often depended on a mock epic format and on metaphor and allusion to lend a greater sense of depth to his perceptions, for example, calling Nabby Adams (*The Malayan Trilogy*) 'a Prometheus with the eagles of drink and debt pecking at his liver', or reducing Aeneas to the bumbling sergeant of *A Vision of Battlements* and his Mediterranean wandering to exploring Gibraltar. His histories involve a form of gamesmanship, with puns and neologisms, acronyms and deflations, with lavatorial and masturbatory humour, with chaos and ambiguity mixed with old-fashioned values and with repetitive cycles that switch from despair to hope and back again.

In other words, Burgess impressed his own personality on history, revelled in a high flown rhetorical style, casually debunked the past and just as casually captured the anguish and the humour of the human condition. He was one of the greatest English language writers this century.

—Andrew and Gina Macdonald

BURGH, Anita.
Pseudonym: Annie Leith. **Born:** Gillingham, Kent, 9 June 1937. **Education:** Chatham Grammar School for Girls, Kent, 1948–55; student nurse, University College Hospital, London, 1955–57. **Relations:** married Alex Leith, Lord Burgh, in 1957 (divorced); two sons and two daughters. **Agent:** Sheil Land Associates Ltd, 43 Doughty Street, WC1N 2LF, London, England. **Address:** Ceneuil, 43800 St Vincent, France.

ROMANCE AND HISTORICAL PUBLICATIONS

Novels (series: Daughter of a Granite Land; Tales from Sarson Magna)

Distinctions of Class. London, Chatto and Windus, 1987.
Love: The Bright Foreigner. London, Chatto and Windus, 1988.
Daughter of a Granite Land:
   The Azure Bowl. London, Chatto and Windus, 1989.
   The Golden Butterfly. London, Chatto and Windus, 1990.
   The Stone Mistress. London, Chatto and Windus, 1991.
Tales from Sarson Magna:
   Molly's Flashings (as Annie Leith). London, Chatto and Windus, 1991.
Advances. London, Macmillan, 1992.
Overtures. London, Macmillan, 1993.

*

Anita Burgh comments:

I was a working class child, evacuated for five war years to a stately home. I returned afterwards to a not-too-happy childhood in a terraced home where I remained until I married a Lord with a millionairess mother. In consequence the themes of my novels are influenced by this background.

I often write of the parental rejection of a child and the long term effects; my heroines tend to be in need—they search for love but are afraid of it. The British class system fascinates and infuriates me in equal parts. I tell of the difficulties of breaking through its barriers. I'm also interested in the effect upon a child of removing it from its natural environment. Too much money too soon is another theme;

the chaos it can cause in someone's life and those that he/she comes into contact with. The selfishness of the super-rich recurs. Frequently there is a large house which appears like a character and is central to the book. It appears in many disguises but it is still the house to which I was evacuated—Lanhydroch, in Cornwall.

My home, in Cornwall, is at Lands End on a cliff and so the sea and weather also feature strongly.

*   *   *

Anita Burgh's first novel became a bestseller and was short-listed for the Romantic Novelists' Association Best Romantic Novel of the Year award, and she has gone on producing popular, though immensely varied novels.

Distinctions of Class is the story of Jane, a student nurse from a working-class background, who marries a lord. Faced with the prejudice and hostility of some of his family, the marriage fails. Jane has to start again, and after another marriage builds up a successful commercial empire.

The original interest in this book may have had something to do with the fact that Leith had been a student nurse who married a lord and then divorced him. But that by no means explains the vast success of the book, and others since. One book may become a bestseller because of publicity, but unless there is intrinsic merit the second will fail dismally. What is the merit in Leith's books? Primarily she is a compulsive, magnificent storyteller, providing that elusive, difficult to analyse page-turning quality, and superb, believable characters.

Love: The Bright Foreigner is a very different story, about an older woman whose life is shattered when she is suddenly widowed. Love can be found again, though, and Ann is whisked off to Greece and initially to blissful happiness, then facing doubt and fear before finding fulfilment.

The next three books form a trilogy, 'Daughter of a Granite Land', set in the first instance in 19th-century Cornwall, centring on a big, granite house, and two women, Alice and Ia. In *The Azure Bowl* the story moves between Cornwall, London and New York, and in *The Golden Butterfly*, which features Alice's granddaughter Juniper, a spoilt American heiress, moves also to Paris. The final book, *The Stone Mistress*, continues Juniper's story as she searches for satisfaction. These books are magnificent in their scope, exploring the relationships of members of two linked families, and the ties they feel to the Cornish house.

Quite different and utterly contemporary is *Advances*. This is a book which was just waiting to be written, and who better to write it than Leith, who dares to poke wicked, sharply observed fun at the publishing world. It is a compelling story in its own right, exciting and amusing, featuring Kate, aspiring writer, her agent Joy and editor Gloria. For anyone who has ever belonged to a writers' group or knows a little about the world of publishing it has several extra dimensions, beautifully satirical, with many people worried or pleased to think that some part of them might have been the model for one of the characters. It is doubtful whether the publishing industry can ever again be quite as it was.

Overtures tells the poignant story of two sisters whose lives are blighted by their ambitious mother. Kitty, unloved and scorned, becomes an opera diva, while Lana, for whom the appalling Amy predicts stardom almost from the moment of the child's birth, takes the path of pop music. Leith is as much at home in the world of gigs and pop culture as she is in the great opera houses of the world. The two girls follow their ambitions, by turns ruthless and doubting. These are fascinating studies of women driven by ambition yet vulnerable to the influences of those they love and those who hate them. In the end, has either of them learned anything?

Molly's Flashing, written as Annie Leith, is the first book in a series set in a typical English village, 'Tales from Sarson Magna'.

The protagonist, Molly Parminter, devises ways of paying for the Hall's leaking roof. The village abounds in amusing, annoying, avaricious characters, and is predictably split by a proposal for an Elizabethan Theme Park. This book is lighter in style, but is far from lightweight. *Hector's Hobbies*, due to be published in 1994, will continue the fortunes of this wickedly but accurately observed slice of rural England.

What makes a bestseller? A blend of sharp observation, humour, compassion, insight into people's feelings and motives, and most of all the ability to set this all down in a spell-binding story told in a racy style and with enviable pace, all qualities displayed in Burgh's books.

—Marina Oliver

BURGHLEY, Rose. See 2nd edition, 1990.

BURGIN, G(eorge) B(rown).
Nationality: British. **Born:** Croydon, Surrey, 15 January 1856. **Education:** Totteridge Park Public School. **Relations:** married Georgina Benington in 1893 (died 1940). **Career:** private secretary to Baker Pasha and accompanied him to Asia Minor in 1880s; subeditor, the *Idler*, to 1899; general editor, New Vagabond Library, 1896–97. Secretary, Authors' Club, 1905–08. Fellow, Institute of Journalists. **Died:** 20 June 1944.

ROMANCE AND HISTORICAL PUBLICATIONS

Novels

The Dance at the Four Corners. Bristol, Arrowsmith, 1894.
Tuxter's Little Maid. London, Cassell, 1895; as *At Tuxter's*, New York, Putnam, 1895.
Gascoigne's Ghost. London, Beeman, and New York, Harper, 1896.
The Judge of the Four Corners. London, Innes, 1896.
Tomalyn's Quest. London, Innes, and New York, Harper, 1896.
Fortune's Footballs. London, Pearson, and New York, Appleton, 1897.
'Old Man's' Marriage. London, Richards, 1897.
The Cattle Man. London, Richards, 1898.
Settled Out of Court. London, Pearson, 1898.
The Bread of Tears. London, Long, 1899.
The Hermits of Gray's Inn. London, Pearson, 1899.
The Tiger's Claw. London, Pearson, 1900.
The Person in the House. London, Hurst and Blackett, 1900.
The Way Out. London, Long, 1900.
A Goddess of Gray's Inn. London, Pearson, 1901.
A Son of Mammon. London, Long, 1901.
A Wilful Woman. London, Long, 1902.
The Man Who Died. London, Everett, 1903.
The Ladies of the Manor. London, Richards, 1903; New York, Smart Set, 1904.
The Hermit of Bonneville. London, Richards, 1904.
The Land of Silence. London, Nash, 1904.
The Devil's Due. London, Hutchinson, 1905.
The Marble City. London, Hutchinson, 1905.
The Belles of Vaudroy. London, Hutchinson, 1906.
The Only World. London, Richards, 1906.
Peggy the Pilgrim. London, Richards, 1907.
Which Woman?. London, Nash, 1907.

Fanuela. London, Hutchinson, 1907.
Flowers of Fire. London, Nash, 1908.
Galahad's Garden. London, Nash, 1908.
A Woman's Way. London, Hutchinson, 1908.
Simple Savage. London, Hutchinson, 1909.
The Slaves of Allah. London, Hutchinson, 1909.
The Trickster. London, Stanley Paul, 1909.
Diana of Dreams. London, Hutchinson, 1910.
The King of Four Corners. London, Hutchinson, 1910.
This Son of Adam. London, Hutchinson, 1910.
The Belle of Santiago. London, Hutchinson, 1911.
A Lady of Spain. London, Hutchinson, 1911.
The Vision of Balmaine. London, Hutchinson, 1911.
Dickie Dilver. London, Hutchinson, 1912.
Varick's Legacy. London, Hutchinson, 1912.
The Love That Lasts. London, Hodder and Stoughton, 1913.
The 'Second-Sighter's' Daughter. London, Hutchinson, 1913.
The Duke's Twins. London, Hutchinson, 1914.
Within the Gates. London, Hutchinson, 1914.
A Game of Hearts. London, Hutchinson, 1915.
The Herb of Healing. London, Hutchinson, 1915.
The Girl Who Got Out. London, Hutchinson, 1916.
The Hut by the River. London, Hutchinson, 1916.
The Greater Gain. London, Hutchinson, 1917.
The Puller of Strings: An Ottawa Valley Romance. London, Hutchinson, 1917.
Lady Mary's Money. London, Hutchinson, 1918.
The Throw-Back. London, Hutchinson, 1918.
A Gentle Despot. London, Hutchinson, 1919.
A Rubber Princess. London, Hutchinson, 1919.
Pilgrims of Circumstance. London, Hutchinson, 1920.
Uncle Jeremy. London, Hutchinson, 1920.
The Faithful Fool. London, Books, 1921.
The Man from Turkey. London, Hutchinson, 1921.
Cyrilla Seeks Herself. London, Hutchinson, 1922.
Love and the Locusts. London, Hutchinson, 1922.
Manetta's Marriage. London, Hutchinson, 1922.
The Man Behind. London, Hutchinson, 1923.
Sally's Sweetheart. London, Hutchinson, 1923.
The Kiss. London, Hutchinson, 1924.
The Lord of Little Langton. London, Hutchinson, 1924.
The Spending of the Pile. London, Hutchinson, 1924.
The Young Labelle. London, Hutchinson, 1924.
Fleurette of Four Corners. London, Hutchinson, 1925.
The Hate That Lasts. London, Hutchinson, 1925.
Mariette's Lovers. London, Hutchinson, 1925.
The Forest Lure. London, Hutchinson, 1926.
Young Deloraine. London, Hutchinson, 1926.
The Dale of Dreams. London, Hutchinson, 1927.
The Hundredth Man. London, Hutchinson, 1927.
The House of Fiske. London, Hutchinson, 1927.
Allandale's Daughters. London, Hutchinson, 1928.
The Final Test. London, Hutchinson, 1928.
Nitana. London, Hutchinson, 1928.
All Things Come Round. London, Hutchinson, 1929.
Out of the Swim. London, Wright and Brown, 1930.
The Woman Without a Heart. London, Alexander Ouseley, 1930.
The Duke's Stratagem. London, Wright and Brown, 1931.
One Traveller Returns. London, Wright and Brown, 1931.
Eternal Justice. London, Wright and Brown, 1932.
When Dreams Come True. London, Wright and Brown, 1932.
The Wrong Woman. London, Wright and Brown, 1932.
The Wheels of Fate. London, Wright and Brown, 1933.
A Poor Millionaire. London, Wright and Brown, 1933.
A Fateful Fraud. London, Wright and Brown, 1934.
The Honour of Four Corners. London, Wright and Brown, 1934.

Pierrepont's Daughters. London, Wright and Brown, 1935.
Who Loses Pays. London, Wright and Brown, 1935.
Slaves of the Ring. London, Hutchinson, 1936.
Uncle Patterley's Money. London, Wright and Brown, 1936.
The Golden Penny. London, Wright and Brown, 1937.
The Ills Men Do. London, Wright and Brown, 1937.
A Pious Fraud. London, Wright and Brown, 1938.
The Man in the Corner. London, Wright and Brown, 1939.

Short Stories

His Lordship, and Others. London, Henry, 1893.

OTHER PUBLICATIONS

Other

Memoirs of a Clubman. London, Hutchinson, 1921; New York, Dutton, 1922.
More Memoirs (and Some Travels). London, Hutchinson, and New York, Dutton, 1922.
Many Memories. London, Hutchinson, 1922; New York, Dutton, 1923.
Some More Memoirs. London, Hutchinson, 1924.

Editor, *The Vagabond's Annual*. Bristol, Arrowsmith, 1893.

*   *   *

Behind the initials of G.B. Burgin lurks that rarity among romantic novelists—the male writer. Working from the mid-1890s until the late-1930s Burgin produced 100 novels. Other male novelists of the period, such as P.C. Wren and Rafael Sabatini, mixed up the love element with a fair amount of adventure, escapism, travel, and excitement, rather than concentrating only on matters of the heart. G.B. Burgin is openly sentimental about love, and keeps his heroines firmly on their pedestals. Suitors declare their love with vigorous, straightforward ardour:

'Cyrilla, you are divinely, most exquisitely beautiful. You are so beautiful that I am afraid of you. You hurt me ... Don't you see, Cyrilla, don't you know, that you are the embodiment of all that is sweetest and dearest in the world to me? You're heaven's explanation on earth. You know what I mean?' The heroine wanted to be swept off her feet, held tightly in strong arms, and perhaps even to be very slightly maltreated. Frankly, she liked men and their society. There was ... an unconscious brutality with most of them, which gave a girl something to think about.

The sentimental nonsense of tales like *The Kiss* or *Cyrilla Seeks Herself* is harmless daydreaming; however the dissemination of the belief that some girls actually *like* being brutalized is more questionable.

—Rachel Anderson

BURNS, Sheila.   See **BLOOM, Ursula.**

BUSBEE, Shirlee.
Nationality: American. **Born:** Shirlee Egan, San José, California. 9 August 1941. **Relations:** married Howard Leon Busbee, 22 June

1963. **Education:** Burbank Business College, certificate, 1962. **Career:** receptionist and secretary, Marin County Title and Abstract Company, 1962–63; plant supervisor, Fairfield Title Company, 1963–66; clerk and drafting technician, Solano County Assessor's Office, 1966. From 1974, drafting technician and secretary, County Parks Department, Fairfield, California. **Agent:** John Payne, Lenniger Literary Agency, 437 Fifth Avenue, New York, NY 10016, USA.

ROMANCE AND HISTORICAL PUBLICATIONS

Novels

Gypsy Lady. New York, Avon, and London, Fontana, 1977.
Lady Vixen. London, Fontana, and New York, Avon, 1980.
While Passion Sleeps. New York, Avon, 1983; London, Corgi, 1984.
Deceive Not My Heart. London, Corgi, and New York, Avon, 1984.
The Tiger Lily. London, Piatkus, and New York, Avon, 1985.
The Spanish Rose. New York, Avon, 1986; London, Severn House, 1991.
Midnight Masquerade. London, Severn House, and New York, Avon, 1988.
Whisper to Me of Love. London, Severn House, 1992.
Each Time We Love. New York, Avon, 1993.

*   *   *

Shirlee Busbee began her impressive career as a novelist in 1977, with the publication of *Gypsy Lady*. In the following 16 years a further eight novels have appeared. Busbee's work is not easy to classify or place in one genre, and it would be misleading to describe her works as either romance or historical fiction.

Busbee's great strength as a novelist lies in her ability to create highly believable, developed, and well-drawn characters who are subjected to the vagaries of life through complex plots. Her novels are racy, pacy, gripping, and well constructed. Her intricate and tangled plots revolve around mistaken identities, abductions, murders, revenge, rapes, seductions, and, above all, an underlying sensuality. Busbee's depiction of sex, although graphic, is always sensuous, but never pornographic.

Deceive Not My Heart is set in New Orleans in the late 18th-/early 19th-centuries, against a background of revolution and decay. The Chateau Saint-André, the American family home of the Saint-André family, refugees from revolutionary France, is a crumbling estate which has fallen into debt and subsequent disrepair because of the profligacy of Claude Saint-André. Claude is the grandfather of Leonie, the heroine of the book. She is forced into marriage by her grandfather who threatens to send Yvette, her bastard half-sister, to a brothel. Like all of Busbee's heroines, Leonie does not wish to get married, but she needs money and wants to claim the substantial dowry that her grandfather will give her husband. The money will be enough to restore the chateau to its former glory.

Leonie agrees to marry a man whom she thinks is Morgan Slade, the hero. However, Slade has had his life thrown into turmoil by the desertion and subsequent murder of his first wife and child, and has sworn never to trust another woman, or to remarry. She actually marries Ashley, Morgan's English cousin, the villain of the book. This case of mistaken identity by Leonie, is the pivot of the book. Leonie and Ashley draw up a marriage contract which states that they will have nothing to do with each other after the wedding night and that Ashley will repay Leonie's dowry within five years. Ashley, of course, has no intention of doing this, and Leonie goes in search of him, only to discover the real Morgan Slade. She falls in love with Morgan.

Ashley is a successful spy who wins the favour of Napoleon himself. Napoleon promises to return the French Saint-André estates to Ashley and his wife. The climax of the novel is complicated, but centres around Ashley's attempts to persuade Leonie to return to France with him. Needless to say, the reader is gripped until the last page—if not the last sentence of the book.

The background of *Deceive Not My Heart* is colonial America as seen in Spanish controlled New Orleans. The political upheavals of the late 18th-/early 19th-centuries are frequently referred to. The revolutions in both America and France, and the Napoleonic War are impressively highlighted, and reflect the turmoil of the society that the author describes. The characters' desire for independence is mirrored in the political climate, which in turn acts as a metaphor of the tensions felt by Busbee's protagonists. Busbee conveys an impression of the period by creating a sense of time and place rather than launching into great descriptive passages.

Money is an important theme in all of Busbee's work. Leonie would not have married Ashley but for her need of the dowry promised to her by the marriage contract. The lack of independent financial control for women is the prime reason why they marry in Busbee's books. They are forced into it by a society that refuses to acknowledge their rights. This is also seen in *Midnight Masquerade* in which Melissa, the heroine, can only get access to her trust before her brother's 21st birthday if she marries first. She prefers to make herself unattractive by wearing glasses and putting her hair up in a bun. Whenever men come near her she behaves like a shrew.

One of the most interesting developments of Busbee's work is the way in which characters from previous novels form the basis of subsequent ones. Dominic Slade, the hero of *Midnight Masquerade* made his first appearance in *Deceive Not My Heart*. In an interview Busbee admits to having a fondness for Dominic and 'thought he should have his own novel'. Royce Manchester, described by Busbee as '. . . my first blonde hero. All the others were black haired. He's also golden eyed! . . . I fell in love with him' is the hero of a subsequent novel. Adam St Clair, his sister, and Justin Savage, originally from *Gypsy Lady* reappear in Busbee's 1993 novel *Each Time We Love*. The recognition of these characters is part of the attraction to the reader and part of the excitement of reading Busbee.

Busbee's novels are well written and well researched. The whole array of human experience and emotion are present in her works. Evil people jostle for power and success with good people. The novels, above all, are consistently enjoyable and thrilling reads.

—Charmaine Moldrich

———

BUTLER, Gwendoline. British. 1922—. See 2nd edition, 1990.

———

BUTTERWORTH, Michael.   See SALISBURY, Carola.

———

BYATT, A(ntonia) S(usan).
Nationality: British. **Born:** Antonia Susan Drabble, Sheffield, Yorkshire, 24 August 1936. Sister of the writer Margaret Drabble; sister-in-law of writer Michael Holroyd. **Education:** Sheffield High School; The Mount School, York; Newnham College, Cambridge (open scholarship), B.A. (honours) in English, 1957; Bryn Mawr College, Pennsylvania (English-Speaking Union fellow), 1957–58; Somerville College, Oxford, 1958–59, B.A. **Relations:** married 1) I.C.R. Byatt in 1959 (divorced 1969), one daughter and one son (deceased); 2) Peter J. Duffy in 1969, two daughters. **Career:** teacher, Westminster Tutors, London, 1962–65; lecturer, Central School of

Art and Design, London, 1965–69; extra-mural lecturer, 1962–71, lecturer, 1972–81, and senior lecturer in English, 1981–83, University College, London (assistant tutor, 1977–80, and tutor for admissions, 1980–82, Department of English). British Council lecturer in Spain, 1978, India, 1981, and Korea, 1985. Deputy chairman, 1986, and chairman, 1986–88, Society of Authors Committee of Management; member, Kingman Committee, on the teaching of English, 1988–89. Associate, Newnham College, 1977–88. **Recipient:** Arts Council grant, 1968; PEN Silver Pen, 1986; Booker prize, 1990, for *Possession*; *Irish Times-Aer Lingus* prize, 1990, for *Possession*. D.Litt.: University of Bradford, Yorkshire, 1987; University of York, 1991; University of Durham, 1991. Fellow, Royal Society of Literature, 1983. CBE (Commander, Order of the British Empire), 1990. **Address:** 37 Rusholme Road, London SW15 3LF, England.

ROMANCE AND HISTORICAL PUBLICATIONS

Novels

Possession: A Romance. London, Chatto and Windus, and New York, Random House, 1990.

OTHER PUBLICATIONS

Novels

The Shadow of a Sun. London, Chatto and Windus, and New York, Harcourt Brace, 1964.
The Game. London, Chatto and Windus, 1967; New York, Scribner, 1985.
The Virgin in the Garden. London, Chatto and Windus, 1978; New York, Knopf, 1979.
Still Life. London, Chatto and Windus, 1985; New York, Random House, 1990.

Short Stories

Sugar and Other Stories. London, Chatto and Windus, and New York, Random House, 1990.
Angels and Insects (novellas). London, Chatto and Windus, 1992.
The Matisse Stories. London, Chatto and Windus, 1994.

Other

Degrees of Freedom: The Novels of Iris Murdoch. London, Chatto and Windus, and New York, Barnes and Noble, 1965.
Wordsworth and Coleridge in Their Time. London, Nelson, 1970; New York, Crane Russak, 1973; as *Unruly Times: Wordsworth and Coleridge in Their Time*, London, Hogarth Press, 1989.
Iris Murdoch. London, Longman, 1976.
Passions of the Mind (essays). London, Chatto and Windus, 1991; New York, Turtle Books, 1992.

Editor, *The Mill on the Floss*, by George Eliot. London, Penguin, 1979.
Editor, with Nicholas Warren, *Selected Essays, Poems, and Other Writings*, by George Eliot. London, Penguin, 1990.
Editor, *George Eliot: Selected Essays*. London, Penguin, 1990.

*   *   *

For A.S. Byatt, the lines between realism and romance, and between history and invention, are particularly problematic. Both her fiction and her criticism, in fact, often make the overlapping of these categories part of their subject. Byatt has said that she writes about 'the nature of the imagination, the ways in which different people take in the world, and the uses they make of what they think or see'. In many of her short stories and novels the interplay between fact and fabrication, and between experience and the language that both embodies and distorts it, is metafictionally foregrounded. Theoretical issues never overshadow Byatt's concern with concrete human experience, however: she often quotes Iris Murdoch (in 'Against Dryness') on the importance of fidelity to 'real people'. Her historical romance, *Possession*, and two novellas which comprise *Angels and Insects*, explore these issues in unique ways, as do several stories in the *Sugar* volume ('The July Ghost' and 'The Next Room', feature ghosts; another, 'Precipice-Encurled', combines historical characters with invented ones).

Possession, Byatt's most substantial achievement so far in the fictional re-creation of history, is subtitled 'A Romance'. One of its epigraphs is Hawthorne's definition of romance, which aptly describes Byatt's own project. Hawthorne stresses that the writer of romance must never 'swerve aside from the truth of the human heart', although claiming the 'latitude' of choosing or creating the circumstances in which that truth will be presented. The circumstances of *Possession* move between the 19th and the late-20th centuries. In the 19th century, the main characters are two poets, Randolph Henry Ash (modelled on Browning) and Christabel La Motte (resembling both Christina Rossetti and Emily Dickinson), and in the 20th century, two scholars, Roland Michell and Maud Bailey, who are working, respectively, on Ash and La Motte. The plot brilliantly fuses elements of mystery, detective story, academic satire, epistolary novel, and love story, through a multiplicity of texts, including fairytale and myth (in the story itself and in the poems which Byatt creates for Ash and Christabel); private letters (some hidden in a Victorian doll's bed; some buried in Ash's grave and exhumed by the 20th-century scholars in a comic gothic grave-robbing scene); scholarly and critical prose. In search of the 'truth,' Roland and Maud make some gratifying discoveries—the secret love affair which linked their subjects, the resulting child who became one of Maud's ancestors, and their own love for each other—but they also discover the elusiveness of truth. So does the reader, although we are allowed to know more of the reality of the Victorian characters, including the sad, hidden life of Ellen, Ash's wife, and a privileged glimpse of Ash and Christabel's daughter. The book explores forms of possession (Byatt describes the title as a 'layered pun'): demonic, sexual, and, most important of all, textual. It ends by celebrating both the dense richness of language and reality and the silence and incompleteness which lie beyond all our versions.

Angels and Insects continues Byatt's probing of the problems of the 19th-century mind which (describing Browning's preoccupations) she defines as 'the relation of time to history, of science to religion, of fact in science or history to fiction, or lies, in both, and of art to all these'. This time, however, there are no 20th-century characters. The first novella, *Morpho Eugenia*, presents a Darwinian entomologist, William Adamson, who, returning to England after years in the Amazon jungle, falls in love with the apparently innocent, virginal Eugenia Alabaster, daughter of William's host and temporary patron. Their fairytale wedding, beautifully heralded by a cloud of butterflies, occurs early in the book. It leads to William's half-enchanted, half-resentful imprisonment in the Alabaster household, to a series of intense debates on evolution between William and his clergyman father-in-law and ultimately to the exposure of the gothic secret of Eugenia's incest with her half-brother. The marriage is over, and William, released from his thralldom, begins a new voyage of scientific and emotional exploration in a more solidly based romance with the household's dependent relation, Matilda. The plot thus both subverts and, in the end, upholds the conventions of romance.

The second novella, *The Conjugial Angel*, is set later in the century. It is linked to *Morpho Eugenia* by one character, Arturo Papagay, captain of the ship on which William and Matilda set sail. Papagay is presumed to have drowned on his latest voyage, and the story introduces his putative widow and her friend Sophy Sheekhy, both professional spiritualists. The book plays historical characters (Alfred Tennyson, his sister Emily, Emily's husband Richard Jesse, and—as a ghost—her dead fiancé and her brother's close friend, Arthur Hallam) against invented ones. It again demonstrates the persistence—sometimes benign, sometimes morbid—of the past in the present. Here the fairytale romance between Emily and Hallam has been cut short by death, with Tennyson and Emily beginning a long mourning which even Emily's marriage to Richard has not wholly assuaged—until Hallam's ghost proclaims to Sophy in a seance that he and Emily are to be 'one Angel' in eternity. In a tender moment of recognition Emily (now an old woman) declares her preference for her flesh-and-blood husband. Completing the pattern of restoration, Papagay comes home alive to his rejoicing wife. Both novellas problematize categories: natural/unnatural/supernatural; Darwinian/Christian; biologically determined/morally free. Both examine the imagination and its limits, its power to falsify as well as to liberate, and both end with moments of happiness which, by being both hard-won and contingent, escape the banality of more simplistic romantic endings.

Byatt's less realistic fiction, then, extends the concerns of her earlier novels. Although Byatt is obviously fascinated by the challenges of romance and historical writing, her primary subject remains the shaping work of the imagination. Here Captain Papagay can be her spokesman: 'As long as you are alive, everything is surprising, rightly seen'.

—Jane Campbell

BYRNE, Donn.
Pseudonym for Brian Oswald Donn-Byrne. **Nationality:** Irish. **Born:** New York City, 20 November 1889; brought up in Ireland. **Education:** Royal University of Ireland, 1907–10, B.A. 1910; University College, Dublin; studied at the Sorbonne, Paris, and in Leipzig, Germany. **Relations:** married Dorothea Cadogan in 1911. Lived in New York after 1911. **Died:** 18 June 1928.

ROMANCE AND HISTORICAL PUBLICATIONS

Novels

Messer Marco Polo. New York, Century, 1921; London, Sampson Low, 1922.
The Wind Bloweth. New York, Century, and London, Sampson Low, 1922.
Blind Raftery and His Wife Hilaria. New York, Century, 1924; London, Sampson Low, 1925.
O'Malley of Shanganagh. New York, Century, 1925; as *An Untitled Story*. London, Sampson Low, 1925.
Hangman's House. New York, Century, and London, Sampson Low, 1926.
Brother Saul. New York, Century, and London, Sampson Low, 1927.
Crusade. Boston, Little Brown, and London, Sampson Low, 1928.
Field of Honor. New York, Century, 1929; as *The Power of the Dog*. London, Sampson Low, 1929.
A Party of Baccarat. New York, Century, 1930; as *The Golden Goat*. London, Sampson Low, 1930.

Short Stories

Stories Without Women. New York, Hearst, 1915; London, Sampson Low, 1931.

Changeling and Other Stories. New York, Century, 1924; London, Sampson Low, 1925.

Destiny Bay. Boston, Little Brown, and London, Sampson Low, 1928.

Rivers of Damascus and Other Stories. London, Sampson Low, and New York, Century, 1931.

The Island of Youth and Other Stories. London, Sampson Low, 1932; New York, Century, 1933.

Sargasso Sea and Other Stories. London, Sampson Low, 1932; as *A Woman of the Shee and Other Stories*. New York, Century, 1932.

An Alley of Flashing Spears and Other Stories. London, Sampson Low, 1933; New York, Appleton Century, 1934.

A Daughter of the Medici and Other Stories. London, Sampson Low, 1933; New York, Appleton Century, 1935.

The Hound of Ireland and Other Stories. London, Sampson Low, 1934; New York, Appleton Century, 1935.

OTHER PUBLICATIONS

Novels

The Stranger's Banquet. New York, Harper, 1919.

The Foolish Matrons. New York, Harper, 1920; London, Sampson Low, 1923.

Poetry

Poems. London, Sampson Low, 1934.

Other

Ireland: The Rock Whence I Was Hewn (memoirs). Boston, Little Brown, and London, Sampson Low, 1929.

*

Manuscript Collection: New York Public Library.

Bibliography: *Donn Byrne: A Descriptive Bibliography 1912–1935* by Henry S. Bannister, New York, Garland, 1982.

Critical Studies: *Donn Byrne: His Place in Literature* by Paul Mellon, New York, Century, 1927; *Donn Byrne: Bard of Armagh* by Thurston Macauley, New York, Century, 1929; London, Sampson Low, 1931.

*   *   *

Donn Byrne's books are full of lyrical language, chivalric heroes, and fiercely noble heroines. He weaves his stories in such a way as to make the reader want them never to end. Byrne's obvious love for and respect of his native Ireland can be seen in his use of the country, language, and people in his various books. Even *Messer Marco Polo*, the story of Marco Polo's life, is narrated through the eyes of a charming old Irish man Malachi Campbell. Byrne's male characters are often wanderers: Knights of the Cross in foreign lands; sailors journeying the world; Americans travelling to France; or Saul finding his way to Christ. His heroines are spirited women with much knowledge of the world and an enduring love for their men.

This is seen best in *Messer Marco Polo* in which Brian Oge is visited in New York by Malachi Campbell of the Long Glen. Malachi tells Brian the story of Marco Polo's adventures which lead him to China to tell Kubla Khan of Christ's life, death, and Resurrection, and to find his love, Golden Bells. The book is written in fluid language, and Marco's story is told in an Irish colloquial dialect which

leads Kubla Khan to say to him, 'Well, now, laddie . . . '. The love affair of Golden Bells and Marco Polo is a sad one which leads Marco to enjoy three years of happy married life and 14 of solitude spent mourning her death. The book ends with Kubla Khan requesting that Marco return to Venice and live again, and Golden Bells's sign that she wishes it so. *Messer Marco Polo* was received to critical acclaim and a critic in *The Daily Telegraph* wrote, 'Pretty work this, Mr Donn Byrne. Mayhap old Malachi has some more tales to tell. If so, we would gladly hear them'.

Another love story is told in *Crusade*, the tale of Sir Miles O'Neill, a Knight of the Cross taken prisoner by the Saracens. He finds his captors more civilized than his peers and falls in love with Kothra, the daughter of his imprisoner. Released by Kothra's father he returns to Jerusalem to disillusionment. Nothing is as he remembered and all sense of honour and order has gone—as half Norman/half Celt honour is the most important thing to him. This book is as much about Miles's search for his own happiness as about depicting Jerusalem during this time. Kothra comes to Jerusalem to find him and the two end up fleeing the remaining Knights of the Cross who think that she is a spy and he 'an apostate to El Islam'. Miles realizes that Islam is more honourable and saves both of their lives by saying the *Fatha* before escaping by swimming out to some boats in the sea. Kothra is a warrior-woman more than capable of fending for herself, and fighting for the man whom she loves.

The Wind Bloweth also finds its hero far from his own land. Shane loves Ireland but sails away to find lands anew. He is tricked into marrying a very cold Irish woman who obliges him by dying; he then falls tragically in love with a beautiful French girl; he takes a Muslim wife and loses her because he doesn't understand that she loves him because he is weak; and he finally finds himself in Buenos Aires with the Swedish Hedda who tells him that despite all of his encounters, he knows nothing about women!

Hangman's House is set in Dublin. It evokes the poetry of Ireland and is very much a human story. 'People will return to the pages of *Hangman's House* as they return to the masterpieces of Blackmore and Hardy', a critic wrote in *The Sunday Times*. Connaught is forced to marry John D'Arcy, a man with a good political future, but who ends up as a crook. There are long descriptions of hunts and races, and passages devoted to evoking the Irish countryside. Ireland is also seen through the eyes of De Bourke O'Malley of Shanganah, an old man who can be found in the pubs of Dublin. O'Malley's story is a tragic one, the reader finds out that as a young and gallant man recently retired from the army, he decides to become a country gentleman but falls in love with an Anglican nun instead. Although they run away together, they find nothing but unhappiness and she eventually returns to her convent. It is a fascinating mix of poetry and irony.

Byrne writes beautifully scribed books, depicting a world in which pain, sadness, love, and laughter go hand in hand.

—P. Campbell

———

CABELL, James Branch. American. 1879–1958. See 2nd edition, 1990.

———

CADE, Robin. See **NICOLE, Christopher.**

———

CADELL, (Violet) Elizabeth.
Pseudonym: Harriet Ainsworth. **Nationality:** British. **Born:** Calcutta, India, 10 November 1903. **Relations:** married H.D.R.M.

Cadell in 1928 (died); one son and one daughter. **Died:** 9 October 1989.

ROMANCE AND HISTORICAL PUBLICATIONS

Novels

My Dear Aunt Flora. London, Hale, 1946.
Last Straw for Harriet. New York, Morrow, 1947; as *Fishy, Said the Admiral*, London, Hale, 1948.
River Lodge. London, Hale, 1948.
Gay Pursuit. New York, Morrow, 1948; London, Hale, 1950; as *Family Gathering*, Hale, 1979.
Iris in Winter. New York, Morrow, 1949; London, Hale, 1951.
Brimstone in the Garden. New York, Morrow, 1950.
The Greenwood Shady. London, Hodder and Stoughton, 1951.
Enter Mrs Belchamber. New York, Morrow, 1951; as *The Frenchman and the Lady*, London, Hodder and Stoughton, 1952.
Men and Angels. London, Hodder and Stoughton, 1952.
Crystal Clear. New York, Morrow, 1953; as *Journey's Eve*, London, Hodder and Stoughton, 1953.
Spring Green. London, Hodder and Stoughton, 1953.
The Cuckoo in Spring. New York, Morrow, and London, Hodder and Stoughton, 1954.
Around the Rugged Rock. New York, Morrow, 1954; as *The Gentlemen Go By*, London, Hodder and Stoughton, 1954.
The Lark Shall Sing. New York, Morrow, and London, Hodder and Stoughton, 1955; as *The Singing Heart*, New York, Berkley, 1959.
The Blue Sky of Spring. London, Hodder and Stoughton, 1956.
I Love a Lass. New York, Morrow, 1956.
Bridal Array. London, Hodder and Stoughton, 1957; Toronto, Harlequin, 1959.
The Green Empress. London, Hodder and Stoughton, 1958.
Sugar Candy Cottage. London, Hodder and Stoughton, 1958.
Alice, Where Art Thou? London, Hodder and Stoughton, 1959.
The Yellow Brick Road. London, Hodder and Stoughton, and New York, Morrow, 1960.
Honey for Tea. London, Hodder and Stoughton, 1961; New York, Morrow, 1962.
Six Impossible Things. London, Hodder and Stoughton, and New York, Morrow, 1961.
Language of the Heart. London, Hodder and Stoughton, 1962; as *The Toy Sword*, New York, Morrow, 1962.
Letter to My Love. London, Hodder and Stoughton, 1963.
Mixed Marriage: The Diary of a Portuguese Bride. London, Hodder and Stoughton, 1963.
Be My Guest. London, Hodder and Stoughton, 1964; as *Come Be My Guest*, New York, Morrow, 1964.
Canary Yellow. London, Hodder and Stoughton, and New York, Morrow, 1965.
The Fox from His Lair. London, Hodder and Stoughton, 1965; New York, Morrow, 1966.
The Corner Shop. London, Hodder and Stoughton, 1966; New York, Morrow, 1967.
The Stratton Story. London, Hodder and Stoughton, 1967.
Mrs Westerby Changes Course. New York, Morrow, 1968.
The Golden Collar. London, Hodder and Stoughton, and New York, Morrow, 1969.
The Friendly Air. London, Hodder and Stoughton, 1970; New York, Morrow, 1971.
The Past Tense of Love. London, Hodder and Stoughton, and New York, Morrow, 1970.
Home for the Wedding. London, Hodder and Stoughton, 1971; New York, Morrow, 1972.

The Haymaker. London, Hodder and Stoughton, 1972.
Royal Summons. New York, Morrow, 1973.
Deck with Flowers. London, Hodder and Stoughton, 1973; New York, Morrow, 1974.
The Fledgling. London, Hodder and Stoughton, and New York, Morrow, 1975.
Game in Diamonds. London, Hodder and Stoughton, and New York, Morrow, 1976.
Parson's House. London, Hodder and Stoughton, and New York, Morrow, 1977.
Round Dozen. London, Hodder and Stoughton, and New York, Morrow, 1978.
Return Match. London, Hodder and Stoughton, and New York, Morrow, 1979.
The Marrying Kind. London, Hodder and Stoughton, and New York, Morrow, 1980.
Any Two Can Play. New York, Morrow, 1981.
A Lion in the Way. London, Hodder and Stoughton, and New York, Morrow, 1982.
Remains to Be Seen. London, Hodder and Stoughton, and New York, Morrow, 1983.
The Waiting Game. London, Hodder and Stoughton, and New York, Morrow, 1985.
The Empty Nest. London, Hodder and Stoughton, and New York, Morrow, 1986.
Out of the Nest. London, Hodder and Stoughton, and New York, Morrow, 1987.
Out of the Rain. London, Hodder and Stoughton, 1987.

Novels as Harriet Ainsworth

Consider the Lilies. London, Hodder and Stoughton, 1956.
Shadows on the Water. London, Hodder and Stoughton, 1958; (as Elizabeth Cadell) New York, Morrow, 1958.
Death among Friends. London, Hodder and Stoughton, 1964.

OTHER PUBLICATIONS

Other

Sun in the Morning (for children). New York, Morrow, 1950; London, Hodder and Stoughton, 1951.

*   *   *

Normality is the essence of Elizabeth Cadell's popular novels. Her heroines are usually intelligent, practical, efficient, their faults the result of impulsiveness and warm-heartedness. Sometimes their suitors will chafe as this impulsiveness brings in its wake a stream of young nephews, eccentric old ladies, and lovable animals to interfere with their courtship. But even imperious suitors accept this, ultimately, or are replaced by more understanding young men.

Beyond this, the novels are substantially middle class. There are few Cinderellas swept away by titled millionaires. Alexandra (*The Cuckoo in Spring*) is one of Cadell's most humbly circumstanced heroines, yet she is self-supporting, a secretary with a firm of solicitors. On some level, the Cadell hero and heroine must meet as equals, since her basic plot shows two people of the same class finding each other and overcoming obstacles that are mildly amusing, to the reader if not to the protagonists.

Often giving her books a Spanish or Portuguese setting, Cadell provides a good read, a piece of escapism where the crucial phone call does not go unanswered and even the rejected suitor is not too crushed by his rejection. Like another prolific writer of romances, D.E. Stevenson, Cadell has a limpid charm of writing that, with the many bizarre subsidiary characters, turns the best of her romances, like *Honey for Tea*, into comedies of manners. And this comic tone allows Cadell to be more realistic than similar authors in areas where her characters are less than perfect. Lucille in *The Lark Shall Sing* is frankly bossy; her beautiful sister tends to ineffectual tears. Kerry's long-lost mother has spent 20 years as mistress to a series of successful men in *The Past Tense of Love*.

Another example of Cadell's realistic streak in the midst of romantic fantasy is her clear-eyed portrayal of children. The three youngest Waynes in *The Lark Shall Sing* are individualized, charming to read about, but possibly less than charming to have to live with. The epitome of the objective portrayal of the child is Tory Brooke in *The Fledgling*. Eponymous heroine though she may be, Tory's determination to recast her circumstances to suit herself shows her as too deliberate and calculating to be altogether attractive. As she waits for her widowed father and the woman of his, and her, choice to announce the happy ending she has contrived for them all, she can be seen, whether or not Cadell intends it, as too cold-blooded for comfort.

At the other end of the scale, particularly in some of her earlier books, Cadell shows an attractive middle-aged woman involved in romantic or family problems. In *Last Straw for Harriet* it is Harriet who holds stage centre, not the romantic young people. The eye that Cadell turns on the aged, like the eye she turns on the young, is sympathetic but not sentimental.

Mrs Westerby Changes Course and *Canary Yellow* may veer in the direction of the suspense story; *Brimstone in the Garden* has a supernatural slant; but Cadell's real genre is clearly romance in perhaps its safest, most wholesome form. If 'life isn't like that', it is clearly life's fault, not Cadell's.

—Susan Branch

CAINE, (Thomas Henry) Hall.
Nationality: British. **Born:** Runcorn, Cheshire, 14 May 1858 (or 1853). **Education:** attended schools on the Isle of Man and in Liverpool. **Relations:** married Mary Chandler in 1882; two sons. **Career:** architect's clerk; schoolmaster; journalist, Liverpool *Mercury*; companion-secretary to D.G. Rossetti, in London, until Rossetti's death, 1882, then lived on the Isle of Man. Lecturer, Royal Institution, London, 1892; Justice of the Peace, and member of the House of Keys, Isle of Man. Freeman of Douglas, Isle of Man, 1928. **Recipient:** Officer of the Order of Leopold, Belgium; Companion of Honour, 1922. Knighted, 1918. **Died:** 31 August 1931.

ROMANCE AND HISTORICAL PUBLICATIONS

Novels

The Shadow of a Crime. London, Chatto and Windus, 3 vols, and New York, Harper, 3 vols, 1885.
She's All the World to Me. New York, Harper, 1885.
The Deemster. London, Chatto and Windus, 3 vols, 1887; New York, Appleton, 1 vol, 1888.
A Son of Hagar. London, Chatto and Windus, 1887; New York, Fenno, 1895.
The Bondman: A New Saga. New York, Lovell, 1889; London, Heinemann, 3 vols, 1890.
The Scapegoat. London, Heinemann, 2 vols, 1891; New York, Lovell, 1 vol, 1891.
The Manxman. London, Heinemann, and New York, Appleton, 1894.
The Mahdi; or, Love and Race. New York, Appleton, and London, Clarke, 1894.

The Christian. London, Heinemann, and New York, Appleton, 1897.
The Eternal City. London, Heinemann, and New York, Appleton, 1901.
The Prodigal Son. London, Heinemann, and New York, Appleton, 1904.
Drink: A Love Story on a Great Question. London, Newnes, 1906; New York, Appleton, 1907.
The White Prophet. London, Heinemann, 2 vols, 1909; New York, Appleton, 1 vol, 1909; revised edition, Heinemann, 1 vol, 1911.
The Woman Thou Gavest Me. London, Heinemann, and Philadelphia, Lippincott, 1913.
The Master of Man. London, Heinemann, and Philadelphia, Lippincott, 1921.
The Woman of Knockaloe: A Parable. London, Cassell, and New York, Dodd Mead, 1923.

Short Stories

Capt'n Davy's Honeymoon, The Last Confession, The Blind Mother. London, Heinemann, 1892; *Capt'n Davy's Honeymoon* published New York, Appleton, 1892; *The Last Confession, The Blind Mother* published New York, Tait, 1892.

OTHER PUBLICATIONS

Plays

The Ben-my-Chree, with Wilson Barrett (produced London, 1888).
The Good Old Times, with Wilson Barrett (produced London, 1889).
The Bondman, (produced Bolton, Lancashire, 1892; London, 1906). London, Daily Mail, 1906.
The Christian, adaptation of his own novel (produced Liverpool and London, 1899; revised version, produced London, 1907). London, Collier, 1907.
Yan, The Icelander; or, Home Sweet Home (produced Hartlepool, 1900; as *The Quality of Mercy*, produced Manchester, 1911). Privately printed, 1896.
The Eternal City, adaptation of his own novel (produced London and New York, 1902). Privately printed, 1902.
The Prodigal Son, adaptation of his own novel (produced London and New York, 1905). Privately printed, 1905.
Pete, with Louis N. Parker, adaptation of the novel *The Manxman* by Caine (produced London, 1908). London, Collier, 1908.
The Fatal Error (produced London, 1908).
The Bishop's Son, adaptation of his novel *The Deemster* (produced London, 1910). Privately printed, 1910.
The Eternal Question, adaptation of his novel *The Eternal City* (produced London, 1910). Privately printed, 1910.
The Prime Minister (produced Atlantic City, 1916; as *Margaret Schiller*, produced New York, 1916; as *The Prime Minister*, produced London, 1918). Privately printed, 1918.
The Iron Hand (produced London, 1916).
The Woman Thou Gavest Me, adaptation of his own novel (produced Boston, 1917).

Screenplays: *Victory and Peace*, 1918; *Darby and Joan*, 1919.

Other

Richard III and Macbeth . . .: A Dramatic Study. London, Simpkin Marshall, 1877.
Recollections of Dante Gabriel Rossetti. London, Stock, 1882; Boston, Roberts, 1883; revised edition, London, Cassell, 1928; as *Recollections of Rossetti*, London, Century, 1990.

Cobwebs of Criticism. London, Stock, 1883; New York, Dutton, 1908.

Life of Samuel Taylor Coleridge. London, Scott, 1887; New York, Scribner, n.d.

The Prophet: A Parable. London, Heinemann, 1890.

The Little Manx Nation. London, Heinemann, and New York, United States Book Company, 1891.

Mary Magdalene: The New Apocrypha. Privately printed, 1891.

The Little Man Island: Scenes and Specimen Days in the Isle-of-Man. Douglas, Steam Packet Company, 1894.

My Story. London, Heinemann, 1908; New York, Appleton, 1909.

Why I Wrote 'The White Prophet'. Privately printed, 1909.

King Edward: A Prince and a Great Man. London, Collier, 1910.

The Drama of Three Hundred Sixty Five Days: Scenes in the Great War. London, Heinemann, and Philadelphia, Lippincott, 1915.

Our Girls: Their Work for the War. London, Hutchinson, 1916.

Life of Christ, edited by Sir Derwent Hall Caine. London, Collins, and New York, Doubleday, 1938.

Editor, *Sonnets of Three Centuries.* London, Stock, 1882; Boston, Clarke, 1883.

Editor, *King Albert's Book: A Tribute to the Belgian King and People.* London, Daily Telegraph, 1914.

*　　　*　　　*

Hall Caine was one of the great names of popular fiction at the turn of the century and continued to be so for three decades afterwards. He mingled with the great, was championed by other writers and poets of the time, fought vociferously for the cause of the one-volume (as against the cumbersome three-volume) novel in order that cheaper and more manageable fiction, including his own, could reach a wider public. Thus, his enthusiastic readership included not only the highly literate, but the great uneducated masses. He wrote with moral passion on great and noble subjects and saw himself as 'the Shakespeare of the novel'. With the decline of religious authority, it seemed necessary for writers such as he to take on themselves the mammoth task of maintaining among the reading masses the moral standards which he felt to be lacking. Today his name is almost forgotten. What is astonishing is that a writer who was so pretentious, so self-important, and whose skill was so inadequate for the task he set himself should have ever been taken seriously in the first place.

The most popular of his 20th-century novels was *The Woman of Knockaloe,* set, like many, on the Isle of Man. He was a pacifist for most of his life, and this romance, written shortly after the end of World War I telling of the forbidden and unacceptable love between a Manxwoman and a German prisoner-of-war, is an impassioned anti-war cry. As Claud Cockburn pointed out in *Best Seller,* the Great War, for all its horror, provided excellent literary food for the popular writers. It was 'a gift, a natural, manna from heaven. It furnished him with a range of fictional and dramatic equipment such as had been ready to hand in the workshops of the Greek classical dramatists'.

The noble intentions of the author of *The Woman of Knockaloe,* the fine motives of his driving force, the proper care to try to end all future war by the power of his pen, contrast strongly with the banality of treatment. The love between Mona and Oskar is necessarily furtive, but utterly pure. Their affair is hopelessly doomed from the start, for the rest of the world is against them. They are driven to a mutual suicide pact. At dawn, they climb a heather-clad mountain to make their love leap from the top, to the 'heaving and singing' sea below. They agree that their leap must be simultaneous, so, as in some ludicrous charade, they solemnly strap themselves together with Oskar's long coat belt. 'They are now eye to eye, breast to breast, heart to heart'.

Hall Caine's lifelong enemy was the equally popular romantic novelist, Marie Corelli, whose own first novel he had turned down for publication. She, too, believed herself to be a Shakespeare of the prose form. They had much in common. Q.D. Leavis, in *Fiction and the Reading Public,* said that their novels 'make play with the key words of the emotional vocabulary which provoke the vague warm surges of feeling associated with religion and religion substitutes—e.g., life, death, love, good, evil, sin, home, mother, noble, gallant, purity, honour. These responses can be touched off with a dangerous ease'.

—Rachel Anderson

———

CAIRD, Janet. British. 1913—. See 2nd edition, 1990.

———

CALDWELL, (Janet Miriam) Taylor (Holland). **Pseudonym:** Max Reiner. **Nationality:** American. **Born:** Prestwich, Manchester, 7 September 1900. **Education:** University of Buffalo, New York (now State University of New York) A.B. 1931. **Military Service:** United States Naval Reserve, 1918–19. **Relations:** married 1) William Fairfax Combs in 1919 (divorced 1931), one daughter; 2) Marcus Reback in 1931 (died 1970), one daughter; 3) William E. Stancell in 1972 (divorced 1973); 4) William Robert Prestie in 1978. **Career:** court reporter, New York State Department of Labor, Buffalo, 1923–24; member of the Board of Special Inquiry, Department of Justice, Buffalo, 1924–31. **Recipient:** National League of American Pen Women gold medal, 1948; Buffalo *Evening News* award, 1949; Grand Prix Chatrain, 1956. D.Litt.: D'Youville College, Buffalo, 1964; St Bonaventure College, New York, 1977. **Died:** 30 August 1985.

ROMANCE AND HISTORICAL PUBLICATIONS

Novels (series: Barbours and Bouchards)

Dynasty of Death (Barbours and Bouchards). New York, Scribner, 1938; London, Collins, 1939.

The Eagles Gather (Barbours and Bouchards). New York, Scribner, and London, Collins, 1940.

Time No Longer (as Max Reiner). New York, Scribner, 1941.

The Earth Is the Lord's. New York, Scribner, and London, Collins, 1941.

The Strong City. New York, Scribner, and London, Collins, 1942.

The Arm and the Darkness. New York, Scribner, and London, Collins, 1943.

The Turnbulls. New York, Scribner, 1943; London, Collins, 1944.

The Final Hour (Barbours and Bouchards). New York, Scribner, 1944; London, Collins, 1945.

The Wide House. New York, Scribner, 1945; London, Collins, 1946.

This Side of Innocence. New York, Scribner, 1946; London, Collins, 1947.

There Was a Time. New York, Scribner, 1947; London, Collins, 1948.

Melissa. New York, Scribner, 1948; London, Collins, 1949.

Let Love Come Last. New York, Scribner, 1948; London, Collins, 1950.

The Balance Wheel. New York, Scribner, 1951; as *The Beautiful Is Vanished,* London, Collins, 1951.

The Devil's Advocate. New York, Crown, 1952.

Maggie, Her Marriage. New York, Fawcett, 1953; London, Muller, 1954.

Never Victorious, Never Defeated. New York, McGraw Hill, and London, Collins, 1954.

Your Sins and Mine. New York, Fawcett, 1955; London, Muller, 1956.

Tender Victory. New York, McGraw Hill, and London, Collins, 1956.

The Sound of Thunder. New York, Doubleday, 1957; London, Collins, 1958.

Dear and Glorious Physician. New York, Doubleday, and London, Collins, 1959.

The Listener. New York, Doubleday, 1960; as *The Man Who Listens*, London, Collins, 1961.

A Prologue to Love. New York, Doubleday, 1961; London, Collins, 1962.

Grandmother and the Priests. New York, Doubleday, 1963; as *To See the Glory*, London, Collins, 1963.

The Late Clare Beame. New York, Doubleday, 1963; London, Collins, 1964.

A Pillar of Iron. New York, Doubleday, 1965; London, Collins, 1966.

Wicked Angel. New York, Fawcett, 1965; London, Coronet, 1966.

No One Hears But Him. New York, Doubleday, and London, Collins, 1966.

Testimony of Two Men. New York, Doubleday, 1968; London, Collins, 1969.

Great Lion of God. New York, Doubleday, and London, Collins, 1970.

Captains and the Kings. New York, Doubleday, 1972; London, Collins, 1973.

Glory and the Lightning. New York, Doubleday, 1974; London, Collins, 1975.

To Look and Pass. London, White Lion, 1974.

The Romance of Atlantis, with Jess Stearn. New York, Morrow, 1975; London, Fontana, 1976.

Ceremony of the Innocent. New York, Doubleday, 1976; London, Collins, 1977.

I, Judas, with Jess Stearn. New York, Atheneum, 1977; London, New English Library, 1978.

Bright Flows the River. New York, Doubleday, 1978; London, Collins, 1979.

Answer As a Man. New York, Putnam, and London, Collins, 1981.

OTHER PUBLICATIONS

Other

Dialogues with the Devil. New York, Doubleday, 1967; London, Collins, 1968.

On Growing Up Tough. Old Greenwich, Connecticut, Devin Adair, 1971; as *Growing Up Tough*, London, Stacey, 1971.

*

Film Adaptations: *Captains and the Kings*, 1976; *Testimony of Two Men*, 1977.

Critical Study: *In Search of Taylor Caldwell* by Jess Stearn, New York, Stein and Day, 1981.

*   *   *

Taylor Caldwell's long list of successes as a popular author began only in 1938 with the wide acceptance of her first published novel.

However, she had a life-long interest in writing having completed her first novel at the age of 12. Caldwell's published works reflect her views and wide-ranging interests. They include historical novels in settings as disparate as ancient Greece and Rome and Richelieu's France; Biblical novels interpreting the events and figures of the Gospels; one detective tale; and novels which discuss the author's religious views. However, Caldwell's most characteristic works, both bestselling and critically acclaimed, are her epic novels about the growth and influence of American political and industrial dynasties and the lives and loves of the families that comprise them. The continuing appeal of these long, complex, and often didactic works lies in their evaluation of the American Dream in terms of domestic and moral values. In over 20 novels of monumental scope and length, Caldwell demonstrates that the glamour, prestige, and beauty of the social elite must be governed by the moral values of the home if it is to be a meaningful or happy world for the people who inhabit it. In Caldwell's fiction, women's love as wives and mothers provides the basis for the moral continuity her industrialist heroes too often ignore or reject.

Caldwell's first novel, *Dynasty of Death*, and its two sequels, *The Eagles Gather* and *The Final Hour*, develop the saga of two French-American families, the Barbours and the Bouchards, whose power in the armaments industry can shape world policy and economics, elect and defeat presidents, and begin and end world wars in the interests of family wealth and influence. The marriages between the 52 members of the Barbour and Bouchard clan become political alliances, often loveless, often betrayed, and producing an increasingly refined line of American aristocrats, absorbed in their own superiority and power. The absolute power of the Barbour/Bouchard dynasty ends as the last scion admits, however grudgingly, the merits of democracy, forces the members of his clan to support the American effort against Nazi Germany, and marries for love, amid plots, counterplots, adultery, heartbreak, and scandal.

Caldwell's powerful industrialists are typically self-made men of pronounced ethnic background; the heroes of *The Strong City* and *The Beautiful is Vanished*, for example, are German immigrants. In addition, Caldwell's novels tend to trace the fortunes of the families they discuss through more than one generation, like the Irish political dynasty of *Captains and the Kings*. Favourite Caldwell themes are ethnic, religious, and personal intolerance (*The Wide House*), the failure of parental discipline (*Let Love Come Last*), and the conflict between the desire for power and money and the humane values of love, marital love, parental love, and Christian *carita* (*Melissa*, *A Prologue to Love*, *Bright Flows the River*, *Answer As a Man*). The victories Caldwell grants love and virtue over greed, self-indulgence, and decadence are few and reserved. She parallels the conflict between power and action to love and contemplation in ancient times to the same conflict in the 19th and 20th centuries: the post-industrial age is inevitably the moral loser. Caldwell's good and generous women suffer; her self-made men are consumed morally and spiritually by selfish delusions, blighting the larger world they themselves consume.

Despite her gloomy themes, wordy and often platitudinous prose, and stylized characterization, Caldwell is an expert storyteller who plays on themes popular with readers, especially with women readers, since the popularity of the domestic novel of the 19th century. In Caldwell's fiction, women represent the good, even if they must suffer for it; sexuality and sexual purity represent personal power; money, the root of all evil, is a masculine addition; harmonious relations between the generations are the duty and the reward of mothers; and powerful dynasties must be based on convoluted conspiracies and moral seduction. Caldwell adapted her formula to a variety of painstakingly researched American settings and periods, and her novels, despite their slow development, carefully evoke time and place. Most important, and most fascinating to Caldwell's mass audience, she presents the equally glamorous and repellent world of the American Dream, a world in which women are, although not politically powerful without men, at least moral victors in their own right.

—Katherine Staples

———

CAMERON, Ann. See **RIEFE, Barbara.**

———

CARNEGIE, Sacha. British. 1920—. See 2nd edition, 1990.

———

CARR, Jolyon. See **PARGETER, Edith.**

———

CARR, Philippa. See **PLAIDY, Jean.**

———

CARR, Roberta. See **ROBERTS, Irene.**

———

CARR, Robyn.
Nationality: American. **Born:** St Paul, Minnesota, 25 July 1951. **Education:** Arthur B. Anker School of Nursing, St Paul, 1969–71. **Relations:** married James R. Carr; two sons. **Address:** c/o St Martin's Press, 175 Fifth Avenue, New York, New York 10010, USA.

Romance and Historical Publications

Novels

Chelynne. Boston, Little Brown, 1980.
The Blue Falcon. Boston, Little Brown, 1981.
The Bellerose Bargain. Boston, Little Brown, 1982.
The Braeswood Tapestry. Boston, Little Brown, 1984.
The Troubadour's Romance. Boston, Little Brown, 1985.
By Right of Arms. Boston, Little Brown, 1986.
The Everlasting Covenant. Boston, Little Brown, 1987.
Tempted. London, Bantam, 1987
Rogue's Lady. New York, Windsor, 1988.
Informed Risk. New York, Silhouette, 1989.
The Armstrong Woman. London, Piatkus, 1990.
Woman's Own. New York, St Martin's Press, 1990.
Mind Tryst. New York, St Martin's Press, 1991; London, Chapmans, 1992.

*   *   *

Since her debut with *Chelynne* in 1980, Robyn Carr has established a solid reputation as a leading author of historical romances. Set primarily in England and France in mediaeval times or the Restoration, Carr's novels feature strong heroines, whose pride and independence are sources of that inner strength they must exhibit to overcome the obstacles thrown against them.

In most of the historical novels, the heroine is matched to her lord by unusual circumstances, and only after respect and trust develop does love grow. Both Chelynne and Felise Scelfton (*The Troubadour's Romance*) enter into arranged marriages, while Jocelyn Cut-

ler (*The Braeswood Tapestry*) is Sir Trent Westcott's mistress before marrying him. Alicia (*The Bellerose Bargain*) is hired to impersonate another, while Lady Aurelie (*By Right of Arms*) is a prize of war won by Sir Hyatt Laidley. In spite of rocky beginnings, however, these strong individuals, tempered by trials, become true partners, equal to the task of founding and holding dynasties.

In general, Carr's novels have intricate and often suspense ridden plots, a strong sense of time and place, and well-developed, likeable characters. *The Blue Falcon* is less satisfying because she fails to develop fully her characters and intertwine their stories. These characters are stiff and their dialogue is stilted, as if Carr is not truly at home in the England of King Richard and the Crusaders. The inclusion of a hint of the occult in the person of the clairvoyant Giselle is not successful. Carr cannot seem to make up her mind to believe in her own creation here and fails fully to exploit the possibilities. *The Everlasting Covenant*, set during the War of the Roses, also is slow-paced but succeeds in holding the reader's interest more fully. Anne Gifford and Dylan deFrayne are lovers torn apart by a family feud and civil war. Their star-crossed love changes but ultimately endures over a quarter of a century as they themselves mature and change.

Woman's Own, set in late-19th-century America is a departure from Carr's other historical romances in several ways. Not only are the location and time different, but the focus of the story has broadened from the traditional couple in romantic conflict to a more generational scope. The story of three generations of women in a Philadelphia family, the novel features strongly drawn, interesting characters. The Armstrong women are determined to live life on their own terms. Amanda, the matriarch, has been married and widowed several times. Her daughter, Emily, abused and abandoned by her husband, forges a new life for herself. Emily's daughters, Patricia and Lilly, also seem cursed in their relationships with men. Moulded by their bad experiences, Emily, Patricia and Lilly all come into their own independence, learning not to rely on a man for support and protection. Carr skilfully engages the reader's interest and emotions in the survival of these women in a man's world.

With *Mind Tryst*, Carr moved into the psychological suspense genre. Although romance is not the main theme, elements of romantic relationships remain, and Jackie Sheppard, the heroine, continues Carr's string of strong, independent women. Trying to leave behind the memory of her son's death, Jackie moves to Colorado. As part of her new life, she begins a relationship with a local handyman, Tom Wahl. Gradually she comes to realize that things are just not right. The situation grows more and more tense as Tom's obsessiveness increases. Although Jackie has the help of the local sheriff and her ex-husband, her fate is ultimately in her own hands.

Carr's most successful romances and historical novels, however, remain those which are more focused and faster-paced. Here, one can appreciate the modern feeling of a woman's power of self-identity and determination in spite of the contemporary mores which might limit her life. Carr has the ability and talent to strike the right balance between romance and authentic historical detail. Her skilfully developed characters are guided by a strong sense of honour and duty, and they engage the reader's emotions in their troubles and triumphs. Although she is not among the most prolific romance authors, Carr's move into more contemporary romances and other genres is an indication of her strength and growth as a writer.

—Barbara E. Kemp

———

CARSTENS, Netta. See **LAFFEATY, Christina.**

———

CARTER, Angela. British. 1940–1992. See 2nd edition, 1990.

CARTER, Ashley. See **HORNER, Lance, Kyle ONSTOTT, and Ashley CARTER.**

CARTER, Elizabeth Eliot. See **HOLLAND, Cecelia.**

CARTLAND, (Mary) Barbara (Hamilton).
Pseudonym: Barbara McCorquodale. **Nationality:** British. **Born:** 9 July 1901. **Education:** Malvern Girls' College; Abbey House, Netley Abbey, Hampshire. **Relations:** married 1) Alexander George McCorquodale in 1927 (divorced 1933), one daughter; 2) Hugh McCorquodale in 1936 (died 1963), two sons. **Career:** freelance writer since 1925. Honorary junior commander, Auxiliary Territorial Service, and Bedfordshire welfare officer and librarian, 1941–49; Bedfordshire cadet officer, St John Ambulance Brigade, 1943–47, and County vice-president cadets, 1948–50; Hertfordshire vice-president, nursing cadets, 1951; Hertfordshire Chairman, St John Council; county councillor, Hertfordshire, 1955–64; President, Hertfordshire branch of Royal College of Midwives, 1957. Editor, Library of Love series. Vice-president, Romantic Novelists Association and Oxfam; president, National Association of Health, 1966. **Recipient:** Certificate of Merit, Eastern Command, 1946; Dame of Grace, St John of Jerusalem; Fellow Royal Society of Arts, 1984; Gold medal of the City of Paris for Achievement, 1988; DBE (Dame, Order of the British Empire), 1991. **Address:** Camfield Place, Hatfield, Hertfordshire, England.

ROMANCE AND HISTORICAL PUBLICATIONS

Novels

Jig-Saw. London, Duckworth, 1925.
Sawdust. London, Duckworth, 1926.
If the Tree Is Saved. London, Duckworth, 1929.
For What? London, Hutchinson, 1930.
Sweet Punishment. London, Hutchinson, 1931; New York Pyramid, 1973.
A Virgin in Mayfair. London, Hutchinson, 1932; as *An Innocent in Mayfair*, New York, Pyramid, 1976.
Just Off Piccadilly. London, Hutchinson, 1933; as *Dance on My Heart*, London, Arrow, 1977.
Not Love Alone. London, Hutchinson, 1933.
A Beggar Wished . . . . London, Hutchinson, 1934; as *Rainbow to Heaven*, London, Arrow, 1976.
Passionate Attainment. London, Hutchinson, 1935.
First Class, Lady? London, Hutchinson, 1935; as *Love and Linda*, London, Arrow, 1976.
Dangerous Experiment. London, Hutchinson, 1936; as *Search for Love*, New York, Greenberg, 1937.
Desperate Defiance. London, Hutchinson, 1936; New York, Pyramid, 1977.
The Forgotten City. London, Hutchinson, 1936.
Saga at Forty. London, Hutchinson, 1937; as *Love at Forty*, London, Arrow, 1977.
But Never Free. London, Hutchinson, 1937; as *The Adventurer*, London, Arrow, 1977.
Broken Barriers. London, Hutchinson, 1938; New York, Pyramid, 1977.
Bitter Winds. London, Hutchinson, 1938; as *Bitter Winds of Love*, London, Arrow, 1976; New York, Berkley, 1978.

The Gods Forget. London, Hutchinson, 1939; as *Love in Pity*, London, Arrow, 1977.
The Black Panther. London, Rich and Cowan, 1939; as *Lost Love*, New York, Pyramid, 1970.
Stolen Halo. London, Rich and Cowan, 1940; as *The Audacious Adventuress*, London, Hutchinson, 1971; New York, Pyramid, 1973.
Now Rough—Now Smooth. London, Hutchinson, 1941.
Open Wings. London, Hale, 1942.
The Leaping Flame. London, Hale, 1942.
The Dark Stream. London, Hutchinson, 1944; as *This Time It's Love*, London, Arrow, 1977; New York, Berkley, 1979.
After the Night. London, Hutchinson, 1944; as *Towards the Stars*, London, Arrow, 1971.
Yet She Follows. London, Hale, 1944; as *A Heart Is Broken*, New York, Pyramid 1977.
Escape from Passion. London, Hale, 1945.
Armour Against Love. London, Hutchinson, 1945; New York, Pyramid, 1974.
Out of Reach. London, Hutchinson, 1945.
The Hidden Heart. London, Hutchinson, 1946; New York, Pyramid, 1970.
Against the Stream. London, Hutchinson, 1946; New York, Pyramid, 1977.
The Dream Within. London, Hutchinson, 1947; New York, Pyramid, 1976.
If We Will. London, Hutchinson, 1947; as *Where Is Love?*, London, Arrow, 1971; New York, Jove, 1972.
Again This Rapture. London, Hutchinson, 1947; New York, Pyramid, 1977.
No Heart Is Free. London, Rich and Cowan, 1948; New York, Pyramid, 1975.
A Hazard of Hearts. London, Rich and Cowan, 1949; New York, Pyramid, 1969.
The Enchanted Moment. London, Rich and Cowan, 1949; New York, Pyramid, 1977.
A Duel of Hearts. London, Rich and Cowan, 1949; New York, Pyramid, 1970.
The Knave of Hearts. London, Rich and Cowan, 1950; New York, Pyramid, 1971.
The Little Pretender. London, Rich and Cowan, 1951; New York, Pyramid, 1971.
Love Is an Eagle. London, Rich and Cowan, 1951; New York, Pyramid, 1975.
A Ghost in Monte Carlo. London, Rich and Cowan, 1951.
Love Is the Enemy. London, Rich and Cowan, 1952; New York, Pyramid, 1970.
Cupid Rides Pillion. London, Hutchinson, 1952; as *The Lady and The Highwayman*. London, Pan, 1952.
Elizabethan Lover. London, Hutchinson, 1953; New York, Pyramid, 1971.
Love Me for Ever. London, Hutchinson, 1953; as *Love Me Forever*, New York, Pyramid, 1970.
Desire of the Heart. London, Hutchinson, 1954; New York, Pyramid, 1969.
The Enchanted Waltz. London, Hutchinson, 1955; New York, Pyramid, 1971.
The Kiss of the Devil. London, Hutchinson, 1955; New York, Jove, 1981.
The Captive Heart. London, Hutchinson, 1956; as *The Royal Pledge*, New York, Pyramid, 1970.
The Coin of Love. London, Hutchinson, 1956; New York, Pyramid, 1969.
Sweet Adventure. London, Hutchinson, 1957; New York, Pyramid, 1970.

Stars in My Heart. London, Hutchinson, 1957; New York, Pyramid, 1971.

The Golden Gondola. London, Hutchinson, 1958; New York, Pyramid, 1971.

Love in Hiding. London, Hutchinson, 1959; New York, Pyramid, 1969.

The Smuggled Heart. London, Hutchinson, 1959; as *Debt of Honor*, New York, Pyramid, 1970.

Love under Fire. London, Hutchinson, 1960; New York, Pyramid, 1972.

Messenger of Love. London, Hutchinson, 1961; New York, Pyramid, 1971.

The Wings of Love. London, Hutchinson, 1962; New York, Pyramid, 1971.

The Hidden Evil. London, Hutchinson, 1963; New York, Pyramid, 1971.

The Fire of Love. London, Hutchinson, 1964; New York, Avon, 1970.

The Unpredictable Bride. London, Hutchinson, 1964; New York, Pyramid, 1969.

Love Holds the Cards. London, Hutchinson, 1965; New York, Pyramid, 1970.

A Virgin in Paris. London, Hutchinson, 1966; New York, Pyramid, 1971.

Love to the Rescue. London, Hutchinson, 1967; New York, Pyramid, 1970.

Love Is Contraband. London, Hutchinson, 1968; New York, Pyramid, 1970.

The Enchanting Evil. London, Hutchinson, 1968; New York, Pyramid, 1969.

The Unknown Heart. London, Hutchinson, 1969; New York, Pyramid, 1971.

Innocent Heiress. New York, Pyramid, 1970.

The Reluctant Bride. London, Hutchinson, 1970; New York, Pyramid, 1970.

The Royal Pledge. New York, Pyramid, 1970.

The Secret Fear. London, Hutchinson, 1970; New York, Pyramid, 1971.

The Secret Heart. New York, Pyramid, 1970.

The Pretty Horse-Breakers. London, Hutchinson, 1971; New York, Pyramid, 1975.

The Queen's Messenger. New York, Pyramid, 1971.

Stars in Her Eyes. New York, Pyramid, 1971.

Innocent in Paris. New York, Pyramid, 1971.

The Audacious Adventuress. London, Hutchinson, 1971; New York, Pyramid, 1972.

A Halo for the Devil. London, Arrow, 1972.

The Irresistible Buck. London, Arrow, 1972.

The Complacent Wife. London, Hutchinson, 1972.

Lost Enchantment. London, Hutchinson, 1972; New York, Pyramid, 1973.

The Odious Duke. London, Arrow, 1973.

The Little Adventure. London, Hutchinson, 1973; New York, Bantam, 1974.

The Daring Deception. London, Arrow, 1973.

The Wicked Marquis. London, Hutchinson, 1973; New York, Bantam, 1974.

No Darkness for Love. London, Hutchinson, and New York, Bantam, 1974.

The Ruthless Rake. London, Pan, and New York, Bantam, 1974.

The Glittering Lights. New York, Bantam, 1974; London, Corgi, 1975.

A Sword to the Heart. New York, Bantam, 1974; London, Corgi, 1975.

The Penniless Peer. London, Pan, and New York, Bantam, 1974.

The Magnificent Marriage. London, Corgi, 1974; New York, Bantam, 1975.

Lessons in Love. London, Arrow, and New York, Bantam, 1974.

The Karma of Love. London, Corgi, 1974; New York, Bantam, 1975.

The Bored Bridegroom. London, Pan, and New York, Bantam, 1974.

The Castle of Fear. London, Pan, and New York, Bantam, 1974.

The Cruel Count. London, Pan, 1974; New York, Bantam, 1975.

The Dangerous Dandy. London, Pan, and New York, Bantam, 1974.

Journey to Paradise. London, Arrow, and New York, Bantam, 1974.

Call of the Heart. London, Pan, and New York, Bantam, 1975.

Love Is Innocent. London, Hutchinson, and New York, Bantam, 1975.

Shadow of Sin. London, Corgi, 1975.

Bewitched. London, Corgi, and New York, Bantam, 1975.

The Devil in Love. London, Corgi, and New York, Bantam, 1975.

Fire on the Snow. London, Hutchinson, 1975; New York, Bantam, 1976.

The Flame Is Love. London, Pan, 1975.

The Frightened Bride. London, Pan, and New York, Bantam, 1975.

The Impetuous Duchess. London, Corgi, and New York, Bantam, 1975.

The Mask of Love. London, Corgi, and New York, Bantam, 1975.

The Tears of Love. London, Corgi, and New York, Bantam, 1975.

A Very Naughty Angel. London, Pan, and New York, Bantam, 1975.

Say Yes, Samantha. London, Pan, and New York, Bantam, 1975.

As Eagles Fly. London, Pan, and New York, Bantam, 1975.

A Frame of Dreams. London, Pan, 1975; New York, Bantam, 1976.

An Arrow of Love. London, Pan, 1975; New York, Bantam, 1976.

A Gamble with Hearts. London, Pan, 1975; New York, Bantam, 1976.

A Kiss for the King. London, Pan, 1975; New York, Bantam, 1976.

The Elusive Earl. London, Hutchinson, and New York, Bantam, 1976.

The Blue-Eyed Witch. London, Hutchinson, 1976.

An Angel in Hell. London, Pan, 1976.

A Dream from the Night. London, Corgi, and New York, Bantam, 1976.

The Fragrant Flower. London, Pan, and New York, Bantam, 1976.

The Golden Illusion. London, Pan, and New York, Bantam, 1976.

The Heart Triumphant. London, Corgi, and New York, Bantam, 1976.

Hungry for Love. London, Corgi, and New York, Bantam, 1976.

The Husband Hunters. London, Pan, and New York, Bantam, 1976.

The Incredible Honeymoon. London, Pan, and New York, Bantam, 1976.

Moon over Eden. London, Pan, and New York, Bantam, 1976.

Never Laugh at Love. London, Corgi, and New York, Bantam, 1976.

No Time for Love. London, Pan, and New York, Bantam, 1976.

Passions in the Sand. London, Pan, and New York, Bantam, 1976.

The Proud Princess. London, Corgi, and New York, Bantam, 1976.

The Secret of the Glen. London, Corgi, and New York, Bantam, 1976.

The Slaves of Love. London, Pan, and New York, Bantam, 1976.

The Wild Cry of Love. London, Pan, and New York, Bantam, 1976.

The Disgraceful Duke. London, Corgi, and New York, Bantam, 1976.

Conquered by Love. New York, Bantam, 1976; London, Pan, 1977.

The Mysterious Maid-Servant. London, Hutchinson, and New York, Bantam, 1977.

The Dragon and the Pearl. London, Hutchinson, and Williamsport, Pennsylvania, Duron, 1977.

The Curse of the Clan. London, Pan, and Williamsport, Pennsylvania, Duron, 1977.

The Dream and the Glory. London, Pan, and New York, Bantam, 1977.

A Duel with Destiny. London, Pan, and New York, Bantam, 1977.

Kiss the Moonlight. London, Pan, 1977.

Look, Listen, and Love. London, Pan, and Williamsport, Pennsylvania, Duron, 1977.

Love Locked In. London, Pan, and New York, Dutton, 1977.

The Magic of Love. London, Pan, and New York, Bantam, 1977.

The Marquis Who Hated Women. London, Pan, and Williamsport, Pennsylvania, Duron, 1977.

The Outrageous Lady. London, Pan, and Williamsport, Pennsylvania, Duron, 1977.

The Sign of Love. Williamsport, Pennsylvania, Duron, 1977; London, Pan, 1978.

A Rhapsody of Love. London, Pan, 1977.

The Taming of Lady Lorinda. London, Pan, and New York, Bantam, 1977.

Vote for Love. London, Corgi, and New York, Bantam, 1977.

The Wild, Unwilling Wife. London, Pan, and New York, Dutton, 1977.

The Castle Made for Love. London, Pan, and Williamsport, Pennsylvania, Duron, 1977.

The Love Pirate. Williamsport, Pennsylvania, Duron, 1977; London, Corgi, 1978.

Punishment of a Vixen. Williamsport, Pennsylvania, Duron, and London, Corgi, 1977.

A Touch of Love. Williamsport, Pennsylvania, Duron, 1977; London, Corgi, 1978.

The Temptation of Torilla. Williamsport, Pennsylvania, Duron, 1977; London, Corgi, 1978.

Love and the Loathsome Leopard. Williamsport, Pennsylvania, Duron, 1977; London, Corgi, 1978.

The Hell-Cat and the King. Williamsport, Pennsylvania, Duron, 1977; London, Pan, 1978.

No Escape from Love. Williamsport, Pennsylvania, Duron, 1977; London, Corgi, 1978.

The Saint and the Sinner. Williamsport, Pennsylvania, Duron, 1977; London, Corgi, 1978.

The Naked Battle. Williamsport, Pennsylvania, Duron, 1977; London, Hutchinson, 1978.

Love Leaves at Midnight. London, Hutchinson, and Williamsport, Pennsylvania, Duron, 1978.

The Passion and the Flower. London, Pan, and New York, Dutton, 1978.

Love, Lords, and Lady-Birds. London, Pan, and New York, Dutton, 1978.

A Fugitive from Love. London, Pan, and Williamsport, Pennsylvania, Duron, 1978.

The Problems of Love. London, Corgi, and Williamsport, Pennsylvania, Duron, 1978.

The Twists and Turns of Love. London, Arrow, and Williamsport, Pennsylvania, Duron, 1978.

Magic or Mirage? London, Corgi, and Williamsport, Pennsylvania, Duron, 1978.

The Ghost Who Fell in Love. London, Pan, and New York, Dutton, 1978.

The Chieftain Without a Heart. London, Corgi, and New York, Dutton, 1978.

Lord Ravenscar's Revenge. London, Corgi, and Williamsport, Pennsylvania, Duron, 1978.

A Runaway Star. London, Pan, and Williamsport, Pennsylvania, Duron, 1978.

A Princess in Distress. London, Pan, and Williamsport, Pennsylvania, Duron, 1978.

The Judgement of Love. Williamsport, Pennsylvania, Duron, 1978; London, Hutchinson, 1979.

Lovers in Paradise. Williamsport, Pennsylvania, Duron, 1978; London, Pan, 1979.

The Race for Love. Williamsport, Pennsylvania, Duron, 1978; London, Corgi, 1979.

Flowers for the God of Love. London, Pan, 1978; New York, Dutton, 1979.

The Irresistible Force. London, Arrow, and Williamsport, Pennsylvania, Duron, 1978.

Alone in Paris. London, Arrow, 1978; Williamsport, Pennsylvania, Duron, 1979.

Love in the Dark. London, Hutchinson, and Williamsport, Pennsylvania, Duron, 1979.

The Duke and the Preacher's Daughter. London, Corgi, and Williamsport, Pennsylvania, Duron, 1979.

The Drums of Love. London, Pan, and Williamsport, Pennsylvania, Duron, 1979.

The Prince and the Pekingese. London, Pan, and Williamsport, Pennsylvania, Duron, 1979.

A Serpent of Satan. London, Pan, and Williamsport, Pennsylvania, Duron, 1979.

Love in the Clouds. London, Corgi, and New York, Dutton, 1979.

The Treasure Is Love. London, Arrow, and Williamsport, Pennsylvania, Duron, 1979.

Imperial Splendour. London, Pan, and New York, Dutton, 1979.

Light of the Moon. London, Pan, and Williamsport, Pennsylvania, Duron, 1979.

The Prisoner of Love. London, Arrow, and Williamsport, Pennsylvania, Duron, 1979.

The Duchess Disappeared. London, Pan, and Williamsport, Pennsylvania, Duron, 1979.

Love Climbs In. London, Corgi, and Williamsport, Pennsylvania, Duron, 1979.

A Nightingale Sang. London, Corgi, and Williamsport, Pennsylvania, Duron, 1979.

Terror in the Sun. London, Pan, and New York, Bantam, 1979.

Who Can Deny Love? London, Corgi, and Williamsport, Pennsylvania, Duron, 1979.

Bride to the King. London, Corgi, 1979; New York, Dutton, 1980.

Only Love. London, Arrow, 1979; New York, Bantam, 1980.

The Dawn of Love. London, Corgi, 1979; New York, Dutton, 1980.

Love Has His Way. London, Corgi, 1979; New York, Dutton, 1980.

A Gentleman in Love. London, Pan, 1979.

Women Have Hearts. London, Pan, 1979; New York, Bantam, 1980.

The Explosion of Love. New York, Bantam, 1979; London, Hutchinson, 1980.

A Heart Is Stolen. London, Corgi, 1980.

The Power and the Prince. London, Pan, 1980.

Free From Fear. London, Pan, and New York, Bantam, 1980.

A Song of Love. London, Pan, and New York, Jove, 1980.

Love for Sale. London, Corgi, and New York, Dutton, 1980.

Little White Doves of Love. London, Pan, and New York, Bantam, 1980.

The Perfection of Love. London, Corgi, and New York, Bantam, 1980.

Lost Laughter. London, Pan, and New York, Dutton, 1980.

Punished with Love. London, Pan, and New York, Bantam, 1980.

Lucifer and the Angel. London, Hutchinson, 1980.

Ola and the Sea Wolf. London, Arrow, and New York, Bantam, 1980.

The Prude and the Prodigal. London, Pan, and New York, Bantam, 1980.

The Goddess and the Gaiety Girl. London, Pan, and New York, Bantam, 1980.

Signpost to Love. London, Corgi, 1980; New York, Bantam, 1981.
Money, Magic, and Marriage. London, Arrow, 1980.
Love in the Moon. London, New English Library, 1980.
The Horizons of Love. London, Pan, 1980.
Pride and the Poor Princess. London, Corgi, 1980; New York, Bantam, 1981.
The Waltz of Hearts. London, Pan, 1980; New York, Bantam, 1981.
From Hell to Heaven. London, Corgi, and New York, Bantam, 1981.
The Kiss of Life. London, Hutchinson, 1981.
Afraid. London, Arrow, and New York, Bantam, 1981.
Dreams Do Come True. London, Pan, 1981.
In the Arms of Love. London, Hutchinson, 1981.
For All Eternity. New York, Berkley, 1981; London, Corgi, 1982.
Pure and Untouched. London, Arrow, and New York, Everest House, 1981.
Count the Stars. London, New English Library, 1981.
The Wings of Ecstasy. London, Pan, and New York, Jove, 1981.
A Night of Gaiety. London, Pan, and New York, Bantam, 1981.
The River of Love. London, Pan, and New York, Bantam, 1981.
Gift of the Gods. London, Pan, and New York, Bantam, 1981.
The Heart of the Clan. London, Arrow, and New York, Jove, 1981.
Love Wins. London, Pan, 1981; New York, Jove, 1982.
The Light of Love. New York, Dell, 1981.
An Innocent in Russia. London, Pan, and New York, Bantam, 1981.
Winged Magic. London, Corgi, and New York, Bantam, 1981.
Dollars for the Duke. London, Corgi, and New York, Bantam, 1981.
The Lioness and the Lily. London, Corgi, and New York, Bantam, 1981.
A Miracle in Music. New York, Berkley, 1982; London, Corgi, 1983.
A King in Love. New York, Everest House, 1982.
A Portrait of Love. London, Corgi, and New York, Bantam, 1982.
A Shaft of Sunlight. London, Corgi, and New York, Bantam, 1982.
Caught by Love. London, Arrow, 1982.
Kneel for Mercy. London, New English Library, 1982.
Looking for Love. London, Hutchinson, and New York, Bantam, 1982.
Love and the Marquis. London, Pan, 1982.
Love Rules. London, New English Library, and New York, Bantam, 1982.
Lucky in Love. London, Pan, 1982.
Moments of Love. London, Pan, 1982.
Music from the Heart. London, Pan, 1982.
Riding to the Moon. New York, Everest House, 1982; London, Arrow, 1983.
Secret Harbour. London, Corgi, and New York, Bantam, 1982.
The Call of the Highlands. London, Hutchinson, 1982.
The Poor Governess. New York, Berkley, 1982; London, Corgi, 1983.
Touch a Star. London, Corgi, 1982.
The Vibrations of Love. London, Corgi, and New York, Bantam, 1982.
Winged Victory. London, Pan, and New York, Berkley, 1982.
A Duke in Danger. London, Pan, 1983.
A Marriage Made in Heaven. London, Corgi, 1983.
Diona and a Dalmation. London, Hutchinson, 1983.
Fire in the Blood. London, Pan, 1983.
Gypsy Magic. London, Pan, 1983.
From Hate to Love. London, New English Library, 1983.
Lies for Love. London, Corgi, 1983.
Lights, Laughter and a Lady. London, New English Library, 1983.
Love and Lucia. London, Pan, 1983.
Love on the Wind. London, Pan, 1983; New York, Severn House, 1986.
Mission to Monte Carlo. London, Corgi, 1983.

Tempted to Love. London, Pan, 1983.
Wish for Love. London, Corgi, 1983.
The Scots Never Forget. London, Corgi, 1984.
Theresa and a Tiger. London, New English Library, 1984.
The Unbreakable Spell. London, Corgi, 1984.
The Unwanted Wedding. London, Corgi, 1984.
The Island of Love. London, Pan, 1984.
Journey to a Star. London, Corgi, 1984.
The Peril and the Prince. London, New English Library, 1984.
Moonlight on the Sphinx. London, Hutchinson, 1984.
Bride to a Brigand. London, New English Library, and New York, Berkley, 1984.
Love Comes West. London, Pan, and New York, Berkley, 1984.
A Witch's Spell. London, Corgi, and New York, Berkley, 1984.
White Lilac. London, Pan, and New York, Berkley, 1984.
Miracle for a Madonna. London, Hutchinson, 1984.
Royal Punishment. London, Severn House, 1984.
Revenge of the Heart. London, Pan, 1984.
A Very Unusual Wife. London, Pan, 1984.
The Duke Comes Home. London, Corgi, 1984.
Help from the Heart. London, Arrow, 1984.
Light of the Gods. London, Corgi, 1984.
Love Is Heaven. London, Pan, 1984.
Love Is a Gamble. London, Pan, 1985.
A Rebel Princess. London, Corgi, 1985.
Safe at Last. London, Pan, 1985; New York, Jove, 1986.
The Devilish Deception. London, New English Library, 1985.
Escape. London, Severn House, 1985; New York, Jove, 1986.
The Storms of Love. London, Corgi, 1985.
Temptation for a Teacher. London, Pan, 1985.
Look with Love. London, Pan, 1985.
A Victory for Love. London, Pan, 1985.
Alone and Afraid. London, Pan, 1985.
Crowned with Love. London, Eaglemoss, 1985; New York, Jove, 1986.
The Devil Defeated. London, Eaglemoss, 1985; New York, Jove, 1986.
Secrets. London, Corgi, 1985.
The Secret of the Mosque. London, Pan, 1986.
Haunted. London, Pan, and New York, Jove, 1986.
The Love Trap. London, Pan, and New York, Jove, 1986.
Paradise Found. London, Arrow, 1986.
Never Forget Love. London, New English Library, 1986.
Love Casts out Fears. London, Severn House, 1986.
An Angel Runs Away. London, Pan, 1986; New York, Berkley, 1987.
Helga in Hiding. London, Arrow, and New York, Jove, 1986.
A Dream in Spain. London, Pan, and New York, Jove, 1986.
Love Joins the Clan. London, Pan, and New York, Jove, 1986.
The Golden Cage. New York, Jove, 1986.
The Perfume of the Gods. London, New English Library, 1987; New York, Jove, 1989.
The Goddess of Love. London, Pan, 1987; New York, Jove, 1989.
A Herb for Happiness. London, Pan, 1987; New York, Jove, 1988.
Lovers in Lisbon. London, Pan, 1987; New York, Jove, 1988.
Sapphires in Siam. London, Pan, 1987.
Saved by Love. London, Pan, 1987.
A Circus for Love. London, Pan, 1987.
A Revolution of Love. London, Pan, 1987.
Dancing on a Rainbow. New York, Jove, 1987.
Love and Kisses. New York, Jove, 1987.
The Love Puzzle. New York, Jove, 1987.
The Earl Escapes. New York, Jove, 1987.
Forced to Marry. New York, Jove, 1987.
Starlight over Tunis. New York, Jove, 1987.
Wanted—a Wedding Ring. New York, Jove, 1987.

The Temple of Love. London, Pan, 1988; New York, Jove, 1989.
A Revolution of Love. London, Pan, 1988; New York, Jove, 1990.
A Chieftain finds Love. London, Pan, 1988; New York, Jove, 1989.
The Lovely Liar. London, Pan, 1988; New York, Jove, 1989.
Revenge Is Sweet. London, Pan, 1988; New York, Jove, 1989.
The Passionate Princess. London,Pan, 1988; New York, Jove, 1989.
Little Tongues of Fire. New York, Jove, 1988.
Riding to the Sky. New York, Jove, 1988.
Love Is Invincible. New York, Jove, 1988.
Only a Dream. New York, Jove, 1988.
An Adventure in Love. New York, Jove, 1988.
The Curse of the Clan. New York, Jove, 1989.
A Knight in Paris. London, Pan, 1989.
Heart Triumphant. London, Hale, 1989.
The Bargain Bride. New York, Jove, 1989.
The Perfect Pearl. London, New English Library, and New York, Jove, 1989.
Solita and the Spies. London, Pan and New York, Jove, 1989.
Love Is a Maze. London, New English Library, and New York, Jove, 1989.
Paradise in Penang. London, Pan, 1989.
Necklace of Love. London, Pan, 1989; New York, Jove, 1990.
Real Love or Fake?. London, Pan, and New York, Jove 1990.
A Game of Love. London, Severn House, 1990.
Love at First Sight. London, Pan, 1989; New York, Jove, 1990.
The Haunted Heart. London, New English Library, 1990.
A Kiss from a Stranger. London, Pan, 1990.
Heaven in Hong Kong. London, Severn House, 1990.
A Very Special Love. London, Pan, 1990.
Beauty or Brains?. London, Pan, 1990.
The Taming of the Tigress. New York, Jove, 1990.
Love Is the Key. New York, Jove, 1990; London, Mandarin, 1991.
The Marquis Wins. London, Pan, 1990.
A Miracle in Mexico. London,Pan, 1990.
Safe in Paradise. London, New English Library 1990.
Love Strikes Satan. London, Mandarin, 1991.
Stand and Deliver Your Heart. London, Mandarin, 1991.
The Magic of Paris. London, Mandarin, 1991.
Seek the Stars. London, Severn House, 1991.
The Sleeping Princess. London, Mandarin, 1991.
A Theatre of Love. London, Mandarin, 1991.
Too Precious to Lose. London, Mandarin, 1991.
A Wish Comes True. London, Mandarin, 1991.
The Scent of Roses. London, Mandarin, 1991.
A Dynasty of Love. London, Mandarin, 1991.
Magic from the Heart. London, Mandarin, 1991.
Warned by a Ghost. London, Mandarin 1991.
Two Hearts in Hungary. London, Mandarin, 1991.
The Earl Rings a Belle. London, Mandarin, 1991.
The Queen Saves the King. London, Mandarin, 1992.
Hidden by Love. London, Mandarin, 1992.
Loved for Himself. London, Mandarin, 1992.
Love Lifts the Curse. London, Mandarin, 1992.
A Tangled Web. London, Mandarin, 1992.
The Windmill of Love. London, Mandarin, 1992.
Hiding. London, Mandarin, 1992.
Just Fate. London, Mandarin, 1992.
Love at the Ritz. London, Mandarin, 1992.
Queen of Hearts. London, Mandarin, 1992.
Drena and the Duke. London, Severn House, 1992.
A Kiss in Rome. London, Mandarin, 1992.
No Disguise for Love. London, Mandarin, 1992.
Walking to Wonderland. London, Mandarin, 1992.
Wonderful Dream. London, Mandarin, 1993.
The Duke Is Trapped. London, Mandarin, 1993.

Love and a Cheetah. London, Mandarin, 1993.
A Dog, a Horse, and a Heart. London, Mandarin, 1993.
Duel of Jewels. London, Severn House, 1993.

Novels as Barbara McCorquodale

Sleeping Swords. London, Hale, 1942.
Love Is Mine. London, Rich and Cowan, 1952; (as Barbara Cartland) New York, Pyramid, 1972.
The Passionate Pilgrim. London, Rich and Cowan, 1952.
Blue Heather. London, Rich and Cowan, 1953.
Wings on My Heart. London, Rich and Cowan, 1954.
The Kiss of Paris. London, Rich and Cowan, 1956.
The Thief of Love. London, Jenkins, 1957.
Love Forbidden. London, Rich and Cowan, 1957.
Lights of Love. London, Jenkins, 1958; (as Barbara Cartland) New York, Pyramid, 1973.
Sweet Enchantress. London, Jenkins, 1958.
A Kiss of Silk. London, Jenkins, 1959.
The Price Is Love. London, Jenkins, 1960.
The Runaway Heart. London, Jenkins, 1961.
A Light to the Heart. London, Ward Lock, 1962.
Love Is Dangerous. London, Ward Lock, 1963.
Danger by the Nile. London, Ward Lock, 1964.
Love on the Run. London, Ward Lock, 1965; (as Barbara Cartland) New York, Pyramid, 1973.
Theft of the Heart. London, Ward Lock, 1966.

OTHER PUBLICATIONS

Plays

Blood Money (produced London, 1925).
French Dressing, with Bruce Woodhouse (produced London, 1943).

Radio Plays: *The Rose and the Violet*, music by Mark Lubbock, 1942; *The Caged Bird*, 1957.

Poetry

Lines on Life and Love. London, Hutchinson, 1972.

Other

Touch the Stars: A Clue to Happiness. London, Rider, 1935.
Ronald Cartland. London, Collins, 1942; as *My Brother, Ronald*, London, Sheldon Press, 1980.
The Isthmus Years 1919–1939 (autobiography). London, Hutchinson, 1943.
You—in the Home. London, Standard Art, 1946.
The Years of Opportunity 1939–1945 (autobiography). London, Hutchinson, 1948.
The Fascinating Forties: A Book for the Over-Forties. London, Jenkins, 1954; revised edition, London, Corgi, 1973.
Marriage for Moderns. London, Jenkins, 1955.
Bewitching Women. London, Muller, 1955.
The Outrageous Queen: A Biography of Christina of Sweden. London, Muller, 1956.
Polly—My Wonderful Mother. London, Jenkins, 1956.
Be Vivid, Be Vital. London, Jenkins, 1956.
Love, Life and Sex. London, Jenkins, 1957; revised edition, London, Corgi, 1973.
The Scandalous Life of King Carol. London, Muller, 1957.
The Private Life of Charles II: The Women He Loved. London, Muller, 1958.
Look Lovely, Be Lovely. London, Jenkins, 1958.

Vitamins for Vitality. London, Foyle, 1959.

The Private Life of Elizabeth, Empress of Austria. London, Muller, 1959; New York, Pyramid, 1974.

Husbands and Wives. London, Barker, 1961; revised edition, as *Love and Marriage,* London, Thorsons, 1971.

Josephine, Empress of France. London, Hutchinson, 1961; New York, Pyramid, 1974.

Diane de Poitiers. London, Hutchinson, 1962.

Etiquette Handbook. London, Hamlyn, 1963; revised edition, as *Book of Etiquette,* London, Hutchinson, 1972.

The Many Facets of Love. London, W.H. Allen, 1963.

Metternich, The Passionate Diplomat. London, Hutchinson, 1964.

Sex and the Teenager. London, Muller, 1964.

Living Together. London, Muller, 1965.

The Pan Book of Charm. London, Pan, 1965.

Woman: The Enigma. London, Frewin, 1965; New York, Pyramid, 1974.

I Search for Rainbows 1946–1966 (autobiography). London, Hutchinson, 1967; New York, Bantam, 1977.

The Youth Secret. London, Corgi, 1968.

The Magic of Honey. London, Corgi, 1970; revised edition, 1976.

We Danced All Night 1919–1929 (autobiography). London, Hutchinson, 1970; New York, Pyramid, 1972.

Health Food Cookery Book. London, Hodder and Stoughton, 1971.

Book of Beauty and Health. London, Hodder and Stoughton, 1972.

Men Are Wonderful. London, Corgi, 1973.

Food for Love. London, Corgi, 1975.

The Magic of Honey Cookbook. London, Corgi, 1976.

Love at the Helm (Mountbatten Memorial Trust volume). London, Weidenfeld and Nicolson, 1977; New York, Everest House, 1981.

Recipes for Lovers, with Nigel Gordon. London, Corgi, 1977.

I Seek the Miraculous (autobiography) London, Sheldon Press, and New York, Dutton, 1978.

Book of Love and Lovers. London, Joseph, and New York, Ballantine, 1978.

Romantic Royal Marriages. New York, Beaufort, 1981.

Keep Young and Beautiful (selections), with Elinor Glyn. London, Duckworth, 1982.

The Romance of Food. London, Hamlyn, and New York, Doubleday, 1984.

Getting Older, Growing Younger. London, Sidgwick and Jackson, and New York, Dodd Mead, 1984.

Etiquette for Love and Romance. New York, Pocket Books, 1984; Bath, Firecrest, 1985.

Princess to the Rescue (for children). London, Hamlyn, and New York, Watts, 1984.

Book of Health (for children). Poole, Dorset, Blandford Press, 1985.

Year of Royal Days. Luton, Bedfordshire, Lennard, 1988.

The Royal Series (*Royal Jewels, Royal Lovers, Royal Eccentrics*). Milton Keynes, Marwain, 3 vols, 1989.

Editor, *The Common Problem,* by Ronald Cartland. London, Hutchinson, 1943.

Editor, *Book of Useless Information.* London, Corgi and New York, Bantam, 1977.

Editor, *The Light of Love: A Thought for Every Day.* London, Sheldon Press; as *The Light of Love: Lines to Live by Day by Day,* New York, Elsevier Nelson, 1980.

Editor, *Written with Love* (letters). London, Hutchinson, 1982.

*

Film Adaptations: *The Flame is Love,* 1979; *A Hazard of Hearts,* 1987; *The Lady and the Highwayman,* 1990, from the novel *Cupid Rides Pillion*; *A Ghost in Monte Carlo,* 1990; *Duel of Hearts,* 1991.

Critical Studies: *Barbara Cartland, Crusader in Pink* by Henry Cloud, London, Weidenfeld and Nicolson, 1979; *Barbara Cartland: An Authorised Biography* by Gwen Robyns, London, Sidgwick and Jackson, 1984, New York, Doubleday, 1985.

* * *

It is a daunting task to assess the work of Barbara Cartland, whose prodigious output of more than 500 books, sales of several million copies, and reputation as the *queen* of the genre are overwhelming. Each branch of 20th-century English light fiction has its phenomenon—and the achievements of Cartland are to romantic fiction what those of Charles Hamilton ('Frank Richards') are to the school story, or those of Agatha Christie are to detective fiction.

Her reputation as an unsurpassed contributor to the genre became established by the end of the 1960s; since then she has gone from strength to strength and there seems no slackening in the pace of her production of romantic stories. Still the innocent but exotically named heroines—the Deloras, Magnolias, Darcias, and Udelas—flare into vivid and passionate life, fresh from the Cartland typewriter or dictating-machine, and still they are avidly received by millions of readers all over the world. The books, though one might have thought them a peculiarly English caprice, have been translated into many languages. They are flagrantly escapist and unconcerned with social issues; they are class-ridden and anti-feminist—the apotheosis, in fact, of attitudes that are today condemned by trendy critics—but their success speaks for itself. Cartland provides for her millions of loyal readers the confirmation that romance is alive and well, even in our materialistic society, and that the individual is still important in this age of group-causes and group-lobbying and group-consciousness. Her confidence in her beliefs is magnificent; her passion for the quintessential English gentleman or aristocrat is idealistic but engaging; and her feelings for innocence, for the feminine aspects of life, and for simple decency are deep-rooted and sincere.

In literary terms, of course, one can find flaws in the Cartland canon. Inevitably, in a writing career that has spanned over half a century, she has established a formula on which she falls back with increasing dependence. The more recent books have a facile quality, a carelessness, which is not evident in her early works. The novels now are slim, and often issued immediately in paperback. They are unlikely to be preserved for posterity in the collections of public or university libraries, although these institutions will almost certainly retain many of her earlier, more substantial hard-backed novels. Her heroines, despite their distinctive and gloriously feminine, romantic names, are, in fact, interchangeable and without individualization. Similarly, her heroes are now symbolic embodiments of masculine strength, magnetism, and charisma rather than real human beings.

It is an intriguing exercise, however, to look back at Cartland's early novels, and to savour their freshness, incisive and occasionally acerbic comments, and sheer storytelling skill. One hopes that the author might one day pause in the production line of 20-plus novels every year to read once again her own early books, and to create, from the vitality of these and the light of her later expertise and experience one or two romances that will become Cartland classics for posterity.

Her first novel, *Jig-Saw,* has charm and conviction as well as an appropriate freshness. It starts on a spring day, with 'excitements, sensations—all palpitating to be discovered', with 'a poignancy in the atmosphere as a catch of breath before a tremendously thrilling experience . . . '. *And* it is Paris which abounds in the *gaité de coeur* for which the city is celebrated. Mona Vivien, as English as they come despite her 'strikingly beautiful' resemblance to the 'type beloved of Botticelli', is packing up after her last day as a pupil at a St Cloud convent-school to return to London. She is on the tremulous threshold of young womanhood, which Cartland conveys so well.

Back in Belgrave Square, life is 'a fairy cinematograph . . . of hectic sensations', a cultural and social round which thrills Mona, and, of course, produces for her the young Marquis who turns out to be her true and upright love—despite the rival claims of his mysterious, fascinating and worldly half-brother, who one day whisks her off unchaperoned 'to see the sunrise in a fairyland of silver birches'. This turns out, rather prosaically perhaps to those who know its much-trodden picnic-littered paths, to be Wimbledon Common at dawn. But Cartland acknowledges the elusive quality of such magically romantic excursions when Mona reflects, on her return to Belgrave Square and disillusioning daytime brightness, that 'Romance, criticized with the hideous sanity of breakfast-time, droops its wings and slinks away'.

Nevertheless this, like the other early novels, has a reflective and lyrical quality that has sadly disappeared from the recent books. In *Jig-Saw,* for example, Mona's love of London, of poetry, and her joy and eagerness in new experiences come across with sensitivity and conviction. Innocence in the stories of the 1920s and 1930s was filled out and made persuasive by passionate questioning of the darker areas of life. Her heroines then were distinctive personalities who were, in a sympathetic and believable way, awakened to broader and deeper areas of experience, passion, and wonder by the heroes.

A look at the recent books shows that although this awakening through romance still continues for the leading Cartland ladies, it has settled firmly into a pattern. The dialogue at the end of each book is, one feels, interchangeable with that of any of the others. When Seldon, the handsome, aristocratic and arrogant Duke of Otterburn, and the American heiress Magnolia Vandevilt acknowledge their love, after a lot of time and languishing looks, at the end of *Dollars for the Duke*, their final clinch predictably carries them 'on waves of ecstasy into the starlit sky'. At the end of *Love for Sale* another worldly-wise Duke and his innocent teenage beloved share a kiss which, she felt, 'carried her up towards the stars that were now shining in the sky outside'. And the heroines share the same tremulous, breathless, and ecstatic manner of speech: 'I have . . . always wanted to . . . have your . . . children,' says Darcia in a whisper at the end of *The Perfection of Love*, while Udela husks in *Love for Sale*, ' . . . when I have been awake in the darkness I have . . . pretended that you were . . . kissing me'; Magnolia caps it all in *Dollars for the Duke* by her whispered and wondering affirmation of passion: 'I love . . . you and everything you do . . . will be perfect and . . . also . . . divine.'

Really, perhaps, it is greedy to ask more from Cartland than this superb romanticism—but one feels that she is capable of something very much more searching, sympathetic 'and . . . also . . . ' real.

—Mary Cadogan

———

CASE, David. American. 1937—. See 2nd edition, 1990.

———

CASTLE, Jayne.   See **KRENTZ, Jayne Ann.**

———

CATHER, Willa (Sibert).
Nationality: American. **Born:** Wilella, Back Creek Valley, Virginia, 7 December 1873. **Education:** Red Cloud High School, graduated 1890; Latin School, Lincoln, Nebraska, 1890–91; University of Nebraska, Lincoln, 1891–95, A.B. 1895. **Career:** columnist, *Lincoln State Journal*, 1893–95; editor, *Home Monthly*, Pittsburgh, 1896–97; telegraph editor and drama critic, Pittsburgh

Daily Leader, 1897–1900; Latin and English teacher, Central High School, Pittsburgh, 1901–03; English teacher, Allegheny High School, Pittsburgh, 1903–06; staff writer, later managing editor, *McClure's* magazine, New York, 1906–11; full-time writer from 1912. **Recipient:** Pulitzer prize, 1923; American Academy Howells medal, 1930, and Gold Medal, 1944; Prix Fémina Américaine, 1932. D.Litt.: University of Nebraska, Lincoln, 1917; University of Michigan, Ann Arbor, 1922; Columbia University, New York, 1928; Yale University, New Haven, Connecticut, 1929; Princeton University, New Jersey, 1931; D.L.: Creighton University, Omaha, Nebraska, 1928; LL.D.: University of California, Berkeley, 1931; L.H.D.: Smith College, Northampton, Massachusetts, 1933. **Member:** American Academy. **Died:** 24 April 1947.

ROMANCE AND HISTORICAL PUBLICATIONS

Novels

Alexander's Bridge. Boston, Houghton Mifflin, 1912; as *Alexander's Bridges*, London, Heinemann, 1912.
O Pioneers!. Boston, Houghton Mifflin, 1913; London, Heinemann, 1913.
The Song of the Lark. Boston, Houghton Mifflin, 1915; London, Murray, 1916.
My Antonia, illustrated by W.T. Bends. Boston, Houghton Mifflin, 1916; London, Heinemann, 1919.
One of Ours. New York, Knopf, and London, Heinemann, 1922.
A Lost Lady. New York, Knopf, 1923; London, Heinemann, 1924.
The Professor's House. New York, Knopf, and London, Heinemann, 1925.
My Mortal Enemy. New York, Knopf, 1926; London, Heinemann, 1928.
Death Comes for the Archbishop. New York, Knopf, and London, Heinemann, 1927.
Shadows on the Rock. New York, Knopf, 1931; London, Cassell, 1932.
Lucy Gayheart. New York, Knopf, 1932; London, Cassell, 1935.
Sapphira and the Slave Girl. New York, Knopf, 1940; London, Cassell, 1941.

OTHER PUBLICATIONS

Short Stories

The Troll Garden. New York, McClure, Philips, 1905; valorium edition, edited by James Woodress, 1983.
Youth and the Bright Medusa. New York, Knopf, 1920; London, Heinemann, 1921.
The Fear That Walks by Noonday, with Dorothy Canfield. New York, Knopf, 1931.
Obscure Destinies. New York, Knopf, and London, Cassell, 1932.
The Old Beauty and Others. New York, Knopf, 1948; London, Cassell, 1956.
Five Stories. New York, Vintage, 1956.
Father Juniper's Holy Family. Lexington, Kentucky, Anvil Press, 1956.
Early Stories of Willa Cather, edited by Mildred R. Bennett. New York, Dodd Mead, 1957.
Collected Short Fiction 1892–1912, edited by Virginia Faulkner. Lincoln, University of Nebraska Press, 1970.
Uncle Valentine and Other Stories: Uncollected Fiction 1915–1929, edited by Bernice Slote. Lincoln, University of Nebraska Press, 1973.
The Short Stories, edited by Hermione Lee. London, Virago Press, 1989.

Poetry

April Twilights (as Willa Sibert Cather). Boston, Badger, 1903; London, Heinemann, 1924; revised edition (as Willa Cather) edited by Bernice Slote, Lincoln, University of Nebraska Press, 1962.

Other

The Life of Mary Baker G. Eddy, and the History of Christian Science, by Georgine Milmine (ghostwritten by Cather). New York, Doubleday, 1909.

My Autobiography, by S.S. McClure (ghostwritten by Cather). New York, Doubleday, 1914.

Not Under Forty (essays and criticism). New York, Knopf, and London, Cassell, 1936.

On Writing: Critical Studies on Writing in Art. New York, Knopf, 1949.

Writings from Cather's Campus Years, edited by James R. Shively. Lincoln, University of Nebraska Press, 1950.

Willa Cather's Apprenticeship: A Collection of Her Writings in the Nebraska State Journal, 1891–1895, edited by Harold Norton White. Austin, Texas, University of Texas, 1955.

Willa Cather in Europe: Her Own Story of the First Journey, edited by George N. Kates. New York, Knopf, and London, Cassell, 1956.

The Kingdom of Art: Cather's First Priciples and Critical Principles 1893–1896, edited by Bernice Slote. Lincoln, University of Nebraska Press, 1967.

The World and the Parish: Cather's Articles and Reviews 1893-1902, edited by William M. Curtin. Lincoln, University of Nebraska Press, 2 vols, 1970.

Willa Cather in Person: Interviews, Speeches, and Letters, edited by L. Brent Bohlke, University of Nebraska Press, 1986.

Editor, *The Best Stories of Sarah Orne Jewett*. Boston, Houghton Mifflin, 2 vols, 1925.

*

Film Adaptations: *A Lost Lady*, 1934; *O Pioneers!*, 1992.

Bibliography: *Cather: A Bibliography*, by Joan Crane. Lincoln, University of Nebraska, 1982.

Critical Studies: *World of Willa Cather* by Mildred R. Bennett, New York, Dodd Mead, 1951, revised edition, Lincoln, University of Nebraska Press, 1961; *Cather: A Critical Biography* by E.K. Brown, completed by Leon Edel, New York, Knopf, 1953; *The Landscape and the Looking Glass: Cather's Search for Value* by John H. Randall III, Boston, Houghton Mifflin, 1960; *Willa Cather: The Paradox of Success* by Leon Edel, Washington DC, Library of Congress, 1960; *Cather's Gift of Sympathy* by Edward and Lilian Bloom, Carbondale, South Illinois University Press, 1962; *Cather and Her Critics* edited by James Schroeter, New York, Cornell University Press, 1967; *Cather: Her Life and Her Art*, Lincoln, University of Nebraska Press, 1970, and *Cather: A Literary Life*, Lincoln, University of Nebraska Press, 1987, both by James Woodress; *Cather* by Dorothy McFarland Tuck, New York, Ungar, 1972; *Cather: A Pictorial Memoir* by Bernice Slote, Lincoln, University of Nebraska Press, 1973, and *The Art of Cather*, edited by Bernice Slote and Virginia Faulkner, Lincoln, University of Nebraska Press, 1974; *Five Essays on Cather*, North Andover, Massachusetts, Merrimack College, 1974, and *Critical Essays on Cather*, North Andover, Massachusetts, Merrimack College, 1984, both edited by John J. Murphy; *Cather's Imagination* by Davide Souck, Lincoln, University of Nebraska Press, 1975; *Willa Cather: A Critical Intro-*duction by David Daiches, Boston, Twayne, 1975; *Chrysalis: Cather in Pittsburgh 1896–1906* by Kathleen D. Byrne and Richard C. Snyder, Pittsburgh, Historical Society of Western Pennsylvannia, 1982; *Willa: The Life of Cather* by Phyllis C. Robinson, New York, Doubleday, 1983; *The Voyage Perilous: Cather's Romanticism* by Susan Rosowski, Lincoln, University of Nebraska Press, 1986; *Willa Cather: The Emerging Voice* by Sharon O'Brien, New York, Oxford University Press, 1987; *Willa Cather: Writing at the Frontier*, by Jamie Ambrose, Oxford, Berg, 1988; *Willa Cather and France: In Search of the Lost Language* by Robert J. Nelson, Champaigne, University of Illinois Press, 1988; *Willa Cather: A Life Saved Up*, by Hermione Lee, London, Virago, 1989, as *Willa Cather: Double Lives*, New York, Pantheon, 1989; *Willa Cather* by Susie Thomas, London, Macmillan, 1989; *Willa Cather: A Memoir*, by Elizabeth Shepley Sergeant, Athens, University of Ohio, 1992; *Willa Cather* by Edward Wagenknecht, New York, Continuum, 1993.

*   *   *

Willa Cather was adept at writing both romances and historical fiction, and she was equally adept at combining the two. But perhaps what is most remarkable about her skill with both types of fiction was her ability to use standard types of fiction in such a way as to seem at once to follow the traditions while at the same time adding her own particular slant. Her fiction seems both old-fashioned and modern in theme and in style.

The early plains novels set in Nebraska have romantic heroines who follow many of the stereotypes. Alexandra Bergson of *O Pioneers!* typifies the strong capable woman who stands alone until the very end. Yet she is made different by Cather's extraordinary ability to tie her characters to the setting and define them through parallel and related stories that defy conventions of plot. Antonia Shimerda, in *My Antonia*, is a kind of earth mother who is at one with her world, a fact given added meaning because she and her family are immigrants to Nebraska. The telling of her story is given distance and colour by a romantic and sentimental male narrator who tells her story with his own special emphasis and memories. Here the story is not that of the boy who gets the girl, except in the special realm of the imagination. Years later the narrator returns to Nebraska to find Antonia married with several children, a woman much used by her hard frontier life. Almost immediately as he talks with Antonia his imagination recreates the woman whom he once knew. The story relates to the narrator's past but more than this, it tells of what the imagination can do with the past. The third most important of Cather's romantic heroines is Marian Forrester of *A Lost Lady*. In the traditional sense she is the fallen woman, and to make it worse, a woman who is unfaithful to a venerable and worthy old gentleman. Perhaps the most striking aspect of the novel is the fact that though the woman falls in absolute terms, Cather manages to keep the reader's sympathy for her undiminished. This is accomplished through the eyes of her male narrator, who while he clearly sees his heroine's faults is unable to forget his earlier reverence of her. He offers a remarkable and human insight that is able to combine strong condemnation with an equally if not stronger admiration for his 'fallen' lady.

Unlike Cather's romantic plains novels, which are similar in tone and substance with their dual focus on prairie settings and women heroines, Cather's most important historical novels are quite different from one another. The first of these, *Death Comes for the Archbishop*, is set in the mid-19th century in the American southwest and is based on the experiences of Roman Catholic priests in the settlement of the area. Loosely episodic, the novel relies on tone and setting rather than plot as its centre. Priestly devotion to calling is rendered against the backdrop of the barren beauty of the landscape. A second historical novel, *Shadows on the Rock*, is set in late 17th-century and early 18th-century Quebec. Like *Death Comes for the Archbishop* the novel is episodic and relies more on setting and tone than plot. The difference in the setting dictates a difference in tone. As opposed to the expansive openness of the desert southwest, Quebec is seen quite literally as a rock surrounded and enclosed by a dense and forbidding wilderness. While the earlier novel attempts to tell the story of the imposition of European culture and religion on a foreign soil, *Shadows on the Rock* is the story of an attempt to cling to the old ways—the ways of the French—in the face of a new world that would have its way with its puny human inhabitants. Against these threats the novel's central characters—the apothecary Euclide Auclair and his daughter, Cecile—cling to old values, religious morality and most of all to the order of domestic life. In this novel the most important matters are how one cooks a meal or cleans a room.

The final historical novel, the last novel that Cather was to complete, *Sapphira and the Slave Girl*, goes back to her own family history in ante-bellum Virginia. The novel's qualities are in many ways the qualities of the gothic, historical romance so popular with writers about the period. There is a plantation with an assortment of black slaves with a suggestion of miscegenation and other dark secrets, there is a flight and much later return of a slave woman, and there is an out-and-out rakish villain who has his cousins in the most sensational novels of the type. Yet these elements aside, the most important and vital theme of the novel focuses on the character of the lady of the manor house, Sapphira Colbert. As a strong leading female figure she suggests the earlier characters Alexandra Bergson and Antonia Shimerda, but about her there is a darkness and suggested evil that is lacking in the other two. Sapphira is a difficult character to classify or to dismiss. She is evil and she is good, and finally she is an enigma. This is of course the very stuff of gothic fiction, and perhaps it is right that Cather should end her writing career with a character so hard to define since her own fiction, as many a critic has said, defies classification. At the end of *Sapphira and the Slave Girl*, Cather takes the unusual step of appearing as a character herself in what seems to be a final attempt at meaning, but no definitive answer comes. This is as it should be. For both Cather and her most fully rendered characters, there is a residue of meaning that is difficult, if not impossible, to fully describe, but what is not difficult to discern is that she was above all a master storyteller.

—Larry Olpin

CATO, Nancy (Fotheringham).
Nationality: Australian. **Born:** Adelaide, South Australia, 11 March 1917. **Education:** Presbyterian Girls' College, Adelaide, 1923–34; Adelaide University, 1938–39; South Australian School of Arts, 1954–55. **Relations:** married Eldred de Bracton Norman in 1941 (died 1971); one daughter and two sons. **Career:** journalist, 1936–41, and art critic, 1957–58, Adelaide *News.* Assistant editor, *Poetry Australia,* Lucindale, South Australia, 1947–48; founding member, *Lyrebird Writers,* Sydney, 1949; advisory editor, *Overland,* Melbourne, 1960–62. Vice president, South Australian Fellowship of Writers; member of council, Australian Society of Authors. **Recipient:** Farmer's Poetry prize, 1963; Commonwealth Literature Fund fellowship, 1968; Society of Women Writers award, 1988. D.Litt.: University of Queensland, 1990. **Member:** Order of Australia, 1984. **Agent:** David Higham Associates, 5–8 Lower John Street, London, England. **Address:** P.O. Box 47, Noosa Heads, Queensland 4567, Australia.

ROMANCE AND HISTORICAL PUBLICATIONS

Novels (series: All the Rivers Run)

All the Rivers Run. New York, St Martin's Press, 1978; London, New English Library, 1981.
    All the Rivers Run. London, Heinemann, 1958.
    Time, Flow Softly. London, Heinemann, 1960.
    But Still the Stream. London, Heinemann, 1962.
Green Grows the Vine. London, Heinemann, 1960.
North-West by South. London, Heinemann, 1965.
Brown Sugar. London, Heinemann, 1974; New York, St Martin's Press, 1975.
Queen Truganini, with Vivienne Rae Ellis. London, Heinemann, 1976.
Forefathers. New York, St Martin's Press, 1982; London, New English Library, 1983.
The Lady Lost in Time. Sydney, Collins, 1985.
A Distant Island. London, New English Library, 1988.
The Heart of the Continent. London, New English Library, and New York, St Martin's Press, 1989.
Marigold. London, Hodder and Stoughton, 1992.

Short Stories

The Sea Ants and Other Stories. London, Heinemann, 1964.

OTHER PUBLICATIONS

Play

Travellers Through the Night (produced Noosa Heads, Queensland, 1979).

Poetry

The Darkened Window. Sydney, Lyre Bird Writers, 1950.
The Dancing Bough. Sydney, Angus and Robertson, 1957.

Other

Nin and the Scribblies (for children). Milton, Queensland, Jacaranda Press, 1976.
Mister Maloga; Daniel Matthews and His Mission. St Lucia, University of Queensland Press, 1976; revised edition, St Lucia, University of Queensland Press, 1993.
The Noosa Story: A Study in Unplanned Development. Milton, Queensland, Jacaranda Press, 1979.

Editor, *Jindyworobak Anthology.* St Lucia, University of Queensland Press, 1950.

*

Film Adaptations: *All The Rivers Run,* 1983.

Manuscript Collections: National Library of Australia, Canberra; Oxley Library, Brisbane.

Nancy Cato comments:

I write mainly historical fiction based on Australian history and historical characters. One of my novels is set in 17th-century London. *All the Rivers Run,* originally a trilogy, has been made into a television series and is a world bestseller. I enjoy researching and strive for absolute accuracy. *Brown Sugar,* the story of kanaka (slave) labour in Queensland, is also to be filmed. I have also written short stories, verse, and a non-fiction historical biography.

* * *

Nancy Cato's novels are mostly set in her native Australia, and the vast majority take place in the past; they are thoroughly researched and imbued with Cato's obvious fascination with the history of her country.

This shows most clearly in *All the Rivers Run*, a novel set at the end of the last century and the beginning of this. It describes the life of Philadelphia Gordon from her emergence from the sea, the sole survivor of a shipwreck which killed her parents, to an enigmatic ending, again in the sea, at the end of a long and fulfilling life. The story takes place around the Murray and Darling Rivers and describes in detail the communities which have grown up on their banks. A constant theme is the flowing of the river and the parallel currents in the lives of the characters, the people inhabiting these communities. Philadelphia, an artist by temperament and training, is fascinated by the river and, untypically for a woman at that time, buys part ownership of a riverboat. This forms the vehicle not only for her own wanderings but also for the plot, and it enables the author to incorporate vivid descriptions of the surrounding countryside. The many relationships which the heroine forms are as fluid as the river, and throughout the novel we are led to draw parallels between the progression of the river and Philadelphia's character as it develops. She grows in stature and independence and eventually, after an accident which deprives her husband of the use of his legs, she successfully becomes the first woman master of a river steamboat. Cato originally wrote this story as three shorter novels but there is no doubt that the continuity provided by their republication in one volume lends strength to the metaphor used to develop the plot and characterizations.

The same potential exists in the subject matter of *North-West by South*, a novel set in Tasmania in the first half of the 19th century. The main characters are Sir John Franklin (governor of Van Diemen's Land, as Tasmania was then known) and his second wife Jane, another emancipated and intelligent woman. Extensively researched, the novel explores the lives and relationships of the English men and women sent to govern and administer the island; the style is terse, even journalistic, and unfortunately this detracts from the undoubtedly fertile material. An immense amount of information is packed into a novel of only average length and even the descriptions of the beautiful countryside have a certain breathlessness. The occasional flashes of humour (when Lady Franklin has been attacked in the press her husband suspects that she has been 'wounded by the slings and arrows of outrageous journalism') are buried in the concise recital of events.

In *A Distant Island* Cato tells the story of Tasmania's famous botanist Ronald Gunn, who is a minor character in *North-West by South*; there is indeed a certain amount of overlap with the earlier novel, and thus Lady Franklin and various other familiar personages reappear.

Another novel describing some of these characters and events is *Queen Truganini*, written jointly with Vivienne Rae Ellis and published some 11 years after *North-West by South*. This expands on one of the themes of the earlier novel, the shameful and degrading extermination of the natives of Tasmania (Truganini was the last surviving member of her tribe). Here again the style is intense; though not entirely satisfactory in a work of fiction it does indicate something of the crusading spirit in which this book was obviously written. The contrast between this book and *North-West by South*, although they are somewhat similar in scope, lies in their emphasis. The latter might have benefited from a stylistic expansion, as the relationships (often unsatisfactorily described) form an important part of the whole. To give this treatment to *Queen Truganini* would have resulted no doubt in a powerful novel, but would probably have diminished the portrayal of the outrageous events and attitudes which form the basis of the story.

The award-winning *Forefathers* and its companion volume *Brown Sugar* are set a few years later and, like *All the Rivers Run*, are completely fictional. Also like *All the Rivers Run*, they are more successful stylistically, and describe in detail an interesting facet of Australia's economic and social development. Again, in *The Heart of the Continent*, Cato produces a novel set in the saga mould, spanning over 40 years and detailing the lives of Alix Macfarlane and her daughter Caro. Both women are nurses, and we are given an impressive amount of presumably authentic medical detail.

A complete contrast to all these books is *Green Grows the Vine*. This is a short novel covering a brief period of time (barely two months) and the characters hardly have time to be introduced to us, let alone to develop. Here again is the raw material for a stronger novel; instead this tale of three girls grape picking in South Australia is superficial and disappointing. The most satisfying reading is provided by the verses from the *Rubaiyat of Omar Khayyam* which head every chapter; that Cato herself is a poet is demonstrated in all her books by the strength of her descriptive prose when she allows herself to elaborate upon the landscape and scenery. The same strengths and weaknesses are also evident in *Marigold*, another disappointingly brief novel, in which the determined and independent heroine is a reporter. A breathless and thus unrealistic sequence of events is counterpointed by beautiful descriptive passages and, by a demonstration of Cato's knowledge of art and art history (Cato studied art, and has worked as an art critic).

There is no doubt whatsoever that Cato is an extremely talented and versatile woman, however, writing interesting and/or impassioned novels is but one of her skills. It is primarily in those books in which she allows time for both plot and characters to develop at a more leisurely pace that her true strengths are demonstrated.

—Judith Rhodes

CHACE, Isobel.   See HUNTER, Elizabeth.

CHAMBERS, Catherine E.   See ST JOHN, Nicola.

CHAMBERS, Kate.   See ST JOHN, Nicola.

CHAMBERS, Robert W(illiam).   American. 1865–1933. See 2nd edition, 1990.

CHANDOS, Fay.
Pseudonym for Irene Maude Swatridge. **Other Pseudonyms:** Theresa Charles, with Charles Swatridge; Leslie Lance; Virginia Storm; Jan Tempest. **Nationality:** British. **Born:** Irene Maude Mossop, Woking, Surrey. **Education:** privately educated. **Relations:** married Charles John Swatridge in 1934. **Died:** 1993.

ROMANCE AND HISTORICAL PUBLICATIONS

Novels

No Limit to Love. London, Mills and Boon, 1937.
No Escape from Love. London, Mills and Boon, 1937.

Man of My Dreams. London, Mills and Boon, 1937.
Before I Make You Mine. London, Mills and Boon, 1938.
Wife for a Wager. London, Mills and Boon, 1938.
Gay Knight I Love. London, Mills and Boon, 1938.
All I Ask. London, Mills and Boon, 1939.
Another Woman's Shoes. London, Mills and Boon, 1939.
When Three Walk Together. London, Mills and Boon, 1939.
The Man Who Wasn't Mac. London, Mills and Boon, 1939.
Husband for Hire. London, Mills and Boon, 1940.
You Should Have Warned Me. London, Mills and Boon, 1940.
When We Two Parted. London, Mills and Boon, 1940.
Substitute for Sherry. London, Mills and Boon, 1940.
Women Are So Simple. London, Mills and Boon, 1941.
Only a Touch. London, Mills and Boon, 1941.
Awake, My Love! London, Mills and Boon, 1942.
A Letter to My Love. London, Mills and Boon, 1942.
Eve and I. London, Mills and Boon, 1943.
A Man to Follow. London, Mills and Boon, 1943.
Away from Each Other. London, Mills and Boon, 1944.
Made to Marry. London, Mills and Boon, 1944.
Just a Little Longer. London, Mills and Boon, 1944.
Last Year's Roses. London, Mills and Boon, 1945.
A Man for Margaret. London, Mills and Boon, 1945.
Three Roads to Romance. London, Mills and Boon, 1945.
When Time Stands Still. London, Mills and Boon, 1946.
Home Is the Hero. London, Mills and Boon, 1946.
Because I Wear Your Ring. London, Mills and Boon, 1947.
Cousins May Kiss. London, Mills and Boon, 1947.
Lost Summer. London, Mills and Boon, 1948.
Since First We Met. London, Mills and Boon, 1948.
June in Her Eyes. London, Mills and Boon, 1949.
For a Dream's Sake. London, Mills and Boon, 1949.
Fugitive from Love. London, Mills and Boon, 1950.
There Is a Tide . . . . London, Mills and Boon, 1950.
The Ugly Prince (as Virginia Storm). New York, Arcadia House, 1950.
This Time It's Love. London, Mills and Boon, 1951.
First and Favourite Wife. London, Mills and Boon, 1952.
Families Are Such Fun. London, Mills and Boon, 1952.
Leave It to Nancy. London, Mills and Boon, 1953.
The Other One. London, Mills and Boon, 1953.
Find Another Eden. London, Mills and Boon, 1953.
Just Before the Wedding. London, Mills and Boon, 1954.
Doctors Are Different. London, Mills and Boon, 1954.
Husbands at Home. London, Mills and Boon, 1955.
Hibiscus House. London, Mills and Boon, 1955; as *Nurse Incognito*, Toronto, Harlequin, 1964.
So Nearly Married. London, Mills and Boon, 1956.
The Romantic Touch. London, Mills and Boon, 1957.
Partners Are a Problem. London, Mills and Boon, 1957.
Model Girl's Farm. London, Mills and Boon, 1958.
Nan—and the New Owner. London, Mills and Boon, 1959.
Wild Violets. London, Mills and Boon, 1959.
When Four Ways Meet. London, Mills and Boon, 1961.
Sister Sylvan. London, Mills and Boon, 1962.
Two Other People. London, Mills and Boon, 1964.
Don't Give Your Heart Away. London, Mills and Boon, 1966.
Stranger in Love. London, Mills and Boon, 1966.
Farm by the Sea. London, Mills and Boon, 1967.
The Three of Us. London, Mills and Boon, 1970.
Sweet Rosemary. London, Mills and Boon, 1972.
Mistress of Martinscombe (as Virginia Storm). London, Mills and Boon, 1973

Novels as Theresa Charles (with Charles Swatridge)

The Distant Drum. London, Longman Green, 1940.
My Enemy and I. London, Longman Green, 1941.
To Save My Life. London, Longman Green, 1946.
Happy Now I Go. London, Longman Green, 1947; as *Dark Legacy*, New York, Dell, 1968.
Man-Made Miracle. London, Longman Green, 1949.
First I Must Forget. New York, Arcadia House, 1951.
At a Touch I Yield. London, Cassell, 1952.
Fairer Than She. London, Cassell, 1953; New York, Dell, 1968.
My Only Love. London, Cassell, 1954.
The Kinder Love. London, Cassell, 1955.
The Burning Beacon. London, Cassell, 1956; New York, Lancer, 1966.
The Ultimate Surrender. London, Cassell, 1958.
A Girl Called Evelyn. London, Hale, 1959.
No Through Road. London, Hale, 1960.
House on the Rocks. London, Hale, 1962; New York, Paperback Library, 1966.
Ring for Nurse Raine. London, Hale, 1962.
Widower's Wife. London, Hale, 1963; as *Return to Terror*, New York, Paperback Library, 1966.
Patient in Love. London, Hale, 1963.
Nurse Alice in Love. London, Hale, 1964; as *Lady in the Mist*, New York, Ace, 1966.
The Man for Me. London, Hale, 1965; as *The Shrouded Tower* (as Theresa Charles), New York, Ace, 1966.
How Much You Mean to Me. London, Hale, 1966.
Proud Citadel. London, Hale, and New York, Dell, 1967.
The Way Men Love. London, Hale, 1967.
The Shadowy Third. London, Hale, 1968.
From Fairest Flowers. London, Hale, 1969.
Wayward as the Swallow. London, Hale, 1970.
Second Honeymoon. London, Hale, 1970.
My True Love. London, Hale, 1971.
Therefore Must Be Loved. London, Hale, 1972.
Castle Kelpiesloch. London, Hale, 1973.
Nurse by Accident. London, Hale, 1974.
The Flower and the Nettle. London, Hale, 1975.
Trust Me, My Love. London, Hale, 1975.
One Who Remembers. London, Hale, 1976.
Rainbow after Rain. London, Hale, 1977.
Crisis at St Chad's. London, Hale, 1977.
Just for One Weekend. London, Hale, 1978.
Surgeon's Reputation. London, Hale, 1979.
With Somebody Else. London, Hale, 1981.
Surgeon's Sweetheart. London, Hale, 1981.
No Easier Road to Love. London, Hale, 1983.
Always in My Heart. London, Severn House, 1985.

Novels as Jan Tempest

Stepmother of Five. London, Mills and Boon, 1936.
Someone New to Love. London, Mills and Boon, 1936.
Be Still, My Heart! London, Mills and Boon, 1936.
Kiss—and Forget. London, Mills and Boon, 1936.
Believe Me, Beloved. London, Mills and Boon, 1936.
All This I Gave. London, Mills and Boon, 1937.
If I Love Again. London, Mills and Boon, 1937.
No Other Man—. London, Mills and Boon, 1937.
Grow Up, Little Lady! London, Mills and Boon, 1937.
Carey, Come Back! London, Mills and Boon, 1937.
Face the Music—for Love. London, Mills and Boon, 1938.
Man—and Waif. London, Mills and Boon, 1938.

Because My Love Is Come. London, Mills and Boon, 1938; as *Because My Love Is Coming*, 1958.
When First I Loved . . . . London, Mills and Boon, 1938.
Hilary in His Heart. London, Mills and Boon, 1938.
Say You're Sorry. London, Mills and Boon, 1939.
My Only Love. London, Mills and Boon, 1939.
Uninvited Guest. London, Mills and Boon, 1939.
I'll Try Anything Once. London, Mills and Boon, 1939.
Top of the Beanstalk. London, Mills and Boon, 1940.
The Broken Gate. London, Mills and Boon, 1940.
Why Wouldn't He Wait?. London, Mills and Boon, 1940.
Little Brown Girl. London, Mills and Boon, 1940.
Always Another Man. London, Mills and Boon, 1941.
The Moment I Saw You. London, Mills and Boon, 1941.
The Unknown Joy. London, Mills and Boon, 1941.
Ghost of June. London, Mills and Boon, 1941.
No Time for a Man. London, Mills and Boon, 1942.
Romance on Ice. London, Mills and Boon, 1942.
If You'll Marry Me. London, Mills and Boon, 1942.
A Prince for Portia. London, Mills and Boon, 1943.
Wife after Work. London, Mills and Boon, 1943.
The Long Way Home. London, Mills and Boon, 1943.
'Never Again!' Said Nicola. London, Mills and Boon, 1944.
The One Thing I Wanted. London, Mills and Boon, 1944.
Utility Husband. London, Mills and Boon, 1944.
Westward to My Love. London, Mills and Boon, 1944.
Love While You Wait. London, Mills and Boon, 1944.
Not for This Alone. London, Mills and Boon, 1945.
To Be a Bride. London, Mills and Boon, 1945.
The Orange Blossom Shop. London, Mills and Boon, 1946.
Happy with Either. London, Mills and Boon, 1946.
House of the Pines. London, Mills and Boon, 1946; New York, Ace, 1967; as *House of Pines*, Ace, 1975.
Bachelor's Bride. London, Mills and Boon, 1946.
Lovely, Though Late. London, Mills and Boon, 1946.
Close Your Eyes. London, Mills and Boon, 1947.
Teach Me to Love. London, Mills and Boon, 1947.
How Can I Forget? London, Mills and Boon, 1948; as *First I Must Forget* (as Virginia Storm), New York, Arcadia House, 1951.
Cinderella Had Two Sisters. London, Mills and Boon, 1948; (as Virginia Storm) New York, Arcadia House, 1950.
Short-Cut to the Stars. London, Mills and Boon, 1949.
Never Another Love. London, Mills and Boon, 1949; New York, Arcadia House, 1950.
Promise of Paradise. New York, Gramercy, 1949.
Nobody Else—Ever. London, Mills and Boon, 1950.
A Match Is Made. London, Mills and Boon, 1950.
Now and Always. New York, Arcadia House, 1950.
Until I Find Her. New York, Arcadia House, 1950; London, Mills and Boon, 1951.
Two Loves for Tamara. London, Mills and Boon, 1951.
Open the Door to Love. London, Mills and Boon, 1952.
Without a Honeymoon. London, Mills and Boon, 1952.
Happy Is the Wooing. London, Mills and Boon, 1952.
Meet Me by Moonlight. London, Mills and Boon, 1953.
Give Her Gardenias. London, Mills and Boon, 1953.
Enchanted Valley. London, Mills and Boon, 1954.
First-Time of Asking. London, Mills and Boon, 1954.
Ask Me Again. London, Mills and Boon, 1955.
Where the Heart Is. London, Mills and Boon, 1955.
For Those in Love. London, Mills and Boon, 1956.
Wedding Bells for Willow. London, Mills and Boon, 1956.
Craddock's Kingdom. London, Mills and Boon, 1957.
. . . Will Not Now Take Place. London, Mills and Boon, 1957.
The Youngest Sister. London, Mills and Boon, 1958.
Because There Is Hope. London, Mills and Boon, 1958.

Romance for Rose. London, Mills and Boon, 1959.
Stranger to Love. London, Mills and Boon, 1960.
Mistress of Castlemount. London, Mills and Boon, 1961.
The Turning Point. London, Mills and Boon, 1961.
That Nice Nurse Nevin. London, Mills and Boon, and Toronto, Harlequin, 1963.
The Madderleys Married. London, Mills and Boon, 1963.
The Flower and the Fruit. London, Mills and Boon, 1964.
Nurse Willow's Ward. Toronto, Harlequin, 1965.
The Way We Used to Be. London, Mills and Boon, 1965.
Jubilee Hospital. Toronto, Harlequin, 1966.
The Lonesome Road. London, Mills and Boon, 1966.
Meant to Meet. London, Mills and Boon, 1967.
Lyra, My Love. Chicago, Moody Press, 1969.
Mistress of Martinscombe. London, Mills and Boon, 1973.

Novels as Leslie Lance

Alice, Where Are You?. London, Hodder and Stoughton, 1940.
Take a Chance. London, Hodder and Stoughton, 1940.
The Dark Stranger. London, Sampson Low, 1946.
Man of the Family. London, Hurst and Blackett, 1952.
Spun by the Moon. London, Ward Lock, 1960.
Sisters in Love. London, Ward Lock, 1960.
A Summer's Grace. London, Ward Lock, 1961.
Springtime for Sally. London, Ward Lock, 1962.
Spreading Sails. London, Ward Lock, 1963.
The Young Curmudgeon. London, Ward Lock, 1964.
I'll Ride Beside You. London, Ward Lock, 1965.
Bright Winter. London, Ward Lock, 1965.
No Summer Beauty. London, Ward Lock, 1967.
Return to King's Mere. London, Hale, 1967.
Bride of Emersham. New York, Pyramid, 1967.
Nurse in the Woods. London, Hale, 1969.
The Summer People. London, Hale, 1969.
Nurse Verena in Weirwater. London, Hale, 1970.
No Laggard in Love. London, Hale, 1971.
The New Lord Whinbridge. London, Hale, 1973.
Now I Can Forget. London, Hale, 1973.
The Love That Lasts. London, Hale, 1974.
The Maverton Heiress. London, Hale, 1975.
The Return of the Cuckoo. London, Hale, 1976.
Romance at Wrecker's End. London, Hale, 1976.
Island House. London, Hale, 1976.
Cousins by Courtesy. London, Hale, 1977.
The Family at the Farm. London, Hale, 1978.
Orchid Girl. London, Hale, 1978.
The Girl in the Mauve Mini. London, Hale, 1979.
The Rose Princess. London, Hale, 1979.
Doctor in the Snow. London, Hale, 1980.
The House in the Woods. New York, Ace, 1980.
Hawk's Head. London, Hale, 1981.
Someone Who Cares. London, Hale, 1982.
Dear Patience. London, Hale, 1983.
Heiress to the Isle. London, Hale, 1987.

OTHER PUBLICATIONS (for children) as Irene Mossop

Fiction

Well Played, Juliana!. London, Sampson Low, 1928.
Prunella Plays the Game. London, Sampson Low, 1929.
Freesia's Feud. London, Warne, 1930.
The Luck of the Oakleighs. London, Warne, 1930.
Chris in Command. London, Sampson Low, 1930.

Sylvia Sways the School. London, Sampson Low, 1930.
Theresa's First Term. London, Nisbet, 1930.
Vivien of St Val's. London, Shaw, 1931.
Charm's Last Chance. London, Nisbet, 1931.
Nicky—New Girl. London, Sampson Low, 1931.
Rona's Rival. London, Warne, 1931.
A Rebel at Rowans. London, Sampson Low, 1932.
Barbara Black-Sheep. London, Warne, 1932.
Una Wins Through. London, Warne, 1932.
Feud in the Fifth. London, Sampson Low, 1933.
Hilary Leads the Way. London, Warne, 1933.
The Taming of Pickles. London, Shaw, 1933.
Fifth at Cliff House. London, Warne, 1934.
Four V's. London, Warne, 1934.
The Fourth at St Faith's. London, Shaw, 1934.
Play Up, Pine House! London, Sampson Low, 1934.
Theresa on Trial. London, Warne, 1935.
Theda Marsh. London, Shaw, 1935.
The Gay Adventure. London, Warne, 1937.

*   *   *

Irene Mossop began writing at the end of the 1920s and has produced some 240 novels. However, her books, mostly romantic stories, have managed to retain their sense of crisp inventiveness. Her pen names—particularly Virginia Storm and Jan Tempest—are well chosen and appropriate for the exciting and atmospheric moods of many of her romantic adventures. The titles also endorse the flavour of the books—*No Limit to Love, Husband for Hire, Meant to Meet*, etc.

Several of the author's heroines start out in a rather calculating way, going to the lengths of participating in forced or fake marriages in order to improve their circumstances, or those of someone dear to them. But, by the final pages of each novel, these phoney marriages have generally focused satisfyingly into liaisons of true love.

There are also accounts of steady and happy marriages that begin to misfire because the heroine becomes insensitive to her spouse's psychological needs. In *The Way We Used to Be*, for instance, Leonie's parents suddenly make a lot of money, and Leonie fails to recognize that the resultant parental subsidy is damaging her hard-working veterinary-surgeon husband's masculine pride—and, of course, their marriage. But happily she comes to her senses, and a realistic appraisal of the illogical qualities of married interdependence just in time to salvage her romantic relationship with her husband.

Variations on these married and romantic themes are deftly handled in the flow of novels by this writer. She is also skilled at manipulating the romantic thriller story, as in *The Girl in the Mauve Mini*, for example. (Her children's stories, written as Irene Mossop, are also rich in excitement and suspense.)

She writes as Theresa Charles in collaboration with her husband, Charles John Swatridge, and as co-authors in the romantic genre they have the briskness and colour that remind one of the flavour of stories by the earlier husband and wife partnership of C.N. and A.M. Williamson. *Nurse by Accident* introduces an intriguing new angle on romance—that of the accident-prone heroine whose love life, as well as her career, is threatened by her habit of unintentionally making things go cockeyed. Nurse Nicola Warren falls in love in this accident-prone way—always with the wrong man, of course—until she meets an almost-too-charming-to-be-true solicitor, who knows that the solution to her problem is for him to gather her into his arms with the unoriginal but, in this case, extremely apt comment: 'You need a husband to keep an eye on you . . .'.

—Mary Cadogan

CHAPMAN, Hester W(olferstan).
Nationality: British. **Born:** Hester Pellatt, London, 26 November 1899. **Education:** privately educated. **Military Service:** worked for the American Red Cross during World War II. **Relations:** married 1) N.K. Chapman in 1926 (died); 2) R.L. Griffin in 1938 (died). **Career:** model in Paris and as a telephone operator, secretary, governess, and schoolmistress in London. **Died:** 6 April 1976.

ROMANCE AND HISTORICAL PUBLICATIONS

Novels

She Saw Them Go By. London, Gollancz, and Boston, Houghton Mifflin, 1933.
To Be a King: A Tale of Adventure. London, Gollancz, 1934.
Long Division. London, Secker and Warburg, 1943.
I Will Be Good. London, Secker and Warburg, 1945; Boston, Houghton Mifflin, 1946.
Worlds Apart. London, Secker and Warburg, 1946.
Ivor Novello's King's Rhapsody (novelization of stage play). London, Harrap, 1950; Boston, Houghton Mifflin, 1951.
Ever Thine. London, Cape, 1951.
Falling Stream. London, Cape, 1954.
The Stone Lily. London, Cape, 1957.
Eugenie. London, Cape, and Boston, Little Brown, 1961.
Lucy. London, Cape, 1965; New York, Reynal, 1966.
Fear No More. London, Cape, and New York, Reynal, 1968.
Limmerston Hall. London, Cape, 1972; New York, Coward McCann, 1973.

OTHER PUBLICATIONS

Other

Great Villiers: A Study of George Villiers, Second Duke of Buckingham. London, Secker and Warburg, 1949.
Mary II, Queen of England. London, Cape, 1953; Westport, Connecticut, Greenwood Press, 1976.
Queen Anne's Son: A Memoir of William Henry, Duke of Gloucester. London, Deutsch, 1954.
The Last Tudor King: A Study of Edward VI. London, Cape, 1958; New York, Macmillan, 1959.
Two Tudor Portraits: Henry Howard, Earl of Surrey, and Lady Katherine Grey. London, Cape, 1960; Boston, Little Brown, 1963.
Lady Jane Grey. London, Cape, 1962; Boston, Little Brown, 1963.
The Tragedy of Charles II in the Years 1630–1660. London, Cape, and Boston, Little Brown, 1964.
Privileged Persons: Four Seventeenth-Century Studies. London, Cape, and New York, Reynal, 1966.
The Sisters of Henry VIII: Margaret Tudor, Queen of Scotland . . . Mary Tudor, Queen of France and Duchess of Suffolk. London, Cape, 1969; as *The Thistle and the Rose*, New York, Coward McCann, 1971.
Caroline Matilda, Queen of Denmark. London, Cape, 1971; New York, Coward McCann, 1972.
Anne Boleyn. London, Cape, 1974; as *The Challenge of Anne Boleyn*, New York, Coward McCann, 1974.

Four Fine Gentlemen. London, Constable, and Lincoln, University of Nebraska Press, 1977.

Editor, with Princess Romanovsky-Pavlovsky, *Diversion.* London, Collins, 1946.

* * *

Although at first sight Hester W. Chapman's books are very different from each other (historical novels, costume romances, old-fashioned gothic, modern comedies of manners), they are in fact a homogeneous whole because each of them explores in a different way the effect of a strong, overpowering woman on the people round her. To my mind her best books are her historical novels, and the best of all is *Fear No More.* This is a book of quite extraordinary power which stays in the mind long after it is finished. It is the story of the downfall of the French monarchy and all the events that led up to the revolution, but it is seen entirely through the eyes of the little Dauphin. Everything is described in the strange half-comprehending way that things appear to a child with little things magnified and big things trivialized. The total picture that emerges thus amazes. The strong woman of this book is, of course, Marie Antoinette who is always seen obliquely.

Another historical novel, *Lucy,* is set in 17th-century London. It is primarily about the effect of Lucy's devastating personality on the people around her, but because these people are all actors and courtiers it is also the story of the Restoration theatre. *The Stone Lily* is about the revolution in Sicily in 1848, a subject which appealed to Chapman for she wrote two more books about revolution—*To Be a King* and *She Saw Them Go By*—but she created imaginary countries and situations for these books and used characters with an English point-of-view to enable her to comment on the decadence and pretension of old ruling families. She also wrote a novelized version of Ivor Novello's romantic musical *King's Rhapsody.*

All these books feature strange, strong women, but her strangest female characters are reserved for her gothic novels. In *Ever Thine,* set in a boy's prep school, there is Victoire, a woman who ruins the lives of two men and two children through her wilfulness. The heroine of *Limmerston Hall,* a Victorian gothic piece, behaves with almost decorous impropriety in her unrequited passion for the man who she believes may have killed her sister and may, even as she tries to attract him, be attempting to kill her nephew and niece. But although this book promises much with its hints and foreshadowing, it delivers little. *I Will Be Good* is a book of almost stupefying dullness even though its murder plot is potentially gripping. *Falling Stream* is a surprising modern novel, lightly written, but featuring a strong wilful woman masquerading as a weak invalid and spoiling the lives of everyone with whom she comes into contact—a delightful light read.

An air of sadness hangs over all Chapman's books—'how splendid things might have been', they seem to say, but the strongly drawn, overpowering women are there to put a stop to that. Her style changes to fit the period portrayed. Her pace is perhaps a little leisurely for today's taste, except for the exquisite *Fear No More*—that has an air of timelessness and the power to haunt.

—Pamela Cleaver

CHAPPELL, Mollie.
Nationality: British. **Born:** Rhymney, Wales, 16 August 1913.
Education: Hengood County School for Girls; Cardiff University, B.A. **Relations:** married R.G. Chappell in 1939 (died); one daughter. Lived in Southern Rhodesia (now Zimbabwe), 1946–61. **Agent:** Curtis Brown, 162–168 Regent Street, London W1R 5TB, England.

ROMANCE AND HISTORICAL PUBLICATIONS

Novels

The Widow Jones. London, Collins, 1956.
Endearing Young Charms. London, Collins, 1957.
Bachelor Heaven. London, Collins, 1958.
A Wreath of Holly. London, Collins, 1959.
One Little Room. London, Collins, 1960.
A Lesson in Loving. London, Collins, 1961; New York, Fawcett, 1975.
The Measure of Love. London, Collins, 1961.
Caroline. London, Collins, 1962; New York, Fawcett, 1975.
Come by Chance. London, Collins, 1963.
The Garden Room. London, Collins, 1964.
The Ladies of Lark. London, Collins, 1965.
Bright Promise. London, Collins, 1966.
Bid Me Live. London, Collins, 1967.
Since Summer. London, Collins, 1967.
The Wind in the Green Trees. London, Collins, 1969.
The Hasting Day. London, Collins, 1970.
Summer Story. London, Collins, 1972.
Valley of Lilacs. London, Collins, 1972.
Family Portrait. London, Collins, 1973.
Cressy. London, Collins, 1973.
Five Farthings. London, Collins, 1974.
A Letter from Lydia. London, Collins, 1974.
Seton's Wife. London, Collins, 1975.
In Search of Mr Rochester. London, Collins, 1976.
The Loving Heart. London, Collins, 1977; New York, Fawcett, 1979.
Country Air. London, Collins, 1977.
The Romantic Widow. London, Collins, 1978; New York, Fawcett, 1979.
Wintersweet. London, Collins, 1978.
Serena. London, Hale, 1980.
Dearest Neighbour. London, Hale, 1981.
Cousin Amelia. London, Hale, 1982.
Springtime for Sophie. London, Hale, 1983.
The Yellow Straw Hat. London, Hale, 1983.
Stepping Stones. London, Hale, 1985.
The Family at Redburn. London, Severn House, 1985.

OTHER PUBLICATIONS

Fiction (for children)

Little Tom Sparrow. Leeds, E.J. Arnold, 1950.
Tusker Tales. Leeds, E. J. Arnold, 1950.
Rhodesian Adventure. London, Collins, 1950.
The Gentle Giant. Leeds, E.J. Arnold, 1951.
The House on the Kopje. London, Collins, 1951.
The Sugar and Spice. London, Collins, 1952.
St Simon Square. London, Nelson, 1952.
The Fortunes of Frisk. London, Collins, 1953.
Cat with No Fiddle. London, Collins, 1954.
The Mystery of the Silver Circle. London, Collins, 1955.
Kit and the Mystery Man. London, Collins, 1955.

* * *

Mollie Chappell has evolved from being a writer of short stories for children, as in *Tusker Tales,* and for young girls, as in *Rhodesian Adventure* (both with African settings) via the light comedy of *Bachelor Heaven* to being a writer of romantic novels suitable for mature women.

Chappell's novels form a district species in the romantic class and, in their rather whimsical way, go against the general run. Romance in her novels is very controlled and chaste, and is seen vicariously rather than experienced in the first person. The world of her books is the world of comfortably off middle-aged womanhood in Southern England in the present, though some of the novels are set in mid-19th-century England. Her stories do not contain much action and plots are modest. The stories are, however, overburdened with characters, many dead or unmet, but ranging from the occasional odd and seedy type, such as Jacko in *The Hasting Day*, to the more common cool and crisp young woman, such as Lucy in *Summer Story*. Most characters are somewhat ordinary and there is often little opportunity for them to be developed.

In *Country Air* one sees the variations between brothers in their life achievements with careful gradation. This book contains many of the elements to be found in Chappell's other works: a setting in the English country towns of Clout and Carvel, careful assessment of strangers and relatives, including their clothes. On a rather deeper level is the presence of orphans who have lost both parents, as also occurs in *In Search of Mr Rochester*, *Serena*, and *Dearest Neighbour*.

Settings are predictable, being either a rather vague and wearisome London and pretty villages such as Wintersweet (*Wintersweet*) as well as the frequently occurring Clout and Carvel. Family relationships are often complex and difficult to work out exactly, and involve distantly related members of the same family. Other relationships often include not-so-close friends and also those with a special closeness such as secretaries and housekeepers.

Chappell has also written historical romances, such as *Serena* and *Dearest Neighbour,* and the well-established themes of orphaned children are dealt with at length. The setting of a genteel mid-Victorian England helps to add to the pathos and sentimentality of the treatment. While in *Dearest Neighbour* there is a setting of rectories and solid country houses, there is nevertheless a controlled amount of melodrama and tragedy. It is largely a feminine world of daughters 'coming out', and ends in a chaste pledging of love between hero and heroine. True to the Chappell style there is an approving eye cast on these proceedings by the girl's former governess. In *Serena* a stronger moral attitude (similar to that in *Seton's Wife*) is developed when the courage of the heroine is combined with love to defeat despair when the girl achieves the serenity befitting her name. A serenity does, in fact, pervade most of Chappell's work through the detached posture of the narrators. The essence of the main characters is that they look out on life from an observing viewpoint rather than from actual experience. Many of the minor characters are very shallow indeed; gossip rather than passion rules. The style of writing is often flat and simple. While it is almost naive, at times it also has the effect of producing a 'stream of consciousness' type of prose fitting the very internalized thoughts and action.

—P.R. Meldrum

CHARD, Judy.
Pseudonym: Lyndon Chase. **Nationality:** British. **Born:** Judy Gordon, Tuffley, Gloucestershire, 8 May 1916. **Education:** Kippington House Junior School, Sevenoaks, Kent; Elstree Junior School and St Winifred's Senior School, both Eastbourne, Sussex. **Relations:** married Maurice Noel Chard in 1942. **Career:** assistant secretary, Guy Motors, Wolverhampton, West Midlands, 1939–42; editor, *Devon Life*, Exeter, 1979–82; course leader for Writers News Correspondence College; tutor, creative writing, Devon County Council, Exeter. Since 1989 director of studies, David and Charles Writing College, Newton Abbot, Devon. **Address:** Morley Farm, Morley Road, Highweek, Newton Abbot, Devon TQ12 6NA, England.

Romance and Historical Publications

Novels

Through the Green Woods. London, Hale, 1974.
The Weeping and the Laughter. London, Hale, 1975.
Encounter in Berlin. London, Hale, 1976.
The Uncertain Heart. London, Hale, 1976.
The Other Side of Sorrow. London, Hale, 1977.
In the Heart of Love. London, Hale, 1978.
Out of the Shadows. London, Hale, 1978.
All Passion Spent. London, Hale, 1979.
Seven Lonely Years. London, Hale, 1980.
The Darkening Skies. London, Hale, 1981.
When the Journey's Over. London, Hale, 1981.
Haunted by the Past. London, Hale, 1982.
Sweet Love Remembered. London, Hale, 1982.
Where the Dream Begins. London, Hale, 1982.
Rendezvous with Love. London, Hale, 1983.
Hold Me in Your Heart. London, Hale, 1983.
Tormentil (as Lyndon Chase). London, Hale, 1984.
To Live with Fear. London, Hale, 1985.
Wings of the Morning. London, Hale, 1985.
A Time to Love. London, Hale, 1987.
Wild Justice. London, Hale, 1987.
For Love's Sake Only. London, Hale, 1988.
Person Unknown. London, Hale, 1988.
To Be So Loved. London, Hale, 1988.
Enchantment. London, Hale, 1989.
Appointment with Danger. London, Hale, 1990.
Betrayed. London, Hale, 1991.

Other Publications

Other

Along the Lemon. Bodmin, Cornwall, Bossiney, 1978.
Along the Dart. Bodmin, Cornwall, Bossiney, 1979.
About Widecombe. Bodmin, Cornwall, Bossiney, 1979.
Devon Mysteries. Bodmin, Cornwall, Bossiney, 1979.
The South Hams. Bodmin, Cornwall, Bossiney, 1980.
Along the Teign. Bodmin, Cornwall, Bossiney, 1981.
Devon County Companion. London, Cadogan, 1984.
Tales of the Unexplained in Devon. Exeter, Devon, Obelisk, 1986.
Devon Air Book of Haunted Happenings. Exeter, Devon, Obelisk, 1988.

Editor, *Traditional Devonshire Recipes*. Exeter, Obelisk, 1985.
Editor, with Chips Barber, *Burgh Island and Bigbury Bay*. Exeter, Devon, Obelisk, 1988.
Editor, with Chips Barber, *Tales of the Teign*. Exeter, Devon, Obelisk, 1990.

*

Judy Chard comments:
My romantic novels always include some suspense and mystery as well as the romantic angle. I find it impossible to write what I would describe as a straight romance; there must be some suspense whether it be smuggling, kidnapping or even murder. I enjoyed writing my one historical novel, *Tormentil* (under the name of Lyndon

Chase), about Victorian Devon and Exeter including Dartmoor, and would have liked to continue in this genre. I would also like to write more straight crime.

I like to use a wide range of backgrounds, from my own native Devon to East Berlin and Bolivia, all of which takes a great deal of research as I am very careful to make these as authentic as possible. I do considerable preliminary work on my characters for they are the basis of my novels, the raw material. The plot comes later.

*   *   *

Judy Chard is an exciting and versatile writer of romances that contain a hint of something just a little bit different from the normal formula romance. Chard's characters often find themselves in interesting locations dealing with highly unusual situations. The hero may find himself having to smuggle a daughter out of East Germany, or the heroine may find herself dealing with war criminals or collaborators, murders, or kidnappings.

In one of Chard's earlier novels, *The Uncertain Heart*, Julie Newton, a club hat-check girl, finds herself on the run after witnessing the murder of a policeman. Julie is a tough cookie, and is used to fending for herself, however the murder leads her to take refuge in a church where she confesses what she has seen to a priest. Julie finds herself hiding as a novice in a convent. One wonders if the highly successful film *Sister Act* is based on this book. Julie is befriended by an ex-show business nun who is recovering from the tragic death of her daughter. The love interest is supplied by a local farmer, Nick Stanbury, whose love and trust give Julie the confidence to go to the police and give her evidence.

Alastair Donaldson finds himself involved with an ex-lover when he returns to Berlin on business in *Encounter in Berlin*. Alastair fell in love with Karen while stationed in Berlin during the war. They planned to marry but Alastair returned to England and became immersed in life there. Years later and married to Sandra he gets the chance to look up his old love and takes it. On their first encounter he finds a disinterested woman who contacts him later and meets him looking like a new woman. She confesses that she has a daughter Ilse who is also Alastair's, but who is trapped in East Berlin—only Alastair can help. An unlikely choice for a hero as an older, more staid man, Alastair finds himself meeting his daughter and smuggling her out of East Berlin. It is only after he overhears a conversation between Ilse and her mother that he realizes that he has been tricked. Ilse is a communist who wants to get out of East Germany and Karen is being blackmailed by her ex-husband who has custody of their little girl. Alastair for old times sake agrees to help Karen get her daughter back; he escorts Ilse to England but then turns her in at customs. On his return he finds out that his wife knew about Karen all along and had always thought that Alastair didn't really love her. However, the encounter in Berlin has made him realize how much he loves and values her.

In one of her latest books, *Betrayed*, Caroline Baker goes to Nantes, France after hearing that her favourite aunt is seriously ill after being run over by a car. She arrives to find that her aunt has been leading a double life and has been meeting a man, Pierre Bertillon, for the last 15 years. With the help of a gendarme, Gaston Lejeune, Caroline discovers about her aunt's secret past. Trained as part of FANY (First Aid Nursing Yeomanry) during World War II, Caroline's aunt Lilian was also trained to be a saboteur and was dropped into Nazi dominated France to work with the Resistance. Pierre was head of the local Resistance and although married, he and Lilian (or Bernadette, the name she adopted in France) fell in love. Lilian became pregnant but lost the baby following an incident with the Nazis which led to her and Pierre being arrested and a Resistance meeting being interrupted and later fire-bombed by the Nazis. Someone betrayed the Resistance and Pierre is arrested years later. Lilian can't remember exactly what happened as she has blacked

that day out, and she is too ill to be questioned. With Gaston and Mark's (a journalist-friend) help, Caroline helps to prove Pierre's innocence and discovers that another man was collaborating. Unfortunately they also discover that Pierre's wife had betrayed them in a fit of jealousy.

A surprising aspect of Chard's novels is their brutality. In *Betrayed* we are told that the Nazis burnt to death all the Resistance people in the meeting that they interrupted, and in *The Uncertain Heart*, Julie is informed that her old friend, Tessa Peterson, has been murdered quite brutally and had obviously suffered a lot before her death. This adds to the realism of Chard's books. The author deals with true-life situations—the problems of getting out of East European countries, drug-smuggling, extra-marital affairs, and Nazi war criminals—and the frankness with which she depicts the nastiness of these situations helps to create more credible books. If one likes reading interesting and different suspense-romances Chard is an author well worth reading.

—P. Campbell

———

CHARLES, Theresa.   See **CHANDOS, Fay.**

———

CHARTERS, Lowell.   See **LOWELL, Elizabeth.**

———

CHASE, Elaine Raco.
Nationality: American. **Born:** Schenectady, New York, 31 August 1949. **Education:** Mohonasen High School, Rotterdam, New York, graduated 1967; Albany Business College, New York, 1967–68, A.A. in computing; State University of New York, Albany, 1977. **Relations:** married Gary D. Chase in 1969; one daughter and one son. **Career:** secretary, Narcotic Addiction Control Commission, Albany, 1967–68; audio visual librarian, WGY-WRGB Television, Schenectady, 1968–70; copywriter, Beckman Advertising, Albany, 1970–71; taught creative writing, John D. Rockefeller Cultural Center, Ormond Beach, Florida. Since 1980, chaired various writer's workshops and conferences. **Recipient:** *Romantic Times* lifetime achievement award, 1987. **Agent:** Denise Marcil Agency, 685 West End Avenue, New York, New York 10025, USA. **Address:** 4333 Majestic Lane, Fairfax, Virginia 22030, USA.

Romance and Historical Publications

Novels (series: Roman Cantrell and Nikki Holden)

Rules of the Game. New York, Dell, 1980.
Tender Yearnings. New York, Dell, 1981; London, Corgi, 1983.
A Dream Come True. New York, Dell, 1982.
Double Occupancy. New York, Dell, 1982.
Designing Woman. New York, Dell, 1982.
Calculated Risk. New York, Silhouette, 1983.
No Easy Way Out. New York, Dell, 1983.
Video Vixen. New York, Dell, 1983.
Best Laid Plans. New York, Avon, 1984.
Lady Be Bad. New York, Silhouette, 1984.
Special Delivery. New York, Dell, 1985.
Dare the Devil. New York, Dell, 1986.
Dangerous Places (Cantrell and Holden). New York, Bantam, 1987.
Dark Corners (Cantrell and Holden). New York, Bantam, 1988.

Rough Edges (Cantrell and Holden). New York, Bantam, 1994.

*

Critical Study: in *Love's Leading Ladies* by Kathryn Falk, New York, Pinnacle, 1982.

Elaine Raco Chase comments:

When I first started writing contemporary romance novels I felt three things were missing: 1) strong intelligent heroines, 2) male point of view for heroes, and 3) humour. I was delighted to see the readers thought so as well. I've also enjoyed doing role reversals; using humour to highlight important topics such as dyslexia, drunken drivers, and orthopedic injury recovery. In my current romantic suspense series, my heroine was an abused and sexually battered child who proves a strong survivor.

*   *   *

Elaine Raco Chase has her feet firmly planted in the 20th century. The heroines of her contemporary romances are bright, capable, and talented. Most have active careers which are satisfying in themselves. They work in fields such as business (*Tender Yearnings*, *Special Delivery*, *Calculated Risk*), entertainment or media (*Video Vixen*, *Dare the Devil*, *Double Occupancy*), and science (*No Easy Way Out*, *Designing Woman*). They do not *need* a man to be complete, although a loving relationship is not to be denied if it develops.

One distinguishing characteristic of Chase's novels is a sense of humour, often displayed in the situations in which the main characters are first introduced. When Thor Devlin finds a cave-woman accompanied by a sabre-toothed tiger and a woolly mammoth on his ranch in *Dare the Devil* he is understandably startled. He does manage to recover rapidly and coolly states, 'You, the hairy elephant, and the cat with the overbite are not the norm in Montana'. Things become even more comic when the tiger, whose name is Pumpkin, loses his teeth and the mammoth is introduced as Ramon. It all is explained when the cave-woman admits she is movie stuntwoman, Cam Stirling. In *No Easy Way Out*, brilliant physicist Dr Virginia Farrell attends a Halloween party as a very sexy bunny and loses her inhibitions. Roxanne Murdoch, in *Special Delivery*, delivers a 'belly-gram' to the vice-president of a bank and ends up stranded with him in the bank during a blizzard. Abigail Wetherby, heroine of *Tender Yearnings*, creates havoc with Nick Maxwell's company computer when she tries to cancel her store's acceptance of credit cards.

Chase also often uses the device of disguises and illusions distorting and altering reality. In addition to the Halloween party in *No Easy Way Out*, there are several instances of masquerades. Brandy Abbott (*Designing Woman*) is an architect but masquerades as a night-time *femme fatale*. Nick Maxwell hides his true identity from Abigail, and Cam Stirling deals in the illusions of the film world. Vikki Kirkland, in *Video Vixen*, plays two roles: one as a soap opera siren and another in her personal life. Kit Forrester of *A Dream Come True* also lives in a world of illusions. A rare romance heroine, she is very insecure and vulnerable. Lacking self-esteem, she fantasizes about a different life, yet views herself as a liar. Fantasy and reality join when she begins to play the role of Rafe Morgan's fiancée.

Recently Chase has branched out of the category romance field into detective fiction. Although there still is an important element of romance, the mystery and action components are more prominent. *Dangerous Places* introduces Nikki Holden and Roman Cantrell. She is a journalist and he is a private investigator. Both have scarred pasts, but Nikki's is particularly dark. An abused child and former juvenile delinquent, she is extremely distrustful of any relationship. Starting as rivals on a murder case, they eventually join forces to solve it and in the process fall in love. Nikki and Roman return in *Dark Corners*. They start with different assignments, but their cases converge. Again the mystery and action take centre stage, but one also can see the relationship between the lovers deepening.

Chase's contemporary romances are good fun and enjoyable reading with enough humour to make them livelier than the average formula romance. However, her move to the detective/romance fiction field holds great promise for the future. She shows real talent in plotting complicated, suspenseful stories an her development of Nikki's and Roman's characters and their relationship truly involves the reader.

—Barbara E. Kemp

CHASE, Lyndon.   See **CHARD, Judy.**

CHAUCER, Daniel.   See **FORD, Ford Madox.**

CHESNEY, Marion.
Pseudonyms: M.C. Beaton; Helen Crampton; Ann Fairfax; Jennie Tremaine. **Nationality:** British. **Born:** Glasgow, Scotland, 10 June 1936. **Address:** c/o St Martin's Press, 175 Fifth Avenue, New York, New York 10010, USA.

ROMANCE AND HISTORICAL PUBLICATIONS

Novels (series: A House for the Season; School for Manners; Six Sisters; Westerbury)

Lady Margery's Intrigues. New York, Fawcett, and London, Macdonald, 1980.
Regency Gold. New York, Fawcett, and London, Macdonald, 1980.
The Constant Companion. New York, Fawcett, 1980; London, Macdonald, 1982.
My Lords, Ladies, and Marjorie. New York, Fawcett, 1981; London, Severn House, 1993.
Quadrille. New York, Fawcett, 1981; London, Macdonald, 1982.
Love and Lady Lovelace. New York, Fawcett, 1982.
The Marquis Takes a Bride (as Helen Crampton). London, Macdonald, 1982.
The Westerbury Inheritance. New York, Pinnacle, 1982.
Six Sisters:
   Minerva. New York, St Martin's Press, 1982; London, Macdonald, 1983.
   The Taming of Annabelle. New York, St Martin's Press and London, Macdonald, 1983.
   Deirdre and Desire. New York, St Martin's Press, 1983; London, Macdonald, 1984.
   Daphne. New York, St Martin's Press, and London, Macdonald, 1984.
   Diana the Huntress. New York, St Martin's Press, and London, Macdonald, 1985.
   Frederica in Fashion. New York, St Martin's Press, and London, Macdonald, 1985.
Duke's Diamonds. New York, Fawcett, 1983; London, Hale, 1988.
The Highland Countess. London, Macdonald, 1983.
The Viscount's Revenge. New York, New American Library, 1983.
The Westerbury Sisters. New York, Pinnacle, 1983.
The French Affair. New York, Fawcett, and London, Macdonald, 1984.

The Poor Relation. New York, New American Library, 1984.
Rake's Progress. New York, St Martin's Press, 1984; Bath, Firecrest, 1988.
Sweet Masquerade. New York, Fawcett, 1984.
The Education of Miss Paterson. New York, New American Library, 1985; London, Severn House, 1992.
The Flirt. New York, Fawcett, 1985; London, Hale, 1988.
The Original Miss Honeyford. New York, St Martin's Press, 1986; Bath, Firecrest, 1987.
Those Endearing Young Charms. New York, Fawcett, 1986; London, Hale, 1987.
To Dream of Love. New York, Fawcett, 1986.
A House for the Season:
   The Miser of Mayfair. New York, St Martin's Press, 1986; Bath, Firecrest, 1987.
   Plain Jane. New York, St Martin's Press, 1986; Bath, Firecrest, 1987.
   The Wicked Godmother. New York, St Martin's Press, 1987; Bath, Firecrest, 1988.
   The Adventuress. New York, St Martin's Press, 1987; Bath, Firecrest, 1989.
   Rainbird's Revenge. New York, St Martin's Press, 1988; Bath, Firecrest, 1989.
   Milady in Love. New York, Ballantine, 1987; London, Severn House, 1989.
Lessons in Love. New York, Fawcett, 1987.
Miss Fiona's Fancy. New York, New American Library, 1987; London, Severn House, 1988.
At the Sign of the Golden Pineapple. New York, Fawcett, 1987; London, Severn House, 1990.
The Perfect Gentleman. New York, Ballantine, 1988.
The Savage Marquess. New York, New American Library, 1988.
Love and Lady Lovelace. London, Hale, 1988.
School for Manners:
   Refining Felicity. New York, St Martin's Press, 1988.
   Finessing Clarissa. New York, St Martin's Press, 1989.
   Perfecting Fiona. New York, St Martin's Press, 1990.
   Enlightening Delilah. New York, St Martin's Press, 1990.
   Animating Maria. New York, St Martin's Press, 1990; Bath Chivers, 1991.
   Marrying Harriet. St Martin's Press, 1990; Bath, Chivers, 1992.
Silken Bonds. New York, Fawcett, 1989.
Pretty Polly. London, Severn House, 1989.
Emily Goes to Exeter. New York, St Martin's Press, 1990.
The Scandalous Lady Wright. New York, Fawcett, 1990; London, Hale, 1991.
Viscount's Revenge. London, Severn House, 1991.
The Love Match. London, Hale, 1992.
Her Grace's Passion. London, Hale, 1992.
Lady Lucy's Lover. London, Severn House, 1992.
The Glitter and the Gold. New York, Fawcett, 1993.

Novels as Ann Fairfax

My Dear Duchess. New York, Berkley, and London, Macdonald, 1979.
Henrietta. New York, Berkley, 1979; London, Macdonald, 1980.
Annabelle. New York, Berkley, 1980; London, Macdonald, 1981.
Penelope. New York, Berkley, 1982; London, Macdonald, 1983.

Novels as Jennie Tremaine

Ginny. New York, Dell, 1980.
Kitty. New York, Dell, 1980.
Molly. New York, Dell, 1980.
Lucy. New York, Dell, 1980.

Polly. New York, Dell, 1980.
Susie. New York, Dell, 1981.
Tilly. New York, Dell, 1981.
Poppy. New York, Dell, 1982.
Sally. New York, Dell, 1982.
Maggie. New York, Dell, 1984.
Lady Anne's Deception. New York, Fawcett, 1986.

OTHER PUBLICATIONS

Novels as M.C. Beaton

Death of a Gossip. New York, St Martin's Press, 1985; Sutherland, Charles Bravos, 1989.
Death of a Cad. New York, St Martin's Press, 1986; Sutherland, Charles Bravos, 1990.
Death of an Outsider. New York, St Martin's Press, 1988.
Death of a Perfect Wife. New York, St Martin's Press, 1989.
Death of a Glutton. New York, St Martin's Press, 1993.

*   *   *

Marion Chesney writes Regencies with a difference. She is amazingly prolific, publishing half a dozen or more novels a year, and while admiring the fertility of her imagination this can lead to hasty, inadequately revised or edited books, shown by minor infelicities of phrasing and repeated words.

The Regency genre is expected to be, above all, entertaining. There are social conventions which have to be obeyed, giving scope for plots such as those involving arranged marriages, which would not be treated in so light a fashion in any other novel. Many of the plots are highly unlikely, but with the well written Regency the reader can normally suspend disbelief and be carried along by the sheer enjoyment of the story, ignoring such unlikely acrobatic feats as the heroine being carried up and down drainpipes and across roofs, and diving into the Thames from a bridge, as in *The French Affair*.

Chesney's books are frothy, light-hearted, fun and amusing, but perhaps more than any other writer of Regency novels she uses contemporary events to good effect in weaving her plots and painting in the background setting. Unlike most authors she often portrays the lower life, the upstairs-downstairs contrast of high society and the servants' hall. There is real appreciation of the feelings of the poor and downtrodden.

Settings are the expected Regency ones, London of course, Bath and Brighton and the squire's houses in the countryside. However, she has set some books in Victorian or Edwardian England, in places like Hampstead in North London.

In *Kitty*, which is set in Hampstead, a poor but genteel and snobbish mother plans to give her daughter a Season in the West End and find her a rich husband; to this end she employs a delightfully outspoken lady to sponsor Kitty. Needing money Lord Chesworth marries Kitty, and the misunderstandings begin—she loves him but he assumes all she wants is his title. After a hilariously raucous wedding reception, a quarrel on their wedding night, mistresses, and attempts on Kitty's life, all is resolved and the lovers are reunited.

Society is well portrayed, but with the added reality of the effects of a dense crowd at a ball, with collisions and trapped waiters that are not recognized in the idealized situations normally described.

Chesney has developed the concept of a series of novels in several ways. *Frederica in Fashion* is the sixth and last of the 'Six Sisters' series, featuring the Armitage family. The youngest, dowdiest sister runs away from school when her father plans to marry his housemaid Sarah, and finds a job as a chambermaid in a duke's household. He is having a house party, and because his mistress and Frederica's godmother clash, Frederica is unmasked, and taken to London where the jealous mistress, collaborating with the villain, organizes her kidnap and disgrace. All ends happily, however, as it must. The other happily married sisters feature briefly in this book. For readers who have followed their earlier adventures the author cleverly and satisfyingly brings their stories up to date in a few sentences.

The importance of manners in Regency novels, often referred to as 'Comedies of Manners', is recognized by producing a whole series called the 'School for Manners'. *Animating Maria* is the fifth in this series, featuring two sisters who specialize in sponsoring 'difficult' debutantes. There are some rather unlikely situations that turn the book into farce, such as an episode in which one of the middle-aged sisters dresses as a man and fights a duel, however, it is inventive and fun, and does not depend solely on the life of the *ton* for its plot.

Another interesting series is the 'House for the Season', in which the sub-plot is an important thread throughout, telling the stories of the servants in the house. *Plain Jane* is the second book of this series. It begins with the servants chained to the house by an unscrupulous agent who steals their wages and utters threats. Then the house is let to Captain and Mrs Hart. He is a naval hero who has been forced to sell out by an ambitious wife. She rents 67 Clarges Street for the coming out of her daughters Euphemia, blonde and lovely, and Jane, small and dark. Jane dreams of a man she saw eight years ago, Beau Tregarthan, and the two are drawn together by the mystery death of a former tenant. Adventure, threats, and an elopement add up to a very satisfying story.

It is followed by *The Wicked Godmother*. Harriet, 25 years old, alone and poor, is left in control of 18-year-old twins. Unknown to her they hate her and are jealous, but manage to conceal their enmity. She takes them to London and their adventures begin. Through the intervention of Beauty, an amusing but vicious pet dog that Harriet insists accompanies them, she meets two exceedingly eligible men and the twins begin to preen themselves on having attracted rich and handsome suitors. It is, however, not the twins that the men admire, and both the twins and a jealous mistress plot vengeance on Harriet. Tricked into venturing into one of London's worst slums at Seven Dials, the endangered Harriet is rescued by the hero and both are rewarded in love.

One of the more unusual episodes in a Regency is when Harriet takes the servants on a day trip to Brighton, where the butler, Rainbird, discovers that his lady love has married. Similarly, because of Harriet's urging the kitchen maid, Lizzie, is taught to read.

An example of Chesney's single title novel is *The Love Match*. Felicity has been adopted and brought up by a feminist, and feels betrayed when her peers marry. However, she is left a house and a fortune, and writes a scandalous novel. She pretends to be her own aunt so as to provide herself with a chaperone, and uses the apparent licence of age to be very forthright. Excitement is provided by a plot to steal some jewels, the search for Felicity's parentage, and a jealous mistress just to complicate matters.

If anyone has inherited Georgette Heyer's mantle, Chesney has the strongest claim.

—Marina Oliver

CHESTERTON, Denise. See **ROBINS, Denise.**

CHETWYND, Berry. See **RAYNER, Claire.**

CHILD, Philip.
Nationality: Canadian. **Born:** Hamilton, Ontario, 9 January 1898. **Education:** Trinity College, University of Toronto, B.A. 1921; Cambridge University, 1921–22; Harvard University, Cambridge, Massachusetts, A.M. 1923, Ph.D. 1929. **Military Service:** served in the Canadian Royal Garrison Artillery during World War I: lieutenant. **Relations:** married Gertrude Helen Potts in 1924; one son and one daughter. **Career:** lecturer, 1923–26 and 1941–42, and professor of English from 1942, Trinity College, University of Toronto; assistant professor of English, University of British Columbia, Vancouver, 1928–29; tutor, Harvard University, 1929–36. Member of the Editorial Board, *University of Toronto Quarterly*, 1940–49. **Recipient:** Ryerson fiction award, 1945, 1949; Governor-General's award, 1950. **Died:** 1978.

ROMANCE AND HISTORICAL PUBLICATIONS

Novel

The Village of Souls. London, Butterworth, 1933.

OTHER PUBLICATIONS

Novels

God's Sparrows. London, Butterworth, 1937.
Blow Wind Come Wrack. London, Jarrolds, 1945.
Day of Wrath. Toronto, Ryerson Press, 1945.
Mr Ames Against Time. Toronto, Ryerson Press, 1949.

Poetry

The Victorian House and Other Poems. Toronto, Ryerson Press, 1951.
The Wood of the Nightingale. Toronto, Ryerson Press, 1965.

Other

Dynamic Democracy, with John W. Holmes. Toronto, Canadian Association for Adult Education and Canadian Institute of International Affairs, 1941.

*   *   *

History is of keen importance to the writing of Philip Child. He has confirmed this not only by writing historical non-fiction but also by producing a number of imaginative works that are historically-specific in their settings. His book-length narrative poem *The Wood of the Nightingale* is set during World War I, as is much of the novel *God's Sparrows*; *Day of Wrath* takes place in Nazi Germany. His first novel, *The Village of Souls*, however, is the only piece of fiction set in a historical period before his own lifetime.

The Village of Souls portrays several months of life in the 17th-century colony of New France and includes commentary on Indian ways of life and differences between Indians and Europeans. While the overwhelming wilderness is perhaps the most powerful presence in the novel, primarily the narrative is focused on the polarized contrasts between individuals. Jornay, the male protagonist, is a well-born but poor young immigrant from France—with a marked tendency towards introspection and a conscious search for self-knowledge—who has become a *coureur de bois*. Lys, his wife of only a few weeks, has, although she is also aristocratic, come to New France as a *fille du roi* (as were known the single women imported to ease the shortage of potential wives) and is fearful of sharing what is to her a terrible secret. Titange is a violent and unreliable *métis*, or half-breed, a brutal figure with only the crudest of consciences. Anne is a young Indian runaway, initially a primitive following the message of a dream but gradually becoming indoctrinated into Christianity and the white man's ways. And Father Bernard is a devout Jesuit missionary, committed to the saving of souls and lured by the prospect of discovering a river to the west.

In this presentation of human spirits and their torments, *The Village of Souls* is typical of all of Child's work. Certainly, it is emblematic of his common concerns and themes in its demonstration of modernist humanism. Jornay and the two women are engaged in the pursuit of inner peace and happiness, and all come eventually to adopt a faith founded in human relations in the face of a cosmically ironic universe. Interestingly, Lys, the white woman, both explains her understanding of this modernist 'truth' and parallels the narrative itself by telling Jornay an Indian story in which a man must choose between a charm from his past that commits him to 'the village of souls' and a female guide who cannot live in this land of the dead. As the narrator's final appraisal makes clear, 'only in the consummation of love can a man share his loneliness with another and make for himself a dust-speck world within the infinite wilderness, forgetting for a little its pressure which never entirely ceases upon a man's spirit'. Even so, the future holds no guarantees; Jornay knows only that life will go on.

As historical realist fiction, the novel is deliberately situated in a specific setting and time. Quotations from contemporary documents, such as *The Jesuit Relation*, as chapter epigrams contribute to its sense of authenticity, and generally the narrative strives to reproduce a genuine flavour of the time. Although the narrator's 20th-century philosophical concerns at times seem imposed upon characters to whom mere physical survival is so clearly paramount, the novel accords well with other Canadian works describing this historical period. In addition, the author protects himself in a prefacing 'note' admitting some variations in historical fact and claiming a story-teller's license to 'treat imaginatively the character and passions of individuals'.

The Village of Souls is considered by many readers to be Child's most finely developed novel. It is perhaps flawed by an uneven portrayal of its female characters and a tendency to define Indians as a race of subhuman savages. (Notably, Anne, who is permitted to rise above this evaluation, is also suspected of being at least part white.) Notwithstanding these problems, however, the novel is carefully crafted and presents an interesting example of the modernist rewriting of early Canadian history.

—M. Jeanne Yardley

———

CHOLMONDELEY, Alice. See ARNIM, Elizabeth von.

———

CHRISTIAN, Frederick H. See NOLAN, Frederick.

———

CHRISTIE, Agatha. See WESTMACOTT, Mary.

———

CHURCHILL, Winston.
Nationality: American. **Born:** St Louis, Missouri, 10 November 1871. **Education:** Smith Academy, St Louis, 1879–88; United States Naval Academy, Annapolis, Maryland, 1890–94; naval cadet on the cruiser *San Francisco*, New York Navy Yard, 1894.

Relations: married Mabel Harlakenden Hall in 1895 (died 1945); one daughter and two sons. **Career:** editor, *Army and Navy Journal*, New York, 1894; managing editor, *Cosmopolitan*, New York, 1895; full-time writer from 1895; Republican member for Cornish, New Hampshire Legislature, 1903–05; delegate for New Hampshire, Republican National Convention, Chicago, 1904; Progressive Party candidate for the New Hampshire governorship, 1912; toured European battle fronts, and wrote for *Scribner's*, New York, 1917–18. President, Authors League of America, 1913. **Died:** 12 March 1947.

ROMANCE AND HISTORICAL PUBLICATIONS

Novels

Richard Carvel. New York and London, Macmillan, 1899.
The Crisis. New York and London, Macmillan, 1901.
The Crossing. New York and London, Macmillan, 1904.

OTHER PUBLICATIONS

Novels

The Celebrity: An Episode. New York and London, Macmillan, 1898.
Coniston. New York and London, Macmillan, 1906.
Mr Crewe's Career. New York and London, Macmillan, 1908.
A Modern Chronicle. New York and London, Macmillan, 1910.
The Inside of the Cup. New York and London, Macmillan, 1913.
A Far Country. New York and London, Macmillan, 1915.
The Dwelling-Place of Light. New York and London, Macmillan, 1917.

Short Stories

Mr Keegan's Elopement. New York and London, Macmillan, 1903.

Plays

The Crisis, adaptation of his own novel (produced New York, 1902). New York, French, 1927.
The Title-Mart (produced London, 1905; New York, 1906). New York, Macmillan, 1905.
The Crossing, with Louis Evan Shipman, adaptation of the novel by Churchill (produced New York, 1906).
Dr Jonathan. New York, Macmillan, 1919.

Other

A Traveller in War-Time, With an Essay on the American Contribution and the Democratic Idea. New York, Macmillan, 1918.
The Green Bay Tree. New York, Macmillan, 1920.
The Uncharted Way: The Psychology of the Gospel Doctrine. Philadelphia, Dorrance, 1940.

*

Bibliography: *Winston Churchill: A Reference Guide* by Eric Steinbaugh, Boston, Hall, 1985.

Critical Studies: *The Romantic Compromise in the Novels of Winston Churchill* by Charles C. Walcutt, Ann Arbor, University of Michigan, 1951; *Winston Churchill* by Warren I. Titus, New York, Twayne, 1963; *Novelist to a Generation: The Life and Thought of Winston Churchill* by Robert W. Schneider, Bowling Green, Ohio, Popular Press, 1976.

* * *

Winston Churchill (no relation to the British statesman) has apparently always seemed a little old-fashioned. In 1911 a contemporary labeled him a mid-Victorian who had not recognized an advance or change in the art of fiction since the work of William Makepeace Thackeray. If he seemed old-fashioned in his own day he must seem doubly so today. Indeed he rather smells of Victorian houses and mothballs, and he makes one think of reading triple-decker novels aloud on the porch or in the sitting room in the evening.

This old-fashionedness is especially apparent in Churchill's three historical romances written early in his career. The first, *Richard Carvel*, is set in pre-Revolutionary War Maryland with a long episode in London and a short but adventurous episode on the high seas. The second, *The Crisis*, is set mostly in Civil War St Louis. The third, *The Crossing*, deals with westward expansion and has the broadest scope of all, ranging from South Carolina to the Kentucky wilderness, and from the old Northwest to New Orleans.

Churchill took particular care to be historically accurate in his novels. He always did his homework, reading the historical material available to him and carefully checking historical facts. He paid special attention to biographies and used them to benefit his fiction. Famous people are liberally sprinkled throughout his novels in both minor and major roles. In *Richard Carvel* such notables as George Washington, John Paul Jones, Horace Walpole, and Charles Fox play roles of varying importance. In *The Crisis* Lincoln is an important character and Generals Grant and Sherman make brief appearances. In *The Crossing* with its theme of exploration of the wilderness and battles for the territories such predictable historical figures as Daniel Boone, Andrew Jackson, and George Rogers Clark play significant roles.

In general Churchill's skill in portraying historical figures is better when the figures are minor characters rather than major ones, something that is also true of his fictive characters. For example, in *The Crisis* his picture of Lincoln, a major character much praised by the critics, is not entirely satisfactory. He is too much the grand figure of legend, too much the genial but tragic jokester to emerge as fully realized. In fact *The Crisis* is brought to a symbolic and highly predictable end by Lincoln serving as a go-between for the marriage of the hero, a Union officer, and a pro-Confederate Southern belle as a symbolic healing gesture. Although this surely has pleased many readers it is more cliché than literary art.

Churchill's historical novels all have the strong mark of their author, and thus the reader will receive a good introduction to his work by reading any of the three. They certainly have the same strengths and weaknesses. Churchill is almost always good at evoking atmosphere and scene. His portrayal of history seems accurate, and he is able to capture the essence of a minor character whether from history or totally from his imagination quickly and effectively. In contrast, his weaknesses are all too glaring to the modern reader. His plotting is loose and episodic and he relies too heavily on coincidence. His handling of romance is sentimental and awkward. He also has difficulty drawing major characters who are almost always entirely virtuous and noble or villainous and ignoble, and what is worse he cannot refrain from making this point repeatedly. Finally, Churchill tries to do too much in each novel. His novels are too long and too broad in their scope given his constant repetitions and his penchant for seeing everything through the restricted sense of absolute right and wrong.

Although it is easy to find fault with Churchill's novels, in each of them there are moments rendered with considerable skill. In *Richard Carvel* both 18th-century Maryland and London are effectively portrayed in detail. *The Crisis* is an outstanding depiction of Civil War St Louis with its conflict between the pro-Union mostly Dutch-German population and the pro-Confederate aristocrats of the city. *The Crossing* has effective wilderness scenes and battles and creates a memorable picture of New Orleans during a particularly volatile time.

Although Churchill originally planned to follow *The Crossing* with other historical romances, other interests intervened, and he shifted to other genres never to return to the historical novel. However, between 1899 and 1904 he wrote three of the most popular historical novels ever produced in America, and in doing so he created two avenues into the American past. First, his novels as highly successful bestsellers are important barometers of public taste in reading at the turn of the century, and second and more importantly in their historical accuracy and skilful evocation of important events and scenes from American history, these novels do what all good historical fiction does, that is create a strong sense of the atmosphere of the past.

—Larry Olpin

CLARE, Ellen. See **SINCLAIR, Olga.**

CLARKE, Brenda.
Pseudonyms: Brenda Honeyman; Kate Sedley. **Nationality:** British. **Born:** Brenda Margaret Lilian Honeyman, Bristol, 30 July 1926. **Education:** Red Maids' School, Westbury-on-Trym, Bristol. **Relations:** married Ronald John Clarke in 1955; one son and one daughter. **Career:** civil service clerical officer, Bristol, 1943–55. **Agent:** David Grossman Literary Agency, 110–114 Clerkenwell Road, London EC1M 5SA, England. **Address:** 25 Torridge Road, Keynsham, Bristol, Avon BS18 1QQ, England.

ROMANCE AND HISTORICAL PUBLICATIONS

Novels

The Glass Island. London, Collins, 1978.
The Lofty Banners. New York, Fawcett, 1979; London, Hamlyn, 1980.
The Far Morning. London, Hamlyn, and New York, Fawcett, 1982.
All Through the Day. London, Hamlyn, 1983.
A Rose in May. London, Hutchinson, 1984.
Three Women. London, Hutchinson, 1985.
Winter Landscape. London, Century Hutchinson, 1986.
Under Heaven. London, Bantam Press, 1988.
An Equal Chance. London, Bantam Press, 1989; as *Riches of the Heart*, New York, Pinnacle, 1991.
Sisters and Lovers. London, Bantam Press, 1990; New York, Pinnacle, 1992.
Beyond the World. London, Bantam Press, 1991.
A Durable Fire. London, Bantam Press, 1993.

Novels as Brenda Honeyman

Richard by Grace of God. London, Hale, 1968.
The Kingmaker. London, Hale, 1969.
Richmond and Elizabeth. London, Hale, 1970; New York, Pinnacle, 1973.
Harry the King. London, Hale, 1971; as *The Warrior King*, New York, Pinnacle, 1972.
Brother Bedford. London, Hale, 1972.
Good Duke Humphrey. London, Hale, 1973.
The King's Minions. London, Hale, 1974.
The Queen and Mortimer. London, Hale, 1974.

Edward the Warrior. London, Hale, 1975.
All the King's Sons. London, Hale, 1976.
The Golden Griffin. London, Hale, 1976.
At the King's Court. London, Hale, 1977.
The King's Tale. London, Hale, 1977.
Macbeth, King of Scots. London, Hale, 1977.
Emma the Queen. London, Hale, 1978.
Harold of the English. London, Hale, 1979.

OTHER PUBLICATIONS

Novels as Kate Sedley

Death and the Chapman. London, HarperCollins, and New York, St Martin's Press, 1991.
The Plymouth Cloak. London, HarperCollins, and New York, St Martin's Press, 1992.

*   *   *

As Brenda Honeyman, Brenda Clarke wrote about a dozen historical novels, set mostly in the 14th to 16th centuries. Stylistically, these works are well-crafted and readable, but contain little to distinguish them from the many others written within this framework. In her attempts to encompass a complex period of history, and to portray as many of the characters and events as possible (within the restrictions of the brief formulaic novel), Clarke achieves only a superficial treatment of her subject. A review of *Harry the King* says that 'Brenda Honeyman leaves no royal relation unmentioned nor any royal relationship unexplained'; this may have been intended as a compliment, but in fact can be seen as a disadvantage in the context of a relatively brief novel.

Edward the Warrior deals with the reign of Edward III, a period attractive to chroniclers of mediaeval history; the events are described in a straightforward fashion, and the dialogue is mercifully unembellished with prithees or sithees. However, in introducing the full range of major personages of the period, and in describing numerous events in a fairly brief narrative, Honeyman does not give her characters a chance to develop and does not give the reader any real understanding of those characters or of the situations. The rare introduction of non-essential description (for example, 'Her hands beat together on her lap, two white birds, hovering frustratedly in a silken cage') strikes the reader as incongruous and a trifle extravagant.

In turning to a different type of fiction, written under her married name, Brenda Clarke did both herself and her readers a great service, and turned to advantage her predilection for broad canvasses and large casts of characters. All of her novels have strong central female characters but these do vary markedly—there are those who were born independent, and those who achieve independence (and even one who has independence thrust upon her!).

The first type is exemplified by Elizabeth Evans in *Three Women*, who even at the age of 14 acts independently of her parents to defy her older sister's employer. She goes on to query the role of women and takes a job which has traditionally always been performed by men, eventually starting her own money lending business, flying in the face of her staunch Methodist background. Integral to the plot is a veritable waltz of romantic partners: Lizzie is loved by Jack but she herself loves Ben, who becomes the second husband of Lizzie's cousin Helen. Lizzie eventually marries Jack, but only after both of them have been widowed (he by Lizzie's sister Mary, she by her sister Mary's stepson). Confused? Who wouldn't be! the whole delicate counterpoint is marred only by the too-convenient deaths of the two unpleasant and redundant (to the plot) male characters. These

deaths, while admittedly very useful, strike a contrived note in a novel in which nothing else has come easily, and it is Lizzie's own fierce independence which has contributed to the complications in her own and other people's romantic relationships.

In a similar vein, *The Far Morning*, while being a novel built round a vast complexity of characters and relationships, also tackles all the issues traditional to novels written about the first half of this century—the effect of World War I, the role of women, and changes in society and the class system. This scenario is now very common in romantic fiction and for a sound reason, as all the components listed above provide an ideal background against which to portray a thoughtful and intelligent heroine.

Winter Landscape and *All Through the Day* both have heroines who at the beginning of their respective stories are subordinate characters, and who by the end are independent, perhaps even dominant. Sally in *Winter Landscape* has our sympathy from the very beginning when, aged 16, she is dominated and overshadowed by her extremely bitchy and totally selfish mother. Sally loves two men: the German prisoner of war Werner and the older married Charles. As in many romantic novels Sally has what seems to be the best of both worlds, and marries the two men in turn, but both she and her two respective husbands go through much unhappiness and self denial.

In contrast, Emily, in *All Through the Day*, is initially selfish and weak, but becomes a strong, independent, and even manipulative businesswoman, although the reader's credulity is somewhat strained when she quotes Nietzsche. In both this novel and *Three Women* the heroine's strength contrasts with the weakness of virtually all the other female characters, and the two novels also have in common an immensely complicated web of relationships. Many of Clarke's characters reveal left-wing leanings, and nowhere is this better handled than in *Sisters and Lovers*, yet another novel of intricately interlocking family and romantic relationships. Here, without proselytizing, Clarke depicts a socialist family background as a lively, challenging environment in which the four sisters of the title grow up.

It is obvious from the name of the heroine of *An Equal Chance* (Harriet Chance-Canossa-Contarini-Cavendish-Georgiadis-Wingfield) that this lady has had more married partners than the average person has had hot dinners. Taken to the United States as a pregnant G.I. bride, Harriet is abandoned by her husband and is forced to become self-reliant, and this she achieves despite, rather than because of, her succession of husbands and other partners. Although in most of Clarke's novels the complexities of the relationships defy belief, the books nevertheless remain interesting and readable. Only when her heroine starts as a comparative nonentity and does not develop in the course of the novel (Katherine in *Under Heaven*), does the narrative ever lack pace and fail to capture the reader's interest.

Under the name of Kate Sedley, Clarke has turned to a different genre, that of crime fiction. Yet, this is not a complete departure for her, as in *Death and the Chapman*, she returns to the 15th century (the setting for some of her earlier novels), in order to swell the ever-growing ranks of bygone amateur detectives. Roger Chapman, pedlar and eponymous sleuth, is a human and likeable character, but without the charm of Ellis Peters' Brother Cadfael (against whom mediaeval detectives must of necessity find themselves measured). As in her previous historical novels, Clarke's style is clear and straightforward, but she is hampered by the necessity to set the scene and fill in the background—the novel is heavily larded with historical and political references; these are interesting, certainly, but do limit the pace of the novel.

Death and the Chapman is obviously destined to be the first of a series, as Roger, telling the story in the first person, twice uses the phrase 'my first case'. Future novels would certainly be stronger, and would fit more comfortably into the mystery genre (this book is, after all, published under a crime imprint), if the fascinating but completely extraneous details of food, drink and clothing were omitted.

—Judith Rhodes

CLAVELL, James (du Maresq).
Nationality: American. **Born**: England, 10 October 1942; moved to the United States in 1953; became citizen, 1963. **Education:** Portsmouth Grammar School; University of Birmingham, 1946-47. **Military Service:** Royal Artillery, 1940–46; prisoner of war in the Far East, 1941–45. **Relations:** married April Stride in 1953; two daughters. **Career:** carpenter, 1953–54. Since 1954 screenwriter, director, and producer. **Recipient:** Writers Guild award, for screenplay, 1964. Ph.D.: University of Maryland, College Park, 1980; D.Litt.: University of Bradford, 1986. **Address:** c/o Foreign Rights Inc, 200 West 57th Street, Suite 1007, New York, New York 10019, USA.

ROMANCE AND HISTORICAL PUBLICATIONS

Novels

Tai-Pan: A Novel of Hong Kong. New York, Atheneum, 1966; London, Joseph, 1967.
Shōgun. New York, Atheneum, and London, Hodder and Stoughton, 1975.
Noble House: A Novel of Contemporary Hong Kong. New York, Delacorte Press, and London, Hodder and Stoughton, 1981.
Whirlwind. New York, Morrow, and London, Hodder and Stoughton, 1986.
Gai-Jin. London, Hodder and Stoughton, 1993.

OTHER PUBLICATIONS

Novel

King Rat. Boston, Little Brown, 1962; London, Joseph, 1963.

Plays

Screenplays: *The Fly*, 1958; *Watusi*, 1959; *Five Gates to Hell*, 1959; *Walk Like a Dragon*, with Daniel Mainwaring, 1960; *The Great Escape*, with W.R. Burnett, 1963; *633 Squadron*, with Howard Koch, 1964; *The Satan Bug*, with Edward Anhalt, 1965; *To Sir, With Love*, 1967; *Where's Jack*, 1968; *The Last Valley*, 1970; *Children's Story . . . But Not for Children*, 1982.

Other

Children's Story, with Michaela Clavell Crisman. New York, Delacorte Press, 1981; London, Hodder and Stoughton, 1982.
Thrump-o-moto, with G. Sharp and Ken Wilson. New York, Delacorte Press, and London, Hodder and Stoughton, 1986.

Editor, *The Art of War*, by Sun Tzu. London, Hodder and Stoughton, 1981; New York, Delacorte Press, 1983.

*

Film Adaptations: *King Rat*, 1965; *Shōgun*, 1981; *Tai-Pan*, 1986; *Noble House*, 1988.

Theatrical Activities:
Director: **Films**—*Five Gates to Hell*, 1959; *Walk Like a Dragon*, 1960; *To Sir, With Love*, 1967; *Where's Jack?*, 1969; *The Last Valley*, 1970; *Children's Story . . . But Not for Children*, 1982.

*   *   *

James Clavell writes a film writer's books—epic, panoramic, swift, with constantly changing viewpoints, intrigue at every level of society, good and evil, broad, vivid washes of colour, conflicts of character and circumstance, startling dramatic effects, and love and sex. Huge in every sense, his multiple plots are demanding, compulsive reading. It takes half a decade to prepare each opus packed with a density and wealth of factual and historical detail.

Throughout his work his prime purpose is to examine the nature of morality and its juxtaposition with pragmatism. How far will a man (almost invariably a man) compromise his principles, if he has any? To what extent should he adapt his own creed, or dignity, or acknowledge that other ways of life may be viable? Adopting a different code of behaviour in order to win, or just survive, may be justifiable, in the short or long term. How much should a man offer to an antipathetic enemy, associate, or lover, in order to achieve his purpose while keeping the relationship in safe balance? For balance read control. Though wry, the author is deeply concerned at the gulf between individuals, sexes, peoples, and cultures, at the clashes between codes and creeds. His design is to get inside, to explain each to the others before time runs out. How far he succeeds is indicated by the huge shift in western attitudes towards everything Japanese after *Shōgun* appeared, first as a record-breaking blockbuster then as a 12-hour television film.

His first novel, *King Rat*, aroused immense public interest, causing establishment anxiety because it appeared to question current codes of morality—which it did not. While undoubtedly cathartic, it is also an incisive metaphysical investigation of how far codes of morality shift under extreme stress. Full of autobiographical material from the author's own nightmares of internment in Changi, from which only one in 15 emerged alive, its theme, as with all Clavell's work, is survival. This novel sears and chills as human values and decencies are stripped away to reveal the raw cruelty and innate selfishness of almost every individual, and a curious, compassionate acceptance of the sins. Another favourite theme, the ambivalence of evil, set intellectual debate rolling. In novelistic terms this is not a good book, with no progression of character, these having already been changed by circumstance. They are stereotypes, but they foretell a development rare in modern writing, and by the time *Whirlwind* appeared he was using some characters allegorically.

Tai-pan has a multi-level, gripping plot about the founding of Hong Kong and the Scot who rose to the top of the pile using guile, merciless manipulation, and the opium trade. Though fictional, historians conceded its vivid portrayal was veracious. Critics began to acknowledge a writer of stature, not literary but commanding as a storyteller courageously investigating alien cultures. His ability to live inside another man's skin forced readers to re-examine their own attitudes and shake their complacency. *Shōgun* consolidated respect for his growing ability to describe both sides of a culture clash, this time in mediaeval Japan. A shipwrecked Englishman is forced, for his own survival, to review all his own tenets of conduct when he becomes amanuensis to a warlord. The density of detail, the deep and accurate depiction of feudal Japan and its outlandish way of thought provoked a public willingness to try to bridge the span of ignorance.

In *Noble House*, during ten days in Hong Kong in 1963, life for Tai-pan descendants is just as cut-throat and barbaric. The intricate struggle between rival companies involves spying, sexual jealousy, murder, double-dealing, and a remarkably vivid evocation of atmosphere. This huge book appears to be written more for entertainment than his other works. Yet there is a distinct development of style and technique, a feature of Clavell's writing. Emotions have almost become characters in their own right, claustrophobia, revenge, yearning, isolation, greed, ruthlessness. In the same year an oddity appeared, *The Children's Story*, a 30 minute lesson in which children's thoughts are poisoned by propaganda. Criticized as a simplistic scrap, it contains the core idea of all Clavell's work—that the human mind is vulnerable, not only in childhood. Where a moral code deteriorates or fragments, where it has been followed blindly or without intelligent justification, there is immense danger of other codes, flawed or inappropriate, taking over, a dated idea but none the less immediate, true and permanent.

The critics were answered chillingly in *Whirlwind*. It describes three terrifying weeks in Iran, when the revolution was at its most chaotic. Noble House and Shōgun descendants struggle to rescue their oil-support helicopters and personnel before mayhem destroys them. Nobody knows who will dominate the splatter of conflicting factions, some indigenous, some puppeteered from abroad, many following tenets riddled with inaccurate misreadings of doctrines or creeds. Progression towards allegory has become disturbingly and insistently philosophical. Clavell is not prophetic but in the highly professional handling of this book he reaches a high standard of clarity and caring, again showing deep concern about the dangers inherent in a clash of cultures. In contrast to *King Rat*'s reception, this book's efforts to enter the minds and souls of non-Western, non-Christian characters have brought few diatribes against the interpretations. All too human, the stereotypes and allegories drive sobering messages home, planting apocalyptic warnings which Clavell urgently defies all civilizations to ignore.

His most recent work, *Gai-Jin*, is yet another big book in which descendants of Shōgun fight modern business battles with the Noble House.

—Margaret Woodward

* * *

CLAYTON, C(olin) Guy.
Nationality: British. **Born:** Horsham, Sussex, 5 November 1936. **Education:** Collyer's Grammar School, Horsham, 1947–55; Hertford College, Oxford, 1958–61, M.A. in English 1961. **Military Service:** Royal Army Education Corps, 1956–58. **Relations:** married Linda-Jane Pashley in 1970; two sons. **Career:** teacher at a boys grammar school, Ashby de la Zouch, Leicestershire, 1961–63, and at Devonport High School for Boys, Plymouth, 1963–76. Since 1976 teacher, St Ninians High School, Douglas, Isle of Man. **Agent:** London Management, 235 Regent Street, London W1A 2JT, England. **Address:** Davian, Main Road, Foxdale, Isle of Man, United Kingdom.

ROMANCE AND HISTORICAL PUBLICATIONS

Novels (series: Blakeney Papers in all books)

Daughters of the Revolution. London, Macdonald, 1984.
Such Mighty Rage. London, Macdonald, 1985.
Bordeaux Red. London, Macdonald, 1986.

*

C. Guy Clayton comments:
The initial idea for the Blakeney papers came in a single moment. I happened to glance through a copy of *The Scarlet Pimpernel* I came upon while sorting out a school stock cupboard and two separate compartments of my mind came together with a click. Why, I asked myself was all fiction of the French Revolution ignorant of

any development in historical knowledge since Lamartine and Carlyle? What was needed was an energetic series of novels showing at least some sympathy with the revolutionary point of view. Baroness Orczy's heroine was a potential gem, provided of course one stripped away the sentimental façade and exposed the woman she really was; an actress in the Comédie Française who knew real people and lived through the most extraordinary political event of the past thousand years. So that was my purpose; to write living stories of the revolutionary period, while at the same time remaining true to the real events as the 20th century sees them rather than a 19th-century myth.

* * *

There are as many versions of history as there are authors. Historians rewrite truths—certain occurrences cannot be denied, but their significance is open to interpretation, after which the events themselves sink into comparative oblivion. C. Guy Clayton adapts this process, presenting the already invented world of the Scarlet Pimpernel as historical fact, based on a contemporary manuscript complete with editorial notes. It becomes impossible to distinguish the fiction, and his resulting trilogy is richer than the original Baroness Orczy story and more realistic than a bare listing of the highlights of the French Revolution.

The narrator and central character is Marie Callot, daughter of a small-town lawyer who changes her identity and sex at the drop of a powdered wig. En route she writes the history of France, England, and the rest of Europe too. She first makes her mark when, as a teenager, she composes a poem on behalf of Robespierre enabling him to join the Societé des Rosati and thus further his career, becomes a member of the Jacobin Club agitating for a new France, and eventually even marries Percy Blakeney to spy for her country. What she fails to do is create herself with similar gusto.

Marie is intelligent, but never considers the academic reasons or future effects of her actions. Theory and speechifying have always precipitated the most crucial events in her life and consequently she has no great faith in the books she reads. Living for the moment means she can never be a full person with a developed philosophy of how she got there, why, and where to now, but her strength is this simplicity. Immediate reality is all that matters and without this lack of self-awareness she would become tangled in doubt and end up guillotined with the people she hates.

Altering appearance and personality leads occasionally to inconsistency. It seems hard to reconcile the honoured figure who was present at the storming of the Bastille with the coquette who later devotes herself to redecorating her new husband's stately home and complains about the ineptitude of English plasterers, but, thanks to the narrator's skills, this reconciliation happens. Marie exemplifies the flightiness of the stereotypical irrational female (albeit with a more developed instinct for self-preservation then most) but is accepted by us because of her style.

She tells her story in lively ingenuous language, with enough self-deprecation to hover this side of false modesty. She claims that everyone is equal and later scorns her husband's common touch with inn-keepers and ostlers, but we remain charmed. Marie's disgust with the two tramps scavenging the smouldering remains of a convent is our disgust because we see the scene through her eyes, and like her we dismiss it because we too realise that the Revolution has solved few problems. She expresses her cynicism with a witty remark, and consequently we remain on her side and at one with her perceptions.

Marie is bullied, raped, insulted, beaten, pursued, imprisoned, and virtually drowned. She betrays, commits sacrilege, murders, steals, fights, and impersonates her way through life. It's gory, but we are reminded of this only occasionally when she interrupts her pacy tale with a chilling phrase or sentence. At the height of her success at the Comédie Française for example, she announces in a new, hollow tone that 'one night after the performance I had a caller at the theatre' thus heralding a change for the worse. Despite her enthusiastic descriptions, danger is never very far away, but her humour generally protects us from it.

In addition, the bloodiness of the Revolution itself is kept in perspective by high comedy. The account of her wedding night, the coach-trip she shares with her lover, former paramour, and husband crammed into a confined space getting along famously and the constant bumbling of the francophobic Dewhurst are some of many moments of pure farce which belie the violence of the times. Marie is not only the prima donna of the French theatre, she is very much Clayton's leading lady, playing a part worthy of Racine on the stage of one of the most important events of the 18th century.

Marie's view of history is that it only justifies the Revolution. The author is equally dismissive. He uses history to achieve objectivity (which is the legitimate stance of the genuine historian) and then treats events and chronology with the manipulation of the novelist and the disdain of the farceur. What happens when is less important than what it signifies—a means of distancing themes. Issues such as the role of women in a society where their only access to power is through deceit or seduction and the nature of violence as a revolutionary tool appear frequently, but no solutions are offered.

England's answer is rule by the vapid and fatuous Prinny, and a parliamentary process which depends on the appearance of Whig or Tory on ball invitation lists for its effectiveness—an unacceptable compromise of democracy. France fares no better, because the successors to the aristocratic order prove that mastery still belongs to human imperfection. Robespierre is paranoid and every provincial civil servant is bureaucratic, corrupt, or just plain stupid. This is what Marie should oppose, but tragically she lacks the analytical skills to see it, and the position to do anything about it. However, our disappointment never lasts for long because of Clayton's skill in blending so many disparate elements—history, fiction, myth, drama, and adventure with very stylish wit.

—L.M. Quinn

CLEEVE, Brian (Brendan Talbot).
Nationality: Irish. Born: Thorpe Bay, Essex, England, 22 November 1921. Education: Selwyn House, Broadstairs, Kent, 1930–35; St Edward's School, Oxford, 1935–38; University of South Africa, Johannesburg, 1951–53, B.A. 1953; National University of Ireland, Dublin, 1954–56, Ph.D. 1956. Relations: married Veronica McAdie in 1945; two daughters. Career: served in the British Merchant Navy, 1938–45; freelance journalist in South Africa, 1948–54, and in Ireland since 1954. Broadcaster, Radio Telefis Eireann, Dublin, 1962–72. Address: 60 Heytesbury Lane, Ballsbridge, Dublin 4, Ireland.

ROMANCE AND HISTORICAL PUBLICATIONS

Novels

Cry of Morning. London, Joseph, 1971; as The Triumph of O'Rourke, New York, Doubleday, 1972.
Sara. London, Cassell, and New York, Coward McCann, 1976.
Kate. London, Cassell, and New York, Coward McCann, 1977.
Judith. London, Cassell, and New York, Coward McCann, 1978.
Hester. London, Cassell, 1979; New York, Coward McCann, 1980.
The House on the Rock. London, Watkins, 1980.
The Seven Mansions. London, Watkins, 1980.
The Fourth Mary. Dublin, Co-op, 1982.

A Woman of Fortune. Dingle, Kerry, Brandon, 1993.

OTHER PUBLICATIONS

Novels

The Far Hills. London, Jarrolds, 1952.
Portrait of My City. London, Jarrolds, 1952.
Birth of a Dark Soul. London, Jarrolds, 1953; as The Night Winds, Boston, Houghton Mifflin, 1954.
Assignment to Vengeance. London, Hammond, 1961.
Death of a Painted Lady. London, Hammond, 1962; New York, Random House, 1963.
Death of a Wicked Servant. London, Hammond, 1963; New York, Random House, 1964.
Vote X for Treason. London, Collins, 1964; New York, Random House, 1965; as Counterspy, London, Lancer, 1966.
Dark Blood, Dark Terror. New York, Random House, 1965; London, Hammond, 1966.
The Judas Goat. London, Hammond, 1966; as Vice Isn't Private, New York, Random House, 1966.
Violent Death of a Bitter Englishman. New York, Random House, 1967; London, Corgi, 1969.
You Must Never Go Back. New York, Random House, 1968.
Exit from Prague. London, Corgi, 1970; as Escape from Prague, New York, Pinnacle, 1973.
Tread Softly in This Place. London, Cassell, and New York, Day, 1972.
The Dark Side of the Sun. London, Cassell, 1973.
A Question of Inheritance. London, Cassell, 1974; as For Love of Crannagh Castle, New York, Dutton, 1975.

Short Stories

The Horse Thieves of Ballysaggert and Other Stories. Cork, Mercier Press, 1966.

Other

Colonial Policies in Africa. Johannesburg, St Benedict's House, 1954.
Dictionary of Irish Writers. Cork, Mercier Press, 3 vols, 1967–71; revised edition, with Anne M. Brady, as A Biographical Dictionary of Irish Writers, Mullingar, Westmeath, Lilliput Press, and New York, St Martin's Press, 1 vol, 1985.
1938: A World Vanishing. London, Buchan and Enright, 1982.
A View of the Irish. London, Buchan and Enright, 1983.

Editor, W.B. Yeats and the Designing of Ireland's Coinage. Dublin, Dolmen Press, 1972.

*

Manuscript Collection: Mugar Memorial Library, Boston University.

Brian Cleeve comments:
I began writing romantic fiction by mistake. I meant to write a historical family saga covering the 19th century, beginning with a Spanish gypsy orphan in the Peninsular War. She took over the book and the whole novel became her story, as Sara. People liked the book, and I wrote three more, with vaguely similar themes, and young heroines in extravagant, romantic, yet historically accurate (I hope) situations. I thought of them as historical novels rather than as romances. I wanted to explore the idea of young women striving for personal liberation at a period when this was becoming even more difficult to achieve than it had been a hundred years earlier.

* * *

Irish writer Brian Cleeve has achieved international attention for his hard-hitting, sometimes brutal analyses of national and international conflicts in his spy and murder novels, and some of these same qualities and concerns are also reflected in his romances. Therein he has been particularly concerned with man, government, and religion's cruelty to women. His hard-boiled crime novels begin the pattern of rape and sadism, hypocrisy, racism, class conflicts, and 'machismo' that his romances continue to explore from a historical perspective.

Cleeve's Regency romances continue past concerns, but with a new twist, following Dickensian patterns to expose the horrors of 19th-century life (the wars and revolutions, the poverty and crime, the prisons and insane asylums) and to provide a vivid picture of the daily life of young people trapped and initially defenceless amid the follies of their day. There are vivid descriptions of the snares and seductions of Regency London: gaming houses and gentlemen's clubs, sparring rings and cockpits, country-house weekends and an underworld of pickpockets and assassins. These works are also Dickensian in their sentimentality and their emphasis on class differences as a major source of evil. Their villains are ruthless and powerful, their heroines initially naive and vulnerable.

In *Judith*, a young lady, pressured by her father's illness and the resultant financial necessity, consorts with smugglers and suffers the consequences—choosing the brutal horrors of Bedlam and the unforgiving poverty of London streets over a loveless, shameful marriage to a rich pervert. The description of Bedlam is particularly grim and terrible. The heroine of *Sara*, a gypsy girl trained in rural witchcraft, works in a disreputable gambling house, while that of *Kate*, an actress by trade and a rebel by heart, consorts with the London 'Upright Men' to promote smuggling operations. Sara has witnessed her parents' slaughter by Bonaparte's soldiers in Spain, while Kate is the sole survivor of a political massacre; both barely escape the London white slave market. The female protagonists in *Hester* are caught up in the monstrosities and injustices of the French Revolution, its glories and insanities, and act on principles, not necessity; Hester herself learns to ride, fight and kill like a man, to accept discomfort and daily knowledge of possible death, and yet to retain her feminine allure and self-respect.

Each of these works focuses on women from the past who are swept along by history, trapped by sexual roles, and forced into choices that can destroy them; they must learn to deal with human cruelty, prejudice, hypocrisy, and greed. Their histories are a tangled web of love and intrigue, class conflicts, and sexual battles, as they seek to liberate themselves from the strictures of a hypocritical society and learn to trust instinct, to reassess old values, and finally to seize their destiny like a man. Writing in a feminist tradition, Cleeve depicts women who are as passionate, proud, resourceful, and daring as men, tossed by fate, bound by social manacles, oppressed by brutal males, but capable of rising above their psychological, economic, and sometimes physical chains to find meaning, purpose, and strength. It is as if he sees in the abuse of women the same mentality at work that he depicts so vividly in his treatment of racism in South Africa.

Cleeve captures the nuances of street slang and dialect, and includes highly sensory, detailed descriptions of place. His historical details are accurate and credible, and vividly reflect an interplay of culture and values and opposing philosophies. His main characters are alienated from each other and their world; absurdist figures, out of place and out of step in a sinister universe, a world gone mad, one that sweeps them blindly and helplessly toward the unknown, sometimes disastrously, sometimes successfully. Ultimately what makes life endurable are the human touchstones; his heroines' sense of personal responsibility for the weak, the injured, the vulnerable lends them strength and helps them survive and thrive. Through his romances Cleeve provides graphic and realistic images of man's inhumanity to man, to take a moral stance against political and social oppression and against inhumanity in its varied forms. He faces pain and human misery head on, vividly evoking the shivers of a malaria attack or the pangs of chronic dysentery. His heroine, Sara, is a shining model of goodness set against the wickedness and degradation of most of Cleeve's characters; an orphan herself, she burdens her life with caring for orphans, and finds it a joy, as she argues, 'When you see a child cold and hungry and naked and afraid, it is quite a natural thing to wish to take care of it'.

Cleeve's Irish works at their best are novels of manners, capturing shifting Irish scenes, interweaving sub-themes and sub-plots, interspersing social commentary, and drawing a variety of vivid character portraits: fanatical communist, radical priest, itinerant tinker, posing artist, real estate tycoon, television commentator, small-town girl made good. *Cry of Morning*, in particular, has been called 'one of the best recent novels in modern Ireland', partly because of its rendering of Ireland's metamorphosis from a 19th-century holdover to a 20th-century economically important nation and its questioning of values that place country above citizens. Ultimately, Cleeve's vision of Ireland and its people is one of paradox—a charming mix of good and bad.

Cleeve's most recent efforts, controversial religious studies that have become bestsellers in Ireland, are the stories of people who lived in Jerusalem at the time of the Crucifixion. Written to convey an unorthodox, though Catholic, spiritual view, they defy classification. *The Fourth Mary* in particular has a striking point of view: that of a servant girl attached to the High Priestess of a sado-masochistic cult, Judas's lover; in other words, it is the Crucifixion story told from the viewpoint of Christ's enemies, enemies who planned it and consider it a triumph. The other two books, *The House on the Rock* and *The Seven Mansions*, provide the historical background preparatory to the Crucifixion. Despite its religious focus, this trilogy graphically portrays the hatred, sadism, and sexuality of characters caught up in events of historical moment.

Cleeve brings to history and romance a social conscience and raises questions of social justice, national character, and personal responsibility. Even his religious histories powerfully dramatize the excuses that ordinary men and women invent to avoid involvement and to deny the realities of suffering and oppression. In sum, the key lesson of Cleeve's canon is that any violation of human dignity and freedom, whether race against race, class against class, or man against woman, is a reversion to the animal savagery of man's Darwinian origins, and must be fought tooth and claw if civilization and mankind are to endure.

—Gina Macdonald

CLEUGH, Sophia.
Nationality: American. **Relations:** married Dennis Cleugh.

ROMANCE AND HISTORICAL PUBLICATIONS

Novels

Matilda, Governess of the English. New York, Macmillan, 1924; London, Butterworth, 1925.
Ernestine Sophie. New York, Macmillan, 1925; London, Butterworth, 1926.
Jeanne Margot. New York, Macmillan, and London, Butterworth, 1927.
A Common Cheat. New York, Macmillan, and London, Butterworth, 1928.

Spring. New York, Macmillan, and London, Hodder and Stoughton, 1929.
Song Bird. Boston, Houghton Mifflin, and London, Hodder and Stoughton, 1930.
Enchanting Clementina. London, Hodder and Stoughton, 1930; Boston, Houghton Mifflin, 1931.
The Daisy Boy. London, Hodder and Stoughton, 1931; as *Young Jonathan*, Boston, Houghton Mifflin, 1932.
Loyal Lady. London, Hodder and Stoughton, 1932; as *Anne Marguerite*, Boston, Houghton Mifflin, 1932.
The Hazards of Belinda. London, Hodder and Stoughton, and Boston, Houghton Mifflin, 1933.
Lindy Lou. London, Hodder and Stoughton, 1934.
The Angel Who Couldn't Sing. London, Hodder and Stoughton, and New York, Doubleday, 1935.
Wind Which Moved a Ship. London, Newnes, and New York, Doubleday, 1936.

*   *   *

Sophia Cleugh, a romance writer of the 1920s and 1930s, plunges the modern reader into another world. Few things can reveal the changes that have occurred in gothic romances as vividly as actually reading material written over half a century ago. Two aspects disturb the modern reader. Cleugh's persistent habit of alternating lengthy involved and often convoluted sentences with sentence fragments is particularly jarring. Frequent rereading for sense is essential for the reader unfamiliar with this style. Also disturbing to most modern readers are the lengthy descriptive passages as well as detailed discussions of the most minute details of daily life accompanied by thorough relating of all accompanying emotional responses.

In *The Daisy Boy* numerous pages are devoted to desultory descriptions and idle chatter during an afternoon tea while Jonathan is assiduously digging daisies from the lawn. An even greater impasse to the plot is apparent in *Matilda, Governess of the English* during numerous exchanges between the Duchess and her maid, Mrs Kincaid. In *Spring* the initial descriptions and the languorous pace of the novel recall another more leisurely time and place when the reader could luxuriate in a novel that was much ado about little.

Yet, while Cleugh's plots move at the same pace as do those of Henry James, her fine wit more than compensates for the absence of fast-paced action or heady romance, or even great mystery. A multitude of aphorisms and clichés only serve to add a special charm and authenticity to these early works ('But, as we have heard time and again, tread on the veriest worm too often, and the creature will turn').

Romantic names such as Sweet William, Gilliflower, Larkspur, Nina, and various titles of nobility abound in Cleugh's novels. She also shows a rather 19th-century interest in children. Children of various ages figure prominently in all of her books, and they are not just property and appendages of their parents but complete personages in their own rights and often described with great wit and clarity.

Although reading aloud is no longer in vogue, were it a habit to which we might someday return, Cleugh, with her often clever turning of a phrase, should be read aloud. While the plot lines—of young maidens seeking a romance not guided by their Mamas or poor young people making good—are not original, a novel which treats language as if it were a treasure has lasting value. In addition, Sophia Cleugh's novels remain as representative novels of manners of another time and place.

—Joan Hinkemeyer

———

CLEVELAND, John.   See **McELFRESH, Adeline.**

———

COATES, Sheila.   See **LAMB, Charlotte.**

———

COCKRELL, Marian.
Nationality: American. **Born**: Marian Brown, Birmingham, Alabama, 15 March 1909. **Education:** Sophie Newcomb College, New Orleans, 1926–29; Metropolitan Art School, New York, 1929–30. **Relations:** married Francis Marian Cockrell in 1931; one daughter. **Agent**: Oliver G. Swan, Collier Associates, 280 Madison Avenue, New York, New York 10016, USA. **Address:** 6118 Circle Creek Drive, Boones Mill, Virginia 24065, USA.

ROMANCE AND HISTORICAL PUBLICATIONS

Novels

Yesterday's Madness. New York, Harper, 1943.
Lillian Harley. New York, Harper, 1943.
Dark Waters, with Frank Cockrell. Cleveland, World, 1944.
Something Between. New York, Harper, 1946.
The Revolt of Sarah Perkins. New York, McKay, 1965; London, Hurst and Blackett, 1966.
Mixed Blessings. New York, Times Books, 1978.
The Misadventures of Bethany Price. New York, Times Books, 1979.
Mixed Company. New York, Popular Library, 1979.

OTHER PUBLICATIONS

Plays

Screenplay: *Dark Waters*, with Joan Harrison, 1945.

Television Plays: scripts for *Alfred Hitchcock* series.

Other

Shadow Castle (for children). New York, McGraw Hill, 1945.

*

Manuscript Collection: Mugar Memorial Library, Boston University.

Marian Cockrell comments:
I enjoy writing. I write to interest and entertain, with life-like characters and amusing conversation. The protagonists are all women, and tend to develop a sense of independence in trying to solve their own problems in their particular time and circumstances. I now prefer to write about the past—early 1900s or 1870s. There is always a love story, but the books are not *about* the love story, but about the difficulties of the heroine, of which the love story is a part.

*   *   *

Marian Cockrell writes well-written books with fully developed plots about community life in rural America. Her novels contain details about life in small towns, and her protagonists are very much a part of a greater picture. Her attention to detail and her interest in depicting the lives of her secondary characters help to paint a broader canvas and make her books an enjoyable read.

Although Cockrell wrote a number of contemporary romances in the 1940s, her historical romances are more interesting. Her heroines are women who have to deal with the *problem* of being female in a world in which the options open to them are limited. Thus, Bethany, in *The Misadventures of Bethany Price*, finds herself married to a much older man when she is 16, and is raped by her stepson. Finding that doing things according to convention doesn't work in her favour, she runs away to a small town—and although she makes friends she also finds that her waywardness attracts hostility.

Sarah, the independent heroine of *The Revolt of Sarah Perkins*, is also a woman who learns to know her own mind. Trapped into living a life of drudgery with her brother and his family, Sarah responds to an advertisement for a job as a schoolteacher in a small mining community. Sarah doesn't realize that she has been picked for her lack of looks as the schoolmistresses keep getting married—the town has had 51 teachers in two years. She arrives to find her school in shambles and she immediately comes into conflict with Lucas (Luke) Ferguson, a 37-year-old widow with a young son.

Life in a growing frontier town is depicted in glorious detail through the eyes of Sarah who has to live in a different household each month. She slowly emerges from being a pale girl, lacking in confidence, into a independent strong-minded and opinionated woman who fights hard for what she thinks is right. She comes into conflict with the town over her decision to allow a half-Indian child to attend school. Most of the community has lost someone to the Indians and the hostility that the people feel is almost tangible. Luke comes to support Sarah and begins to court her.

Sarah is on the verge of calling a town meeting when there is an Indian raid. Cockrell describes the build-up to the incident and the reactions of different town members to it. Many people are killed including most of the men in town at the time. The happier side of the incident is that the town accepts Redbird, the half-Indian child, because of her behaviour during the raid.

Cockrell creates minor characters depicting their eccentricities and bigotries in glorious detail. She humorously tells the reader of the town's mad behaviour when Fish Williams, the local trader comes to town, and recounts the events of the town meetings called for seemingly small events. We also learn of the extra-marital affair between Alice and George Bailey. Alice is one of Sarah's closest friends and is a fierce ally when Sarah decides to teach Redbird; she is one of the few people who allows her son to continue attending school. The reader soon learns that Georgie is not Alice's son but her nephew and that she had run away with him rather than let him fall into the hands of his grandfather. When Georgie's grandfather comes to find him it is Sarah's intervention and calm sensibility that prevents tragedy.

Sarah gets engaged to Martin Pope, the local newsman, when she is seen kissing him by two of the town's most malicious gossips. Although she initially believes herself in love with Martin, she knows he is love with someone else. However, it is only when Luke comes storming in to declare his love for Sarah and his disbelief over her engagement that she realizes how much she cares for him. As she explains to Martin later, 'When I think of being with Luke, I seem to settle down like a cat on a cushion in front of a fire. I'm where I belong'.

Mixed Blessings tells the story of a young woman trying to make a living for herself and her brother in a small southern town at the turn of the century. Like Sarah Perkins, she finds herself involved in the lives of the people around her. This ability to draw the reader into community life is what makes Cockrell's books so appealing—this and the feeling that the main protagonists exist in a real world in which laughter, love, and sadness exist.

—P. Campbell

———

COFFIN, Geoffrey. See **MASON, F. Van Wyck.**

———

COFFMAN, Virginia (Edith). 1914—. See 2nd edition, 1990.

———

COGHLAN, Peggie. See **STIRLING, Jessica.**

———

COLLIN, Marion.
Nationality: British. **Born:** Marion Cripps, Aylesbury, Buckinghamshire, 12 May 1928. **Relations:** married to John W. H. Collin; two children. **Career:** student nurse, Isle of Wight, 1945–48; medical secretary, London, 1948–52; secretary, 10th International Congress of Dermatologists, London; fiction editor, *Woman's Own*, London, 1952–56; lecturer in business and commerce, West Kent College of Further Education, Tonbridge, Kent, 1973–88. **Agent:** Elaine Greene Ltd, 31 Newington Green, London N16 9PU, England. **Address:** 20 Eridge Road, Tunbridge Wells, Kent TN4 8HJ, England.

ROMANCE AND HISTORICAL PUBLICATIONS

Novels

Nurse Maria. London, Mills and Boon, 1963.
Nurse at the Top. London, Mills and Boon, and Toronto, Harlequin, 1964.
Doctors Three. London, Mills and Boon, 1964; Toronto, Harlequin, 1965.
Nurse in the Dark. London, Mills and Boon, 1965.
The Doctor's Delusion. London, Mills and Boon, 1967; Toronto, Harlequin, 1968.
The Shadow of the Court. London, Mills and Boon, 1967.
The Man on the Island. London, Mills and Boon, 1968.
Sun on the Mountain. London, Mills and Boon, 1969.
Nurse on an Island. London, Mills and Boon, 1970.
Calling Dr Savage. London, Mills and Boon, 1970.
House of Dreams. London, Mills and Boon, 1971.
Sawdust and Spangles. London, Mills and Boon, 1972.
Nurses in the House. London, Mills and Boon, 1989.
A Catch of the Day. Toronto, Harlequin, 1990.
A Sparrow Falls. New York, Ballantine, 1990.

OTHER PUBLICATIONS

Other

Romantic Fiction, with Anne Britton. London, Boardman, 1960.
Hospital Office Practice. London, Ballière Tindall, 1981; 5th edition, with Michael Drury, as *The Medical Secretary's and Receptionist's Handbook*, 1986.

*

Marion Collin comments:

As most of my titles indicate, I have a predilection for medical romances, but I also enjoy the research entailed in historical and foreign settings. While the former is the basis for future work, I do not rule out the occasional foray into a more exotic field.

* * *

In *Romantic Fiction* Marion Collin and Anne Britton presented their formula for the successful love story: *girl meets boy, girl gets boy, girl loses boy, girl gets boy.* Having arrived at her formula, Collin used it for her first novel, *Nurse Maria*, and thereafter rang the changes upon it. Her principal medium is the doctor/nurse romance (recognizable by title), with the splendid variant of the doctor/doctor romance in which the heroine is also a doctor (*Doctors Three* and *The Doctor's Delusion*). The atmosphere of the hospital, even of the operating theatre, pervades these books. The descriptions of disease, treatments, and surgery are convincing, and are frequently not for the faint-hearted ('The rotting appendix reared us easily, and ... she severed it from the bowel'—*The Doctor's Delusion*). The smaller details of hospital life are there too—nurses chatting in the sluice, the eternal bedpan, etc. There is a certain incongruity, no doubt occurring in real life, about love and the hospital ('She could never rid herself of guilt when he kissed her in uniform.' 'She had created love out of a dream. The real thing had been under her nose up on Men's Surgical'—*Nurse at the Top*). We have to assume that as hospitals can produce medically dramatic situations endlessly they can also produce *romantically* dramatic situations in considerable profusion (while still functioning perfectly).

All of Collin's novels except one are set in modern times (*The Shadow of the Court* is set in the Crimean War). Locations range from an industrial English city (notably St Luke's Infirmary, later General Hospital, in Manchester), to exotic islands in the Caribbean, to tea-plantations in Ceylon. Some later novels have non-medical settings and non-medical heroines: Jo in *House of Dreams* is a model, Kate in *Sawdust and Spangles* is Girl Friday in a circus, and Jan in *Sun on the Mountain* is P.A. in her father's tea company. However, the lure of the stethoscope is strong and the characters in these novels are never too far from medicine: Jo suffers from a burst appendix, accidents happen in the circus, and in Ceylon Jan meets a glamorous woman doctor and her widowed father takes up with a lapsed nurse.

The heroines of Collin's novels are capable, honest, serious young women who are conscious of their responsibilities. Her medical heroines are dedicated, competent professionals, sometimes almost cases of Lamp Fever; they always put their patients first, even when their private lives are turmoils of emotion (which they are most of the time, until a happy conclusion is reached). If Collin's heroines do have a fault, it is their naivety which, helped along by their dedication to medicine and other responsibilities, makes them unaware of their physical attractiveness. The heroine is frequently contrasted with some predatory pussycat *femme fatale* who wreaks havoc in her romantic life. But this is all part of the growing-up process which accompanies each heroine's progress towards true love as she resists or sees through the attractions of some spurious (or merely less earnest) charmer who temporarily impedes her path to the worthier man. Collin is particularly good at providing male red herrings, so that the reader is as much in two minds about possible husbands as the heroine.

—Jean Buchanan

COLT, Zandra.   See **STEVENSON, Florence.**

CONWAY, Celine.   See **BLAIR, Kathryn.**

CONLEE, Jaelyn.   See **PRESTON, Fayrene.**

COOKSON, Catherine.
Pseudonym: Catherine Marchant. **Nationality:** British. **Born:** Catherine Ann McMullen, Tyne Dock, County Durham, 20 June 1906. **Relations:** married Thomas H. Cookson in 1940. **Recipient:** Royal Society of Literature Winifred Holtby prize, for *The Round Tower*, 1968. M.A.: University of Newcastle upon Tyne, 1983; D.Litt.: University of Sunderland, 1992. OBE (Officer, Order of the British Empire), 1985; DBE (Dame, Order of the British Empire), 1993. **Agent:** Anthony Sheil Associates Ltd, 43 Doughty Street, London WC1N 2LF, England. **Address:** White Lodge, 23 Glastonbury Grove, Jesmond, Newcastle upon Tyne, NE2 2HB, England.

ROMANCE AND HISTORICAL PUBLICATIONS

Novels (series: Bill Bailey; Hamilton; Mallen; Mary Ann; Tilly Trotter)

Kate Hannigan. London, Macdonald, 1950; New York, Bantam, 1972.
The Fifteen Streets. London, Macdonald, 1952; New York, Bantam, 1973.
Colour Blind. London, Macdonald, 1953; New York, New American Library, 1977.
A Grand Man. London, Macdonald, 1954; New York, Macmillan, 1955.
Maggie Rowan. London, Macdonald, 1954; New York, New American Library, 1975.
The Lord and Mary Ann. London, Macdonald, 1956; New York, Morrow, 1975.
Rooney. London, Macdonald, 1957; New York, Bantam, 1976.
The Devil and Mary Ann. London, Macdonald, 1958; New York, Morrow, 1976.
The Menagerie. London, Macdonald, 1958; New York, Bantam, 1975.
Slinky Jane. London, Macdonald, 1959; New York, New American Library, 1976.
Fanny McBride. London, Macdonald, 1959; New York, Bantam, 1976.
Fenwick Houses. London Macdonald, 1960; New York, Bantam, 1973.
Love and Mary Ann. London, Macdonald, 1961; New York, Morrow, 1976.
The Garment. London, Macdonald, 1962; New York, New American Library, 1974.
Life and Mary Ann. London, Macdonald, 1962; New York, Morrow, 1977.
The Blind Miller. London, Macdonald, 1963; New York, New American Library, 1974.
Marriage and Mary Ann. London, Macdonald, 1964; New York, Morrow, 1978.
Hannah Massey. London, Macdonald, 1964; New York, New American Library, 1973.
Mary Ann's Angels. London, Macdonald, 1965; New York, Morrow, 1978.
The Long Corridor. London, Macdonald, 1965; New York, New American Library, 1976.
The Unbaited Trap. London, Macdonald, 1966; New York, New American Library, 1974.
Mary Ann and Bill. London, Macdonald, 1967; New York, Morrow, 1979.
Katie Mulholland. London, Macdonald, and Indianapolis, Bobbs Merrill, 1967.
The Round Tower. London, Macdonald, 1968; New York, New American Library, 1975.

The Glass Virgin. Indianapolis, Bobbs Merrill, 1969; London, Macdonald, 1970.

The Nice Bloke. London, Macdonald, 1969; as *The Husband*, New York, New American Library, 1976.

The Invitation. London, Macdonald, 1970; New York, New American Library, 1974.

The Dwelling Place. London, Macdonald, and Indianapolis, Bobbs Merrill, 1971.

Feathers in the Fire. London, Macdonald, 1971; Indianapolis, Bobbs Merrill, 1972.

Pure as the Lily. London, Macdonald, 1972; Indianapolis, Bobbs Merrill, 1973.

The Mallen Novels. London, Heinemann, 1979.

    The Mallen Girl. New York, Dutton, 1973; London, Heinemann, 1974.

    The Mallen Streak. London, Heinemann, and New York, Dutton, 1973.

    The Mallen Lot. New York, Dutton, 1974; as *The Mallen Litter*, London, Heinemann, 1974.

The Invisible Cord. London, Heinemann, and New York, Dutton, 1975.

The Gambling Man. London, Heinemann, and New York, Morrow, 1975.

The Tide of Life. London, Heinemann, and New York, Morrow, 1976.

The Girl. London, Heinemann, and New York, Morrow, 1977.

The Cinder Path. London, Heinemann, and New York, Morrow, 1978.

The Man Who Cried. London, Heinemann, and New York, Morrow, 1979.

Tilly Trotter. London, Heinemann, 1980; as *Tilly*, New York, Morrow, 1980.

Tilly Trotter Wed. London, Heinemann, 1981; as *Tilly Wed*, New York, Morrow, 1981.

Tilly Trotter Widowed. London, Heinemann, 1982; as *Tilly Alone*, New York, Morrow, 1982.

The Whip. London, Heinemann, and New York, Summit, 1983; as *The Spaniard's Gift*, New York, Summit, 1989.

Hamilton. London, Heinemann, 1983.

The Black Velvet Gown. London, Heinemann, and New York, Summit, 1984.

Goodbye Hamilton. London, Heinemann, 1984.

A Dinner of Herbs. London, Heinemann, 1985; as *The Bannaman Legacy*, New York, Summit, 1985.

Harold (Hamilton). London, Heinemann, 1985.

The Moth. London, Heinemann, and New York, Summit, 1986.

Bill Bailey. London, Heinemann, 1986.

The Parson's Daughter. London, Heinemann, and New York, Summit, 1987.

Bill Bailey's Lot. London, Bantam, 1987.

The Cultured Handmaiden. London, Heinemann, 1988.

Bill Bailey's Daughter. London, Bantam, 1988.

The Harrogate Secret. New York, Summit, 1988; London, Bantam, 1989.

The Bailey Chronicles. New York, Summit, 1989.

The Black Candle. London, Bantam, 1989; New York, Summit, 1990.

The Wingless Bird. London, Bantam, 1990.

The Gillyvors. London, Bantam, 1990.

The Rag Nymph. London, Bantam, 1991.

My Beloved Son. London, Bantam, 1991.

The House of Women. London, Bantam, 1992.

The Maltese Angel. London, Bantam, 1992.

The Year of the Virgins. London, Bantam, 1993.

The Golden Straw. London, Bantam, 1993.

Novels as Catherine Marchant

Heritage of Folly. London, Macdonald, 1962; New York, Lancer, 1965.

The Fen Tiger. London, Macdonald, 1963; as *The House on the Fens*, New York, Lancer, 1965.

House of Men. London, Macdonald, 1963; New York, Lancer, 1965.

The Mists of Memory. New York, Lancer, 1965.

Evil at Roger's Cross. New York, Lancer, 1966; as *The Iron Facade*, London, Heinemann, 1976.

Miss Martha Mary Crawford. London, Heinemann, 1975; New York, Morrow, 1976.

The Slow Awakening. London, Heinemann, 1976; New York, Morrow, 1977.

OTHER PUBLICATIONS

Play

Screenplay: *Jacqueline*, with others, 1956.

Other

Matty Doolin (for children). London, Macdonald, 1965; New York, New American Library, 1976.

Joe and the Gladiator (for children). London, Macdonald, 1968; New York, New American Library, 1977.

Our Kate: An Autobiography. London, Macdonald, 1969; Indianapolis, Bobbs Merrill, 1971; revised edition, Macdonald, 1982.

The Nipper (for children). London, Macdonald, and Indianapolis, Bobbs Merrill, 1970.

Blue Baccy (for children). London, Macdonald, 1972; Indianapolis, Bobbs Merrill, 1973; as *Rory's Fortune*, London, Futura, 1988.

Our John Willy (for children). London, Macdonald, and Indianapolis, Bobbs Merrill, 1974.

Mrs Flannagan's Trumpet (for children). London, Macdonald and Jane's, 1976; New York, Lothrop, 1980.

Go Tell It to Mrs Golightly (for children). London, Macdonald and Jane's, 1977; New York, Lothrop, 1980.

Lanky Jones (for children). London, Macdonald, and New York, Lothrop, 1981.

Nancy Nutall and the Mongrel (for children). London, Macdonald, 1982; New York, Simon and Schuster, 1990.

Catherine Cookson Country. London, Heinemann, 1986.

Let Me Make Myself Plain. London, Bantam, 1988.

*

Film Adaptations: *Rooney*, 1958; *The Mallens*, 1979; *The Black Velvet Gown*, 1991; *The Fifteen Streets*, 1991; *The Black Candle*, 1991.

Manuscript Collection: Boston University.

*   *   *

Catherine Cookson is a literary phenomenon: not only is she a prolific and exceedingly popular author (for ten consecutive years she has earned the highest Public Lending Right payments), but from the early 1950s when her first novels were published, she has turned the world of popular fiction on its head. She was the first popular writer consistently to use working-class scenarios and to feature serious working-class heroes and heroines. Previous writers had written about the working classes, of course, but usually from the outside, and frequently treating individuals as somewhat comic characters; the nearest many writers ever got to the working class was, by misconception, in fact the manufacturing class. Cookson has spawned a long line of 'clog and shawl' imitators (Marie Joseph, Jessica Stirling, Lena Kennedy, etc.), and it is a tribute not only to their own capabilities but also to Cookson's success that these writers have become popular.

The settings of Cookson's novels range from the early-19th century to the late-20th century, and from rural Northumberland to industrial Tyneside. She writes multi-volume historical sagas and domestic tales, single-volume stories dealing with the development of an individual character or the complexities of a single relationship—and even a couple of novels in the gothic mode, written under her pseudonym of Catherine Marchant. All her novels have two things in common—the authenticity of their background and the careful attention to literary style, grammar and language. Unlike that of many purveyors of popular fiction, Cookson's style is never sloppy, her syntax seldom inaccurate. Although it must be said that the standard of her work varies, even at her worst she is never less than a competent storyteller—and at her best she is a very good novelist indeed.

Her first novel, *Kate Hannigan*, depicts a scenario which becomes familiar to readers of Cookson and her many imitators: Kate, a working-class girl in the early years of the 20th century, becomes pregnant by an upper-middle-class man. The child is brought up by Kate's parents and believes them to be her real parents, and Kate to be her sister; of course, this is Cookson's own story, as revealed in her autobiography *Our Kate*, which is as much the story of Cookson's mother, Kate, as of herself. Cookson's actual life and the life of her novels began on Tyneside, and she writes with unassailable authority about the conditions in the working-class terraced houses of Jarrow, Hebburn, Tyne Dock and Shields, and of the Irish Catholic communities and the firm grip which their religion has on them. Occasionally one of Cookson's characters speaks out against this grip (for example, outsider Dr Rodney Prince in *Kate Hannigan* and insider Kate herself), but in general her working-class characters are completely dominated by their religious faith. Kate talks of Father O'Malley, the domineering and interfering parish priest, as being 'only a man' and her mother Sarah is horrified and rebukes her—'... "He's a priest, lass" ... with as much reproach as she could find it in her heart to use to her daughter'. This is important, a vital feature even of present-day Tyneside, and certainly of all the periods Cookson deals with.

In her novels, Cookson has created some outstanding heroines. Her 'Mary Ann' books are a series of eight short novels following the career of Mary Ann Shaughnessy, aged eight in *A Grand Man*, and 19 years later at the end of the series in *Mary Ann and Bill*, being the mother of twins. In the earlier books Mary Ann bounces through her own and other people's lives like a cross between a deus (or dea) ex machina and a gremlin, interfering in situations and people with blithe impartiality, generally for the benefit of her beloved, drunken father Mike Shaughnessy. Although the novels are primarily about Mary Ann, and in the earlier ones of the sequence a child's perceptions are very successfully portrayed, these same novels also chart the development of a man. Mike Shaughnessy, the 'grand man' of the opening novel, is weak, his character undermined by his fondness for drink; through the not always welcome intervention of his daughter he finds strength and independence of character, and by the final novel (in which Mary Ann has to cope with a daughter who promises to be a small clone of herself) is a wise father and father-in-law. Few of Cookson's other novels demonstrate her capacity for comedy as this series does; not only does Mary Ann herself create a number of amusing situations, but her grannie McMullen, (an evil-minded old besom if ever there was one, and in all probability not entirely a figment of the author's imagination) is a wonderful comic character.

In *Tilly Trotter*, Cookson has created a woman who inspires intense emotions of love, friendship and loyalty. Tilly is viewed by the local villagers as a witch, and the fear and hatred that this belief engenders follows her from England to America and back again, and through all the very varied circumstances of her career. When her first job, as a nurserymaid, finishes, Tilly is forced to work down the pit to earn money; trapped in an underground accident, she saves the life of the mine-owner, Mark Sopwith, although he is crippled in the accident. He instates her as his housekeeper and she later becomes his mistress and bears his posthumous child. Dismissed by Mark's daughter, she has a loyal friend in his youngest son, and later marries his eldest son Matthew; they go to live in America, where after a couple of years Matthew is killed by Indians. Tilly returns to England with her son (who is gradually losing his sight owing to a childhood injury—as a baby he deflected a blow intended for Tilly) and a small girl of mixed blood, whose mother gave Matthew to understand that the child was his. Eventually Tilly marries a solid, worthy, working-class chap who has loved her from the time he was a young boy, but not before she has received and turned down other offers (including one from Mark Sopwith's middle son), assisted in another rescue at the mine which she now owns, and seen her son in turn become involved in a tragic affair. The scale and scope of all these events is breathtaking, and it seems incredible that they could all happen to one woman; but such is Cookson's skill as a storyteller that as one reads the three novels (*Tilly Trotter*, *Tilly Trotter Wed* and *Tilly Trotter Widowed*) which make up this saga there seems nothing untoward in Tilly's transition from one class and status to another, in the amazing attraction she holds for so many men, the hatred she inspires in so many women or the loyalty she creates in the Drew family, whose many members love and support Tilly as she works her way up and down (and back up again) the social scale.

Not all Cookson's women, however, are quite so admirable. Mary Ann's grannie McMullen is only one of a range of vitriolic, interfering old women, most of them working class, but a few (for example Mrs Vidler in the 'Bill Bailey' series) middle class. Some are not only interfering by nature but also wield the financial or moral power to dominate their families (for example Emma Funnell in *The House of Women*) and some, it is revealed, are selfish and demanding only because they in their turn have had demands made upon them, often by a self-centred and sexually dominating male. One thing that many of Cookson's heroines have in common is that they tend to act and react against the current trend: her 19th-century characters often think little or nothing of living with their men without the benefit of wedlock or of bearing illegitimate children, yet ironically it is the heroines of the permissive 1970s who balk at doing this. Pat Ridley, in *Pure as the Lily*, leaves university and eschews the freedom she has as a modern woman— 'All this piffle about equality, ... there's something in me that doesn't want to be equal ...'

Few of Cookson's heroines marry the conventional dashing heroes of romance fiction—rather, they marry solid, worthy, often low-key types who are usually picking up the pieces left by a previous relationship, Cookson's definition of 'happy ever after' generally (but by no means always) being 'safe and secure'. Although in general the men are fairly stalwart types both physically and in character, many of them acquire physical defects through war or accident, ranging from losing part of a hand in a man-trap (Ned Ridley in *The Girl*) to the loss of a foot and an arm and severe facial disfigurement in World War I (Reginald Farrier in *The Wingless Bird*). This particular plot device (usually occasioning bitterness followed by increased sensitivity) is not, of course, unique to Cookson, but she does provide a particularly large selection of maimed males for her heroines. In some of the men the flaws are not physical, but are inherent character defects; of course, the villains have a wide range of these—her novels contain bigots, cruel, selfish, sadistic, womanizing, miserly men—most vices are represented. However, some of the sympathetic characters too are flawed—for example by extreme sensitivity. *The Man Who Cried* is an unusual novel; Abel Mason, who has been a conscientious objector in World War I, seeks refuge from a shrewish wife firstly in an affair then, when his mistress is killed, by running away with his small son. At first his sensitivity seems a commendable trait, but as the novel progresses it begins to be seen as a weakness and at the end he is seen by his second wife as 'a child seeking comfort and protection'. Similarly Charlie McFell in *The Cinder Path*, the sensitive son of a sadistic father, describes himself at the end of the novel as ' . . . not easygoing and quiet. I am lazy and weak-willed and vindictive'.

A recurrent theme in all Cookson's novels is the difference between male and female needs in sexual relationships. Time and again we are told that men have physical needs which must be satisfied, and if they cannot be satisfied within matrimony then it is quite acceptable for the man to seek his satisfaction elsewhere. Mark Sopwith in *Tilly Trotter* says, 'I am a man, I have bodily needs . . . . .' and Angus Cotton in *The Round Tower* says ' . . . it was different for a man. A fellow had to have it; . . . ' and 'I'm a man, I need somebody, ... '. While such statements might not seem out of place in those novels set in the 19th century, when such attitudes were widely held—were indeed the norm—they do not sit quite so well when incorporated in novels set well into the 20th century and held even by sympathetic and sensitive men. Dr Rodney Prince, in *Kate Hannigan*, is married to Stella, a self-centred woman with artistic pretensions, who dislikes the physical side of their marriage. He, being a decent chap, does not, it seems, force himself upon her very often, but clearly both Rodney and Cookson feel that Stella's attitude is both unreasonable and unjustifiable—there is no suggestion here that there may be some underlying mental or physical cause, or that such an attitude is not necessarily abnormal. Rodney 'knew the course he should have adopted long ago . . .' (i.e. he should have sought physical satisfaction elsewhere) and, moreover, when he finds out that Stella has been using a contraceptive device he is furious, and asks himself 'Of how many sons had she deprived him?' (Sons, of course, not daughters!) And yet this is one of Cookson's more sympathetic male characters! It is not only in sexual matters that these men dominate: Bill Bailey says to the mother of the woman whom he is about to marry and in whose house he lodges 'I'm master in this house now whether I'm married or not'. The thoughtful woman reader of the late-20th century is forced to ask many questions of such aspects of Cookson's novels, for it is hard to discern whether the attitudes of the characters are those of the author, and if Cookson sets these figures up in order to shoot them down she sometimes fails to make this clear.

Cookson frequently addresses moral issues in her novels, although it must be said that the answers to the questions she raises are frequently ambiguous. In *The Long Corridor*, murder is virtually condoned as a means of bringing about what is seen as natural justice—a wife is killed in order to free her husband to marry the woman he loves. And in *The House of Women*, just as shockingly, incest and child abuse are if not actually condoned by a character, at least allowed to happen. Peggy Jones does nothing to halt her husband's unnatural affection for their daughter, and an act of physical incest is only narrowly averted; yet Peggy sees her husband take up with another woman who has two small girls and does nothing.

Far more clear-cut are the issues of social class which Cookson continually raises in her novels, and in which lie her great strength. For much of the dramatic tension in her books comes not from the personal relationships but from the conflict between social classes and the struggles of individuals as they strive to change their social status. The conditions in which the lower classes of the 19th and early-20th centuries live and work are described dispassionately enough, but with conviction, and the conditions endured by Tilly Trotter down the mine and Biddy Millican (*The Black Velvet Gown*) in a laundry, have the dreadful ring of authenticity about them. But equally unspeakable is the individual treatment meted out by the middle and upper classes, every verbal and personal contact based on the premise that the lower classes are inferior in every respect. It is frequently by the means of education that a Cookson character crosses the class barrier: Tilly Trotter is taught to read and write by the parson's daughter, and is thus able to act as nurserymaid to her employer's children, Kate Hannigan is educated in history and literature by a kindly employer, and Biddy Millican (already literate thanks to her miner father) actually is taught French and Latin, in addition to literature, by her mother's employer—her education brings her to the attention of her employers and begins her rise through the social hierarchy. The upper classes have an unpleasant tendency to resent any show of learning in their inferiors—understandably, as even the dimmer members of the upper echelons can grasp that such knowledge engenders power, and that their own status is thereby threatened. (Cookson is of course firmly allied with the lower classes, educated or not, and the reader experiences immense frustration at the intractability of the middle- and upper-class characters). Acts of violence are frequently the concrete symptoms of the class conflict; men from differing backgrounds beat each other up of course (this is to be expected), but Cookson's women too frequently suffer, and not only the usual physical attack ending in rape. Biddy Millican, for example, is whipped and beaten and strung up, suspended from a drying rack by two adolescent members of the family for whom she works—and this happens basically because her education has brought her to their attention.

Cookson's oeuvre is amazingly rich; she has produced novels, aimed at readers of popular fiction, which contain a wealth of social history, dramatic plots and some memorable characters. It is hardly surprising that her output is mixed, that some of her novels have weak plots or unbelievable characters; frequently it is impossible to feel unalloyed sympathy for particular individuals—*The Maltese Angel*, for example, hinges on whether Ward Gibson was justified in jilting Daisy Mason, whom he had led to believe he loved. Ward is dull as a hero and unpleasant as a man, Daisy is vengeful and ultimately demented, and Ward's wife Fanny is insipid—for a sizeable part of the book it is hard to find a sympathetic character with whom to identify. Contrast with this *The Black Candle*, a powerful historical saga which sums up everything which has come to be identified with the best in Cookson's work. The background is mainly industrial; the novel starts in the very best tradition with a young girl becoming pregnant by the 'young squire' (who gives her a paltry five sovereigns for the privilege) and ends happily half a century later with the reconciliation of an estranged couple; there is social injustice (a man is wrongly hanged) and the novel is fraught with family and social tensions. As a specimen of Cookson's recent work this book is important, demonstrating her technique, style, imagination and insight at the peak of her powers; as an example of a genre it encapsulates all that one would expect (with the possible exception of a torrid sex scene—Cookson handles such scenes with delicacy, without in any way being priggish). Cookson has found a milieu in which she flourishes and which has brought her notable success; she produces popular novels at an amazing rate and generally of a high standard. It is unlikely that she will have a serious rival within the foreseeable future.

—Judith Rhodes

———

COOMBS, Ann.   See **PYKARE, Nina.**

———

COOMBS, Nina.   See **PYKARE, Nina.**

———

COOPER, Jilly.

Nationality: British. **Born:** Jilly Sallitt, Hornchurch, Essex, 21 February 1937. **Education:** Godolphin School, Salisbury. **Relations:** married Leo Cooper in 1961; one son and one daughter. **Career:** reporter, *Middlesex Independent*, Brentford, 1957–59; worked as account executive, copywriter, publisher's reader, receptionist, model, and typist; columnist, *The Sunday Times*, London, 1969–82. Since 1982 columnist, *Mail on Sunday*, London. **Agent:** Desmond Elliot, 15–17 King Street, London S.W.1., England. **Address:** c/o Bantam, 61–63 Uxbridge Road, London W5 5SA, England.

ROMANCE AND HISTORICAL PUBLICATIONS

Novels

Emily. London, Arlington, 1975.
Bella. London, Arlington, 1976.
Harriet. London, Arlington, 1976.
Octavia. London, Arlington, 1977.
Imogen. London, Arlington, 1978.
Prudence. London, Arlington, 1978.
Riders. London, Arlington, 1985; New York, Ballantine, 1986.
Rivals. London, Bantam, 1988; as *Players*, New York, Ballantine, 1989.
Polo. London, Bantam, 1991.
The Man who Made Husbands Jealous. London, Bantam, 1993.

OTHER PUBLICATIONS

Other

How to Stay Married. London, Methuen, 1969; New York, Taplinger, 1970.
How to Survive from Nine to Five. London, Methuen, 1970.
Jolly Super. London, Methuen, 1971.
Men and Super Men. London, Eyre Methuen, 1972.
Jolly Super Too. London, Eyre Methuen, 1973.
Women and Super Women. London, Eyre Methuen, 1974.
Jolly Superlative. London, Eyre Methuen, 1975.
Super Men and Super Women (omnibus). London, Eyre Methuen, 1976.
Work and Wedlock (omnibus). London, Magnum, 1977.
Superjilly. London, Eyre Methuen, 1977.
Class: A View from Middle England. London, Eyre Methuen, 1979.
Supercooper. London, Eyre Methuen, 1980.
Little Mabel (for children). London, Granada, 1980.
Little Mabel's Great Escape (for children). London, Granada, 1981.
Love and Other Heartaches. London, Arlington, 1981.
Intelligent and Loyal: A Celebration of the Mongrel, photographs by Graham Wood. London, Methuen, 1981.
Jolly Marsupial. London, Methuen, 1982.
Little Mabel Wins the Day (for children). London, Granada, 1982.
Animals in War. London, Heinemann, 1983.
The Common Years: The Country Diary of an Urban Lady. London, Methuen, 1984.
On Rugby, with Leo Cooper. London, Bell and Hyman, 1984.
On Cricket, with Leo Cooper. London, Bell and Hyman, 1985.
Little Mabel Saves the Day (for children). London, Granada, 1985.
Hotfoot to Zabriskie Point, photographs by Patrick Lichfield. London, Constable, 1985.

Horse Mania, with Leo Cooper. London, Bell and Hyman, 1986.
How to Survive Christmas. London, Methuen, 1986.
Turn Right at the Spotted Dog and Other Diversions. London, Methuen, 1987.
Angels Rush In: The Best of Jilly Cooper's Satire and Humour. London, Methuen, 1990.

Editor, with Tom Hartman, *Violets and Vinegar: An Anthology of Women's Writings and Sayings*. London, Allen and Unwin, 1980.
Editor, *The British in Love*. London, Arlington, 1980.

*

Film Adaptations: *Riders*, 1993.

*   *   *

The discernment and observation that have sharpened many of the love stories of the last decade have reached an apex in Jilly Cooper's accounts of heroines who are romantically inclined but also wry, gutsy, earthy, and at times anarchic. Her stories are at the far end of the spectrum from, say, those of Barbara Cartland which are in the classic and sentimental mould. Jilly Cooper (like Mabel St John in 1908) gives the romantic novel a fresh, invigorating, and frequently funny slant. With her stories, one feels that the genre is on the brink of a breakthrough into an exciting and still uncharted new lease of life.

She has her own highly individual style and method of packaging her novels, of course. The title of each book is the name of its heroine, and possibly every heroine reflects certain aspects of her author. (It is the representation of Cooper's own face—in many moods—that provides cover illustrations for the stories and no other picture would seem more relevant to the different plots.) Sometimes rueful, sometimes racy, but always romantically persuasive, the narratives are at their most stylish when in the first person (*Emily*, *Prudence*, and *Octavia*, for example). Her novels are extremely inventive and occasionally outrageous. They present a glittering mosaic of misunderstandings and changing partners, idealism and disillusionment, glamour and good nature, in settings as varied as colleges, canal barges, and haunted Highland castles.

With the publication of *Riders*, *Rivals*, and *Polo* there has been a considerable enlargement of Cooper's canvas, although romance remains a strong ingredient. *Riders* has as its setting the tensely glittering world of show jumping. When the book first appeared, a reviewer wrote 'Sex and horses: who could ask for more?' Certainly in the hands of Cooper these two themes are handled invigoratingly enough to make entertaining reading even for those who might normally have little feeling for the mystique of equestrian endeavours. Ambition and the fear of failure spill over from field events into romantic relationships, and bitter rivalries between the hard-up, half-gypsy Jake and the promiscuous upper-class cad Rupert Campbell-Black are played out in a riot of horsey happenings from home-counties gymkhanas to the Los Angeles Olympics.

Rivals is another romantic block-buster in which the now divorced and still dissolute Rupert pursues a political career. The book's vital atmosphere is provided by the conflict between warring groups and individuals who seek the franchise of a Cotswolds television company. Here, as in *Riders*, cut-throat ambition crosses the divide between business and personal affairs. Cooper is at her most deliciously barbed in these bed-to-boardroom exploits, and, despite the general frothiness of the story there are some moments of serious social challenge.

—Mary Cadogan

COOPER, Lettice.
Nationality: British. **Born:** Eccles, Lancashire, 3 September 1897. Educated at St Cuthbert's School, Southbourne; Lady Margaret Hall, Oxford, 1916–18, B.A. **Career:** editorial assistant and drama critic, *Time and Tide*, London, 1939–40; public relations officer, Ministry of Food, London, 1940–45. President, Robert Louis Stevenson Club, 1958–74; Vice Chairman, 1975–78, and President, 1979–81, English PEN Club. **Recipient:** Arts Council bursary, 1968, 1979; Eric Gregory travelling scholarship, 1977. OBE (Officer, Order of the British Empire), 1980. **Agent:** A. P. Watt Ltd, 20 John Street, London WC1N 2DL, England. **Address:** 4 Wherry Quayside, Anchor Street, Coltishall, Norwich, Norfolk NR12 7AQ.

ROMANCE AND HISTORICAL PUBLICATIONS

Novels

The Lighted Room. London, Hodder and Stoughton, 1925.
The Old Fox. London, Hodder and Stoughton, 1927.
Good Venture. London, Hodder and Stoughton, 1928.
Likewise the Lyon. London, Hodder and Stoughton, 1928.
The Ship of Truth. London, Hodder and Stoughton, and Boston, Little Brown, 1930.
Private Enterprise. London, Hodder and Stoughton, 1931.
Hark to Rover! London, Hodder and Stoughton, 1933.
We Have Come to a Country. London, Gollancz, 1935.
The New House. London, Gollancz, and New York, Macmillan, 1936.
National Provincial. London, Gollancz, and New York, Macmillan, 1938.
Black Bethlehem. London, Gollancz, and New York, Macmillan, 1947.
Fenny. London, Gollancz, 1953.
Three Lives. London, Gollancz, 1957.
A Certain Compass. London, Gollancz, 1960.
The Double Heart. London, Gollancz, 1962.
Late in the Afternoon. London, Gollancz, 1971.
Tea on Sunday. London, Gollancz, 1973.
Snow and Roses. London, Gollancz, 1976.
Desirable Residence. London, Gollancz, 1980.
Unusual Behaviour. London, Gollancz, 1986.

OTHER PUBLICATIONS

Novels (for children)

Blackberry's Kitten. Leicester, Brockhampton Press, 1961; New York, Vanguard Press, 1963.
The Bear Who Was Too Big. London, Parrish, 1963; Chicago, Follett, 1966.
Bob-a-Job. Leicester, Brockhampton Press, 1963.
Contadino. London, Cape, 1964.
The Twig of Cypress. London, Deutsch, 1965; New York, Washburn, 1966.
We Shall Have Snow. Leicester, Brockhampton Press, 1966.
Robert the Spy Hunter. London, Kaye and Ward, 1973.
Parkin. London, Harrap, 1977.

Other (for children)

Great Men of Yorkshire (West Riding). London, Lane, 1955.
The Young Florence Nightingale. London, Lane, 1960; New York, Roy, 1961.

The Young Victoria. London, Parrish, 1961; New York, Roy, 1962.
James Watt. London, A. and C. Black, 1963.
Garibaldi. London, Methuen, 1964; New York, Roy, 1966.
The Young Edgar Allan Poe. London, Parrish, 1964; New York, Roy, 1965.
The Fugitive King. London, Parrish, 1965.
A Hand upon the Time: A Life of Charles Dickens. New York, Pantheon, 1968; London, Gollancz, 1971.
Robert Louis Stevenson. London, Burns and Oates, 1969.
Gunpowder: Treason and Plot. London, Abelard Schuman, 1970.

Other

Robert Louis Stevenson. London, Home and Van Thal, 1947; Denver, Alan Swallow, 1948.
Yorkshire: West Riding. London, Hale, 1950.
George Eliot. London, Longman, 1951; revised editions, 1960, 1964.

*

Manuscript Collection: Eccles Public Library, Lancashire.

*   *   *

Mary Welburn in *National Provincial* is just what Lettice Cooper herself must have been like at a similar age—a clever girl who went to university, moved away from her northern roots and became involved in a new life and the new ideas that surrounded her, held down an involving and exciting job, was tolerant, broadminded, fascinated by other people, and open to every new experience. She is a brilliant and born writer. Her books read so effortlessly that it is easy to overlook the superb writing that makes the reading such a pleasure.

Cooper has a clarity of mind, a breadth of learning, and a depth of understanding that enable her to describe other people's lives with immense sympathy and appreciation. She understands what makes people tick: their worries, fears, and indecisions; the little things that concern them, and their bewilderment and feelings of inadequacy when faced with big issues and problems they don't really understand. Cooper makes one feel for the unhappy *nouveau riche* Ward children in *National Provincial*, and sympathize as Stephen Harding wrestles with his awakening political consciousness, which sets him apart from his wife and family, and everything he was brought up to think right. And you know from the beginning that there is no future for them. The character of Fenny (in the book of the same name), also stays in the mind; she loses the first man she loves because she is too inexperienced and nice, and cannot see, until it is too late, what is happening. And the reader hopes that Rhoda, in *The New House*, will find the courage to break away from the gentle but vice-like clutches of her mother and at last live her own life; that the new house will, in fact, mean a new beginning for them all; and that she will not become a mirror image of her Aunt Ellen. She deserves better.

What is striking about Cooper's novels is that despite the fact that they were written 50 years ago, the issues they confront and the way in which they are written are as relevant today as they were then. And her places are as alive as her characters; for example the Florence she so lovingly portrays in *Fenny*.

Cooper, in her new introduction to the reissue of *National Provincial*, published in honour of her 90th birthday, describes the book as 'a piece of Yorkshire tapestry'. However, all her novels weave together the strands of politics and philosophy, love and friendship, hatred and jealousy. She says of Mary Welburn that 'it was impossible for her to go on a railway journey without feeling that at the other end of it there was likely to be something interesting'. Her readers feel the same about beginning a Cooper novel.

—Dorothy Wood

CORCORAN, Barbara.
Pseudonyms: Paige Dixon; Gail Hamilton. **Nationality:** American. **Born:** Hamilton, Massachusetts, 12 April 1911. **Education:** Wellesley College, Massachusetts, 1929–33, B.A. in English 1933; University of Montana, Missoula, 1954–55, M.A. in English 1955. **Career:** electronics inspector in the United States Navy and a code clerk in the United States Army Signal Corps during World War II; researcher, Celebrity Service, Hollywood, 1945–53; copywriter, Station KGVO, Missoula, 1953–54; instructor in English, University of Kentucky, Covington, 1956–57; researcher, CBS Television story department, Hollywood, 1957–59; English teacher, Marlboro School, Los Angeles, 1959–60; instructor in English, University of Colorado, Boulder, 1960–65, and Palomar College, San Marcos, California, 1965–69. **Recipient:** William Allen White award, 1972; National Science Teachers' award-Children's Book Council award, 1974, 1977; National Endowment for the Arts grant, 1978. **Agent:** McIntosh and Otis, 310 Madison Avenue, New York, New York 10017, USA. **Address:** PO Box 4394, Missoula, Montana 59806, USA.

ROMANCE AND HISTORICAL PUBLICATIONS

Novels

Abbie in Love. New York, Ballantine, 1981.
Abigail. New York, Ballantine, 1981.
Beloved Enemy. New York, Ballantine, 1981.
By the Silvery Moon. New York, Ballantine, 1981.
Call of the Heart. New York, Ballantine, 1981.
A Husband for Gail. New York, Ballantine, 1981.
Love Is Not Enough. New York, Ballantine, 1981.
Song for Two Voices. New York, Ballantine, 1981.
Stay Tuned. New York, Atheneum, 1991.
Family Secrets. New York, Atheneum, 1992.

OTHER PUBLICATIONS (for children)

Fiction

Sam. New York, Atheneum, 1967.
A Row of Tigers. New York, Atheneum, 1969.
Sasha, My Friend. New York, Atheneum, 1969.
The Long Journey, with Bradford Angier. New York, Atheneum, 1970.
A Star to the North, with Bradford Angier. New York, Nelson, 1970.
The Lifestyle of Robie Tuckerman. New York, Nelson, 1971.
This Is a Recording. New York, Atheneum, 1971.
Don't Slam the Door When You Go. New York, Atheneum, 1972.
A Trick of Light. New York, Atheneum, 1972.
All the Summer Voices. New York, Atheneum, 1973.
A Dance to Still Music. New York, Atheneum, 1974.
The Winds of Time. New York, Atheneum, 1974.
The Clown. New York, Atheneum, 1975; as *I Wish You Love*, Scholastic, 1977.
Meet Me at Tamerlane's Tomb. New York, Atheneum, 1975.
Axe-Time, Sword-Time. New York, Atheneum, 1976.
Cabin in the Sky. New York, Atheneum, 1976.

Faraway Island. New York, Atheneum, 1977.
Make No Sound. New York, Atheneum, 1977.
Ask for Love, and They Give You Rice Pudding, with Bradford Angier. Boston, Houghton Mifflin, 1977.
Hey, That's My Soul You're Stomping On. New York, Atheneum, 1978.
Me and You and a Dog Named Blue. New York, Atheneum, 1979.
The Person in the Potting Shed. New York, Atheneum, 1980.
Rising Damp. New York, Atheneum, 1980.
Making It. Boston, Little Brown, 1981.
You're Allegro Dead. New York, Atheneum, 1981.
Child of the Morning. New York, Atheneum, 1982.
A Watery Grave. New York, Atheneum, 1982.
Strike! New York, Atheneum, 1983.
Which Witch Is Which? New York, Atheneum, 1983.
August, Die She Must. New York, Atheneum, 1984.
The Woman in Your Life. New York, Atheneum, 1984.
Face the Music. New York, Atheneum, 1985.
Mystery on Ice. New York, Atheneum, 1985.
The Shadowed Path. New York, Archway, 1985.
When Darkness Falls. New York, Archway, 1985.
A Horse Named Sky. New York, Atheneum, 1986.
I Am the Universe. New York, Atheneum, 1986.
The Hideaway. New York, Atheneum, 1987.
The Sky Is Falling. New York, Atheneum, 1988.
The Private Wars of Lillian Adams. New York, Atheneum, and London, Macmillan, 1989.
The Potato Kid. New York, Atheneum, and London, Macmillan, 1989.
You Put Up With Me, I'll Put Up With You. Camelot, Avon, 1989.
Annie's Monster. New York, Atheneum, and London, Macmillan, 1990.

Fiction as Paige Dixon

Lion on the Mountain. New York, Atheneum, 1972.
Silver Wolf. New York, Atheneum, 1973.
Promises to Keep. New York, Atheneum, 1974.
The Young Grizzly. New York, Atheneum, 1974.
May I Cross Your Golden River? New York, Atheneum, 1975.
A Time To Love, A Time To Mourn. New York, Scholastic, 1975.
Pimm's Cup for Everybody. New York, Atheneum, 1976.
The Search for Charlie. New York, Atheneum, 1976.
Summer of the White Goat. New York, Atheneum, 1977.
The Loner: A Story of the Wolverine. New York, Atheneum, 1978.
The Mustang and Other Stories. New York, Atheneum, 1978.
Skipper. New York, Atheneum, 1979.
Walk My Way. New York, Atheneum, 1980.

Fiction as Gail Hamilton

A Candle to the Devil. New York, Atheneum, 1975.
Titania's Lodestone. New York, Atheneum, 1975.
Love Comes to Eunice K. O'Herlihy. New York, Atheneum, 1977.

*

Manuscript Collection: de Grummond Collection, University of Southern Mississippi, Hattiesburg; Central Missouri State University, Warrensburg.

*   *   *

Perhaps Barbara Corcoran's experience in writing novels for young adults influences her historical and romance fiction to an undue extent. Her books for this age level, to which she has largely confined herself in recent years, like her adult novels are most concerned with the process by which a young person breaks free of family ties and gains some independence. In this newly independent state, her protagonist may love some family members more than ever, but it is a love based on understanding rather than on duty.

Also perhaps a reminder of her young adult novels is her tendency to focus on one central character. Even though the subsidiary characters are important to the plot, they tend to be insubstantial when regarded closely. In *Call of the Heart*, one of her most conventionally romantic historic novels, even the hero, Tom Weatherby, a self-made industrialist, is presented in a fragmented way: his character does not develop organically. Doty Connor-Jones, the heroine, is a young governess for a wealthy family as America enters World War I. Her Irish charm wins the hearts of Weatherby and also of young Sam Winchester, her employer's brother. Doty's engagement to Sam and her care for his elderly parents when he is killed as a Canadian pilot make a poignant story, although the novel also clearly shows Corcoran's major failing as a writer of historical novels—her inability to give a true period feeling to her stories. The historical characters always seem like modern people in period costume. The aristocratic episcopalean Winchesters make no complaint about Sam's sudden engagement to an Irish Catholic girl who attends Mass with some regularity.

Similarly, Abigail, the eponymous heroine of Corcoran's novel about Civil War New England, goes as a schoolteacher to a small village. Even her stodgy, proper mother accepts the need for Abigail to make a living working outside the home. Abigail is seduced by the school board president, a rich man whose wife is addicted to opium. She goes home, pregnant and in disgrace. But her mother calmly accepts her condition, and her brother writes 'As for your child, I shall love it like my own'. Apparently no one in her home community, among her relatives or even among the local church congregation, audibly disapproves of her illegitimate baby. While details like the brief meeting with Henry Cabot Lodge in the Old Corner Book Store may be true to period, the attitudes and opinions of the characters are atypical of their eras. Perhaps this provides some reassurance to readers who would be dismayed by changing standards of tolerance between our day and earlier times.

Some of Corcoran's work straddles the line between adult novels and those written for young adults. *Skipper* has a protagonist who goes to an ancestral estate to find a long-lost father, meeting enemies and unexpected friends. But Skipper is not a typical gothic heroine, but a high school student looking for his roots in the wake of his beloved brother's death. Instead of love, he finds the understanding that he must live his own life while continuing to cherish his brother's memory.

It is, in fact, not unusual for romance to be secondary. In *Axe-Time, Sword-Time*, a girl with learning disabilities finds a way to help the United States war effort in the early 1940s, while defining her independence from her conventional mother. Elinor is in love with a neighbour but their relationship is a stable background to her life, rather than an exciting novelty. In *Abigail*, the heroine takes her baby west to make a new life in Colorado, leaving behind a young man who cares for her, after one last bitter encounter with her wealthy seducer, who is still trying to convince her he is serious about getting a divorce someday. Abigail and her baby will be, one is to assume, sufficient unto themselves. Abigail has finally defined herself in such a way that she is a woman who may not need a lover—not as a romantic heroine after all.

—Susan Branch

CORDELL, Alexander.
Nationality: British. **Born:** George Alexander Graber, Colombo, Ceylon (now Sri Lanka), 9 September 1914. **Education:** privately educated, and at Marist Brothers' College, 1921–30. **Military Service:** served in the British Army, 1932–36; Royal Engineers, 1939–45: Major. **Relations:** married 1) Rosina Wells in 1937 (died 1972), one daughter; 2) Elsie May Donovan. **Career:** quantity surveyor in Wales, 1936–68. Since 1968, full-time writer. **Address:** The Conifers, Railway Road, Rhosddu, Wrexham, Clwyd, Wales.

ROMANCE AND HISTORICAL PUBLICATIONS

Novels (series: The Welsh Trilogy)

A Thought of Honour. London, Museum Press, 1954; as *The Enemy Within*, London, Coronet, 1974.
The Welsh Trilogy. Sevenoaks, Coronet, 1986.
   Rape of the Fair Country. London, Gollancz, and New York, Doubleday, 1959.
   The Hosts of Rebecca. London, Gollancz, 1960; as *Robe of Honor*, New York, Doubleday, 1960.
   Song of the Earth. London, Gollancz, 1969; New York, Simon and Schuster, 1970.
Race of the Tiger. London, Gollancz, 1963.
The Sinews of Love. London, Gollancz, 1965; New York, Doubleday, 1966.
The Bright Cantonese. London, Gollancz, 1967; as *The Deadly Eurasian*, New York, Weybright and Talley, 1968.
The Fire People. London, Hodder and Stoughton, 1972.
If You Believe the Soldiers. London, Hodder and Stoughton, 1973; New York, Doubleday, 1974.
The Dream and the Destiny. London, Hodder and Stoughton, and New York, Doubleday, 1975.
This Sweet and Bitter Earth. London, Hodder and Stoughton, 1977; New York, St Martin's Press, 1978.
To Slay the Dreamer. London, Hodder and Stoughton, and New York, St Martin's Press, 1980.
Rogue's March. London, Hodder and Stoughton, 1981.
Land of My Fathers. London, Hodder and Stoughton, 1983.
Peerless Jim. London, Hodder and Stoughton, 1984.
Tunnel Tigers. London, Weidenfeld and Nicolson, 1986.
This Proud and Savage Land. London, Weidenfeld and Nicolson, 1987.
Requiem for a Patriot. London, Weidenfeld and Nicolson, 1988.
Moll Walbee. London, Weidenfeld and Nicolson, 1989; as *Moll*, London, Weidenfeld and Nicolson, 1990.
Dreams of Fair Women. London, Piatkus, 1993.
Beloved Exile. London, Piatkus, 1993.

Short Stories

Tales from Tiger Bay. Abergavenny, Monmouth, Blorenge Press, 1986.

OTHER PUBLICATIONS (for children)

Fiction

The White Cockade. Leicester, Brockhampton Press, and New York, Viking Press, 1970.
Witches' Sabbath. Leicester, Brockhampton Press, and New York, Viking Press, 1970.
The Healing Blade. Leicester, Brockhampton Press, and New York, Viking Press, 1971.
The Traitor Within. Leicester, Brockhampton Press, 1971; Nashville, Nelson, 1973.

Sea-Urchin. London, Collins, 1979.

*

Manuscript Collection: Boston University.

*   *   *

You have to appreciate Wales and the Welsh to enjoy fully Alexander Cordell's stirring novels, because his writing is so deeply steeped in Welsh idiom and the lilting speech of the valleys. Probably best known for his famous trilogy, *Rape of the Fair Country*, *The Hosts of Rebecca*, and *Song of the Earth*, he likes a big canvas on which he can paint large, and industrial Wales in the 19th century provides him with a wonderful backcloth for his history of the industrial revolution, and the rise of the trades union and Chartist movements. His sweeping lyrical novels are a wonderful way to learn history.

It was Benjamin Disraeli who first described Britain as a nation divided (between the rich and the poor) and the division has never been shown more clearly than in Wales at this time. The thriving Welsh industrial towns were a magnet for a rich stew of people: they came from the North of England, Ireland, and Scotland to earn a pitiful living in the mills and mines of Wales, while the mine owners and iron masters grew rich and prosperous. Cordell has based many of his stories on the folk memories of the people he has met, and he pulls no punches. The conditions the ordinary people lived and worked in were appalling: cholera was rampant, two out of every three children died by the age of five, and those who survived were employed down the pits, put there by their desperate parents so that they could feed them. The employers thought nothing of cutting wages, or laying off workers when times were hard. But what comes through Cordell's novels is the amazing resilience and humour of the ordinary working people, and their charity and compassion to one another.

Some of Cordell's most memorable characters are the martyrs of the Chartist movement—Dic Penderyn in *The Fire People*; the legendary martyr of the Welsh working class who was wrongfully hanged and in *Requiem for a Patriot*, John Frost—the idealistic Mayor of Newport and the acknowledged leader of the Chartist rebellion, who survived deportation to Van Dieman's Land, and who was greeted by a crowd of 20 thousand people when he finally returned to England in 1857 still preaching against parliament and the economic and social prejudices still so widespread.

There is also a less-Welsh side to Cordell; it comes through in two of his most readable novels. *Peerless Jim* is the fictionalized account of the life of Jim Driscoll—British and European featherweight boxing champion, and unofficial champion of the world, known as 'Peerless' for his incomparable left hand—a generous man and a great fighter, probably one of the greatest the British Isles has ever produced, Irish by birth, but Welsh by adoption.

Jim McAndrew in *Rogue's March*, is one of Cordell's most engaging characters—a bawdy, brilliant, drunken, womanizing artist. Jim is cashiered from the army for breaking into the regimental museum and dressing up as an officer, striking a superior, and persistent desertion. He lives in Paris and befriends Toulouse-Lautrec, marries a woman who doesn't even like him very much but thinks he will be good for her business, and paints day and night. It is refreshing to read a novel of Cordell's that is so different, though still with its roots in the period he knows so well.

Cordell, like Peerless Jim, is Welsh by adoption, but if you want to immerse yourself in 19th-century Wales, you will find no finer guide than this writer.

—Dorothy Wood

———

CORELLI, Marie.
Nationality: British. **Born:** Marie MacKay, Bayswater, London, 1 May 1855. **Education:** privately educated; studied music and made debut as a pianist, London, 1884. **Career:** writer from 1885; settled in Stratford-on-Avon, 1901. **Died:** 21 April 1924.

Romance and Historical Publications

Novels

A Romance of Two Worlds. London, Bentley, 2 vols, 1886; New York, Ivers, 1 vol, n.d.
Vendetta; or, The Story of One Forgotten. London, Bentley, 3 vols, 1886; New York, Ivers, 1 vol, n.d.
Thelma: A Society Novel. London, Bentley, 3 vols, 1887; New York, Ivers, 1 vol, n.d.
Ardath: The Story of a Dead Self. London, Bentley, 3 vols, 1889; New York, Ivers, 1 vol, n.d.
My Wonderful Wife: A Study in Smoke. London, White, 1889; New York, Ivers, 1890.
Wormwood: A Drama of Paris. London, Bentley, 3 vols, 1890; New York, Munro, 1 vol, 1890.
The Soul of Lilith. London, Bentley, 3 vols, 1892; New York, Lovell, 1 vol, 1892.
Barabbas: A Dream of the World's Tragedy. London, Methuen, 3 vols, 1893; Philadelphia, Lippincott, 1 vol, 1893.
The Sorrows of Satan; or, The Strange Experiences of One Geoffrey Tempest, Millionaire: A Romance. London, Methuen, 3 vols, 1895; Philadelphia, Lippincott, 1 vol, 1896.
Silence of the Maharajah. New York, Merriam, 1895.
The Distant Voices, A Fact or Fancy. Philadelphia, Lippincott, 1896.
The Murder of Delicia. London, Skeffington, and Philadelphia, Lippincott, 1896; as *Delicia*, London, Constable, 1917.
The Mighty Atom. London, Hutchinson, and Philadelphia, Lippincott, 1896.
Ziska. Bristol, Arrowsmith, and Chicago, Stone and Kimball, 1897.
Jane: A Social Incident. London, Huchinson, and Philadelphia, Lippincott, 1897.
Boy. London, Hutchinson, and Philadelphia, Lippincott, 1900.
The Master-Christian. London, Methuen, and New York, Dodd Mead, 1900.
Angel's Wickedness: A True Story. New York, Beers, 1900.
Temporal Power: A Study in Supremacy. London, Methuen, and New York, Dodd Mead, 1902.
God's Good Man: A Simple Love Story. London, Methuen, and New York, Dodd Mead, 1904.
The Strange Visitation of Josiah McNason: A Christmas Ghost Story. London, Newnes, 1904; as *The Strange Visitation*, London, Hodder and Stoughton, 1912.
The Treasure of Heaven: A Romance of Riches. London, Constable, and New York, Dodd Mead, 1906.
Holy Orders. London, Methuen, and New York, Stokes, 1908.
The Devil's Motor. London, Hodder and Stoughton, and New York, Doran, 1910.
The Life Everlasting: A Reality of Romance. London, Methuen, and New York, Doran, 1911.
The Philosopher and the Sentimentalist. New York, Paget, 1911.
Innocent: Her Fancy and His Fact. London, Hodder and Stoughton, and New York, Doran, 1914.
The Young Diana: An Experience of the Future. London, Hutchinson, and New York, Doran, 1918.
My 'Little Bit'. London, Collins, and New York, Doran, 1919.
The Secret Power. London, Methuen, and New York, Doubleday, 1921.
Love—and the Philosopher: A Study in Sentiment. London, Methuen, and New York, Doran, 1923.

Short Stories

The Hired Baby and Other Stories and Social Sketches. Leipzig, Tauchnitz, 1891; New York, Optimus, 1894.
Three Wise Men of Gotham. Philadelphia, Lippincott, 1896.
Cameos. London, Hutchinson, and Philadelphia, Lippincott, 1896.
The Song of Miriam and Other Stories. New York, Munro, 1898.
The Love of Long Ago and Other Stories. London, Methuen, 1920; New York, Doubleday, 1921.

OTHER PUBLICATIONS

Poetry

Poems, edited by Bertha Vyver. London, Hutchinson, 1925; New York, Doran, 1926.

Other

The Silver Domino; or, Side-Whispers, Social and Literary. London, Lamley, 1892.
Patriotism or Self-Advertisement? A Social Note on the War. London, Greening, and Philadelphia, Lippincott, 1900.
The Greatest Queen in the World: A Tribute to the Majesty of England 1837–1900. London, Skeffington, 1900.
An Open Letter to His Eminence Cardinal Vaughan. London, Lamley, 1900.
A Christmas Greeting of Various Thoughts, Verses, and Fancies. London, Methuen, 1901; New York, Dodd Mead, 1902.
The Passing of the Great Queen. London, Methuen, and New York, Dodd Mead, 1901.
The Vanishing Gift: An Address on the Decay of the Imagination. Edinburgh, Philosophical Institution, 1902.
The Plain Truth of the Stratford-upon-Avon Controversy. London, Methuen, 1903.
Free Opinions Freely Expressed on Certain Phases of Modern Social Life and Conduct. London, Constable, and New York, Dodd Mead, 1905.
Faith Versus Flunkeyism: A Word on the Spanish Royal Marriage. London, Rapid Review, 1906.
Woman or Suffragette? A Question of National Choice. London, Pearson, 1907.
America's Possession in Shakespeare's Town. Edinburgh, Morrison and Gibb, 1909.
Is All Well with England? London, Jarrolds, 1917.
Eyes of the Sea (on the Grand Fleet). London, Marshall, 1917.
Mistaken Both Ways. New York, Paget, 1922.
Praise and Prayer: A Simple Home Service. London, Methuen, 1923.
Open Confession to a Man from a Woman. London, Hutchinson, 1924; New York, Doran, 1925.
Harvard House Guide Book, with Percy S. Brentnall and Bertha Vyver. Privately printed, 1931.

*

Bibliography: by Richard L. Kowdczyk, in *Bulletin of Bibliography* (Boston), 1973.

Critical Studies: *The Writings of Marie Corelli* by S. Boswin, Bombay, Examiner Press, 1907; *Marie Corelli: The Life and Death of a Best-Seller* by George Bullock, London, Constable, 1940; *Marie Corelli: The Woman and the Legend* by Eileen Bigland, London, Jarrolds, 1953; *Marie Corelli: The Story of a Friendship* by William Stuart Scott, London, Hutchinson, 1955; *Now Barabbas Was a Rotter: The Extraordinary Life of Marie Corelli* by Brian Masters, London, Hamish Hamilton, 1978.

*   *   *

Marie Corelli has been claimed as the first modern 'bestseller' author for the reading public expanded by Forster's 1870 Education Act. At the time of her death *The Sorrows of Satan* and *Thelma* had gone through 60 and 56 editions respectively. In the face of mainly hostile reception from the literary establishment, she refused after 1893 to send out review copies, but this did nothing to lessen her popularity: Richard Hoggart has noted that his aunts in working-class Leeds considered *The Sorrows of Satan* 'a classic'; it was also praised by Queen Victoria. The huge popularity of her novels makes her of social interest, but her writing itself has the fascination of an intense, emotive imagination almost totally uninhibited by considerations of style, taste, or factual reality.

Her life itself was an elaborately cultivated fantasy. Born in London in May 1855, the illegitimate daughter of Charles Mackay, a songwriter, and Ellen Mills, she claimed to be born in 1854 of aristocratic Italian blood. In 1884 she made a well-received debut as an *improvatrice* pianist in London—a character to emerge, thinly disguised, as the heroine of her first novel, *A Romance of Two Worlds*, who, on the verge of a nervous breakdown, was released through the help of a Parisian scientist Heliobas to discover her 'personal electricity' and so explore the spiritual realm. This curious blend of mysticism and pseudo-science was to become one hallmark of her writing. It gave comforting assurance to those disturbed by the impact of science—in particular Darwinism—on the thought and life of the period. Wireless telegraphy and light-rays, she informed readers of *The Life Everlasting*, were known to Egyptian priests and the Hermetic Brethren 'ages before the coming of Christ', and the mystic Heliobas, who appears in several of her works, was a Chaldean descended from the Wise Men from the East.

The Soul of Lilith combines the myths of Frankenstein and Pygmalion. El-Râmi, an Egyptian sage, uses a chemical elixir to bring to life a child who grows up as Lilith. Controlling her body, he wishes to possess her soul, considering a female soul a minor entity. Although warned of his error by Heliobas, he professes to Lilith his love for her, and she dissolves to dust. The horror of a scientific view of life was even more sensationally attacked in *The Mighty Atom*, which owes a possible debt to J.S. Mill's *Autobiography* (1873). The 11-year-old Lionel Valliscourt is told by his materialist teacher, Professor Cadman-Gore, that the basis of all existence is the atom. Lionel pertly argues with his mentor; nevertheless when his child love Jessamine, daughter of the local sexton, dies, he determines to find out whether there is life after death and hangs himself. (Combe-Martin, the setting for the story, became a minor place of pilgrimage due to the popularity of the novel.)

In *Barabbas* she pioneered the Biblical epic. Spiced with a subplot showing Judas Iscariot to have betrayed Christ under the prompting of his sister Judith Escariot, who is a lover of Caiaphas, and with accounts of the Crucifixion that in emotionalism border on the pornographic, the book could be attacked but not ignored. *The Master-Christian* is a more subdued work. It tells how Christ returned to earth as Manuel, a street urchin discovered outside the Cathedral in Rouen. Rejected by the Roman Catholic Church, Manuel is taken in by Cardinal Felix Bonport who, in a sensational scene, is received up into heaven.

Throughout her work she savagely attacked both the established churches and the society of the day whose attentions she in private life courted with paranoiac intensity. *Thelma* concerns a pure and mystic Norwegian girl discovered on a visit to that country by Sir Philip Bruce-Errington, and brought back to England to be his wife. She is more than a match in debate for the sensual, hypocritical Anglican clergyman Charles Dyceworthy, but when the evil Lady Winsleigh has her husband suspect her of unchastity, she retires to Norway, finally to be recovered by the penitent Sir Philip. Apart from the account of corrupt London society life, the novel is remarkable for its evocation of the wild Norse landscape and religion that is set against it. Although Corelli had never been to Norway, guides were soon showing visitors Thelma's rock.

Corelli is, however, most likely to be remembered for *The Sorrows of Satan*. The hero, Geoffrey Tempest, is mysteriously left five million pounds by an uncle, and is befriended by Prince Lucio Ramanez. It is soon clear that the Prince is Satan, after Tempest's soul. The contest is complicated by the two women in his life, the wicked Lady Sibyl Elton and the brilliant, spiritual Mavis Clare, author, who as critics were quick to point out, had the same initials as her creator. The originality of this Faust story is that Prince Lucio himself hopes for Tempest's salvation—forced to expiate his fall from heaven, when man ceases to worship him, he will be free to return to grace. A strong story line and the melodramatic life of the main characters made it deservedly her most popular work.

Corelli saw herself as fulfilling a mission to assert 'the underlying spiritual quality of life as it really is', and her work was widely quoted by both fashionable and popular preachers. Her success points to an undoubted thirst for religious literature. She also made it comfortable: the only evil was that willed by man, and every reader had the power for spiritual growth towards total goodness. She embodied this message in fiction that is vulgar in the fullest sense, clichéd, melodramatic, uninformed; yet with an imaginative flair, theatricality, and self-conviction that ultimately defies criticism by literary conventions.

—Louis James

CORNWELL, Bernard.

Pseudonym: Susannah Kells. **Nationality:** British. **Born:** London, 23 February 1944. **Education:** University of London, B.A. 1967. **Relations:** married Judy Acker in 1980. **Career:** producer, London, 1969–76, and head of current affairs, Belfast, 1976–79, BBC Television; news editor, Thames Television, London, 1979–80. **Agent:** Toby Eady, Toby Eady Associates Ltd, 7 Gledhow Gardens, London SW5 0BL, England.

ROMANCE AND HISTORICAL PUBLICATIONS

Novels (series: Richard Sharpe)

Sharpe's Eagle. London, Collins, and New York, Viking Press, 1981.
Sharpe's Gold. London, Collins, 1981; New York, Viking Press, 1982.
Sharpe's Company. London, Collins, and New York, Viking Press, 1982.
Sharpe's Sword. London, Collins, and New York, Viking Press, 1983.
Sharpe's Enemy. London, Collins, and New York, Viking, 1984.
Sharpe's Honour. London, Collins, and New York, Viking, 1985.
Sharpe's Regiment. London, Collins, and New York, Viking, 1986.
Sharpe's Siege. London, Collins, and New York, Viking, 1987.
Redcoat. London, Joseph, 1987; New York, Viking, 1988.
Sharpe's Rifles. London, Collins, and New York, Viking, 1988.
Sharpe's Revenge. London, Collins, and New York, Viking, 1989.
Sharpe's Waterloo. London, Collins, and New York, Viking, 1990.
Crackdown. New York, HarperCollins, 1990; London, Joseph, 1991.
Sharpe's Devil. London and New York, HarperCollins, 1992.
Stormchild. London, Joseph, 1991; New York, HarperCollins, 1992.
Scoundrel. London, Joseph, 1992.

Rebel. London, HarperCollins, 1993.
Copperhead. London, HarperCollins, 1993.

Novels as Susannah Kells (series: Campion)

A Crowning Mercy. London, Collins, 1983.
The Fallen Angels. London, Collins, 1984.
Coat of Arms (based on an idea by Richard Gregson). London, Collins, 1986.

OTHER PUBLICATIONS

Novels

Wildtrack. London, Joseph, and New York, Putnam, 1988.
Sea Lord. London, Joseph, and New York, Putnam, 1989.
Killer's Wake. New York, Putnam, 1989.

*

Film Adaptation: *Sharpe*, 1993, based on several of the Sharpe books; *Sharpe's Rifles*, 1993.

*   *   *

Over the past decade, Bernard Cornwell has proved himself to be a novelist of remarkable ability, whose literary skill is equalled only by his versatility. Already acknowledged as a leading figure—under two separate names—in the field of the historical novel, he has more recently begun to build a new reputation for himself outside the genre. His continuing sequence of modern adventure stories, of which *Wildtrack* is the first and most famous, reveal an expert blend of nautical background and compelling action, usually involving terrorism of some kind, whether the PLO (*Scoundrel*), or the sinister quasi-religious Genesis organization (*Stormchild*). Each novel stands on its own merits, and together they have earned their author a secure place among contemporary adventure writers. This said, the fact remains that Cornwell's most impressive contribution is to be found in the large number of historical novels he has produced under his own name, or as Susannah Kells.

The three works written under the Susannah Kells pseudonym provide a fresh and interesting insight into the nature of their author. All of them portray the changing fortunes of British aristocrats during successive historical periods, and are more openly romantic—indeed gothic, on occasion—than the Cornwell novels. The first two, *A Crowning Mercy*, and *The Fallen Angels*, are directly linked through their leading protagonists, members of the landowning Lazender family of Lazen Castle. The former describes the adventures of Campion Slythe, a beautiful young girl released from her repressive Puritan background by her love for the Royalist Toby Lazender, and interweaves their search for a mysterious fortune with a convincing Civil War background. In *The Fallen Angels*, another Campion Lazender and her brother Toby, aided by a handsome gypsy, manage to thwart a sinister cult—the Fallen Angels of the title—from spreading the horrors of the French Revolution to England. Once more the atmosphere of the September Massacres and the Terror are evoked, together with some memorably gothic scenes as the Angels perform their grim initiation rites in the Mad Duke's derelict temple. Cornwell, as Kells, achieves a compelling vision of both the Civil War and French Revolutionary periods, his powerful and exciting narratives aided by strong characterization, and some very authentic-sounding dialogue. He also manages to convey, in an uncomfortably convincing manner, the almost routine brutality and squalor that are linked with the art and culture of the time, the grim spectacle of a public execution presented with the same visual force as the splendour of a court ball. The rather stereotypical view of Puritans and French Revolutionaries, who are invariably shown as not only wicked but ugly and coarse into the bargain, is a minor flaw that in no way spoils the strength of these two novels as fine examples of the romantic historical genre. This is less true of *Coat of Arms*, where a similar aristocratic family are driven to desperate measures—including a climactic game of cards—to save their country house. Set in the post-war period, it contains good scenes and some strong characters, but lacks the overall coherence of its predecessors, and it is difficult to give credence to some of the extreme views presented. Even a writer of Cornwell's skill is taxed to make the reader believe his glamorized picture of property speculation, while the constant whingeing of his characters about the National Health Service, and the post-war Labour government, quickly becomes tiresome. *Coat of Arms*, sadly, falls short of the novels which precede it.

Without a doubt, however, the peak of Cornwell's achievement is the magnificent sequence of novels featuring his rifleman hero Richard Sharpe, which span the entire period of the Napoleonic Wars, from the viewpoint of the frontline soldier. This monolithic task has now been accomplished, and is an altogether impressive achievement, a memorable portrayal of Wellington's army worthy of comparison with the naval Hornblower novels of C.S. Forester, from whom its author drew his original inspiration.

Cornwell's painstaking research, his sure grasp of authentic period detail, enable him to bring home to the reader the scent and feeling of those vanished times, forcing him to witness afresh the savage butchery of the battles, the squalor and corruption that marks life in the early-19th century.

In the character of Richard Sharpe, the grim, scarred rifle officer commissioned from the ranks, Cornwell has created a fitting hero for his canon. Low-born and illegitimate, a ruthless professional soldier, Sharpe is convincingly presented as a man of strong and complex desires, his unremitting hatred for the enemy counter-balanced by his fierce attachment to the men under his command, his physical lusts matched by an austere code of honour from which he never deviates. While it is possible to cite the figure of Hornblower, and perhaps the rifleman Matthew Dodd in Forester's *Death to the French* as his spiritual precursors, Sharpe impresses as a powerful individual creation in his own right.

It is with Sharpe, and his giant Irish comrade Patrick Harper, that Cornwell follows the fortunes of the Peninsular Army from Moore's retreat at Corunna to Wellington's final expulsion of the French from Spain. Each novel has a particular campaign as its background, over which is superimposed Sharpe's personal mission. Cornwell excels in scenes of action, with individual duels merged into the engulfing carnage of the Napoleonic battles. The strength of his narrative impels the reader along with Sharpe and Harper and the men of the South Essex Regiment through the murderous storm of Badajoz, or the vicious closequarter fighting at the capture of the French Eagle standard at Talavera in *Sharpe's Eagle*. Cornwell recreates the fearful destruction of the citadel at Almeida (*Sharpe's Gold*), the struggle for Salamanca (*Sharpe's Sword*), and the incredible riches of Napoleon's plundered baggage train after the battle of Vitoria (*Sharpe's Honour*). Each is perfectly complemented by Sharpe's own encounters—his duel with the French swordsman Leroux, his fight to the death with the crazed bandit El Catolico outside Almeida, his love-hate relationship with the beautiful but faithless Marquesa. In every case, the work is enhanced by the wealth of minor characters, briefly but expertly drawn, whose presence helps to bring Cornwell's Napoleonic universe to life. So high is the standard of the writing, it seems invidious to single out any one novel from the rest. Suffice it to say that, for all the excellence of the earlier books, the later novels display a greater imagination and maturity. Particularly striking is *Sharpe's Regiment*, where Sharpe and Harper return to England in search of a regiment appropriated by milit-

ary speculators. Cornwell's presentation of the corruption and privilege of the army administration at this period is both salutary and utterly believable. *Sharpe's Rifles*, which chronologically predates the other novels, and *Sharpe's Siege*, which describes an ill-advised invasion of France in 1814, are almost equally good.

The last three novels of the sequence rank with the author's finest. *Sharpe's Revenge* has a graphic portrayal of the siege of Toulouse, and Sharpe's final encounter with his enemy Major Ducos on a remote villa in Naples, while *Sharpe's Waterloo* presents a superbly detailed and riveting account of the last great campaign against Napoleon. *Sharpe's Devil*, set in the aftermath of war, has Sharpe and Harper involved in a struggle for Chilean independence, and the last ambitious plans of the exiled French emperor. The exciting resolution leaves both men free to return home to their families and to settle down to a life at peace. After all the enjoyment they have given to readers, they have surely earned it!

With *Redcoat*, Cornwell ventures beyond the confines of the Napoleonic age to depict an episode from the American Revolution. Set in and around Philadelphia in the years 1777 and 1778, the novel describes the bitter conflict between the British and their erstwhile colonists, from the viewpoint of a disillusioned British soldier. Cornwell's knowledge of 18th-century warfare is thorough and accomplished, and brings home the brutality of this savage family dispute. Sam Gilpin's struggle with his divided loyalties, and his final choice, are rendered more poignant and credible by the author's masterly evocation of a forgotten place and time. *Redcoat* is an excellent historical novel, and gives further evidence of Cornwell's versatile talent.

This said, it is the Sharpe stories which provide a basis for Cornwell's reputation, and which serve to establish him as a leading historical novelist. Sharpe is one of the best fictional creations of recent years, and his adventures yield fresh insights into the Napoleonic period. With him the reader re-lives a vanished age, learning the techniques of skirmish and ambush, the handling of the deadly Baker rifle and its fearsome sword-bayonet. Cornwell brings the time alive in a manner unrivalled since Forester. On the evidence of what he has already written, he is deserving of such exalted company.

—Geoffrey Sadler

COSTAIN, Thomas B(ertram).
Nationality: American. **Born:** Brantford, Ontario, Canada, 8 May 1885. **Education:** attended schools in Brantford. **Relations:** married Ida Randolph Spragge in 1910; two daughters. **Career:** reporter, Brantford *Courier*; editor, Guelph *Daily Mercury*, Ontario, 1908–10, and *Maclean's*, Toronto, 1914–20; chief associate editor, *Saturday Evening Post*, Philadelphia, 1920–34; story editor, Twentieth Century-Fox, 1934–36; advisory editor, Doubleday, publishers, New York, 1939–46. Founding editor, *American Cavalcade* magazine, Chicago, 1937. D. Litt.: University of Western Ontario, London. **Died:** 8 October 1965.

ROMANCE AND HISTORICAL PUBLICATIONS

Novels

For My Great Folly. New York, Putnam, 1942.
Ride with Me. New York, Doubleday, 1944.
The Black Rose. New York, Doubleday, 1945; London, Staples Press, 1947.
The Moneyman. New York, Doubleday, 1947; London, Staples Press, 1948.

High Towers. New York, Doubleday, and London, Staples Press, 1949.
Son of a Hundred Kings. New York, Doubleday, 1950.
The Silver Chalice. New York, Doubleday, 1952; London, Hodder and Stoughton, 1953.
The Tontine. New York, Doubleday, 2 vols, 1955; London, Collins, 1956.
Below the Salt. New York, Doubleday, 1957; London, Collins, 1958.
The Darkness and the Dawn. New York, Doubleday, 1959; London, Collins, 1960.
The Last Love. New York, Doubleday, 1963; London, W.H. Allen, 1964.

OTHER PUBLICATIONS

Other

Joshua, Leader of a United People, with Rogers MacVeagh. New York, MacVeagh, 1943.
The Conquerors. New York, Doubleday, 1949; as *The Conquering Family,* 1962.
The Magnificent Century. New York, Doubleday, 1951.
The White and the Gold: The French Regime in Canada. New York, Doubleday, 1954; London, Collins, 1957.
The Mississippi (for children). New York, Random House, 1955.
The Three Edwards. New York, Doubleday, 1958.
William the Conqueror (for children). New York, Random House, 1959; as *All about William the Conqueror,* London, W.H. Allen, 1961.
The Chord of Steel: The Story of the Invention of the Telephone. New York, Doubleday, 1960.
The Last Plantagenets. New York, Doubleday, 1962.

Editor, with John Beecroft, *Stories* [*More Stories, 30 Stories to Remember*]. New York, Doubleday, 5 vols, 1956–61.
Editor, *Twelve Short Novels.* New York, Doubleday, 1961.
Editor, *Read with Me.* New York, Doubleday, 1965.

*

Film Adaptations: *The Black Rose,* 1950; *The Silver Chalice,* 1954.

Manuscript Collections: University of California, San Diego; University of Pennsylvania, Philadelphia; University of Texas, Austin.

*   *   *

Thomas B. Costain's historical romances combine a fascination with historical minutiae with a deep-seated desire to expose tyranny in all its facets and to promote democracy as the only truly humanistic form of government. At their best (*The Black Rose, Below the Salt, For My Great Folly*) his novels integrate historical events of great moment with the romantic frustrations of a young couple, usually separated by rank and family. The historical events range from Attila the Hun's final assault on Rome to Genghis Khan's invasion of China, from the Norman Conquest to the Magna Carta, from the founding of New Orleans to the final days of Napoleon. At their weakest, history is superimposed on romance to produce digressions and references inexplicable in terms of plot and character (*Son of a Hundred Kings, The Last Love, High Towers*). Costain's favourite digressions trace linguistic origins of words like 'rubbernecking', relate the personal history of obscure associates of famous personalities, or expostulate on democratic theories. Costain's historical evaluations are always in terms of modern American democratic values and perspectives rather than historical necessities, expectations, and sensibilities. The result is, despite the wealth of fact, ancients who talk like moderns, adolescents who could be your neighbours, and past cultures and conflicts that seem to foreshadow present democratic concepts.

His Plantagenet tetralogy is vital to understanding the virtues and vices of his historical romances. A moving pageant of history, rich in humanizing details and anecdotes ordinary histories so often ignore, it is marred by disrupted chronology necessitating repetition and by an all too modern interpretation of historical actions and relationships; Costain tries to right the record and show how even the best of kings is but a tyrant, his good acts undercut by cruelty and indifference, and how, even in mediaeval times, the democratic spirit was at work as peasants rebelled for more rights, freedom, and privilege. Such a stance leads to his justifying even their destructive acts, deploring the nobility that punished them, eulogizing the Wat Tylers and John Balls of the past. In a way this historical account verges on romance, for it pays special tribute to Richard II's love for Isabel, Henry V's for Katherine, Richard III's for Anne. Its panoramic sweep and plethora of characters and events, its attempts to reinterpret the past from a modern perspective are typical of Costain's fictive technique.

Often his heroes are men out of time who have come to view their culture—its customs, politics, and values—with disdain or disgust. Frequently they meet a visionary who looks forward to an age of democracy, fairness, and scientific advancement (Roger Bacon, Galileo, St Peter). Occasionally there are anachronisms: an awestruck 17th-century youth musing over 'the elevated conversations, the universal truths', propounded by Shakespeare, Jonson, Dekker, and Sly in the Mermaid Tavern, or the first Christians talking like 20th-century protestants. These heroes take pride in the competitive skills of their culture, and eventually match them against experts, proving they can make the longest shot, produce the fastest horse, or make a chalice worthy of Christ's last cup. They break bad laws in the name of justice and suffer long journeys and separation as self-made outcasts.

The scene frequently moves back and forth from the steppes to Rome, from Jerusalem to Antioch, from London to Peking, from Montreal to New Orleans. Ultimately these men find their destiny in a noble woman, sometimes met on journeys (*The Black Rose, Ride with Me, The Silver Chalice*), but more often a rich neighbour, loved since childhood (*Son of a Hundred Kings, For My Great Folly, High Towers, The Darkness and the Dawn, Below the Salt*). Romance thrives despite differences of race, culture, loyalty, or creed: Christian loves pagan; Norman, Saxon; orphaned factory worker, wealthy heiress. The man, always lower ranked, achieves position through courage, industry, and initiative; the factory worker turns star reporter, the lowly Saxon gains knighthood and wealth, the waif turns architectural genius.

Costain strives to integrate historical pageant with the trials and tribulations of his lovers. *The Darkness and the Dawn* traces the last years of Attila the Hun, particularly his final unsuccessful assault on Rome, to contrast the effete decadence of Roman culture with the hearty practicality of Mongolian hordes, to emphasize the dehumanizing effects of both extremes, and to eulogize the rebelliousness of spirited plainsmen who must toy with tyranny ultimately to be free—play Rome against Hun for their own advantage. To win his Norman lady's hand, in *The Black Rose,* a Saxon noble, his fortune lost to Norman invaders, seeks fame and fortune in a daring trip to China where he meets, rescues, and falls in love with the captive daughter of a Saxon crusader. To save her, he must outwit slave traders and Mongols alike, and put his trust in a Chinese legend about pale visitors who foretell the will of gods. In *Below the Salt,* a novel mix of modern and mediaeval, an American senator employs a young writer to help him write his biography, trace the Plantagenet line in Ireland, uncover a Saxon document that inspired the Magna Carta, and confirm his Saxon past and 20th-century present. The story moves from the sadistic tortures, dank cells, and limited horizons that Costain always associates with tyrannies to a modern romance involving descendants of the ghost who walks their hills. *For My Great Folly* is a convincing portrait of the Free Rovers, brave and lusty English sea captains like John Ward, who, despite James I's opposition, modelled their seamanship on Sir Walter Raleigh and fought to keep the lanes open for English ships—attacking Spanish vessels, freeing slaves, and taking rich booty. The tale sweeps through the Mediterranean and captures the grim horrors of sea life (rickets, scurvy, death-in-a-basket, becalmed seas) as well as the pride in seamanship and craftsmanship that made English sailors great. Its central character spurns court posturing for the romance and patriotism of the high seas, and acts with courage to force a foolish king to act for England's honor and safety. *Ride with Me* follows the romantic adventures of a lame newspaper man, who uses his paper to goad the government into decisive action against Napoleon; who initiates the use of carrier pigeons, war correspondents, 'special' editions, and the power press to improve news service; and who pursues his vivacious French mistress, a Royalist turned Bonapartist, through the major steps in the Napoleonic saga: Spain, Russia, escape from Elba, defeat at Waterloo, and bloody reprisal therafter. Doubtful of his prowess and ability, the hero discovers his strengths as, separated by distance, by scandal, by political conviction, he seeks his beloved. As is clear from each of these books, it is the amalgam of beautiful women, idealistic men, and tyrannical threats that most interests Costain. However, in an attempt to make a political point, too often Costain makes his heroes and heroines sacrificial idealists, his villains self-centred sadists.

Several of Costain's books involve the history of important merchant families. *The Moneyman* focuses on the influence of wealthy merchant Jacques Coeur and his family on trade and politics during the reign of Charles VII; *The Tontine* involves two families entangled in an annuity-lottery-insurance scheme; *High Towers* traces the LeMoyne family's willing sacrifice of individual members for a greater cause—conquering the wilderness and building an empire for France; their success in driving out hostile Indians, frustrating greedy countrymen, and manipulating a hesitant king to found New Orleans and control the Mississippi seems to justify this stance. *Son of a Hundred Kings* deals with one of Costain's many orphans who seek their heritage, but its main thrust is the conflicts, competitions, and hatreds of a wealthy, turn-of-the-century Canadian family that rose to fame and wealth through investments in journalism and motorcars.

When Costain is content to focus on plot and character and to discuss historical events only as they relate to his central focus, his books have a compelling force that commands interest, but when he lets his fascination with detail lead him to wander from the plot, his novels degenerate into a disconnected patchwork of anecdotes. *The Last Love* is typical of his attempts to do too much, for it tries to recreate Napoleon's drive, power, triumph, and genius; humanize him; characterize those important figures around him, including past loves; summarize his significant acts and battles; and follow the metamorphosis of his final, would-be mistress from childhood to womanhood. Thus, Costain must be evaluated in terms of how well he reconciles his different but ambitious goals, the extremes of depicting detailed history, creating exciting plot, indulging in sentimental romance, and defending democratic idealism.

—Gina Macdonald

———

COULSON, Juanita (Ruth). American. 1933—. See 2nd edition, 1990.

———

COULTER, Catherine.
Pseudonym for Jean Coulter Pogony. **Nationality:** American. **Born:** Texas. **Education:** University of Texas, Austin, B.A.; Boston College, Massachusetts, M.A. **Relations:** married Anton Coulter. **Career:** worked in human resources for firms in New York City and San Francisco. Writer. Lives in Mill Valley, California. **Recipient:** *Romantic Times* award for best historical author, 1989. **Agent:** Robert Gottlieb, William Morris Agency, 1350 Avenue of the Americas, New York, New York 10019, USA.

ROMANCE AND HISTORICAL PUBLICATIONS

Novels (series: Bride Trilogy; Welles; Magic Trilogy; Night Trilogy; Delaney Saxton; Song Trilogy; Star Trilogy)

The Rebel Bride. New York, New American Library, 1979; revised edition, New York, Topaz, 1993.
The Autumn Countess. New York, New American Library, 1979.
Lord Harry's Folly. New York, New American Library, 1980.
Lord Deverill's Heir. New York, New American Library, 1980.
The Generous Earl. New York, New American Library, 1981.
An Honorable Offer. New York, New American Library, 1981.
Devil's Embrace (Welles). New York, New American Library, 1982.
An Intimate Deception. New York, New American Library, 1983.
Sweet Surrender (Saxton). New York, New American Library, 1984.
Chandra. New York, New American Library, 1984.
Devil's Daughter (Welles). New York, New American Library, 1985.
Aftershocks. New York, Silhouette, 1985; Toronto, Harlequin, 1993.
Song Trilogy:
    Fire Song. New York, New American Library, 1985; London, Severn House, 1990.
    Earth Song. New York, New American Library, 1990; London, Severn House, 1993.
    Secret Song. New York, Severn House, 1991.
The Aristocrat. New York, Silhouette, 1986; Toronto, Harlequin, 1990.
Texas Spitfire. New York, Zebra, 1986.
Scoundrel's Bride. New York, Zebra, 1986.
Rapture's Rogue. New York, Zebra, 1986.
Surrender to Desire. New York, Zebra, 1986.
Texas Bride. New York, Zebra, 1986.
Wild Texas Loving. New York, Zebra, 1986.
Star Trilogy:
    Midnight Star (Saxton). New York, New American Library, 1986.
    Wild Star. New York, Onyx, 1986.
    Jade Star. New York, New American Library, 1987.
Afterglow. New York, Silhouette, 1987; Toronto, Harlequin, 1992.
Magic Trilogy:
    Midsummer Magic. New York, New American Library, 1987.
    Moonspun Magic. New York, New American Library, 1988.
    Calypso Magic. New York, New American Library, 1988.
False Pretenses. New York, New American Library, 1988; London, Sphere, 1989.
Night Trilogy:
    Night Shadow. New York, Avon, 1989.
    Night Fire. New York, Avon, 1989.
    Night Storm. New York, Avon, 1990.
    Impulse. London, Piatkus, and New York, New American Library, 1990.
Season of the Sun. New York, Dutton, 1991.

Bride Trilogy:
Sherbrooke Bride. New York, Putnam, 1992; London, Orion, 1993.
The Hellion Bride. New York, Putnam, 1992; London, Orion, 1993.
The Heiress Bride. New York, Putnam, 1993; London, Orion, 1993.
Beyond Eden. New York, Dutton, 1992.
Lord of Hawkfell Island. New York, Jove, 1993.
The Whyndham Legacy. New York, Putnam, 1994.

*   *   *

A prolific author of historical romances, Catherine Coulter has set her works in several historical periods and locations, but she favours 19th-century England. No matter the time or place, however, she creates a believable environment for her characters to inhabit.

Like many romance authors, Coulter connects titles, usually by employing the same characters in several books. Some of these links are looser than others since at times the reappearance of a character is no more than a walk-on role. The strongest connection between books is seen in those linked by family. Anthony and Cassandra, of *Devil's Embrace*, are parents of Arabella, the heroine of *Devil's Daughter*. Coulter's 'Bride Trilogy' features members of the Sherbrooke family, Douglas Sherbrooke, Earl of Northcliffe, is the hero of *The Sherbrooke Bride*. His brother, Ryder, takes centre stage in *The Hellion Bride*. Their spirited sister, Sinjun (Joan), is the heroine of *The Heiress Bride*. Although there is a third brother, Tysen, it seems his career choice as a clergyman makes him too stuffy to be considered as a hero in his own book.

Coulter has published several more loosely linked series, such as the 'Song', 'Night', 'Magic', and 'Star' Trilogies. *Earth Song, Fire Song,* and *Secret Song* are set in 13th-century England and tell the stories of several women fighting not to be barter in the dealings of men and for their own rights. The 'Night Trilogy' (*Night Fire, Night Shadow,* and *Night Storm*) takes place in 19th-century England and America and again features women battling for their rights and a place in a man's world. *Midsummer Magic, Calypso Magic,* and *Moonspun Magic* involve a group of friends in plots set in England and the West Indies of the 1800s. *Midnight Star, Wild Star,* and *Jade Star* are set in the American West of the same time period. *Midnight Star* is also linked to an earlier novel, *Sweet Surrender,* by the character of Delaney Saxton. Coulter's Regency novels include *An Intimate Deception, Lord Harry's Folly,* and *The Rebel Bride.*

In 1985, Coulter made a successful entry into the ranks of contemporary romance authors with *Aftershocks* in the Silhouette Intimate Moments line. Dr Elliot Mallory and model Georgina 'George' Hathaway are an engaging couple, and their somewhat rocky relationship is depicted with style and humour by Coulter. They are quickly attracted to one another when they meet, but Elliot eventually breaks up with George because he feels he is too old for her and would only hold her back in her career. He also does not trust her to recognize true love and tries to prevent future pain if she were to find someone closer to her own age. George, on the other hand, knows precisely what she wants and that is Elliot. Although she is deeply hurt by Elliot's decision, she has the courage to fight for her love. Coulter is at her best with this story, showing her talent for developing characters in depth and a deft comic touch in several scenes. George's practical joke on the ski slopes and her later alcoholic binge are amusingly described by Coulter. She also demonstrates a flair for witty dialogue. *Afterglow,* published in the same line, shows many of these same qualities.

Although she is obviously capable of writing a good light-hearted contemporary romance, when Coulter moved to hardcover editions, she also moved on to incorporating darker themes with her stories of romance and suspense. *False Pretenses, Impulse,* and *Beyond Eden*

all present more complex stories of intrigue in which romance often takes a back seat to a tangled plot, often with mixed results. Coulter seems much less confident in developing elements of mystery and suspense than she is in simply writing a good love story.

Coulter obviously has a wide following, but she also is somewhat controversial and has enjoyed a mixed critical reception. She often is praised for creating likeable, dynamic characters and putting them in a spicy, adventure-filled story. On the other hand, she is criticized for seeming to dwell on a dark, often painful view of sex. Anthony Welles (*Devil's Embrace*) is so taken by young Cassandra that he kidnaps her, taking her on a ship to his home in Italy. Mistakenly believing her to be experienced, he is jealous and rapes her. This basically hostile relationship continues throughout the voyage. Later, a pregnant Cassandra is kidnapped again, this time by a member of an Italian secret society. They repeatedly rape and brutalize her. She loses her child as a direct result of this experience. In *Devil's Daughter*, Arabella, their daughter, is kidnapped and kept as a harem love-slave by Kamal, Bey of Oran. In *Season of the Sun*, Magnus, a Viking, arranges to take Zarabeth as his slave and mistress in revenge for a perceived rejection of his courtship of her. Similar scenes of sexual violence appear in all of the historical romances. Coulter's women are subjected to abuse and humiliation but end up loving their tormentors. She seems to say that such actions are exciting if taken by 'Mr Right'.

Coulter walks a fine line in developing these themes, but it is apparent from her following that her graphic descriptions of these sorts of relationships are popular with her readers, if not the critics.

—Barbara E. Kemp

COURTNEY, Caroline. Address: c/o Arlington Books, 15–17 King Street, London S.W.1. England.

ROMANCE AND HISTORICAL PUBLICATIONS

Novels

Duchess in Disguise. New York, Warner, and London, Arlington, 1979.
A Wager for Love. New York, Warner, and London, Arlington, 1979.
Love Unmasked. New York, Warner, and London, Arlington, 1979.
Guardian of the Heart. New York, Warner, 1979; London, Arlington, 1980.
Dangerous Engagement. New York, Warner, 1979; London, Arlington, 1980.
The Fortunes of Love. New York, Warner, and London, Arlington, 1980.
Forbidden Love. New York, Warner, 1980; London, Arlington, 1982.
Love Triumphant. New York, Warner, 1980.
Heart of Honour. London, Arlington, 1980.
The Romantic Rivals. New York, Warner, and Arlington, 1980.
Love's Masquerade. London, Arlington, 1981.
Love of My Life. New York, Warner, 1981; London, Arlington, 1983.
Libertine in Love. London, Arlington, 1982.
Abandoned for Love. Boston, Hall, 1982; London, Arlington, 1983.
Destiny's Duchess. London, Arlington, 1983.
The Tempestuous Affair. London, Arlington, 1983; Boston, Hall, 1985.
The Daring Heart. Boston, Hall, 1983; London, Arlington, 1985.
The Masquerading Heart. London, Arlington, 1984.
A Lover's Victory. London, Arlington, 1984.

Love in Waiting. London, Arlington, 1984.
The Courier of Love. London, Arlington, 1984; Boston, Hall, 1986.
Hearts or Diamonds. London, Arlington, 1985.
Prisoner of Passion. London, Arlington, 1985.
Dual Enchantment. London, Arlington, 1985.
Conspiracy of Kisses. London, Arlington, 1986.

*   *   *

Of all the contemporary romance novelists, Caroline Courtney is the most likely to succeed Barbara Cartland as the grande dame of the formula romance. Her characters and style recall the early Cartland at her best, before her heroines became too breathless or incoherent to speak in complete sentences. The plots are simplistic and focus on the heroine and her emotions. The innocent heroines and stalwart heroes are likable people who display all the requisite virtues, such as sensitivity, fidelity, tenderness, and self-sacrifice. Even the names are right: Clorinda, Davinia, Candida, Serenity, Valeria; Julian, Gilles, Justin, Greville, Auberon. Whatever the names, however, the hero and heroine are clearly meant for each other from the moment they meet, although there are always problems to overcome before they can be united and love triumph over all.

One of her earliest novels, *Duchess in Disguise*, exhibits the general characteristics and themes found in her other books. Clorinda, a pure, young country miss, weds a notorious rake, the Duke of Westhampton. Dismissed to one of his country estates, she resolves to seek revenge. She disguises herself and poses as yet another virginal innocent, and in this guise she wins his love. He learns the value of true love and is ready to sacrifice his reputation to pursue this ideal. Mutual love is revealed and everyone lives happily ever after.

The idea of the masquerade or disguise appears in about half of Courtney's novels, and is directly reflected in several titles. Similarly the theme of the disillusioned rake redeemed by pure love occurs frequently (*A Wager for Love, Guardian of the Heart, Forbidden Love, Libertine in Love*). Obviously none of this is particularly original. Fans of Barbara Cartland and Georgette Heyer will undoubtedly recognize many of the elements in Courtney's plots. However, Courtney has polished the romance formula to a fine sheen. For sheer escapist, romantic fantasy, she is hard to beat.

—Barbara E. Kemp

COWEN, Frances.
Pseudonym: Eleanor Hyde. **Nationality:** British. **Born:** Oxford, 27 December 1915. **Education:** Ursuline Convent, Oxford, 1920–28; Milham Ford School, Oxford, 1928–35. **Relations:** married George Heinrich Munthe in 1938 (died 1941); one daughter. **Career:** worked for Blackwell, publishers, Oxford, 1938–39; member of Air Raid Precautions staff, Dartmouth, Devon, 1940–44; assistant secretary, Royal Literary Fund, London, 1955–66. **Address:** c/o Robert Hale Ltd, 45–47 Clerkenwell Green, London EC1R 0HT, England.

ROMANCE AND HISTORICAL PUBLICATIONS

Novels

The Little Heiress. London, Gresham, 1961.
The Balcony. London, Gresham, 1962.
A Step in the Dark. London, Gresham, 1962.
The Desperate Holiday. London, Gresham, 1962.
The Elusive Quest. London, Gresham, 1965.
The Bitter Reason. London, Gresham, 1966.

Scented Danger. London, Gresham, 1966.
The One Between. London, Hale, 1967.
The Gentle Obsession. London, Hale, 1968.
The Fractured Silence. London, Hale, 1969.
The Daylight Fear. London, Hale, 1969; New York, Ace, 1973.
The Shadow of Polperro. London, Hale, 1969; New York, Ace, 1973.
Edge of Terror. London, Hale, 1970.
The Hounds of Carvello. London, Hale, 1970; New York, Ace, 1973.
The Nightmare Ends. London, Hale, 1970; New York, Ace, 1972.
The Lake of Darkness. London, Hale, 1971; New York, Ace, 1974.
The Unforgiving Moment. London, Hale, 1971.
The Curse of the Clodaghs. London, Hale, 1973; New York, Ace, 1974.
Shadow of Theale. London, Hale, and New York, Ace, 1974.
The Village of Fear. New York, Ace, 1974; London, Hale, 1975.
The Secret of Weir House. London, Hale, 1975.
The Dangerous Child. London, Hale, 1975.
The Haunting of Helen Farley. London, Hale, 1976.
The Medusa Connection. London, Hale, 1976.
Sinister Melody. London, Hale, 1976.
The Silent Pool. London, Hale, 1977.
The Lost One. London, Hale, 1977.
Gateway to Nowhere. London, Hale, 1978.
The House Without a Heart. London, Hale, 1978.
House of Larne. London, Hale, 1980.
Wait for Night. London, Hale, 1980.
The Elusive Lover. London, Hale, 1981.
Sunrise at Even. London, Hale, 1982.

Novels as Eleanor Hyde (series: Tudor)

Tudor Maid. London, Hale, 1972.
Tudor Masquerade. London, Hale, 1972.
Tudor Mayhem. London, Hale, 1973.
Tudor Mystery. London, Hale, 1974.
Tudor Myth. London, Hale, 1976.
Tudor Mausoleum. London, Hale, 1977.
Tudor Murder. London, Hale, 1977.
Tudor Mansion. London, Hale, 1978.
Tudor Malice. London, Hale, 1979.
The Princess Passes. London, Hale, 1979.

OTHER PUBLICATIONS

Other (for children)

In the Clutch of the Green Hand. London, Nelson, 1929.
The Wings That Failed. London, Collins, 1931; abridged edition, as *The Plot That Failed*, 1933.
The Milhurst Mystery. London, Blackie, 1933.
The Conspiracy of Silence. London, Sheldon Press, 1935.
The Perilous Adventure. London, Queensway Press, 1936.
Children's Book of Pantomimes. London, Cassell, 1936.
Laddie's Way: The Adventures of a Fox Terrier. London, Lutterworth Press, 1939.
The Girl Who Knew Too Much. London, Lutterworth Press, 1940.
Mystery Tower. London, Lutterworth Press, 1945.
Honor Bound. London, Lutterworth Press, 1946.
Castle in Wales. Huddersfield, Schofield and Sims, 1947.
The Secret of Arrival. Huddersfield, Schofield and Sims, 1947.
Mystery at the Walled House. London, Lutterworth Press, 1951.
The Little Countess. London, Thames, 1954.
The Riddle of the Rocks. London, Lutterworth Press, 1956.

Clover Cottage. London, Blackie, 1958.
The Secret of Grange Farm. London, Children's Press, 1961.
The Secret of the Loch. London, Children's Press, 1963.

*   *   *

Frances Cowen is adept at producing emotional suspense stories—for children in full-length books and tales published in the *Girl's Own Paper* and in adult detective fiction and thriller romances. She has been writing for more than five decades but her feeling for the romantic gothic mood is as intense as ever. *The Secret of Weir House* combines the flavours of Edwardian and modern life with English and American interest. Gisele—from the USA—inherits a Thames-side Victorian house from a remote English relative, but when she arrives to claim her property, it is not only occupied by squatters but overhung with a ghostly mystery that is linked to the death by drowning of a great-aunt just before World War I. Stephen, a London social worker, however, not only helps Gisele to unravel the mystery but, of course, to find love.

Cowen is most strongly associated with romance when she writes historical novels as Eleanor Hyde. There are nine of these books in the 'Tudor' series, with vivid conveyance of the period by discerning use of historical trappings, ritual pageantry and splendours. There are the sights and sounds of viol, lute, and recorder playing in the musicians' gallery of great houses; the herb garden of a country manor; the 'chaotic medley' of men-at-arms, ladies-in-waiting, and courtiers attending 'Gloriana' on one of her journeys—and so on. Events in the first of these novels (*Tudor Maid*) clearly illustrate the dramatic and romantic nature of the series. Ann de Chaubriez, the illegitimate daughter of a French marquis and an English mother, is brought up in France. Eventually, orphaned abruptly by her father's murder, and unprovided for, she is taken to England to work ostensibly as a governess in the home of an unscrupulous plotter against the Queen: he tries to use Ann's auburn-haired, pale-faced resemblance to the Queen in a scheme to overthrow her.

Ann undergoes some hair-raising adventures before being rescued from these intrigues by Richard Davenant—a young Englishman who not only clears her reputation but marries her. Similar themes recur in the books. In the last novel of the series, *Tudor Malice*, there is another orphaned heroine, Isobelle, who finds herself exposed to black magic as well as court intrigues. In her case too, romantic love—in the shape of a miller's son, Matthew Holborn—lifts her out of the hazards of association with magic and majesty.

—Mary Cadogan

———

COX, Josephine.
Pseudonym: Jane Brindle. **Nationality:** British. **Born:** England, 15 July 1938. **Education:** Ragged School, Blackburn, Lancashire, 1943–45; St Anne's, Blackburn, Lancashire, 1945–54; Bletchley Centre of Further Education, 1968–73; Bedford Teacher Training, 1973–76. **Relations:** married Kenneth George in 1956; two sons. **Career:** typist, 1970–72, personnel officer, 1972–73, MKDC, Milton Keynes; teacher, 1976–88, Bedfordshire Council. Since 1987, full-time writer. **Agent:** Anthony Shiel, 43 Doughty Street, London, England. **Address:** 11, Burrows Close, Woburn Sands, Milton Keynes, MK1 85S, England.

Romance and Historical Publications

Novels (series: Emma Grady)

Her Father's Sins (Grady). London, Macdonald, 1987.

Let Loose the Tigers (Grady). London, Macdonald, 1987.
Angels Cry Sometimes (Grady). London, Macdonald, 1988.
Take This Woman (Grady). London, Macdonald, 1988; New York, Evans, 1991.
Whistledown Woman (Grady). London, Macdonald, 1989; New York, Evans, 1990.
Outcast (Grady). London, Macdonald, 1989.
Alley Urchin (Grady). London, Macdonald, 1990.
Vagabonds (Grady). London, Macdonald, 1990.
Don't Cry Alone. London, Headline, 1992.
Scarlet (as Jane Brindle). London, Sphere, 1992.
No Mercy (as Jane Brindle). London, Sphere, 1992.
Jessica's Girl. London, Headline, 1993.
Nobody's Darling. London, Headline, 1993.

*

Manuscript Collection: Anthony Sheil, Sheil Land, 43 Doughty Street, London.

Josephine Cox comments:
All of my work reflects the tapestry of life itself—love, fear, and all the emotions that touch the heart. Many of my characters are drawn from my own life experience, and almost all of the settings are authentic. Between the pages of any one of my novels, the reader can experience life's struggles, joys and the deep satisfaction that comes with love and achievement. Conversely, there is also greed, hatred and possessiveness. One facet always—must—balance another. Because most of my work is historical, it is necessary to travel back over documentation and available research, in order to bring alive the history in the story. More than that, it is the characters themselves that speak and act in the 'colourful' way of our forefathers. Each book I write is, not only a labour of love for me, but a great joy and privilege.

*   *   *

Josephine Cox draws on her own experience to describe the struggle and hardship of family life. Setting novels in familiar terrain, she successfully transcends the present with excellent recreations of domestic life in other eras. The affinity she clearly feels for honest people is apparent in her characters. The desire to avenge the injustices wrought by amoral people upon the powerless is strong in her plots. Maternal instinct too is unwavering in her heroines, who will do anything necessary to protect and foster their children.

Cox's eighth novel *Vagabonds*, is the concluding volume of the Emma Grady series. Set in Lancashire, in 1885–1887, it describes the struggle of a young woman with three children to establish a stable loving family. In great need of emotional and financial support, and companionship she searches for her husband, Jack. She loves him faithfully and accepts his almost total neglect of her and their children's needs until he leaves her again after the birth of their third child. A love triangle develops—Molly loves Jack, Jack can't grow up, and kind, constant Mick loves Molly. Alone in the world, Molly's only link to her past is the alcoholic tramp who brought her up, and the clasp of a timepiece. She is hounded by a corrupt judge, (Justice Crowther), who wrongfully accused her of kidnapping his grandson. When she is forced to flee, she is constantly hounded by different men, drawn to her because of her beauty, eager to capitalize on her vulnerability. Emma Grady's bitterness at the loss of her daughter when sentenced to a term in Australia—by her relative the evil Justice—is exacerbated by the death of her son. Justice not only took Emma's liberty, but her inheritance. He is wealthy, but is morally poor; indeed he is a totally corrupt and despicable figure. Emma fights evil, so he must be punished. Every character holds a part of the jigsaw of the family, which is very satisfactorily put into place at the end.

Jessica's Girl is set in Lancashire in 1925–26. Phoebe, a beautiful young woman of poor background, is forced to live with a recently found uncle after the death of her beloved mother. She leaves her home and friends in the East End of London for Lancashire. Her uncle, Edward Dickens, a self made businessman (a gentleman's outfitter, but no gentleman himself), lives in a grand house with his meek wife, Noreen, and his spoilt daughter, Margaret. Mr Dickens gradually shows himself to be a sadistic and dangerous man, keen on duty and delivering 'fire and brimstone' sermons. He inflicts a reign of terror upon the members of his household—all women.

Phoebe must be strong to survive the abuse she encounters, recalling the Trollope quotation at the beginning of the novel: 'Those who have courage to love should have courage to suffer'. It is hard to envisage that Phoebe will ever attain peace, happiness, and an independent life with the man she loves. However after much suffering, finally she does.

Cox also writes as Jane Brindle. *Scarlet* starts in New York, in 1937, and moves to the English West Country. A promising young artist, Cassie's past and identity have been destroyed by the unforgiving rich man she thought was her father. She leaves America behind to find the mother she has just recently learnt of. The only connection she has to her real mother is a desperate note sent from the West Country of England, signed Scarlet Pengally. Much darker than the novels written under her own name, the novels written as Jane Brindle tell of lurking menace, constant dread, tragic death, and unhealthy relationships—within, and out the family. Desire, conflict, and passion are the themes that run throughout *Scarlet*—a name loaded with romantic associations. The world is a cruel and frightening place for this young woman trapped in an old isolated family home, with just her kind and loving, but weakened mother as her ally. Her father, and his young worker in the smithy, are both the source of consuming desire, conflict, and passion. The house itself exerts a strong influence over Scarlet, almost as though it was a sentient entity.

Nature too draws Scarlet. The wild moors console and pacify her, but unseen, threatening things are there, as are tragic deaths. Scarlet's struggle for survival is hard, the sustaining love of her mother and daughter the only support to motivate her—but both fall short, in physical presence, to over balance the scales of good over evil. Cassie determines the identity of her mother, and of herself and her past, and is resolved to make a happy future from a tragic past. The moral ambiguity of the main protagonist's lover makes for fascinating reading. The reader is uncertain of his true nature and intent. This is a cryptic suspenseful novel with a surprising climax.

—Iris Wakulenko

COYLE, William.   See **KENEALLY, Thomas.**

CRAMPTON, Helen.   See **CHESNEY, Marion.**

CRAVEN, Sara.
Nationality: British. **Born:** Anne Bushell. **Address:** c/o Mills and Boon Ltd, Eton House, 18–24 Paradise Road, Richmond, Surrey TW9 1SR, England.

ROMANCE AND HISTORICAL PUBLICATIONS

Novels

The Garden of Dreams. London, Mills and Boon, 1975.

A Gift for a Lion. London, Mills and Boon, 1977.
A Place of Storms. London, Mills and Boon, 1977.
Strange Adventure. London, Mills and Boon, 1977.
Temple of the Moon. London, Mills and Boon, 1977.
Wild Melody. London, Mills and Boon, 1977.
Dragon's Lair. London, Mills and Boon, 1978.
High Tide at Midnight. London, Mills and Boon, 1978.
Past All Forgetting. London, Mills and Boon, 1978.
The Devil at Archangel. London, Mills and Boon, 1978.
Flame of Diablo. London, Mills and Boon, 1979.
Moth to the Flame. London, Mills and Boon, 1979.
Solitaire. London, Mills and Boon, 1979.
Fugitive Wife. London, Mills and Boon, 1980.
Moon of Aphrodite. London, Mills and Boon, 1980.
Shadow of Desire. London, Mills and Boon, 1980.
Dark Summer Dawn. London, Mills and Boon, 1981; Toronto, Harlequin, 1982.
Summer of the Raven. London, Mills and Boon, 1981.
Witching Hour. London, Mills and Boon, 1981.
Counterfeit Bride. London, Mills and Boon, 1982; Toronto, Harlequin, 1983.
Unguarded Moment. London, Mills and Boon, 1982; Toronto, Harlequin, 1982.
A Bad Enemy. London, Mills and Boon, and Toronto, Harlequin, 1983.
Pagan Adversary. London, Mills and Boon, and Toronto, Harlequin, 1983.
Sup with the Devil. London, Mills and Boon, 1983, and Toronto, Harlequin, 1983.
Dark Paradise. London, Mills and Boon, 1984.
Alien Vengeance. London, Mills and Boon, 1985.
Act of Betrayal. London, Mills and Boon, 1985.
Escape Me Never. London, Mills and Boon, 1985.
Promise of the Unicorn. London, Mills and Boon, 1985.
A High Price to Pay. London, Mills and Boon, 1986.
The Marriage Deal. London, Mills and Boon, 1986.
Night of the Condor. London, Mills and Boon, 1987; Toronto, Harlequin, 1989.
Outsider. London, Mills and Boon, 1987.
Witch's Harvest. London, Mills and Boon, 1987.
Flawless. London, Mills and Boon, 1989; Toronto, Harlequin, 1990.
Storm Force. London, Mills and Boon, 1989.
King of Swords. London, Mills and Boon, 1988; Toronto, Harlequin, 1989.
Island of the Heart. London, Mills and Boon, 1989; Toronto, Harlequin, 1990.
When the Devil Drives. London, Mills and Boon, 1991.
Dark Ransom. London, Mills and Boon, 1992; Toronto, Harlequin, 1993.
Desperate Measures. London, Mills and Boon, 1992.
Tower of Shadows. London, Mills and Boon, 1993.
Dawn Song. London, Mills and Boon, 1993.

*   *   *

Sara Craven's romances are reminiscent of the novels of the 1920s and 1930s in which the heroine is forced into a relationship with the hero against her better judgement, but then comes to realize how much she has misunderstood him and how much she loves him.

This is shown in its weakest form in *Wild Melody*, in which Catriona Muir, a young and very naive Scottish girl, travels to London to find the man with whom she had a brief romance. Instead she encounters his uncle, Jason Lord, a rich, sophisticated, and extremely attractive television producer. Catriona's first disillusionment comes when Jason takes her to a party at his sister's house to be reunited with his nephew Jeremy, and it turns out to be a celebration of Jeremy's engagement to another woman. Catriona pretends to be Jason's girlfriend to save face, and arouses Jeremy's interest again. However, she realizes how much more attractive, sensitive, and worthy of her love Jason is—and falls in love with him. Jason in turn, refuses to treat her like the women in his past, and decides to marry her instead of just taking her to his bed.

Alain de Courcy, in *Desperate Measures*, offers Philippa Roscoe a chance to save her dying father's life. He asks her to marry him in exchange for paying for her father's medical expenses. Alain needs a wife because his involvement with the spouse of a prominent French politician is in danger of affecting his career. His uncle wants Alain's resignation, and only marriage to Philippa can save his face. Unfortunately, the wedding night scene involves Philippa being raped by her husband, while secretly wanting him to make love to her. The beautiful Marie-Laure de Sommerville-Resnais is the rival love interest whom Alain, of course, actually doesn't love at all. Philippa, also an art student, realizes how much she loves him when she sketches him—in a very clichéd scene. After dissolving into each other's arms, Philippa and Alain realize how much they love each other. Only the author's writing skill saves the book from being anachronistic.

Dark Ransom features a heroine who, while holidaying in the Brazilian interior, agrees, due to her slightly gullible but caring personality, to deliver a package for a woman whom she meets on a boat. She finds herself 'kidnapped' by some men and delivered into the hands of the noble, and seemingly gorgeous hero, Riago da Santana. The package contains a silk dressing gown, and Charlie, the heroine, finds herself propositioned, and eventually seduced by Riago. Realizing that she is a virgin (as are most of Craven's female protagonists), Riago demands that she marry him. The plot is further complicated by the entrance of an extremely sick man, Philip, who turns out to be the nephew of one of Charlie's care patients in England, and who is also a crook. She realizes that she is in love with Riago, who, in turn, is in love with his sister-in-law. Charlie thus decides to leave with Philip. The complicated delivery of a baby prevents Charlie from leaving and she finds herself back at Riago's plantation— and back in her hero's arms.

Saul Kingsland, the hero of *Flawless*, finds himself falling in love with a woman bent on revenge. Carly has transformed herself from the shy gawky girl who once had a crush on Saul, into a gorgeous international model. Unfortunately she has lost most of her softness—and reason!—in the process. She wins a lucrative modelling deal by catching Saul's attention, and decides to use it to ruin her reputation as a photographer. Fortunately Saul 'saves' her by wrecking her plans—and by loving her so much that the fact that she has behaved in a seemingly distasteful way doesn't matter at all. The plot of this book is interesting as Craven creates a heroine who is not immediately likeable, reasonable, or rational; Carly is willing to wreck both her own and her hero's lives because of a misunderstanding from her past. However, the essential message in this and the author's other books is: if you love someone enough things will always work out.

Craven's later books feature capable heroines with careers who ultimately need the help or backing of a man to help them achieve success or happiness. This can be seen in *The Marriage Deal*, in which the heroine, Ashley, is a successful business woman whose company is in danger of a take-over bid. Only the intervention of Jago Marrick, her ex-fiancé and businessman extraordinaire, saves the business. It also stops Ashley from being the cold, 'frigid' woman she is in danger of becoming at the beginning of the book. The protagonists marry but only later do Jago and Ashley realize how much they really love each other.

The essential ingredients of a successful formula romance writer include a strong, attractive, and dominant hero, and a heroine who, in spite of her various capabilities, needs a man to make her life complete. Craven undoubtedly binds her mixture well, adding interesting locations—including France, her home—and well-written dialogue as added spice. However, her predilection for masterful men who 'overpower' their women in the bedroom could be deemed outdated, and in the hands of a less skilled writer could be seen as offensive. Craven does remain one of Mills and Boon's most successful writers proving that her scenarios and characters are still popular among romance fans today.

—P. Campbell

CRAWFORD, Robert. See **STIRLING, Jessica.**

CRICHTON, Lucilla. See **ANDREWS, Lucilla.**

CROSBY, Caroline. See **STIRLING, Jessica.**

CROWE, Cecily.
Nationality: American. **Born:** Cecily Teague, New York City. **Education:** St Agatha School, New York; Columbia University, New York. **Relations:** married 1) Richard H. Crowe (died), one daughter; 2) James A. Bentley in 1975. **Agent:** Harold Ober Associates, 40 East 49th Street, New York, New York 10017, USA. **Address:** Brick House, Mirror Lake, New Hampshire 03853, USA.

ROMANCE AND HISTORICAL PUBLICATIONS

Novels

Miss Spring. New York, Random House, 1953.
The Tower of Kilraven. New York, Holt Rinehart, 1965.
Northwater. New York, Holt Rinehart, 1968.
The Twice-Born. New York, Random House, 1972.
Abbeygate. New York, Coward McCann, 1977.
The Talisman. New York, St Martin's Press, 1979.
Bloodrose House. New York, St Martin's Press, 1985.

*

Manuscript Collection: Boston University Library.

*   *   *

It is obvious that Cecily Crowe honed her novelistic skills by writing short stories. Her prose style is exquisitely crafted and tight as befits the short story, which must reveal much in a confined space. Crowe's novels burst with highly detailed, almost practised descriptive passages. One feels that she knows every secret of the lives of even her minor characters.

While these novels fall into the category of romantic suspense their true emphasis is on romance, in the sense that both the characters and the reader are transported to a world remote from ordinary life. The heroines are as a rule rather unglamorous women, often older than the average romantic heroine. For the most part they are widows or in some manner losers at love. When these women are transplanted into exotic environments like castles and brought into contact with traditionally brooding gothic heroes their adventures are escapist entertainment of the highest order. Crowe's sense of humour saves her work from being merely frothy. There is a tongue-in-cheek feeling about much of her work that seems lovingly to parody the style that she has chosen. Her humour is evident in *The Tower of Kilraven* when she first describes the frankly sexual allure of one of the heroes and then describes him as mounted upon a 'tall, self-centred-looking horse'. Flashes of such humour and mockery as this run through most of her work.

The characters in Crowe's writing are so painstakingly delineated that they stand out against the rich backgrounds like beautifully detailed miniatures. Even children, who often get very short shrift in romances, are treated as full characters rather than plot devices. Thomas, Maggie, and Anne in *Abbeygate* are memorable for their complete naturalness. They are neither perfect creatures nor monsters, but believably troubled children. The secondary characters in all the novels are drawn with somewhat broader strokes, like Dottie in *The Talisman*, whose passion for costumes like a Hawaiian print skirt, shocking pink sweater, and Tartan shawl is a metaphor for her personality. The heroes are perhaps the least realistic of all the characters since they are made in the Heathcliff—Mr Rochester mould. Nevertheless, they are human and attractive in their flaws so that the reader can hardly fail to respond to their charms.

Crowe's training in the short story emerges again in the endings of her books. She avoids the over-writing and the sensation of winding down that is often found in romances. In *The Tower of Kilraven* the love story is left hanging as the heroine leaves the castle without having made a choice between two prospective lovers. A less confident author might have written this ending to death. The crispness and finality of these denouements leave the reader satisfied rather than sated.

—Susan Quinn Berneis

CUNNINGHAM, E.V.   See **FAST, Howard.**

CURRIE, Katy.   See **PALMER, Diana.**

CURRY, Avon.   See **BARCLAY, Tessa.**

CURTIN, Philip.   See **LOWNDES, Marie Belloc.**

CURTIS, Peter.   See **LOFTS, Norah.**

CURZON, Lucia.   See **STEVENSON, Florence.**

DAILEY, Janet.
Nationality: American. **Born:** Storm Lake, Iowa, 21 May 1944. **Education:** Independence High School, Iowa, graduated 1962. **Relations:** married William Dailey; two stepchildren. **Career:** sec-

retary, Omaha, Nebraska, 1963–74. **Recipient:** Romance Writers of America Golden Heart award, 1981; *Romantic Times* contemporary award, 1983. **Agent:** Janbill Ltd, Star Route 4, Box 2197, Branson, Missouri 65616, USA.

ROMANCE AND HISTORICAL PUBLICATIONS

Novels (series: Calder)

No Quarter Asked. London, Mills and Boon, 1974; Toronto, Harlequin, 1976.

Savage Land. London, Mills and Boon, 1974; Toronto, Harlequin, 1976.

Something Extra. London, Mills and Boon, 1975; Toronto, Harlequin, 1978.

Fire and Ice. London, Mills and Boon, 1975; Toronto, Harlequin, 1976.

Boss Man from Ogallala. London, Mills and Boon, 1975; Toronto, Harlequin, 1976.

After the Storm. London, Mills and Boon, 1975; Toronto, Harlequin, 1976.

Land of Enchantment. London, Mills and Boon, 1975; Toronto, Harlequin, 1976.

Sweet Promise. London, Mills and Boon, 1976; Toronto, Harlequin, 1979.

The Homeplace. London, Mills and Boon, and Toronto, Harlequin, 1976.

Dangerous Masquerade. London, Mills and Boon, 1976; Toronto, Harlequin, 1977.

Show Me. London, Mills and Boon, 1976; Toronto, Harlequin, 1977.

Valley of the Vapours. London, Mills and Boon, 1976; Toronto, Harlequin, 1977.

The Night of the Cotillion. London, Mills and Boon, 1976; Toronto, Harlequin, 1977.

Fiesta San Antonio. London, Mills and Boon, and Toronto, Harlequin, 1977.

Bluegrass King. London, Mills and Boon, and Toronto, Harlequin, 1977.

A Lyon's Share. London, Mills and Boon, and Toronto, Harlequin, 1977.

The Widow and the Wastrel. London, Mills and Boon, and Toronto, Harlequin, 1977.

The Ivory Cane. London, Mills and Boon, 1977; Toronto, Harlequin, 1978.

Six White Horses. London, Mills and Boon, 1977; Toronto, Harlequin, 1979.

To Tell the Truth. London, Mills and Boon, 1977; Toronto, Harlequin, 1978.

The Master Fiddler. London, Mills and Boon, 1977; Toronto, Harlequin, 1978.

Giant of Medabi. London, Mills and Boon, and Toronto, Harlequin, 1978.

Beware of the Stranger. London, Mills and Boon, and Toronto, Harlequin, 1978.

Darling Jenny. London, Mills and Boon, and Toronto, Harlequin, 1978.

The Indy Man. London, Mills and Boon, and Toronto, Harlequin, 1978.

Reilly's Woman. London, Mills and Boon, and Toronto, Harlequin, 1978.

For Bitter or Worse. London, Mills and Boon, 1978; Toronto, Harlequin, 1979.

Tidewater Lover. London, Mills and Boon, 1978; Toronto, Harlequin, 1979.

The Bride of the Delta Queen. London, Mills and Boon, 1978; Toronto, Harlequin, 1979.

Green Mountain Man. London, Mills and Boon, 1978; Toronto, Harlequin, 1979.

Sonora Sundown. London, Mills and Boon, and Toronto, Harlequin, 1978.

Summer Mahogany. London, Mills and Boon, 1978; Toronto, Harlequin, 1979.

The Matchmakers. London, Mills and Boon, and Toronto, Harlequin, 1978.

Big Sky Country. London, Mills and Boon, and Toronto, Harlequin, 1978.

Low Country Liar. London, Mills and Boon, and Toronto, Harlequin, 1979.

Strange Bedfellow. London, Mills and Boon, and Toronto, Harlequin, 1979.

For Mike's Sake. London, Mills and Boon, and Toronto, Harlequin, 1979.

Sentimental Journey. London, Mills and Boon, and Toronto, Harlequin, 1979.

Sweet Promise. London, Mills and Boon, and Toronto, Harlequin, 1979.

Bed of Grass. London, Mills and Boon, 1979; Toronto, Harlequin, 1980.

That Boston Man. London, Mills and Boon, 1979; Toronto, Harlequin, 1980.

Kona Winds. London, Mills and Boon, 1979; Toronto, Harlequin, 1980.

A Land Called Deseret. London, Mills and Boon, and Toronto, Harlequin, 1979.

Touch the Wind. New York, Pocket Books, 1979; London, Fontana, 1980.

Difficult Decision. London, Mills and Boon, and Toronto, Harlequin, 1980.

Enemy in Camp. London, Mills and Boon, and Toronto, Harlequin, 1980.

Heart of Stone. London, Mills and Boon, and Toronto, Harlequin, 1980.

Lord of the High Lonesome. London, Mills and Boon, and Toronto, Harlequin, 1980.

The Mating Season. London, Mills and Boon, and Toronto, Harlequin, 1980.

Southern Nights. London, Mills and Boon, and Toronto, Harlequin, 1980.

The Thawing of Mara. London, Mills and Boon, and Toronto, Harlequin, 1980.

One of the Boys. London, Mills and Boon, and Toronto, Harlequin, 1980.

The Rogue. New York, Pocket Books, and London, Fontana, 1980.

Wild and Wonderful. London, Mills and Boon, 1980; Toronto, Harlequin, 1981.

Ride the Thunder. New York, Pocket Books, and London, Fontana, 1981.

The Travelling Kind. London, Mills and Boon, and Toronto, Harlequin, 1981.

Dakota Dreamin'. London, Mills and Boon, and Toronto, Harlequin, 1981.

The Hostage Bride. New York, Silhouette, 1981.

With a Little Luck. London, Mills and Boon, and Toronto, Harlequin, 1981.

That Carolina Summer. London, Mills and Boon, and Toronto, Harlequin, 1981.

Night Way. New York, Pocket Books, and London, Futura, 1981.

The Lancaster Men. New York, Silhouette, 1981; London, Hodder and Stoughton, 1982.

This Calder Sky. New York, Pocket Books, 1981; London, Futura, 1982.

For the Love of God. New York, Silhouette, 1981; London, Hodder and Stoughton, 1982.

A Tradition of Pride. London, Mills and Boon, and Toronto, Harlequin, 1982.

Northern Magic. London, Mills and Boon, and Toronto, Harlequin, 1982.

Terms of Surrender. New York, Silhouette, and London, Hodder and Stoughton, 1982.

Wildcatter's Woman. New York, Silhouette, and London, Hodder and Stoughton, 1982.

This Calder Range. New York, Pocket Books, 1982; London, Hodder and Stoughton, 1983.

Stands a Calder Man. New York, Pocket Books, 1982; London, Hodder and Stoughton, 1983.

Foxfire Light. New York, Silhouette, 1982; Bath, Firecrest, 1985.

The Second Time. New York, Silhouette, 1982; London, Hodder and Stoughton, 1983.

Mistletoe and Holly. New York, Silhouette, 1982; London, Hodder and Stoughton, 1983.

Separate Cabins. New York, Silhouette, 1983; Bath, Chivers, 1984.

Western Man. New York, Silhouette, and London, Hodder and Stoughton, 1983.

The Best Way to Lose. New York, Silhouette, 1983; London, Hodder and Stoughton, 1984.

Calder Born, Calder Bred. New York, Pocket Books, 1983; London, Hodder and Stoughton, 1984.

Leftover Love. New York, Silhouette, and London, Hodder and Stoughton, 1984.

Silver Wings, Santiago Blue. New York, Poseidon Press, 1984.

The Pride of Hannah Wade. New York, Pocket Books, and London, Hodder and Stoughton, 1985.

The Glory Game. New York, Poseidon Press, 1985; London, Joseph, 1986.

The Great Alone. New York, Poseidon Press, and London, Joseph, 1986.

Heiress. Boston, Little Brown, and London, Joseph, 1987.

Rivals. Boston, Little Brown, and London, Joseph, 1989.

Masquerade. Boston, Little Brown, and London, Joseph, 1990.

Aspen Gold. Boston, Little Brown, and London, Joseph, 1990.

Tangled Vines. London, Joseph, 1992.

*

Janet Dailey comments:

I consider myself to be a teller of stories about the interrelationships of people whether it be in the multi-character form of my major novels or the one-on-one, man/woman relationships of my romance stories. To me, it is extremely important that each story be uniquely different, even if they retain common elements such as conflicts that are resolved to 'happy endings'. I write my stories to entertain. That is their purpose for being. It's very rewarding for an author artistically to learn of the hours of enjoyment people have derived from reading his or her works. I know it's been true for me.

*   *   *

In her category romance career Janet Dailey hit the record books for two reasons: she was the first American romance writer to find success with the British publishing house Mills and Boon and she celebrated her native country by writing one book set in every state in the union, later re-issued by Harlequin Books in North America as the 'Janet Dailey Americana' series.

The short romances, which made Dailey's name, are punchy reads with plenty of passion. Always fast-paced, with lots of sparky dialogue between the central characters, they are notable for strong, independent heroines who give as good as they get and epitomize the confident American career girl, whether they work in the urban business world or on a ranch in the Mid-West. Attractive, intelligent, and articulate, they invariably know what they want and go straight for it. If they don't already have money and success it won't be long before they achieve it—with or without the hero's help. The power of positive thinking goes a long way; it is rare to encounter a Dailey heroine who lets life get her down for very long.

Dailey's heroes are equally assured; tough, laid-back men with clipped, no-nonsense names like Brad, Judd, and Josh, who do not waste time on idle chatter, but who can hold their own in any argument that matters—especially with the feisty heroine. They may have inherited money, but more often they are self-made men who have struggled in their early days before reaching their current position as head of their own corporation or as a successful ranch-owner. Ruggedly good-looking, they are in their element in the Great Outdoors where being the boss never prevents them from showing off their skills on horseback. Even in a corporate setting a Dailey hero carries with him the slightly raffish air of a Western cowboy with his own code of honour, and a feeling that a man must fulfil his destiny whatever the cost.

The story is very much a clash of strong personalities between hero and heroine and the plot is usually a fairly simple one. Yet Dailey was one of the first authors to challenge the conventions of romantic fiction. For example, tradition had always dictated that a heroine suffering any physical handicap should have it put right with a miracle cure which succeeded against all odds. Dailey cleverly reversed this situation in *The Ivory Cane* in which the blind heroine is told she has no chance of regaining her sight and is then persuaded by the hero to see one more doctor. She undergoes tests, but finally must accept that there can be no cure. No fairytale ending, but readers seemed equally happy with the reassurance that the heroine would still have a wonderful future with a hero who would continue to love her regardless of her physical limitations.

Dailey's move out of category and into longer, more demanding reads has not meant her abandoning the ingredients which brought her initial success. Although her longer stories are more complex, they still rely on fast pace and the interaction of strong characters, many of whom are familiar types from her early works. The series of interlinked books about the Calder clan, written during the 1980s for Pocket Books, give a clear indication of no radical change of style, rather the opportunity for the author to spread herself across a wider canvas and to explore a greater cast of characters than she had formerly had the chance to use. The Calder books make use of a favourite Dailey background—a cattle ranch in Montana—and span different generations. But the essential struggle between feisty heroine and strong, sexy, uncompromising hero is still centre stage, even against a backdrop of family feuds and local passions.

Dailey has always excelled at exposing the strengths and weaknesses of family life (she was one of the first category writers to abandon the notion that the heroine should be bereft of close family ties) and it is interesting to note how often her long books dwell on this area. *The Glory Game*, for example, details the breakdown of the mature heroine's apparently secure marriage and the impact of her divorce not just on her but on the rest of her family and especially on her two near-adult children. The hero is an outsider from a different background who successfully challenges the heroine's subservience to her family and encourages her to make her own life (not surprisingly in a Dailey novel the link between them is forged through a mutual love of horses). A similar pattern underlies *Masquerade* in which the heroine's amnesia means that she has to rely on instinct rather than facts to weigh the motives of the hero against those of her family.

Dailey's families belong to the world of the super-rich, often with an echo of a real life parallel; for example, the pressurized, over-achieving Kincaids, in *The Glory Game*, headed by a matriarch who had a philandering husband, invite initial comparisons with the Kennedys. Their life-style offers the reader vicarious enjoyment of the haunts of the wealthy across continents, while their problems simultaneously confirm that the rich are no happier than anyone else. This lesson is carried to its logical conclusion in *Aspen Gold*, when the heroine, on the verge of movie stardom, realizes the divide between the famous and the rest of the world and the unhappiness it can bring, eventually opting for the real values offered by her childhood sweetheart. As with her category stories Dailey does her homework on the background detail and drops the right names and places. However competent the research, one feels that it is not Dailey's first love and the result can be a little laboured (as in what seems to be her least successful book, *The Great Alone*, an epic saga of Alaska ranging over two centuries).

Dailey can be counted on for an entertaining read and fully merits her position as one of America's leading mass market talents.

—Frances Whitehead

DANBURY, Iris. British. Died. See 2nd edition, 1990.

DANE, Clemence.
Nationality: British. **Born:** Winifred Ashton, Blackheath, London, in 1887. **Education:** private schools, and at the Slade School of Art, London, 1904–06; studied art in Dresden, 1906–07. **Career:** French teacher in Geneva, 1903, and in Ireland, 1907–13; teacher at a girls' school during World War I; actress, as Diana Portis, 1913–18; literary critic, *Good Housekeeping*, London, early 1930s. General editor, Novels of Tomorrow series, Michael Joseph, publishers, London, from 1955. President, Society of Women Journalsts, 1941. **Recipient:** Oscar, for screenplay, 1947. CBE (Commander, Order of the British Empire), 1953. **Died:** 28 March 1965.

ROMANCE AND HISTORICAL PUBLICATIONS

Novels

Regiment of Women. London, Heinemann, and New York, Macmillan, 1917.
First the Blade: A Comedy of Growth. London, Heinemann, and New York, Macmillan, 1918.
Legend. London, Heinemann, 1919; New York, Macmillan, 1920.
Wandering Stars, Together with The Lover. London, Heinemann, and New York, Macmillan, 1924.
The Dearly Beloved of Benjamin Cobb. London, Benn, 1927.
The Babyons: A Family Chronicle. London, Heinemann, and New York, Doubleday, 1928.
Broome Stages. London, Heinemann, and New York, Doubleday, 1931.
The Moon Is Feminine. London, Heinemann, and New York, Doubleday, 1938.
He Brings Great News. London, Heinemann, 1944; New York, Random House, 1945.
The Flower Girls. London, Joseph, 1954; New York, Norton, 1955.
The Godson: A Fantasy. London, Joseph, and New York, Norton, 1964.

Short Stories

The King Waits. London, Heinemann, 1929.

Fate Cries Out: Nine Tales. London, Heinemann, and New York, Doubleday, 1935.

OTHER PUBLICATIONS

Novels

Enter Sir John, with Helen Simpson. London, Hodder and Stoughton, and New York, Cosmopolitan, 1928.
Printer's Devil, with Helen Simpson. London, Hodder and Stoughton, 1930; as *Author Unknown*, New York, Cosmopolitan, 1930.
The Floating Admiral, with others. London, Hodder and Stoughton, 1931; New York, Doubleday, 1932.
Re-Enter Sir John, with Helen Simpson. London, Hodder and Stoughton, and New York, Farrar and Rinehart, 1932.
The Arrogant History of White Ben. London, Heinemann, and New York, Doubleday, 1939.

Plays

A Bill of Divorcement (produced London and New York, 1921). London, Heinemann, and New York, Macmillan, 1921.
The Terror (produced Liverpool, 1921).
Will Shakespeare: An Invention (produced London, 1921; New York, 1923). London, Heinemann, 1921; New York, Macmillan, 1922.
The Way Things Happen: A Story, adaptation of her novel *Legend* (produced Newark, New Jersey, 1923; New York and London, 1924). London, Heinemann, and New York, Macmillan, 1924.
Shivering Shocks; or, The Hiding Place: A Play for Boys. London, French, 1923.
Naboth's Vineyard. London, Heinemann, 1925; New York, Macmillan, 1926.
Granite (produced London, 1926; New York, 1927). London, Heinemann, and New York, Macmillan, 1926.
Mariners (produced New York, 1927; London, 1929). London, Heinemann, and New York, Macmillan, 1927.
Mr Fox: A Play for Boys. London, French, 1927.
A Traveller Returns. London, French, 1927.
Adam's Opera, music by Richard Addinsell (produced London, 1928). London, Heinemann, 1928; New York, Doubleday, 1929.
Gooseberry Fool, with Helen Simpson (produced London, 1929).
Wild Decembers (produced London, 1933). London, Heinemann, 1932; New York, Doubleday, 1933.
Come of Age, music by Richard Addinsell (produced New York, 1934). New York, Doubleday, 1934; London, Heinemann, 1938.
L'Aiglon, music by Richard Addinsell, adaptation of the play by Rostand (produced New York, 1934; London, 1936). New York, Doubleday, 1934.
Moonlight Is Silver (also director: produced London, 1934). London, Heinemann, 1934.
Richard of Bordeaux (produced New York, 1934).
The Laughing Woman (produced New York, 1936).
The Happy Hypocrite, adaptation of the story by Max Beerbohm (produced London, 1936).
Herod and Mariamne, adaptation of the play by Friedrich Hebbel (produced Pittsburgh, 1938). New York, Doubleday, 1938; London, Heinemann, 1939.
England's Darling, music by Richard Addinsell. London, Heinemann, 1940.
Cousin Muriel (produced London, 1940). London, Heinemann, 1940.
The Saviours: Seven Plays on One Theme (includes *Merlin, The Hope of Britain, England's Darling, The May King, The Light of Britain, Remember Nelson, The Unknown Soldier*), music by Richard Addinsell (broadcast 1940–41). London, Heinemann, and New York, Doubleday, 1942.
The Golden Reign of Queen Elizabeth (produced York, 1941). London, French, 1941.
Cathedral Steps (produced London, 1942).
Alice's Adventures in Wonderland and Through the Looking-Glass, music by Richard Addinsell, adaptation of the novels by Lewis Carroll (produced London, 1943). London, French, 1948.
The Lion and the Unicorn (produced Thame, Oxfordshire, 1959). London, Heinemann, 1943.
Call Home the Heart (produced London, 1947). London, Heinemann, 1947.
Scandal at Coventry (broadcast 1958). Included in *The Collected Plays*, 1961.
Eighty in the Shade (produced Newcastle-upon-Tyne, 1958; London, 1959). London, Heinemann, 1959.
Till Time Shall End (televised 1958). Included in *The Collected Plays*, 1961.
The Collected Plays of Clemence Dane (includes *Scandal at Coventry, Granite, A Bill of Divorcement, Till Time Shall End*). London, Heinemann, 1961.

Screenplays: *The Lame Duck*, 1921; *The Tunnel (Transatlantic Tunnel)*, with Curt Siodmak and L. DuGarde Peach, 1935; *Anna Karenina*, with Salka Viertel, 1935; *The Amateur Gentleman*, with Edward Knoblock, 1936; *Fairwell Again (Troopship)*, with Patrick Kirwan, 1937; *Fire over England*, with Sergei Nolbandov, 1937; *St Martin's Lane (Sidewalks of London)*, 1938; *Salute John Citizen*, with Elizabeth Baron, 1942; *Perfect Strangers (Vacation from Marriage)*, with Anthony Pelissier, 1945; *Bonnie Prince Charlie*, 1948; *Bride of Vengeance*, with Cyril Hume and Michael Hogan, 1949; *The Angel with the Trumpet*, with Karl Hartl and Franz Tassie, 1950.

Radio Plays: *The Scoop* (serial), with others, 1931; *The Saviours* (7 plays), 1940–41; *Henry VIII*, from the play by Shakespeare, 1954; *Don Carlos*, from the play by Schiller, 1955; *Scandal at Coventry*, 1958.

Television Play: *Till Time Shall End*, 1958.

Poetry

Trafalgar Day 1940. London, Heinemann, 1940; New York, Doubleday, 1941.
Christmas in War-Time. New York, Doubleday, 1941.

Other

The Woman's Side. London, Jenkins, 1926; New York, Doran, 1927.
Tradition and Hugh Walpole. New York, Doubleday, 1929; London, Heinemann, 1930.
Recapture: A Clemence Dane Omnibus. London, Heinemann, 1932.
Claude Houghton: Appreciations, with Hugh Walpole. London, Heinemann, 1935.
Mozart's Così fan Tutte: Essays, with Edward J. Dent and Eric Blom. London, Lane, 1945.
Approaches to Drama (address). London, English Association, 1961.
London Has a Garden (on Covent Garden). London, Joseph, and New York, Norton, 1964.

Editor, *A Hundred Enchanted Tales.* London, Joseph, 1937.
Editor, *The Shelter Book: A Gathering of Tales, Poems, Essays, Notes and Notions for Use in Shelters, Tubes, Basements and Cellars in War-Time.* London, Longman, 1940.

Editor, *The Nelson Touch: An Anthology of Lord Nelson's Letters*. London, Heinemann, 1942.

*

Film Adaptations: *Murder*, 1930, from the novel *Enter, Sir John*; *A Bill of Divorcement*, 1932, 1940.

Theatrical Activities:
Director: **Play**—*Moonlight Is Silver*, London, 1934.
Actress (as Diana Portis): **Plays**—Vera Lawrence, in *Eliza Comes to Stay* by H.V. Esmond, London, 1913; Baroness des Herbettes, in *This Way* by Sydney Blow and Douglas Hoare, London, 1913; Sidonie in *Oh, I Say!* by Sydney Blow and Douglas Hoare, toured 1914.

Critical Studies: *'Therefore Imagine': The Works of Clemence Dane* by David Waldron Smithers, Tunbridge Wells, Dragonfly, 1988.

*   *   *

Clemence Dane is best remembered for her play *A Bill of Divorcement* in which Meggie Albanesi made a great success on the London stage and Katharine Hepburn obtained her first film part in Hollywood. She also wrote several historical works mostly set in the Elizabethan period.

Her first novel, *Regiment of Women*, has a delicately handled lesbian theme. Clare Hartill, a gifted teacher, enslaves a pretty junior mistress aged 19 and is loved by a talented girl of 13 whom she coaches. The girl kills herself falling from a window because she feels rejected, and the junior mistress marries, leaving Clare angry and lonely with a partnership in the school and her teaching to console her. This well written, sensitive study was presented at a time when discussion of such relationships was rare. It was bold, controversial, and perceptive, dealing with 'a lot of women at close quarters all enthusiasm and fussing and importance'.

Legend is one of Dane's most successful works. It covers one evening meeting of a literary circle to which news arrives of the death in childbirth of one of their number, Madala Grey, a successful novelist they all admired, were jealous of, used to their own advantage, but never really knew. They quarrel, make sharp remarks, and discuss their work while the reader learns about Madala Grey. The reader also comes to understand each member of the circle just by listening to their conversation and observing their behaviour. It is a minor triumph.

First the Blade is a sad little 'comedy' about a neglected young woman devoted to her fiancé, a self-centred, humourless, spoiled young man ruled by a passion for collecting birds' eggs. In desperation she smashes his collection trying to divert his attention without success. It has similarities to Somerset Maugham's story 'The Kite', in which Herbert Sunbury's wife breaks up his much loved kite which has become an obsession, with a similar lack of success. *The Babyons* is a four-part family chronicle with hauntings, suicide, murder, and baleful family influences. The best section is 'Creeping Jenny' in which Robert Thistledallow's daughter by a gypsy girl, slighted by his relations for her illegitimacy, triumphs over the family, inherits her father's fortune and becomes Lady Babyon.

Wandering Stars, *Broome Stages*, and *The Flower Girls* are three theatrical novels. *Broome Stages*, Dane's most famous novel, is still popular today. It starts with the foundation of the Broome family's theatrical ventures in 1715 and continues with their domination of the English theatre for 200 years. In a curious arrangement the family parallels the names and characteristics of the Plantagenet Kings of England. The Broomes are great actor-managers whose family loyalty is permeated by a ruthless pursuit of fame and a jealousy of the success of their own children as they challenge for dominance and authority. One kills himself in his theatre when his son triumphs as Shylock after tricking him out of his leading position in management and depriving him of leading roles. His son also dies in the theatre of a heart attack at his own son's debut. There are some well drawn, effective female members of the clan. It is a big book and a tour de force. *The Flower Girls*, written 23 years later, follows another theatrical family, less dramatically but with charm, humour, and many fine characters, some in the minor parts, and some clearly drawn from the great stage performers of the day.

The Moon Is Feminine begins as a pleasant fantasy with Henry Cope who believes in his green ancestors from St Martin's Land, based on William of Newburgh's story of the green children who arrived in East Anglia in 1150, and a beguiling, mysterious, dangerous boy who has a second life as a seal. It is well told and keenly observed but has a totally unexpected, violent, and horrifying ending for which the reader has not been adequately prepared.

The Arrogant History of White Ben is an allegory 'about a Hitleresque personage' who starts and ends as a scarecrow, and a combination of power, stupidity, hatred, and the use of rhetoric to inflame and dominate a crowd. *The Godson* tells of Sir William Davenant, Shakespeare's godson, who wrote an opera, became a Lieutenant General and the Poet Laureate. On Shakespeare's birthday in Stratford, Will Davenant, as a boy, presents his own production of *A Midsummer Night's Dream* in which he plays Puck. His mother almost admits that he is really Shakespeare's son in one of Dane's fancifully suggested versions of Elizabethan history. *He Brings Great News* is a novel about the arrival of the news of the victory of Trafalgar, dealing with Nelson, one of Dane's particular heroes.

Dane's work is always well written and is a pleasure to read. The best is quite outstanding, inventive, and richly deserving of a revival in interest.

—David Waldron Smithers

———

DANE, Eva.   See **DRUMMOND, Emma.**

———

DANIELS, Dorothy.   American. 1915—. See 2nd edition, 1990.

———

DANIELS, Max.   See **GELLIS, Roberta.**

———

DANIELS, Olga.   See **SINCLAIR, Olga.**

———

DARBY, Catherine.   See **PETERS, Maureen.**

———

DARCY, Clare.
Nationality: American. **Address:** c/o Walker, 720 Fifth Avenue, New York, New York 10019, USA.

ROMANCE AND HISTORICAL PUBLICATIONS

Novels

Georgina. New York, Walker, 1971; London, Wingate, 1974.

Cecily; or, A Young Lady of Quality. New York, Walker, 1972; London, Wingate, 1975.

Lydia; or, Love in Town. New York, Walker, 1973; London, Wingate, 1976.

Victoire. New York, Walker, 1974; London, Wingate, 1976.

Allegra. New York, Walker, 1975; London, Wingate, 1976.

Lady Pamela. New York, Walker, 1975; London, Wingate, 1977.

Regina. New York, Walker, 1976; London, Raven, 1977.

Elyza. New York, Walker, 1976; London, Raven-Macdonald and Jane's, 1977.

Cressida. New York, Walker, 1977; London, Raven, 1978.

Eugenia. New York, Walker, 1977; London, Raven, 1978.

Gwendolen. New York, Walker, 1978; London, Raven, 1979.

Rolande. New York, Walker, 1978; London, Raven, 1979.

Letty. New York, Walker, and London, Futura, 1980.

Caroline and Julia. New York, Walker, and London, Macdonald, 1982.

*   *   *

Cinderella is one of the world's best-known stories, and Clare Darcy is one of its most assiduous popularizers. Of course, the eponymous heroines of Darcy's popular Regency novels differ in many respects. However, almost all of them are penniless, most are orphans or have ineffective parents, and they are set adrift in a Regency world that is hospitable only to the rich and the well-connected. While some of these women are a few years past the age of their London season and regard themselves as mature women of the world, all are comparatively young (most no older than their early twenties), spirited and usually reluctant to admit that they are falling in love with a man who is older, harsh-featured but attractive, socially usually superior and also usually very rich.

The formula is subject to changes and alterations, or it would be difficult for Darcy to plot her stories. In *Georgina*, for instance, the love interest, Mr Shannon, is the bastard son of an earl, rich only because he has inherited the estate of his first wife, Georgina's cousin, but he is not their social equal. Much of the novel is set in Ireland where his estate is located. The *local*, as opposed to the London, gentry will accept him in time. After all, Georgina would have been the heiress had it not been for her cousin's marriage, so a member of the old family will still be in residence.

In *Eugenia*, the schoolgirl heroine helps her cousin, Richard, to prove his legitimacy so that he can inherit her late father's entailed estates. Although this provides Richard with a small income (and he is still socially inferior as his mother was a farmer's daughter) it does provide Eugenia with the means to marry the man she loves and also live on the rural estate where she spent a happy childhood.

Caroline and Julia, one of Darcy's rare double romances, shows Julia Daventry, respectable widow and vicar's daughter (although she is an actress), and her teenage ward, Caroline, receiving the devotion of Neville Deveraux and his young cousin, Lord Revers. Other Darcy heroines are connected to the wicked world of the theatre. The female protagonist of *Cecily* is also an actress, though not as talented as Julia, until her distant kinsman, Robert Ranleigh, finds out about her plight, and sends her to be trained as a governess. A sinister man-about-town tries to blackmail Cecily into becoming his mistress, and afraid that chivalry rather than love will force Ranleigh to offer her marriage, she resolves to return to the stage, thereby putting herself beyond the pale. Letty, in the book of the same name, sings in Henry's gambling house at the Congress of Vienna, until her efforts reinstate him to the good graces of his wealthy great-uncle. The heroine of *Rolande* is a professional actress, hired to impersonate a missing heir, who ends up assuming several identities before her employer realizes that he is in love with her. Thus, the

social significance of being an actress is more ambiguous than it first appears.

Allegra and her young sister, Hillary, in *Allegra*, brave the Continent and flee to their old governess who runs a school in Brussels, on the eve of the Battle of Waterloo. They meet the wealthy cousin whom Allegra had rejected in England. One way in which this story, *Caroline and Julia*, and *Gwendolyn* differ from Darcy's other novels is the way in which the ends are neatly stitched together. All too often, Darcy leaves sub-plots unresolved and secondary characters unmatched. *Lady Pamela*, one of the most fully plotted romances, has an exciting story with a spy component added to the romance, and a rare wealthy and independent heroine (rivalled in this respect by the heroine of *Cressida*). Pamela's masquerade as a lady's maid adds suspense and piquancy, although the lack of real confrontation with any of the several villains and traitors, as well as Pamela's inexplicable failure to question her own servants, certainly weaken the 'mystery' component. However, more noticeably, neither the ingenue, Pamela's jilted fiancé, nor her younger brother are provided with alternate sweethearts.

If one does not read Darcy for the plot, what of her characters? One thinks first of her women. While they may be similar (and of course, are uniformly charming and spunky), it is Darcy's ability to differentiate between them that makes her books special. For instance, she can present Regina trying to cope with her wayward Irish relatives and conceal the fact that she finds her cousin's beau, Lord Wrexham, more attractive than a chaperon should, as totally different to the similarly situated Gwendolyn, who falls in love with her sister's would-be fiancé, the Marquis of Lyndale.

With her heroes, Darcy sets herself even higher hurdles. After all, they are, with few exceptions, handsome though harsh-featured, sardonic but humorous, wealthy sportsmen, admired by their peers. The Marquis of Tarr, in *Victoire*, is an example of the younger, carefree and irresponsible hero who nonetheless feels it is his gentlemanly duty to protect Victoire's reputation by proposing to her, only to realize that he is actually in love with her. Lyndale, in *Gwendolyn*, makes up his mind to move more quickly—at their first meeting, in fact. However, he finds himself obliged to find a suitable position for her sister Jane's true love, while evading the wiles of her hoydenish youngest sister. Jane's lover, in a secondary role, is one of Darcy's few attempts at a more poetic, sensitive hero.

Aside from the main love interests, Darcy has painted some interesting villains in those novels that include active villains. Croil and Honoria, Lady Prest, in *Rolande*, are two who come to mind. A few commanding grande-dames, like Baroness Lebanoff in the same book, add a humorous touch.

Darcy's books are set in a familiar Regency world, although fewer days are spent receiving callers and refusing politely to waltz at Almack's, and more trips are made to Bristol by heroines disguised as boys (*Elyza*), and ventures to Ned Trice's gin mill, The Fighting Cock (*Eugenia*). Despite her extensive research, Darcy's history is perhaps more functional than ornamental. While the Battle of Waterloo plays an important role in *Allegra*, or in *Lydia*, in *Love in Town* the Fourth Viscount of Northover, shortly after Waterloo, makes the acquaintance of three money-hungry but charming Louisianans, without referring to the recent War of 1812. If Darcy doesn't need an historical event for plot purposes, it isn't mentioned. Description is not limited to dresses and furniture. In fact, Darcy frequently gets out of the drawing rooms and into the streets of Vienna (*Letty*), the fields of Ireland (*Regina*, *Georgina*), or the English countryside. The wider scope of the novels, as well as the often tomboyish nature of the youthful heroines, brings a refreshing breath of fresh air to the conventions of the genre.

Darcy has a clear, appropriate prose style, the kind that provides readers with no distractions that might cause a suspension of belief. Typically, a last minute clinch, lasting for several pages and described only in the vaguest terms, is the only indication of sex.

Darcy gives her readers a pleasant reading experience, with a happy ending and something to fantasize about, while offending no-one.

—Susan Branch

———

DARCY, Emma.
Pseudonym for Wendy and Frank Brennan. **BRENNAN, Wendy. Nationality:** Australian. **Born:** Dorrigo, New South Wales, 28 November 1940. **Education:** St Joseph's College, Lochinvar, New South Wales; Sydney Teachers' College, Teacher's Certificate, 1959. **Relations:** married Frank Brennan in 1964; three sons. **Career:** French/English teacher, department of education, Wingham, New South Wales, 1960–61; English teacher, department of education, Macksville, New South Wales, 1962, 1963; computer programmer, IBM, Sydney, 1963–66, and CAS, Sydney, 1966–67. Acted in amateur dramatic productions; also paints. Full-time writer. **BRENNAN, Frank. Nationality:** Australian. **Born:** Gosford, New South Wales, 2 October 1940. **Education:** St Edward's College, Gosford; Sydney University, Sydney, Bachelor of Pharmacy, 1963; Society of Australian Genealogists, diploma of family historical studies, 1986. **Career:** pharmacist, Reily's Pharmacy, Darlington, Sydney, 1963–65, and Wyong, New South Wales (own business), 1965–84. President of local historical society. Since 1981, full-time writer. **Address:** *Greener Pastures*, 1 Woods Road, Wyee 2259, New South Wales, Australia.

ROMANCE AND HISTORICAL PUBLICATIONS

Novels

A World Apart. Sydney, Harlequin, 1983; London, Mills and Boon, 1984; Toronto, Harlequin, 1986.
Twisting Shadows. London, Mills and Boon, 1983; Toronto, Harlequin, 1984.
Tangle of Torment. London, Mills and Boon, 1983; Toronto, Harlequin, 1984.
Don't Play Games. London, Mills and Boon, and Toronto, Harlequin, 1985.
Fantasy. London, Mills and Boon, and Toronto, Harlequin, 1985.
Song of a Wren. London, Mills and Boon, 1985; Toronto, Harlequin, 1986.
Point of Impact. London, Mills and Boon, 1985; Toronto, Harlequin, 1986.
The Impossible Woman. London, Mills and Boon, 1985; Toronto, Harlequin, 1986.
Woman of Honour. London, Mills and Boon, 1986; Toronto, Harlequin, 1987.
Man in the Park. London, Mills and Boon, 1986; Toronto, Harlequin, 1987.
Blind Date. London, Mills and Boon, 1986; Toronto, Harlequin, 1988.
Don't Ask Me Now. London, Mills and Boon, 1986; Toronto, Harlequin, 1987.
The Wrong Mirror. London, Mills and Boon, 1986; Toronto, Harlequin, 1987.
The Unpredictable Man. London, Mills and Boon, 1986; Toronto, Harlequin, 1987.
Whirlpool of Passion. London, Mills and Boon, and Toronto, Harlequin, 1987.
The One that Got Away. London, Mills and Boon, 1987; Toronto, Harlequin, 1988.
Strike at the Heart. London, Mills and Boon, 1987; Toronto, Harlequin, 1988.

The Positive Approach. London, Mills and Boon, 1987; Toronto, Harlequin, 1988.
Mistress of Pillatoro. London, Mills and Boon, 1987; Toronto, Harlequin, 1988.
Always Love. London, Mills and Boon, 1988; Toronto, Harlequin, 1989.
A Priceless Love. London, Mills and Boon, 1988; Toronto, Harlequin, 1989.
The Aloha Bride. London, Mills and Boon, 1988; Toronto, Harlequin, 1989.
The Falcon's Mistress. London, Mills and Boon, 1988; Toronto, Harlequin, 1990.
The Ultimate Choice. London, Mills and Boon, 1989; Toronto, Harlequin, 1990.
The Power and the Passion. London, Mills and Boon, 1989; Toronto, Harlequin, 1990.
Pattern of Deceit. London, Mills and Boon, 1989; Toronto, Harlequin, 1990.
Too Strong to Deny. London, Mills and Boon, 1990; Toronto, Harlequin, 1991.
One Woman Crusade. London, Mills and Boon, 1990; Toronto, Harlequin, 1991.
The Colour of Desire. London, Mills and Boon, 1990; Toronto, Harlequin, 1991.
Bride of Diamonds. London, Mills and Boon, 1990; Toronto, Harlequin, 1991.
Ride the Storm. Toronto, Harlequin, 1991; London, Mills and Boon, 1992.
Breaking Point. Toronto, Harlequin, 1992; London, Mills and Boon, 1993.
High Risk. Toronto, Harlequin, 1992; London, Mills and Boon, 1993.
To Tame a Wild Heart. Toronto, Harlequin, 1992; Toronto, Mills and Boon, 1993.
The Wedding. Toronto, Harlequin, 1992; London, Mills and Boon, 1993.
The Seduction of Keira. Toronto, Harlequin, 1992; London, Mills and Boon, 1993.
The Velvet Tiger. Toronto, Harlequin, 1992.
Dark Heritage. Toronto, Harlequin, 1992.
Heart of the Outback. Toronto, Harlequin, 1993; London, Mills and Boon, 1994.
The Upstairs Lover. Toronto, Harlequin, 1993.
An Impossible Dream. Toronto, Harlequin, 1993.
No Risks, No Prizes. Toronto, Harlequin, 1993.
A Very Stylish Affair. Toronto, Harlequin, 1993.
The Last Grand Passion. Toronto, Harlequin, 1993.

OTHER PUBLICATIONS

Other books by Frank Brennan

A History of Gosford. Wyong, New South Wales, Wyong Shire Historical Society, 1970.

*

Emma Darcy comments:
We have tried to create unique, individual books that do not follow traditional story patterns. Unlike other authors in the genre, we have never kept to one or two themes, nor to a highly ordered pattern. The emotional range varies from very light to intense, bringing a smile or a tear, sometimes both. Characterization varies with plot, but is never plastic and is frequently very deep. Straightline motivation is an essential ingredient of every book. Over the years there has

been a tendency towards apparent simplification which reflects an increased mastery over book construction.

From early on, as Emma Darcy, we have challenged the boundaries of the category romance genre, and have successfully re-established the limits of the permissable. Mystery, intrigue, paranormal, surprising and unpredictable plot-twists, and other unusual and less traditional elements are all part of the Emma Darcy technique. Our aim is to create something new, exciting, compelling, and satisfying. A huge readership response attests to the fresh and invigorating voice of Emma Darcy.

* * *

In the past decade the romantic fiction publisher Mills and Boon has published several successful Australasian writers among whom Susan Napier, Robyn Donald, Lindsay Armstrong, and Emma Darcy are the most popular. Emma Darcy is a pseudonym for the writing team, Frank and Wendy Brennan, and the couple have written some of the most interesting and innovative scenarios in contemporary romantic fiction today. Darcy's earlier novels, written at the beginning of the 1980s, conform to the more traditional formula romance: girl and boy meet, they fall in love, problems arise (usually from a misunderstanding from the past), problem is resolved, boy and girl marry. Of course, Darcy's books elaborate on this storyline, setting the plots in exotic and beautiful countries—Australia, Fiji, Hawaii, South East Asia—and creating characters who are interesting and independent.

In *Twisting Shadows* Jo Standish believes that Mark and Michael Hunter are responsible for the death of her sister, Carol. She meets them years after the incident when she agrees to install a new computer system at Michael's company. Jo fights fiercely against her growing attraction to Michael but loses, and the couple end up together by the end of the book. Similarly, *Tangle of Torment* takes the formula theme and embellishes on it. Both protagonists are engaged to 'nice' people, but the strong attraction that both feel proves too hard to fight; when the heroine falls pregnant, it is inevitable that everything will be resolved.

Most of Darcy's books centre around an almost instantaneous attraction between the hero and heroine, one that defies words and rationale. Thus the serious female protagonist of *Blind Date*, Peggy Dean, ends up falling for pop star Adam Gale, and their first fiery encounter is watched by millions of Australian viewers; bubbly Judy is immediately intrigued by the tanned stranger she meets in *The Impossible Woman*; and school teacher Elizabeth falls quickly under the spell of lawyer Prince Domenico in *Too Strong to Deny*. The fact that one or both of the characters fights this attraction provides the entertainment, anguish, and plot for these books.

Darcy's heroines tend to be normal women who hold down careers and have had to struggle to overcome some major obstacle to get to their present status in life. Elizabeth, in *Too Strong to Deny*, has overcome her complex about feeling stupid (the result of a dominating husband and father telling her so) to be part of a degree programme, and to have a career as a teacher. Similarly, secret songwriter Jenny Wren, in *Song of a Wren*, initially thinks she is ordinary and insignificant, but comes to realize that she is a talented artist; and Kate, in *Don't Play Games*, emerges from an abusive marriage to take control of her own life. All of these women possess great honesty and integrity, and these qualities attract their heroes who tend to be, at least initially, disillusioned and cynical. However, while the heroine may lead a comparatively ordinary life, Darcy's hero is a dream-come-true. Rich, handsome, charismatic, he has a successful career—as a lawyer, a pop star, an architect, a journalist, or a businessman among others—which leads him to have an interesting and glamorous life. He is also slightly wearied by the people that he meets. Pop star Adam, in *Blind Date*, can never be sure if people want to know Adam-the-star, or Adam-real-person; Morgan

Llewellyn, in *The Colour of Desire*, is a world famous composer whose cynicism is destroyed by the belief and trust of his protégée, Katherine; and Joel Faber, in *Ride the Storm*, has been driven by the hatred of the island where he grew up, the death of his childhood sweetheart, and the need to prove that he is worth something—all of which make him mix in a world full of strangers who view him on his looks and wealth alone.

Serious issues are also tackled, and are used as a background for Darcy's books. In *The Wrong Mirror*, the infertility of Karen's husband is a major problem exacerbated when Karen adopts her twin sister's child; their marriage is destroyed as a result. Karen's twin, Kirsty, is also killed in a terrorist bombing in Tel Aviv, at the beginning of the book. Julian Lassiter's brother, Davey, is a brilliant scientist who is dying, in *The Aloha Bride*, the heroine Robyn agrees to marry Davey and have his child so that his genius won't be lost; and Tiffany, the heroine of *Ride the Storm*, goes to ex-islander Joel Faber, in a bid to save the flagging economy of Haven Bay. The island needs the tourism that can be generated with Joel's help, the consequent employment and income generated from it would stop the youth of the island leaving for the mainland. Many of the heroines in Darcy's books have also been physically or mentally abused, or are the products of foster homes.

Unlike many other formula romance writers, Darcy's books are not variations on the same theme. Her protagonists may possess many of the same redeeming (and sometimes annoying) qualities, but the scenarios in which they appear alter. The hero may find himself taking part in a television dating game (*Blind Date*), or may find himself injured in a bombing (*The Wrong Mirror*): he may be an outrageous entrepreneur (*The Unpredictable Man*), or the ruler of a foreign land (*The Falcon's Mistress*)—however, wherever he appears, as the hero of a Darcy book it will always be in an exciting and unpredictable plot, and he will always encounter a woman who is more than worthy of him.

—P. Campbell

D'ARCY, Pamela. See **ROBY, Mary Linn.**

DARK, Eleanor.
Nationality: Australian. **Born:** Eleanor O'Reilly, Sydney, New South Wales, 26 August 1901. **Education:** Redlands, Neutral Bay, Sydney. **Relations:** married Eric Dark in 1927; one son. **Recipient:** Australian Literature Society gold medal, 1934, 1936, Officer, Order of Australia, 1977. **Died:** 1985.

ROMANCE AND HISTORICAL PUBLICATIONS

Novels (series: Mannion and Prentice families appear in all books)

The Timeless Land. London, Collins, and New York, Macmillan, 1941.
Storm of Time. London, Collins, 1945; New York, McGraw Hill, 1950.
No Barrier. London, Collins, 1953.

OTHER PUBLICATIONS

Novels

Slow Dawning. London, Lane, 1932.

Prelude to Christopher. Sydney, Stephenson, 1934; London, Collins, 1936.
Return to Coolami. London, Collins, and New York, Macmillan, 1936.
Sun Across the Sky. London, Collins, and New York, Macmillan, 1937.
Waterway. London, Collins, and New York, Macmillan, 1938.
The Little Company. London, Collins, and New York, Macmillan, 1945.
Lantana Lane. London, Collins, 1959.

*

Bibliography: 'Eleanor Dark: A Handlist of Her Books and Critical References' by Hugh Anderson, in *Biblio News* (Sydney), 1954.

Critical Study: *Eleanor Dark* by A. Grove Day, Boston, Twayne, 1976.

*   *   *

The most noticeable characteristic of Eleanor Dark's writing is a stream-of-consciousness technique, through which the reader is drawn into the most intimate thoughts of the protagonists. Although this suggests a concentration on individuals, in later books Dark writes about the actions and attitudes of her characters in a social and political context. She is a novelist of ideas, who writes about women and men, families and love as an interrogator seeking out patterns and connections between individual lives and the wider society.

Dark is best known for *The Timeless Land*, the first novel in an historical trilogy set in the earliest years of white settlement in Australia from 1788 to 1814. This trilogy is her only historical work, all other novels having contemporary settings, although links between the style and subject of the trilogy and novels such as *Prelude to Christopher*, *Sun Across the Sky*, *Waterway*, and *The Little Company* are strong. In the tradition of convict novels, a central theme in *The Timeless Land* is freedom, and Dark sets liberty as the principal component of human happiness. In this overtly political novel, black and white society are contrasted in order to argue that all the Europeans, jailers and convicts alike, are shackled by their supposed rationality and dependence on possessions. Dark suggests that a society which elevates men of wealth over those rich in inner resources and strength will inevitably weaken. It is obvious that in choosing to look at the beginnings of her own society, Dark was exploring the deficiencies of the present—that is the 1930s world depression and looming world war—although what she has to say about Western society seems no less relevant today. The protagonists, the Aboriginal songmaker Bennilong and the British Governor Arthur Phillip, are depicted as strong but flawed men who hold to a high personal code while around them the precarious white settlement and the original inhabitants are threatened by disease, starvation, and moral degradation. Dark quotes the authentic diaries and letters of her historical characters and goes behind these records to create characters who are believable and varied in their reactions to the 'timeless land!' She also takes up the challenge of writing from the inside of the black society, and although some of her interpretations of Aboriginal philosophy might be debatable, the result is artistically satisfying. There is little action in the novel and for most readers, particularly for Australians, part of the drama comes from knowing the outcome of the story and the fate of the Aboriginals who so generously help the Europeans, thinking that the white people, like a dream, will soon go away.

The sequels, *Storm of Time* and *No Barrier*, take up the stories of two families from *The Timeless Land*, the wealthy Mannions and the convict Prentices. Both these families have links to the native community through Johnny Prentice, who as a boy ran away from home and lives a tribal life, and through Dilboong, daughter of Bennilong, who is a servant in the Mannion household. All of these characters are fictional although their lives are certainly no more extraordinary than the historical figures in these two novels such as the Governors William Bligh and Hunter, or the sheep baron Macarthur. After the wise government of Phillip, the colony is now functioning at the whim of the greedy large landholders. Governor Hunter, in a moment of what he considers near insanity, reflects that perhaps chains are on the wrong people. It is a point that Dark returns to often. The greatest crime, these two novels suggests, is the loss of an opportunity to build a better society, that the men in power are guilty of a deficiency of imagination and compassion. Generally women characters play a minor role although the majority are depicted as having considerably more insight into the nature of their society than their menfolk and, most particularly, an awareness of the special characteristics of the land itself. Strong characterization, a feel for the landscape, drama based on historical fact together with political insight make all three novels compelling reading.

—Kerry White

_____

DARRELL, Elizabeth.   See DRUMMOND, Emma.

_____

DAVENPORT, Marcia.   American. 1903—. See 2nd edition, 1990.

_____

DAVIS, Dorothy Salisbury. American. 1916—. See 2nd edition, 1990.

_____

DAVIS, Julia.   See WOODWARD, Lilian.

_____

DAVIS, Lindsey.
Nationality: British. **Born:** Birmingham in 1949. **Education:** studied English at Oxford University. **Career:** civil service; full-time writer. **Address:** c/o Century Publishing Ltd, Random House, 20 Vauxhall Bridge Road, London SW1V 2SA, England.

ROMANCE AND HISTORICAL PUBLICATIONS

Novels (series: Marcus Didius Falco appears in all books)

The Silver Pigs. London, Pan, and New York, Crown, 1989.
Shadows in Bronze. London, Sidgwick and Jackson, and New York, Crown, 1990.
Venus in Copper. London, Hutchinson, and New York, Crown, 1991.
The Iron Hand of Mars. London, Hutchinson, 1992.
Poseidon's Gold. London, Century, 1993.

*   *   *

Imagine Philip Marlowe in ancient Rome . . . and meet Marcus Didius Falco, the hero of Lindsey Davis's romantic historical novels. Or are they really detective thrillers? An important element of their complex plots is that of a mystery. Ancient Rome is the setting chosen by Davis—the Rome of Vespasian and Titus, but also a city full of intrigue, political scandal, financial skulduggery, and murder.

The reader is first introduced to Falco in *The Silver Pigs*. An ex-legionary turned private informer, he finds himself rescuing the charming Sosia from an abduction. When she is murdered he is drawn into a much more complicated case involving fraud against the State (and therefore the Emperor) which eventually takes him undercover to Britain. He meets and falls in love with the lovely, but redoubtable Helena Justina. A hard stint in the British silver mines eventually provides Falco with the evidence he needs to solve his case. The trail leads him back to Rome but Helena's uncle, her ex-husband, and the Emperor's younger son, Domitian, are all implicated in the affair. Davis develops the love affair between Falco and Helena as counterpoint to the headlong excitement and intricacies of Falco's investigation.

Davis's second novel, *Shadows in Bronze*, picks up the narrative almost at the point at which *Silver Pigs* comes to an end. Beginning in the late spring of A.D. 79, Falco, now an official informer to Vespasian, finds himself commissioned to discover the whereabouts of a missing senator. Once more undercover (this time as a dealer in lead piping), and accompanied by his closest friend, L. Petronius Longus, and his family, Falco arrives in the district of Pompeii and Naples. Again, he finds himself embroiled in a complicated plot to overthrow Vespasian. Helena behaves strangely and the reappearance of her ex-husband, Pertinax, with whom Falco has old scores to settle, complicates matters further. This is the longest of the Falco novels and possibly the least successful. Similarly, the complexities of the plot—or rather plots, for Davis juggles several stories at the same time—the crowded canvas, the Latin names, and the unfamiliar settings do not make this book easy to read.

Such criticism is less applicable to the remaining titles—*Venus in Copper*, *The Iron Hand of Mars*, and *Poseidon's Gold*, all of which are shorter and less diffuse. In the first, Falco finds himself in need of a job. Reverting to his former role of private informer he undertakes an investigation into the background of a 'professional' bride. The lady's previous husbands have all died in suspicious circumstances. The task brings him into contact with some exotic but improbable characters. There is a particularly nasty protection racket as well as two murders to solve. However, with his usual tenacity and perseverance—and thanks to the help of Helena—Falco is able to reach the right conclusion and produce a reasonably happy, if somewhat ironic ending.

The Iron Hand of Mars takes Falco out of Rome and into the provinces again, this time to Germany and to the scene of one of Rome's worst defeats, the Varus disaster in A.D. 6. The area is still recovering from a rebellion led by Civilis in which the XVI Legion had been involved dishonourably. Falco has to discover the fates of both Civilis, and of a missing legate. Complications soon arise in the form of the exotic Xanthus, the murdered bodies of the leaders of a local guild, and the disappearance of another officer. Solving these mysteries takes Falco out of the Empire across the Rhine and into the clutches of the Germanic Tribes.

The latest title in the Falco canon, *Poseidon's Gold*, maintains Davis's high standards in terms of a lively plot and of colourful characters. Having returned to Rome Falco and Helena find themselves heavily implicated in the affairs of Falco's recently deceased elder brother, Festus, who died heroically in the Judaean wars. However, Falco finds himself accused of his brother's murder. His search for the true killer brings him into contact with his estranged father, the larger than life Geminus. The denouement is thoroughly satisfying with a humorous Davis twist to add piquancy. The Falco/Helena romance continues to unfold and develop to an almost satisfying conclusion allowing scope for further instalments in the saga.

Davis's novels are an interesting combination of history and romantic thriller. Falco bears more than a little resemblance to Philip Marlowe while Helena is a strong-minded feminist contributing more than a little to her lover's success. Their love affair provides an added dimension and depth to the adventures that Falco is involved in and the very close-knit nature of the five titles enables the reader to follow the development of their relationship from the initial stormy exchanges, through the trauma of Helena's miscarriage, to a more settled if still volatile status, with interest.

Each title introduces a different aspect of life in Ancient Rome—*Silver Pigs* takes the reader to Britain, and the reader learns how a province was governed and run, as well as being introduced to aspects of trade and economy; *The Iron Hand of Mars* also has a provincial setting, this time of Germany, and the unsettled nature of the frontier is shown. In *Shadows in Bronze*, the reader samples life in Naples and also learns about the complications of the senatorial system, while *Venus in Copper* takes place against a background of property deals and profiteering, and allows the reader a glimpse of the world of slaves and freedmen.

These five close-knit novels establish Davis as an interesting and enjoyable writer who manages to combine successfully the demands of the historical novel with those of the romantic genre while introducing the further dimension of a detective mystery. Though sometimes this results in a rather too intricate and crowded plot, the reader's interest rarely wanes. Even the difficulties inherent in unfamiliar Roman names and places diminish in the face of Davis's enthusiasm (she always provides a *dramatis personae* for the more faint-hearted). Davis is an attractive author for readers who want romantic excitement and unassuming but convincing scholarship.

—Ferelith Hordon

DAVIS, Robert Hart. See **HORNER, Lance, Kyle ONSTOTT, and Ashley CARTER**.

DAWES, Edna. See **DRUMMOND, Emma**.

DEAN, Shelley. See **WALKER, Lucy**.

DE BLASIS, Celeste (Ninette).
Nationality: American. **Born:** Santa Monica, California, 8 May 1946. **Education:** Wellesley College, Massachusetts, 1964–65; Oregon State University, Corvallis, 1965–66; Pomona College, Claremont, California, B.A. (cum laude) in English 1968. Lives in California. **Agent:** Jane Rotrosen Agency, 318 East 51st Street, New York, New York 10022, USA.

ROMANCE AND HISTORICAL PUBLICATIONS

Novels (series: Swan)

The Night Child. New York, Coward McCann, and London, Millington, 1975.
Suffer a Sea Change. New York, Coward McCann, 1976.
The Proud Breed. New York, Coward McCann, 1978; London, Arrow, 1979.
The Tiger's Woman. New York, Delacorte Press, 1981; London, Granada, 1982.

Wild Swan. New York, Bantam, and London, Bantam, 1984.
Swan's Chance. New York, Bantam, 1985; London, Bantam, 1987.
A Season of Swans. New York, Bantam, and London, Bantam, 1989.

OTHER PUBLICATIONS

Other

Graveyard Peaches. New York, St Martin's Press, 1991.

*

Celeste De Blasis comments:

My name is unfortunate. It sounds wildly romantic to Anglo-Saxon ears, but it is no more than the result of having an Italian father. I write historical novels based on solid research from hundreds, often thousands of primary and secondary sources. The books are not 'bodice rippers', though they contain romance in the old sense of the heroic, the adventurous, the emotional lives of human beings depicted on a broad canvas. There is love in the books—love between men and women, between generations, love for friends, for ideas, for a particular piece of earth or a particular way of life. There are also hatred, prejudice, envy, greed—all the counterweights of love. Surely, good fiction explores the light and dark of the human spirit, and good historical novels should expand that exploration to include the light and dark of the collective heart people form to govern themselves and others. In the best combination, readers are both informed and entertained, and I hope that is what my novels do.

*   *   *

Three themes run through Celeste De Blasis's works: love of the sea; love of animals, especially horses; and the intense love of two human beings which overpowers everything else.

The Night Child is her only book which does not express the author's love of the sea, but horses and dogs are there. The setting is the interior of Maine in 1869. This is an old-fashioned gothic romance with a heroine who has plenty of backbone, though De Blasis tries to mislead the reader by making Brandy appear more timorous than she is. Brandy is hired by Grey King to care for his daughter Missy, who has exhibited autistic behavior since her mother's death. As the child begins to respond to Brandy's experiments, strange and sometimes dangerous things begin to happen to Brandy. The knowledge that Missy's mother died in a stable fire two years earlier makes Brandy wonder who is trying to kill her. Clues to the miscreant are placed throughout until, by the finale, all the loose ends are tied up, and love vanquishes evil.

Suffer a Sea Change owes more than a little to Shakespeare's *The Tempest.* Jess is Miranda, Winston St James her Caliban, etc. Although animals are not of great import here, the sea is. Jess accepts a trip to Bermuda from an avuncular gentleman she does not really know very well. He not only insists she join the tour group, he directs her to wear an ornate emerald ring while she is there. No sooner does the plane land than Jess is compelled to assist an obviously terrified native man whom she sees again at the resort. She is drawn toward the American, Kyre Tarkington, even as she is frightened by the Englishman, St James. Despite the danger, Jess is pulled deeper into the mystery. She almost loses her life to ocean-going drug smugglers before the criminal activities are resolved, and she accepts the love of the right man. This is a page-turner even if the opening premise is unrealistic.

In *The Proud Breed* the animals take centre stage in the form of palomino horses. Tessa's family raises them in the 1840's. Of mixed Spanish and American heritage, Tessa marries Yankee Gavin Ramsey after almost killing him. Disaster follows disaster (flood, drought, rape, Indian raids, war, and attempted abortion among others) as the history of California is related through three generations of the Ramsey family. Lots of violence and sex underscore the deep love between the characters in this long, satisfying read.

The Tiger's Woman brings all of the author's loves into full flower. Jason Drake owns ships, logging camps, property in San Francisco, and several businesses. The one thing he is not interested in is a woman to replace his dead wife. Mary Smith is only interested in his protection and feels safe only on his island off the coast of Seattle. Neither Jason nor the reader becomes privy to her horrible secret until much further in their relationship. In fact, Mary withholds information from Jason until it is almost too late. But the love they finally recognize as binding them together keeps them alive when survival seems impossible. Again, violence and sex are major parts of the plot.

Wild Swan and *Swan's Chance* span 50 years and detail the lives of Alexandria Thaine and Rane Falconer. Beginning in 1813 in Devon, England, Rane falls in love with Alex while she is still a child. Unaware of his feelings, or even her own, she returns home and weds her dead sister's husband, moving to Maryland to legitimize the marriage. The couple establish a tavern and a breeding farm for race horses, both named Wild Swan. St John is killed in a fall from a horse, and some years later Alex and Rane marry. In the sequel, Rane has founded a Baltimore shipyard and builds clipper ships, while Alex breeds and races her horses. Their love is strong but tempestuous, and their children and grandchildren have their own adventures, following the examples of their elders. The underground railroad, women's rights, the relocation of the Cherokee Indians, the Civil War, and improvements in medical care all become important issues in a dramatic and interesting tale.

De Blasis keeps meticulous notes on each of her characters, even the animals. She records physical descriptions, psychological profiles, and genealogical charts for each. She believes in happy endings, too, so love always wins in the end, regardless of the amount of sex and violence which precede the victory. Her work shows growth from one book to the next, and this bodes well for future novels.

—Andrea Lee Shuey

———

de CRESPIGNY, Charles.   See **WILLIAMSON, C.N. and A.M.**

———

DEEPING, (George) Warwick.
Nationality: British. **Born:** Southend, Essex, 28 May 1877. **Education:** Merchant Taylors' School, London; Trinity College, Cambridge, B.A., M.A., M.B.; studied medicine at Middlesex Hospital, London. **Military Service:** served in the Royal Army Medical Corps, 1915–18. **Relations:** married Maude Phyllis Merrill. **Career:** practiced as a doctor for one year. **Died:** 20 April 1950.

ROMANCE AND HISTORICAL PUBLICATIONS

Novels

Uther and Igraine. London, Richards, and New York, Outlook, 1903.
Love among the Ruins. London, Richards, and New York, Macmillan, 1904.
The Seven Streams. London, Nash, 1905; New York, Fenno, 1909.
The Slanderers. New York, Harper, 1905; London, Cassell, 1907.
Bess of the Woods. London and New York, Harper, 1906.

A Woman's War. London and New York, Harper, 1907.

Bertrand of Brittany. London and New York, Harper, 1908.

Mad Barbara. London, Cassell, 1908; New York, Harper, 1909.

The Red Saint. London, Cassell, 1909; New York, McBride, 1940.

The Return of the Petticoat. London and New York, Harper, 1909; revised edition, London, Cassell, 1913.

The Lame Englishman. London, Cassell, 1910.

The Rust of Rome. London, Cassell, 1910.

Fox Farm. London, Cassell, 1911; as *The Eyes of Love*, New York, McBride, 1933.

Joan of the Tower. London, Cassell, 1911; New York, McBride, 1941.

Sincerity. London, Cassell, 1912; as *The Strong Hand*, 1912; as *The Challenge of Love*, New York, McBride, 1932.

The House of Spies. London and New York, Cassell, 1913.

The White Gate. London, Cassell, 1913; New York, McBride, 1914.

The King Behind the King. London, Cassell, and New York, McBride, 1914.

The Pride of Eve. London, Cassell, 1914.

Marriage by Conquest. London, Cassell, and New York, McBride, 1915.

Unrest. London, Cassell, 1916; as *Bridge of Desire*, New York, McBride, 1916.

Martin Valliant. London, Cassell, and New York, McBride, 1917.

Valour. London, Cassell, 1918; New York, McBride, 1934.

Second Youth. London, Cassell, 1919; New York, Grosset and Dunlap, 1932.

The Prophetic Marriage. London, Cassell, 1920; New York, Grosset and Dunlap, 1932.

The House of Adventure. London, Cassell, 1921; New York, Macmillan, 1922.

Lantern Lane. London, Cassell, 1921.

Orchards. London, Cassell, 1922; as *The Captive Wife*, New York, Grosset and Dunlap, 1933.

Apples of Gold. London, Cassell, 1923.

The Secret Sanctuary; or, The Saving of John Stretton. London, Cassell, 1923.

Suvla John. London, Cassell, 1924.

Three Rooms. London, Cassell, 1924.

Sorrell and Son. London, Cassell, 1925; New York, Knopf, 1926.

Doomsday. London, Cassell, and New York, Knopf, 1927.

Kitty. London, Cassell, and New York, Knopf, 1927.

Old Pybus. London, Cassell, and New York, Knopf, 1928.

Roper's Row. London, Cassell, and New York, Knopf, 1929.

Exiles. London, Cassell, 1930; as *Exile*, New York, Knopf, 1930.

The Road. London, Cassell, 1931; as *The Ten Commandments*, New York, Knopf, 1931.

Old Wine and New. London, Cassell, and New York, Knopf, 1932.

Smith. London, Cassell, and New York, Knopf, 1932.

Two Black Sheep. London, Cassell, and New York, Knopf, 1933.

The Man on the White Horse. London, Cassell, and New York, Knopf, 1934.

Seven Men Came Back. London, Cassell, and New York, Knopf, 1934.

Sackcloth into Silk. London, Cassell, 1935; as *The Golden Cord*, New York, Knopf, 1935.

No Hero—This. London, Cassell, and New York, Knopf, 1936.

Blind Man's Year. London, Cassell, and New York, Knopf, 1937.

These White Hands. New York, McBride, 1937.

The Woman at the Door. London, Cassell, and New York, Knopf, 1937.

The Malice of Men. London, Cassell, and New York, Knopf, 1938.

Fantasia. London, Cassell, 1939; as *Bluewater*, New York, Knopf, 1939.

Shabby Summer. London, Cassell, 1939; as *Folly Island*, New York, Knopf, 1939.

The Man Who Went Back. London, Cassell, and New York, Knopf, 1940.

The Shield of Love. London, Cassell, and New York, McBride, 1940.

Corn in Egypt. London, Cassell, 1941; New York, Knopf, 1942.

The Dark House. London, Cassell, and New York, Knopf, 1941.

I Live Again. London, Cassell, and New York, Knopf, 1942.

Slade. London, Cassell, and New York, Dial Press, 1943.

Mr Gurney and Mr Slade. London, Cassell, 1944; as *The Cleric's Secret*, New York, Dial Press, 1944.

Reprieve. London, Cassell, and New York, Dial Press, 1945.

The Impudence of Youth. London, Cassell, and New York, Dial Press, 1946.

Laughing House. London, Cassell, 1946; New York, Dial Press, 1947.

Portrait of a Playboy. London, Cassell, 1947; as *The Playboy*, New York, Dial Press, 1948.

Paradise Place. London, Cassell, 1949.

Old Mischief. London, Cassell, 1950.

Time to Heal. London, Cassell, 1952.

Man in Chains. London, Cassell, 1953.

The Old World Dies. London, Cassell, 1954.

Caroline Terrace. London, Cassell, 1955.

The Serpent's Tooth. London, Cassell, 1956.

The Sword and the Cross. London, Cassell, 1957.

Short Stories

Countess Glika and Other Stories. London, Cassell, 1919.

Martyrdom, with *The House Behind the Judas Tree* by Gilbert Frankau and *Forbidden Music* by Ethel Mannin. London, Readers Library, 1929; as *Three Stories of Romance*, 1936.

The Short Stories of Warwick Deeping. London, Cassell, 1930.

Stories of Love, Courage, and Compassion. New York, Knopf, 1930.

Two in a Train and Other Stories. London, Cassell, 1935.

*

Film Adaptation: *Sorrell and Son*, 1934, 1984.

* * *

Traditionalist Warwick Deeping turned out 70 novels in an effort to keep alive the pastoral vision of Edwardian England in the years after World War I; but only his early *Sorrell and Son* (1925) became a mass audience favourite in the United States as well as the British Empire. This harrowing tale of an aristocratic World War I veteran's returning to find himself destitute and deserted by his wife recounts Stephen Sorrell's successful struggle to emerge from a demeaning position to regain dignity and wealth, while continuing to command the loyalty of his son. Throughout his travails, Sorrell's obsession is to remain a gentleman and have his son educated as befits a gentleman. The reviewer for *The New Statesman* complained that 'it is difficult to understand how a man so wisely determined when he reaches bottom could have fallen so low' (31 October 1925); but the criticism misses the source of the novel's enduring popularity. *Sorrell and Son* is no Samuel Smiles success story, but rather a secularized allegory in the tradition of *Pilgrim's Progress*. The author arbitrarily reduces Sorrell to a Job-like state so that he can describe the sort of person who can rehabilitate himself in a fictional reincarnation of the 'stiff upper lip' tradition that kept Britons going through demoralizing times. His son, Christopher, even becomes a doctor, not just because the position is properly genteel, but so that in a heart-rending conclusion he can administer an overdose of morphine that ends his father's physical sufferings after this man has triumphed over moral defeats the world has administered to him. *Sorrell and Son* appeared the same year as *The Great Gatsby*; and it can be read as an unintended reply to Fitzgerald's cynical, ironic tale of father-son relationships destroyed in a squalid world. Deeping's tribute to the triumph of the old verities was enormously more popular than Fitzgerald's novel at the time of their publication; but Deeping never again found the formula to shape his nostalgic vision into a popular myth.

—Warren French

de GUISE, Elizabeth.   See HUNTER, Elizabeth.

DELAFIELD, E.M.

Nationality: British. **Born:** Edmée Elizabeth Monica De la Pasture in Aldrinton, Sussex, 9 June 1890; daughter of the writer Mrs Henry De la Pasture. Educated at convent schools; postulant with religious order in Belgium, 1911–12. **Military Service:** served in the Voluntary Aid Detachment, 1914–17; Ministry of National Service, Bristol, 1917–18. **Relations:** married Arthur Paul Dashwood in 1919; one son and one daughter. **Career:** journalist: regular contributor to *Time and Tide* and *Punch*. Justice of the Peace, Cullompton, Devon. **Died:** 2 December 1943.

ROMANCE AND HISTORICAL PUBLICATIONS

Novels (series: Provincial Lady)

Zella Sees Herself. London, Heinemann, and New York, Knopf, 1917.
The War-Workers. London, Heinemann, and New York, Knopf, 1918.
The Pelicans. London, Heinemann, 1918; New York, Knopf, 1919.
Consequences. London, Hodder and Stoughton, and New York, Knopf, 1919.
Tension. London, Hutchinson, and New York, Macmillan, 1920.
The Heel of Achilles. London, Hutchinson, and New York, Macmillan, 1921.
Humbug. London, Hutchinson, 1921; New York, Macmillan, 1922.
The Optimist. London, Hutchinson, and New York, Macmillan, 1922.
A Reversion to Type. London, Hutchinson, and New York, Macmillan, 1923.
Mrs Harter. London, Hutchinson, 1924; New York, Harper, 1925.
Messalina of the Suburbs (includes story and play). London, Hutchinson, 1924.
The Chip and the Block. London, Hutchinson, 1925; New York, Harper, 1926.
Jill. London, Hutchinson, 1926; New York, Harper, 1927.
The Way Things Are. London, Hutchinson, 1927; New York, Harper, 1928.
The Suburban Young Man. London, Hutchinson, 1928.
What Is Love? London, Macmillan, 1928; as *First Love*, New York, Harper, 1929.
Turn Back the Leaves. London, Macmillan, and New York, Harper, 1930.
Diary of a Provincial Lady. London, Macmillan, 1930; New York, Harper, 1931.
Challenge to Clarissa. London, Macmillan, 1931; as *House Party*, New York, Harper, 1931.
Thank Heaven Fasting. London, Macmillan, 1932; as *A Good Man's Love*, New York, Harper, 1932.

The Provincial Lady Goes Further. London, Macmillan, 1932; as *The Provincial Lady in London*, New York, Harper, 1933.
Gay Life. London, Macmillan, and New York, Harper, 1933.
The Provincial Lady in America. London, Macmillan, and New York, Harper, 1934.
The Bazalgettes: A Tale (published anonymously). London, Hamish Hamilton, 1935.
Faster! Faster! London, Macmillan, and New York, Harper, 1936.
Nothing Is Safe. London, Macmillan, and New York, Harper, 1937.
The Provincial Lady in War-Time. London, Macmillan, and New York, Harper, 1940.
No One Now Will Know. London, Macmillan, and New York, Harper, 1941.
Late and Soon. London, Macmillan, and New York, Harper, 1943.

Short Stories

The Entertainment. London, Hutchinson, and New York, Harper, 1927.
Women Are Like That: Short Stories. London, Macmillan, 1929; New York, Harper, 1930.
When Women Love. New York, Harper, 1938; as *Three Marriages*, London, Macmillan, 1939.
Love Has No Resurrection and Other Stories. London, Macmillan, 1939.

OTHER PUBLICATIONS

Plays

To See Ourselves: A Domestic Comedy (produced London, 1930; New York, 1935). London and New York, French, 1932.
The Glass Wall (produced London, 1933). London, Gollancz, 1933.

Screenplays: *Crime on the Hill*, with others 1933; *Moonlight Sonata* (*The Charmer*), with Edward Knoblock and Hans Rameau, 1937.

Radio Plays: *The Little Boy*, 1934; *Case for the Defense; Vice Versa*, from the novel by F. Anstey; *Home Life Relayed* (sketches); *Home Is Like That* (sketches), 1938.

Other

Man, Proud Man, with Mary Borden and Susan Ertz. London, Hamilton, 1932.
General Impressions. London, Macmillan, 1933.
Ladies and Gentlemen in Victorian Fiction. London, Hogarth Press, and New York, Harper, 1937.
As Others Hear Us: A Miscellany. London, Macmillan, 1937.
Straw Without Bricks: I Visit Soviet Russia. London, Macmillan, 1937; as *I Visit the Soviets: The Provincial Lady Looks at Russia*, New York, Harper, 1937.
People You Love. London, Collins, 1940.
This War We Wage. New York, Emerson, 1941.

Editor, *The Time and Tide Album.* London, Hamish Hamilton, 1932.
Editor, *The Brontës: Their Lives Recorded by Their Contemporaries.* London, Hogarth Press, 1935; Westport, Connecticut, Meckler, 1980.

*

Bibliography: in *Ten Contemporaries*, 2nd series by John Gawsworth, London, Benn, 1933.

Critical Study: *The Life of a Provincial Lady: A Study of E.M. Delafield* by Violet Powell, London, Heinemann, 1988.

*   *   *

A prolific writer whose work spans three decades, E.M. Delafield explores the human capacity for self-deception and self-love, often revealed in affairs of the heart. These aspects are present in her first novel—appropriately titled *Zella Sees Herself*—and recur constantly in later books. Nowadays Delafield is best known for her superb comic masterpiece *Diary of a Provincial Lady*, a work justly famous for its sardonic wit and shrewd insights into human nature. Its popularity led to a number of sequels, all of which are amusing without matching the excellence of their original. Unfortunately the fame of the 'Provincial Lady' has tended to detract from other novels of a different kind, where the humour is muted, and the author approaches various facets of life and love in a witty but serious manner.

Delafield's best novel in this style is generally thought to be *Thank Heaven Fasting*, where the heroine experiences and rejects romantic passion for the staid affections of a reliable middle-aged suitor. The pressures of upper-class society, where marriage is regarded as all-important and spinsterhood a fate worse than death, is admirably portrayed. So, too, is the heroine's ability to think herself in love at each encounter. This, though, is to give too cynical an interpretation of Delafield's motives. Though gothic elements are occasional and slight—her study of a female criminal in *Messalina of the Suburbs*, and parts of *When Women Love (Three Marriages)* are exceptions—romance figures largely in her work. Delafield is no stranger to passion, though her recounting of it is often dispassionate. The early novel *The Heel of Achilles* concentrates on the possessive self-love of Lydia Raymond, who throughout her life ruthlessly claims the centre of the stage for herself under the guise of caring for others. Lydia, who marries without love, is brought to her downfall by her daughter Jennie, the one person for whom she cares. Her selfishness and hypocrisy are laid bare at last in her vain struggle to usurp the life experience of Jennie for herself. Though the ending has rather too much of the sermon about it, its character studies go deeper than those of *Thank Heaven Fasting*. Like many of Delafield's novels, it is unjustly neglected.

Turn Back the Leaves centres on the growth to womanhood of Stella, child of an illicit liaison, who is brought up as a 'cousin' in the household of the wronged husband. Delafield describes her impact on the family, and its eventual break-up. The story is interesting, but an uneasy shift of focus from Stella to her 'cousins' near the end weakens the book as a whole. More effective is *When Women Love* which views three different relationships in 1857, 1897, and 1937 respectively. The first, 'The Wedding of Rose Barlow', deals with the young bride in a marriage of convenience who falls in love with her French cousin, and is finally reunited with him after surviving the horrors of the Cawnpore massacre, in which her husband dies. 'A Girl of the Period' looks satirically at a 'modern' girl of 1897, who is engaged without being in love, and openly scorns sentiment. When her fiancé falls for someone else she strikes a noble pose in 'releasing' him, but when she herself becomes infatuated by the rakish Courtenay, promised to her friend, Violet fights viciously with her rival rather than give him up. 'We Meant to Be Happy' describes an ill-fated extra-marital affair where disillusion sets in, and the husband's illness serves to blackmail the erring wife into submission. The three stories are skilfully related, the tone varied in each case.

In *No One Now Will Know* the author explores Rosalie Meredith's love for the Creole Lucian Lempriere, her illicit passion for his brother Fred, and her violent death. This central theme—described in retrospect over three generations—is paralleled by Rosalie's friend Kate, and her unrequited love for Lucian. There is an ironic echo a generation later, when Rosalie's daughter Callie loses her own lover to her best friend, Elisabeth. The tangle of relationships is adroitly presented, the author refraining from comment to let the reader draw his own conclusions.

Late and Soon is Delafield's last novel, and ranks among her best. The story takes place over a winter weekend in 1942, at the country home of Valentine, Lady Arbell. A group of soldiers are billeted there, and Valentine recognizes their Colonel—Rory Lonergan—as the young Irish artist with whom she fell in love as a girl, but was prevented from marrying. Now he re-enters her life as the lover of her worldly daughter, Primrose. The re-awakening of their love and its traumatic resolution are brilliantly depicted by Delafield, who eyes her characters with a wry affection. *Late and Soon* is a worthy conclusion to her career, marred as it was by her premature death.

Delafield's work extends beyond the novel. She produced three collections of short stories, which display all her familiar talents. *Love Has No Resurrection* is typical, with tales ranging from the tragic to the comic and mundane, often touching on the deluding power of passion and its consequences. Other works include plays, sociopolitical commentaries, and literary criticism. Her articles for *Punch* and *Time and Tide*, many of them masterly examples of humorous dialogue, are collected in *As Others Hear Us*. Delafield's vision is broad as it is deep, her analyses of human character at once sharp and sympathetic. Her writing reveals a natural warmth, a wary fondness for the human heart, no matter how often it deceives.

—Geoffrey Sadler

DELANEY, Denis. See **GREEN, Peter.**

---

de la ROCHE, Mazo (Louise).
Nationality: Canadian. **Born:** Newmarket, Ontario, 15 January 1879. **Education:** schools in Galt, Ontario, and Toronto; Parkdale Collegiate Institute, Toronto; University of Toronto; school of art, Toronto. **Relations:** two adopted daughters. **Career:** full-time writer from childhood; lived in Windsor, England, 1929–39; thereafter lived in Toronto. **Recipient:** Lorne Pierce medal, 1938; University of Alberta National award, 1951. D.Litt.: University of Toronto, 1954. **Died:** 12 July 1961.

ROMANCE AND HISTORICAL PUBLICATIONS

Novels (series: Whiteoaks of Jalna)

Possession. New York and London, Macmillan, 1923.
Delight. New York and London, Macmillan, 1926.
Jalna. Boston, Little Brown, and London, Hodder and Stoughton, 1927.
Whiteoaks of Jalna. Boston, Little Brown, 1929; as *Whiteoaks*, London, Macmillan, 1929.
Finch's Fortune (Jalna). Boston, Little Brown, and London, Macmillan, 1931.
Lark Ascending. Boston, Little Brown, and London, Macmillan, 1932.
The Thunder of New Wings, in *Chatelaine* (Toronto), June–December 1932.
The Master of Jalna. Boston, Little Brown, and London, Macmillan, 1933.
Beside a Norman Tower. Boston, Little Brown, and London, Macmillan, 1934.
Young Renny (Jalna). Boston, Little Brown, and London, Macmillan, 1935.

Whiteoak Harvest (Jalna). Boston, Little Brown, and London, Macmillan, 1936.

The Very House. Boston, Little Brown, and London, Macmillan, 1937.

Growth of a Man. Boston, Little Brown, and London, Macmillan, 1938.

Whiteoak Heritage (Jalna). Boston, Little Brown, and London, Macmillan, 1940.

Wakefield's Course (Jalna). Boston, Little Brown, 1941; London, Macmillan, 1942.

The Two Saplings. London, Macmillan, 1942.

The Building of Jalna. Boston, Little Brown, 1944; London, Macmillan, 1945.

Return to Jalna. Boston, Little Brown, 1946; London, Macmillan, 1948.

Mary Wakefield (Jalna). Boston, Little Brown, and London, Macmillan, 1949.

Renny's Daughter (Jalna). Boston, Little Brown, and London, Macmillan, 1951.

The Whiteoak Brothers (Jalna). Boston, Little Brown, and London, Macmillan, 1953.

Variable Winds at Jalna. Boston, Little Brown, and London, Macmillan, 1955.

Centenary at Jalna. Boston, Little Brown, and London, Macmillan, 1958.

Morning at Jalna. Boston, Little Brown, and London, Macmillan, 1960.

Short Stories

Explorers of the Dawn. New York, Knopf, and London, Cassell, 1922.

The Sacred Bullock and Other Stories of Animals. Boston, Little Brown, and London, Macmillan, 1939.

A Boy in the House and Other Stories. Boston, Little Brown, and London, Macmillan, 1952.

Selected Stories, edited by Douglas Daymond. Ottawa, University of Ottawa Press, 1979.

OTHER PUBLICATIONS

Plays

Low Life: A Comedy in One Act (produced Montreal, 1925). Toronto, Macmillan, 1925; in *Low Life and Other Plays*, 1929.

Come True (produced Toronto, 1927). Toronto, Macmillan, 1927; in *Low Life and Other Plays*, 1929.

The Return of the Emigrant (produced Toronto, 1928). Included in *Low Life and Other Plays*, 1929.

Low Life and Other Plays. Toronto, Macmillan, and Boston, Little Brown, 1929.

Whiteoaks, adaptation of her own novel (produced London, 1936; New York, 1938), with Nancy Price. Boston, Little Brown, and London, Macmillan, 1936.

The Mistress of Jalna (produced London, 1951).

Other

Portrait of a Dog: a Novel. Boston, Little Brown, and London, Macmillan, 1930.

Quebec, Historic Seaport. New York, Doubleday, 1944; London, Macmillan, 1946.

The Song of Lambert (for children). Boston, Little Brown, and London, Macmillan, 1955.

Ringing the Changes: An Autobiography. Boston, Little Brown, and New York, Macmillan, 1957.

Bill and Coo (for children). Boston, Little Brown, and London, Macmillan, 1958.

*

Critical Studies: *Mazo de la Roche of Jalna* by Ronald Hambleton, New York, Hawthorn, 1966; *Mazo de la Roche* by George Hendrick, New York, Twayne, 1970; *Mazo de la Roche: A Hidden Life*, by Joan Givner, Toronto, Oxford University Press, 1989.

*   *   *

Mazo de la Roche was a writer of novels, short stories, plays, children's books, and a volume of autobiography. Yet it is doubtful whether any of her works would still be read were it not for the remarkable success of her 'Whiteoaks of Jalna' series.

Her earlier novels contained little to distinguish them from the normal run of the mill sentimental romance stories written in large quantities in the late-19th century and the first quarter of this. *Delight*, for example, is the over-emotional story of Delight Mainprize (de la Roche's penchant for bizarre names remained with her throughout her writing career), a young girl emigrating from England to Canada. The plot is melodramatic and the characters are cardboard, detailed physical descriptions fail to compensate for the lack of any depth or insight. Moreover, the characters speak with dreadfully overdone accents and brogues; in this and other respects this novel is a little reminiscent of those of Gene Stratton Porter, but without the latter's fey, if sporadic, charm.

But close on the heels of *Delight* followed *Jalna*, and with the publication of this de la Roche's style was set for the next 30 years. The first of a total of 16 books telling the story of four generations of the Whiteoaks family, farming and breeding horses in Canada, *Jalna* was originally intended to stand alone. However, such was the popular and critical acclaim with which the novel was received that sequels and prequels ensued at a steady rate for the rest of de la Roche's life.

This first novel is set in the 1920s, roughly three-quarters of the way through the 100-year span of the saga, and we join the family a year or so before the 100th birthday of its matriarch, Adeline Whiteoak, who is immediately established as the most strong-willed, demanding member of a family which has more than its fair share of such personalities. The family at this stage consists of Adeline, three of her four children, and her six grandchildren, together with various spouses, ex-spouses, and spouses-to-be; the individual characters are all drawn in skilful and humorous detail, but more importantly it is made clear that the family is much more than the sum of its constituent members. The family has an all too overpowering identity, as some of those who marry into it (or narrowly escape marriage into it), find out to their cost. In particular Alayne, the wife first of Adeline's grandson Eden and then of Eden's half-brother Renny (the Master of Jalna himself) finds it hard to come to terms with this. And indeed any bride might justifiably be irate when her new (albeit second) husband continues to share his bedroom—and in fact his bed—with his young brother, rather than with her. Even after a few years of marriage, and the birth of her first child, Alayne thinks '. . . It took the individuality out of one; one could put up only a losing fight against the power of the Whiteoaks'. Years later her son, Archer, preparing to depart for Oxford, remarks:

This family has been the structure of all our lives. We don't think about it. It's like the air we breathe. It's sacred to us. I wake up in the morning, feeling myself a part of the family. I go to bed at night, knowing that I'm a part of it. It's time I went away into another country. But I daresay I shall come home again.

And there Archer, who even as a small boy was very astute, sums up the whole Whiteoaks saga!

Renny is the dominant character in most of the books but, although virtually all the women he encounters find him attractive, he is not always particularly likeable. This remarkable family throws up some unusually talented members, and of Renny's four half-brothers one is a poet, one becomes a concert pianist, and one a monk and then later an actor—but Renny himself shows scant tolerance for these artistic pursuits. Of his step-mother, Mary Wakefield, he 'recalled vividly the fact that when he had come upon her she had nearly always been reading. Poetry, too. What a mother for men!' And of his half-brother Finch—' . . . in his heart he was deeply ashamed for Finch . . . . It was humiliating that he should be such a cissy—wanting to own a canary, of all things!' The books are peppered with such comments, disparaging of any male who demonstrates an atom of sensitivity. One can only speculate as to what his reaction might have been had one of his brothers or uncles turned out to be gay, but they all seem to be reassuringly (from Renny's point of view) heterosexual.

Although the first-written novel is self-contained, the backgrounds of the family and its members, and of the house of Jalna itself, are so thoroughly documented that when, after producing several sequels, de la Roche started to write the novels dealing with the years before our entry into the saga, these prequels fitted quite seamlessly into the tale. From *The Building of Jalna*, set in 1850, to *Centenary at Jalna* the family expands rather like an amoeba, absorbing in-laws and intended in-laws, occasionally spitting them out but often re-embracing them in re-marriage to another member of the family. The Whiteoaks do have a convenient habit of picking up each other's rejects—although often, it must be said, having precipitated that rejection. And as for Jalna itself, the mansion-cum-farm housing this family: 'always he [Renny] was convinced of the elasticity of Jalna and its capacity to shelter all the family'. Newly-wed couples who come to live under its roof, may depart (amicably or otherwise) to a nearby house or cottage, and then return, perhaps permanently, or at least for sufficient time to work out a marital or other familial problem.

And in the course of all this exchanging of partners and of habitations, the characters themselves develop. Of Renny's half-brothers, Finch, initially a gawky, clumsy youth with no social graces whatsoever, becomes a sensitive, withdrawn concert pianist; Wakefield grows from a lying, thieving, manipulative small boy into an attractive (although still manipulative—it's a Whiteoak family trait) adult; and the boorish insensitive Piers mellows into a vastly more pleasant individual, engaging the reader's sympathy with his sarcastic verbal sparring with his selfish (and manipulative!) half-sister Meg. Even the philistine Renny develops a certain warmth and sensitivity; *Centenary at Jalna* finds him as a 60-year-old conducting his eight-year-old niece on a tour of the various Whiteoak-inhabited dwellings. Of course, the whole point of this exercise is to inculcate the child with a sense of 'family' in this centenary year of Jalna, but in so doing Renny reveals a hitherto unsuspected sense of humour, and a very warm and human relationship is depicted. Only Renny's wife Alayne remains as she was at the beginning—resentful of the continual intrusion of Whiteoaks and their hangers-on into her life with her husband and children.

Even in the 1920s, when de la Roche began the 'Whiteoaks of Jalna' series, the family saga was a well-established formula, but few writers could create such a self-engrossed family with such extravagantly disparate members, and to write to such a consistent standard about these same characters for 30 years demonstrates a particular talent. For there are only the characters and their relationships to hold the reader's interest; outside events rarely impinge, and even two world wars, in which several of the brothers fight, do not really encroach much upon the family. Any drama, and there is plenty, comes from within.

Towards the end of her life, de la Roche wrote a volume of autobiography, *Ringing the Changes*, and in it regressed to her former style; it is unstructured and full of novelistic clichés, and some of the members of her family would seem to have been even more improbable than the Whiteoaks. Her writing in this book springs to life only when she is describing her and her family's dogs, and indeed in all her novels she is particularly skilful at depicting animals and children with immense warmth and humour. Somehow in Jalna she discovered the milieu to exploit her talents to the full, and this saga stands out not only against the remainder of her own writing, but also against most others in the genre.

—Judith Rhodes

DELDERFIELD, R(onald) F(rederick).
Nationality: British. **Born:** Greenwich, London, 12 February 1912. **Education:** attended West Buckland School, Devon. **Military Service:** served in the Royal Air Force, 1940–45: public relations officer, 1944–45. **Relations:** married May Evans in 1936; one son and one daughter. **Career:** reporter, sub-editor, and editor, *Exmouth Chronicle*, Devon, 1929–39 and 1945–47, then freelance writer. **Died:** 24 June 1972.

ROMANCE AND HISTORICAL PUBLICATIONS

Novels (series: Craddocks of Shallowford; Swann)

All over the Town. London, Bles, 1947; New York, Simon and Schuster, 1977.
Seven Men of Gascony. London, Laurie, and Indianapolis, Bobbs Merrill, 1949.
Farewell the Tranquil Mind. London, Laurie, 1950; as *Farewell the Tranquil*, New York, Dutton, 1950.
The Avenue Story. London, Hodder and Stoughton, 1964; as *The Avenue*, New York, Simon and Schuster, 1969.
  The Dreaming Suburb. London, Hodder and Stoughton, 1958.
  The Avenue Goes to War. London, Hodder and Stoughton, 1958.
There Was a Fair Maid Dwelling. London, Hodder and Stoughton, 1960; as *Diana*, New York, Putnam, 1960.
Stop at a Winner. London, Hodder and Stoughton, 1961; New York, Simon and Schuster, 1978.
The Unjust Skies. London, Hodder and Stoughton, 1962.
The Spring Madness of Mr Sermon. London, Hodder and Stoughton, 1963; as *Mr Sermon*, New York, Simon and Schuster, 1970.
Too Few for Drums. London, Hodder and Stoughton, 1964; New York, Simon and Schuster, 1971.
A Horseman Riding By (Craddocks). London, Hodder and Stoughton, 1966; New York, Simon and Schuster, 1967.
Cheap Day Return. London, Hodder and Stoughton, 1967; as *Return Journey*, New York, Simon and Schuster, 1974.
The Green Gauntlet (Craddocks). London, Hodder and Stoughton, and New York, Simon and Schuster, 1968.
Come Home Charlie and Face Them. London, Hodder and Stoughton, 1969; as *Charlie Come Home*, New York, Simon and Schuster, 1976.
God Is an Englishman (Swann). London, Hodder and Stoughton, and New York, Simon and Schuster, 1970.
Their Was the Kingdom (Swann). London, Hodder and Stoughton, and New York, Simon and Schuster, 1971.
To Serve Them All My Days. London, Hodder and Stoughton, and New York, Simon and Schuster, 1972.
Give Us This Day (Swann). London, Hodder and Stoughton, and New York, Simon and Schuster, 1973.

Post of Honor. New York, Ballantine, 1974.
Long Summer Days. New York, Pocket Books, 1974.

OTHER PUBLICATIONS

Plays

Spark in Judaea (produced London, 1937). Boston, Baker, 1951; London, de Wolfe and Stone, 1953.
Twilight Call (produced Birmingham, 1939).
Printer's Devil (produced London, 1939).
This Is My Life, with Basil Thomas (as *Matron*, produced Wolverhampton, 1942). London, Fox, 1944.
Worm's Eye View (produced London, 1945). In *Embassy Successes 1*, London, Sampson Low, 1946; New York, French, 1948.
The Spinster of South Street (produced London, 1945).
Peace Comes to Peckham (produced London, 1946). London, French, 1948.
All over the Town, adaptation of his own novel (produced London, 1947). London, French, 1948.
The Queen Came By (produced London, 1948). London, Deane, and Boston, Baker, 1949.
Sailors Beware: An Elizabethan Improbability. London, Deane, 1950.
The Elephant's Graveyard (produced Chesterfield, 1951).
Waggonload o' Monkeys: Further Adventures of Porter and Taffy (produced London, 1951). London, Deane, 1952.
Golden Rain (produced Windsor, 1952). London, French, 1953.
Miaow! Miaow! London, French, 1952.
The Old Lady of Cheadle. London, Deane, 1952.
Made to Measure (broadcast 1953). London, French, 1952.
The Bride Wore an Opal Ring (broadcast 1954). London, French, 1952.
Follow the Plough (produced Leatherhead, Surrey, and London, 1953).
The Testimonial (broadcast 1953). London, French, 1953.
Glad Tidings (produced 1953).
The Offending Hand (produced Northampton, 1953). London, Deane, 1955.
The Orchard Walls (produced Aldershot, Hampshire, and London, 1953). London, French, 1954.
Absent Lover: A Plantagenet Improbability. London, French, 1953.
Smoke in the Valley (broadcast 1954). London, French, 1953.
The Guinea-Pigs. London, Deane, 1954.
Home Is the Hunted. London, French, 1954.
Musical Switch. London, de Wolfe and Stone, 1954.
The Rounderlay Tradition. London, Deane, 1954.
Ten till Five. London, de Wolfe and Stone, 1954.
Where There's a Will. London, French, 1954.
And Then There Were None (broadcast 1955). London, French, 1954.
Uncle's Little Lapse. London, de Wolfe and Stone, 1955.
The Mayerling Affair (produced Pitlochry, 1957). London, French, 1958.
Duty and the Beast, adaptation of a work by Hans Keuls (produced Worthing, Sussex, 1957).
Flashpoint. London, French, 1958.
Once Aboard a Lugger. London, French, 1962.
Wild Mink. London, French, 1962.
My Dearest Angel (produced Pitlochry, 1963).

Screenplays: *All over Town*, with others, 1949; *Worm's Eye View*, with Jack Marks, 1951; *Value for Money*, with William Fairchild, 1955; *Where There's a Will*, 1955; *Now and Forever*, with Michael Pertwee, 1956; *Keep It Clean*, with Carl Nystrom, 1956; *Home and Away*, with Vernon Sewell, 1956; *On the Fiddle*, with Harold Buchman, 1961.

Radio Plays: *The Cocklemouth Comet*, 1938; *The Comet Covers a Wedding*, 1939; *Made to Measure*, 1953; *The Testimonial*, 1953; *The Bride Wore an Opal Ring*, 1954; *Smoke in the Valley*, 1954; *And Then There Were None*, 1955; *This Happy Brood*, 1956; *Midal Beach*, 1960; *Napoleon in Love*, 1960; *The Avenue Goes to War*, from his own novel, 1961; *The Dreaming Suburb*, from his own novel, 1962; *A Horseman Riding By*, from his own novel, 1967.

Television Plays: *The Day of the Sputnik*, 1963; *Jezebel*, 1963 (USA).

Other

These Clicks Made History: The Stories of Stanley ('Glorious') Devon, Fleet Street Photographer. Exmouth, Devon, Raleigh Press, 1946.
Nobody Shouted Author (autobiography). London, Laurie, 1951.
Bird's Eye View: An Autobiography. London, Constable, 1954.
The Adventures of Ben Gunn (for children). London, Hodder and Stoughton, 1956; Indianapolis, Bobbs Merrill, 1957.
Napoleon in Love. London, Hodder and Stoughton, 1959; Boston, Little Brown, 1960.
The March of the Twenty-Six: The Story of Napoleon's Marshals. London, Hodder and Stoughton, 1962; as *Napoleon's Marshals*, Philadelphia, Chilton, 1966.
Under an English Sky. London, Hodder and Stoughton, 1964.
The Golden Millstones: Napoleon's Brothers and Sisters. London, Weidenfeld and Nicolson, 1964; New York, Harper, 1965.
The Retreat from Moscow. London, Hodder and Stoughton, and New York, Atheneum, 1967.
Imperial Sunset: The Fall of Napoleon 1813–1814. Philadelphia, Chilton, 1968; London, Hodder and Stoughton, 1969.
For My Own Amusement (autobiography). London, Hodder and Stoughton, 1968; New York, Simon and Schuster, 1972.
Overture for Beginners (autobiography). London, Hodder and Stoughton, 1970.
R.F. Delderfield, 1912–72. London, Coronet, 1979.

Editor, *Tales Out of School: An Anthology of West Buckland Reminiscences 1895–1963*. St Austell, Cornwall, H.E. Warne, 1963.

*

Film Adaptations: *Worm's Eye View*, 1951; *Glad Tidings*, 1953; *Where There's A Will*, 1955; *Now and Forever*, 1955, from the play *The Orchard Walls*; *Carry on Sergeant*, 1958, from the play *The Bull Boys*; *On the Fiddle*, 1961, from the novel *Stop at a Winner*; *To Serve Them All My Days*, 1980; *Diana*, 1983, from the novels, *There was a Fair Maid Dwelling* and *The Unjust Skies*; *Come Home Charlie and Face Them*, 1990.

Critical Study: *R.F. Delderfield* by Sanford Sternlicht, Boston, Twayne, 1988.

*   *   *

R.F. Delderfield's novels are not so much classic love stories as family sagas punctuated by strong romantic impulses. In *The Avenue Goes to War*, for instance, the hard-bitten, self-seeking Elaine abandons affluence and security with a rich lover to live with the impoverished and disgraced Archie. In *God Is an Englishman* Adam Swann makes a sudden and surprising decision to marry the fiercely independent but terribly vulnerable 18-year-old Henrietta.

Broader canvasses of the English country or suburban scene, and astute socio-political comment adds realism and drama to Delderfield's romantic relationships, which are basically straightforward and described strictly from a masculine stance—something that is unusual in the general run of romantic novels. There is none of the tremulous, long-winded lead up and final-scene-only clinch that forms the love story pattern when the narrative viewpoint is that of the traditional heroine of the genre. Delderfield's emphasis is on married love and mutuality, not only of passion but of various levels of experience. In *God Is an Englishman* Adam's and Henrietta's relationship only really begins to flower when, after seven years of marriage, Henrietta is forced to become actively involved in her husband's work commitments. David Powlett-Jones, the boarding-school headmaster hero of *To Serve Them All My Days*, far from wanting a merely ornamental or domesticated wife, encourages Chris in her career ambitions. She is his second wife, as David marries once in his youth and again in middle-age.

Romantic relationships in Delderfield's books are in fact often of the second-time-around, middle-aged, or even elderly variety. In *The Dreaming Suburb* Jim Carver loses his first wife almost as soon as he returns home from the trenches at the end of World War I. He does not marry his second wife, Edith—a spinster neighbour he has known for over 25 years—until the end of World War II (in the closing pages of *The Avenue Goes to War*, the sequel to *The Dreaming Suburb*). Edith and Jim are in their sixties; they have suffered bombing and bereavement, and each is sustained by the friendship of the other and by the helpfulness of neighbours. (There is always a strong community feeling in Delderfield's novels, even when his heroes and heroines go against the tide of popular opinion.) Their marriage is a satisfying one. Even though love is often expressed by the brewing of pots of tea and the filling of hot water bottles for each other rather than by acts of passion, theirs is nevertheless a romantic story.

Second or late marriages, of course, add variety to any novel, and particularly to those of the family saga type which the author handled so well. (At least three of the leading male characters in *The Avenue Goes to War* marry twice.) Although Delderfield's emphasis is on very much married love, there is, however, always a place in his novels for the realistic extramarital affair. In *The Dreaming Suburb* Archie Carver, as a teenage errand boy during World War I, engages in grocery black-marketeering which brings him, as well as a great deal of extra cash, a satisfying sexual initiation with the lovely and full-blooded wife of an officer who is away at the front. Archie is a go-getter, and so—in the sequel—is Elaine Frith. Delderfield is at his best when writing of non-conformist characters of a complex disposition, and particularly about their romantic involvements. Elaine quickly discards the claustrophobic morality of her narrow-minded upbringing, and as a very young girl begins to exploit her sexual power over men. Later on, she purposefully harnesses this to further her clearly defined material ambitions, and she is untroubled by the strictures of neighbours on her activities: 'Marvellous what some women'll do nowadays for a pound of granulated and a tin of pineapple chunks, isn't it?' (The provider of wartime black-market goodies is once again Archie Carver.)

Generally speaking, however, in Delderfield's novels the brief affair or sexual encounter, whatever its intensity, is prevented by its tucked away nature from having deep significance in the hero's life. He cannot achieve with a mistress the mutuality at all levels of experience that he might (hopefully) know with a wife.

Love and war are inextricably intertwined in these several-generational sagas in a way that is inevitable when the influence of the two world wars plays such an important part in the author's assessment of life. Delderfield's most poignant vignette of a romantic encounter in a war setting occurs in *A Horseman Riding By*. Paul Craddock, an army officer at the Western Front in 1915, has a chance meeting on the road to Messines with his ex-wife, Grace, who is serving as an ambulance driver. They meet again by mutual consent, and amid the mud and carnage and disillusionment they communicate with a completeness that they never managed to achieve in their once comfortable life in England. The residual bitterness of his breakup with Grace is wiped away for Paul—and the encounter helps him to understand aspects of his present marriage to Claire, a much younger woman. But his new found and comradely closeness to Grace is soon shattered. She is killed by the blast of an enemy bomb on one of her ambulance runs. In the hands of a less skilful storyteller, this encounter could have been embarrassing or banal—but it works, in the unsentimental and robust manner in which all Delderfield's fictional romantic situations do.

—Mary Cadogan

DELINSKY, Barbara.
Pseudonyms: Billie Douglass; Bonnie Drake. **Nationality:** American. **Born:** Barbara Ruth Greenberg, Boston, Massachusetts, 9 August 1945. **Education:** Tufts University, Medford, Massachusetts, B.A. in psychology 1967; Boston College, M.A. in sociology 1969. **Relations:** married Stephen R. Delinsky in 1967; three sons. **Career:** researcher, Children's Protective Services, Boston, 1968–69; photographer and reporter, Belmont *Herald*, Massachusetts. **Recipient:** Writers of America golden medallion, 1988. Lives in Needham, Massachusetts. **Address:** c/o Harlequin Enterprises Ltd, 225 Duncan Mill Road, Don Mills, Ontario M3B 3K9, Canada.

ROMANCE AND HISTORICAL PUBLICATIONS

Novels (series: The Crosslyn Trilogy)

A Special Something. London, Mills and Boon, and Toronto, Harlequin, 1984.
Bronze Mystique. Toronto, Harlequin, 1984.
Finger Prints. Toronto, Worldwide, 1984.
The Forever Instinct. Toronto, Harlequin, 1985.
First Things First. Toronto, Harlequin, 1985; London, Mills and Boon, 1989.
Secret of the Stone. London, Mills and Boon, and Toronto, Harlequin, 1985.
Chances Are. Toronto, Harlequin, 1985.
Threats and Promises. Toronto, Harlequin, 1986.
First, Best and Only. Toronto, Harlequin, and London, Mills and Boon, 1986.
Straight from the Heart. Toronto, Harlequin, 1986.
Within Reach. Toronto, Worldwide, 1986.
Jasmine Sorcery. Toronto, Harlequin, 1986.
The Real Thing. Toronto, Harlequin, 1987.
Twelve Across. Toronto, Harlequin, 1987.
A Single Rose. Toronto, Harlequin, 1987.
Twilight Whispers. New York, Warner, 1987.
Cardinal Rules. Toronto, Harlequin, 1987.
Heatwave. Toronto, Harlequin, 1987; London, Mills and Boon, 1989.
Fulfillment. Toronto, Harlequin, 1988; London, Mills and Boon, 1989.
Commitments. New York, Warner, 1988; London, Severn House, 1990.
TLC. Toronto, Harlequin, 1988.
Through My Eyes. Toronto, Harlequin, 1989; London, Mills and Boon, 1990.
Heart of the Night. New York, Warner, 1989; London, Severn House, 1990.

Montana Man. Toronto, Harlequin, 1989; London, Mills and Boon, 1991.
Having Faith. Toronto, Harlequin, 1990.
Cross My Heart. Toronto, Harlequin, 1990.
The Crosslyn Trilogy:
    The Dream. Toronto, Harlequin, 1990; London, Mills and Boon, 1991.
    The Dream Unfolds. Toronto, Harlequin, 1990; London, Mills and Boon, 1991.
    The Dream Comes True. Toronto, Harlequin, 1990; London, Mills and Boon, 1991.
Facets. London, Piatkus, 1991.
The Passions of Chelsea Kane. London, Piatkus, 1992.
A Woman Betrayed. London, Piatkus, 1992
More Than Friends. New York, HarperCollins, 1993.
Suddenly. New York, HarperCollins, 1993.
The Outsider. London, Mills and Boon, 1993.

Novels as Bonnie Drake

The Passionate Touch. New York, Dell, 1981.
Surrender by Moonlight. New York, Dell, 1981.
Sweet Ember. New York, Dell, 1981.
Sensuous Burgundy. New York, Dell, 1981.
The Ardent Protector. New York, Dell, 1982.
Whispered Promise. New York, Dell, 1982.
Lilac Awakening. New York, Dell, 1982.
Amber Enchantment. New York, Dell, 1982.
Lover from the Sea. New York, Dell, 1983.
The Silver Fox. New York, Dell, 1983.
Passion and Illusion. New York, Dell, 1983.
Gemstone. New York, Dell, 1983.
Moment to Moment. New York, Dell, 1984.

Novels as Billie Douglass

Search for a New Dawn. New York, Silhouette, 1982.
A Time to Love. New York, Silhouette, 1982.
Knightly Love. New York, Silhouette, 1982.
Sweet Serenity. New York, Silhouette, 1983.
Fast Courting. New York, Silhouette, 1983.
Flip Side of Yesterday. New York, Silhouette, 1983.
Beyond Fantasy. New York, Silhouette, 1983.
An Irresistible Impulse. New York, Silhouette, 1983.
The Carpenter's Lady. New York, Silhouette, 1983.
Variation on a Theme. New York, Silhouette, 1985.

*   *   *

Originally known for her category romances that she wrote under the names Bonnie Drake and Billie Douglass, Barbara Delinsky has made an impressive and successful transition to writing longer, more complex, mainstream novels. Her popularity is such that many of her earlier novels are being re-released, this time under her own name. This will be likely to introduce her to even more readers and broaden her appeal.

The earlier, shorter novels focus on the romantic relationship of the hero and heroine, often with some interesting quirks. In *A Special Something*, model Oliver Ames is 'given' to Leslie Parish by her brother as a 30th-birthday present because she jokingly pointed to his picture in a magazine when asked what she wanted. Chelsea Ross, finder of missing and runaway children is hired by a Boston socialite to bring home her son, a 40-year old runaway executive (*First Things First*). Delinsky's ability to add an unusual touch to an otherwise standard plot enlivens her work and makes her

books stay in the reader's mind. Some of her stories have gone beyond simply adding an uncommon element by developing a unique situation to drive the plot. An example is *The Outsider*. The title alone might lead the reader to think that it is about a typical loner in society. However, Cameron Divine, the hero, is actually an alien research scientist from the planet Cyteron. He comes to earth to locate Summer VanVorn, a healer, whose great-great-grandmother was born on Cyteron. Unaware of her alien background, Summer has always felt apart from others and has been especially lost since the death of her mother. Gradually she comes to accept the reality of her heritage and leaves with Cameron for a new home. In a nice epilogue, Delinsky brings another scientist to Earth, who also brings news of Summer's happiness.

While these category romances are entertaining, Delinsky's longer, more complex books are a better indication of the depth and quality of her writing. They are much more sophisticated, involving intricate plots and strongly developed characters. There are often strong elements of suspense. In *Finger Prints*, the heroine, Carly Quinn, is in the Federal Witness Protection Program. Not only must she cope with her new life but she must deal with a new relationship and the threat of disclosure of her identity to the criminals. The search by an adopted woman for her past is the theme of *The Passions of Chelsea Kane*. Returning to the tiny New Hampshire town where she was born and given up for adoption, Chelsea stirs up old memories for many of the townspeople, including someone who wants to keep her true identity hidden. She also falls in love with a man, only to discover that she is pregnant by a former lover. Although it is relatively easy for the reader to spot the villain and predict one major plot twist, Delinsky skilfully and sympathetically develops her characters so that the reader truly cares about them and their futures.

Others of the longer novels focus even more on the psychology of the characters and situations. In *A Woman Betrayed*, Laura Frye, a successful wife and mother, suddenly faces the loss of everything when her husband of 20 years disappears. As his guilty secrets are brought to light, she must rebuild her life. Ultimately she finds more strength within herself than she ever thought possible. *Facets* is the story of an obsessive love and the revenge that follows when it is betrayed. Successful writer, Hillary Cox, has maintained a long-term affair with John St George, a powerful businessman who has always said he would never marry. She finds out that he is engaged to another woman when it is announced on television. Vowing to revenge herself publicly, she plans to write an expose of his life. She uncovers an unsavoury mix of theft, violence, blackmail and other sordid actions that bring St George down. Here Delinsky opts for a more ambiguous but probably more realistic ending when St George is repaid by losing his power rather than by being prosecuted or by dying. It is unfortunate, but also quite possible, that at the end Hillary confesses she still loves him. *More Than Friends* is an even more complex story. A momentary indiscretion tears at the fabric of a more than 20-year-long friendship between the Maxwells and the Popes, as well as shaking the two marriages and families. Love, friendship, forgiveness, and personal growth are all explored by Delinsky in this story. Again, she avoids the trite 'happily ever after' ending as she develops a moving and realistic outcome for the two couples.

It is interesting to note that these psychological explorations involve both long-term relationships under stress and more mature characters. Not idealized creations, these people make mistakes that are not easily correctable and that may have even lasting effects. This allows Delinsky to probe more deeply into complex, universal emotions and puts her more into mainstream fiction than most romance authors. She writes with great compassion, sensitivity, and style and maintains both the rhythm and flow of multiple narrative lines. Like many of her characters, Delinsky has demonstrated growth. Both her writing and choice of subjects have matured over time. A true professional with great talent, she should be considered in the top echelon of contemporary romance writers.

—Barbara E. Kemp

———

DELL, Belinda.   See **BARCLAY, Tessa.**

———

DELL, Ethel M(ary).
Nationality: British. **Born:** Streatham, London, 2 August 1881. **Education:** Streatham College for Girls, 1893–98. **Relations:** married Gerald Tahourdin Savage in 1922. **Died:** 19 September 1939.

ROMANCE AND HISTORICAL PUBLICATIONS

Novels

The Way of an Eagle. New York, Putnam, 1911; London, Unwin, 1912.
The Knave of Diamonds. London, Unwin, and New York, Putnam, 1913.
The Rocks of Valpré. New York, Putnam, 1913; London, Unwin, 1914.
The Desire of His Life (includes 'Her Compensation'). London, Holden and Hardingham, 1914; New York, Burt, 1927.
The Keeper of the Door. London, Unwin, and New York, Putnam, 1915.
The Bars of Iron. London, Hutchinson, and New York, Putnam, 1916.
The Hundredth Chance. London, Hutchinson, and New York, Putnam, 1917.
The Rose of Dawn. New York, Putnam, 1917.
Greatheart. London, Unwin, and New York, Putnam, 1918.
The Lamp in the Desert. London, Hutchinson, and New York, Putnam, 1919.
The Top of the World. London, Cassell, and New York, Putnam, 1920.
The Princess's Game. London, Hardingham, 1920.
The Lucky Number. New York, Putnam, 1920.
The Obstacle Race. London, Cassell, and New York, Putnam, 1921.
Charles Rex. London, Hutchinson, and New York, Putnam, 1922.
Tetherstones. London, Hutchinson, and New York, Putnam, 1923.
The Unknown Quantity. London, Hutchinson, and New York, Putnam, 1924.
A Man under Authority. London, Cassell, 1925; New York, Putnam, 1926.
The Black Knight. London, Cassell, and New York, Putnam, 1926.
By Request. London, Unwin, 1927; as *Peggy by Request*, New York, Putnam, 1928.
The Gate Marked 'Private'. London, Cassell, and New York, Putnam, 1928.
The Altar of Honour. London, Hutchinson, 1929; New York, Putnam, 1930.
Storm Drift. London, Hutchinson, 1930; New York, Putnam, 1931.
Pullman (omnibus). London, Benn, 1930.
The Silver Wedding. London, Hutchinson, 1932; as *The Silver Bride*, New York, Putnam, 1932.
The Prison Wall. London, Cassell, 1932; New York, Putnam, 1933.
Dona Celestis. London, Benn, and New York, Putnam, 1933.
The Electric Torch. London, Cassell, and New York, Putnam, 1934.
Where Three Roads Meet. London, Cassell 1935; New York, Putnam, 1936.

Honeyball Farm. London, Hutchinson, and New York, Putnam, 1937.
The Juice of the Pomegranate. London, Cassell, and New York, Doubleday, 1938.
The Serpent in the Garden. London, Cassell, and New York, Doubleday, 1938.
Sown among Thorns. London, Cassell, and New York, Doubleday, 1939.

Short Stories

The Swindler and Other Stories. London, Unwin, and New York, Putnam, 1914.
The Safety-Curtain and Other Stories. London, Unwin, and New York, Putnam, 1917.
The Tidal Wave and Other Stories. London, Cassell, 1919; New York Putnam, 1920.
Rosa Mundi and Other Stories. London, Cassell, and New York, Putnam, 1921.
The Odds and Other Stories. London, Cassell, and New York, Putnam, 1922.
The Passerby and Other Stories. London, Hutchinson, and New York, Putnam, 1925.
The House of Happiness and Other Stories. London, Cassell, and New York, Putnam, 1927.
The Live Bait and Other Stories. London, Benn, and New York, Putnam, 1932.

OTHER PUBLICATIONS

Poetry

Verses. London, Hutchinson, and New York, Putnam, 1923.

*

Critical Study: *Nettie and Sissie: The Biography of Ethel M. Dell and Her Sister Ella* by Penelope Dell, London, Hamish Hamilton, 1977.

*   *   *

Absurd though they may at first seem, the novels of Ethel M. Dell have nonetheless a boisterous power, an irresistible quality about them, defined by Queenie Leavis as sheer luxuriant vitality: 'Even the most critical reader who brings only an ironical appreciation to their work cannot avoid noticing a certain power, the secret of their success with the majority. Bad writing, false sentiment, sheer silliness, and a preposterous narrative are all carried along by the magnificent vitality of the author, as they are in *Jane Eyre*'.

Such gripping tales as *The Way of an Eagle*, *The Lamp in the Desert*, *The Hundredth Chance*, *The Black Knight*, and *The Knave of Diamonds* are a highly readable mixture which combines quasi-religious themes with drama, action, and full-blooded adventure. Dashing officer heroes with murky pasts, exercising gallantry and bravery, are reminiscent of some of the 19th-century heroes of a Ouida or a Rhoda Broughton novel. The heroines, sensitive and virginal, strong but innocent, are no longer tormented by urgent doctrinal doubt, misgivings about the 39 Articles or the meaning of the original sin. For, as interest in orthodox Christianity gradually waned, it was replaced, in popular romantic fiction, by a new, less clearly defined spiritual quest. The heroines are driven by passions which are simultaneously of an earthly and a heavenly nature. Their vague, mystical uncertainty runs a parallel course to their difficulties and sufferings of mortal love. Thus, for example, Ann Carfax is tormented by the need for a prayerful life, but, in her darkest hour finds total inability to pray: 'Powerless, she sank upon her knees by the open window, striving painfully, piteously, vainly, to pray. But no words came to her, no prayer rose from her wrung heart. It was as though she knelt in outer darkness before a locked door'. (This is from *The Knave of Diamonds*, the title referring to the ambiguous, but probably sinful, nature of the hero.) Stella, similarly, in *The Way of an Eagle*, is beset by intense inner doubts and fears, not specifically religious, but rather, spiritually worthy 'feelings': 'And again, very deep down in her soul there stirred that blind, unconscious entity, of the existence of which she herself had so vague a knowledge, feeling upwards, groping outwards, to the light'.

Ill-defined though such feelings may be, the implication is that they have a worth, a value, which is as good, if not better, than orthodox religion. Heroines (less often heroes) grapple with their doubt for a couple of hundred pages, before the ultimate discovery of some symbol in their lives which represents for them a renewal and refreshment of the spirit. In *The Lamp in the Desert* that symbol is clear. Christ is the lamp, which lights up the Desert of the World: 'Her halting feet were now guided by God's Lamp. She had come to realise that the wanderers in the wilderness are ever His especial care, and that she would come at last into the Presence of God Himself'. Her acceptance of her Creator after such a prolonged period of confusion, occurs at the same time as her rediscovery of her love for her long-lost husband.

In *The Way of an Eagle* that symbolic bird refers less to our Lord, more to the primeval, bird-like nature of the fierce husband whom she both fears, and dreams of longingly. He is the eagle who will gather her up, and bear her swiftly through wide spaces to his eyrie in the mountains. The eagle-hero is not without his acknowledgement of one greater than he. When hero and heroine, thwarted pair, uncover their mutual passion while communing with nature at the top of the mountain, it is the man who decides that prayer would be appropriate: 'Do you know what we are going to do as soon as we are married, sweetheart? We are going to climb the highest mountain in the world, to see the sun rise, and to thank God'.

The searing, or burning, or scorching, kiss became one of the hallmarks of romance; and Dell was an early perfectionist at hot literary embraces. 'His quick breath scorched her face, and in a moment almost before she knew what was happening, his lips were on her own. He kissed her as she had never been kissed before—a single fiery kiss that sent all the blood in tumult to her heart'. Or 'There was sheer unshackled savagery in the holding of his arms, and dismay thrilled her through and through'. And 'Again his lips pressed hers, and again from head to foot she felt as if a flame had scorched her'. Today, Barbara Cartland may declare that what readers want is innocence and chastity. In the 1930s what they wanted was hot kissing and unbridled passion. Ray Smith's Twopenny Library reported in 1933 that the three women authors most in demand were Ethel M. Dell, Elinor Glyn, and Marie Corelli, in that order.

Despite the 'religious' content, the novels are full of blood, guts, and thunder. Dell included tempests, infant deaths, runaway horses, wife-beating, men going violently mad, fine young lovers crippled for life, an electric storm, falling meteors, and a mutiny at the Northwest frontier. During times of chaos, men are aware of the importance of risking life to protect the honour of the heroine. This bravery results in a number of hand-to-hand fights to the death: 'So long as his heart should beat he would defend that one precious possession that yet remained—the honour of the woman who loved him and whom he loved as only the few knew how to love'.

Dell did not have the pretensions of some other popular novelists of her era. She was not seeking literary glory; nor did she continually complain, as did Marie Corelli or Elinor Glyn, that her work was misunderstood by the critics. She did not hold herself out as some female latter-day Shakespeare like Ouida or Hall Caine. The loyalty of her readers was the reward she sought and enjoyed. She

repaid them by dedicating to them one of her novels, *By Request*, a gesture which signals the importance, for popular writers, of a close reader/writer relationship. Those who do not have it, aspire to it; those who do, rightly nurture it.

—Rachel Anderson

———

DELMAR, Viña.
Nationality: American. **Born:** Viña Croter, New York City, 29 January 1905. **Education:** public schools in New York. **Relations:** married Eugene Delmar in 1921; one child. **Career:** typist, switchboard operator, usher, actress, and theatre manager, then freelance writer. **Died:** 19 January 1990.

Romance and Historical Publications

Novels

Bad Girl. New York, Harcourt Brace, 1928; London, Allan, 1929.
Kept Woman. New York, Harcourt Brace, 1929; as *The Other Woman*, London, Allan, 1930.
Women Live Too Long. New York, Harcourt Brace, and London, Allan, 1932; as *The Restless Passion*, New York, Avon, 1947.
The Marriage Racket. New York, Harcourt Brace, and London, Allan, 1933.
Mystery at Little Heaven. Los Angeles, Times Mirror Press, 1933.
The End of the World. New York, International Magazine Company, 1934.
The Love Trap. New York, Avon, 1949.
New Orleans Lady. New York, Avon, 1949.
About Mrs Leslie. New York, Harcourt Brace, 1950; London, Hale, 1952.
Strangers in Love. New York, Dell, 1951.
The Marcaboth Women. New York, Harcourt Brace, 1951; London, Hale, 1953.
The Laughing Stranger. New York, Harcourt Brace, 1953; London, Hale, 1954.
Ruby. New York, Pocket Books, 1953.
Beloved. New York, Harcourt Brace, 1956; London, Hale, 1957.
The Breeze from Camelot. New York, Harcourt Brace, 1959; London, Davies, 1960.
The Big Family. New York, Harcourt Brace, 1961.
The Enchanted. New York, Harcourt Brace, 1965.
Grandmère. New York, Harcourt Brace, 1967.
The Freeways. New York, Harcourt Brace, 1971.
A Time for Titans. New York, Harcourt Brace, 1974.
McKeever. New York, Harcourt Brace, 1976.

Short Stories

Loose Ladies. New York, Harcourt Brace, 1929; as *Women Who Pass By*, London, Allan, 1929.

Other Publications

Plays

Bad Girl, with Brian Marlowe, adaptation of the novel by Delmar (produced New York, 1930).
The Rich, Full Life (produced New York, 1945). New York, French, 1945.
Mid-Summer (produced New York, 1953). New York, French, 1954.

Warm Wednesday. New York, French, 1959.
The Rest Is Silence, adaptation of her screenplay *Make Way for To-morrow* (produced Moscow, 1970).

Screenplays: *A Soldier's Plaything*, with Perry Vikroff, 1930; *The Awful Truth*, with Dwight Taylor, 1937; *Make Way for Tomorrow*, *1937*.

Other

The Becker Scandal: A Time Remembered (autobiography). New York, Harcourt Brace, 1968.

*   *   *

Viña Delmar's novels range from period pieces about complicated relationships to well-researched, historically accurate works. Although the author died in 1990, her books will be remembered for their depiction of lower-middle and middle-class life; her real talent lay in creating sympathetic, realistic characters who encounter and overcome the problems that life throws at them.

Delmar's first novel, *Bad Girl*, set the precedent for her other works. The main characters meet and marry quickly only to discover later that they have a real problem communicating with each other. This theme is also taken up in a much later work, *The Breeze from Camelot*, which begins with the sudden and swift break-up of a marriage. Ward and Myra Galvin wake up one day to find that they just don't understand each other any more. Ward meets a young, aristocratic girl, Trina Macklyn, whom he falls in love with and quickly marries.

Trina and Myra are complete opposites: Trina is young, innocent, and surprisingly unworldly; Myra is older, more tired, and less willing to jump into situations in the same way that Trina does. One quality that both women share is the will to survive. Just as Myra quietly accepts that her marriage is over, so Trina offers Ward a divorce when she finds out that he has made Myra pregnant after a post-divorce fling. Ward seems to drift into situations: he is lured into the Macklyn household, and it seems that a web is slowly woven to keep him there.

Trina offers him a quick way out of their marriage, but he can't keep out of her life after he remarries Myra. He professes to love Trina and is completely thrown when she marries someone else. *The Breeze from Camelot* ends in the unhappiness of all the main characters—Ward and Trina both married to other people, and Myra aware that Ward has only remarried her because she is pregnant.

Lilian Cory, the mistress in *Kept Woman* is also a strong character. She is set up by Hubert Scot, a retired, extravagant man who sells his business and proceeds to spend all the money on impressing Lilian. He is thrown out by his wife but Lilian remains with him until the end of the book. She is unlike Ruby, the young, selfish wife of Simon Marcaboth, in *The Marcaboth Women*, whose birthday brings the other women in the family to certain realizations about their lives and marriages. Ruby is a careless character, adored by her much older husband, whose presence inflicts change on the Maraboth family life.

However, it is in *Beloved* that Delmar reaches the pinnacle of her literary success. Set in New Orleans, New Haven, London, and Paris, this book tells the life story of politician, Judah P. Benjamin, who was one of the leading figures in Confederacy. *Beloved* is an extremely well-researched work, and Delmar paints the historical background beautifully. We follow Benjamin's life from his birth in the West Indies to Charleston, from Yale, New Haven to New Orleans where he determines, 'I will make New Orleans mine'. He marries a beautiful and promiscuous young woman, Natalie, and the book tells as much their love story as of the politics of the time, and of Benjamin's journey to becoming a senator and the leading light of the bar in America. In his last years, Benjamin goes to live in London and then Paris, knowing that he is going to die. He hides it from Natalie but their relationship is passionate to the end. Although he is a Jew, Natalie insists that he have the last rites before he dies, she says, 'Let him rest where I can go to him when a world without him is more that I can bear'. *Beloved* is written in a clear, succinct style which captures the reader's attention from the beginning of the book till the very end.

Delmar wrote several examples of historical and romance literature at its very best. She is a writer who will be sorely missed.

—P. Campbell

———

DERLETH, August (William). American. 1909–71. See 2nd edition, 1990.

———

de SALVALLO, Donna Teresa. See **WILLIAMSON, C.N. and A.M.**

———

DEVERAUX, Jude.
Nationality: American. **Born:** Jude Gilliam, Louisville, Kentucky, 20 September 1947. **Education:** Murray State University, Murray, Kentucky, B.S. 1970; College of Santa Fe, New Mexico, teaching certificate 1973; University of New Mexico, Albuquerque, 1976. **Relations:** married 1) Richard Sides in 1967 (divorced 1969); 2) Claude White in 1970. **Career:** elementary school teacher, Santa Fe, 1973–77. **Address:** 1937 Tijeras Road, Sante Fe, New Mexico 87501, USA.

ROMANCE AND HISTORICAL PUBLICATIONS

Novels (series: James River; Montgomery; Twin).

The Enchanted Land. New York, Avon, 1978; London, Hamlyn, 1979.
The Black Lyon. New York, Avon, 1980.
The Temptress. New York, Pocket Books, 1980; London, Century, 1988.
The Velvet Promise (Montgomery). New York, Pocket Books, 1981; London, Arrow, 1984.
Casa Grande. New York, Avon, 1982.
Highland Velvet (Montgomery). New York, Pocket Books, 1982; London, Arrow, 1984.
Song of Promise. New York, Pocket Books, 1983.
Sweetbriar. New York, Pocket Books, and London, Hodder and Stoughton, 1983.
Velvet Angel (Montgomery). New York, Pocket Books, 1983; London, Arrow, 1984.
Velvet Song (Montgomery). New York, Pocket Books, 1983; London, Arrow, 1984.
Counterfeit Lady (James River). New York, Pocket Books, 1984; Bath, Firecrest, 1985.
Lost Lady (James River). New York, Pocket Books, 1985; Bath, Firecrest, 1986.
Twin of Fire. New York, Pocket Books, 1985.
Twin of Ice. New York, Pocket Books, 1985.
River Lady. (James River). New York, Pocket Books, 1985; Bath, Firecrest, 1986.

The Awakening. New York, Pocket Books, 1987; London, Century, 1989.

The Raider. New York, Pocket Books, 1987.

The Princess. New York, Pocket Books, and London, Century, 1988.

The Maiden. New York, Pocket Books, 1988; London, Century, 1990.

The Taming. New York, Pocket Books, 1989; London, Century, 1991.

A Knight in Shining Armor. New York, Pocket Books, 1989.

Enchanted Land. London, Severn House, 1989.

Wishes. New York, Pocket Books, 1989.

Mountain Laurel. New York, Pocket Books, 1990.

The Conquest. New York, Pocket Books, 1991.

The Duchess. New York, Pocket Books, 1992.

Eternity. New York, Pocket Books, 1992.

Sweet Liar. New York, Pocket Books, 1993.

*

Jude Deveraux comments:

More than a writer, I consider myself a storyteller. To me the story is everything. Too often romance novels are merely sex scenes stuck together with a little literary glue. I write stories about love. I try to explain why people love each other so that when the readers close the book they will feel they know the people and know that they love each other. Also, my books are funny. I can't imagine loving someone who didn't make me laugh so all my books have a lot of humour in them.

Overall, I write amusing, adventurous love stories with a smart heroine and a hero who is smart enough to recognize the heroine's uniqueness.

*   *   *

After publishing her less than successful modern novel *Casa Grande*, Jude Deveraux stated 'God gave me the ability to write. He didn't extend it very far. All I want to do is write the very best historical romances that I possibly can—and historicals seem to be all I'm capable of. I don't want to write family sagas or occult books, and I have no intention of again trying to ruin the contemporary market'.

Having outlined this ambition, albeit in a very limited field, Deveraux sets out with verve, gusto, and every plot device known to woman to create a very large number of light but nevertheless entertaining historical romances, often known more colloquially as 'bodice rippers'.

The plots tend to contain similar elements—man, woman, other woman, kidnapping, class barriers, abduction (there's a lot of this), forced marriages, mistaken identities—the list is almost, but not quite, endless. However, a definite redeeming feature of her work is the distinct glint of humour that appears in many of the books; enough, at times, to make the reader suspect that the whole novel is actually written tongue-in-cheek.

For example, a common theme in such romantic fiction (we have only to think of the Scarlet Pimpernel) is that of the bold crusading hero cunningly concealed inside the persona of the least likely (and usually most effeminate) male character. In *The Raider*, Deveraux takes this device to extremes (and even beyond) as she endows Alexander Montgomery not only with effeminate mannerisms, but also with a badly fitting wig and vast amounts of padding—the prime use of the latter is to make him appear mundane and unheroic but it is also extremely useful for concealing his gun, his mask, and the other tools of his trade. This character is of course the Raider, and when not actively engaged in raiding he conducts a passionate although intermittent relationship with the heroine; unfortunately

for this lady (and also for the story's credibility) she does not detect any similarity between her secret lover and the overweight and balding gentleman whom she is forced to marry.

This is only one of many novels dealing with the Montgomery clan in its many manifestations. These range from the Velvet series, all set in correctly romantic periods of history, to *The Princess* which brings us almost up to date. In *Velvet Song* the current member of the Montgomery clan is a Robin Hood-type figure (many of the male Montgomerys seem to model themselves on heroes of romantic fiction!) into whose convenient arms the heroine, Alyx, flees, hotly pursued by an evil squire. Our hero, of course, falls in love with her instantly and only later pauses to consider the wisdom of this reaction, as Alyx is disguised as a boy. Her lot is actually fairly reasonable compared with that of the female Montgomerys, who, in this and other books, regularly suffer pursuit, kidnap, and humiliation, not to mention the inevitable fate worse than death.

These vicissitudes are not confined to Montgomery women, however, and in *The Enchanted Land*, the heroine, Morgan Wakefield, is careless enough to be kidnapped not just once but *three* times (although as the third abduction is a mock one, performed by her husband, Seth Colter, perhaps this one does not count). Here too are the obligatory misunderstandings—Morgan believes Seth to be dead, Seth believes Morgan to be unfaithful; all par for the course, as is the fact that the marriage is one of convenience, yet each partner has, completely unknown to the other, been head-over-heels in love from the word go. The reader worked this one out by the ninth page, so why on earth didn't the protagonists?

Having discovered most of the plot devices in popular use, Deveraux obviously aimed to assemble as many as she could in *The Princess*. This is set during World War II at a time when America's shortage of vanadium deposits was seriously endangering the war effort. By an amazing coincidence one small desert island becomes temporary accommodation for an American naval officer (handsome, heroic, rich—and a Montgomery) and a princess (beautiful and strong-willed—whose native Lanconia just happens to be rich in vanadium). The following events happen in fairly quick succession—a kidnap, a rescue, a romantic interlude, a forced marriage, an unromantic interlude, mistaken identities, a happy ending—and while all this has been going on the vanadium is helping America to win the war.

The 'James River' trilogy (*River Lady*, *Counterfeit Lady*, and *Lost Lady*) is relatively, but alas not totally, free of Montgomerys; but each novel does contain a forced marriage followed by an estrangement, during which time the respective heroines have time to develop hitherto unsuspected talents. One manages a grain mill, one becomes a weaver, and the third enterprising lady runs a tavern—while using all the clichés under the sun, Deveraux is certainly not short of a fresh idea or two!

These three books do not run consecutively, but are interlocking, a device which the author also utilizes in *Twin of Ice* and *Twin of Fire*. These two books tell the simultaneous stories of twins Houston (ice) and Blair (fire) Chandler, and their respective husbands Kane Taggert (uncouth hunk) and Leander Westfield (relative wimp). Apart from the by now expected kidnapping, forced marriage, estrangement, misunderstandings, and mistaken identity (don't forget we have twins in this novel!), there are also several added ingredients. One heroine is a newly qualified doctor, the other is involved in undercover activities bringing aid to the families of oppressed miners; and both attend secret meetings of The Sisterhood, whose social and political gathering develops into a hen party which is enlivened by the presence of a male stripper—all pretty strong stuff for the 1890s!

Deveraux's novels are probably taken totally seriously by many of her millions of readers, but one cannot help feeling that they miss a lot of enjoyment. The novels have a drive and gusto which lift them out of the normal run of such works; one can only admire

Deveraux for her ability to incorporate some rather sly digs at the genre while exploiting it to the full.

—Judith Rhodes

———————

de VERE, Jane. See **HAMILTON, Julia.**

———————

DEVINE, Raynard. See **TRESSILIAN, Richard.**

———————

DILL, W.S. See **MACBETH, Madge.**

———————

DINGWELL, Joyce. Australian. 1912—. See 2nd edition, 1990.

———————

DIVER, (Katherine Helen) Maud.
Nationality: British. **Born:** Murree, India, in 1867 (?). **Education:** England. Spent early years in India and Ceylon. **Relations:** married T. Diver in 1896 (died 1941); one son. Lived in England after 1896: journalist. **Died:** 14 October 1945.

ROMANCE AND HISTORICAL PUBLICATIONS

Novels

Capt. Desmond, V.C. Edinburgh, Blackwood, 1907; New York, Lane, 1908; revised edition, New York, Putnam, 1914; Blackwood, 1915.
The Great Amulet. Edinburgh, Blackwood, and New York, Lane, 1908.
Desmond's Daughter. Edinburgh, Blackwood, and New York, Putnam, 1916.
Candles in the Wind. Edinburgh, Blackwood, and New York, Lane, 1909.
Lilamani. London, Hutchinson, 1911; as *Awakening*, New York, Lane, 1911.
The Hero of Herat. London, Constable, 1912; New York, Putnam, 1913.
The Judgement of the Sword. London, Constable, 1913; New York, Putnam, 1914.
Unconquered. London, Murray, and New York, Putnam, 1917.
Strange Roads. London, Constable, 1918.
The Strong Hours. London, Constable, and Boston, Houghton Mifflin, 1919.
Far to Seek. Edinburgh, Blackwood, and Boston, Houghton Mifflin, 1921.
Lonely Furrow. London, Murray, and Boston, Houghton Mifflin, 1923.
Coombe St Mary's. Edinburgh, Blackwood, and Boston, Houghton Mifflin, 1925.
But Yesterday—. London, Murray, and New York, Dodd Mead, 1927.
Together. London, Newnes, 1928.
A Wild Bird. London, Murray, and Boston, Houghton Mifflin, 1929.
The Men of the Frontier Force. London, Newnes, 1930.
Ships of Youth. Edinburgh, Blackwood, and Boston, Houghton Mifflin, 1931.

The Singer Passes. Edinburgh, Blackwood, and New York, Dodd Mead, 1934.
The Dream Prevails. London, Murray, and Boston, Houghton Mifflin, 1938.
Sylvia Lyndon. Edinburgh, Blackwood, and Boston, Houghton, Mifflin, 1940.

Short Stories

Sunia and Other Stories. Edinburgh, Blackwood, and New York, Putnam, 1913.
Siege Perilous and Other Stories. London, Murray, and Boston, Houghton Mifflin, 1924.

OTHER PUBLICATIONS

Other

The Englishwoman in India. Edinburgh, Blackwood, 1909.
Kabul to Kandahar. London, Davies, 1935.
Honoria Lawrence: A Fragment of Indian History. London, Murray, and Boston, Houghton Mifflin, 1936.
Royal India: A Descriptive and Historical Study of India's Fifteen Principal States and Their Rulers. London, Hodder and Stoughton, and New York, Appleton Century, 1942.
The Unsung: A Record of British Services in India. Edinburgh, Blackwood, 1945.

* * *

Maud Diver's early life in India and Ceylon provided her with the background for many of her tales. 'I don't know how or why I am so successful in getting the Indian quality of my characters so true. I have really known very few Indians: One didn't know them in my day. It is some sort of sympathetic insight that guides me—and guides me right'.

Her first novel, *Capt. Desmond, V.C.*, is set in and around the Punjab cavalry regiment, and at the frontier station of Kohat. With its alluring mixture of exotica, passion, and reassuring confirmation of all the clichés about life, men, love, marriage, and sex, it established her reputation as a popular writer. Diver specialized in marvelously voluptuous overwriting. Even minor descriptive passages which have no bearing on plot, characters, or theme are given full rein, the same weight. Thus, a sunrise: 'By now the moon's last rim formed a golden sickle behind a blunt shoulder of rock; while over the eastward levels the topaz-yellow of an Indian dawn rushed at one stride to the zenith of heaven'. This is what her readers wanted—that soothing mixture of accepted generalizations, with a daring, foreign feel. However, lest the background material prove too exotic for her less well-travelled readers, the text is lightly spattered with footnotes explaining the meaning of some less familiar Indian terms (*chuprassee*, a government servant; *chota hazri*, a small breakfast) which add still more to the eastern flavour without confusing. Any obscurity in her novels is caused, less by the foreign setting, more by the luxuriant enthusiasm of her over-written style.

The Hero of Herat was another 'frontier biography', and *The Judgement of the Sword* is set in Kabul. At the end of the Great War, she attempted two companion novels, *Strange Roads* and *The Strong Hours*, an ambitious attempt at the family saga story, which tries to show the effects of war on the lives and loves of the Blounts of Avonleigh, 'an ancient family dating back to the days of Coeur de Lion'. To give the prose more importance, she was partial to the conceit of attaching a literary (and sometimes not so literary) heading or quotation to the start of each brief chapter. These appear to have been selected almost at random, some so trite as to be more like cracker mottos, some popular philosophical tags, others from Emerson, E.M. Forster, Shakespeare, and St Luke's Gospel.

The lack of any sense of proportion is the biggest limitation to many romantic novelists. Most writers get to a point where they realize that there is something that they cannot do in their work. Second-rate novelists such as Diver never reach this point. Nothing is beyond her sublime confidence. She did not relinquish the attempt to ask important moral questions, to tackle impossibly large themes.

—Rachel Anderson

DIXON, Paige.   See CORCORAN, Barbara.

DIXON, Thomas.
Nationality: American. **Born:** Shelby, North Carolina, 11 January 1864. Invalid from 1937. **Education:** Shelby Academy, North Carolina, 1877; Wake Forest College, North Caroline, M.A. 1883; The Johns Hopkins University, Baltimore, Maryland, 1883–84; graduate, law school, Greensboro, North Carolina, 1885. **Relations:** married 1) Harriet Bussey in 1886 (died 1937); 2) Madelyn Donovan in 1937. **Career:** lawyer, 1884; Baptist minister, Dudley Street Church, Boston, Massachusetts, and Twenty Third Street Church, New York, 1889–95; lecturer, 1889–95; resigned from Baptish Church, and founded nondenominational Church of the People, 1895–99 (returned to Baptist Church in 1899); toured USA with dramatic productions, 1907; actor, 1910; motion picture producer, Hollywood, 1915–19; founded real estate project, North Carolina, 1925. Appointed to the federal court, Raleigh, North Carolina, 1937. Lost fortunes on the stock market, 1907, 1929. **Died:** 3 April 1946.

ROMANCE AND HISTORICAL PUBLICATIONS

Novels (series: Reconstruction Trilogy; Socialism Trilogy)

Reconstruction Trilogy:
The Leopard's Spots: A Romance of the White Man's Burden, illustrated by C.D. Williams. New York, Doubleday Page, 1902.
The Clansman: An Historical Romance of the Ku Klux Klan. London, Heinemann, and New York, Doubleday Page, 1905.
The Traitor: A Story of the Fall of the Invisible Empire, illustrated by C.D. Williams. New York, Doubleday Page, 1907.
Socialism Trilogy:
The One Woman: A Story of Modern Utopia. New York, Doubleday Page, 1903.
Comrades: A Story of Social Adventure in California, illustrated by C.D. Williams. London, and New York, Doubleday Page, 1909.
The Roots of Evil. Garden City, Doubleday Page, 1911.
The Fall of a Nation: Sequel to Birth of a Nation. New York, Appleton, 1911.
The Sins of the Father: A Romance of the South, illustrated by John Cassell. New York, Appleton, 1912.
The Southerner: A Romance of the Real Lincoln, illustrated by John Cassell. London, Appleton, and New York, Grossett and Dunlap, 1913.
The Sun Virgin. London, Stanley Paul, and New York, Stanley Liveright, 1913.

The Victim: A Romance of the Real Jefferson Davis. London, Appleton, and New York, Grossett and Dunlop, 1914.
The Foolish Virgin. New York, D. Appleton, 1915.
The Way of Man: A Story of the New Woman. New York, Appleton, 1919.
A Man of the People: A Drama of Abraham Lincoln. New York, Appleton, 1920.
The Man in Gray: A Romance of North and South. New York, Appleton, 1921.
The Black Hood. London, Appleton, and New York, Grossett and Dunlop, 1924.
The Love Complex. New York, Boni and Liveright, 1925.
Companions. New York, Cleveland, Otis, 1931.
The Dreamer in Portugal: The Story of Bernarr Macfadden's Mission to Continental Europe. New York, Covici Friede, 1934.
The Flaming Sword. Atlanta, Monarch, 1939.

OTHER PUBLICATIONS

Screenplays: Clansman, adaptation of his novel, 1905; The Sins of the Father, 1907; The Traitor, adaptation of his novel, 1907; Old Black Joe, 1912; The Almighty Dollar, 1913; Red Dawn, adaptation of his novel Comrades, 1919; A Man of the People, 1920.

Other

Living Problems in Religion and Social Science. New York, Dillingham, 1889.
Dixon on Ingersoll: Ten Discourses Delivered in Association Hall. New York, Ogilvie, 1892.
The Failure of Protestantism in New York and its Causes. New York, Strauss, 1896.
Dixon's Sermons, Delivered in the Grand Opera House 1898–1899. New York, Bussey, 1899.
The Life Worth Living: A Personal Experience (autobiography). London, Doubleday Page, 1905.
What is Religion? An Outline of Vital Ritualism. New York, The Scott, 1918.
Wildacres: In the Land of the Sky. Little Switzerland, The Mount Mitchell Association of Arts and Sciences, 1926.
The Inside Story of the Harding Tragedy, with H.M. Dougherty. New York, Churchill, 1932.

*

Film Adaptations: Birth of a Nation, 1915, from the novel The Clansman; The One Woman, 1918; Comrades, 1919 (originally titled Bolshevism on Trial); The Mark of the Beast, 1923, from the novel The Foolish Virgin.

Critical Studies: As to the Leopard's Spots—an Open Letter to T. Dixon Jr. by Kelly Miller, n.p., 1903; Fire from the Flint, Winston-Salem, North Carolina, John F. Blair, 1968; Thomas Dixon by R.A. Cook, New York, Twayne, 1974.

*   *   *

Thomas Dixon Jr is usually mentioned in passing today only as the bigoted author of rabble-rousing novels hymning the praises of the original Ku Klux Klan (KKK) founded by disgruntled southerners after the American Civil War—particularly those on which D.W. Griffith based his first epic feature film, The Birth of a Nation (1914). The distortions of history, motivated by the virulent race hatred of this self-styled 'reactionary individualist' need to be viewed, however, against the ups and downs of a long career, in order to understand how his clumsily plotted, and often crudely written romances, could at times have inflamed thousands of readers.

By the time Dixon was selected, in 1906, for inclusion, with other trendsetters of the new century, in the prestigious *National Cyclopedia of American Biography*, he had already achieved distinction in the three enterprises that exert greatest influence in shaping American public opinion. After graduating from college at the age of 19, he entered a seminar at Johns Hopkins University, where he became a friend of Woodrow Wilson. He was then elected to the North Carolina legislature before he was old enough to vote. He became disillusioned with politics and was ordained a Baptist minister in 1886. His dynamic preaching in small southern churches soon attracted enough attention for him to be called to important pulpits in Boston and New York; but, in 1895, he left the Baptists to form his own 'People's Church', which reputedly had the largest protestant congregation in the country. During this period he published four books on theology; but, in 1899, he became impatient with the constraints of the church and left it to devote himself to secular writing and lecturing against the evils of the time.

The first book of his trilogy about the Ku Klux Klan during the Reconstruction appeared in 1902. *The Leopard's Spots* 'sought to preserve ... the letter and the spirit of this remarkable period' from the viewpoint of a southern traditionalist. Reviewers found the writing vulgar, but the fiery melodrama appealed to a public who responded even more enthusiastically to *The Clansman* in 1905, although national reviewers objected that Dixon appealed to the public's worst passions. That same year Dixon also published *The Life Worth Living*, a personal account illustrated with his own photographs, of the beauty of nature, and the joys of country life, away from 'the horrors of the city'; but this was little noticed.

In 1907 his fortunes began to fall when he completed his KKK trilogy with *The Traitor: A Story of the Fall of the Invisible Empire*, which took to task 'unscrupulous men' who after the dissolution of the original order used 'its garbs and methods for personal ends'. Reviewers dismissed it as 'yellow journalism', and Dixon decided he had better find new targets. He poured out in rapid succession lurid novels warning against the dangers of miscegenation, socialism, pacifism, and women's emancipation; but most of these were greeted with derision rather than enthusiasm, because of their virulence and unbelievable plots.

His fortunes took a turn for the better when Griffith converted *The Clansman*, and some additional material, into the improbable story of romances between the children of the leader of the Northern Radical Republicans, who imposed Reconstruction upon the South after Lincoln's assassination, and those of a kindly southern planter, victimized by former slaves and urged on by carpetbaggers. The relationships almost lead to the death of the children until the northern leader realizes that he has 'fallen victim to the wiles of a yellow vampire housekeeper'. His repentance makes it possible to proclaim that 'Civilization has been saved, and the South redeemed from shame'.

Dixon had always sensed the value of theatrical productions, and had been involved with Griffith at a time when he had earlier begun turning some of his novels into plays. When he enjoyed little success with fictionalized biographies of Lincoln and Jefferson Davis, he decided to try his own hand at filmmaking with a sequel to Griffith's epic, a futuristic *The Fall of a Nation*, about the redemption of a degenerate, defeated United States after World War I by a Klan-like secret society. A typical reviewer found it 'difficult to discover anything more futile and foolish'.

The 1920s were not prosperous times for Dixon, though bigotry flourished in the United States. His earlier followers turned on him when he attacked the revived Ku Klux Klan that was attracting a new generation, as a betrayal of the principles of the original in *Black Hood*. He wrote scripts for forgotten films, and engaged in land speculation which left him bankrupt in 1929. His message

throughout his career had been that anyone who differed from him in the slightest detail, genetically, psychologically, or ideologically was a menace to civilization, which he equated with the ante-bellum southern plantation. His vicious attacks on blacks were motivated by a mindset that they were not a primitive people—as progressive reformers of the time often maintained—but a degenerate race fit only for bondage, a dogma probably derived from the biblical account of the dispersion of Noah's family. The only value of his works today is their demonstration of how tenaciously persons with rhetorical skills may promote socially demoralizing fanaticism. It is hard to believe, however, that Dixon's career from any viewpoint provides a model anyone might wish to emulate.

—Warren French

DOBSON, William.   See SALISBURY, Carola.

DOCTOROW, E(dgar) L(aurence).
Nationality: American. **Born:** New York City, 6 January 1931. **Education:** Bronx High School of Science; Kenyon College, Gambier, Ohio, A.B. (honours) in philosophy 1952; Columbia University, New York, 1952–53. **Military service:** United States Army, 1953–55. **Relations:** married Helen Setzer in 1954; two daughters and one son. **Career:** script reader, Columbia Picture Industries Inc, New York; senior editor, New American Library, New York, 1960–64; editor-in-chief, 1964–69, and publisher, 1969, Dial Press, New York; member of the faculty, Sarah Lawrence College, Bronxville, New York, 1971–78; adjunct professor of English, 1982–86, New York University. Since 1987, Glucksman professor of American and English Letters. Writer-in-residence, University of California, Irvine, 1969–70; creative writing fellow, Yale School of Drama, New Haven, Connecticut, 1974–75; visiting professor, University of Utah, Salt Lake City, 1975; visiting senior fellow, Princeton University, New Jersey, 1980–81. Director, Authors Guild of America, and American PEN. **Recipient:** Guggenheim fellowship, 1972; Creative Artists Publish Service grant, 1973; National Book Critics Circle award, 1976, 1990; American Academy award, 1976; American Book award, 1986; PEN Faulkner award, 1990; Howells award, 1990. L.H.D.: Kenyon College, 1976; Brandeis University, Waltham, Massachusetts, 1989; D.Litt.: Hobart and William Smith Colleges, Geneva, New York, 1979. **Member:** American Academy, 1984. Lives in New Rochelle, New York. **Agent:** International Creative Management, 40 West 57th Street, New York, New York 10022, USA. **Address:** c/o Random House Inc, 201 East 50th Street, New York, New York 10022, USA.

ROMANCE AND HISTORICAL PUBLICATIONS

Novels

Welcome to Hard Times. New York, Simon and Schuster, 1960; as *Bad Man from Bodie*, London, Deutsch, 1961.
The Book of Daniel. New York, Random House, 1971; London, Macmillan, 1972.
Ragtime. New York, Random House, and London, Macmillan, 1975.
Loon Lake. New York, Random House, and London, Macmillan, 1980.
World's Fair. New York, Random House, 1985; London, Joseph, 1986.
Billy Bathgate. New York, Random House, and London, Macmillan, 1989.

OTHER PUBLICATIONS

Short Stories

Lives of the Poets: Six Stories and a Novella. New York, Random House, 1984; London, Joseph, 1985.

Plays

Drinks before Dinner (produced in New York, 1978). New York, Random House, 1979; London, Macmillan, 1980.

Screenplay: *Daniel*, 1983.

Other

Big as Life. New York, Simon and Schuster, 1966.
American Anthem, photographs by Jean-Claude Suarès. New York, Stewart Tabori and Chang, 1982.
Eric Fischl: Scenes and Sequences: Fifty-Eight Monotypes (text by Doctorow). New York, Abrams, 1990.

*

Film Adaptations: *Welcome to Hard Times*, 1967 (as *Killer on a Horse*, 1967); *Ragtime*, 1981; *Billy Bathgate*, 1991.

Bibliography: *E.L. Doctorow: An Annotated Bibliography* by Michelle M. Tokarczyk, New York, Garland, 1988.

Critical Studies: *E.L. Doctorow: Essays and Conversations*, edited by Richard Trenner, Princeton, New Jersey, Ontario Review Press, 1983; *E.L. Doctorow* by Paul Levine, London, Methuen, 1985; *E.L.Doctorow* by Carol C. Harter and James R. Thompson, Boston, Twayne, 1990; *E.L. Doctorow* by John G. Parks, New York, Continuum Press, 1991; *Models of Misrepresentation: The Fiction of E.L. Doctorow* by Christopher D. Morris, Jackson, University Press of Mississippi, 1991.

*　　*　　*

Young Edgar buries a time capsule in E.L. Doctorow's semi-autobiographical *World's Fair*. It contains objects which will summon, he hopes, the spirit of the 1930s for whoever finds it in the future. So he puts into it a Tom Mix badge, an essay on Roosevelt, a harmonica, a torn silk stocking. The works of that other Edgar, Doctorow himself, are also time capsules. They repackage the familiar signs and symbols of the past.

However, the history with which he fills his novels is distorted. In *The Book of Daniel*, his most political work, the events leading to the execution of the Rosenbergs, in 1951, are tampered with. The Rosenbergs, who sold atomic bomb secrets to the Russians, become the Isaacsons, a name which suggests that they are sacrificed to salve American fears about global communist domination. Although Doctorow's recreation of the social climate of the 1930s and 1950s is convincing, the implied parallel between fiction and fact is constantly skewed. Crucial episodes prior to the trial, for instance, are seen from the point of view of the Isaacsons' children, Daniel and Susan. This re-routes attention away from the historical controversy. We see the accused as harried parents, and not as heinous criminals.

These events are further trivialized by the various games Doctorow plays with the material. *The Book of Daniel* pastiches the form of a dissertation submitted by Daniel for a doctorate in the 1960s. It contains reminders about subjects to be researched at a later date and brief notes about forms of execution in other areas. Daniel's self-consciousness about the act of writing deflects interest away from the factual core, too. 'This is a Thinline felt tip marker, black', he tells us early on. 'This is Composition Notebook 79C made in USA by Long Island Paper Products Inc'. Later, when he describes physically abusing his wife with a lighter, he harangues the reader directly: 'Who told you you could read this?' Such histrionics cannot help but obscure the history.

If the past is seen through a glass darkly in *The Book of Daniel*, the pane is shattered in several of Doctorow's other works. His approach has little in common with the techniques of Sir Walter Scott, founder of the historical novel, who was famed for his painstaking realism and research. Instead, Doctorow markets the past like a consumer product. Rough edges are smoothed out, and history is made glossy and digestible.

Ragtime, set in the early decades of this century, topped the best-seller lists for a while. It concerns the downfall of a middle-class New Rochelle family who trade in flags and fireworks. They help black ragtime musician Coalhouse Walker, Jr (a Scott Joplin devotee, and suitor to their maid Sarah) when he becomes involved in a dispute over damage done to his Model 'T' Ford by white racists. Unable to obtain justice, Walker turns terrorist. He threatens to blow up J.P. Morgan's priceless art collection if demands about the restoration of his car are not met.

The verisimilitude of *Ragtime* is severely compromised by the way that Doctorow mixes-and-matches the most unlikely of real-life couples. Anarchist Emma Goldman, (accused of playing a part in McKinley's assassination in 1901) gives an erotic massage to Evelyn Nesbit (the former chorus girl involved in a sex-scandal with husband Harry Thaw and architect Stanford White). J.P. Morgan and Henry Ford prattle about Rosicrucian theories or reincarnation after a fine lunch. Sigmund Freud and Carl Jung go through the Tunnel of Love together at Coney Island, and Harry Houdini meets Archduke Franz Ferdinand on a German airfield. Houdini is a suitable symbol for a book in which Doctorow's legerdemain produces only the illusion of its past and not its substance.

Contemporary writers, it seems, love the surface gleam of the past, and disregard its depth. The 1920s? That's the Jazz Age. The 1960s? Flower Power. A label for every decade. So it is to Doctorow's credit that he at least seeks to see beyond the dazzle. However, even in a book like *Loon Lake*, which appears to document the Depression, well-worn images are shuffled. It begins with that most cinematic of clichés: a hobo, Joe, jumps aboard a rail-car to hitch a free ride to the Adirondacks. Most of the stock types of the era are introduced. Roustabouts, bolshy union men, evil capitalists, even a pioneering female pilot based on Amelia Earhart—each panders to our preconceptions. *Billy Bathgate*, inspired by the criminal career of Dutch Schultz, follows a pedictable Hollywood-inspired path, too, by compiling many hackneyed gangster motifs. The members of Schultz's bootlegging gang are all caricatures. Lulu Rosenkrantz is the wildman; Irving, the calm professional; Abbadabba Berman, the brains of the outfit. There's even a 'moll', Lola Drew, who is befriended by the young boy Billy Bathgate when her double-crossing lover, Bo Weinberg, is murdered by the 'concrete slipper' method.

Why does Doctorow repackage history as myth in this way? Is he complicit with the advertisers, who glean their history from the silver screen? No. The *Book of Daniel, Ragtime, Loon Lake, World's Fair, Billy Bathgate*—and even his early novel about the Wild West, *Welcome to Hard Times*—undoubtedly contribute to an extent to our contemporary amnesia about the way things *really* were. They also, though, critically engage with postmodern anxieties about the truth or representations. In a fax society, facts have lost their grip. The image is king. But Doctorow is canny enough to realize that even if his time capsules only contain ideas about the past, and not the past itself, that's no reason not to plant them in the soil. Let the future understand our present, even if our present cannot understand its past. Meanwhile, we can but gawp at the impeccable prose.

—Barry Lewis

———————

DONALD, Robyn.
Pseudonym for Robyn Kingston. **Nationality:** New Zealander. **Born:** Robyn Elaine Hutching, Auckland, New Zealand, 14 August, 1940. **Education:** Warkworth Primary School, Auckland; Warkworth District High School, Auckland; Auckland Teachers Training College, 1961. **Relations:** married Donald James Kingston in 1960; one son and one daughter. **Career:** primary school teacher, Warkworth, 1960–64, and Kerikeri, 1971–72; teacher of remedial reading, Kerikeri, 1974–77. Since 1973, secondary school teacher, Kerikeri. **Address:** Kerikeri Road, RD3 Kerikeri, New Zealand.

ROMANCE AND HISTORICAL PUBLICATIONS

Novels

Bride at Whangatapu. London, Mills and Boon, 1977; Toronto, Harlequin, 1978.
Dilemma in Paradise. London, Mills and Boon, 1978; Toronto, Harlequin, 1978.
Summer at Awakopu. London, Mills and Boon, 1978; Toronto, Harlequin, 1979.
Wife in Exchange. London, Mills and Boon, 1978; Toronto, Harlequin, 1979.
Shadow of the Past. London, Mills and Boon, and Toronto, Harlequin, 1979.
Bay of Stars. London, Mills and Boon, 1980; Toronto, Harlequin, 1981.
Iceberg. London, Mills and Boon, 1980; Toronto, Harlequin, 1981.
The Interloper. London, Mills and Boon, and Toronto, Harlequin, 1981.
The Dark Abyss. London, Mills and Boon, 1981; Toronto, Harlequin, 1982.
An Old Passion. London, Mills and Boon, 1982; Toronto, Harlequin, 1983.
Mansion for My Love. London, Mills and Boon, 1982; Toronto, Harlequin, 1983.
The Guarded Heart. London, Mills and Boon, and Toronto, Harlequin, 1983.
Return to Yesterday. London, Mills and Boon, and Toronto, Harlequin, 1983.
The Gates of Rangitatau. London, Mills and Boon, 1983; Toronto, Harlequin, 1984.
A Durable Fire. London, Mills and Boon, 1983; Toronto, Harlequin, 1984.
An Unbreakable Bond. London, Mills and Boon, and Toronto, Harlequin, 1986.
Captives of the Past. London, Mills and Boon, 1986; Toronto, Harlequin, 1987.
Long Journey Back. London, Mills and Boon, and Toronto, Harlequin, 1986.
A Willing Surrender. London, Mills and Boon, and 1986; Toronto, Harlequin, 1987.
Country of the Heart. London, Mills and Boon, 1987; Toronto, Harlequin, 1988.
A Late Loving. London, Mills and Boon, 1987; Toronto, Harlequin, 1988.
Smoke in the Wind. London, Mills and Boon, 1987; Toronto, Harlequin, 1988.

The Sweetest Trap. London, Mills and Boon, and Toronto, Harlequin, 1988.
Love's Reward. London, Mills and Boon, 1989; Toronto, Harlequin, 1990.
A Matter of Will. London, Mills and Boon, 1989; Toronto, Harlequin, 1991.
A Bitter Homecoming. London, Mills and Boon, 1989; Toronto, Harlequin, 1990.
No Guarantees. London, Mills and Boon, and Toronto, Harlequin, 1990.
The Darker Side of Paradise. London, Mills and Boon, 1990; Toronto, Harlequin, 1991.
Summer Storm. London, Mills and Boon, 1990; Toronto, Harlequin, 1991.
No Place Too Far. London, Mills and Boon, 1990; Toronto, Harlequin, 1992.
Some Kind of Madness. London, Mills and Boon, 1991; Toronto, Harlequin, 1992.
Storm Bluer Paradise. London, Mills and Boon, 1991; Toronto, Harlequin, 1992.
The Stone Princess. London, Mills and Boon, 1991; Toronto, Harlequin, 1993.
Once Bitten, Twice Shy. London, Mills and Boon, 1992; Toronto, Harlequin, 1993.
The Golden Mask. London, Mills and Boon, 1992; Toronto, Harlequin, 1993.
Such Dark Magic. London, Mills and Boon, 1993.
Pagan Surrender. London, Mills and Boon, 1993.
Dark Fire. London, Mills and Boon, 1994.

*

Robyn Donald comments:
I consider myself an entertainer and I write to give my readers pleasure. I write romances because I enjoy reading them and because I believe a happy marriage to be the state in which people attain the greatest felicity. I write about strong men and strong women who fall in love and learn to trust each other. I set my novels in New Zealand and the South Pacific because I love my country and nothing is more beautiful or evocative than an island in the south seas.

* * *

Since her debut in 1977 Robyn Donald has produced some 40 romances. All of them have been set in the South Pacific region, with most featuring New Zealand, and Donald is widely recognized as a Kiwi writer, although her work far from reflects the conventional outsider's view of a country set in a 1950s time warp whose inhabitants all have something to do with sheep. Donald has used sheep stations as backgrounds and she certainly feels comfortable describing the local flora and fauna—for example, her leading characters always have well-stocked and beautifully maintained gardens—but the picture she gives of everyday life in her native country is far from dull. Her stories are absorbing, fast-paced reads with plenty of passion. A battle of wills between the strong central characters, often arising from a past encounter which has left unfinished business between them, forms Donald's usual plot and her mood is often a dark one, reflecting the baser human emotions such as jealousy, physical obsession, the desire for revenge and the need to manipulate (and also to be manipulated) which are more often kept hidden.

Donald's heroine is an attractive character with whom it is easy to identify. An ordinary woman in the sense that she rarely has a high-powered career (*Country of the Heart* is unique among Donald's stories in presenting the dilemma of a doctor heroine whose job is so important to her that she must force the hero to compromise if they are to find happiness together), she is intelligent and articulate, with a fairly practical approach to life. She can be relied upon to rally round in a crisis, whether it is helping refloat stranded whales on a local beach, or giving a hand with the cooking when the hero's housekeeper is called away unexpectedly. Her talents do not intimidate and every reader could see her as a would-be friend. Early books such as *Bride at Whangatapu* present a less assured figure than the feisty, independent heroine of more recent stories, such as Eden, in *The Golden Mask*, but they share a common theme in the heroine's domination by and ultimate submission to the hero. Quite simply she acknowledges at an early stage in the relationship that she has met her destiny and that her subsequent struggles to avoid involvement are fated to end in failure. Even at their first meeting there is an instant recognition of the hero's hold over her and the part he will play in her future; 'the heady compound of attraction and dislike held her in thrall'(*A Matter of Will*), 'No emotion stirred the strong beauty of his face; it could have been a bronze mask turned towards her, yet Clary shivered, suddenly afraid' (*A Willing Surrender*). Her fears are those of a normal woman dealing with a man who is beyond the bounds of her experience, both emotionally and sexually.

The physical relationship between the main characters is always dynamite. Which is hardly surprising when we consider the heroine's counterpart. Every romantic hero is larger than life, but the Donald hero must surely represent the ultimate female fantasy. Wealthy, sexy, sophisticated, confident, with charismatic good looks and a sense of humour, he turns female heads wherever he goes. His flaws are those of the best romantic heroes from Mr Darcy onwards; pride, arrogance and a tendency to judge others (especially the heroine) by his own high standards—and find them wanting. In the matter of selecting a mate he naturally prefers to do the chasing and when, after some initial confusion between lust and love, he decides that the heroine is the woman he wants, he pursues her with a predatory single-mindedness which scares her as much as it excites her. He is a possessive lover and sometimes even a cruel one, although his ultimate admission that it is his obsessive love for the heroine which drives him to extremes usually serves as adequate justification. Kieran Sinclair, in *Pagan Surrender*, echoes every Donald hero when he explains, 'It's selfish, but I wanted a woman who'd love me more than anything else, who would put me first. I'd begun to lose hope of ever finding someone like that.' He will be a doting father, but the reader feels that he will always wish his wife to see herself primarily as his partner rather than as mother to their children, although it is interesting to note that his own mother—usually still on the scene and taking an active interest in the progress of his romance with the heroine—has a closer than normal relationship with him and, like a latter-day Coriolanus, he bends to her wishes when he might be inclined otherwise.

The circle of minor characters surrounding the central couple are often family members, and blind loyalty to relatives or close friends can be a major cause of misunderstanding between hero and heroine. For example, Lora, in *A Matter of Will*, resents the hero for hounding her half-brother from the country and Tegan, the heroine of *Pagan Surrender*, is despised by the hero for jilting his best friend. Often the friends who act as matchmakers or counsellors for the hero and heroine are themselves the central characters from previous books, thus allowing readers the reassurance that their marriages have turned out successfully.

Donald gives her readers the preferred fantasy of an ordinary woman swept off her feet by an extraordinary man. Her great strength is the power and passion with which she is able to recreate the mixture afresh with every book.

—Frances Whitehead

DONNELLY, Jane.

Nationality: British. **Relations:** married twice; one daughter. **Career:** reporter, Birmingham *Gazette* group; television critic, feature writer, and women's page editor. **Address:** Mill Cottage, Lower Quinton, Stratford-on-Avon, Warwickshire, CV37 8RY, England.

ROMANCE AND HISTORICAL PUBLICATIONS

Novels

A Man Apart. London, Mills and Boon, and Toronto, Harlequin, 1968.

Don't Walk Alone. London, Mills and Boon, and Toronto, Harlequin, 1969.

Shadows from the Sea. London, Mills and Boon, and Toronto, Harlequin, 1970.

Take the Far Dream. London, Mills and Boon, and Toronto, Harlequin, 1970.

Halfway to the Stars. London, Mills and Boon, and Toronto, Harlequin, 1971.

Never Turn Back. London, Mills and Boon, and Toronto, Harlequin, 1971.

The Man in the Next Room. London, Mills and Boon, and Toronto, Harlequin, 1971.

The Mill in the Meadow. London, Mills and Boon, and Toronto, Harlequin, 1972.

A Stranger Came. London, Mills and Boon, and Toronto, Harlequin, 1972.

The Long Shadow. London, Mills and Boon, and Toronto, Harlequin, 1973.

Rocks Under Shining Water. London, Mills and Boon, and Toronto, Harlequin, 1973.

A Man Called Mallory. London, Mills and Boon, and Toronto, Harlequin, 1974.

Collision Course. London, Mills and Boon, and Toronto, Harlequin, 1975.

The Man Outside. London, Mills and Boon, and Toronto, Harlequin, 1975.

Ride Out the Storm. London, Mills and Boon, and Toronto, Harlequin, 1975.

Dark Pursuer. London, Mills and Boon, and Toronto, Harlequin, 1976.

The Silver Cage. London, Mills and Boon, and Toronto, Harlequin, 1976.

Dear Caliban. London, Mills and Boon, and Toronto, Harlequin, 1977.

Four Weeks in Winter. London, Mills and Boon, and Toronto, Harlequin, 1977.

The Intruder. London, Mills and Boon, and Toronto, Harlequin, 1977.

Forest of the Night. London, Mills and Boon, 1978; Toronto, Harlequin, 1979.

Love for a Stranger. London, Mills and Boon, and Toronto, Harlequin, 1978.

Spell of the Seven Stones. London, Mills and Boon, and Toronto, Harlequin, 1978.

The Black Hunter. London, Mills and Boon, and Toronto, Harlequin, 1978.

Touched by Fire. London, Mills and Boon, and Toronto, Harlequin, 1978.

A Man to Watch. London, Mills and Boon, 1979; Toronto, Harlequin, 1980.

A Savage Sanctuary. London, Mills and Boon, and Toronto, Harlequin, 1979.

Behind a Closed Door. London, Mills and Boon, and Toronto, Harlequin, 1979.

No Way Out. London, Mills and Boon, and Toronto, Harlequin, 1980.

When Lightning Strikes. London, Mills and Boon, and Toronto, Harlequin, 1980.

Flash Point. London, Mills and Boon, 1981; Toronto, Harlequin, 1982.

So Long a Winter. London, Mills and Boon, and Toronto, Harlequin, 1981.

The Frozen Jungle. London, Mills and Boon, and Toronto, Harlequin, 1981.

Diamond Cut Diamond. London, Mills and Boon, and Toronto, Harlequin, 1982.

A Fierce Encounter. London, Mills and Boon, and Toronto, Harlequin, 1983.

Call up the Storm. London, Mills and Boon, and Toronto, Harlequin, 1983.

Face the Tiger. London, Mills and Boon, and Toronto, Harlequin, 1983.

Moon Lady. London, Mills and Boon, and Toronto, Harlequin, 1984.

Ring of Crystal. London, Mills and Boon, and Toronto, Harlequin, 1985.

To Cage a Whirlwind. London, Mills and Boon, and Toronto, Harlequin, 1985.

Force Field. London, Mills and Boon, and Toronto, Harlequin, 1987.

Ride a Wild Horse. London, Mills and Boon, and Toronto, Harlequin, 1987.

The Frozen Heart. London, Mills and Boon, and Toronto, Harlequin, 1988.

No Place to Run. London, Mills and Boon, 1987; Toronto, Harlequin, 1988.

Fetters of Gold. London, Mills and Boon, and Toronto, Harlequin, 1988.

When We're Alone. London, Mills and Boon, 1989; Toronto, Harlequin, 1990.

The Devil's Flower. London, Mills and Boon, 1990; Toronto, Harlequin, 1991.

Jewels of Helen. London, Mills and Boon, 1990; Toronto, Harlequin, 1991.

Once a Cheat. London, Mills and Boon, 1991; Toronto, Harlequin, 1992.

The Trespasser. London, Mills and Boon, 1992; Toronto, Harlequin, 1993.

Hold Back the Dark. London, Mills and Boon, 1993.

Shadow of a Tiger. London, Mills and Boon, 1994.

*

Jane Donnelly comments:

My novels, as with all Mills and Boon books, are happy escapist reading. My heroines are smart girls, with minds of their own and nobody's fool. Although part of the fun of the book is in the awful things that happen to them on the way, I try to leave the reader feeling that the future is bright, and really fancying the hero!

*   *   *

Jane Donnelly's protagonists often work in the media or the arts, reflecting the author's own career background. They are journalists, actors, television producers—and are interesting, independent people who are capable of dealing with most situations. Donnelly's books are straight forward romances in which the hero meets the heroine and they encounter the problems that any normal couple would have during the course of their relationship. Thus, it is perfectly understandable that Philippa, in *The Silver Cage*, should wonder why such an attractive, charismatic hero should want to marry the nondescript girl that she perceives herself to be; that Kate, in *The Trespasser*, should use Mark to help her get over a failed love affair; and that Rosalyn, in *Once a Cheat*, should continue to see Jeremy despite being warned off by a family friend.

Philippa Roscoe is 20 years old when she falls in love with a friend of her parents in *The Silver Cage*. Kern is a witty, sophisticated writer who seemingly loves her too. However, Philippa has never thought of herself as beautiful, and has always been put down by her glamorous actor mother and aristocratic father. She does not think she can compete with Kern's ex-lover and listening to the advice of her parents and 'friends' she eventually leaves Kern, fleeing to the cottage where they had their honeymoon. He proves his worth by following her and declaring his love for her. Kern is a smouldering, very masculine hero who believes that actions speak louder than words. He is the quintessential Donnelly hero.

Similarly, James Halloran, hero of *Once a Cheat*, is a successful lawyer who assumes rather too much about the heroine Rosalyn. Encountering her as the new and unsuitable girlfriend of his neighbour, James takes it upon himself to warn Rosalyn off. Rosalyn is an actress and actually doesn't like Jeremy Hiatt but decides to let James believe she wants to see him in order to spite him. Before she can do anything, she and Jeremy are involved in a car crash—she ends up saving Jeremy by pushing him out of the automobile before it explodes and is immediately welcomed into the bosom of his family. James is not too happy, especially when her beloved, but crooked brother Ben turns up. Despite this everything is resolved and the hero and heroine end the book in each other's arms.

Similarly Kerry Holland, in *Force Field*, is an actress invited to play Rosalind in *As You Like It*, in Cornwall. She encounters David Caradoc, a sculptor and artist, who is the stepson of the woman who invited her to act. She sits for David and gradually falls in love with him. The reader realizes that she is a compassionate woman when she risks her life to save a dog from a mine-shaft. Although the interest of a female rival complicates matters, Kerry eventually wins David's love.

Joanne, the heroine of *Behind A Closed Door*, one of Donnelly's earlier novels, is also a kind and compassionate woman who is landed with other people's cast-offs. Joanna runs a second hand clothes shop and encounters Peter Craig, a lawyer and the boss of a good friend of hers, at a dinner at which she cooks. Peter persuades her to cater for a supper party that he is having, and uses her also to get rid of an unwanted lover. After a dramatic fire in her shop, Peter realizes that he cares for her and invites her to Paris. Although she is not 'that sort of girl' she agrees but returns when she finds out that Peter hasn't mentioned that his father has died. She takes this to mean that he doesn't care for her—Peter proves his love by buying her late father's paintings at more than their worth so that she can pay off her debts, and following her back from Paris.

Kate uses Mark to help her get over her lover's betrayal in *The Trespasser*. Kate is a journalist in local radio and meets Mark when she looks around his home, a tower. Mark is a local photographer and lets her stay in the tower while she recovers. She invites Mark to stay with her so that all of her friends will think that they are an item. Although she is deceiving Mark, she objects when she finds out that he has deceived her—far from being a local small-time photographer, he is internationally known. However, Kate is in love, and love conquers all.

Donnelly's books are simply constructed but well written books with long descriptive passages and comparatively little dialogue. Her heroes are of the quintessential tall, dark, and handsome mould, and her heroines are spirited young women who lead independent lives.

—P. Campbell

_____

DOUGLAS, Barbara. See **LAKER, Rosalind.**

_____

DOUGLAS, Lloyd C(assell).
Nationality: American. **Born:** Columbia City, Indiana, 27 August 1877. **Education:** Wittenberg College, Springfield, Ohio, A.B. **Relations:** married Bessie Porch in 1904. **Career:** Lutheran minister. **Recipient:** LL.D.: Gettysburg College, Pennsylvania, 1935; D. Litt.: Northeastern University, Boston, 1936. **Died:** 13 February 1951.

ROMANCE AND HISTORICAL PUBLICATIONS

Novels

Magnificent Obsession. Boston, Houghton Mifflin, 1929; London, Allen and Unwin, 1932.
Forgive Us Our Trespasses. Boston, Houghton Mifflin, 1932; London, Lovat Dickson, 1937.
Precious Jeopardy: A Christmas Story. Boston, Houghton Mifflin, 1933; London, Davies, 1949.
Green Light. Boston, Houghton Mifflin, and London, Dickson and Thompson, 1935.
White Banners. Boston, Houghton Mifflin, and London, Lovat Dickson, 1936.
Home for Christmas. Boston, Houghton Mifflin, and London, Lovat Dickson, 1937.
Disputed Passage. Boston, Houghton Mifflin, and London, Lovat Dickson, 1939.
Dr Hudson's Secret Journal. Boston, Houghton Mifflin, 1939; London, Davies, 1940.
Invitation to Live. Boston, Houghton Mifflin, 1940; London, Davies, 1941.
The Robe. Boston, Houghton Mifflin, 1942; London, Davies, 1943.
The Big Fisherman. Boston, Houghton Mifflin, 1948; London, Davies, 1949.

OTHER PUBLICATIONS

Other

The Fate of the Limited. New York, Associated Press, 1919.
Wanted: A Congregation. Chicago, Christian Century Press, 1920.
An Affair of the Heart. Akron, Ohio, Summit, 1922.
The Minister's Everyday Life. New York, Scribner, 1924.
These Sayings of Mine: An Interpretation of the Teachings of Jesus. New York, Scribner, 1926.
Those Disturbing Miracles. New York, Harper, 1927.
The College Student Facing a Muddled World. Sackville, New Brunswick, Mount Allison University, 1933.
A Time to Remember (autobiography). Boston, Houghton Mifflin, 1951; London, Davies, 1952.
The Living Faith: Selected Sermons. Boston, Houghton Mifflin, and London, Davies, 1955.

*

Film Adaptations: *The Robe*, 1953; *The Big Fisherman*, 1959.

Critical Study: *The Shape of Sunday: An Intimate Biography of Lloyd C. Douglas* by Virginia Douglas Dawson and Betty Douglas Wilson, Boston, Houghton Mifflin, 1952.

*   *   *

If Lloyd C. Douglas is still read it will be for his two historical novels, *The Robe* and *The Big Fisherman*. Both share the same background, the New Testament world of Palestine and Rome and both are concerned with the events surrounding the founding of the early Christian Church including the last days of Christ. It may be that their survival owes at least as much to their appearance on the lists of the subscription book clubs of the day and to the fact that they were both made into films, as to their literary merit. The interest aroused by the subject of the books and the use of the gospel narratives must also have contributed.

Naturally the two books overlap in the events they describe and they have many characters in common. *The Robe* is the story of how the robe of Christ, won in a dice game at the foot of the cross by Marcellus, changes his life; *The Big Fisherman* follows the ministry of Christ and the life of Peter. However, despite many similarities, the two novels are quite different. In the first place, *The Robe*, the earlier of the two, is the more readable. The hero, Marcellus, is an attractive, talented young man whose outspoken behaviour in Rome causes him to be sent to Palestine to command the notorious Gaza fort. Visiting Jerusalem during the Passover and in his capacity as Commander of Gaza, he is assigned the task of crucifying Christ. The event is traumatic and under the influence of the strange robe Marcellus finds himself searching for the truth about Jesus and for peace of mind. This he will find only in the arena of the Colosseum in Rome. By focusing on one character Douglas maintains interest and it is easy for the reader to feel sympathy for Marcellus, both in his quest and in his love for the beautiful Diana.

The Big Fisherman is a more diffuse novel pursuing several stories—the story of Esther, daughter of an Arabian princess and Antipas, son of Herod; the romance between Esther and Voldi; the ministry of Christ and the story of Peter, the big fisherman. The crowded plot makes it difficult for the reader to feel particularly involved with any one character, although the portrayal of Peter is human and far from saintly.

The two novels achieved popularity when first published, although today, their style, both stilted and tendentious, severely limits their attraction. Although not lacking historical accuracy—the Roman world of the early Christian Church is carefully drawn—a sense of period is curiously absent from the books. Rather Douglas maintains an unrelievedly modern style in both dialogue and description. One can hear his characters speaking with American accents. Despite this approach his characters fail to achieve a sense of vitality. While Douglas's attempt to clothe the shadowy figures familiar to us from the gospels is interesting, these characters do not become memorable. The young lovers Marcellus and Diana, Esther and Voldi, fare no better. They are sympathetically portrayed but little more than stereotypes of romantic fiction—handsome, exquisitely beautiful, brave, and true. In fact Douglas's main purpose is to present a Christian thesis in the form of a novel by expanding the rather austere gospel narratives to include the human interest of a romance. The form allows him to introduce a wide range of characters, various viewpoints, and to indulge in speculative dialogue. However, the reader cannot help but feel that these novels succeed better translated to the movement and colour of the cinema screen.

The serious purpose of both *The Robe* and *The Big Fisherman* is the presentation of Christ and the Christian faith. This preoccupation underlies all Douglas's other novels—though in these it is the author's own particular thesis which is put forward. They are mostly romances and, though dated, are enjoyable, however their didactic approach, lacking the warmth and humanity present in Elizabeth Goudge's books, must have helped to prevent them from surviving.

Douglas's first novel, *Magnificent Obsession*, is very readable and introduces themes that reappear in later books—a medical setting (appropriate to Douglas's view that religion can be seen as a science); the wealthy background; the conversion of the atheist hero to a practising Christian, all within the framework of the traditional romantic novel. Several of the books share characters—*Green Light* introduces Dean Harcourt who appears in subsequent novels in the role of father confessor and inspiration, but even he remains a shadowy figure, as do the other characters who in the final analysis are still very much stereotypes of the genre.

—Ferelith Hordon

DOUGLAS, O.

Pseudonym for Anna Buchan. **Nationality:** British. **Born:** Pathhead, near Kirkcaldy, Fife, Scotland. Sister of the writer, John Buchan, *q.v.* **Education:** Hutcheson's school, Fife; private school in Edinburgh; Queen's Margaret College, Edinburgh. **Career:** teacher, Sunday school, Kirkcaldy, Fife; assisted her brother John at Band of Hope meetings. Moved to Bank House, Peebles in 1906. Visited her brother Willie in India, 1907–08. Full-time writer. **Died:** 24 November 1948.

ROMANCE AND HISTORICAL PUBLICATIONS

Novels

Olivia in India: The Adventures of a Chota Sahib. London, Hodder and Stoughton, 1913; as *Olivia*, London, Hodder and Stoughton, 1918.
The Setons. London, Hodder and Stoughton, 1917; New York, Doran, 1920.
Penny Plain. London, Hodder and Stoughton, 1920; New York, Doran, 1922.
Anna and Her Mother. London, Hodder and Stoughton, and New York, Doran, 1922.
Pink Sugar. London, Hodder and Stoughton, and New York, Doran, 1924.
The Proper Place. London, Hodder and Stoughton, and New York, Doubleday Doran, 1926.
Eliza for Common. London, Hodder and Stoughton, and New York, Doubleday Doran, 1928.
The Day of Small Things. London, Hodder and Stoughton, and New York, Doubleday Doran, 1930.
Priorsford. London, Hodder and Stoughton, and New York, Kinsey, 1932.
Taken by the Hand. London, Hodder and Stoughton, 1935.
Jane's Parlour. London, Hodder and Stoughton, 1937.
People Like Ourselves (includes *Penny Plain*; *Pink Sugar*; *Priorsford*). London, Hodder and Stoughton, 1938.
The House that Is Our Own. London, Hodder and Stoughton, 1940.

OTHER PUBLICATIONS

Other

Unforgettable, Unforgotten (autobiography). London, Hodder and Stoughton, 1945.
Farewell to Priorsford. London, Hodder and Stoughton, 1950.

*   *   *

O. Douglas was the pen-name of Anna Buchan. She wrote, in her autobiography *Unforgettable, Unforgotten* about her decision to use a pseudonym: 'John [Buchan] had given lustre to the name of Buchan which any literary efforts of mine would not be likely to add to.' John was, of course, the brilliantly successful writer and statesman who started life as the poor son from a Scottish manse and ended it as Lord Tweedsmuir, one-time governor-general of Canada. Anna, who had always hero-worshipped her older brother, saw her own career as an author as almost insignificant compared with his. She relied on him for advice, deferred to his judgement of the final work, and bemoaned the ease with which he wrote while she struggled. Nevertheless, between the wars, her gentle stories of small-town life in the Scottish Borders brought pleasure to millions.

John Buchan's tales of romantic adventure were an escape for author and reader alike: often hampered by ill health, he took vicarious pleasure in creating larger than life, physically courageous heroes who could cope with anything that life threw at them. His sister offered her readers a different kind of escapism based on the philosophy which she absorbed from their minister father: her talent was to lighten dark days for her readers by reminding them of happier, more cheerful times of the sort that they might themselves have experienced. There are no heroes or villains in O. Douglas's books, just ordinary people presented in various shades of grey with warmth, sympathy and a good deal of humour.

O. Douglas wrote about what she knew and many of her stories were pure autobiography. Of her first book, *Olivia in India*, an account of her own visit to her brother, William, who was working in the Indian Civil Service, she wrote; 'It did not strike me at the time that it was rather a daring thing to publish a book in which practically all the incidents were true and in which the characters could all recognize themselves and each other; in some cases the names were not even altered.' Complaints from those who had unwittingly figured in the story taught her to be more cautious thereafter, but many episodes are culled from her own experiences of life as a minister's daughter. Members of the Buchan family appear thinly disguised in stories such as *The Setons*, *Anna and Her Mother*, and *Eliza for Common*. Priorsford, the fictional Border town where many of Douglas's novels were set is easily identifiable as Peebles, the Tweeddale town in which she spent most of her life.

O. Douglas bemoaned her inability to create a strong plot. 'My brother John used to say that when he wrote stories he invented, but that I in my books was always remembering.' It is true that her stories are vignettes of everyday life rather than page-turning reads leading to a breath-taking denouement. Romance, although always important, is only one strand in a series of engagingly sharp observations of human nature at all levels of society. Who can fail to laugh at the pretensions of small-town social climber, Mrs Duff-Whalley or sympathize with the plight of Rebecca Brand, the lonely, unloved spinster who keeps house for her minister brother, but longs for a home of her own? A large cast of minor characters surrounds, yet does not swamp, the heroine and it is through her reactions to the people around her that she gains the reader's sympathy. Kirsty Gilmour, the heroine of *Pink Sugar* has spent an unhappy life being dragged around Europe by an egotistical stepmother. On the latter's death Kirsty returns to her Border homeland determined, at the age of 30, to enjoy herself at last. She is not rich, but, like all Douglas heroines, she has enough for her current needs. When a worldly friend hears that Kirsty's landlord is single, she observes: 'I can see the end from the beginning. Of course you will marry Colonel Home'. And, although Kirsty dismisses such speculation as the product of too much reading of 'silly novels', this is precisely what happens in a quiet, orderly way as the couple get to know one another against a background of Kirsty's decision to open her home to three lively children who are temporarily fatherless.

The Douglas heroine does not need a man to make her life complete; he is the icing on the cake, but not essential for happiness which she finds in the company of friends, children, good works and the Border countryside. Nevertheless, once identified, he is the only man for her. Nicole Rutherford, a central figure in several Douglas stories, finds love, but then her man is killed. Despite several attractive offers from compatible men she prefers to remain single and is presented making the best of her life without complaint—perhaps typical of many women of the post-World War I generation. Contrasted with the heroine's warmth and openness the Douglas hero can seem enigmatic and remote. Archie Home, in *Pink Sugar*, is a war hero who has suffered and finds it hard to unbend; Lord Bidborough, in *Penny Plain*, is distanced from the heroine, Jean Jardine, by his title and worldly possessions. Always an honourable county type with a responsible attitude to life the hero will ensure in his quiet way that his wife will lack neither material benefits nor emotional support. Yet, both hero and heroine will always put duty before personal pleasure: in *Priorsford*, Lord Bidborough, now safely married to his Jean, leaves her and their children for five months while he accompanies a wartime comrade on an overseas trip which may restore him to health; Jean entirely understands his decision.

Douglas was perhaps too modest about her talents. Her stories have dated a little (although perhaps less than those of her brother!), but her strength of characterization and her ability to capture dialogue mean that they remain eminently readable.

—Frances Whitehead

DOUGLASS, Billie.   See DELINSKY, Barbara.

DOYLE, (Sir) Arthur Conan.
Nationality: British. **Born:** Edinburgh, Scotland, 22 May 1859. **Education:** Hodder School, Lancashire, 1868–70, Stonyhurst College, Lancashire, 1870–75, and the Jesuit School, Feldkirch, Austria (editor, *Feldkirchian Gazette*), 1875–76; studied medicine at the University of Edinburgh, 1876–81, M.B. 1881, M.D. 1885. **Military Service:** senior physician at a field hospital in South Africa during the Boer War, 1899–1902: knighted, 1902. **Relations:** married 1) Louise Hawkins in 1885 (died 1906), one daughter and one son; 2) Jean Leckie in 1907, two sons and one daughter. **Career:** assistant to physician in Birmingham, 1879; ship's surgeon on a voyage to Arctic, 1880, and west coast of Africa, 1881–82; doctor, Southsea, Hampshire, 1882–90; full-time writer from 1891; stood for Parliament as Unionist candidate for Central Edinburgh, 1900, and tariff reform candidate for the Hawick Burghs, 1906. **Member:** Society for Psychical Research, 1893–1930 (resigned). **Recipient:** LL.D.: University of Edinburgh, 1905. Knight of Grace of the Order of St John of Jerusalem. **Died:** 7 July 1930.

ROMANCE AND HISTORICAL PUBLICATIONS

Novels (series: Sir Nigel Loring)

Micah Clarke. London, Longman, and New York, Harper, 1889.
The White Company (Sir Nigel). London, Smith Elder, 3 vols, 1891; New York, Lovell, 1 vol, 1891.
The Great Shadow. New York, Harper, 1892.
The Great Shadow, and Beyond the City. Bristol, Arrowsmith, 1893; New York, Ogilvie, 1894.
The Refugees. London, Longman, 3 vols, 1893; New York, Harper, 1 vol, 1893.

Rodney Stone. London, Smith Elder, and New York, Appleton, 1896.
Uncle Bernac: A Memory of the Empire. London, Smith Elder, and New York, Appleton, 1897.
Sir Nigel. London, Smith Elder, and New York, McClure, 1906.

Short Stories (series: Brigadier Gerard)

The Exploits of Brigadier Gerard. London, Newnes, and New York, Appleton, 1896.
Adventures of Gerard. London, Newnes, and New York, McClure, 1903.
The Last Galley: Impressions and Tales. London, Smith Elder, and New York, Doubleday, 1911.
Tales of Pirates and Blue Water. London, Murray, 1922; as *The Dealings of Captain Sharkey and Other Tales of Pirates*, New York, Doran, 1925.
Tales of Long Ago. London, Murray, 1922; as *The Last of the Legions and Other Tales of Long Ago*, New York, Doran, 1925.
The Conan Doyle Historical Romances. London, Murray, 2 vols, 1931–32.

OTHER PUBLICATIONS

Novels

A Study in Scarlet. London, Ward Lock, 1888; Philadelphia, Lippincott, 1890.
The Mystery of Cloomber. London, Ward and Downey, 1888; New York, Fenno, 1896(?).
The Firm of Girdlestone. London, Chatto and Windus, and New York, Lovell, 1890.
The Sign of Four. London, Blackett, 1890; New York, Collier, 1891.
The Doings of Raffles Haw. London, Cassell, and New York, Lovell, 1892.
The Parasite. London, Constable, and New York, Harper, 1894.
The Stark Munro Letters. London, Longman, and New York, Appleton, 1895.
The Tragedy of Korosko. London, Smith Elder, 1898; as *A Desert Drama*, Philadelphia, Lippincott, 1898.
A Duet, with an Occasional Chorus. London, Grant Richards, and New York, Appleton, 1899; revised edition, London, Smith Elder, 1910.
The Hound of the Baskervilles. London, Newnes, and New York, McClure, 1902.
The Lost World. London, Hodder and Stoughton, 1912; New York, Doran, 1915.
The Poison Belt. London, Hodder and Stoughton, and New York, Doran, 1913.
The Valley of Fear. New York, Doran, and London, Smith Elder, 1915.
The Land of Mist. London, Hutchinson, 1925; New York, Doran, 1926.

Short Stories

Mysteries and Adventures. London, Scott, 1889; as *The Gully of Bluemansdyke and Other Stories*, 1892.
The Captain of the Polestar and Other Tales. London, Longman, 1890; New York, Munro, 1894.
The Adventures of Sherlock Holmes. London, Newnes, and New York, Harper, 1892.
My Friend the Murderer and Other Mysteries and Adventures. New York, Lovell, 1893.
The Memoirs of Sherlock Holmes. London, Newnes, 1893; New York, Harper, 1894.

The Great Keinplatz Experiment and Other Stories. Chicago, Rand McNally, 1894.

Round the Red Lamp, Being Facts and Fancies of Medical Life. London, Methuen, and New York, Appleton, 1894.

The Man from Archangel and Other Stories. New York, Street and Smith, 1898.

Hilda Wade (completion of work by Grant Allen). London, Richards, and New York, Putnam, 1900.

The Green Flag and Other Stories of War and Sport. London, Smith Elder, and New York, McClure, 1900.

The Return of Sherlock Holmes. London, Newnes, and New York, McClure, 1905.

Round the Fire Stories. London, Smith Elder, and New York, McClure, 1908.

His Last Bow: Some Reminiscences of Sherlock Holmes. London, Murray, and New York, Doran, 1917.

Danger! and Other Stories. London, Murray, 1918; New York, Doran, 1919.

Tales of the Ring and Camp. London, Murray, 1922; as *The Croxley Master and Other Tales of the Ring and Camp*, New York, Doran, 1925.

Tales of Terror and Mystery. London, Murray, 1922; as *The Black Doctor and Other Tales of Terror and Mystery*, New York, Doran, 1925.

Tales of Twilight and the Unseen. London, Murray, 1922; as *The Great Keinplatz Experiment and Other Tales of Twilight and the Unseen*, New York, Doran, 1925.

Tales of Adventure and Medical Life. London, Murray, 1922; as *The Man from Archangel and Other Tales of Adventure*, New York, Doran, 1925.

The Case-Book of Sherlock Holmes. London, Murray, and New York, Doran, 1927.

The Maracot Deep and Other Stories. London, Murray, and New York, Doubleday, 1929.

The Field Bazaar. Privately printed, 1934; Summit, New Jersey, Pamphlet House, 1947.

The Professor Challenger Stories. London, Murray, 1952.

Great Stories, edited by John Dickson Carr. London, Murray, and New York, London House and Maxwell, 1959.

The Annotated Sherlock Holmes, edited by William S. Baring-Gould. New York, Potter, 2 vols, 1967; London, Murray, 2 vols, 1968.

The Adventures of Sherlock Holmes (facsimile of magazine stories). New York, Schocken, 1976; as *The Sherlock Holmes Illustrated Omnibus*, London, Murray-Cape, 1978.

The Best Supernatural Tales of Arthur Conan Doyle, edited by E. F. Bleiler. New York, Dover, 1979.

Sherlock Holmes: The Published Apocrypha, with others, edited by Jack Tracy. Boston, Houghton Mifflin, 1980.

The Final Adventures of Sherlock Holmes, edited by Peter Haining. London, W. H. Allen, 1981.

The Edinburgh Stories. Edinburgh, Polygon, 1981.

The Best Science Fiction of Arthur Conan Doyle, edited by Charles G. Waugh and Martin H. Greenberg. Carbondale, Southern Illinois University Press, 1981.

Uncollected Stories, edited by John Michael Gibson and Richard Lancelyn Green. London, Secker and Warburg, and New York, Doubleday, 1982.

The Best Horror Stories of Arthur Conan Doyle, edited by Martin H. Greenberg and Charles G. Waugh. Chicago, Academy, 1988.

The Supernatural Tales of Sir Arthur Conan Doyle, edited by Peter Haining. Slough, Berkshire, Foulsham, 1988.

Plays

Jane Annie; or, The Good Conduct Prize, with J.M. Barrie, music by Ernest Ford (produced London, 1893). London, Chappell, and New York, Novello Ewer, 1893.

Foreign Policy, adaptation of his story 'A Question of Diplomacy' (produced London, 1893).

Waterloo, adaptation of his story 'A Straggler of 15' (as *A Story of Waterloo*, produced Bristol, 1894; London, 1895; as *Waterloo*, produced New York, 1899). London, French, 1907; in *One-Act Plays of To-day*, 2nd series, edited by J.W. Marriott, Boston, Small Maynard, 1926.

Halves, adaptation of the story by James Payn (produced Aberdeen and London, 1899).

Sherlock Holmes, with William Gillette, adaptation of works by Doyle (produced Buffalo and New York, 1899; Liverpool and London, 1901).

A Duet (A Duologue) (produced London, 1902). London, French, 1903.

Brigadier Gerard, adaptation of his own stories (produced London and New York, 1906).

The Fires of Fate: A Modern Morality, adaptation of his novel *The Tragedy of Korosko* (produced Liverpool, London, and New York, 1909).

The House of Temperley, adaptation of his novel *Rodney Stone* (produced London, 1910).

The Pot of Caviare, adaptation of his own story (produced London, 1910).

The Speckled Band: An Adventure of Sherlock Holmes (produced London and New York, 1910). London, French, 1912.

The Crown Diamond (produced Bristol and London, 1921). Privately printed, 1958.

It's Time Something Happened. New York, Appleton, 1925.

Poetry

Songs of Action. London, Smith Elder, and New York, Doubleday, 1898.

Songs of the Road. London, Smith Elder, and New York, Doubleday, 1911.

The Guards Came Through and Other Poems. London, Murray, 1919; New York, Doran, 1920.

The Poems of Arthur Conan Doyle: Collected Edition (includes play *The Journey*). London, Murray, 1922.

Other

The Great Boer War. London, Smith Elder, and New York, McClure, 1900.

The War in South Africa: Its Cause and Conduct. London, Smith Elder, and New York, McClure, 1902.

Works (Author's Edition). London, Smith Elder, 12 vols, and New York, Appleton, 13 vols, 1903.

The Fiscal Question. Hawick, Roxburgh, Henderson, 1905.

An Incursion into Diplomacy. London, Smith Elder, 1906.

The Story of Mr George Edalji. London, Daily Telegraph, 1907.

Through the Magic Door (essays). London, Smith Elder, 1907; New York, McClure, 1908.

The Crime of the Congo. London, Hutchinson, and New York, Doubleday, 1909.

Divorce Law Reform: An Essay. London, Divorce Law Reform Union, 1909.

Sir Arthur Conan Doyle: Why He Is Now in Favour of Home Rule. London, Liberal Publication Department, 1911.

The Case of Oscar Slater. London, Hodder and Stoughton, 1912; New York, Doran, 1913.

Divorce and the Church, with Lord Hugh Cecil. London, Divorce Law Reform Union, 1913.

Great Britain and the Next War. Boston, Small Maynard, 1914.

In Quest of Truth, Being a Correspondence Between Sir Arthur Conan Doyle and Captain H. Stansbury. London, Watts, 1914.

To Arms! London, Hodder and Stoughton, 1914.

The German War. London, Hodder and Stoughton, 1914; New York, Doran, 1915.

Western Wanderings (travel in Canada). New York, Doran, 1915.

The Outlook on the War. London, Daily Chronicle, 1915.

An Appreciation of Sir John French. London, Daily Chronicle, 1916.

A Petition to the Prime Minister on Behalf of Sir Roger Casement. Privately printed, 1916.

A Visit to Three Fronts: Glimpses of British, Italian, and French Lines. London, Hodder and Stoughton, and New York, Doran, 1916.

The British Campaign in France and Flanders. London, Hodder and Stoughton, 6 vols, 1916–20; New York, Doran, 6 vols, 1916–20; revised edition, as *The British Campaigns in Europe 1914–1918*, London, Bles, 1 vol, 1928.

The New Revelation. London, Hodder and Stoughton, and New York, Doran, 1918.

The Vital Message (on spiritualism). London, Hodder and Stoughton, and New York, Doran, 1919.

Our Reply to the Cleric. London, Spiritualists' National Union, 1920.

A Public Debate on the Truth of Spiritualism, with Joseph McCabe. London, Watts, 1920; as *Debate on Spiritualism*, Girard, Kansas, Haldeman Julius, 1922.

Spiritualism and Rationalism. London, Hodder and Stoughton, 1920.

The Wanderings of a Spiritualist. London, Hodder and Stoughton, and New York, Doran, 1921.

Spiritualism: Some Straight Questions and Direct Answers. Manchester, Two Worlds, 1922.

The Case for Spirit Photography, with others. London, Hutchinson, 1922; New York, Doran, 1923.

The Coming of the Fairies. London, Hodder and Stoughton, and New York, Doran, 1922.

Three of Them: A Reminiscence. London, Murray, 1923.

Our American Adventure. London, Hodder and Stoughton, and New York, Doran, 1923.

Our Second American Adventure. London, Hodder and Stoughton, and Boston, Little Brown, 1924.

Memories and Adventures. London, Hodder and Stoughton, and Boston, Little Brown, 1924.

Psychic Experiences. London and New York, Putnam, 1925.

The Early Christian Church and Modern Spiritualism. London, Psychic Bookshop, 1925.

The History of Spiritualism. London, Cassell, 2 vols, and New York, Doran, 2 vols, 1926.

Pheneas Speaks: Direct Spirit Communications. London, Psychic Press, and New York, Doran, 1927.

What Does Spiritualism Actually Teach and Stand For? London, Psychic Bookshop, 1928.

A Word of Warning. London, Psychic Press, 1928.

An Open Letter to Those of My Generation. London, Psychic Press, 1929.

Our African Winter. London, Murray, 1929.

The Roman Catholic Church: A Rejoinder. London, Psychic Press, 1929.

The Edge of the Unknown. London, Murray, and New York, Putnam, 1930.

Works (Crowborough Edition). New York, Doubleday, 24 vols, 1930.

Strange Studies from Life, edited by Peter Ruber. New York, Candlelight Press, 1963.

Arthur Conan Doyle on Sherlock Holmes. London, Favil, 1981.

Essays on Photography, edited by John Michael Gibson and Richard Lancelyn Green. London, Secker and Warburg, 1982.

Letters to the Press: The Unknown Doyle, edited by John Michael Gibson and Richard Lancelyn Green. London, Secker and Warburg, and Iowa City, University of Iowa Press, 1986.

Editor, *D.D. Home: His Life and Mission*, by Mrs Dunglas Home. London, Kegan Paul Trench Trubner, 1921.

Editor, *The Spiritualists' Reader.* Manchester, Two Worlds, 1924.

Translator, *The Mystery of Joan of Arc*, by Léon Denis. London, Murray, 1924; New York, Dutton, 1925.

*

Film Adaptations: *The Speckled Band*, 1931; *The Hound of the Baskervilles*, 1932, 1939, 1959, 1977; *The Sign of Four*, 1932, 1983, 1988; *The Study in Scarlet*, 1933; *The Triumph of Sherlock Holmes*, 1935, from the novel *The Valley of Fear*; *Silver Blaze*, 1937; *The Adventures of Sherlock Holmes*, 1939 (*Sherlock Holmes*, 1939), 1984; *His Last Bow*, 1942; *The Pearl of Death*, 1944, from the novel *The Six Napoleons*; *House of Fear*, 1945, from the novel *Adventure of the Five Orange Pips*; *The Man with the Twisted Lip*, 1951; *The Lost World*, 1960; *The Adventures of Gerard*, 1970, from the short stories *The Exploits of Brigadier Gerard*; *Return of Sherlock Holmes*, 1988; *Tales from the Darkside: the Movie*, 1990, from the novel *Cat From Hell*.

Bibliography: *The World Bibliography of Sherlock Holmes and Dr. Watson* by Ronald Burt De Waal, Boston, New York Graphic Society, 1975; *A Bibliography of A. Conan Doyle* by Richard Lancelyn Green and John Michael Gibson, Oxford, Clarendon Press, 1983.

Manuscript Collection: Humanities Research Center, University of Texas, Austin.

Critical Studies (selection): *The Private Life of Sherlock Holmes* by Vincent Starrett, New York, Macmillan, 1933, London, Nicholson and Watson, 1934, revised edition, Chicago, University of Chicago Press, 1960, London, Allen and Unwin, 1961; *Conan Doyle: His Life and Art* by Hesketh Pearson, London, Methuen, 1943, New York, Walker, 1961; *The Life of Sir Arthur Conan Doyle* by John Dickson Carr, London, Murray, and New York, Harper, 1949; *Conan Doyle: A Biography* by Pierre Nordon, London, Murray, 1966, New York, Holt Rinehart, 1967; *Conan Doyle: A Biography of the Creator of Sherlock Holmes* by Ivor Brown, London, Hamish Hamilton, 1972; *The Adventures of Conan Doyle: The Life of the Creator of Sherlock Holmes* by Charles Higham, London, Hamish Hamilton, and New York, Norton, 1976; *The Encyclopedia Sherlockiana* by Jack Tracy, New York, Doubleday, 1977, London, New English Library, 1978; *Conan Doyle: A Biographical Solution* by Ronald Pearsall, London, Weidenfeld and Nicolson, 1977; *Sherlock Holmes and His Creator* by Trevor H. Hall, London, Duckworth, 1978, New York, St. Martin's Press, 1983; *Conan Doyle: Portrait of an Artist* by Julian Symons, London, G. Whizzard, 1979; *Sherlock Holmes: The Man and His World* by H.R.F. Keating, London, Thames and Hudson, and New York, Scribner, 1979; *The Quest for Sherlock Holmes: A Biographical Study of the Early Life of Sir Arthur Conan Doyle* by Owen Dudley Edwards, Edinburgh, Mainstream, and Totowa, New Jersey, Barnes and Noble, 1983; *Arthur Conan Doyle* by Don Richard Cox, New York, Ungar, 1985; *The Unrevealed Life of Doctor Arthur Conan Doyle: A Study in Southsea* by Geoffrey Stavert, Horndean, Hampshire, Milestone, 1987; *Arthur Conan Doyle* by Jacqueline A. Jaffe, Boston, Twayne, 1987; *The Quest for Sir Arthur Conan Doyle: Thirteen Biographers in Search of a Life* edited by Jon L. Lellenberg, Carbondale, Southern Illinois University Press, 1987.

*   *   *

Arthur Conan Doyle was a successful doctor, a war correspondent, a military historian, a champion of prisoners doubtfully convicted or too severely punished, and twice stood for Parliament. His fame rests on his creation of Sherlock Holmes but there are many people, including Winston Churchill and Doyle himself, who preferred his historical romances.

Doyle sought a greater literary standing than he thought the Holmes stories provided. His love of adventure resulted in the first, longest, and best of his romances, *Micah Clarke*. This was a gratifying and immediate success, fully repaying the two years of research Doyle put into it. The book was praised by Oscar Wilde and went to four editions in the first year. Micah Clarke, the hero, passes from childhood to participation in Monmouth's rebellion, to capture, trial by Judge Jeffreys and escape secured by the great character of the tale, the soldier of fortune Decimus Saxon. The account of the battle of Sedgemoor and the portrait of Jeffreys are the high points. It is a fine cloak and dagger adventure story for any age, even if best met for the first time as a child.

Other stories of history, chivalry, and romance followed: *The White Company*, *The Refugees*, *The Exploits of Brigadier Gerard*, *Rodney Stone*, *Uncle Bernac*, and *Sir Nigel*, all steeped in action and adventure and located in a variety of times and places.

The White Company, set in the Middle Ages, is one of the best, though you may weary of 'By Saint Paul!', 'My fair lord', 'By my hilt!', 'Pest take him!', 'In sooth', etc. Three companions, Alleyne Edricson, a clerk fresh from the Abbey at Beaulieu, Hordle John, a vast, red-headed forester, and Samkin Aylward, a war-hardened archer, join Sir Nigel to march into Spain. There are so many adventures along the way that it is nearly the end of the book before the company arrives. An engagement with a pirate ship, a jousting at which an unidentified French knight arrives at its close to challenge five Knights to meet him each with the weapon of his own choice and beats them all except Sir Nigel, an escape from a burning castle taken by a mob, desperate fighting, slaughter, chivalry, and love enliven Sir Nigel's journey.

The White Company is a sequel to *Sir Nigel* although the earlier story was written 15 years later. In *Sir Nigel*, our hero serves in France for Edward III as squire to Sir John Chandos and vows to perform three great and noble deeds before claiming the Lady Mary as his bride. The mixture of ruthless slaughter and generous chivalry is a fair reflection of the times, indeed much of the tale is taken from life and confirmed by contemporary sources. The reality of those times required little embellishment.

The Refugees is told in two halves, the first is placed in France with the Court of Louis XIV and persecution of the Huguenots, the second, set in America, is concerned with the Huguenots' flight and their struggles both with a harsh new environment and with the Indians. *Uncle Bernac* takes Louis de Laval from Kent to intrigue and danger in France where his Uncle Bernac has acquired his family estates. It contains a fine study of Napoleon. *The Exploits of Brigadier Gerard* presents that dashing, swashbuckling character, who was one of the most popular of Doyle's creations.

Rodney Stone is a story of prize-fighters, Bucks, Corinthians, wagers, and perfection in cravats. It is a grand tale in which, as in *The White Company*, an unknown challenger, Boy Jim, appears at a supper party given for the fancy and offers to take on anyone they may choose from among all the great fighters present. It also contains a grand account of a great match between Crab Wilson and the representative of Sir Charles Tregellis; the old Champion Harrison throws his hat into the ring with one minute to spare when Boy Jim, brought up by him to work in his forge, is called away on finding that he is really the heir to Lord Avon.

Doyle's historical novels certainly varied in quality but *Micah Clarke*, *The White Company*, and *Rodney Stone* stand high in any list of such romances; in their own field they equal and indeed outshine some of the works of Rider Haggard and Anthony Hope.

—David Waldron Smithers

———

DOYLE, John.   See **GRAVES, Robert.**

———

DOZIER, Zoe.   See **BROWNING, Dixie.**

———

DRAKE, Bonnie.   See **DELINSKY, Barbara.**

———

DRAKE, Connie.   See **FINCH, Carol.**

———

DRAKE, Shannon.   See **POZZESSERE, Heather Graham.**

———

DREW, Eleanor.   See **DRUMMOND, Emma.**

———

DRINKROW, John.   See **HARDWICK, Mollie.**

———

DRUMMOND, Emma.
Pseudonym for Edna Dawes. **Other Pseudonyms:** Eva Dane; Elizabeth Darrell; Eleanor Drew. Also writes as Edna Dawes. **Nationality:** British. **Address:** c/o Gollancz Ltd, 14 Henrietta Street, London WC2E 8QJ, England.

ROMANCE AND HISTORICAL PUBLICATIONS

Novels

Burn All Your Bridges (as Eleanor Drew). London, Macdonald and Jane's, 1976.
Scarlet Shadows. London, Troubadour, and New York, Dell, 1978.
The Burning Land. London, Macdonald and Jane's, and New York, Dell, 1979.
The Rice Dragon. London, Macdonald, 1980; New York, Dell, 1982.
Beyond All Frontiers. London, Gollancz, and New York, St Martin's Press, 1983.
Forget the Glory. London, Gollancz, and New York, St Martin's Press, 1985.
The Bridge of a Hundred Dragons. London, Gollancz, and New York, St Martin's Press, 1986.
A Captive Freedom. London, Gollancz, and New York, St Martin's Press, 1987.
Some Far Elusive Dawn. London, Gollancz, 1988.
That Sweet and Savage Land. London, Gollancz, 1990.
A Question of Honour. London, Gollancz, 1991.

Novels as Elizabeth Darrell (series: Sheridan Family)

The Jade Alliance. New York, Putnam, 1979; London, Hodder and Stoughton, 1980.

The Gathering Wolves. New York, Coward McCann, 1980; London, Hodder and Stoughton, 1981.
At the Going Down of the Sun (Sheridan). London, Century, 1984; New York, St Martin's Press, 1985.
And in the Morning (Sheridan). London, Century, 1986; New York, St Martin's Press, 1987.
The Flight of the Flamingo. London, Century, 1989.

Novels as Eva Dane

A Lion by the Mane. London, Macdonald and Jane's, 1975.
Shadows in the Fire. London, Macdonald and Jane's, 1975.
The Vaaldorp Diamond. London, Macdonald and Jane's, 1978.

Novels as Edna Dawes

Dearest Tiger. London, Hale, 1975.
Pink Snow. London, Hale, 1975.
A Hidden Heart of Fire. London, Hale, 1976.
Fly with My Love. London, Hale, 1978.

*   *   *

Emma Drummond chronicles the lives of individuals and societies wracked by the horrors of war. Employing settings familiar to her from her foreign travel and periods of residence abroad, she often examines tensions that occur when men and women from different cultures fall in love. Drummond is also known for her novels written under her own name, Edna Dawes, and as Elizabeth Darrell.

In *A Captive Freedom*, Vivian Veasy-Hunter, a soldier recently returned to London from the Ashanti wars, falls in love with actress Leila Dawes. Their different social backgrounds and secrets from their pasts generate numerous misunderstandings. However, their paths converge in South Africa. With death looming during the siege of Kimberley, they declare the love that has bound them for years. One theme that Drummond explores in *A Captive Freedom* is that a person can hold incorrect views of family members. Vivian comes to recognize the weakness of his mother and brother and appreciate his decisive grandfather, whom he had previously regarded as a bully.

The patriarchal grandfather, Sir Gilliard Ashleigh, in *A Question of Honour* runs the lives of his grandchildren as though they were soldiers in his command. Idolizing his grandson, Vorne, who had died a hero near Khartoum in 1885, he is certain his remaining grandsons fall short. He views artistic Vere, the elder, as little more than a vehicle for begetting heirs. Spurned by his fiancée, Vere enlists with forces bound for Khartoum. Along the way, he discovers the real Vorne had left gambling debts, mistresses, and an illegitimate child. Vere's own heroism and artistry earn him respect. Younger brother Valentine draws his grandfather's wrath for wanting to enlist in the cavalry against the Ashleigh tradition. Although the emphasis on military glory runs high, the novel reveals the personal costs exacted from military men and their families, from one generation to the next.

The costs of war figure prominently in *Some Far Elusive Dawn* set in Singapore in 1920. Two men must deal with World War I after the fighting has ended. Martin Linwood, who lost his family and suffers from shell shock, enters the civil service for a new life. Wealthy Alex Beresford, whose parents blocked his enlistment, engages in foolhardy feats to prove his manhood while waiting for his father to give him some role in the family shipping business. Both men fall in love with Thea du Lessier, an eccentric captivating novelist trying to deal with betrayal from her own past. Although echoes of military conflicts fill the pages, the battles lie more in economic, social, and psychological areas.

Beyond All Frontiers and *That Sweet and Savage Land* draw on 19th-century British military exploits in India. In the latter Elizabeth Delacourt learns of India's sweetness and savagery first-hand when she joins the husband who had left her with his family while he sought military adventure. Because her plan involves the desire to escape entanglements with an officer she had come to love in England, she is appalled to discover him at her husband's frontier post. Lovers' misunderstandings take second place to battles with the Sikhs, however.

The themes that run through the books written as Elizabeth Darrell are similar to those running through Drummond's work. For example, Drummond's *The Burning Land* and *A Captive Freedom* centre on British soldiers who fight in the Boer war as had Andrew Stanton in Darrell's *The Jade Alliance*.

The Jade Alliance begins with the aristocratic Brusilovs fleeing from Russia after the head of their family is murdered by revolutionaries in 1905. Settling in Hong Kong, they build up a thriving jade business. To Ivan Brusilov, the heir who intends to return to Russia, such involvement in trade is abhorrent. Maintaining his aristocratic outlook, he misreads the unfamiliar culture around him. This myopia brings disaster after he seduces the daughter of a powerful Hong Kong comprador.

Ivan's twin sister Nadia does not share his desire to return to Russia, especially after she falls in love with Andrew Stanton, a British agent, who had been posted to Hong Kong to quiet scandals surrounding his wife's accidental death. Andrew's attraction to Nadia threatens both his position in society and career because of British distrust of Russia.

The Gathering Wolves also concerns the relationship between the British and Russians. Set in a slightly later period, the novel deals with the turmoil following the Bolshevik Revolution. British soldiers, including engineer Paul Anderson, have been sent to aid the White Russians. Paul's task is to keep the railway line open between Murmansk and Petrograd by constructing a bridge. Assisting in the project is a contingent of White Russians commanded by Alexander (Sasha) Swarovsky, a member of the aristocracy. Tension about authority runs high between Paul and Sasha as sabotage delays construction. Paul completes the bridge only to receive orders to escape north and destroy his work to stop the Red Army's advance.

After portraying foreign conflicts, Darrell turned to her native England for the companion volumes *At the Going Down of the Sun* and *And in the Morning*, set during World Wars I and II respectively. Of all her novels, *At the Going Down of the Sun* is the most moving, with an overpowering sense of loss of an innocent, carefree life that can never be recaptured. Darrell concentrates on brothers Roland, Rex, and Christopher Sheridan, who have lived in comfort. Their father's gambling debts and suicide ruin them financially just as Europe plunges into war. Too poor to finish medical school, Roland, the eldest, stays to raise crops on the estate in support of the war effort. However, as casualties mount, community pressure forces him to enlist. Joining the medical corps, he enters the netherworld of the trenches, where he heroically saves lives until losing his own.

Rex becomes a flying ace, downing German fighter planes. As he sees scores of young men die, his disillusionment with war increases, especially when he realizes many have enlisted to emulate his exploits. Only his passion for a London actress sustains him, and their fairy-tale romance, marriage and deaths provide fodder for the tabloids.

A brilliant scholar, Christopher, the youngest, must relinquish his chance to enroll at Cambridge after he impregnates the local doctor's daughter. Forced to marry Marion to legitimize the child, 18-year-old Chris cannot face a loveless life in payment for one afternoon of passion. Fleeing wife and son, he enlists in the army, where his talent for languages leads him to intelligence work. At Gallipoli he endures such horror that his mind snaps, and he spends years struggling to remember and deal with his past. At the war's end, he and Marion agree to save their marriage for their son's sake.

Europe enters war again 20 years later. In *And in the Morning*, Christopher and Marion lead separate lives, Marion devoting herself to their son, David. He hates his father for having deserted him but idolizes his uncle Rex, a legend in the Royal Air Force, of which David is a member. His artist sister Vesta has been closer to her father although Christopher has spent long periods away from home on secret government missions.

This war draws more women, including Vesta, into active service. Both she and David encounter senseless death and destruction. His torture by the Japanese scars him but leads to reassignment in the secret service, where Chris has devoted his energy. Father and son reconcile. A brilliant artist brings Chris the romantic love that had never been part of his forced marriage.

The Flight of the Flamingo, about the British aircraft industry's development of World War II transport planes depends more on aerial acrobatics than romance to hold readers' attention. The novel's weaknesses are apparent when juxtaposed with the companion novels about the Sheridans.

Drawing on the far-flung British empire, Drummond seems unlikely to run out of subjects or settings. Her willingness to explore human relationships and her command of military history combine effectively in her tales.

—Kathy Piehl

DRYDEN, Lennox. See **STEEN, Marguerite.**

DRYDEN, Pamela. See **ST JOHN, Nicola.**

DUDLEY, Nancy. See **ELIOT, Anne.**

DUFFIELD, Anne.
Nationality: American. **Born:** Anne Tate, Orange, New Jersey, 20 November 1893. **Education:** private school in Toronto; the Sorbonne, Paris. **Relations:** married Edgar Duffield in 1922.

ROMANCE AND HISTORICAL PUBLICATIONS

Novels

Miss Mayhew and Ming Yun: A Story of East and West. New York, Stokes, 1928.
The Lacquer Couch. London, Murray, 1928.
Predestined. London, Murray, 1929.
Passionate Interlude. London, Murray, 1931.
Phantasy. London, Cassell, 1932.
Lantern-Light. London, Cassell, 1933; New York, Arcadia House, 1943.
Fleeing Shadows. London, Cassell, 1934; as *Stamboul Love*, New York, Knopf, 1934.
Flaming Felicia. London, Cassell, 1934; New York, Arcadia House, 1941.
Golden Horizons. London, Cassell, 1935; New York, Arcadia House, 1942.
Silver Peaks. London, Cassell, 1935; New York, Arcadia House, 1941.

Wild Memory. London, Cassell, 1935; as *Love's Memory*, New York, Arcadia House, 1936.
Glittering Heights. London, Cassell, 1936.
Moon over Stamboul. London, Cassell, 1936; New York, Arcadia House, 1937.
Paradise. London, Cassell, 1936; as *Brief Rapture*, New York, Arcadia House, 1938.
Bitter Rapture. London, Cassell, 1937.
Enchantment. New York, Curl, 1937.
The House on the Nile. London, Cassell, 1937; as *Gossip*, New York, Curl, 1938.
Gay Fiesta. New York, Arcadia House, 1938; as *The Dragon's Tail*, London, Cassell, 1939.
Grecian Rhapsody. London, Cassell, 1938; as *High Heaven*, 1939.
Desert Moon. London, Cassell, 1939; New York, Arcadia House, 1940.
False Star. New York, Arcadia House, 1939.
Karen's Memory. London, Cassell, and New York, Arcadia House, 1939.
Bubbling Springs. London, Cassell, and New York, Arcadia House, 1940.
The Sweeping Tide. London, Cassell, and New York, Arcadia House, 1940.
The Shadow of the Pines. London, Cassell, 1940; New York, Arcadia House, 1941.
A Bevy of Maids. London, Cassell, 1941; as *Volunteer Nurse*, New York, Arcadia House, 1942.
Old Glory. London, Cassell, 1942; New York, Arcadia House, 1943.
The Inscrutable Nymph. London, Cassell, 1942; as *This Alien Heart*, New York, Arcadia House, 1942.
Sunrise. London, Cassell, 1943; New York, Arcadia House, 1944.
Out of the Shadows. London, Cassell, 1944; as *Turn to the Sun*, New York, Arcadia House, 1944.
Taffy Came to Cairo. London, Cassell, 1944; New York, Arcadia House, 1945.
Repent at Leisure. London, Cassell, 1945; New York, Arcadia House, 1946.
Forever To-morrow. London, Cassell, 1946; New York, Arcadia House, 1951.
Song of the Mocking Bird. London, Cassell, 1946; as *The Lonely Bride*, New York, Arcadia House, 1947.
Wise Is the Heart. New York, Arcadia House, 1947.
Arkady. London, Cassell, 1948.
Dusty Dawn. London, Cassell, 1949; New York, Arcadia House, 1953.
Lovable Stranger. Philadelphia, Macrae Smith, 1949.
Beloved Enemy. London, Cassell, 1950.
Love Deferred. Philadelphia, Macrae Smith, 1951; as *Tomorrow Is Theirs*, London, Cassell, 1952.
Sugar Island. London, Cassell, 1951.
Harbour Lights. London, Cassell, 1953; New York, Arcadia House, 1954.
The Golden Summer. London, Cassell, 1954; New York, Arcadia House, 1955.
The Grand Duchess. London, Cassell, and New York, Arcadia House, 1954.
Come Back, Miranda. London, Cassell, 1955; New York, Berkley, 1974.
Fiametta. London, Cassell, 1956; New York, Arcadia House, 1958.
Castle in Spain. London, Cassell, 1958.
Violetta. London, Cassell, 1960.

*   *   *

Anne Duffield wrote from the 1920s until 1960. The appeal of her books lies in their settings which invariably involve foreign travel on ships. The romance of her world is pretty dated by modern standards and the consistency of the formula which Duffield applies means that her books will have less and less appeal. Duffield belongs to the ocean liner age, and features of that age have disappeared completely, such as the Anglo-Egyptian community, plantation colonies, and plentiful servants. The romance of being abroad and being in love abroad, however, is a very enduring theme in Duffield's books. Whereas in *Flaming Felicia* the setting is Egypt, in the novels from the 1950s the settings move closer to home. The mystery of the orient as seen in *Moon over Stamboul* gives way to a more conventional holiday setting of Spain in her novel of 1958, *Castle in Spain*. The traditional mystery settings of romantic novels give way to summer-holiday settings agreeable to conventional young girls. The very foreignness of the men the girls fall in love with, such as Don Eduardo in *Castle in Spain*, makes them that much more attractive. Mixed in with the excitement of foreign environs is an element of danger and mystery, such as unexpected encounters with snakes in *Bitter Rapture* and *Bubbling Springs*. Voodoo appears in *Sugar Island*.

The girls in Duffield's books are charmingly flirtatious, attractive, and lively. Yet they are coy about revealing their true feelings for the man they love until they are ready to fall into his arms. Indeed the progression from initial repulsion from a man (for various reasons) to eventual falling in love with him forms the main interest of these novels. Other matters, such as the second man who is also in love with the heroine and the eventual outcome of his relationship with her, are inevitably incidental. The plots are drawn out and slight. They also include rather contrived incidents, such as the use of a car crash or falls from cliffs. Duffield is good at drawing the minutiae of the social relationships of various groups in the middle ranges of society, such as West Indies planter types and the expatriate British. She is very skilful with description of the clothes her heroines and other female characters wear.

Duffield's best attribute is her ability to depict local colour in foreign lands. There is, however, something dated about this as well as the clothes. Even though her 1950s novels were reprinted as late as the 1970s, to the young reader Paris and Spain are no longer romantic in themselves.

—P.R. Meldrum

DUGGAN, Alfred (Leo).
Nationality: British. **Born:** Buenos Aires, Argentina, in 1903.
Education: Balliol College, Oxford. **Military Service:** Territorial Army in Norway, 1938–41. **Relations:** married Laura Hill in 1953; one son. **Died:** 1964.

ROMANCE AND HISTORICAL PUBLICATIONS

Novels

Knight with Armour. London, Faber, and New York, Coward McCann, 1950.
Conscience of the King. London, Faber, and New York, Coward McCann, 1951.
The Little Emperors. London, Faber, 1951; New York, Coward McCann, 1953.
The Lady for Ransom. London, Faber, and New York, Coward McCann, 1953.
Leopards and Lilies. London, Faber, and New York, Coward McCann, 1954.
God and My Right. London, Faber, 1955; as *My Life for My Sheep*, New York, Coward McCann, 1955.

Winter Quarters. London, Faber, and New York, Coward McCann, 1956.
Three's Company. London, Faber, and New York, Coward McCann, 1958.
Founding Fathers. London, Faber, 1959; as *Children of the Wolf*, New York, Coward McCann, 1959.
The Cunning of the Dove. London, Faber, and New York, Pantheon, 1960.
Family Favourites. London, Faber, 1960; New York, Pantheon, 1961.
The King of Athelrey. London, Faber, 1961; as *The Right Line of Cedric*, New York, Pantheon, 1961.
Lord Geoffrey's Fancy. London, Faber, and New York, Pantheon, 1962.
Elephants and Castles. London, Faber, 1963; as *Besieger of Cities*, New York, Pantheon, 1963.
Count Bohemond. London, Faber, 1964; New York, Pantheon, 1965.

OTHER PUBLICATIONS

Other

Thomas Becket of Canterbury. London, Faber, 1952; as *The Falcon and the Dove: A Life of Thomas Becket of Canterbury*, New York, Pantheon, 1966.
Julius Caesar: A Great Life in Brief (biography). London, Hutchinson, and New York, Knopf, 1955.
Devil's Brood: The Angevin Family. London, Faber, and New York, Coward McCann, 1957.
Historical Fiction. Cambridge, Cambridge University Press, 1957.
He Died Old: Mithradates Eupator, King of Pontus. London, Faber, 1958; as *King of Pontus: The Life of Mithradates Eupator*, New York, Coward McCann, 1959.
The Story of the Crusades 1097–1291. London, Faber, 1963; New York, Pantheon, 1964.

Other (for children)

Look at Castles. London, Hamish Hamilton, 1960; as *The Castle Book*, New York, Pantheon, 1960.
Look at Churches. London, Hamish Hamilton, 1961; as *Arches and Spires: A Short History of English Churches from Anglo-Saxon Times*, New York, Pantheon, 1962.
Growing Up in the Thirteenth Century. London, Faber, 1962; as *Growing Up in Thirteenth-Century England*, New York, Pantheon, 1962.
The Romans. Cleveland, World, 1964.
Growing Up with the Norman Conquest. London, Faber, 1965; New York, Pantheon, 1966.

* * *

Irony, wit and a strong sense of the ridiculous distinguish the works of Alfred Duggan, and may well reflect the apparent incongruities in the life of their author. An adopted Briton, of Irish-Argentinian and American parentage, he proved extremely patriotic, enlisting in a commando unit at the outbreak of war, and working at a factory bench when invalided out of the service. Displaying little promise in a hedonistic, adventurous youth, he emerged suddenly in his late forties as a leading historical novelist, writing with remarkable energy and skill over the next 14 years. The inhabitant of a century he did not pretend to understand, and for which he had scant regard, he delved passionately back into the far reaches of history to bring the spokesmen of ancient worlds to vigorous life on the page. The brief, concentrated span of his career as a writer produced 15 novels, and a further 11 factual works for adults and younger readers. Small wonder that paradox and humour should surface so frequently in his writing.

The most impressive single aspect of all Duggan's novels is their maturity of expression. Coming late to the form after a wide-ranging experience of life, he displays from the beginning a polished, assured style which blends genuine enthusiasm for his subject with a wry, amused distancing from characters and events. The precision of utterance shows most clearly in his dialogue, whose slangy modernisms serve him perfectly in defining the action and the innermost feelings of his creations. Duggan's battle scenes, although they reveal an expert eye for the minutiae of combat, are terse and understated, describing in a coldly efficient manner what is an essentially repellent activity.

His first novel, *Knight with Armour*, shows its author to be the master of a full-fledged, distinct and personal style. Through the eyes of Roger de Bodeham, the landless younger son of a Sussex knight, Duggan presents a downbeat, unromantic vision of the first crusade. Tracking his idealistic hero through battles and sieges, he reveals the constant squabbling and intrigue among the Western leaders, and the hand-to-mouth existence of Roger himself as the youngster suffers poverty, disease, and the betrayal and humiliation of his errant wife. The unpleasant underside of a holy war is convincingly rendered, heroic swordplay far outweighed by starvation, dysentery, corns and rheumatism. Duggan views the passage of events from a distance, avoiding any intrusive moral comment. When Roger, weakened by illness, falls to his death from the walls of Jerusalem, the novel closes with the laconic statement: 'The pilgrimage was accomplished'. *Conscience of the King* is even more assured, and must rank as one of its author's finest works. Here Duggan probes deep into the Dark Ages to the Saxon conquest of Britain, and the founding of the kingdom of Wessex by the legendary Cerdic, who tells his own story as a garrulous old man in his eighties. A ruthless, cynical survivor with a total lack of scruples, Cerdic recalls his desertion of home and family to join the barbarian invaders, his murder of brothers and wives, and the numerous dirty tricks that have brought him to power. Towards the end of his life, a late flicker of conscience prompts him to wonder if there might have been some truth in the Christian nonsense his brother once spouted; if so, he is doubtless destined for Hell, but 'it has been fun while it lasted'. One senses Duggan's wry smile as he describes the undeserved success of an old rogue, and the irony that links Cerdic to today's royal family. *Conscience of the King* manages to present a shadowy historical figure as a credible human being through a first-person narrative that shows the author at the height of his power.

The novels that follow attain a uniform level of excellence, and display much the same literary skills. Later works are notable for a refining of elements already present, rather than any radical departure from previous models. Duggan's main areas of interest are the Middle Ages (especially the time of the Crusades), the Roman period, and the further edge of antiquity containing the Hellenic civilization. In his writings he explores these past ages and their great concerns with a keenly dispassionate eye, probing beneath the avowed ideals of his characters to their less laudable motives. A staunch Catholic whose faith was genuine and deep, Duggan identifies strongly with the pledges of Crusaders and early Christian kings, but is also aware of human frailty; more than most authors, he marks the point at which the desire to liberate fellow-Christians is undermined by pride, ambition and greed. His portrayal of the warring complexities within his subjects is readily shown in such works as *God and My Right*, where the power struggle between church and state is personalized in the figures of Henry II and Thomas à Becket. Nor are his choices confined to conventionally heroic models. Roger, in *Knight with Armour*, is the first of several well-meaning but ineffectual losers whose fortunes the author follows with the

same blend of sympathy and detachment. Felix, the staid civil servant who finds himself dragged into a web of murder and intrigue in *The Little Emperors*, and the ill-fated Norman adventurer Roussel de Balliol in *The Lady for Ransom*, are men of higher position, but of similar ineptitude, whose efforts appear doomed to failure. At the other end of the spectrum, Duggan examines those who have grown so powerful that they regard themselves as above the law. In *Elephants and Castles* he traces the astonishing career of Demetrius Poliorcetes, the brilliant general who flouted the canons of Hellenic religion by declaring that 'there are no more gods', while by a supreme irony being worshipped as Saviour God in his own lifetime. *Elephants and Castles* is a superbly achieved portrait of an unusual individual, and contains some of Duggan's sharpest exchanges of dialogue between the characters. Although men predominate in his work, his women are far from being overshadowed by them; Phila, the wife of Demetrius, more than holds her own in their many verbal duels, and elsewhere, the formidable, comic Lady Matilda of *The Lady for Ransom*, and the unlucky, twice-married Margaret Fitz-Gerold, of *Leopards and Lilies*, demand the reader's attention, as much as their spouses. Perhaps the most engaging of Duggan's heroines is the lovely Melisande, wife of the narrator of *Lord Geoffrey's Fancy*, who, in what is arguably the author's most imaginative work of fiction, takes the measure of the handsome, heroic but ultimately unreliable Sir Geoffrey. Melisande alone is able to see through the bravery and chivalrous charm of the paragon and, while still liking him, to make the perceptive comment that: 'He will never love a lady. He has no love to spare, for he loves himself only. Or rather, not exactly himself, but the image of the best knight in all Romanie that walks about Carytena blazoned with his arms'. Lord Geoffrey, like Demetrius, is deluded by his vision of himself into thinking that the rules do not apply to him, and thus he is able to pose as the knightly ideal while betraying his lord and his comrades and eloping with another man's wife. His tragic end, by drinking tainted water, makes a sad mockery of his gallant pretensions, but it is difficult not to feel sorry for him. After all, he has fooled himself quite as much as anyone else.

The two most sympathetic 'heroes' of Duggan's novels are surely his namesake Alfred the Great, and Edward the Confessor, given keen but sensitive treatment in *The King of Athelney*, and *The Cunning of the Dove*. Alfred, the pious soldier-scholar, is shown as a noble but flawed human being, capable of personal and local prejudice as well as the better-known high-minded traits; Edward emerges as a far stronger personality than the saintly milksop familiar to most readers, ultimately defying the hardbitten lords around him by guile, and force of character rather than military might. The most idealistic of Duggan's historical re-creations, the Saxon kings, impress as truly exceptional men, the more so for their evident shortcomings.

This said, it is to the period of the Crusades that Duggan returns most often, and his fascination with the forays and campaigns of the Western lords in the kingdoms of the East is the basis of many of his best novels. *Knight with Armour* began the cycle, and *Count Bohemund* closes it, the first crusade once more the theme for its author's final work, this time seen through the eyes of Bohemund of Antioch, the greatest fighter of the age. Duggan displays all the old strengths refined to near-perfection, the dialogue crisp and assured, the action scenes neatly handled, the subtle examination of character and motive as purposeful as ever. *Count Bohemund* is a fitting end to his impressive corpus of novels, outdone only by *Lord Geoffrey's Fancy*, where Duggan's inspired picture of the mediaeval world finds its most heightened form.

Duggan's simple apparently effortless style is in fact a marvel of economical precision and strength. A novelist of considerable psychological depth, he reveals the natures of his characters through their own words. His exploration is keen and unsparing, often sardonic, but if his tone lacks sentiment it also lacks any hint of malice.

One feels that Duggan rather likes his creations, regarding their failures with a rueful, half-amused tolerance, and his work evokes a similar response from his readers. Although his death undoubtedly robbed the modern historical novel of one of its greatest talents, the sustained excellence of the work he had already accomplished is more than enough to confirm his position at the forefront of the genre.

—Geoffrey Sadler

---

du MAURIER, Daphne.
Nationality: British. **Born:** London, 13 May 1907. Daughter of the actor/manager Sir Gerald du Maurier; granddaughter of the writer George du Maurier. **Education:** privately and in Paris. **Relations:** married Lieutenant-General Sir Frederick Browning in 1932 (died 1965); two daughters and one son. **Recipient:** Mystery Writers of America Grand Master award, 1977. Fellow, Royal Society of Literature, 1952. DBE (Dame Commander, Order of the British Empire), 1969. **Died:** 19 April 1989.

ROMANCE AND HISTORICAL PUBLICATIONS

Novels

The Loving Spirit. London, Heinemann, and New York, Doubleday, 1931.
I'll Never Be Young Again. London, Heinemann, and New York, Doubleday, 1932.
The Progress of Julius. London, Heinemann, and New York, Doubleday, 1933.
Jamaica Inn. London, Gollancz, and New York, Doubleday, 1936.
Rebecca. London, Gollancz, and New York, Doubleday, 1938.
Frenchman's Creek. London, Gollancz, 1941; New York, Doubleday, 1942.
Hungry Hill. London, Gollancz, and New York, Doubleday, 1943.
The King's General. London, Gollancz, and New York, Doubleday, 1946.
The Parasites. London, Gollancz, 1949; New York, Doubleday, 1950.
My Cousin Rachel. London, Gollancz, 1951; New York, Doubleday, 1952.
Mary Anne. London, Gollancz, and New York, Doubleday, 1954.
The Scapegoat. London, Gollancz, and New York, Doubleday, 1957.
Castle Dor, by Arthur Quiller-Couch, completed by du Maurier. London, Dent, and New York, Doubleday, 1962.
The Glass-Blowers. London, Gollancz, and New York, Doubleday, 1963.
The Flight of the Falcon. London, Gollancz, and New York, Doubleday, 1965.
The House on the Strand. London, Gollancz, and New York, Doubleday, 1969.
Rule Britannia. London, Gollancz, 1972; New York, Doubleday, 1973.

Short Stories

Happy Christmas (story). New York, Doubleday 1940; London, Todd, 1943.
Come Wind, Come Weather. London, Heinemann, 1940; New York, Doubleday, 1941.
Nothing Hurts for Long, and Escort. London, Todd, 1943.
Consider the Lilies (story). London, Todd, 1943.
Spring Picture (story). London, Todd, 1944.
Leading Lady (story). London, Vallancey Press, 1945.
London and Paris (two stories). London, Vallancey Press, 1945.
The Apple Tree: A Short Novel, and Some Stories. London, Gollancz, 1952; as *Kiss Me Again, Stranger: A Collection of Eight Stories, Long and Short*, New York, Doubleday, 1953; as *The Birds and Other Stories*, London, Penguin, 1968.
Early Stories. London, Todd, 1954.
The Breaking Point: Eight Stories. London, Gollancz, and New York, Doubleday, 1959; as *The Blue Lenses and Other Stories*, London, Penguin, 1970.
The Treasury of du Maurier Short Stories. London, Gollancz, 1960.
The Lover and Other Stories. London, Ace, 1961.
Not after Midnight and Other Stories. London, Gollancz, 1971; as *Don't Look Now*, New York, Doubleday, 1971.
Echoes from the Macabre: Selected Stories. London, Gollancz, 1976; New York, Doubleday, 1977.
The Rendezvous and Other Stories. London, Gollancz, 1980.
Classics of the Macabre. London, Gollancz, and New York, Doubleday, 1987.

OTHER PUBLICATIONS

Plays

Rebecca, adaptation of her own novel (produced Manchester and London, 1940; New York, 1945). London, Gollancz, 1940; New York, Dramatists Play Service, 1943.
The Years Between (produced Manchester, 1944; London, 1945). London, Gollancz, 1945; New York, Doubleday, 1946.
September Tide (produced Oxford and London, 1948). London, Gollancz, 1949; New York, Doubleday, 1950.

Screenplay: *Hungry Hill*, with Terence Young and Francis Crowdry, 1947.

Television Play: *The Breakthrough*, 1976.

Other

Gerald: A Portrait (on Gerald du Maurier). London, Gollancz, 1934; New York, Doubleday, 1935.
The du Mauriers. London, Gollancz, and New York, Doubleday, 1937.
The Infernal World of Branwell Brontë. London, Gollancz, 1960; New York, Doubleday, 1961.
Vanishing Cornwall, photographs of Christian Browning. London, Gollancz, and New York, Doubleday, 1967.
Golden Lads: Sir Francis Bacon, Anthony Bacon and Their Friends. London, Gollancz, and New York, Doubleday, 1975.
The Winding Stair: Francis Bacon, His Rise and Fall. London, Gollancz, 1976; New York, Doubleday, 1977.
Growing Pains: The Shaping of a Writer (autobiography). London, Gollancz, 1977; as *Myself When Young*, New York, Doubleday, 1977.
The Rebecca Notebook and Other Memories (includes short stories). New York, Doubleday, 1980; London, Gollancz, 1981.
Enchanted Cornwall: Her Pictorial Memoir, edited by Piers Dudgeon. London, Joseph, 1990.
Daphne Du Maurier: Letters from Menabilly, edited by Oriel Malett, London, Orion, 1993.

Editor, *The Young George du Maurier: A Selection of His Letters 1860–1867*. London, Davies, 1951; New York, Doubleday, 1952.
Editor, *Best Stories*, by Phyllis Bottome. London, Faber, 1963.

*

Film Adaptations: *Jamaica Inn*, 1939, 1983; *Rebecca*, 1940; *Frenchman's Creek*, 1944; *The Years Between*, 1946; *The Hungry Hill*, 1947; *My Cousin Rachel*, 1952; *The Scapegoat*, 1959; *The Birds*, 1963; *Don't Look Now*, 1973.

Critical Studies: *The Private World of Daphne Du Maurier* by Martyn Shallcross, London, Robson, 1991, New York and St Martin's Press, 1992; *Daphne: The Life of Daphne Du Maurier* by Judith Cook, London, Bantam, 1991; *Daphne Du Maurier* by Margaret Forster, London, Chatto and Windus, 1993.

*   *   *

Daphne du Maurier was obsessed with the past. She intensively researched the lives of Francis and Anthony Bacon, the history of Cornwall, the Regency Period, and 19th-century France and England. Above all, however, she was obsessed with her own family history, which she chronicled in *Gerald: A Portrait*, the biography of her father, the famous actor; *The du Mauriers*, a study of her family; *The Glass-Blowers*, a novel based upon the lives of her du Maurier ancestors; and *Growing Pains*, an autobiography that ignores nearly 50 years of her life in favour of the joyful and more romantic period of her uninhibited youth. Du Maurier can best be understood in terms of her remarkable and paradoxical family, the ghosts which haunted and shaped her life and fiction.

While her contemporaries were dealing critically in their fiction with such subjects as the war, alienation, religion, poverty, Marxism, psychology, and art, and experimenting with new techniques, such as stream of consciousness, du Maurier committed herself to writing 'old fashioned' novels with straightforward narratives that appealed to a conventional audience's love of fantasy, adventure, sexuality, and mystery. At an early age she recognized that her principal readership was comprised of women, and she cultivated their loyal following through several decades by embodying their desires and dreams in her novels and short stories.

Although best remembered today for her novel *Rebecca*, which was made into an Oscar winning film by Alfred Hitchcock, and her short story 'The Birds', also made into a film by Hitchcock, du Maurier wrote numerous best-selling novels, including *The Progress of Julius, Jamaica Inn, Frenchman's Creek, The King's General, The Parasites, My Cousin Rachel, Mary Anne, The Scapegoat*, and *The House on the Strand*. Most of these novels take the form of romantic melodramas decked out with smugglers, pirates, mysterious houses, and strong-willed, independent heroines.

In some of her novels, however, du Maurier goes beyond the techniques of the formulaic romance to achieve a powerful psychological realism reflecting her intense feelings about her father and, to a lesser degree, about her mother. The vision that underlies *The Progress of Julius, Rebecca*, and *The Parasites* is that of an author overwhelmed by her obsession with her father's authoritarian presence. In *The Progress of Julius* and *The Parasites* she introduces the image of a domineering but deadly father and the daring subject of incest. In *Rebecca*, on the other hand, du Maurier fuses psychological realism with a sophisticated version of the Cinderella story. The nameless heroine of her novel has been saved from a life of drudgery and marries a handsome, wealthy aristocrat, but unlike the prince in 'Cinderella', Maxim de Winter is old enough to be the narrator's father. The narrator, thus, must do battle with the Other Woman—the dead Rebecca and her witch-like surrogate, Mrs Danvers—to win the love of her husband and father figure. The fantasy of this novel is fulfilled when Maxim confesses to the narrator that he never loved Rebecca—indeed, he hated her, a confession that allows the narrator to emerge triumphantly from the Oedipal triangle.

The Freudian subtext of Rebecca is embodied in a form that represents the first major gothic romance in the twentieth century and perhaps the finest written to this day. The novel contains most of the trappings of the typical gothic romance: a mysterious and haunted mansion (Manderley/Menabilly), violence, murder, a sinister villain, sexual passion, a spectacular fire, brooding landscapes, and a version of the mad woman in the attic. Du Maurier's novel, however, is much more than a simple thriller or mystery. It is a profound and fascinating study of an obsessive personality, of sexual dominance, of human identity, and of the liberation of the hidden self. The real power of the novel derives from du Maurier's obsession with her charismatic father and her resolution of that obsession through the fantasy structure of the story.

Du Maurier's last five novels, *The Scapegoat, The Glass-Blowers, The Flight of the Falcon, The House on the Strand*, and *Rule Britannia*, reveal her growing interest in psychology and the question of identity. Each of these works takes a different perspective on psychodynamics as du Maurier explores the theme of the double in *The Scapegoat*, the shaping influence of family history upon one's identity in *The Glass-Blowers*, the nature of the demonic self in *The Flight of the Falcon*, the influence of mind-altering drugs upon one's sense of reality in *The House on the Strand*, and the importance of family, regional, and national identity in *Rule Britannia*.

Despite her limitations as a stylist, du Maurier is a master storyteller who knows how to manipulate female fantasies. She creates in her fiction a world that is simple, romantic, usually unambiguous, adventuresome, mysterious, dangerous, erotic, picturesque, and emotionally satisfying. It is a world that sharply contrasts with the mundane realities of ordinary existence, and it is a world that does not require the reader to suffer the pains of introspection and analysis.

Rebecca, however, stands out among her novels as a landmark in the development of the modern gothic romance. Du Maurier has breathed new life into the old forms of the gothic novel to come up with a classic tale of the Other Woman. Millions of women have identified with the plain, nameless narrator of *Rebecca*, a woman who defines her personality by overcoming the mother figure of Rebecca to win the lasting love of her father-lover.

Few writers have created more magical and mysterious places than Jamaica Inn and Manderley, buildings invested with a rich and brooding character that gives them memorable lives of their own. Although du Maurier does not subscribe to a conventional religious belief, she has transformed the places she inhabited, such as Jamaica Inn and Menabilly, into gothic paradises, sacred structures of the imagination shaped by the elusive and erotic figure of her father and by the violent and mysterious history of Cornwall.

—Richard Kelly

———

DUNNETT, Dorothy.
Also writes as Dorothy Halliday. **Nationality:** British. **Born:** Dorothy Halliday, Dunfermline, Fife, 25 August 1923. **Education:** James Gillespie's High School, Edinburgh; Edinburgh College of Art; Glasgow School of Art. **Relations:** married Alastair M. Dunnett in 1946; two sons. **Career:** assistant press officer, Scottish government departments, Edinburgh, 1940–46; member of the Board of Trade Scottish Economic Research Department, Glasgow, 1946–55. Since 1950 professional portrait painter; since 1979 non-executive director, Scottish Television plc, Edinburgh; trustee, National Library of Scotland, 1979–92. Since 1988, director, Edinburgh Book Festival, Edinburgh. **Recipient:** Scottish Arts Council award, 1976, for *Checkmate*; award for literature, St Andrews Presbyterian College, Laurinburg, 1993. OBE (Officer of the Order of the British Empire) 1992. Fellow, Royal Society of Arts, 1986.

Agent: Curtis Brown, 162–168 Regent Street, London W1R 5TB, England. **Address:** 87 Colinton Road, Edinburgh EH10 5DF, Scotland.

ROMANCE AND HISTORICAL PUBLICATIONS

Novels (series: Johnson Johnson—Dolly books prior to *Bird of Paradise* published as Dorothy Halliday in UK; Lymond; Niccolò)

The Game of Kings (Lymond). New York, Putnam, 1961; London, Cassell, 1962.

Queens' Play (Lymond). London, Cassell, and New York, Putnam, 1964.

The Disorderly Knights (Lymond). London, Cassell, and New York, Putnam, 1966.

Johnson Johnson series:

> *Dolly and the Singing Bird*. London, Cassell, 1968; as *The Photogenic Soprano*, Boston, Houghton Mifflin, 1968; as *Rum Affair* (as Dorothy Dunnett) London, Arrow, 1968.
> *Dolly and the Cookie Bird*. London, Cassell, 1970; as *Murder in the Round*, Boston, Houghton Mifflin, 1970; as *Ibiza Surprise* (as Dorothy Dunnett), London, Arrow, 1991.
> *Dolly and the Doctor Bird*. London, Cassell, 1971; as *Match for a Murderer*, Boston, Houghton Mifflin, 1971; as *Operation Nassau* (as Dorothy Dunnett), London, Arrow, 1993.
> *Dolly and the Starry Bird*. London, Cassell, 1973; as *Murder in Focus*, Boston, Houghton Mifflin, 1973; as *Roman Nights* (as Dorothy Dunnett), London, Arrow, 1991.
> *Dolly and the Nanny Bird*. London, Joseph, 1976; New York, Knopf, 1982; as *Split Code* (as Dorothy Dunnett), London, Arrow, 1991.
> *Dolly and the Bird of Paradise*. London, Joseph, 1983; New York, Knopf, 1984; as *Tropical Issue*, London, Arrow, 1991.
> *Moroccan Traffic*. London, Chatto and Windus, 1991; as *Take a Fax to the Kasbah*, London, Arrow, 1992; New York, Harcourt Brace Jovanovich, 1993.

Pawn in Frankincense (Lymond). London, Cassell, and New York, Putnam, 1969.

The Ringed Castle (Lymond). London, Cassell, 1971; New York, Putnam, 1972.

Checkmate (Lymond). London, Cassell, and New York, Putnam, 1975.

King Hereafter. London, Joseph, and New York, Knopf, 1982.

Niccolò Rising. London, Joseph, and New York, Knopf, 1986.

The Spring of the Ram (Niccolò). London, Joseph 1987; New York, Knopf, 1988.

Race of Scorpions (Niccolò). London, Joseph, 1989; New York, Knopf, 1990.

Scales of Gold (Niccolò). London, Joseph, 1991; New York, Knopf, 1992.

The Unicorn Hunt (Niccolò). London, Joseph, 1993.

OTHER PUBLICATIONS

Other

The Scottish Highlands, with Alastair M. Dunnett, photographs by David Paterson. Edinburgh, Mainstream, 1988.

*

Bibliography: in *Book and Magazine Collector 53* (London), August 1988.

*   *   *

Dorothy Dunnett's historical novels were once described by a reviewer as 'a stylish blend of high romance and high camp'. This is true, but there is more than this to them: they are long, complex books, full of action and violence, wit and surprises. Her descriptions are always vivid and her period knowledge is vast, but above all her characters are alive and memorable: even the minor characters are real enough to step off the page.

King Hereafter, the 11th-century tale of Thorfinn, Earl of Orkney who was also known as Macbeth, stands apart from her series books. Thorfinn and his wife are totally unlike their counterparts in Shakespeare's play, but probably closer to reality. Thorfinn is a difficult man—courageous and skilful, a wonderful lover, a Viking sea-rover as well as a prince who, in the end, sacrifices himself for his people. The story is told in stark, saga-like language but this doom-laden book is less appealing than her others.

The six-book Lymond stories chart ten years in the life of Francis Crawford of Lymond, Comte de Sevigny, one of the most attractive heroes in all historical fiction. He has a talent for getting into scrapes and out again, he is a leader of men and a charmer of women: 'a man of wit and crooked felicities, born to luxury and heir to a fortune'. There is a mystery about his parentage which tantalizes the reader throughout the series until it is finally solved by Philippa Somerville in *Checkmate*.

Philippa is an unlikely heroine, starting off in *The Game of Kings* as a stolid child who hates Lymond. After a country upbringing in Northumberland, because of her concern for Lymond's bastard child, she travels to the Middle East in *Pawn in Frankincense* because of her concern for Lymond's illegitimate baby caught up in a feud. There, Philippa has the harem of Suleiman the Magnificent as her finishing school and is married to Lymond for convention's sake. Lymond falls in love with her in *Ringed Castle* but goes to Russia to avoid being near her, as he is sure that he will be bad for her. In *Checkmate* Philippa and Lymond acknowledge their love for each other just when she can't bear him to touch her because of a hideous experience during her search for his origins. When all seems lost, everything is resolved and it ends happily.

As the Lymond books take their hero travelling from Scotland to the courts of France, Russia and Istanbul in the 16th century, the Niccolò books take their hero trading from Bruges to Italy, Trebizond, Cyprus, and Africa in the 15th century. Unlike Lymond, born with a silver spoon in his mouth, Claes vander Poel (also known as Nicholas and Niccolò) is an apprentice, his hands blue with dye. He is 'good natured, randy and innocent'. He is also an accomplished mimic and clown, clever at making models and toys, brilliant at figures and loyal to his employer, Marian de Charretty, who took him in aged ten, the bastard of a distant relative.

In *Niccolò Rising* Claes falls foul of an arrogant Scottish nobleman, Simon St Pol of Kilmarren who, although he was married to the boy's mother, denies Claes is his son. A feud between Nicholas and the St Pol family runs through the books, aggravated by Claes taking the virginity of Katelina van Borselen at her request. She marries Simon and bears Nicholas a son allowing Simon to think that it is his.

During *Niccolò Rising* our hero travels and acquires martial skills and sophistication. On his return to Bruges he faces malice, jealousy, and danger but obtains power and status by marrying Marian de Charetty. She sends him to Trebizond, in *The Spring of the Ram*, where he sets up as a merchant adventurer and charts his adventures among the Byzantine Greeks. He learns painful lessons about himself and his relationships with others. After many adventures he returns to Europe to find himself a widower and a rich man. He founds the Bank of Niccolò in Venice.

Race of Scorpions takes him to Cyprus where he deals in sugar and is courted for his Machiavellian mind and his mercenary company. Katelina is there and works against him only to be reconciled on her deathbed. In *Scales of Gold*, he goes to Africa to find gold to recoup the fortunes of his bank accompanied by Gelis, Katelina's vindictive sister. After amazing adventures and vicissitudes, Nicholas and Gelis are married and the book ends on their wedding night with Gelis revealing that to avenge her sister she has become pregnant by Simon.

What next? We are more than half way through the eight-book series. Should Dunnett fail to complete it, we are told a paper locked in her publisher's safe will unravel all Nicholas's mysteries.

Although Nicholas and Lymond come from very different backgrounds, there are similarities. Both of them are brilliant leaders but have an arrogance that makes them disliked and at times mistrusted; they develop as the books progress through meeting brutal challenges and having to make difficult choices. Both of them are accomplished lovers, both are pitted against suave villains who are cruel, ruthless and have venomous tongues; both have mysteries in their lineage and both have to cope with other men's children—cuckoos in their nests. Several times both heroes are brought close to death, and several of their friends die simply because of their association with Lymond and Niccolò.

These elegantly crafted books are a joy to read and so intricately plotted that they can be read and reread with undiminished pleasure.

—Pamela Cleaver

———

DWIGHT, Allan.   See ELIOT, Anne.

———

DWYER-JOYCE, Alice.
Nationality: British. **Born:** Alice Louise Myles, in Birr, Offaly, Ireland, 7 September 1913. **Education:** Birr Model School; Alexandra College, Dublin; Royal College of Surgeons, Dublin, medical degree 1936; Richmond Hospital, Dublin. **Relations:** married Robert Dwyer-Joyce in 1936; one son. **Career:** in general medical practice with her husband, 1936–78, Histon, Cambridgeshire; medical officer, Midfield Children's Home, Oakington, Cambridgeshire, for 20 years. **Died:** 9 February 1986.

ROMANCE AND HISTORICAL PUBLICATIONS

Novels (series: Dr Esmond Ross)

Price of Inheritance. London, Hale, 1963.
The Silent Lady. London, Hale, 1964.
Dr Ross of Harton. London, Hale, 1966.
The Story of Doctor Esmond Ross. London, Hale, 1967.
Verdict on Doctor Esmond Ross. London, Hale, 1968.
Dial Emergency for Dr Ross. London, Hale, 1969.
Don't Cage Me Wild. London, Hale, 1970.
For I Have Lived Today. London, Hale, 1971.
Message for Doctor Ross. London, Hale, 1971.
Cry the Soft Rain. London, Hale, 1972; New York, St Martin's Press, 1974.
Reach for the Shadows. London, Hale, 1972; New York, St Martin's Press, 1973.
The Rainbow Glass. London, Hale, and New York, St Martin's Press, 1973.
The Brass Islands. London, Hale, 1974.
Prescription for Melissa. London, Hale, 1974.
The Moonlit Way. London, Hale, and New York, St Martin's Press, 1974.
The Strolling Players. London, Hale, and New York, St Martin's Press, 1975.

The Diamond Cage. London, Hale, and New York, St Martin's Press, 1976.
The Master of Jethart. London, Hale, and New York, St Martin's Press, 1976.
The Gingerbread House. London, Hale, and New York, St Martin's Press, 1977.
The Banshee Tide. London, Hale, 1977.
The Storm of Wrath. London, Hale, 1977; New York, St Martin's Press, 1978.
The Glitter-Dust. London, Hale, and New York, St Martin's Press, 1978.
Lachlan's Woman. London, Hale, and New York, St Martin's Press, 1979.
Danny Boy. London, Hale, 1979.
The Swiftest Eagle. London, Hale, and New York, St Martin's Press, 1979.
The House of Jackdaws. London, Hale, and New York, St Martin's Press, 1980.
The Chieftain. London, Hale, 1980.
The Penny Box. London, Hale, and New York, St Martin's Press, 1980.
The Glass Heiress. London, Hale, 1981; New York, St Martin's Press, 1982.
The Cornelian Strand. London, Hale, 1982.
The Unwinding Corner. London, Hale, and New York, St Martin's Press, 1983.
Gibbet Fen. London, Hale, and New York, St Martin's Press, 1984.

*

Alice Dwyer-Joyce commented (1982):
I started to write in about 1960, in the midst of a life full of activity, and I was glad of it in 1978 when I got severe arthritis. The authorship has been my escape from the ferocity of disablement.

*   *   *

Alice Dwyer-Joyce brings the stuff of dreams to an everyday world. A touch of magic gilds the remote island communities of her novels, with their ruined castles and half-remembered ancestral ghosts. Elements of folklore and fairytale seem always present—whether the wicked stepmother of *The Gingerbread House*, or the hero of princely lineage who appears in so many of her works. The line between good and evil is sharply drawn—heroes are perfect and unflawed, villains irredeemably wicked. The morality, as in most fairy tales, is Old Testament, with such crimes as adultery and deception punished by death and the wrongdoers irrevocably damned. The shadow of old wrongs remains to haunt later generations, and her books abound with talismans to ward off the unappeased spirits—'The Penny Box', the waterfall in *The Rainbow Glass*, the woolly monkey in *The Master of Jethart*.

A natural prose poet, Dwyer-Joyce is also a qualified doctor, and in many of her works the roles of artist and healer are given an equal emphasis. The early 'Dr Ross' novels which helped to establish her popularity made effective use of her medical knowledge, and the hospital environment serves as background for the novels featuring Dr Catriona Chisholm—*For I Have Lived Today* and *Prescription for Melissa*. The missionary figure of the doctor martyred in Third World revolution is also a recurrent theme, notably in *Lachlan's Woman*, whose story includes a princely hero betrayed by a faithless wife. There are other works with exotic locations, for example *The Swiftest Eagle*, where action moves from Malaya to Cambodia and its exodus of refugees. Always, though, the author returns to those bleak coastal settings—Ireland or the Western Isles—where her atmosphere is strongest, and her Celtic gifts as a storyteller are allowed their fullest expression. Such works as *The Banshee Tide*, with its picture of rural Ireland, or *The Brass Islands* are typical, the highly poeticized speech of the characters in keeping with the landscape they inhabit. *The Chieftain* follows an Irish-American tycoon in search of his roots, evoked by the diary of an ancestor in the 1850s, and *The Glass Heiress* explores the theme of a ghostly past. Essentially her message remains the same: the determined heroine struggling against evil or circumstance, fulfilled at last by the love of the noble prince-hero come out of the West, who will help her rebuild the fallen castle and bring back the greatness to their house.

—Geoffrey Sadler

DYMOKE, Juliet.
Pseudonym for Juliet Dymoke de Schanschieff. **Nationality:** British. **Born:** Enfield, Middlesex, 28 June 1919. **Education:** Chantry Mount School. **Relations:** married Hugo de Schanschieff in 1942; one daughter. **Career:** worked for the Bank of England, London, 1937–42, and for the Canadian army medical records department, London, 1942–44; script reader, Ealing Film Studios, Paramount Films, and Samuel Bronston Productions, 1950–63. Lives near Ashdown Forest, Sussex. **Address:** c/o Severn House Publishers, 35 Manor Road, Wallington, Surrey SM6 0BW, England.

ROMANCE AND HISTORICAL PUBLICATIONS

Novels (series: French Revolution; Henry I; Hollanders; Plantagenets)

The Orange Sash. London, Jarrolds, 1958.
Born for Victory. London, Jarrolds, 1960.
Treason in November. London, Jarrolds, 1961.
Bend Sinister. London, Jarrolds, 1962.
The Cloisterman. London, Dobson, 1969.
Henry I:
    Of the Ring of Earls. London, Dobson, 1970.
    Henry of the High Rock. London, Dobson, 1971.
    The Lion's Legacy. London, Dobson, 1974.
Serpent in Eden. London, Wingate, 1973.
Shadows on a Throne. London, Wingate, 1976.
Plantagenet:
    A Pride of Kings. London, Dobson, 1978.
    The Royal Griffin. London, Dobson, 1978; New York, Ace, 1980.
    Lady of the Garter. London, Dobson, 1979; New York, Ace, 1980.
    The Lion of Mortimer. London, Dobson, 1979; New York, Ace, 1980.
    The Lord of Greenwich. London, Dobson, 1980.
    The Sun in Splendour. London, Dobson, 1980.
French Revolution:
    The White Cockade. London, Dobson, 1979.
    The Queen's Diamond. London, Severn House, 1983.
    March to Corunna. London, Severn House, 1985.
    Two Flags for France. London, Severn House, 1986.
A Kind of Warfare. London, Dobson, 1981.
A Border Knight. London, Severn House, 1987.
Ride to Glencoe. London, Kimber, 1989.
Portrait of Jenny. London, Piatkus, 1990.
Hollanders House (Hollanders). London, Piatkus, 1991.
Cry of the Peacock (Hollanders). London, Piatkus, 1992.
Winter's Daughter (Hollanders). London, Piatkus, 1993.

OTHER PUBLICATIONS

Other (for children)

The Sons of the Tribune: An Adventure on the Roman Wall. London, Arnold, 1956.
London in the 18th Century. London, Longman, 1958.
Prisoner of Rome. London, Dobson, 1975.
Aboard the Mary Rose. London, Severn House, 1985.
The Spanish Boy (sequel to *Aboard the Mary Rose*). London, Severn House, 1987.

*

Juliet Dymoke comments:
My work as an historical novelist naturally includes a great deal of research, and this perhaps is the most exacting as well as a very pleasurable part of my work. I write mainly about England as I know and love England, and I try not to start on a description of a place I do not know without making every effort to see it—it is so easy to be caught out! I am passionately interested in history, European as well as English, but it is the past of these islands that interests me most, and I am fascinated by the lives of our forebears, and how they are similar to and dissimilar from our own. I can trace my own ancestry back to the Norman Conquest and perhaps this was the spur, or the inheritance, that set me on my career. I hope through my work to reach a large number of people, to interest them in the history that has made this country, perhaps in some way to influence them for good—as I myself was influenced by the historical writers I once read.

*   *   *

Juliet Dymoke's works of historical fiction range over several centuries of mainly English history, though she occasionally ventures over the border to Scotland or over the Channel to France. Her style is characterized by both simplicity and historical authenticity. Romance features strongly, often driving forward the historical action; in her most recent works romance is central, with a historical milieu providing the backdrop.

Dymoke mingles fact and fiction to varying degrees in all her works. In her early novel *Treason in November* she recounts actual events with the focus on a central, fictitious character. Piers Mallory becomes implicated in the Gunpowder Plot of 1605 through a chance acquaintance with one of its instigators, Robert Catesby. Romance is something of a sideline, the central theme being Piers's journey of self-discovery and the restoring of his good name. Similarly, *The Cloisterman* shows Dymoke's own creations coexisting and interacting with historical figures. However, *The Cloisterman* is less reliant upon fact: it is the tale of a fictitious individual in the historical milieu of the early reign of Henry VIII. It opens with Sir Thomas More, awaiting execution and writing a farewell note to Julian, the central character. The origin and development of their friendship, in flashback, forms the story.

The 'Plantagenet' series of six novels is Dymoke at her most ambitious and, possibly, at her best. Along with historical detail and continuity there is an interesting variety of theme and character. For example, in the first of the series, *A Pride of Kings*, there are two parallel stories: the career of William Marshall as he serves the successive monarchs Henry III, Richard the Lionheart, and John, and that of his relationship in middle-age to a 16-year-old girl, a story which is sensitively portrayed. *The Royal Griffin* is the tale of King John's daughter, Eleanor, who marries her first husband for security and her second, Simon de Montfort, for excitement. Alongside a comparison of these two marriages, de Montfort's career from commoner to duke is followed to its tragic end. *The Lion of Mortimer* explores the relationship between Edward II and Piers Gaveston, while *The Lord of Greenwich* shows the extremes of scholasticism and sensuousness in the personality of Humfrey of Gloucester. In the latter novel the reader is also taken through the campaigns against France, including an account of the Battle of Agincourt.

The Queen's Diamond, set mainly in France during the latter stages of the revolution, involves some of the descendants of characters in Dymoke's 18th-century Scottish novel *The White Cockade* and depends for much of its theme on the tension between political and personal allegiances. This issue is taken up again in *Two Flags for France*, set some 20 years later, though in the latter novel the relationship between Louis de la Rouelle and his ward, Julie, throws the associated dilemmas into much sharper focus. The political situation and Napoleon's attempt to reassert power serve not merely as a backdrop, but come to be inextricably linked to the course of Louis and Julie's relationship.

Though the period and location are typically well-researched, *Portrait of Jenny* is a romantic story which could have been set whenever and wherever political allegiances are divided. The setting is 18th-century Scotland, shortly following the Jacobite uprisings. The heroine, Jenny, sets out to avenge the deaths of her parents and finds romance in the process. Moving ever closer to the present day, *Hollanders House* and *Cry of the Peacock* also move further into the realms of romantic fiction. Forming two of a series of which there may well be more to follow, both are set in and around the Romney Marshes, the former in the very early-19th century and the latter in the middle of the same. Even with the added interest of smugglers, *Hollanders House* and its successor are basically straightforward stories of a central female character thwarted in love, mostly by male thoughtlessness but occasionally through her own indecision. In the final chapters, true love and common sense prevail. All of this is not to say that the novels lack colourful characters and incident, all in keeping with the period. Essentially they are fine romances.

—Anne M. Shields

EAGLES, Cynthia Harrod. See **HARROD-EAGLES, Cynthia.**

EATON, Evelyn (Sybil Mary).
Nationality: American; became United States citizen, 1944. **Born:** Montreux, Switzerland, 22 December 1902. **Education:** Sorbonne, Paris, 1920–21. **Relations:** married Ernst Paul Richard Viedt in 1928 (divorced 1934); one daughter. **Career:** war correspondent, 1945; lecturer, Columbia University, New York, 1949–51, for the arts programme of the Association of American Colleges, 1950–60, at Sweet Briar College, Virginia, 1951–60, Adult Education Centers, Virginia, 1955–60, Mary Washington College, Fredericksburg, Virginia, 1957–59, Montalvo Association, 1960 and 1963, Hartford Foundation, 1960 and 1962, Deep Springs College, 1961, Ohio University, Athens, 1962, and Pershing College, 1967. Member, Board of Directors, Draco Foundation of Virginia, 1958; founder, Draco Foundation of California Inc, 1965, and Deepest Valley Theater, Owens Valley, California, 1965. Vice-president, Canadian Authors Association, 1940–41. **Recipient:** John Masefield award, 1923.

ROMANCE AND HISTORICAL PUBLICATIONS

Novels (series: Acadian Trilogy)

The Hours of Iris. London, Baskerville, 1928.

Summer Dust. London, Bles, 1936.
Pray to the Earth. Boston, Houghton Mifflin, 1938; London, Cassell, 1946.
Canadian Circus. London, Nelson, 1939.
Acadian Trilogy:
    Quietly My Captain Waits. New York, Harper, and London, Cassell, 1940.
    Restless Are the Sails. New York, Harper, 1941; London, Cassell, 1942.
    The Sea Is So Wide. New York, Harper, 1943; London, Cassell, 1944.
In What Torn Ship. New York, Harper, 1944; London, Cassell, 1946.
Heart in Pilgrimage, with E.R. Moore. New York, Harper, 1948.
Give Me Your Golden Hand. New York, Farrar Straus, 1951.
Flight. Indianapolis, Bobbs Merrill, and London, Gollancz, 1954.
I Saw My Mortal Sight. New York, Random House, 1959; London, Cassell, 1960.
The King Is a Witch. London, Cassell, 1965; New York, St Martin's Press, 1974.
Go Ask the River. New York, Harcourt Brace, and London, Cassell, 1969.

OTHER PUBLICATIONS

Novels

Desire—Spanish Version. London, Chapman and Hall, 1932; New York, Morrow, 1933.
Canadian Circus. London, Nelson, 1939.
By Just Exchange. London, Cassell, 1952.

Poetry

Stolen Hours. London, Selwyn and Blount, 1923.
The Interpreter. London, Selwyn and Blount, 1925.
The Encircling Mist (includes prose). London, Selwyn and Blount, 1935.
Birds Before Dawn. Toronto, Ryerson Press, 1943.
The Small Hour. Francis Town, New Hampshire, Golden Quill Press, 1955.
Love Is Recognition. Georgetown, California, Dragon's Teeth Press, 1971.

Other

Every Month Was May (autobiography), with Edward Roberts Moore. New York, Harper, 1947; London, Gollancz, 1949.
The North Star Is Nearer (autobiography). New York, Farrar Straus, and London, Gollancz, 1949.

*   *   *

In her historical writings Evelyn Eaton specialized in the European and Canadian scene during the first three-quarters of the 18th century. *Every Month Was May* and *The North Star Is Nearer*, Eaton's two autobiographical volumes, indicate that she used historical settings with which she was personally familiar in their present day character: Nova Scotia, New England, England, Paris, southern France, and Corsica. Indeed, her life story seems to have provided the background material for most of her fiction.

Two novels, *Canadian Circus*, a kidnapping mystery located in Nova Scotia, and *Desire—Spanish Version*, based on Eaton's experiences at the Paramount studios near Paris, are not historical, strictly speaking, but provide documentation of events that are of interest to the reader who sees the text as historical in itself. The latter novel provides a wealth of detail for anyone interested in film production in the early 1930s.

Pray to the Earth and *In What Torn Ship* derive their sense of immediacy from Eaton's knowledge of the Callian-in-the-Var region of southern France and of Corsica, respectively. *Pray to the Earth*, apart from describing the rural conditions at the time of the Spanish Civil War, also concerns itself with scenes from the life of the main character, Louis-Jean Jacquier, variously a herdsman and farm hand, a member of the Carpathian Knights Templar, and a reluctant fighter with the Spanish leftists. Covering the period from 1755 to 1769, *In What Torn Ship* follows the generalship of Pascal Paoli who attempted to unite Corsica against the Genoese, losing the island in the end to France. Again, Eaton's knowledge of the land allows her to draw the landscape with a fine hand.

Two very different novels characterize her later work in the 1950s and 1960s. The main character in *Give Me Your Golden Hand* is Axford Daigle, eldest son of George III of England and a Quaker girl whom he married when he was underage, who emigrates and settles in the American colonies at the outbreak of the American revolution. *Go Ask the River*, Eaton's last historical novel, reflects the interest in China she developed during a visit there as a news correspondent shortly after becoming an American citizen. The main character is a Tang dynasty courtesan, Hsueh T'ao, and the novel presents her life from A.D. 760 to 824. This novel is rich in philosophical and cultural detail and is Eaton's most densely and skilfully written book.

But ultimately Eaton's reputation as a writer of fine historical fiction rests on three novels written in the middle of her career. *Quietly My Captain Waits* is set mainly in Fort Port Royal, New France, between 1691–1710, and focuses on the life of Madame Freneuse and her love for Pierre de Bonaventure. *Restless Are the Sails* covers 1744–1746, and deals with the siege and fall of Louisbourg from France to England. *The Sea Is So Wide* forcefully presents the expulsion of the Acadians by the English in 1755. Close attention to historical detail is present in each of these novels in the form of maps, transcriptions, and translations by the author of evidence ranging from official dispatches to personal letters. Such documentation, skilfully worked into the narrative, rather than set aside in a preface or notes, adds to the sense of period and locale given in detailed descriptions of buildings, persons, costumes, manners, conveyances, and landscape. However, historical verisimilitude in these novels serves to heighten the sense of the atrocities around which the plots are built rather than to distance them through nostalgia or romance.

Apart from the 'Acadian Trilogy', Eaton's most successful historical novel is *Heart in Pilgrimage*, which presents the life of Elizabeth Ann Seton, who founded the Sisters of Charity and became Mother Superior of the Convent of the Sisters of St Joseph in New York City, from her marriage in 1794 to her death in 1821. The novel is filled with the details of both the prosperous household of her husband's shipping family and the austere conditions of Elizabeth's life after her conversion to Catholicism. The novel successfully persuades us to accept this abrupt change as Elizabeth's response to the poverty into which she was thrown upon the death of her husband; the most significant alteration to her circumstances was her move to a house that faced the wharves where the poorest immigrants landed and were temporarily housed. Eaton's compelling fictionalization of Elizabeth's history approaches the best work in her Acadian novels.

Eaton's touch is not a delicate one in that she graphically depicts violent actions with an eye to a very human sort of cruelty and pathetic scenes of the filth of bodily processes, natural and diseased, with unsettling but memorable images. But her emphasis on the strength of the spirit in her characters balances the picture and lends a poign-

ancy to the fleeting romantic element in her work frequently missing from less thorough historical realist fiction.

—Heather Iris Jones

EBEL, Suzanne.   See **GOODWIN, Suzanne.**

EBERHART, Mignon G(ood). American. 1899—. See 2nd edition, 1990.

EDEN, Dorothy (Enid).
Pseudonym: Mary Paradise. **Nationality:** British. **Born:** Canterbury Plains, near Christchurch, New Zealand, 3 April 1912. **Education:** village school and a secretarial college. **Career:** secretary, 1929–39; lived in London from the 1950s. **Died:** 4 March 1982.

Romance and Historical Publications

Novels

Singing Shadows. London, Stanley Paul, 1940.
The Laughing Ghost. London, Macdonald, 1943; New York, Ace, 1968.
We Are for the Dark. London, Macdonald, 1944.
Summer Sunday. London, Macdonald, 1946.
Walk into My Parlour. London, Macdonald, 1947.
The Schoolmaster's Daughters. London, Macdonald, 1948; as *The Daughters of Ardmore Hall*, New York, Ace, 1968.
Crow Hollow. London, Macdonald, 1950; New York, Ace, 1967.
The Voice of the Dolls. London, Macdonald, 1950; New York, Ace, 1971.
Cat's Prey. London, Macdonald, 1952; New York, Ace, 1967.
Lamb to the Slaughter. London, Macdonald, 1953; as *The Brooding Lake*, New York, Ace, 1966.
Bride by Candlelight. London, Macdonald, 1954; New York, Ace, 1972.
Darling Clementine. London, Macdonald, 1955; as *The Night of the Letter*, New York, Ace, 1967.
Death Is a Red Rose. London, Macdonald, 1956; New York, Ace, 1970.
The Pretty Ones. London, Macdonald, 1957; New York, Ace, 1966.
Listen to Danger. London, Macdonald, 1958; New York, Ace, 1967.
The Deadly Travellers. London, Macdonald, 1959; New York, Ace, 1966.
The Sleeping Bride. London, Macdonald, 1959; New York, Ace, 1969.
Samantha. London, Hodder and Stoughton, 1960; as *Lady of Mallow*, New York, Coward McCann, 1962.
Sleep in the Woods. London, Hodder and Stoughton, 1960; New York, Coward McCann, 1961.
Face of an Angel (as Mary Paradise). London, Hale, 1961; New York, Ace, 1966.
Shadow of a Witch (as Mary Paradise). London, Hale, 1962; New York, Ace, 1966.
Whistle for the Crows. London, Hodder and Stoughton, 1962; New York, Ace, 1964.
Afternoon for Lizards. London, Hodder and Stoughton, 1962; as *The Bridge of Fear*, New York, Ace, 1966.

The Bird in the Chimney. London, Hodder and Stoughton, 1963; as *Darkwater*, New York, Coward McCann, 1964.

Bella. London, Hodder and Stoughton, 1964; as *Ravenscroft*, New York, Coward McCann, 1965.

The Marriage Chest. London, Hodder and Stoughton, 1965; (as Mary Paradise) New York, Coward McCann, 1966.

Never Call It Loving. London, Hodder and Stoughton, and New York, Coward McCann, 1966.

Siege in the Sun. London, Hodder and Stoughton, and New York, Coward McCann, 1967.

Winterwood. London, Hodder and Stoughton, and New York, Coward McCann, 1967.

The Shadow Wife. London, Hodder and Stoughton, and New York, Coward McCann, 1968.

The Vines of Yarrabee. London, Hodder and Stoughton, and New York, Coward McCann, 1969.

Melbury Square. London, Hodder and Stoughton, 1970; New York, Coward McCann, 1971.

Waiting for Willa. London, Hodder and Stoughton, and New York, Coward McCann, 1970.

Afternoon Walk. London, Hodder and Stoughton, and New York, Coward McCann, 1971.

A Linnet Singing. New York, Pocket Books, 1972.

Speak to Me of Love. London, Hodder and Stoughton, and New York, Coward McCann, 1972.

The Millionaire's Daughter. London, Hodder and Stoughton, and New York, Coward McCann, 1974.

The Time of the Dragon. London, Hodder and Stoughton, and New York, Coward McCann, 1975.

The Salamanca Drum. London, Hodder and Stoughton, and New York, Coward McCann, 1977.

The Storrington Papers. New York, Coward McCann, 1978; London, Hodder and Stoughton, 1979.

Depart in Peace. London, Hodder and Stoughton, 1979.

The American Heiress. London, Hodder and Stoughton, and New York, Coward McCann, 1980.

An Important Family: A Novel About New Zealand. New York, Morrow, and London, Hodder and Stoughton, 1982.

Short Stories

Yellow Is for Fear and Other Stories. New York, Ace, 1968; London, Coronet, 1976.

The House on Hay Hill and Other Stories. London, Coronet, and New York, Fawcett, 1976.

*

Manuscript Collection: Mugar Memorial Library, Boston University.

*   *   *

Dorothy Eden published steadily from the 1940s until the early 1980s. Since 1970 more than five million copies of her books have been sold and she now numbers more than 30 books in print. These figures alone place her as one of the *grande dames* of romance/gothic.

Her plots are traditional in that the heroines must meet the challenge of 1) finding the right mate, 2) being poor and becoming rich or the reverse, and 3) coping with a frontier land. Her typical heroine is content to find and secure her true mate and run his house, mansion, or castle correctly and well. She must be prepared to repel or charm the threatening natives, survive disasters, and protect other women, children, and dependants.

Eden's heroines are usually without family and are poor, or they have lost the wealth they once had. Briar, in *Sleep in the Woods*, was found in a ditch as a baby, clasped in the arms of the dead woman presumed to be her mother. Raised and educated beyond her station by a poor schoolmaster, she goes out as a ladies' maid to New Zealand, facing the untamed frontier and capturing the most eligible bachelor in Wellington. After moving to the bush, she must wrestle with a recalcitrant husband, the man-eating Maori, and her own lies about her non-existent family in England. Briar has a sister in Harriet 'Hetty' Brown in *The American Heiress*, published 20 years later in 1980.

Also born on the wrong side of the blanket, Hetty is left on her natural father's doorstep by her poor and dying mother. Her father takes her in but then dies; so the wicked stepmother trains Hetty as her daughter's maid. The trick here is that Hetty is a look-alike for Clemency, her half-sister, so much so that she substitutes for Clemency on dates with her more dull suitors. Therein lies the tale. Hetty, Clemency, and mother sail for England and Clemency's elegant marriage on the *Lusitania*. Briar lies about her non-existent family; Hetty, the lone survivor of this trio, takes Clemency's place, marrying the dashing Major Hugo, Lord Hazzard, heir to one of England's most venerable titles. She, like Briar, must continually struggle with her conscience and wonder when and if she will be found out. For both of them the motivation is, at first, possession of a house/castle and social position. They eventually come to love their husbands, however, but only after trials which reveal their mates' worthiness. Both Hetty and Briar suffer for their lies and both are discovered, though in Hetty's case it takes the next generation to reveal her impersonation. Both characters are saved from triviality by their independent spirit. Eden handles the Cinderella story with controlled realism in the areas of sexual implication and setting.

The famous *The Vines of Yarrabee*, perhaps Eden's most widely read novel, tells of the Australian outback, convict labour, and violence mixed with the background of grape-growing and wine-making. In this case, a genteel Eugenia marries Gilbert Massingham and goes to Australia, a most ungenteel place. She, unlike Briar and Hetty, is legitimately of fine English breeding and possesses impeccable social sense, for which quality Gilbert has married her. Eugenia's struggles are concerned with finding her true mate and coping with the frontier. She must adjust to the Australian outback without the prior toughening experiences of Briar and Hetty. Rough times develop character whether rich or poor. Shady financial schemes and love triangles complicate Eugenia's search for her happy ending.

In the Eden canon, *Melbury Square* and *Never Call It Loving* should be singled out as exceptional. In the former, a fashionable portrait artist rules his Kensington Square house, crippling the emotional lives of both his wife and daughter. Maud Lucie, the daughter and protagonist, is a beautiful Edwardian debutante afflicted with a father fixation. Maud carelessly drifts through her youth being her father's favourite model and finds any search on her part for love and happiness thwarted by her dominating father. A selfish and obtuse Maud represents a reality not usually found in gothic/romance heroines. Maud's moment of truth comes only in her crotchety old age when, her father dead, herself tricked, swindled, and poor, she finally finds her independence: 'The one left might be old and ugly, but at least she was entirely herself'.

Never Call It Loving fictionalizes the real love affair between Charles Stewart Parnell and Katherine O'Shea. In reality their affair ruined Parnell's reputation, which indirectly destroyed the chances for Irish Home Rule and ultimately drove Parnell to an early death. A historical novel *par excellence*, this sensitive recounting proves Eden's ability to write successfully outside the romance/gothic formula.

Eden has been universally praised for her well-researched backgrounds—Australia, Peking, Denmark, New Zealand, Ireland. No country or time period was too remote if it interested the author. There has been some faint carping about unoriginal and artificial plots but for a prolific and successful writer such problems are bound to occur. On the whole, an Eden story is a reliable source of entertainment, well told and well researched.

—Marilynn Motteler

EDGAR, Josephine. See **HOWARD, Mary.**

EDGINTON, May. British. 1883–1912. See 1st edition, 1982.

EDMONDS, Walter D(umaux).
Nationality: American. **Born:** Boonville, New York, 15 July 1903. **Education:** Cutler School, New York, 1914–16; St Paul's School, Concord, New Hampshire, 1916–19; Choate School, Wallingford, Connecticut, 1919–21; Harvard University, Cambridge, Massachusetts (staff member from 1922, secretary, 1924–25, and president, 1925–26, *Harvard Advocate*), 1921–26, A.B. 1926 (Phi Beta Kappa). **Relations:** married 1) Eleanor Livingston Stetson in 1930 (died 1956), one son and two daughters; 2) Katharine Howe Baker-Carr in 1956. Member of the Board of Overseers, Harvard College, 1945–50; director, 1955–72, and president and publisher, 1957–66, *Harvard Alumni Bulletin*. **Recipient:** (for children's books): American Library Association Newbery medal, 1942; National Book award, 1976; Christopher award, 1976. D.Litt.: Union College, Schenectady, New York, 1936; Rutgers University, New Brunswick, New Jersey, 1940; Colgate University, Hamilton, New York, 1947; Harvard University, 1952. Member, American Academy of Arts and Sciences. **Agent:** Harold Ober Associates, 424 Madison Avenue, New York, New York 10017, USA. **Address:** 27 River Street, Concord, Massachusetts 01742, USA.

ROMANCE AND HISTORICAL PUBLICATIONS

Novels

Rome Haul. Boston, Little Brown, and London, Sampson Low, 1929.
The Big Barn. Boston, Little Brown, 1930; London, Sampson Low, 1931.
Erie Water. Boston, Little Brown, 1933; London, Hurst and Blackett, 1934.
Drums Along the Mohawk. Boston, Little Brown, and London, Jarrolds, 1936.
Chad Hanna. Boston, Little Brown, and London, Collins, 1940.
Young Ames. Boston, Little Brown, and London, Collins, 1942.
In the Hands of the Senecas. Boston, Little Brown, and London, Collins, 1947; as *The Captive Woman*, New York, Bantam, 1962.
The Wedding Journey. Boston, Little Brown, 1947.
The Boyds of Black River. New York, Dodd Mead, and London, Collins, 1953.
The South African Quirt. Boston, Little Brown, 1985.

Short Stories

Mostly Canallers: Collected Stories. Boston, Little Brown, 1934.

OTHER PUBLICATIONS

Fiction (for children)

The Matchlock Gun. New York, Dodd Mead, 1941.

Tom Whipple. New York, Dodd Mead, 1942.
Two Logs Crossing: John Haskell's Story. New York, Dodd Mead, 1943.
Wilderness Clearing. New York, Dodd Mead, 1944.
Cadmus Henry. New York, Dodd Mead, 1949.
Mr Benedict's Lion. New York, Dodd Mead, 1950.
Corporal Bess. New York, Dodd Mead, 1952.
Hound Dog Moses and the Promised Land. New York, Dodd Mead, 1954.
Uncle Ben's Whale. New York, Dodd Mead, 1955.
They Had a Horse. New York, Dodd Mead, 1962.
Time to Go House. Boston, Little Brown, 1969.
Seven American Stories. Boston, Little Brown, 1970.
Wolf Hunt. Boston, Little Brown, 1970.
Beaver Valley. Boston, Little Brown, 1971.
The Story of Richard Storm. Boston, Little Brown, 1974.
Bert Breen's Barn. Boston, Little Brown, 1975.
The Night Raider and Other Stories. Boston, Little Brown, 1980.

Other

Moses. Privately printed, 1939.
The First Hundred Years, 1848–1948: 1848, Oneida Community; 1880, Oneida Community Limited; 1935, Oneida Ltd. Oneida, New York, Oneida Ltd, 1948; revised edition, 1958.
They Fought with What They Had: The Story of the Army Air Forces in the Southwest Pacific 1941–1942. Boston, Little Brown, 1951.
The Erie Canal: The Story of the Digging of Clinton's Ditch. Utica, New York, Munson Williams Proctor Institute, 1960.
The Musket and the Cross: The Struggle of France and England for North America. Boston, Little Brown, 1968.

*

Film Adaptation: *Drums Along the Mohawk*, 1939; *The Farmer Takes a Wife*, 1953, from the novel *Rome Haul*.

Critical Study: *Walter D. Edmonds, Storyteller* by Lionel D. Wyld, Syracuse, New York, Syracuse University Press, 1982.

*   *   *

Walter D. Edmonds is known, among readers of historical novels, almost exclusively for his *Drums Along the Mohawk* (made into a film in 1939). He is also known for his children's books, for which he has won several awards. His strengths as a novelist are abundantly and clearly displayed in his first novel, *Rome Haul. Drums Along the Mohawk* and *Rome Haul* reveal his natural abilities to recreate specific historical periods with teeming, well-rendered detail; to delineate character through external action; and to blend history and fiction with an authority so finely managed as to blur the distinction between the two. Edmonds's latest novel, *The South African Quirt*, is quite different from his other fiction.

Rome Haul reveals at once Edmonds's ability to create with fidelity and Dickensian realism the life on the Erie Canal during its halcyon days in the 1850s, before railroads made them nearly obsolete. Edmonds convinces the reader that these brief years were as uniquely American and as important as the old New England whaling days or the frontier years following the Civil War; it was a distinct culture, and Edmonds makes it resonate with vibrant detail: the sweaty horses and mules, the barge ropes, the bawdy language, the shapes and noises of freight-laden boats, the itinerant pedlars and the bullies. The life among the 'canawlers' is suffused with a thick and satisfying atmospheric reality. The story is told against a richly textured background.

While the novel is fully peopled, at times the narrative is loose. The two main narrative threads—the chase of Gentleman Joe Calash by the Justice Department, and the love story of Dan Harrow and Mollie Larkin (the main characters of the novel)—do not always intertwine or relate tightly enough. Mollie is the most fully realized character, perhaps because she is the most thoroughly and realistically treated; she is both cook and near-roustabout with the men, and also their lover. Her amorality is the most believable characteristic in the entire novel. The story sometimes rambles, but is always alive and convincing.

Drums Along the Mohawk, though more panoramic, hardly advances the talent so evident in *Rome Haul*, and that is more than acceptable because Edmonds's abilities are immense. Like *Rome Haul*, the setting is specific—northern New York State in 1782. The historical occasion is the 'war' during the American Revolution when the farmers of the Mohawk Valley were separated from the Continental forces and had to fight both the British and the Indians. But the fighting, often dramatically rendered, is not the real focus or intent of the novel.

Edmonds tries to subordinate action to character. Though he does not probe the 'inner' realities of his men and women, he does define their lives in terms of their dailiness and their rough virtues, especially the courage they display in clearing the land and making it serve their purposes. The principal characters—Gilbert Martin, a poor backwoods farmer and a member of the militia from Deerfield settlement, and his wife Lana with whom he makes a life out of the wilderness—are strong presences in the novel, but their conflicts remain unexplored, though never sentimentalized. The problem is one of omission; he also fails to register horror at the increasing brutality of the Indian attacks.

Again, as in *Rome Haul*, Edmonds makes his characters eminently real, but he does not provide them with enough force to make them fully realized. Perhaps this is partly due to Edmonds introducing too many episodic elements into this longish tale. But it should be reiterated that his characters, given the kind of novel *Drums Along the Mohawk* is, are utterly believable, as evidenced by the equally realistic treatment given historic and fictional characters—they are indistinguishable throughout the novel. Edmonds deals here with the frontier men and women whose enduring strengths made America possible. He teaches us about the national character, almost to the point of illustrating an American philosophy.

The South African Quirt, has little in common with his earlier novels, perhaps because it is autobiographical and deals with childhood rites-of-passage, a common enough theme in American literature, but not for Edmonds (although some might want to place his *Chad Hanna* in the same category). The book seems to be more concerned with personal purgation than with exploration of character or the influence of locale, although the setting is specific, the Mohawk Valley region of New York in the 1830s.

The story centres on a 12-year-old boy, Natty Dunston, and his cruel father who is given to blinding, uncontrollable rages. Mr Dunston receives a gift of a South African quirt (a riding crop made of rhinoceros hide); the reader immediately feels there is, inevitably, going to be violence, perhaps inflicted on Natty's mongrel dog Bingo, perhaps on Natty himself. The father is a terrifying presence throughout the novel, but in the absence of any attribual motivation for Mr Dunston's behaviour, the novel has nowhere to go and lacks substance. Here the flaw is almost fatal because there are no rich background, interesting characters, or action to divert the reader, who merely wants to see Mr Dunston die or suffer. The novel is somewhat redeemed by the boy's revenge against his father, but the ending is inconclusive and murky, though arresting and surprising.

Edmonds's abilities are considerable, and his talent is unquestionable. He might have been even more notable had he not been so strict an heir of the local colourists and the early American realists.

—Peter Desy

———

EDWARDS, Anne. American. 1927—. See 2nd edition, 1990.

———

EDWARDS, June. See **FORRESTER, Helen.**

———

ELDERSHAW, M. Barnard. Pseudonym for Marjorie Barnard (1897—) and Flora Eldershaw (1897–56). Australian. See 2nd edition, 1990.

———

ELGIN, Mary.
Pseudonym for Dorothy Mary Stewart. **Nationality:** British. **Born:** Dorothy Mary Okell, in Douglas, Isle of Man, 7 October 1917. **Education:** St Felix School, Southwold, Suffolk, 1928–34; London University, 1934–35; Mrs Hoster's Secretarial School, 1938. **Relations:** married Walter Stewart in 1947; one son and one daughter. **Career:** secretary, Short Brothers; manager in an aircraft repair organization, Cambridge, 1940–45; secretary to the director, Wellcome Foundation Laboratories, London, 1945–47. **Recipient:** Romantic Novelists Association award, 1964. **Died:** 23 March 1965.

ROMANCE AND HISTORICAL PUBLICATIONS

Novels

Visibility Nil. London, Hodder and Stoughton, 1963; as *A Man from the Mist*, New York, Mill, 1965.
Return to Glenshael. London, Hodder and Stoughton, 1965; as *Highland Masquerade*, New York, Mill, 1966.
The Wood and the Trees. London, Hodder and Stoughton, and New York, Mill, 1967.

*

Manuscript Collection: Boston University Libraries.

*   *   *

Mary Elgin's gothic romances displayed her unique ability to create and use a setting to inform a story. For *Visibility Nil* and *Return to Glenshael* she created a mythical region in the Highlands of north-west Scotland. The country around Anacher and Glenshael is wild and mysterious, but inevitable signs of modernization create tension. Old mansions have been bought by rich newcomers. A massive hydroelectric scheme changes the landscape and creates jobs. A river is dammed, but salmon runs preserve the native fish. One character in both books is clan chief to the neighbours but also a hardworking engineer.

The novels are domestic gothic, relying upon family history, impostures, feuds, and the exoticism of the Highlands for their suspense rather than upon genuine villains or violence. There are mysteries to solve, but they are neither life-threatening nor complex. More important is the heroines' emerging sense of self as they learn to live in the changing environment and come to love the heroes.

Elgin's ability to evoke the language of the Highlands was unusually fine; in one novel she describes the regional speech as a derivation of Scots Gaelic rather than a literal translation from it. Her heroines in these first-person novels are lively and strong, speaking in a charming but astringently honest voice.

Because the hero and heroine of one book recur as secondary characters in another, Elgin's works contain a rare picture of a romantic hero and heroine after marriage. The characters have changed and matured, and their relationship is stable; but they are still interesting, acerbic, and witty. Her output may have been meagre; but the quality of Elgin's work is consistently high.

—Kay Mussell

————

ELIOT, Anne.
Pseudonym for Lois Dwight Taylor. **Other Pseudonyms:** Caroline Arnett; Lynn Avery; Nancy Dudley; Allan Dwight; Anne Lattin. **Nationality:** American. **Born:** Lois Dwight Cole, New York City, 1903. **Education:** Smith College, Northampton, Massachusetts, B.A. 1924. **Relations:** married Turney Allan Taylor (died 1968); one son and one daughter. **Career:** associate editor, Macmillan, New York; editor, Whittlesey House and Putnam's Sons, New York; senior editor, William Morrow and Walker and Company, New York. **Died:** 20 July 1979.

ROMANCE AND HISTORICAL PUBLICATIONS

Novels

Return to Aylforth. New York, Meredith Press, 1967.
Shadows Waiting. New York, Meredith Press, 1969.
Stranger at Pembroke. New York, Hawthorn, 1971.
Incident at Villa Rahmana. New York, Hawthorn, 1972; London, Hale, 1975.
The Dark Beneath the Pines. New York, Hawthorn, 1974; London, Hale, 1976.

Novels as Caroline Arnett

Melinda. New York, Fawcett, 1975.
Clarissa. New York, Fawcett, 1976.
Theodora. New York, Fawcett, 1977.
Claudia. New York, Fawcett, 1978.
Stephanie. New York, Fawcett, 1979.
Christina. New York, Fawcett, 1980.

OTHER PUBLICATIONS (for children)

Fiction as Allan Dwight, with Turney Allan Taylor

Spaniards' Mark. New York, Macmillan, 1933.
Linn Dickson, Confederate. New York, Macmillan, 1934.
The First Virginians. New York, Nelson, 1936; London, Nelson, 1938.
Drums in the Forest. New York, Macmillan, 1936.
Kentucky Cargo. New York, Macmillan, 1939.
The Silver Dagger. New York, Macmillan, 1959; London, Collier Macmillan, 1963.
Guns at Quebec. New York, Macmillan, 1962; London, Collier Macmillan, 1963.
To the Walls of Cartegena. Williamsburg, Virginia, Colonial Williamsburg, 1967.

Fiction as Nancy Dudley

Linda Goes to the Hospital [*Travels Alone, Goes to a TV Studio, Goes on a Cruise*]. New York, Coward McCann, 4 vols, 1953–58.
Linda's First Flight. New York, Coward McCann, 1956.
Cappy and the River (as Lynn Avery). New York, Duell, 1960.
Jorie of Dogtown Common (as Anne Eliot). New York, Abingdon Press, 1962.
The Mystery of the Vanishing Horses (as Lynn Avery). New York, Duell, 1963.

Fiction as Anne Lattin

Peter Liked to Draw. Chicago, Wilcox and Follett, 1953.
Peter's Policeman. Chicago, Follett, 1958.
Sparky's Fireman. Chicago, Follett, 1968.

Other

Soldier and Patriot: The Life of General Israel Putnam (as Allan Dwight, with Turney Allan Taylor). New York, Washburn, 1965.

Editor (i.e., adaptor), *Timothy's Shoes and Two Other Stories*, by Mrs Ewing. New York, Macmillan, 1932.

*   *   *

Anne Eliot is the pseudonym for children's writer Lois Dwight Taylor. She is also well known as a writer of regency romances under her other pseudonym of Caroline Arnett.

Eliot's novels fall into the gothic-romance/suspense-romance category. Her heroines are young, charming women with independent spirits who encounter among other things, murder, kidnapping, and fake deaths in exotic locations. Her heroes are slightly more experienced, debonair men, who are terribly inscrutable (and attractive because of it) and who end up saving the heroine's life at some point in the book.

In *Incident at Villa Rahmana*, Kate Haskell meets three inscrutable men in the beautiful and picturesque location of Morocco when she accepts the job as an assistant to a famous interior decorator working on a luxury hotel there. She encounters romance, suspense, and intrigue—and falls in love with Laird Ferrin in the process. *The Dark Beneath the Pines* also finds heroine Andrea Wilmot embroiled in trouble. Andrea goes to the house of her recently deceased favourite uncle to help find his hidden fortune. She meets her uncle's business partner, John Claiborne, and together they discover that her uncle is alive, and that someone has stolen his money.

One of the most interesting things about this book is the way in which Andrea behaves. Set in turn-of-the-century America, Andrea is a forward thinking woman who spouts endlessly on the role of women in upper-class society. 'We aren't allowed to do anything but go to school, or to stupid little parties to practice our manners, or to a matinee of a nice, safe play'. Her own behaviour is extraordinary for a woman of her class and upbringing: she encounters a stranger on the train and has an intimate, flirtatious conversation with him—and she wanders off alone into danger. However, this gives her the opportunity to get into situations from which the hero can rescue her, and, of course, fall in love.

As Caroline Arnett, the author writes entertaining, humorous Regency novels with vivacious heroines who surprise the reader—and the hero—at every turn. This is shown in *Clarissa* in which the heroine of the same name goes from virtual slavery as a paid-companion to being the wife of one of the most sought after men in London. Jason, Lord Lynburn, is everything that a hero should be—tall, dark, and handsome, he is suitably sardonic and sarcastic. Added plot twists are introduced by the presence of the 'other man' and 'other woman'. While the 'other woman' is quickly dismissed as a potential threat to the protagonists' relationship, the 'other man', Jeffrey Rowlan, remains a disruptive influence to the end. Rowlan is both an old friend of Jason's and an old flame of Clarissa's; he is a nice, handsome, honourable man who falls in love with Clarissa, and bows out of the picture when he realizes that she is in love with her husband. Jason, however, thinks that his wife is leaving him for his best friend until the very end of the book.

In *Theodora* the heroine finds herself the co-heir to a stately manor and a potential fortune. Taking an instant dislike to the other heir, Myles Chilot, Lord Devron, 'one of the handsomest men she had ever seen', Theodora quickly embarks on the task of keeping her inheritance. The conditions of the will state that the couple either have to get married within six months or find the famous Zamara emeralds. The search for the emeralds brings a variety of adventurers and long lost relatives to the house. Theodora encounters an intruder who turns out to be an aristocrat, Laurent Brainend, Lord Bourne with whom she eventually falls in love. Theodora, like Clarissa, is transformed from a plain, thin miss, into a beauty. Eventually Theodora and Myles make friends and Myles offers her marriage, Bourne overhears and mistakenly thinks that she has accepted. The twist in the story comes when having found the emeralds the couple donate them to the descendant of the woman from whom they were originally stolen. In doing so both Myles and Theodora break the conditions of the will, as the money from the emeralds would have saved the estate. However, all is not lost, Bourne whisks Theodora away to get married at the end of the book. *Theodora* contains several humorous episodes including the arrival of another supposed relative, 'Ariel', who has hidden powers, and manages to locate some gold by waving a strange instrument around the room. Ariel is an adventurer who absconds with Theodora's booty, however, the irony is that in doing this she fails to find the emeralds which are hidden in the fireplace above the gold.

All of the author's books are well-researched, with particular attention paid to historical details of social manners and customs. The reader gets a good sense, through the Arnett novels especially, of the way in which men and women of a certain class conducted themselves. The author's books as both Anne Eliot and Caroline Arnett are a sure bet for an interesting, entertaining, and engaging read.

—P. Campbell

ELIZABETH.   See **ARNIM, Elizabeth von.**

ELLERBECK, Rosemary (Anne L'Estrange).
Pseudonyms: Anna L'Estrange; Nicola Thorne; Katherine Yorke. **Nationality:** British. **Born:** Cape Town, South Africa. **Education:** London School of Economics, B.Sc. in sociology. **Career:** publisher's reader and editor until 1975, then full-time writer. **Agent:** Richard Scott Simon, 32 College Cross, London N1 1PR, England. **Address:** 96 Townshend Court, Mackennal Street, London NW8 6LB, England.

ROMANCE AND HISTORICAL PUBLICATIONS

Novels

Inclination to Murder. London, Hodder and Stoughton, 1965.
Hammersleigh. New York, McKay, and London, Hale, 1976.
Return to Wuthering Heights (as Anna L'Estrange). New York, Pinnacle, 1977; London, Corgi, 1978.

Rose, Rose, Where Are You? London, Hale, and New York, Coward McCann, 1978.

Novels as Katherine Yorke (series: Enchantress Saga)

Enchantress Saga (revised edition; as Nicola Thorne). London, Granada, 1985.
  The Enchantress. London, Futura, and New York, Pocket Books, 1979.
  Falcon Gold. London, Futura, 1980; New York, Pinnacle, 1981.
  Lady of the Lakes. London, Futura, 1981.
A Woman's Place. London, Macdonald, 1983.
The Pair Bond. London, Macdonald, 1984.
Swift Flows the River. London, Macdonald, 1988.
The People of This Parish. London, Heinemann, 1991.
A Wind in Summer. London, Heinemann, 1991.

Novels as Nicola Thorne (series: Askham Quartet)

The Girls. London, Heinemann, and New York, Random House, 1967.
Bridie Climbing. London, Mayflower, 1969.
In Love. London, Quartet, 1974.
A Woman Like Us. London, Heinemann, and New York, St Martin's Press, 1979.
The Perfect Wife and Mother. London, Heinemann, 1980; New York, St Martin's Press, 1981.
The Daughters of the House. London, Granada, and New York, Doubleday, 1981.
Where the Rivers Meet. London, Granada, 1982; as *Cashmere*, New York, Doubleday, 1982.
Affairs of Love. London, Granada, 1983; New York, Doubleday, 1984.
Askham Quartet:
  Never Such Innocence. London, Granada, 1985.
  Yesterday's Promises. London, Grafton, 1986.
  Bright Morning. London, Grafton, 1986.
  A Place in the Sun. London, Grafton, 1987.
Champagne. London, Bantam, 1989; New York, HarperCollins, 1990.
Pride of Place. London, Grafton, 1989.
Bird of Passage. London, Grafton, 1990.
Champagne Gold. London and New York, HarperCollins, 1992.
The Rector's Daughter. London, Heinemann, 1992.

*   *   *

In the author's note at the beginning of the revised edition of *Enchantress Saga* (*The Enchantress*, *Falcon Gold*, and *Lady of the Lakes*) Rosemary Ellerbeck writing as Nicola Thorne comments that it is a great opportunity for an author to be able to revise published novels. The *Enchantress Saga* originally appeared under Ellerbeck's other pseudonym, Katherine Yorke. The author states that just as Yorke's style changed from writing historical novels to more modern works, Thorne moved from contemporary fiction to historical.

Ellerbeck describes these books as being full of 'fun, adventure and intrigue'; however, the heroine does lead an exciting life, but her lot cannot really be described as 'fun'. Analee, a gypsy who becomes Marchioness, is kidnapped and forcibly married, raped, and almost killed by her second husband, the Marquess of Falconer, imprisoned, and rejected by her eldest child.

Analee is an attractive character—a wild, free spirit, with too much beauty and sensuality for her own good. She glides through life, felling men like trees, and through good fortune ends up mixing with both French and English royalty. This trilogy revolves around her relationship with Brent Delamain, an aristocrat whom she meets within the opening pages of the first book, *The Enchantress*. Although she does not marry Brent until the last pages of the third book, their relationship is an ongoing one which moves from England to Paris and back again. Analee saves Brent when he is accused of treason by getting her husband to intervene. However, it is only after Falconer's death that she can acknowledge the special feeling between them, and the presence of her daughter, who was brought up in ignorance of Analee's identity by Brent's mother.

Even more intriguing given the recent penchant for sequels is *Return to Wuthering Heights*, written by Ellerbeck as Anna L'Estrange. This, as the title suggests, is the follow-up book to Emily Brontë's famous work. Ellerbeck commented (author's note)

So, why attempt a sequel at all? Mainly, I think, because the novel cries out for it. It is a tribute to Emily's genius that after so many years, it [*Wuthering Heights*] is still such a powerful force. Despite its faults it lives in the hearts of all who have read it; it has an urgency and a dynamism that transcends time.

The story takes up from where Brontë's novel finished with the marriage of Hareton Earnshaw and Cathy (Catherine Earnshaw's daughter). Cathy falls in love with Captain Jack Ibbotson who rents Wuthering Heights, only to find out that Jack is the illegitimate son of Heathcliff. Cathy dies giving birth to Jack's son and Anthony, their child, is brought up by Hareton. Years later, Margaret (Cathy and Hareton's daughter), falls in love and marries Jack, only to be terrorized by him, and continually compared to her mother. Anthony later falls in love with Jessica (Margaret's sister-in-law), and the two live together at Wuthering Heights.

Return to Wuthering Heights is an extremely well written book, if a little confusing. For those readers unfamiliar with the original Brontë work, the relationships will probably be extremely confusing. The author has tried to follow a similar structure to *Wuthering Heights*, and the story is told through the eyes of Tom Lockwood, Agnes, the servant of the younger Cathy Earnshaw, and Cathy's daughter, Margaret. Ellerbeck also read newspapers and historical textbooks to make her style of writing as authentic and close to Brontë's as possible. While it would be difficult to create a book as worthy as the original, *Return to Wuthering Heights* is an extremely credible work.

Ellerbeck has written several books which combine history with the supernatural. *Hammersleigh* tells the story of the forbidden love between monk Abbot Roderick and the beautiful Prioress of Hammersleigh, Agatha. Roderick travelled abroad to seek permission for their marriage and Agatha died in mysterious circumstances. Their tale is taken up 500 years later when they begin to affect the lives of recently widowed Karen Blackwood and Hugh Fullerton, the master of Hammersleigh Hall. Karen begins to wonder if psychic influences have led her back to Hammersleigh. Joan of Arc's curse on a French family forms the plot of *Rose, Rose, Where Are You?*. Clare Trafford gets involved when she goes to Port St Pierre to work on a biography of the woman and encounters the DeFrigecourts.

The author has also written several historical novels as Nicola Thorne.

—P. Campbell

ELLIS, Julie.
Pseudonyms: Alison Lord; Jeffrey Lord; Susan Marino; Julie Marvin; Susan Marvin; Susan Richard. **Nationality:** American. **Born:** Columbus, Georgia, 21 February 1933. **Relations:** married (husband deceased); two children. Lives in New York City. **Agent:** Jane

Gelfman, John Farquharson Ltd, 250 West 57th Street, New York, New York 10107. **Address:** c/o William Morrow Inc, 105 Madison Avenue, New York, New York 10016, USA.

ROMANCE AND HISTORICAL PUBLICATIONS

Novels (series: Hampton)

Deedee (as Alison Lord). New York, Pyramid, 1969; as *The Strip*, London, Sphere, 1970.
Jeb (as Jeffrey Lord). New York, Pyramid, and London, New English Library, 1970.
Evil at Hillcrest. New York, Avon, 1971.
Vendetta Castle (as Susan Marino). New York, Avon, 1971.
The Jeweled Dagger. New York, Dell, 1973.
Walk into Darkness. New York, Dell, 1973.
Kara. New York, Dell, 1974.
Eden. New York, Simon and Schuster, 1975.
Walk a Tightrope. New York, Dell, 1975.
Eulalie. New York, Avon, 1976.
The Magnolias. New York, Simon and Schuster, 1976.
The Girl in White. New York, Pocket Books, 1976.
Rendezvous in Vienna. New York, Dell, 1976.
Wexford. New York, Pocket Books, 1976.
Savage Oaks. New York, Simon and Schuster, 1977.
Long Dark Night of the Soul. New York, Pocket Books, 1978.
The Hampton Heritage. New York, Simon and Schuster, 1978; London, Severn House, 1992.
The Hampton Women. New York, Simon and Schuster, 1980; London, Grafton, 1992.
Glorious Morning. New York, Arbor House, 1982; London, Grafton, 1989.
East Wind. New York, Arbor House, 1983; London, Grafton, 1988.
Maison Jennie. New York, Arbor House, 1984; London, Grafton, 1991.
Rich Is Best. New York, Arbor House, 1985; London, Sidgwick and Jackson, 1989.
The Only Sin. New York, Arbor House, and London, Sidgwick and Jackson, 1986.
The Velvet Jungle. New York, Arbor House, 1987; London, Sidgwick and Jackson, 1988.
A Daughter's Promise. New York, Arbor House, and London, Sidgwick and Jackson, 1988.
Loyalties. New York, Morrow, and London, Grafton, 1990.
No Greater Love. New York, Morrow, and London, Grafton, 1991.
Trespassing Hearts. New York, Putnam, and London, HarperCollins, 1992.

Novels as Susan Marvin

The Secret of the Villa Como. New York, Lancer, 1966.
Chateau in the Shadows. New York, Dell, 1969.
Summer of Fear. New York, Dell, 1971.
The Secret of Chateau Laval. New York, Avon, 1973; (as Susan Richard), 1975.
Where Is Holly Carleton? New York, Beagle, 1974.
Chateau Bougy-Villars. New York, Zebra, 1975.

Novels as Susan Richard

Ashley Hall. New York, Paperback Library, 1967.
Intruder at Maison Benedict. New York, Paperback Library, 1967.
The Secret of Chateau Kendall. New York, Paperback Library, 1967.
Chateau Saxony. New York, Paperback Library, 1970.

Terror at Nelson Woods. New York, Paperback Library, 1973.

OTHER PUBLICATIONS

Other

The Women Around R.F.K. New York, Lancer, 1967.
Revolt of the Second Sex (as Julie Marvin). New York, Lancer, 1970.

*   *   *

The most striking aspect of Julie Ellis's novels, particularly the later ones, is their sheer volume. The reader is left asking could the story have been told in less than the average 500 pages that an Ellis novel spans. Unfortunately, the answer is yes every time. The time period explored, usually 20 to 30 years, is far too short, the cast of characters limited, and the main theme fairly straightforward. This tends to slow down the pace of the story, especially as the characters' basic longings and goals do not change dramatically during this space of time. Ellis is compelled to reiterate their underlying motivations every 100 or so pages.

Ellis captivates her audience by taking them through a variety of situations—from the theatre to a shipyard business—and these form the background for her stories. However, her creation of the historical setting is not particularly imaginative. For one thing, she does not indulge in minutiae; her method is to aggregate events of a particular period around the main character. In *Glorious Morning*, for example, the main character lives in East Europe at the turn of the century, and is Jewish—and of course a pogrom occurs. There are lynchings, and campus riots to create a credible setting. There are moments when this technique, when used subtly, works to advantage. In *Loyalties*, a secondary character exults over the Pill—and the reader is catapulted into the tumultuous age of the 1960s. In a sense, Ellis posits history on her characters rather than blending them into a fact-fictitious re-creation of the time.

This is understandable as Ellis's approach to storytelling is fundamentally character-oriented. Her focus is on the men and women in her tales, the turmoils of their inner world, and their interaction with each other. Her cameo characters are mainly women, who bear remarkable similarities to one another. They are extraordinarily good looking, often Jewish, and they have unhappy childhoods, either as orphans or as unloved children. Ellis portrays them as victims of their situation which they surmount, through sheer determination and grit, to become mistresses of their own lives and fates. Her women are bright and independent, but they have strong family and interpersonal ties, are devoted to their children, and Ellis does not think it déclassé for her heroines to bear three children, or sometimes even more. All in all, she strives to present a harmonious image of her heroine as a hard-headed career woman, a sentimental 'mom', and a doyenne of haute-couture.

There is also a strong cast of secondary characters whose identities are established in their relationship to the central character. One is the man to whom the heroine is passionately committed. Infidelity, and sometimes divorce, may follow, yet the nature of her feelings is a strong stimulus for her metamorphosis into a mature woman. Another recurring character is the confidante, normally a close woman friend, who has a pragmatic view of the world.

The unusual make-up of her characters emphasizes the prominent theme in her love stories. Ellis questions the significance given by most writers of the genre to 'romantic-love' in the quest for personal fulfilment. She presents heroines as complex creatures for whom contentment involves a multi-dimensional understanding; and her relationship with men is but one of these. Ellis summarizes her sentiments on this in the words of one of her characters in *East Wind*—

'Life is a series of rooms, [Connie] . . . we've shared a small but precious one'. Ellis's stories also impress upon her readers the element of continuity in life. There is a constant overshadowing of the past on the present and the present into the future. Actions are not isolated events—motives have deep origins and far reaching implications. This particular theme is adequately elaborated in a recent novel, *Loyalties*, the story of two sisters growing up in the lumber business in the early 20th century. One of them, Naomi, deceives and usurps her sister Rachel's inheritance. Decades later, both Naomi's and Rachel's offspring are brought together to manage the same business through a binding clause in Naomi's will. There is a consistent relationship with the past as the daughters strive to both fulfil their personal ambitions for complete control of the business, and to redeem a legacy that rightfully belonged to one of their grandmothers.

Ellis's novels have several secondary storylines that interweave with the main story. The Jewish sentiment, environmental concerns, homosexuality, materialism among the elite are among the minor themes she introduces, but rarely develops. Ellis's primary shortcoming lies in the fact that her text is steeped in banalities. Yet, her stories can be captivating because of their unconventional characterization.

—Rachel Kumar

———

ELSNA, Hebe. British. See 2nd edition, 1990.

———

ELTON, John. See **WOODWARD, Lilian.**

———

EMSLEY, Clare. British. 1912–80. See 2nd edition, 1990.

———

ERICSON, Walter. See **FAST, Howard.**

———

ERSKINE, John. American. 1878–1951. See 2nd edition, 1990.

———

ERSKINE-LINDOP, Audrey (Beatrice Noël).
Nationality: British. **Born:** London, 26 December 1920. **Education:** Convent of Our Lady of Lourdes, Hatch End, Middlesex; Blackdown School, Wellington, Somerset. **Relations:** married Dudley Gordon Leslie in 1945. **Career:** actress with Worthing Repertory Company; then screenwriter in England and Hollywood. **Recipient:** Prix Roman Policier, 1968. **Died:** 7 November 1986.

ROMANCE AND HISTORICAL PUBLICATIONS

Novels

Fortune My Foe. New York, Harper, 1947; as *In Me My Enemy*, London, Harrap, 1948.
Soldiers' Daughters Never Cry. New York, Simon and Schuster, 1948; London, Heinemann, 1949.
The Tall Headlines. London, Heinemann, and New York, Macmillan, 1950.

Out of the Whirlwind. London, Heinemann, 1951; New York, Appleton Century Crofts, 1952.
The Singer Not the Song. London, Heinemann, and New York, Appleton Century Crofts, 1953; as *The Bandit and the Priest*, New York, Pocket Books, 1953.
Details of Jeremy. London, Heinemann, 1955; as *The Outer Ring*, New York, Appleton Century Crofts, 1955.
The Judas Figures. London, Heinemann, and New York, Appleton Century Crofts, 1956.
Mist over Talla. New York, Doubleday, 1957; as *I Thank a Fool*, London, Collins, 1958.
Nicola. New York, Doubleday, 1959; London, Collins, 1964.
The Way to the Lantern. London, Collins, and New York, Doubleday, 1961.
I Start Counting. London, Collins, and New York, Doubleday, 1966.
Sight Unseen. London, Collins, and New York, Doubleday, 1969.
Journey into Stone. New York, Doubleday, 1972; London, Macmillan, 1973.
The Self-Appointed Saint. London, Macmillan, and New York, Doubleday, 1975.

OTHER PUBLICATIONS

Plays

Let's Talk Turkey, with Dudley Leslie (produced Windsor, 1954).
Beware of Angels, with Dudley Leslie (produced London, 1959).

Screenplays: *Blanche Fury*, with Hugh Mills and Cecil McGivern, 1948; *Tall Headlines* (*The Frightened Bride*), with Dudley Leslie, 1952; *The Rough and the Smooth* (*Portrait of a Sinner*), with Dudley Leslie, 1959.

Other

The Adventures of the Wuffle (for children). London, Methuen, 1966; New York, McGraw Hill, 1968.

*   *   *

It is arguable whether Erskine-Lindop can be fittingly described as a romantic novelist. Her books certainly deal with love in its different aspects, but the central theme usually offers the reader far more than a single male/female relationship and there is very rarely a simplistic or conventionally happy ending. Erskine-Lindop's early training in the theatre and her subsequent career in the film world ensure that drama is never absent from her stories (indeed some, such as *The Tall Headlines* and *Mist over Talla*, verge on the melodramatic) and often they can be viewed almost as theatrical pieces with one or two well-rounded leading characters, a colourful backdrop, a strong supporting cast of minor players, a central issue for debate rather than a complex plot with twists and turns which might confuse the audience and a succession of well-paced scenes which build up the tension satisfactorily.

The Singer Not the Song, probably Erskine-Lindop's best book, typifies this approach. Father Keogh, an idealistic Catholic priest, and Malo, a young bandit who vehemently opposes the church and its teachings, duel over a period of several years for the hearts and minds of the inhabitants of a small Mexican village. The opposing central figures are surrounded by a large cast of minor characters whose individual quirks contribute lightness and humour: Locha, the young girl whose adolescent love centres first on one man, then on the other; Sam, the good-hearted town drunk, who befriends the priest; Father Gomez, Keogh's timid predecessor, who plays a

small, but significant role in setting the scene for Malo's first entrance; Miss Finch, Locha's spinster governess from England, who strongly disapproves of the Church of Rome, but comes to develop a whole-hearted respect for its representative; Uncle Joaquin, Malo's surrogate father, who still clings to his religious beliefs. The main theme of the need for good to triumph over evil, even if it means the sacrifice of a life, is skilfully drawn and Erskine-Lindop adds spice to the battle between the two men by enlisting reader sympathy on each side in turn. Father Keogh is young and attractive enough not to appear priggish in his devotion to his faith and we can empathize with his moments of self-doubt. Malo, despite his nickname, is not entirely bad and his fondness for cats certainly shows him in a positive light. Like Milton's Lucifer, whom he resembles, he has a charm and attraction which is easily understood.

The author is particularly good at presenting love under various guises. In *The Singer Not the Song* there is more than a hint of homosexual feeling in the central relationship, especially in the shared death scene, although both men are portrayed as heterosexual (the priest's feelings for the young girl whom he knows first as a child are described with great delicacy and insight). The *Way to the Lantern*, a picaresque novel set against the backdrop of the French Revolution, offers an object lesson to the actor hero of the different types of emotion which all masquerade as love: the adoptive father/son relationship which he has with his rogue of a manager, Lambert Smith; the single-minded materialism of Lizzy Weldon who thinks that she can use her wealth to buy him as the dream lover she wants; physical love as offered by the aristocratic Marie-Clarice and finally the love-hate relationship with the child 'Puce', who sees through the hero's flaws, but is nevertheless determined to marry him one day. 'Puce' is one of many studies in Erskine-Lindop of adolescent love treated with an understanding that such feelings are not always merely a teenage crush. Wynne, the 14-year-old central figure in *I Start Counting*, carries her love for an older man, George, to the extreme of covering up for him when she suspects him of being a murderer; the story line might be judged to be implausible, but instead works well because of the author's ability to get inside a teenage mind and show a mixture of naivety and maturity which often emerges as a quaint mouthing of adult comments which have been picked up and not entirely assimilated.

Erskine-Lindop has a strong sense of social values. She is careful to avoid easy descriptions of the purely picturesque in order to highlight the hopelessness and apathy of peasant life in Mexico or a drab housing estate in the English Midlands. She is in her element commenting on the French Revolution and personalizing the issues behind it. *The Way to the Lantern*, unlike many novels about the period, does not romanticize the aristocrats and during the story the hero's initial preference for the republicans based purely on his own social background hardens into real conviction as he observes the poverty and need around him and notes with horror an undernourished child, 'old before her time and dead before she had lived'. Religion and comment upon it are strangely absent in this book, although catholicism features in most of the author's stories.

Erskine-Lindop's intelligence and sensitivity shine through in all her books. She has the ability to round out and motivate her characters in such a way that her reader comes to care about them and willingly follows them to the end of the story.

—Frances Whitehead

———————

ERTZ, Susan.
Nationality: British. **Born:** Walton-on-Thames, Surrey, in 1894 of American parents; taken to the United States as an infant. **Education:** privately educated in England, 1901–06, and in California, 1906–12. **Military Service:** worked in England and France

during World War I. **Relations:** married John Ronald McCrindle in 1932 (died 1977). **Career:** Fellow, Royal Society of Literature. **Died:** 11 April 1985.

ROMANCE AND HISTORICAL PUBLICATIONS

Novels

Madam Claire. London, Unwin, and New York, Appleton, 1923.
Nina. London, Unwin, and New York, Appleton, 1924.
After Noon. London, Unwin, and New York, Appleton, 1926.
Now East, Now West. London, Benn, and New York, Appleton, 1927.
The Galaxy. London, Hodder and Stoughton, and New York, Appleton, 1929.
Julian Probert. London, Hodder and Stoughton, 1931; as *The Story of Julian*, New York, Appleton, 1931.
The Proselyte. London, Hodder and Stoughton, and New York, Appleton Century, 1933.
Now We Set Out. London, Hodder and Stoughton, 1934; New York, Appleton Century, 1935.
Woman Alive. London, Hodder and Stoughton, 1935; New York, Appleton Century, 1936.
No Hearts to Break. London, Hodder and Stoughton, and New York, Appleton Century, 1937.
One Fight More. New York, Appleton Century, 1939; London, Hodder and Stoughton, 1940.
Anger in the Sky. London, Hodder and Stoughton, and New York, Harper, 1943.
Two Names under the Shore. London, Hodder and Stoughton, 1947; as *Mary Hallam*, New York, Harper, 1947.
The Prodigal Heart. London, Hodder and Stoughton, and New York, Harper, 1950.
The Undefended Gate. London, Hodder and Stoughton, 1953; as *Invitation to Folly*, New York, Harper, 1953.
Charmed Circle. London, Collins, and New York, Harper, 1956.
In the Cool of the Day. New York, Harper, 1960; London, Collins, 1961.
Devices and Desires. London, Collins, 1972; as *Summer's Lease*, New York, Harper, 1972.
The Philosopher's Daughter. London, Collins, and New York, Harper, 1976.

Short Stories

And Then Face to Face and Other Stories. London, Unwin, 1927; as *The Wind of Complication*, New York, Appleton, 1927.
Big Frogs and Little Frogs. London, Hodder and Stoughton, 1938; New York, Harper, 1939.

OTHER PUBLICATIONS

Other

Man, Proud Man, with Mary Borden, and E.M. Delafield. London, Hamilton, 1932.
Black, White and Caroline (for children). London, Hodder and Stoughton, and New York, Appleton Century, 1938.

*

Film Adaptation: *In the Cool of the Day*, 1962.

*   *   *

Susan Ertz enjoyed a long and cosmopolitan career as a writer of fiction. Although her novels may be said to fall into the general category of 'romance', this description does not really to justice to her range and originality. Her books rarely follow an established formula, though they may contain formulaic elements; the central interest lies not in plot, but rather in the psychology of individual characters. In this respect, her works often strike one as essentially gothic in tone, and, occasionally, as excessively ingenious.

Nina, the story of a woman's hopeless infatuation for an unfaithful husband, exemplifies the author's approach to romantic love. Her novels are filled with examples of romances which end unhappily, or which contain elements of selfishness, manipulation, or cruelty. A recurring theme is the unhealthy influence of families upon their members, and the difficulty experienced by individuals in escaping from what the title of one novel refers to, ironically, as a *Charmed Circle*. The effectiveness of this theme is sometimes blurred, however, by a tendency to present secondary characters as caricatures: *Charmed Circle* is narrated by one son who manages to escape the clutches of his family, who appear to have no redeeming qualities whatever. There is often an element of mystery in the novels, usually associated with an event which occurred in the past. However, as she is essentially unconcerned with plot, this element results in some rather unconvincing convolutions. In *The Philosopher's Daughter*, for example, a girl falls in love with the man she assumes to be her long-lost half-brother. Although generally free from the fascination with exotic locale which characterizes the work of many romance writers, the novels frequently present some version of what might be called the 'international theme'. *Now East, Now West* presents a contrast between the societies of England and America; *In the Cool of the Day* provides a combination of high romance and travelogue; and *Devices and Desires* is the story of an English woman, unhappily married to a faithless American husband, who is loved by a Frenchman and an American professor, and who, sacrificing herself to her son, loses the love of both. This plot illustrates both the weaknesses and the strengths of the author, who once declared that she preferred 'a new idea . . . to a diamond watch'.

—Joanne Harack Hayne

———

ESSEX, Mary.   See **BLOOM, Ursula.**

———

ESTEVEN, John.   See **SHELLABARGER, Samuel.**

———

EVANS, Tabor.   See **HORNER, Lance, Kyle ONSTOTT, and Ashley CARTER.**

———

EYRE, Annette.   See **WORBOYS, Anne.**

———

FAIRE, Zabrina. See **STEVENSON, Florence.**

FAIRFAX, Ann. See **CHESNEY, Marion.**

FARNES, Eleanor. British. Died. See 2nd edition, 1990.

FARNOL, (John) Jeffery.
Nationality: British. **Born:** Warwickshire, 10 February 1878.
Education: privately schooled; apprenticed briefly to a brass foundry in Birmingham; studied at Westminster School of Art, London.
Relations: married 1) Blanche V.W. Hawley in 1900 (divorced 1938), one daughter; 2) Phyllis Clarke in 1938, one adopted daughter. **Career:** worked in his father's business; lived in the USA, 1902–10: scene painter, Astor Theatre, New York, for two years; lived in England after 1910. **Died:** 9 August 1952.

ROMANCE AND HISTORICAL PUBLICATIONS

Novels

My Lady Caprice. London, Stevens and Brown, and New York, Dodd Mead, 1907; as *The Chronicles of the Imp*, London, Sampson Low, 1915.
The Broad Highway. London, Sampson Low, 1910; Boston, Little Brown, 1911.
The Money Moon. London, Sampson Low, and Boston, Little Brown, 1911.
The Oubliette. London, Watt, 1912.
The Amateur Gentleman. London, Sampson Low, and Boston, Little Brown, 1913.
The Honourable Mr Tawnish. London, Sampson Low, and Boston, Little Brown, 1913.
Beltane the Smith. London, Sampson Low, and Boston, Little Brown, 1915.
The Definite Object. London, Sampson Low, and Boston, Little Brown, 1917.
Our Admirable Betty. London, Sampson Low, and Boston, Little Brown, 1918.
The Geste of Duke Jocelyn. London, Sampson Low, 1919; Boston, Little Brown, 1920.
Black Bartlemy's Treasure. London, Sampson Low, and Boston, Little Brown, 1920.
Martin Conisby's Vengeance. London, Sampson Low, and Boston, Little Brown, 1921.
Peregrine's Progress. London, Sampson Low, and Boston, Little Brown, 1922.
Sir John Dering. London, Sampson Low, and Boston, Little Brown, 1923.
The Loring Mystery. London, Sampson Low, and Boston, Little Brown, 1925.
The High Adventure. London, Sampson Low, and Boston, Little Brown, 1926.
The Quest of Youth. London, Sampson Low, and Boston, Little Brown, 1927.
Gyfford of Weare. London, Sampson Low, 1928; as *Guyfford of Weare*, Boston, Little Brown, 1928.
Over the Hills. London, Sampson Low, and Boston, Little Brown, 1930.
The Jade of Destiny. London, Sampson Low, 1931; as *A Jade of Destiny*, Boston, Little Brown, 1931.

Charmian, Lady Vibart. London, Sampson Low, and Boston, Little Brown, 1932.
The Way Beyond. London, Sampson Low, and Boston, Little Brown, 1933.
Winds of Fortune. London, Sampson Low, 1934; as *Winds of Chance*, Boston, Little Brown, 1934.
A Portrait of a Gentleman in Colours: The Romance of Mr Lewis Berger. London, Sampson Low, 1935.
John o' the Green. London, Sampson Low, and Boston, Little Brown, 1935.
A Pageant of Victory. London, Sampson Low, and Boston, Little Brown, 1936.
The Crooked Furrow. London, Sampson Low, 1937; New York, Doubleday, 1938.
The Lonely Road. London, Sampson Low, and New York, Doubleday, 1938.
The Happy Harvest. London, Sampson Low, 1939; New York, Doubleday, 1940.
Adam Penfeather, Buccaneer. London, Sampson Low, 1940; New York, Doubleday, 1941.
Murder by Nail. London, Sampson Low, 1942; as *Valley of Night*, New York, Doubleday, 1942.
The King Liveth. London, Sampson Low, 1943; New York, Doubleday, 1944.
The 'Piping Times'. London, Sampson Low, 1945.
Heritage Perilous. London, Sampson Low, 1946; New York, McBride, 1947.
My Lord of Wrybourne. London, Sampson Low, 1948; as *Most Sacred of All*, New York, McBride, 1948.
The Fool Beloved. London, Sampson Low, 1949.
The Ninth Earl. London, Sampson Low, 1950.
The Glad Summer. London, Sampson Low, 1951.
Waif of the River. London, Sampson Low, 1952.
Justice by Midnight, completed by Phyllis Farnol. London, Sampson Low, 1956.

Short Stories

The Shadow and Other Stories. London, Sampson Low, and Boston, Little Brown, 1929.
Voices from the Dust, Being Romances of Old London. London, Macmillan, and Boston, Little Brown, 1932.
A Matter of Business and Other Stories. London, Sampson Low, and Boston, Little Brown, 1940.

OTHER PUBLICATIONS

Play

The Honourable Mr Tawnish, adaptation of his own novel (produced Manchester, 1920; London, 1924).

Other

Some War Impressions. London, Sampson Low, 1918; as *Great Britain at War,* Boston, Little Brown, 1918.
Epics of the Fancy. London, Sampson Low, 1928; as *Famous Prize Fights; or, Epics of 'The Fancy'.* Boston, Little Brown, 1928.
Hove. Privately printed, 1937.
A Book [New Book] for Jane (for children). London, Sampson Low, 2 vols, 1937–39.

*

Film Adaptation: *The Amateur Gentleman,* 1936.

Critical Studies: *Jeffery Farnol*, Beaminster, Cox, 1964, and *More Memories of My Brother Jack: Jeffery Farnol*, Beaminster, Cox, 1966, both by E.E. Farnol.

*   *   *

Jeffery Farnol provides a link between the major writers of the 19th century and the popular romancers of the present. While no one could call him a serious writer like Scott or Dickens, one can easily note traces of both these writers in his works. The quaint lower-class characters, the concern for social evils speak of Dickens; the heroes who were 'out with the Jacobites' look back to Scott. Yet the moral purpose of the earlier writers is lacking; the whole cumbersome plot mechanism merely provides the opportunity to get two young people together and let them get on with their own business.

Even the formulas that Farnol uses are not really formulas; they are more like convention in which he felt comfortable letting his imagination work. For instance, the hero and heroine are often disguised when they meet. Either he does not know who she is, so he can unwittingly disparage her public persona (as in *John o' the Green*, where John tells the girl 'Lia' that the Duchess Ippolita's name 'tis neigh of horse, 'tis sneeze, 'tis hiccough'); or she fails to recognize that he is a member of the family with whom her family have feuded (Lady Joan Brandon in *Black Bartlemy's Treasure*). She is usually quicker than he to realize the truth, however. Farnol's women are slow only to realize that they are falling in love; other than that, they are independent, intelligent, and only too likely to try to take control from the heroes when those gentlemen are moving too slowly. In *The Money Moon*, however, a modern dress version of Farnol's favourite tale, the hero recognizes what is happening sooner than Anthea; he is also the one in disguise, and it is not until the end that she discovers he is really at once Prince Charming and millionaire *deus ex machina* come to pay off the mortgage.

What makes all this foolishness pleasant is Farnol's innocent enthusiasm. The whole-heartedness with which his characters fall into and out of their scrapes and their insistence on doing what they perceive of as the right thing are curiously endearing. Even the villainous Mr Dartry (in *The Lonely Road*) can have a change of heart when Jason reminds him of his mother. It's sentimental, of course; but it is still reassuring, on some level. Even conventional romances today do not guarantee quite this level of escapism.

Farnol's prose may be too rich for the modern reader, but his crazy vehicles of plots do carry the reader along willy-nilly, dialogues full of ellipses and dashes, fevered but chaste passions, poetic descriptions of scenery, broadly rendered accents and all. At his best—in *The Crooked Furrow* and *The Happy Harvest*—Farnol presents genuinely attractive characters in a model of what a picaresque novel should be. That descendant of the Roundheads, Oliver, and his cousin, the impulsive 'cavalier' Roland, go off at the behest of their stern guardian uncle to find out how well they can live on a guinea a week in an Arcadian Georgian England, where friendly gypsies, honourable highwaymen, and faithful servants abound. Oliver, a complete romantic at heart, adopts an abused child and helps his uncle find the wife he had mistakenly cast off years before. But the beautiful heroine prefers Roland. Despite his broken heart, Oliver finds comfort in the fact that he and Roland are finally reconciled, the friends their mothers hoped they would become. And in the sequel Oliver's virtues find their reward. The little foundling, grown to be a bewitching young woman, overcomes her fears about her unknown parentage and Oliver's fears about the difference in their ages and her informal engagement to his other ward, Robin. Clia redeems her promise at the end of *The Crooked Furrow* to marry Oliver when she is old enough. Clia is not really one of Farnol's happiest female creations; she is as cloying as a child, and as full of imperious wiles as an adult. Yet she's what Oliver wants and for Oliver, through the third person narration of *The Crooked Fur-*

row and the rather stuffy first person narration of *The Happy Harvest*, one develops a fondness. Oliver's ward Robin, incidentally, decides that, despite his own love for Clia, the passion that she and Oliver share is so perfect that he cannot sully it with jealousy. Thus Farnol provides an all-around happy ending without the necessity of sketching a second female lead, always a chore for him (the tearful Angela in *Gyfford of Weare* is one example).

Oliver and Roland find adventures, in both books, in the midst of the crime and poverty of London, which is relieved in part by the work of the ladies of 'The Jolly Young Waterman', running the equivalent of a settlement house in a pub in the roughest part of the vast city. London is not present in all Farnol's books, except as an implicit contrast to the idyllic scenes of the southern English countryside. Urban criminals may be misguided louts; rural gypsies, complete with Romany vocabularies, are noble and charming, and cant-spouting highwaymen are helpful to the causes of right.

Farnol's ventures away from his favourite, though vaguely delineated, Regency period are not always happy; that adult fairytale without magic, *John o' the Green*, is set mistily 'in King Tristan's day'; we are always aware of the disparity between modern life as we know it and the picture presented to us in *The Money Moon*. The linked short stories of *Voices from the Dust* follow the reincarnation of two lovers through English history; they vary from the entertaining ('White Friars') to the absurd ('The White Tower').

Ultimately, what Farnol brings to his chosen genre is the unusual viewpoint of a man writing for women. In Farnol's world women are beautiful but mysterious creatures, the repository of exalted ideals about family and sanctity. But his men never really understand them very well. Women can read his books with bemused condescension at how like children the men in his books are. Men can read his books with fellow feeling, and because there is always a share of fighting and swordplay. Contemporary romances are usually written either by a woman or from a woman's point of view; and they are read almost exclusively by women. Reading Farnol reminds us that this is not the way things have to be, and makes us wonder if something has been lost to us that we used to have.

—Susan Branch

FARRELL, J(ames) G(ordon).
Nationality: British. **Born:** Liverpool, Lancashire, 23 January 1935. **Education:** Rossall School, Fleetwood, Lancashire, 1947–53; Brasenose College, Oxford, 1956, 1957–60, B.A. in French and Spanish 1960. **Career:** teacher in Dublin, 1954–55; labourer, fireman, and clerk for Early Warning Defence System, Baffin Island, Northwest Territories, Canada, 1955–56; language teacher in France, 1961–63; teacher of English as a foreign language and publisher's reader, London, 1964–66; lived in New York, 1966–68, London, 1969–78, and County Cork, Ireland, 1979. Contracted polio, 1956. **Recipient:** Harkness fellowship, 1966; Arts Council award, 1970; Faber Memorial prize, 1971; Booker prize, 1973, for *The Siege of Krishnapur*. **Died:** 12 August 1979.

<small>ROMANCE AND HISTORICAL PUBLICATIONS</small>

Novels

Troubles. London, Cape, 1970; New York, Knopf, 1971.
The Siege of Krishnapur. London, Weidenfeld and Nicolson, 1973; New York, Harcourt Brace, 1974.
The Singapore Grip. London, Weidenfeld and Nicolson, 1978; New York, Knopf, 1979.

OTHER PUBLICATIONS

Novels

A Man from Elsewhere. London, Hutchinson, 1963.
The Lung. London, Hutchinson, 1965.
A Girl in the Head. London, Cape, 1967; New York, Harper, 1969.
The Hill Station: An Unfinished Novel, and An Indian Diary, edited by John Spurling. London, Weidenfeld and Nicolson, 1981.

*

Film Adaptation: *Troubles*, 1989.

Manuscript Collection: Trinity College, Dublin.

Critical Study: *J.G. Farrell* by Ronald Binns, London, Methuen, 1986.

*   *   *

The works of J.G. Farrell—notably *Troubles* and *The Siege of Krishnapur*—provide a brave contribution to this century's historical fiction. His is a distinctive and courageous voice.

Farrell was fascinated by historical problems and problematic historical periods; times when the issues appear black and white, when people are called on to 'take sides', but where the reality is inevitably more complex. This fascination is evident in Farrell's most accomplished book, *Troubles*, which is set in a post-1916 Ireland, as the sectarian struggle between Protestants and Catholics is beginning to emerge in its modern form. The situation is further complicated by the looming 'threat' of partition, and the nervous British presence, as personified by the novel's protagonist Major Brendan.

In *The Siege of Krishnapur* Farrell explores the 19th-century Indian Mutiny in Krishnapur, presenting it as the inevitable expression of native outrage against a colonial and exploitative power. As Farrell states in his Afterword: 'The reality of the Indian Mutiny constantly defies imagination', and so his 'fiction' is based on: 'Actual events, taken from the mass of diaries, letters and memoirs written by eye witnesses'.

Civilization versus a native culture, high art and primitivism, materialism, and spiritualism, these are some of the dichotomies the novel explores and eventually explodes, arguing for an integrated notion of humanity, one that defies the crippling logic of oppositions.

It is a tribute to Farrell's skill that throughout all his works the narrative voice is controlled yet passionate, refusing to take sides. His is not a partisan voice. Another courageous feature of the writing lies in its innovative structures and eclectic style.

The Siege is a relatively straightforward narrative that maps out the experience of a British community administering British justice, culture, and religion to the Indian town of Krishnapur. Fleury and his sister Miriam arrive from England as the first signs of revolt break out. While the Maharaja and his son vainly try to mimic the British way of life the native uprising gains momentum until the town is placed under self-imposed siege. Starvation and cholera ravage the community: 'India itself was now a different place, the fiction of happy natives being led forward along the road to civilization could no longer be sustained'. Episodes of savage realism chart the community's fall from 'respectable' behaviour in its fight for survival. At points Farrell is graphic and disturbing. Relief finally arrives, but the novel closes with ironic portraits of the major characters many years on: people who have chosen to forget their experiences.

Troubles is a more daring narrative which moves in and out of domestic realism, with surreal humour reminiscent of Flann O'Brien, and journalistic news coverage of both the Irish and Indian struggles for self-determination in the post-colonial, modern world.

Major Brendan is a British soldier, shattered by his experience of World War I. He arrives at the Majestic Hotel in Ireland to find out if his rash engagement to Angela made years previously still holds true. Gradually this nervous, eager-to-please man is drawn into the family's various obsessions and intrigues and the situation in Ireland. Angela dies, but Sarah, a wild and independent woman, emerges as his doomed lover. The struggles and troubles bubble away in the background until the novel finally reaches its powerful climax: the Major nearly loses his life at the hands of the Sinn Feiners, the Hotel lies ransacked and abandoned, the family disrupted and the country partitioned.

The title is intriguing: the novel suggests the modern 'troubles' need to be understood in the light of their earlier history in the 1920s. The language of the media is under close scrutiny: as the story line is continually interrupted by press flashes from around the world, we see the human consequences of these historical movements enacted by a small cast of individuals.

—Catherine S. Wearing

———

FARRELL, M.J.   See **KEANE, Molly.**

———

FAST, Howard (Melvin).
Pseudonyms: E.V. Cunningham; Walter Ericson. **Nationality:** American. **Born:** New York City, 11 November 1914. **Education:** George Washington High School, New York, graduated 1931; National Academy of Design, New York. **Military Service:** Office of War Information, 1942–43, and the Army Film Project, 1944. **Relations:** married Bette Cohen in 1937; one daughter and one son, the writer Jonathan Fast. **Career:** war correspondent in the Far East for *Esquire* and *Coronet* magazines, 1945. Teacher, Indiana University, Bloomington, Summer 1947; imprisoned for contempt of Congress, 1947; owner, Blue Heron Press, New York, 1952–57. Since 1989 weekly columnist, New York, *Observer*. Founder, World Peace Movement, and member, World Peace Council, 1950–55; currently, member of the Fellowship for Reconciliation. American-Labor Party candidate for Congress for 23rd District of New York, 1952. **Recipient:** Bread Loaf Writers Conference award, 1933; Schomburg Race Relations award, 1944; Newspaper Guild award, 1947; Jewish Book Council of America award, 1948; Stalin International Peace prize (now Soviet International Peace prize), 1954; Screenwriters award, 1960; National Association of Independent Schools award, 1962; Emmy Award, for television play, 1976. **Agent:** Sterling Lord Literistic Inc, 1 Madison Avenue, New York, New York 10010, USA.

ROMANCE AND HISTORICAL PUBLICATIONS

Novels (series: The Immigrants)

Two Valleys. New York, Dial Press, 1933; London, Dickson, 1934.
Strange Yesterday. New York, Dodd Mead, 1934.
Conceived in Liberty: A Novel of Valley Forge. New York, Simon and Schuster, and London, Joseph, 1939.
The Last Frontier. New York, Duell, 1941; London, Lane, 1948.
The Unvanquished. New York, Duell, 1942; London, Lane, 1947.
The Tall Hunter. New York, Harper, 1942.
Citizen Tom Paine. New York, Duell, 1943; London, Lane, 1945.
Freedom Road. New York, Duell, 1944; London, Lane, 1946.
The American: A Middle Western Legend. New York, Duell, 1946; London, Lane, 1949.

Clarkton. New York, Duell, 1947.
My Glorious Brothers. Boston, Little Brown, 1948; London, Lane, 1950.
The Proud and the Free. Boston, Little Brown, 1950; London, Lane, 1952.
Spartacus. Privately printed, 1951; London, Lane, 1952.
Moses, Prince of Egypt. New York, Crown, 1958; London, Methuen, 1959.
April Morning. New York, Crown, and London, Methuen, 1961.
Agrippa's Daughter. New York, Doubleday, 1964; London, Methuen, 1965.
Torquemada. New York, Doubleday, 1966; London, Methuen, 1967.
The Crossing. New York, Morrow, 1971; London, Eyre Methuen, 1972.
The Hessian. New York, Morrow, 1972; London, Hodder and Stoughton, 1973.
The Immigrants:
  The Immigrants. Boston, Houghton Mifflin, 1977; London, Hodder and Stoughton, 1978.
  Second Generation. Boston, Houghton Mifflin, and London, Hodder and Stoughton, 1978.
  The Establishment. Boston, Houghton Mifflin, 1979; London, Hodder and Stoughton, 1980.
  The Legacy. Boston, Houghton Mifflin, and London, Hodder and Stoughton, 1981.
  The Immigrant's Daughter. Boston, Houghton Mifflin, 1985; London, Hodder and Stoughton, 1986.
The Call of Fife and Drum: Three Novels of the Revolution (includes *The Unvanquished, Conceived in Liberty, The Proud and the Free*). Secaucus, New Jersey, Citadel Press, 1987.

Short Stories

Patrick Henry and the Frigate's Keel and Other Stories of a Young Nation. New York, Duell, 1945.
Departures and Other Stories. Boston, Little Brown, 1949.
The Last Supper and Other Stories. New York, Blue Heron Press, 1955; London, Lane, 1956.

OTHER PUBLICATIONS

Novels

Place in the City. New York, Harcourt Brace, 1937.
The Children. New York, Duell, 1947.
Fallen Angel (as Walter Ericson). Boston, Little Brown, 1952; as *The Darkness Within*, New York, Ace, 1953; as *Mirage* (as Howard Fast), New York, Fawcett, 1965.
Silas Timberman. New York, Blue Heron Press, 1954; London, Lane, 1955.
The Story of Lola Gregg. New York, Blue Heron Press, 1956; London, Lane, 1957.
The Winston Affair. New York, Crown, 1959; London, Methuen, 1960.
The Golden River, in *The Howard Fast Reader*. New York, Crown, 1960.
Power. New York, Doubleday, 1962; London, Methuen, 1963.
The Hunter and the Trap. New York, Dial Press, 1967.
Max. Boston, Houghton Mifflin, 1982; London, Hodder and Stoughton, 1983.
The Outsider. Boston, Houghton Mifflin, 1984; London, Hodder and Stoughton, 1985.
The Dinner Party. Boston, Houghton Mifflin, and London, Hodder and Stoughton, 1987.
The Pledge. Boston, Houghton Mifflin, 1988; London, Hodder and Stoughton, 1989.

The Confession of Joe Cullen. Boston, Houghton Mifflin, 1989; London, Hodder and Stoughton, 1990.

Novels as E.V. Cunningham

Sylvia. New York, Doubleday, 1960; London, Deutsch, 1962.
Phyllis. New York, Doubleday, and London, Deutsch, 1962.
Alice. New York, Doubleday, 1963; London, Deutsch, 1965.
Lydia. New York, Doubleday, 1964; London, Deutsch, 1965.
Shirley. New York, Doubleday, and London, Deutsch, 1964.
Penelope. New York, Doubleday, 1965; London, Deutsch, 1966.
Helen. New York, Doubleday, 1966; London, Deutsch, 1967.
Margie. New York, Morrow, 1966; London, Deutsch, 1968.
Sally. New York, Morrow, and London, Deutsch, 1967.
Samantha. New York, Morrow, 1967; London, Deutsch, 1968; as *The Case of the Angry Actress*, New York, Dell, 1984.
Cynthia. New York, Morrow, 1968; London, Deutsch, 1969.
The Assassin Who Gave Up His Gun. New York, Morrow, 1969; London, Deutsch, 1970.
Millie. New York, Morrow, 1973; London, Deutsch, 1975.
The Case of the One-Penny Orange. New York, Holt Rinehart, 1977; London, Deutsch, 1978.
The Case of the Russian Diplomat. New York, Holt Rinehart, 1978; London, Deutsch, 1979.
The Case of the Poisoned Eclairs. New York, Holt Rinehart, 1979; London, Deutsch, 1980.
The Case of the Sliding Pool. New York, Delacorte Press, 1981; London, Gollancz, 1982.
The Case of the Kidnapped Angel. New York, Delacorte Press, 1982; London, Gollancz, 1983.
The Case of the Murdered Mackenzie. New York, Delacorte Press, 1984; London, Gollancz, 1985.
The Wabash Factor. New York, Delacorte Press, 1986; London, Gollancz, 1987.

Short Stories

The Edge of Tomorrow. New York, Bantam, 1961; London, Corgi, 1962.
The General Zapped an Angel. New York, Morrow, 1970.
A Touch of Infinity. New York, Morrow, 1973; London, Hodder and Stoughton, 1975.
Time and the Riddle: Thirty-One Zen Stories. Pasadena, California, Ward Ritchie Press, 1975.

Plays

The Hammer (produced New York, 1950).
Thirty Pieces of Silver (produced Melbourne, 1951; London, 1984). New York, Blue Heron Press, and London, Lane, 1954.
General Washington and the Water Witch. London, Lane, 1956.
The Crossing (produced Dallas, 1962).
The Hill (screenplay). New York, Doubleday, 1964.
David and Paula (produced New York, 1982).
Citizen Tom Paine, adaptation of his own novel (produced Williamstown, Massachusetts, 1985). Boston, Houghton Mifflin, 1986.
The Novelist (produced Williamstown, Massachusetts, 1987).
The Second Coming (produced Greenwich, Connecticut, 1991).

Screenplay: *The Hessian*, 1971.

Television Plays: *What's a Nice Girl Like You ...?*, 1971; *The Ambassador* (*Benjamin Franklin* series), 1974; *21 Hours at Munich*, with Edward Hume, 1976.

Poetry

Never to Forget the Battle of the Warsaw Ghetto, with William Gropper. New York, Jewish Peoples Fraternal Order, 1946.
Korean Lullaby. New York, American Peace Crusade, n.d.

Other

The Romance of a People (for children). New York, Hebrew Publishing Company, 1941.
Lord Baden-Powell of the Boy Scouts. New York, Messner, 1941.
Haym Salomon, Son of Liberty. New York, Messner, 1941.
The Picture-Book History of the Jews, with Bette Fast. New York, Hebrew Publishing Company, 1942.
Goethals and the Panama Canal. New York, Messner, 1942.
The Incredible Tito. New York, Magazine House, 1944.
Intellectuals in the Fight for Peace. New York, Masses and Mainstream, 1949.
Tito and His People. Winnipeg, Manitoba, Contemporary Publishers, 1950.
Literature and Reality. New York, International Publishers, 1950.
Peekskill, USA.: A Personal Experience. New York, Civil Rights Congress, and London, International Publishing Company, 1951.
Korean Lullaby. New York, American Peace Crusade, n.d.
Tony and the Wonderful Door (for children). New York, Blue Heron Press, 1952; as *The Magic Door*, Culver City, California, Peace Press, 1979.
Spain and Peace. New York, Joint Anti-Fascist Refugee Committee, 1952.
The Passion of Sacco and Vanzetti: A New England Legend. New York, Blue Heron Press, 1953; London, Lane, 1954.
The Naked God: The Writer and the Communist Party. New York, Praeger, 1957; London, Bodley Head, 1958.
The Howard Fast Reader. New York, Crown, 1960.
The Jews: Story of a People. New York, Dial Press, 1968; London, Cassell, 1970.
The Art of Zen Meditation. Culver City, California, Peace Press, 1977.
Being Red: A Memoir. Boston, Houghton, Mifflin, 1991.
War and Peace (essays). Armonk, New York, Sharpe, 1991.

Editor, *The Selected Work of Tom Paine*. New York, Modern Library, 1946; London, Lane, 1948.
Editor, *Best Short Stories of Theodore Dreiser*. Cleveland, World, 1947.

*

Film Adaptations: *Rachel*, 1948; *Spartacus*, 1960; *Man in the Middle*, 1963, from the novel *The Winston Affair*; *The Immigrants*, 1978; *Freedom Road*, 1980; *April Morning*, 1988.

Manuscript Collections: University of Pennsylvania Library, Philadelphia; University of Wisconsin, Madison.

*   *   *

Howard Fast is a prolific writer (two or more books a year) whose works, with their quickly sketched characterization, their clear, simple dialogue, their straightforward plots, their sequence of dramatic scenes embodying conflicts of ideals, their sentimentality, and their sometimes heavy-handed, black-and-white treatment of morality, transfer easily to the movie screen. Fast's works vary in quality from the highly effective and gripping to the melodramatic and propagandistic, but they are almost always interesting. Fast has always believed, since he began writing at age 18, that his works should both teach and please, that behind every romance should be a lesson

and that every treatment of historical events should reduce the monumental to the personal, the understandable, the human. He is a master at trivializing the great and in turn at showing the great in the commonplace; his most common historical theme is how men of seemingly little note can be transformed by circumstances into men of great accomplishments and great ideals. Fast brings a social conscience to his historical fiction, with works that expose the pitfalls of power and wealth and the virtues of the simple life, of family, and of personal human concern. He has been praised for his life-like characters and action-packed narratives, but it is his commitment to liberal and humanitarian values that marks his canon as special. His works sympathetically treat women as courageous, witty, intuitive, and reasonable; they project an empathy with cultural outcasts, an understanding of the pressures that sometimes force decent men to conform, and a disdain for prejudice, hypocrisy, and abuse of power. In sum, Fast combines political statement with enjoyable entertainment.

Fast, in his early novels, focuses primarily on the American Revolutionary War, exploring how harassed human beings paid the price for liberty. His first book, *Two Valleys*, captures the terrors and the potentials of life on the edge of civilization. Among his most compelling treatments of the American Revolution and its heroes are *Conceived in Liberty*, a grimly realistic study of Valley Forge, *The Unvanquished*, an analysis of how a 'confused, humble, indecisive foxhunter' (George Washington) slowly developed into 'a leader of men', and *Citizen Tom Paine*, a complex portrait of Paine as a foolish, weak, incompetent politician, and yet a committed visionary, and a great radical. These provocative works try to humanize history and historical figures, admitting their weaknesses, reversing conventional perspectives, and demonstrating the processes that led such men to greatness. They vividly evoke the stormy background of the times. Of a similar quality and concern is *The Last Frontier*, a work which has received particular praise as a taut and moving story of the abuse and extermination of 300 Cheyenne, an incident indicative of how any violation of principle paves the way for abuse.

In the 1940s Fast's anti-fascist feeling led him to communism and to one-dimensional, doctrinaire works with capitalist villains and proletarian heroes. He continued to write historical fiction, but increasingly with a Marxist focus. *Freedom Road*, for example, portrays virtuous blacks struggling against Simon Legree whites during the traumas of post-Civil War Reconstruction, and in particular one slave's rise to statesman and martyr; *Clarkton* provides a socialist view of a Massachusetts mill town; *The American* explores why a midwestern politician pardoned three anarchists convicted of the Haymarket bombings in 1886; and *Silas Timberman*, and *The Story of Lola Gregg* depict the good (communists or fellow travelers) battling the bad (strike-breakers or FBI agents). *Spartacus*, written while Fast was serving a prison term for contempt of Congress, is a controversial treatment of the great slave revolt of 71 B.C., one Anthony Manousos calls a metaphor for all oppressed people's struggle to throw off the shackles of their inhuman oppressors. Its slaves are proletarian heroes; its Romans capitalist villains; its arena a symbol of the life-and-death struggles between the oppressors and the oppressed. A bestseller and a movie, it brought Fast the Stalin International Peace prize in 1954 and the Screenwriters award in 1960. *My Glorious Brothers* is a similar treatment of the Maccabean uprising against Greek tyrants. Most of the works of this period gloss over historical realities and rewrite events to suit Fast's message, but, ironically, only *The Passion of Sacco and Vanzetti* comes close to expressing any coherent communist dream. By 1957, tired of communist pressures to change his works to please party functionaries and disenchanted overall with the Party, Fast wrote *The Naked God* to recant clearly and completely.

Since then he has turned out a book a year of historical fiction (mainly about the American Revolution and Civil War days, immigrants, and biblical figures), science fiction, and thrillers. These vary greatly in quality, teaching less about politics than in the past, and more about the personal and the religious; in other words, the doctrinal has given way somewhat to the compassionate and the humanistic. Fast always includes people tinged with prejudice but convinced they have none: prejudice against blacks, Jews, Catholics, Nisei, and outsiders of all sorts. He is particularly disturbed by anti-Jewish sentiments, having, early in his career, written a semi-fictional life of a Polish-Jewish broker/financier who helped the American Revolutionary cause, as well as a picture-book history of the Jews. *Torquemada* predictably addresses what motivates men to do evil in the name of good. His biblical stories, like *Moses, Prince of Egypt*, and *Agrippa's Daughter*, trace the development of Jewish heroes from spoiled youths to rebels to compassionate and competent leaders. Among his most popular works in this later period is his tetralogy: *The Immigrants*, *Second Generation*, *The Establishment*, *The Legacy*, and *The Immigrant's Daughter*. Criticized for 'milking emotions' and for reading like 'soap history', they trace the changes wrought in four immigrant families (Protestant, Catholic, Jewish, and Chinese) as they fight to become established members of a new San Francisco society. The novels focus, in particular, on a poor Italian-French immigrant, who ambitiously builds a corporate empire in the first novel, only to lose it more quickly than he gained it. The last two in the series concern the hardships of reestablishment and of dual identities. The novels play off the legitimate but selfish Nob Hill family of the founder against his kinder, more humane illegitimate Chinese offspring. Also notable are *April Morning* (a teenager's coming of age at the Battle of Lexington), *The Hessian* (Quakers struggling with conscience over a Hessian youth sought by irate and vengeful townsmen and later tried in a kangaroo court), and *The Crossing* (Washington's famous 1776 Christmas crossing of the Delaware). Always an idealist, Fast believes that books 'open a thousand doors, they shape lives and answer questions, they widen horizons, they offer hope for the heart and food for the soul'.

Fast's prolific writing in his later years retains the general political and moral interests of the earlier novels, returning to unresolved matters in some cases but also confronting new issues as well, often in somewhat experimental literary forms. *The Outsider* straddles both early and late interests, using the town of Leighton Ridge, Connecticut, to examine the effects of all the major political events of post-war America, from McCarthyism to Vietnam, on the career of David Hartman, a rabbi in a small WASP town. *The Immigrant's Daughter* follows the later years of Barbara Lavette of Fast's earlier series, tracing her campaign for Congress (clearly based on Fast's own 1952 try in New York) and her reporting of the war in El Salvador. The concern for Central America continues in *The Dinner Party*, a play-like novel that takes place in a single day and location, dealing with a US Senator's attempt to help the cause of Latin American refugees as he confronts the turmoil in the life of his own family. *The Confession of Joe Cullen* is told by the title character as a series of 'confessions' to the murder of a priest in Central America, and the repercussions of Cullen's acceptance of guilt. Only *The Pledge* returns to a much earlier event, the post World War II years of McCarthyism and the imprisonment of Bruce Bacon in a prison very like that which held Fast for a similar refusal to cooperate with the House Un-American Activities Committee. *Being Red: A Memoir* is an interesting non-fiction commentary on the work of the 1940s and 1950s, since Fast's fiction is so often based on real events.

In the main Fast's writing is straightforward, simple, and unadorned. What often gives it its greatest strength is his handling of point of view. Fast describes the retreat from New York in 1776 through the eyes of Washington himself in order to, as Malcolm Cowley points out, bring alive the meaning of a phrase like 'the soul of the Revolution'. Fast's description of the defiant journey of the Cheyenne from their reservations to the Montana Territory that had been their home depends totally on biased white points of view, perspectives that end up lending the Indians more dignity and suggesting more of a sense of their right than would the same story told through the Indians' own eyes. Fast can also be experimental with form, though in a conservative way that never troubles the reader's progress through the work or the basic narrative coherence.

Basically, Fast's canon reflects his concern with man's historical and present struggles for liberty and for a government that recognizes the rights and needs of the individual. Fast disapproves of all that reduces man to a catchphrase, a class, an ideology, a nonentity. For him struggle, self-awareness, love and affection, family, privacy, and humanitarian values give life meaning. He disapproves of any group, no matter what the governmental system, that tries to force the human into mechanical categories or that denies genuine emotion. His politics move from committed Marxism in the 1940s and 1950s to more religious and humanitarian values later on, although Fast has never apologized for his passionate and sometimes extravagant defences of what he found right. Extreme emotion has informed his political outlook, and thus in his writing his message outweighs all else; as Fast himself says, 'His [an artist's] only obligation is to truth'.

—Andrew and Gina Macdonald

FECHER, Constance. See **HEAVEN, Constance.**

FEDDERSEN, Connie. See **FINCH, Carol.**

FELIX, Jennie. See **SAXTON, Judith.**

FELLOWS, Catherine.
Recipient: Romantic Novelists Association Netta Muskett award, 1970. **Address:** c/o Hodder and Stoughton, Mill Road, Dunton Green, Sevenoaks, Kent TN13 2YA, England.

ROMANCE AND HISTORICAL PUBLICATIONS

Novels

Leonora. London, Hurst and Blackett, 1972; New York, Fawcett, 1974.
The Marriage Masque. London, Hodder and Stoughton, and New York, Dell, 1974.
The Heywood Inheritance. London, Hodder and Stoughton, 1975; as *The Love Match*, New York, Dell, 1977.
Vanessa. New York, Dell, 1978.
Entanglement. London, Hodder and Stoughton, and New York, Fawcett, 1979.

*   *   *

The addition of Catherine Fellows to the ranks of light historical romantic fiction writers has been welcomed by many devotees of Georgette Heyer to whom she is most frequently compared. One of the reasons for this may lie in the similarity of their spirited heroines, who manage to single-mindedly pursue their own goals and aims in a series of light-hearted adventures and farcical misunderstandings set against a background of a highly rigid and morally intransigent society where women's behaviour is heavily circumscribed.

In all of her period novels, Fellows's constant theme is with the sexism imposed upon women by the mores of a male-oriented society. Her heroines need to be quick-witted and intelligent in order to achieve the highly desirable marital state recognized by the society of the time as being the only suitable state for a respectable woman. At the same time, they also manage to achieve the aim of a love match. Fellows brings into her novels society's obsession with the need for one or other of the party's (preferably both) to bring a big dowry with them, this being considered a successful match. Fellows's descriptive style is witty, with precise attention paid to period details. The action is consistently fast-paced and the characters finely drawn.

In *Leonora*, Fellows's first novel, the author highlights one aspect of the marriage theme when the heroine suspects that the hero wishes to marry her because he doesn't want her to reveal his dark secret to the world. This relates to the fact that a wife, at that time, could not give evidence against her husband. Notwithstanding the possible bleakness which could have underscored the plot, the issue is handled with a light touch and the heroine is settled happily at the end. The theme of marriage is considered again in *The Marriage Masque*, in which the heroine is asked to oversee the coming out of a young, beautiful, and naive girl. The protégée serves as a useful device to describe the importance of the coming out procedure increasing marriage prospects of a young girl in society. This was one of the few respectable ways in which an unattached female could meet her future husband. The subsequent trials and adventures that the heroine goes through as a result of her chaperoning her young charge are skilfully handled. The heroine has to use her considerable resourcefulness to protect her charge from having her reputation ruined—a woman's reputation being regarded by society at that time as one of her most precious attributes, but easily tarnished if society's rigid rules were ignored or broken. Fellows cleverly highlights the hypocrisy of this attitude when the protégée's would-be seducer has an entrée to most of society's houses, despite having an unsavoury reputation. Another feature of the story is that the heroine is relatively ordinary-looking; by the standards of the day, this would have been regarded as a severe handicap unless the woman had a substantial dowry to make her eminently more marriageable. The heroine accepts her own shortcomings as far as her physical appearance is concerned with good-humoured self-deprecation, and it is her common sense and spirit which win her the hero's love. Fellows's characterization serves to highlight the advantages of commonsense and intelligence over mere vapid beauty, and the former attributes serve to help the heroine achieve a satisfactory marriage for both her young charge and herself.

Fellows adopts a slightly more gothic, darker style, but with the same underlying light touch, in *The Heywood Inheritance*. The heroine of this book is bequeathed a substantial family home and inheritance—to her own and her family's deep shock. As a result of the inheritance she finds herself in personal danger, and it is mainly through her own resourcefulness and intelligence that she survives the various attempts on her life. She comes to realize that appearances can be deceptive as her own initial antagonistic feelings to the hero develop into love. The many family members brought together for the reading of the will (who are all subsequently stranded in the family home) are carefully described with some humour—particularly the heroine's elderly dowager aunt. Even a situation in which the latter is injured by a wardrobe falling on her (the heroine initially believes this to be an attempt on her aunt's life) is described in a light-hearted way, and an element of farce is thereby introduced into an atmosphere of menace.

The emphasis that Fellows places on the heroine being the strong main character, to the extent of perhaps overshadowing the hero's part in the adventures that occur, is followed through in both *Vanessa* and *Entanglement*. In the former, the heroine's determination to arrange desirable marriages for both herself and her sister is successful despite a sequence of comic deceptions and misunderstandings that are primarily brought about by the wealthy hero's anxieties to achieve a match with someone who loves him for himself and not for his wealth and status. Fellows interestingly focuses on the eligible bachelor's point of view as far as the marriage stakes are concerned. An interesting mix of characters is encountered along the way, including a rather blowsy actress with a heart of gold who acts as a fairy godmother to join the various sundry hearts together. Not the least of Fellows's careful characterization is her depiction of two dogs who befriend the heroine and her sister. In *Entanglement*, Fellows uses her deft touch to bring together both romantic and thriller elements again, as in *The Heywood Inheritance*. This time a murder plot against one of the heroes is foiled, and two romances are brought to a satisfactory conclusion.

—Sobhana Rowland

FERBER, Edna.

Nationality: American. **Born:** Kalamazoo, Michigan, 15 August 1885. **Education:** Ryan High School, Appleton, Wisconsin, graduated 1902. **Career:** reporter, Appleton *Daily Crescent*, 1902–04, *Milwaukee Journal*, 1905–08, and *Chicago Tribune*; full-time writer from 1910; lived in New York after 1912; served with the Writers War Board and as a war correspondent with the United States Army Air Force during World War II. Member of the literary Algonquin Round Table which met at the Algonquin Hotel, New York. **Recipient:** Pulitzer prize, 1924, for *So Big*. D.Litt.: Columbia University, New York; Adelphi College, Garden City, New York, USA. **Member:** American Academy. **Died:** 16 April 1968.

ROMANCE AND HISTORICAL PUBLICATIONS

Novels

Dawn O'Hara, The Girl Who Laughed. New York, Stokes, 1911; London, Methuen, 1925.
Fanny Herself. New York, Stokes, 1917; London, Methuen, 1923.
The Girls. New York, Doubleday, 1921; London, Heinemann, 1922.
So Big. New York, Doubleday, and London, Heinemann, 1924.
Show Boat. New York, Doubleday, and London, Heinemann, 1926.
Cimarron. New York, Doubleday, and London, Heinemann, 1930.
American Beauty. New York, Doubleday, and London, Heinemann, 1931.
Come and Get It. New York, Doubleday, and London, Heinemann, 1935.
Nobody's in Town (includes *Trees Die at the Top*). New York, Doubleday, and London, Heinemann, 1938.
Saratoga Trunk. New York, Doubleday, 1941; London, Heinemann, 1942.
Great Son. New York, Doubleday, and London, Heinemann, 1945.
Giant. New York, Doubleday, and London, Gollancz, 1952.
Ice Palace. New York, Doubleday, and London, Gollancz, 1958.

Short Stories (series: Emma McChesney)

Buttered Side Down. New York, Stokes, 1912; London, Methuen, 1926.
Roast Beef, Medium: The Business Adventures of Emma McChesney and Her Son, Jock. New York, Stokes, 1913; London, Methuen, 1920.

Personality Plus: Some Experiences of Emma McChesney and Her Son, Jock. New York, Stokes, 1914.
Emma McChesney & Co. New York, Stokes, 1915.
Cheerful, By Request. New York, Doubleday, 1918; London, Methuen, 1919.
Half Portions. New York, Doubleday, 1920.
Gigolo. New York, Doubleday, 1922; as *Among Those Present,* London, Nash and Grayson, 1923.
Mother Knows Best. New York, Doubleday, and London, Heinemann, 1927.
They Brought Their Women. New York, Doubleday, and London, Heinemann, 1933.
No Room at the Inn. New York, Doubleday, 1941.
One Basket: Thirty-One Stories. New York, Simon and Schuster, 1947.

OTHER PUBLICATIONS

Plays

Our Mrs McChesney, with George V. Hobart (produced New York, 1915).
$1200 a Year, with Newman Levy. New York, Doubleday, 1920.
Minick, with George S. Kaufman, adaptation of the story 'Old Man Minick' by Ferber (produced New York, 1924). *As Old Man Minick: A Short Story ... Minick: A Play*, New York, Doubleday, 1924; London, Heinemann, 1925.
The Eldest: A Drama of American Life. New York, Appleton, 1925.
The Royal Family, with George S. Kaufman (produced New York, 1927). New York, Doubleday, 1928; as *Theatre Royal* (produced London, 1935), London, French, 1936.
Dinner at Eight, with George S. Kaufman (produced New York, 1932; London, 1933). New York, Doubleday, 1932; London, Heinemann, 1933.
Stage Door, with George S. Kaufman (produced New York, 1936; London, 1946). New York, Doubleday, 1936; London, Heinemann, 1937.
The Land Is Bright, with George S. Kaufman (produced New York, 1941). New York, Doubleday, 1941.
Bravo!, with George S. Kaufman (produced New York, 1948). New York, Dramatists Play Service, 1949.

Screenplay: *A Gay Old Dog*, 1919.

Other (autobiography)

A Peculiar Treasure. New York, Doubleday, and London, Heinemann, 1939.
A Kind of Magic. New York, Doubleday, and London, Gollancz, 1963.

*

Film Adaptations: *Cimarron*, 1930, 1960; *So Big*, 1932, 1953; *Showboat*, 1936, 1951; *Come and Get It*, 1936; *Saratoga Trunk*, 1945; *Giant*, 1956; *Ice Palace*, 1960.

Manuscript Collection: State Historical Society of Wisconsin, Madison.

Critical Studies: *Women and Success in American Society in the Works of Edna Ferber* by Mary Rose Shaughnessy, New York, Gordon Press, 1977; *Edna Ferber: A Biography* by Julie Goldsmith Gilbert, New York, Doubleday, 1978.

*   *   *

Though she was also a successful short story writer and playwright, Edna Ferber's greatest literary works are her novels in which she variously combines four major elements: intense and often difficult love affairs; strong, able female protagonists; dramatic portraits of intriguing American locales; and serious, if not always profound, examinations of American values. 'The American Dream' she dissects theoretically includes not only professional success and economic security but also genuine personal fulfilment within a successful marriage and applies to women as well as to men.

In *Saratoga Trunk* Ferber creates tolerance for her tough, angry heroine, Clio Dulaine, a stunning beauty of mixed blood, not only through Clio's decision to marry impecunious gambler Clint Maroon for love but also by distancing Clio's story amid the garish 'elegance' of the racing set of the 1880s. Thus Clio and Clint become acceptable prototypes of Americans who overcome class bias by exploiting their cleverness and guile, for they achieve the 'Dream'.

But within the Ferber canon, dream usually differs sharply from the gritty reality that she depicts and which takes into account racial prejudice, class snobbery, and sexism. Few of her heroines make happy, lasting marriages; professional success tends to be more attainable largely because they can achieve it by themselves, by means of personal determination.

At times, Ferber hangs her crowded plots upon exciting historical books; *Cimarron* sweeps from the Land Rush of 1899 into the 1920s attempting to encapsulate Oklahoma history. Against this background, the marriage of Sabra and Yancey Cravat is both enlarged (they symbolize divergent responses to frontier life) and diminished (place sometimes briefly over-shadows character). *Ice Palace*, a family saga set in Alaska, capitalizes on characters' memories of such early events as the Gold Rush as well as on the territory's thrust toward statehood, using heroine Chris Storm's choice of a mate—dashing outsider or stalwart Alaskan—to reflect conflicting political and economic impulses. In *Giant* the love between cultured Leslie Benedict and her brash husband, Bick, is threatened by tension between her more traditional values and his pragmatic ones. Their personal conflict parallels the struggle between cattle and oil interests in Texas. These stories are vigorous, brisk, and exciting, though the symbolism is a bit obvious.

Show Boat, Ferber's most famous novel, contrasts the pain in the lives of two pairs of lovers—Julie and Steve, victims of the miscegenation legislation, and Magnolia and Gaylord Ravenal, victims of conflicting standards—to the glittering, romantic façade of river life. Similarly, *So Big*, a Pulitzer prize winner, undercuts the myth of idyllic farm life through the account of Selina Peake's struggle to earn a living. Both novels touch upon the problems of single motherhood.

While Ferber clearly depicts the tremendous power of passionate love, she generally demonstrates that romance alone is an inadequate basis for marriage; this theme united with her examination of the American Dream results in worthy, vivid, compelling fiction.

—Jane S. Bakerman

FIELD, Rachel (Lyman).
Nationality: American. **Born:** New York City, 19 September 1894. **Education:** Springfield High School, Massachusetts; Radcliffe College, Cambridge, Massachusetts, 1914–18. **Relations:** married Arthur Siegfried Pederson in 1935; one adopted daughter. **Career:** member of the editorial department, Famous Players-Lasky film company, Hollywood, 1918–23. **Recipient:** Drama League of America prize, 1918; American Library Association Newbery medal, for children's book, 1930. **Died:** 15 March 1942.

ROMANCE AND HISTORICAL PUBLICATIONS

Novels

Time Out of Mind. New York, Macmillan, 1935; London, Macmillan, 1937.
To See Ourselves, with Arthur Pederson. New York, Macmillan, 1937; London, Collins, 1939.
All This and Heaven Too. New York, Macmillan, 1938; London, Collins, 1939.
And Now Tomorrow. New York, Macmillan, 1942; London, Collins, 1943.

Short Story

Christmas in London. Privately printed, 1946.

OTHER PUBLICATIONS

Fiction (for children)

Eliza and the Elves. New York, Macmillan, 1926.
The Magic Pawnshop: A New Year's Eve Fantasy. New York, Dutton, 1927; London, Dent, 1928.
Little Dog Toby. New York, Macmillan, 1928.
Polly Patchwork. New York, Doubleday, 1928.
Hitty, Her First Hundred Years. New York, Macmillan, 1929; as *Hitty: The Life and Adventures of a Wooden Doll*, London, Routledge, 1932.
Pocket-Handkerchief Park. New York, Doubleday, 1929.
Calico Bush. New York, Macmillan, 1931; London, Collier Macmillan, 1966.
The Yellow Shop. New York, Doubleday, 1931.
The Bird Began to Sing. New York, Morrow, 1932.
Hepatica Hawkes. New York, Macmillan, 1932.
Just Across the Street. New York, Macmillan, 1933.
Susanna B. and William C. New York, Morrow, 1934.
The Rachel Field Story Book (includes *The Yellow Shop, Pocket-Handkerchief Park, Polly Patchwork*). New York, Doubleday, 1958; Kingswood, Surrey, World's Work, 1960.

Plays (for children)

Everygirl, in *St Nicholas* (New York), October 1913.
Three Pills in a Bottle (produced Cambridge, Massachusetts, 1917; New York, 1923). Included in *Six Plays*, 1924.
Rise Up, Jennie Smith (produced Cambridge, Massachusetts, 1918). New York, French, 1918.
Time Will Tell (produced Cambridge, Massachusetts, 1920).
The Fifteenth Candle. New York, French, 1921.
Six Plays (includes *Cinderella Married, Three Pills in a Bottle, Columbine in Business, The Patchwork Quilt, Wisdom Teeth, Theories and Thumbs*). New York, Scribner, 1924; *The Patchwork Quilt* published in *One-Act Plays of Today*, edited by J. W. Marriott, London, Gollancz, 1928.
The Cross-Stitch Heart and Other Plays (includes *Greasy Luck, The Nine Days' Queen, The Londonderry Air, At the Junction, Bargains in Cathay*). New York, Scribner, 1927.
Patchwork Plays (includes *Polly Patchwork; Little Square-Toes; Miss Ant, Miss Grasshopper*, and *Mr Cricket; Chimney Sweeps' Holiday; The Sentimental Scarecrow*). New York, Doubleday, 1930.
First Class Matter. New York, French, 1936.
The Bad Penny. New York, French, 1938.

Poetry

The Pointed People: Verses and Silhouettes (for children). New Haven, Connecticut, Yale University Press, and London, Oxford University Press, 1924.
An Alphabet for Boys and Girls (for children). New York, Doubleday, and London, Heinemann, 1926.
Taxis and Toadstools: Verses and Decorations (for children). New York, Doubleday, and London, Heinemann, 1926.
A Little Book of Days (for children). New York, Doubleday, and London, Heinemann, 1927.
Points East: Narratives of New England. New York, Brewer and Warren, 1930.
A Circus Garland. Washington, D.C., Winter Wheat Press, 1930.
Branches Green. New York, Macmillan, 1934.
Fear Is the Thorn. New York, Macmillan, 1936.
Christmas Time (for children). New York, Macmillan, 1941.
Poems (for children). New York, Macmillan, 1957.
Poems for Children. Kingswood, Surrey, World's Work, 1978.

Other

Fortune's Caravan (for children), from translation by Marion Saunders of a work by Lily Jean-Javal. New York, Morrow, 1933; London, Oxford University Press, 1935.
God's Pocket: The Story of Captain Samuel Hadlock, Junior, of the Cranberry Isles, Maine. New York, Macmillan, 1934; London, Macmillan, 1937.
Ave Maria: An Interpretation from Walt Disney's 'Fantasia' Inspired by the Music of Franz Schubert. New York, Random House, 1940.
All Through the Night (for children). New York, Macmillan, 1940; London, Collins, 1954.
Prayer for a Child. New York, Macmillan, 1944.

Editor, *The White Cat and Other Old French Fairy Tales*, by Marie Catherine d'Aulnoy. New York, Macmillan, 1928.
Editor, *American Folk and Fairy Tales*. New York and London, Scribner, 1929.
Editor, *People from Dickens: A Presentation of Leading Characters from the Books of Charles Dickens*. New York and London, Scribner, 1935.

*

Film Adaptations: *All This and Heaven Too*, 1940; *And Now Tomorrow*, 1944; *Time Out of Mind*, 1947.

*　　　*　　　*

In August, 1847, Paris rocked with scandal: the brutal murder of the Duchesse de Praslin was in every headline, on every lip. It was a *cause célèbre* of the juiciest kind, involving as it did a ducal household, a handsome, mysterious governess, identified only as Mlle. D, nine orphaned children, and all the titillation, bloodied handprints, and the Duc's botched suicide by arsenic could provide. Obviously, it was a scandalmonger's delight.

Nearly a century later, the great-niece by marriage of that scarlet lady, Mlle D, told her version of the famous affair in *All This and Heaven Too*, her most successful novel. The almost forgotten players in the 19th-century tragedy are brought back to life by the author's possibly partisan interest in the ancestress on whose tombstone she cracked nuts in her childhood. To Rachel Field, Henriette Deluzy-Desportes was a figure of family legend, not of suggestive headlines. She tells the story of a young governess unfortunate enough to find herself trapped between the unpredictable passions of the half-mad, vindictive Duchesse, and her estranged husband, the blondely Byronic Duc. The truth of the sad story will never now be known, and scarcely matters; but in its day the Praslin murder had an unexpected effect upon the fate of an entire nation, for the scandal helped to topple a shaky monarchy.

Henriette's life took a turn for the better when, hoping to leave notoriety behind, she left Europe to make a new life in America as a schoolmistress. Here she forged her link with the future when she married the novelist's great-uncle, the Rev Henry M. Field, and became for her remaining, happier years, a respected if mildly quirky matron. The closing chapters of her life, and her relations with her husband's famous family (brother Cyrus laid the first Trans-Atlantic cable) are not as fascinating as the earlier, unhappy years—but such is life. In this novel, as in none of her others, Field created a fully rounded, flawed, but sympathetic character in Mlle D. Perhaps she and her great-aunt are each in the other's debt, one for her inspiration, the other for an impassioned defender.

—Joan McGrath

FINCH, Carol.
Pseudonym for Connie Feddersen. **Other Pseudonyms:** Connie Drake, Gina Robins. Also writes as Connie Feddersen. **Nationality:** American. **Born:** Oklahoma, 6 June 1948. **Education:** Oklahoma State University, Stillwater, Oklahoma (tennis scholarship) B.Sc. 1969; Southwestern University, Weatherford, Oklahoma. **Relations:** married Ed Feddersen in 1969; two daughters and one son. **Career:** health and physical education teacher, Scott City, Kansas, 1970–74, biology and geology teacher, Union City, Oklahoma, 1980–83, writing teacher, Yukon Community College, Yukon, Oklahoma, 1984, Redlands College, El Reno, Oklahoma, 1990. Oklahoma and Texas State Doubles Tennis Champion, 1965, 1966, 1967, 1968; National Tennis Team Champions, 1967. **Recipient:** six national awards from *Romantic Times*. **Address:** Rt 1, Box 260, Union City, OK 73090, USA.

ROMANCE AND HISTORICAL PUBLICATIONS

Novels

Rapture's Dream. New York, Zebra, 1982.
Endless Passion. New York, Zebra, 1983.
Dawn's Desire. New York, Zebra, 1983.
Passion's Vixen. New York, Zebra, 1984.
Midnight Fires. New York, Zebra, 1984.
Ecstasy's Embrace. New York, Zebra, 1985.
Wildfire. New York, Zebra, 1986.
Satin Surrender. New York, Zebra, 1986.
Texas Angel. New York, Zebra, 1987.
Captive Bride. New York, Zebra, 1987.
Angel Fire (as Connie Drake). New York, Zebra, 1987.
Beloved Betrayal. New York, Zebra, 1988.
Lone Star Surrender. New York, Zebra, 1988.
Stormfire. New York, Zebra, 1989.
Thunder's Tender Touch. New York, Zebra, 1989.
Love's Hidden Treasure. New York, Zebra, 1990.
Montana Moonfire. New York, Zebra, 1990.
Wild Mountain Honey. New York, Zebra, 1991.
Moonlight Enchantress. New York, Zebra, 1992.
Promise Me Moonlight. New York, Zebra, 1993.
Apache Wind. New York, Zebra, 1993.
Wild Apache Night. New York, Zebra, 1994.

Novels as Gina Robins

Diamond Fire. New York, Pinnacle, 1986.

Secret Splendor. New York, Pinnacle, 1988.
Love's Reckless Rebel. New York, Pinnacle, 1988.
Captive Enchantress. New York, Pinnacle, 1989.
Texas Temptation. New York, Pinnacle, 1989.
Deception's Sweet Kiss. New York, Pinnacle, 1990.
Mississippi Mistress. New York, Pinnacle, 1990.
Love's Sweetest Secret. New York, Pinnacle, 1991.
Whispers of Love. New York, Pinnacle, 1991.
Always and Forever. New York, Pinnacle, 1992.
Wyoming Ecstasy. New York, Pinnacle, 1993.
Forbidden. New York, Pinnacle, 1994.

OTHER PUBLICATIONS

Novels as Connie Feddersen

Dead in the Water. New York, Zebra, 1993.
Dead in the Cellar. New York, Zebra, 1994.
Dead in the Hay. New York, Zebra, 1994.

*

Carol Finch comments:

Rich in historical detail my romances stretch the limits of the traditional genre to include fast-paced action, humour, mystery, and suspense. My novels and those written under my other pseudonym, Gina Robins, vary in era, ranging from mediaeval England, the American Revolution, the War of 1812, the Oklahoma Land Run, to the Old West. The heroines in these books are the hallmark of modern woman establishing herself in male-dominated society. The main focus is on the development of a strong, lasting relationship between the hero and the heroine, the joint efforts of resolving both internal and external conflicts. All of these books are well known for their humour and suspense, as well as lively dialogue. I have written 38 novels and three short stories as both Carol Finch and Gina Robins, all of which are under contract to Zebra and Pinnacle book publishers in New York City.

Under my real name, Connie Feddersen, I have penned the first three mysteries in a series, plus a Christmas mystery short story, which are all set in a small, rural community in Oklahoma. These novels include not only mystery and suspense, but also humour and lively dialogue between the heroine, Amanda Hazard, and the hero, Nick Thorn. I have been recognized for my contribution to love and laughter in historical romance, and have received numerous awards and nominations in the last decade.

*   *   *

For three years the romance writer Gina Robins's true identity was one of the best kept secrets of the publishing world—however, in 1988, Robins finally revealed herself to be the writer Carol Finch, also known as Connie Drake and Connie Feddersen. This respected novelist writes light historical romances as Robins, Finch, and Drake, and has recently launched into mystery-romances under her real name, Connie Feddersen. The author explains why she adopted the other writing names in the *Romantic Times*, '. . . I write at least five 150,000 word historicals a year, and because Carol Finch could only release two books per year without flooding the market, Gina Robins and Connie Drake were hatched'.

The author stopped writing as Connie Drake after publishing *Angel Fire* in 1987, concentrating instead on her other pseudonyms. Lady Meagan Lowell, the heroine of *Angel Fire*, is a volatile Saxon who is pledged to the Norman 'Dark Prince', Trevor Burke, as part of a peace settlement. Meagan is unhappy with this decision, and although Burke has not planned to marry, he finds himself interested by Meagan's spirit. The humour of this book, which is also a feature of the author's other works, captivates the reader, and the witty dialogue between the main characters makes this an interesting read.

As Finch the author has written several enjoyable books, featuring fun-loving heroes, independent heroines, and adventure, set against well described locations. In *Lone Star Surrender*, the author combines suspense, adventure, and romance in a historical setting. Tara Winslow, the heroine, comes to Texas to help her father put a rich and corrupt rancher in jail. Her first encounter with the hero (and her future lover) Sloane Prescott, is when Sloane finds her lying unconscious by the roadside. Tara is the daughter of his partner, and Sloane is afraid that she will reveal his secret—that he is the Night Rider of Pal Duro Canyon, the legendary local phantom who steals horses. Tara decides to help him, not only by keeping quiet but also by helping him to find a missing locket which will solve a 30-year old mystery.

Finch/Robins/Drake is a very sensual writer, indulging in frank and sexy love scenes between the main characters. In *Captive Bride* the heroine Rozalyn DuBois has some sensual encounters with her hero. She gets more than she bargains for when she asks trapper Dominic Baudeliar to help her in a harmless deception. Anxious to grant her 'dying' grandmother's request that she get engaged, Rozalyn chooses Dominic to help in her masquerade. Unfortunately Rozalyn is the daughter of Dominic's rival, and he kidnaps her to force her father to trade fairly. The book contains some farcical encounters, including one in which Rozalyn is given to the Sioux Indians, who promptly return her as she causes so much trouble! The story travels from St Louis to the Wind River mountains, and contains some evocative descriptions of the landscape. Stranded in a cabin in the wilderness, Rozalyn and Dominic finally give in to the strong attraction between them. They acknowledge their love for each other but realize that the family feud which exists must be sorted out before they can have any future together.

Montana Moonfire finds Victoria 'Tory' Flemming Cassidy about to marry Hubert Carrington Frazier II, when she is kidnapped by her father's business partner. Tory is a very proper young lady, and Dru Sullivan is a rugged rancher used to hard ways and hard living. Both gradually learn a lot from each other, and eventually marry. The book is filled with fast-paced dialogue, action, and wit. *Apache Wind* brings a beautiful but wilful lawyer, the appropriately named Tempest Litchfield, into contact with a half-breed Apache who has been accused of murder. She realizes that he is innocent and sets out to prove it, only to have love, and the fact that he kidnaps her, complicate matters.

The author has received much publicity and success as Gina Robins. As Robins she uses witty one-liners, farcical situations, and a vivid imagination to create well-written historical romances. In *Diamond Fire*, Brant Diamond, an American privateer, agrees to help in a raid on St Mary's island. He ends up abducting a youth who tries to warn the British of his plans. The youth is actually a strong willed woman, Catrina Hamilton, who has escaped from an arranged marriage. The action takes place in Scotland, France, and the Bermuda Triangle. Both characters are fiercely independent and proud, and both fight their sexual attraction at great length, before submitting to it, and finally admitting that they are in love. The 'Terror of Texas', Jacqueline Reid is the heroine of *Love's Reckless Rebel*. Jacqueline falls in love with the business rival of her grandfather, after initially mistaking him for the man who is supposed to accompany her to Texas from New Orleans. Jacqueline and Mason 'Mace' Gallagher travel home together, fighting to outwit, and outlive, the stranger who wants Jacqueline dead.

Finch has now been asked to write for a new romantic series featuring characters in the over 45 age group. A critic for the *Romantic Times* commented that this series aims to show that 'love is even more sensual when a mature hero understands a woman of experi-

ence'. This will provide Finch with a new challenge—but one that she will undoubtedly meet with her usual style and humour.

—P. Campbell

FINDLEY, Timothy.
Nationality: Canadian. **Born:** Toronto, Ontario, 30 October 1930. **Education:** Rosedale Public School, Toronto; St Andrews College, Aurora, Ontario; Jarvis Collegiate, Toronto; Royal Conservatory of Music, Toronto, 1950–53; Central School of Speech and Drama, London. **Career:** stage, television, and radio actor, 1951–62; charter member, Stratford Shakespearean Festival, Ontario, 1953; contract player with H.M. Tennent, London, 1953–56; toured USA in *The Matchmaker*, 1956–57; studio writer, CBS, Hollywood, 1957–58; copywriter, CFGM Radio, Richmond Hill, Ontario. Playwright-in-residence, National Arts Centre, Ottawa, 1974–75; writer-in-residence, University of Toronto, 1979–80, Trent University, Peterborough, Ontario, 1984, and University of Winnipeg, 1985. Chairman, Writers Union of Canada, 1977–78. President, English Canadian Centre, International PEN, 1986–87. **Recipient:** Canada Council award, 1968, 1978; Armstrong award, for radio writing, 1971; ACTRA award, for television documentary, 1975; Toronto Book award, 1977; Governor General's award, 1977; Senior Arts award, 1978, 1983; Ontario Arts Council award, 1977–78; Anik award, for television writing, 1980; Canadian Booksellers award, 1984; Canadian Authors Association prize, 1985, 1991; Trillium award, 1989; Mystery Writers of America Edgar award, 1989; National Radio award, 1989, 1990. D.Litt.: Trent University, 1982; University of Guelph, Ontario, 1984; York University, Ontario, 1989. Officer, Order of Canada, 1986; Order of Ontario, 1991. **Agent:** Virginia Barber Literary Agency, 353 West 21st Street, New York, New York 10011, USA. **Address:** Stone Orchard, Box 419, Cannington, Ontario L0E IEO, Canada.

ROMANCE AND HISTORICAL PUBLICATIONS

Novels

The Butterfly Plague. New York, Viking Press, 1969; London, Deutsch, 1970.
The Wars. Toronto, Clarke Irwin, 1977; New York, Delacorte Press, and London, Macmillan, 1978.
Famous Last Words. Toronto, Clarke Irwin, and New York, Delacorte Press, 1981; London, Macmillan, 1987.
Not Wanted on the Voyage. Toronto, Viking, 1984; New York, Delacorte Press, and London, Macmillan, 1985.
The Telling of Lies. Toronto, Penguin, 1986; New York, Dell, 1988.

Short Stories

Dinner Along the Amazon. Toronto and London, Penguin, 1984; New York, Penguin, 1985.
Stones. Toronto, Penguin, and London, Viking, 1988; New York, Delta, 1990.

OTHER PUBLICATIONS

Novels

The Last of the Crazy People. New York, Meredith Press, and London, Macdonald, 1967.
The Telling of Lies. Toronto, Penguin, 1986; London, Macmillan, and New York, Dell, 1988.

Plays

The Paper People (televised 1968). Published in *Canadian Drama* (Toronto), vol 9, no 1, 1983.
The Journey (broadcast 1971). Published in *Canadian Drama* (Toronto), vol 10, no 1, 1984.
Can You See Me Yet? (produced Ottawa, 1976). Vancouver, Talonbooks, 1977.
John A, Himself music by Berthold Carriere (produced London, Ontario, 1979).
Strangers at the Door (radio script), in *Quarry* (Kingston, Ontario), 1982.
Daybreak at Pisa: 1945, in *Tamarack Review* (Toronto), Winter 1982.
Inside Memory: Pages from a Writer's Workbook. Toronto, HarperCollins, 1990.
The Stillborn Lover (produced London and Ottawa, 1993). Winnipeg, Blizzard, 1993.

Screenplays: *Don't Let the Angels Fall*, 1970; *The Wars*, 1983.

Radio Plays and Documentaries: *The Learning Stage* and *Ideas* series, 1963–73; *Adrift*, 1968; *Matinee* series, 1970–71; *The Journey*, 1971; *Missionaries*, 1973.

Television Plays and Documentaries: *Umbrella* series, 1964–66; *Who Crucified Christ?*, 1966; *The Paper People*, 1968; *The Whiteoaks of Jalna* (7 episodes), from books by Mazo de la Roche, 1971–72; *The National Dream* series (8 episodes), with William Whitehead, 1974; *The Garden and the Cage*, with William Whitehead, 1977; *1832* and *1911* (*The Newcomers* series), 1978–79; *Dieppe 1942*, with William Whitehead, 1979; *Other People's Children*, 1981; *Islands in the Sun* and *Turn the World Around* (*Belafonte Sings* series), with William Whitehead, 1983.

Other

Imaginings, with Janis Rapaport, illustrated by Heather Cooper. Toronto, Ethos, 1982.

*

Critical Studies: 'Timothy Findley Issue' of *Canadian Literature* (Vancouver), Winter 1981; *Timothy Findley* by Wilfred Cude, Toronto, Dundurn Press, 1982; *Introducing Timothy Findley's 'The Wars'*, Toronto, ECW Press, 1990, and *Front Lines: The Fiction of Timothy Findley*, Toronto, ECW Press, 1991, both by Lorraine M. York; *Moral Metafiction: The Novels of Timothy Findley* by Donna Pennee, Toronto, ECW Press, 1991.

*   *   *

One of Canada's most successful novelists today, Timothy Findley began his career as an actor and scriptwriter, working on various stage, television, and radio productions. By 1962 he began to write full-time resulting in a short story collection, *Dinner Along the Amazon*. His first novel, *The Last of the Crazy People*, is set in southern Ontario, and, like his early stories, is strongly autobiographical. It concerns a lonely child's struggle for survival in a mad and strange world. The demise and disintegration of one eccentric family is told with terrifying horror.

Findley's second novel, *The Butterfly Plague*, was praised by Rex Reed as 'the best book about Hollywood' he had ever read, but did not gain the author critical acclaim. Illustrating Findley's fascination with decadence and corruption, the book is set in the early decades of the 20th century and deals with the movie industry, film directors, and superstars. It shows the brutality of the real world in

comparison to cinematic ideals and illusions. As one critic pointed out, North American 'dreams of immortality, . . . of dynasties, . . . of peace, and . . . beauty' are analogous to 'monarch butterflies: beautiful and ostensibly fragile creatures whose annual migration' in thousands is like a 'plague of dreams'.

In the early 1970s Findley received critical recognition for his work on radio and television documentaries. As playwright-in-residence at the National Arts Centre, Ottawa, he wrote *Can You See Me Yet?*, produced in March 1976. This play, set in an insane asylum in southern Ontario in 1938, is a psychodrama that asks the question posed in the title: Is there anyone there to see the life of the inmate Cassandra Wakelin? Does anyone care enough to know and accept her as she is? Many of Findley's works deal with madness which the author believes can give us access to a form of reality that is stimulating and magical. His works invite us to look again through the mad person's eyes at what might be there.

The need to pay attention to another human being is an issue that Findley brings out repeatedly. In his two historical novels set during war-time, *The Wars* and *Famous Last Words*, Findley asserts the validity of an individual's experience in the midst of chaos, senseless violence, and confusion. In both of these novels the reader is made to see how history and factual or newspaper accounts of events do not necessarily tell the 'truth' about any incident. Both these novels have been labelled by critics as examples of postmodern fiction; *Famous Last Words* specifically as 'historiographic metafiction'.

The Wars describes the emotional and psychological breakdown of a soldier during World War I. John Moss remarks that 'other novelists have conveyed the terrors of the battlefield with more authority, but none has so vividly portrayed the sheer carnage and waste, the desolation and depravity of corpse piled upon corpse upon corpse, the mutilations and putrefaction of flesh, and always the mud, and the shifting earth, the flames, the gas'. There are several powerfully emotional scenes—one where a well-meaning, innocent German soldier is shot erroneously as he reaches for his binoculars, and another where Robert Ross is raped and sodomized in a public bath by his fellow soldiers. The novel climaxes with Ross trapped in a burning barn with about 50 horses, which conjures up images of the fiery apocalypse, and is a fitting culmination of the hellish experience of war.

Famous Last Words is a larger, panoramic historical novel focusing on the events surrounding the Duke and Duchess of Windsor between 1910 and 1945. The novel includes characters from both literature and real life: the hero, Hugh Selwyn Mauberley, is a fictionalization of a character found in Ezra Pound's 13-part poem of the same name published in 1920. Non-fictional personages, such as Rudolf Hess, Ezra Pound, Joachim von Ribbentrop, and Sir Harry Oakes seem indistinguishable from Findley's own fictional characters. Mauberley, a minor writer, becomes involved in a complicated and dangerous plot composed of high-ranking figures from both the Allied and Axis causes. He becomes the key witness and the reporter of a secret cabal that aimed at restoring the Windsors to the throne as puppet rulers after the destruction of the two world forces. Flirting with the splendour of wealth, power, and elitist fascism, Mauberley, 'out of key with his time', slowly becomes entangled in the web of corruptions, betrayals, and failures of the power-hungry glittery people with whom he associates. A brilliant line found scrawled on the walls of the Grand Elysium Hotel illustrates the paradoxical nature of writing: 'All I have written here is true; except the lies'.

One of Findley's greatest strengths as an artist lies in his retelling and re-working of old tales. Critics have found intertextual relations between Findley's war stories and the memoirs of Siegfried Sassoon, Robert Graves, and Edmund Blunden. Lorraine York argues that in Findley's novels war is a central trope that mirrors 'a larger network of aggression—sexual, familial, intellectual . . . . Timothy Findley's fiction is not only haunted by the spectre of war; it is a compulsive testament to the infinite repetitions of war in our domestic, gender and class conflicts'. Aside from war stories, Findley has also re-told other crucial texts of Western culture. *Not Wanted on the Voyage*, is a historical fable based on the Biblical story of Noah and the great flood. It has been read as an allegory of the nuclear age. In *Headhunter* Findley reworks Joseph Conrad's *Heart of Darkness* to create a parallel between late-20th century North American society and the colonizing and rapacious tendencies of late 19th century Europe. Both use civilization to gain wealth, to ruin and enslave others. The literary and historical 'ghosts' in the novel—characters such as Emma Bovary, Susanna Moodie, Gatsby, and Kurtz, are there to demonstrate the repetitive tendency of history. Breaking down the boundaries between the literary, the mythic, the factual, and the political in his novels, Findley reminds us that as our culture is approaching its millennium, it is in danger of destroying all the things that we consider beautiful and valuable.

—Eleanor Ty

FINLAY, Fiona. See **STUART, Vivian.**

FINLEY, Glenna. American. 1925—. See 2nd edition, 1990.

FISKE, Sharon. See **HILL, Pamela.**

FITZGERALD, Ellen. See **STEVENSON, Florence.**

FITZGERALD, Julia. See **HAMILTON, Julia.**

FITZGERALD, Valerie.
Nationality: Canadian. **Born:** India in 1927. **Education:** India and England. **Relations:** married E.P. Fitzgerald; one daughter and one son. Left India in 1947; has lived in England, Switzerland, Ireland, Kenya, and Italy; now lives in Ottawa. **Recipient:** Georgette Heyer award, 1981, for *Zemindar*; Romantic Novelists Association Major award, 1982, for *Zemindar*; Elizabeth Goudge Historical trophy, 1982, for *Zemindar*. **Address:** c/o Bodley Head Ltd, 20 Vauxhall Bridge Road, London SW1V 2SA, England.

ROMANCE AND HISTORICAL PUBLICATIONS

Novel

Zemindar. London, Bodley Head, 1981.

*   *   *

Valerie Fitzgerald's sprawling but adroitly executed novel, *Zemindar*, deservedly won the 1981 Georgette Heyer award for a historical novel. It is a romantic story of unusual discernment, set against the dramatic background of India during the 1857 mutiny. The plot is a traditional one, with the heroine, Laura, becoming involved in hazardous exploits and, in the process, discovering truths about herself, and her feelings for the hero Oliver.

The novel's strong strand of romance is enhanced by the vivid realism in which this is rooted, and from which it flowers. The refulgent descriptions of the Indian landscape, and the conveyance of life in the villages and bazaars are authoritative and compelling. They arise from the author's personal memories of growing up in India on a zemindari estate similar to the one featured in the book, and there is throughout a feeling for the 'real India' which so deeply appeals to both Laura and Oliver. As the zemindar (landowner) of a vast estate, Oliver has a passionate sense of responsibility for his land and his people. He is a believable and fleshed-out character, although it is amusing to trace in his contradictory moods of glinting appeal and brooding arrogance a combination of certain characteristics of both Heathcliff and Darcy. Fitzgerald, as an 'enthusiastic Austenite', acknowledges the possible influence of Jane Austen in her work, if not that of Emily Brontë. Her own heroine is able to demolish social hypocrisies with something of Elizabeth Bennet's wit and economy of style. Laura is both reflective and robust: she reads Marcus Aurelius for pleasure, studies Urdu as part of her effort to understand the real nature of India, but also learns how to handle a revolver to protect herself against the possible 'ultimate outrage'.

Despite its length of almost 800 pages, *Zemindar* sustains its romantic interest and suspense until the end. In the convention of romantic fiction, the author manages to keep the couple at arms' length until the book's later stages. She does this convincingly by making the first frightening eruptions of the Mutiny curtail Laura's stay at the zemindari estate. It is only after a series of terrifying happenings that Laura, caught up in the five-month siege of Lucknow, recognizes her feelings for Oliver.

In this satisfying novel Fitzgerald illustrates her capacity to present the panoramic as well as an intimate view of events; she knows exactly when to use succinctness in the expression of human emotions, and—most of all—when and how to harness the lusher images of romance.

—Mary Cadogan

FLANAGAN, Thomas (James Bonner).
Nationality: American. **Born:** Greenwich, Connecticut, 5 November 1923. **Education:** Amherst College, Massachusetts, B.A. 1945; Columbia University, New York, M.A. 1948, Ph.D. in English 1958. **Military Service:** United States Naval Reserve, 1942–44. **Relations:** married Jean Parker in 1949; two daughters. **Career:** instructor, 1949–52, and assistant professor, 1952–59, Columbia University; assistant professor, 1960–67, associate professor, 1967–73, professor, 1973–78, and chair of the department of English, 1973–76, University of California, Los Angeles. Since 1978 professor of English, State University of New York, Stony Brook. **Recipient:** American Council of Learned Societies grant, 1962; Guggenheim fellowship, 1962; National Book Critics Circle award, 1979. **Address:** Department of English, State University of New York, Stony Brook, New York 11794, USA.

ROMANCE AND HISTORICAL PUBLICATIONS

Novels

The Year of the French. New York, Holt Rinehart, and London, Macmillan, 1979.
The Tenants of Time. New York, Dutton, and London, Bantam, 1988.

OTHER PUBLICATIONS

Other

The Irish Novelists 1800–1850. New York, Columbia University Press, 1959.

*   *   *

Thomas Flanagan's novels *The Year of the French* and *The Tenants of Time* span three centuries of Irish history, from the invasion of Cromwell to 1908. Each book focuses on a specific act of rebellion, each relies on a dizzying array of narrative voices, each blends historical and fictional characters, and each ultimately views the study of history as a romance, but the living of it as a perplexing and often tragic burden. To some extent his characters make history, but most are unmade by it, caught in the dangerous vortex of crosscurrents that is the sad, often merciless, history of Ireland.

The central event in *The Year of the French* is the brief series of battles in 1798 between Irish-speaking peasants of County Mayo, led by an army from republican France, and a huge English force commanded by Lord Cornwallis. The skeletal history is simple: the English were victorious, the French were deported, the Irish were massacred or hanged, and the Act of Union was forced upon the farcical Irish Parliament. It is, however, the flesh and blood history that Flanagan seeks, the story of the internal and external forces that led men to lift pikes in rebellion or to hang rebels for king and country.

Flanagan explores his characters' motives by allowing them to narrate most of the book (there is also a nameless general narrator which provides a matrix for their stories). The most important voices are those of Owen McCarthy and Reverend Mr Broome, Anglican vicar of Killala, County Mayo.

McCarthy speaks Gaelic and English and, in a sense, straddles two worlds. He is an itinerant schoolmaster, teaching English, Latin, and other subjects. He is also an accomplished Gaelic poet, drunkard, and seducer. He sees himself as carrying on the ancient bardic tradition, and, indeed, he recites his verses throughout the west and south, where Irish was the dominant tongue until the Great Famine. Hearing about his countrymen in Munster rising up to fight the English at 'Tara of the Kings', and seeing the gradual decline of the Gaelic language and culture that give meaning to his work and life, he joins in the Mayo revolt and is hanged.

Reverend Mr Broome is a loyal English subject who spends years trying to reconcile his distaste for what he deems to be a barbarous Irish culture with the shame he feels for the unchristian treatment of the Irish by absentee landlords and their agents. Broome attempts to write what he calls an 'Impartial Narrative' of the rebellion, and he succeeds up to a point. He sets aside racial and religious prejudice, but he does not and cannot learn of the inner lives of the peasants for whom he has sympathy; he does not speak their language, either literally or figuratively. McCarthy and Broome are assisted by other narrators. Together, they help recreate and juxtapose a collection of images that for a time give the reader the illusion of knowing what 1798 was like.

The Tenants of Time is a darker book, a kaleidoscopic remembrance of the dismal Fenian rebellion of 1867, the subsequent rise of the Land League, and the rise and fall of Charles Stewart Parnell (1846–91). In Kilpeder, County Cork, the principal setting for the novel, a small band of rebels attack a police barracks, skirmish in Clonbrony Wood, and surrender in the face of a cavalry onslaught. The surviving rebels are jailed and mistreated, and spend the rest of their lives trying to understand and give meaning to their one moment of youthful bravado. Once again, Flanagan relies on a variety of narrators, among them Hugh McMahon, a gentle schoolmaster and former Fenian; Patrick Prentiss, son of a Catholic barrister and self-styled historian; and Lionel Forrester, cousin to the Earl of Ardmor, 'owner' of Kilpeder. Through them and a nameless narrative voice, we hear others—Ned Nolan, Fenian rebel and IRA assassin; Lord and Lady Ardmor, the latter the lover of Robert Delaney, former rebel and MP for Cork; the great Parnell himself; and many others.

Although there are light moments, the interrelated stories of the demise of the Fenians and those close to them, the ruthless infighting among the Irish politicians, and the duplicity of the English government are sombre reading. The underlying message, that we are all time's tenants on a lease of unknown length or dubious purpose, haunts the self-conscious characters and the reader as well.

Flanagan's books are pro-Irish, but the clouded definition of exactly who is Irish makes this an uncertain pronouncement. He lavishes sympathy and scorn on Catholics, Anglo-Irish Protestants, and Englishmen alike. Ireland is both a place and a state of mind. Flanagan attempts with great success to give us history as experienced by the diverse religious, economic, political, and social groupings that have for centuries had a stake in Ireland.

—Thomas J. Morrisey

———

FLEMING, Caroline. See **MATHER, Anne.**

———

FLETCHER, Inglis.
Nationality: American. **Born:** Inglis Minna Clark, Alton, Illinois, in 1888. **Education:** St Louis School of Fine Arts; Washington University, St Louis; University of California, Berkeley. **Relations:** married John George Fletcher (deceased); one son. **Career:** member of the North Carolina Governor's Commission for the Restoration of Governor Tryon's Palace; full-time writer. **Recipient:** Sir Walter Raleigh award, 1953; North Carolina Governor's Gold medal. D.Litt.: Greensboro College, North Carolina. **Died.**

ROMANCE AND HISTORICAL PUBLICATIONS

Novels (series: Carolina)

Carolina:
   Raleigh's Eden. Indianapolis, Bobbs Merrill, 1940; London, Hutchinson, 1941.
   Men of Albemarle. Indianapolis, Bobbs Merrill, 1942; London, Hutchinson, 1943.
   Lusty Wind for Carolina. Indianapolis, Bobbs Merrill, 1944; London, Hutchinson, 1947.
   Toil of the Brave. Indianapolis, Bobbs Merrill, 1946; London, Hutchinson, 1948.
   Roanoke Hundred. Indianapolis, Bobbs Merrill, 1948; London, Hutchinson, 1949.
   Bennett's Welcome. Indianapolis, Bobbs Merrill, 1950; London, Hutchinson, 1952.
   Queen's Gift. Indianapolis, Bobbs Merrill, 1952; London, Hutchinson, 1953.
The Young Commissioner. London, Hutchinson, 1951.
The Scotswoman. Indianapolis, Bobbs Merrill, 1955; London, Hutchinson, 1956.
The Wind in the Forest. Indianapolis, Bobbs Merrill, 1957; London, Hutchinson, 1958.
Cormorant's Brood (Carolina). Philadelphia, Lippincott, 1959.
Wicked Lady (Carolina). Indianapolis, Bobbs Merrill, 1962.
Rogue's Harbor (Carolina). Indianapolis, Bobbs Merrill, 1964.

OTHER PUBLICATIONS

Novels

The White Leopard. Indianapolis, Bobbs Merrill, and London, Hodder and Stoughton, 1931.

Red Jasmine. Indianapolis, Bobbs Merrill, 1932; London, Hutchinson, 1933.

Other

Pay, Pack, and Follow (autobiography). New York, Holt, 1959.

*   *   *

Although Inglis Fletcher began her writing career with two novels about Africa (*The White Leopard* and *Red Jasmine*), her reputation as a historical romance writer rests upon her numerous works about the Carolinas. Her 'Carolina' series comprises seven novels detailing the development of the Albemarle region of North Carolina from its earliest settlement through the days immediately following the American Revolution. Additionally, Fletcher wrote several more Carolina novels not officially included in the 'Carolina' series.

Fletcher's interest in the turbulent birth of the Carolinas stems from her family history; her genealogical researches were the springboard for the intensive historical studies that produced her books. In her novels she combines actual historical personages with fictional characters, some of them bearing the names of her own ancestors. Her talent as a writer meshes perfectly with her talent as an historical researcher, for her plots weave believably in and out of the events of her chosen period with both fact and fiction ringing equally true. It is the case that on occasion, to speed the development of a plot, she rearranges the dates of some historical occurrences; but, as in *Lusty Wind for Carolina*, she takes care to admit a compression of period so that the reader might be well-informed as well as entertained.

The characters in Fletcher's work are three-dimensional; she does not allow history to do her work in developing her more famous characters, but takes the trouble to show them as personalities. It would be incorrect to say that her books have heroes and heroines as do many historical-romantic novels. Rather, the realistic nature of the stories dictates that the characters be real people with human problems stemming on the one hand from their personal relationships and on the other from their participation in the creation of a new country. The heroes and heroines of these volumes are the human focus of the times. This is not to deny the romance in the Carolina novels, for there are multiple romantic entanglements in each book. The love affairs are true to life rather than larger than life, even when dealing with such near-mythic figures as Flora Mac-Donald (*The Scotswoman*) or Anne Bonney. It is interesting to note that much of the romance involved in the books is between married partners; while courtship is not neglected, Fletcher paints a charming but real picture of married love again and again. The characters that she creates (and recreates) are thinking people who set more store by reason than by pure emotion.

In each book the history is vividly detailed. Fletcher has a great facility for providing historical background necessary to the plot without becoming bogged down in lengthy exposition. Instead, she uses the devices of letters or conversation to provide information while advancing the plot at a crisp, steady pace. The reader who prefers the romantic side to the historical is not forgotten, however, for the books have plenty of adventure, from pirate attacks to thwarted love. The dialogue has a 'period' feel without being stilted or static. Likewise, the dialect of the slaves is understandable and not overdone. Fletcher treats all social classes, from aristocrats to slaves, as individuals. Her view of the place of each social class in daily life has the feel of truth.

For the reader of all Fletcher's books there is a sense of continuity. In the 'Carolina' series, the families of her fictional characters are followed through several generations, and, of course, the contemporary historical personalities appear from one book to the next.

It is a bit unnerving for the reader who completes *Queen's Gift*, the last volume of the 'Carolina' series, and then reads *Wicked Lady*, a non-series title published a few years later. The two books read like different treatments of the same plot, with variances in some characters and dates. In view of Fletcher's inventiveness, this duplication is inexplicable. Both books are quite readable, with the earlier volume being much more detailed, and consequently the superior tale. Aside from this anomaly, Fletcher's novels provide a chronicle of life in early America as it probably was lived.

—Susan Quinn Berneis

———

FOOTE, Shelby.
Nationality: American. **Born:** Greenville, Mississippi, 17 November 1916. **Education:** University of North Carolina, Chapel Hill, 1935–37. **Military Service:** United States Army, 1940–44: captain; and Marine Corps, 1944–45. **Relations:** married Gwyn Rainer in 1956 (second marriage); two children. **Career:** novelist-in-residence, University of Virginia, Charlottesville, November 1963; playwright-in-residence, Arena Stage, Washington, DC, 1963–64; writer-in-residence, Hollins College, Virginia, 1968. **Recipient:** Guggenheim fellowship, 1955, 1956, 1957; Ford fellowship, for drama, 1963; Fletcher Pratt award, for non-fiction, 1964, 1974; University of North Carolina award, 1975; Mississippi Historical Society Wailes award, 1992; St Louis University literary award, 1992; National Endowment for the Humanities Frankel prize, 1992. D.Litt.: University of the South, Sewanee, Tennessee, 1981; Southwestern University, Memphis, Tennessee, 1982; Christian Brothers University, Memphis, Tennessee, 1991; University of South Carolina, 1991; University of North Carolina, 1991. **Address:** 542 East Parkway South, Memphis, Tennessee 38104, USA.

ROMANCE AND HISTORICAL PUBLICATIONS

Novels

Tournament. New York, Dial Press, 1949.
Follow Me Down. New York, Dial Press, 1950; London, Hamish Hamilton, 1951.
Love in a Dry Season. New York, Dial Press, 1951.
Shiloh. New York, Dial Press, 1952.
Jordan County: A Landscape in Narrative (includes stories). New York, Dial Press, 1954.
September September. New York, Random House, 1978.

OTHER PUBLICATIONS

Play

Jordan County: A Landscape in the Round (produced Washington, DC, 1964).

Other

The Civil War: A Narrative:
   1. *Fort Sumter to Perryville*. New York, Random House, 1958.
   2. *Fredericksburg to Meridian*. New York, Random House, 1963.
   3. *Red River to Appomattox*. New York, Random House, 1974.
The Novelist's View of History. Winston-Salem, North Carolina, Palaemon Press, 1981.
Conversations with Shelby Foote, edited by William C. Carter. Jackson, University Press of Mississippi, 1989.

*

Film Adaptation: *September, September*, 1992.

Manuscript Collection: Southern Historical Collection, Chapel Hill, North Carolina.

Critical Studies: 'Shelby Foote Issue' (includes bibliography) of *Mississippi Quarterly* (State College), October 1971, and *Delta* (Montpellier, France), 1977; *Shelby Foote* by Helen White and Reading Sugg, Boston, Twayne, 1982; *Shelby Foote: Novelist and Historian* by Robert L. Philips, Jackson, University of Mississippi Press, 1992.

*   *   *

Shelby Foote is probably better known as a historian rather than as a novelist. This seems a strange state of affairs for the man who is seen in France to be the 'next William Faulkner', and who has produced some of the best literature to come out of the American South this century. His novels are beautifully crafted, extensively researched, and detailed works which inform the reader about specific events in the character's life or history.

Foote has said that the novel is the literary genre that he prefers most. He also commented that he could see no distinction between novel writing and history writing as both make considerable demands on the narrative skill of the writer. By the time he wrote *Shiloh* in 1952, Foote had formulated his views on how one should write a historical novel. In an interview with Harvey Breit in the *New York Times Book Review*, the author said 'In this one [*Shiloh*] no historical character says or does anything except what I have accurate evidence of his having said or done'. For his 'evidence' Foote turned to the memoirs of Grant and Sherman, and the records of the men who had been at the battle. *Shiloh* was subsequently hailed by Walker Percy as 'an American Iliad, a unique work writing the scholarship of the historian and the high readability of the first-class novelist'. The book is a powerful account of two days in a battle that took place in Tennessee, in April 1862, between Union and Confederacy troops. Foote creates a complete picture of the events of those days through the monologues of several of the men present—from officers to foot soldiers.

The use of monologue is also seen in *Follow Me Down*, a vivid account of a religious crime of passion. Foote cleverly divides the book into three sections; the first and last sections involve the accounts of dispassionate witnesses to both the crime and the court case, however, the middle section involves the accounts of the protagonists—Luther Eustis, the murderer, and Beulah, his victim. Starting with the discovery of a woman's body in a river, and the subsequent arrest and confession of Eustis, as recounted initially by a court clerk, a journalist, and a deaf and dumb boy (who was in love with Beulah), the author slowly builds up a picture of the events leading up to the tragedy. In the second section we find the god-fearing Eustis 'tempted' by the seductive Beulah into leaving his wife and children. Eustis hears a voice which he believes to be God (but later identifies as the devil) telling him how wrong he has been, and he eventually realizes that his only solution is to kill Beulah. He lures her out to the lake, where they have previously made love, and strangles her.

Through Beulah's account, however, we learn a more tragic tale. Sold by her mother for 400 dollars to a man much older than herself, Beulah embarks on a sordid life of prostitution and easy sex. Despite this she secretly waits for the man of her dreams to turn up. When finally she meets Eustis she falls in love and goes away with him believing that she has found the man who is right for her. Instead she is killed.

In a later novel, *September September*, Foote uses the framework of the kidnapping of a young black boy from Memphis to relate two important historical events—the trouble at the Central High in Little Rock and the Russian crisis which both occur in the month of September. Foote skilfully presents a black bourgeois family dealing with this trauma.

Shelby Foote cites Tacitus, Marcel Proust, Tolstoy, and Stendhal among the writers who have influenced him most. His style of writing is succinct, and his plots contain just the right blend of detail, accuracy, and interest necessary to make them outstanding works of literature.

—P. Campbell

———

FORBES, Esther.
Nationality: American. **Born:** Westborough, Massachusetts, 28 June 1891. **Education:** Bradford Junior College, graduated 1912; University of Wisconsin, Madison, 1916–18. **Relations:** married Albert Learned Hoskins in 1926 (divorced 1933). **Career:** staff member, Houghton Mifflin Company, publishers, Boston, 1920–26, 1942–46. **Recipient:** Pulitzer prize, for history, 1943; American Library Association Newbery medal, for children's book, 1944. D.Litt.: Clark University, Worcester, Massachusetts, 1943; University of Maine, Orono, 1943; University of Wisconsin, 1949; Northeastern University, Boston, 1949; Wellesley College, Massachusetts, 1959; LLD.: Tufts University, Medford, Massachusetts. **Member:** American Academy of Arts and Sciences. **Died:** 12 August 1967.

ROMANCE AND HISTORICAL PUBLICATIONS

Novels

O Genteel Lady!. Boston, Houghton Mifflin, 1926; London, Heinemann, 1927.
Miss Marvel. Boston, Houghton Mifflin, 1935.
Paradise. New York, Harcourt Brace, and London, Chatto and Windus, 1937.
The General's Lady. New York, Harcourt Brace, 1938; London, Chatto and Windus, 1939.
Johnny Tremain. Boston, Houghton Mifflin, 1943; London, Chatto and Windus, 1944.
The Running of the Tide. Boston, Houghton Mifflin, 1948; London, Chatto and Windus, 1949.
Rainbow on the Road. Boston, Houghton Mifflin, 1954; London, Chatto and Windus, 1955.

OTHER PUBLICATIONS

Other

Ann Douglas Sedgwick: An Interview. Boston, Houghton Mifflin, 1928.
A Mirror for Witches, in Which Is Reflected the Life, Machinations, and Death of Famous Doll Bilby, Who, with a More Than Feminine Perversity, Preferred a Demon to a Mortal Lover. Boston, Houghton Mifflin, and London, Heinemann, 1928.
Paul Revere and the World He Lived In. Boston, Houghton Mifflin, 1942.
America's Paul Revere (for children). Boston, Houghton Mifflin, 1946.
The Boston Book. Boston, Houghton Mifflin, 1947.

*

Film Adaptation: *Johnny Tremaine*, 1957.

Manuscript Collections: American Antiquarian Society, Worcester, Massachusetts; Clark University Library, Worcester, Massachusetts.

Critical Study: *Esther Forbes* by Margaret Erskine, Worcester, Massachusetts, Worcester Bicentennial Committee, 1976.

*   *   *

Following her earlier adult historical romance novels, and building on her 1942 Pulitzer prize-winning non-fiction research into the life of Paul Revere and the British-American War of Revolution, Esther Forbes was moved by the events of World War II to write her only novel for children, *Johnny Tremain*, which may be the book for which she will be remembered.

It is worth stressing that although written and published as a 'children's book', there is nothing 'childish' about it. In some editions it is subtitled, 'A novel for young and old'. There is only one real 'child' in the book, a foolish spoiled little girl, Isannah, yet she is matched with an equally foolish, vain, and spoiled young adult woman, Lavinia Lyte. Johnny may be just a young teenager at the beginning, but at that time adult behaviour was expected of all but mere infants. *Johnny Tremain* is no more a children's book than, for example, *Treasure Island*, or Leon Garfield's stories of 18th-century apprentices. Indeed one of its great strengths is its appeal to adult and child reader alike. *Johnny Tremain* is a book about being a sensitive, responsible human in a terrifying, beautiful world.

Johnny is directly involved in the early actions of the American rebellion when he joins in with the crowd dressed as Indians, chopping open crates of heavily-taxed tea and hurling the contents into Boston Harbour—the famous Boston Tea Party! For the most part, he observes, rides with messages, and reports to others who are more directly active.

Forbes's narrative is plainly written, with no attempt to invoke the prose of the period, nor the older, more formal spoken style of the protagonists, except where non-fictional leaders of the rebellion deliver weighty, highly charged public speeches. Forbes creates the sights, sounds, and even the smells of late 18th-century Boston, drawing effortlessly on her research to select precise details (such as the narrow streets, simple food, the cheek-by-jowl living of animals among humans, the buckets of water from a public stand-pump, and hand-rolled paper cartridges of lead ball and gun powder) that evoke the way that life used to be.

For a 'classic' narrative, dealing with pivotal issues and events, *Johnny Tremain* seems curiously understated. Although concerned with the beginning of an arguably justified war, it is strikingly anti-war, refusing to offer any glorification of violence. With horror Johnny witnesses the execution of a British deserter, one whom Johnny had helped to flee from the army. Much later he sees a little American girl, jubilant with a grenadier bearskin hat, and he can only think of the grenadier who is by now most likely dead, possibly another of the soldiers Johnny knew. Crippled for most of the book, Johnny is little more than an observer. Forbes stops the book as the sun sets on the day after fighting began, leaving Johnny hopeful, but stunned by the inglorious agonized death of his closest friend.

The point of *Johnny Tremain*—'That a man can stand up'—was intensely relevant in the struggle for democracy against the appalling tyranny and brutality of both Nazi Germany and Imperial Japan. It continued to be relevant during the grey decades of the Cold War, when western democracy was pitted against Soviet and Chinese socialism. More than 50 years later it continues to be relevant when countries released from repressive centralized control, doctrinaire dictatorship, and one-party brutality, struggle to let their men and women 'stand up'. Forbes has achieved something far more significant than just a 'historical novel'.

Currently only two other books by Forbes remain in print (recently reprinted within the United States). The first, *A Mirror for Witches*, might now be described as 'faction' or factual fiction. It is an account, from the point of view of one of the alleged witches, of the Salem witch-hunting hysteria, and consequent trials. One of Forbes's ancestors was accused of being a witch and died in prison. Another was troubled by visions of the devil, and of black imps biting her feet. The story, of a jealous wife's accusations of witchcraft against the young girl that her husband has adopted, was in fact turned into a Sadler's Wells ballet in 1952, choreographed by Andrée Howard, with music by Dennis Aplvor.

The other book still in print, *O, Genteel Lady!*, written in the year of her marriage, is the story of a young lady who rebels against the 19th-century conventions of her time. With the rise of feminist consciousness, this book should be much more widely read.

The out-of-print Bantam edition of *Paradise* reminds us that there were indeed pioneers and Indians 100 years before the days of James Fenimore Cooper's 'Leatherstocking' sagas, and that there was much more to the Puritans and the Pilgrim Fathers than religious bigotry and witch-hunting. Jazan Parre, an independent young woman in a male-dominated world of Puritan elders, marries the religiously high-minded Forethought Fearing, and struggles to preserve her identity. Indian wars, religious intolerance, and restrictions rage around her, and she is one of Forbes's most fascinating achievements, an excellent match for Johnny, or Fenimore Cooper's 'Leatherstocking'.

Forbes's last book, *Rainbow on the Road*, deserves to be much better known. It tells of one long New England ante-bellum summer in the life of 13-year-old orphan Eddy Creamer, travelling with his adoptive 'uncle', Jude Rebough, an itinerant commercial artist cum made-to-order portrait painter. Like Johnny Tremaine, Jude is potentially a true artist. His fantastic pictures of an orchestra of dressed crickets, or a factory of flies and spiders weaving spiders' webs on power looms have great naive charm, and the portrait of his would-be love Emma Faucett leaning, in a state of New England undress, from an upstairs window is redolent of Rubens. Jude is a most appealing character, kicking against the restrictions of his society, itching to amuse his fellows, even to the extent of hinting to a gullible housewife they meet along the road that he and Eddy are body-snatchers!. As they ramble, free from the restrictions of their small home town, they encounter a travelling broadsheet and ballad pedlar, Phineas Sharp, who helps to construct a legend (and make a profit on the proceeds) about a roving Robin Hood-figure, Ruby Lambkin, with a spitting resemblance to Jude.

Finally it should be noted that Forbes began work as an editor with Houghton Mifflin, and always prided herself on 'discovering' Rafael Sabatini—for that alone she deserves to be remembered with gratitude. But her own books are a significant literary achievement that far exceeds anything by Sabatini. She must not be forgotten, or neglected as only a one good book, and that a 'children's' book, writer. It is time to reclaim her to the ranks of the greatest.

—John Gough

———

FORD, Elbur.   See **PLAIDY, Jean.**

———

FORD, Elizabeth.   See **GIBBS, Mary Ann.**

———

FORD, Ford Madox.
Pseudonyms: Daniel Chaucer; Fenil Haig. **Nationality:** British.
Born: Ford Hermann Hueffer in Merton, Surrey, 17 December

1873; grandson of the artist Ford Madox Brown; changed name to Ford Madox Ford, 1919 (work published under this name from 1923). **Education:** privately in Folkestone, Kent; at University College School, London. **Military Service:** officer in the Welch Regiment in France, 1915–17. **Relations:** married Elsie Martindale in 1894 (separated 1909); two daughters. **Career:** writer from 1892; collaborated with Joseph Conrad, 1898–1906; founding editor, *English Review*, London 1908–10; moved to Paris, 1922; founding editor, *Transatlantic Review*, Paris, 1924; in later years lived in the south of France and in New York City. **Recipient:** D.Litt.: Olivet College, Michigan, 1938. **Died:** 26 June 1939.

ROMANCE AND HISTORICAL PUBLICATIONS

Novels (series: The Fifth Queen Trilogy)

Romance, with Joseph Conrad. London, Smith Elder, 1903; New York, McClure, 1904.
The Fifth Queen Trilogy:
  The Fifth Queen and How She Came to Court. London, Rivers, 1906.
  Privy Seal: His Last Venture. London, Rivers, 1907.
  The Fifth Queen Crowned: A Romance. London, Nash, 1908.
The Half Moon: A Romance of the Old World and the New. London, Nash, and New York, Doubleday, 1909.
The Portrait. London, Methuen, 1910.
Ladies Whose Bright Eyes: A Romance. London, Constable, 1911; New York, Doubleday, 1912; revised edition, Philadelphia, Lippincott, 1935.
The Young Lovell: A Romance. London, Chatto and Windus, 1913.
A Little Less Than Gods: A Romance. London, Duckworth, and New York, Viking Press, 1928.

OTHER PUBLICATIONS

Novels

The Shifting of the Fire. London, Unwin, and New York, Putnam, 1892.
The Inheritors: An Extravagant Story, with Joseph Conrad. New York, McClure Philips, and London, Heinemann, 1901.
The Benefactor: A Tale of a Small Circle. London, Brown Langham, 1905.
An English Girl: A Romance. London, Methuen, 1907.
Mr Apollo: A Just Possible Story. London, Methuen, 1908.
A Call: The Tale of Two Passions. London, Chatto and Windus, 1910.
The Simple Life Limited (as Daniel Chaucer). London and New York, Lane, 1911.
The Panel: A Sheer Comedy. London, Constable, 1912; revised edition, as *Ring for Nancy*, Constable, and Indianapolis, Bobbs Merrill, 1913.
The New Humpty-Dumpty (as Daniel Chaucer). London and New York, Lane, 1912.
Mr Fleight. London, Latimer, 1913.
The Good Soldier: A Tale of Passion. London and New York, Lane, 1915.
The Marsden Case: A Romance. London, Duckworth, 1923.
The Nature of a Crime, with Joseph Conrad. London, Duckworth, and New York, Doubleday, 1924.
Parade's End (The Tietjens Tetralogy). New York, Knopf, 1950.
  Some Do Not. London, Duckworth, and New York, Seltzer, 1924.
  No More Parades. London, Duckworth, and New York, Boni, 1925.

A Man Could Stand Up. London, Duckworth, and New York, Boni, 1926.
The Last Post. New York, Boni, 1928; as *Last Post*, London, Duckworth, 1928.
When the Wicked Man. New York, Liveright, 1931; London, Cape, 1932.
The Rash Act. New York, Long and Smith, and London, Cape, 1933.
Henry for Hugh. Philadelphia, Lippincott, 1934.
Vive le Roy. Philadelphia, Lippincott, 1936; London, Allen and Unwin, 1937.

Plays

The Fifth Queen Crowned, with F.N. Connell, adaptation of the novel by Ford (produced London, 1909).
Mister Bosphorus and the Muses; or, A Short History of Poetry in Britain. London, Duckworth, 1923.

Poetry

The Questions at the Well, with Sundry Other Verses for Notes of Music (as Fenil Haig). London, Digby Long, 1893.
Poems for Pictures and for Notes of Music. London, MacQueen, 1900.
The Face of the Night: A Second Series of Poems for Pictures. London, MacQueen, 1904.
From Inland and Other Poems. London, Rivers, 1907.
Songs from London. London, Mathews, 1910.
High Germany: Eleven Sets of Verse. London, Duckworth, 1912.
Collected Poems. London, Goschen, 1913.
Antwerp. London, Poetry Bookshop, 1915.
On Heaven, and Poems Written on Active Service. London, Lane, 1918.
A House. London, Poetry Bookshop, 1921.
New Poems. New York, Rudge, 1927.
Collected Poems. New York, Oxford University Press, 1936.
Buckshee. Cambridge, Massachusetts, Pym Randall Press, 1966.
Selected Poems, edited by Basil Bunting. Cambridge, Massachusetts, Pym Randall Press, 1971.

Other

The Brown Owl: A Fairy Story (for children). London, Unwin, and New York, Stokes, 1892.
The Feather (for children). London, Unwin, and New York, Cassell, 1892.
The Queen Who Flew: A Fairy Story (for children). London, Bliss Sands and Foster, 1894.
Ford Madox Brown: A Record of His Life and Work. London, Longman, 1896.
The Cinque Ports: A Historical and Descriptive Record. Edinburgh, Blackwood, 1900.
Rossetti: A Critical Essay on His Art. London, Duckworth, and New York, Dutton, 1902.
Hans Holbein the Younger: A Critical Monograph. London, Duckworth, and New York, Dutton, 1905.
England and the English: An Interpretation. New York, McClure, 1907.
  The Soul of London: A Survey of a Modern City. London, Rivers, 1905.
  The Heart of the Country: A Survey of a Modern Land. London, Rivers, 1906.
  The Spirit of the People: An Analysis of the English Mind. London, Rivers, 1907.
Christina's Fairy Book (for children). London, Rivers, 1906.
The Pre-Raphaelite Brotherhood: A Critical Monograph. London, Duckworth, and New York, Dutton, 1907.

Ancient Lights and Certain New Reflections. London, Chapman and Hall, 1911; as *Memories and Impressions: A Study in Atmospheres*, New York, Harper, 1911.

The Critical Attitude. London, Duckworth, 1911.

This Monstrous Regiment of Women. London, Minerva, 1913.

The Desirable Alien: At Home in Germany, with Violet Hunt. London, Chatto and Windus, 1913.

Henry James: A Critical Study. London, Secker, 1914; New York, Boni, 1915.

When Blood Is Their Argument: An Analysis of Prussian Culture. London, Hodder and Stoughton, 1915.

Between St Dennis and St George: A Sketch of Three Civilizations. London, Hodder and Stoughton, 1915.

Zeppelin Nights: A London Entertainment, with Violet Hunt. London, Lane, 1915.

Thus to Revisit: Some Reminiscences. London, Chapman and Hall, and New York, Dutton, 1921.

Women and Men. Paris, Three Mountain Press, 1923.

Joseph Conrad: A Personal Remembrance. London, Duckworth, and Boston, Little Brown, 1924.

A Mirror to France. London, Duckworth, and New York, Boni, 1926.

New York Is Not America. London, Duckworth, and New York, Boni, 1927.

New York Essays. New York, Rudge, 1927.

No Enemy: A Tale of Reconstruction. New York, Macaulay, 1929.

The English Novel from the Earliest Days to the Death of Conrad. Philadelphia, Lippincott, 1929; London, Constable, 1930.

Return to Yesterday (Reminiscences 1894–1914). London, Gollancz, 1931; New York, Liveright, 1932.

It Was the Nightingale (reminiscences). Philadelphia, Lippincott, 1933; London, Heinemann, 1934.

Provence: From Minstrels to the Machine. Philadelphia, Lippincott, 1935; London, Allen and Unwin, 1938.

Great Trade Route. New York, Oxford University Press, and London, Allen and Unwin, 1937.

Portraits from Life: Memories and Criticisms. Boston, Houghton Mifflin, 1937; as *Mightier Than the Sword*, London, Allen and Unwin, 1938.

The March of Literature from Confucius' Day to Our Own. New York, Dial Press, 1938; as *The March of Literature from Confucius to Modern Times*, London, Allen and Unwin, 1939.

The Bodley Head Ford Madox Ford, edited by Graham Greene. London, Bodley Head, 4 vols, 1962–63.

Critical Writings, edited by Frank MacShane. Lincoln, University of Nebraska Press, 1964.

Letters of Ford Madox Ford, edited by Richard M. Ludwig. Princeton, New Jersey, Princeton University Press, 1965.

Your Mirror to My Times (reminiscences), edited by Michael Killigrew. New York, Holt Rinehart, 1971; as *Memories and Impressions* (not same as 1911 book), London, Penguin, 1979.

Pound/Ford: The Story of a Literary Friendship (correspondence with Ezra Pound), edited by Brita Lindberg-Seyersted. London, Faber, and New York, New Directions, 1982.

The Ford Madox Ford Reader, edited by Sondra J. Stang. Manchester, Carcanet, 1986.

A History of Our Own Times, edited by Solon Beinfeld and Sondra J. Stang. Bloomington, Indiana University Press, 1988.

Translator, *The Trail of the Barbarians*, by Pierre Loti. London, Longman, 1917.

*

Bibliography: *Ford Madox Ford 1873–1939: A Bibliography of Works and Criticism* by D.D. Harvey, Princeton, New Jersey, Princeton University Press, 1962; by P. Armato, in *English Literature in Transition 10* (Greensboro, North Carolina), 1967.

Manuscript Collections: Princeton University Library, New Jersey; Yale University Library, New Haven, Connecticut; University of Virginia Library, Charlottesville.

Critical Studies: *Ford Madox Ford: A Study of His Novels* by Richard A. Cassell, Baltimore, Johns Hopkins University Press, 1961, and *Ford: Modern Judgements* edited by Cassell, London, Macmillan, 1972; *Ford Madox Ford's Novels: A Critical Study* by John A. Meixner, Minneapolis, University of Minnesota Press, 1962; *Novelist of Three Worlds: Ford Madox Ford* by Paul L. Wiley, Syracuse, New York, Syracuse University Press, 1962; *Ford Madox Ford: The Essence of His Art* by R. W. Lid, Berkeley, University of California Press, 1964; *Ford Madox Ford: From Apprentice to Craftsman* by Carol Burke Ohmann, Middletown, Connecticut, Wesleyan University Press, 1964; *The Life and Work of Ford Madox Ford* by Frank MacShane, New York, Horizon Press, and London, Routledge, 1965, and *Ford: The Critical Heritage* edited by MacShane, Routledge, 1972; *The Limited Hero in the Novels of Ford* by Norman Leer, East Lansing, Michigan State University Press, 1966; *Ford Madox Ford* by Charles G. Hoffmann, New York, Twayne, 1967; *The Alien Protagonist of Ford Madox Ford* by H. Robert Huntley, Chapel Hill, University of North Carolina Press, 1970; *The Saddest Story: A Biography of Ford Madox Ford* by Arthur Mizener, New York, World, 1971, London, Bodley Head, 1972; *Ford Madox Ford* by Sondra J. Stang, New York, Ungar, 1977, and *The Presence of Ford Madox Ford* edited by Stang, Philadelphia, University of Pennsylvania Press, 1981; *The Life in the Fiction of Ford Madox Ford* by Thomas C. Moser, Princeton, New Jersey, Princeton University Press, 1980; *Ford Madox Ford: Prose and Politics* by Robert Green, London, Cambridge University Press, 1981; *Ford Madox Ford and the Voice of Uncertainty* by Ann Barr Snitow, Baton Rouge, Louisiana State University Press, 1984; *Fairy Tale and Romance in Works of Ford Madox Ford* by Timothy Weiss, Lanham, Maryland, University Press of America, 1984; 'Ford Madox Ford Issue' of *Antaeus* (New York), Spring 1986; *Critical Essays on Ford Madox Ford* edited by Richard A. Cassell, Boston, Hall, 1987; *Ford Madox Ford* by Alan Judd, London, Collins 1990, and Cambridge, Massachusetts, Harvard University Press, 1991.

*   *   *

Ford Madox Ford wrote more than 70 books, including several volumes of outstanding poetry. He is better known for his work in genres other than historical fiction, for example his personal favourite *The Good Soldier*, and the Tietjens books (*Some Do Not*, *No More Parades*, *A Man Could Stand Up*, and *The Last Post*).

However, a significant proportion of the oeuvre does come under Ford's own title of 'romance' and 'The Fifth Queen Trilogy' is a vast and important work of historical fiction. Together, they make up a significant part of his corpus and cast an intriguing light on the better known work.

In the trilogy Ford experiments with his historical knowledge, bringing a psychological realism and human motive to the material. This was commented on when the trilogy first appeared. A reviewer for the *Daily News* wrote: 'There is a power and thought in the characterization, and the whole work has an astonishing effect in revealing to us the flesh and blood side of history'. These qualities are still evident and remain the chief sources of the trilogy's abiding interest for readers.

The tale of Katharine Howard's career at court, culminating in her becoming Henry VIII's fifth wife and eventual fifth victim in the tower, surrounded as it is by Machiavellian intrigue and religious reformations, in the hands of a less skilful writer could so easily have become merely a series of factional plots and counter plotting, of little interest to contemporary readers. But Ford, while placing his cast of thousands within a huge historical setting, actually keeps the narrative focus small, preferring rather to explore in detail the lives of a few principal characters. Ford produced what amounts to an historical whodunnit, where suspense and danger are the key. The works exploit an obvious fascination with a crisis moment in English history: the 'Old Faith' is set against the 'New Learning', religion against heresy, the ideas of the infamous Machiavelli are evident in the culture, 'the walls have ears' and: 'God hath withdrawn himself . . . and all mankind goeth a-mumming' (*Privy Seal*).

'The Fifth Queen Trilogy' begins with Henry's unhappy marriage to Anne of Cleves, and the burgeoning Protestant movement that is sweeping the land. Into this world arrives the poor, yet learned Catholic, Katharine Howard, who steadily gains influence at court, and with the king. This narrative line is the link between the three volumes, around which several other narratives are interwoven—Thomas Cromwell's rise and demise, the schism between Church and State, the tragic tale of Sir Thomas Culpepper who loves Katharine yet unwittingly becomes the source of her downfall.

Privy Seal follows the progress of Katharine's career, Henry's proposal, and Anne of Cleves agreeing to the annulment of her marriage to the king. Ford weaves a powerful love story for the ageing king and young queen against the intrigue of Cromwell's world: 'He played upon people's fear, troubled them with apprehensions. It was part of the tradition that Cromwell had given all his men. He ruled England by such fears'.

In the final volume the focus is a familial one: a tender peace has returned as Katharine tries to heal the wounds within Henry's warring brood. Yet her integrity proves her downfall, a tragic end for a powerful woman: 'I must be the same make of Queen that I am as a woman'.

The trilogy remains the most compelling of Ford's works. His other 'romances' tend to be sketchy and less interesting. In *The Young Lovell* he returns to Tudor times; *Ladies Whose Bright Eyes* is a dream narrative in which the publisher Mr Sorrell travels back to 1326 and falls in love with a woman '600 years dead'. The most interesting of these novels is *An English Girl* with its Citizen Kane-like tale of corruption and insightful investigation of the culture clash when a young English heroine falls in love with the all-American boy.

—Catherine S. Wearing

FORESTER, C(ecil) S(cott).
Nationality: British. **Born:** Cairo, Egypt, 27 August 1899; grew up in the London suburbs. **Education:** Alleyne's School, London, and Dulwich College, London, 1910–17; studied medicine at Guy's Hospital, London, but left without qualifying. **Relations:** married 1) Kathleen Belcher in 1926 (divorced 1944), two sons; 2) Dorothy Ellen Foster in 1947. **Career:** writer from 1917; screenwriter in Hollywood, 1932; war correspondent for *The Times*, London, in Spain, 1936–37, and subsequently in Czechoslovakia during the Nazi occupation; in later life lived in Berkeley, California. **Recipient:** James Tait Black memorial prize, 1940. **Died:** 2 April 1966.

ROMANCE AND HISTORICAL PUBLICATIONS

Novels (series: Horatio Hornblower)

The Shadow of the Hawk. London, Lane, 1928; as *The Daughter of the Hawk*, Indianapolis, Bobbs Merrill, 1928.

Death to the French. London, Lane, 1932; as *Rifleman Dodd*, with *The Gun*, Boston, Little Brown, 1943.
The Gun. London, Lane, and Boston, Little Brown, 1933.
The Happy Return (Hornblower). London, Joseph, 1937; as *Beat to Quarters*, Boston, Little Brown, 1937.
Flying Colours (Hornblower). London, Joseph, 1938; Boston, Little Brown, 1939.
A Ship of the Line (Hornblower). London, Joseph, 1938; as *Ship of the Line*, Boston, Little Brown, 1938.
The Captain from Connecticut. London, Joseph, and Boston, Little Brown, 1941.
The Commodore. London, Joseph, 1945; as *Commodore Hornblower*, Boston, Little Brown, 1945.
Lord Hornblower. London, Joseph, and Boston, Little Brown, 1946.
Mr Midshipman Hornblower. London, Joseph, and Boston, Little Brown, 1950.
Lieutenant Hornblower. London, Joseph, and Boston, Little Brown, 1952.
Hornblower and the Atropos. London, Joseph, and Boston, Little Brown, 1953.
Hornblower in the West Indies. London, Joseph, 1958; as *Admiral Hornblower in the West Indies*, Boston, Little Brown, 1958.
Hornblower and the Hotspur. London, Joseph, and Boston, Little Brown, 1962.
Hornblower and the Crisis: An Unfinished Novel (includes story 'The Last Encounter'). London, Joseph, 1967.

Short Stories

Two-and-Twenty. London, Lane, and New York, Appleton, 1931.
The Nightmare. London, Joseph, and Boston, Little Brown, 1954.
The Man in the Yellow Raft. London, Joseph, and Boston, Little Brown, 1969.
Gold from Crete. Boston, Little Brown, 1970; London, Joseph, 1971.

OTHER PUBLICATIONS

Novels

A Pawn Among Kings. London, Methuen, 1924.
Payment Deferred. London, Lane, 1926; Boston, Little Brown, 1942.
Love Lies Dreaming. London, Lane, and Indianapolis, Bobbs Merrill, 1927.
The Wonderful Week. London, Lane, 1927; as *One Wonderful Week*, Indianapolis, Bobbs Merrill, 1927.
Brown on Resolution. London, Lane, 1929; as *Single-Handed*, New York, Putnam, 1929.
Plain Murder. London, Lane, 1930; New York, Dell, 1954.
The Peacemaker. London, Heinemann, and Boston, Little Brown, 1934.
The African Queen. London, Heinemann, and Boston, Little Brown, 1935.
The General. London, Joseph, and Boston, Little Brown, 1936.
The Ship. London, Joseph, and Boston, Little Brown, 1943.
The Sky and the Forest. London, Joseph, and Boston, Little Brown, 1948.
Randall and the River of Time. Boston, Little Brown, 1950; London, Joseph, 1951.
The Good Shepherd. London, Joseph, and Boston, Little Brown, 1955.
Hunting the Bismarck. London, Joseph, 1959; as *The Last Nine Days of the Bismarck*, Boston, Little Brown, 1959; as *Sink the Bismarck!*, New York, Bantam, 1959.

Short Stories

The Paid Piper. London, Methuen, 1924.

Plays

U 97. London, Lane, 1931.
Nurse Cavell, with C.E. Bechhofer Roberts (produced London, 1934). London, Lane, 1933.

Screenplays: *Forever and a Day*, with others, 1944; *Captain Horatio Hornblower*, with others, 1951.

Other

Napoleon and His Court. London, Methuen, and New York, Dodd Mead, 1924.
Josephine, Napoleon's Empress. London, Methuen, and New York, Dodd Mead, 1925.
Victor Emmanuel II and the Union of Italy. London, Methuen, and New York, Dodd Mead, 1927.
Louis XIV, King of France and Navarre. London, Methuen, and New York, Dodd Mead, 1928.
Nelson (biography). London, Lane, 1929; as *Lord Nelson*, Indianapolis, Bobbs Merrill, 1929.
The Voyage of the Annie Marble. London, Lane, 1929.
The Annie Marble in Germany. London, Lane, 1930.
Marionettes at Home. London, Joseph, 1936.
The Earthly Paradise. London, Joseph, 1940; as *To the Indies*, Boston, Little Brown, 1940.
Poo-Poo and the Dragons (for children). London, Joseph, and Boston, Little Brown, 1942.
The Barbary Pirates (for children). New York, Random House, 1953; London, Macdonald, 1956.
The Age of Fighting Sail: The Story of the Naval War of 1812. New York, Doubleday, 1956; as *The Naval War of 1812*, London, Joseph, 1957.
The Hornblower Companion. London, Joseph, and Boston, Little Brown, 1964.
Long Before Forty (autobiography). London, Joseph, 1967; Boston, Little Brown, 1968.

Editor, *The Adventures of John Wetherell*. New York, Doubleday, 1953; London, Joseph, 1954.

*

Film Adaptations: *Brown on the 'Resolution'*, 1935; *Captain Horatio Hornblower, RN*, 1951, from the novel *Captain Hornblower, R.N.*; *The African Queen*, 1951; *The Pride and the Passion*, 1957, from the novel *The Gun*; *Sink the Bismarck*, 1960, from the novel *Hunting the Bismarck*.

Critical Study: *C.S. Forester* by Sanford Sternlicht, Boston, Twayne, 1981.

*   *   *

He never won a Nobel prize or a Pulitzer or any major literary award, but when Cecil Scott Forester died in 1966 his obituary commenced on the front page of the *New York Times*, eight million copies of his books had been sold, and the name of his great creation, the 20th-century superhero of historical fiction was a household word: Captain Horatio Hornblower. Paperback editions, the film *Captain Horatio Hornblower*, and serialization in the *Saturday Evening Post* ensured that Hornblower was in the public eye for more than 30 years. Not until Ian Fleming's James Bond smashed

his way into the collective consciousness of the Anglo-American reading public in the 1950s was Hornblower's primacy in escapist fiction challenged. That a 19th-century British naval officer was ultimately replaced by a contemporary British undercover agent as the nonpareil fantasy hero of the general reading public indicated a shift in values during the last half of the 20th century. Hornblower was a hero of and for the World War II generation, and Bond was the darling of the Cold War generation.

Forester was a genuinely great storyteller who loved the creative, imaginative process that turned words into the illusion of a past reality. Forester's strengths are sharp, swift, sometimes Dickensian characterization, carefully thought-out plots, and, most of all, accurate historical details. Forester was an avid reader of naval history. He studied all aspects of life at sea in the age of sail, and masterfully integrated accurate technical information into a fascinating narrative. Particularly, he based the character of Hornblower on his deep knowledge of the life and times of Admiral Horatio Nelson, and of another real-life British naval hero of the Napoleonic Wars, Captain Thomas, Lord Cochrane. Furthermore, he created a historical naval milieu by studying the once popular nautical novels of Captain Frederick Marryat, like *Mr Midshipman Easy* (1836).

The 11-novel Hornblower saga is best read and enjoyed in historical order, not in the order of writing. In *Mr Midshipman Hornblower* the 17-year-old Hornblower reports aboard HMS *Justinian*, becomes seasick (a weakness he never shakes in 30 years at sea), is involved in a duel, but fortunately is transferred to the frigate *Indefatigable*, under the command of the dashing Captain Sir Edward Pellew, his mentor and model. Hornblower gets his first taste of command when he brings a prize to port. Along the way he is captured by the Spanish but released after an heroic act.

Four years pass and in *Lieutenant Hornblower* Horatio serves under the Queeg-like Captain Sawyer and his pusillanimous successor. He saves the day for England by planning and executing a courageous action against a Spanish fort. He returns to England with a prize, but is then a lieutenant without a billet, waiting for war with France to break out again. In this work the reader meets two major architectonic characters in the saga: Hornblower's life-long friend and shipmate, Lieutenant William Bush, and Maria Mason, dumpy and not quite young, the daughter of his landlady, to whom he proposes as war erupts and he receives a command.

In *Hornblower and the Hotspur*, Horatio is in command of the sloop *Hotspur*. He marries Maria and Bush is his first lieutenant. Hornblower attacks French shore installations and then defeats a much larger French warship. Maria has a son and then becomes pregnant again when her husband returns to Portsmouth. As the novel ends Hornblower is promoted to captain.

In *Hornblower and the Crisis*, unfinished at Forester's death, Hornblower is preparing for the French invasion of Britain. He captures some documents that help him to force the French to sea where Nelson can get at them. Voilà: Trafalgar!

Hornblower and the Atropos is post-Trafalgar. Maria is pregnant again, and Horatio, a junior captain, gets the *Atropos*. A daughter is born as Hornblower finishes directing Nelson's funeral. After cruising successfully with the *Atropos* in the Mediterranean, Hornblower loses the ship, for it is given to the King of the Two Sicilies. Disgusted, Hornblower returns home to seek command of a new frigate. In Portsmouth he learns that his children are ill with smallpox.

Six months later he is at sea again, captain of the frigate *Lydia*, in *The Happy Return* (*Beat to Quarters*). Again Bush is his first lieutenant, and we meet Lady Barbara Wellesley, who will be Hornblower's second wife. Meanwhile, his children have died of smallpox. Hornblower must help an odious rebel band capture a Spanish ship of the line, which he turns over to the dictator El Supremo. Learning that Spain has quit Napoleon and joined the Allies, he must recapture the *Natividad* even though Lady Barbara is aboard the *Lydia*. The battle is vicious and the victorious *Lydia* is badly battered. Lady Barbara succours the wounded while Horn-blower repairs his ship. He falls in love with the beautiful aristocrat but cannot bring himself, a married man, to make love to her. She angrily, if temporarily, sweeps out of his life, and Horatio returns home to Maria, seemingly relieved at having escaped commitment and scandal.

A Ship of the Line finds Hornblower in command of the battleship *Sutherland*. Bush is still his first lieutenant. Lady Barbara has married an admiral, Hornblower's superior. Horatio saves a fleet of East Indiamen from French privateers through brilliant shiphandling. Then he attacks the Spanish coast and routs with his batteries a French army marching down a road. Not surprisingly, he does not get on well with Barbara's husband, who orders him to attack a French fort, an effort doomed to failure. The *Sutherland* winds up fighting four French ships of the line. Hornblower is taken prisoner and faces years of captivity.

Flying Colours, however, finds Hornblower escaping in France, building a small boat, having an affair with a French girl, and rowing down the Loire to Nantes, where disguised as Dutch officers loyal to the French, he and the maimed Bush recapture a British cutter and sail her to the British Channel fleet. He soon learns that Lady Barbara's husband is dead, and that Maria too has died giving birth to a son who survived. Hornblower the hero is honoured by the Prince Regent. Now affluent and famous, Hornblower takes his infant son to Lady Barbara and the yarn ends with Hornblower knowing she is his for the asking.

The Commodore (*Commodore Hornblower*) opens with Horatio and Barbara married. Hornblower is promoted to commodore and sent to the Baltic to harass French shipping and exert diplomatic pressure on the Swedes and the Russians. He is now a major player on the stage of world events. After victorious sea fights directed from his flagship, the *Nonsuch*, Hornblower the diplomat sails to Russia where he stiffens Czar Alexander's resolve to defy Napoleon. He prevents an assassination of the Czar, gets drunk for the first time, and has sex with the countess Caterine, who gives him fleas. At the siege of Riga, Hornblower on horseback saves the Russian defenders by leading a counter-attack. The Russian army and the British fleet check the French while Napoleon meets his destiny at Moscow. Hornblower gets the Prussians to desert Napoleon, and thus he is instrumental in the overthrow of the despot, but then the hero falls ill with typhus (the fleas!). He recovers at home in Barbara's arms.

Lord Hornblower finds the hero suppressing a mutiny and accepting the surrender of Le Havre. He becomes provisional governor (like MacArthur in Japan). His friend Bush is killed in action while Hornblower is elevated to a peerage. He returns to England, but soon goes back to France to rescue his former mistress, who dies in the attempt. Hornblower is captured and sentenced to death, but is saved by Waterloo.

Hornblower in the West Indies (*Admiral Hornblower in the West Indies*) has the hero a rear admiral, commanding the British West Indies squadron long after the end of the Napoleonic War. He thwarts an attempt to rescue his old nemesis from St Helena. On the way home from his last command Hornblower saves his wife and the other passengers of the ship they are embarked in, through superior seamanship in a storm. Lady Barbara tells her husband that she has never loved anyone but him, and Hornblower has been made happy forever.

The short story, 'The Last Encounter' published with *Hornblower and the Crisis*, concludes the saga. In 1848 the 72-year-old Hornblower, now Admiral of the Fleet and retired, is visited by a madman who turns out to be the future Napoleon III. Thus the saga ends on a humorous note.

The theme of the Hornblower saga is the man alone. Forester discourses on the problems of independent command and its stresses on character, honour, integrity, and courage. For Forester the ulti-mate source of virtue is a well-developed conscience.

The key to the success of Forester's historical novels lies in his training as a film writer. The works are episodic, vivid, and easily visualized. Characterization is unambiguous and emphasis is decidedly on entertainment.

Forester's historical novels about the Peninsular War, *Death to the French* (*Rifleman Dodd*) and *The Gun*, are well worth the read. In *The Captain from Connecticut* Forester tried to introduce an American Hornblower, Captain Joshua Peabody, USN, but failed. It is Hornblower who sails on.

—Sanford Sternlicht

FORRESTER, Helen.
Pseudonyms: Jamunadevi Bhatia; June Bhatia; June Edwards; J.Rana. **Nationality:** Canadian. **Born:** Hoylake, Cheshire, 6 June 1919. **Education:** privately in England; Liverpool evening institutes, 1933–40. **Relations:** married Avadh Behari Bhatia in 1950; one son. **Career:** writer, since 1953. **Recipient:** Beaver awards, 1970, for *Liverpool Daisy*, and 1977, for the then unpublished book, *The Moneylenders of Shahpur*; literary excellence citation, Edmonton, 1977; Government of Alberta achievement award, 1979. **Address:** Suite 209, 11826–100 Avenue, Edmonton, Alberta T5K 0K3, Canada.

ROMANCE AND HISTORICAL PUBLICATIONS

Novels

Alien There Is None (as J. Rana). London, Hodder and Stoughton, 1959; (as Helen Forrester) as *Thursday's Child*, London, Collins, 1985.
The Latchkey Kid (as June Bhatia). Don Mills, Ontario, Longman, 1971; (as Helen Forrester), London, Hale, 1985.
Most Precious Employee (as June Edwards). London, Hale, 1976.
Liverpool Daisy (as June Bhatia). London, Hale, 1979; (as Helen Forrester) London, Fontana, 1984.
Three Women of Liverpool. London, Hale, 1984.
Lime Street at Two. London, Bodley Head, 1985.
The Moneylenders of Shahpur. London, Collins, 1987.
Yes, Mama. London, Collins, 1988.
The Lemon Tree. London, Collins, 1990.
The Liverpool Basque. London, HarperCollins, 1993.

OTHER PUBLICATIONS

Other

Twopence to Cross the Mersey (autobiography). London, Jonathan Cape, 1974.
Minerva's Stepchild (autobiography). London, Bodley Head, 1979; New York, Beaufort, 1981; as *Liverpool Miss*, London, Fontana, 1982.
By the Waters of Liverpool. London, Bodley Head, 1981.

*   *   *

Love is a vital, controlling force in Helen Forrester's work, governing the destiny of her central characters and influencing many of their decisions. Forrester examines love and life within all levels of society, often utilizing her fascination with the industrial city of Liverpool by using it as a setting for her plots. Forrester's work is characteristic in that while she explores her characters and their lives, she also details the social and economic conditions in which they grow and mature. This combination of personal and social histories gives her characters fully-developed personalities, and highlights their strength of spirit to seek love despite the unpleasant hardships generated by social conditions.

Three Women of Liverpool, set in 1941, is close to Forrester's own experience of living in Liverpool. By constructing three parallel plots that constantly interlink, Forrester uses these women to represent conflicting social attitudes and class differences that persist even in a time of war. The most attractive character, Emmie, although finally released from caring for her aged parents, is emotionally barren and still economically trapped. Having acquired a measure of her own independence so late in life, Emmie's swift romance and engagement to a sailor is viewed disparagingly by Gwen, her sister-in-law. Gwen represents the lower-middle class, intent on bettering herself socially by cutting all ties with the working class. While Emmie endures her economic hardship and is rewarded with a sincere love, Gwen cultivates a starchy, snobbish attitude that overpowers her ability to love: her obsessiveness with her spotless house and its material contents drains her of any emotional support for her husband and her daughter. When Ellen, the mother of a working-class family living temporarily next door, is killed by shrapnel, Gwen slowly reasserts her priorities as she cares for Ellen's dirty, untamed children. The savage bombing of Liverpool brings individual tragedy to each of these women, but it also ends their alienation from one another and tears down the divides created by society so that they learn to love more freely.

Economic and physical hardship test almost every character in Forrester's novels. Polly, in *Yes, Mama*, links the cultivated upper classes with the deprived slums of late-19th century Liverpool. Polly signifies the horror that poor women faced at that time: if a woman was lucky enough to gain a measure of security by marrying, she was still faced with endless childbirth, disease, and suffering. *Liverpool Daisy* focuses even more intently upon this fate—Daisy Gallagher prostitutes herself as the only means of caring for her poverty-stricken family. Polly, however, betters herself by gaining employment in the Woodman household. Despite realizing a deeply satisfying love with the second son, Edward Woodman, Polly accepts that she can never marry him. Her charge, Alicia, is the unloved illegitimate daughter of Elizabeth Woodman, a spoilt, attractive woman caught in a loveless marriage. Alicia is faced with the paradox of being born into a wealthy family yet denied its status and opportunities. Ironically, she falls in love with Polly's brother who has made his own escape from the slums of Liverpool by settling in the Canadian outback.

The settling of English, French, and Scottish immigrants features in several of Forrester's works. Canada, for Forrester, is a place of physical hardship, but has immense potential for individual freedom. Helena Wallace, Forrester's strongest heroine, encapsulates a hybrid of identities in *The Lemon Tree*: an intelligent, educated girl from a rich Lebanese family who escapes from the Turkish invasion of Lebanon in 1860 to Hudson Bay in Canada. She matures into a vigorously independent woman who learns to farm the rough terrain, smoke with the men, and ignore social etiquette. She is also free from classist, racist, and social attitudes, and when she falls in love with her stepfather's black partner, Joe Black, the purity and naturalness of their love is one of the strongest themes in the book. When Helena is invited to Liverpool to take over her uncle's soap factory, she confronts a grimy, rigidly conformist society. Yet Liverpool attracts Helena—as it does Manuel Echaniz, in *The Liverpool Basque*, who has also made his home in Canada—this world offers to pamper her, refresh her cultured mind, and gives her the chance to run a business. When Helena discovers she is carrying an illegitimate child, it is not society's intolerance of her own condition that she fears, but its condemnation of her child's coloured skin.

Sacrificing the temptation to run her factory, she follows the convictions of her heart and returns to Joe.

The internal unrest and political change in India in 1945 provides a metaphor for the personal relationships between characters in two of Forrester's novels. *Alien There is None* (*Thursday's Child*) explores the difficulties and complications of interracial love and marriage. Liverpudlian Peggie falls in love with sincere, courteous Ajit Singh, who takes her to live in India. Spurned by his disapproving family, who suggest that Peggie remain in England while they arrange a traditional Indian marriage for Ajit, Peggie is shocked further by her husband's lapse into male chauvinism. Gradually she learns to cope with a country and its customs that she has accepted in return for love.

The Moneylenders of Shahpur is a novel about the tragedy of a love that is smothered by traditional Indian values. An unwilling Anasyabehn is forced into an arranged marriage, and though she declares her mutual love for Dr Tilak, he has not the wealth and social status of the moneylending Desai family. The tragic failure of Anasyabehn and Tilak to escape is heightened when an impoverished beggar attempts to stab Anasyabehn's husband and kills Tilak instead.

The inadequacies of a loveless society are also explored in *The Latchkey Kid*. This work marks a change in style for Forrester, with its amusingly wicked exposé of life in small-town Tollemarche, Alberta, in the 1950s and 1960s. Forrester cuts through the hypocritical social lifestyle of upwardly-mobile families to reveal a decaying family life. Reacting against his neglected childhood, Hank Stych publishes a novel that shatters the smooth veneer of society, and seeks his own unconventional love. Love is pivotal to Forrester's work, and she explores its many facets with sensitivity and honesty.

—Susannah Steel

FORTINA, Martha.   See LAFFEATY, Christina.

FOWLES, John (Robert).
Nationality: British. **Born:** Leigh-on-Sea, Essex, 31 March 1926. **Education:** Bedford School, 1940–44; Edinburgh University, 1944; New College, Oxford, B.A. (honours) in French 1950. **Military Service:** Royal Marines, 1945–46. **Relations:** married Elizabeth Whitton in 1956. **Career:** lecturer in English, University of Poitiers, France, 1950–51; teacher, Anargyrios College, Spetsai, Greece, 1951–52, and in London, 1953–63. Lives in Lyme Regis, Dorset. **Recipient:** Silver Pen award, 1969; W.H. Smith literary award, 1970; Christopher award, 1981. **Agent:** Anthony Sheil Associates, 43 Doughty Street, London WC1N 2LF, England. **Address:** c/o Jonathan Cape Ltd, 20 Vauxhall Bridge Road, London SW1V 2SA, England.

ROMANCE AND HISTORICAL PUBLICATIONS

Novels

The French Lieutenant's Woman. London, Cape, and Boston, Little Brown, 1969.
A Maggot. London, Cape, and Boston, Little Brown, 1985.

OTHER PUBLICATIONS

Novels

The Collector. London, Cape, and Boston, Little Brown, 1963.

The Magus. Boston, Little Brown, 1965; London, Cape, 1966; revised edition, Cape, 1977; Little Brown, 1978.
Daniel Martin. Boston, Little Brown, and London, Cape, 1977.
Mantissa. London, Cape, and Boston, Little Brown, 1982.

Short Stories

The Ebony Tower: Collected Novellas. London, Cape, and Boston, Little Brown, 1974.

Plays

Don Juan, adaptation of the play by Molière (produced London, 1981).
Lorenzaccio, adaptation of the play by Alfred de Musset (produced London, 1983).
Martine, adaptation of a play by Jean Jacques Bernard (produced London, 1985).

Screenplay: *The Magus*, 1968.

Poetry

Poems. New York, Ecco Press, 1973.
Conditional. Northridge, California, Lord John Press, 1979.

Other

The Aristos: A Self-Portrait in Ideas. Boston, Little Brown, 1964; London, Cape, 1965; revised edition, London, Pan, 1968; Little Brown, 1970.
Shipwreck, photographs by the Gibsons of Scilly. London, Cape, 1974; Boston, Little Brown, 1975.
Islands, photographs by Fay Godwin. London, Cape, 1978; Boston, Little Brown, 1979.
The Tree, photographs by Frank Horvat. London, Aurum Press, 1979; Boston, Little Brown, 1980.
The Enigma of Stonehenge, photographs by Barry Brukoff. London, Cape, and New York, Summit, 1980.
A Brief History of Lyme. Lyme Regis, Dorset, Friends of the Lyme Regis Museum, 1981.
A Short History of Lyme Regis. Wimborne, Dorset, Dovecote Press, 1982; Boston, Little Brown, 1983.
Of Memoirs and Magpies. Austin, Texas, Taylor, 1983.
Land, photographs by Fay Godwin. London, Heinemann, and Boston, Little Brown, 1985.

Editor, *Steep Holm: A Case History in the Study of Evolution.* Sherborne, Dorset, Allsop Memorial Trust, 1978.
Editor, with Rodney Legg, *Monumenta Britannica*, by John Aubrey. Sherborne, Dorset Publishing Company, 2 vols, 1980–82; vol.1, Boston, Little Brown, 1981.
Editor, *Thomas Hardy's England*, by Jo Draper. London, Cape, and Boston, Little Brown, 1984.
Editor, *Lyme Regis Camera.* Stanbridge, Dorset, Dovecote Press, 1990; Boston, Little Brown, 1991.

Translator, *Cinderella*, by Perrault. London, Cape, 1974; Boston, Little Brown, 1975.
Translator, *Ourika*, by Claire de Durfort. Austin, Texas, Taylor, 1977.

*

Film Adaptations: *The Collector*, 1965; *The Magus*, 1968; *The French Lieutenant's Woman*, 1981; *The Ebony Tower*, 1984.

Bibliography: 'John Fowles: An Annotated Bibliography 1963–76' by Karen Magee Myers, in *Bulletin of Bibliography* (Boston), vol 33, no 4, 1976; *John Fowles: A Reference Guide* by Barry N. Olshen and Toni A. Olshen, Boston, Hall, 1980; 'John Fowles: A Bibliographical Checklist' by Ray A. Roberts, in *American Book Collector* (New York), September–October, 1980; 'Criticism of John Fowles: A Selected Checklist' by Ronald C. Dixon, in *Modern Fiction Studies* (Lafayette, Indiana), Spring 1985.

Manuscript Collection: University of Tulsa, Oklahoma.

Critical Studies: *The Fiction of John Fowles: Tradition, Art, and the Loneliness of Selfhood* by William J. Palmer, Columbia, University of Missouri Press, 1974; *John Fowles, Magus and Moralist* by Peter Wolfe, Lewisburg, Pennsylvania, Bucknell University Press, 1976, revised edition, 1979; *Etudes sur 'The French Lieutenant's Woman' de John Fowles* edited by Jean Chevalier, Caen, University of Caen, 1977; *John Fowles* by Barry N. Olshen, New York, Ungar, 1978; *John Fowles* by Robert Huffaker, New York, Twayne, 1980; 'John Fowles Issue' of *Journal of Modern Literature* (Philadelphia), vol.8, no.2, 1981; *John Fowles* by Peter J. Conradi, London, Methuen, 1982; *The Timescapes of John Fowles* by H.W. Fawkner, Rutherford, New Jersey, Fairleigh Dickinson University Press, 1983; *Male Mythologies: John Fowles and Masculinity* by Bruce Woodcock, Brighton, Harvester Press, 1984; *The Romances of John Fowles* by Simon Loveday, London, Macmillan, 1985; 'John Fowles Issue' of *Modern Fiction Studies* (Lafayette, Indiana), Spring 1985; *The Fiction of John Fowles: A Myth for Our Time* by Carol M. Barnum, Greenwood, Florida, Penkevill, 1988; *The Art of John Fowles* by Katherine Tarbok, Athens, University of Georgia Press, 1988; *Form and Meaning in the Novels of John Fowles* by Susan Onega, Ann Arbor, Michigan, UMI Research Press, 1989; *John Fowles: A Reference Companion* by James R. Aubrey, New York, Greenwood Press, 1991; *Point of View in Fiction and Film, Focus on John Fowles* by Charles Garard, New York, Lang, 1991; *Something and Nothingness, Fiction of John Updike and John Fowles* by John Neary, Carbondale, Southern Illinois University Press, 1992.

*   *   *

Despite the fact that two of his six novels are clearly grounded in English history, John Fowles does not wish to be considered a historical novelist. Of *The French Lieutenant's Woman*, he wrote: 'I don't think of it as a historical novel, a genre in which I have very little interest', and the epilogue to *A Maggot* informs the reader that those 'who know something of what that Manchester baby was to become will not need telling how little this is a historical novel'. Given the meticulous recreation of Victorian England of 1867 to 1869 in the former and the similar concern for historical details in portraying Devonshire in 1736 in the latter, Fowles's novels, whatever the author's disclaimers, have a rich sense of historical period, created by careful research, even though their first allegiance is to fiction. His own interest in history outside fiction is even more firmly established by his several landscape and monument books, including *A Short History of Lyme Regis*.

The French Lieutenant's Woman, Fowles's best-known and certainly his most successful novel, carefully examines certain aspects of the Victorian period at a crucial moment in time, 1867, when a new age begins to emerge. The novel is a stunningly successful pastiche of Victorian fiction, in particular a homage to Thomas Hardy. Virtually every major convention of the fiction of Dickens, Thackeray, Eliot, Meredith, Hardy, and other Victorian novelists is replicated, but then refracted through a 20th-century perspective. Like Lawrence, Fowles is particularly drawn to the English landscape, and his descriptions of the landscape of Dorset and the architecture of the houses are no less detailed than his exploration of the relationship of masters and mistresses and servants, between the powerful mercantile and the aristocratic classes, and of their language, ideas, medicines, amusements, and dress than are the probing comments about the thoughts of Karl Marx and Charles Darwin, the two major voices in the period for gradual evolution. The story focuses on Charles Smithson's love for Ernestina Freeman and Sarah Woodruff, a typical Victorian triangle, but with Ernestina's conformity to Victorian society reducing her to the status of an object and with Sarah's rebellion ultimately casting her out of society. Charles's relationships with the two women free him, but leave him at a point where the prospect of a free, authentic, new life almost paralyzes him. The novel's most notorious feature, its three endings, allows the reader to measure himself or herself in order to determine if he or she is a Victorian, an Edwardian, or a modern existentialist. Throughout the novel, Fowles establishes a dialogue between the Victorian and the modern periods, using each as a critique of the other.

A Maggot, idiosyncratically titled and considerably less popular than Fowles's earlier novels, tells a mystery story about the disappearance of a Duke's son and the finding of the hanged body of his devoted servant, with violets growing from his mouth. The son had hired two actors and a prostitute from London to impersonate his uncle and companions on a ride from London to Bideford on the Devon coast, without telling them the exact purposes of the journey. The novel consists of Henry Ayscough's interrogations of eight individuals knowing something of the trip, six letters from Ayscough to the Duke, several letters from individuals contributing information about the Duke's son, six sections of third-person narrative, reproductions from the *Historical Register* from April 1736 to October 1736, and an epilogue by Fowles informing the reader that the pregnancy of Rebecca Lee, the reformed prostitute, resulted in the birth of Ann Lee (1736–84), also known as Mother Ann, the leader of the Shakers and 'the female principle in Christ'. After being imprisoned in England several times for crimes against established religion, Ann Lee migrated to Watervliet, New York, and spent the rest of her life preaching and faith-healing among the Shakers.

Fowles's novel is a 'maggot', that is, a 'whim or quirk' born 'out of obsession with a theme'. The theme concerns Fowles's interest throughout his career with the freedom of the individual, the eruptions of the irrational, even the supernatural, into human life, and the human response to these eruptions. In its opening section, the novel quite accurately describes the clothing of rural England in 1736, the conditions of the roads, the riding equipment, the breeds of animals popular at the time, and the inns, all the while reproducing Devon dialect. The rest of the novel, however, consists of static interrogation scenes, which, depending on the reader's interest in solving the mystery of what actually happened in the Devon cavern from which the missing lord seems never to have emerged, will be intellectually challenging or needlessly evasive.

—David Leon Higdon

FOWLIS, Hugh. See **MUNRO, Neil.**

FRANKAU, Gilbert.
Nationality: British. **Born:** London, 21 April 1884; son of the writer Julia Davis Frankau (i.e., Frank Danby). **Education:** Eton College. **Military Service:** 9th East Surrey Regiment, 1914; transferred to the Royal Field Artillery; adjutant to the 107th Brigade; invalided out, 1918: captain; recommissioned in 1939; invalided out, 1941: squadron leader. **Relations:** married 1) Dorothea Frances Black in 1905 (divorced), two daughters, including the writer Pamela Frankau; 2) Aimée de Burgh in 1922 (divorced); 3) Susan Lorna Harris in 1932. **Career:** joined his father's wholesale cigar business in 1904; managing director; full-time writer after World War I: editor, *Britannia*, 1928. **Died:** 4 November 1952.

ROMANCE AND HISTORICAL PUBLICATIONS

Novels

The Woman of the Horizon: A Romance of Nineteen-Thirteen. London, Chatto and Windus, 1917; New York, Century, 1923.
Peter Jackson, Cigar Merchant: A Romance of Married Life. London, Hutchinson, 1920; as *Peter Jameson: A Modern Romance*, New York, Knopf, 1920.
The Seeds of Enchantment. London, Hutchinson, and New York, Doubleday, 1921.
The Love-Story of Aliette Brunton. London, Hutchinson, and New York, Century, 1922.
Gerald Cranston's Lady: A Romance. London, Hutchinson, and New York, Century, 1924.
Life—and Erica: A Romance. New York, Century, 1924; London, Hutchinson, 1925.
Masterson: A Study of an English Gentleman. London, Hutchinson, and New York, Harper, 1926.
So Much Good. London, Hutchinson, and New York, Harper, 1928.
Dance, Little Gentleman! London, Hutchinson, 1929; New York, Harper, 1930.
Martin Make-Believe: A Romance. London, Hutchinson, 1930; New York, Harper, 1931.
Christopher Strong: A Romance. London, Hutchinson, and New York, Dutton, 1932.
The Lonely Man: A Romance of Love and the Secret Service. London, Hutchinson, 1932; New York, Dutton, 1933.
Everywoman. New York, Dutton, 1933; London, Hutchinson, 1934.
Three Englishmen: A Romance of Married Lives. London, Hutchinson, and New York, Dutton, 1935.
Farewell Romance. London, Hutchinson, and New York, Dutton, 1936.
The Dangerous Years: A Trilogy. London, Hutchinson, 1937; New York, Dutton, 1938.
Royal Regiment: A Drama of Contemporary Behaviours. London, Hutchinson, 1938; New York, Dutton, 1939.
Winter of Discontent. London, Hutchinson, 1941; as *Air Ministry, Room 28*, New York, Dutton, 1942.
World Without End. London, Hutchinson, and New York, Dutton, 1943.
Michael's Wife. London, Macdonald, and New York, Dutton, 1948.
Son of the Morning. London, Macdonald, 1949.
Oliver Trenton, K.C. London, Macdonald, 1951.
Unborn Tomorrow: A Last Story. London, Macdonald, 1953.

Short Stories

Men, Maids, and Mustard-Pot: A Collection of Tales. London, Hutchinson, 1923; New York, Century, 1924.
Twelve Tales. London, Hutchinson, 1927.
The House Behind the Judas Tree, with *Martyrdom* by Warwick Deeping and *Forbidden Music* by Ethel Mannin. London, Readers Library, 1929; as *Three Stories of Romance*, 1936.
Concerning Peter Jackson and Others. London, Hutchinson, 1931.
Wine, Women, and Waiters. London, Hutchinson, 1932.
Secret Services. London, Hutchinson, 1934.
Experiments in Crime and Other Stories. London, Hutchinson, and New York, Dutton, 1937.

Escape to Yesterday: A Miscellany of Tales. London, Hutchinson, 1942.

OTHER PUBLICATIONS

Poetry

Eton Echoes: A Volume of Humorous Verse. Eton, New, 1901.
The XYZ of Bridge. London, King, 1906.
One of Us: A Novel in Verse. London, Chatto and Windus, 1912; as *Jack—One of Us*, New York, Doran, 1912.
'Tid' apa' (What Does It Matter?). New York, Huebsch, 1914; London, Chatto and Windus, 1915.
The Guns. London, Chatto and Windus, 1916; as *A Song of the Guns*, Boston, Houghton Mifflin, 1916; as *A Song of the Guns in Flanders*, New York, Federal, 1916.
How Rifleman Brown Came to Valhalla. New York, Federal, 1916.
The City of Fear and Other Poems. London, Chatto and Windus, 1917.
One of Them: A Novelette in Verse. London, Hutchinson, 1918.
The Judgement of Valhalla. London, Chatto and Windus, and New York, Federal, 1918.
The Other Side and Other Poems. New York, Knopf, 1918.
The Poetical Works of Gilbert Frankau. London, Chatto and Windus, 2 vols., 1923.
More of Us, Being the Present-Day Adventures of 'One of Us': A Novel in Verse. London, Hutchinson, and New York, Dutton, 1937.
Selected Verses. London, Macdonald, 1943.

Other

The Dominant Type of Man. London, Dorland Agency, 1925.
My Unsentimental Journey. London, Hutchinson, 1926.
Gilbert Frankau's Self-Portrait: A Novel of His Own Life. London, Hutchinson, and New York, Dutton, 1940.

Editor, *A Century of Love Stories.* London, Hutchinson, 1935.

*

Film Adaptation: *Christopher Strong*, 1933.

*   *   *

The novels of Gilbert Frankau are almost unreadable outside the context of his times. He was deeply concerned with the place in society, still far from being determined, of 'the Modern Woman' of the 1920s and 1930s. The reader must constantly re-adjust contemporary assumptions to the confinements of a day, not so very distant in time, but incredibly so in flavour, in which even persons in circumstances far from affluent had *such* problems with their servants' upstart independent ideas; when for a woman, as now in an odd reversal for a man, cutting or not cutting one's hair was a 'statement' of sorts; when it was a daring step for any young woman to attempt to earn a living outside the home or to live apart from her family; and above all, at a time when iron divorce laws could still crush the lives of those unhappy enough to fall afoul of them, as Frankau himself did.

His bright young things, with their snappy conversations, affectations, and nicknames, are all so impossibly dated now that it will re-

quire at least another generation before their true charm will begin to reveal itself to the literary researcher's penetratingly anthropological eye. For the present, they are simply too tediously outdated to be readable, not yet antique enough to have attained the period charm of, for example, Regency chit-chat, which was equally as slangy and colloquial.

Above all, Frankau was a product of an age in which the double standard of sexual morality was in fullest flower, and he spends a good deal of time and thought on the exploration of this theme. He appears to accept the premise without question, while deploring the damaging results upon mere fallible human beings unable to uphold unrealistic standards of conduct. Mildly daring in their day, his are the works of a man strictly of his time and milieu—and both have passed.

—Joan McGrath

———

FRANKEN, Rose (Dorothy).
Pseudonyms: Margaret Grant; Franken Meloney. **Nationality:** American. **Born:** Rose Dorothy Lewin in Gainesville, Texas, 28 December 1895. **Education:** Ethical Culture School, New York. **Relations:** married 1) S.W.A. Franken in 1914 (died 1932), three sons; 2) William Brown Meloney in 1937 (died 1970). **Died:** 22 June 1988.

ROMANCE AND HISTORICAL PUBLICATIONS

Novels (series: Claudia)

Pattern. New York, Scribner, 1925.
Twice Born. New York, Scribner, 1935; London, W.H. Allen, 1969.
Call Back Love (as Margaret Grant, with W.B. Meloney). New York, Farrar and Rinehart, 1937.
Of Great Riches. New York, Longman, 1937; as *Gold Pennies*, London, Constable, 1938.
Claudia: The Story of a Marriage. New York, Farrar and Rinehart, 1939; London, W.H. Allen, 1946.
Claudia and David. New York, Farrar and Rinehart, 1940; London, W.H. Allen, 1946.
Another Claudia. New York, Farrar and Rinehart, 1943; London, W.H. Allen, 1946.
Young Claudia. New York, Rinehart, 1946; London, W.H. Allen, 1947.
The Marriage of Claudia. New York, Rinehart, and London, W.H. Allen, 1948.
From Claudia to David. London, W.H. Allen, 1949; New York, Harper, 1950.
The Fragile Years. New York, Doubleday, 1952; as *Those Fragile Years*, London, W.H. Allen, 1952; as *The Return of Claudia*, London, W.H. Allen, 1957.
Rendezvous. New York, Doubleday, 1954; as *The Quiet Heart*, London, W.H. Allen, 1954.
Intimate Story. New York, Doubleday, and London, W.H. Allen, 1955.
The Antic Years. New York, Doubleday, 1958.

Novels as Franken Meloney (with W.B. Meloney)

Strange Victory. New York, Farrar and Rinehart, 1939.
When Doctors Disagree. New York, Farrar and Rinehart, 1940.
American Bred. New York, Farrar and Rinehart, 1941.

OTHER PUBLICATIONS

Plays

Another Language (produced New York and London, 1932). New York, French, 1932; London, Rich and Cowan, 1933.

Mr Dooley, Jr (for children), with Jane Lewin. New York, French, 1932.

Claudia, adaptation of her own novel (produced New York, 1941; London, 1942). New York, Farrar and Rinehart, 1941.

Outrageous Fortune (produced New York, 1943). New York, French, 1944.

Doctors Disagree, adaptation of her own novel *When Doctors Disagree* (produced New York, 1943).

Soldier's Wife (produced New York, 1944; London, 1946). New York, French, 1945.

The Hallams (produced New York, 1948). New York, French, 1948.

Screenplays: *Alias Mary Dow*, 1935; *Beloved Enemy*, with John Balderston and William Brown Meloney, 1936; *Made for Each Other*, with Jo Swerling, 1939; *Claudia and David*, with William Brown Meloney and Vera Caspary, 1946; *The Secret Heart*, with others, 1946.

Other

When All Is Said and Done (autobiography). London, W.H. Allen, 1962; New York, Doubleday, 1963.

You're Well Out of Hospital. London, W.H. Allen, and New York, Doubleday, 1966.

*

Film Adaptations: *Another Language*, 1933; *Claudia*, 1943; *Claudia and David*, 1946.

*   *   *

Once upon a time—not all that long ago—a story of young, innocent love won the hearts of a nation. Within the charmed circle of Claudia's wedding ring, it seemed, were contained all warmth and love, the ideals, hopes, and virtues, of a country in the flower of its youth and promise. Claudia and her David embodied innocence. It was one of Claudia's greatest charms in her husband's eyes, as well as her mother's and (all too obviously) her creator's, that she *was* such an innocent. Married practically out of the schoolroom, to a young man she regarded as being mature and worldly, but who was in fact only 25, the child-bride was launched upon a career of wedded bliss that was to last for nine volumes, in magazine serials, on stage and screen, on radio and television, and in translations all over the world. Plainly the world adored Claudia, through episode after episode. Franken believed that it was a woman's perception of a love story that carried the emotional wallop, and wrote accordingly, on and on and on; apparently the world agreed with her.

Sadly, to return to Claudia's world decades later is to find it a tarnished paradise. The youth of the central characters excuses much, but not all of their smugness, their comfortable wealth that sees itself as straitened circumstances, and their self-consciously 'special' carryings-on. It was only to be expected, in Claudia's world, for example, that everyone would adore the young bride, and that domestic servants would gladly set aside their own lives to provide a comfortable background for hers and David's. It is quite impossible now to take seriously this sweetly two-dimensional creation once glowingly described as 'one of the classical characters of American literature'.

Franken wrote in a style that belonged to the golden era of serialization for magazines with enormous mass circulation—most of them now dead and gone. She wrote prolifically, at great speed, without reading, let alone rewriting, and it shows. Times and tastes have changed. Even her more 'hard-hitting' works, daring in their day (*Twice Born* dared to hint at the existence and problems of homosexuality) have long been overtaken and forgotten. Franken was an author who spoke clearly and compellingly to a particular, specific audience; the lonely service wives of World War II, who waited anxiously for their men to return. Their gallantly held ideals of home and fireside, their special war-born reverence for a threatened way of life, lent Franken's work an enormous popularity; but today, *Claudia*, the once so dearly beloved, has faded to a footnote in the history of American popular literature.

—Joan McGrath

———————

FRASER, Christine Marion.
Pseudonym for Christian Marion Ashfield. **Nationality:** Scottish. **Born:** Glasgow, 24 March 1946. **Education:** formal education ended when the author was ten due to illness; tutored between hospitalizations. **Relations:** married Kenneth Cameron Ashfield in 1964; one daughter. **Member:** Society of Authors. **Agent:** Jennifer Luithlen, *The Rowans*, 88 Holmfield Road, Leicester LE2 ISB, England.

ROMANCE AND HISTORICAL PUBLICATIONS

Novels (series: King; Rhanna)

Rhanna:
Rhanna. London, Blond and Briggs, 1978.
Rhanna at War. London, Blond and Briggs, 1980.
Children of Rhanna. London, Fontana, 1983.
Return to Rhanna. London, Fontana, 1984.
Song of Rhanna. London, Fontana, 1985.
Storm over Rhanna. London, Collins, 1988.
Stranger on Rhanna. London: HarperCollins, 1992.
King:
King's Croft. London, Collins, 1986.
King's Acre. London, Collins, 1987.
King's Exile. London, Collins, 1989.
King's Close. London, Collins, 1991.
King's Farewell. London, Collins, 1993.

OTHER PUBLICATIONS

Other

Blue Above the Chimneys (autobiography). London, Hutchinson, 1985.

Roses Round the Door (autobiography). London, Fontana, 1986.

Green Are My Mountains (autobiography). London, Fontana, 1990.

*

Christine Marion Fraser comments:

Having a fertile imagination, I began telling my brothers and sisters stories that I made up as a four to five-year-old. As soon as I learned to read and write, I began to write stories, especially from the age of ten when I was diagnosed as having a very rare bone and muscular disease that curtailed my education and left me, at 12 years old, confined to a wheelchair. In later years when just married, my able-bodied husband who was an artist, encouraged me to write my story, *Blue Above the Chimneys*, which was rejected by publishers. Leaving Glasgow to live in Argyll, I wrote the first Rhanna book for fun, and was most surprised when Blond and Briggs accepted it for publication with a request for more in the series. The 'Rhanna' series are now world bestsellers in many foreign languages. After the first two 'Rhanna' books, Hutchinson published *Blue Above the Chimneys*, and later when Fontana/Collins began publishing my books, they reluctantly agreed to publish it in paperback. They were astounded by its success and requested more autobiographical books. *Roses Round the Door* and *Green Are My Mountains* followed, a fourth book is planned. I have written the 'King' series for Collins/Fontana, now complete with the publication of *King's Farewell*, and I am now working on a new series. HarperCollins published the first two Rhanna books in the USA, just as the American recession started and they are not doing as well as expected. However, my agent has sold my books to Scandinavia, Holland, Germany, Poland, and some East European countries. Scottish television have voted me top selling Scottish fiction writer. For someone who was disabled as a child, lacking in education, and who has reared a family, I feel I have proved myself. I have many more books in the pipeline, including some Scottish crime, and books for children. But, due to popular demand, I will have to produce the occasional 'Rhanna' title also.

*   *   *

The imaginary Hebridean island of Rhanna is the setting for Christine Marion Fraser's first multi-volume family saga—and an amazingly fertile setting it proves to be. Against a rich background of comic characters the protagonists play out their extremely dramatic lives: the males suffer from broken or amputated limbs, alcoholism and drowning, the females from birth defects, stillborn babies and death in childbed; both sexes suffer from broken love affairs, misunderstandings—and from the fatal inability to grasp the opportunity to explain all these misunderstandings. In the latter, of course, they are not alone; this is the crux of many a romance novel.

Centre-stage in this saga, and indeed on the island itself, most often the reader finds a McKenzie: Fergus and his second wife Kirsteen; their sons Grant, Lorn and Lewis and their wives or lovers; Fergus's daughter Shona and her husband Niall McLachlan. The McKenzie family has a reputation on Rhanna for being argumentative and strong-willed, and its members do need great strength of will and character to overcome the obstacles strewn so lavishly in their path to happiness by Christine Marion Fraser. Fergus's first wife Helen dies in childbirth, and for many years he is a lonely, bitter man, blaming the doctor (formerly his friend), Lachlan McLachlan, for her death. Fergus falls in love with his daughter's teacher, Kirsteen and they have an affair, Fergus then loses his arm in an accident and finally makes his peace with Lachlan, Kirsteen (by now pregnant) leaves the island and is not persuaded to return and marry Fergus until their child Grant is five years old. By this time Fergus's daughter Shona has grown up, fallen pregnant, heard that her fiancé, Niall McLachlan, is missing in the war, given birth to a stillborn child, and then received the news that Niall is safe, and relatively sound. It is Shona and Niall who play the leading roles in the second book, *Rhanna at War*, and Fergus and Kirsteen's twin sons Lewis and Lorn in *Children of Rhanna*. In each successive novel some or all of the McKenzies tackle life's joys and sorrows head-on, and as the saga progresses they begin to lead rather more settled lives and to move aside slightly to enable other characters, both natives of, and incomers to the island, to come to the fore.

The constants throughout the novels are the island itself (its rocks, heather, sunshine, and storms), and the comic characters—Behag Beag, the inquisitive and malicious postmistress, Dodie, the island's none too fragrant eccentric, and various amusing and warm-hearted elderly gossips of both sexes, many of whom are related by blood or marriage to the McKenzies. From *Rhanna*, set in 1923, to the later novels, *Storm over Rhanna*, *Stranger on Rhanna* etc., set in the 1960s, their doings and sayings are documented in highly entertaining detail. There are births, marriages and normal, non-violent deaths aplenty, and in this close-knit community each event affects every inhabitant to a greater or lesser extent. This island and its people are easily credible, for the characters in the 'Rhanna' series are warm, natural human beings; their personalities are skilfully and consistently outlined by description, word, and deed. The only thing that really stretches the reader's imagination is the thought that one family has to cope with such a range of accidents and disasters, so much mental and physical trauma and angst.

Fraser's next saga (the 'King' sequence of novels) tells the story of the Grant family, and primarily of Evelyn, the seventh child and youngest daughter of Maggie and Jamie King Grant, from her childhood, through her promising adolescence, young womanhood, and an adult life of drudgery, to an eventual happy fulfilment. *King's Croft*, the first book in the series, sets the scene and gives the background of the family: Jamie King Grant is a gypsy (and as his seventh child Evelyn inherits his second sight), Maggie is the illegitimate daughter of Lord Lindsay Ogilvie. Unpromising as this union sounds, the couple settle down in an Aberdeenshire croft and raise their family in a secure and loving environment in the years before World War I. From the first, it is clear that these novels contain all the traditional ingredients of a working-class family saga: a drunken father, rape, poverty, illegitimate children, social class divide, unrequited love, separation by war—and in the course of the five novels we do get all these elements in varying quantities.

For an intelligent and sensible girl, blessed moreover with second sight, Evelyn is singularly inept when it comes to choosing her men. After her childhood sweetheart is accidentally drowned, she rejects the kind, sensitive Gillan Forbes (son of the family at 'the big house'—and also her cousin). She falls in love with the charming, faithless, jealous Davie Grainger, has an illegitimate child by him, marries him, has four more children and is widowed. By this time Gillan, after having wooed her at various stages in the books, has long since given up, married on the rebound, and gone to live in South Africa. To escape from a life of poverty, Evelyn unwisely (inexplicably, even) marries a much older man, the father-in-law of one of her sisters; he turns out to be a brutal husband who abuses not only Evelyn but virtually any other female he can lay his hands on. While still married to this man she meets Gillan (by now separated from his wife, but about to return to South Africa) and conceives a child by him. And although it is not long before Evelyn's husband meets a suitably unpleasant end, it is a further seven years before Gillan returns (now divorced) and finally claims Evelyn as his wife.

However, Evelyn is not the only member of the Grant family to encounter a few ups and downs. Jamie King Grant spends time in prison for the attempted murder of Whisky Jake (the latter having raped Evelyn's sister Nellie when she was a child, his attempted rape of Evelyn herself being the cause of Jamie's attack on him); Evelyn's sister Murn, obsessed with the man who marries Nellie, eventually goes completely mad and drowns herself; in *King's Acre* another sister, Grace, loses her husband in World War I but refuses to believe that he is dead—quite rightly, as it turns out, for three volumes and some 20 years later he reappears, but with a new face courtesy of plastic surgery.

To view these novels as a series of disasters with a happy ending is unfair; one expects neither unrelieved happiness nor unmitigated tragedy in a family saga, and in both her series Fraser achieves a judicious blend of the two. Her characters, some sympathetic, some comic, some brutal, some downright infuriating, interact successfully—although one might question the wisdom of some of their decisions. A pleasing blend of drama and domestic scenes, a variety of settings, and a wide range of characters combine to form two well-written and enjoyable family stories.

—Judith Rhodes

FRASER, George MacDonald.
Nationality: British. **Born:** Carlisle, Cumberland, 2 April 1925. **Education:** Carlisle Grammar School, 1932–38; Glasgow Academy, 1938–43. **Military Service:** British Army, 1943–47: lieutenant. **Relations:** married Kathleen Margarette Hetherington in 1949; two sons and one daughter. **Career:** reporter, Carlisle *Journal*, 1947–49, and Regina *Leader-Post*, Saskatchewan, 1949–50; reporter and sub-editor, Cumberland *News*, Carlisle, 1950–53; deputy editor, *Glasgow Herald*, 1953–69. Lives on the Isle of Man. **Recipient:** Arts Council award, 1972; Screenwriters Guild award, 1973; *Playboy* award, 1974, 1975; Krug award, 1980. **Agent:** John Farquharson Ltd, 162–168 Regent Street, London W1R 5TB, England.

ROMANCE AND HISTORICAL PUBLICATIONS

Novels (series: Flashman)

Flashman. London, Jenkins, and New York, World, 1969.
Royal Flash (Flashman). London, Barrie and Jenkins, and New York, Knopf, 1970.
Flash for Freedom! (Flashman). London, Barrie and Jenkins, 1971; New York, Knopf, 1972.
Flashman at the Charge. London, Barrie and Jenkins, and New York, Knopf, 1973.
Flashman in the Great Game. London, Barrie and Jenkins, and New York, Knopf, 1975.
Flashman's Lady. London, Barrie and Jenkins, 1977; New York, Knopf, 1978.
Mr American. London, Collins, and New York, Simon and Schuster, 1980.
Flashman and the Redskins. London, Collins, and New York, Knopf, 1982.
The Pyrates. London, Collins, 1983; New York, Knopf, 1984.
Flashman and the Dragon. London, Collins, and New York, Knopf, 1986.
Flashman and the Mountain of Light. London, Collins, 1990; New York, Knopf, 1991.
The Candlemass Road. London, Harvill, 1993.

Short Stories

The General Danced at Dawn. London, Barrie and Jenkins, 1970; New York, Knopf, 1973.
McAuslan in the Rough. London, Barrie and Jenkins, and New York, Knopf, 1974.
The Sheikh and the Dustbin. London, Collins, 1988.

OTHER PUBLICATIONS

Plays

Screenplays: *The Three Musketeers*, 1973; *The Four Musketeers*, 1974; *Royal Flash*, 1975; *The Prince and the Pauper* (*Crossed Swords*), 1977; *Octopussy*, with Richard Maibaum and Michael G.

Wilson, 1983; *Red Sonja*, with Clive Exton, 1984; *Return of the Musketeers*, 1989.

Television Play: *Casanova*, 1987.

Other

The Steel Bonnets: The Story of the Anglo-Scottish Border Reivers. London, Barrie and Jenkins, 1971; New York, Knopf, 1972.
The Hollywood History of the World. London, Joseph, and New York, Morrow, 1988.
The World of the Public School. New York, St Martin's Press, 1977.
Quartered Safe Out of Here: A Recollection of the War in Burma. London, Harvill, 1992; New York, HarperCollins, 1993.

*

Film Adaptation: *Royal Flash*, 1975.

George MacDonald Fraser comments:

The Flashman novels purport to be the adult memoirs of the school bully of *Tom Brown's School Days*, and describe his adventures in various campaigns and episodes of Victorian history. The three volumes of short stories are based on my experience as a subaltern in a Highland regiment. *The Pyrates* is a historical fantasy, and *Mr American* is a conventional novel set in England before World War I.

*   *   *

Like his fellow-novelists Angus Wilson, Andrew Sinclair, and Graham Swift, George MacDonald Fraser is a historian, quite comfortable with writing a book such as *The Steel Bonnets*, his study of Anglo-Scottish border counties, which garnered praise from the distinguished historian, Hugh Trevor-Roper, for being 'a splendid book, both scholarly and readable, accurate and alive'. His contributions to historical fiction, however, have come in the form of nine novels, equally grounded in history, known collectively as 'The Flashman Papers', so called because this vast personal memoir is identified as the papers of the late Harry Paget Flashman, discovered 'during a sale of household furniture at Ashby, Leicestershire in 1965' and given to Fraser to 'edit'. The nine volumes which have appeared so far have hewed so closely to actual historical events and persons and have maintained such an authentic tone, that the first volume duped more than one reviewer into treating it as an actual memoir, an eyewitness account of many of the 19th-century's significant historical events, an impression Fraser's publisher hurried to correct.

The volumes easily fall into two groupings. In *Flashman, Royal Flash, Flash for Freedom!*, and, to a certain extent, *Flashman at the Charge*, Fraser has turned literary history upside-down because he has invaded *Tom Brown's Schooldays*, *The Prisoner of Zenda*, *Uncle Tom's Cabin*, and much *Charge* literature, has appropriated their characters, actions, and occasionally themes, making them totally his own and has presented the 'real historical truth' glibly muddled or deliberately obscured by Thomas Hughes, Anthony Hope, and Harriet Beecher Stowe. The novels are more than parodies; they so skilfully replicate and are so adroitly interwoven into the interstices of history that a reader can quickly find himself or herself believing that Flashman was actually a Victorian gentleman, that the Schleswig-Holstein affair, Otto von Bismarck, and Lola Montez are the true life figures behind the characters in *The Prisoner of Zenda*, and that Flashman was actually sold into slavery in the American South. In these novels, Fraser is doing more than guying Victorian novels and debunking Victorian beliefs; he is participating in one of the most obvious activities of postmodernism: that of impeaching an earlier book's authority and creating a counter-book such as William Golding, Brian Aldiss, Jean Rhys, and John Fowles have done in *Lord of the Flies*, *Frankenstein Unbound*, *Wide Sargasso Sea*, and *The French Lieutenant's Woman*. One is tempted to see the early Flashman volumes as parasites fastened tightly on a host text and draining life from it, but they should more accurately be viewed as successful acts of colonization in which a text or a military campaign has been annexed in the name of colonialism and imperialism, and rendered uniquely British.

The volumes since *Flashman at the Charge* have not always had specific targets and, as a result, have somewhat looser, more picaresque structures; they do maintain and at times refine the enormous energy and comic vitality of the earlier books, but do not always enjoy the same narrative drive. Only *Flashman's Lady* may actually be said to disappoint, and it signals a slightly darker turn in the novels which followed it. All in all, the later novels have unrolled a panorama of 19th-century Asian, African, and North American history, presenting Flashman during the Sikh war in the Punjab (1845–46), the Indian Mutiny (1857–58), in James Brooke's Borneo and Queen Ranavalona I's Madagascar (1842–45), the American gold rush and the infamous Battle of Little Bighorn (1849–50, 1875–76), and the Taiping Rebellion in China and the burning of the Summer Palace in 1860. Yet to come are promised volumes on Flashman's exploits in the American Union Army, with Emperor Maximilian of Mexico, and in the South African Zulu Wars, incidents mentioned in Flashman's *Who's Who* entry.

The novels surely attract readers because of their clear philosophy of history and their irrepressible anti-hero. Both Fraser and Flashman believe that the romantic school of history which glamorizes and the historical specialist school which documents lack perspective and have forgotten the force of human personality. For Flashman, history is more often made by 'some aristocratic harlot waggling her backside', some sailor getting drunk, or some forgetful encounter which ultimately 'perhaps shaped the destiny of British India'. Fraser's agenda involves revealing the 'truth' hidden behind the Victorian masks called honour, duty, bravery, and patriotism, the values lauded in Thomas Hughes's *Tom Brown's Schooldays*, an author and a book which Flashman attacks throughout the papers. He sees human beings as governed by two main forces: the desire to survive at all costs no matter what values must be compromised or sacrificed—the first principle to Flashman whether facing a pit full of serpents in Afghanistan, a Dahomey cannibal, Sioux warriors, or Chinese torture—and the desire to get what one can, sexually, financially and socially.

Harry Paget Flashman is truly one of the 'other' Victorians. Fraser has taken the notorious bully of *Tom Brown's Schooldays* and allowed him to admit to being 'a scoundrel, a liar, a cheat, a thief, a coward—and, oh yes, a toady'. Flashman is all these and more as he strives to escape whatever danger confronts him, but his sexual energies, his audacious impostures, his unbelievable luck, his disarming frankness, his candid criticism of the heroes of the age, his unvarnished look at the corruption of man's actions, and his sheer vitality transform him into an ultimate anti-hero. Best of all, the reader is constantly in on the joke. As each of the volumes has depicted Flashman in yet more swashbuckling adventures, his complexity has increased and so has the awareness of the effect his father's rejection has had on his life. The father-son tensions culminate in a moving confrontation between Flashman and his own illegitimate Indian son during the Battle of Little Bighorn.

—David Leon Higdon

FRASER, Jane. See **PILCHER, Rosamunde.**

FRASER, (Sir Arthur) Ronald.   1888–1974. See 2nd edition, 1990.

FREEMAN, Cynthia.
Pseudonym for Bea Feinberg. **Nationality:** American. **Born:** New York City in 1915. **Education:** University of California, Berkeley. **Relations:** married Herman Feinberg in 1933; one son and one daughter. **Career:** interior designer. **Died:** 22 October 1988.

ROMANCE AND HISTORICAL PUBLICATIONS

Novels

A World Full of Strangers. New York, Arbor House, 1975; London, Corgi, 1976.
Fairytales. New York, Arbor House, 1977; London, Bantam, 1978.
The Days of Winter. New York, Arbor House, 1978; London, Corgi, 1979.
Portraits. New York, Arbor House, 1979; Loughton, Essex, Piatkus, 1980.
Come Pour the Wine. New York, Bantam, and Loughton, Essex, Piatkus, 1981.
No Time for Tears. New York, Arbor House, and Loughton, Essex, Piatkus, 1981.
Catch the Gentle Dawn. New York, Arbor House, 1983.
Illusions of Love. New York, Putnam, and London, Collins, 1984.
Seasons of the Heart. New York, Putnam, and London, Collins, 1986.
The Last Princess. New York, Putnam, and London, Collins, 1988.
Always and Forever. New York, Putnam, 1990.
To Everything a Season. New York, Putnam 1991.

*   *   *

Romance is always a strong element in Cynthia Freeman's novels, though these fall into the category of the family saga as well as the love story, and their main concerns are with rootseeking and power.

Freeman's books tend to have the flavour of travelogues through place and time with action ranging through diversely colourful settings (from Polish ghetto to Californian expansiveness in *Portraits*), as well as through several generations. The author occasionally over-indulges her vivid feeling for place, though often she skilfully harnesses it to accentuate the moods of her characters and the impact of events.

Several of the novels have backgrounds of displacement and disorientation (*A World Full of Strangers*, *Fairytales*, *Portraits*), and immigrant characters who are engaged in seeking social identity and racial roots. Their approach to this is romantic rather than realistic, but nevertheless compelling. It is *Portraits*, her four-generational chronicle of a Jewish immigrant family, that most clearly illustrates Freeman's storytelling skill, through its intense and well-realized relationships, and her characters' convincing struggles to cling to their spiritual heritage in an alien environment.

Perversely, this passionate identification with a specific racial group that gives *Portraits* its vitality produces a serious flaw in her more conventional love story, *Come Pour the Wine*. Allan, a middle-aged Jewish hero, is rather artificially introduced during the book's later stages in order to give heroine Janet the deep and sensitive love that her gentile husband, Bill, lacks the maturity to provide. Bill's inadequacies are carefully rehearsed but—though this is almost certainly not the author's intention—despite his shortcomings he still emerges as a more appealing character than Allan. Janet, however, eventually settles for the duller but more determined of the two men. (Her pairing off with Allan is a literary let-down similar to that produced by Louisa Alcott in *Little Women*, when she made Jo reject lively handsome Laurie for the protective but prosaic Professor Bhaer.)

Apart from this weakness of plot, *Come Pour the Wine* represents the romantic story at its most persuasive. The action unfolds believably from the viewpoint of the intelligent heroine; the 'will-he, won't he' themes, although repetitive and lengthy, are enlivened by Freeman's capacity to get beneath the skin of her characters, and to enlist her readers' sympathy for their inadequacies and approbation of their strengths.

—Mary Cadogan

* * *

FRENCH, Ashley. See **ROBINS, Denise.**

* * *

GAINES, Ernest J(ames).
Nationality: American. **Born:** Oscar, Louisiana, 15 January 1933.
Education: Vallejo Junior College; San Francisco State College, 1955–57, B.A. 1957; Stanford University, California (Stegner fellow, 1958), 1958–59. **Military Service:** United States Army, 1953–55. **Career:** writer-in-residence, Denison University, Granville, Ohio, 1971, Stanford University, Spring 1981, and Whittier College, California, 1982. Since 1983 Professor of English and writer-in-residence, University of Southwestern Louisiana, Lafayette.
Recipient: San Francisco Foundation Joseph Henry Jackson award, 1959; National Endowment for the Arts grant, 1966; Rockefeller grant, 1970; Guggenheim grant, 1970; Black Academy of Arts and Letters award, 1972; San Francisco Art Commission award, 1983; American Academy award, 1987. D.Litt.: Denison University, 1980; Brown University, Providence, Rhode Island, 1985; Bard College, Annandale-on-Hudson, New York, 1985; Louisiana State University, 1987. D.H.L.: Whittier College, 1986. **Agent:** JCA Literary Agency Inc, 242 West 27th Street, New York 10001, USA.
Address: Department of English, University of Southwestern Louisiana, East University Avenue, Lafayette, Louisiana 70504, USA.

ROMANCE AND HISTORICAL PUBLICATIONS

Novels

Catherine Carmier. New York, Atheneum, 1964; London, Secker and Warburg, 1966.
Of Love and Dust. New York, Dial Press, 1967; London, Secker and Warburg, 1968.
The Autobiography of Miss Jane Pittman. New York, Dial Press, 1971; London, Joseph, 1973.

OTHER PUBLICATIONS

Novels

In My Father's House. New York, Knopf, and London, Prior, 1978.
A Gathering of Old Men. New York, Knopf, 1983; London, Heinemann, 1984.
A Lesson Before Dying. New York, Knopf, 1993.

Short Stories

Bloodline. New York, Dial Press, 1968.

Other

A Long Day in November (for children). New York, Dial Press, 1971.
Porchtalk with Ernest Gaines by Marcia Gaudet and Carl Wooton. Baton Rouge, Louisiana State University Press, 1990.

*

Film Adaptations: *The Autobiography of Miss Jane Pittman*, 1974; *A Gathering of Old Men*, 1987.

Manuscript Collection: Dupree Library, University of Southwestern Louisiana, Lafayette.

* * *

Ernest J. Gaines is one of the most respected African American writers to emerge this century. The popularity of his books lies in his ability to capture, through his use of dialect, setting, and characterization, the experiences of black people in the rural South. Much of Gaines's success lies in his creation of authentic characters whose experiences are drawn from his own past. His novels are deeply rooted in African American culture and history, and the folktraditions of rural Louisiana where Gaines was raised. One of his earliest influences was his aunt, Augusteen Jefferson, a strong, religious woman who brought him up, in spite of her own invalidity. Augusteen became the model for the recurrent character of the aunt in Gaines's novels, most significantly seen as Jane Pittman in *The Autobiography of Miss Jane Pittman*. The aunt figure shows strength, dignity, and makes it possible for the next generation to have a better future.

Gaines shows the dehumanizing effects of racism on both the community and on individual relationships. He charts social and economic change through the lives of his characters, using important historical events as backdrops to his fiction. While the aunt figure often endures much hardship, she clings to the traditions of the past, found in the church and the community. It is essentially through the strong black male characters that change occurs. Accepted traditions and social structures are challenged and fought against—to this end, the male characters often die, but they die with dignity. Hence the themes of dignity, loyalty, and strength are important and recurrent in all of Gaines's work.

Catherine Carmier, the author's first book, follows the story of a young black man, Jackson Bradley, who returns to the fictional Bayonne after educating himself elsewhere. Jackson immediately comes into conflict with his community whose traditions he no longer accepts, and with a black Creole farmer with whose daughter he falls in love. Catherine Carmier is beautiful and light skinned, her father believes her to be superior to other black people and refuses to acknowledge any of her relationships with black men. Following the path of a true love story, Catherine and Jackson fall in love, however, Catherine is torn between her lover and her father. Unfortunately when the book ends the reader is unsure if Jackson has lost Catherine. Gaines admits that his writing has been influenced by the great 19th-century Russian writers, and *Catherine Carmier* is fashioned after Turgenev's *Fathers and Sons*. This is Gaines's most pessimistic book and did not achieve much critical recognition.

Of Love and Dust, Gaines's next novel, fared better. Gaines described it as 'the same story you find in Romeo and Juliet', a tale of forbidden love—in this case based on race. It tells the story of Marcus Payne, a black man bonded out of prison by a white landowner. Marcus comes into conflict with his supervisor, Sidney Bonbon; he also offends his community who cannot understand why he cannot keep the existing status quo.

The theme of miscegenation is explored through the relationship that develops between Marcus and Bonbon's thwarted wife, Louise.

Bonbon, much to his wife's chagrin, openly keeps a black mistress, thus Louise enters a relationship with Marcus as revenge. Vengeance is also the main reason for Marcus's initial pursuit of Louise. He hates Bonbon who tries to break his spirit, and he has also been rejected by Bonbon's mistress. However, feelings of bitterness are overcome, and Marcus and Louise fall in love. They plan to escape but are betrayed by the white plantation owner, and Marcus is killed by Bonbon. Louise goes mad, and Bonbon and his mistress leave together. The whole story is told through the first person narrative of Jim Kelly, a middle-aged black man who commands respect on the plantation. Although Kelly does not understand the boy at the beginning of the book, he gradually comes to respect Marcus's spirit and courage. By the end of the book Jim Kelly has learned that he has been too willing to accept the existing racial power relationship; he gains dignity and finally begins to explore who he really is. In spite of the unhappy fate of Marcus and Louise, the book ends on an uplifting note—the beginning of Jim Kelly's self discovery.

The use of the first person narrative allows the reader to gain a deep feeling for life in rural Louisiana. It is a device that Gaines uses again in his most successful novel *The Autobiography of Miss Jane Pittman* which spans African-American history from the Civil War to the Civil Rights Movement of the 1960s. Gaines began the book as a communal biography, however, Jane Pittman's character emerged and found its own extremely successful voice, and the reader perceives a realistic character who renders the folk history of black experience more accessible.

The book is divided into four sections and follows the life of an 110-year-old African-American women. Her life is recorded by a black history teacher (Gaines) who wants his students to have a real perspective on their own past. He persuades Jane to tell her story and through her narrative the history and experience of millions of illiterate black people is told in rich detailed language. The book begins with the emancipation of the slaves in Louisiana, Jane and her fellow slaves begin their epic march to freedom by renaming themselves, casting off the slave names given to them by their white masters. The White-Black power relationship is less easy to discard and most of Jane's companions are killed by a party of white men who object to emancipation. Jane becomes surrogate mother to Ned whose mother is one of those killed. Ned is the first of three important men in Jane's life. She is the focal point from which these men can attain their ideals. Ned becomes a teacher who fights for better conditions for the rural black population; consequently, he is murdered. Joe Pittman is the man whom Jane marries, he is an independent man who works hard to change his future but is killed while doing so. Jane turns to the Church, and becomes spiritual mother. The spirituality of the black community is clearly important in shaping the third important man in Jane's life, Jimmy Aaron or 'the One'. Jimmy is recognized from birth as being special, the religious black community invest all of their hopes and dreams in him. While Jimmy does seek better conditions for his people he tries to achieve it politically, through the Civil Rights Movement, and rejects religion as being the way forward. When Jimmy is killed in the Bayonne Jane Pittman finally finds her time has come to stand up and fight. She finds the courage to lead her friends and community in the struggle against segregation. Thus the book ends as it begins with Jane embarking on a journey towards self-discovery, and a new future for herself and her people.

Gaines does not compromise in his writing, he creates a positive, interesting, and true-to-life image of his culture, his history, and his people. 'Gaines is mellow with historical reflection, supple with wit, relaxed and expansive because he does not equate his people with failure', said Alice Walker in the *New York Times Book Review*, and this comment does much to explain the author's great popularity.

—P. Campbell

GALLAGHER, Patricia.
Nationality: American. **Born:** Patricia Bienek in Lockhart, Texas. Educated at Trinity University, San Antonio, Texas, 1951. **Relations:** married James D. Gallagher (died 1966); one son. **Career:** staff member, KTSA Radio, San Antonio, 1950–51. **Agent:** Scott Meredith Literary Agency, 845 Third Avenue, New York, New York, 10022, USA. **Address:** 3111 Clearfield Drive, San Antonio, Texas 78230, USA.

ROMANCE AND HISTORICAL PUBLICATIONS

Novels

The Sons and the Daughters. New York, Messner, and London, Muller, 1961.
Answer to Heaven. London, Muller, 1962; New York, Avon, 1964.
The Fires of Brimstone. New York, Avon, 1966.
Shannon. New York, Avon, 1967.
Shadows of Passion. New York, Avon, 1971.
Summer of Sighs. New York, Avon, 1971.
The Thicket. New York, Avon, 1973.
Castles in the Air. New York, Avon, 1976; London, Corgi, 1984.
Mystic Rose. New York, Avon, 1977; London, Hamlyn, 1978.
No Greater Love. New York, Avon, 1979; London, Corgi, 1984.
All for Love. New York, Avon, 1981; London, Corgi, 1987.
Echoes and Embers. New York, Avon, 1983; London, Corgi, 1986.
Love Springs Eternal. New York, Berkley, 1985.
On Wings of Dreams. New York, Berkley, 1985.
A Perfect Love. New York, Berkley, 1987.

*   *   *

Patricia Gallagher is a romance novelist who employs the conventions of the genre for unusual goals. This generalization is appropriate to any of her novels (compared to many of her contemporaries she has not written a great deal); it is particularly apt of *Castles in the Air*, her most famous, most popular, work.

Suspend expectation. Devon Marshall, the heroine, does not pursue the hero; he pursues her—and gets her within the first 20 pages, in less than exalted circumstances. Devon is a penniless refugee from post-Civil War Virginia, trying to make her way north; she has worked for her father, a newspaper proprietor, before his death; she hopes to get work as a journalist in New York City. Keith, a wealthy Wall Street banker, allows her to stow away in his private railway car, then demands recompense: he rapes her. Gallagher doesn't mince her scenes. That this one seems credible is a compliment to her powers in conveying the desperation of the times; that she causes both Devon and the reader to subsequently care for, then admire, Keith is a credit to the breadth of her sympathies, her cunning in conveying his own desperation, and her view of the contrariness of human life. Keith loves at first sight, but he is trapped in a hopeless and in some ways despicable marriage by society, his position, and his own conscience. After her initial resistance, Devon and Keith become lovers—passionate, selfless, honourable adulterers; they produce a son, live in the second home that Keith provides for them, then, in the end, after five years, part when it becomes apparent that Keith's now half-crazed wife will never release him or conveniently die. They part at Devon's instigation: she agrees to marry a man she does not love, gives up the man and child she does love, and prepares to go to live with her new husband half a continent away. A story that begins with a violent passion, then deals with its refinement, ends with its defeat. And lest the reader console himself that Devon may find happiness after the last page—that expectation is firmly squelched, as the novel ends, in Devon's dreams, fevered, horrible dreams of the world to which she has exiled herself.

The novel provokes respect. Not only for this vision of the destruction of happy and fulfilling love by society but also for its undoubted expertise as a novel—in its construction, in its handling of time, and in its characterizations. Gallagher's talent is immediately obvious: the first chapter introduces the main characters, vividly renders Devon's situation in post-war Richmond, establishes the themes that will be developed throughout the book—and does so not in laborious exposition but in a very few seemingly random conversations. Her setting of scene is also admirable: New York City, though its elegance is finely conveyed, is for much of the novel not a world of romance but of seedy rooming houses, dirt, and human greed, poverty and squalor. Most impressive, the love story is not the only story or perhaps even the main one. For castles in the air are the dreams of women; and if love, children and family are some of those dreams, so too, and just as important, is the dream of achieving self-hood, of being an entity—as a man may be. Devon's goal is a simple-sounding one: she wishes to be a good journalist; and the main plot of *Castles in the Air* is really of the struggle and hardships such a goal involves—if one is a woman. This quest also ends in defeat.

Devon asks herself early on, trying to make her own way without Keith, whether it is possible for any woman to survive on her own terms without dissembling and mendacity and guile. Thwarted in her main ambition, she takes a series of servile jobs in order to stay alive, does all of them well, then discovers that she's been given chances because she's physically desirable. Finally, she succumbs to Keith, to the kind of help and comfort his money can provide, and also becomes a protégée of one of Boss Tweed's men, whose influence gains her access to a newspaper. She's successful: she becomes a society reporter (appropriate journalistic work for a woman), excels at her work, eventually becomes known to the best New York society, and earns the right to move from coverage of that society to that of the presidential party in Washington. Still, in any real sense, she never wins. Keith, loving in all other ways, never conceives her work or her aspirations to another kind of reportage as anything other than exercise for exasperatingly attractive high spirits. Her benefactor waits for her to weary. The world—even other women engaged in the same kind of work—fail to take her or (it is implied) each other very seriously.

Early in the story Devon befriends Mally, a poor Irish girl at the rooming house where they both live in less than genteel poverty. Considering Devon's ambitions, Mally says to her: 'But you can't marry a dream . . . . And what else is there for a girl? Marriage and children. That's all there is for us'. Devon asks: 'But why, Mally? *Why* must it be all there is for us'. Mally replies: 'Because we're female'. Devon sets out to prove Mally wrong—but in fact proves something else. What separates Mally from her is not the difference in their ambitions or even in their capacity for vision; the difference is in how well each can survive in a marketplace in which the currency is physical attractiveness. Devon is beautiful; Mally is not; Devon is loved by a rich man and desired by a politically powerful one, they provide her with her opportunities; Mally, conversely, is plain, she has nothing to barter: she never moves from poverty and hopelessness, she falls for the wrong man, her life ends tragically. Mally is not regarded; but then neither is Devon, except as an object of love and passion who, in return for inspiring lust, is allowed to play. The world to which Devon finally gains entrance is described as beautiful because it *is* beautiful—but not for a woman. For if she aspires to being something more than one of the beautiful things, she will be defeated—in the definition of self, in any kind of moral or intellectual fulfilment.

Gallagher is too good a writer to labour any of these points (indeed, within so obviously feminist a novel, she is scrupulously fair to men: some are rats, some are decent). She presents situation, leaves moral reflection to her readers. And this interest in something beyond a conventional romantic plot, this use of romantic devices to convey her own themes, is common to many of her novels. Yet one puts down any of them with a mild but gnawing dissatisfaction. The problem is language.

Castles in the Air—any of the novels—provides rich examples. The very names of her main characters are risible. And they stare into a dense opacity. They feel like mice on a treadmill to oblivion. In conveying information, women sound like a teacher who has presented the same lecture too many times. In being masculine, men reach for the diction and cadences of the King James Bible. If her plots are the antithesis of cliché, her language falls into all the traps.

And yet. The criticism, once made, seems wrong. For every three scenes of bad dialogue, there is one good one. Some of her descriptions are downright embarrassing; some are masterful. She allows some of her physical scenes to become mawkish—but, in any of her books, there is sex which is stylishly described, pleasantly torrid. Often—too often—she conveys the emotional relations between people in ways that are, frankly, corny; other times, she invokes feeling with such exactness as to be genuinely affecting and profound. It is as if she is not so much unskilful as lazy with language—or, perhaps, that she devotes such time and effort to getting it right in plot, setting, scene, that she has little energy left for words themselves. The result is hit or miss. If she can now refine language as she has perfected the other aspects of her craft, Gallagher can almost certainly set a standard against which other romance novelists will be measured.

—George Walsh

———

GALLANT, Jennie.   See SMITH, Joan.

———

GALWAY, Robert Conington.   See McCUTCHAN, Philip.

———

GANN, Ernest K(ellogg).
Nationality: American. **Born:** Lincoln, Nebraska, 13 October 1910. **Education:** Culver Military Academy; Yale University, New Haven, Connecticut, 1930–32. **Military Service:** United States Air Force Air Transport Command, 1942–46: captain. **Relations:** married 1) Eleanor Michaud in 1933 (divorced), two sons (one deceased) and one daughter; 2) Dodie Post in 1966. **Recipient:** H.H.D.: University of California, 1979. **Died:** 21 December 1991.

ROMANCE AND HISTORICAL PUBLICATIONS

Novels

The Antagonists. New York, Simon and Schuster, 1970; London, Hodder and Stoughton, 1971.
The Triumph. New York, Simon and Schuster, and London, Hodder and Stoughton, 1986.

OTHER PUBLICATIONS

Novels

Island in the Sky. New York, Viking Press, 1944; London, Joseph, 1945.
Blaze at Noon. New York, Holt, 1946; London, Aldor, 1947.
Benjamin Lawless. New York, Sloane, 1948.

Fiddler's Green. New York, Sloane, 1950; London, Hodder and Stoughton, 1954.

Twilight for the Gods. New York, Sloane, 1950; London, Hodder and Stoughton, 1956.

The High and the Mighty. New York, Sloane, and London, Hodder and Stoughton, 1953.

Soldier of Fortune. New York, Sloane, 1954; London, Hodder and Stoughton, 1955.

Trouble with Lazy Ethel. New York, Sloane, 1958; London, Hodder and Stoughton, 1959.

Of Good and Evil. New York, Simon and Schuster, and London, Hodder and Stoughton, 1963.

In the Company of Eagles. New York, Simon and Schuster, 1966; London, Hodder and Stoughton, 1967.

The Song of the Sirens. New York, Simon and Schuster, 1968; London, Hodder and Stoughton, 1969.

Band of Brothers. New York, Simon and Schuster, 1973; London, Hodder and Stoughton, 1974.

Brain 2000. New York, Doubleday, and London, Hodder and Stoughton, 1980.

The Aviator. New York, Arbor House, and London, Hodder and Stoughton, 1981.

The Magistrate. New York, Arbor House, 1982; London, Hodder and Stoughton, 1983.

Gentlemen of Adventure. New York, Arbor House, 1983; London, Hodder and Stoughton, 1984.

The Bad Angel. New York, Arbor House, 1987; London, Hodder and Stoughton, 1988.

Plays

Screenplays: *The Raging Tide*, 1951; *Island in the Sky*, 1953; *The High and the Mighty*, 1954; *Soldier of Fortune*, 1955; *Twilight for the Gods*, 1958.

Other

Sky Roads. New York, Crowell, 1940.
All American Aircraft. New York, Crowell, 1941.
Getting Them into the Blue. New York, Crowell, 1942.
Fate Is the Hunter (memoirs). New York, Simon and Schuster, and London, Hodder and Stoughton, 1961.
Flying Circus. New York, Macmillan, 1974; London, Hodder and Stoughton, 1976.
A Hostage to Fortune (autobiography). New York, Knopf, 1978; London, Hodder and Stoughton, 1979.
The Black Watch: America's Spy Pilots and Their Planes. New York, Random House, 1989.

*

Film Adaptations: *Blaze of Noon*, 1947; *The Raging Tide*, 1951, based on the novel *Fiddler's Green*; *Island in the Sky*, 1953; *The High and the Mighty*, 1954; *Soldier of Fortune*, 1955; *Twilight for the Gods*, 1958; *Fate Is the Hunter*, 1964; *Masada*, 1981, from the novel, *The Antagonists*; *The Aviator*, 1985.

*   *   *

To think of Ernest K. Gann is to conjure up the John Waynes and Clark Gables of Hollywood flying high and mighty in the clouds, for Gann's novels, nearly all bestsellers, have been primarily about airplanes and pilots, and have succeeded on screen as well as in bookstores. Until 1970 his historical fiction took place in the 20th century. As a pilot himself, it is little wonder that his first book *Island in the Sky*, and many subsequent ones dealt with flying. How

then can we explain *The Antagonists* after some 12 books and many years later? In his autobiography, *A Hostage to Fortune* Gann explained how this came about. While taking a vacation from writing he came across Israel's Yigael Yadin's archaeological report on Masada, the mountain fortress in the Judaean desert where the last battle between the Romans and Jews was waged in the first century A.D. He became fascinated by the lore of the Judaean desert and the siege that took place there 1900 years before. With research a joyous prelude to writing, Gann threw himself into the exploration of the siege that precious little had been written about in this century before Yadin. His Jewish friends had heard about Masada, but knew very little about it. Though Gann had studied the 'hearsay' account of Josephus, the Jewish general turned Roman who was a contemporary of the antagonists General Flavius Silva and Eleazar ben Yair, he based his fictional tale more closely on the Yadin archaeological findings. Josephus was not present at Masada—but the ruins of Herod's once impregnable stronghold still are.

The Antagonists is a marvellous novel. The situation itself is very dramatic—a three-year siege by Silva's famed Roman 10th legion attempting to capture the Jewish stronghold and the 960 zealots led by Eleazar; the ancient machines of war—catapults and attack towers moving up the giant ramp built with slave labour, all described as if Gann could actually see it. We can't truly know what Silva and Eleazar were like, but it is easy enough to accept Gann's portrayal of the two men as they hurl sardonic insults at each other from far above and far below. The natural acoustics of the place make this believable. The final scene is both exhilarating and tragic—as the Romans scale the mountain fortress only to discover the mass suicide of the zealots who preferred death to captivity.

Though Gann believed, in 1970, that Silva had disappeared from history after Masada (according to his preface to *The Antagonists*) he obviously continued his research, fascinated perhaps by both the historical Silva and the Silva of his own creation, for that same patrician general appears 16 years later as the main character in his second historical novel, *The Triumph*. This is indeed a sequel to *The Antagonists* as it begins just where the Masada tale left off—with Silva weary and sick at heart at his hollow victory. But time heals, and so does the love of a woman, Domitillia, daughter of the aging Emperor Vespasian and childhood friend to Silva. *The Triumph* is very different from its predecessor save that the same detail of archaeological research is evident, but spread over a much wider area, primarily the city of Rome. This is a story of love, intrigue, and adventure from A.D.74 to 79, when Vespasian's sons, Titus and Domitian, vied to succeed him. Gann has chosen Titus as his favourite (as did the historical Silva who reappeared in history for a few years more) while treating Domitian much less kindly than many historians have done. Gann does not pretend to recreate the facts accurately in this novel, but he vividly pictures the street scenes of teeming slums and magnificent palaces, glimpses of the Christians praying to their unseen God, the building of the Colosseum and the horror of the bloodletting that went on in it and in other arenas. Most colourful of all is the description of the 'triumph', the magnificent parade planned to honour the aging Emperor which instead became his funeral procession. But it was glorious: 200 pipers led the way, followed by trumpeters, mourning women (who were forbidden by law to tear out their hair), flute players, actors, mimes, and buffoons, machines of war, gladiators, beasts in cages, and the surviving family, wending their way through the narrow streets to the forum to set fire to the funeral pyre. A fitting end to Vespasian and to Gann's second historical novel.

With *The Bad Angel* Gann returned to the USA, and to contemporary history. This action-packed novel was also an impassioned treatise against drug pushers and traders. Gann's protagonist, Lee Rogers, is an unsophisticated rancher from the West whose beloved son dies tragically, seduced by cocaine. Lee wins his bid to Congress to wage war against the drug trade, and his single-minded campaign shakes up a lot of people both in Washington and abroad. Though the plot loses credibility, the background does not. The enormity and the intricacies of the drug problem are clearly examined, as is the futility of one man's crusade to alleviate it. Gann also returned to the air in *The Bad Angel*. It seems that he could not allow his fictional pilot turned drug smuggler to be all bad so he used Lee, the 'cowboy Congressman' to redeem himself by the force of his own character and mission, and with challenging flying escapades.

Though Gann's last book, *The Black Watch*, can not be classified as fiction, many of the names and events portrayed in this story of the men who fly America's secret spy planes are disguised—for obvious reasons.

—Marion Hanscom

———

GARNETT, David. British. 1892–1981. See 2nd edition, 1990.

———

GARVICE, Charles.
Pseudonyms: Charles Gibson; Caroline Hart. **Nationality:** British. **Born:** 1833. **Career:** journalist; county councillor, Northam, Devon. President, Institute of Lecturers, and Farmers and Landowners Association. Fellow, Royal Society of Literature. **Died:** 1 March 1920.

ROMANCE AND HISTORICAL PUBLICATIONS

Novels

Maurice Durant. London, Smith, 3 vols, 1875; New York, Ogilvie, n.d.; as *Eyes of Love*, New York, Street and Smith, n.d.
On Love's Altar. New York, Munro, 1892; London, King, 1908; as *A Wasted Love* (as Caroline Hart), Cleveland, Westbrook, n.d.
Paid For! New York, Munro, 1892; London, Hutchinson, 1909.
Married at Sight. New York, Munro, 1894.
The Price of Honour (as Charles Gibson). Cleveland, Westbrook, n.d.
His Love So True. New York, Munro, 1896.
The Marquis. New York, Munro, 1896.
Just a Girl. London, Bowden, 1898; as *An Innocent Girl*, New York, Munro, 1898.
She Loved Him. New York, Street and Smith, 1899; London, Hutchinson, 1909.
Claire. New York, Street and Smith, 1899.
Lorrie. New York, Street and Smith, 1899; London, Hodder and Stoughton, 1910.
Modern Juliet. New York, Street and Smith, 1900; London, Pearson, 1910.
Nell of Shorne Mills. New York, Street and Smith, 1900; London, Hutchinson, 1908.
Nance. London, Sands, 1900.
Her Heart's Desire. London, Sands, 1900; New York, Hurst, 1903.
An Outcast of the Family. London, Sands, 1900.
A Coronet of Shame. London, Sands, 1900; New York, Ogilvie, n.d.
Leola Dale's Fortune. New York, Street and Smith, 1901; London, Hutchinson, 1910.
Maida. New York, Street and Smith, 1901.
Only a Girl's Love. New York, Street and Smith, 1901; London, Hodder and Stoughton, 1911.
For Her Only. New York, Street and Smith, 1902; London, Hodder and Stoughton, 1911.
The Lady of Darracourt. New York, Street and Smith, 1902; London, Hodder and Stoughton, 1911.

Jeanne. New York, Street and Smith, 1902.
Heir of Vering. New York, Street and Smith, 1902; London, Hutchinson, 1910.
Woman's Soul. New York, Street and Smith, 1902.
So Nearly Lost. New York, Street and Smith, 1902; as *The Spring-Time of Love*, London, Hodder and Stoughton, 1910.
So Fair, So False. New York, Street and Smith, 1902.
Love's Dilemma. New York, Street and Smith, 1902; London, Hodder and Stoughton, 1917; as *For an Earldom*, New York, Ogilvie, n.d.
Martyred Love. New York, Street and Smith, 1902.
My Lady Pride. New York, Street and Smith, 1902.
Olivia. New York, Street and Smith, 1902.
In Cupid's Chains. London, Sands, 1902.
Woven on Fate's Loom, and The Snowdrift. New York, Street and Smith, 1903.
Staunch of the Heart. New York, Street and Smith, 1903; as *Adrien Leroy*, London, Newnes, 1912.
Her Ransom. New York, Hurst, 1903.
Led by Love. New York, Street and Smith, 1903.
Staunch as a Woman. New York, Street and Smith, 1903; London, Hodder and Stoughton, 1910.
A Jest of Fate. New York, Munro, 1904; London, Newnes, 1909.
Her Humble Lover. Cleveland, Westbrook, 1904; as *The Usurper*, Chicago, Donohue, n.d.
Love Decides. London, Hutchinson, 1904.
Linked by Fate. London, Hutchinson, 1905.
Love, The Tyrant. London, Hutchinson, 1905.
Edna's Secret Marriage. New York, Street and Smith, 1905.
The Other Woman. New York, Street and Smith, 1905.
When Love Meets Love. New York, Street and Smith, 1906.
A Girl of Spirit. London, Hutchinson, 1906; New York, Street and Smith, n.d.
Diana and Destiny. London, Hodder and Stoughton, 1906; as *Diana's Destiny*, New York, Burt, n.d.
Where Love Leads. London, Hutchinson, 1907.
The Gold in the Gutter. London, Hutchinson, 1907.
Sacrifice to Art. Chicago, Stein, 1908.
Sample of Prejudice. Chicago, Stein, 1908.
Slave of the Lake. Chicago, Stein, 1908.
Taming of Princess Olga. Chicago, Stein, 1908.
Woman Decides. Chicago, Stein, 1908.
My Lady of Snow. Chicago, Stein, 1908.
Linnie. Chicago, Stein, 1908.
Olivia and Others. London, Hutchinson, 1908.
A Love Comedy. Chicago, Stein, 1908; London, Hodder and Stoughton, 1912.
Marcia Drayton. London, Newnes, 1908.
Female Editor. Chicago, Stein, 1908.
Leave Love to Itself. Chicago, Stein, 1908.
First and Last. Chicago, Stein, 1908.
In the Matter of a Letter. Chicago, Stein, 1908.
Farmer Holt's Daughter. Chicago, Stein, 1908.
Story of a Passion. London, Hutchinson, 1908; New York, Burt, n.d.
Kyra's Fate. London, Hutchinson, 1908; New York, Burt, n.d.
The Rugged Path. London, Hodder and Stoughton, 1908.
In Wolf's Clothing. London, Hodder and Stoughton, 1908.
Queen Kate. London, Hodder and Stoughton, 1909.
The Scribblers' Club. London, Hodder and Stoughton, 1909.
The Fatal Ruby. London, Hodder and Stoughton, and New York, Doran, 1909.
By Dangerous Ways. London, Amalgamated Press, 1909; New York, Burt, n.d.
A Fair Imposter. London, Newnes, 1909.
A Heritage of Hate. London, Amalgamated Press, 1909.

The Mistress of Court Regina. London, Hutchinson, 1909; Philadelphia, Royal, n.d.
At Love's Cost. London, Hutchinson, 1909; New York, Burt, n.d.
Ashes of Love. New York, Ogilvie, 1910.
Barriers Between. London, Hodder and Stoughton, 1910.
The Beauty of the Season. London, Hodder and Stoughton, 1910.
Better Than Life. London, Hodder and Stoughton, 1910.
Dulcie. London, Hodder and Stoughton, 1910.
The Earl's Daughter. London, Hodder and Stoughton, 1910; as *The Earl's Heir*, Chicago, Donohue, n.d.
A Girl from the South. London, Cassell, 1910.
The Heart of a Maid. London, Hodder and Stoughton, 1910.
Once in a Life. London, Hodder and Stoughton, 1910.
Only One Love. London, Hodder and Stoughton, 1910; New York, Street and Smith, n.d.
A Passion Flower. London, Hodder and Stoughton, 1910; New York, Street and Smith, n.d.
With All Her Heart. London, Newnes, 1910.
Floris. London, Hutchinson, 1910.
Signa's Sweetheart. London, Hutchinson, 1910.
Sweet as a Rose. London, Hutchinson, 1910.
Leslie's Loyalty. London, Hodder and Stoughton, 1911; New York, Street and Smith, n.d.; as *Her Love So True*, Philadelphia, Royal, n.d.
Miss Estcourt. London, Hutchinson, 1911.
My Love Kitty. London, Hutchinson, 1911.
That Strange Girl. London, Hutchinson, 1911.
Violet. London, Hutchinson, 1911.
Doris. London, Newnes, 1911.
Elaine. London, Newnes, 1911; New York, Street and Smith, n.d.
He Loves Me, He Loves Me Not. London, Hodder and Stoughton, 1911; New York, Street and Smith, n.d.
His Guardian Angel. London, Newnes, 1911; New York, Street and Smith, n.d.
Lord of Himself. London, Hodder and Stoughton, 1911.
The Other Girl. London, Hodder and Stoughton, 1911.
Sweet Cymbeline. London, Newnes, 1911; New York, Street and Smith, n.d.
A Wilful Maid. London, Newnes, 1911; New York, Street and Smith, n.d.; as *Phillippa*, Chicago, Donohue, n.d.
The Woman in It. London, Hodder and Stoughton, 1911.
Wounded Heart. New York, Ogilvie, 1911.
Breta's Double. New York, Street and Smith, n.d.
His Perfect Trust. Philadelphia, Royal, n.d.
Imogene. New York, Street and Smith, n.d.
Love of a Life Time. Philadelphia, Royal, n.d.
Lucille. Chicago, Donohue, n.d.
Out of the Past. New York, Street and Smith, n.d.
Price of Honor. Philadelphia, Royal, n.d.
Pride of Her Life. New York, Street and Smith, n.d.
Royal Signet. Philadelphia, Royal, n.d.
The Spider and the Fly. New York, Street and Smith, n.d.
Sydney. New York, Street and Smith, n.d.
'Twix Smile and Tear. New York, Street and Smith, n.d.
Wasted Love. New York, Street and Smith, n.d.
Love in a Snare. London, Hodder and Stoughton, 1912.
Fate. London, Newnes, 1912; New York, Ogilvie, 1913.
Fickle Fortune. London, Newnes, 1912.
In Fine Feathers. London, Hodder and Stoughton, 1912.
Stella's Fortune. London, Hodder and Stoughton, 1912; New York, Street and Smith, n.d.; as *Sculptor's Wooing*, New York, Ogilvie, n.d.
Two Maids and a Man. London, Hodder and Stoughton, 1912; as *Two Girls and a Man*, London, Wright and Brown, 1937.
The Verdict of the Heart. London, Newnes, 1912.
Country Love. London, Hutchinson, 1912.

Reuben. London, Hutchinson, 1912.
Nellie. London, Hutchinson, 1913; (as Caroline Hart) Cleveland, Westbrook, n.d.
The Loom of Fate. London, Newnes, 1913.
The Woman's Way. London, Hodder and Stoughton, 1914.
Iris. London, Newnes, 1914.
The Call of the Heart. London, Hodder and Stoughton, 1914.
In Exchange for Love. London, Hodder and Stoughton, 1914.
The One Girl in the World. London, Hodder and Stoughton, 1915.
Love, The Adventurous. London, Hodder and Stoughton, 1917.
Creatures of Destiny. New York, Burt, n.d.
Heart for Heart. New York, Burt, n.d.
Love and a Lie. New York, Burt, n.d.
Shadow of Her Life. New York, Burt, n.d.
'Twas Love's Fault. New York, Burt, n.d.
When Love Is Young. New York, Burt, n.d.
The Waster. London, Lloyds, 1918.
The Girl in Love. London, Skeffington, 1919.
Wicked Sir Dare. London, Hutchinson, 1938.

Novels as Caroline Hart

A Hidden Terror. Cleveland, Westbrook, 1910.
Angela's Lover. Cleveland, Westbrook, n.d.
For Love or Honor. Cleveland, Westbrook, n.d.
From Want to Wealth. Cleveland, Westbrook, n.d.
From Worse Than Death. Cleveland, Westbrook, n.d.
Game of Love. Cleveland, Westbrook, n.d.
Haunted Life. Cleveland, Westbrook, n.d.
Hearts of Fire. Cleveland, Westbrook, n.d.
Her Right to Love. Cleveland, Westbrook, n.d.
Lil, The Dancing Girl. Cleveland, Westbrook, n.d.
Lillian's Vow. Cleveland, Westbrook, n.d.
Little Princess. Cleveland, Westbrook, n.d.
Love's Rugged Path. Cleveland, Westbrook, n.d.
Madness of Love. Cleveland, Westbrook, n.d.
Nameless Bess. Cleveland, Westbrook, n.d.
Nobody's Wife. Cleveland, Westbrook, n.d.
Redeemed by Love. Cleveland, Westbrook, n.d.
Rival Heiresses. Cleveland, Westbrook, n.d.
She Loved Not Wisely. Cleveland, Westbrook, n.d.
Strange Marriage. Cleveland, Westbrook, n.d.
That Awful Scar. Cleveland, Westbrook, n.d.
Vengeance of Love. Cleveland, Westbrook, n.d.
Women Who Came Between. Cleveland, Westbrook, n.d.
Woman Wronged. Cleveland, Westbrook, n.d.
Working Girl's Honor. Cleveland, Westbrook, n.d.

Short Stories

The Girl Without a Heart and Other Stories. London, Newnes, 1912.
A Relenting Fate and Other Stories. London, Newnes, 1912.
All Is Not Fair in Love and Other Stories. London, Newnes, 1913.
The Tessacott Tragedy and Other Stories. London, Newnes, 1913.
The Girl in the 'bacca Shop. London, Skeffington, 1920.
Miss Smith's Fortune and Other Stories. London, Skeffington, 1920.

OTHER PUBLICATIONS

Plays

The Fisherman's Daughter (produced London, 1881).
A Life's Mistake. London, Hutchinson, 1910.

Marigold, with Allan F. Abbott (produced Glasgow, 1914).

Poetry

Eve and Other Verses. Privately printed, 1873.

Other

A Farm in Creamland: A Book of the Devon Countryside. London, Hodder and Stoughton, 1911; New York, Doran, 1912.

Editor, *The Red Budget of Stories*. London, Hodder and Stoughton, 1912.

* * *

Charles Garvice was an English writer of the early 1900s. His novels actually became popular in the mid-1890s and were so well received by American readers that many of his works were printed by American publishers in pirated editions even after the 1891 international copyright agreement.

Garvice's style and his frequent diversions into social commentary would tend to put modern readers off from fully enjoying his works today. Often his stories begin by drawing comparisons between his developing characters and the common people of the poorer sections of London. Frequently his characters display a deep and unusual social consciousness that makes them aware of changes in the economy that worked to the detriment of the working classes. In fact, the theme of helping the working classes, or of accepting people for themselves remains a solid underlying force throughout many of his novels. On another level it is his consistent emphasis on natural, instinctive qualities within the lower classes that make these people just as socially acceptable as those from the upper ranks. Often the reader finds phrases such as 'He had the instincts of a gentleman' or 'She moved and spoke in the manner born' applied to characters from the working classes. The fact that these qualities could be found in the lower classes made that person even more exceptional and valued. For this element in his novels alone, one can understand why they appealed so greatly to American readers.

That is not, however, the major cause of his popularity. For Garvice had an unusual ability to weave fast-paced, intricate, and believable plots that do not need to rely on coincidence to succeed. Missing jewels or treasures are combined with missing or lost heiresses. His plots usually centre on the hero of the story, and the action is told from his viewpoint. He is often from a titled family and he usually succeeds to the title or is reinstated into his father's good graces. In *The Gold in the Gutter* Clive Harvey is the third son of a family of notable rakes and spendthrifts who becomes a radical thinker and wins a seat in the House of Commons. Basically, the development of Garvice's stories rests on the hero's ability to overcome obstacles and in the process, of course, to win the girl who has captured his heart. If any major flaw emerges in Garvice's writing, it is his tendency to draw his characters larger than life; even the hero's faults assume a virtuous glow so that one does not come to grips with the real person Garvice is attempting to characterize. He is too good, too virtuous, too everything to be readily acceptable to today's readers. In spite of this drawback, one must conclude that his writings fall very definitely into the romance genre. Actually Garvice is within the traditional guidelines of the misunderstood hero who faces all sorts of trials before he succeeds in achieving his goal.

Dialogue is often cleverly used to round out a character. It is sharp, and frequently colourful and rich, adding to the speaker's overall character. Description is not always kept as short as one would like, but from the period in which he was writing, that cannot be considered a fault. Certainly he mastered the technique of telling a good, moving story that kept readers waiting for the next chapter.

His writing apparently appealed to men as well as women, for some of his works actually could be classified as adventure stories rather than straight romances. For example, in *The Rugged Path* Jack, the son of Sir William Morton, leaves home after disagreeing with his father. He is literally cut off from his father and any money his father would leave him. The prospect certainly does not upset him, for he sails to Australia and undertakes a whole new life for himself. The Australian scenes are quite well presented by Garvice, indicating careful research to lend accuracy to his works. The scene shifts back to England, with the death of his father and the arrival of the villain in the person of his cousin, Hesketh Carton. Contested wills, fetching girls of the new breed, and the hero's own queer sense of honour add to an intriguing story and eventual happiness.

It is difficult to summarize Garvice as a romance writer. Barring stylistic elements that certainly date his work, he still can be enjoyably read by anyone. In fact, careful editing and the presentation of his works as historical novels might make them appealing even now. Yet, he was not an outstanding writer. He may not have had that special spark that would allow for such liberties to be taken. Perhaps it would make no difference, for romance writers tend to want to tell a good story and to make people experience, just for a moment, someone else's life and happiness. The fact that Garvice wrote well over 150 novels indicates that he may have achieved his purpose and did not particularly care for lasting fame.

—Arlene Moore

GASCOIGNE, Marguerite. See **GILBERT, Anna.**

GASKIN, Catherine.
Nationality: Irish. **Born:** Dundalk, County Louth, 2 April 1929. **Education:** Holy Cross College, Sydney, Australia; Conservatorium of Music, Sydney, 1943–48, piano studies. **Relations:** married Sol Cornberg in 1955. **Career:** lived in London, 1948–55, New York, 1955–65, the Virgin Islands 1965–67, and Ireland 1967–81. **Address:** White Rigg, East Ballaterson, Maughold, Isle of Man, United Kingdom.

ROMANCE AND HISTORICAL PUBLICATIONS

Novels

This Other Eden. London, Collins, 1947.
With Every Year. London, Collins, 1949.
Dust in the Sunlight. London, Collins, 1950.
All Else Is Folly. London, Collins, and New York, Harper, 1951.
Daughter of the House. London, Collins, 1952; New York, Harper, 1953.
Sara Dane. London, Collins, and Philadelphia, Lippincott, 1955.
Blake's Reach. London, Collins, and Philadelphia, Lippincott, 1958.
Corporation Wife. London, Collins, and New York, Doubleday, 1960.
I Know My Love. London, Collins, and New York, Doubleday, 1962.
The Tilsit Inheritance. London, Collins, and New York, Doubleday, 1963.
The File on Devlin. London, Collins, and New York, Doubleday, 1965.

Edge of Glass. London, Collins, and New York, Doubleday, 1967.
Fiona. London, Collins, and New York, Doubleday, 1970.
A Falcon for a Queen. London, Collins, and New York, Doubleday, 1972.
The Property of a Gentleman. London, Collins, and New York, Doubleday, 1974.
The Lynmara Legacy. London, Collins, 1975; New York, Doubleday, 1976.
The Summer of the Spanish Woman. London, Collins, and New York, Doubleday, 1977.
Family Affairs. London, Collins, and New York, Doubleday, 1980.
Promises. London, Collins, and New York, Doubleday, 1982.
The Ambassador's Women. London, Collins, 1985; New York, Scribner, 1986.
The Charmed Circle. London, Collins, 1988; New York, Scribner, 1989.

*

Film Adaptation: *The File on Devlin*, 1969.

Catherine Gaskin comments:
I write to entertain and I expend enormous effort on my writing so that the end product will appear effortless.

*   *   *

Catherine Gaskin has created her own niche in the world of the romance novel. Her works contain the familiar gothic elements—disputed inheritance, forbidden love, mysterious strangers, ancestral homes and their hidden skeletons, and the culminating act of violence. What sets her apart is her ability to integrate these elements into the fabric of a modern world so convincingly drawn as to anchor the fantastic firmly to earth. *This Other Eden*, the first novel she later rewrote as *The Lynmara Legacy*, reveals the talent as already fully formed. Its theme, of an American girl's succession to an English inheritance, is basically the same in both versions, and displays Gaskin's skill in blending realism and romance.

Since then, Gaskin's writing is roughly divisible into two main streams: modern stories with gothic ingredients, and historical romances. The latter tend to be longer, and sometimes more ambitious; viewed critically, they are often less satisfying. Though immensely popular, *Sara Dane* lacks the sense of solid reality that marks even the earliest of Gaskin's contemporary novels. Without the social background so ably provided in the modern works, its events seem unnecessarily theatrical and shorn of conviction. The story—of a transported servant girl who rises to wealth and power in colonial Australia—moves uncertainly from one crisis to another, with the arrivals and departures of Sara's prospective lovers rendered improbably convenient. Comparison with Susan Taite, the sophisticated and sensual fashion editor of *All Else Is Folly*, reveals Sara's deficiencies; she is merely a character in a book, while Susan impresses as a living woman evoked by words. *Blake's Reach*, a story of smuggling adventure off the Romney marshes in the 18th century, and *I Know My Love* with its historical Australian setting, both suffer from the same defects. Although they are exciting period tales, they do not possess the depth of penetration found in other works. Measured beside Gaskin's finest creations, the romances are costume dramas rather than portrayals of life. Later attempts in the genre, notably *A Falcon for a Queen*, achieve a greater degree of success, but serve as exceptions that prove the rule.

Corporation Wife, one of Gaskin's most satisfying books, explores the lives of four women in a small town taken over by an industrial company. Gaskin studies the women—two executive wives and two natives—in terms of their loves and ambitions, and the differing ways in which each adapts to the pressures of the corporation in her life. Her touch is sure, romance and tragedy made part of a convincing social scene, the characters perfectly and subtly realized. Equally skilled are *The Tilsit Inheritance*, where a pottery business provides the background for a disputed legacy and love for a dark stranger, and the imaginative spy mystery *The File on Devlin*. Gaskin shows a keen awareness of various crafts and their commercial applications, and this knowledge is effectively used in most of her works. Examples include the mechanics of glass production in *Edge of Glass*, fashion in *All Else Is Folly*, and viticulture in *The Summer of the Spanish Woman*. Presentation of her characters at work is a major factor in the authenticity of Gaskin's best novels.

The Property of a Gentleman displays the aspects of the Gaskin novel in perfect balance. Against a background of art auctioneering, the heroine falls in love with the heir to a Lakeland mansion. Action revolves around the discovery of a skeleton and related art treasures, and the book has a violent denouement. This novel shares another factor with many of Gaskin's works, the emphasis on the family and the ancestral home. This last theme forms the core of *The Lynmara Legacy*, whose self-reliant, determined heroine is typical of the Gaskin woman in other novels. This theme is a significant aspect of more recent books, longer contemporary family chronicles reminiscent of the historical romances, into which the violent, gothic items are more fitfully inserted. Such works present a larger world-view, and usually depict an elite, privileged group of people, whether financial (*The Ambassador's Women*), political (*Family Affairs*), artistic (*The Charmed Circle*), or industrial (*Promises*). Each contains the recurrent theme of the outsider, adopted by the powerful head of the family, coming into her inheritance, usually after rivalry and death. Gaskin's storytelling gift is undiminished, but the later sagas lack the coherence and balance of previous works, the gothic elements somehow more intrusive and less integral than before. Gaskin has produced an impressive body of work, unique of its kind. More than most, she has brought a modern dimension to the gothic romance.

—Geoffrey Sadler

GAVIN, Catherine (Irvine).
Nationality: British. **Born:** Aberdeen, Scotland, in 1907. **Education:** University of Aberdeen, M.A. (honours) 1928, Ph.D. 1931. **Relations:** married John Ashcraft in 1948. **Career:** lecturer in History, University of Aberdeen, 1932–34, 1941–43, and University of Glasgow, 1934–36; editorial writer, European bureau chief, and war correspondent, Kemsley Newspapers, 1943–45; correspondent in the Middle East and Ethiopia, *Daily Express*, London, 1945–47; staff member, *Time*, New York, 1950-52; public lecturer in the USA, 1952–60. Active in Scottish politics in the 1930s: Conservative candidate for Parliament twice. D.Litt.: University of Aberdeen, 1986. **Address:** 1201 California Street, San Francisco, California 94109, USA.

ROMANCE AND HISTORICAL PUBLICATIONS

Novels (series: Napoleon; Second Empire Quartet; Second World War Trilogy)

Clyde Valley. London, Barker, 1938.
The Hostile Shore. London, Methuen, 1940.
The Black Milestone. London, Methuen, 1941.
The Mountain of Light. London, Methuen, 1944.

Second Empire Quartet:

>*Madeleine.* New York, St Martin's Press, 1957; London, Macmillan, 1958.
>
>*The Cactus and the Crown.* London, Hodder and Stoughton, and New York, Doubleday, 1962.
>
>*The Fortress.* London, Hodder and Stoughton, and New York, Doubleday, 1964.
>
>*The Moon into Blood.* London, Hodder and Stoughton, 1966.

The Devil in Harbour. London, Hodder and Stoughton, and New York, Morrow, 1968.

The House of War. London, Hodder and Stoughton, and New York, Morrow, 1970.

Give Me the Daggers. London, Hodder and Stoughton, and New York, Morrow, 1972.

The Snow Mountain. London, Hodder and Stoughton, 1973; New York, Pantheon, 1974.

Second World War Trilogy:

>*Traitors' Gate.* London, Hodder and Stoughton, and New York, St Martin's Press, 1976.
>
>*None Dare Call It Treason.* London, Hodder and Stoughton, and New York, St Martin's Press, 1978.
>
>*How Sleep the Brave.* London, Hodder and Stoughton, and New York, St Martin's Press, 1980.

The Sunset Dream. London, Hodder and Stoughton, 1983; New York, St Martin's Press, 1984.

A Light Woman. London, Grafton, 1986.

The Glory Road. London, Grafton, 1987.

A Dawn of Splendour (Napoleon). London, Grafton, 1989.

The French Fortune (Napoleon). London, Grafton, 1991.

OTHER PUBLICATIONS

Other

Louis Philippe, King of the French. London, Methuen, 1933.

Britain and France: A Study of Twentieth Century Relations, The Entente Cordiale. London, Cape, 1941.

Edward the Seventh: A Biography. London, Cape, 1941.

Liberated France. London, Cape, and New York, St Martin's Press, 1955.

*   *   *

The closer a historical novelist sets her books to the present day, the more she puts her scholarship on the line and invites criticism, for many readers will remember the events and will be quick enough to say 'this did not happen' or 'this did happen but not for that reason' if she is wrong. Catherine Gavin passes this test with flying colours in what she calls her 'war novels'—four about World War I and a trilogy about World War II—all of which will have readers who lived through the events portrayed. They will agree that not only does she get her history right but that she has a masterly way of evoking the atmosphere of a given place at a precise moment in time. Thus having found her accounts of times we are competent to judge trustworthy, we feel she must be right, too, when she tells us about earlier periods of history.

Her 'Second Empire Quartet' is a series of books set in the 19th century and loosely connected by their theme: they set out to explore various revolutionary struggles, mixing fictional characters with historical personalities. *The Fortress* tells of the naval campaign in the Baltic, in 1885, through the eyes of an American in the Royal Navy and adumbrates Finland's struggles through his Finnish wife; *The Moon into Blood* is about the Risorgimento in Italy with a fictional American hero who works with Cavour and Garibaldi; *Madeleine* is about the Second Empire in France, and *The Cactus and the Crown* the ill-fated Hapsburg intervention in Mexico. While not

part of this series, *The Glory Road* belongs here, the story of a young man's serach for 'La Gloire' in the French army in the late-19th century.

The French Revolution and Bonaparte's rise to power is seen obliquely through the eyes of Marie Fontaine, a young woman who wants to be the first woman apothecary, and is dazzled by Napoleon in *A Dawn of Splendour*, and *The French Fortune*. The romance in these two books is overpowered by the historical detail, although the characterization of both the fictional and real people is strong and interesting.

The theme of the World War I novels is that the pressures distort normal behaviour patterns. *The Devil in Harbour* is concerned with spying, divided loyalties, and the battle of Jutland. *The Snow Mountain* is a poignant recreation of the fall of the Romanovs, in which Gavin's interpretations of the Czar and Czarina's motives is interesting; the fictitious characters who share the story are extremely believable. *Give Me the Daggers* tells of General Mannerheim's fight for Finnish independence in 1918, but it is also about a young man coming to terms with a disfiguring wound and a spoiled young girl learning unselfishness. Kemal Ataturk's struggle for Turkish freedom is explored in *The House of War* set against the break up of a marriage.

In all of these books the history is well integrated into the fiction, and the descriptions of places evocative. A felicitous touch which adds verity is the way a character who plays a major part in one novel gets a walk-on part in another; descendants of people in *The Fortress* turn up in *Give Me the Daggers*, and Joe Calvert, the American consul in *The Snow Mountain*, appears as godfather to the heroine of *None Dare Call It Treason*, one of the World War II novels.

This remarkable trilogy is arguably Gavin's best writing. *Traitors' Gate*, set in London and Brazil, evokes the atmosphere and emotions of 1940 exactly; *None Dare Call It Treason* takes place in the unoccupied zone of France, mainly in Nice and Menton, and explores different kinds of loyalty and betrayal. *How Sleep the Brave* takes the story through the liberation to the end of the war, and includes an understated yet unforgettably horrific description of the massacre at Oradour-sur-Glane.

The Sunset Dream is a saga, covering 100 years of life in San Francisco, 'phoenix of American cities, born in conflict and rising again and again from its own ashes' through the story of four generations of Spanish and American families, interlinked by marriage, friendship, and rivalry. The Californian countryside is the real star of this book, just as the Mexican scene stars in *The Cactus and the Crown*.

Occasionally the reader may feel that Gavin is giving them too big a chunk of history to digest, however, Gavin's stories are so entertaining that the reader is impatient to know what will happen next.

—Pamela Cleaver

GELLIS, Roberta.
Pseudonyms: Max Daniels; Priscilla Hamilton; Leah Jacobs. **Nationality:** American. **Born:** Roberta Leah Jacobs in New York City, 27 September 1927. **Education:** Hunter College, New York, 1943–47, B.A. 1947; Brooklyn Polytechnic Institute, 1949–52, M.A. 1952; New York University, 1953–58, M.A. **Relations:** married Charles Gellis in 1947; one son. **Career:** chemist, Foster D. Snell Inc, New York, 1947–53; editor, McGraw-Hill Book Company, New York, 1953–56; then freelance editor, for Macmillan Company, New York, 1956–58 and since 1971, and for Academic Press, New York, 1956–70. **Recipient:** several awards from *Romantic Times*, including gold medal Porgy. **Address:** P.O. Box 483, Roslyn Heights, New York 11577, USA.

ROMANCE AND HISTORICAL PUBLICATIONS

Novels (series: Heiress; The Roselynde Chronicles; Royal Dynasty)

Knight's Honor. New York, Doubleday, 1964; London, Mayflower, 1979.
Bond of Blood. New York, Doubleday, 1965; London, Mayflower, 1979.
The Psychiatrist's Wife (as Leah Jacobs). New York, New American Library, 1966.
Sing Witch, Sing Death. New York, Bantam, 1975.
The Sword and the Swan. Chicago, Playboy Press, 1977; London, Mayflower, 1979.
The Dragon and the Rose. Chicago, Playboy Press, 1977; London, Mayflower, 1979.
The Roselynde Chronicles:
  1. *Roselynde*. Chicago, Playboy Press, 1978; London, Hamlyn, 1979.
  2. *Alinor*. Chicago, Playboy Press, 1978; London, Hamlyn, 1979.
  3. *Joanna*. Chicago, Playboy Press, 1978; London, Hamlyn, 1979.
  4. *Gilliane*. Chicago, Playboy Press, and London, Hamlyn, 1979.
  5. *Rhiannon*. Chicago, Playboy Press, 1982; Bath, Chivers, 1985.
  6. *Sybelle*. New York, Berkley, 1983; Bath, Chivers, 1985.
Love Token (as Priscilla Hamilton). Chicago, Playboy Press, 1979.
Heiress:
  The English Heiress. New York, Dell, 1980.
  The Cornish Heiress. New York, Dell, 1981.
  The Kent Heiress. New York, Dell, 1982.
  Fortune's Bride. New York, Dell, 1983.
  A Woman's Estate. New York, Dell, 1984.
Royal Dynasty:
  Siren Song. Chicago, Playboy Press, 1981.
  Winter Song. New York, Playboy Press, 1982.
  Fire Song. New York, Berkley, 1984.
  A Silver Mirror. New York, Berkley, 1989.
A Tapestry of Dreams. New York, Berkley, 1985.
The Rope Dancer. New York, Berkley, 1986.
Fires of Winter. New York, Berkley, 1987.
Masques of Gold. New York, Berkley, 1988.
A Delicate Balance. New York, Leisure, 1993.

*

Roberta Gellis comments:

Perhaps in reaction against the cynical attitudes and impersonal horrors perpetrated by humankind on humankind, I have always been fascinated by the past. In mediaeval times, there was a passionate belief in honour, truth, courage, and loyalty. This is not to say that I think men and women at that time were different or better; they were not. However, when they diverged from the path, when they were dishonourable or cowardly, they knew they had done wrong; they did not tell themselves that 'everybody does it'. And, although cruelty and slaughter were as rife then as now, one at least had to face one's victim; there were no bombs that killed faceless thousands impersonally.

The combination of these high standards and my awareness that people are people in any place or time has led me to attempt to present the social and political history of the mediaeval period, especially mediaeval England, in human terms. In any time the two great desires of human beings are for love and power. Thus, I try to weave together a strong love story and the political events, showing the latter through the eyes of the people affected. Most of my books are in continuing series, which permits me to give a chronological history not only of the nation but also of a family.

'The Roselynde Chronicles', for example, begin with the young heiress, Alinor of Roselynde, and detail, through her two marriages, the reign of Richard the Lionhearted and the early years of King John. In *Joanna* I deal with the marriage of Alinor's daughter and the last four years of John's reign, showing how Joanna's marriage increased both the power and the responsibilities of the family. The spread of influence of the Roselynde clan is increased still further in Volume 4 of the Chronicles, when Alinor's eldest son marries another heiress, twice widowed. Through all the books I attempt to show the conditions, both physical and social, in which these people lived. Moreover, I try to present events as *these* people saw and felt them by the use of chronicles written at the time rather than by the use of modern history books, although I also consult modern texts. Historical events and historical personages are presented as accurately as possible, although the central characters of my books are almost always fictional.

However, I do not want any reader to believe that I am writing historical texts. To my characters, as to any human being, their own personal affairs are of essential importance, of far greater importance than any political event—unless that political event affects them directly. It is, thus, the love story in each book that is the central theme, not political and social history. To each man and woman personal need and desire are not only of overriding importance, but these emotions colour all other events. So I emphasize the personal element, for in real life that is how we frail humans perceive our world, and that is how my characters perceived theirs.

*   *   *

When one reads a Roberta Gellis novel, one should be prepared to enter an historical world of great vitality. Her stories are carefully researched and are loaded with details of the life and manners of the period. Historical figures wander easily into the narrative or may even take centre stage, as does Henry VII, the central figure in *The Dragon and the Rose*. In some of her novels Gellis has extended her scope from the world of the nobility to that of other classes such as the travelling players in *The Rope Dancer*, and the guilds of *Masques of Gold*. No matter the status of the protagonists, however, there is a wealth of detail that immerses the reader in another time and place. Although that same detail might seem overwhelming at times, Gellis creates such real characters that they bring all the facts into focus and make history a living thing rather than a collection of dry dates and events. The underlying love stories serve to point out how historical events affect individuals.

In contrast, Gellis's contemporary romance, *A Delicate Balance*, lacks her usual sharp character development and sense of place or ambience. Therefore, it is less successful in engaging the reader's interest. Although published in 1993, the story of an unhappy rich girl seeking to prove herself by working as a companion seems almost anachronistic or outdated. It has the bland innocence of the early Harlequin novels, so that the one rather explicit description of a sexual encounter, an earthy reality in the historical novels, is jarringly out of place in the present day. Gellis also fails to create a real sense of mystery or suspense in spite of the supposed attempts on the old woman's life. It is simply hard to care much about these people.

Most of Gellis's prolific output has been devoted to the mediaeval period. *A Tapestry of Dreams* and *Fires of Winter* are set during the struggles of Stephen and Matilda for the throne of England and are linked by some characters who appear in both. The popular 'Roselynde' series takes the reader through one of the most tumultuous eras of English history. Action in the first two volumes, *Roselynde* and *Alinor*, moves to the Crusades and into the rebellion against King John. Later volumes involve the characters in events leading to the Magna Carta, war with France, and later rebellions against Henry III. No less historically accurate than the 'Roselynde' series, *The English Heiress*, *The Cornish Heiress*, and *The Kent Heiress* are set in the 18th and 19th centuries more familiar to readers of Regency-based historical novels.

Perhaps the most striking thing about Gellis's creations is the courage, strength, and integrity shown by her female characters. Alinor, first of the exceptional Roselynde women, is not only beautiful and intelligent, but has the almost mystical bond to the land that is usually reserved for males. She may be caught up in great events, but her love for and protection of her land and family remain paramount. Indeed, it is a measure of the importance of the women in these stories that the great estate of Roselynde is passed on through the female line. Alinor's daughter and granddaughter, Joanna and Sybelle, are worthy successors to the dynasty. Even Alinor's sons, Adam and Simon, search for and find strong, independent women in *Gilliane* and *Rhiannon*. Although some critics feel that endowing mediaeval women with such modern sensibilities is historically inaccurate, Gellis makes it clear that she is dealing with extraordinary, rather than average, women. It is to her credit that she is able to portray such strong women so believably. It would be a mistake, however, to think that these women dominate their male companions. The women may be the central focus, but the men are their equals. They too are extraordinary: fiercely independent, passionate, and devoted to duty and honour. Secure in themselves, they are not threatened by the Roselynde women.

Gellis creates a broad political canvas on which she paints domestic stories of love and romance. She excels in developing vibrant characters and integrating their stories with the historical period's events. The same strength and independence of the men and women is seen in all of her historical novels, although the focus may shift somewhat to the male characters, as it does in the Heiress books or from the nobility to other classes. Gellis's view of men and women as individuals who are equal, who are able to maintain their individuality and equality in their male-female relationships, sets a different tone in the historical romance genre and places Gellis well ahead of many other authors in terms of quality.

—Barbara E. Kemp

GIBBS, Mary Ann.
Pseudonym for Marjory Elizabeth Sarah Bidwell. **Other Pseudonym:** Elizabeth Ford. **Nationality:** British. **Born:** Marjory Elizabeth Sarah Lambe in Seaford, Sussex. **Education:** secondary schools in Seaford. **Relations:** married Thomas Edward Palmer Bidwell (died 1965); one son. **Died:** January 1985.

ROMANCE AND HISTORICAL PUBLICATIONS

Novels

A Young Man with Ideas. London, Davies, 1950.
Enchantment: A Pastoral. London, Davies, 1952.
A Bit of a Bounder: An Edwardian Trifle. London, Davies, 1952.
The Guardian. London, Hurst and Blackett, 1958; New York, Beagle, 1974.
Young Lady with Red Hair. London, Hurst and Blackett, 1959; New York, Beagle, 1974; as *The Penniless Heiress*, London, Coronet, 1975.
Horatia. London, Hurst and Blackett, 1961; New York, Beagle, 1973.
The Apothecary's Daughter. London, Hurst and Blackett, 1962; New York, Beagle, 1974.
Polly Kettle. London, Hurst and Blackett, 1963; New York, Beagle, 1973; as *The Nursery Maid*, London, Coronet, 1975.
The Amateur Governess. London, Hurst and Blackett, 1964; as *The House of Ravensbourne*, New York, Pyramid, 1965.

The Sugar Mouse. London, Hurst and Blackett, 1965; New York, Beagle, 1974.
The Romantic Frenchman. London, Hurst and Blackett, 1967; New York, Beagle, 1973.
The Sea Urchins. London, Hurst and Blackett, 1968; New York, Beagle, 1973.
A Parcel of Land. London, Hurst and Blackett, 1969; New York, Beagle, 1973.
A Lady in Berkshire. London, Hurst and Blackett, 1970; New York, Beagle, 1973.
The Year of the Pageant. London, Hurst and Blackett, 1971; New York, Beagle, 1973.
The Moon in a Bucket. London, Hurst and Blackett, 1972; New York, Beagle, 1973.
The Glass Palace. London, Hurst and Blackett, 1973; New York, Mason Charter, 1975.
A Wife for the Admiral. London, Hurst and Blackett, 1974; as *The Admiral's Lady*, New York, Mason Charter, 1975.
A Most Romantic City. London, Hurst and Blackett, and New York, Mason Charter, 1976.
The Tempestuous Petticoat. London, Hurst and Blackett, and New York, Mason Charter, 1977.
A Young Lady of Fashion. London, Hurst and Blackett, 1978; New York, Fawcett, 1979.
The Tulip Tree. London, Hurst and Blackett, and New York, Fawcett, 1979.
Dinah. Loughton, Essex, Piatkus, and New York, Fawcett, 1981.
The Milliner's Shop. Loughton, Essex, Piatkus, 1981; as *Renegade Girl*, New York, Fawcett, 1981.
The Marquess. Loughton, Essex, Piatkus, 1982.

Novels as Elizabeth Ford (series: Maplechester)

Fog. London, Chapman and Hall, 1933.
The House with the Myrtle Trees. London, Lutterworth Press, 1942.
The Blue Cockade: A Romantic Novel of 1780. London, Lutterworth Press, 1943.
Queen's Harbour. London, Hurst and Blackett, 1944.
The Young Ladies' Room. London, Hurst and Blackett, 1945.
The Irresponsibles. London, Hurst and Blackett, 1946.
Mountford Show. London, Hurst and Blackett, 1948.
Spring Comes to the Crescent. London, Hurst and Blackett, 1949.
So Deep Suspicion. London, Hurst and Blackett, 1950.
Four Days in June. London, Hurst and Blackett, 1951.
Just Around the Corner. London, Hurst and Blackett, 1952.
English Rose. London, Hurst and Blackett, 1953.
One Fine Day. London, Hurst and Blackett, 1954.
Meeting in the Spring. London, Hurst and Blackett, 1954.
Outrageous Fortune. London, Hurst and Blackett, 1955.
That Summer at Bacclesea. London, Hurst and Blackett, 1956.
The Empty Heart. London, Hurst and Blackett, 1957.
The Cottage at Drimble. London, Hurst and Blackett, 1957.
Butter Market House. London, Hurst and Blackett, 1958.
Heron's Nest. London, Hurst and Blackett, 1960.
A Week by the Sea. London, Hurst and Blackett, 1962.
A Holiday Engagement (Maplechester). London, Hurst and Blackett, 1963.
No Room for Joanna (Maplechester). London, Hurst and Blackett, 1964.
A Country Holiday. London, Hurst and Blackett, 1966; as *Dangerous Holiday*, New York, Ace, 1967.
The Turbulent Messiters. London, Hurst and Blackett, 1967.
Limelight for Jane. London, Hurst and Blackett, 1970.
The Day of the Storm. London, Hurst and Blackett, 1971.
The Green Beetle. London, Hurst and Blackett, 1972.
The Belvedere. London, Hurst and Blackett, 1973.

Young Ann. London, Hurst and Blackett, 1973.
A Charming Couple. London, Hurst and Blackett, 1975.
The Amber Cat. London, Hurst and Blackett, 1976.
Open Day at the Manor. London, Hurst and Blackett, 1977.

OTHER PUBLICATIONS

Other

The Years of the Nannies. London, Hutchinson, 1960.

*

Mary Ann Gibbs commented (1982):

I am meticulous as to research and always do my own. I find that only by reading journals, diaries, letters, guides, and fiction of the era in which my books are set, and by studying minutely dress, jewellery, maps, transport, etc., can I recreate the atmosphere of the time. I never use what I call 'gadsookery' in dialogue, as I have often found that many of the expressions used today were used as a matter of course at the beginning of the last century, and a word here and there will be enough to bring the reader back to the years in which the books are set. I never dictate my books. I do not think I could even use a dictaphone. I type them out as a first draft, which is then scribbled over and re-typed several times before I embark on the final typing, and even then I change phrases and sometimes characters, as I go. In other words I live in and with the book while I am writing.

*   *   *

A plucky girl with a zest for life and a refusal to let its adversities overwhelm her characterize the type of heroine always present in a Mary Ann Gibbs romance. The fact that the girl is usually not a stunning beauty and might even be considered plain does not prevent her from winning one of society's more desirable bachelors. She lives in a place and time (19th-century England) where morals and manners are applied rigidly. A Gibbs heroine often finds it necessary to abandon conventional manners in order to survive catastrophe while still remaining a lady and keeping a sense of self-worth. In *The Apothecary's Daughter* Susanna becomes the recipient of expensive gifts from Lord Vigilant, a much older man with a rakish past. That she is his long lost illegitimate daughter is kept secret at the insistence of her foster father, the apothecary. The scandal threatens to ruin Susanna's good name forever, but in the end the truth comes out. Meanwhile a man of position, Hugo Vigilant, the Lord's cousin and heir, has come to love her and finally wins her hand.

Often the young ladies of Gibbs's romances are left destitute by a negligent father and must give up the dream of marrying an eligible man of society, their impoverishment making them no longer acceptable. In *The Amateur Governess* Catherine finds herself penniless after the sudden death of a father from whom she inherits nothing but debts. Taking the job of governess to the young daughter of a wealthy tradesman, Catherine solves the mystery of the child's mistreatment by a cruel aunt and wins the love of the little girl's father. Similarly, Vicky Langford of *The Milliner's Shop* must make her own way when her father leaves the country, the charge of fraud following in his wake. She provides for herself and her brother by taking a job as a clerk in a milliner's shop; she does not feel sorry for herself when all of her proper society friends cross her permanently off their lists. All, that is, except for a very few, one of whom is Sebastian, whose love for this young lady knows no bounds.

A novel by Gibbs tells of old-fashioned romance in which love has a special tenderness. There often exists an element of mystery—in fact Gibbs wrote suspense novels as Elizabeth Ford—but the stories mainly centred on the many obstacles the lovers must overcome in order to live happily ever after.

—Patricia Altner

———

GIBSON, Charles.   See GARVICE, Charles.

———

GILBERT, Anna.
Pseudonym for Marguerite Lazarus. **Other Pseudonym:** Marguerite Gascoigne. **Nationality:** British. **Born:** Durham, 1 May 1916. **Education:** Durham University, B.A. (honours) 1937, M.A. 1945. **Relations:** married Jack Lazarus in 1956. **Career:** grammar school English teacher, 1941–73. **Recipient:** Romantic Novelists Association major award, 1976, for *The Look of Innocence*. **Agent:** Watson Little Ltd, 12 Egbert Street, London NW1 8LJ, England. **Address:** Oakley Cottage, Swainsea Lane, Pickering, North Yorkshire, England.

ROMANCE AND HISTORICAL PUBLICATIONS

Novels

Images of Rose. London, Hodder and Stoughton, and New York, Delacorte Press, 1974.
The Look of Innocence. London, Hodder and Stoughton, and New York, St Martin's Press, 1975.
A Family Likeness. London, Hodder and Stoughton, 1977; New York, St Martin's Press, 1978.
Remembering Louise. London, Hodder and Stoughton, and New York, St Martin's Press, 1978.
The Leavetaking. London, Hodder and Stoughton, 1979; New York, St Martin's Press, 1980.
Flowers for Lilian. London, Hodder and Stoughton, 1980; New York, St Martin's Press, 1981.
Miss Bede Is Staying. Loughton, Essex, Piatkus, 1982; New York, St Martin's Press, 1983.
The Long Shadow. Loughton, Essex, Piatkus, 1983; New York, St Martin's Press, 1985.
A Walk in the Wood. New York, St Martin's Press, and London, Piatkus, 1989.
The Wedding Guest. New York, St Martin's Press, 1993.

OTHER PUBLICATIONS

Fiction (for children)

The Song of the Gipsy (as Marguerite Gascoigne). London, Warne, 1953.

*

Anna Gilbert comments:

My books are romantic in atmosphere in so far as romanticism implies a selection of the pleasing and picturesque rather than an insistence on the harsher aspects of reality. My aim is to charm and intrigue the reader, and to create tension by other means than the use of sensational material. I hope to appeal to women who want the reassurance of traditional values in stories which involve convincing characters in experiences of universal interest: love, loss, sadness, fear, forgiveness resolving into happiness, though the ultimate happiness is not always unalloyed. The stories depend upon a strong plot and are set in Victorian England: a society near enough in time to be well documented but far enough away to offer escape from the complications of contemporary life; or in the first half of the 20th century. I choose close-knit, claustrophobic situations and relationships. Tension arises from some element of mystery and the gradual accumulation of significant detail leading to its disclosure: secrecy, deception, illusion—created and dispelled. I am particularly interested in the way innocence and generosity are exploited by selfishness and greed.

My favourite setting is the English countryside: remote hamlets and villages, woods and moors, small market towns: a country in itself mysterious, beautiful, and menacing, and for me constantly interfused with haunting glimpses of the ideal.

*   *   *

Anna Gilbert's first book, *Images of Rose*, was shortlisted for the 1974 Romantic Novelists Association major award. In 1976 she won the award with her second book, *The Look of Innocence*. She writes Victorian stories with a strong element of mystery—classics of their kind. Gilbert's plots are intricate and subtle. Her favourite theme is the quiet but relentless manipulation of people by each other, and the helplessness of the good and innocent in the face of ruthless egotism and jealousy. The manner, as much as the matter, is important. Her work is stylish and elegant. She writes with fastidious care, making every word count (not for nothing has she taught English to a high level), and she is past mistress at the art of heightening tension by placing a gentle finger on the reader's nerves.

In *Remembering Louise*, for example, the story begins in a deceptively low key, carefully setting the scene and filling in the heroine's background with loving detail, with little more than a hint of underlying unease. Character, place, and small, apparently trivial, incidents dominate the early pages and absorb the attention. Even when Hesther, the narrator, becomes involved in a shockingly violent incident, it at first seems peripheral to the story. Hesther is the daughter of a jeweller and watchmaker in the small north-country town of Wickborough. She is overjoyed when her pretty sister who has lived for many years in Scotland comes home unexpectedly. But from the moment she arrives Louise, sweet, docile, and housewifely though she is, has a disrupting influence. Without lifting a finger, or her eyes, she manages, apparently unwittingly, to destroy not only Hesther's present contentment, but her lovingly planned future too. However, Hesther continues to love her, and as her world crumbles around her she worries about the mysterious stranger in black whose life she might have saved, but didn't.

Gilbert returns again and again (notably in *Flowers for Lilian*) to this theme of a relationship in which one person, usually a woman, remorselessly dominates and takes advantage of another in order to get her own way. The plots differ and the stories are far from repetitious, but Gilbert's pre-occupation with the subject is a continuing thread throughout her work.

Her understanding of the period about which she writes, and the countryside in which her stories are set, the northeast of England, are inherent in everything she writes. She brings the landscape to life graphically and memorably. Her insight into rural life in that part of the world in the 19th century is in some measure explained by her deep interest in the literature, history, diaries, memoirs, letters, and biographies of the time, which results in minute, almost eyewitness descriptions of everyday dress and household objects, as well as the daily routine of those who lived in small, often remote, communities in those days. The vividness with which Gilbert conveys their lives and surroundings draws the reader inexorably into the atmosphere of her novels.

—Elizabeth Grey

GILES, Janice Holt.
Nationality: American. **Born:** Altus, Arkansas, 28 March 1909. **Education:** University of Arkansas, Fayetteville; Transylvania University, Lexington, Kentucky. **Relations:** married 1) Otto Moore in 1927 (divorced 1939), one daughter; 2) Henry Giles in 1945. **Career:** assistant to the Dean, Presbyterian Seminary, Louisville, 1941–50; director of religious education, Pulaski Heights Community Church, and director of children's work for Arkansas Board of Missions, both Little Rock. **Died:** 1 June 1979.

ROMANCE AND HISTORICAL PUBLICATIONS

Novels

The Enduring Hills. Philadelphia, Westminster Press, 1950.
Miss Willie. Philadelphia, Westminster Press, 1951.
Tara's Healing. Philadelphia, Westminster Press, 1951.
Harbin's Ridge, with Henry Giles. Boston, Houghton Mifflin, 1951.
40 Acres and No Mule. Philadelphia, Westminster Press, 1952.
The Kentuckians. Boston, Houghton Mifflin, 1953.
The Plum Thicket. Boston, Houghton Mifflin, 1954.
Hannah Fowler. Boston, Houghton Mifflin, 1956.
The Believers. Boston, Houghton Mifflin, 1957.
The Land Beyond the Mountains. Boston, Houghton Mifflin, 1958.
Johnny Osage. Boston, Houghton Mifflin, 1960.
Savanna. Boston, Houghton Mifflin, 1961.
Voyage to Santa Fe. Boston, Houghton Mifflin, 1962.
Find Me a River. Boston, Houghton Mifflin, 1964.
Time of Glory. Boston, Houghton Mifflin, 1966.
Special Breed. Boston, Houghton Mifflin, 1966.
The Great Adventure. Boston, Houghton Mifflin, 1966.
Shady Grove. Boston, Houghton Mifflin, 1968.
Six-Horse Hitch. Boston, Houghton Mifflin, 1969.

Short Stories

Wellspring. Boston, Houghton Mifflin, 1975.

OTHER PUBLICATIONS

Other

A Little Better Than Plumb: The Biography of a House, with Henry Giles. Boston, Houghton Mifflin, 1963.
The Damned Engineers. Boston, Houghton Mifflin, 1970.
Around Our House, with Henry Giles. Boston, Houghton Mifflin, 1971.
The Kinta Years (autobiography). Boston, Houghton Mifflin, 1973.

Editor, *The G.I. Journal of Sergeant Giles*, by Henry Giles. Boston, Houghton Mifflin, 1965.

*   *   *

It is impossible to think of Janice Holt Giles's work without envisioning her own particular part of the world. A regional writer in the best sense, her novels project the spirit of the pioneers who first tamed the rugged forest country of Kentucky and the westward wilderness. Her best tales unfold the continuing saga of a pioneering family, the Fowlers, through several generations, beginning with her most truly memorable fictional heroine, Hannah Fowler. Hannah is a true child of the new world. Born and raised among the hills by a restlessly wandering father, she dimly remembers a town-bred mother who tried out but could not learn to love the new life Hannah needs if she is to thrive. Where her mother pined for company of her own kind, Hannah shies from it like any forest creature; her ideal home is a cabin in a clearing, out of sight of the nearest neighbour folk, for she holds with the old frontier saying that 'If you can see their smoke, they're too close'. Alone in the world after her father's death, which is as hard and lonely as the life he has chosen to lead, Hannah is forced to marry, against her independent inclinations. Women are scarce and sought-after, here at the back of the beyond, and men need strong and capable wives who will give them the children the country life requires. Hannah can have her pick of the single men of the fort, for all come courting in the abrupt and unromantic fashion of the time and place—but Hannah has chosen her own mate, Tice, and the matter is soon settled.

In Giles's hands this oddly arranged marriage of convenience becomes one of the deepest and most touching, if most understated, love stories of the frontier. Two less articulate people would be hard to find, but speech is scarcely necessary to Hannah and Tice; they completely understand one another. Through the vicissitudes of a very hard life, they become steadily more devoted, and from their strength and understanding grow new generations of the Fowler family, the subjects of further adventures as the country continues to open westward.

Giles is a writer who knows her subject and her setting absolutely. The day-to-day detail of her peoples' lives is as fascinating as their encounters with marauding Indians, ferocious weather, and the incredible privations that were a part of life at the outermost edge of civilization. It is humbling for a city-bred 20th-century reader to realize the proud self-sufficiency of these people of the not-so-long-ago, who could survive in the trackless forest equipped only with a knife and a flintlock gun; make a home and raise a family, and see the accomplishment as nothing remarkable. They had an independence that their remote descendants have long since exchanged for comforts and luxuries undreamt of by Hannah. How heartily she would have despised so poor an example of horse trading: a birthright frittered away for a mess of inferior pottage.

—Joan McGrath

————

GILLEN, Lucy.   See STRATTON, Rebecca.

————

GLADSTONE, Maggie.   See SEBASTIAN, Margaret.

————

GLASGOW, Ellen (Anderson Gholson).
Nationality: American. **Born:** Richmond, Virginia, 22 April, 1873 (some sources 21 April 1874). Began to lose her hearing at the age of 16, and eventually went deaf. **Education**: privately, and at home in Richmond. **Relations:** companion, Anne Virginia Bennett during 1940s. **Career:** writer from 1896. Lived in New York, 1911–16; president, Richmond Society for the Prevention of Cruelty to Animals, 1924–25. Literary circle included Allen Tate, Stark Young, James Branch Cabell, and Marjorie Kinnan Rawlings. **Recipient:** American Academy Howells medal, 1941; Pulitzer prize, 1942, for *In This Our Life*. D.Litt.: University of North Carolina, Chapel Hill, 1930; LL.D.: University of Richmond, 1938; Duke University, Durham, North Carolina, 1938; College of William and Mary, Williamsburg, Virginia, 1939. **Member:** American Academy, 1938. **Died:** 21 November 1945.

ROMANCE AND HISTORICAL PUBLICATIONS

Novels

The Voice of the People. New York, Doubleday Page, and London, Heinemann, 1900.
The Battle-Ground. New York, Doubleday Page, and London, Constable, 1902.
The Deliverance. New York, Doubleday Page, and London, Constable, 1904.
The Wheel of Life. New York, Doubleday Page, and London, Constable, 1906.
The Ancient Law. New York, Doubleday Page, and London, Constable, 1908.
The Romance of a Plain Man. New York, Macmillan, and London, Murray, 1909.
The Miller of Old Church. New York, Doubleday Page, and London, Murray, 1911.
Virginia. New York, Doubleday Page, and London, Heinemann, 1913.
Life and Gabriella. New York, Doubleday Page, and London, Murray, 1916.
The Builders. New York, Doubleday Page, and London, Murray, 1919.

OTHER PUBLICATIONS

Novels

The Descendant (published anonymously). New York, Harper, 1897.
Phases of an Inferior. New York, Harper, and London, Heinemann, 1898.
One Man in His Time. New York, Doubleday Page, and London, Murray, 1922.
Barren Ground. New York, Doubleday Page, and London, Murray, 1925.
The Romantic Comedians. New York, Doubleday Page, 1926; London, Murray, 1927.
They Stooped To Folly. New York, Doubleday Doran, and London, Heinemann, 1929.
The Sheltered Life. New York, Doubleday Doran, 1932; London, Heinemann, 1933.
Vein of Iron. New York, Harcourt Brace, 1935; London, Cape, 1936.
In This Our Life. New York, Harcourt Brace, and London, Cape, 1941.
Beyond Defeat: An Epilogue to an Era, edited by Luther Y. Gore. Charlottesville, University Press of Virginia, 1966.

Short Stories

The Shadowy Third and Other Stories. New York, Doubleday Page, 1923; as *Dare's Gift and Other Stories*, London, Murray, 1924.
The Collected Stories of Ellen Glasgow edited by Richard K. Gore. Charlottesville, University Press of Virginia, 1966.

Poetry

The Freeman and Other Poems. New York, Doubleday Page, 1902.

Other

Works (Old Dominion Edition). New York, Doubleday Doran, 8 vols, 1929–33.
Works (Virginia Edition). New York, Scribners, 12 vols, 1938.

A Certain Measure: An Interpretation of Prose Fiction. New York, Harcourt Brace, 1943.
The Woman Within (autobiography). New York, Harcourt Brace, 1954; London, Eyre and Spottiswoode, 1955.
Letters of Ellen Glasgow, edited by Blair Rouse. New York, Harcourt Brace, 1958.
Ellen Glasgow's Reasonable Doubts: A Collection of Her Writings, edited by J.R. Raper. Baton Rouge and London, Louisiana State University Press, 1988.

*

Film adaptations: *In This Our Life*, 1942.

Bibliography: *An Ellen Glasgow Bibliography* by William W. Kelly, Charlottesville, University Press of Virginia, 1963; *A Catalogue of the Library of Ellen Glasgow* by Carrington C. Tutwiler, Charlottesville, Bibliographical Society of the University of Virginia, 1969; *Ellen Glasgow: A Reference Guide* by Edgar E. MacDonald, Boston, Hall, 1986.

Critical Studies: *Of Ellen Glasgow: An Inscribed Portrait* by James Branch Cabell, New York, Maverick Press, 1938; *Ellen Glasgow and the Ironic Art of Fiction* by Frederick P.W. McDowell, Madison, University of Wisconsin Press, 1960; *Ellen Glasgow, Romancière* by Monique Parent, Paris, Nizet, 1962; *Ellen Glasgow* by Blair Rouse, New York, Twayne, 1962; *Ellen Glasgow* by Louis Auchincloss, Minneapolis, University of Minnesota Press, 1964; *Ellen Glasgow's American Dream* by Joan Foster Santas, Charlottesville, University Press of Virginia, 1965; *Without Shelter: The Early Career of Ellen Glasgow*, Baton Rouge, Louisiana State University Press, 1971, and *From the Sunken Garden: The Fiction of Ellen Glasgow, 1916–1945*, Baton Rouge, Louisiana State University Press, 1980, both by J.R. Raper; *Ellen Glasgow's Development as a Novelist* by Marion K. Richards, The Hague, Mouton, 1971; *Ellen Glasgow and the Woman Within* by E. Stanly Godbold, Jr, Baton Rouge, Louisiana State University Press, 1972; *Ellen Glasgow: Centennial Essays*, edited by M. Thomas Inge, Charlottesville, University Press of Virginia, 1976; *The Social Situation of Women in the Novels of Ellen Glasgow* by Elizabeth Gallup Myer, Hickeville, Exposition Press, 1978; *The End of a Legend: Ellen Glasgow as History of Southern Women* by Barbro Ekman, Uppsala and Stockholm, Almquist and Wiksell, 1979; *Ellen Glasgow* by Marcelle Thiébaux, New York, Ungar, 1982; *Ellen Glasgow, Beyond Convention* by Linda W. Wagner, Austin, University of Texas Press, 1982.

Manuscript Collections: Alderman Library, University of Virginia, Charlottesville.

*   *   *

When measured against standard definitions, little of Ellen Glasgow's work can be labelled either romance or historical fiction. However, seen in the light of her own well-articulated delineations, her fiction exemplifies both of these genres in unique and significant ways. Having eschewed the sentimentalism which dominated southern American fiction during the post-Civil War decades, Glasgow maintained that what the literature of her region needed was 'blood and irony'—the former because the South had grown 'thin and pale' from artificial depictions; the latter because it is 'an indispensable ingredient of the critical vision . . . [and] the safest antidote to sentimental decay'. Glasgow's own contribution to this antidote was a series of six novels that constitute a social history of Virginia from a decade before the Civil War to the eve of World War I.

The first of these is *The Battle-Ground*, her only novel treating the late antebellum and Civil War periods in Virginia and perhaps the best vantage point she provides for viewing her approach to history and romance. Disavowing the traditional labels of both realist and romancer, Glasgow characterized herself in *A Certain Measure* as a *verist*, i.e. one whose depiction of truth 'must embrace the interior world as well as external appearances'. Contrary to the majority of fiction inspired by the Civil War, which idealized colourful personalities and military action, Glasgow's approach held that 'the chief aim of the novel is to create life', and that, secondly, there is an obligation to 'reflect the movement and tone of its age'. Therefore, in rebutting the charge that she had romanticized the era in which *The Battle-Ground* is set, she noted that 'realism of that period in Virginia was tinctured with romantic illusion'.

Although Glasgow was a scion of the aristocracy, which had been the slave-owning class in the antebellum South, the major theme of her fictional social history is the rise of the middle class, as she believed that this caste was 'the dominant force in southern democracy'. This focus is all but unique in the fictional annals of the Lost Cause, for between the strata of master and slave there is characteristically a void. These polarities exist in the early chapters of *The Battle-Ground*. The action centres around two aristocratic families who live on adjoining plantations in the Shenandoah Valley (where the author's paternal ancestors had settled in the 18th century). The patriarch of one family is Peyton Ambler, a former Virginia governor and a Unionist in an era of threatening schism. His household at Uplands consists of his wife, Julia; two daughters, Virginia and Betty; and an elderly maiden aunt, Lydia. Their neighbours, at Chericoke, are: Major Lightfoot, a veteran of the war of 1812, and a fiery states-rightist who quotes Addison and Horace; his wife, Molly; his nephew, Champe; and his grandson, Dan Montjoy. Both families are sustained by large retinues of slaves, whose care by kind, if paternalistic masters, is emphasized. The only major character with questionable aristocratic credentials is Dan, whose mother eloped years before with Jack Montjoy, a bounder and, apparently, a commoner. Although a vehement defender of his way of life ('Without slavery, where is our aristocracy, sir?') the Major had been a blade in his youth and sees himself reflected in Dan.

In the half of *The Battle-Ground* dealing with the war itself the focus is upon the major characters, their involvement with the trials of war, and the impact of the conflict on a society that was effectively dealt a mortal wound with the first volley at Fort Sumter. There are no dates given; legendary Confederate leaders such as Robert E. Lee, 'Stonewall' Jackson, and J.E.B. Stuart make only cameo appearances. Even the expanse of major battles such as First Manassas, Antietam, and Gettysburg are presented as shadowings upon the perceptions of the principal characters. In other words, this is not a 'historical' novel in the sense that, say, *War and Peace* or *Gone with the Wind* is. Rather, it presents the 'movement and tone' of an era, as reflected in the lives and perceptions of the major characters. Neither do the romantic sensibilities that certain of these fictional beings express appear as they do conventionally in Civil War fiction. Warfare is presented as anything but a cavalier enterprise. Though Governor Ambler enlists and proclaims that 'a gentleman fights for his country as he pleases, a plebeian as he must', Dan Montjoy, following an argument with his grandfather, and a petulant departure from Chericoke, becomes one of Jackson's foot-sore infantry and suffers wounds and disease. More importantly, he comes to recognize the military as a leveller of antebellum social stratification. The son of a poor-white 'rascal', 'unfit to black [his] boots' in pre-war civilian society, becomes Dan's lieutenant. One of the best drawn characters is Pinetop, an illiterate mountain man whom Dan comes to admire and love, thereby illustrating Glasgow's critical and (for the times) radical conviction that the strength of southern society lay not in the hegemony of an inbred aristocracy, but in the hitherto submerged middle class. Though Dan and Pinetop bid a poignant farewell after Appomattox, each to return to the class he had left, their bond is unbreakable. During the war Virginia Ambler, the beautiful but pale elder daughter of the governor, dies in childbirth, and Dan returns to the ruins of Chericoke to reconciliation, and to the arms of Betty, Virginia's younger sister who, like Dan, possesses far more common sense and derring-do than aristocratic pretension.

In no other novel does Glasgow deal with material so susceptible to romantic transformation. Southern romancers might indulge in retrospective treatments of the tragic, if legendary, Confederacy; Glasgow now directed her own focus to what followed its demise. The post-bellum era was not nearly as attractive or so inspiring. It is foreshadowed by the scene that greets Dan Montjoy's return to Chericoke: the main house in ashes, its master living in an overseer's cottage; the work force depleted; fields in weeds, provisions exhausted, families decimated, fortunes depleted, spirits broken. Subsequent Glasgow novels feature the tensions between those who are able to adapt to the realities of the new order and those who, like the elderly (and symbolically blind) Mrs Blake in *The Deliverance*, vicariously continue a way of life that is gone forever. Such characters are made to look ridiculous, their delusions seen not as innocent nostalgia, but as lies.

The future belonged not to the beleaguered and inbred aristocracy, but to the emerging middle class, often embodied by lawyer/politicians (*The Voice of the People, The Builders*) or parvenus in trade (*The Romance of a Plain Man*), who are strong, intelligent, and worldly wise to an extent that leaders of the old order never were. The new people occasionally marry the old (*The Deliverance, The Romance of a Plain Man, The Miller of Old Church*), and the best of these alliances (*The Romance of A Plain Man*) produce a viable hybrid. Beginning with *Life and Gabriella* Glasgow's perspective began to shift from social history to character, as embodied in a lineage of redoubtable heroines that would dominate the remainder of her work. But they ply their strengths in a time and place that has a fictional history, and it is portrayed ably and memorably in this early cycle of novels.

—Welford Dunaway Taylor

GLASS, Amanda. See **KRENTZ, Jayne Ann.**

GLOVER, Judith.
Nationality: British. **Born:** Wolverhampton, West Midlands, 31 March 1943. **Education:** Wolverhampton High School for Girls, 1954–59; Aston Polytechnic, Birmingham, 1960. **Relations:** married 1) Anthony Rowley in 1961 (marriage annulled); 2) Stanley Martin in 1966 (died), two daughters. **Career:** journalist, Wolverhampton *Express and Star*, 1960–61; freelance feature writer, 1962–74. **Agent:** Artellus Ltd, 30 Dorset House, Gloucester Place, London NW1 5AD, England. **Address:** Oaklands House, Llanteg, Narberth, Dyfed SA67 8QG, Wales.

ROMANCE AND HISTORICAL PUBLICATIONS

Novels (series: Sussex Quartet)

Sussex Quartet:
   The Stallion Man. London, Hodder and Stoughton, 1982; New York, St Martin's Press, 1983.
   Sisters and Brothers. London, Hodder and Stoughton, and New York, St Martin's Press, 1984.
   To Everything a Season. London, Hodder and Stoughton, 1986.
   Birds in a Gilded Cage. London, Hodder and Stoughton, 1988.
   The Imagination of the Heart. London, Hodder and Stoughton, 1989; New York, St Martin's Press, 1990.

Tiger Lilies. London, Hodder and Stoughton, and New York, St Martin's Press, 1991.
Mirabelle. London, Hodder and Stoughton, and New York, St Martin's Press, 1993.

OTHER PUBLICATIONS

Other

The Place Names of Sussex. London, Batsford, 1974.
The Batsford Colour Book of Sussex. London, Batsford, 1975.
The Batsford Colour Book of Kent. London, Batsford, 1976.
Sussex in Photographs, photographs by Anthony Kersting. London, Batsford, 1976.
The Place Names of Kent. London, Batsford, 1976.
Drink Your Own Garden (on wine making). London, Batsford, 1979.

*

Judith Glover comments:
History is people—all the drama of their individual lives creates the tapestry of the past. By writing historical romantic fiction, it is ever my intention to recreate the colours of that tapestry, weaving stories which come vividly alive through the everyday events of Victorian and Edwardian England, in the lives of those men and women who are my characters.

*   *   *

Although each of Judith Glover's first four historical romances can be read independently, they form a continuing saga of the intertwined lives of several families in Sussex. The series spans the time from the 1850s, when Frank Morgan, *The Stallion Man*, indiscriminately sires children during his travels through the countryside, to 1912, when Europe is poised on the brink of war.

For the most part Frank Morgan's sexual liaisons are as casual as those of his stallion, which he mates with mares for a living. His pursuit of women, married and unmarried, reveals his arrogance and lack of morality. *The Stallion Man* centres on his attempts to seduce Rachel Bates, the wife of a curate who is unable to consummate his marriage because of psychological problems. Esmond Bates had been denied a normal childhood because of the rigid fundamentalism of his father, who delighted in flogging his servants, pupils, wife, and son for any impropriety.

Mistakenly convinced that Rachel has welcomed Frank's advances, Esmond attacks Morgan in a fight that results in both men's deaths under the hooves of Morgan's stallion. Released from her husband's insane domination, Rachel eventually marries widower George Bashford, a well-to-do farmer.

Morgan's descendants populate the pages of the three sequels. Two of his children, Frank and Isabelle Flynn, form one of the pairs of *Sisters and Brothers*. Like his father, Frank lets his violence and sexual appetites cause his downfall. Although he marries wealthy Rosannah Weldrake after she tricks him into fathering a child, he continues an affair with Lizzie Newbrook despite the fact that she is already married. Tom Newbrook's attempt to defend his honour ends in his death at Frank's hands. The murder trial brings more horror when Frank and Lizzie learn that they are both Frank Morgan's children.

Isabelle's involvement with unscrupulous Harry Weldrake ends in her imprisonment in a brothel, from which she is rescued by Alec Bethway, a parson who eventually marries her. Their children continue the family tradition of unhappy love affairs. For example, daughter Dinah loses her husband of a few months when he dies in the Boer War in *To Everything a Season*, and is duped into marrying a bigamist before recognizing the steadfast love of Stephen Moore (*Birds in a Gilded Cage*). Francis Bethway inherits his grandfather's penchant for promiscuity, eventually adopting the name Frank Morgan as he and his mistress undertake a doomed voyage to the United States on the *Titanic*.

The first two books of the series contain a good deal of violence, including harsh sexual relationships. Esmond finally consummates his marriage to Rachel only when his enraged jealousy drives him to rape her. Rosannah Weldrake is attracted to Frank Flynn because of his violent nature. She tells her brother, 'I need the kind of man who'll abuse me, hurt me, exact my submission by violence . . . oh, how I love it when he mistreats me'. Their mother had been beaten to death in a sado-masochistic encounter. Although Glover's later characters remain duplicitous in their sexual relationships, the violence in her books decreases.

For the most part, the women in Glover's books have little control over their own lives. An independent income provides some leverage, as Adelaide Winter discovers when she successfully uses threats of withdrawing her family's support if her errant husband Harry Weldrake continues to gamble in *Sisters and Brothers*. But Dinah Garland finds no legal remedy to stop her gambler husband from depleting her resources, in *Birds in a Gilded Cage*.

Catherine March, the central character in *The Imagination of the Heart*, initially appears cast from the same mould. Wealthy Oliver van der Kleve selects her for her beauty and sends her abroad to complete her education. Oliver makes the investment to prepare Catherine as a suitable second wife for him as his first wife had died without bearing a son. Pride of possession characterizes Oliver's attitude towards Catherine, who is systematically excluded from running the household by Oliver's self-righteous sister Beatrice and tormented by his teenage daughter Angelina.

Longing for romance, Catherine commits adultery with the artist commissioned to paint her portrait. Her plans to marry him are dashed when he abandons her once their liaison is discovered. Only the revelation of Oliver's own infidelity and his fear of scandal keep the marriage together. Yet, Catherine's developing confidence and independence earn Oliver's admiration. 'A little steel had entered into her soul, forged there by the tragedy and sorrow which had followed so hard one upon the heels of the other'. They both grow in tolerance throughout the novel, and tolerance deepens to love.

In this exploration of a Victorian marriage of convenience, Glover exhibits her best writing. She deftly incorporates sub-plots such as Beatrice's relentless pursuit of the local minister and Angelina's ill-fated romance with a seemingly respectable young man who betrays her. Glover captures the destructive power of gossip and the social strictures of the era.

In *Tiger Lilies* the links between the two major plots are often tenuous and sometimes contrived. Spanning the period from 1905 to the early 1920s, the novel follows the fortunes of Flora Dennison, the daughter of wealthy entrepreneur George Dennison, and Roseen O'Connor, the daughter of his mistress. Although Roseen is not George's child, he prefers her beauty, liveliness, and spunk to Flora's conventional appearance and goodness. Roseen's pursuit of wealth and pleasure lead her to a succession of love affairs and a brief marriage that ends with her husband's death in World War I. The man Flora loves, Robert Wells, survives the war. However, his marriage stands between them from the time they meet at college through her own marriage and widowhood. Only an intervention by Roseen makes Robert realize that his plans for divorce will lead only to eventual unhappiness for him and Flora. Many of the connections

between Flora and Roseen seem contrived as their lives intersect in various ways. The contrast of their approaches to life never quite succeeds. Yet Glover's willingness to venture beyond the territory and era she explored successfully in her 'Sussex Quartet' demonstrates her desire to grow as a writer.

—Kathy Piehl

GLUYAS, Constance.
Nationality: British. **Born:** England in 1920. **Military Service:** British Women's Auxiliary Air Force during World War II. **Relations:** married Donald Gluyas in 1944. **Career:** full-time writer. Lives in California. **Address:** c/o Robert Hale Ltd, 45–47 Clerkenwell Green, London EC1R 0HT, England.

ROMANCE AND HISTORICAL PUBLICATIONS

Novels

The King's Brat. Englewood Cliffs, New Jersey, Prentice Hall, 1972; London, Hale, 1974.
Born to Be King. Englewood Cliffs, New Jersey, Prentice Hall, 1974; London, Hale, 1976.
My Lady Benbrook. Englewood Cliffs, New Jersey, Prentice Hall, 1975.
Brief Is the Glory. New York, McKay, 1975.
The House on Twyford Street. New York, McKay, 1976; London, Magnum, 1978.
My Lord Foxe. New York, McKay, 1976; London, Magnum, 1980.
Savage Eden. New York, New American Library, 1976; London, Sphere, 1978.
Rogue's Mistress. New York, New American Library, 1977; London, Sphere, 1978.
Woman of Fury. New York, New American Library, 1978; London, Hale, 1980.
Flame of the South. New York, New American Library, 1979; London, Sphere, 1981.
Madame Tudor. New York, New American Library, 1979.
Lord Sin. New York, New American Library, 1980; London, Sphere, 1985.
The Passionate Savage. New York, New American Library, 1980; London, Sphere, 1982.
The Bridge to Yesterday. New York, New American Library, 1981; London, Sphere, 1983.
Brandy Kane. London, Hale, 1985.

*   *   *

Constance Gluyas depicts a universe of romantic violence. Her novels have historical settings, and are notable for the turbulent passions of their heroines and the torture and humiliation to which they are subjected. Whether struggling for a crust in the gutters of Restoration London, or slaving on a tobacco plantation, Gluyas's ladies undergo brutal punishment, and display a breath-taking sexual vigour. Strong in endurance, they challenge all that a cruel world flings at them. It follows that the man of their choice must be even stronger and more masterful.

The King's Brat is typical. Its urchin heroine is imprisoned in Newgate for theft. Freed by Charles II, the intrepid angel quickly works her way into society. Sought after by the King, she chooses the artist Nicholas Tavington instead. Though the course of their love is difficult, they survive the horrors of the Great Plague to find wedded bliss. *The King's Brat* is a touch long-winded (verbosity is a familiar Gluyas failing), but the story is lively, and the action is full-blooded, the author dwelling equally on the delights of love and the squalor of poverty and prison in the 1660s.

Born to Be King is set during the 1745 Jacobite rebellion, with Elizabeth Drummond disguising herself as a man to join the rebels. The novel centres on her love-affair with an Englishman, Moncrieff, who intends to betray the prince but is later won over to his cause. The fortunes of the Jacobites are followed to Culloden, and final exile. Faster-moving than *The King's Brat*, *Born to Be King* contains the usual ingredients—wilful heroine, dark satanic hero, and their fierce love-hate relationship—that recur constantly in Gluyas's work.

Woman of Fury, with its witch-finder villain, is closer to fantasy than most. The perverted lustful Matthew Lorne, who covets his adopted daughter and kills wife and son with casual brutality, is so incredibly evil he teeters on the edge of absurdity. Some of the coincidences, too, are scarcely to be believed. But Gluyas's creations do not inhabit the real world. Theirs is the fevered kingdom of the imagination, where subtleties of character and plot give way to the garish visions of nightmare and dream. This accepted, the fast and furious action helps to suspend disbelief. *Flame of the South* deals with similar leading characters who combine passion with their efforts to free black slaves from the southern plantations, while the fever-pitch plot of *The Passionate Savage* has settler Lucien Marsh torn between the demands of an Indian maiden and an earthy English lady trapped in a loveless marriage. Physical passion and tragedy cram the pages, Gluyas's doomed characters endlessly raging and lusting until cut down by sudden death. *Brandy Kane* transfers the same extreme appetites to a modern setting, centring on the fraught love-hate relationship of the beautiful Brandy, daughter of a Texan millionaire, for the arrogant but handsome Dr Cameron Phillips. Brandy survives the incestuous attentions of her father, her bond with Cameron suitably consummated in feverish prose to reach a climactic resolution. Though the scene shifts, the story remains unchanged, the action swift and savage as ever, the appetites unquenchable.

Among the most famous Gluyas novels are *Savage Eden* and *Rogue's Mistress*, with their central characters of Justin 'Rogue' Lawrence and Caroline Fane. The works follow Lawrence and Caroline in their adventures as robbers in England, and later as convict settlers in the United States. The ferocity of love and hate is continually present. Like other Gluyas heroes and heroines, Justin and Caroline quarrel frequently, and their very lovemaking partakes of violence.

Gluyas's creations—fiery heroines and formidable heroes—are of a world other than our own. Though a far from satisfactory stylist—sometimes prolix, at other times cramming the action into too short a compass—her writing drives home the one unvarying theme: the clash of strong woman with stronger man, and their physical union. The battle of the sexes becomes tedious, but on its own gothic grounds it remains valid. Gluyas writes with animal vigour, and shows herself fully aware of the beast beneath the skin.

—Geoffrey Sadler

GLYN, Elinor.
Nationality: British. **Born:** Elinor Sutherland, Jersey, Channel Islands, 17 October 1864, of Canadian parents; grew up in Ontario and Jersey. **Education:** privately. **Relations:** married Clayton Glyn in 1892 (died 1915); two daughters. **Career:** canteen worker and war correspondent during World War I. Lived in the USA, 1920–29; film producer, writer, and director. **Died:** 23 September 1943.

ROMANCE AND HISTORICAL PUBLICATIONS

Novels (series: Elizabeth)

The Visits of Elizabeth. London, Duckworth, 1900; New York, Lane, 1901.
The Reflections of Ambrosine. London, Duckworth, and New York, Harper, 1902; as *The Seventh Commandment*, New York, Macaulay, n.d.
The Damsel and the Sage. London, Duckworth, and New York, Harper, 1903.
The Vicissitudes of Evangeline. London, Duckworth, and New York, Harper, 1905; as *Red Hair*, New York, Macaulay, n.d.
Beyond the Rocks. London, Duckworth, and New York, Harper, 1906.
Three Weeks. London, Duckworth, and New York, Business Press, 1907.
Elizabeth Visits America. London, Duckworth, and New York, Duffield, 1909.
His Hour. London, Duckworth, and New York, Appleton, 1910; as *When His Hour Came*, London, Newnes, 1915.
The Reason Why. London, Duckworth, and New York, Appleton, 1911.
Halcyone. London, Duckworth, and New York, Appleton, 1912; as *Love Itself*, Auburn, New York, Author's Press, 1924 (?).
The Sequence 1905–1912. London, Duckworth, 1913; as *Guinevere's Lover*, New York, Appleton, 1913.
The Man and the Moment. New York, Appleton, 1914; London, Duckworth, 1915.
The Career of Katherine Bush. New York, Appleton, 1916; London, Duckworth, 1917.
The Price of Things. London, Duckworth, 1919; as *Family*, New York, Appleton, 1919.
Man and Maid—Renaissance. London, Duckworth, 1922; as *Man and Maid*, Philadelphia, Lippincott, 1922.
The Great Moment. London, Duckworth, and Philadelphia, Lippincott, 1923.
Six Days. London, Duckworth, and Philadelphia, Lippincott, 1924.
This Passion Called Love. London, Duckworth, and Auburn, New York, Author's Press, 1925.
Love's Blindness. London, Duckworth, and Auburn, New York, Author's Press, 1926.
The Flirt and the Flapper. London, Duckworth, 1930.
Love's Hour. London, Duckworth, and New York, Macaulay, 1932.
Glorious Flames (novelization of screenplay). London, Benn, 1932; New York, Macaulay, 1933.
Sooner or Later. London, Rich and Cowan, 1933; New York, Macaulay, 1935.
Did She?. London, Rich and Cowan, 1934.
The Third Eye. London, Long, 1940.

Short Stories

The Contract and Other Stories. London, Duckworth, 1913; *The Point of View* published separately, New York, Appleton, 1913.
It and Other Stories. London, Duckworth, and New York, Macaulay, 1927.
Saint or Satyr? and Other Stories. London, Duckworth, 1933; as *Such Men Are Dangerous*, New York, Macaulay, 1933.

OTHER PUBLICATIONS

Plays

Three Weeks, adaptation of her own novel (produced London, 1908).

Screenplays: *The Great Moment*, with Monte M. Katterjohn, 1921; *The World's a Stage*, with Colin Campbell and George Bertholon, 1922; *His Hour*, with King Vidor and Maude Fulton, 1924; *Three Weeks (The Romance of a Queen)*, with Carey Wilson, 1924; *How to Educate a Wife*, with Douglas Z. Doty and Grant Carpenter, 1924; *Man and Maid*, 1925; *The Only Thing*, 1925; *Love's Blindness*, 1926; *Ritzy*, with others, 1927; *It*, with others, 1927; *Three Week-Ends*, with others, 1928; *The Man and the Moment*, with Agnes Christine Johnston and Paul Perez, 1929; *Such Men Are Dangerous*, with Ernst Vajda, 1930; *Knowing Men*, with Edward Knoblock, 1930.

Other

The Sayings of Grandmama and Others. London, Duckworth, and New York, Duffield, 1908.
Letters to Caroline. London, Duckworth, 1914; as *Your Affectionate Godmother*, New York, Appleton, 1914.
Three Things. London, Duckworth, and New York, Hearst, 1915.

Destruction. London, Duckworth, 1918.
Points of View. London, Duckworth, 1920.
The Philosophy of Love. London, Duckworth, 1920.
The Elinor Glyn System of Writing. Auburn, New York, Author's Press, 4 vols, 1922.
The Philosophy of Love (different from 1920 book). Auburn, New York, Author's Press, 1923; as *Love—What I Think of It*, London, Readers Library, 1928.
Letters from Spain. London, Duckworth, 1924.
The Wrinkle Book; or, How to Keep Looking Young. London, Duckworth, 1927; as *Eternal Youth*, New York, Macmillan, 1928.
Romantic Adventure (autobiography). London, Nicholson and Watson, 1936; New York, Dutton, 1937.
Keep Young and Beautiful (selections), with Barbara Cartland. London, Duckworth, 1982.

*

Critical Studies: *Elinor Glyn: A Biography* by Anthony Glyn, London, Hutchinson, 1955, revised edition, 1968; *The 'It' Girls: Lucy, Lady Duff Gordon, the Couturière 'Lucile' and Elinor Glyn, Romantic Novelist* by Meredith Etherington-Smith and Jeremy Pilcher, London, Hamish Hamilton, 1986, New York, Harcourt Brace, 1987.

Theatrical Activities:
Director: **Films**—*Knowing Men*, 1930; *The Price of Things*, 1930.
Actress: **Play**—The Queen in *Three Weeks*, London, 1908.

*   *   *

Elinor Glyn always felt that writing should stress feeling rather than ideas. Perhaps this explains why, when she addressed the 1931 International PEN Congress as a best-selling author of 30 years' standing, she described herself as 'A society person of no particular brains or talents'. She added, 'I can't think why my books sell and make so much money'. Glyn's loyal readers found both intelligence and appeal in her romances, and the fantasy world of rank, beauty, breeding, passion, and heroic self-restraint these works created.

Glyn's first novel, *The Visits of Elizabeth*, is a naughty epistolary romance featuring a pert, charming ingenue narrator who observes the eccentricities and extra-marital adventures of French and English nobility at a series of house-parties she attends. The novel created a great stir among Glyn's society acquaintances, on whom it was based. The tone, form, and malicious good humour appeared in *Elizabeth Visits America*, and 'Elizabeth's Daughter'. The Eliza-

beth novels reflect Glyn's views, travels, and preoccupation with good breeding and physical beauty.

A second romance formula appears in a series of novels based on mismatches, marriages between sensitive, beautiful aristocrats and unfeeling, unmannered newly rich. *The Reflections of Ambrosine, The Vicissitudes of Evangeline*, and *Beyond the Rocks* are representative. The titled half of the pair finds a true soul mate in a handsome and titled suitor. However, sorely tempted by adulterous passion, the heroines of these tales resist until their moneyed louts die and they are free to marry again. These novels reflect a mistrust of money and a snobbish insistence on rank difficult for the modern reader to accept.

Glyn's greatest success, the one work which best displays her style, her characters, and her favourite themes of elegant snobbery and spiritual/sexual attraction is *Three Weeks*—a purple prose hymn to aristocratic soul passion. Roughly inspired by the assassination of Queen Draga of Serbia, *Three Weeks* describes the spiritual and sensual awakening of a handsome young English noble, Paul, by an unnamed, dark, wilful Slavic beauty of noble rank—the Lady. After their meeting in Switzerland, Paul presents the Lady with a gift that he feels reflects her untamed and splendid spirit: a tigerskin. When he next calls on the Lady, he sees:

a bright fire burnt in the grate, and some palest mauve curtains were drawn . . . . And loveliest sight of all, in front of the fire, stretched at full length, was his tiger—and on him—also at full length—reclined his lady, garbed in some strange clinging garment of heavy purple crepe, one white arm resting on the beast's head, her back supported by a pile of velvet cusions and a heap of rarely bound books at her side, while between her lips was a rose not redder than they—an almost scarlet rose.

The relationship between Paul and the Lady soon blossoms into a short but intense affair that takes them to Venice, where they part, never to meet again. The Lady, however, has conceived a son who will some day inherit the throne of Russia.

Despite its heady mixture of eroticism and exoticism, *Three Weeks* remains remarkably moral in tone. The adulterous love of Paul and the Lady is based on a mutually lofty recognition of beauty and nobility; their physical union represents a small portion of their spiritual experience. Denied each other by fate, the lovers are punished for their adultery by the Lady's brutal murder at the hands of her degenerate husband. Critical response to *Three Weeks* was favourable but guarded; popular response was spectacular. Glyn became a household word and all of her works bestsellers. Moral objection was voiced largely in America, where the novel was banned in several states. However, readers on both sides of the Atlantic were drawn by the image of passion blazing beyond sexuality in *Three Weeks*; 'It', sexuality and attraction, was delineated, but never so vividly, in Glyn's later films and fiction.

Glyn's travels in the United States and her work in the developing American film industry modified her rigid early views on noble blood and gentle breeding. Her later works, notably *The Career of Katherine Bush*, show that independent, handsome, disciplined men and women can train themselves for social standing. This theme demonstrates that character can triumph over circumstances to allow a hero or heroine to find ennobling love.

The shortcomings of Glyn's 25 romances—the defence of snobbery, the equation of character with physical beauty, the remarkable combination of bourgeois prudishness and aristocratic passion—are the very elements that made her romances so appealing to her readers. Glyn herself described romance as 'spiritual disguise created by the imagination with which to envelop material happenings with desires and thus bring them into greater harmony with the soul'. Glyn's novels created a romance world which her readers could otherwise never know. With her and through her work, generations of readers lived this fantasy of romance.

—Katherine Staples

————

GODDEN, (Margaret) Rumer.
Nationality: British. **Born:** Sussex, 10 December 1907. **Education:** privately and at Moira House, Eastbourne, Sussex. **Relations:** married 1) Laurence Sinclair Foster in 1934 (died), two daughters; 2) James Lesley Haynes Dixon in 1949 (died 1973). **Career:** director of a children's ballet school, Calcutta, 1930s. **Recipient:** Whitbread award, for children's book, 1973. **Agent:** Curtis Brown, 162–168 Regent Street, London W1R 5TA, England; or, 10 Astor Place, New York, New York 10003, USA. **Address:** Ardnacloich, Moniaive, Thornhill, Dumfries and Galloway DG3 4HZ, Scotland.

ROMANCE AND HISTORICAL PUBLICATIONS

Novels

Chinese Puzzle. London, Davies, 1936.
The Lady and the Unicorn. London, Davies, 1937.
Black Narcissus. London, Davies, and Boston, Little Brown, 1939.
Gypsy, Gypsy. London, Davies, and Boston, Little Brown, 1940.
Breakfast with the Nikolides. London, Davies, and Boston, Little Brown, 1942.
A Fugue in Time. London, Joseph, 1945; as *Take Three Tenses: A Fugue in Time*, Boston, Little Brown, 1945.
The River. London, Joseph, and Boston, Little Brown, 1946.
A Candle for St Jude. London, Joseph, and New York, Viking Press, 1948.
A Breath of Air. London, Joseph, 1950; New York, Viking Press, 1951.
Kingfishers Catch Fire. London, Macmillan, and New York, Viking Press, 1953.
An Episode of Sparrows. New York, Viking Press, 1955; London, Macmillan, 1956.
The Greengage Summer. London, Macmillan, and New York, Viking Press, 1958.
China Court: The Hours of a Country House. London, Macmillan, and New York, Viking Press, 1961.
The Battle of the Villa Fiorita. London, Macmillan, and New York, Viking Press, 1963.
In This House of Brede. London, Macmillan, and New York, Viking Press, 1969.
The Peacock Spring. London, Macmillan, 1975; New York, Viking Press, 1976.
Five for Sorrow, Ten for Joy. London, Macmillan, and New York, Viking Press, 1979.
The Dark Horse. London, Macmillan, 1981; New York, Viking Press, 1982.
Thursday's Children. London, Macmillan, and New York, Viking, 1984.
Coromandel Sea Change. London, Macmillan, 1990; New York, Morrow, 1991.

Short Stories

Mooltiki and Other Stories and Poems of India. London, Macmillan, and New York, Viking Press, 1957.
Swans and Turtles: Stories. London, Macmillan, 1968; as *Gone: A Thread of Stories*, New York, Viking Press, 1968.

Indian Dust. London, Macmillan, 1989.
Mercy, Pity, Peace and Love, with Jon Godden. London, Macmillan, 1989; New York, Morrow, 1990.

OTHER PUBLICATIONS

Fiction (for children)

The Doll's House. London, Joseph, 1947; New York, Viking Press, 1948; as *Tottie*, London, Penguin, 1983.
The Mousewife. London, Macmillan, and New York, Viking Press, 1951.
Four Dolls. London, Macmillan, 1983; New York, Greenwillow, 1984.
    Impunity Jane: The Story of a Pocket Doll. New York, Viking Press, 1954; London, Macmillan, 1955.
    The Fairy Doll. London, Macmillan, and New York, Viking Press, 1956.
    The Story of Holly and Ivy. London, Macmillan, and New York, Viking Press, 1958.
    Candy Floss. London, Macmillan, and New York, Viking Press, 1960.
Mouse House. New York, Viking Press, 1957; London, Macmillan, 1958.
Miss Happiness and Miss Flower. London, Macmillan, and New York, Viking Press, 1961.
Little Plum. London, Macmillan, and New York, Viking Press, 1963.
Home Is the Sailor. London, Macmillan, and New York, Viking Press, 1964.
The Kitchen Madonna. London, Macmillan, and New York, Viking Press, 1967.
Operation Sippacik. London, Macmillan, and New York, Viking Press, 1969.
The Old Woman Who Lived in a Vinegar Bottle. London, Macmillan, and New York, Viking Press, 1972.
The Diddakoi. London, Macmillan, and New York, Viking Press, 1972.
Mr McFadden's Hallowe'en. London, Macmillan, and New York, Viking Press, 1975.
The Rocking Horse Secret. London, Macmillan, 1977; New York, Viking Press, 1978.
A Kindle of Kittens. London, Macmillan, 1978; New York, Viking Press, 1979.
The Dragon of Og. London, Macmillan, and New York, Viking Press, 1981.
The Valiant Chatti-Maker. London, Macmillan, and New York, Viking Press, 1983.
Fu-Dog. London, MacRae, 1989.
Listen to the Nightingale. 1992.
Great Grandfather's House. 1992.

Plays

Screenplays: *The River*, with Jean Renoir, 1951; *Innocent Sinners*, with Neil Patterson, 1958.

Poetry (for children)

In Noah's Ark. London, Joseph, and New York, Viking Press, 1949.
St Jerome and the Lion. London, Macmillan, and New York, Viking Press, 1961.

Other

Rungli-Rungliot (Thus Far and No Further). London, Davies, 1943;

as *Rungli-Rungliot Means in Paharia, Thus Far and No Further*, Boston, Little Brown, 1946; as *Thus Far and No Further*, London, Macmillan, 1961.

Bengal Journey: A Story of the Part Played by Women in the Province 1939–1945. London, Longman, 1945.

Hans Christian Andersen: A Great Life in Brief. London, Hutchinson, and New York, Knopf, 1955.

Two Under the Indian Sun (autobiography), with Jon Godden. London, Macmillan, and New York, Knopf, 1966.

The Tale of Tales: The Beatrix Potter Ballet. London, Warne, 1971.

Shiva's Pigeons: An Experience of India, with Jon Godden. London, Chatto and Windus, and New York, Viking Press, 1972.

The Butterfly Lions: The Story of the Pekingese in History, Legend, and Art. London, Macmillan, 1977; New York, Viking Press, 1978.

Gulbadan: Portrait of a Rose Princess at the Mughal Court. London, Macmillan, 1980; New York, Viking Press, 1981.

A Time to Dance, No Time to Weep (autobiography). London, Macmillan, and New York, Morrow, 1987.

A House With Four Rooms (autobiography). London, Macmillan, and New York, Morrow, 1989.

Editor, *Round the Day, Round the Year, The World Around: Poetry Programmes for Classroom or Library*. London, Macmillan, 6 vols, 1966–67.

Editor, *A Letter to the World: Poems for Young Readers*, by Emily Dickinson. London, Bodley Head, 1968; New York, Macmillan, 1969.

Editor, *Mrs Manders' Cookbook*, by Olga Manders. London, Macmillan, and New York, Viking Press, 1968.

Editor, *The Raphael Bible*. London, Macmillan, and New York, Viking Press, 1970.

Translator, *Prayers from the Ark* (verse), by Carmen de Gasztold. New York, Viking Press, 1962; London, Macmillan, 1963.

Translator, *The Creatures' Choir* (verse), by Carmen de Gasztold. New York, Viking Press, 1965; as *The Beasts' Choir*, London, Macmillan, 1967.

*

Film Adaptations: *Black Narcissus*, 1947; *Enchantment*, 1948, from the novel *A Fugue in Time*; *The River*, 1951; *Innocent Sinners*, 1957, from the novel *An Episode of Sparrows*; *Loss of Innocence*, 1961, from the novel *Greengage Summer*; *The Battle of the Villa Fiorita*, 1964 (as *Affair at the Villa Fiorita*, 1964); *In This House of Brede*, 1975; *Kizzie*, 1976, from the novel *The Diddakoi*; *Tottie*, 1982, from the novel *The Doll's House*.

Manuscript Collection: Mugar Memorial Library, Boston University.

Critical Study: *Rumer Godden* by Hassell A. Simpson, New York, Twayne, 1973.

*   *   *

'Theirs seems to me to be a love story that transcends all ordinary love stories', Rumer Godden has said about one of the recurrent themes in her novels, that of the nun and conventual life. The romance of the Brides of Christ is one that has intrigued her for many years: her early success, *Black Narcissus*, explored the disastrous consequences of transplanting a cell of nuns trained in an Edwardian British tradition to a disused Indian palace high in the Himalayas. Nuns occur again, most notably in *In This House of Brede*, and *Five for Sorrow, Ten for Joy*. 'Writing about nuns is exceedingly diffi-

cult—if they are to be true nuns (so often in books their stories are distorted)'—but Godden makes these women enormously real; their loves, joys, sorrows, and struggles are treated with the dignity, the humour, and the preceptive eye which are the hallmarks of this author.

None of Godden's novels could be termed a conventional romance. Her characters are flawed and human, and don't fit into stereotypical moulds. They react as imperfect people do—brittle Louise in *Breakfast with the Nikolides*, reunited because of the war with Charles, the husband she had left years before, lashes out when her daughter's affections are engaged by a dog, for example, or Mrs Manning, resorting to any device she can think of to stay near the man she loves in *Coromandel Sea Change*.

There are straightforward, boy-meets-girl, happy ever after romantic stories in Godden's novels. The stories of Tracy and Peter in *China Court*, or Grizel and Pax in *A Fugue in Time*, could be so described. But they are only part of a much more complex narrative: Rollo cannot have a military career and marry Lark in *A Fugue in Time*: and although Ripsie, Borowis and John Henry in *China Court* are all in love, the decisions they make do not lead to starry-eyed bliss. In her latest novel, *Coromandel Sea Change*, Blaise and Mary seem to be a conventionally happy young couple. However, staying at the Patna Hall hotel, under the benevolent wise eye of Auntie Sanni, during an Indian election, has a liberating effect on Mary. An important part of the plot deals with Blaise's reaction, and whether he is strong enough to let his marriage grow to accommodate Mary's personal development.

Another major and potent strand in Godden's novels is her use of children. *The Greengage Summer* is related by the child Cecil, trying to cope on holiday in France with her mother sick in hospital, the younger children to worry about, and her elder sister Joss behaving very oddly. What is happening between Joss and handsome, sophisticated Eliot? Is Eliot at all what he seems to be? Tip Malone and Lovejoy Mason in *An Episode of Sparrows* are poor London children. Their story is about making a garden, and is not a romance at all—or is it? What happens when children, upset and confused by their mother's divorce, fight to get her back? Fanny and Rob, in *The Battle of the Villa Fiorita*, are very much in love. The children—Caddie in particular—have only blundering, innocent vulnerability to fight with.

The agonies of first love are particularly poignantly portrayed in *The Peacock Spring*. Una, torn from her beloved school to live with her diplomat father in Delhi, is angry and resentful. She resents being used as a cover for his romance with the 'governess', Eurasian Alix, and angry at her father's total failure to understand her needs and hopes. Una is highly susceptible to the romantic lure of India. When she meets a beautiful young man, Ravi, who is temporarily her father's gardener, but also a student, revolutionary and poet, Una falls desperately in love. The author conveys the fresh intensity of Una's love, while also conveying the certainty that the romance is hopeless and must be doomed.

One of the very attractive features of Godden's work is that she has time for characters who might in other circumstances be considered marginal. Children have already been mentioned. The curious world of the Eurasian is described with humour in *The Peacock Spring*—Alix's old mother is a splendid comic creation. This world can also be cruel: in the Delhi of the 1930s John loves and marries Eurasian Dahlia (*The Dark Horse*) but he has to resign from his regiment as a consequence, and live a life of semi-ostracism. Even the unmarried woman is allowed to play a part. For example, the sisters Angela and Olivia, in *An Episode of Sparrows*, make an interesting contrast as a study of what a couple of spinsters can do with their lives.

Settings are important in all Godden's novels. There are a wide range: a house in a Kensington square, Lake Garda, the Marne river valley—and in many novels, India; a country the author knows extremely well, in all its infinite variety. Each location is one the author knows, and she builds up a picture of it with clear and loving detail. In this way the reader can experience the busy quiet of a convent, or hear the endless sound of the wind in the Himalayas.

Godden is above all a storyteller, with the ability to weave an intriguing narrative together, constructing a tale to entrance and absorb the reader. Her stories may have two or three strands plaited together in an apparently simple way: the doings of the family in *The River*, for example, with the arrival of the wounded Captain John and the effect this has on Harriet growing up. They can also be multi-layered and complete, like *China Court*, or *A Fugue in Time*, where several stories that occur at different times are told together. One of the most characteristic features of the author's work is her ability to spring surprises on the reader. It must never be assumed that the plot is heading towards the obvious, logical ending. There will always be something quite unexpected: harshness, maybe violence even, which will pull the story right away from sentiment, or conventionality, and raise it to a new and memorable level.

For those readers who enjoy a real story—the sort of book that will absorb them completely: a good plot, authentic background, colourful and well-observed characters, but above all a beautifully told and written narrative—Godden's work cannot be too highly recommended.

—Felicity Trotman

GOLDING, (Sir) William (Gerald).
Nationality: British. **Born:** St Columb Minor, Cornwall, 19 September 1911. **Education:** Marlborough Grammar School; Brasenose College, Oxford, B.A. 1935. **Military Service:** Royal Navy, 1940–45. **Relations:** married Ann Brookfield in 1939; one son and one daughter. **Career:** writer, actor, and producer in small theatre companies, 1934–40; schoolmaster, Bishop Wordsworth's School, Salisbury, Wiltshire, 1945–61; visiting professor, Hollins College, Virginia, 1961–62. **Recipient:** James Tait Black memorial prize, 1980; Booker prize, 1980; Nobel prize for literature, 1983. M.A.: Oxford University, 1961; D.Litt.: University of Sussex, Brighton, 1970; University of Kent, Canterbury, 1974; University of Warwick, Coventry, 1981; the Sorbonne, Paris, 1983; Oxford University, 1983; LLD.: University of Bristol, 1984. Honorary Fellow, Brasenose College, 1966. Fellow, 1955, and Companion of Literature, 1984, Royal Society of Literature. CBE (Commander, Order of the British Empire), 1966. Knighted, 1988. **Died:** 19 June 1993.

ROMANCE AND HISTORICAL PUBLICATIONS

Novels (series: Sea Trilogy)

The Inheritors. London, Faber, 1955; New York, Coward McCann, 1956.
The Spire. London, Faber, and New York, Harcourt Brace, 1964.
To the Ends of the Earth: A Sea Trilogy. London, Faber and Faber, 1991.
    Rites of Passage. London, Faber, and New York, Farrar Straus, 1980.
    Close Quarters. London, Faber, and New York, Farrar Straus, 1987.
    Fire Down Below. London, Faber, and New York, Farrar Straus, 1989.

Short Stories

The Scorpion God: Three Short Novels. London, Faber, 1971; New York, Harcourt Brace, 1972.

OTHER PUBLICATIONS

Novels

Lord of the Flies. London, Faber, 1954; New York, Coward, McCann, 1955.
Pincher Martin. London, Faber, 1956; as *The Two Deaths of Christopher Martin*, New York, Harcourt Brace, 1957.
Free Fall. London, Faber, 1959; New York, Harcourt Brace, 1960.
The Pyramid. London, Faber, and New York, Harcourt Brace, 1967.
Darkness Visible. Faber, and New York, Farrar Straus, 1979.
The Paper Men. London, Faber, and New York, Farrar Straus, 1984.

Plays

The Brass Butterfly, adaptation of his story 'Envoy Extraordinary' (produced London, 1958; New York, 1970). London, Faber, 1958; Chicago, Dramatic Publishing Company, n.d.

Radio Plays: *Miss Pulkinhorn*, 1960; *Break My Heart*, 1962.

Poetry

Poems. London, Macmillan, 1934; New York, Macmillan, 1935.

Other

The Hot Gates and Other Occasional Pieces. London, Faber, 1965; New York, Harcourt Brace, 1966.
Talk: Conversations with William Golding, with Jack I. Biles. New York, Harcourt Brace, 1970.
A Moving Target (essays). London, Faber, and New York, Farrar Straus, 1982.
An Egyptian Journal. London, Faber, 1985.

*

Film Adaptations: *Lord of the Flies*, 1963, 1990.

Bibliography: *William Golding: A Bibliography* by R.A. Gekoski and David Hughes, London, Deutsch, 1990.

Critical Studies: (selection): *William Golding* by Samuel Hynes, New York, Columbia University Press, 1964; *William Golding: A Critical Study* by James R. Baker, New York, St Martin's Press, 1965, and *Critical Essays on William Golding* edited by Baker, Boston, Hall, 1988; *The Art of William Golding* by Bernard S. Oldsey and Stanley Weintraub, New York, Harcourt Brace, 1965; *William Golding* by Bernard F. Dick, New York, Twayne, 1967; *William Golding: A Critical Study* by Mark Kinkead-Weekes and Ian Gregor, London, Faber, 1967, New York, Harcourt Brace, 1968, revised edition, Faber, 1984; *William Golding* by Leighton Hodson, Edinburgh, Oliver and Boyd, 1969, New York, Putnam, 1971; *The Novels of William Golding* by Howard S. Babb, Columbus, Ohio State University Press, 1970; *William Golding: The Dark Fields of Discovery* by Virginia Tiger, London, Calder and Boyars, and Atlantic Highlands, New Jersey, Humanities Press, 1974; *William Golding* by Stephen Medcalf, London, Longman, 1975; *William Golding: Some Critical Considerations* edited by Jack I. Biles and Robert O. Evans, Lexington, University Press of Kentucky, 1978; *Of Earth and Darkness: The Novels of William Golding* by Arnold Johnston, Columbia, University of Missouri Press, 1980; *A View from the Spire: William Golding's Later Novels* by Don Crompton, Oxford, Blackwell, 1985; *William Golding: The Man and His Books: A Tribute on His 75th Birthday* edited by John Carey, London, Faber, 1986, New York, Farrar Straus, 1987; *William Golding: A Structural Reading of His Fiction* by Philip Redpath, London, Vision Press, 1986; *The Novels of William Golding* by Stephen Boyd,

Brighton, Sussex, Harvester Press, and New York, St Martin's Press, 1988; *William Golding* by James Gindin, London, Macmillan, and New York, St Martin's Press, 1988; *William Golding Revisited: A Collection of Original Essays*, edited by B.L. Chakoo. Bangalore, Arnold, 1989; *The Modern Allegories of William Golding* by L.L. Dickson, Tampa, University of South Florida Press, 1990; *William Golding's Use of Symbolism* by Nicola C. Dicken-Fuller, Lewes, Book Guild, 1990.

*   *   *

William Golding's fiction embraces a time-span that ranges from the world of Neanderthal man (*The Inheritors*) to more contemporary times (*The Paper Men*), and includes three novels (*Free Fall, The Pyramid*, and *Darkness Visible*) which are specifically concerned with the periods immediately before and after World War II. However, whatever the period in which they are set, all his novels are explorations of certain basic Christian themes, in particular the Fall of Man, the vain quest to recover lost innocence, and the possibilities of supernatural redemption. Allied to these is a repeated insistence on the limitations of human knowledge, which expresses itself in a literary technique designed to keep the reader guessing. The novels are, to a greater or lesser extent, puzzles that seem to call for a solution; but in each case the puzzle turns out to be a mystery in which the 'solution' only serves to open up new perspectives upon the experiences described. Golding was not concerned simply with the world of time and, either in their wholes or in their parts, his novels contain moments which enshrine a vision of an eternal, transcendent order of being.

To this extent, therefore, it is misleading to label any of Golding's fiction 'historical' as the term is generally understood. Even in those novels set in verifiable past times (*The Spire, Rites of Passage, Close Quarters, Fire Down Below*) it is not historical accuracy as such that was his main concern. Nevertheless, these four novels do exhibit an intuitive understanding of past ways of life. *Rites of Passage, Close Quarters*, and *Fire Down Below* constitute Golding's 'Sea Trilogy' *To the Ends of the Earth*; *The Spire*, however, a work of great humanity and verve, exists as a satisfying entity on its own. The Sea trilogy, an account of a voyage to the Antipodes in an early-19th century sailing vessel, is heavily laced with contemporary nautical terms and is transmitted through the journal of an ambitious, self-sufficient young man of the period, whose thought processes and instinctive responses are convincingly of their time. The inner, hidden significance of the story, however, is conveyed to the reader in a characteristically indirect and elliptical manner, and is not an intrinsic aspect of the period the books describe.

In *The Spire* subject matter, theme, and style are more closely approximated. The novel is a thinly disguised account of the building of the 14th-century spire of Salisbury Cathedral, at 404 feet the highest in England. The action is seen through the eyes of Jocelyn, dean of the cathedral and originator of the spire, whose dreams and ambitions are bound up with its construction. As in all Golding's work, one has to be alert for clues as to what is actually going on, and to interpret the inner meaning of events: Jocelyn's own point of view is in question and not necessarily to be trusted. But the enigmatic nature of the story does not prevent Golding from giving a brilliant account of the spire's construction, a gripping descriptive feat that shows an understanding of the mechanical problems involved and a knowledge of mediaeval building methods. The erection of the spire is both convincingly authentic at the material level and also symbolically appropriate, for its rise coincides with the physical and nervous breakdown of its instigator, Jocelyn, as his motives in insisting on its completion are sifted and variously assessed.

The book provides a graphic picture not only of the workings of the cathedral clergy but also of the lives and superstitious beliefs of the semi-pagan workmen who actually build the spire. The historical details are recorded unobtrusively as things which Jocelyn himself sees and takes for granted; one is not so much being shown past time by an instructive author as being imaginatively transported into it. Golding demonstrated in this book how the supernaturalizing of natural events was a characteristic process of the mediaeval mind, and, as in *The Inheritors*, he was thus able to comment on the assumptions of his own age from the point of view of another one. Indeed, *The Spire* is as much fable as a piece of realistic historical fiction; but this in no way detracts from its impression of historical accuracy.

In *The Inheritors*, and in the novella 'The Scorpion God' (a remarkable evocation of an Egyptian community 3000 years ago) Golding relied still more on imaginative intuition; he referred engagingly to this faculty in 'Digging for Pictures', an essay on his archaeological interests which he reprinted in the collection *The Hot Gates. The Inheritors* is certainly a *tour de force* in its presentation of the pre-rational mind, and calls for the kind of attentive reading that not everyone finds it easy to give. It is a historical novel by implication, attempting to capture the innocence of a community whose endowments and experience preclude any sense of history in a rational sense. Another tale to throw an ironic light upon notions of historical progress is the relatively light-hearted 'Envoy Extraordinary'. Easily the most amusing of Golding's stories, this was adapted to make his only publicly performed play, *The Brass Butterfly*. The story tells of the premature invention of printing, steam navigation, and explosives in a Roman world unwilling to adopt them, the only thing that interests the world-weary Emperor being a pressure-cooker. The tale appears in *The Scorpion God* collection, as does 'Cronk Cronk', an almost mimetic description of a prehistoric African tribe.

Golding's interest in anthropology gives a clue to the nature of his historical concerns, and in this respect he was a writer who extended the boundaries of the historical novel and helped to incorporate it into the mainstream of 20th-century English fiction.

—Glen Cavaliero

GOODWIN, Suzanne.

Pseudonyms: Suzanne Ebel; Cecily Shelbourne. **Nationality:** British. **Born:** London. **Education:** Roman Catholic schools in England and Belgium. **Marriages:** John Goodwin in 1948. One daughter and two sons. **Career:** journalist, *The Times*, London; public relations director, Young and Rubicam, advertising agency, London, 1950–72. **Recipient:** Romantic Novelists Association major award, 1964; British Travel Association award, 1986. **Agent:** Curtis Brown, 162–168 Regent Street, London W1R 5TB, England. **Address:** 52-A Digby Mansions, Hammersmith Bridge Road, London W6 9DF, England.

ROMANCE AND HISTORICAL PUBLICATIONS

Novels

The Winter Spring. London, Bodley Head, 1978; as *Stage of Love* (as Cecily Shelbourne), New York, Putnam, 1978.
The Winter Sisters. London, Bodley Head, 1980.
Emerald. London, Magnum, 1980.
Floodtide. London, Severn House, and New York, St Martin's Press, 1983.
Sisters. London, Severn House, 1984; New York, St Martin's Press, 1985.
Cousins. New York, St Martin's Press, 1985; London, Severn House, 1986.

Daughters. New York, St Martin's Press, and London, Joseph, 1987.

Lovers. London, Joseph, 1988.

To Love a Hero. London, Joseph, 1989.

A Change of Season. London, Joseph, 1991.

The Rising Storm. London, Macdonald, 1992.

While the Music Lasts. London, Little Brown, 1992.

Novels as Suzanne Ebel (series: Sir Robert Waring)

Love, The Magician. London, Muller, 1956.

Journey from Yesterday. London, Collins, 1963.

The Half-Enchanted. London, Collins, 1964.

The Love Campaign. London, Collins, 1965.

The Dangerous Winter. London, Collins, 1965.

A Perfect Stranger. London, Collins, 1966.

A Name in Lights (Waring). London, Collins, 1968; New York, Fawcett, 1975.

A Most Auspicious Star (Waring). London, Collins, 1968.

Somersault. London, Collins, 1971.

Portrait of Jill. London, Collins, 1972.

Dear Kate. London, Collins, 1972; New York, Fawcett, 1974.

To Seek a Star. London, Collins, 1973; New York, Fawcett, 1975.

The Family Feeling. London, Collins, 1973; New York, Fawcett, 1975.

Girl by the Sea. London, Collins, 1974; New York, Fawcett, 1976.

Music in Winter. London, Collins, 1975.

A Grove of Olives. London, Collins, 1976.

River Voices. London, Collins, 1976.

The Double Rainbow. London, Collins, 1977.

A Rose in Heather. London, Collins, 1978.

Provencal Summer. London, Ulverscroft, 1980

Julia's Sister. London, Severn House, 1982.

The House of Nightingales. London, Severn House, 1985.

The Clover Field. London, Severn House, 1987.

Reflections in a Lake. Bath, Firecrest, 1988.

OTHER PUBLICATIONS

Play

Radio Play: *Chords and Discords*, 1975.

Other

Explore the Cotswolds by Bicycle, with Doreen Impey. London, Ward Lock, 1973.

London's Riverside, from Hampton Court in the West to Greenwich Palace in the East, with Doreen Impey. London, Luscombe, 1975; New York, Ballantine, 1976; revised edition, as *A Guide to London's Riverside: Hampton Court to Greenwich*, London, Constable, 1985.

Godfrey: A Special Time Remembered (on Godfrey Seymour Tearle), with Jill Bennett. London, Hodder and Stoughton, 1983.

*   *   *

Suzanne Goodwin's romances, which sometimes have a historic coloration, have capable, talented heroines who are determined to make their way in the world. Covering different, comparatively recent periods of English history, they are strongly concerned with the sexual nature of love, and with various highly coloured events in the lives of the heroine. The nobility described are usually haughty and snobbish, but women of humble birth can use their inborn abilities to rise above the contempt of those better born.

Goodwin's sensuous *Cousins*, set in the period just before World War II, is perhaps most convincing in its evocation of place, time lost, experience altered. Elizabeth, one of her youngest and most naive heroines, is the penniless cousin of the heir to a Devonshire estate. Elizabeth and her cousin, Peter, have grown up together there and she loves Peter only slightly less than she cares for the estate. However, beautiful Sylvia steals Peter's heart, and as Sylvia's selfish ways take over the estate as well, Elizabeth marries *nouveauriche* Ted. A short affair with Peter gives Elizabeth a taste of the sexual pleasure she's never had with Ted. When Peter is killed in an accident, Sylvia takes Ted away from Elizabeth as well—but Elizabeth is not a Bidwell for nothing. With the aid of Sylvia's mysterious godfather, Elizabeth takes over the running of the estate. In the stormy days before the war starts, she finds a new love and a new future. The description of the Devon countryside and the interplay of characters make this one of Goodwin's most successful novels.

Only slightly later in the period, *Sisters*, covers the romantic adventures of three daughters of a London physician during the Blitz, and up until the end of World War II. The eldest, Elaine, marries, loses her baby, and is widowed. The only one to do substantial war work, she is the sensible one, and glue for the rest of the family. Even her grief is ignored or underrated as her sisters' more dramatic lives take centre stage. Philippa rejects her American sweetheart when she finds that he has slept with her youngest sister, then forgives him and marries him. She follows him from base to base as he and the other American volunteers fight in the skies, and sustains their marriage through his injury and recuperation. Trix, the youngest, lives for and by men. Her marriage and divorce leave the way clear for her ex-husband to marry Elaine. Trix goes off to America with yet another man. Her sisters admit that they do not expect the marriage to last, or Trix to return to England. They decide England is no place for Trix. These amours are played out against an essentially suburban London setting and their father's gradual involvement with a French refugee. However, the major issues of the day, and the war, aren't discussed.

Daughters, presents two half-sisters, Catherine and Sara, competing for the love of their father and then for their share of his international art auction house. Catherine, an aristocrat, feels her background and legitimacy should give her an advantage, but it is feisty, half-American Sara who learns the business and whom we are meant to admire. Sara is also the character in whom Goodwin's theory of sexual obsession is most clearly realized. Sara makes love with a mysterious stranger in the closing days of World War I. When she meets him again as her father's banker, she is in his sexual thrall and resumes their relationship even when she finds that her best friend is in love with him. His sudden last minute realization that he must break through his war-imposed restraints and love her emotionally as well as physically is never convincing. Another interesting point is that Goodwin characterizes their father as half French and half Jewish, but Catherine is referred to as English and Sara as American, the nationalities of their mothers.

Set partly in the artistic milieu of the Left Bank in Paris during the closing days of the 19th-century, *Lovers* presents another career-woman heroine, Nelly Briggs, who climbs from abject poverty—her best job is as a maid in a brothel—and through a series of reversals of fate, becomes an acclaimed actress. After many tribulations, she receives a proposal from Matthew, whose illegitimate child she bore many years ago in Paris. Nelly also exposes the pretender to her lover's estate. In a novel that features strong women characters, one of the more interesting is Matthew's American wife, an heiress who—with the support of her lover and her sister—is able to get an annulment of their Catholic marriage, leaving the way clear for Matthew and Nelly to marry.

In much the same time period and a similar setting, *Floodtide* follows Stella from her life on a Boer farm through her insistence on marrying the British Officer whose life she saved and who has made her pregnant. However, Stella is not at home with the British nobility, and her in-laws do not make her welcome. After her husband's untimely death, she flees to London with her young child and becomes a singing star. Her affair with her brother-in-law and her efforts to help her sister-in-law break away from her oppressive mother further estrange her from the family. Eventually, her son learns of his heritage. Alone, she turns to her other long-term lover, the American Theo, who has always helped her with her career and whose wife has just conveniently died. This is perhaps the only novel in which Goodwin's protagonist clearly chooses something other than sexual passion, however hopeless, and looks for a future of contentment, not ecstasy.

Set in a post World War II period, the more ambitious *A Change of Season*, follows the fortunes of an orphaned brother and sister, virtually penniless after the rigours of the war, who return to England from the Far East. Charles, the brother, is a ladies' man and gambler; he elopes with a young heiress and is cast off by her father. He leaves her in turn for fateful, beautiful actress Gemma, who is married to Tom, the lover of Charles' sister Lisa years ago in India. Lisa has always loved Tom, and is ready to marry him, but he is afraid Gemma will try to keep the custody of her son. The background of this is Stratford, and the Stratford Repertory Theatre features prominently, but it also includes a portrayal of genteel poverty as the siblings try to live on Lisa's scant earnings as a sales assistant in an antique store, until a friend discovers unexpected value in one of their father's seemingly futile investments. Charles is sexually obsessed with Gemma, who comes to an untimely end when she dies in a skiing accident. Of course, this frees Tom to marry Lisa and lets Charles return to his pregnant wife.

These novels feature some strong characters, but the plot lines are extravagant, and full of improbabilities. The intrinsically interesting topics of travel, money, jewellery, and sex rather than convincing plot provide the impetus that leads readers to seek out and read these books. While Goodwin's style is more than adequate for the descriptions that she delights in, her work remains within distinct limits beyond which she does not choose to venture.

—Susan Branch

GORDON, Deborah.   See **HASTINGS, Brooke.**

GORDON, Diana.   See **ANDREWS, Lucilla.**

GORDON, Ethel Edison.
Nationality: American. **Born:** New York City, 5 May 1915. **Education:** Washington Square College, New York University, B.A. (cum laude) 1936 (Phi Beta Kappa). **Relations:** married Herman Gordon in 1936; one son. **Agent:** John Schaffner Associates, 264 Fifth Avenue, New York, New York 10001, USA. **Address:** c/o Dell, 1540 Broadway, New York, New York 10036, USA.

ROMANCE AND HISTORICAL PUBLICATIONS

Novels

Freer's Cove. New York, Coward McCann, 1972.
The Chaperone. New York, Coward McCann, 1973; London, Barker, 1974.
The Birdwatcher. New York, McKay, 1974; London, Barker, 1975.

The Freebody Heiress. New York, McKay, and London, Barker, 1974.
The French Husband. New York, Crowell, 1977.
The Venetian Lover. New York, Dell, 1982.

OTHER PUBLICATIONS

Fiction (for children)

Where Does the Summer Go. New York, Crowell, 1967.
So Far From Home. New York, Crowell, 1968.

*

Ethel Edison Gordon comments:
I have always enjoyed using an interesting foreign locale—foreign to me in America, that is—as a background for my fiction. Usually an American girl finds herself in a suspenseful situation in an environment that is different from her own. She moves from one continent to the other, to unravel the romantic but hostile predicament. This gives me a chance to re-visit the places I've enjoyed through fiction—from the Shetland Isles to the mountains of France to the lagoons of Venice.

*   *   *

Ethel Edison Gordon's compact well-crafted suspense novels are agreeably easy to read. After writing two fiction works for young audiences, she wrote her first novel *Freer's Cove*. A pregnant protagonist attempts to resolve the mystery of the death of Ernest Freer's wife, thereby endangering her own life. In Gordon's subsequent novels, the well-designed plots lead her contemporary heroines to locales exotic to the United States. This is the world of intelligent, well-educated, young American women.

The Chaperone is written in the first person. Carrie Belding, a 28-year-old art tutor at Burns Junior College for Women in Lower Manhatten , gets a fateful letter on 'handsome vellum' from her employer. She is entreated to use the subtle judgement of a 'mature sensitive woman' to determine if Egan, the suitor of Miss Burns's ward (Maria Waldron) would marry her if she were penniless. The contemporary American setting—the tutor is reminded of watching *Perry Mason* on television as a girl—is replaced by an isolated country inn perched high in the mountains in the South of France.

Upon arrival at the neglected inn, La Ferme, there is an immediate sense of threat—a car hurriedly leaving, mud on Egan's slippers, and an ominous conversation with Conor, Egan's attractive brother. The housekeeper, the difficult Mademoiselle Sophie, a reminder of the family's former wealth and standing, refers to 'foul money'. When the Turkish visitors Armad and Anna Abdykian arrive, with Laure, Conor Macklyn's married lover, Carrie realizes that she has a more than platonic interest in Conor. Strange things begin to occur—movement in the passageways after people retire to bed; Maria's dresses are slashed, and a razor is embedded in her bath soap; and Mademoiselle Sophie becomes ill, while insisting that 'this hotel [is a] façade for their dirty business'. Surviving an attempt on her life, Carrie eventually delivers Maria back safely to New York.

America during the war in Vietnam is the backdrop to *The Birdwatcher*. The familiar worries of America are lost in this strained journey to the remote and exotic shores of the Shetlands. Written in the first person, this tense tale features Lisette, a 24-year-old, working in an office in mid-town Manhattan. She is working with information on 'smart bombs'—military secrets—when she gets news of her fiancé's death. Shocked and sickened, she leaves work but the confidential papers she has been working on disappear. The familiar landscape of Bloomingdale's and Queensboro bridge are replaced with the isolated Shetland Islands when Lisette receives a plea from her cousin Irene to visit her. She is accompanied on her journey by Jim Baird of Atico Oil, who knew Irene and her husband Eugene in the Middle East. Irene appears ill and unhappy, seeming to entertain a passion for a husband who no longer loves her. The austerity and isolation of their house, and the forbidding environment seem to generate a series of denials, accidents, and attacks. The events overtake Lisette's personal loss, and, cautiously she finds herself in love, amid betrayal and murder.

The Freebody Heiress refers to Iris Freebody, a reclusive heiress living on the family estate in East Vermont. Ian Sexton comes to teach at the college endowed by the Freebody estate. Searching for a place of his own, he comes across the gate-house of a Freebody Estate, and enquires if he may rent it. He meets Iris, who is engaged to Ralph, a Harvard law student. Iris is recovering from a nervous breakdown following the suicide of Robbie, the gatekeeper's son. Ian's arrival coincides with Iris's desire to move back into the wider world. He offers to tutor her privately and their friendship develops to the extent that she puts her pending marriage to Ralph on hold. The hesitant steps that Iris takes to gain some control and independence are threatened by some attempts on her life. Iris decides to distance herself from her past, and free of the burden of her identity, she has a chance to reflect on her life. She realizes that she fears the effect of her money upon the people who are attracted to her—that her fortune, like the power that it represents, corrupts those who come close to it.

Gordon portrays her characters clearly and sympathetically, placing them in convincing landscapes of dramatic action—both private and external—and delivers a characteristic quality narrative.

—Iris Wakulenko

GOUDGE, Elizabeth (de Beauchamp).
Nationality: British. **Born:** Wells, Somerset, 24 April 1900. **Education:** Grassendale School, Southbourne, Hampshire; Reading University School of Art. **Career:** teacher of design and applied art, Ely and Oxford, 1922–32. Vice-president, Romantic Novelists Association, 1966–84. **Recipient:** Library Association Carnegie medal, 1947, for *The Little White Horse*. Fellow, Royal Society of Literature, 1945. **Died:** 1 April 1984.

ROMANCE AND HISTORICAL PUBLICATIONS

Novels (series: Eliots of Damerosehay)

Island Magic. London, Duckworth, and New York, Coward McCann, 1934.
The Middle Window. London, Duckworth, 1935; New York, Coward McCann, 1939.
A City of Bells. London, Duckworth, and New York, Coward McCann, 1936.
Towers in the Mist. London, Duckworth, and New York, Coward McCann, 1938.
The Eliots of Damerosehay. London, Hodder and Stoughton, 1957.
    The Bird in the Tree. London, Duckworth, and New York, Coward McCann, 1940.
    The Herb of Grace. London, Hodder and Stoughton, 1948; as *Pilgrim's Inn*, New York, Coward McCann, 1948.
    The Heart of the Family. London, Hodder and Stoughton, and New York, Coward McCann, 1953.
The Castle on the Hill. London, Duckworth, and New York, Coward McCann, 1941.

Green Dolphin Country. London, Hodder and Stoughton, 1944; as *Green Dolphin Street*, New York, Coward McCann, 1944.
Gentian Hill. London, Hodder and Stoughton, and New York, Coward McCann, 1949.
The Rosemary Tree. London, Hodder and Stoughton, and New York, Coward McCann, 1956.
The White Witch. London, Hodder and Stoughton, and New York, Coward McCann, 1958.
The Dean's Watch. London, Hodder and Stoughton, and New York, Coward McCann, 1960.
The Scent of Water. London, Hodder and Stoughton, and New York, Coward McCann, 1963.
The Child from the Sea. London, Hodder and Stoughton, and New York, Coward McCann, 1970.

Short Stories

The Fairies' Baby and Other Stories. London, Foyle, 1919.
A Pedlar's Pack and Other Stories. London, Duckworth, and New York, Coward McCann, 1937.
The Golden Skylark and Other Stories. London, Duckworth, and New York, Coward McCann, 1941.
The Ikon on the Wall and Other Stories. London, Duckworth, 1943.
The Reward of Faith and Other Stories. London, Duckworth, 1950; New York, Coward McCann, 1951.
White Wings: Collected Short Stories. London, Duckworth, 1952.
The Lost Angel. London, Hodder and Stoughton, and New York, Coward McCann, 1971.

OTHER PUBLICATIONS

Fiction (for children)

Sister of the Angels: A Christmas Story. London, Duckworth, and New York, Coward McCann, 1939.
Smoky-House. London, Duckworth, and New York, Coward McCann, 1940.
The Well of the Star. New York, Coward McCann, 1941.
Henrietta's House. London, University of London Press-Hodder and Stoughton, 1942; as *The Blue Hills*, New York, Coward McCann, 1942.
The Little White Horse. London, University of London Press, 1946; New York, Coward McCann, 1947.
Make-Believe. London, Duckworth, 1949; Boston, Bentley, 1953.
The Valley of Song. London, University of London Press, 1951; New York, Coward McCann, 1952.
Linnets and Valerians. Leicester, Brockhampton Press, and New York, Coward McCann, 1964.
I Saw Three Ships. Leicester, Brockhampton Press, and New York, Coward McCann, 1969.

Plays

The Brontës of Haworth (produced London, 1932). Included in *Three Plays*, 1939.
Joy Will Come Back (produced London, 1937).
Suomi (produced London, 1938). Included in *Three Plays*, 1939.
Fanny Burney (produced Oldham, Lancashire, 1949). Included in *Three Plays*, 1939.
Three Plays: Suomi, The Brontës of Haworth, and Fanny Burney. London, Duckworth, 1939.

Poetry

Songs and Verses. London, Duckworth, 1947; New York, Coward McCann, 1948.

Other

The Elizabeth Goudge Reader, edited by Rose Dobbs. New York, Coward McCann, 1946; as *At the Sign of the Dolphin: An Elizabeth Goudge Anthology*, London, Hodder and Stoughton, 1947.
God So Loved the World: A Life of Christ (for children). London, Hodder and Stoughton, and New York, Coward McCann, 1951.
Saint Francis of Assisi. London, Duckworth, 1959; as *My God and My All: The Life of St Francis of Assisi*, New York, Coward McCann, 1959.
The Chapel of the Blessed Virgin Mary, Buckler's Hard, Beaulieu. Privately printed, 1966.
A Christmas Book (anthology). London, Hodder and Stoughton, and New York, Coward McCann, 1967.
The Ten Gifts (anthology), edited by Mary Baldwin. London, Hodder and Stoughton, and New York, Coward McCann, 1969.
The Joy of the Snow: An Autobiography. London, Hodder and Stoughton, and New York, Coward McCann, 1974.
Pattern of People: An Elizabeth Goudge Anthology, edited by Muriel Grainger. London, Hodder and Stoughton, 1978; New York, Coward McCann, 1979.

Editor, *A Book of Comfort: An Anthology*. London, Joseph, and New York, Coward McCann, 1964.
Editor, *A Diary of Prayer*. London, Hodder and Stoughton, and New York, Coward McCann, 1966.
Editor, *A Book of Peace: An Anthology*. London, Joseph, 1967; New York, Coward McCann, 1968.
Editor, *A Book of Faith*. London, Hodder and Stoughton, and New York, Coward McCann, 1976.

*

Film Adaptation: *Green Dolphin Street*, 1947.

*   *   *

More than 20 years since her last novel was published Elizabeth Goudge is in serious danger of being forgotten. For many decades her novels came out in paperback 'women's romance' editions, often with lurid irrelevant covers. Her children's books were always old-fashioned, and even *The Little White Horse*, (winner of the 1947 Carnegie medal) suffers from undeserved neglect—it is a superb story, mixing a fantasy conflict between good and evil in a Jane Austen world, peopled with the larger-than-life eccentrics of Dickens! The best-sellerdom and Hollywood fame of *Green Dolphin Country* (*Green Dolphin Street*) has long since passed.

Goudge has never been properly understood. It is time to reconsider what she achieved, to recognize the substance behind the enthusiasms of faithful fans. Many of her novels, when written, were set in earlier historical times: *Island Magic*, *Green Dolphin Country*, and *The Dean's Watch*, all set during the 19th century; *Towers in the Mist* concerns the early years of Elizabeth I; *The White Witch* is set during the English Civil War; *The Child from the Sea* is about Lucy Walter, the first love of Charles II and mother of the Duke of Monmouth; *Gentian Hill* is located in Devon in the time of Nelson; and *A City of Bells* is set at the beginning of the 20th century. Obviously these are 'historical' novels, however others dealing contemporaneously with the period of the 1930s to 1960s are now becoming 'historical', by default, simply because they were written in and about earlier times than now, near the turn of the millennium. Historical by intention, or not, they are all, also, 'romance' novels, concerned with affairs of the heart and the relationships between men and women, rather than with great deeds of exploration, upheavals of war, science fiction and speculative fantasy, murder and mystery, and other genres apart from 'romance'. Yet in Goudge's

case the label 'romance' is too restrictive, and has been at least partly responsible for her work having been misunderstood for so long.

Her first published novel, *Island Magic*, is based loosely on her maternal grandparents, her mother as a child, and their life on Guernsey. All the elements that are typical of Goudge's writing can be seen in this first story. Intense observation of landscape, emotions that soar and plunge, references to earlier writers, such as Shakespeare, Keats, Browning, and Hopkins, a narrative full of characters from a richly varied community, from domineering upper-class society, down to the bitterly exploited working class.

At the heart of *Island Magic* are the du Frocqs, a tempestuous, loving family, celebrating seasons and festivals with riotous, joyful energy. Typically for Goudge, the du Frocq children play a significant part in the larger concerns of the adults. For Goudge, adults and children alike share the same driving hungers, and are equally close to the book's central moral issues such as the paradox of freedom and obedience (that we are most truly free when we accept or choose constraints tantamount to imprisonment), or the paradox of good and evil (that a wicked creature may be able to discern the paths through heaven that are hidden from the good people inside), or the paradox of Christian faith sitting comfortably beside ancient pagan belief (as does the church-going Islanders' belief in the water fairies of their Island and their legend of their own fairy ancestors). Yet through the book they squabble, lie, and behave like typically boisterous, annoying, loving children, in much the same way the adults squabble and lie.

One of Goudge's later novels, *The Dean's Watch*, also exemplifies her view of life. Set during the 1870s in an unnamed English fen city, whose heart is a mediaeval cathedral, it tells what happens when an old clock-maker, Isaac Peabody, mistakenly places a printed motto in the antique pocket watch of the grim cathedral Dean, Adam Ayscough, and subsequently meets the dean. Isaac is a tradesman and an atheist, brutalized by the hell-fire faith of his father who had been a Church of England priest in one of the city's churches. He is terrified of the cathedral itself, and would never dare presume to speak with such an elevated member of the gentry as the dean. Yet, a man of profound faith and enormous compassion for the suffering poor, the dean himself is himself emotionally crippled by shyness. He is as lonely, and as isolated in his marriage to his unloving wife, as Isaac is in the household he shares with his embittered sister.

Many other characters are pulled into the events of a few months. Goudge also does not hesitate to throw in vigorous chapters of cathedral and town history, and many flashbacks and reminiscences of the earlier years of her characters. The book is packed with incident, character, and landscape, despite its immediate action being comparatively slight and covering a short span of present narrative time.

The creation of mechanically intricate and faithful watches and clocks, decorated lovingly with charming filigree, or Dresden figurines, or secret illuminated manuscripts, stands as a covert metaphor of the highest to which humans can aspire in the dark world that Goudge evokes. At the same time the ticking of a watch and its sheer mechanical longevity stand as an implicit reminder of the morality of its maker, who labours to make the watch despite foreknowledge of his own death. Even the title has several meanings: the actual heirloom watch, which triggers the story; the Dean's 'ticker' or heart, which physically beats uncertainly, yet passionately loves behind the shyness; the Dean's 'watch', as a navy term, in which he faithfully steers the ship of the city and cares for her people.

Goudge's ability to handle a more distant historical setting can be seen in *Towers in the Mist*, originally published for adults, but much later reissued as a Peacock paperback for 'young adults'. Indeed it is an anybody book. Set in Oxford during the early years of Queen Elizabeth I, in 16th-century England, during a peaceful interlude in the conflict between Catholic and Protestant that ripped 'Merrie' England apart, *Towers in the Mist* is a double love story.

Interestingly, like *Island Magic*, her only bestseller, *Green Dolphin Country*, is also based on an intriguing event in the lives of her Guernsey Island ancestors. Her maternal grandfather's brother found himself in trouble, and escaped to a kind of exile in the antipodes. When he began to prosper he wrote back to the island to propose to his childhood sweetheart. But, with a Goudgeian poor memory for names, in his letter he proposed to the older sister of the girl he loved. When she finally arrived to marry him he was agonized, but he never told her. What may seem far-fetched in this rich, romantic, novel actually happened, and knowing this makes the book all the more readable.

All of Goudge's novels are 'romances' in one important aspect: they hinge on moments of visionary insight for her characters, filled with that romantic longing for a strange beauty and joy. Dreams, glimpses of landscape, moments of weather, the sound of a voice or melody when no one else is present, sudden remembering of lost experience, or a poetry quote which stabs to the heart. These are frequently counterbalanced against moments of evil, terror, despair, emotional collapse, irrational rage or blinding hate. Most of her central characters are well educated and intellectually or emotionally gifted, although many are presented as frail, and absentminded. Yet not only are they bound up in everyday tasks, they are surrounded by salt-of-the-earth uneducated workers, heroic peasants, people of utter reliability and ancient Hardyesque virtue.

Goudge has been criticized for what might appear to be cosy over-sentimentality, and for writing about a world which is alleged to be unreal. But this fundamentally misunderstands her moral vision. Her novels, historical or modern, are always about two worlds—our own everyday world, as it once was, intensely realized, full of the brutal and tender facts of reality, as well as being about another world, of poetry, music, faith, or a child's vision. Her lasting achievement is to present these two worlds so that they are convincingly part of each other, two aspects of one larger, richer world that transforms and transcends what we take for granted as 'ordinary', limited, flawed, violent, painful, terrifying, awe-full, and beautiful. Her achievement is unique and to be treasured.

—John Gough

GOWER, Iris.

Pseudonym for Iris Davies. **Nationality:** British. **Born:** Swansea, West Glamorgan, Wales, 4 February 1939. **Education:** Swansea Technical College; Swansea College of Art. **Relations:** married W.T. Davies in 1957; two daughters and two sons. **Agent:** June Hall, 5th Floor, The Chambers, Chelsea Harbour, Lots Road, London SW10 0XF, England. **Address:** c/o Bantam, 61–63 Uxbridge Road, London W5 5SA, England.

ROMANCE AND HISTORICAL PUBLICATIONS

Novels (series: Sweyn's Eye)

Beloved Captive. London, Macdonald, 1981.
Beloved Traitor. London, Macdonald, 1981.
Copper Kingdom (Sweyn). London, Century, and New York, St Martin's Press, 1983.
Proud Mary (Sweyn). London, Century, 1984; New York, St Martin's Press, 1985.
Spinner's Wharf (Sweyn). London, Century, and New York, St Martin's Press, 1985.
The Loves of Catrin. London, Century 1986.
The Copper Cloud. London, Hale, 1976.
Return to Tip Row. London, Hale, 1977.
Morgan's Woman (Sweyn). London, Century, 1986.
Fiddler's Ferry (Sweyn). London, Century, 1987; New York, St Martin's Press, 1988.
Black Gold (Sweyn). London, Century, 1988.
Sins of Eden. London, Century, 1990.
The Shoemaker's Daughter. London, Bantam, 1991.
Honey's Farm. London, Bantam, 1993.

*   *   *

Because Iris Gower's series of novels set in Wales is narrowly focused both in time and place, they form a rich tapestry of stories that examine different aspects of society. The six books span approximately 15 years before, during, and after World War I. Although some of the characters travel to England, Europe, and the United States, Gower's focus remains on Sweyn's Eye (old Swansea).

In the first book of the series, *Copper Kingdom*, Gower introduces three women whose lives weave in and out of the pages of the subsequent novels. Mali Llewelyn, the daughter of a widowed copper worker, leads a meagre life in a cottage along Copperman's Row. Next door live Katie Murphy and her family, who run a fresh fish shop. Both Mali and Katie work at the Canal Street laundry, under the supervision of Mary Jenkins.

After her mother's death, Mali attracts the attention of Sterling Richardson, the young heir to the copper works. Their romance provides the main narrative line of *Copper Kingdom*, but, as in all the books in the series, numerous sub-plots contribute to the novel's complexity. Katie is used and abandoned by William Owen, a young copperman unworthy of the love she lavishes upon him. Sterling has an affair with Bea Cardigan, a woman from his own class, who turns out to be his half-sister. Sterling's unscrupulous younger brother Rickie plots against him to gain control of the family fortune. Rickie, Will Owen, and others rig an explosion they hope will devastate Sterling's fortunes and possibly kill him. However, Will dies in the attempt while Sterling survives and marries Mali.

Mali's and Sterling's marriage remains strong throughout the series despite the class differences that divided them at first. Mali never forgets her life of poverty and remains kind to her old friends. She works with unwed mothers in *Fiddler's Ferry* and serves nourishing meals at a soup kitchen during the coal strike in *Black Gold*. Although Mali has times of worry, as when Sterling is away at war in *Spinner's Wharf*, for the most part, her life and marriage contain undiminished joy. As Mary tells her in *Black Gold*, 'Yours is one marriage that has never faltered—not for you and Sterling doubts and infidelities'.

Mary's years are not as calm. *Proud Mary* concentrates on her rise as a successful businesswoman in the city, and her business acumen is apparent in other novels as well. Although she eventually amasses a fortune, wealth cannot buy her family happiness. The first years of her marriage to Brandon Sutton bring increasing unhappiness as she remains childless. When she hears that Brandon is missing in action and presumed dead shortly after leaving for war, she seeks comfort in the arms of Dr Paul Soames (*Spinner's Wharf*). Shortly thereafter, she discovers she is pregnant but cannot be certain of the child's father.

When Brandon returns, Mary confesses her infidelity. He leaves her and refuses to acknowledge the boy, even though Stephan resembles Brandon more and more as he grows up. A car accident with Mary at the wheel results in Stephan's blindness. Mary and Brandon reunite and travel to the United States, Brandon's home. After his lingering illness and death, Mary returns to Sweyn's Eye, where she marries Paul Soames, who still loves her (*Black Gold*).

Katie Murphy is less fortunate in love than either Mali or Mary. Will Owen's death in *Copper Kingdom* is followed by more tragedy. Her husband of a few months, Mark, drowns at sea as the pair return from France (*Morgan's Woman*). Katie miscarries as a result of that same accident. She rejects the love of Ceri Llewelyn, (Mali's cousin in *Fiddler's Ferry*), only to fall in love with a married man, Luke Proud, in *Black Gold*. Luke, who insists on keeping his coal mine operating, is stoned by strikers and dies in Katie's arms.

The last scene of *Black Gold* closely resembles that of *Copper Kingdom*. In each, an unmarried pregnant women rushes to a mine to learn her lover's fate. Mali finds Sterling and achieves a happy marriage; Katie receives yet another disappointment.

Friends and families of the three women inhabit the pages of all the books. Each volume examines one family in some detail while drawing strands from many other lives. For example, *Fiddler's Ferry* considers the family of Siona Llewelyn, Mali's uncle. In the course of the novel he meets and marries Nerys Beynon, who had cared for Stephan Sutton.

The book most removed from others in the series is *Morgan's Woman*, in part because it is set in the countryside, not the city. Although each book can stand alone, they are best read as a set. In fact, in the later volumes Gower sometimes gets bogged down in explaining the complex histories she has created. But she needs to provide such information for those unfamiliar with earlier books.

One of Gower's strengths is the lilting speech of her characters that gives even everyday conversations a pleasant rhythm. Another is her ability to incorporate history into a story without turning a novel into a textbook.

In contrast, her far-fetched romance *Beloved Captive* is filled with contrived situations and shopworn language. Among other tribulations, the heroine is shipwrecked, captured by a primitive Russian tribe, then rescued only to be drugged and forced to be the Tsar's mistress. Gower is on much firmer authorial ground when she writes of her native Wales.

—Kathy Piehl

GRAHAM, Heather.   See POZZESSERE, Heather Graham.

GRAHAM, Winston (Mawdsley).
Nationality: British. **Born:** Victoria Park, Manchester, Lancashire. **Relations:** married Jean Mary Williamson in 1939; one son and one daughter. **Career:** chair, Society of Authors, London, 1967–69. **Recipient:** Crime Writers Association prize, 1956. Fellow, Royal Society of Literature, 1968. OBE (Officer, Order of the British Empire), 1983. **Agent:** A.M. Heath, 79 St Martin's Lane, London WC2N 4AA, England. **Address:** Abbotswood House, Buxted, East Sussex, England.

ROMANCE AND HISTORICAL PUBLICATIONS

Novels (series: Ross Poldark in all Cornwall novels)

The Forgotten Story. London, Ward Lock, 1945; as *The Wreck of the Grey Cat*, New York, Doubleday, 1958.
Ross Poldark: A Novel of Cornwall 1783–1787. London, Ward Lock, 1945; as *The Renegade*, New York, Doubleday, 1951.
Demelza: A Novel of Cornwall 1788–1790. London, Ward Lock, 1946; New York, Doubleday, 1953.
Cordelia. London, Ward Lock, 1949; New York, Doubleday, 1950.
Jeremy Poldark: A Novel of Cornwall 1790–1791. London, Ward Lock, 1950; as *Venture Once More*, New York, Doubleday, 1954.

Warleggan: A Novel of Cornwall 1792–1793. London, Ward Lock, 1953; as *The Last Gamble*, New York, Doubleday, 1955.
The Grove of Eagles. London, Hodder and Stoughton, 1963; New York, Doubleday, 1964.
The Black Moon: A Novel of Cornwall 1794–1795. London, Collins, 1973; New York, Doubleday, 1974.
The Four Swans: A Novel of Cornwall 1795–1797. New York, Doubleday, 1977.
The Angry Tide: A Novel of Cornwall 1798–1799. London, Collins, 1977; New York, Doubleday, 1978.
The Stranger from the Sea: A Novel of Cornwall 1810–1811. London, Collins, 1981; New York, Doubleday, 1982.
The Miller's Dance: A Novel of Cornwall 1812–1813. London, Collins, 1982; New York, Doubleday, 1983.
The Loving Cup: A Novel of Cornwall 1813–1815. London, Collins, 1984; New York, Doubleday, 1985.
The Twisted Sword: A Novel of Cornwall 1815–1816. London, Chapmans, 1990; New York, Carroll and Graf, 1991.
Stephanie. London, Chapmans, 1992; New York, Carroll and Graf, 1993.

Short Stories

The Japanese Girl and Other Stories. London, Collins, 1971; New York, Doubleday, 1972.
The Cornish Farm. Bath, Chivers, 1982.

OTHER PUBLICATIONS

Novels

The House with the Stained-Glass Windows. London, Ward Lock, 1934.
Into the Fog. London, Ward Lock, 1935.
The Riddle of John Rowe. London, Ward Lock, 1935.
Without Motive. London, Ward Lock, 1936.
The Dangerous Pawn. London, Ward Lock, 1937.
The Giant's Chair. London, Ward Lock, 1938.
Strangers Meeting. London, Ward Lock, 1939.
Keys of Chance. London, Ward Lock, 1939.
No Exit: An Adventure. London, Ward Lock, 1940.
Night Journey. London, Ward Lock, 1941; New York, Doubleday, 1968.
My Turn Next. London, Ward Lock, 1942.
The Merciless Ladies. London, Ward Lock, 1944; revised edition, London, Bodley Head, 1979; New York, Doubleday, 1980.
Take My Life. London, Ward Lock, 1947; New York, Doubleday, 1967.
Night Without Stars. London, Hodder and Stoughton, and New York, Doubleday, 1950.
Fortune Is a Woman. London, Hodder and Stoughton, and New York, Doubleday, 1953.
The Little Walls. London, Hodder and Stoughton, and New York, Doubleday, 1955; abridged edition, as *Bridge to Vengeance*, New York, Spivak, 1957.
The Sleeping Partner. London, Hodder and Stoughton, and New York, Doubleday, 1956.
Greek Fire. London, Hodder and Stoughton, and New York, Doubleday, 1958.
The Tumbled House. London, Hodder and Stoughton, 1959; New York, Doubleday, 1960.
Marnie. London, Hodder and Stoughton, and New York, Doubleday, 1961.
After the Act. London, Hodder and Stoughton, 1965; New York, Doubleday, 1966.

The Walking Stick. London, Collins, and New York, Doubleday, 1967.
Angell, Pearl and Little God. London, Collins, and New York, Doubleday, 1970.
Woman in the Mirror. London, Bodley Head, and New York, Doubleday, 1975.
The Green Flash. London, Collins, 1986; New York, Random House, 1987.
Cameo. London, Collins, 1988.

Plays

Shadow Play (produced Salisbury, 1978).
Circumstantial Evidence (produced Guildford, Surrey, 1979).

Screenplays: *Take My Life*, with Valerie Taylor and Margaret Kennedy, 1948; *Night Without Stars*, 1951.

Television Play: *Sleeping Partner*, 1967.

Other

The Spanish Armadas. London, Collins, and New York, Doubleday, 1972.
Poldark's Cornwall, photographs by Simon McBride. London, Bodley Head, 1983.

*

Film Adaptations: *Take My Life*, 1947; *Night Without Stars*, 1951; *Fortune Is a Woman*, 1956; *The Sleeping Partner*, 1961; *Marnie*, 1964; *The Walking Stick*, 1970.

*   *   *

Winston Graham brings to the history and romance genres a versatility and variety that breaks formulas, that mixes history, romance, adventure, politics, murder, and intrigue, and that explores the deeply-rooted motives and deeds of the past that have produced the conflicts, doubts, hesitations, and peculiarities of the present. Graham enjoys exposing seething passions beneath cold exteriors. Critics praise Graham's works for their 'tense, dramatic realism', 'their crisp narrative style', their 'understatement which . . . gives . . . sensitivity and depth'. It is his good solid writing, interesting characterization, clever and sensitive psychoanalysis, and vivid images of Cornish life that have won the most praise.

Graham has made the coast of Cornwall, with its cliffs and caves, sea, and sky, his hallmark. In fact, Poldark's Cornwall gives a good sense of Graham's literary territory. Though he never includes travelogues or lengthy descriptions for their own sake, Graham has an eye for those particulars that bring a scene to life. His method is to focus on quality of detail, with setting illuminating character and conflict. Memorable are scenes of drudgery and terrors of 18th-century life, the conspiracies and illegal trafficking, the wary fellowship of local taverns where a wrong word breeds ill-will but the right gesture can elicit acceptance, and camaraderie. *The Forgotten Story* captures the dangers of the Cornish coast as it tells of a shipwreck, a rescue attempt, and an old love rekindled, while the 'Poldark' series in particular focuses on the people of Cornwall, their struggles against an unforgiving land, their economic troubles, their social conflicts, their patriotism, treachery, loves, and lies.

The 'Poldark' series (1783–1816) (starring Robin Ellis in the BBC production) reflects the concern with social, economic, and political relationships that lies behind all Graham's works. It traces the adventures of Captain Ross Poldark, a man who 'lives on a knife edge', as he returns to his rundown estate in Cornwall at the end of the American Revolution, finds his beloved engaged to his cousin, and, making the best of it, plunges wholeheartedly into restoring his estate, and championing the cause of the lower classes of the area. It is a story of secret love, warring families, and social conflicts. Captain Ross Poldark partakes of the dour strength of his land; he plays a lone hand and does not suffer fools. One act, misunderstood by all, involves transforming Demelza, the mistreated daughter of a miner, from scullerymaid to lady of the manor in a pattern perhaps more Victorian than 18th century. Demelza embodies the strength of Cornwall: its tenacious hold on life despite the bitter struggles ordained by nature. The novel *Demelza* continues the story begun in *Ross Poldark* as the Poldarks struggle to cope with social disdain, class consciousness, and the ever-present economic conflicts of the grim Cornish coast as it shares in the trouble and tensions of the French Revolution. A New York Times reviewer rightly praised its 'realistic and sombre descriptions of Cornish farmers, fishermen, and miners pushed to the verge of revolution by unjust laws' and in particular the scene of 'an illegal raid on a prison in which innocent and guilty are left to die of disease and starvation, and another of the looting of two wrecked ships by the starving population'. *Jeremy Poldark* finds Poldark preparing for the birth of his son, dealing with an attempted take-over of the local copper mines, and facing charges of instigating locals to plunder and riot. *Warleggan*, in turn, manages four plots, bound together by rich images of seacoast life and characters, as Poldark flees revenue agents and deals with possible bankruptcy and marital strife. *The Black Moon* and *The Four Swans* continue the saga, with old relationships and old feuds motivating present behaviour and present passions. The past impinges on the present as the smoldering rivalry between Poldark and Warleggan is passed on to their children in *The Stranger from the Sea*, a story centred on the relationship between young Jeremy, his sister, Clowance, and a stranger rescued from a shipwreck. Hatred begets hatred, and rivalry works itself out in fiery competitions for land, power, and love.

The Miller's Dance, *The Loving Cup*, and *The Twisted Sword* continue the saga with a new generation of Poldarks and Warleggans who must deal as their parents did with the effects of money and social position on love and with an emerging new social order, the changing morality of their age, and the growing turbulence of the Industrial Revolution. As the Napoleonic wars wind down, Ross Poldark serves in the House of Commons to bring progress without revolution, and to offset the greed and the insensitivity of his colleagues. He ends up with a title for his troubles. Poldark's cousin brings back a Spanish bride; his daughter Clowance becomes entangled in a troubled romance with Stephen Carrington, the shipwrecked stranger of *The Stranger from the Sea*, a man with neither position nor wealth, whose behaviour both attracts Clowance and gives her pause; and his son Jeremy proves he has his father's penchant for trouble, outlawry, romance—and reform. The final book in the series, *The Twisted Sword*, follows Ross and Demelza to Paris, records Napoleon's triumphant return to France, and Jeremy's discovery on the battlefield of Waterloo that he shares his father's heroic mettle as a leader of men in crisis. Demelza's secret knowledge of Jeremy's youthful misdeeds adds tension to the final exposition as do the marital conflicts and tragedies of the younger generation.

The 'Poldark' series are almost novels of manners as they trace family and relationships through a period of social change, and provide insights into the expectations and social behaviour of the period. They graphically capture the horrors of poverty and war, and the effects of major historical events on the private lives of individuals. Poldark is, as Richard Match describes him, 'a kind of Heathcliffian Mr Rochester'. The story of his life and loves, his fiery defiance of convention, and his sympathy for the working classes is one of growth and transformation but also of recurring patterns and rivalries that endure into the second and third generation.

Graham's other historical works include *The Grove of Eagles*, a fictionalized history of the Elizabethan years, packed with local lore and the minutiae of daily life, but all from a safe perspective of an outsider, and *The Spanish Armadas*, popular historiography focused on the Elizabethan war with Spain, particularly Grenville's fight with a flota, the Lisbon and Cadiz raids, and the five true armadas. The first novel is told from the point of view of a Cornish man, Maugham Killigrew, who survived the Spanish Inquisition, fought with Raleigh at the capture of Cadiz, and the defeat of the second Armada, and was tried before the Queen's Privy Council. The second covers some of the same territory in a more scholarly way, but avoiding technicalities to focus on a fluent narrative and a clear record.

Graham's romances, though not purely so, are interesting psychological studies, sensitive portraits of the restraints and compulsions, the tensions and metamorphoses of personal and sexual relationships. *The Walking Stick* makes credible a young polio victim's transformation from wallflower to dancer, skater, and robber through skilfully interweaving her past and present experiences with life and love. In turn, the seemingly cold, unreachable Marnie, in the novel of the same title, must discover and face the secret fears of her childhood if she is ever to cope normally with life and love. In *The Green Flash*, lover and con man David Abden must do the same; only the death by misadventure (a fencing accident) of an unloved wife forces him to face his part in the untimely death of his drunken father and allows him to come to terms with his self-destruction and self-punishment, his Scottish ancestry, and his love for a vibrant Russian emigré 33 years his senior, the founder of an exclusive line of perfume and the only true love of his life. *Stephanie* begins as a torrid romance set in Goa, India, but turns into a mystery when the youthful and lively heroine chooses moral right over love, and her lame father, a war hero turned nemesis, unrelentingly ferrets out and damns the lover and drug dealers who feared her. Throughout his canon Graham explores the way experience transforms and shapes a person and the way individuals act as catalysts moulding and changing human relationships. His characters and their relationships take on a compelling life of their own, a mixture of good and bad that rings psychologically true.

In sum, Graham's novels derive their success in part from the psychological, from class conflict, and from the deep-seated spirit of rebellion they portray—rebellion against demeaning social conditions, unjust rulers, the demands of convention, and fickle fate. They derive it in part too from a strong sense of place and atmosphere, but most of all from the moral dilemmas, the images of men and women caught up in circumstances beyond their control, not knowing how to act nor to whom to turn, acting impetuously according to the moment and finding themselves thereby trapped in patterns that separate them further and further from what they want most. At their best his characters discover that they must look within, find their hidden reservoirs of strength, and face their deepest fears about themselves, and their relationships before they can turn outward and deal with the ever more pressing problems around them. Graham provides poignant images of failures of humanity, indifference to others, betrayals of trust or of need, obsessions with the past, with the land, with social position, with one's heritage, set against images of love and passion and human obligation.

—Gina Macdonald

GRANGE, Peter.   See NICOLE, Christopher.

GRANT, Joan. British. 1907—. See 2nd edition, 1990.

GRANT, Margaret.   See FRANKEN, Rose.

GRAVEL, Fern.   See NORDHOFF, Charles, and HALL, James Norman.

GRAVES, Robert (von Ranke).
Pseudonyms: John Doyle; Barbara Rich, with Laura Riding. **Nationality:** British. **Born:** Wimbledon, London, 24 July 1895. **Education:** King's College School and Rokeby School, Wimbledon; Copthorne School, Sussex; Charterhouse School, Surrey, 1907–14; St John's College, Oxford (exhibitioner; editor, the *Owl*, from 1919, and *Winter Owl*, 1923), 1919–25, B.Litt. 1925. **Military Service:** Royal Welch Fusiliers, 1914–19: captain; was refused admittance into the armed forces in World War II. **Relations:** married 1) Nancy Nicholson in 1918 (divorced 1949), two daughters and two sons; 2) Beryl Pritchard in 1950 (lived with her from 1939), three sons and one daughter. **Career:** professor of English, Egyptian University, Cairo, 1926; with Laura Riding established the Seizin Press, 1928, and *Epilogue* magazine, 1935; lived in Deyá, Mallorca, 1929–36, the USA, 1936, England, 1937–46, and Deyá after 1946. Clark lecturer, Trinity College, Cambridge, 1954–55; professor of poetry, Oxford University, 1961–66; Arthur Dehon Little memorial lecturer, Massachusetts Institute of Technology, Cambridge, 1963. **Recipient:** bronze medal for poetry, Olympic Games, Paris, 1924; Hawthornden prize, for fiction, 1935; James Tait Black memorial prize, for fiction, 1935; Femina Vie Heureuse prize, for fiction, 1939; Loines award, for poetry, 1958; National Poetry Society of America gold medal, 1960; Foyle poetry prize, 1960; Arts Council award, 1962; Italia prize, for radio play, 1965; gold medal for poetry, Cultural Olympics, Mexico City, 1968; Queen's gold medal for poetry, 1969. M.A.: Oxford University, 1961. Honorary member, American Academy of Arts and Sciences, 1970; Honorary Fellow, St John's College, 1971. **Died:** 7 December 1985.

ROMANCE AND HISTORICAL PUBLICATIONS

Novels (series: Claudius; Sergeant Lamb)

My Head! My Head!. London, Secker, and New York, Knopf, 1925.
The Real David Copperfield. London, Barker, 1933; as *David Copperfield by Charles Dickens, Condensed by Robert Graves*, edited by Merrill P. Paine, New York, Harcourt Brace, 1934.
I, Claudius . . . . London, Barker, and New York, Smith and Haas, 1934.
Claudius the God and His Wife Messalina . . . . London, Barker, 1934; New York, Smith and Haas, 1935.
Count Belisarius. London, Cassell, and New York, Random House, 1938.
Sergeant Lamb of the Ninth. London, Methuen, 1940; as *Sergeant Lamb's America*, New York, Random House, 1940.
Proceed, Sergeant Lamb. London, Methuen, and New York, Random House, 1941.
The Story of Marie Powell: Wife to Mr Milton. London, Cassell, 1943; as *Wife to Mr Milton*, New York, Creative Age Press, 1944.
The Golden Fleece. London, Cassell, 1944; as *Hercules, My Shipmate*, New York, Creative Age Press, 1945.
King Jesus. New York, Creative Age Press, and London, Cassell, 1946.
Watch the North Wind Rise. New York, Creative Age Press, 1949; as *Seven Days in New Crete*, London, Cassell, 1949.
The Islands of Unwisdom. New York, Doubleday, 1949; as *The Isles of Unwisdom*, London, Cassell, 1950.

Homer's Daughter. London, Cassell, and New York, Doubleday, 1955.

They Hanged My Saintly Billy. London, Cassell, and New York, Doubleday, 1957.

Short Stories

¡Catacrok! Mostly Stories, Mostly Funny. London, Cassell, 1956.

Collected Short Stories. New York, Doubleday, 1964; London, Cassell, 1965; as *The Shout and Other Stories*, London, Penguin, 1978.

OTHER PUBLICATIONS

Novel

Antigua, Penny, Puce. Deyá, Mallorca, Seizin Press, and London, Constable, 1936; as *The Antigua Stamp*, New York, Random House, 1937.

Short Story

The Shout. London, Mathews and Marrot, 1929.

Plays

John Kemp's Wager: A Ballad Opera. Oxford, Blackwell, and New York, Edwards, 1925.

Nausicaa (opera libretto), adaptation of his novel *Homer's Daughter*, music by Peggy Glanville-Hicks (produced Athens, 1961).

Television Documentary: *Greece: The Inner World*, 1964 (USA).

Poetry

Over the Brazier. London, Poetry Bookshop, 1916; New York, St Martin's Press, 1975.

Goliath and David. London, Chiswick Press, 1916.

Fairies and Fusiliers. London, Heinemann, 1917; New York, Knopf, 1918.

The Treasure Box. London, Chiswick Press, 1919.

Country Sentiment. London, Secker, and New York, Knopf, 1920.

The Pier-Glass. London, Secker, and New York, Knopf, 1921.

Whipperginny. London, Heinemann, and New York, Knopf, 1923.

The Feather Bed. Richmond, Surrey, Hogarth Press, 1923.

Mock Beggar Hall. London, Hogarth Press, 1924.

Welchman's Hose. London, The Fleuron, 1925.

(Poems). London, Benn, 1925.

The Marmosite's Miscellany (as John Doyle). London, Hogarth Press, 1925.

Poems (1914–1926). London, Heinemann, 1927; New York, Doubleday, 1929.

Poems (1914–1927). London, Heinemann, 1927.

Poems 1929. London, Seizin Press, 1929.

Ten Poems More. Paris, Hours Press, 1930.

Poems 1926–1930. London, Heinemann, 1931.

To Whom Else? Deyá, Mallorca, Seizin Press, 1931.

Poems 1930–1933. London, Barker, 1933.

Collected Poems. London, Cassell, and New York, Random House, 1938.

No More Ghosts: Selected Poems. London, Faber, 1940.

Work in Hand, with Alan Hodge and Norman Cameron. London, Hogarth Press, 1942.

(Poems). London, Eyre and Spottiswoode, 1943.

Poems 1938–1945. London, Cassell, 1945; New York, Creative Age Press, 1946.

Collected Poems (1914–1947). London, Cassell, 1948.

Poems and Satires 1951. London, Cassell, 1951.

Poems 1953. London, Cassell, 1953.

Collected Poems 1955. New York, Doubleday, 1955.

Poems Selected by Himself. London, Penguin, 1957; revised edition, 1961, 1966, 1972.

The Poems of Robert Graves. New York, Doubleday, 1958.

Collected Poems 1959. London, Cassell, 1959.

More Poems 1961. London, Cassell, 1961.

Collected Poems. New York, Doubleday, 1961.

New Poems 1962. London, Cassell, 1962; as *New Poems*, New York, Doubleday, 1963.

The More Deserving Cases: Eighteen Old Poems for Reconsideration. Marlborough, Wiltshire, Marlborough College Press, 1962.

Man Does, Woman Is 1964. London, Cassell, and New York, Doubleday, 1964.

Love Respelt. London, Cassell, 1965.

Collected Poems 1965. London, Cassell, 1965.

Seventeen Poems Missing from 'Love Respelt'. Privately printed, 1966.

Collected Poems 1966. New York, Doubleday, 1966.

Colophon to 'Love Respelt'. Privately printed, 1967.

(Poems), with D.H. Lawrence, edited by Leonard Clark. London, Longman, 1967.

Poems 1965–1968. London, Cassell, 1968; New York, Doubleday, 1969.

Poems About Love. London, Cassell, and New York, Doubleday, 1969.

Love Respelt Again. New York, Doubleday, 1969.

Beyond Giving. Privately printed, 1969.

Poems 1968–1970. London, Cassell, 1970.

Advice from a Mother. London, Poem-of-the-Month Club, 1970.

The Green-Sailed Vessel. Privately printed, 1971.

Corgi Modern Poets in Focus 3, with others, edited by Dannie Abse. London, Corgi, 1971.

Poems 1970–1972. London, Cassell, 1972; New York, Doubleday, 1973.

Deyá. London, Motif, 1973.

Timeless Meeting. London, Rota, 1973.

At the Gate. London, Rota, 1974.

Collected Poems 1975. London, Cassell, 1975; New York, Oxford University Press, 1988.

New Collected Poems. New York, Doubleday, 1977.

Eleven Songs. Deyá, Mallorca, Seizin Press, 1983.

Selected Poems, edited by Paul O'Prey. London, Penguin, 1986.

Poems About War. London, Cassell, 1988.

Love Poems, edited by Sue Bradbury. London, Folio, 1990.

Recordings: *Robert Graves Reading His Own Poems*, Argo and Listen, 1960; *Robert Graves Reading His Own Poetry and The White Goddess*, Caedmon; *The Rubaiyat of Omar Khayyam*, Spoken Arts.

Other

On English Poetry. New York, Knopf, and London, Heinemann, 1922.

The Meaning of Dreams. London, Cecil Palmer, 1924; New York, Greenberg, 1925.

Poetic Unreason and Other Studies. London, Cecil Palmer, 1925.

Contemporary Techniques of Poetry: A Political Analogy. London, Hogarth Press, 1925.

Another Future of Poetry. London, Hogarth Press, 1926.

Impenetrability; or, The Proper Habit of English. London, Hogarth Press, 1926.

The English Ballad: A Short Critical Survey. London, Benn, 1927; revised edition, as *English and Scottish Ballads*, London, Heinemann, and New York, Macmillan, 1957.

Lars Porsena; or, The Future of Swearing and Improper Language. London, Kegan Paul Trench Trubner, and New York, Dutton, 1927; revised edition, as *The Future of Swearing and Improper Language*, Kegan Paul Trench Trubner, 1936.

A Survey of Modernist Poetry, with Laura Riding. London, Heinemann, 1927; New York, Doubleday, 1928.

Lawrence and the Arabs. London, Cape, 1927; as *Lawrence and the Arabian Adventure*, New York, Doubleday, 1928.

A Pamphlet Against Anthologies, with Laura Riding. London, Cape, 1928; as *Against Anthologies*, New York, Doubleday, 1928.

Mrs Fisher; or, The Future of Humour. London, Kegan Paul Trench Trubner, 1928.

Goodbye to All That: An Autobiography. London, Cape, 1929; New York, Cape and Smith, 1930; revised edition, New York, Doubleday, and London, Cassell, 1957; London, Penguin, 1960.

But It Still Goes On: A Miscellany. London, Cape, and New York, Cape and Smith, 1930.

No Decency Left (as Barbara Rich, with Laura Riding). London, Cape, 1932.

T.E. Lawrence to His Biographer Robert Graves. New York, Doubleday, 1938; London, Faber, 1939.

The Long Week-end: A Social History of Great Britain 1918–1939, with Alan Hodge. London, Faber, 1940; New York, Macmillan, 1941.

The Reader over Your Shoulder: A Handbook for Writers of English Prose, with Alan Hodge. London, Cape, 1943; New York, Macmillan, 1944.

The White Goddess: A Historical Grammar of Poetic Myth. London, Faber, and New York, Creative Age Press, 1948; revised edition, Faber, 1952, 1966; New York, Knopf, 1958.

The Common Asphodel: Collected Essays on Poetry 1922–1949. London, Hamish Hamilton, 1949.

Occupation: Writer (includes the play *Horses*). New York, Creative Age Press, 1950; London, Cassell, 1951.

The Nazarene Gospel Restored, with Joshua Podro. London, Cassell, 1953; New York, Doubleday, 1954.

The Crowning Privilege: The Clark Lectures 1954–1955; Also Various Essays on Poetry and Sixteen New Poems. London, Cassell, 1955; as *The Crowning Privilege: Collected Essays on Poetry*, New York, Doubleday, 1956.

Adam's Rib and Other Anomalous Elements in the Hebrew Creation Myth: A New View. London, Trianon Press, 1955; New York, Yoseloff, 1958.

The Greek Myths. London, Penguin, 2 vols, 1955; Mount Kisco, New York, Moyer Bell, 1 vol, 1988.

Jesus in Rome: A Historical Conjecture, with Joshua Podro. London, Cassell, 1957.

5 Pens in Hand. New York, Doubleday, 1958.

Steps: Stories, Talks, Essays, Poems, Studies in History. London, Cassell, 1958.

Food for Centaurs: Stories, Talks, Critical Studies, Poems. New York, Doubleday, 1960.

The Penny Fiddle: Poems for Children. London, Cassell, 1960; New York, Doubleday, 1961.

Greek Gods and Heroes (for children). New York, Doubleday, 1960; as *Myths of Ancient Greece*, London, Cassell, 1961.

Selected Poetry and Prose, edited by James Reeves. London, Hutchinson, 1961.

The Siege and Fall of Troy (for children). London, Cassell, 1962; New York, Doubleday, 1963.

The Big Green Book (for children). New York, Crowell Collier, 1962; London, Penguin, 1978.

Oxford Addresses on Poetry. London, Cassell, and New York, Doubleday, 1962.

Nine Hundred Iron Chariots: The Twelfth Arthur Dehon Little Memorial Lecture. Cambridge, Massachusetts Institute of Technology, 1963.

The Hebrew Myths: The Book of Genesis, with Raphael Patai. New York, Doubleday, and London, Cassell, 1964.

Ann at Highwood Hall: Poems for Children. London, Cassell, 1964.

Majorca Observed. London, Cassell, and New York, Doubleday, 1965.

Mammon and the Black Goddess. London, Cassell, and New York, Doubleday, 1965.

Two Wise Children (for children). New York, Harlin Quist, 1966; London, W.H. Allen, 1967.

Poetic Craft and Principle. London, Cassell, 1967.

The Poor Boy Who Followed His Star (for children). London, Cassell, 1968; New York, Doubleday, 1969.

The Crane Bag and Other Disputed Subjects. London, Cassell, 1969.

On Poetry: Collected Talks and Essays. New York, Doubleday, 1969.

Poems: Abridged for Dolls and Princes (for children). London, Cassell, and New York, Doubleday, 1971.

Difficult Questions, Easy Answers. London, Cassell, 1972; New York, Doubleday, 1973.

An Ancient Castle (for children), edited by W.D. Thomas. London, Owen, 1980; New York, Kesend, 1981.

Selected Letters of Robert Graves, edited by Paul O'Prey:
1. *In Broken Images: 1914–1946.* London, Hutchinson, 1982; Mount Kisco, New York, Moyer Bell, 1988.
2. *Between Moon and Moon: 1946–1972.* London, Hutchinson, 1984.

Conversations with Robert Graves, edited by Frank Kersnowki. Jackson, University Press of Mississippi, 1989.

Dear Robert, Dear Spike: The Graves-Milligan Correspondence, edited by P. Scudamore. Stroud, Sutton, 1991.

Editor, with Alan Porter and Richard Hughes, *Oxford Poetry 1921.* Oxford, Blackwell, 1921.

Editor, *John Skelton (Laureate), 1460(?)–1529.* London, Benn, 1927.

Editor, *The Less Familiar Nursery Rhymes.* London, Benn, 1927.

Editor, *English and Scottish Ballads.* London, Macmillan, 1957.

Editor, *The Comedies of Terence.* New York, Doubleday, 1962; London, Cassell, 1963.

Translator, with Laura Riding, *Almost Forgotten Germany*, by Georg Schwarz. Deyá, Mallorca, Seizin Press, London, Constable, and New York, Random House, 1936.

Translator, *The Transformation of Lucius, Otherwise Known as The Golden Ass*, by Apuleius. London, Penguin, 1950; New York, Farrar Straus, 1951.

Translator, *The Cross and the Sword*, by Manuel de Jésus Galván. Bloomington, Indiana University Press, 1955; London, Gollancz, 1956.

Translator, *The Infant with the Globe*, by Pedro Antonio de Alarcón. London, Trianon Press, 1955; New York, Yoseloff, 1958.

Translator, *Winter in Majorca*, by George Sand. London, Cassell, 1956.

Translator, *Pharsalia: Dramatic Episodes of the Civil Wars*, by Lucan. London, Penguin, 1956.

Translator, *The Twelve Caesars*, by Suetonius. London, Penguin, 1957.

Translator, *The Anger of Achilles: Homer's Iliad.* New York, Doubleday, 1959; London, Cassell, 1960.

Translator, with Omar Ali-Shah, *Rubaiyat of Omar Khayyam*. London, Cassell, 1967; New York, Doubleday, 1968.

Translator, *The Song of Songs*. New York, Potter, and London, Collins, 1973.

*

Film Adaptation: *I, Claudius*, 1976,

Bibliography: *A Bibliography of the Works of Robert Graves* by Fred H. Higginson, London, Vane, 1966, revised edition, as *Robert Graves: A Bibliography*, by W. P. Williams, Winchester, St Paul's, and Charlottesville, University Press of Virginia, 1987; *Robert Graves: An Annotated Bibliography* by Hallman Bell Bryant, New York, Garland, 1986.

Manuscript Collections: Lockwood Memorial Library, State University of New York, Buffalo; University of Victoria, British Columbia; New York City Public Library; University of Texas Library, Austin.

Critical Studies (selection): *Robert Graves*, London, Longman, 1956, revised edition, 1965, 1970, and *Robert Graves: His Life and Work*, London, Hutchinson, 1982, New York, Holt Rinehart, 1983, both by Martin Seymour-Smith; *Robert Graves* by J. M. Cohen, Edinburgh, Oliver and Boyd, 1960, New York, Barnes and Noble, 1965; *Robert Graves* by George Stade, New York, Columbia University Press, 1967; *Robert Graves, Peace-Weaver* by James S. Mehoke, The Hague, Mouton, 1975; *Robert Graves* by Katherine Snipes, New York, Ungar, 1979; *Robert Graves* by Robert H. Canary, Boston, Twayne, 1980; *Robert Graves: The Assault Heroic 1895–1926* by Richard Perceval Graves, London, Weidenfeld and Nicolson, 1986.

*   *   *

Although Robert Graves denigrated his own historical fiction, saying that 'all I really care about is poetry', it is an ironic fact that his novels are now more widely read and acclaimed both by critics and the general public than are his many collections of poems. Graves was an accomplished, and invariably contentious, historian; the backgrounds of his novels are researched so exhaustively that, no matter how unlikely the incidents related, they are always plausible. When applying his research to fiction, he practised what he described as the 'analeptic method: the intuitive recovery of forgotten events by a deliberate suspension of time'. He immersed himself totally in his subject, becoming so deeply entranced at times that he imagined his protagonists to be physically present in the room with him. The result of this fusion of painstaking research and imaginative projection is a series of historical fiction in which the reader is engaged in the beliefs, thoughts, and realities of a previous time. No other historical writer this century has been as successful in bringing the past to a contemporary audience.

I, Claudius and *Claudius the God* combine as a diptych portrait of one of the most enigmatic figures in history. Claudius was an outsider in his own Imperial family, reckoned a fool and a coward by each successive ruler. The first book describes his tenuous survival through the reigns of Augustus, Tiberius, and Caligula, each more tyrannical, suspicious, and dangerous than his predecessor. It comes to a climax during the last days of Caligula's power, as the insane Emperor creates a nightmarish environment of terror and surreal cruelty. Claudius has survived, almost the sole member of the Augustan dynasty left alive, by becoming Caligula's court jester. As the novel ends, with a desperate assassination removing the monstrous Caligula, Claudius is declared Emperor almost by accident. The subsequent book relates his reign as Emperor, an honourable though pragmatic man in harsh and ambitious times. As his power

wanes even he succumbs to the Imperial disease and becomes a tyrant; masterfully, Graves has the reader come to perceive this though the narrative never makes this tyranny explicit.

As exciting as the story is in itself, as fascinating as the detail becomes in the developing narrative, the greatest achievement of these books is the portrayal of the protagonist and narrator, Claudius. It is he who is telling the tale, to be sealed in a lead casket and 'found again some nineteen hundred years hence'. His official autobiography, he tells us, has been made deliberately dull; this is 'myself writing as I feel ... a confidential history'. To this central premiss the books remain faithful, and the result is a narrative that remains as convincing as it is speculative. Claudius becomes the reader's confidant, describing the events of his amoral world with calm irony; only he can afford to do so, being a survivor of the political intrigue. In the second book he becomes triumphant, winning the last frontier conquest of the Empire of Britain. The latter half of *Claudius the God*, however, is much darker in tone, as he prepares his children for his inevitable demise. From the epic black farce of the first volume, and the first half of the second, develops a more sombre and tragic story. All through his reign he plans to restore the Republic; finally he abandons this ambition and accepts the inevitability of his own death, and with it the last hopes of republicanism.

Count Belisarius takes up the story of the Empire from its last days in the 6th century. Belisarius is the commander of the army of Emperor Justinian, who comes to hate his general for the heroic reputation he gains in his defence of the Empire. Although the story is provided with the customary amount of period detail and incident, it remains rather lacklustre in comparison to the Claudius novels, if only because these show a greater development in the central character. Here Belisarius, noble forerunner of the medieval knight, is flat; by contrast the literally Byzantine workings of the court politics are almost incomprehensible in their subtlety.

Following his explorations of Roman history, though pressed to write a novel based on the life of Nero, Graves ranged closer to home in search of subjects. Two adventure yarns relate the life of Sergeant Lamb during the American War of Independence: *Sergeant Lamb of the Ninth* and *Proceed, Sergeant Lamb*. The research into even these rather simple tales is thorough and detailed; but the novelistic imagination seems rarely to have been engaged. Only with *The Story of Marie Powell: Wife to Mr Milton* did Graves recapture the immediacy of his earlier novels. This is the story of a young countrywoman who, because of her father's debt, was made to marry John Milton. The exact details of the marriage, apart from its disastrous unsuitability, remain unknown today; but Graves reconstructs the life of Marie through her memoirs, presenting a less than flattering portrait of Milton. As their marriage falls apart, the country falls prey to Civil War. Milton's fortune is in the ascendant with that of parliament, but Marie's family declines as their royalist faction loses the day. Graves's contentious statement that Milton suffered from 'trichomania', a morbid obsession with hair, is not the least of the charges that Diana Trilling and other critics objected to. Milton is made out to be an opportunist, prepared to use the chaos of war to further his ambition. In contrast to their awkward, hostile marriage, Marie maintains a protracted and platonic affair with a royalist officer, Sir Edmund ('Mun') Verney. Their love, free from the gruesome realities of the time, continues on an etheric plane as the Milton marriage becomes harsher. This dichotomy, as with the larger narrative, is presented entirely in 17th-century idiom, which prevents the more fantastic conceits of the relationships from lapsing entirely into absurdity. Graves confessed that he made use of this device so that the assumptions of 20th-century psychology did not interfere with the vivid air of authenticity. Marie Powell stands out as one of his greatest characters, a convincing voice who speaks for the obscure and vulnerable in a cataclysmic time.

The subject matter of his next novels was influenced radically by the research undertaken for his great work of comparative theology,

The White Goddess. The thesis of this work is that the original religions of mankind were matriarchal in nature, and that traces of this goddess-worship still survive in existing scriptures, mythology, and archaeology. *The Golden Fleece* recounts the Argonaut legend, borrowing heavily from the version by Apollonius of Rhodes. In it the Orphic myth becomes a potent symbol of death and rebirth, an offering to the goddess on whom society depended for fertility. *King Jesus* was a bolder recasting of myth, a re-examination of the legend at the heart of our culture. Graves takes the view that Jesus was a secret grandson of Herod, equipped both spiritually and temporally for the Messiahship to which Herod also aspired. The narrative follows broadly the accounts given in the canonical gospels, but the result is a version of Christ that proved unacceptable to Christian orthodoxy. To take just one example, the book explains the term Christos (the anointed one) as Chrestos (the fool); the early church embraces this gladly and become the sect of fools. Jesus attempts to remove all traces of the archaic and ecstatic goddess religions from Judaism, allying himself with the Pharisees. In his attempt he plans to become the Messiah Son of David, a political and spiritual leader; but his attempt fails and he becomes instead the lowly shepherd, groom and sacrifice to the vestigial goddess. The gentler nature of the religion that results is, ironically, the means whereby it takes over the Roman empire: the outcast and lowly of civilization come to claim this aristocratic Messiah as their own. The combination of historical event and prophetic symbol becomes inexorably powerful, and his deification is assured. *King Jesus* is a fascinating exposition of the problematic identity of the most significant figure in history, though the complexity of detail is sometimes allowed to overwhelm the narrative; at times the story becomes lost in Graves's passionate concern to prove his case.

The last three novels of the author's career are altogether less momentous, more worthy of the 'potboiler' disclaimer that Graves applied to the Claudius novels. *The Islands of Unwisdom* describes the sea adventures of Isabelle de Baretto, privateer and explorer in the age of discovery and piracy. *Homer's Daughter* is set in Sicily around 750 B.C. and relates the exploits of a conjectural Nausicaa. *They Hanged My Saintly Billy* examines the evidence in the celebrated case of Dr William Palmer of Rugely, convicted for poisoning and hanged in 1857; characteristically, Graves ignores the accepted guilt of his subject and finds him not guilty. Though widely diverse in content, the books share a view of humanity we might associate with Claudius: tolerant, non-judgemental, and disputatious. William Palmer, for instance, might be a cheat, liar, and thief, but Graves (or his anonymous narrator) evinces an affection for him, and considers him incapable of murder. The same robust and elastic sensibility informs all of Graves's work.

For all their varied milieux, Graves's novels all take place in times of radical transformation, underscoring the dangerous nature of human existence by reference to exceptional circumstances. If they are adventure stories, it is not only because they portray sensational incidents, but because the author is adventuring in the human personality. Graves himself appeared to believe he was in some way travelling to the past; his great achievement is that he convincingly performed the same magic on the reader, the supreme illusion of bringing the dead to life.

—Alan Murphy

GRAY, Caroline.   See NICOLE, Christopher.

GRAY, Ellington.   See JACOB, Naomi.

GRAY, Harriet.   See ROBINS, Denise.

GREAVES, Richard.   See McCUTCHEON, George Barr.

GREEN, Peter (Morris).
Pseudonym: Denis Delaney. **Nationality:** British. **Born:** London, 22 December 1924. **Education:** Charterhouse School, Surrey; Trinity College, Cambridge (Craven scholar and student, 1950), 1947–52, B.A. (honours) in classics 1950; M.A. and Ph.D. 1954. **Military Service:** Royal Air Force Volunteer Reserve, 1943–47: with Burma Command, 1944–46. **Relations:** married 1) Lalage Isobel Pulvertaft in 1951 (marriage dissolved), two sons and one daughter; 2) Carin Margreta Christensen in 1975. **Career:** editor, *Cambridge Review,* 1950–51; director of studies in Classics, Selwyn College, Cambridge, 1951–52; fiction critic, *Daily Telegraph,* London, 1953–63; literary adviser, Bodley Head Ltd, publishers, London, 1957–58; consultant editor, Hodder and Stoughton Ltd, publishers, London, 1960–63; television critic, the *Listener,* London, 1961–63; film critic, *John o' London's,* 1961–63; full-time writer in Greece, 1963–71: teacher of Greek history and literature, College Year in Athens, 1966–71. Visiting professor, 1971–72, since 1973 professor of Classics, and since 1982 James R. Dougherty Jr Centennial professor of Classics, University of Texas, Austin. Visiting professor of Classics, University of California, Los Angeles, 1976; Mellon professor of Humanities, Tulane University, New Orleans, 1986. **Recipient:** Royal Society of Literature Heinemann award, 1958; National Endowment for the Humanities fellowship, 1983. Fellow, 1956, and member of the Council, 1958–63, Royal Society of Literature. **Address:** Department of Classics, University of Texas, 123 Waggener Hall, Austin, Texas 78712, USA.

ROMANCE AND HISTORICAL PUBLICATIONS

Novels

Achilles His Armour. London, Murray, 1955; New York, Doubleday, 1967.
The Sword of Pleasure. London, Murray, 1957; Cleveland, World, 1958.
The Laughter of Aphrodite. London, Murray, 1965; New York, Doubleday, 1966.

OTHER PUBLICATIONS

Novel

Cat in Gloves (as Denis Delaney). London, Gryphon, 1956.

Short Stories

Habeas Corpus and Other Stories. London, Hamish Hamilton, 1962; Cleveland, World, 1963.

Other

The Expanding Eye: A First Journey to the Mediterranean. London, Dobson, 1953; New York, Abelard Schuman, 1957.
Sir Thomas Browne. London, Longman, 1959.
Kenneth Grahame 1859–1932: A Study of His Life, Work and Times. London, Murray, 1959; as *Kenneth Grahame: A Biography,* Cleveland, World, 1959; abridged edition, as *Beyond the*

Wild Wood: The World of Kenneth Grahame, Exeter, Devon, Webb and Bower, 1982; New York, Facts on File, 1983.

Essays in Antiquity. London, Murray, and Cleveland, World, 1960.

John Skelton. London, Longman, 1960.

Look at the Romans (for children). London, Hamish Hamilton, 1963.

Alexander the Great: A Biography. London, Weidenfeld and Nicolson, and New York, Praeger, 1970.

Armada from Athens. New York, Doubleday, 1970; London, Hodder and Stoughton, 1971.

The Year of Salamis 480–479 B.C. London, Weidenfeld and Nicolson, 1970; as *Xerxes at Salamis*, New York, Praeger, 1970.

The Shadow of the Parthenon: Studies in Ancient History and Literature. London, Temple Smith, and Berkeley, University of California Press, 1972.

A Concise History of Ancient Greece to the Close of the Classical Era. London, Thames and Hudson, 1973; as *Ancient Greece: An Illustrated History*, New York, Viking Press, 1973.

The Parthenon, with the Editors of Newsweek. New York, Newsweek, and London, Readers Digest, 1973.

Alexander of Macedon 356–323 B.C.: A Historical Biography. London, Penguin, 1974.

Classical Bearings: Interpreting Ancient History and Culture. London, Thames and Hudson, 1989.

Alexander to Actium: The Hellenistic Age. London, Thames and Hudson, 1990; *Alexander to Actium: The Historical Evolution of the Hellenistic Age*, Berkeley, University of California Press, 1990.

Editor, *Poetry from Cambridge, 1947–1950.* London, Fortune Press, 1951.

Editor, *Appreciations: Essays*, by Clifton Fadiman. London, Hodder and Stoughton, 1962.

Translator, *The Fountain at Marlieux*, by Claude Aveline. London, Dobson, and New York, Roy, 1954.

Translator, *Tanguy: The Story of a Child of Our Time*, by Michel del Castillo. London, Muller, 1958; as *A Child of Our Time*, New York, Knopf, 1958.

Translator, *The Lottery*, by Paul Guimard. London, Faber, 1958; as *House of Happiness*, Boston, Houghton Mifflin, 1960.

Translator, *The Lion*, by Joseph Kessel. London, Hart Davis, and New York, Knopf, 1959.

Translator, *Antoine*, by Marie Gisèle Landes. London, Muller, 1959.

Translator, *The Children of Lilith*, by Guy Piazzini. London, Hodder and Stoughton, and New York, Dutton, 1960.

Translator, *Journey into the Blue*, by Gusztáv Rab. London, Sidgwick and Jackson, and New York, Pantheon, 1960.

Translator, *A Room in Budapest*, by Gusztáv Rab. London, Sidgwick and Jackson, 1961.

Translator, *Destiny of Fire*, by Zoe Oldenbourg. London, Gollancz, and New York, Pantheon, 1961.

Translator, *Massacre of Montségur: A History of the Albigensian Crusade*, by Zoe Oldenbourg. London, Weidenfeld and Nicolson, 1961; New York, Pantheon, 1962.

Translator, *The Novice*, by Giovanni Arpino. London, Hodder and Stoughton, 1961; New York, Braziller, 1962.

Translator, *The Prime of Life*, by Simone de Beauvoir. London, Deutsch-Weidenfeld and Nicolson, and Cleveland, World, 1962.

Translator, *The Black Dove*, by Enrico Emanuelli. London, Macdonald, 1962.

Translator, *Innocence*, by Diane Giguère. London, Gollancz, 1962.

Translator, *Douchka: The Story of a Dog*, by Colette Andry. London, Souvenir Press, 1963; as *Behind the Bathtub: The Story of a French Dog*, Boston, Little Brown, 1963.

Translator, *Diamond River*, by Sadio Garavini de Turno. London, Hamish Hamilton, and New York, Harcourt Brace, 1963.

Translator, *Love Without Grace*, by Luciana d'Arad. London, Muller, 1963.

Translator, *Calvary Street*, by Miklós Bátori. London, Constable, 1963.

Translator, *Okapi Fever*, by Philippe Diolé. London, Souvenir Press, and New York, Viking Press, 1965.

Translator, *Cordelia and Other Stories*, by Françoise Mallet-Joris. New York, Farrar Straus, and London, W.H. Allen, 1965.

Translator, *The Novel Computer*, by Robert Escarpit. London, Secker and Warburg, 1966.

Translator, *The Flood*, by J.M.G. Le Clézio. London, Hamish Hamilton, 1966; New York, Atheneum, 1968.

Translator, *The Sixteen Satires of Juvenal.* London, Penguin, 1967.

Translator, *The Sardinian Smile*, by Petru Dumitriu. London, Collins, and New York, Holt Rinehart, 1968.

Translator, *Ovid: The Erotic Poems.* London, Penguin, 1982; New York, Penguin, 1983.

Translator of other historical and biographical works.

*　　*　　*

Peter Green is probably best known as a historian, an expert in classical literature, and a translator. However, Green is also a talented novelist of some repute. Three of his novels are set in the ancient world, and are full of evocative descriptions and minute detail.

His first book, *Achilles His Armour*, follows the life of Alcibiades, an Athenian hero—and traitor. Green possesses a clear and concise style which makes his vivid descriptions of the time and place fascinating. Green's success as an ancient historian is shown in the skill with which he sets his stage: the historical setting is painted with the knowledge of an expert. It is, however, with *The Sword of Pleasure* that the author achieves success in creating a well-written and evocative historical novel. Written as the testament of a Roman dictator, the book reflects the life of a disillusioned but powerful man of his time. Lucius Cornelius Sulla recounts his version of historical events—real and fictional—as a worldly bystander with a deep insight into the politics and society of his day. Sulla's memoirs are always written in the style of a leading figure of the ancient world commenting on the events of his time—and this is an accomplishment in itself, allowing the reader to sustain his/her interest and belief in the character.

The interesting figure of the poet Sappho is presented in *The Laughter of Aphrodite*. This is probably the most ambitious of Green's fictional works, but also offers the most imaginative scope of all of the subjects tackled by him, as almost nothing is known about Sappho. The result is a fascinating and well conceived book that is always interesting, sometimes shocking, but which leaves the reader wanting to know more about the subject.

Green is an articulate and talented writer who tackles out-of-the-ordinary subjects with verve and style. His re-creation of the ancient world, his characterization, and his imagination, help to create outstanding examples of historical fiction.

—P. Campbell

GREGORY, Philippa.
Nationality: British. **Born:** Kate Wedd, Nairobi, Kenya, 9 January 1954. **Education:** University of Sussex, Brighton, B.A., 1978; University of Edinburgh, M.Litt. 1980, Ph.D. 1984. **Relations:** one daughter. **Career:** provincial journalist for newspapers in England, 1971–75; radio journalist, BBC-Radio, Southampton, 1978–80, and

1984; columnist for *The Guardian*, London (pseudonym Kate Webb). Founding member, and vice-president of *Hartlepool People*, a community centre for the unemployed and homeless. **Agent:** Rogers, Coleridge and White Ltd, 20 Powis Mews, London W11 1JN, England. **Address:** c/o HarperCollins Publishers, 71–85 Fulham Palace Road, London W6 8JB, England.

ROMANCE AND HISTORICAL PUBLICATIONS

Novels (series: Wideacre Trilogy)

Wideacre Trilogy:
Wideacre. London, Viking, 1987; New York, Simon and Schuster, 1988.
The Favoured Child. London, Viking, and New York, Pocket Books, 1989.
Meridon. London, Viking, and New York, Pocket Books, 1990.
Wise Woman. London, Viking, 1992.
Fallen Skies. London, HarperCollins, 1993.

OTHER PUBLICATIONS

Novel

Mrs Hartley and the Growth Centre. London, Penguin, 1992.

Other (for children)

Princess Florizella. London, Viking, 1988.
Florizella and the Wolves. London, Walker, 1991.
Florizella and the Giant. London, Walker, 1992.

*   *   *

Philippa Gregory, novelist, children's writer, academic, and journalist, is the author of several highly successful historical novels which have achieved massive worldwide sales and have propelled her into the forefront of the genre. Critics have described her writing as pacey, compelling, passionate, and versatile. The novelist and critic Peter Ackroyd said of her: 'she writes from instinct, not out of calculation and it shows'.

Gregory's first novel, *Wideacre*, part of a trilogy featuring the Lacey family, explores the power and danger of a passionate love. The novel was published to universal acclaim and described as a 'gripping novel of power and passion' by the *Mail on Sunday*. The London *Evening Standard* commented on the vividness of the central character in equally glowing terms: 'amid . . . the social upheaval strides Beatrice Lacey, who, for singlemindedness, tempestuousness, passion, amorality and plain old-fashioned evil, knocks Scarlett O'Hara into short cotton socks'.

The reader consistently feels the presence of Beatrice ('the witch of Wideacre'), and it is her lust for power which eventually leads to both her own death, and that of her brother, and the destruction of Wideacre. Beatrice is so superbly drawn that even when she is referred to in subsequent novels, the reader expects her to make an entrance. Not only is Beatrice strong on the page but her legacy passes itself genetically through her descendants, giving them the Lacey skills of horsemanship, agriculture, and foresight.

The Favoured Child, the second novel in the series, is set in the 18th century against a background of rising social tension and near revolution. The system of enclosures (which Beatrice introduced to the villages of Wideacre), was a system used to appropriate land, and was an agrarian method used during the 18th and 19th centuries which led directly to an increase in poverty among the lower classes. The French Revolution and the political ideals of the London radicals are subjects which find voice through the novel's characters and events. The historical veracity of this book is impeccable.

Julia Lacey and Richard MacAndrew are raised by Julia's mother, Celia. They believe themselves to be cousins (they are in fact brother and sister but this is only revealed near the end of the book). As children they are close and promise to marry. Both Richard and Julia are to inherit Wideacre. Richard's father, John MacAndrew (Beatrice's husband) returns home from India determined to remove the Lacey curse from the history of Acre. He wishes to turn the estate into a profit sharing co-operative with the villagers of Acre, and hires Ralph Megson, a cripple, ex-smuggler, and bread-rioter as estate manager. Megson tells Julia (in whom he sees more than a passing resemblance to Beatrice) that he led the uprising against Wideacre, the riot that resulted in the death of his lover, Beatrice. Together Ralph, John, and Julia transform Wideacre into a highly profitable business. Richard does not care for this new approach (which lowers his possible income), and is determined that when he inherits he will revert Wideacre back to a more traditional set-up.

Richard despises the villagers and Megson for not being aristocrats, landowners or 'quality'. Jealous of Julia's abilities as a farmer and her growing popularity within the village, Richard forces her into marriage after raping her, and then murders his father and aunt, so they can both inherit the estate.

The ensuing battle (whether Richard will succeed in undermining the achievements of his father) demonstrates clearly to the reader the absolute power of an 18th-century landowner. The villagers cannot fight back against Richard (in whom the law as well as the land resides). In these historically accurate passages of the novel, Gregory is always instructive and informative, without once being didactic. At the climax of the novel, Julia, determined to end the rule of the Lacey's, gives away her only child, Sarah, the heir to Wideacre, to a convoy of travelling gypsies and looks on passively as Megson kills Richard.

The return of Sarah Lacey to Wideacre forms the plot of Gregory's concluding novel in the series, *Meridon*. Once again the relationship between landowner and worker is at the heart of the book.

The estate of Wideacre has been run as a trust (along the lines originally proposed by MacAndrew, Megson, and Julia) and is compared favourably with Havering, the neighbouring estate. Havering is run under the auspices of Lady Clare Havering for her and her family's profit. The Havering workers live in squalor and poverty. The crops of Havering are sent to market and sold for the best possible price which results in low wages for the workers and high food prices for everyone else. The situation is typical of the period which saw the introduction of the Corn Laws. At one point in the novel, Lady Havering is so disgusted at the state her villagers live in that she determines to have their properties razed to the ground with the consequent result that the workers are made homeless and have to rely on Parish Relief, (if any Parish will accept them), or are arrested for vagrancy and thrown into the poorhouse—a more likely alternative. In contrast, Wideacre is a model estate, run by the workers for the workers, who invest profits into buying new machinery. The village boasts a school in which the children of both sexes are taught to read and write so they will not remain ignorant, a charity fund, and a community spirit totally lacking in Havering. The central plot of the novel is Lady Havering's attempt to unite Wideacre and Havering through the marriage of Sarah Lacey to the drunken gambler, Lord Perrywith—also the heir to Havering.

The 'Wideacre Trilogy' is rightly the focus of any appraisal of Gregory's work. Her other novels, namely the wickedly satirical *Mrs Hartley and the Growth Centre*, and her latest work, *Fallen*

Skies, only serve to demonstrate Gregory's power, talent and above all, the sheer readability of her novels.

—Kate Thompson

———

GREIG, Maysie.
Pseudonym for Jennifer Greig-Smith. **Other Pseudonyms:** Jennifer Ames; Ann Barclay; Mary Douglas Warre; Mary Douglas Warren. **Nationality:** Australian. **Born:** Sydney, New South Wales, in 1902. **Education:** Presbyterian Ladies' College, Pymble, New South Wales. **Relations:** married 1) the writer Delano Ames; 2) the writer Maxwell Murray in 1937 (died 1956); 3) Jan Sopoushek in 1959. **Career:** journalist, Sydney *Sun*, 1919–20; moved to London: contributor *Westminster Gazette*, *Daily Sketch*, and *Mirror*; also worked in New York and Boston. Vice-President, New South Wales PEN. **Died:** 10 June 1971.

ROMANCE AND HISTORICAL PUBLICATIONS

Novels

Peggy of Beacon Hill. Boston, Small Maynard, 1924; London, Jenkins, 1926.
The Luxury Husband. London, Long, and New York, Dial Press, 1928.
Ragamuffin. London, Long, 1929.
Satin Straps. London, Long, and New York, Dial Press, 1929.
Jasmine—Take Care! or, A Girl Must Marry. London, Benn, 1930; as *A Girl Must Marry*, New York, Dial Press, 1931.
Lovely Clay. London, Benn, 1930; New York, Doubleday, 1933.
A Nice Girl Comes to Town. London, Long, and New York, Dial Press, 1930.
The Man She Bought. New York, Dial Press, 1930.
This Way to Happiness. London, Long, 1931; New York, Dial Press, 1932; as *Janice*, Cleveland, World, 1947.
One-Man Girl. London, Benn, and New York, Dial Press, 1931.
The Women Money Buys. New York, Dial Press, 1931.
Faint Heart, Fair Lady. London, Long, 1932.
Laughing Cavalier. London, Long, 1932.
Little Sisters Don't Count. London, Benn, 1932; New York, Doubleday, 1934.
Cake Without Icing. London, Benn, and New York, Dial Press, 1932; revised edition, as *Marriage Without a Ring*, London, Collins, 1972.
Professional Lover. London, Benn, and New York, Doubleday, 1933; as *Screen Lover*, London, Collins, 1969.
Parents Are a Problem. London, Hodder and Stoughton, 1933; as *Love, Honour, and Obey*, New York, Doubleday, 1933.
A Bad Girl Leaves Town. New York, Doubleday, 1933.
Men Act That Way. New York, Doubleday, 1933.
Heart Appeal. London, Hodder and Stoughton, 1934; New York, Doubleday, 1935.
She Walked into His Parlour. London, Hodder and Stoughton, 1934.
Ten Cent Love. New York, Doubleday, 1934.
I Lost My Heart. London, Hodder and Stoughton, 1935; New York, Doubleday, 1936; as *The Sinister Island* (as Jennifer Ames), London, Collins, 1968.
Love and Let Me Go. New York, Doubleday, 1935; London, Hodder and Stoughton, 1936; as *Love Me*, London, Collins, 1971.
Marry in Haste. London, Hodder and Stoughton, and New York, Doubleday, 1935.
Rich Man, Poor Girl. London, Hodder and Stoughton, and New York, Doubleday, 1935.

Challenge to Happiness. London, Hodder and Stoughton, 1936; New York, Doubleday, 1937.
The Girl from Nowhere. Hanley, Staffordshire, Locker, 1936; New York, Doubleday, 1942; as *The Girl Who Wasn't Welcome*, London, Collins, 1969.
Odds on Love. London, Hodder and Stoughton, and New York, Doubleday, 1936.
Workaday Lady. London, Hodder and Stoughton, and New York, Doubleday, 1936.
Touching the Clouds. New York, Doubleday, 1936.
New Moon Through a Window. London, Hodder and Stoughton, and New York, Doubleday, 1937.
Retreat from Love. London, Hodder and Stoughton, 1937; (as Jennifer Ames) New York, Doubleday, 1937.
The Pretty One. London, Hodder and Stoughton, 1937; (as Jennifer Ames) New York, Doubleday, 1937.
The Girl Men Talked About. London, Hodder and Stoughton, 1938; as *Stopover in Paradise*, New York, Doubleday, 1938; as *The Golden Garden*, London, Collins, 1968.
Young Man Without Money. London, Hodder and Stoughton, 1938; as *Debutante in Uniform*, New York, Doubleday, 1938.
Stepping under Ladders. London, Hodder and Stoughton, 1938; New York, Doubleday, 1939; as *Girl in Jeopardy*, London, Collins, 1967.
Other Women's Beauty. London, Hodder and Stoughton, 1938.
Strange Beauty. New York, Doubleday, 1938.
Ask the Parlourmaid. London, Hodder and Stoughton, 1939; as *Unmarried Couple*, New York, Doubleday, 1940.
Girl on His Hands. London, Hodder and Stoughton, and New York, Doubleday, 1939.
A Man to Protect You. London, Hodder and Stoughton, and New York, Doubleday, 1939.
Grand Relations. London, Hodder and Stoughton, 1940; as *A Fortune in Romance*, New York, Doubleday, 1940; as *A Girl and Her Money*, London, Collins, 1971.
The Man Is Always Right. London, Hodder and Stoughton, and New York, Doubleday, 1940.
Rich Twin, Poor Twin. London, Hodder and Stoughton, and New York, Doubleday, 1940.
Girl Without Credit. New York, Doubleday, 1941; London, Hodder and Stoughton, 1942.
This Desirable Bachelor. London, Hodder and Stoughton, and New York, Doubleday, 1941.
Heaven Isn't Here. New York, Doubleday, 1941.
No Retreat from Love. New York, Doubleday, 1942; Hanley, Staffordshire, Locker, 1947.
Salute Me Darling. London, Hodder and Stoughton, 1942; as *Heartbreak for Two*, New York, Doubleday, 1942.
The Wishing Star. New York, Doubleday, 1942; (as Mary Douglas Warre) London, Hutchinson, 1943.
Pathway to Paradise. New York, Doubleday, 1942; London, Collins, 1943.
Professional Hero. London, Collins, and New York, Doubleday, 1943.
I've Always Loved You. New York, Doubleday, 1943.
Reluctant Millionaire. London, Collins, 1944; New York, Random House, 1945.
One Room for His Highness. London, Collins, 1944.
Girl with a Million. London, Collins, 1945.
I Loved Her Yesterday. London, Collins, 1945.
Darling Clementine. London, Collins, 1946; as *Candidate for Love*, New York, Random House, 1947.
Table for Two. London, Collins, and New York, Random House, 1946.
Castle in the Air. London, Collins, 1947.
The Thirteenth Girl. Hanley, Staffordshire, Locker, 1947.

Take This Man. London, Collins, 1947.

I Met Him Again. London, Collins, 1948.

Yours Forever. London, Collins, and New York, Random House, 1948.

Whispers in the Sun. London, Collins, and New York, Random House, 1949; as *The Reluctant Cinderella* (as Jennifer Ames), New York, Avalon, and Collins, 1952.

Dark Carnival. New York, Random House, 1950; (as Jennifer Ames) London, Collins, 1951.

My Heart's Down Under. London, Collins, 1951; (as Jennifer Ames) New York, Avalon, 1951.

It Happened One Flight. London, Collins, 1951; New York, Macfadden, 1966.

London, Here I Come. London, Collins, 1951; as *Assignment to Love* (as Jennifer Ames), New York, Avalon, 1953.

Wagon to a Star. London, Collins, 1952; (as Jennifer Ames) New York, Avalon, 1953.

Lovers under the Sun. London, Collins, 1954; as *Passport to Happiness*, New York, Avalon, 1955; as *Ship's Doctor*, Collins, 1966.

That Girl in Nice. London, Collins, 1954; as *Love Is a Gamble* (as Jennifer Ames), New York, Avalon, 1954.

Cloak and Dagger Lover. London, Collins, 1955; as *Moon over the Water* (as Mary Douglas Warren), New York, Arcadia House, 1956.

Kiss in Sunlight. London, Collins, 1956; New York, Avalon, 1957.

Girl Without Money. London, Collins, 1957.

No Dowry for Jennifer. New York, Avalon, 1957.

Love Is a Gambler. London, Collins, 1958.

Love Is a Thief. London, Collins, 1959; New York, Macfadden, 1966.

Send for Miss Marshall. London, Collins, 1959.

Follow Your Love. New York, Avalon, 1959.

Doctor in Exile. London, Collins, 1960; New York, Avalon, 1961.

Catch Up to Love. New York, Avalon, 1960.

Kiss of Promise. New York, Avalon, 1960.

Cherry Blossom Love. London, Collins, 1961; New York, Macfadden, 1967.

Every Woman's Man. London, Collins, 1961; New York, Macfadden, 1966.

The Doctor Is a Lady. London, Collins, 1962.

Nurse at St Catherine's. London, Collins, 1963.

French Girl in Love. London, Collins, 1963.

Every Woman's Doctor. London, Collins, 1964.

Married Quarters. London, Collins, 1964; New York, Macfadden, 1966.

Nurse in Danger. London, Collins, 1964.

The Doctor and the Dancer. London, Collins, 1965.

Doctor on Wings. London, Collins, 1966.

Never the Same. London, Collins, 1970.

Novels as Jennifer Ames

Pandora Lifts the Veil. New York, Dial Press, 1932; London, Hodder and Stoughton, 1933.

Anything But Love. London, Hodder and Stoughton, 1933.

Cruise. London, Hodder and Stoughton, 1934; as *Romance on a Cruise* (as Maysie Greig), New York, Doubleday, 1935.

Good Sport. London, Hodder and Stoughton, 1934; (as Maysie Greig) New York, Doubleday, 1934; as *Love Will Win*, London, Fontana, 1969.

Romance for Sale. London, Hodder and Stoughton, 1934; (as Maysie Greig) New York, Doubleday, 1934.

I'll Get over It. London, Hodder and Stoughton, 1935; (as Maysie Greig) New York, Doubleday, 1936; as *Jilted* (as Jennifer Ames), London, Collins, 1968.

Sweet Peril. London, Hodder and Stoughton, 1935; as *Sweet Danger* (as Maysie Greig), New York, Doubleday, 1935.

I Seek My Love. London, Hodder and Stoughton, 1936; as *Dreams Get You Nowhere* (as Maysie Greig), New York, Doubleday, 1937.

Tinted Dream. London, Hodder and Stoughton, 1936; as *Doctor's Wife* (as Maysie Greig), New York, Doubleday, 1937; as *Doctor Brad's Nurse*, London, Collins, 1966.

Her World of Men. London, Hodder and Stoughton, 1937; (as Maysie Greig) New York, Doubleday, 1938.

Elder Sister. London, Hodder and Stoughton, 1938; New York, Doubleday, 1939.

Stranger Sweetheart. London, Hodder and Stoughton, 1938; as *Honeymoons Arranged* (as Maysie Greig), New York, Doubleday, 1938.

Bury the Past. London, Hodder and Stoughton, 1939; (as Maysie Greig) New York, Doubleday, 1939.

Dangerous Holiday. London, Hodder and Stoughton, 1939; as *Dangerous Cruise* (as Maysie Greig), New York, Doubleday, 1940.

Not One of Us. London, Hodder and Stoughton, 1939; (as Maysie Greig) New York, Doubleday, 1939.

Make the Man Notice You. London, Hodder and Stoughton, 1940; (as Maysie Greig) New York, Doubleday, 1940.

Honeymoon Alone. London, Hodder and Stoughton, 1940; (as Maysie Greig) New York, Doubleday, 1941; as *Honeymoon for One*, London, Collins, 1971.

Ring Without Romance. London, Hodder and Stoughton, 1940; (as Maysie Greig) New York, Doubleday, 1941.

Too Many Women. London, Hodder and Stoughton, 1941; (as Maysie Greig) New York, Doubleday, 1941.

Diplomatic Honeymoon. London, Collins, 1942; (as Maysie Greig) New York, Doubleday, 1942.

Dark Sunlight. London, Collins, 1943.

The Impossible Marriage. London, Collins, 1943.

At the Same Time Tomorrow. London, Collins, 1944; (as Maysie Greig) New York, Doubleday, 1944.

Restless Beauty. London, Collins, 1944.

I Married Mr Richardson. London, Collins, 1945.

Journey in the Dark. London, Collins, 1945.

Lovers in the Dark. London, Collins, 1946.

Take Your Choice, Lady. London, Collins, 1946.

Fear Kissed My Lips. London, Collins, 1947.

Heart in Darkness. New York, Arcadia House, 1947.

Shadow Across My Heart. London, Collins, 1948; (as Mary Douglas Warren) New York, Arcadia House, 1952.

She'll Take the High Road. London, Collins, 1948.

Danger Wakes My Heart. London, Collins, 1949; as *Danger in Eden*, New York, Avalon, 1950.

Lips for a Stranger. London, Collins, 1949.

Too Much Alone. London, Collins, 1950.

Flight to Happiness. New York, Avalon, 1950.

After Tomorrow. New York, Avalon, 1951; as *Overseas Nurse*, New York, Ace, 1961.

The Frightened Heart. London, Collins, 1952; as *Date with Danger* (as Maysie Greig), New York, Random House, 1952.

The Fearful Paradise. London, Collins, 1953; as *This Fearful Paradise* (as Maysie Greig), New York, Random House, 1953.

Flight into Fear. London, Collins, and New York, Avalon, 1954.

Shadows Across the Sun. London, Collins, 1955; as *Shadow over the Island* (as Mary Douglas Warren), New York, Arcadia House, 1955.

Rough Seas to Sunrise. London, Collins, 1956; as *Winds of Fear* (as Maysie Greig), New York, Avalon, 1956.

Night of Carnival. London, Collins, 1956.

Love on Dark Wings. London, Collins, 1957.

Follow Your Dream. New York, Avalon, 1957.

Beloved Knight. London, Collins, 1958; New York, Avalon, 1959.
Doctor's Nurse. London, Collins, 1959.
Love in a Far Country. London, Collins, 1960; New York, Avalon, 1965.
Love in the East. London, Collins, 1960.
Perilous Quest. New York, Avalon, 1960.
Her Heart's Desire. New York, Avalon, 1961.
Diana Goes to Tokyo. London, Collins, 1961.
It Started in Hongkong. London, Collins, 1961.
The Timid Cleopatra. London, Collins, 1962.
Honeymoon in Manila. London, Collins, 1962.
Geisha in the House. London, Collins, 1963.
Sinners in Paradise. London, Collins, 1963.
The Two of Us. London, Collins, 1964.
Happy Island. London, Collins, 1964.
Nurse's Holiday. London, Collins, 1965.
Nurse's Story. London, Collins, 1965.
Doctor Ted's Clinic. London, Collins, 1967.
The Doctor Takes a Holiday. London, Collins, 1969.
Write from the Heart. London, Hale, 1972.

Novels as Ann Barclay

Other Men's Arms. London, Collins, 1936.
Swing High, Swing Low. London, Collins, 1936.
Men as Her Stepping Stones. London, Collins, 1937; (as Maysie Greig) New York, Doubleday, 1938.

Novels as Mary Douglas Warren

Reunion in Reno. New York, Carlton House, 1941.
The Rich Are Not Proud. New York, Carlton House, 1942.
Southern Star. New York, Arcadia House, 1950.
The Manor Farm. New York, Arcadia House, 1951.
The Sunny Island. New York, Arcadia House, 1952.
Salt Harbor. New York, Arcadia House, 1953.
The High Road. New York, Arcadia House, 1954.
The Doctor Decides. London, Collins, 1963.

*   *   *

Maysie Greig, writing prolifically under several names, favoured a heroine who was pert and petite rather than philosophical and introspective. Unlike the romantic heroines of only a very few years earlier, Greig's do not believe in a personal God, nor are they stirred by Christian doubt or reflection, although some of the activities usually associated with belief in a deity are practised by hero and heroine, particularly at times of great stress or sexual tension. Thus, for example, in *Love and Let Me Go* we see Sally and Red, an unreliable wandering artist, rush into a marriage against the wishes of Sally's beastly family who believe in 'duty above love'. Sally's dad won't let them sleep together even after marriage. Having originally met on a camping holiday (hiking, cycling, walking, and the great outdoors were much in vogue in the mid-1930s), Sally and Red finally manage to consummate that marriage while camping in the Lake District. As Red carries his girlish bride into their honeymoon tent, he is moved to pray to an un-named deity. '"I'm not a religious man but I feel like going down on my knees right now and praying that our love will always be as glorious as it is now." She nodded slowly'. This camping scene is not typical. On the whole, Greig liked her heroines to be sophisticated, elegant, languid, fascinated by good clothes and firm men. While it used to be a girl's soul that counted for so much, now it is her clothes and make-up. Greig's girls spend a great deal of time getting ready to go out, wondering what to wear to suit the surroundings: 'I'll wear it tonight when he takes me out to dinner somewhere swish.' While being courted, a girl liked to be taken out to dine in Soho or Knightsbridge, followed by a show or a visit to a nightclub. Occasionally, beneath her desire for would-be glamorous outings with urban lustre, a girl showed a wide-eyed, breathless spirit, questing for adventure, which could be absorbed by a variation on background. Greig tried out various settings—the hospital romance, travel, a forest fire, a romance set in 'Jamaica's fashionable Montego Bay', and even a political romance, *Rich Twin, Poor Twin.*

Although some of the girls hold down jobs—Jennifer Prudence in *Anything But Love* is a successful magazine illustrator, Annette in *Kiss in Sunlight* a restless nurse, while the occupation of the heroine of *The Doctor Is a Lady* is self-explanatory—the chief occupation of these girls is to preserve reputation and to find a man, preferably as described in the title *A Man to Protect You*. Such chaps are lean and hard: 'Jason, lean, dark-skinned, was very distinctive in full dress kit. Jenny felt all the other women in the dining room must be envying her. Or if they weren't they should be!' Nigel, we read, looked very attractive in his well-cut dark blue suit. And on another occasion, we see how the cut accentuated his height and powerful shoulders. But despite many jutting jaws and powerful shoulders, the heroes conform to an ideal of middle-class gentility and prim pleasantness. The ideal man is a soft-centred savage in city clothes.

In the 1920s and 1930s new ideas on sexual freedom, on allowing the biological urge to follow its natural course, were being advocated by more serious writers and philosophers, while practical advice was being offered by Marie Stopes. Despite alluringly daring titles like *Too Many Women, Anything But Love, Professional Lover,* or *Fear Kissed My Lips,* sexual freedom (either before or after marriage) was not sought by a Greig girl. There was still one man for one woman. Chastity was a much prized virtue, and virginity, although not openly named as such, was 'something very precious'. It was, as a heroine who has narrowly avoided seduction, observes: 'Something which she had kept locked inside her for years. Something which, once broken, could never be repaired. Something he probably didn't know about, couldn't even guess at'.

Any critique of Greig's approach to her craft, is best summed up in her own resumé of her philosophy.

> I write happy love stories because I believe happiness is the greatest virtue in the world and misery the greatest sin. You can so infect people with your own misery that you can make them miserable when they were quite happy and contented before. To be happy is as though you opened every window in your mind and let in strong, clean sunlight. That is why I think everyone should try to be happy, and read stories that make one happy, rather than those that increase one's sense of futility and despair. If I tried to write a really miserable story I think I should end up by committing suicide!

This happiness was only to be found in the discovery of a true and lasting love. That love, once established, carried a sanctity. One must revere happy love. Her own beliefs were echoed by her characters.

> 'Happiness is the most important thing', he said quietly, 'and love. Not only love of a woman, but love of the whole world you are living in. Why waste time scrambling for wordly goods when but to live happily and simply gives one such an intense pleasure?... Do you think that God intended any of us to lead a life of miserable self-sacrifice for the sake of others? Do you think He would have given us the power of love if He meant us to deny that love when it came to us? No, your first duty lies to our love, because that's the most important thing in the world.'

Mediaeval courtly love may have held that true love was only possible through a passion created by suffering, continual partings and re-unions, and ultimate separation. Greig, however, held that true love could, and should, be happy love, and that this happiness was a beginning and an end in itself. This was not only what she believed, but what her reading public wanted. She gave it to them, and 'won the affection of a great and admiring public', who shared her view that 'Love is the most fascinating, inspiring, complete emotion in the world. Happiness is the greatest virtue, and misery the greatest sin in the world.' Shallow, vacuous statements to some, but indisputable and convincing dogma to her and her readership.

—Rachel Anderson

GREY, Belinda.   See **PETERS, Maureen.**

GREY, Brenda.   See **MACKINLAY, Leila.**

GREY, Georgina.   See **ROBY, Mary Linn.**

GRIMSTEAD, Hettie. British. See 2nd edition, 1990.

GRUNDY, (Mrs) Mabel (Sarah) Barnes.

ROMANCE AND HISTORICAL PUBLICATIONS

Novels

A Thames Camp. Bristol, Arrowsmith, 1902; as *Two in a Tent—and Jane*, 1913.
The Vacillations of Hazel. Bristol, Arrowsmith, 1905.
Marguerite's Wonderful Year. Bristol, Arrowsmith, 1906.
Hazel of Heatherland. New York, Baker and Taylor, 1906.
Dimbie and I—and Amelia. New York, Baker and Taylor, 1907.
Hilary on Her Own. New York, Baker and Taylor, and London, Hutchinson, 1908.
Gwenda. New York, Baker and Taylor, 1910; as *Two Men and Gwenda*, 1910.
The Third Miss Wenderby. New York, Baker and Taylor, and London, Hutchinson, 1911.
Patricia Plays a Part. London, Hutchinson, 1913; New York, Dodd Mead, 1914.
Candytuft—I Mean Veronica. London, Hutchinson, 1914.
An Undressed Heroine. London, Hutchinson, 1916.
Her Mad Month. London, Hutchinson, 1917.
A Girl for Sale. London, Hutchinson, 1920.
The Great Husband Hunt. London, Hutchinson, 1922.
The Mating of Marcus. London, Hutchinson, 1923.
Sleeping Dogs. London, Hodder and Stoughton, 1924; New York, Stokes, 1926.
Three People. London, Hodder and Stoughton, 1926.
The Strategy of Suzanne. London, Hutchinson, 1929.
Pippa. London, Hutchinson, 1932.
Sally in a Service Flat. London, Hutchinson, 1934.
Private Hotel—Anywhere. London, Hutchinson, 1937.
Paying Pests. London, Hutchinson, 1941.
Mary Ann and Jane. London, Hutchinson, 1944.

The Two Miss Speckles. London, Hutchinson, 1946.

*   *   *

A novel by Mabel Barnes Grundy reads like a breath of fresh air. This author, whose 24 books were published between 1902 and 1946, writes with verve, enthusiasm, and energy in a distinctive style which is characterized by its ease and wit. Grundy's novels are mostly of the 'roads to matrimony' type. They move along at a brisk pace with plenty of action and ingenious plots. Their atmosphere is gently romantic rather than loaded with emotion. Their heroines are charming, enterprising, high-spirited, independent-minded, witty, modern enough to smoke and drink cocktails (in the 1920s and 1930s), but ultimately traditionalist in that they marry solid, reliable, *nice* men whom they will allow to take care of them. The personality of the heroine is strongly established, particularly in those novels in which the heroine is narrator, as Peronelle, the heroine/narrator of *The Great Husband Hunt*, and Sally of *Sally in a Service Flat*, who describes one morning's post thus: '*July 7* Another repulsive Income Tax paper has arrived and of the same sticky hue. I suppose those who perpetuate these abominable documents imagine that we will be reminded of sunshine when we catch sight of their yellow envelopes, but nothing of the sort, jaundice or yellow-fever is nearer the mark'.

Grundy's characters are endearing, good-humoured people, sometimes benignly eccentric (and consequently good at helping the plot along) as, for instance, the uncle in *The Great Husband Hunt* who offers £1,000 and a substantial dowry to the first of his four dependent nieces to get engaged. The dialogue is consistently light-hearted and amusing, as this exchange between Hazel and her pompous, over-aesthetic fiancé, Eustace: 'There is a little book on monistic and genetic philosophy I want to read to you', he said. 'I think it will help you to feel happier'. 'Is it about monasteries?' I inquired (*The Vacillations of Hazel*; Eustace later asks to be released from their engagement, and Hazel marries nice, comfortable Mr Ickworth, her devoted admirer for many years).

The wit with which Grundy habitually treats her plots, characters, and dialogue extends also to the titles of her novels, which are alliterative, eyecatching, and intriguing. Sometimes they may even appear rather risqué, though of course they prove to be entirely respectable. The *Undressed Heroine* is simply a dowdily dressed young woman whose romantic prospects improve no end when she is provided with artistic and beautiful clothes by Mrs Clinton Tomkins, an eccentric well-wisher. *Her Mad Month* is the time spent in Harrogate by an independent-minded heroine who runs away in her stern grandmother's absence and incidentally 'meets her fate'. The heroine of *A Girl for Sale* is the enterprising and modern Whiff Woffran who finds herself without a job after the Armistice and in desperation advertises in the newspaper for a new employer (whom she marries).

Grundy's delightful novels brought her many admirers, including *Times Literary Supplement* reviewers, and although they would today be regarded as period pieces it is a shame that they are so difficult to come by.

—Jean Buchanan

HAGGARD, (Sir) H(enry) Rider.
Nationality: British. **Born:** Bradenham, Norfolk, 22 June 1856. **Education:** Ipswich Grammar School, Suffolk; Lincoln's Inn, London, 1881–85: called to the Bar 1885. **Relations:** married Louisa Mariana Margitson in 1880; one son and three daughters. **Career:** lived in South Africa, as secretary to Sir Henry Bulwer, lieutenant-governor of Natal, 1875–77, member of the staff of Sir Theophilus

Shepstone, special commissioner in the Transvaal, 1877, and master and registrar of the High Court of the Transvaal, 1877–79; returned to England, 1879; managed his wife's estate in Norfolk, from 1880; worked in chambers of Henry Bargave Deane, 1885–87; unionist and agricultural candidate for East Norfolk, 1895; co-editor, *African Review*, 1898; travelled throughout England investigating condition of agriculture and the rural population, 1901–02; British Government special commissioner to report on Salvation Army settlements in the USA, 1905; chairman, Reclamation and Unemployed Labour Committee, Royal Commission on Coast Erosion and Afforestation, 1906–11; travelled around the world as a member of the Dominions Royal Commission, 1912–17. Chair of the Committee, Society of Authors, 1896–98; vice-president Royal Colonial Institute, 1917. **Recipient:** knighted, 1912; KBE (Knight Commander, Order of the British Empire), 1919. **Died:** 14 May 1925.

Romance and Historical Publications

Novels (series: Chaka; Allan Quatermain; She)

Dawn. London, Hurst and Blackett, 3 vols, 1884; New York, Appleton, 1 vol, 1887.
The Witch's Head. London, Hurst and Blackett, 3 vols, 1884; New York, Appleton, 1 vol, 1885.
King Solomon's Mines (Quatermain). London and New York, Cassell, 1885.
She: A History of Adventure. New York, Harper, 1886; London, Longman, 1887.
Allan Quatermain. London, Longman, and New York, Harper, 1887.
Jess. London, Smith Elder, and New York, Harper, 1887.
A Tale of Three Lions, and On Going Back. New York, Munro, 1887.
Mr Meeson's Will. New York, Harper, and London, Spencer Blackett, 1888.
Maiwa's Revenge. New York, Harper, and London, Longman, 1888.
My Fellow Laborer (includes 'The Wreck of the Copeland'). New York, Munro, 1888.
Colonel Quaritch, V.C. New York, Lovell, 1888; London, Longman, 3 vols, 1888.
Cleopatra. London, Longman, and New York, Harper, 1889.
Beatrice. London, Longman, and New York, Harper, 1890.
The World's Desire, with Andrew Lang. London, Longman, and New York, Harper, 1890.
Eric Brighteyes. London, Longman, and New York, United States Book Company, 1891.
Nada the Lily. New York and London, Longman, 1892.
Montezuma's Daughter. New York and London, Longman, 1893.
The People of the Mist. London and New York, Longman, 1894.
Heart of the World. New York, Longman, 1895; London, Longman, 1896.
Joan Haste. London and New York, Longman, 1895.
The Wizard. Bristol, Arrowsmith, and New York, Longman, 1896.
Doctor Therne. London and New York, Longman, 1898.
Swallow. New York and London, Longman, 1899.
The Spring of a Lion. New York, Neeley, 1899.
Lysbeth. New York and London, Longman, 1901.
Pearl-Maiden. London and New York, Longman, 1903.
The Brethren. London, Cassell, and New York, Doubleday, 1904.
Stella Fregelius: A Tale of Three Destinies. London and New York, Longman, 1904.
Ayesha: The Return of She. London, Ward Lock, and New York, Doubleday, 1905.
Benita: An African Romance. London, Cassell, 1906; as *The Spirit of Bambatse*, New York, Longman, 1906.

The Way of the Spirit. London, Hutchinson, 1906.
Fair Margaret. London, Hutchinson, 1907; as *Margaret*, New York, Longman, 1907.
The Lady of the Heavens. New York, Authors and Newspapers Association, 1908; as *The Ghost Kings*, London, Cassell, 1908.
The Yellow God. New York, Cupples and Leon, 1908; London, Cassell, 1909.
The Lady of Blossholme. London, Hodder and Stoughton, 1909.
Morning Star. London, Cassell, and New York, Longman, 1910.
Queen Sheba's Ring. London, Nash, and New York, Doubleday, 1910.
The Mahatma and the Hare: A Dream Story. London, Longman, and New York, Holt, 1911.
Red Eve. London, Hodder and Stoughton, and New York, Doubleday, 1911.
Marie (Chaka). London, Cassell, and New York, Longman, 1912.
Child of Storm (Chaka). London, Cassell, and New York, Longman, 1913.
The Wanderer's Necklace. London, Cassell, and New York, Longman, 1914.
The Holy Flower. London, Ward Lock, 1915; as *Allan and the Holy Flower*, New York, Longman, 1915.
The Ivory Child. London, Cassell, and New York, Longman, 1916.
Finished (Chaka). London, Ward Lock, and New York, Longman, 1917.
Moon of Israel. London, Murray, and New York, Longman, 1918.
Love Eternal. London, Cassell, and New York, Longman, 1918.
When the World Shook. London, Cassell, and New York, Longman, 1919.
The Ancient Allan. London, Cassell, and New York, Longman, 1920.
She and Allan. New York, Longman, and London, Hutchinson, 1921.
The Virgin of the Sun. London, Cassell, and New York, Doubleday, 1922.
Wisdom's Daughter. London, Hutchinson, and New York, Doubleday, 1923.
Heu-Heu; or, The Monster (Quatermain). London, Hutchinson, and New York, Doubleday, 1924.
Queen of the Dawn. New York, Doubleday, and London, Hutchinson, 1925.
The Treasure of the Lake. New York, Doubleday, and London, Hutchinson, 1926.
Allan and the Ice-Gods. London, Hutchinson, and New York, Doubleday, 1927.
Mary of Marion Isle. London, Hutchinson, and New York, Doubleday, 1929.
Belshazzar. London, Paul, and New York, Doubleday, 1930.

Short Stories

Allan's Wife and Other Tales. London, Blackett, and New York, Harper, 1889.
Black Heart and White Heart, and Other Stories. London, Longman, 1900; as *Elissa, and Black Heart and White Heart*, New York, Longman, 1900.
Smith and the Pharaohs and Other Tales. Bristol, Arrowsmith, 1920; New York, Longman, 1921.
The Best Short Stories of Rider Haggard, edited by Peter Haining. London, Joseph, 1981.

Other Publications

Other

Cetywayo and His White Neighbours; or, Remarks on Recent

Events in Zululand, Natal, and the Transvaal. London, Trübner, 1882; revised edition, 1888; reprinted in part, as *The Last Boer War*, London, Kegan Paul, 1899; as *A History of the Transvaal*, New York, New Amsterdam, 1899.

Church and the State: An Appeal to the Laity. Privately printed, 1895.

A Farmer's Year, Being His Commonplace Book for 1898. London and New York, Longman, 1899.

The New South Africa. London, Pearson, 1900.

A Winter Pilgrimage: . . . Travels Through Palestine, Italy, and the Island of Cyprus. London and New York, Longman, 1901.

Rural England. London and New York, Longman, 2 vols, 1902.

A Gardener's Year. London and New York, Longman, 1905.

Report on the Salvation Army Colonies. London, His Majesty's Stationery Office, 1905; as *The Poor and the Land*, London and New York, Longman, 1905.

Regeneration, Being an Account of the Social Work of the Salvation Army in Great Britain. London, Longman, 1910; New York, Longman, 1911.

Rural Denmark and Its Lessons. London and New York, Longman, 1911.

A Call to Arms to the Men of East Anglia. Privately printed, 1914.

The After-War Settlement and the Employment of Ex-Service Men in the Oversea Dominions. London, Saint Catherine Press, 1916.

The Days of My Life: An Autobiography, edited by C. J. Longman. London and New York, Longman, 2 vols, 1926.

The Private Diaries of Sir H. Rider Haggard 1914–1925, edited by D.S. Higgins. London, Cassell, and New York, Stein and Day, 1980.

*

Film Adaptations: *She*, 1935, 1965, 1985; *King Solomon's Mines*, 1937, 1950, 1959, 1985; *King Solomon's Treasure*, 1979, from the novel *Allan Quatermain*; *Allan Quatermain and the Lost City of Gold*, 1987, based on several of the novels featuring Alain Quartermain.

Bibliography: *A Bibliography of the Writings of Sir Henry Rider Haggard* by J.E. Scott, London, Elkin Mathews, 1947; *H. Rider Haggard: A Bibliography* by D.E. Whatmore, London, Mansell, 1987.

Critical Studies: *The Cloak That I Left* (biography) by Lilias Rider Haggard, London, Hodder and Stoughton, 1951; *Rider Haggard: His Life and Works* by Morton N. Cohen, London, Hutchinson, 1960, New York, Walker, 1961, revised edition, London, Macmillan, 1968; *H. Rider Haggard: A Voice from the Infinite* by Peter Berresford Ellis, London, Routledge, 1978; *Rider Haggard, The Great Storyteller* by D.S. Higgins, London, Cassell, 1981, New York, Stein and Day, 1983; *Rider Haggard and the Fiction of Empire: A Critical Study of British Imperial Fiction* by Wendy R. Katz, Cambridge, Cambridge University Press, 1988; *Rider Haggard and the Lost Empire* by Tom Pocock, London, Weidenfeld and Nicolson, 1993.

*   *   *

King Solomon's Mines is rather patronizingly dedicated by Allan Quatermain, its fictive narrator, to 'all the big and little boys who read it'. However, since its first publication in 1885, this story has been both thrilling youngsters with its adventure and delighting adults with the skill its author displays in relating it. It is a childhood classic that never loses its power to enthral, even nowadays when attitudes towards the native peoples of Africa and the environment in which they live have changed radically.

In writing the story, H. Rider Haggard followed the wise course of writing about what he knew well and responded to emotionally himself. Fortunately for him his readers in the second-half of the Victorian period were ready to welcome his presentation of the romance of Southern Africa. The opening up of the territory ranked high on the European agenda at the time, and Rider Haggard had personal experience of colonial administration in Natal and the Transvaal. He was particularly impressed, as was British opinion generally, by the military vigour of the Zulus who had inflicted notable defeats even on regular troops, and the finding of enigmatic traces of ancient civilizations, such as the extensive ruins at Grand Zimbabwe which some scholars linked with the semi-mythical Queen of Sheba, stirred an imagination already fired by the discovery of unimagined deposits of gold and diamonds in southern Africa. Rider Haggard brings all these fabulous elements together in an account, told by the tight-lipped and experienced hunter Allan Quatermain, of the quest by the English aristocrat Sir Henry Curtis for his brother, who, rather like David Livingstone, has disappeared in the interior without a trace. The other white member of the search party is Captain John Good RN, whose fastidious keeping up of standards adds humour and even a little love interest—which is not, however, allowed to develop very far. Gradually, as the Europeans press on and enter the sinister native kingdom of Kukuanaland, they come to realize that their servant Umbopa, a magnificent figure of a man, is Ignosi, the legitimate heir to its throne. In Rider Haggard's respect for what Ignosi represents and the society he is called to rule there is sympathy and understanding that offsets, to some extent at least, the imperialist and white-suprematist assumptions that disturb some who read the novel. Before all the problems are resolved the travellers have to endure extreme privations and fight desperately for their lives; worse still, these Europeans who set out confident in the power of rationality begin to sense that mysterious forces are ranged against them, especially when the hideous old hag Gagool starts her witch hunt.

Though *King Solomon's Mines* is, in large measure, a reflection of a fertile imagination's response to life in Southern Africa at an exciting time, the novel owes much of its success to the dexterity with which it is presented. Rider Haggard wrote it in just six weeks, apparently on the spur of the moment, but that does not mean that the execution is in any way slap-dash. Perhaps the fact that *Treasure Island* had just shown how romances could be handled may be one reason why he was able to work so quickly, though it is unfair to exaggerate the importance of the undoubted influence of R.L. Stevenson, for there are many obvious differences between the technique of the two stories and their subjects. Rider Haggard does, however, follow Stevenson in taking a handful of characters who are clearly differentiated, creating adventure fast on the heels of adventure, and, above, in making his narrative style calmly matter-of-fact with realistic detail, sometimes in an almost pedantic way, which makes it very easy to believe everything.

Had Rider Haggard written nothing except *King Solomon's Mines*, he would still be famous. In fact he was the author of some 60 other works, ranging from factual accounts of the Zulus and of farming in East Anglia, where he lived much of his life, to novels in a variety of styles and set in many different locations. *Allan Quatermain* is another African adventure, this time in search of a lost white civilization, and *She*, almost as a counterpart to the masculine orientation of *King Solomon's Mines*, features Ayesha, a terrifying Persian priestess 2,000 years old who tyrannizes a central African society as she awaits the reincarnation of her former lover. Rider Haggard's imagination played on similar themes of female power in *Allan's Wife* and *Cleopatra*, which is set in ancient Egypt. There is a change of scene for the Viking story of *Eric Brighteyes*, but *Nada the Lily* takes us back to Africa again. Critics, who discount Rider Haggard's attempts at sustained novel writing, have been inclined to see most of his later romances as attempts to find fresh life in the sort of material he exploited so cleverly in his first successes. When he does cogitate on such themes as the relationships between societies at different stages of development or else to explore ideas such as the cyclical return of the personality in different guises, it is doubtful whether this amounts to genuine intellectual curiosity, rather than an attempt to give some depth to his tale. Hard as he tried, Rider Haggard did not in his later years manage to produce works that equalled *King Solomon's Mines* and *She* in the estimation of the general public.

—Christopher N. Smith

HAIG, Fenil.   See **FORD, Ford Madox.**

HAINES, Pamela (Mary).
Nationality: British. **Born:** Harrogate, Yorkshire, 4 November 1929. **Education:** St Joseph's Convent, Tamworth, Staffordshire, 1938; Newnham College, Cambridge, 1949–52, M.A. in English. **Relations:** married Tony Haines in 1955; three daughters and two sons. **Recipient:** *Spectator* New Writing prize, 1971; Yorkshire Art award, 1975. **Died.**

ROMANCE AND HISTORICAL PUBLICATIONS

Novels

Tea at Gunter's. London, Heinemann, 1974.
A Kind of War. London, Heinemann, 1976.
Men on White Horses. London, Collins, 1978.
The Kissing Gate. London, Collins, and New York, Doubleday, 1981.
The Diamond Waterfall. London, Collins, and New York, Doubleday, 1984.
The Golden Lion. London, Collins, and New York, Scribner, 1986.
Daughter of the Northern Fields. London, Collins, 1987.

OTHER PUBLICATIONS

Other

Hastings in Old Photographs. Stroud, Sutton, 1989.

*   *   *

The novels of Pamela Haines share a nucleus of common themes. All portray the growth of a young girl to womanhood, the fight for independence from the smothering shadow of the past, the idealized love for the flawed love object. All are pervaded by a strong tragic sense and the lurking threat of violence. From the first there are indications that the early balanced precision will be foresaken in favour of a greater breadth of vision, a wider compass. It seems inevitable that their author should eventually come to the full-scale family saga of *The Kissing Gate*.

Tea at Gunter's focuses on the heroine's attempts at self-realization, which are threatened by the pervasive dream-world of her mother, still living in a romanticized past of love for her effete stepbrother Gervase. When Lucy herself falls in love, her freedom is achieved only at a terrible cost. A poised, subtle work, *Tea at Gun-*

ter's is the most perfect of Haines's creations, the author displaying a mastery of tone and considerable psychological penetration. *A Kind of War* explores the minds of three women, each of a different generation, whose lives lack a fulfilling relationship. Skilfully the novel traces each through past and present, moving towards the concluding tragedy in a clean underplayed style which reveals the nature of the differing characters, the grief tinged with welcome touches of humour. Already in *A Kind of War* one senses a movement outward from the confines of the work, a yearning for larger forms.

Men on White Horses describes Edwina's growth from childhood to maturity in Edwardian Yorkshire. Beginning with a brilliant portrayal of her early years, the author reveals the threat to her selfhood posed by her mother, and later by a domineering school friend. Physically and spiritually scarred by life, her one secret love tragically killed, Edwina finds fulfilment in her music and its related symbol, the sea. When at last she feels life return in waves in her pianist's hands, the reader knows that her spirit remains unconquered by its suffering. Some of the later chapters are less satisfying, but the novel as a whole is a remarkable achievement.

The Kissing Gate, which combines gothic romance with the psychological subtlety of the previous novels, is the most ambitious of Haines's works, and follows the Rawson family through three generations of the last century. The kissing gate of the title—symbol of love and death—is central to the book. Here Sarah Rawson rescues the squire's son, and begins the involvement between the Rawsons and the aristocratic Inghams which spans the course of the novel. The story is continued through Sarah's children, and ends with her granddaughter, another Sarah, leaving the kissing gate for a new life. Most of the action, though, is dominated by two Catherines—both outsiders brought to Downham by Sarah's son John. Catriona Drummond, who marries him, and Kate the Irish girl he saves from starvation in the Great Famine. Their personalities overshadow the plot, and give the work its direction. Violence flares throughout, and the railway runs a dark thread through the story, instrument of disgrace and death. A huge epic novel, *The Kissing Gate* lacks the perfect balance of Haines's earlier works. There are flaws in the fabric—too many unhappy marriages, unfortunate accidents, fortuitous deaths—but interest is sustained to such an extent that they are scarcely noticed. In its vast scale and the sureness of its insights, this is the most impressive of Haines's novels.

The subsequent novels are similar in form to *The Kissing Gate*, and cover several generations. In *The Diamond Waterfall* the reader follows three heroines from Edwardian times to 1945, exploring their luckless marriages and joyful, forbidden loves. *The Golden Lion* examines the relationship between a Sicilian girl raised by a Yorkshire family, and her own adopted daughter. These works, too, plunge deep into the darker side of pre-war life, uncovering the repressed violence and sexuality seething beneath the respectable façade. Such an interest sometimes appears obsessive, but there is no doubting the author's assured control, or her mastery of detail. *Daughter of the Northern Fields* pursues a new direction, telling the story of Christabel, natural daughter of Branwell Brontë. Its theme—the destructive force of illicit love—and the device of the internal narrative recall the Brontë novels, but it impresses as a strong, intriguing story in its own right.

Haines's writing shows an excellent period sense. Whether contemporary or historical, the feel of the time is splendidly caught. Her grasp of character is sure, her dialogue superb. Her books present the essence of life, its tragedy leavened by sharp flashes of humour. With a clear but sympathetic eye she depicts the transient joys, the harrowing griefs, the slow poignant awakening of love.

—Geoffrey Sadler

HALL, James Norman.   See NORDHOFF, Charles and HALL, James Norman.

HALL, (Marguerite) Radclyffe.

Pseudonym: Marguerite Radclyffe-Hall. **Nationality:** British. **Born:** Bournemouth, Hampshire, 12 August 1880 (or 1886?). Called John by intimate friends. **Relations:** lived with her lover, Mabel Veronica Batten, 1908–16 (died 1916); 2) lover, Lady Una Vincent Troubridge, 1916–43. **Career:** full-time writer. Council member, Society for Psychical Research, 1916–24. Inherited a fortune from her grandfather, 1901. **Recipient:** James Tait Black memorial prize, 1927; Prix Femina Vie Heureuse, 1927, for *Adam's Breed*. **Died:** 11 October 1943.

ROMANCE AND HISTORICAL PUBLICATIONS

Novels

The Forgotten Island (as Marguerite Radclyffe-Hall). London, Chapman and Hall, 1915.
The Forge. London, Arrowsmith, 1924.
The Unlit Lamp. London, Cassell, 1924; New York, Cape, 1929.
A Saturday Life. London, Arrowsmith, 1925.
Adam's Breed. London, Cassell, and New York, Doubleday Page, 1926.
The Well of Loneliness. London, Cape, and New York, Covici Friede, 1928.
The Master of the House. London, Cape, 1932.
The Sixth Beatitude. London, Heinemann, and New York, Harcourt Brace, 1936.

OTHER PUBLICATIONS

Short Stories

Miss Ogilvy Finds Herself. London, Heinemann, and New York, Harcourt, Brace, 1934.

Poetry

Twixt Earth and Stars (as Marguerite Radclyffe-Hall). London, John and Edward Bumpas, 1906.
A Sheaf of Verses. London, John and Edward Bumpas, 1908.
Poems of the Past and Present (as Marguerite Radclyffe-Hall). London, Chapman and Hall, 1910.
Songs of Three Counties and Other Poems. London, Chapman and Hall, 1913.
The Forgotten Island. London, Chapman and Hall, 1915.

Other

Policeman of the Land: A Political Satire. London, Sophistocles Press, 1928.

*

Critical Studies: *The Life and Death of Radclyffe Hall* by Una Vincent Troubridge, London, Femina Books, 1945; *Hall: A Case of Obscenity?* by Vera Brittain, London, Hammond, 1968; *Hall at the Well of Loneliness: A Sapphic Chronicle* by Lovat Dickson, London, Collins, 1975; *Beyond the Well of Loneliness: The Fiction of Hall* by Claudia Stillman Franks, Amersham, Avebury, 1982; *Our Three Selves: A Life Of Hall* by Michael Baker, London, Hamilton, 1985; *Reflecting on the Well of Loneliness* by Rebecca O'Rourke, London, Routledge, 1989.

*   *   *

Radclyffe Hall is undoubtedly best remembered for her novel *The Well of Loneliness*—partly because of the obscenity trial and banning to which the book was subjected (lifted in 1948), and partly because, as Alison Hennegan points out in the 1982 Virago edition, it became known as *the* lesbian novel—and even as 'the Bible of lesbianism'. It is, thus, a book which has often had a reputation, moreover, for being either salacious or radical—or both. In fact, it is not salacious and its status as a radical *text* is not immediately self-evident (apart from the subject matter, which was, in effect, what was being censored at the book's trial).

It is, in many respects, a very conventional novel (even a conservative one), and one which draws firmly on romance traditions, though usually centred on the 'masculine' rather than 'feminine' romantic consciousness which its notably named female protagonist Stephen Gordon possesses (Stephen is masculine in the way men are envisaged in romance). Its central themes are the desire of its protagonist, Stephen Gordon, to love, and the obstacles that stand in the way. The narrative technique is similarly straightforward: an omniscient 'authorial' narrator can range without any sense of disjunction over external and internal viewpoints at will, and is able to give complete accounts of characters' thoughts, feelings and actions:

> Anna Gordon held her child to her breast, but she grieved while it drank, because of her man who longed so much for a son. And seeing her grief, Sir Philip hid his chagrin, and he fondled the baby and examined its fingers.

However, this seeming conformity to generic and technical 'norms' is transformed by a simple device at the level of *content* rather than form. The device is simply to locate what the novel clearly sees as a 'masculine' psyche in a female body, and then to trace what difference this 'fact' does make to this individual and to their experience of social existence.

In terms of the romance quest for love and identity, the first obstacles present themselves early in childhood—indeed at her very birth—because her mother, Anna, is disappointed that she is a girl (a disappointment based on her total acceptance of her husband's desire for a male child). She finds it impossible to love the child, and the child is never able to love her. In the more-or-less Freudian terms which underpin much of the novel's psychological discourse, the nature of the protagonist's desire thereafter could be seen as largely motivated by the need to replace this 'bad' mother figure by a female figure who can be loved. The child's strong identification with her father reinforces this by making him—and other men—a figure who is loved in a way strongly categorized as non-erotic:

> At about this time Stephen first became conscious of an urgent necessity to love. She adored her father, but that was quite different; he was part of herself, he had always been there, she could not envisage the world without him—it was other with Collins the housemaid.

The strong identification of the reader with a protagonist who is seen as definitively masculine, which the narrative establishes by conventional means, makes the obstacles and paradoxes met by Stephen shocking precisely to a conservative sense of 'normality'. Even her name functions not as a sign of sexual difference, but as a sign of her membership of normality—a sign insisted upon by her father—because we do not perceive any disjunction between name and gender. Thus curiously the novel asserts Stephen's 'normality' by associating her with norms which would normally reject her. A good illustration of this is provided by a romance-style scene in which friendship becomes love, as Martin Hallam proposes to her; this is Stephen's reaction:

She was staring at him a kind of dumb horror, staring at his eyes that were clouded by desire, while gradually over her colourless face there was spreading an expression of the deepest repulsion ... and ... a look as of outrage.

Stephen is clearly reacting here as a 'normal' heterosexual male to an unexpected declaration of erotic love from a close male friend.

Many other episodes in the novel function in similar ways—for example, Stephen's general attitude to gay men such as Jonathon Brockett is to see them as 'effeminate', and her competition with Martin Hallam at the end of the novel for the love of Mary Llewellyn is seen very much as if between two 'conventional' male friends. This could be seen as part of what Alison Hennegan suggests is a 'repugnantly masochistic' attitude in the novel towards the kinds of sexuality it appears to speak for. Its location of Stephen (almost) wholly in terms of 'constant reference to heterosexual standards and masculine values' could, however, also be seen as a strategic device to construct a 'normal' reader to whom the absurdities of contemporary definitions of gender and sexuality would be unavoidable (the charge that this fundamentally regards 'inversion' as 'unnatural' is not, of course, disposed of by this argument).

In her six other novels Radclyffe Hall treated a range of issues (particularly those concerning various kinds of social entrapment or alienation), often using romance modes, and showed, as with *The Well of Loneliness*, that conventions can be used to challenge convention, and that highly readable novels can also be challenging.

—Chris Hopkins

HALLIDAY, Dorothy. See **DUNNETT, Dorothy.**

HAMILTON, Gail. See **CONCORAN, Barbara.**

HAMILTON, Hervey. See **ROBINS, Denise.**

HAMILTON, Julia.
Pseudonym for Julia Watson. **Other Pseudonyms:** Jane de Vere; Julia Fitzgerald. Also wrote as Julia Watson. **Nationality:** British. **Born:** Bangor, North Wales, 18 September 1943. **Education:** Elland Grammar School, and Huddersfield College of Art, both in Yorkshire. **Relations:** married and divorced twice; one daughter and one son. **Career:** artist, jewellery designer, model, and historical adviser to Sphere Books. **Died:** 1991.

ROMANCE AND HISTORICAL PUBLICATIONS

Novels as Julia Hamilton (series: Habsburg)

The Scarlet Women (as Jane de Vere). London, Corgi, 1969.
The Last of the Tudors. London, Hale, 1971.
Katherine of Aragon. London, Sphere, and New York, Beagle, 1972; as *Katherine the Tragic Tudor.* London, Hale, 1974.
Anne of Cleves. London, Sphere, and New York, Beagle, 1972.
Son of York. London, Sphere, 1973.
Habsburg:
    The Changeling Queen. London, Hale, 1977.
    The Emperor's Daughter. London, Hale, 1978.

The Pearl of the Habsburgs. London, Hale, 1978.
The Snow Queen. London, Hale, 1978.
The Habsburg Inheritance. London, Hale, 1980.

Novels as Julia Fitzgerald (series: Astromance)

Royal Slave. London, Futura, and New York, Ballantine, 1978.
Scarlet Woman. London, Futura, 1979; New York, Nordon, 1981.
Slave Lady. London, Futura, 1980.
Salamander. London, Futura, 1981.
Fallen Woman. London, Futura, 1981.
Venus Rising. London, Futura, 1982.
The Princess and the Pagan. London, Futura, 1983; as *Silken Captive.* New York, Pinnacle, 1986.
Firebird. London, Century, 1983; n.p., Leisure Circle, 1988.
The Jewelled Serpent. London, Century, 1984; as *Beyond Ecstasy,* New York, Pinnacle, 1985.
Taboo. London, Century, 1985; New York, Bart, 1988.
Desert Queen. London, Century, 1986; New York, Bart, 1988.
Astromance:
    1. *Flame of the East.* London, Macdonald, 1986; New York, Bart, 1988.
    2. *Daughter of the Gods.* London, Macdonald, 1986; New York, Bart, 1988.
    3. *Pasadoble.* London, Futura, 1986; New York, Bart, 1988.
    4. *A Kiss from Aphrodite.* London, Futura, 1987; New York, Bart, 1988.
    5. *Castle of the Enchantress.* London, Futura, 1987; New York, Bart, 1988.
    6. *Jade Moon.* New York, Bart, 1988.
    7. *Devil in My Arms.* New York, Bart, 1989.
    8. *Temple of Butterflies.* New York, Bart, 1989.
    9. *Glade of Jewels.* New York, Bart, 1989.
    10. *Bridge of Rainbows.* New York, Bart, 1989.
    11. *Pagan Blossoms.* New York, Bart, 1989.
Beauty of the Devil. London, Century, 1988.
Earth Queen, Sky King. London, Century, 1989.
Rich in Paradise. London, Century, 1992.

Novels as Julia Watson (series: Gentian Trilogy)

The Lovechild. London, Hale, 1967; New York, Bantam, 1968.
Medici Mistress. London, Corgi, 1968.
The Gentian Trilogy:
    A Mistress for the Valois. London, Hale, 1969.
    The King's Mistress. London, Corgi, 1970.
    The Wolf and the Unicorn. London, Corgi, 1971.
Winter of the Witch. London, Corgi, 1971; New York, Bantam, 1972.
The Tudor Rose. London, Hale, 1972.
Saffron. London, Corgi, 1972.
Love Song. London, Futura, 1981.

OTHER PUBLICATIONS

Other

Healthy Signs. London, Arrow, 1989; Wallingford, Pennsylvania, Middle Atlantic Press, 1989.

*

Julia Hamilton commented (1990):
    'Live dangerously in print' is my motto for today's women readers who are so often tied down by both jobs and families. The pas-

sionate, epic love stories that I create are a feast which won't make my readers overweight and which won't have any unpleasant repercussions (unless the dinner's allowed to burn while they're being read). I believe implicitly in love, that it is everything, that it can conquer all, that life would be empty and meaningless without it; and this is also the opinion of my strong-minded, spirited, and undaunted heroines—although my heroes take a little longer to be persuaded! Despite trials and adversities, my heroes and heroines find they can't live without one another, which is exactly the point of love, in my opinion. They are also sensual characters with strong appetites for each other, whose love story is played out against an authentic deeply researched background. Turkey, Venice, London, Arabia, Egypt, India, Dublin and Tipperary, Algiers, Yorkshire, Liverpool, and Greece are just some of the settings featured in my books. Pirates, sultans, pashas, renegades, princes, dukes, kings and queens, magicians, astrologers, and royal intriguers feature among my characters, as do ladies of fashion, princesses, courtesans, gypsies, daughters of dukes, and wilful heiresses.

*   *   *

The late author Julia Watson enjoyed a successful career as a romance and historical writer. Under three separate pseudonyms—Julia Hamilton, Jane de Vere, and Julia Fitzgerald, the author created enjoyable and lively books.

As Julia Hamilton, the author combined her best talents of a good imagination, the ability to write steamy scenes, and a penchant for detailed, opulent backgrounds to create the 'Habsburg series'. The series examines the lives of the children and grandchildren of Maximilian, the Holy Roman Emperor. *The Changeling Queen*, the first in the series, reconstructs the life of the volatile Juana of Castile. Beautiful, wilful, and moody the young Juana is married to Philip the Handsome, a spoilt, self-indulgent king, who loves her passionately at first and then discards her callously. His treatment of her and his open extra-marital affairs drive what little sanity Juana has away, leaving her an unstable and sad character by the end of the book. Philip has her incarcerated in a fortress castle near Medina del Campo, and takes away almost all of her children.

Marguerite of Austria is the main protagonist of *The Pearl of the Habsburgs*. Recently widowed, Marguerite hides herself away in her château, only to emerge when she is needed by Juana of Castile's children. Juana's children are neglected, and a Regent is desperately needed to govern Flanders. Marguerite has to overcome her grief, and do her duty to the Empire and her family.

Similarly the mistreated and abused Queen Isabella of Denmark suffers her foul husband, Christian, because of her duty to her grandfather, Maximilian, and her children in *The Snow Queen*. Isabella, the sweetest and most delicate of all of the Holy Roman Emperor's grandchildren, is bartered off as part of a political alliance. No one realizes just how perverted and brutal Christian of Denmark is. He flaunts his mistress, Sigritt Valloms, in Isabella's face, and makes Sigritt the most powerful woman in Denmark. She takes away Isabella's son and places her own daughter in the queen's chambers as a spy. In contrast to this, the plot moves to the Spanish court where Juana is still imprisoned with her youngest daughter, Catalina. The book ends with Maximilian's death and Charles V's accession.

In all of these books the author recreated historic events with considerable artistic licence—dwelling more on the sexual exploits of Christian of Denmark, for example, than on the political games of the time. Her female characters are all exploited and governed by men; thus, Juana of Castile and Isabella are auctioned off in order to gain the best treaty or alliance for their parents/grandparents.

As Julia Fitzgerald, the author wrote a mixture of lengthy, steamy sagas set in exotic locations, and also a series of highly innovative Astromances, which unites romance and astrology. She said of the Astromance series, 'There is a wide belief that some signs are in-compatible but I hope to show that love can conquer all, a possibility that I believe implicitly'. Indeed *Flame of the East*, the first of the series, sees a Sagittarian heroine (adventurous, loving, full of adventure) and a Scorpio hero (intense, sensual, and possessive) link horns and then fall in love. The setting is the exotic North African desert which finds Star Kempton trekking, and Zack Barclay leading the trek. He objects to her presence but gradually changes his mind about her abilities and her character. Although this series is fun and lighthearted it is disappointing given the more detailed historical novels that the author wrote.

Hamilton also had the ability to create realistic scenes of poverty and brutality. This is best seen in *Scarlet Woman* in which the ten-year-old heroine, Meggie, finds herself living in terror because of her physically and sexually abusive stepfather. She puts up with it for the sake of her weak mother until she herself is raped and she overhears her stepfather planning a 'gang-bang' for his friends. Although she tries hard to survive she eventually realizes that prostitution is her only option. The author portrays slum-London in glorious detail evoking the dirty dwellings from which Meggie comes.

Cassia, the heroine of *Royal Slave* is also raped by her fiancé—and then by a series of other men. Unfortunately, she ends up as the Sultan's favourite in a harem, and is rescued only to fall into even worse straits. Similarly *The Jewelled Serpent* is set in the Muslim world of North Africa, and the heroine who journeys there to rescue her sister also has gruelling encounters.

Although Hamilton/Fitzgerald/de Vere's characters sometimes find themselves in seemingly unbelievable positions, the author's books are always an interesting and well-researched read.

—P. Campbell

HAMILTON, Mollie.   See **KAYE, M.M.**

HAMILTON, Priscilla.   See **GELLIS, Roberta.**

HAMPSON, Anne.
Nationality: British. **Education:** left school at age 14; later attended Manchester College of Education, teaching certificate. **Relations:** married for 14 years; one son. **Career:** café owner, sewing factory worker, and milk deliverer; teacher for four years, then full-time writer. **Address:** c/o Hodder and Stoughton Ltd, Mill Road, Dunton Green, Sevenoaks, Kent TN13 2YA, England.

ROMANCE AND HISTORICAL PUBLICATIONS

Novels

Eternal Summer. London, Mills and Boon, 1969; Toronto, Harlequin, 1970.
Precious Waif. London, Mills and Boon, 1969; Toronto, Harlequin, 1970.
Unwary Heart. London, Mills and Boon, 1969; Toronto, Harlequin, 1970.
The Autocrat of Melhurst. London, Mills and Boon, 1969; Toronto, Harlequin, 1970.
Gates of Steel. London, Mills and Boon, 1970; Toronto, Harlequin, 1973.
By Fountains Wild. London, Mills and Boon, 1970; Toronto, Harlequin, 1973.

Heaven Is High. London, Mills and Boon, 1970; Toronto, Harlequin, 1972.

Love Hath an Island. London, Mills and Boon, 1970; Toronto, Harlequin, 1971.

The Hawk and the Dove. London, Mills and Boon, 1970; Toronto, Harlequin, 1973.

Beyond the Sweet Waters. London, Mills and Boon, 1970; Toronto, Harlequin, 1971.

When the Bough Breaks. London, Mills and Boon, 1970; Toronto, Harlequin, 1971.

An Eagle Swooped. London, Mills and Boon, 1970; Toronto, Harlequin, 1974.

Isle of the Rainbows. London, Mills and Boon, 1970; Toronto, Harlequin, 1972.

Dark Hills Rising. London, Mills and Boon, 1971; Toronto, Harlequin, 1975.

The Rebel Bride. London, Mills and Boon, 1971; Toronto, Harlequin, 1973.

Stars of Spring. London, Mills and Boon, and Toronto, Harlequin, 1971.

Wings of the Night. London, Mills and Boon, 1971; Toronto, Harlequin, 1973.

Follow a Shadow. London, Mills and Boon, 1971; Toronto, Harlequin, 1977.

Gold Is the Sunrise. London, Mills and Boon, 1971; Toronto, Harlequin, 1972.

Petals Drifting. London, Mills and Boon, 1971; Toronto, Harlequin, 1974.

South of Mandraki. London, Mills and Boon, 1971; Toronto, Harlequin, 1973.

Waves of Fire. London, Mills and Boon, 1971; Toronto, Harlequin, 1973.

The Fair Island. London, Mills and Boon, 1972; Toronto, Harlequin, 1975.

Enchanted Dawn. London, Mills and Boon, 1972; Toronto, Harlequin, 1976.

Beloved Rake. London, Mills and Boon, 1972; Toronto, Harlequin, 1974.

The Plantation Boss. London, Mills and Boon, 1972; Toronto, Harlequin, 1973.

There Came a Tyrant. London, Mills and Boon, and Toronto, Harlequin, 1972.

Dark Avenger. London, Mills and Boon, 1972; Toronto, Harlequin, 1973.

Wife for a Penny. London, Mills and Boon, 1972; Toronto, Harlequin, 1974.

Hunter of the East. London, Mills and Boon, 1973; Toronto, Harlequin, 1974.

Boss of Bali Creek. London, Mills and Boon, 1973; Toronto, Harlequin, 1977.

Blue Hills of Sintra. London, Mills and Boon, 1973; Toronto, Harlequin, 1974.

Dear Stranger. London, Mills and Boon, and Toronto, Harlequin, 1973.

Stormy the Way. London, Mills and Boon, 1973; Toronto, Harlequin, 1974.

When Clouds Part. London, Mills and Boon, 1973; Toronto, Harlequin, 1974.

Master of Moonrock. Toronto, Harlequin, 1973.

Windward Crest. London, Mills and Boon, 1973.

A Kiss from Satan. Toronto, Harlequin, 1973.

The Black Eagle. London, Mills and Boon, 1973; Toronto, Harlequin, 1975.

Dear Plutocrat. London, Mills and Boon, 1973; Toronto, Harlequin, 1976.

After Sundown. Toronto, Harlequin, 1974.

Stars over Sarawak. London, Mills and Boon, and Toronto, Harlequin, 1974.

Fetters of Hate. London, Mills and Boon, 1974; Toronto, Harlequin, 1975.

Pride and Power. London, Mills and Boon, 1974; Toronto, Harlequin, 1975.

The Way of a Tyrant. London, Mills and Boon, and Toronto, Harlequin, 1974.

Moon Without Stars. London, Mills and Boon, 1974; Toronto, Harlequin, 1977.

Not Far from Heaven. London, Mills and Boon, 1974.

Two of a Kind. London, Mills and Boon, 1974.

Autumn Twilight. London, Mills and Boon, 1975; Toronto, Harlequin, 1976.

Flame of Fate. London, Mills and Boon, 1975.

Jonty in Love. London, Mills and Boon, 1975.

Reap the Whirlwind. London, Mills and Boon, 1975.

South of Capricorn. London, Mills and Boon, 1975.

Sunset Cloud. London, Mills and Boon, 1976; New York, Oxford University Press, 1979.

Song of the Waves. London, Mills and Boon, 1976; Toronto, Harlequin, 1977.

Dangerous Friendship. Toronto, Harlequin, 1976.

Satan and the Nymph. London, Mills and Boon, 1976.

A Man to Be Feared. London, Mills and Boon, and Toronto, Harlequin, 1976.

Isle at the Rainbow's End. London, Mills and Boon, 1976; Toronto, Harlequin, 1977.

Hills of Kalamata. London, Mills and Boon, 1976; Toronto, Harlequin, 1977.

Fire Meets Fire. London, Mills and Boon, 1976.

Dear Benefactor. London, Mills and Boon, 1976.

Call of the Outback. London, Mills and Boon, 1976; Toronto, Harlequin, 1977.

Call of the Veld. London, Mills and Boon, 1977; Toronto, Harlequin, 1978.

Harbour of Love. London, Mills and Boon, 1977; Toronto, Harlequin, 1979.

The Shadow Between. London, Mills and Boon, 1977; Toronto, Harlequin, 1978.

Sweet Is the Web. London, Mills and Boon, 1977; Toronto, Harlequin, 1978.

Moon Dragon. London, Mills and Boon, 1978.

To Tame a Vixen. London, Mills and Boon, 1978.

Master of Forrestmead. London, Mills and Boon, 1978.

Under Moonglow. London, Mills and Boon, and Toronto, Harlequin, 1978.

For Love of a Pagan. London, Mills and Boon, 1978.

Leaf in the Storm. London, Mills and Boon, and Toronto, Harlequin, 1978.

Above Rubies. Toronto, Harlequin, 1978.

Fly Beyond the Sunset. Toronto, Harlequin, 1978.

Isle of Desire. Toronto, Harlequin, 1978.

South of the Moon. Toronto, Harlequin, 1979.

Bride for a Night. London, Mills and Boon, 1979; Toronto, Harlequin, 1981.

Chateau in the Palms. London, Mills and Boon, 1979.

Coolibah Creek. London, Mills and Boon, 1979.

A Rose from Lucifer. London, Mills and Boon, 1979.

Temple of Dawn. London, Mills and Boon, 1979.

Call of the Heathen. London, Mills and Boon, 1980.

The Laird of Locharrun. London, Mills and Boon, 1980.

Pagan Lover. London, Mills and Boon, 1980.

The Dawn Steals Softly. New York and London, Silhouette, 1980.

Stormy Masquerade. New York and London, Silhouette, 1980.

Second Tomorrow. London, Silhouette, 1980.

Man of the Outback. New York, Silhouette, 1980; London, Silhouette, 1981.

Where Eagles Nest. New York, Silhouette, 1980; London, Silhouette, 1981.

Payment in Full. New York and London, Silhouette, 1980.

Beloved Vagabond. Toronto, Harlequin, 1981.

Man Without a Heart. New York, Silhouette, 1981.

Shadow of Apollo. New York, Silhouette, 1981.

Fascination. New York, Silhouette, 1981.

Desire. New York, Silhouette, 1981; London, Hodder and Stoughton, 1982.

Bitter Harvest. Toronto, Harlequin, 1982.

Unwanted Bride. Toronto, Harlequin, 1982.

Enchantment. London, Hodder and Stoughton, and New York, Silhouette, 1982.

Too Hot to Handle. Toronto, Harlequin, 1982.

A Kiss and a Promise. London, Hodder and Stoughton, 1982.

Man Without Honour. London, Hodder and Stoughton, 1982.

Realm of the Pagans. London, Hodder and Stoughton, 1982.

Stardust. London, Hodder and Stoughton, and New York, Silhouette, 1982.

Strangers May Marry. London, Hodder and Stoughton, 1982; New York, Silhouette, 1983.

Another Eden. New York, Silhouette, 1982; London, Hodder and Stoughton, 1983.

The Tender Years. New York, Silhouette, 1982; London, Hodder and Stoughton, 1983.

Devotion. London, Hodder and Stoughton, 1983.

The Dawn Is Golden. London, Hodder and Stoughton, 1983; New York, Silhouette, 1984.

Love So Rare. New York, Silhouette, 1983.

Dreamtime. London, Hodder and Stoughton, 1983.

Spell of the Island. New York, Silhouette, 1983; London, Hodder and Stoughton, 1984.

Soft Velvet Night. New York, Silhouette, 1983.

To Buy a Memory. London, Hodder and Stoughton, 1983.

When Love Comes. London, Hodder and Stoughton, and New York, Silhouette, 1983.

There Must Be Showers. New York, Silhouette, 1983; London, Hodder and Stoughton, 1984.

Sweet Second Love. New York, Silhouette, 1984.

Destiny. Bath, Firecrest, 1988.

A Touch of Romance. Bath, Firecrest, 1988.

*　　　*　　　*

As a well-known and prolific writer of romantic fiction, Anne Hampson has developed a style of writing peculiar to her own interpretation of romance as a battle between the sexes. The emphasis in her writing is on what may be described as a 'state of warfare' between the hero and heroine—as in warfare, neither side is initially prepared to compromise. Hostilities are often exacerbated by the fact that the main characters come from completely different social and cultural backgrounds. An example of this can be seen in *Bitter Harvest* when the heroine, Raine, meets a rich and arrogant Greek, Darius, at her engagement party. Through his machinations Raine's engagement is called off and she is determined to seek revenge by marrying him, and then deserting him. During the course of their marriage of convenience Raine falls in love with Darius, but various misunderstandings have to be cleared up before they achieve a happy ending. Throughout the book the heroine's emotions are made clear to the reader, in contrast to the hero who remains an enigma to the heroine, though not to the discerning reader. Indeed, it is essential to the plot that the heroine fails to understand the hero. Invariably the heroine is placed in situations of physical intimacy with the hero before she even understands him as a person. Hampson is one of the major writers in her genre who manages to detail the physical aspects of a relationship both skilfully and tastefully.

Some critics may perceive Hampson as an apologist for male violence, as violence of some kind is a common thread running through her novels. In *Bitter Harvest*, the hero says to the heroine, 'You, wife, owe me total fidelity! It would be fatal for you to let me down in this way . . . because I'd not hesitate to strangle you!' These violent emotions are frequently expressed physically through shakings and spankings, and what might even constitute rape, despite being carried out within marriage. However, the author deliberately creates this type of physical and emotional tension in a scenario where the reader knows that the heroine is physically attracted to the hero (albeit reluctantly at the beginning of their relationship). Hampson also ensures that the reader is aware that the hero is drawn to the heroine, although both characters have to overcome a variety of prejudices and misunderstandings arising from their different backgrounds and cultures before either is sure of the other's true feelings. In the end love overcomes these barriers, and a new, more tender, relationship is reached.

Hampson plays upon the average female reader's preference for the enigmatic, tall, dark, handsome stranger in the 'Valentino' mould. Her heroines are young, beautiful, and also invariably strong-willed. This latter characteristic creates a tension between the heroine and the equally strong-minded hero, thus enabling Hampson to control the narrative pace. The hero is usually Greek, or of a similar Mediterranean background: 'She noted the classical features, the strong determined chin and firm, implacable jaw. His mouth was equally firm, but sensuous, for all that' (*Bitter Harvest*). The hero in *Destiny* is to all intents and purposes English, but still has 'teak brown features', and 'a skin that was still firm and clear, tightly-drawn over high cheekbones and out-thrust jaw'. Her heroes cannot be classified as 'New Men', and one certainly cannot imagine any of them performing mundane household chores. Instead, they are characteristically successful businessmen. This appears to be an essential prerequisite for her heroes, perhaps on the basis that power is an aphrodisiac. For example, in *Destiny* the hero owns and runs a successful chain of hotels, and although he and the heroine are divorced, he manages to trick her into working for him on an exotic island in the Seychelles. He also manages to persuade a rival suitor to work for him, thereby acting as the puppet master and pulling the strings to his advantage. By contrast, Hampson's heroines are not usually successful career women who regard their career as an important aspect of their lives.

Hampson is an author who prefers to set her story in an exotic location, frequently Greece or South Africa. She describes the scenery in beautiful expressive prose which declares her love of nature. She appears to regard a romantic, beautiful setting as a prerequisite for a romance. Thus, in *Destiny* the scenery is an important instrument in shedding the heroine's resistance to the hero: 'The sea was all around, with three tiny islands off-shore, and the reef where starlit water cascaded down into the lagoon, lazy and dark and truly romantic beneath the stars'. The physical expression of love is an important component of Hampson's works, but Hampson does remind us through her characters that it is not completely fulfilling on its own—love also has to be present in order to achieve a truly satisfying and enriching experience.

—Sobhana Rowland

HARDIN, J.D. See **RIEFE, Barbara.**

HARDWICK, Mollie.

Pseudonyms: Mary Atkinson; John Drinkrow. **Nationality:** British. **Born:** Mollie Greenhalgh in Manchester. **Education:** Manchester High School for Girls. **Relations:** married the writer Michael Hardwick in 1961; one son. **Career:** announcer, Manchester, 1940–45, and drama script editor and producer, London, 1946–62, BBC Radio; then freelance writer. **Recipient:** Romantic Novelists Association major award, 1977, for *Beauty's Daughter.* Fellow, Royal Society of Arts. **Died:** 1991.

ROMANCE AND HISTORICAL PUBLICATIONS

Novels (series: Atkinson Heritage; Duchess of Duke Street; Upstairs, Downstairs)

Upstairs, Downstairs (novelization of television series):
  Sarah's Story. London, Sphere, 1973; New York, Pocket Books, 1975.
  The Years of Change. London, Sphere, and New York, Dell, 1974.
  Mrs Bridges' Story. London, Sphere, 1975.
  The War to End Wars. London, Sphere, and New York, Dell, 1975.
  Thomas and Sarah. London, Sphere, 1978.
The Duchess of Duke Street (novelization of television series). New York, Holt Rinehart, 1977.
  The Way Up. London, Futura, 1976.
  The Golden Years. London, Futura, 1976.
  The World Keeps Turning. London, Futura, 1977.
Beauty's Daughter: The Story of Lady Hamilton's 'Lost' Daughter. London, Eyre Methuen, 1976; New York, Coward McCann, 1977.
Charlie Is My Darling. London, Eyre Methuen, and New York, Coward McCann, 1977.
The Atkinson Heritage:
  The Atkinson Heritage. London, Futura, 1978.
  Sisters in Love. London, Futura, 1979.
  Dove's Nest. London, Futura, 1980; as *The Atkinson Century*, London, Severn House, 1980.
Lovers Meeting. London, Eyre Methuen, and New York, St Martin's Press, 1979.
Willowwood. London, Eyre Methuen, and New York, St Martin's Press, 1980.
Monday's Child. London, Macdonald, 1981; New York, St Martin's Press, 1982.
I Remember Love. London, Macdonald, 1982; New York, St Martin's Press, 1983.
The Shakespeare Girl. London, Methuen, and New York, St Martin's Press, 1983.
By the Sword Divided (novelization of television series). London, Century, 1983; New York, Penguin, 1986.
The Merry Maid. London, Methuen, 1984; New York, St Martin's Press, 1985.
The Girl with the Crystal Dove. London, Methuen, and New York, St Martin's Press, 1985.
Malice Domestic. London, Century, and New York, St Martin's Press, 1986.
Parson's Pleasure. London, Century, and New York, St Martin's Press, 1987.
Uneaseful Death. London, Century, and New York, St Martin's Press, 1988.
Blood Royal. London, Methuen, 1988; New York, St Martin's Press, 1989.
The Bandersnatch. London, Century, 1989; New York, St Martin's Press, 1990.
Perish in July. London, Century, 1989; New York, St Martin's Press, 1990.

The Dreaming Damozel. London, Century, 1990; New York, St Martin's Press, 1991.

OTHER PUBLICATIONS

Novels (novelizations)

The Private Life of Sherlock Holmes, with Michael Hardwick. London, Mayflower, 1970; New York, Bantam, 1971.
The Gaslight Boy, with Michael Hardwick. London, Weidenfeld and Nicolson, 1976.
Juliet Bravo. London, Pan, 2 vols, 1980.
Calling Juliet Bravo. London, BBC Publications, 1981.
Juliet Bravo 2. London, Severn House, 1981.

Plays

Four [and *Four More*] *Sherlock Holmes Plays*, with Michael Hardwick. London, Murray, 2 vols, 1964–73; New York, French, 2 vols, 1964–74.
The Game's Afoot: Sherlock Holmes Plays, with Michael Hardwick. London, Murray, 1969; New York, French, 1970.
Plays from Dickens, with Michael Hardwick. London, Murray, and New York, French, 1970.
Alice in Wonderland, adaptation of the story by Lewis Carroll. London, Davis Poynter, 1974.
A Christmas Carol, adaptation of the story by Dickens. London, Davis Poynter, 1974.
The Hound of the Baskervilles and Other Sherlock Holmes Plays, with Michael Hardwick. London, Murray, 1982.

Radio Plays: *The Corpse in the Case*, 1962; *Going Concern*, 1963; *The Prisoner's Friend*, from a work by Andrew Garve, 1964; *A Shadow of Doubt*, 1964; *Mrs Thompson*, 1965; *Sarah Churchill*, 1966; *Dear Miss Prior*, from a story by Thackeray, 1970; *The French Lieutenant's Woman*, from the novel by John Fowles, 1974; and others.

Television Plays: *A Question of Values*, with Michael Hardwick, 1976; *The Cedar Tree*; *The Dickens of a Christmas*; *Charles Dickens, Storyteller Extraordinary*; and others.

Other with Michael Hardwick

The Jolly Toper. London, Jenkins, 1961; New York, State Mutual Books, 1978.
The Sherlock Holmes Companion. London, Murray, 1962; New York, Doubleday, 1963.
Sherlock Holmes Investigates. New York, Lothrop, 1963.
The Man Who Was Sherlock Holmes. London, Murray, and New York, Doubleday, 1964.
The Charles Dickens Companion. London, Murray, 1965; New York, Holt Rinehart, 1966.
The Plague and the Fire of London. London, Parrish, 1966.
Writers' Houses: A Literary Journey in England. London, Phoenix House, 1968; as *A Literary Journey*, South Brunswick, New Jersey, A. S. Barnes, 1970.
Alfred Deller: A Singularity of Voice. London, Cassell, 1968; New York, Praeger, 1969.
Dickens's England. London, Dent, and South Brunswick, New Jersey, A.S. Barnes, 1970.
Charles Dickens . . . As They Saw Him. London, Harrap, 1970.
The Vintage Operetta Book (as John Drinkrow). London, Osprey, 1972.
The Charles Dickens Encyclopedia. London, Osprey, and New York, Scribner, 1973.

The Bernard Shaw Companion. London, Murray, 1973; New York, St Martin's Press, 1974.
The Vintage Musical Comedy Book (as John Drinkrow). London, Osprey, 1974.
The Charles Dickens Quiz Book. London, Luscombe, and New York, Larousse, 1974.

Editor, *The World's Greatest Sea Mysteries.* London, Odhams Press, 1967.

Other

Emma, Lady Hamilton. London, Cassell, 1969; New York, Holt Rinehart, 1970.
Mrs Dizzy: The Life of Mary Ann Disraeli. London, Cassell, and New York, St Martin's Press, 1972.
The Thames-Side Book (as Mary Atkinson). London, Osprey, 1973.
The World of Upstairs, Downstairs. Newton Abbot, David and Charles, and New York, Holt Rinehart, 1976.

Editor, *Stories from Dickens.* London, Arnold, 1968.

*

Mollie Hardwick commented (1990):

I would describe myself as an historical, rather than a romantic/gothic novelist. My novels grew out of my non-fiction works (i.e. *Emma, Lady Hamilton*), by way of a request from Sphere Books to write an original novel based on the character of Sarah the housemaid from *Upstairs, Downstairs*. I write, in general, out of my personal enthusiasms (the age of Nelson, the Jacobite Rising of 1745, the Regency theatre, cricket, etc.). In general I stick to the 18th century and the early 19th, disliking Victoriana as such; though *Monday's Child* is set in the 1880s. My next novel is set much farther back in time, beginning during the Wars of the Roses. I might one day write a gothic novel, with a strong supernormal element—who knows? My motivation in writing fiction is to tell a story that will entertain my readers (and incidentally myself) and perhaps provide them with a temporary escape from everyday life.

*   *   *

Perhaps because Mollie Hardwick began her prolific and diverse career in radio her written work was projected towards the inner ear and intended for the individual reader. Even her biographical and discursive work, while displaying strength and authority, bears a directness of expression.

Hardwick thought of herself primarily as a historical writer; certainly this element is present in everything she did. With her husband she wrote many dramas and non-fiction literary companion books mainly on late Victorian subjects. In her own fiction, however, she avoided the period except in *Monday's Child* and *The Girl with the Crystal Dove*, although elements common in Victorian drama crept in—sparks of sorcery, brief wallows in pathos, vulnerable young heroines made of steel, unexpected good fortune. Characters cede morality to practicality, and Hardwick made cavalier use of coincidence to help the plot along or to counterbalance uncharacteristic reactions.

Her first independent venture was a biography, *Emma, Lady Hamilton*, which brought critical approval, confirmed by *Mrs Dizzy*, a touching life of Disraeli's wife. In 1977 she won the Romantic Novelists Association major award for *Beauty's Daughter*, about Emma's 'lost' child, putting earlier research to good use in what is probably the best of her self-generated fiction. A succession of historical romances highlight her gift for characterization. Repeatedly it is speech, cleverly multi-layered, which is most significant, re-laying what the author wants us most keenly to understand. Motivations and emotions are projected even before the protagonists guess at them, yet Hardwick's style has a deceptive simplicity. Plot, however, is subordinate to characters, a weakness in her pure fiction which is unashamedly romantic, not only in the strong love interest but also in complete approach.

In historical fiction there is a valid division that Hardwick accepted, writing for both sides of the divide. Telling a fictitious tale set in the past requires no more than recreating atmosphere, using what detail one has to hand to embellish a plot of choice. Once a feel for the time is acquired a writer may choose to make his/her characters be and do whatever he/she wants. For example, *The Merry Maid* is a lively, attractive tale set in Tudor England, rosy rather than realistic, with the dark side of the times barely sketched on the backcloth. Frank storytelling permits licence to enhance with gentle humour, touches of the supernatural, and occasional shafts of gothic melodrama. History recreated is altogether more demanding. The writer is obliged to research thoroughly and, more crucially, to consider the motivation of real characters in real situations. In *Blood Royal*, a powerful depiction of the story of Anne Boleyn and her family, Hardwick returned to her strongest field. Everybody knows the basic details, however, only when Hardwick had checked every possible detail from every available source did she begin to write, with the details at her fingertips, and the story already immutably established. Her only creative freedom was to live inside her character's head and heart.

Hardwick's best-known works are novels based on television serials, at which she is unmatched. *Upstairs, Downstairs* was a benchmark, stirring public interest in turn of the century life. Along with *The Duchess of Duke Street* it provided Hardwick with material for eight books, which in turn spawned the historical saga fashion still flourishing. She concentrated on her real skills, vividly recreating a class-bisected England, subtly analysing social stresses which would eventually destroy the Victorian way of life and turn their values upside down. *The Atkinson Heritage* she brought wonderfully alive on the page. Again, however, she hesitated to underscore the brutishness and depression inherent in industrial life. Satanic mills are described almost cinematically rather than making the reader feel the heat inside or smell the stinking hovels. In her novelization of *By the Sword Divided* Hardwick again sanitized the battle gore, concentrating on the emotional stresses. Those interested in detailed accounts of battles can find them in military volumes.

Even in the novelization of the television series *Juliet Bravo*, superficially no more than one of the better modern police soaps, she captured the spirit of contemporary social attitudes. Her venture into detective fiction was dense with titbits gleaned from past research, and full of historical and literary allusions. Particularly delightful is the way Hardwick buried a potted biography, Keats in one book, Rossetti and his nasty clique in another, or a historical summary of churches and their artefacts, or a particular category of antique. Often the titbits provide a surprising insight into another period, and the information is always convincing. Hardwick was nothing if not a thorough and careful researcher.

—Margaret Woodward

———

HARDY, Laura.   See **LAMB, Charlotte.**

———

HARDY, W(illiam) G(eorge).
Nationality: Canadian. **Born:** Oakwood, Ontario, 3 February 1895. **Education:** University of Toronto, B.A. 1917, M.A. 1920; University of Chicago, Ph.D. 1922. **Relations:** married Llewella May Son-

ley in 1919 (died), two daughters and one son. **Career:** lecturer in Classics, University of Toronto, 1918–20; lecturer, 1920–22, assistant professor, 1922–28, associate professor, 1928–33, and professor of Classics, 1933–65, University of Alberta, Edmonton. President, 1930, and play producer, Edmonton Little Theatre. President, Canadian Authors Association, 1950–52; member of the Council, Classical Association of Canada. **Recipient:** University of Alberta National award, 1962. **Died:** 1979.

ROMANCE AND HISTORICAL PUBLICATIONS

Novels (series: Roman Trilogy)

Abraham, Prince of Ur. New York, Dodd Mead, 1935; as *Father Abraham*, London, Lovat Dickson, 1935.
Turn Back the River. New York, Dodd Mead, and London, Lovat Dickson, 1938.
All the Trumpets Sounded. New York, Coward McCann, 1942; London, Macdonald, 1946.
The Unfulfilled. Toronto, McClelland and Stewart, 1951; New York, Appleton Century Crofts, 1952.
Roman Trilogy:
    The City of Libertines. Toronto, McClelland and Stewart, and New York, Appleton Century Crofts, 1957; London, Heinemann, 1959.
    The Scarlet Mantle: A Novel of Julius Caesar. Toronto, Macmillan, 1978.
    The Bloodied Toga: A Novel of Julius Caesar. Toronto, Macmillan, 1979.

OTHER PUBLICATIONS

Other

Education in Alberta. Calgary, Calgary Herald, 1946.
From Sea unto Sea: Canada 1850–1920: The Road to Nationhood. New York, Doubleday, 1960.
The Greek and Roman World: Ten Radio Talks. Toronto, Canadian Broadcasting Corporation, 1960; revised edition, Cambridge, Massachusetts, Schenkman, 1962, 1970.
Our Heritage from the Past. Toronto, McClelland and Stewart, 1964.
Journey into the Past, with J.W.R. Gwyne-Timothy. Toronto, McClelland and Stewart, 1965.
Origins and Ordeals of the Western World. Cambridge, Massachusetts, Schenkman, 1968.

Editor, *The Alberta Golden Jubilee Anthology.* Toronto, McClelland and Stewart, 1955.
Editor, *Alberta: A Natural History.* Edmonton, Hurtig, 1967.

*   *   *

The early works of W.G. Hardy were based upon social commentary on the Canada of the day: *The Unfulfilled* examined Canadian/British Canadian/American relations. These novels were flavoured by what was for the day a surprising emphasis on explictly sexual carryings-on; but even so, Hardy's first few books made relatively little stir. His fame rests in large part upon his 'Roman Trilogy', three massive volumes which are not precisely a series, since they are readable as self-sufficient works, but sharing certain elements, most notably the presence of Julius Caesar.

The City of Libertines examines the politics and decadence of Roman life in the latter days of the Republic. The plot hinges upon the destructive adoration of the poet Catullus for his faithless 'Lesbia'. She was in real life Clodia Pulcher, sister of that Clodius Pulcher who created the scandal of a scandalous era by profaning the sacred rites of the Good Goddess, a religious ceremony forbidden to men. The uproar caused by his blasphemous act, and the subsequent manipulation of the Roman population by the self-seeking libertines of the title, provide a jolting comparison with the political manipulation of peoples of the 20th century. Although not the central figure in this novel, Caesar plays a significant role as a presence on the periphery, watchfully prepared to seize any opportunity the fates may afford him.

The Scarlet Mantle covers the mid-period of the life of Julius Caesar. Here is the warrior, the renegade, who led his troops, more loyal to himself than to Rome, across the Rubicon, thus casting his personal challenge in the teeth of the Republic. Parallel with Caesar's story runs another thread, that of the life of a humble soldier, Fadius, a fictional character whose changing life and perceptions reflect the effects of Caesar's career upon his times and countrymen.

The 'Roman Trilogy' concludes with *The Bloodied Toga*, telling of the climax of Caesar's life and reign, and of his relations with the voluptuous Egyptian queen Cleopatra.

Hardy certainly was comfortably familiar with the historic accounts that provide a basis for his Roman stories, and included the facts as a comprehensible and coherent chain of events in a convincing fashion, but the baldly contemporary language of his Romans is obtrusive and tends to undercut the effect of his ease and familiarity with the intricacies of ancient history.

Apparently jealous of the commercial success of the 'slick' novels of the era, some of which his writer persona scornfully lists in *The Unfulfilled*, Hardy seems to have resolved to conquer cheap fiction from within. His obsessive emphasis on sexual relations, in particular sex as a manipulative weapon especially though not exclusively of women, becomes tiresomely repetitive and predictable. Let any man and woman occupy adjacent space in any of his Roman titles, and inevitably their clothing will shortly slither to the floor to the accompaniment of a good deal of embarrassingly adolescent bedroom badinage. Though his work would have benefited by the attentions of a ruthless editor, Hardy's later novels won for him an extensive public who may, at intervals, have learned something about ancient Rome backstage.

—Joan McGrath

———

HARLAND, Christina.   See PEMBERTON, Margaret.

———

HARLE, Elizabeth.   See ROBERTS, Irene.

———

HARLEY, John.   See WOODWARD, Lilian.

———

HARRIS, Lavinia.   See ST JOHN, Nicola.

———

HARRIS, Marilyn.
Nationality: American. **Born:** Oklahoma City, Oklahoma, 4 June 1931. **Education:** Cottey College, Nevada, Missouri, 1949–51; University of Oklahoma, Norman, B.A. 1953, M.A. 1955. **Relations:** married Edgar V. Springer, Jr, in 1953; one son and one

daughter. **Recipient:** University of Carolina literary award, 1970; Lewis Carroll shelf award, 1973, for *The Runaway's Diary.* **Address:** 1846 Rolling Hills, Norman, Oklahoma 73069, USA.

ROMANCE AND HISTORICAL PUBLICATIONS

Novels (series: Eden)

Bledding Sorrow. New York, Putnam, 1976.
This Other Eden. New York, Putnam, 1977; London, Futura, 1980.
The Prince of Eden. New York, Putnam, 1978; London, Futura, 1980.
The Eden Passion. New York, Putnam, 1979; London, Macdonald, 1981.
The Women of Eden. New York, Putnam, 1980.
The Portent. New York, Putnam, 1980.
The Last Great Love. New York, Putnam, 1981.
Eden Rising. New York, Putnam, 1982.
The Diviner. New York, Putnam, 1983.
Warrick. New York, Doubleday, 1985.
Night Games. New York, Doubleday, 1987.
American Eden. New York, Doubleday, 1987.
Eden and Honor. New York, Doubleday, 1989.
Lost and Found. New York, Crown, 1991.

OTHER PUBLICATIONS

Novels

In the Midst of Earth. New York, Doubleday, 1969.
Hatter Fox. New York, Random House, 1973; London, Gollancz, 1974.
The Conjurers. New York, Random House, 1974; London, Panther, 1977.

Short Stories

King's Ex. New York, Doubleday, and London, Gollancz, 1967.

Other (for children)

The Peppersalt Land. New York, Four Winds Press, 1970.
The Runaway's Diary. New York, Four Winds Press, 1971.

*

Film Adaptation: *The Girl Called Hatter Fox,* 1977, from the novel *Hatter Fox.*

*   *   *

In Marilyn Harris's first gothic romance, *Bledding Sorrow,* a three-century-old drama of imprisonment, madness, adultery, mutilation, and murder slowly and plausibly repeats itself in the present. In her masterpiece of historical romance, the Eden novels, Harris also sounds, believably, the rest of the painful notes in the scale of passion: abandonment, exile, bastardy, betrayal, incest, rape, and sado-masochism. *This Other Eden,* set in the 1790s, begins when Thomas Eden has his servant girl, Marianne, stripped and flogged for insubordination. The book chronicles his attacks of remorse and his attempts to possess her, which include persuading her sister to abet a kidnapping, and also a sham marriage. They finally plunge together into 'the whole ecstatic process of domination and submission'. But when a child, Edward, is born, Thomas suffers another personality change and rejects them both. In order to get Marianne back this time, he has *himself* flogged. She nurses him back to health, they marry, and a legitimate son, James, is born. Harris turns

history to good account with frequent and bizarre appearances by Beckford (author and builder, of an early gothic novel and castle) and by Lord Nelson's mistress Emma Hamilton, who gains social acceptance for Marianne.

The Prince of Eden, however, is less love story than tragedy of circumstance. The 'Prince', Edward, as a result of his parents' marriage settlement, owns Eden. He is selling it off piecemeal to finance various rescue operations among the poor and criminal classes of London in the 1830s. Opium addiction (learned from De Quincey, practised with Branwell Brontë) and a grand passion for his brother's intended bride, Harriet, drive Edward farther outside the bounds of bourgeois respectability. Harriet refuses to run off with Edward. Unfortunately, she is pregnant and must feign a long illness before her wedding; fortunately, Edward learns of this in time to rescue his son, John.

Edward's revulsion from the charade of respectability is further underlined by his involvement with the radical causes of the day. When he proposes to use half the Eden estate on a friend's system of Ragged Schools, James sues for the right to the property. He loses, but Edward, in a typical act of self-immolation, gives it up. He is subsequently killed in an industrial accident, leaving John with nothing but the dream of Eden.

In *The Eden Passion* John realizes this dream, but ironically at the cost of rejecting all his father's beliefs. With this novel, in fact, Harris begins to undermine the conventions of her genre: she creates no more romantic heroes. John, bastard of a bastard, returns to Eden and has for the first and only love of his life his own mother, Harriet, and the rest of the Eden novels chart the pathology of his exile from this love. Although this is gothic romance at its source, Harris's increased attention to themes of social injustice and crimes of imperialism ultimately debunks the myth of the Great Family Estate. When the doomed lovers learn the truth, Harriet blinds and imprisons herself, while John flees to commerce in the City, in the Crimea (where his war wounds are tended by Florence Nightingale), and to India, in search of fortune. He returns to England with an Indian woman who has had her tongue cut out while rescuing him during the 1857 mutiny in Delhi. With Dhari's and Harriet's mutilation, Harris says more than 'Passion is dangerous'. While John, in his pain, amasses a great fortune, marries, and acquires Eden at last, his women have no consolation but that of being among his valued acquisitions.

In *The Women of Eden* Harris develops this theme. The title is that of a painting of John's wife Lila, Dhari, Harriett's daughter Mary, and Elizabeth, the former prostitute who raised him. An observer says they look sick to their stomachs. Certainly John's behaviour becomes increasingly sickening. His wife is repeatedly subjected to marital rape and dies in grotesque agony of a neglected uterine cancer. Dhari is brutalized. Mary is at first a wretched prisoner of his idea of her as a pure maiden; when he sees her in her American lover's embrace, he arranges to have her raped by a gang of thugs. John hates women (especially suffragettes—Elizabeth, by the way, is one), radicals, the poor, Americans, and those he terms Sodomites, whom he also plots to victimize. John's frustrated desire for social acceptance is, he thinks, blocked by a newspaper columnist's attack: 'Eden present[s] a contradiction of material splendour and moral bankruptcy, though unwittingly he serve[s] as the most polished mirror ever held to English society in recent times'. Eden is denied revenge upon the writer, who is Mary's lover. They escape to America, Dhari and John's lawyer marry and leave for Canada, and Elizabeth joins the French feminists. So much for the Women of Eden and for English society in 1870. Harris has ended the Eden series by accusing a society of providing gothic materials.

—Sally Allen McNall

HARRIS, Rosemary (Jeanne). British. 1923—. See 2nd edition, 1990.

HARRISON, Elizabeth (Francourt).
Nationality: British. **Career:** hospital administration; script editor, and researcher, Chest, Heart, and Stroke Foundation, London. **Address:** c/o Mills and Boon Ltd, Eton House, 18–24 Paradise Road, Richmond, Surrey TW9 1SR, England.

ROMANCE AND HISTORICAL PUBLICATIONS

Novels (series: Central Hospital is featured in all books except for *Coffee at Dobree's*, and *The Surgeon She Married*)

Coffee at Dobree's. London, Ward Lock, 1965.
The Physicians. London, Ward Lock, 1966.
The Ravelston Affair. London, Ward Lock, 1967.
Corridors of Healing. London, Ward Lock, 1968.
Emergency Call. London, Hurst and Blackett, 1970.
Accident Call. London, Hurst and Blackett, 1971.
Ambulance Call. London, Hurst and Blackett, 1972.
Surgeon's Call. London, Hurst and Blackett, 1973.
On Call. London, Hurst and Blackett, 1974.
Hospital Call. London, Hurst and Blackett, 1975.
Dangerous Call. London, Hurst and Blackett, 1976.
To Mend a Heart. London, Hurst and Blackett, 1977.
Young Doctor Goddard. London, Hurst and Blackett, 1978.
A Doctor Called Caroline. London, Hurst and Blackett, 1979.
A Surgeon Called Amanda. London, Hale, 1982.
A Surgeon's Life. London, Hale, 1983.
Marrying a Doctor. London, Hale, 1984.
A Surgeon's Affair. London, Mills and Boon, 1985.
A Surgeon at St Mark's. London, Mills and Boon, 1986.
The Surgeon She Married. London, Mills and Boon, 1988.
The Faithful Type. London, Mills and Boon, 1993.

* * *

Elizabeth Harrison is probably best known for her series of medical romances based around the Central Hospital. Unlike Betty Neels or Lucilla Andrews, Harrison has no nursing experience and this is reflected in her novels. Harrison offers her reader a wider perspective of the nurse/doctor's world and we are allowed to see how the protagonists deal in an environment much wider than the hospital in which they work.

Despite writing medical romances Harrison depicts a seemingly unromantic world, describing medical operations and procedure with great attention to detail. Issues such as interracial marriage, drunk-driving, and the effect of having a job that takes one or both partners away from home are tackled in the author's books with sensitivity and sensibility.

To Mend a Heart finds the staid, no-nonsense hero, James Leyburn, nursing a broken heart and dealing with his ex-girlfriend's sister, Emily. James is the assistant to the leading heart surgeon of the Cardio-Thoracic ward of the Central and finds after getting to know Emily that he is in love with her. Emily and her sister are depicted as complete opposites and both are allegories for 'purity' and 'decadence' respectively. Whereas Melissa is seen from the outset as a vain, selfish creature, who tries to 'corrupt' her younger sister from her arrival in London, Emily is incorruptible—despite witnessing her sister's adultery, involvement in drugs, and general 'loose' lifestyle. Through Melissa's boyfriend, Emily is introduced to a group of troubled children with whom he is working. This leads her to an unfortunate encounter with a psychopathic ten-year-old

who stabs her so badly that she almost dies. This does, however, give James the opportunity to save her life as she is taken to his ward.

Amanda, in the aptly titled *A Surgeon Called Amanda*, is a successful doctor who finds herself having to make the choice between love and her career. Amanda emerges from her chrysalis to become a gorgeous woman who attracts the attention of her previously uninterested colleagues. She finally settles on the widowed Simon. She, of course, sacrifices her career for her man at the end.

Hugh Ravelston also finds himself in a great dilemma when he is involved in a drunk-driving accident that kills another person and ruins his career. He disgraces his family and takes a research post in a smaller town. He becomes friendly with a junior consultant, Colin Warr, who is dying of a terminal illness and falls in love with Colin's wife. Although Colin gives his blessing *The Ravelston Affair* closes with Hugh seeing off Judith as she goes to teach summer-school. The implication is that they will see each other again.

Gabrielle Vereker, a doctor with a promising career becomes engaged to a Sikh doctor, Paul Singh. Unfortunately, Paul's family have arranged his marriage to someone of his own religion, and matters are complicated when his Sikh fiancée turns up. The reader witnesses the problems of being involved with a doctor when Gabrielle has to spend most of her engagement party alone as Paul is too busy to attend. Gabrielle gradually turns to Robert Scorer, the director of her unit, who asserts himself as a strong, much more dependable figure in contrast to Paul.

Harrison handles seemingly difficult themes with panache and perception. Her books are good, extremely readable examples of the medical romance.

—P. Campbell

HARRISON, Sarah.
Nationality: British. **Born:** Sarah Martyn, Exeter, Devon, 7 August 1946. **Education:** University of London, B.A. (honours) 1967. **Relations:** married Jeremy Harrison in 1969; one son and two daughters. **Career:** journalist, International Publishing Corporation, London, 1967–70. **Agent:** Carol Smith, 25 Hornton Court, Kensington High Street, London W8 7RT, England.

ROMANCE AND HISTORICAL PUBLICATIONS

Novels (series: Harriet Blair)

The Flowers of the Field. London, Futura, and New York, Coward McCann, 1980.
A Flower That's Free. London, Futura, and New York, Simon and Schuster, 1984.
Hot Breath (Blair). London, Futura, 1985.
An Imperfect Lady. London, Futura, 1988; New York, Warner, 1989.
Cold Feet (Blair). London, Macdonald, 1989.
Forests of the Night. London, Futura, 1991.
Foreign Parts (Blair). London, Macdonald, 1992.
Be An Angel. London, Little Brown, 1993.

OTHER PUBLICATIONS (for children)

Other

In Granny's Garden. London, Cape, and New York, Holt Rinehart, 1980.

Laura and Edmund [*Old Lumber, the Lady, the Squire*]. London, Hutchinson, 4 vols, 1986.

* * *

In her first two novels, *The Flowers of the Field* and *A Flower That's Free*, Sarah Harrison treats us to a total of almost 1400 pages of a family saga, spanning the obligatory 50 years and three generations. Although this format is something of a cliché, and the period covered (1890s–1940s) one of the most frequently written about, Harrison handles her subject in a deft and professional manner.

With settings as diverse as the Kentish Weald, Paris, Berlin, Malta, and Kenya, and a period which includes both world wars, these novels could truly be described as panoramic, and one has the feeling that Harrison has indeed had this adjective in mind. It is hard to think of any character type or any aspect of social life which does not make an appearance in one or the other of these two novels. Had this been Harrison's brief she could not have succeeded better. This in no way detracts from a compelling story fluently and interestingly told.

The heroine of the first book, Thea Tennant, is very much a 20th-century woman, becoming involved in the suffragette movement and later serving as an ambulance driver in France. As a young girl she falls in love with Jack Kingsley, but their burgeoning romance encounters a slight setback when he is successfully seduced by her younger sister Dulcie. The two girls travel to Vienna where Thea meets a new love, Josef von Crieff; Dulcie again disrupts her sister's life, this time by eloping to Paris with the tutor of Josef's younger brother. (Dulcie does at least put her experiences to good use when she becomes the 'whore with a heart of gold', offering hospitality to British soldiers in Paris during World War I.) By the very long arm of coincidence so beloved of romance writers, Jack and Josef meet in the trenches without knowing of their mutual acquaintances and exchange tokens. Josef is later killed and Thea does eventually marry Jack. More briefly, but in fact far more movingly portrayed is the unrequited love between Thea's cousin Maurice, a conscientious objector during the war, and Primmy, the maidservant. These and other characters seen against the turbulence not only of the war, but also of social conditions prevailing at home, give depth to a fulfilling and stirring tale.

The second book, *A Flower That's Free*, has as its main character Thea's adopted (and Dulcie's actual) daughter, Kate. Brought up by Jack and Thea in Kenya, Kate knows that she is adopted, but has no idea who her mother is, and in fact does not find out until after Dulcie's death. Here again we have a heroine who is very much her own woman, and who ultimately has to make the choice between her loving and fairly unexceptional husband, and an older man who (just to complicate matters a little) has in fact been her mother's (i.e. Dulcie's) lover. And once more the backdrop of a world war provides opportunities for the novelist to introduce the extra tensions of brief relationships, contributing to a fast moving plot.

One receives the impression that Harrison was perhaps thankful to turn away from the conventionalities of a family saga to her far from conventional third novel *Hot Breath*. Harrison assures us that she is not portraying herself in the person of Harriet Blair, historical novelist and heroine of *Hot Breath*—does the lady perhaps protest too much? Whatever the truth of the matter she provides us with an outrageously funny and immensely original romance novel, in which the heroine has an extramarital affair with Kostaki Ghikas, a good looking, oversexed and unfortunately not quite credible Greek doctor. Meanwhile Harriet's husband George is in his turn having an affair with Ghikas' mother, who is 'a marine archaeologist with a man in every port'. Not really believable is it? But great fun, and so enjoyable that one readily forgives the basic improbability.

Both the fun and the improbability continue at full strength in *Cold Feet* and *Foreign Parts*, Harrison's two further novels featur-ing Harriet Blair. The rampant Ghikas is mercifully absent in the first of these, although he reappears, together with a bizarre assortment of fresh characters, in *Foreign Parts*. In *Cold Feet* his place in Harriet's affections (and eventually in her bed) is taken by Edward Lethbridge, the editor of a right-wing political journal; apparently austere, Edward turns out to have distinctly sadistic sexual tendencies, which Harrison depicts amusingly enough to make the reader overlook the basic tastelessness of such a scenario.

With *An Imperfect Lady* Harrison returns to the family saga, giving us this time an even wider sweep in both time (more than 70 years) and space (the West Country to the Caribbean, taking in France and Ireland on the way). Again we are offered a very independent-minded heroine, Adeline Gundry, who certainly needs her immense strength of character in order to overcome the constant emotional obstacles and challenges which life throws at her.

Her first marriage (at the age of 18, to a childhood friend of her brother) ends after only a couple of years when her husband commits suicide. She finds out later that the wounds he had received in World War I were self-inflicted, and that he was beset by doubts and uncertainties. Following a happy four years at the Slade School of Art, Adeline embarks upon a lesbian relationship; she later marries, has a child and then is divorced. After a third marriage Adeline has a stillborn baby; this marriage deteriorates as her husband's gambling problems become insurmountable. This would daunt many a lesser woman, but Adeline (by now a much sought-after portrait painter) also manages to cope with the scandal when her lesbian relationship becomes public knowledge many years after the event, and with the ultimate demise of her husband, who dies as they are about to become reconciled.

Forests of the Night is a complete departure from both Harrison's previous styles; unusually for her, all the major *dramatis personae* are male, and the complexities of their characters and the sexual ambivalence of several of the men are central to the development of the story. With the settings including an English public school in the 1920s, a Japanese prison camp during World War II, and Jerusalem in 1989, this novel intrigues with its jigsaw of interlocking relationships and tantalizingly half-revealed identities. With this novel, Sarah Harrison demonstrates versatility, and indicates that she should no longer be regarded solely as a writer of family sagas and light-hearted comedies.

—Judith Rhodes

HARRISON, Whit. See **HORNER, Lance, Kyle ONSTOTT, and Ashley CARTER.**

HARROD-EAGLES, Cynthia.
Pseudonyms: Elizabeth Bennett; Emma Woodhouse. **Nationality:** British. **Born:** London, 13 August 1948. **Education:** Burlington Grammar School, London, 1959–66; Edinburgh University 1966–67; University College, London, 1969–72, B.A. (honours) 1972. **Recipient:** Romantic Novelists Association award, 1993, for *Emily*. **Address:** c/o Macdonald and Company (Publishers) Ltd, 165 Great Dover Street, London SE1 4YA, England.

ROMANCE AND HISTORICAL PUBLICATIONS

Novels (series: Dynasty; Kirov Saga)

The Waiting Game. London, New English Library, 1972.
Shadows on the Mountain. London, New English Library, 1973.

Hollow Night. London, Magnum, 1980.
Dynasty:

1. *The Founding.* London, Macdonald, and New York, Dell, 1980.
2. *The Dark Rose.* London, Macdonald, and New York, Dell, 1981.
3. *The Princeling.* London, Macdonald, 1981; as *The Distant Wood*, New York, Dell, 1981.
4. *The Oak Apple.* London, Macdonald, 1982; as *The Crystal Crown*, New York, Dell, 1982.
5. *The Black Pearl.* London, Macdonald, and New York, Dell, 1982.
6. *The Long Shadow.* London, Macdonald, and New York, Dell, 1983.
7. *The Chevalier.* London, Macdonald, 1984.
8. *The Maiden.* London, Macdonald, 1985.
9. *The Flood-Tide.* London, Macdonald, 1986.
10. *The Tangled Thread.* London, Macdonald, 1987.
11. *The Emperor.* London, Macdonald, 1988.
12. *The Victory.* London, Macdonald, 1989.
13. *The Regency.* London, Macdonald, 1990.
14. *The Campaigners.* London, Macdonald, 1991.
15. *The Reckoning.* London, Macdonald, 1992.

Deadfall. London, Methuen, 1982.
The Orange Tree Plot. London, Sidgwick and Jackson, 1989.
Kirov Saga:

1. *Anna.* London, Sidgwick and Jackson, 1990.
2. *Fleur.* London, Sidgwick and Jackson, 1990.
3. *Emily.* London, Sidgwick and Jackson, 1992.

Enchanted Isle. London, Severn House, 1993.

Novels as Emma Woodhouse

A Rainbow Summer. London, Mayflower, 1976.
A Well-Painted Passion. London, Mayflower, 1976.
Romany Magic. London, Mayflower, 1977.
Love's Perilous Passage. London, Sphere, 1978.
On Wings of Love. London, Sphere, 1978.
Never Love a Stranger. London, Sphere, 1978.

Novels as Elizabeth Bennett

Title Role. London, New English Library, 1980.
The Unfinished. London, New English Library, 1983.
Even Chance. London, New English Library, 1984.
Last Run. London, New English Library, 1984.

OTHER PUBLICATIONS

Novels (crime)

Orchestrated Death. London, Macdonald, 1991.
Death Watch. London, Little Brown, 1992; New York, Scribner, 1992.

*

Cynthia Harrod-Eagles comments:

The Dynasty series was conceived as a kind of history without tears, a saga following the fortunes of the late Middle Ages to the present day. While the Morland family is purely fictional, the background to their lives is the real history of England, carefully researched and accurately recorded, so that the reader should emerge with a good overview of the flow of social development during the last 500 years: how people lived, what they ate, what they wore, how they viewed the world they lived in. Originally commissioned as a 12-book series, it now has been extended to at least 17.

*   *   *

Cynthia Harrod-Eagles is a highly acclaimed historical novelist, who won the Romantic Novelists Association award for *Emily*, in 1993. She had already achieved much recognition for the 'Dynasty' series which features the Morland family, and takes the reader from the Wars of the Roses through to the Napoleonic era. Her latest books, the 'Kirov Saga', (*Anna*, *Fleur*, and *Emily*) concentrate on 19th-century Russia, from the Napoleonic invasion of the Crimea to Sarajevo, and the Bolshevik Revolution

The first of the Morland novels, *The Founding*, introduces the family established through the marriage of Eleanor Courtney to Robert Morland the younger son of a Yorkshire sheep farmer. Spanning the years 1434 to 1486 and crowded with characters, it sets the formula for the subsequent books. For though Harrod-Eagles manages to avoid writing quite the same novel throughout the series, thus maintaining interest in the fortunes of the Morlands, nevertheless her readers can enjoy the security engendered by recurring themes and situations and characters. The changes are adroitly rung; different historical periods, varying viewpoints, each book with a different time span—some of them encompass several generations of the family (*The Founding*, *The Princeling*), others—*The Emperor* for example—a mere decade, sometimes more than one volume follow the careers of one generation, as is the case with her four latest novels in the 'Dynasty' series, while the 'Kirov Saga' concentrates on two generations of the Kirov family in the 19th century.

As a historian Harrod-Eagles includes a short list of source material with each title thus ensuring her work can be seen in a more serious light than mere historical romance. Further weight is added to this creation of a dynastic family by a family tree relevant to the particular generation in each volume. The final touch is a plan of Morland Place of that period. For it is Morland Place built under the aegis of the first Eleanor Morland that provides the link between the increasingly farflung elements of the family, a central point to return to, reflecting as it grows in grandeur their rise in fortune and at the same time providing the key to their status. For it is the status of the Morlands as landed gentry that ensures the dynastic marriages that are a central and repeated feature of the saga—marriages that ensure their progress upwards. And it is their status that allows Harrod-Eagles to introduce the great events and prominent historical figures of each period into the action, while the marriages also ensure that her characters move further afield than Yorkshire. Thus the alliance of Lettice Morland to the Scottish Lord, Robert Hamilton (*The Princeling*), introduces the court of Mary, Queen of Scots, and the murders of Rizzio and Darnley; while *The Flood-Tide* transports the reader to pre-revolutionary France and also to America on the eve of the War of Independence. Nor is it just the action that is wide ranging. The whole gamut of political opinion and allegiance is represented—Lancastrian and Yorkist, Cavalier and Roundhead, Catholic and Protestant, British and American patriot.

The 'Kirov Saga', in some ways more romantic than the Morland series, opens with Anna, orphaned and unemployed, arriving in Russia to take up the position of governess to the Kirov family. This device allows Harrod-Eagles to describe Russian society and life without seeming didactic or halting the flow of the narrative. The background—as with the Morland series—is aristocratic; thus the reader is introduced to the glittering social gatherings of St Petersburg and Moscow, to the grandeur of the summer estates, to the hierarchy of Russian society, and of course to the great historic events of the time: Napoleon's invasion of Moscow, the Crimea, the Charge of the Light Brigade, the Great Exhibition, and the 1917 Uprising.

However, Harrod-Eagles does not rely on major events alone to set the historical background to each title. Details of dress, food, architecture, the occasional nuance of speech—all of these touches allow each period to be differentiated, though without the exuberant immediacy of a Georgette Heyer. By and large the narrative and dialogue are modern in tone. Period excesses may be avoided but much is made of such social details as the position of women, the frequency of pregnancies, and the high rate of infant mortality. For though attention is paid to the many male characters (frequently sharing the same first name to the confusion of the inattentive reader), it is the women who emerge as the more memorable and most distinctive. It is indicative that her latest three novels are all called after their heroines—Anna, leaving her familiar background to face a strange society, and the ambivalent position of being a governess; well-bred Fleur who is prepared to defy convention and follow the dictates of her heart; and Emily, again from a conventional background, who has to meet new challenges and face great dangers. Similarly although Morland Place is handed down from father to son in the traditional manner, in the end it is the ladies of Morland Place who emerge as the dominant and enduring characters—the first Eleanor, Nanette, Annunciata, Jemima. The Morland dynasty is, in the final analysis, a matriarchy, and history is seen from the woman's point of view.

The 'Dynasty' series may be designed to unfold the panorama of English history—the Morland family fortunes in their rise from sheep farmer to the aristocracy, mirroring the ascendancy of the country through trading superiority to military success and the acquisition of an empire, while the 'Kirov Saga' rests firmly on the grand sweep of European events in the 19th and early-20th centuries. But they are also romances and it is the interest generated by the relations between the characters, their progress in love and hate, their interraction as members of an increasingly complex family that holds the reader's attention. Harrod-Eagles's technique is to present the action from a multiplicity of viewpoints thus ensuring the widest variety of characteristics and the inclusion of many aspects of the social scene from the court to the world of the strolling players. However, though none of her characters is outstanding and they are frequently stereotypes of the romance genre, when she allows them enough space in the action to develop, Harrod-Eagles can create enjoyable and distinctive people who enlist sympathy and add depth to the relentless progress of both sagas.

—Ferelith Hordon

HART, Caroline.   See **GARVICE, Charles.**

HARVEY, Caroline.   See **TROLLOPE, Joanna.**

HARVEY, Kathryn.   See **WOOD, Barbara.**

HARVEY, Rachel.   See **BLOOM, Ursula.**

HARWOOD, Alice.
Nationality: British. **Born:** West Bromwich, Staffordshire. **Education:** King Edward VI School and Edgbaston College, both Birmingham; Bedford College, University of London, B.A. 1932. **Career:** assistant editor, *New Chronicle of Christian Education*, London, 1933–35; staff member, British Red Cross Education Department, Oxford, 1943–45. **Died:** 19 December 1985.

ROMANCE AND HISTORICAL PUBLICATIONS

Novels

Caedmon: A Lyrical Drama. London, S.P.C.K., 1937.
So Merciful a Queen, So Cruel a Woman. New York, Hutchinson, 1939; as *The Star of the Greys*, London, Hutchinson, 1939.
She Had to Be Queen. London, Bodley Head, 1948; as *The Lily and the Leopards*. Indianapolis, Bobbs Merrill, 1949.
Merchant of the Ruby. London, Bodley Head, and Indianapolis, Bobbs Merrill, 1951.
The Strangeling. London, Bodley Head, and Indianapolis, Bobbs Merrill, 1954.
Seats of the Mighty. Indianapolis, Bobbs Merrill, 1956; as *At Heart a King*, London, Bodley Head, 1957.
No Smoke Without Fire. Indianapolis, Bobbs Merrill, 1964.
The Living Phantom. London, Hale, 1973.
The Clandestine Queen. London, Hale, 1979.
The Uncrowned Queen. London, Hale, 1983.

*   *   *

In Alice Harwood's *The Strangeling*, Michal, the main protagonist, comments at one point 'those who write books live others' lives'. If this is so then Harwood herself is inconsistent with such an avowed principle because the last thing her work concerns is anyone's life. She wrote instead about the various actual political and social situations which occurred in the past to which the people were simply adjuncts. Consequently her books are one-dimensional and totally factual narratives. Harwood is thereby more true to the concept of an historical novel than many writers who claim to belong to the same school but who in fact write novels in an historical setting.

The difference is subtle but nevertheless exists, and Harwood has purity of purpose and a cast iron integrity in handling her data. Her stories are well researched and extremely detailed, and the readers' familiarity with the central events and figures from history lends a certain security to reading the novels. We already know the outcome, and Harwood never contradicts us, but she does encourage speculation on the what-might-have-beens had the circumstances been different.

Harwood raises many historical questions which she doesn't really go on to answer. They are, however, purely rhetorical, and suggest new perceptions which we might not have thought about before, but at the same time she promotes many other preconceptions. Darnley, in *No Smoke Without Fire*, is the archetypal insecure wimp of popular myth, so that our picture of him, built up from common sources already is ratified instead of being queried.

Although Harwood does occasionally try to explore and develop her characters through frequent soliloquies or stream of consciousness passages, they fail to come across as real, believable, and fully fleshed out figures. Our pre-knowledge of the characters can prevent our acceptance of a new interpretation, and Harwood is more concerned with making us contemplate other possible historical scenarios than with making us understand the people responsible for them. Even focusing on one small group like the Grey family, as she does frequently (providing a loose link between the books) fails to convey any intimate knowledge of their individuality. They are simply playing their part in history and relating themselves into the greater social order.

In *So Merciful a Queen, So Cruel a Woman*, for example, Harwood concentrates on comparatively minor figures like Kathryn, Lady Jane Grey's younger sister. Kathryn is a relatively unknown historical figure so one would expect there to be more scope for creative development than with the major well-known kings, queens, and politicians. Kathryn is not, however, the angst-ridden 13-year-old adolescent one would expect considering her life so far, and she therefore rings false, untrue to her experiences and unable to provoke our sympathy. There are exceptions of course; Michal is a more believable character because she is not immediately identifiable as an historical personage and the author is therefore free to expand her creation in any chosen direction.

For Harwood, then, history provides boundaries to the fictional elements of plot and characterization. However, it also supplies her with the opportunity to exploit her strong sense of place and contemporary atmosphere. Kinross village in *Seats of the Mighty* (*At Heart a King*) and the London of *So Merciful a Queen, So Cruel a Woman* are equally evocative of the 16th century and there are also some brilliant passages of archaic dialect in *Merchant of the Ruby*. Features like these lighten the otherwise ponderous style crammed as it is with the occasional touches of tongue-in-cheek cynicism—in *She Had to Be Queen* we meet the bored and worldly-wise Winchester receiving Elizabeth 'hardened by this time to the spectacle of princesses in trouble'.

Harwood also exhibits a keen eye for human failings. Mary in *The Strangeling* is more than a little uneasy at her first ever train journey, although she has survived for years abroad in much less civilized places than Lime Street railway station. There are occasional strokes of drama where the unexpected can happen—well-known literary figures—the Brontës, Erasmus, Thomas More—wander in and out of the pages, purely for effect.

The net result is a very idiosyncratic approach to the historical novel, which Harwood justifies as fact being stranger than fiction. This is her excuse for poking into obscure corners of the past, but not into the human psyches of the inhabitants. She brushes the dust off forgotten but important figures like Elizabeth Woodville and places them in our already existing historical knowledge. We reassess accepted truths as a consequence, and this is a refreshingly original treatment of a well established genre.

—L.M. Quinn

HASTINGS, Brooke.
Pseudonym for Deborah Hannes Gordon. **Other Pseudonym:** Deborah Gordon. **Nationality:** American. **Born:** New York City, 31 May 1946. **Education:** Yorktown High School, Yorktown Heights, New York, graduated 1964; Brandeis University, Waltham, Massachusetts, B.A. in political science, 1968 (Phi Beta Kappa). **Relations:** married David W. Gordon in 1967; one daughter and one son. **Career:** research assistant, Columbia University, New York, 1968–70; secretary, Huron Institute and *Working Papers* magazine, Cambridge, Massachusetts, 1971–73; researcher and writer, CARD Consultants, Sacramento, California, 1979. **Recipient:** Romantic Writers of America golden medallion, 1982, for *Winner Take All*. **Agent:** Mel Berger, William Morris Agency Inc, 1350 Avenue of the Americas, New York, NY 10021, USA. **Address:** 1240 Noonan Drive, Sacramento, California 95822, USA.

Romance and Historical Publications

Novels

Desert Fire. New York, Silhouette, 1980.
Innocent Fire. New York, Silhouette, 1980.
Playing for Keeps. New York, Silhouette, 1980.
Island Conquest. New York, Silhouette, 1981.
Winner Take All. New York, Silhouette, 1981; London, Hodder and Stoughton, 1982.
A Matter of Time. New York, Silhouette, 1982.
Intimate Strangers. New York, Silhouette, 1982.
Rough Diamond. New York, Silhouette, 1982.

An Act of Love. New York, Silhouette, 1983.
Interested Parties. New York, Silhouette, 1984.
Reasonable Doubts. New York, Silhouette, 1984.
Tell Me No Lies. New York, Silhouette, 1984.
Hard to Handle. New York, Silhouette, 1985.
As Time Goes By. New York, Silhouette, 1986.
Double Jeopardy. New York, Silhouette, 1986.
Forward Pass. New York, Silhouette, 1986.
Too Close for Comfort. New York, Silhouette, 1987.
Forbidden Fruit. New York, Silhouette, 1987.
Both Sides Now. New York, Silhouette, 1988.
Catch a Falling Star. New York, Silhouette, 1988.
So Sweet a Sin. New York, Silhouette, 1989.
Reluctant Mistress. New York, Silhouette, 1990.
Beating the Odds (as Deborah Gordon). New York, Harper, 1990.
Seduction. New York, Silhouette, 1991.

*

Brooke Hastings comments:

I see my typical reader as a woman who's probably juggling two or three or four very demanding roles—homemaker, student, wife, mother, paid employee and/or volunteer, for example. She probably has more stress in her life than she can handle. I hope my books will entertain her . . . that they'll provide a few hours of escape from the daily grind, an evening or two of emotion, adventure, and mystery. I want to leave her with a warm feeling in her heart, a smile on her face, and even a few joyful tears in her eyes. And if in the process, I can say a few things about subjects such as the importance of a woman being able to stand up for herself and take care of herself financially if she has to . . . of men and women caring for each other, trusting each other and bringing out what's best in each other . . . of love, family, and charity being far more meaningful and fulfilling than fancy cars, clothing, and condos . . . well, then, so much the better.

*　　*　　*

Brooke Hastings has written more than 20 contemporary romance novels for Silhouette's Romance, Special Edition, and Intimate Moments lines. Her *Winner Take All* won the Romance Writers of America's golden medallion.

Hastings uses a variety of settings for her stories, from the United States to Hong Kong to the fictitious Jammipur. Her characters' livelihoods are diverse, too. *A Matter of Time* features thoroughbred racing, and whiskey distilling; *Intimate Strangers*, gourmet cooking; and *Rough Diamond*, baseball.

Hastings's heroes and heroines usually come from wealthy backgrounds. Their families are very much a part of the story. Sometimes there are so many characters that one wishes for a cast list to help keep track. Often, one of these relatives creates a situation that initially throws the two lovers together. For example, in *Intimate Strangers*, Rachel Grant is hired by Olivia Bennett to cook for her writer son, Jason Wilder. Rachel does not know that Jason is the man who wrote a controversial book about her own past. In *Rough Diamond*, Dani Ronsard inherits millions from her father, but only if she agrees to manage his baseball team, of which Ty Morgan is the star. In *Innocent Fire*, Julia Harcourt's father threatens to withdraw his financial support from a college unless she is allowed to take an art course from professor Derek Veblen, and in *Desert Fire*, Jenny Ross's father contrives to have her employed as Nick Butler's housekeeper.

These manipulative relatives then drop conveniently into the background while the hero and heroine fall in love and struggle with their conflicts. However, they may surface when needed to keep the plot moving. For example, in *Innocent Fire*, *Desert Fire*, and *Both*

Sides Now, the father steps in and demands marriage when he thinks his daughter has been compromised.

Relatives also provide sub-plots which contribute to the conflict between hero and heroine. *Hard to Handle* has Doug Hunter disapproving of Melanie, the woman his best friend Edward has chosen to marry. This complicates Doug's falling in love with Melanie's sister, Cassie Valdenberg. In *An Act of Love*, Luke Griffin is angry because heroine Miranda Dunne's sister is having an affair with his brother-in-law. *Both Sides Now* shows Bradley Fraser's favourite aunt involved with the rakish father of heroine Sabrina Lang.

The plethora of characters and sub-plots results in variety but also in plots that lack unity. In *Both Sides Now*, the first part of the story focuses on the conflict over Brad's aunt's relationship with Sabrina's father, while the second part features the rescue of Sabrina's friend, a prisoner in Jammipur. In *Reasonable Doubts*, Laura Silver initially is repelled by Gregory Steiger because she feels he is indirectly responsible for her father's death. As the story progresses, this issue is lost as new sub-plots develop. *Seduction* has Diana Van Slyke and Marc Rochard running off on a treasure hunt to Madagascar that seems superfluous to include, since the amount of booty discovered is negligible.

Conflicts between the lovers almost always include an unhappy past relationship. Sylvie Kruger's attorney husband was unfaithful (*A Matter of Time*). Sabrina Lang was married to the domineering king of Jammipur (*Both Sides Now*), and Rachel Grant's former spouse was a corrupt South American dictator (*Intimate Strangers*).

Other conflicts are also those commonly found in series romance novels; for example, the wife-mother versus career woman theme in *Seduction*. However, *Reluctant Mistress* delves into a deeper theme by pitting Leilani Howe's belief in Hawaiian myth against Paul Lindstrom's more pragmatic outlook. No matter what the conflicts, as the story nears its end, the issues are rather simply resolved, usually by one of the characters changing his mind so that an agreement may be reached. Sometimes both characters give a little to effect a compromise.

During the story the heroine and hero engage in much self analysis as they attempt to work through their emotional pain. This preoccupation creates a rather depressing atmosphere. Even when the lovers make love it is with a joyless desperation. Often, during their first attempts at lovemaking, one or the other experiences sexual dysfunction and they must resort to substitute expressions of sexuality. However, as their relationship progresses, this problem magically disappears, and they achieve more conventional fulfilment.

In the early stories, true to genre demands, the heroine suffers at the hands of the arrogant, mercurial hero. But, she has fallen in love with him, and thus endures his harsh treatment. At some point, usually near the crisis, she is reduced to tears and utterly humiliated. Then, she flees to find solace with one of the sympathetic relatives or friends. At the end, the man explains the reason for his behaviour (i.e. an unhappy past relationship), and all is forgiven. These early heroes do have some decency and sensitivity, but the effectiveness of these positive traits is diminished because they are told rather than shown.

In the later stories, in keeping with genre changes, heroes are more sensitive and heroines stronger. In *Both Sides Now*, Brad is the one who wants to marry Sabrina, now that she is pregnant with his child, but she wants to maintain her freedom. *Seduction*'s Diana Van Slyke refuses to let Marc Rochard manipulate her into the mould of wife and mother that he so desires.

Too Close for Comfort has a lighter tone than most of Hastings's novels. To keep her safe from manipulative relatives, Jessica Lawrence's fiancé has her spirited away by private detective Griff Marshall. The humour is clever and the characters display a refreshing frivolity. Also, hero Griff is much more mellow and likeable than earlier heroes.

Hastings steps outside the confines of category romance with *Beating the Odds*, a romantic-suspense novel published under her legal name, Deborah Gordon. Heroine Laura Miller helps FBI agent Mike Clemente solve the murder of a client of the insurance agent for whom she works. While some of the mystery's solution relies on contrivance, the story's lively pace does keep the reader's interest. Despite the happy romantic ending, Laura appears a victim of men as she suffers sexual harassment by her employer, manipulation by her soon-to-be ex-husband, and intimidation by her FBI agent-lover.

—Linda Lee

HASTINGS, Harrington. See **WOODWARD, Lilian.**

HASTINGS, Phyllis.
Pseudonyms: John Bedford; Julia Mayfield. **Nationality:** British. **Born:** Phyllis Dora Hodge, in Bristol. **Education:** Edgebaston Church of England College for Girls. **Relations:** married Philip Norman Hastings in 1938; one child. **Career:** ballet dancer as a child; later operator of a dairy farm, and an antique business. **Recipient:** Romantic Novelists Association Historical award, 1973. **Address:** c/o Robert Hale Ltd, 45–47 Clerkenwell Green, London EC1R 0HT, England.

ROMANCE AND HISTORICAL PUBLICATIONS

Novels (series: Sussex)

As Long as You Live. London, Jenkins, 1951.
Far from Jupiter. London, Jenkins, 1952.
Crowning Glory. London, Jenkins, 1952.
Rapture in My Rags. London, Dent, and New York, Dutton, 1954; as *Scarecrow Lover*, London, Pan, 1960; as *Rapture*, London, Consul, and New York, Popular Library, 1966.
Dust Is My Pillow. London, Dent, and New York, Dutton, 1955.
The Field of Roses. London, Dent, 1955; as *Her French Husband*, New York, Dutton, 1956.
The Black Virgin of the Gold Mountain. London, Dent, 1956.
The Innocent and the Wicked. New York, Popular Library, 1956.
The Signpost Has Four Arms. London, Dent, 1957.
The Forest of Stone (as Julia Mayfield). London, Hale, 1957.
A Time for Pleasure. New York, Popular Library, 1957.
The Happy Man. London, Hutchinson, 1958.
Golden Apollo. London, Hutchinson, 1958.
The Fountain of Youth. London, Hutchinson, 1959.
Sandals for My Feet. London, Hutchinson, 1960.
Long Barnaby. London, Hodder and Stoughton, 1961; as *Hot Day in High Summer*, London, May Fair, 1962.
The Night the Roof Blew Off. London, Hodder and Stoughton, 1962.
Their Flowers Were Always Black. London, Hale, 1967; as *The Harlot's Daughter*, London, New English Library, 1967.
The Swan River Story. London, Hale, 1968.
The Sussex Saga:
　All Earth to Love. London, Corgi, 1968.
　Day of the Dancing Sun. London, Corgi, 1971.
An Act of Darkness. London, Hale, 1969; as *The House on Malador Street*, New York, Putnam, 1970.
The Stars Are My Children. London, Hale, 1970.
The Temporary Boy. London, Hale, 1971.
When the Gallows Is High. London, Hale, 1971.

The Conservatory. London, Hale, 1973; New York, Pocket Books, 1974.
The Gates of Morning. London, Corgi, 1973.
Bartholomew Fair. London, Hale, 1974.
House of the Twelve Caesars. London, Hale, 1975; New York, Berkley, 1976.
The Image-Maker. London, Hale, 1976.
The Candles of the Night. London, Cassell, 1977.
The Death-Scented Flower. London, Hale, 1977.
Field of the Forty Footsteps. London, Cassell, 1978; New York, St Martin's Press, 1979.
The Stratford Affair. London, Hale, 1978.
The Feast of the Peacock. London, Cassell, 1978.
Running Thursday. London, Hale, 1980.
Buttercup Joe. London, Hale, 1980.
Tiger's Heaven. London, Hale, 1981.
A Delight of Angels. London, Hale, 1981.
The Overlooker. London, Hale, 1982.
Blackberry Summer. London, Hale, 1982.
The Lion at the Door. London, Hale, 1983.
The Free Traders. London, Hale, 1984.
My Four Uncles. London, Hale, 1984.
The Women Barbers of Drury Lane. London, Hale, 1985.
The Julian Maze. London, Hale, 1986.
The Naked Runner. London, Hale, 1987.

*

Film Adaptation: *Rapture*, 1970.

*   *   *

One of Phyllis Hastings's earlier novels, *Rapture in My Rags*, was described in the *New York Times Book Review* (18 July 1954) as 'A touching story of a girl's search for affection, her achieving a kind of protective maturity, and her revolt to preserve her new found identity.' Many of the author's female characters fit this very description although their personalities and their predicaments vary widely. Endeavoring to overcome loneliness in the midst of coping with peculiar situations is a hallmark of Hastings's heroines. From the confused Anna in *Dust Is My Pillow*, gullible Rose in *The Field of Roses* (US title *Her French Husband*), and responsible Ellie in *The Conservatory* to stalwart Melita in *The Swan River Story*, warped Victoria in *An Act of Darkness* (US title *The House on Malador Street*), and even the indomitable Caroline Dyke in *The Gates of Morning*, the author relentlessly examines the problems and powers of being female in largely male-dominated situations.

While the trials of women dealing with men in their lives is the primary focus of romance and gothic fiction, Hastings's style is distinctly her own. She can dispose of years in a sentence or two and describe wide-ranging adventures in understated terms as she does in *The Stars Are My Children*. One delights in the bright bits of humour that crop up sometimes in the most unlikely situations. She distinctively crafts her stories around characters or circumstances that are slightly offbeat, a shade removed from the normal. Hastings has a flair for portraying the neurotic character, such as the obsessed patriarch Isaac Shipton in *Dust Is My Pillow* and religious fanatic Stand Fast Dyke in *The Gates of Morning* as well as the evil sister Margaret in *The Conservatory*. She is also a master at portraying the growing sexual awareness of her heroines. Repressed sexuality accounts for the tension in many of her novels, and she also explores the touchy area of relationships between older women and younger men with humour in *The Stars Are My Children* and sensitivity in *The Gates of Morning*.

Hastings is an insightful student of human nature, always in control of her narrative, often lyrical in her descriptions of country life,

but it is her original characters and her taste for the unusual that make her repertoire of stories truly entertaining. A minor character in *The Stars Are My Children* expresses what might well be the author's own philosophy. After Arthur Balmer relates the fantastic tale of his rescue from slavery by a woman who gave him her infant daughter before perishing in a shipwreck and his later 15-year separation from the girl after his impressment, the listener, an old sailor, proclaims, ''Tis a mighty strange story though I have heard stranger. The earth teems with strange stories, it being the dwelling place of such odd creatures as human beings.'

—Allayne C. Heyduk

HATHAWAY, Vesta. See **OLIVER, Marina.**

HAWKES, Zachary. See **RIEFE, Barbara.**

HAYGOOD, Arnold G. See **SLAUGHTER, Frank G.**

HEATH, Sharon. See **RITCHIE, Claire.**

HEAVEN, Constance.
Pseudonyms: Constance Fecher; Christina Merlin. **Nationality:** British. **Born:** Enfield, Middlesex, 6 August 1911. **Education:** The Convent, Woodford Green, Essex, 1921–28; King's College, London, 1928–31, B.A. (honours) 1931; London College of Music, Licentiate 1931. **Relations:** married William Heaven in 1939 (died 1958). **Career:** actress, 1939–66; operated theatre companies at Henley-on-Thames with her husband; tutor in English literature, history, and creative writing, City Literary Institute, London, 1967–79. Chair, Romantic Novelists Association, 1981. **Recipient:** Romantic Novelists Association Major award, 1973, for *The House of Kuragin*. **Address:** 37 Teddington Park Road, Teddington, Middlesex TW11 8NB, England.

ROMANCE AND HISTORICAL PUBLICATIONS

Novels (series: Kuragin; Ravensley)

The House of Kuragin. London, Heinemann, and New York, Coward McCann, 1972.
The Astrov Inheritance (Kuragin). London, Heinemann, 1973; as *The Astrov Legacy*, New York, Coward McCann, 1973.
Castle of Eagles. London, Heinemann, and New York, Coward McCann, 1974.
The Place of Stones. London, Heinemann, and New York, Coward McCann, 1975.
The Fires of Glenlochy. London, Heinemann, and New York, Coward McCann, 1976.
The Queen and the Gypsy. London, Heinemann, and New York, Coward McCann, 1977.
Lord of Ravensley. London, Heinemann, and New York, Coward McCann, 1978.
Heir to Kuragin. London, Heinemann, 1978; New York, Coward McCann, 1979.

The Spy Concerto (as Christina Merlin). London, Hale, and New York, St Martin's Press, 1980.
The Wildcliffe Bird. London, Heinemann, 1981; New York, Coward McCann, 1983.
The Ravensley Touch. London, Heinemann, and New York, Coward McCann, 1982.
Sword of Mithras (as Christina Merlin). London, Hale, 1982.
Daughter of Marignac. London, Heinemann, 1983; New York, Putnam, 1984.
Castle of Doves. London, Heinemann, 1984; New York, Putnam, 1985.
Larksghyll. London, Heinemann, 1986.
The Craven Legacy. New York, Putnam, 1986.
The Raging Fire. London, Heinemann, 1987; New York, Putnam, 1988.
The Fire Still Burns. London, Heinemann, 1989.
The Wind from the Sea. London, Heinemann, 1991.
Love's Shadow. London, Heinemann, 1994.

Novels as Constance Fecher (series: Tudor Trilogy)

Tudor Trilogy:
  Queen's Delight. London, Hale, 1966; as *Queen's Favorite*, New York, Dell, 1974.
  Traitor's Son. London, Hale, 1967; New York, Dell, 1976.
  King's Legacy. London, Hale, 1967; New York, Dell, 1976.
Player Queen. London, Hale, 1968; as *The Lovely Wanton*, New York, Dell, 1977.
Lion of Trevarrock. London, Hale, 1969.
The Night of the Wolf. London, Hale, 1972; New York, Delacorte Press, 1974.
By the Light of the Moon. London, Hale, 1985.

OTHER PUBLICATIONS

Other (for children)

Venture for a Crown. New York, Farrar Straus, 1968.
Heir to Pendarrow. New York, Farrar Straus, 1969.
Bright Star: A Portrait of Ellen Terry. New York, Farrar Straus, 1970; London, Gollancz, 1971.
The Link Boys (as Constance Fecher). New York, Farrar Straus, 1971.
The Last Elizabethan: A Portrait of Sir Walter Raleigh. New York, Farrar Straus, 1972.
The Leopard Dagger (as Constance Fecher). New York, Farrar Straus, 1973.

*

Constance Heaven comments:

I came to writing late after some 25 years in the theatre with my husband and then alone after his early death. A lifelong interest in history gave me my first inspiration—a biographical novel about Sir Walter Raleigh which turned into a trilogy covering his son and grandson. From choosing real historical characters I turned to fictional heroes and heroines, and my first true romance was *The House of Kuragin* set in pre-revolutionary Russia. Quite small incidents often spark off a story: a holiday in the Highlands rich in family feuds, a fascination with the Camargue in southern France, an abiding interest in the Fen country—and before I know where I am I'm deep in research and inventing a plot to fit the scene. I cannot write to any formula. Plot and people have to come out of the circumstances and often develop in their own way, sometimes against my will. I am of a practical turn of mind so my characters tend to fol-

low suit and I'm not given to the wilder flights of romance. My two modern tales (as Christina Merlin) are a relief and contrast to my usual work. Basically I think I write to please myself. It's what I enjoy reading and I hope that others will find the same interest.

*   *   *

The writing of Constance Heaven has strong links with the Brontës. For the most part it inhabits the same 19th century, and uncovers the same dark passions, violence simmering beneath Victorian respectability. Her heroes are formidable and proud, with a definite streak of ruthlessness. Her heroines are spirited, often artistic, their quiet natures masking their inner strength. To this world Heaven brings her own individual voice.

As Constance Fecher she wrote the 'Tudor Trilogy'—*Queen's Delight*, *Traitor's Son*, *King's Legacy*—where historical characters and events are given a fictional treatment. *Queen's Delight* follows the life of Sir Walter Raleigh from his youth to final execution in the reign of James I. The work is perfectly achieved, the understated style honed to essentials. The author presents the complex nature of Raleigh, his varying fortunes, the triumph and tragedy of his life, without glamour or false dramatics. *Queen's Delight* is a remarkable novel, its restrained skill typical of the trilogy as a whole. *Lion of Trevarrock* and *The Night of the Wolf* are more conventionally gothic stories, well written though lacking the depth of the Tudor novels. The latter, with its Russian setting, indicates the future course of her work.

The House of Kuragin marks her debut as Constance Heaven, and describes her governess heroine's adventures with the Kuragin family in Tsarist Russia. Her love for the proud Andrei provides the central thread of the story. Quarrels over an inheritance, the sensual Natasha with her murky past, the steward who proves to be the old count's bastard son—all are skilfully interwoven, and the Russian setting beautifully evoked. *The Astrov Inheritance* is an effective sequel.

Castle of Eagles and *The Place of Stones* retain heroes and heroines of the gothic type, the settings respectively Vienna and Napoleonic France. Both are ably written, though they somehow lack the spark of the Kuragin novels. Better is *The Fires of Glenlochy*, set in the Scottish Highlands. The atmosphere is excellently caught, the plot exciting with secret passages and sudden discoveries, the brooding violence erupting in a climax of destruction.

The Queen and the Gypsy is outstanding. A return to Elizabethan history, it presents the tragic figure of Robert, Earl of Leicester, torn between ambition and love, for his wife and his queen. Tracking through time, Heaven focuses on the sequence of events that leads to final tragedy. All the old skills are displayed, the characters brought brilliantly to life.

Later writings display considerable period research, with precise historical dates and authentic—predominantly 19th-century—backgrounds. There is, too, a continual and intriguing contrast between the down-to-earth and the exotic in Heaven's locations. The Fen country provides a landscape for *Lord of Ravensley* and its sequel *The Ravensley Touch*, while *The Wildcliffe Bird*, one of her most impressive novels, is imaginatively set in Victorian Staffordshire. *Larksghyll* has a Yorkshire setting, its impoverished heroine working as a teacher in a mill town of the 1840s. Like *Wildcliffe Bird*, *Larksghyll* and its successor *The Craven Legacy* compel belief, the characters and the world they inhabit drawn with strength and conviction. The same is true of the more obviously 'romantic' stories like *Heir to Kuragin*, where the second Kuragin generation is followed to the Caucasus, and where the standard of authentic background and existing plot is maintained.

Castle of Doves and *Daughter of Marignac* explore 19th-century Continental locations, the former set in Spain during the Carlist rebellion, the latter following its aristocratic heroine and her

American lover through the Franco-Prussian war to the siege of Paris. Heaven returns to pre-revolution Russia with *The Raging Fire*, which depicts the interwoven lives of the English doctor Richard Aylsham and the beautiful peasant girl Galina Palova. The stormy passage of their love survives imprisonment, separation in loveless marriages, and the horrors of the 1914–18 war, and Tsarist and Bolshevik atrocities. Heaven brings the period to life with memorable snapshot scenes of the Russian landscape and people, the action culminating in the flight of the lovers and their children to safety in England. A sequel, *The Fire Still Burns*, follows the loves of a second generation in settings which include the Côte d'Azur, England, Russia, and Nazi Germany, but although a worthy effort it lacks the strengths of *The Raging Fire*.

Altogether more impressive is *The Wind from the Sea*, in which the aristocratic Isabelle de Sauvigny and her brother, Guy, flee the excesses of the French Revolution to find grudging sanctuary with their British aunt and uncle, at High Willows, in the Romney Marshes. Their subsequent adventures involve smuggling and revolutionary spies, and Isabelle's struggle to decide between two rival lovers. Characters and plot hold the reader's attention throughout, while the setting of the Romney Marshes comes alive on the page in brief but effective descriptions. *The Wind from the Sea* confirms the skill of its author in combining romantic themes with historical backgrounds, its atmosphere capably evoked, the period detail captured without strain. As with all her work, the central story recurs, of hero and heroine locked in a battle of the sexes, their conflict eventually resolved by love.

—Geoffrey Sadler

HEWLETT, Maurice (Henry).
Nationality: British. **Born:** Addington, Kent, 22 January 1861.
Education: London International College; studied law, 1879–91.
Relations: married Hilda Beatrice Herbert in 1888. **Career:** lecturer in Mediaeval Art, South Kensington University, London; keeper of the Land Revenue Records and Enrollments for the Record Office, London, 1898–1900. **Died:** 16 June 1923.

ROMANCE AND HISTORICAL PUBLICATIONS

Novels (series: John Maxwell Senhouse)

The Forest Lovers. London, Macmillan, and New York, Scribner, 1898.
The Life and Death of Richard Yea-and-Nay. London, Macmillan, 1900.
The Queen's Quair. London, Macmillan, 1904.
The Fool Errant. London, Heinemann, and New York, Macmillan, 1905.
The Stooping Lady. London, Macmillan, and New York, Dodd Mead, 1907.
The Spanish Jade. London, Cassell, and New York, Doubleday, 1908.
Halfway House: A Comedy of Degrees (Senhouse). London, Chapman and Hall, and New York, Scribner, 1908.
Letters to Sanchia. Privately printed, 1908.
Open Country: A Comedy with a Sting (Senhouse). London, Macmillan, and New York, Scribner, 1909.
Rest Harrow: A Comedy of Resolution (Senhouse). London, Macmillan, and New York, Scribner, 1910.
Brazenhead the Great. London, Smith Elder, and New York, Scribner, 1911.
The Song of Renny. London, Macmillan, and New York, Scribner, 1911.

Mrs Lancelot: A Comedy of Assumptions. London, Macmillan, and New York, Century, 1912.
Bendish: A Study of Prodigality. London, Macmillan, and New York, Scribner, 1913.
The Little Iliad. London, Heinemann, and Philadelphia, Lippincott, 1915.
A Lovers' Tale. London, Ward Lock, 1915; New York, Scribner, 1916.
Frey and His Wife. London, Ward Lock, and New York, McBride, 1916.
Love and Lucy. London, Macmillan, and New York, Dodd Mead, 1916.
Thorgils of Treadholt. London, Ward Lock, 1917; as *Thorgils*, New York, Dodd Mead, 1917.
Gudrid the Fair. London, Constable, and New York, Dodd Mead, 1918.
The Outlaw. London, Constable, 1919; New York, Dodd Mead, 1920.
Flowers in the Grass: Wiltshire Plainsong. London, Constable, 1920.
The Light Heart. London, Chapman and Hall, and New York, Holt, 1920.
Mainwaring. New York, Dodd Mead, 1920; London, Collins, 1921.

Short Stories

Little Novels of Italy. London, Chapman and Hall, and New York, Macmillan, 1899.
New Canterbury Tales. London, Constable, and New York, Macmillan, 1901.
Fond Adventures. London, Macmillan, and New York, Harper, 1905.
The Ruinous Face. New York, Harper, 1909.
The Birth of Roland. Chicago, Seymour, 1911.

OTHER PUBLICATIONS

Poetry

A Masque of Dead Florentines. London, Dent, 1895; Portland, Maine, Mosher, 1911.
Songs and Meditations. London, Constable, 1896.
Pan and the Young Shepherd. London, Lane, 1898; New York, Macmillan, 1906.
Artemision: Idylls and Songs. London, Mathews, and New York, Scribner, 1909.
The Agonists: A Trilogy of God and Man. London, Macmillan, and New York, Scribner, 1911.
Songs of Loss (published anonymously). Privately printed, 1911.
Helen Redeemed and Other Poems. London, Macmillan, and New York, Scribner, 1913.
Sing-Songs of the War. London, Poetry Bookshop, 1914.
The Wreath. Privately printed, 1914.
A Ballad of The Gloster and The Goeben. London, Poetry Bookshop, 1914.
Gai Saber: Tales and Songs. London, Mathews, and New York, Putnam, 1916.
The Song of the Plow. London, Heinemann, and New York, Macmillan, 1916.
The Loving History of Peridore and Paravail. London, Collins, 1917.
The Village Wife's Lament. London, Secker, and New York, Putnam, 1918.
Selected Poems. London, Benn, 1926.

Other

Earthwork Out of Tuscany. London, Dent, 1895; revised edition, 1899, 1901; New York, Putnam, 1899; revised edition, 1900.
The Road in Tuscany (travel). London, Macmillan, 2 vols, 1904.
Lore of Proserpine (essays and stories). London, Macmillan, and New York, Scribner, 1913.
In a Green Shade: A Country Commentary. London, Bell, 1920.
Wiltshire Essays. London, Oxford University Press, 1921.
Extemporary Essays. London, Oxford University Press, 1922.
Last Essays. London, Heinemann, and New York, Scribner, 1924.
The Letters of Maurice Hewlett: To Which Is Added a Diary in Greece, edited by Lawrence Binyon. London, Methuen, 1926.

Translator, *The Iliad: The First Twelve Stanzas.* London, Cresset Press, 1928.

* * *

Maurice Hewlett was a deservedly popular historical novelist who was scrupulous about the factual background to his books and who took pride in his precise use of evocative language. His ambition was to win recognition as a poet, and rather perversely he claimed to have been disappointed that the public kept on demanding prose romances from him. Certainly the diversity of his work is some indication of his unwillingness to continue ploughing the same furrow time and again.

The Forest Lovers is a remarkable achievement in the creation of atmosphere and tone. Hewlett drew on his deep knowledge and instinctive sympathy with Malory's *Le Morte d' Arthur* to devise a romance of his own. The story is basically simple, and Hewlett wrote in one of his letters that his aim was always to invent plots in which everything, however disparate the elements might seem as they occurred, would knit together into a seemingly inevitable unity. Prosper Le Gai rides out on his horse into a great forest which may, another of Hewlett's letters states, be best identified with the New Forest in Hampshire. The young man discovers a mysterious damsel in distress. He is kindly, she is smitten, but the two part, and it is only after many complications, which seem to be reflected in the long journeys through the shady ways of the forest, that the pair come together at the end. Menace is ever-present, made all the worse because it is connected with the church, which has spiritual and secular power and few hesitations about the way it uses it. Origins in particular are always doubtful and pose endless threats to the present and the future. Permeating all this, as in so much gothic fiction, is powerful sensuality, and Hewlett conveys a strong sense of the sexuality which is always just below the surface of this superficially chaste romance.

In *The Life and Death of Richard Yea-and-Nay* there are equally strong passions. But the scene changes: Hewlett offers here an account of the life of Richard Coeur de Lion which is set in Anjou and the Levant. Possibly smarting from the accusation that in that book he had twisted historical accuracy a little too much to make it serve his theme of the conflict between human passions and religious obligations, Hewlett took special care to ensure that the facts were accurate in his next novel, *The Queen's Quair.* The queen referred to is Mary, Queen of Scots, whose inner nature had in Hewlett's view never been properly understood before, and 'quair' is a word meaning 'book' (a sense which is preserved in the stationer's term 'a quire of paper'). First appearing in serial form in the *Pall Mall, The Queen's Quair* was a great commercial success, but failed to gain Hewlett the critical appreciation he craved. He was similarly disappointed by the reception of *The Fool Errant*, which is set in 18th-century Italy.

Towards the end of his life Hewlett turned to the Vikings as a final source of inspiration. Once again he informed himself fully about stirring times, and *Gudrid the Fair*, for instance, focuses on the great adventure of the Viking discovery of the shores of North America. In these novels Hewlett seems short of details of everyday life to give substance to his characters and fails to offer much psychological insight into them. The style lacks the distinction of his earlier works, which, though perhaps somewhat dated and mannered, can still give a lot of pleasure to readers who are prepared to accept a fairly leisurely style of narration.

—Christopher N. Smith

———

HEYER, Georgette.
Pseudonym: Stella Martin. **Nationality:** British. **Born:** Wimbledon, Surrey, 16 August 1902. **Education:** seminary schools and Westminster College, London. **Relations:** married George Ronald Rougier in 1925; one son. Lived in Tanganyika (now Tanzania), 1927–28, Yugoslavia, 1928–29, Sussex 1930–42, and London after 1942. **Died:** 5 July 1974.

Romance and Historical Publications

Novels

The Black Moth. London, Constable, and Boston, Houghton Mifflin, 1921.
The Great Roxhythe. London, Hutchinson, 1922; Boston, Small Maynard, 1923.
The Transformation of Philip Jettan (as Stella Martin). London, Mills and Boon, 1923; as *Powder and Patch* (as Georgette Heyer), London, Heinemann, 1930; New York, Dutton, 1968.
Instead of the Thorn. London, Hutchinson, 1923; Boston, Small Maynard, 1924.
Simon the Coldheart. London, Heinemann, and Boston, Small Maynard, 1925.
These Old Shades. London, Heinemann, and Boston, Small Maynard, 1926.
Helen. London and New York, Longman, 1928.
The Masqueraders. London, Heinemann, 1928; New York, Longman, 1929.
Beauvallet. London, Heinemann, 1929; New York, Longman, 1930.
Pastel. London and New York, Longman, 1929.
Barren Corn. London and New York, Longman, 1930.
The Conqueror. London, Heinemann, 1931; New York, Dutton, 1966.
The Convenient Marriage. London, Heinemann, 1934; New York, Dutton, 1966.
Devil's Cub. London, Heinemann, 1934; New York, Dutton, 1966.
Regency Buck. London, Heinemann, 1935; New York, Dutton, 1966.
The Talisman Ring. London, Heinemann, 1936; New York, Doubleday, 1937.
An Infamous Army. London, Heinemann, 1937; New York, Doubleday, 1938.
Royal Escape. London, Heinemann, 1938; New York, Doubleday, 1939.
The Spanish Bride. London, Heinemann, and New York, Doubleday, 1940.
The Corinthian. London, Heinemann, 1940; as *Beau Wyndham*, New York, Doubleday, 1941.
Faro's Daughter. London, Heinemann, 1941; New York, Doubleday, 1942.
Friday's Child. London, Heinemann, 1944; New York, Putnam, 1946.

The Reluctant Widow. London, Heinemann, and New York, Putnam, 1946.

The Foundling. London, Heinemann, and New York, Putnam, 1948.

Arabella. London, Heinemann, and New York, Putnam, 1949.

The Grand Sophy. London, Heinemann, and New York, Putnam, 1950.

The Quiet Gentleman. London, Heinemann, 1951; New York, Putnam, 1952.

Cotillion. London, Heinemann, and New York, Putnam, 1953.

The Toll-Gate. London, Heinemann, and New York, Putnam, 1954.

Bath Tangle. London, Heinemann, and New York, Putnam, 1955.

Sprig Muslin. London, Heinemann, and New York, Putnam, 1956.

April Lady. London, Heinemann, and New York, Putnam, 1957.

Sylvester; or, The Wicked Uncle. London, Heinemann, and New York, Putnam, 1957.

Venetia. London, Heinemann, 1958; New York, Putnam, 1959.

The Unknown Ajax. London, Heinemann, 1959; New York, Putnam, 1960.

A Civil Contract. London, Heinemann, 1961; New York, Putnam, 1962.

The Nonesuch. London, Heinemann, 1962; New York, Dutton, 1963.

False Colours. London, Bodley Head, 1963; New York, Dutton, 1964.

Frederica. London, Bodley Head, and New York, Dutton, 1965.

Black Sheep. London, Bodley Head, 1966; New York, Dutton, 1967.

Cousin Kate. London, Bodley Head, 1968; New York, Dutton, 1969.

Charity Girl. London, Bodley Head, and New York, Dutton, 1970.

Lady of Quality. London, Bodley Head, and New York, Dutton, 1972.

My Lord John. London, Bodley Head, and New York, Dutton, 1975.

Short Stories

Pistols for Two and Other Stories. London, Heinemann, 1960; New York, Dutton, 1964.

OTHER PUBLICATIONS

Novels (crime)

Footsteps in the Dark. London, Longman, 1932.

Why Shoot a Butler? London, Longman, 1933; New York, Doubleday, 1936.

The Unfinished Clue. London, Longman, 1934; New York, Doubleday, 1937.

Death in the Stocks. London, Longman, 1935; as *Merely Murder*, New York, Doubleday, 1935.

Behold, Here's Poison!. London, Hodder and Stoughton, and New York, Doubleday, 1936.

They Found Him Dead. London, Hodder and Stoughton, and New York, Doubleday, 1937.

A Blunt Instrument. London, Hodder and Stoughton, and New York, Doubleday, 1938.

No Wind of Blame. London, Hodder and Stoughton, and New York, Doubleday, 1939.

Envious Casca. London, Hodder and Stoughton, and New York, Doubleday, 1941.

Penhallow. London, Heinemann, 1942; New York, Doubleday, 1943.

Duplicate Death. London, Heinemann, 1951; New York, Dutton, 1969.

Detection Unlimited. London, Heinemann, 1953; New York, Dutton, 1969.

Plays

Radio Play: *The Toll Gate*, from her own novel, 1974.

*

Film Adaptation: *The Reluctant Widow*, 1950.

Critical Studies: *The Private World of Georgette Heyer* by Jane Aiken Hodge, London, Bodley Head, 1984; *Georgette Heyer's Regency England* by Teresa Chris, London, Sidgwick and Jackson, 1989.

*   *   *

"'I'm going back to London!" answered the Viscount (in *Friday's Child*). "And I'm going to marry the first woman I see!"' This perilous declaration is rendered merely fortunate by the fairytale element in Georgette Heyer's world of Regency romance: the first woman the Viscount encounters is a suitably born heroine who has loved him since childhood.

Although best known for her Regency novels, Heyer's work covers a greater range of history with books set in the mediaeval period (*Simon the Coldheart*), the Civil War (*Royal Escape*) and Elizabethan piracy (*Beauvallet*). For much of her career, she was working on a never completed mediaeval piece, posthumously published as *My Lord John*. Though Heyer developed her themes from interest in relationships between men in early works, to those between men and women, she never lost her fascination with war, culminating in the meticulous portrayal of the Battle of Waterloo, complete with Wellington, in *An Infamous Army*.

Three broad periods in Heyer's writing can be discerned: the early swashbuckling romances (*Beauvallet*); Regency comedy of manners, sometimes combined with a mystery story (*The Reluctant Widow*); and the late comedies of humour and feeling (*Frederica*). Her distinctive, essentially inimitable style (though many tried) combines remarkable historical accuracy with high quality literary artifice in plot, characters, and social code. No plagiarist could equal Heyer's precision on fashion, and the material world of Regency London, nor on the slang of the characters drawn from contemporary records.

Yet it is the artificial world she created that is most recognizably hers, structured on the importance of birth, decorum, and manners. Characters are either Quality or are willing to serve, and society is run happily by males born to privilege and duty while females are confined to the domestic and the romantic spheres. Contrary to recorded history, no voice is allowed to challenge these restrictions. Many of the novels contain a chorus of blithe devoted servants and however bold the heroines, their independence always proves a chimera when they find true love.

Tragedy is banished from Heyer's golden world and sex (never depicted) reserved for marriage except for the 'muslin company' allowed to unmarried males but never foregrounded in the theme of aristocratic romance. For Heyer, 'fallen' women do not exist as characters and irredeemably bad men are rare, decently dying or removing themselves from the ensemble. The recurrent motif of a sometimes dangerous lone male initiated into a domestic world of family relationships by romance with the heroine. This pattern is established as early as 1926 with *These Old Shades*, in which the mysterious Leonie reconciles all the estranged members of the Duke of Avon's family and continues to the end, notably in *Venetia*, in which the rake, Damerel, courts the heroine by becoming a better brother to her disabled sibling, Aubrey.

Some lovers, such as Damerel and Venetia, continue the distancing role of manners by use of quotations. Religion is discounted as a motivating force in Heyer's world and strong passions become increasingly subject to irony by the author and late heroes and heroines. A natural consequence is the employment of a restricted range of characters for comic purposes. Heyer herself spoke of her Mark 1 and Mark 2 heroes: the first a rakish 'Mr Rochester' type, ripe for reformation, the second a 'Corinthian' urbane, usually wealthy, man of fashion.

Heroines can similarly be divided into older, ironic, strong minded ladies, and the more innocent pliable types prone to family pressure. Other stock creations include the selfish mother, the boring suitor, immature romantic young men, and magnificent comic flourishes such as Mrs Floore, in *Bath Tangle*, and Mr Chawleigh, in *A Civil Contract*.

In addition, Heyer ironized romantic conventions by doubling the pair of lovers with the older pair consciously parodying youthful passions. *The Talisman Ring* provides the romantic Eustacie who very properly flees when her betrothed, Sir Tristram, refuses to ride 'ventre à terre' to her deathbed. Thereafter she meets a more romantic figure in smuggler and fugitive, Lord Lavenham, while Sir Tristram and Miss Thane enact a humorous counterpoint to their ardours. Sir Tristram refuses romantic vocabulary and Miss Thane assumes the role of a distressed damsel with clandestine assignations to deceive some ludicrous Bow Street Runners.

For later novels, Heyer even re-examined her own romantic clichés, for example in *A Civil Contract* in which the 'story book' passion is explicitly discounted, and Heyer's most unromantic heroine proves a devoted and loving wife. By the time of *The Nonesuch*, the beautiful girl proves heartless and the humorous but exceptionally well born governess acquires the matrimonial prize in a comedy reminiscent of *Jane Eyre*.

Despite her command of witty dialogue, Heyer had problems with her plots. Earlier romances tended to be duly frustrated until resolution by mystery or aristocratic crime. An example is *Regency Buck*, in which the spirited heroine, Judith, and the reader are tempted to confuse the potential murderer of her brother with the hero. Later works might depend upon comic misunderstanding or even a dash of social realism to temper the love story. Squalid social conditions are no real part of Heyer's world but provide interludes to demonstrate true worth in a mis-represented main character. *Arabella* wins the heart of wealthy Mr Beaumaris by rescuing a chimney sweep; the frivolous man of fashion in *The Nonesuch* proves a benefactor of orphans. By the time of *Frederica*, Heyer had developed family conflicts as effective in frustrating and promoting love affairs in one of her most successful comedies of feeling.

Essentially a writer of adult fairytales in a credible historical setting, Heyer created a unique world of delightful artifice, permitting of humour and irony due to its coherence. Not a writer of realism, passion or social criticism, she was a true artist of comedy where laughter and love (not sex) always prevailed. She is sorely missed.

—S.A. Rowland

HICHENS, Robert (Smythe).
Nationality: British. **Born:** Speldhurst, Kent, 14 November 1864. **Education:** Clifton College, Bristol; Royal College of Music, London; London School of Journalism. **Career:** music critic, the *World*. Fellow, Royal Society of Literature, 1926. **Died:** 20 July 1950.

ROMANCE AND HISTORICAL PUBLICATIONS

Novels

The Green Carnation (published anonymously). London, Heinemann, and New York, Appleton, 1894.
After Tomorrow, and The New Love. New York, Merriam, 1895.

An Imaginative Man. London, Heinemann, and New York, Appleton, 1895.
Flames: A London Phantasy. London, Heinemann, and Chicago, Stone, 1897.
The Londoners: An Absurdity. London, Heinemann, and Chicago, Stone, 1898.
The Daughters of Babylon, with Wilson Barrett. London, Macqueen, and Philadelphia, Lippincott, 1899.
The Slave. London, Heinemann, and Chicago, Stone, 1899.
The Prophet of Berkeley Square: A Tragic Extravaganza. London, Methuen, and New York, Dodd Mead, 1901.
Felix: Three Years of a Life. London, Methuen, 1902; New York, Stokes, 1903.
The Garden of Allah. London, Methuen, and New York, Stokes, 1904.
The Women with the Fan. London, Methuen, and New York, Stokes, 1904.
The Call of the Blood. London, Methuen, and New York, Harper, 1906.
Barbary Sheep. New York, Harper, 1907; London, Methuen, 1909.
A Spirit in Prison. London, Hutchinson, and New York, Harper, 1908.
Bella Donna. London, Heinemann, and Philadelphia, Lippincott, 1909.
The Knock on the Door. London, Heinemann, and Philadelphia, Lippincott, 1909.
The Dweller on the Threshold. London, Methuen, and New York, Century, 1911.
The Fruitful Vine. London, Unwin, and New York, Stokes, 1911.
The Way of Ambition. London, Methuen, and New York, Stokes, 1913.
In the Wilderness. London, Methuen, and New York, Stokes, 1917.
Mrs Marden. London, Cassell, and New York, Doran, 1919.
The Spirit of the Time. London, Cassell, and New York, Doubleday, 1921.
December Love. London, Cassell, and New York, Doran, 1922.
After the Verdict. London, Methuen, and New York, Doran, 1924.
The God Within Him. London, Methuen, 1926; as *The Unearthly*, New York, Cosmopolitan, 1926.
The Bacchante and the Nun. London, Methuen, 1927; as *The Bacchante*, New York, Cosmopolitan, 1927.
Dr Artz. London, Hutchinson, and New York, Cosmopolitan, 1929.
On the Screen. London, Cassell, 1929.
The Bracelet. London, Cassell, and New York, Cosmopolitan, 1930.
The First Lady Brendon. London, Cassell, and New York, Doubleday, 1931.
Mortimer Brice: A Bit of His Life. London, Cassell, and New York, Doubleday, 1932.
The Paradine Case. London, Benn, and New York, Doubleday, 1933.
The Power to Kill. London, Benn, and new York, Doubleday, 1934.
'Susie's' Career. London, Cassell, 1935; as *The Pyramid*, New York, Doubleday, 1936.
The Sixth of October. London, Cassell, and New York, Doubleday, 1936.
Daniel Airlie. London, Cassell, and New York, Doubleday, 1937.
The Journey Up. London, Cassell, and New York, Doubleday, 1938.
Secret Information. London, Hurst, and Blackett, and New York, Doubleday, 1938.
That Which Is Hidden. London, Cassell, 1939; New York, Doubleday, 1940.
The Million: An Entertainment. London, Cassell, 1940; New York, Doubleday, 1941.
Married or Unmarried. London, Cassell, 1941.

A New Way of Life. London, Hutchinson, and New York, Double-day, 1942.

Veils. London, Hutchinson, 1943; as *Young Mrs Brand*, Philadelphia, Macrae Smith, 1944.

Harps in the Wind. London, Cassell, 1945; as *The Woman in the House*, Philadelphia, Macrae Smith, 1945.

Incognito. London, Hutchinson, 1947; New York, McBride, 1948.

Too Much Love of Living. Philadelphia, Macrae Smith, 1947; London, Cassell, 1948.

Beneath the Magic. London, Hutchinson, 1950; as *Strange Lady*, Philadelphia, Macrae Smith, 1950.

The Mask. London, Hutchinson, 1951.

Nightbound. London, Cassell, 1951.

Short Stories

The Folly of Eustace and Other Stories. London, Heinemann, and New York, Appleton, 1896.

Byeways. London, Methuen, and New York, Dodd Mead, 1897.

Tongues of Conscience. London, Methuen, and New York, Stokes, 1900.

The Black Spaniel and Other Stories. London, Methuen, and New York, Stokes, 1905.

The Hindu. New York, Ainslee, 1917.

Snake-Bite and Other Stories. London, Cassell, and New York, Doran, 1919.

The Last Time and Other Stories. London, Hutchinson, 1923; New York, Doran, 1924.

The Streets and Other Stories. London, Hutchinson, 1928.

The Gate of Paradise and Other Stories. London, Cassell, 1930.

My Desert Friend and Other Stories. London, Cassell, 1931.

The Gardenia and Other Stories. London, Hutchinson, 1934.

The Afterglow and Other Stories. London, Cassell, 1935.

The Man in the Mirror and Other Stories. London, Cassell, 1950.

OTHER PUBLICATIONS

Plays

The Medicine Man, with H.D. Traill (produced London, 1898). New York, De Vinne Press, 1898.

Becky Sharp, with Cosmo Gordon-Lennox, adaptation of the novel *Vanity Fair* by Thackeray (produced London, 1901; as *Vanity Fair*, produced New York, 1911).

The Real Woman (produced London, 1909).

The Garden of Allah, with Mary Anderson, adaptation of the novel by Hichens (produced New York, 1911; London, 1920).

The Law of the Sands (produced London, 1916).

Black Magic (produced London, 1917).

Press the Button! (produced London, 1918).

The Voice from the Minaret (produced London 1919; New York, 1922).

Screenplay: *Bella Donna*, with Ouida Bergère, 1923.

Other

The Coastguards Secret (for children). London, Sonnenschein, 1886.

Homes of the Passing Show, with others. London, Savoy Press, 1900.

Egypt and Its Monuments. London, Hodder and Stoughton, and New York, Century, 1908; as *The Spell of Egypt*, Hodder and Stoughton, 1910; Century, 1911.

The Holy Land. London, Hodder and Stoughton, and New York, Century, 1910.

The Near East. London, Hodder and Stoughton, and New York, Century, 1913.

Yesterday: The Autobiography of Robert Hichens. London, Cassell, 1947.

*

Film Adaptations: *Bella Donna*, 1934; *Temptation*, 1935, from the novel *Bella Donna*; *The Garden of Allah*, 1936.

*   *   *

Although Robert Hichens had written earlier material, he first achieved fame with *The Green Carnation*, a very amusing takeoff on Oscar Wilde and the Aesthetic Movement, filled with bon mots, strokes of wit, and comic touches. Its intrinsic merit can be seen from the fact that it retained its popularity after the Wilde scandals and is still in print.

A more commercial phenomenon was *The Garden of Allah*, Hichens's best-known work. It sold close to a million copies, was staged, and was filmed at least three times. Although superficially it is a sentimental romance, in substructure (like much of Hichens's other work) it is antisexual, anticipating the earlier versions of *Lady Chatterley's Lover* in its concept of the loathly bridegroom. It is the story of Domini Enfilden, a lonely masculine British spinster who comes to a minor tourist town in North Africa and forces herself upon the only other tourist, the gauche Androvsky. Under the influence of the desert (the garden of Allah) they experience passion and marry. But Androvsky is a run-away monk from a Trappist monastery. He and Domini agree that he must return to his vows, and Domini, after bearing his child, settles in the area without him. The narrative, however, is less significant than the background. Hichens went all out to create North African local colour, with the result that for the close reader a remarkable picture emerges of landscape, Arab personality types, and Franco-Arabic social life, all much more interesting than the narrative.

Hichens's next two important works also deal with impermissible love, in this case, adultery. In *The Call of the Blood*, set in Sicily, when Maurice Delarey becomes irritated because his wife has returned to England for a visit, he has an affair with Maddalena, a peasant girl. He is murdered by the girl's father, but his wife never learns what had happened. A sequel, *A Spirit in Prison*, set 16 years later, is concerned with Ruffino, the by-blow of Delarey's affair. In both novels Italian local colour is applied almost obsessively.

Most of Hichens's other work is romantic fiction of this sort, usually based on a theme of sex gone astray. His stories usually deal with a formalized upper society group, and his treatment of potentially sensational matter always remained restrained and polite. While he outgrew the tendency to fill pages with painterly detail of exotic landscapes and authorial reflections, he substituted for these highly detailed descriptions of events, and his fiction was often overdeveloped and word-choked.

In the 1920s and 1930s Hichens applied himself occasionally to crime situations. Although such fiction was undoubtedly intended to meet the market demand for detective stories, there is little mystery or detection in such stories, but much about the psychological surroundings of crime. *After the Verdict* describes a society man who has been tried and found innocent of murdering his mistress. But, like Androvsky in *The Garden of Allah*, he cannot tolerate his role in marriage and confesses to his wife that he had been an accomplice to suicide. The most important of these crime-romances is *The Paradine Case*, based on a triangle of psychologies: vicious intellect (Justice Horfield), foolish sentiment and emotion (Keane, a barrister), and selfish, ruthless sensuality (Mrs Paradine). Keane, who is defending Mrs Paradine in her trial for the murder of her husband, has the misfortune to fall in love with her. His case and his ego both collapse when his thoughtlessness and passion cause him to take the wrong line during the trial. The characters in this novel are better drawn than is usual with Hichens, but it must be admitted that a reader who has seen the motion picture made from it may see Horfield as enlarged by Charles Laughton.

Hichens also wrote a fair amount of supernatural and occult fiction. The most important works are: 'The Return of the Soul' (*The Folly of Eustace*), dealing with the reincarnation of an abused cat as a vengeful woman; *Flames*, a very long novel about black magic, personality interchange, and redemption by love; *Tongues of Conscience*, short stories in which obsessions are portrayed in terms of fantasy; and *The Dweller on the Threshold*, a novel concerned with psychic research and spiritual vampirism of a sort.

Since little is known about Hichens as a man, it is not possible to say why he failed to realize his early promise. His technical virtuosity, his facility, his remarkable eye for picturesque detail, his originality of thought should have produced better work than overblown society romances. Only a little of the large corpus of his work is still vital: *The Green Carnation*, for its exuberant wit and *roman à clef* elements; *The Garden of Allah*, for its rich evocation of Africa; and perhaps the motion picture version of *The Paradine Case*.

—E.F. Bleiler

HILL, Grace Livingston. American. 1865–1947. See 2nd edition, 1990.

HILL, James.   See JAMESON, Storm.

HILL, Pamela.
Pseudonym: Sharon Fiske. **Nationality:** British. **Born:** Nairobi, Kenya, 26 November 1920. **Education:** Hutchesons' Grammar School, Glasgow; Glasgow School of Art, D.A. 1943; Glasgow University. **Career:** pottery and biology teacher in Glasgow and Edinburgh, 1958–74, and in Galloway, Scotland, 1965–70; also worked as a mink farmer. **Address:** 89-A Winchester Street, London SW1V 4NU, England.

ROMANCE AND HISTORICAL PUBLICATIONS

Novels

Flaming Janet: A Lady of Galloway. London, Chatto and Windus, 1954; as *The King's Vixen*, New York, Putnam, 1954.
Shadow of Palaces: The Story of Françoise d'Aubigné, Marquise de Maintenon. London, Chatto and Windus, 1955; as *The Crown and the Shadow*, New York, Putnam, 1955.
Marjorie of Scotland. London, Chatto and Windus, and New York, Putnam, 1956.
Here Lies Margot. London, Chatto and Windus, 1957; New York, Putnam, 1958.
Maddalena. London, Cassell, 1963.
Forget Not Ariadne. London, Cassell, 1965; South Brunswick, New Jersey, A.S. Barnes, 1967.
Julia. London, Cassell, 1967.
The Devil of Aske. London, Hodder and Stoughton, 1972; New York, St Martin's Press, 1973.
The Malvie Inheritance. London, Hodder and Stoughton, 1973; New York, St Martin's Press, 1974.

The Incumbent. London, Hodder and Stoughton, 1974; as *The Heatherton Heritage*, New York, St Martin's Press, 1976.
Whitton's Folly. London, Hodder and Stoughton, and New York, St Martin's Press, 1975.
Norah Stroyan. London, Hodder and Stoughton, 1976; as *Norah*, New York, St Martin's Press, 1976.
The Green Salamander. London, Hodder and Stoughton, and New York, St Martin's Press, 1977.
Tsar's Woman. London, Hale, 1977; New York, St Martin's Press, 1985.
Strangers' Forest. London, Hale, and New York, St Martin's Press, 1978.
Daneclere. London, Hale, 1978; New York, St Martin's Press, 1979.
Homage to a Rose. London, Hale, 1979.
Daughter of Midnight. London, Hale, 1979.
Fire Opal. London, Hale, and New York, St Martin's Press, 1980.
A Place of Ravens. London, Hale, 1980; New York, St Martin's Press, 1981.
Summer Cypress (as Sharon Fiske). London, Hale, 1981.
Knock at a Star. London, Hale, 1981.
This Rough Beginning. London, Hale, 1981.
The House of Cray. London, Hale, and New York, St Martin's Press, 1982.
The Fairest One of All. London, Hale, 1982.
Duchess Caine. London, Hale, 1983.
Bride of Ae. London, Hale, and New York, St Martin's Press, 1983.
The Copper-Haired Marshal. London, Hale, 1983.
Still Blooms the Rose. London, Hale, 1984.
Children of Lucifer. London, Hale, 1984.
The Governess. London, Hale, 1985.
Sable for the Count. London, Hale, 1985.
My Lady Glamis. London, Hale, 1985; New York, St Martin's Press, 1987.
Venables. London, Hale, 1986.
The Sisters. London, Hale, 1986; Boston, Hall, 1988.
Digby. London, Hale, 1987.
Fenfallow. London, Hale, 1987.
The Sutburys. London, Hale, and New York, St Martin's Press, 1988.
Jeannie Urquhart. London, Hale, 1988.
The Woman in the Cloak. London, Hale, 1988; New York, St Martin's Press, 1990.
Artemia. London, Hale, 1989; New York, St Martin's Press, 1990.
Trevithick. London, Hale, 1989.
The Loves of Ginerva. London, Hale, 1990.
Vollands. London, Hale, 1990.
The Brocken. London, Hale, 1990.
A Dark Star Passing. London, Hale, 1990.
The Sword and the Flame. London, Hale, 1991.
Mercer. London, Hale, 1992.
The Silver Runaways. London, Hale, 1992.
Angell and Sons. London, Hale, 1992.
Aunt Lucy. London, Hale, 1993.
O Madcap Duchess. London, Hale, 1993.
The Parson's Children. London, Hale, 1994.

*   *   *

Pamela Hill says that she got the idea for her first story—'The One Night', written in 1951—on a bus travelling between Glasgow and Edinburgh. Her imagination—and her pen—have been in the fast lane ever since, speeding through more than 50 historical romance/gothic novels since then.

Hill endows the heroines of her romances with equal stamina. In fact, many of them are practically Amazonian—true daughters of

Queen Boadicea, the 1st-century British ruler who led the revolt against the Romans—in their courage, strength, and physical abilities (in Hill's world, the *heroes* play the supportive roles): *Flaming Janet: A Lady of Galloway*; Françoise d'Aubigné, Marquis of Maintenon (in *Shadow of Palaces*); *Marjorie of Scotland*; the ruthless and iron-willed Madame of Aske (*The Devil of Aske*); Livia (*The Malvie Inheritance*), who survives a house of correction to become a guiding force at the Doon estate; the headstrong Primrose Tebb, who at the age of 12 marries Andrew Farquhar (*Strangers' Forest*); the courageous and ambitious Margaret Douglas, mother of Lord Darnley, who in turn was to become the husband of Mary, Queen of Scots in *The Green Salamander;* Fiona/Fiametta in *Fire Opal*, whose extraordinarily powerful swimming ability saves her from the Turks and helps the Knights of Malta in their defence of Christianity; Marfa Skavronsky, the orphaned Russian peasant girl who escapes from poverty by marrying a soldier, goes on to marry the Tsar (and indeed shaves her head, dons a helmet, and is at his side on the front lines of battle), and upon Peter's death becomes Catherine I, empress of the Russian people ('Marfa Skavronskaya . . . there is nothing you cannot do if you set your mind to it', she was told as a girl); Sara Ryder (*Bride of Ae*), who, in order to escape the dreary milliner's shop where she is apprenticed makes a marriage of convenience with the ill-tempered Francis Atherstone, squire of Ae ('one of the oldest—though not the largest—properties in England [whose] particulars go back to the Domesday Book'); and the beautiful Jonet Douglas (*My Lady Glamis*), who bravely rejects the advances of a captive (and very determined) King James V of Scotland. Several of Hill's heroines—Marjorie of Scotland; Margaret Douglas and her sister Jonet; Françoise d'Aubigné, Marquise of Maintenon; Catherine I of Russia—are actual historical (though highly dramatized) figures.

In *The Sutburys*, Hill's characters are more believable, perhaps, but their lives and predicaments are just as fantastic. A feud between the two Sutbury brothers results in a family curse, bringing with it the birth of a grossly handicapped child, the birth of a black child (to a seemingly white couple), deathbed confessions vital to the plot, and, as we have by now proceeded into the age of the railroad, several tragically relevant train accidents.

The heroines of Hill's most recent novels are notable for their Amazonian sexual appetites as well. Artemia Wivenhoe, the eponymous 'plain, downtrodden' companion to a Victorian lady of the 1850s, carries on a long-standing affair with her mistress's married son, and bears him two children, including a daughter, Rose, who is abducted from boarding school and brutally raped by a lusty neighbour. She is pursued by him thereafter, and tragically spoiled for men of a lesser sexual endowment and vigour. Melanie von Reichmansthal, the insatiable heroine of the Rabelaisian *The Brocken*, seduces the satyrical Nicholas Crowbetter, returns to her wealthy husband pregnant with Nicholas's child—a boy whom she cannot help seducing when he grows up.

As though she were still looking out of the window of that bus, Hill sets her gothic adventures primarily in her native Scotland, crossing the border into England from time to time, now and then dreaming of more exotic realms, her inner eye seeing the people and places of centuries past (most often, the 17th and 18th). Her pen is swift, her characters vividly drawn, and her adventures highly suspenseful.

—Marcia G. Welsh

HILL, Susan (Elizabeth).
Nationality: British. **Born:** Scarborough, Yorkshire, 5 February 1942. **Education:** grammar schools in Scarborough and Coventry; King's College, University of London, B.A. (honours) in English 1963. **Relations:** married the writer and editor Stanley Wells in 1975; three daughters (one deceased). **Career:** since 1963 full-time writer: since 1977 monthly columnist, *Daily Telegraph*, London. Presenter, *Bookshelf* radio programme, 1986–87. **Recipient:** Maugham award, 1971, for *I'm the King of the Castle*; Whitbread award, 1972, for *The Bird of Night*; Rhys memorial prize, 1972. Fellow, Royal Society of Literature, 1972, and King's College, 1978. **Address:** Midsummer Cottage, Church Lane, Beckley, Oxfordshire OX3 9UT, England.

ROMANCE AND HISTORICAL PUBLICATIONS

Novel

Mrs de Winter. London, Sinclair Stevenson, and New York, Morrow, 1993.

OTHER PUBLICATIONS

Novels

The Enclosure. London, Hutchinson, 1961.
Do Me a Favour. London, Hutchinson, 1963.
Gentleman and Ladies. London, Hamish Hamilton, 1968; New York, Walker, 1969.
A Change for the Better. London, Hamish Hamilton, 1969.
I'm the King of the Castle. London, Hamish Hamilton, and New York, Viking Press, 1970.
Strange Meeting. London, Hamish Hamilton, 1971; New York, Saturday Review Press, 1972.
The Bird of Night. London, Hamish Hamilton, 1972; New York, Saturday Review Press, 1973.
In the Springtime of the Year. London, Hamish Hamilton, and New York, Saturday Review Press, 1974.
The Woman in Black: A Ghost Story. London, Hamish Hamilton, 1983; Boston, Godine, 1986.
Air and Angels. London, Sinclair Stevenson, 1991.

Short Stories

The Albatross and Other Stories. London, Hamish Hamilton, 1971; New York, Saturday Review Press, 1975.
The Custodian. London, Covent Garden Press, 1972.
A Bit of Singing and Dancing. London, Hamish Hamilton, 1973.
Lanterns Across the Snow (novella). London, Joseph, 1987.

Plays

Lizard in the Grass (broadcast 1971; produced Edinburgh, 1988). In *The Cold Country and Other Plays for Radio*, 1975.
The Cold Country and Other Plays for Radio (includes *The End of Summer, Lizard in the Grass, Consider the Lilies, Strip Jack Naked*). London, BBC Publications, 1975.
On the Face of It (broadcast 1975). In *Act I*, edited by David Self and Ray Speakman, London, Hutchinson, 1979.
The Ramshackle Company (for children; produced London, 1981).
Chances (broadcast 1981; produced London, 1983).

Radio Plays: *Taking Leave*, 1971; *The End of the Summer*, 1971; *Lizard in the Grass*, 1971; *The Cold Country*, 1972; *Winter Elegy*, 1973; *Consider the Lilies*, 1973; *A Window on the World*, 1974; *Strip Jack Naked*, 1974; *Mr Proudham and Mr Sleight*, 1974; *On the Face of It*, 1975; *The Summer of the Giant Sunflower*, 1977; *The Sound That Time Makes*, 1980; *Here Comes the Bride*, 1980; *Chances*, 1981; *Out in the Cold*, 1982; *Autumn*, 1985; *Winter*, 1985.

Television Play: *Last Summer's Child*, from her story 'The Badness Within Him', 1981.

Other (for children)

One Night at a Time. London, Hamish Hamilton, 1984; as *Go Away, Bad Dreams!*, New York, Random House, 1985.
Mother's Magic. London, Hamish Hamilton, 1986.
Can It Be True? A Christmas Story. London, Hamish Hamilton, and New York, Viking Kestrel, 1988.
Suzy's Shoes. London, Hamish Hamilton, 1989.
Septimus Honeydew. London, Walker Books, 1990.
Stories from Codling Village. London, Walker Books, 1990.
I Won't Go There Again. London, Walker Books, 1990.
The Glass Angels. London, Walker Books, 1991.
Pirate Poll. London, Walker Books, 1991.

Other

The Magic Apple Tree: A Country Year. London, Hamish Hamilton, 1982; New York, Holt Rinehart, 1983.
Through the Kitchen Window. London, Hamish Hamilton, 1984.
Through the Garden Gate. London, Hamish Hamilton, 1986.
Shakespeare Country, photographs by Rob Talbot. London, Joseph, 1987.
The Lighting of the Lamps. London, Hamish Hamilton, 1987.
The Spirit of the Cotswolds, photographs by Nick Meers. London, Joseph, 1988.
Family. London, Joseph, 1989; New York, Viking, 1990.

Editor, *The Distracted Preacher and Other Tales*, by Thomas Hardy. London, Penguin, 1979.
Editor, with Isabel Quigly, *New Stories 5*. London, Hutchinson, 1983.
Editor, *People: Essays and Poems*. London, Chatto and Windus, 1983.
Editor, *Ghost Stories*. London, Hamish Hamilton, 1983.
Editor, *The Walker Book of Ghost Stories*. London, Walker Books, 1990.
Editor, *The Parchment Moon: An Anthology of Modern Women's Short Stories*. London, Joseph, 1990; as *The Penguin Book of Modern Women's Short Stories*, 1991.

*

Manuscript Collection: Eton College Library, Windsor, Berkshire.

*   *   *

A prolific and professional author, Susan Hill has written in a wide range of genres, from autobiography and children's tales to topographical works and ghost stories. While she is probably best known for the latter (*The Woman in Black*, for example, is something of a modern classic, and has run successfully in the West End as a stage play for several years) she has produced a number of novels that can be described as containing elements of romantic/historical fiction. With the recent publication of *Mrs de Winter* Hill looks set to confirm her reputation in this field: a reputation, if not of greatness, then of superb craftsmanship and expertise.

A typical Hill novel opens in autumn, often at a graveside, and proceeds to tell a story that is set in the not-too-distant past, and which involves, usually, some form of haunting. This is as true of Hill's romantic/historical works as it is of her ghost stories: there is, in fact, a strong unity of themes and imagery in all these books, a unity particularly evident in *Mrs de Winter*. The haunting in the romantic/historical pieces is not so much literal as metaphoric—

characters are obsessed, and transfixed by memories of love. In *Strange Meeting*, for example, one of Hill's earlier works, two young British officers stationed at the Front in 1916 develop an intense (though platonic) relationship: only one survives the war, but he carries with him forever painful memories of his passion. *Air and Angels*, a more recent book, tells a similar story of romantic obsession, only here the canvas is much larger (England and India) and the obsession lasts a lifetime. If neither piece succeeds wholly— there is, for all Hill's skill, an odd lack of emotional force in her romantic-historical writing—each is none the less superbly crafted: in *Strange Meeting*, for example, the physical environment of war-torn northern France (lush, autumnal countryside, muddy, verminous trenches) is vividly and expertly evoked, while in *Air and Angels* the airless, claustrophobic world of Victorian Cambridge is conveyed beautifully. Such exact re-creation of the past is, of course, the secret of Hill's success; by persuading her readers so artfully of the reality of her settings she convinces them equally of the reality of the emotions (love and hate, joy and fear) she creates.

Mrs de Winter, Hill's most recent work, is something of a new departure, not least because it is not an original idea but a sequel to Daphne du Maurier's *Rebecca*. It is a brave writer who attempts a follow-up to such a classic tale, but Hill succeeds. She does so because she has studied *Rebecca*. All the familiar characters appear: desperate, haunted Maxim, sinister Mrs Danvers, and always, just out of sight, but never out of mind, the teasing, malicious spirit of Rebecca—in fact the whole Manderley world recreated not just in broad outline but in the very words and cadences of du Maurier's novel. Even more potent than this, however, is the fact that Hill has given her work an emotional charge lacking in her other fiction by writing it, in effect, as a ghost story. Like *The Woman in Black*, *Mrs de Winter* begins in autumn, by a graveside; like *The Woman in Black* it charts the vain attempts of the narrator and his/her loved ones to escape the vengeful persecution of a sable shade. The final scene, in which Maxim's young wife confronts the black-clad Mrs Danvers in her lair, is hair-raising in the best traditions of the ghost story; purists may cavil at the mixing of two genres, but the effect is powerful.

In *Mrs de Winter* Hill has written her best romantic/historical novel to date. It will be interesting to see what she does next.

—John O'Leary

———

HILTON, Margery.
Nationality: British. **Relations:** married. **Address:** c/o Mills and Boon Ltd, Eton House, 18–24 Paradise Road, Richmond, Surrey TW9 1SR, England.

ROMANCE AND HISTORICAL PUBLICATIONS

Novels

The Dutch Uncle. London, Mills and Boon, 1966.
Young Ellis. London, Mills and Boon, 1966.
Darling Radamanthas! London, Mills and Boon, 1966.
The Grotto of Jade. London, Mills and Boon, 1967.
Girl Crusoe. London, Mills and Boon, 1969.
Interlude in Arcady. London, Mills and Boon, 1969.
The Flower of Eternity. London, Mills and Boon, 1970.
Bitter Masquerade. London, Mills and Boon, 1970.
The House of the Amulet. London, Mills and Boon, 1970.
Frail Sanctuary. London, Mills and Boon, 1970.
The Inshine Girl. London, Mills and Boon, 1970.
Miss Columbine and Harley Quinn. London, Mills and Boon, 1970.

A Man Without Mercy. London, Mills and Boon, 1971.
The Whispering Grove. London, Mills and Boon, 1971.
Trust in Tomorrow. London, Mills and Boon, 1971.
Dear Conquistador. London, Mills and Boon, 1972.
The Spell of the Enchanter. London, Mills and Boon, 1972.
Miranda's Marriage. London, Mills and Boon, 1973.
The Beach of Sweet Returns. London, Mills and Boon, 1975.
Time of Curtain Fall. London, Mills and Boon, 1976.
The House of Strange Music. London, Mills and Boon, 1976.
The Dark Side of Marriage. London, Mills and Boon, 1978.
Snow Bride. London, Mills and Boon, 1979.
The Velvet Touch. London, Mills and Boon, 1979.
Way of a Man. London, Mills and Boon, 1981.

*   *   *

Margery Hilton has written a string of successful romances, some of which are considered classics of the genre. Although adept at creating strongly male and fervently feminine stereotypes, she manages to inject these with shafts of subtlety and sharpness which lift her books from conventional ordinary-girl-meets-glamorous-Mr-Right romances into interesting complexes of challenge and response.

One of her most powerful stories is *A Man Without Mercy*. In this her heroine, Gerda, has to face some fearful situations. Her marriage to a very sick man is a tragic business: then, widowed and grappling with career problems, she finds that her romantic aspirations become terribly tangled with misunderstandings, intrigues, and an obsessive desire for vengeance on the part of the man to whom she gives her at first unrequited passion. Hatred from the past threatens to overwhelm the present, but Gerda's responses show that, as befits her robust business-girl image, she is far more than a mere shuttlecock in the winds of fate.

The leading character in *Girl Crusoe* is similarly resilient. Jan, a skilled commercial photographer, gets stranded on an uninhabited Pacific island with Nick Redfern the irritatingly superior pilot of the small plane in which she has been travelling. Of course it is inevitable that enforced proximity and the struggle for survival will eventually throw each into the other's arms, but, true to the traditions of the genre Hilton contrives, by means of some compelling psychological sparring between girl and boy, to defer the truly passionate clinches until the end of the book (when rescue provides the possibility of respectable matrimony).

Girl Crusoe embodies some of Hilton's most atmospheric description of locations, as the delights and difficulties of the island terrain are uncovered. Strong local colour is an enlivening feature of many of her stories, whether it embraces 'the romantic island of Salamander in the Indian Ocean' (to which Toni retreats after an accident has ended her ballet-dancing career in *The Whispering Grove*), the steamy Peruvian jungle in *The Flower of Eternity* (which lures Gail into the search for a lost valley *and* a lover among 'those strong, silent explorer types'), or simply the London of flat-sharing working girls in *Miss Columbine and Harley Quinn*. Whatever the setting, Hilton can be relied upon to provide engaging characters and lively plots as well as the expected dollops of romance.

—Mary Cadogan

———

HINES, Jeanne. See SHERWOOD, Valerie.

———

HINTZE, Naomi A(gans).   American. 1909—. See 2nd edition, 1990.

———

HODGE, Jane Aiken.
Nationality: British. **Born:** Watertown, Massachusetts, 4 December 1917; daughter of the writer Conrad Aiken; sister of Joan Aiken, *q.v.* **Education:** Hayes Court, Kent, 1929–34; Somerville College, Oxford (Lefevre fellow), 1935–38, B.A. (honours) 1938; Harvard University, Cambridge, Massachusetts, 1938–39, A.M. 1939. **Relations:** married the writer Alan Hodge in 1948 (died 1979); two daughters. **Career:** British Board of Trade, Washington, DC, 1941–44, and the British Supply Council of North America, 1944–45; researcher, Time Inc, New York, 1945–47, and for *Life* magazine, in London, 1947–48; reader for film companies and publishers, and freelance reviewer, 1950s and 1960s. **Agent:** David Higham Associates, 5–8 Lower John Street, London W1R 4HA, England. **Address:** 23 Eastport Lane, Lewes, East Sussex BN7 1TL, England.

ROMANCE AND HISTORICAL PUBLICATIONS

Novels

Maulever Hall. London, Hale, and New York, Doubleday, 1964.
The Adventurers. New York, Doubleday, 1965; London, Hodder and Stoughton, 1966.
Watch the Wall, My Darling. New York, Doubleday, 1966; London, Hodder and Stoughton, 1967.
Here Comes a Candle. London, Hodder and Stoughton, and New York, Doubleday, 1967; as *The Master of Penrose*, New York, Dell, 1968.
The Winding Stair. London, Hodder and Stoughton, 1968; New York, Doubleday, 1969.
Marry in Haste. London, Hodder and Stoughton, 1969; New York, Doubleday, 1970.
Greek Wedding. London, Hodder and Stoughton, and New York, Doubleday, 1970.
Savannah Purchase. London, Hodder and Stoughton, and New York, Doubleday, 1971.
Strangers in Company. London, Hodder and Stoughton, and New York, Coward McCann, 1973.
Shadow of a Lady. New York, Coward McCann, 1973; London, Hodder and Stoughton, 1974.
One Way to Venice. London, Hodder and Stoughton, 1974; New York, Coward McCann, 1975.
Rebel Heiress. London, Hodder and Stoughton, and New York, Coward McCann, 1975.
Runaway Bride. New York, Fawcett, 1975; London, Coronet, 1976.
Judas Flowering. London, Hodder and Stoughton, and New York, Coward McCann, 1976.
Red Sky at Night: Lovers' Delight? New York, Coward McCann, 1977; London, Hodder and Stoughton, 1979.
Last Act. London, Hodder and Stoughton, and New York, Coward McCann, 1979.
Wide Is the Water. London, Hodder and Stoughton, and New York, Coward McCann, 1981.
The Lost Garden. London, Hodder and Stoughton, and New York, Coward McCann, 1982.
Secret Island. London, Hodder and Stoughton, and New York, Putnam, 1985.
Polonaise. London, Hodder and Stoughton, and New York, Putnam, 1987.
First Night. London, Hodder and Stoughton, and New York, Putnam, 1989.
Leading Lady. London, Hodder and Stoughton, and New York, Putnam, 1990.
Windover. London, Hodder and Stoughton, and New York, St Martin's Press, 1992.

Escapade. London, Hodder and Stoughton, and New York, St Martin's Press, 1993.

OTHER PUBLICATIONS

Other

The Double Life of Jane Austen. London, Hodder and Stoughton, 1972; as *Only a Novel: The Double Life of Jane Austen*, New York, Coward McCann, 1972.
The Private World of Georgette Heyer. London, Bodley Head, 1984.

*

Jane Aiken Hodge comments:

I would rather be called a writer of romance than of gothic. The term gothic now seems to imply a kind of violent horror that I think out of place in books written as entertainment. There is too much violence and horror in real life, and they should be written about seriously, not to titillate. Besides, I prefer the tension of feeling to the spurious kind provided by violence. I hope to keep my reader happily hooked without ever making her (or him) shocked, or sick. This is one reason why I write mainly historical romance, in which it is easier to indulge in moral standards, and a happy ending. A reviewer once said of one of my early books that it was a blend of Jane Austen and the Brontës, and I think this is the comment that has pleased me most in my writing career. I also owe a vast debt to Georgette Heyer, whose impeccable historical accuracy I have always tried to emulate. The background research is part of the pleasure, and so is the tension between historical fact and the vagaries of one's characters. I have, however, also written three novels of modern romantic suspense, enjoyed them very much, and hope to do more. In them, too, I aim for excitement without excessive violence. There seems to be a terrible dearth, just now, of the kind of civilized light reading provided by writers like Dorothy Sayers, Georgette Heyer, or Mary Stewart. It is my immodest ambition to be classed with them.

*   *   *

Jane Aiken Hodge's heroines are engaged on a journey that will change their lives, whether or not they know that the change is coming. This prolific writer, whose work can be roughly divided into historical novels and works of romantic suspense, excels in both fields. In modern dress or the period from the American Revolution to the end of the Napoleonic era—her chosen period—her novels show women changing in more ways than their physical location. The challenges and mysteries they meet force them to look within themselves to find a strength and a capacity for growth of which they were unaware.

Like her sister, the writer Joan Aiken, Hodge is an author of dazzling imagination. Her novels sometimes seem to begin where a lesser writer's would end. In *Greek Wedding*, for instance, the first chapter marks Phyllida's escape from the harem of the Sultan during riots marking the Greek War of Independence. Her voyage across the Atlantic, her capture and her father's death at the hands of pirates—these are relegated to the past, as she starts the yacht trip from Istanbul to the isles of Greece that will be her journey. Juliet and her scheming cousin Josephine have all but literally been through the Napoleonic wars—Bonaparte himself is on St Helena—when they arrive separately in Georgia in *Savannah Purchase*.

The theme of family life, although far from idealized, is always strong in Hodge's books. Phyllida is in Greece to find her brother, fighting with the Greek independence movement. Henrietta crosses the Atlantic in *Rebel Heiress* to find her long-lost father. But Hodge is also interested in more political themes, as well as the intimate theme of personal identity.

The sweeping *Polonaise*, a saga covering several countries and numerous historic as well as fictional characters, shows the development of Jenny Peverel, who comes to Poland from England as a companion to Princess Isobel Ovinska. Jenny's passion for Englishman Glynde seems lost in Glynde's devotion to Isobel. But Isobel's main loyalty is to her son, Casimir, whom she sees as Poland's hope of unification, not as a child at all. Her concerns are dynastic; she turns first to the Emperor of Russia and then to the Emperor of France, depending on who seems more willing to listen to Poland's plea for an independent state. Jenny, not Isobel, realizes that the true Poland is in the people, not in the whims of the upper classes. Polish-American Jan learns to love the no-longer beautiful, stubbornly independent Jewish former mistress of Isobel's husband. Glynde, who has crossed Europe in the service of the British, learns that his true father is really French.

This too is typical of Hodge. Her characters are located on the borderlines of nationality, as Camille Foret, in *Marry in Haste*, becomes English Camilla Forest, or as Kate, in *Here Comes a Candle*, changes into an American after her staunchly English upbringing. Just as the period Hodge writes of is one of changing alliances and shifts in the balance of power, so do her characters develop and change, often under the influence of political ideas, as Hart Purchis, in *Judas Flowering*, begins as a loyal subject of King George III and ends as an American sea captain.

Her books about the Purchis family of Georgia are the closest Hodge comes to a family saga. Hart and the printer's daughter Mercy, whom he rescues from a mob in *Judas Flowering*, reappear in *Wide Is the Water*, where they are again separated, this time by the Atlantic. Hart is captured by the British, in the person of his distant cousin. Mercy assumes responsibility for an orphan traumatized by an Indian attack, and eventually lands in England as well, where the newly recovered orphan finds and marries Hart's cousin. It is their foster daughter who becomes the mother of Caroline, heroine of *The Lost Garden*. Another Purchis descendant, in Georgia, weds first Josephine and then Juliet, in *Savannah Purchase*. Only in the first two books, however, does the story show continuity. True, the reader who follows Hodge can pick up hints and clues that connect the stories, but these are not necessary to enjoy the later two novels. The connection of the Purchis family to *The Lost Garden* is very slight, and so much else happens in this book that even Hodge enthusiasts may not notice. This gallimaufry includes illegitimacy, emotional incest, women's rights, witchcraft and a proposed invasion of England. The important thing about Caroline's mother is that she is mistress of a duke, not that she has been a Purchis connection. Caroline is fostered out in a minister's family, but eventually received in her true father's household, where she develops an affectionate relationship with her unacknowledged half brother. She is forced into a marriage with an untalented young poet, and shipped off with him to be a vicar's wife in a town that proves to be a hotbed of superstition and sedition. She rewrites her husband's verses until he is famous; when the cabal of smugglers and French sympathizers he belongs to is broke up, he is killed and she is left to pen his posthumous poems to satisfy her publisher, her long-lost foster brother. Only the intervention of an unlikely hero, the former lover of her father's late duchess, saves her from the publisher's designs on her purse and person.

The ambiguous role played by brothers and other family members may be mentioned here. The only reliable relative seems to be a dead one, and the heroine in *Red Sky at Night: Lover's Delight*, finds that reports of her brother's death are not reliable either. Caroline's half brother was kind to her, but her foster brother is deceptive, and her mother can be actively hostile. Mercy in the Purchis books is an orphan. Henrietta, in *Rebel Heiress*, finds her father is loving, but they have been separated most of her life by her scheming aunt, and she also gains an unfriendly stepmother and an unreliable step-brother. Kathryn, in the recent *Windover*, has a feeble, hysterical mother, a lecherous stepfather, uninteresting brats of half brothers, a religiously obsessed mother-in-law and a lover with amnesia. Camilla, in *Marry in Haste*, and Phyllida, in *Greek Wedding*, have brothers who prove at best neglectful of their sisters, and at worst, actively hostile to their best interests.

In her romantic fiction, set in the present day, one finds Hodge returning to her beloved Greece in *Secret Island* and the popular *Strangers in Company*. The latter is notable especially for the heroine, Marian Frenche, a woman in her thirties who finds danger as well as opportunity for a new, happier life when she accepts a job as companion to a neurotic young woman who wants to tour Greece. The top tourist attractions of modern Greece are described in Hodge's usual delightful prose, although the excitement of the last-minute rescue on Aegina is powerful enough to pull readers from the scenery. Similarly, *The Lost Garden* is less successful than other novels. *Secret Island* narrates Daphne's visit to her hitherto unknown aunt, where she finds herself involved with world politics, three men including her estranged husband, an unknown archaeological site, and a secret of mind control that her father discovered but which he cannot quite remember. Add several murders, incest, the politics of matriarchy, and a mysterious healing effect on her aunt's island home, and the mixture becomes too rich. As is often the case with Hodge, less is more. The abundance of material has weakened the story. *One Way to Venice*, because it is more focused, is more successful although it is improbable in its own right. Julia tries to find the child she gave up for adoption years before as her husband's Gothic family reaches out from America to thwart her. *Last Act* is set in a tiny European principality, where dying opera singer Anne Page is to perform in an unknown opera by Beethoven. This would seem to be enough plot for one book, but Hodge adds more—conflict in the ruling family, not one but two plots against the security of the state, an errant prince and high explosives. Still, perhaps because Hodge so enjoys writing about music, the reader can accept the disparate elements, however implausible.

Her faults, however, are minor compared to her strengths. Despite traditional weaknesses assigned to this genre, Hodge consistently delivers well-researched period pieces with strong-willed feminine characters whose interests range beyond dancing at Almack's. These and other characters grow and develop in exciting, usually convincing and always suspenseful plots, their actions described in supple, enjoyable prose. Since her characters have assumptions that can often challenge the conventional, and since readers may find the background events as important as the actual romances, Hodge may not have the popularity of some more formulaic writers. But the informed reader looks for the new Hodge with confidence and pleasure.

—Susan Branch

HOHL, Joan.   See **LORIN, Amii.**

HOLLAND, Cecelia (Anastasia).
Pseudonym: Elizabeth Eliot Carter. **Nationality:** American. **Born:** Henderson, Nevada, 31 December 1943. **Education:** Pennsylvania State University, University Park, 1961–62; Connecticut College, New London, B.A. 1965. **Career:** visiting professor of English, Connecticut College, 1979. **Recipient:** Guggenheim fellowship, 1981. **Address:** c/o Houghton Mifflin Company, One Beacon Street, Boston, Massachusetts 02108, USA.

ROMANCE AND HISTORICAL PUBLICATIONS

Novels

The Firedrake. New York, Atheneum, 1966; London, Hodder and Stoughton, 1967.
Rakóssy. New York, Atheneum, and London, Hodder and Stoughton, 1967.
The Kings in Winter. New York, Atheneum, and London, Hodder and Stoughton, 1968.
Until the Sun Falls. New York, Atheneum, and London, Hodder and Stoughton, 1969.
Antichrist. New York, Atheneum, 1970; as *The Wonder of the World*, London, Hodder and Stoughton, 1970.
The Earl. New York, Knopf, 1971; as *Hammer for Princes*, London, Hodder and Stoughton, 1972.
The Death of Attila. New York, Knopf, 1973; London, Hodder and Stoughton, 1974.
Great Maria. New York, Knopf, 1974; London, Hodder and Stoughton, 1975.
Two Ravens. New York, Knopf, and London, Gollancz, 1977.
Valley of the Kings (as Elizabeth Eliot Carter). New York, Dutton, 1977; (as Cecelia Holland), London, Gollancz, 1978.
City of God. New York, Knopf, and London, Gollancz, 1979.
The Sea Beggars. New York, Knopf, and London, Gollancz, 1982.
The Belt of Gold. New York, Knopf, and London, Gollancz, 1984.
Pillar of the Sky. New York, Knopf, and London, Gollancz, 1985.
The Lords of Vaumartin. Boston, Houghton Mifflin, 1988; London, Gollancz, 1989.
The Bear Flag. Boston, Houghton Mifflin, and London, Gollancz, 1990.
Pacific Street. London, Gollancz, 1992.

OTHER PUBLICATIONS

Novels

Floating Worlds. New York, Knopf, and London, Gollancz, 1976.
Home Ground. New York, Knopf, and London, Gollancz, 1981.

Other (for children)

Ghost on the Steppe. New York, Atheneum, 1969.
The King's Road. New York, Atheneum, 1970.

*   *   *

Cecelia Holland had been out of college only a year when her first novel, *The Firedrake* was published in 1966. Since then, hardly a year has gone by without a Holland novel offered to hungry historical fiction buffs. Her time and place settings range from pre-history with *Pillar of the Sky*, set at Stonehenge on England's Salisbury plain, to 16th-century Hungary with *Rakóssy*, a rough, uncultured Magyar nobleman, and *The Sea Beggars*, the story of Dutch Calvinists fighting the heretic-hunting Spanish for their religious freedom—with one unsuccessful foray into science fiction (*Floating Worlds*) and one contemporary novel (*Home Ground*).

Holland's historical novels have received mixed reviews, but weighted heavily on the positive side. Her first novel was criticized for the use of very short, plain, often abrupt language and simple sentence structure, but praised for the sound research about England just before the Norman conquest. Those early reviews clearly did not disturb Holland unduly, for 20 years later, her style has not changed and in fact her disdain for the ornate language often found in historical novels has become a hallmark of her work, which is now frequently praised for the immediacy her prose brings to her stories. Some reviewers have taken a different tack in their criticism by challenging her facts while praising her imagination. Though she is obviously intrigued by primitive cultures and remote historical periods, these only set the stage for her tales. Holland is above all a storyteller who has a wonderful way of transporting herself back in time and taking us along with her. One can feel the eerie and terrifying atmosphere in a scene from *City of God* (a story of the Borgias in early 16th-century Rome), which takes place at the Vatican where Pope Alexander sports with his mistress on his lap while his illegitimate son, Valentino, also known as Cesare Borgia, turns his pet leopard loose on drunken palace revellers. Or the reader can experience the joy and frivolity of a May Day celebration in Norman England with the young men and girls singing and dancing and leading 'a creature made of leaves, strutting from side to side. Green boughs covered it from its pointed head to the ground'. This description of the King of the Green is a bright spot in the rather grim story *Two Ravens* about the wanderings of an 11th-century Icelander estranged from his cruel father who returns home to wreak his revenge.

Another Holland signature is the frequent use and description of animals, especially horses who play roles in most of her novels, including the contemporary *Home Ground*. As for characterizations, she is at her best and most believable when free to create imaginary characters. Frequently the protagonists in her novels are colleagues, companions, or servants to the more wooden historical folk whose actions and personalities have been documented. Read history books to learn the facts about a given age, but read Holland to soak up the atmosphere.

In 1990, Holland delved into American history for the first time with *The Bear Flag*. This novel is perhaps more accessible than her earlier ones as it deals with familiar territory and historic characters known from books, films, and television. School children sing about Kit Carson, and young adults have studied the maps and explorations of John Charles Fremont. The protagonist, Catherine Reilly, survives a miraculous winter crossing of the Sierra mountains into Mexican controlled California, though her husband does not. She manages to make a life for herself, and grows to love her new land—so much that she joins the others settlers in revolt against the Mexican dons. For 24 days their Bear Flag Republic stands alone with allegiance to neither the United States nor Mexico. Cat Reilly is a fictional character, but the Bear Flag revolt of 1846 is fact. Both Kit Carson and John Fremont are treated less heroically by Holland than they are by other historians. Though brave and clever, they were also savage and cruel, particularly to Indians in the territory. The pastimes of both the Mexican and American settlers were also merciless as illustrated by scenes of bear baiting and cockfighting. Confusion reigned about the political climate in the United States, and it is still not clear if Fremont knew that war against Mexico had been declared when he took up with the rebels. In both fact and fiction, the Bear Flag uprising began when the settlers stole a large string of horses from the Mexicans. Holland has maintained her considerable talents for research and writing in this tale of an incident in the conquest of California.

—Marion Hanscom

HOLLAND, Isabelle.   American. 1920—. See 2nd edition, 1990.

HOLLAND, Kel.   See **HORNER, Lance, Kyle ONSTOTT, and Ashley CARTER.**

HOLLAND, Sheila.   See **LAMB, Charlotte.**

HOLT, Victoria.   See **PLAIDY, Jean.**

HOLTBY, Winifred.
Nationality: British. **Born:** Rudstone, Yorkshire, 23 June 1898. **Education:** Queen Margaret's School, Scarborough, Yorkshire; Somerville College, Oxford, 1917, 1919–21, B.A. 1921. **Military Service:** Women's Auxiliary Army Corps Signals Unit in France, 1918–19. **Relations:** lived with the writer Vera Brittain, 1921–25, and with Brittain and her husband, 1926–35. **Career:** part-time tutor, and lecturer for the feminist Six Point Group and Open Door Council, early 1920s; active in the Friends of Africa organization from 1926, and in supporting the South African Industrial and Commercial Workers' Union; lecturer for the League of Nations, South Africa, 1926; contributor, from 1924, and director, from 1926, *Time and Tide*, London; regular contributor to the Manchester *Guardian*, *Yorkshire Post*, and *News Chronicle*; feature writer, *Radio Times*, London, and the *Schoolmistress* (journal of the National Union of Women Teachers); literary critic, *Good Housekeeping*, London, 1933–35. **Recipient:** James Tait Black memorial prize, 1937, for *South Riding*. **Died:** 29 September, 1935.

ROMANCE AND HISTORICAL PUBLICATIONS

Novels

Anderby Wold. London, John Lane, 1923.
The Crowded Street. London, John Lane, 1924.
The Land of Green Ginger: A Romance. London, Cape, and New York, McBride, 1927.
Poor Caroline. London, Cape, and New York, McBride, 1931.
Mandoa Mandoa! A Comedy of Irrelevance. London, Collins, and New York, Macmillan, 1933.
South Riding: An English Landscape. London, Collins, and New York, Macmillan, 1936.

OTHER PUBLICATIONS

Short Stories

Truth is Not Sober. London, Collins, and New York, Macmillan, 1934.

Play

Take Back Your Freedom, completed by Norman Ginsbury. London, Cape, 1939.

Poetry

My Garden and Other Poems. London, Brown, 1911.
The Frozen Earth and Other Poems. London, Collins, 1935.

Other

Eutychus; or, The Future of the Pulpit. London, Kegan Paul, and New York, Dutton, 1928.
A New Voter's Guide to Party Programmes: Political Dialogues. London, Kegan Paul, 1929.
Virginia Woolf. London, Wishart, 1932.

The Astonishing Island. London, Lane, and New York, Macmillan, 1933.

Women and a Changing Civilization. London, Lane, and New York, Longman, 1935.

Letters to a Friend, edited by Alice Holtby and Jean McWilliam. London, Collins, 1937.

Selected Letters of Winifred Holtby and Vera Brittain 1920–1935, edited by Vera Brittain and Geoffrey Handley-Taylor. London, Brown, 1937.

Pavements at Anderby: Tales of 'South Riding' and other regions, edited by H.S. Reid and Vera Brittain. London, Collins, 1937; New York, Macmillan, 1937.

Testament of a Generation: The Journalism of Vera Brittain and Winifred Holtby, edited by Paul Berry and Alan Bishop. London, Virago Press, 1985.

*

Film adaptations: *South Riding,* 1937, 1974.

Bibliography: *Winifred Holtby: A Concise and Selected Bibliography, Together with Some Letters* by Geoffrey Handley-Taylor, London, Brown, 1955.

Manuscript Collections: Bridlington Public Library, East Yorkshire; Central Library, Kingston upon Hull, East Yorkshire; City of Leeds Central Reference Library, Yorkshire.

Critical Studies: *Winifred Holtby as I Knew Her* by Evelyn E.M. White, London, Collins, 1938; *Testament of a Friendship: The Story of Winifred Holtby* by Vera Brittain, London, Macmillan, 1940; *Vera Brittain and Winifred Holtby: A Working Partnership* by Jean E. Kennard, London, University Press of New England, 1989.

*　　*　　*

Each of Winifred Holtby's six novels pays lip-service to a romance plot although their central concerns are with wider social and moral issues. Relatively unscathed by World War I, and one of the first generation of women to receive the vote, Holtby was conscious of what she regarded as her 'immunity' from hardship and suffering, and was dedicated to the notion of the 'woman citizen' with duties towards a career in the public world outside the home. Her novels reflect these feminist preoccupations but they also make use of a love interest which usually provides a structure for the narrative, and is also a vehicle for contemporary debates concerning women's needs and responsibilities. Most of the romances in her novels are unsuccessful, and the typical Holtby heroine survives a failed love relationship to live an unromantic, although not unsatisfied, useless or inactive life. Of the two novels which end in a marriage, *Poor Caroline* does so with emphatic reservations: 'She would not become an unpaid curate-housekeeper in Bermondsey. She would marry him and go off, just as she had intended . . . to America', and *Mandoa, Mandoa!*, Holtby's African novel, confines its heroine's unexpected and compassionate marriage to a postscript.

Holtby's first novel, *Anderby Wold,* takes its setting from her childhood as a farmer's daughter in Yorkshire, and its heroine is based on her dominating mother who held matriarchal sway over village life. Mary Robson in *Anderby Wold* must learn to accommodate her ideals to human frailty and by the end of the novel her energies and passion have been cruelly limited to the care of an invalid husband. The suffering that has taught her humility is her unfulfilled love for a young socialist who travels the country urging labourers to join a trade union, and who is killed subsequently in a village quarrel. The rural setting and the heroine's situation are developed in *The Land of Green Ginger,* Holtby's third novel, but here the heroine, Joanna, is freed by her invalid husband's death and the novel ends with her undaunted departure, with her children, for South Africa.

The heroines of Holtby's two most successful novels, *The Crowded Street* and the renowned *South Riding,* published posthumously in 1936, are spinsters, a topic Holtby wrote about frequently in her journalism, vigorously countering popular fascist and Freudian claims that such 'surplus' women, of whom there were upwards of a million-and-a-half during the inter-war period, were pathetic social burdens. In *The Crowded Street,* Muriel's life in her middle-class, suburban parents' home is dominated by 'sex-success', the ability to attract a respectable man into marriage. When Muriel finally achieves sex-success, she finds she doesn't want to marry: 'I've got an idea . . . [an] idea of service—not just vague and sentimental, but translated into quite practical things . . . if I married you I'd have to give up every new thing that has made me a person'. The 'idea of service' finds full and detailed expression in *South Riding* both as a novel which addresses a wide range of social problems and in the life of its headmistress heroine, Sarah Burton, who has 'unlimited confidence in the power of the human intelligence and will to achieve order, happiness, health and wisdom'. *South Riding,* contemporaneous in its setting, and perhaps the only English novel to make use of the genuinely democratic although unglamorous topic of local government, exemplifies the concerns of inter-war feminists like Holtby with birth control, maternity clinics, housing, the care of the mentally ill, and the education of girls. Expansively realist in style, the novel's plot dynamics derive from the antagonism between socialist and feminist ideals and the traditional customs and power relations of a rural community. Related to this is the love story of Sarah Burton and Robert Carne, the local landowner. The initial hostility between them—'I dislike, I oppose everything he stands for—feudalism, patronage, chivalry, exploitation', Sarah says—gives way, in typical romance fashion, to attraction yet there is no happy-ever-after ending to their love story (although the 1937 film version provided one). In a scene bordering on farce, Carne collapses as he enters Sarah's bedroom; the moment of grand passion is avoided and the novel restored to its social purpose. Carne's death leaves Sarah grief-stricken yet combative in the battle against 'poverty, madness, sickness and old age'.

Although Holtby knew and admired the modernist novel (in 1932 she wrote the first study of Woolf in English), her own novels are conventional in form, and *South Riding,* in particular, looks back to a 19th-century predecessor like *Middlemarch.* Yet the ideas in *South Riding* are modern and it goes beyond the ending of *Middlemarch* to explore not only alternatives to marriage for women but also alternatives to romantic love; 'to belong to a community . . . to be a people' is what will sustain Sarah Burton into old age, not love for one man.

—Marion Shaw

———

HONEYMAN, Brenda. See **CLARKE, Brenda.**

———

HOOPER, Kay.
Pseudonym: Kay Robbins. **Nationality:** American. **Address:** c/o Dell Publishing, 666 Fifth Avenue, New York, New York 10103, USA.

ROMANCE AND HISTORICAL PUBLICATIONS

Novels (series: Delaneys; Hagen; Men of Mysteries Past; Shamrock)

Lady Thief. New York, Dell, 1981.
Breathless Surrender. New York, Dell, 1982.
Mask of Passion. New York, Dell, 1982.
Breathless Summer. New York, Dell, 1982.
On the Wings of Magic. New York, Dell, 1983.
C. J.'s Fate. New York, Bantam, 1984.
If There Be Dragons. New York, Bantam, 1984.
Pepper's Way. New York, Bantam, 1984.
Something Different. New York, Bantam, 1984.
Illegal Possession. New York, Bantam, 1985.
Rafe the Maverick (Shamrock). New York, Bantam, 1986.
Rebel Waltz. New York, Bantam, 1986.
Time after Time. New York, Bantam, 1986.
Larger than Life. New York, Bantam, 1986.
Adelaide the Enchantress (Delaneys). New York, Bantam, 1987.
In Serena's Web (Hagen). New York, Bantam, 1987.
Raven on the Wing (Hagen). New York, Bantam, 1987.
Rafferty's Wife (Hagen). New York, Bantam, 1987.
Zach's Law (Hagen). New York, Bantam, 1987.
Summer of the Unicorn. New York, Bantam, 1988.
The Fall of Lucas Kendrick (Hagen). New York, Bantam, 1988.
Unmasking Kelsey (Hagen). New York, Bantam, 1988.
Outlaw Derek (Hagen). New York, Bantam, 1988.
Shades of Gray (Hagen). New York, Bantam, 1988.
Captain's Paradise (Hagen). New York, Bantam, 1988.
Summer of the Unicorn. New York, Bantam, 1988.
Golden Flames (Delaneys). New York, Bantam, 1988.
Velvet Lightning (Delaneys). New York, Bantam, 1988.
It Takes a Thief (Hagen). New York, Bantam, 1989.
Aces High (Hagen). New York, Bantam, 1989.
Golden Threads. New York, Doubleday, 1989; London, Bantam, 1990.
The Glass Shoe. New York, Doubleday, 1989; London, Bantam, 1990.
Star-Crossed Lovers. London, Bantam, 1991.
What Dreams May Come. London, Bantam, 1991.
Crime of Passion. New York, Avon, 1991.
House of Cards. New York, Avon, 1991.
The Trouble with Jared (Men of Mysteries Past). Toronto, Harlequin, 1993.
The Touch of Max (Men of Mysteries Past). New York, Bantam Press, 1993.
All for Quinn (Men of Mysteries Past). Toronto, Harlequin, 1993.
Hunting the Wolfe (Men of Mysteries Past). New York, Bantam Press, 1993.
The Wizard of Seattle. New York, Bantam Press, 1993.

Novels as Kay Robbins

Return Engagement. New York, Berkley, 1982.
Elusive Dawn. New York, Berkley, 1983.
Kissed by Magic. New York, Berkley, 1983.
Taken by Storm. New York, Berkley, 1983.
Moonlight Rhapsody. New York, Berkley, 1984.
Eye of the Beholder. New York, Berkley, 1985.
Belonging to Taylor. New York, Berkley, 1986.
On Her Doorstep. New York, Berkley, 1986.

*   *   *

One of the Loveswept series' prolific authors, Kay Hooper is also one of the best of the contemporary romance writers now at work.

She has created some memorable characters and placed them in intriguing circumstances. She also has shown a willingness to expand the limits of romance fiction and succeeded in her attempt.

Hooper has created two series of books that have delighted readers. One, connected by the machinations of a wily government agent, Hagen, ended with ten titles: *Raven on the Wing, Rafferty's Wife, Zach's Law, The Fall of Lucas Kendrick, Unmasking Kelsey, Outlaw Derek, Shades of Gray, Captain's Paradise, It Takes a Thief,* and *Aces High*. While *In Serena's Web* is not technically in the Hagen series, it does introduce the first of Hagen's 'victims', Josh Long, who is the hero in *Raven on the Wing*. He falls in love with a woman who seems to be a criminal but is in reality one of Hagen's undercover agents. Josh is a wealthy, powerful man himself, but he and his carefully selected cadre of top aides are, one by one, drawn into Hagen's net. While each takes centre stage in turn, the others always return to help in the newest assignment. One standing joke among the closely knit circle of friends is that Hagen is an inadvertent matchmaker. Most of the adventures lead to the development of romance for one of his agents so that he runs the risk of losing them all to love. Hagen himself remains very much in the background throughout, although he gradually emerges as a character as opposed to remaining simply a name. He is manipulative and secretive, often sending agents into the field without all the available information. This understandably upsets the agents, and makes them reluctant to work for him. Hooper gets a measure of revenge in *Aces High* by pairing Hagen off with another agent.

The other series, 'Men of Mysteries Past', revolves around the planned exhibition of a collection of fabulous gems and efforts to protect it from thieves. Several couples meet and fall in love under these dangerous circumstances. *The Touch of Max, Hunting the Wolfe, The Trouble with Jared,* and *All for Quinn* all display Hooper's standard of great characters, intriguing plots and just the right amount of humour. She even waits until the last of these titles to explain fully the plot and characters linking the stories.

Along with Iris Johansen and Fayrene Preston, Kay Hooper has collaborated on several trilogies focusing on the Delaney family. She wrote *Rafe the Maverick* for the 'Shamrock Trilogy', the story of the Delaney brothers. For the 'Delaneys of Killaroo', the stories of three sisters in the Australian branch of the family, she wrote *Adelaide the Enchantress*. Based on the success of these trilogies, the three authors developed two Delaney 'prequel' trilogies: 'The Untamed Years' and 'The Untamed Years II'. Both *Golden Flames* and *Velvet Lightning*, Hooper's contributions to these series, tell the story of Falcon Delaney and Victoria Fontaine, but the second book branches out to an intriguing story about the fate of Abraham Lincoln as seen through the eyes of Marcus Tyrone and Catherine Waltrip. Hooper contributed 'Christmas Future' to *The Delaney Christmas Carol*, a collection of novellas by the three collaborators.

In 1988, Hooper experimented with a longer fantasy/science-fiction romance, *Summer of the Unicorn*. Set in some indefinite future and beginning on another planet, it is the story of a quest for a myth and dreams, as personified by the unicorn. The hero, Hunter Morgan, is on a quest to find the mythical beast in order to win a throne. The heroine, Siri, daughter of a mermaid, is guardian of the unicorns and other mythical or supposedly extinct animals. Together, they fight Hunter's evil brother who would destroy the last unicorns. They also must find a way in which they will be able to exist together, since according to legend, Siri cannot live outside the Valley of the Unicorns. In *The Wizard of Seattle*, Hooper returns to fantasy and adds in the element of time travel. Richard Merlin and Serena Smyth, master and apprentice wizard respectively, journey back from present-day Seattle to Atlantis to discover the reasons behind the traditions preventing the training of female wizards and the barriers male wizards erect against any female. They find that together they complement one another and are stronger so they can overcome the obstacles in their way.

Hooper has also tried her hand at mysteries, with heroine Lane Montana becoming involved with murder and police lieutenant Trey Fortier in *Crime of Passion* and *House of Cards*. While the emphasis in these books is on solving the crimes, Hooper realistically portrays a developing romance between Lane and Trey.

Hooper writes with humour and passion, develops her characters well, and is adept at creating intriguing plots. Her continued willingness to experiment and expand the limits of the genre contribute to her status and importance in the field.

—Barbara E. Kemp

HOPE, Anthony.

Pseudonym for Sir Anthony Hope Hawkins. **Nationality:** British. **Born:** London, 9 February 1863. **Education:** St John's Foundation School, London and subsequently in Leatherhead, Surrey; Marlborough School, 1876–81; Balliol College, Oxford (exhibitioner, then scholar), 1881–85, graduated with honours; Middle Temple, London, called to the Bar, 1887. **Military Service:** government service in the Editorial and Public Branch Department, 1914–18. **Relations:** married Elizabeth Somerville Sheldon in 1903; two sons and one daughter. **Career:** lawyer in London, 1887–94, then full-time writer. Liberal Parliamentary candidate for South Buckinghamshire, 1892. Chair of the Committee, 1900–03, 1907, and founder of the pension scheme, Society of Authors. **Recipient:** Knighted, 1918. **Died:** 8 July 1933.

ROMANCE AND HISTORICAL PUBLICATIONS

Novels

A Man of Mark. London, Remington, 1890; New York, Holt, 1895.
Father Stafford. London and New York, Cassell, 1891.
Mr Witt's Widow. London, Innes, and New York, United States Book Company, 1892.
A Change of Air. London, Methuen, 1893; New York, Holt, 1894.
Half a Hero. London, Innes, 2 vols, 1893; New York, Harper, 1 vol, 1893.
The Dolly Dialogues. London, Westminster Gazette, and New York, Holt, 1894.
The God in the Car. London, Methuen, 2 vols, 1894; New York, Appleton, 1 vol, 1894.
The Indiscretion of the Duchess. Bristol, Arrowsmith, and New York, Holt, 1894.
The Prisoner of Zenda. Bristol, Arrowsmith, and New York, Holt, 1894.
The Lady of the Pool. New York, Appleton, 1894.
The Chronicles of Count Antonio. London, Methuen, and New York, Appleton, 1895.
Phroso. London, Methuen, and New York, Stokes, 1897.
Rupert of Hentzau. Bristol, Arrowsmith, and New York, Holt, 1898.
Simon Dale. London, Methuen, and New York, Stokes, 1898.
The King's Mirror. London, Methuen, and New York, Appleton, 1899.
Quisanté. London, Methuen, and New York, Stokes, 1900.
Captain Dieppe. New York, Doubleday, 1900; London, Skeffington, 1918.
Tristam of Blent. London, Murray, and New York, McClure, 1901.
The Intrusions of Peggy. London, Smith Elder, and New York, Harper, 1902.
Double Harness. London, Hutchinson, and New York, McClure, 1904.

A Servant of the Public. London, Methuen, and New York, Stokes, 1905.
Sophy of Kravonia. Bristol, Arrowsmith, and New York, Harper, 1906.
Tales of Two People. London, Methuen, 1907.
Helena's Path. New York, McClure, 1907.
The Great Miss Driver. London, Methuen, and New York, McClure, 1908.
Second String. London, Nelson, and New York, Doubleday, 1910.
Mrs Maxon Protests. London, Methuen, and New York, Harper, 1911.
A Young Man's Year. London, Methuen, and New York, Appleton, 1915.
Beaumaroy Home from the Wars. London, Methuen, 1919; as *The Secret of the Tower*, New York, Appleton, 1919.
Lucinda. London, Hutchinson, and New York, Appleton, 1920.
Little Tiger. London, Hutchinson, and New York, Doran, 1925.

Short Stories

Sport Royal and Other Stories. London, Innes, 1893; New York, Holt, 1895.
Lover's Fate, and A Friend's Counsel. Chicago, Neely, 1894.
Frivolous Cupid. New York, Platt Bruce, 1895.
Comedies of Courtship. London, Innes, and New York, Scribner, 1896.
The Heart of Princess Osra and Other Stories. London, Longman, and New York, Stokes, 1896.
A Man and His Model (includes 'An Embassy'). New York, Merriam, n.d.
A Cut and a Kiss. Boston, Brown, 1899.
Love's Logic and Other Stories. New York, McClure, 1908.

OTHER PUBLICATIONS

Plays

The Adventure of Lady Ursula (produced New York, and London, 1898). New York, Russell, and London, French, 1898.
When a Man's in Love, with Edward Rose (produced London, 1898).
Rupert of Hentzau, adaptation of his own novel (produced Glasgow, 1899; London, 1900).
English Nell, with Edward Rose, adaptation of the novel *Simon Dale* by Hope (produced London, 1900).
Pilkerton's Peerage (produced London, 1902). London, French, 1909.
Captain Dieppe, with Harrison Rhodes (produced New York, 1903; London, 1904).
Helena's Path, with Cosmo Gordon-Lennox (produced London, 1910).
In Account with Mr Peters, in *Windsor Magazine* (London), December 1914.
Love's Song (produced London, 1916).
The Philosopher in the Apple Orchard: A Pastoral. New York, French, 1936.

Other

Dialogue (address). Privately printed, 1909.
The New—German—Testament: Some Texts and a Commentary. London, Methuen, 1914; New York, Appleton, 1915.
Militarism, German and British. London, Darling, 1915.
Why Italy Is with the Allies. London, Clay, 1917.

Selected Works. London, Harrap, 10 vols, 1925.
Memories and Notes. London, Hutchinson, 1927; New York, Doubleday, 1928.

*

Film Adaptations: *Prisoner of Zenda*, 1837, 1852, 1979, 1984.

Critical Studies: *Anthony Hope and His Books* by Charles Mallet, London, Hutchinson, 1935; 'The Prisoner of the Prisoner of Zenda: Hope and the Novel of Society' by S. Gorley Putt, in *Essays in Criticism 6* (Brill, Buckinghamshire), 1956.

*   *   *

Anthony Hope is best known for *The Prisoner of Zenda*, yet he was a man of several parts, both in his career and as a writer. The son of a clergyman, he became a Balliol College Scholar, was elected President of the Oxford Union, and took a First Class degree. He was called to the Bar in 1887, and faced a brilliant legal career. Interested in politics, he made a respectable stand as a Liberal against the incumbent Conservative member in 1892. Although he was to become a prolific novelist with over 30 works of fiction to his credit, he remained ambivalent to this profession. He called his popular romance *Phroso* 'tosh', while taking most pains over a serious novel such as *Quinsanté* which he did not expect the public to notice. In 1918 he was knighted for his war work.

He began his published writing with social satire and political fiction. *The Dolly Dialogues*, first published in *The Westminster Review*, received wide attention as a witty and pointed dramatization of fashionable foibles. *The God in the Car*, which still has interest as a sensitive study of political life, achieved some notoriety for its parallel with the career of Cecil Rhodes. Willy Rushton, chief founder of the Great Omofaga Company, rides roughshod over his colleagues and suppresses his own humanity in his quest for power. Maggie Dennison, who loves him, finally refuses to interpose in his life, recognizing this will compromise his real desires. In *Quinsanté* Hope was to portray another odious but brilliant politician who is himself exploited for his popularity, and dies of heart failure after making a speech.

But in 1890, in *A Man of Mark*, a privately printed collection of short stories, he had experimented with adventure set in an imaginary world—in this case the South American state of Aurentland. At the end of 1893, exuberant with winning a legal case, he imagined a tale set in a middle European country, Ruritania, and wrote *The Prisoner of Zenda* in spare moments during four weeks. When it appeared the following year its immediate and overwhelming success made him abandon the law for a full-time writing career—perhaps to the detriment of his fiction, for he never recaptured the fresh immediacy of this early work.

The appeal of *The Prisoner of Zenda* lies both in its high spirits and in the way in which its world of Ruritania is at once contemporary and antique. A world of feudal ceremony, it can be reached by train (although once there Rassendyll tends to ride on horseback). The castle is half modern residence and half gothic pile with fearful mysteries. In the world of firearms, honour can still be defended in a duel, and political struggles are fought out in romantic adventure. Uniting the two worlds is Rudolph Rassendyll, himself a genetic throwback to a romantic *alliance*, in 1733, of the redheaded Rudolph the Third of Ruritania. He is a modern Cavalier, brave, excellent horseman and swordsman, yet with a hint of self-mockery in his heroism. His narrative voice seduces the reader into willing complicity with the absurd story. The plot itself has some archetypal patterns—double identity, the conflict between Black Michael and Red Ephberg, the love for an unreachable princess. But any sub-

merged symbolism is contained within the rapidly moving narrative.

Rupert of Hentzau returns to Ruritania some years later. Black Michael is dead, and Rudolph's red hair shows streaks of grey. The danger is now from Rupert, who captures a compromising letter from Queen (earlier Princess) Flavia. Rudolph destroys the letter and saves the Queen's honour—at the cost of his life. The theme of chivalry present in the earlier work here becomes overworked; the basis for the plot is thin, and the narrator is the old retainer Fritz von Tarlehein, who is no substitute for Rudolph. But the narrative pace is still fast, the swashbuckling is exhilarating. Hope wrote other tales of Ruritania, none of them wholly successful. *The Heart of Princess Osra*, for instance, is a series of tales from the country in olden times, in which Osra is educated through five loves—from Stephen the silversmith to the Grand Duke of Mittenheim—into the meanings of the passion. But what the first readers found charming the modern audience is likely to consider heavy-handed and sentimental.

Hope had a weak historical imagination. In *Simon Dale*, for example, he explores his theme of chivalry in 17th-century England. Dale, a country boy, goes to London and enters the employ of Charles I. He offers his pure love to Nell Gwyn against that of the dissolute monarch. Later he leaves the King, respectfully telling him that he pays too high a price for his power. He lives to bring up his own children honourably. By comparison *Sophy of Kravonia* also has an incredible plot. Sophy, an Essex kitchen maid, rises to become for a few days Queen of Kravonia, a Balkan state split into warring parties, and to revenge her dead royal husband. Yet, although Hope had not been to the Balkans, the novel gives a convincing sense of present-day eastern Europe, and it remains one of his most readable novels. It was one of the books that turned Graham Greene to a life of travel.

Hope was one of the group of adventure story writers that included Robert Louis Stevenson, Rider Haggard and Conan Doyle. But he never achieved a consistent narrative style, and he remains notable for *The Prisoner of Zenda* alone. This introduced 'Ruritania' into the English language; it was directly reflected in prose imitations, dramatizations, and film: more remarkably, it entered into the popular consciousness. It established the romantic image of middle Europe for England and America.

—Louis James

———

HORNER, Lance, Kyle ONSTOTT, and Ashley CARTER.
HORNER, Lance. Nationality: American. **Born:** Kenric Lancaster Horner in Stateville, New York, 5 August 1902. **Education:** Boston University. **Career:** commercial art director, advertising copywriter, and antique dealer. **Died:** 1973. **ONSTOTT, Kyle. Nationality:** American. **Born:** DuQuoin, Illinois, 12 January 1887. **Relations:** one son. **Career:** licensed by the American Kennel Club as an all-breeds judge. **Died:** 1966. **CARTER, Ashley. Pseudonyms:** Robert Hart Davis; Tabor Evans; Whit Harrison; Kel Holland; Harriet Kathryn Myers; Blaine Stevens; Clay Stuart; Hondo Wells; Harry White; Hallam Whitney; also wrote as Harry Whittington. **Nationality:** American. **Born:** Harry Benjamin Whittington in Ocala, Florida, 4 February 1915. **Education:** Florida public schools and extension and night classes. **Military Service:** United States Navy, 1945–46: petty officer. **Relations:** married Kathryn Lavinia Odom in 1936; one daughter and one son. **Career:** copywriter, Griffith Advertising Agency, St Petersburg, Florida, 1932–33; assistant manager and advertising manager, Capitol Theatre, St Petersburg, 1933–34; post office clerk, St Petersburg, 1934–45; editor, *Advocate*, St Petersburg, 1938–45; freelance writer, 1946–68; editor, US Department of Agriculture, 1968–75; from

1975 freelance writer: author of many stories for King Features Syndicate, 1948–57, and *Man from UNCLE*, *Dime Detective*, *Manhunt*, *Bluebook*, *Mantrap*.

ROMANCE AND HISTORICAL PUBLICATIONS

Novels by Lance Horner (series: Falconhurst)

The Street of the Sun. New York, Abelard Schuman, 1956.
The Tattooed Road, with Kyle Onstott. Middleburg, Virginia, Denlinger, 1960; London, Souvenir Press, 1962; as *Santiago Road*, London, Pan, 1967.
Rogue Roman. New York, Pyramid, 1965; London, W.H. Allen, 1969.
Child of the Sun, with Kyle Onstott. London, W.H. Allen, 1966.
Falconhurst Fancy. New York, Fawcett, 1966; London, W.H. Allen, 1967.
The Black Sun, with Kyle Onstott. New York, Fawcett, 1967; London, W.H. Allen, 1968.
The Mustee. New York, Fawcett, 1967; London, W.H. Allen, 1968.
Heir to Falconhurst. New York, Fawcett, 1968; London, W.H. Allen, 1969.
The Mahound. New York, Fawcett, 1969.
Flight to Falconhurst. New York, Fawcett, 1971; London, W.H. Allen, 1972.
Mistress of Falconhurst. New York, Fawcett, and London, W.H. Allen, 1973.
Golden Stud, with Kyle Onstott. New York, Fawcett, 1975; as *Six-Fingered Stud*, London, W.H. Allen, 1975.

Novels by Kyle Onstott (series: Falconhurst)

Mandingo. Richmond, Virginia, Denlinger, 1957; London, Longman, 1959.
Drum. New York, Dial Press, 1962; London, W.H. Allen, 1963.
Master of Falconhurst. New York, Dial Press, 1964; London, W.H. Allen, 1965.
Strange Harvest (unfinished; completed by Ashley Carter). London, W.H. Allen, 1986.

Novels by Ashley Carter (series: Blackoaks; Falconhurst)

Master of Blackoaks. New York, Fawcett, 1976; London, W.H. Allen, 1977.
The Sword of the Golden Stud (Falconhurst). New York, Fawcett, 1977; London, W.H. Allen, 1978.
Secret of Blackoaks. New York, Fawcett, 1978; London, W.H. Allen, 1980.
Panama. New York, Fawcett, 1978; London, Pan, 1980.
Taproots of Falconhurst. New York, Fawcett, 1978; London, W.H. Allen, 1979.
Scandal of Falconhurst. New York, Fawcett, 1980; London, W.H. Allen, 1981.
Heritage of Blackoaks. New York, Fawcett, 1981; London. W.H. Allen, 1982.
Against All Gods. London, W.H. Allen, 1982.
Rogue of Falconhurst. New York, Fawcett, 1983.
Road to Falconhurst. London, W.H. Allen, 1983.
A Farewell to Blackoaks. London, W.H. Allen, 1984.
The Outlanders. London, W.H. Allen, 1983.
A Darkling Moon. London, W.H. Allen, 1985.
Embrace the Wind. London, W.H. Allen, 1985.
Falconhurst Fugitive. London, W.H. Allen, 1985.
Miz Lucretia of Falconhurst. London, W.H. Allen, 1985.

Mandingo Mansa (Falconhurst). London, W.H. Allen, 1986.

OTHER PUBLICATIONS by Kyle Onstott

Other

Your Dog as a Hobby, with Irving C. Ackerman. New York, Harper, 1940.
Beekeeping as a Hobby. New York, Harper, 1941.
The Art of Breeding Better Dogs. Washington, DC, Denlinger, 1946.

For other publications by Ashley Carter, see Harry Whittington entry in *Twentieth-Century Crime and Mystery Writers*, 2nd edition, 1991.

*

Film Adaptation: *Mandingo*, 1975.

*   *   *

Bound by a harsh code of 'honour', the American South of the 'slave' novels of Lance Horner and Kyle Onstott is bleak and joyless: slavery is a god-given norm, and slaves are bred like horses and dogs for prime blood-lines (though the animal breeder does not normally merge his own genetic material with the pedigree blood-line). These books are to the 'romantic' and 'realistic' traditions of 'Southern Gothic' both a *reductio ad absurdam* and a stripping of the veils of ambiguity and half-understood symbolism. Ostentatiously avoided by 'respectable' readers, they sold in vast quantities.

Their publishing history is complicated by the involvement of three different hands. The first 'Falconhurst' novel *Mandingo*, was published by Kyle Onstott, whose name also appears on *Drum*, and *Master of Falconhurst* as well as unrelated historical novels. Onstott wrote several books about dog-breeding; one suspects that this was one of the roots of the series' obsession with human bloodlines. During the late 1960s and early 1970s Horner set more books on the Falconhurst plantation. After his death, the baton of the 'Lance Horner novel' was taken up by Ashley Carter (Harry B. Whittington) whose parallel 'Blackoaks' saga retrod much of the same ground.

Mandingo introduces old Warren Maxwell, the owner of the human stud farm, and his son, Ham. Dramatically if not socially equal is Lucrezia Borgia, the cook (yes, there is a joke here). Ham, an ignorant bigot occasionally warped (as he sees it) by feelings he would call 'kindness' finds white women repellent. His wife Blanche turns to Mede, the Mandingo fighting slave, for sexual comfort. Ham poisons her and kills Mede horribly, a murder which haunts him in later books. Dino de Laurentis's film of *Mandingo* allegedly became something of a 'gay' cult movie. Certainly the book focuses extensively upon male bodies. (Whether this was specifically homoerotic or designed to attract the series female readers, further novels feature more explicit homosexual encounters.) Readership grew for reasons not unconnected with inter-racial sex, the physical cruelty of slave-owning, and the bitter drama inherent in so much Southern literature where, as a character in Harper Lee's *To Kill a Mockingbird* remarks, 'once you have a drop of Negro blood, that makes you all black'. Having to 'pass' at the cost of the terror of discovery powers most of the plots.

Herman, in *The Mustee*, must masquerade as white to save the plantation when Warren Maxwell dies. Meanwhile in *Taproots of Falconhurst*, Ham, without any major qualms, returns his own light-skinned, slave-born son who has fled to Texas. The 'six-fingered stud' Tommy Verder (pursued through several books) is only black 'on the inside'. The irony of Wade Cameron, cutting cane for his bitterest enemy in *Taproots of Falconhurst* is that he *is* white.

However, any moral dimension is almost pure plot device. There is some ironic depth in *Heir to Falconhurst*, where Drum Maxwell is ostracized in the post-Civil War North once his black ancestry is discovered, and there are some relatively sympathetic black characters—notably the homosexual 'Lucy'. But Drum *can* pass for white (except in the paranoid South) and his achievement is to turn Falconhurst into a benevolent dictatorship. The most important truly black character is the intelligent and forceful Lucrezia Borgia of earlier books. She effectively runs Falconhurst, manipulating her masters in her rise to the status of a 'person'. Even so, her solution is to trade humiliation for moral power. A trustee who works the system for her allies, rather then a rebel, she is nevertheless responsible for whatever changes happen to Ham Maxwell. Her attempted suicide in *Taproots of Falconhurst* does seem to bring him to consider their respective places in the *status quo*, leaving an uncharacteristic sense of poignancy in the implied message of the tiny scraps of survival possible in a hellish world.

Other novels, such as *The Street of the Sun*, *The Tattooed Road* and *Rogue Roman*, follow a similar formula in different times. Broader viewpoints are given in *Strange Harvest* by Onstott (completed by Carter), which describes the colonial relationship between modern American landowners and Mexican workers, and especially *The Black Sun*, by Onstott and Horner, which shows an exceptionally open picture of the Haitian Slave Rebellion following the French Revolution. Although the main character is white, the story is of his growing friendship and identification with Henry Christophe, one of the rebel leaders and, briefly, King of Haiti. Beneath the obligatory sex is a relatively humane message that skin colour is not the true measure of a person's worth. After Falconhurst, this liberal truism here strikes the reader with a freshness its status as a cliché scarcely warrants.

However, structural ineptitudes are normally more apparent than nods to liberal sensibilities. Throughout both 'Falconhurst' and 'Blackoaks' sagas are the quirks of any series writers condemned to spread an initial idea over a longer time than is good for it. Past events are summarized almost identically. In book after book, the same unhygienic fondlings, the same sensory impressions appear. Reader-demand overcame originality. Twice, a child is born to a slave in the plantation household under circumstances which cause her to be named 'Scandal'—*Master of Blackoaks* and *Scandal of Falconhurst*. The hard-bitten slave dealer Baxter Simon of *Blackoaks* is merely an analogue of Ham Maxwell, from his belief that his slaves are talking animals to his impotence with white women.

This apart, the Lance Horner novels are well-researched in the history of the slave trade and New Orleans. At times, when the storytelling pauses to reflect on situation, we even sense the tragic Southern ambiguity where individuals such as plantation-owner Tom Verder and his slave Nero (*Falconhurst Fancy*) like and respect each other but are unable to articulate such a concept as 'friendship'. Generally, though, most of the characters are sex object. Any rage arising from the injustice of the situation is dispelled by another sexual encounter. Throughout most of the books black slaves are ignorant savages or sexual superhumans, and this stereotyping undercuts any possibility of them being allowed their own voices. Almost with exception, any anti-slavery opinion comes from fools and hypocrites.

If Hammond Maxwell's moral dilemma had been stressed to show him either more evil or self-questioning, the series may have overcome even this. But despite those instances where he acts humanely even though he 'knows' this to be wrong, the confused nihilism of the background swamps any ironic potential. It can certainly be claimed for the 'slave' books that they mercilessly strip aside both reactionary and liberal myths of the relations between slave and slave owner, but they do so as entertainment rather than exposé.

The passion behind this flaying of façades proceeds little further than the act of stripping aside and laying bare.

—Andy Sawyer

HOUSTON, R.B.   See **STIRLING, Jessica.**

HOWARD, Audrey.
Nationality: British. **Born:** Worthington, Liverpool, Lancashire, 23 October 1929. **Education:** Queen Mary School, St Anne's. **Relations:** divorced; one son. **Career:** variety of jobs, including model, shop assistant, hairdresser, cleaner, and civil servant. Now a full time writer. Lives in St Anne's, Lancashire. **Recipient:** Boots romantic novel of the year award, 1988, for *The Juniper Bush*. **Agent:** The Peters Fraser and Dunlop Group Ltd, Chelsea Harbour, Lots Road, London SW10 0XF, England.

ROMANCE AND HISTORICAL PUBLICATIONS

Novels (series: Liverpool family in all books)

The Skylark's Song. New York, St Martin's Press, and London, Fontana, 1984.
The Morning Tide. London, Century, and New York, St Martin's Press, 1985.
Ambitions. London, Century, and New York, Macmillan, 1986.
The Juniper Bush. London, Century, 1987.
Between Friends. London, Century, 1988.
The Mallow Years. London, Hodder and Stoughton, 1989.
Shining Threads. London, Hodder and Stoughton, 1990.
A Day Will Come. London, Hodder and Stoughton, 1992.
All the Dear Faces. London, Hodder and Stoughton, 1992.
There Is No Parting. London, Hodder and Stoughton, 1993.

*

Audrey Howard comments:

After working at many jobs, mostly clerical, and becoming unemployed I decided to try my hand at writing. I had done none before and had no inclination towards 'scribbling'. I emigrated to Australia in 1981 and it was there that my first book was completed. I sent it, not to a publisher, but to a competition being held in England by Hodder and Stoughton, and June Hall Literary Agency, I didn't win the competition but June Hall liked it and wrote to me to say that if I was prepared to work on it she thought she could find a publisher. The book was published in February 1984.

I like to write about relationships, between men and women and also women and women (not sexual). My female character is usually a strong woman fighting for her place in a man's world, Victorian or Edwardian. I do a vast amount of research which is no hardship as I love the history of that period.

*   *   *

Most of Audrey Howard's books are set in Liverpool or in industrial Lancashire in the 19th or early 20th centuries, and against these backgrounds a wide range of family dramas are played out. Although the settings of the individual novels vary, from the turbulent marriage of Christy Emmerson and Alexander Buchanan (*The Juniper Bush*) to the fortunes of slum child Zoe (*The Skylark's Song*), or the problems of both mill-owners and mill-workers in the Industrial

Revolution (*The Mallow Years* and its sequel, *Shining Threads*), there are many themes common to several novels.

For example, extreme poverty and degradation are contrasted either with comfortable middle-class life (when central characters move from one to the other, and sometimes back again) or with a wealthy upper-class or manufacturing-class background, in which case a member of one class woos and ultimately weds someone from the other. Each novel is centred on a strong-minded young woman, in many instances setting up a business (Meg Hughes in *Between Friends* has the energy and drive to progress from being a scullery maid to running her own hotel—and incidentally learns to fly and develops a motor-cycle manufacturing business inherited from her lover), or taking over a business when the man currently running it is killed (the heroine's father in *The Mallow Years*, uncle in *Shining Threads*) or incapacitated (husband Alex Buchanan in *The Juniper Bush*). In the latter two novels, especially, the reader is privy to the struggles undergone by the respective heroines in learning the business and in dealing with their resentful male colleagues and employees.

For men, particularly in the books set in the 19th century, are most emphatically men. Martin Hunter in *Between Friends* is ' . . . a beautiful young man! And yet his beauty was completely and absolutely male with an earthiness about it which was instantly appealing to women'. And throughout *The Juniper Bush* we receive reminders of Alex Buchanan's masculinity— '. . . his strong, golden muscular body, eternally masculine, proud, savage and determined . . .', '. . . he took her to bed . . . putting his masculine mark on what was his'. Alex has his way with his wife Christy rather a lot (until he is paralysed in a mining accident) and the element of choice on her part is absent much of the time, although as she ultimately enjoys all these episodes one is apparently supposed to condone this macho male behaviour. It was, of course, de rigeur in the part of the 19th century in which this story is set, but here it is described without any apparent intention of arousing outrage in the 20th-century reader.

As if it were not enough for men to be men, in Audrey Howard's novels villains are very definitely villains—except where they are heroes, as in the case of Luddite Joss Greenwood in *The Mallow Years*; the destruction of buildings and machinery is normally the action of a villain rather than of a hero, but we are prepared to make an exception in the case of Joss. Joss meets heroine Katherine (Kit) Chapman up on the moors above the manufacturing town where she lives—and here is another recurrent theme, that of the meeting alone on the moors, which serves to establish the heroine right from her first appearance as an independent, strong-willed individual who relishes personal freedom. *The Mallow Years* does have an authentic villain, Harry Atherton, who is arrogant and patronizing to our heroine, who fathers a child on a mill girl and who later, in revenge for being dismissed from his involvement in the mills by Kit, attempts blackmail, commits perjury, incites rape and murder, and steals his illegitimate child. But the villain to end all villains is Benjamin Harris in *Between Friends*—cruel, grasping, vicious, vindictive (one runs out of adjectives) and thoroughly repellent, he emerges from prison, whence he has been sent on information provided by heroine Meg, and confronts her. As he has previously attempted to coerce her into sleeping with him, she is naturally apprehensive, but must presumably feel reassured by his assertion that while he was in prison he lost his taste for female flesh! In the very best traditions of melodrama, Benjamin Harris is omnipresent, and spends the rest of the novel popping up sporadically to threaten Meg and her friends and family. He meets a suitably sticky end— Meg's husband Tom murders him with a garden fork, before himself committing suicide by undressing and lying down naked in a blizzard (it should be pointed out that Tom's mind has been unhinged by his experiences in World War I).

Several of Howard's novels do end in a rather downbeat fashion: where the heroine has to choose between two men, how is the reject to be disposed of? Tom's suicide puts an end to his increasingly sad and bewildered life, leaving Meg free to marry Martin, her lover and the father of her child; in *Shining Threads* heroine Tessa Greenwood is enabled to marry her lover Will Broadbent by the death from cholera of her unstable husband Drew (his mind was unhinged by the death of his twin Pearce in the Crimean war). Not all the rival males are disposed of quite so dramatically, however—in *The Skylark's Song*, Zoe Taylor simply rejects her fiancé, kindly solicitor Ned Fitzgerald, when her former lover Sir Jonathan, father of her illegitimate child, is free to marry her after his crippled wife's death from cancer.

It is clear from many of the characters and situations cited above that Howard's works have much in common with the many melodramatic novels written at the end of the 19th and the beginning of the 20th century. A particularly endearing scenario used on more than one occasion is that in which the recovery of a sick or injured man is speeded by the physical embrace of a loved one, a device beloved of such novelists as Florence L. Barclay ('author of *The Rosary*'). Both Will Broadbent in *Shining Threads* and Alex Buchanan in *The Juniper Bush* benefit immeasurably from the embrace or even the mere presence of their respective women.

But there is another side to Howard's novels, and that is the vivid way in which she brings to life the settings in which the heroines function. Whether it is the domestic background of sisters Kate and Jenny Fowler in *The Morning Tide*, Kit Chapman's mills in *The Mallow Years*, or Alex Buchanan's mines which his wife Christy runs in *The Juniper Bush*, the description is detailed, historically accurate, never less than interesting and (something which is not always achieved by novelists) forms an integral part of the development of the novel. The wealth of technical detail does not intrude, and never deflects interest from the romantic or other strands of the plot; indeed, the reader feels a real sense of outrage when Alex Buchanan seeks to take over from the capable Christy as soon as he is on the road to recovery—she has succeeded in getting to grips with his business, and he now expects her to resume her former role as a breeding machine (as soon as his paralysis is completely cured, that is). But that is not, and can never be, the sole role of a Howard heroine.

This is well illustrated by *Ambitions* and its sequels *All the Dear Faces* and *There Is No Parting*; in the first novel heroine Lacy Hemingway overcomes a whole series of adversities—betrayal by her lover, the abortion of his child, rejection by her family and indeed the whole of polite Liverpool society. Determined and independent, a true prototype feminist, Lacy, with the help of her close companion, Rose O'Malley, overcomes social and physical degradation to become a successful businesswoman and thanks to her husband James Osborne re-enters society. But now she encounters a fresh problem—how to balance her all-absorbing business interests with her married life; in addition, Lacy is now barren, a source of great grief to her and James. Rose, whose intense love for James preceded even Lacy's, makes love with him on a single occasion, the end results of which are Rose's death in childbirth and Lacy's undertaking to bring the child up as her own.

All the Dear Faces starts in 1910, James is recently dead, Lacy an old lady, and Rose's infant son Sean (known as Johnny) the father of three adolescent children of whom one, Elizabeth, is one of the three heroines of this novel. Elizabeth is the well-brought-up child of a wealthy family, her behaviour and prospects seemingly bound by the social mores of the day; but she gradually attains a fair measure of independence, first of thought then of action, defies her appalling mother, and somehow manages to balance her love for her husband Harry Woodall (boyhood friend of her brother James) and her lover Michael O'Shaughnessy (Harry's groom) and to have offspring by both men. The other two heroines are sisters—Mara O'Shaughnessy, a beautiful, scheming and totally selfish young woman who marries Elizabeth Osborne's brother James (and the description of the wedding is excellent, encompassing every detail from the bride's underwear to the shocked reactions of her new mother-in-law), and Caitlin O'Shaughnessy, a militant suffragette. Both Mara and Caitlin cause great distress to their very Irish, very Roman Catholic parents by their actions, Mara by eloping with and then marrying a Protestant, and Caitlin by her involvement in marches and demonstrations and her repeated imprisonment.

In *There Is No Parting*, the next generation of Osbornes, Woodalls, and O'Shaughnessys take the saga forward into the 1930s and 1940s; again there are two heroines, Maris Woodall and Rose Osborne, and again the marriages and other relationships connecting these three families (all powerful in their different ways) are far from straightforward. These novels have less melodrama and fewer clichés than some of Howard's other works, and are much better for that. The characters interact successfully, with none of the hate-at-first-sight which the reader knows to be in reality love-at-first-sight, and in Caitlin O'Shaughnessy in particular Howard has created a heroine who is actually heroic, who sacrifices her health and is prepared to sacrifice her happiness for a cause she believes in.

—Judith Rhodes

HOWARD, Linda.
Pseudonym for Linda S. Howington. **Nationality:** American. **Born:** Gadsden, Alabama, 3 August 1950. **Relations:** married Gary F. Howington. **Career:** secretary, Bowman Transportation, Gadsden, 1969–86. **Agent:** Robin Rue, Anita Diamant Agency, 310 Madison Avenue, New York, New York 10017, USA. **Address:** 116 Louise Avenue, Gadsden, Alabama 35903, USA.

ROMANCE AND HISTORICAL PUBLICATIONS

Novels (series: Midnight Rainbow; Sarah's Child)

All That Glitters. New York, Silhouette, 1982.
An Independent Wife. New York, Silhouette, 1982.
Against the Rules. New York, Silhouette, 1983.
Come Lie with Me. New York, Silhouette, 1984.
Tears of the Renegade. New York, Silhouette, 1985.
Sarah's Child. New York, Silhouette, 1985.
The Cutting Edge. New York, Silhouette, 1985.
Midnight Rainbow. New York, Silhouette, 1986.
Almost Forever (Sarah's Child). New York, Silhouette, 1986.
Diamond Bay (Midnight Rainbow). New York, Silhouette, 1987.
Bluebird Winter (Sarah's Child). New York, Silhouette, 1987.
Heartbreaker (Midnight Rainbow). New York, Silhouette, 1987.
White Lies (Midnight Rainbow). New York, Silhouette, 1988.
MacKenzie's Mountain. New York, Silhouette, 1989.
Against the Rules. New York, Silhouette, 1989.
A Lady of the West. New York, Pocket Books, 1990.
Duncan's Bride. New York, Silhouette, 1991.
Angel Creek. New York, Pocket Books, 1991.
The Touch of Fire. New York, Pocket Books, 1992.
Mackenzie's Mission. New York, Silhouette, 1992.
Heart of Fire. New York, Pocket Books, 1993.

*

Linda Howard comments:
I work with two aims in mind. One is to write for myself, period. The other is to entertain the reader. That's what writers are for.

*   *   *

Linda Howard's work is distinguished by strong character devel-opment and fast-paced, well-developed action. Her heroines are determined, independent women, and her heroes are powerful, often dangerous men. While such portrayals can easily degenerate into romance stereotypes, Howard's skill as a writer breathes real life into the characters and saves them from becoming mere clichés. Writing somewhat longer novels, she has the time to develop her characters fully, providing them with context and meaning.

The high pressure world of business is a favourite setting for Howard's contemporary romances. The heroes in these stories wield great power and tend to be both ruthless and possessive. Their attempts to manipulate and even dominate their women lead to deep rifts in their relationships that are difficult to heal. Nikolas Constantinos is willing to take Jessica Stanton as his mistress in *All That Glitters*, as long as he gets some shares of stock he wants from her. Wrongly assuming that she had 'sold' herself to an older, wealthy husband for security, he punishes her with cruelty, in part because he despises himself for wanting her. In *Sarah's Child*, widower Rome Matthews, also a strong businessman, marries Sarah but refuses to have children. When she does become pregnant, he puts her in an almost untenable position by refusing to have anything to do with the child. Rome's right-hand man, Max Conroy, uses his charm to insinuate himself into the good graces of Claire Westbrook (*Almost Forever*) before taking over the company for which she works. In *The Cutting Edge*, Brett Rutland puts Tessa Conway through hell, almost destroying her emotionally, when he mistakenly believes she is guilty of embezzlement. Like Nikolas, he despises himself for still loving her even though he believes she is a criminal.

Howard has also created several heroes who are even more hard-edged and dangerous. Government agents, they move in situations presenting physical danger as well as emotional turmoil between men and women. In *Midnight Rainbow*, retired agent Grant Sullivan must rescue Jane Greer from Central American rebels. In *Diamond Bay*, Grant's boss, Kell Sabin, is rescued and cared for by Rachel Jones. She, in turn, is critically wounded in a shoot-out with Kell's pursuers. Another of Sabin's agents, Lucas Stone, involves Jay Granger in a deadly charade to trap a dangerous criminal (*White Lies*). These men, living in the shadows, find it difficult to admit their need of anyone, which makes their developing relationships even more tenuous. Wolf MacKenzie (*MacKenzie's Mountain*) and his son, Joe (*MacKenzie's Mission*), are cast in this same mould of the dangerous loner, gentled by the right woman. Several longer novels set in the Old West (*Angel Creek, A Lady of the West, The Touch of Fire*) feature the same ruthless, determined hero. In *Heart of Fire*, Ben Lewis seems at first to be one of Howard's typical lone-wolf heroes. Hired to guide archaeologist Jillian Sherwood's expedition into the Amazonian jungle, Ben hides his dangerous nature behind an easy-going, somewhat crude façade. What makes Ben and Jillian different from Howard's other lovers is the amount of humour and teasing that exists between them almost from the beginning. Jillian delights in thwarting Ben's attempts at seduction, which is in contrast to the usual romance action. Contrary to most of Howard's heroines, Jillian does not patiently wait for Ben to accept her love. She is in charge and in control. This subtle shift in the heroine's behaviour and the addition of a lighter tone in no way lessens the sexual tension between them nor does it detract from the passion and danger of the story. It will be interesting to see if Howard continues to incorporate these elements in future novels.

Howard's heroes are often in pain over past mistakes and betrayals and must learn to leave a bitter past behind in order to build a future. They fight to protect themselves from further pain but become torn by their very possessiveness and protectiveness when they discover that in hurting someone they love, they hurt themselves too.

Howard's heroines face men who make their own rules and laws. These women must, therefore, be even stronger than the men since they often endure great hurt and humiliation before healing the wounds in the souls of their men. Tessa chooses honour and integrity over the legally easy way out offered by Brett. Sarah finds great inner strength to continue loving Rome when he rejects their unborn child and proposes an abortion. Mary faces the anti-Indian prejudices of an entire town and the danger of an unbalanced foe to fight for her love for Wolf and to give Joe the opportunities he deserves. Later, an adult Joe believes the worst of the woman he loves based on circumstantial evidence. Like Brett Rutland, he strikes out at her even more because he is angry at himself for still being attracted to her when he believes she is a traitor.

Howard's women have much to forgive, but the men they win are worthy of their pain. In less skilful hands, such stories could become stereotypes of masochistic, self-sacrificing love in which the woman does all of the sacrificing. Howard prevents this from happening, however, by showing her characters as strong individuals and vividly painting their emotions and motivations. The hero may not be likeable for his actions, but he is at least understandable. For the reader, as for the heroine, understanding can then lead to forgiveness.

—Barbara E. Kemp

HOWARD, Linden. See **MANLEY-TUCKER, Audrie.**

HOWARD, Mary.
Pseudonym for Mary Mussi. **Pseudonym:** Josephine Edgar. **Nationality:** British. **Born:** Mary Edgar, London, 27 December 1907. **Education:** privately. **Relations:** married Rudolph F. Mussi in 1934; one son and one daughter. Past chairwoman, Society of Women Writers and Journalists. **Recipient:** Romantic Novelists Association major award, 1960, for *More Than Friendship*, 1979, for *Mr Rodriguez*, and 1980, for *Countess*; Elinor Glyn award, 1961. **Died:** 2 March 1991.

ROMANCE AND HISTORICAL PUBLICATIONS

Novels

Windier Skies. London, Long, 1930.
Dark Morality. London, Lane, 1932.
Partners for Playtime. London, Collins, 1938.
Stranger in Love. London, Collins, 1939; New York, Doubleday, 1941.
It Was Romance. London, Collins, 1939.
The Untamed Heart. London, Collins, 1940.
Far Blue Horizons. London, Collins, 1940; New York, Doubleday, 1942.
Uncharted Romance. New York, Doubleday, 1941.
Devil in My Heart. London, Collins, and New York, Doubleday, 1941.
To-morrow's Hero. London, Collins, 1941; New York, Doubleday, 1942.
Reef of Dreams. London, Collins, 1942.
Gay Is Life. London, Collins, and New York, Doubleday, 1943.
Have Courage, My Heart. London, Collins, 1943.
Anna Heritage. London, Collins, 1944; New York, Arcadia House, 1945.
The Wise Forget. London, Collins, 1944; New York, Arcadia House, 1945.
Family Orchestra. London, Collins, and New York, Arcadia House, 1945.
The Man from Singapore. London, Collins, 1946.

Return to Love. New York, Arcadia House, 1946.
Weave Me Some Wings. London, Collins, 1947.
The Clouded Moon. New York, Arcadia House, 1948.
Strange Paths. London, Collins, 1948.
Star-Crossed. London, Collins, 1949.
There Will I Follow. London, Collins, and New York, Arcadia House, 1949.
Two Loves Have I. London, Collins, 1950; as *Mist on the Hills*, New York, Arcadia House, 1950.
Bow to the Storm. London, Collins, 1950; as *The Young Lady*, New York, Arcadia House, 1950.
Sixpence in Her Shoe. London, Collins, 1950; New York, Arcadia House, 1954.
Promise of Delight. London, Collins, and New York, Arcadia House, 1952.
The Gate Leads Nowhere. London, Collins, 1953.
Fool's Haven. London, Collins, 1954; New York, Arcadia House, 1955(?).
Sew a Fine Seam. London, Hale, 1954.
Before I Kissed. London, Collins, 1955.
The Grafton Girls. London, Collins, 1956.
A Lady Fell in Love. London, Hale, 1956.
Shadows in the Sun. London, Collins, 1957.
Man of Stone. London, Collins, 1958.
The Intruder. London, Collins, 1959.
The House of Lies. London, Collins, 1960; as *The Crystal Villa*, New York, Lenox Hill Press, 1970.
More Than Friendship. London, Collins, 1960.
Surgeon's Dilemma. London, Collins, 1961.
The Pretenders. London, Collins, 1962.
The Big Man. London, Collins, 1965.
The Interloper. London, Collins, 1967.
The Repeating Pattern. London, Collins, 1968.
The Bachelor Girls. London, Collins, 1968.
The Pleasure Seekers. London, Collins, 1970.
Home to My Country. London, Collins, 1971.
A Right Grand Girl. London, Collins, 1972.
The Cottager's Daughter. New York, Dell, 1972.
Soldiers and Lovers. London, Collins, 1973.
Who Knows Sammy Halliday? London, Collins, 1974.
The Young Ones. London, Collins, 1975.
The Spanish Summer. London, Collins, 1977.
Mr Rodriguez. London, Collins, 1979.
Success Story. London, Piatkus, 1984.

Novels as Josephine Edgar

My Sister Sophie. London, Collins, 1964; New York, Pocket Books, 1974.
The Dark Tower. London, Collins, 1966; New York, Dell, 1969.
The Dancer's Daughter. London, Collins, 1968; New York, Dell, 1970.
Time of Dreaming. London, Collins, 1968; New York, Pocket Books, 1974.
The Devil's Innocents. London, Collins, 1972; New York, Dell, 1975.
The Stranger at the Gate. London, Collins, 1973; New York, Pocket Books, 1975.
The Lady of Wildersley. London, Macdonald and Jane's, 1975; New York, Pocket Books, 1977.
Duchess. London, Macdonald and Jane's, and New York, St Martin's Press, 1976.
Countess. London, Macdonald and Jane's and New York, St Martin's Press, 1978.
Margaret Normanby. Loughton, Essex, Piatkus, 1982; New York, St Martin's Press, 1983.

Bright Young Things. London, Piatkus, and New York, St Martin's Press, 1986.

*

Mary Howard commented (1982):

Until 1961 I wrote in the conventional light, popular romantic style, but with *The Big Man* I began my series of more realistic romantic stories under the Mary Howard name, trying to combine a 'good read' with a feeling of contemporary life, and avoiding the clichés of boy meets girl, boy is separated from girl, boy finds girl again/is reconciled after explanations/happy ending. This series culminated with *The Spanish Summer* and *Mr Rodriguez.*

I also began the Josephine Edgar books, set in the 19th century, and developed the family saga in *Duchess* and *Countess*, which begin in 1900 and end in the early 1920s.

*   *   *

Mary Howard was a well known and much respected author of romance and historical literature. During a long and illustrious writing career in which she won four awards (an Elinor Glyn award, and three of the Romantic Novelists Association's major awards), Howard wrote over 60 highly successful books including the award winning *Mr Rodriguez.*

Howard's earlier novels were straightforward stories, often set in exotic locales. *Far Blue Horizons* sees the heroine Cecilia Marden walk from her father's death bed into a job which takes her to exotic Cairo. Cecilia is highly principled, loyal, with great integrity—qualities which attract her unhappily married employer's attention. His highly strung wife, Myra, is both a kleptomaniac and a drug addict. Eventually Myra tries to kill herself but ends up unable to walk. Cecilia distances herself from the man she loves, but he comes to find her when his wife dies.

Howard's success as a writer is illustrated in her ability to keep up with the times. Her books always include contemporary issues, and her characters are never anachronistic—her heroines are intelligent women, who have mature sexual relationships. The heroes are not infallible, and often they prove themselves to be far more weak than their female counterparts.

In *Before I Kissed*, Jany Meredith is an ambitious wife who drives her beloved husband away by trying to promote his career. Duncan is an actor, a straightforward rather solid man, who falls passionately in love with his fickle co-star, Leonie, and has an affair with her. The story takes an unexpected twist when Leonie's jealous husband attacks her, and attempts to kill Duncan. Both Jany and Duncan work out their problems, and the strength and durability of their marriage is shown because it survives all of these disruptions.

Gillian, in *The Bachelor Girls*, is an unexpected character in a romantic novel. One of four girls who share a flat, Gillian has a fantasy life which disturbs Daisy Armitage, the heroine of the story. Gradually Daisy discovers that Gillian's childish but malicious behaviour is far more dangerous than she suspected, and Daisy places herself in danger when she falls in love with a man whom Gillian covets. This culminates in Gillian trying to attack her with a knife, and Dave, the hero, saving her. Despite the twisting plot, the narrative is, for the most part, cocky, and humorous in tone—and the reader comes away from the book with a good sense of 1960s London.

Kit Murdoch, the younger of the heroines of *The Big Man*, finds herself the subject of an unhealthy obsession. Following her sister to London, Kit finds out that Anthea is having an affair with a married but powerful man, Bernard Ryan. He takes an unhealthy interest in Kit, despite the fact that she is in love with, and eventually marries, someone else. Luckily, Anthea's boss, Tony Franconeri, is on the scene to comfort Anthea when she realizes how nasty her lover is, and how much she has been deceived.

Howard's plots are always interesting, and always well written containing unexpected twists in the plot, and realistic characters who have to deal with true-to-life crises.

—Marion Hatchard

————

HOWATCH, Susan.
Nationality: British. **Born:** Susan Elizabeth Sturt, Leatherhead, Surrey, 14 July 1940. **Education:** King's College, London, LL.B. 1961. **Relations:** married Joseph Howatch in 1964 (separated); one daughter. **Career:** law clerk, Masons of London, 1961–62; secretary, RCA Victor Record Corporation, 1964–65. **Recipient:** Winifred Mary Stanford memorial prize, 1991, for *Scandalous Risks.* **Agent:** Harold Ober Associates, 40 East 49th Street, New York, New York 10017, USA; or, Aitken and Stone, 29 Fernshaw Road, London SW10 0TG, England. **Address:** c/o HarperCollins, 77–85 Fulham Palace Road, London W6 8JB, England.

ROMANCE AND HISTORICAL PUBLICATIONS

Novels

The Dark Shore. New York, Ace, 1965; London, Hamish Hamilton, 1972.
The Waiting Sands. New York, Ace, 1966; London, Hamish Hamilton, 1972.
Call in the Night. New York, Ace, 1967; London, Hamish Hamilton, 1972.
The Shrouded Walls. New York, Ace, 1968; London, Hamish Hamilton, 1972.
April's Grave. New York, Ace, 1969; London, Hamish Hamilton, 1973.
The Devil on Lammas Night. New York, Ace, 1970; London, Hamish Hamilton, 1973.
Penmarric. New York, Simon and Schuster, and London, Hamish Hamilton, 1971.
Cashelmara. New York, Simon and Schuster, and London, Hamish Hamilton, 1974.
The Rich Are Different. New York, Simon and Schuster, and London, Hamish Hamilton, 1977.
Sins of the Fathers. New York, Simon and Schuster, and London, Hamish Hamilton, 1980.
The Wheel of Fortune. New York, Simon and Schuster, and London, Hamish Hamilton, 1984.
Glittering Images. New York, Knopf, and London, Collins, 1987.
Glamorous Powers. New York, Knopf, and London, Collins, 1988.
Ultimate Prizes. New York, Knopf, and London, Collins, 1989.
Scandalous Risks. New York, Knopf, and London, HarperCollins, 1990.
Mystical Paths. New York, Knopf, and London, HarperCollins, 1992.

*   *   *

Susan Howatch began writing as a child and started submitting her work for publication as a teenager. Her first novel, *The Dark Shore*, was published when she was in her twenties. Despite her surprise at critics' classification of it as a 'modern gothic', *The Dark Shore* launched her career as a writer in this genre. She then produced, in rapid succession, five more modern gothics and two gothic epics or sagas.

Although she's been a resident in the United States since 1964, Howatch's love of Scotland and England, especially Cornwall, is reflected in the British settings of many of her novels. As Howatch commented in *The Writer* in 1974, she believes that settings should provide more than just 'scenic glamour'; location should be integral to the story both in terms of plot and atmosphere. So *April's Grave* is set in a remote part of Scotland reachable only by boat; in this novel, and in *The Waiting Sands*, the remoteness itself becomes psychologically unnerving and suspenseful.

Howatch's interest in realism and mystery is also seen in her plots and her characterizations. She shows a fondness for such plot devices as anonymous phone calls, missing characters, shallow graves, surprise murderers, and touches of the occult. Her characters are as three-dimensional as possible, given the constraints of this genre. Howatch says she pays more attention than other gothic writers to her heroes' characterizations, trying to show them as more than just a 'splendid façade'. Howatch's heroines are spunky, sensible, and risk-taking, as the genre demands, but also can be vulnerable when the occasion arises. Her realistic characters are portrayed with a range of traits—both positive and negative—and interests, including sexual interests and desires. But, they also fit the gothic 'formula' enough to move the plot along and provide mystery and suspense as well as romance.

Howatch's six gothics contain all of the above elements, in various mixes and with varying degrees of success. She perceived *The Dark Shore* originally as the story of the hero, for example. Jon was 'burdened with loneliness' and his problems were triggered, to some extent, by an anonymous phone call about his dead wife. Howatch tells us, however, that her editor saw this first book as a romantic mystery about a girl in distress at a sinister house by the sea and—'instant gothic'.

April's Grave, *Call in the Night*, and *The Waiting Sands* all offer the reader sexual entanglements along with missing characters and shallow graves to advance the plot. Karen, the heroine of *April's Grave*, is introduced to the hero, an English professor, and turned, '. . . expecting to see a white-haired, stooping scholar, and had come face to face with all six foot of the charm and grace and frank sexual interest which emanated from Neville Bennett'. To get the mystery started, however, is not quite so easy. Not only is April's grave missing but, as one reviewer in *Best Seller* noted, 'April herself has been missing for three years without causing the slightest ripple of concern'. Eventually, though, April's buried suitcases are accidentally discovered and the web of mystery grows, culminating in another killing and a surprise murderer.

Just as Karen, April's twin, initiated the search for April, so Claire sets off to Europe to find her missing sister, in *Call in the Night*. Here again are shallow graves, broken engagements, and entangled relationships! Claire persists in searching for Gina despite her growing fascination with Garth (the hero) and despite her qualms that he may be not only a murderer, but also a womanizer.

Sexual entanglements also dominate *The Waiting Sands*. Decima invites her oldest friend, Rachel (the heroine), to her 21st birthday party at remote Roshven off the coast of Scotland. But the invitation carries with it a plea for protection from a suspected murder plot by her husband Charles. Decima is due to inherit Roshven on her birthday—if she lives that long! Unusual plot twists involve Charles's sexual liaison with a house guest, gossip and innuendo, suspense, quicksand, and a double murder.

In *The Shrouded Walls* Howatch builds suspense with a surprise heir, a marriage of convenience, murder, and a touch of the occult—a local witch who supplies potions and poisons. She also uses the heroine's persistent curiosity to trigger the plot resolution. This novel, however, is not regarded as one of Howatch's better gothics. A reviewer in *Best Seller* terms it 'strictly a ho-hum affair', and another critic in *Library Journal*, credits Howatch with producing interesting characters propelled by believable motives but criticizes her for 'sometimes melodramatic prose'.

Black magic, only a secondary theme in *The Shrouded Walls*, becomes central in *The Devil on Lammas Night*. Howatch's skilful interweaving of realistic characters and complex situations makes a bizarre theme plausible and frightening. The plot involves Nicola and Elan (former lovers) and their possible reconciliation. The action focuses primarily around the sinister Tristan Poole who has leased Colwyn Court (Elan's ancestral home). Poole's Society for the Propagation of Nature Foods is in actuality a witches' coven—and Poole, a warlock. Howatch provides supernatural occurrences, convenient 'accidental' deaths, and a celebration of Lammas Night featuring a plot to use the heroine in a Satanic wedding.

Despite considerable success with these modern gothics, Howatch's reputation as a writer of note was not firmly established until the publication of her bestselling gothic epic or saga *Penmarric* in 1971. It was followed by another highly acclaimed saga, *Cashelmara*. In *Penmarric*, set in Cornwall, and *Cashelmara*, set in Ireland, England, and America, the sprawling and complex tale of several generations of a family is told in turn by each of the characters from their own moral and emotional perspective. These two novels set the style for her family sagas (but not gothics), *The Rich Are Different*, *Sins of the Fathers*, and *The Wheel of Fortune*. It may be that the sagas offer Howatch a more flexible vehicle for pursuing her love of realism. Certainly they allow her more exploration of sexual themes and more complex character development, especially of the male characters who tend to dominate her sagas.

Howatch's career entered a new phase in the late 1980s with the publication of *Glittering Images* and *Glamorous Powers* (the first two books of six books about the Church of England in the 20th century). The last, *Absolute Truths*, is forthcoming. Each novel is narrated by an Anglican clergyman, with the first and last novel in the series narrated by the same character. In *Scandalous Risks*, Howatch breaks this male-centred pattern and presents us with a female narrator and central character. Although these books are independent, the central characters often carry over from novel to novel. The time frame of the first two novels in this series is pre-World War II; the third is set after the war, the fourth and fifth are set in 1963 and 1968 respectively, and the sixth and final novel will take place in 1965, three years before the main events described in *Mystical Paths*.

In this series, Howatch continues her exploration of human relationships, sexual themes, and male character development. Her interest in the supernatural and matters of faith are also evident. Through her characters and plot lines, Howatch examines the conflict between illusions and reality, and the often large disparity between public image and private self, the penchant for sexual obsession, and the likelihood that disaster is lying in wait. Since these novels focus principally on male central characters, the female characters are not terribly well developed. They are somewhat sexually stereotyped, possibly because the reader sees the women's images only through the viewpoint of the male narrator, or some other male character.

With this set of six novels and its three predecessors, Howatch seems to have left the romance novel behind, and replaced it with a vehicle which explores relationships and human foibles, as well as struggles with issues of faith and public images versus private behaviour.

—Josephine A. Ruggiero and Louise C. Weston

HOY, Elizabeth.
Pseudonym for (Alice) Nina Conarain. **Nationality:** Irish. **Born:** Dublin. **Relations:** married. **Career:** worked as a nurse, and as a secretary-receptionist; staff member, *Daily News*, London. **Address:** c/o Mills and Boon Ltd, Eton House, 18–24 Paradise Road, Richmond, Surrey TW9 1SR, England.

Novels

Love in Apron Strings. London, Hodder and Stoughton, 1933.
Roses in the Snow. London, Mills and Boon, 1936.
Crown for a Lady. London, Mills and Boon, 1937.
Sally in the Sunshine. London, Mills and Boon, 1937.
Shadow of the Hills. London, Mills and Boon, 1938.
Stars over Egypt. London, Mills and Boon, 1938.
You Belong to Me. London, Mills and Boon, 1938.
Mirage for Love. London, Mills and Boon, 1939.
Runaway Bride. London, Mills and Boon, 1939.
You Took My Heart. London, Mills and Boon, 1939; Toronto, Harlequin, 1959.
Enchanted Wilderness. London, Mills and Boon, 1940.
Heart, Take Care! London, Mills and Boon, 1940.
It Had to Be You. London, Mills and Boon, 1940.
You Can't Lose Yesterday. London, Mills and Boon, 1940.
I'll Find You Again. London, Mills and Boon, 1941.
Take Love Easy. London, Mills and Boon, 1941.
Come Back My Dream. London, Mills and Boon, 1942; Toronto, Harlequin, 1959.
Hearts at Random. London, Mills and Boon, 1942.
Proud Citadel. London, Mills and Boon, 1942; Toronto, Harlequin, 1975.
Ask Only Love. London, Mills and Boon, 1943.
One Step from Heaven. London, Mills and Boon, 1943.
You Can't Live Alone. London, Mills and Boon, 1944.
Give Me New Wings. London, Mills and Boon, 1944; New York, Arcadia House, 1945.
Sylvia Sorelle. London, Mills and Boon, 1944.
Heart's Haven. London, Mills and Boon, 1945; as *The Heart Remembers*, New York, Arcadia House, 1946.
It's Wise to Forget. London, Mills and Boon, 1945; as *Shatter the Rainbow*, New York, Arcadia House, 1946.
Dear Stranger. London, Mills and Boon, 1946; New York, Arcadia House, 1947.
Sword in the Sun. London, Mills and Boon, 1946.
To Win a Paradise. London, Mills and Boon, 1947; Toronto, Harlequin, 1960.
The Dark Loch. London, Mills and Boon, 1948.
Though I Bid Farewell. London, Mills and Boon, 1948.
Background to Hyacinthe. London, Mills and Boon, 1949.
Immortal Morning. London, Mills and Boon, 1949.
June for Enchantment. London, Mills and Boon, 1949.
The Vanquished Heart. London, Mills and Boon, 1949.
For Love's Sake Only. New York, Arcadia House, 1951.
Silver Maiden. London, Mills and Boon, 1951.
When You Have Found Me. London, Mills and Boon, and New York, Arcadia House, 1951.
White Hunter. London, Mills and Boon, 1951; Toronto, Harlequin, 1961.
The Enchanted. London, Mills and Boon, 1952.
The Web of Love. London, Mills and Boon, 1952.
Fanfare for Lovers. London, Mills and Boon, 1953.
If Love Were Wise. London, Mills and Boon, 1954; Toronto, Harlequin, 1970.
So Loved and So Far. London, Mills and Boon, 1954; Toronto, Harlequin, 1965.
Snare the Wild Heart. London, Mills and Boon, 1955; Toronto, Harlequin, 1966.
Who Loves Believes. London, Mills and Boon, 1955; Toronto, Harlequin, 1965.
Young Doctor Kirkdene. London, Mills and Boon, 1955; Toronto, Harlequin, 1959.
Because of Doctor Danville. London, Mills and Boon, 1956; Toronto, Harlequin, 1958.
My Heart Has Wings. London, Mills and Boon, 1957; Toronto, Harlequin, 1959.
Do Something Dangerous. London, Mills and Boon, 1958; Toronto, Harlequin, 1959.
City of Dreams. London, Mills and Boon, 1959; Toronto, Harlequin, 1960.
Dark Horse, Dark Rider. London, Mills and Boon, 1960; Toronto, Harlequin, 1967.
Dear Fugitive. London, Mills and Boon, and Toronto, Harlequin, 1960.
The Door into the Rose Garden. London, Mills and Boon, 1961.
Heart, Have You No Wisdom? London, Mills and Boon, 1962.
Her Wild Voice Singing. London, Mills and Boon, 1963.
Homeward the Heart. London, Mills and Boon, 1964; Toronto, Harlequin, 1965.
Flowering Desert. London, Mills and Boon, 1965; Toronto, Harlequin, 1966.
The Faithless One. London, Mills and Boon, 1966; Toronto, Harlequin, 1967.
My Secret Love. London, Mills and Boon, 1967.
Honeymoon Holiday. London, Mills and Boon, 1967; Toronto, Harlequin, 1968.
Be More Than Dreams. London, Mills and Boon, 1968; Toronto, Harlequin, 1969.
Music I Hear with You. London, Mills and Boon, 1969; Toronto, Harlequin, 1970.
It Happened in Paris. London, Mills and Boon, 1970; Toronto, Harlequin, 1971.
African Dream. London, Mills and Boon, 1971.
Into a Golden Land. London, Mills and Boon, and Toronto, Harlequin, 1971.
Immortal Flower. London, Mills and Boon, and Toronto, Harlequin, 1972.
That Island Summer. London, Mills and Boon, and Toronto, Harlequin, 1973.
The Girl in the Green Valley. London, Mills and Boon, 1973; Toronto, Harlequin, 1974.
Shadows on the Sand. London, Mills and Boon, and Toronto, Harlequin, 1974.
The Blue Jacaranda. London, Mills and Boon, and Toronto, Harlequin, 1975.
When the Dream Fades. London, Mills and Boon, 1980.

OTHER PUBLICATIONS

Other

Editor (as Nina Conarain), with Kay Boyle and Laurence Vail, *365 Days*. New York, Harcourt Brace, and London, Cape, 1936.

*   *   *

Elizabeth Hoy's novels reflect her Irish childhood and her early fondness for writing which later evolved into a journalistic career with the London *Daily News*. From this, it was a short step to writing romance novels which she began publishing in the 1930s. She is one of those writers who feels that she can only write about things she has experienced herself, and that her characters, although imaginary, must have some 'foundation in reality'. Consequently, her novels often reflect experiences with incidents, background, and people in her life. She spent some time in nurse's training before she had to leave it, but the experiences remained with her, lending a greater degree of authenticity to her early doctor/nurse novels.

A holiday trip to Australia provided her with sufficient material for her to use in her writing and she describes the people and the country with comfortable familiarity. Besides Australia, Hoy uses Ireland, England, and Africa as settings for her other novels.

Because of her own inclination and, perhaps, because of the period she wrote in, Hoy's romances have a more traditional outlook as she describes her heroines and heroes. She also has a touch of the true romantic's ability to make her readers believe the unbelievable. Not, however, without some very genuine soul searching by the heroine.

The Blue Jacaranda illustrates this and offers a good example of her writing ability. In this novel, Lena Shannon travels from England to Queensland, Australia, to stay with her Uncle Tom. Before her arrival, he dies, leaving a will that thoroughly insures impossible complications. She is to live on his estate for six months with the other inheritor, Rod Carron, and his daughter. By the end of six months, he expects them to marry each other or both lose any inheritance. The fact that Rod has a daughter is an added difficulty, although Lena and she become friends immediately. Both Lena and Rod resent the conditions and are extremely suspicious of each other for they can't feel that such a marriage would work. The estate stands between them as each wonders about the other's willingness to marry for money. Personality clashes and instinctive efforts at self-defence continue to complicate matters until a devastating cyclone strikes the estate. The cyclone is the final touch and shows them the way to resolve their differences.

Shadows on the Sand has an entirely different mood. Alison Gray is sent by a research institution to Cairo to substitute for an elderly secretary. Her arrival instantly brings Scott Crane, her temporary boss, storming down on her as he refuses to let her stay. He is forced to wait for a replacement and he does let her work. Alison's fresh sweetness is not so ingrained that she cannot stand up for herself and frequent clashes occur between her and Scott. The novel takes place against the background of scientific research, primitive desert country, and the excitement of new archaeological findings. Secondary characters such as other members of the team and an old girlfriend play their roles in furthering the plot complications, as do sand storms, antagonistic natives, and unexpected dangers such as falling rocks near the excavation.

Romance readers find Hoy's novels satisfyingly filled with the right mixture of romance, danger, and suspense. Her heroines are well drawn, and not the conventional naive or helpless romance heroine. Her heroes are also a complex assortment; they keep their feet firmly on the ground, their hands and minds in control of every tiniest detail but their hearts, which unaccountably refuse to behave. It is this constant source of amusement which keeps her readers so involved as they wonder just how the 'mighty will fall' under Hoy's adept connivance.

—Arlene Moore

HUFFORD, Susan.
Nationality: American. **Born:** Cincinnati, Ohio, 15 December 1940. **Education:** DePauw University, Greencastle, Indiana, B.A. 1960; Temple University, Philadelphia, M.A. 1961. **Career:** actress and singer. **Agent:** Jane Jordan Browne, 410 South Michigan Avenue, Room 828, Chicago, Illinois 60615, USA.

Romance and Historical Publications

Novels

Midnight Sailing. New York, Popular Library, 1975.

The Devil's Sonata. New York, Popular Library, 1976.
A Delicate Deceit. New York, Popular Library, 1976.
Cove's End. New York, Popular Library, 1977.
Satan's Sunset. New York, Popular Library, 1977.
Skin Deep. New York, Popular Library, 1978.
Trial of Innocence. New York, Popular Library, 1978.
Melody of Malice. New York, Popular Library, 1979.
Going All the Way. New York, New American Library, 1980.
Reflections. New York, Seaview, 1981; London, Methuen, 1982.
Miracles. New York, Dutton, 1989; London, Piatkus, 1990.

*   *   *

Susan Hufford tells fast-paced stories of beautiful women plunged into frightening situations and familiar, seemingly tranquil surroundings; surface peace is disrupted by evil and death, and even friends and lovers cannot escape suspicion, as heroines seek to come to terms with their family, their past, and their tenuous future.

Her tetralogy, *Midnight Sailing, The Devil's Sonata, A Delicate Deceit*, and *Satan's Sunset*, traces the changing adventures of 25-year-old Hilda Hughes, a petite, beautiful university professor from Ann Arbor, Michigan, as she deals with terror on romantic cruise ships, amid tropical paradises, and in stunning mansions. Old friends and new acquaintances always seem involved in strange conspiracies that seek to use and abuse her wealth and her psychic sensitivity; handsome psychotic males play power games that end in sadism and death; and her newly discovered sister, Ursula, proves a neurotic, murderous tool of diabolical schemers, both male and female. Her father's sins are visited upon his daughters, who are pursued by vengeful madmen and cultists. The father's adultery endangers both sisters as a psychotic returns from the grave to bring more madness and death in *The Devil's Sonata*. Hilda's love for a crippled but forceful pianist draws her into greater danger in *Satan's Sunset*, wherein a mad artist and a rejected lover plot her demise. Sensitive to threatening atmospheres, but unsure of whom to trust, Hilda usually makes bad judgements, believing the smooth tales of villains and fearing the contradictions and hesitations of friends.

In *Cove's End* New York's top model, a popular jet-setter, escapes to her grandparents' home in Maine, seeking peace and quiet and a new sense of self, only to find a childhood friend murdered, her inheritance a mystery, and her own life threatened. Her lover's acts make him a suspect, despite the absence of motive, and her only relative proves no relative at all.

Hufford's most compelling work, *Trial of Innocence*, set in the 19th century, records the nightmarish experiences of a young girl who leaves a beloved aunt to follow a desperate but cryptic call for aid from her dead sister's husband; but the invitation proves a hoax, and she is left a penniless stranger in a strange land where in-laws believe her a scheming fortune hunter and where, amid Victorian elegance in a rambling Tudor home, an intricate web of lies threatens sanity and life. The naive and innocent heroine must learn to cope with her own unexpected fascination with a cynical, worldly man who both frightens and allures; to compete with a beautiful, catty adventuress whose feminine wiles seem to have already ensnared both love and wealth; and to deal with amoral children whose feigned innocence and make-believe fantasies hide a murderous reality. Here, and throughout Hufford's canon, the secret compulsions of the seeming innocent endanger the truly innocent.

—Gina Macdonald

HULL, E(dith) M(aude).
Nationality: British. **Relations:** married a pig farmer. Lived in Derbyshire. **Died.**

ROMANCE AND HISTORICAL PUBLICATIONS

Novels

The Sheik. London, Nash, 1919; Boston, Small Maynard, 1921.
The Shadow of the East. London, Nash, and Boston, Small Maynard, 1921.
The Desert Healer. London, Nash, and Boston, Small Maynard, 1923.
The Sons of the Sheik. Boston, Small Maynard, 1925; London, Nash, 1926.
The Lion-Tamer. London, Nash, and New York, Dodd Mead, 1928.
The Captive of Sahara. London, Methuen, and New York, Dodd Mead, 1931.
The Forest of Terrible Things. London, Hutchinson, 1939; as *Jungle Captive*, New York, Dodd Mead, 1939.

OTHER PUBLICATIONS

Other

Camping in the Sahara. London, Nash, 1926; New York, Dodd Mead, 1927.

*

Film Adaptation: *The Sheik*, 1921.

*   *   *

Robert Hichens, writing a decade earlier, first made a romantic speciality out of deserts. So, too, Elinor Glyn sent a heroine to consult with a sphinx in the desert (in *His Hour*, 1909). Katharine Rhodes, popular in the 1910s, wrote tales of 'the fire and passion of the relentless desert'. But it was E.M. Hull who, with *The Sheik* in 1919, first put the desert on the map as a fine place for sexual encounter. The heroine, beautiful but haughty Diana Mayo, a pale-skinned but spirited English aristocrat, is the first romantic heroine to be physically assaulted, to learn in the course of 300 pages to enjoy it, and to marry the man who kept on doing it. The morality of whether a man guilty of rape should be ultimately rewarded is highly questionable. Diana's adventures with the Sheik were, possibly, a compensation for E.M. Hull's own lack of amorous excitement, for she was married to a dull pig-breeder called Percy, and, though her real name was Edith Maude, preferred to be called Diana like her ravished heroine.

At the time of writing *The Sheik*, Hull had never set foot in a desert. But this was no disadvantage, for her imagination filled in the background of sunsets, dust, and thirst. The excitement of nightly struggles in the sheik's barbarous yet luxurious tent in the oasis is interspersed with other 'eastern' thrills—attacks by rebel Arabs, horse-taming, horse-shooting, servant beating, escapes on horseback into the cruel and inhospitable wastes, the threat of death by vulture or by sandstorm, attempted suicide by the heroine, attempted rape by a rival sheik which proves to be far worse than submission to Diana's own regular assaulter, murder, and many violent deaths of the expendable natives. Erotic passion is linked with fear and pain, and there is a streak of sado-masochism running through the book. The rival rapist is seized by the sheik and throttled to death before Diana's eyes:

> With the terrible smile always on his lips, he choked him slowly to death, till the dying man's body arched and writhed in his last agony, till blood burst from his nose and mouth, pouring over the hands that held him like a vice.

The initial rape is distanced, and thus made more discreet, by being reported in the past historic:

> She *had* fought until the unequal struggle *had* left her exhausted and helpless in his arms, until her whole body was one agonized ache from the brutal hands that forced her to compliance, until her courageous spirit was crushed by the realization of her own powerlessness.

And subsequent struggles are conveyed by constant repetition of crush, kiss, hot, fierce, fire, lips, thrill. In one dialogue between Diana and the sheik, the author finds no less than 11 different variations on 'he said' and 'she said'. Thus, on a single page of text, Diana burst out passionately, and she choked furiously. Then she began desperately. He replied drily. She gasped. He went on evenly. She whispered with dry lips. His reply was given carelessly. She whispered again, but this time jerkily. He continued sarcastically. She murmured faintly.

When she has given up gasping and learned to obey and love, he expresses himself more tenderly. The pinnacle of his passion is a kiss on the upturned palm of her hands. This act of devotion had already been performed in previous romances (e.g. by the blind hero of Florence Barclay's *The Rosary*) but it was in *The Sheik* that it became an established convention, and a gesture which Rudolph Valentino, star of the film version of *The Sheik*, borrowed from the script and used as his trade-mark of passion in other roles.

Diana's relationship with the desert echoes her relationship with the man. The desert both repels and lures her, it tames and brutalizes her.

> It was the desert at last, the desert that she felt she had been longing for all her life. It was welcoming her softly with the faint rustle of the whispering sand, the mysterious charm of its billowy, shifting surface that seemed beckoning her to penetrate further and further into its unknown obscurities.

Hull followed her highly successful first novel with *The Sons of the Sheik*, but the sons lacked their father's strength and brutality, and the work is sentimental rather than passionate or violent. Hull visited Algeria to produce the non-fiction *Camping in the Sahara* and a small handful of other eastern/desert romance novels, but none had the same impact as her first, which was responsible for sparking off a whole series of sandy romances from other writers, and established the convention of desert passion whose basic elements have remained almost unchanged to the present day. Time and again, never seeming to learn from the experience of others, a spirited girl goes off into the desert and is captured by a mysterious and cruel Arab who tames her. Love blossoms, whereupon it transpires that, for all his foreign ways, he is no Arab, but as white-skinned and safely European as herself.

A contemporary, but rival, novelist, Philip Gibbs, wished to make quite clear the distinction between Hull's books, and his own novels, which, while selling well, never reached the peak of *The Sheik*: 'My own view is that such freak sales as those of *The Sheik* are not representative of the general reading public of average intelligence—a public which is steadily growing larger and more critical'.

—Rachel Anderson

HUNT, Donna.   See **OLIVER, Marina.**

HUNTER, Elizabeth.
Pseudonym for Elizabeth Mary Teresa de Guise. **Other Pseudonyms:** Isobel Chace; also writes as Elizabeth de Guise. **Born:** Eli-

zabeth Mary Teresa Scott, Nairobi, Kenya, 1934. **Education:** Open University, London. **Career:** landowner in Kent, 1952–58; English teacher to Arab students in Folkestone, Kent, 1958–62. Since 1960, full-time writer. **Agent:** June Hall, The June Hall Literary Agency Ltd, 504 The Chambers, Chelsea Harbour, Lots Road, London SW10 0XF, England; **Address:** 113 Nun Street, St David's, Haverford West, Dyfed SA62 6BP, Wales.

ROMANCE AND HISTORICAL PUBLICATIONS

Novels

Cherry-Blossom Clinic. London, Mills and Boon, 1961; Toronto, Harlequin, 1962.
Spiced with Cloves. London, Mills and Boon, 1962; Toronto, Harlequin, 1966.
Watch the Wall My Darling. London, Mills and Boon, 1963.
No Sooner Met. London, Mills and Boon, 1965.
There Were Nine Castles. London, Mills and Boon, 1967.
The Crescent Moon. London, Mills and Boon, 1973; Toronto, Harlequin, 1974.
The Tree of Idleness. London, Mills and Boon, 1973; Toronto, Harlequin, 1974.
The Tower of the Winds. London, Mills and Boon, 1973; Toronto, Harlequin, 1974.
The Beads of Nemesis. London, Mills and Boon, 1974; Toronto, Harlequin, 1975.
The Bride Price. London, Mills and Boon, 1974; Toronto, Harlequin, 1976.
The Bonds of Matrimony. London, Mills and Boon, and Toronto, Harlequin, 1975.
The Spanish Inheritance. London, Mills and Boon, and Toronto, Harlequin, 1975.
The Voice in the Thunder. London, Mills and Boon, and Toronto, Harlequin, 1975.
The Sycamore Song. London, Mills and Boon, 1975; Toronto, Harlequin, 1976.
The Realms of Gold. London, Mills and Boon, 1976; Toronto, Harlequin, 1977.
Pride of Madeira. Toronto, Harlequin, 1977.
Bride of the Sun. New York, Silhouette, 1980.
The Lion's Shadow. New York, Silhouette, 1980.
A Touch of Magic. New York, Silhouette, 1981.
One More Time. London, Hodder and Stoughton, and New York, Silhouette, 1982.
Written in the Stars. London, Hodder and Stoughton, and New York, Silhouette, 1982.
A Silver Nutmeg. New York, Silhouette, 1982.
A Tower of Strength. New York, Silhouette, 1983; London, Hodder and Stoughton, 1984.
Fountains of Paradise. New York, Silhouette, 1983.
London Pride. New York, Silhouette, and London, Hodder and Stoughton, 1983.
Shared Destiny. New York, Silhouette, 1983; London, Hodder and Stoughton, 1984.
A Time to Wed. New York, Silhouette, 1984.
Rain on the Wind. New York, Silhouette, 1984.
Eye of the Wind. New York, Silhouette, 1984
Kiss of the Rising Sun. New York, Silhouette, 1984
Song of Surrender. New York, Silhouette, 1984.
Loving Relations. New York, Silhouette, 1984.
Legend of the Sun. New York, Silhouette, 1985.
The Painted Veil. New York, Silhouette, 1986.
The Tides of Love. New York, Silhouette, 1988.

Dance of the Peacocks (as Elizabeth de Guise). London, Grafton, 1988.

Novels as Isobel Chace

The African Mountain. London, Mills and Boon, 1960.
The Japanese Lantern. London, Mills and Boon, 1960; Toronto, Harlequin, 1966.
Flamingoes on the Lake. London, Mills and Boon, 1961; Toronto, Harlequin, 1965.
The Song and the Sea. London, Mills and Boon, 1962; Toronto, Harlequin, 1963.
The Hospital of Fatima. London, Mills and Boon, 1963; Toronto, Harlequin, 1975.
The Wild Land. London, Mills and Boon, 1963; Toronto, Harlequin, 1964.
A House for Sharing. London, Mills and Boon, 1964; Toronto, Harlequin, 1965.
The Rhythm of Flamenco. London, Mills and Boon, and Toronto, Harlequin, 1966.
The Spider's Web. London, Mills and Boon, 1966; as *The Secret Marriage*, London, Mills and Boon, 1966.
The Land of the Lotus-Eaters. London, Mills and Boon, 1966; Toronto, Harlequin, 1971.
A Garland of Marigolds. London, Mills and Boon, and Toronto, Harlequin, 1967.
Brittany Blue. London, Mills and Boon, 1967.
Oranges and Lemons. London, Mills and Boon, 1967; Toronto, Harlequin, 1968.
The Saffron Sky. London, Mills and Boon, and Toronto, Harlequin, 1968.
The Damask Rose. London, Mills and Boon, 1968; Toronto, Harlequin, 1969.
A Handful of Silver. London, Mills and Boon, 1968; Toronto, Harlequin, 1969.
The Legend of Katmandu. London, Mills and Boon, 1969.
Flower of Ethiopia. London, Mills and Boon, 1969.
Sugar in the Morning. London, Mills and Boon, 1969; Toronto, Harlequin, 1970.
The Day That the Rain Came Down. London, Mills and Boon, and Toronto, Harlequin, 1970.
The Flowering Cactus. London, Mills and Boon, 1970; Toronto, Harlequin, 1971.
To Marry a Tiger. London, Mills and Boon, 1971; Toronto, Harlequin, 1972.
The Wealth of the Islands. London, Mills and Boon, 1971; Toronto, Harlequin, 1972.
Home Is Goodbye. London, Mills and Boon, 1971; Toronto, Harlequin, 1972.
The Flamboyant Tree. London, Mills and Boon, 1972; Toronto, Harlequin, 1973.
The English Daughter. London, Mills and Boon, 1972.
Cadence of Portugal. London, Mills and Boon, 1972; Toronto, Harlequin, 1973.
A Pride of Lions. London, Mills and Boon, 1972; Toronto, Harlequin, 1973.
The Tartan Touch. London, Mills and Boon, 1972; Toronto, Harlequin, 1973.
The House of Scissors. London, Mills and Boon, 1972; Toronto, Harlequin, 1974.
The Dragon's Cave. London, Mills and Boon, 1972; Toronto, Harlequin, 1974.
The Edge of Beyond. London, Mills and Boon, 1973; Toronto, Harlequin, 1974.
A Man of Kent. London, Mills and Boon, 1973; Toronto, Harlequin, 1974.

The Cornish Hearth. London, Mills and Boon, and Toronto, Harlequin, 1975.
A Canopy of Rose Leaves. London, Mills and Boon, 1976; Toronto, Harlequin, 1977.
The Clouded Veil. London, Mills and Boon, and Toronto, Harlequin, 1976.
The Desert Castle. Toronto, Harlequin, 1976.
Singing in the Wilderness. London, Mills and Boon, and Toronto, Harlequin, 1976.
The Whistling Thorn. Toronto, Harlequin, 1977.
The Mouth of Truth. Toronto, Harlequin, 1977.
The Undesirable Wife. London, Mills and Boon, 1978.

*   *   *

Elizabeth Hunter has long been a popular romance writer with a particularly individual style of writing that is quite distinctive, although she also writes under the name of Isobel Chace.

She enjoys taking an improbable situation and making her readers believe it. She must—for she is a past master at 'once upon a time' beginnings and 'they lived happily ever after' endings. Her novels are 'happy novels' regardless of the trials and suspense the heroine must encounter before she finds that strongest of havens, her loved one's arms.

In *The Bonds of Matrimony* Hero Kaufman needs to gain British nationality in order to migrate to Britain. To achieve it, she offers her farm in the drought-stricken part of Kenya to Benedict Carmichael in exchange for a wedding ring. Morag Grant meets Pericles Holmes and his two children in *The Beads of Nemesis* while she is on a walking holiday in Greece. He takes her in charge so that she can mind the children, but, with true Greek thoroughness, he marries her out of hand before she really knows what is going on. These are typical of the stories that she writes as Elizabeth Hunter.

Writing under the name of Isobel Chace, she devises plots equally daring. *To Marry a Tiger* finds Ruth Arnold trying to protect her flighty sister and ending by being forced into marriage by Mario Verdecchio, a Sicilian. Although the encounter was innocent enough, she still had stayed the night in his home without a chaperon. Finally, Kirsty MacTaggart in *The Tartan Touch* finds herself married to Andrew Fraser, a stranger, within days of her father's death. He has come to Scotland from Australia to research family records, and, once he finds what he is looking for, he seems to sweep Kirsty along with him.

In each of these novels, the writer develops strong motivation, believable characters, and an added touch of romance. She has a special knack of describing the backgrounds that she portrays in her novels as she uses Scotland, the Mediterranean countries, and Australia as locales. She also includes special scenes and descriptions of each country in such a way that the reader has a sense of authenticity in the things she mentions. Certainly she depends heavily on various customs in these countries to help her make the story work. For instance, Ruth in *To Marry a Tiger* is unaware of the Sicilian concept of honour so that, when the marriage takes place, she believes it is solely because of the antiquated beliefs of the people and not because Mario is attracted to her.

Improbable as some of her plots seem, it is impossible for the reader not to become absorbed in the story almost immediately. Her characters emerge quite naturally as they move and speak against the background of the unfolding plot. Perhaps it is this element of characterization that makes her novels work, for she has a delicacy of touch in this facet of writing that few romance writers can match. She is able to make her heroines come alive in the nicest way as they meet and fall in love with the man in the story. Depth of character is woven lightly but effectively through her novels as both the girl and man react to the situation they find themselves in.

Hunter has recently stepped out of the standard romance formula. This departure has resulted in glowing reviews of her latest novel in the Silhouette line.

In *The Tides of Love*, Ruth Gaynor, an up-and-coming actress is accused of murder! The murder happens in a crowded pub. During the confusion, Ruth receives a slash on her arm because she had been standing very close to the victim. She is held in custody temporarily and is finally released through the efforts of Aidan Wakefield, a barrister who represents her. Charges are eventually dropped for lack of evidence and Ruth retreats to Lindisfarne Island where she has inherited a cottage. A notorious 'resting' actress is not quite in demand for new work, especially if she might yet be charged with the crime.

Aidan traces her there for he is anxious to help clear her of the charge. Predictably, he falls in love with her. Mysterious events about the cottage, a hidden art collection, and a not so subtle attempt on her life lend more than enough conflict and confusion to the story line. What is enjoyable about this novel is the fact that Hunter has been able to maintain the sense of a typical romance, but has also added this new dimension to it. The combination of romance and mystery/murder, in this instance, does not take the novel out of Hunter's usual series. It can't be mistaken for a Harlequin Intrigue for instance. There are enough pending troubles, missing keys, and unknown phone callers to give it heightened suspense and excitement but the emphasis is on romance. General opinion is that Hunter has a winning combination going for her.

—Arlene Moore

HUNTER, Hall.   See **MARSHALL, Edison.**

HURST, Fannie.
Nationality: American. **Born:** Hamilton, Ohio, 18 October 1887. **Education:** Washington University, St Louis, B.A. 1909; Columbia University, New York, 1910. **Relations:** married Jacques S. Danielson in 1915 (died 1952). **Career:** actress in New York before becoming full-time writer. Chair, Woman's National Housing Commission, 1936–37; member of the National Advisory Committee of the WPA, 1940–41; USA delegate to the UN World Health Assembly, Geneva. President, 1936–37, and vice-president, 1944–46, and 1947, Authors League; trustee, Heckscher Foundation, 1940–60. **Recipient:** D.Litt.: Washington University, 1953; Fairleigh Dickinson University, Rutherford, New Jersey. **Died:** 23 February 1968.

Romance and Historical Publications

Novels

Star-Dust: The Story of an American Girl. New York, Harper, 1921.
Lummox. New York, Harper, 1923; London, Cape, 1924.
Appassionata. New York, Knopf, and London, Cape, 1926.
Mannequin. New York, Knopf, 1926.
A President Is Born. New York, Harper, and London, Cape, 1928.
Five and Ten. New York, Harper, and London, Cape, 1929.
Back Street. New York, Cosmopolitan, and London, Cape, 1931.
Imitation of Life. New York, Harper, 1933.
Anitra's Dance. New York, Harper, and London, Cape, 1934.
Great Laughter. New York, Harper, 1936; London, Cape, 1937.
Sister Act. New York, Longmans, 1941.
Lonely Parade. New York, Harper, and London, Cape, 1942.

White Christmas. New York, Doubleday, 1942.
Hallelujah. New York, Harper, 1944.
The Hands of Veronica. New York, Harper, and London, Lane, 1947.
Anywoman. New York, Harper, and London, Cape, 1950.
The Name Is Mary. New York, Dell, 1951.
The Man with One Hand. London, Cape, 1953.
Family! New York, Doubleday, 1960.
God Must Be Sad. New York, Doubleday, 1961.
Fool—Be Still. New York, Doubleday, 1964; London, Hale, 1966.

Short Stories

Just Around the Corner: Romance en Casserole. New York, Harper, 1914.
Every Soul Hath Its Song. New York, Harper, 1916.
Gaslight Sonatas. New York, Harper, and London, Hodder and Stoughton, 1918.
Humoresque: A Laugh on Life with a Tear Behind It. New York, Harper, 1919.
The Vertical City. New York, Harper, 1922.
Song of Life. New York, Knopf, and London, Cape, 1927.
Procession. New York, Harper, and London, Cape, 1929.
We Are Ten. New York, Harper, 1937.

OTHER PUBLICATIONS

Plays

The Land of the Free, with Harriet Ford (produced New York, 1917).
Back Pay (produced New York, 1921).
Humoresque (produced New York, 1923).
It Is to Laugh (produced New York, 1927).

Screenplays: *The Younger Generation,* with Sonya Levien and Howard J. Green, 1929; *Lummox,* with Elizabeth Meehan, 1930.

Other

No Food with My Meals. New York, Harper, 1935.
Today Is Ladies' Day. New York, Home Institute, 1939.
Anatomy of Me: A Wonderer in Search of Herself. New York, Doubleday, 1958; London, Cape, 1959.

*

Film Adaptations: *Five and Ten,* 1931; *Symphony of Six Million* (*Melody of Life*), 1932; *Back Street,* 1932, 1941, 1961; *Anatomy of Me,* 1934, 1959; *Four Daughters,* 1938, from the novel *Sister Act*; *Humoresque,* 1946; *Young at Heart,* 1956.

Manuscript Collections: Olin Library, Washington University, St Louis; Goldfarb Library, Brandeis University, Waltham, Massachusetts; University of Texas, Austin.

Critical Study: *Myths About Love and Women: The Fiction of Fannie Hurst* by Mary Rose Shaughnessy, New York, Gordon Press, 1980.

*   *   *

Fannie Hurst may be the worst writer ever to have become an internationally famous bestseller. In her heyday, she earned the more-or-less affectionate sobriquet 'Queen of the Sob Sisters', but the only aspect of her work likely to inspire tears today would be its truly abysmal style and grammar.

Hurst's stock in trade was the ill-advised golden-hearted woman who gives her all to some unworthy man, and is not thereafter rewarded, in this world at any rate. Of all her many short stories and novels, probably the quintessential Hurst title was *Back Street,* a real tear jerker, later translated into a 'three-hankie' moving picture. It is the long-drawn-out, painful story of Ray Schmidt, a flashily attractive young working girl of the turn of the century. Courted and admired by many men, Ray chooses to waste her young womanhood as the guilty secret of an ostensibly respectable married man's life. Her lover, Walter Saxel, is a pillar of the community, blessed with a lovely wife and three adored children. In the 'back street' of his life, content to live on stolen bits and scraps of his affection and time, Ray lives a life of seclusion and degradation redeemed only by her lifelong devotion to the man she loves.

Walter loves too, in a selfish and possessive way—but he fails to make any provision for the woman he has kept hidden in a stuffy 'love-nest', isolated from the world; and after his untimely death, Ray's declining years are a decrescendo of misery and privation. The moral lesson couldn't be plainer—and could scarcely be wordier, lasting as it does for hundreds of tear-soaked pages.

Hurst was a product of an age in which the double standards of conduct for men and women remained for the most part unchallenged; and she well understood the effects upon high spirited youth of censoriousness, continual, critical surveillance, and lack of guidance. If present day readers can still find a lesson worth learning in her writings, it must surely be that of gratitude that they live in a less puritanical era, one in which both men and women have greater freedom to shape their own lives than Hurst or her creation, Ray Schmidt, ever dreamed of.

—Joan McGrath

———

HUTTEN, Baroness von.
Nationality: American. **Born:** Betsey Riddle in Erie, Pennsylvania, 14 February 1874. **Education:** New York. **Relations:** married Freiherr von Hutten zum Stolzenberg in 1897 (divorced 1909; regained American nationality, 1938); two sons and two daughters. **Died:** 26 January 1957.

ROMANCE AND HISTORICAL PUBLICATIONS

Novels (series: Pam)

Miss Carmichael's Conscience: A Study in Fluctuations. Philadelphia, Lippincott, 1900; London, Pearson, 1902.
Marr'd in Making. Philadelphia, Lippincott, and London, Constable, 1901.
Our Lady of the Beeches. Boston, Houghton Mifflin, 1902; London, Heinemann, 1907.
Violett: A Chronicle. Boston, Houghton Mifflin, 1904.
Pam. London, Heinemann, 1904; New York, Dodd Mead, 1905.
Araby. New York, Smart Set, 1904.
He and Hecuba. New York, Appleton, 1905.
What Became of Pam. London, Heinemann, 1906; as *Pam Decides,* New York, Dodd Mead, 1906.
The One Way Out. New York, Dodd Mead, 1906.
The Halo. New York, Dodd Mead, and London, Methuen, 1907.
Beechy; or, The Lordship of Love. New York, Stokes, 1909; as *The Lordship of Love,* London, Hutchinson, 1909.
Kingsmead. London, Hutchinson, and New York, Dodd Mead, 1909.
The Green Patch. London, Hutchinson, and New York, Stokes, 1910.

Sharrow. London, Hutchinson, and New York, Appleton, 1910.
Mrs Drummond's Vocation. London, Heinemann, 1913.
Maria. London, Hutchinson, and New York, Appleton, 1914.
Birds' Fountain. London, Hutchinson, and New York, Appleton, 1915.
Mag Pye. London, Hutchinson, and New York, Appleton, 1917.
The Bag of Saffron. London, Hutchinson, 1917; New York, Appleton, 1918.
Happy House. London, Hutchinson, 1919; New York, Doran, 1920.
Mothers-in-Law. London, Cassell, and New York, Doran, 1922.
Pam at Fifty. London, Cassell, and New York, Doran, 1924.
Julia. London, Hutchinson, and New York, Doran, 1924.
Eddy and Edouard. London, Hutchinson, 1928; New York, Doubleday, 1929.
The Loves of an Actress. London, Readers Library, 1929.
Pam's Own Story. London, Hutchinson, 1930; Philadelphia, Lippincott, 1931.
Swan House. London, Hutchinson, 1930.
Monkey-Puzzle. London, Long, 1932.
Mice for Amusement. London, Hutchinson, 1933; New York, Dutton, 1934.
The Mem. London, Hutchinson, 1934; as *Lives of a Woman,* New York, Dutton, 1935.
Die She Must. London, Hutchinson, 1934; New York, Dutton, 1936.
Cowardly Custard. London, Hutchinson, 1936; as *Gentlemen's Agreement,* New York, Dutton, 1936.
The Elgin Marble. London, Hutchinson, 1937; as *Youth Without Glory,* New York, Dutton, 1938.
What Happened Is This. London, Hutchinson, 1938; New York, Dutton, 1939.

Short Stories

Helping Hersey. New York, Doran, 1914; London, Skeffington, 1918.
Candy and Other Stories. London, Mills and Boon, 1925.
Flies. London, Mills and Boon, 1927.
The Curate's Egg: A Volume of Stories. London, Mills and Boon, 1930; Freeport, New York, Books for Libraries, 1961.
In the Portico and Others. London, Mills and Boon, 1931.
The Notorious Mrs Gatacre and Other Stories. London, Hutchinson, 1933.

OTHER PUBLICATIONS

Other

The Courtesan: The Life of Cora Pearl. London, Davies, 1933.

Translator, *The Rocket to the Moon,* by Thea von Harbou. New York, World Wide, and London, Readers Library, 1930.

*   *   *

Baroness von Hutten produced some 40 novels and collections of short stories, published on both sides of the Atlantic in the first four decades of the century. Her first novel, *Miss Carmichael's Conscience,* was a conventional high-society romance. It was with *Pam* a few years later that resounding success came. *Pam* was immensely popular—it is the story of a society scandal, of the romantic elopement of a beautiful aristocratic English lady and a handsome Italian tenor, who settle in Italy (where people understand about these things and the landscape is romantic); Pam is their illegitimate child, and her story so enthralled readers that Baroness von Hutten produced several sequels, *What Became of Pam, Pam at Fifty,* and

Pam's Own Story. After *Pam,* Baroness von Hutten's next great success was *Kingsmead* whose charming, wistful young hero, Tommy, Earl of Kingsmead, was much admired.

Hutten appeared never to be at a loss for a plot. Her cosmopolitan background allowed her to set her books in Britain, America, and Europe, and her characters came from all levels of society from the highest to the lowest. Some of her settings are very sleazy indeed: Margaret Pye (*Mag Pye*) the daughter of a gentleman fallen on reduced circumstances, is brought up in the Chelsea Workmen's Dwellings, and the central character of *Monkey-Puzzle* is the transparently named Jess Lightfoot, a prostitute who attempts to maintain a respectable front for the sake of her son, the son of a lord. (About the same time as *Monkey-Puzzle,* Hutten also produced a biography of Cora Pearl, *The Courtesan*).

Hutten wrote at a great rate, and her writing was frequently praised for its crispness, facility and assurance. Her range as a writer was considerable. Although she made her name as a writer of romance novels and 'family novels' of a fairly melodramatic nature, she also included some psychological portraiture, particularly in *Mothers-in-Law* in which are contrasted the characters of two mothers-in-law (one American, one Italian) of very different upbringing and outlook who meet with the marriage of their children, and in *Eddy and Edouard* in which the hero, the son of a French aristocrat and her American husband, finds himself torn between two countries and two identities.

With an astute eye to changing tastes in fiction, Hutten included in her repertoire from the late 1920s onwards elements of the murder story and the detective story. Most of the short stories in *Flies* are about murders or murderers, whereas the previous volume of short stories, *Candy,* was 'a collection of pretty and sentimental tales' (*Times Literary Supplement*). *Die She Must* and *What Happened Is This* included elements of the thriller/detective story, though it is characteristic of Hutten's capacity to manoeuvre plot and character that neither of these is a straightforward example of its kind.

—Jean Buchanan

———

HYDE, Eleanor.   See COWEN, Frances.

———

IBBOTSON, Eva.
Nationality: British. **Born:** Maria Charlotte Michele Wiesner in Vienna, Austria, 21 January 1925. **Education:** private schools in Vienna; Dartington Hall School, Devon, 1934–41; Bedford College, University of London, 1941–45, B.Sc. (honours) in physiology; University of Durham, diploma in education 1965. **Relations:** married Alan Ibbotson in 1948; one daughter and three sons. **Career:** lecturer, University of London, 1946–48; teacher, department of Education, Newcastle upon Tyne. **Recipient:** Romantic Novelists Association major award, 1983. **Agent:** Curtis Brown, 162–168 Regent Street, London W1R 5TB, England. **Address:** 2 Collingwood Terrace, Jesmond, Newcastle upon Tyne NE2 2JP, England.

ROMANCE AND HISTORICAL PUBLICATIONS

Novels

A Countess Below Stairs. London, Macdonald, 1981.
Magic Flutes. London, Century, and New York, St Martin's Press, 1982.
A Company of Swans. London, Century, and New York, St Martin's Press, 1985.

Madensky Square. London, Century, and New York, St Martin's Press, 1988.
The Morning Gift. London, Century, 1993.

Short Stories

A Glove Shop in Vienna. London, Century, 1984; New York, St Martin's Press, 1991.

OTHER PUBLICATIONS

Fiction (for children)

The Great Ghost Rescue. London, Macmillan, and New York, Walck, 1975.
Which Witch?. London, Macmillan, 1979.
The Worm and the Toffee Nosed Princess. London, Macmillan, 1983.
The Haunting of Hiram C. Hopgood. London, Macmillan, 1987.
Not Just a Witch. London, Macmillan, 1989.

Play

Television Play: *Linda Came Today*, 1965.

*

Eva Ibbotson comments:

As the child of a broken home, growing up in a country (Austria before the war) soon to be destroyed; I found myself pursuing security in love and 'happy endings', with a particular assiduity, both as a writer and a person. My long and fulfilling marriage has convinced me that there is nothing false or absurd in the belief that two people can give each other abiding love. This doesn't mean that I have found writing romantic novels easy: the simpler the story, the more difficult (for me) the technique.

*   *   *

Eva Ibbotson's very first romance novel is in fact a story written for children, *Which Witch?* This should not be dismissed as merely a tale of witches, wizards and spells, for it sets the style for her later novels for adults, and contains a similar set of ingredients: a beautiful and vulnerable heroine (in this particular case vulnerable because she is a white witch in a community of black witches, her spells producing pots of begonias when in preference she would have a nest of vipers), a cast of eccentric and entertaining minor characters and an exceedingly attractive hero (Arriman the Awful, Loather of Light, and Wizard of the North). The story is told with gentle humour and a romanticism which is rather difficult to describe without using such overworked phrases as 'heart-warming'. Reviews of Ibbotson's novels have used such words as 'sparkling', 'delicious', 'magical' and 'enchanting', and while these words convey quite accurately the style of her writing, they do the novels rather less than justice and are in fact a little off-putting. Admittedly the romanticism of the writing is a little lush at times, but the style is uniquely fresh and witty, and Ibbotson's powers of observation and perception are extremely sharp.

Her first two novels for adults are rather similar to each other: both *A Countess Below Stairs* and *Magic Flutes* have impoverished aristocratic heroines, working willingly at menial tasks and beloved of all their temporary colleagues. Both novels have dark, brooding heroes, trapped in engagements to females beautiful in looks but repellent in character, from which they must somehow escape with honour. Anna Grazinsky, the eponymous heroine of the first novel,

has been orphaned in the Russian Revolution, has fled to England, and in order to send her young brother to school takes employment as a housemaid; armed with *The Domestic Servant's Compendium* by Serena Strickland (2003 pages of arcane and obsolete advice), she bursts upon the household of the Earl of Westerholme. The comparison with Flora Poste in Stella Gibbons's *Cold Comfort Farm*, descending upon the Starkadder family armed with a copy of the Pensées of the Abbé Fausse-Maigre, is inescapable and Anna, just like Flora, sets a number of lives and careers on the right path. Tessa of *Magic Flutes* (in reality Princess Theresa-Maria of Pfaffenstein, Princess of Breganzer, Duchess of Unterthur, Countess of Malk, of Zeeburg, and of Freischule), works as junior wardrobe mistress, assistant lighting engineer, deputy wig maker, assistant stage manager, prompter and errand girl for an opera company; just like Anna, she takes innumerable minor characters under her passionately altruistic wing. Anna and Tessa are entirely satisfactory heroines, and the respective objects of their adoration eminently heroic, but it is Ibbotson's casts of lesser characters which help to mark her novels out. From the irascible, bed-ridden Mrs Proom (*A Countess Below Stairs*), who hurls pots of geraniums out of her window and keeps her appendix in a jar above her bed, to Boris (*Magic Flutes*), a gloomy Bulgarian wig-maker devoted to a revolting yoghurt culture ('it lived in a jam-jar, ... smelling vilely, flocculating, turning blue and generally showing all the signs of artistic temperament'), characters like these are found in the pages of no other romance novelist.

Ibbotson's next heroine is a little different: Harriet is 'Professor Morton's clever daughter; Miss Morton's biddable niece'. In *A Company of Swans*, this quiet but determined girl flees her repressive upbringing in the Cambridge of 1912 to dance with a classical ballet company in a legendary opera house in the Amazon jungle. But again there is an array of fascinating minor characters, a most attractive hero, and a fair selection of the sort of misunderstandings without which no self-respecting romance novel is complete.

Ibbotson's style in all these novels is very distinctive. Not an author to use one word where two or three are available, she is generous with adverbs and adjectives, and occasionally her prose only just falls short of being florid. But it does fall short, and the intensity of her prose style encourages her readers to pay close attention to every word, lest they miss such joyous and totally apt descriptions as 'its ... painted ceiling of obese and ecstatic nymphs' (in the Klostern Theatre in Vienna), or the succinct character summary of Harriet Morton's Aunt Louisa, who 'kept in her bedroom a box labelled "String too short to tie"'.

The heroine of *Madensky Square*, Susanna Weber, is somewhat different from Anna, Tessa, and Harriet, being a mature, comfortably-off woman, the mother of an illegitimate child, and the mistress of a middle-aged, pessimistic, married Field Marshall with whom she is totally besotted. This novel, told in the first person, covers a year in the lives of Susanna and her acquaintances, and is written in a somewhat calmer style; the torrent of adjectives and adverbs has abated somewhat, although the prose is still unmistakably Ibbotson's. Susanna has much the same penchant for helping lame ducks (while herself being vulnerable) as Ibbotson's other heroines, although her lover is not quite the same mould as Anna's Rupert, Tessa's Guy or Harriet's Rom, and cannot really be said to be the book's hero—an ingredient which this novel surprisingly lacks. But the minor characters are as inspired as ever—Herr Egger with his Nasty Little Habit, Frau Schultzer who on her honeymoon reads Goethe's *Trilogy of Passion* while her new husband waits downstairs.

A Glove Shop in Vienna is a book of short stories, all with the customary Ibbotson stamp upon them, but with a variety of themes, from 'The Great Carp Ferdinand', which would not be out of place in a collection of stories for children, to 'The Little Countess' with its clever parodies of Chekhov. Some of the settings recur throughout Ibbotson's writings; the legendary opera house in Manaus, for example, features in both *A Company of Swans* and the short story 'A Rose in Amazonia', and Ibbotson's native Vienna is the setting for a number of her writings. St Petersburg, too, figures more than once, and in all these cities the world of the theatre, of opera and ballet, assume great importance.

But amid the light-hearted short stories, the sentimental novels, Ibbotson does deal with serious subjects; she creates unpleasant characters—selfish women, boorish or insensitive men—and condemns the social mores they uphold. Some of her sympathetic characters will never have truly happy endings; for example, Susanna, in *Madensky Square*, suffers the life-long anguish of having had to give her illegitimate daughter up for adoption, and in *The Morning Gift*, Ibbotson's most recent novel, Ruth Berger flees from Vienna after the Nazi Anschluss and then has to adapt to an alien way of life in England. But the gloom can never be all-pervading, and this latest book, although rather more serious than its predecessors, is just as sharp in its observations and as gentle in its humour.

—Judith Rhodes

———————

IDRIESS, Ion L(lewellyn).
Nationality: Australian. **Born:** Sydney, New South Wales, in 1890. **Career:** jobs included working as a miner and a drover. **Died:** 1979.

ROMANCE AND HISTORICAL PUBLICATIONS

Novels

Lasseter's Last Ride: An Epic of Central Australian Gold Discovery. Sydney, Angus and Robertson, 1931; London, Cape, 1936.
Flynn of the Inland. Sydney, Angus and Robertson, 1932.
Drums of Mer. Sydney, Angus and Robertson, 1933.
The Great Boomerang. Sydney, Angus and Robertson, 1941.
Headhunters of the Coral Sea. Sydney, Angus and Robertson, 1941.
Isles of Despair. Sydney, Angus and Robertson, 1947.
The Red Chief. Sydney, Angus and Robertson, 1953.
Our Living Stone Age. Sydney, Angus and Robertson, 1963.

Short Stories

The Yellow Joss and Other Tales. Sydney, Angus and Robertson, 1934.

OTHER PUBLICATIONS

Other

Madman's Island. Sydney, Cornstalk, 1927.
Prospecting for Gold. Sydney, Angus and Robertson, 1931.
The Desert Column: Leaves from the Diary of an Australian Trooper in Gallipoli, Sinai, and Palestine. Sydney, Angus and Robertson, 1932.
Men of the Jungle (memoirs). Sydney, Angus and Robertson, 1932.
Gold-Dust and Ashes: The Romantic Story of the New Guinea Gold-fields. Sydney, Angus and Robertson, 1933.
Man Tracks. Sydney, Angus and Robertson, 1933; London, Cape, 1937.
The Cattle King: The Story of Sir Sidney Kidman. Sydney, Angus and Robertson, 1936.
Forty Fathoms Deep. Sydney, Angus and Robertson, 1937.
Over the Range. Sydney, Angus and Robertson, 1937.
Must Australia Fight? Sydney, Angus and Robertson, 1939.

Cyaniding for Gold. Sydney, Angus and Robertson, 1939.
Lightning Ridge, The Land of Black Opals (autobiography). Sydney, Angus and Robertson, 1940.
Nemarluk, King of the Wilds. Sydney, Angus and Robertson, 1941.
Australian Guerilla series (military handbooks)
    Shoot to Kill. Sydney, Angus and Robertson, 1942.
    Sniping. Sydney, Angus and Robertson, 1942.
    Guerilla Tactics. Sydney, Angus and Robertson, 1942.
    Trapping the Jap. Sydney, Angus and Robertson, 1942.
    The Scout. Sydney, Angus and Robertson, 1943.
Onward Australia: Developing a Continent. Sydney, Angus and Robertson, 1944.
The Silent Service: Action Stories of the Anzac Navy, with T.M. Jones. Sydney, Angus and Robertson, 1944.
Horrie the Wog-Dog. Sydney, Angus and Robertson, 1945; as *Dog of the Desert*, Indianapolis, Bobbs Merrill, 1945.
In Crocodile Land: Wandering in Northern Australia. Sydney, Angus and Robertson, 1946.
Stone of Destiny. Sydney, Angus and Robertson, 1948; as *The Diamond: Stone of Destiny*, 1969.
The Opium Smugglers. Sydney, Angus and Robertson, 1948.
One Wet Season. Sydney, Angus and Robertson, 1949.
The Wild White Man of Badu: A Story of the Coral Sea. Sydney, Angus and Robertson, 1950.
Across the Nullarbor: A Modern Argosy. Sydney, Angus and Robertson, 1951.
Outlaws of the Leopolds. Sydney, Angus and Robertson, 1952.
The Nor-Westers (memoirs). Sydney, Angus and Robertson, 1954.
The Vanished People. Sydney, Angus and Robertson, 1955.
The Silver City (memoirs). Sydney, Angus and Robertson, 1956.
Coral Sea Calling. Sydney, Angus and Robertson, 1957.
Back O'Cairns. Sydney, Angus and Robertson, 1959.
The Tin Scratchers. Sydney, Angus and Robertson, 1960.
The Wild North. Sydney, Angus and Robertson, 1960.
Tracks of Destiny. Sydney, Angus and Robertson, 1961.
My Mate Dick. Sydney, Angus and Robertson, 1962.
Our Stone Age Mystery. Sydney, Angus and Robertson, 1964.
Opals and Sapphires: How to Work, Mine, Class, Cut, Polish and Sell Them. Sydney, Angus and Robertson, 1967; Palo Alto, California, Pacific, 1970.
Challenge of the North: Wealth from Australia's Northern Shores. Sydney, Angus and Robertson, 1969.

*   *   *

Are the books of Ion L. Idriess fact or fiction? He himself claimed that all of them were 'true'. Even the highly imaginative romance *Drums of Mer* is announced as 'in all essentials historical fact', and many of his works are expressly biographical or autobiographical.

It must be conceded that for Idriess plot and character development count for less than the authentic evocation of a time, place, culture, or event. Yet regardless of how libraries choose to catalogue them, even his most 'factual' books, like *The Cattle King*, a biography of Sid Kidman, and *The Silver City*, a history of Broken Hill, read like novels. Idriess may base his writing on documentary evidence—even quote it at length to give the flavour of authenticity—but around the framework of the bare facts he invariably weaves a thick fabric of invented conversation, interior monologue, and dramatic—often melodramatic—incident.

Though born in Sydney, Idriess spent most of the first 30 years of his life as a wanderer and casual worker in remote areas of Australia and New Guinea. His experience of these, together with his war service in the Middle East, supplied most of the raw material for his subsequent career as a prolific and popular writer.

His favourite settings, Torres Strait and Central Australia, were among the last areas to be conquered by Europeans, and Idriess is therefore fairly characterized as a writer of the final phase of colonial advance in the Pacific. He writes from the point of view of the colonist, but because his knowledge is intimate and his sympathies wide, his view is complicated. Possibly the clearest sign of the colonial mentality in his writing is the prominence of the 'dreamer', the individual who struggles to achieve a great goal against the odds. Sometimes, like the prospector in *Lasseter's Last Ride*, the dreamer is doomed to failure, but just as often he (it is always *he*) succeeds gloriously, like Sid Kidman, or the founder of the outback Flying Doctor Service, *Flynn of the Inland*. Idriess himself had a dream: the rerouting of coastal rivers to make fertile pasture of the dry outback, which he advocated passionately in *The Great Boomerang*.

Idriess is most interesting for his treatment of the other side of colonialism. He is fascinated by indigenous peoples and their clash with 'civilization', and his books provide some of the most vivid descriptions of tribal life in popular literature. It is true that these are seriously marred by the author's pervasive racism. Not only does he depict native peoples as emotionally and intellectually immature: to be fair, his characterization of Europeans is also simplistic. Indigenous peoples—especially Australians—are made the butt of crude jokes and slurs. But for all that, he is capable at times of forcefully conveying the moral strains of colonialism. And it is also true that by the 1950s the earlier derision had been replaced by a benign paternalism and even romanticized admiration (*The Red Chief*, *Our Living Stone Age*).

The aspect of tribal life most intriguing to him is its 'savage' religion—the dark world of magic, witchcraft, and sorcery. The priest C'Zarcke (*sic!*) in *Drums of Mer* is the most complete rendition of the 'Witch Doctor', a figure who recurs almost obsessively. (Probably such a person had profoundly impressed Idriess's imagination when he was 'a lad in a strange new world sailing the Coral Sea in a cockroach infested cutter.') Idriess depicts the Witch Doctor as the bearer of the deepest values of tribal culture. He is thus the natural enemy of Europeans and, being closer to the source of an uncorrupted spirituality, in a sense superior to them. At the same time he, the wild spirituality he embodies, and the people he represents, are doomed.

The complement to the Witch Doctor is the lone white man or woman stranded in the midst of tribal culture. This situation dramatically reverses the terms of colonialism. Here it is the European who is in an inferior and dependent position. This is another theme which Idriess returned to many times. At one extreme there is Lasseter, eventually left to die by the group which had rescued him from starvation, at the other Wongai, the 'wild white man of Badu', who becomes a feared chieftain. In between are those who adapt but later return to their own society: Jakara in *Drums of Mer*, the two boys in *Headhunters of the Coral Sea*, Barbara Thomson in *Isles of Despair*.

The authorial personality which Idriess's work conveys conforms to the Australian 'type' which continues to live in popular prejudice and the mass media, though Australian literature has long since shunned it. He displays both its strengths and its weaknesses: a friendly but complacent egalitarianism—at least towards fellow whites; a warm curiosity about people and their doings which can be insensitive; a zest for action which easily becomes jingoistic; a wry humour which can turn nasty. For as long as this cultural type lives, people will read him with pleasure. *Drums of Mer*, his most enduringly popular book, may also be his best. Besides evoking memorably a (no doubt overdone) atmosphere of 'superstition and savage power', it is a suspenseful and fast-moving adventure, written with considerable dash.

—Paul Gillen

INGLIS, Susan. See 2nd edition, 1990.

INNES, Jean.   See SAUNDERS, Jean.

IRWIN, Margaret (Emma Faith).
Nationality: British. **Born:** London in 1889. **Education:** Clifton School, Bristol; Oxford University. **Relations:** married the artist John Robert Monsell in 1929. **Died:** 11 December 1967.

ROMANCE AND HISTORICAL PUBLICATIONS

Novels (series: Elizabeth I Trilogy; Seventeenth Century)

How Many Miles to Babylon? London, Constable, 1913.
Come Out to Play. London, Constable, 1914; New York, Doran, 1915.
Out of the House. London, Constable, and New York, Doran, 1916.
Still She Wished for Company. London, Heinemann, 1924.
Who Will Remember? New York, Seltzer, 1924.
These Mortals. London, Heinemann, 1925.
Knock Four Times. London, Heinemann, and New York, Harcourt Brace, 1927.
Fire Down Below. London, Heinemann, and New York, Harcourt Brace, 1928.
None So Pretty. London, Chatto and Windus, and New York, Harcourt Brace, 1930.
Seventeenth Century:
    Royal Flush: The Story of Minette. London, Chatto and Windus, and New York, Harcourt Brace, 1932.
    The Proud Servant: The Story of Montrose. London, Chatto and Windus, and New York, Harcourt Brace, 1934.
    The Stranger Prince: The Story of Rupert of the Rhine. London, Chatto and Windus, and New York, Harcourt Brace, 1937.
    The Bride: The Story of Louise and Montrose. London, Chatto and Windus, and New York, Harcourt Brace, 1939.
The Gay Galliard: The Love Story of Mary Queen of Scots. London, Chatto and Windus, 1941; New York, Harcourt Brace, 1942.
Elizabeth I Trilogy:
    Young Bess. London, Chatto and Windus, 1944; New York, Harcourt Brace, 1945.
    Elizabeth, Captive Princess. London, Chatto and Windus, and New York, Harcourt Brace, 1948.
    Elizabeth and the Prince of Spain. London, Chatto and Windus, and New York, Harcourt Brace, 1953.

Short Stories

Madame Fears the Dark: Seven Stories and a Play. London, Chatto and Windus, 1935.
Mrs Oliver Cromwell and Other Stories. London, Chatto and Windus, 1940.
Bloodstock and Other Stories. London, Chatto and Windus, 1953; New York, Harcourt Brace, 1954.

OTHER PUBLICATIONS

Plays

The Happy Man: A Sketch for Acting. London, Oxford University Press, 1921; Boston, Baker, 1938.
Check to the King of France (for children). London, French, 1933.

Minette (for children). London and New York, French, 1933.
Save the Children (for children). London, French, 1933.
The King's Son, in *Nash's* (London), February 1934.
Madame Fears the Dark (produced London, 1936). London, Chatto and Windus, 1936.

Other

South Molton Street. London, Mate, 1927.
The Great Lucifer: A Portrait of Sir Walter Raleigh. London, Chatto and Windus, 1936; New York, Harcourt Brace, 1960.

*   *   *

Margaret Irwin's fame was founded primarily on her series of longish, leisurely-paced novels focusing on notable figures from the Tudor and Stuart periods. Although many of these are nominally centred around female figures, such as Elizabeth I in the trilogy *Young Bess, Elizabeth, Captive Princess, Elizabeth and the Prince of Spain*, and the Princess Minette in *Royal Flush*, she had a marked predilection for dashing, military heroes: Thomas Seymour threatens to steal the scene from the nominal heroine in *Young Bess*, a gallant, charming, and improbably altruistic Earl of Bothwell is the eponymous hero of *The Gay Galliard*, and a glamorous, wronged prince Rupert of the Rhine takes centre stage in *The Stranger Prince*. Despite this preference for strong, romantic heroes, however, the actual descriptions of romantic interludes in her work are chaste and brief, and completely eclipsed in importance by her worthy but often rather muddled attempts to recount the Machiavellian political intrigues which beset the lives of all those of whom she writes.

Perhaps because of this emphasis, her works have not come well out of the test of time. Long since out of print, her novels are available only in second-hand book shops and libraries. But if they no longer speak to our time, they nevertheless have something to tell us about Irwin's own.

Irwin's work is marked by attempts at serious novel-writing in the style of the 1930s and 1940s—taut, nervous dialogue, briefly sketched characters, and much use of interior monologue verging at times on stream-of-consciousness, and even some elementary acknowledgement of Freudian theories of character, in the recurrent emphasis on men's relationships with their mothers. This, however, sits rather awkwardly alongside the historical settings. She is not of the 'blood and thunder' school, though sensational events are occasionally forced on her by her choice of narrative; her interest is in the interior life of her characters, which is conveyed through the methods and language of her own time. Alongside this urge, however, lies an implicit respect for historical accuracy which effectively hamstrings her by forcing her to incorporate into her books any details which her research has unearthed, no matter how awkward their introduction may be. Even more disastrously, it also leads her to intersperse her characters' habitual 20th-century comments with verbatim quotations from their own letters or from historical documents about them. A classical example can be found in *Young Bess* by the Duchess of Somerset—a very modern-sounding Duchess, in many ways more of a Wallis Simpson than an Anne Seymour—on a letter received from her brother-in-law: 'What in the name of God are "rudder beaste"? And "urne"?' To which her husband conscientiously but most improbably replies with a mini-lecture on historical semantics which enables this supposedly 16th-century character to understand a piece of 16th-century prose. A similarly incongruous moment occurs in *The Gay Galliard* when all illusionism and drama are forfeited while Irwin interrupts the flow of the narrative to reveal that the source for her re-creation of this scene is Knox's own historical account of it, and to speculate rather unimaginatively that had Bothwell left us a similar set of comments they might perhaps have been different.

Alongside this linguistic and narrative incompetence there also runs a lack of any real feel for the period. Totally dependent on what her admittedly copious researches have taught her, Irwin never projects herself imaginatively into the different culture or attitudes of the past: her characters remain essentially 1930s and 1940s English men and women, going through the motions of situations which their own behaviour patterns would never have produced. Her concentration on interiority even ensures the lack of the customary descriptions of physical appearance or material surroundings, which further accentuates the sense of the psychological equivalent of 'modern dress' history rather than costume drama. Detailed description occurs only where there is precise historical evidence of it, as in *The Gay Galliard* in which various details of the room in which David Rizzio was killed are specified, once again highlighting Irwin's absolute dependence on sources rather than on imaginative engagement with the characters and period.

Indeed such interest as the books retain resides primarily in the ways in which Irwin reads the past through the mirror of her present. This is never more obviously the case than in a passage in *Young Bess* in which Thomas Seymour fulminates against his brother's decision to employ German mercenaries: he has, he tells him, seen for himself in Hungary the devastating effects of the Germans' obsessive insistence on racial purity. However badly this may relate to the likely mentality of the historical Thomas Seymour, it does of course fit very well with the book's first publication date of 1944; and such a homogenizing attitude to the past is pervasive in Irwin's work. Where they still speak to us, they do so not about the period in which she set them, but, above all, about the period in which she wrote them.

—Lisa Hopkins

————

JACKSON, Shirley (Hardie). American. 1919–65. See 2nd edition, 1990.

————

JACOB, Naomi (Ellington).
Pseudonym: Ellington Gray. **Nationality:** British. **Born:** Ripon, Yorkshire, 1 July 1884. **Education:** Middlesbrough High School. **Career:** teacher in a Middlesbrough school; secretary and companion to Marguerite Broadfoot and Eva Moore, music hall entertainers; actress; supervisor in munitions factory during World War I; welfare officer in Overseas Service during World War II. After 1930 lived in Sirmione, Italy. **Died:** 26 August 1964.

ROMANCE AND HISTORICAL PUBLICATIONS

Novels (series: Broad Acres; Gollantz Saga)

Jacob Ussher. London, Butterworth, 1925.
Rock and Sand. London, Butterworth, 1926.
Power. London, Butterworth, 1927.
The Plough. London, Butterworth, 1928.
Saffroned Bridesails (as Ellington Gray). London, Butterworth, 1928.
The Man Who Found Himself. London, Butterworth, 1929; revised edition, London, Pan, 1952.
The Beloved Physician. London, Butterworth, 1930.
Gollantz Saga:
   1. *The Founder of the House*. London, Hutchinson, 1935; New York, Macmillan, 1956.
   2. *That Wild Lie—*. London, Hutchinson, 1930.

3. *Young Emmanuel*. London, Hutchinson, 1932; New York, New American Library, 1973.
4. *Four Generations*. London, Hutchinson, and New York, Macmillan, 1934.
5. *Private Gollantz*. London, Hutchinson, 1943.
6. *Gollantz: London, Paris, Milan*. London, Hutchinson, 1948.
7. *Gollantz and Partners*. London, Hutchinson, 1958.
Tales of the Broad Acres. London, Hutchinson, 1955.
> *Roots*. London, Hutchinson, 1931.
> *The Loaded Stick*. London, Hutchinson, 1934; New York, Macmillan, 1935.
> *Sally Scarth*. London, Hutchinson, 1940.
Seen Unknown . . . . London, Hutchinson, 1931.
Props. London, Hutchinson, 1932.
Groping. London, Hutchinson, 1933.
Poor Straws! London, Hutchinson, 1933.
Honour Comes Back—. London, Hutchinson, and New York, Macmillan, 1935.
Time Piece. London, Hutchinson, 1936; New York, Macmillan, 1937.
Barren Metal. London, Hutchinson, and New York, Macmillan, 1936.
Fade Out. London, Hutchinson, and New York, Macmillan, 1937.
The Lenient God. London, Hutchinson, 1937; New York, Macmillan, 1938.
Straws in Amber. London, Hutchinson, 1938; New York, Macmillan, 1939.
No Easy Way. London, Hutchinson, 1938.
Full Meridian. London, Hutchinson, 1939; New York, Macmillan, 1940.
This Porcelain Clay. London, Hutchinson, and New York, Macmillan, 1939.
They Left the Land. London, Hutchinson, and New York, Macmillan, 1940.
Under New Management. London, Hutchinson, 1941.
The Cap of Youth. London, Hutchinson, and New York, Macmillan, 1941.
Leopards and Spots. London, Hutchinson, 1942.
White Wool. London, Hutchinson, 1944.
Susan Crowther. London, Hutchinson, 1945.
Honour's a Mistress. London, Hutchinson, 1947.
A Passage Perilous. London, Hutchinson, 1948.
Mary of Delight. London, Hutchinson, 1949.
Every Other Gift. London, Hutchinson, 1950.
The Heart of the House. London, Hutchinson, 1951.
A Late Lark Singing. London, Hutchinson, 1952.
The Morning Will Come. London, Hutchinson, 1953.
Antonia. London, Hutchinson, 1954.
Second Harvest. London, Hutchinson, 1954.
The Irish Boy: A Romantic Biography. London, Hutchinson, 1955.
Wind on the Heath. London, Hutchinson, 1956.
What's to Come. London, Hutchinson, 1958.
Search for a Background. London, Hutchinson, 1960.
Three Men and Jennie. London, Hutchinson, 1960.
Strange Beginning. London, Hale, 1961.
Great Black Oxen. London, Hale, 1962.
Yolanda. London, Hale, 1963.
Long Shadows. London, Hale, 1964.
Flavia. London, Hale, 1965.

OTHER PUBLICATIONS

Play

The Dawn (produced Glasgow, 1923).

Other

Me: A Chronicle about Other People. London, Hutchinson, 1933.
Me—in the Kitchen. London, Hutchinson, 1935.
Our Marie: Marie Lloyd: A Biography. London, Hutchinson, 1936.
Me—Again. London, Hutchinson, 1937.
More about Me. London, Hutchinson, 1939.
Shadow Drama, by Nina Abbott, completed by Jacob. London, Duckworth, 1940.
Me—In War-Time. London, Hutchinson, 1940.
Balance Suspended, by Nina Abbott, completed by Jacob. London, Duckworth, 1942.
Me and the Mediterranean. London, Hutchinson, 1945.
Me—Over There. London, Hutchinson, 1947.
Opera in Italy, with James C. Robertson. London, Hutchinson, 1948; Freeport, New York, Books for Libraries, 1970.
Me and Mine, You and Yours. London, Hutchinson, 1949.
Me—Looking Back. London, Hutchinson, 1950.
Impressions from Italy. London, Hutchinson, 1952.
Robert, Nana, and—Me. London, Hutchinson, 1952.
Just about Us. London, Hutchinson, 1953.
Me—Likes and Dislikes. London, Hutchinson, 1954.
Prince China. London, Hutchinson, 1955.
Me—Yesterday and To-day. London, Kimber, 1957.
Me—and the Stags. London, Kimber, 1962.
Me—and the Swans. London, Kimber, 1963.
Me—Thinking Things Over. London, Kimber, 1964.

*

Critical Study: *Naomi Jacob: The Seven Ages of 'Me'* by James Norbury, London, Kimber, 1965.

Theatrical Activities:
Actress: **Plays**—Julia Cragworthy in *The Young Idea* by Noël Coward, London, 1923; Mrs Hackitt in *The Ringer* by Edgar Wallace, London, 1926; Ma Gennochio in *The Nutmeg Tree* by Margery Sharp, London, 1941; Nurse in *Love for Love* by Congreve, London, 1943.

* * *

The full list of Naomi Jacob's output over the years is staggering. How could any writer have had so much to say? She accomplished her impressive feat by recording the ordinary, but by doing so in a generously florid style that ran to untold pages. She tended to become infatuated with the characters of her own invention—the 'good' ones, at any rate. Grudgingly she would sometimes allow some tiny defect or character flaw to one of her pets, such as Emmanuel Gollantz, patriarch of her popular multi-generational family saga, but would hasten to better than redeem it with heaped-up evidence of her dear one's excellence. Her villains, by contrast, are of deepest dye. Julian Gollantz, one of the black sheep, is a near approach to the mustachio-twirling 'bad guys' of the early cinema: relentlessly evil, unmotivated in his Iago-like malice, and a foil for the many virtuous Gollantz characters.

For all her broad and sweeping strokes, Jacob was somehow unable, though infinitely willing, to create a convincingly *important* character. Good or bad (and some of them are indeed quite interesting and/or likeable; one wants to learn their eventual fates), her people do not live up to her own obviously high opinion of them. They remain—ordinary. Like the rest of us, they are earthbound with family concerns of enormous complication and difficulty; though usually quite comfortably fixed, the occasional one must pinch and scrape a little; all are deeply concerned with the mechanics of making a living, with their feet solidly planted on the commercial ground. This does indeed set them apart from the creations of a great many other authors of the romance novel, whose characters appear to exist like the lilies of the field, neither toiling nor spinning, living only for love.

As well as working, Jacob's people do love, however. Intensely, burningly, with enormous fervour, self-sacrifice, and dedication: each of them adores—some other ordinary creation. Jacob has a habit of overburdening little characters with giant, heroic emotions that they cannot gracefully sustain. Although this inevitably flattens the sought-after effect of romantic magnificence, it may be that this very quality of 'commonplaceness' served to endear her undeniably popular novels to a large, faithful, and 'ordinary' public, after all.

—Joan McGrath

JACOBS, Leah. See **GELLIS, Roberta.**

JAGGER, Brenda.
Nationality: British. **Born:** Yorkshire in 1936. **Relations:** married; three daughters. **Career:** worked in Paris and as a probation officer in the north of England. **Recipient:** Romantic Novelists Association major award, 1986. **Died:** 1986.

ROMANCE AND HISTORICAL PUBLICATIONS

Novels (series: Barforth)

Antonia. London, Hodder and Stoughton, 1978.
The Clouded Hills (Barforth). London, Macdonald, 1980.
Verity. New York, Doubleday, 1980.
Daughter of Aphrodite. London, Constable, 1981.
Flints and Roses (Barforth). London, Macdonald, 1981.
The Sleeping Sword (Barforth). London, Macdonald, 1982.
The Barforth Women. New York, Doubleday, 1982.
An Independent Woman. New York, New American Library, 1983.
Days of Grace. London, Collins, 1983; New York, Morrow, 1984.
A Winter's Child. London, Collins, and New York, Morrow, 1984.
A Song Twice Over. London, Collins, and New York, Morrow, 1985.
Distant Choices. London, Collins, and New York, Morrow, 1986.

*   *   *

Brenda Jagger's two early novels *Antonia* and *Daughter of Aphrodite* are set in Ancient Rome. The characters, and the atmosphere of the courts of Tiberius and Galba, form a fascinating setting for the stories, both of which centre around young girls whose lives and loves develop against a time-honoured background of power, treachery, murder, and money. The heroines differ in their positions in society: Antonia is an heiress whose wealth makes her a political pawn in the intrigue following Nero's death, Danae a rich courtesan who has fought her way up from the slums of Subura. Each bears the hallmarks of a Jagger heroine; tenacity, a strong sense of survival, and a capacity to develop and to learn from all the experiences that life and the author throw at them. This description would encompass a typical heroine of most traditional historical and romantic novels, but what is unusual about Jagger's work is the interesting way in which she describes in some detail the socio-political structures of the period about which she writes.

However, it is not until her first trilogy—*The Clouded Hills*, *Flints and Roses*, and *The Sleeping Sword*—that her real strength in this area emerges. These three books, set in the 19th century, chart the uneven progress of a mill-owning family as it faces industrialization, riots, and subsequently the implementation of the Reform Act. Many novels have been written about this period, but few offer such a compelling blend of love and politics, or deal so convincingly with the development of the role of women. None of the heroines, who become increasingly militant as the books progress, is outrageous or unbelievable; rather, each is developed in a sympathetic and moving way. The restrictions of the conventions of Victorian England are skilfully drawn, and in each novel the tension gradually builds as the individuality of the strong-minded female character develops to a point where rebellion in some form becomes inevitable. Verity, in *The Clouded Hills*, accepts a marriage of convenience which she uses to give her a freedom to find love elsewhere; Grace Agbrigg in *The Sleeping Sword* resists her natural emotions and marries as expected, but she breaks free and defies convention to become the only divorcee in Cullingford.

Throughout the trilogy, the plight of the homeless and working conditions in the cities are described graphically, and form not a mere adjunct to the plot but an integral part of the action. For example, in *The Clouded Hills* Hannah is involved in improving social conditions in the worst working areas, while in *Flints and Roses* Dr Giles Ashburn, the heroine's first husband, dies fighting a cholera epidemic in the slums. Contrasting starkly with the grim realities of these authentically drawn situations are Jagger's vivid descriptions of the Yorkshire countryside.

In *Days of Grace* Jagger extends her geographical range to Paris and London but returns once again to her native Yorkshire for the denouement of the story. She uses the atmosphere of the moors and the emotions and ambitions of the strong-willed women (and men) who people them, to depict the tensions of those turbulent times.

Several of the themes only touched upon in her trilogy are developed in her later novels. In *A Winter's Child*, set in the years following World War I, Clare, having experienced the freedom ironically offered to many women during those years, is now forced to return from nursing in France to the closed society of a Yorkshire town. She is unable to accept the position that society offers her, and chooses to use the money left to her by her husband (killed in the trenches) to set up a house of her own, living a 'bohemian' lifestyle. She is allowed to follow this course of action only as a result of the somewhat unexpected acquiescence of Benedict (the trustee of her father-in-law's estate and thus the holder of the purse-strings). Less unexpected is the development of their relationship despite the constraints still in force at the time.

The overall theme of a woman's freedom to choose her destiny is also present in Jagger's later novels *A Song Twice Over* and *Distant Choices*. The barriers are still there—the expectations of society, social background, and convention—as are the strengths to overcome these barriers. Jagger's powerful writing brings to life the often agonizing and painful choices inflicted upon Victorian women from all social backgrounds, and offers a picture of their emotional plight no less vivid than in her earlier works.

—Judith Rhodes

JAKES, John (William).
Pseudonyms: William Ard; Alan Payne; Rachel Ann Payne; Jay Scotland. **Nationality:** American. **Born:** Chicago, Illinois, 31 March 1932. **Education:** DePauw University, Greencastle, Indiana, A.B. 1953; Ohio State University, Columbus, M.A. in American literature 1954. **Relations:** married Rachel Ann Payne in 1951; three daughters and one son. **Career:** copywriter, then promotion manager, Abbott Laboratories, North Chicago, 1954–60; copywriter, Rumrill Company, Rochester, New York, 1960–61; freelance writer, 1961–65; copywriter, Kircher Helton and Collett, Dayton, Ohio,

1965–68; copy chief, then vice-president, Oppenheim Herminghausen and Clarke, Dayton, 1968–70; creative director, Dancer Fitzgerald Sample, Dayton, 1970–71. Since 1971 freelance writer; writer-in-residence, DePauw University, Fall 1979. Research fellow, department of History, University of South Carolina, Columbia, 1989. **Recipient:** Ohio Governor's award, 1977, 1989. LLD.: Wright State University, Dayton, Ohio, 1976; D.Litt.: DePauw University, 1977; L.H.D.: Winthrop College, 1985. Research Fellow, department of History, University of South Carolina, Columbia. **Address:** c/o Rembar and Curtis, Attorneys, 19 West 44th Street, New York, New York 10036, USA.

ROMANCE AND HISTORICAL PUBLICATIONS

Novels (series: Kent Family Chronicles; North and South Trilogy)

Kent Family Chronicles:
 The Bastard. New York, Pyramid, 1974; as *Fortune's Whirlwind* and *To an Unknown Shore*, London, Corgi, 2 vols, 1975.
 The Rebels. New York, Pyramid, 1975; London, Corgi, 1979.
 The Seekers. New York, Pyramid, 1975; London, Corgi, 1979.
 The Furies. New York, Pyramid, 1976; London, Corgi, 1979.
 The Titans. New York, Pyramid, 1976; London, Corgi, 1979.
 The Warriors. New York, Pyramid, 1977; London, Corgi, 1979.
 The Lawless. New York, Berkley, 1978; London, Corgi, 1979.
 The Americans. New York, Berkley, 1980.
North and South Trilogy:
 North and South. New York, Harcourt Brace, and London, Collins, 1982.
 Love and War. New York, Harcourt Brace, 1984; London, Collins, 1985.
 Heaven and Hell. San Diego, Harcourt Brace, and London, Collins, 1987.
California Gold. New York, Random House, and London, Collins, 1989.
Homeland. New York, Doubleday, 1993; London, Warner, 1994.

Novels as Jay Scotland

Strike the Black Flag. New York, Ace, 1961.
Sir Scoundrel. New York, Ace, 1962; revised edition, as *King's Crusader*, New York, Pinnacle 1977.
Veils of Salome. New York, Avon, 1962.
Arena. New York, Ace, 1963.
Traitors' Legion. New York, Ace, 1963; revised edition, as *The Man from Cannae*, New York, Pinnacle, 1977.

OTHER PUBLICATIONS

Novels

Gonzaga's Woman. New York, Universal, 1953.
Wear a Fast Gun. New York, Arcadia House, 1956; London, Ward Lock, 1957.
A Night for Treason. New York, Bouregy, 1956.
The Devil Has Four Faces. New York, Bouregy, 1958.
This'll Slay You (as Alan Payne). New York, Ace, 1958.
The Seventh Man (as Jay Scotland). New York, Bouregy, 1958.
I, Barbarian (as Jay Scotland). New York, Avon, 1959; revised edition (as John Jakes), New York, Pinnacle, 1976.
The Imposter. New York, Bouregy, 1959.
Johnny Havoc. New York, Belmont, 1960.
Johnny Havoc Meets Zelda. New York, Belmont, 1962.
Johnny Havoc and the Doll Who Had 'It'. New York, Belmont, 1963.

G.I. Girls. Derby, Connecticut, Monarch, 1963.
Ghostwind (as Rachel Ann Payne). New York, Paperback Library, 1966.
When the Star Kings Die. New York, Ace, 1967.
Making It Big. New York, Belmont, 1968.
The Asylum World. New York, Paperback Library, 1969; London, New English Library, 1978.
Brak Versus the Mark of the Demons. New York, Paperback Library, 1969; as *Brak the Barbarian—The Mark of the Demons*, London, Tandem, 1970.
Brak the Barbarian Versus the Sorceress. New York, Paperback Library, 1969; as *Brak the Barbarian—The Sorceress*, London, Tandem, 1969.
The Hybrid. New York, Paperback Library, 1969.
The Last Magicians. New York, New American Library, 1969.
The Planet Wizard. New York, Ace, 1969.
Tonight We Steal the Stars. New York, Ace, 1969.
Black in Time. New York, Paperback Library, 1970.
Mask of Chaos. New York, Ace, 1970.
Master of the Dark Gate. New York, Lancer, 1970.
Monte Cristo 99. New York, Curtis, 1970.
Six-Gun Planet. New York, Paperback Library, 1970; London, New English Library, 1978.
Mention My Name in Atlantis. New York, DAW, 1972.
Witch of the Dark Gate. New York, Lancer, 1972.
Conquest of the Planet of the Apes (novelization of screenplay). New York, Award, 1972.
On Wheels. New York, Paperback Library, 1973.
Brak: When the Idols Walked. New York, Pocket Books, 1978.
Excalibur!, with Gil Kane. New York, Dell, 1980.

Novels as William Ard

Make Mine Mavis. Derby, Connecticut, Monarch, 1961.
And So to Bed. Derby, Connecticut, Monarch, 1962.
Give Me This Woman. Derby, Connecticut, Monarch, 1962.

Short Stories

Brak the Barbarian. New York, Avon, 1968; London, Tandem, 1970.
The Best of John Jakes, edited by Martin H. Greenberg and Joseph D. Olander. New York, DAW, 1977.
Fortunes of Brak. New York, Dell, 1980.
In the Big Country, the Best Western Stories of John Jakes. New York, Bantam, 1993.

Plays

Dracula, Baby (lyrics only). Chicago, Dramatic Publishing Company, 1970.
Wind in the Willows. Elgin, Illinois, Performance, 1972.
A Spell of Evil. Chicago, Dramatic Publishing Company, 1972.
Violence. Elgin, Illinois, Performance, 1972.
Stranger with Roses, adaptation of his own story. Chicago, Dramatic Publishing Company, 1972.
For I Am a Jealous People, adaptation of the story by Lester del Rey. Elgin, Illinois, Performance, 1972.
Gaslight Girl. Chicago, Dramatic Publishing Company, 1973.
Pardon Me, Is This Planet Taken? Chicago, Dramatic Publishing Company, 1973.
Doctor, Doctor!, music by Gilbert M. Martin, adaptation of a play by Molière. New York, McAfee Music, 1973.
Shepherd Song. New York, McAfee Music, 1974.
A Christmas Carol, adaptation of the novel by Dickens (produced, 1989–93).

Other

The Texans Ride North (for children). Philadelphia, Winston, 1952.
Tiros: Weather Eye in Space. New York, Messner, 1966.
Famous Firsts in Sports. New York, Putnam, 1967.
Great War Correspondents. New York, Putnam, 1968.
Great Women Reporters. New York, Putnam, 1969.
Secrets of Stardeep (for children). Philadelphia, Westminster Press, 1969.
Time Gate (for children). Philadelphia, Westminster Press, 1972.
The Bastard Photostory. New York, Berkley, 1980.
Susanna at the Alamo: A True Story (for children). San Diego, Harcourt Brace, 1986.

*

Film Adaptations: *The Bastard*, 1978; *The Rebels*, 1979; *North and South*, 1985; *North and South: Book II*, 1986, from the novel, *Love and War*.

Manuscript Collection: University of Wyoming, Laramie. Thomas Cooper Library, The University of South Carolina, Columbia.

Critical Study: *The Kent Family Chronicles Encyclopedia* edited by Robert Hawkins, New York, Bantam, 1979.

John Jakes comments:

An early interest in historical novels and films, as well as the study of history, led to a series of paperback historical novels in the 1960s. These in turn perhaps presaged the enormous success of the eight-volume 'Kent Family Chronicles' and then the 'North and South Trilogy'. In historical fiction I found, at last, my strength and my real audience. I was gratified when the Los Angeles *Times* referred to me as the 'godfather of historical novelists'.

*   *   *

Few writers have succeeded in popularizing the American Civil War as John Jakes has. He has now joined the ranks of the likes of Margaret Mitchell and James A. Michener in re-creating a highly evocative portrayal of a particular period of history through the eyes of memorable characters. Jakes is probably best known to the general public for his best-selling series of novels chronicling the histories of the Kent family, and for his famous trilogy of the Civil War (*North and South*, *Love and War*, and *Heaven and Hell*).

The 'Kent Family Chronicles' is a series of eight novels covering the lives of several generations of an American family. The first book, *The Bastard*, does not in fact begin in America. The main character, Philippe Charboneau, is the illegitimate son of the Duke of Kentland and a French actress. He travels from his birth place in France to England to claim his heritage but is thwarted by his father's family. Having to fall back on his own resources, he becomes an apprentice printer. Thus, from an inauspicious beginning, the foundations of the Kent publishing house are laid, and a turning point in the fortunes of the Kent family is reached. Philippe decides to change his name to Philip Kent when he travels to America.

The running of the publishing business is an obsession with various members of the Kent family, both male and female. The 'Chronicles' document the turbulent fortunes of the Kent family's publishing concern over the decades against a background of equal turbulence in America's socio-economic and political history. For example, in *The Furies*, the fourth book in the series, the story covers the first half of the 19th century, and centres on an intrepid female member of the Kent family, Amanda de la Gura (née Kent), who is a survivor of the Alamo massacre. She becomes obsessed by the idea of recouping the fortunes of the Kent publishing house, and

in the process of attempting to do so incurs the emnity of a formidable adversary. Jakes convincingly portrays Amanda as a strong, liberated, and intelligent woman who manages to dominate her male contemporaries through force of character—a particularly tough feat in an age when women did not have the vote and were still regarded as their husband's property. A fascinating feature of these books is the involvement of the main Kent character with some legendary historical figures—in Amanda's case, Davy Crockett and Jim Bowie. Jakes somewhat amusingly says of the former: 'The tales about his prowess as a frontiersman—spread throughout the United States in campaign biographies—had been craftily designed, often by Crockett himself, to help him win his races for Congress'.

The Titans, continues the story of Amanda's son, Louis, who is the antithesis of all that Amanda holds dear, being a spoilt and greedy man who intends to profit from both the North and South's involvement in the American Civil War. The book also follows the fortunes of Jeptha Kent, Amanda's cousin's son, who has resigned from his vocation as a minister. Having been forced to leave Lexington because of his pro-abolitionist views, he finds a job as a reporter on a Unionist newspaper in Washington, just prior to the onset of the American Civil War. Jakes uses Jeptha's role as a reporter as a device to set down the events which led to the outbreak of war. It is clear from the immense, but precise detail that Jakes has researched meticulously into the military aspects of the war, ranging from the mundane, abstract details of the numbers of men involved in the various battles to the more personal accounts of the characters involved in the war. One of these characters is Jeptha's son, Gideon, who enlists in the Confederate cavalry. The novel describes war in all its inglorious, destructive form through the eyes of Gideon, who is initially estranged from his father. By the end of the book Gideon is reconciled with his father. Jakes takes the reader through the political thinking of the day and the ideas posited by both the North (the pro-abolitionists) and the South (the pro-secessionists) and the tragedy of civil war. The purging of wrong by blood is a constant theme underlying all the 'Kent Chronicles'. The series finally ends in 1890, the author having maintained a consistently high standard of factual historical accuracy while retaining the reader's interest.

In his well-known trilogy of the Civil War—*North and South*, *Love and War*, and *Heaven and Hell*—Jakes covers the fortunes of two families, the Hazards from Pennsylvania, and the Mains from South Carolina. The first two books in the trilogy were serialized as a mini-series on television. The main protagonists from each family, George Hazard and Orry Main, become firm friends at West Point (their military academy), in 1842. They are from different social backgrounds, and their friendship is tested during the Civil War—a time when brother turned against brother. As in the 'Kent Chronicles', the interesting plot line is interspersed with a minutiae of historical details.

—Sobhana Rowland

———

JAMES, Margaret.   See BENNETTS, Pamela.

———

JAMES, Norah (Cordner).
Nationality: British. **Born:** London, England. **Education:** Francis Holland, London; Slade School of Art, London. **Military service:** Auxiliary Territorial Service. **Career:** former designer of book covers; organizing secretary for Civil Service Clerical Association, England; advertising and publicity manager, Jonathan Cape Ltd, London. Borough councillor for Finsbury, 1945–46. From 1929, a full-time writer. **Member:** National Book League. **Died:** 1979.

ROMANCE AND HISTORICAL PUBLICATIONS

Novels

Sleeveless Errand. London, Scholartis, and New York, Morrow, 1929.
Hail! All Hail!. London, Scholartis, 1929.
Shatter the Dream. London, Constable, 1930; New York, Morrow, 1931.
To the Valiant. New York, Morrow, 1930.
The Wanton Way. New York, Morrow, 1931; as *Wanton Ways*, London, Duckworth, 1931.
Hospital. London, Duckworth, 1932.
Nurse Adriane. London, Duckworth, and New York, Covici Friede, 1933.
Jealousy. New York, Covici Friede, 1933.
Sacrifice. New York, Covici Friede, 1934; as *The Strap-Hangers*, London, Duckworth, 1934.
The Return. London, Duckworth, 1935.
The Lion Beat the Unicorn. London, Duckworth, 1935.
By a Side Wind. London, Jarrolds, 1936.
Two Divided by One. New York, Macauley, 1936.
Sea View. London, Jarrolds, 1936.
The Stars are Fire. London, Cassell, 1937.
Women Are Born to Listen. New York, Macauley, 1937.
As High as the Sky. New York, Macauley, 1938.
The House by the Tree. London, Cassell, 1938.
Mighty City. London, Cassell, 1939.
The Gentlewoman. London, Cassell, 1940.
The Hunted Heart. London, Cassell, 1941.
The Long Journey. London, Cassell, 1941.
Two Selfish People. London, Cassell, 1942.
Enduring Adventure. London, Cassell, 1944.
One Bright Day. London, Cassell, 1945.
The Father. London, Cassell, 1946.
Penny Trumpet. London, Macdonald, 1947.
Brittle Glory. London, Macdonald, 1948.
Swift to Sever. London, Macdonald, 1949.
There Is Always To-morrow. London, Macdonald, 1949.
Pay the Piper. London, Macdonald, 1950.
Pedigree of Honey. London, Macdonald, 1951.
So Runs the River. London, Macdonald, 1952.
A Summer Storm. London, Macdonald, 1953.
Silent Corridors. London, Hutchinson, 1953.
Over the Windmill. London, Hutchinson, 1954.
Wed to Earth. London, Hutchinson, 1955.
Mercy in Your Hands. London, Hutchinson, 1956.
The Flower and the Fruit. London, Hutchinson, 1957.
The True and the Tender. London, Hutchinson, 1958.
The Shadow Between. London, Hutchinson, 1959.
Portrait of a Patient. London, Hutchinson, 1959; as *Tangled Destiny*, London, Hamilton, 1961.
The Uneasy Summer. London, Hutchinson, 1960.
The Wind of Change. London, Hurst and Blackett, 1961.
A Sense of Loss. London, Hutchinson, 1962.
The Green Vista. London, Hurst and Blackett, 1963.
Sister Veronica Greene. London, Hurst and Blackett, 1963.
Bright Day Renewed. London, Hurst and Blackett, 1964.
Small Hotel. London, Hurst and Blackett, 1965.
Hospital Angles. London, Hurst and Blackett, 1966.
Double Take. London, Hurst and Blackett, 1967.
Point of Return. London, Hurst and Blackett, 1968.
There is No Why. London, Hurst and Blackett, 1970.
Ward of Darkness. London, Hurst and Blackett, 1971.
The Doctor's Marriage. London, Hurst and Blackett, 1972.
If Only. London, Hurst and Blackett, 1975.

The Bewildered Heart. London, Hurst and Blackett, 1973.
Love. London, Hurst and Blackett, 1975.

OTHER PUBLICATIONS

Novels (for children)

Tinker the Cat: An Animal Story. London, Dent, 1932.
Jake the Dog: An Animal Story. London, Dent, 1933.
Mrs Piffy. London, Dent, 1934.

Other

Cottage Angles, with engravings by Gwendolyn Raverat. London, Dent, 1935.
I Live in a Democracy (autobiography). London, Longmans, and New York, Longmans, Green, 1939.
Greenfingers and the Gourmet, with Barbara Beauchamp. London, Nicholson and Watson, 1949.
Cooking in Cider. London, World's Work, 1952.

* * *

English writer Norah James achieved notoriety with her first novel *Sleeveless Errand*—which was banned in Britain in 1929 for, among other things, its shocking depravity and blasphemous language.

Considering that *Sleeveless Errand* was written in 1929, it is a frank and brutal depiction of upper-class decadent society. The female protagonist, Paula, lived with her lover for a year before he tells her that he is in love with someone else. 'She would not listen to what Philip was saying; she would not remember that he had ceased to be her lover; that she would never sleep with him again; never feel his weight upon her eager limbs; or his lips moving from her mouth to her breasts'.

Paula goes to a café where she plans her suicide. She meets Bill, the other main character, who has found his wife in bed with his best friend. Paula takes him on a two-day journey of discovery. She introduces him to a society that he has never seen before—one in which the standards of morality that he is used to don't exist. He meets bisexual men and women, he goes to drinking clubs, and is introduced to whores.

Paula and Bill exchange stories. Paula has done everything that would make her seem in the eyes of the reader a 'loose woman'— and her background explains her present situation. Her father started an affair with a local village girl and lived with her secretly in London, Paula's mother drank herself to death. Paula then became involved in the suffrage movement, took up sculpture, and hung around with Irish Sinn Fein artists, before the man whom she loved briefly was killed in the war. She worked as a journalist but then had a severe nervous breakdown. She became financially independent because of a legacy, and then met Philip. Bill's life, in contrast, is normality itself—he comes from a stable home, and married the woman whom he adored.

The couple end up in a hotel where Paula finally decides to kill herself by driving her car off a cliff. Bill intends to go back to his wife whom he realizes he loves despite what she has done. Paula wakes him up and says, 'since last night you must have realized that your wife's simply like a lot of other women. No worse'. She makes a very radical speech about how difficult it is for the women of her generation—the post-war generation—who were given freedom because of the war, were expected to sleep with their men because of the 'tomorrow we die' ethic, who are used to freedom but are now damned because of the lack of available men, and the lives that they have to lead because of this fact. It is an interesting speech, all the more so because of the time in which it was written.

Paula is a much stronger and more clearly defined character than Bill—she decides early on in the book that she wants to die, and the whole work is, in a sense, a journey towards this end. In fact James devotes five pages to Paula's death. Bill is a much weaker character. He cheats death at the end, and returns to his wife instead. He wants to do this all along, but needs Paula to show him the way back to his old life.

James's female characters are strong, independent women; 'free spirits' with a sexual and moral code that is different from the norm, and they are often ostracized or treated badly because of this. Thus, Anna Bond's mother, in *The Flower and the Fruit*, has to live her life with her mentally ill man as penance for an extra-marital affair which resulted in Anna's conception; Judith, in *Hospital Angles*, has to live in the United States after leaving her husband for another man—she is subsequently abandoned by her lover; and Paula pays for her extraordinary life with her death in *Sleeveless Errand*.

While James's male characters are more worthy, they are also less appealing. Ambrose Logan appears dull and mundane in comparison to his flighty wife, Valerie, in *One Bright Day*; both Elizabeth Pellon and Rose, the mother and wife of Matthew Pellon, in *Small Hotel*, are far more interesting than the artistic, dreamy man who is abused and manipulated by the scheming, drinking, promiscuous Rose; and Dennis Rutherford, in *Hospital Angles*, may be an honest, consistent character but his wife, Judith, is more exciting because she has had an affair and has brought up a child independently.

Thus, James tackles subjects avoided by other writers, writing about sexual relationships and morality in a frank but attention-grabbing way. She is always honest, and never sensational in her depiction of women (mostly) who live on the periphery of society. Although James wrote several hospital romances, and other notable books, she is a much forgotten writer—this is a great shame as her work tells the reader a great deal about the life of the privileged classes and society in inter-war Britain.

—P. Campbell

JAMES, Robin.   See **LONDON, Laura.**

JAMES, Sally.   See **OLIVER, Marina.**

JAMES, Stephanie.   See **KRENTZ, Jayne Ann.**

JAMESON, (Margaret) Storm.
Pseudonyms: James Hill, William Lamb. **Nationality:** British. **Born:** Whitby, Yorkshire, 8 January 1891. **Education:** private school, one year at Municipal School, Scarborough, and Leeds University, first class honours in English Language and Literature, B.A. 1912; King's College, London, M.A. 1914. **Relations:** married 1) Clark, in 1914 (divorced 1924); 2) Guy Chapman, in 1926 (died 1972); one son. **Career:** copywriter, advertising agency, 1919; editor, *New Commonwealth*; English representative, publishers, London, 1923–25, and then co-manager, with Guy Patterson Chapman, Alfred Knopf, London; first woman president of British section of international PEN, 1938–45; delegate to UNESCO conference of Arts, Venice, 1952. **Recipient:** International PEN award,

1974, for *There Will Be a Short Interval*. D.Litt.: Leeds University, 1943. **Died:** 30 September 1986.

ROMANCE AND HISTORICAL PUBLICATIONS

Novels (series: Mirror in Darkness; Triumph of Time trilogy; Women Against Men trilogy)

The Pot Boils. London, Constable, 1919.
The Happy Highways. London, Heinemann, and New York, Century, 1920.
The Clash. London, Heinemann, and New York, Little Brown, 1922.
The Pitiful Wife. London, Constable, 1923; New York, Knopf, 1924.
Lady Susan and Life: An Indiscretion. London, Chapman and Dodd, 1924.
Three Kingdoms. London, Constable, and New York, 1926.
Farewell to Youth. London, Heinemann, and New York, Knopf, 1928.
The Triumph of Time: A Trilogy. London, Heinemann, 1932.
　The Lovely Ship. London, Heinemann, and New York, 1927.
　The Voyage Home. London, Heinemann, and New York, Knopf, 1930.
　A Richer Dust. London, Heinemann and New York, Knopf, 1931.
That Was Yesterday (Hervey). London, Heinemann, and New York, Knopf, 1932.
No Time Like the Present. London, Cassell, and New York, Knopf, 1933.
Women Against Men. New York, Knopf, 1933.
　The Single Heart. London, Nicholson and Watson, 1933.
　A Day Off. London, Nicholson and Watson, 1933.
　Delicate Monster. London, Nicholson and Watson, 1937.
Mirror in Darkness (Hervey):
　Company Parade. London, Cassell, and New York, Knopf, 1935.
　Love in Winter. London, Cassell, and New York, Knopf, 1935.
　None Turn Back. London, Cassell, 1936.
　Before the Crossing. New York, Macmillan, 1947.
　The Black Laurel. London, Macmillan 1947; New York, Macmillan, 1948.
The Soul of Man in the Age of Leisure. London, Nott, 1935.
In the Second Year. London, Cassell, and New York, Macmillan, 1936.
The World Ends (as William Lamb). London, Dent, 1937.
Loving Memory (as James Hill). London, Collins, and Boston, Little Brown, 1937.
The Moon Is Making. London, Cassell, 1937; New York, Macmillan, 1938.
No Victory for the Soldier (as James Hill). London, Collins, 1938; New York, Doubleday Doran, 1939.
Here Comes the Candle. London, Cassell, 1938; New York, Macmillan, 1939.
Farewell, Night; Welcome, Day (Hervey). London, Cassell, 1939; as *The Captain's Wife*, New York, Macmillan, 1939.
Cousin Honoré. London, Cassell, 1940; New York, Macmillan, 1941.
The Fort. London, Cassell, and New York, Macmillan, 1942.
Then Shall We Hear Singing: A Fantasy in C Major. London, Cassell, and New York, Macmillan, 1942.
Cloudless May. London, Macmillan, 1943; New York, Macmillan, 1944.
The Journal of Mary Hervey Russell (Hervey). London, Macmillan, and New York, Macmillan, 1945.
The Other Side. London, Macmillan, and New York, Macmillan, 1946.

The Moment of Truth. New York, Macmillan, 1949.
The Green Man. London, Macmillan, 1952; New York, Harper, 1953.
The Hidden River. London, Macmillan, and New York, Harper, 1955.
The Intruder. London, Macmillan, and New York, St Martin's Press, 1956.
A Cup of Tea for Mr Thorgill. New York, Harper, 1957; and London, Macmillan, 1965.
A Ulysses Too Many. London, Macmillan, 1958; as *One Ulysses Too Many*, New York, Harper, 1958.
The Road from the Monument. London, Macmillan, and New York, St Martin's Press, 1962.
A Month Soon Goes. London, Macmillan, and New York, St Martin's Press, 1963.
The Aristide Case. London, Macmillan, 1964; as *The Blind Heart*, New York, Harper and Row, 1964.
The Early Life of Stephen Hind. London, Macmillan, and New York, Harper and Row, 1964.
The White Crow. London, Macmillan, and New York, Harper and Row, 1968.
There Will be a Short Interval. London, Harvill, and New York, Harper and Row, 1973.
The Intruder. London, White Lion, 1977.

OTHER PUBLICATIONS

Short Stories

Europe to Let: The Memoirs of an Obscure Man (novellas). New York, Macmillan, 1941.
A Day Off: Two Short Novels and Some Stories. London, Macmillan, 1959.

Plays

Full Circle: A Play in One Act. Oxford, Blackwell, 1928.

Other

Modern Drama in Europe. London, Collins, and New York, Harcourt, Brace and Howe, 1920.
The Georgian Novel and Mr Robinson. London, Heinemann, and New York, Morrow, 1929.
The Decline of Merry England. London, Cassell, and New York, Bobbs-Merrill, 1930.
The Novel in Contemporary Life. Boston, Writer, 1938.
Civil Journey. London, Cassell, 1939.
The End of This War. London, Allen and Unwin, 1941.
The Writer's Situation and Other Essays. London, Macmillan, 1950; Westport, Connecticut, Greenwood Press, 1977.
Morley Roberts: The Last Eminent Victorian. London, Unicorn, 1961.
Last Score: Or, The Private Life of Sir Richard Ormston. London, Macmillan, and New York, Harper, 1961.
Journey from the North (autobiography), in two vols. London, Collins, 1969, 1970; 1 vol, New York, Harper and Row, 1973.
Parthian Words. London, Collins, 1970; New York, Harper and Row, 1971.
Speaking of Stendhal. London, Gollancz, 1979.

Editor, *Challenge to Death: A Symposium on War and Peace.* London, Constable, 1934; New York, Dutton, 1935.
Editor, *London Calling: A Salute to America*, by Rebecca West, and others. London, Harper, and New York, Harper, 1942.
Editor, *A Kind of Survivor: The Autobiography of Guy Chapman*, by Guy Chapman. London, Gollancz, 1975.

Translator, *Yvette and Other Stories*, by Guy de Maupassant. New York, Knopf, 1924.
Translator, *Mont-Oriol*, by Guy de Maupassant. New York, Knopf, 1924.
Translator, with Ernest Boyd, *Eighty-Eight Short Stories*, by Guy de Maupassant. London, Knopf, 1934.
Translator, with Ernest Boyd, *88 More Stories*, by Guy de Maupaussant. London, Cassell, 1950.

*

Manuscript collections: University of Texas, Austin; Wellesley College, Wellesley, Massachusetts.

*   *   *

Storm Jameson is a prolific novelist who has enjoyed a long career. In some editions of her novels which appeared during the 1940s her fictional oeuvre up to that period was listed under two distinct categories: 'Novels of Personal Life' and 'Novels of the Crisis'. This categorization aptly sums up two main strands in her work, but obscures the way in which her novels of public or political life in fact attempt to show its impact on personal life, particularly by using romance modes to portray her central (normally female) characters.

It is these 'Novels of the Crisis' which show Storm Jameson at her most characteristic, and indeed, it is their combination of public and private worlds, their attempt to give a view of modernity which is both panoramic and personal that makes her work distinctive. For Jameson 'the Crisis' starts with World War I: in her novels the dislocated conditions of modern life thus established have continued ever since.

Her best remembered work is the 'Mirror in Darkness' series (this was originally proposed as a continuation of *The Triumph of Time* trilogy; after writing the first three books, *Company Parade*, *Love in Winter*, *None Turn Back*, Jameson took a break and only returned to the series in 1945). Elaine Feinstein's introduction to the Virago edition of the first of these novels argues that Jameson had 'little time for modernism'. In fact, though, she deploys a range of modernist styles and references to particular modernist works (alongside a range of more traditional devices) as a central strategy in her portrayal of the intersection of personal and public life. Thus there are frequent passages clearly located in characters' minds which give access to thought (particularly that of the female protagonist Hervey Russell) in a way related to a Woolfian 'stream of consciousness', though they are never as freely associative. An example can be seen in the following passage from *Company Parade*:

> ... and so the moment an imagined event emerges into the real world, time seizes on it and gives it a twist that deforms everything. A spring you had supposed dry overflows, the imagined ground gives way, and down you go. How could I have guessed I should cry every night for a year?, she said.

Moreover, the whole trilogy is deeply influenced by T.S. Eliot's *The Waste Land* (1922)—a poem which in her cultural/political essays in *Civil Journey*, Storm Jameson argues is the only 20th-century work of literature able to cope with the representation of the crisis of the modern. A number of sections in the trilogy are given Eliotesque titles ('Rats are Underneath the Piles', 'Unreal City', 'Ebb', 'Und Flutt') and the character Evelyn Lamb, in *Company Parade*, at times draws markedly on the woman in 'A Game of Chess': 'I look old this evening ... Tell me, what shall I do? What shall I ever do?' Images of decay, sterility, dryness, water, and spring also provide constant references to Eliot's poem and to its ideas of cultural crisis. It is notable that two of the men in the series—William Gary and Nicholas Roxby—are literally impotent (like the Fisher King), that another, David Rann, has a serious war-wound in the thigh, that Julian Swann is lame, and that yet two more, George Ling and Penn Vane, are feeble, neurotic, and childish.

These images of post-war masculinity have a large impact on the sequence's use of romance modes. Though it is clearly a romance in terms of many stylistic features and in terms of its central concern with a woman seeking love, there is no straightforwardly 'masculine' man who is available and desirable. Traditionally 'powerful' men are seen as utterly brutal (Thomas Harben, Captain Hunt), and others who are desirable are 'weak' in a number of ways in both their own and women's estimation. Thus Hervey is married first to the childish Penn (who is an emotional and economic parasite), and then to Nicholas Roxby. Nicholas is the 'true love' of romance, but only in a complex way: he fails to provide any clear meaning or stability for Hervey. In fact, it is almost as if Hervey acts the traditional part of the strong partner for him. This 'modified' romance pattern is in itself part of the representation of crisis. However, the trilogy does not simply lament the loss of meaning and meaningful masculinity: it also celebrates Hervey's discovery of her own strong identity in a world of precarious identities.

Storm Jameson sometimes felt that her attempts to treat the 'public' and 'private' together were failures. Indeed, as Elaine Feinstein says in her introduction to *None Turn Back*, Jameson abandoned her original plan of creating a sequence of six novels because she felt that, 'no single novel of the series had a clear centre'. Nevertheless, her attempts to combine romance with politics, modernism with realism give her novels a distinctive feel which is all their own.

—Chris Hopkins

JARMAN, Rosemary Hawley.
Nationality: British. **Born:** Rosemary Josephine Smith in Worcester, 27 April 1935. **Education:** Alice Ottley School, Worcester, 1946–52; studied opera in London, 1952–55. **Relations:** married David C. Jarman in 1958 (divorced 1970). Lives with the writer P.T. Plumb. **Career:** local government officer, Worcester, 1962–68; receptionist, Midlands Electricity, Worcester, 1969; secretary, Rural District Council, Upton on Severn, Worcestershire, 1970. **Recipient:** Silver Quill award, 1971. **Agent:** A.M. Heath, 79 St Martin's Lane, London, WC2N 4AA, England. **Address:** Llanungar Cottage, Whitchurch, Solva, Haverfordwest, Dyfed SA62 6UD, Wales.

ROMANCE AND HISTORICAL PUBLICATIONS

Novels (series: Wars of the Roses)

We Speak No Treason (Wars of the Roses). London, Collins, and Boston, Little Brown, 1971.
The King's Grey Mare (Wars of the Roses). London, Collins, and Boston, Little Brown, 1973; as *Crown of Glory*, New York, Berkley, 1987.
Crown in Candlelight. London, Collins, and Boston, Little Brown, 1978.
The Courts of Illusion (Wars of the Roses). London, Collins, and Boston, Little Brown, 1983.

OTHER PUBLICATIONS

Other

Crispin's Day: The Glory of Agincourt. London, Collins, and Boston, Little Brown, 1979.

*

Rosemary Hawley Jarman comments:

25 years ago I discovered my literary métier—history as it was lived—when I fell totally and irrevocably in love with King Richard III.

Now history became real, the characters fully fleshed, the climate of the times oddly familiar as if I drew upon past experience. To me the 15th century, in which all my work to date is set, was a time for flowers and blood, swords and viols, when courtly manners rode in tandem with dreadful punishments. This was a world which, although light years away in morals and manners, seemed somehow keyed to modern living. Good men went unrewarded even then, and corruption flourished, yet candles bloomed in dusky abbeys, lovers met, and music was made in heaven.

I have always been totally convinced that Richard Plantagenet's historical reputation was the result of a careful propaganda exercise begun by the Tudors and perpetuated by the world's greatest playwright. Academic rehabilitation of this monarch is slowly taking place, but my obsession, when writing *We Speak No Treason*, was to state his case in the best way I could. Research was profound, and intuition flourished as I sought to inform through entertainment; the cause was paramount.

The King's Grey Mare dealt with the Wars of the Roses—seen from the sinister side. The chief protagonist, Elizabeth Woodville, Queen of Edward IV, was responsible in many ways for the machinations which caused Richard's downfall. I gained enough insights to find understanding of, if not sympathy for this 'Witch Queen', and later, summoned enough impartiality to write *Crown in Candlelight*. This novel describes the extraordinary career of Owen ap Tydier, a Welsh esquire who, by his seduction of Henry V's widow, was destined to found the powerful dynasty of Tudor.

The Courts of Illusion rounds off the quartet and is in a way a sequel to the first book. Some of the old characters reappear and the tale is told by the son of the Man of Keen Sight, one of the three principal narrators in *We Speak No Treason*. The novel is crueller, more abrasive than its predecessors, which to me is aptly significant, since its action takes place during the reign of Henry VII, when the golden age of Plantagenet was over. It is also the summation of my defence of Richard, as it shows that Perkin Warbeck (whose character forms the hub of the plot) was indeed no pretender to the English throne but one of the allegedly murdered Princes in the Tower—alive and well.

*   *   *

A turbulent period in England's history known as the Wars of the Roses is brought to life in the works of Rosemary Hawley Jarman. The debate over its most famous participant, Richard III, concerning whether he was truly the callous, evil king portrayed by Shakespeare, has been rekindled in recent years by a spate of fictional accounts—many of which support his innocence. The fact that the man who defeated him at Bosworth, Henry VII, gained more by the deaths of the young princes (in the Tower) than did Richard has given writers such as Jarman much material for speculation.

In the novel *We Speak No Treason*, the reader discovers the compassionate and loyal nature of Richard as seen through the eyes of three narrators. First a young maiden in the service of the Woodvilles comes to love the young Richard, Duke of Gloucester, the confidant of his brother Edward IV. Unfortunately, this young maiden, never named by the author, is betrayed by someone she thought was her friend, and she is forced into a convent where she gives birth to Gloucester's daughter. From another perspective we see Richard through the eyes of the court jester, a young man named Patch. It is

Patch who watches the dogged determination with which Richard finds Anne Neville, the woman that he loves, who has been hidden away by his other brother George, Duke of Clarence. The third narrator, a young soldier when he first meets Richard, finds him to be a kind, generous and inspiring leader.

Richard III was defeated and killed at Bosworth field in 1485. The victor, Henry VII, was the first Tudor king. In *The Courts of Illusion* Jarman portrays life for the defeated Yorkists under Henry through the life of Nicholas Archer, son of a knight loyal to Richard and a man hideously executed for that loyalty. All family properties were forfeit, and Nicholas, along with his family, survives on the charity of relatives. He eventually becomes a follower of a pretender calling himself Richard Plantagenet, one of the young princes purportedly killed by their uncle Richard III. Young Nicholas witnesses the horror of war and lives through the emotional turmoil of losing his family and eventually the Yorkist cause for which so many gave their lives. His travels take him from England to France and to Flanders where the beauty of the lush countryside and the old mediaeval cities is gloriously brought to life through lush descriptions of the locales and their people. Eventually young Nicholas finds a certain peace within himself, and retires to live with the Grey Friars of Leicester, close to the tomb of Richard III.

The author has intertwined the characters of these two novels. The maiden of *We Speak No Treason* makes an appearance as a nun maddened by grief, following Richard's body as it is taken from Bosworth Field. And the court jester Patch, now an old man and nearly blind, comes to know Nicholas through the young man's friendship with Patch's sons.

To understand the downfall of the House of York one must understand Elizabeth Woodville, wife to Edward IV, and her highly ambitious family. In *We Speak No Treason*, Jarman portrays Elizabeth's mother, Jacquetta, as a sorceress who uses her special herbs and incantations to cause Edward IV to marry her widowed daughter. In *The King's Grey Mare*, Elizabeth's story from the time she is a young girl to her death as Dowager Queen sweeps through much of England's bloodiest history. Her first husband, a Lancastrian knight, dies in battle, but not long after she snares the heart of the victorious Yorkist king, Edward IV. Her world comes undone after Edward's death when Richard of Gloucester declares himself king and her children to be illegitimate. For this she embraces the cause of Henry Tudor, but this does not bring her peace. Jarman, in a bit of historical revisionism, shows Henry Tudor to be the culprit in the slaying of the young princes and not the much maligned Richard.

The Wars of the Roses began with Richard II—a Lancastrian, and ended with Richard III—a Yorkist. This historic panorama has been fertile ground for Jarman's rich imagination and evocative prose. *Crown and Candlelight* gives insight into the beginning as well as the end of this terrible war. Isabelle, a daughter of the mad French king, Charles VI, is second wife to Richard II of England. Henry Bolingbroke usurps the throne and has Richard killed. He is succeeded by his son, Henry V, who marries Katherine, another daughter of the French king. Katherine soon finds herself a widow, and her infant son, the future Henry VI. A young and lonely young woman she begins a liaison with a landless Welshman, Owen Tudor. It is their grandson who is victorious at Bosworth.

The Byzantine intrigues of the English and French courts can be mindboggling. Add to this the number of major players all with the same name and the confusion can overwhelm the most passionate history buff. Jarman is a writer of great clarity who can juggle all the machinations of the various characters, give each a distinctive personality, and weave the threads of an intricate plot, all the while keeping the reader absorbed to the end. The author's detailed research into her subject comes across on every page. Not that she overwhelms or shows off her knowledge, she simply keeps the reader firmly planted in that long ago time.

In addition to these works of fiction, Jarman has written *Crispin's*

Day: The Glory of Agincourt, a detailed and lucid account of Henry V's surprising victory over the French.

—Patricia Altner

JASON, Veronica.   See **JOHNSTON, Velda.**

JENNINGS, Gary.
Pseudonym: Gabriel Quyth. **Nationality:** American. **Born:** Buena Vista, Virginia, 20 September 1928. **Education:** Art Students' League, New York, 1949–51. **Military Service:** United States Army Infantry, 1952–54: Bronze Star. **Relations:** one son. **Career:** advertising copywriter and account executive, New York, 1947–52, 1954–58; newspaper reporter, California and Virginia, 1958–61; managing editor, *Duke* and *Gent* magazines, New York, 1962–63. **Agent:** McIntosh and Otis Inc, 310 Madison Avenue, New York, New York 10017, USA. **Address:** PO Box 1371, Lexington, Virginia 24450, USA.

ROMANCE AND HISTORICAL PUBLICATIONS

Novels

Sow the Seeds of Hemp. New York, Norton, 1976.
Aztec. New York, Atheneum, 1980; London, Macdonald, 1981.
The Journeyer. New York, Atheneum, and London, Hutchinson, 1984.
Spangle. New York, Atheneum, 1987; London, Muller, 1988.
Raptor. New York, Doubleday, and London, Hutchinson, 1992.

OTHER PUBLICATIONS

Novels

The Terrible Teague Bunch. New York, Norton, 1975.
The Lively Lives of Quentin Mobey (as Gabriel Quyth). New York, Atheneum, 1988.

Other (for children)

March of the Robots. New York, Dial Press, 1962.
The Movie Book. New York, Dial Press, 1963.
Black Magic, White Magic. New York, Dial Press, 1964; London, Hart Davis, 1967.
Parades! Philadelphia, Lippincott, 1966.
The Killer Storms. Philadelphia, Lippincott, 1970.
The Teenager's Realistic Guide to Astrology. New York, Association Press, 1971.
The Shrinking Outdoors. Philadelphia, Lippincott, 1972.
The Earth Book. Philadelphia, Lippincott, 1974.
March of the Heroes. New York, Association Press, 1975.
The Rope in the Jungle. Philadelphia, Lippincott, 1976.
March of the Gods. New York, Association Press, 1976.
March of the Demons. New York, Association Press, 1977.

Other

Personalities of Language. New York, Crowell, 1965; London, Gollancz, 1967; as *World of Words*, New York, Atheneum, 1984.

The Treasure of the Superstition Mountains. New York, Norton, 1973.

*

Manuscript Collection: Boston University, Massachusetts.

Gary Jennings comments:

I choose for my novels a subject, an historical incident, or an era that has never before been treated in fiction—or that I believe has not been *adequately* treated. Each of my novels involves a journey of both extent and duration, and (I hope) illustrates and celebrates the perdurability of human beings. That theme appears to have a fairly universal appeal.

*　　*　　*

Initially a non-fiction for youth writer, Gary Jennings later turned to adult fiction. These novels display marked characteristics of his early work, including well-researched historical times and events; a well-told story (often encircling on a young hero whose rite of passage involves undergoing an arduous life-journey with consequent loss of innocence and gain of mature, less idealistic *Weltanschauung*); and themes of betrayal and survival.

Following *The Terrible Teague Bunch*, a comic western about a turn-of-the-century Texas cowpuncher who ineptly attempts train robbery, the earliest representative example of Jennings's fiction is *Sow the Seeds of Hemp*. The factual story brings Virgil Stewart, a young 1830s tradesman, to a Mississippi town where, at the urgings of a self-seeking prospective father-in-law, he becomes a spy in the thieving band of notorious John Murrell, to bring him to justice for operating a slave-stealing network along the Gulf Coast. During a harrowing journey, Steward witnesses sufficient wrongdoings to betray the robber chieftain, who has befriended him. However, finding himself subsequently betrayed and impoverished by the 'good people' who prove inferior to the charismatic Murrell, the now wiser hero must begin life anew. Characterization and period detail are better developed in later work.

A similarly swiftly-paced story with an odyssey-surviving hero and theme of betrayal is the basis of Jennings's finest novel, *Aztec*. This monumental work unfolds the drama of the 16th-century Aztec civilization and Spanish conquest as told by an elderly Mexicatl, Mixtl (Dark Cloud), who, commanded by the victorious Spaniards' priest to be a chronicler of the past, is burned at the stake as a heretic after his tale is told. Born in his people's capital a half-century before Cortes's arrival, Mixtl recounts travels thorough Mexico as scribe, merchant, warrior, and finally advisor to Montezuma. On his way, Mixtl encounters betrayal and treachery, a variety of sexual adventures, and life-threatening episodes involving such cruelty and violence as, for example, reluctant servitude to a princess who makes sculptures of murdered lovers' corpses. Amidst treachery and disloyalty, Mixtl reaches manhood as a survivor. His life-journey ends with the arrival of sadistic, gold-hungry, horse-mounted conquistadors who ravage and plunder, quelling thousands of spear-carrying Aztecs by cannon, cross-bow, smallpox and treachery. The novel allows the amiable narrator with his undertone of obsequious defiance to draw ironic parallels between Aztec and Spanish customs and inhumanity. *Aztec* possesses abundant detail about the culture, customs, daily life, and religion reflecting Jennings's meticulous research. Moreover, his story never loses momentum or suspense. Filled with lively, picaresque adventures, interlaced with episodes of eroticism and violence which commonly serve constructive story telling purpose, *Aztec* is a gripping work of historical fiction whose narration evokes an exotic culture existing for two centuries before the Conquest.

Less brilliant, but also absorbing, is *The Journeyer*, effectively evoking Marco Polo's personal story from the interstices of his own historical account. Having been banished from Venice at the age of 17 after an unjust accusation of murder, Marco accompanies his father and uncle to the Orient, undertaking maturing experiences and gaining a position of importance with Kublai Khan. While the elders dedicate themselves to trading, Marco adventurously journeys through Italy, the Middle East, Central and Southeast Asia. The impressive account delineates a wide variety of cultural and social life with finely detailed descriptions of the landscape, climes, flora and fauna, mixed with hazards in the bleak Gobi desert, in Asian jungles, or in the chamber of the Great Khan's official torturer. The first-person narrative is replete with bizarre sexual and violence-filled episodes, yet Jennings does not idealize violence (Marco is disgusted by it), nor does he stoop to fake mysticism and solemnity, but instead frequently offers a tone of irreverence and satirical observation. Jennings combines extensive research with the yarn-spinner's art, drawing a distinctive portrait of Marco as he methodically accomplishes his development toward maturity while retaining a certain naiveté. A compelling story of derring-do, *The Journeyer* has humour, vivid detail, and sustained narrative drive.

With a more contemporary setting, *Spangle* centres on a collective protagonist, an impoverished circus. Initially stranded in Virginia after the American Civil War, the circus sails for Europe, where it gradually recoups its fortunes and arrives in Paris after six years, to be trapped in that city's siege during the Franco-Prussian War. Jennings creates a lively 19th-century world of circus lore, exotic locales, and a characteristic plenitude of violence and sex. The multitude of characters are rather sketchily drawn in this tangled yet entertaining tale of the Big Top.

More successful is the 1992 novel *Raptor*. It spins an exciting saga of a 5th-century Goth wanderer and hermaphrodite Thorn, who becomes friend and counsellor to Theodoric the Great, the Ostrogoth king who temporarily revitalized the decaying Empire upon becoming Emperor of Rome. The orphan hero's dual sexuality, discovered at the age of 12 when raped in a monastery, generates many graphically described, barely credible, sexual encounters and adventurous escapades. Exiled from the monastery, Thorn becomes a travelling companion to an old Roman centurion, poses as a rich merchant while learning to exploit both his male and female aspects, encounters an evil 'twin' who shares his sexual duality, and finally joins his fellow Ostrogoths in the cause of the young king Theodoric, serving him throughout his historical conquest. The ability of the hero, whom the novel takes from youth to middle age, to act either as a man or woman serves him and his king well, and furnishes him with a nature providing interesting perspectives of events. This impressive epic richly re-creates the world of fifth-century Europe through the eyes of a hero uncommon in fact or fiction. Here again, Jennings's power as a storyteller shines through.

In a 1987 article, Jennings advised that the achievement of verisimilitude and the knowledge of every detail of a story's time, place, and characters are essential for writers of historical fiction. He practises what he preaches. He is a historical novelist of the first order.

—Christian H. Moe

———

JENNINGS, Sara.   See **SEGER, Maura.**

———

JHABVALA, Ruth Prawer.
Nationality: American. **Born:** Cologne, Germany, 7 May, 1927; sister of the writer S.S. Prawer. Moved to England as a refugee, 1939; became British citizen, 1948. Lived in India, 1951–75, and in New York from 1975; now an American citizen. **Education:** Hendon County School, London; Queen Mary College, University

of London, 1945–51, M.A. in English literature, 1951. **Relations:** married Cyrus S.H. Jhabvala in 1951; three daughters. **Career:** Since 1951, full-time writer. Close working relationship with the producers and directors James Ivory and Ismail Merchant. **Recipient:** Booker prize, 1975, for *Heat and Dust*; Guggenheim fellowship, 1976; Neil Gunn international fellowship, 1978; MacArthur fellowship, 1984; Oscar for best screen adaptation, 1987, for *A Room with a View*, and, 1993, for *Howard's End*. **Agent:** Harriet Wasserman, 137 East 36th Street, New York, New York 1001, USA. **Address:** 400 East 52nd Street, New York, New York 10022, USA.

ROMANCE AND HISTORICAL PUBLICATIONS

Novels

To Whom She Will. London, Allen and Unwin, 1955; as *Amrita*, New York, Norton, 1956.
The Nature of Passion. London, Allen and Unwin, 1956; New York, Norton, 1957.
Esmond in India. London, Allen and Unwin, 1957; New York, Norton, 1958.
The Householder. London, Murray, and New York, Norton, 1960.
Get Ready for Battle. London, Murray, 1962; New York, Norton, 1963.
A Backward Place. London, Murray, and New York, Norton, 1965.
A New Dominion. London, Murray, 1972; as *Travelers*, New York, Harper, 1973.
Heat and Dust. London, Murray, 1975; New York, Harper, 1976.
In Search of Love and Beauty. London, Murray, and New York, Morrow, 1983.
Three Continents. London, Murray, and New York, Morrow, 1987.
Poet and Dancer. London, Murray, 1993.

OTHER PUBLICATIONS

Short Stories

Like Birds, Like Fishes and Other Stories. London, Murray, 1963; New York, Norton, 1964.
A Stronger Climate: Nine Stories. London, Murray, 1968; New York, Norton, 1969.
An Experience of India. London, Murray, 1971; New York, Norton, 1972.
How I Became a Holy Mother and Other Stories. London, Murray, and New York, Harper, 1976.
Out of India: Selected Stories. New York, Morrow, 1986; London, Murray, 1987.

Plays

Shakespeare Wallah: A Film, with James Ivory, with *Savages*, by James Ivory. London, Plexus, and New York, Grove Press, 1973.
Autobiography of a Princess, Also Being the Adventures of an American Film Director in the Land of Maharajas, with James Ivory and John Swope. London, Murray, and New York, Harper, 1975.
A Call from the East (produced New York, 1981).

Screenplays: *The Householder*, 1963; *Shakespeare Wallah*, with James Ivory, 1965; *The Guru*, 1968; *Bombay Talkie*, 1970; *Autobiography of a Princess*, 1975; *Roseland*, 1976; *Hullabaloo over Georgie and Bonnie's Pictures*, 1978; *The Europeans*, 1979; *Jane Austen in Manhattan*, 1980; *Quartet*, 1981; *Heat and Dust*, 1983; *The Bostonians*, 1984; *A Room with a View*, 1986; *Madame Sousatzka*, with

John Schlesinger, 1988; *Mr and Mrs Bridge*, 1990; *Howard's End*, 1991; *The Remains of the Day*, 1992.

Television Play: *The Place of Peace*, 1975.

Other

Meet Yourself at the Doctor (published anonymously). London, Naldrett Press, 1949.

*

Film adaptations: *Shakespeare Wallah*, 1965; *Heat and Dust*, 1982.

Critical Studies: *The Fiction of Ruth Prawer Jhabvala* by H.M. Williams, Calcutta, Writer's Workshop, 1973; 'A Jewish Passage to India' by Renee Winegarten, in *Midstream* (New York), March 1974; *Ruth Prawer Jhabvala* by Vasant A. Shahane, New Delhi, Arnold-Heinemann, 1976; *Silence, Exile and Cunning: The Fiction of Ruth Prawer Jhabvala* by Yasmine Gooneratne, New Delhi, Orient Longman and London, Sangam, 1983; *Cross-Cultural Interaction in Indian Fiction: An Analysis of the Novels of Ruth Prawer Jhabvala and Kamala Markandaya* by Ramesh Chadha, New Delhi, National Book Organisation, 1988; *The Fiction of Ruth Prawer Jhabvala* by Laurie Sucher, London, Macmillan, 1988; *The Novels of Kamala Markandaya and Ruth Prawer Jhabvala* by Rekha Jha, New Delhi, Prestige, 1990.

*   *   *

The basis for the majority, and certainly the most significant works of Ruth Prawer Jhabvala is, first and foremost, the *contemporary* history of India as seen through the lives of Indians and Westerners who live there. In common with many other ancient lands India is a country where that which appears to be contemporary is in reality antique, and it is this conceit that forms the core of her work as a novelist.

Jhabvala's childhood was moulded and marked by the historical events in Germany of the 1930s, which culminated in her move to England in 1939. Her survival there as a teenager was in the knowledge that her friends and relations had been annihilated in the Holocaust. As she noted in an interview with Eamlal Agarwal in 1974: 'I was practically born a displaced person, and all anybody ever wanted was a travel document and a residential permit. One just didn't care so long as one was allowed to live somewhere'.

In 1951 she married Parsi architect Cyrus Jhabvala, who brought her to India for the first time—an accident not without historical resonance. The Parsis, Zoroastrian immigrants to India from ancient Persia have a history of displacement, and ironically enough, it was Cyrus the Great, the Persian ruler who freed the Jews held captive in Babylonia, who is a historical figure particularly dear to Jewish tradition. Thus, with her personal history of displacement Jhabvala appears to be a writer whose own life is representative of the times in which we live, a period of history that will no doubt be typified in future ages by the figure of the wanderer and the refugee.

Jhabvala's canon can be divided, broadly speaking, into three distinct phases, thus establishing a pattern which bears a distinct resemblance to the European 'cycle of experience' outlined and discussed in her autobiographical essay 'Myself in India':

There is a cycle that Europeans—by Europeans I mean all Westerners, including Americans—tend to pass through. It goes like this: first stage, tremendous enthusiasm—everything Indian is marvellous; second stage, everything Indian is not so marvellous; third stage, everything Indian abominable.

Her early novels, including *Esmond In India, To Whom She Will*, and *The Nature of Passion*, present a vivid and colourful picture of the East, where 'everything Indian' clearly fired the young author's imagination, and where a plethora of Indian protagonists form a favourable contrast to their less numerous and unimpressive western counterparts. Despite the skilful use of irony and comedy, which serves to distance Jhabvala from her protagonists, Jhabvala is firmly and willingly immersed in the history, culture, and climate of the Indian landscape. Conflict between West and East, or future and past, when it figures at all, is often envisaged as the unpleasant result of a process of 'westernization'—an influence which is continually undermined and discredited.

With the publication of *Like Birds, Like Fishes* and *A Backward Place*, however, Jhabvala clearly entered a new creative phase. Her narrative focus expanded to include a far greater proportion of western protagonists whose mixed impressions of India create a spectrum of possible western attitudes. *A Backward Place*, with its emphasis on unsatisfactory western role playing, and its oblique criticism of surrendering to a specifically eastern type of mental stagnation, suggests that Jhabvala's evident dissatisfaction with the conventional western novel as a means of conveying Eastern experience, stems, ironically, from her growing recognition of, and unconscious alignment with, a distinct and 'alien' set of western cultural standards and traditions. The novels of this period accordingly reinforce the validity of a separate western perspective, and set up the possibility of the traditional East/West conflict so dominant in *A New Dominion* and *A Stronger Climate*.

Here Jhabvala is clearly in retreat from an abominable India; a personal position which produces, in creative terms, the most bitter and damaging of her eastern portraits to date. Hostile and remote, Jhabvala appears to focus with a mixture of scorn, resignation, and compassion upon the machinations and antics of her characters—a collection of pitiful and naive western protagonists, whose Indian adventures inexorably end in disaster, and whose function seems reduced at times to the symbolic representation of the different aspects of the author's own pronounced disillusionment. Still further light is shed upon the intolerable personal toll of the struggle between East and West, so dominant in Jhabvala's work by her eventual departure from India in 1975.

Heat and Dust explores, more than any other of Jhabvala's works, not only the East/West divide, but also the conceit that the contemporary, especially in the case of ancient India, is to be found deeply rooted in the past. The theme of endurance and survival, so central to *Heat and Dust*'s immediate literary antecedents, is present more than ever.

The plot intertwines the life of a young woman, in the 1970s, who has come to India on a whim to find out more about her relative Olivia Rivers, who, in the 1920s left her English civil-servant husband for a local ruler. The novel contrasts a period of British culture when involvement with natives was avoided and when it was romantic to defy such social conventions, with a more contemporary setting, when hippies and drop-outs litter the Indian scene. Jhabvala's nameless narrator records objectively the romance of colonial India and her own, fairly flat existence there. She assumes Indian dress and customs, has an affair with her Indian landlord, and, pregnant, travels up to the mountains to visit the place where Olivia spent the last years of life, seeking to understand the undocumented conclusion of her life.

In her rejection of England for 'a simpler and more natural way of life' in India, Jhabvala's narrator moves her romanticization from the past to the present: her 'isolation' in London is contrasted with her sense of the 'community' in India. In essence the narrator has been driven to India by her own sense of failure, and she is ultimately driven to despair as she confuses romantic myths with the poverty, indifference, and cruelty of Indian life. As a final frantic gesture she escapes to the snow-covered mountains in an effort to find *sanyasi*, the fourth stage of life granted after withdrawal from the hurly burly of worldly activity.

Whether referring to her earlier films like *Shakespeare Wallah*, *Bombay Talkie*, *The Guru*, or any of her later novels there is a sense that a line is being drawn not merely along the boundary of contemporary and ancient India but between the timeless and the ephemeral. The simple fact that Jhabvala ostensibly chooses (almost) consistently throughout her work to turn her back on the great Indian *issues*—Independence, the Raj, colonial England—and focus on *people*, reveals a very credible and sustainable understanding of India, both past and present, and the Westerner's relationship to it. As V.S. Naipaul points out in *An Area of Darkness*, 'The only writer who, while working from within the society, is yet able to impose on it a vision which is an acceptable type of comment, is Ruth Prawer Jhabvala'. Naipaul considered the contemporary crisis of India as 'the larger crisis of a wounded old civilization that has at last become aware of its inadequacies and is without the intellectual means to move ahead'. In that context, Jhabvala, ironic observer *par excellence*, provides via her fiction an India with a strong mysterious presence, half-mediaeval, half modern, immensely old, intensely spiritual, scarred by unimaginable cruelties, blessed with indescribable beauty and burdened by inescapable poverty.

—Mike Downey

JOHANSEN, Iris.
Nationality: American. **Address:** c/o Bantam Publishing, 666 Fifth Avenue, New York, New York 10103, USA.

ROMANCE AND HISTORICAL PUBLICATIONS

Novels (series: Delaneys; Shamrock; Wind Dancer Trilogy)

Stormy Vows. New York, Bantam, 1983.
Tempest at Sea. New York, Bantam, 1983.
The Reluctant Lark. New York, Bantam, 1983.
The Bronzed Hawk. New York, Bantam, 1983.
The Lady and the Unicorn. New York, Bantam, 1984.
The Golden Valkyrie. New York, Bantam, 1984.
The Trustworthy Redhead. New York, Bantam, 1984.
Return to Santa Flores. New York, Bantam, 1984.
No Red Roses. New York, Bantam, 1984.
Capture the Rainbow. New York, Bantam, 1984.
Touch the Horizon. New York, Bantam, 1984.
The Forever Dream. New York, Bantam, 1985.
White Satin. New York, Bantam, 1985.
Blue Velvet. New York, Bantam, 1985.
A Summer Smile. New York, Bantam, 1985.
And the Desert Blooms. New York, Bantam, 1986.
Always. New York, Bantam, 1986.
Everlasting. New York, Bantam, 1986.
York the Renegade (Shamrock). New York, Bantam, 1986.
'Til the End of Time. New York, Bantam, 1987.
Matilda the Adventuress (Delaneys). New York, Bantam, 1987.
Last Bridge Home. New York, Bantam, 1987.
Across the River of Yesterday. New York, Bantam, 1987.
The Spellbinder. New York, Bantam, 1987.
Magnificent Folly. New York, Bantam, 1987.
Wild Silver (Delaneys). New York, Bantam, 1988.
Satin Ice (Delaneys). New York, Bantam, 1988.
One Touch of Topaz. New York, Bantam, 1988.
Star Light, Star Bright. New York, Bantam, 1988.
This Fierce Splendor. New York, Bantam, 1988.
Man from Half Moon Bay. New York, Bantam, 1988.
Blue Skies and Shining Promises. New York, Bantam, 1988.

Strong, Hot Winds. New York, Bantam, 1988.
Notorious. New York, Bantam, 1990.
Wicked Jake Darcy. New York, Bantam, 1990.
Tender Savage. New York, Bantam, 1991.
Wind Dancer Trilogy:
    The Wind Dancer. New York, Bantam, 1991.
    Storm Winds. New York, Bantam, 1991
    Reap the Wind. New York, Bantam, 1991.
The Golden Barbarian. New York, Bantam, 1992.
The Tiger Prince. New York, Bantam, 1993.
Star Spangled Bride. New York, Bantam, 1993.
The Magnificent Rogue. New York, Bantam, 1993.
The Beloved Scoundrel. New York, Bantam, 1994.

*   *   *

Iris Johansen is one of the most prolific and innovative writers of romance fiction. She has stretched the boundaries of the standard formulas in the category romance field and has written some of the best historical romance novels.

Beginning with her first Loveswept novel in 1983, *Stormy Vows*, Johansen has linked many of her novels with recurring characters. *The Golden Valkyrie* introduced the first in a long line of interconnected stories about the inhabitants of two imaginary present-day countries. The Middle Eastern kingdom of Sedikhan is featured most prominently, but the Balkan kingdom of Tamrovia is occasionally used as a locale. They are linked through the royal families, the Ben Raschids and the Rubinoffs. Even some of the characters from the first novels make brief appearances or are mentioned in these subsequent books. Although other novels intervene, Johansen returns time and again to Sedikhan and Tamrovia. Some of these stories are especially poignant. David Bradford, a recovering drug addict introduced in *The Trustworthy Redhead*, is shown to have found peace and finds love in *Touch the Horizon*. His love is Billie Callahan, a generous waif, who played a major role in *Capture the Rainbow*. Later, in *A Summer Smile*, Johansen tells the story of Zilah, a young girl who had been sold into prostitution but was rescued by David. She finds her peace and happiness with Daniel Seifert, who himself appeared earlier in *Blue Velvet*. Gradually Johansen has created a far-flung, but related world. Sedikhan also figures in two novels in which Johansen crosses over into fantasy. Both *Last Bridge Home* and *Star Light, Star Bright* use Sedikhan as a refuge for the Clanad, people with very special powers who are persecuted by a shadowy government agency. In *The Golden Barbarian*, she returns to tell the story of the founding of the Sedikhan dynasty.

Johansen has collaborated with two other romance writers, Kay Hooper and Fayrene Preston, on a series of novels. Each author wrote one book in the 'Shamrock Trilogy', which tells the story of the Delaney brothers. Johansen's contribution is *York the Renegade*. The family series was continued when the three authors created the 'Delaneys of Killaroo' series. This time the focus was on three sisters in the Australian branch of the family, with Johansen contributing *Matilda the Adventuress*. Obviously having developed a real winner in the romance field, the three writers have continued with two Delaney 'prequel' trilogies: 'The Untamed Years' and 'The Untamed Years II'. Johansen's contributions in these series are, respectively, *Wild Silver* and *Satin Ice*. Both follow the story of Silver Delaney and the Russian Prince Nicholas Savron. Johansen also wrote a longer novel, *This Fierce Splendor*, which is the story of Dominic Delaney and Elspeth MacGregor, the first of the Delaney clan. Her novella, 'Christmas Past', appears in the collection, *The Delaney Christmas Carol*.

Johansen's solo 'Wind Dancer Trilogy' (*The Wind Dancer*, *Storm Winds*, *Reap the Wind*) follows the fortunes of the Andreas family across the centuries as they pursue the legendary golden statue of Pegasus called the Wind Dancer. The first two novels, set in 16th-century Italy and the French Reign of Terror, are fast-paced and have well-drawn characters. Lorenzo Vasaro (*The Wind Dancer*), in particular, is one of her most moving and memorable characters. Although he is a secondary character, he is so vividly drawn that he almost eclipses the hero, Lionello Andreas. Lorenzo's tragic love for Caterina seems to cry out for a happier ending for him in another novel, but Johansen merely alludes to his life in *Storm Winds*, which takes place 300 years after his lifetime. The last volume of the trilogy, set in the contemporary world, is less satisfying. The introduction of the KGB, CIA, rogue agents, and terrorist plots to destabilize Europe all seem forced in the context of the romance. However, a disappointing novel by Johansen is still far better than the work of many other authors.

Most of Johansen's novels feature at least one lengthy seduction scene of the heroine by the hero. At times there is an element of punishment in the hero's actions as when Ruel MacClaren misuses Jane Barnaby in *The Tiger Prince*, or Galen Ben Raschid, in *The Golden Barbarian*, disciplines Princess Theresa Rubinoff. Johansen, however, makes it clear that even when the woman is being humiliated by her vulnerability to the man's seduction and her inability to resist him, she is in no real danger of physical harm. Deep down, he cannot hurt her because he loves her. However, the uncertainty of remaining safely on the edge of possible pain adds sexual tension to the stories.

Johansen's skill as a romance writer and her willingness to experiment with new storylines and formats has firmly established her as one of the leading authors of romance fiction writing today. Her ability to create memorable characters who live in the minds of her readers is among the best in the genre. Her reputation as one of the stars of romance fiction is well-deserved.

—Barbara E. Kemp

———

JOHN, Nancy. See **BUCKINGHAM, Nancy.**

———

JOHNSON, Barbara Ferry.
Nationality: American. **Born:** Grosse Pointe, Michigan, 7 July 1923. **Education:** Northwestern University, Evanston, Illinois, B.S. 1945; Clemson University, South Carolina, M.A. 1964. **Relations:** married William David Johnson in 1947; one son and two daughters. **Career:** associate editor, *American Lumberman* magazine, Chicago, 1945–48; high school English teacher, Myrtle Beach, South Carolina, 1960–62. Since 1964, member of the English department, Columbia College, South Carolina. **Agent:** Writers House Inc, 21 West 26th Street, New York, New York 10010, USA. **Address:** 4207 Sequoia Road, Columbia, South Carolina 29206, USA.

ROMANCE AND HISTORICAL PUBLICATIONS

Novels

Lionors. New York, Avon, 1975; London, Sphere, 1977.
Delta Blood. New York, Avon, 1977; London, Sphere, 1978.
Tara's Song. New York, Avon, 1978; London, Sphere, 1980.
Homeward Winds the River. New York, Avon, 1979; London, Sphere, 1980.
The Heirs of Love. New York, Avon, 1980.
Echoes from the Hills. New York, Warner, 1983; London, Sphere, 1984.

* * *

Barbara Ferry Johnson is most interested in the confrontation of men and women from alien cultures and alien backgrounds; she depicts the way love helps them transcend personal prejudices and personal limitations to come to terms with another's values and to learn to see with new eyes. In *Tara's Song* an English earl's daughter, taken from a convent in a Viking raid, learns to love a Viking prince and his family, appreciate their values, and fight for their causes. In *Lionors* King Arthur's first love must learn from Merlin and Arthur to see with Nature's eyes, and to sacrifice personal need for a nation's vision as her lover is transformed from an orphan of little significance to King of England. In *Delta Blood* and *Homeward Winds the River* a New Orleanean octoroon, Leah, attempts to escape the restrictions imposed by her black blood, but love and war transform her perceptions and lead her to defend southern values and southern traditions against Union barbarism and hypocrisy, to work uncomplainingly as a nurse comforting wounded Confederate soldiers, and to help save both them and a plantation (the symbol of the slave tradition which has constricted and limited her life) from death and destruction. In *Homeward* she moves north to fulfil her life-long dream—to pass for white, only to learn that each person is trapped in some way, if not by skin colour, then by differences in values and ways of life, and that her heritage, though black, is also southern. The final book in this trilogy, *The Heirs of Love*, traces her children's attempts to come to terms with their white/black heritage, and to discover who and what they are and where they truly belong. In *Echoes from the Hills* a young Belgian girl, Alys Prevou, in love with a resistance fighter killed by the Germans, must first come to terms with her rape by arrogant, vengeful German officers, and then with the child that it produces. Later she chances loss of family and execution to save, protect, and nurture a comatose, then aphasic and amnesiac American soldier, knowing all the while that his recovery of memory will mean his loss of all knowledge of her and her love and aid. In each of these books Johnson's heroines must adapt to changing conditions of war and conflict, death, disease, and drudgery, and somehow maintain their spirit and inspire their men to endure seemingly impossible difficulties. Johnson's women are strong and enduring. Despite their emotional conflicts, they learn to cope, to survive, and to lend strength and courage to those around them. Where others would yield, they determinedly and selflessly persist.

Mystic elements play important roles in these sagas: magic runes embodying ancient secrets in *Tara's Song*, seers and magicians in *Lionors*, voodoo rites and voodoo princesses in the New Orleans trilogy, and deep-seated, subconscious psychological responses in *Echoes from the Hills*. Yet each is down-to-earth in its specific detailing of the difficult day-to-day skills women in different ages have had to master, particularly skills vital to the continuation of life and comfort, work borne of necessity in hard times—learning to cultivate the land, organize help, preserve and store food, sew, redecorate, rear children, nurse, and even fight. Typical is the heroine of *Echoes from the Hills*, who, her world a no-man's land dominated by Americans and Germans in turn, none-the-less manages to produce and raise two children, support her aging parents, teach and tend the children of her war-torn neighbourhood, and nurse the wounded of both sides. Intrigued by the genetic complexities that reproduce, modify, and mould each generation, Johnson examines child-parent conflicts, advocates different approaches to child-rearing for different psychologies, and suggests the difficulty of ever predicting the final results of environment and genes.

The focus of her books is the psychology of women's love—Lionors who must hide her love despite her deep romantic yearnings; Tara who fears love's betrayal, and learns its selflessness only after suffering slavery, imprisonment, and culture shock in Turkey; Leah whose emotional and physical needs lead her to become a rich plantation owner's mistress when her deeper longing is to be a wife and mother; and Alys, whose husband has totally forgotten not only their love but her very existence, but who keeps silent to protect his privacy and to free him to choose with a whole mind. Each of Johnson's heroines is threatened by or endures brutal attack by libidinous males; each finds strength and comfort in a deeply romantic and sexually satisfying love that demands sacrifice and understanding. Each must deal with rivals in love; and each must help her beloved regain his sense of vitality and manhood which injury and humiliation threaten.

Though Johnson makes occasional minor slips in locale and custom, in the main her books conjure up past times with delightful detail, clearly and carefully evoking the hardships and pleasures of bygone ages to make the alien familiar. Although they vividly depict the psychology of men in war and conflict, they focus most particularly on the psychology of women, abandoned, maltreated, loved, or disdained, and are a tribute to the strengths that have made men and women and love endure, despite the insanities that beset them.

—Gina Macdonald

JOHNSON, Susan.
Nationality: American. **Born:** Hibbing, Minnesota, 7 June 1939. **Education:** University of Minnesota, Minneapolis, B.A. in studio art 1960, M.A. in art history 1969. **Relations:** married 1) Pat MacKay in 1957, two children; 2) Craig Johnson in 1966, one child. **Career:** librarian, University of Minnesota, 1966–79. **Agent:** Oscar Collier, 2000 Flat Run Road, Seaman, Ohio 45679, USA. **Address:** Route 2, Box 85, North Branch, Minnesota 55056, USA.

R**OMANCE AND** H**ISTORICAL** P**UBLICATIONS**

Novels (series: Braddock-Black; Kuzan)

Seized by Love (Kuzan). New York, Playboy Press, 1979.
Love Storm (Kuzan). New York, Playboy Press, 1981.
Sweet Love, Survive (Kuzan). New York, Berkley, 1985.
Blaze (Braddock-Black). New York, Berkley, 1986.
The Play. New York, Fawcett, 1987.
Silver Flame (Braddock-Black). New York, Berkley, 1988.
Golden Paradise. Toronto, Harlequin, 1990
Sinful. New York, Bantam, 1991.

O**THER** P**UBLICATIONS**

Other

Editor, with Mary Roberts, *Latitudes: New Writing from the North.* Brisbane, University of Queensland Press, 1987.

*

Susan Johnson comments:
It does not take great maestri, Danilo Kiš noted, to describe life as hell. I agree. What I hope to do instead is entertain, but also inform, seduce, perhaps even astonish and disturb, all with a painter's eye for atmospheric reality and lyrical detail. Within this reality I strive to make my characters come alive—so you can hear them breathe.

* * *

In Susan Johnson's historical romance *Silver Flame* the heroine, Empress Jordan, accuses the hero, Trey Braddock-Black, of being scandalous. 'But entertaining', he adds with a grin. One might say the same of Johnson.

She began her writing career with Playboy Press which placed no editorial restrictions on her erotic imagination. Consequently, her first three novels, a Russian trilogy set from 1874 to 1920, featuring the sexual and military exploits of three generations of the Kuzan family men, are spicy well beyond the limits of most historical romances. The second in the Russian series, *Love Storm*, is a masterpiece of erotica. A particularly lavish scene set in a Turkish encampment, complete with hypnotic music, hashish, richly woven Persian carpets, aphrodisiacs, sexual teasing, and purple plums earned Johnson the nickname 'Plum Lady' in some romance reading circles. Sex, in Johnson's novels, is pure delight for both men and women, an intensely pleasurable physical experience devoid of guilt or cloying sentimentality.

Johnson's next two historical novels, set predominantly in the American west from 1861 to 1890, are less daring in sexual content, although sexuality is still an essential part of their focus and appeal. *Blaze* is about the love affair between Jon Hazard Black, an Absarokee Indian chief, and Blaze Braddock, a beautiful, spoiled Bostonian debutante; *Silver Flame* is the story of their son, Trey. A third novel featuring Jon Hazard Black's natural daughter, Daisy, is in the works.

Although a reader may initially focus only on the sexuality in Johnson's novels, her work has other qualities that recommend it. One of the major challenges facing writers of popular historical fiction is finding a balance between 'history' and 'the story'. Johnson never lets historical detail overwhelm her story; yet, she clearly loves history. Trained in art history, she is a frequent speaker at regional and national romance conferences on historical research. Each of her novels is a blend of fictional and real historical characters and events which she smoothly incorporates in the text or describes in endnotes which provide fascinating information on a wide range of subjects from frontier political corruption and Indian customs to the sleeping and drinking habits of Alexander II and Erik Satie.

Besides the vividly portrayed sex and history, Johnson's novels are notable for their wry wit. For example, in *Silver Flame*, she makes the following simple but damning observation about a rather sleazy villain: 'Duncan's intrigues occasionally outstripped his intelligence'. Her humour also enlivens the sex scenes, as in this description of a 'hot and steamy' glance exchanged by the hero and heroine: 'The look he gave her could have boiled every coffee pot in Montana for a month'.

Her fictional style, which has steadily developed since her first novel, *Seized by Love*, is an interesting combination of Regency romance, erotica, and 'glitz and glamour'. The fantasy she constructs is reinforced by her use of multiple points of view—the hero, heroine, or even a minor character, an onlooker—which draw the reader into the story.

Johnson favours 'larger than life' characters rather than realistic 'boy/girl-next-door' characters. Her heroes, the real focus of her stories, are invariably rich aristocrats—charming and arrogant men who make love, ride horses, hunt wild game, play politics, plan military strategy, gamble, and drink with graceful expertise. The heroines are not quite the match of the heroes although the heroes think they are. Certainly the heroines are not mere simpering misses or delicate flowers. They put up a good fight and manage to cure the hero of a little of his arrogance by the story's end.

—Margaret Jensen

JOHNSTON, Mary.
Nationality: American. **Born:** Buchanan, Virginia, 21 November 1870. **Education:** privately at home. **Died:** 9 May 1936.

ROMANCE AND HISTORICAL PUBLICATIONS

Novels

The Prisoners of Hope: A Tale of Colonial Virginia. Boston, Houghton Mifflin, 1898; as *The Old Dominion*, London, Constable, 1899.
To Have and to Hold. Boston, Houghton Mifflin, 1900; as *By Order of the Company*, London, Constable, 1900.
Audrey. Boston, Houghton Mifflin, and London, Constable, 1902.
Sir Mortimer. New York, Harper, and London, Constable, 1904.
Lewis Rand. Boston, Houghton Mifflin, and London, Constable, 1908.
The Long Roll. Boston, Houghton Mifflin, 1911.
Cease Firing. Boston, Houghton Mifflin, and London, Constable, 1912.
Hagar. Boston, Houghton Mifflin, and London, Constable, 1913.
The Witch. Boston, Houghton Mifflin, and London, Constable, 1914.
The Fortunes of Garin. Boston, Houghton Mifflin, and London, Constable, 1915.
Foes. New York, Harper, 1918; as *The Laird of Glenfernie*, London, Constable, 1919.
Michael Forth. New York, Harper, 1919; London, Constable, 1920.
Sweet Rocket. New York, Harper, and London, Constable, 1920.
Silver Cross. Boston, Little Brown, and London, Butterworth, 1922.
1492. Boston, Little Brown, 1922; as *Admiral of the Ocean-Sea*, London, Butterworth, 1923.
Croatan. Boston, Little Brown, 1923; London, Butterworth, 1924.
The Slave Ship. Boston, Little Brown, 1924; London, Butterworth, 1925.
The Great Valley. Boston, Little Brown, and London, Butterworth, 1926.
The Exile. Boston, Little Brown, and London, Butterworth, 1927.
Hunting Shirt. Boston, Little Brown, 1931; London, Butterworth, 1932.
Miss Delicia Allen. Boston, Little Brown, and London, Butterworth, 1933.
Drury Randall. Boston, Little Brown, 1934; London, Butterworth, 1935.

Short Stories

The Wanderers. Boston, Houghton Mifflin, and London, Constable, 1917.
Collected Short Stories, edited by Annie and Hensley C. Woodbridge. Troy, New York, Whitston, 1982.

OTHER PUBLICATIONS

Play

The Goddess of Reason (produced New York, 1909). Boston, Houghton Mifflin, and London, Constable, 1907.

Other

An Address Read at Vicksburg . . . . Privately printed, 1907.

The Status of Women. Richmond, Virginia, Equal Suffrage League of Virginia, 1909.
The Reason Why. Privately printed, 1910 (?).
To the House of Governors (address). New York, National American Women's Suffrage Association, 1912.
Pioneers of the Old South: A Chronicle of English Colonial Beginnings. New Haven, Connecticut, Yale University Press, 1918.

*

Bibliography: in *Three Virginia Writers: A Reference Guide* by George C. Longest, Boston, Hall, 1978.

Manuscript Collection: Alderman Library, University of Virginia, Charlottesville.

Critical Study: *Mary Johnston* by C. Ronald Cella, Boston, Twayne, 1981.

*   *   *

For all practical purposes, Mary Johnston's career began in 1898 with publication of *The Prisoners of Hope*, a romance of colonial Virginia. That initial historical romance acts as a paradigm of her work in the genre: superior story-telling and romantic sensitivity to landscape are wedded to an acute interest in colonial Virginian history. Although frequently compared by early reviewers to Thackeray, Johnston lacked Thackeray's insight into human nature. In the first romance, her portrait of Sir William Berkeley, for example, is wooden, her dialogue artificial. Emphasis in her romances clearly falls on action born of quest. Character, at best, is the by-product of quest, or the by-product of a Victorian ideal.

The most successful of her historical romances, however, was *To Have and to Hold*, a considerably more refined romance than *The Prisoners of Hope*, and the number one bestseller for 1900. Grounded in Virginia history, the romance involves the 1622 Indian massacre of Jamestown. It owes its appeal, however, as Ronald Cella has observed, to the love story of Captain Ralph Percy and Lady Jocelyn Smith and the triangle created by her former suitor, the villainous Lord Carnal. The romance, melodramatic though it may be, remains her best-known work.

Audrey, a romance set in colonial Virginia, capitalizes on the vogue created by *To Have and to Hold*. Emphasizing manners, customs, and history, the romance, as *The Independent* observed on 20 November 1902, made a 'romantic rainbow of colonial civilization in Virginia'. Replacing the traditional forest scene with a colourful town scene, the setting of *Audrey* becomes 'illustrative of character' (*New York Times*, 22 February 1902).

Sir Mortimer, set in late 16th-century England; *The Fortunes of Garin*, set in 11th-century France, *Foes*, set in Jacobite Scotland during the 1745 uprising; and *Silver Cross*, set in Tudor England, suggest Johnston's continued exploitation of the genre and her diminishing talent for it. In the European romances the history is superficial and the characterization too frequently 'ideal'. *Silver Cross*, however, is the most important work in the European corpus. Johnston's mixture of superstition and mysticism in *Silver Cross* creates, as William Rose Benét early perceived, a 'telegraphic' style bordering on pointillism (*New York Evening Post*, 18 March 1922). The style, although inappropriate to the romance, does, however, document Johnston's conflicting interests in romance and novel genres.

Croatan, *The Great Valley*, and *Hunting Shirt* mark Johnston's return to her best mode. In all three romances, setting is of major importance, historical event is motivation, character is ideal, and quest suggests the coherence and definition of the plot. *Croatan* achieves a James Fenimore Cooper suspense in its rendering of pursuit and escape. As *The Athenaeum* reviewer observed in 1926, *The Great Valley* owes its success to its depiction of the effect of wilderness on 'natures marked out by a poetic mysticism of Celtic birth'. Somewhat similarly, *Hunting Shirt* creates a highly successful view of the link between American Indians and Scottish settlers. All these romances are considerably strengthened by the author's familiarity with the Virginia setting.

—George C. Longest

————

JOHNSTON, Norma. See **ST JOHN, Nicola.**

————

JOHNSTON, Velda.
Pseudonym: Veronica Jason. **Nationality:** American. **Education:** schools in California. **Address:** c/o Dodd Mead, 79 Madison Avenue, New York, New York, 10016, USA.

ROMANCE AND HISTORICAL PUBLICATIONS

Novels

Along a Dark Path. New York, Dodd Mead, 1967; Aylesbury, Buckinghamshire, Milton House, 1974.
House above Hollywood. New York, Dodd Mead, 1968; Aylesbury, Buckinghamshire, Milton House, 1974.
A Howling in the Woods. New York, Dodd Mead, 1968; London, Hale, 1969.
I Came to the Castle. New York, Dodd Mead, 1969; as *Castle Perilous*, London, Hale, 1971.
The Light in the Swamp. New York, Dodd Mead, 1970; London, Hale, 1972.
The Phantom Cottage. New York, Dodd Mead, 1970; London, Hale, 1971.
The Face in the Shadows. New York, Dodd Mead, 1971; London, Hale, 1973.
The People on the Hill. New York, Dodd Mead, 1971; as *Circle of Evil*, London, Hale, 1972.
The Mourning Trees. New York, Dodd Mead, 1972; Aylesbury, Buckinghamshire, Milton House, 1974.
The Late Mrs Fonsell. New York, Dodd Mead, 1972; Aylesbury, Buckinghamshire, Milton House, 1974.
The White Pavilion. New York, Dodd Mead, 1973; Aylesbury, Buckinghamshire, Milton House, 1974.
Masquerade in Venice. New York, Dodd Mead, 1973; Aylesbury, Buckinghamshire, Milton House, 1974.
I Came to the Highlands. New York, Dodd Mead, 1974; Aylesbury, Buckinghamshire, Milton House, 1975.
The House on the Left Bank. New York, Dodd Mead, 1975.
A Room with Dark Mirrors. New York, Dodd Mead, 1975; London, Prior, 1976.
Deveron Hall. New York, Dodd Mead, 1976; London, Prior, 1977.
The Frenchman. New York, Dodd Mead, and London, Prior, 1976.
The Etruscan Smile. New York, Dodd Mead, 1977; London, W.H. Allen, 1980.
The Hour Before Midnight. New York, Dodd Mead, 1978; London, W.H. Allen, 1981.
The Silver Dolphin. New York, Dodd Mead, 1979; London, Prior, 1981.
The People from the Sea. New York, Dodd Mead, 1979.
A Presence in an Empty Room. New York, Dodd Mead, 1980; London, W.H. Allen, 1982.

The Stone Maiden. New York, Dodd Mead, 1980; Bath, Chivers, 1983.
The Fateful Summer. New York, Dodd Mead, 1981; Bath, Chivers, 1983.
So Wild a Heart (as Veronica Jason). New York, New American Library, 1981.
The Other Karen. New York, Dodd Mead, 1983.
Voice in the Night. New York, Dodd Mead, 1984; Bath, Chivers, 1985.
Shadow Behind the Curtain. New York, Dodd Mead, 1985; London, Severn House, 1986.
The Crystal Cat. New York, Dodd Mead, 1985; London, Severn House, 1987.
Fatal Affair. New York, Dodd Mead, 1986; Bath, Firecrest, 1988.
The House on Bostwick Square. New York, Dodd Mead, 1987; Bath, Firecrest, 1988.
The Girl on the Beach. New York, Dodd Mead, 1987.
The Man at Windmere. New York, Dodd Mead, 1988.
Flight to Yesterday. New York, St Martin's Press, 1988.
The Underground Stream. Boston, Hall, 1992.

*   *   *

From the prolific pen of Velda Johnston come historical and contemporary romance mysteries in which young, vulnerable women find their lives plunged into perilous circumstances. Often an unsolved murder has occurred and the heroine, sometimes innocently but often because of her own amateur sleuthing, becomes the killer's next target.

In the historical novel *The Late Mrs Fonsell* Irene is forced into a marriage with the dark, brooding Jason Fonsell. Many years before, Jason's stepmother had been mysteriously and brutally murdered. Irene, intrigued by this mystery, brings the killer's unwelcome attentions upon herself. Meanwhile, the marriage of convenience to Jason eventually becomes one of love. In the end it is Jason who comes to Irene's rescue as she is stalked by the killer. The novel, *A Presence in an Empty Room*, has an added touch of the supernatural. The evil antagonist whom the newly married Susan Summerslee must overcome is the spirit of her husband's first wife, a woman who had plotted the death of her husband by paying someone to sabotage his private plane, but instead dies in the fiery crash. In *The Other Karen*, aspiring actress Kathy Mayhew is hired to impersonate a young woman who disappeared years ago. This 'acting assignment' almost leads to her death.

What makes Johnston's characters so appealing is their believability. Most of the women are attractive without being overwhelmingly beautiful, and the men, while virile, do not necessarily carry a heavy macho image. Her contemporary heroines are firmly rooted in their middle-class origins and usually have a career, while those of the historical periods belong to the genteel class but have families often skirting the edge of poverty. Many of these women have suffered some recent tragedy or mishap. In *The House on Bostwick Square*, the recently widowed Laura Harmon, an American with a six-year-old daughter, must turn to her wealthy English in-laws when she finds herself without resources. There is little welcome for her or her daughter in this grim household. Diana (*The People from the Sea*) must take a leave of absence from her job as a children's book editor to recover from a breakdown following divorce. In the historical novel *I Came to the Highlands* Elizabeth, thinking she has lost the love of John, allows herself to succumb to the charms of Charles Stuart, pretender to the English throne, and gives birth to his illegitimate son. Sara Hargreaves, of *Flight to Yesterday*, is wrongly accused of murdering her lover and must find the real killer in order to prove her innocence.

Another attraction of Johnston's novels is the richness of her settings, which come from her obviously intimate knowledge of the location of her stories. Often the mystery unfolds in an isolated area of wild beauty along eastern Long Island. This is the setting for *The Underground Stream*, a contemporary story with the heroine Gail living alone in a Victorian era house with a haunted past. Time travel, a recently popular phenomenon in romance literature, plays an important part in solving the mystery at the heart of this novel.

For all the romance and mystery that are the hallmarks of a Johnston story there is little emphasis on sex (much taking place by innuendo), and there is minimal description of violence. However this emphasis changes when she writes historical romances as Veronica Jason. These novels have a theme of male/female antagonism as their basis, but unlike so many of this genre the characters are well developed, the plots believable, and the sexual tension of the hero and heroine is handled in good taste. *Never Call It Love* her first book under this pen name is an excellent example. The heroine Elizabeth Montlow finds herself pregnant by the Anglo-Irish Lord Patrick Stanford, who because he blamed her for allowing his young ward's killer to go free, in an uncharacteristic moment of savagery, raped her. After their hasty marriage Elizabeth finds herself living first as a lady of social standing and later as a fugitive fleeing Britain with her husband; Patrick has been denounced as a secret organizer in Ireland's fight for independence.

Whether writing as Johnston or Jason, this author is an excellent story teller. All of her novels are well plotted with neat twists and turns that give an element of drama and excitement all the way through.

—Patricia Altner

JORDAN, Laura. See **BROWN, Sandra.**

JORDAN, Penny.
Nationality: British. **Born:** Preston, Lancashire, 24 November 1946. **Relations:** married. **Career:** since early 1980s, full-time writer. Lives in a 14th-century house in Cheshire. **Address:** c/o Mills and Boon Ltd, Eton House, 18–24 Paradise Road, Richmond, Surrey TW9 1SR, England.

ROMANCE AND HISTORICAL PUBLICATIONS

Novels

Tiger Man. London, Mills and Boon, 1981; Toronto, Harlequin, 1982.
Falcon's Prey. London, Mills and Boon, and Toronto, Harlequin, 1981.
Marriage Without Love. London, Mills and Boon, 1981; Toronto, Harlequin, 1982.
Northern Sunset. London, Mills and Boon, and Toronto, Harlequin, 1982.
Blackmail. London, Mills and Boon, and Toronto, Harlequin, 1982.
Bought with His Name. London, Mills and Boon, 1982; Toronto, Harlequin, 1983.
The Caged Tiger. London, Mills and Boon, and Toronto, Harlequin, 1982.
Daughter of Hassan. London, Mills and Boon, and Toronto, Harlequin, 1982.
Island of the Dawn. London, Mills and Boon, 1982; Toronto, Harlequin, 1983.
Long Cold Winter. London, Mills and Boon, and Toronto, Harlequin, 1982.
Escape from Desire. London, Mills and Boon, 1982; Toronto, Harlequin, 1983.

Desire's Captive. London, Mills and Boon, and Toronto, Harlequin, 1982.

An Unbroken Marriage. London, Mills and Boon, and Toronto, Harlequin, 1982.

Passionate Protection. London, Mills and Boon, and Toronto, Harlequin, 1983.

Forgotten Passion. London, Mills and Boon, 1983; Toronto, Harlequin, 1984.

Phantom Marriage. London, Mills and Boon, and Toronto, Harlequin, 1983.

The Flawed Marriage. London, Mills and Boon, and Toronto, Harlequin, 1983.

Rescue Operation. London, Mills and Boon, and Toronto, Harlequin, 1983.

Man-Hater. London, Mills and Boon, 1983.

A Sudden Engagement. London, Mills and Boon, and Toronto, Harlequin, 1983.

Savage Atonement. London, Mills and Boon, and Toronto, Harlequin, 1983.

The Friendship Barrier. London, Mills and Boon, 1984; Toronto, Harlequin, 1985.

Rules of the Game. London, Mills and Boon, 1984; Toronto, Harlequin, 1985.

Campaign for Loving. London, Mills and Boon, 1984; Toronto, Harlequin, 1985.

Response. London, Mills and Boon, and Toronto, Harlequin, 1984.

Wanting. London, Mills and Boon, and Toronto, Harlequin, 1984.

Shadow Marriage. London, Mills and Boon, and Toronto, Harlequin, 1984.

Darker Side of Desire. London, Mills and Boon, and Toronto, Harlequin, 1984.

The Inward Storm. London, Mills and Boon, 1984.

Injured Innocent. London, Mills and Boon, 1985; Toronto, Harlequin, 1986.

The Hard Man. London, Mills and Boon, 1985; Toronto, Harlequin, 1986.

Permission to Love. London, Mills and Boon, 1985; Toronto, Harlequin, 1986.

Desire for Revenge. London, Mills and Boon, 1985; Toronto, Harlequin, 1987.

Exorcism. London, Mills and Boon, 1985; Toronto, Harlequin, 1986.

The Only One. London, Mills and Boon, and Toronto, Harlequin, 1985.

Fire with Fire. London, Mills and Boon, 1985; Toronto, Harlequin, 1986.

Time Fuse. London, Mills and Boon, and Toronto, Harlequin, 1985.

The Six-Month Marriage. London, Mills and Boon, and Toronto, Harlequin, 1985.

Taken Over. London, Mills and Boon, and Toronto, Harlequin, 1985.

What You Made Me. London, Mills and Boon, and Toronto, Harlequin, 1985.

You Owe Me. London, Mills and Boon, and Toronto, Harlequin, 1985.

A Man Possessed. London, Mills and Boon, 1986; Toronto, Harlequin, 1987.

Stronger than Yearning. Toronto, Worldwide, 1986.

Capable of Feeling. London, Mills and Boon, and Toronto, Harlequin, 1986.

Desire Never Changes. London, Mills and Boon, 1986; Toronto, Harlequin, 1987.

Return Match. London, Mills and Boon, 1986.

A Reason for Marriage. London, Mills and Boon, 1986; Toronto, Harlequin, 1988.

Loving. London, Mills and Boon, 1986; Toronto, Harlequin, 1988.

Research into Marriage. Toronto, Harlequin, 1987.

Passionate Relations. Toronto, Harlequin, 1987.

For One Night. London, Mills and Boon, 1987; Toronto, Harlequin, 1989.

A Savage Adoration. London, Mills and Boon, 1987; Toronto, Harlequin, 1988.

Substitute Lover. London, Mills and Boon, 1987; Toronto, Harlequin, 1988.

Too Short a Blessing. London, Mills and Boon, and Toronto, Harlequin, 1987.

Fight for Fight. Toronto, Harlequin, 1988.

Levelling the Score. Toronto, Harlequin, 1988.

Potential Danger. London, Mills and Boon, 1988; Toronto, Harlequin, 1989.

Without Trust. London, Mills and Boon, 1988; Toronto, Harlequin, 1989.

Special Treatment. London, Mills and Boon, 1988.

Power Play. London, Worldwide, and Toronto, Harlequin, 1988.

Love's Choices. Toronto, Harlequin, 1988.

Stronger than Yearning. Toronto, Harlequin, 1988.

Lovers' Touch. London, Mills and Boon, 1988; Toronto, Harlequin, 1989.

So Close and No Closer. London, Mills and Boon, 1989; Toronto, Harlequin, 1991.

Valentine's Night. London, Mills and Boon, 1989; Toronto, Harlequin, 1990.

Power Play Sampler. Toronto, Harlequin, 1989.

Force of Feeling. Toronto, Harlequin, 1989.

Equal Opportunities. London, Mills and Boon, 1989; Toronto, Harlequin, 1990.

A Reason for Being. London, Mills and Boon, and Toronto, Harlequin, 1989.

A Rekindled Passion. London, Mills and Boon, 1989; Toronto, Harlequin, 1990.

Beyond Compare. London, Mills and Boon, 1989; Toronto, Harlequin, 1990.

Bitter Betrayal. London, Mills and Boon, 1989; Toronto, Harlequin, 1991.

Free Spirit. London, Mills and Boon, 1989; Toronto, Harlequin, 1990.

Silver. Toronto, Worldwide, 1989.

An Expert Teacher. Toronto, Harlequin, 1989; London, Mills and Boon, 1991.

Payment in Kind. Toronto, Harlequin, 1990.

Unspoken Desire. London, Mills and Boon, 1990; Toronto, Harlequin, 1991.

Rival Attractions. London, Mills and Boon, 1990; Toronto, Harlequin, 1991.

Breaking Away. London, Mills and Boon, 1990; Toronto, Harlequin, 1991.

Time for Trust. London, Mills and Boon, 1990; Toronto, Harlequin, 1991.

Out of the Night. London, Mills and Boon, 1990; Toronto, Harlequin, 1992.

The Hidden Years. Toronto, Worldwide, 1990.

Game of Love. London, Mills and Boon, 1990; Toronto, Harlequin, 1992.

Second Time Loving. London, Mills and Boon, 1990.

A Kind of Madness. London, Mills and Boon, 1990; Toronto, Harlequin, 1992.

A Time to Dream. London, Mills and Boon, 1991; Toronto, Harlequin, 1993.

A Cure for Love. London, Mills and Boon, 1991; Toronto, Harlequin, 1993.

Second-Best Husband. London, Mills and Boon, 1991; Toronto, Harlequin, 1993.

Dangerous Interloper. London, Mills and Boon, 1991; Toronto, Harlequin, 1993.

A Forbidden Loving. London, Mills and Boon, 1991; Toronto, Harlequin, 1992.

Payment Due. London, Mills and Boon, 1991; Toronto, Harlequin, 1992.

Stranger from the Past. London, Mills and Boon, 1992.

Tug of Love. Mills and Boon, 1992.

Lingering Shadows. Toronto, Harlequin, 1992.

Law of Attraction. London, Mills and Boon, 1992.

Lesson to Learn. London, Mills and Boon, 1992.

A Matter of Trust. London, Mills and Boon, 1992.

Mistaken Adversary. London, Mills and Boon, 1992; Toronto, Harlequin, 1994.

Past Passion. London, Mills and Boon, 1992.

Yesterday's Echoes. London, Mills and Boon, 1993.

Lingering Shadows. Toronto, Worldwide, 1993.

For Better, for Worse. Toronto, Worldwide, 1993.

*   *   *

While genre fans may applaud Penny Jordan's formulaic productions, her works represent many of the aspects of the romantic genre that repel non-fans. Her series of girl meets boy, love conquers all novels are set in modern-day England, but none-the-less seem to reflect an earlier period. Causes of this curiously old-fashioned air are hard to isolate. While it is true that her heroines typically have a career, often at the fringes of the artistic world (Holly in *Beyond Compare* is an interior designer, Tasha in *Game of Love* is a fabric dealer) or in the world of business (Charlotte in *Rival Attractions* is an estate agent, Somer in *Desire Never Changes* is a computer programmer), they also regard their careers as secondary to their husbands and putative offspring.

In Jordan's world, attractive women typically are convinced that they are somehow unwomanly, unattractive. This skilfully allows her readers a way to identify with the insecure heroines, who are in 'reality' (the reality of the novel) more attractive, intelligent, sexy and charming than women in the actual world can be. Often a previous involvement with an insensitive, unappreciative male has destroyed the heroine's confidence in her essential femininity—the egregious Andrew in *Desire Never Changes*, who becomes engaged to Somer for her father's fortune and who pursues her even after her marriage to Chase Lorimer is one notable example. In many of the novels, the first man is merely sketched in as a former boyfriend, rather than characterized fully.

When she first meets the Jordan hero—handsome, wealthy, successful, and above all virile—the Jordan heroine decides first that he couldn't be interested in someone as unfeminine as she is. Then she decides that his interest in her is caused by ulterior motives—in *Rival Attractions*, that Oliver is trying to get real estate business away from Charlotte's firm, in *Northern Sunset* that Brett needs Catriona's approval for the oil depot he wants to build. Or even, she may assume, he is interested only in sex. Of course, like a proper romantic heroine, she tries to ignore the animal magnetism that arises between them. Then she admits her attraction but decides that a relationship based on sex is not for her. Even when she finally admits that she truly loves him, she is sure for some reason or another that he doesn't return her love. Her reason can be as slender as Hazel's, who spends more than half of *A Forbidden Loving* thinking that Simon is the lover of her daughter, an idea that both he and her daughter would have found absurd.

The Jordan hero, too, has his blind spots. Luke, in *Game of Love*, decides on the basis of a fashionable dress, and a reported assignation, that Tasha is sexually irresponsible. Never mind that it is none of his business—just because his cousin is going to marry her cousin—his opinion seems to justify him treating her with contempt even as he tries to seduce her. His view of her as sexually experienced also gives the virginal Tasha an excuse to avoid acting on the passion she feels for him—it would be too embarrassing for her if he learns that she is really so unsophisticated.

As the characters introspectively discuss, or just think over, their feelings, they are usually too occupied to interact much with other people in their lives. Notably in *A Forbidden Love*, nothing much happens in the way of plot and other than Hazel's daughter Katie there are few other characters. An attempted rape, and the problems of the heroine's friends make *Rival Attractions* more heavily peopled than some of the other novels. *Beyond Compare* has a number of characters, although they are only lightly sketched in, and a convoluted plot that focuses on Holly's attempts to make her ex-boyfriend Howard, and his new fiancée, Drew's former girlfriend, jealous by pretending that she and Drew are in love. Imagine Holly's surprise when she finds out that she no longer loves the wimpish Howard, and that Drew has secretly loved her for years, and has also become prosperous enough to marry her.

Northern Sunset has an unusual sub-plot, with Catriona's brother recovering from the emotional effects of his oil-rig accident and proposing to his long-time flame Fiona. The secondary couple is quite clearly secondary, however; they don't even have any love scenes. And love scenes between the two main characters in all the books tend to be remarkably erotic, more carefully described than any other element of the story, and interspersed frequently throughout the narrative. While not explicit, they are quite graphic (and quite similar from book to book), more so than in many romantic novels. The only elements described with anything like the same amount of care are clothes and, sometimes, food. Items like houses and scenery take a decided second place. While travel, usually within the United Kingdom, is frequent, the places the characters go to seem fairly homogenous, differentiated more by name than by any other feature.

The love scenes include episodes that are saved from being rape only because, whatever lip service to her principles the heroine may utter, we share her secret: that she is willing. She may tear herself away, half nude, or yield to the hero's importunities, saying 'no' all the while, but the hero has not the reader's knowledge, only his own sense of her passion to signal acceptance of his suit. Perhaps even more dismaying—since the genre must presumably be allowed its conventions—is the clearly caddish behaviour of some of the heroes. Chase blackmails Somer into a marriage she insists be one in name only, by threatening to use nude photos of her to sabotage her father's much-desired appointment as ambassador to a puritanical near-eastern state. Brett insults the hapless Catriona at their first meeting and, subsequently, is both deliberately and thoughtlessly insulting. Drew, one of the pleasanter Jordan heroes, deceives Holly about how long it will take her car to be repaired (a ploy that Holly never realizes, though a friendly mechanic gives the readers enough information so that they will know what is happening—perhaps Jordan's tacit indication that her readers are more aware than her characters). Luke Chalmers, in *A Time to Dream*, is perhaps more liberated than most, and Matt, in *Past Passion*, is actually courteous to his lovelorn secretary Nicola. Perhaps, as these two are recent books, this shows a trend toward more nearly equal relationships.

Beyond the hero's treatment of the heroine, however, earlier loves of the hero's are referred to in a disparaging way, after serving the purpose of showing that, unlike men, women who have been sexually active without love will find no happy endings.

The manly man and the womanly woman—nominally updated for the last quarter of the 20th century—reign triumphant in these novels. The man may be reluctant to believe that this is, at last, true love—he may fight against his overwhelming passionate attraction; the woman, in her modern armour of career and independence, may pretend not to feel the throb of unbridled passion, but sooner or later all the insignificant—and they are insignificant—problems disappear, and they unite forever. Sex may not wait for the wedding bells, but they are always in prospect as Jordan completes her final chapter.

—Susan Branch

JOSEPH, Marie.
Nationality: British. **Born:** Blackburn, Lancashire. **Education:** Girls High School, Blackburn, Lancashire. **Relations:** married Frank Joseph in 1942; two daughters. **Career:** civil servant; clerical officer, Post Office Telephones, Blackburn, 1938–44. **Recipient:** Romantic Novelists' award, 1987, for *A Better World Than This*. **Agent:** Mary Irvine, 4 Coombe Gardens, Wimbledon, London, England. **Address:** Studio, Green Lane, Stanmore, Middlesex, England.

ROMANCE AND HISTORICAL PUBLICATIONS

Novels

Maggie Craig. New York, St Martin's Press, 1980.
A Leaf in the Wind. London, Arrow, and New York, St Martin's Press, 1981.
Emma's Sparrow. London, Arrow, and New York, St Martin's Press, 1982.
The Listening Silence. London, Arrow, 1982; New York, St Martin's Press, 1983.
Footsteps in the Park. London, Arrow, 1982.
Gemini Girls. London, Arrow, 1983.
Lisa Logan. London, Arrow, 1984.
Polly Pilgrim. London, Arrow, 1984.
Clogger's Child. London, Arrow, 1986.
A Better World Than This. London, Century, 1986.
A World Apart. London, Century, 1988.
Ring-a-Roses. Bath, Chivers, 1990.
Travelling Man. London, Arrow, 1990.
Since He Went Away. London, Century, 1992.

Short Stories

Passing Strangers and Other Stories. London, Arrow, 1989.
When Love Was Like That and Other Stories. London, Century, 1991.

OTHER PUBLICATIONS

Other

The House Through the Trees (for children), illustrated by Will Nickless. London, Nelson, 1964.
One Step at a Time (autobiography). New York, St Martin's Press, 1977.

*   *   *

For many years Marie Joseph was one of the most popular writers of short stories for women's magazines in Britain. Hardly a week went by without her by-line appearing in one magazine or another. In more recent years she has turned to writing novels, something she once thought she would never attempt. However, she has been even more successful with novels than she was with her sensitive and evocative shorter works.

A number of her short stories have been assembled in two collections under the titles, *Passing Strangers and Other Stories* and *When Love Was Like That*. These illustrate the wide variety of emotional situations she has dealt with in her stories, and the depth she was able to achieve within the restricted length of a few hundred words.

The viewpoints vary from that of a man who is concerned for the safety of his teenage daughter, to that of a young unmarried mother being visited by her parents immediately after the birth of her child. The latter story ends with the echoing thoughts of the girl after her parents have left. 'But no-one, not one single person, told me how lonely, how *desperately* lonely I would be . . . '. The stories always have the ring of truth. The reader feels to have been taken into the confidence of the narrator.

Having already established herself as a novelist, Joseph published an autobiographical book under the title *One Step at a Time*. This gives a serious but at the same time light-hearted account of her lifelong struggle against rheumatoid arthritis. Having described one particularly depressing stay in hospital, she writes, 'I made up my mind that . . . my letters to him [her husband, Frank] would be gay and carefree, the kind of letters he'd loved to receive all through the war'. This is typical of all her writing. It is never depressing. Her characters, like herself, always look for the brighter side, rarely complain about their lot. This quality has no doubt made a contribution to the popularity of her writing.

A Better World Than This won the Romantic Novelists Association major award in 1987. One critic remarked that Joseph was a witty and humorous writer rather than a purely romantic one. This was a well deserved prize for a writer whose work is always comforting, reassuring and often amusing, as well as being thought provoking. The main character in *A Better World Than This*, Daisy Bell, lives and works with her widowed mother, the owner of a bakery in a Lancashire town. At 26, Daisy, although reasonably attractive, is already resigned to being an old maid. Then a man walks into her shop and transforms her life. He's a Clark Gable look-alike and Daisy immediately falls in love. Regular visits to the cinema have provided an escape from her humdrum life. She imagines that her life could be similar to that on the screen, if she was given the chance.

She builds a fantasy existence around the man she has met, Sam Barnet, a Londoner, in town briefly because of his job. He is a chauffeur. The knowledge that he is married with two young children, and the fact that they can meet only rarely does nothing to diminish Daisy's passion.

When her mother dies, Daisy sells the bakery and accompanied by Florence, who has been a friend for many years, she buys a boarding house in Blackpool. Florence, although intelligent and able, suffers moods of black depression and is jealous of Daisy's association with Sam. Despite a variety of setbacks, the boarding house business prospers, almost entirely due to Daisy's unflagging efforts. She has some support from a widowed teacher, one of two permanent guests she took over with the business. Joshua Penny gradually falls in love with Daisy and becomes her confidant. Sam's son, Jimmy, stays with Daisy for a while, but when Sam's wife comes to visit, Daisy realizes that her love affair with Sam has been a fantasy. Another death of someone close hits Daisy badly. Joshua increases his support and is about to ask Daisy to marry him. Her remark, that he reminds her of the father she loved, leads him to the conclusion that she can never love him in the way he would wish. One misunderstanding leads to another and it is not until almost the end of the novel that Daisy's future happiness is secured.

A number of minor characters, each one distinctly and clearly depicted, are woven into the storyline. The atmosphere of the depressed Lancashire mill towns of the 1930s, contrasted with the annual holiday week in Blackpool, are subtly, but none the less clearly created. The hard slog of running a boarding house in the holiday period, with a narrow profit margin, is also handled with bleak realism. Throughout the story the indomitable courage and determined cheerfulness of Daisy shines thorough like a beacon. Few readers could fail to feel great affection for the sometimes naive, but always loveable, Daisy Bell.

Her apprenticeship in short story writing has taught Joseph to be economical but effective with words. The first two sentences of another of her novels, *Footsteps in the Park*, illustrates this quality. 'Stanley was late and it wasn't like him. Usually he was there before her'. These few words set the scene, giving the reader an immediate mental picture. They also provide an initial indication of the personalities of the characters and raise questions in the reader's mind, providing the incentive to read on. This is just one example of the way in which Joseph, both in her short stories and her novels, makes every word work.

—W.H. Bradley

KANE, Julia.   See **ROBINS, Denise.**

KANTOR, MacKinlay.
Nationality: American. **Born:** Webster City, Iowa, 4 February 1904. **Education:** Webster City High School. **Relations:** married Florence Irene Layne in 1926; two sons. **Career:** reporter, Webster City *Daily News*, 1921–24; advertiser in Chicago, 1925–26; reporter, Cedar Rapids *Republican*, Iowa, 1927; columnist, Des Moines *Tribune*, Iowa, 1930–31; scenario writer for Hollywood studios; war correspondent for United States and British air forces, 1943, 1950, and technical consultant to the United States Air Force, 1951–53; member of the uniformed division, New York City Police, 1948–50. Member of the National Council, Boy Scouts of America; trustee, Lincoln College, Illinois, 1960–68. **Recipient:** Pulitzer prize, 1956; National Association of Independent Schools award, 1956. D.Litt.: Grinnell College, Iowa, 1957; Drake University, Des Moines, 1958; Lincoln College, 1959; Ripon College, Wisconsin, 1961; LL.D.: Iowa Wesleyan College, Mount Pleasant, 1961. Fellow, Society of American Historians. **Died:** 11 October 1977.

ROMANCE AND HISTORICAL PUBLICATIONS

Novels (series: Civil War Trilogy)

Long Remember. New York, Coward McCann, and London, Selwyn and Blount, 1934.
Civil War Trilogy:
    The Voice of Bugle Ann. New York, Coward McCann, and London, Selwyn and Blount, 1935.
    Arouse and Beware. New York, Coward McCann, 1936; London, Gollancz, 1937.
    The Romance of Rosy Ridge. New York, Coward McCann, 1937.
Cuba Libre. New York, Coward McCann, 1940.
Gentle Annie: A Western Novel. New York, Coward McCann, 1942; London, Hale, 1951; as *The Goss Boys*, London, Corgi, 1958.
Wicked Water: An American Primitive. New York, Random House, 1949; London, Falcon Press, 1950.
Warwhoop: Two Short Novels of the Frontier (includes *Behold the Brown-Faced Man* and *Missouri Moon*). New York, Random House, 1952.
The Daughter of Bugle Ann. New York, Random House, 1953.
Andersonville. Cleveland, World, 1955; London, W.H. Allen, 1956.
Spirit Lake. Cleveland, World, 1961; London, W.H. Allen, 1962.

If the South Had Won the Civil War. New York, Bantam, 1961.
Beauty Beast. New York, Putnam, 1968.
Valley Forge. New York, Evans, 1975.

Short Stories

Author's Choice: 40 Stories. New York, Coward McCann, 1944.
Silent Grow the Guns and Other Tales of the American Civil War. New York, New American Library, 1958.
Again the Bugle. New York, American Weekly, 1958.
Frontier: Tales of the American Adventure. New York, New American Library, 1959.
The Gun-Toter and Other Stories of the Missouri Hills. New York, New American Library, 1963.
Story Teller. New York, Doubleday, 1967.

OTHER PUBLICATIONS

Novels

Diversey. New York, Coward McCann, 1928.
El Goes South. New York, Coward McCann, 1930.
The Jaybird. New York, Coward McCann, 1932.
The Noise of Their Wings. New York, Coward McCann, 1938; London, Hale, 1939.
Valedictory. New York, Coward McCann, 1939.
Happy Land. New York, Coward McCann, 1943.
Glory for Me (in verse). New York, Coward McCann, 1945.
Midnight Lace. New York, Random House, 1948; London, Falcon Press, 1949.
The Good Family. New York, Coward McCann, 1949.
One Wild Oat. New York, Fawcett, 1950; London, W.H. Allen, 1952.
Signal Thirty-Two. New York, Random House, 1950.
Don't Touch Me. New York, Random House, 1951; London, W.H. Allen, 1952.
God and My Country. Cleveland, World, 1954.
The Work of St Francis. Cleveland, World, 1958; as *The Unseen Witness*, London, W.H. Allen, 1959.
I Love You, Irene. New York, Doubleday, 1972; London, W.H. Allen, 1973.
The Children Sing. New York, Hawthorn, 1973; London, Hale, 1974.

Short Stories

The Boy in the Dark. Webster Groves, Missouri, International Mark Twain Society, 1937.
It's About Crime. New York, New American Library, 1960.

Plays

Screenplays: *Gun Crazy* (*Deadly Is the Female*), with Millard Kaufman, 1950; *Hannah Lee*, with Rip Von Ronkel, 1953.

Poetry

Turkey in the Straw: A Book of American Ballads and Primitive Verse. New York, Coward McCann, 1935.

Other

Angleworms on Toast (for children). New York, Coward McCann, 1942.
But Look, the Morn: The Story of a Childhood (reminiscences). New York, Coward McCann, 1947; London, Falcon Press, 1951.

Lee and Grant at Appomattox (for children). New York, Random House, 1950.

Gettysburg (for children). New York, Random House, 1952.

Three Views of the Novel, with John O'Hara and Irving Stone. Washington, DC, Library of Congress, 1957.

Lobo (reminiscences). Cleveland, World, 1957; London, W.H. Allen, 1958.

Mission with LeMay: My Story, with General Curtis LeMay. New York, Doubleday, 1965.

The Historical Novelist's Obligation to History (lecture). Macon, Georgia, Wesley College, 1967.

The Day I Met a Lion. New York, Doubleday, 1968.

Missouri Bittersweet (reminiscences). New York, Doubleday, 1969; London, Hale, 1970.

Hamilton County, photographs by Tim Kantor. New York, Macmillan, 1970.

*

Film Adaptations: *The Voice of Bugle Ann*, 1936; *The Man from Dakota*, 1940, from the novel *Arouse and Beware*; *Happy Land*, 1943; *Gentle Annie*, 1944; *The Best Years of Our Lives*, 1946, from the novel *Glory for Me*; *The Romance of Rosie Ridge*, 1947; *Deadly Is the Female*, 1949, from the novel *Gun Crazy*; *Follow Me Boys!*, 1966, from the novel *God and My Country*.

Manuscript Collections: Library of Congress, Washington, DC; University of Iowa Library, Iowa City.

Critical Study: *My Father's Voice: MacKinlay Kantor Long Remembered* by Tim Kantor, New York, McGraw Hill, 1988.

*   *   *

A prolific, versatile author whose novel *Glory for Me* was made into the award-winning film *The Best Years of Our Lives*, MacKinlay Kantor has nevertheless come to be regarded primarily as a historical writer, and as such ranks high among the chroniclers of the American past. The bitter, divisive War between the States is the event which dominates most of his fiction in this genre—Kantor was the descendant of a Civil War veteran—and to this recurring scenario he applies a strongly individual style which breaks down the narrative to a fragmented sequence of incident and reflection, combining humour, reportage and interior monologue. It is a style already discernible in Kantor's first important novel, *Long Remember*, and one which is developed in later works.

In *Long Remember*, which depicts the carnage of the Gettysburg campaign, Kantor eschews the illusory glamour of warfare to present a grimmer reality where the humdrum and the horrific maintain an uneasy co-existence. Subsequent writings, especially the trilogy *The Voice of Bugle Ann*, *Arouse and Beware*, and *The Romance of Rosy Ridge*, show a continuing exploration of the Civil War theme in the context of human relationships and desires, and a further stylistic development. As in *Long Remember*, conventional heroics are ignored, sometimes to the extent of sidestepping the battles.

Arouse and Beware, for instance, focuses on two escaped Union prisoners and their hazardous trek to freedom through a hostile Virginia landscape. Narrated by one of the main characters, the novel incorporates interior monologue and flashback with descriptions of the terrain and dramatic action passages. The result is an impressive work, whose central image of the starving, half-crazed men, wandering in a malevolent wilderness with their mysterious female companion, lingers powerfully in the mind. The trilogy is a milestone in Kantor's growth as a writer, and is excelled only by his masterpiece, *Andersonville*.

This monolithic novel, which occupied its author for several years, and for which he was awarded a Pulitzer prize, recounts the history of the infamous Georgia prison camp from its initial surveying to its demolition at the end of the Civil War. Kantor builds up each scene gradually to attain a relentless momentum, switching his vision from one set of characters to another to present a convincing microcosm of the life inside the prison. Captives, guards, and onlookers are shown as individuals, their lives and deaths described soberly and almost without comment, in a manner which renders the endless catalogue of starvation and disease all the more appalling. Kantor lays bare the mind of the camp commandant, whose inadequacies express themselves in severity and neglect of the prisoners, and counters him with the dedicated prison surgeon, whose love for a local planter's daughter is an important strand of the novel. The fragmented, incident-based style enables Kantor to construct his prison-universe in a memorable, and often shocking, narrative. A novel of compelling realism, and deep psychological insights, *Andersonville* is justifiably recognized as Kantor's greatest achievement.

With *Spirit Lake* and *Beauty Beast*, Kantor delves further back into American history, exploring pioneer and plantation life in the 1850s. While neither novel equals the power and scope of *Andersonville*, each has definite merits. In *Spirit Lake* particularly Kantor approaches his earlier masterpiece, using the same broken, multifaceted style to describe the massacre of Iowa settlers by the renegade Inkpaduta and his band. As with *Andersonville*, he follows his characters through their past lives to the final nemesis. The writing shows comparable skill, and individuals are strikingly realized, but *Spirit Lake* does not have the coherence of *Andersonville*, and lacks any obvious unifying theme. A flawed major work, it fails to achieve its considerable promise. *Beauty Beast*, which examines racism, slavery, and sexual desire in the ante-bellum south, is less ambitious but possibly more successful. The story centres on the unrequited love of a female plantation owner for her cultured black house servant, and its eventual tragic outcome. Kantor investigates the many subtle varieties of enslavement—the white mistress in thrall to her uncontrollable passion, the black servant's vision of the great composers as slaves of their patrons—and although the ending is predictable, many of the novel's conclusions are original and unexpected. *Beauty Beast*, like *Spirit Lake*, is less satisfying than some of Kantor's earlier works. All the same, both are worthy of mention as part of an impressive body of fiction by one of America's foremost historical writers.

—Geoffrey Sadler

KAYE, M(ary) M(argaret).
Pseudonyms: Mollie Hamilton; Mollie Kaye. **Nationality:** British. **Born:** Simla, India, 21 August 1908. **Education:** Lawn School, Clevedon, Somerset. **Relations:** married Geoffrey John Hamilton in 1942 (died 1985); two daughters. **Career:** writer and painter. **Recipient:** Fellow, Royal Society of Literature. **Agent:** David Higham Associates, 5–8 Lower John Street, London W1R 4HA, England.

ROMANCE AND HISTORICAL PUBLICATIONS

Novels

Shadow of the Moon. London, Longman, and New York, Messner, 1957.

Trade Wind. London, Longman, 1963; New York, Coward McCann, 1964.

The Far Pavilions. London, Allen Lane, and New York, St Martin's Press, 1978.

OTHER PUBLICATIONS

Novels

Strange Island. Calcutta, Thacker Spink, n.d.
Six Bars at Seven. London, Hutchinson, 1940.
Death Walked in Kashmir. London, Staples Press, 1953; as *Death in Kashmir*, New York, St Martin's Press, 1984.
Death Walked in Berlin. London, Staples Press, 1955; as *Death in Berlin*, New York, St Martin's Press, 1983.
Death Walked in Cypress. London, Staples Press, 1956; as *Death in Cypress*, New York, St Martin's Press, 1984.
Later than You Think. London, Longman, 1958; (as Mollie Hamilton), New York, Coward McCann, 1959; as *It's Later than You Think*, Manchester, World Distributors, 1960; as *Death in Kenya*. London, Allen Lane, 1983.
The House of Shade. London, Longman, and New York, Coward McCann, 1959; as *Death in Zanzibar*, London, Allen Lane, 1983.
Night on the Island. London, Longman, 1960; as *Death in the Andamans*, New York, Viking, 1985.

OTHER PUBLICATIONS

Fiction (for children) as Mollie Kaye

Potter Pinner series (*Potter Pinner Meadow*, *Black Bramble Wood*, *Willow Witches Brook*, *Gold Gorse Common*). London, Collins, 4 vols, 1937–45.
The Ordinary Princess. London, Kestrel, 1980; New York, 1984.
Thistledown. London, Quartet, 1981.

Play

Radio Play: *England Wakes*, 1941.

Other

The Sun in the Morning: My Early Years in India and England (autobiography). London, Viking, and New York, St Martin's Press, 1990.

Editor, *The Golden Calm: An English Lady's Life in Moghul Delhi*, by Emily Bayley and Thomas Metcalfe. New York, Viking Press, and Exeter, Devon, Webb and Bower, 1980.
Editor, *Moon and Other Days: M.M. Kaye's Kipling: Favourite Verses*. London, Hodder and Stoughton, 1988.
Editor, *Picking Up Gold and Silver: A Selection of Kipling's Short Stories*. London, Macmillan, 1989.

*

Film Adaptation: *The Far Pavilions*, 1983.

*   *   *

If you want to be immersed in the sights, sounds, and scents of the gorgeous East, to understand the thoughts of mid-Victorian men and women, to enjoy lush, melodramatic romance against a background of authentic history, then read M.M. Kaye's historical romances.

The Far Pavilions is probably her best-known book. It tells the story of Ash, a man who is 'two people in one skin'. Born to English parents in India, he grows up believing he is Indian because at the time of the Indian Mutiny his Hindu nurse disguises him as her son, and he remains so until he is 12 when she dies, revealing the truth on her death-bed. Reluctantly he goes to England to be trained as a Sahib, an incident that is pure *Kim*, as is the way Ash can easily pass as a native. In all three books, it is the love story that captures the

imagination and sometimes makes one impatient with the copious historical detail.

As a grown man in the Indian army, Ash is deputed to escort two princesses to their wedding in a far-off province. He discovers that one of them is Ann-Juli with whom he played as a child when he and his mother were servants at her brother's court. They fall in love, only to part because Ann-Juli has promised her younger sister she will never leave her. When the Rana to whom the princesses were married dies, Ash sets out to rescue them from Suttee, the custom of burning widows on their husbands' funeral pyres. After many adventures, Ash and Ann-Juli get their happy ending.

The Shadow of the Moon, similarly, has a key character born in India and sent to England to be educated—Winter Ballasteros, the heroine. Like Ash, she has a miserable time in England and longs to return to India. Winter is an orphaned heiress who is betrothed, while still a child, to Conway Barton, a District Commissioner in India, who has fooled her grandfather into thinking him a paragon, in fact he is a dissolute fortune hunter. Winter, at 19, goes to India to marry Conway, escorted by his assistant, Alex Randall, who tries to warn her and her kinfolk what Barton is like. Her relatives want her out of the way and Winter has idealized her fiancé as St George, and refuses to believe he is a dragon. As soon as the experienced romance reader sees Alex and Winter irritating each other she knows they will fall in love.

However, Winter, blind to his faults, marries Conway, is raped on her wedding night, and leads a miserable life. Then comes the mutiny and Conway's death. Winter, Alex, and two other women escape from the beleaguered residence into the jungle where they lead a simple but strangely happy life until there is a forest fire and in running for safety they are recaptured. Their durance is far from vile as they end up in the palace of Winter's relatives in Lucknow where Winter and Alex are finally married.

We are still in the gorgeous East in the 1850s in *Trade Wind*, but this time in Zanzibar with an American heroine, Hero Hollis, niece of the American consul. She has been pronounced 'the best lookin' gal in Boston and the biggest goddamned bore' for she is self-opinionated, a relentless do-gooder who acts without thinking things through, secure in her belief that she is right. On her journey to Zanzibar, she is washed overboard in a storm and rescued by Rory Frost, an Englishman who is said to be a slave trader, gun runner, and womanizer. Again the reader knows as soon as they meet and quarrel that Rory will teach Hero the lessons she needs to learn and that they will end the book in each others arms. Before that can happen, Hero misguidedly gets involved in aiding and abetting rebellion; she is kidnapped and raped, she nurses Frost's bastard child through typhoid; has a miscarriage, and during a cholera epidemic sets up an orphanage for the babies of cholera victims.

All three books are long and move at a stately pace; sub-plots are plentiful and well devised but sometimes the details of history and long passages of introspection slow down the action and overwhelm the plot. The descriptions are graphic and lyrical, the characters lively and well-drawn, and the romance is absorbing. Although the final outcome of these romances is predictable, the twists and turns of the plots are not. The writing is of a high quality and the books are extremely enjoyable.

—Pamela Cleaver

———

KEANE, Molly (Mary Nesta).
Pseudonym: M.J. Farrell. **Nationality:** Irish. **Born:** Mary Nesta Skrine, County Kildare, 4 July 1904. **Relations:** married Robert Lumley Keane, 1938 (died 1947). **Agent:** Murray Pollinger, 222 Old Brompton Road, London SW5 0BZ, England. **Address:** Dysert, Ardmore, County Waterford, Ireland.

Novels

Good Behaviour. London, Deutsch, and New York, Knopf, 1981.
Time After Time. London, Deutsch, 1983; New York, Knopf, 1984.
Loving and Giving. London, Deutsch, 1988; as *Queen Lear*, New York, Dutton, 1989.

Novels as M.J. Farrell

The Knight of the Cheerful Countenance. London, Mills and Boon, 1928.
Young Entry. London, Mathews and Marrot, 1928; New York, Holt, 1929.
Taking Chances. London, Mathews and Marrot, 1929; Philadelphia, Lippincott, 1930.
Mad Puppetstown. London, Collins, 1931; New York, Farrar and Rinehart, 1932.
Conversation Piece. London, Collins, 1932; as *Point-to-Point*, New York, Farrar, 1933.
Devoted Ladies. London, Collins, and Boston, Little, Brown, 1934.
Full House. London, Collins, and Boston, Little, Brown, 1935.
The Rising Tide. London, Collins, 1937; New York, Macmillan, 1938.
Two Days in Aragon. London, Collins, 1941.
Loving Without Tears. London, Collins, 1951; as *The Enchanting Witch*, New York, Crowell, 1951.
Treasure Hunt. London, Collins, 1952.

Plays as M.J. Farrell

Spring Meeting, with John Perry (produced London, 1938; New York, 1939). London, Collins, 1938.
Ducks and Drakes, with John Perry (produced London, 1941).
Guardian Angel (produced Dublin, 1944).
Treasure Hunt, with John Perry (produced London, 1949). London, Collins, 1950.
Dazzling Prospect, with John Perry. London, French, 1961.

Other

Red Letter Days, with Snaffles (as M.J. Farrell; on hunting). London, Collins, 1933.
Molly Keane's Nursery Cooking. London, Macdonald, 1985.
Molly Keane's Ireland: An Anthology, edited by Sally Phipps. London, HarperCollins, 1993.

*

Film Adaptation: *Spring Meeting*, 1940; *Treasure Hunt*, 1952.

Critical Studies: 'Three Writers of the Big House: Elizabeth Bowen, Molly Keane and Jennifer Johnston' by Bridget O'Toole, in *Across a Roaring Hill: The Protestant Imagination in Modern Ireland* edited by Gerald Dawe and Edna Longley, Belfast, Blackstaff Press, 1985; 'The Persistent Pattern; Molly Keane's Recent Big House Fiction' by Vera Kreilkamp, in *Massachusetts Review* (Amherst), Autumn 1987.

*   *   *

The background of Molly Keane's novels is always Ireland—the vanishing, nearly gone Ireland of the Ascendancy, of the great country houses, of the Anglo-Irish gentry. Charming, feckless, passionate about horses and hunting, as exasperating and appealing as the Ranevsky household in Chekhov's *The Cherry Orchard*, her characters pass before our eyes caught in their last moments of glory (as in the hunt ball in *Good Behaviour*, which ends so disastrously for Aroon), and displayed mercilessly in their downfall, most notably perhaps in the descriptions of the Swifts' kitchen in *Time After Time*, and of the desolation of Deer Forest in *Loving and Giving*.

It is hard to tell whether Keane loves her heroes and heroines, as she too adheres to their code of good behaviour, of the stiff upper lip, banning any unseemly display of emotion. She certainly understands them, their love of horses, of dogs (tellingly referred to as 'the little terrier people'), and of unaffordable luxury. They will order from Harrods even when they are penniless, and their delight in good tweeds, fine silks, well-made shoes, and hunting-books is quite obviously understood and shared by the author. Naturally she also shares their love of their old houses, of the old, inherited, beautiful things in them (look for example at her rapturous descriptions of Hepplewhite chairs and an Adam fireplace in *Conversation Piece*).

Behind the façade of good breeding there are emotions deep enough perhaps to qualify Keane's novels for entry in this volume. There is love, certainly—in *Loving and Giving* Nicandra's hopeless unrewarded love first for her flighty Maman, then for her shallow, spoilt husband; Aroon's hopeless adoration of Richard in *Good Behaviour*; the compelling physical passion between Mary and Rowley in *Taking Chances*. There are other passions, too, equally powerful if unacknowledged: Jasper Swift's dream of a garden in *Time After Time*, the destructive hatred between Aroon St Charles and her mother in *Good Behaviour*.

Mother love, the excess or the lack of it, plays a significant part in many of Keane's novels. Nicandra Forester is an emotional cripple for all of her short life because her pretty, frivolous mother had never really loved her and abandoned her in the end; the four Swifts, all marked physically in different ways, have been crippled emotionally by their over-protective, over-possessive 'darling Mummie'; and Aroon St Charles, mocked for her size and clumsiness by her delicate beauty of a mother, learns through her own bitter experiences the art of bullying by sweet words and is ready to practise it on her mother when their roles are reversed.

Significantly perhaps sexual love, passion, is introduced by an outsider: the exotic Leda in *Time After Time*, the wayward English girl Mary Fuller in *Taking Chances*, the whippet-like, greedy Lal in *Loving and Giving*. Referred to obliquely and fastidiously as 'light behaviour', sexual passion is seen as destructive, incomprehensible, alien to good breeding, to be regretted perhaps, but never to be underrated, certainly not by a writer who understands her people so well.

Keane writes about the Anglo-Irish, Protestant gentry as an insider, and therefore, by definition, of the Irish people as placed on the other side of the barrier. With the breaking up of the old order this barrier can be broken down too. In the earlier novels the Irish, referred to as 'the people', are not forgotten, if only because appearances have to be kept up when they are present: it would not do for a lady to be seen smoking by 'the people' (*Young Entry*). In the later novels the relationship between the former masters and the former subjugated is quite different. Rose, the former cook and maid, is Aroon's powerful adversary in *Good Behaviour*; Silly-Willie in *Loving and Giving* conspires with Aunt Tossie to keep the well-meaning Nicandra at bay; in *Time After Time* Baby June relies on Christy Lucey to help her run the farm.

The marked change in the tone and spirit of her later novels is signalled by Molly Keane herself in a manner that may be unique in present-day fiction. Her early novels, ten in number, all published under a pseudonym, M.J. Farrell, were witty, amusing, and deeply preoccupied with fox-hunting. After the sudden death of her husband Keane gave up her writing, and returned to her craft some 20 years later, writing now under her own name, and writing of a world no longer so very amusing, and viewed perhaps more charitably. A comparison between Aunt Edythe in *Taking Chances*, grotesque in her 'lust for self-bedizenment', and the deaf April Swift in *Time After Time*, so religiously—and so successfully—at work on retaining her beauty in old age, is illuminating.

The sobering pity, the awareness of people's pathetic reasons for their foolish pretences are new, but the wit and the brilliance of Keane's writing have remained with her, polished to perfection. Her descriptions of people, of the old houses and of the Irish countryside are superb, giving credence yet again to the claim that the best writing in English comes from across the Irish Sea.

—Hana Sambrook

KELL, Joseph. See **BURGESS, Anthony.**

KELLOW, Kathleen. See **HOLT, Victoria.**

KELLS, Susannah. See **CORNWELL, Bernard.**

KEMP, Sarah. See **SALISBURY, Carola.**

KENEALLY, Thomas (Michael).
Pseudonym: William Coyle. **Nationality:** Australian. **Born:** Sydney, New South Wales, 7 October 1935. **Education:** St Patrick's College, Strathfield, New South Wales; studied for the priesthood, 1953–60, and studied law. **Military Service:** Australian Citizens Military Forces. **Relations:** married Judith Mary Martin in 1965; two daughters. **Career:** high school teacher in Sydney, 1960–64; lecturer in drama, University of New England, Armidale, New South Wales, 1968–69; visiting professor of English, University of California, Irvine, 1985; Berg professor of English, New York University, 1988. Member, Australia-China Council, 1978–83; member of the advisory panel, Australian Constitutional Commission, 1985–88; member, Australian Literary Arts Board, 1985–88; president, National Book Council of Australia, 1985–89. Since 1987, Chair, Australian Society of Authors. **Recipient:** Commonwealth Literary Fund fellowship, 1966, 1968, 1972; Miles Franklin award, 1968, 1969; Captain Cook Bi-Centenary prize, 1970; Royal Society of Literature Heinemann award, 1973; Booker prize, 1982, for *Schindler's Ark*; *Los Angeles Times* award, 1983. Fellow, Royal Society of Literature, 1973; Officer, Order of Australia, 1983. **Agent:** Tessa Sayle Agency, 11 Jubilee Place, London SW3 3TE, England.

ROMANCE AND HISTORICAL PUBLICATIONS

Novels

Bring Larks and Heroes. Melbourne, Cassell, 1967; London, Cassell, and New York, Viking Press, 1968.
The Chant of Jimmie Blacksmith. Sydney and London, Angus and Robertson, and New York, Viking Press, 1972.
Blood Red, Sister Rose. London, Collins, and New York, Viking Press, 1974.
Moses the Lawgiver (novelization of television play). London, Collins-ATV, and New York, Harper, 1975.

Gossip from the Forest. London, Collins, 1975; New York, Harcourt Brace, 1976.
A Victim of the Aurora. London, Collins, 1977; New York, Harcourt Brace, 1978.
Confederates. London, Collins, 1979; New York, Harper, 1980.
The Playmaker. London, Hodder and Stoughton, and New York, Simon and Schuster, 1987.

OTHER PUBLICATIONS

Novels

The Place at Whitton. Melbourne and London, Cassell, 1964; New York, Walker, 1965.
The Fear. Melbourne and London, Cassell, 1965.
Three Cheers for the Paraclete. Sydney, Angus and Robertson, 1968; London, Angus and Robertson, and New York, Viking Press, 1969.
The Survivor. Sydney, Angus and Robertson, 1969; London, Angus and Robertson, and New York, Viking Press, 1970.
A Dutiful Daughter. Sydney and London, Angus and Robertson, and New York, Viking Press, 1971.
Season in Purgatory. London, Collins, 1976; New York, Harcourt Brace, 1977.
Passenger. London, Collins, and New York, Harcourt Brace, 1979.
The Cut-Rate Kingdom. Sydney, Wildcat Press, 1980; London, Allen Lane, 1984.
Schindler's Ark. London, Hodder and Stoughton, 1982; as *Schindler's List*, New York, Simon and Schuster, 1982.
A Family Madness. London, Hodder, and Stoughton, 1985; New York, Simon and Schuster, 1986.
Act of Grace (as William Coyle). London, Chatto and Windus, 1988.
Firestorm (as William Coyle). Boston, G.K. Hall, 1989.
Towards Asmara. London, Hodder and Stoughton, 1989; as *To Asmara*, New York, Warner, 1989.
Flying Hero Class. London, Hodder and Stoughton, and New York, Warner, 1991.
Chief of Staff (as William Coyle). London, Chatto and Windus, 1991.
A Woman of the Inner Sea. London, Hodder and Stoughton, 1992.

Plays

Halloran's Little Boat, adaptation of his novel *Bring Larks and Heroes* (produced Sydney, 1966). Published in *Penguin Australian Drama 2,* Melbourne, Penguin, 1975.
Childermass (produced Sydney, 1968).
An Awful Rose (produced Sydney, 1972).
Bullie's House (produced Sydney 1980; New Haven, Connecticut, 1985). Sydney, Currency Press, 1981.
Our Country's Good (adaptation of his novel *The Playmaker*). London, Methuen, 1988.

Screenplay: *The Priest* (episode in *Libido*), 1973; *Silver City*, with Sophia Turkiewicz, 1988.

Television writing (UK): *Essington,* 1974; *The World's Wrong End* (documentary: *Writers and Places* series), 1981; *Australia* series, 1987.

Other

Ned Kelly and the City of Bees (for children). London, Cape, 1978; Boston, Godine, 1981.
Outback, photographs by Gary Hansen and Mark Lang. Sydney and London, Hodder and Stoughton, 1983.

Australia: Beyond the Dreamtime, with Patsy Adam-Smith and Robyn Davidson. London, BBC Publications, 1987; New York, Facts on File, 1989.
Child of Australia, with music by Peter Sculthorpe. London, Faber Music, 1987.
The Place Where Souls Are Born (travel). London, Hodder and Stoughton, 1991.
By the Line. London, Sceptre, 1992.
Now and in Time to Be: Ireland and Irish, photographs by Patrick Pendergast. London, Ryan Press, 1991; New York, Norton, 1992.

*

Film Adaptations: *The Chant of Jimmie Blacksmith,* 1981; *Schindler's List,* 1993, from the novel *Schindler's Ark.*

Critical Study: *Thomas Keneally* by Peter Quartermaine, London, Arnold, 1991.

Manuscript Collections: Mitchell Library, Sydney; Australian National Library, Canberra.

Theatrical Activities:
Actor: **Films**—*The Devil's Playground,* 1976; *The Chant of Jimmie Blacksmith,* 1978.

* * *

Much of Thomas Keneally's work is historical fiction, plotting the lives of fictional characters against large events, or representing people who existed. Several novels deal with different phases of the Australian past. *Blood Red, Sister Rose* reconstructs the life of Joan of Arc. *Schindler's Ark* and *A Family Madness* tell stories connected with Nazi Europe and the Holocaust. *Gossip from the Forest* is about the Armistice negotiations in 1918. *Confederates* is about the American Civil War. *A Victim of the Aurora* uses an Edwardian expedition to the Antarctic as the setting for a murder mystery.

Keneally is interested in the eruption of history into people's lives. He looks at the distances across which history carries people, the transformations it makes, the loyalties that survive its interventions. He is concerned with the mystery, from the viewpoint of late 20th-century suburban safety, of the horrors and miracles of the past. Keneally brings to this a transferred and secularized version of a Catholic sense of mystery. He works with mystery in both its religious and its thriller-story sense. He sets up mysteries of origin, and, especially, mysteries of goodness and evil.

Two sorts of heroism recur: a jovial, imperfect and usually male heroism, and a mystical, superficially serene and generally female heroism, frequently ending in martyrdom. Oskar Schindler and Joan of Arc are the clearest examples. The chatty, confiding male version has much more in common with the characteristic narrative sensibility. The female version is a kind of Other, and is erotically constructed by male observers—male characters in the novels and at times the male narrative viewpoint. Important in several novels is a contemplative, sympathizing male admiration for the grace of women under torture. Sometimes this admiration is acknowledged to contain strong elements of desire.

Central to the Australian novels is the white settler's disturbed and vengeful sense of the strangeness of the land and the people he has appropriated. Women settlers are unstably positioned, sometimes holding the settler's viewpoint, sometimes viewed as mysterious like the new land. In *Bring Larks and Heroes,* and more recently in *The Playmaker,* the narrative focus is on the inscrutability of the new land for convict settlers and the officers, marines, and missionaries who rule them. This inscrutability resembles that of the convicts for their rulers, and becomes the general inscrutability and

otherness of a human psyche from which savagery and kindness emerge with equal unexpectedness. Momentarily there are reversals: constructions of other points of view, revealing the inscrutability of the whites for the aborigines, the men for the women, the gentry for the convicts. These other viewpoints demand acknowledgement but resist represention; the novels want to acknowledge female subjectivity, black subjectivity and convict subjectivity, but cannot sufficiently break down the dominant viewpoint. Generally, Keneally's pragmatically anecdotal narratives do not allow such moments of impasse to be more than momentary, providing instead a rich but largely unbroken surface of description, and forms of closure which allow the reader to disengage easily as a chapter ends.

The Chant of Jimmie Blacksmith is the story of a half-aboriginal Australian, in the first decade of this century, who is so tormented by the ideas of himself he is given by the whites that he murders the wives and children of his employers, and is hunted. The third-person narrative mainly takes Jimmie Blacksmith's viewpoint, but is unable to inhabit this to any depth, and so has to impose a pace too fast for extensive reflection. The interspersing of this with a voice resembling that of newspaper reports provides an alienating effect, but this too is not allowed to develop sufficiently to stall the thriller-like pace.

Keneally's typical central characters are the male heroes, whose idiom and mood his narrative voice can more confidently share. Often they will have some reason to keep ahead of their feelings, some doubt or fear that threatens to well up and incapacitate them and the narrative. They keep on the move; Keneally's narratives are often travel-narratives given urgency by the pressure of plot. Frequently these heroes have reluctantly accepted a mission for which they feel inadequate, and they seem to look to the process of narrative, to some implicit reader, for reassurance.

Matthias Erzberger was a German plenipotentiary sent to negotiate the Armistice in November 1918. In *Gossip from the Forest,* Keneally constructs him as a small-town rationalist, a man of human weaknesses, of practical cunning rather than an intellectual. Indeed, he has a specific sort of decency and awareness which in Keneally tends to be at odds with abstraction. Overtaken, in his provincial life, by a terrible logic of history, Erzberger keeps down his terror by observing, and struggles to gain a provisional sense. He becomes a secular martyr.

In Oskar Schindler, the Sudeten-German factory owner in occupied Cracow who set up a fake labour camp and saved over a thousand Jewish prisoners, Keneally finds the apotheosis of this type. His Schindler is a more heroic version of his Erzberger, a secular saviour who in saving others found an unexpected, latent self. Certain kinds of reflection would endanger this: 'An existentialist would have been defeated by the numbers at Prokocim, stunned by the equal appeal of all the names and voices. But Herr Schindler was a philosophic innocent. He knew the people he knew'.

Keneally sets up a bemused sense of the similarities between Schindler and Amon Goeth, a concentration camp commander. Like Oskar, Goeth is often referred to by his first name, and at times the narrative goes so far as to construct for him a viewpoint. This runs no risk of implying a kind of complicity with him, as it might if his crimes were smaller, and throughout this novel Keneally's narrative has a paradoxical freedom because of the enormity of the events concerned; in relation to them it clearly can only be a small, contingent voice. This narrative notes the ordinariness of these two men, and the mysterious smallness of their difference that was so absolute.

—Richard Kerridge

KENNEDY, Margaret (Moore).

Nationality: British. **Born:** London, 23 April 1896. **Education:** Cheltenham Ladies College, Gloucestershire, 1912–15; Somerville College, Oxford, B.A. in history. **Relations:** married David (later Sir David) Davies in 1925 (died 1964); one son and two daughters. **Recipient:** James Tait Black memorial prize, 1954, for *Troy Chimneys*. Fellow, Royal Society of Literature. **Died:** 31 July 1967.

Romance and Historical Publications

Novels

The Ladies of Lyndon. London, Heinemann, 1923; New York, Doubleday, 1925.
The Constant Nymph. London, Heinemann, 1924; New York, Doubleday, 1925.
Red Sky at Morning. London, Heinemann, and New York, Doubleday, 1927.
The Fool of the Family. London, Heinemann, and New York, Doubleday, 1930.
Return I Dare Not. London, Heinemann, and New York, Doubleday, 1931.
A Long Time Ago. London, Heinemann, and New York, Doubleday, 1932.
Together and Apart. London, Cassell, 1936; New York, Random House, 1937.
The Midas Touch. London, Cassell, 1938; New York, Random House, 1939.
The Feast. London, Cassell, New York, Rinehart, 1950.
Lucy Carmichael. New York, Rinehart, and London, Macmillan, 1951.
Troy Chimneys. New York, Rinehart, 1952; London, Macmillan, 1953.
The Oracles. London, Macmillan, 1955; as *Act of God*, New York, Rinehart, 1955.
The Heroes of Clone. London, Macmillan, 1957; as *The Wild Swan*, New York, Rinehart, 1957.
A Night in Cold Harbour. London, Macmillan, and New York, St Martin's Press, 1960.
The Forgotten Smile. London, Macmillan, 1961; New York, Macmillan, 1962.
Not in the Calendar. London, Macmillan, and New York, Macmillan, 1964.

Short Stories

A Long Week-End. London, Heinemann, and New York, Doubleday, 1927.
Dewdrops. London, Heinemann, 1928.
The Game and the Candle. London, Heinemann, 1928.
Women at Work. London, Macmillan, 1966.

Other Publications

Plays

The Constant Nymph, with Basil Dean, adaptation of the novel by Kennedy (produced London and New York, 1926). London, Heinemann, and New York, Doubleday, 1926.
Come with Me, with Basil Dean (produced London, 1928; New York, 1935). London, Heinemann, 1928.
Jordan (produced London, 1928).
Escape Me Never!, adaptation of her novel *The Fool of the Family* (produced Manchester and London, 1933). London, Heinemann, 1934; New York, Doubleday, 1935.

Autumn, with Gregory Ratoff, adaptation of a play by Ilya Surguchev (produced Manchester and London, 1937). London, Nelson, 1940.
Who Will Remember? Chicago, Dramatic Publishing Company, 1946.
Happy with Either (produced London, 1948).

Screenplays: *The Constant Nymph*, with Basil Dean and Dorothy Farnum, 1933; *The Old Curiosity Shop*, with Ralph Neale, 1934; *Little Friend*, with Christopher Isherwood and Berthold Viertel, 1934; *Whom the Gods Love (Mozart)*, 1936; *Dreaming Lips*, with Carl Mayer and Cynthia Asquith, 1937; *Prison Without Bars*, with Hans Wilhelm and Arthur Wimperis, 1938; *Stolen Life*, with George Barraud, 1939; *Return to Yesterday*, with others, 1940; *Rhythm Serenade*, with others, 1943; *The Man in Grey*, with Doreen Montgomery and Leslie Arliss, 1943; *One Exciting Night (You Can't Do Without Love)*, with others, 1944; *Take My Life*, with Winston Graham and Valerie Taylor, 1947.

Other

A Century of Revolution 1789–1920. London, Methuen, 1922.
Where Stands a Wingèd Sentry. New Haven, Connecticut, Yale University Press, 1941.
The Mechanized Muse (on film). London, Allen and Unwin, 1942.
Jane Austen. London, Barker, 1950; Denver, Swallow, 1952; revised edition, Barker, 1957.
The Outlaws on Parnassus (on the novel). London, Cresset Press, 1958; New York, Viking Press, 1960.

*

Film Adaptations: *The Constant Nymph*, 1933, 1943; *Escape Me Never*, 1935, 1947; *That Dangerous Age*, 1948, from the play *Autumn*.

Critical Study: *The Constant Novelist: A Study of Margaret Kennedy 1896–1967* by Violet Powell, London, Heinemann, 1983.

*   *   *

The Constant Nymph was the literary sensation of an era. *Everyone* read it; everyone was bowled over. The compulsively readable tale of a sprawling family of genius left its mark indelibly upon a generation of young writers—but no one ever matched its triumph, not even Margaret Kennedy herself.

In this famous story, the ill-disciplined brood of an expatriate British composer is notorious among its victims as 'Sanger's Circus'. Here and there across Europe, at home everywhere and nowhere, they lead a straggling, unpredictable life: they were wild, amoral, and dishonest in all ways but one; to each of them music alone is sacred and apart, not to be treated as lightly as mere matters of life, love, or death. Suddenly Albert Sanger, the father whose larger-than-life personality has been the sun around which the wild family circles in orbit, collapses and dies. What is to become of his uncouth children?

Into their gypsy life, on a mission of mercy, comes respectability in the person of a determined female cousin with conventional ideas. The rest of the novel, and its sequel, *The Fool of the Family*, explores the inevitable clash between self-willed artistic temperament and law-abiding society. Little Tessa, the nymph whose constancy causes her death, is the pathetic and unforgettable victim crushed between the irresistible force of her love, and the immovable object that is her respectable cousin's determination that she shall conform to a code she can never understand.

The fame of this one stunningly successful book has somewhat obscured the fact that Kennedy was the author of other novels, one of the most notable being the prize-winning *Troy Chimneys*. The haunting tale of a dual personality, half sensitive, penniless charmer, half self-seeking, conscienceless political climber, is told in a series of brief flashes, as his correspondence is discovered and interpreted years after his untimely death. Miles Lufton, the hero, is a complex creation, slave to the conventions of his age and the ugly necessities of his poverty, but always conscious within himself that he is capable of better things. This tragi-comedy of a man who gained *almost* everything he ever wanted, but found that the price had been too high, and his soul lost in the endeavour, is a beautifully crafted and memorable example of Kennedy's artistry.

—Joan McGrath

KENT, Alexander.

Pseudonym: Douglas Reeman. **Nationality:** British. **Born:** Thames Ditton, Surrey, 15 October 1924. **Education:** attended local schools in England, 1928–39. **Relations:** married Kimberley Jordan. **Career:** Royal Navy from 16, served on destroyers and small craft during World War II, lieutenant, 1940–46; constable, and detective in Criminal Investigation Division, 1946–50; children's welfare officer, London County Council, 1950–60. Since 1946, full-time writer. **Address:** Blue Posts, Eaton Park Road, Cobham, Surrey, England.

ROMANCE AND HISTORICAL PUBLICATIONS

Novels (series: Richard Bolitho in all books)

Captain Richard Bolitho, RN. London, Hutchinson, 1978.
  To Glory We Steer. London, Hutchinson, and New York, Putnam, 1968.
  Sloop of War. London, Hutchinson, and New York, Putnam, 1972.
  Command a King's Ship. London, Hutchinson, and New York, Putnam, 1973.
Form Line of Battle. London, Hutchinson, and New York, Putnam, 1969.
Enemy in Sight!. London, Hutchinson, and New York, Putnam, 1970.
The Flag Captain. London, Hutchinson, and New York, Putnam, 1971.
Signal: Close Action! (sequel to *The Flag Captain*). London, Hutchinson, 1974; New York, Putnam, 1976.
Richard Bolitho: Midshipman. London, Hutchinson, 1975; New York, Putnam, 1976.
Passage to Mutiny. London, Hutchinson, and New York, Putnam, 1976.
In Gallant Company. London, Hutchinson, and New York, Putnam, 1977.
The Inshore Squadron. London, Hutchinson, 1978; New York, Putnam, 1979.
Midshipman Bolitho and the Avenger. London, Hutchinson, and New York, Putnam, 1978.
Stand into Danger. London, Hutchinson, and New York, Putnam, 1980.
Tradition of Victory. London, Hutchinson, 1981.
Success to the Brave. London, Hutchinson, 1983.
Colours Aloft!. London, Hutchinson, and New York, Putnam, 1986.
Bolitho. London, Heinemann, 1993.
  Honour this Day. London, Heinemann, 1987.
  With All Dispatch. London, Heinemann, 1988.
  The Only Victor. London, Methuen, 1990.

Beyond the Reef. London, Heinemann, 1992.
Darkening Sea. London, Heinemann, 1993.

Novels as Douglas Reeman

A Prayer for the Ship. London, Jarrolds, 1958; New York, Putnam, 1973.
High Water. London, Jarrolds, 1959.
Send a Gunboat. London, Jarrolds, 1960; New York, Putnam, 1961; as *Escape from Santu*, New York, Panther, 1962.
Dive in the Sun. London, Jarrolds, and New York, Putnam, 1961.
The Hostile Shore. New York, Jarrolds, 1962.
The Last Raider. London, Jarrolds, 1963; New York, Putnam, 1964.
With Blood and Iron. London, Jarrolds, 1964; New York, Putnam, 1965.
HMS Saracen. London, Jarrolds, 1965; New York, Putnam, 1966.
Path of the Storm. London, Hutchinson, 1966; New York, Putnam, 1967.
The Deep Silence. London, Hutchinson, 1967; New York, Putnam, 1968.
The Pride and the Anguish. London, Hutchinson, 1968; New York, Putnam, 1969.
To Risks Unknown. London, Hutchinson, 1969; New York, Putnam, 1970.
The Greatest Enemy. London, Hutchinson, 1970; New York, Putnam, 1971.
Rendezvous: South Atlantic. London, Hutchinson, and New York, Putnam, 1972.
Go In and Sink. London, Hutchinson, 1973.
His Majesty's U-Boat. New York, Putnam, 1973.
The Destroyers. London, Hutchinson, and New York, Putnam, 1974.
Winged Escort. London, Hutchinson, and New York, Putnam, 1975.
Surface with Daring. New York, Putnam, 1977.
Strike from the Sea. London, Hutchinson, and New York, Morrow, 1978.
A Ship Must Die. London, Hutchinson, and New York, Morrow, 1979.
Torpedo Run. London, Hutchinson, and New York, Morrow, 1981.
Badge of Glory. London, Hutchinson, 1982; New York, Morrow, 1984.
The Iron Pirate. New York, Putnam, 1986.
The White Guns. London, Heinemann, 1989.

OTHER PUBLICATIONS

Other

Adventures in the High Seas: True Stories from Captain Bligh to the Nautilus. New York, Walker, 1971.
The First To Land. London, Hutchinson, and New York, Morrow, 1984.

*   *   *

Alexander Kent is this generation's outstanding author of naval romances. They are set in the stirring period of Britain's history that is linked in the public imagination with the daring deeds and enigmatic personality of Lord Nelson, and it is quite easy to see reflections of his career and character in Kent's fictional hero, Richard Bolitho. It is not difficult to find parallels with Horatio Hornblower, and discerning critics have hailed Kent as the true heir to the highly successful C.S. Forester.

One way to read the Richard Bolitho novels would be to start at the beginning of the chronological sequence and continue straight through them as he gradually wins promotion to ever higher rank. There is, however, no obligation to do this. Just as their author wrote the stories out of order for the sake of freshness and to present himself with a greater challenge, so too his readers may get more from them, become more involved in the stories and, more importantly, in the characterization of their hero if they pick up any one of the novels and make the effort to piece together all the fragments of information that are enticingly provided, little by little. For what matters are not just all the exciting events that occur and Bolitho's numerous courageous deeds, but the way in which his responses are continuously influenced by a past that is always, to some degree, problematic, and a future that is never certain.

The son of a naval officer, Richard Bolitho was born in Falmouth in 1756. He commands a sloop by the time of the American Revolution and has command of larger ships in the conflicts with the French after 1789. His Cornish origins are reflected not only in recurrent dreams of returning to his home there and his ready sympathy for others who hail from those parts, but also his distaste for London and his unease about society in general. It is aboard ship that he is in his element, and Bolitho's personality is portrayed within the closed and strictly organized hierarchy of a man-of-war. We can trace his career from midshipman upwards. He is fortunate in comparison to others who serve with him, who find their promotion blocked at various levels, provided, that is, they are not mangled by a cannon ball, or felled by a musket bullet, or a cutlass slash. However, like any other serving officer, Bolitho must accept the limitations imposed on his freedom of action by senior officers, most of whom do not inspire or, indeed, merit his total confidence. In some instances that is because they lack professional competence or are so hidebound that they have no imagination. On other occasions personal factors intervene, either on account of weakness of character on their part, or as a result of their animosity towards Bolitho. In some cases his seniors find motives for doubting his total commitment on account of the questionable loyalty of his brother Hugh, or else they have personal scores to settle, sometimes over rivalry for the favours of women.

We soon become aware of the complexity of Bolitho's relationships with those who serve under him in his various commands. His officers are an interestingly varied set of human beings. Some are devoted to him, but others, often with more complex personalities, seek their own advancement, and their harsh treatment of others shows Bolitho in a good light, especially when it comes to sympathizing with the plight of midshipmen who are as yet unused to the rigours of war at sea. There is a strong sense that officers and crew belong to different worlds, but, again, Bolitho is remarkable because of his concern for his men; he is loath to mete out the savage punishments that were considered normal in those rough times. His reward is his men's constant support, and his personal servants are almost dog-like in their devotion.

The Bolitho stories are set against the background of the navy in Nelson's day. There is meticulously recorded detail of the various types of vessels employed by the Royal Navy in that period, of the drills of ship handling on passage and in battle, and of the ceremonies and customs of naval life. Equally impressive are the battle scenes with their noise and confusion, their appalling carnage and the frightful suffering that follows even success in battle. Bolitho's reactions of disgust and horror mirror those of his modern readers. They also make it even more remarkable that Bolitho invariably takes the lead when the time comes for close quarters fighting again and again, without a second thought, even though in the later novels he might as a senior officer be justified in entrusting perilous duties to his juniors. Since Alexander Kent places his tales within the grand panorama of war across the seven seas over several decades, we witness Bolitho as he faces up to a great variety of problems, in different situations. His response is always brave and ingenious, and

his success is typically achieved against the odds, with scant help from his superiors.

Further complexities are added for Bolitho, as for Hornblower and indeed Nelson himself, by relationships with women. These are not explored in any great psychological depth, but there is a lot of passion. This adds an extra dimension to these novels which, with all the realism of their factual and historical background, dwells above all on the loneliness of a sensitive hero in a world of appalling cruelty and violence.

—Christopher N. Smith

KEPPEL, Charlotte.   See BLACKSTOCK, Charity.

KEVERN, Barbara.   American. 1932—. See 2nd edition, 1990.

KEYES, Frances Parkinson.
Nationality: American. **Born:** Francis Parkinson Wheeler, Charlottesville, Virginia, 21 June 1885. **Education:** Miss Carroll's School and Winsor School, Boston; Mlle. Dardelle's School, Switzerland. **Relations:** married Henry Wilder Keyes (governor of New Hampshire, 1917–19, and United States Senator, 1919–31) in 1904 (died 1938); three sons. **Career:** associate editor, *Good Housekeeping*, New York, 1923–35; editor, *National Historical Magazine*, 1937–39. **Recipient:** Siena medal, 1946; Christopher medal, 1953. D.Litt.: George Washington University, Washington, DC, 1921; Bates College, Lewiston, Maine, 1934; L.H.D.: University of New Hampshire, Durham, 1951. Légion d'honneur, 1962. **Died:** 3 July 1970.

ROMANCE AND HISTORICAL PUBLICATIONS

Novels

The Old Gray Homestead. Boston, Houghton Mifflin, and London, Hodder and Stoughton, 1919; as *Sylvia Cary*, New York, Paperback Library, 1962.
The Career of David Noble. New York, Stokes, 1921; London, Nash, 1923.
Queen Anne's Lace. New York, Liveright, 1930; London, Eyre and Spottiswoode, 1940.
Lady Blanche Farm: A Romance of the Commonplace. New York, Liveright, 1931; London, Eyre and Spottiswoode, 1940.
Senator Marlowe's Daughter. New York, Messner, 1933; as *Christian Marlowe's Daughter*, London, Eyre and Spottiswoode, 1934.
The Safe Bridge. New York, Messner, 1934; London, Eyre and Spottiswoode, 1935.
Honor Bright. New York, Messner, and London, Eyre and Spottiswoode, 1936.
Parts Unknown. New York, Messner, 1938; as *The Ambassadress*, London, Eyre and Spottiswoode, 1938.
The Great Tradition. New York, Messner, and London, Eyre and Spottiswoode, 1939.
Fielding's Folly. New York, Messner, and London, Eyre and Spottiswoode, 1940.
All That Glitters. New York, Messner, and London, Eyre and Spottiswoode, 1941.
Crescent Carnival. New York, Messner, 1942; as *If Ever I Cease to Love*, London, Eyre and Spottiswoode, 1943.

Also the Hills. New York, Messner, 1943; London, Eyre and Spottiswoode, 1944.

The River Road. New York, Messner, 1945; as *The River Road* and *Vail d'Alvery*, London, Eyre and Spottiswoode, 2 vols, 1946–47.

Came a Cavalier. New York, Messner, 1947; London, Eyre and Spottiswoode, 1948.

Dinner at Antoine's. New York, Messner, 1948; London, Eyre and Spottiswoode, 1949.

Joy Street. New York, Messner, 1950; London, Eyre and Spottiswoode, 1951.

Steamboat Gothic. New York, Messner, 1952; as *Steamboat Gothic* and *Larry Vincent*, London, Eyre and Spottiswoode, 2 vols, 1952–53.

The Royal Box. New York, Messner, and London, Eyre and Spottiswoode, 1954.

Blue Camellia. New York, Messner, and London, Eyre and Spottiswoode, 1957.

Victorine. New York, Messner, 1958; as *The Gold Slippers*, London, Eyre and Spottiswoode, 1958.

Station Wagon in Spain. New York, Farrar Straus, 1959; as *The Letter from Spain*, London, Eyre and Spottiswoode, 1959.

The Chess Players. New York, Farrar Straus, 1960; London, Eyre and Spottiswoode, 1961.

Madame Castel's Lodger. New York, Farrar Straus, 1962; London, Eyre and Spottiswoode, 1963.

The Explorer. New York, McGraw Hill, 1964; London, Eyre and Spottiswoode, 1965.

I, The King. New York, McGraw Hill, and London, Eyre and Spottiswoode, 1966.

The Heritage. New York, McGraw Hill, and London, Eyre and Spottiswoode, 1968.

Short Stories

The Restless Lady and Other Stories. New York, Liveright, 1963; London, Eyre and Spottiswoode, 1964.

OTHER PUBLICATIONS

Poetry

The Happy Wanderer. New York, Messner, 1935.

Other

Letters from a Senator's Wife. New York, Appleton, 1924.

Silver Seas and Golden Cities: A Joyous Journey Through Latin Lands. New York, Liveright, 1931.

Capital Kaleidoscope: The Story of a Washington Hostess. New York, Harper, 1937.

Written in Heaven: The Life on Earth of the Little Flower of Lisieux. New York, Messner, and London, Eyre and Spottiswoode, 1937; as *Therese, Saint of a Little Way*, Messner, 1950; as *St Teresa of Lisieux*, Eyre and Spottiswoode, 1950.

Pioneering People in Northern New England: A Series of Early Sketches. Washington, DC, Judd and Detweiler, 1937.

Along a Little Way. New York, Kenedy, and London, Burns Oates, 1940; revised edition, New York, Hawthorn, 1962.

Bernadette, Maid of Lourdes. New York, Messner, 1940; revised edition, as *The Sublime Shepherdess*, Messner, and London, Burns Oates, 1940; revised edition, as *Bernadette of Lourdes: Shepherdess, Sister, and Saint*, Messner, 1953; London, Hollis and Carter, 1954.

The Grace of Guadalupe. New York, Messner, 1941; London, Burns Oates, 1951.

Once an Esplanade: A Cycle of Two Creole Weddings (for children). New York, Dodd Mead, 1947; London, Hollis and Carter, 1949.

All This Is Louisiana. New York, Harper, 1950.

The Cost of a Best Seller (memoirs). New York, Messner, 1950; London, Eyre and Spottiswoode, 1953.

The Frances Parkinson Keyes Cookbook. New York, Doubleday, 1955; London, Muller, 1956.

St Anne: Grandmother of Our Saviour. New York, Messner, 1955; London, Wingate, 1956; revised edition, New York, Hawthorn, 1962.

Guadalupe to Lourdes (omnibus). St Paul, Catechetical Guild Educational Society, 1957.

The Land of Stones and Saints (on Spain). New York, Doubleday, 1957; London, Davies, 1958.

Christmas Gift. New York, Hawthorn, 1959; London, Davies, 1960.

Mother Cabrini, Missionary to the World. New York, Farrar Straus, and London, Burns Oates, 1959.

Roses in December (autobiography). New York, Doubleday, and London, Davies, 1960; revised edition, New York, Liveright, 1966.

The Rose and the Lily: The Lives and Times of Two South American Saints. New York, Hawthorn, 1961; London, Davies, 1962.

Three Ways of Love. New York, Hawthorn, 1963; London, Davies, 1964.

Tongues of Fire. New York, Coward McCann, 1966.

All Flags Flying: Reminiscences. New York, McGraw Hill, 1972.

Editor, *A Treasury of Favorite Poems.* New York, Hawthorn, 1963.

Translator, *The Third Mystic: The Self Revelation of María Vela of Avila.* New York, Farrar Straus, and London, Davies, 1960.

*   *   *

Frances Parkinson Keyes, the favourite novelist of many American readers during the middle third of this century, received only a few sympathetic and understanding criticisms during her lifetime. In the most notable of these, 'The Queens of Fiction' (*Life*, 6 April 1959), Robert Warnick compared her with Taylor Caldwell and Edna Ferber, noting that then all the fiction of all three was in print. By 1980, the situation had changed; nearly all of Caldwell and Ferber's epics remained available, but almost all of Keyes's had disappeared from print. How could a popular favourite so soon lose her place in readers' affections? The mystery of this 'generation gap' poses an important problem in changing tastes, much like the elusive problems that often provide the leisurely momentum for this lady's tales.

One of Warnick's distinctions between these three practitioners of the 'big, old-fashioned novel' suggests an answer; he sharply contrasts the 'strident world' of Edna Ferber's tales and 'the nightmare world' of Taylor Caldwell's with the 'gentle and aristocratic world' of Keyes's. As television epics like *Dallas* and *Dynasty* that are the descendants of the work of these novelists show, the Ferber/Caldwell tradition of violence and nightmare has appropriated an audience that increasingly confuses aristocracy with just being rich.

Although Keyes wrote popular novels about rural New England, Boston, Washington, DC, and London, among the many places to which her extensive travels had taken her, she discovered the ambience that best suited her talents and led to her greatest successes when friends lured her to New Orleans in the late 1930s. She lived in a fine old house in the restored French Quarter and elsewhere about Louisiana off and on for the rest of her life, absorbing the unique atmosphere that provided the groundwork for the intricately designed tapestries of her eight tales of traditional Creole society from *Crescent Carnival* to *The Chess Players.* Whether she was creating a tale that spanned three generations (*Crescent Carnival*, *Steamboat Gothic*) or only a few days that brought to a head years of frustration (*Dinner at Antoine's*, *Victorine*), whether she was writing nostalgically for children (*Once an Esplanade*) or with more chic for her contemporaries (*The River Road*), whether she moved out of the magic city to the back country (*Blue Camellia*) or to other exotic ports of call around the world (*The Chess Players*), Keyes's legends, to the delight of her lending-library readers and the despair of fashionable reviewers, were richly decorated with the fruits of long and careful research into the culture—in both the artistic and anthropological senses—of the regions that intrigued her.

Reviewers who faulted her indifferent plotting, rambling narratives, flabby style, overindulgence in background material, and long, confidential prefaces shaping her struggles in creating the books and acknowledging the help of those who befriended her missed altogether the source of her appeal. Reading a novel by Keyes was not a way to pass the time restlessly on idle days, it was rather like a chatty visit from an old and welcome friend who had just returned from fabulous places, brimming over with their quaint lore and exciting gossip.

Since the pattern of all her works—too imprecise to be labelled a formula—is similar, one provides a model for all these local colour tales. *Dinner at Antoine's* remains of possibly most interest because of the ever increasing fame of the titular restaurant the characters frequent. Although built around a mysterious murder, it is no detective story, as fans of that genre complained. Too little of the tale concerns the improbable crime and its solution; the event serves simply to hold together a knowing account of the resorts and activities of the glamorous characters as they either adjust to the increasingly commercial society that is destroying their elegant world or simply fade out of the changing picture. The weakness of the novel, like others of the same weave, is that Keyes never quite finds the skill to blend the conventionalized foreground figures into the overpowering background; but this lack of sophisticated technique didn't bother readers who liked to enjoy each page for itself and regretted reaching the drawn-out endings of the meandering tales.

Length and detail alone do not distinguish Keyes's novels from Ferber's and Caldwell's. The reason for the comparative impermanence of Keyes's fabrications is most likely that the societies she portrayed have faded with the passing years. Although neither Keyes nor her readers would probably have thought of themselves as decadent, they were profoundly so; and this fascination with decadence suggests the reason that Creole Louisiana and its hothouse culture provided the ideal vehicle for rewarding their tastes. Keyes has since failed to attract readers that still revel in the lusty works of Ferber and Caldwell; but she would not have cared for such vulgarians or their affection. She had the joy of writing for a fastidious class that loved her and whose fantasy world can now only be recaptured through her works.

—Warren French

KIDD, Flora.
Nationality: Canadian. **Born:** England. **Education:** University of Liverpool, 1944–49, B.A. **Relations:** married Robert Kidd; four children. **Career:** teacher, London. **Address:** Sandy Point Road, Saint John, New Brunswick, Canada.

ROMANCE AND HISTORICAL PUBLICATIONS

Novels

Visit to Rowanbank. London, Mills and Boon, 1966.

Whistle and I'll Come. London, Mills and Boon, 1966; Toronto, Harlequin, 1967.

Nurse at Rowanbank. Toronto, Harlequin, 1966; London, Mills and Boon, 1967.

Love Alters Not. London, Mills and Boon, 1967; Toronto, Harlequin, 1968.

Wind So Gay. London, Mills and Boon, 1968.

Strange as a Dream. London, Mills and Boon, 1968; Toronto, Harlequin, 1969.

When Birds Do Sing. London, Mills and Boon, 1970; Toronto, Harlequin, 1971.

Love Is Fire. London, Mills and Boon, 1971; Toronto, Harlequin, 1972.

My Heart Remembers. London, Mills and Boon, and Toronto, Harlequin, 1971.

The Dazzle on the Sea. London, Mills and Boon, and Toronto, Harlequin, 1971.

If Love Be Love. London, Mills and Boon, and Toronto, Harlequin, 1972.

Remedy for Love. London, Mills and Boon, and Toronto, Harlequin, 1972.

The Taming of Lisa. London, Mills and Boon, 1972; Toronto, Harlequin, 1973.

The Cave of the White Rose. London, Mills and Boon, 1972; Toronto, Harlequin, 1973.

Beyond the Sunset. London, Mills and Boon, and Toronto, Harlequin, 1973.

Night on the Mountain. London, Mills and Boon, 1973.

The Legend of the Swans. London, Mills and Boon, 1973; Toronto, Harlequin, 1974.

Gallant's Fancy. London, Mills and Boon, and Toronto, Harlequin, 1974.

The Paper Marriage. London, Mills and Boon, and Toronto, Harlequin, 1974.

Stranger in the Glen. London, Mills and Boon, and Toronto, Harlequin, 1975.

Enchantment in Blue. London, Mills and Boon, and Toronto, Harlequin, 1975.

The Bargain Bride. London, Mills and Boon, 1976; Toronto, Harlequin, 1979.

The Black Knight. London, Mills and Boon, 1976; Toronto, Harlequin, 1977.

The Dance of Courtship. London, Mills and Boon, and Toronto, Harlequin, 1976.

The Summer Wife. London, Mills and Boon, 1976; Toronto, Harlequin, 1976.

Dangerous Pretence. London, Mills and Boon, and Toronto, Harlequin, 1977.

Night of the Yellow Moon. London, Mills and Boon, 1977; Toronto, Harlequin, 1978.

To Play with Fire. London, Mills and Boon, 1977; Toronto, Harlequin, 1978.

Jungle of Desire. London, Mills and Boon, Toronto, Harlequin, 1977.

Marriage in Mexico. London, Mills and Boon, and Toronto, Harlequin, 1978.

Castle of Temptation. London, Mills and Boon, and Toronto, Harlequin, 1978.

Sweet Torment. London, Mills and Boon, and Toronto, Harlequin, 1978.

Canadian Affair. London, Mills and Boon, 1979.

Passionate Encounter. London, Mills and Boon, and Toronto, Harlequin, 1979.

Stay Through the Night. London, Mills and Boon, and Toronto, Harlequin, 1979.

Tangled Shadows. London, Mills and Boon, 1979; Toronto, Harlequin, 1980.

Together Again. London, Mills and Boon, and Toronto, Harlequin, 1979.

The Arranged Marriage. London, Mills and Boon, and Toronto, Harlequin, 1980.

The Silken Bond. London, Mills and Boon, and Toronto, Harlequin, 1980.

Wife by Contract. London, Mills and Boon, and Toronto, Harlequin, 1980.

Beyond Control. London, Mills and Boon, and Toronto, Harlequin, 1981.

Passionate Stranger. London, Mills and Boon, and Toronto, Harlequin, 1981.

Personal Affair. London, Mills and Boon, and Toronto, Harlequin, 1981.

Meeting at Midnight. London, Mills and Boon, 1981; Toronto, Harlequin, 1982.

Bride for a Captain. London, Mills and Boon, and Toronto, Harlequin, 1981.

Makebelieve Marriage. London, Mills and Boon, and Toronto, Harlequin, 1982.

Between Pride and Passion. London, Mills and Boon, and Toronto, Harlequin, 1982.

Tempted to Love. London, Mills and Boon, 1982; Toronto, Harlequin, 1983.

Dangerous Encounter. London, Mills and Boon, 1983; Toronto, Harlequin, 1984.

Dark Seduction. London, Mills and Boon, 1983; Toronto, Harlequin, 1984.

Tropical Tempest. London, Mills and Boon, 1983; Toronto, Harlequin, 1984.

Desperate Desire. London, Mills and Boon, 1984; Toronto, Harlequin, 1985.

The Open Marriage. London, Mills and Boon, 1984; Toronto, Harlequin, 1985.

Passionate Pursuit. London, Mills and Boon, 1984; Toronto, Harlequin, 1985.

A Secret Pleasure. London, Mills and Boon, 1985; Toronto, Harlequin, 1986.

Passionate Choice. London, Mills and Boon, 1986; Toronto, Harlequin, 1987.

The Arrogant Lover. London, Mills and Boon, 1986; Toronto, Harlequin, 1987.

Beloved Deceiver. London, Mills and Boon, 1987; Toronto, Harlequin, 1988.

The Married Lovers. London, Mills and Boon, 1987; Toronto, Harlequin, 1988.

Masquerade Marriage. London, Mills and Boon, 1987; Toronto, Harlequin, 1988.

When Lovers Meet. London, Mills and Boon, 1987; Toronto, Harlequin, 1988.

The Loving Gamble. London, Mills and Boon, 1988.

A Risky Affair. London, Mills and Boon, 1989.

*   *   *

Flora Kidd is an English writer who now lives in Canada. The change in country did not occur immediately for she first spent several years living in Scotland. She has also visited several South American countries and later used them as backgrounds for her novels. *Sweet Torment* takes place in Colombia, while *Enchantment in Blue* takes place in the Caribbean. For the most part, however, Kidd is most known for her novels with Scottish settings. Here she excels in bringing the country and people to life for her readers.

Sandy Phillips, in *The Black Knight*, journeys to Scotland to help a cousin. Her trip takes her through many historic places such as Carlisle, Gretna Green, and on into the Galloway part of Scotland. Juliet Grey in *The Cave of the White Rose* is able to travel on into the Highlands and the story is developed against the backgrounds of the moors and mists of Scotland.

Kidd provides a subtle blending that lessens the impact of the physical surroundings and concentrates on the development of character and plot instead. Her heroines tend to be rather young, with a fresh, engaging manner to them. Sandy has just completed a university degree in history and is considering going on for an advanced degree. Juliet, on the other hand, is virtually alone except for relatives who do not care for her. Both have been sheltered, though, and both are unaware of themselves as women. It is this aspect of Kidd's heroines that makes her stories so readable. Slowly and quite cleverly, she lets her heroines grow up and become aware of their capacity to love.

In developing her male characters, she gives them just the right level of experience to help them eventually win their loved ones. They are naturally older and have more experience, but one does not feel that they are too sophisticated and completely out of reach of the heroines.

In a way, it is difficult to categorize Kidd as a romance writer, for she balances everything so well that glaring differences are not found in her novels. Background stays that way, while character and plot support each other easily. She is intensely creative in developing her characters so that each emerges as a rounded figure.

Her later novels, however, are more dramatic and have an added touch of sophistication and maturity in them that her earlier romances lack. Although her heroines are yet naive and unsure of themselves, they face more emotional turmoil throughout the story, and the endings are more suspenseful than in her earlier novels. In these books the heroine is faced with a hopeless love for a man who is far beyond her reach, and it is not until the very end of the novel that she learns that her love is returned.

The hero is often cynical and hardened. His treatment of the heroine at times borders on cruelty and contempt. The emotional overtones in these novels are heightened and the 'despairing' sort of reaction leaves the reader in a turmoil at the end of the novel, for the change of pace is often abrupt.

Kidd is one of the more prolific novelists who publishes in the Harlequin Presents Series. It is this type of novel that dominates this series. It is of particular note that Kidd is able to adapt her style of writing to both kinds of novels, that is, the familiar 'sweet' romance and the more modern 'sophisticated' ones. Certainly she has developed an avid readership for both types over the last few years.

—Arlene Moore

————

KIMBROUGH, Katheryn. American. 1929——. See 2nd edition, 1990.

————

KIRK, Alexandra.   See **WOODS, Sherryl.**

————

KIRK, Russell (Amos). American. 1918——. See 2nd edition, 1990.

————

KNIGHT, Alanna. British. See 2nd edition, 1990.

————

KNOX, Gilbert. See **MACBETH, Madge.**

———

KOESTLER, Arthur. British. 1905–1983. See 2nd edition, 1990.

———

KRENTZ, Jayne Ann.
Pseudonyms: Jayne Bentley; Jayne Castle; Amanda Glass; Stephanie James; Amanda Quick; Jayne Taylor. **Nationality:** American. **Born:** San Diego, California, 28 March 1948. **Education:** University of California, Santa Cruz, B.A. (honours) in history; San Jose State University, California, M.A. in librarianship, 1971. **Relations:** married. **Career:** librarian; now a full-time writer. Lives in Seattle. **Agent:** The Axelrod Agency, 66 Church Street, Lenox, Massachusetts, MA 01240, USA.

ROMANCE AND HISTORICAL PUBLICATIONS

Novels (series: Katherine, Sarah, and Margaret; Verity Ames and Jonas Quarrel)

Whirlwind Courtship (as Jayne Taylor). New York, Tiara, 1979.
Uneasy Alliance. Toronto, Harlequin, 1984; London, Mills and Boon, 1985.
Call It Destiny. Toronto, Harlequin, 1984; London, Mills and Boon, 1991.
Ghost of a Chance. Toronto, Harlequin, 1984; London, Mills and Boon, 1985.
Man with a Past. Toronto, Harlequin, 1985.
Witchcraft. Toronto, Harlequin, 1985; London, Mills and Boon, 1986.
Legacy. Toronto, Harlequin, 1985.
The Waiting Game. Toronto, Harlequin, 1985.
True Colors. Toronto, Harlequin, and London, Mills and Boon, 1986.
Ties That Bind. Toronto, Harlequin, 1986; London, Mills and Boon, 1987.
Between the Lines. Toronto, Harlequin, 1986; London, Mills and Boon, 1987.
Sweet Starfire. New York, Popular Library, 1986.
Crystal Flame. New York, Popular Library, 1986; London, Worldwide, 1988.
Twist of Fate. Toronto, Worldwide, 1986; London, Severn House, 1991.
The Family Way. Toronto, Harlequin, 1987.
The Main Attraction. Toronto, Harlequin, 1987.
A Coral Kiss. New York, Popular Library, 1987; London, Severn House, 1992.
Chance of a Lifetime. Toronto, Harlequin, 1987.
Midnight Jewels. New York, Popular Library, 1987; London, Worldwide, 1989.
Test of Time. Toronto, Harlequin, 1987.
Full Bloom. Toronto, Harlequin, 1988; London, Mills and Boon, 1989.
Joy. Toronto, Harlequin, 1988; London, Mills and Boon, 1989.
Gift of Gold (Ames and Quarrel). New York, Popular Library, 1988; London, Worldwide, 1990.
Dreams 1–2. Toronto, Harlequin, 2 vols, 1988.
Gift of Fire (Ames and Quarrel). New York, Popular Library, 1989.
A Woman's Touch. Toronto, Harlequin, and London, Mills and Boon, 1989.
Lady's Choice. Toronto, Harlequin, 1989; London, Mills and Boon, 1990.
Shield's Lady (as Amanda Glass). New York, Popular Library, 1989.

The Main Attraction. London, Mills and Boon, 1989.
The Golden Chance. New York, Pocket Books, 1990.
The Pirate (Katherine). Toronto, Harlequin, and London, Mills and Boon, 1990.
The Adventurer (Sarah). Toronto, Harlequin, 1990; London, Mills and Boon, 1990.
A Chance of a Lifetime. Toronto, Harlequin, 1990.
The Cowboy (Margaret). Toronto, Harlequin, and London, Mills and Boon, 1991.
Silver Linings. New York, Pocket Books, 1991.
Too Wild to Wed. London, Mills and Boon, 1991.
Sweet Fortune. New York, Pocket Books, 1991.
Family Man. New York, Pocket Books, 1992.
Perfect Partners. New York, Pocket Books, 1992.
Hidden Talent. New York, Pocket Books, 1993.
Wildest Dreams. New York, Pocket Books, 1993.
Grand Passion. New York, Pocket Books, 1994.

Novels as Jayne Bentley

A Moment Past Midnight. New York, Macfadden, 1979.
Turning Towards Home. New York, Macfadden, 1979.
Maiden of the Morning. New York, Macfadden, 1979.

Novels as Jayne Castle (series: Guinevere Jones)

Vintage of Surrender. New York, Macfadden, 1979.
Queen of Hearts. New York, Macfadden, 1979.
The Gentle Pirates. New York, Dell, 1980.
Bargain with the Devil. New York, Dell, 1981; London, Corgi, 1983.
Right of Possession. New York, Dell, 1981; London, Corgi, 1983.
Wagered Weekend. New York, Dell, 1981; London, Corgi, 1983.
A Man's Protection. New York, Dell, 1982.
A Negotiated Surrender. New York, Dell, 1982.
Affair of Risk. New York, Dell, 1982.
Power Play. New York, Dell, 1982.
Relentless Adversary. New York, Dell, 1982.
Spellbound. New York, Dell, 1982.
Conflict of Interest. New York, Dell, 1983.
Double Dealing. New York, Dell, 1984.
Trading Secrets. New York, Dell, 1985.
The Desperate Game (Jones). New York, Dell, 1986.
The Chilling Deception (Jones). New York, Dell, 1986.
The Sinister Touch (Jones). New York, Dell, 1986.
The Fatal Fortune (Jones). New York, Dell, 1986.

Novels as Stephanie James

A Passionate Business. New York, Silhouette, 1981.
The Dangerous Magic. New York, Silhouette, 1982.
Stormy Challenge. New York, Silhouette, 1982.
Corporate Affair. New York, Silhouette, 1982.
Velvet Touch. New York, Silhouette, 1982.
Lover in Pursuit. New York, Silhouette, 1982.
Renaissance Man. New York, Silhouette, 1982.
A Reckless Passion. New York, Silhouette, 1982.
The Price of Surrender. New York, Silhouette, 1983.
To Tame the Hunter. New York, Silhouette, 1983.
Affair of Honor. New York, Silhouette, 1983.
Gamesmaster. New York, Silhouette, 1983.
The Silver Snare. New York, Silhouette, 1983.
Battle Prize. New York, Silhouette, 1983.
Bodyguard. New York, Silhouette, 1983.
Serpent in Paradise. New York, Silhouette, 1983.
Gambler's Woman. New York, Silhouette, 1984.

Fabulous Beast. New York, Silhouette, 1984.
Devil to Pay. New York, Silhouette, 1984.
Night of the Magician. New York, Silhouette, 1984.
Nightwalker. New York, Silhouette, 1984.
Raven's Prey. New York, Silhouette, 1984.
Golden Goddess. New York, Silhouette, 1985.
Wizard. New York, Silhouette, 1985.
Cautious Lover. New York, Silhouette, 1985.
Green Fire. New York, Silhouette, 1986.
Second Wife. New York, Silhouette, 1986.
Challoner Bride. New York, Silhouette, 1987.
Saxon's Lady. New York, Silhouette, 1987.

Novels as Amanda Quick

Seduction. New York, Bantam, 1990.
Surrender. New York, Bantam, 1990.
Scandal. New York, Bantam, 1991.
Rendezvous. New York, Bantam, 1992.
Ravished. New York, Bantam, 1992.
Reckless. New York, Bantam, 1992.
Dangerous. New York, Bantam, 1993.
Deception. New York, Bantam, 1993.

OTHER PUBLICATIONS

Other

Editor, *Dangerous Men and Adventurous Women: Romance Writers on the Appeal of the Romance*. Pennsylvania, University of Pennsylvania Press, 1992.

*　　*　　*

Jayne Ann Krentz is one of the best and most popular authors of romances. Using several pseudonyms as well as her own name, she is also one of the most varied and prolific. She has published in several series and has many single-title releases. Although most of her novels are contemporary romances, she sometimes introduces elements of fantasy or the occult (*Gift of Gold, Gift of Fire, Dreams 1–2*). Jonas Quarrel of the Gift books has exceptional psychic powers but has not known how to control them until meeting Verity Ames. Only with her can he harness and direct his gift. The two *Dreams* books are unusual both in format and content. Published as Parts One and Two and issued separately, they are a sort of miniseries or cliffhanger since the story begun in Part One is not completed until Part Two. The story itself also includes a powerful psychic element as the present-day lovers find they are caught up in a past legend.

Often Krentz incorporates a strong element of suspense as in *The Desperate Game, The Chilling Deception, The Sinister Touch*, and *The Fatal Fortune*, titles in the detective series that she wrote as Jayne Castle and which features female detective Guinevere Jones. Krentz also has experimented with futuristic romances (*Shield's Lady, Sweet Starfire, Crystal Flame*). As Amanda Quick she regularly publishes Regency romances such as *Dangerous, Ravished, Reckless, Scandal*, and *Seduction*.

Krentz's heroines are unusually strong and determined. They also display a healthy sense of selfworth. They are managing although they are not manipulative. Rather, they delight in solving problems and organizing the lives of the people around them. Many times their unsolicited advice is less than welcome but they persist because they are supremely confident in their abilities. Perhaps the ultimate example is Hannah Jesset in *Twist of Fate*. She has the audacity to seek out tycoon, Gideon Cage, in order to offer him career counselling in exchange for something she wants. To anyone else, including Gideon, this would seem to be the last thing he needs since he is a rich and powerful man. Hannah, however, has analysed his career and decided that he is growing bored and needs a change. As a counsellor she knows just how to rearrange his life to give him a challenge. She is ready to step in and manage him.

The contemporary novels usually show the heroine as running a business successfully, either as an owner or as the guiding power in the background. In *Perfect Partners*, Letitia Thornquist is a midwestern librarian who inherits a family-owned sporting goods store based in the Pacific Northwest. She learns the ropes of the business, and successfully engineers changes in the way it is run. Katy Wade of *Family Man* is the executive assistant who organizes and manages the dysfunctional family which owns a chain of restaurants. She is the one called upon to bring the family black sheep back into the fold and save the family business.

The hero often represents some challenge to the heroine's authority or livelihood. Joel Blackstone (*Perfect Partners*) has no intention of yielding power to anyone, let alone a librarian. When Simon Kendrick (*The Gentle Pirates*) takes over a business, he threatens to eliminate Kirsten Mallory's department unless she can justify its existence. Krentz's women, however, fight for more than a job or even love. For them, respect is as important as love. Any relationship is an equal partnership and anything less is not acceptable. These same modern feelings are displayed by Krentz's Regency heroines.

The typical hero in a Krentz novel is a hard-headed leader or businessman, who is instantly intrigued by the heroine, if somewhat irritated by her insistence on equality. He often stresses the need for trust in a relationship but thinks primarily in terms of her trusting him. Some of these men are wary of commitment or at least of saying the words. Others are immediately drawn to the women and carefully plot out a pursuit. The heroes can be less than physically perfect, which is a welcome touch of reality. For example, Simon Kendrick has a hook in place of one hand and Case Garrett (*Affair of Risk*) wears an eyepatch. Even Gideon Cage is described as being less than the normally requisite six-feet tall. What counts for Krentz is the innate power and self-confidence of the male, not his physical appearance.

Krentz always presents a romance with sparks between the hero and heroine, snappy dialogue, vividly drawn characters and lots of humour thrown in. She also creates very sensual situations for her characters. Verity and Jonas of the Gift books are especially inventive, and Verity's 'revenge' on Jonas in *Gift of Fire* is unique in romance fiction. Krentz knows the wide range of possibilities in the romance genre and seems comfortable working in all of them. As editor of *Dangerous Men and Adventurous Women*, she has gathered essays by romance writers on the appeal of romance fiction and taken a positive step in justifying or legitimizing the genre to a broader audience. It is clear that much of her success results from the respect she has for both the genre and her readers.

—Barbara E. Kemp

————

KUCZKIR, Mary. See **MICHAELS, Fern.**

————

KYLE, Susan. See **PALMER, Diana.**

————

LAFFEATY, Christina.
Pseudonyms: Netta Carstens, Martha Fortina. **Born:** South Africa.
Education: attended 12 different schools between the ages of seven

and fifteen. **Relations:** married; two children. **Career:** clerical jobs. Full-time writer. **Address:** 50 Glen Road, Wadebridge, Cornwall, PL27 7PE, England.

ROMANCE AND HISTORICAL PUBLICATIONS

Novels

The Reluctant Bride. London, Hale, 1966.
Island of Storm. London, Hale, 1966.
The Dark Pursuer. London, Hale, 1967.
Too Many Brides. London, Hale, 1967.
Dark Beneath the Moon. London, Hale, 1968.
Midnight of Madness. London, Hale, 1968.
Stormy Oasis. London, Hale, 1968.
This Heart So Wild. London, Hale, 1968.
The Desolation and the Dream. London, Gresham, 1969.
Dangerous Claim. London, Gresham, 1969.
Man of Destiny. London, Gresham, 1969.
The Revealing Moment. London, Gresham, 1969.
Road to Destiny. London, Hale, 1969.
Stormy Haven. London, Gresham, 1969.
The Heart Must Pause. London, Gresham, 1969.
If Tomorrow Ever Comes. London, Gresham, 1969.
In Another's Footsteps. London, Gresham, 1969.
Valley of Heartache. London, Gresham, 1969.
Broken Journey (as Martha Fortina). London, Gresham, 1969.
Prisoner of Fate (as Martha Fortina). London, Hale, 1969.
Uneasy Eden. London, Hale, 1970.
Dream of a Shadow. London, Gresham, 1970.
Cold Shine the Stars. London, Hale, 1970.
Heart of a Stranger. London, Hale, 1970.
Mistress of Mooralee. London, Hale, 1972.
The Sugar Angel. London, Hale, 1972.
Cry Pity, Cry Love. London, Hale, 1972.
Village of Secrets. London, Hale, 1973.
Clouds over Castile. London, Hale, 1973.
The Beckoning Dream. London, Hale, 1974.
The Brides of Bunyon. London, Hale, 1975.
Stranger Among the Stars. London, Hale, 1975.
Prisoner in Paradise. London, Hale, 1976.
The Blue Scarab. London, Hale, 1977.
Lamorna. London, Hale, 1977.
The Rage of Heaven. London, Hale, 1977.
The Windleton Conspiracy. London, Hale, 1978.
The Stranger in the Mirror. London, Hale, 1979.
The House in Lavender Grove. London, Hale, 1979.
To Reap a Bitter Harvest. London, Hale, 1980.
Zulu Sunset. London, Mills and Boon, 1980.
Count Antonov's Heir. London, Mills and Boon, 1980.
For Love or Lorenzo. London, Hale, 1981.
Caradon's Castle. London, Hale, 1982.
Date with Destiny. London, Hale, 1983.
The Heirs of Polyrayne. London, Hale, 1983.
Land of Living Waters. London, Hale, 1983.
Diamonds in the Dust. London, Mills and Boon, 1984.
All the Hills Moved. London, Hale, 1984.
The Khan of Shapoora. London, Hale, 1984.
Twenty-Sovereign Bride. London, Mills and Boon, 1984.
The Haunting Stranger. London, Hale, 1985.
The Andalusian Affair. London, Hale, 1985.
Love Undefeated. London, Mills and Boon, 1986.
Illicit Obsession. Toronto, Worldwide, 1987.
Trelawney's Woman. London, Mills and Boon 1988.
Far Forbidden Plains. London, Hodder and Stoughton, 1989.

Where the Hills Reply. London, Hodder and Stoughton, 1991.

Novels as Netta Carstens

The Passion and the Pain. London, Hale, 1970.
Nor Pride nor Pity. London, Hale, 1972.
Katherine of Tamerlaine. London, Hale, 1974.
House of Whispers. London, Hale, 1975.
By Sun and Candlelight. London, Hale, 1976.
Ridge of White Waters. London, Hale, 1976.
While the Gentleman Go By. London, Hale, 1977.
Romany of the Marshes. London, Hale, 1978.

*   *   *

Whether writing historical romances, romantic suspense, or romantic gothic fiction, Christina Laffeaty's books are always extremely well written, with tight interesting plots, and good characterization and setting. Laffeaty's heroines are feisty young women who are independent and opinionated, with a strong sense of right and wrong. Her heroes are dark, moody characters, with a brooding masculinity that is inherently attractive. Her plots often involve children who bring out the loyal and moral qualities in her protagonists.

In *The Reluctant Bride* Sadie takes her young brother to Australia in order to retain custody of him. She arrives to find that Aunt Jessie, who had offered them a home, has died. Sadie thus becomes embroiled in a wild scheme in order to keep her brother. She agrees to marry Adam Preston, the dying brother of a man who gives her a lift in a storm. Adam, however, recovers from his illness, and Sadie is left in a strange country with a husband who does not want anything to do with her. To complicate matters, Adam is rumoured to have strangled his first wife six months earlier. However, Sadie gradually realizes that she is in love with him. Someone tries to strangle Sadie, and she thinks it is Adam; although she realizes her mistake quickly, Adam is too hurt and frustrated to believe her. *The Reluctant Bride* has a complicated plot, but it is successful as a romantic suspense novel because of Laffeaty's skill as a writer.

The Brides of Bunyoni is, similarly, a romantic suspense novel. The book begins in London where the heroine, Lyn, lives with her stepson. Receiving an invitation to her Aunt Pearl's wedding, Lyn realizes that the bridegroom is her ex-husband, Justin, a confidence trickster and hustler. In order to save her aunt she travels to Bunyoni, in the eastern Transvaal. She encounters Sebastian, the nephew of her aunt's late husband who informs her that her aunt is dead. There is an immediate antagonism between them, which, of course, masks a deep abiding attraction. The will leaving the estate to Sebastian has disappeared; Lyn inherits instead. She intends to return the land to Sebastian but realizes on closer inspection that her aunt had overextended herself financially and that the estate could be lost to pay the debts. Lyn, showing her independent and moral spirit, decides to get the estate back on its feet before returning it to Sebastian. Sebastian and Lyn marry, but the latter discovers that not only is she not divorced from Justin, but that he killed Pearl. Justin tries to kill her, but crashes his car, and kills himself instead.

Cold Shine the Stars is set in Edmonton, during a Canadian winter. It revolves around a group of people who are trapped in a cabin by the snow. Katherine is left to look after the children of her late brother-in-law Johnnie. She is set to marry Brett Stephens, a local, when Johnnie's cousin, the appropriately named Adam Storm, turns up and claims custody of the children. The snow prevents Katherine from leaving, and the ensuing situation reveals tensions, and intricate relationships. Katherine and Adam realize that they love each other.

Uneasy Eden and *Cry Pity, Cry Love* also revolve around adult relationships with children. In *Uneasy Eden* Beth goes to see her mother and discovers Timothy, a small boy, who decides he wants her to marry his father. Beth, of course, ends up falling in love with Timothy's father. *Cry Pity, Cry Love*, however, deals with the serious issue of fostering children. The heroine, Kate, is an ex-foster child, turned successful career woman. She 'inherits' a brood of foster children from her ex-foster mother on the latter's death. Each child has his/her own problem which is treated with sensitivity and understanding. Kate, through her relationship with the children, emerges from the tough shell that she has built to protect herself, and allows herself to care for the children and for her boss.

Laffeaty's later books are longer, more weighty tomes. They contain accurate historical detail, and long descriptive passages that give the reader a good sense of time and place. *Far Forbidden Plains* is set in the Transvaal and deals with the relationship between Petronella and Marcus Cohen. The book begins in the period leading up to the Boer war and the historical background is thoroughly researched and presented. Laffeaty makes the reader aware of the harsher realities of the war: concentration camps set up by the British to house Boer women and children, the dysentery and measles that wiped out many people, and the British attitude to the war is reflected through reports from British newspapers.

Where the Hills Reply is also set in South Africa at the turn of the century. It features long passages describing the African wildlife and landscape. Sabella is the central character, who, following her father's death, takes her siblings to stay with her aunt. Finding her aunt has died, she ends up marrying her cold cousin, Hendrik, in order to keep her family together. However, she falls in love with his half-brother Sebastian. While pregnant with Sebastian's child, Sabella loses her husband in an accident. Sebastian has married someone else in the meantime, and Sabella ends up marrying a trickster, Pierre Le Roux. Sabella's efforts to keep her family together go unrewarded when her brother Anton turns against her and joins the banned neo-nazi movement, *Ossewa Brandwag*. Love triumphs in the end and Sebastian and Sabella end up together on Mooikrantz, the farm that Sabella has fought so hard to keep.

Laffeaty is a popular writer fundamentally because of her well written and impeccably researched books. Whether it be Transvaal, Australia, or England, Laffeaty creates authentic settings against which her interesting, and often complicated, plots are played out.

—P. Campbell

LAKE, Rozella. See **LINDSAY, Rachel.**

LAKER, Rosalind.
Pseudonym for Barbara Øvstedal. **Other Pseudonyms:** Barbara Douglas; Barbara Paul. **Recipient:** Elizabeth Goudge historical award, 1986. **Agent:** Laurence Pollinger Ltd, 18 Maddox Street, London W1R 0EU, England. **Address:** c/o Doubleday, 666 Fifth Avenue, New York, New York 10103, USA.

ROMANCE AND HISTORICAL PUBLICATIONS

Novels (series: Warwyck)

Sovereign's Key. London, Hale, 1969.
Far Seeks the Heart. London, Hale, 1970.
Sail a Jeweled Ship. London, Hale, 1971.
The Shripney Lady. London, Hale, 1972.
Fair Wind of Love. London, Hale, 1974; (as Barbara Douglas) New York, Doubleday, 1980.

The Smuggler's Bride. New York, Doubleday, 1975; London, Hale, 1976.
Ride the Blue Riband. New York, Doubleday, 1977; London, Hale, 1978.
Warwyck's Woman. New York, Doubleday, 1978; as *Warwyck's Wife*, London, Eyre Methuen, 1979.
Claudine's Daughter (Warwyck). New York, Doubleday, and London, Eyre Methuen, 1979.
Warwyck's Choice. New York, Doubleday, 1980; as *The Warwycks of Easthampton*, London, Eyre Methuen, 1980.
Banners of Silk. New York, Doubleday, 1981; London, Methuen, 1982.
Gilded Splendor. New York, Doubleday, and London, Methuen, 1982.
Jewelled Path. London, Methuen, and New York, Doubleday, 1983.
What the Heart Keeps. London, Methuen, and New York, Doubleday, 1984.
This Shining Land. London, Methuen, and New York, Doubleday, 1985.
Tree of Gold. London, Methuen, and New York, Doubleday, 1986.
The Silver Touch. London, Methuen, and New York, Doubleday, 1987.
To Dance with Kings. London, Methuen, 1988; New York, Doubleday, 1989.
Circle of Pearls. London, Doubleday, and New York, Doubleday, 1990.
The Golden Tulip. London, Doubleday, and New York, Doubleday, 1991.
The Venetian Mask. London, Doubleday, and New York, Doubleday, 1992.
The Sugar Pavilion. London, Doubleday, and New York, Doubleday, 1993.

Novels as Barbara Øvstedal

Red Cherry Summer. London, Hale, 1973.
Valley of the Reindeer. London, Hale, 1973.
Souvenir from Sweden. London, Hale, 1974.

Novels as Barbara Paul

The Seventeenth Stair. London, Macdonald and Jane's, and New York, St Martin's Press, 1975.
The Curse of Halewood. London, Macdonald and Jane's, 1976; as *Devil's Fire, Love's Revenge*, New York, St Martin's Press, 1976.
The Frenchwoman. London, Macdonald and Jane's, and New York, St Martin's Press, 1977.
A Wild Cry of Love. London, Macdonald and Jane's, 1978; as *To Love a Stranger*, New York, St Martin's Press, 1978.

OTHER PUBLICATIONS

Other

Norway (as Barbara Øvstedal). London, Batsford, and New York, Hastings House, 1973.

*   *   *

Since the appearance of her very first novel, Rosalind Laker has presented her readers with a broad range of offerings from period gothics to fictionalized biography. As might be expected with such a variety of periods and settings, she achieves varying degrees of success while on the whole providing well-written, tightly woven books.

The Smuggler's Bride begins with the typical premiss of an orphan turned governess for the spoiled daughters of a snobbish wealthy family whose grown son considers the attractive new employee fair game. When the young woman sees and hears strange goings-on from the adjoining home of a reclusive neighbour, she attempts to dispel the children's fear that the house is haunted, and finds the occupant alone and injured. She agrees to stay on as his nurse and housekeeper, and when he has sufficiently recovered the man offers her marriage as a means of salvaging her reputation. She finds herself well-provided for from the proceeds of her husband's unsavoury former occupation.

Set in 19th-century England, *Claudine's Daughter* deals with events in the life of Lucy di Castelloni, orphaned at a young age, raised in an Italian convent, and married off to a wealthy elderly landowner. Now widowed, Lucy travels to Easthampton seeking freedom and a home, but unprepared for love or the revival of a scandal from past decades which involved another beautiful woman and holds the key to Lucy's past and future.

Warwyck's Choice continues recounting the relationship of love, hate, rivalry, jealousy, and loyalty of three generations of the wealthy Radcliffe and Warwycke families whose saga began in the earlier *Warwyck's Woman*.

A fictionalized biography of Thomas Chippendale, *Gilded Splendor*, details the life of a carpenter's apprentice with dreams of becoming a master cabinet-maker, and the genteel woman determined to become his patroness, and to assure that his dreams come true.

Another portrayal of the spectacular European playgrounds and pastimes of the rich and famous at the turn of the century unfolds in *Jewelled Path*. The daughter of an eminent London jeweller seeks to make her own mark in the world of jewellery design despite her father's preferring to see her safely married and his opposition to her exciting new designs being promoted by Tiffany and Fabergé.

Abandoning the glitz and glamour of such period pieces, *What the Heart Keeps* follows Lisa Shaw, a 'home' child sent from an English orphanage to the freedom of an adoptive home in North America—a freedom which is, in fact, the equivalent of indentured servitude. With determination and strength of character, she overcomes all obstacles finally to fulfil her destiny in life and love.

In what is perhaps Laker's strongest work, *This Shining Land* is set in Norway during the German occupation and provides the reader with a genuine sense of the horrors and degradation facing the ordinary citizen in such extraordinary circumstances, and the quiet courage and determination with which they strove to survive as individuals and as a nation. She offers a grim portrait of the experiences of the concentration camps without excessively gruesome detail nor gratuitous violence or presenting her protagonists as superhuman heroes.

The Napoleonic Wars and France's silk industry serve as a backdrop for the seemingly doomed love of the heirs of the feuding silk houses of Roche and Deveaux in *Tree of Gold*.

The *Golden Tulip* recounts Francesca Vesser's attempts to become a Master Painter in the face of the financial, personal, and political difficulties facing her family, and 17th-century Holland.

Set in 18th-century Venice, *The Venetian Mask* combines the traditions of music, masks, political intrigue, and personal vendettas as it follows the fortunes of three friends, brought together at the renowned musical conservatory for orphaned girls, the Ospedale de la Pieta, and destined to share a lifetime of joy and sorrow.

All of Laker's novels are carefully researched and meticulously crafted, but it is in the more recent settings, rather than those of centuries past, that her characters most successfully rise above the tend- ency to be interchangeable stock types and take on life as real individuals.

—Judith A. Gifford

LAMB, Charlotte.
Pseudonym for Sheila Holland. **Other Pseudonyms:** Sheila Coates; Laura Hardy; Sheila Lancaster; Victoria Woolf. Also writes as Sheila Holland. **Nationality:** British. **Born:** Sheila Coates in London, 22 December 1937. **Education:** Ursuline Convent, Ilford, Essex. **Relations:** married Richard Holland in 1959; two sons and three daughters. **Career:** secretary, Bank of England, London, 1954–56, and BBC, London, 1956–58. **Agent/Address:** Richard Holland, Crogga, Santon, Isle of Man, United Kingdom.

ROMANCE AND HISTORICAL PUBLICATIONS

Novels (series: Barbary Wharf)

Follow a Stranger. London, Mills and Boon, and Toronto, Harlequin, 1973.
Carnival Coast. London, Mills and Boon, 1973; Toronto, Harlequin, 1974.
A Family Affair. London, Mills and Boon, and Toronto, Harlequin, 1974.
Star-Crossed. London, Mills and Boon, 1976; New York, Oxford University Press, 1978.
Sweet Sanctuary. London, Mills and Boon, and Toronto, Harlequin, 1976.
Festival Summer. London, Mills and Boon, and Toronto, Harlequin, 1977.
Florentine Spring. London, Mills and Boon, and Toronto, Harlequin, 1977.
Hawk in a Blue Sky. London, Mills and Boon, 1977; Toronto, Harlequin, 1978.
Kingfisher Morning. London, Mills and Boon, 1977.
Master of Comus. London, Mills and Boon, 1977; Toronto, Harlequin, 1978.
Call Back Yesterday. London, Mills and Boon, and Toronto, Harlequin, 1978.
Desert Barbarian. London, Mills and Boon, and Toronto, Harlequin, 1978.
Disturbing Stranger. London, Mills and Boon, 1978; Toronto, Harlequin, 1979.
Autumn Conquest. London, Mills and Boon, 1978.
The Long Surrender. London, Mills and Boon, 1978.
The Cruel Flame. London, Mills and Boon, 1978; Toronto, Harlequin, 1980.
Duel of Desire. London, Mills and Boon, 1978.
The Devil's Arms. London, Mills and Boon, 1978; Toronto, Harlequin, 1979.
Pagan Encounter. London, Mills and Boon, 1978; Toronto, Harlequin, 1979.
Sweet Compulsion (as Victoria Woolf). London, Mills and Boon, and Toronto, Harlequin, 1979.
Forbidden Fire. London, Mills and Boon, 1979.
The Silken Trap. London, Mills and Boon, 1979; Toronto, Harlequin, 1980.
Dark Dominion. London, Mills and Boon, 1979.
Fever. London, Mills and Boon, 1979; Toronto, Harlequin, 1980.
Dark Master. London, Mills and Boon, 1979.
Temptation. London, Mills and Boon, and Toronto, Harlequin, 1979.

Twist of Fate. London, Mills and Boon, 1979; Toronto, Harlequin, 1980.

Possession. London, Mills and Boon, 1979.

Love Is a Frenzy. London, Mills and Boon, 1979; Toronto, Harlequin, 1980.

Frustration. London, Mills and Boon, 1979.

Sensation. London, Mills and Boon, 1979; Toronto, Harlequin, 1980.

Compulsion. London, Mills and Boon, 1980; Toronto, Harlequin, 1981.

Crescendo. London, Mills and Boon, 1980; Toronto, Harlequin, 1981.

Stranger in the Night. London, Mills and Boon, 1980; Toronto, Harlequin, 1981.

Storm Centre. London, Mills and Boon, and Toronto, Harlequin, 1980.

Seduction. London, Mills and Boon, 1980; Toronto, Harlequin, 1981.

Savage Surrender. London, Mills and Boon, and Toronto, Harlequin, 1980.

A Frozen Fire. London, Mills and Boon, and Toronto, Harlequin, 1980.

Man's World. London, Mills and Boon, 1980; Toronto, Harlequin, 1981.

Night Music. London, Mills and Boon, 1980; Toronto, Harlequin, 1981.

Obsession. London, Mills and Boon, 1980.

Retribution. London, Mills and Boon, and Toronto, Harlequin, 1981.

Illusion. London, Mills and Boon, and Toronto, Harlequin, 1981.

Heartbreaker. London, Mills and Boon, and Toronto, Harlequin, 1981.

Desire. London, Mills and Boon, and Toronto, Harlequin, 1981.

Dangerous. London, Mills and Boon, and Toronto, Harlequin, 1981.

Abduction. London, Mills and Boon, and Toronto, Harlequin, 1981.

The Girl from Nowhere. London, Mills and Boon, 1981.

Midnight Lover. London, Mills and Boon, 1982.

A Wild Affair. London, Mills and Boon, 1982.

Betrayal. London, Mills and Boon, 1983.

The Sex War. London, Mills and Boon, 1983.

Haunted. London, Mills and Boon, 1983.

Darkness of the Heart. London, Mills and Boon, 1983.

A Secret Intimacy. London, Mills and Boon, 1983.

A Violation. London, Fontana, and Toronto, Harlequin, 1983.

Infatuation. London, Mills and Boon, 1984.

Scandalous. London, Mills and Boon, 1984.

For Adults Only. London, Mills and Boon, 1984.

Love Games. London, Mills and Boon, 1984.

A Naked Flame. London, Mills and Boon, 1984.

Man Hunt. London, Mills and Boon, 1985.

Who's Been Sleeping in My Bed? London, Mills and Boon, 1985.

Sleeping Desire. London, Mills and Boon, 1985.

The Bride Said No. London, Mills and Boon, 1985.

Explosive Meeting. London, Mills and Boon, 1985.

Heat of the Night. London, Mills and Boon, 1986; Toronto, Harlequin, 1987.

Love in the Dark. London, Mills and Boon, 1986; Toronto, Harlequin, 1987.

Hide and Seek. London, Mills and Boon, and Toronto, Harlequin, 1987.

Circle of Fate. London, Mills and Boon, and Toronto, Harlequin, 1987.

Kiss of Fire. London, Mills and Boon, 1987; Toronto, Harlequin, 1988.

Whirlwind. London, Mills and Boon, 1987; Toronto, Harlequin, 1988.

You Can Love a Stranger. London, Mills and Boon, 1988.

Echo of Passion. London, Mills and Boon, 1988.

Out of Control. London, Mills and Boon, 1988.

No More Lonely Nights. London, Mills and Boon, 1988; Toronto, Harlequin, 1989.

Seductive Stranger. London, Mills and Boon, 1989; Toronto, Harlequin, 1990.

Desperation. London, Mills and Boon, and Toronto, Harlequin, 1989.

Runaway Wife. London, Mills and Boon, and Toronto, Harlequin, 1990.

Dark Music. London, Mills and Boon, 1990.

Dark Pursuit. London, Mills and Boon, 1990.

Rites of Possession. London, Mills and Boon, 1990.

The Threat of Love. London, Mills and Boon, 1990.

Spellbinding. London, Mills and Boon, 1990.

Heart on Fire. London, Mills and Boon, 1991.

Sleeping Partners. London, Mills and Boon, 1991.

Forbidden Fruit. London, Mills and Boon, 1991.

Shotgun Wedding. London, Mills and Boon, 1991.

Barbary Wharf:
1. *Besieged*. London, Worldwide, 1992.
2. *Battle for Possession*. London, Worldwide, 1992.
3. *Too Close for Comfort*. London, Worldwide, 1992.
4. *Playing Hard to Get*. London, Worldwide, 1992.
5. *A Sweet Addiction*. London, Worldwide, 1992.
6. *Surrender*. London, Worldwide, 1992.

Dreaming. London, Mills and Boon, 1993.

Fire in the Blood. London, Mills and Boon, 1993.

Falling in Love. London, Mills and Boon, 1993.

Wounds of Passion. London, Mills and Boon, 1993.

Guilty Love. London, Mills and Boon, 1994.

Novels as Sheila Holland

Love in a Mist. London, Hale, 1971.

Prisoner of the Heart. London, Hale, 1972.

A Lantern in the Night. London, Hale, 1973.

Falcon on the Hill. London, Hale, 1974.

Shadows at Dawn. London, Hale, 1975; Chicago, Playboy Press, 1979.

The Growing Season. London, Hale, 1975.

The Gold of Apollo. London, Hale, 1976.

Caring Kind. London, Hale, 1976.

The Devil and Miss Hay. London, Hale, 1977.

Eleanor of Aquitaine. London, Hale, 1978.

Maiden Castle. Chicago, Playboy Press, 1978.

Love's Bright Flame. Chicago, Playboy Press, 1978.

Dancing Hill. Chicago, Playboy Press, 1978.

Folly by Candlelight. London, Hale, 1978; Chicago, Playboy Press, 1979; as *The Notorious Gentleman*, Playboy Press, 1980.

Sophia. Chicago, Playboy Press, 1979.

The Masque. New York, Zebra, 1979.

The Merchant's Daughter. Chicago, Playboy Press, 1980.

Miss Charlotte's Fancy. Chicago, Playboy Press, 1980.

Secrets to Keep. Chicago, Playboy Press, 1980.

Secrets. London, Fontana, 1983; Toronto, Harlequin, 1984.

A Woman of Iron. London, Collins, 1985.

Novels as Sheila Coates

A Crown Usurped. London, Hale, 1972.

The Queen's Letter. London, Hale, 1973.

The Flight of the Swan. London, Hale, 1973.

The Bells of the City. London, Hale, 1975.

Novels as Sheila Lancaster

Dark Sweet Wanton. London, Hodder and Stoughton, 1979; New York, Berkley, 1980.
The Tilthammer. London, Hodder and Stoughton, 1980.
Mistress of Fortune. London, Hodder and Stoughton, 1982.

Novels as Laura Hardy

Burning Memories. London, Silhouette, 1981.
Playing with Fire. London, Silhouette, 1981.
Dream Master. London, Silhouette, 1982.
Tears and Red Roses. London, Silhouette, 1982.
Dark Fantasy. London, Silhouette, 1983.
Men Are Dangerous. London, Silhouette, 1984.

*

Charlotte Lamb comments:

I try to write romantic novels which have very real characters and situations, but which never lose sight of the basic truth about romantic fiction—that we are creating dreams for our readers, dreams which must be rooted in real life if they are to be intensely powerful. The more closely a reader can identify with the book, the more she can respond to it and enjoy it. Women are both highly practical and deeply emotional, and what they want in their fiction is a mixture of warmly observed life and powerful emotion. All fiction is invented; the best fiction is close to reality yet with that added dimension of an escape into dreams.

*   *   *

Charlotte Lamb's series romances are characterized by energy and sensation despite their large number. For a considerable period of time, Lamb published one novel per month. Often identified by highly charged one-word titles (*Obsession, Desire, Frustration, Infatuation, Scandalous*), her novels detail the romantic entanglements of characters with deep-seated problems, often related to sexuality.

Although Lamb's heroines are occasionally country girls, their most typical milieu is London. Some are secretaries to playboy businessmen; others are actresses, singers, or artists. They are usually young, occasionally naive, and always more inhibited than other women in the books. Her heroes are older, highly successful, and domineering without being excessively brutal. She knows how to suggest an appealing vulnerability in traditionally 'macho' men. Unlike some other series writers, however, Lamb has not significantly altered her formula to appeal to a more contemporary audience. Where some series writers have changed the balance of knowledge and power between male and female characters to suggest a more equal relationship, Lamb's women remain less assertive, less accomplished, and less independent than many more recent heroines.

Lamb often writes about heroines who have been victims of sexual trauma. In *Stranger in the Night* and *Seduction* her women are unwillingly seduced and are marked by the experience. She writes about troubled marriages in *Sensation* and *A Frozen Fire*. In *Dark Dominion* the hero is almost pathologically jealous. In *Frustration* the heroine is debilitated by the death of her husband. Most heroines need to be shown how to express sexuality; most heroes need to be taught fidelity. Although Lamb's topics are often more potentially sensational than those of other series writers, she handles the material with circumspection. Any author as prolific as Lamb will pro-

duce uneven work, but despite her productivity she is unusually inventive within the restricted range of series romance formulas.

—Kay Mussell

———

LAMB, William.   See JAMESON, Storm.

———

LAMONT, Marianne.   See MANNERS, Alexandra.

———

LAMPITT, Dinah.
Nationality: British. **Born:** Essex, 6 March 1937. **Education:** Putney High School, London, 1947–52; Regent Street Polytechnic, London, 1952–54. **Relations:** L.F. Lampitt, 1959 (died 1981). Two children. **Career:** junior journalist, *Woman*, London, 1954–55; assistant to news editor, *The Times*, London, 1956–57; assistant to fiction editor, *The Evening News*, London, 1957–59. Director, theatre productions in South-East England. **Agent:** Shirley Russell, Rupert Crew Ltd, Kings Mews, London WC1N 2JA, England. **Address:** Fairlight Cottage, Rushers Cottage, Mayfield, Sussex TN20 6PU, England.

ROMANCE AND HISTORICAL PUBLICATIONS

Novels (series: Sutton Place Trilogy)

Sutton Place Trilogy:
    Sutton Place. London, Muller, 1983.
    The Silver Swan. London, Muller, 1984.
    Fortune's Soldier. London, Muller, 1985.
To Sleep No More. London, Joseph, 1987; New York, St Martin's Press, 1988.
Pour the Dark Wine. London, Joseph, 1989.
The King's Women. London, New English Library, 1992; New York, New American Library, 1993.
As Shadows Haunting. London, New English Library, 1993; New York, New American Library, 1994.

*

Dinah Lampitt comments:

My historical novels are not all they would appear to be, for an element of the supernatural, a dalliance with the paranormal, haunts the pages of each and every one. Painstakingly researched, vividly bringing to life the people and events of the past, they all have a gothic quality that has earned me an ever-increasing readership. Recently reviewed as 'the best writer' of my kind, my fascination with the world unseen continues unabated.

*   *   *

In writing her historical novels, Dinah Lampitt combines her interest in history with her fascination with the supernatural; she has a vivid imagination, and tells a good tale. She has an exact sense of period and a great feeling for colour.

In her 'Sutton Place Trilogy' she tells the story of a house and estate, doomed by the curse of Queen Edith, neglected wife of Edward the Confessor. The curse falls on the heirs of the owners, and in *Sutton Place* we learn how it affects Francis, the eldest son of the Weston family, who was accused of adultery with Ann Boleyn, and subsequently was executed. Interwoven with the Westons' story is that of Dr Zachary Fitzhoward, a powerful astrologer and clairvoyant, who was the natural son of the Duke of Norfolk, and a gypsy.

Throughout the book, both the ghosts of people who have been affected by the anguish of the dead queen appear to the bewildered Tudor inhabitants, and the apparitions of those who will live in the house in the 20th century, such as Paul Getty and Lord Northcliffe.

Sutton Place in the early-18th century is explored in *The Silver Swan* in which descendants of the Westons and the Fitzhowards are again juxtaposed. In a tale of love and betrayal, of selfishness and magic, the Silver Swan is the beautiful Melior Mary, heir to the Catholic, Jacobite Westons. Her hair turns white in childhood when the ghosts of the house persecute her; she discovers a secret to keep her youthful looks so she is the most beautiful woman of her times. The book tells of her part in rescuing the Old Pretender's bride from prison, and of her love affair with the Young Pretender. However, the curse finally defeats her as she dies alone and unloved, allowing the house to fall into ruin.

Fortune's Soldier tells how dilapidated Sutton Place in the early-19th century caused the Webbe Westons to lose all their money, and drives their heir, John Joseph, to become a soldier in the Austrian Army. His great friend, Jackdaw, is a Fitzhoward descendant, and both men are in love with Lady Horatia Waldegrove. This is the most melodramatic of the three books; there are too many coincidences and prophetic dreams for credibility but in all three a gripping story is told, and the doom-laden atmosphere is deliciously spine-chilling.

To Sleep No More is a saga set in the Sussex village of Mayfield. In the 14th century a young girl is married to the idiot brother of the Archbishop of Canterbury, and is loved by a Gascon squire. The three of them form a touching bond and when they meet untimely deaths their spirits cannot rest. They are reincarnated in the 17th century and become embroiled in a witch trial, again meeting early deaths. In the final part of the story they are involved in the lawless 18th-century world of smuggling and highwaymen.

In *Pour the Dark Wine*, Lampitt returns to the Tudor court. This time it is the story of the Seymour family, although she interweaves into it Dr Zachary Fitzhoward's astrology. She explores two interesting theories: firstly, that Edward VI was born to Jane Seymour by caesarian section, which resulted in her death soon afterwards, and secondly, that Queen Elizabeth I remained 'virgin queen' because of an anatomical malformation that made it impossible for her to have intercourse.

She gives this same malformation to Joan of Arc in *The King's Women*. Charles VII is the king in question, and the women in his life are his mother, Isabeau of Bavaria, the most dissolute queen since Messalina; Yolande of Aragon, a strong dominant woman who, Lampitt suggests, was secretly the mother of the Maid of Orleans; Charles's wife, Marie; Joan, *la Pucelle*; and finally, Agnes Sorel, Charles's mistress, the most beautiful woman of her time. This is an ambitious book, well written and well researched, telling a fascinating and compelling story.

Lampitt is at home in all the periods she writes about, having a sure hand with the details of the social life of the past. Although her writing is occasionally a little too lush and fulsome, her stories are always absorbing, and well worth reading.

—Pamela Cleaver

LANCASTER, Sheila. See **LAMB, Charlotte.**

LANCE, Leslie. See **CHARLES, Theresa.**

LANE, Jane.

Pseudonym for Elaine Dakers. **Nationality:** British. **Born:** Ruislip, Middlesex, in 1905. **Education:** attended schools in Middlesex. **Relations:** married the publisher Andrew Dakers in 1937; one son. **Died:** 6 January 1978.

ROMANCE AND HISTORICAL PUBLICATIONS

Novels

Undaunted. London, Heath Cranton, 1934.
Be Valiant Still. London, Rich and Cowan, 1935.
King's Critic. London, Rich and Cowan, 1936.
Prelude to Kingship. London, Rich and Cowan, 1936.
Come to the March. London, Rich and Cowan, 1937.
Sir Devil-May-Care. London, Methuen, 1937.
You Can't Run Away. London, Methuen, 1940.
He Stooped to Conquer. London, Dakers, 1943.
England for Sale. London, Dakers, 1943.
Gin and Bitters. London, Dakers, 1945; as *Madame Geneva*, New York, Rinehart, 1946.
His Fight Is Ours. London, Dakers, 1946.
London Goes to Heaven. London, Dakers, 1947.
Parcel of Rogues. London, Dakers, and New York, Rinehart, 1948.
Fortress in the Forth. London, Dakers, 1950.
Dark Conspiracy. London, Hale, 1952.
The Sealed Knot. London, Hale, 1952.
The Lady of the House. London, Hale, 1953; as *Countess at War*, London, Davies, 1974.
The Phoenix and the Laurel. London, Hale, 1954.
Thunder on St Paul's Day. London, Hale, and Westminster, Maryland, Newman Press, 1954.
Conies in the Hay. London, Hale, 1957; as *Rabbits in the Hay*, Westminster, Maryland, Newman Press, 1958.
Command Performance. London, Hale, 1957.
Queen of the Castle. London, Hale, 1958.
Cat among the Pigeons. London, Hale, 1959.
Sow the Tempest. London, Muller, 1960.
Ember in the Ashes. London, Muller, 1960.
Farewell to the White Cockade. London, Muller, 1961.
The Crown for a Lie. London, Muller, 1962.
A State of Mind. London, Muller, 1964.
A Wind Through the Heather: A Novel of the Highland Clearances. London, Muller, 1965.
From the Snare of the Hunter. London, Muller, 1968.
The Young and Lonely King. London, Muller, 1969.
The Questing Beast. London, Muller, 1970.
A Call of Trumpets. London, Muller, 1971.
The Severed Crown. London, Davies, 1972; New York, Simon and Schuster, 1973.
Bridge of Sighs. London, Davies, 1973; New York, Day, 1975.
Heirs of Squire Harry. London, Davies, 1974.
A Summer Storm. London, Davies, 1976.
A Secret Chronicle. London, Davies, 1977.

OTHER PUBLICATIONS

Fiction (for children)

The Escape of the King. London, Evans, 1950.
The Escape of the Prince. London, Evans, 1951.
Desperate Battle. London, Evans, 1953.
The Escape of the Queen. London, Evans, 1957.
The Escape of the Duke. London, Evans, 1960.
The Escape of the Princess. London, Evans, 1962.

The Trial of the King. London, Evans, 1963.
The Return of the King. London, Evans, 1964.
The March of the Prince. London, Evans, 1965.
The Champion of the King. London, Evans, 1966.

Other

The Last of the Hales; For Church and King (articles). London,
 Manresa Press, 1931.
King James the Last. London, Dakers, 1942.
Titus Oates: A Biography. London, Dakers, 1949; Westport, Con-
 necticut, Greenwood Press, 1971.
Puritan, Rake and Squire. London, Evans, 1950.
The Reign of King Convenant (on Scotland 1633–61). London,
 Hale, 1956.

*   *   *

The output of historical novels by Elaine Dakers, who wrote as
Jane Lane, was prolific. She enjoyed great popularity and most of
her books were reprinted many times. She wrote three different
kinds of book—straight historical novels, social histories of a short
period of time when a way of life was changing, and a third kind in
which an historical story is told in the form of extracts from diaries,
memoirs, and letters.

All her books were exhaustively researched and every tiny detail
of the life of the time is crammed in to show how people lived. If, as
one critic has said, there are two kinds of historical novels—those
that show our ancestors as very like us and those that show what
strange lives they led—Lane was definitely of the second school of
thought.

She set many of her books in the 17th and 18th centuries and was
very pro-Stuart. Typical of her straight historical novels are her
Scottish stories. *He Stooped to Conquer* tells the shameful story of
the Massacre of Glencoe when William III tried to have the Glencoe
sept of the Macdonalds treacherously wiped out. In *His Fight Is
Ours* the story of the years between the 1715 and 1745 uprisings is
told by the chief of the Macdonalds from his poverty-stricken exile
in Paris. These books are beautifully written and read as if they are
translated from the Gaelic and are full of details of Highland life.

The Questing Beast tells of the run up to the Civil War, concentrating on Pym, the Parliamentarian leader. *A Call of Trumpets*
shows the Royalist cause in the Civil War doomed by the feud between Queen Henrietta Maria and Prince Rupert, with King Charles
sitting on the fence between them. Lane also wrote novels set in the
16th century: *Parcel of Rogues* is about Mary Queen of Scots and
Heirs of Squire Harry about Henry VIII's children.

Another straight historical novel but with a very different subject
is *From the Snare of the Hunter*, a moving, detailed account of
Jesus's last days from the entry to Jerusalem to the finding of the
empty tomb.

Her 'social history' novels are typified by *London Goes to
Heaven* and *Gin and Bitters.* In the first we see the Interregnum from
the day of Charles I's beheading to the day of Charles II's restoration through the bewildered eyes of Samuel Guffin, a London innkeeper. He cannot come to terms with the times and we see many
shades of opinion and behaviour through his family. His daughter
runs after every religious sect, Levellers, Ranters, Friends, and
Diggers and his son is a hell-fire bigot in the Roundhead army.

A similar formula is used in *Gin and Bitters* covering the years
from 1688 to 1720. Nathaniel Vance can no more accept the new
ideas of his time than can Guffin. He does not understand his son
who wins money in a lottery and becomes a banker only to lose
everything in the South Sea Bubble. He doesn't understand the fever
for oblivion from cheap gin that seduces his wife and many others
from his good ale nor the Jacobite plotting of his bookkeeper and his

apprentice. In these books the story is slight, merely a vehicle to
show off the minutiae of the life and thought of the times, but absorbing nonetheless.

Lane's third type of book tells stories through what purport to be
documents of the time. Although these are all good stories, they are
harder to read for they are written 'forsoothly', as Josephine Tey
used to refer to language supposed to be contemporary with the time
portrayed. *A Secret Chronicle* is the story of Edward II's miserable
death as discovered for his daughter, the Queen of Scots, by her
chronicler. It has testimony from people who knew him—his old
nurse, his Queen's Lady-in-Waiting and a Welsh Bard whose 'Look
you, boyo' contribution is hard to take. *Fortress in the Forth* uses
letters and diaries to tell the story of Jacobite prisoners immured
there. *The Severed Crown* uses letters, memoirs, and diaries to tell of
Charles I's last days from the time he ran away from Oxford to join
the Scottish army who basely sold him to the Parliamentarians, to
his imprisonment and his execution.

All of Lane's books are filled with accurate historical detail. All
are fiercely partisan towards the characters she favours but they are
so well written and so powerfully told that, even knowing the outcome, one is still gripped by them and still one hopes as one reads
that *this* time history will turn out differently and that this time the
story will end happily.

—Pamela Cleaver

———

LANE, Roumelia. British. 1927—. See 2nd edition, 1990.

———

LANGLEY, Tania. See **ALEXANDER, Kate.**

———

LA TOURRETTE, Jacqueline. American. 1926—. See 2nd edition, 1990.

———

LATTIN, Anne. See **ELIOT, Anne.**

———

LAW, Elizabeth. See **PETERS, Maureen.**

———

LAWRENCE, Irene. See **WOODWARD, Lilian.**

———

LEE, Elsie. American. 1912–1987. See 2nd edition, 1990.

———

LEHMANN, Rosamond (Nina).
Nationality: British. **Born:** Bourne End, Buckinghamshire, 3 February 1901. **Education:** privately; Girton College, Cambridge
(scholar), 1919–22. **Relations:** married 1) Leslie Runciman in 1924
(marriage dissolved, 1942); 2) Wogan Philipps, later Lord Milford,
in 1928, one daughter (died 1958). Longterm friendship with the
poet, C. Day Lewis. **Career:** co-director, John Lehmann Ltd, publishers, London, 1946–53. Past-president, PEN English Centre, and
international vice-president, PEN; council member, Society of Au-

thors; vice-president, College of Psychic Studies. **Recipient:** Denyse Clairouin prize, for translation, 1948. Honorary fellow, Girton College, 1986; CBE (Commander, Order of the British Empire), 1982; Companion of Literature, Royal Society of Literature, 1987. **Died:** 12 March 1990.

ROMANCE AND HISTORICAL PUBLICATIONS

Novels

Dusty Answer. London, Chatto and Windus, and New York, Grossett and Dunlap, 1927.
A Note in Music. London, Chapman and Hall, and New York, Holt, 1930.
Invitation to the Waltz. London, Chatto and Windus, and New York, Holt, 1932.
The Ballad and the Source. London, Collins, and New York, Harcourt, Brace, 1944.
The Sea-Grape Tree. London, Collins, 1976.

OTHER PUBLICATIONS

Novels

The Weather in the Streets. London, Collins, 1936.
The Echoing Grove. London, Collins, and New York, Harcourt Brace Jovanovich, 1953.

Short stories

The Gypsy's Baby and Other Stories. London, Collins, 1946.

Play

No More Music (produced, 1939). London, Collins, 1939.

Other

A Letter to a Sister. London, Woolf, 1931.
A Man Seen Afar, with W. Tudor Pole. London, Neville Spearmann, 1965.
The Swan in the Evening: Fragments of an Inner Life (autobiography). London, Collins, 1967; revised edition, 1982.
Letters from Our Daughters, with Cynthia Sandys. London, College of Psychic Science Press, 1972.
My Dear Alexis: Letters from Wellesley Tudor Pole to Rosamond Lehmann, edited by Elizabeth Gythorpe. St Helier, Jersey, Spearmann, 1979.

Editor, with E. Muir, Denys Kilham Roberts, and C. Daniel Day Lewis, *Orion: A Miscellany 1–3*. London, Nicholson and Watson, 1945–46.
Editor, *The Awakening Letters*, with Cynthia Sandys. St Helier, Jersey, Spearmann, 2 vols, 1978.

Translator, *Geneviève* by Jacque Lemarchand. London, John Lehmann, 1947.
Translator, *Children of the Game*, from the novel *Les Enfants Terribles* by Jean Cocteau. London, Harvill, 1955; as *The Holy Terrors*, New York, New Directions, 1957.

*

Film Adaptations: *The Weather in the Streets*, 1984.

Critical studies: *Subjective Vision and Human Relationships in the Novels of Rosamond Lehmann* by W. Dorosz; *Feminine Conscious-* *ness in the Modern British Novel* by S.J. Kaplan; *Rosamond Lehmann* by Diana E. Le Stourgeon. 1965; *Rosamond Lehmann: An appreciation* by Gillian Tindall, London, Chatto and Windus, 1985; *Rosamond Lehmann* by Judy Simons, London, Macmillan, 1992.

*   *   *

Rosamond Lehmann's fiction, if it does lend itself to a single sentence summary, may be described as singularly concerned with exploring the variations in the nexus between the human and love. Her first novel, *Dusty Answer*, tells the story of Judith Earle, beginning with her childhood, taking us through her years at Cambridge, and culminating with the months immediately after her coming down from Cambridge when she sustains a profound romantic disappointment. Judith Earle's Cambridge years contain arguably one of the strongest depictions of emotional lesbianism in fiction. Perhaps the strong conjunction of lesbian and heterosexual yearnings may have been too much for some of her readers, for in Lehmann's words, her work was perceived in some quarters as the 'outpourings of a sex-maniac', although she herself terms it, in *The Swan in the Evening*, as an 'impassioned but idealistic' creation.

Lehmann's claim is entirely justifiable, since *Dusty Answer* is the site of the disjuncture between an imaginative, idealistically-driven subjectivity, that of Judith Earle, and an exteriority increasingly at variance with it. Intimations of disjuncture reach us in the adolescent Judith's awareness of the probable lack of coincidence between dreams and reality, which does not necessarily mitigate the possibilities for confusing the two. Given the discrepancy between subjective awareness and reality, the appropriation of exteriority within the scope of a comforting and self-validating dream is inevitably doomed to disappointment. Invariably the passionate overtures of the heart, springing from such dreams, meet with a rude and disdainful response, which shakes all the assumed certainties attached to the very processes of perception. The title, *Dusty Answer*, derived from Meredith's 'Ah, what a dusty answer gets the soul/When hot for certainties in this our life!', reflects the consequent sense of desolation. As the proliferating mismatch in the novel between desiring lover and unreceptive beloved shows, the vulnerability to dreams is not confined to Judith Earle, but afflicts all as a condition of their subjectivity.

In providing this novel with a central protagonist with strong propensities for both lesbian and heterosexual attachment, Lehmann probably sees bisexuality as a natural orientation, limited by social taboos and prejudices and by the exclusivity demanded by sexual attachments. The latter factor especially makes it difficult to pursue a homosexual attachment alongside a heterosexual one. Consequently, singular sexual attachments may not be a matter of affective determination so much as a by-product of the exclusivity of romantic liaisons.

The 17-or-so years following the publication of *Dusty Answer* were the most prolific in Lehmann's chequered career as a novelist. These years culminated with the publication, in 1944, of what is arguably her best work of fiction, *The Ballad and the Source*. In this novel, she represents the consequences on narrative form of the relativity of human perception. Accordingly, the novel is the product of diverse narrations from individuals who have confided their tales to Rebecca Landon, our most immediate narrator, at various points during her childhood and young adolescence. The discrepancies in the various narrations and the multiple tellings and retellings on which each tale is based produces a novel whose internal inconsistencies erect a counter-claim to the facile assumption of authorial omniscience.

The residual narrative, that survives the variations in the telling, raises significant questions about women's rights to their erotic life, and the relationship between female eroticism and motherhood. The questions themselves are the product of the way in which patriarchy organizes women's lives, giving the husband ownership over his wife's sexuality as well as the right to define the form her motherhood should take. In *The Ballad and the Source*, the challenge to patriarchal control occurs when Sibyl Jardine, one of the central characters, asserts her rights to her sexuality, by taking off with her lover. Her husband and society punish her by depriving her of her maternal rights. The implicit assumption here is that the woman has no independent right to motherhood or to her sexuality. Furthermore, by relieving Sibyl of her maternity, the courts and her husband perceive an incompatibility between maternity and woman's right to erotic expression. There is an answering resonance in Sibyl to such a profound division of female functions and identities, and it is seen in her inability to reconcile her roles of mother and lover. The story of Sibyl, reconstructed from a variety of sources, covers the span of her life from youth to old age. Sibyl's romantic attachment in old age to the young sculptor Gil, calls into question assumptions about the asexuality of older women.

The *Ballad and the Source* was swiftly succeeded by a collection of short stories, *The Gypsy's Baby*, followed after a longer interval by *The Echoing Grove*, in 1953. Then, after a lapse of 23 years, Lehmann published her last novel, *The Sea-Grape Tree*, in 1976. The immense gap in her fictional production coincided with the death of her daughter, and her subsequent exploration into psychic phenomena. In *The Swan in the Evening*, published in 1967, she describes the mystical experiences in which she encountered her dead daughter.

Lehmann's venture into the mystical realm resulted in a redefinition of the boundaries of fiction to include characters who had died, with the resultant representation of what she described, in *The Swan in the Evening*, as 'expanded consciousness' that came with death. In *The Sea-Grape Tree*, Lehmann returns to some of the characters of *The Ballad and the Source*, particularly Rebecca Landon and Sibyl Jardine. Rebecca visits a Caribbean island where Mrs Jardine spent her last years, and subsequently had died. Rebecca and Mrs Jardine make contact across the dividing line between life and death. *The Sea-Grape Tree* also returns to the theme of the sexuality of the older woman, through allusions to the attraction Johnny, a young handicapped pilot, had for Mrs Jardine. She had taken him under her wing and worked to achieve his rehabilitation. It is Rebecca who completes the task when she and Johnny fall in love, and she becomes pregnant. Johnny, who had felt that he was an accident in time, thus has once more a stake in the passage of generations. In *The Sea-Grape Tree*, Rosamond Lehmann finally dissolves the polarization of motherhood and female eroticism by representing motherhood (and necessarily fatherhood) as the completion of heterosexual love.

Presumably, Lehmann's fiction may be subsumed under a variety of organizing perspectives. One of these, as this essay has indicated, is her exploration of the vicissitudes and triumphs entailed in loving. In *Dusty Answer*, at the beginning of her career, Lehmann painted a disconcerting picture of the reiterated theme of unrequited love, which made love look like a joke played by an unfeeling deity upon an unsuspecting world. At the end of her career, in *The Sea-Grape Tree*, love is life-giving, transcends material proximity, and is ultimately not dependent on physicality, though it may express itself in physical terms. It is possible that Lehmann sees in the overestimation of physical signs the reason for much of the confusion and disarray which attends lovers. When love is mutual, as in *The Sea-Grape Tree*, the lovers also recognize the spiritual genesis of their passion.

—Doreen D'Cruz

LEIGH, Roberta. See **LINDSAY, Rachel.**

LEITH, Annie. See **BURGH, Anita.**

LENANTON, C. See **OMAN, Carola.**

LESLIE, Doris.
Nationality: British. **Born:** Doris Oppenheim, London, c1902. **Education:** privately in London, and in Brussels; studied art in Florence. **Relations:** married 1) John Leslie (died); 2) Sir Walter Fergusson Hannay in 1936 (died 1961). **Career:** Civil Defence, 1941–45. **Died:** 31 May 1982.

ROMANCE AND HISTORICAL PUBLICATIONS

Novels

The Starling. London, Hurst and Blackett, and New York, Century, 1927.
Fools in Mortar. London, Hurst and Blackett, and New York, Century, 1928.
The Echoing Green. London, Hurst and Blackett, 1929.
Terminus. London, Hurst and Blackett, 1931.
Puppets Parade. London, Lane, 1932.
Full Flavour. London, Lane, and New York, Macmillan, 1934.
Fair Company. London, Lane, and New York, Macmillan, 1936.
Concord in Jeopardy. London, Hutchinson, and New York, Macmillan, 1938.
Another Cynthia: The Adventures of Cynthia, Lady Ffulkes 1780–1850. London, Hutchinson, and New York, Macmillan, 1939.
Royal William: The Story of a Democrat. London, Hutchinson, 1940; New York, Macmillan, 1941.
House in the Dust. London, Hutchinson, and New York, Macmillan, 1942.
Polonaise. London, Hutchinson, 1943.
Folly's End. London, Hutchinson, 1944.
The Peverills. London, Hutchinson, 1946.
Wreath for Arabella. London, Hutchinson, 1948; New York, Popular Library, 1973.
That Enchantress. London, Hutchinson, 1950; New York, Popular Library, 1973.
A Toast to Lady Mary. London, Hutchinson, 1954; New York, Popular Library, 1973.
Peridot Flight. London, Hutchinson, 1956.
Tales of Grace and Favour (omnibus). London, Hutchinson, 1956.
As the Tree Falls. London, Hodder and Stoughton, 1958; as *The King's Traitor*, New York, Popular Library, 1973.
The Perfect Wife. London, Hodder and Stoughton, 1960; as *The Prime Minister's Wife*, New York, Doubleday, 1961.
I Return. London, Hodder and Stoughton, 1962; as *Vagabond's Way*, New York, Doubleday, 1962.
This for Caroline. London, Heinemann, 1964; New York, Popular Library, 1973.
Paragon Street. London, Heinemann, 1965.
The Sceptre and the Rose. London, Heinemann, 1967.
The Marriage of Martha Todd. London, Heinemann, 1968.
The Rebel Princess. London, Heinemann, 1970; New York, Popular Library, 1973.
A Young Wives' Tale. London, Heinemann, 1971.
The Desert Queen. London, Heinemann, 1972.

The Dragon's Head. London, Heinemann, 1973.
The Incredible Duchess. London, Heinemann, 1974.
Call Back Yesterday. London, Heinemann, 1975.
Notorious Lady. London, Heinemann, 1976.
The Warrior King. London, Heinemann, 1977.
Crown of Thorns. London, Heinemann, 1979.

OTHER PUBLICATIONS

Other

The Great Corinthian: A Portrait of the Prince Regent. London,
Eyre and Spottiswoode, 1952; New York, Oxford University
Press, 1953.

*   *   *

Doris Leslie has an impressive list of titles to her credit, both
novels and 'biographical studies'. Her period research was intensive; seldom if ever can she be faulted in any detail, and she projects a
real sense of history. She wrote of people important to her who,
through her, become so to the reader. It is the day-to-dayness of ordinary life that animates her novels, rather than engrossing plot or
suspense. Events do occur, but in an apparently formless, accidental
way as in most lives, only forming recognizable patterns in retrospect. Her characters, though convincing and well-rounded, seem
all to speak in the same voice, however their circumstances may differ; and while it is a voice worth hearing, it provides little variety.

She is best known for her biographical studies, in part perhaps because she ventured into territories heretofore the province of the
scholar only. Readers of the romantic-historical genre have at their
command literally dozens of titles based upon the familiar story of
Elizabeth Tudor, her tragic mother and monstrous golden father;
similarly, there are scores of works based on the lives of Queen Victoria, Empress Josephine, Louis XIV, and others of that category of
historical personage whose own vividly dramatic lives attract the romance novelist as a lightning rod draws the thunderbolt. But what
other author has seen the possibilities inherent in the relatively unfamiliar stories of Lady Blessington, bluff and foolish William IV, or
Queen Anne's beloved Lady Masham? Though Leslie has traversed
more popularly familiar terrain with her stories of the Prince Regent, Caro Lamb, and Chopin, it is the lesser historical personages in
her pageant of fortune's fools and favourites that best hold the reader's interest.

A failing in her work is the recurring tendency to suggest the
workings of incomprehensible providence at work in a tiresomely
portentous manner; as in making reference, quite out of context to
the story in hand, to the fact that even as the action takes place,
across the dark city, that selfsame night, a young girl is untimely
called from her bed in Kensington Palace . . . Victoria! (She is also in
the habit of referring to her own other novels in asterisked
footnotes.)

In spite of a few such annoying mannerisms, as well as a propen-
sity for documenting the facts of a life in essay form, interpolating
patches of very readable dialogue, and renaming it a study, Leslie
has earned her popularity, if for no other reason than as the author of
a painless mini-course in history. She proves that history is peopled
with characters any one of whom, if singled out by a sympathetic,
period-conscious writer, provides a fresh perspective on familiar,
often-worked literary and historical ground.

—Joan McGrath

_____

L'ESTRANGE, Anne. See ELLERBECK, Rosemary.

_____

LEWIS, Janet.
Nationality: American. **Born:** Chicago, Illinois, 17 August 1899.
Education: Lewis Institute, Chicago, A.A. 1918; University of Chicago, Ph.B. 1920. **Relations:** married the writer Yvor Winters in
1926 (died 1968); one daughter and one son. **Career:** passport Bureau clerk, American Consulate, Paris, 1920; proof reader, *Redbook*
magazine, Chicago, 1921; English teacher, Lewis Institute,
1921–22; editor, with Howard Baker and Yvor Winters, *Gyroscope*,
Palo Alto, California, 1929–30. Lecturer, writers workshop, University of Missouri, Columbia, 1952, and University of Denver,
1956; visiting lecturer, then lecturer in English, Stanford University, California, 1960, 1966, 1970. **Recipient:** Friends of American
Literature award, 1932; Shelley memorial award, for poetry, 1948;
Guggenheim fellowship, 1950; Los Angeles *Times* Kirsch award,
1985. **Member:** American Academy, 1992. **Address:** 143 West
Portola Avenue, Los Altos, California 94022, USA.

ROMANCE AND HISTORICAL PUBLICATIONS

Novels

*The Invasion: A Narrative of Events Concerning the Johnston Fam-
ily of St Mary's.* New York, Harcourt Brace, 1932.
The Wife of Martin Guerre. San Francisco, Colt Press, 1941; Lon-
don, Rapp and Carroll, 1967.
The Trial of Sören Qvist. New York, Doubleday, 1947; London,
Gollancz, 1967.
The Ghost of Monsieur Scarron. New York, Doubleday, and Lon-
don, Gollancz, 1959.

OTHER PUBLICATIONS

Novel

Against a Darkening Sky. New York, Doubleday, 1943.

Short Stories

Goodbye, Son, and Other Stories. New York, Doubleday, 1946.

Plays (opera libretti)

The Wife of Martin Guerre, music by William Bergsma, adaptation
of the novel by Lewis (produced New York, 1956). Denver,
Swallow, 1958.
The Last of the Mohicans, adaptation of the novel by Cooper, music
by Alva Henderson (produced Wilmington, Delaware, 1976).
A Birthday of the Infanta, adaptation of the story by Wilde, music by
Malcolm Seagrave (produced Carmel, California, 1977). Los An-
geles, Symposium Press, 1979.
Mulberry Street, music by Alva Henderson. Onset, Massachusetts,
Dermont, 1981.
The Ancient Ones (cantata), music by Alva Henderson (produced
1983).
The Swans. Santa Barbara, California, Daniel, 1986.
The Legend (cantata), music by Brian Murray (produced Cleveland,
1987).
West of Washington Square, music by Alva Henderson (produced
San Jose, 1988).

Poetry

The Indians in the Woods. Bonn, Germany, Monroe Wheeler, 1922;
Palo Alto, California, Matrix Press, 1980.

The Wheel in Midsummer. Lynn, Massachusetts, Lone Gull Press, 1927.
The Earth-Bound 1924–1944. Aurora, New York, Wells College, 1946.
The Hangar at Sunnyvale 1937. San Francisco, Book Club of California, 1947.
Poems 1924–1944. Denver, Swallow, 1950.
The Ancient Ones. Portola Valley, California, No Dead Lines, 1979.
Poems Old and New 1918–1978. Athens, Ohio University Press-Swallow Press, 1981.
Late Offerings. New York, Barth, 1989.

Other

The Friendly Adventure of Ollie Ostrich (for children). New York, Doubleday, 1923.
Keiko's Bubble (for children). New York, Doubleday, 1961; Kingswood, Surrey, World's Work, 1963.
The U.S. and Canada, with others. Green Bay, University of Wisconsin Press, 1970.

*

Manuscript Collection: Stanford University Library, California.

Critical Study: 'The Historical Novels of Janet Lewis' by Donald Davie, in *Southern Review* (Baton Rouge, Louisiana), January 1966.

*   *   *

Janet Lewis is admired as one of the purest stylists in contemporary fiction, and as a novelist who continued to write quietly probing dramas of psycho-moral ambiguity with almost total disregard for the changing fashions of American fiction. She is to be compared, in the quiet integrity of her art, with Willa Cather, Caroline Gordon, and her friend Elizabeth Madox Roberts. Only her modest volume of short stories (*Goodbye, Son*) and the slow-paced, intelligent, at times dreary *Against a Darkening Sky* are contemporary in scene. Her reputation rests instead on her four historical novels, one related to her own part-Indian background, the others set in remote European times.

The Invasion occupies a surprisingly satisfying border region between fiction and history, and contains some of the loveliest prose in modern American literature. Its singular achievement is to present without pretentiousness or strain an Indian culture from within (the Ojibway of the Lake Superior area), and its gradual change and slow obliteration over a century and a half. The family chronicle extends from 1791, when we meet the 14-year-old Woman of the Glade, who married the trader John Johnston, to the death in 1944 of Anna Maria Johnston, the Red Leaf. The novel is the work of a poet recording delicate nuances of landscape and mood, and of a scrupulous historian contemplating with equanimity the inevitable outrages of human passion and eroding time. It combines with remarkable success an intimate immersion in scene (a succession of lived moments) and a flow of time that is calm as well as swift. The chronicle's exceptional authenticity is strengthened by the fact that the famous ethnologist, linguist, and Indian agent Henry Rowe Schoolcraft is a central figure in the family history.

Three very different historical novels are based on incidents recorded in Phillips's *Famous Cases of Circumstantial Evidence*, an early 19th-century work. *The Trial of Sören Qvist*, set in 17th-century Denmark, is the story of a saintly pastor executed for a crime he did not commit. This is a spare and dramatic novel, but meditative too, like everything Lewis has written. *The Ghost of Monsieur Scarron* is the product of years of research, some of it in a part of Paris that has not greatly changed since 1694. It is the minutely realistic story of a bookbinder falsely accused of authoring a libellous pamphlet directed against Louis XIV and Madame de Maintenon. The evocation of the Paris of that time is remarkable.

The best of these novels, one of the greatest short novels in American literature, is *The Wife of Martin Guerre*, a quietly authentic, immaculately written story of a man whose physical 'double' (but far more considerate and more loving than the original) returns to claim the wife of a soldier supposed dead in the wars of 16th-century France. Here as in her other two novels of ambiguous crime and punishment Lewis dramatizes, always calmly, situations exerting extreme pressure on her characters. The marriage of Martin Guerre and Bertrande de Rols, at 11, is of its time, and so too the execution 21 years later. A sentence from Lewis's Foreword suggests the human understanding underlying all her work: 'The rules of evidence vary from century to century, and the morality which compels many of the actions of men and women varies also, but the capacities of the human soul for suffering and for joy remain very much the same.'

—Albert Guerard

———

LEWIS, Maynah.
Nationality: British. **Born:** Maynah McIntire, Liverpool, Lancashire, 14 April 1919. **Education:** schools in Scotland. **Relations:** married Victor Lewis in 1936; one son. **Career:** professional musician and teacher; full-time writer from 1958. **Recipient:** Romantic Novelists Association Ayres award, 1962, and major award, 1967, 1972. **Died:** 16 July 1988.

ROMANCE AND HISTORICAL PUBLICATIONS

Novels

No Place for Love. London, Hurst and Blackett, 1963.
Give Me This Day. London, Hurst and Blackett, 1964.
See the Bright Morning. London, Hurst and Blackett, 1965.
Make Way for Tomorrow. London, Hurst and Blackett, 1966; New York, Beagle, 1973.
The Long, Hot Days. London, Hurst and Blackett, 1966.
The Future Is Forever. London, Hurst and Blackett, 1967.
Till Then, My Love. London, Hurst and Blackett, 1968.
Of No Fixed Abode. London, Hurst and Blackett, 1968.
Symphony for Two Players. London, Hurst and Blackett, 1969.
A Corner of Eden. London, Hurst and Blackett, 1970.
A Pride of Innocence. London, Hurst and Blackett, 1971; New York, Beagle, 1973.
Too Late for Tears. London, Hurst and Blackett, 1972.
The Town That Nearly Died. London, Collins, 1973.
The Miracle of Lac Blanche. London, Collins, 1973.
The Unforgiven. London, Collins, 1974; New York, Ace, 1976.
The Other Side of Paradise. London, Collins, 1975.
Yesterday Came Suddenly. London, Collins, 1975.
A Woman of Property. London, Collins, 1976.
These My Children. London, Collins, 1977.
Love Has Two Faces. London, Hamlyn, 1981.
Barren Harvest. London, Hale, 1981.
Hour of the Siesta. London, Hale, 1982.
Whisper Who Dares. London, Hale, 1983.

*   *   *

Maynah Lewis, a professional musician turned prolific novelist, no doubt had little time to be idle, and this is reflected in the activity and diversity of her novels. Her heroes and heroines are all working (though not necessarily 'working-class') people, deeply involved in their jobs or careers, be they in the legal or medical professions, or running a corner store. Each novel is set in different and definite surroundings: a Caribbean island (*The Other Side of Paradise*), a small industrial Northern town (*A Woman of Property*), a home for handicapped children (*Love Has Two Faces*). The characters are not on the whole seekers of experience. Often they are settled, rather staid people forced into action by tangible problems: the loss of memory, the forces of big business, the difficulties of dealing with a delinquent child. Neither do they long for romance: love creeps up on them accidentally after an acquaintanceship, or reappears from a long-distant past.

Nowhere is this better illustrated than in *Yesterday Came Suddenly*, where the hero, Edward, a 38-year-old right-wing lawyer who has taken a public stand against declining moral standards, is approached out of the blue by the girlfriend of his university days, the mysterious, dark-eyed, apparently widowed Eleanor. Eleanor begs him to defend her delinquent son David, who, while driving a stolen car with a gang of friends, has run over and badly injured an elderly man. When Edward discovers that Eleanor has never been married and that David is indeed his own illegitimate son, he is thrown into confusion. Suddenly on the other side of the moral fence he flounders between his desire to protect his son, his renewed passion for Eleanor, and his unwillingness to be seen as a hypocrite in the eyes of his colleagues, his clinging mother, and his beautiful, clever, undemanding too-good-to-be-true doctor fiancée. But in typical Lewis style, his problems are sorted out as neatly as they happened: his colleagues rally round him, David is given a suspended sentence, his fiancée, retaining her pride, goes off to South Africa, sparing him even the ordeal of making a clean break with her, and Edward is reunited with his one real love, with the approval of her mother if not his own. Although Edward's dilemma is a real one, and well set up, he remains a dislikeable character throughout the book, shirking responsibility wherever he can. One at times feels that this learned lawyer should, at his age, be a bit more grown-up.

Also guilty of shirking parental responsibility is Robert, the lawyer hero of *These My Children* who, until the death of his forceful wife prompts him into action, has taken no interest in the upbringing of his children. Now alone and lonely, Robert sets out to reestablish contact with his grown-up daughters and son. The theme of child/parent conflict re-emerges often in Lewis's books. More often than not the young are striking out by themselves in the face of parental opposition, either to pursue an 'unsuitable' partner (Hilary and Carol in *These My Children*) or to take a stand against something they believe to be morally wrong (Veronica and Stuart in *A Woman of Property*). Any guilty feelings they may have about hurting or leaving an aged relative are, in the end, exonerated: Lewis's predilection for happy endings for all ensures a reunion in the end, by which time the parent is well on the way to forming a lasting relationship with someone of his or her own generation.

It is difficult to sum up work of such diversity as Lewis's. She is at her best in devising interesting plots and settings for her characters though one might wish, at times, that the tensions inherent in these situations could have been more fully explored. However, the richness of her novels has ensured her continuing popularity, and is the reason, no doubt, why she has twice been winner of Romantic Novelists Association awards.

—Judith Summers

LEWTY, Marjorie.

Nationality: British. **Born:** Marjorie Lobb, Wallasey, Cheshire, 8 April 1906. **Education:** Queen Mary High School, Liverpool.

Relations: married Richard Arthur Lewty in 1933 (died); one son and one daughter. **Career:** secretary, District Bank Ltd, Liverpool, 1923–33. **Address:** c/o Mills and Boon Ltd, Eton House, 18–24 Paradise Road, Richmond, Surrey TW9 1SR, England.

ROMANCE AND HISTORICAL PUBLICATIONS

Novels

Never Call It Loving. London, Mills and Boon, 1958; Toronto, Harlequin, 1968.
The Million Stars. London, Mills and Boon, 1959.
The Imperfect Secretary. London, Mills and Boon, 1959; Toronto, Harlequin, 1967.
The Lucky One. London, Mills and Boon, 1961; Toronto, Harlequin, 1968.
This Must Be for Ever. London, Mills and Boon, 1962.
Alex Rayner, Dental Nurse. London, Mills and Boon, and Toronto, Harlequin, 1965.
Dental Nurse at Denley's. London, Mills and Boon, 1968; Toronto, Harlequin, 1969.
Town Nurse—Country Nurse. London, Mills and Boon, 1970; Toronto, Harlequin, 1971.
The Extraordinary Engagement. London, Mills and Boon, 1972; Toronto, Harlequin, 1973.
The Rest Is Magic. London, Mills and Boon, 1973; Toronto, Harlequin, 1974.
All Made of Wishes. London, Mills and Boon, and Toronto, Harlequin, 1974.
Flowers in Stony Places. London, Mills and Boon, and Toronto, Harlequin, 1975.
The Fire in the Diamond. London, Mills and Boon, and Toronto, Harlequin, 1976.
To Catch a Butterfly. London, Mills and Boon, and Toronto, Harlequin, 1977.
The Time and the Loving. London, Mills and Boon, 1977; Toronto, Harlequin, 1978.
The Short Engagement. London, Mills and Boon, and Toronto, Harlequin, 1978.
A Very Special Man. London, Mills and Boon, 1979.
A Certain Smile. London, Mills and Boon, 1979; Toronto, Harlequin, 1980.
Prisoner in Paradise. London, Mills and Boon, 1980.
Love Is a Dangerous Game. London, Mills and Boon, 1980.
Beyond the Lagoon. London, Mills and Boon, 1981.
A Girl Bewitched. London, Mills and Boon, 1981; Toronto, Harlequin, 1982.
Makeshift Marriage. London, Mills and Boon, 1982.
One Who Kisses. London, Mills and Boon, 1983; Toronto, Harlequin, 1983.
Dangerous Male. London, Mills and Boon, 1983.
Riviera Romance. London, Mills and Boon, 1984.
A Lake in Kyoto. London, Mills and Boon, 1985.
Acapulco Moonlight. London, Mills and Boon, 1985.
Villa in the Sun. London, Mills and Boon, 1986.
In Love with the Man. London, Mills and Boon, 1986.
Honeymoon Island. London, Mills and Boon, 1987.
Falling in Love Again. London, Mills and Boon, 1988.
A Kiss is Still a Kiss. London, Mills and Boon, 1989.
Bittersweet Honeymoon. London, Mills and Boon, and Toronto, Harlequin, 1989.
Man-Trap. London, Mills and Boon, 1990.
Lightning Strike. London, Mills and Boon, 1990.
Little White Lies. London, Mills and Boon, 1992.
The Beginning of the Affair. London, Mills and Boon, 1992.

Deep Water. London, Mills and Boon, 1992.

*

Marjorie Lewty comments:

All I can say about my work is that I write to please the reader, as well as myself. I believe the purpose of fiction is to tell a story, and that a story is what most people enjoy. I write romantic novels because I was born and brought up in a romantic age, the age of the 1920s, when there was still optimism in the world. I don't think romantic stories are necessarily 'escapist', using the word in its pejorative sense, any more than a trip into the countryside is 'escapist'. I think the 'romantic' formula corresponds to the basic myth of all time: the descent into despair, followed by the rise again to happiness—the happy ending. This myth is built into our culture, which would account for the popularity of the romantic novel through the ages.

*   *   *

Whether writing about Japan, France, England, or Grand Cayman Marjorie Lewty is at home creating romantic stories against authentic backgrounds. A Mills and Boon writer of some repute, Lewty's love stories involve attractive dynamic men, often with some secret, and healthy, lively heroines.

In *Deep Water*, Anthea meets Charles Ravenscroft, a hero in his mid-thirties, with whom she fell in love after a brief meeting five years earlier. Charles is a changed man, embittered by a failed love affair, he wants nothing to do with Anthea, especially as his sister, and Philippa, Anthea's sister, keep throwing them together. Set in Grand Cayman, the couple decide to join up to foil their sisters' attempts, and just enjoy their holiday as friends. Their relationship inevitably develops into something more, and Anthea is heartbroken when Charles disappears. Charles returns later to declare his love for her—he left because his cousin had involved him in a scandal, and as a good and moral hero he has to clear his name before he can claim Anthea.

Sara Bennett, in *Man-Trap*, believes that Rafe Jordan is in love with his ex-wife. Rafe is a brooding, dark hero with hidden demons. He treats Sara badly when he finds her working for his firm as she reminds him of his ex-wife. The couple are thrown together when Sara's designs for the atrium-gallery of a château are accepted and they have to travel to France together. Their relationship is tense with frustrated passion and sexual desire, initially Rafe's and then later Sara's. Denise, Rafe's gorgeous ex-wife, turns up with her young son Philip (Flip), who as it turns out is Rafe's son. Rafe ends up getting both his son and his girl. He declares: 'I don't know what love is, after all these years, but I know I can't go on without you, I want you with me every minute of the day and night, to look at, to talk to, to laugh with, to work with, to go to bed with. When you're not there the sun seems to go out'. This is the key to Lewty's books, the hero and heroine are both drawn into a deep, passionate, and often dark love, against both their wills—but it is a love that will last.

Similarly, in *A Lake in Kyoto*, Sue Larkin finds herself with the dilemma of being proposed to, by a lake in Japan, by the man she is in love with, but who is still in love with his ex-wife. Luke Masters takes pity on Sue, whom he perceives as young, charming, and a 'babe in the woods' type of girl. He needs someone to look after his son and is attracted to Sue. They engage in an affair but matters are complicated by the fact that Luke's ex-wife, Vanessa, turns up. Eventually Sue makes friends with Luke's son and Vanessa shows how unworthy she is by losing her son. Sue finds the boy and true love at the end of the book.

Emma also works for her hero in *A Girl Bewitched*. Strong and masterful, Trent Marston appears to Emma initially as a wicked seducer as Emma's cousin Lisa tells her that she and Trent were in-volved. Lisa marries someone else seemingly on the rebound, and later tells Emma that it is because Trent made her pregnant. Trent and Emma fall in love with each other in Mexico (he is of Mexican/ Spanish blood), and although Lisa tries to ruin their relationship Emma eventually realizes that she is lying and that her love for Trent is all that matters.

In *Little White Lies*, one of Lewty's most recent titles, the heroine Kate Lovell declares that she 'can cope with any man'. This is, of course, before she meets writer Will Raven. Kate goes to her aunt's hotel in Normandy, after the death of her mother. Although meant to be holidaying, Kate finds herself looking after the hotel and the 'guest', Will, whom she initially mistakes for the new manager. Will, who speaks fluent French, helps Kate to run things while her aunt is in hospital and Will declares his love for her early on in the book. Matters are complicated by the fact that Kate has a hang-up about her father who left her when she was 15 for another woman. The woman was Will's mother who was dying of a terminal illness. Kate realizes that no matter what, she loves Will and is reconciled with both him and her father at the end of the book.

Lewty often uses the death of a parent, usually the heroine's father or mother, to explain the heroine's circumstances. Thus, Sue, in *A Lake in Kyoto*, finds herself in Japan via Australia, after the death of her father; Kate, in *Little White Lies*, goes to France after her mother's death; Sara Bennett gives up her job to move to London following her father's death in *Man-Trap*; and Philippa, in *The Beginning of the Affair*, is left her father's printing business after he dies. This is an interesting device as it immediately provokes the reader's sympathy, and makes the heroine seem both vulnerable and human.

—P. Campbell

LEY, Alice Chetwynd.
Nationality: British. **Born:** Alice Chetwynd Humphrey, Halifax, Yorkshire, 12 October 1913. **Education:** King Edward VI Grammar School, Birmingham; London University, diploma in sociology 1962. **Relations:** married Kenneth James Ley in 1945; two sons. **Career:** tutor in creative writing, Harrow College of Further Education, Middlesex 1963–84. Past chair, Romantic Novelists Association. **Recipient:** Gilchrist award. **Agent:** Curtis Brown, 162–168 Regent Street, London W1R 5TB, England. **Address:** 42 Cannonbury Avenue, Pinner, Middlesex HA5 1TS, England.

ROMANCE AND HISTORICAL PUBLICATIONS

Novels (series: Justin Rutherford and Anthea)

The Jewelled Snuff Box. London, Hale, 1959; New York, Beagle, 1974.
The Georgian Rake. London, Hale, 1960; New York, Beagle, 1974.
The Guinea Stamp. London, Hale, 1961; as *The Courting of Joanna*, New York, Ballantine, 1976.
Master of Liversedge. London, Hale, 1966; as *The Master and the Maiden*, New York, Ballantine, 1977.
The Clandestine Betrothal. London, Hale, 1967; New York, Ballantine, 1976.
The Toast of the Town. London, Hale, 1969; New York, Ballantine, 1976.
Letters for a Spy. London, Hale, 1970; as *The Sentimental Spy*, New York, Ballantine, 1977.
A Season at Brighton. London, Hale, 1971; New York, Ballantine, 1976.
Tenant of Chesdene Manor. London, Hale, 1974; as *Beloved Diana*, New York, Ballantine, 1977.

The Beau and the Bluestocking. London, Hale, 1975; New York, Ballantine, 1977.
At Dark of the Moon. London, Hale, 1977; New York, Ballantine, 1978.
An Advantageous Marriage. London, Hale, 1977; New York, Ballantine, 1978.
A Regency Scandal. New York, Ballantine, and London, Futura, 1979.
A Conformable Wife. New York, Ballantine, 1981; London, Severn House, 1988.
The Intrepid Miss Hayden. New York, Fawcett, 1983; London, Severn House, 1987.
A Reputation Dies (Rutherford and Anthea). London, Methuen, 1984; New York, St Martin's Press, 1985.
A Fatal Assignation (Rutherford and Anthea). London, Severn House, and New York, St Martin's Press, 1987.
Masquerade of Vengeance (Rutherford and Anthea). London, Severn House, 1989.

OTHER PUBLICATIONS

Plays

Radio Play: *The Georgian Rake* (produced London, 1962).

Alice Chetwynd Ley comments:
My novels are set in the late Georgian period, i.e., 1760–1816. Several are in the Regency period. I made a study of the period when working on the social history section of my diploma course, and have always been a devotee of Jane Austen. This gives an authentic background to my work, but my novels are essentially romantic.

*   *   *

In a career spanning more than two decades, Alice Chetwynd Ley has proven herself to be one of the finest, most consistent authors of historical romances. In tone, style, and qualities her work is reminiscent of that of Georgette Heyer, yet she remains much less widely known.
Most of Ley's books are Regency romances, with a few taking place in the Georgian period. Like Heyer, she concentrates on developing her characters and giving them life. The care she takes in portraying even minor characters brings a depth to her stories not often found in formula romances, which frequently feature one- or two-dimensional figures.
Under Ley's pen, the aristocratic worlds of Georgian and Regency fashionable society comes to life. Enough movement to keep a story briskly paced is supplied, but the real focus is on the characters and their relationships. Feverish action is not necessary to interest the reader in the lovers of *The Clandestine Betrothal* or *The Beau and the Bluestocking.* Even in the more eventful novels, such as *Tenant of Chesdene Manor* or *The Jewelled Snuff Box,* the people are more important than specific events. The most action-filled of Ley's novels are those set against the background of the war with France. *The Guinea Stamp, At Dark of the Moon,* and *Letters for a Spy* all draw on the English fears of a French invasion and Napoleonic spies, yet most of the problems remain on a personal level for the protagonists. The heroes of these books are double agents or counter spies, and confusion of identities and mistaken motives lead to much of the action. Ley does manage to slip a few slightly unexpected twists into these plots when Elizabeth is the one suspected of being a spy in *Letters for a Spy* and the double agent, Captain Jackson, in *The Guinea Stamp,* is revealed as also leading a double life in England.
The 1981 Ballantine edition of *A Conformable Wife* proclaims Alice Chetwynd Ley 'the new queen of Regency romance'. While

in the main such a statement is accurate, it is somewhat misleading. It is true that she has authored many quality romances, yet her long career hardly qualifies her for a title as a *new* leader of the genre. Instead, real devotees of historical romances will recognize her as one of their best kept secrets.

—Barbara E. Kemp

————

LEYTON, Sophie.   See WALSH, Sheila.

————

LIBBEY, Laura Jean.
Nationality: American. **Born:** New York City in 1862. **Education:** privately. **Relations:** married Von Mater Sitwell in 1898. **Career:** editor, *Fashion Bazaar,* New York, 1881–94; correspondent, New York *Evening World,* 1899–1901. **Died:** 25 October 1924.

ROMANCE AND HISTORICAL PUBLICATIONS

Novels

Madolin Rivers; or, The Little Beauty of Red Oak Seminary. New York, Munro, 1885.
Junie's Love Test. New York, Ogilvie, 1886.
Miss Middleton's Lover; or, They Parted on Their Bridal Tour. New York, American News, 1888.
A Forbidden Marriage; or, In Love with a Handsome Spendthrift. New York, American News, 1888.
A Fatal Wooing. New York, Lovell, 1888.
Little Rosebud's Lovers; or, A Cruel Revenge. New York, Munro, 1888.
That Pretty Young Girl. New York, American News, 1889; London, Milner, 1902.
Daisy Brooks; or, A Perilous Love. New York, Munro, 1889; as *A Bride for a Day,* Cleveland, Westbrook, n.d.
The Heiress of Cameron Hall. New York, Munro, 1889.
All for the Love of a Fair Face; or, Broken Betrothal. New York, Munro, 1889.
A Struggle for a Heart; or, Crystabel's Fatal Love. New York, Munro, 1889.
Leonie Locke; or, The Romance of a Beautiful New York Working-Girl. New York, Munro, 1889.
Pretty Freda's Lovers; or, Married by Mistake. New York, Munro, 1889.
The Flirtations of a Beauty; or, A Summer's Romance at Newport. New York, Munro, 1890.
Ione: A Broken Love Dream. New York, Bonner, 1890.
A Mad Betrothal; or, Nadine's Vow. New York, Bonner, 1890.
Parted by Fate. New York, Bonner, 1890.
Willful Gaynel; or, The Little Beauty of the Passaic Cotton Mills. New York, Munro, 1890.
My Sweetheart Idabell; or, The Romance of a Pretty Coquette. Cleveland, Westbrook, 1890.
He Loved but Was Lured Away. New York, Ogilvie, 1891.
Little Leafy, The Cloakmaker's Beautiful Daughter. New York, Munro, 1891.
The Crime of Hallo-e'en; or, The Heiress of Graystone Hall. New York, Ogilvie, 1891.
We Parted at the Altar. New York, Bonner, 1892.
Florabel's Lover; or, Rival Belles. New York, Bonner, 1892; London, Milner, n.d.
Beautiful Ione's Lover. New York, Munro, 1892.

Lyndall's Temptation; or, Blinded by Love. New York, Munro, 1892.

A Master Workman's Oath; or, Coralie, The Unfortunate. New York, Ogilvie, 1892.

Only a Mechanic's Daughter. New York, Munro, 1892.

Olive's Courtship. New York, American News, 1892.

The Alphabet of Love. New York, Munro, 1892.

The Beautiful Coquette; or, The Love That Won Her. New York, Munro, 1892.

Daisy Gordon's Folly; or, The World Lost for Love's Sake. New York, Munro, 1892.

Dora Miller; or, A Young Girl's Love and Pride. New York, Munro, 1892.

The Romance of Enola. Cleveland, Westbrook, 1893.

When His Love Grew Cold. New York, Ogilvie, 1895.

When Lovely Maiden Stoops to Folly. New York, American News, 1896.

Garnetta, The Silver King's Daughter; or, The Startling Secret of the Old Mine. Cleveland, Westbrook, 1897.

Sweet Kitty Clover. New York, Street and Smith, 1898.

Sweetheart Will You Be True? or, Lovely Corine, The Queen of the Golf-Links. New York, Street and Smith, 1901.

True Love's Reward. New York, Weekly Budget Novels, 1904.

Shadows and Sunshine. New York, Weekly Budget Novels, 1904.

Only Love's Cross for Her; or, Shadow of the Cross. Brooklyn, Eagle Press, 1908.

The Clutch of the Marriage Tie; or, Jilbett, The Story of the Second Class. Brooklyn, Eagle Press, 1920.

Wooden Wives. New York, Publisher's Printing, 1923.

Cora, The Pet of the Regiment. Cleveland, Westbrook, n.d.

A Dangerous Flirtation; or, Did Ida May Sin? Cleveland, Westbrook, n.d.

Della's Handsome Lover; or, A Hasty Ballroom Betrothal. Cleveland, Westbrook, n.d.

A Fatal Elopement; or, A Too Hasty Love Match. Cleveland, Westbrook, n.d.

Flora Garland's Courtship; or, The Race for a Young Girl's Heart. Cleveland, Westbrook, n.d.

Flora Temple; or, All for Love's Sake. Cleveland, Westbrook, n.d.

Aleta's Terrible Secret; or, The Strange Mystery of a Wedding Eve. Cleveland, Westbrook, n.d.

The Girl He Forsook; or, The Young Doctor's Secret. Cleveland, Westbrook, n.d.

Gladiola's Two Lovers. Cleveland, Westbrook, n.d.

A Handsome Engineer's Flirtation; or, How He Won the Hearts of Girls. Cleveland, Westbrook, n.d.

Happy-Go-Lucky Lotty. New York, Ogilvie, n.d.

Jolly Sally Pendleton; or, The Wife Who Was Not a Wife. Cleveland, Westbrook, n.d.

Little Romp Edda. New York, Ogilvie, n.d.

The Loan of a Lover; or, Vera's Flirtation. Cleveland, Westbrook, n.d.

Pretty Madcap Dorothy; or, How She Won a Lover. Cleveland, Westbrook, n.d.

Was She Sweetheart or Wife? or, Pretty Gualda's Love. Cleveland, Westbrook, n.d.

*   *   *

Few modern readers will recognize the name Laura Jean Libbey. However, 90 years ago, most readers of story newspapers would have eagerly reached for their weekly issue of the *Family Story Paper* or the *Fireside Companion* to read the latest instalment of Libbey's current novel.

She was an extremely popular novelist who was avidly read by female audiences from the late 1880s through to the early 1920s. Be-cause she wrote for the story newspapers, her novels enjoyed enormous reprinting runs due to publishing practices of that period. Her income was reported to have been over $50,000 a year during much of her writing career. At least one novel, *We Parted at the Altar*, netted her $10,000 when it appeared in the *Fireside Companion* during 1892.

Libbey specialized in romance stories that appealed to young working girls as well as to women of the middle classes. Her plots were extremely predictable and very melodramatic. The heroine was always a young, working girl or a girl suddenly left penniless and homeless. The course of the novel followed the heroine through countless adversities and misunderstandings. These adversities were compounded by villainous machinations or were temporarily relieved by the quick intervention of the hero.

The narratives are a succession of calamities, each fore-shadowing the next dire threat and barely accounting for the previous difficulty in her heroine's life. Phrases such as 'I am only a poor working girl ... ', and 'God can take care of unprotected working girls', are typical expressions uttered by her heroines.

The last few years have seen a reevaluation of Libbey's place in early 20th-century fiction. Her novels are being studied as examples of feminist literature or as examples of reform movement advocacy. However, neither position can be supported by historical data or by the contents of her stories. This conclusion is based on two facts. First, editorial control of the novels effectively limited an author's ability to take definite stands on specific social problems. It was the willingness of editors to recognize the problems of social conditions and to encourage the writers to use them in their novels that prompted stories similar to Libbey's.

The second factor is Libbey's own strongly conservative attitudes. Her heroines did not necessarily seek to change working conditions, they merely wanted to escape such conditions by the only socially accepted way—marriage. To this end, the heroines did attempt to show initiative, especially when getting themselves out of grave difficulties. For instance, in *Leonie Locke* the heroine is kidnapped and held by a ruthless man determined to marry her. Leonie thinks nothing of climbing out of a window and descending a narrow fire ladder fastened to the wall. In most other situations, the heroines were content to wait for rescue with an attitude of appealing helplessness, or they tried to improve their situation by doing something that was so unrealistic that it was sure to fail.

In depicting working girls Libbey lets her heroine's reactions speak for her. Generally, the working companions of the heroine do not emerge very well. There is the occasional 'friend', but for the most part, they are most definitely 'working class'. Their interests and standards are sharply if briefly illustrated and the contrast between them and the heroine is quite distinct. The reader is aware that the heroine is different from the other girls. There is always that illusive 'something' about her.

Modern readers will find her novels difficult to believe, given the improbability of many of the incidents in her stories. In *We Parted at the Altar*, Girelda Northrup goes to the house of her former fiancé, Hubert Varrick. He believed her to be dead and had fallen in love with Jessie Bain. Girelda is only slightly disguised, yet she works as a seamstress in the house for several weeks without being recognized. Frequently Hubert makes hurried journeys that should take many hours or even several days. He makes them in two or three hours at the most. In another incident, Jessie has a letter mailed for her by a nurse just before lunch and it is delivered to Hubert by mid-afternoon. Coincidence plays a major role in keeping Libbey's conflicts going, which, especially for modern readers, reduces the believability of her novels. In *Pretty Madcap Dorothy* the heroine is accidentally lost overboard from an excursion boat to Staten Island. She is rescued and pulled back aboard. Suddenly, an elderly man notices a birth mark on her chest and identifies her as the daughter of his ward who had died years ago.

It is unfortunate that the deficiencies of Libbey's style and her improbable plots are so evident, as these serve to relegate her novels to curiosities. Their value is mainly to students of publishing history and popular culture. One must be cautious in reading too much of social or cultural significance into them.

—Arlene Moore

LIDE, Mary.

Also writes as Mary Lomer. **Nationality:** British. **Born:** Mary Lomer, Cornwall, England. **Education:** St Hugh's College, Oxford, B.A. 1953, M.A. 1960. **Relations:** two sons, and one daughter. **Career:** historian and English teacher at universities in the USA, and other countries; administrative assistant, International Monetary Fund, Washington DC, 1981–84; teacher of creating writing, The Writer's Center, Bethesda, Maryland. Lives in Cornwall. **Recipient:** Avery Hopwood award for poetry, 1954; *Romantic Times* New Historical Writer award, 1984, for *Ann of Cambray*. **Agent:** Goodman Associates, 500 West End Avenue, New York, New York 10024, USA.

ROMANCE AND HISTORICAL PUBLICATIONS

Novels (series: Sedgemont Trilogy)

The Bait (as Mary Lomer). London, Murray, 1961.
Sedgemont Trilogy:
  Ann of Cambray. London, Sphere, and New York, Warner Books, 1984.
  Gifts of the Queen. London, Sphere, and New York, Warner Books, 1985.
  A Royal Quest. London, Sphere, and New York, Warner Books, 1987; as *Hawks of Sedgemont*, London, Sphere, 1988.
Isobelle. New York, Warner Books, 1988; as *Diary of Isobelle*, London, Grafton, 1988.
Tregaran. London, Grafton, and New York, St Martin's Press, 1989.
Command of the King. London, Grafton, 1990; New York, St Martin's Press, 1991.
The Legacy. London, Grafton, 1991; as *The Legacy of Tregaran*, New York, St Martin's Press, 1991.
Robert of Normandy (as Mary Lomer). London, Headline, 1991.
The Homecoming. London, HarperCollins, and New York, St Martin's Press, 1992.
Fortune's Knave (as Mary Lomer). London, Headline 1992; New York, St Martin's Press, 1993.

*   *   *

Mary Lide is a versatile writer creating historical novels of great detail and accuracy as easily as she does more contemporary works.

The successful 'Sedgemont Trilogy' brought Lide much critical acclaim. Chronicling the lives of a mediaeval noble family in 12th-century Britain, the books are extremely passionate, well-written historical novels. *Ann of Cambray* begins just after Henry I's death: England is war-torn, and the Lady Ann, the heroine of the book, is caught in the middle of the conflict. Ann becomes Lord Raoul of Sedgemont's ward, and almost inevitably, she falls in love with him. The book is as much about their turbulent but passionate relationship as it is about the war, and life during this volatile period of history. *Gifts of the Queen*, and *A Royal Quest* (*Hawks of Sedgemont*) continue the story of Ann and Raoul, following their lives through marriage, and the subsequent births and marriages of their children.

In *A Royal Quest*, Olwen, their bronze-haired, brown-eyed wild daughter falls in love with a Celtic prince. Taliesin of Afron is a sworn enemy of Henry II because his three elder brothers were executed by the king—subsequently, he swears revenge on Henry. Like the other books, Lide takes the reader from war-torn England, to the exotic French courts, painting the contrast between the glamorous foreign court, and the more savage English landscape. Prince Taliesin and Gervaise of Walran compete for Olwen's hand, though it is evident from the first meeting between Taliesin and Olwen that they are meant for each other. In contrast to the love story, Lide explores the relationship between Olwen's brothers, calm Lord Robert, and impetuous and angry Lord Hue, who are torn by their differing ambitions and loyalties to the crown, and to their family.

Robert of Normandy and *Fortune's Knave* tell the story of William I, and his father. Told with the same precision and interest as the 'Sedgemont Trilogy' these books allow the reader into the minds of one of the most famous English kings. Lide used contemporary records and monks' chronicles to help create a realistic sense of time, place, and language.

For *Tregaran* and *The Legacy* (*The Legacy of Tregaran*), Lide moves to her native Cornwall in the early-20th century. Both books follow the fortunes of two families, confusingly called the Tregarns and the Tregarans. The narrator of *Tregaran*, Jocelyn Tregaran, is ten years old at the beginning of the book, and a changeling. Born into a gentrified family, Jocelyn feels immediate empathy with Phil Tregarn when she meets him on her birthday. Their relationship grows and changes, until she leaves her home to be with him. Although Phil is deemed an unsuitable mate, Jocelyn finds out that her grandmother was once in love with Zack Tregarn, Phil's uncle.

Paul Craddock, a mild-mannered barrister, is the narrator in *The Legacy*. Leaving London to find some peace in Cornwall, he finds himself drawn quickly into village affairs, and the enmity between the Tregarns and the Tregarans. Zack Tregarn is the over-protective brother of Alice. Nigel and John Tregaran compete for Alice's love, although it is always John that holds her affection. In a rather complicated plot, Nigel rapes Alice while John is away at war, she falls pregnant, and Nigel is forced to marry her, and they live separately after the marriage. It is only when John returns from the war gravely injured that he and Alice find happiness finally.

Lide's novels are essential reading for any fan of the romance and historical genres. They are extremely well-written, interesting, and extensively researched books, and have brought the author well-deserved acclaim.

—Marion Hatchard

LINDOP, Audrey Erskine.   See ERSKINE-LINDOP, Audrey.

LINDSAY, Jack.
Pseudonym: Richard Preston. **Nationality:** Australian. **Born:** Melbourne, Victoria, 20 October 1900; son of the writer and artist Norman Lindsay. **Education:** Brisbane Grammar School; University of Queensland, Brisbane, 1918–21, B.A. (honours) in classics 1921. **Military Service:** British Army, 1941–45, in the Royal Corps of Signals, 1941–43, and as a scriptwriter in the War Office, 1943–45. **Relations:** married 1) Janet Beaton; 2) Ann Davies (died 1954); 3) Meta Waterdrinker in 1958, one son and one daughter. **Career:** editor, with Kenneth Slessor and F. Johnson, *Vision*, Sydney, 1923–24; moved to England, 1926; proprietor and director, Fanfrolico Press, London, 1927-30; editor, with P.R. Stephensen, *London Aphrodite*, 1928–29; editor, *Poetry and the People*, London, 1938–39; editor, *Anvil*, London, 1947; editor, with John Davenport

and Randall Swingler, *Arena*, London, 1949–51. **Recipient:** Australian Literature Society Couch Gold Medal, 1960; Order of Merit (USSR), 1968. D.Litt.: University of Queensland, 1973. Fellow, Royal Society of Literature, 1945, Ancient Monuments Society, 1961 and, Australian Academy of Humanities; Member, Order of Australia, 1981. **Died:** 8 March 1990.

ROMANCE AND HISTORICAL PUBLICATIONS

Novels (series: Roman Republic)

Cressida's First Lover: A Tale of Ancient Greece. London, Lane, 1931; New York, Long and Smith, 1932.
Rome for Sale (Roman Republic). London, Mathews and Marrot, and New York, Harper, 1934.
Caesar Is Dead (Roman Republic). London, Nicholson and Watson, 1934.
Last Days with Cleopatra (Roman Republic). London, Nicholson and Watson, 1935.
Despoiling Venus. London, Nicholson and Watson, 1935.
Storm at Sea. London, Golden Cockerel Press, 1935.
The Wanderings of Wenamen: 1115–1114 B.C.. London, Nicholson and Watson, 1936.
Shadow and Flame (as Richard Preston). London, Chapman and Hall, 1936.
Adam of a New World. London, Nicholson and Watson, 1936.
Sue Verney. London, Nicholson and Watson, 1937.
End of Cornwall (as Richard Preston). London, Cape, 1937.
1649: A Novel of a Year. London, Methuen, 1938.
Brief Light: A Novel of Catullus. London, Methuen, 1939.
Lost Birthright. London, Methuen, 1939.
Giuliano the Magnificent, adapted from a work by Dorothy Johnson. London, Dakers, 1940.
Light in Italy. London, Gollancz, 1941.
Hannibal Takes a Hand. London, Dakers, 1941.
Men of Forty-Eight. London, Methuen, 1948.
Fires in Smithfield. London, Lane, 1950.
The Passionate Pastoral. London, Lane, 1951.
The Great Oak: A Story of 1549. London, Bodley Head, 1957.
Thunder Underground: A Story of Nero's Rome. London, Muller, 1965.

Short Stories

Come Home at Last and Other Stories. London, Nicholson and Watson, 1936.
Death of a Spartan King and Two Other Stories of the Ancient World. London, Inca, 1974.

OTHER PUBLICATIONS

Novels

The Stormy Violence. London, Dakers, 1941.
We Shall Return: A Novel of Dunkirk and the French Campaign. London, Dakers, 1942.
Beyond Terror: A Novel of the Battle of Crete. London, Dakers, 1943.
The Barriers Are Down: A Tale of the Collapse of a Civilization. London, Gollancz, 1945.
Hullo Stranger. London, Dakers, 1945.
Time to Live. London, Dakers, 1946.
The Subtle Knot. London, Dakers, 1947.
Betrayed Spring: A Novel of the British Way. London, Lane, 1953.
Rising Tide. London, Lane, 1953.
The Moment of Choice. London, Lane, 1955.

A Local Habitation: A Novel of the British Way. London, Bodley Head, 1957.
The Revolt of the Sons. London, Muller, 1960.
All on the Never-Never: A Novel of the British Way of Life. London, Muller, 1961.
The Way the Ball Bounces. London, Muller, 1962.
Masks and Faces. London, Muller, 1963.
Choice of Times. London, Muller, 1964.
The Blood-Vote. St Lucia, University of Queensland Press, 1985; New York, University of Queensland Press, 1986.

Plays

Marino Faliero: A Verse-Play. London, Fanfrolico Press, 1927.
Helen Comes of Age: Three Original Plays in Verse (includes *Ragnhild* and *Bussy d'Amboise*). London, Fanfrolico Press, 1927.
Hereward: A Verse Drama, music by J. Gough. London, Fanfrolico Press, 1930.
The Whole Armour of God (produced London, 1944).
Robin of England (produced London, 1945).
The Face of Coal, with B. L. Coombes (produced London, 1946).
Iphigeneia in Aulis, adaptation of a play by Euripides (produced London, 1967).
Hecuba, adaptation of a play by Euripides (produced London, 1967).
Electra, adaptation of a play by Euripides (produced London, 1967).
Orestes, adaptation of a play by Euripides (produced London, 1967).
Nathan the Wise, adaptation of a play by Lessing (produced London, 1967).

Poetry

Fauns and Ladies. Sydney, Kirtley, 1923.
The Pleasante Conceited Narrative of Panurge's Fantastic Ally Brocaded Codpiece. Sydney, Panurgean Society, 1924.
The Spanish Main and Tavern. Sydney, Panurgean Society, 1924.
The Passionate Neatherd. London, Fanfrolico Press, 1926.
Into Action: The Battle of Dieppe. London, Dakers, 1942.
Second Front. London, Dakers, 1944.
Clue of Darkness. London, Dakers, 1949.
Peace Is Our Answer. London, Collet, 1950.
Three Letters to Nikolai Tikhonov. London, Fore, 1951.
Three Elegies. Sudbury, Suffolk, Myriad Press, 1957.
Faces and Places. Toronto, Basilike, 1974.
Collected Poems. Lake Forest, Illinois, Cheiron, 1981.

Other

William Blake: Creative Will and the Poetic Image. London, Fanfrolico Press, 1927; revised edition, 1929; New York, Haskell House, 1971.
Dionysos; or, Nietzsche contra Nietzsche: An Essay in Lyrical Philosophy. London, Fanfrolico Press, 1928.
The Romans. London, A and C Black, 1935.
Runaway (for children). London, Oxford University Press, 1935.
Rebels of the Goldfields (for children). London, Lawrence and Wishart, 1936.
Marc Antony: His World and His Contemporaries. London, Routledge, 1936; New York, Dutton, 1937.
John Bunyan: Maker of Myths. London, Methuen, 1937; New York, Kelley, 1969.
The Anatomy of Spirit: An Enquiry into the Origins of Religious Emotions. London, Methuen, 1937.
To Arms! A Story of Ancient Gaul (for children). London, Oxford University Press, 1938.

England, My England. London, Fore, 1939.

A Short History of Culture. London, Gollancz, 1939; revised edition, London, Studio, 1962; New York, Citadel Press, 1964.

The Dons Sight Devon: A Story of the Defeat of the Invincible Armada (for children). London, Oxford University Press, 1942.

Perspective for Poetry. London, Fore, 1944.

British Achievement in Art and Music. London, Pilot Press, 1945.

Mulk Raj Anand: A Critical Essay. Bombay, Hind Kitabs, 1948; revised edition, as *The Elephant and the Lotus*, Bombay, Kutub Popular, 1954.

Song of a Falling World: Culture During the Break-up of the Roman Empire (A.D. 350–600). London, Dakers, 1948; Westport, Connecticut, Hyperion Press, 1979.

Marxism and Contemporary Science; or, The Fulness of Life. London, Dobson, 1949.

A World Ahead: Journal of a Soviet Journey. London, Fore, 1950.

Charles Dickens: A Biographical and Critical Study. London, Dakers, and New York, Philosophical Library, 1950.

Byzantium into Europe: The Story of Byzantium as the First Europe (362–1204 A.D.) and Its Further Contribution till 1453 A.D. London, Lane, 1952.

Rumanian Summer: A View of the Rumanian People's Republic, with Maurice Cornforth. London, Lawrence and Wishart, 1953.

Civil War in England: The Cromwellian Revolution. London, Muller, 1954; New York, Barnes and Noble, 1967.

George Meredith: His Life and Work. London, Lane, 1956; New York, Kraus, 1973.

The Romans Were Here: The Roman Period in Britain and Its Place in Our History. London, Muller, 1956; New York, Barnes and Noble, 1969.

After the Thirties: The Novel in Britain and Its Future. London, Lawrence and Wishart, 1956.

Life Rarely Tells (autobiography). Ringwood, Victoria, Penguin, 1982.

Life Rarely Tells: An Autobiographical Account Ending in the Year 1921 and Situated Mostly in Brisbane, Queensland. London, Bodley Head, 1958.

The Roaring Twenties: Literary Life in Sydney, New South Wales, in the Years 1921–26. London, Bodley Head, 1960.

Fanfrolico and After. London, Bodley Head, 1962.

Arthur and His Times: Britain in the Dark Ages. London, Muller, 1958; New York, Barnes and Noble, 1966.

The Discovery of Britain: A Guide to Archaeology. London, Merlin Press, 1958.

1764: The Hurly-Burly of Daily Life Exemplified in One Year of the 18th Century. London, Muller, 1959.

The Writing on the Wall: An Account of Pompeii in Its Last Days. London, Muller, 1960.

Death of the Hero: French Painting from David to Delacroix. London, Studio, 1960.

William Morris: Writer. London, William Morris Society, 1961.

Our Celtic Heritage. London, Weidenfeld and Nicolson, 1962.

Daily Life in Roman Egypt. London, Muller, 1963; New York, Barnes and Noble, 1964.

Nine Days' Hero: Wat Tyler. London, Dobson, 1964.

The Clashing Rocks: A Study of Early Greek Religion and Culture, and the Origins of Drama. London, Chapman and Hall, 1965.

Leisure and Pleasure in Roman Egypt. London, Muller, 1965; New York, Barnes and Noble, 1966.

Our Anglo-Saxon Heritage. London, Weidenfeld and Nicolson, 1965.

J.M.W. Turner: His Life and Work: A Critical Biography. London, Adams and MacKay, and Greenwich, Connecticut, New York Graphic Society, 1966.

Our Roman Heritage. London, Weidenfeld and Nicolson, 1967.

Meetings with Poets: Memories of Dylan Thomas, Edith Sitwell, Louis Aragon, Paul Eluard, Tristan Tzara. London, Muller, 1968; New York, Ungar, 1969.

Men and Gods on the Roman Nile. London, Muller, and New York, Barnes and Noble, 1968.

The Ancient World: Manners and Morals. London, Weidenfeld and Nicolson, and New York, Putnam, 1968.

Cézanne: His Life and Art. London, Adams and MacKay, and Greenwich, Connecticut, New York Graphic Society, 1969.

The Origins of Alchemy in Graeco-Roman Egypt. London, Muller, and New York, Barnes and Noble, 1970.

Cleopatra. London, Constable, and New York, Coward McCann, 1971.

Origins of Astrology. London, Muller, and New York, Barnes and Noble, 1971.

Gustave Courbet: His Life and Work. Bath, Adams and Dart, 1973; New York, Harper, 1974.

Helen of Troy: Woman and Goddess. London, Constable, and Totowa, New Jersey, Rowman and Littlefield, 1974.

Blast-Power and Ballistics: Concepts of Force and Energy in the Ancient World. London, Muller, and New York, Barnes and Noble, 1974.

The Normans and Their World. London, Hart Davis MacGibbon, 1974; New York, St Martin's Press, 1975.

William Morris: His Life and Work. London, Constable, 1975; New York, Taplinger, 1979.

Decay and Renewal: Critical Essays on Twentieth Century Writing. Sydney, Wild and Woolley, 1976; London, Lawrence and Wishart, 1977.

The Troubadours and Their World of the Twelfth and Thirteenth Centuries. London, Muller, 1976.

Hogarth: His Art and World. London, Hart Davis MacGibbon, 1977; New York, Taplinger, 1979.

William Blake: His Life and Work. London, Constable, 1978; New York, Braziller, 1979.

The Monster City: Defoe's London 1688–1730. London, Hart Davis MacGibbon, and New York, St Martin's Press, 1978.

Thomas Gainsborough: His Life and Art. London, Granada, and New York, Universe, 1981.

The Crisis in Marxism. Bradford on Avon, Wiltshire, Moonraker Press, and New York, Barnes and Noble, 1981.

Turner: The Man and His Art. London, Granada, and New York, Watts, 1985.

Editor, with Kenneth Slessor, *Poetry in Australia*. Sydney, Vision Press, 1923.

Editor, with P. Warlock, *Loving Mad Tom: Bedlamite Verses of the XVI and XVII Centuries*. London, Fanfrolico Press, 1927; New York, Kelley, 1970.

Editor, *The Metamorphosis of Aiax*, by Sir John Harington. New York, McKee, 1928.

Editor, *The Parlement of Pratlers*. London, Fanfrolico Press, 1928.

Editor, (as Peter Meadows), *Delighted Earth*, by Robert Herrick. London, Fanfrolico Press, 1928.

Editor, *Inspiration*. London, Fanfrolico Press, 1928.

Editor, *Letters of Philip Stanhope, Second Earl of Chesterfield*. London, Fanfrolico Press, 1930.

Editor, with Edgell Rickword, *A Handbook of Freedom: A Record of English Democracy Through Twelve Centuries*. London, Lawrence and Wishart, and New York, International Publishers, 1939.

Editor, with Maurice Carpenter and Honor Arundel, *New Lyrical Ballads*. London, Editions Poetry, 1945.

Editor, *Anvil: Life and the Arts: A Miscellany*. London, Meridian, and New York, Universal Distributors, 1947.

Editor, *New Development Series*. London, Lane, 1947–48.

Editor, *Herrick: A Selection*. London, Grey Walls Press, 1948.

Editor, *William Morris: A Selection*. London, Grey Walls Press, 1948.

Editor, with Randall Swingler, *Key Poets*. London, Fore, 1950.

Editor, *Barefoot*, by Z. Stancu. London, Fore, 1950.

Editor, *Paintings and Drawings of Leslie Hurry*. London, Grey Walls Press, 1952.

Editor, *The Sunset Ship: Poems of J.M.W. Turner*. Lowestoft, Suffolk, Scorpion Press, 1966.

Editor, *The Autobiography of Joseph Priestley*. Bath, Adams and Dart, 1970; Teaneck, New Jersey, Fairleigh Dickinson University Press, 1971.

Translator, *Lysistrata*, by Aristophanes. Sydney, Kirtley, 1925; London, Fanfrolico Press, 1926.

Translator, *Propertius in Love*. London, Fanfrolico Press, 1927.

Translator, *Satyricon and Poems*, by Petronius, London, Fanfrolico Press, 1927; revised edition, London, Elek, 1960.

Translator, *Homage to Sappho*. London, Fanfrolico Press, 1928.

Translator, *Complete Poems of Theocritus*. London, Fanfrolico Press, 1929.

Translator, *Hymns to Aphrodite*, by Homer. London, Fanfrolico Press, 1929.

Translator, *Women in Parliament*, by Aristophanes. London, Fanfrolico Press, 1929.

Translator, *The Mimiambs of Herondas*. London, Fanfrolico Press, 1929.

Translator, *The Complete Poetry of Gaius Catullus*. London, Fanfrolico Press, 1930; revised edition, London, Sylvan Press, 1948.

Translator, *Sulpicia's Garland: Roman Poems*. New York, McKee, 1930.

Translator, *Patchwork Quilt: Poems by Ausonius*. London, Fanfrolico Press, 1930.

Translator, *The Golden Ass*, by Apuleius. New York, Limited Editions Club, 1931; revised edition, London, Elek, and Bloomington, Indiana University Press, 1960.

Translator, *I Am a Roman*. London, Mathews and Marrot, 1934.

Translator, *Medieval Latin Poets*. London, Mathews and Marrot, 1934.

Translator, *Daphnis and Chloe*, by Longus. London, Daimon Press, 1948.

Translator, with S. Jolly, *Song of Peace*, by V. Nezval. London, Fore, 1951.

Translator, *Poems of Adam Mickiewicz*. London, Sylvan Press, and New York, Transatlantic Arts, 1957.

Translator, *Russian Poetry 1917–1955*. London, Lane, 1957; Chester Springs, Pennsylvania, Dufour, 1961.

Translator, *Asklepiades in Love*. Twinstead, Essex, Myriad Press, 1960.

Translator, *Modern Russian Poetry*. London, Vista, 1960.

Translator, *Cause, Principle, and Unity: 5 Dialogues*, by Giordano Bruno. London, Daimon Press, 1962; New York, International Publishers, 1964.

Translator, *Ribaldry of Ancient Greece*. London, Elek, and New York, Ungar, 1965.

Translator, *Ribaldry of Ancient Rome*. London, Elek, and New York, Ungar, 1965.

Translator, *The Elegy of Haido*, by Tefcros Anthias. London, Anthias Publications, 1966.

Translator, *The Age of Akhenaten*, by Eleonore Bille-de-Mot. London, Adams and MacKay, 1967; New York, McGraw Hill, 1968.

Translator, *Greece, I Keep My Vigil for You*, by Tefcros Anthias. London, Anthias Publications, 1968.

Translator, *The Twelve, and The Scythians*, by Alexander Blok. London, Journeyman Press, 1982.

*

Bibliography: *Jack Lindsay: A Catalogue of First Editions* by Harry F. Chaplin, Sydney, Wentworth Press, 1983.

Manuscript Collection: University of Queensland, St Lucia.

Critical Studies: *Mountain in the Sunlight* by Alick West, London, Lawrence and Wishart, 1958; *A Garland for Jack Lindsay* edited by Edgell Rickword, London, Piccolo Press, 1980; *Jack Lindsay: The Thirties and Forties* edited by Robert Mackie, London, Institute of Commonwealth Studies, 1984; *Culture and History: Essays Presented in Honour of Jack Lindsay* edited by Bernard Smith, Sydney, Hale and Iremonger, 1984.

*   *   *

Before the 1930s Jack Lindsay's abundant energies were concentrated on poetry, translation, cultural criticism, editing, and publishing. In Sydney he and his father, the artist Norman Lindsay, created the shortlived but influential magazine *Vision*, and later in London he and P.R. Stephensen, another Australian expatriate, founded the literary periodical *London Aphrodite* and the upmarket Fanfrolico Press.

Lindsay's historical fiction belongs mainly to the middle period of his long literary career. He wrote 16 examples before 1941 and five thereafter. His later output shifted to contemporary fiction and biographical and historical studies, which he continued to write into the 1980s. Between 1934 and 1941 Lindsay produced seven other prose works, six volumes of verse and verse translation, and a large quantity of short stories and critical essays. The historical novels thus belong to a phase of phenomenal literary output, possibly surpassed only by Lindsay's own postwar production.

Lindsay's writing is shaped by an idiosyncratic philosophy—a Romanticism influenced by Blake and Nietzsche, blended with Marxist historicism. He himself characterized his work as being concerned primarily with 'alienation . . . and the struggle against alienation'. But these abstract concerns seldom detract from the readability of his novels, which are vividly descriptive and dramatic. At one level the struggle for and against alienation means Tyranny versus Liberty. But it also refers to the efforts of individuals to achieve awareness, freedom, and fulfilment in their private lives. This passage from confinement to freedom recurs throughout Lindsay's novels, with many different resolutions: mystical ecstasy; self-destructive despair; joyous acceptance of life and work; death.

His stories are usually set in periods of fundamental crisis. They convey an intense feeling for history as an organic force which drives people to act in ways they scarcely understand, with consequences they cannot fathom. Often the cycle of a year is used as a narrative frame to stress the interconnection of natural, ritual, and social elements. Connected with this is a focus on the 'irrational'—poetry, sex, religion, dancing, and drunkenness. And while he takes great pains to ensure historical authenticity (to reproduce, in his own words, 'the particular intonation of an age, its coloration and resonance') he is also driven to uncover deep universals in human experience: 'the effect should be simultaneously: how like ourselves, how unlike'. This makes for a characteristic tension which is often dark and disturbing.

Lindsay has his weaknesses. Although well crafted, the great speed with which his novels were written is betrayed by an occasional slackness of style, while their sheer quantity exposes a certain repetitiveness of theme and technique. At times, especially in the novels of the late 1930s and 1940s, he is prone to tendentious rhetoric and simplistic analysis, though this hardly amounts to the 'crude propaganda' he has been accused of. On the whole, these works do not deserve the relative obscurity into which they have fallen, and it is to be hoped that critical interest will help spark a revival.

Lindsay's career as a classicist gave him an easy familiarity with Graeco-Roman antiquity, and it was to this period that he turned when he began writing novels. *Rome for Sale* announces the major preoccupations of his maturity. Concerned with the abortive rebellion of Catalina in the dying days of the Roman Republic, it evokes a delirious atmosphere of sophisticated corruption, religious fanaticism, perverse sexuality, poetry, violence, honour, and futility. It was followed quickly by *Caesar Is Dead*, a particularly successful recreation of the explosive political situation following the dictator's assassination. The more conventional *Last Days with Cleopatra* completed a trilogy on the Caesarian revolution.

Lindsay soon began to write novels with an English setting. In 1939 he completed a trilogy on English revolutionary periods, using the techniques he had developed in the Roman novels—the yearly cycle, the interweaving of multiple viewpoints, the use of contemporary writings, and the linking of political change with religious ideology and personal life.

1649 is set in the year following the execution of Charles I, memorably depicting the relations between the fervently religious Puritans, the idealistic radicalism of the Levellers and the individualism and commercialism of the rising middle class. According to a normally unsympathetic critic (David Smith), this novel 'gave to Marxist ideology a life and conviction that few British novelists had so far been able to do'. *Lost Birthright* deals with the Wilkesite disturbances of 1769, contrasting the lives of two brothers cheated of their inheritance; *Men of Forty-Eight* is concerned with the Chartist movement.

The English novels met with a cooler critical reception than the Roman novels. Conservatives considered them provokingly radical, while most of the left felt they were too concerned with culture and personality at the expense of political and economic issues. The width of critical opinion about Lindsay can be judged by the contrast between Edith Sitwell's verdict on *Men of Forty-Eight* as 'profoundly impressive and as moving as it is impressive', and David Smith's comment on the same novel: 'too much like a Left Wing history textbook'.

During the war Lindsay worked as a scriptwriter for the army Theatre Unit and afterwards began the 'British Way' series of contemporary novels. Only in 1950 did *Fires in Smithfield* appear. Concerned with the political and religious disturbances of 1558, it is one of his best and most characteristic works. Of the many remaining historical novels, the most important is *Adam of a New World*, an account of the trial and execution of Giordano Bruno, who was for Lindsay a symbol of the yearning for human freedom and unity. Widely read as a parable of fascism—which was part of its author's intention—it remains both a fierce condemnation of institutionalized repression and a troubled reflection on the nature of power and freedom, ideology, and truth.

By the mid 1950s the exposure of Stalin's crimes and the Russian invasion of Hungary produced unresolvable stresses in Lindsay's never smooth relationship with the Communist movement. The simplifications and enthusiasms which tempted him in earlier decades were no longer possible. Significantly, in his last historical novel, *Thunder Underground*, there is a conspicuous return to the period and atmosphere of his early novels. Rebellion against Nero and the Empire smoulders undirected in the social depths, surfacing in the religious cults of the populace and the artistic fashions of the intelligentsia. Throughout his writings Lindsay adverted to cycles—of decay and renewal, becoming and return. This masterly conclusion to his career as a novelist also closes a cycle, coming back to a symbolic point of origin in the history of culture and in Lindsay's own work: the turmoil of Ancient Rome at the height of its power.

—Paul Gillen

LINDSAY, Rachel.
Pseudonyms: Rozella Lake; Roberta Leigh; Janey Scott. **Nationality:** British. **Address:** c/o Mills and Boon Ltd, Eton House, 18–24 Paradise Road, Richmond, Surrey TW9 1SR, England.

ROMANCE AND HISTORICAL PUBLICATIONS

Novels

The Widening Stream. London, Hutchinson, 1952.
Alien Corn. London, Hutchinson, 1954; Toronto, Harlequin, 1973.
Healing Hands. London, Hutchinson, 1955.
Mask of Gold. London, Hutchinson, 1956; Toronto, Harlequin, 1974.
Castle in the Trees. London, Hurst and Blackett, 1958; Toronto, Harlequin, 1974.
House of Lorraine. London, Mills and Boon, 1959; Toronto, Harlequin, 1966.
The Taming of Laura. London, Mills and Boon, 1959; Toronto, Harlequin, 1966.
Business Affair. London, Mills and Boon, 1960; Toronto, Harlequin, 1974.
Heart of a Rose. London, Mills and Boon, 1961; Toronto, Harlequin, 1965.
Song in My Heart. London, Mills and Boon, 1961.
Lesley Forrest, M.D. New York, Berkley, 1962.
Moonlight and Magic. London, Mills and Boon, 1962; Toronto, Harlequin, 1972.
Design for Murder. London, Mills and Boon, 1964.
No Business to Love. London, Mills and Boon, 1966.
Love and Lucy Granger. London, Mills and Boon, 1967; Toronto, Harlequin, 1972.
Price of Love. London, Mills and Boon, 1967; Toronto, Harlequin, 1974.
Love and Dr Forrest. London, Mills and Boon, 1971; Toronto, Harlequin, 1978.
The Latitude of Love. London, Mills and Boon, 1971.
A Question of Marriage. London, Mills and Boon, 1972; Toronto, Harlequin, 1973.
Cage of Gold. London, Mills and Boon, 1973; Toronto, Harlequin, 1974.
Chateau in Provence. London, Mills and Boon, 1973; (as Rozella Lake), Toronto, Harlequin, 1975.
Food for Love. Toronto, Harlequin, 1974; London, Mills and Boon, 1975.
Affair in Venice. London, Mills and Boon, and Toronto, Harlequin, 1975.
Love in Disguise. London, Mills and Boon, and Toronto, Harlequin, 1975.
Innocent Deception. London, Mills and Boon, and Toronto, Harlequin, 1975.
Prince for Sale. London, Mills and Boon, and Toronto, Harlequin, 1975.
The Marquis Takes a Wife. London, Mills and Boon, 1976; Toronto, Harlequin, 1977.
Roman Affair. London, Mills and Boon, 1976; Toronto, Harlequin, 1977.

Secretary Wife. London, Mills and Boon, and Toronto, Harlequin, 1976.

Tinsel Star. London, Mills and Boon, 1976; Toronto, Harlequin, 1977.

A Man to Tame. London, Mills and Boon, 1976; Toronto, Harlequin, 1977.

Forbidden Love. London, Mills and Boon, and Toronto, Harlequin, 1977.

Prescription for Love. London, Mills and Boon, and Toronto, Harlequin, 1977.

Rough Diamond Lover. Toronto, Harlequin, 1978; London, Mills and Boon, 1979.

An Affair to Forget. London, Mills and Boon, and Toronto, Harlequin, 1978.

Forgotten Marriage. Toronto, Harlequin, 1978; (as Roberta Leigh), London, Mills and Boon, 1978.

Brazilian Affair. Toronto, Harlequin, 1978.

My Sister's Keeper. London, Mills and Boon, 1979.

Man of Ice. London, Mills and Boon, and Toronto, Harlequin, 1980.

Untouched Wife. Toronto, Harlequin, 1981.

Novels as Roberta Leigh

In Name Only. London, Falcon Press, 1951; Toronto, Harlequin, 1973.

Dark Inheritance. London, Hutchinson, 1952; Toronto, Harlequin, 1968.

The Vengeful Heart. London, Hutchinson, 1952; Toronto, Harlequin, 1970.

Beloved Ballerina. London, Hutchinson, 1953; Toronto, Harlequin, 1974.

And Then Came Love. London, Hutchinson, 1954; Toronto, Harlequin, 1974.

Pretence. London, Hutchinson, 1956; Toronto, Harlequin, 1969.

Stacy. London, Heinemann, 1958.

My Heart's a Dancer. London, Mills and Boon, 1970; Toronto, Harlequin, 1973.

Cinderella in Mink. London, Mills and Boon, 1973; Toronto, Harlequin, 1974.

If Dreams Came True. London, Mills and Boon, 1974; (as Rozella Lake), Toronto, Harlequin, 1975.

Shade of the Palms. London, Mills and Boon, and Toronto, Harlequin, 1974.

Heart of the Lion. London, Mills and Boon, and Toronto, Harlequin, 1975.

Man in a Million. London, Mills and Boon, 1975; Toronto, Harlequin, 1976.

Temporary Wife. London, Mills and Boon, and Toronto, Harlequin, 1975.

Cupboard Love. London, Mills and Boon, and Toronto, Harlequin, 1976.

To Buy a Bride. London, Mills and Boon, and Toronto, Harlequin, 1976.

The Unwilling Bridegroom. London, Mills and Boon, 1976; Toronto, Harlequin, 1977.

Man Without a Heart. London, Mills and Boon, 1976; Toronto, Harlequin, 1977.

Girl for a Millionaire. London, Mills and Boon, and Toronto, Harlequin, 1977.

Too Young for Love. Toronto, Harlequin, 1977.

Facts of Love. London, Mills and Boon, 1978.

Night of Love. London, Mills and Boon, 1978; New York, Fawcett, 1979.

The Savage Aristocrat. London, Mills and Boon, 1978; New York, Fawcett, 1979.

Not a Marrying Man. Toronto, Harlequin, 1978.

Love in Store. New York, Fawcett, 1978.

Flower of the Desert. New York, Fawcett, 1979; London, Mills and Boon, 1983.

Love and No Marriage. London, Mills and Boon, 1980.

Rent a Wife. London, Mills and Boon, 1980; (as Rachel Lindsay), Toronto, Harlequin, 1980.

Wife for a Year. London, Mills and Boon, 1980; (as Rachel Lindsay), Toronto, Harlequin, 1981.

Love Match. New York, Fawcett, 1980.

Confirmed Bachelor. London, Mills and Boon, and Toronto, Harlequin, 1981.

No Time for Marriage. London, Mills and Boon, 1985.

An Impossible Man to Love. London, Mills and Boon, 1987.

Too Bad to Be True. London, Mills and Boon, 1987.

It All Depends on Love. London, Mills and Boon, 1987.

Not Without Love. London, Mills and Boon, 1989.

No Man's Mistress. London, Mills and Boon, 1989.

Man on the Make. London, Mills and Boon, 1989.

A Most Unsuitable Wife. London, Mills and Boon, 1990.

One Girl at a Time. London, Mills and Boon, 1990.

Two-Faced Woman. London, Mills and Boon, 1991.

Not His Kind of Woman. London, Mills and Boon, 1992.

Bachelor at Heart. London, Mills and Boon, 1992.

Two-Timing Man. London, Mills and Boon, 1993.

Novels as Janey Scott

Memory of Love. London, Mills and Boon, 1959.

Melody of Love. London, Mills and Boon, 1960.

A Time to Love. London, Mills and Boon, 1960; revised edition, as *Unwanted Wife* (as Rachel Lindsay) Mills and Boon, 1976; Toronto, Harlequin, 1978.

Sara Gay—Model Girl [*in Mayfair, in New York, in Monte Carlo*]. London, World, 4 vols, 1961.

*   *   *

Rachel Lindsay's primary theme is how much easier it is to love than it is to trust. Her stories show passionate physical attraction between people from vastly different backgrounds, holding vastly different beliefs and values. Usually the girl is innocent and ordinary, while the man is rich, arrogant, and sexually experienced. Another standard motif is the patient Griselda story: an arrogant man assumes the innocent heroine to be devious and scheming and therefore treats her brutally and insultingly. She naturally falls in love with him and patiently puts up with his abuse until he realizes her innocence and abases himself before her. There is more sex in her novels than in most Harlequins, though heavy petting always stops short of consummation.

In *The Widening Stream* two people who love each other without knowing each other very well are pushed apart by the lies of a scheming woman. *The Taming of Laura* is a Cinderella story. Eric Berne suggested that after Cinderella married the prince she would still spend her time sweeping up the cinders. In this novel and in *Affair in Venice* and *Secretary Wife*, Lindsay's Cinderellas have this problem of adjusting to their new position and wealth. *Forgotten Marriage* is the patient Griselda story par excellence. The heroine has the double disadvantage of being accused of vile actions, and having amnesia and therefore being unable to disprove the accusations. While her falling in love with her accuser is incomprehensible, his subsequent grovelling is satisfying to heroine and reader alike. In *A Time to Love* a refugee from an iron curtain country seeks her English husband only to find he is under the impression she has divorced him, and is planning to marry again. Since the heroine is blonde and beautiful, one can tell the difference between her and the doormat, though with some difficulty. Other patient Griselda stories include *Roman Affair* and *Man of Ice*. *An Affair to Forget* concerns a rock singer and a sweet country girl whose values are so different that only total surrender by one of them (guess who?) will make this relationship possible. *Song in My Heart* deals with a pop singer who falls in love with a married man. When his wife conveniently dies, the story becomes a murder mystery. *Price of Love* reverses the normal situation; an arrogant woman doctor loves a man she regards as hopelessly frivolous and unreliable, and she is the one who has to change. *Design for Murder* is a murder mystery and love story set in the world of high fashion. In *A Man to Tame* a woman doctor overcomes sex discrimination, demonstrates her courage, and wins the heart of an arrogant man. In *Prescription for Love* neither hero nor heroine is sufficiently self-confident to admit their love. Were there no intermediary to resolve this romance, no doubt they would have pined genteely for each other for the rest of their lives. In *My Sister's Keeper* the heroine deeply distrusts the man she loves because of her preconceptions of his values. In *Love and No Marriage* a successful dress designer allows the hero to continue to believe she is a professional housekeeper, albeit a not very good one. *Wife for a Year* is another one of those books where only an intermediary can make the romance happen at all.

Bizarre and unlikely things happen in Lindsay's world: heroines rescue people from burning buildings and emerge with nary an unsightly scar; 22-year-old women own their own fabulously successful businesses; opera singers become rock singers; worst of all, her heroines live in a peculiarly friendless vacuum. Nevertheless, between her heroes and heroines, there is great emotional realism. Though some of her heroines do silly, irrational things, and several of her men are brutal and insensitive, most of her characters are reasonable people, trying to reconcile their differences and to develop trust and understanding as well as love.

—Marylaine Block

LINDSEY, Johanna.
Nationality: American. **Born:** Frankfurt, Germany, 10 March 1952. **Education:** high schools in Kailua and Hawaii. **Relations:** married Ralph B. Lindsey in 1970; three sons. **Career:** full-time writer. Lives in Kaneohe, Hawaii. **Address:** c/o Avon Books, 1350 Avenue of the Americas, New York, New York 10019, USA.

ROMANCE AND HISTORICAL PUBLICATIONS

Novels

Captive Bride. New York, Avon, 1977; London, Hamlyn, 1978.
A Pirate's Love. New York, Avon, 1978; London, Hamlyn, 1979.
Fires of Winter. New York, Avon, 1980; London, Hamlyn, 1981.
Paradise Wild. New York, Avon, 1981; London, Hamlyn, 1982.
Glorious Angel. New York, Avon, 1982; London, Corgi, 1985.
So Speaks the Heart. New York, Avon, and London, Corgi, 1983.
Heart of Thunder. New York, Avon, 1983; London, Corgi, 1984.
A Gentle Feuding. New York, Avon, and London, Corgi, 1984.
Brave the Wild Wind. New York, Avon, 1984; London, Corgi, 1985.
Love Only Once. New York, Avon, 1985; London, Corgi, 1986.
Tender Is the Storm. New York, Avon, and London, Corgi, 1985.
A Heart So Wild. New York, Avon, 1986; London, Corgi, 1987.
When Love Awaits. New York, Avon, and London, Corgi, 1986.
Hearts Aflame. New York, Avon, and London, Corgi, 1987.
Secret Fire. New York, Avon, 1987.
Tender Rebel. New York, Avon, 1988.
Silver Angel. New York, Avon, 1988.
Defy Not the Heart. New York, Avon, 1989; London, Corgi, 1991.

Savage Thunder. New York, Avon, 1989.
Warrior's Woman. New York, Avon, 1990.
Gentle Rogue. New York, Avon, 1990.
Once a Princess. New York, Avon, 1991.
Man of My Dreams. New York, Avon, 1992.
Angel. New York, Avon, 1992; London, Corgi, 1993.
The Magic of You. New York, Avon, 1993.
Keeper of the Heart. New York, Avon, 1993.

*

Johanna Lindsey comments:

My writing career began in 1977 when my first historical romance was published. My success as a writer wouldn't have been possible without the loyalty and support of my many readers, who have enjoyed my characters' adventures in love and folly, and my many different settings, from pirate ships and Viking strongholds to mediaeval castles and the American west. Each time I learn that I have made someone laugh, or cry a little, or just feel good for a while, I am deeply gratified and hopeful that in the years ahead I will continue to touch others lives with my stories.

*   *   *

Johanna Lindsey's novels feature a wide variety of locations and historical periods. Although England, Scotland, and the American West in the 19th century are among her favourite settings (*Glorious Angel*, *Heart of Thunder*, *Brave the Wild Wind*, *Tender Is the Storm*, *Love Only Once*, *A Heart So Wild*, and *Tender Rebel*), Lindsey also has written several stories set in mediaeval times or in exotic locations. *Captive Bride* and *Silver Angel* are set in the Middle East, *Fires of Winter* and *Hearts Aflame* treat the Viking raids of England, while *Secret Fire* takes place primarily in Russia. *Warrior's Woman* takes place in another star system in the 22nd century. No matter the time or place, however, Lindsey's books almost always provide an accurate sense of place.

There are common plot devices and themes to be seen throughout Lindsey's work. Abduction of the heroine, usually by the hero, is a familiar ploy used to throw the leading characters together in a situation destined to spark with hostility. Often the abduction involves some mistaken identity such as the belief that the young noblewoman is of lower class or is a male. Some variation of the heroine-held-prisoner figures prominently in many of the works, including *Captive Bride*, *Fires of Winter*, *A Gentle Feuding*, *Love Only Once*, *Secret Fire*, *Silver Angel*, and *Warrior's Woman*.

A basic violence, both in external events and the male-female relationships is found throughout, as is a strong aura of sensuality. Sex can become the ultimate weapon. Love, as seen by Lindsey, has a dark side which shows itself in distrust, misunderstandings, and violent physical love. The latter even extends to the rape of the heroine, although a passionate love affair develops in which the woman usually becomes a demanding partner. This sexual violence and cruelty creates a deep tension and lets the relationship teeter on a point between destruction and total fulfilment. A romance, of course, will veer towards the latter, but the heroine endures humiliation before attaining happiness. In *Prisoner of My Desire*, it seems as if women may have some measure of revenge when Lord Warrick deChaville is captured, and suffers the sexual humiliation of being 'raped' by Lady Rowena Belleme, but he quickly turns the tables and imprisons her for his own revenge. Sex can also be seen as a method of punishment. Fearing they might inadvertently harm their women in disciplining them for some infraction of rules, the warrior barbarians in *Warrior's Woman* have developed a system of punishment in which they engage a woman in extended foreplay, raising her to the point of fulfilment, then withhold from her the ultimate satisfaction of sexual release. Similarly, Tony Malory uses sexual seduction to punish Roslynn Chadwick when she displeases him (*Tender Rebel*). Many may view this portrayal of women accepting physical violence and sexual abuse as perpetuating a harmful myth of rape, but it seems clear that Lindsey's readers expect such scenes. As long as the perpetrator is the hero, the effect is arousing rather than truly painful or humiliating.

In general, the characters in these novels are well developed and believable. At times, however, credibility is strained. This is true in *Silver Angel*, in which the hero, Derek Sinclair, the Earl of Mulbury, also is the twin brother of Jamil, a Barbary Coast Dey. The relationship is explained but is more than usually difficult to accept. Nevertheless, Derek is an appropriately brooding and masterful hero. Tedra De Arr and Challen Ly-San-Ter of *Warrior's Woman* are among Lindsey's least believable characters. She is a shrieking parody of feminist-turned-love-slave, while he is a stereotypical 'civilized' barbarian. Neither character is helped by Lindsey's failure to create a believable world for them to inhabit.

Like many other romance authors, Lindsey also writes linked books with related or continuing characters. Kristen, the young Viking woman of *Hearts Aflame* is the daughter of Brenna and Garrick (*Fires of Winter*). Both Kristen's parents and her brother, Selig, return to help her in the later story. Hank Chavez, the enigmatic bandit of *Glorious Angel*, returns as the hero of *Heart of Thunder*, and the gunfighter, Angel, who appeared briefly in *Savage Thunder*, reappears as the title character in *Angel*, Lindsey's 25th romance for Avon. The volatile Malory family appear in *Gentle Rogue*, *Tender Rebel*, *Love Only Once*, and *The Magic of You*.

Although the explicit sensuality and frequent abusiveness found in Lindsey's works may disturb some readers, her well thought out, fast moving stories appeal to many more. In her skilled hands, the standard battle of strong-willed individuals comes to life. Anchored by authentic descriptions and historical detail and focusing on the turbulent passions in the battle of the sexes, her books are among the best of the sensuous historical novels.

—Barbara E. Kemp

LLOYD, Levanah. See **PETERS, Maureen.**

LLYWELYN, Morgan. Irish. 1937—. See 2nd edition, 1990.

LOCKRIDGE, Ross.
Nationality: American. **Born:** Bloomington, Indiana, 25 April 1914. **Education:** Indiana University, Bloomington, 1931–35, B.A. (summa cum laude) in English 1935 (Phi Beta Kappa); postgraduate study, Harvard University, Cambridge, Massachusetts, 1940–41. **Relations:** married Vernice Baker in 1937; four children. **Career:** instructor in English, Indiana University, 1936–40, and Simmons College, Boston, 1941–45. **Died:** (suicide) 6 March 1948.

ROMANCE AND HISTORICAL PUBLICATIONS

Novel

Raintree County. Boston, Houghton Mifflin, 1948; London, Macdonald, 1949.

*

Critical Study: *Ross and Tom: Two American Tragedies* (on Lockridge and Thomas Heggen) by John Leggett, New York, Simon and Schuster, 1974.

*   *   *

Ross Lockridge is known for only one book, *Raintree County*, published in 1948 to acclaim and financial success. The novel, 1066 pages long and dense with history, event, and personality, is a conscious attempt to create and profit from creating 'the Great American Novel'—the novel at last deep and wide enough to encompass the entire USA in its development and nature.

Warning the reader in the front matter of *Raintree County* that the county 'is not the country of perishable fact. It is the country of the enduring fiction', Lockridge nevertheless built his novel upon knowledge of Indiana, that central state of the USA which might be thought the most typical of the nation's people and history. Son of a talented amateur historian and a Christian Science mother obsessed with having one of her children become an outstanding American, Lockridge, after university and while teaching at college, tried to meet the challenge of his parents by becoming what would most please them: a historical novelist with national acclaim and great prosperity.

Deciding that he would in *Raintree County* narrate the history of his main character and his nation at once, Lockridge chose one day in his hero's life—4 July 1892, the nation's Independence Day—for detailed narration of the present, this one day's events to be expanded into historical and national scope by the addition of 52 flashbacks to describe critical experiences in his hero's life and his nation's life. These flashbacks cover the life of the major character, John Wickliff Shawnessy, from 1844, when he was very young, to the recent past, when his wife and daughter reflect their pride in their husband and father. They round out the life of a typical young American from his boyhood in Indiana, near the National Road leading westward, into the maturity of the character at 53, rich in experience and exemplary of the best qualities of his countrymen.

Lockridge, being trained by his historian father for the writing and interpreting of history, worked into his novel the story of his nation, giving, for example, the first settlement of the area of Raintree County by Indians, their replacement by whites, the frontier nature of the area, the crisis over slavery, the involvement of the citizens in the Civil War over that slavery, the assassination of President Lincoln, the corruption of the government in the gilded age after that war, and the optimism of the citizens as the new century approached, with its hint and promise of even greater success, individual and national.

In the *Bildungsroman* aspects of *Raintree County* Shawnessy is made by idealistic parents into a reflective youth, soon tempted and educated toward maturity through love of an unattainable local blonde goddess, then a fire-scarred, dark-haired southern slave holder, then a worldly, beautiful, and confident New York City actress, and finally a youthful and fine average Indiana girl. At every stage of his life Shawnessy is contrasted with his contemporaries in Raintree County: Cassius P. Carney, who goes eastward to become a financial mogul; Garwood B. Jones, who goes eastward to become a leading senator in the federal government; and—most important of all—Jerusalem Webster Stiles, who becomes an educator, a journalist, a war reporter, and always an alter ego to John Wickliff Shawnessy (note the identical initials of the two names). Stiles is the cynical, worldly, realistic, deterministic counterforce to the romantic philosophizing hero, who all his life seeks for the mythical 'raintree' that would reign in the ideal garden of human life and that represents the unknowable secret of that human life.

Epic in concept and achievement, *Raintree County* was chosen immediately at publication for the members of the Book-of-the-Month Club subscription company, excerpted in *Life* magazine, and won for its author $150,000 from the MGM film company for rights to make the novel into a movie. Despite this success, Lockridge, diagnosed as clinically depressed amid success, having pleased his ambitious parents, committed suicide weeks after his one novel was published.

—Ray Lewis White

LOFTS, Norah.
Pseudonym: Juliet Astley; Peter Curtis. **Nationality:** British. **Born:** Norah Robinson, Shipdham, Norfolk, 27 August 1904. **Education:** West Suffolk County School; Norwich Training College, teaching diploma 1925. **Relations:** married 1) Geoffrey Lofts in 1933 (died 1948), one son; 2) Robert Jorisch in 1949. **Career:** taught English and history at Guildhall Feoffment Girl's School, 1925–36. **Recipient:** Georgette Heyer prize, for historical novel, 1978. **Died:** 10 September 1983.

ROMANCE AND HISTORICAL PUBLICATIONS

Novels (series: Suffolk Trilogy)

Here Was a Man: A Romantic History of Sir Walter Raleigh. London, Methuen, and New York, Knopf, 1936.
White Hell of Pity. London, Methuen, and New York, Knopf, 1937.
Requiem for Idols. London, Methuen, and New York, Knopf, 1938.
Out of This Nettle. London, Gollancz, 1938; as *Colin Lowrie*, New York, Knopf, 1939.
Blossom Like the Rose. London, Gollancz, and New York, Knopf, 1939.
Hester Roon. London, Davies, and New York, Knopf, 1940.
The Road to Revelation. London, Davies, 1941.
The Brittle Glass. London, Joseph, 1942; New York, Knopf, 1943.
Michael and All the Angels. London, Joseph, 1943; as *The Golden Fleece*, New York, Knopf, 1944.
Jassy. London, Joseph, and New York, Knopf, 1944.
To See a Fine Lady. London, Joseph, and New York, Knopf, 1946.
Silver Nutmeg. London, Joseph, and New York, Doubleday, 1947.
A Calf for Venus. London, Joseph, and New York, Doubleday, 1949; as *Letty*, New York, Pyramid, 1968.
Esther. New York, Macmillan, 1950; London, Joseph, 1951.
The Lute Player. London, Joseph, and New York, Doubleday, 1951.
Bless This House. London, Joseph, and New York, Doubleday, 1954.
Winter Harvest. New York, Doubleday, 1955.
Queen in Waiting. London, Joseph, 1955; as *Eleanor the Queen*, New York, Doubleday, 1955; as *Queen in Waiting*, Doubleday, 1958.
Afternoon of an Autocrat. London, Joseph, and New York, Doubleday, 1956; as *The Devil in Clevely*, Leeds, Morley Barker, 1968.
Scent of Cloves. New York, Doubleday, 1957; London, Hutchinson, 1958.
Suffolk Trilogy:
The Town House. London, Hutchinson, and New York, Doubleday, 1959.
The House at Old Vine. London, Hutchinson, and New York, Doubleday, 1961.
The House at Sunset. New York, Doubleday, 1962; London, Hutchinson, 1963.
The Concubine: A Novel Based upon the Life of Anne Boleyn. New York, Doubleday, 1963; London, Hutchinson, 1964; as *Concubine*, London, Arrow, 1965.

How Far to Bethlehem? London, Hutchinson, and New York, Doubleday, 1965.
The Lost Ones. London, Hutchinson, 1969; as *The Lost Queen*, New York, Doubleday, 1969; London, Corgi, 1970.
Madselin. London, Corgi, 1969; New York, Bantam, 1970.
The King's Pleasure. New York, Doubleday, 1969; London, Hodder and Stoughton, 1970.
Lovers All Untrue. London, Hodder and Stoughton, and New York, Doubleday, 1970.
A Rose for Virtue. London, Hodder and Stoughton, and New York, Doubleday, 1971.
Charlotte. London, Hodder and Stoughton, 1972; as *Out of the Dark*, New York, Doubleday, 1972.
Nethergate. London, Hodder and Stoughton, and New York, Doubleday, 1973.
Crown of Aloes. London, Hodder and Stoughton, and New York, Doubleday, 1974.
Walk into My Parlour. London, Corgi, 1975.
Knight's Acre. London, Hodder and Stoughton, and New York, Doubleday, 1975.
The Homecoming. London, Hodder and Stoughton, 1975; New York, Doubleday, 1976.
Checkmate. London, Corgi, 1975; New York, Fawcett, 1978.
The Fall of Midas (as Juliet Astley). New York, Coward McCann, 1975; London, Joseph, 1976.
The Lonely Furrow. London, Hodder and Stoughton, 1976; New York, Doubleday, 1977.
Gad's Hall. London, Hodder and Stoughton, 1977; New York, Doubleday, 1978.
Copsi Castle (as Juliet Astley). London, Joseph, and New York, Coward McCann, 1978.
Haunted House. London, Hodder and Stoughton, 1978; as *The Haunting of Gad's Hall*, New York, Doubleday, 1979.
The Day of the Butterfly. London, Bodley Head, 1979; New York, Doubleday, 1980.
A Wayside Tavern. London, Hodder and Stoughton, and New York, Doubleday, 1980.
The Old Priory. London, Bodley Head, 1981; New York, Doubleday, 1982.
The Claw. London, Hodder and Stoughton, 1981; New York, Doubleday, 1982.
Pargeters. London, Hodder and Stoughton, 1984; New York, Doubleday, 1986.

Novels as Peter Curtis

Dead March in Three Keys. London, Davies, 1940; as *No Question of Murder*, New York, Doubleday, 1959; as *The Bride of Moat House*, New York, Dell, 1969.
You're Best Alone. London, Macdonald, 1943; with *Requiem for Idols*, in *Two by Norah Lofts*, New York, Doubleday, 1981.
Lady Living Alone. London, Macdonald, 1945.
The Devil's Own. London, Macdonald, and New York, Doubleday, 1960; as *The Witches*, London, Pan, 1966; as *The Little Wax Doll*, London, Hodder and Stoughton, and New York, Doubleday, 1970.

Short Stories

I Met a Gypsy. London, Methuen, and New York, Knopf, 1935.
Heaven in Your Hand and Other Stories. New York, Doubleday, 1958; London, Joseph, 1959.
Is Anybody There? London, Corgi, 1974; as *Hauntings: Is Anybody There?*, New York, Doubleday, 1975.
Saving Face and Other Stories. London, Hodder and Stoughton, 1983; New York, Doubleday, 1984.

OTHER PUBLICATIONS

Other

Women in the Old Testament: Twenty Psychological Portraits. London, Sampson Low, and New York, Macmillan, 1949.
Eternal France: A History of France 1789-1944, with Margery Weiner. New York, Doubleday, 1968; London, Hodder and Stoughton, 1969.
The Story of Maude Reed (for children). London, Transworld, 1971; as *The Maude Reed Tale*, New York, Nelson, 1972.
Rupert Hatton's Story (for children). London, Carousel, 1972.
Domestic Life in England. London, Weidenfeld and Nicolson, and New York, Doubleday, 1976.
Queens of Britain. London, Hodder and Stoughton, 1977; as *The Queens of England*, New York, Doubleday, 1977.
Emma Hamilton. London, Joseph, and New York, Coward McCann, 1978.
Anne Boleyn. New York, Coward McCann, and London, Orbis, 1979.

*

Norah Lofts commented (1982):

Strictly speaking I don't think I belong in the romance or gothic class. I write books about ordinary people some of whom happen to live in the past. The love story is never dominant; most of my people are concerned with earning a living, achieving an ambition, holding their own in a harsh world. And gothic I never understood—I thought it was a form of architecture. I do tend to write about old houses because they fascinate me. Some of my houses are haunted—but never with spectres—mainly by emotions that have made impact on the atmosphere. Some of my houses are said to be cursed; but it is the people themselves who bring the bad luck into operation.

*   *   *

Norah Lofts wrote historical romances for 50 years and has innumerable admirers. Above all, Lofts can tell a story: her inventive power, her very real gift of narrative, and her instinct for a story have been much praised. Her vigorous style of storytelling, whether in the first or the third person, carries the reader along as a multiplicity of events unfolds. Often in one historical romance the stories of several lives are told, sometimes down along the generations, and we see how these lives, socially or geographically remote from each other though they may be, touch and intertwine so as to affect each other irretrievably, for good or ill. Sometimes the stories span continents and oceans, as *Blossom Like the Rose* and *The Road to Revelation*, both set in England and the American colonies in the 17th century, and *Silver Nutmeg* and *Scent of Cloves*, both set in Europe and in the Dutch East Indies in the 17th century and involving 'glove marriages' of girls sent out from Europe to marry unseen Dutch traders. Lofts's wide historical knowledge, which includes small social details as well as the details of great events, enables her to place her stories at home and abroad from the Anglo-Saxon period onwards. Her sense of history and her capacity to transmit the fascination of the past are remarkable, though it must be said that the first-person narrators in her historical romances have their narrative styles firmly rooted in the 20th century, regardless of the times in which they operate.

Lofts's first book was *I Met a Gypsy*, a collection of short stories which are linked by the gypsy blood which flows in the veins of a dominant character in each story. The stories range in time and location from the dissolution of the monasteries in England to a British mission in China in the 1930s. There is much in this book which is found again and again in Lofts's work: the fascination with gypsies

and their association with the supernatural; the dynastic or sequential ideas implicit in the arrangement of the stories which show a connection through history and through the generations; and the refusal to gloss over the brutality, nastiness, and squalor of previous ages. Stylistically, the inter-linking of several first-person narratives into one book is a technique which Lofts uses very successfully in many novels.

Lofts has a strong sense of time and a strong sense of place. Many of her historical novels are set in Suffolk, and many of them are set around houses. Both landscape and houses have a permanency which their occupants lack, although the occupants may leave impressions. The 'Suffolk Trilogy' (*The Town House*, *The House at Old Vine*, and *The House at Sunset*) spans 600 years in the history of a house, from its beginnings as the home of a mediaeval wool-merchant to the present day, and *Bless This House* tells the story of the fortunes of a beautiful Elizabethan house in Suffolk in eight episodes, each narrated by a different character who plays a part in its history.

Lofts portrays with skill and sympathy the economic and social positions of women from highest to lowest. Indeed, her women characters are her most interesting. We see their reactions to chance and opportunities; we see what they make of their successes and failures, whether they make the best of their lot or become indifferent or embittered. There is an idea of 'what you get and what you're prepared to pay for it' in the stories of many of Lofts's heroines, from Walter Raleigh's wife, Beth (in *Here Was a Man*), who has to share her husband with the ageing, coquettish Queen and with his own political and seafaring ambitions, to Hester (in *Hester Roon*) and the heroine of *The Day of the Butterfly* who rise from the most abject and squalid poverty by their own efforts. Such women as these last two who are prepared to take their destinies into their own hands contrast sharply with, for instance, poor little Emmie in *White Hell of Pity*, who refuses the opportunity of further schooling out of an over-nice conscience and ends her days prematurely as an exhausted skivvy.

—Jean Buchanan

LOGAN, Jake. See **RIEFE, Barbara.**

LOGAN, Mark. See **NICOLE, Christopher.**

LOMER, Mary. See **LIDE, Mary.**

LONDON, Laura.
Pseudonym for Thomas Dale Curtis and Sharon Curtis. **Other Pseudonym:** Robin James. **CURTIS, Thomas Dale. Nationality:** American. **Born:** Antigo, Wisconsin, 11 November 1952. **Education:** University of Wisconsin, Madison. **Relations:** married Sharon Curtis in 1970; one son and one daughter. **Career:** has worked as a professional musician, newswriter, television reporter, actor, and truck driver. **CURTIS, Sharon. Nationality:** American. **Born:** Dahran, Saudi Arabia, 6 March 1951. **Education:** schools in Turkey, Pakistan, and Iran; Marymount School for Girls, Kingston-on-Thames, Surrey; University of Wisconsin, Madison. **Address:** c/o Berkley, 200 Madison Avenue, New York, New York 10016, USA.

ROMANCE AND HISTORICAL PUBLICATIONS

Novels

A Heart Too Proud. New York, Dell, 1978.
The Bad Baron's Daughter. New York, Dell, 1978.
Moonlight Mist. New York, Dell, 1979.
Love's a Stage. New York, Dell, 1980.
The Gypsy Heiress. New York, Dell, 1981.
The Golden Touch (as Robin James). New York, Berkley, 1982.
The Windflower. New York, Dell, 1984.
Lightning Lingers (as Tom and Sharon Curtis). New York, Bantam, 1986.
Sunshine and Shadow (as Tom and Sharon Curtis). New York, Bantam, 1986.
Keepsake (as Tom and Sharon Curtis). New York, Jove, 1987.
The Testimony (as Sharon Curtis). New York, Bantam, 1993.

*

Laura London comments:

We've always wanted to be writers, and for us our career has been like a pleasant drift into a dream. Our finished works can be described as long conversations between the co-authors from which the interruptions have been edited. We believe in the romantic point of view and try to give our readers the quality craftsmanship they deserve.

We enjoy the research end of our work, and feel best when we can share some obscure fact with our readers in an original way. We read as many as 30 books to gain the background for one Regency romance.

*   *   *

The hallmark of books by Sharon and Tom Curtis, who write most often as Laura London and Robin James, is the humour displayed in the exchanges between the hero and heroine. Certainly the basic plots used in the Regency-style novels of Laura London conform to the formula of the genre: a lively virginal heroine and a strong, handsome hero confront perilous situations. Yet when the verbal sparring begins, it is difficult not to smile or even laugh out loud at the dialogue, which has a very modern quality that verges on the sarcastic.

In *The Bad Baron's Daughter*, Katie (who has been found in a low tavern called The Merry Maidenhead) rebels against Lord Linden's plans and tells him that she would rather 'lose my maidenhead fifty times first'. His cool response is to tell her that that is 'an anatomical impossibility' and that her reputation cannot get any worse anyway. Frances, in *Love's a Stage*, melodramatically protests David's lovemaking, 'Because I intend to marry a virgin'. David laughingly confesses that he, unfortunately, can no longer meet that requirement. In a longer novel, *The Windflower*, the heroine, Merry Wilding, is kidnapped in error and taken aboard a pirate ship, appropriately named Black Joke. When in an argument she bites Devon, her pirate captor, he inquires, 'Do you want to speak . . . or gnaw?' This mocking style carries over to the embellishments given to the standard romance plots by the Curtises. How else to explain an experienced nobleman (who also happens to be 'The Bard of the Lakeland') who lets his bride bring her twin sister on their honeymoon (*Moonlight Mist*), a mysterious highwayman whose claim to a title is supported by the strange physical characteristic of one blue eye and one brown (also in *Moonlight Mist*), or a villain who keeps a wolf on a leash and lets it loose to attack his enemies once every four years (*The Gypsy Heiress*)?

The deft comic touch also is apparent in the modern novels written under the name Robin James like *The Golden Touch* and *The Testimony* and those issued under the Curtis's own names

(*Lightning That Lingers, Sunshine and Shadow*). *Lightning That Lingers* is very much a modern Regency, with its shy, virginal heroine, Jennifer, who is a children's librarian. She falls in love with Philip, a wildlife biologist who moonlights as a male dancer in the Cougar Club in order to earn money to support his wildlife preserve. In *The Golden Touch*, Kathy Carter is a widow, but in relation to rock star Neil Stratton's experience, she is very much a beginner. She is a quick learner, however, and even manages to pursue Neil after a break-up by bribing his fans to throw her on stage at one of his concerts. The underlying theme of *The Testimony* is more sombre in that it deals with the adjustments and problems facing a couple after the husband, a journalist, spends six months in jail. In spite of the seriousness, however, there is a thread of humour in the sharp dialogue of the characters. *Sunshine and Shadow*, a longer contemporary romance, features another unusual pair of lovers: Susan Peachey, a young Amish widow, and Alan Wilde, a cynical Hollywood director.

The contemporary romances, along with *The Windflower*, all feature more explicit lovemaking, but there is laughter as well as passion. After the diet of saccharin prose and seduction scenes verging on rape which are found in so many 'romance' novels, it is refreshing to find characters who enjoy themselves and one another, even as they work through their problems.

—Barbara E. Kemp

————

LONDON, Nancy. See BUCKINGHAM, Nancy.

————

LONG, William Stuart. See STUART, Vivian.

————

LORD, Alison. See ELLIS, Julie.

————

LORD, Jeffrey. See ELLIS, Julie.

————

LORIN, Amii.
Pseudonym for Joan M. Hohl. **Other Pseudonyms:** Paula Roberts. Also writes as Joan Hohl. **Nationality:** American. **Address:** c/o Silhouette Books, 300 East 42nd Street, New York, New York 10017, USA.

ROMANCE AND HISTORICAL PUBLICATIONS

Novels

Morning Rose, Evening Savage. New York, Dell, 1980; as *Morning Rose*, London, Mills and Boon, 1982.
The Tawny Gold Man. New York, Dell, 1980.
Breeze off the Ocean. New York, Dell, 1980; London, Corgi, 1983.
Come Home to Love (as Paula Roberts). New York, Tower, 1980.
Morgan Wade's Woman. New York, Dell, 1981.
The Game Is Played. New York, Dell, 1981.
Snowbound Weekend. New York, Dell, 1982.
Gambler's Love. New York, Dell, 1982.
Candleglow. London, Mills and Boon, 1983.
While the Fire Rages. New York, Dell, 1984; as *While the Fire Rages, the Game is Played*, New York, Dorchester, 1989.

Night Striker. New York, Dell, 1985.
Power and Seduction. New York, Dell, 1985.

Novels as Joan Hohl (series: Sharp Family; Vanzant Family; Window)

Thorne's Way. New York, Silhouette, 1982.
Moments Harsh, Moments Gentle. New York, Silhouette, 1984.
A Taste for Rich Things. New York, Silhouette, 1984.
A Much Needed Holiday. New York, Silhouette, 1986.
Someone Waiting. New York, Silhouette, 1986.
The Scent of Lilacs. New York, Silhouette, 1986.
Texas Gold (Sharp). New York, Silhouette, 1986.
California Copper (Sharp). New York, Silhouette, 1986.
Nevada Silver (Sharp). New York, Silhouette, 1987.
Lady Ice (Vanzant). New York, Silhouette, 1987.
One Tough Hombre (Vanzant). New York, Silhouette, 1987.
Falcon's Flight. New York, Silhouette, 1987.
Forever Spring (Vanzant). New York, Silhouette, 1988.
Window on Yesterday. New York, Berkley, 1988.
Window on Today. New York, Berkley, 1989.
Window on Tomorrow. New York, Berkley, 1989.
The Gentleman Insists. New York, Silhouette, 1989.
Silver Thunder. New York, Dell, 1992.
Shadow's Kiss. New York, Dell, 1994.
Wolfe Waiting. New York, Silhouette, 1994.

*   *   *

Amii Lorin, who also writes under her real name, Joan Hohl, is a prolific, bestselling author under both names. A Lorin title, *The Tawny Gold Man*, was chosen to start Dell's 'Candlelight Ecstasy Romance' series, which signalled the arrival of an important new author of romantic fiction.

Lorin's novels usually feature arrogant, commanding men who frequently try to dominate the heroine. Their success in getting their way depends largely on the strength and independence of the heroines. Often they clash over a serious misunderstanding. In *The Tawny Gold Man*, Jud Cammeron suspects his stepsister of a liaison with his own father and of conspiring to have him banished from his family, yet he still loves her. He marries her but remains cold and distant since he does not fully trust her. Samantha and Morgan (*Morgan Wade's Woman*) hurt one another badly because they cannot seem to communicate. Both are proud and arrogant and see yielding as losing. Sam, one of Lorin's strongest women, resists Morgan's domineering behaviour but this proves as destructive in its intensity as his response to her defiance. Samantha's cousin, Courtney, has a similar problem with the enigmatic Rio McCord, an ex-agent and mercenary in *Night Striker*.

A serious, but ultimately unbelievable, problem caused by lack of communication is the focal point in *Breeze off the Ocean*. Micki Durrant is forced into marriage with Wolf Renniger because, believing she had a voluntary abortion, he feels 'owes' him a child. In actual fact she miscarried early in her pregnancy, but in talking to Wolf, she uses the technical term 'abortion' rather than the more common 'miscarriage'. Even if one accepts the fact that Micki would not simply say she miscarried, the situation could be easily resolved, but she does not explain until after marrying Wolf, and suffering a cruel rejection at his hands. Wolf's brother, Brett, is equally cruel to Jo Lawrence (*While the Fire Rages*) when he mistakenly believes that she has had an affair with Wolf after his marriage to Micki. Lorin manages to treat such foolish behaviour so realistically, however, that it rarely seems outrageous or unconvincing as one reads it. It is only later that the reader questions the underlying premiss.

Many of the novels written as Joan Hohl are linked by related characters. *Texas Gold* and *California Copper* feature twin brothers,

Thackery and Zackery Sharp, who were separated as children, each raised by one of their divorced parents. *Nevada Silver* tells the story of their half sister, Kit Aimsley, and also introduces Flint Falcon, who later is the hero of *Falcon's Flight*. Another character from *Texas Gold*, Peter Vanzant, began another related series with *Lady Ice*. His sister's story is continued in *One Tough Hombre*. The Vanzants' father, Paul, is then the hero of *Forever Spring*. These novels are entertaining but not outstanding. Nevertheless, the linking of novels provides a certain continuity which satisfies the reader's desire to know what happens beyond the end of a single story.

Hohl experimented with the traditional romance formula in a trilogy of stories centred on three older college roommates in which she added a touch of the unexplained. In *Window on Yesterday*, a history student seems to travel back in time where she becomes her own ancestor and meets the ancestor of her contemporary love. The love affair in *Window on Today* seems to follow standard lines, but in *Window on Tomorrow*, Hohl hints at an extraterrestrial connection. She strongly implies that the perfect hero of the story is really from outer space, and that the heroine leaves with him in the end. Hohl later moved on to a true time-travel story with 'Footsteps in the Snow', a novella in the 1992 Avon *A Christmas Collection*. Writing as Joan Hohl, she made an impressive debut into historical romance with *Silver Thunder*, a sensual western with an appropriately enigmatic hero and feisty, independent heroine. Duncan Frazer, Earl of Rayburne, returns to his childhood home in Wyoming to protect his land and that of friends from criminals. In disguise as the Segundo, a ranch foreman, he also enters into a duel of wills with fiercely independent Jessica Randall. Part Scot, part English, and part American Indian, Duncan is an imposing but exotic hero.

Whether writing as Amii Lorin or under her own name, Joan Hohl has developed a solid reputation for providing light, but satisfying stories. With her move into other subgenres of romance fiction, she promises to broaden her appeal and increase her following.

—Barbara E. Kemp

———————

LORING, Emilie.
Pseudonym: Josephine Story. **Nationality:** American. **Born:** Emilie Baker, Boston, Massachusetts. **Education:** privately. **Relations:** married Victor J. Loring; two sons. **Died:** 14 March 1951.

ROMANCE AND HISTORICAL PUBLICATIONS

Novels

The Trail of Conflict. Philadelphia, Penn, 1922; London, Unwin, 1923.
Here Comes the Sun! Philadelphia, Penn, 1924.
The Dragon-Slayer. London, Unwin, 1924.
A Certain Crossroad. Philadelphia, Penn, 1925.
The Solitary Horseman. Philadelphia, Penn, 1927.
Gay Courage. Philadelphia, Penn, 1928; London, Long, 1929.
Swift Water. Philadelphia, Penn, 1929.
Lighted Windows. Philadelphia, Penn, 1930; London, Hale, 1974.
Fair Tomorrow. Philadelphia, Penn, 1931; London, Stanley Paul, 1932.
Uncharted Seas. Philadelphia, Penn, 1932; London, Hale, 1975.
Hilltops Clear. Philadelphia, Penn, 1933; London, Stanley Paul, 1934.
Come On, Fortune! London, Stanley Paul, 1933.
We Ride the Gale! Philadelphia, Penn, 1934; London, Stanley Paul, 1935.
With Banners. Philadelphia, Penn, 1934; London, Stanley Paul, 1935.

It's a Great World! Philadelphia, Penn, 1935.
Give Me One Summer. Philadelphia, Penn, 1936.
As Long as I Live. Philadelphia, Penn, 1937; London, Hale, 1972.
Today Is Yours. Boston, Little Brown, 1938.
High of Heart. Boston, Little Brown, 1938.
Across the Years. Boston, Little Brown, 1939.
There Is Always Love. Boston, Little Brown, 1940; London, Foulsham, 1951.
Stars in Your Eyes. Boston, Little Brown, 1941; London, Nicholson and Watson, 1943.
Where Beauty Dwells. Boston, Little Brown, 1941.
Rainbow at Dusk. Boston, Little Brown, 1942; London, Hale, 1976.
When Hearts Are Light Again. Boston, Little Brown, 1943; London, Foulsham, 1953.
Keepers of the Faith. Boston, Little Brown, 1944; London, Hale, 1975.
Beyond the Sound of Guns. Boston, Little Brown, 1945.
Bright Skies. Boston, Little Brown, 1946; London, Hale, 1984.
Beckoning Trails. Boston, Little Brown, 1947; London, Foulsham, 1952.
I Hear Adventure Calling. Boston, Little Brown, 1948; London, Hale, 1976.
Love Came Laughing. Boston, Little Brown, 1949; London, Foulsham, 1951.
To Love and to Honor. Boston, Little Brown, 1950; London, Foulsham, 1951.
For All Your Life. Boston, Little Brown, 1952; London, Hale, 1970.
I Take This Man. Boston, Little Brown, 1954; London, Foulsham, 1955.
My Dearest Love. Boston, Little Brown, 1954; London, Hale, 1972; as *My Love*, London, Foulsham, 1955.
The Shadow of Suspicion. Boston, Little Brown, 1955; London, Hale, 1965.
What Then Is Love. Boston, Little Brown, 1956; London, Hale, 1965.
Look to the Stars. Boston, Little Brown, 1957; London, Hale, 1966; as *Scott Pelham's Princess*, London, Foulsham, 1958.
Behind the Cloud. Boston, Little Brown, 1958; London, Hale, 1967.
With This Ring. Boston, Little Brown, 1959; London, Hale, 1966.
How Can the Heart Forget. Boston, Little Brown, 1960; London, Hale, 1966.
Throw Wide the Door. Boston, Little Brown, 1962.
Follow Your Heart. Boston, Little Brown, 1963; London, Hale, 1964.
A Candle in Her Heart. Boston, Little Brown, 1964; London, Hale, 1969.
Forever and a Day. Boston, Little Brown, 1965.
Spring Always Comes. Boston, Little Brown, 1966; London, Hale, 1968.
A Key to Many Doors. Boston, Little Brown, 1967; London, Hale, 1969.
In Times Like These. Boston, Little Brown, 1968; London, Hale, 1976.
Love with Honor. Boston, Little Brown, 1969; London, Hale, 1970.
No Time for Love. Boston, Little Brown, 1970; London, Hale, 1971.
Forsaking All Others. Boston, Little Brown, 1971; London, Hale, 1973.
The Shining Years. Boston, Little Brown, 1972; London, Hale, 1974.

OTHER PUBLICATIONS

Play

Where's Peter? Philadelphia, Penn, 1928.

Other as Josephine Story

For the Comfort of the Family: A Vacation Experiment. New York, Doran, 1914.
The Mother in the House. Boston, Pilgrim Press, 1917.

*   *   *

Emilie Loring was an American writer of patriotic, moralistic romances that comment upon some of the major socio-political events occurring in the United States during the period in which they were published. Loring's version of the romance formula has had an enduring appeal, for, although her books were written in the first half of the century, their multiple printings up to the present day attest to their continued popularity.

Strong pro-Americanism is the most striking feature of Loring's fiction. Her books constitute a resounding defence of democratic capitalism. The heroines declare themselves to be fierce patriots ('my country, right or wrong'), and the heroes are either benevolent industrialists, war heroes, lawyers, and politicians fighting for the 'American Way', or 'trouble-shooters for Uncle Sam'. Whenever the American system of business or government is under attack, as is usually the case in Loring's plots, the main characters respond with impassioned speeches and may even burst into the Pledge of Allegiance to the Flag. Anyone who disagrees with this creed is considered to be a weak, inadequate person who blames society for his personal failures.

The moral tone of Loring's romances is consistent with her patriotic conservativeness. She bemoans the loosening of morals of the modern world, particularly the increase of divorce, and wishes for a return to stricter ethics. She continually attacks idleness, cheapness, spinelessness, selfishness, and pessimism, and admires integrity, modesty, graciousness, loyalty, sweetness, self-discipline, and a sense of humour.

Loring philosophizes most about marriage. Characters are apt to quote from the marriage service and discuss the components of a good marriage, as in *Swift Water*:

> . . . marriage fundamentally is a matter of sympathetic companionship shot through and through with gleams of passion, love. It should be productive of fidelity, loyalty, responsibility, of the stamina to see a difficult situation through if necessary. It is not just the business of two persons. A marriage which breaks down threatens the institution.

When marriage breaks down, Loring adds elsewhere, society breaks down. Many romance writers portray love and courtship but stop short of portraying real marriages. Loring does not shirk this task. In fact, she frequently portrays even very unhappy marriages. These she uses to convey moral lessons. Loring advocates a 'bite the bullet' approach to marriage. Once married, partners are irrevocably committed to each other, no matter what. Faithful spouses are always ultimately rewarded in Loring's novels. If one lives by a code of honour, 'Things have a marvelous, unbelievable way of coming right'. Thus, Loring's romances are optimistic and 'up-lifting'.

Loring differs from many writers of romances in another way as well. She describes and comments on crucial, contemporary social events such as World War I and II, the Korean conflict, Red scares, unionization, racketeer crime, wide-scale immigration, urbanization, and the Great Depression. Once again, her political conservatism is noticeably evident. For example, all union organizing is attributed to outside agitators, parasites, and ungrateful aliens. One hero (in *The Shadow of Suspicion*) tells a group of striking workers: 'You've been getting a dose of propaganda. And do you know who paid for it? The Reds!' He proceeds to outline the evils of Russian communism. Loring's novels are full of traitors, spies, and subversives against whom one must be ever vigilant. Throughout her romances, Loring openly supports McCarthy-era tactics, the Cold War hostility, and the armaments race.

In addition to the romance and political intrigue, Loring's novels blend a number of stylistic and plot devices like humour, dialects, colloquialisms, and details of local colour to make them distinctive. Every novel features amusing incidents which usually involve innocent but embarrassingly outspoken children or servants, or cute pets. Gay repartee also provides a sense of high spirits. Loring also has fun with characters' names which often reveal the nature of the character. Thus, a detective is called Tom Search; a formal butler is named Propper; a religious fanatic is Luther Calvin. These are rather heavy-handed and obvious, of course, but Loring apparently delights in them as they are a consistent pattern. Loring's minor characters (servants, farmers, and foreigners) speak in pronounced dialect with stereotypical mannerisms. For example, in *Across the Years* Loring describes a typical plump 'Southern mammy' who talks like this: 'Ah sure is glad to see yo', Mistuh Duke. . . . Let me tak' dat coat, honey-girl'. While this technique adds 'colour' to Loring's writing style and is probably not intended to be racist, it is simplistic and condescending.

Loring has a fine eye for detail and she can skilfully create vivid scenes. However, she frequently relies too heavily on naming colours to evoke a mood. In addition, she sometimes gets trapped in a repetitive series of descriptive phrases that end up being irritating as in the following: 'She darted in and out of a drove of bleating black-faced sheep; did a running high jump over a squealing pig; ducked under the nose of a pawing colt; skirted a dog fight and shooed away a flock of cackling geese . . .' (*High of Heart*).

One final criticism of Loring's style stems from her moral lessons and patriotic lectures which result in some very stilted dialogue. One does not usually break into the Pledge of Allegiance in a casual, social conversation. Loring's flair for the dramatic leads her astray in these cases.

—Margaret Jensen

LORING, Peter. See SHELLABARGER, Samuel.

LORRIMER, Claire.
Pseudonym for Patricia Denise Clark. **Other Pseudonym:** Patricia Robins. **Nationality:** British. **Born:** Patricia Denise Robins, Hove, Sussex, 1 February 1921; daughter of Denise Robins, *q.v.* **Education:** Parents' National Educational Union, Burgess Hill, Sussex, 1927–30; Effingham House, Bexhill-on-Sea, Sussex, 1930–35; Institut Prealpina, Switzerland, 1935–37; and in Munich, 1937–38. **Military Service:** radar filter room, Women's Auxiliary Air Force, 1940–45: flight officer. **Relations:** married D.C. Clark in 1948 (divorced); two sons and one daughter. **Career:** sub-editor, *Woman's Illustrated*, London, 1938–40. **Agent:** Anthea Morton Saner, Curtis Brown, 162–168 Regent Street, London W1R 5TB. **Address:** Chiswell Barn, Christmas Mill Lane, Marsh Green, Edenbridge, Kent TN8 5AP, England.

Romance and Historical Publications

Novels (series: Rochford)

A Voice in the Dark. London, Souvenir Press, 1967; New York, Avon, 1968.
The Shadow Falls. New York, Avon, 1974.
Relentless Storm. New York, Avon, 1975; London, Arlington, 1979.

The Secret of Quarry House. New York, Avon, 1976; London, Century, 1988.
Mavreen. London, Arlington, 1976; New York, Bantam, 1977.
Tamarisk. London, Arlington, 1978; New York, Bantam, 1979.
Chantal. London, Arlington, 1980; New York, Bantam, 1981.
The Chatelaine (Rochford). London, Arlington, 1981; New York, Ballantine, 1982.
The Wilderling (Rochford). London, Arlington, 1982; New York, Ballantine, 1983.
Last Year's Nightingale. London, Century, 1984.
Frost in the Sun. London, Century, 1986.
House of Tomorrow. London, Corgi, 1987.
The Spinning Wheel. London, Bantam, 1990.
Ortolans. London, Bantam, 1990.
The Calverley Inheritance. London, Doubleday, 1990.

Novels as Patricia Robins

To the Stars. London, Hutchinson, 1944.
See No Evil. London, Hutchinson, 1945.
Statues of Snow. London, Hutchinson, 1947.
Three Loves. London, Hutchinson, 1949.
Awake My Heart. London, Hutchinson, 1950.
Beneath the Moon. London, Hutchinson, 1951.
Leave My Heart Alone. London, Hutchinson, 1951.
The Fair Deal. London, Hutchinson, 1952.
Heart's Desire. London, Hutchinson, 1953.
So This Is Love. London, Hutchinson, 1953.
Heaven in Our Hearts. London, Hutchinson, 1954.
One Who Cares. London, Hutchinson, 1954.
Love Cannot Die. London, Hutchinson, 1955.
The Foolish Heart. London, Hutchinson, 1956.
Give All to Love. London, Hutchinson, 1956.
Where Duty Lies. London, Hutchinson, 1957.
He Is Mine. London, Hurst and Blackett, 1957.
Love Must Wait. London, Hurst and Blackett, 1958.
Lonely Quest. London, Hurst and Blackett, 1959.
Lady Chatterley's Daughter. London, Consul, and New York, Ace, 1961.
The Last Chance. London, Hurst and Blackett, 1961.
The Long Wait. London, Hurst and Blackett, 1962.
The Runaways. London, Hurst and Blackett, 1962.
Seven Loves. London, Consul, 1962.
With All My Love. London, Hurst and Blackett, 1963.
The Constant Heart. London, Hurst and Blackett, 1964.
Second Love. London, Hurst and Blackett, 1964.
The Night Is Thine. London, Consul, 1964.
There Is But One. London, Hurst and Blackett, 1965.
No More Loving. London, Consul, 1965.
Topaz Island. London, Hurst and Blackett, 1965.
Love Me Tomorrow. London, Hurst and Blackett, 1966.
The Uncertain Joy. London, Hurst and Blackett, 1966.
Forbidden. London, Mayflower, 1967.
The Man Behind the Mask. London, Sphere, 1967.
Sapphire in the Sand. London, Arrow, 1968.
Return to Love. London, Hurst and Blackett, 1968.
Laugh on Friday. London, Hurst and Blackett, 1969.
No Stone Unturned. London, Hurst and Blackett, 1969.
Cinnabar House. London, Hurst and Blackett, 1970.
Under the Sky. London, Hurst and Blackett, 1970; New York, Atlantic Monthly Press, 1988.
The Crimson Tapestry. London, Hurst and Blackett, 1971; New York, Atlantic Monthly Press, 1988.
Play Fair with Love. London, Hurst and Blackett, 1972; New York, Atlantic Monthly Press, 1988.
None But He. London, Hurst and Blackett, 1973.

Forever. London, Severn House, 1991.

Short Stories

Variations: A Collection of Short Stories. London, Bantam Press, 1991.

OTHER PUBLICATIONS

Poetry as Patricia Robins

Seven Days Leave. London, Hutchinson, 1943.

Other (for children) as Patricia Robins

The Adventures of the Three Baby Bunnies. London, Nicholson and Watson, 1934.
Tree Fairies. London, Hutchinson, 1945.
Sea Magic. London, Hutchinson, 1946.
The Heart of a Rose. London, Hutchinson, 1947.
The £100 Reward. Exeter, Wheaton, 1966.

Other

The Garden. London, Arlington, 1980.
House of Tomorrow. London, Century, 1987.

*

Claire Lorrimer comments:

When I decided to become a freelance writer after World War II, it seemed natural to continue writing the kind of light romantic fiction I had been associated with as a junior sub-editor on a magazine before the war. It did not occur to me to change to anything else until the 1970s when my agent, Desmond Elliott, suggested I could improve the standard of my work. I wrote *Mavreen* in 1975 and when it went immediately into the best-seller list in the USA, I decided to make a permanent change and virtually begin a new career. I like to think the standard of my work is improving with each book and the critical reviews I have been receiving suggest this is so. I prefer the relative realism of my Claire Lorrimers in which I try to make certain that no one says or does anything that in real life they might not have done or said, and although the stories are full of action and adventure I hope to convince my reader that these characters really could have existed and have led the lives I have given them. I often end up believing them real myself. Of all my reviews, I am most satisfied by George Thaw's (*Daily Mirror*) in which he concludes the *Chatelaine* review with the words: 'A slice of life'. I am never satisfied with the finished product. Of everything I have written in my life, my favourite is *The Garden*.

*   *   *

To date, Claire Lorrimer has enjoyed two separate and highly successful careers as a romantic novelist. The 44 light romances, written under her maiden name, Patricia Robins, and published over a 30-year period between 1944 and 1973, established her as a leading figure in the genre, while the late phase of epic romantic/historical novels under the Lorrimer byline has won her an even greater measure of critical fame. Lorrimer is the daughter of Denise Robins, and some of the Patricia Robins stories, while strongly individual, reveal a certain affinity with the work of her mother. Both writers use controversial subjects as themes for their novels, and each displays a refreshing honesty in her treatment of physical passion, neither over-glamorizing nor sensationalizing what is a basic

fact of life. As Patricia Robins, Lorrimer notes the gradual change in moral attitudes that becomes most marked in her fiction of the 1960s and 1970s. *Forbidden* gives a balanced, sympathetic portrayal of illicit love, while in *Forever* the heroine is forced to resolve the conflict of adulterous passion with pity for a husband who has recently gone blind. The unsentimental presentation of the dilemma, and the complex personalities of the characters themselves, lend added interest to an otherwise conventional love story. With *Return to Love* the author explores the pain of lost love, her former model character holidaying in Austria as she attempts to come to terms with the scar that destroyed her beauty, and the deeper psychological trauma of rejection. The story of her recovery, her finding of new love and exorcism of the past, is smoothly and skilfully told, the writer moving easily within the confines of the genre while providing her material with an interesting and personal treatment. Several of the Patricia Robins novels are now being reissued, and confirm the mastery of their author in the conventional romantic field.

Claire Lorrimer adopted her most recent pseudonym in the late 1960s, when *A Voice in the Dark* was published. This and the three novels which follow it show a clear attempt to explore other literary worlds, notably the fields of suspense and gothic horror, while retaining a romantic theme at the centre, but in each case the success is less than total. *Relentless Storm*, in particular, fails to satisfy, its characters and their forbidden passions the very stuff of gothic dream, but unable to sustain what is basically a short story stretched out to novel length. *A Voice in the Dark*, though, is more effective. A gothic romance, which describes the adventures of a young girl on holiday in Florence and her involvement with Italian aristocrats at their ancestral home, is not without flaws. The long arm of coincidence is virtually dislocated in the opening pages, but the story moves more rapidly than *Relentless Storm*, the characters deliver their speeches promptly, the required climaxes are reached without delay, and a happy ending secured at last. The other two books in this sequence, *The Shadow Falls* and *The Secret of Quarry House*, display similar unevenness of execution, and may be fairly judged as the early work of an author establishing herself in a new and unfamiliar genre. This task Lorrimer abandoned in favour of novels on an altogether more epic scale, which featured the lives of tempestuous and striking heroines against a strongly drawn historical background. It proved to be an inspired decision, and the characters of *Mavreen*, *Tamarisk*, and *Chantal* established Lorrimer's reputation, the former becoming an immediate bestseller in the United States. Mavreen sets the pace, and is the dominating presence of the trilogy. Natural daughter of an English nobleman, raised as a child by Sussex farmers, she enters into passionate love affairs with the French aristocrat Gerard de Valle and the titled highwayman Sir Perry Waite, taking part in the latter's robberies. She, together with Tamarisk and Chantal, tastes triumph and disaster in the aristocratic world of the Regency and enjoys the friendship of the great. The three heroines overshadow their men, although Gerard and Sir Perry are ably drawn. The novels are stories of individuals rather than a picture of the times—the Regency atmosphere is less strong than in the 'Haggard' novels of Nicole—but this is unimportant. The characters compel and convince.

The Chatelaine is set in the early part of this century. Willow, daughter of an American millionaire, marries Rowell Rochford, not knowing the impoverished English nobleman is after her money. The Rochford mansion with its dominant matriarch, the dark secret of hereditary illness, and the imprisonment of Rowell's crippled sister all bring back gothic echoes of *A Voice in the Dark*. *The Chatelaine* is one of the most impressive of Lorrimer's novels to date, compact and well crafted. Willow, in her gradual assertion of independence from Rowell and his dragon of a mother, is at once interesting and credible. Her presence throws her male counterparts into the shade, but secondary characters are more fully realized in this work. Lorrimer continues the story of the Rochfords in *The Wilder-*

ling. Covering the period 1911 to 1918, the novel deals with the trials and tribulations of the younger generation of Rochfords during World War I. With her latest work, Lorrimer has moved onto another successful family saga. *Frost in the Sun* is set in Spain and concentrates on two rival families, the Costains and the Monteros, during the first half of this century. With *Ortolans* and *The Calverley Inheritance* Lorrimer undertakes another ambitious family saga centring on the Calverleys and their ancestral Sussex home, which after an Elizabethan prologue, begins in the late-18th century, and continues up to modern times. A measure of continuity between the different love stories is achieved by the device of a family diary which links the separate episodes together, but unfortunately the strength of the stories varies considerably, the 18th century and Victorian incidents far more compelling than the adventures of the modern-day protagonists. This is a pity, as the former are excellent examples of gothic/romantic writing which evoke a strong sense of period, Lorrimer drawing on her knowledge of her beloved Sussex countryside to present an authentic picture of figures and landscape alike. More coherent and more impressive is *The Spinning Wheel*, which ranks with *The Chatelaine* as among Lorrimer's finest novels. The story of Harry Keynes, the illegitimate child of an aristocrat, raised by the family of a gardener at a country house, has echoes of *Mavreen*, but there the resemblance ends. The involved tale of Harry's infatuation with Madelaine, spoilt child of his father's employers, the unrequited love of his 'sister' Alice, and their eventual struggle to success and fulfilment, show the author writing at the peak of her form. Her depiction of rural Sussex life in the period before World War I is superb, equalled only by her convincing presentation of Alice's career as a fashion designer in Paris. Mastery of characters and plot is matched by a strength of period detail and atmosphere only rarely encountered in her earlier books.

Aside from her novels, Lorrimer has written a number of short stories, the best of which have recently been collected as *Variations: A Collection of Short Stories*. It is a fitting title, whose contents display the range of its author's talents in the shorter form. 'Trust Me' is a story of marital infidelity with an unexpected sharp ending, 'The Patient in Number Twenty-Two', a perceptive treatment of mental breakdown, and its hidden causes, while in 'Progress' Lorrimer provides a humorous and balanced account of the change in a rural village invaded by yuppies. Several of the stories show a marked insight into the minds of children, and their relationships with adults. This quality is perhaps most movingly achieved in 'The Garden', a touching ghost story which Lorrimer rates as her own favourite creation.

—Geoffrey Sadler

———

LOW, Dorothy Mackie. British. 1916—. See 1st edition, 1982.

———

LOWELL, Elizabeth.
Pseudonym for Ann Maxwell. **Other Pseudonyms:** Lowell Charters, A.E. Maxwell, Ann Maxwell, and Annalise Sun, all with Evan Lowell Maxwell. **Nationality:** American. **Born:** Milwaukee, Wisconsin, 5 April 1944. **Education:** University of California, Davis, 1962–63, and Riverside, 1963–66, B.A. in English. **Relations:** married Evan Lowell Maxwell in 1966; one son and one daughter. **Agent:** Dominick Abel, Dominick Abel Literary Agency, Inc, 146 W. 82nd Street, Apt. 1B, New York, New York 10024, USA. **Address:** P.O. Box 464, Three Rivers, CA 93271, USA.

ROMANCE AND HISTORICAL PUBLICATIONS

Novels (series: Western Trilogy)

Golden Empire (as A.E. Maxwell). New York, Fawcett, 1979.
Summer Thunder. New York, Silhouette, 1983.
The Danvers Touch. New York, Silhouette, 1983.
Forget Me Not. New York, Silhouette, 1984.
Lover in the Rough. New York, Silhouette, 1984.
Summer Games. New York, Silhouette, 1984.
A Woman Without Lies. New York, Silhouette, 1985.
The Valley of the Sun. New York, Silhouette, 1985.
Traveling Man. New York, Silhouette, 1985.
Fires of Eden. New York, Silhouette, 1986.
Sequel. New York, Silhouette, 1986.
The Fire of Spring. New York, Silhouette, 1986.
Too Hot to Handle. New York, Silhouette, 1986.
Tell Me No Lies. Toronto, Worldwide, 1986.
Redwood Empire (as A.E. Maxwell). Toronto, Worldwide, 1987.
Love Song for a Raven. New York, Silhouette, 1987.
Sweet Wind, Wild Wind. New York, Silhouette, 1987.
Fever. New York, Silhouette, 1988.
Chain Lightning. New York, Silhouette, 1988.
Dark Fire. New York, Silhouette, 1988.
The Golden Mountain (as Annalise Sun, with Evan Lowell Maxwell).
New York, Pocket Books, 1990.
Reckless Love. Toronto, Harlequin, 1990.
Fire and Rain. New York, Silhouette, 1990.
Outlaw. New York, Silhouette, 1991.
Granite Man. New York, Silhouette, 1991.
Warrior. New York, Silhouette, 1991.
Western Trilogy:
    Only His. New York, Avon, 1991.
    Only Mine. New York, Avon, 1992.
    Only You. New York, Avon, 1992.
Untamed. New York, Avon, 1993.
Forbidden. New York, Avon, 1993.

OTHER PUBLICATIONS

Novels as Ann Maxwell

Change. New York, Popular Library, 1975.
The Singer Enigma. New York, Popular Library, 1976.
A Dead God Dancing. New York, Avon, 1979.
Name of a Shadow. New York, Avon, 1980.
The Jaws of Menx. New York, New American Library, 1981.
Fire Dancer. New York, New American Library, and London, Orbit, 1982.
Dancer's Luck. New York, New American Library, and London, Orbit, 1983.
Dancer's Illusion. New York, New American Library, and London, Orbit, 1983.
Timeshadow Rider. New York, Tor, 1986.
Thunderheart (as Lowell Charters, with Evan Lowell Maxwell). New York, Avon, 1992.
The Diamond Tiger (with Evan Lowell Maxwell). New York, Harper, 1992.
The Secret Sisters (with Evan Lowell Maxwell). New York, Harper, 1993.

Novels as A.E. Maxwell (with Evan Lowell Maxwell)

Steal the Sun. New York, Marek, 1981.
Just Another Day in Paradise. New York, Doubleday, 1985.

The Frog and the Scorpion. New York, Doublday, 1986.
Gatsby's Vineyard. New York, Doubleday, 1987.
Just Enough Light to Kill. New York, Doubleday, 1989.
The Art of Survival. New York, Doubleday, 1989.
Money Burns. New York, Villard, 1991.
The King of Nothing. New York, Villard, 1992.
Murder Hurts. New York, Villard, 1993.

Other

The Year-Long Day (as A. E. Maxwell, with Evan Maxwell), with
Ivar Ruud. Philadelphia, Lippincott, 1976; London, Gollancz,
1977.

*

Elizabeth Lowell comments:

I enjoy writing romance fiction because it is the only area of modern fiction in which an author is permitted to celebrate the beauty
that a man and a woman can bring to each other. To me, romance fiction is an extension of a mythic tradition that began long before our
present dour Existential age and will endure long after Existen-
tialism is little more than a footnote in the history of humanity.

*   *   *

Many of Elizabeth Lowell's contemporary romances have been
published in category romance series, but the quality of her writing
is much higher than the average formula romance. She also has written several longer novels set in the Old West and a few longer contemporary novels of romantic suspense. All of her work is
distinguished by strong, well-developed characters, well-constructed plots, and a use of language that frequently borders on the
poetic.

Not surprisingly, Lowell's heroines are strong, intelligent, and independent women. They are distinguished, however, by a seemingly infinite capacity to love, even in the face of the greatest odds
against having their love returned. Often they have been hurt in
some way but find the strength to go on and love again. In doing so,
they demonstrate to the heroes that love is not a potentially dangerous weakness but a powerful positive force and a source of strength.
After losing her fiancé in a car crash just before their wedding, Angel manages to create a new life for herself in *A Woman Without
Lies.* Although it is painful for her, she comes to love Hawk but is
brutally rejected by him. However, her softness, strength, and courage reach beneath his protective shell to find the gentleness he has
hidden. Rio, the drifter and water witcher in *The Valley of the Sun,*
finds his own dreams and peace in Hope Gardeners's determination
to create her dream. Cat Cochran (*The Danvers Touch*) almost loses
everything before the embittered Travis Danvers finally accepts the
reality of her love. He, in turn, must draw on his newly discovered
love for her to bring her back from the edge of destructive despair.
Doubting herself after a disastrous marriage, Janna Moran can still
find the strength to love Carlson Raven (*Love Song for a Raven*) and
convince him of her love. Lowell's 'Western Trilogy' (*Only His,
Only Mine, Only You*) features the same courageous women who
risk everything to prove the value of love and the bleak, formidable
men who almost lose everything before recognizing the value of the
women and their love. With *Untamed,* Lowell moved her basic
themes of a cold, hardened warrior and a strong woman into a new
era and location. Set at the disputed border of England and Scotland
in the 12th century, the novel also includes a hint of the occult with
witches, and an ancient curse which can only be overcome by deep,
abiding love.

In contrast to Lowell's heroines, her heroes are emotionally
scarred, cynical men, who do not believe in love or dreams. They

have difficulty in offering or accepting love. Loving another is taking a risk which opens the giver to betrayal, loss and pain. Frequently, the man rejects the woman's love because in his ignorance
or isolation he cannot recognize it for what it is. His rejection may be
gentle or cruel, but it nearly always strips the woman's feelings to
her soul.

Lowell also writes widely in other genres, especially science fiction and mysteries, under her own name, Ann Maxwell, and with her
husband as A.E. Maxwell. Her experience in developing action
plots is apparent in the romance thriller of international intrigue,
Tell Me No Lies. A shadowy, shifting world of dangerous conspiracies and smuggling of Chinese artifacts is an effective setting for a
more complex contemporary romance. In fact, the action is the
primary focus, but Lowell develops a solid romance for the main
characters, Lindsay Danner and Jacob Catlin. *The Diamond Tiger*
and *The Secret Sisters,* also by Maxwell, are romantic suspense
novels, but they lack the intensity and complexity of *Tell Me No
Lies.*

Lowell's romance novels focus on the power and beauty of love
and love that is worthy of trust. She excels in describing the emotions of her characters, who find that although loving is taking a risk,
loving another brings a new kind of freedom and strength. Her couples share a love that is all the stronger for having been tempered in a
fire of pain and disillusionment. As Lowell writes in the last line of *A
Woman Without Lies,* Hawk and Angel can now sleep deeply, 'their
pain transformed into peace by the surpassing beauty of love'.

—Barbara E. Kemp

LOWNDES, Marie (Adelaide) Belloc.
Pseudonym: Philip Curtin. **Nationality:** British. **Born:** 1868; sister
of the writer Hilaire Belloc. **Relations:** married the writer Frederic
Sawrey Lowndes (died 1940); one son and two daughters. **Died:** 14
November 1947.

Romance and Historical Publications

Novels (series: Duchess Laura)

The Heart of Penelope. London, Heinemann, 1904; New York, Dut-
ton, 1915.
Barbara Rebell. London, Heinemann, 1905; New York, Dodge,
1907.
The Pulse of Life. London, Heinemann, 1908; New York, Dodd
Mead, 1909.
The Uttermost Farthing. London, Heinemann, 1908; New York,
Kennerley, 1909.
When No Man Pursueth. London, Heinemann, 1910; New York,
Kennerley, 1911.
Jane Oglander. London, Heinemann, and New York, Scribner,
1911.
The Chink in the Armour. London, Methuen, and New York,
Scribner, 1912; as *The House of Peril,* London, Readers Library,
1935.
Mary Pechell. London, Methuen, and New York, Scribner, 1912.
The Lodger. London, Methuen, and New York, Scribner, 1913.
The End of Her Honeymoon. New York, Scribner, 1913; London,
Methuen, 1914.
Good Old Anna. London, Hutchinson, 1915; New York, Doran,
1916.
The Red Cross Barge. London, Smith Elder, 1916; New York,
Doran, 1918.
Lilla: A Part of Her Life. London, Hutchinson, 1916; New York,
Doran, 1917.

Love and Hatred. London, Chapman and Hall, and New York, Doran, 1917.

Out of the War? London, Chapman and Hall, 1918; as *Gentleman Anonymous*, London, Philip Allan, 1934.

From the Vasty Deep. London, Hutchinson, 1920; as *From Out the Vasty Deep*, New York, Doran, 1921.

The Lonely House. London, Hutchinson, and New York, Doran, 1920.

What Timmy Did. London, Hutchinson, 1921; New York, Doran, 1922.

The Terriford Mystery. London, Hutchinson, and New York, Doubleday, 1924.

What Really Happened. London, Hutchinson, and New York, Doubleday, 1926.

The Story of Ivy. London, Heinemann, 1927; New York, Doubleday, 1928.

Thou Shalt Not Kill. London, Hutchinson, 1927.

Cressida: No Mystery. London, Heinemann, 1928; New York, Knopf, 1930.

Duchess Laura: Certain Days of Her Life. London, Ward Lock, 1929; as *The Duchess Intervenes*, New York, Putnam, 1933.

Love's Revenge. London, Readers Library, 1929.

One of Those Ways. London, Heinemann, and New York, Knopf, 1929.

Letty Lynton. London, Heinemann, and New York, Cape and Smith, 1931.

Vanderlyn's Adventure. New York, Cape and Smith, 1931; as *The House by the Sea*, London, Heinemann, 1937.

Jenny Newstead. London, Heinemann, and New York, Putnam, 1932.

Love Is a Flame. London, Benn, 1932.

The Reason Why. London, Benn, 1932.

Duchess Laura: Further Days from Her Life. New York, Longman, 1933.

Another Man's Wife. London, Heinemann, and New York, Longman, 1934.

The Chianti Flask. New York, Longman, 1934; London, Heinemann, 1935.

Who Rides on a Tiger. New York, Longman, 1935; London, Heinemann, 1936.

And Call It Accident. New York, Longman, 1936; London, Hutchinson, 1939.

The Second Key. New York, Longman, 1936; as *The Injured Lover*, London, Hutchinson, 1939.

The Marriage-Broker. London, Heinemann, 1937; as *The Fortune of Bridget Malone*, New York, Longman, 1937.

Motive. London, Heinemann, 1938; as *Why It Happened*, New York, Longman, 1938.

Lizzie Borden: A Study in Conjecture. New York, Longman, 1939; London, Hutchinson, 1940.

Reckless Angel. New York, Longman, 1939.

The Christine Diamond. London, Hutchinson, and New York, Longman, 1940.

Before the Storm. New York, Longman, 1941.

She Dwelt with Beauty. London, Macmillan, 1949.

Short Stories

Studies in Wives. London, Heinemann, 1909; New York, Kennerley, 1910.

Studies in Love and Terror. London, Methuen, and New York, Scribner, 1913.

Why They Married. London, Heinemann, 1923.

Bread of Deceit. London, Hutchinson, 1925; as *Afterwards*, New York, Doubleday, 1925.

Some Men and Women. London, Hutchinson, 1925; New York, Doubleday, 1928.

What of the Night? New York, Dodd Mead, 1943.

A Labour of Hercules. London, Todd, 1943.

OTHER PUBLICATIONS

Plays

The Lonely House, with Charles Randolph, adaptation of the novel by Lowndes (produced Eastbourne, Sussex, 1924).

The Key: A Love Drama (as *The Second Key*, produced London, 1935). London, Benn, 1930.

With All John's Love. London, Benn, 1930.

Why Be Lonely?, with F.S.A. Lowndes. London, Benn, 1931.

What Really Happened, adaptation of her own novel (produced London, 1936). London, Benn, 1932.

Her Last Adventure (produced London, 1936).

The Empress Eugenie. New York, Longman, 1938.

Other

H.R.H. the Prince of Wales: An Account of His Career (published anonymously). London, Richards, and New York, Appleton, 1898; revised edition, as *His Most Gracious Majesty King Edward VII* (as Mrs Belloc Lowndes), Richards, 1901.

The Philosophy of the Marquise (sketches and dialogues). London, Richards, 1899.

T.R.H. the Prince and Princess of Wales (published anonymously). London, Newnes, 1902.

Noted Murder Mysteries (as Philip Curtin). London, Simpkin Marshall, 1914.

Told in Gallant Deeds: A Child's History of the War. London, Nisbet, 1914.

I, Too, Have Lived in Arcadia: A Record of Love and of Childhood. London, Macmillan, 1941; New York, Dodd Mead, 1942.

Where Love and Friendship Dwelt (autobiography). London, Macmillan, and New York, Dodd Mead, 1943.

The Merry Wives of Westminster (autobiography). London, Macmillan, 1946.

A Passing World (autobiography). London, Macmillan, 1948.

The Young Hilaire Belloc. New York, Kenedy, 1956.

Editor and Translator, with M. Shedlock, *Edmond and Jules de Goncourt, with Letters and Leaves from Their Journals.* London, Heinemann, and New York, Dodd Mead, 2 vols, 1895.

*   *   *

Marie Belloc Lowndes's romances capture changing moral values from Victorian elders to Edwardian youth, from pre-war idealists to post-war cynics, the sense of propriety, respectability, and practicality in love of the one, the more liberal, convention-breaking affairs of the other. Frequently her love stories involve elements of the supernatural, with seances, forewarnings, and apparitions, or criminal activities that involve the reputations of young innocents caught in a web of treachery. Staid and proper members of society find themselves unexpectedly seized by alien feelings of jealousy and shameless desire; young men and women sacrifice their reputations and virtue for love or money, find themselves manipulated and abused, their honesty questioned, their beloved driven into the arms of devious rivals. Occasionally the situation is an adulterous one, pregnant with mixed feelings of love and remorse. Always Lowndes portrays the joys and horrors of the every day. Her forte is a compassionate understanding of the diversity and complexity of human motives, the shades of grey, the unspoken and the hidden. Her novels are replete with sad adventuresses, rich but eccentric relatives, gossipy neighbours, potential scandals, driving hatreds, and surprising human generosity. Her historical romance *She Dwelt with Beauty* is typical of her domestic interests, focusing on the courtship and marriage of Eugenie de Montijo and Louis Napoleon, not for the historical repercussions, but for the human conflicts that grow out of the failure of the sexes to understand their differing natures and needs: Napoleon's sexually rampant nature; Eugenie's naivety, her shock at his infidelities, her mixture of love and abhorrence.

Occasionally Lowndes's tales seem conventionally Victorian: a cold-hearted, rich, young man, rejected by a kind-hearted beauty, seeks revenge on his rival, a generous and much-admired new arrival with a dark past, only to find his own aunt aiding the young lovers' escape. Such novels usually feature a decaying manor, family scandal, and scheming relatives. But more frequently Lowndes depends on psychological portraits and ironic twists: an unexpected call announcing death traps a philanderer who has seduced his best friend's wife; another philanderer, dependent on the security of a bedridden wife to protect him from his various conquests' demands for marriage, finds one lover who takes his toying all too seriously, murders his wife, and leaves him to face the consequences; a betrayed wife realizes her own responsibility for her divorced husband's acts and, upon the death of his second wife, hesitantly returns to his arms; a wealthy widow, upon learning her ex-lover has seduced her daughter into a secret engagement, executes their mutual lover—for her daughter's sake; a greedy woman, obsessed by money, starves herself to death; thereafter, her bereaved husband squanders the hard-earned wealth on a poor, young, neighbouring beauty (*Some Men and Women*). Often they verge on the gothic: a spoiled, self-righteous prude seeking revenge for her husband's infidelity in an illicit affair is warned from the act by the ghost of a woman whose illicit love she had once condemned; her insane husband having decapitated his rival in love, a terrified wife must return the head to the scene of horror to hide her shame and protect her family; a submarine captain and his mistress share a final farewell as the ship sinks, and the proud and loveless husband must use his wits to hide the scandal and preserve his honour (*Studies in Love and Terror*). The last focuses on the husband's guilt in the affair, and the cold self-possession that clearly alienated his gentle wife and allowed him to take the horror of her death so calmly. Always secret sins have public repercussions, and reputation is almost as important as survival.

Duchess Laura and *Duchess Laura: Further Days from Her Life*, sum up the contrast in generations, the first focusing on the very proper romance and marriage of a Victorian lady, the second, portraying episodically her forced readjustment to a changing world as she saves her son from a loveless marriage, helps an adventuress afford her true love, rescues a cynical young girl from the loathsome advances of a rich lecher, brings together an overprotected blind girl and a bitter, horribly scarred heir, prevents a repressed niece from poisoning her cantankerous old aunt, and faces the shock of her son wedding a poor, unattractive, roadhouse worker for her kindness and intelligence rather than family or beauty. Her difficulties in adjusting to the new morality and the breakdown of class differences among the younger generation are typical of the conflicts facing many of Lowndes's characters. *The Christine Diamond*, like many of her crime romances, deals with love beyond class bounds and the social patterns and taboos of upstairs/downstairs, as a rich young playboy takes pity on, then falls in love with, his aunt's secretary, to find he can win her love only by finding a stolen diamond and a clever thief. In *Reckless Angel* a spoiled debutante, moving in a rich, fast crowd, develops a reputation for carefree, thoughtless acts, yet becomes enamoured of a steady, puritanical naval officer whose only flaw is moral bondage to a grasping older woman; only in-

volvement in murder and theft, and the near loss of love and reputation finally teach her to be more careful of her loyalties. In *Love Is a Flame*, an unusual mixture of the highly cynical and highly romantic, a hard-working young woman's honesty sends her lover into the arms of a spoiled and petulant acquaintance who marries him on a whim, then sends him to possible death; only after blackmail, murder, suicide, and a blinding, crippling war injury does true love win out.

Thus, Lowndes portrays sympathetically domestic conflicts between generations, classes, and sexes; the misunderstandings and rationale of love; the attraction of opposites; the disillusionment of the naive; and the rewards of the faithful. With its commonplace horrors and its focus on the contradictory impulses of individuals, her canon reflects the war-induced breakdown of moral codes and the consequent confusion of decent characters caught in a morass of dimly understood shifting values. As a result, her work speaks to our time as well as her own.

—Gina Macdonald

LURGAN, Lester.   See **WYNNE, May.**

LUTYENS, Mary.   See **WYNDHAM, Esther.**

LYALL, David.   See **SWAN, Annie S.**

LYNN, Margaret. British. Died. See 2nd edition, 1990.

LYNTON, Ann.   See **RAYNER, Claire.**

LYTLE, Andrew (Nelson).
Nationality: American. **Born:** Murfreesboro, Tennessee, 26 December 1902. **Education:** Sewanee Military Academy, Tennessee; Exeter College, Oxford, 1920; Vanderbilt University, Nashville, B.A. 1925 (Phi Beta Kappa); Yale University School of Drama, New Haven, Connecticut, 1927–29. **Relations:** married Edna Langdon Barker in 1938 (died 1963); three daughters. **Career:** professor of history, Southwestern College, Memphis, Tennessee, 1936; professor of history, University of the South, Sewanee, Tennessee, and managing editor, *Sewanee Review*, 1942–43; lecturer, 1946–48, and acting head, 1947–48, University of Iowa School of Writing, Iowa City; lecturer in creative writing, University of Florida, Gainesville, 1948–61; lecturer in English, 1961–67, and professor of English, 1968–73, University of the South, and editor, *Sewanee Review*, 1961–73. **Recipient:** Guggenheim fellowship, 1940, 1941, 1960; National Endowment for the Arts grant, 1966; University of the South Brown fellowship, 1978, 1981; Lyndhurst Foundation prize, 1985; Ingersoll Foundation prize, 1986. D.Litt.: Kenyon College, Gambier, Ohio, 1965; University of Florida, 1970; University of the South, 1973; D.H.L.: Hillsdale College, Michigan, 1985. **Address:** Department of English, University of the South, Sewanee, Tennessee 37375, USA; or, Log Cabin, Monteagle, Tennessee 37356, USA.

ROMANCE AND HISTORICAL PUBLICATIONS

Novels

The Long Night. Indianapolis, Bobbs Merrill, 1936; London, Eyre and Spottiswoode, 1937.
At the Moon's Inn. Indianapolis, Bobbs Merrill, 1941; London, Eyre and Spottiswoode, 1943.
A Name for Evil. Indianapolis, Bobbs Merrill, 1947.
The Velvet Horn. New York, McDowell Obolensky, 1957.

Short Stories

A Novel, A Novella and Four Stories. New York, McDowell Obolensky, 1958.
Alchemy. Winston-Salem, North Carolina, Palaemon Press, 1979.
Stories: Alchemy and Others. Sewanee, Tennessee, University of the South, 1984.

OTHER PUBLICATIONS

Other

Bedford Forrest and His Critter Company (biography). New York, Minton Balch, 1931; London, Eyre and Spottiswoode, 1939; revised edition, New York, McDowell Obolensky, 1960.
The Hero with the Private Parts: Essays (literary criticism). Baton Rouge, Louisiana State University Press, 1966.
A Wake for the Living: A Family Chronicle. New York, Crown, 1975.
The Lytle/Tate Letters, with Allen Tate, edited by Thomas Daniel Young and Elizabeth Sarcone. Jackson, University Press of Mississippi, 1987.
Southerners and Europeans: Essays in a Time of Disorder. Baton Rouge, Louisiana State University Press, 1988.
From Eden to Babylon: The Social and Political Essays of Andrew Nelson Lytle. San Francisco, Gateway, 1989.

Editor, *Craft and Vision: The Best Fiction from The Sewanee Review*. New York, Delacorte Press, 1971.

*

Bibliography: *An Andrew Lytle Checklist* by Jack De Bellis, Charlottesville, Bibliographical Society of the University of Virginia, 1960; *Andrew Nelson Lytle: A Bibliography 1920-1982* by Stuart Wright, Sewanee, Tennessee, University of the South, 1982; *Andrew Lytle, Walker Percy, Peter Taylor: A Reference Guide* by Victor A. Kramer, Boston, Hall, 1983.

Manuscript Collections: Joint University Libraries (Vanderbilt University), Nashville, Tennessee; University of Florida Library, Gainesville.

Critical Studies: 'Andrew Lytle Issue' of *Mississippi Quarterly* (State College), Fall 1970; *The Form Discovered: Essays on the Achievement of Andrew Lytle* edited by M.E. Bradford, Jackson, University and College Press of Mississippi, 1973; 'Novels as History: The Art of Andrew Lytle' by Gregory Wolfe, in *Continuity* (Bryn Mawr, Pennsylvania), Fall 1984.

*   *   *

Influenced by both the Fugitive and Agrarian movements of the early 20th century in America, Andrew Lytle was intensely south-ern, his works often speaking for the nature and quality of the southern way of life, past and present, antebellum and modern. In the largest sense his historical novels constitute direct or subliminal defences of the southern identity in the presence of a threatening but blandly homogenous American one. *The Long Night*, which suggests the novelist's familiarity with Senecan drama, is a revenge tragedy set during the Civil War. Unified by the narrator Pleasant McIvor, the novel, with particularly moving Civil War battle scenes, is the history of family duty, including revenge for a murdered father. The plot for the novel was suggested by Lytle's friend, historian Frank Owsley.

The novel, however, transcends the limitations of Senecan convention in its theme of moral responsibility which is brought sharply to focus in Pleasant McIvor's conflict between a family duty of personal revenge and his larger responsibility in the war ... symbolic of the war's destruction of the code-sanctioned values of the Old South.

At the Moon's Inn which chronicles the quest of DeSoto in 16th-century Florida, speaks in a theme consistent with southern thought. In 1938 Lytle, for example, wrote to his editor D.L. Chambers that 'the new world will be seen as the old world's sin, even its destruction'. The relationship of past to present, though subliminal in the novel, may be viewed as the clash between the Agrarians of the south and contemporary American industrialization and commerce. In his materialistic quest DeSoto violates all the Agrarian sentiments, destroying much that was beautiful in the native tradition of the Seminoles.

A Name for Evil may well be the least effective novel Lytle wrote. It is, none the less, as one critic noted, an 'unflinching look at the ambiguities of a Southern allegiance that craves the past' as well as a criticism of betrayal of land and family. When the troubled narrator buys and restores a country house, he becomes obsessed with the past (the psychological ghost of the house) and order. Obsession with the past results in the narrator's wife's death, a psychology reminiscent, as critics further note, of James's 'The Turn of the Screw'.

The Velvet Horn is Lytle's masterpiece. Set in rural, late 19th-century Tennessee, the novel follows Lucius Cree's maturation into the attainment of harmony and a recognition of how to live with others. The novel, however, is not limited to maturation alone, since it epitomizes yearning for paradise, for innocence and wholeness. The hero's real growth is consequently dependent upon his acceptance of man's fallen condition and redemption in Christ.

With its rich symbolism and myth, clearly developed character, and acute historical awareness, *The Velvet Horn* remains Lytle's greatest achievement in historical writing. Its adroit intermingling of past and present and subtle and direct references to incest—literal and symbolic—make it a classic in the southern canon.

—George C. Longest

———

MACARDLE, Dorothy (Margaret Callan). Irish. 1899–1958. See 2nd edition, 1990.

———

MACAULAY, (Emilie) Rose.
Nationality: British. **Born:** Rugby, Warwickshire, 1 August 1881; lived with her family in Varazze, Italy, 1887–94. **Education:** Oxford High School for Girls, 1894–99; Somerville College, Oxford, 1900–03. **Career:** full-time writer from 1903; lived in Wales, 1903–05, Cambridgeshire, 1905–16, Beaconsfield, 1916–25, and London from 1925; worked in a hospital, as a land girl, in the War Office, and in the Ministry of Information, during

World War I; publisher's reader, Constable, London, 1919; special reporter, London *Daily Chronicle*, in Geneva, 1925; columnist ('Marginal Comments'), *Spectator*, London, 1935–36. **Recipient:** Femina-Vie Heureuse prize, 1922; James Tait Black memorial prize, 1957. D.Litt.: Cambridge University, 1951. DBE (Dame Commander, Order of the British Empire), 1958. **Died:** 30 October 1958.

ROMANCE AND HISTORICAL PUBLICATIONS

Novel

They Were Defeated. London, Collins, 1932; as *The Shadow Flies*, New York, Harper, 1932.

OTHER PUBLICATIONS

Novels

Abbots Verney. London, Murray, 1906.
The Furnace. London, Murray, 1907.
The Secret River. London, Murray, 1909.
The Valley Captives. London, Murray, and New York, Holt, 1911.
Views and Vagabonds. London, Murray, and New York, Holt, 1912.
The Lee Shore. London, Hodder and Stoughton, and New York, Doran, 1912.
The Making of a Bigot. London, Hodder and Stoughton, 1914.
What Not: A Prophetic Comedy. London, Constable, 1918.
Potterism: A Tragi-Farcical Tract. London, Collins, and New York, Boni and Liveright, 1920.
Dangerous Ages. London, Collins, and New York, Boni and Liveright, 1921.
Mystery at Geneva. London, Collins, 1922; New York, Boni and Liveright, 1923.
Told by an Idiot. London, Collins, and New York, Boni and Liveright, 1923.
Orphan Island. London, Collins, 1924; New York, Boni and Liveright, 1925.
Crewe Train. London, Collins, and New York, Boni and Liveright, 1926.
Keeping Up Appearances. London, Collins, 1928; as *Daisy and Daphne*, New York, Boni and Liveright, 1928.
Staying with Relations. London, Collins, and New York, Liveright, 1930.
Going Abroad. London, Collins, and New York, Harper, 1934.
I Would Be Private. London, Collins, and New York, Harper, 1937.
And No Man's Wit. London, Collins, and Boston, Little Brown, 1940.
The World My Wilderness. London, Collins, and Boston, Little Brown, 1950.
The Towers of Trebizond. London, Collins, 1956; New York, Farrar Straus, 1957.

Short Stories

Non-Combatants and Others. London, Hodder and Stoughton, 1916.

Poetry

The Two Blind Countries. London, Sidgwick and Jackson, 1914.
Three Days. London, Constable, 1919.
(Poems). London, Benn, 1927.

Other

A Casual Commentary (essays). London, Methuen, 1925; New York, Boni and Liveright, 1926.
Catchwords and Claptrap (essays). London, Hogarth Press, 1926.
Some Religious Elements in English Literature. London, Hogarth Press, and New York, Harcourt Brace, 1931.
Milton. London, Duckworth, 1934; New York, Harper, 1935; revised edition, Duckworth, and New York, Macmillan, 1957.
Personal Pleasures. London, Gollancz, 1935; New York, Macmillan, 1936.
An Open Letter to a Non-Pacifist. London, Peace Pledge Union, 1937.
The Writings of E.M. Forster. London, Hogarth Press, and New York, Harcourt Brace, 1938.
Life Among the English. London, Collins, 1942.
They Went to Portugal. London, Cape, 1946.
Fabled Shore: From the Pyrenees to Portugal. London, Hamish Hamilton, 1949; New York, Farrar Straus, 1951.
Pleasure of Ruins. London, Weidenfeld and Nicolson, 1953; New York, Walker, 1966; edited by Constance Babington Smith, London, Thames and Hudson, and New York, Holt Rinehart, 1977.
Letters to a Friend 1950–1952 and *Last Letters to a Friend 1952–1958* (to J.H.C. Johnson), edited by Constance Babington Smith. London, Collins, 2 vols, 1961–62; New York, Atheneum, 2 vols, 1962–63.
Letters to a Sister (to Jean Macaulay), edited by Constance Babington Smith. London, Collins, and New York, Atheneum, 1964.

Editor, *The Minor Pleasures of Life*. London, Gollancz, 1934; New York, Harper, 1935.
Editor, with Daniel George, *All in a Maze: A Collection of Prose and Verse*. London, Collins, 1938.

*

Critical Studies: *Rose Macaulay* by Alice R. Bensen, New York, Twayne, 1969; *Rose Macaulay* (biography) by Constance Babington Smith, London, Collins, 1972; *Eros and Androgyny: The Legacy of Rose Macaulay* by Jeanette N. Passty, Rutherford, New Jersey, Fairleigh Dickinson University Press, 1988; *Rose Macauley: A Writer's Life* by James Emery, London, Trafalgar Square, 1992.

*   *   *

Rose Macaulay's one historical novel, *They Were Defeated*, was her own favourite among her works, and testifies to her love for and knowledge of the early 17th century, a knowledge equally apparent in her anthology, *The Minor Pleasures of Life*, published two years later. The story of *They Were Defeated* takes place during the period immediately prior to the outbreak of the English Civil War, and centres on the fortunes and aspirations of Julian Conybeare, the 15-year-old daughter of a country doctor, who comes to Cambridge from Devonshire to visit her undergraduate brother, only to fall in love with his tutor, the cynical and worldly poet John Cleveland. The novel contrasts the backward life of the rural West Country with the intellectual tumult of a university divided in its political and religious allegiances. The central section of the book is dense with discussion and debate, the historian rather than the novelist being most in evidence; and the narrative emphasizes the continuing relevance of the issues which move and divide the characters. The latter include such well-known individuals as John Milton, Andrew Marvell, Richard Crashaw, John Suckling, Abraham Cowley, Kenelm Digby, and Henry More, and at times the text becomes implausibly burdened with celebrities. But there is a feeling of genuine authenticity where physical settings and domestic details are concerned, and

Macauley claimed that she had not given her characters any words to speak that would not have been in use at the time.

The Devonshire scenes are equally persuasive. Here the central character is Robert Herrick, vicar of Dean Prior; he is presented as very much a man of his time in his conservatism, yet full of commonsense, wary of the superstition of his parishioners, and attempting to succour the victim of a witch-hunt while remaining resistant to the open scepticism of Julian's father. Julian's brother, on the other hand, becomes a Roman Catholic; and the activities of the Jesuits in Cambridge form a significant thread in a narrative that also takes into account the happenings in London, such as the calling of the Long Parliament, the attainder of Strafford, and the arrest of Land, which determine directly or indirectly the fates of all the characters.

Julian's father, the doctor, is a humanitarian sceptic, whose easygoing attitude to belief brings disaster on those he loves; the origins of this subtly drawn portrait may be found in the social and religious radicalism of the time of Macaulay's youth. Her own sympathies with the Anglican ideals of liberal catholicism, of moderation and intellectual integrity, are in evidence throughout. In the character of Julian, Macaulay provides a portrait of a girl whose intellectual and artistic gifts are thwarted and tragically frustrated by the age in which she lives; in this respect *They Were Defeated* could be described as a feminist historical novel. Cleveland's refusal to take Julian's poems and treatise seriously makes familiarly painful reading. Another feminist aspect is seen in the character of Julian's tomboy friend, the squire's granddaughter, chafing against the relentless social customs which entrap her. One of the merits of the novel is the way in which the relationships between the characters are themselves seen as aspects of the time: Macaulay's people are not so much perennial types as such as modifications of those types in 17th century terms.

Macaulay makes telling use of the conflict in Herrick's own character, as evident in his two collections of poems, the secular *Hesperides* and the sacred *Noble Numbers;* she quotes from them in the text and even ascribes the 'Elegy on Strafford' (one of Cleveland's doubtfully authentic poems) to her fictional heroine. Accounts of clothing, furnishing, food, and household work are slipped in at every turn in the story, rather in the style of the 19th-century historical novelist Anne Manning, whose *The Household of Sir Thomas More* (1852) and *Mary Powell* (1849) appeared in Everyman's Library in 1906 and 1908 respectively, and which Macaulay would probably have known. A similar blend of sympathy and unpedantic learning characterizes her own work in the field.

—Glen Cavaliero

MACBETH, Madge (Hamilton).
Pseudonyms: W.S. Dill; Gilbert Knox. **Nationality:** Canadian. **Born:** Philadelphia, Pennsylvania, in 1878. **Education:** privately; at Helmuth College, London, Ontario. **Relations:** married Charles Macbeth; two sons. **Career:** past president of the Canadian Authors Association.

ROMANCE AND HISTORICAL PUBLICATIONS

Novels

The Winning Game. New York, Broadway, 1910.
Kleath. Boston, Small Maynard, 1917.
The Patterson Limit. Toronto, Hodder and Stoughton, 1923.
The Land of Afternoon (as Gilbert Knox). Ottawa, Graphic, 1925.
Shackles. Ottawa, Graphic, 1926; New York, Waterson, 1927.

The Great Fright; Onesiphore, Our Neighbor, with A.B. Conway. Montreal, Carrier, 1929; *Onesiphore, Our Neighbor* published as *Your Neighbour*, London, Stanley Paul, 1929.
The Kinder Bees (as Gilbert Knox). London, Dickson and Thompson, 1935.
Wings in the West. London, John Hamilton, 1937.
Shreds of Circumstance. London, W.H. Allen, 1947.
Lost: A Cavalier. London, W.H. Allen, 1948.

OTHER PUBLICATIONS

Play

Curiosity Rewarded (as Gilbert Knox). Ottawa, Graphic, 1926.
The Goose's Sauce. Toronto, French, 1935.

Other

The Long Day (reminiscences of the Yukon; as W.S. Dill). Ottawa, Graphic, 1926.
Over the Gangplank to Spain. Ottawa, Graphic, 1931.
Over My Shoulder (autobiography). Toronto, Ryerson, 1953.
Boulevard Career. Toronto, Kingswood House, 1957.

*   *   *

Madge Macbeth stretched the idea of the 'historical' novel to include the history of the idea of femininity and its impact on women's lives in the first half of the 20th century. Although documenting her own times, an historical perspective forms the core of all her novels. Macbeth uses plot twists and fine psychological detail to construct and then to question the conventions which determine the reader's expectations. She does this by denying the comic ending, the anticipated happy marriage of the central female character. Romance conventions are undermined further by frank references to women's sexual desire and experience and to the hypocritical social and cultural mores which repress women's natural physicality. *The Great Fright* and *Wings in the West* excepted, her novels develop a plot and psychological framework in which a female character is central.

Kleath and *Wings in the West* are adventure novels of the Canadian Klondike and of northern Ontario, respectively. *Wings in the West*, an action-oriented novel is not particularly effective. In concrete description of winter in a northern Canadian forest and in reference to the newly discovered potential of the uranium deposits, however, the novel does succeed in giving the reader a sense of the still unexplored north of this period. *Wings in the West* and *The Great Fright*, episodic and written in French-Canadian dialect, are Macbeth's least satisfying novels. *Kleath*, a very enjoyable novel of gold rush days, is based on the mystery surrounding Kleath's past. Conflict develops between Clare and Goldie. While these latter two characters are represented mainly within a conventional angel/monster dualism, the narrator's commentary does not allow complacent acceptance of this contrast. A third female character, Kleath's wife recently released from prison, disrupts our expectations and gives the marriage of Goldie and Kleath, reported on the last page, a sense of closure that is technically, but not emotionally, achieved.

The Kinder Bees and *The Land of Afternoon* are bitingly witty satires of politics and culture in Canada's capital city, Ottawa. In using a masculine pseudonym, Gilbert Knox, perhaps Macbeth had in mind Sara Jeannette Duncan's *The Imperialist* (1904), which was ridiculed from the position that, as a woman, the author could not understand political issues and, therefore, should not have attempted to represent them. A permanent resident of Ottawa, Macbeth was able to pack these two well-crafted novels with local detail and a sense of moment that are fundamental to the historical novel form. In both novels, Macbeth's critique of the government, the sphere of men, is balanced by an equally acerbic view of the social hierarchy, the sphere of women.

The Patterson Limit and *The Winning Game* explore the boundaries of women's sphere. In both novels the main characters are given sexually indeterminate names, Ray Lane and Leslie Loring, respectively. *The Winning Game*, Macbeth's first novel, presents a woman's life as determined by her relationship to men; *The Patterson Limit* presents a woman determining her life in terms of her own ideas and desires. Both novels are skilfully constructed and powerfully evoke contrasting and specific historical moments in women's thinking about themselves.

Shreds of Circumstance stretches the conventions of romance writing insofar as the central female character, Dagmar Kalany, has several sexual encounters, enjoys them all, and remains unmarried and happy at the end. Dagmar, her mother Nena, and friend Ellen, each represent different ideas of femininity. For all three characters, social and cultural expectations of women conflict with each woman's sense of personal happiness. Through Dagmar's cosmopolitanism, Macbeth avoids promoting any one national cultural or social model and suggests, therefore, the shared frustrations facing women in Europe and North America at the time between the two world wars.

Lost: A Cavalier and *Shackles*, Macbeth's best work, deal with women writers. Both novels are finely-wrought and develop excruciating tension. Both present female characters, Stephanie Barstow and Naomi Lennox, respectively, trapped by a man in an intolerable relationship that is both a perfection and perversion of accepted social and cultural conventions, including those of realist fiction. Prefacing *Shackles*, Macbeth notes that 'Woman is passing though a cultural transition. Instinctively, she is bound to the old order of things; intellectually, she clamours for the new. And vacillating, she stands between them'. Thus her female characters are estranged psychologically from the femininity they must enact. Macbeth not only achieves the idea of objective distance required to give the reader a sense of history revisited necessary to the historical novel form but also makes us aware that, in her own work, this distance is both because of and made problematic by a woman's point of view.

—Heather Iris Jones

MacGILL, Mrs Patrick
Nationality: British. **Born:** Margaret Gibbons. **Died.**

ROMANCE AND HISTORICAL PUBLICATIONS

Novels

The Rose of Glenconnel. London, Thomson, 1916.
An Anzac's Bride. London, Jenkins, 1917.
Whom Love Hath Chosen. London, Jenkins, 1919.
The Bartered Bride. London, Jenkins, 1920.
Each Hour a Peril. London, Thomson, 1921.
The Flame of Life. London, Jenkins, 1921.
Hidden Fires. London, Jenkins, 1921.
The Highest Bidder. London, Thomson, 1921.
His Dupe. London, Thomson, 1922.
Molly of the Lone Pine. London, Thomson, 1922.
Shifting Sands. London, Jenkins, 1922.
A Lover on Loan. London, Jenkins, 1923.

Her Undying Past. London, Jenkins, 1924.
Love—and Carol. London, Jenkins, 1925.
Her Dancing Partner. London, Jenkins, 1926.
Love's Defiance. London, Thomson, 1926.
The Ukelele Girl. London, Jenkins, 1927; as *His Ukelele Girl*, London, Thomson, 1927.
Dancers in the Dark. London, Jenkins, 1929.
Painted Butterflies. London, Jenkins, 1931.
Hollywood Madness. London, Jenkins, 1936; as *Hollywood Star Dust*, New York, Chelsea House, 1936.

OTHER PUBLICATIONS

Other

The 'Good-Night' Stories (for children; as Margaret Gibbons). London, Year Book Press, 1912.

*   *   *

Mrs Patrick MacGill's first book, *The 'Good-Night' Stories*, was a collection of stories for children. It has a stories-within-a-story framework, and is set in the Vane household whose numerous children are told bedtime stories by their mother before the Golden Dustman comes to throw magic dust on their eyes and send them to the enchanted realm of Slumberland. The stories are chiefly about fairies—'The bluebells tinkle merrily, and the fairies and elves form a ring round the Queen, who always sailed down in the moon to these gatherings (*sc.* on Hampstead Heath)'.

MacGill went from writing fairy stories for children to writing fairy stories for adults. Her romantic novels, which appeared between 1916 and 1936, are highly melodramatic, as their titles suggest. The plots are packed with incident—the result of genteel poverty, gambling fathers, spendthrift siblings, rascally employers, false accusations, bankruptcy, intrigue, treachery, deceit, gangsters—so that the hero and heroine are kept well apart until the final chapters.

The heroines of the earlier novels tend to be either unprotected orphan girls (such as the Rose of Glenconnel, born Rosalie Moran, who was brought up on a mining and lumber camp in the Yukon and turns out to be the grand-daughter of a baronet) or young wives having trouble with their husbands (through shell-shock or a forced marriage). The heroines of the later novels (with an eye to changing social conditions) are in paid employment, doing jobs which are quite advanced for the time, glamorous, or even daring—'girl clerk' assistant in a Bond Street hat shop, society dress designer, Exhibition Dancer in a night club, film actress. Though the heroines do not vary much in type, their settings do, from the Canadian backwoods, to titled circles in London, to Hollywood. MacGill seems to have been particularly smitten by 'the Tinsel Kingdom, Filmdom's capital', and much of the action in her last two novels takes place in Hollywood, where (of course) two of her earlier works, *The Flame of Life* and *Hidden Fires*, are being turned into films. A *Times Literary Supplement* reviewer had already accused her of having an eye to 'another mode of presentation than that of print' (1924 review of *Her Undying Past*).

Her literary style was as melodramatic as her plots, and did not change much over 20 novels: 'She was shy now, this fragrant, beautiful little bride, and a burning, blushing face was pressed close to Ronald's breast. But the young trapper, with eyes and heart aflame, bent down and raised his wife's face to his own ...' (*The Rose of Glenconnel*, 1916); or '"Let me look after you, sweetheart." The low, deep voice was vibrant with passion, but very kindly and tender ... as, stemming the tide of his own desire to press wild ecstatic kisses on the soft red mouth, he said, "You are afraid of love, Peggy ..." ' (*Hollywood Madness*, 1936).

—Jean Buchanan

___

MacINNES, Colin.
Nationality: British. **Born:** Colin McInnes in London, 20 August 1914; son of the writer Angela Thirkell and the singer James Campbell McInnes; moved to Australia, 1920. **Education:** Grimwade House and Scotch College, both Melbourne. **Military Service:** British Army, 1939–40, and the Intelligence Corps, 1941–46: sergeant. **Career:** returned to England, 1930; staff member, Imperial Continental Gas Association, Antwerp and Brussels, 1931–36; studied painting, Chelsea Polytechnic and Euston Road School of Painting and Drawing, both London, 1936–38; freelance journalist and broadcaster in London, 1946–69, and in Folkestone, Kent, from 1970. **Died:** 23 April 1976.

Romance and Historical Publications

Novels

Westward to Laughter. London, MacGibbon and Kee, 1969; New York, Farrar Straus, 1970.
Three Years to Play. London, MacGibbon and Kee, and New York, Farrar Straus, 1970.

Other Publications

Novels

To the Victors the Spoils. London, MacGibbon and Kee, 1950.
June in Her Spring. London, MacGibbon and Kee, 1952.
Visions of London. London, MacGibbon and Kee, 1969; as *The London Novels*, New York, Farrar Straus, 1969.
  City of Spades. London, MacGibbon and Kee, 1957; New York, Macmillan, 1958.
  Absolute Beginners. London, MacGibbon and Kee, 1959; New York, Macmillan, 1960.
  Mr Love and Justice. London, MacGibbon and Kee, 1960; New York, Dutton, 1961.
All Day Saturday. London, MacGibbon and Kee, 1966.
Out of the Garden. London, Hart Davis MacGibbon, 1974.

Other

England, Half English (essays). London, MacGibbon and Kee, 1961; New York, Random House, 1962.
London: City of Any Dream, photographs by Erwin Fieger. London, Thames and Hudson, 1962.
Australia and New Zealand, with the editors of *Life*. New York, Time, 1964.
Sweet Saturday Night. London, MacGibbon and Kee, 1967.
Loving Them Both: A Study of Bisexuality and Bisexuals. London, Martin Brian and O'Keeffe, 1974.
No Novel Reader. London, Martin Brian and O'Keeffe, 1975.
Out of the Way: Later Essays. London, Martin Brian and O'Keeffe, 1979.
Absolute MacInnes: The Best of Colin MacInnes, edited by Tony Gould. London, Allison and Busby, 1985.

*

Film Adaptation: *Absolute Beginners*, 1985.

Critical Study: *Inside Outsider: The Life and Times of Colin MacInnes* by Tony Gould, London, Chatto and Windus, 1983.

*   *   *

It is likely that Colin MacInnes will always be best remembered for his novels of swinging London of the 1950s, especially for *Absolute Beginners*, which was made into a film, and *June in Her Spring*, a more or less autobiographical romance set in Australia where the author spent a formative part of his youth.

The historical fiction of MacInnes has not been so well received, but it has a distinct quality and flavour of its own. *Westward to Laughter* is an intriguing work, in part a parody of children's adventure fiction and in part a philosophical fable. Alexander Nairn is a Scottish 16-year-old who is left an orphan after the Jacobite Rebellion of 1745 and turns to his rascally uncle for help. In no time at all he is embarked on a slave ship which crosses the Atlantic, making for the British West Indian Island of St Laughter (hence travelling 'westwards to Laughter'). The irony and the humour in the name are typical of the novel as a whole. A naive and seemingly irrepressibly optimistic observer of a world whose horrors are all too apparent to the reader, Alexander owes, as the author admits, much to Candide, the youthful hero of Voltaire's philosophical tale which is a devastating critique of 18th-century society. The first-person narration conveys a strange lack of awareness of horrors on every side, and so it is artfully left to the reader to respond in a more appropriate way. The language is not by any means a full-scale recreation of authentic period style, but words are used sparingly, in a manner which is often thought to be characteristic of the tight-lipped Scots, and the odd touch of historical colour—just spelling the adjective 'pathetick' with that extra letter at the end, for instance—goes a long way to convey a sense of the past. The object is not so much to give an impression that this is indeed an 18th-century narration as to make it clear that this essentially tragic tale is in fact a comment on the predicaments of modern man. Alexander's faith in humanity and justice is assailed at every turn as he finds himself betrayed again and again, and his fate is to be hanged at the age of 19. There seems no escaping the conclusion that the world is in the grip of evil, and Alexander's faith in providence is shown to be quite vain. The juxtaposition of surface cheerfulness and deep-seated despair about the human condition is a very powerful device.

A young man is also the hero of MacInnes's second—and distinctly longer—historical novel, *Three Years to Play*, which appeared a year after *Westward to Laughter*, in 1970. The setting is England towards the end of the Elizabethan era, and MacInnes is, not unexpectedly, especially successful in recreating the atmosphere of the London underworld. The 'Three Years to Play' of the title refer to the period of time during which the young Aubrey has to learn his skills as a boy-actor in the Shakesperean theatre and gain his fame. As well as some reflection of political conditions, the novel offers a portrayal of Shakespeare himself who finds in Aubrey's adventures the situations he was to develop in *As You Like It*, and this is the starting point for some consideration of the mechanisms of artistic production. MacInnes, who found much to admire in the freer moral attitudes of England in the late Renaissance, also takes the opportunity of exploring aspects of bisexuality. As in *Westward to Laughter* there is some control of language and style, if not to imitate the idiom of the day exactly, then at least to convey a pervading sense of the era in which the novel is set.

—Christopher N. Smith

MACKENZIE, Lee. See **BARCLAY, Tessa.**

MacKENZIE, Pierce. See **RIEFE, Barbara.**

MACKINLAY, Leila (Antoinette Sterling).
Pseudonym: Brenda Grey. **Nationality:** British. **Born:** London, 5 September 1910. **Education:** Camden House School, London; trained as a singer and actress. **Career:** music critic, *Dancing Times*, 1935–39, and from 1946 for *Amateur Stage;* publisher's reader, and drama and verse adjudicator. **Recipient:** Romantic Novelists Association president's prize, 1966. **Address:** 4-N Portman Mansions, Chiltern Street, London W1M 1LF, England.

ROMANCE AND HISTORICAL PUBLICATIONS

Novels

Little Mountebank. London, Mills and Boon, 1930.
Fame's Fetters. London, Mills and Boon, 1931.
Madame Juno. London, Mills and Boon, 1931.
An Exotic Young Lady. London, Mills and Boon, 1932.
Willed to Wed. London, Mills and Boon, 1933.
The Pro's Daughter. London, Ward Lock, 1934.
Shadow Lawn. London, Ward Lock, 1934.
Love Goes South. London, Ward Lock, 1935.
Into the Net. London, Ward Lock, 1935.
Night Bell. London, Ward Lock, 1936.
Young Man's Slave. London, Ward Lock, 1936.
Doubting Heart. London, Ward Lock, 1937.
Apron-Strings. London, Ward Lock, 1937.
Caretaker Within. London, Ward Lock, 1938.
Theme Song. London, Ward Lock, 1938.
Only Her Husband. London, Ward Lock, 1939.
The Reluctant Bride. London, Ward Lock, 1939.
Man Always Pays. London, Ward Lock, 1940.
Woman at the Wheel. London, Ward Lock, 1940.
Ridin' High. London, Ward Lock, 1941.
None Better Loved. London, Ward Lock, 1941.
Time on Her Hands. London, Ward Lock, 1942.
The Brave Live On. London, Ward Lock, 1942.
Green Limelight. London, Ward Lock, 1943.
Lady of the Torch. London, Ward Lock, 1944.
Two Walk Together. London, Ward Lock, 1945.
Piper's Pool. London, Ward Lock, 1946.
Piccadilly Inn. London, Ward Lock, 1946.
Blue Shutters. London, Ward Lock, 1947.
Echo of Applause. London, Ward Lock, 1948.
Peacock Hill. London, Ward Lock, 1948.
Restless Dream. London, Ward Lock, 1949.
Pilot's Point. London, Ward Lock, 1949.
Six Wax Candles. London, Ward Lock, 1950.
Spider Dance. London, Ward Lock, 1950.
Guilt's Pavilions. London, Ward Lock, 1951.
Five Houses. London, Ward Lock, 1952.
Unwise Wanderer. London, Ward Lock, 1952.
Cuckoo Cottage. London, Ward Lock, 1953.
She Married Another. London, Ward Lock, 1953.
Midnight Is Mine. London, Ward Lock, 1954.
Fiddler's Green. London, Ward Lock, 1954.
Vagabond Daughter. London, Ward Lock, 1955.
Riddle of a Lady. London, Ward Lock, 1955.
Man of the Moment. London, Ward Lock, 1956.

She Moved to Music. London, Ward Lock, 1956.
Divided Duty. London, Ward Lock, 1957.
Mantle of Innocence. London, Ward Lock, 1957.
Love on a Shoestring. London, Ward Lock, 1958.
The Secret in Her Life. London, Ward Lock, 1958.
Seven Red Roses. London, Ward Lock, 1959.
Uneasy Conquest. London, Ward Lock, 1959.
Food of Love. London, Ward Lock, 1960.
Spotlight on Susan. London, Ward Lock, 1960.
Beauty's Tears. London, Ward Lock, 1961.
Spring Rainbow. London, Ward Lock, 1961.
Vain Delights. London, Ward Lock, 1962.
Broken Armour. London, Ward Lock, 1963.
False Relations. London, Ward Lock, 1963.
Fool of Virtue. London, Ward Lock, 1964.
Practice for Sale. London, Ward Lock, 1964.
Ring of Hope. London, Ward Lock, 1965.
No Room for Loneliness. London, Ward Lock, 1965.
An Outside Chance. London, Ward Lock, 1966.
The Third Boat. London, Ward Lock, 1967.
Mists of the Moor. London, Ward Lock, 1967.
Frost at Dawn. London, Ward Lock, 1968.
Homesick for a Dream. London, Ward Lock, 1968.
Wanted—Girl Friday. London, Ward Lock, 1968.
Farewell to Sadness. London, Hale, 1970.
The Silken Purse. London, Hale, 1970.
Bridal Wreath. London, Hale, 1971.
Strange Involvement. London, Hale, 1972.
Birds of Silence. London, Hale, 1974.
Fortune's Slave. London, Hale, 1975.
Twilight Moment. London, Hale, 1976.
The Uphill Path. London, Hale, 1979.

Novels as Brenda Grey

Modern Micawbers. London, Eldon Press, 1933.
Stardust in Her Eyes. London, Gresham, 1964.
Girl of His Choice. London, Gresham, 1965.
How High the Moon. London, Gresham, 1966.
Throw Your Bouquet. London, Gresham, 1967.
A Very Special Person. London, Gresham, 1967.
Shadow of a Smile. London, Gresham, 1968.
Tread Softly on Dreams. London, Gresham, 1970.
Son of Summer. London, Gresham, 1970.
Mixed Singles. London, Gresham, 1971.
Husband in Name. London, Hale, 1972.

OTHER PUBLICATIONS

Other

Musical Productions. London, Jenkins, 1955.

*   *   *

Leila Mackinlay has had one of the longest careers of living romantic fiction writers. Her first novel, *Little Mountebank*, came out in 1930, and she continued writing until the late 1970s. She has also written fiction under the name of Brenda Grey and drama criticism. She received the Romantic Novelists Association president's prize in 1966.

Most of Mackinlay's novels concern the world of the theatre or singing, and her own training and involvement in the stage have served as a source of inspiration. Many of her books concern pupils or young entertainers. *An Exotic Young Lady*, for instance, is set in a popular environment of an Italian singing school in London and contains a very convincing description of this milieu.

The promotion of young and obscure theatrical talent has become a familiar theme, but there is a wide variety of plots, and love invariably is involved. In *Food of Love* the singer is a young miner and he has to be helped to overcome the disadvantages of his background and the jealous opposition of his small town fiancée. After the breaking off of the hero's engagement, a love triangle results between the hero's lady agent and her younger friend. The book is saved from being clichéd by a very sympathetic drawing of character, especially of the older woman whose attraction stirs in her long dormant feelings. A classic British theme of the time, the conflict between a rising hero and his working-class background is convincingly handled.

The world of the professional theatre can be inward looking but Mackinlay is able to give the reader a perspective on the life of a stage family in *An Outside Chance*. The position of second-team actors and actresses is convincingly summarized. The principal character, a young actress, is well drawn and shows us that she is quite normal and stable, somewhat against our expectations. True to a tradition in romance writing, glamour is pointed up by the grotesque: the heroine is the object of romantic advances from her fiancé's hideously crippled brother. The men are weak but the women are strong, and the heroine is able to cope with difficult situations and becomes the lynch pin of her own family.

True to the theatrical tradition, careers have their ups and downs. In *The Uphill Path* the heroine is able to turn round her fortunes and rebuild her career; although painful memories are recalled, she rediscovers and renews her original love affair.

As well as a very accurate background setting of the theatre, Mackinlay gives a considerable credibility in her novels to her characters. Unexpected depths are found in people and she shows the hard work necessary for success. Ordinary people outside show business come across very well, too, and display a mature and steady attitude to emotional relationships despite being, in some cases, just out of their teens. Some minor characters, for instance in *Fool of Virtue*, are glaring exceptions to this rule.

Dialogue does not overburden her books and is neither trite nor silly. The plots are interesting and credible. The narrative is well written although occasionally slow.

The great achievement of Mackinlay is to be able to keep her books up to date for each decade. The heroine in *An Exotic Young Lady* of 1932 is an orthodox girl of the decade. *None Better Loved* of 1941 has an appropriate setting of air raid shelters. In *The Uphill Path* the modern post-1960s pop scene, its mores and attendant problems for a girl, is very well drawn as is the character of the girl herself.

As befits the tradition of romantic novels, Mackinlay's have a moral but it is palatable and does not spoil a good story.

—P.R. Meldrum

MACLAGAN, Bridget. See **BORDEN, Mary.**

MacLEOD, Charlotte (Matilda). American. 1922—.

MacLEOD, Jean S.
Pseudonym: Catherine Airlie. **Nationality:** British. **Born:** Glasgow, Scotland, 20 January 1908. **Education:** Bearsden Academy, near Glasgow; High School for Girls, Swansea, Wales. **Relations:**

married Lionel Walton in 1935; one son. **Career:** secretary, British Ministry of Labour, Newcastle-upon-Tyne, 1930–35. **Recipient:** Cartland Historical Novel award, 1962. **Address:** c/o Mills and Boon Ltd, Eton House, 18–24 Paradise Road, Richmond, Surrey TW9 1SR, England.

ROMANCE AND HISTORICAL PUBLICATIONS

Novels

Life for Two. London, Mills and Boon, 1936.
Human Symphony. London, Mills and Boon, 1937.
Summer Rain. London, Mills and Boon, 1938.
Sequel to Youth. London, Mills and Boon, 1938.
Mist Across the Hills. London, Mills and Boon, 1938; Toronto, Harlequin, 1967.
Dangerous Obsession. London, Mills and Boon, 1938; Toronto, Harlequin, 1962.
Run Away from Love. London, Mills and Boon, 1939; Toronto, Harlequin, 1961.
Return to Spring. London, Mills and Boon, 1939; Toronto, Harlequin, 1971.
The Rainbow Isle. London, Mills and Boon, 1939.
The Whim of Fate. London, Mills and Boon, 1940.
Silent Bondage. London, Mills and Boon, 1940; Toronto, Harlequin, 1961.
The Lonely Farrow. London, Mills and Boon, 1940.
Heatherbloom. London, Mills and Boon, 1940.
The Reckless Pilgrim. London, Mills and Boon, 1941.
The Shadow of a Vow. London, Mills and Boon, 1941.
One Way Out. London, Mills and Boon, 1941.
Forbidden Rapture. London, Mills and Boon, 1941.
Penalty for Living. London, Mills and Boon, 1942.
Blind Journey. London, Mills and Boon, 1942.
Bleak Heritage. London, Mills and Boon, 1942; Toronto, Harlequin, 1970.
Reluctant Folly. London, Mills and Boon, 1942.
Unseen To-morrow. London, Mills and Boon, 1943.
The Rowan Tree. London, Mills and Boon, 1943.
Flower o' the Broom. London, Mills and Boon, 1943.
The Circle of Doubt. London, Mills and Boon, 1943.
Lamont of Ardgoyne. London, Mills and Boon, 1944.
Two Paths. London, Mills and Boon, 1944; Toronto, Harlequin, 1966.
Brief Fulfilment. London, Mills and Boon, 1945.
The Bridge of Years. London, Mills and Boon, 1945.
This Much to Give. London, Mills and Boon, 1945; Toronto, Harlequin, 1961.
One Love. London, Mills and Boon, 1945; Toronto, Harlequin, 1970.
The Tranquil Haven. London, Mills and Boon, 1946.
Sown in the Wind. London, Mills and Boon, 1946; Toronto, Harlequin, 1970.
The House of Oliver. London, Mills and Boon, 1947; Toronto, Harlequin, 1968.
And We in Dreams. London, Mills and Boon, 1947.
The Chalet in the Sun. London, Mills and Boon, 1948.
Ravenscrag. London, Mills and Boon, 1948.
Above the Lattice. London, Mills and Boon, 1949.
To-morrow's Bargain. London, Mills and Boon, 1949.
Katherine. London, Mills and Boon, 1950.
The Valley of Palms. London, Mills and Boon, 1950; Toronto, Harlequin, 1963.
Roadway to the Past. London, Mills and Boon, 1951.
Once to Every Heart. London, Mills and Boon, 1951.

Cameron of Gare. London, Mills and Boon, 1952; Toronto, Harlequin, 1961.

Music at Midnight. London, Mills and Boon, 1952.

The Silent Valley. London, Mills and Boon, 1953; Toronto, Harlequin, 1958.

The Stranger in Their Midst. London, Mills and Boon, 1953; Toronto, Harlequin, 1961.

Dear Doctor Everett. London, Mills and Boon, 1954; Toronto, Harlequin, 1958.

The Man in Authority. London, Mills and Boon, 1954.

After Long Journeying. London, Mills and Boon, 1955.

Master of Glenkeith. London, Mills and Boon, 1955; Toronto, Harlequin, 1969.

The Way in the Dark. London, Mills and Boon, 1956; Toronto, Harlequin, 1960.

My Heart's in the Highlands. London, Mills and Boon, 1956; Toronto, Harlequin, 1963.

Journey in the Sun. London, Mills and Boon, 1957; Toronto, Harlequin, 1960.

The Prisoner of Love. London, Mills and Boon, 1958; Toronto, Harlequin, 1960.

The Gated Road. London, Mills and Boon, 1959; Toronto, Harlequin, 1960.

Air Ambulance. London, Mills and Boon, and Toronto, Harlequin, 1959.

The Little Doctor. London, Mills and Boon, and Toronto, Harlequin, 1960.

Nurse Lang. Toronto, Harlequin, 1960.

The White Cockade. London, Mills and Boon, 1960.

The Silver Dragon. London, Mills and Boon, 1961; Toronto, Harlequin, 1962.

Slave of the Wind. London, Mills and Boon, 1962; Toronto, Harlequin, 1969.

The Dark Fortune. London, Mills and Boon, 1962.

Mountain Clinic. Toronto, Harlequin, 1962.

Sugar Island. London, Mills and Boon, and Toronto, Harlequin, 1964.

The Black Cameron. London, Mills and Boon, and Toronto, Harlequin, 1964.

Crane Castle. London, Mills and Boon, and Toronto, Harlequin, 1965.

The Wolf of Heimra. London, Mills and Boon, 1965; Toronto, Harlequin, 1966.

Doctor's Daughter. Toronto, Harlequin, 1965.

The Tender Glory. London, Mills and Boon, 1965; Toronto, Harlequin, 1967.

The Drummer of Corrae. London, Mills and Boon, and Toronto, Harlequin, 1966.

Lament for a Lover. London, Mills and Boon, and Toronto, Harlequin, 1967.

The Master of Keills. London, Mills and Boon, 1967; Toronto, Harlequin, 1968.

The Bride of Mingalay. London, Mills and Boon, and Toronto, Harlequin, 1967.

The Moonflower. London, Mills and Boon, 1967; Toronto, Harlequin, 1968.

Summer Island. London, Mills and Boon, 1968; Toronto, Harlequin, 1969.

The Joshua Tree. London, Mills and Boon, 1970.

The Fortress. London, Mills and Boon, 1970.

The Way Through the Valley. London, Mills and Boon, and Toronto, Harlequin, 1971.

The Scent of Juniper. London, Mills and Boon, 1971.

Light in the Tower. London, Mills and Boon, and Toronto, Harlequin, 1971.

Moment of Decision. London, Mills and Boon, and Toronto, Harlequin, 1972.

Adam's Wife. London, Mills and Boon, 1972; Toronto, Harlequin, 1973.

The Rainbow Days. London, Mills and Boon, and Toronto, Harlequin, 1973.

Over the Castle Wall. London, Mills and Boon, 1974.

Time Suspended. London, Mills and Boon, 1974; Toronto, Harlequin, 1975.

The Phantom Pipes. London, Mills and Boon, 1975.

Journey into Spring. London, Mills and Boon, and Toronto, Harlequin, 1976.

Island Stranger. London, Mills and Boon, 1977; Toronto, Harlequin, 1978.

Viking Song. London, Mills and Boon, 1977.

The Ruaig Inheritance. London, Mills and Boon, 1978.

Search for Yesterday. London, Mills and Boon, and Toronto, Harlequin, 1978.

Meeting in Madrid. London, Mills and Boon, 1979.

Brief Enchantment. London, Mills and Boon, 1979.

Black Sand, White Sand. London, Mills and Boon, 1981.

Moreton's Kingdom. London, Mills and Boon, and Toronto, Harlequin, 1981.

Cruel Deception. London, Mills and Boon, and Toronto, Harlequin, 1981.

Zamora. London, Mills and Boon, and Toronto, Harlequin, 1983.

A Distant Paradise. London, Mills and Boon, and Toronto, Harlequin, 1984.

Beyond the Reef. London, Mills and Boon, and Toronto, Harlequin, 1984.

Valley of the Snows. London, Mills and Boon, and Toronto, Harlequin, 1985.

The Apollo Man. London, Mills and Boon, 1986.

The Olive Grove. London, Mills and Boon, 1986.

After the Hurricane. London, Mills and Boon, and Toronto, Harlequin, 1987.

Call Back the Past. London, Mills and Boon, and Toronto, Harlequin, 1988.

Legacy of Doubt. London, Mills and Boon, and Toronto, Harlequin, 1989.

Shadow on the Hills. London, Mills and Boon, and Toronto, Harlequin, 1989.

Flame of Avila. London, Mills and Boon, 1990.

Tidal Wave. London, Mills and Boon, 1991.

Home To the Hills. London, Mills and Boon, 1992.

A Handful of Shells. London, Mills and Boon, 1993.

The Jade Pagoda. London, Mills and Boon, 1993.

Novels as Catherine Airlie

The Wild Macraes. London, Mills and Boon, 1948.

From Such a Seed. London, Mills and Boon, 1949.

The Restless Years. London, Mills and Boon, 1950.

Fabric of Dreams. London, Mills and Boon, 1951.

Strange Recompense. London, Mills and Boon, 1952; Toronto, Harlequin, 1960.

The Green Rushes. London, Mills and Boon, 1953; Toronto, Harlequin, 1968.

Hidden in the Wind. London, Mills and Boon, 1953.

A Wind Sighing. London, Mills and Boon, 1954; Toronto, Harlequin, 1969.

Nobody's Child. London, Mills and Boon, 1954; Toronto, Harlequin, 1968.

The Valley of Desire. London, Mills and Boon, 1955; Toronto, Harlequin, 1967.

The Ways of Love. London, Mills and Boon, 1955; Toronto, Harlequin, 1970.
The Mountain of Stars. London, Mills and Boon, 1956; Toronto, Harlequin, 1969.
The Unguarded Hour. London, Mills and Boon, 1956.
Land of Heart's Desire. London, Mills and Boon, 1957; Toronto, Harlequin, 1968.
Red Lotus. London, Mills and Boon, 1958; Toronto, Harlequin, 1968.
The Last of the Kintyres. London, Mills and Boon, 1959; Toronto, Harlequin, 1969.
Shadow on the Sun. London, Mills and Boon, 1960.
One Summer's Day. London, Mills and Boon, 1961; Toronto, Harlequin, 1966.
The Country of the Heart. London, Mills and Boon, 1961; Toronto, Harlequin, 1964.
The Unlived Year. London, Mills and Boon, 1962; Toronto, Harlequin, 1971.
Passing Strangers. London, Mills and Boon, 1963.
The Wheels of Chance. London, Mills and Boon, 1964.
The Sea Change. London, Mills and Boon, 1965.
Doctor Overboard. Toronto, Harlequin, 1966.
Nurse Jane in Tenerife. Toronto, Harlequin, 1967.

*

Jean S. MacLeod comments:

After writing romantic and historical fiction for over 50 years I have come to the conclusion that I am happily employed in my chosen career which, even now, I would not like to be without. I have been most fortunate in my connection with Mills and Boon Ltd. and all the women's magazine editors with whom I have worked in that time.

* * *

Jean S. MacLeod is a writer who captivates the reader with unusual stories in exotic settings. It is obvious that she has thoroughly researched the background to her novels. Her characters seem to be equally at home in the mountains of Norway and the warmth of the Canary Islands as in her own native Scotland. More than mere settings, her milieux form an intrinsic part of the action, with unobtrusive descriptions of customs and natural phenomena providing an air of authenticity.

The majority of the novels are set in some part of Scotland: amid the cliffs and seas (*The Prisoner of Love*), in the Hebrides (*The Bride of Mingalay*), or in the Western Highlands (*Above the Lattice*). And in these books it is clear that the writer is in her element. However, there is an equal feeling of affinity in the novels which deal with less familiar places. The description of the Norwegian mountains in *The Mountain of Stars* (Catherine Airlie), for example, include many references to real places. The characters' observance of customs, such as that of the 'bridal veil', whether real or not, also give an air of authenticity. This feeling of reality is also conveyed by the dialogues and interaction between the characters, such as that between Felicity and Philip in *Red Lotus*, whose relationship is moving and very plausible.

The force of the elements is strongly felt in all MacLeod's works, and one may even say that natural forces seem to influence events at times or at least to be in sympathy with them. In *Music at Midnight* Kay goes to Norway to take her dead sister's son to his grandparents. The writer manages to portray very convincingly the weighty fear of an avalanche, and in *Red Lotus* the volcanic eruption that traps Felicity and Philip on the mountain plays a frightening part in the action. *The Man in Authority* also contains a strong feeling of the power of places and the elements. Here, as in a number of these

novels, the main character comes to possess a feeling of 'belonging' to a location which was alien when the story began. Perhaps significantly, many of the novels (e.g. *After Long Journeying*) begin with someone standing on a quayside or waving from the deck of a ship at the commencement of a journey.

This travel element is often combined with a medical setting, a tried and tested favourite for romances of this kind. The formula is obviously well chosen in this case. The romances which MacLeod invents are often characterized by misunderstanding or lack of communication between the parties concerned. Margaret and Thor marry (in *The Mountain of Stars*) although each believes that their love is not reciprocated. In *Time Suspended* Ruth at first thinks Logan could be either 'a gentleman or a pirate', but they finally settle happily together in Antigua. So, too, in *The Bride of Mingalay* Rowena ends up marrying Andrew Fenwick despite her initial detestation.

In conclusion, it may be said that MacLeod, whether writing under this name or her pseudonym of Catherine Airlie, has written carefully researched romances with some depth. The well chosen settings combine effectively with the events of the plot to give an unusual and entertaining final product.

—Kim F. Paynter

———

MacNEIL, Duncan. See McCUTCHAN, Philip.

———

MacNEILL, Anne. See SEGER, Maura.

———

MADDOCKS, Margaret (Kathleen Avern).
Nationality: British. **Born:** Caversham, Berkshire, 10 August 1906. **Education:** St Helen's School, Northwood, Middlesex, and in Dresden. **Relations:** married Richard Maddocks in 1937 (died 1970). **Recipient:** Romantic Novelists Association major award, 1962, 1965 (for *The Silver Answer*), 1970, 1976. **Address:** 40 Heathfield Green, Midhurst, West Sussex GU29 9QA, England.

ROMANCE AND HISTORICAL PUBLICATIONS

Novels

Come Lasses and Lads. London, Hurst and Blackett, 1944.
The Quiet House. London, Hurst and Blackett, 1947.
Remembered Spring. London, Hurst and Blackett, 1949.
Fair Shines the Day. London, Hurst and Blackett, 1952; as *The Open Door*, London, Hamlyn, 1980.
Piper's Tune. London, Hurst and Blackett, 1954.
A Summer Gone. London, Hurst and Blackett, 1957.
The Frozen Fountain. London, Hurst and Blackett, 1959.
Larksbrook. London, Hurst and Blackett, 1962.
The Green Grass. London, Hurst and Blackett, 1963.
November Tree. London, Hurst and Blackett, 1964.
The Silver Answer. London, Hurst and Blackett, 1965.
Dance Barefoot. London, Hurst and Blackett, 1966.
Fool's Enchantment. London, Hurst and Blackett, 1968.
Thea. London, Hurst and Blackett, 1969; New York, Ace, 1973.
The Weathercock. London, Hurst and Blackett, 1971; New York, Ace, 1973.
A View of the Sea. London, Hurst and Blackett, 1973.

The Moon Is Square. London, Hurst and Blackett, 1975.

OTHER PUBLICATIONS

Other

An Unlessoned Girl (autobiography). London, Hutchinson, 1977.

*

Margaret Maddocks comments:

Any writer must find it difficult to assess her own work honestly and objectively, so I can only say that I hope my books may be considered as well-written. They appear to be popular among all age groups in the nine countries where they have been published. This is probably because the reader can believe in the characters and the plot holds the interest to the end. They tend to cheer rather than depress.

*   *   *

The heroines of Margaret Maddocks's novels are less concerned with finding true love than with finding themselves. The last thing on their minds is falling in love; rather they are concerned with rebuilding their lives after a time of great unhappiness, for example, the death of a spouse. Going it alone, after having depended on someone else to deal with the practicalities of life, may be tough, but Maddocks's heroines cope admirably. In fact they flourish, growing in spirit and personality as they meet and surmount the obstacles in their way. It is almost as if, in a brief but passionate marriage or a too-close relationship with a child, they have suppressed part of themselves. The constraints of adapting their temperaments to suit that of someone else are lifted, and the women are free to be, in fact they are forced to be, themselves. Such freedom brings its own difficulties, emotional and physical isolation being the most pressing. The characters yearn not for passion and romance, which they have experienced in the past, but for companionship and understanding, and someone to laugh with them at the problems that come their way. In short, the ability to make love seems a less important quality to look for in a lover than the ability to make a good joke.

Despite strong elements of realism in some novels, elements of clichéd romanticism are still to be found. Jane, the attractive young heroine of *The Silver Answer* (winner of the Romantic Novelists Association major award—one of four such awards that Maddocks has received), has been widowed after a brief passionate year of marriage. We meet her two years on, having recovered from the nervous breakdown and miscarriage that followed Alan's death, setting out over one summer to write a book about the mountaineering expedition in which he was tragically killed. Before long she has won the hearts of not one, not two, but three men! Two of these, the artistic, humorous Mike Harling and the sensible, understanding Lawrence Stafford, were friends of Alan's, and companions on the fatal expedition. The third is an untruthful actor, the hairy, 'bear-like' egoistic Aubrey Charles. Though Jane declares that she could never fall in love again, and that she holds Mike and Lawrence responsible for Alan's death and thus 'hates' them, her actual behaviour shows little evidence of this, and she spends the entire summer vacillating between the three men. After having a brief affair with the attractive/repulsive Aubrey, she ends up, rather predictably, with the man we knew she would end up with on page one. Still, elements of realism creep into the rather thin plot: the book that Jane writes over the summer turns out to be a rather self-indulgent failure, and is even rejected by her friends and former employers, who run a literary agency; and Jane's relationship with her aging, tight-lipped parents casts a gloomy shadow over the summer months.

The theme of child/parent relationships is one that obviously concerns Maddocks, and she deals with it admirably. The heroine of *Thea*, one of her most moving works, has recently been widowed after a long, superficially happy marriage to a man more than 20 years her senior. Not only must she now build a new life for herself but she must also cope with the problems of her two daughters, the rather remote and volatile Harriet whose stormy marriage is going through a crucial phase, and the endearing warm-hearted 18-year-old Lizzy, Thea's 'other-self'. When Harriet walks out on her husband and arrives back on her mother's doorstep with her three-year-old son, and Lizzy falls in love with Jonah, a man Thea's age, Thea is forced to re-examine her marriage, which she finds to have had many faults, and is torn between concern for her children's futures and the need to explore and assert her own new-found independence. When she expresses her fears that Lizzy will, by marrying a man in a different generation, miss out on much of her youth, as she herself did, a rift forms for the first time between mother and daughter. Things are further complicated when Lizzy accuses Thea of wanting Jonah herself. *Thea* is a rich novel, realistic in plot and execution. The characters are all the more believable for having their imperfections (bad temper, insensitivity, Thea's obsession with feeding extra mouths), and the central portrait of a woman struggling for the first time in her life to put herself before her children is a convincing one.

The relationship between child and parent, or rather the lack of it, forms the basis of *The Moon Is Square*. In this case the 'child' in question, teenage Stephen, far from needing his widowed mother Judith, disappears from home on the brink of the university career for which she has such high hopes. Left with no information of his whereabouts other than the fact that he is 'walking to India', Judith, who had in the past turned down a proposal of marriage in order to devote herself to her son (or so she tells herself), is shocked, worried, and confused. Suddenly she realizes that she had not really known Stephen as a person, so involved has she been in the world of romantic fiction, which she has been writing for financial reasons during her long widowhood. As in many of Maddocks's novels, the feeling of isolation predominates: the heroine has few friends, lives in an isolated country cottage, and has no one to turn to who understands her mixed reactions to Stephen's departure. The reappearance of her rejected suitor, Paul, and the rewarding if uneasy friendship she forms with one of Stephen's 'drop-out' friends, Jan, through whom she begins to understand her son, lead her to reject the idea of forming a relationship with the attractive Paul, who treats her as 'an unreasonable child', and towards a union of compassionate understanding with Jan's father, Ross.

As in most romantic fiction, Maddock's hero and heroine get together in time for a happy, or at least hopeful, ending, however what draws them together is companionship rather than passion, and far more important, and best explored, is what happens to them on the way.

—Judith Summers

MAJORS, E.B. See **RIEFE, Barbara.**

MALPASS, Eric.
Nationality: British. **Born:** Derby, 14 November 1910. **Education:** King Henry VIII School, Coventry. **Military Service:** Royal Air Force Volunteer Reserve, 1941–46. **Relations:** married Muriel Gladys Barnett in 1936; one son. **Career:** cashier, Barclays Bank, Nottingham, 1926–66. **Agent:** Campbell Thomson and McLaughlin Ltd, 1 Kings Mews, London WC1N 2JA, England. **Address:** 216 Breedon Street, Long Eaton, Nottingham NG10 4FD, England.

ROMANCE AND HISTORICAL PUBLICATIONS

Novels (series: Shakespeare Trilogy)

Shakespeare Trilogy:
  Sweet Will. London, Macmillan, 1973; New York, St Martin's Press, 1974.
  The Cleopatra Boy. London, Macmillan, 1974; New York, St Martin's Press, 1975.
  A House of Women. London, Macmillan, and New York, St Martin's Press, 1975.
The Wind Brings Up the Rain. London, Heinemann, and New York, St Martin's Press, 1978.
The Lamplight and the Stars. London, Hamlyn, 1985.
Of Human Frailty. London, Hale, 1987.

OTHER PUBLICATIONS

Novels

Beefy Jones. London, Longman, 1957.
Morning's at Seven. London, Heinemann, 1965; New York, Viking Press, 1966.
At the Height of the Moon. London, Heinemann, 1967.
Fortinbras Has Escaped. London, Pan, and New York, Transworld, 1970.
Oh My Darling Daughter. London, Eyre and Spottiswoode, 1970.
Summer Awakening. London, Corgi, 1978.
The Long Long Dances. London, Corgi, 1978.

*

Eric Malpass comments:
  My subjects present the attractive side of life: good humoured family unity, traditional values, appreciation of nature and the English countryside.

*   *   *

Eric Malpass had his first novel published in Germany, and—in spite of a growing recognition of his achievement by British readers—remains far more celebrated a writer on the Continent than in his native land. Never a 'fashionable' author, his work displays those virtues of the storyteller's art which, in an age where innovation and experiment are often lauded, have tended to be undervalued. The early success of *Morning's at Seven* and his other humorous novels featuring the Pentecost family has been followed by an altogether more lasting and substantial reputation as one of today's leading writers of historical fiction. It is a reputation which he has more than earned in the last decade.

  Foremost of his works in the genre, and arguably the peak of his achievement as a novelist, is the 'Shakespeare' trilogy—*Sweet Will, The Cleopatra Boy*, and *A House of Women*—in which Malpass provides an inspired fictional treatment of the Bard's life from early boyhood to death. The first volume concentrates on the Elizabethan period, detailing Will's courtship and marriage to Anne Hathaway, and his rise to fame as an actor and playwright in London. It also presents a convincing account of Shakespeare's dangerous involvement with Essex and Southampton, and his narrow escape from punishment after their failed rebellion against Elizabeth I. *The Cleopatra Boy* follows the mature writer through his creation of *Hamlet* and *Antony and Cleopatra* during the uneasy days of James I's accession, and his friendship with the catholic Peyre family, which almost implicates him in the Gunpowder Plot of Guy Fawkes and his associates. *A House of Women* describes Shakespeare's last years in Stratford, and the writing of his final plays against a background of

his daughters' enmities, loves, and marriages. Using a strong, often almost poetic prose style, Malpass captures the atmosphere of the Elizabethan and Jacobean ages, contrasting in memorable fashion the robust life of the common people and its precarious nature, continually menaced by filth and plague, and the chilling cruelty of the state.

  The intensity of a knife-edge existence is brilliantly conveyed throughout the trilogy, and from this superbly evoked background Malpass moves in closer to enter the mind of Shakespeare himself. Each novel explores the complexities of this quiet, affable man possessed by the overwhelming need to write, the respectable Stratford burgher and social climber who at the same time contains within himself the soul of a farsighted, supremely gifted artist. Shakespeare's conflicting 'halves' are effectively mirrored by the shifting of focus between rural Stratford and the anthill universe of the capital, each of which exerts its spell on the Bard at different periods of his life. A magnificent achievement, the Shakespeare trilogy places Malpass unmistakably in the front rank of historical novelists.

  With *The Lamplight and the Stars* Malpass leaves the Elizabethan age to describe the fortunes of a Midland family at the turn of this century. Action centres on Nathan Cranswick's move from an industrial town to a rural village on the estate of a local landowner, Robert Heron. The nonconformist preacher's country idyll is threatened by his sister's illicit love for a clergyman who later commits suicide, and is then caught in the upheaval of the Boer War, in which Robert Heron dies. The novel ends with the Cranswick's chastened return to the town, choosing domesticity rather than an illusory retreat from the world. Characters are ably presented, and the 1890s Midland landscape caught to perfection, but with all its merits *The Lamplight and the Stars* fails to achieve the heights of the Shakespeare novels. Somehow it veers rather too closely to family sagaland for total conviction, and falls short of Malpass's finest work.

  Far more impressive, and worthy of comparison with the trilogy, is *Of Human Frailty*, Malpass's 'biographical novel' of Thomas Cranmer, where the author returns to the Tudor period for fictional treatment of another eminent personality of the age. Once more, Malpass investigates the complex nature of a Renaissance man, the shy, unambitious scholar who by a chance meeting rises to power at the court of Henry VIII, and eventually becomes Archbishop of Canterbury. Malpass explores the flawed, yet heroic figure of Cranmer, and through him the palace intrigues and dynastic plots that interweave with England's emergence from domination by Rome. His final, tragic fall, another victim of the merciless Tudor state machine, is quietly but sympathetically rendered. *Of Human Frailty* is a worthy addition to an already excellent body of work, and gives further proof of Malpass's mature skill as a writer of historical fiction.

—Geoffrey Sadler

MANLEY-TUCKER, Audrie.
Pseudonym: Linden Howard. **Nationality:** British. **Born:** 1924. **Died:** 1983.

ROMANCE AND HISTORICAL PUBLICATIONS

Novels (series: Julie Barden)

Leonie. London, Mills and Boon, 1958.
Lost Melody. London, Mills and Boon, 1959.
A Love Song in Springtime. London, Mills and Boon, 1960.
Piper's Gate. London, Mills and Boon, 1960.

Dark Bondage. London, Mills and Boon, 1961.
A Memory of Summer. London, Mills and Boon, 1961; New York, Paperback Library, 1966.
The Promise of Morning. London, Mills and Boon, 1962.
Candlemas Street. London, Mills and Boon, 1963.
The Loved and the Cherished. London, Mills and Boon, 1964.
A Rainbow in My Hand. London, Mills and Boon, 1965.
Shadow of Yesterday. London, Mills and Boon, 1965.
Champagne Girl. London, Mills and Boon, 1967.
Love, Spread Your Wings. London, Mills and Boon, 1967; Toronto, Harlequin, 1973.
Door Without a Key. London, Mills and Boon, 1967; Toronto, Harlequin, 1973.
Julie Barden, District Nurse. London, Mills and Boon, 1968.
Return to Sender. London, Mills and Boon, 1968.
Julie Barden, Doctor's Wife. London, Mills and Boon, 1969.
A Room Without a Door. London, Mills and Boon, 1970.
Assistance Unlimited. London, Mills and Boon, 1971.
Every Goose a Swan. London, Mills and Boon, 1972.
Shetland Summer. London, Mills and Boon, 1973; New York, Pinnacle, 1980.
The Piper in the Hills. London, Mills and Boon, 1974.
Life Begins Tomorrow. London, Mills and Boon, 1975.
Foxglove Country (as Linden Howard). New York, St Martin's Press, 1977; London, Millington, 1978.
Two for Joy. London, Mills and Boon, 1979.
The Devil's Lady (as Linden Howard). London, Millington, and New York, St Martin's Press, 1980.
Tamberlyn. London, Mills and Boon, 1981.
The Lonely Road. London, Mills and Boon, 1983.

*   *   *

Audrie Manley-Tucker's romantic novels fulfil their function—to give enjoyment. It is one of her attributes that she makes really nice people interesting. The heroines are bright modern girls who tackle their problems with courage and spirit. The reader identifies with them straightaway because they have to deal with difficulties that face every girl. Serena, in *Shetland Summer*, for instance, is in love with a married man but is realistic enough to see there is no (happy) future in that. With characteristic courage she decides to make a clean break and goes off to Shetland.

Another bonus of Manley-Tucker's novels is her excellent use of description: 'That hat in the milliner's window looked like an upturned rush basket spilling artificial daises and had two long streamers of pale green ribbon hanging down the back'. An unusual little shop, a village garden, or the Scottish Highlands become vivid verbal paintings. The descriptions are so deftly inserted that they never hold up the narrative but enhance it.

As topical as today's news is the problem of the adopted child. Should she try to find her 'real' mother and risk hurting her adoptive parents or stifle her curiosity and be content with her present environment? Sandy Drummond, in *Every Goose a Swan* is determined to seek out her 'mother', and she carries the reader along in her search.

With very few exceptions none of Manley-Tucker's heroines has glamorous jobs or goes to exotic places. They have ordinary jobs and mostly live at home with their parents. The same could be said of the men, the majority of whom are likeable and worthy of the heroines. The few children appearing are life-like and not at all angelic.

Gothic novels by Manley-Tucker are written under the name of Linden Howard. These conform to the usual gothic tradition of a young girl facing a new life in an ancient mansion set in the country, and also facing, although she does not know it, hostility and danger. Manley-Tucker shows her adaptability in being able to tackle con-

vincingly novels with so many restricted plot conventions. *Foxglove Country* and *The Devil's Lady* are excellent examples of this genre. The former novel has a powerful character (the grandfather) and a charming heroine in Sara Pryce. The background of the desolate Welsh Beacons adds to the tension and menace. There are accidents, death, and love stories woven into this fast-moving and convincing book. Manley-Tucker's descriptive gifts and perceptive insight into character makes this gothic compelling reading.

—Lucy Rogers and Peggy York

————

MANN, Deborah. See **BLOOM, Ursula.**

————

MANNERS, Alexandra.
Pseudonym for Anne Rundle. **Other Pseudonyms:** Georgianna Bell; Marianne Lamont; Joanne Marshall; Jeanne Saunders. **Nationality:** British. **Born:** Anne Lamb, Berwick-on-Tweed, Northumberland. **Education:** army schools, and Berwick High School for Girls. **Relations:** married Edwin Charles Rundle in 1949; one daughter and two sons. **Career:** civil servant, Berwick, Newcastle-upon-Tyne, and London, to 1951. **Recipient:** Romantic Novelists Association Netta Muskett award, 1967, and major award, 1970, 1971. **Agent:** John McLaughlin, Campbell Thomson and McLaughlin, 1 Kings Mews, London WC1N 2JA, England.

ROMANCE AND HISTORICAL PUBLICATIONS

Novels (series: Island)

Passionate Jade (as Georgianna Bell). London, Fontana, 1969; New York, Pocket Books, 1981.
The Stone Maiden. New York, Putnam, 1973; London Millington, 1974.
Spindrift (as Jeanne Saunders). London, Hale, 1974.
Candles in the Wood. New York, Putnam, 1974; London, Millington, 1975.
The Singing Swans. New York, Putnam, 1975; London, Millington, 1976.
Sable Hunter. New York, Putnam, 1977; London, Collins, 1978; as *Cardigan Square*, New York, Berkley, 1977.
Wildford's Daughter. New York, Putnam, 1978; as *The White Moths*, London, Collins, 1979.
Echoing Yesterday (Island). London, Corgi, 1981.
Karran Kinrade (Island). London, Corgi, 1982.
The Red Bird (Island). London, Corgi, 1984.
The Gaming House (Island). London, Corgi, 1984.

Novels as Anne Rundle

The Moon Marriage. London, Hurst and Blackett, 1967.
Swordlight. London, Hurst and Blackett, 1968.
Forest of Fear. London, Hurst and Blackett, 1969.
Rakehell. London, Hurst and Blackett, 1970.
Lost Lotus. London, Hale, 1972.
Amberwood. London, Hale, 1972; New York, Bantam, 1974.
Heronbrook. New York, Bantam, 1974; London, Hale, 1975.
Judith Lammeter. London, Hale, 1976.
Grey Ghyll. London, Hale, 1978; New York, St Martin's Press, 1979.
Moonbranches. New York, Macmillan, 1986.

Novels as Joanne Marshall

Cuckoo at Candlemas. London, Jenkins, 1968.

Cat on a Broomstick. London, Jenkins, 1969.
The Dreaming Tower. London, Jenkins, 1969.
Flower of Silence. London, Mills and Boon, 1970; New York, Avon, 1974.
Babylon Was Dust. London, Mills and Boon, 1971.
Wild Boar Wood. London, Mills and Boon, 1972; New York, Avon, 1973.
The Trellised Walk. London, Mills and Boon, 1973.
Sea-Song. London, Mills and Boon, 1973.
Follow a Shadow. London, Collins, and New York, Putnam, 1974.
Valley of Tall Chimneys. London, Collins, 1975.
The Peacock Bed. London, Collins, and New York, St Martin's Press, 1978.

Novels as Marianne Lamont

Dark Changeling. London, Hurst and Blackett, 1970; New York, Avon, 1973.
Green Glass Moon. London, Hurst and Blackett, 1970.
Bitter Bride-Bed. London, Hurst and Blackett, 1971.
Nine Moons Wasted. London, Constable, and New York, Putnam, 1977.
Horns of the Moon. London, Constable, 1979.
A Serpent's Tooth. London, Constable, 1983.

OTHER PUBLICATIONS

Other (for children)

Dragonscale. London, Hutchinson, 1969.
Tamlane. London, Hutchinson, 1970.
Last Act (as Joanne Marshall). London, Collins, and New York, Putnam, 1976.

* * *

The early books by Alexandra Manners are gothic romances but, after three novels, she ceased to use as many gothic elements and began to write historical romances. History plays a major role in each of her works, and she portrays the times and places realistically. She also shows an ability to depict children well, a theme appearing in most of her books.

The Stone Maiden is a Victorian gothic set near Stirling in Scotland. The title comes from an island rock formation which broods over the area. Now orphaned, Maggie comes to live with her father's relatives. She is entangled in the undercurrents of the past as well as the present, and is simultaneously welcomed and rejected by her new family. The neighbour's son, Buck, provides the romantic interest, and is compared to Heathcliff throughout the novel. However, aside from his brooding good looks, there seems little resemblance. The reader discovers early on who really wants to harm Maggie. There are many overheard conversations—a device exploited in most of Manners's works. The story is somewhat overwritten, and at times the plot appears too contrived to convince fully.

Candles in the Wood opens with the seven-year-old daughter of a servant to the Scottish Grants of Gallowmerry as the narrator. One night, Helen's mother runs away with a valet, her father is transported for illegal whisky smuggling, and Helen is traumatized by the discovery of a fake body in a mediaeval torture device in the dungeon of the castle. Years later, having been educated with the money her father made in Australia, Helen returns to the Grant's house incognito. She is accepted as a friend, proving herself worthy of the family's sanction before her real identity is revealed. The child Manners features in this novel is the ghost of a girl allegedly buried in the foundations of the castle centuries earlier and who,

using Helen, acts as a catalyst affecting all the characters' lives. The youngest son provides the romantic element. The complicated plot holds the reader's interest, and the evil-doer is too obvious to be immediately suspected.

In *The Singing Swans,* ten-year-old Meraud's prostitute mother is murdered in Paris. Her Scottish father, who may or may not be the killer, takes Meraud to his home on the Island of Skye, where she tries to win his love. She absorbs the superstitious customs and legends of the villagers and attempts to discover who is trustworthy, other than the neighbouring 13-year-old boy who rescues her after one of two attempts are made on her life. This eerie story is permeated with evil but is not wholly convincing or enjoyable.

As a child Sable Martin (in *Sable Hunter*), a young servant girl in late 18th-century England, watches the Hunter family through their mansion windows and falls in love with the younger son Morgan. She becomes a companion to an elderly woman and learns how to speak and conduct herself properly. Eventually, Sable is driven away by an insidious plot and rescued by Adam Hunter, a member of parliament. Proving herself to be intelligent, she becomes his assistant and works to eliminate the practice of kidnapping young children for prostitution. Morgan's reappearance results in a duel, pregnancy, and Sable's marriage to Adam. Sable's increasing love for her unresponsive husband fails to impress him until danger threatens them both. This political romance teaches as well as entertains.

Wildford's Daughter is Emma, the spoiled only child of banker Luke Wildford. His frigid wife flees her womanizing husband, who thinks he can buy whatever he desires, and Emma elects to stay with her father. By the time she is 18 Emma has acquired some of her father's worst traits: arrogance, stubbornness, and jealousy—but she has a tender heart too. She helps the quaker Elizabeth Fry alleviate some of the suffering of the female inmates of Newgate prison. Even there, her naivety gets her into trouble when a blackmailer promises to remain silent about a murder Emma has tried to cover up. Her youth and inexperience also cause problems in her love life; she falls for a ruthless, ambitious man, but refuses to accept the truth about him. Her father's overseer rescues her from one dangerous escapade after another. Interesting, complex characters enhance a well told tale.

The 'Island' series charts the trials and tribulations of Karran Kinrade. *Echoing Yesterday*, the first in the series, sets the scene and depicts the passionate courtship between Clemence and Luke, Karran's parents. *Karran Kinrade*, *The Red Bird*, and *The Gaming House* follow Karran through a turbulent childhood to adulthood, with all the problems of growing up in a small community where suspicion is rife and 'outsiders' are barely tolerated. Manners's gripping saga is full of romance, excitement, and tragedy.

Manners seems entranced with the underside of life and her works have an air of melancholy. She shows both the dark and the good sides of her characters, and contrasts the elegance and poverty of the times. Her works are uneven in quality but are often interesting particularly for their depiction of local customs and settings.

—Andrea Lee Shuey

———

MANTEL, Hilary (Mary).
Nationality: British. **Born:** Glossop, Derbyshire, 6 July 1952.
Education: London School of Economics, 1970; Sheffield University, Yorkshire, B. Jurisprudence, 1973. **Relations:** married Gerald McEwen in 1972. **Career:** social worker in a geriatric hospital, 1974–75; English teacher, Botswana, 1977, and Lobatse Secondary School, 1979–80; lived in Jeddah, Saudi Arabia, 1981–86. **Recipient:** Naipaul memorial prize, for travel writing, 1987; Winifred Holtby prize, 1990; Cheltenham fiction prize, 1991; *Sunday Express* award, for *A Place of Greater Safety*, 1992. Fellow,

Royal Society of Literature, 1990. **Agent:** Bill Hamilton, A.M. Heath, 79 St Martin's Lane, London WC2N 4AA, England.

ROMANCE AND HISTORICAL PUBLICATIONS

Novels

Every Day Is Mother's Day. London, Chatto and Windus, 1985.
Vacant Possession. London, Chatto and Windus, 1986.
Eight Months on Ghazzah Street. London, Viking, and New York, Viking, 1988.
Fludd. London, Viking, 1989.
A Place of Greater Safety. London, Viking, 1992.

OTHER PUBLICATIONS

Novel

A Change of Climate. London, Viking, 1994.

*   *   *

What strikes the reader of Hilary Mantel's novels most forcibly is the remarkable versatility of her writing. True, her first two novels, *Every Day Is Mother's Day* and *Vacant Possession*, share not just their mood of black comedy, but also their main characters and, most unusually, to some extent their plots. Though they may be enjoyed (if that is the word for such a catalogue of horrors) separately, only when read in sequence do they offer clarification of some of the obscure and alarming happenings chronicled there. Having read both novels, the reader is then able to appreciate the economy of the author's writing and the neatness with which apparently chance incidents illuminate one another, and demonstrate the clear line of inevitability of the dreadful events taking place.

With her third novel, *Eight Months on Ghazzah Street*, however, we find a complete change—of style, of construction, and of mood. Written from Mantel's own experiences in Saudi Arabia, the novel may be seen as a personal catharsis. Mantel uses her novelist's craft to get rid of her feelings of shock and indignation at the way in which Westerners—and western women in particular—are regarded and treated in an arab kingdom. (Very likely the Westerners' inevitable awareness that they are living there, and putting up with the humiliating restrictions purely for the sake of money, plays some part in their sense of mortification, deepening their resentment.) Undoubtedly, this is Mantel's most personal novel, based on something she had experienced and could not distance herself from. Involved personally, she is unable to find anything amusing in the events, and so the comic element of her first two novels is missing. Instead, we find ourselves sharing the claustrophobic terrors of a western woman virtually imprisoned in her silent apartment, constantly aware of being watched, and also experiencing incomprehensible incidents. The indefinable terrors are reflected in the shadowy story line. Wilfully, what promises to be a recognizable form of entertainment, that of a conventional thriller, offers no satisfactory conclusion, no neat tying up of threads. Instead, mirroring the heroine's disintegration under the relentless pressure of the alien heat and a hostile culture, there are vague explanations, sudden disappearances, figures noticed briefly, and seen no more. Given Mantel's skill in constructing a neat plot, we can only assume that the uncertainties and the inconclusive tailings off are a deliberate strategy to reproduce the distressing confusions of a disintegrating mind.

This sharp realism, employed to record obliquely the break-up of the Shores's marriage, and of the disintegration of their personalities, is very different from the matter-of-fact reporting of macabre events in Mantel's earlier novels. In these, the realism of familiar details heightens the readers' shocked recognition of evil personified by Muriel Axon. In Mantel's third book her main preoccupation is not with the nature of evil, or the possibility of satanic possession (as the title of the second novel makes clear, Muriel's empty mind and heart lie open to be taken over by the forces of evil), but with the stresses and distress of a woman's mind. The realism here is centred on Frances's feelings and thoughts against an alien background that affects her deeply yet remains shadowy: there is no need to flesh it out in detail, as it is merely a background, however cataclysmatic in its effect.

Mantel's fourth novel, *Fludd*, breaks new ground again. Though she stresses that her north country village of Fetherhoughton is a product of her imagination (and thereby obliquely claims that her intention had been to create a convincing picture of a real village), realism is not her aim, and her novel is a fairy tale. In her first two novels she was concerned with evil, but in *Fludd* her concern is with goodness. There are various miracles in this tale, brought about by the visitation of Fludd, the mysterious curate, who is perhaps a reincarnation of a 17th-century alchemist and scholar, and the greatest of these miracles is the liberation of the young nun, Philomena, through her brief love affair with Fludd. It is a strangely joyful, even merry tale, and if it mocks the readers' bafflement, it comforts them and makes them laugh as well.

A Place of Greater Safety is yet another departure for her. It takes as its heroes historical figures of the French Revolution: Camille Desmoulins, Danton, and Robespierre. As the author herself points out, there is little known of their lives before the Revolution, which gives Mantel the freedom to use her imagination in order to elaborate on what little is known of their early years. She uses her imagination equally freely to describe their thoughts and feelings, and to report their conversations during the terrible years when they were in power, and during the last days and hours before they too went to the guillotine.

She employs a large cast to play out the drama of the Terror, and the metaphor of a play seems peculiarly apt in this vast novel which contains almost no description, and in which the main action is reported almost entirely through conversation. The result is an odd dryness, particularly striking in the last two parts of the novel, almost as if the events described were too appalling to be evoked visually. No black comedy here, no occasion for laughter, no juxtaposition of good and evil. Mantel passes no judgement, singles out no villains. The novel is strange—unexpected in its methods and achievements, leaving the reader to wonder which direction Mantel's undoubted talent will take next.

—Hana Sambrook

————

MARCHANT, Catherine.   See **COOKSON, Catherine.**

————

MARCUS, Joanna.   See **ANDREWS, Lucilla.**

————

MARINO, Susan.   See **ELLIS, Julie.**

————

MARLOWE, Katherine.   See **ALLEN, Charlotte Vale.**

————

MARLOWE, Michael. See **SALISBURY, Carola.**

———

MARSH, Jean.

Pseudonym for Evelyn Marshall. **Other Pseudonym:** Lesley Bourne. **Nationality:** British. **Born:** Pershore, Worcestershire, 2 December 1897. **Education:** Bournville High School; Halesowen Grammar School, Worcestershire; Oxford Senior Certificate for teaching. **Relations:** married Gerald Eric Marshall in 1917 (died 1964); one son (deceased) and one daughter. **Career:** teacher in Halesowen until 1919, then journalist for Thomson and Leng groups until late 1920s; contract writer for Amalgamated Press group until 1939; broadcaster during World War II; writer for *Children's Hour* until 1956. **Died:** 6 April 1991.

ROMANCE AND HISTORICAL PUBLICATIONS

Novels

Sand Against the Wind. London, Hale, 1973.
Loving Partnership. London, Hale, 1978; Rolling Meadows, Illinois, Aston Hall, 1979.
The Family at Castle Trevissa. London, Hale, 1979.
Sawdust and Dreams. London, Hale, 1980.
Mistress of Tanglewood. London, Hale, 1981.
Unbidden Dream. London, Hale, 1981.
The Rekindled Flame. London, Hale, 1982.
The Foolish Love. London, Hale, 1982.
The Divided Heart. London, Hale, 1983.
Sanctuary for Louise. London, Hale, 1983.
Quest for Love. London, Hale, 1984.
Destiny at Castle Rock. London, Hale, 1985.
Pride of Vallon. London, Hale, 1985.
The Golden Parakeet. London, Hale, 1986.
Loving Heritage. London, Hale, 1987.
Island of Dreams. London, Hale, 1987.
Mission to Argana. London, Hale, 1988.
Love in Hazard. London, Hale, 1989.
The Wayward Heart. London, Hale, 1989.
Shades of Aphrodite. London, Hale, 1992.

OTHER PUBLICATIONS

Novels

The Shore House Mystery. London, Hamilton, 1931.
Murder Next Door. London, Long, 1933.
Death Stalks the Bride. London, Long, 1943.
Identity Unwanted. London, Long, 1951.
Death Visits the Circus. London, Long, 1953.
The Pattern Is Murder. London, Long, 1954.
Death Among the Stars. London, Long, 1955.
Death at Peak Hour. London, Long, 1957.

Plays

Radio Serials: *Mystery of Castle Rock Zoo*, 1945; *On the Trail of the Albatross*, 1949; *Judith and the Dolls*, 1950; *Secret of the Pygmy Herd*, 1951; *Adventure with a Boffin*, 1952; *Death Visits the Circus*, 1952; *Ghost Ship*, 1952; *Helen Had a Daughter*, 1953; *Johnny Pilgrim Again*, 1953; *The Small Beginning*, 1954; *Valley of Silent Sound*, 1956; *The White Sapphire*, 1956; *Pocahontas*.

Other (for children)

On the Trail of the Albatross (adaptation of radio serial). London, Burke, 1950.
Secret of the Pygmy Herd (adaptation of radio serial). London, Burke, 1951.
Trouble for Tembo (as Lesley Bourne). London, University of London Press, 1958.
Adventure with a Boffin (adaptation of radio serial). London, University of London Press, 1962.
The Valley of Silent Sound (adaptation of radio serial). London, University of London Press, 1962.

Other

Bewdley, XV Century Sanctuary Town, Kinver, Staffordshire, Halmar, 1979.
All Saints' Centenary, Kinver, Staffordshire, Halmar, 1980.

*

Jean Marsh commented (1982):

I began my writing career at the end of World War I with the object, of necessity, of making a living at it. Being fortunate enough to have a contract with the multi-magazine publishers Amalgamated Press, this was possible. Short stories and serials were turned out as required by the group editor. With the advent of the 1939 war, most writings and broadcast talks were geared to the war effort both on home and overseas programmes. But at this time I discovered the delight of writing the kind of detective novels I had always wanted to write. These paved the way to writing adventure serials for BBC *Children's Hour* when the war ended. This was also the period when I wrote a number of adult radio plays and documentaries. After *Children's Hour* closed, I returned to the romantic novels written earlier as magazine serials. But now they have a country background, many of them featuring animals as well as human characters. These have proved popular first as series in *Woman's Story Magazine*, later in book form. I am still doing them. Fortunately even in one's eighties the creative urge is as strong as ever. It's the fingers that become a little stiff on the typewriter keys.

*   *   *

Jean Marsh's novels are a blend of the magazine fiction she cut her teeth on in the early part of her lengthy career, and the detective fiction which she took to writing during World War II. They are set in small, inward-looking and closely-knit communities crowded with a multitude of characters whose lives and problems form the core of her plots. Romance takes second place to outside events, such as business problems, and to friendship. Her heroes and heroines are drawn together less by an immediate passion than by a particular situation in which they find themselves allied. As the situation unfolds, so their alliance develops into a stronger tie to which there is no real opposition.

Her heroines are usually professional women: veterinary surgeons (*Unbidden Dream*), nurses (*Island of Dreams*, *The Golden Parakeet*), or accountants (*The Rekindled Flame*), If they are seeking fulfilment, it is not necessarily through romance. For example, nurse Amanda Hicks in *The Golden Parakeet*, who takes a job with a large construction company's hospital in the Andes, is in reality setting out on a private pilgrimage to revisit the country where she was brought up and where her father died in a tragic earthquake accident. This immediately unites her with Dr Mark Donnelly, whose own brother has apparently died in a more recent earthquake. However, while handling her notoriously difficult boss, Dr Ettrick, with aplomb, Amanda hangs back from any involvement with

Mark, almost as if she does not feel herself worthy of him. Believing him to be involved with the beautiful Della Marchant, she selflessly helps him unravel the mystery of his brother's disappearance, showing her worth through her skills as a nurse and an interpreter.

Amanda is typical of Marsh's heroines in being more confident in her professional role than in her 'role' as a woman. For in relation to men, Marsh's heroines are passive, content for the men in their lives to do the running and, later, to decide their fate. This old-fashioned attitude is echoed by her careful heroes, who will not make a move towards the women they secretly love until any complicated emotional or financial situations of their own have been fully sorted out. Matt Erskine, the hero of *Island of Dreams*, is involved in an uncomfortable business deal with his widowed sister-in-law Anthea, who, unknown to him, is scheming to trick him out of a fair share of the Corfu estate he owned jointly with his late brother. He is attracted to Claire, a private nurse who comes to Corfu to care for his invalid aunt Flora, but makes no move towards her. It is only when Flora and Claire, through their own detective work, uncover Anthea's duplicity, thus freeing Matt from his financial burdens, that he feels free to declare his love for Claire.

Pride of Vallon illustrates another important Marsh trait: the synonymity of relationship and marriage, particularly in the hero's eyes. Melita Kane accompanies her famous film-star aunt, Lorna, to the Camargue in southern France, where Lorna hopes to persuade her ex-lover, composer Maurice Delorme, to let her film at Vallon, his ranching estate. But Maurice's adopted son, Antoine, heir to Vallon, is against such a venture, and Melita finds herself torn between agreeing with him and supporting her aunt, who is also her employer. Eventually Melita earns Antoine's love by helping him uncover a ring of horse thieves. Still she is uncertain if they have a future, and she tells him openly that it is up to him to decide their fate. Given this go-ahead, he immediately announces their engagement at a large party—without giving Melita the chance to say yes or no.

Melita is more at home nursing a new-born foal in a stable than in the glamorous world of show business, and in her ability to relate to animals she is similar to many Marsh heroines. Marsh's settings are predominantly rural: farms (*Loving Heritage*), wild-life parks (*Unbidden Dream*), and riding schools (*Mistress of Tanglewood*); her characters often work in professions which bring them in close contact with a wide variety of animals. In *Sawdust and Dreams* the story of Melissa, the teenage daughter of a circus-owning family, who is suddenly called upon to take over her sister-in-law's elephant act, we encounter the joys and difficulties of dealing with animals which are, though apparently tame, still wild at heart. In *Unbidden Dream* the heroine, Sue, a veterinary surgeon, has to cope with anything from a wounded lion to a baby giraffe. *The Family at Castle Trevissa* features, among other animals, a sick dolphin and a shoal of stranded seals. Though she tends at times towards a sentimental attitude to her animals (piglets are being fattened up for market on the farm in *The Rekindled Flame*, but there's not so much as a whisper of the word abattoir), one feels at times that it is only in their relationship to animals that the characters dare reveal their true warmth. Marsh deals with the problems of caring for animals with compassion and authority, and this lends a great deal of weight to her work.

Marsh's description of people and settings was, at times, sketchy, but the twists and turns of plot were important to her.

For many years Marsh was a writer of detective fiction; it seems that she was unable to stop herself placing her characters under some kind of threat. Yet the denouements of these mysteries are sometimes disappointingly handled, and might well have benefited from some further twist at the end.

—Judith Summers

MARSH, Joan. See **WOODWARD, Lilian.**

MARSH, John. See **WOODWARD, Lilian.**

MARSHALL, Edison (Tesla).
Pseudonym: Hall Hunter. **Nationality:** American. **Born:** Rensselaer, Indiana, 28 August 1894. **Education:** University of Oregon, Eugene, 1913–16. **Military Service:** United States Army Ordnance Field Services, 1918: lieutenant; educational film writer for Department of Defense during World War II. **Relations:** married Agnes Sharp Flythe in 1920; one son and one daughter. **Career:** hunter and explorer; freelance writer. **Recipient:** O. Henry award, for short story, 1921. M.A.: University of Oregon, 1941. **Died:** 29 October 1967.

ROMANCE AND HISTORICAL PUBLICATIONS

Novels

Benjamin Blake. New York, Farrar and Rinehart, 1941.
Great Smith. New York, Farrar and Rinehart, 1943; London, Aldor, 1947.
The Upstart. New York, Farrar Straus, 1945; London, World Distributors, 1959.
Yankee Pasha: The Adventures of Jason Starbuck. New York, Farrar Straus, 1948; London, Redman, 1950.
Castle in the Swamp: A Tale of Old Carolina. New York, Farrar Straus, 1948; London, Muller, 1949.
Gypsy Sixpence. New York, Farrar Straus, 1949; London, Muller, 1950.
The Infinite Woman. New York, Farrar Straus, 1950; London, Muller, 1951.
The Viking. New York, Farrar Straus, 1951; London, Muller, 1952.
The Bengal Tiger: A Tale of India (as Hall Hunter). New York, Doubleday, 1952; as *Rogue Gentleman* (as Edison Marshall), New York, Popular Library, 1963.
American Captain. New York, Farrar Straus, 1954; as *Captain's Saga*, London, Muller, 1955.
Caravan to Xanadu: A Novel of Marco Polo. New York, Farrar Straus, 1954; London, Muller, 1955.
The Gentleman. New York, Farrar Straus, and London, Muller, 1956.
The Inevitable Hour: A Novel of Martinique. New York, Putnam, 1957; London, Muller, 1958.
Princess Sophia. New York, Doubleday, 1958; London, Muller, 1959.
The Pagan King. New York, Doubleday, 1959; London, Muller, 1960.
Earth Giant. New York, Doubleday, 1960; London, Muller, 1961.
West with the Vikings. New York, Doubleday, 1961.
The Conqueror. New York, Doubleday, 1962.
Cortez and Marina. New York, Doubleday, 1963.
The Lost Colony. New York, Doubleday, 1964.

Short Stories

The Heart of Little Shikara and Other Stories. Boston, Little Brown, 1922; London, Hodder and Stoughton, 1924.
Love Stories of India. New York, Farrar Straus, 1950.

OTHER PUBLICATIONS

Novels

The Voice of the Pack. Boston, Little Brown, and London, Hodder and Stoughton, 1920.
The Strength of the Pines. Boston, Little Brown, and London, Hodder and Stoughton, 1921.
The Snowshoe Trail. Boston, Little Brown, and London, Hodder and Stoughton, 1921.
Shepherds of the Wild. Boston, Little Brown, and London, Hodder and Stoughton, 1922.
The Sky Line of Spruce. Boston, Little Brown, 1922; as *The Sky-Line*, London, Hodder and Stoughton, 1922.
The Land of Forgotten Men. Boston, Little Brown, 1923; London, Hodder and Stoughton, 1924.
The Isle of Retribution. Boston, Little Brown, and London, Hodder and Stoughton, 1923.
The Death Bell. New York, Garden City, 1924.
Seward's Folly. Boston, Little Brown, and London, Hodder and Stoughton, 1924.
The Sleeper of the Moonlit Ranges. New York, Cosmopolitan, and London, Hodder and Stoughton, 1925.
Child of the Wild: A Story of Alaska. New York, Cosmopolitan, and London, Hodder and Stoughton, 1926.
The Deadfall. New York, Cosmopolitan, and London, Hodder and Stoughton, 1927.
The Far Call. New York, Cosmopolitan, and London, Hodder and Stoughton, 1928.
The Fish Hawk. New York, Cosmopolitan, and London, Hodder and Stoughton, 1929.
Singing Arrows. London, Hodder and Stoughton, 1929.
The Missionary. New York, Cosmopolitan, and London, Hodder and Stoughton, 1930.
The Doctor of Lonesome River. New York, Cosmopolitan, and London, Hodder and Stoughton, 1931.
The Deputy at Snow Mountain. New York, Kinsey, and London, Hodder and Stoughton, 1932.
Forlorn Island. New York, Kinsey, and London, Hodder and Stoughton, 1932.
The Light in the Jungle. New York, Kinsey, 1933; as *Victory in the Jungle*, London, Hodder and Stoughton, 1933.
The Splendid Quest. New York, Kinsey, 1934.
Ogden's Strange Story. New York, Kinsey, 1934.
Dian of the Lost Land. New York, Kinsey, 1935; as *The Lost Land*, New York, Curtis, 1966.
Sam Campbell, Gentleman. New York, Kinsey, 1935; London, Hodder and Stoughton, 1936.
The Stolen God. New York, Kinsey, 1936; London, Hodder and Stoughton, 1937.
The White Brigand. New York, Kinsey, 1937; London, Hodder and Stoughton, 1938.
Darzee, Girl of India. New York, Kinsey, 1937; as *The Flower Dancer*. London, Hodder and Stoughton, 1937.
The Jewel of Malabar. New York, Kinsey, and London, Hodder and Stoughton, 1938.

Other

Ocean Gold (for children). New York, Harper, 1925.
Campfire Courage: The Woodsmoke Boys in the Canadian Rockies (for children). New York, Harper, 1926.
Shikar and Safari: Reminiscences of Jungle Hunting. New York, Farrar Straus, 1947; London, Museum Press, 1950.
The Heart of the Hunter (autobiography). New York, McGraw Hill, 1956; London, Muller, 1957.

*

Film Adaptations: *Son of Fury*, 1942, from the novel *Benjamin Blake*; *Treasure of the Golden Condor*, 1953, from the novel *Jewel of Mahabar*; *Yankee Pasha*, 1954; *The Viking*, 1958, from the novel *The Vikings*.

*   *   *

Edison Marshall's long career was a sweeping curve upward to the position of the foremost historical novelist of the 1940s and 1950s, but since his death the reputation of his fiction has not so much declined as that fiction has simply been ignored. In spite of his success, including ten films based upon his works, he perhaps expected his fate when he said, 'I am an anachronism, and my career is *contre tempes*'.

His work falls neatly into two groups on the basis of both chronology and subject matter. Until the late 1930s, most of his writing consisted of short stories and magazine serials in the adventure-thriller genre. Many were based upon his own hunting expeditions around the world, especially in southern Asia and Alaska. 'The Heart of Little Shikara', winner of the O. Henry prize in 1921, *The Light in the Jungle*, and *The Jewel of Malabar* are examples of the Asian stories. Even more prevalent are those set in Alaska or the American northwest; there are more than a dozen. Marshall stated that he was 'Obsessed by nature to a degree of passion that would floor Freud,' and these works are filled with close and accurate descriptions of nature, often to emphasize its redeeming power of various city types who find themselves suddenly amidst its wonders, as in *The Voice of the Pack, Shepherds of the Wild*, and *The Isle of Retribution*. Though the plots are often repetitive, these works can still have appeal for lovers of adventure and admirers of nature.

Even more successful with readers than these adventure stories were the historical novels beginning with *Benjamin Blake*. Ranging throughout history and varied in locale, they were novels of action and romance. Some centred on actual persons, as *Great Smith* (Captain John Smith) and *The Infinite Woman* (based on Lola Montez), while the central characters of others were imaginary: *Yankee Pasha* and *Gypsy Sixpence*. A major success was *The Viking*, with the legendary Ogier the Dane as its hero. Whether set in early America, India, the Caribbean, or Norseland, and whatever the time period, Marshall's novels were well-researched, fast-paced, and colourful in the presentation of customs and sights. The heroes and heroines were generally noble in deed, if not in title, and the sexual element was treated conservatively. With Marshall's many excellent qualities as a historical novelist, it may be that the lack of explicit sex is the reason for his being replaced by other novelists of lesser talent who provide titillation in historical guise for their readers. If so, that says more about the readers about than Marshall's ability as novelist.

—Earl F. Bargainnier

———

MARSHALL, Joanne.   See **MANNERS, Alexandra.**

———

MARSHALL, Rosamond (Van der Zee).
Nationality: American. **Born:** New York City, 17 October 1902. **Education:** Miss Eaton's School, Pasadena, California; Lycée des Jeunes Filles, Dijon; Real Gymnasium, Vienna; University of Munich. **Relations:** married Albert Earl Marshall (second marriage); one daughter. **Career:** amateur mountaineer. **Died:** 13 November 1957.

Novels

Kitty. New York, Duell, 1943; London, Redman, 1956.
Duchess Hotspur. New York, Prentice Hall, 1946; London, Redman, 1958.
Celeste. New York, Prentice Hall, 1949.
Laird's Choice. New York, Prentice Hall, 1951; London, Redman, 1952.
Bond of the Flesh. New York, Doubleday, 1952; London, Redman, 1953.
Jane Hadden. New York, Prentice Hall, 1952; London, Redman, 1953.
The Temptress. New York, New American Library, 1952.
The General's Wench. New York, Prentice Hall, 1953; London, Redman, 1954.
The Dollmaster. New York, Prentice Hall, 1954; London, Redman, 1955; as *Mistress of Rogues*, New York, Popular Library, 1956.
The Loving Meddler. New York, Doubleday, 1954; London, Redman, 1955.
Rogue Cavalier. New York, Doubleday, 1955; London, Redman, 1956.
The Rib of the Hawk. New York, Appleton Century Crofts, 1956; London, Redman, 1957.
Captain Ironhand. New York, Appleton Century Crofts, and London, Redman, 1957.
The Bixby Girls. New York, Doubleday, 1957; London, Redman, 1958.

Other novels (in French): *L'Enfant du Cirque*, 1930; *La Main d'Acier*, 1931; *Plaisirs d'Amour*, 1932; *Le Vaisseau Fanôme*, 1933; *Vengeance du Sheik*, 1934; *Mystères de Chinatown*, 1934; *Mystères de Londres*, 1935.

Other (for children)

None But the Brave: A Story of Holland. Boston, Houghton Mifflin, 1942; London, Hutchinson, 1946.
The Treasure of Shafto. New York, Messner, 1946.

*   *   *

The traditional Horatio Alger 'rags to riches' success story based upon hard work and righteous living has long been a favourite in the world of adult fairy tales, but Rosamond Marshall gave the old theme a surprising new twist with her best-selling period romance *Kitty.* This quite different success story tells of a nameless child of the 18th-century London gutters, her virginity sold for a few pence to a lecherous sexton when she was but eight years old by the heartless bawd who holds her bond. Kitty lives by petty theft and prostitution, until one day her gamin charm catches the eye of a great painter in want of a model. Thomas Gainsborough recognizes great beauty disguised by dirt, and the bath and arbitrary surname he provides for the lovely waif are her keys to a new life. Working her way up from man to man, finally attaining a peak of success as a duchess, Kitty has something the 'Moll Flanders' version of fictional harlot lacked—a heart. She never forgets her own miserable beginnings, nor ceases to pity the plight of other child victims. At the height of her triumph, Kitty risks her own safety and happiness for the benefit of the wretched mill-children on her inherited estate.

As though to prove that a rake can progress in either direction, Marshall followed the success of *Kitty* with another lighthearted romp, *Duchess Hotspur,* the tale of a high-born lady with an eclectic taste in lusty men, who falls in love at last with a penniless journalist. Duchess Percy thinks at first that it will be a simple matter to bring her scruffy lover up to a standard of appearances acceptable to her privileged circle by means of a few judicious gifts, but not so. He is a proud fellow, who regards such treatment as an insult to his manhood. A compromise must be reached between the wanton, lovely duchess and the stiff-necked quill-pusher, and it makes for a rousing tale.

Marshall's books, considered daring in their day, are unlikely now to raise any eyebrows. Good humoured pre-Regency fun and games, they make cheerfully diverting bedtime stories.

—Joan McGrath

———

MARTIN, Rhona.
Nationality: British. **Born:** London, 3 June 1922. **Education:** private schools; Redland High School, Bristol; West of England College of Art, 1937–39. **Relations:** married 1) Peter Wilfrid Alcock in 1941 (divorced 1957), two daughters; 2) Thomas Neighbour in 1959 (divorced). **Career:** fashion artist, Willsons Ltd, Bristol, 1940–41; clerk, Fire Guard Office, Weston-super-Mare, 1942–45; freelance theatrical designer, 1946–48; catering manager, Club Labamba, Tunbridge Wells, 1963–68; assistant manager, Odeon, Sevenoaks, 1968–72; accounts secretary and office manager, Crown Chemical Company, Lamberhurst, Kent, 1972–79; then full-time writer. **Recipient:** Georgette Heyer prize, for historical novel, 1978. **Agent:** John McLaughlin, Campbell Thomson and McLaughlin Ltd, 1 Kings Mews, London WC1N 2JA, England. **Address:** c/o Bodley Head, 20 Vauxhall Bridge Road, London SW1V 2SA, England.

Novels

Gallows Wedding. London, Bodley Head, 1978; New York, Coward McCann, 1979.
Mango Walk. London, Bodley Head, 1981; New York, Bantam, 1982.
The Unicorn Summer. London, Bodley Head, 1984.

Novel

Goodbye, Sally. London, Bodley Head, 1987.

Other

Writing Historical Fiction. London, A. and C. Black, and New York, St Martin's Press, 1988.

*

Rhona Martin comments:
I am not sure that I would classify my writing as either romance or gothic—but then classification is in any case best left to the reader. With me, a novel comes from first one idea and then two, usually a character and a situation, which interact and grow in darkness until they are gnawing a hole in me and have to be got out of my system. I am blessed or cursed with a fertile imagination to which these tiny seeds of thought cling and germinate like mushroom spores, some-

times with little awareness on my part. Suddenly there they are, refusing to be suppressed or ignored, thrusting upwards towards the light and pushing up pavingstones if need be to get there. I prefer not to be tied to a category, modern, historical or whatever; it is people who interest me, their reactions to each other and to the situations in which they find themselves, and to explore these fascinating avenues one must be free. *Gallows Wedding* happened as a result of wondering how a girl would feel who is reduced to buying a stranger from the gallows for the sake of his protection . . . and how would the couple fare afterwards? As I could find no book to tell me, I had to write it myself in order to find out. *Mango Walk* sprang from a dream I was unable to shake off; the figures in it remained to haunt me until I gave in and put their story down on paper. From here my work could go in any direction. I have to write what fires me, and to quote from one of my own verses, 'joy's a nymph, not captured one way twice'.

*   *   *

Anyone expecting that a Georgette Heyer 'read-alike' would win the first Historical Novel prize in her memory was in for a shock. Rhona Martin's *Gallows Wedding* is stark, grim reality, exploring without any sanitization the terrifying world of the poor and homeless in 16th-century England, a country driven by fear of witchcraft.

Unlike most historical novels, this book depicts the lives of mean, desperate wretches rather than the glamour of the rich and powerful. The opening is harsh and uncompromising. Hazel, in danger from her very birth because she is 'witchmarked', sees her mother tortured, and her new-born sibling tossed heedlessly on the fire. Alone, homeless, she is robbed, betrayed, raped, and scorned. Then she saves Black John from the gallows, as the local custom dictates that on May Day, any man condemned to die can be saved if a girl is willing to marry him. The rest of the book relates their love story, however without the conventional happy ending.

Gallows Wedding is a very powerful book, peopled with a fantastic but real cast of characters. Whether tinkers or villagers, they all have their fears and preoccupations, loves and hates. The research is formidable, and the reader is transported into this terrifying world, and held there by the sheer skill of the narrative.

Martin began publishing novels relatively late, and in nine years has published only four. Each one, however, is distinctive and remarkable. *Mango Walk*, her second book, begins in 1940, when Sam, a seaman, finds a child, Honey. Both are alone, and destitute because of the blitz. The novel traces their relationship as Honey grows from child to woman, relating the story of lovers facing the prejudices of the time, defying the taboos, far stronger then than today, against marriage between people of different race, and greatly differing age.

The Unicorn Summer returns to the 16th century, continuing the story which began with Hazel and Black John, but moving this time between the low life of the tinkers and travelling folk, and wealthy upper-class circles. It is the story of another unlikely pair of lovers, the dispossessed Joanna and the gentle, witchmarked Angel.

Goodbye, Sally, finds Zoe puzzled at the manner of the death of Sally, her mother. She stays behind after the funeral to read her mother's letters. Gradually she discovers the facts behind her mother's life, and begins to understand her. Sally's early life with her old but childish mother Aimée, and her father, the American Erik, 15 years younger, is one of repression in which she is trained to be good, to obey, and always give in. She has no friends because of constant moves, and when her adored father leaves, unable to tolerate life with the fretful and demanding Aimée any more, Aimée is furious and resentful of her. She makes Sally leave school to look after her, then marries her off to a friend's son, Gerald, a sexless emotionless solicitor. The twins Zoe and Gerald are born, and although Sally appears to be submissive, she has a wild secret affair

with Adam, a foreign correspondent who vanishes in South America. Sally is accustomed to getting the blame for everything, and it is inevitable that when she meets an old friend, George, who is unable to forget his love for a woman who died just before their wedding, she falls under his influence. When Gerald divorces her she marries George, and his late fiancée's brother, Mark, stays with them. He is in love with Sally but eventually turns to Zoe. Alone once more, without any formal qualifications, Sally begins to write of her experiences and becomes a very successful magazine journalist, advising others on their problems. By now confident and rich, it seems inconceivable that Sally should simply walk out into the path of fast traffic.

This book is highly perceptive about emotions, and very subtle in its delicate portrayal of Sally, deliberately too perfect in her tolerance and refusal to take action, while permitting things to happen to her.

All Martin's books are beautifully and fluently written, with excellently researched backgrounds, perceptive characterization, suspense, and pace. They are thoroughly satisfying.

—Marina Oliver

MARTIN, Ruth.   See **RAYNER, Claire.**

MARTIN, Stella.   See **HEYER, Georgette.**

MARTINES, Julia.   See **O'FAOLAIN, Julia.**

MARVIN, Susan.   See **ELLIS, Julie.**

MASEFIELD, John (Edward). British. 1878–1967. See 2nd edition, 1990.

MASON, A(lfred) E(dward) W(oodley).
Nationality: British. **Born:** Camberwell, London, 7 May 1865. **Education:** Dulwich College, London, 1878–84; Trinity College, Oxford (exhibitioner in classics, 1887), 1884–87, degrees in classics 1886, 1888. **Military Service:** Royal Marine Light Infantry in World War I, and involved in Naval Intelligence Division secret service missions in Spain, Gibraltar, Morocco, and Mexico. **Career:** actor in provincial touring companies, 1888–94 (appeared in first performance of *Arms and the Man*, 1894); Liberal member of Parliament for Coventry, 1906–10. **Recipient:** honorary fellow, Trinity College, 1943. **Died:** 22 November 1948.

ROMANCE AND HISTORICAL PUBLICATIONS

Novels

The Courtship of Morrice Buckler. London, Macmillan, 1896; New York, Macmillan, 1903.
Lawrence Clavering. London, Innes, and New York, Dodd Mead, 1897.

Parson Kelly. London and New York, Longman, 1900.
Clementina. London, Methuen, and New York, Stokes, 1901.
Fire over England. London, Hodder and Stoughton, and New York, Doubleday, 1936.
Königsmark. London, Hodder and Stoughton, 1938; New York, Doubleday, 1939.
Musk and Amber. London, Hodder and Stoughton, and New York, Doubleday, 1942.

OTHER PUBLICATIONS

Novels

A Romance of Wastdale. London, Mathews, and New York, Stokes, 1895.
The Philanderers. London and New York, Macmillan, 1897.
Miranda of the Balcony. London and New York, Macmillan, 1899.
The Watchers. Bristol, Arrowsmith, and New York, Stokes, 1899.
The Four Feathers. London, Smith Elder, and New York, Macmillan, 1902.
The Truants. London, Smith Elder, and New York, Harper, 1904.
The Broken Road. London, Smith Elder, and New York, Scribner, 1907.
Running Water. London, Hodder and Stoughton, and New York, Century, 1907.
At the Villa Rose. London, Hodder and Stoughton, and New York, Scribner, 1910.
The Turnstile. London, Hodder and Stoughton, and New York, Scribner, 1912.
The Witness for the Defence. London, Hodder and Stoughton, 1913; New York, Scribner, 1914.
The Summons. London, Hodder and Stoughton, and New York, Doran, 1920.
The Winding Stair. London, Hodder and Stoughton, and New York, Doran, 1923.
The House of the Arrow. London, Hodder and Stoughton, and New York, Doran, 1924.
No Other Tiger. London, Hodder and Stoughton, and New York, Doran, 1927.
The Prisoner in the Opal. London, Hodder and Stoughton, and New York, Doubleday, 1928.
The Dean's Elbow. London, Hodder and Stoughton, 1930; New York, Doubleday, 1931.
The Three Gentlemen. London, Hodder and Stoughton, and New York, Doubleday, 1932.
The Sapphire. London, Hodder and Stoughton, and New York, Doubleday, 1933.
They Wouldn't Be Chessmen. London, Hodder and Stoughton, and New York, Doubleday, 1935.
The Drum. London, Hodder and Stoughton, and New York, Doubleday, 1937.
The House in Lordship Lane. London, Hodder and Stoughton, and New York, Dodd Mead, 1946.

Short Stories

Ensign Knightley and Other Stories. London, Constable, and New York, Stokes, 1901.
The Clock. New York, Paget, 1910.
Making Good. New York, Paget, 1910.
The Four Corners of the World. London, Hodder and Stoughton, and New York, Scribner, 1917.
The Episode of the Thermometer. New York, Paget, 1918.
Dilemmas. London, Hodder and Stoughton, 1934; New York, Doubleday, 1935.

The Secret Fear. New York, Doubleday, 1940.

Plays

Blanche de Malètroit, adaptation of the story 'The Sire de Malètroit's Door' by Robert Louis Stevenson (produced London, 1894). London, Capper and Newton, 1894.
The Courtship of Morrice Buckler, with Isabel Bateman, adaptation of the novel by Mason (produced London, 1897).
Marjory Strode (produced London, 1908).
Colonel Smith (produced London, 1909). London, privately printed, 1909; revised version, as *Green Stockings* (produced New York, 1911), New York and London, French, 1914.
The Princess Clementina, with George Pleydell Bancroft, adaptation of the novel *Clementina* by Mason (produced Cardiff and London, 1910).
The Witness for the Defence, adaptation of his own novel (produced London and New York, 1911). Privately printed, 1911.
Open Windows (produced London, 1913).
At the Villa Rose, adaptation of his own novel (produced London, 1920). London, Hodder and Stoughton, 1928.
Running Water (produced London, 1922).
The House of the Arrow, adaptation of his own novel (produced London, 1928).
No Other Tiger, adaptation of his own novel (produced Leicester and London, 1928).
A Present from Margate, with Ian Hay (produced London, 1933). London, French, 1934.

Other

The Royal Exchange. London, Royal Exchange, 1920.
Sir George Alexander and the St James' Theatre. London, Macmillan, 1935.
The Life of Francis Drake. London, Hodder and Stoughton, 1941; New York, Doubleday, 1942.

*

Film Adaptations: *The Four Feathers*, 1929, 1939, *Storm over the Nile*, 1955, all from the novel *The Four Feathers*; *The House of the Arrow*, 1930, 1940, 1953; *Fire Over England*, 1937; *The Drum*, 1938; *At the Villa Rosa*, 1939.

Critical Study: *A.E.W. Mason: The Adventures of a Story Teller* by Roger Lancelyn Green, London, Parrish, 1952.

*   *   *

Though A.E.W. Mason is perhaps primarily known today for his near-contemporary adventure story *The Four Feathers*, and his detective stories about Inspector Hanaud, such as *At the Villa Rose*, his reputation as one of the best and most popular storytellers in the first half of the 20th century also derived to a great extent from his skill as a writer of historical romances, which he produced at the beginning and end of his career.

Through the work of Scott and Dumas, and their followers, the popularity of the historical tale was in full flood at the end of the 19th century when Mason began to write. Stevenson's masterpieces *Treasure Island* and *Kidnapped* were still on everyone's lips, and a host of successors—Quiller-Couch, Conan Doyle, Stanley Weyman, Samuel Rutherford Crockett—sought to emulate him.

Mason, who turned to writing in his late twenties after appearing on the stage for several years, worked in this established tradition of the tale of adventure set in the historical past, which was sometimes called the costume novel. His novels are usually set somewhere between the Elizabethan age and the middle of the 18th century, where Mason's acting experience gave him considerable facility in period dialogue as well as an understanding of costume and manners, and his plots usually deal with intrigues and romances among kings and princesses, aristocrats and statesmen. This is the world of Handel and Walsingham—not Hogarth and Mother Courage.

A characteristic plot involves a handsome young hero setting out on a difficult mission—to work for the Jacobite rising or to spy on the Spanish Armada. He is then caught up in political intrigues and personal feuds, and manipulated by older and unscrupulous figures. There is plenty of action with the hero having to defend himself with swashbuckling sword-play as Charles Wogan does in *Clementina*, or destroying with gunpowder a Spanish galleon as Robin Aubrey does in *Fire over England*. Duels are not uncommon, and there is many a desperate gallop by night. There is nearly always a love-element in Mason's romances, but the hero is not always fortunate, for though Robin does win his sweetheart, both Wogan and Philip von Königsmark fall passionately in love with women forbidden to them, and end unhappily.

There is indeed a curious awareness of betrayal and failure present in all the novels. Lawrence feels that he has accidentally betrayed Herbert and must atone for it with his life, if necessary, in *Lawrence Clavering*. Wogan and his princess feel guilty about their love in *Clementina*; Robin's father accidentally betrays his own son and commits suicide in *Fire over England;* and Philip is brought down by the envy of his friend Anthony in *Königsmark*.

In the end, in fact, a mood of romantic sadness pervades most of the tales. Though Lawrence outwits his villainous cousin and escapes to France at the conclusion of the very Stevensonian *Lawrence Clavering*, the treachery of his cousin and the failure of the Jacobite cause create a sombre tone. Similarly, although *Clementina* achieves a rattling pace after a clumsy expository beginning, and the hero outwits his Hanoverian enemies enabling Clementina to marry James III, a sense of doom is created, not only by the unhappy failure of that marriage but by the hero's forebodings of disaster.

Fire over England is the one exception to this melancholy pattern, for although the young hero fails to rescue his father, he does help to defeat the Spanish Armada and is happily re-united with Cynthia. But the atmosphere of *Königsmark* is overcast from the beginning when young Philip is imprisoned and humiliated by a political enemy, and though he grows up to become a dashing military hero, he is haunted by memories of his shameful past, so that, when he does find true love, it is too late.

Finally, in *Musk and Amber*, which Roger Lancelyn Green has described as Mason's 'highest point . . . on the very snow-line of great literature', the hero is doomed from the beginning. Young Julian, Earl of Linchcombe, and heir to the beautiful 18th-century estate of Grest, is kidnapped by relations, and passed to Italian peasants who have him castrated and then trained as an opera singer. Though Julian achieves great success and uses his power and wealth to return to England and take his revenge, the novel ends with him renouncing his title and returning to live in obscurity in Italy.

There is an individual flavour about Mason's best work, and, though his historical romances come very close to 'tushery' at times, his craftsmanship and zest usually enable him to avoid the worst excesses. In *Fire over England* and *Musk and Amber* there are moments of pain and sadness unusual in the genre for the period.

—Dennis Butts

MASON, F(rancis) Van Wyck.
Pseudonyms: Geoffrey Coffin (with Helen Brawner); Frank W. Mason; Ward Weaver. **Nationality:** American. **Born:** Boston, Massachusetts, 11 November 1901. **Education:** Berkshire School, 1919–20; Harvard University, Cambridge, Massachusetts, B.S. 1924. **Military Service:** Allied Expeditionary Forces in France, 1918–19: second lieutenant; New York National Guard Cavalry, 1924–29: sergeant; Maryland National Guard Field Artillery, 1930–33: first lieutenant; general staff corps officer and chief historian, Civil and Military Government Section, 1942–45; Supreme Headquarters, Allied Expeditionary Force, 1943–45: colonel. **Relations:** married 1) Dorothy Louise Macready in 1927 (died 1958), two children; 2) Jeanne-Louise Hand in 1958. **Career:** importer; after 1928 self-employed writer. Lived in Bermuda, 1956–78. **Recipient:** Medaille de Sauvetage, Croix de Guerre with two palms; Légion d'honneur; Valley Forge foundation medal, 1953; Society of Colonial Wars Citation of Honour, 1960. **Died:** 29 August 1978.

ROMANCE AND HISTORICAL PUBLICATIONS

Novels

Captain Nemesis. New York, Putnam, 1931; London, Hale, 1959.
Three Harbours. Philadelphia, Lippincott, 1938; London, Jarrolds, 1939.
Stars on the Sea. Philadelphia, Lippincott, and London, Jarrolds, 1940.
Hang My Wreath (as Ward Weaver). New York, Funk and Wagnalls, 1941; London, Jarrolds, 1942.
Rivers of Glory. Philadelphia, Lippincott, 1942; London, Jarrolds, 1944.
End of Track (as Ward Weaver). New York, Reynal, 1943.
Eagle in the Sky. Philadelphia, Lippincott, 1948; London, Jarrolds, 1949.
Cutlass Empire. New York, Doubleday, 1949; London, Jarrolds, 1950.
Valley Forge: 24 December 1777. New York, Doubleday, 1950.
Proud New Flags. Philadelphia, Lippincott, 1951; London, Jarrolds, 1952.
Golden Admiral: A Novel of Sir Francis Drake and the Armada. New York, Doubleday, 1953; London, Jarrolds, 1954.
Wild Drums Beat. New York, Pocket Books, 1954.
The Barbarians. New York, Pocket Books, 1954; London, Hale, 1956.
Blue Hurricane. Philadelphia, Lippincott, 1954; London, Jarrolds, 1955.
Silver Leopard. New York, Doubleday, 1955; London, Jarrolds, 1956.
Captain Judas. New York, Pocket Books, 1955; London, Hale, 1957.
Our Valiant Few. Boston, Little Brown, 1956; as *To Whom Be Glory*, London, Jarrolds, 1957.
Lysander. New York, Pocket Books, 1956; London, Hale, 1958.
The Young Titan. New York, Doubleday, 1959; London, Hutchinson, 1960.
Return of the Eagles. New York, Pocket Books, 1959.
Manila Galleon. Boston, Little Brown, and London, Hutchinson, 1961.
The Sea'venture. New York, Doubleday, 1961; London, Hutchinson, 1962.
Rascals' Heaven. New York, Doubleday, and London, Hutchinson, 1965.
Wild Horizon. Boston, Little Brown, 1966.
Harpoon in Eden. New York, Doubleday, 1969.
Brimstone Club. Boston, Little Brown, 1971; London, Hutchinson, 1972.
Roads to Liberty (includes *Three Harbours, Stars on the Sea, Eagle in the Sky*). Boston, Little Brown, 1972.

Guns for Rebellion. New York, Doubleday, 1977; London, Hutchinson, 1978.
Armored Giants. Boston, Little Brown, 1980; London, Hutchinson, 1981.

OTHER PUBLICATIONS

Novels

Seeds of Murder. New York, Doubleday, 1930; London, Eldon Press, 1937.
The Vesper Service Murders. New York, Doubleday, 1931; London, Eldon Press, 1935.
The Fort Terror Murders. New York, Doubleday, 1931; London, Eldon Press, 1936.
The Yellow Arrow Murders. New York, Doubleday, 1932; London, Eldon Press, 1935.
The Branded Spy Murders. New York, Doubleday, 1932; London, Eldon Press, 1936.
Spider House. New York, Mystery League, 1932; London, Hale, 1959.
The Shanghai Bund Murders. New York, Doubleday, 1933; London, Eldon Press, 1934; revised edition, as *The China Sea Murders*, New York, Pocket Books, 1959; London, Consul, 1961.
The Sulu Sea Murders. New York, Doubleday, 1933; London, Eldon Press, 1936.
Oriental Division G-2 (omnibus). New York, Reynal, n.d.
The Budapest Parade Murders. New York, Doubleday, and London, Eldon Press, 1935.
Murder in the Senate (as Geoffrey Coffin, with Helen Brawner). New York, Dodge, 1935; London, Hurst and Blackett, 1936.
The Washington Legation Murders. New York, Doubleday, 1935; London, Eldon Press, 1937.
The Forgotten Fleet Mystery (as Geoffrey Coffin, with Helen Brawner). New York, Dodge, 1936; London, Jarrolds, 1943.
The Seven Seas Murders (novelets). New York, Doubleday, 1936; London, Eldon Press, 1937.
The Castle Island Case. New York, Reynal, 1937; London, Jarrolds, 1938; revised edition, as *The Multi-Million Dollar Murders*, New York, Pocket Books, 1960; London, Hale, 1961.
The Hong Kong Airbase Murders. New York, Doubleday, 1937; London, Jarrolds, 1940.
The Cairo Garter Murders. New York, Doubleday, and London, Jarrolds, 1938.
The Singapore Exile Murders. New York, Doubleday, and London, Jarrolds, 1939.
The Bucharest Ballerina Murders. New York, Stokes, 1940; London, Jarrolds, 1941.
Military Intelligence—8 (omnibus). New York, Stokes, 1941.
The Rio Casino Intrigue. New York, Reynal, 1941; London, Jarrolds, 1942.
The Man from G-2 (omnibus). New York, Reynal, n.d.
Saigon Singer. New York, Doubleday, 1946; London, Barker, 1948.
Dardanelles Derelict. New York, Doubleday, 1949; London, Barker, 1950.
Himalayan Assignment. New York, Doubleday, 1952; London, Hale, 1953.
Two Tickets to Tangier. New York, Doubleday, 1955; London, Hale, 1956.
The Gracious Lily Affair. New York, Doubleday, 1957; London, Hale, 1958.
Secret Mission to Bangkok. New York, Doubleday, 1960; London, Hale, 1961.
Trouble in Burma. New York, Doubleday, 1962; London, Hale, 1963.
Zanzibar Intrigue. New York, Doubleday, 1963; London, Hale, 1964.
Maracaibo Mission. New York, Doubleday, 1965; London, Hale, 1966.
The Deadly Orbit Mission. New York, Doubleday, and London, Hale, 1968.

Novels as Frank W. Mason

Q-Boat. Philadelphia, Lippincott, 1943.
Pilots, Man Your Planes! Philadelphia, Lippincott, 1944.
Flight into Danger. Philadelphia, Lippincott, 1946.

Other

The Winter at Valley Forge (for children). New York, Random House, 1953; as *Washington at Valley Forge*, Eau Claire, Wisconsin, E.M. Hale, 1953.
The Battle of Lake Erie (for children). Boston, Houghton Mifflin, 1960.
The Battle for New Orleans (for children). Boston, Houghton Mifflin, 1962.
The Battle for Quebec (for children). Boston, Houghton Mifflin, 1965.
The Maryland Colony (for children). New York, Macmillan, 1969.

Editor, *The Fighting American*. New York, Reynal, 1943; London, Jarrolds, 1945.
Editor, *American Men at Arms*. Boston, Little Brown, 1964.

*   *   *

F. Van Wyck Mason retired from a successful business career in the 1920s, a dedicated advocate of the American free enterprise system and American military superiority, to write a series of detective stories featuring a US Army intelligence officer named North, which he continued to produce at intervals throughout his career. These mystery stories never achieved the reputation, or sales, of those of S.S. Van Dine, Ellery Queen, or Erle Stanley Gardner; but Mason found the métier in which he would triumph in the historical romance. A first venture into this field—*Captain Nemesis*, about Caribbean pirates—attracted few reviews or sales in the depression year of 1931, when the book business was suffering badly; but in 1938, as improved economic conditions resulted in improved book sales and the hoopla attendant upon the celebration of the sesquicentennial of the American Constitution led to an unprecedented demand for romances of national glory, Mason hit the bestseller lists with *Three Harbours*. This rousing tale of Norfolk, Boston, and Bermuda (as well as Salem and Philadelphia), is the first of a tetralogy on the founding of the American Navy in 1774–75 as the Revolution was brewing. *Stars on the Sea*, *Rivers of Glory*, and *Eagle in the Sky* carried readers forward to the defeat of Cornwallis in 1781.

In a foreword Mason set forth his concept of the historical novel that set the pattern for more than a dozen volumes to follow:

> ... the main facts, dates, and figures are as nearly correct as a painstaking and selective research can make them. The same also applies to such details as uniforms, military movements, legal proceedings, customs, currency, and documents. The writer of a novel which employs a historical setting is, I believe, to the careful historian somewhat as a landscape painter to an architect .... Therefore, in the selection of incidents used in this tale I have necessarily omitted or glossed over some historical events of great importance which unfortunately did not bear on the story.

Contemporary reviewers were not much impressed, however, observing that Mason was not in a league with such respected historical novelists as Kenneth Roberts and Esther Forbes. Holmes Alexander, in the *Saturday Review of Literature*, labelled productions like Mason's 'costume novels', noteworthy for their excitement and colour. Readers were intrigued, however, by Mason's vivid rendition of incidents designed to further his 'underlying purpose' of telling how 'the early merchants of America's Eastern Coast lived, to show what they did and, on occasion, what they suffered' in order to 'be reasonably free in the conduct of a business'. 'They met a crisis and defeated it without the aid of a paternalistic regime', Mason concludes, expressing the hope that should contemporary merchants meet such a challenge, they would act 'as courageously as did their forebears'.

At a time when highbrow intellectuals were attacking bourgeois American traditions and trying to proselytize readers with 'proletarian' novels, Mason was offering patriotic audiences the comfortable message that though their ancestors wore funny clothes, they spoke the same language and dreamed the same dream as their descendants. Although the trappings of his tales are 18th century, the sentiments and even the language are straight from the 'go-getter' stories of Clarence Buddington Kelland in the *Saturday Evening Post*: as Mason's hero exclaims, for example, at a crucial point in the action, 'Well, it stands to reason that without merchants to do her business, America can never amount to anything . . . . Fortunes will be made by those who get started early, but they'll have to run risks no assurance underwriter would cover'.

Not all Mason's romances were bestsellers, but the tales that he spun from his formula at his Bermuda retreat continued to entertain readers enjoying historical sanction for their booster philosophy. Since Mason's novels remained remarkably consistent in quality, one's preferences among them may depend upon their historical backgrounds ranging from modern Europeans' first quest for colonial empire to the little-known struggle to keep the Mississippi River open for trade during the Civil War. Since his titles are not self-explanatory, a listing of the order for reading his major works chronologically by setting is useful: *Silver Leopard* (the First Crusade), *Golden Admiral* (Sir Francis Drake and the Spanish Armada), *Cutlass Empire* (Sir Henry Morgan, Caribbean pirate), *The Sea 'venture* (British colonies in Jamestown and Bermuda), *The Young Titan* (New England during the French and Indian Wars), *Manila Galleon* (the British in the Pacific in the 1840s), *Proud New Flags*, *Blue Hurricane*, and *Our Valiant Few* (the navy in the Civil War). Mason also reworked some of his old material with new in books intended to interest teenagers in history, especially that of America's mercantile princes.

—Warren French

MASON, Frank W. See **MASON, F. Van Wyck.**

MASTERS, John.
Nationality: American. Born with British nationality, became US citizen, 1954. **Born:** Calcutta, India, 26 October 1914. **Education:** Wellington School, Somerset; Royal Military College, Sandhurst, Surrey. **Relations:** married Barbara Allcard; one son and two daughters. **Career:** British Army, 1934 until his retirement as lieutenant colonel in 1948: commissioned 2nd lieutenant, Indian Army, 1934; served in the 2nd Battalion, 4th Prince of Wales's Own Gurkha Rifles, 1935; served on the North West Frontier, 1936–37; adjutant, 1939; served in Iraq, Syria, and Persia, 1941; brigade major, 114th Indian Infantry Brigade, 1942, and 111th Indian Infantry

Brigade, 1943; commandant, 3rd Battalion, 1944; served in Burma, 1944–45; general staff officer-1, 19th Indian Division, 1945; general staff officer-2, Staff College, Camberley, Surrey, 1947. Lived many years in Santa Fe, New Mexico. **Recipient:** DSO (Companion, Distinguished Service Order), 1944; OBE (Officer, Order of the British Empire), 1945. **Died:** 7 May 1983.

ROMANCE AND HISTORICAL PUBLICATIONS

Novels (series: An Indian Trilogy; Loss of Eden Trilogy; Savage Family)

An Indian Trilogy (Savage). London, Joseph, 1978.
  Nightrunners of Bengal. London, Joseph, and New York, Viking, 1951.
  The Deceivers. London, Joseph, and New York, Viking, 1952.
  Bhowani Junction. London, Joseph, and New York, Viking, 1954.
The Lotus and the Wind (Savage). London, Joseph, and New York, Viking, 1953.
Coromandel! (Savage). London, Joseph, and New York, Viking, 1955.
Far, Far the Mountain Peak (Savage). London, Joseph, and New York, Viking, 1957.
The Venus of Konpara. London, Joseph, and New York, Harper, 1960.
The Rock. London, Joseph, and New York, Putnam, 1970.
Loss of Eden Trilogy:
  Now, God Be Thanked. London, Joseph, and New York, McGraw Hill, 1979.
  Heart of War. London, Joseph, and New York, McGraw Hill, 1980.
  By the Green of the Spring. London, Joseph, and New York, McGraw Hill, 1981.

OTHER PUBLICATIONS

Novels

Fandango Rock. London, Joseph, and New York, Harper, 1959.
To the Coral Strand. London, Joseph, and New York, Harper, 1962.
Trial at Monomoy. London, Joseph, and New York, Harper, 1964.
Fourteen Eighteen. London, Joseph, 1965.
The Breaking Strain. London, Joseph, and New York, Delacorte Press, 1967.
The Ravi Lancers. London, Joseph, and New York, Doubleday, 1972.
Thunder at Sunset. London, Joseph, and New York, Doubleday, 1974.
The Field-Marshal's Memoirs. London, Joseph, and New York, Doubleday, 1975.
The Himalaya Concerto. London, Joseph, and New York, Doubleday, 1976.
Man of War. London, Joseph, 1983; as *High Command*, New York, Morrow, 1984.

Other

The Compleat Indian Angler. London, Country Life, 1938.
Bugles and a Tiger: A Personal Adventure (autobiography). London, Joseph, and New York, Viking, 1956.
The Road Past Mandalay (autobiography). London, Joseph, and New York, Viking, 1961.
Casanova. London, Joseph, and New York, Geis, 1969.
Pilgrim Son: A Personal Odyssey (autobiography). London, Joseph, and New York, Putnam, 1971.

*

Film Adaptations: *Bhowani Junction*, 1955; *The Deceivers*, 1988.

Critical Study: *John Masters: A Regimented Life* by John Clay, London, Joseph 1992.

*   *   *

John Masters's India is a place where the constraints of European civilization can be shrugged off, where (in the words of Joseph Conrad's narrator in *Heart of Darkness*) the white man is liberated 'by the awakening of forgotten and brutal instincts, by the memory of gratified and monstrous passions'. In his first novel, a character complains that the English occupy only the surface of India; in the course of his tales the protagonist ventures beneath this surface and encounters himself, transmogrified into the savage.

Ironically, it is the Savage family whose adventures Masters intended to chronicle in his projected series of 30 or more novels. The scope of his ambition can be gauged by the fact that the series would encompass all of the years of the English presence in India, from around 1600 to Independence in 1947. In the end, he completed only a few of these, and collected three of them as *An Indian Trilogy: Nightrunners of Bengal*, *The Deceivers*, and *Bhowani Junction*. Of these, the latter falls outside the scope of this essay as it deals with the events immediately prior to Independence.

Nightrunners of Bengal is in many ways Masters's most accomplished novel; despite the overindulgences of gothic melodrama, it displays most eloquently his fascination with the exotic and horrific essence of the subcontinent. The novel is set in 1857—the year of the Great Mutiny of the sepoys, and the centenary of British rule in India. Rodney Savage, the protagonist, is a workhorse of Anglo-Indian administration, an officer of the East India Company. He is in charge of a company of sepoys whom he trusts implicitly, but whose minds and imaginations he realizes are closed to him. The devastating tedium of garrison life is portrayed with bitter accuracy; Masters himself was an officer in charge of native troops, and describes the petty rivalries, intrigues, and snobberies in astonishing detail. Savage sees his life as a colonial functionary stretch into infinity: promotion by slow degrees, retirement to England, death. But two events, linked in a byzantine plot, disrupt the humdrum stability. The first is a conspiracy to murder the prince of a neighbouring 'independent' state. Savage, sent to police the subsequent disturbance, becomes involved in a passionate affair with its new ruler. The proud, cruel, beautiful harlot-queen Sumitra is an index to the author's notion of one aspect of India, as a repository of an exotic sensuality to which the civilized man is barred. Savage is tempted by her offer to become lord both of her and her state, but finds himself unable to cross over into 'the other room' as a dominant metaphor describes it.

He returns to the bloodless, enervated Anglo-India to which he belongs, the incident apparently finished. But the second event occurs, abruptly, but foreshadowed by signals to which the English have been oblivious. The sepoys rise up and in one bloody night manage to murder, rape, and destroy all trace of British rule in Savage's garrison. This scene is rendered in all the brutal detail the author can muster; interestingly, it breaks with the straightforward linear course of the narrative so far and becomes a dizzying montage of horrific chaos. The experience turns Savage's mind, and when he escapes with his badly injured son and another survivor, he retreats into murderous paranoid fantasies of revenge and apocalypse. The remainder of the novel relates their escape to safe territory, and the climactic battle with the mutinous sepoys. It is a fast-paced, exhilarating, and sometimes brutal tale, flavoured with the melodramatic passion of a story narrated at a high pitch of emotion. It addresses the problem of independence through the device of Savage's love affair with Sumitra, whose ardent nationalism is revealed to have engineered the uprising. Confronted, after the gruesome death of his wife, with the choice between Sumitra and the other English survivor, Caroline Langford, he chooses the latter; through the workings of the labyrinthine plot, he is revealed to have saved all India from revolt by this decision. This far-reaching (or far-fetched) consequence is characteristic of Masters's novels, where the plot is tightly bound and few actions are without effects.

The Deceivers, though published a year later, relates the events of a previous generation. Rodney Savage's father William infiltrates and destroys the *thugee* organization, who are the deceivers of the title. The thugs, who are estimated to have killed over a million people, were a religious sect who devoted themselves to robbery and murder in the service of the destroyer-goddess Kali. Masters freely admits to using the novelist's freedom to create a new situation, and there is no doubt that he employs this licence to glamorize the historical facts behind the suppression of *thugee*. William Savage, on learning of a series of unexplained murders in his district, adopts the identity of a thug, travelling with a band and participating in their murders until he gains enough evidence to present to the administration. So good is he at impersonating the devoted killer, he actually takes command of the band; more dangerously, he begins to lose his previous identity and finds his true vocation as a thug. Only a massive act of will enables him to return to Anglo-Indian life and expose the corruption below the apparent surface of the country. For he has been a poor 'paper administrator', clumsy, inarticulate, and inept when dealing with administrative routine; his only skill has been a profound empathy with the land and native population. Once again, the foray into Indian life, crossing over into 'the other room', has provided the protagonist with the kind of existential freedom to confront terrible aspects of his own self. Masters has been accused of subtle racism in his portrayal of the squalid aspects of Indian life and culture; but in fact he suggests that at his centre 'civilized' man harbours the same horror-driven impulses toward unlimited destruction and sexual fulfilment. Moreover, the situations he portrays in these books are, to say the least, extreme. Despite his claim that he understands the Indians 'better than Kipling', Masters feels under no obligation to present ordinary Indian life.

Other historical works include *The Lotus and the Wind*, set in the troubled times of tension with Russia in the 1880s; *Far, Far the Mountain Peak*, which relates the adventure of a group of mountaineers in a Himalayan expedition; and *The Venus of Konpara*, in which a young prince discovers his exotic love and her exact double graven in rock thousands of years beforehand. This latter book cleverly exploits the dichotomy hinted at in earlier works, in which Indian comes to stand for erotic gratification and English for sexual inhibitions. The remarkable heroine of this book becomes the focus of a multiple sexual rivalry between the young prince, educated in Eton and Sandhurst, his mentor Mr Kendrick (revealed to be impotent), his wife, and others. Although the book aims at a grand tragic conclusion, Masters succumbs to the demands of an excessively romanticized plot and schematic symbolism.

It would be absurd to claim that Masters has created works of subliminal beauty; to make comparisons with D.H. Lawrence (as some have done) would be fatuous at best. But his novels are adventure stories in the classic mould, laden with excitement, historical detail, and melodramatic sensibility, vastly enjoyable and compelling. At his fantastic best, he presents lurid images of the self which reflect, as do all gothic fantasies, a bizarre truth about the self. He aims, with his India, to offer an alternative realm of the unlimited for his European reader.

—Alan Murphy

MATHER, Anne.
Pseudonym: Caroline Fleming. **Address:** c/o Mills and Boon Ltd,
Eton House, 18–24 Paradise Road, Richmond, Surrey TW9 1SR,
England.

ROMANCE AND HISTORICAL PUBLICATIONS

Novels

Caroline. London, Hale, 1965.
Beloved Stranger. London, Hale, 1966; as *Legacy of the Past*, London, Mills and Boon, 1975; Toronto, Harlequin, 1974.
Design for Loving. London, Hale, 1966.
Masquerade. London, Hale, 1966; Toronto, Harlequin, 1972.
The Arrogance of Love. London, Hale, 1968; Toronto, Harlequin, 1976.
Dark Venetian (as Caroline Fleming). London, Hale, 1969; (as Anne Mather) Toronto, Harlequin, 1976.
The Enchanted Island. London, Hale, 1969.
Dangerous Rhapsody. London, Hale, 1969; Toronto, Harlequin, 1977.
Legend of Lexandros. London, Mills and Boon, 1969; Toronto, Harlequin, 1973.
Dangerous Enchantment. London, Mills and Boon, 1969; Toronto, Harlequin, 1974.
Tangled Tapestry. London, Mills and Boon, 1969.
The Arrogant Duke. London, Mills and Boon, and Toronto, Harlequin, 1970.
Charlotte's Hurricane. London, Mills and Boon, 1970; Toronto, Harlequin, 1971.
Lord of Zaracus. London, Mills and Boon, 1970; Toronto, Harlequin, 1972.
Sweet Revenge. London, Mills and Boon, 1970; Toronto, Harlequin, 1973.
Who Rides the Tiger. London, Mills and Boon, 1970; Toronto, Harlequin, 1973.
Moon Witch. London, Mills and Boon, 1970; Toronto, Harlequin, 1974.
Master of Falcon's Head. London, Mills and Boon, 1970; Toronto, Harlequin, 1974.
The Reluctant Governess. London, Mills and Boon, 1971; Toronto, Harlequin, 1972.
The Pleasure and the Pain. London, Mills and Boon, 1971; Toronto, Harlequin, 1973.
The Sanchez Tradition. London, Mills and Boon, 1971; Toronto, Harlequin, 1973.
Storm in a Rain Barrel. London, Mills and Boon, 1971; Toronto, Harlequin, 1973.
Dark Enemy. London, Mills and Boon, 1971; Toronto, Harlequin, 1973.
All the Fire. London, Mills and Boon, 1971; Toronto, Harlequin, 1976.
The High Valley. London, Mills and Boon, 1971; Toronto, Harlequin, 1976.
The Autumn of the Witch. London, Mills and Boon, 1972; Toronto, Harlequin, 1973.
Living with Adam. London, Mills and Boon, 1972; Toronto, Harlequin, 1973.
A Distant Sound of Thunder. London, Mills and Boon, 1972; Toronto, Harlequin, 1973.
Monkshood. London, Mills and Boon, 1972; Toronto, Harlequin, 1973.
Prelude to Enchantment. London, Mills and Boon, 1972; Toronto, Harlequin, 1974.
The Night of the Bulls. London, Mills and Boon, 1972; Toronto, Harlequin, 1974.

Jake Howard's Wife. London, Mills and Boon, 1973; Toronto, Harlequin, 1974.
A Savage Beauty. London, Mills and Boon, 1973; Toronto, Harlequin, 1974.
Chase a Green Shadow. London, Mills and Boon, 1973; Toronto, Harlequin, 1974.
White Rose of Winter. London, Mills and Boon, 1973; Toronto, Harlequin, 1974.
Mask of Scars. London, Mills and Boon, 1973; Toronto, Harlequin, 1975.
The Waterfalls of the Moon. London, Mills and Boon, 1973; Toronto, Harlequin, 1975.
The Shrouded Web. London, Mills and Boon, 1973; Toronto, Harlequin, 1976.
Seen by Candlelight. Toronto, Harlequin, 1974.
Leopard in the Snow. London, Mills and Boon, and Toronto, Harlequin, 1974.
The Japanese Screen. London, Mills and Boon, 1974; Toronto, Harlequin, 1975.
Rachel Trevellyan. London, Mills and Boon, 1974; Toronto, Harlequin, 1975.
Silver Fruit upon Silver Trees. London, Mills and Boon, 1974; Toronto, Harlequin, 1975.
Dark Moonless Night. London, Mills and Boon, 1974; Toronto, Harlequin, 1975.
Witchstone. London, Mills and Boon, 1974; Toronto, Harlequin, 1975.
No Gentle Possession. Toronto, Harlequin, 1975.
Pale Dawn, Dark Sunset. London, Mills and Boon, and Toronto, Harlequin, 1975.
Take What You Want. London, Mills and Boon, 1975; Toronto, Harlequin, 1976.
Come the Vintage. London, Mills and Boon, 1975; Toronto, Harlequin, 1976.
Dark Castle. London, Mills and Boon, 1975; Toronto, Harlequin, 1976.
Country of the Falcon. London, Mills and Boon, 1975; Toronto, Harlequin, 1976.
For the Love of Sara. London, Mills and Boon, 1975; Toronto, Harlequin, 1976.
Valley Deep, Mountain High. London, Mills and Boon, 1976; Toronto, Harlequin, 1977.
The Smouldering Flame. London, Mills and Boon, 1976; Toronto, Harlequin, 1977.
Wild Enchantress. London, Mills and Boon, 1976; Toronto, Harlequin, 1977.
Beware the Beast. London, Mills and Boon, 1976; Toronto, Harlequin, 1977.
Devil's Mount. London, Mills and Boon, 1976; Toronto, Harlequin, 1977.
Forbidden. London, Mills and Boon, 1976; Toronto, Harlequin, 1978.
Come Running. London, Mills and Boon, 1976; Toronto, Harlequin, 1978.
Alien Wife. London, Mills and Boon, and Toronto, Harlequin, 1977.
The Medici Lover. London, Mills and Boon, and Toronto, Harlequin, 1977.
Born Out of Love. London, Mills and Boon, and Toronto, Harlequin, 1977.
A Trial Marriage. London, Mills and Boon, and Toronto, Harlequin, 1977.
Devil in Velvet. London, Mills and Boon, 1977; Toronto, Harlequin, 1978.
Loren's Baby. London, Mills and Boon, and Toronto, Harlequin, 1978.

Rooted in Dishonour. London, Mills and Boon, and Toronto, Harlequin, 1978.

Proud Harvest. London, Mills and Boon, and Toronto, Harlequin, 1978.

Scorpions' Dance. London, Mills and Boon, and Toronto, Harlequin, 1978.

Captive Destiny. London, Mills and Boon, 1978; Toronto, Harlequin, 1981.

Fallen Angel. London, Mills and Boon, 1978; Toronto, Harlequin, 1979.

Apollo's Seed. London, Mills and Boon, 1979; Toronto, Harlequin, 1980.

Hell or High Water. London, Mills and Boon, 1979.

The Judas Trap. London, Mills and Boon, 1979.

Lure of Eagles. London, Mills and Boon, and Toronto, Harlequin, 1979.

Melting Fire. London, Mills and Boon, 1979.

Images of Love. London, Mills and Boon, and Toronto, Harlequin, 1980.

Sandstorm. London, Mills and Boon, and Toronto, Harlequin, 1980.

Spirit of Atlantis. London, Mills and Boon, and Toronto, Harlequin, 1980.

Whisper of Darkness. London, Mills and Boon, and Toronto, Harlequin, 1980.

Castles of Sand. London, Mills and Boon, 1981.

Forbidden Flame. London, Mills and Boon, and Toronto, Harlequin, 1981.

A Haunting Compulsion. London, Mills and Boon, and Toronto, Harlequin, 1981.

Innocent Obsession. London, Mills and Boon, and Toronto, Harlequin, 1981.

Duelling Fire. London, Mills and Boon, 1981.

Edge of Temptation. London, Mills and Boon, and Toronto, Harlequin, 1982.

Stormspell. London, Mills and Boon, and Toronto, Harlequin, 1982.

Impetuous Masquerade. London, Mills and Boon, 1982.

A Passionate Affair. London, Mills and Boon, 1982.

Smokescreen. London, Mills and Boon, 1982.

Season of Mist. London, Mills and Boon, 1982.

Cage of Shadows. London, Mills and Boon, 1983.

Green Lightning. London, Mills and Boon, 1983.

An Elusive Desire. London, Mills and Boon, 1983.

Sirocco. London, Mills and Boon, 1983.

Wild Concerto. London, Mills and Boon, and Toronto, Harlequin, 1983.

Moondrift. London, Mills and Boon, 1984.

Pale Orchid. London, Mills and Boon, 1985.

Act of Possession. London, Mills and Boon, 1985.

An All Consuming Passion. London, Mills and Boon, 1985.

Stolen Summer. London, Mills and Boon, 1985.

Hidden in the Flame. London, Mills and Boon, and Toronto, Worldwide, 1985.

The Longest Pleasure. Toronto, Harlequin, 1986.

Burning Inheritance. London, Mills and Boon, 1987.

Night Heat. London, Mills and Boon, and Toronto, Harlequin, 1987.

Dark Mosaic. London, Mills and Boon, 1989.

A Fever in the Blood. London, Mills and Boon, 1989.

A Relative Betrayal. London, Mills and Boon, 1990.

Indiscretion. London, Mills and Boon, 1990.

Betrayed. London, Mills and Boon, 1991.

Blind Passion. London, Mills and Boon, 1991.

Diamond Fire. London, Mills and Boon, 1991.

Such Sweet Poison. London, Mills and Boon, 1991.

Rich as Sin. London, Mills and Boon, 1992.

Tidewater Seduction. London, Mills and Boon, and Toronto, Harlequin, 1993.

OTHER PUBLICATIONS

Play

Screenplay: *Leopard in the Snow*, with Jill Hyem, 1978.

* * *

Among the most prolific of the series romance writers, Anne Mather writes novels that are more complex than those of her contemporaries. Her books have more sub-plots and she employs more texture and mood in her stories. Occasionally, her books have subtle gothic overtones, with brooding heroes, who live in inaccessible and mysterious places, and have secret problems for the heroine to solve. In *Whisper of Darkness* the hero is maimed and convinced no one could love him. The heroine liberates him from his self-imposed exile and helps his troubled daughter, much as do the heroines in 'governess gothics' although Mather's heroine has no mystery to solve.

Mather's plots frequently centre on romantic triangles and potentially illicit sexual relations. In *Edge of Temptation*, *Come Running*, and *Diamond Fire*, the hero is a married man whose wife must be disposed of before the characters can come together. For a series writer, such a plot situation can be tricky to justify, especially if the heroine's marriage is made possible by a divorce. Mather's usual stratagem is to portray the first wife as an inadequate wife or a cruel mother in order to rationalize the extreme solution of divorce and remarriage. In *A Relative Betrayal*, the characters had divorced because of the hero's relationship with the heroine's cousin. Mather's heroines often seem less passive than those of other series romance writers. Although most of her novels are set in England, Mather occasionally employs exotic locations abroad to provide romantic suspense. Because of her richer plots, her characters are occasionally kept apart by outside forces rather than by the internal conflicts and misunderstandings of most series romances.

Mather was one of the first series writers to use premarital sex and divorce as themes in her novels and one of the few whose heroines fell in love with married men. But despite her innovations that move beyond the usual situations of series romances, Mather always handles potentially scandalous material with care and taste.

—Kay Mussell

MATTHEWS, Patricia.
Pseudonyms: P.A. Brisco; Patty Brisco, with Clayton Matthews; Laura Wylie. **Nationality:** American. **Born:** Patricia Anne Ernst, San Fernando, California, 1 July 1927. **Education:** Pasadena Junior College, California; Mt San Antonio Junior College, California; California State University, Los Angeles. **Relations:** married 1) Marvin Owen Brisco in 1946 (divorced 1961), two sons; 2) Clayton Hartley Matthews in 1971. **Career:** secretary and administrator, California State University, 1959–77. **Recipient:** *West Coast Review of Books* award, 1979, 1983. **Agent:** Jay Garon Booke Associates, 101 West 55th, Suite 8D, New York, NY 10019-5348, USA.

ROMANCE AND HISTORICAL PUBLICATIONS

Novels

Love's Avenging Heart. New York, Pinnacle, and London, Corgi, 1977.

Love's Wildest Promise. New York, Pinnacle, 1977; London, Corgi, 1978.

Love, Forever More. New York, Pinnacle, 1977; London, Corgi, 1978.

Love's Daring Dream. New York, Pinnacle, 1978; London, Corgi, 1979.
Love's Pagan Heart. New York, Pinnacle, 1978; London, Corgi, 1979.
Love's Magic Moment. New York, Pinnacle, and London, Corgi, 1979.
Love's Golden Destiny. New York, Pinnacle, 1979; London, Corgi, 1980.
The Night Visitor (as Laura Wylie). New York, Bantam, 1979; as Patricia Matthews, London, Severn House, 1987.
Love's Raging Tide. New York, Pinnacle, and London, Corgi, 1980.
Love's Bold Journey. New York, Pinnacle, 1980; London, Corgi, 1981.
Love's Sweet Agony. New York, Pinnacle, 1980; London, Corgi, 1981.
Tides of Love. New York, Bantam, and London, Corgi, 1981.
Midnight Whispers, with Clayton Matthews. New York, Bantam, 1981; London, Corgi, 1982.
Embers of Dawn. New York, Bantam, and London, Corgi, 1982.
Empire, with Clayton Matthews. New York, Bantam, 1982; London, Corgi, 1983.
Flames of Glory. New York, Bantam, and London, Corgi, 1983.
Dancer of Dreams. New York, Bantam, and London, Century, 1984.
Gambler in Love. New York, Bantam, and London, Corgi, 1985.
Midnight Lavender, with Clayton Matthews. New York, Bantam, 1985; London, Corgi, 1986.
Tame the Restless Heart. New York, Bantam, 1986.
Enchanted. Toronto, Worldwide, 1987.
Thursday and the Lady. Toronto, Worldwide, 1987.
Mirrors. Toronto, Worldwide, 1988.
Oasis. Toronto, Worldwide, 1988; London, Severn House, 1989.
The Dreaming Tree. Toronto, Worldwide, and London, Severn House, 1989.
Sapphire. Toronto, Worldwide, 1989.
The Death of Love. London, Severn House, 1990.
The Unquiet. London, Severn House, 1991.
The Scent of Fear, with Clayton Matthews. London, Severn House, 1992.
Vision of Death, with Clayton Matthews. London, Severn House, 1993.

Novels as Patty Brisco, with Clayton Matthews

Horror at Gull House. New York, Belmont, 1970.
House of Candles. New York, Manor, 1973.
The Crystal Window. New York, Avon, 1973.
Mist of Evil. New York, Manor, 1976; (as Patricia Matthews) London, Severn House, 1990.

OTHER PUBLICATIONS

Novel as P.A. Brisco

The Other People. Reseda, California, Powell, 1979.

Poetry

Love's Many Faces. New York, Bantam, 1979.

Other (for children)

Destruction at Dawn. Belmont, California, Lake, 1986.
Twister. Belmont, California, Lake, 1986.

Other (for children) as Patty Brisco

Merry's Treasure. New York, Avalon, 1970.

The Carnival Mystery. New York, Scholastic, 1974.
The Campus Mystery. New York, Scholastic, 1977.
Raging Rapids. Minneapolis, Creative Education, 1979.
Too Much in Love. New York, Scholastic, 1979.

*

Manuscript Collection: California State College, Fullerton.

Patricia Matthews comments:

To me there are a magic and mystery in the past. During my more than 30 years of writing I have written, and enjoyed writing, many different types of fiction; however, the historical novel has the firmest grip upon my imagination. The past is like a huge jigsaw puzzle, with millions of fascinating pieces. Through anthropology, archaeology, and historical research, we find some of these pieces, and in putting them together, begin to understand our world and the sort of people we once were. I have written over 20 historical novels so far, but I never grow tired of them. Each book I research teaches me more, and gives me more pieces of that marvellous puzzle; the nature of mankind.

*　　*　　*

With a powerful blending of passion, violence, and intrigue, Patricia Matthews has perfected her distinctive formula for the historical romance. Her heroines are sensual and wildly spirited, which is fortunate as they are usually subjected to a physical and psychological assault that would destroy less resilient characters. Unlike the leading ladies of traditional romance novels, Matthews's heroines rarely retain their virginity beyond the opening chapters. There is none of the conventional slow build-up to physical contact, and the girls have to endure sadistic beatings and rapes, enforced prostitution, and slavery.

Male characters from different backgrounds and occupations have astounding depths of brutality—even missionaries turn out to be lecherous! It is surprising, after suffering so much degradation at the hands of men, that Matthews's heroines are always able, eventually, to attain not only romantic but rapturous fulfilment. However, in spite of the hardships and humiliations that are heaped on them, they are not merely passive victims of circumstances. In *Love's Pagan Heart*, for example, a half-Hawaiian, half-English innocent has tremendous resilience; the teenage American heroine of *Love's Avenging Heart* is not only tough and voluptuous but calculating; and the leading character of *Love's Golden Destiny* is a late-Victorian New Yorker with intelligence and career ambitions.

Matthews's robustness of style triumphantly carries not only her heroines but her readers through her long and lusty books, which are modern romantic variants of the 'colonial adventure'. The author says that she is 'a history buff' who refuses 'to believe that love has gone out of style', and her novels certainly endorse her publisher's claim that historical backgrounds do not have to be textbookish! As Patty Brisco, she has written several successful and atmospheric gothic stories.

—Mary Cadogan

———

MAXWELL, A. E. See **LOWELL, Elizabeth.**

———

MAXWELL, Ann. See **LOWELL, Elizabeth.**

———

MAXWELL, Patricia. See **BLAKE, Jennifer.**

———

MAXWELL, Vicky. See **WORBOYS, Anne.**

———

MAY, Wynne (Winifred Jean May).
Nationality: South African. **Born:** North Rand, Transvaal.
Education: Rand College, Johannesburg; studied journalism at
technical college, Durban. **Relations:** married Douglas Claude May
in 1944; two sons. **Career:** worked for African Explosives and
Chemical Industries Ltd, North Rand, and African Consolidated
Films Ltd, and South African Broadcasting Corporation, both
Johannesburg. **Address:** Shalimar, 43 Cotham Road, Moseley,
Natal 4093, South Africa.

ROMANCE AND HISTORICAL PUBLICATIONS

Novels

A Cluster of Palms. London, Mills and Boon, 1967.
The Highest Peak. London, Mills and Boon, 1967.
The Valley of Aloes. London, Mills and Boon, and Toronto, Harle-
    quin, 1967.
Tawny Are the Leaves. London, Mills and Boon, 1968; Toronto,
    Harlequin, 1969.
Tamboti Moon. London, Mills and Boon, and New York, Golden
    Press, 1969.
Where Breezes Falter. London, Mills and Boon, 1970.
Sun, Sea and Sand. London, Mills and Boon, 1970.
The Tide at Full. London, Mills and Boon, 1971.
A Grain of Gold. London, Mills and Boon, 1971.
A Slither of Silk. London, Mills and Boon, 1972.
A Bowl of Stars. London, Mills and Boon, and Toronto, Harlequin,
    1973.
Pink Sands. London, Mills and Boon, and Toronto, Harlequin,
    1974.
A Plume of Dust. London, Mills and Boon, and Toronto, Harlequin,
    1975.
The Sky At Night. London, Mills and Boon, 1975.
A Plantation of Vines. London, Mills and Boon, and Toronto, Harle-
    quin, 1977.
Island of Cyclones. London, Mills and Boon, 1979.
A Scarf of Flame. London, Mills and Boon, 1979.
Peacock in the Jungle. London, Mills and Boon, 1982; Toronto,
    Harlequin, 1983.
Wayside Flower. London, Mills and Boon, 1982; Toronto, Harle-
    quin, 1983.
Iceberg in the Tropics. London, Mills and Boon, 1983.
Fire in the Ash. London, Mills and Boon, 1984.
The Leopard's Lair. London, Mills and Boon, 1984.
A Boma in the Bush. London, Mills and Boon, 1985.
A Flaunting Cactus. London, Mills and Boon, 1986.
Peak of the Furnace. London, Mills and Boon, 1986.
Tomorrow's Sun. London, Mills and Boon, 1989.
Diamonds and Daisies. London, Mills and Boon, 1989.
Filigree of Fancy. London, Mills and Boon, 1990.
Moon over Mombasa. London, Mills and Boon, 1991; Toronto,
    Harlequin, 1992.
Desert Rose. London, Mills and Boon, 1993.

*

Wynne May comments:
    I knew from the day I started school that I wanted to write. Mar-
riage and the problems which this state of affairs often brings
about—in my case the tragic loss of our first two children—left me
feeling 'stranded' and, although I became active in other spheres, I
did not write. That had to come later, when I was ready for it. My
aim, at this stage, was to write for women. I only wish I had started
earlier—but, at least I started. I realise that to 'escape' in the form of
romance fiction is important to many women. Who wants to be confronted with stark reality all the time?

*   *   *

    Wynne May is a South African romance writer of some repute.
Her books are always enjoyable primarily because of May's predilection for exotic locations—usually Africa or an island in the Indian Ocean. The reader is always aware of the geography, society,
or culture of the location when he/she finishes a May book.
    In her long career as a romance writer, May's plots have
developed from the straight-forward plot—innocent girl meets man;
falls madly in love; man falls in love with girl; rival/s interfere; and
finally everything is resolved—to a more complicated version
involving heroines who are not necessarily virgins, who do embark
on affairs with their loved ones, and who do have minds which they
are quite happy to use.
    For the most part the May heroine is beautiful, loyal, and is in-
volved with someone else when she meets her true hero. Carol Tra-
cey, in *The Valley of Aloes*, travels to South Africa to marry a man
whom she has never met, and instead ends up falling in love with the
domineering man who meets her at the airport, Michael Copeland.
Carol believes that Michael is in love with Maxine, the 'other woman', but matters are neatly taken care of when the reader discovers
at the end of the book that Maxine is really in love with Carol's
fiancé, Laine. This device is used again in *Island of Cyclones* when
Jade falls in love with Laurent Sevigny, a rich and charismatic businessman, while engaged to Marlow. She believes that Laurent is in
love with another woman—instead we find that Marlow is really in
love with Laurent's supposed lover.
    In May's more recent novels her heroine is a much more feisty,
independent creature. In *Diamonds and Daisies* Syrie flies out to
beautiful Mauritius (a popular location) to find the man whom she
wishes to marry—instead she finds his attractive business partner.
Ceil Downing goes to Kenya, against the wishes of her family, to
live in the legacy left to her by her great-aunt in *Moon over Mombasa*. Trasi King is a successful fashion designer in *Filigree of
Fancy*, and Alix is a safari guide in *Tomorrow's Sun*. All of these
women are head strong, and do not accept male-domination. Ceil, in
Moon over Mombasa, commissions architect Jonathon Caister to
help renovate her house, and refuses to marry him because she is so
concerned about giving her house up to live with him. Fashion designer, Trasi, gives Matt Laveridge, her competitor, a hard time for
supposedly stealing her staff.
    May's heroes are strong willed, domineering, intelligent men
who demand the total loyalty and attention of their women. They are
hard men, slightly world weary and sardonic, but when they fall in
love their love endures.
    May's books have attracted a large audience among the fans of
the formula romance, and she is one of Mills and Boons most popular authors to date.

—Marion Hatchard

———

MAYBURY, Anne.
Pseudonym for Anne Buxton. **Other Pseudonym:** Katherine Troy.
Nationality: British. **Relations:** married Charles Burdon Buxton.

Career: vice-president, Society of Women Journalists, and Romantic Novelists Association. **Agent:** A.M. Heath, 79 St Martin's Lane, London WC2N 4AA, England.

ROMANCE AND HISTORICAL PUBLICATIONS

Novels

The Best Love of All. London, Mills and Boon, 1932.
The Enchanted Kingdom. London, Mills and Boon, 1932.
The Love That Is Stronger Than Life. London, Mills and Boon, 1932.
Love Triumphant. London, Mills and Boon, 1932.
The Way of Compassion. London, Mills and Boon, 1933.
The Second Winning. London, Mills and Boon, 1933.
Farewell to Dreams. London, Mills and Boon, 1934.
Harness the Winds. London, Mills and Boon, 1934.
Catch at a Rainbow. London, Mills and Boon, 1935.
Come Autumn—Come Winter. London, Mills and Boon, 1935.
The Garden of Wishes. London, Mills and Boon, 1935.
The Starry Wood. London, Mills and Boon, 1935.
The Wondrous To-Morrow. London, Mills and Boon, 1936.
Give Me Back My Dreams. London, Mills and Boon, 1936.
Lovely Destiny. London, Mills and Boon, 1936.
The Stars Grow Pale. London, Mills and Boon, 1936.
This Errant Heart. London, Mills and Boon, 1937.
This Lovely Hour. London, Mills and Boon, 1937.
I Dare Not Dream. London, Mills and Boon, 1937.
Oh, Darling Joy! London, Mills and Boon, 1937.
Lady, It Is Spring! London, Mills and Boon, 1938.
The Shadow of My Loving. London, Mills and Boon, 1938.
They Dreamed Too Much. London, Mills and Boon, 1938.
Chained Eagle. London, Mills and Boon, 1939.
Gather Up the Years. London, Mills and Boon, 1939.
Return to Love. London, Mills and Boon, 1939.
The Barrier Between Us. London, Mills and Boon, 1940.
Dare to Marry. London, Mills and Boon, 1940.
I'll Walk with My Love. London, Mills and Boon, 1940.
Dangerous Living. London, Mills and Boon, 1941.
The Secret of the Rose. London, Collins, 1941.
All Enchantments Die. London, Collins, 1941.
To-Day We Live. London, Collins, 1942.
Arise, Oh Sun! London, Collins, 1942.
A Lady Fell in Love. London, Collins, 1943.
Journey into Morning. London, Collins, 1944; New York, Arcadia House, 1945.
Can I Forget You? London, Collins, 1944.
The Valley of Roses. London, Collins, 1945.
The Young Invader. London, Collins, 1947.
The Winds of Spring. London, Collins, 1948.
Storm Heaven. London, Collins, 1949.
The Sharon Women. London, Collins, 1950.
First, The Dream. London, Collins, 1951.
Goodbye, My Love. London, Collins, 1952.
The Music of Our House. London, Cherry Tree, 1952.
Her Name Was Eve. London, Collins, 1953.
The Heart Is Never Fair. London, Collins, 1954.
Prelude to Louise. London, Collins, 1954.
Follow Your Hearts. London, Collins, 1955.
The Other Juliet. London, Collins, 1955.
Forbidden. London, Collins, 1956.
Dear Lost Love. London, Collins, 1957.
Beloved Enemy. London, Collins, 1957.
The Stars Cannot Tell. London, Collins, 1958.
My Love Has a Secret. London, Collins, 1958.

The Gay of Heart. London, Collins, 1959.
The Rebel Heart. London, Collins, 1959.
Shadow of a Stranger. London, Collins, 1960; New York, Ace, 1966.
Bridge to the Moon. London, Collins, 1960.
Stay Until Tomorrow. London, Collins, 1961; New York, Ace, 1967.
The Night My Enemy. London, Collins, 1962; New York, Ace, 1967.
I Am Gabriella! London, Collins, 1962; New York, Ace, 1966; as *Gabriella*, London, Fontana, 1979.
Green Fire. London, Collins, 1963; New York, Ace, 1965.
My Dearest Elizabeth. London, Collins, 1964; as *The Brides of Bellenmore*, New York, Ace, 1964.
Pavilion at Monkshood. New York, Ace, 1965; London, Fontana, 1966.
Jessica. London, Collins, 1965.
The Moonlit Door. London, Hodder and Stoughton, and New York, Holt Rinehart, 1967.
The Minerva Stone. London, Hodder and Stoughton, and New York, Holt Rinehart, 1968.
Ride a White Dolphin. London, Hodder and Stoughton, and New York, Random House, 1971.
The Terracotta Palace. London, Hodder and Stoughton, and New York, Random House, 1971.
Walk in the Paradise Garden. New York, Random House, 1972; London, Collins, 1973.
The Midnight Dancers. New York, Random House, 1973; London, Collins, 1974.
Jessamy Court. New York, Random House, 1974; London, Collins, 1975.
The Jewelled Daughter. London, Collins, and New York, Random House, 1976.
Dark Star. New York, Random House, 1977; London, Collins, 1978.
Radiance. New York, Random House, 1979.
Invitation to Alannah. Loughton, Essex, Piatkus, 1983.

Novels as Katherine Troy

Someone Waiting. London, Collins, 1961; (as Anne Maybury) New York, Ace, 1966.
Whisper in the Dark. London, Collins, 1961; (as Anne Maybury) New York, Ace, 1966.
Enchanter's Nightshade. London, Collins, 1963; as *The Winds of Night* (as Anne Maybury), New York, Ace, 1967.
Falcon's Shadow. London, Collins, 1964; (as Anne Maybury) New York, Ace, 1967.
The House of Fand. London, Collins, 1966; (as Anne Maybury) New York, Ace, 1966.
The Night of the Enchantress. London, Hodder and Stoughton, 1967.
Farramonde. New York, McKay, 1968.
Storm over Roseheath. London, Hodder and Stoughton, 1969; as *Roseheath*, New York, McKay, 1969.

*   *   *

Anne Maybury has attracted a steady number of fans with her gothic novels, though she had earlier written many romances. Since about 1968 she has published approximately a book a year, and has never failed her audience in their expectations of a good gothic/romance, sensuously and delicately well-told. Maybury rises above the strait jacket of formula with well-conceived plots, sympathetic characters, and lushly described settings.

In Maybury's stories, the person under the most suspicion is the husband or the fiancé of the heroine, whom she both loves and suspects of foul deeds at the same time. The situation is complicated by the presence of a dependant, usually a child of nine or ten, or a friend for whom the heroine feels responsible. These relationships are complicated and tenuous, involving excruciating decisions for the heroine, often *for* the dependent and *against* the loved male. For example, Cathy Mountavon in *The Midnight Dancers* is responsible for Pippa, aged nine, her husband's child by his first wife. Pippa worships her father while innuendos abound that he is responsible for her mother's death. These tangled relationships are always complicated by the heroine's doubt about her prospective/actual mate. The true male mate for the heroine usually emerges only at the conclusion as misunderstood and gallantly heroic, a Galahad who has been searching for the truth all along and trying to defend the heroine, all unknown to her or the reader. But these are not the males' stories; they belong to the woman as she independently explores both dangerous situations and her own emotions. The plots center on her ability not only to endure a threatening environment, but also to rise above situations bordering on the tragic.

Setting is always significant, varied, and expertly invoked. Maybury specializes in atmosphere, with the result that whether the setting is a castle in England or Rome, a pavilion in Hong Kong, or a house on a Greek island, the beauty or each serves as a contrast to the threatening atmosphere of the unknown—the unknown culture and the unfamiliar place. A fine balance is maintained between the heightened emotions of love and fear in a suffocating atmosphere of suspicion and the delicious beauty of each setting.

Maybury's heroines have come a long way from the fainting innocents of the first gothic fiction. Most are at the least able to support themselves; moreover, in *The Jewelled Daughter* Sarah Brendt is a trained gemologist and in *The Midnight Dancers* Cathy Mountavon is an artist trained in stained glass. That these heroines have professions introduces a new thread to the formulaic plot of new gothic, exploring the complications and rewards of further female independence. The villains are brilliant, but power mad. Insanity is the result of their being thwarted in whatever Machiavellian plans they have secretly laid throughout the novel. Of course, the twist is that they may be either male or female, the loved male of the female friend.

Maybury's stories represent the best and newest of the genre and can be counted on for vivid characters, basically sound plots, and carefully researched and lusciously described settings.

—Marilynn Motteler

MAYFIELD, Julia. See **HASTINGS, Phyllis.**

McBAIN, Laurie (Lee).
Nationality: American. **Born:** Riverside, California, 15 October 1949. **Education:** San Bernardino Valley College, California, and California State University, San Bernardino, 1967–72. **Address:** c/o Avon Book, 1350 Avenue of the Americas, New York, New York 10019, USA.

ROMANCE AND HISTORICAL PUBLICATIONS

Novels

Devil's Desire. New York, Avon, 1975.
Moonstruck Madness. New York, Avon, 1977; London, Futura, 1978.
Tears of Gold. New York, Avon, and London, Futura, 1979.
Chance the Winds of Fortune. New York, Avon, 1980.
Dark Before the Rising Sun. New York, Avon, 1982.
Wild Bells to the Wild Sky. New York, Avon, 1983; London, Piatkus, 1984.
When the Splendor Falls. New York, Avon, 1985; London, Inner Circle, 1986.

*   *   *

Laurie McBain's novels are the type that often are described as 'sweeping sagas', in which the heroine moves from adventure to adventure, usually in dire peril and in conflict with the hero. The action may take place in England, but often moves to other, more exotic locations. Mara O'Flynn (*Tears of Gold*) travels from England to California in Gold Rush days, and finally to Louisiana before embarking again for England. Sabrina Verrick (*Moonstruck Madness*) supports her family as a Robin Hood style highwayman. Later she appears as Rhea Dominick's mother in *Chance the Winds of Fortune*, a less than staid duchess, who agonizes over her daughter's adventures. Rhea is sold as an indentured servant in the colonies and roams about the lush Caribbean before returning home. Lily Christian (*Wild Bells to the Wild Sky*), daughter of an English privateer and his willing Spanish conquest, is involved in intrigue in England and the West Indies. Leigh Travers (*When the Splendor Falls*) survives the American Civil War and travels to the New Mexico Territory before winning through to happiness.

Description of period dress and mannerisms fill the books, while much of the dialogue in the earlier works is laced with colloquialisms. It is all meant to help the reader 'experience' the period, but at times the obsolete terms and phrases get in the way. In her more recent works, especially *Wild Bells to the Wild Sky* and *When the Splendor Falls*, McBain has gone a long way in correcting the occasional stiltedness which marred the early novels.

In spite of the locations and historical details, the main interest in McBain's novels remains the romance and its attendant problems. The course of true love is never allowed to run smoothly since there is hostility or tension between the hero and heroine. The hero is strong, older, more experienced, usually cynical, and preferably titled (or the American equivalent, wealthy). The heroine is young, relatively innocent, and something of a spitfire. The conflict between them allows for many twists and turns of the plot before she is tamed (but not broken) and he surrenders and confesses his love for her. The characters and plots are pretty standard fare, but McBain succeeds in developing her characters within the limitations of the genre and inventing some interesting stories and subplots. Another plus for McBain is that she allows her heroines to mature. The original 'spitfire' often seems to be little more than a spoiled brat rather than a woman fighting for independence, but McBain manages to alter the strident overtones as the romantic conflict is resolved.

Although her body of work remains relatively small, McBain has developed a solid reputation for delivering a satisfying romance.

—Barbara E. Kemp

McCORQUODALE, Barbara. See **CARTLAND, Barbara.**

McCULLOUGH, Colleen.
Nationality: Australian. **Born:** Wellington, New South Wales, in 1937. **Education:** East Holy Cross College, Woolahra, New South Wales; University of Sydney; Institute of Child Health, London University. **Relations:** married Ric Robinson in 1984. **Career:** neu-

rophysiologist, Sydney, London, and Medical School, Yale University, New Haven, Connecticut, 1967–76. Since 1976, full-time writer. Lives on Norfolk Island, South Pacific. **Address:** c/o Century, 20 Vauxhall Bridge Road, London SW1V 2SA, England.

ROMANCE AND HISTORICAL PUBLICATIONS

Novels (series: Masters of Rome)

Tim. New York, Harper, 1974; London, Angus and Robertson, 1975.
The Thornbirds. New York, Harper, and London, Raven, 1977.
An Indecent Obsession. New York, Harper, and London, Macdonald, 1981.
The Ladies of Missalonghi. New York, Harper, and London, Hutchinson, 1987.
Masters of Rome:
    The First Man In Rome. New York, Morrow, and London, Century, 1990.
    The Grass Crown. New York, Morrow, and London, Century, 1991.
    Fortune's Favourites. London, Century, 1993.

OTHER PUBLICATIONS

Novels

A Creed for the Third Millennium. New York, Harper, and London, Macdonald, 1987.

Other

Cooking with Colleen McCullough and Jean Easthope. New York, Harper, and London, Macdonald, 1982.

*   *   *

Colleen McCullough gained international recognition with her racy second novel, *The Thornbirds*, set in outback Australia, although all her other books have had considerable success by any standards. *The Thornbirds, An Indecent Obsession*, and *The Ladies of Missalonghi* are historical novels, and *Tim* is a modern romance. *A Creed for the Third Millennium*, an unconvincing exploration of the basis of faith, is set in the future, as the title might suggest. The publication, in 1990, of *The First Man in Rome*, followed by *The Grass Crown*, the first two of a projected series of six novels, marks a new and major undertaking chronicling the political manoeuvring and personal lives of powerful men in Ancient Rome, from 110 B.C.

McCullough's first three books, and *The Ladies of Missalonghi*, feature an Australian woman who, at some point in her life, has to make a decision to pursue a course of conduct contrary to what society dictates is acceptable. In *Tim* a middle-aged spinster decides to marry a young mentally-retarded man who loves her. The beautiful heroine, Meggie, in *The Thornbirds*, has a child by a priest. Nurse Langtry, in *An Indecent Obsession*, chooses between career and marriage, and in *The Ladies of Missalonghi*, the heroine Missy tricks a man into marrying her. Frequently plots turn on taboo subjects such as the sexual needs of priests, older women, and the mentally retarded. A motif is the transformation of a dull or insignificant woman into someone spirited and outgoing. Money, particularly the freedom it can bring a single woman, is a central concern and often there is a progression from poverty to riches.

Although plot summaries might suggest otherwise, McCullough's books are not feminist in tone. Relationships between men and women are depicted in a cliché-ridden manner. Despite heroines achieving a degree of autonomy, the status quo is maintained and they are more or less dependent on relationships with men. Even Nurse Langtry's choice suggests the cloister rather than liberty. McCullough's chief talent is in her description of landscape and in depicting vivid scenes such as the deathbed of Mary Carson in *The Thornbirds* which is both gruesome and memorable. In the same novel, the author casts a wide net and convincingly covers subjects as diverse as Vatican politics to sugar cane cutting in Queensland.

McCullough uses well-worn plots in all her novels but has the ability to make even hackneyed situations fresh and appealing. She was a voracious reader as a child, and it is apparent that many situations from childhood reading have stayed with her. *The Ladies of Missalonghi* attracted comment on publication when it was alleged the novel was a rewrite of Canadian novelist's L.M. Montgomery's *The Blue Castle*. Despite numerous similarities between the two books, the actions of McCullough's heroine alter the entire tone of the tale. Montgomery's heroine is a victim of circumstance whereas Missy, once off the leash, takes an active part in determining her future. However, in this and other novels McCullough's characters are one-dimensional and she cannot create convincing dialogue. A reader's faith is sorely tested by the sudden changes in the various heroines, and by such unlikely lines as 'Sweet suffering rock oysters' and 'Holy man-eating toads!', only two examples from a repertoire of expressions given to Mary's boss (a professional man) in *Tim*. Also often commented on by critics is the author's addiction to florid metaphors drawn out to absurd lengths. It is perhaps a tribute to McCullough's storytelling ability that her novels are still immensely readable despite very apparent flaws in technique.

Not all fans of McCullough's earlier romances will enjoy the Rome series which require considerable staying power from the readers due to their immense length and formidable historical detail. Both *The First Man in Rome* and *The Grass Crown* have extensive glossaries and numerous maps in addition to the wealth of information in the novels. The themes are government and power, and unlike the earlier novels, female characters have only minor roles. The two major characters, Gaius Marius and Lucius Cornelius Sulla, are memorable creations, and readers will recognize, only too readily, modern equivalents to these power hungry men, and their unscrupulous ways of achieving their ends. Again, there are faults with dialogue—'Ooooops, sorry!' says Sulla to Gaius Marius, the most powerful man in Rome. The domestic scenes are fascinating as are many of the political debates, but bodies in bed are outnumbered by the piles of dead in battlefields, and particularly, in *The Grass Crown*, by marching legions.

—Kerry White

McCUTCHAN, Philip (Donald).
Pseudonyms: Robert Conington Galway; Duncan MacNeil; T.I.G. Wigg. **Nationality:** British. **Born:** Cambridge, 13 October 1920. **Education:** St Helens' College, Southsea, Hampshire, 1926–34; studied for H.M. Forces entry examination, 1934–38; Royal Military College, Sandhurst, Surrey, 1938. **Military Service:** Royal Naval Volunteer Reserve, 1939–46: lieutenant. **Relations:** married Elizabeth May Ryan in 1951; one son and one daughter. **Career:** assistant purser, Orient Steam Navigation Company, London, 1946–49; accounts assistant, Anglo-Iranian Oil Company, London, 1949–52; teacher in preparatory schools, 1952–54; owner of a teashop, 1954–60. Full-time writer since 1960. Chair, Crime Writers Association, 1965–66. **Address:** 107 Portland Road, Worthing, West Sussex BN11 1QA, England.

ROMANCE AND HISTORICAL PUBLICATIONS

Novels (series: Lieutenant St Vincent Halfhyde in all books)

Beware, Beware the Bight of Benin. London, Barker, 1974; as *Beware the Bight of Benin*, New York, St Martin's Press, 1975.
Halfhyde's Island. London, Weidenfeld and Nicolson, 1975; New York, St Martin's Press, 1976.
The Guns of Arrest. London, Weidenfeld and Nicolson, and New York, St Martin's Press, 1976.
Halfhyde to the Narrows. London, Weidenfeld and Nicolson, and New York, St Martin's Press, 1977.
Halfhyde for the Queen. London, Weidenfeld and Nicolson, and New York, St Martin's Press, 1978.
Halfhyde Ordered South. London, Weidenfeld and Nicolson, 1979; New York, St Martin's Press, 1980.
Halfhyde and the Flag Captain. London, Weidenfeld and Nicolson, 1980; New York, St Martin's Press, 1981.
Halfhyde on the Yangtze. London, Weidenfeld and Nicolson, 1981.
Halfhyde on Zanatu. London, Weidenfeld and Nicolson, and New York, St Martin's Press, 1982.
Halfhyde Outward Bound. London, Weidenfeld and Nicolson, 1983; New York, St Martin's Press, 1984.
The Halfhyde Line. London, Weidenfeld and Nicolson, 1984; New York, St Martin's Press, 1985.
Halfhyde and the Chain Gangs. London, Weidenfeld and Nicolson, 1985; New York, St Martin's Press, 1986.
Halfhyde Goes to War. London, Weidenfeld and Nicolson, 1986; New York, St Martin's Press, 1987.
Halfhyde on the Amazon. London, Weidenfeld and Nicolson, and New York, St Martin's Press, 1988.
Halfhyde and the Admiral. London, Weidenfeld and Nicolson, 1990.
The Last Farewell. London, Weidenfeld and Nicolson, and New York, St Martin's Press, 1991.
Flood. London, Hale, 1991.
Halfhyde and the Fleet Review. London, Weidenfeld and Nicolson, 1991; New York, St Martin's Press, 1992.
Cameron's Crossing. London, Weidenfeld and Nicolson, 1993.
Kidnap. London, Hodder and Stoughton, 1993.

Novels as Duncan MacNeil (series: James Ogilvie in all books)

Drums Along the Khyber. London, Hodder and Stoughton, 1969; New York, St Martin's Press, 1973.
Lieutenant of the Line. London, Hodder and Stoughton, 1970; New York, St Martin's Press, 1973.
Sadhu on the Mountain Peak. London, Hodder and Stoughton, 1971; New York, St Martin's Press, 1974.
The Gates of Kunarja. London, Hodder and Stoughton, 1972; New York, St Martin's Press, 1974.
The Red Daniel. London, Hodder and Stoughton, 1973; New York, St Martin's Press, 1974.
Subaltern's Choice. London, Hodder and Stoughton, and New York, St Martin's Press, 1974.
By Command of the Viceroy. London, Hodder and Stoughton, and New York, St Martin's Press, 1975.
The Mullah from Kashmir. London, Hodder and Stoughton, 1976; New York, St Martin's Press, 1977.
Wolf in the Fold. London, Hodder and Stoughton, and New York, St Martin's Press, 1977.
Charge of Cowardice. London, Hodder and Stoughton, and New York, St Martin's Press, 1978.
The Restless Frontier. London, Hodder and Stoughton, 1979; New York, St Martin's Press, 1980.
Cunningham's Revenge. London, Hodder and Stoughton, 1980; New York, Walker, 1985.

The Train at Bundarbar. London, Hodder and Stoughton, 1981; New York, Walker, 1986.
A Matter for the Regiment. London, Hodder and Stoughton, 1982.

OTHER PUBLICATIONS

Novels

Whistle and I'll Come. London, Harrap, 1957.
The Kid. London, Harrap, 1958.
Storm South. London, Harrap, 1959.
Gibraltar Road. London, Harrap, 1960; New York, Berkley, 1965.
Redcap. London, Harrap, 1961; New York, Berkley, 1965.
Hopkinson and the Devil of Hate. London, Harrap, 1961.
Bluebolt One. London, Harrap, 1962; New York, Berkley, 1965.
Leave the Dead Behind Us. London, Harrap, 1962.
Marley's Empire. London, Harrap, 1963.
The Man from Moscow. London, Harrap, 1963; New York, Day, 1965.
Warmaster. London, Harrap, 1963; New York, Day, 1964.
Moscow Coach. London, Harrap, 1964; New York, Day, 1966.
Bowering's Breakwater. London, Harrap, 1964.
Sladd's Evil. London, Harrap, 1965; New York, Day, 1967.
A Time for Survival. London, Harrap, 1966.
The Dead Line. London, Harrap, and New York, Berkley, 1966.
Skyprobe. London, Harrap, 1966; New York, Day, 1967.
Poulter's Passage. London, Harrap, 1967.
The Day of the Coastwatch. London, Harrap, 1968.
The Screaming Dead Balloons. London, Harrap, and New York, Day, 1968.
The Bright Red Businessmen. London, Harrap, and New York, Day, 1969.
The All-Purpose Bodies. London, Harrap, 1969; New York, Day, 1970.
Hartinger's Mouse. London, Harrap, 1970.
Man, Let's Go On. London, Harrap, 1970.
Half a Bag of Stringer. London, Harrap, 1971.
This Drakotny. London, Harrap, 1971.
The German Helmet. London, Harrap, 1972.
The Oil Bastards. London, Harrap, 1972.
Pull My String. London, Harrap, 1973.
Coach North. London, Harrap, 1974; New York, Walker, 1975.
Call for Simon Shard. London, Harrap, 1974.
A Very Big Bang. London, Hodder and Stoughton, 1975.
Blood Run East. London, Hodder and Stoughton, 1976.
The Eros Affair. London, Hodder and Stoughton, 1977.
Blackmail North. London, Hodder and Stoughton, 1978.
Sunstrike. London, Hodder and Stoughton, 1979.
Corpse. London, Hodder and Stoughton, 1980.
Cameron, Ordinary Seaman. London, Barker, 1980.
Cameron Comes Through. London, Barker, 1980; New York, St Martin's Press, 1986.
Cameron of the Castle Bay. London, Barker, 1981.
Lieutenant Cameron RNVR. London, Barker, 1981; New York, St Martin's Press, 1985.
Shard Calls the Tune. London, Hodder and Stoughton, 1981.
Werewolf. London, Hodder and Stoughton, 1982.
Cameron's Convoy. London, Barker, 1982.
Cameron in the Gap. London, Barker, 1982; New York, St Martin's Press, 1983.
Orders for Cameron. London, Barker, and New York, St Martin's Press, 1983.
Cameron in Command. London, Barker, 1983; New York, St Martin's Press, 1984.
The Hoof. London, Hodder and Stoughton, 1983.

Rollerball. London, Hodder and Stoughton, 1984.

Cameron and the Kaiserhof. London, Barker, and New York, St Martin's Press, 1984.

Cameron's Raid. London, Weidenfeld and Nicolson, and New York, St Martin's Press, 1985.

Shard at Bay. London, Hodder and Stoughton, 1985.

The Executioners. London, Hodder and Stoughton, 1986.

Cameron's Chase. London, Weidenfeld and Nicolson, and New York, St Martin's Press, 1986.

The Convoy Commodore. London, Weidenfeld and Nicolson, 1986; New York, St Martin's Press, 1987.

Greenfly. London, Hodder and Stoughton, 1987.

Cameron's Troop Lift. London, Weidenfeld and Nicolson, and New York, St Martin's Press, 1987.

Convoy North. London, Weidenfeld and Nicolson, 1987; New York, St Martin's Press, 1988.

Overnight Express. London, Hodder and Stoughton, 1988.

Convoy South. London, Weidenfeld and Nicolson, and New York, St Martin's Press, 1988.

The Boy Who Liked Monsters. London, Hodder and Stoughton, 1989.

Cameron's Commitment. London, Weidenfeld and Nicolson, and New York, St Martin's Press, 1989.

Convoy East. London, Weidenfeld and Nicolson, and New York, St Martin's Press, 1989.

Convoy of Fear. London, Weidenfeld and Nicolson, and New York, St Martin's Press, 1990.

Convoy Homeward. London, Weidenfeld and Nicolson, and New York, St Martin's Press, 1992.

The Abbott of Stockbridge. London, Hodder and Stoughton.

A Lady of the Line. London, Weidenfeld and Nicolson, 1992.

Novels as T.I.G. Wigg

A Job with the Boys. London, Dobson, 1958.

For the Sons of Gentlemen. London, Dobson, 1960.

A Rum for the Captain. London, Dobson, 1961.

Novels as Robert Conington Galway

Assignment New York. London, Hale, 1963.

Assignment London. London, Hale, 1963.

Assignment Andalusia. London, Hale, 1965.

Assignment Malta. London, Hale, 1966.

Assignment Gaolbreak. London, Hale, 1968.

Assignment Argentina. London, Hale, 1969.

Assignment Fenland. London, Hale, 1969.

Assignment Seabed. London, Hale, 1969.

Assignment Sydney. London, Hale, 1970.

Assignment Death Squad. London, Hale, 1970.

The Negative Man. London, Hale, 1971.

Plays

Radio Plays and Features: *The Proper Service Manner,* 1954; *Unlawful Occasions,* 1954; *First Command,* 1954; *The Feast of Lanterns,* 1955; *Thirty-Four for Tea,* 1955; *A Run Ashore,* 1956; *Flash Point,* 1956; *The Great Siege,* 1956; *In Partnership.* 1958; *O'Flynn of UBI* (for children), 1963.

Other

On Course for Danger (for children). London, Macmillan, and New York, St Martin's Press, 1959.

Tall Ships: The Golden Age of Sail. London, Weidenfeld and Nicolson, and New York, Crown, 1976.

Great Yachts. London, Weidenfeld and Nicolson, and New York, Crown, 1979.

*

Philip McCutchan comments:

My main work falls into six series. Two of these series are historical: under the pseudonym Duncan MacNeil I write an army series based on a fictitious Highland Regiment fighting on the North-West Frontier of India in the 1890s, and I write a naval series featuring Lieutenant St Vincent Halfhyde, also set in the 1890s. Four series are set in more modern times. One features Commander Esmonde Shaw, ex-Naval Intelligence; one features Detective Chief Superintendent Simon Shard, attached to a special-special branch in the Foreign Office; and two are naval series set in World War II, featuring Donald Cameron and Commodore John Mason Kemp. I have also written a number of non-series adventure thrillers. I am tending more and more to concentrate on naval fiction.

*   *   *

Variety, as opposed to versatility, is the mark of Philip McCutchan's novels. From a Pitlochry industrial estate to Australia's Barrier Reef to the Kola Penninsula of Russia, various heroes, differentiated only in name, battle evil. Shaw, Shard, Cameron, and Mason Kemp become involved in fascism, terrorism, blackmail (nuclear and otherwise), theft, treason, and espionage, travelling anywhere from Yorkshire to Valparaiso in under 200 pages. The female side-kick is an optional, but always the villains are of the classic school and work for abbreviated agencies like WUSWIPP. Although the picture is as simple as an early Hollywood gangster film, the elements are rooted in the late 1980s.

The destruction of the ozone layer, brain-washing in a Libyan gaol, a Belfast bomber's threat to blow up a chemical defence establishment—these are likely scenarios but perhaps not appropriate material for a writer like McCutchan. He trivializes these issues which are close to the hearts of many, and unless they are handled with thoughtfulness and sensitivity it would be better not to exploit such topics at all. Writers like Ian Fleming do succeed with similar concepts because they move completely into fantasy with tongue firmly in cheek, but McCutchan lacks this redeeming characteristic. In trying to mix the headlines of the daily newspaper with the requirement of a gripping thriller, he flounders.

McCutchan comes home when he writes about the past, when the pressure to be 'relevant' lessens. His element is the sea, with sailing ships a way of life and every sailor a hero. The best of these is the 'Halfhyde' series. Set in the late 1800s and early 20th century, it tells of the adventures of St Vincent Halfhyde, first in the Royal Navy and later as commander of a merchant vessel. The detail reflects the author's knowledge of seamanship and military matters, but not to the extent that it overshadows the basic story line. Some jargon creates an atmosphere of authenticity so that his narrative rings true and renders what he has to say more plausible. What he has to say is a severe indictment of the times.

Although the books are chronological, Halfhyde's persona remains constant from volume to volume. Even his failed marriage to Mildred and his subsequent passionate affair with Victoria Penn leave him spiritually unchanged and he gains nothing more than memories from his scrapes. He reminds the reader of Horatio Hornblower, but without Hornblower's increasing maturity as he advances in rank. Halfhyde's immutability is not necessarily a bad thing in this context, however. McCutchan has pitted him against the British Empire and all that was wrong with it, represented by his commanding officers and their landbound puppeteers. Because Halfhyde's foe is his own side he cannot afford the luxury of developing his own self-awareness. He must be left inviolate to stand firm against this pervasive, close, and domineering force, and if stability means stasis then that is the sacrifice McCutchan makes. Otherwise the focus would be split between Halfhyde's growing consciousness and his role as righter of imperial wrong—a juggling act which is wisely avoided.

McCutchan is not anti-imperialist as such, but he does object to a society which places small-minded, well-connected men in positions of power for which they are ill-qualified. In *Halfhyde and the Flag Captain*, Watkiss, Halfhyde's senior officer, exacerbates an already volatile situation with an act of aggression without considering the possible consequences. The diplomatic corps has the opposite blind-spot, making well-planned decisions in London which prove impractical on the high seas.

The ordinary seaman is held responsible for any resulting errors of command judgment, despite the fact that they simply carry out orders. Halfhyde for one refuses to be a pawn in this type of power game, and he constantly challenges his superiors' decisions, forcing them either to modify their original demands or at least momentarily to question their own convictions. Later, when he himself is in a position of authority, he consults his men (most notably his first lieutenant) and considers all options before acting. The result is invariably a success, having been brought about through his natural leadership abilities.

Halfhyde's chief function is to confront the moguls who try to manipulate his destiny. McCutchan uses the ensuing conflict to expose the status of a power which relies on tradition for its potency, not on the intrinsic value of its individuals. This conflict disappears and takes with it much of the thematic content once Halfhyde quits the Royal Navy as he does in *Halfhyde Outward Bound*. Suspended on half-pay, he joins the crew of a merchant ship bound for Sydney. The conditions are disgusting, and the first mate, appropriately named Bullock, turns out to be a tyrannical bully with the obligatory sadistic tendencies. Halfhyde's enemy from previous books appears again, this time with a personal vendetta to capture Halfhyde and present him as a prisoner to the Kaiser. Luckily he fails.

The elements are there as previously—chases, battles, skulduggery, and general excitement, but it rings hollow because the context is different. Halfhyde, having left the navy behind him, is now not fighting against his own side to preserve his integrity, nor is he even defending queen and country except in a very general way. He has lost all his thematic purpose as a figure once that framework was taken away, and what is left, random grappling with random evil, is far from satisfactory. The British government and naval command continue to make cameo appearances, in *The Halfhyde Line* for example, where a large arms cache is smuggled into Ireland through the ineptitude of officialdom. Bureaucracy is here an object which precipitates events rather than the subject of commentary as it would have been earlier in the series. It certainly contributes to the plot, but is no longer McCutchan's main concern.

This is characteristic of a less than successful historical novel. The background of history—its institutions and events—is the ideal vehicle to explore the past and what has gone into making the present. However when history becomes just another aspect of the story-line, its potency is wasted and the reader is left with just another cheap adventure yarn. Swashbuckling stories have many merits and are great fun to read, but in the case of the Halfhyde books the reader is left cheated out of the thoughtfulness the early work promised.

—L.M. Quinn

McCUTCHEON, George Barr.
Pseudonym: Richard Greaves. **Nationality:** American. **Born:** near Lafayette, Indiana, 26 July 1866. **Education:** Purdue University, Lafayette, two years. **Relations:** married Marie Fay in 1904; one stepson. **Career:** reporter, *Journal*, 1889, columnist, *Sunday Journal*, 1890, and city editor, 1893 and part-time staff member until 1905, *Courier*, all in Lafayette. President, Authors League, 1924–26. **Died:** 23 October 1928.

ROMANCE AND HISTORICAL PUBLICATIONS

Novels (series: Graustark)

Graustark: The Story of a Love Behind a Throne. Chicago, Stone, 1901; London, Richards, 1902.
Castle Craneycrow. Chicago, Stone, 1902; London, Richards, 1903.
Brewster's Millions (as Richard Greaves). Chicago, Stone, 1903; London, Collier, 1907.
The Sherrods. New York, Dodd Mead, 1903; London, Ward Lock, 1905.
Beverly of Graustark. New York, Dodd Mead, and London, Stevens and Brown, 1904.
The Day of the Dog. New York, Dodd Mead, 1904; revised edition, 1916.
Nedra. New York, Dodd Mead, and London, Stevens and Brown, 1905.
The Purple Parasol. New York, Dodd Mead, 1905.
Cowardice Court. New York, Dodd Mead, 1906.
Jane Cable. New York, Dodd Mead, and London, Hodder and Stoughton, 1906.
The Flyers. New York, Dodd Mead, and London, Stevens and Brown, 1907.
The Husbands of Edith. New York, Dodd Mead, 1908; London, Holden and Hardingham, 1912.
The Man from Brodney's. New York, Dodd Mead, and London, Hodder and Stoughton, 1908.
The Alternative. New York, Dodd Mead, 1909.
Truxton King: A Story of Graustark. New York, Dodd Mead, and London, Stevens and Brown, 1909.
The Butterfly Man. New York, Dodd Mead, 1910.
The Rose in the Ring. New York, Dodd Mead, and London, Everett, 1910.
Mary Midthorne. New York, Dodd Mead, and London, Stevens and Brown, 1911.
What's-His-Name. New York, Dodd Mead, and London, Stevens and Brown, 1911.
The Hollow of Her Hand. New York, Dodd Mead, and London, Stevens and Brown, 1912.
A Fool and His Money. New York, Dodd Mead, and London, Stevens and Brown, 1913.
Black Is White. New York, Dodd Mead, 1914; London, Everett, 1915.
The Prince of Graustark. New York, Dodd Mead, and London, Stevens and Brown, 1914.
Mr Bingle. New York, Dodd Mead, and London, Stevens and Brown, 1915.
From the Housetops. New York, Dodd Mead, and London, Stevens and Brown, 1916.
The Light That Lies. New York, Dodd Mead, 1916; London, Jenkins, 1917.
Green Fancy. New York, Dodd Mead, 1917; London, Hodder and Stoughton, 1918.
The City of Masks. New York, Dodd Mead, 1918; as *The Court of New York*, London, Melrose, 1919.
Shot with Crimson. New York, Dodd Mead, 1918; London, Jenkins, 1920.
Sherry. New York, Dodd Mead, 1919.

West Wind Drift. New York, Dodd Mead, 1920; London, Nash, 1921.

Quill's Window. New York, Dodd Mead, 1921; London, Nash, 1922.

Yollop. New York, Dodd Mead, 1922.

Viola Gwyn. New York, Dodd Mead, and London, Nash, 1922.

Oliver October. New York, Dodd Mead, 1923; London, Harrap, 1924.

East of the Setting Sun: A Story of Graustark. New York, Dodd Mead, 1924; London, Harrap, 1925.

Romeo in Moon Village. New York, Dodd Mead, 1925; London, Nash, 1926.

The Inn of the Hawk and Raven: A Tale of Old Graustark. New York, Dodd Mead, 1926; London, Lane, 1927.

Kindling and Ashes; or, The Heart of Barbara Wayne. New York, Dodd Mead, 1926; London, Lane, 1927.

Blades. New York, Dodd Mead, and London, Lane, 1928.

The Merivales. New York, Dodd Mead, 1929.

Short Stories

Her Weight in Gold. Privately printed, 1911; revised edition, New York, Dodd Mead, 1912.

OTHER PUBLICATIONS

Novel

The Daughter of Anderson Crow. New York, Dodd Mead, and London, Hodder and Stoughton, 1907.

Short Stories

Anderson Crow, Detective. New York, Dodd Mead, 1920.

Anderson, The Joker, in *Three Yarns*, with Booth Tarkington and G. K. Chesterton. Chicago, Blue Ribbon, 1924.

Plays

Brood House. Privately printed, 1910.

One Score and Ten. Privately printed, 1919.

Daddy Dumplings, with Earl Carroll (produced New York, 1920).

Other

Books Once Were Men: An Essay for Booklovers. New York, Dodd Mead, 1931.

The Young Mathematician Series. Skokie, Illinois, National Textbook, 6 vols, 1968–70.

*

Film Adaptation: *Brewster's Millions*, 1916, 1921, 1935, 1945 (*Three on a Spree*, 1961), 1985.

Critical Study: *Beyond Graustark: George Barr McCutcheon: Playwright Discovered*. by A.L. Lazarus and Victor H. Jones, Port Washington, New York, Kennikat Press, 1981.

*   *   *

George Barr McCutcheon wrote more than 40 novels, a number of plays and novelettes, and several essays, but he is best remembered for six popular romances, the Graustark stories.

A product of the turn-of-the-century midwestern American imagination, McCutcheon reflected both America's attraction to Euro-

pean culture and its self-conscious pride in her own youth and independence during years when she was becoming a world power. McCutcheon's work attempts to resolve this tension, yet gives America the edge in the argument. A faith in the wholesomeness, ingenuity, and democracy of the optimistic American hero characterizes McCutcheon's most important work.

Related to adventure-romances like Anthony Hope's *Prisoner of Zenda*, and influenced by his early reading in 19th-century dime novels, McCutcheon's Graustark books were predominantly departures from the domestic female-protagonist romances of the 19th century and excursions into a world of male action and resourcefulness. The Graustark novels are all set in a mythical Balkan state and in and around Edelweiss, its central city. Most of the six novels are male versions of the familiar Cinderella formula, but the commoner hero's reward for valour is not money or Christian salvation, but acceptance by the aristocratic community. Sometimes charmingly innocent before formal European ways, McCutcheon's heroes are over-simplified Jamesian Americans abroad. Unlike Henry James's realistic characters, however, McCutcheon's heroes overcome countless obstacles and manage to save beautiful aristocratic women from European villains and to bring them home to New York or Washington, DC.

The Graustark novels tend to begin slowly with background to the hero's search for love and adventure, then pick up with his sudden, undermotivated attraction for a beautiful, mysterious woman who leads him into a labyrinth of improbable intrigues and through a lengthy catalogue of obstructions that increase in difficulty until the plot reaches a culminating action and the hero's triumph. With his victory comes the defeat of evil forces and less worthy suitors for his lover's hand, the stability of marriage, and the respect of the aristocrats who doubted his abilities.

In the best-selling *Graustark*, the first of the series, Count Halfont finds it difficult to accept commoner hero Grenville Lorry's proposal of marriage to Graustark's Princess Yetive, even though Halfont finds Lorry to be 'the soul of honour, of courage, of manliness'. Lorry's reply summarizes the democratic American bias throughout McCutcheon's books.

> ... every born American may become ruler of the greatest nation in the world—the United States. His home is his kingdom; his wife, his mother, his sisters are his queens and princesses; his fellow citizens are his admiring subjects if he is wise and good. In my land you will find the poor man climbing to the highest pinnacle side by side with the rich man.... We recognize little as impossible. Until death destroys this power to love and to hope I must say to you that I shall not consider Princess Yetive beyond my reach.

Love triumphs: Lorry married the Princess, and with that marriage begins the saga that includes the continuing story of Yetive and Lorry in *Beverly of Graustark*, the tale of Prince Robin, the Lorry's son and his protectors in *Truxton King*, Robin's courtship and marriage to an American woman in *The Prince of Graustark*, and the postwar adventures of an American writer in Graustark in *East of the Setting Sun*. The final Graustark novel, *The Inn of the Hawk and Raven*, returns to the years before Yetive's marriage to Lorry.

Although McCutcheon made his name on the Graustark books, he wrote 40 additional novels; many were similar formula romances with robust American heroes, but most were set in the United States. The best known of these, *Brewster's Millions*, published under the pseudonym Richard Greaves, became a popular film. In the American romances McCutcheon experimented more with realistic techniques, paying greater attention to local colour settings, regional dialects, and humour.

McCutcheon's style and most of his characterizations are flat and pedestrian, his plot construction competent, but slow moving. His achievement comes in his clever conceptions for stories and most importantly in his creation of likeable, democratic American heroes of near-mythical proportions.

—Nancy H. Pogel

————

McELFRESH, (Elizabeth) Adeline.
Pseudonyms: Jennifer Blair; John Cleveland; Jane Scott; Elizabeth Wesley. **Nationality:** American. **Born:** Indiana, 28 May 1918. **Education:** high school in Bruceville, Indiana. **Career:** proofreader, 1936–42, and feature editor, 1943–56, Vincennes *Sun-Commercial*, Indiana; reporter, Troy *Daily News*, Ohio, 1942–43; reporter and editor, 1973–1978; managing editor, 1978–81; feature writer, 1981–83. Since 1966, director of public relations, Good Samaritan Hospital, Vincennes. **Address:** R.R.3, Vincennes, Indiana, USA.

ROMANCE AND HISTORICAL PUBLICATIONS

Novels (series: Dr Jane; Jill Nolan)

Charlotte Wade. New York, Arcadia House, 1952.
Homecoming. New York, Arcadia House, 1953.
The Old Baxter Place. New York, Arcadia House, 1954.
Doctor Jane. New York, Avalon, 1954; London, Corgi, 1958.
Ann and the Hoosier Doctor. New York, Avalon, 1955; as *Hill Country Nurse,* New York, Bantam, 1959.
Young Doctor Randall. New York, Avalon, 1957.
Nurse Kathy. New York, Avalon, 1957.
Calling Doctor Jane. New York, Avalon, 1957; London, Corgi, 1959.
Dr Jane's Mission. New York, Avalon, 1958.
Dr Jane Comes Home. New York, Avalon, 1959; London, Corgi, 1961.
Kay Manion, MD. New York, Dell, 1959; as *Kay Mannion, MD,* London, Corgi, 1960.
Team-Up for Ann. London, Ward Lock, 1959.
Wings for Nurse Bennett. New York, Dell, 1960.
Ann Kenyon, Surgeon. New York, Dell, 1960.
Dr Jane's Choice. New York, Avalon, 1961.
To Each Her Dream. Indianapolis, Bobbs Merrill, 1961.
Night Call. New York, Dell, 1961.
Hospital Hill. New York, Dell, 1961.
Romantic Assignment. London, Ward Lock, 1961.
Jeff Benton, MD. New York, Dell, 1962; London, Mayflower, 1964.
Jill Nolan, Surgical Nurse. New York, Dell, 1962.
Jill Nolan, RN. New York, Dell, 1962.
Challenge for Dr Jane. New York, Avalon, 1963.
Jill Nolan's Choice. New York, Dell, 1963.
The Magic Scalpel of Dr Farrer. New York, Avalon, 1965.
Nurse Nolan's Private Duty. New York, Dell, 1966.
Dr Jane, Interne. New York, Bantam, 1966.
Nurse for Mercy's Mission. New York, Belmont, 1976.
If Dreams Were Wild Horses. Toronto, Harlequin, 1988.
Murphy Goes A-Courtin'. Toronto, Harlequin, 1990.

Novels as Elizabeth Wesley (series: Dr Dee)

Nora Meade, MD. New York, Avalon, 1955; London, Corgi, 1958.
Ann Foster, Lab Technician. New York, Avalon, 1956.
Sharon James, Free-lance Photographer. New York, Avalon, 1956.
Polly's Summer Stock. New York, Avalon, 1957; as *Summer Stock Romance,* New York, Berkley, 1961.

Doctor Barbara. New York, Avalon, 1958.
Nurse Judy. New York, Avalon, 1958.
Jane Ryan, Dietician. New York, Avalon, 1959.
Doctor Dee. New York, Avalon, 1960.
Dr Dee's Choice. New York, Avalon, 1962.
Dr Dorothy's Choice. New York, Paperback Library, 1963.

Novels as Jane Scott

Barbara Owen, Girl Reporter. New York, Avalon, 1956.
Kay Rogers, Copy Writer. New York, Avalon, 1956.
A New Love for Cynthia. New York, Avalon, 1958.
Nurse Nancy. New York, Avalon, 1959.
A Nurse for Rebels' Run. New York, Avalon, 1960.

Novels as Jennifer Blair

Assignment in the Islands. New York, Dell, 1970.
Skye Harbour. New York, Dell, 1971.
Danger at Olduvai. New York, Dell, 1972.
Evil Island. New York, Dell, 1974.
Kanesbrake. New York, Dell, 1975.
Dangerous Assignments. New York, Dell, 1975.
The Longshadow. New York, Dell, 1976.
To Last a Lifetime. New York, Dell, 1977.
Safe Harbor. New York, Dell, 1977.

OTHER PUBLICATIONS

Novels

My Heart Went Dead. New York, Phoenix Press, 1949.
Murder with Roses. New York, Phoenix Press, 1950; London, Foulsham, 1953.
Keep Back the Dark. New York, Phoenix Press, 1951.
Minus One Corpse (as John Cleveland). New York, Arcadia House, 1954.
Shattered Halo. New York, Avalon, 1956; London, Ward Lock, 1960.

Other (for children)

Career for Jenny. New York, Avalon, 1958.
Summer Change. Indianapolis, Bobbs Merrill, 1960.

*   *   *

Adeline McElfresh was a prolific writer of romance and mystery novels who finally found her perfect writing form in medical romances.

Set in small, rural towns in America (southern Indiana is a favourite setting), McElfresh's books detail the minutiae of living in a close-knit community. Her protagonists usually work in the medical or journalistic professions, and her heroines are independent, spirited women with high standards of morality.

In *Shattered Halo*, Bess Nolan becomes engaged to the rich and charismatic Porter Dale, much to the horror of her colleague, Al Hanover, who is also in love with her. From the beginning of the book the reader is aware that there is something not quite trustworthy about Porter. Bess receives strange phone calls asking her to meet and investigate various people. As Porter begins to fulfil his political ambitions he starts to use Bess as a tool for his campaign. He is revealed as corrupt and callous, and Bess realizes that she is really in love with Al.

Similarly, Jeff, the hero of *Jeff Benton MD*, is also disillusioned about someone that he loves. He finds out that his father, a well-respected doctor has sanctioned an abortion. Given that this book was written in 1962, McElfresh was extremely courageous in introducing such a sensitive issue. One of Jeff's old flames, Carolee Meriden, becomes pregnant by her fiancé (a man whom the reader finds out is a murderer), and goes to Jeff for help. When he refuses, she turns to his father who 'advises' her on the best method to abort a child. The exploitation of workers, the need for adequate and protective housing policies, and the plight of impoverished miners and their families are other social issues that handled with sensitivity and care in the author's books.

In *Sharon James, Free-lance Photographer* (written as Elizabeth Wesley) the heroine has to face up to whether her career or her love life are more important. In the end she gives up her rich beau in favour of a much more sympathetic man.

In all of McElfresh's books love takes second place to more important issues—the career of one or both protagonists, an important social matter, or a natural disaster (for example, flooding and an outbreak of typhoid in *Kay Manion, MD*). It is this ability to depict a world outside of the romance of the hero and heroine that makes McElfresh's novels more than run-of-the mill formula romances. Her books are always a good reflection of the social and moral issues of the time in which they are set.

—Marion Hatchard

McEVOY, Marjorie. British. See 2nd edition, 1990.

McKAY, Simon.   See NICOLE, Christopher.

McKENNA, Lindsay.
Pseudonym for Ruth Eileen Nauman. **Other Pseudonyms:** Beth Brookes, Eileen Nauman, Ai Gvhdi Waya. **Nationality:** American. **Born:** San Diego, California, 24 May 1946. **Education:** Medford Senior High School, Medford, Oregon, 1952–64; Kent State University, 1978; National Center of Homeopathy, Alexandria, Washington, 1985–89. **Military Service:** United States Navy, 1964–67: aerographer's mate 3rd class, and meteorologist. **Relations:** married David G. Nauman in 1973. **Career:** teletype operator for stock market, legal secretary, and paralegal in contracts, 1967–80; teacher, creative writing and manuscript evaluation, Akron University, Akron, Ohio, 1975–80; teacher, creative writing, Uranian and medical astrology, Kent State University, Canton, Ohio, 1975–79; fire-fighter, West Point Volunteer Fire Department, West Point, Ohio, 1980–83; adjunct professor, Union Institute, Cincinnati, Ohio, 1992. Since 1975, medical astrologer. **Agent:** Jay Acton, 928 Broadway, New York, New York 10010, USA. **Address:** PO Box 2513, Cottonwood, Arizona 86326, USA.

ROMANCE AND HISTORICAL PUBLICATIONS

Novels (series: Kincaid; Love and Glory; Moments of Glory; Morgan's Mercenaries Travis; Women of Glory)

Captive of Fate. New York, Silhouette, 1983.
Chase the Clouds. New York, Silhouette, 1983.
Love Me Before Dawn. New York, Silhouette, 1984.
Too Near the Fire. New York, Silhouette, 1984.
Wilderness Passion. New York, Silhouette, 1984.
Texas Wildcat. New York, Silhouette, 1985.

Red Tail (Travis). New York, Silhouette, 1985.
Heart of the Eagle (Kincaid). New York, Silhouette, 1986.
A Measure of Love (Kincaid). New York, Silhouette, 1987.
Solitaire (Kincaid). New York, Silhouette, 1987.
Heart of the Tiger. New York, Silhouette, 1988.
A Question of Honor (Love and Glory). New York, Silhouette, 1989.
No Surrender (Love and Glory). New York, Silhouette, 1989.
Return of a Hero (Love and Glory). New York, Silhouette, 1989.
Come Gentle the Dawn. New York, Silhouette, 1989.
Dawn of Valor (Love and Glory). New York, Silhouette, 1991.
Sun Woman. Toronto, Harlequin, 1991.
No Quarter Given (Women of Glory). New York, Silhouette, 1991.
The Gauntlet (Women of Glory). New York, Silhouette, 1991.
Under Fire (Women of Glory). New York, Silhouette, 1991.
Lord of Shadowhawk. Toronto, Harlequin, 1992.
Ride the Tiger (Moments of Glory). New York, Silhouette, 1992.
One Man's War (Moments of Glory). New York, Silhouette, 1992.
Off Limits (Moments of Glory). New York, Silhouette, 1992.
King of Swords. Toronto, Harlequin, 1992.
Brave Heart. Toronto, Harlequin, 1993.
Heart of the Wolf (Morgan's Mercenaries). New York, Silhouette, 1993.
The Rogue (Morgan's Mercenaries). New York, Silhouette, 1993.
Commando (Morgan's Mercenaries). New York, Silhouette, 1993.
Point of Departure. New York, Silhouette, 1993.

Novels as Eileen Nauman (series: Travis)

Dare to Love (Travis). Toronto, Harlequin, 1985.
The Right Touch (Travis). Toronto, Harlequin, 1986.
Hostage Heart. New York, Avon, 1987.
Beginnings. New York, Popular Library, 1989.
Night Flight. New York, Popular Library, 1990.
My Only One. Toronto, Harlequin, 1991.

Novels as Beth Brookes

Hold Fast 'Til Morning. New York, Berkley, 1982.
Untamed Desire. New York, Berkley, 1983.
On Wings of Passion. New York, Berkley, 1983.
Torrid Nights. New York, Silhouette, 1984.
Where Enchantment Lies. New York, Berkley, 1986.

OTHER PUBLICATIONS

Screenplay: *Beginnings*, 1993.

Other

Interpreting Your Novien Moon (as Eileen Nauman). San Diego, California, Van Nuys, 1978.
Colored Stones and Healing (as Eileen Nauman), with Ruth Gent. Cottonwood, Arizona, Blue Turtle, 1990.
Soul Recovery and Extraction (as Ai Gvhdi Waya). Cottonwood, Arizona, Blue Turtle, 1992.
The American Book of Nutrition and Medical Astrology (as Eileen Nauman). San Diego, California, Astro-Computing, 1980; revised edition as *Medical Astrology*, Cottonwood, Arizona, Blue Turtle, 1993.

*

Lindsay McKenna comments:
My books, whether fiction or non-fiction, ultimately reflect me, my experience, my philosophy toward living life, and observing

people and situations around me. I don't believe any writer can write outside themselves, but rather, the wealth of information and creativity comes from within on both a conscious and subconscious level.

Because of my wide breadth of experience with life I was given a wonderful opportunity to observe people, religions, philosophies, and life. I've always been mesmerized by how people cope with situations, particularly life-altering kinds where there is pain involved on some level—because, we only change when pain is applied to us in some way.

Because I believe in hope, I want my writing to reflect that key point—that no matter how many bad cards life deals us, there is always hope to make the best of the situation and come out victorious through that experience. I also believe that Love is the strongest, most positive emotion we have on the face of Mother Earth, and that if we are to survive as a species and with one another, that it is the only emotional resource we have up our sleeve to accomplish this feat. Love, to me, is like light. When there is light, there can be no darkness. These themes are constantly interwoven throughout my writing now, and will be in the future. I always combine adventure, danger, or intrigue into my stories because I like seeing my characters not only dealing with internal situations, but external ones at the same time. I believe this makes for a far more riveting book for the reader.

I want my books to educate, and to teach my reader something about life. I try to put my experience, my observations of the human condition both in general and specific terms, into my work. For instance, due to my USA Navy/military background, I write about men and women in the military. I consequently created a sub-genre in romance known as the 'military romance'. I've been a fire-fighter, so I write about that. My love of nature and horses comes from my Cherokee/Irish background, and all of these topics are written about in my books.

More than anything, I want my books to give the reader hours of enjoyment, of being able to 'check out' of our harsh reality, and deliver a good story wrapped with love and hope. The bottom line on my books to the reader is: don't EVER give up—keep trying, keep struggling because in the end, you will be rewarded for having the courage to move forward instead of remaining where you're at, or retreating. Courage is never rewarded with defeat. Having the courage to love another person, to me, is one of the most fearful and challenging things in the world—yet, if we can gather our courage, despite our own woundings by life, and love someone outside of ourselves, there is no greater gift waiting for us because of it. The world could use a lot more love that it is presently getting. I believe that love can end the hatred and prejudice that infect our world, and that's why I write books that give us hope in that direction.

*　　*　　*

The writer Lindsay McKenna specializes in the romance for the modern woman in which the heroine, far from being a shrinking violet, actively participates in 'a man's world'. Many of her books have an army background (McKenna was in the United States Navy)—and the setting is an important part of the action—the ranks, the procedures, the attitudes, and the stresses are all emphasized, and provide a reassuringly solid framework for the romance between the protagonists. Her characters must also face the tension, difficulties, and excitement of active service, whether it be Korea in the 1950s, or Vietnam in the 1960s.

If the background of McKenna's books is not a military one, the situation is predominantly male, and involves action and stress. *Too Near the Fire*, for example, features a heroine, Leah, embarking on a career as a fire-fighter—the only woman in the department. Male chauvinism in the face of female endeavour is a prominant theme in McKenna's books, and her heroines have to prove themselves,

which they all do admirably without compromising their desirability or femininity.

As is obligatory in the romantic genre, her heroines are always beautiful, and whether tall or petite they are nearly always fine-boned, with heart shaped faces, and green eyes (Tess Ramsey in *One Man's War*; Rachel in *Dawn of Valor*; Leah in *Too Near the Fire* are examples). They are presented as intelligent, active, and strong-minded. Alexandrea Vance, in *Off Limits*, is prepared to defy her congressman father over the alleged desertion of marine Jim Mackenzie, the man she loves; she stands by Jim when he is sentenced to hard labour, and goes to live with him later. Similarly, Leah, in *Too Near the Fire*, stands up to the hostile chief of the Fire Fighting Department, and then has to endure the hostility of the men on her team; she has 'brains, aggressiveness, and good looks'.

Similarly, the men in McKenna's books are for the most part tall, broad-shouldered, with strong chins, and have 'piercing blue eyes'. Although they are very tough, as befits their active jobs (marine, helicopter pilot, fire-fighter), they can be very gentle when the occasion demands, usually concealing their feelings behind a granite exterior. When Alex, in *Off Limits*, first meets Jim:

> Her gaze clung to his harsh tense features. Under any other circumstances she would have thought Jim made of granite, his face not handsome at all. But the way he pursed his mouth, as if to hold back his own barrage of feelings told her he was a man of conscience.

Her heroes always do their duty, however unpleasant. Above all they are American patriots.

McKenna's style is colloquial, and she uses dialogue to enhance the immediacy of the situation. Descriptions are kept to a minimum, and are used to reinforce the technical background to her stories. Her characters do not inhabit the rarified world of the moneyed classes typical of this genre. The combination of action-packed stories, the element of excitement, and the emphasis on the less glamorous aspects of life lend an air of solid reality to McKenna's books—and this is why McKenna is a particularly attractive writer to the modern reader of romance.

—Ferelith Hordon

McNAUGHT, Judith.
Nationality: American. **Born:** California, 10 May 1944. **Education:** Northwestern University, Evanston, Illinois, 1962–66, B.S. in business administration. **Relations:** married 1) Michael McNaught (died 1983); 2) Don Smith (separated in 1993); one daughter and one son from an earlier marriage. **Career:** stewardess and personnel interviewer, United Airlines, Chicago, 1966–67; executive producer, KMOX-CBS Radio, St Louis, 1970–73; assistant director and motion picture director, Moritz Inc, St Louis, 1973–76; legal administrator, Sommers Schwartz Inc, Detroit, 1976–78; controller, U.S. Transportation Company, Detroit, 1978; president, Pro-Temps Inc, St Louis, 1979–85. **Agent:** Perry Knowlton, Curtis Brown, 10 Astor Place, New York, New York 10003, USA. **Address:** 5237 West Plano Parkway, Plano, Texas 75093, USA.

ROMANCE AND HISTORICAL PUBLICATIONS

Novels

Tender Triumph. Toronto, Harlequin, 1983; New York, Pocket Books, 1986.
Double Standards. Toronto, Harlequin, 1984; New York, Pocket Books, 1986.

Whitney, My Love. New York, Pocket Books, 1985; London, Corgi, 1986.
Once and Always. New York, Pocket Books, 1987; London, Corgi, 1988.
Something Wonderful. New York, Pocket Books, 1988; London, Severn House, 1989.
A Kingdom of Dreams. New York, Pocket Books, 1989; London, Corgi, 1991.
Almost Heaven. New York, Pocket Books, 1990; London, Corgi, 1992.
Paradise. New York, Pocket Books, 1991; London, Simon and Schuster, 1992.
Perfect. London, Simon and Schuster, 1993; New York, Pocket Books, 1994.

*

Judith McNaught comments:

I believe the success of my novels lies in the fact that each of them seems to be able to make readers laugh and cry—and then leave them smiling. I try to appeal to reader's emotions; to make readers really *feel* the joy, the sorrow, the tension experienced by all my characters.

*   *   *

Judith McNaught has a strong and well-deserved following among romance readers which increases with each new novel. Averaging a book a year, her total output of books is not great in comparison to many other writers, but her fans anticipate each new title impatiently. McNaught delivers a solid, well-crafted story, sympathetic, believable characters, and great chemistry between the hero and heroine. Moving easily between historical and contemporary romances, she seems to improve with each new book.

Her heroines are intelligent, proud, and independent. When faced with a difficult situation, they take action, often in the face of anticipated pain or retribution. Alexandra, in *Something Wonderful*, protects her husband physically in spite of his distrust of her. Jennifer Merrick (*A Kingdom of Dreams*) plans and executes a daring escape from her captors, showing all the finesse of a born soldier. The heroes of McNaught's novels are strong, determined men, who are distinguished by an innate sensitivity. Although they may appear hard, and even ruthless to others, they are capable of deep emotion. In many ways the main characters demonstrate the most admirable virtues of the opposite sex, which only increases the deep emotional bonds which develop between them.

McNaught does not rely solely on the common ploy of a simple clash of personalities to create dramatic conflict. Her couples are certainly strong-willed individuals, but there are often serious issues that divide the lovers so the substantive tensions between them must be resolved. It is in facing these concerns that the lovers find strength since the resolution is not so much a question of taming or yielding, as it is of understanding and compromise. In her first novel, *Tender Triumph*, McNaught tackled the basic question of a contemporary woman's role. Katie is very much a modern woman with a good job, and a bad marriage in her past. Falling in love with Ramon, she is unprepared to accept his traditional, 'old world' view of their relationship. She expects to be his equal, sharing his problems and victories, while he believes that she should be shielded and protected by him at all costs. This basic philosophical difference is exacerbated by a clash of cultures, when Katie and Ramon return to his home in Puerto Rico to be married. Similar conflicts in culture occur in the historical romances *Once and Always*, and *A Kingdom of Dreams*. In the former, American Victoria comes to England to live, while in the latter, Jennifer, a fiery Scot, must marry her English enemy and, eventually, choose between him and her beloved

clan. McNaught makes it clear that these women face difficult choices, but their situations are made a little easier by their husbands'/lovers' ability to make concessions in their own beliefs, proving that such romantic clashes do not have to result in winners and losers. In *Perfect* McNaught moves from the problems of individuals alone to tackle an important social problem. Adult illiteracy plays an important role in the story, and McNaught convincingly describes the problems of its victims and the triumphs they feel when they overcome their handicap.

In *A Kingdom of Dreams* McNaught joined many other romance authors in linking stories through related characters. In what is now popularly known as a 'prequel', readers are introduced to Royce Westmoreland, the first Duke of Claymore. It is his descendant, Clayton Westmoreland, the ninth Duke of Claymore, who is the hero of *Whitney, My Love*. Similarly, Jordan and Alexandra Townsende of *Something Wonderful* also appear in *Almost Heaven*.

McNaught has continued to develop the promise shown in her early novels. With *Paradise* she began to publish in hardcover, a sure sign of mainstream approval and popularity. Her novels are eagerly awaited and often appear on bestseller lists. Much of her appeal can be traced to the realistic bases she gives to her stories. Her couples think and act much more like real individuals than do the more fantasy-based couples in many other romances. Her novels provide support and reaffirmation of the existence of passion, tenderness, and love rather than simple escapism. At the same time she can be counted on to provide a fast-paced story with well-developed engaging characters, written with elegance and imbued with great emotional energy.

—Barbara E. Kemp

MEADMORE, Susan.   See **SALLIS, Susan.**

MELONEY, Franken.   See **FRANKEN, Rose.**

MELVILLE, Anne.
Pseudonym for Margaret Edith Potter. **Other Pseudonyms:** Anne Betteridge; Margaret Newman. Also writes as Margaret Potter. **Nationality:** British. **Born:** Margaret Edith Newman, Harrow, Middlesex, 21 June 1926. **Education:** Harrow County School for Girls, 1937–44; St Hugh's College, Oxford (major scholar), 1944–47, B.A. 1947, M.A. 1952. **Relations:** married Jeremy Potter in 1950; two children. **Career:** teacher, Egypt and England, 1947–50; editor, *King's Messenger* children's magazine, London, 1950–55; adviser, Citizen's Advice Bureau, Twickenham, Middlesex, 1962–70. **Recipient:** Romantic Novelists Association major award, 1966. **Agent:** Peters Fraser and Dunlop, 5th Floor, The Chambers, Chelsea Harbour, Lots Road, London SW10 0XF, England.

ROMANCE AND HISTORICAL PUBLICATIONS

Novels (series: Hardie; Lorimer)

The Lorimer Line. London, Heinemann, and New York, Doubleday, 1977.
The Lorimer Legacy. London, Heinemann, 1979; as *Alexa*, New York, Doubleday, 1979.
Blaize. New York, Doubleday, 1981.

Lorimers at War. London, Heinemann, 1980.
Lorimers in Love. London, Heinemann, 1981.
The Last of the Lorimers. London, Heinemann, 1983.
Lorimer Loyalties. London, Heinemann, 1984.
Family Fortunes (Lorimer). New York, Doubleday, 1984.
The House of Hardie. London, Grafton, 1987.
Grace Hardie. London, Grafton, 1988.
The Hardie Inheritance. London, Grafton, 1990.

Novels as Anne Betteridge

The Foreign Girl. London, Hurst and Blackett, 1960.
The Young Widow. London, Hurst and Blackett, 1961.
Spring in Morocco. London, Hurst and Blackett, 1962; New York, Beagle, 1973.
The Long Dance of Love. London, Hurst and Blackett, 1963.
The Younger Sister. London, Hurst and Blackett, 1964.
Return to Delphi. London, Hurst and Blackett, 1964.
Single to New York. London, Hurst and Blackett, 1965; New York, Beagle, 1973.
The Chains of Love. London, Hurst and Blackett, 1965; New York, Beagle, 1973.
The Truth Game. London, Hurst and Blackett, 1966; New York, Beagle, 1973.
A Portuguese Affair. London, Hurst and Blackett, 1966; New York, Beagle, 1973.
A Little Bit of Luck. London, Hurst and Blackett, 1967; New York, Beagle, 1973.
Shooting Star. London, Hurst and Blackett, 1968.
Love in a Rainy Country. London, Hurst and Blackett, 1969.
Sirocco. London, Hurst and Blackett, 1970; New York, Beagle, 1973.
The Girl Outside. London, Hurst and Blackett, 1971; New York, Beagle, 1973.
Journey from a Foreign Land. London, Hurst and Blackett, 1972.
The Sacrifice. London, Hurst and Blackett, 1973.
The Stranger on the Beach. London, Hurst and Blackett, 1974.
The Temp. London, Hurst and Blackett, 1976.
The Tiger and the Goat. London, Hurst and Blackett, 1978.

Short Stories

A Time of Their Lives. London, Hurst and Blackett, 1974.
A Place for Everyone. London, Hurst and Blackett, 1977.
Snapshots. London, Severn House, 1990.

OTHER PUBLICATIONS

Novels

Murder to Music (as Margaret Newman). London, Long, 1959.
Unto the Fourth Generation (as Margaret Potter). London, W.H. Allen, 1986.
Lochandar (as Margaret Potter). London, W.H. Allen, 1988.
The Dangerfield Diaries. London, Grafton, 1989.
The Tantivy Trust. London, HarperCollins, 1992.
A Clean Break. London, Piatkus, 1993.

Other (for children) as Margaret Potter

The Touch-and-Go Year. London, Dobson, 1968; New York, Meredith Press, 1969.
The Blow-and-Grow Year. London, Dobson, 1969.
Sandy's Safari. London, Dobson, 1971.
The Story of the Stolen Necklace. London, Dobson, 1974.

Trouble on Sunday. London, Methuen, 1974.
Smoke over Shap. London, BBC Publications, 1975.
The Motorway Mob. London, Methuen, 1976.
Tony's Special Place. London, Bodley Head, 1977.
The Boys Who Disappeared. London, Hodder and Stoughton, 1985.
Tilly and the Princess. London, Methuen, 1987.

*   *   *

Not so much a saga writer as a creator of fictional biographies, Anne Melville uses her writing as a medium for debating topics of social and philosophical significance. Experiences from her travels and teaching enrich her early works, colourful, gently scribed romances culminating in 1966 with winning the major Romantic Novelists Association award. Delphi, Morocco, New York, Portugal, and many other locations are evoked with growing skill as she tries new styles and avenues to satisfy a changing market, interspersing her novels with short stories and children's books.

Melville handles the position of women in awkward social situations with care and understanding, controlling the pace of her plot, balancing joy and sorrow, teasing from her characters the motives which drive them to fight against the restrictions of convention and prejudice to win independence, inside or outside accepted relationships. In doing so she tilts at the windmills of established British life, particularly at pretensious patrician classes. Every individual needs fulfilment of his or her own choosing, she insists, but throughout history most women have been doomed to conform or to pay bitterly if they do not. She concentrates on those who find their way through the maze, eventually, often opting for the unexpected, those who grow stronger through their mistakes but who, above all else, remain true to themselves. Her men, too, are real, thankfully too complex to be true heroes or villains.

She is good at children, having the rare ability to enter a small child's mind. Her depictions of childhood have a near fairy-tale quality which contrarily brings children alive. Grace Hardie, aged three, puts butter on her feet as was done to her kitten, Pepper, and licks it off, dust included, so that she will never stray too far from her new home. In *The Hardie Inheritance* curious Trish climbs into 'the hole', a stone sculpture which she declares represents Greystones. Her perspicacity earns her a lump of clay and the readers enjoy a perfect vignette of a child's doubtful exploration of a new medium, squashing the result with, 'It's more fun making things than having them'.

The theme of the Hardie sagas is happiness, 'when what you are is what you do', carrying sensitive, dedicated but often painfully nonconforming characters through the century. The descriptions of different periods are strong, though the early decades are drawn with slightly too feudal an emphasis on the gulf between the classes even after acknowledging the need for paternalistic care in an interdependent community. Her keenest eye is on World War I, and the slow dawning of comprehension by the home population of the horror unfolding in Europe. Deeply moving are the counterpoints she draws; as when letters of condolence say a soldier 'died instantaneously', to be crassly denied when torn, bloodied uniforms cut from the body are returned to families showing the clear nature of the wounds, resulting in inevitable rage and disaffection. The horror of war itself is described indirectly in terms of its results, through the maimed and insane, the imbalance of the sexes, the civil upheaval and truncating of old ways, beliefs and aspirations. Only rarely does she depict direct suffering, such as the choking claustrophobia inside a gas-mask. The brutality of war is not shirked, for she makes the reader acutely aware of permanent changes evoked in individuals, society, politics, and even ethics, for moral viewpoints change too.

Frequently Melville traces how an incident in childhood proves seminal. Pepper is shot accidently by Grace's least favourite brother, with whom, she realizes in adulthood, she will never be wholly reconciled. In her grief she upsets the new baby's cot. She thinks that the baby died, but when her own child is born a mongol in *The Hardie Inheritance* Grace has to struggle against a feeling of retribution. Her baby brother had been another, as she knew by then, and was put into permanent care. His reappearance is a difficult co-incidence to swallow, even more so when followed by the rediscovery of the parents' first child born, lost and fostered in China. Such things are easier to accept in fact than in fiction. The compassion Grace shows for her homosexual husband is also unusually benign for the period, even for someone as unorthodox as she.

That weakness apart, in this series and in the preceding Lorimer saga, the vivacity with which Edwardian times and the frenetic inter-war years are brought alive in sight, sound, and smell deepens our understanding. Attitudes convince, for she can capture the spirit of a period, especially in rural settings. Atmosphere is tangible, and she attends just as carefully to recent eras. In encapsulating so meticulously the protocol in a 1988 hospital ward in *The Dangerfield Diaries* she inadvertently startles us when we realize how much has changed even in the last five years. This book is also a study of the protection of personal privacy even beyond death, concluding that the control lies ultimately in the hands of the individual. Allowing for the exigencies of the plot, a life story told in diary-assisted flashbacks while the teller is in hospital for surgery, she mounts an absorbing investigation into the nature of truth. The use of the present tense for the hospital scenes is uneasy but it does help 'fix' the reader in the intended time, past or present.

Ainslie begins her recording in 1917 when her brother sets off to war after giving her a handsome leather diary, 'a selfish present' to be written for him to share. She is to include 'everything', though instinctively both feel he may not return to read it; a 'secret between you and me. It's the only way to be straight. If you suspect there's the slightest chance that someone else might see, then you'll leave out things which might offend them or make you feel ashamed. Or else you'll put things in that you want them to believe'. After her brother's death she records secrets, of others as well as herself which inevitably leads to conflict, not least between silence and outright lying, because she has an obligation to protect these secrets.

Spanning several decades, Melville's sagas chart changing attitudes, to abortion, sexuality, illegitimacy, racism, the position of women, the function of art in human life, personal responsibility, the sacrosanctity of law or medical responsibility, and much more. AIDS is barely mentioned, and then only as a push to the pendulum which she sees as constantly swinging. But these are the questions at the roots of every society. It takes a special writer to deal with philosophy so palatably, while avoiding the deadening taint of moralizing.

—Margaret Woodward

MERLIN, Christina. See **HEAVEN, Constance.**

MERTZ, Barbara G. See **MICHAELS, Barbara.**

METALIOUS, Grace.
Nationality: British. **Born:** Grace Repentigny, Manchester, Lancashire, 8 September 1924. **Relations:** married George Metalious in 1942; two daughters and one son. **Died:** 25 February 1964.

ROMANCE AND HISTORICAL PUBLICATIONS

Novels (series: Peyton Place)

Peyton Place. New York, Messner, 1956; London, Muller, 1957.
Return to Peyton Place. New York, Messner, 1959; London, Muller, 1960.
The Tight White Collar. New York, Messner, and London, Muller, 1960.
No Adam in Eden. New York, Trident, 1963; London, Muller, 1964.

*

Film Adaptations: *Peyton Place*, 1957; *Return to Peyton Place*, 1960.

Critical Studies: *The Girl from Peyton Place* (biography) by George Metalious and June O'Shea, New York, Dell, 1965.

* * *

At the height of its prestige as America's showcase community, Peyton Place—its townscape drawn from Gilmanton, New Hampshire; its name evoked by nearby but otherwise uninvolved Potter Place—was the setting and subject of the second bestselling novel in the United States up to that time, of a hit film that was nominated for several Academy awards, and of the first prime time television soap opera, beamed three nights a week into millions of homes. Today the book is out of print, the soap opera is a fading memory, and the movie and a sequel are revived occasionally for nostalgic old-timers.

The meteoric rise and rapid fizzling-out of Metalious's success were the result of her having both the fortune and misfortune to produce her masterpiece at just the time that its titillating genre was at the peak of its appeal—before being replaced by an offspring that made the parent look pale indeed. *Peyton Place* was the culmination of the fictional exposures of small-town American life whose authors inched their way along in efforts to see how far they could go in chronicling the cycle of the seasons in towns 'rampant with murder, incest, adultery, and general disagreeableness', as an anonymous reviewer for *Library Journal* put it, before censors suppressed the works and the authors were punished for libel and obscenity.

The genre originated late in the 19th century with Joseph Kirkland's and E.M. Howe's vindictive but veiled accounts of the meanness and frustration of life in mid-western small towns. It flourished especially in the iconoclastic 1920s in the avidly read and bitterly denounced *Winesburg, Ohio* by Sherwood Anderson and *Main Street* by Sinclair Lewis and climaxed in Henry Bellaman's probe of *King's Row*, to which *Peyton Place* is often compared. William Faulkner and Erskine Caldwell instituted a southern sub-genre, but the Currier-and-Ives villages of New England had remained off-limits, despite some grim glimpses in Edith Wharton's *Ethan Frome*, and some of Robert Frost's poems. Metalious's penetration of the heavily draped and shuttered windows of the staid communities where those like laconic President Calvin Coolidge kept any secrets inviolate outraged this last stronghold of national propriety and elated scandal-mongers everywhere.

Metalious's daring proved, however, her downfall. Although her first novel perilously walked the narrow line that bordered permissible tale-telling, it went just far enough to help tumble down the crumbling barriers of legal pre-restraint on fiction and film in the United States.

Metalious was never able to repeat her early success. Reviewers complained that *Return to Peyton Place* was a laboured tale that added nothing to the original except self-pitying details of an author's attempt to write and publish a book like *Peyton Place* in the face of community hostility. Having apparently exhausted her personal experiences, Metalious tried to draw upon limited powers of invention for *The Tight White Collar*, another tale of small town life, and *No Adam in Eden*, an episodic history of three generations of French Canadian women's search for love. Reviewers complained that these were 'pallid stuff', lacking any central theme or direction.

The most cogent summary of the reasons for Metalious's fleeting celebrity comes, as often such judgements do, from a distant source that could view her real and fictional worlds objectively. A London *Times* reviewer observed that she was 'expert at evoking sex-ridden adolescence—the permanent condition of most of her characters', but that she was 'addicted to a strident and ultimately risible vulgarity that infects much of what she writes'.

—Warren French

MICHAELS, Barbara.

Pseudonym for Barbara (Louise) G(ross) Mertz. Also writes as Barbara G. Mertz. **Other Pseudonym:** Elizabeth Peters. **Nationality:** American. **Born:** Canton, Illinois, 29 September 1927. **Education:** University of Chicago Oriental Institute, Ph.B 1947, M.A. 1950, Ph.D. 1952. **Relations:** married Richard R. Mertz in 1950 (divorced 1968); one daughter and one son. **Agent:** Dominick Abel, 146 West 82nd, New York 10001, USA.

ROMANCE AND HISTORICAL PUBLICATIONS

Novels

The Master of Blacktower. New York, Appleton Century Crofts, 1966; London, Jenkins, 1967.
Sons of the Wolf. New York, Meredith, 1967; London, Jenkins, 1968; as *Mystery on the Moors*, New York, Paperback Library, 1968.
Ammie, Come Home. New York, Meredith, 1968; London, Jenkins, 1969.
Prince of Darkness. New York, Meredith, 1969; London, Hodder and Stoughton, 1971.
The Dark on the Other Side. New York, Dodd Mead, 1970; London, Souvenir Press, 1973.
Greygallows. New York, Dodd Mead, 1972; London, Souvenir Press, 1974.
The Crying Child. New York, Dodd Mead, and London, Souvenir Press, 1973.
Witch. New York, Dodd Mead, 1973; London, Souvenir Press, 1975.
House of Many Shadows. New York, Dodd Mead, 1974; London, Souvenir Press, 1976.
The Sea King's Daughter. New York, Dodd Mead, 1975; London, Souvenir Press, 1977.
Patriot's Dream. New York, Dodd Mead, 1976; London, Souvenir Press, 1978.
Wings of the Falcon. New York, Dodd Mead, 1977; London, Souvenir Press, 1979.
Wait for What Will Come. New York, Dodd Mead, 1978; London, Souvenir Press, 1980.
The Walker in Shadows. New York, Dodd Mead, 1979; London, Souvenir Press, 1981.
The Wizard's Daughter. New York, Dodd Mead, 1980; London, Souvenir Press, 1982.
Someone in the House. New York, Dodd Mead, 1981; London, Souvenir Press, 1983.
Black Rainbow. New York, Congdon and Weed, 1982; London, Souvenir Press, 1983.

Here I Stay. New York, Congdon and Weed, 1983; London, Souvenir Press, 1985.
Dark Duet (includes *Ammie, Come Home* and *Prince of Darkness*). New York, Congdon and Weed, 1983.
The Grey Beginning. New York, Congdon and Weed, 1984; London, Souvenir Press, 1986.
Be Buried in the Rain. New York, Atheneum, 1985; London Piatkus, 1986.
Shattered Silk. New York, Atheneum, 1986; London, Piatkus, 1987.
Search the Shadows. New York, Atheneum, 1987; London, Piatkus, 1988.
Smoke and Mirrors. New York, Simon and Schuster, and London, Piatkus, 1989.
Into the Darkness. New York, Simon and Schuster, and London, Piatkus, 1990.
Vanish with the Rose. New York, Simon and Schuster, and London, Piatkus, 1992.
Houses of Stone. New York, Simon and Schuster, 1993.

Novels as Elizabeth Peters (series: Vicky Bliss; Jacqueline Kirby; Amelia Peabody)

The Jackal's Head. New York, Meredith, 1968; London, Jenkins, 1969.
The Camelot Caper. New York, Meredith, 1969; London, Cassell, 1976.
The Dead Sea Cipher. New York, Dodd Mead, 1970; London, Cassell, 1975.
The Night of Four Hundred Rabbits. New York, Dodd Mead, 1971; as *Shadows in the Moonlight*, London, Coronet, 1975.
The Seventh Sinner (Kirby). New York, Dodd Mead, 1972; London, Coronet, 1975.
Borrower of the Night (Bliss). New York, Dodd Mead, 1973; London, Cassell, 1974.
The Murders of Richard III (Kirby). New York, Dodd Mead, 1974; London, Piatkus, 1989.
Crocodile on the Sandbank (Peabody). New York, Dodd Mead, 1975; London, Cassell, 1976.
Legend in Green Velvet. New York, Dodd Mead, 1976; as *Ghost in Green Velvet*, London, Cassell, 1977.
Devil-May-Care. New York, Dodd Mead, 1977; London, Cassell, 1978.
Street of the Five Moons (Bliss). New York, Dodd Mead, 1978; London, Piatkus, 1988.
Summer of the Dragon. New York, Dodd Mead, 1979; London, Souvenir Press, 1980.
The Love Talker. New York, Dodd Mead, 1980; London, Souvenir Press, 1981.
The Curse of the Pharaohs (Peabody). New York, Dodd Mead, 1981; London, Souvenir Press, 1982.
The Copenhagen Connection. New York, Congdon and Lattès, 1982; London, Souvenir Press, 1983.
Silhouette in Scarlet (Bliss). New York, Congdon and Weed, 1983; London, Souvenir Press, 1984.
Die for Love (Kirby). New York, Congdon and Weed, 1984; London, Souvenir Press, 1985.
The Mummy Case (Peabody). New York, Congdon and Weed, 1985; London, Souvenir Press, 1986.
Lion in the Valley (Peabody). New York, Atheneum, 1986; London, Piatkus, 1987.
Trojan Gold (Bliss). New York, Atheneum, and London, Piatkus, 1987.
The Deeds of the Disturber (Peabody). New York, Atheneum, and London, Piatkus, 1988.
Naked Once More (Kirby). New York, Warner, 1989; and London, Piatkus, 1990.

The Last Camel Died at Noon (Peabody). New York, Warner, and London, Piatkus, 1991.
The Snake, the Crocodile, and the Dog (Peabody). New York, Warner, 1992.

OTHER PUBLICATIONS

Other as Barbara G. Mertz

Temples, Tombs, and Hieroglyphs: The Story of Egyptology. New York, Coward McCann, and London, Gollancz, 1964; revised edition, New York, Dodd Mead, 1978.
Red Land, Black Land: The World of the Ancient Egyptians. New York, Coward McCann, 1966; London, Hodder and Stoughton, 1967; revised edition, New York, Dodd Mead, 1978.
Two Thousand Years in Rome, with Richard Mertz. New York, Coward McCann, 1968; London, Dent, 1969.

*

Manuscript Collections: Mugar Memorial Library, Boston University.

Barbara Michaels comments:

I do not consider myself a writer of romances and I abhor the word 'gothic' as applied to anything except the novels of Mrs Radcliffe and 'Monk' Lewis. The Elizabeth Peters books are mysteries; so are the Barbara Michaels novels. Both are written from the point of view of a female protagonist, and both incorporate romantic plot elements; in my opinion, this does not make them romance novels any more than the presence of a romance between Richard Hannay and Mary makes *Mr Standfast* by John Buchan a romance novel.

'Romantic Suspense' is another term which has been applied to my books and those of other women writers. It is marginally more acceptable than gothic, but the question remains—why is it applied only to suspense novels by *women*? Most mystery and suspense novels include a love story—even tough private eyes maintain a romantic or sexual relationship with one or more women, so why make this distinction contingent upon the gender of the author? As Peters, I write straight mysteries; as Michaels I write suspense novels. I like and use a strong romantic element, but I don't believe that word should label my books.

*   *   *

The writer Barbara Michaels is also Elizabeth Peters, and both are in reality Barbara Mertz, who writes exceedingly readable books on archaeology and Egyptology. Michaels's novels combine romance, history, suspense and usually more than a touch of the supernatural; Peters's, on the other hand, generally feature romance, ancient history, suspense and more than a touch of humour.

The heroines in the novels written as Barbara Michaels are in general less pragmatic, less stalwart, and a good deal less humorous, and although Michaels herself eschews the word 'gothic', her publishers do not scorn to use it. Her first novel, *The Master of Blacktower*, is certainly very much in what is thought of as the gothic tradition. For a start, the heroine's name is Damaris, and as if this were not enough, she takes a job as secretary/librarian to a tall, scarred gent, and is governess to his crippled daughter. Add to this such details as an agd retainer's 'goblin laughter', an edifice known as the Black Tower, and wind which obligingly howls atmospherically, and the assembled ingredients are complete. It will, incidentally, come as no surprise that Damaris and the tall, scarred gent fall in love. Michaels's second novel, *Sons of the Wolf*, features a similarly predictable set of ingredients—two orphaned cousins, a manor on the edge of the Yorkshire Moors, the cousins' crippled

guardian, Mr Wolfson ('my friends—when I had friends—used to call me "Wolf"'), taciturn Yorkshiremen, laudanum, the odd ruin, etc.

But with the next book, *Ammie, Come Home*, Michaels turns to a new formula, and one which serves her well in many more novels, although she does occasionally return to the more traditional form. This is set in Washington's Georgetown district, where Ruth, a civil servant in her forties, lives in a beautiful old house which she has inherited. Ruth's young student cousin, Sara, who boards with her, is gradually possessed by the spirit of a young girl who was murdered in the 18th century. It takes Sara, Ruth, and their respective boyfriends (Ruth's being a professor of anthropology who happens to be an expert on black magic) much research, a seance or two, and quite a few very unpleasant experiences including physical injury, before the mystery is solved.

Often Michaels's heroine has suffered an illness, a bereavement, or has had a bad marriage. In the framework of the novel the twin threads of romance and suspense are generally woven in the setting of a large old house, often inherited by the heroine, and usually haunted by some previous tragedy. (The presence of the supernatural is signalled by the appearance of the words dark, darkness, shadow, grey or black in the titles of many of these novels). Solving the mystery, whether it is supernatural or merely unnatural, generally involves the partnership of hero and heroine in some historical and/or genealogical research, often giving rise to good-natured (or sometimes rather bad-natured) disagreements, as one partner frequently has a greater belief in the supernatural than the other. To reduce these novels to a formula this way is not, however, to denigrate the individual novels; each is entertaining and the historical background, as uncovered by the protagonists, is always most interesting. However, occasionally the supernatural element intrudes upon an otherwise ordinary (in no deleterious sense of the word) novel of mystery and romance, and for the reader with no interest or belief in the supernatural can mar an otherwise enjoyable story.

However, Michaels has written several novels which conform to neither of these patterns. *The Sea King's Daughter*, set in the Aegean, is rather reminiscent of the scenarios used by Mary Stewart, featuring as it does a mystery resulting from old wartime hostilities and betrayal, and the only elements of the supernatural being a religious cult, and the heroine's mythology-inspired dreams. In complete contrast, *Wings of the Falcon* is set in the Italy of the Risorgimento, and features a mysterious masked horseman known as 'The Falcon' (his true identity is Stefano, the embittered lame cousin of the heroine Francesca, and he is of course in reality neither embittered nor lame, but dashing and heroic). This is a melodramatic adventure story, set against an unusual background, and giving an interesting flavour of the political situation which influences the hero's actions, and thus the action of the novel.

It becomes evident that the past is a very dominant theme in Michaels's books, and even those set in the present look backwards to some ancient crime or tragedy. Some of her most interesting novels are those where the past is evoked not only by supernatural happenings or historical research, but by the physical trappings of earlier times, be they archaeological finds or more recent artefacts. In *Shattered Silk*, heroine Karen Nevitt opens an antique clothing shop, and in *Into the Darkness* Meg Venturi inherits an antique jewellery store; both these novels contain detailed descriptions of the respective antiques, and form a pleasing extra ingredient to the otherwise standard mix of romance and suspense.

Smoke and Mirrors is an interesting variation upon some of the above generalizations. Erin Hartsock joins the campaign staff of a senatorial election candidate, and as she comes to grips with the complicated world of politics she also helps (as in many Michaels novels) to uncover the truth about an old tragedy. The difference here is that the political setting, and the lack of a supernatural or other atmospheric element deprive the story of most of the Michaels trade marks—thereby demonstrating that these components are not essential to the production of an interesting and exciting novel with just the right amounts of romance and the humour.

Michael's other pseudonym Elizabeth Peters has created a most remarkable heroine. Amelia Peabody Emerson burst upon a startled world in *Crocodile on the Sandbank*, and in this and six successive novels to date has entertained and informed her readers. The books' readers are indeed Amelia's readers, for the stories are told by her in the first person, and the later volumes contain a foreword purporting to be by the editor of the 'memoirs' which constitute the succeeding chapters. The independent female to end all independent females, at the very start of the series Amelia Peabody is a 32-year old Victorian spinster travelling in Egypt. There she encounters archaeology, adventure, and the tall, dark, handsome, brooding hero to end all tall, dark, handsome, brooding heroes, archaeologist Radcliffe Emerson. From the very beginning their relationship is marked by verbal warfare (the word 'sparring' would be totally inadequate) and, once they are married, by intense physical enjoyment of each other—the latter is, of course, very delicately handled! As the series progresses, the plots become ever more fantastic—and ever less relevant to the reader's enjoyment of the books. The enjoyment lies in Amelia's narration of events, in her portrayal of the main characters, of their dialogue, and of the reaction of the lesser characters to Amelia, Radcliffe, and their unique (for which God be praised!) son, Ramses. This child, highly intelligent, frighteningly articulate (although encumbered in his early years with a rather nauseating lisp) is described by his mother thus: 'Oh, I grant you, no-one mummifies mice or mixes explosives better than Ramses, but those skills have limited utility. As for the social graces . . . '. His parents dote upon him, while being aware that his presence is a commodity to be avoided. In the course of the novels Amelia acquires considerable archaeological expertise (and by proxy the reader gains considerable interesting information), courtesy not only of Radcliffe Emerson, but also of Flinders Petrie, Howard Carter, and various other famous and infamous names from the period, many of whom have walk-on roles in the novels. An advocate of 'rational dress', Amelia devises a costume 'to combine utility with womanly modesty', and thus attired, and equipped with a belt hung with various knives, tools, and, above all, her trusty parasol, she takes on all comers, not least the series villain and her ardent admirer, the 'Master Criminal'. Amelia recounts her adventures with great verve, and the style of her amanuensis, Elizabeth Peters, is a wicked parody of Victorian melodramatic novels.

Peters's other two series heroines, Vicky Bliss and Jacqueline Kirby, are mere shadows of the redoubtable Amelia, but are nevertheless fine characters in their own right, and the novels themselves are just as entertaining. Vicky is an art historian, Jacqueline the 'assistant head librarian of Coldwater College, B.A., M.A., scholar and self confessed intellectual snob'—and a highly entertaining lady, moreover. She does bear certain resemblances to Amelia, both in character (both women are always, quite unequivocally, right—in their own eyes, at least), and in habits, Jacqueline's handbag being the equivalent of Amelia's trusty belt and parasol. In *Die for Love*, Jacqueline attends a Romance Writers' Convention in Manhattan—not out of any great interest in the subject, but in order to get a tax-deductible stay in New York. By the end of the conference (a glorious send-up of the bodice-ripper genre and its accompanying hype), she has solved two murders and conceived a new style of bodice-ripper—or rather, a deerskin-ripper, the hero and heroine being Cro-Magnon Man and Woman. And at the beginning of the next Kirby novel, *Naked Once More*, we learn that this novel has been published, been successful, and has spawned a sequel, despite being intended as a joke. Peters is at her very best when writing about the milieux she knows so well—Egyptology and romance fiction—and Amelia and Jacqueline, both true originals, flourish against these backgrounds.

Vicky Bliss is not in herself such an entertaining character, but she turns a very sardonic eye upon the situations and above all the people whom she encounters in her adventures which are told, like Amelia's, in the first person. These novels are set in various European countries, and elements common to them all are lost or stolen antiquities or works of art, and large amounts of skulduggery and/or thuggery—often perpetrated by 'Sir' John Smythe, master art-forger and thief, and Vicky's lover. A slippery but exceedingly attractive character, Smythe romps across Europe in a highly entertaining fashion with Vicky.

Peters has also written several non-series novels, usually with archaeological settings ranging from Mexico (*The Night of Four Hundred Rabbits*) to Scotland (*Legend in Green Velvet*, where the hero is a young man bearing a startling resemblance to Prince Charles). All are interesting, many are amusing, with lively heroines, but in none of these does she attain the high standards she has set for herself in *Die for Love* or *Crocodile on the Sandbank*.

Michaels is perhaps one of the most versatile of the novelists writing genre fiction today. With at least three distinct strands to her writings under the name of Elizabeth Peters, and a wide variety within the vast number of works in the Michaels canon, she seems incapable of producing a story which is less than entertaining, and most of them are a good deal more than that. The Peters novels have a harder edge—in general the heroines are more acerbic, their humour more sardonic; the Michaels stories generally have more vulnerable heroines, some of whom rather more on their male rescuers than do their Peters counterparts—most of the latter can take care not only of themselves but also of any vulnerable heroes who happen to be around. The variety within the two lists is remarkable, and if some of the earlier novels are a little too melodramatic, and if occasionally the supernatural element is hard to accept, these are more than compensated for by the many truly original, and highly entertaining, characters and settings in many of the more recent books.

—Judith Rhodes

MICHAELS, Fern.
Pseudonym for Roberta Anderson and Mary Kuczkir. From 1989, pseudonym for Mary Kuckzir only. **ANDERSON, Roberta. Nationality:** American. **Born:** New Jersey, 22 August 1942. **Relations:** married Alfred P. Anderson; one daughter and one son. **Career:** supervisor and freelance jobber in market research. **KUCZKIR, Mary. Nationality:** American. **Born:** Hastings, Pennsylvania, 9 April 1933. **Relations:** married Michael Kuczkir in 1952; three daughters and two sons. **Address:** c/o Ballantine, 201 East 50th Street, New York, New York 10022, USA.

<small>ROMANCE AND HISTORICAL PUBLICATIONS</small>

Novels (series: Captive; Coleman)

Pride and Passion. New York, Ballantine, 1975.
Vixen in Velvet. New York, Ballantine, 1976.
Captive Passions. New York, Ballantine, 1977.
Valentina. New York, Ballantine, 1978.
Captive Embraces. New York, Ballantine, 1979.
Captive Splendors. New York, Ballantine, 1980.
The Delta Ladies. New York, Pocket Books, 1980.
Golden Lasso. New York, Silhouette, 1980.
Sea Gypsy. Boston, Hall, 1980; London, Silhouette, 1981.
Beyond Tomorrow. London, Hodder and Stoughton, 1981; Boston, Hall, 1985.

Captive Innocence. New York, Ballantine, 1981.
Whisper My Name. New York, Silhouette, 1981.
Without Warning. New York, Pocket Books, 1981.
Nightstar. Boston, Hall, 1982.
Paint Me Rainbows. Boston, Hall, and London, Hodder and Stoughton, 1982.
Wild Honey. New York, Pocket Books, 1982; London, Arrow, 1984.
All She Can Be. New York, Ballantine, 1983; London, Severn House, 1990.
Free Spirit. New York, Ballantine, 1983; London, Severn House, 1991.
Tender Warrior. New York, Ballantine, 1983.
Cinders to Satin. New York, Ballantine, and London, Futura, 1984.
Texas Rich (Coleman). New York, Ballantine, 1985; London, Severn House, 1989.
Texas Heat (Coleman). New York, Ballantine, 1986; London, Severn House, 1989.
To Taste the Wine. New York, Ballantine, 1987; London, Severn House, 1991.
Texas Fury (Coleman). New York, Ballantine, 1989; London, Severn House, 1991.
Sins of Omission. New York, Ballantine, 1989.

Novels by Mary Kuczkir as Fern Michaels

Captive Passions. New York, Ballantine, 1987; London, Severn House, 1992.
Sins of the Flesh. New York, Ballantine, 1990.
For All Their Lives. New York, Ballantine, and London, Headline, 1992.
Texas Sunrise (Coleman). New York, Ballantine, 1993.

OTHER PUBLICATIONS

Novels

Without Warning. New York, Pocket Books, 1981.
Panda Bear Is Critical. London, Macmillan, 1982; New York, Pocket Books, 1984.

Other by Mary Kuczkir

My Dish Towel Flies at Half Mast. New York, Ballantine, 1979.

*   *   *

Writing as a team during the 1970s, Roberta Anderson and Mary Kuczkir generated erotic historical romance novels typical of the 'bodice rippers' of the period (e.g. *Vixen in Velvet*, *Captive Passions*), stories filled with piracy, passion, and possession, with the occasional rape thrown in to season a brew already boiling with rebellious heroines bent on adventure and self-determination. It was this quality of nonconformity, in fact, that sets these stories and heroines apart from other, more submissive and domestic, women of their time. In the process they changed romance formula conventions by redefining the admirable traits associated with romance heroines, reflecting the social changes taking place in American society during the late 1960s, 1970s, and early 1980s. As a result, the American romance novel has developed roots in native soil from which it takes shape and substance, and now follows a different path from its British sister.

In the early 1980s, when the romance market began to focus on the concerns of contemporary women, Anderson and Kuczkir produced two short novels—*Free Spirit* and *All She Can Be*—which

were issued as titles in an avant garde series published by Ballantine, titled 'Love and Life: Women's Stories for Today', in which the heroines all develop a strong, conscious sense of self. *All She Can Be* constitutes a landmark in the evolution of the genre, in reflecting the personal experiences and fantasies of so many women who came of age during the 1960s and 1970s—one of the most turbulent periods of social change in this century. It is also the more incisively developed story of the two titles—no mean achievement in this novelette form—about a middle-aged woman's attempt to redefine herself as an individual and as a woman rather than as a wife and a mother, after her husband leavers her for a younger woman. She must deal with her feelings about her former husband (who is starting a second family with a younger woman), and also change the 'rules' for her relationships with her three adult children, while continuing to work at a career that is denigrated by just about everyone (writing romance novels!) even though it has brought her financial independence. After a new man appears in her life, who is ten years her junior, she eventually comes to realize that he is the only kind of man possible for the woman she has become. He is, in fact, the 'new hero'—strong, supportive, and sexually secure enough to be a partner rather than the boss—demanded by the 'new heroine', who at last has emerged as a whole woman, possessing intellectual and professional talents as well as emotions, and capable of being both mother and a sexual being. *Free Spirit* is the story of a successful magazine editor who decides to go all out for domesticity, giving in to the pull of society's traditional socialization of females because she is unsure of the validity of her own newfound values and goals in life. It is a decision that turns disastrous, and in the end she realizes she not only misread but distrusted both herself and the man she loves.

By the mid-1980s, Anderson and Kuczkir had moved on to glitz, glamour, and dynasty novels such as *Texas Rich* (echoing Edna Ferber's *Giant*, except for an embarrassing lack of regional authenticity), followed by *Texas Heat*, and *Texas Fury*. In 1989 Kuczkir obtained full legal right to use the Fern Michaels name, bringing this collaboration to an end.

With the historical romance market burgeoning again, several earlier titles have been reissued with new covers, and in 1991, Michaels added a new title to her Captive series. *Captive Secrets* features the daughter of Sirena, the infamous Sea Siren, a virgin who is about to give herself up to the life she has always desired in a convent when she decides to indulge in 'one night of passion'. Both the story and the characterization lack imagination and sophistication, while the writing sounds curiously old-fashioned, if not ungrammatical: 'The warmth of his body and the rippling muscles beneath her hands so delighted her, she crushed her lips to his, demanding he return her ardor'. Since popular romances are social documents that exude the sensibilities of their time, and this one sounds so untimely, one is left wondering if it might have been 'recaptured' from a dusty closet shelf. Would that Michaels had retrieved instead the more intelligent efforts and fluid style of her 'Love and Life' novels, which remain as thought-provoking today as they were a decade ago.

—Carol Thurston

MICHENER, James A(lbert).
Nationality: American. **Born:** 3 February 1907; brought up by foster parents. **Education:** Doylestown High School, Pennsylvania; Swarthmore College, Pennsylvania, A.B. (summa cum laude) 1929 (Phi Beta Kappa); University of Northern Colorado, Greeley, A.M. 1935; University of St Andrews, Scotland. **Military Service:** United States Navy, 1944–45: lieutenant commander. **Relations:** married 1) Patti Koon in 1935 (divorced 1948); 2) Vange Nord in

1948 (divorced 1955); 3) Mari Yoriko Sabusawa in 1955. **Career:** master, Hill School, Pottstown, Pennsylvania, 1929–31, and George School, Newtown, Pennsylvania, 1934–36; professor, University of Northern Colorado, 1936–40; visiting professor, Harvard University, Cambridge, Massachusetts, 1940–41; associate editor, Macmillan Company, New York, 1941–49. Since 1949 freelance writer. Member, Advisory Committee on the Arts, United States Department of State, 1957; chair, President Kennedy's Food for Peace Program, 1961; secretary, Pennsylvania Constitution Convention, 1967–68; member of the Advisory Committee, United States Information Agency, 1970–76, and NASA, 1980–83. Since 1983 member of the board, International Broadcasting. **Recipient:** Pulitzer prize, 1948; National Association of Independent Schools award, 1954, 1958; Einstein award, 1967; National Medal of Freedom, 1971; golden badge, Order of Merit, 1988; D.H.L.: Rider College, Lawrenceville, New Jersey, 1950; Swarthmore College, 1954; LLD.: Temple University, Philadelphia, 1957; D.Litt.: Washington University, St Louis, 1967; Yeshiva University, New York, 1974; D.Sc.: Jefferson Medical College, Philadelphia, 1979. **Address:** 2719 Mount Laurel, Lincoln, Austin, Texas, TX 78703, USA.

ROMANCE AND HISTORICAL PUBLICATIONS

Novels

Hawaii. New York, Random House, 1959; London, Secker and Warburg, 1960.

The Source. New York, Random House, and London, Secker and Warburg, 1965.

Centennial. New York, Random House, and London, Secker and Warburg, 1974.

Chesapeake. New York, Random House, and London, Secker and Warburg, 1978; selections published as *The Watermen*, Random House, 1979.

The Covenant. New York, Random House, and London, Secker and Warburg, 1980.

Poland. New York, Random House, and London, Secker and Warburg, 1983.

Texas. New York, Random House, and London, Secker and Warburg, 1985.

Legacy. New York, Random House, and London, Secker and Warburg, 1987.

Alaska. New York, Random House, and London, Secker and Warburg, 1988.

Journey. New York, Random House, and London, Secker and Warburg, 1989.

Caribbean. New York, Random House, and London, Secker and Warburg, 1989.

Chesapeake Bay. New York, Abrams, and London, Secker and Warburg, 1990.

The Eagle and the Raven. Austin, Texas, State House Press, 1990; London, Secker and Warburg, 1991.

OTHER PUBLICATIONS

Novels

The Fires of Spring. New York, Random House, 1949; London, Corgi, 1960.

The Bridges at Toko-Ri. New York, Random House, and London, Secker and Warburg, 1953.

Sayonara. New York, Random House, and London, Secker and Warburg, 1954.

The Bridge at Andau. New York, Random House, and London, Secker and Warburg, 1957.

Caravans. New York, Random House, 1963; London, Secker and Warburg, 1964.

The Drifters. New York, Random House, and London, Secker and Warburg, 1971.

Space. New York, Random House, and London, Secker and Warburg, 1982.

The Novel. New York, Random House, and London, Secker and Warburg, 1991.

Short Stories

Tales of the South Pacific. New York, Macmillan, 1947; London, Collins, 1951.

Return to Paradise. New York, Random House, and London, Secker and Warburg, 1951.

Creatures of the Kingdom: Stories of Animals and Nature. New York, Random, and London, Secker and Warburg, 1993.

Other

The Unit in the Social Studies, with Harold M. Long. Cambridge, Massachusetts, Harvard University Graduate School of Education, 1940.

The Voice of Asia. New York, Random House, 1951; as *Voices of Asia,* London, Secker and Warburg, 1952.

The Floating World (on Japanese art). New York, Random House, 1954; London, Secker and Warburg, 1955.

Rascals in Paradise, with A. Grove Day. New York, Random House, and London, Secker and Warburg, 1957.

Selected Writings. New York, Modern Library, 1957.

Report of the County Chairman. New York, Random House, and London, Secker and Warburg, 1961.

The Modern Japanese Print: An Introduction. Rutland, Vermont, Tuttle, 1962.

Iberia: Spanish Travels and Reflections. New York, Random House, and London, Secker and Warburg, 1968.

The Subject Is Israel: A Conversation Between James A. Michener and Dore Schary. New York, Anti-Defamation League of B'nai B'rith, 1968.

Presidential Lottery: The Reckless Gamble in Our Electoral System. New York, Random House, and London, Secker and Warburg, 1969.

The Quality of Life. Philadelphia, Lippincott, 1970; London, Secker and Warburg, 1971.

Facing East: A Study of the Art of Jack Levine. New York, Random House, 1970.

Kent State: What Happened and Why. New York, Random House, and London, Secker and Warburg, 1971.

A Michener Miscellany 1950–1970, edited by Ben Hibbs. New York, Random House, 1973; London, Corgi, 1975.

About 'Centennial': Some Notes on the Novel. New York, Random House, 1974.

Sports in America. New York, Random House, 1976; as *Michener on Sport,* London, Secker and Warburg, 1976.

Testimony. Honolulu, White Knight, 1983.

Collectors, Forgers—and a Writer: A Memoir. New York, Targ, 1983.

Six Days in Havana, with John Kings. Austin, Texas, University of Texas Press, and London, Souvenir Press, 1990.

Pilgrimage: A Memoir of Poland and Rome. Emmaus, Pennsylvannia, Rodale Press, 1990.

The World Is My Home (autobiography). New York, Random, and London, Secker and Warburg, 1992.

Editor, *The Future of the Social Studies: Proposals for an Experimental Social-Studies Curriculum.* New York, National Council for the Social Studies, 1939.

Editor, *The Hokusai Sketch Books: Selections from the Manga*. Rutland, Vermont, Tuttle, 1958.

Editor, *Japanese Prints from the Early Masters to the Modern*. Rutland, Vermont, Tuttle, and London, Paterson, 1959.

Editor, *Firstfruits: A Harvest of 25 Years of Israeli Writing*. Philadelphia, Jewish Publication Society of America, 1973.

*

Film Adaptations: *Return to Paradise*, 1953, *Until They Sail*, 1957, from the story *Return to Paradise*; *The Bridges at Toko-Ri*, 1954; *Sayonara*, 1957; *Hawaii*, 1966; *Dynasty*, 1976; *Caravans*, 1978; *Centennial*, 1979; *Kent State*, 1981, from the book *Kent State: What Happened and Why*; *Space*, 1985.

Manuscript Collection: Library of Congress, Washington, DC.

Critical Studies: *James Michener* by A. Grove Day, New York, Twayne, 1964, revised edition, 1977; *James Michener* by George J. Becker, New York, Ungar, 1983; *James A. Michener: A Biography* by John P. Hayes, Indianapolis, Bobbs Merrill, 1984.

*   *   *

Dr Cullinane, the archaeologist hero of *The Source*, forms a fitting cipher for James A. Michener himself. His skill is not in artistic creation, but rather in careful examination and presentation of the past. Michener is remarkable among novelists for his exploitation of the old truism that truth can be stranger, and more dramatic, than fiction. History by definition, then, contains stories more momentous and extraordinary than do novels.

Michener combs history for these stories, and makes them accessible to his readers. Whereas many historical novels use history merely as background, to lend colour to a plot that is, in essence, driven by the forces of adventure or romance, for Michener history forms the very stuff of most of his novels. His titles—*Texas, Hawaii, Alaska*—suggest reference works rather than fiction. They also hint at the epic scale of his subjects.

Michener's grasp of history is nothing if not sweeping. *The Source* tells the story of Israel since neolithic times, while the opening of *Alaska*, set in the Ice Age, has no human characters at all, its heroine being a woolly mammoth. As such vast spans of time imply, these are epic works—running up to over a thousand pages in length. And like primary epics, these novels set out the stories of whole nations through chronicles of heroic deeds. Michener's vision of heroism, though, is one focused not on towering legends but on ordinary people. Despite his attraction to characters extraordinary and grotesque (such as Herod in *The Source* or General Santayana in *The Eagle and the Raven*) most of his heroes are ordinary people, and his novels focus on those times of crisis—wars, famines, persecutions when ordinary people commit acts of extraordinary bravery. Through such characters, past and present, Michener sets out to tell the stories of nations. Thus we witness the lives of imagined characters caught up in the real events at moments of crisis in a nation's life: documentary unfolded by means of a series of fictions, chiefly revolving around love and courtship. His heroes are thus inevitably short lived—a character's life may last only a few chapters before it is superseded by another generation or another century.

Lacking the space to develop his characters psychologically, Michener relies on other devices to give them identity. One is to mark them with some distinctive physical feature—hence the profusion of extremely tall, or strong, or fat people in his pages. Another device is that of the family line which passes a name or a set of traits from generation to generation (in *The Source* we follow the ancestors of a Palestinian Arab all the way from the stone age).

Other linking threads are provided by motifs and artifacts which continue down the centuries—a building, or a piece of jewellery, which remain familiar to his readers.

As a writer who occupies something of a middle-ground between the creators of text books and fiction, the success of Michener's work is dependent upon the efficiency of his research: not just into 'state' history but into the domestic and social history which supplies the everyday details of how his characters live. Michener's reader is subject to education as well as entertainment (the author works as a college teacher), and this education extends to fairly arcane details: techniques of shipbuilding, and mediaeval cookery are explained painstakingly. The same urge to educate underlies the inclusion in his books of maps, diagrams, and drawings—even of a chart of Polish pronunciation in the midst of *Poland*. By the nature of his subjects, his stories are often bloody, and Michener does not shrink from this, listing, for example, the tortures of the Spanish Inquisition in detail. Michener's zeal for research can become intrusive and at times, fairly bizarre—almost suggesting a terror of leaving anything out. The story of a Polish woman who is shot by the Nazis for hoarding a flour quern is robbed of its pathos by the interruption of a lengthy explanation of the quern's mechanism. When his characters attend a piano concert, Michener takes us step by step through the score, listing, and notating the chords. Again, some subjects such as the mysteries of Siberian shamanism or early middle eastern religion are simply not amenable to Michener's techniques of careful summary and simplification, resulting in hollowness or bathos.

Michener's later work moves from military and political history to literary history—as though trying to bridge the gap between high and popular art. In his introduction to *The Eagle and the Raven* he reveals that he draws his inspiration for his blockbusters from Keats's poetic urgency and Milton's sense of duty. The latter half of *Journey*, a tale of frontier adventure, becomes an anthology of, and commentary on, selected pieces from English literature. These books prefigure *The Novel* in which, again, the developing history of the novel as a cultural form is discussed as part of a series of contemporary dramas.

In the last analysis, Michener's mission of education must serve as his greatest achievement. It offers a completeness of vision that is unique in modern fiction, leading us to the inescapable conclusion that we may only know and understand the present by understanding the forces which have shaped us in the previous ages. The narrative voice which steers us through these dramas is liberal, humane, and international, one which seeks the truth of the present through fictions of the past.

—Edmund Cusick

MILES, Lady.
Nationality: British. **Born:** Favell Mary Hill, Bath, Somerset. **Relations:** married Sir Charles Miles in 1912 (died 1966); two sons. **Died:** 3 January 1969.

ROMANCE AND HISTORICAL PUBLICATIONS

Novels

The Red Flame. London, Hutchinson, 1921.
Red, White, and Grey. London, Hutchinson, 1921.
Ralph Carey. London, Hutchinson, 1922.
Stony Ground. London, Hutchinson, 1923.
The Fanatic. London, Hutchinson, 1924.
Tread Softly. London, Hutchinson, 1926.

Love's Cousin. London, Hutchinson, 1927.
Dark Dream. London, Hutchinson, 1929.
Lorna Neale. London, Hutchinson, 1932.
This Flower. London, Hutchinson, 1933.
The Second Lesson. London, Hutchinson, 1936.

*   *   *

Lady Miles's first novel, *The Red Flame*, appeared in 1921. Her heroine is a red-haired *femme fatale* with a strange childhood in India behind her. She is 'a lovely scrap of a disreputable thing, who'd look well à la mode on a tiger skin', and she goes through life (and her marriage) bringing unhappiness. The novel presents a picture of an unlovely character and her effect on others. The *Times Literary Supplement* reviewer pointed out that this novel 'does not succeed in absorbing the attention of the reader', and this criticism continued to be made of subsequent novels, although reviewers acknowledged the care with which Miles wrote.

Miles's characters tend to be unsympathetic creations who lead unhappy lives, frequently as the result of dismal and unloving childhoods. Consequently, the stories of their lives abound in frustrated or misplaced affections, unfortunate marriages (of which they may or may not attempt to make the best), and cycles of failure in the capacity to love. Various ways of ensuring unhappiness are examined—obsession with religion (*The Fanatic*), obsession with spiritual forces communicating mysteriously à la Joan of Arc (*Dark Dream*), obsession with introspective questionings after an unhappy childhood (*Ralph Carey*), and vast over-sensitiveness and over-imagination (*Lorna Neale*).

Emotions and motives are examined and analysed at considerable length both by the author (as narrator) and by the characters who think and talk a great deal about their relationships with one another ('What must Michael be thinking of her? Granted the courage of a mouse, she would not have deserted him, but she hadn't a mouse's courage. She always deserted those she loved ... Glen? Glen had trusted her. She had led him to believe that she could save them both. The spirit is willing but the flesh is weak. The flesh is weak because the spirit is not willing enough; because, beneath a show of strength, the spirit is fatally weak, too. She had thrust Glen away... He, not Michael, needed her'. *Lorna Neale*).

Plot, consequently, tends to arise from character, or to be a demonstration of character, and in some of the novels nothing much happens. The novels variously end unhappily, when the heroine falls down a quarry (*Dark Dream*) or walks into the sea in a religious ecstasy (*The Fanatic*), or with qualified happiness, when the hero and heroine decide to make the best of their lot or when (as the *TLS* said of *The Second Lesson*) disaster is averted but not very convincingly.

—Jean Buchanan

MILLAR, Margaret. American. 1915—. See 2nd edition, 1990.

MILLHISER, Marlys. American. 1938—. See 2nd edition, 1990.

MILLER, Linda Lael.
Nationality: American. **Born:** Spokane, Washington, 10 June 1949. **Relations:** married Rick M. Miller in 1968 (divorced 1987); two daughters. **Career:** clerk, Rockwood Clinic, Spokane, Washington, 1968–71, Aetna Insurance Company, Spokane, 1978–79,

and Pan American World Airways, Bangor, Washington, 1980–81. **Agent:** Irene Goodman, Irene Goodman Literary Agency, 521 Fifth Avenue, 17th Floor, New York, NY 10017, USA. **Address:** 2295 Woods Road, South East, Port Orchard, Washington 98366, USA.

ROMANCE AND HISTORICAL PUBLICATIONS

Novels (series: Beyond the Threshold; Corbin; Orphan Train Trilogy)

Fletcher's Woman. New York, Pocket Books, 1983; London, Coronet, 1984.
Snowflakes on the Sea. New York, Silhouette, and Toronto, Harlequin, 1984.
Desire and Destiny. New York, Pocket Books, and London, Coronet, 1984.
Banner O'Brien (Corbin). New York, Silhouette, 1984.
Willow. New York, Silhouette, 1984.
Part of the Bargain. New York, Silhouette, and Toronto, Harlequin, 1985.
Corbin's Fancy. New York, Silhouette, 1985.
State Secrets. Toronto, Harlequin, 1985; New York, Silhouette, 1986.
Ragged Rainbows. New York, Silhouette, and Toronto, Harlequin, 1986.
Memory's Embrace (Corbin). New York, Silhouette, 1986.
Lauralee. New York, Pocket Books, 1987.
Wanton Angel. New York, Silhouette, 1987.
Moonfire. New York, Pocket Books, 1988.
Used-To-Be Lovers. New York, Silhouette, and Toronto, Harlequin, 1988.
Angelfire. New York, Silhouette, 1989.
Only Forever. New York, Silhouette, and Toronto, Harlequin, 1989.
Just Kate. Toronto, Harlequin, 1989; New York, Silhouette, 1990.
My Darling Melissa (Corbin). New York, Silhouette, 1990.
Daring Moves. New York, Silhouette, and Toronto, Harlequin, 1990.
Mixed Messages. New York, Silhouette, and Toronto, Harlequin, 1990.
Orphan Train Trilogy:
   Lily and the Major. New York, Silhouette, 1990.
   Emma and the Outlaw. New York, Silhouette, 1991.
   Caroline and the Raider. New York, Silhouette, 1992.
Escape from Cabiz. Toronto, Harlequin, 1990; New York, Silhouette, 1991.
Glory, Glory. Toronto, Harlequin, 1990; New York, Silhouette, 1991.
Wild About Harry. Toronto, Harlequin, 1991; New York, Silhouette, 1992.
There and Now (Beyond the Threshold). New York, Silhouette, and Toronto, Harlequin, 1992.
Here and Then (Beyond the Threshold). New York, Silhouette, and Toronto, Harlequin, 1992.
Daniel's Bride. New York, Pocket Books, 1992.
Taming Charlotte. New York, Pocket Books, 1993.
Yankee Wife. New York, Pocket Books, 1993.

*   *   *

As an author of both historical and contemporary romances, Linda Lael Miller is acknowledged to write some of the genre's most explicitly sensual love scenes. She incorporates humour in both the dialogue and situations so that her books are generally fun to read.

Most of Miller's historical romances are set in the Pacific Northwest of the late 1800s. The 'Corbin' series (*Banner O'Brien, Cor-*

bin's Fancy, Memory's Embrace, My Darling Melissa), the 'Orphan Train Trilogy' (Lily and the Major, Emma and the Outlaw, Caroline and the Raider), Daniel's Bride and Yankee Wife are all set in Miller's favourite locale and follow a familiar storyline of romance novels. A feisty heroine and a proud, hard-headed man meet, and are paired into an unlikely couple. Sparks begin to fly when she insists on declaring or maintaining her independence, no matter how superficially. They disagree on just about everything and seem incompatible except in bed. They are so involved in mutual pleasure that they forget their differences. Miller elevates this fairly standard formula with her vividly drawn characters, often witty dialogue and humorous situations, and the especially sizzling chemistry that develops between the hero and heroine.

Banner O'Brien and Yankee Wife are typical of Miller's romances. In the former, Dr Banner O'Brien moves to Washington Territory to assume the practice of an injured physician. She meets her competition, Dr Adam Corbin, and eventually they marry, but their battle of wills continues. In addition to their personal differences, Miller throws in significant external obstacles from their pasts. His secretiveness leads Banner to believe he is still involved with other women, when in fact he is trying to keep the secret of his father's leprosy. Banner's past threatens when her violent ex-husband turns up and accuses her of bigamy.

Similarly in Yankee Wife, Lydia McQuire answers an ad for a wife in the Washington Territory. She agrees to go but only discovers on the voyage there that her husband-to-be is not Devon Quade, the charming man who interviewed her, but his irascible brother, Brigham. Arriving at their home, she discovers the widowed Brigham is even less enthusiastic about the marriage than she is. There are inevitable clashes between the two, especially about Brigham's establishment of a brothel for his lumberjacks, and his neutral stance during the Civil War. Although Brigham does not frequent the brothel, Lydia cannot condone its presence in town. The more serious obstacle for her, however, is the fact that he had sold lumber to both the North and South, refusing to take sides. This seems unforgivable to Lydia who had been a nurse, and saw all the pain and suffering first-hand. Although they marry, they continue to battle, with Lydia refusing to live with him. They eventually reconcile, but Lydia never gets the concessions she had demanded. In essence they agree to disagree, and get on with loving one another and building a new family.

Many of Miller's characters are shedding a less than glorious past and grasping at a chance to build a new life. That past is destined to reappear as a threat to the new and still tentative future. Devon Quade's new wife, Polly, is discovered to have been a con artist in collaboration with a former lover (Yankee Wife) and Jolie McKibbin (Daniel's Bride) must save her husband who is threatened by her former companions (thieves and murderers). Like Banner O'Brien, these women defeat the ghosts of the past with courage and strength and earn the right to a new life.

Miller seems to be willing to experiment more with some of her contemporary novels. In Wild About Harry, Amy Ryan is visited by the ghost of her beloved husband, Tyler, who tells her that she is holding up a master plan by refusing to get on with her life. He 'arranges' a date for her with his best friend, Australian tycoon, Harry Griffith, and reappears from time to time to keep the romance on target. Miller shows a light comic touch in dealing with the serious themes of grief and personal growth. Her dialogue sparkles and is loaded with sly references to in-jokes like the movies Ghost Busters and It's a Wonderful Life.

In her 'Beyond the Threshold' books Miller uses time-travel as a plot device. There and Now is the story of Elisabeth McCartney, who with the aid of a magic necklace travels back to 1892, where she meets Dr Jonathan Fortner. Unhappy in her modern-day life, she decides to stay with him. Here and Then takes up the story with Rue Claridge's search for Elisabeth, her cousin. She finds the necklace

and travels back in time. She locates Elisabeth and Jonathan and also meets US Marshall Farley Haynes. Like Elisabeth and Jonathan, Rue and Farley sample each other's centuries, and toy with changing history. Eventually they settle in the present.

No matter the time, place, or characters, however, the most distinguishing feature of Miller's work remains her lengthy, graphic descriptions of lovemaking. Often, the hero torments the heroine with several bouts of extended foreplay seen as 'putting her through her paces'. Once consummated, the relationship flares into passion at almost every opportunity. With several such scenes in each book, Miller gives free rein to her imagination in creating these situations. They are more likely to take place on a coffee table or kitchen counter, in a small airplane, or in a treehouse than they are in a bed. Miller revels in these descriptions of physical love mixed with tenderness. Occasionally, the heroine gets to take charge and torment her man to the point of exhaustion, but usually he controls the situation. With such a style it is no wonder that Miller was named 'the Most Outstanding Writer of Sensual Romance'.

—Barbara E. Kemp

MORGAN, Alice. American. See 2nd edition, 1990.

MITCHELL, Margaret (Munnerlyn).
Nationality: American. Born: Atlanta, Georgia, 8 November 1900. Education: Washington Seminary, Atlanta, 1914–18; Smith College, Northampton, Massachusetts, 1918–19. Relations: married 1) Berrien Kinnard Upshaw in 1922 (divorced); 2) John R. Marsh in 1925. Career: feature writer and reporter, Atlanta Journal and Constitution and Sunday Journal Magazine, 1922–26. Recipient: Pulitzer prize, 1937; Bohmenberger Memorial award, 1938. M.A.: Smith College, 1939. Died: 16 August 1949.

ROMANCE AND HISTORICAL PUBLICATIONS

Novel

Gone with the Wind. New York and London, Macmillan, 1936.

OTHER PUBLICATIONS

Other

Margaret Mitchell's Gone with the Wind Letters 1936–1949, edited by Richard Harwell. New York, Macmillan, and London, Collier Macmillan, 1976.
Margaret Mitchell, A Dynamo Going to Waste: Letters to Allen Edee 1919–1921, edited by Jane Peacock. Atlanta, Peachtree, 1985.

*

Film Adaptation: Gone with the Wind, 1939.

Manuscript Collections: University of Georgia, Athens; Atlanta Public Library.

Critical Studies: Margaret Mitchell of Atlanta by Finis Farr, New York, Morrow, 1965; The Road to Tara: The Life of Margaret Mitchell by Anne Edwards, New Haven, Connecticut, Ticknor and

Fields, and London, Hodder and Stoughton, 1983; *Gone with the Wind as Book and Film* edited by Richard Harwell, Columbia, University of South Carolina Press, 1983.

*   *   *

From its conception, Mitchell had intended *Gone with the Wind* to fulfil two functions. Firstly, the treatment of the content resulted in a prosaic eulogy. Like the many 'plantation' novels that preceded it, the book was an ode to the bygone era of the South on the eve of the American Civil War, and a commendation for the travails that the genteel were compelled to endure in its aftermath. Secondly, the novel was also, on a more subtle plane, a didactic treatise. Mitchell took on the task of giving her readers the correct perspective with which to view the history of the time. Consequently, as her critics have pointed out, her descriptions of scenes and characters, which at times reach the extremities of caricature, are not free from the bias of her social and racial politics. However, it was not, because it captured one—or rather, several—generations' empathy, that the single Mitchellian novel became a phenomenal success. In fact, despite the limitations imposed by the projection of a southerner's world-view, the story is actually a delightful experience in which the characters come alive by the sheer richness of imagery and passionate emotions they embody.

At the heart of the story is Scarlett O'Hara who, with her 17-inch waist, flaming hair, green eyes and pretty dresses like 'the rose organdie with the long pink sash', is introduced to the reader in the opening pages of the book. She is an unlikely candidate for a heroine—vain and winsome, flirtatious and hot-headed, and above all, totally self-engrossed. Neither is Rhett Butler, known for his cynicism and unscrupulous ways—saved only by his swarthy good looks—a model hero. Their tale is indisputably filled with romance, but less certainly, with love. The 12 years of life in pre-and post-war Atlanta that Mitchell charts, elucidates the dramatic events that move Scarlett's personal world. As a 16 year old, Scarlett is deeply infatuated with the married Ashley Wilkes while being responsive to the friendship offered by his wife Melanie. Her meeting with Rhett Butler is in the first few pages of the book, and apart from her impression that 'she had never seen a man with such wide shoulders, so heavy with muscles', she is oblivious to the interest she arouses in him. Her two brief and inconsequential marriages, first to Charles Hamilton. and later to George Kennedy, fail to alter her adoration for the vacillating Ashley. And always, in the background, is Rhett, his dark looks disapproving and rigid silence beseeching. The Civil War reaches Georgia. Participating in the war effort, Scarlett faces hazards far worse than any she has known before. For the first time, she is confronted with hunger, lack of protection, and unaccustomed vulnerability. Above all, her home, Tara, is in ruins. Her privations during this period engender a sense of insecurity that endures to the end. Her consequent actions, some unprincipled, stem from her determination never to relive these horrifying moments. Meanwhile, her infrequent brushes with Rhett are the most sensuous she has experienced: 'she had a wild thrill such as she had never known'. The twice-widowed Scarlett becomes Rhett's wife only after nearly two-thirds of the story is over. Her years with Rhett are marked with the same obduracy that only widens the chasm between them. When finally, in the closing pages of the book, the death of their daughter doesn't appear to move her, Rhett reciprocates in kind. Her own actions have destroyed his love for her, but as realization dawns, the marriage can no longer be saved. Rhett departs with the unforgettable words: 'My dear, I don't give a damn'.

As a novel, the writing offers little by way of an original style. In fact, coming, as it did, in a period dominated by modernist strains of literature, the ready acceptance of the relatively conventional text has left its status, in the world of literary taxonomy, suspect. However, what Mitchell lacks in style she makes up in story telling. Un-

doubtedly, she has effectively employed various techniques open to a writer to produce a story refreshingly devoid of characters stereotyped by genre or dialogues replete with clichés. Thus, her story swings along a range of moods so that the burlesque can be found alongside the nostalgic, and the heartwarming followed almost immediately by the chilling, and the cruel.

The plot is far removed from the standard formula prescribed for romantic fiction. Scarlett, for most part of the book, is enamoured with Ashley, while her own understanding of her feelings for Rhett borders only on the sensual. Rarely is it that a heroine is twice married before she enters into a conjugal relationship with the hero in this type of book. And marriage between the hero, and heroine, contrary to the laws of romance, does not assure contentment. In fact, its culmination is the most unexpected part of the book. Mitchell's departure from the norm, and the element of unpredictability, worked with finesse at every point in the story, has been responsible for producing the most compelling piece of romance fiction written this century.

The magic of *Gone with the Wind* is enhanced by the multifarious interpretations that may be derived on various levels of analysis. While at the outset, the story deals with the emotions of individuals, it is impossible not to draw parallels with the historical events that dominated the period. Mitchell had always upheld her rationale for fashioning her characters and the way she did this was to preserve the typicality of the inhabitants of the time. However, in a deeper perspective, her characters are subtle symbolisms portraying a social order that was doomed to decadence long before the Civil War accelerated the inevitable process of transformation. Scarlett's struggle for survival in post-war Atlanta was no less the echo of an entire community. What Mitchell has so movingly captured has been the struggle between two civilizations: an Old South in painful transition to the New. Some critics, inclined to Freudian reasoning, have not failed to identify expressions of the author's own unstable early adulthood in the principal character's dilemmas. Mitchell's own unfulfilled relationship with her mother has been seen in Scarlett's continuing quest for tranquillity, and the latter's intense attachment to her home—she feels with conviction that everything will be all right, once at Tara.

It is, ultimately, its unorthodox plot that has given *Gone with the Wind* a longer life span than any other popular romance. Clearly, the imaginative writing of the original book has already assured a growing popularity for the sequel *Scarlett*. Whether this book too will carve a unique place in romantic fiction, only time will tell.

—Rachel Kumar

MITCHISON, Naomi.
Nationality: British. **Born:** Naomi Margaret Haldane, Edinburgh, Scotland, 1 November 1897; daughter of the scientist John Scott Haldane; sister of the writer J.B.S. Haldane. **Education:** Lynam's School, Oxford; St Anne's College, Oxford. **Military Service:** volunteer nurse, 1915. **Relations:** married G.R. Mitchison (who became Lord Mitchison, 1964) in 1916 (died 1970); three sons and two daughters. **Career:** Labour candidate for parliament, Scottish Universities constituency, 1935; member, Argyll County Council, 1945–66; member, Highland Panel, 1947–64, and Highlands and Islands Development Council, 1966–76. Tribal adviser, and Mmarona (Mother), to the Bakgatla of Botswana, 1963–89. **Recipient:** D.Univ.: University of Stirling, Scotland, 1976; University of Dundee, Scotland, 1985; D.Litt.: University of Strathclyde, Glasgow, 1983. Honorary fellow, St Anne's College, 1980, and Wolfson College, 1983, both Oxford. Officer, French Academy, 1924. CBE (Commander, Order of the British Empire), 1985. **Address:** Carradale House, Campbeltown, Argyll, Scotland.

ROMANCE AND HISTORICAL PUBLICATIONS

Novels

The Conquered. London, Cape, and New York, Harcourt Brace, 1923.

Cloud Cuckoo Land. London, Cape, 1925; New York, Harcourt Brace, 1926.

The Corn King and the Spring Queen. London, Cape, and New York, Harcourt Brace, 1931; as *The Barbarian*, New York, Cameron, 1961.

The Blood of the Martyrs. London, Constable, 1939; New York, McGraw Hill, 1948.

Behold Your King. London, Muller, 1957.

Short Stories

When the Bough Breaks and Other Stories. London, Cape, and New York, Harcourt Brace, 1924.

Black Sparta: Greek Stories. London, Cape, and New York, Harcourt Brace, 1928.

Barbarian Stories. London, Cape, and New York, Harcourt Brace, 1929.

Beyond This Limit: Selected Shorter Fiction of Naomi Mitchison, edited by Isobel Murray. Edinburgh, Scottish Academic Press, 1986.

OTHER PUBLICATIONS

Novels

The Powers of Light. London, Cape, and New York, Peter Smith, 1932.

Beyond This Limit. London, Cape, 1935.

We Have Been Warned. London, Constable, 1935; New York, Vanguard Press, 1936.

The Bull Calves. London, Cape, 1947.

Lobsters on the Agenda. London, Gollancz, 1952.

Travel Light. London, Faber, 1952.

To the Chapel Perilous. London, Allen and Unwin, 1955.

Memoirs of a Spacewoman. London, Gollancz, 1962.

When We Become Men. London, Collins, 1965.

Cleopatra's People. London, Heinemann, 1972.

Solution Three. London, Dobson, and New York, Warner, 1975.

Not by Bread Alone. London, Boyars, 1983.

The Oath Takers. Nairn, Balnain, 1991.

Sea-Green Ribbons. Nairn, Balnain, 1991.

Short Stories

The Delicate Fire: Short Stories and Poems. London, Cape, and New York, Harcourt Brace, 1933.

The Fourth Pig: Stories and Verses. London, Constable, 1936.

Five Men and a Swan: Short Stories and Poems. London, Allen and Unwin, 1958.

Images of Africa. Edinburgh, Canongate, 1980.

What Do You Think Yourself? Scottish Short Stories. Edinburgh, Harris, 1982.

Early in Orcadia. Glasgow, Drew, 1987.

A Girl Must Live. Glasgow, Drew, 1990.

Plays

Nix-Nought-Nothing: Four Plays for Children (includes *My Ain Sel'*, *Hobyah! Hobyah!*, *Elfen Hill*). London, Cape, 1928; New York, Harcourt Brace, 1929.

Kate Crackernuts: A Fairy Play. Oxford, Alden Press, 1931.

The Price of Freedom, with L. E. Gielgud (produced Cheltenham 1949). London, Cape, 1931.

Full Fathom Five, with L. E. Gielgud (produced London, 1932).

An End and a Beginning and Other Plays (includes *The City and the Citizens*, *For This Man Is a Roman*, *In the Time of Constantine*, *Wild Men Invade the Roman Empire*, *Charlemagne and His Court*, *The Thing That Is Plain*, *Cortez in Mexico*, *Akbar*, *But Still It Moves*, *The New Calendar*, *American Britons*). London, Constable, 1937; as *Historical Plays for Schools*, 2 vols, 1939.

As It Was in the Beginning, with L.E. Gielgud. London, Cape, 1939.

The Corn King, music by Brian Easdale, adaptation of the novel by Mitchison (produced Glasgow, 1951). London, French, 1951.

Spindrift, with Denis Macintosh (produced Glasgow, 1951). London, French, 1951.

Poetry

The Laburnum Branch. London, Cape, 1926.

The Alban Goes Out. Harrow, Middlesex, Raven Press, 1939.

The Cleansing of the Knife and Other Poems. Edinburgh, Canongate, 1978.

Other (for children)

The Hostages and Other Stories for Boys and Girls. London, Cape, 1930; New York, Harcourt Brace, 1931.

Boys and Girls and Gods. London, Watts, 1931.

The Big House. London, Faber, 1950.

Graeme and the Dragon. London, Faber, 1954.

The Swan's Road. London, Naldrett Press, 1954.

The Land the Ravens Found. London, Collins, 1955.

Little Boxes. London, Faber, 1956.

The Far Harbour. London, Collins, 1957.

Judy and Lakshmi. London, Collins, 1959.

The Rib of the Green Umbrella. London, Collins, 1960.

The Young Alexander the Great. London, Parrish, 1960; New York, Roy, 1961.

Karensgaard: The Story of a Danish Farm. London, Collins, 1961.

The Young Alfred the Great. London, Parrish, 1962; New York, Roy, 1963.

The Fairy Who Couldn't Tell a Lie. London, Collins, 1963.

Alexander the Great. London, Longman, 1964.

Henny and Crispies. Wellington, New Zealand, Department of Education, 1964.

Ketse and the Chief. London, Nelson, 1965; New York, Nelson, 1967.

A Mochudi Family. Wellington, New Zealand, Department of Education, 1965.

Friends and Enemies. London, Collins, 1966; New York, Day, 1968.

The Big Surprise. London, Kaye and Ward, 1967.

Highland Holiday. Wellington, New Zealand, Department of Education, 1967.

African Heroes. London, Bodley Head, 1968; New York, Farrar Straus, 1969.

Don't Look Back. London, Kaye and Ward, 1969.

The Family at Ditlabeng. London, Collins, 1969; New York, Farrar Straus, 1970.

Sun and Moon. London, Bodley Head, 1970; Nashville, Nelson, 1973.

Sunrise Tomorrow. London, Collins, and New York, Farrar Straus, 1973.

The Danish Teapot. London, Kaye and Ward, 1973.

Snake! London, Collins, 1976.

The Little Sister, with works by Ian Kirby and Keetla Masogo. Cape Town, Oxford University Press, 1976.

The Wild Dogs, with works by Megan Biesele. Cape Town, Oxford University Press, 1977.
The Brave Nurse and Other Stories. Cape Town, Oxford University Press, 1977.
The Two Magicians, with Dick Mitchison. London, Dobson, 1978.
The Vegetable War. London, Hamish Hamilton, 1980.

Other

Anna Comnena. London, Howe, 1928.
Comments on Birth Control. London, Faber, 1930.
The Home and a Changing Civilization. London, Lane, 1934.
Vienna Diary. London, Gollancz, and New York, Smith and Haas, 1934.
Socrates, with Richard Crossman. London, Hogarth Press, 1937; Harrisburg, Pennsylvania, Stackpole, 1938.
The Moral Basis of Politics. London, Constable, 1938; Port Washington, New York, Kennikat Press, 1971.
The Kingdom of Heaven. London, Heinemann, 1939.
Men and Herring: A Documentary, with Denis Macintosh. Edinburgh, Serif, 1949.
Other People's Worlds (travel). London, Secker and Warburg, 1958.
A Fishing Village on the Clyde, with G.W.L. Paterson. London, Oxford University Press, 1960.
Presenting Other People's Children. London, Hamlyn, 1961.
Return to the Fairy Hill (autobiography and sociology). London, Heinemann, and New York, Day, 1966.
The Africans: A History. London, Blond, 1970.
Small Talk: Memories of an Edwardian Childhood. London, Bodley Head, 1973.
A Life for Africa: The Story of Bram Fischer. London, Merlin Press, and Boston, Carrier Pigeon, 1973.
Oil for the Highlands? London, Fabian Society, 1974.
All Change Here: Girlhood and Marriage (autobiography). London, Bodley Head, 1975.
Sittlichkeit (lecture). London, Birkbeck College, 1975.
You May Well Ask: A Memoir 1920–1940. London, Gollancz, 1979.
Mucking Around: Five Continents over Fifty Years. London, Gollancz, 1981.
Margaret Cole 1893–1980. London, Fabian Society, 1982.
Among You, Taking Notes: The Wartime Diary of Naomi Mitchison 1939–1945, edited by Dorothy Sheridan. London, Gollancz, 1985.
Naomi Mitchison (autobiographical sketch). Edinburgh, Saltire Society, 1986.
As It Was. Glasgow, Drew, 1988.

Editor, *An Outline for Boys and Girls and Their Parents*. London, Gollancz, 1932.
Editor, with Robert Britton and George Kilgour, *Re-Educating Scotland*. Glasgow, Scoop, 1944.
Editor, *What the Human Race Is Up To*. London, Gollancz, 1962.

*

Critical Study: *Naomi Mitchison: A Century of Experiment in Life and Letters* by Jill Benton, London, Pandora Press, 1990.

Manuscript Collections: National Library of Scotland, Edinburgh; University of Texas, Austin.

*   *   *

'Friendships were such lovely, brittle things, they broke unless one was very, very careful'. This sentence from *Cloud Cuckoo Land* holds the key to much of Naomi Mitchison's historical fiction. The complex fragility of human relationships is continually emphasized in her writing, and underlies all the other major themes—flight and exile, culture clash, the search for fulfilment and its tragic failure—inherent in her work. Beneath them all, one feels the unifying thread of shared lives, of communal and individual love and loss. The significance of such relationships, their frailty and abuse, pervades the early stories in *Black Sparta*, where on several occasions an unrequited love is used by the beloved for personal advantage, and the lover promptly abandoned. Already, in these stories, one senses the attraction of ancient Greece for Mitchison, and her ability to enter a vanished age at will.

Mitchison's fame was established with the historical novels and stories she produced during the 1920s, and which remain among the finest of her creations. In them she depicts the interaction of opposing cultures, observing from the viewpoint of the vanquished underdog the disintegration and painful adjustment that follow in the wake of conquest. Her narrators are invariably victims, decent but unheroic individuals obliged to compromise in order to fit the changed circumstances of their lives. Robbed of stability and self-respect, their only recourse is to adapt, or to flee to exile. Through their eyes, Mitchison chronicles the fall of civilizations, the wrecking of families, the undermining of communal tribal faiths by newer, secular systems which lead to questioning and discontent. Her exploration of the inner lives of her characters shows her art at its subtlest, capturing the human sensibilities of another time. To each of these historical works, Mitchison brings a contemporary voice, employing a modern, colloquial style with current patterns of speech and thought. By these apparently anachronistic means, she succeeds totally in evoking the remote past in all its multilayered complexity and emotional depth.

Mitchison's first novel, *The Conquered*, is set in Gaul at the time of Caesar's campaigns, where Meromic, son of a local chieftain, witnesses the tribe's defeat and the death of his family. Taken prisoner by the Romans, he subsequently fights with them against the Gallic army of Vercingetorix. Meromic's conflicting loyalties—to his former people, and to his Roman master—are adroitly displayed by Mitchison, who presents each scene clearly and without undue comment, leaving readers to judge for themselves. Her understated, contemporary style conveys to perfection the world of the volatile, feuding Celts, where fact and magic mingle indissolubly together. Such a world cannot endure the impact of the practical, ordered universe of the Romans, whose methodical skill in battle proves too much for the foolhardy heroism of the Gauls. Vercingetorix dies, and the hopelessly torn Meromic finds his own solution by retreating into tribalism and mystery, metamorphosing into the wolf totem of the Veneti. Mitchison traces the decline, the reduction of a proud people to vassal status, with a vision at once sympathetic and pared of sentiment. Her ability to get inside the mind of Meromic, seeing the tragedy through his eyes, renders that vision all the more moving. *The Conquered* is a powerful story, whose exploration of the psychology of its main characters is a foretaste of things to come. Its insights are surpassed in *Cloud Cuckoo Land*, where the author examines an ancient Greece fallen from its previous greatness.

Cloud Cuckoo Land follows the fortunes of the central character, Alxenor, who with his sweetheart Moiro flees his native island after a Spartan coup. Forced into a life of exile, the illfated lovers spend time in the three dominant states of the period, with tragic consequences. Moiro is seduced into a love affair with a Spartan warrior, and dies in childbirth. Alxenor returns to help liberate his own island, but finds the place still beset with factions and intrigue. He ends the book an exile, serving as a mercenary in the wars of the Persian king. Mitchison charts the progress of her hounded, amiable 'hero' through an intricate weave of political manoeuvre, violence, and domestic turmoil. The familiar style accommodates some beautiful descriptive passages, but its main strength is its presentation of the varying states of mind of Mitchison's creations. The seemingly casual brutality, heartlessness even, of some scenes—Moiro's taking of a lover, her exposure of an unwanted child, her eventual death—is counterbalanced by extreme sensitivity in the treatment of relationships, and of the complex mass of contradictions that constitute a human personality. It is this network of individual lives and feelings that provides the core of the book, and against which the fall of nations strikes a more cosmic resonance. *Cloud Cuckoo Land* marks an advance on *The Conquered*, its insights more skilfully developed, its psychology more subtle. It brings, too, a fuller evocation of the Greece of *Black Sparta*, a landscape of the mind to which Mitchison was to return in an even more memorable work of fiction.

The Corn King and the Spring Queen is Mitchison's masterpiece, the crown of her achievement as a historical novelist. Set in Marob, a farming kingdom ruled by the fertility ritual of Corn King and Spring Queen, characters and action move to Sparta and Ptolemaic Egypt before a return to Marob brings final resolution. Once again the novel is centred on individual relationships, from which the author works outward to examine other, universal themes. Action focuses on Tarrik and Erif Der—the King and Queen of the title—and the effect of outside pressures on their lives. Their personalities, and the world of tribal magic and religion which they represent, are exposed to the challenge of new ideas from Greece, where the gods no longer rule, and Kleomenes of Sparta posits a theory of 'the good life' based on secular idealism and democracy. Questioning of their beliefs brings inward conflict in both Tarrik and Erif that amounts to psychological disturbance, and which for a time expresses itself in violence and cruelty. Flight to, and eventual escape from, the hierarchical but directionless kingdom of Egypt, where the despot Ptolemy seeks vainly to create his own pantheon of gods, and where the defeated Kleomenes meets his death, brings about their return to Marob. Here the old beliefs are shown to endure in a second generation, albeit infused with the refined version of sacrifice and renewal exemplified by Kleomenes himself. Mitchison enters the hearts and minds of her characters, presenting sensitively and with conviction states of possession and contemplation, the shifting perceptions of the world and each other. Through the precarious equilibrium of human relationships, she investigates the many varieties of love—from platonic friendship to sexual hunger—in a penetrating, clear-sighted manner free from moralistic comment. Her novel explores religion, psychology and art to their roots, indicating through ritual and conversation the potency of the idea whose time has come. In Kleomenes, a well-meaning king who dies for his people, she appears to hint at later Christian beliefs. The story of individuals in a particular place and time, *The Corn King and the Spring Queen* examines a multiplicity of themes, and rewards successive readings with deeper layers of meaning. It is without doubt one of the most significant historical novels.

Later works which might be classed as historical tend to reveal an overt religious belief, and while often excellent, lack the complexity and depth of the earlier novels. *Blood of the Martyrs*, which describes the persecution of Christians in Nero's Rome, and *Behold Your King*, an account of the Crucifixion, are both skilfully constructed, with events viewed by several different characters to give varying perspectives on the action. Once more Mitchison uses a no-nonsense modern style, and effectively presents the thoughts and feelings of her creations, but the specific religious theme robs these books of the multi-faceted power of *The Corn King and the Spring Queen*, or even *Cloud Cuckoo Land*.

A powerful, seminal writer and an innovative stylist, Mitchison remains a major influence on the modern historical novel. Her use of contemporary speech patterns and expressions in historic contexts suggests similarities with Alfred Duggan, while her exploration of inner thoughts and feelings and the visual force of her scenes recall Henry Treece. In her ability to convey deep psychological and religious perceptions, and to show them at work in the minds of her

characters, Mitchison has few rivals. On the basis of her early writings, she is unquestionably one of the great historical novelists.

—Geoffrey Sadler

MONTGOMERY, L(ucy) M(aud).
Nationality: Canadian. **Born:** Clifton (now New London), Prince Edward Island, 30 November 1874. **Education:** schools in Cavendish, Prince Edward Island, and Prince Albert, Saskatchewan; Prince of Wales College, Charlottetown, Prince Edward Island, teacher's certificate 1894, teacher's license 1895; Dalhousie College, Halifax, Nova Scotia, 1895–96. **Relations:** married Ewan Macdonald in 1911; two sons. **Career:** schoolteacher, Bideford, 1894–95, 1896–97, and Lower Bedeque, 1897–98, both in Prince Edward Island; assistant postmistress, Cavendish, 1898–1911; staff member, Halifax *Echo*, 1901–02. **Recipient:** fellow, Royal Society of Arts, 1923; OBE (Officer, Order of the British Empire), 1935. **Died:** 24 April 1942.

ROMANCE AND HISTORICAL PUBLICATIONS

Novels (series: Anne; Emily; Pat)

Anne of Green Gables. Boston, Page, and London, Pitman, 1908.
Anne of Avonlea. Boston, Page, and London, Pitman, 1909.
Kilmeny of the Orchard. Boston, Page, and London, Pitman, 1910.
The Story Girl. Boston, Page, and London, Pitman, 1911.
The Golden Road. Boston, Page, 1913; London, Cassell, 1914.
Anne of the Island. Boston, Page, and London, Pitman, 1915.
Anne's House of Dreams. New York, Stokes, and London, Constable, 1917.
Rainbow Valley (Anne). Toronto, McClelland and Stewart, and New York, Stokes, 1919; London, Constable, 1920.
Rilla of Ingleside (Anne). Toronto, McClelland and Stewart, New York, Stokes, and London, Hodder and Stoughton, 1921.
Emily of New Moon. New York, Stokes, and London, Hodder and Stoughton, 1923.
Emily Climbs. New York, Stokes, and London, Hodder and Stoughton, 1925.
The Blue Castle. Toronto, McClelland and Stewart, New York, Stokes, and London, Hodder and Stoughton, 1926.
Emily's Quest. New York, Stokes, and London, Hodder and Stoughton, 1927.
Magic for Marigold. Toronto, McClelland and Stewart, New York, Stokes, and London, Hodder and Stoughton, 1929.
A Tangled Web. New York, Stokes, 1931; as *Aunt Becky Began It*, London, Hodder and Stoughton, 1931.
Pat of Silver Bush. New York, Stokes, and London, Hodder and Stoughton, 1933.
Mistress Pat: A Novel of Silver Bush. New York, Stokes, and London, Harrap, 1935.
Anne of Windy Poplars. New York, Stokes, 1936; as *Anne of Windy Willows*, London, Harrap, 1936.
Jane of Lantern Hill. Toronto, McClelland and Stewart, New York, Stokes, and London, Harrap, 1937.
Anne of Ingleside. New York, Stokes, and London, Harrap, 1939.

Short Stories

Chronicles of Avonlea. Boston, Page, and London, Sampson Low, 1912.
Further Chronicles of Avonlea. Boston, Page, 1920; London, Harrap, 1953.

The Road to Yesterday. Toronto, McGraw Hill Ryerson, 1974; London, Angus and Robertson, 1975.

The Doctor's Sweetheart and Other Stories, edited by Catherine McLay. Toronto, McGraw Hill Ryerson, and London, Harrap, 1979.

Akin to Anne: Tales of Other Orphans, edited by Rea Wilmshurst. Toronto, McClelland and Stewart, 1988.

OTHER PUBLICATIONS

Poetry

The Watchman and Other Poems. Toronto, McClelland and Stewart, 1916; New York, Stokes, 1917; London, Constable, 1920.

The Poetry of Lucy Maud Montgomery, edited by Kevin McCabe and John Ferns. Markham, Ontario, Fitzhenry and Whiteside, 1987.

Other

Courageous Women, with Marian Keith and Mabel Burns McKinley. Toronto, McClelland and Stewart, 1934.

The Green Gables Letters to Ephraim Weber 1905–1909, edited by Wilfrid Eggleston. Toronto, Ryerson Press, 1960.

The Alpine Path: The Story of My Career. Don Mills, Ontario, Fitzhenry and Whiteside, 1974.

My Dear Mr M: Letters to G.B. MacMillan, edited by Francis W. P. Bolger and Elizabeth R. Epperly. Toronto, McGraw Hill Ryerson, 1980.

Spirit of Place: L.M. Montgomery and Prince Edward Island, edited by Francis W.P. Bolger. Toronto, Oxford University Press, 1982.

The Selected Journals 1: 1889–1910 2: 1910–1921, edited by Mary Rubio and Elizabeth Waterston. Toronto, Oxford University Press, 2 vols, 1985–87.

*

Bibliography: *L.M. Montgomery: A Preliminary Bibliography* by Ruth Weber Russell, Waterloo, Ontario, University of Waterloo Library, 1986.

Critical Studies: *The Years Before 'Anne'* by Francis W.P. Bolger, Charlottetown, Prince Edward Island Heritage Foundation, 1975; *The Wheel of Things: A Biography of L.M. Montgomery* by Mollie Gillen, Don Mills, Ontario, Fitzhenry and Whiteside, 1975, London, Harrap, 1976; *L.M. Montgomery: An Assessment* edited by John Robert Sorfleet, Guelph, Ontario, Canadian Children's Press, 1976; *Kindred Spirit: Biography of L.M. Montgomery* by Catherine M. Andronik, New York, Atheneum, 1993.

*   *   *

L.M. Montgomery is celebrated for novels like *Anne of Green Gables* and *Emily of New Moon* which have become classics of children's literature on both sides of the Atlantic. However, these are read avidly by adults as well as children, and indeed their sequels, in which the young and rapturous heroines mature, have a distinctly adult appeal. Montgomery's short stories (collected in *Chronicles of Avonlea, Further Chronicles of Avonlea, The Road to Yesterday,* and *The Doctor's Sweetheart*), though sometimes tenuously linked to the Green Gables characters, are set firmly in an adult world and contain little with which child readers would identify.

Whatever the age group Montgomery meant to address, her fiction always includes strong elements of romance. This is at one extreme cosily domestic and at the other ecstatically spiritual. Physical intensity plays little part in the books. It is significant that whenever a young man snatches his first kiss, the typical Montgomery heroine is likely to slap his face in fury. Despite the vividness of the girls' emotional response to life, they inhabit a well ordered housewifely world of newpin neatness where, one feels (to use one of Montgomery's own expressions) it must be a heinous sin to allow fluffrolls to build up on one's linoleum. And so bodily sex, being a disorderly experience, is not allowed to disrupt the social tidiness of the stories. There is plenty of passion; it is sometimes folksy, sometimes fey—but never physical.

Anne, Emily, and other leading ladies have high flown flights of fantasy which spring from their passion for natural beauty. Emily, for example, has an extremely mobile soul which, we are told, slips easily away from mundane matters into 'eternity' so that she can say with conviction: 'I washed my soul free from dust in the aerial bath of a spring twilight'. Similarly Susette in *The Road to Yesterday* refreshes her inner being by 'bathing her soul in dawn'.

Montgomery's pattern of young love is predictable. After the heroine's initial and dramatic renunciation of romance ('I will not love—to love is to be a slave'), it creeps up from behind like a game of Grandma's Footsteps, catches her unawares, and explodes in a burst of ecstasy that is eventually consummated in happily married fecundity.

Fortunately, Anne, for example, never allows the claims of her many offspring and a very busy doctor-husband completely to eclipse her joy in her Lake of Shining Waters or the White Way of Delight. And Emily—who is on the threshold of marriage at the end of the trilogy that features her—will, one feels certain, not let domesticity radically dim her mystical 'flashes', or her enjoyment of the sun-steeped ferns in her Land of Uprightness.

It must be said that Montgomery handles these tricky transitions from nature-waif to great-earth-mother far more skilfully than many authors who allow their juvenile heroines to mature in the course of a series. She is not only adept at tackling the theme of young love, but of middle-aged romance. (Significantly, perhaps, she did not marry until she was 36, as she devoted many years of her life to looking after an elderly relative, and the rival claims of love and duty are often featured in her books.) Later flowering love is a recurring theme in her story collections (particularly *The Road to Yesterday* and *The Doctor's Sweetheart*). These are full of misunderstandings, jiltings, estrangements, and nostalgia for what might have been; but also there are reconciliations and endeavours to resurrect romance in relationships that are—at least ostensibly—no longer touched by passion. There are also touches of ironic realism when, for example, Montgomery writes of fine but fading ladies who hold out against the attentions of male admirers for one or even two decades, until they find their own 'air of distinction getting a little shopworn'.

The complex processes of courtship and consummation in Montgomery's fiction are, as she says of the Canadian spring, 'long and fickle and reluctant' but full of 'unnameable' and haunting—'charm'.

—Mary Cadogan

MOORE, Doris (Elizabeth) Langley.
Nationality: British. **Born:** Liverpool, Lancashire, in 1903. **Education:** convent schools in South Africa, and privately. **Relations:** married Robin Sugden Moore in 1926 (divorced 1942); one daughter. **Career:** author and specialist in costume: founder and adviser, Museum of Costume, Bath, 1955–74; designer of costumes for films. **Recipient:** British Academy Crawshay prize, for non-fiction, 1975. Fellow, Royal Society of Literature, 1973. OBE (Officer, Order of the British Empire), 1971. **Died:** 24 February 1989.

ROMANCE AND HISTORICAL PUBLICATIONS

Novels

A Winter's Passion. London, Heinemann, 1932.
The Unknown Eros. London, Secker, 1935.
They Knew Her When: A Game of Snakes and Ladders. London,
    Rich and Cowan, 1938; as *A Game of Snakes and Ladders*, Lon-
    don, Cassell, 1955.
Not at Home. London, Cassell, 1948.
All Done by Kindness. London, Cassell, 1951; Philadelphia, Lip-
    pincott, 1952.
My Caravaggio Style. London, Cassell, and Philadelphia, Lip-
    pincott, 1959.

OTHER PUBLICATIONS

Poetry (for children)

Doris Langley Moore's Book of Scraps. London, Deutsch, 1984.

Other

The Technique of the Love Affair (as A Gentlewoman). London,
    Howe, and New York, Simon and Schuster, 1928; revised edi-
    tion, (as Doris Langley Moore) London, Rich and Cowan, 1936;
    New York, Knickerbocker, 1946.
Pandora's Letter Box, Being a Discourse on Fashionable Life. Lon-
    don, Howe, 1929.
The Bride's Book; or, Young Housewife's Compendium (with June
    Moore, as Two Ladies of England). London, Howe, 1932; revised
    edition, as *Our Loving Duty*, (as Doris Langley Moore and June
    Moore) London, Rich and Cowan, 1936.
The Pleasure of Your Company: A Text-Book of Hospitality, with
    June Moore. London, Howe, 1933; revised edition, London, Rich
    and Cowan, 1936.
E. Nesbit: A Biography. London, Benn, 1933; revised edition, Phila-
    delphia, Chilton, 1966; Benn, 1967.
*The Vulgar Heart: An Enquiry into the Sentimental Tendencies of
    Public Opinion.* London, Cassell, 1945.
*Gallery of Fashion 1790–1822: From Plates by Heideloff and Ack-
    ermann.* London, Batsford, 1949.
The Woman in Fashion. London, Batsford, 1949.
Pleasure: A Discursive Guide Book. London, Cassell, 1953.
The Child in Fashion. London, Batsford, 1953.
The Great Byron Adventure. Philadelphia, Lippincott, 1959.
The Late Lord Byron: Posthumous Dramas. London, Murray, and
    Philadelphia, Lippincott, 1961.
*Marie and the Duke of H—: The Daydream Love Affair of Marie
    Bashkirtseff.* London, Cassell, and Philadelphia, Lippincott,
    1966.
Fashion Through Fashion Plates 1771–1970. London, Ward Lock,
    1971; New York, Potter, 1972.
Lord Byron: Accounts Rendered. London, Murray, and New York,
    Harper, 1974.
Ada, Countess of Lovelace: Byron's Legitimate Daughter. London,
    Murray, 1977.

Editor, *Good Fare: A Code of Cookery*, by Édouard de Pomiane,
    translated by Blanche Bowes. London, Howe, 1932.

Translator, *Anacreon: 29 Odes.* London, Howe, 1926.
Translator, *Carlotta Grisi*, by Serge Lifar. London, Lehmann, 1947.

*   *   *

Doris Langley Moore's novels celebrate the pleasures of connois-

seurship and the satisfactions of art, the collector's world, 'the little
world where beauty was permanent and craftsmanship worth while'
(*They Knew Her When*). Her novels, while not at all conventional
romances, are comedies which frequently end in marriage, and
which seriously investigate the nature of love, often from a contemporary woman's point of view. They complement her biographical
and critical works and are worthy and stylish artifacts from the author of *Pleasure: A Discursive Guide Book*.

The Unknown Eros sets out most schematically Moore's concerns with the nature of love—maternal, erotic, intellectual, religious, aesthetic—and gives primacy to the aesthetic. Her heroine,
because she is an honest artist, is granted a vision of Eros when the
disparate faces of love merge into one figure, that of a schoolboy
singing at a speech day. The aesthetic impulse also redeems the betrayals of the narrator of *A Winter's Passion*, for Caroline's lust for
her sister's lover is sparked by her unsatisfied artistic ambitions.
These novels are more overtly serious than the dazzlingly plotted
comedies that follow.

In these, every turn of the plot, rooted in tics of character, is both
surprising and inevitable. *All Done by Kindness* is a merry chase after a recently discovered cache of Renaissance masterpieces. The
heroine's disinterested love, her honest connoisseurship, is the force
which leads to the defeat of the band of aesthetic pretenders, chief
among them a dishonest art critic, and to her own marriage.

The narrator of *My Caravaggio Style* is brought to betray his aesthetic principles and his love for Byron by jealousy of his fiancée's
attraction to the poet dead more than a hundred years. Quentin's preparations for his forgery of the lost Byron memoirs have the obsessive, hypnotic quality of preparations for a murder.

As *My Caravaggio Style* reprises the pattern and concerns of *All
Done by Kindness*, so *Not at Home* repeats the romance pattern of
They Knew Her When—the story of an actress stranded in Egypt after World War I who is reduced to the position of box office clerk in
a cinema in Alexandria by the disastrous charity of a hypocritical
friend. The comic resolution, Lucy's marriage to a duke, is dee-
pened by the precise detailing of her slip from her class and the
frightening despair engendered by poverty and exile. A similar confrontation between honesty and hypocrisy is repeated in *Not at
Home*. This postwar novel recounts a domestic invasion in which
the unlikely heroine, a middle-aged, botanical artist, Miss Mac-
Farren, is rescued from a tendency toward spiritual smugness by her
suffering at the hands of a slovenly and self-deluding tenant. Here is
the most satisfying of Moore's investigations of beauty, friendship,
and love, and the heroine's repossession of her solitary domain has
overtones of a civilization restored.

—Karen Robertson

———————

MOORE, Gwyneth.   See **VERYAN, Patricia.**

———————

MORRISON, Toni (Chloë Anthony).
Nationality: American. **Born:** Chloë Anthony Wofford, Lorain,
Ohio, 18 February 1931. **Education:** Howard University, Washington, DC, B.A. 1953; Cornell University, Ithaca, New York, M.A.
1955. **Relations:** married Harold Morrison in 1958 (divorced
1964); two sons. **Career:** instructor in English, Texas Southern
University, Houston, 1955–57, and Howard University, 1957–64;
senior editor, Random House, publishers, New York, 1965–84;
associate professor, State University of New York, Purchase,
1971–72; visiting lecturer, Yale University, New Haven, Connecticut, 1976–77, Rutgers University, New Brunswick, New Jersey, 1983–84, and Bard College, Annandale-on-Hudson, New

York, 1986–88; Schweitzer professor of humanities, State University of New York, Albany, 1984–89; Regents' lecturer, University of California, Berkeley, 1987; Santagata lecturer, Bowdoin College, Brunswick, Maine, 1987. Since 1989 professor of humanities, Princeton University, New Jersey. **Recipient:** American Academy award, 1977; National Book Critics Circle award, 1977; New York State Governor's award, 1985; Book of the Month Club award, 1986; Before Columbus Foundation award, 1988; Robert F. Kennedy award, 1988; Melcher award, 1988; Pulitzer prize, 1988; Nobel prize for literature, 1993. Honorary degree: College of Saint Rose, Albany, 1987. **Agent:** International Creative Management, 40 West 57th Street, New York, New York 10019. **Address:** Department of Creative Writing, Princeton University, Princeton, New Jersey 08544, USA.

ROMANCE AND HISTORICAL PUBLICATIONS

Novels

Beloved. New York, Knopf, and London, Chatto and Windus, 1987.
Jazz. New York, Knopf, and London, Chatto and Windus, 1992.

OTHER PUBLICATIONS

Novels

The Bluest Eye. New York, Holt Rinehart, 1970; London, Chatto and Windus, 1980.
Sula. New York, Knopf, and London, Allen Lane, 1974.
Song of Solomon. New York, Knopf, and London, Chatto and Windus, 1981.
Tar Baby. New York, Knopf, and London, Chatto and Windus, 1981.

Play

Dreaming Emmett (produced Albany, New York, 1986).

Other

Playing in the Dark: Whiteness and the Literary Imagination. New York, Harvard University Press, 1992.
Editor, *Race-ing Justice, En-gendering Power.* London, Chatto and Windus, 1993.

*

Bibliography: *Toni Morrison: An Annotated Bibliography* by David L. Middleton, New York, Garland, 1987.

Critical Studies: *New Dimensions of Spirituality: A Biracial and Bicultural Reading of the Novels of Toni Morrison* by Karla F.C. Holloway, Westport, Connecticut, Greenwood Press, 1987; *The Crime of Innocence in the Fiction of Toni Morrison* by Terry Otten, Columbia, University of Missouri Press, 1989; *Toni Morrison* by Wilfred D. Samuels, Boston, Twayne, 1990; *The Dilemma of 'Double-Consciousness': Toni Morrison's Novels* by Denise Heinz, Athens, University of Georgia Press, 1993.

*   *   *

Toni Morrison's six novels are historical to varying degrees; more importantly, they fundamentally transform fictional use of the historical. In Morrison's work, the historical is not limited to or by realism, but becomes reality—to characters and readers—through image, magic, spectres, folk tales, gossip, and spirit presence of the dead, the oral histories and metaphoric understanding of communities. The process of discovering history—of making known and coming to terms with the past's secrets—is for Morrison a process of both understanding and negotiation. To know the past, to reconcile the spirits, to resolve repressed memories, means acknowledging that the past only can be understood if one grants its phantoms. In *Playing in the Dark*, Morrison remarks: 'It has been suggested that romance is an evasion of history . . . but I am more persuaded by arguments that find in it the head-on encounter with very real, pressing historical forces and the contradictions inherent in them'.

Morrison takes her characters on journeys to personal and communal historical authenticity. Their natural and supernatural experience of the past is contoured by Morrison's remarkable use of image, multiple voices, movements in narrative time, and transformations of contemporary life through storytelling, myth, and memory. In this fusion Morrison creates a distinctive fictional style that forms an ongoing quest for individual and racial identity.

Morrison weaves her stories of black girls and women through shared voices of black culture. The novels present women coming to self in a 'historically racialized' society (*Playing in the Dark*). Slavery has marked these women's lives: in their personal experience, in the tales told to them that shape their communities, in the knowledge of evil that is both self and other. Morrison does not pose singular responses to, or evocations of, the forces of racism and sexism. The personae and plots of the novels converge doubleness and multiplicity. Girls become women, changing in and over time—personal identity colliding with growing knowledge of (and often rejection by) her shapes, actively intervenes, not only in characters' minds and memories but also as a representation in the present. Each girl and woman also is paired, often multiply paired, with friend, mother, daughter so that their characteristics of strength and love and evil and survival become both individual and a reflection of the other. And each has connection to a past and knowledge that is both literal and magical—a supernatural intelligence of the world that racism has often made unnatural.

Critics continually remark that readers' ability to share this knowledge comes from the blending of techniques and spirits in Morrison's novels—the grounding in highly articulated historical reality along with the voices of folk wisdom and magic, metaphor which goes beyond verbal image to become plot and wisdom, language which captures the tradition of black music and a knowledge beyond literal language's precise saying and knowing. The voices of belief, of gossip, of stories of past and present evil are often voices from the larger community's margins—voices of those who like the title character of *Sula* 'had discovered years before that they were neither white nor male'.

Morrison's first novel, *The Bluest Eye*, explores a young girl's destructive desire for blue eyes, a colour which represents a flight from blackness and isolation, a desire for the sign of beauty the community seems to admire. Like Morrison's later novels, *The Bluest Eye* establishes the quest for the loss of self within an historically knowable community, pairing the title quest with the understanding of a surviving narrator, another young girl who gradually fathoms the destruction of her friend's quest to become another.

Sula, Morrison's second novel, also follows a pair of friends, through adulthood and Sula's increasing separation from the community. Sula's uniqueness, resistance, perhaps evil, is unacceptable to a community which makes her its outcast. At Sula's early, isolated death, the shared secrets of girlhood, horrible knowledge of many pasts, the experience and consciousness of black women, come together with the power of friendship for a keening cry, 'loud and long . . . it had no bottom and it had no top, just circles and circles of sorrow': 'Sula . . . girl, girl, girlgirlgirl'.

Song of Solomon, Morrison's next novel, takes knowledge beyond circles of sorrow. Milkman, its central character, is a child of privilege in the black middle class. Searching for a self beyond the material ambition and possessive sexuality of his father, Milkman sets out to know the other side of town and the family his father will not acknowledge—an aunt with seemingly supernatural powers, love that makes jealousy both terror and metaphor, and a black identity in organized resistance and covert revenge for racism. Coming to terms with a racial and community past moves Milkman out of the particular past of family secrets and into engagement with the history and presence of racism.

Tar Baby, Morrison's fourth novel, has a contemporary Caribbean and European setting. Yet, like her other novels, its principal characters—Jadine, an educated, privileged, westernized model, and Son, a poor African-American who longs for his home in a black Florida town—discover in themselves secrets of the past. Meeting on an island where legendary African horsemen refused to be slaves, Jadine and Son cannot reconcile their different views of past or future. However, their growing sense of racial history becomes plotted authenticity when Son returns to the island's wild side, where nature and the spectral horsemen wait for him.

The Pulitzer prize winning *Beloved*, is the most expressly historical in purpose of all Morrison's novels, as well as the most fantastic in its representation of a world both past and beyond the plotted time. Germinating in historical records of an escaped slave woman who killed her daughter rather than see her returned to slavery, *Beloved* is set in post-Civil War America and follows Sethe, a former slave, her surviving family, and the spirit of her murdered child as they come to terms with each other, their past, and the community's rejection of an act too horrible to know and bear. Sethe lives in the house with her surviving daughter and the spirit of her murdered child, a living and sometimes destructive presence embodied in the house and their lives. With the coming of Paul D, another former slave from the plantation, Sethe and Paul D move through loving, memory, and rememory recreating their past and the history of slavery in a metaphoric and literal exorcism of evil, in a sometimes tentative retelling of what both know and fear to remember.

Morrison's recent novel *Jazz* continues her achievement with its lyrical, metaphorical treatment of historically, racially, inscribed culture. In a society haunted by the phantom of slavery, by racism, and sexism, Morrison represents phantom and evil on the page—taking readers beyond and within historicity towards the transformation of new history through new selves.

—Carol Klimick Cyganowski

MORTIMER, Carole.
Nationality: British. **Born:** Bedfordshire, in the early 1960s. **Relations:** married; three sons. **Career:** full-time writer. Lives on the Isle of Man. **Address:** c/o Mills and Boon Ltd, Eton House, 18–24 Paradise Road, Richmond, Surrey, TW9 1SR, England.

Romance and Historical Publications

Novels

The Passionate Winter. London, Mills and Boon, 1978; Toronto, Harlequin, 1979.
Savage Interlude. London, Mills and Boon, 1979; Toronto, Harlequin, 1980.
Only Lover. London, Mills and Boon, 1979; Toronto, Harlequin, 1982.
The Tempestuous Flame. London, Mills and Boon, 1979; Toronto, Harlequin, 1980.
Tempted by Desire. London, Mills and Boon, and Toronto, Harlequin, 1979.

Yesterday's Tears. London, Mills and Boon, and Toronto, Harlequin, 1980.
Brand of Possession. London, Mills and Boon, 1980; Toronto, Harlequin, 1981.
Engaged to Jarrod Stone. London, Mills and Boon, and Toronto, Harlequin, 1980.
Deceit of a Pagan. London, Mills and Boon, and Toronto, Harlequin, 1980.
Fear of Love. London, Mills and Boon, 1980.
Satan's Master. London, Mills and Boon, and Toronto, Harlequin, 1981.
Living Together. Toronto, Harlequin, 1981.
First Love, Last Love. London, Mills and Boon, and Toronto, Harlequin, 1981.
Devil Lover. London, Mills and Boon, and Toronto, Harlequin, 1981.
The Flame of Desire. London, Mills and Boon, and Toronto, Harlequin, 1981.
Freedom to Love. London, Mills and Boon, and Toronto, Harlequin, 1981.
Point of No Return. London, Mills and Boon, 1981; Toronto, Harlequin, 1982.
Ice in His Veins. London, Mills and Boon, and Toronto, Harlequin, 1981.
Love's Duel. Toronto, Harlequin, 1982.
Red Rose for Love. London, Mills and Boon, and Toronto, Harlequin, 1982.
Forbidden Surrender. London, Mills and Boon, 1982.
Forgotten Lover. London, Mills and Boon, and Toronto, Harlequin, 1982.
Burning Obsession. London, Mills and Boon, and Toronto, Harlequin, 1982.
Elusive Lover. London, Mills and Boon, and Toronto, Harlequin, 1982.
Golden Fever. London, Mills and Boon, 1982; Toronto, Harlequin, 1983.
Hidden Love. London, Mills and Boon, 1982; Toronto, Harlequin, 1983.
Passion from the Past. London, Mills and Boon, 1982; Toronto, Harlequin, 1983.
Perfect Partner. London, Mills and Boon, 1982; Toronto, Harlequin, 1983.
A Shadowed Stranger. London, Mills and Boon, and Toronto, Harlequin, 1982.
Love's Due. London, Mills and Boon, 1982.
A Subtle Revenge. London, Mills and Boon, and Toronto, Harlequin, 1983.
Sensual Encounter. London, Mills and Boon, 1983; Toronto, Harlequin, 1984.
Pagan Enchantment. London, Mills and Boon, Toronto, Harlequin, 1983.
Captive Loving. London, Mills and Boon, and Toronto, Harlequin, 1983.
Lifelong Affair. Toronto, Harlequin, 1983.
The Failed Marriage. London, Mills and Boon, 1983; Toronto, Harlequin, 1984.
Love's Only Deception. London, Mills and Boon, 1983; Toronto, Harlequin, 1984.
Fantasy Girl. London, Mills and Boon, and Toronto, Harlequin, 1983.
Love Unspoken. Toronto, Harlequin, 1983.
Undying Love. London, Mills and Boon, and Toronto, Harlequin, 1983.
Untamed. London, Mills and Boon, 1983; Toronto, Harlequin, 1984.

Heaven Here on Earth. London, Mills and Boon, and Toronto, Harlequin, 1983.

Trust in Summer Madness. London, Mills and Boon, 1983; Toronto, Harlequin, 1984.

Everlasting Love. London, Mills and Boon, and Toronto, Harlequin, 1984.

Hard to Get. London, Mills and Boon, and Toronto, Harlequin, 1984.

A Lost Love. Toronto, Harlequin, 1984.

An Unwilling Desire. London, Mills and Boon, 1984; Toronto, Harlequin, 1985.

Gypsy. London, Worldwide, 1985; Toronto, Harlequin, 1986.

The Devil's Price. London, Mills and Boon, 1985; Toronto, Harlequin, 1986.

Cherish Tomorrow. Toronto, Harlequin, 1985.

A No Risk Affair. London, Mills and Boon, and Toronto, Harlequin, 1985.

Trust in Tomorrow. London, Mills and Boon, 1985.

A Past Revenge. Toronto, Harlequin, 1985.

Tempestuous Affair. Toronto, Harlequin, 1985.

Lovers in the Afternoon. London, Mills and Boon, and Toronto, Harlequin, 1985.

A Passionate Lover. London, Mills and Boon, and Toronto, Harlequin, 1985.

Lady Surrender. Toronto, Harlequin, 1986.

Knight's Possession. Toronto, Harlequin, 1986.

Darkness into Light. Toronto, Harlequin, 1986; London, Mills and Boon, 1992.

Glass Slippers and Unicorns. London, Mills and Boon, 1986.

Velvet Promise. London, Mills and Boon, 1986; Toronto, Harlequin, 1987.

No Longer a Dream. London, Mills and Boon, and Toronto, Harlequin, 1986.

A Rogue and A Pirate. London, Mills and Boon, 1986; Toronto, Harlequin, 1987.

Elusive as a Unicorn. London, Mills and Boon, 1986.

Wade Dynasty. London, Mills and Boon, and Toronto, Harlequin, 1986.

Hawk's Prey. Toronto, Harlequin, 1987.

Merlyn's Magic. Toronto, Harlequin, 1987.

Witchchild. London, Worldwide, 1987.

After the Loving. London, Mills and Boon, and Toronto, Harlequin, 1987.

Tangled Hearts. London, Mills and Boon, 1987; Toronto, Harlequin, 1988.

Taggart's Woman. London, Mills and Boon, and Toronto, Harlequin, 1988.

Secret Passion. Toronto, Harlequin, 1988; London, Mills and Boon, 1992.

Wish for the Moon. Toronto, Harlequin, 1988.

Just One Night. Toronto, Harlequin, 1988.

Uncertain Destiny. Toronto, Harlequin, 1988.

One Chance at Love. London, Mills and Boon, and Toronto, Harlequin, 1988.

To Love Again. Toronto, Harlequin, 1988.

The Loving Gift. Toronto, Harlequin, 1989.

Elusive as the Unicorn. Toronto, Harlequin, 1990.

A Christmas Affair. London, Mills and Boon, and Toronto, Harlequin, 1990.

Romance of a Lifetime. London, Mills and Boon, 1991; Toronto, Harlequin, 1992.

Dreveilion Surprise. Toronto, Harlequin, 1991.

Memories of the Past. London, Mills and Boon, 1991; Toronto, Harlequin, 1992.

The Jilted Bridegroom. London, Mills and Boon, 1992; Toronto, Harlequin, 1993.

Mother of the Bride. London, Mills and Boon, 1992; Toronto, Harlequin, 1993.

Private Lives. London, Mills and Boon, 1992; Toronto, Harlequin, 1993.

Elusive Obsession. London, Mills and Boon, 1992.

Fated Attraction. London, Mills and Boon, 1992.

Gracious Lady. London, Mills and Boon, 1993.

Saving Grace. London, Mills and Boon, and Toronto, Harlequin, 1993.

The Sheik's Captive. Toronto, Harlequin, 1993.

Return Engagement. London, Mills and Boon, 1993.

*   *   *

In the last decade Carole Mortimer has written an impressive number of titles for avid readers of romance. All of her novels fall into the category of the light romantic, from her first titles in the late 1970s, to one of her latest books *Gracious Lady.* At first glance Mortimer's books conform to the limits of the genre—beautiful heroines, glamorous and virile heroes, antagonistic first encounters, misunderstandings, and final declarations; however, a second examination reveals that her books display a distinct liveliness, and her dialogue is refreshingly coherent and natural.

In one of her early novels, *Engaged to Jarrod Stone*, the heroine, Brooke, is the instigator of a practical joke. She has been so incensed by the chauvinistic attitude of her boss, Jarrod Stone, that she decides to dent his ego by placing an embarrassing (and false) announcement of their engagement in the newspaper.

The reader may find many of the ingredients that reappear in Mortimer's novels in this book. The author's heroine is always young, her age is in the eighteen to early twenties range. Brooke, in *Engaged to Jarrod Stone*, is 20, as are Regan in *Devil Lover* and Diana in *Elusive Obsession*; Rachel in *Hidden Love* is 18. The heroine is usually described as being small and petite, hence Cynara in *The Devil's Price*, is 'dwarfed' by six-foot Zak Buchanan, and Finn in *Private Lives* stands 'barely five feet in height even in her white trackshoes'.

Mortimer's heroes, on the other hand, are tall and invariably in their mid-to-late thirties. Rick Howarth, in *A Shadowed Stranger*, is a typical Mortimer male. 'He was a handsome man, although rather unkempt-looking, his hair long and out of style, although it gleamed with a clean black sheen, his eyes grey and piercing, his nose long and straight . . . He was very leanly built, although firmly muscled'. The hero often has grey hair 'to lend distinction to his bearing'. Green or blue are favourite alternative eye colourings, and his gaze nearly always displays a hint of steel.

Unlike many of her peers, Mortimer is not afraid to let her characters make love although they are usually married, or at least engaged, before doing so. Cynara, in *The Devil's Price*, is an exception, although it is made clear to the reader that her liaison with Zak will end in marriage. A frequent motif used to conclude books is the expectation or arrival of a baby (or babies, as in *Burning Obsession*) which puts a final seal on the romance. Another favourite device which adds interest to the plot, or love affair, is to provide one or both of the protagonists with a secret past. In *Devil Lover*, the father of heroine Regan has apparently seduced the wife of Andreas Vatis, this leads Andreas to want to revenge himself by marrying Regan; similarly Darcy, in *Glass Slippers and Unicorns*, was involved in a bank robbery, and subsequently suffered a nervous breakdown; and Sophie (*Gracious Lady*) hides the fact that she had been married (albeit disastrously) from her employer, the wealthy and autocratic Maximillian. *Gracious Lady* also includes a possible poisoning, and the threatened kidnapping of Maximillian's racehorse.

Mortimer's prose is lively. Dialogue abounds but is usually consistent with the genre. Characters rarely speak—they exclaim, rasp, are scornful, in fact do anything but talk normally. Action is fairly static, mainly concentrating on encounters between the main characters, although there are exceptions. In *Devil Lover* the spirited heroine Regan climbs out of a window with the help of a rope made from blankets and indulges in a flight across the country, from Cornwall to Scotland to escape the attentions of the hero; Darcy, in *Glass Slippers and Unicorns*, has a panic attack, and is involved in a bank robbery and a fire, while her lover Reed attempts to find out who is defrauding him; and Maximillian, the hero of *Gracious Lady*, suffers from an attempted poisoning by his daughter, however in most cases the action is less volatile. Venues range from Italy to Cornwall, Canada to London, although Mortimer is not really interested in location except as a background, and this is used as a foil for her characters, or to emphasize their status or culture.

Characterization is minimal, again consistent with the romance genre, through heroes and heroines are never vapid. They may be difficult to distinguish from book to book, but they are lively and spirited. The heroines often have careers that the reader can identify with—Robyn, in *A Shadowed Stranger*, is a librarian; Natalie, in *Fantasy Girl*, runs a modelling agency; and Laura, in *First Love, Last Love*, is a typist. There are more exotic occupations—a filmstar, model, singer, but on the whole there is a reassuring 'reality' about Mortimer's heroines. Her heroes, however, are all rich and successful with the assurance that this state brings them. Indeed Mortimer's characters have no need to worry about the stress of poverty, or the strain that lack of money can place on a relationship. Whatever vicissitudes the protagonists' love affair encounters, it is against a background of casual luxury and comfort.

Though writing within the prescribed limits of her chosen genre, Mortimer's books display a certain individuality that is refreshing and enjoyable, and which ensures that she will continue to attract new readers to the romance genre.

—Ferelith Hordon

MOTLEY, Annette. Address: c/o Little, Brown and Company (UK) Ltd, 165 Great Dover Street, London SE1 4YA, England.

ROMANCE AND HISTORICAL PUBLICATIONS

Novels

My Lady's Crusade. London, Futura, 1977.
The Sins of the Lion. London, Hutchinson, and New York, Stein and Day, 1979.
The Quickenberry Tree. London, Macdonald, 1983; New York, St Martin's Press, 1984.
Green Dragon, White Tiger. London, Macdonald, and New York, Macmillan, 1986.
Men on White Horses. London, Macdonald, 1988.

*　　*　　*

It is always a pleasure to find an author who can write intelligent historical fiction as well as romantic adventure. Annette Motley is such a writer. Here is an author who has thoroughly researched the widely diverse periods covered in her five novels, *The Sins of the Lion*, *My Lady's Crusade*, *The Quickenberry Tree*, *Green Dragon, White Tiger*, and *Men on White Horses*. Motley weaves history very cleverly into natural sounding dialogue allowing the flow of words and ideas to explain events to the reader.

As in other tales of romance fiction, war, with all its passions and cruelties, serves as a background for handsome heroes and enticingly beautiful heroines. But in Motley's novels this background takes on an aspect of gritty reality. With clear insight she describes the horrors of war as it is experienced by the participants. For Richard the Lionheart (*My Lady's Crusade*) war becomes a way of life, a way to display his ruthless and bloodthirsty courage. For others, such as his more humanitarian lieutenant, Tristan de Jarnac, engagement in battle is necessary only when the cause is just. Killing then becomes an essential but unpleasant duty. In *The Sins of the Lion* the Renaissance Prince Leone de Montevalenti desperately wishes to keep a hard-won peace for his city, but when war with his traitorous brother-in-law becomes inevitable, he reluctantly reverts to his warrior role. Feeling like nothing less than a killing machine, completely devoid of fear for himself or compassion for his adversaries he leads his army to victory. In contrast Tom Herron (*The Quickenberry Tree*) when facing his most loathsome enemy, holds to the highest standards of a Royalist cavalier and refuses to take unfair advantage.

In each novel it is the heroine's story that weaves all other events together. The lovely Lady Eden of Hawkhurst (*My Lady's Crusade*) sets out to find her young husband Stephen who had left England years before to fight the Saracens in the Holy Land. Seen through her eyes the sights and sounds of the exotic and often barbarous Outremer pulsate with life. She suffers much privation in her lonely quest before aid and love come in the form of the chivalrous Knight Tristan. *The Sins of the Lion* is the story of Tulla an exotically beautiful half-Greek, half-Turkish slave bought for the pleasure of Il Leone. As the aristocratic daughter of a Pasha, she possesses a pride that cannot allow her to become the willing mistress to the golden Prince, but eventually even this strong-minded lady falls under the spell of this complex man. In *The Quickenberry Tree* Oliver Cromwell's army plunges England into years of civil strife, all of which is viewed through the eyes of Lucy Herron and members of her Royalist family. Lucy is a young teenager when the story begins and a mature woman at its close 16 years later. During those years, along with agony and fear engendered by civil war, she knew the love of two men, Irish charmer Cathal O'Connor and worldly wise Will Staunton. Seventh-century China forms the setting of *Green Dragon, White Tiger*, based on the life of Empress Wu, the only woman to rule this vast country from the exalted Dragon throne. Known throughout most of her life as Black Jade, this highly intelligent, strong-minded lady began her climb to power as the favourite concubine of Emperor Shin-min. She continued her ascent by marrying his weak-willed son, and ruthlessly eliminating her many powerful enemies until she acquired absolute control. *Men on White Horses* tells the story of Sophie, daughter of the ambitious Princess Joanna of Anhalt-Zerbst. Sophie's dream is to become Empress of Russia, a land she sees as full of romance and adventure. With the help of her mother Sophie initially wins the favour of Empress Elisabeth who arranges a marriage with her heir. The novel traces Sophie's journey through life and the Russian court set against a background of religious and political turbulence.

The characters in Motley's novels have flesh and blood reality. For example Eden's anguish is graphically described when she learns that her husband has been seduced into a homosexual relationship with his Saracen captor. The reader sympathizes with both Lucy and Will over the pain each suffers because of Lucy's brief adulterous liaison with Cathal.

Detailed historical background intertwined with a tale of romance characterizes Motley's fiction.

—Patricia Altner

MULLINS, Edwin (Brandt).
Nationality: British. **Born:** London, 14 September 1933. **Education:** Midhurst Grammar School; Oxford University, B.A.

(honours) in English 1957, M.A. 1958. **Military Service:** British Army, 1952–54. **Relations:** married 1) Gillian Brydone in 1960 (died 1982), two daughters and one son; 2) Anne Kelleher in 1984. **Career:** editorial assistant, Medici Society, 1957–58; London, editor, *Two Cities*, London, 1958–60; art correspondent, *Illustrated London News*, 1958–62; sale-room correspondent, *Financial Times*, London, 1962–67; art critic, *Sunday Telegraph*, London, 1962–69; art correspondent and adviser, *Daily Telegraph Magazine*, London, 1964–86. Since 1967 broadcaster and presenter of television documentaries. **Agent:** Curtis Brown, 162–168 Regent Street, London W1R 5TB, England. **Address:** 7 Lower Common South, London SW15 1BP, England.

ROMANCE AND HISTORICAL PUBLICATIONS

Novels

The Golden Bird. London, Collins, 1987.
The Lands of the Sea. London, Collins, 1988; as *The Master Painter*, New York, Doubleday, 1989.

OTHER PUBLICATIONS

Novels

Angels on the Point of a Pin. London, Secker and Warburg, 1979.
Sirens. London, Secker and Warburg, 1983.

Other

F.N. Souza: An Introduction. London, Blond, 1962.
Alfred Wallis: Cornish Primitive Painter. London, Macdonald, 1967.
Josef Herman. London, Adams and McKay, 1967.
Braque. London, Thames and Hudson, 1968; as *The Art of Georges Braque*, New York, Abrams, 1968.
The Art of Elisabeth Frink. London, Lund Humphries, 1972.
The Pilgrimage to Santiago. London, Secker and Warburg, and New York, Taplinger, 1974.
A Love Affair with Nature. Oxford, Phaidon Press, 1985.
The Painted Witch: Female Body, Male Art. London, Secker and Warburg, and New York, Carroll and Graf, 1985.
The Royal Collection. London, Channel Four Publications, 1992.

Editor, *Great Paintings*. London, BBC Publications, and New York, St Martin's Press, 1981.
Editor, *The Arts of Britain*. Oxford, Phaidon Press, 1983.

*

Edwin Mullins comments:
My historical novels have been attempts to bring to life through fiction certain periods of history which have particularly fascinated me as an art historian and as a traveller. Historical fiction as a genre does not interest me at all.

*   *   *

Edwin Mullins has written two highly successful historical novels—*The Golden Bird*, and *The Lands of the Sea* (US title *The Master Painter*). Both books are extremely well researched, detailed works that explore the dawn and dusk of the Age of Chivalry.
The Golden Bird is set in AD1000, in Northern France. The hero, Fulk, a young and extraordinary looking stonemason, creates in-

credible buildings, first of all for God, and then for Count Fulk 'the Black' (great-great-great-grandfather of the first Plantagenet English king). Rollo travels from his sheltered existence at the abbey of Jumièges to the count's court at Anjou where he creates indestructable fortresses, castles, and garrisons. His vision of the violence, slaughter, and suffering caused by the prevailing war is so strong that he is driven to question God's existence, and to use his creative vision to prevent further bloodshed.
Rollo falls in love with a good and beautiful woman—however, Fulk suffers a much sadder fate. Believing lies about his wife, Fulk has her burnt as a witch and then goes to the Holy Lands on a pilgrimage. *The Golden Bird* spans two-and-a-half years in Rollo and Fulk's lives, and Mullins manages to convey the horror and brutality of living during such a war-torn period.
The Lands of the Sea has an artistic main character, the painter Jan van Eyck, whose tranquil character is contrasted to the larger than life Philip of Burgundy. The capture of Joan of Arc and Burgundy's alliance with England provide the background historical detail for the book.
Both *The Golden Bird* and *The Lands of the Sea* provide a successful overview of this turbulent but magnificent period in history.

—P. Campbell

———

MUNRO, Neil.
Pseudonym: Hugh Fowlis. **Nationality:** British. **Born:** Inveraray, Argyllshire, 3 June 1864. **Relations:** married. **Career:** journalist, *Scottish News*, 1881–93, Greenock *Advertiser*, 1893, and Glasgow *News;* editor, Glasgow *Evening News*, 1918–27. **Recipient:** LL.D.: University of Glasgow, 1908. **Died:** 22 December 1930.

ROMANCE AND HISTORICAL PUBLICATIONS

Novels

John Splendid: The Tale of a Poor Gentleman and the Little Wars of Lorns. Edinburgh, Blackwood, and New York, Dodd Mead, 1898.
Gilian the Dreamer. London, Isbister, and New York, Dodd Mead, 1899.
Doom Castle: A Romance. Edinburgh, Blackwood, and New York, Doubleday, 1901.
The Shoes of Fortune. London, Isbister, and New York, Dodd Mead, 1901.
Children of the Tempest: A Tale of the Outer Isles. Edinburgh, Blackwood, 1903.
The New Road. Edinburgh, Blackwood, 1914.

Short Stories

The Lost Pibroch and Other Sheiling Stories. Edinburgh, Blackwood, 1896.
Jaunty Jock and Other Stories. Edinburgh, Blackwood, 1918.

OTHER PUBLICATIONS

Novels

The Daft Days. Edinburgh, Blackwood, 1907; as *Bud*, New York, Harper, 1907.
Fancy Farm. Edinburgh, Blackwood, 1910.
Ayrshire Idylls. London, A. and C. Black, 1912.

Jimmy Swan, The Joy Traveller. Edinburgh, Blackwood, 1917.

Short Stories as Hugh Fowlis

Erchie My Droll Friend. Edinburgh, Blackwood, 1904.
The Vital Spark and Her Queer Crew. Edinburgh, Blackwood, 1906.
In Highland Harbours with Para Handy, S.S. Vital Spark. Edinburgh, Blackwood, 1911.
Hurricane Jack of the Vital Spark. Edinburgh, Blackwood, 1923.
Para Handy and Other Tales. Edinburgh, Blackwood, 1931.

Poetry

Bagpipe Ballads and Other Poems. Edinburgh, Blackwood, 1917.
The Poetry of Neil Munro. Edinburgh, Blackwood, 1931.

Other

The Clyde: River and Firth, with M.Y. and J.Y. Hunter. London, A. and C. Black, 1907.
The History of the Royal Bank of Scotland 1727–1927. Privately printed, 1928.
The Brave Days: A Chronicle from the North. Edinburgh, Porpoise Press, 1931.
The Looker-on. Edinburgh, Porpoise Press, 1933.

*   *   *

Neil Munro creates a complete picture of the Scottish Highlands in the past. It is not only the old words, the speech, half Gaelic and half English according to the character, and the tartans that convincingly create a sense of the past but also the way of thinking. The power of the Presbyterian Church in the 17th century is demonstrated in *John Splendid* as kirk and court of law act together excommunicating defaulters for crimes great and small, even forbidding women to keep their plaids over their heads during the sermon as it made it impossible to tell if they were asleep or not. Respect is shown for the minister who follows the Campbells in their fighting and takes water to the wounded.

The story keeps up a good pace in recounting the barbaric warfare between the Campbells and the MacDonalds supported by Montrose, with the fury of vengeance wreaked on young and old alike. The people must endure the looting and burning of their homes, as well as intervals of tense waiting, hiding in the hills. Through it all runs a code of hospitality to any wayfarer and a concern for children. Montrose on hearing a child's cry passes by with a wave of his bonnet without searching the building. Everyone wears easily recognizable tartan kilts; a blind woman claims that she can tell the clan by the feel of the cloth. John Splendid himself, a cousin of the Marquis of Argyll, a fierce fighter just returned from fighting with Gustavus in Germany, gets on well with others by claiming that they do everything better than he does. He says the highlanders keep themselves warm by quarrelling with each other.

'It's a gossiping community this, long lugged and scandal loving', says the villain in *Doom Castle*. The power of rumour and scurrilous songs pervades all the novels. This novel is set in 1755, ten years after the failure of Bonnie Prince Charlie's uprising when the Highlands were a prey to spies. A Frenchman comes to Argyll seeking revenge. Everyone is very free with their swords and daggers. Tartans are forbidden to the Jacobites, so the heroine's father wears his kilt only in secret in the attic of Doom Castle, a sinister building on the edge of the sea. Admiration of Highland scenery is another recurring feature: 'To the north brooded enormous hills, seen dimly by the stars, couchant terrors, vague vast shapes of dolours and alarums'. This story has comic relief in the form of the garrulous dwarf

retainer at the Castle who playacts the soldier he was never able to become.

Exhilarating descriptions of wild weather where 'the ford was gulping full', details of the women's talk, and the whole way of life among the Catholics of South Uist 50 years after Bonnie Prince Charlie's departure fill *Children of the Tempest*. Here again gossip is all powerful but only on an island could singing a song taunting Duncan that he was only courting the angelic Ann, the virtuous priest's sister, because of her possible fortune, drive him away to the mainland. His half brother Col has the courage to rescue an old man from the sea but, the sea cheated of its prey, takes the old man in the end. At one point in the story the Sergeant takes to his English, a sign that he saw some need for lying. The heroine Ann, much loved by the people, is nearly lost returning one terrible dark night from a funeral and is later kidnapped.

General Wade's roads built across the Highlands after the 1715 Jacobite uprising were unpopular with the Clans. *The New Road* is full of the intrigues between Inveraray and Inverness, the violence among the cattle stealers and the men who traffic in arms. The Duke of Argyll sends Ninian Campbell to Inverness to check up on Jacobites. With him goes young Aeneas to start up business for his uncle. The mystery of his father's death adds to his problems, marauding gangs steal the pay chest meant for the road builders. The two men are followed by Col who has Virgilian tags engraved on his sword but was a 'kite and trembling things went clapping in the heather when he hovered, blackmail he lifted like a rent on quarter day'. The road builders found the Highlands 'dark and deep and cunning' more loyal to their chiefs who held state 'in gaunt old keeps where pipers blew from turrets' than to the crown. Aeneas is finally nearly deported to the West Indies for knowing too much.

Between writing his historical novels Munro (as Hugh Fowlis) wrote a number of short humorous tales about the captain and crew of the *Vital Spark*, a steam puffer on the Clyde before World War I.

—Margaret Campbell

MURRAY, D(avid) L(eslie).
Born: 1888. Died: 1962.

ROMANCE AND HISTORICAL PUBLICATIONS

Novels

The Bride Adorned. London, Constable, and New York, Harcourt Brace, 1929.
Stardust: A Tale of the Circus. London, Constable, and Boston, Little Brown, 1931.
The English Family Robinson: A Tale for the New Poor. London, Constable, 1933; as *Once They Were Rich*, New York, Dutton, 1933.
Regency: A Quadruple Portrait. London, Hodder and Stoughton, and New York, Knopf, 1936.
Trumpeter, Sound! London, Hodder and Stoughton, 1933; New York, Knopf, 1934.
Commander of the Mists. London, Hodder and Stoughton, and New York, Knopf, 1934.
Tale of Three Cities: A Novel in Baroque. London, Hodder and Stoughton, and New York, Knopf, 1940.
Enter Three Witches. London, Hodder and Stoughton, 1942.
Folly Bridge: A Romantic Tale. London, Hodder and Stoughton, 1945.
Leading Lady. London, Hodder and Stoughton, 1947.
Royal Academy: A Victorian Picture Show. London, Hodder and Stoughton, 1950.

Outrageous Fortune: An Edwardian Adventure. London, Hodder and Stoughton, 1952.
Come Like Shadows: A Romance in Three Ages. London, Hodder and Stoughton, 1955.
Roman Cavalier. London, Hodder and Stoughton, 1958.
Hands of Healing. London, Hodder and Stoughton, 1961.

OTHER PUBLICATIONS

Other

Pragmatism. London, Constable, 1912.
Reservation: Its Purpose and Method. London, Mowbray, and Milwaukee, Morehouse, 1923.
Scenes and Silhouettes. London, Cape, 1926; as *Candles and Crinolines*, 1930.
Benjamin Disraeli. London, Benn, and Boston, Little Brown, 1927.
Fortune's Favourite: The Life and Times of Franz Lehár, with W. Macqueen-Pope. London, Hutchinson, 1953.

*   *   *

D.L. Murray wrote on a variety of subjects—from 19th-century Papal Rome (*The Bride Adorned*), race courses and gambling dens in Edwardian London (*Outrageous Fortune: An Edwardian Adventure*), to life in a travelling circus (*Stardust*).

The Bride Adorned, like Murray's other work, is a long, extremely detailed book that draws on original sources to create realistic picture of the political and religious tensions existing in Rome in the 19th century. Angela Craven, a young English girl, moves to Rome to live with her uncle, and finds herself torn between her love for a handsome count who supports the papacy, and her friendship with anti-papists who oppose everything her lover stands for. The problem of loving someone of a different religion is raised: Angela is Protestant and Count Camillo Ursi is Catholic, and although she tries to convert to catholicism, she finds it impossible in the end. While the protagonists come into conflict over their differing definitions of 'freedom' ('freedom means expressing the voice of God' says Camillo in opposition to Angela's more romantic notion of freeing the masses from oppression), they find that their love is more powerful than all of the obstacles thrown into their paths. The jealous love of Princess Valloscura for Camillo adds further complications to the plot.

Showing his versatility as a writer, Murray set *Stardust* in a circus. It follows the fortunes of Georgina Dufay, who begins the book as the penniless daughter of a bankrupt circus owner, but then establishes herself in the circus after she marries Otto Riegelmann, the 'elephant man'. After their marriage starts to founder, Otto begins to drink and womanize. Georgina finds true love with Darrell Carless, whom she eventually marries at the end of the book. *Stardust* contains lots of descriptive detail about the difficulties of living and working in a circus—the pressures, the hard work, and the joy when things go right.

War and soldiers frequently feature in Murray's books—George Masterman, in *Outrageous Fortune: An Edwardian Adventure*, was involved in the Boer war; Deodatus, in *Tale of Three Cities*, fights in the Franco-Prussian war; Count Camillo Ursi is part of the Noble Guard in 19th-century Rome (*The Bride Adorned*); and Mark, in *Trumpeter, Sound!*, joins the army, and goes off to fight in the Crimean war with his half-brother.

Trumpeter, Sound is probably one of Murray's most popular works. Depicting in glorious detail life in the less salubrious districts of mid-19th-century London, as well as the Duke of Wellington's funeral, and the Charge of the Light Brigade.

Tale of Three Cities moves from Rome, to London, and finally to Metz. It follows the story of Deodatus, who ends up as a soldier in the Franco-Prussian war. Deodatus finds love with a beautiful Italian girl, Ludovico.

Murray was particularly good at creating a strong historic background against which his plots take place. He painted his canvasses with layer upon layer of rich detail, until the smells, sounds, and atmosphere of the period and place seemed real, and his characters' actions and lives were completely believable.

—P. Campbell

————

MURRAY, Fiona.   See **BEVAN, Gloria.**

————

MURRAY, Frances.
Pseudonym for Rosemary Booth. **Nationality:** British. **Born:** Rosemary Sutherland, Glasgow, Scotland, 10 February 1928. **Education:** University of Glasgow, 1945–47; University of St Andrews, Fife, M.A. 1965, diploma in education 1966. **Relations:** married Robert Edward Booth in 1950; three daughters. History teacher, Perth Academy, Scotland, 1966–72. Since 1972 principal teacher of history, Linlathen High School, Dundee. School scriptwriter for BBC radio. **Recipient:** Romantic Novelists Association major award, 1974, and Elgin prize, 1974. **Agent:** David Higham Associates, 5–8 Lower John Street, London W1R 4HA, England.

ROMANCE AND HISTORICAL PUBLICATIONS

Novels

The Dear Colleague. London, Hodder and Stoughton, and New York, St Martin's Press, 1972.
The Burning Lamp. London, Hodder and Stoughton, and New York, St Martin's Press, 1973.
The Heroine's Sister. London, Hodder and Stoughton, and New York, St Martin's Press, 1975.
Red Rowan Berry. London, Hodder and Stoughton, 1976; New York, St Martin's Press, 1977.
Castaway. London, Hodder and Stoughton, 1978; New York, St Martin's Press, 1979.
Payment for the Piper. London, Hodder and Stoughton, 1983.
The Belchamber Scandal. London, Hodder and Stoughton, and New York, St Martin's Press, 1985.

OTHER PUBLICATIONS

Other (for children)

Ponies on the Heather. London, Collins, 1966; revised edition, 1973.
Ponies and Parachutes. London, Hodder and Stoughton, 1975.
White Hope. London, Hodder and Stoughton, 1978.
Shadow over the Islands. London, Hodder and Stoughton, 1986.

*   *   *

If you like your history lessons presented in an easily comprehended manner aided by lots of romance and adventure, then Frances Murray is a safe bet. Her novels are always enjoyable, briskly paced, and set in unusual and interesting times and places. No matter where or when, her heroines are always spirited, liberated females who take command of their destinies with or without the hero's help.

Her first historical novel, *The Dear Colleague*, involved cloak and dagger politics in the British Foreign Office in Paris during Louis Napoleon's bid for emperor. The hero, Hector, and the heroine, Elizabeth, become husband and wife in an arranged marriage of convenience, naturally falling in love by the story's end. The grand finale includes a shoot-out at the Opera House in Paris where, thanks to Britain's intervention, Louis Napoleon escapes unharmed.

The Burning Lamp, almost more of a young adult title, again involves a liberated woman, Euphemia Witherspoon, who has trained as a nurse with Florence Nightingale and sets out for the Wild West to try to establish a hospital. In spite of Comanches, chauvinist townsmen, and incompetent doctors, Phemie still manages to get the hospital built and find herself a man.

The setting for *The Heroine's Sister*, a well-written romance adventure, is Venice in 1868, when it is still under Austrian rule. Again skulduggery and intrigue are the themes as the heroine, a wonderfully resourceful and courageous Victorian lady, foils the military and saves her tall dark Italian nobleman.

Red Rowan Berry is the least historical of her novels. Nineteenth-century Scotland provides the background for the romantic story of Janet Laidlaw and her quest through many trials and tribulations, including a bigamous marriage, to be reunited with her true love.

Another unusual setting occurs in *Castaway*, the tale of a young girl who is shipwrecked off the coast of Guernsey in 1804 at a time when Napoleon is readying troops to invade England. History takes precedence over romance as she finds it difficult to recognize friend from foe on an island filled with spies and smugglers. A lieutenant in Her Majesty's Royal Navy provides the brief love interest.

Payment for the Piper begins in 1850 and unfolds into a generational saga centring on Hannah Lindsay. Hannah leaves her home in Scotland against the wishes of her parents who have arranged her marriage with the local minister. Undaunted, Hannah sails, alone, in search of her brother to a remote New Zealand sheep farm. Adventures follow quickly, culminating 150 years later in Hannah's great-great-grandson's musical triumph at an Edinburgh festival. Through each generation Hannah's spirit is the dominant force carrying her descendants through grief, despair, the misery of war, and finally happiness and success.

Murray fills a much-needed niche in the historical romance category. Being neither straight historical nor a sweet-savage saga that uses historical settings to tell an erotic story of love, her novels fall comfortably in between, granting readers the best of both worlds by giving them true historical romance.

—Marilyn Lockhart

MUSKETT, Netta (Rachel).
Nationality: British. **Born:** 1887. **Career:** former vice-president, Romantic Novelists Association. **Died.**

ROMANCE AND HISTORICAL PUBLICATIONS

Novels

The Jade Spider. London, Hutchinson, 1927.
The Open Window. London, Hutchinson, 1930.
After Rain. London, Hutchinson, 1931.
The Flickering Lamp. London, Hutchinson, 1931.
A Mirror for Dreams. London, Hutchinson, 1931.
Nor Any Dawn. London, Hutchinson, 1932.
The Shallow Cup. London, Hutchinson, 1932.
Wings in the Dust. London, Hutchinson, 1933.
Plaster Cast. London, Hutchinson, 1933.

Painted Heaven. London, Hutchinson, 1934.
Silver-Gilt. London, Hutchinson, 1935; New York, Berkley, 1978.
Tamarisk. London, Hutchinson, 1935.
Winter's Day. London, Hutchinson, 1936.
Misadventure. London, Hutchinson, 1936.
Alley-Cat. London, Hutchinson, 1937.
Middle Mist. London, Hutchinson, 1937.
Happy To-Morrow. London, Hutchinson, 1938.
The Shadow Market. London, Hutchinson, 1938.
Blue Haze. London, Hutchinson, 1939; New York, Berkley, 1978.
To-Day Is Ours. London, Hutchinson, 1939.
Wide and Dark. London, Hutchinson, 1940.
Scarlet Heels. London, Hutchinson, 1940.
Twilight and Dawn. London, Hutchinson, 1941.
The Gilded Hoop. London, Hutchinson, 1941.
Love in Amber. London, Hutchinson, 1942.
Candle in the Sun. New York, Liveright, 1943; London, Hutchinson, 1960.
The Quiet Island. London, Hutchinson, 1943.
Time for Play. London, Hutchinson, 1943.
The Wire Blind. London, Hutchinson, 1944.
Golden Harvest. London, Hutchinson, 1944.
The Patchwork Quilt. London, Hutchinson, 1946.
Fire of Spring. London, Hutchinson, 1946.
The Clency Tradition. London, Hutchinson, 1947.
A Daughter for Julia. London, Hutchinson, 1948.
The Durrants. London, Hutchinson, 1948.
Living with Adam. London, Hutchinson, 1949.
Cast the Spear. London, Hutchinson, 1950; New York, Berkley, 1978.
House of Many Windows. London, Hutchinson, 1950.
No May in October. London, Hutchinson, 1951.
The Long Road. London, Hale, 1951.
Rock Pine. London, Hale, 1952.
Safari for Seven. London, Hale, 1952.
Brocade. London, Hutchinson, 1953.
Red Dust. London, Hutchinson, 1954.
Philippa. London, Hutchinson, 1954.
Give Back Yesterday. London, Hutchinson, 1955.
Flowers from the Rock. London, Hutchinson, 1956.
Light from One Star. London, Hutchinson, 1956.
The Crown of Willow. London, Hutchinson, 1957.
The Fettered Past. London, Hutchinson, 1958.
Flame of the Forest. London, Hutchinson, 1958.
The High Fence. London, Hutchinson, 1959.
Through Many Waters. London, Hutchinson, 1961.
The Touchstone. London, Hutchinson, 1962.
The Weir House. London, Hutchinson, 1962.
Love and Deborah. London, Hutchinson, 1963.
Cloudbreak. London, Hutchinson, 1964.

*   *   *

Blue Haze, After Rain, Happy To-Morrow, Flame of the Forest, Through Many Waters, Painted Heaven—behind a succession of such pretty, light-hearted sounding titles lies the urgent attempt to deal conscientiously with serious human problems. After the 1914–18 war, a number of romantic novelists tackled those ethical problems which war had engendered. Netta Muskett looked, for instance, at the 'surplus million' women, left on the shelf because of the huge numbers of young men killed in action. The heroine of *Painted Heaven* has the misfortune to lose fiancé, brothers, parents. The orphaned heroine, utterly alone in the world, is of course a much used device, since pathos can be added to her many other predicaments. Doomed to spinsterhood, with no chance of ever finding a husband, this heroine resolves to find 'another kind of happiness' through an illegitimate child, only to discover that this offers false security, a false happiness which is no more than a 'painted heaven'.

By the mid 1950s, with changing social mores, and increasing sexual freedom, there were new problems to be solved. The dreaded peril of permissiveness was threatening to sweep away all that romantic novelists held to be most noble, dear, and beautiful. The reaction of some writers to the increased liberation going on in real life was to tighten up fictional virtue still more, to place their heroines on still higher pedestals. 'The romantic novelist is almost alone in presenting a picture of true love, decent and honourable conduct, and the happiness which is the result of these "old-fashioned things"', explained a spokeswoman for the Romantic Novelists Association.

While some ignored the new problems, Muskett seized upon them. Not for her the happy-ever-after ending with marriage at the last chapter. Marital unrest, failed marriage, middle-aged marriages, even unconsummated marriages, could provide daring food for thought, an opportunity for psychological insight into human difficulties. *Light from One Star* concerns the marital problems encountered by the older, thoughtful type of man if he mistakenly marries a younger woman. She is a glamorous, extroverted, television personality. This gives the clue to her flighty selfish behaviour as a bride. Career women, particularly in glamorous, self-advertising work, are not to be trusted. She accepts her husband's generous presents, and continental holidays, but refuses to sleep with him. Time and again, she 'denies him his rights'. And when, at long last, she finally resolves to give in/be a good wife/allow him to make love to her, which she does 'with a pretty little lift of her head and an inviting look in her eyes', and the crude words, 'Well—how, about it?', her husband has lost interest. He sadly, but wisely, tells her, 'I'm not blaming you, my dear. I ought to have known. As a doctor, I ought to have realised *before it was too late*'. Has the poor chap become impotent? Discretion prevents Muskett delving any further into the problem.

Muskett treats her problem novels to a special style of writing. Verbs are left out, random adverbs stuck in, commas here and there. This can be interpreted either, as one critic suggested, as 'sloppy writing and false sentiment', or as a specially constructed, neo-realistic, semi-documentary prose appropriate to the important topic.

—Rachel Anderson

MYERS, Harriet Kathryn.   See **HORNER, Lance, Kyle ONSTOTT, and Ashley CARTER.**

NAPIER, Susan.
Pseudonym for Susan Potter. **Nationality:** New Zealander. **Born:** Auckland, New Zealand, 14 February 1954. **Education:** Papatoetoe High School, Auckland. **Relations:** married Anthony Potter, 1973; two sons. **Career:** journalist, *The Auckland Star*, 1970–72; scriptwriter, Reynolds Film Productions, Auckland, 1974–77. **Address:** 105 Grand Drive, Remuera, Auckland 5, New Zealand.

ROMANCE AND HISTORICAL PUBLICATIONS

Novels

Sweet Vixen. London, Mills and Boon, 1983; Toronto, Harlequin, 1985.

Love in the Valley. London, Mills and Boon, 1984; Toronto, Harlequin, 1985.
Sweet as My Revenge. London, Mills and Boon, 1985; Toronto, Harlequin, 1986.
The Counterfeit Secretary. London, Mills and Boon, 1985; Toronto, Harlequin, 1986.
The Lonely Season. London, Mills and Boon, and Toronto, Harlequin, 1986.
True Enchanter. London, Mills and Boon, 1987; Toronto, Harlequin, 1988.
Reasons of the Heart. London, Mills and Boon, 1987; Toronto, Harlequin, 1988.
Another Time. London, Mills and Boon, and Toronto, Harlequin, 1989.
The Love Conspiracy. London, Mills and Boon, 1989; Toronto, Harlequin, 1990.
Bewitching Compulsion. London, Mills and Boon, 1989; Toronto, Harlequin, 1990.
Fortune's Mistress. London, Mills and Boon, 1990; Toronto, Harlequin, 1991.
No Reprieve. London, Mills and Boon, 1990; Toronto, Harlequin, 1991.
Deal of a Lifetime. London, Mills and Boon, 1991; Toronto, Harlequin, 1992.
Devil to Pay. London, Mills and Boon, 1991; Toronto, Harlequin, 1992.
Tempt me Not. London, Mills and Boon, 1991; Toronto, Harlequin, 1993.
Winter of Dreams. London, Mills and Boon, 1992; Toronto, Harlequin, 1993.
Secret Admirer. London, Mills and Boon, 1992; Toronto, Harlequin, 1993.
The Hawk and the Lamb. London, Mills and Boon, 1993.

*   *   *

Susan Napier is one of Mills and Boon's more recent authors. Writing popular, contemporary books, Napier sets her plots in or around her native New Zealand. Her heroines are strong, independent women, often with important careers that they care about. Falling in love is the last thing on most of their minds. Her male characters also adhere to type: they are depicted as arrogant, masculine men who show their vulnerability through falling in love. Just as Napier's women are voluptuous, striking, but not necessarily beautiful characters, who combine integrity, sensuality, and liveliness, her men are also of a certain physical type—powerfully built, hard-featured men with striking eyes, who exude the lethal combination of sex and power. Victoria West, in *Tempt me Not*, describes the hero Lucas Grey as 'the man [who] was *very* everything'. This aptly sums up Napier's heroes who are *very* successful, *very* attractive, and *very* irresistible. All of her characters are believable people, they are the sort of men and women that we would all like to fall in love with.

Many of the themes and stylistic quirks that feature in Napier's books can be seen in her first novel, *Sweet Vixen*. The heroine, Sarah Carter, is an editorial assistant on a New Zealand fashion magazine, *Rags and Riches*. Max Wilde comes to revolutionize the rag, and consequently brings havoc into Sarah's life. Their first meeting involves an incident of mistaken identity when sent to the airport to meet the new boss, Sarah thinks that Max is trying to pick her up, however, Max has guessed her identity. This confused encounter is repeated in Napier's later books: the hero often believes the heroine to be someone, or something, other than she actually is—and she becomes etched on his memory as a result. Sarah, at the beginning of the book, is a very restrained woman, who takes little interest in her physical appearance. Max, of course, through his pursuit of her, helps her to change and she emerges as a beautiful, confident woman worthy of his interest. She, in turn, helps Max to redefine his image of women, and he becomes a hero worthy of his heroine.

The roles are reversed in *Love in the Valley*, Napier's next book. Julia Fry is an extremely confident, funny woman who falls in love with the seemingly taciturn (and tall!) Hugh Walton. He is the adopted elder son of Julia's employers, the Marlows (a very colourful theatrical family who feature in *True Enchanter*). Hugh and Julia's relationship is characterized by farcical encounters, and it is the element of humour in both the plot and in the characters themselves that makes Napier such a successful writer. Napier tackles an extremely topical subject by making Hugh the subject of physical child abuse, a fact that colours his attitude towards women. Julia overcomes Hugh's fear of losing control through her love for him, and shows him that far from being a violent man like his father, he is actually extremely caring and sensitive.

Napier tackles important subjects. Matthew Grieve, the hero of *Sweet as My Revenge*, was impotent as a result of a particularly nasty divorce; Leo Sterne in *The Lonely Season* struggles to come to terms with his deaf son, and Gina Bennett, the heroine of this book, is extremely insecure both because of a motorbike accident that almost killed her, and because of a previous nightmare relationship; Clare, in *Bewitching Compulsion*, is the mother of a child prodigy, and encounters all of the problems that come with having a musical genius as a son; and Jake Jackson in *No Reprieve* is a man trying to find his missing daughter. All of these subjects are handled with sensitivity and seriousness.

Many of the author's heroines are sexually inexperienced, waiting consciously or not, for the right man to come along. In this respect Napier conforms to the traditional formula romance; however, she has broken new ground by introducing a new aspect to the virgin scenario. In one of her most recent titles, *Secret Admirer*, the heroine is a widow and the *hero* is a virgin waiting for his perfect woman to come along. It will be interesting to see if this device proves a popular one and is used by other Mills and Boon writers in the future.

Napier allows the reader a greater understanding of her male characters by switching between her hero and heroine's perception of events. Hence her plots are given greater credibility and depth as the reader becomes aware of the hero's vulnerability and feelings towards the emerging love relationship; an interesting characteristic of these books is that the hero often admits that he is in love well before the heroine does. Thus in Napier's books love becomes a much more egalitarian emotion, experienced by both the hero and the heroine.

Napier is a successful romance writer. She creates stories involving believable and likeable characters, and uses humour, serious social situations, and innovative plots to weave interesting and enjoyable novels. Napier is one of an emerging generation of romance authors who write about believable independent characters falling in love in contemporary settings.

—P. Campbell

NAUMAN, Eileen.   See **McKENNA, Lyndsay.**

NEAL, Hilary.   See **NORWAY, Kate.**

NEELS, Betty.
A pseudonym. **Nationality:** British. **Relations:** married; one daughter. **Career:** nurse in the Netherlands and England. Lives in

Dorset. **Address:** c/o Mills and Boon Ltd, Eton House, 18–24 Paradise Road, Richmond, Surrey TW9 1SR, England.

ROMANCE AND HISTORICAL PUBLICATIONS

Novels

Amazon in an Apron. London, Mills and Boon, 1969.
Blow Hot, Blow Cold. London, Mills and Boon, 1969; as *Surgeon from Holland*, Toronto, Harlequin, 1970.
Sister Peters in Amsterdam. London, Mills and Boon, 1969; Toronto, Harlequin, 1970.
Nurse in Holland. Toronto, Harlequin, 1970.
Fate Is Remarkable. London, Mills and Boon, 1970; Toronto, Harlequin, 1971.
Nurse Harriet Goes to Holland. Toronto, Harlequin, 1970.
Damsel in Green. London, Mills and Boon, 1970; Toronto, Harlequin, 1972.
The Fifth Day of Christmas. London, Mills and Boon, 1971; Toronto, Harlequin, 1972.
Tangled Autumn. London, Mills and Boon, 1971; Toronto, Harlequin, 1972.
Tulips for Augusta. London, Mills and Boon, and Toronto, Harlequin, 1971.
Uncertain Summer. London, Mills and Boon, 1972; Toronto, Harlequin, 1974.
Victory for Victoria. London, Mills and Boon, and Toronto, Harlequin, 1972.
Saturday's Child. London, Mills and Boon, 1972; Toronto, Harlequin, 1973.
Tabitha in Moonlight. London, Mills and Boon, 1972; Toronto, Harlequin, 1975.
Wish with the Candles. London, Mills and Boon, and Toronto, Harlequin, 1972.
Three for a Wedding. London, Mills and Boon, and Toronto, Harlequin, 1973.
Winter of Change. London, Mills and Boon, and Toronto, Harlequin, 1973.
Enchanting Samantha. London, Mills and Boon, 1973; Toronto, Harlequin, 1974.
Cassandra by Chance. London, Mills and Boon, and Toronto, Harlequin, 1973.
Stars Through the Mist. London, Mills and Boon, 1973; Toronto, Harlequin, 1974.
Cruise to a Wedding. London, Mills and Boon, 1974; Toronto, Harlequin, 1975.
The End of the Rainbow. London, Mills and Boon, 1974; Toronto, Harlequin, 1975.
The Gemel Ring. London, Mills and Boon, and Toronto, Harlequin, 1974.
The Magic of Living. London, Mills and Boon, 1974; Toronto, Harlequin, 1975.
Henrietta's Own Castle. London, Mills and Boon, 1975; Toronto, Harlequin, 1976.
A Small Slice of Summer. London, Mills and Boon, 1975; Toronto, Harlequin, 1977.
Heaven Is Gentle. Toronto, Harlequin, 1975.
Tempestuous April. London, Mills and Boon, 1975.
Cobweb Morning. London, Mills and Boon, 1975; Toronto, Harlequin, 1976.
Roses for Christmas. London, Mills and Boon, 1975; Toronto, Harlequin, 1976.
A Star Looks Down. London, Mills and Boon, 1975; Toronto, Harlequin, 1976.
The Edge of Winter. London, Mills and Boon, 1976; Toronto, Harlequin, 1977.

The Moon of Lavinia. Toronto, Harlequin, 1976.
Gem of a Girl. London, Mills and Boon, 1976; Toronto, Harlequin, 1977.
Esmeralda. London, Mills and Boon, and Toronto, Harlequin, 1976.
The Hasty Marriage. London, Mills and Boon, and Toronto, Harlequin, 1977.
A Matter of Chance. London, Mills and Boon, and Toronto, Harlequin, 1977.
Grasp a Nettle. London, Mills and Boon, and Toronto, Harlequin, 1977.
The Little Dragon. London, Mills and Boon, 1977; Toronto, Harlequin, 1978.
Britannia All at Sea. London, Mills and Boon, and Toronto, Harlequin, 1978.
Never While the Grass Grows. London, Mills and Boon, 1978; Toronto, Harlequin, 1979.
Philomela's Miracle. London, Mills and Boon, and Toronto, Harlequin, 1978.
Ring in a Teacup. London, Mills and Boon, 1978.
Pineapple Girl. London, Mills and Boon, and Toronto, Harlequin, 1978.
Midnight Sun's Magic. London, Mills and Boon, 1979; Toronto, Harlequin, n.d.
The Promise of Happiness. London, Mills and Boon, 1979.
Sun and Candlelight. London, Mills and Boon, 1979.
Winter Wedding. London, Mills and Boon, 1979; Toronto, Harlequin, 1980.
Caroline's Waterloo. London, Mills and Boon, 1980; Toronto, Harlequin, 1981.
Hannah. London, Mills and Boon, 1980; Toronto, Harlequin, 1981.
Last April Fair. London, Mills and Boon, 1980.
The Silver Thaw. London, Mills and Boon, 1980; Toronto, Harlequin, 1981.
When May Follows. London, Mills and Boon, 1980; Toronto, Harlequin, 1981.
Not Once but Twice. London, Mills and Boon, and Toronto, Harlequin, 1981.
An Apple from Eve. London, Mills and Boon, 1981; Toronto, Harlequin, 1982.
Heaven round the Corner. London, Mills and Boon, 1981.
Judith. London, Mills and Boon, and Toronto, Harlequin, 1982.
All Else Confusion. London, Mills and Boon, 1982; Toronto, Harlequin, 1983.
A Dream Come True. London, Mills and Boon, 1982; Toronto, Harlequin, 1983.
A Girl to Love. London, Mills and Boon, and Toronto, Harlequin, 1982.
Midsummer Star. London, Mills and Boon, 1983.
Never Say Goodbye. London, Mills and Boon, 1983.
Never Too Late. London, Mills and Boon, 1983.
Roses and Champagne. London, Mills and Boon, 1983; Toronto, Harlequin, 1984.
Once for All Time. London, Mills and Boon, 1984.
A Summer Idyll. London, Mills and Boon, 1984.
Year's Happy Ending. London, Mills and Boon, 1984.
Polly. London, Mills and Boon, 1984; Boston, Hall, 1986.
Magic in Vienna. London, Mills and Boon, 1985.
Never the Time and the Place. London, Mills and Boon, 1985.
The Secret Pool. London, Mills and Boon, 1986.
A Girl Named Rose. London, Mills and Boon, 1986.
Two Weeks to Remember. London, Mills and Boon, 1986.
The Doubtful Marriage. London, Mills and Boon, 1987.
Stormy Springtime. London, Mills and Boon, 1987.
Off with the Old Love. London, Mills and Boon, 1987.
The Gentle Awakening. London, Mills and Boon, 1987.
When Two Paths Meet. London, Mills and Boon, 1988.

The Course of True Love. London, Mills and Boon, 1988.
Paradise for Two. London, Mills and Boon, 1988.
Fateful Bargain. London, Mills and Boon, 1989.
No Need to Say Goodbye. London, Mills and Boon, 1989.
The Chain of Destiny. London, Mills and Boon, 1989.
Hilltop Tryst. London, Mills and Boon, 1989.
Roses Have Thorns. London, Mills and Boon, 1990.
The Girl with Green Eyes. London, Mills and Boon, 1990.
A Suitable Match. London, Mills and Boon, 1990.
The Convenient Wife. London, Mills and Boon, 1991.
The Most Marvellous Summer. London, Mills and Boon, 1991.
A Little Moonlight. London, Mills and Boon, 1991.
A Kind of Magic. London, Mills and Boon, 1991.
The Final Touch. London, Mills and Boon, 1991.
An Unlikely Romance. London, Mills and Boon, 1992.
A Romantic Encounter. London, Mills and Boon, 1992.
A Happy Meeting. London, Mills and Boon, 1992.
The Quiet Professor. London, Mills and Boon, 1993.
An Old Fashioned Girl. London, Mills and Boon, 1993.

*   *   *

Betty Neels's novels are most often based in England and Holland. The author has a very good feel for medical life in both countries, and her heroes or heroines are normally involved in this profession. The detailed descriptions of Dutch scenery and life are very well portrayed, and family features strongly in her books.

Neels's heroines fall into two basic types. Firstly, there is the attractive, intelligent, and sometimes fiery woman, who is unaware of her natural attributes. She is usually surrounded by a loving and caring family. The hero in this type of novel is normally committed to a glamorous, but coldly-calculating fashion plate. This is illustrated in *The Most Marvellous Summer* when the heroine, Mathilda, falls in love at first sight, with James Scott Thurlow, an eminent surgeon. James is engaged to Rhoda, whom he feels fits perfectly into his wealthy lifestyle. The fact that there is no love or mutual empathy between them is immaterial to both James and Rhoda; both of them understand the situation and each other completely. James is happy until Mathilda comes along and throws his ordered existence into chaos. James, of course, falls in love with Mathilda, and they eventually sort out their misunderstandings and true feelings.

The second type of heroine is the 'plain and mousey' woman, whose strength is her calm and unflappable nature. She is unlikely to disturb her hero's life. This heroine stays in the background, yet manages to sort out the day-to-day problems in the hero's life without intruding or irritating him. A prime example of this type of woman is Beatrice (known as Trixie to her close friends), the heroine of *An Unlikely Romance*. She is described as 'a small girl, nicely plump with a face which was hardly pretty; her nose was too short and her mouth too large, but it curved up at the corners and her smile was charming'. The hero, Professor van der Brink Schaaksma, only notices Beatrice because he catches her when she trips over in front of him. The professor is typical of Neels's heroes. He is a tall, broad man and is aristocratically handsome in looks; he is also around ten years older than Beatrice. He comes from a wealthy Dutch family and is considered to be a 'catch'. He has all of the sophistication and experience that Beatrice lacks: he is Mr Rochester to Beatrice's Jane. The professor sees Beatrice as the ideal candidate to organize his social and personal life, to act as a buffer between him and all the 'matchmaking mammas' who seem to cross his path. This gives the professor the peace he needs to finish his medical thesis without distraction. He consequently asks Beatrice to agree to a marriage of convenience. Beatrice, as part of the arrangement, will receive a life of comfort and security, but this plays little part in her decision to marry him: Beatrice has fallen in love with the professor. Neither character thinks through the long term consequences of their relationship (a typical factor in formula romances). However, Beatrice fits into his lifestyle perfectly, and completely understands the professor's needs. Love blossoms between them in this cosy, but somewhat sterile environment. It might not be the most exciting kind of romance, but they live happily ever after.

Throughout Neels's novels her heroes and heroines retain a refreshing purity of both thought and feeling that is unusual in most contemporary romantic fiction. The old fashioned values ingrained in the author's books are reminiscent of another era. Perhaps it is this that make Neels one of Mills and Boons most popular authors to date.

—Naya Quin

NEILAN, Sarah.

Nationality: British. **Born:** Newcastle-upon-Tyne, Northumberland. **Education:** Oxford University, M.A. **Relations:** married; four children. **Career:** book editor for 12 years. **Recipient:** Mary Elgin award, 1976. **Agent:** Peters Fraser and Dunlop, 5th Floor, The Chambers, Chelsea Harbour, Lots Road, London SW10 0XF, England.

ROMANCE AND HISTORICAL PUBLICATIONS

Novels

The Braganza Pursuit. London, Hodder and Stoughton, and New York, Dutton, 1976.
An Air of Glory. London, Hodder and Stoughton, and New York, Morrow, 1977.
Paradise. London, Hodder and Stoughton, 1981; New York, St Martin's Press, 1982.
The Old Enchantment. London, Hodder and Stoughton, 1990; New York, St Martin's Press, 1991.

*

Sarah Neilan comments:

I am primarily a storyteller, and try to produce a strong, exciting, fast-moving narrative, full of suspense (two of my novels have been serialized), set against an authentic, unusual, and carefully researched historical background.

'A cheerful adventure gothic' was how one American reviewer described my first novel, *The Braganza Pursuit*, which was a governess story set in England and Brazil. My second novel, *An Air of Glory*, was about early immigrants to Nova Scotia; the book retraced a real journey (though with fictional characters). *Paradise*, my third novel, is a family saga set among British frontier settlers in what is now southern Ontario, at the time of the war of 1812 between Canada and the USA. *The Old Enchantment* follows the fortunes of a group of young people who grow up during World War I.

*   *   *

The settings for Sarah Neilan's novels of romantic adventure span the Atlantic Ocean. While her first books rely on swift-moving action to hold readers' interest, her maturing power of expression is apparent in the growing complexity of her later novels.

In *The Braganza Pursuit*, 19-year-old Adelaide Smith unexpectedly finds she must earn her own living after her father's business failures and his death. She secures a post as governess for Bonita and Baltasar, the children of the Portuguese ambassador to London. Their mother Dona Ines is a member of the Braganza family, part of the Portuguese nobility that had ruled until forced to flee

by Napoleon. Unexpectedly Dona Ines orders Adelaide to take the children to their uncle Martim, the wealthy Duque de Miranda in Brazil. The necessity of such flight becomes apparent as they are pursued by Dona Ines's other brother, Duarte, intent on murdering all Braganzas who stand in the way of his inheritance. The melodramatic plot depends on one close escape after another. Fights on ship, a tremendous storm at sea, escape by rowboat, pursuit through the jungle and over mountains are followed by a brief respite in Dom Martin's care until he too must flee the plots of his insane brother. Ultimately Duarte is killed and Adelaide and Martim can seal in marriage the love that has grown inevitable through their adventures.

Like Adelaide, Polly Forster's poverty offers few prospects for the future in *An Air of Glory*. Steeped in Jacobite lore and eager to escape the stifling charity of an elderly cousin, Polly is easily duped by the promise of marriage offered by handsome but mysterious Lucian. She agrees to carry a message to Jacobite sympathizers in Nova Scotia, and trusts Lucian's promise that they will marry once she arrives. With her on the Atlantic crossing are dozens of refugees driven from their homes in the Scottish Highlands by landowners anxious to acquire more space to raise sheep. Also on board ship is August Fenwick, whom Polly fears is a British agent. However, distrust changes to respect and love as the two nurse the steerage passengers through an outbreak of smallpox. Polly's discovery that Lucian has used her to carry a message for Napoleon, not the Jacobites, impels her to undertake a desperate journey to reach the Governor by iceboat once her ship reaches Nova Scotia.

Neilan based *An Air of Glory* on stories she heard from a descendant of a woman who had made a similar ocean voyage in 1801 from Fort William to Pictou, Nova Scotia. Indeed, the Canadian ties of the last three of Neilan's books can be attributed to her fascination with the country of her husband's family.

In *Paradise* she chronicles the hardships inherent in the early settlement of Canada. Charles and Rose Clare meet Anne and Vivian O'Mara as both families travel to Talbot Settlement on Lake Erie. Unfortunately, their arrival in 1812 quickly embroils them in war with the Americans, and dreams of prosperous farm life are delayed. The fates of the two families intertwine in numerous ways, particularly the lives of Quality Clare and Patrick O'Mara, who eventually marry but only after major misunderstandings. Quality spends much of her life trapped by her sense of duty in a loveless marriage to Jem Scott, who had made her his wife through deception.

Neilan's evocation of pioneer life encompasses the importance of neighbours and community as well as the hard work and danger. Patrick and Quality share the dream of a united Canada, and that political goal seems close to fulfilment as their marriage brings family peace through union of Clares and O'Maras.

One sub-plot of *Paradise* involves the attempt to save the Clare farm from foreclosure after Charles and Rose had devoted much of their adult lives to the back-breaking work of clearing the land and building a home. A similar threat of foreclosure overshadows Neilan's entire fourth novel, *The Old Enchantment*. By far Neilan's most complex and best-written book, *The Old Enchantment* excels in her creation of place through the rich descriptions of Old Hall, the Northumberland estate of the Delmaynes and the abundant life of its inhabitants. The story is told from the viewpoint of their cousin Lizzie who spends extended visits at the estate from the time she is six years old. Those golden days early in the century are changed utterly by hasty marriages and untimely deaths brought by World War I. The Delmaynes' constant love and boundless energy fill a space left by the distant correctness of Lizzie's own parents. However, overshadowing all other relationships is Lizzie's unspoken love for Peregrine Fenwick, a frequent visitor to Old Hall.

At 17 Lizzie enters a disastrous marriage to Charles McIver, and emigrates to his Nova Scotian farm, isolated and primitive. Like

Quality Clare, she endures the situation because of her faithfulness to marriage vows. Worn down by unending work and poverty, Lizzie is swept away by her cousin Zinnia to England on the eve of World War II, when she and Peregrine finally find freedom to marry one another. However, the secrets and entanglements of the Delmayne family are not totally revealed for several more decades when Lizzie must search desperately to find a way to secure Old Hall for her impoverished aunt and cousins.

Although the layers of relationships demand readers' attention, the rewards are worth the effort. In her longest and most complex novel, Neilan succeeds in recreating the ties of love that bind one generation to the next. Rather than relying on chase scenes and melodrama as in her first novels, she takes time to explore the complexities of relationships among family and friends.

—Kathy Piehl

NEWMAN, Margaret. See **MELVILLE, Anne.**

NEWMAN, Sharan. American. 1949—. See 2nd edition, 1990.

NICHOLSON, C.R. See **NICOLE, Christopher.**

NICHOLSON, Christina. See **NICOLE, Christopher.**

NICHOLSON, Jane. See **STEEN, Marguerite.**

NICHOLSON, Robin. See **NICOLE, Christopher.**

NICOLE, Christopher (Robin).
Pseudonyms: Leslie Arlen; Robin Cade; Peter Grange; Caroline Gray; Mark Logan; Simon McKay; C.R. Nicholson; Christina Nicholson; Robin Nicholson; Alan Savage; Alison York; Andrew York. **Nationality:** British. **Born:** Georgetown, British Guiana (now Guyana), 7 December 1930. **Education:** Harrison College, Barbados; Queen's College, Guyana. **Relations:** married 1) Jean Barnett in 1951 (divorced), two sons and two daughters; 2) Diana Bachmann. **Career:** clerk, Royal Bank of Canada, the West Indies, 1947–56. Lives in Guernsey. **Agent:** David Higham Associates, 5–8 Lower John Street, Golden Square, London W1R 4HA, England.

ROMANCE AND HISTORICAL PUBLICATIONS

Novels (series: Amyot; Barclay; Black Majesty; China Trilogy; Dawson; Haggard; Hilton and Warner; Japan Trilogy; Mackinder; The New Americans; Sword; United States Navy)

Off White. London, Jarrolds, 1959.
Shadows in the Jungle. London, Jarrolds, 1961.
Ratoon. London, Jarrolds, and New York, St Martin's Press, 1962.

Dark Noon. London, Jarrolds, 1963.
Amyot's Cay. London, Jarrolds, 1964.
Blood Amyot. London, Jarrolds, 1964.
The Amyot Crime. London, Jarrolds, 1965; New York, Bantam, 1974.
White Boy. London, Hutchinson, 1966.
The Self-Lovers. London, Hutchinson, 1968.
The Thunder and the Shouting. London, Hutchinson, and New York, Doubleday, 1969.
The Longest Pleasure. London, Hutchinson, 1970.
The Face of Evil. London, Hutchinson, 1971.
Lord of the Golden Fan. London, Cassell, 1973.
Heroes. London, Corgi, 1973.
Caribee (Hilton and Warner). London, Cassell, and New York, St Martin's Press, 1974.
The Devil's Own (Hilton and Warner). London, Cassell, and New York, St Martin's Press, 1975.
Mistress of Darkness (Hilton and Warner). London, Cassell, and New York, St Martin's Press, 1976.
Black Dawn (Hilton and Warner). London, Cassell, and New York, St Martin's Press, 1977.
Sunset (Hilton and Warner). London, Cassell, and New York, St Martin's Press, 1978.
The Secret Memoirs of Lord Byron. Philadelphia, Lippincott, and London, Joseph, 1978; as *Lord of Sin*, London, Corgi, 1980.
The Fire and the Rope (as Alison York). London, W.H. Allen, and New York, Berkley, 1979.
The Scented Sword (as Alison York). London, W.H. Allen, 1980.
Haggard. London, Joseph, and New York, New American Library, 1980.
The Friday Spy (as C.R. Nicholson). London, Corgi, 1980; as *A Passion for Treason* (as Robin Nicholson), New York, Jove, 1981; as *The Friday Spy* (as Christopher Nicole), London, Severn House, 1989.
Haggard's Inheritance. London, Joseph, 1981; as *The Inheritors*, New York, New American Library, 1981.
The New Americans:
  Brothers and Enemies. New York, Berkley, 1982; London, Corgi, 1983.
  Lovers and Outlaws. New York, Berkley, 1982.
The Young Haggards. London, Joseph, and New York, New American Library, 1982.
China Trilogy:
  The Crimson Pagoda. New York, New American Library, 1983; London, Joseph, 1984.
  The Scarlet Princess. New York, New American Library, 1984; London, Joseph, 1985.
  Red Dawn. London, Joseph, 1985.
Japan Trilogy:
  The Sun Rises. London, Hamlyn, 1984.
  The Sun and the Dragon. London, Hamlyn, 1985.
  The Sun on Fire. London, Arrow, 1985.
The Seeds of Rebellion (Black Majesty). London, Severn House, 1984.
Wild Harvest (Black Majesty). London, Severn House, 1985; New York, Severn House, 1987.
United States Navy:
  1. *Old Glory.* London, Severn House, 1986; New York, Severn House, 1988.
  2. *The Sea and the Sand.* London, Severn House, 1986; New York, Severn House, 1988.
  3. *Iron Ships, Iron Men.* London, Severn House, 1987.
  4. *The Wind of Destiny.* London, Severn House, 1987.
  5. *Raging Seas, Seering Skies.* London, Severn House, 1988.
  6. *The Power and the Glory.* London, Severn House, 1988.
  7. *The Passion and the Glory.* London, Severn House, 1989.

The Ship with No Name. London, Severn House, 1987.
The High Country. London, Century, 1988.
The Regiment. London, Century, 1988; New York, St Martin's Press, 1989.
Singapura. London, Century, 1988.
Pearl of the Orient. London, Century, 1988.
The Happy Valley. London, Century, 1989.
The Command. London, Century, 1989.
Dragon Blood. London, Century, 1989.
The Triumph. London, Century, 1989.
Dark Sun. London, Century, 1990.
Caribee. London, Severn House, 1990.
Sword of Fortune. London, Century, 1990.
Sword of Empire. London, Century, 1991.
Days of Wine and Roses. London, Severn House, 1991.
The Titans. London, and New York, Severn House, 1992.
Resumptions. London, and New York, Severn House, 1992.
The Last Battle. London, and New York, Severn House, 1993.
Bloody Sunrise. London, and New York, Severn House, 1993.

Novels as Peter Grange

King Creole. London, Jarrolds, 1966.
The Devil's Emissary. London, Jarrolds, 1968.
The Tumult at the Gate. London, Jarrolds, 1970.
The Golden Goddess. London, Jarrolds, 1973.

Novels as Mark Logan

Tricolour. London, Macmillan, and New York, St Martin's Press, 1976; as *The Captain's Woman*, New York, New American Library, 1977.
Guillotine. London, Macmillan, and New York, St Martin's Press, 1976; as *French Kiss*, New York, New American Library, 1978.
Brumaire. London, Wingate, and New York, St Martin's Press, 1978; as *December Passion*, New York, New American Library, 1979.

Novels as Christina Nicholson

The Power and the Passion. London, Corgi, and New York, Coward McCann, 1977; (as Christopher Nicole) London, Severn House, 1983.
The Savage Sands. London, Corgi, and New York, Coward McCann, 1978.
The Queen of Paris. London, Corgi, 1979; (as Christopher Nicole) London, Severn House, 1982.

Novels as Leslie Arlen (series: Borodins in all books)

Love and Honor. New York, Berkley, and London, Futura, 1980.
War and Passion. New York, Berkley, and London, Futura, 1981.
Fate and Dreams. New York, Berkley, and London, Futura, 1981.
Destiny and Desire. New York, Berkley, 1982.
Rage and Desire. New York, Berkley, 1982.
Hope and Glory. New York, Berkley, 1984.

Novels as Caroline Gray

First Class. London, Joseph, 1984; as *Treasures*, New York, Fawcett, 1984.
Hotel De Luxe. London, Joseph, 1985; as *So Grand*, New York, Fawcett, 1985.
White Rani. London, Joseph, and New York, Fawcett, 1986.
Victoria's Walk. London, Joseph, 1986; New York, Fawcett, 1988.
The Third Life. London, Joseph, and New York, St Martin's Press, 1988.

The Shadow of Death. London, Severn House, 1989.
Blue Water, Black Depths. London, Severn House, 1990.
The Daughter. London, and New York, Severn House, 1992.
Golden Girl. London, and New York, Severn House, 1992.
Spares. London, and New York, Severn House, 1993.

Novels as Alan Savage (series: Ottoman)

Ottoman. London, Macdonald, 1990.
Moghul. London, Macdonald, 1991.
The Eight Banners. London, Little Brown, 1992.
Queen of the Night. London, Little Brown, 1993.
The Last Bannerman. London, Little Brown, 1993.
Queen of Lions. London, Little Brown, 1994.

Novels as Simon McKay (both books feature the Anderson Line)

The Seas of Fortune. London, Severn House, 1984.
The Rivals. London, Severn House, 1985.

OTHER PUBLICATIONS

Novels as Andrew York

The Eliminator. London, Hutchinson, 1966; Philadelphia, Lippincott, 1967.
The Co-Ordinator. London, Hutchinson, and Philadelphia, Lippincott, 1967.
The Predator. London, Hutchinson, and Philadelphia, Lippincott, 1968.
The Deviator. London, Hutchinson, and Philadelphia, Lippincott, 1969.
The Dominator. London, Hutchinson, 1969.
The Infiltrator. London, Hutchinson, and New York, Doubleday, 1971.
The Expurgator. London, Hutchinson, 1972; New York, Doubleday, 1973.
The Captivator. London, Hutchinson, 1973; New York, Doubleday, 1974.
The Fear Dealers (as Robin Cade). London, Cassell, and New York, Simon and Schuster, 1974.
The Fascinator. London, Hutchinson, and New York, Doubleday, 1975.
Dark Passage. New York, Doubleday, 1975; London, Hutchinson, 1976.
Tallant for Trouble. London, Hutchinson, and New York, Doubleday, 1977.
Tallant for Disaster. London, Hutchinson, and New York, Doubleday, 1978.
The Combination. New York, Doubleday, 1983; London, Severn House, 1984.

Other (for children) as Andrew York

The Doom Fishermen. London, Hutchinson, 1969; as *Operation Destruct*, New York, Holt Rinehart, 1969.
Manhunt for a General. London, Hutchinson, 1970; as *Operation Manhunt*, New York, Holt Rinehart, 1970.
Where the Cavern Ends. London, Hutchinson, and New York, Holt Rinehart, 1971.
Appointment in Kiltone. London, Hutchinson, 1972; as *Operation Neptune*, New York, Holt Rinehart, 1972.

Other

West Indian Cricket. London, Phoenix House, 1957.

The West Indies: Their People and History. London, Hutchinson, 1965.
Introduction to Chess. London, Corgi, 1973.

*

Christopher Nicole comments:

I am a romantic or a gothic writer simply because those are names currently in vogue for historical novels. I regard myself as an historical novelist. I also happen to be a romantic by nature and aim to re-tell history as entertainingly as possible.

*   *   *

Christopher Nicole denies the primacy of the intellect to stress the physical. Natural forces, the promptings of the senses, savage instincts in individuals and societies, are essentials of his work. His upbringing as a white man in the West Indies with their history of slavery, rebellion, and natural disaster is also evident. Much of his early work is set in the Caribbean, his native Guyana being a favourite location, and this part of the world serves as a background for several of his later novels.

Off White, his first book, revolves around racial tensions in a Caribbean setting, and has an earthquake as its climax. *Ratoon* is, if anything, more accomplished. Based upon the Demerara slave insurrection of 1823, the book describes the relationship between a white woman planter and the black rebel who for a time holds her captive. The two share physical passion, and, though in the end they part, both are changed by the experience. The theme is skilfully handled by Nicole, who uses a pared understated style to bring out the nature of his characters. *Ratoon* has a pristine quality, and the strength of the writing is impressive.

Off White and *Ratoon* earned their author a measure of critical praise, but his popularity was established with the first of his series the 'Amyot Trilogy'—*Amyot's Cay*, *Blood Amyot*, and *The Amyot Crime*—which describes the adventures of a white family through several generations in the Bahamas. Nicole's protagonists are shown as hard, ruthless, and determined, carving out their own territory in a conquered land. Their natural unpleasantness is at its worst in *The Amyot Crime*, in which a racist family member murders an inoffensive black, and the clan closes ranks to hush up the crime. The 'Amyot Trilogy' contains some strong action writing, but is a flawed conception with characters who are, for the most part, decidedly unlovable. More impressive is his longer five-volume saga depicting the fortunes of the Hiltons and Warners—*Caribee*, *The Devil's Own*, *Mistress of Darkness*, *Black Dawn*, and *Sunset*. Like the Amyot novels, this longer sequence features a succession of despots with undisputed power over the subjects of their plantation world. Often such power brings out their worst instincts, but a few characters combine strong desires with equally strong ideals. Some critics have seen the influence of Edgar Mittelholzer in Nicole's work, but while there are some similarities—the dominant matriarchs are reminiscent of the *Kaywana* novels—the debt is overstressed. Nicole's writing, for all its ruthlessness, displays greater warmth and humanity, a fact that is evident to the reader from *Ratoon* onwards.

Lord of the Golden Fan describes the adventures of Will Adams, the first Englishman to set foot in Japan. Nicole outlines his rise as the friend of Prince Ieyeyasu, and his involvement in the struggle against the ruthless Princess Yodogimi. The story lacks nothing in excitement, with fearsome battle scenes and descriptions of Will's love for the half-caste Pinto Magdalena, consummated after an earthquake destroys Osaka. The differing lifestyles of puritan Europe and Japan are adroitly presented. *Lord of the Golden Fan* is a fine novel, its story compelling and its characters memorable. The vigour of the narrative cannot conceal its subtler insights. A rare non-series novel, it ranks alongside *Off White* and *Ratoon* with the best of its author's early work.

Nicole's preference, however, is clearly for the series or novel sequence, and over the past decade he has produced an astonishing body of work, as varied as it is impressive. No less than ten separate series have appeared under his own name since 1980, and at least two more have been written under pseudonyms. Two of the finest, 'Haggard' and 'Black Majesty', re-explore the author's beloved Caribbean to memorable effect. In *Haggard* and *Haggard's Inheritance*, Nicole follows two generations from plantation wealth in Barbados to the Derbyshire squirearchy, where their personalities bring them into conflict with the social order. *Black Majesty*, a two-volume sequence which presents the Haitian rebellion, and the tragic story of Henri Christophe from the viewpoint of a white family newly arrived on the island, displays the same pacy narrative style and is equally accomplished. In a blend of action, history, and romance, Nicole depicts the overthrow of plantation slavery, the cruelty of the landowners, and the horrors of rebellion, as backcloth to the interracial love story of Christophe and Richilde de Mortmain. No attempt is made to gloss over the atrocities, but the abiding impression left with the reader is an awareness of the courage of the black leaders, and the nobility of their ideas. *Seeds of Rebellion* and *Wild Harvest* are excellent examples of Nicole's return to his Caribbean roots.

He has also explored less familiar ground. In his trilogy, *The Sun Rises*, *The Sun and the Dragon*, and *The Sun on Fire*, Nicole views the gradual assimiliation of American Ralph Freeman and his descendants into the society of Japan, from the 1860s to World War II. His fascination with Japanese culture, encountered in *Lord of the Golden Fan* presents the reader with some unexpected revelations. A similar examination of Chinese history is made in *The Crimson Pagoda*, *The Scarlet Princess*, and *Red Dawn*; here, as elsewhere, Nicole utilizes the theme of exile, and the clash of western and oriental cultures, contrasting the acquisitive puritanism of the former with the subtlety and open sexuality of the host nation. The same is true of *Dark Sun* and *Singapura*, non-series but related novels which show the adventures of European newcomers in Hong Kong and Singapore. In the 'Sword' series, which deals with the British Raj in colonial India, Nicole provides an interesting departure from his normal method by alternating action scenes with letters written by another leading character. *Sword of Fortune* follows East India Company clerk Richard Bryant to a love affair with the Begum Sombre, and military glory at the siege of Seringapatam, his exploits interspersed with the effusively romantic epistles of Miss Barbara Smythe. With *Sword of Empire* the roles are reversed, the American heroine Laura Dean lives through similar erotic and dangerous adventures before eventually choosing the safe (if stuff-shirted) Captain Bartlett, whose pompous correspondence again fills alternate chapters. It is an amusing and inventive tactic, which adds a wry humour to the customary action-packed narrative.

Three other series show clear similarities, and are best judged together. In *The High Country* and *The Happy Valley* Nicole describes the experiences of two generations of the Barclay family in colonial Kenya and Tanganyika, from the turn of the century to the Mau Mau uprising. His 'Mackinder' series'—*The Regiment*, *The Command*, and *The Triumph*—follows the redoubtable Murdoch Mackinder, scion of a British army family, through service in the Boer war, to death in the 1980s, while in *Days of Wine and Roses*, *The Titans*, *Resumptions*, and *The Last Battle* successive generations of the Dawson clan encounter similar adventures at sea during the both world wars. At times, the similarities between the series are a little too close for comfort—all three include a fraught love-hate relationship between a British hero and a sinister, sadistic German, and each also features a *femme fatale* (again German) who threatens to bring about the hero's downfall. This criticism aside, and taken on their own merits, all of the novels are well-written, exciting adventure stories with a genuine period atmosphere, real-life figures from the past mingling easily with the fictional characters. *Resumptions* and *The Last Battle*, in particular, enable Nicole to tie several strands together in his tale of Jack Dawson Jr, and his brushes with the Japanese in China and the Pacific, the author's knowledge of Oriental cultures lending a further dimension to a powerful historical adventure story.

Nicole's longest series, the 'United States Navy' sequence of six novels, is ironically his least satisfying. The atmosphere is capably evoked in each case, and real characters, such as Decatur, and John Paul Jones, are rendered with some conviction, but there is a sameness to the storylines that leads to predictability. With such a prodigious output achieved in so short a time, it is perhaps inevitable that repetition should creep in, but in some of the series the author appears to be retelling the same story in different periods. This is unfortunate as all the other series produced by Nicole over the past decade are excellent examples of historical adventure writing.

Aside from the mass of novels written under his own name, Nicole has brought out a pseudonymous body of work which is almost as large. Among his numerous disguises are Simon McKay (the 'Anderson Line' series), Leslie Arlen (the 'Borodin' series), and Mark Logan (*Tricolour*, *Guillotine*, and *Brumaire*), all 'authors' in the historical adventure field. As Caroline Gray, he varies his output between stylish, racy thrillers (*Blue Water*, *Black Depths*, *The Daughter*, *Spares*), and historical novels with heroines rather than heroes—*The Shadow of Death*, set in turn of the century St Vincent, is a fine example of the latter. Nicole is rarely less than good, but the pick of his pseudonymous writing is surely the epic series of novels under the byline of Alan Savage—*Ottoman*, *Moghul*, and *The Eight Banners*—in which the great empires of Turkey, India, and Manchu China are traced from their first days of power to eventual tragic decline, the events viewed through the eyes of several generations of British adventurers. These novels are written with tremendous power and verve, the period detail neatly matched to a compelling, fast-moving plot which as usual allows for a fair amount of sex and violence. Nicole spares the reader nothing in his accounts of impalings, flayings, and the death of a thousand cuts, but these are minor aspects of a novel sequence which ranks with his best. Nicole, whether as himself or Alan Savage, remains one of the most talented and vigorous exponents of the historical adventure story.

—Geoffrey Sadler

NIVEN, Frederick (John).
Nationality: British. **Born:** Valparaiso, Chile, 31 March 1878; moved to Scotland, 1883. **Education:** Hutchesons Grammar School, Glasgow; Glasgow School of Art. **Military Service:** Ministry of Food, and the Ministry of Information during World War I. **Relations:** married Pauline Thorne-Quelch in 1911. **Career:** worked in the textile business briefly, then a librarian in Glasgow and Edinburgh; worked in construction camps in western Canada; journalist: worked for Glasgow *Weekly Herald*, papers in Edinburgh and Dundee, and reviewer for *Observer*, *Pall Mall Gazette*, and *Bookman*, all London; after 1920 lived in Nelson and Vancouver, British Columbia. **Died:** 30 January 1944.

ROMANCE AND HISTORICAL PUBLICATIONS

Novels

The Island Providence. London, Lane, 1910.
Dead Men's Bells. London, Secker, 1912.
The Flying Years. London, Collins, 1935.
Mine Inheritance. London, Collins, and New York, Macmillan, 1940.
Brothers in Arms. London, Collins, 1942.
Under Which King. London, Collins, 1943.
The Transplanted. London, Collins, 1944.

OTHER PUBLICATIONS

Novels

The Lost Cabin Mine. London, Lane, 1908; New York, Lane, 1909.
A Wilderness of Monkeys. London, Secker, and New York, Lane, 1911.
Hands Up! London, Secker, and New York, Lane, 1913.
Ellen Adair. London, Nash, 1913; New York, Boni and Liveright, 1925.
The Porcelain Lady. London, Secker, 1913.
Justice of the Peace. London, Nash, 1914; New York, Boni and Liveright, 1923.
The SS Glory. London, Heinemann, 1915; New York, Doran, 1916.
Cinderella of Skookum Creek. London, Nash, 1916.
Two Generations. London, Nash, 1916.
Penny Scot's Treasure. London, Collins, 1918.
The Lady of the Crossing: A Novel of the New West. London, Hodder and Stoughton, and New York, Doran, 1919.
A Tale That Is Told. London, Collins, and New York, Doran, 1920.
The Wolfer. New York, Dodd Mead, 1923.
Treasure Trail. New York, Dodd Mead, 1923.
Queer Fellows. London, Lane, 1927; as *Wild Honey*, New York, Dodd Mead, 1927.
The Three Marys. London, Collins, 1930.
The Paisley Shawl. London, Collins, and New York, Dodd Mead, 1931.
The Rich Wife. London, Collins, 1932.
Mrs Barry. London, Collins, and New York, Dutton, 1933.
Triumph. London, Collins, and New York, Dutton, 1934.
Old Soldier. London, Collins, 1936.
The Staff at Simson's. London, Collins, 1937.
The Story of Their Days. London, Collins, 1939.

Short Stories

Above Your Heads. London, Secker, 1911.
Sage-Brush Stories. London, Nash, 1917.

Poetry

Maple-Leaf Songs. London, Sidgwick and Jackson, 1917.
A Lover of the Land and Other Poems. New York, Boni and Liveright, 1925.

Other

Go North, Where the World Is Young (on Alaska and the Yukon). Privately printed, n.d.
The Story of Alexander Selkirk. London, Wells Gardner, 1929.
Canada West. London, Dent, 1930.
Colour in the Canadian Rockies, with Walter J. Phillips. Toronto, Nelson, 1937.
Coloured Spectacles. London, Collins, 1938.

*   *   *

Frederick Niven, a prolific and popular author of his day, was a man whose own background offered him unusual insight into a problem he very often addressed in his writings: that of the dispossessed and heartsick exile.

For Niven, as for others who suffer from a divided heart, the problem was that of a kind of internalized dual citizenship. When he was in Scotland, he pined for Canada's sweeping plains and egalitarian society; but when in Canada, he yearned for his beloved 'country of the mind', with its glorious, bloody history and its heather-scented hills. To compound all this, Niven was actually born in Valparaiso, Chile.

Niven's early work, such as *The Porcelain Lady* was that of a minor but promising writer; readable enough, but totally unmemorable. Subsequent books following in rapid succession were, not to put too fine a point on it, potboilers written 'To keep the wolf from the wife'. Nevertheless, the urge to write drove him on, and with practice came polish. There was *something* there that suggested more than the mere acquisition of a cheque to pay the rent.

He had a decided flair for dialect, a talent more admired at the turn of the century than it is today; and his skilful use of finely differentiated regional accents helped him to flesh out believable characters. He particularly excelled in the portrayal of 'ordinary' little lives, unremarkable until subjected to the close scrutiny he afforded them, in stories set in Glasgow such as those of the warehouse workers in *The Staff at Simson's*, of the struggling artist at odds with a narrowly religious family in *Justice of the Peace*, and in *Mrs Barry*.

His *Mrs Barry* exemplifies the understated gallantry Niven most admired; that of a once-prosperous woman now widowed and fallen upon very hard times, who nevertheless makes no concessions to her altered circumstances. She prefers to go down with her poor little flag flying if tattered, rather than to appeal to a cold and uncaring world for sympathy, fearing pity more than she does poverty or even death; genteel privation to subsiding into the working-class milieu in which she now must live.

Niven's best work was transatlantic in its setting. His 'Canadian side' if so it may be described, inspired his major historic output, notably the thematically related trilogy consisting of *Mine Inheritance*, *The Flying Years*, and *The Transplanted*.

Mine Inheritance tells of the fierce struggle of the Selkirk settlers to establish their infant colony on the bleak and unwelcoming prairie that was so unlike the Scottish homes they had left behind, against a flaming background of the fur trade wars. *The Flying Years*, the broadly panoramic story of a man's life between the 1850s and the 1920s links the two lands Niven loved, and has been hailed as his greatest achievement. It is a novel of considerable scope and power, and is the only one of his novels currently available in the country of which it is a celebration.

The years that pass so rapidly are those of Angus Munro, the son of Scots crofters driven out of their beloved home of Loch Brendan by the heartless Highland Clearances, in which people were forced out by the great landowners to make way for sheep and deer. With his father and mother Angus comes to the empty new land; but while at 16 he is young and adaptable enough to transplant, his parents, particularly his mother, are not. Although she tries very hard to make a new home for her family, her yearning heart is broken, and she soon dies. Not long afterward, her husband too is buried in the alien ground. Alone now, young Angus becomes almost a native; indeed he marries a lovely Cree, Minota; but he too is poisoned by homesickness that gives him no rest; and he leaves his wife to return to Scotland, promising that he will return to her one day.

It is in the passages describing Angus's unhappy sojourn in the land of his fathers that Niven most poignantly reveals the dilemma of the exile. Angus tries to fit in to the old, cap-in-hand life of a shop clerk, the best his old country has to offer him; but he is haunted by memories of a land where 'Jack is as good as his master', and where he tugged his forelock to no man. A chance meeting with Indian

visitors to Scotland forces his decision; part of his heart will always remain in Scotland, but he knows now that he will live out his life in Canada.

The Transplanted, which closely parallels Niven's own life, portrays the development of a British Columbia settlement from its first beginnings as a lumbering, mining, ranching area to its emergence as a thriving new city; the history of the West encapsulated. This, Niven's final novel, posthumously published in 1944, sums up his own story. In his lifetime he worked through the trauma of exile, bringing with him to his final home the riches of a British literary tradition, an immigrant rather than a colonial writer, and a significant figure among those who have brought Canada's history to fictional life.

—Joan McGrath

NOLAN, Frederick.
Pseudonyms: Frederick H. Christian; Danielle Rockfern; Donald Severn. **Nationality:** British. **Born:** Liverpool, Lancashire, in 1931. **Education:** Aberayron County School, Wales; Liverpool Collegiate. **Relations:** married Heidi Wümli in 1962; two sons. **Career:** editor, Corgi Books, London; sales representative, Penguin Books, London; worked in publicity, Fontana Books, and marketing, Granada Publishing, London, and Ballantine Books, New York; publisher, Warner Communications, London. **Agent:** Arthur Pine Associates, 1780 Broadway, New York, New York 10019, USA.

ROMANCE AND HISTORICAL PUBLICATIONS

Novels (series: Call to Arms)

Carver's Kingdom. London, Macmillan, 1978; New York, Warner, 1980.
White Nights, Red Dawn. New York, Macmillan, 1980; London, Hutchinson, 1981.
A Promise of Glory (Call to Arms). London, Arrow, 1983; New York, Bantam, 1984.
Blind Duty (Call to Arms). London, Arrow, 1983; New York, Bantam, 1985.
Field of Honour (as Danielle Rockfern). London, Hamlyn, 1985.
Maximum Demolition. London, Century, 1991.
Soft Target. London, Century, 1992.

OTHER PUBLICATIONS

Novels

The Oshawa Project. London, Barker, 1974; as *The Algonquin Project*, New York, Morrow, 1974; as *Brass Target*, New York, Jove, 1979.
NYPD, No Place to Be a Cop. London, Barker, 1974; as *No Place to Be a Cop*, London, Futura, 1975.
The Ritter Double-cross. London, Barker, 1974; New York, Morrow, 1975.
Kill Petrosino! London, Barker, 1975.
The Mittenwald Syndicate. London, Cassell, and New York, Morrow, 1976.
Wolf Trap. London, Piatkus, 1983; New York, St Martin's Press, 1984.
Red Centre. London, Grafton, and New York, St Martin's Press, 1987.

The Garrett Dossier:

Sweet Sister Death. London, Arrow, 1989; as *A Time to Die* (as Donald Severn), New York, Lynx, 1989.

Alert State Black (as Donald Severn). New York, Lynx; (as Frederick Nolan) London, Century, 1990.

Designated Assassin. London, Century, 1990.

Rat Run. London, Century, 1991.

Novels as Frederick H. Christian

Sudden Strikes Back. London, Corgi, 1966.

Sudden—Troubleshooter. London, Corgi, 1967.

Sudden at Bay. London, Corgi, 1968.

Sudden—Apache Fighter. London, Corgi, 1969.

Sudden—Dead or Alive!. London, Corgi, 1970.

Kill Angel. London, Sphere, 1972; New York, Pinnacle, 1974; as *Bad Day at Agua Caliente*, Los Angeles, Pinnacle, 1979.

Send Angel. London, Sphere, 1972; New York, Pinnacle, 1974; as *Ride Clear of Daranga*, New York, Pinnacle, 1979.

Find Angel. London, Sphere, 1973; New York, Pinnacle, 1974; as *Ride Out to Vengeance*, Los Angeles, Pinnacle, 1979.

Trap Angel. London, Sphere, 1973; New York, Pinnacle, 1974; as *Ambush in Purgatory*, Los Angeles, Pinnacle, 1979.

Frame Angel. New York, Pinnacle, 1974; London, Sphere, 1975; as *Shoot-Out at Silver King*, Los Angeles, Pinnacle, 1980.

Hunt Angel. London, Sphere, and New York, Pinnacle, 1975; as *Massacre in Madison*, Los Angeles, Pinnacle, 1980.

Hang Angel. London, Sphere, and New York, Pinnacle, 1975; as *Showdown in Trinidad*, Los Angeles, Pinnacle, 1979.

Take Angel. London, Sphere, 1975; as *Warn Angel*, New York, Pinnacle, 1975.

Stop Angel!. London, Sphere, and New York, Pinnacle, 1976.

Plays

Screenplay: *Brass Target*, 1978.

Radio Plays: *The Richard Rodgers Story* (six one-hour programmes), 1976.

Television Plays: *Hemingway's 'Fiesta'*, *New Horizons* series, 1970; *Westerns* and *Spies and Secret Service Agents*, both 1980; *Thrillers* and *Bestsellers*, 1981; *A Better Read* series.

Other (for children)

Jesse James. London, Macdonald, 1973.

Cowboys. London, Macdonald, 1974.

Lewis and Clark. London, Macdonald, 1974.

The Wagon Train. London, Macdonald, 1974.

Geronimo. London, Macdonald, 1975.

The Pilgrim Fathers. London, Macdonald, 1975.

Battle of the Alamo. London, Macdonald, 1978.

Other

The Life and Death of John Henry Tunstall. Albuquerque, University of New Mexico Press, 1965.

Jay J. Armes: Detective (by Jay J. Armes, as told to Frederick Nolan). New York, Macmillan, 1976; London, Macdonald, 1977.

Rodgers and Hammerstein: The Sound of Their Music. London, Dent, and New York, Walker, 1978.

An Eyewitness History of the Lincoln County War. Norman, University of Oklahoma Press, 1989.

Editor (as Frederick H. Christian), *The Authentic Life of Billy the Kid*, by Pat Garrett. London, Sphere, 1973.

Translator, *Lucky Luke* series (*The Stage Coach, Jesse James, Dalton City, The Tenderfoot, Western Circus*) (for children) by R. Goscinny. Leicester, Brockhampton Press, 5 vols, 1972–74.

Translator, *Gideon* [*And His Friends, On the Riverbank*] *Gideon's House* (for children) by Benjamin Rabier. London, Hodder and Stoughton, 4 vols, 1979.

Translator, *The Black Forest Clinic*, by Peter Heim. London, Sphere, 1987.

*

Film Adaptation: *Brass Target*, 1978, from the novel *The Oshawa Project*.

Frederick Nolan comments:

Historical fiction is one of my favourite disciplines—indeed it might be said that practically everything I have written for adults under my own name falls into that category. Of all that I write I would like to think I take my cue from Trevelyan, who said that 'what is important about history is not what happened, but how people felt when it was happening'.

*   *   *

A writer whose fame was established with such popular contemporary thrillers as *The Mittenwald Syndicate* and *The Oshawa Project*, Frederick Nolan has begun to earn a second—and equally valid—reputation as a historical novelist. His interest in the events of the previous two centuries, especially those affecting the United States, is always evident—among his nonfiction works is an account of the battle of the Alamo—and the novels he has so far produced testify to his ability as a fictional chronicler of the American past. As befits the creations of an 'action adventure' writer, Nolan's historical books display a terseness of delivery and a brooding atmospheric power, together with scenes of shocking brutality.

The least typical of his novels, *White Nights, Red Dawn*, is set in Tsarist Russia on the eve of its collapse into war and revolution. Against the background of a regime tottering on the verge of destruction, Nolan explores the love-hate relationship of his heroine Tatiana for the playboy Vladimir Smirnoff, and the more unwelcome attentions of the secret policeman Boris Abrikosov. A further strand of sub-plot involves a series of vicious child-murders, and the final unmasking of the killer. The effect of political developments on the lives of the characters is skilfully portrayed, Tsar and peasant alike caught in the gradual, inexorable slide into dissolution and chaos. Nolan recreates the atmosphere of a land in turmoil, fixing in turn on individuals and huddled city crowds, ruthlessly presenting the Tsarist torture-chambers, the intrigues of Lenin and the German High Command, the hypnotic debauchery of Rasputin. In memorable, panoramic scenes he evokes the agony of Russia, the horrifying slaughter of her armies by the Germans, the wholesale butchery of the Bolshevik executions. Though at times the welter of savagery threatens to overwhelm, the overall vision is sure, and utterly convincing. *White Nights, Red Dawn* is perhaps the most unusual of Nolan's creations; it is also one of the most satisfying.

More typical, and altogether more ambitious, is the 'Call to Arms' series of novels, where the history of the United States from the War of Independence onwards is traced through the lives of the Strong family. At present, the sequence is unfinished, with two novels completed. *A Promise of Glory* follows the adventures of David Strong, an exiled Englishman won over to the American cause, through the campaigns of Washington against British and Indians in the 1770s. Characterization is thin—there is a touch of pasteboard about the villainous Wellbeloveds, for instance—but Nolan compensates for this with the power of his battle scenes, and his detailed reconstruction of 18th-century life and death. Sensational incidents abound, and the sickening brutality is excessive at times, but the pace of the work is compelling. Although the most flawed of Nolan's historical works, *A Promise of Glory* has considerable merit. More impressive is its sequel, *Blind Duty*, where a later generation of Strongs find themselves involved in the American Civil War, and divided loyalties threaten to break up the family. In this novel Nolan's characters show greater depth and credibility, and his descriptive writing is at its most inspired. His portrayal of the Civil War itself—whether in its broader sweep, or in the snapshot-image recollections of individual battles—is outstanding, and as ever he excels in the action scenes. Imaginary episodes are neatly interwoven with the actual events of the period, with real-life generals and politicians sharing the stage with Nolan's own creations. *Blind Duty* marks a further advance on its predecessor, and bodes well for subsequent works in the series.

Carver's Kingdom ranks highest of all Nolan's historical novels to date. In this account of the financial empire founded by the Carver brothers, and their personal and business lives, the author at the same time presents a capsule history of the United States during the period 1849 to 1873. Ranging from the Californian goldfields to the plantations of Virginia, from the high society of New York and Washington to the western frontier settlements, Nolan conjures up a vivid picture of America's industrial growth, and through the Carver brothers exemplifies the ruthless determination of its pioneers. His compelling narrative involves the fictional characters and their real-life counterparts without undue strain, providing neat vignettes of such worthies as Jim Fisk, J. C. Fremont, James King, and Andrew Carnegie. Nolan's mastery of detail is always apparent, and there are several epic scenes as he pursues his characters through Gold Rush and Civil War, and the 1871 Chicago fire, to the final shootout and trial in Wichita, Kansas. *Carver's Kingdom* is a major achievement, a significant historical novel which confirms Nolan's reputation in the genre. It is to some extent paralleled by his recent non-fiction venture into the history of the American West, *An Eyewitness History of the Lincoln County War*, which may well prove to be the definitive work on this legendary conflict. Nolan's latest fictional writings have been his series of adventure thrillers—*Sweet Sister Death*, *Alert State Black*, *Designated Assassin*, and *Rat Run* (collectively known as *The Garrett Dossier*), but *Carver's Kingdom* and *The Lincoln County War* are clear indications that he retains his interest in historical themes.

—Geoffrey Sadler

NORCROSS, Lisabet. See **SEBASTIAN, Margaret.**

NORDHOFF, Charles and **HALL, James Norman.**
NORDHOFF, Charles (Bernard). Nationality: American. **Born:** London, England, 1 February 1887. **Education:** Harvard University, Cambridge, Massachusetts, 1906–09, B.A. 1909. **Military Service:** ambulance driver in France, 1916; pilot in United States Air Service: lieutenant. **Relations:** married 1) Pepe Teara in 1920 (divorced), four daughters and two sons; 2) Laura Whiley in 1941. Worked on a sugar plantation, Mexico, 1909–11; secretary and treasurer, Tile and Fine Brick Company, California, 1911–16. **Died:** 11 April 1947. **HALL, James Norman. Pseudonym:** Fern Gravel. **Nationality:** American. **Born:** Colfax, Iowa, 22 April 1887. **Education:** public schools in Colfax; Grinnell College, Iowa, graduated 1910. **Military Service:** 9th Battalion Royal Fusiliers, 1914–16; pilot in the United States Air Service. **Relations:** married Sarah Winchester in 1925; one son and one daughter. **Career:** social worker, Society for the Prevention of Cruelty to Children, Boston, 1910–14. **Died:** 5 July 1951.

ROMANCE AND HISTORICAL PUBLICATIONS

Novels (series: Bounty Trilogy)

Bounty Trilogy. Boston, Little Brown, 1936.
    Mutiny on the Bounty. Boston, Little Brown, 1932; as *Mutiny!*, London, Chapman and Hall, 1933.
    Men Against the Sea. Boston, Little Brown, 1933; London, Chapman and Hall, 1934.
    Pitcairn's Island. Boston, Little Brown, 1934; London, Chapman and Hall, 1935.
Botany Bay. Boston, Little Brown, 1941; London, Chapman and Hall, 1942.

OTHER PUBLICATIONS

Novels

Faery Lands of the South Seas. New York, Harper, 1921.
Falcons of France: A Tale of Youth and the Air. Boston, Little Brown, 1929; London, John Hamilton, 1931.
The Hurricane. Boston, Little Brown, 1936.
The Dark River. Boston, Little Brown, 1938.
No More Gas. Boston, Little Brown, 1940.
Men Without Country. Boston, Little Brown, and London, Chapman and Hall, 1942.
The High Barbaree. Boston, Little Brown, 1945; London, Faber, 1946.
The Far Lands. Boston, Little Brown, 1950; London, Faber, 1951.

Other

The Lafayette Flying Corps. Boston, Houghton Mifflin, 1920.

OTHER PUBLICATIONS

by Charles Nordhoff

Novels

The Fledgling. Boston, Houghton, Mifflin, 1919.
The Pearl Lagoon. Boston, Atlantic Monthly Press, 1924.
Picarò. New York, Harper, 1924.
The Derelict. Boston, Little Brown, 1928.

Other

In Yankee Windjammers. New York, Dodd Mead, 1940; as *I Served in Windjammers*, London, Chapman and Hall, 1941.

OTHER PUBLICATIONS

by James Norman Hall

Novels

Kitchener's Mob. Boston, Houghton Mifflin, and London, Constable, 1916.
High Adventure. Boston, Houghton Mifflin, and London, Constable, 1918.
On the Stream of Travel. Boston, Houghton Mifflin, 1926.
Mid-Pacific. Boston, Houghton Mifflin, 1928.
Under the South. London, Chapman and Hall, 1928.
Flying with Chaucer. Boston, Houghton Mifflin, 1930.

Oh Millersville (as Fern Gravel). Muscatine, Iowa, Prairie Press, 1940.
Under a Thatched Roof. Boston, Houghton Mifflin, 1942.
Lost Island. New York, Sundial Press, 1945.

Short Stories

The Forgotten One and Other True Tales of the South Sea. Boston, Little Brown, 1952.

Poetry

A Word for His Sponsor. Boston, Little Brown, 1928.

Other

Mother Goose Land (for children). Boston, Houghton Mifflin, 1930.
The Tale of a Shipwreck (for children). Boston, Houghton Mifflin, 1934.
The Friends (for children). Muscatine, Iowa, Prairie Press, 1939.
Dr Dogbody's Leg (for children). Boston, Little Brown, 1940.
My Island Home (autobiography). Boston, Little Brown, 1952.

*

Film Adaptations: *Mutiny on the Bounty*, 1935, 1962, *The Bounty*, 1984, from the novel *Mutiny on the Bounty*; *The Hurricane*, 1937, 1979; *The Turtles of Tahiti*, 1942, from the novel *No More Gas*; *High Barbaree*, 1947; *Botany Bay*, 1952.

*   *   *

The collaborative team of Charles Nordhoff and James Norman Hall exemplifies the working out of that puzzling anomaly, 'a whole that is greater than the sum of its parts'. Both men had written competent material on various subjects before they came together to work on the history of the World War I Lafayette Flying Corps of which both had been members, and later on a fictional account, *Falcons of France*. Their writing partnership proved so smoothly agreeable, they debated the possibility of finding other work upon which they could profitably pool their efforts; eventually Hall suggested the story of a mutiny aboard a British ship in 1789 as a possible subject for a novel—perhaps even three novels, if the first proved successful.

It was a true story almost forgotten except by those few people who had read the account published in 1831 by John Barrows, Secretary of the British Admiralty, in a work largely unknown to the general public. The story of the mutiny and its aftermath was so sensational that had it not been demonstrably based upon fact, the events recounted would have seemed incredible. The authors decided to allow the now elderly Captain Roger Byam, once a lowly midshipman under Captain Bligh, to tell his own well-remembered story of *Mutiny on the Bounty*.

In 1787 the HMS *Bounty* proceeded upon orders to collect a cargo of breadfruit trees from Tahiti for an experimental transplantation in the West Indies. The delicate plants depended upon speedy delivery if they were to survive the voyage, and the officer in command, Captain William Bligh, was absolutely determined that the mission should be a notable success that would redound to his credit.

At a time when ordinary seamen expected and received harsh treatment almost as a matter of course, Bligh's inhumanity was so extreme that it was more than his crew were prepared to endure. Most of them, under the charismatic leadership of mate Fletcher Christian, rose in mutiny against Bligh's tyranny. Bligh himself, and those few men aboard who refused to join the mutineers, were set adrift at sea in an open longboat. The chances of their survival, as they well knew, were slim indeed.

Men Against the Sea describes the almost miraculous safe return of the castaways to landfall at Timor in the East Indies, thanks to the navigational skill of Captain Bligh. He was a hard man with an abusive tongue, ambitious and overbearing even by the standards of his day; but he was a masterful seaman by *any* standards.

Meanwhile the mutineers, all too well aware that they were certain to be hanged if captured, provisioned the *Bounty*, and after persuading a handful of friendly Polynesians to accompany them, set sail to find eventual refuge on Pitcairn's Island, an uninhabited speck in mid-ocean.

Men outnumbered the women marooned on the island after the deliberate destruction of the *Bounty*, and the sexual tensions and jealousy aroused by this disparity led to a murderous uprising of the outraged Polynesians. Those who survived were finally discovered in 1808, living peacefully on the island still inhabited by their descendants. Of the mutineers who had refused to flee with Christian on the stolen *Bounty*, three were tried and executed in England.

The *Bounty Trilogy* surpassed the authors' fondest hopes with its enormous success, which they were never to repeat, although they continued to work together. The trilogy was the result of a coming together of well-matched talents perfectly suited to the subject matter; their bold, distinctly masculine style of prose was exactly right for the story they had to tell. *Mutiny on the Bounty*, which has been filmed repeatedly, is familiar to millions more than ever read the bestselling books, and remains Nordhoff and Hall's joint masterpiece.

It was said of Nordhoff and Hall that 'their friendship was the mainspring of their collaboration'. Two very different types, Nordhoff ambitious, sceptical, handsome; Hall more of the plain, homespun dependable sort, together created what neither could accomplish alone: a landmark work of fiction in which a sordid mutiny against authority in the person of a petty tyrant won for both captain and mutineers alike a place in the annals of courage, endurance, and adventure.

—Joan McGrath

———

NORRIS, Kathleen (Thompson).
Nationality: American. **Born:** San Francisco, California, 16 July 1880. **Education:** University of California, Berkeley, 1905. **Relations:** married the writer Charles Gilman Norris in 1909 (died 1945); one son and two daughters. **Career:** bookkeeper, saleswoman, and teacher; society editor, *Evening Bulletin*, and reporter, *Call*, both San Francisco, 1907–09; freelance writer from 1909. **Died:** 18 January 1966.

Romance and Historical Publications

Novels

Mother. New York, Macmillan, 1911.
The Rich Mrs Burgoyne. New York, Macmillan, 1912.
Saturday's Child. New York, and London, Macmillan, 1914.
The Treasure. New York, Macmillan, 1914.
The Story of Julia Page. New York, Doubleday, and London, Murray, 1915.
The Heart of Rachael. New York, Doubleday, and London, Murray, 1916.
Martie, The Unconquered. New York, Doubleday, 1917; London, Murray, 1918.
Undertow. New York, Doubleday, and London, Curtis Brown, 1917.
Josselyn's Wife. New York, Doubleday, 1918; London, Murray, 1919.

Sisters. New York, Doubleday, and London, Murray, 1919.
The Works. New York, Doubleday, 11 vols, 1920.
Harriet and the Piper. New York, Doubleday, and London, Murray, 1920.
The Beloved Woman. New York, Doubleday, and London, Murray, 1921.
Little Ships. New York, Doubleday, 1921; London, Murray, 1925.
Certain People of Importance. New York, Doubleday, and London, Heinemann, 1922.
Lucretia Lombard. New York, Doubleday, and London, Curtis Brown, 1922.
Butterfly. New York, Doubleday, 1923; as *Poor Butterfly*, London, Heinemann, 1923.
Uneducating Mary. New York, Doubleday, 1923.
Rose of the World. New York, Doubleday, and London, Murray, 1924.
The Callahans and the Murphys. New York, Doubleday, and London, Heinemann, 1924.
The Black Flemings. New York, Doubleday, and London, Murray, 1926; as *Gabrielle*, New York, Paperback Library, 1965.
Hildegarde. New York, Doubleday, and London, Murray, 1926.
Barberry Bush. New York, Doubleday, 1927; London, Murray, 1929.
My Best Girl. New York, Burt, and London, Readers Library, 1927.
The Sea Gull. New York, Doubleday, 1927; London, Murray, 1938.
Beauty and the Beast. New York, Doubleday, 1928; as *Outlaw Love*, London, Murray, 1928.
The Foolish Virgin. New York, Doubleday, and London, Murray, 1928.
Storm House. New York, Doubleday, and London, Murray, 1929.
Red Silence. New York, Doubleday, and London, Murray, 1929.
The Lucky Lawrences. New York, Doubleday, and London, Murray, 1930.
Passion Flower. New York, Doubleday, and London, Murray, 1930.
Margaret Yorke. New York, Doubleday, 1930; London, Murray, 1931.
Belle-Mère. New York, Doubleday, 1931; London, Murray, 1932.
The Love of Julie Borel. New York, Doubleday, and London, Murray, 1931.
Treehaven. New York, Doubleday, and London, Murray, 1932.
Younger Sister. New York, Doubleday, 1932; as *Make Believe Wife*, London, Murray, 1947.
Second Hand Wife. New York, Doubleday, 1932; London, Murray, 1933.
Young Mother Hubbard. London, Benn, 1932.
Tangled Love. London, Murray, 1933.
The Angel in the House. New York, Doubleday, 1933.
Walls of Gold. New York, Doubleday, and London, Murray, 1933.
Wife for Sale. New York, Doubleday, 1933; London, Murray, 1934.
False Morning. London, Murray, 1934.
Maiden Voyage. New York, Doubleday, 1934.
Manhattan Love Song. New York, Doubleday, 1934.
Three Men and Diana. New York, Doubleday, and London, Murray, 1934.
Beauty's Daughter. New York, Doubleday, and London, Murray, 1935.
Shining Windows. New York, Doubleday, and London, Murray, 1935.
Woman in Love. New York, Doubleday, 1935; as *Tamara*, London, Murray, 1935.
The Mystery of Pine Point. London, Murray, 1936.
Secret Marriage. New York, Doubleday, and London, Murray, 1936.
The American Flaggs. New York, Doubleday, 1936; as *The Flagg Family*, London, Murray, 1936.

Bread into Roses. New York, Doubleday, and London, Murray, 1937.
You Can't Have Everything. New York, Doubleday, and London, Murray, 1937.
Heartbroken Melody. New York, Doubleday, and London, Murray, 1938.
Mystery House. New York, Doubleday, 1939.
Lost Sunrise. New York, Doubleday, and London, Murray, 1939.
The Runaway. New York, Doubleday, and London, Murray, 1939.
The Secret of the Marshbanks. New York, Doubleday, and London, Murray, 1940.
The World Is Like That. New York, Doubleday, and London, Murray, 1940.
April Escapade. London, Murray, 1941.
The Venables. New York, Doubleday, and London, Murray, 1941.
An Apple for Eve. New York, Doubleday, 1942; London, Murray, 1943.
Come Back to Me, Beloved. New York, Sun Dial Press, 1942; London, Murray, 1953; as *Motionless Shadows*, New York, Bart House, 1945.
Dina Cashman. New York, Doubleday, 1942; London, Murray, 1943.
Corner of Heaven. New York, Doubleday, 1943; London, Murray, 1944.
Love Calls the Tune. New York, Sun Dial Press, 1944; London, Murray, 1945.
Burned Fingers. New York, Doubleday, 1945; London, Murray, 1946.
Mink Coat. New York, Doubleday, and London, Murray, 1946.
The Secrets of Hillyard House. New York, Doubleday, 1947; as *Romance at Hillyard House*, London, Murray, 1948.
Christmas Eve. London, Murray, 1949.
High Holiday. New York, Doubleday, 1949.
Shadow Marriage. New York, Doubleday, and London, Murray, 1952.
Miss Harriet Townshend. New York, Doubleday, and London, Murray, 1955.
The Best of Kathleen Norris. Garden City, New York, Hanover House, 1955.
Through a Glass Darkly. New York, Doubleday, 1957; as *Cherry*, London, Murray, 1958.

Short Stories

Poor, Dear Margaret Kirby and Other Stories. New York, Macmillan, 1913.
Baker's Dozen. New York, Doubleday, 1938; as *Plain People*, London, Murray, 1938.
Star-Spangled Christmas. New York, Doubleday, 1942.
Over at the Crowleys'. New York, Doubleday, 1946.

OTHER PUBLICATIONS

Plays

The Kelly Kid, with Dan Totheroh. Boston, Baker, 1926.
Victoria. New York, Doubleday, 1934.

Screenplay: *Lucretia Lombard* (*Flaming Passion*), with Bertram Millhauser and Sada Cowan, 1923.

Poetry

One Nation Indivisible. New York, Doubleday, 1942.

Other

Noon: An Autobiographial Sketch. New York, Doubleday, 1925.
The Fun of Being a Mother. New York, Doubleday, and London, Heinemann, 1927.
Herbert Hoover as Seen by Kathleen Norris. Washington, DC, Republican National Committee, 1928.
Home. New York, Dutton, 1928.
What Price Peace? A Handbook of Peace for American Women. New York, Doubleday, 1928.
After the Honey Moon What? New York, Paulist Press, n.d.
Mother and Son. New York, Dutton, 1929.
Beauty in Letters. New York, Doubleday, 1930.
Hands Full of Living: Talks with American Women. New York, Doubleday, 1931.
My San Francisco. New York, Doubleday, 1932.
My California. New York, Doubleday, 1933.
Dedications. Privately printed, 1936.
These I Like Best: The Favorite Novels and Stories of Kathleen Norris, Chosen by Herself. New York, Doubleday, 1941.
Companionate Marriage. New York, Paulist Press, n.d.
Morning Light (for children). New York, Doubleday, 1950; as *Mary-Jo*, London, Dent, 1952.
Family Gathering (memoirs). New York, Doubleday, and London, Murray, 1959.

*   *   *

Kathleen Norris has, unfortunately, been lumped together with the masses of popular magazine writers of the period from 1910 to 1950, and this, while appropriate for much of her work, does a disservice to her best novels. Possibly a bit defensive about her work because of the more 'serious' (but utterly forgotten) work of her husband, Charles Norris (brother of Frank), she saw herself as a professional writer, doing two or three serials a year for leading magazines, even cutting back on her fiction when income tax made it appropriate to do so. But she said in her autobiography: 'Most of the critics did not take my work seriously, but then neither did I take the critics too seriously. My writing I took with deadly seriousness'.

Certainly the critics were just to ignore much of her work. Norris's central mood hovers between the sentimental and the didactic; together they are a dangerous combination. It often leads to works which point a threadbare moral at the expense of much exploration of character. *The Treasure* (1914) is a 'modern' story about social insecurity, 'domestic science', and progress. The characters are used as counters in the thematic game—and the result is a 'hard' story with little life to it. Usually Norris allows herself more space, but even so many of the novels centre on obvious conflicts between ordinary folk and smart or rich people, usually with a romantic plot to keep the theme moving. *Rose of the World* contrasts a socially unacceptable girl with a rich snobbish family, but the girl is given the chance to have the last word, and marry the son of the family after all. *Mink Coat* contrasts a playboy New Yorker with an honest westerner by their effect on one woman. Other novels show rich or shiftless men damaging young susceptible girls. Perhaps a sacrifice has to be made to protect a relative or friend (*Lost Sunrise*)—but the long-term effect is usually a triumph for the heroine.

Norris emphasized her interest in 'the fearful power of money upon human lives', and her stories are full of spendthrifts, unworkable household budgets, bank loans, wills, and middle-aged women who don't understand the principle of insurance. But another prime interest is the family itself, and her best novels are those which centre on the family or clan as a preserver of traditional right action, even as an expression of the healthy melting pot of America itself.

Norris was from a prosperous Irish family from San Francisco, and many of her works use this background. She was not afraid to use simple or even slight themes: 'I have no knowledge of those dark forces which fascinate modern writers. I write for people with simple needs and motives because I am like that myself'. Her very first long story, *Mother*, brought her fame, and it initiates a constant Norris theme by having a strong sense of family—centred on the unassuming Mrs Paget—act as a stabilizing force against the false values of a 'smart' idle life: 'the old beauty that had been hers was chiselled to a mere pure outline now, but there was a contagious serenity in Mrs Paget's smile, a clear steadiness in her calm eyes, and her forehead, beneath an unfashionably plain sweep of hair, was untroubled and smooth'. Other volumes also centre on strong mothers (*Over at the Crowleys'*, *The Callahans and the Murphys*, *Little Ships*), though sometimes the theme is reversed, so that a weak mother yields to a daughter who learns strength elsewhere (*The Venables*).

The two novels which most convincingly posit Norris's fictional values are *Certain People of Importance* and *The Flagg Family*, and the two books neatly represent two consecutive generations. The 'certain people of importance' of the first novel are the members of the Crabtree family. The novel traces the Crabtrees in detail from their arrival in San Francisco in 1849 through the 40 or 50 years to the death of Reuben Crabtree. We see a family begun, a group of traditions started, rivalries and intimacies, financial and spiritual losses and gains—and life continues to surprise Reuben's daughters May and Fannie to the very end. The Flaggs represent the next generation, but their novel covers a shorter span of time (about 10 years) and has a firmer plot. The Flaggs are a large rich clan in northern California, the symbol of tradition and aristocracy to outsiders. Norris allows the clan to be penetrated by an outsider, not in order to debunk the Flaggs, but to show the value of the traditions the Flaggs have built up and learned to accept as part of their future, the richness of the strains that have fed them (English, Indian, Jewish, Italian, Dutch), the compromises that keep them afloat. Even the rather melodramatic plot superimposed on the more substantial edifice—should the newcomer Penelope divorce the spoiled Jeff Flagg to marry the more sedate cousin Tom Flagg?—is worked out in terms of the family theme.

Norris in these two books keeps her sentiments and nostalgia uncontaminated with didacticism, and the results are probing. She represents a second-generation American writer with second-generation American themes, and these are interesting yet today (vulgarized into sentimental myths as pervasive as Ozzie and Harriet or the Kennedys)—and presented with directness and precision.

—George Walsh

NORTON, Bess.   See **NORWAY, Kate.**

NORWAY, Kate.
Pseudonym for Olive Marion Norton. **Other Pseudonyms:** Hilary Neal; Bess Norton. **Nationality:** British. **Born:** Olive Marion Claydon, 13 January 1913. **Education:** King Edward's School, Birmingham; Birmingham Children's Hospital; Manchester Royal Infirmary. **Relations:** married George Norton in 1938; one son and three daughters. **Career:** nurse, 1930–36: in charge of first aid post during World War II; columnist, Birmingham *News*, 1954–59. Counsellor, Citizens Advice Bureau. **Died:** 1973.

Romance and Historical Publications

Novels

Sister Brookes of Bynd's. London, Mills and Boon, 1957; as *Nurse Brookes*, Toronto, Harlequin, 1958.

The Morning Star. London, Mills and Boon, and Toronto, Harlequin, 1959.
Junior Pro. London, Mills and Boon, and Toronto, Harlequin, 1959.
Nurse Elliot's Diary. London, Mills and Boon, and Toronto, Harlequin, 1960.
Waterfront Hospital. London, Mills and Boon, 1961.
The White Jacket. London, Mills and Boon, 1961; Toronto, Harlequin, 1962.
Goodbye, Johnny. London, Mills and Boon, 1962.
The Night People. London, Mills and Boon, 1963.
Nurse in Print. London, Mills and Boon, 1963.
The Seven Sleepers. London, Mills and Boon, 1964.
A Professional Secret. London, Mills and Boon, 1964.
The Lambs. London, Mills and Boon, 1965.
The Nightingale Touch. London, Mills and Boon, 1966.
Be My Guest. London, Mills and Boon, 1966; as *Journey in the Dark*, London, Corgi, 1973.
Merlin's Keep. London, Mills and Boon, 1966.
A Nourishing Life. London, Mills and Boon, 1967.
The Faithful Failure. London, Mills and Boon, 1968.
Dedication Jones. London, Mills and Boon, 1969; Toronto, Harlequin, 1970.
To Care Always. London, Mills and Boon, 1970.
Reluctant Nightingale. London, Mills and Boon, 1970.
Paper Halo. London, Mills and Boon, 1970; Toronto, Harlequin, 1971.
The Bedside Manner. London, Mills and Boon, 1971.
Casualty Speaking. London, Mills and Boon, 1971.
The Dutiful Tradition. London, Mills and Boon, 1971.
The Gingham Year. London, Mills and Boon, 1973.
Voices in the Night. London, Mills and Boon, 1973.

Novels as Bess Norton

The Quiet One. London, Mills and Boon, 1959; Toronto, Harlequin, 1960.
Night Duty at Dukes. London, Mills and Boon, 1960.
The Red Chalet. London, Mills and Boon, 1960.
The Summer Change. London, Mills and Boon, 1961.
The Waiting Room. London, Mills and Boon, 1961; Toronto, Harlequin, 1962.
A Nurse Is Born. London, Mills and Boon, 1962; Toronto, Harlequin, 1963.
The Green Light. London, Mills and Boon, 1963.
The Monday Man. London, Mills and Boon, 1963.
St Luke's Little Summer. London, Mills and Boon, 1964.
A Miracle at Joe's. London, Mills and Boon, 1965.
St Julian's Day. London, Mills and Boon, 1965.
What We're Here For. London, Mills and Boon, 1966.
Night's Daughters. London, Mills and Boon, 1966.
The Night Is Kind. London, Mills and Boon, 1967.

Novels as Hilary Neal

Factory Nurse. London, Mills and Boon, 1961; Toronto, Harlequin, 1964.
Tread Softly, Nurse. London, Mills and Boon, and Toronto, Harlequin, 1962.
Star Patient. London, Mills and Boon, 1963.
Love Letter. London, Mills and Boon, 1963.
Houseman's Sister. London, Mills and Boon, 1964.
Nurse Off Camera. London, Mills and Boon, 1964.
Mr Sister. London, Mills and Boon, 1965.
The Team. London, Mills and Boon, 1965.
Charge Nurse. London, Mills and Boon, 1965.
A Simple Duty. London, Mills and Boon, 1966.

Nurse Meg's Decision. London, Mills and Boon, 1966.

OTHER PUBLICATIONS

Novels as Olive Norton

A School of Liars. London, Cassell, 1966.
Now Lying Dead. London, Cassell, 1967.
The Speight Street Angle. London, Corgi, 1968.
Dead on Prediction. London, Cassell, 1970.
The Corpse-Bird Cries. London, Cassell, 1971.

Play

Radio Play: *Rose*, 1962.

Other as Olive Norton

Bob-a-Job Pony (for children). London, Heinemann, 1961.

*   *   *

The hospital romance has become a popular and fertile branch of novel writing. It dates from 1948 in Britain—the start of the National Health Service, but Kate Norway has established herself as the most successful practitioner of this genre as well as being a crime writer.

Material for her many books is based on first-hand experience of hospital nursing in Britain, and on the whole the pictures she provides of hospitals are very truthful and realistic to the point of being workaday. There is, as a result, much technical medical detail, as well as clear examples of administrative systems, and much of the interest for many readers is contained in those two areas. The romance in many of her novels is intimately mixed with the work; it is even possible to see the romance aspect as subsidiary. Thus, a young reader contemplating a nursing career would read her novels for an inside picture of hospital life which will also be entertaining. *The Gingham Year*, in fact, deals with the transition of a girl from school to nursing. *The Lambs* concerns a group of student nurses.

Plots tend to follow a well-established pattern. They usually revolve around a young female nurse (occasionally doctor) who is dedicated, competent, and attractive. The nurse is attracted to several doctors and surgeons in the hospital, and can be warm and loving. Much of the interest in the plots is produced by a complicating of romantic situations involving the heroine. She is often disturbed in an initially inexplicable way by her attraction to a particular male. This attraction is often despite herself, and directed towards an unpromising suitor. At the same time she is involved with an ostensibly better candidate. Generally the least promising situation turns out to bring true love. Romantic plots are thus normally triangular: a little variety is added by including a subsidiary mystery involving crime. In *The White Jacket*, for instance, there is a masquerading murderer working in the hospital.

Another device used by Norway to add variety to plots is the accident which happens to nurse or doctor. In *Reluctant Nightingale* the nurse herself ends up needing nursing by those intruders, male nurses. Male nurses were once a controversial issue, and this remains true for the world in Norway's books, which is primarily a female one.

An interesting device occurs in *Voices in the Night* where the chapters form separate diaries written in a *sotto voce* style belonging to five characters. They are inter-related, and one sees hospital life from the view of the elderly spinster sister as well as the young nurse and young doctor. This device adds poignancy to the fact that one doctor is loved by two nurses.

Minor issues which appear in several books are motor car, and especially motor bike, accidents. Settings are commonly the English Midlands. The style of writing is simple with much lively dialogue, but with a good deal of narrative in the first person; descriptive passages are not overlong. Character is not probed too deeply and judgements are often made in a snappy, personnel-management style.

—P.R. Meldrum

NYE, Robert.

Nationality: British. **Born:** London, 15 March 1939. **Education:** Dormans Land, Surrey; Hamlet Court, Westcliff, Essex; Southend High School, Essex. **Relations:** married 1) Judith Pratt in 1959 (divorced 1967), three sons; 2) Aileen Campbell in 1968, one daughter, one stepdaughter, and one stepson. **Career:** since 1961 freelance writer: since 1967 poetry editor, the *Scotsman;* since 1971 poetry critic, *The Times.* Writer-in-residence, University of Edinburgh, 1976–77. **Recipient:** Eric Gregory award, 1963; Scottish Arts Council bursary, 1970, 1973, and publication award, 1970, 1976; James Kennaway memorial award, 1970; *Guardian* fiction prize, 1976; Hawthornden prize, 1977. Fellow, Royal Society of Literature, 1977; Society of Authors travel scholarship, 1991. **Agent:** Sheil Land Associates, 43 Doughty Street, London WC1N 2LF, England; or, Wallace, Aitken, and Sheil Inc, 118 East 61st Street, New York, New York 10021, USA. **Address:** 2 Westbury Crescent, Wilton, Cork, Ireland.

ROMANCE AND HISTORICAL PUBLICATIONS

Novels

Falstaff. London, Hamish Hamilton, and Boston, Little Brown, 1976.
Merlin. London, Hamish Hamilton, 1978; New York, Putnam, 1979.
Faust. London, Hamish Hamilton, 1980; New York, Putnam, 1981.
The Voyage of the Destiny. London, Hamish Hamilton, and New York, Putnam, 1982.
The Memoirs of Lord Byron. London, Hamish Hamilton, 1989.
The Life and Death of My Lord Gilles de Rais. London, Hamish Hamilton, 1990.
Mrs Shakespeare: The Complete Works. London, Sinclair Stevenson, 1993.

OTHER PUBLICATIONS

Novel

Doubtfire. London, Calder and Boyars, and New York, Hill and Wang, 1968.

Short Stories

Tales I Told My Mother. London, Calder and Boyars, 1969; New York, Hill and Wang, 1970.
Penguin Modern Stories 6, with others. London, Penguin, 1970.
The Facts of Life and Other Fictions. London, Hamish Hamilton, 1983.

Plays

Sawney Bean, with Bill Watson (produced Edinburgh, 1969; London, 1972; New York, 1982). London, Calder and Boyars, 1970.

Sisters (broadcast 1969; produced Edinburgh, 1973). In *Penthesilea, Fugue, and Sisters,* 1975.
Penthesilea, adaptation of the play by Heinrich von Kleist (broadcast 1971; produced London, 1983). In *Penthesilea, Fugue, and Sisters,* 1975.
The Seven Deadly Sins: A Mask, music by James Douglas (produced Stirling, 1973). Rushden, Northamptonshire, Omphalos Press, 1974.
Mr Poe: A Public Lecture with Private Illustrations (produced Edinburgh and London, 1974).
Penthesilea, Fugue, and Sisters. London, Calder and Boyars, 1975.

Radio Plays: *Sisters,* 1969; *A Bloody Stupit Hole,* 1970; *Reynolds, Reynolds,* 1971; *Penthesilea,* 1971; *The Devil's Jig,* music by Humphrey Searle, from a work by Thomas Mann, 1980.

Poetry

Juvenilia 1. Northwood, Middlesex, Scorpion Press, 1961.
Juvenilia 2. Lowestoft, Suffolk, Scorpion Press, 1963.
Darker Ends. London, Calder and Boyars, and New York, Hill and Wang, 1969.
Agnus Dei. Rushden, Northamptonshire, Sceptre Press, 1973.
Two Prayers. Richmond, Surrey, Keepsake Press, 1974.
Five Dreams. Rushden, Northamptonshire, Sceptre Press, 1974.
Divisions on a Ground. Manchester, Carcanet, 1976.
A Collection of Poems 1955–1988. London, Hamish Hamilton, 1988.

Other (for children)

Taliesin. London, Faber, 1966; New York, Hill and Wang, 1967.
March Has Horse's Ears. London, Faber, 1966; New York, Hill and Wang, 1967.
Bee Hunter: Adventures of Beowulf. London, Faber, 1968; as *Beowulf: A New Telling,* New York, Hill and Wang, 1968; as *Beowulf, The Bee Hunter,* Faber, 1972.
Wishing Gold. London, Macmillan, 1970; New York, Hill and Wang, 1971.
Poor Pumpkin. London, Macmillan, 1971; as *The Mathematical Princess and Other Stories,* New York, Hill and Wang, 1972.
Cricket: Three Stories. Indianapolis, Bobbs Merrill, 1975; as *Once upon Three Times,* London, Benn, 1978.
Out of the World and Back Again. London, Collins, 1977; as *Out of This World and Back Again,* Indianapolis, Bobbs Merrill, 1978.
The Bird of the Golden Land. London, Hamish Hamilton, 1980.
Harry Pay the Pirate. London, Hamish Hamilton, 1981.
Three Tales (includes *Beowulf, Wishing Gold, Taliesin*). London, Hamish Hamilton, 1983.

Other

Masculinity and Male Codes of Honour in Modern France. London, Oxford University Press, 1993.

Editor, *A Choice of Sir Walter Ralegh's Verse.* London, Faber, 1972.
Editor, *William Barnes of Dorset: A Selection of His Poems.* Oxford, Carcanet, 1972.
Editor, *A Choice of Swinburne's Verse.* London, Faber, 1973.
Editor, *The Faber Book of Sonnets.* London, Faber, 1976; as *A Book of Sonnets,* New York, Oxford University Press, 1976.
Editor, *The English Sermon 1750–1850.* Cheadle, Cheshire, Carcanet, 1976.
Editor, *PEN New Poetry.* London, Quartet, 1986.
Editor, with Elizabeth Freidman and Alan J. Clark, *First Awakenings: The Early Poems of Laura Riding.* Manchester, Carcanet, and New York, Persea Press, 1992.

*

Manuscript Collections: University of Edinburgh; University of Texas, Austin; Colgate University, Hamilton, New York; National Library of Scotland, Edinburgh.

* * *

'There's always another version' said Faust . . .
'another way of telling it'.

The gulf between the official and the secret version of history provides the imaginative space within which Robert Nye works. It is history in the sense of story, rather than of chronicle, which inspires Nye—his histories being made of tours de force of the story-tellers art: bawdy, tragic, and moving. They are inspired by those who have passed out of history into legend. Nye's historical novels present a series of dazzling encounters with these half-mythic figures: Merlin, Ralegh, Shakespeare. His greatest work creates the illusion of barely being writing at all in the conventional sense, but rather of being spoken stories. The voices we hear are often those of characters whose public faces are well known to us, who approach us to tell the secret tale of their own lives, flattering us with their confidences—even their confessions. Those 'other' versions are, inevitably, subversions of the public myths, and so seem the more convincing. (The secret sexual 'histories' of Queen Elizabeth I, of Shakespeare, and of Byron are thus exposed.)

The illusion of the spoken voice, or the soliloquy overheard, creates a sense of the speaker's presence in which the style is indeed the man. The nature of his speakers emerges in their pace and diction: Byron's detached intelligence and saturnine wit, Falstaff's immensely energetic bawdry, Ralegh's painful self awareness and moral rigour. The relationship offered to their readers—or listeners—is an intimate one: Nye frequently slips from the first person into the second, drawing us into the process of narration. And as his tellers are aware of their readers, so they are conscious of their role as mythmakers. Their memoirs are half conscious attempts to discover and understand the meaning of their lives. At the same time, we observe characters in the process of actively constructing their own myth: Faust through drunken self aggrandizement, Gilles de Rais through heroic and costly pageants in which he plays himself.

As his characters construct a version of the past, however, they are interrupted by events in the present. The original story may be disrupted and compromised—as in *Falstaff* where Falstaff's own scribes interrupt his narrative. Nye makes the narrative perspective of the deathbed confession his own. Through the act of continued reflection comes a sense of the greater imperatives which have driven his characters to lead the life they have.

Another trait which unites his characters is the urge to transgress or defy the ordered limits of their world. One manifestation of this is in their prodigious sexual repertoires. Another emerges in an interest in the supernatural: illustrated in Nye's haunting retelling of the tale of Thomas the Rhymer.

The same interest can be seen beneath Nye's obsession with the myths or histories of Joan of Arc and Gilles de Rais. Having made an early appearance in *Doubtfire* it erupts again in *Falstaff*, where Falstaff encounters Joan in the shape of a white hind. The complex finds its nexus in *The Life and Death of My Lord Gilles de Rais*. This intensely poetic work draws its reader deeper and deeper into spiritual concerns—from initial sensuous fascination with Gilles's earthly paradise to eventual horror at the terrors which underlie it. Its final chapters almost cease from narrative, to become an intense meditation on the mysteries of good and evil, damnation and grace; a child murderer who is 'the perfect Christian'. Nye's dazzling narrative skill finds its apotheosis in Gilles's story, told through another story—that of the priest whose life Gilles has shattered.

Nye's use of language exhibits an intensity and versatility which betray his first calling—as a poet. His style adapts effortlessly to his subject—in Falstaff's gloriously inflated bombast, in Mrs Shakespeare's keen reductive wit, in Kit Wagner's abrupt obscenity. The poet is evident, too, in images bearing the force of haunting epiphanies: a snake climbing a bell rope, tolling the bell, or the golden man that fascinates Ralegh—images standing as portents to the meaning of their lives.

Nye's most complete synthesis of poetry and prose, reality and magic, comes in *Merlin*. Merlin's story is at one time the record of his thoughts and of events at Arthur's court. Thus, we see the power of magic in operation: images conceived in the magician's mind are passed through a web of word and spell, fantasy and suggestion, to take root in the characters' lives. The energy which charges his magic is that of sexual desire: 'an erotic nerve below everything, a source for all manner of imaginations and enchantments'.

Merlin shows most vividly the erotic energy which emerges in sexual fantasy in many of Nye's novels. Merlin argues that words hold the essence of the thing they name, while his father, the devil, says 'everything is a book'. Nye's reverence for words emerges in delight in verbal play and parody, in a story simply about the marginalia of a rare first edition, and in Ralegh's famous act of chivalry with his cloak, which he describes as a 'poem'.

—Edmund Cusick

OATES, Joyce Carol. American. 1938—. See 2nd edition, 1990.

O'BRIAN, Patrick.
Nationality: British. **Relations:** married Mary in 1940s. **Education:** studied Classics and Philosophy in England and France in 1930s. **Career:** full-time writer. Lives in Roussillon, France. **Address:** c/o HarperCollins, 77–85 Fulham Palace Road, Hammersmith, London W6 8JB, England.

ROMANCE AND HISTORICAL PUBLICATIONS

Novels (series: Jack Aubrey and Stephen Maturin)

Three Bear Witness. London, Secker and Warburg, 1952; as *Testimonies*, New York, Harcourt Brace, 1952.
The Catalans. New York, Harcourt Brace, 1953; as *The Frozen Flame*, London, Hart Davis, 1953.
The Road to Samarcand. London, Hart Davis, 1954.
The Golden Ocean. London, Hart Davis, 1956; New York, Day, 1957; revised edition, London, Macmillan, 1970.
The Unknown Shore. London, Hart Davis, 1959.
Richard Temple. London, Macmillan, 1962.
Aubrey and Maturin:
  1. *Master and Commander*. Philadelphia, Lippincott, 1969; London, Collins, 1970.
  2. *Post Captain*. London, Collins, 1972.
  3. *HMS Surprise*. London, Collins, and Philadelphia, Lippincott, 1973.
  4. *The Mauritius Command*. London, Collins, 1977; New York, Stein and Day, 1978.
  5. *Desolation Island*. London, Collins, 1978; New York, Stein and Day, 1979.
  6. *The Fortune of War*. London, Collins, 1979.
  7. *The Surgeon's Mate*. London, Collins, 1980.
  8. *The Ionian Mission*. London, Collins, 1981.

9. *Treason's Harbour*. London, Collins, 1983.
10. *The Far Side of the World*. London, Collins, 1984.
11. *The Reverse of the Medal*. London, Collins, 1986.
12. *The Letter of Marque*. London, Collins, 1988; New York, Norton, 1990.
13. *The Thirteen Gun Salute*. London, Collins, 1989; New York, Norton, 1991.
14. *The Nutmeg of Consolation*. London, HarperCollins, 1991.
15. *Clarissa Oakes*. London, HarperCollins, 1992; as *The True-love*, New York, Norton, 1992.
The Wine-Dark Sea. London, HarperCollins, 1993.

Short Stories

The Last Pool and Other Stories. London, Secker and Warburg, 1950.
The Walker and Other Stories. New York, Harcourt Brace, 1955; as *Lying in the Sun and Other Stories*, London, Hart Davis, 1956.
The Chian Wine and Other Stories. London, Collins, 1974.

OTHER PUBLICATIONS

Other

Men-of-War. London, Collins, 1974.
Pablo Ruiz Picasso: A Biography. London, Collins, 1976; as *Picasso: A Biography*, New York, Putnam, 1976.
Joseph Banks: A Life, with David R. Godine. London, Collins, 1987.

Editor, *A Book of Voyages*. London, Home and Van Thal, 1947.

Translator, *The Daily Life of the Aztecs on the Eve of the Spanish Conquest*, by Jacques Soustelle. London, Weidenfeld and Nicolson, 1961.
Translator, *Daily Life in Palestine at the Time of Christ*, by Daniel-Rops. London, Weidenfeld and Nicolson, 1962; as *Daily Life in the Time of Jesus*, New York, Hawthorn, 1962.
Translator, *St Bartholomew's Night: The Massacre of Saint Bartholomew*, by Philippe Erlanger. London, Weidenfeld and Nicolson, and New York, Pantheon, 1962.
Translator, *The Wreathed Head*, by Christine de Rivoyre. London, Hart Davis, 1962.
Translator, *From the New Freedom to the New Frontier: A History of the United States from 1912 to the Present*, by André Maurois. New York, McKay; as *A History of the USA: From Wilson to Kennedy*, London, Weidenfeld and Nicolson, 1964.
Translator, *A History of the USSR: From Lenin to Kruschchev*, by Louis Aragon. London, Weidenfeld and Nicolson, and New York, McKay, 1964.
Translator, *A Letter to Myself*, by Françoise Mallet-Joris. London, W.H. Allen, and New York, Farrar Straus, 1964.
Translator, *When the Earth Trembles*, by Haroun Tazieff. London, Hart Davis, and New York, Harcourt Brace, 1964.
Translator, *Munich; or, The Phoney Peace*, by Henri Noguères. London, Weidenfeld and Nicolson, 1965; as *Munich: Peace in Our Time*, New York, McGraw Hill, 1965.
Translator, *The Uncompromising Heart: A Life of Marie Mancini, Louis XIV's First Love*, by Françoise Mallet-Joris. London, W.H. Allen, and New York, Farrar Straus, 1966.
Translator, *A Very Easy Death*, by Simone de Beauvoir. London, Deutsch-Weidenfeld and Nicolson, and New York, Putnam, 1966.
Translator, *The Delights of Growing Old*, by Maurice Goudeket. New York, Farrar Straus, 1966; London, Joseph, 1967.

Translator, *The Italian Campaign*, by Michel Mohrt. London, Weidenfeld and Nicolson, and New York, Viking Press, 1967.
Translator, *Memoirs*, by Clara Malraux. London, Bodley Head, and New York, Farrar Straus, 1967.
Translator, *The Quicksand War: Prelude to Vietnam*, by Lucien Bodard. Boston, Little Brown, and London, Faber, 1967.
Translator, *The Horsemen*, by Joseph Kessel. London, Barker, and New York, Farrar Straus, 1968.
Translator, *Les Belles Images*, by Simone de Beauvoir. London, Collins, and New York, Putnam, 1968.
Translator, *Louis XVI; or, The End of a World*, by Bernard Faÿ. London, W.H.Allen, and Chicago, Regnery, 1968.
Translator, *The Woman Destroyed*, by Simone de Beauvoir. London, Collins, and New York, Putnam, 1969.
Translator, *The Japanese Challenge*, by Robert Guillian. Philadelphia, Lippincott, and London, Hamish Hamilton, 1970.
Translator, *A Life's Full Summer*, by André Martinerie. London, Collins, and New York, Harcourt Brace, 1970.
Translator, *Papillon* by Henri Charrière. London, Hart Davis, 1970.
Translator, *Old Age*, by Simone de Beauvoir. London, Deutsch-Weidenfeld and Nicolson, 1972; as *The Coming of Age*, New York, Putnam, 1972.
Translator, *The Assassination of Heydrich: 27 May 1942*, by Miroslav Ivanov. London, Hart Davis, 1973.
Translator, *Banco: Further Adventures of Papillon*, by Henri Charrière. London, Hart Davis, and New York, Morrow, 1973.
Translator, *All Said and Done*, by Simone de Beauvoir. London, Deutsch-Weidenfeld and Nicolson, and New York, Putnam, 1974.
Translator, *The Paths of the Sea*, by Pierre Schoendoerffer. London, Collins, 1977.
Translator, *Obsession: An American Love Story*, by Yves Berger. New York, Putnam, 1978.
Translator, *When Things of the Spirit Come First: Five Early Tales*, by Simone de Beauvoir. London, Deutsch-Weidenfeld and Nicolson, and New York, Pantheon, 1982.
Translator, *Adieux: A Farewell to Sartre*, by Simone de Beauvoir. London, Deutsch-Weidenfeld and Nicolson, and New York, Pantheon, 1984.

*

Bibliography: *Patrick O'Brian: A Bibliography of First Printings and First British Printings* by A. E. Cunningham, York, Thrommett, 1986.

*   *   *

Patrick O'Brian said in a note to *Master and Commander*, the first of his sequence of historical novels, 'When one is writing about the Royal Navy of the 18th and early-19th centuries it is difficult to avoid understatement; it is difficult to do full justice to one's subject, for so very often the improbable reality outruns fiction'.

As the series has progressed, the author has reiterated his sense of debt to the rich legacy of log-books, dispatches, letters, memoirs, and contemporary reports. 'All these ... form a wonderfully rich pasture, and one in which I have grazed with great pleasure this many a year'. But interesting stories and unexpected details about your chosen subject don't in themselves make a novel, and certainly not the elegant, witty, polished novels with which O'Brian regales his reader.

In two early novels, *The Golden Ocean* and *The Unknown Shore*, (both originally written for children, but wholly enjoyable for adults) some of the characteristics that particularize O'Brian's fiction can be seen. Both deal with Anson's circumnavigation of the world in 1740: in *The Golden Ocean*, we have the complete voyage, full of trials and tribulations but ending happily and successfully. *The Unknown Shore* is a darker book altogether, dealing with the *Wager*'s shipwreck, and the fearful problems of survival on the bleak and inhospitable coast of southern Chile.

The Unknown Shore is of particular interest, because the two chief characters are a prototype for another pair of friends. Jack Byron and Tobias Barrow, midshipman and surgeon's mate, might be in embryo the more developed and more colourful friends Jack Aubrey and Stephen Maturin, whose adventures now span 15 novels.

In *The Unknown Shore* midshipman Jack Byron is a historic person. 'Foulweather' Jack Byron ended up as an admiral, and was the poet Byron's grandfather. His early adventures make thrilling reading, but O'Brian did not continue them in a fictional form. Can one guess that it proved not entirely satisfactory to have to bend a narrative round the rigidity of known fact? That's a problem that has exercised many a writer.

Jack Aubrey, one of the heroes of O'Brian's major novel sequence, being fictional, is more flexible. His exploits bear more than a passing resemblance to the real-life actions of Lord Cochrane (later Earl of Dundonald). For example, in *Master and Commander*, Jack takes his 14-gun *Sophie* into action against the 32-gun Spanish xebecfrigate *Cacafuego* and wins—just as Cochrane captured the *Gamo* with his *Speedy*. Jack is brought to trial (in *The Reverse of the Medal*) for a fraud on the stock exchange, as Cochrane was in 1816. But Cochrane was imprisoned for a year, and spent the rest of his life trying to prove his innocence. O'Brian uses the pain and distress Jack experiences on being ejected from the navy he loves to good effect: we are introduced to the twilight world of the private ship of war in *The Letter of Marque*, and see something of the plotting, intrigues, and squalid in-fighting of politicians when faced with undeniable proof that an innocent man has been found guilty. When Jack's heroism wins him his longed-for reinstatement (*The Thirteen Gun Salute*) we share his joy.

Stephen Maturin, Jack's close friend, is a remarkable creation. He may have his antecedents in Tobias Barrow, a dedicated natural philosopher brought up on a unique educational principle, but he far surpasses Tobias. Stephen is a physician (rare enough by land, exceptional at sea), a man of wide interests, well-read, cultured, and highly intelligent. His work as a naval surgeon is fascinating, his work as an intelligence agent adds an extra dimension to the plots, for we see not only the tension and danger of that important, lonely profession, but also the political in-fighting and bungling of the vying intelligence services in Whitehall and overseas. Stephen is, however, an outsider in naval matters—at least insofar as they involve actually sailing ships. His attempts to enlighten himself allow us, the readers, to discover what is going on—a simple but effective way of explaining some notoriously obscure activities!

Stephen is at home on land as Jack is not, and one of the most interesting features of the books is the changing balance of the relationship between the two men from sea to shore. At sea Jack is in his element; he is knowledgable, competent, and absolutely to be trusted. On land he is gullible and vulnerable, and it is usually Stephen who rescues him from his troubles, whether emotional entanglement, debt, projectors, or political conspiracy.

The friendship between the two is a fascinating relationship between complete opposites: it is made the more believable because it is often strained. This is most clearly seen when they both contend for Diana Villiers in *Post Captain*. Jack draws off and finally marries his first love, Diana Villiers's cousin Sophie Williams, but Diana remains as a sensitive area between them. Stephen seems doomed to unhappiness: his persistent devotion to Diana causes him to abuse himself by taking laudanum to endure the torment of his emotions. Even when he succeeds in marrying Diana there is no major change in his circumstances, for Diana yearns for more fulfilment in her life than the world can offer her. In *Clarissa Oakes* (*The*

Truelove in USA), we learn that all is not well with Diana at home. Stephen, in the South Pacific, must wait patiently for news of his tempestuous wife, and so must the reader. The length of time that letters or other communications take to reach their destination is one of the small details that mark the vast difference between O'Brian's period and our own.

O'Brian is an urbane, well-informed writer: intelligent and expecting intelligence from his readers. His stories embrace broad sweeps of canvas, very richly detailed. One incident from a novel by O'Brian might form the entire plot of another author's book. He is familiar with the smallest details of the construction and sailing methods of ships of the period, but is also at home in many other areas, including literature, natural history, medicine, philosophy, politics, law, and the classics. This erudition is leavened by a strong sense of humour, which is one of the most engaging features of his writing. He falls easily and fluently into speech patterns that are completely of their period, he can describe a technical operation, or a storm at sea, a soirée, or a single-ship engagement, and never waver or falter. He is there, and so are we. For first-class adventure in the days of Nelson's navy, O'Brian's books can be unhesitatingly recommended. However, each book is so much more than simple adventure that the reader who embarks upon them can be assured of a rich and unforgettable experience.

—Felicity Trotman

O'BRIEN, Kate.
Nationality: Irish. **Born:** Limerick, Ireland, 3 December 1897. **Education:** Laurel Hill Convent, Limerick, 1903–15; University College, Dublin, from 1916. **Relations:** married the Dutch journalist, Gustaaf Renier, in 1923 (separated after a few months). **Career:** staff journalist, the Manchester *Guardian*, during World War I; teacher at a convent school, Hampstead, London, 1920–21; governess, Bilbao, Spain, 1922–23; secretary, London, 1924–26; freelance writer from 1926; journalist, Bilbao, in 1930s. Lived in England until 1949, Galway, Ireland, 1950–64, and Boughton, Kent, 1965–74. **Recipient**: James Tait Black memorial prize, 1932, and Hawthornden prize, 1932, both for *Without My Cloak*. Fellow, Royal Society of Literature, 1947. **Member:** Irish Academy of Letters. **Died:** 13 August 1974.

ROMANCE AND HISTORICAL PUBLICATIONS

Novels

Without My Cloak. London, Heinemann, and New York, Doubleday Doran, 1931.
The Ante-Room. London, Heinemann, and New York, Doubleday Doran, 1934.
Mary Lavelle. London, Heinemann, and New York, Doubleday Doran, 1936.
Pray for the Wanderer. London, Heinemann, and New York, Doubleday Doran, 1938.
The Land of Spices. London, Heinemann, and New York, Doubleday Doran, 1941.
The Last of Summer. London, Heinemann, and New York, Doubleday Doran, 1943.
That Lady. London, Heinemann, 1946; New York, Harper, 1949; as *For One Sweet Grape*, New York, Doubleday, 1946.
The Flower of May. London, Heinemann, and New York, Harper, 1953.
As Music and Splendour. London, Heinemann, and New York, Harper, 1958.

OTHER PUBLICATIONS

Plays

Distinguished Villa (produced London, 1926). London, Benn, 1926.
The Bridge (produced London, 1927).
The Ante-Room, with W.A. Carot and Geoffrey Gomer, from the novel by O'Brien (produced London, 1936).
The Schoolroom Window (produced London, 1937).
The Last of Summer, with John Perry, from the novel by O'Brien (produced London, 1944).
That Lady: A Romantic Drama, from the novel by O'Brien (produced London, 1949).

Other

Farewell, Spain (travel). London, Heinemann, and New York, Doubleday Doran, 1937.
English Diaries and Journals. London, Collins, 1943.
Teresa of Avila. London, Parrish, and New York, Sheed and Ward, 1951.
My Ireland. London, Batsford, 1962.
Presentation Parlour (autobiography). London, Heinemann, 1963.

*

Film Adaptations: *That Lady*, 1955.

Critical Studies: *Kate O'Brien: A Literary Portrait* by L. Reynolds, Scottsdale, Arizona, B. and M. Exports, 1987; *O'Brien: A Critical Study* by Adele M. Dalsimer, Dublin, Gill and Macmillan, 1990.

*   *   *

Arguably one of the first female writers to promote female autonomy and sexual freedom in Irish literature, Kate O'Brien exposes the frustrations of middle- and upper-class women who, while part of the leisured classes, were trapped within suffocating traditional domestic life-roles. Evocative in her analysis of the texture of women's lives, O'Brien focuses on love—and inevitably the failure of that love by oppressive family and social forces—as a means of self-enlightenment and definition.

O'Brien based the majority of her novels in Ireland, and a fictionalized Limerick—known as Mellick—provides both an historical and social backdrop for her characters, and a metaphor for a complacent Ireland that O'Brien felt had betrayed her as an artist and a woman. Her first novel, *Without My Cloak*, deals most obviously with the Irish conventions that O'Brien raged against. She depicts a wealthy Catholic merchant class that has survived the Irish famine and bettered itself to the point of over-indulgence and deep dissatisfaction. The love affairs of brother and sister Denis and Caroline Considine are both destructive and fruitless: Caroline falls in love with a wealthy Protestant Londoner, yet her identity has only ever been as a Catholic wife of 20 years to her husband Jim. Although we learn little of her lover, Richard Fronde, O'Brien suggests that both he and the constricting moral codes of society deny her any real romantic passion. Her brother, Denis, although only physically attracted to his illegitimate peasant lover, also retracts his love and succumbs to a socially respectable lifestyle.

O'Brien's second work, *The Ante-Room*, set in Mellick in 1880, picks up the threads of *Without My Cloak* as Agnes Mulqueen fails to discommunicate herself from her family and country by renouncing her love; her faith is ultimately seen as a regressive and repressive force. In this book, O'Brien begins to conceptualize and internalize the main themes and conventions of Irish society within her characters, so that they take on a striking power and presence.

Published in 1938, *Pray for the Wanderer* is a vitriolic attack by O'Brien on the deepening conservatism of Ireland at a time of European political unrest. Matt Costello, a successful writer living in London, returns to Mellick after a failed love affair anticipating emotional restoration within the comfort of his brother's family home. O'Brien initially juxtaposes the uncertain political undercurrents of the Oxford Group, communists, and fascists in fashionable London with the apparent fecundity and renewing spirit of Ireland. Tom's family is the epitome of a Catholic family in 1930s Ireland: Una, his wife, is pretty, plump, passive; content with her lifestyle and abundant children. Una is O'Brien's only positive domestic female character—even the mother-figure, Hannah, in *The Last of Summer* is depicted as greedy, self-centred, and resentful, perverting her son Tom's affection so that he is tied inexorably to her. Ironically, Una's relationship with her husband is viewed as merely a 'happy accident of match-making'. Una's sister Nell represents the 'new' Irish woman. Self-supporting, she smokes and drives her own car, but when Matt seeks consolation by proposing, Nell only expresses old values in a new way. She denies herself a route out of her stultifying lifestyle because Matt does not love her completely. Matt realizes that it is the suffocating charms of Mellick, rather than his failed affair, that overcomes him with its intolerance of his autonomy as a writer, and its censorship of his work.

This direct attack by O'Brien parallels the Irish banning of her book *Mary Lavelle* in 1938. At a time when the rest of Europe was in the midst of pre-war political upheavals, her irritation as a creative writer with a lethargic and isolated Ireland increased, despite her empathy for Irish Nationalism.

Written in 1936, on the eve of the Spanish Civil War, *Mary Lavelle* signifies a move away from the confines of Ireland to the freedom and individualism of Spain. Ireland and Spain are personified by Mary's complacent fiancé, and her passionate lover. Her self-awakening at a bullfight provides the central core to the book, as well as signifying the social issues and violence that confronted modern Spain. The sexual passion and beauty of *Mary Lavelle* were not expounded so openly again. Her subsequent heroines are strong, independent women afflicted by the confines or failures of society.

Also set in Spain, *That Lady* is based on the historical figure Ana de Mendoza, a friend of Philip II, and her affair with his secretary Don Antonio Perez. Ana is one of O'Brien's most forceful characters, already a self-assured woman as the book begins, but what starts as a light-hearted dalliance with Perez soon turns into a passionate love affair. Perez, a confirmed agnostic, lives the very life of indulgence and sensual pleasure and he releases basic emotions in Ana that she, as a refined noble woman, has been taught to suppress. Philip, the tortured, dutiful Catholic who loses touch with his people by taking on the sins of the world, is angered by their affair and maliciously destroys their love and lives. Through the increasing physical limitations and restricted lifestyle of Ana, the diseased, withering nation of Spain is played out—two mistresses fighting to retain their dignity while their power is eroded by one weak, obsessed man. Ana finally wins the battle: in having to reject the world, she liberates her inner self and ultimately becomes free.

Family ties and religion again feature in *The Land of Spices* and *The Flower of May*, but the failure of men to provide a stable, loving relationship—either by dying or by deception—causes the female relationships between Helen Archer and Anna, and Fanny Morrow and Lucille, to appear far stronger and more satisfying than those between men and women.

Such profound, unexplained relationships between women are exposed in O'Brien's final work, *As Music and Splendour*, in which she openly defies the taboos of her time by writing of lesbian feelings and female autonomy. As Clare Halvey and Rose Lennane pursue their operatic careers through Europe, O'Brien 'normalizes' their developing relationship with references to their potential fate in Ireland; of Clare quelling flesh and spirit as a nun, and of Rose lapsing into the role of a traditional Irish wife.

Ultimately, this book conveys a message that is present in all O'Brien's work; that it is possible for women to choose freely in life and love while still maintaining their own integrity.

—Susannah Steel

———

O'FAOLAIN, Julia.

Also writes as Julia Martines. **Nationality:** Irish. **Born:** London, England, 6 June 1932; daughter of the writer Sean O'Faolain. **Education:** Sacred Heart Convent, Dublin, B.A. in 1952, in French and Italian, M.A. in 1953; University of Rome; the Sorbonne, Paris. **Relations:** married Lauro Martines in 1957; one son. **Career:** translator, Council of Europe; supply teacher and cook, London, 1955–57; instructor in French, Reed College, Portland, Oregon, and teacher, Italian evening classes, Portland State University, 1957–61; teacher, Scuola Interpreti, Florence, 1962–65. Lives in London. **Recipient:** Arts Council of Great Britain bursary, 1981. **Agent:** Deborah Rogers, Rogers Coleridge and White Ltd, 20 Powis Mews, London, W11 1JN, England; or, International Creative Management, 40 West 57th Street, New York, New York 10010, USA.

ROMANCE AND HISTORICAL PUBLICATIONS

Novels

Woman in the Wall. London, Faber, and New York, Viking Press, 1975.
No Country for Young Men. London, Allen Lane, 1980; New York, Carroll and Graf, 1987.
The Obedient Wife. London, Allen Lane, 1982; New York, Carroll and Graf, 1985.
The Irish Signorina. London, Viking, 1984; Bethesda, Maryland, Adler, 1986.
The Judas Cloth. London, Sinclair Stevenson, 1992.
The Heather Blazing. London, Picador, 1992.

OTHER PUBLICATIONS

Novels

Godded and Codded. London, Faber, 1970; as *Three Lovers*, New York, Coward McCann, 1971.

Short Stories

We Might See Sights! and Other Stories. London, Faber, 1968.
Man in the Cellar. London, Faber, 1974.
Melancholy Baby and Other Stories. Dublin, Poolbeg Press, 1978.
Daughters of Passion. London, Penguin, 1982.

Other

Editor, with Lauro Martines, *Not in God's Image: Women in History from the Greeks to the Victorians.* London, Temple Smith, and New York, Harper, 1973.

Translator (as Julia Martines), *Two Memoirs of Renaissance Florence: The Diaries of Buonaccorso Pitti and Gregori Dati*, edited by Gene Brucker. New York, Harper, 1967.

Translator, *A Man of Parts*, by Piero Chiara. Boston, Little, Brown, 1968.

*

Critical Studies: *Two Decades of Irish Writing*, edited by Douglas Dunn, Manchester, Carcanet, and Philadelphia, Dufour, 1975; *Irish Women Writers* by Ann Owens Weekes, Lexington, University Press of Kentucky, 1990.

*   *   *

The Introductory Note of Julia O'Faolain's second novel, *Woman in the Wall* introduces fragmentation as an issue in the book:

Almost all the characters in this story lived in Gaul 13 centuries ago and left behind odd, slivered images of themselves. I have tried to put these together as one might, taking a few surviving sherds, try for shape of a lost and curious pot . . .

My setting is the Wild West of an age often called 'Dark'. It was a world as fissile and fragmented as our own and its end was often thought to be in sight. Unlike ourselves, thinking people then did not embrace the fragmentary quality of experience but reacted by trying to contain bolting certitudes under grids of inflexible belief. They have longed for coherence. In retelling this story, I too have tried for it. But it is, I repeat, a story.

Fragmentation is both a central literary technique, and an essential topic in O'Faolain's work.

This interest in the fragmentary is very much a modernist one, which sees the fragmented narrative as the only way of representing genuine personal experience, but also as a disturbing sign of a lack of wholeness in the world. This is as much the case in her novel about sixth-century Gaul as it is in her novels about 19th-century Italy, and 20th-century Ireland. A second notable feature in her fiction (which is suggested by O'Faolain's choice of settings and themes) is the sense of Europe having a continuous shared Catholic heritage and philosophy. A profound (if often sceptical) interest in the promise of wholeness contained in Catholicism as a system of belief, underlies the concern with the fragmentary nature of actual experience.

Thus, *Woman in the Wall* is concerned with a group of women who attempt to achieve in this life a wholeness lacking in the unstable and murderous world of the Frankish kingdoms. Radegunda, a Frankish queen, leaves her husband, Clotair, to become a nun and to found a convent. Her motivation can be seen clearly in her past: Radegunda was forcibly married to Clotair after he killed her family in a raid; she wishes to escape the only world she has experience of—one in which women are raped, captured, or killed, and in which the male members of their families reciprocate in the same way, thus perpetuating an endless cycle of violence. However, escape from this world is not that simple. The novel traces the internal and external pressures on the convent which make the retreat from worldliness temporary and incomplete. Some of these pressures are simply external (the threat of marauding armies, the interference of hostile kings), but others arise in the apparently safe haven of the convent itself, and bring in aspects of the outside world. Love, jealousy, and violence exist in both worlds: the abbess Agnes craves and finds love but is forced to renounce it when she enters the convent, and Radegunda's own spiritual vision becomes increasingly physical as she begins to torture her own body. Moreover, when Radegunda's visions tell her that the convent must be used for the greater glory of God, she becomes involved in the planned overthrow of a Frankish king by a group of bishops—eventually this leads to the convent's destruction.

However, the character who epitomizes the ultimately destructive nature of the withdrawal into a wholly defined space is the nun Ingunda (the illegitimate daughter of abbess Agnes). After taking a vow to become an anchorite, Ingunda has herself walled up. This act is praised by her community as an example of spiritual courage, but in fact Ingunda's motivation is a wish to atone for the sin of her own birth. The novel opens with Ingunda's thoughts as she sits in her prison:

The mad cannot sin.
Darkness chews at my brain. Chinks multiply. It seeps in.

Thus Radegunda's attempt to construct a safe and wholly regulated world becomes for Ingunda a madhouse where all freedom is denied.

It is far from incidental that the narrative of *Woman in the Wall* is fragmentary and chronologically disordered. Despite the idea of wholeness there can be no experience of integration for either the characters or the reader, since the convent itself is in the end part of the fragmentation which it eschews.

Both *No Country for Young Men* (set in modern Eire) and *The Judas Cloth* (set in 19th-century Italy) share the relation of the systematic and public to the personal and fragmentary (in the first book there is also a character who, like Ingunda, has been put into a convent both to protect her and to imprison her). However, the world created in both of these novels is different. Each novel deploys a brilliantly varied range of distinctive voices to create a sense of the 'odd slivered images of themselves' which each character has to assert as his/her only way of claiming some kind of personal integrity in worlds which deny any possibility of a complete and transparent narrative.

—Chris Hopkins

OGILVIE, Elisabeth (May).
Nationality: American. **Born:** 20 May 1917. **Education:** North Quincy High School, Massachusetts. Lives in Cushing, Maine. **Agent:** Watkins/Loomis Agency, 133 East 35th Street, New York, New York 10016. **Address:** c/o Down East Books, PO Box 679, Camden, Maine 04843, USA.

ROMANCE AND HISTORICAL PUBLICATIONS

Novels (series: Jennie)

High Tide at Noon. New York, Crowell, 1944; London, Harrap, 1945.
Storm Tide. New York, McGraw Hill, 1945; London, Harrap, 1947.
Honeymoon (novelization of screenplay). New York, Bartholomew House, 1947.
The Ebbing Tide. New York, Crowell, 1947; London, Harrap, 1948.
Rowan Head. New York, McGraw Hill, 1949; London, Harrap, 1950.
The Dawning of the Day. New York, McGraw Hill, 1954.
No Evil Angel. New York, McGraw Hill, 1956; London, Harrap, 1957.
The Witch Door. New York, McGraw Hill, 1959; London, W.H. Allen, 1961.
Call Home the Heart. New York, McGraw Hill, 1962.
There May Be Heaven. New York, McGraw Hill, 1966.
The Seasons Hereafter. New York, McGraw Hill, 1966.
Waters on a Starry Night. New York, McGraw Hill, 1968.
Bellwood. New York, McGraw Hill, 1969.

The Face of Innocence. New York, McGraw Hill, 1970.
A Theme for Reason. New York, McGraw Hill, 1970.
Weep and Know Why. New York, McGraw Hill, 1972.
Strawberries in the Sea. New York, McGraw Hill, 1973.
Image of a Lover. New York, McGraw Hill, 1974.
Where the Lost Aprils Are. New York, McGraw Hill, 1975.
The Dreaming Swimmer. New York, McGraw Hill, 1976.
An Answer in the Tide. New York, McGraw Hill, 1978.
A Dancer in Yellow. New York, McGraw Hill, 1979.
The Devil in Tartan. New York, McGraw Hill, 1980.
The Silent Ones. New York, McGraw Hill, 1981; Bath, Chivers, 1983.
The Road to Nowhere. New York, McGraw Hill, 1983.
Jennie About to Be. New York, McGraw Hill, 1984.
The World of Jennie G. New York, McGraw Hill, 1986.
The Summer of the Osprey. New York, McGraw Hill, 1987.
When the Music Stopped. New York, McGraw Hill, 1989.
Jennie Glenroy. Maine, Down East, 1993.

OTHER PUBLICATIONS

Other (for children)

My World Is an Island (for adults; reminiscences). New York, McGraw Hill, 1950; London, Harrap, 1951.
Whistle for a Wind: Maine 1820. New York, Scribner, 1954.
Blueberry Summer. New York, McGraw Hill, 1956.
The Fabulous Year. New York, McGraw Hill, 1958.
How Wide the Heart. New York, McGraw Hill, 1959.
The Young Islanders. New York, McGraw Hill, 1960.
Becky's Island. New York, McGraw Hill, 1961.
Turn Around Twice. New York, McGraw Hill, 1962; as *Mystery on Hopkins Island*, 1966.
Ceiling of Amber. New York, McGraw Hill, 1964.
Masquerade at Sea House. New York, McGraw Hill, 1965.
The Pigeon Pair. New York, McGraw Hill, 1967.
Come Aboard and Bring Your Dory. New York, McGraw Hill, 1969; as *Nobody's Knows about Tomorrow*, London, Heinemann, 1971.
Too Young to Know. London, Hippo, 1983.

*   *   *

Elisabeth Ogilvie is a writer in love with landscape. Her passion has been primarily directed toward the coastal islands of Maine, although she has extended it to England, and to her ancestral home of Scotland in her recent works. Her descriptions of the physical surroundings of her novels are so detailed and portrait-like that the setting almost becomes another character. By the final chapter of each of her books one is so minutely acquainted with every mood and view of the environment that one could be transported to that place and never feel lost. This sensitivity to scene gives these novels an immediacy and reality not often found in romantic novels today.

It is easy to call Ogilvie's works romantic novels; it is not easy to characterize them more specifically as each of her many works is different. Some, like *The Devil in Tartan*, could be classified as gothics, while others, like *A Dancer in Yellow*, are nearly pure suspense. Many of her books are not classifiable beyond the feeling that a thread of romance binds the plot together. Her plots are rich and complex but at the same time easy for the reader to follow. The characters are as vivid as the settings. One feels that these people have lives apart from the span of time covered in the book, that the novel is merely a fascinating slice of a larger life. This feeling is reinforced by the author's ability to use the same characters in a later work as is the case with *Weep and Know Why*, *The Dreaming Swimmer*, and

The Summer of the Osprey. She repeats this success with her historical novels *Jennie About to Be* and *The World of Jennie G*. The successive works might be called sequels, but they are stronger than mere sequels with none of the flavour of afterthought. Ogilvie is an author who observes and notices; her eye for detail is unerring. For this reason, she is skilled at evoking sudden menace in everyday situations. In such works as *The Summer of the Osprey* and *The Road to Nowhere* the secrets that people try to keep and the failure of communication between even the closest people show how life can suddenly change for worse as well as for better.

Even Ogilvie's use of the elements of romance cannot be described in general terms. Often her books conclude at a point that may be the germination of a romantic relationship rather than its culmination. She has also chosen, in the series beginning with *Weep and Know Why*, to follow a romance from earliest courtship through comfortable married life. Yet there is no emphasis here on happy endings, nor does culmination automatically bring happiness. Her characters must work hard to make their relationships work; sometimes the relationships are not of their own choosing (as in the Jennie books) but are expedient for one reason or another.

If there is an area of consistency in these novels it is in the characters of the heroes. Ogilvie seems to admire the taciturn, unemotional male who is deeply sensitive beneath a terse exterior. This is not to say that these men lack individuality or realism. Rather it seems that the writer began with a general type and fleshed him out to meet the demands of the story. These men are consistent with their stations in life. Ogilvie does not focus on people of glamour, so sophistication and wit would be jarring characteristics to find in her heroes. Instead, they are workers and survivors, men to lean on. If the heroines do not lean on them very often it is because they are formed by the same forces that shaped their men. They must be strong rather than clinging to survive.

Perhaps the strongest appeal to the reader in Ogilvie's work is the ordinariness of her characters. Even the pseudo-Egyptian princess of *The Face of Innocence* is a normal girl grown into an unremarkable wife and mother. It is the sudden twistings and rearranging of the common events of life that give rise to the plots. One can identify with these everyday people as they deal with upheavals that may be frightening but are also somehow familiar.

—Susan Quinn Berneis

O'GRADY, Rohan. Canadian. 1922—. See 2nd edition, 1990.

OLDFIELD, Pamela.
Born: London, in 1931. Relations: one son and one daughter. Career: teacher and secretary. Lives in Kent. Address: c/o Michael Joseph Ltd, 27 Wright's Lane, London W8 5TZ, England.

ROMANCE AND HISTORICAL PUBLICATIONS

Novels (series: Heron Saga; Kent Trilogy)

Heron Saga:
 The Rich Earth. London, Futura, 1980.
 This Ravished Land. London, Futura, 1980.
 After the Storm. London, Futura, 1981.
 White Water. London, Futura, 1982.
Kent Trilogy:
 Green Harvest. London, Century Hutchinson, 1983.
 Summer Song. London, Century Hutchinson, 1984.

Golden Tally. London, Century Hutchinson, 1985.
The Gooding Girl. London, Century Hutchinson, 1985.
The Stationmaster's Daughter. London, Century Hutchinson, 1986.
Lily Golightly. London, Century Hutchinson, 1987.
The Turn of the Tide. London, Century Hutchinson, 1988.
A Dutiful Wife. London, Joseph, 1989.
Sweet Sally Lunn. London, Joseph, 1990.
The Halliday Girls. London, Joseph, 1991.
Long Dark Summer. London, Joseph, 1992.
The Passionate Exile. London, Joseph, 1993.

OTHER PUBLICATIONS (for children)

Other

Melanie Brown Goes to School. London, Faber, 1970.
Melanie Brown Climbs a Tree. London, Faber, 1972.
Melanie Brown and the Jar of Sweets. London, Faber, 1974.
The Halloween Pumpkin. London, Hodder and Stoughton, 1974; Chicago, Children's Press, 1976.
The Adventures of Sarah and Theodore Bodgitt. Leicester, Brockhampton Press, 1974.
Simon's Extra Gran. London, Knight, 1974; Chicago, Children's Press, 1976.
A Witch in the Summer House. London, Hodder and Stoughton, 1976.
The Terribly Plain Princess and Other Stories. London, Hodder and Stoughton, 1977.
The Adventures of the Gumby Gang. London, Blackie, 1978.
The Gumby Gang Again. London, Blackie, 1978.
Katy and Dom. Brighton, Angus and Robertson, 1978.
Children of the Plague. London, Hamish Hamilton, 1979.
More About the Gumby Gang. London, Blackie, 1979.
The Princess May-I-Well. London, Hodder and Stoughton, 1979.
The Gumby Gang Strikes Again. London, Blackie, 1980.
The Rising of the Wain. London, Abelard, 1980.
The Riverside Cat. London, Hamish Hamilton, 1980.
Cloppity. London, Hamish Hamilton, 1981.
The Willerbys and the Burglar [*Haunted Mill, Old Castle, Sad Clown, Bank Robbers, Mystery Man*]. London, Blackie, 6 vols, 1981–84.
Parkin's Storm. London, Abelard, 1982.
The Gumby Gang on Holiday. London, Blackie, 1983.
Tommy Dobbie and the Witch-Next-Door. London, Hodder and Stoughton, 1983.
Ghost Stories. London, Blackie, 1984.
Barnaby Bell and the Lost Button. London, Piccadilly, 1985.
Barnaby Bell and the Birthday Cake. London, Piccadilly, 1985.
The Christmas Ghost. London, Blackie, 1985.
Ginger's Nine Lives. London, Blackie, 1986.
The Return of the Gumby Gang. London, Blackie, 1986.
Toby and the Donkey. London, Methuen, 1986.
The Ghosts of Bellering Oast. London, Blackie, 1987.
Spine Chillers. London, Blackie, 1987.
Stories from Ancient Greece. London, Kingfisher, 1988; as *Tales from Ancient Greece*, New York, Doubleday, 1989.
Sam, Sue and Cinderella. London, Methuen, 1989.
Bomb Alert. London, Armada, 1989.
Secret Persuader. London, Armada, 1989.
A Shaggy Dog Story. London, Blackie, 1990.
The Mill Pond Ghost. London, HarperCollins, 1993.
The Haunting of Wayne. London, HarperCollins, 1993.
The Haunting of Briggs. London, HarperCollins, 1993.

Editor, *Helter Skelter: Stories for Six-Year-Olds*. London, Blackie, 1983.

Editor, *Hurdy Gurdy*. London, Blackie, 1984; as *Merry-Go-Round: Stories for Seven-Year-Olds*, Sevenoaks, Kent, Knight, 1985.
Editor, *Roller Coaster*. London, Blackie, 1986.

* * *

The novels of Pamela Oldfield inhabit a world midway between historical fiction and family saga. In most of her works, the Tudor or Edwardian setting and the often precise chronology are far outweighed by such gothic elements as inheritance and scandal, illicit passion, and violent death. Oldfield fixes on individual lives, sketching in the movement of history behind them. Her first important novel-sequence—*The Rich Earth, This Ravished Land, After the Storm*, and *White Water*—has been collectively titled the 'Heron Saga'. Although these novels cover the period from Henry VII's accession to Elizabeth I's war with Spain, the 'Heron Saga' is far from being a portrayal of the Tudor age; rather, it chronicles four successive generations of the Kendal family, owners of the Heron estate and its tin-mining concerns in Devonshire, recounting their lives, their loves and deaths. Drama and tragedy stalk through the work, with the various protagonists dogged by witchcraft, madness, murder, and guilt. Historic events—the Dissolution of the Monasteries, the sinking of the *Mary Rose*—impinge fleetingly on the story, but are secondary to the fortunes of the Kendals throughout. The 'Heron Saga' is a fast-moving, exciting sequence of novels which are best judged not as historical works, but as excellent examples of their own particular hybrid genre.

The trilogy of novels set in the hopfields of turn-of-the-century Kent—*Green Harvest, Summer Song*, and *Golden Tally*—marks a substantial advance on the 'Heron Saga' in every respect. Charting the rise of her heroine, Vinnie Harris, from a childhood in the Whitechapel slums to wealth and happiness as mistress of the Foxearth estate, Oldfield achieves greater depth of characterization and captures the sense of the period more effectively than in previous works. Personalities rather than events remain in the foreground, but the social atmosphere of the 1890s and 1900s is presented with conviction, and there are some fine descriptive scenes. Though melodramatic incidents occur, their frequency is less than in the 'Heron Saga', and is more than balanced by the periods of domestic routine. While there are a number of fortuitous deaths, and at times an overabundance of minor characters and sub-plots, the 'Kent Trilogy' brings the people and their age memorably to life, and must be counted as one of Oldfield's finest achievements.

The Stationmaster's Daughter and *The Gooding Girl*, set in Kent in the early part of the 20th century, once more combine an authentic re-creation of their period with the gothic drama of scandal and inheritance. The former describes the emergence of Amy Turner, daughter of the stationmaster in a remote country district, as a fulfilled individual and a successful writer, and incorporates the customary lust, suicide, and violent death. *The Gooding Girl*, the most modern of Oldfield's novels in that it covers the first three decades of this century, is the story of Julia Coulsden, heiress of a fishing business, and evokes a picture of life in the Kentish fishing towns of the period. Though perhaps overlong, both novels succeed on their own terms, and manage an effective blend of drama and domesticity.

Lily Golightly tells the story of a parson's daughter who follows her husband to the goldfields of California in 1849. The rigours of her journey with a wagon train across the wilds of America are ably described by the author, who creates a strong, interesting narrative and a group of living characters with whom the reader identifies at once. *Lily Golightly* is one of the most impressive of Oldfield's works, and once more emphasizes the ironic fact that her sense of history is most convincing in those works nearest to our own time. The standard is more than maintained in her most recent writings, where strength of social background matches that of her characters

and themes. *The Halliday Girls* follows the varied fortunes of three sisters and their feckless, racehorse-owning father during the 1890s, while *The Turn of the Tide* presents a compelling household romance between master and nurse which takes place in the years 1911–12, and has the sinking of the *Titanic* as its climax. In *A Dutiful Wife*, Oldfield explores the Victorian world of match workers, factory disputes, philanthropy, and sensational journalism as a background to her story, where a doctor's marital fidelity leads him to crime. The author's research into the life of the Victorian age shows plainly in her description of the strike by women workers at the Bryant and May match factory, the horrifying details of the lethal 'phossy jaw' suffered by a matchgirl, and her portrait of the brash American reporter Jeff Bannerman, while her central theme of love and murder compels the reader's attention. Perhaps most interesting of all are *Sweet Sally Lunn* and *Long Dark Summer*, in which Oldfield successfully delves back into the 17th century in a way she has never done before, to create two of her most memorable novels. The former describes the adventures of Solange Luyon, a Huguenot refugee from persecution in France, who takes up residence in Bath, and who, as Sally Lunn, earns lasting fame with the teacakes that still bear her name. Sally's life in Georgian Bath, her involvement with the notorious Beau Nash, and her eventual success, are convincingly portrayed. *Long Dark Summer* is, if anything, even better. Her story of a woman betrayed by a faithless husband, who is left alone to safeguard her family at the time of the Great Plague of London, ranks among her finest work, and brings this terrible year alive on the page. Oldfield's authentic presentation of the folklore connected with the Plague, the futile remedies, the 'protective clothing' of the physicians, lends solidarity and depth to the powerful narrative. With *Sweet Sally Lunn* and *Long Dark Summer* she has made her most impressive forays into the distant past, and may well continue this exploration in future novels.

—Geoffrey Sadler

OLIVER, Marina (Yvonne).
Pseudonyms: Vesta Hathaway; Donna Hunt; Sally James; Yvonne Oliver; Bridget Thorn. **Nationality:** British. **Born:** Marina Yvonne Stroud, Walsall, 18 December 1934. **Education:** Queen Mary's High School, Walsall; Keele University, 1953–57. **Relations:** married Christopher Brookes Oliver, in 1958; three daughters, and one son. **Career:** lecturer, various further education colleges, 1966–81; treasurer, 1986–91, chair, Romantic Novelists Association, 1991–93. **Agent:** Sally Molloy, A.M. Heath and Co Ltd, 79 St Martin's Lane, London WC2N 4AA, England. **Address:** Half Hidden, West Lane, Bledlow, Princes Risborough, Buckinghamshire, HP27 9PF, England.

Romance and Historical Publications

Novels (series: Lord Hugo)

Cavalier Courtship. London, Hale, 1974.
Restoration Affair. London, Hale, 1975.
A Civil Conflict. London, Hale, 1975.
Sibylla and the Privateer. London, Hale, and New York, New English Library, 1976.
Courtesan of the Saints. London, Hale, 1976.
Campaign for a Bride. London, Hale, 1977.
Charms of a Witch. London, Hale, 1977.
Strife Beyond Tamar. London, Hale, 1977.
Gavotte. London, Hale, 1978.
Masquerade for the King. London, Hale, 1978; New York, Thorpe, 1992.

Highland Destiny. London, Hale, 1979.
Players Wench. London, Hale, 1979.
Forbidden Love (as Donna Hunt). London, Macdonald, 1981.
Lord Hugo's Bride. London, Hale, 1981.
Lord Hugo's Wedding. London, Hale, 1981.
Fires in the Forest (as Bridget Thorn). London, Hale, 1983.
Highwayman's Hazard. London, Hale, 1983.
The Cobweb Cage. London, Penguin, 1984.
A Question of Love (as Bridget Thorn). London, Hale, 1985.
Rebel Heart. London, Hale, 1986.
The Baron's Bride. London, Hale, 1986.
Hospital Heartbreaker (as Bridget Thorn). London, Hale, 1988.
Honor and Passion (as Vesta Hathaway). New York, Dime, 1992.

Novels as Sally James

Miranda of the Island. London, Hale, 1977.
The Golden Gypsy. London, Hale, 1978.
Mask of Fortune. London, Hale, 1978.
A Clandestine Affair. London, Hale, 1980.
Petronella's Waterloo. London, Hale, 1980.
Heir to Rowanlea. London, Hale, 1981.
Fortune at Stake. London, Hale, 1981.
Lord Fordington's Offer. London, Hale, 1982.

*

Marina Oliver comments:

From childhood when I was not reading I was usually writing something. Any group I joined which did not have a magazine or newsletter soon acquired one, written by me! I am also passionate about history, so it was perhaps inevitable that I would eventually write historical novels. Many of these have been inspired by a particular event or character, and I try to make the details, historical and geographical, as accurate as possible. I frequently have to restrain my absorption in the research and get on with the story. I hope my books are primarily good stories which can capture the readers' imaginations. They all include a love story (and very little fiction totally ignores this vital aspect of life) but I also enjoy creating adventure, mystery and suspense, and using many different locations. I began with the 17th century, to me one of the most fascinating and varied periods of English history, and most of the ones by Marina Oliver are in that period. As Sally James I write Regencies, and as Bridget Thorn, contempory fiction. *The Cobweb Cage*, is a regional saga set at the beginning of the 20th century in Staffordshire and Birmingham.

*   *   *

Marina Oliver has written many novels set in different times, and with different settings. Most of them are historical romances set during and after the English Civil War (as Marina Oliver); others are set in the early part of the 19th century (as Sally James); and there are also a handful of historical novels set in other periods, and a trio of modern romances.

The Civil War novels reflect a great deal of detailed research about political events of the day. Each novel focuses on a specific event, or person. Thus *Restoration Affair* is set just before and during the Great Fire of London; *Charms of a Witch* deals with witch hunts in Essex at the start of the Civil War and the activities of Matthew Hopkins, witchfinder general; *Campaign for a Bride* is set at the time of the Battle of Worcester; and *Highland Destiny* deals with the activities of Montrose and the MacDonald Clan in Scotland in the 1640s. These events and people are dealt with only so far as they affect the romantic theme or the adventures of the main characters. Usually Oliver presents the facts unobtrusively, allowing the reader to feel how the characters are personally affected by the events of the day.

Politics is much less evident in most of the novels set during the restoration, and the romantic themes are allowed to dominate the plot. *Gavotte*, for example, deals sympathetically with a lady hurt by a previous suitor, who eventually finds love in an unexpected source. The reader can empathize with Isabella as she works through her own hurts and follows her destiny.

Lord Hugo's Bride and *Lord Hugo's Wedding* are the only novels to be linked in any way. They deal with the adventures of an aristocrat who reluctantly seeks the hand in marriage of an equally reluctant young lady. Howvever eventually he falls in love with her identical cousin, and many adventures follow. Humour, adventure, and suspense are as important here as the strong romantic story.

There is a strong element of mystery in Oliver's novels which appears to be almost as important as the romantic theme. Sometimes the heroine has a mysterious past, such as the reason why the heroine of *Miranda of the Island* is kept secluded, and has been told she is mad since childhood. In other novels, the mystery concerns the hero: is he really the cheat at cards who ruined the reputation of the heroine's father? (*Mask of Fortune*); can he truly be an ogre who beats his ward and attempts to kill her? (*A Clandestine Affair*). The heroines fall in love despite these apparent lapses from honour, but it is only in the light of the truth that the way is clear for a mutual declaration of love. In *Heir to Rowanlea*, in contrast, the mystery is whether the suddenly rediscovered heir is really who he says he is; the romantic interest is of secondary importance here.

The exciting climax of these novels usually features a chase, usually involving the hero or the heroine, who is either running away or being taken against his/her will. Frequently Oliver's books end with a declaration of love by the hero (and of course a proposal of marriage), numerous prevarications by the heroine, who cannot believe her good fortune, and finally the kiss which seals their love.

Oliver's modern novels are less successful, as the settings are not altogether credible. Romantic fiction is a form of escapism, true, but ordinary people do not often go to Minorca to be secretary to an aging Hollywood star (*A Question of Love*). The author seems more at ease in historical settings, where her knowledge is precise and assured. Every detail is a little too perfect in the modern novels—the clothes, the food, the houses, and above all the heroes!

The heroines, in these more contemporary works, are attractive people, but they have their bad points as well as good ones. In some cases, they seem as much to blame for their tribulations as the villains. The author does not make the mistake, however, of putting women with 20th century ideas into 17th-or 19th-century costumes and settings. The characters are true to their times and upbringings. What happens to them may seem extraordinary, but not completely impossible, given their personalities and circumstances.

The Cobweb Cage, one of Oliver's more recent works, is a family saga set in and around the Midlands in the early part of this century. The reliable use of historical details and the ability to draw realistic and sympathetic characters are talents which the author has shown in previous works, and puts to good effect in this work.

Oliver's novels are very enjoyable to read, immersing the reader gently into other places and especially other times. They lack the details and minutiae of daily life that are found in much longer novels, but she is adept at creating an atmosphere of being in a time not one's own, conveyed largely through the conversations and thoughts of the characters. The reader follows the adventures of the protagonists closely, sometimes with crossed fingers that things will turn out well, but always with a contented smile at the finish because the lovers have sorted out their misunderstandings and overcome adversity, so that they can live happily ever after.

—Jackie Stopyra

OLIVER, Yvonne. See **OLIVER, Marina.**

OLIVIERI, David. See **WHARTON, Edith.**

OMAN, Carola (Mary Anima).
Also wrote as C. Lenanton. **Nationality:** British. **Born:** Oxford, 11 May 1897; daughter of the historian Sir Charles Oman. **Education:** Wychwood School, Oxford. **Military Service:** British Red Cross Service, 1916–19 and 1938–58 (president, Hertfordshire Branch, 1947–58). **Relations:** married Sir Gerald Lenanton in 1922 (died 1952). **Recipient:** *Sunday Times* prize, 1947, for biography; James Tait Black memorial prize, 1954. Fellow, Royal Historical Society, Society of Antiquaries, and Royal Society of Literature. CBE (Commander, Order of the British Empire), 1957. **Died:** 11 June 1978.

ROMANCE AND HISTORICAL PUBLICATIONS

Novels

Princess Amelia. London, Unwin, and New York, Duffield, 1924.
The Road Royal. London, Unwin, and New York, Duffield, 1924.
King Heart. London, Unwin, 1926.
Mrs Newdigate's Window (as C. Lenanton). London, Unwin, and New York, Appleton, 1927.
The Holiday (as C. Lenanton). London, Unwin, and New York, Appleton, 1928.
Crouchback. London, Hodder and Stoughton, and New York, Holt, 1929.
Miss Barrett's Elopement (as C. Lenanton). London, Hodder and Stoughton, 1929; New York, Holt, 1930.
Fair Stood the Wind (as C. Lenanton). London, Hodder and Stoughton, 1930.
Major Grant. London, Hodder and Stoughton, 1931; New York, Holt, 1932.
The Empress. London, Hodder and Stoughton, and New York, Holt, 1932.
The Best of His Family. London, Hodder and Stoughton, 1933.
Over the Water. London, Hodder and Stoughton, 1935.
Nothing to Report. London, Hodder and Stoughton, 1940.

OTHER PUBLICATIONS

Poetry

The Menin Road and Other Poems. London, Hodder and Stoughton, 1919.

Other

Prince Charles Edward. London, Duckworth, 1935.
Henrietta Maria. London, Hodder and Stoughton, and New York, Macmillan, 1936.
Elizabeth of Bohemia. London, Hodder and Stoughton, 1938; revised edition, 1964.
Britain Against Napoleon. London, Faber, 1942; as *Napoleon at the Channel*, New York, Doubleday, 1942.
Somewhere in England. London, Hodder and Stoughton, 1943.
Nelson. New York, Doubleday, 1946; London, Hodder and Stoughton, 1947.
Sir John Moore. London, Hodder and Stoughton, 1953.
Lord Nelson. London, Collins, 1954; Hamden, Connecticut, Archon, 1968.

David Garrick. London, Hodder and Stoughton, 1958.
Mary of Modena. London, Hodder and Stoughton, 1962.
Ayot Rectory (biography of Mary Sneade Brown). London, Hodder and Stoughton, 1965.
Napoleon's Viceroy: Eugène de Beauharnais. London, Hodder and Stoughton, 1966; New York, Funk and Wagnalls, 1968.
The Gascoyne Heiress: The Life and Diaries of Frances Mary Gascoyne-Cecil 1802–1839. London, Hodder and Stoughton, 1968.
The Wizard of the North: The Life of Sir Walter Scott. London, Hodder and Stoughton, 1973.
An Oxford Childhood (autobiography). London, Hodder and Stoughton, 1976.

Other (for children)

Ferry the Fearless. London, Pitman, 1936.
Johel. London, Pitman, 1937.
Robin Hood, The Prince of Outlaws: A Tale of the Fourteenth Century from the Lytell Geste. London, Dent, and New York, Dutton, 1937.
Alfred, King of the English. London, Dent, 1939; New York, Dutton, 1940.
Baltic Spy. London, Pitman, 1940.

*   *   *

As a daughter of a distinguished historian, Sir Charles Oman, who was Chichele professor of History at Oxford, Carola Oman grew up in an atmosphere steeped in history, and it would seem that the example of two popular historical novelists, Mary Martha Sherwood (1775–1851) and Charlotte Yonge (1823–1901), counted almost as much with her as the massive scholarship of her erudite father. It is hardly surprising that even without the benefits of systematic education she became a remarkably well-informed person, aware of the social detail, manners and linguistic usage of the past and of its development from age to age. What is more remarkable is that her imagination was always fired by the great figures of the past, in Britain and in France too, and that she responded to them warmly as human beings all through her life. It was between the two world wars that she published a succession of substantial historical novels, and as early as 1935 she brought out *Prince Charles Edward*, the first of the considerable number of biographies that are now generally seen as constituting her main claim to fame. Her decision to switch from fiction, solidly based on fact, to history, with scrupulously documented facts interpreted with sympathetic human insight, cannot really be considered to be anything other than Oman's own verdict on her historical novels as her confidence in her own abilities developed over the years. All the same, her novels, which were well received in the 1930s, still have merit and charm, for both their period flavour and their human interest.

Though not quite so wide-ranging a writer as her father, who published authoritative works on periods as disparate as Ancient Greece, the Byzantine Empire and the 19th century, Oman cut an impressive swathe through British history, and she was not afraid to tackle well-known figures. *The Empress* takes us back to the 12th century when Mathilda was in conflict with King Stephen, and *Crouchback*, an account of the character and reign of Richard III, was much praised for its depiction of the Wars of the Roses. Stirring episodes from Scottish history are evoked in *King Heart*, which is an account of the life and times of James IV, and in *The Road Royal*, which tells the tragic story of Mary Queen of Scots from her departure from France to her imprisonment at Loch Leven.

The Best of His Family presents William Shakespeare, setting his entire career against the background of the Elizabethan Age. It provides some useful insights into his dramatic writing, even if the interpretation of the well-known incidents of his private life is, to some degree, fanciful. Placing Shakespearean quotations in the mouths of some of the people whom he meets as he goes about his business also begs some interesting questions about the way his verbal imagination really worked when he settled down to composing his plays. There is, however, some indication of how seriously Oman went about writing historical fiction in what she, perhaps rather pointedly, calls a 'short bibliography' that was printed as an appendix to the 300-page novel; from material on the historical and theatrical background of a well-known figure in a period that would be quite familiar to most of her readers she consulted some 60 scholarly sources. Oman moved on to the Georgian period with *Princess Amelia*, and *Major Grant* is set in the time of the Napoleonic Wars. *Miss Barrett's Elopement* brings Robert Browning on to the scene, and the time is the early-Victorian era. *Fair Stood the Wind* sounds as if it ought to be about the Agincourt campaign, but it is in fact a story about a motoring holiday on the continent in the late 1930s, which may explain why it was published under Oman's married name, Carola Lenanton.

Oman's chief interest in historical fiction was not so much in public events, though these are not neglected, or in the more profound intellectual issues of the periods under consideration, but rather in the re-creation of the every-day life of the protagonists, especially the female ones, at the time. Every detail of costume, household furnishing and behaviour is evoked, sometimes delaying the development of the story. A sense of period is conveyed by passing allusions to happenings and personalities which may occasionally puzzle readers not quite so familiar with the background as the author is. Similar difficulties can occur in the conversations between Oman's characters in which archaic speech and, as in the case of her Scottish novels, dialect is used. The motivation here is both understandable and praiseworthy, but employing this sort of language in what might well be the most lively parts of the tales sometimes demands rather too much of the reader. All the same, though Oman's historical novels are not always very exciting, they still offer attractions as vivid and seriously researched depictions of important episodes from Britain's past.

—Christopher N. Smith

ONIONS, (George) Oliver. British. 1873–1961. See 2nd edition, 1990.

ONSTOTT, Kyle. See **HORNER, Lance, Kyle ONSTOTT, and Ashley CARTER.**

ORCZY, Baroness (Emma Magdalena Rosalia Maria Josefa Barbara Orczy).
Nationality: British. **Born:** Tarna-Ors, Hungary, 23 September 1865. **Education:** Brussels and Paris; West London School of Art; Heatherley School of Art, London. **Relations:** married Montagu Barstow in 1894 (died 1943); one son. **Career:** artist: exhibited work at the Royal Academy, London. **Died:** 12 November 1947.

ROMANCE AND HISTORICAL PUBLICATIONS

Novels (series: Sir Percy Blakeney, The Scarlet Pimpernel)

The Emperor's Candlesticks. London, Pearson, 1899; New York, Doscher, 1908.

The Scarlet Pimpernel. London, Greening, and New York, Putnam, 1905.

By the Gods Beloved. London, Greening, 1905; as *Beloved of the Gods*, New York, Knickerbocker Press, 1905; as *The Gates of Kamt*, New York, Dodd Mead, 1907.

A Son of the People. London, Greening, and New York, Putnam, 1906.

I Will Repay (Pimpernel). London, Greening, and Philadelphia, Lippincott, 1906.

In Mary's Reign. New York, Cupples and Leon, 1907.

The Tangled Skein. London, Greening, 1907.

Beau Brocade. Philadelphia, Lippincott, 1907; London, Greening, 1908.

The Elusive Pimpernel. London, Hutchinson, and New York, Dodd Mead, 1908.

The Nest of the Sparrowhawk. London, Greening, and New York, Stokes, 1909.

Petticoat Government. London, Hutchinson, 1910; as *Petticoat Rule*, New York, Doran, 1910.

A True Woman. London, Hutchinson, 1911; as *The Heart of a Woman*, New York, Doran, 1911.

Meadowsweet. London, Hutchinson, and New York, Doran, 1912.

Fire in the Stubble. London, Methuen, 1912; as *The Noble Rogue*, New York, Doran, 1912.

Eldorado: A Story of the Scarlet Pimpernel. London, Hodder and Stoughton, and New York, Doran, 1913.

Unto Caesar. London, Hodder and Stoughton, and New York, Doran, 1914.

The Laughing Cavalier. London, Hodder and Stoughton, and New York, Doran, 1914.

A Bride of the Plains. London, Hutchinson, and New York, Doran, 1915.

The Bronze Eagle. London, Hodder and Stoughton, and New York, Doran, 1915.

Leatherface: A Tale of Old Flanders. London, Hodder and Stoughton, and New York, Doran, 1916.

A Sheaf of Bluebells. London, Hutchinson, and New York, Doran, 1917.

Lord Tony's Wife: An Adventure of the Scarlet Pimpernel. London, Hodder and Stoughton, and New York, Doran, 1917.

Flower o' the Lily. London, Hodder and Stoughton, 1918; New York, Doran, 1919.

The League of the Scarlet Pimpernel. London, Cassell, and New York, Doran, 1919.

His Majesty's Well-Beloved. London, Hodder and Stoughton, and New York, Doran, 1919.

The First Sir Percy: An Adventure of the Laughing Cavalier. London, Hodder and Stoughton, 1920; New York, Doran, 1921.

Nicolette. London, Hodder and Stoughton, and New York, Doran, 1922.

The Triumph of the Scarlet Pimpernel. London, Hodder and Stoughton, and New York, Doran, 1922.

The Honourable Jim. London, Hodder and Stoughton, and New York, Doran, 1924.

Pimpernel and Rosemary. London, Cassell, 1924; New York, Doran, 1925.

The Celestial City. London, Hodder and Stoughton, and New York, Doran, 1926.

Sir Percy Hits Back: An Adventure of the Scarlet Pimpernel. London, Hodder and Stoughton, and New York, Doran, 1927.

Blue Eyes and Grey. London, Hodder and Stoughton, 1928; New York, Doubleday, 1929.

Marivosa. London, Cassell, 1930; New York, Doubleday, 1931.

A Child of the Revolution. London, Cassell, and New York, Doubleday, 1932.

A Joyous Adventure. London, Hodder and Stoughton, and New York, Doubleday, 1932.

The Way of the Scarlet Pimpernel. London, Hodder and Stoughton, 1933; New York, Putnam, 1934.

A Spy of Napoleon. London, Hodder and Stoughton, and New York, Putnam, 1934.

The Uncrowned King. London, Hodder and Stoughton, and New York, Putnam, 1935.

Sir Percy Leads the Band. London, Hodder and Stoughton, 1936.

The Divine Folly. London, Hodder and Stoughton, 1937.

No Greater Love. London, Hodder and Stoughton, 1938.

Mam'zelle Guillotine: An Adventure of the Scarlet Pimpernel. London, Hodder and Stoughton, 1940.

Price of Race. London, Hodder and Stoughton, 1942.

Will-o'-the-Wisp. London, Hutchinson, 1947.

Short Stories

The Traitor. New York, Paget, 1912.

Two Good Patriots. New York, Paget, 1912.

The Old Scarecrow. New York, Paget, 1916.

A Question of Temptation. New York, Doran, 1925.

Adventures of the Scarlet Pimpernel. London, Hutchinson, and New York, Doubleday, 1929.

In the Rue Monge. New York, Doubleday, 1931.

OTHER PUBLICATIONS

Short Stories

The Case of Miss Elliott. London, Unwin, 1905.

The Old Man in the Corner. London, Greening, 1909; as *The Man in the Corner*, New York, Dodd Mead, 1909; edited by E.F. Bleiler, New York, Dover, 1980.

Lady Molly of Scotland Yard. London, Cassell, 1910; New York, Arno, 1976.

The Man in Grey, Being Episodes of the Chouan Conspiracies in Normandy During the First Empire. London, Cassell, and New York, Doran, 1918.

Castles in the Air. London, Cassell, 1921; New York, Doran, 1922.

The Old Man in the Corner Unravels the Mystery of the Khaki Tunic. New York, Doran, 1923.

The Old Man in the Corner Unravels the Mystery of the Pearl Necklace, and The Tragedy in Bishop's Road. New York, Doran, 1924.

The Old Man in the Corner Unravels the Mystery of the Russian Prince and of Dog's Tooth Cliff. New York, Doran, 1924.

The Old Man in the Corner Unravels the Mystery of the White Carnation, and The Montmartre Hat. New York, Doran, 1925.

The Old Man in the Corner Unravels the Mystery of the Fulton Gardens Mystery, and The Moorland Tragedy. New York, Doran, 1925.

The Miser of Maida Vale. New York, Doran, 1925.

Unravelled Knots. London, Hutchinson, 1925; New York, Doran, 1926.

Skin o' My Tooth. London, Hodder and Stoughton, and New York, Doubleday, 1928.

Plays

The Scarlet Pimpernel, with Montagu Barstow (produced Nottingham, 1903; London, 1905; New York, 1910).

The Sin of William Jackson, with Montagu Barstow (produced London, 1906).

Beau Brocade, with Montagu Barstow, adaptation of the novel by Orczy (produced Eastbourne, Sussex, and London, 1908).

The Duke's Wager (produced Manchester, 1911).

The Legion of Honour, adaptation of her novel *A Sheaf of Bluebells* (produced Bradford, 1918; London, 1921).

Leatherface, with Caryl Fiennes, adaptation of the novel by Orczy (produced Portsmouth and London, 1922).

Other

Les Beaux et les Dandys des Grands Siècles en Angleterre. Monaco, Société des Conférences, 1924.

The Scarlet Pimpernel Looks at the World (essays). London, John Heritage, 1933.

The Turbulent Duchess: H.R.H. Madame le Duchesse de Berri. London, Hodder and Stoughton, 1935; New York, Putnam, 1936.

Links in the Chain of Life (autobiography). London, Hutchinson, 1947.

Editor and Translator, with Montagu Barstow, *Old Hungarian Fairy Tales.* London, Dean, and Philadelphia, Wolf, 1895.

Editor and Translator, *The Enchanted Cat* (fairy tales). London, Dean, 1895.

Editor and Translator, *Fairyland's Beauty* (*The Suitors of Princess Fire-fly*). London, Dean, 1895.

Editor and Translator, *Uletka and the White Lizard* (fairy tales). London, Dean, 1895.

*   *   *

Romance in Baroness Orczy's stories is on more than one level, for she tackles with panache the romanticism of historical and improbably heroic adventures as well as sexual love. The shadow of the guillotine seems an unlikely breeding ground for the tender passion, but this is most potently conveyed in *The Scarlet Pimpernel* and its sequels which had as their background the French Revolution. Orczy's books are highly wrought and intensely atmospheric. There are vivid contrasts between the rabble-ridden, blood-running, and squalid streets of revolutionary Paris and the glittering splendour of the court of King George III in England.

Sir Percy Blakeney seems to have been equally at home in both, ringing the changes from appearing at London balls and supper-parties as one of the Prince of Wales's favourite associates, to disguising himself as a 'loathsome' looking old 'jew trader', or some smelly market-hag or fisherman in order to whisk innocent potential victims away from the fury of the French mob, and the ever-devouring 'Mam'zelle Guillotine'. Those whom he rescued were more often than not aristocratic, and he drew his band of helpers—'The League of the Scarlet Pimpernel'—from the same class (Sir Andrew Ffoulkes, Lord Antony Dewhurst, Lord Hastings, etc.).

Generally speaking, artisans and even middle-class people did not show up too well in Orczy's stories. In spite of her attraction to strongly chivalric ideas, she writes about the 'lower orders' with a distinct air of patronage and condescension, especially if they step out of line and fail to respect their 'betters'. (And, of course, nothing could be more disrespectful than putting the heads of these betters under the guillotine!)

Sir Percy, however, falls heavily in love with someone from a different class *and* a foreigner to boot—Marguerite St Just, a French actress of considerable beauty and accomplishment who, until she recognizes the ruthless nature of the Revolution, is a republican. Naturally their married relationship is at first fraught with misunderstandings, and to conceal from Marguerite—as well as the rest of the world—that he is the Scarlet Pimpernel, Sir Percy assumes the role of inept but fashionable fop. Readers, of course, suspect his secret from the early stages of the first book, mainly because the foppish exterior never quite conceals his inner reserves of strength, humour, and compassion, or his romantic but slightly sardonic sense of chivalry: 'The commands of a beautiful woman are binding on all mankind, even Cabinet Ministers...'.

The action of the plot demands that the identity of the Scarlet Pimpernel, intrepid arch-enemy of the French Revolutionary government, *has* to be revealed to his friends and enemies at the end of the first book. Those that followed never quite achieved the same sense of drama or splendid style—but they were always rich in romantic interest. In different books from those in the 'Scarlet Pimpernel' series, Orczy created other gallant and upright English aristocrats but they lacked the charisma of Sir Percy and his associates.

Strangely enough, everything that worked so well in Orczy's creation of Sir Percy seems to have misfired when a little later on she produced a female righter-of-wrongs. In *Lady Molly of Scotland Yard*, the heroine from whom the book derives its name is, like Sir Percy, aristocratic, enigmatic, plucky, and adept at assuming disguises. But whereas Sir Percy remains a complex and endearing character, Lady Molly comes across as an arch and self-indulgent poseuse. However, although her place in literature is in the detective genre rather than the love-story, she is as much a romantic as Sir Percy. Unlike him, she never actually has to rescue her spouse from the threat of the guillotine—but she *does* vindicate his honour and secures his release from unjust imprisonment.

Orczy was adept not only in different literary genres but with different literary forms. *The Scarlet Pimpernel* was originally a successful play co-authored by Orczy and her husband Montagu Barstow. It was then re-written by the Baroness as a beautifully balanced and, of course, bestselling novel. All the other novels in the series are entertaining and dramatic, especially *The Elusive Pimpernel* and *I Will Repay*. In *Adventures of the Scarlet Pimpernel* she skillfully manipulates the romantic/suspense short story.

—Mary Cadogan

ØVSTEDAL, Barbara.   See LAKER, Rosalind.

PALMER, Diana.
Pseudonym for Susan (Eloise Spaeth) Kyle. **Other Pseudonyms:** Diana Blayne; Katy Currie; also writes as Susan Kyle. **Nationality:** American. **Born:** Cuthbert, Georgia, 12 December 1946. **Education:** Chamblee High School, Georgia, 1964; Famous Writers School, Westport, Connecticut, graduated 1968. **Relations:** married James Edward Kyle in 1972; one son. **Career:** legal secretary, Oliver and Oliver, Clarkesville, Georgia, 1965–66, and Crawford and Crawford, Cornelia, Georgia, 1966; clerk, Carwood Manufacturing Company, 1971–72; reporter, *Tri-County Advertiser*, Clarkesville, 1972–82, and Gainesville *Times*, Georgia, 1969–85; freelance journalist, 1986. **Agent:** Maureen Walters, Curtis Brown, 10 Astor Place, New York, New York 10003, USA. **Address:** PO Box 844, Cornelia, Georgia 30531, USA.

ROMANCE AND HISTORICAL PUBLICATIONS

Novels (series: Long Tall Texan; Mercenary)

Now and Forever. New York, Macfadden, 1979.
Storm over the Lake. New York, Macfadden, 1979.
To Have and to Hold. New York, Macfadden, 1979.
Sweet Enemy. New York, Macfadden, 1979.
Bound by a Promise. New York, Macfadden, 1979.
To Love and to Cherish. New York, Macfadden, 1979.
Dream's End. New York, Macfadden, 1979.

If Winter Comes. New York, Macfadden, 1979.
At Winter's End. New York, Macfadden, 1979.
The Cowboy and the Lady. New York, Silhouette, 1982.
September Morning. New York, Silhouette, 1982.
Heather's Song. New York, Silhouette, 1982.
Darling Enemy. New York, Silhouette, 1983.
Friends and Lovers. New York, Silhouette, 1983.
Fire and Ice. New York, Silhouette, 1983.
Snow Kisses. New York, Silhouette, 1983.
Diamond Girl. New York, Silhouette, 1984.
Lady Love. New York, Silhouette, 1984.
Roomful of Roses. New York, Silhouette, 1984.
Heart of Ice. New York, Silhouette, 1984.
Passion Flower. New York, Silhouette, 1984.
The Rawhide Man. New York, Silhouette, 1984.
Blind Promises (as Katy Currie). New York, Silhouette, 1984.
The Cattleman's Choice. New York, Silhouette, 1985.
Love by Proxy. New York, Silhouette, 1985.
Soldier of Fortune (Mercenary). New York, Silhouette, 1985.
The Tender Stranger (Mercenary). New York, Silhouette, 1985.
The Australian. New York, Silhouette, 1985.
Loveplay. New York, Silhouette, 1986.
Eye of the Tiger. New York, Silhouette, 1986.
After the Music. New York, Silhouette, 1986.
Champagne Girl. New York, Silhouette, 1986.
Unlikely Lover. New York, Silhouette, 1986.
Betrayed by Love. New York, Silhouette, 1987.
Rage of Passion. New York, Silhouette, 1987.
Rawhide and Lace. New York, Silhouette, 1987.
Fit for a King. New York, Silhouette, 1987.
Enamored (Mercenary). New York, Silhouette, 1988.
Calhoun (Texan). New York, Silhouette, 1988.
Justin (Texan). New York, Silhouette, 1988.
Tyler (Texan). New York, Silhouette, 1988.
Hoodwinked. New York, Silhouette, 1989.
Reluctant Father. New York, Silhouette, 1989.
Woman Hater. New York, Silhouette, 1989.
His Girl Friday. New York, Silhouette, 1989.
Sutton's Way (Texan). New York, Silhouette, 1989.
Connal (Texan). Toronto, Harlequin, 1990.
Ethan (Texan). New York, Silhouette, 1990.
Nelson's Brand. New York, Silhouette, 1991.
Lacy. New York, Fawcett, 1991.
The Best Is Yet to Come. New York, Silhouette, 1991.
Hunter. New York, Silhouette, 1991.
The Case of the Mesmerising Boss. New York, Silhouette, 1992.
The Case of the Confirmed Bachelor. New York, Silhouette, 1992.
The Case of the Missing Secretary. New York, Silhouette, 1993.
Amelia. New York, Fawcett, 1993.
Night of Love. New York, Silhouette, 1993.
King's Ransom. New York, Silhouette, 1993.
Trilby. New York, Fawcett, 1993.
Emmett (Texan). New York, Silhouette, 1993.

Novels as Diana Blayne

A Waiting Game. New York, Dell, 1982.
A Loving Arrangement. New York, Dell, 1983.
White Sand, Wild Sea. New York, Dell, 1983.
Dark Surrender. New York, Dell, 1983.
Color Love Blue. New York, Dell, 1984.
Tangled Destinies. New York, Dell, 1986.
Denim and Lace. New York, Dell, 1990.

Novels as Susan Kyle

The Diamond Spur. New York, Warner, 1988.

Fire Brand. New York, Warner, 1989.
Night Fever. New York, Warner, 1990.
True Colors. New York, Warner, 1991.
Escapade. New York, Warner, 1992.
After Midnight. New York, Warner, 1993.

Short Stories

Silhouette Summer Sizzlers, with Sherryl Woods, and Patricia Coughlin. New York, Silhouette, 1991.

OTHER PUBLICATIONS

Novel (as Susan S. Kyle)

The Morcai Battalion. New York, Manor, 1980.

*

Diana Palmer comments:

I draw heavily from my background as a journalist when researching my books. Even though they deal, for the most part, with romance, the factual portions require every bit as much detail as non-fiction works. My books are hallmarked by their regional settings, old-fashioned morality and virtues, spirited heroines, and rugged, uncompromising heroes. I prefer to write books set in the American west and have become known primarily for such books. I have a diverse and loyal reading audience, some of whom have been with me since the very start of my career. I owe everything I am to those wonderful readers and booksellers. I never forget their part in my success. I was orphaned last year, and my readers have become my family-at-large. I am the luckiest lady in the world to have received so much love and loyalty.

*   *   *

One of the most prolific authors of contemporary romances, Diana Palmer has a special talent for developing disagreeable heroes, then letting them be changed by love. Although her novels are generally short, she manages to make this reversal of character believable. She is one of the strongest proponents of moral values, often letting her characters make a case for traditional virtues.

Palmer's men usually are cold, distant, and sarcastic. They seem bent on maintaining self-isolation rather than risk any emotional trauma. A typical Palmer hero has insulated himself against the pain of loving, pain which he has felt first hand. Often he has had the misfortune of being a mature adult attracted to a much younger girl. In fighting this attraction, he appears to have brutally rejected her when he has really rejected himself. Since the girl is not yet sophisticated or worldly enough to understand the difference, she runs from him. Palmer usually picks up their story when the girl has grown to womanhood and is ready to accept a man's love, although she might still be frightened of the past. This scenario or a variation of it is featured in such works as *Heather's Song*, *Calhoun*, *September Morning*, *The Cowboy and the Lady*, *Eye of the Tiger*, and *Betrayed by Love*.

Another common reason for the hero's coldness is a previous lack of love. Betrayal and abandonment by a mother, wife, or fiancée leads to a condemnation of all women, which is then focused on the heroine. In *After the Music*, Thorn almost destroys Sabina because of his biased view of women. Even after learning the truth, he stays away, helping her in order to make up for hurting her but still unwilling to try a real relationship. It takes an accident to break down the walls he has so effectively built and maintained. In the appropriately named *Woman Hater*, Nicole must contend with the ghost of

Winthrop's former love, who had walked out on him. Blake Donovan in *Reluctant Father* was hit doubly hard by not knowing his mother and by marrying the wrong woman, who eventually walked out on him.

Like many romance authors, Palmer sometimes uses characters from one book to another. One of her most intriguing creations along this line links the stories of several mercenaries. The leader of the group, now a criminal lawyer, is introduced in *Soldier of Fortune*. He comes out of retirement to rescue his sister from terrorists, taking his secretary Gabby along with him. Knowing her innocence, he tries to stay away. He manages to scare her away with deliberately crude foreplay but then realizes that he really wants her love. In *The Tender Stranger*, the enigmatic mercenary Eric meets and marries Dani St Clair but leaves her to fend for herself for a long time. He re-enters her life shortly before his child is to be born. A third 'team' member, Diego Laremos, suddenly finds his former wife in dire straits and in need of his help (*Enamored*). Although these three men are in different stages of male-female relationships, it is apparent that each must cope with his own basic impulse to stay separated from emotion. It is not surprising, however, that they eventually, and happily, succumb to love and learn to trust and accept love. The 'Long Tall Texan' series is another of Palmer's extremely popular creations with many memorable heroes.

Palmer is one of the few romance novelists who places a sharper focus on the hero than on the heroine. The stories are not told from the male point of view, but as a general rule her male characters are more interestingly developed. She has been unique in often having a hero who is not very experienced with women, which is understandable given their predilection for emotional isolation and their previous bad experiences. However, she is probably the first romance author to have a contemporary adult hero, Quinn Sutton, confess that he is a virgin (*Sutton's Way*).

Palmer, who also writes as Diana Blayne and Susan Kyle, her real name, has also written some longer novels (*Escapade*, *The Diamond Spur*, *Night Fever*, *Fire Brand*, *Lacy*, *Trilby*). Most are set in the contemporary world, but with *Lacy*, Palmer moved back in time to the Roaring Twenties. Cole Whitehall, the forebear of Jason Whitehall (*The Cowboy and the Lady*), is another of Palmer's vulnerable males. He suffers from deep scars caused by World War I. In *Trilby*, the scene shifts to the Southwest in 1910. There Thorn Vance and Trilby Lang spar in the shadow of raids by Mexican revolutionaries. These longer stories are more leisurely paced than the category romances and consequently are less dynamic and seem to lack the sharper focus she has developed in her shorter novels.

Palmer's real strength in romantic fiction remains her willingness and ability to keep alive the values of virtue, celibacy, and true commitment. Her stories lack the detailed descriptions of sex found in many best-selling authors, but that is precisely her appeal to her many readers. Her insistence on morality might seem old-fashioned and illusionary to some in today's world, but such a fantasy can be a refuge in an increasingly ambiguous sexual world.

—Barbara E. Kemp

PARADISE, Mary. See **EDEN, Dorothy.**

PARGETER, Edith (Mary).
Pseudonyms: Peter Benedict; Jolyon Carr; Ellis Peters; John Redfern. **Nationality:** British. **Born:** Horsehay, Shropshire, 28 September 1913. **Education:** Dawley Church of England Elementary School, Shropshire; Coalbrookdale High School for Girls,

Oxford School and Higher School Certificate. **Military Service:** Women's Royal Navy Service, 1940–45: British Empire medal, 1944. **Career:** chemist's assistant, Dawley, 1933–40. **Recipient:** Mystery Writers of America Edgar Allan Poe award, 1963; Czechoslovak Society for International Relations gold medal, 1968; Crime Writers Association Silver Dagger award, 1981. Fellow, International Institute of Arts and Letters, 1961. **Agent:** Deborah Owen, 78 Narrow Street, London E14 8BP, England. **Address:** 3, Lee Dingle, Madeley, Telford, Shropshire TF7 5TW, England.

ROMANCE AND HISTORICAL PUBLICATIONS

Novels (series: Brothers of Gwynedd Quartet; War Trilogy)

Hortensius, Friend of Nero. London, Lovat Dickson, 1936; New York, Greystone Press, 1937.
Iron-Bound. London, Lovat Dickson, 1936.
Day Star (as Peter Benedict). London, Lovat Dickson, 1937.
The City Lies Foursquare. London, Heinemann, and New York, Reynal, 1939.
Freedom for Two (as Jolyon Carr). London, Jenkins, 1939.
Masters of the Parachute Mail (as Jolyon Carr). London, Jenkins, 1940.
Ordinary People. London, Heinemann, 1941; as *People of My Own,* New York, Reynal, 1942.
She Goes to War. London, Heinemann, 1942.
War Trilogy:
   The Eighth Champion of Christendom. London, Heinemann, 1945.
   Reluctant Odyssey. London, Heinemann, 1946.
   Warfare Accomplished. London, Heinemann, 1947.
The Fair Young Phoenix. London, Heinemann, 1948.
By Firelight. London, Heinemann, 1948; as *By This Strange Fire,* New York, Reynal, 1948.
Lost Children. London, Heinemann, 1951.
Holiday with Violence. London, Heinemann, 1952.
This Rough Magic. London, Heinemann, 1953.
Most Loving Mere Folly. London, Heinemann, 1953.
The Soldier at the Door. London, Heinemann, 1954.
A Means of Grace. London, Heinemann, 1956.
The Heaven Tree. London, Heinemann, and New York, Doubleday, 1960.
The Green Branch. London, Heinemann, 1962.
The Scarlet Seed. London, Heinemann, 1963.
A Bloody Field by Shrewsbury. London, Macmillan, 1972; New York, Viking Press, 1973.
Brothers of Gwynedd Quartet:
   1. *Sunrise in the West.* London, Macmillan, 1974.
   2. *The Dragon at Noonday.* London, Macmillan, 1975.
   3. *The Hounds of Sunset.* London, Macmillan, 1976.
   4. *Afterglow and Nightfall.* London, Macmillan, 1977.
The Marriage of Meggotta. London, Macmillan, and New York, Viking Press, 1979.

Short Stories

The Lily Hand and Other Stories. London, Heinemann, 1965.

OTHER PUBLICATIONS

Novels as Ellis Peters

Murder in the Dispensary (as Jolyon Carr). London, Jenkins, 1938.

Death Comes by Post (as Jolyon Carr). London, Jenkins, 1940.
Fallen into the Pit (as Edith Pargeter). London, Heinemann, 1951.
Death Mask. London, Collins, 1959; New York, Doubleday, 1960.
The Will and the Deed. London, Collins, 1960; New York, Avon, 1966; as *Where There's a Will,* New York, Doubleday, 1960.
Death and the Joyful Woman. London, Collins, 1961; New York, Doubleday, 1962.
Funeral of Figaro. London, Collins, 1962; New York, Morrow, 1964.
Flight of Witch. London, Collins, 1964.
A Nice Derangement of Epitaphs. London, Collins, 1965; as *Who Lies Here?,* New York, Morrow, 1965.
The Piper on the Mountain. London, Collins, and New York, Morrow, 1966.
Black Is the Colour of My True-Love's Heart. London, Collins, and New York, Morrow, 1967.
The Grass-Widow's Tale. London, Collins, and New York, Doubleday, 1968.
The House of Green Turf. London, Collins, and New York, Morrow, 1969.
Mourning Raga. London, Macmillan, 1969; New York, Morrow, 1970.
The Knocker on Death's Door. London, Macmillan, 1970; New York, Morrow, 1971.
Death to the Landlords! London, Macmillan, and New York, Morrow, 1972.
City of Gold and Shadows. London, Macmillan, 1973; New York, Morrow, 1974.
The Horn of Roland. London, Macmillan, and New York, Morrow, 1974.
Never Pick Up Hitch-Hikers! London, Macmillan, and New York, Morrow, 1976.
A Morbid Taste for Bones: A Mediaeval Whodunnit. London, Macmillan, 1977; New York, Morrow, 1978.
Rainbow's End. London, Macmillan, 1978; New York, Morrow, 1979.
One Corpse Too Many. London, Macmillan, 1979; New York, Morrow, 1980.
Monk's-Hood. London, Macmillan, 1980; New York, Morrow, 1981.
Saint Peter's Fair. London, Macmillan, and New York, Morrow, 1981.
The Leper of Saint Giles. London, Macmillan, 1981; New York, Morrow, 1982.
The Virgin in the Ice. London, Macmillan, 1982; New York, Morrow, 1983.
The Sanctuary Sparrow. London, Macmillan, and New York, Morrow, 1983.
The Devil's Novice. London, Macmillan, 1983; New York, Morrow, 1984.
Dead Man's Ransom. London, Macmillan, 1984; New York, Morrow, 1985.
The Pilgrim of Hate. London, Macmillan, 1984.
An Excellent Mystery. London, Macmillan, 1985; New York, Morrow, 1986.
The Raven in the Foregate. London, Macmillan, and New York, Morrow, 1986.
The Rose Rent. London, Macmillan, and New York, Morrow, 1986.
The Hermit of Eyton Forest. London, Headline, 1987; New York, Mysterious Press, 1988.
The Confession of Brother Haluin. London, Headline, 1988; New York, Mysterious Press, 1989.
The Heretic's Apprentice. London, Headline, 1989.
The Potter's Field. London, Headline, 1989.
The Summer of the Danes. London, Headline, 1991.
The Holy Thief. London, Headline, 1993.

Short Stories

The Assize of the Dying (includes *The Assize of the Dying, Aunt Helena*). London, Heinemann, and New York, Doubleday, 1958.
A Rare Benedictine. London, Headline, 1989; New York, Mysterious Press, 1989.

Other

The Coast of Bohemia. London, Heinemann, 1950.

Translator, *Tales of the Little Quarter: Stories*, by Jan Neruda. London, Heinemann, 1957; New York, Greenwood Press, 1976.
Translator, *The Sorrowful and Heroic Life of John Amos Comenius*, by Frantisek Kosík. Prague, State Educational Publishing House, 1958.
Translator, *A Handful of Linden Leaves: An Anthology of Czech Poetry*. Prague, Artia, 1958.
Translator, *Don Juan*, by Josef Toman. London, Heinemann, and New York, Knopf, 1958.
Translator, *The Abortionists*, by Valja Stýblová. London, Secker and Warburg, 1961.
Translator, *Granny*, by Bozena Nemcová. Prague, Artia, 1962; New York, Greenwood Press, 1976.
Translator, with others, *The Linden Tree* (anthology). Prague, Artia, 1962.
Translator, *The Terezin Requiem*, by Josef Bor. London, Heinemann, and New York, Knopf, 1963.
Translator, *Legends of Old Bohemia*, by Alois Jirásek. London, Hamlyn, 1963.
Translator, *May*, by Karel Hynek Mácha. Prague, Artia, 1965.
Translator, *The End of the Old Times*, by Vladislav Vancura. Prague, Artia, 1965.
Translator, *A Close Watch on the Trains*, by Bohumil Hrabal. London, Cape, 1968.
Translator, *Report on My Husband*, by Josefa Slánská. London, Macmillan, 1969.
Translator, *A Ship Named Hope*, by Ivan Klíma. London, Gollancz, 1970.
Translator, *Mozart in Prague*, by Jaroslav Seifert. Prague, Orbis, 1970.

*

Critical Study: *The Cadfael Companion: The World of Brother Cadfael* by Robin Whiteman, London, Macdonald, 1991.

*   *   *

Many readers are familiar with the works of this author through her popular mysteries written under the pseudonym of Ellis Peters. Set in 12th-century Britain these stories feature the resourceful sleuth, Brother Cadfael, a Benedictine monk, who tends his herbal garden when not solving intricate mysteries. The locations for these stories, as well as many others by the author, are Shropshire, and Wales. Pargeter's love for this part of Britain comes passionately through in the vivid descriptions of this wild and wonderful land.

After publishing *The Marriage of Megotta*, Pargeter revealed that in writing historical novels she seems 'to have retreated into the 13th century for keeps'. This statement has the ring of truth since so many of her tales take place in that turbulent time.

The realistic depiction of daily hardships suffered by the common people, as well as of political intrigues among the nobility, in her stories, speaks clearly of thorough research. She writes in the melodic prose often associated with mediaeval historical fiction and carries it off well. Pargeter manages also to create in each character a distinct personality and a unique voice.

Her stories are not those of knights in shining armour riding out to rescue fair maidens but of real people caught in tragic events often not of their doing. *The Marriage of Megotta* offers the poignant tale of two young people, Meggotta and Richard, whose love has the purity and innocence reminiscent of Romeo and Juliet. But the scheming world of Henry III's court tears them apart and eventually causes the death of Meggotta. In *The Heaven Tree* Harry Talvace discovers the cruelty of King John's character when the monarch orders the death of a young boy, Owen, foster son of the Welsh Prince Llewelyn Fawr, also known as the Great. Harry's intense sense of justice will not allow him to stand by while this sentence is carried out. At the risk of his own life he engineers Owen's safe return to Wales. Later Llewelyn shows his gratitude by offering sanctuary to Harry's wife and infant son. In her epic saga the 'Brothers of Gwynedd Quartet', she evokes the tumultuous reign of Llewelyn ap Griffith, grandson of Llewelyn the Great, and the first true Prince of Wales. With political skill and a warrior spirit Llewelyn brought the fractious Welsh together in order to face the English foe. The soldiers of this small, poor nation were no match for the wealthier, better armed English. First they battled the troops of Henry III then later those of his son Edward I. It is Edward who cruelly destroyed the Welsh forces along with their Prince and his brother, David. But the feisty Welsh are not easily put aside. They continue their harassment of English monarchs as depicted in *A Bloody Field by Shrewsbury,* where Henry IV must contend with the rebellious troops of Owen Glendower.

Recently some of Pargeter's contemporary novels of World War II have been republished. A trilogy comprising *The Eighth Champion of Christendom, Reluctant Odyssey,* and *Warfare Accomplished,* follows the fortunes of young soldier Jim Benison as he leaves behind his small town innocence and matures under the brutality of war. These novels as well as *She Goes to War* give a vivid account of attitudes of the period since they were written and published during war years.

This prolific, versatile author has a knowledge and love of history that she combines with intuitive insight into the human heart.

—Patricia Altner

———

PARGETER, Margaret.
Nationality: British. **Born:** Northumberland. **Relations:** married (husband deceased); two sons. **Address:** c/o Mills and Boon Ltd, Eton House, 18–24 Paradise Road, Richmond, Surrey TW9 1SR, England.

ROMANCE AND HISTORICAL PUBLICATIONS

Novels

Winds from the Sea. London, Mills and Boon, and Toronto, Harlequin, 1975.
The Kilted Stranger. London, Mills and Boon, 1975; Toronto, Harlequin, 1976.
Ride a Black Horse. London, Mills and Boon, 1975; Toronto, Harlequin, 1976.
Stormy Rapture. London, Mills and Boon, and Toronto, Harlequin, 1976.
Hold Me Captive. London, Mills and Boon, and Toronto, Harlequin, 1976.
Blue Skies, Dark Waters. London, Mills and Boon, 1976; Toronto, Harlequin, 1977.
Better to Forget. London, Mills and Boon, 1977; Toronto, Harlequin, 1978.

Never Go Back. Toronto, Harlequin, 1977.
Flamingo Moon. London, Mills and Boon, 1977; Toronto, Harlequin, 1978.
Wild Inheritance. London, Mills and Boon, 1977; Toronto, Harlequin, 1978.
The Jewelled Caftan. London, Mills and Boon, and Toronto, Harlequin, 1978.
A Man Called Cameron. London, Mills and Boon, 1978.
Marriage Impossible. London, Mills and Boon, 1978.
Midnight Magic. London, Mills and Boon, and Toronto, Harlequin, 1978.
The Wild Rowan. London, Mills and Boon, 1978; Toronto, Harlequin, 1979.
Autumn Song. London, Mills and Boon, 1979.
Boomerang Bride. London, Mills and Boon, 1979; Toronto, Harlequin, 1981.
The Devil's Bride. London, Mills and Boon, 1979.
Only You. London, Mills and Boon, 1979.
Savage Possession. London, Mills and Boon, 1979; Toronto, Harlequin, 1980.
Kiss of a Tyrant. London, Mills and Boon, and Toronto, Harlequin, 1980.
Deception. London, Mills and Boon, 1980; Toronto, Harlequin, 1981.
Dark Surrender. London, Mills and Boon, 1980; Toronto, Harlequin, 1981.
The Dark Oasis. London, Mills and Boon, 1980; Toronto, Harlequin, 1981.
The Loving Slave. London, Mills and Boon, 1981; Toronto, Harlequin, 1982.
Captivity. London, Mills and Boon, and Toronto, Harlequin, 1981.
Collision. London, Mills and Boon, 1981.
At First Glance. London, Mills and Boon, 1981.
Substitute Bride. London, Mills and Boon, 1981; Toronto, Harlequin, 1983.
Man from the Kimberleys. London, Mills and Boon, 1982; Toronto, Harlequin, 1983.
Not Far Enough. London, Mills and Boon, and Toronto, Harlequin, 1982.
Prelude to a Song. London, Mills and Boon, 1982; Toronto, Harlequin, 1983.
Storm Cycle. London, Mills and Boon, 1982.
Storm in the Night. London, Mills and Boon, 1983; Toronto, Harlequin, 1984.
Clouded Rapture. London, Mills and Boon, 1983.
Chains of Regret. London, Mills and Boon, 1983.
Caribbean Gold. London, Mills and Boon, and Toronto, Harlequin, 1983.
The Demitrious Line. London, Mills and Boon, and Toronto, Harlequin, 1983.
The Silver Flame. London, Mills and Boon, 1983.
Born of the Wind. London, Mills and Boon, 1984.
The Odds Against. London, Mills and Boon, 1984.
Captive of Fate. London, Mills and Boon, 1985.
Impasse. London, Mills and Boon, 1985.
Total Surrender. London, Mills and Boon, 1985.
Lost Enchantment. London, Mills and Boon, 1985.
Model of Deception. London, Mills and Boon, 1985.
The Other Side of Paradise. London, Mills and Boon, 1985.
Beyond Reach. London, Mills and Boon, 1986.
A Scarlet Woman. London, Mills and Boon, 1986.

*   *   *

Margaret Pargeter is a relatively new British romance writer. She began being published in the mid-1970s and has continued since then to develop her own style of writing. It is a style that has instantly made her one of the more popular romance writers in years.

She is also one of the 'new' romance writers who aims for realism by drawing on modern 'literary' techniques of writing. Her plots are generally complicated as are her characters. Inner turmoil plays a constant counter-point as the heroine reacts to events in the novel and her own hopeless love for her hero. Tension, pathos, and despair provide constant reaction for her readers as she maintains near melodramatic levels of stress.

Her early novels do not have this heightened emotionalism, although they do have refreshing plots and well-balanced characters. *Better to Forget* and *Ride a Black Horse* are both in this traditional vein. Liza Dean in *Better to Forget* helps to prevent a fire in the large department store she works in. The shock of the accident and her own emotional problems cause Liza to lose her memory. She is taken care of by Grant Latham, the wealthy owner of the store. Jane Brown in *Ride a Black Horse* applies for a job in an exclusive stables and riding school at High Linton. She gets the job by falsifying her background. She eventually runs away after falling in love with the owner, Karl Grierson. Both of these novels depend on standard reactions and conflicts within the story.

Her later novels have more complicated dimensions that quickly illustrate the complex development of character and Pargeter's development as a writer. In *The Devil's Bride* Sandra is forced by her cousin Alexandra into taking her place after her fiancée, Stein Freeman, is blinded in an accident. He is a well known writer who spends much of his time in Greece. He discovers the deception and forces Sandra to marry him and return to Greece with him. His treatment of her is cruel and vindictive as he takes out his frustrations and anger on her. There is a constant pressure on Sandra as she grows to love him in spite of his action. Conflict is intense, and reader reaction is just as intense, for emotional build up is continued and heightened until the very end of the novel.

Even more intense is *Boomerang Bride*. The character development is extremely complex and shows a wealth of complicated emotional reactions. In fact, it comes close to being a psychological study rather than a romance. The central thrust of the plot centres on the McLeods, an 'Outback' station family. Only Wade McLeod and his grandfather are left, and their relationship is one of extreme dislike that borders on hate. The grandfather almost fanatically wants an heir for the station. In revenge, and hoping to prevent his grandfather's wishes from coming true, Wade marries Vicki. She is a temporary home-help and he considers her very ineligible. He presents his proposition as a business arrangement and Vicki agrees. He is determined not to have children! His passion and Vicki's unconscious provocation end that, however, and she becomes pregnant. Furious, Wade orders her to leave the station and she does—only to be brought back four years later with their son, Graham. The course of the story picks up their relationship and the final outcome centres on the people as they face the changes that have taken place over these years.

In assessing Pargeter as a writer, one must keep in mind the tremendous changes that have taken place in romance writing over the past few years. Many of these novels are filled with modern writing techniques and have a slightly different frame of reference than just romance. Stream of consciousness plays a much greater part in the novels, as does a more sophisticated outlook. Because of these elements, Pargeter probably appeals to a somewhat different audience from the traditional romance readers. She is also one of the Harlequin Presents writers. These writers tend to show modern love against more complicated and emotional backgrounds.

—Arlene Moore

PARKINSON, C(yril) Northcote.
Nationality: British. **Born:** Barnard Castle, County Durham, 30 July 1909. **Education:** St Peter's School, York; Emmanuel College, Cambridge (Corbett prize), B.A. 1932, M.A., Ph.D. 1935. **Military Service:** British Army, Queen's Royal Regiment, 1940–45: major. **Relations:** married 1) Ethelwyn Graves in 1942 (divorced 1949), one son and one daughter; 2) Ann Fry in 1951 (died 1983), two sons and one daughter; 3) Iris Waters in 1985. **Career:** master, Blundell's School, Tiverton, Devon, 1938–39, and Royal Naval College, Dartmouth, Devon, 1939–40; lecturer in history, University of Liverpool, 1946–50; Raffles professor of history, University of Malaya, Singapore, 1950–58. Visiting professor, Harvard University, Cambridge, Massachusetts, 1958, and University of Illinois, Urbana, and University of California, Berkeley, 1959–60; visiting professor, 1961–62, and since 1970 professor emeritus and honorary president, Troy State University, Troy, Alabama. **Recipient:** LLD: University of Maryland, College Park, 1974; D.Litt.: Troy State University, 1976. Fellow, Royal Historical Society. **Died:** 9 March 1993.

ROMANCE AND HISTORICAL PUBLICATIONS

Novels (series: Richard Delancey in all books except *The Life and Times of Horatio Hornblower*)

The Life and Times of Horatio Hornblower. London, Joseph, and Boston, Little Brown, 1970.
Devil to Pay. London, Murray, and Boston, Houghton Mifflin, 1973.
The Fireship. London, Murray, and Boston, Houghton Mifflin, 1975.
Touch and Go. London, Murray, and Boston, Houghton Mifflin, 1977.
Dead Reckoning. London, Murray, and Boston, Houghton Mifflin, 1978.
So Near so Far. London, Murray, and Boston, Houghton Mifflin, 1981.
The Guernsey Man. London, Murray, and Boston, Houghton Mifflin, 1982.

OTHER PUBLICATIONS

Novel

Jeeves: A Gentleman's Personal Gentleman. London, Macdonald and Jane's, and New York, St Martin's Press, 1979.

Plays

Helier Bonamy (produced Guernsey, 1967).
The Royalist (produced Guernsey, 1969).

Radio Play: *The China Fleet*, 1952 (Singapore).

Other

Edward Pellew, Viscount Exmouth. London, Methuen, 1934.
Trade in the Eastern Seas 1793–1813. London, Cambridge University Press, 1937.
Always a Fusilier: The War History of the Royal Fusiliers. London, Sampson Low, 1949.
The Rise of the Port of Liverpool. Liverpool, University of Liverpool Press, 1952.
War in the Eastern Seas 1793–1815. London, Allen and Unwin, 1954.

Templer in Malaya. Singapore, Moore, 1954.
A Short History of Malaya. Singapore, Moore, 1954; revised edition, 1956.
Britain in the Far East. Singapore, Moore, 1955.
Marxism for Malayans. Singapore, Moore, 1956.
Heroes of Malaya, with Ann Parkinson. Singapore, Moore, 1956.
Parkinson's Law. Boston, Houghton Mifflin, 1957; London, Murray, 1958.
The Evolution of Political Thought. London, University of London Press, and Boston, Houghton Mifflin, 1958.
British Intervention in Malaya. Singapore, University of Malaya Press, 1960.
The Law and the Profits. London, Murray, and Boston, Houghton Mifflin, 1960.
In-Laws and Outlaws. London, Murray, and Boston, Houghton Mifflin, 1962.
East and West. London, Murray, and Boston, Houghton Mifflin, 1963.
Ponies Plot (for children). London, Murray, and Boston, Houghton Mifflin, 1965.
A Law unto Themselves. London, Murray, and Boston, Houghton Mifflin, 1966.
Left Luggage. London, Murray, and Boston, Houghton Mifflin, 1967.
Mrs Parkinson's Law and Other Stories in Domestic Science. London, Murray, and Boston, Houghton Mifflin, 1968.
The Law of Delay: Interviews and Outerviews. London, Murray, 1970; Boston, Houghton Mifflin, 1971.
The Essential Parkinson: Six Lectures in India. New Delhi, Economic and Scientific Research Foundation, 1970.
Incentives and Penalties. Bombay, Shah, 1973.
Big Business. London, Weidenfeld and Nicolson, and Boston, Little Brown, 1974.
How to Get to the Top Without Ulcers, Tranquillisers, or Heart Attacks, with M.K. Rustomji. New Delhi, Macmillan, 1974.
Watch Your Fingers, with M.K. Rustomji. New Delhi, Macmillan, 1976.
Gunpowder, Treason and Plot. London, Weidenfeld and Nicolson, 1976; New York, St Martin's Press, 1977.
Britannia Rules: The Classic Age of Naval History 1793–1815. London, Weidenfeld and Nicolson, 1977.
Communicate: Parkinson's Formula for Business Survival, with Nigel Rowe. Englewood Cliffs, New Jersey, Prentice Hall, 1977.
The Rise of Big Business. London, Weidenfeld and Nicolson, 1977.
The Law; or, Still in Pursuit. London, Murray, 1979; Boston, Houghton Mifflin, 1980.
The Law of Longer Life, with Herman Le Compte. Troy, Alabama, Troy State University Press, 1980.
Realities in Management, with M.K. Rustomji. Bombay, IBH, 1981.
The Fur-Lined Mousetrap. Bolton, Lancashire, Anderson, 1983.
Parkinson: The Law Complete, Part II. London, Ballantine, 1983.
The Management Jungle. New Delhi, Tarang, 1984.
Manhunt: Wartime Adventure on the Isle of Man. Isle of Man, Manx, Experience Publications, 1990.

Editor, *The Trade Winds*. London, Allen and Unwin, 1948.
Editor, *Portsmouth Point: The Navy in Fiction 1793–1815*. Liverpool, University of Liverpool Press, 1948; Cambridge, Massachusetts, Harvard University Press, 1949.
Editor, *Samuel Walters, Lieutenant RN*. Liverpool, University of Liverpool Press, 1949.
Editor, *Industrial Disruption*. Epsom, Surrey, Leviathan House, 1973.
Editor and Translator, *The Journal of a Frenchman in Malayan Waters*. Singapore, Royal Asiatic Society, 1952.

*

C. Northcote Parkinson commented (1990):

My works of historical fiction relate to a period known to me as an historian. Characters and events are close to reality. I did not write these novels until C.S. Forester had died.

*   *   *

Before embarking on a career as a novelist, C. Northcote Parkinson was already well established as a professional historian, as well as being widely known as the originator of 'Parkinson's Law'. His researches into late 18th- and early 19th-century naval history (summarized in *Britannia Rules* and countless other volumes) provided a firm basis for his 'biography' of C.S. Forester's *Horatio Hornblower*.

Parkinson's own novels follow the fortunes of Richard Delancey, a native of Guernsey, who becomes a captain's clerk in the Royal Navy, at the time of the War of American Independence, in order to avoid imprisonment for his accidental involvement in a seamen's riot in Liverpool. Elevated to the quarterdeck as a midshipman, he serves in America during the war with the rebel colonists, sees further service against the French at the 'battle of St Helier' in Jersey in 1781, and against the Spanish at the siege of Gibraltar (all of which events are recounted in *The Guernsey Man*, the opening novel in the sequence). Thereafter, during the revolutionary and Napoleonic wars, Lieutenant Delancey has further adventures—as commander of a revenue cutter, privateer, secret agent, and as a participant in a series of naval battles—before reaching his apotheosis as Sir Richard Delancey, successful frigate captain home from the East Indies in 1811, following numerous, victorious encounters with the French. Romantic and personal interest is provided in the stories by Delancey's marriage to a former actress and by the gradual recovery of his maternal family inheritance, as a landowner and figure of substance in the island of Guernsey.

In terms of their historical detail the novels would be difficult to fault. Parkinson was scrupulous in his use of events and the presentation of facts. His knowledge of the naval world of the Napoleonic era was encyclopaedic; his understanding of ships and seamen, of politics, strategy and trade almost unrivalled. This solid bedding in the reality of the past gives the novels their appeal. They are interesting, too, compared with other novels of their type, in that they cover some unfamiliar ground, Parkinson's use of the Channel Islands, both as a home for Delancey and a setting for action, being a case in point. Elsewhere it is instructive to compare fictional accounts of famous episodes, for example Parkinson's account of the capture of Mauritius (*Dead Reckoning*) with the version of the same event in the career of Patrick O'Brian's Jack Aubrey (in O'Brian's book, *The Mauritius Command*). Parkinson keeps closer in some respects to the historical record (at least in taking fewer liberties with real characters), although critics may feel that O'Brian's is the more successful novel.

This last point leads to what is perhaps the one serious reservation about Parkinson's work. While impeccable as an historian, it has to be admitted that, as a novelist, Parkinson was no great stylist, and that some of his characterization lacks depth. The writing is too often that of the compressed descriptive summary, with a sometimes surprising reluctance on the part of the author to capitalize on the dramatic potential of the material at hand. The novels are intricately and closely plotted, yet all too frequently situations are built up only to be resolved in a matter of a sentence of two, where other writers might have used pages, or even chapters, to good advantage. Dialogue is a further problem. Parkinson's characters make speeches rather than have conversations; their discussions lack the feeling of spontaneity and consequently create an unfortunately stilted effect.

Similarly, while Delancey himself is a credible character (sensitive, artistic, yet authentically concerned with matters of money and promotion), he fails to engage the affections or emotions of the reader. The same is true of minor characters—the officers on Delancey's ships, his smuggler friend Sam Carter, the French spy Fabius. They appear at the right places in the plot but they do not live and breathe in the mind of the reader. Greater success is achieved with pen-portraits of actual historical figures whom Parkinson knows well, for instance Philip D'Auvergne, Duc de Bouillon, and head of an intelligence network based on the Channel Islands, who appears in *Devil to Pay*. Otherwise one misses the camaraderie and interaction of characters provided by other writers of the naval/historical school—the partnership of Aubrey-Maturin, Bolitho and his 'happy few', and the rest.

For all that, Parkinson's novels are faithful to their subject and their period. They display considerable invention and erudition, and they deserve to retain their (somewhat scholarly) place in the gallery of fictional contemporaries created in affectionate imitation of Forester's Hornblower. In chronicling the career of Richard Delancey, Parkinson has painted a realistic picture of the life of a sea-officer of his time. The balance of his literary reputation may rest with his non-fiction work, but that does not mean that the novels themselves are a negligible achievement in their chosen field.

—David Powell

PATERSON, Isabel M. (Bowler).
Nationality: Canadian. **Born:** Manitoulin Island, Alberta, in 1885. **Education:** public schools in Mountain View and Cardston, Alberta. **Relations:** married Kenneth Birrell Paterson. **Career:** clerk, Canadian Pacific Railroad, Calgary; journalist, *American* and *Hearst's Magazine*, both New York; columnist, *New York Herald Tribune*. **Died:** 1961.

ROMANCE AND HISTORICAL PUBLICATIONS

Novels

The Singing Season. New York, Boni and Liveright, 1924; London, Parsons, 1925.
The Fourth Queen. New York, Boni and Liveright, and London, Parsons, 1926.
The Road of the Gods. New York, Liveright, 1930.

OTHER PUBLICATIONS

Novels

The Shadow Riders. London, Lane, 1916.
The Magpie's Nest. London, Lane, 1917.
Never Ask the End. New York, Morrow, 1933.
The Golden Vanity. New York, Morrow, 1934.
If It Prove Fair Weather. New York, Putnam, 1940.

Other

The God of the Machine. New York, Putnam, 1943.

Editor, *A High Wind in Jamaica*, by Richard Hughes. New York, Modern Library, 1932.

*   *   *

Isabel M. Paterson's historical novels form less than half of her fiction titles. Contemporary novels dealing with the romantic adventures of young, urban American men and women between the world wars constitute the larger share of her work. However, romance and youth structure the plots of Paterson's historical novels as well and her style is consistent between her historical and non-historical novels. In Paterson's writing, plot and characterization are not complex nor are they developed in any depth of detail or sophistication. Her novels were well-received in the reviews of the day and their popularity should be acknowledged.

In *The Singing Season* Paterson presents the court and church intrigue in Spain at the time of King Henry and his brother King Pedro. This novel is Paterson's most historically detailed. The plot focuses on the romance between Isabella and Roderigo who become caught up in the larger political forces of the times. Its plot is chronological and the outcome of the romance is predictable, yet Paterson uses historical detail skilfully and rewards the reader's close attention with a fine sense of period and locale. An interesting aspect of her historical novels generally is that archaisms conventionally restricted in the genre to dialogue are carried over into scene description and narrative commentary.

The Fourth Queen is set near the end of the reign of Elizabeth I. The central romance is between Jack, John Philip Sidney Montagu, and Kate, granddaughter of Sir Thomas More. Other major figures presented are Essex and Francis Drake. Again, Paterson's concern is to evoke a sense of court life and the complex web of intrigue and power which ultimately determines the future of nations.

The Road of the Gods is the least conventional of Paterson's three historical novels. It is set in northeastern Europe during the reign of Octavian. She skilfully develops a detailed picture of pre-Christian culture not yet thoroughly penetrated by Roman influence. The novel closes with an impending invasion of the area by Roman forces and the sense that an ancient world is about to give way before the expansion of the Roman empire and the influence of classical civilization. Paterson carefully undermines the conventional view of life in Europe, before Roman military and cultural advancement, as mindless barbarism. Instead she uses plot, the romance between Hoath and Greda, to explore the possible complexity and richness of a culture and society which had evolved over centuries.

While Paterson's historical novels make pleasant, even provocative, reading, they are not her best work. Perhaps the best is her first novel, *The Shadow Riders*, which examines political and social life in a rapidly growing town in pre-World War I Alberta, Canada. The richness of the characters and the complexity of the plot, which follows two intersecting lines, are developed within a sophisticated narrative to an extent that Paterson does not manage to achieve in any of her later work.

—Heather Iris Jones

PATRICK, Maxine.   See **BLAKE, Jennifer.**

PAUL, Barbara.   See **LAKER, Rosalind.**

PAULEY, Barbara Anne.
Nationality: American. **Born:** Barbara Anne Cotton, Nashville, Tennessee, 12 January 1925. **Education:** Wellesley College, Cambridge, Massachusetts, 1942. **Relations:** married Robert Reinhold Pauley in 1946; one daughter and three sons. **Career:** editorial assistant, Ideal Publishing Corporation, then freelance writer.

Agent: Blassingame McCauley and Wood, 432 Park Avenue South, Suite 1205, New York, New York 10016. **Address:** c/o Doubleday, 666 Fifth Avenue, New York, New York 10103, USA.

Romance and Historical Publications

Novels

Blood Kin. New York, Doubleday, 1972.
Voices Long Hushed. New York, Doubleday, 1976.

*   *   *

To capture the passions, conflicts, and terrors of the Civil War, Barbara Anne Pauley focuses on a microcosm, an individual and familial situation, that reflects the broader problems of the times. *Blood Kin* focuses on a young southern miss whose disillusionment and longing for lost relationships and the pleasures of a lost youth lead her to visit neighbouring cousins, Union sympathizers firmly entrenched in a symbol of the dying South—a stately family plantation house. In *Voices Long Hushed* a young New England girl seeks her dubious heritage on a southern plantation, ravaged by war, but kept operative by poor, dependent Southern relations. In both, the conflicts, like those of the war itself, are family conflicts in which distant relatives conspire against the central characters—to acquire land or wealth or love, to hide sins, to work out personal hatreds.

In *Blood Kin* Leslie Hallam, deprived of family, land, and childhood by war, seeks to recreate her lost world of aristocratic and social comforts at Sycamore Knob, a magnificent Nashville plantation. She arrives amid stormy weather, only to find a more terrifying storm within, a frightening psychological turbulence beneath surface calm: a child terrorized by a nameless 'bad thing' that haunts her nights, and leaves her clothing bloodied; a fat, pasty-faced woman, once beautiful, whose greed and passions make her strike out in jealousy; her arrogant brother, a model of decadent aristocratic weakness; a dashing, self-possessed confederate soldier, the family black sheep, seemingly crushed by his own spirited steed; a mysteriously wounded head of house whose wit, spirit, and sexuality capture the heart of a vulnerable cousin; a kindly Union officer who suspects but cannot prove fearful undercurrents and dangerous conspiracies. Nightmarish sequences follow: a deadly game of hide and seek, an attic excursion that nearly ends in death by fire, a mad dash in a swift carriage—fleeing madness only to find secret madness inescapable. Amid such gothic horrors, romance blossoms, first in the sudden, physical passion that draws together an experienced man-of-the-world and an innocent girl, and then a gentler, self-giving love that grows with time and proximity.

In *Voices Long Hushed* an uncle's will shatters a young orphan's tranquillity. The loss of a lover and the discovery of a live mother, possibly a murderess and a madwoman, compel her to seek the truth of her inheritance at St Cloud, her mother's plantation. There Stacy begins to untangle the web of deceit spun by an odd assortment of distant, conniving relatives. Her realization that her mother's innocence means another's guilt awakens the conflicts that produced the first murder 25 years before, and once again murder stalks the balconies and shadowy galleries of the old manor. A chain of gothic horrors ensues: an elevator shaft left open in the dark, a poisonous snake left in a bedroom, a slave dead in a trunk, a locked-room murder, a deadly drug that simulates insanity. As three men try to impose their will on pliable Stacy, relationships prove skewed; family hatreds and pre-war wounds are exposed. Destroying the evil depends on a cryptic journal hidden in a slave cabin and restoration of an amnesiac's memory by recreating childhood terror. Ultimately, the young Northern heiress finds her place in the South, and chooses a relationship tangled forever in the tight emotional knots of love and murder, of father killing father.

Together these novels seek to expose and exorcise the terrors and evils that separate brother from brother—the essence, for Pauley, of Civil War conflict—while suggesting the strength that allows one to build from ties on the shaky ground of old horrors, atrocities, and passions.

—Gina Macdonald

———

PAYE, Robert. See BOWEN, Marjorie.

———

PAYNE, Alan. See JAKES, John.

———

PAYNE, Rachel Ann. See JAKES, John.

———

PEAKE, Lilian (Margaret).
Nationality: British. **Born:** London, 25 May 1924. **Relations:** married; has children. **Career:** secretary, and typist; journalist in High Wycombe; fashion writer in London; writer for *Daily Herald* and *Woman* magazine. Lives in Oxford. **Address:** c/o Mills and Boon Ltd, Eton House, 18–24 Paradise Road, Richmond, Surrey TW9 1SR, England.

ROMANCE AND HISTORICAL PUBLICATIONS

Novels

Man of Granite. London, Mills and Boon, 1971; Toronto, Harlequin, 1975.
This Moment in Time. London, Mills and Boon, 1971; Toronto, Harlequin, 1972.
The Library Tree. London, Mills and Boon, and Toronto, Harlequin, 1972.
Man Out of Reach. London, Mills and Boon, 1972; Toronto, Harlequin, 1973.
The Real Thing. London, Mills and Boon, 1972; Toronto, Harlequin, 1973.
A Girl Alone. London, Mills and Boon, 1972; Toronto, Harlequin, 1978.
Mist Across the Moors. London, Mills and Boon, and Toronto, Harlequin, 1972.
No Friend of Mine. London, Mills and Boon, 1972; Toronto, Harlequin, 1977.
Gone Before Morning. London, Mills and Boon, and Toronto, Harlequin, 1973.
Man in Charge. London, Mills and Boon, and Toronto, Harlequin, 1973.
Familiar Stranger. London, Mills and Boon, 1973; Toronto, Harlequin, 1976.
Till the End of Time. London, Mills and Boon, 1973; Toronto, Harlequin, 1975.
The Dream on the Hill. London, Mills and Boon, 1974; Toronto, Harlequin, 1975.
A Sense of Belonging. London, Mills and Boon, and Toronto, Harlequin, 1974.
Master of the House. London, Mills and Boon, and Toronto, Harlequin, 1974.
The Impossible Marriage. London, Mills and Boon, 1974; Toronto, Harlequin, 1975.

Moonrise over the Mountains. London, Mills and Boon, 1975; Toronto, Harlequin, 1976.
Heart in the Sunlight. London, Mills and Boon, 1975; Toronto, Harlequin, 1976.
The Tender Night. London, Mills and Boon, 1975; Toronto, Harlequin, 1976.
The Sun of Summer. London, Mills and Boon, 1975; Toronto, Harlequin, 1976.
A Bitter Loving. London, Mills and Boon, 1976; Toronto, Harlequin, 1977.
The Distant Dream. London, Mills and Boon, and Toronto, Harlequin, 1976.
The Little Impostor. London, Mills and Boon, 1976; Toronto, Harlequin, 1977.
This Man Her Enemy. London, Mills and Boon, 1976; Toronto, Harlequin, 1977.
Somewhere to Lay My Head. London, Mills and Boon, and Toronto, Harlequin, 1977.
Passionate Involvement. London, Mills and Boon, 1977; Toronto, Harlequin, 1978.
No Second Parting. London, Mills and Boon, 1977; Toronto, Harlequin, 1979.
Across a Crowded Room. London, Mills and Boon, 1977; Toronto, Harlequin, 1981.
Day of Possession. London, Mills and Boon, 1978.
Rebel in Love. London, Mills and Boon, and Toronto, Harlequin, 1978.
Run for Your Love. London, Mills and Boon, 1978; Toronto, Harlequin, 1980.
Dangerous Deception. London, Mills and Boon, 1979; Toronto, Harlequin, 1980.
Enemy from the Past. London, Mills and Boon, and Toronto, Harlequin, 1979.
Stranger on the Beach. London, Mills and Boon, and Toronto, Harlequin, 1979.
Promise at Midnight. London, Mills and Boon, 1980; Toronto, Harlequin, 1981.
A Ring for a Fortune. London, Mills and Boon, and Toronto, Harlequin, 1980.
A Secret Affair. London, Mills and Boon, 1980; Toronto, Harlequin, 1981.
Strangers into Lovers. London, Mills and Boon, and Toronto, Harlequin, 1981.
Gregg Barratt's Woman. London, Mills and Boon, and Toronto, Harlequin, 1981.
Capture a Stranger. London, Mills and Boon, 1981.
Stay Till Morning. London, Mills and Boon, 1982.
Bitter Revenge. London, Mills and Boon, 1982.
No Other Man. London, Mills and Boon, 1982.
Passionate Intruder. London, Mills and Boon, 1982.
Come Love Me. London, Mills and Boon, 1983.
Night of Possession. London, Mills and Boon, 1983.
A Woman in Love. London, Mills and Boon, and Toronto, Harlequin 1984.
Elusive Paradise. London, Mills and Boon, 1985; Toronto, Harlequin 1987.
Ice into Fire. London, Mills and Boon, 1985; Toronto, Harlequin 1986.
Never in a Lifetime. London, Mills and Boon, 1985.
Love in the Moonlight. London, Mills and Boon, 1986; Toronto, Harlequin 1987.
The Bitter Taste of Love. London, Mills and Boon, 1988; Toronto, Harlequin 1989.
Take This Woman. London, Mills and Boon, and Toronto, Harlequin 1988.
Dance to My Tune. London, Mills and Boon, 1989.

Climb Every Mountain. London, Mills and Boon, 1989.
Irresistable Enemy. London, Mills and Boon, 1990.
Forbidden Attraction. London, Mills and Boon, 1990.
Stranger Passing By. London, Mills and Boon, 1992; Toronto, Harlequin, 1994.

*   *   *

Lilian Peake's first romance title was published in 1971, and since then she has proved her staying power in the exacting field of category romance with another 60 books. One of the first Mills and Boon authors to appear in the breakaway Harlequin Presents series in North America, she achieved early popularity on both sides of the Atlantic and, although her output has declined in recent years, she remains a very steady performer.

Peake is not especially strong on different or unusual plots, preferring to use the standard romantic misunderstanding between hero and heroine as a regular device, occasionally combined with another common romantic theme, the engagement or marriage of convenience. Instead she achieves her effects by the creation of larger than life central characters whose psychological profiles dominate the action and involve the reader in the battle of wits between them. Often she stresses the importance of the struggle beween the couple by choosing physically to isolate them from the world for a section of the story in fairly basic accommodation, as for example, in *Stranger on the Beach* in which the hero and heroine share adjoining beach huts on the North Sea coast, or *Passionate Intruder* in which they are thrown together on a remote Scottish island.

A Peake heroine conforms to category romance requirements that she should attract reader sympathy, and be idealistic, principled, loyal, and compassionate. She is reasonably attractive with an outgoing personality, has a fondness for animals, and an affinity with older people, often acting as companion and friend to an elderly person whose family apparently neglects them (*Take This Woman*, *Dance to My Tune*). These admirable qualities are balanced by a quick temper, a tendency to impulsiveness, and a belief in doing what she considers to be the right thing carried to an extreme which can be construed as wilful stubbornness. Usually less able than the hero socially and intellectually, she is conscious of the gap between them and may have a chip on her shoulder when she contrasts his worldly success and formal qualifications with her lack of conventional training. She does have the edge over the hero in her ability to surrender to her emotions. Usually she has to teach the hero how to overcome past hurt and learn to trust again. Unlike most romantic heroines she admits or shows her love for the hero quite early in the book and by so doing leaves herself open to hard-hitting emotional attacks from him. The line between hate and love is a fragile one in Peake's stories.

The Peake hero is cool and assured, confident of his position in life and well aware that he is a good matrimonial catch. He is usually British and, although he looks like the answer to every woman's dream, he is cerebral rather than physical, and often has an academic or artistic slant. It is interesting to note how often Peake's heroes, especially in the earlier part of her career, pursue less glamorous occupations than are usually standard for a romantic hero, for example, head librarian (*The Library Tree*), schools inspector (*This Moment in Time*), acting headmaster (*Mist Across the Moors*), chairman of the education committee (*Rebel in Love*). Usually a loner and invariably a misogynist because of past experiences with materialistic or unprincipled women, he is cynical about love, and is not inclined to let down the emotional barriers. Alaric Stoddart, in *Master of the House* speaks for most Peake heroes when he announces, 'All women are the same. They're after two things and two things only—money and marriage in that order'. He drives himself as hard as the people around him and his standards are impossibly high. The harsh surface eventually cracks to show inner compassion, but initially he can seem breathtakingly arrogant. His subsequent cutting down to size by the heroine must provide a good deal of satisfaction for the reader.

With a central couple whose battle of wills makes such an impact on the reader, it is inevitable that the other characters remain somewhat in the background. Often they are family members and Peake is one of the few writers successfully to tackle sibling rivalry as a regular theme; for example, in *Love in the Moonlight* the heroine's sister courts the hero's affections just as the hero's brother is the focus for the heroine's interest in *Never in a Lifetime*.

Peake's characters inhabit an everyday world that is more often down-to-earth than glamorous. One feels that, left to his own devices, the herò would prefer to wear an anorak rather than a dinner jacket and, although the heroine is quite capable of glamour when the occasion demands it, she is equally adept at roughing it in primitive surroundings. Peake clearly prefers the countryside to the town; the Scottish countryside and the Yorkshire moors are favourite settings—often in the rain or mist. When the author has ventured further afield she has been particularly successful at giving well-researched pictures of countries with less obvious reader appeal such as Switzerland, Norway, and Germany.

Peake is a solid, workman-like writer whose stories, although offering the reader the expected blend oflove and passion combining in a happy ending, are far from the frothy concoctions usually ascribed to producers of category romance. Over her writing career she has deservedly built up an appreciative audience worldwide and fully merits her reputation as a reliable read.

—Frances Whitehead

PEARL, Jack.   See **BLAKE, Stephanie.**

PEARSON, Diane.
Nationality: British. **Born:** Diane Margaret Holker, Croyden, Surrey, 5 November 1931. **Education:** Secondary school, Croyden. **Relations:** Richard Leeper McClelland, 1975. **Career:** book production assistant, Jonathan Cape Ltd, London, 1948–52; associated with local government, 1952–64. Since 1964, copy writer, Corgi Books Ltd. **Address:** c/o Curtis Brown Ltd, 1 Craven Hill, London W2 3EP, England.

ROMANCE AND HISTORICAL PUBLICATIONS

Novels

The Loom of Tancred. London, Hale, 1967; as *The Bride of Tancred*, London, Corgi, 1976.
The Marigold Field. London, Macmillan, and Philadelphia, Lippincott, 1969.
Sarah Whitman. London, Macmillan, 1971; as *Sarah*, Philadelphia, Lippincott, 1971.
Csardas. London, Macmillan, 1975; Greenwich, Connecticut, Fawcett, 1985.
The Summer of the Barshinskeys. London, Macmillan, and New York, Crown, 1984.
Voices of Summer. London, Bantam Press, 1992.

*   *   *

Diane Pearson's books are immensely varied in background, from the gothic house and tormented people of *The Loom of*

Tancred (*Bride of Tancred*), the tranquil country and a lost era of *The Marigold Field*, to various parts of Russia, the realities of London's East End, the missions of India, wartime Hungary, and Austrian musical comedy.

Yet there are common themes throughout Pearson's novels, of strong women rising above sorrows and disadvantages, and the importance of religion, often featuring Quakers. All of them have the page-turning quality of a born storyteller's work.

In *The Loom of Tancred* the Quaker Miriam, outwardly a demure Victorian girl hampered by her illegitimacy, but inwardly rebellious, escapes from her village to go to Tancred, a decaying mansion on the South Downs. She is to be needlewoman and companion, but finds herself involved with a strange, mysterious family dominated by the memory of the dead father, Richard, who ruined and brought shame to the family. The atmosphere created is one of immense tension, fear, and ominous foreboding.

Evoking a particular ambience is something at which Pearson excels. In the early scenes of *Sarah Whitman* one can smell the chalk in the East End schoolroom where Sarah, having fought to raise herself from being a servant to become a teacher, faces her class. In *The Summer of the Barshinskeys* there is a delightful evocation of village life before 1914, with its harsh struggles and simple pleasures, and then the equally brilliant portrayal of the grim reality of war and famine and filth in a Russia torn by war and revolution. Quite different is the frothy operetta plot of *Voices of Summer*, with its high drama, starcrossed lovers, villains, and secrets, a story which is heart warming and charming.

Pearson's best-known book is *Csardas*, which received rave reviews and is compared with both *Gone with the Wind* and *War and Peace*. It is a book of enormous scope, following the fortunes of the Ferenc sisters from the glittering days of the Austro-Hungarian Empire to the totalitarianism of communist rule.

Other books deal with similarly broad canvasses. In *The Summer of the Barshinskeys* a Russian exile and his Kentish wife come to live in a typical village, where they both enchant and infuriate the neighbouring family, the Willoughbys. The youngest children, Sophie and Daisy May, make friends, and the first part is told from Sophie's point of view as she recalls that far-off summer. The eldest girls are very different. Lilian is aloof and superior, destined to make something of her life, while Galina is strange and wild, wants only to dance, and is the apple of her father's eye. Then Galina, rather against her will, is given a job at the Rectory, seduces the curate, runs away and her distraught father follows. The summer has ended.

Years later Edwin Willoughby meets and falls under Galina's spell, and follows her and her rich, indulgent but old lover to St Petersburg by becoming a stoker on a ship. It is 1914, and the ship is trapped. Edwin and Galina manage to survive, despite her foolishness, through war and revolution, until Galina becomes ill and dies. By then Daisy is with the Quakers who are helping refugees in the Caucasus, and she eventually finds Edwin and brings him home.

Pearson's most recent novel, *Voices of Summer* is a romance par excellence, in much lighter mood than Pearson's other novels. There is a small operetta company based in an Austrian town, Hochhauser. The star is Karl Gesner who was born in the town, has a good voice, but is a monster, jealous of good singers, and has destructive affairs with dancers and the second female singer Ingrid. Few sopranos are willing to work with him more than once, but Therese Aschmann is lured back into the world of singing after 20 years in obscurity. As a girl she was brilliant. Then her husband tried to kill her during a performance, creating an immense scandal. She divorced him, but lost both her confidence and her voice. The book follows the fortunes of the cast and others involved, and the townsfolk during the festival, in the manner of light opera. There is an absolutely delightful description of Gesner trying to steal Therese's

scene in the *Count of Luxemburg* while she wittily outflanks him. Then there is almost a tragedy as Gesner manipulates her exhusband into recreating the horrific scene which destroyed her before. But in the proper fashion virtue is rewarded, evil punished, and the lovers pair off satisfactorily.

Pearson creates marvellously memorable characters, she establishes them indelibly in a few lines of dialogue, with great expertise. She conveys the deepest emotions of both men and women equally well, and tackles both tragedy and comedy superbly.

—Marina Oliver

PEDLER, Margaret (Bass).
Nationality: British. **Relations:** married.

ROMANCE AND HISTORICAL PUBLICATIONS

Novels

This Splendid Folly. London, Mills and Boon, 1918; New York, Doran, 1921.
The House of Dreams-Come-True. London, Hodder and Stoughton, and New York, Doran, 1919.
The Hermit of Far End. London, Hodder and Stoughton, 1919; New York, Doran, 1920.
The Lamp of Fate. London, Hodder and Stoughton, 1920; New York, Doran, 1921.
The Moon Out of Reach. London, Hodder and Stoughton, and New York, Doran, 1921.
The Vision of Desire. London, Hodder and Stoughton, and New York, Doran, 1922.
The Barbarian Lover. London, Hodder and Stoughton, and New York, Doran, 1923.
Red Ashes. London, Hodder and Stoughton, 1924; New York, Doran, 1925.
The Better Love. New York, Doran, 1924.
Her Brother's Keeper. New York, Doran, 1924.
Mrs Daventry's Reputation. New York, Doran, 1924.
To-morrow's Tangle. London, Hodder and Stoughton, 1925; New York, Doran, 1926.
Yesterday's Harvest. London, Hodder and Stoughton, and New York, Doran, 1926.
Bitter Heritage. London, Hodder and Stoughton, and New York, Doubleday, 1928.
The Guarded Halo. London, Hodder and Stoughton, and New York, Doubleday, 1929.
Fire of Youth. London, Hodder and Stoughton, and New York, Doubleday, 1930.
Many Ways. London, Hodder and Stoughton, 1931.
Kindled Flame. London, Hodder and Stoughton, and New York, Doubleday, 1931.
Desert Sand. London, Hodder and Stoughton, and New York, Doubleday, 1932.
Pitiless Choice. London, Hodder and Stoughton, 1933.
The Greater Courage. New York, Doubleday, 1933.
Green Judgment. London, Hodder and Stoughton, 1934; as *Distant Dawn*, New York, Doubleday, 1934.
The Shining Cloud. London, Hodder and Stoughton, 1935; New York, Doubleday, 1936.
Flame in the Wind. London, Hodder and Stoughton, and New York, Doubleday, 1937.
No Armour Against Fate. London, Hodder and Stoughton, and New York, Doubleday, 1938.

Blind Loyalty. London, Hodder and Stoughton, and New York, Doubleday, 1940.
Not Heaven Itself. London, Hodder and Stoughton, 1940; New York, Doubleday, 1941.
Then Came the Test. London, Hodder and Stoughton, and New York, Doubleday, 1942.
No Gifts from Chance. London, Hodder and Stoughton, and New York, McBride, 1944.
Unless Two Be Agreed. London, Hodder and Stoughton, and New York, McBride, 1947.

Short Stories

Waves of Destiny. London, Hodder and Stoughton, and New York, Doran, 1924.
Checkered Paths. London, Hodder and Stoughton, 1935.

*   *   *

The stereotyped heroine of the 1930s was uncertain whether she wished to be liberated from man or dominated by him. It is indicative of this confusion (which was replacing the spiritual confusion on matters of the soul of earlier heroines) that she often seeks out a lover who is paradoxically both fierce yet gentle, who can kiss with stormy, sudden passion, while simultaneously maintaining a 'strange and lingering gentleness'. This quality of kissing, difficult thought it may be to achieve, is clearly seen as an attractive characteristic, for it has been adopted by a number of present-day heroes, who manage to kiss with 'fierce yet tender passion'.

Pedler went even further than just fierce tenderness, and invented in *The Barbarian Lover*, a strong, hard, arrogant man with sun-burned hatchet face, and obstinate straight-lipped mouth. He strides about the wide open spaces of the earth in travel-stained riding-kit always on hand to rescue the heroine from whatever dangerous and unlikely situation she has got herself into. His first act of bravery and chivalry is to save her from a man-eating tiger seconds before it gobbles her up. Later, he rescues her when she is struck by lightning in a forest. He saves her from her bolting horse. He finally concludes that she is overcivilized and if only she would go camping with him, this would make a real woman of her.

'Or a savage', retorted Patricia.
'I suppose that's what you set me down for, isn't it?'
'I certainly think you're—primitive', she returned.
'So is God; so is nature. I don't want to be anything else. After all, it's the big primitive things that count'.

The big primitive things in his life are birth, death, and the urgent desire to kiss her. Being a barbarian, he takes what he wants in every fibre of his being: 'There was a fire in his eyes—a flaming light of passion barely held in leash that terrified her. He caught her roughly in his arms. His mouth sought hers, straining against it in fierce, possessive kisses. The love and passion which his iron will had thwarted and held back for months surged over her now in a resistless torrent. The gates had been opened. They could never again be closed'.

Though to some extent afraid of this man's unleashed instincts, the girl ultimately gives in to her growing love for him, and learns to lie back and enjoy that fierce, barbarian, yet strangely gentle kissing, to yield tremulously to the imperious passion.

The Barbarian Lover was sold, in its first, 1923, version as one of 'Hodders Ninepenny Series' in a jaunty jacket showing the barbarian lover himself, clutched at by the girl behind both superimposed over a crossword puzzle. 'First Read the Book', the jacket commands. 'Then do the crossword'. When reissued in 1938; it was abridged.

Pedler's other 30-odd titles share similar tangled emotions, and unleashed passion.

—Rachel Anderson

———

PEMBERTON, Margaret.
Pseudonym: Christina Harland. **Nationality:** British. **Born:** Margaret Hudson, Bradford, Yorkshire, 10 April 1943. **Education:** girls school, Bradford, Yorkshire. **Relations:** married Mike Pemberton in 1968; four daughters, one son. **Agent:** Carol Smith Agency, 25 Hornton Court, Kensington High Street, London W8 7RT, England. **Address:** 13 Manor Lane, London, S.E.13, England.

ROMANCE AND HISTORICAL PUBLICATIONS

Novels

Rendezvous with Danger, edited by Lesley Saxby. London, Macdonald and Jane's, 1974.
The Mystery of Saligo Bay. London, Macdonald and Jane's, 1976.
Tapestry of Fear. London, Hale, 1979.
Vengeance in the Sun. London, Hale, 1979.
The Guilty Secret. London, Hale, and New York, St Martin's Press, 1979.
Pioneer Girl. London, Mills and Boon, 1981.
Harlot. London, Arrow, 1981.
Lion of Languedoc. London, Mills and Boon, 1981.
African Enchantment. London, Mills and Boon, 1982.
The Flower Garden. London, Macdonald, 1982.
Forever. London, Fontana, 1982.
Devil's Palace. London, Mills and Boon, 1983.
Flight to Verechenko. London, Mills and Boon, 1983.
Silver Shadows, Golden Dreams. London, Macdonald, 1985.
Never Leave Me. London, Macdonald, and New York, Bantam, 1986.
A Multitude of Sins. London, Bantam, 1988.
Party in Peking. London, Hale, 1989.
White Christmas in Saigon (as Christina Harland). London, Corgi 1990.
Waiting Wives (as Christina Harland). New York, Bantam, 1991.
An Embarrassment of Riches. London, Bantam Press, 1992.
Moonflower Madness. London, Severn House, 1993.
Zadruga. London, Bantam Press, 1994.

*

Margaret Pemberton comments:

I began writing suspense stories at the age of eight. In my teens I wrote stories for the women's magazines market, abandoning short stories when my first novel, *Rendezvous with Danger*, was published in 1974. This book is a romantic suspense, and like much of my later fiction, is set in a foreign locale well known to me. In 1981, my first historical romance was published by Mills and Boon. A desire to write stories of more depth, and against a background of actual historical events led to the publication of *Never Leave Me*, with its in-depth account of American landings on Omaha Beach. *A Multitude of Sins*, a love story of equal intensity, is set against the drama of the fall of Hong Kong to the Japanese. Friendship with a woman whose husband was a Prisoner of War in Hanoi for six years, led to *White Christmas in Saigon*, a novel of great human emotion centring on the lives of three men missing in action in Vietnam, and the women who love them and who embark on a personal mission to find them. As well as the intense human drama of such storylines, humour is much in evidence in my work, as in *An Embarrassment of Riches* and *Moonflower Madness*.

*   *   *

Margaret Pemberton is a versatile writer, equally at home in the past and the present, in Europe, America, or Asia. She has written thrillers, historical novels, romantic suspense, family sagas, and contemporary novels. Her books are full of deeply felt emotion and sexual tension, her characters are lively, the women beautiful, the men devastatingly attractive and her plots are ingenious: just when you think you know what is going to happen next, she surprises you.

Pioneer Girl is typical of her early historicals, dealing with a burgeoning love affair set against a well-researched historical background with a minimum of minor characters so that she can concentrate on the hero and heroine. A young girl is travelling with the Mormons on the Oregon Trail in 1846. She meets a Cavalry officer who tries to turn the Mormons back but they are determined to go on. Major Dart Richards travels with them, falling in love with Polly. In spite of mutual attraction, misunderstandings keep them apart until Polly is captured by Indians and Dart reveals that he is half Indian and rescues her and sweeps her off into marriage, despite convention.

Silver Shadows, Golden Dreams is typical of her earlier near-contemporary novels. It is a fascinating story set in the early days of Hollywood. Daisy is abandoned in a orphanage as a baby and when she leaves at 17, finds her way to Hollywood where she catches the eye of Vidal a powerful, enigmatic producer. She calls herself Valentina and becomes a screen idol. She loves Vidal who is violently attracted to her but for reasons withheld from the reader for some time, cannot divorce his wife and marry her. The plot twists and turns with many exciting events and misunderstandings until at last Valentina and Vidal achieve happiness.

Longer books with bigger casts of characters and varying locations took her onto the bestseller lists. *Never Leave Me*, is set during World War II and the post-war period and moves from Normandy in wartime to post-war San Francisco. It is the story of Lisette, a young French girl in the Resistance, who succumbs to forbidden love for Dieter, a German officer. When the liberation comes, Dieter dies leaving her pregnant. She rescues Luke, an Englishman, from his burning plane. Luke knowing her predicament, offers her marriage but Lisette refuses him, and thinks she has lost the baby. She falls in love with Greg, an American officer and marries him only to find she is still carrying Dieter's child and that Greg has an implacable hatred of anything German. This causes Lisette much distress and her guilty feelings threaten their marriage. She cannot bring herself to tell Greg in case she loses him: he comes to believe that Luke fathered her child. It is not until Lisette's son Dominic falls in love with Luke's daughter that the truth comes out and Lisette and Greg's marriage comes right, love triumphing.

Pemberton has an excellent grasp of military history and uses it well in her books. The Allied landing on Omaha beach, in June 1944, is graphically portrayed in *Never Leave Me*, and the taking of Hong Kong by the Japanese during World War II is the background to Elizabeth Harland's love story, in *A Multitude of Sins*, and the conflict in Vietnam in the 1960s is starkly depicted as the background to the struggle of three very different women to find the men they love in *White Christmas in Saigon*.

Ireland and America in the turbulent middle years of the 19th-century are the background to her saga, *An Embarrassment of Riches*. Maura Sullivan, a beautiful, illegitimate Irish girl is married, coldly out of hand, by a rich New Yorker merely to spite his snobbish father. How Maura established herself in New York society and finds love makes an absorbing story.

The strong emotions in Pemberton's books make them compelling reading, her descriptions of people and places bring them alive so that the reader feels as if she were seeing them herself. Her books are the sort that are hard to put down and cause one to burn the midnight oil to find out what happens next.

—Pamela Cleaver

———

PEMBERTON, Nan. See **PYKARE, Nina.**

———

PENMAN, Sharon K(ay).
Nationality: American. **Address:** c/o Henry Holt Inc, 115 West 18th Street, New York, New York 10011, USA.

ROMANCE AND HISTORICAL PUBLICATIONS

Novels

The Sunne in Splendour. New York, Holt Rinehart, 1982; London, Macmillan, 1983.
Here Be Dragons. New York, Holt Rinehart, 1985; London, Collins, 1986.
Falls the Shadow. New York, Holt Rinehart, and London, Joseph, 1988.
The Reckoning. New York, Holt Rinehart, and London, Joseph, 1991.

*   *   *

Sharon K. Penman's *The Sunne in Splendour* is a most impressive undertaking for a first work. Exceedingly readable, obviously well researched, this major novel of the life of Richard III brings the 15th century vividly to life. The adjective 'panoramic' springs to mind, but with its implications of a fairly shallow treatment of a broad subject this does the book less than justice.

Many writers of Ricardian novels give the impression of being more than a little in love with the protagonist, so that this work is by no means unique in being unashamedly pro-Richard. He is portrayed as a man with a conscience, swept partly against his will into the political machinations rife in the 15th century; this is not a fresh interpretation of Richard's participation in historical events, but what makes it particularly credible is the way in which all the characters are brought alive, making this complex period in history more readily understandable.

Well written, interesting, and even gripping, *The Sunne in Splendour* is in many ways an exceedingly scholarly work. Penman recognizes that 'While imagination is the heart of any novel, historical fiction needs a strong factual foundation, especially a novel revolving around a man as controversial as Richard III'. She says that she finds herself 'torn between two faiths. The novelist's need for an untrammelled, freeflowing imagination is always at war with the historian's pure passion for verity. I do try to keep fact-tampering to a minimum, but it occasionally is necessary in order to advance the storyline'. *The Sunne in Splendour*, and her other novels do indeed follow the known facts very closely, with embellishments to fill in the blanks. Obviously much must be speculation, but with such integrity does Penman tackle her subjects that these embellishments always have the ring of authenticity. For example, the romance between Anne Neville and Richard is often said to have dated from childhood; this is very handy for the historical novelist but is it true? Romance and history are in this novel integrated in such a way as to make it plausible, and Penman's technique of weaving known details with the projection of possibilities also sows the seeds of Anne's eventual consumption in the period she spent in hiding disguised as a kitchen maid.

As with any retelling of Ricardian history, *The Sunne in Splendour* is overlaid with a sense of doom, as we not only know the end of the story but are also aware of history's verdict. This in no way diminishes the grip which this novel has upon the reader, but instead seems to increase the power that this tragic period in history still exercises.

The hero of Penman's next book, *Here Be Dragons*, is Llewelyn ab Iowerth, Prince of Gwynedd. This novel does not make the same impact as *The Sunne in Splendour*, perhaps because the author's heart was not given to her subject in quite the same way. The telling is not as detailed or realistic and undoubtedly not as committed; however, in being more dispassionate could it perhaps be considered a better novel? There is certainly more of a sense of pure fiction, perhaps because the historical period dealt with is not so well known or so well documented. Penman herself admits 'it was necessary to rely upon imagination to a greater extent than in my earlier novel of 15th-century England, for Llewelyn's world was not as well chronicled as that of the Yorkist kings. But the structure of *Here Be Dragons* is grounded in fact; even the more unlikely occurrences are validated by mediaeval chroniclers'. Thus we are given more detail of personal and romantic interludes, and rather less insight into the broader sweep of history.

The portrayals of major historical characters in this novel and its sequels seem to be borne out by the verdict of history. Henry III was indeed a rather weak, naive, and vacillating king; King John (given a surprisingly sympathetic personality) did in fact have rather more winning ways than many historical novelists would have us believe. *Here Be Dragons*, in dealing with both Simon de Montfort, and Llewelyn ab Iowerth and his descendants, seeks to portray a very confusing period of history. The narrative flow is not made any clearer by a veritable plethora of Nells, Eleanors, Ellens, and Henrys, Harrys or Hals; it is often rather difficult to distinguish the identity of an individual character. The next volume, *Falls the Shadow*, does not seem to work quite as well as *Here Be Dragons*, being more episodic, and fictionalizing more complex situations. Penman, while managing to portray Simon de Montfort sympathetically, makes no bones about his ruthlessness and arrogance; and indeed historians remain divided in their opinions as to both his character and his motivations.

One flaw in the structure of *Falls the Shadow* is the imbalance between the early part of the book, in which the fortunes of de Montfort and the princes of Gwynedd alternate, and the latter part in which the author concentrates primarily on de Montfort. Penman came early to the conclusion that the two characters of de Montfort and Llewelyn ab Gruffydd were too much for one book, and the third novel involving the princes of Gwynedd, *The Reckoning*, seems to redress this. De Montfort is now dead, but the lives and destinies of his widow and children are inextricably bound to those of the Welsh princes. Penman continues, with the judicious addition of well-informed speculation to a broad base of historical fact, to bring to vivid and believable life the complex machinations of these 13th-century rulers and fighters. Some minor flaws of the earlier two novels are overcome, as Penman describes in an afterword, by the way she has deliberately simplified some of the characters' names, and has taken small but valid liberties with one or two of the relationships.

One of the strengths of all Penman's novels is the way in which she avoids the common pitfall (that Waterloo of so many historical novelists) of language. The speech of Penman's characters is informal (but not too colloquial) 20th century, with an occasional slight stiffness which conveys to us that we are in fact in the 13th or the 15th century.

—Judith Rhodes

PETER, Elizabeth O.

ROMANCE AND HISTORICAL PUBLICATIONS

Novels

Confident Tomorrows. London, Hurst and Blackett, 1931.
The Third Miss Chance. London, Hurst and Blackett, 1933.
Familiar Treatment. London, Hurst and Blackett, 1940.
At Professor Chummy's. London, Sampson Low, 1946.
Compromise with Yesterday. London, Sampson Low, 1946.

*   *   *

Elizabeth O. Peter wrote only a few novels in the 1930s and early 1940s. There is, however, considerable development in style and mood between the first (*Confident Tomorrows*, 1931) and the last (*Compromise with Yesterday*, 1946). Both deal with the effects of war on romance. The melodrama and set-piece stiff-upper-lip situations of *Confident Tomorrows* fail to convince, but the unashamedly romantic plot of *Compromise with Yesterday* is skilfully and touchingly manipulated.

The first book was probably partly inspired by R.C. Sherriff's *Journey's End*. Jerry Mainwaring is, like Stanhope in Sherriff's play, only able to see the war through by taking to drink. He survives World War I, but is by then an incurable alcoholic. Thelma ('Tim'), the wife who has adored him ever since they both were children, remains loyal—in spite of Jerry's drunkenness, debts, and degradation. But gradually she and Jerry's friend, Michael, fall in love, though they nobly damp down their feelings until almost the end of the book. Jerry's increasing depravity through drink, and his repeated reconciliations with Thelma lack conviction, mainly because the book's language is so often stilted: 'Timmy . . . take me back. Let me be your husband again, and your lover, and your pal'. But the romantic triangle is ultimately resolved successfully when, after Jerry strikes Thelma, Michael declares his love, and Jerry—as usual the worse for drink—gets killed in an accident.

By contrast, *Compromise with Yesterday* is vivid and compulsive from the beginning. David Allen, a World War I pilot who has become an Air Commodore in the RAF by the time of Hitler's war, represents not only the vulnerability of youthful romance but the potency of remembered love affairs. These are, of course, as Peter writes, 'more powerful, more relentless than the living presence, which might disappoint or cease to enchant'. The author uses the clichés of wartime romantic fiction with aplomb. Her descriptions of snatched meetings between lovers on leave and the fear of sudden death that formed the background of so many people's lives make haunting and memorable reading.

This novel gets as deeply under the emotional skin as, for example, Noël Coward's celebrated drama *Cavalcade*, which was also, like *Compromise with Yesterday*, a family saga of two wars and the years between. Peter uses the sweet-savage images of romance with such impact and intensity that it is surprising she did not follow up her last novel with further love stories.

—Mary Cadogan

PETERS, Elizabeth.   See **MICHAELS, Barbara.**

PETERS, Ellis.   See **PARGETER, Edith.**

PETERS, Maureen.
Pseudonyms: Veronica Black; Catherine Darby; Belinda Grey; Elizabeth Law; Levanah Lloyd; Judith Rothman; Sharon Whitby. **Nationality:** British. **Born:** Caernarvon, Wales, 3 March 1935. **Education:** Caernarvon Grammar School, 1945–52; University College, Bangor, 1952–56, B.A. 1956, Dip.Ed. **Relations:** married and divorced twice; two sons and two daughters. **Address:** c/o Robert Hale Ltd, 45–47 Clerkenwell Green, London EC1R 0HT, England.

ROMANCE AND HISTORICAL PUBLICATIONS

Novels (series: Greys; Vinegar Trilogy)

Elizabeth the Beloved. London, Hale, 1965; New York, Beagle, 1972.
Katheryn, The Wanton Queen. London, Hale, 1967; New York, Beagle, 1971.
Mary, The Infamous Queen. London, Hale, 1968; New York, Beagle, 1971.
Bride for King James. London, Hale, 1968.
Joan of the Lilies. London, Hale, 1969.
The Rose of Hever. London, Hale, 1969; as *Anne, The Rose of Hever*, New York, Beagle, 1971.
Flower of the Greys. London, Hale, 1969.
Princess of Desire. London, Hale, 1970; New York, Pinnacle, 1973.
Struggle for a Crown. London, Hale, 1970.
Shadow of a Tudor. London, Hale, 1971.
Seven for St Crispin's Day. London, Hale, 1971.
The Cloistered Flame. London, Hale, 1971.
Jewel of the Greys. London, Hale, 1972.
The Woodville Wench. London, Hale, 1972.
Henry VIII and His Six Wives (novelization of screenplay). London, Fontana, and New York, St Martin's Press, 1972.
The Peacock Queen. London, Hale, 1972.
The Virgin Queen. New York, Pinnacle, 1972.
The Queen Who Never Was. New York, Pinnacle, 1972.
Royal Escape. Boston, Lincolnshire, Jones Blakey, 1972.
Destiny's Lady. New York, Pinnacle, 1973.
The Gallows Herd. London, Hale, 1973.
The Maid of Judah. London, Hale, 1973.
Flawed Enchantress. London, Hale, 1974.
So Fair and Foul a Queen. London, Hale, 1974.
The Willow Maid. London, Hale, 1974.
The Curse of the Greys. London, Hale, 1974.
With Murder in Mind (as Judith Rothman). London, Hale, 1975.
The Queenmaker. London, Hale, 1975.
Tansy. London, Hale, 1975.
Kate Alanna. London, Hale, 1975.
A Child Called Freedom. London, Hale, 1976.
The Crystal and the Cloud. London, Hale, 1977.
Beggar Maid, Queen. London, Hale, 1980.
I, The Maid. London, Hale, 1980.
The Snow Blossom. London, Hale, 1980.
Night of the Willow. London, Hale, 1981; New York, St Martin's Press, 1982.
Ravenscar. London, Hale, 1981.
Song for a Strolling Player. London, Hale, 1981.

Red Queen, White Queen. London, Hale, 1982.
The Dragon and the Rose. London, Hale, 1982.
Frost on the Rose. London, Hale, 1982.
Imperial Harlot. London, Hale, 1983.
My Lady Troubadour. London, Hale, 1983.
Lackland's Bride. London, Hale, 1983.
Dark Gemini (as Judith Rothman). London, Fontana, 1983.
Alianor. London, Hale, 1984.
A Song for Marguerite. London, Hale, 1984.
My Philippa. London, Hale, 1984.
Fair Maid of Kent. London, Hale, 1985.
Isabella, The She-Wolf. London, Hale, 1985.
Vinegar Trilogy:
    The Vinegar Seed. London, Hale, 1986.
    The Vinegar Blossom. London, Hale, 1986.
    The Vinegar Tree. London, Hale, 1987.
The Luck-Bride. London, Hale, 1987.
Lady for a Chevalier. London, Hale, 1987.
My Catalina. London, Hale, 1988.
The Noonday Queen. London, Hale, 1988.
Incredible, Fierce Desire. London, Hale, 1988.
Wife in Waiting. London, Hale, 1988.
Patchwork. London, Hale, 1989.
Minstrel for a Valois. London, Hale, 1989.
Witch Queen. London, Hale, 1990.
Proud Bess. London, Hale, 1990.
Much Suspected of Me. London, Hale, 1990.
A Masque of Brontës. London, Hale, 1991.
England's Mistress. London, Hale, 1991.
The Flower of Martinique. London, Hale, 1991.
Green Apple Burning. London, Hale, 1993.

Novels as Veronica Black

Dangerous Inheritance. London, Hale, 1969; New York, Paperback Library, 1970.
Portrait of Sarah. London, Hale, 1969; New York, Berkley, 1973.
The Wayward Madonna. London, Hale, and New York, Lenox Hill Press, 1970.
A Footfall in the Mist. London, Hale, and New York, Lenox Hill Press, 1971.
Master of Malcarew. London, Hale, and New York, Lenox Hill Press, 1971.
Enchanted Grotto. London, Hale, 1972; New York, Lenox Hill Press, 1973.
Moonflete. London, Hale, 1972; New York, Lenox Hill Press, 1973.
Fair Kilmeny. London, Hale, and New York, Berkley, 1972.
Minstrel's Leap. London, Hale, 1973.
Spin Me a Shadow. London, Hale, 1974.
The House That Hated People. London, Hale, 1974.
Echo of Margaret. London, Hale, 1978.
Greengirl. London, Hale, 1979.
Pilgrim of Desire. London, Hale, 1979.
Flame in the Snow. London, Hale, 1980.
My Pilgrim Love. London, Hale, 1982.
Bond Wife. London, Hale, 1983.
Lover Dark, Lady Fair. London, Hale, 1983.
Hoodman Blind. London, Hale, 1984.
Last Seen Wearing. London, Hale, 1990.
Vow of Chastity. London, Hale, 1991.
A Vow of Silence. London, Hale, 1991.
My Name is Polly Winter. London, Hale, 1992.

Novels as Sharon Whitby

The Last of the Greenwood. London, Hale, 1975; New York, Pyramid, 1976.

The Unforgotten Face. London, Hale, 1975.
Here Be Dragons. London, Hale, 1980.
The Silky. London, Hale, 1980.
The Houseless One. London, Hale, 1981.
No Song at Morningside. London, Hale, 1981.
The Savage Web. London, Hale, 1982.
Shiver Me a Story. London, Hale, 1982.
Nine Days a-Dying. London, Hale, 1982.
Children of the Rainbow. London, Hale, 1982.

Novels as Catherine Darby (series: Falcon; Moon; Rowan Family; Sabre Family)

Falcon:
  1. *A Falcon for a Witch.* New York, Popular Library, and London, Hale, 1975.
  2. *The King's Falcon.* New York, Popular Library, 1975; as *A Game of Falcons*, London, Hale, 1976.
  3. *Fortune for a Falcon.* New York, Popular Library, 1975; London, Hale, 1976.
  4. *Season of the Falcon.* New York, Popular Library, and London, Hale, 1976.
  5. *Falcon Royal.* New York, Popular Library, 1976; as *A Pride of Falcons*, London, Hale, 1977.
  6. *Falcon Tree.* New York, Popular Library, 1976; London, Hale, 1977.
  7. *The Falcon and the Moon.* New York, Popular Library, 1976; London, Hale, 1977.
  8. *Falcon Rising.* New York, Popular Library, 1976; London, Hale, 1978.
  9. *Falcon Sunset.* New York, Popular Library, 1976; London, Hale, 1978.
  10. *Seed of the Falcon.* New York, Popular Library, 1978; London, Hale, 1981.
  11. *Falcon's Claw.* New York, Popular Library, 1978; London, Hale, 1981.
  12. *Falcon to the Lure.* New York, Popular Library, 1978; London, Hale, 1981.
Moon:
  1. *Whisper Down the Moon.* New York, Popular Library, 1977; London, Hale, 1978.
  2. *Frost on the Moon.* New York, Popular Library, 1977; London, Hale, 1979.
  3. *The Flaunting Moon.* New York, Popular Library, 1977; London, Hale, 1979.
  4. *Sing Me a Moon.* New York, Popular Library, 1977; London, Hale, 1980.
  5. *Cobweb Across the Moon.* New York, Popular Library, 1978; London, Hale, 1980.
  6. *Moon in Pisces.* New York, Popular Library, 1978; London, Hale, 1980.
A Dream of Fair Serpents. London, Hale, and New York, Popular Library, 1979.
Child of the Flesh. London, Hale, 1982.
Lass of Silver, Lad of Gold. London, Hale, 1982.
Rowan Family:
  1. *Rowan Garth.* London, Hale, 1982.
  2. *Rowan for a Queen.* London, Hale, 1983.
  3. *A Scent of Rowan.* London, Hale, 1983.
  4. *A Circle of Rowan.* London, Hale, 1983.
  5. *The Rowan Maid.* London, Hale, 1984.
  6. *Song of a Rowan.* London, Hale, 1984.
Sangreal. London, Hale, 1984.
Sabre Family:
  1. *Sabre.* London, Hale, 1985.
  2. *Sabre's Child.* London, Hale, 1985.

  3. *The Silken Sabre.* London, Hale, 1985.
  4. *House of Sabre.* London, Hale, 1986.
  5. *A Breed of Sabre.* London, Hale, 1987.
  6. *Morning of a Sabre.* London, Hale, 1987.
  7. *Fruit of the Sabre.* London, Hale, 1987.
  8. *Gentle Sabre.* London, Hale, 1988.
Heart of Flame. London, Hale, 1986.
Pilgrim in the Wind. London, Hale, 1988.
The Love Knot. London, Hale, 1989.
Zabillet of the Snow. London, Hale, 1990.
Daffodil Anne. London, Hale, 1991.

Novels as Belinda Grey

The Passionate Puritan. London, Mills and Boon, 1978; Toronto, Harlequin, 1979.
Loom of Love. London, Mills and Boon, 1979; Toronto, Harlequin, 1980.
Sweet Wind of Morning. London, Mills and Boon, 1979; Toronto, Harlequin, 1980.
Moon of Laughing Flame. London, Mills and Boon, and Toronto, Harlequin, 1980.
Daughter of Isis. London, Mills and Boon, and Toronto, Harlequin, 1981.
Glen of Frost. London, Mills and Boon, and Toronto, Harlequin, 1981.
Proxy Wedding. London, Mills and Boon, 1982.
Saraband for Sara. London, Mills and Boon, 1984.

Novels as Levanah Lloyd

A Maid Called Wanton. London, Futura, 1981.
Mail Order Bride. London, Futura, 1981.
Cauldron of Desire. London, Futura, 1981.
Dark Surrender. London, Futura, 1981.

Novels as Elizabeth Law

Double Deception. New York, Walker, 1987.
A Scent of Lilac. New York, Walker, 1988.
Regency Morning. New York, Walker, 1988.

OTHER PUBLICATIONS

Other

Jean Ingelow, Victorian Poetess. Ipswich, Suffolk, Boydell Press, and Totowa, New Jersey, Rowman and Littlefield, 1972.
An Enigma of Brontës. London, Hale, and New York, St Martin's Press, 1974.

Editor, *Wife in Waiting.* London, Hale, 1989.

*   *   *

Aficionados of Maureen Peters will recognize the fact that she is a highly prolific writer. The author has expressed a particular fondness for the Tudor and Plantagenet periods (for example, *Henry VIII and his Six Wives*, *Shadow of a Tudor*, and *The Rose of Hever*).

The Rose of Hever recounts the life of the hapless and ill-fated Anne Boleyn, who was regarded as disposable by Henry VIII because she failed to present him with a son, and only gave birth to a daughter. (Ironically Elizabeth I became one of the most formidable monarchs in English history.) Peters continued to explore her fascination with Henry the VIII's wives, all of whom were remarkable women doomed by the accepted notion that male primogeniture was the necessary state for royal succession. Peters successfully conveys the atmosphere of life being 'short, sharp, and brutish' in the royal court, while at the same time capturing its romance and colour.

Peters has turned to more recent history in *The Vinegar Seed*, *The Vinegar Blossom*, and *The Vinegar Tree*. These constitute a family trilogy detailing the history of the Clares. In *The Vinegar Seed*, the reader is introduced to two Irish sisters, Elizabeth and Moira Clare, impoverished but of good breeding, who migrate to England to escape their poverty-stricken existence in Ireland. The elder sister, Elizabeth, befriends a young aspiring writer, David Rose. When he is posted to America he needs a bride, and because he has no particular preference for either sister he asks them to choose between themselves who will go with him. The sisters throw dice for him and Moira wins the throw. Although Elizabeth had a secret crush on David, she ends up marrying a mill clerk, Shekdon Knight, for love. When he dies, she marries a richer man, Francis Darby, and realizes her dream of living in a house with two front doors so that no one can ever send her again to the tradesman's entrance.

The symbol of Elizabeth's hopes is a sprig of willow brought back from Ireland, and as long as it flourishes she superstitiously believes that her family's fortunes will similarly survive. Elizabeth follows her Gran's advice of 'Marry well and, if you can't marry well, then earn your own bread and take a man with ambition in him so that you can push him to the top'. Peters' description of the sexual act between Elizabeth and her husband, Francis, is almost comical but does in fact describe society's attitude as to how a respectable wife should act: 'My dear, you're my wife. There is no need to force yourself to act like a bad woman in order to please me'. Being a dutiful wife, Elizabeth makes no further attempt to expect sexual gratification herself. The story also follows the different paths taken by the two sisters. On visiting her sister, Elizabeth finds that her brother-in-law has risen rapidly up the ladder and is reluctantly going into politics because of his wife's ambitions. The book details the calamitous, if quasi-comic actions carried out in all innocence by Elizabeth which lead to the abrupt curtailment of the visit. Peters is not afraid to introduce humour into a more serious structure to highlight the differences between the two sisters. Whereas Moira has become more priggish, Elizabeth is determined to ride roughshod over convention in order to satisfy her desires, resulting in her affair with an actor on her return trip to England.

The Vinegar Blossom continues the story of Elizabeth's ongoing affair with the actor to whom she bears a daughter, Marian. The story also chronicles the fortunes of the now adult daughters, Fere-lith and Enid. Elizabeth is shown to be a caring if remote parent. The author illustrates the double life of the heroine—in both her respectable role as a pillar of society and in her life with her lover—through the analogy of the two separate doors of Elizabeth's house.

Peters has a tendency to use a physical object or heirloom to represent a symbol of hope in her later family dramas. In the 'Vinegar Trilogy' it is the sprig of willow; in *Patchwork* the Star of David is taken by a rich Jewish girl, Elana Fellini, as a symbol of both her old, comfortable lifestyle and an emblem of the perpetual Judaic struggle for survival in a hostile world. It is also part of her dowry when she decides to elope with a young, penniless Catholic boy, Giuseppe Bellini. By this act of elopement, the couple unwittingly start a feud which will affect the lives of their descendants. The novel covers recent history, from the turn of the century to the end of World War II, and roams from Italy to Wales and finally to Nazi Germany. The old axiom that 'Old sins have long shadows' is fully explored in this novel.

Peters appears to have a preference for strong, somewhat unconventional heroines who appear to prefer to shape events and make things happen rather than just act in conformity with the mores and rules of society—even if it results in the ruin of their own lives.

Perhaps this is one reason why Peters has remained so popular with her fans.

—Sobhana Rowland

PETERS, Natasha.
Pseudonym for Anastasia N. Cleaver. **Address:** c/o Fawcett, 210 East 50th Street, New York, New York 10022, USA.

ROMANCE AND HISTORICAL PUBLICATIONS

Novels

Savage Surrender. New York, Ace, 1977; London, Arrow, 1978.
Dangerous Obsession. New York, Ace, 1978; London, Arrow, 1979.
The Masquers. New York, Ace, 1979; London, Arrow, 1980.
The Enticers. New York, Fawcett, 1981; London, New English Library, 1983.
The Immortals. New York, Fawcett, 1983.
Darkness into Light. New York, Fawcett, 1984; London, New English Library, 1985.
Wild Nights. New York, Fawcett, 1986; London, New English Library, 1988.
Blues in the Night. London, New English Library, 1989.
Star Dust. New York, Fawcett, 1992.

*   *   *

Historical settings vividly detailed, incredible characters in even more incredible plots, rude talk, and sexual encounters provocatively if not pornographically described—these form the basis of the historical romances of Natasha Peters.

Savage Surrender opens in a French château in the 19th century, where the reader meets the novel's heroine, Elise Lesconflair, the spoiled and headstrong niece of Count Lesconflair, and the goddaughter of Napoleon. Elise grows up quickly when she is betrothed to Baron Friederich Rolland von Meier, whom the willful Elise detests: ' . . . so terribly dull . . . and so ugly . . . Grotesquely ugly! That fat belly and those thin blond wisps of baby hair—yes, he looks just like a gigantic baby! And his breath stinks, too'. In a fit of defiance, Elise runs out into the forest, sheds her clothing, and jumps into a swimming pond, where the villainous Garth McClelland takes advantage of her. Elise's indignant brothers force her to marry McClelland (posing as 'Lord Armand Charles Alexandre Valadon, Marquis de Pellissier') despite her betrothal to the repugnant Baron. McClelland, alternately a 'beast', and a gentle lover, takes his 'hellcat' Elise off to Nantes, where both board a slave ship headed for Africa and the West Indies. Elise is rescued from cruel Garth by pirate Jean Lafitte, who takes her to his home in Louisiana, and installs her as his mistress. Amazingly, Elise and Garth McClelland find each other, villain and hell-cat are reunited, they start a family, and eventually go 'out of the gathering gloom of the forest into the brightness of the afternoon sun'.

The Masquers is set in 18th-century Venice—'the beautiful, the sensual city of Venice' where 'gondolas glide soundlessly through narrow canals, carrying masked lovers to secret trysts, while *cicisbei* (18th century gallants) play court to bored noblewomen'. Fosca Loredan is the beautiful and bored noblewoman heroine. Her husband is the aristocratic Alessandro; her lover, the bold revolutionary Rafaello Leopardi.

Pre-Communist Shanghai in the 1930s is the setting for *The Enticers*, a story of two sisters—Anne Fox, a 'sensitive, passionate woman whose secret past bound her to this enigmatic land and stood between her and love forever', and Kit, Anne's gorgeous sister, 'the queen of a razzle-dazzle social set, who ran from bed to bed savagely trying to fill an empty life'—and the two men they marry—Gilbert Lawrence, Anne's husband, 'a doctor whose lust for his own wife's sister finally drove him to the sweet release of the East—opium', and James Innes, Kit's husband, a rich empire-builder 'whose money bought his fashionable wife but could never pave his way into the high society he pretended to scorn'.

The Immortals returns to Shanghai—and to Anne Fox, who has since married Innes after her husband Lawrence (conveniently) killed her sister Kit and then himself. Anne Innes, who runs the institution for orphans and abandoned children that she founded (her office there, in fact, is in the very room where the murder-suicide took place), is now confronted by her long-lost daughter Amalie, the product of her teenage romance with a Chinese Communist student, Chen. 'Clothed in stunning silk and white-hot hate', the bitter Amalie Berenger (the name of her adoptive parents) has come to Shanghai to seek revenge from the former Nazi soldier who had brutally assaulted her during the war, but she ends up not only meeting her mother (now dying of cancer) but seducing her mother's good friend, a Roman Catholic priest, Father Michael Cassaday.

Wild Nights begins with a postcard from Emma Louise Vaughan, dated September 8, 1952:

Dear Mom and Aunt Louise,
WOW! I finally made it to Cambodia! Trip up the Mekong River was beautiful but scary—boats travel in convoys as protection against pirates on water and guerrillas on land. After I explore Phnom Penh, I'm going to find a way to get to Angkor Wat. This has already been the most fantastic experience of my entire life! Can't wait to see what happens next!
Love, Emma

Emma has left her life as a Nebraska beauty queen to be a foreign correspondent covering the escalating French military presence in Southeast Asia. Alan Hazan, the first man she meets there, falls in love with her ('Beautiful Emma. Emma of the golden hair and the flashing green eyes'). But it is Captain Robert Janvier of the French Foreign Legion who captures Emma's heart and introduces her to the pleasures of opium as well as 'the sensuality of her young body'. (Yes, the title is from the Emily Dickinson poem, recited to Emma by Alan, who perseveres: 'Wild Nights—Wild Nights!/Were I with thee/Wild Nights should be/Our luxury!').

Although the settings for her latest book, *Star Dust*—New York City, Las Vegas, Los Angeles, and Miami—are perhaps cheaply glitzy rather than truly exotic, and the time is contemporary, the characters and plot are as incredible as those in Peters's earlier novels. Here, our heroine, Frankie Fallon, makes her 'stage debut' when her mother gives birth to her on 'The Ed Sullivan Show' (her twin brother, Tommy, is born in the hospital 40 minutes earlier). Thus propelled into show-biz by her stage-mother, Lily, Frankie proceeds to become a child star on a popular television series. By the time she is 15, she is stuffing her bra with cotton and dancing in Reno. On her first date, with Ray Keller, whom she rescues from a mob hit, she is flown to Las Vegas, and taken to see Frank Sinatra. Ray and Frankie go to his uncle's Las Vegas mansion, where the uncle rapes her. She survives the rampages of alcohol, drugs, and cheap sex that follow but goes on to star in an off-Broadway musical, gets both legs broken for resuming her romance with the now married Ray, recovers, and moves to Miami.

Like the author's pseudonym, each 'Natasha' novel dazzles with exoticism, then 'Peters' out in incredulity.

—Marcia G. Welsh

———

PIANKA, Phyllis Taylor. See 2nd edition, 1990.

———

PILCHER, Rosamunde.
Pseudonym: Jane Fraser. **Nationality:** British. **Born:** Rosamunde Scott, Lelant, Cornwall, 22 September 1924. **Education:** St Clares, Polwithen, Cornwall; Howell's School, Llandaff; Miss Kerr-Sanders' Secretarial College. **Military Service:** Women's Royal Naval Service, 1943–46. **Relations:** married Graham Hope Pilcher in 1946; two daughters and two sons. **Agent:** Curtis Brown, 162–168 Regent Street, London W1R 5TB, England. **Address:** Over Pilmore, Invergowrie, Dundee DD2 5EL, Scotland.

Romance and Historical Publications

Novels

A Secret to Tell. London, Collins, 1955.
April. London, Collins, 1957.
On My Own. London, Collins, 1965.
Sleeping Tiger. London, Collins, 1967; New York, St Martin's Press, 1974.
Another View. London, Collins, 1969; New York, St Martin's Press, 1974.
The End of the Summer. London, Collins, 1971; New York, St Martin's Press, 1975.
Snow in April. London, Collins, 1972; New York, St Martin's Press, 1975.
The Empty House. London, Collins, 1973; New York, St Martin's Press, 1975.
The Day of the Storm. London, Collins, and New York, St Martin's Press, 1975.
Under Gemini. New York, St Martin's Press, 1976; London, Collins, 1977.
Wild Mountain Thyme. New York, St Martin's Press, 1978; London, New English Library, 1980.
The Carousel. New York, St Martin's Press, 1982; London, Severn House, 1983.
Voices in Summer. New York, St Martin's Press, 1984; London, Severn House, 1985.
The Shell Seekers. New York, St Martin's Press, and London, Severn House, 1987.
September. London, New English Library, and New York, St Martin's Press, 1990.
The Blackberry Day. London, New English Library, 1991.

Novels as Jane Fraser

Half-way to the Moon. London, Mills and Boon, 1949.
The Brown Fields. London, Mills and Boon, 1951.
Dangerous Intruder. London, Mills and Boon, 1951.
Young Bar. London, Mills and Boon, 1952; Toronto, Harlequin, 1965.
A Day Like Spring. London, Mills and Boon, 1953; Toronto, Harlequin, 1968.
Dear Tom. London, Mills and Boon, 1954.
Bridge of Corvie. London, Mills and Boon, 1956; New York, Fawcett, 1975.

A Family Affair. London, Mills and Boon, 1958.
A Long Way from Home. London, Mills and Boon, 1963; Toronto, Harlequin, 1964.
The Keeper's House. London, Mills and Boon, 1963; Toronto, Harlequin, 1964.

Short Stories

The Blue Bedroom and Other Stories. New York, St Martin's Press, 1985; London, New English Library, 1990.
Flowers in the Rain and Other Stories. London, New English Library, 1991.

OTHER PUBLICATIONS

Plays

The Dashing White Sergeant, with Charles C. Gairdner (produced London, 1955). London, Evans, 1955.
The Piper of Orde, with Charles C. Gairdner. London, Evans, n.d.
The Tulip Major (produced Dundee, 1957).

*

Rosamunde Pilcher comments:

I try in my work to strike a balance between the out-and-out romantic and the serious woman's writing of today. There is a huge market of intelligent women who sometimes wish to read a light novel without necessarily reading a load of out-dated rubbish. Over the 40 years I have been writing and selling, social conditions, behaviour, and expectations have changed drastically, and I have endeavoured always to keep a fresh and modern outlook, accepting the inevitable permissiveness, and incorporating it into my work, without necessarily condoning it nor encouraging the sort of loveless amorality which was prevalent in the 1960s. My short stories are not so much love stories, but more about human relations, i.e. the love which can exist, not simply between two young people, but also between mothers and children, brothers and sisters, old people and young people. If the stories do not have a happy ending, then they always have a hopeful ending. Life is a succession of problems and decisions, and sometimes the best we can do is simply to come to terms with them.

*   *   *

Although Rosamunde Pilcher had published many novels and collections of short stories, both under her own name and under her pseudonym Janet Fraser, it was only with the publication of *The Shell Seekers*, in 1987, that her international reputation as a novelist was established. Pilcher's success lies in her attention to detail, her lengthy narratives, and most of all, in her ability to create credible, interesting characters. As a reviewer in *Cosmopolitan* wrote in 1990, Pilcher 'brings to life small boys who are afraid of being sent away to school, country ladies and restless husbands, with equal insight'.

The Shell Seekers, one of the author's longest novels, focuses on Penelope Keeling, an independent, elderly woman, coming to terms with her life, her relationship with her children, and her approaching death. Her three children are too caught up in their own lives to bother much with their mother. Nancy, the oldest, is the responsible yet martyred child, married with children of her own: she never feels that she has enough, either emotionally or materialistically, from her mother. Noel is Penelope's spoilt and selfish only son: charming but feckless, he does not realize how much he depends on his mother until she dies. Noel also features as a character in *September*. Olivia

probably understands Penelope the most. She is a busy career woman who expects nothing from her mother and although Olivia loves Penelope, she does not spend much time with her.

The title of the book refers to a two-panelled painting owned by Penelope, and left to her by her father, the painter Lawrence Stern. The book is divided into several sections in which each of the main characters tells his/her story: through a series of flashbacks a full picture emerges of Penelope Keeling's life and family. Pilcher grew up in an artist's colony in Cornwall, and the long descriptive passages of Cornwall's beautiful countryside are written with obvious care and affection. Although *The Shell Seekers* is not autobiographical, the author stated in the *New York Times Book Review* that if she 'died the next day after writing (*The Shell Seekers*), everyone would know exactly what happened' in her life.

September is set in Scotland, where the author now lives. The storyline revolves around a group of people who are invited to a 21st birthday party. Part of the book's success lies in the rich characterization and riveting plot. Noel Keeling (Penelope's son) features in this book as a slightly jaded man who has attained the success and money that he longed for in *The Shell Seekers*. Noel's chief realizations are that he misses his mother, and that, in spite of all his success, he is lonely. Noel begins an affair with Alexa, a young, vulnerable woman from a wealthy background. Although Alexa is unlike Noel's usual type of woman, he ends up falling in love with her by the end of the book, and thus redeems himself. Violet Aird, Alexa's grandmother, is a similar character to Penelope Keeling. Older and wiser than the other characters, Violet is the central character who binds the book, with its sub-plots and petty intrigues together.

Both *The Shell Seekers* and *September* were warmly received by critics and were in the European and American best-seller lists. Since their publication, Pilcher's other titles have received greater attention and recognition. Pilcher began her writing career as a Mills and Boon author (as Janet Fraser), and her earlier books, written as Rosamunde Pilcher, adhere more closely to formula romance, and lack the complicated sub-plots and twists of her later works.

Rebecca Bayliss, the heroine in *The Day of the Storm*, travels to Ibiza to her mother's deathbed, and is told about her mother's past. Rebecca travels to a mansion in Cornwall to meet her aged grandfather, a journey which changes her life as she discovers a family she never knew of, and falls in love. Selina Bruce in *Sleeping Tiger* begins the book preparing for her marriage to a staid, upper-crust man. She changes her life course completely by running away to a Spanish island to find George Dyer, the man she thinks is her father, and whom she had previously thought dead. Her 'father' turns out to be a remote cousin of George's and this explains their likeness. Although Selina does not find her father, she is compensated by finding love instead. George saves Selina from a life of mundanity, Selina saves George from a life of cynicism.

Pilcher's plots often involve a change in the heroine/hero's attitude towards love. In *Wild Mountain Thyme*, Victoria Brandewyne finds Oliver Dobbs, the man she has always loved, on her doorstep with his two-year old son. Renewing her affair with him, she travels to Scotland, and discovers that she is in love with a more serious, but worthy man. *The Empty House* is set in Cornwall, and tells the story of a young widow (and her children) who is given a second chance at love with the same man. Jane Marsh, in the *The End of the Summer*, returns to Scotland to find love, and realizes that her life-long infatuation with her cousin is over and that she loves someone else instead.

'I don't ever write about a place or a person or an experience that I don't know a lot about' Pilcher told *Publisher's Weekly*. Hence many of her books are set in either Cornwall where she lived and grew up, or in Scotland, where she now lives, and many of the experiences recounted in her books are ones that the author herself has lived through. Pilcher is a successful and much loved author: her capacity to create realistic, interesting, and intriguing characters in beautifully depicted locations makes her one of the most popular authors writing in the romance genre today.

—P. Campbell

————

PIZZEY, Erin.
Nationality: British. **Born:** Tsiengtao, China, 19 February 1939.
Education: St Antonys, Leweston Manor, Sherborne, Dorset.
Relations: two children. **Career:** family captured by the Japanese in 1942; spent next 20 years in South Africa, Canada, Persia, England, and Hong Kong. Founder, Women's Aid (refuge for battered women and children), Chiswick, London, 1971, and a series of sanctuaries for battered women and children. Lives in Cayman Islands. **Recipient:** Italian peace prize, 1978; Nancy Astor award for journalism, 1983, 1985. Made honorary citizen of St Giovanni D'Asso, Italy, 1992. **Address:** c/o Christopher Little, 49 Queen Victoria Street, London, EC4N 4SA, England.

ROMANCE AND HISTORICAL PUBLICATIONS

Novels

The Watershed. London, Hamish Hamilton, 1983; New York, HarperCollins, 1992.
In the Shadow of the Castle. London, Hamish Hamilton, 1984; New York, HarperCollins, 1992.
First Lady. London, and New York, Collins, 1986.
The Consul General's Daughter. London, and New York, Collins, London, 1987.
The Snow Leopard of Shanghai. London, Collins, 1989.
Other Lovers. London, and New York, Harper Collins, 1989.
Swimming with Dolphins. London, and New York, Harper Collins, 1990.
Morningstar. London, HarperCollins, 1992.
For the Love of a Stranger. London, HarperCollins, 1993.

OTHER PUBLICATIONS

Other

Scream Quietly or The Neighbours Will Hear, edited by Alison Forbes. London, Penguin, 1974; Short Hills, New Jersey, Enslow, 1977; reprinted with postscript, London, Penguin, 1979.
Infernal Child: A Memoir. London, Gollancz, 1978.
The Slut's Cook Book, illustrations by Anny White. London, Macdonald, 1981.
Prone to Violence, with Jeff Shapiro. London, Hamlyn, 1982.
Erin Pizzey Collects. London, Hamlyn, 1983.

Plays

Screenplays: *Requiem*, 1990; *Shadows*, 1993.

Television Plays: *Scream Quietly or the Neighbours Will Hear*, 1974; *That Awful Woman*, 1989; *Sanctuary*, 1989.

*

Erin Pizzey comments:

I write to tell the truth, however unpalatable, of women's lives since the dawn of time. Men have choices, women have children. Men have money, women (there are exceptions, but few) live below the poverty line everywhere. I write not only of the suffering and the tragedy of women's lives, but also in celebration of the power and value of women's relationships with each other. I am fascinated by the process of writing. For me it is like a drug. There are no breaks, no holidays, only my writing!

*   *   *

You might think it strange that a leading feminist, a much needed but often outspoken advocate of important causes, and the founder of refuges for battered women and children in both Europe and North America, should also be known as a successful writer of romantic/blockbuster novels. However, Erin Pizzey's books are not formula romances. Pizzey sets her books in glamorous environs, but her heroes and heroines are normal people who often find love after surviving traumatic experiences (mostly based on the author's own life).

'It took nine years for Bonnie to recognize fully that Angus would probably kill her', the author writes of Bonnie Fraser, the female protagonist of *In the Shadow of the Castle*. Brought up by an abusive mother, Bonnie marries a seemingly perfect man—older, successful, and wealthy. Angus MacPherson also possesses an extremely black side that leads him to physically and emotionally abuse Bonnie. This is the darker side of love, an unhealthy emotion which leads to a mutual dependence between the couple. Bonnie stays in a physically abusive situation for years before she realizes that she has a choice. She eventually takes her children to a refuge, only to return when Angus comes to find her. Pizzey pulls no punches in depicting the desperate life of her heroine. Based loosely on Pizzey's own experiences through her work with abused women and children, Bonnie's life as a battered wife is realistically and frighteningly portrayed. Bonnie flees to America, and briefly finds love, only to return when Angus again tries to find her. Bonnie does find release at the end of the book when Angus kills himself. Unfortunately the majority of women in the refuges are not so lucky.

Pizzey's other books conform more to the traditional romance/historical formula. *First Lady* follows the lives of four generations of women, and begins in late 19th-century America. Reuben and Lilla Braff are Russian immigrants who come to New Jersey to find wealth. Lilla is a beautiful frustrated woman who wants more from life than the successful but boring life Reuben can give her. Lilla leaves her husband to become part of an artistic, high flying, lesbian group of women. Her daughter Nora marries well and has two twin daughters, Esther and Etta. Etta is quite conventional, but Esther is more like her grandmother and craves a more exciting life. She eventually ends up meeting Lilla in Paris. However, it is in the last generation of women that success is really found, Jenny becomes the first lady of New Mexico. The historical setting of the book is well detailed by the author, but the book's fundamental success lies in its action. Jenny is hated by Martin Archuleta, a Mexican who is a fellow student at Cambridge University. Martin pretends to be her friend but, in a bitter twist to the book, arranges for her son, the one person that she really loves, to be killed in front of her.

The Snow Leopard of Shanghai also has a twist at the end. Pizzey portrays the Orient, the last days of Tsarist Russia, and pre-revolution China, in realistic detail. Sophia Oblimova, the female protagonist, is approached by a young journalist to tell her life story. Oblimova has had a colourful, if ambiguous past which has led both she and her sister, the gentle Elena, to flee Russia and take refuge in Shanghai. While her sister marries a British diplomat, Sophia's past is much more interesting, and leads her to, among other things, set up school communes in China. The twist in the novel is that Natasha, the young woman who interviews Oblimova, is her granddaughter.

Most of Pizzey's male protagonists lead dual lives. At first glance the charismatic Michael, in *Morningstar*, appears to be a rich benefactor of charities, however, his charming persona hides the fact that he is really an international drug dealer. Charles, in *The Watershed*, seems to be a faithful husband, but his wife Rachel finds that he is exactly the opposite. Angus, in *In the Shadow of the Castle*, is charming and debonair to the outside world, but at home he beats his wife badly. Each of these men displays his weakness through his attitude, usually one of contempt, towards the women in his life. However, Pizzey's heroines often achieve personal liberation through the actions of men. Rachel in *The Watershed* is freed from a staid marriage and finds herself and love after a journey through despair, promiscuity, and a flirtation with lesbianism. Similarly, Nina Stockton leaves her husband in *Morningstar* after discovering his affair with his secretary, and becomes a person in her own right after years of being the perfect wife. Unfortunately, she falls in love with the mysterious and nasty Michael, but finds true love at the end of the book.

Pizzey's is an important voice in contemporary fiction. She writes about subjects normally avoided in literature, with frankness, and, often, with wry humour. Everything from child abuse to homosexuality is treated seriously in Pizzey's novels, and her ability to create interesting characters in fascinating settings make her a popular author.

—P. Campbell

PLAIDY, Jean.
Pseudonym for Eleanor Alice Hibbert. **Other Pseudonyms:** Eleanor Burford; Phillippa Carr; Elbur Ford; Victoria Holt; Kathleen Kellow; Ellalice Tate. **Nationality:** British. **Born:** Eleanor Alice Burford, London, in 1906. **Education:** privately. **Relations:** married G.P. Hibbert. **Died:** 20 January 1993.

ROMANCE AND HISTORICAL PUBLICATIONS

Novels (series: Catherine de'Medici; Charles II; Georgian; Isabella and Ferdinand; Katharine of Aragon; Louis XV; Lucrezia Borgia; Mary Queen of Scots; Norman; Plantagenet; Queens of England; Stuarts; Victorian)

Together They Ride. London, Swan, 1945.
Beyond the Blue Mountains. New York, Appleton Century, 1947; London, Hale, 1948.
Murder Most Royal. London, Hale, 1949; New York, Putnam, 1972; as *The King's Pleasure*, New York, Appleton Century Crofts, 1949.
The Goldsmith's Wife. London, Hale, and New York, Appleton Century Crofts, 1950; as *The King's Mistress*, New York, Pyramid, 1952.
Catherine de' Medici. London, Hale, 1969.
  Madame Serpent. London, Hale, and New York, Appleton Century Crofts, 1951.
  The Italian Woman. London, Hale, 1952; New York, Putnam, 1975.
  Queen Jezebel. London, Hale, and New York, Appleton Century Crofts, 1953.
Daughter of Satan. London, Hale, 1952; New York, Putnam, 1973; as *The Unholy Woman*, Toronto, Harlequin, 1954.
Mary Queen of Scots:
  Royal Road to Fotheringay. London, Hale, 1955; New York, Putnam, 1968.
  The Captive Queen of Scots. London, Hale, 1963; New York, Putnam, 1970.
The Sixth Wife. London, Hale, 1953; New York, Putnam, 1969.

The Spanish Bridegroom. London, Hale, 1954; Philadelphia, Macrae Smith, 1956.
St Thomas's Eve. London, Hale, 1954; New York, Putnam, 1970.
Gay Lord Robert. London, Hale, 1955; New York, Putnam, 1972.
Charles II. London, Hale, 1972.
  The Wandering Prince. London, Hale, 1956; New York, Putnam, 1971.
  A Health unto His Majesty. London, Hale, 1956; New York, Putnam, 1972.
  Here Lies Our Sovereign Lord. London, Hale, 1957; New York, Putnam, 1973.
Flaunting Extravagant Queen (Marie Antoinette). London, Hale, 1957.
Lucrezia Borgia. London, Hale, 1976.
  Madonna of the Seven Hills. London, Hale, 1958; New York, Putnam, 1974.
  Light on Lucrezia. London, Hale, 1958; New York, Putnam, 1976.
Louis XV:
  Louis, The Well-Beloved. London, Hale, 1959.
  The Road to Compiègne. London, Hale, 1959.
Isabella and Ferdinand. London, Hale, 1970.
  Castile for Isabella. London, Hale, 1960.
  Spain for the Sovereigns. London, Hale, 1960.
  Daughters of Spain. London, Hale, 1961.
Katharine of Aragon. London, Hale, 1968.
  Katharine. The Virgin Widow. London, Hale, 1961.
  The Shadow of the Pomegranate. London, Hale, 1962.
  The King's Secret Matter. London, Hale, 1962.
The Thistle and the Rose. London, Hale, 1963; New York, Putnam, 1973.
Mary, Queen of France. London, Hale, 1964.
The Murder in the Tower. London, Hale, 1964; New York, Putnam, 1974.
Evergreen Gallant. London, Hale, 1965; New York, Putnam, 1973.
The Last of the Stuarts. London, Hale, 1977.
  The Three Crowns. London, Hale, 1965; New York, Putnam, 1977.
  The Haunted Sisters. London, Hale, 1966; New York, Putnam, 1977.
  The Queen's Favourites. London, Hale, 1966; New York, Putnam, 1978.
Georgian Saga:
  1. *The Princess of Celle*. London, Hale, 1967; New York, Putnam, 1985.
  2. *Queen in Waiting*. London, Hale, 1967; New York, Putnam, 1985.
  3. *The Prince and the Quakeress*. London, Hale, 1968; New York, Putnam, 1986.
  4. *Caroline, The Queen*. London, Hale, 1968; New York, Putnam, 1986.
  5. *The Third George*. London, Hale, 1969; New York, Putnam, 1987.
  6. *Perdita's Prince*. London, Hale, 1969; New York, Putnam, 1987.
  7. *Sweet Lass of Richmond Hill*. London, Hale, 1970; New York, Putnam, 1988.
  8. *Indiscretions of the Queen*. London, Hale, 1970; New York, Putnam, 1988.
  9. *The Regent's Daughter*. London, Hale, 1971; New York, Putnam, 1989.
  10. *Goddess of the Green Room*. London, Hale, 1971; New York, Putnam, 1989.
Victorian Saga:
  1. *The Captive of Kensington Palace*. London, Hale, 1972; New York, Putnam, 1976.

2. *Victoria in the Wings*. London, Hale, 1972; New York, Putnam, 1990.
3. *The Queen and Lord M*. London, Hale, 1973; New York, Putnam, 1977.
4. *The Queen's Husband*. London, Hale, 1973; New York, Putnam, 1978.
5. *The Widow of Windsor*. London, Hale, 1974; New York, Putnam, 1978.

Norman Trilogy:
1. *The Bastard King*. London, Hale, 1974; New York, Putnam, 1979.
2. *The Lion of Justice*. London, Hale, 1975; New York, Putnam, 1979.
3. *The Passionate Enemies*. London, Hale, 1976; New York, Putnam, 1979.

Plantagenet Saga:
1. *The Plantagenet Prelude*. London, Hale, 1976; New York, Putnam, 1980.
2. *The Revolt of the Eaglets*. London, Hale, 1977; New York, Putnam, 1980.
3. *The Heart of the Lion*. London, Hale, 1977; New York, Putnam, 1980.
4. *The Prince of Darkness*. London, Hale, 1978; New York, Putnam, 1980.
5. *The Battle of the Queens*. London, Hale, 1978; New York, Putnam, 1981.
6. *The Queen from Provence*. London, Hale, 1979; New York, Putnam, 1981.
7. *Edward Longshanks*. London, Hale, 1979; as *Hammer of the Scots*, New York, Putnam, 1981.
8. *The Follies of the King*. London, Hale, 1980; New York, Putnam, 1982.
9. *The Vow on the Heron*. London, Hale, 1980; New York, Putnam, 1982.
10. *Passage to Pontefract*. London, Hale, 1981; New York, Putnam, 1982.
11. *The Star of Lancaster*. London, Hale, 1981; New York, Putnam, 1982.
12. *Epitaph for Three Women*. London, Hale, 1981; New York, Putnam, 1983.
13. *Red Rose of Anjou*. London, Hale, 1982; New York, Putnam, 1983.
14. *The Sun in Splendour*. London, Hale, 1982; New York, Putnam, 1983.
15. *Uneasy Lies the Head*. London, Hale, 1982; New York, Putnam, 1984.

Queens of England:
1. *My Self, My Enemy*. London, Hale, 1983; New York, Putnam, 1984.
2. *Queen of This Realm: The Story of Queen Elizabeth I*. London, Hale, 1984; New York, Putnam, 1985.
3. *Victoria Victorious*. London, Hale, 1985; New York, Putnam, 1986.
4. *The Lady in the Tower*. London, Hale, and New York, Putnam, 1986.
5. *The Courts of Love*. London, Hale, 1987; New York, Putnam, 1988.
6. *In the Shadow of the Crown*. London, Hale, 1988; New York, Putnam, 1989.
7. *The Queen's Secret*. London, Hale, 1989; New York, Putnam, 1990.
8. *The Reluctant Queen: The Story of Anne of York*. London, Hale, 1990.
9. *William's Wife*. London, Hale, 1990.

The Pleasures of Love. London, Hale, 1991.
Kisses of Death. London, Hale, 1993.

Novels as Eleanor Burford

Daughter of Anna. London, Jenkins, 1941.
Passionate Witness. London, Jenkins, 1941.
The Married Lover. London, Jenkins, 1942.
When All the World Is Young. London, Jenkins, 1943.
So the Dreams Depart. London, Jenkins, 1944.
Not in Our Stars. London, Jenkins, 1945.
Dear Chance. London, Jenkins, 1947.
Alexa. London, Jenkins, 1948.
The House at Cupid's Cross. London, Jenkins, 1949.
Believe the Heart. London, Jenkins, 1950.
The Love Child. London, Jenkins, 1950.
Saint or Sinner? London, Jenkins, 1951.
Dear Delusion. London, Jenkins, 1952.
Bright Tomorrow. London, Jenkins, 1952.
Leave Me My Love. London, Jenkins, 1953.
When We Are Married. London, Jenkins, 1953.
Castles in Spain. London, Jenkins, 1954.
Heart's Afire. London, Jenkins, 1954.
When Other Hearts. London, Jenkins, 1955.
Two Loves in Her Life. London, Jenkins, 1955.
Begin to Live. London, Mills and Boon, 1956.
Married in Haste. London, Mills and Boon, 1956.
To Meet a Stranger. London, Mills and Boon, 1957.
Pride of the Morning. London, Mills and Boon, 1958.
Blaze of Noon. London, Mills and Boon, 1958.
The Dawn Chorus. London, Mills and Boon, 1959.
Red Sky at Night. London, Mills and Boon, 1959.
Night of Stars. London, Mills and Boon, 1960.
Now That April's Gone. London, Mills and Boon, 1961.
Who's Calling. London, Mills and Boon, 1962.

Novels as Philippa Carr (series: Daughters of England)

Daughters of England:
1. *The Miracle at St Bruno's*. London, Collins, and New York, Putnam, 1972.
2. *The Lion Triumphant*. London, Collins, and New York, Putnam, 1974.
3. *The Witch from the Sea*. London, Collins, and New York, Putnam, 1975.
4. *Saraband for Two Sisters*. London, Collins, and New York, Putnam, 1976.
5. *Lament for a Lost Lover*. London, Collins, and New York, Putnam, 1977.
6. *The Love-Child*. London, Collins, and New York, Putnam, 1978.
7. *The Song of the Siren*. London, Collins, and New York, Putnam, 1980.
8. *The Drop of the Dice*. London, Collins, and New York, Putnam, 1981.
9. *The Adultress*. London, Collins, and New York, Putnam, 1982.
10. *Zipporah's Daughter*. London, Collins, 1983; as *Knave of Hearts*, New York, Putnam, 1983.
11. *Voices in a Haunted Room*. London, Collins, and New York, Putnam, 1984.
12. *The Return of the Gypsy*. London, Collins, and New York, Putnam, 1985.
13. *Midsummer's Eve*. London, Collins, and New York, Putnam, 1986.
14. *The Pool of St Branok*. London, Collins, and New York, Putnam, 1987.
15. *The Changeling*. London, Collins, and New York, Putnam, 1989.

16. *The Black Swan*. London, HarperCollins and New York, Putnam, 1991.
17. *A Time for Silence*. London, HarperCollins, and New York, Putnam, 1991.
18. *The Gossamer Cord*. London, HarperCollins, and New York, Putnam, 1992.

Novels as Elbur Ford

Poison in Pimlico. London, Laurie, 1950.
Flesh and the Devil. London, Laurie, 1950.
The Bed Disturbed. London, Laurie, 1952.
Such Bitter Business. London, Heinemann, 1953; as *Evil in the House*, New York, Morrow, 1954.

Novels as Victoria Holt

Mistress of Mellyn. New York, Doubleday, 1960; London, Collins, 1961.
Kirkland Revels. London, Collins, and New York, Doubleday, 1962.
Bride of Pendorric. London, Collins, and New York, Doubleday, 1963.
The Legend of the Seventh Virgin. London, Collins, and New York, Doubleday, 1965.
Menfreya. London, Collins, 1966; as *Menfreya in the Morning*, New York, Doubleday, 1966.
The King of the Castle. London, Collins, and New York, Doubleday, 1967.
The Queen's Confession. London, Collins, 1968; as *The Queen's Confession: A Biography of Marie Antoinette*, New York, Doubleday, 1968.
The Shivering Sands. London, Collins, and New York, Doubleday, 1969.
The Secret Woman. New York, Doubleday, 1970; London, Collins, 1971.
The Shadow of the Lynx. New York, Doubleday, 1971; London, Collins, 1972.
On the Night of the Seventh Moon. New York, Doubleday, 1972; London, Collins, 1973.
The Curse of the Kings. London, Collins, and New York, Doubleday, 1973.
Pride of the Peacock. London, Collins, and New York, Doubleday, 1974.
The House of a Thousand Lanterns. London, Collins, and New York, Doubleday, 1974.
Lord of the Far Island. London, Collins, and New York, Doubleday, 1975.
The Devil on Horseback. London, Collins, and New York, Doubleday, 1977.
My Enemy the Queen. London, Collins, and New York, Doubleday, 1978.
The Spring of the Tiger. London, Collins, and New York, Doubleday, 1979.
The Mask of the Enchantress. London, Collins, and New York, Doubleday, 1980.
The Judas Kiss. London, Collins, and New York, Doubleday, 1981.
The Demon Lover. London, Collins, and New York, Doubleday, 1982.
The Time of the Hunter's Moon. London, Collins, and New York, Doubleday, 1983.
The Landower Legacy. London, Collins, and New York, Doubleday, 1984.
The Road to Paradise Island. London, Collins, and New York, Doubleday, 1985.
Secret for a Nightingale. London, Collins, and New York, Doubleday, 1986.

The Silk Vendetta. London, Collins, and New York, Doubleday, 1987.
The India Fan. London, Collins, and New York, Doubleday, 1988.
The Captive. New York, Doubleday, and London, Collins, 1989.
Snare of Serpents. London, Collins, and New York, Doubleday, 1990.
Daughter of Deceit. London, HarperCollins, 1991.
Seven for a Secret. London, HarperCollins, and New York, Doubleday, 1992.

Novels as Kathleen Kellow

Danse Macabre. London, Hale, 1952.
Rooms at Mrs Oliver's. London, Hale, 1953.
Lilith. London, Hale, 1954; (as Jean Plaidy) New York, Putnam, 1990.
It Began in Vauxhall Gardens. London, Hale, 1955.
Call of the Blood. London, Hale, 1956.
Rochester. The Mad Earl. London, Hale, 1957.
Milady Charlotte. London, Hale, 1959.
The World's a Stage. London, Hale, 1960.

Novels as Ellalice Tate

Defenders of the Faith. London, Hodder and Stoughton, 1956.
The Scarlet Cloak. London, Hodder and Stoughton, 1957.
The Queen of Diamonds. London, Hodder and Stoughton, 1958.
Madame du Barry. London, Hodder and Stoughton, 1959.
This Was a Man. London, Hodder and Stoughton, 1961.

OTHER PUBLICATIONS

Other

The Triptych of Poisoners. London, Hale, 1958.
The Rise [Growth, End] of the Spanish Inquisition. London, Hale, 3 vols, 1959–61; as *The Spanish Inquisition: Its Rise, Growth, and End*, New York, Citadel Press, 1 vol, 1967.
The Young Elizabeth (for children). London, Parrish, and New York, Roy, 1961.
Meg Roper, Daughter of Sir Thomas More (for children). London, Constable, 1961; New York, Roy, 1964.
The Young Mary Queen of Scots (for children). London, Parrish, 1962; New York, Roy, 1963.
Mary, Queen of Scots, The Fair Devil of Scotland. London, Hale, and New York, Putnam, 1975.

*   *   *

Writing under various pseudonyms, Eleanor Burford Hibbert was one of the most prolific and popular romance writers of the 20th century. Most of her Jean Plaidy historical romances are based upon the lives of actual women in history; her Victoria Holt romances sparked a renewed interest in women's gothic; and her Philippa Carr 'historical gothics' made her prominent as a writer of family saga romances. In her long career, which began with the publication of *Daughter of Anna* in 1941, Hibbert has also written as Eleanor Burford, Elbur Ford, and Kathleen Kellow.

As Jean Plaidy, Hibbert dramatizes in her novels the lives of prominent European women since the Renaissance. Although the novels are not uniform in quality, they all follow a similar pattern. She selects a woman in history who was significant because of her relationships with famous or powerful men—as wife, daughter, sister, mother, sister-in-law, or paramour. Most of the women she writes about were connected to Royal families in England, Spain,

Italy, or France. Many of the Plaidy books are in series: the Plantagenet Saga, the Queens of England, the Georgian Saga, the Victorian Saga, the Norman Trilogy, or series about families such as the Medicis, the Tudors, the Stuarts, the Victorians, or the French Royal Family. In each novel, she places her heroine at the centre of the action, writing as if virtually all the public events of the period had a direct effect on the heroine's life. The books are popularized history, employing a relatively unsophisticated level of historical analysis, although Hibbert's knowledge of detail is encyclopaedic. She avoids historical controversy by relying upon standard interpretations of character and event and by defining history as it might have appeared to the woman at the centre of the story. Since rivalries among women and competition for male attention are prominent features of each book, characters (such as Mary Queen of Scots or Anne Boleyn) who recur in more than one novel may seem sympathetic when at the centre of the action and unsympathetic when peripheral. Two of her novels written under her Victoria Holt pseudonym, *My Enemy the Queen* and *The Queen's Confession*, are actually more typical of the Plaidy formula since they are about real women in history rather than fictional characters.

A typical sequence of Plaidy novels is the 'Georgian Saga', published out of historical order, from *The Princess of Celle* to *Goddess of the Green Room*. The novels in the series tell the story of each of the Georgian queens, of several mistresses of the Georgian kings and princes, and of Princess Charlotte (whose early death led to the accession of Queen Victoria). The entire series covers more than a century of British history, told from a domestic point of view. A representative novel is *The Queen's Secret*, which tells the story of Katherine of Valois, daughter and sister of kings of France, wife of Henry V of England, mother of Henry VI of England, and (through her second marriage) ancestor of the Tudor monarchs. In the novel, Katherine is portrayed as a valuable pawn of the most powerful men in both France and England.

Hibbert's Victoria Holt gothics usually divide into one of three plot types: the 'suspicious husband' plot (e.g. *Bride of Pendorric*), 'the governess gothic' (e.g. *Mistress of Mellyn*), and the 'adventuress' plot (e.g. *Daughter of Deceit*). All her Holt novels are set between the French Revolution and the Edwardian era, and she sometimes uses the Pacific Islands or Australia as backgrounds along with her more traditional background of landed estates in England. She is particularly adept at creating terror in a confined space, and at imagining motives for her villains. In her gothics, the past always holds the key to the mystery and the heroine must find out the truth before it is too late.

Hibbert's most fully realized gothics include *Mistress of Mellyn* and *Bride of Pendorric*, both set in Cornwall, one of her favourite locales. *Mistress of Mellyn*, the novel that set off the wide popularity of gothic romances in the ensuing decade and a half, has close narrative and thematic similarities to both *Jane Eyre* and Daphne du Maurier's *Rebecca*. The governess of the tale solves the mystery of the past, nurtures the hero's troubled daughter, and earns the hero's love by redeeming him from his disillusion about women.

Hibbert's Philippa Carr novels, which she called 'historical gothics', follow the fortunes of a family through several generations. The series began with *The Miracle at St Bruno's*, a novel of the English Reformation. Subsequent books pose two women of a later generation against a background of historical controversy, often involving the religious wars of the period. These books have not been as popular as her Plaidy and Holt novels.

Hibbert was prolific, probably too much so for her own good. Her last few years witnessed a significant decrease in the complexity and believability of her plots in all three types. Her best work was probably her first five or six Victoria Holt novels, when she was setting the standards for a host of authors who imitated her formula, although few could match her in the evocation of terror. In recent years, her writing became tired and dull; her plots, diffuse. *Mistress*

of Mellyn, however, deserves a place among the most important gothic romances of the century, placing Hibbert (as Holt) near the top of her field as heiress to Daphne du Maurier, whose *Rebecca* remains the premier gothic romance of the 20th century.

—Kay Mussell

———

PLAGEMANN, Bentz. American. 1913—. See 1st edition, 1982.

———

PLAIN, Belva.
Nationality: American. **Born:** New York City, 9 October, 1918. **Education:** Barnard College, New York, B.A. 1937. **Relations:** married Dr Irving H. Plain in 1940; three children. **Agent:** Janklow and Nesbit Associates, 598 Madison Avenue, New York, New York, New York 10022, USA. **Address:** 77 Slope Drive, Short Hills, New Jersey 07078, USA.

ROMANCE AND HISTORICAL PUBLICATIONS

Novels (series: Anna Friedman)

Evergreen (Anna Friedman). New York, Delacorte Press, and London, Collins, 1978.
Random Winds. New York, Delacorte Press, and London, Collins, 1980.
Eden Burnings. New York, Delacorte Press, and London, Collins, 1982.
Crescent City. New York, Delacorte Press, and London, Collins, 1984.
The Golden Cup (Anna Friedman). New York, Delacorte Press, and London, Collins, 1986.
Tapestry (Anna Friedman). New York, Delacorte Press, and London, Collins, 1988.
Blessings. New York, Delacorte Press, and London, Hodder and Stoughton, 1989.
Harvest (Anna Friedman). New York, Delacorte Press, and Hodder and Stoughton, 1990.
Treasures. New York, Delacorte Press, and London, Hodder and Stoughton, 1992.
Whispers. New York, Delacorte Press, 1993.

OTHER PUBLICATIONS

Play

Television play: *Evergreen*, 1983.

*

Film Adaptation: *Evergreen*, 1985.

Belva Plain comments:
Evergreen began a series about an immigrant family in the United States whose story begins before World War I and contiues through the trauma of the war in Vietnam. These titles are: *The Golden Cup*, *Tapestry*, and *Harvest*.

Other novels are centred on current social issues. *Blessings*, for example, concerned the problem of the availability (to adopted children) of birth records. *Treasures* tells of rampant greed in the financial world of the 1980s. *Whispers* is the story of an upper-middle class battered wife.

*　　*　　*

Belva Plain is among the more popular contemporary romance writers in America. Most of her novels are multi-generational family sagas set during important periods of American history. Her key figures are generally well-drawn and sympathetic. Although she lacks the ability of the best writers to create characters who seem to come fully alive and completely engage the imagination of the reader, nevertheless her characters are unique and consistent enough to maintain interest. More importantly, Plain's creations are much like the average reader of her fiction—commonplace people who possess middle-class values. As Katherine Ramsland in the *New York Times Book Review* put it, the characters who attain wealth or status in Plain's books find that 'wholesome family values offer more true wealth than does an emphasis on status and unbridled accumulation'. Infidelity may provide dramatic tension, but sex takes place behind closed doors. Even her most independent heroines are essentially loyal to their marriages and families in spirit, if not always in deed. Though some may find Plain too tame and predictable for their taste, her books provide a comfortable escape for readers who appreciate her optimism and emphasis on traditional values.

Whether writing period romances or contemporary family sagas, Plain's female protagonists are usually tenacious, independent women who find personal strength in fully meeting, if sometimes reluctantly, life's challenges. Teenage pregnancy (*Blessings*), wife abuse (*Whispers*), and war (*Crescent City*) are but a few of the dark foes which threaten the heroine and her family. True to the tradition of romance novels, Plain is concerned primarily with the effect that interior conflicts or exterior threats have on the domestic scene and the heroine's search for perfect romantic love—and struggle she must to remain true to herself in her search for truth and goodness.

One of Plain's successes as a writer is the care she takes to apply her research into the habitat, culture, and history of her period romances and sagas. Details of clothing and food are accurately rendered and placed in appropriate settings. The accoutrements and mores of a given time and place are skilfully incorporated, and historical events are carefully woven into the plot. Her writing is better than many popular historical novelists whose cardboard characters in paper costumes stand before some historical backdrop, though her characters do not effortlessly emerge as real-life historic persons. At times Plain intrudes on history when one of her characters makes an observation which is entirely too contemporary.

The first novel published by Plain spans the first six decades of 20th-century American history. *Evergreen*, the first book in a series of four about the Roth and Werner families, is a three-generational saga that begins with young Jewish orphan Anna's trek from Poland to America at the turn of the century. Once settled in Manhattan, she falls in love with a rich man, Paul Werner, but marries Joseph Friedman, a poor, hard-working man. They achieve success, but not happiness, as they face numerous family misfortunes through two world wars, and Arab terrorism. *Evergreen* was highly successful, immediately assuring Plain of an audience for her succeeding works.

Random Winds focuses on three generations of New York doctors from the turn of the century to the present. Once again a family endures domestic tragedies and difficult choices. In *Eden Burnings* Plain changes the setting to a Caribbean island. Teresa, a young white woman, is raped by a black man, and a son is conceived. The scene is set for a number of conflagrations, both familial and political. *Eden Burning* is one of Plain's less successful works. The characters are thinly developed and the writing tends to be overdone ('She heard him crashing down the mountain, heard the terror in his

feet. A stone struck a rock; branches snapped. The heavy silence fell again. She stood up. I, I, she thought, and stopped crying. She pulled at the skirt, smoothing, smoothing, reached back then for the ribbon that had fastened her hair'). *Crescent City* is also set against an exotic background, New Orleans before and during the American Civil War; a European Jewish family faces prejudice on all fronts.

In her next three books, Plain picks up the story of *Evergreen*'s Anna Friedman. *The Golden Cup*, *Tapestry*, and *Harvest* follow various branches of the family through World War I, the Holocaust, and into the political unrest of the 1960s, where they reaffirm their Jewish heritage. However, her latest two novels are built around contemporary themes. *Treasures*, set in the 1980s, follows the lives of three siblings from Ohio whose dead father was an alcoholic. In their pursuit of wealth, status, and control, all three eventually discover that lifes true riches are love and good health, a message delivered in a rather heavy-handed manner. In *Whispers* Plain tackles the subject of domestic violence. Robert and Lynn Ferguson seem to be the perfect married couple, complete with children, wealth, and good looks. But behind closed doors they live with an uglier reality. Lynn must come to terms with Robert's physical abuse before she can become her own person. Although many traditional elements of romance are present in *Whispers*, Plain moves a step away from her earlier works towards realism.

However much as some book reviewers may dislike what one critic in *People Weekly* called Plain's 'twaddle', the fact that she remains widely read and reviewed 15 years after the publication of her first novel is a testament to Plain's ability to tell a good story.

—Marcia L. Thomas

POLLAND, Madeleine A(ngela).
Pseudonym: Frances Adrian. **Nationality:** British. **Born:** Madeline Angela Cahill, Kinsale, County Cork, Ireland, 31 May 1918. **Education:** Hitchin Girls' Grammar School, Hertfordshire, 1929–37. **Military Service:** Women's Auxiliary Air Force, 1942–45. **Relations:** married Arthur Joseph Polland in 1946; one daughter and one son. **Career:** assistant librarian, Letchworth Public Library, Hertfordshire, 1939–42 and 1945–46. **Agent:** Clarissa Rushdie, A.P. Watt Ltd., 20 John Street, London WC1N 2DL, England. **Address:** Edificio Hercules 634, Avenida Gamonal, Arroyo de la Miel, Malaga, Spain.

ROMANCE AND HISTORICAL PUBLICATIONS

Novels

Thicker than Water. New York, Holt Rinehart, 1965; London, Hutchinson, 1967.
The Little Spot of Bother. London, Hutchinson, 1967; as *Minutes of a Murder*, New York, Holt Rinehart, 1967.
Random Army. London, Hutchinson, 1969; as *Shattered Summer*, New York, Doubleday, 1970.
Package to Spain. London, Hutchinson, and New York, Walker, 1971.
Double Shadow (as Frances Adrian). New York, Fawcett, and London, Macdonald and Jane's, 1977.
Sabrina. New York, Delacorte Press, and London, Collins, 1979.
All Their Kingdoms. New York, Delacorte Press, and London, Collins, 1981.
The Heart Speaks in Many Ways. New York, Delacorte Press, and London, Collins, 1982.
No Price Too High. New York, Delacorte Press, 1984; London, Piatkus, 1985.

As It Was in the Beginning. London, Piatkus, 1987.
Rich Man's Flowers. London, Piatkus, 1990; New York, Bantam, 1992.
The Pomegranate House. London, Piatkus, 1992.

OTHER PUBLICATIONS

Fiction (for children)

Children of the Red King. London, Constable, 1960; New York, Holt Rinehart, 1961.
The Town Across the Water. London, Constable, 1961; New York, Holt Rinehart, 1963.
Beorn the Proud. London, Constable, 1961; New York, Holt Rinehart, 1962.
Fingal's Quest. New York, Doubleday, and London, Burns Oates, 1961.
The White Twilight. London, Constable, 1962; New York, Holt Rinehart, 1965.
Chuiraquimba and the Black Robes. New York, Doubleday, and London, Burns Oates, 1962.
City of the Golden House. New York, New York, Doubleday, 1963; Kingswood, Surrey, World's Work, 1964.
The Queen's Blessing. London, Constable, 1963; New York, Holt Rinehart, 1964.
Flame over Tara. New York, Doubleday, 1964; Kingswood, Surrey, World's Work, 1965.
Mission to Cathay. New York, Doubleday, 1965; Kingswood, Surrey, World's Work, 1966.
Queen Without Crown. London, Constable, 1965; New York, Holt Rinehart, 1966.
Deirdre. New York, Doubleday, and Kingswood, Surrey, World's Work, 1967.
To Tell My People. London, Hutchinson, and New York, Holt Rinehart, 1968.
Stranger in the Hills. New York, Doubleday, 1968; London, Hutchinson, 1969.
To Kill a King. London, Hutchinson, 1970; New York, Holt Rinehart, 1971.
Alhambra. New York, Doubleday, 1970; London, Hutchinson, 1971.
A Family Affair. London, Hutchinson, 1971.
Daughter to Poseidon. London, Hutchinson, 1972; as *Daughter of the Sea*, New York, Doubleday, 1972.
Prince of the Double Axe. London, Abelard Schuman, 1976.

*

Manuscript Collection: Mugar Memorial Library, Boston University.

*   *   *

Madeleine A. Polland has written some very fine historical novels for children set in distant times and far-off places, but for her adult books, she uses settings she knows well and times not too far distant from our own.

She was born in Ireland, grew up in England, and now lives in Spain. All these settings are used in her books. Her love for Ireland is very strong and her sympathy for its tribulations shows in books like *As It Was in the Beginning*, *Thicker Than Water*, and *The Little Spot of Bother*. Her best, most lyrical descriptions, too, are of the Irish countryside. As she says in one of her books, 'with Irish exiles, Ireland sort of goes thick in them like condensed milk and they're twice as passionate as the people who stay'.

Her beautiful heroines have many difficulties to overcome before they gain the romantic happiness they crave. The heroine of *No Price Too High* suffers a similar fate to Frances Hodgson Burnett's Little Princess; in the 1920s her wealthy father disappears, leaving her school fees unpaid, and she is ill-used by a mercenary headmistress. But she is old enough to go out to work although totally unfitted for it by her upbringing. She suffers dreadfully from horrible employers, is tricked into a loveless marriage, and has a crippled child whom her husband will not even look at before her resurrected father arrives to save her, fortuitously bringing an Irish doctor with him with whom she falls in love.

Another high-born heroine who suffers is Irish Emily who is being 'finished' in Spain at the time of the Civil War. Emily is swept off her feet by aristocratic Alejandro who leaves her literally at the altar. She returns desolate to Ireland, recovers and is about to marry Dermot (a Viscount) when he is whisked off to war and is posted missing. Grieving Emily joins the WAAF (as did the author) and falls improbably for Sam, a humble mechanic with a chip on his shoulder. She keeps enough distance between them so that at the war's end, when Dermot reappears they can marry but she realizes she has ruined Sam's life. Dermot's money has gone so they set out for a new life in Spain.

Orphaned Kate Mary Pearse is a simple Irish girl in *As It Was in the Beginning*, set at the time of the Irish troubles in the 1920s. She suffers the anguish of divided loyalty for her beloved is a sergeant in the Royal Ulster Constabulary whose mission is to capture Kate's cousin, the local Sinn Fein leader. Her dilemma is impossible—'to pray for victory for one meant praying for the almost certain death of the other'. Finally, Kate marries her sergeant after her cousin's execution, but they have to live exiled from their beloved Ireland.

Polland uses conflict of war (especially civil war in both Spain and Ireland), conflict of class, and conflict of cultures in her plotting. Her characters, especially her Irish people are realistic, and she is adept at portraying atmosphere such as the claustrophobic closeness of Irish village life. Her descriptions are evocative and beautiful; her love for the places she describes shines through. Her stories, however, are very slow moving with more emphasis on emotion than action and they are often sad, with more agony than ecstasy. Indeed, a book like *The Little Spot of Bother* could easily be condensed into a short story as far as the action is concerned. However, Polland's romances are truly romantic and although the reader is battered by the stormy seas of emotion during the books, she reaches the safe harbour of the happy ending eventually.

—Pamela Cleaver

———

PONSONBY, D(oris) A(lmon).
Pseudonyms: Doris Rybot; Sarah Tempest. **Nationality:** British. **Born:** Devonport, Devon, 23 March 1907. **Education:** Shrewsbury High School for Girls; Villabelle, Neuchâtel, Switzerland. **Relations:** married John Rybot in 1933 (died 1979). **Career:** subeditor, Oxford *Times*, reporter, Aldershot *Gazette*, and freelance writer for *South China Morning Post*, and Hong Kong *Herald*, 1928–37. **Agent:** Curtis Brown, 162–168 Regent Street, London, W1R 5TB, England.

ROMANCE AND HISTORICAL PUBLICATIONS

Novels (series: Jaspard Family Chronicle)

The Gazebo. London, Hutchinson, 1945; as *If My Arms Could Hold* (as Doris Ponsonby), New York, Liveright, 1947.
Sophy Valentine. London, Hutchinson, 1946.

Merry Meeting. London, Hutchinson, 1948.
Strangers in My House. London, Hutchinson, 1948.
Bow Window in Green Street. London, Hutchinson, 1949.
Family of Jaspard. London, Hutchinson, and New York, Crowell, 1950; as *The General* and *The Fortunate Adventure*, London, White Lion, 2 vols, 1971.
The Bristol Cousins (Jaspard). London, Hutchinson, 1951.
The Foolish Marriage. London, Hutchinson, 1952.
The Widow's Daughters. London, Hutchinson, 1953.
Royal Purple. London, Hutchinson, 1954.
Dogs in Clover. London, Hutchinson, 1954.
Conquesta's Caravan. London, Hutchinson, 1955.
Unhallowed House. London, Hutchinson, 1956.
So Bold a Choice. London, Hurst and Blackett, 1960.
Romany Sister (as Doris Rybot). London, Hale, 1960.
A Japanese Doll (as Doris Rybot). London, Hale, 1961.
A Living to Earn. London, Hurst and Blackett, 1961.
The Orphans. London, Hurst and Blackett, 1962.
Bells along the Neva. London, Hurst and Blackett, 1964.
The Jade Horse of Merle. London, Hurst and Blackett, 1966.
An Unusual Tutor. London, Hurst and Blackett, 1967.
A Winter of Fear (as Sarah Tempest). London, Hurst and Blackett, 1967; New York, Pyramid, 1968.
The Forgotten Heir. London, Hurst and Blackett, 1969.
The Heart in the Sand. London, Hurst and Blackett, 1970.
Mr Florian's Fortune. London, Hurst and Blackett, 1971.
Flight from Hanover Square. London, Hurst and Blackett, 1972.
The Gamester's Daughter. London, Hurst and Blackett, 1974.
The Heir to Holtwood. London, Hurst and Blackett, 1975.
An Unnamed Gentlewoman. London, Hurst and Blackett, 1976.
Kaye's Walk. London, Hurst and Blackett, 1977.
Sir William. London, Hurst and Blackett, 1978.
Exhibition Summer. London, Hale, 1982.
A Woman Despised. London, Hale, 1988.

OTHER PUBLICATIONS

Other

Call a Dog Hervey. London, Hutchinson, 1949.
The Lost Duchess: The Story of the Prince Consort's Mother. London, Chapman and Hall, 1958.
A Prisoner in Regent's Park. London, Chapman and Hall, 1961.

Other as Doris Rybot

The Popular Chow Chow, with Lydia Ingleton. London, Popular Dogs, 1954.
My Kingdom for a Donkey. London, Hutchinson, 1963.
A Donkey and a Dandelion. London, Hutchinson, 1966.
It Began Before Noah (on zoos). London, Joseph, 1972.

*

D.A. Ponsonby comments:

In all my historical stories and romances my main aim (apart from telling a good story) is to be as historically accurate as possible, not only in facts, but concerning manners, dress, social attitudes, and everything else.

*   *   *

It is almost 50 years since D.A. Ponsonby's historical novels were first published, yet there is a freshness about them that makes them hold their attraction today.

Her sense of period is accurate and her shrewd knowledge of people splendidly evokes the time in which the tales are set. *The Gazebo*, her first novel, is a gripping family story revealing a young girl's awakening to love, her marriage and its problems. Much of her fiction is told by means of excellent descriptive passages with the conversations slipping into place effortlessly, avoiding the all-too-common failure of so many of today's writers of using mainly jerky conversations for narration.

The novel *Merry Meeting*, about the love of two orphans, begins in a foundling home in the cruel days of the 18th century. Their future lives are mingled, and the boy's eventual sacrifice fits exactly into the story. The author's ability to bring life to her characters ensures a convincing tale.

Bow Window in Green Street is set in 18th-century Bath, and all the hopes and excitement of Regency living are wonderfully captured. One feels one could again knock on the door of the very house in which they all lived. The Regency, in fact, was a favourite period for Ponsonby who vividly recreated its days in her novels. *The Widow's Daughters* is a more light-hearted story of a silly, scheming widow using her wiles to marry off her four daughters who had their own surprising ideas.

The well-worn themes of regency novels take on a new meaning under this writer's narrative skill; the timelessness of her writing is its strong quality. Her sense of period and the fact that her stories can be read and re-read with ease makes them stand out in the morass of historical fiction. My regret is there are not more of them, though their exclusivity is another charm, making them novels to be treasured.

—Lornie Leete-Hodge

POPE, Dudley (Bernard Egerton).
Nationality: British. **Born:** Ashford, Kent, 29 December 1925. **Education:** Ashford Grammar School, 1934–42. **Relations:** married Kathleen Patricia Hall in 1954; one daughter. **Career:** merchant Navy, 1941–43; sub-editor and deputy foreign editor, London *Evening News*, 1944–59. **Agent:** John McLaughlin, Campbell Thomson and McLaughlin Ltd, 1 King Mews, London WC1N 2JA, England. **Address:** Le Pirate 379, B.P. 677, 97150 Marigot, St Martin, French West Indies.

ROMANCE AND HISTORICAL PUBLICATIONS

Novels (series: Lord Nicholas Ramage; Yorke)

Ramage. London, Weidenfeld and Nicolson, and Philadelphia, Lippincott, 1965.
Ramage and the Drum Beat. London, Weidenfeld and Nicolson, 1967; as *Drumbeat*, New York, Doubleday, 1968.
Ramage and the Freebooters. London, Weidenfeld and Nicolson, 1969; as *Triton Brig*, New York, Doubleday, 1969.
Governor Ramage RN. London, Secker and Warburg, and New York, Simon and Schuster, 1973.
Ramage's Prize. London, Secker and Warburg, 1974; New York, Simon and Schuster, 1975.
Ramage and the Guillotine. London, Secker and Warburg, and New York, Simon and Schuster, 1975.
Ramage's Diamond. London, Secker and Warburg, 1976.
Ramage's Mutiny. London, Secker and Warburg, 1977.
Ramage and the Rebels. London, Secker and Warburg, 1978; New York, Walker, 1985.
The Ramage Touch. London, Secker and Warburg, 1979; New York, Walker, 1984.

Convoy (Yorke). London, Secker and Warburg, 1979; New York, Walker, 1987.

Ramage's Signal. London, Secker and Warburg, 1980; New York, Walker, 1984.

Buccaneer (Yorke). London, Secker and Warburg, 1981; New York, Walker, 1984.

Ramage and the Renegades. London, Secker and Warburg, 1981.

Admiral (Yorke). London, Secker and Warburg, 1982.

Ramage's Devil. London, Secker and Warburg, 1982.

Decoy (Yorke). London, Secker and Warburg, 1983; New York, Walker, 1984.

Ramage's Trial. London, Secker and Warburg, 1984.

Ramage's Challenge. London, Secker and Warburg, 1985.

Galleon (Yorke). London, Secker and Warburg, 1986; New York, Walker, 1987.

Ramage at Trafalgar. London, Secker and Warburg, 1986.

Corsair (Yorke). London, Secker and Warburg, 1987.

Ramage and the Saracens. London, Secker and Warburg, 1988.

Ramage and the Dido. London, Secker and Warburg, 1989.

OTHER PUBLICATIONS

Other

Flag 4: The Battle of Coastal Forces in the Mediterranean. London, Kimber, 1954.

The Battle of the River Plate. London, Kimber, 1956; as *Graf Spee*, Philadelphia, Lippincott, 1957.

73 North: The Battle of the Barents Sea. London, Weidenfeld and Nicolson, and Philadelphia, Lippincott, 1958.

England Expects. London, Weidenfeld and Nicolson; as *Decision at Trafalgar*, Philadelphia, Lippincott, 1959.

At 12 Mr Byng Was Shot. London, Weidenfeld and Nicolson, and Philadelphia, Lippincott, 1962.

The Black Ship: Mutiny on the H.M.S. Hermion 1797. London, Weidenfeld and Nicolson, 1963; Philadelphia, Lippincott, 1964.

Guns. London, Weidenfeld and Nicolson, and New York, Delacorte Press, 1965.

The Great Gamble. London, Weidenfeld and Nicolson, and New York, Simon and Schuster, 1972.

Harry Morgan's Way (biography). London, Secker and Warburg, 1977; as *The Buccaneer King*, New York, Dodd Mead, 1978.

Life in Nelson's Navy. London, Allen and Unwin, and Annapolis, Maryland, Naval Institute Press, 1981.

The Devil Himself: The Mutiny of 1800. London, Secker and Warburg, 1987.

*

Manuscript Collection: Reading University, Berkshire.

Dudley Pope comments:

I have specialized in the history of the Navy in Nelson's time, and realized that the best way of describing it was in fictional form, so I created Nicholas Ramage as a young officer in Nelson's day and wrote the Ramage series.

*   *   *

Dudley Pope is an internationally known writer of British naval history. Besides writing numerous non-fiction works about the Royal Navy, he is also the creator of a series of novels about Lord Nicholas Ramage, a lowly lieutenant in His Majesty's Navy during the Napoleonic period.

Before commenting on Pope's fiction, one must acknowledge his vast store of historical information about the Royal Navy and its history. It is not the kind of knowledge that is found on tediously compiled note-cards. Pope has internalized so much of what he has learned that readers would find it difficult, if not impossible, to detect a false note within his writing. There is no awkward stretch for words, no laborious description, no cut and paste line to show where historical fact blends with narrative need.

Not only does Pope avoid the normal pitfalls inherent in historical writing, he seems effortlessly to weave fact and fiction together. His writing is taut, compelling, and deceptively simple. His characters are works of art, especially Nicholas Ramage.

Ramage is not a super-hero. He doubts, he ponders his decisions. He questions his perceptions and tries to be fair in a world that functioned on patronage, rank, and bribery. He is not a stoic, for he worries. Like other men, he fears the unknowable and the uncontrollable.

The supporting characters in the Ramage series are just as well drawn and uniquely representative of the historical figures Pope brings to life. Finally, one cannot forget the other main character in the Ramage series—the Royal Navy. The ships, the daily tasks of living, the seaman's life of storms and wind, the noise of battles; all carry out their part in making Ramage and his adventures the best historical novels in years.

A look at two of the novels that were written sequentially might help illustrate just how readers become addicted to Lieutenant Ramage and his escapades. In *Governor Ramage, RN.*, the Lieutenant and his crew face daunting odds. They are assigned convoy duty to help escort a fleet of merchant ships to Jamaica. Before they finally reach their destination, Ramage must cope with the following. His ship, the *Triton*, attacks and defeats a French privateer that had slipped into the convoy. He is then caught in a hurricane, and eventually lands near a small Spanish island along with the ship owned by Mr Yorke. The *Triton* is lost as is Mr Yorke's ship, which carried passengers. The crews of both ships accept Ramage as their natural leader and between them, they capture the island. While waiting to capture the Spanish supply ship that is expected, Ramage and his men find buried treasure. They easily capture the ship when it does arrive and eventually reach Jamaica. Ramage's arrival, however, is less than joyous for he is immediately arrested and charged with cowardliness in battle. At the end of the book Ramage confronts his accusers. Tension and suspense do not resolve themselves until the last two or three pages, keeping the reader gripped by the story.

Ramage's Prize is the sequel to *Governor Ramage RN*. In it, Ramage is offered further adventures. He and some of his men are still waiting to be posted on another ship in Jamaica, when he is offered an unusual assignment. What he gets is not another brig, but a mail packet! His charge—to find out how mail packets from England to Jamaica and back are being intercepted and taken. Whatever the answer, events are creating critical problems for government officials as well as military personnel. There is literally no direct communication with the government in Jamaica either to the different military or diplomatic posts or with London. Ramage does, indeed, face a very puzzling mystery when he sets out to learn exactly what is happening to the mail packets.

Readers have a delightful time keeping up with Ramage's razor-sharp mind as he unravels the tangled knot of deception and traitorous guile. Pope's earlier career as a newspaper writer definitely helped him to learn the value of economic writing where one word did the work of three or four. Certainly the recognition of his scholarly publications helped as well. These two aspects of his writing life somehow blended to produce a style of fiction that is uniquely his own. If his style is unique, so are his novels.

—Arlene Moore

PORTER, Eleanor H(odgman).

Pseudonym: Eleanor Stuart. **Nationality:** American. **Born:** Little-
ton, New Hampshire, 19 December 1868. **Education:** New
England Conservatory of Music, Boston. **Relations:** married John
L. Porter in 1892. **Career:** choir and concert singer, then teacher;
full-time writer from 1901. **Died:** 21 May 1920.

ROMANCE AND HISTORICAL PUBLICATIONS

Novels (series: Margaret; Miss Billy; Pollyanna)

Cross Currents: The Story of Margaret. Boston, Wilde, 1907; Lon-
don, Harrap, 1928.
*The Turn of the Tide: The Story of How Margaret Solved Her Prob-
lem.* Boston, Wilde, 1908; London, Harrap, 1928.
The Story of Marco. Cincinnati, Jennings and Graham, 1911; Lon-
don, Stanley Paul, 1920.
Miss Billy. Boston, Page, 1911; London, Stanley Paul, 1914.
Miss Billy's Decision. Boston, Page, 1912; London, Stanley Paul,
1915.
Pollyanna. Boston, Page, and London, Pitman, 1913.
Miss Billy—Married. Boston, Page, 1914; London, Stanley Paul,
1915.
Pollyanna Grows Up. Boston, Page, and London, Pitman, 1915.
Just David. Boston, Houghton Mifflin, and London, Constable,
1916.
The Road to Understanding. Boston, Houghton Mifflin, and Lon-
don, Constable, 1917.
Oh, Money! Money! Boston, Houghton Mifflin, and London, Con-
stable, 1918.
Dawn. Boston, Houghton Mifflin, 1919; as *Keith's Dark Tower*,
London, Constable, 1919.
Mary Marie. Boston, Houghton Mifflin, and London, Constable,
1920.
Sister Sue. Boston, Houghton Mifflin, and London, Constable,
1921.

Short Stories

The Tangled Threads. Boston, Houghton Mifflin, 1919.
Across the Years. Boston, Houghton Mifflin, 1919.
The Tie That Binds. Boston, Houghton Mifflin, 1919.
Money, Love, and Kate, Together with The Story of a Nickel. New
York, Doran, 1923; London, Hodder and Stoughton, 1924.
Hustler Joe and Other Stories. New York, Doran, 1924.
Little Pardner and Other Stories. New York, Doran, 1926; London,
Hodder and Stoughton, 1927.
Just Mother and Other Stories. New York, Doran, 1927.
The Fortunate Mary. New York, Doubleday, 1928.

OTHER PUBLICATIONS

Other (for children)

The Sunbridge Girls at Six Star Ranch (as Eleanor Stuart). Boston,
Page, 1913; as *Six Star Ranch*, London, Stanley Paul, 1916.

*

Film Adaptations: *Pollyanna*, 1960, *Polly*, 1989, from the novel
Pollyanna.

*   *   *

When Eleanor H. Porter died in her early fifties, having given up a

singing career for writing only 20 years before, she left behind her
over 20 volumes of fiction. From this prolific output, posterity has
selected a single novel, *Pollyanna*, and given its name not to one
who sees the best side of a bad situation, but to one who embraces
blind and foolish optimism. As with Harriet Beecher Stowe's Black
Christ, so with Porter's little 'glad' girl who brought happiness into
lives as afflicted as her own—for who today would want to be called
an Uncle Tom or a Pollyanna?

As a writer of children's stories—for and about children—Porter
belongs in that very American line which runs from Mark Twain to
Booth Tarkington. The boys are mischievous, the girls responsible;
the boys disrupt the social order, though they (even Huck)
ultimately conform to it, the girls work on it from within, and restore
it with certain improvements. The boys foment misunderstandings
between unconsenting adults, the girls resolve them. Tom Sawyer is
constantly evading *his* Aunt Polly, Pollyanna nudges *hers* to the
altar. Yet the status quo is not quite safe from either boys or girls:
Porter's social blueprint, happily based upon feminine values, may
be as subversive as Twain's 'boy's' books, though repressed by the
adult reader. For as a perceptive reviewer of 1913 noted, *Pollyanna*
is 'a book for grown-up people who will understand the criticism of
convention; it would be a disaster if many little girls should undertake to imitate the heroine'.

It is this 'criticism of convention', however defused, which may
give Porter some claim to our continuing attention. There is a genuine social conscience in her work which distinguished her from the
Alice Hegan Rices and the Gene Stratton Porters, and brings her
closer to the best of all these 'cheerful' (if not always quite 'glad')
writers, Jean Webster. Porter's first novel, *Cross Currents*, sets the
tone: a poor little rich girl is lost, and grows up in the slums, amid the
sweatshops. The novel vigorously attacks the child labour of its day,
and several of Porter's works at least touch upon social questions.
Pollyanna certainly criticizes the same over-zealous do-gooders
who will be the villains of Griffith's film *Intolerance* three years
later; *Mary Marie*, in which the character's odd name is a compromise agreed upon by warring parents, seriously discusses divorce; and
Pollyanna Grows Up accuses the slum landlord.

Though the Six Star Ranch stories deal with a moderately
mischievous group of six girls—'the happy hexagons'—Porter's
typical heroine, as well as being a marital fixer, is, like Anne of
Green Gables or Rebecca of Sunnybrook Farm, an orphan reaching
for a family; and her arrangements are not always selfless, especially since she is so often poor. The formula works well enough
with the girl at its centre, but two of Porter's more egregiously sentimental works fail by attempting to force the boy into this stereotyped role. *Dawn* finds a 15-year-old youth suddenly stricken with
blindness; he turns away from human contact, but is won back by
the love of the great eye surgeon's stepdaughter, who adopts a false
identity to woo him (one wonders if Lloyd C. Douglas read this
novel). And the hero of *Just David*, as *The Times* not unjustly remarked, 'combines in his pathetic person the shortcomings of Lord
Fauntleroy, Eric, and Humphrey in *Misunderstood*'. Girls could still
be prigs, but boys, after Tom, Huck, and Penrod, could not.

One (or three) of Porter's most effective works is the group of
novels made up of *Miss Billy* (her first major success), *Miss Billy's
Decision*, and *Miss Billy—Married*. Three settled bachelors receive
a letter announcing the arrival of the forgotten godchild of the
eldest. Because of her androgynous name, they assume that *she* is
he, but their settled existence is in for a much greater dis-
combobulation. Each falls in love with her, each proposes, and after
several misunderstandings she marries the youngest. By June 1921,
these three novels had sold 93, 78, and 86 thousand copies (*Pollyanna* at the same time had sold half a million, and, as James D.
Hart has noted, Porter's publishers after her death commissioned
five further writers of 'their' Pollyanna series, which over 40 years
sold two million copies).

Porter had a considerable talent for the short story—her novels tend to be episodic—and her best stories are collected in three volumes published the year before her death: *The Tangled Threads*, *The Tie That Binds*, and *Across the Years*, dealing with the three ages of love. The last collection especially shows her as a benign Mary Wilkins Freeman—the Yankee spareness and satiric bite of Freeman's famous 'The Revolt of Mother' provides a point of comparison, one of many, with Porter's charming but sentimentally lenient 'When Mother and Father Rebelled'.

It is easy to sneer at Porter. A reviewer of 1917, condemning one of her novels, predicted a large sale for it notwithstanding ('take it from a pessimist'). We do better to use as her epitaph the phrase of a reviewer of her second Pollyanna book: 'after all, she has the right idea'.

—Barrie Hayne

PORTER, Gene Stratton (Geneva Grace Stratton Porter).
Nationality: American. **Born:** Wabash County, Indiana, 17 August 1863. **Career:** attended public schools. **Relations:** married Charles Darwin Porter in 1886; one daughter. **Career:** regular contributor, *McCall's* magazine; photographic editor, *Recreation* magazine; member of the natural history department, *Outing* magazine; natural history photography specialist, *Photographic Times Annual Almanac*, four years. Founded Gene Stratton Porter Productions film company, 1922. **Died:** 6 December 1924.

ROMANCE AND HISTORICAL PUBLICATIONS

Novels

The Song of the Cardinal: A Love Story. Indianapolis, Bobbs Merrill, 1903; London, Hodder and Stoughton, 1913.
Freckles. New York, Doubleday, 1904; London, Murray, 1905.
At the Foot of the Rainbow. New York, Outing Publishing Company, 1907; London, Hodder and Stoughton, 1913.
A Girl of the Limberlost. New York, Doubleday, 1909; London, Hodder and Stoughton, 1911.
The Harvester. New York, Doubleday, and London, Hodder and Stoughton, 1911.
Laddie: A True-Blue Story. New York, Doubleday, and London, Murray, 1913.
Michael O'Halloran. New York, Doubleday, and London, Murray, 1915.
A Daughter of the Land. New York, Doubleday, and London, Murray, 1918.
Her Father's Daughter. New York, Doubleday, and London, Murray, 1921.
The White Flag. New York, Doubleday, and London, Murray, 1923.
The Keeper of the Bees. New York, Doubleday, and London, Hutchinson, 1925.
The Magic Garden. New York, Doubleday, and London, Hutchinson, 1927.

OTHER PUBLICATIONS

Play

Screenplay: *A Girl of the Limberlost*, 1924.

Poetry

Morning Face, illustrated by the author. New York, Doubleday, and London, Murray, 1916.

The Fire Bird. New York, Doubleday, and London, Murray, 1922.
Jesus of the Emerald. New York, Doubleday, and London, Murray, 1923.

Other

What I Have Done with Birds: Character Studies of Native American Birds. Indianapolis, Bobbs Merrill, 1907; revised edition, New York, Doubleday, 1917; as *Friends in Feathers*, London, Curtis Brown, 1917.
Birds of the Bible. Cincinnati, Jennings and Graham, 1909; London, Hodder and Stoughton, 1910.
Music of the Wild, illustrated by the author. Cincinnati, Jennings and Graham, and London, Hodder and Stoughton, 1910.
Moths of the Limberlost, illustrated by the author. New York, Doubleday, 1912; London, Hodder and Stoughton, 1913.
After the Flood. Indianapolis, Bobbs Merrill, 1912.
Birds of the Limberlost. New York, Doubleday, 1914.
Homing with the Birds. New York, Doubleday, and London, Murray, 1919.
Wings. New York, Doubleday, 1923.
Tales You Won't Believe (natural history). New York, Doubleday, and London, Heinemann, 1925.
Let Us Highly Resolve (essays). New York, Doubleday, and London, Heinemann, 1927.

*

Film Adaptations: *A Girl of the Limberlost*, 1934; *Keeper of the Bees*, 1935; *Laddie*, 1935; *Freckles*, 1935, 1960.

Critical Studies: *The Lady of the Limberlost: The Life and Letters of Gene Stratton Porter* by Jeanette Porter Meehan, New York, Doubleday, 1928, as *Life and Letters of Gene Stratton Porter*, London, Hutchinson, 1928; *Gene Stratton Porter* by Bernard F. Richards, Boston, Twayne, 1980.

*   *   *

It seems incredible today that Gene Stratton Porter's books were once among the most popular all over the world, both in English and in translation; that they sold out edition after edition; and that several of them were the subjects of motion pictures. Surely never before or since did such cardboard creations capture and hold a more enthusiastic audience. A good many of her major characters were never even named; they were designated and remain The Swamp Angel, The Man of Affairs, The Bird Woman, and so on. Stereotypical characterization surely never has been carried to greater length. Her dialogue is a curious combination of simon-pure, long-winded passion, and quirky lectures on diet and nature study, perpetrated by a writer totally deaf to the cadence of natural, colloquial speech; her code of values defies comprehension, muddling as it does fundamental issues of moral integrity and personal worth with trivial concerns of good form and etiquette relevant only to the turn of the century.

Still, when one has laughed at the quaint set speeches, purer-than-life heroes and positively incandescent heroines, and outmoded, bombastic philosophy, a glimmer of the charm that caught and held Porter's millions of readers remains. She created a world of good, honest (if pompous) people who offered one another whole hearts and an enviable confidence in a wholesome, unspoiled world full of the bounty of nature that was to be theirs and their children's. 'Homely' was to her a word of highest praise. A more cynical generation cannot share this perhaps blinkered simplicity—but it is surely to her credit that it is difficult to believe in the existence of a nuclear arms race while in imagination patrolling the Limberlost

odland trail with Freckles, or keeping bees in the beautiful blue
rden with Jamie MacFarlane and his little Scout.

—Joan McGrath

———

ORTER, Hal.
ationality: Australian. **Born:** Albert Park, Melbourne, Victoria,
February 1911. **Education:** Kensington State School, 1917;
airnsdale State School, Victoria, 1918–21; Bairnsdale High
hool, 1922–26. **Relations:** married Olivia Parnham in 1939
ivorced 1943). **Career:** cadet reporter, Bairnsdale *Advertiser*,
27; schoolmaster, Victorian Education Department, 1927–37 and
40, Queen's College, Adelaide, 1941–42, Prince Alfred College,
ent Town, South Australia, 1943–46, Hutchins School, Hobart,
smania, 1946–47, Knox Grammar School, Sydney, 1947, Balla-
College, Victoria, 1948–49, and Nijimura School, Kure, Japan
ustralian Army Education), 1949–50; manager, George Hotel, St
lda, Victoria, 1949; director, National Theatre, Hobart, 1951–53;
unicipal librarian, 1953–57, and regional librarian, 1958–61,
airnsdale and Shepparton, Victoria; from 1961 full-time writer.
ustralian writers representative, Edinburgh Festival, 1962;
ustralian Department of External Affairs lecturer, Japan, 1967.
ecipient: Sydney Sesquicentenary prize, 1938; Commonwealth
terary Fund fellowship, 1956, 1960, 1964, 1968, 1972, 1974,
77, 1980, and subsidy, 1957, 1962, 1967; Sydney *Morning
erald* prize, 1958; Sydney Journalists' Club prize, for fiction,
59, for drama, 1961; Adelaide *Advertiser* prize, for fiction, 1964,
70, for non-fiction, 1968; Encyclopaedia *Brittanica* award, 1967;
aptain Cook Bi-Centenary prize, 1970; Australia and New Zea-
nd Bank award, for local history, 1977. Member, Order of Austra-
, 1982. **Died:** 29 September 1984.

OMANCE AND HISTORICAL PUBLICATIONS

ovel

e Tilted Cross. London, Faber, 1961.

THER PUBLICATIONS

ovels

Handful of Pennies. Sydney, Angus and Robertson, 1958; London, Angus and Robertson, 1959; revised edition in *Hal Porter*,
1980.
he Right Thing. Adelaide, Rigby, and London, Hale, 1971.

ort Stories

ort Stories. Adelaide, Advertiser Press, 1942.
Bachelor's Children. Sydney and London, Angus and Robertson,
1962.
he Cats of Venice. Sydney, Angus and Robertson, 1965.
r Butterfry and Other Tales of New Japan. Sydney, Angus and
Robertson, 1970.
lected Stories, edited by Leonie Kramer. Sydney and London,
Angus and Robertson, 1971.
redo Fuss Love Life. Sydney, Angus and Robertson, 1974.
n Australian Selection, edited by John Barnes. Sydney, Angus and
Robertson, 1974.
he Clairvoyant Goat and Other Stories. Melbourne, Nelson, 1981.

Plays

The Tower (produced London, 1964). Published in *Three Australian
Plays*, Melbourne and London, Penguin, 1963.
The Professor (as *Toda-San*, produced Adelaide, 1965; as *The Professor*, produced London, 1965). London, Faber, 1966.
Eden House (produced Melbourne, 1969; as *Home on a Pig's Back*,
produced Richmond, Surrey, 1972). Sydney, Angus and Robertson, 1969.
Parker (produced Ballarat, Victoria, 1972). Melbourne, Arnold,
1979.

Screenplay: *The Child* (episode in *Libido*), 1973.

Television Play: *The Forger*, 1967.

Poetry

The Hexagon. Sydney, Angus and Robertson, 1956.
Elijah's Ravens. Sydney, Angus and Robertson, 1968.
In an Australian Country Graveyard. Sydney, Angus and Robert-
son, 1975.

Other

The Watcher on the Cast-Iron Balcony (autobiography). London,
Faber, 1963.
Australian Stars of Stage and Screen. Adelaide, Rigby, 1965.
The Paper Chase (autobiography). Sydney, Angus and Robertson,
1966.
The Actors: An Image of the New Japan. Sydney, Angus and
Robertson, 1968.
The Extra (autobiography). Melbourne, Nelson, 1975.
Bairnsdale: Portrait of an Australian Country Town. Melbourne,
Ferguson, 1977.
Seven Cities of Australia. Sydney, Ferguson, 1978.
Hal Porter (selection), edited by Mary Lord. St Lucia, University of
Queensland Press, 1980.

Editor, *Australian Poetry 1957*. Sydney, Angus and Robertson,
1957.
Editor, *Coast to Coast 1961–1962*. Sydney, Angus and Robertson,
1963.
Editor, *It Could Be You*. Adelaide, Rigby, 1972; London, Hale,
1973.

*

Bibliography: *A Bibliography of Hal Porter* by Janette Finch, Adelaide, Libraries Board of South Australia, 1966; 'A Contribution to
the Bibliography of Hal Porter' by Mary Lord, in *Australian
Literary Studies* (Hobart, Tasmania), October 1970; *Papers of Hal
Porter 1924–1975*, Sydney, Mitchell Library, n.d.

Manuscript Collection: Mitchell Library, Sydney.

Critical Studies: *Hal Porter* by Mary Lord, Melbourne, Oxford
University Press, 1974; *Speaking of Writing* edited by R.D. Walshe
and Leonie Kramer, Sydney, Reed, 1975; *Australian Writers* by
Graeme Kinross Smith, Melbourne, Nelson, 1980.

*   *   *

Hal Porter had been writing for many years before he gained critical recognition and popular acceptance. By the dominant standards
of the Australian literary scene in the 1930s and 1940s his work
appeared precious, even wilfully perverse. But a change of literary

fashion brought him a change of literary fortune, and by the 1960s he was counted with the best Australian authors, his candle dimmed only by Patrick White's.

Short stories dominated his early output and were the basis of his reputation, but later he assayed many forms. His autobiographical classic *The Watcher on the Cast-Iron Balcony* seems likely to remain his best-known book. Porter's writing is distinguished by an arresting and very personal style, intricately decorated, sharp-edged, self-conscious, and archly exact. At its worst this manner can degenerate into an affected sneer, but at its best it does what Porter admired in Katherine Mansfield, representing a 'breathtaking surface texture and, simultaneously, what the x-ray showed'.

Although his play *The Tower* is also set in mid-19th-century Hobart, *The Tilted Cross* is Porter's only extended piece of historical fiction. It is his second novel, and critical consensus ranks it his best because of its narrative tightness, carefully researched historical detailing, and metaphysical import. Though the novel itself consciously parades a Christian analogy, it is perhaps better understood, in common with much of Porter's work, as swinging on a Rousseauistic axis: untutored goodness versus civilized corruption. On the one hand there is the hypocritical world of the mansion of Cindermead, inhabited by the discreetly promiscuous Lady Rose Knight and her husband's cousin Asnetha Sleep, who is rich, malformed, epileptic, and lonely. On the other hand is the crude, passionate underworld of a raw penal colony.

The link between these worlds is the cold, arid figure of Judas Griffin Vaneleigh, at home in both worlds and despising both equally. Vaneleigh is based closely on the real-life Thomas Griffiths Wainwright, a notorious art forger and suspected murderer transported to Van Diemen's Land, who found his way into the pages of Dickens, Hazlitt, Wilde, and many other writers. Vaneleigh, who has been engaged as a portrait painter at Cindermead, is taken up by the simplehearted (and somewhat simpleminded) Queely Sheill, who drops his aitches and never tires of proclaiming his belief in human goodness. Pitying Vaneleigh for his despairing cynicism, Sheill ends up becoming his attendant and proceeds to get into a liaison with Asnetha Sleep. Crushed between Rose Knight's malice and Vaneleigh's moral dissociation, he finally dies a horrible death.

The characters are memorable but lack depth, and the author evidently intends this to be so, for he surrounds them—especially the two central men—with an array of alienation effects (artificial dialogue, ironic authorial comment, dislocated point of view). The aim appears to be a moral parable of universal import. But in this respect Queely Sheill in particular is problematic. While a caricature may effectively represent moral failure, a caricatured impression of goodness tends to undermine the basis of a moral parable.

The morbid action and grotesque characters of *The Tilted Cross* produce a structure of feeling which is piquant or bitter, according to taste: rather more melodramatic than tragic, and rather more sardonic than earnest. The abiding interest of the book will remain the author's extravagantly mannered prose, with its remarkable capacity for disconcerting precision, complexity, and irony.

—Paul Gillen

POTTER, Margaret. See MELVILLE, Anne.

POWERS, Nora. See PYKARE, Nina.

POWYS, John Cowper. British. 1872–1963. See 2nd edition, 1990.

POZZESSERE, Heather Graham.
Pseudonym: Shannon Drake. Also writes as Heather Graham Pozzessere. **Nationality:** American. **Relations:** married Dennis Pozzessere; five children. **Career:** various jobs including bartender, model, and actress. Lives in Florida. **Address:** c/o Silhouette Books, 300 East 42nd Street, New York, New York 10017, USA.

ROMANCE AND HISTORICAL PUBLICATIONS

Novels

Night Moves. New York, Silhouette, 1985.
Double Entendre. New York, Silhouette, 1986.
The DiMedici Bride. New York, Silhouette, 1986.
The Game of Love. New York, Silhouette, 1986.
A Matter of Circumstance. New York, Silhouette, 1987.
All in the Family. New York, Silhouette, 1987; (as Heather Graham) London, Severn House, 1991.
Bride of the Tiger. New York, Silhouette, 1987.
King of the Castle. New York, Silhouette, 1987.
Strangers in Paradise. New York, Silhouette, 1988.
Angel of Mercy. New York, Silhouette, 1988.
Dark Stranger. Toronto, Harlequin, 1988; (as Heather Graham) London, Severn House, 1993.
Lucia in Love. New York, Silhouette, 1988.
Night Moves. New York, Silhouette, 1988.
This Rough Magic. New York, Silhouette, 1988.
Double Entendre. New York, Silhouette, 1989.
A Matter of Circumstance. New York, Silhouette, 1990.
A Perilous Eden. New York, Silhouette, 1991.
Forbidden Fire. New York, Silhouette, 1991.
Wedding Bell Blues. New York, Silhouette, 1991.
Mistress of Magic. New York, Silhouette, 1992.
Borrowed Angel. New York, Silhouette, 1992.
The Last Cavalier. New York, Silhouette, 1993.
Hatfield and McCoy. New York, Silhouette, 1993.
The Trouble with Andrew. New York, Silhouette, 1993.
Between Roc and a Hard Place. New York, Silhouette, 1993.
Snowfire. New York, Silhouette, 1993.

Novels as Heather Graham (series: Civil War Trilogy; Donna Miro and Lorna Doria)

A Season for Love. New York, Dell, 1983.
Forbidden Fruit. New York, Dell, 1983.
Quiet Walks the Tiger. New York, Dell, 1983.
Tempestuous Eden. New York, Dell, 1983.
Tender Taming. New York, Dell, 1983.
When Next We Love. New York, Dell, 1983.
Night, Sea and Stars. New York, Dell, 1983.
Arabian Nights. New York, Dell, 1984.
Hours to Cherish. New York, Dell, 1984.
Red Midnight. New York, Dell, 1984.
Serena's Magic. New York, Dell, 1984.
Tender Deception. New York, Dell, 1984.
Hold Close the Memory. New York, Dell, 1985.
Sensuous Angel (Miro and Doria). New York, Dell, 1985.
An Angel's Share (Miro and Doria). New York, Dell, 1985.
Queen of Hearts. New York, Dell, 1985.
Golden Surrender. New York, Dell, 1985.
Dante's Daughter. New York, Dell, 1986.

Devil's Mistress. New York, Dell, 1986.
Eden's Spell. New York, Dell, 1986.
Handful of Dreams. New York, Dell, 1986.
The Maverick and the Lady. New York, Dell, 1986.
Every Time I Love You. New York, Dell, 1987.
Liar's Moon. New York, Dell, 1987.
Siren from the Sea. New York, Dell, 1987.
Sweet Savage Eden. New York, Dell, 1989.
Rides a Hero. New York, Silhouette, 1989.
Civil War Trilogy:
   One Wore Blue. New York, Dell, and London, Severn House,
      1992.
   And One Wore Gray. New York, Dell, 1992.
   And One Rode West. New York, Dell, 1992.
The Spirit of the Season. New York, Delacorte, 1993.
Lord of the Wolves. New York, Dell, 1993.
The Vikings Woman. New York, Dell, 1993.

Novels as Shannon Drake

Tomorrow the Glory. New York, Pinnacle, 1985.
Blue Heaven, Black Night. New York, Berkley, 1986.
Lie Down in Roses. New York, Charter, 1988.
Ondine. New York, Charter, 1988.
Princess of Fire. New York, Charter, 1989.
Bride of the Wind. New York, Avon, 1992.
Damsel in Distress. New York, Avon, 1992.
Knight of Fire. New York, Avon, 1993.

                    *   *   *

Since the mid-1980s, Heather Graham Pozzessere has been entertaining readers with solid, well-written love stories with lots of
sizzle. Originally writing as Heather Graham and Shannon Drake,
she now publishes mostly under her full name. Pozzessere is equally
adept at developing contemporary and historical romances. Her
characters are sharply defined and their physical and emotional passion frankly described.

Pozzessere seems at home in a wide range of historical periods,
from the Vikings in *Golden Surrender*, to the England of King
Charles (*Bride of the Wind*) and the American Civil War (*One Wore
Blue*, *And One Wore Gray*, and *And One Rode West*). Against a
background of just enough historical details, Pozzessere brings to
life adventure and romance in often violent periods of history. The
setting, however, is primarily a frame for the spirited, spicy romance
between the hero and heroine.

Pozzessere's contemporary novels often incorporate elements of
suspense and danger. *Angel of Mercy* involves a DEA agent in the
Florida swamps. Brad McKenna battles killers, snakes, and
alligators as he tries to survive. He is helped by Wendy Hawk, a
widow, and her Seminole relatives. Naturally, it is Wendy who
proves to be the most dangerous threat to Brad, at least in terms of
his independence. *Sensuous Angel* and *An Angel's Share* are linked
by characters although they were published in two different Ecstasy
series. In the first (*Sensuous Angel*), Donna Miro travels to New
York City to find her long-time friend, Lorna Doria who has disappeared. She is helped in her search by Father Luke Trudeau, an Epis-
copalian priest. Eventually they discover that Lorna is being held in
protective custody as a witness to a murder and is being guarded by
Luke's brother, Andrew. In *An Angel's Share*, they all return to Lorna's Massachusetts home although the murderer is still at large. In
Mistress of Magic, Regina Delaney and her brother, Max, are threatened by an unknown criminal. FBI agent Robert McCoy and
psychic Julie Hatfield are thrown together as they investigate a kidnapping in *Hatfield and McCoy*. Pozzessere's use of the names of

legendary feuding families as the names of her hero and heroine un-
derscores the nature of the lovers' conflict.

'Vanquish the Night', a story by Shannon Drake in *Bewitching
Love Stories*, presents the threat to the heroine as something supernatural. There also is a hint of the unknown in 'Wilde Imaginings', a
story in the Silhouette Shadows collection. When this collection expanded into a new line, Pozzessere was chosen to write the first volume issued, *The Last Cavalier*. Although it is not truly an
exploration of the 'dark side', it is a work of fantasy. In the book,
Pozzessere cleverly blends the present with one of her favourite historical periods by using a time-travel theme. Somehow a tunnel in
time is created so that Vickie Knox, the contemporary heroine, and
her Civil War cavalier, Captain Jason Tarkenton, move between
each other's reality. Tension builds as they try to resolve their relationship before the tunnel closes and they are separated or even
caught in the tunnel between two lives. Pozzessere also devises a
clever way to inform the reader of the ultimate fate of the two lovers
once they travel back to Virginia in the 1860s as Vickie leaves word
for her grandfather to find 'in the future'.

Reincarnation and past betrayals and misunderstandings drive the
plot of *Every Time I Love You*. Gayle Norman and Brent McCauley
are inexplicably drawn to one another, but their passionate relationship just as mysteriously and rapidly deteriorates into distrust and
violence. Through hypnotic regression to the time of the American
Revolution, they discover past lives as lovers who die, each thinking
the other has betrayed their love. Pozzessere effectively alternates
the story of Gayle and Brent with that of Katrina and Percy as the
modern day lovers seek to correct old misunderstandings. A
mistaken belief of betrayal also is the source of conflict in *A Season
for Love* and *Quiet Walks the Tiger*.

Many of Pozzessere's historical novels are loosely connected
through the Cameron family. Lord Jaimie Cameron (*Sweet Savage
Eden*) emigrates to colonial Virginia. Eric Cameron is a rebel general in the Revolutionary War (*Love Not a Rebel*). The 'Civil War'
trilogy features two Cameron brothers and their sister. In *And One
Rode West*, Christa Cameron marries Jeremy McCauley. The
McCauley name then recurs as the name of the hero in *Every Time I
Love You*. This kind of circular symmetry is not readily apparent to
the occasional reader of Pozzessere's work, but her devoted fans undoubtedly appreciate the continuity provided by these connections.

Pozzessere's characters are engaging and vividly drawn. She is
among the best of the romance authors at breathing life into tempestuous characters. She has a knack for developing colourful situations for them to face and gives them witty, sharp dialogue. Steamy
sexual tension, passionate love scenes, action, and intrigue all add to
the mix she so carefully prepares and keeps stirring. Pozzessere
keeps the reader totally involved so that her books are real page-
turners and hard to put down. She understands her readers and her
craft.

—Barbara E. Kemp

————

PREEDY, George.   See BOWEN, Marjorie.

————

PRESCOTT, H(ilda) F(rances) M(argaret).
Nationality: British. **Born:** Latchford, Cheshire, 22 February 1896.
Education: Wallasey High School, Cheshire; Lady Margaret Hall,
Oxford (Jephson scholar), B.A., M.A.; Manchester University,
M.A. Jubilee research fellow, Royal Holloway College, Surrey,
1958–60. **Recipient:** James Tait Black memorial prize, for non-
fiction, 1941; Christopher medal, 1953. D.Litt.: Durham University,
1957. Fellow, Royal Society of Literature, 1953. **Died:** 5 May 1972.

ROMANCE AND HISTORICAL PUBLICATIONS

Novels

The Unhurrying Chase. London, Constable, and New York, Dodd
Mead, 1925.
The Lost Fight. London, Constable, and New York, Dodd Mead,
1928.
Son of Dust. London, Constable, 1932; New York, Macmillan,
1956.
The Man on a Donkey: A Chronicle. London, Eyre and Spot-
tiswoode, 2 vols, 1952; New York, Macmillan, 1952.

OTHER PUBLICATIONS

Novel

Dead and Not Buried. London, Constable, and New York, Macmillan, 1938.

Other

Spanish Tudor: The Life of Bloody Mary. London, Constable, and
New York, Columbia University Press, 1940; revised edition,
London, Eyre and Spottiswoode, and New York, Macmillan,
1953.
*Friar Felix at Large: A Fifteenth-Century Pilgrimage to the Holy
Land.* New Haven, Connecticut, Yale University Press, 1950; as
Jerusalem Journey: Pilgrimage to the Holy Land, London, Eyre
and Spottiswoode, 1954.
Once to Sinai: The Further Pilgrimage of Friar Felix Fabri. Lon-
don, Eyre and Spottiswoode, 1957; New York, Macmillan, 1958.

Translator, *Flamenca,* by Bernardet the Troubadour. London, Constable, 1933.

*   *   *

As an historical novelist H.F.M. Prescott is noteworthy for her
adroit use of scholarly material, her concern with hardship, pain,
and self-denial, and for her Christian outlook. Her first three novels
are set in France during the Middle Ages. The action of *The Unhurrying Chase* takes place in the late-12th century. The main character
is Yves de Rifaucon, dispossessed of his fief and bitterly resentful of
his feudal overlords, in particular the future Richard I of England.
The book traces his misfortunes and ultimate degradation, together
with the love for him of a girl whose loyalty he fails to comprehend,
and is to some extent the study of an obsession; at a religious level it
recalls Francis Thompson's poem 'The Hound of Heaven'. The
background detail is skilfully incorporated into the story; Prescott
also makes powerful use of the devastation of southwestern France
by the mercenary armies of the time. Like its two successors, *The
Lost Fight* (set in Lorraine and Cyprus during the 13th century) and
Son of Dust (11th-century Normandy), *The Unhurrying Chase* combines a swiftly-paced narrative with a meticulous use of detail.
Prescott lays great stress on knightly codes of honour and of duty to
overlords; but the feudal world she depicts is harsh and frequently
brutal, and there is nothing superficially picturesque about it. *Son of
Dust,* indeed, is based on actual events recorded in the *Historia
Ecclesiastica* of Orderic Vitalis, and is, possibly as a result, more
broadly focussed than are its predecessors.

All three novels are primarily love stories written from an overtly
Christian point of view, their theme being the conflict between the
strict rules of chastity imposed by the Church and the importunate
needs and desires of the flesh: in *The Lost Fight* and *Son of Dust* the
lovers are separated by the laws of both God and man, and pay the

price of defying them. (At the same time, lovingly detailed evocations of landscape and of animal and bird life serve as relief from the
unflagging intensities of the human relationships.) Both *The
Unhurrying Chase* and *The Lost Fight* uphold the values of courtly
love celebrated by the Provençal troubadours. The leading male
characters in all three novels are stubborn, confused personalities,
while the women they love are heroically passive and long-
suffering: the sexual sensibility is as much of the late-19th century
as mediaeval, and is presented with great emotional intensity. The
historical settings, skilfully handled though they are, thus seem to be
occasions for the narration of stories whose ideology would be more
difficult to present in a contemporary setting. Both in their themes
and in their resolutions these first three novels by Prescott anticipate
the early and specifically Catholic fiction of Graham Greene.

Her masterpiece, however, is *The Man on a Donkey.* It was long
in preparation, and can fairly claim to be among the most ambitious
and persuasive English historical novels to be written in the 20th
century. The action covers 30 years, between 1509 and 1539, and
reaches its climax with the Pilgrimage of Grace, the rebellion of the
North Country Catholics against the dissolution of the monasteries.
The book consists of a number of parallel stories centering on five
principal characters, whose fortunes are gradually drawn together as
the narrative proceeds. They are Christabel Cowper, the Prioress of
Marrick Abbey, near Richmond in Swaledale; the elderly Lord
Darcy, one of the loyal Catholic nobility; Gilbert Dawe, a Protestant
malcontent whose religious intransigence resembles that of the prot-
agonists of *The Unhurrying Chase* and *Son of Dust;* Robert Aske,
the Yorkshire squire who becomes the leader of the rebellion; and
Julian Savage, a young married woman who loves him. Many historical characters of the period are depicted, including King Henry
VIII, Katherine of Aragon, the Princess Mary and Anne Boleyn;
Thomas Cromwell and Archbishop Cranmer; Cardinal Wolsey and
Sir Thomas More. But their roles are secondary in dramatic terms to
those of the Aske family, of the nuns of Marrick, of Julian's devoted
husband, and of her sister Margaret, who takes a leading part in the
insurrection: this is a novel primarily about people in ordinary walks
of life.

The book is written in the form of a discontinuous chronicle,
which allows the author to shift her scene with ease between Yorkshire and London, and between character and character. The result is
to do away with the artificial and thus distracting element of formal
plot, and to secure a close involvement in events as they build up,
item by item, full of small, unobtrusive details that serve to heighten
the reader's feeling of participation in the life of Tudor England.
Both in style and technique this aspect of the novel resembles Rose
Macaulay's portrait of Caroline England in *They Were Defeated.*

The Man on a Donkey is also impressive for its breadth of outlook
and its humanity. The brooding menace of the rise of a totalitarian
state is contrasted with the many descriptions of domestic life, with
the placid rigours of the monastic round, and with the beauties of the
Yorkshire landscape, all of which lend an element of timelessness to
the story. The account of life in Marrick Priory is especially memorable. Although she portrays the nuns' rivalries and limitations with a
good deal of not unkindly satirical humour, Prescott is sympathetic
to the monastic ideal and to its theological premises. Her Christian
outlook encompasses party divisions and religious controversies
alike in a vision of transcendent divine love—one that is painfully
tested, however, in the account of Aske's death by hanging in chains
from York castle keep, a piece of descriptive writing of haunting
power. The medium used to convey this impression of a supernatural order is the character of a simple-minded serving woman, a visionary whose words both echo and interpret those of the
14th-century mystic, Julian of Norwich. Thanks to the unstrained
and persuasive use of its religious theme, *The Man on a Donkey* is
one historical novel which effortlessly achieves a timeless relevance. But for all its emotional and poetic qualities it is naturalistic

and based on solid scholarship, also evident in Prescott's biography of Mary Tudor and in her two accounts of 15th-century pilgrims, *Jerusalem Journey* and *Once to Sinai*.

—Glen Cavaliero

PRESTON, Fayrene.
Pseudonym: Jaelyn Conlee. **Nationality:** American. **Address:** c/o Bantam, 666 Fifth Avenue, New York, New York 10103, USA.

ROMANCE AND HISTORICAL PUBLICATIONS

Novels (series: Delaneys; Pearls of Sharah; Shamrock; Swan Sea Place)

Satin and Steele (as Jaelyn Conlee). New York, Berkley, 1982.
Silver Miracles. New York, Bantam, 1983.
That Old Feeling. New York, Bantam, 1983.
The Seduction of Jason. New York, Bantam, 1983.
For the Love of Sami. New York, Bantam, 1984.
Mississippi Blues. New York, Bantam, 1985.
Rachel's Confession. New York, Bantam, 1985.
Fire in the Rain. New York, Bantam, 1986.
Burke, The Kingpin (Shamrock). New York, Bantam, 1986.
Mysterious. New York, Bantam, 1986.
A Magnificent Affair. New York, Bantam, 1986.
Allure. New York, Bantam, 1987.
Sydney, The Temptress (Delaneys). New York, Bantam, 1987.
Robin and Her Merry People. New York, Bantam, 1987.
Copper Fire (Delaneys). New York, Bantam, 1988.
Silken Thunder (Delaneys). New York, Bantam, 1988.
Emerald Sunshine. New York, Bantam, 1988.
Sapphire Lightning. New York, Bantam, 1988.
Leah's Story (Sharah). New York, Doubleday, 1989.
Alexandra's Story (Sharah). New York, Doubleday, 1989.
Raine's Story (Sharah). New York, Doubleday, 1989.
The Witching Time. New York, Bantam, 1989.
Swan Sea Place:
    Swan Sea Place. New York, Bantam, 1990.
    Swan Sea Place: The Legacy. New York, Bantam, 1990.
    Swan Sea Place: Deceit. New York, Bantam, 1991.
    Swan Sea Place: Jeopardy. New York, Bantam, 1991.
    Swan Sea Place: The Promise. New York, Bantam, 1991.
The Swan Sea Destiny. New York, Bantam, 1992.
What Emily Wants. New York, Bantam, 1993.
The Princess and the Pea. New York, Bantam, 1993.

*   *   *

Fayrene Preston is one of the leading authors in the Loveswept romance line. Chosen to help launch the line in 1983, she has not become one of the most prolific or varied romance writers, at least in comparison to other writers such as Iris Johansen, and Kay Hooper, with whom she writes, but she has an excellent reputation for providing an entertaining story peopled with believable, likeable characters.

Preston combines a deep sensuality with subtle humour. In *The Seduction of Jason*, the hero, has a somewhat peculiar compliment for Morgan Saunders, the heroine. He tells her she is interesting because, among other things, 'you have a name that could belong to a linebacker—yet you're deliciously feminine'. Anyone who has wondered at the often bizarre or exotic names given to romance characters has to appreciate such a statement. Similarly, Preston

reverses the traditional roles in a seduction when Jason and Morgan are torn apart by a misunderstanding. Morgan pursues Jason in a very open and aggressive manner, loading him down with flowers and declaring her love for him on a billboard.

The story of Morgan and Jason introduces Morgan's eccentric friend, Samuelina (Sami) Adkinson, who gets her own story in *For the Love of Sami*. An abused child, the adult Sami is a free-spirited generous woman with some deep-rooted psychological problems. Her romance with Daniel Parker-St James, a powerful attorney, is a much more gentle story, again told with humour. It shows another facet of Preston's talent since it is written with great poignancy.

Preston's slightly offbeat sense of humour shows in the quirks given to her characters. Ashley Whitfield (*A Magnificent Affair*) makes an unforgettable entrance into Max Hayden's life when she crashes her car into the garden of his inn. In Preston's hands, Ashley is an endearingly vague character who seems to float on another plane.

In 1989 Preston introduced a new trilogy. The stories are woven around a fabled necklace of perfectly matched pearls. Each title in the 'Pearls of Sharah' series begins with the same prologue set in ancient Persia, which explains the origin and legend of the necklace. In *Alexandra's Story*, *Raine's Story*, and *Leah's Story* the necklace is used as a continuing prop. It brings the hero and heroine together, and is the source of tension between them. In the end, however, the necklace keeps them together and then passes on to another since it can never truly be possessed. Another Preston series revolves around Swan Sea, a mansion in New England, and its inhabitants. *The Legacy*, *Deceit*, *The Promise*, and *Jeopardy* were all published as volumes in the Loveswept series. Later Preston published a prequel, *The Swan Sea Destiny* as a single-title release.

Preston has collaborated with two other Loveswept authors, Iris Johansen, and Kay Hooper, in writing a series of trilogies which chronicle the Delaney family. For the first trilogy, the 'Shamrock Trilogy', which focuses on the contemporary American Delaney brothers, Preston wrote *Burke, the Kingpin*. The second trilogy, 'The Delaneys of Killaroo', to which Preston contributed *Sydney, the Temptress*, shifted focus to the Australian Delaney sisters. After the success of these trilogies, Preston, Johansen, and Hooper created two 'prequel' trilogies, 'The Untamed Years' and 'The Untamed Years II'. As her contribution to these series, Preston first tells the story of Briane Delaney and Sloan Lassiter in *Copper Fire*. In *Silken Thunder* their story continues but the main focus is shifted to another couple, Anna Nilsen and Wes McCord, Sloan's enemy.

Working well within the standard romance formula, Preston has not been as innovative as Johansen and Hooper, but she is extremely popular. Her engaging characters are bright and personable without the underlying darkness found in much romance fiction. Preston celebrates romance and tenderness so they are the real focus of her gentle novels. Her books are 'keepers', destined to be read and re-read.

—Barbara E. Kemp

PRESTON, Ivy (Alice).
Nationality: New Zealander. **Born:** Ivy Alice Kinross, Timaru, 13 November 1913. **Education:** Southburn Primary School, 1919–25; Timaru Technical College, 1925–26. **Relations:** married Percival Edward James Preston in 1937 (died 1956); two sons and two daughters. **Address:** 95 Church Street, Timaru, New Zealand.

ROMANCE AND HISTORICAL PUBLICATIONS

Novels

Where Ratas Twine. London, Wright and Brown, 1960.

None So Blind. London, Wright and Brown, 1961.
Magic in Maoriland. London, Wright and Brown, 1962.
Rosemary for Remembrance. London, Hale, 1962.
Island of Enchantment. London, Hale, 1963.
Tamarisk in Bloom. London, Hale, 1963.
Hearts Do Not Break. London, Hale, 1964.
The Blue Remembered Hills. London, Hale, 1965.
Secret Love of Nurse Wilson. London, Hale, 1966.
Enchanted Evening. London, Hale, 1966.
Hospital on the Hill. London, Hale, 1967.
Nicolette. London, Hale, 1967.
Red Roses for a Nurse. London, Hale, 1968.
Ticket of Destiny. London, Hale, 1969.
April in Westland. London, Hale, 1969.
A Fleeting Breath. London, Hale, 1970; New York, Beagle, 1971.
Interrupted Journey. London, Hale, 1970; New York, Beagle, 1971.
Portrait of Pierre. London, Hale, 1971.
Petals in the Wind. London, Hale, 1972.
Release the Past. London, Hale, 1973.
Romance in Glenmore Street. London, Hale, 1974; New York, Ace, 1978.
Voyage of Destiny. London, Hale, 1974.
Moonlight on the Lake. London, Hale, 1976.
The House above the Bay. London, Hale, 1976.
Sunlit Seas. London, Hale, 1977.
Where Stars May Lead. London, Hale, 1978.
One Broken Dream. London, Hale, 1979.
Mountain Magic. London, Hale, 1979.
Summer at Willowbank. London, Hale, 1980.
Interlude in Greece. London, Hale, 1982.
Nurse in Confusion. London, Hale, 1983.
Enchantment at Hillcrest. London, Hale, 1984.
Fair Accuser. London, Hale, 1985.
To Dream Again. London, Hale, 1985.
Flight from Heartbreak. London, Hale, 1986.
Threads of Destiny. London, Hale, 1986.
Stranger from the Sea. London, Hale, 1987.
Tumult of the Heart. London, Hale, 1988.
Spring of Granite Peaks. London, Hale, 1990.

OTHER PUBLICATIONS

Other

The Silver Stream (autobiography). Christchurch, Pegasus Press, 1959.

Editor, with Margaret Smith, *Springbook: Seventy-Five Years of Progress* (on Springbook school). Privately printed, 1970.

*

Ivy Preston comments:

I had always intended to be a writer of romance novels for as long as I can remember but, in the event, I began my writing career the wrong way round with an autobiography. Most people wait until they are successful before venturing to write the story of their life. I wrote mine as an ordinary housewife whom nobody except family, friends and neighbours had ever heard of. Oddly enough it was reasonably successful. It was written as a tribute to my late husband who had died suddenly in 1956 leaving me with four young children to bring up alone. Writing that book helped rid me of the mental block I had suffered since his death and I was able to return to the romance novels I had been trying unsuccessfully to write for several years,

this time with success. I now average one every nine months . . . like having a baby. Most have a New Zealand setting but now that my family have grown up I am able to travel to other countries and occasionally make use of these experiences for a change of background. I write romance stories because I enjoyed a very happy marriage relationship and believe strongly in love and romance.

*   *   *

Ivy Preston's books are normally set in her native New Zealand, a beautiful country with an interesting history, full of exotic flowers, and gorgeous landscapes. Her plots are straight forward romances in which the protagonists meet, initially hate each other, and then fall madly in love. The complication arises in the form of another man or woman who serves to confuse the love issue.

In *The Blue Remembered Hills* Sally Thompson lives on a lovely sheep station, Ngap-Ukeroa. She is content and fulfilled, and her future seems to lie with Russell Blaire, the farmer of the neighbouring station—until the owner of Ngap-Ukeroa dies, and leaves it to his great grand-nephew, Alan Armitage. Sally and Alan knew each other when they were children, and she always disliked him, a fact exacerbated when Alan turns up to claim his inheritance. He succeeds in upsetting Sally's well ordered existence. The book contains long detailed descriptions of New Zealand and illustrates Preston's obvious love for her country.

Poor Rosemary leaves her family when she discovers her fiancé kissing her glamorous cousin in *Rosemary for Remembrance*; she realizes that she is not sure whether her heart or her pride are more hurt by the discovery. New frontiers are opened up as Rosemary moves to a new town in New Zealand and meets a divinity student, Kenneth McLean. The plot revolves around her decision to avoid falling in love with him as she cannot imagine being a vicar's wife. Martine, her cousin, and Rosemary's ex-fiancé reappear to complicate matters. However, Rosemary realizes that Kenneth is the most important thing in her life.

Dawn Calder's problem, in *Where Ratas Twine*, is her idyllic life on Stewart Island—a tourist's idea of paradise. She cannot wait to leave the island for a bigger and brighter city. When her widowed father remarries she gets her opportunity, and tries to ignore the disapproving stance of her new stepbrother, John. Dawn discovers that the city lights aren't as brilliant as her own island, and returns to it to fall in love with John.

For the most part, Preston's novels are well-written, fun books, with ingenuous heroines and stereotypically masculine heroes, and the reader can always be certain that love will triumph over all.

—P. Campbell

———

PRESTON, Richard. See **LINDSAY, Jack.**

———

PRICE, Evadne.
Pseudonym: Helen Zenna Smith. **Nationality:** British. **Born:** at sea, in 1896. **Education:** West Maitland, New South Wales, and in Belgium. **Military Service:** Air Ministry during World War I. **Relations:** married 1) C.A. Fletcher (died); 2) Kenneth A. Attiwill in 1929. **Career:** actress from 1906; columnist, *Sunday Chronicle* and *Sunday Graphic*; feature writer, *Daily Sketch*; war correspondent, the *People*, 1943–45; astrology columnist, *She* magazine, and *Vogue Australia*, Sydney. **Recipient:** Severigne prize. **Died:** 17 April 1985.

ROMANCE AND HISTORICAL PUBLICATIONS

Novels

Diary of a Red-Haired Girl. London, Long, 1932.
The Haunted Light. London, Long, 1933.
Strip Girl. London, Hurst and Blackett, 1934.
Probationer! London, Hurst and Blackett, 1934.
Society Girl. London, Harrap, 1935.
Red for Danger! London, Long, 1936.
Glamour Girl. London, Harrap, 1937.
The Dishonoured Wife. London, Jenkins, 1951.
Escape to Marriage. London, Jenkins, 1952.
My Pretty Sister. London, Jenkins, 1952.
Her Stolen Life. London, Milestone, 1954.
What the Heart Says. London, Hale, 1956.
The Love Trap. London, Hale, 1958.
Air Hostess in Love. London, Gresham, 1962.

Novels as Helen Zenna Smith

Not So Quiet . . . : Stepdaughters of War. London, Marriott, 1930; as
  Stepdaughters of War, New York, Dutton, 1930.
Women of the Aftermath. London, Long, 1931; as *One Woman's
  Freedom*, New York, Longman, 1932.
Shadow Women. London, Long, 1932.
Luxury Ladies. London, Long, 1933.
They Lived with Me. London, Long, 1934.

OTHER PUBLICATIONS

Plays

The Phantom Light, with Joan Roy-Byford (as *The Haunted Light*,
  produced London, 1928; as *The Phantom Light*, produced Lon-
  don, 1937). London, French, 1949.
Red for Danger (produced Richmond, Surrey, 1938).
Big Ben, with Ruby Miller (produced Malvern, Worcestershire,
  1939).
Once a Crook, with Kenneth Attiwill (produced London, 1940).
  London, French, 1943.
Who Killed My Sister?, with Kenneth Attiwill (produced London,
  1942).
Three Wives Called Roland, with Kenneth Attiwill (produced Lon-
  don, 1943).
Through the Door (also director: produced London, 1946).
What Lies Beyond (also director: produced Margate, Kent, 1948).
Cabin for Three, with Kenneth Attiwill (produced Southsea, Hamp-
  shire, 1949).
Blonde for Danger (produced London, 1949).
Wanted on Voyage, with Kenneth Attiwill (produced Wimbledon,
  1949).

Screenplays: *Wolf's Clothing*, with Brock Williams, 1936; *When
the Poppies Bloom Again*, with Herbert Ayres, 1937; *Merry Comes
to Town*, with Brock Williams, 1937; *Silver Top*, with Gerald Elliott
and Dorothy Greenhill, 1938; *Lightning Conductor*, with J. Jefferson Farjeon and Ivor McLaren, 1938; *Not Wanted on Voyage*,
with others, 1957.

Other (for children)

Just Jane. London, John Hamilton, 1928.
Meet Jane. London, Marriott, 1930.
Enter—Jane. London, Newnes, 1932.
Jane the Fourth [*the Sleuth, the Unlucky, the Popular, the Patient,
  Gets Busy, at War*]. London, Hale, 7 vols, 1937–47.

She Stargazes (for adults; on astrology). London, Ebury Press,
  1965.
Jane and Co. (omnibus), edited by Mary Cadogan. London, Macmillan, 1985.

*

Film Adaptations: *Blondes for Danger*, 1938, from the novel *Red
for Danger*; *Once A Crook*, 1941.

Theatrical Activities:
Director: **Plays**—*Through the Door*, London, 1946; *What Lies Beyond*, Margate, Kent, 1948.

Actress: **Plays**—in *Peter Pan* by J.M. Barrie, Sydney, 1906; Nang
Ping in *Mr Wu* by H. M. Vernon and Harold Owen, tour, 1914;
toured in South Africa, and in *Oh, I Say* and *Within the Law*, 1915;
Suzee in *Five Nights*, tour, 1919; Liliha in *The Bird of Paradise*,
London, 1919, 1922; Sua-See in *The Dragon*, London, 1920; Tessie
Kearns in *Merton of the Movies* by George S. Kaufman and Marc
Connelly, London, 1923; Princess Angelica in *The Rose and the
Ring*, London, 1923.

*   *   *

In Evadne Price's lighter books there is often a distinctly draw-
ing-room comedy flavour. (This applies to her 'Jane' books for children.) The heroines of her romantic novels often have theatrical
careers or other glamorous jobs. These give Price ample opportunity
to exploit her flair for lively, dramatic, or 'bitchy' situations and relationships. The larger and more colourful than life quality of her
love stories is enhanced by flashes of wit, and an overall feeling of
exuberance.

Glamour Girl is one of her most incisive theatrical novels in
which the temperamental 'Glama Gaye'—'Britain's Premier Box-
Office Attraction'—rides roughshod over everyone in her orbit—
fellow performers, stage hands, dressers, and, most of all, her husband and secretary, who are eventually driven into each other's
arms as a result of the star's ruthlessness. Theirs is, however, a
triumph of true love—and Glama gets her just deserts in an uneasy
relationship with a male 'limelight idol' who is as fatally attractive
and faithless as herself. The story has a slightly bizarre touch that is
characteristic of Price's books; Glama, the striking beauty, and
Elna, her rather drab secretary, are actually twin sisters, though the
relationship is never publicly acknowledged. But Elna can overcome her mousiness sufficiently to disguise herself as Glama and
'double' for her on assignments that Glama finds too dangerous—or
too dull—to undertake.

Price uses this twin theme again with dramatic effect in *Air Hostess in Love*. Again, the quieter of the sisters, Judy, is a secretary,
while the flashier one, Stella, has the glossy job of air hostess. And
as in *Glamour Girl* the sedate young woman has sometimes to substitute for her sister in hazardous situations before her romantic difficulties with the man she loves can be resolved. Although Price
skilfully enlists her readers' sympathies for conformist and 'ordinary' heroines like these sisters of the high-powered actress or air
hostess, she is at her best with more vivid characters, for example,
the dancer Carole Iden in *The Love Trap*, who has 'a flame of red
hair' and 'the permanent challenge' of 'provocative green eyes'.
Carole in fact needs all the help that her startling good looks can
bring her—because, at the beginning of the story, she has been made
pregnant by a dashing test pilot who gets killed before he can marry
her. She attracts an older and more stable man who offers her one of
those marriages in-name-only that, in the romantic novel genre, always end happily with hero and heroine falling blissfully in love
with each other. In some of her other books, Price persuasively

exploits several inventive variations on the type of situation used in *The Love Trap*, *Glamour Girl*, and *Air Hostess in Love*.

—Mary Cadogan

PROLE, Lozania.   See **BLOOM, Ursula.**

PYKARE, Nina.
Pseudonyms: Ann Coombs; Nina Coombs; Nan Pemberton; Nora Powers; Regina Towers. **Nationality:** American. **Address:** c/o Silhouette Books, 300 East 42nd Street, New York, New York 10017, USA.

ROMANCE AND HISTORICAL PUBLICATIONS

Novels

The Fire Within (as Ann Coombs). New York, Silhouette, 1978.
Love's Promise. New York, Dell, 1979.
The Scandalous Season. New York, Dell, 1979.
Lady Incognita. New York, Dell, 1980.
Love's Delusion (as Nan Pemberton). New York, Pocket Books, 1980.
The Rake's Companion (as Regina Towers). New York, Dell, 1980.
Love's Folly. New York, Dell, 1980.
Love in Disguise. New York, Dell, 1980.
The Dazzled Heart. New York, Dell, 1980.
Man of Her Choosing. New York, Dell, 1980.
Love Plays a Part. New York, Dell, 1981.
The Innocent Heart. New York, Dell, 1981.
A Matter of Honor. New York, Dell, 1982.
Heritage of the Heart. New York, Dell, 1982.
Lost Duchess of Greyden Castle. New York, Zebra, 1990.
Love's Promise. New York, Curley, 1991.

Novels as Nora Powers

Affairs of the Heart. New York, Silhouette, 1980.
Design for Love. New York, Silhouette, 1980.
Promise Me Tomorrow. New York, Silhouette, 1982.
Dream of the West. New York, Silhouette, 1983.
In a Moment's Time. New York, Silhouette, 1983.
Time Stands Still. New York, Silhouette, 1983.
In a Stranger's Arms. New York, Silhouette, 1984.
This Brief Interlude. New York, Silhouette, 1984.
A Different Reality. New York, Silhouette, 1985.
A Woman's Wiles. New York, Silhouette, 1985.
No Man's Kisses. New York, Silhouette, 1986.
Woman of the West. New York, Silhouette, 1989.

Novels as Nina Coombs

Love so Fearful. New York, New American Library, 1983.
Forbidden Joy. New York, New American Library, 1983.
Passion's Domain. New York, New American Library, 1983.
Sun Spark. New York, New American Library, 1984.
Before It's Too Late. New York, New American Library, 1986.

*   *   *

During the early 1980s Nina Pykare wrote a series of novels for the Silhouette Desire line under the name Nora Powers. As Nina Coombs she wrote *Love so Fearful* for Rapture Romances. Ann Coombs, Nan Pemberton, and Regina Towers are also pseudonyms that she has used.

If one had to pick out some of her most enjoyable novels, however, the choice might be surprising. Writing under her own name, Pykare wrote numerous Regency novels in the early Candlelight Regency Specials. These were delightfully done! They were skilfully plotted, and missed the typical pitfalls of many other such novels. Rather than stressing the London Season, she set her hero and heroine in other parts of the country. She also concentrated on plot developments and a strong narrative line. Her characters were believable, if somewhat stereotypical of such stories. To a certain extent, these novels also had definite elements of the gothic interwoven in the rest of the plot. Hidden passages, mysterious noises, flitting ghosts, and dark and mysterious shadows all reinforce the gothic feel in some of her stories. It is difficult to really pin down their appeal because no single element stands out, but a Regency written by Pykare has all the conflict, mystery, and love that a reader could want.

Two novels, *The Rake's Companion* by Regina Towers and *The Dazzled Heart* by Pykare, are good examples of her writing in this genre. *The Rake's Companion* has a tantalizing Cinderella plot. Faith Duncan applies for a position as a nurse-companion to the Countess of Moorshead Castle in Yorkshire. Once she is offered the position and arrives from London, she eventually learns that the Countess is matchmaking, with Faith's hand as the prize as well as the Countess's fortune. The competitors are Felix Kingston and his brother, the Earl of Moorshead, who are both nephews of the Countess. Falling rocks, mysterious intruders, a kidnapping that leaves Faith stranded near deadly bogs all add to the heightened tension. The hero, the earl, is appropriately cynical and suspicious, while Faith is innocence personified, but thankfully bright enough to help find the real culprit. In spite of rigid determination on the parts of the hero and heroine, they fall madly in love which naturally finds them facing a happy-ever-after ending.

The Dazzled Heart is equally enjoyable. Jennifer Whitcomb is hired as a governess by a family living near Dover. The mother is a confirmed hypochondriac, the father is a bluff retired businessman who patiently copes with his wife and their three spoiled children. The plot centres on the hero, Viscount Haverford's search for spies in the area and on a Monsieur Dupen who is both an hypnotist and the spy being sought. Jennifer's unwitting discovery of the plotters puts her right in the centre of things. Only the quick-thinking actions of the hero and the occasional kiss indicate his surrender to love and to Jennifer.

For those readers interested in her contemporary romances, *Time Stands Still* by Nora Powers is a typical example of her work. Libby Collins is a geologist specializing in oil discovery. She works for World Wide Exploration, feeling that this sort of company is just the kind for her. Actually, she is interested in oil discovery, but also in Jared Harper, her ex-husband, who is also part of the company. They eventually meet again on an exploration expedition in Indonesia. Throughout the trip, Libby strives to show Jared that she has grown up, that she is no longer the flighty, immature girl she'd been. Conflicts in the story naturally centre on their relationship. Both are very much in love with each other, but both are afraid of being hurt again.

This novel has certain ambiguities that cause some confusion in characterization. Libby is determined to show how mature and independent she has become. Yet, she says, 'I'm going to follow you. Everywhere. Until you take me back'. Or, 'Please say we can try again. Anyway you want it'. Somehow, this reaction is contradictory. The heroine is determined to be a 'new' woman, yet she ends up acting very 'old' women and definitely a clinging vine. Perhaps it is this ambivalence that creates a sense of contradiction in the novel.

This may have been intentional on Pykare's part to show that a woman need not give up certain traits and characteristics in the modern world. There is enough uncertainty in this particular story to leave readers with mixed messages. In her Regency romances, her heroines fill 'traditional' roles and Pykare seems comfortable in portraying them so. Certainly in these types of novels, her creativity, enthusiasm, and abilities as a writer are well evident to all her readers. In any future contemporary romances, she may need to resolve her heroine's basic character and stick with it.

—Arlene Moore

QUEST, Erica. See **BUCKINGHAM, Nancy.**

QUICK, Amanda. See **KRENTZ, Jayne Ann.**

QUYTH, Gabriel. See **JENNINGS, Gary.**

RADCLYFFE-HALL, Marguerite. See **HALL, Radclyffe.**

RADDALL, Thomas Head.
Nationality: Canadian. **Born:** Hythe, Kent, England, 13 November 1903; emigrated to Canada, 1913. **Education:** St Leonard's School, Hythe; Chebucto School, Halifax, Nova Scotia; Halifax Academy. **Military Service:** wireless operator, Canadian Merchant Marine, 1918–22; 2nd (Reserve) Battalion, West Nova Scotia Regiment, 1942–43; lieutenant. **Relations:** married Edith Margaret Freeman in 1927 (died); two children. **Career:** accountant in the wood pulp and paper industries in Nova Scotia, 1923–38. Full-time writer since 1938. **Recipient:** Governor-General's award, 1944, for non-fiction, 1949; Lorne Pierce medal, 1956; University of Alberta Canadian literature medal, 1977. LL.D.: Dalhousie University, Halifax, 1949; St Francis Xavier University, Antigonish, Nova Scotia, 1973; D.Litt.: St Mary's University, Halifax, 1969; D.C.L.: King's College, Halifax, 1972. Fellow, Royal Society of Canada, 1953. Officer, Order of Canada, 1970. **Address:** 44 Park Street, Liverpool, Nova Scotia, B0T 1K0, Canada.

ROMANCE AND HISTORICAL PUBLICATIONS

Novels

His Majesty's Yankees. Toronto, McClelland and Stewart, and New York, Doubleday, 1942; Edinburgh, Blackwood, 1944.
Roger Sudden. Toronto, McClelland and Stewart, and New York, Doubleday, 1944; London, Hurst and Blackett, 1946.
Pride's Fancy. Toronto, McClelland and Stewart, and New York, Doubleday, 1946; London, Hurst and Blackett, 1948.
The Governor's Lady. New York, Doubleday, 1960; London, Collins, 1961.
Hangman's Beach. New York, Doubleday, 1966.

OTHER PUBLICATIONS

Novels

Saga of the Rover, with C.H.L. Jones. Halifax, Nova Scotia, Royal, 1931.

The Nymph and the Lamp. Toronto, McClelland and Stewart, and Boston, Little Brown, 1950; London, Hutchinson, 1951.
Son of the Hawk. Philadelphia, Winston, 1950.
Tidefall. Toronto, McClelland and Stewart, and Boston, Little Brown, 1953; London, Hutchinson, 1954; as *Give and Take*, New York, Popular Library, 1954.
The Wings of Night. New York, Doubleday, 1956; London, Macmillan, 1957.

Short Stories

Pied Piper of Dipper Creek and Other Tales. Edinburgh, Blackwood, 1939.
Tambour and Other Stories. Toronto, McClelland and Stewart, 1945.
The Wedding Gift and Other Stories. Toronto, McClelland and Stewart, 1947.
A Muster of Arms and Other Stories. Toronto, McClelland and Stewart, 1954.
At the Tide's Turn and Other Stories. Toronto, McClelland and Stewart, 1959.
The Dreamers. Porters Lake, Nova Scotia, Pottersfield Press, 1986.

Other

A Souvenir from the Land of Maple. Liverpool, Nova Scotia, Mersey Paper Company, n.d.
The Markland Sagas, with C.H.L. Jones. Montreal, Gazette Printing, 1934.
Ogomkegea: The Story of Liverpool, Nova Scotia. Liverpool, Nova Scotia, Liverpool Advance, 1934.
Canada's Deep Sea Fighters. Halifax, Government of Nova Scotia, 1936; revised edition, 1937.
West Novas: A History of the West Nova Scotia Regiment. Montreal, Provincial, 1948.
Halifax, Warden of the North. Toronto, McClelland and Stewart, 1948; London, Dent, 1950; revised edition, New York, Doubleday, 1965; McClelland and Stewart, 1971.
The Path of Destiny: Canada from the British Conquest to Home Rule 1763-1850. New York, Doubleday, 1957.
The Rover: The Story of a Canadian Privateer (for children). London, Macmillan, 1958; New York, St Martin's Press, 1959.
Halifax and the World in 1809 and 1959. Halifax, Nova Scotia, Halifax Insurance Company, 1959.
Footsteps on Old Floors: True Tales of Mystery. New York, Doubleday, 1968.
This Is Nova Scotia, Canada's Ocean Playground. Halifax, Nova Scotia, Book Room, 1970.
In My Time: A Memoir. Toronto, McClelland and Stewart, 1976.
The Mersey Story. Liverpool, Nova Scotia, Bowater-Mersey Paper Company, 1979.
Courage in the Storm (for children). Porters Lake, Nova Scotia, Pottersfield, 1987.

*

Bibliography: *Thomas Head Raddall: A Bibliography* by Alan R. Young, Kingston, Ontario, Loyal Colonies Press, 1982; 'Thomas H. Raddall: An Annotated Bibliography' by Alan R. Young, in *The Annotated Bibliography of Canada's Major Authors*, Vol 7, Toronto, ECW Press, 1987.

Manuscript Collections: Killam Memorial Library, Dalhousie University, Halifax; Humanities Center, University of Texas, Austin.

Critical Studies: 'Thomas H. Raddall: The Man and His Work' by W. J. Hawkins, in *Queen's Quarterly* (Kingston, Ontario), Spring

1968; 'Thomas Raddall: The Art of Historical Fiction' by Donald Cameron, in *Dalhousie Review* (Halifax), Winter 1970; *Thomas Head Raddall* by Alan R. Young, Boston, Twayne, 1983; *A Name for Himself* by Joyce Barkhouse, Toronto, Irwin, 1990; *Time and Place: The Life and Works of Thomas H. Raddall* edited by Alan R. Young, Fredericton, New Brunswick, Acadiensis Press, 1991.

*   *   *

Thomas Head Raddall's early historical romances in the 1940s and 1960s, and the three romances with modern settings that he published in the 1950s initially earned him great critical acclaim in Canada. Changing critical tastes have temporarily dimmed his reputation, but a large public in Canada and elsewhere continues to read his work.

From his earliest full-length work, *Saga of the Rover*, Raddall exploited a key formula of historical fiction—the placing of narrative within a historical context that demonstrated the impact of world events upon ordinary people. Raddall's most subtle exploration of this pattern occurs in his historical romance *His Majesty's Yankees*, which depicts the situation of Nova Scotians during the American Revolution. The entire Strang family becomes involved in the conflict when their elected representative in the capital, Halifax, tells the citizens that he has been stripped of his public offices. In a manner typical of historical fiction the Strang family's responses are divided. Matthew, the head of the family, urges non-involvement, but one of his sons joins the rebel cause while another joins the King's forces. David, another son and the hero of the novel, at first has no political position. However, after seeing some of the evils of colonialism and after rescuing a woman from an assault by a British seaman, he takes up with the rebels. The novel then delineates David's growth towards adulthood and political maturity. Eventually, he returns home to embrace a code of domestic values that takes precedence over political causes. Historically, David's point of view is also adopted by Nova Scotia, so that David is to be taken as representative of a people.

Equally typical of historical fiction is Raddall's portrait in this novel of momentous historical transition, in this instance the birth of the American republic and the dissociation of Nova Scotia from its ties with New England, and its shift from neutrality towards loyalty to the crown. Typical too is the manner in which such transitions occasion dramatic conflicts between family members, generations, and societies, the middle way (represented by the hero) ultimately triumphing. As often in historical romance, the political and moral quest of the hero becomes inseparable from the working out of a love plot. David Strang's love is Fear Bingay, daughter of a prominent Tory who marries a British officer. The gulf between David and Fear appears uncrossable, but when her husband dies, the way is open for a marriage that as the novel concludes becomes symbolic of the new social and political balance established between the citizens and the crown. The marriage also symbolizes the triumph of the domestic ideals of peace, marital love, and (typical of Raddall) love for the land that will provide the new family with its livelihood.

To some extent Raddall's subsequent historical romances make use of similar patterns. *Roger Sudden* explores the demise of French imperial power in North America and the simultaneous growth of the British. *Pride's Fancy* explores the conflicts among the traditional planter elite of the West Indies, the supposedly egalitarian society of post-revolution Haiti, the aggressive commercialism of the merchant barons of Nova Scotia, and the different way of life and values espoused by Nathan Cain. The hero of the novel, Cain, ultimately opts for the creative craft of ship-building, domesticity, and love for his native Nova Scotia. *Hangman's Beach* depicts the conflicting forces that transformed the war between Britain and France into something else—the 1812 conflict between Britain and

the United States—and *The Governor's Lady* depicts, though far less effectively than *His Majesty's Yankees*, the American Revolution and the demise of British rule in the rebellious North American colonies. The protagonists of these works are, like David Strang, reluctant participants in these conflicts, and only in *The Governor's Lady*, in which Raddall's protagonists (John and Fannie Wentworth) are real historical personages, does Raddall radically (and not very successfully) veer from the pattern that has served him and other historical fiction writers so well.

Generally, Raddall is highly effective at working within the classic framework of the historical novel. He can also brilliantly create a vivid and colourful sense of place and time, and he is a gifted storyteller with a fine sense of drama. Some of these qualities are carried over into the three romances set in his own time—*The Nymph and the Lamp*, *Tidefall*, and *The Wings of Night*. *Tidefall* and *The Wings of Night*, set in pre- and post-World War II Nova Scotia respectively, are only partial successes, but *The Nymph and the Lamp* is arguably Raddall's finest literary achievement. For this work Raddall chose the remote setting of Marina (Raddall's fictional name for Sable Island, the notorious 'Graveyard of the Atlantic'). The plot concerns a radio operator (Matthew Carney), the woman (Isabel Jardine) he 'marries' while on shore leave from Marina, and her affair with another radio operator (Greg Skane). This triangular love plot is fairly conventional, but Raddall's handling of it is far from ordinary.

As in a number of his historical romances, Raddall presents his protagonist undergoing a long and painful process of self-discovery, culminating in a crucial choice between opposing sets of values. As in the case of David Strang, Roger Sudden, and Nathan Cain, the fulfilment of this quest is achieved simultaneously with the union between hero and heroine. *The Nymph and the Lamp* is, however, far more complex, chiefly because of Raddall's presentation of Isabel Jardine. Once Raddall has delineated the existential state of Carney's psyche and his retreat to the symbolic isolation of Marina, he focuses his attention almost exclusively on Isabel. At first we see her suffering the indefinable malaise of unfulfilled sexuality. We see her inability to throw off her inherited Puritan conscience once on the island, the paradoxical but temporary release she finds with Skane, and then her return to her rural roots in Nova Scotia's Annapolis Valley, a rich and golden land of orchards, blossoms, and fruit, with all of which Isabel becomes symbolically associated. When Skane arrives to claim the 'harvest', however, Isabel rejects his egocentricity and sensuality and chooses the way of loving self-sacrifice (she will be a 'lamp' for Carney who is going blind), leaving behind both the world of her birthplace and the materialistic 'scrabble for cash' that characterizes city life in Halifax.

Raddall's historical fiction and romances are very much part of the literary tradition in which he was nurtured. They look back to a pre-World War I context in which Scott, Cooper, Kipling, Stevenson, Conan Doyle, and Conrad served as preeminent influences. Indeed, all were acknowledged favourites of Raddall in his youth, though he never consciously imitated any of them. Nor does he seem to have imitated any Canadian writer, though he clearly belongs to the same tradition within Canadian literature as John Richardson, Rosanna Mullins, William Kirby, Gilbert Parker, Charles and Theodore Roberts. This is an important (though of neglected) segment of the Canadian literary heritage, and Raddall is one of its finest representatives. Until quite recently, however, it has been somewhat neglected, but as has been shown in the 1991 collection of critical essays on Raddall (*Time and Place: The Life and Works of Thomas H. Raddall*), there are now signs of a renewed interest in both the nature of romance and the contribution to it of this group of Canadian writers. Important in this respect is the work of a number of feminist critics for whom the literary conventions of romance offer an especially challenging subject for interpretative criticism. Where Raddall's work is concerned, these new critical voices are likely to enrich not only our understanding of romance but of much of Raddall's work in particular.

—Alan R. Young

RAE, Hugh C.   See **STIRLING, Jessica.**

RANA, J.   See **FORRESTER, Helen.**

RANDALL, Florence Engel. American. 1917—. See 2nd edition, 1990.

RANDALL, Rona.
Nationality: British. **Born:** Birkenhead, Cheshire. **Education:** Birkenhead High School; Pitman's College, London. **Relations:** married Frederick Walter Shambrook; one son. **Career:** theatre repertory companies, three years, then a journalist; chair, Women's Press Club of London, 1962–63; founder member, Society of Sussex Authors, 1969. **Recipient:** Romantic Novelists Association major award, 1969. **Agent:** Curtis Brown, 162–168 Regent Street, London W1R 5TB, England. **Address:** Conifers, Pembury Road, Tunbridge Wells, Kent TN2 4ND, England.

ROMANCE AND HISTORICAL PUBLICATIONS

Novels (series: Drayton)

The Moon Returns. London, Collins, 1942.
Doctor Havelock's Wife. London, Collins, 1943.
Rebel Wife. London, Collins, 1944.
The Late Mrs Lane. London, Collins, 1945; New York, Arcadia House, 1946.
The Howards of Saxondale. London, Collins, 1946.
That Girl, Jennifer! New York, Arcadia House, 1946.
The Fleeting Hour. London, Collins, 1947.
I Married a Doctor. London, Collins, 1947; as *The Doctor Takes a Wife,* New York, Arcadia House, 1947.
The Street of the Singing Fountain. London, Collins, 1948.
Shadows on the Sand. London, Collins, 1949; New York, Ace, 1973.
Delayed Harvest. London, Collins, 1950.
Young Doctor Kenway. London, Collins, 1950.
The Island Doctor. London, Collins, 1951.
Bright Morning. London, Collins, 1952.
Girls in White. London, Collins, and New York, Arcadia House, 1952.
Young Sir Galahad. London, Collins, 1953.
Journey to Love. London, Collins, 1953; New York, Ace, 1972.
Faith, Hope, and Charity. London, Collins, 1954.
The Merry Andrews. London, Collins, 1954.
Desert Flower. London, Collins, 1955.
Journey to Arcady. New York, Arcadia House, 1955.
Leap in the Dark. London, Collins, 1956; New York, Ace, 1967.
A Girl Called Ann. London, Collins, 1956; New York, Ace, 1973.
Runaway from Love. London, Collins, 1956.
The Cedar Tree. London, Collins, 1957.
The Doctor Falls in Love. London, Collins, 1958.

Nurse Stacey Comes Aboard. London, Collins, 1958; New York, Ace, 1968.
Love and Dr Maynard. London, Collins, 1959.
Enchanted Eden. London, Collins, 1960.
Sister at Sea. London, Collins, 1960.
Hotel De Luxe. London, Collins, 1961; New York, Ace, 1967.
Girl in Love. London, Collins, 1961.
House Surgeon at Luke's. London, Collins, 1962.
Walk into My Parlour. London, Collins, 1962; New York, Ace, 1967; revised edition, as *Lyonhurst,* London, Fontana, and New York, Ballantine, 1977.
Lab Nurse. New York, Berkley, 1962.
The Silver Cord. London, Collins, 1963; New York, Ace, 1968.
The Willow Herb. London, Collins, 1965; New York, Ace, 1967.
Seven Days from Midnight. London, Collins, 1965; New York, Ace, 1967.
Arrogant Duke. London, Collins, 1966; New York, Ace, 1972.
Knight's Keep. London, Collins, and New York, Ace, 1967.
Broken Tapestry. London, Hurst and Blackett, 1969; New York, Ace, 1973.
The Witching Hour. London, Hurst and Blackett, and New York, Ace, 1970.
Silent Thunder. London, Hurst and Blackett, 1971.
Mountain of Fear. New York, Ace, 1972; London, Severn House, 1989.
Time Remembered, Time Lost. New York, Ace, 1973.
Glenrannoch. London, Collins, 1973; as *The Midnight Walker,* New York, Ace, 1973.
Dragonmede. London, Collins, and New York, Simon and Schuster, 1974.
Watchman's Stone. London, Collins, and New York, Simon and Schuster, 1975.
The Eagle at the Gate. New York, Coward McCann, 1977; London, Hamish Hamilton, 1978.
The Mating Dance. London, Hamish Hamilton, and New York, Coward McCann, 1979.
The Ladies of Hanover Square. London, Hamish Hamilton, and New York, Coward McCann, 1981.
Curtain Call. London, Hamish Hamilton, 1983.
The Drayton Legacy. London, Hamish Hamilton, 1985.
The Potter's Niece (Drayton). London, Hamish Hamilton, 1987.
Mountain of Fear. London, Severn House, 1989.
The Rival Potters (Drayton). London, Hamish Hamilton, 1990.

OTHER PUBLICATIONS

Other

Jordan and the Holy Land. London, Muller, 1968.
The Model Wife, Nineteenth Century Style. London, Herbert Press, 1989.
Writing Popular Fiction. London, A. and C. Black, 1992.

*

Rona Randall comments:

I devote myself to writing historical novels now because they seem to come instinctively; I lose myself in them completely. Because the present day seems to be becoming more distasteful? Perhaps. I don't know. But it seems significant that my historical novels bring me more appreciative letters from readers of all ages than my 'modern' ones. I am particularly attracted to the potteries in the 18th and 19th centuries. The reason for this is quoted on the jackets of my Drayton books: 'Rona Randall has herself progressed, through pottery, to become an accomplished modeller in ceramics, and the unusual background for the Drayton novels is one she knows well'.

*   *   *

A common theme found in Rona Randall's novels concerns a young woman who becomes involved with a handsome man unworthy of her love. Often the heroine actually marries this man and shares with him a passionate relationship, all the time believing that they will live happily ever after. At first all goes well, but slowly sinister aspects of his personality emerge. Fortunately there is usually another man around willing to offer the kind of love she deserves. Though not necessarily handsome, he is a robust individual who impresses the heroine with a powerful masculine presence. In what has become standard romantic form, the hero and heroine are initially incompatible, often because of his overbearing personality or sarcastic wit. Typically, he is a medical doctor and, through the tender caring of his patients, Randall shows the reader and the heroine his intrinsic goodness. This format is ideal for the gothic novel of which Randall has written several. Probably one of her best known is *Dragonmede*.

In this Victorian tale Eustacia Rochdale falls in love with the aristocratic Julian Kershaw. Although Eustacia is well educated, her family background (a mother who runs an illegal gambling establishment) leaves much to be desired. However, the young man seems genuinely to love her and eventually proposes marriage. She is ecstatic until she first glimpses the ancestral home, Dragonmede, whereupon a feeling of foreboding engulfs her. Her fears are not unfounded for, although Julian proves to be a passionate husband, he has a brooding, sadistic side that eventually destroys Eustacia's love for him. Other sinister characters abound, and with Julian's murder she finds herself in mortal danger. In the end it is the love of a virile young doctor that saves her life and gives her the happy marriage she has always wanted.

An earlier work with a similar plot but fewer of the gothic trappings is *Shadows on the Sand*. Sorrel Dean, a young architect, journeys to Beirut in order to join her fiancé Richard Baily, an archaeologist working at a desert site. Soon she finds that he is involved in the theft of valuable relics uncovered by the expedition. Although Sorrel is never directly in danger, her innocent association with this dark character causes her a great deal of emotional stress. Again it is a taciturn but basically compassionate medical doctor who proves to be her true love.

Variations on the eternal triangle theme also run through many of Randall's stories. In *Dragonmede* Julian, although married to Eustacia, still keeps the wickedly beautiful Victoria on the side. In *Watchman's Stone* the lovely Elizabeth marries Calum only to discover his affair with her younger sister. In *The Mating Dance* pretty blonde Lucinda finds her worthless husband in bed with her older sister Clemetine, an irrepressible lady whose obvious enjoyment of sex is in sharp contrast to Lucy's more conventional attitude. Things are even worse for Dulcima Howard one of *The Ladies of Hanover Square*. First she loves Sir Charles Ashleigh then later falls for his evil son, Justin, who spurns her even while knowing she carries his child. Her niece Deborah fares better. Although loved by two men she has eyes for only one, but not until he divorces his wife (she is no good) can Deborah marry him.

Randall's fiction contains equal elements of drama and excitement. Her excellent portrayal of the various characters, especially the heroines, makes the reader care what happens to them. With a fluid writing style this author weaves engaging tales of women in love.

—Patricia Altner

RAYNER, Claire (Berenice).
Pseudonyms: Sheila Brandon; Berry Chtwynd; Ann Lynton; Ruth Martin; Isobel Saxe. **Nationality:** British. **Born:** 22 January 1931.

Relations: married Desmond Rayner in 1957; one daughter and two sons. **Career:** nurse in the pediatric department, Whittington Hospital, London, until 1960; television presenter, *Pebble Mill* programme; columnist, as Ruth Martin, 1966–75, and as Claire Rayner, 1975–88, *Woman's Own*, London; columnist, the *Sun*, 1973–80, the *Sunday Mirror*, 1980–88, *Today*, 1988–91, since 1988, *Woman*, all London; presenter, BBC series, *Claire Rayner Casebook*, 1980–84, *A Problem Shared*, Sky TV series; since 1985 TV-AM advice presenter, London. **Agent:** Desmond Rayner, Holly Wood House, Roxborough Avenue, Harrow-on-the-Hill, Middlesex, England; or, Aaron M. Priest, Aaron Priest Literary Agency Inc, 565 Fifth Avenue, New York, New York 10017, USA.

ROMANCE AND HISTORICAL PUBLICATIONS

Novels (series: The Performers; The Poppy Chronicles)

Desperate Remedies (as Isobel Saxe). London, Corgi, 1968.
The Performers:
1. *Gower Street*. London, Cassell, and New York, Simon and Schuster, 1973.
2. *The Haymarket*. London, Cassell, and New York, Simon and Schuster, 1974.
3. *Paddington Green*. London, Cassell, and New York, Simon and Schuster, 1975.
4. *Soho Square*. London, Cassell, and New York, Putnam, 1976.
5. *Bedford Row*. London, Cassell, and New York, Putnam, 1977.
6. *Long Acre*. London, Cassell, 1978; as *Covent Garden*, New York, Putnam, 1978.
7. *Charing Cross*. London, Cassell, and New York, Putnam, 1979.
8. *The Strand*. London, Cassell, and New York, Putnam, 1980.
9. *Chelsea Reach*. London, Weidenfeld and Nicolson, 1982.
10. *Shaftesbury Avenue*. London, Weidenfeld and Nicolson, 1983.
11. *Piccadilly*. London, Weidenfeld and Nicolson, 1985.
12. *Seven Dials*. London, Weidenfeld and Nicolson, 1987.
Family Chorus. London, Hutchinson, 1984.
The Poppy Chronicles:
1. *Jubilee*. London, Weidenfeld and Nicolson, 1987.
2. *Flanders*. London, Weidenfeld and Nicolson, 1988.
3. *Flapper*. London, Weidenfeld and Nicolson, 1989.
4. *Blitz*. London, Weidenfeld and Nicolson, 1990.
5. *Festival*. London, Weidenfeld and Nicolson, 1991.
6. *Sixties*. Weidenfeld and Nicolson, 1992.

Novels as Sheila Brandon

The Final Year. London, Corgi, 1962.
Cottage Hospital. London, Corgi, 1963; (as Claire Rayner), London, Severn House, 1993.
Children's Ward. London, Corgi, 1964.
The Lonely One. London, Corgi, 1965.
The Doctors of Downlands. London, Corgi, 1968.
The Private Wing. London, Corgi, 1971.
Nurse in the Sun. London, Corgi, 1972.

OTHER PUBLICATIONS

Novels

Shilling a Pound Pears. London, Hart Davis, 1964.
The House on the Fen. London, Corgi, and New York, Bantam, 1967.

Starch of Aprons. London, Hale, 1967; as *The Hive,* London, Corgi, 1968.

Lady Mislaid. London, Corgi, 1968.

Death on the Table. London, Corgi, 1969.

The Meddlers. London, Cassell, and New York, Simon and Schuster, 1970.

A Time to Heal. London, Cassell, and New York, Simon and Schuster, 1972.

The Burning Summer. London, Allison and Busby, 1972.

Sisters. London, Hutchinson, 1978.

Reprise. London, Hutchinson, 1980.

The Running Years. London, Hutchinson, 1981; as *The Enduring Years,* New York, Delacorte Press, 1982.

The Virus Man. London, Hutchinson, 1985.

Lunching at Laura's. London, Hutchinson, 1986.

Maddie. London, Joseph, 1988.

Clinical Judgements. London, Joseph, 1989; New York, Viking, 1990.

Other

Mothers and Midwives. London, Allen and Unwin, 1962.

What Happens in the Hospital. London, Hart Davis, 1963.

The Calendar of Childhood: A Guide for All Mothers. London, Ebury Press, 1964.

Your Baby. London, Hamlyn, 1965.

Careers with Children. London, Hale, 1966.

Housework—The Easy Way. London, Corgi, 1967.

Mothercraft (as Ann Lynton). London, Corgi, 1967.

Shall I Be a Nurse? Exeter, Wheaton, 1967.

Home Nursing and Family Health. London, Corgi, 1967.

101 Facts an Expectant Mother Should Know. London, Dickens Press, 1967.

For Children: Equipping a Home for a Growing Family. London, Macdonald, 1967.

Essentials of Out-patient Nursing. London, Arlington, 1967.

101 Key Facts of Practical Baby Care. London, Dickens Press, 1967.

A Parent's Guide to Sex Education. London, Corgi, 1968; New York, Dolphin, 1969.

People in Love: A Modern Guide to Sex in Marriage. London, Hamlyn, 1968; revised edition, as *About Sex,* London, Fontana, 1972.

Woman's Medical Dictionary. London, Corgi, 1971.

When to Call the Doctor—What to Do Whilst Waiting. London, Corgi, 1972.

The Shy Person's Book. London, Wolfe, 1973; New York, McKay, 1974.

Childcare Made Simple. London, W. H. Allen, 1973.

Where Do I Come From? Answers to a Child's Questions about Sex. London, Arlington, 1974.

You Know More Than You Think You Do. London, MIND Council, 1975.

Kitchen Garden, with Keith Fordyce. London, Independent Television Publications, 1976.

More Kitchen Garden, with Keith Fordyce. London, Independent Television Publications, 1977.

Family Feelings: Understanding Your Child from 0 to Five. London, Arrow, 1977.

Claire Rayner Answers Your 100 Questions on Pregnancy. London, BBC Publications, 1977.

The Body Book (for children). London, G. Whizzard, 1978; Woodbury, New York, Barron's, 1980.

Related to Sex. New York and London, Paddington Press, 1979.

Everything Your Doctor Would Tell You If He Had the Time. London, Cassell, and New York, Putnam, 1980.

Claire Rayner's Lifeguide: A Commonsense Approach to Modern Living. London, New English Library, 1980.

Baby and Young Child Care: A Practical Guide for Parents of Children Aged 0–5 Years. Maidenhead, Berkshire, Purnell, 1981.

Growing Pains: And How to Avoid Them. London, Heinemann, 1984.

Claire Rayner's Marriage Guide: How to Make Yours Work. London, Macmillan, 1984.

The Getting Better Book (for children). London, Deutsch, 1985.

Woman. London, Hamlyn, 1986.

Safe Sex. London, Sphere, 1987.

The Don't Spoil Your Body Book (for children). London, Bodley Head, 1989.

Postscripts. London, Joseph, 1991.

Dangerous Things. London, Joseph, 1993.

Editor (as Ruth Martin), *Before the Baby—and After.* London, Hurst and Blackett, 1958.

Editor, *The Mitchell Beazley Atlas of the Body and Mind.* London, Mitchell Beazley, 1976; as *Rand McNally Atlas of the Body and Mind,* Chicago, Rand McNally, 1976.

Editor, *When I Grow Up: Children's Views on Adulthood.* London, Virgin, 1986.

*   *   *

Claire Rayner's first series of 12 novels, known collectively as 'The Performers', focuses on the theatre: operating theatres and the more traditional variety. Both doctors and thespians are portrayed to some extent as performers within their own setting. The novels concentrate on the Lucas and Lackland families, Lilith Lucas and Abel Lackland. Lilith and Abel start powerful family traditions of theatrical and medical success that continues through their children, grandchildren and great-grandchildren. The families also come together through a relationship between Lilith and Abel, and relationships between the two families (successful and unsuccessful) carry on through their descendants.

The Victorian period—the background against which Rayner's characters act out their lives—is a rich period for any novelist and Rayner selects her material with care. The creation of modern medicine and modern pharmacy begins in this period and Rayner carefully arranges the plot of the books to enable the doctors Lackland to be at the forefront of these discoveries. Abel is far ahead of his time in his attitude towards sanitation, surgery and the rights, enshrined in the hippocratic oath, of good healthcare for all—regardless of social station. The most notable characteristic of the Lackland's is their open-minded attitude towards change. While they may not, in the strictest sense, be innovators, they do see the need for change and welcome it.

The depiction of an unequal society is likewise one of the strengths of the books, and the way in which both medicine and theatre represent ways out of a rigid social structure is cleverly portrayed. Neither profession is particularly respectable in the mind of the upper class but they are an escape route for the industrious and hard-working.

The relationships between the characters do not always demand happy endings and this is the fundamental strength of Rayner's writing, (and what we would expect from an agony aunt). Greed, hatred, a desire for revenge, or wealth, or power are human emotions and while they may not be particularly pleasant they can be offset by love, altruism, and philanthropy. The difficulties human beings have in talking to each other, in communicating their needs, fears, and desires to their friends, families and lovers is all too often the reason why these relationships fail.

Rayner's portrayal of the Victorian theatre is alternatively attractive and repellent. London productions vie with working-class productions and provide many notable comparisons. The skill and nerve that Rayner shows in describing medical matters is especially worthy of note, as is her depiction of sensitive topics such as abortion and Celia Lackland's decline into madness.

'The Performers' series is an uncompromising and accurate portrayal of Victorian life, written with a compassion and sensitivity that never degenerates into sentimentality.

Rayner's second series of novels, 'The Poppy Chronicles', covers the majority of the 20th century. As with the performers series, the 'Poppy Chronicles' concentrates on a family, headed by Poppy herself, and her Aunt Jessie. This time scale offers Rayner many opportunities and she doesn't shirk from embracing them. World War I and World War II, the increased use of technology and the incredible advances in scientific learning that have helped to create the modern world, are all dealt with in these books.

Flanders, the second novel in the series, opens with Poppy, aged 16, full of excitement at a life that promises to afford her so much. Poppy becomes concerned with the role of women in society and attends, regularly, Suffragette meetings. The Great Cause, as it is known to the woman working for the vote, is portrayed convincingly and one scene, in which Sir Winston Churchill attends a 'votes for women' meeting, pays tribute to Rayner's use of material. The use of real characters in fiction can often be done badly, undermining the rest of the novel, but not so here. The developing war helps, amidst terrible suffering, to achieve equality for women. Poppy, working abroad, discovers freedom and gains her independence.

As with 'The Performers' series, 'The Poppy Chronicles' do not always have happy endings. Again Rayner explores the full range of human emotions and behaviour. Herbie, the black marketeer: the selfishness of Poppy's stepdaughter, Chloe, described by her stepsister Robin as 'the nastiest sister—well half sister—anyone could possible have'; and the dedicated, starry-eyed matchmaker Aunt Jessie are just three notable characters among many. All the characters, whether they be 'walk-ons' or not, are persuasive and contribute to the unfolding drama.

The details of these novels, as well as the characterization, help to create a sense of time, place, and history, against which the travails of human existence can be played out. The fourth novel in the series, *Blitz*, is set against a backdrop of World War II. The effect of rationing is explored when Poppy and Jessie receive a dubious offer from the ex-prisoner (and lover of Chloe), Bernie. The moral dilemma of gaining food to eat is treated sympathetically. The following passage is indicative of Rayner's ability to generate a credible atmosphere:

> Even the shops had cheeky signs on them; 'Special Sale, Courtesy the Nasties' read one in a shoe shop and on a china shop, 'Business as usual. To hell with Adolf.' With that sort of attitude in everyone around her, it was all right, she [Robin] decided, to feel tolerably good.

Moral issues are regularly dramatized in 'The Poppy Chronicles'. In *Flanders*, the details of Poppy's birth are unravelled (she is illegitimate) and her treatment at the hands of Edwardian society is shameful. In *Flapper*, set during the 1920s, the treatment of workers during the General Strike of 1926 sets out clearly the tensions in a society dominated by the reasonably-to-very-prosperous. *Blitz* portrays an interesting moral battle for Robin (Poppy's daughter), a nurse, between her affections for Hamish Todd a conscientious objector, and the friendly Doctor Landow, considered a saviour by society at large.

Rayner's merits as a novelist lie with her unrivalled commitment to her subjects and her characters. Her understanding of human nature is exceptional and she is never dogmatic or preachy. These talents combine to form a novelist who is consistently brilliant and her success is richly deserved.

—Kate Thompson

REDFERN, John.   See **PARGETER, Edith.**

REEMAN, Douglas.   See **KENT, Alexander.**

REID, Henrietta. British. See 2nd edition, 1990.

REINER, Max.   See **CALDWELL, Taylor.**

RENAULT, Mary.

Pseudonym for Eileen Mary Challans. **Nationality:** British. **Born:** London, 4 September 1905. **Education:** Clifton High School, Bristol, 1921–24; St Hugh's College, Oxford, 1924–27, B.A. (honours) in English 1928, M.A.; Radcliffe Infirmary, Oxford, SRN (State Registered Nurse) 1937. **Career:** nurse in brain surgery ward, Radcliffe Infirmary, 1938–45. Moved to South Africa, 1948: lived in Cape Town. National President, PEN Club of South Africa, 1961. **Recipient:** MGM award, 1946; National Association of Independent Schools award (USA), 1963; Silver Pen award, 1971. Fellow, Royal Society of Literature, 1959; honorary fellow, St Hugh's College, 1982. **Died:** 13 December 1983.

ROMANCE AND HISTORICAL PUBLICATIONS

Novels (series: Alexander trilogy; Theseus)

The Last of the Wine. London, Longman, and New York, Pantheon, 1956.
The King Must Die (Theseus). London, Longman, and New York, Pantheon, 1958.
The Bull from the Sea (Theseus). London, Longman, and New York, Pantheon, 1962.
The Mask of Apollo. London, Longman, and New York, Pantheon, 1966.
The Alexander Trilogy. London, Penguin, 1984.
   Fire from Heaven. New York, Pantheon, 1969; London, Longman, 1970.
   The Persian Boy. London, Longman, and New York, Pantheon, 1972.
   Funeral Games. London, Murray, and New York, Pantheon, 1981.
The Praise Singer. New York, Pantheon, 1978; London, Murray, 1979.

OTHER PUBLICATIONS

Novels

Purposes of Love. London, Longman, 1939; as *Promise of Love*, New York, Morrow, 1939.

Kind Are Her Answers. London, Longman, and New York, Morrow, 1940.
The Friendly Young Ladies. London, Longman, 1944; as *The Middle Mist*, New York, Morrow, 1945.
Return to Night. London, Longman, and New York, Morrow, 1947.
North Face. New York, Morrow, 1948; London, Longman, 1949.
The Charioteer. London, Longman, 1953; New York, Pantheon, 1959.

Other

The Lion in the Gateway: The Heroic Battles of the Greeks and Persians at Marathon, Salamis, and Thermopylae (for children). London, Longman, and New York, Harper, 1964.
The Nature of Alexander. London, Allen Lane, and New York, Pantheon, 1975.

*

Critical Studies: *Mary Renault* by Peter Wolfe, New York, Twayne, 1969; *The Hellenism of Mary Renault* by Bernard F. Dick, Carbondale, Southern Illinois University Press, 1972; *Mary Renault, a Biography* by David Sweetman, London, Chatto and Windus, 1993.

*   *   *

Mary Renault's training as a nurse shaped her early work, much of it set in and around hospitals. *Purposes of Love* and *The Friendly Young Ladies* however, bear no resemblance to ordinary 'nurse' romances; rather, they plumb the intricacies of complex, often murky and unorthodox relationships, a theme the author was to explore throughout her distinguished career. *Return to Night*, the story of a forbidden love affair between a female doctor and her much younger male patient, won the 1946 MGM award of $150,000, and although it was never in fact filmed (indeed, it is difficult to imagine the product if it *had* been), this resounding success brought Renault's work to the world's attention.

Renault came into her own as a star of the first magnitude when she turned from her accomplished novels of contemporary lives and loves to the stunning recreation of a classic Hellenistic world compounded of legendary, shadowy and contradictory history, and the patent Renault enchantment.

The twin Theseus novels, *The King Must Die* and *The Bull from the Sea*, had the impact of a thunderbolt. They were unique; never before had the time-honoured tale of the hero Theseus, Ariadne his forsaken love, the Amazon Queen Hippolyta, the dreaded man-eating Minotaur and all the rest been presented as more than highly-coloured fairytale figures, half-remembered from stories told by innumerable firesides.

Now Renault breathed new life into these stock figures. The familiar lumbering, herculean figure of a giant Theseus became an undersized, quicksilver daredevil of uncertain birth, seizing control of his own destiny rather than tamely submitting to the apparent will be the Olympians until, at last in *The Bull from the Sea*, the aging king tries the patience of the unrelenting gods too far and suffers the terrible punishment he has brought upon himself and his house.

The Theseus stories have a pagan majesty of the Bronze Age, yet the cast of finely-detailed characters, whose names are so familiar in song and legend, have a life and vigour that is entirely Renault's contribution. No reader of her work can ever again imagine the world of the Hellenes except as touched by her triumphant imagination.

Farther from legend, closer to history, but still magically transmuted from the chilly recital of battles and conquests, *Fire from*

Heaven recreates the formative years of Alexander the Great, from childhood in his father's turbulent court to young manhood at the threshold of mastery of the known world.

Alexander is a complex figure, shaped by the bitterness of the mother he both loves and hates, and by the barbarian King Philip of Macedon, the father he half-unwillingly admires.

Even as a child, Alexander was not as others; focused always to luminescence, and possessed of an uncanny ability to bind others to him in lifelong loyalty. In the years in which lesser children play and daydream, young Alexander planned and trained, under the cruel tutor who kept the boy ill-fed and shivering with the cold. By cruel necessity he learned early to disregard physical comfort, as he was to do throughout his short, meteoric life. Renault skilfully weaves a tapestry of known fact, educated surmise, and a generous measure of her own unmatched storytelling magic, to achieve a masterpiece of historical fiction.

Magnificent as it was, *Fire from Heaven* was to be followed by a still more triumphant creation. Acclaimed by many critics as Renault's masterpiece is the sequel in which the second half of Alexander's story is related by Bagoas, *The Persian Boy*. The court eunuch was castrated by slavers to preserve his youthful beauty from coarsening into manhood, and to make him an attractive, saleable sexual toy for the Persian King, Darius. The despairing lad sees a life of futile emptiness and degradation stretching endlessly before him. All too clearly he realizes that he will be used and discarded like any other frivolous, outworn plaything.

Then the might of Darius, the Great King, is utterly, humiliatingly defeated by the strong young warrior king out of the despised, half-civilized West, Alexander of Macedon. Bagoas is offered to the new barbarian king as a part of the conqueror's tribute. Surely now, he fears, he is worse off than before; the only eunuch among a fierce, wild people who scarcely know what a eunuch *is*, and are therefore contemptuously curious, supposing that 'one had been cut down to the shape of a woman'.

Amazingly, beyond his expectation, beyond even his hope, Bagoas has found the one with whom he can be whole again, if only Alexander can be made to love him: but Alexander has, and has always had, Hephaistion, his boyhood lover, almost his other self.

The tug-of-war, never openly acknowledged, but fierce and determined, between Alexander's lifelong lover and the Persian boy who is 'Alexander's dog' is amazingly vivid. A situation utterly alien to Western readers, and repugnant in some of its aspects to the unaccustomed, is rendered most affectingly and effortlessly believable; an enduring love story. *The Persian Boy* transcends time and mores to bring to life not merely a romance, but a true love story that takes its inspiration from the fateful beauty that is both Bagoas's undoing and his salvation.

Another astonishing work, *The Last of the Wine*, is a story of the waning years of the long-drawn-out Peloponnesian War, as told by Alexias, son of Myron, a young Athenian of good family, who is the lover of Lysis, a member of Socrates's circle.

The responsibility for one another that commitment entailed has a great deal to do with the nature of their passionate relationship. Theirs was not an adventure to be taken lightly, nor their love an empty affair. The love pledged between Alexias and Lysis was as meaningful and as binding as a marriage vow.

Alexias and his family, Lysis, the girl who would one day become his wife, their fellow Athenians, are well-rounded and wholly believable characters. Again it is amazing how through the persuasive conviction of the author, the reader comes readily to accept without shock or question the correctness, in the circumstances, of practices abhorrent to modern thought, such as the father's right of life or death over his children. One even understands Alexias's pangs of conscience in failing to obey his father's instructions that his newborn sibling be exposed on the hillside, should it prove to be a daughter.

The characters of Alexias and Lysis have been compared with those of Andrew and Laurie, heroes of *The Charioteer*, a tale of contemporary Britain; or rather, of Britain only yesterday.

Laurie is convalescing from wounds suffered at Dunkirk; Andrew is a 'Conchie', a conscientious objector doing orderly duty in the service hospital. Laurie is finally, unwillingly, forced to face the fact of his homosexuality by his love for Andrew, who sees Laurie only as a valued friend. A rakish figure from Laurie's schooldays, Ralph, brings brisk pragmatism to bear upon the increasingly difficult situation. Ralph has come to terms with his own homosexuality, is perfectly content to be what he is, and has made a satisfactory life for himself. He is more than willing to do the same for Laurie, if and when he can abandon his dream of ideal love with the unconscious object of his devotion.

It is an unusual 'triangle', but one in which each of the three men involved is a sympathetic, indeed an admirable character. A work of this nature was a breakthrough at the time of its publication: portraying a forbidden love as simply that, a love, even a selfless love, was a bold step.

In all of Renault's work, so much of which is concerned with various configurations of homosexuality or bisexuality, there is absolutely nothing to shock even the prudish; nothing to suggest a plea for pity or indulgence as for an aberrant condition; merely an understanding and heartfelt portrayal of people acting and being acted upon, with whose problems the reader cannot but be deeply, personally involved.

Other titles, such as *The Mask of Apollo*, the story of Nikeratos, actor and servant of the god, *The Praise Singer*, Simonides the bard, even *Funeral Games*, the third book in *The Alexander Trilogy*, the confused and confusing account of the chaotic years following the untimely death in Babylon, lack the fire and impact of earlier work; all are cooler, sombre, and autumnal in tone. But it is not on these lesser, though quite readable works, that her enduring reputation will be founded. Her accomplishment in bringing new life to a glorious age of hot-blooded men and women to replace the impression of broken statuary and crumbling temples that had for many been all that was known of Ancient Greece, should be saluted as long as readers dare to be swept out of the known and ordinary into the land of enchantment.

—Joan McGrath

RENIER, Elizabeth.
Pseudonym for Betty Doreen Baker. **Nationality:** British. **Born:** Betty Flook, Bristol, 22 November 1916. **Education:** Collegiate School, and Merchant Venturers College, both Bristol. **Military Service:** Voluntary Aid Detachment, attached to the Royal Army Medical Corps, 1940–42. **Relations:** married Frank Edward Baker (died). **Career:** doctor's secretary; volunteer, Family Planning Association, 1958–62. **Recipient:** Romantic Novelists Association Warwick award, 1962. **Address:** 4 Cranford Close, Exmouth, Devon EX8 2EY, England.

ROMANCE AND HISTORICAL PUBLICATIONS

Novels

The Generous Vine. London, Hurst and Blackett, 1962; New York, Ace, 1972.
The House of Water. London, Hurst and Blackett, 1963; New York, Ace, 1972.
Blade of Justice. London, Hurst and Blackett, 1965; New York, Ace, 1972.

If This Be Treason. London, Hurst and Blackett, 1965; as *If This Be Love*, New York, Ace, 1971.
Valley of Nightingales. London, Hurst and Blackett, 1966.
A Singing in the Woods. London, Hurst and Blackett, 1966; New York, Ace, 1972.
Prelude to Freedom. London, Hurst and Blackett, 1967; as *Prelude to Love*, New York, Ace, 1972.
The House of Granite. London, Hurst and Blackett, 1968; New York, Ace, 1971.
By Sun and Candlelight. London, Hurst and Blackett, 1968; New York, Ace, 1973.
Tomorrow Comes the Sun. London, Hurst and Blackett, 1969; New York, Ace, 1971.
The Spanish Doll. London, Hurst and Blackett, 1970; New York, Ace, 1972.
Valley of Secrets. London, Hurst and Blackett, 1970; New York, Ace, 1972.
Woman from the Sea. London, Hurst and Blackett, 1971; New York, Ace, n.d.
The Renshawe Inheritance. London, Hurst and Blackett, 1972; New York, Ace, 1973.
A Time for Rejoicing. London, Hurst and Blackett, and New York, Ace, 1973.
Ravenstor. London, Hurst and Blackett, 1974.
Yesterday's Mischief. London, Hurst and Blackett, 1975.
The Moving Dream. London, Hurst and Blackett, 1977; New York, Fawcett, 1978.
Landscape of the Heart. London, Hurst and Blackett, 1978; New York, Fawcett, 1979.

OTHER PUBLICATIONS

Other (for children)

The Lightkeepers. London, Hamish Hamilton, 1977.
The Stone People. London, Hamish Hamilton, 1978.
The Dangerous Journey. London, Hamish Hamilton, 1979.
The Post-rider. London, Hamish Hamilton, 1980.
The Mail-Coach Drivers. London, Hamish Hamilton, 1985.
The Night of the Storm. London, Hamish Hamilton, 1986.
The Hiding Place. London, Hamish Hamilton, 1987.
The Secret Valley. London, Hamish Hamilton, 1988.

*   *   *

'Do not hit those children like that as if you were herding cattle'. 'Cattle'd fetch a better price, m'lady'. These lines from Elizabeth Renier's *A Singing in the Woods* typify a dominant theme in her works, that of the wealthy heroine dedicating herself to improving conditions among the less fortunate. This egalitarian theme echoes her own avocational interest in working with deprived children. What is particularly impressive about Renier's novels, however, is a second theme, that of a young heiress pitted against the male dominance which surrounds her in the Devonshire area during the Georgian period. She masterfully creates the spirited innocence of the wealthy heroine of the time, allowing her lady to become a formidable challenge for the male counterpart. She effortlessly depicts the prosaic figure of a lovely woman amidst the splendour of her affluence but at the same time provides her with more than a superficial personality. Renier's heroine is eager to know about the world which surrounds her; she is an amalgam of feistiness, tenaciousness, and strength. Renier captures the rebellious nature of a woman with power during this period without losing the harmony of the poignantly described period setting. The lady always possesses a strong feeling for the grandeur of her homeland, whether it be Stant

Lydeard of *A Singing in the Woods*, Merriott of *The Renshawe Inheritance*, or similar settings. The reader can trust the character to be true to her ideals throughout the novel.

Renier's writing is refreshingly free from affectation, simply paced. The plot usually presents an energetic promenade of adventures which entangle the heroine and the hero (frequently land disputes create the dilemmas); but the potentially intolerable wooing scenes are pruned to crisp-in-form but tender-in-content meetings, punctuated with convincing descriptions of historical and graphical details. The heroes range from engaging swashbucklers to the more diffident gentlemen whose psychological strength outperforms their physical strength. Even Renier's minor characters are effective and memorable sketches.

Renier is an equal master in creating the ambience of the period, providing the reader with an almost illustrated tour, a topocosmography of the Devonshire area with detailed descriptions that almost allow the reader to scent the aroma of the salt air.

Using these themes and style, Renier consistently writes well. With efficacy she creates a stimulating romance novel.

—W.M. von Zharen

REVERE, M.P. See **WILLIAMSON, C.N. and A.M.**

RHODES, Elvi.
Nationality: British. **Born:** West Yorkshire, 1930s. **Education:** scholarship to Bradford Grammar School. **Relations:** widow; two sons. Lives in Sussex. **Address:** c/o Jenny Dufton, Transworld Publishers, 61–63 Uxbridge Road, London W5 5SA, England.

ROMANCE AND HISTORICAL PUBLICATIONS

Novels

Opal. London, Century, 1984.
Doctor Rose. London, Century, 1984.
Ruth Appleby. London, Corgi, 1987.
The Golden Girls. London, Bantam, 1988.
Madeleine. London, Bantam, 1989.
The House of Bonneau. London, Bantam, 1990.
Cara's Land. London, Bantam Press, 1991.
The Rainbow Through the Rain. London, Bantam Press, 1993.

Short Stories

Summer Promises and Other Stories. London, Bantam, 1990.

*   *   *

Elvi Rhodes was a prolific and accomplished writer of short stories, published mainly in magazines, before she began to write novels. Her plots range widely, but are always amusing, tender, funny, and delightful. Usually Rhodes takes a simple situation and tells the story with great economy of words. It is a spare and remarkably effective style, without superfluous detail yet everything necessary is there to satisfy the readers. She has a delicate method of inserting crucial information at precisely the right moment. Her stories are told equally successfully from the varied viewpoints of young and old, men and women. Some of her short stories have a twist, beautifully misleading the reader. The characters find love or freedom, not always the predictable sort. A selection of her short stories is contained in the volume *Summer Promises and Other Stories*.

In her novels Rhodes takes her native Yorkshire as the background for both books which have a historical setting, and for those with a more contemporary backdrop. Her heroines are all strong, determined women with more than their fair share of Yorkshire grit and determination, fighting against ill fortune or prejudice to emerge triumphant at the end, even if it is not always the end one might expect.

In *Opal*, the heroine is married to a weaver, but he is unemployed; thus, like many women in similar circumstances Opal starts a shop in her front room. Unlike most of these enterprises her shop develops into a department store, changing her life, and the lives of everyone about her.

Doctor Rose takes place in the 1920s, and tells the story of one of the earliest woman doctors. Rose works with women and children, and tries to give advice on birth control, a practice which offends both her professional colleagues and many other men, not least the husbands of the women involved. She loses her job in the clinic because she helps a young mother with a bully of a husband. Rose marries a local journalist, Alec, although she is in love with John, a rich married man. Secure financially she starts her own practice and clinics, carrying on the work, through her own pregnancy and motherhood, with Alec's support; this continues through the failure of her marriage, and her eventual attainment of love.

In *The Golden Girls* the heroine is a young widowed mother, struggling to bring up her daughters. It takes many hard times and the trauma of war before this love story can come to fruition.

A daughter, rather than a mother, is the focal character of *Ruth Appleby*. Set in the 19th century, Ruth's mother dies when she is 12, and she has to care for the rest of her family. This book expands beyond Yorkshire, as Ruth leaves for America, where she makes a success of her business.

Madeleine is set in a mill town, and contains much description of the processes of cloth making. This book was shortlisted for the Romantic Novelists' Association romantic novel of the year award. The mill girl who marries the boss and comes to run the business is a fairly common theme, but in Rhodes's hands such a story transcends the normal story. It is a strong enough story to permit a very successful sequel, *The House of Bonneau*. In addition to having problems with her marriage, her husband's resentful family, and a jealous childhood sweetheart, Madeleine has other serious problems to solve. This book moves out of Yorkshire, and includes a most exciting description of when Madeleine is trapped during the siege of Paris.

The most modern setting yet is *Cara's Land*. The heroine, Cara, is a landgirl during World War II; she marries Edward, a widowed man 15 years older than her, who has two children. The wedding scene includes a beautiful cameo of a ghastly aunt being rude and embarrassing. Cara's father dislikes the wedding, but he is a pompous bore. Cara's stepdaughter Susan is angry and rude, and the honeymoon is ruined by an over-friendly couple. Worried whether Edward hankers for his first wife, Cara discovers that she had been about to leave him when she was killed by a bomb. Then Edward dies in an accident. Cara has to choose between the other men in her life—Grant Fawcett, a neighbour, Kit Marsden, the half-gypsy horse dealer, and Johann, an Austrian prisoner of war.

Rhodes's characters are immensely real people, and the heroines have foibles and faults that simply make the reader like them more. The novels have fluency and pace, but above all they are gripping stories which are difficult to put down.

—Marina Oliver

RHYS, Jean.

Nationality: British. **Born:** Ella Gwendolyn Rees Williams in Roseau, Dominica, West Indies, 24 August 1890. **Education:** The Convent, Roseau; Perse School, Cambridge, England, 1907–08; Academy (now Royal Academy) of Dramatic Art, London, 1909. **Relations:** married 1) Jean Lenglet in 1919 (divorced 1932), one son and one daughter; 2) Leslie Tilden Smith in 1934 (died 1945); 3) Max Hamer in 1947 (died 1966). Also had a close relationship with the writer Ford Madox Ford. **Career:** toured England in chorus of *Our Miss Gibbs*, 1909–10; volunteer worker in soldiers canteen, 1914–17, and worked in a pension office, 1918, both London; lived in Paris, 1919 and 1923–27, and Vienna and Budapest, 1920–22; lived mainly in England after 1927: in Maidstone, Kent, 1950–52, London, 1952–56, Bude and Perranporth, Cornwall, 1956–60, and Cheriton Fitzpaine, Devon, from 1960. **Recipient:** Arts Council bursary, 1967; W.H. Smith award, 1967; Royal Society of Literature Heinemann award, 1967; Séguier prize, 1979. CBE (Commander, Order of the British Empire), 1978. **Died:** 14 May 1979.

ROMANCE AND HISTORICAL PUBLICATIONS

Novel

Wide Sargasso Sea. London, Deutsch, 1966; New York, Norton, 1967.

OTHER PUBLICATIONS

Novels

Postures. London, Chatto and Windus, 1928; as *Quartet*, New York, Simon and Schuster, 1929.
After Leaving Mr Mackenzie. London, Cape, and New York, Knopf, 1931.
Voyage in the Dark. London, Constable, 1934; New York, Morrow, 1935.
Good Morning, Midnight. London, Constable, 1939; New York, Harper, 1970.

Short Stories

The Left Bank and Other Stories. London, Cape, and New York, Harper, 1927.
Tigers Are Better-Looking, with a Selection from The Left Bank. London, Deutsch, 1968; New York, Harper, 1974.
Penguin Modern Stories 1, with others. London, Penguin, 1969.
Sleep It Off Lady. London, Deutsch, and New York, Harper, 1976.
Tales of the Wide Caribbean, edited by Kenneth Ramchand. London, Heinemann, 1985.
The Collected Short Stories. New York, Norton, 1987.

Other

My Day (essays). New York, Hallman, 1975.
Smile Please: An Unfinished Autobiography. London, Deutsch, 1979; New York, Harper, 1980.
Jean Rhys Letters 1931–1966, edited by Francis Wyndham and Diana Melly. London, Deutsch, and New York, Viking, 1984.
The Early Novels. London, Deutsch, 1984.
The Complete Novels. New York, Norton, 1985.

Translator, *Perversity*, by Francis Carco. Chicago, Covici, 1928 (translation attributed to Ford Madox Ford).
Translator, *Barred*, by Edward de Nève. London, Harmsworth, 1932.

*

Film Adaptations: *Quartet* 1981; *Wide Sargasso Sea*, 1993.

Bibliography: *Jean Rhys: A Descriptive and Annotated Bibliography of Works and Criticism* by Elgin W. Mellown, New York, Garland, 1984.

Manuscript Collection: University of Tulsa, Oklahoma.

Critical Studies: *Jean Rhys* by Louis James, London, Longman, 1978; *Jean Rhys: A Critical Study* by Thomas F. Staley, London, Macmillan, and Austin, University of Texas Press, 1979; *Jean Rhys* by Peter Wolfe, Boston, Twayne, 1980; *Jean Rhys, Woman in Passage: A Critical Study of the Novels* by Helen E. Nebeker, Montreal, Eden Press, 1981; *Difficult Women: A Memoir of Three* by David Plante, London, Gollancz, and New York, Atheneum, 1983; *Jean Rhys* by Arnold E. Davidson, New York, Ungar, 1985; *Jean Rhys* by Carole Angier, London, Viking, 1985; *Jean Rhys: The West Indian Novels* by Teresa F. O'Connor, New York, New York University Press, 1986; *Jean Rhys and the Novel as Women's Text* by Nancy R. Harrison, Chapel Hill, University of North Carolina Press, 1988; *The Rhys Woman* by Paul le Gallez, London, Macmillan, 1990; *Critical Perspectives in Jean Rhys* edited by Pierrette Frickey, New York, Three Continents Press, 1990; *Jean Rhys: A Life and Work* by Carole Angiers, London, Deutsch, 1990; *Jean Rhys* by Carol Ann Howells, London, Harvester Wheatsheaf, 1991.

*   *   *

Critics often view Jean Rhys's fiction as a chronology of the writer's own decline into despair, a biographical focus that relegates the texts to the margins of the literary canon. Yet Rhys insistently transformed biography into metaphor, the personal into the political. Beyond her central figures of women rendered passive by men resonate metonymic images of familial, racial, economic, and linguistic oppression. Thus turning to historical fiction in her last novel represents, not a departure from earlier themes, but a foregrounding of Rhys's lifelong obsession with the collusion in Western culture of imperialism, capitalism, religion, racism, classism, and sexism.

Since *Wide Sargasso Sea* precipitated the 'resurrection' of Rhys, it has received more critical attention than her other four novels combined. A prologue to *Jane Eyre* which centres the character of Rochester's mad West Indian wife, Rhys's last novel obviously reflects the author's racial and sexual identification with Charlotte Brontë's minor character. Angry at the silencing of Brontë's Bertha, Rhys sought to give voice to the madwoman in the attic. *Wide Sargasso Sea* creates for Bertha a past in the West Indies of the early-19th century when emancipation disrupted the colonial plantation life. Drawing on family history and her own childhood memories of Dominica, Rhys fictionalizes the untenable Creole position of belonging neither to the British colonial regime nor to the black ex-slave majority.

Called by her French first name, Antoinette Bertha Cosway (later Mason) suffers from childhood an awareness of the fragility of her identity. Rhys expands Rochester's cursory allusion in *Jane Eyre* to Bertha's genetic insanity by portraying Antoinette as witness as well as heir to her mother Annette's disintegration. Widow of a slave-owner, Annette is not only despised by the blacks but scorned by the white Jamaicans for her Martinique background. Her marriage to the British Mr Mason only exacerbates her decline as his refusal to recognize racial hostility results in the burning by blacks of the Coulibri estate, and the consequent death of the favoured child Pierre. The first part of the novel traces from Antoinette's retrospective viewpoint, her early rejection by Annette, and by her black friend Tia; her terror at Annette's mad degradation; her illicit passion for her black cousin, Saudi; and her reluctant, arranged marriage to the British Edward Rochester. Antoinette's foreboding dreams parallel those of Brontë's Jane, suggesting Rhys's view of Bertha Antoinette as a double rather than a nemesis of Jane.

The second part shifts the narrating voice to Rochester, whom Rhys strove to portray not as malicious but as tormented. Like Brontë's character, Rhys's Edward is constrained, as a younger son, to marry Antoinette for her inheritance, which he soon appropriates as he does her voice in the novel. Rhys's portrayal thus does not reflect a mono-dimensional victimization, for Edward, too, suffers familial and national displacement. His fevered disorientation peaks on their Dominican honeymoon in his lust/love for Antoinette; however, a letter from a black, who claims to be Antoinette's illegitimate half-brother, revives Edward's British censorious reserve. The desperate Antoinette, whose voice periodically interrupts her husband's, obtains an *obeah* love potion from her black surrogate mother Christophine; but she cannot be saved by the black culture and, in fact, is finally driven mad when Edward begins to flaunt his relationship with a black servant. Yet, though Edward's imperialistic/male script has objectified his wife into the grey ghost he insists on calling Bertha, Rhys's narrative technique elaborates Edward's agonizing recognition that her madness stems from her desire to convey to him 'the secret: ... she belonged to the magic and the loveliness. She had left me thirsty and all my life would be thirst and longing for what I had lost before I had found it'.

Antoinette's narration is retrieved in the third part of the novel only after opening with a passage narrated by Grace Poole, Antoinette's money-counting, drunken warden in the English tower. Such a device further evinces Rhys's determination to preclude a dualistic male/female, white/black, rich/poor, British/Caribbean portrayal of oppression. Antoinette's dream of setting fire to the house and jumping to her death at Tia's beckoning coalesces the foreshadowed destruction of Thornfield with the remembered destruction of Coulibri by the blacks. Yet the victimized blacks had victimized her, offering no more place to the Creole Antoinette than does the white culture; nor does the Caribbean (contrary to critical consensus) represent to Antoinette (or to Rhys) an antidotal opposite to England.

Rhys's one historical novel, then, broadens paradigmatically a recurrent Rhys theme. *Wide Sargasso Sea* enunciates the wideness of the gap between Rhys and Brontë, but Rhys had repeatedly subverted the romance plot in her first four novels. Like Antoinette, the early protagonists also fail to navigate the gap in a civilization that posits them as other, their passivity the byproduct of a thwarted active desire. The historical context of Rhys's last novel reveals that the Sargasso seaweed which entangles the characters is a multilayered morass inexorably reproduced. Antoinette's envisioned apocalypse images Rhys's vision of all sexes, all classes, all races as entrapped and self-immolating in civilization's dualistic structures.

—Janet Haedicke

RICH, Barbara. See GRAVES, Robert.

RICHARD, Susan. See ELLIS, Julie.

RICHARDS, Emilie.
Nationality: American. **Education:** Florida State University, Tallahassee; M.A. in family development. **Relations:** married to a minister, Michael; four children. **Career:** therapist, mental health centre; Head Start coordinator; community organizer, VISTA (domestic peace corps), Ozark mountains, Arkansas. Has lived in Florida, Virginia, Pennsylvannia, and Australia. Now lives in Bay Village, Ohio. **Recipient:** *Romantic Times* award for best new series writer, 1986. **Address:** c/o Silhouette Books, 300 East 42nd Street, New York, New York 10017, USA.

ROMANCE AND HISTORICAL PUBLICATIONS

Novels (series: Runaway; Sonny's Girls; Tales of the Pacific)

Brendan's Song. Toronto, Harlequin, 1985.
Sweet Georgia Gal. Toronto, Harlequin, 1985; New York, Silhouette, 1993.
Gilding the Lily. Toronto, Harlequin, 1985.
The Unmasking. Toronto, Harlequin, 1985.
Lady of the Night. Toronto, Harlequin, 1986.
Sweet Sea Spirit. New York, Silhouette, and New York, Silhouette, 1986.
Angel and the Saint. New York, Silhouette, and Toronto, Harlequin, 1986.
Sweet Mockingbird's. New York, Silhouette, and Toronto, Harlequin, 1986.
Good Time Man. New York, Silhouette, and Toronto, Harlequin, 1986.
Sweet Mountain Magic. New York, Silhouette, and Toronto, Harlequin, 1986.
Seasons of Miracles. Toronto, Harlequin, 1986.
Something so Right. Toronto, Harlequin, 1986; London, Worldwide, 1989.
Sweet Homecoming. New York, Silhouette, and Toronto, Harlequin, 1987.
Bayou Midnight. Toronto, Harlequin, 1987; New York, Silhouette, 1991.
Aloha Always. New York, Silhouette, and Toronto, Harlequin, 1987.
Sweet Homecoming. Toronto, Harlequin, 1987; New York, Silhouette, 1988.
Outback Nights. Toronto, Harlequin, 1987; New York, Silhouette, 1988.
Tales of the Pacific:
  From Glowing Embers. Toronto, Harlequin, 1987; New York, Silhouette, 1988.
  Smoke Screen. New York, Silhouette, 1988.
  Rainbow Fire. Toronto, Harlequin, 1989; New York, Silhouette, 1992.
  Out of the Ashes. Harlequin, 1989; New York, Silhouette, 1992.
All the Right Reasons. New York, Silhouette, and Toronto, Harlequin, 1988.
A Classic Encounter. New York, Silhouette, and Toronto, Harlequin, 1988.
Island Glory. New York, Silhouette, and Toronto, Harlequin, 1989.
Runaway (Runaway). New York, Silhouette, and Toronto, Harlequin, 1990.
The Way Back Home. New York, Silhouette, and Toronto, Harlequin, 1990.
Fugitive. New York, Silhouette, and Toronto, Harlequin, 1990.
The Way Back Home (Runaway). New York, Silhouette, 1990.

Labor Dispute. Toronto, Harlequin, 1990.

All Those Years Ago (Sonny's Girls). New York, Silhouette, and Toronto, Harlequin, 1991.

Desert Shadows. New York, Silhouette, and Toronto, Harlequin, 1991.

Twilight Shadows. New York, Silhouette, and Toronto, Harlequin, 1991.

From a Distance. New York, Silhouette, and Toronto, Harlequin, 1992.

One Perfect Rose. New York, Silhouette, and Toronto, Harlequin, 1992.

Somewhere Out There. New York, Silhouette, and Toronto, Harlequin, 1993.

Dragonslayer: American Heroes. New York, Silhouette, and Toronto, Harlequin, 1993.

The Trouble with Joe. New York, Silhouette, 1994.

Short Stories

To Mother with Love, with Jennifer Greene and Karen Keast. New York, Silhouette, 1992.

*　　*　　*

As an author of contemporary category romances, Emilie Richards has developed a reputation for providing love stories laced with intrigue and strong emotion. Many of Richards's characters are in disguise or hiding, running from physical danger, or a painful past.

In *Lady of the Night* Joshua Martane, a psychologist and minister, tries to help a 'Jane Doe' brought to the hospital where he works. Gravely injured, she is a suspected prostitute-victim of a serial killer. After she awakens from a five month long catatonic state, her past remains hidden by hysterical amnesia caused by her trauma. While Joshua is helping Maggie, as he comes to call her, cope with her problems, he discovers he also is beginning to heal from the pain of a bad marriage.

The 'Tales of the Pacific' series again shows many characters running, hiding, and eventually confronting the past. In the first title in the series, *From Glowing Embers*, Julie Ann has hidden from her husband, Gray Sheridan, for ten years, angry and bitter over the death of their child, but also in the belief that he did not really love her. Overwhelmed by his own guilt, Gray let her stay hidden, but finally he begins to search for her in Hawaii, where they have a confrontation over their painful past which allows them finally to bury their old ghosts. Paige Duvall returns to her mother's home in New Zealand (*Smoke Screen*). There she learns that her own past has been hidden from her. She discovers her Maori heritage, learning to embrace it as she falls in love with Adam Tamoana. Kelsey Donovan travels to the Australian Outback, in *Rainbow Fire*, to find her father, Jake, who has hidden from her and her mother for more than 20 years. Dillon Ward, Jake's partner, helps her overcome her lonely past and uncover some of Jake's secrets. In the final volume of the series, *Out of the Ashes*, Alexis Whitham seeks refuge from an abusive ex-husband on a remote Australian island. She struggles to overcome her past, and helps Matthew Haley confront his own tragic past. Characters from all of the books are introduced in the first book, and reappear in the last.

Runaway introduces another of Richards's masqueraders. Krista Jensen, who is searching for her sister, Rosie, poses as a teenage runaway on the streets of New Orleans. Jess Cantrell, an investigative reporter, becomes her protector and helps her in her search. Although they do not find Rosie, they do 'adopt' Tate, another runaway. *The Way Back Home* continues the story of the two sisters. In both, Richards displays real talent as she movingly describes the plight of these children, and the lengths to which they often must go in order to survive in a hostile and dangerous world.

Richards has also shown a talent for incorporating suspense into her romances. In *Desert Shadows*, Felice Cristy, a private investigator, goes undercover in a convent to protect a nun who has led the fight for human rights in a small Caribbean country. Felice meets Joshua Gallagher, an FBI agent, also undercover to protect the nun. Richards keeps things nicely confused as Gallagher and Felice each try to decide if the other is a threat. They also are puzzled, as is the reader, by seemingly inconsistent actions of the villains. It is not until the end that Richards reveals that there really are two sets of villains and two targets. She displays a light comic touch in describing the unusual encounters between Felice and Gallagher. Needless to say that they fall in love, and their wedding is the starting point for *Twilight Shadows*, in which gunmen disrupt the ceremony by spraying the guests with bullets. Felice's partner, Kelley Samuels, is hired to protect Griff Bryant, a movie star, who might have been the target. Richards keeps things stirred up with more questions about Kelley's secret past, just who the intended victim is, and what the motive is.

In *Smoke Screen*, Richards introduced some mystical elements when describing Paige's encounter with the spirits of her ancestors. In *From a Distance*, she maintains a mystical feeling of awe in a very moving love story with an unusual twist. Brilliant neurosurgeon, Stefan Daniels and his ex-wife, Lindsey, are reunited under unusual circumstances. She insists that she has had a close encounter with an alien spaceship, while he fears she may be losing her mind. What becomes irrefutable is that Lindsey is dying of some unknown cause. As her condition deteriorates, Stefan works frantically to find a cure and the two draw closer together. Richards does an excellent job of describing the frightening ordeal which finally teaches them to communicate and admit their love. The caring alien who comes to help heal Lindsey is, in many ways, more a spiritual being than a mere fantasy. The story continues in *Somewhere Out There*. After helping Lindsey, the alien, who has taken human form, is separated from his ship. Injured and stranded in the Australian Dry, he is rescued and cared for by Mackenzie Conroy. Having lost his memory, he takes the name Patrick. Gradually he falls in love with Mackenzie, but he also begins to rediscover his powers and recover his memory. Increasingly torn between his love for her and his longing for his home, he finally realizes that he must leave earth. Although the discovery that the captain of the ship returning for Patrick is actually Mackenzie's father is too coincidental, it does allow a satisfying end to an unusual and poignant romance.

Richards has proven herself as an author who creates memorable characters in intriguing, often provocative romances. She invites the reader to recognize that image and reality are not always the same and that tangled emotions can disguise the truth. By her vivid descriptions of emotional pain and its consequences, she encourages the reader to look beyond differences separating people to the possibilities and beauty of really connecting with another.

—Barbara E. Kemp

RICHARDSON, Henry Handel.
Nationality: Australian. **Born:** Ethel Florence Lindesay Richardson, Melbourne, Victoria, 3 January 1870. **Education:** Presbyterian Ladies' College, Melbourne, 1883–86; studied music at the Leipzig Conservatorium, 1889–92. **Relations:** married J.G. Robertson in 1895 (died 1933). **Career:** full-time writer. Lived in Strasbourg, 1896–1903, London, 1903–32, and Sussex from 1933. Visited Australia 1912. **Recipient:** Australian Literature Society gold medal, 1929. **Died:** 20 March 1946.

ROMANCE AND HISTORICAL PUBLICATIONS

Novels

Maurice Guest. London, Heinemann, and New York, Reynolds, 1908.
The Getting of Wisdom. London, Heinemann, and New York, Duffield, 1910.
The Fortunes of Richard Mahony. London, Heinemann, and New York, Norton, 1930.
  The Fortunes of Richard Mahony. London, Heinemann, 1917; as *Australia Felix.* New York, Norton, 1917.
  The Way Home. London, Heinemann, and New York, Norton, 1925.
  Ultima Thule. London, Heinemann, and New York, Norton, 1929.
Two Studies. London, Ulysses Press, 1931.
The Young Cosima. London, Heinemann, 1939.

Short Stories

The End of a Childhood and Other Stories. London, Heinemann, and New York, Norton, 1934.
The Adventures of Cuffy Mahony and Other Stories. Sydney, Angus and Robertson, and London, Heinemann, 1979.

OTHER PUBLICATIONS

Other

Myself When Young (unfinished autobiography). London, Heinemann, and New York, Norton, 1948.
Letters to Nettie Palmer, edited by Karl-Johan Rossing. Cambridge, Harvard University Press, 1953.

Translator, *Siren Voices*, by J.P. Jacobsen. London, Heinemann, 1896.
Translator, *The Fisher Lass*, by B. Bjornson. London, Heinemann, 1896.

*

Bibliography: *Richardson 1870–1949: A Bibliography to Honour the Centenary of Her Birth* by Gay Howells, 1970.

Critical Studies: *Henry Handel Richardson: A Study* by Nettie Palmer, Sydney, Angus and Robertson, 1950; *Henry Handel Richardson* by Vincent Buckley, Melbourne, Lansdowne Press, 1961; *Ulysses Bound: Richardson and Her Fiction* by Dorothy Green, Canberra, Australian National University Press, 1973, revised edition, as *Richardson and Her Fiction*, 1986; *Art and Irony, the Tragic Vision of Henry Handel Richardson, a Discussion of the Relationship of Theme and Technique in Fiction* by J.R. Nichols, Washington DC, University Press of America, 1982; *The Portrayal of Women in the Fiction of Henry Handel Richardson* by Eva Jarring Corones, Lund, Gleerup, 1983; *Henry Handel Richardson: A Critical Study* by Karen McLeod, Cambridge, Cambridge University Press, 1985; *Henry Handel Richardson: Fiction in the Making* by Axel Clark, Brookvale, New South Wales, Simon and Schuster, 1990.

*   *   *

Henry Handel Richardson was the pseudonym for the Australian novelist, essayist, and short story writer Ethel Florence Lindesay Richardson Robertson. Born in Melbourne, Australia, in 1810, Richardson left her native country to attend the Conservatorium in Leipzig, and it was here that she met her husband, the respected German and Scandinavian scholar J.G. Robertson, who encouraged her to write.

Richardson's most famous works—*Maurice Guest* and *The Fortunes of Richard Mahony*—are based closely on events in her life. *Maurice Guest* is a study of the destructive obsessive nature of love and draws heavily on Richardson's experiences in Leipzig; Laura's childhood, in *The Getting of Wisdom*, is close to Richardson's own; and *The Fortunes of Richard Mahony* is based loosely on the life of her doctor father. A.D. Hope wrote in an essay (1955) '. . . all Henry Handel Richardson's books, except *Young Cosima*, are in one sense or another about herself'.

Maurice Guest is a book about a great and destructive passion—and studies the degrading nature of love. The protagonist is ruined by both his hopeless obsession for a woman of little principle and his sense of inadequacy and failure as a musician (like Richardson herself). The book is imbued with Nietzschean ideas—the most important being the belief in the existence of two types of people in society: 'free spirits' who exist in a artistic, intellectual, but morally depraved world, and the 'herd' or masses who are incapable of ascending above society's conventions. Maurice's failure as a lover and an artist stem from his lack of morbidity and power to break away from the herd. Louise, the woman whom he adores, fits into the 'free spirit' mould, and has no sense of good or evil.

The Fortunes of Richard Mahony (*Australia Rex*, *The Way Home*, and *Ultima Thule*) are filled with minutiae about the colonization of Australia in the nineteenth century. J.G. Robertson wrote in 1929 that *Richard Mahony*

. . . is a very terrible book, this history of a mind diseased, one of the great tragic books of our time. Looking back over the three volumes one realizes how firm and spacious was the plan of Richard Mahony: how his life-history, with the inevitableness of an impersonal fate, has been forged. One becomes aware of the constructive strength of its creator, of the art which never falters, which never fails to rise through a thousand pages to a fuller tragic music. Harrowing and poignant as are Mahony's sufferings from the beginning . . . there are always deeper depths, and greater tragic heights to come.

Mahony suffers a mental breakdown, but as he sinks into depression Mary, his wife, emerges as a courageous, positive woman. She begins to work, supports her family, and manages to get her husband admitted to a private hospital. When he is finally transferred to an asylum, Mary fights for him—in many ways Mahony's madness is Mary's making.

The publication of the third volume of the trilogy, *Ultima Thule*, brought Richardson the critical acclaim and commercial success that she deserved. Although criticized for her rich, often florid prose, Richardson has been called the 'greatest British naturalist' and is still considered to be one of Australia's most influential novelists.

—Marion Hatchard

———

RICHMOND, Grace. See **WOODWARD, Lilian.**

———

RIEFE, A.R. See **RIEFE, Barbara.**

———

RIEFE, Alan.   See **RIEFE, Barbara.**

———

RIEFE, Barbara.
Pseudonym for Alan Riefe. **Other Pseudonyms:** Ann Cameron; J.D. Hardin; Zachary Hawkes; Jake Logan; Pierce MacKenzie; E.B. Majors; A.R. Riefe; also writes as Alan Riefe. **Nationality:** American. **Born:** Waterbury, Connecticut, 18 May 1925. **Education:** Colby College, Waterville, Maine, B.A. 1950. **Military Service:** United States Army during World War II. **Relations:** married 1) Martha Daggett in 1948 (died 1949); 2) Barbara Dube in 1955; four children. **Career:** freelance writer. **Agent:** Sharon Jarvis, RR2, Box 16B, Laceyville, Pennsylvannia 18623, USA.

ROMANCE AND HISTORICAL PUBLICATIONS

Novels (series: Dandridge Trilogy)

Barringer House. New York, Popular Library, 1976.
Rowleston. New York, Popular Library, 1976.
Auldearn House. New York, Popular Library, 1976.
Dandridge Trilogy
  This Ravaged Heart. Chicago, Playboy Press, 1977; London, Sphere, 1979.
  Far Beyond Desire. Chicago, Playboy Press, 1978; London, Sphere, 1980.
  Fire and Flesh. Chicago, Playboy Press, 1978; London, Sphere, 1980.
Tempt Not This Flesh. Chicago, Playboy Press, 1979; London, Sphere, 1981.
Black Fire. Chicago, Playboy Press, 1980; London, Sphere, 1982.
So Wicked the Heart. Chicago, Playboy Press, 1980; London, Sphere, 1982.
Olivia. Chicago, Playboy Press, 1981.
Wild Fire. Chicago, Playboy Press, 1981; London, Sphere, 1983.
Julia. Chicago, Playboy Press, 1982.
Lucretia. Chicago, Playboy Press, 1982.
Wicked Fire. New York, Berkley, 1983; London, Sphere, 1985.
This Proud Love. New York, Berkley, 1985.
A Woman of Dreams. New York, Berkley, 1986.
Vipor. New York, Diamond Books, 1990.
Second, to Death. New York, Diamond Books, 1991.
Visiting Hours (as Ann Cameron). New York, Diamond Books, 1992.
The Woman who Fell from the Sky. New York, Tor, 1993.

OTHER PUBLICATIONS

Novels as Alan Riefe

The Lady Killers. New York, Popular Library, 1975; London, New English Library, 1976.
The Conspirators. New York, Popular Library, 1975; London, New English Library, 1977.
The Black Widower. New York, Popular Library, 1975.
The Silver Puma. New York, Popular Library, 1975.
The Bullet-Proof Man. New York, Popular Library, 1975.
The Killer with the Golden Touch. New York, Popular Library, 1975.
Tyger at Bay. New York, Popular Library, 1976.
Tyger by the Tail. New York, Popular Library, 1976.
The Smile on the Face of the Tyger. New York, Popular Library, 1976.
Tyger and the Lady. New York, Popular Library, 1976.

Hold That Tyger. New York, Popular Library, 1976.
Tyger, Tyger, Burning Out. New York, Popular Library, 1976.

Novels as Jake Logan

Bloody Trail to Texas. Chicago, Playboy Press, 1976.
White Hell. Chicago, Playboy Press, 1977.
Iron Mustang. Chicago, Playboy Press, 1978.
Montana Showdown. Chicago, Playboy Press, 1978.
See Texas and Die. Chicago, Playboy Press, 1979.

Novels as J.D. Hardin

The Slick and the Dead. Chicago, Playboy Press, 1979.
Blood, Sweat, and Gold. Chicago, Playboy Press, 1979.
The Good, The Bad and the Deadly. Chicago, Playboy Press, 1979.
Bullets, Buzzards, Boxes of Pine. Chicago, Playboy Press, 1980.
Face Down in a Coffin. Chicago, Playboy Press, 1980.
The Man Who Bit Snakes. Chicago, Playboy Press, 1980.
Bloody Time in the Blacktower. New York, Berkley, 1983.
The Man with No Face. New York, Berkley, 1983.
Queens over Deuces. New York, Berkley, 1984.
Carnival of Death. New York, Berkley, 1984.
Tombstone in Deadwood. New York, Berkley, 1984.
The Great Jewel Robbery. New York, Berkley, 1985.
Apache Trail. New York, Berkley, 1985.
Hell's Belle. New York, Berkley, 1985.
The Swindler's Trail. New York, Berkley, 1987.
Thunder Mountain Massacre. New York, Berkley, 1987.
Raider. New York, Berkley, 1987.
The Yuma Roundup. New York, Berkley, 1987.
The Cheyenne Fraud. New York, Berkley, 1988.
Silver City Ambush. New York, Berkley, 1988.

Novels as Zachary Hawkes

Fancy Hatch. New York, Pinnacle, 1984.
The Case Deuce. New York, Pinnacle, 1984.
Solomon King's Mine. New York, Pinnacle, 1984.
The Odds Against Sundown. New York, Pinnacle, 1985.

Novels as E.B. Majors

Slaughter and Son. New York, Warner, 1985.
Nightmare Trail. New York, Warner, 1986.
Hair Trigger and Kill. New York, Warner, 1986.
Death in Durango. New York, Warner, 1986.

Novels as Pierce MacKenzie

The Stolen White Eagle. New York, New American Library, 1987.
The Fleecing of Fodder City. New York, New American Library, 1987.
Winner Take Nothing. New York, New American Library, 1987.
The Spanish Monte Fiasco. New York, New American Library, 1987.
Double Trouble in Skagway. New York, New American Library, 1987.
The Cockeyed Coyote. New York, New American Library, 1987.

Novels as A.R. Riefe

Tucson. New York, New American Library, 1988.
Cheyenne. New York, New American Library, 1989.
San Francisco. New York, New American Library, 1989.
Salt Lake City. New York, New American Library, 1989.

Short Stories

Tales of Horror (as Alan Riefe). New York, Pocket Books, 1965.

Plays (as Alan Riefe)

Television Writing: *Masquerade Party* series, 8 years; *Keep Talking* series, 2 years; and scripts for *Pulitzer Prize Playhouse* and *Studio One* series.

Other

Vip's Illustrated Woman Driver's Manual. New York, Fawcett, 1966.

*   *   *

Since 1976, Alan Riefe, writing under the pseudonym of Barbara Riefe, has turned his writing skills to the genre of historical romance with varying success. Riefe has a solid understanding of those elements which are of interest to the romance reader—true love, adventure in foreign lands, fast-paced action, and a sprinkling of spicy sex, all set in a time period gone by, and eventually leading to the beloved 'happy ending'.

Riefe's plots are often based on the separation of loved ones by unfortunate circumstances and the ensuing struggle by the loved ones against nearly impossible odds to become reunited. Riefe is at his best when he sends his characters on adventures, most often by sea. His sense of geographical detail—ranging from the United States to Capri to Tasmania to the Far East—and his knowledge of the sea and seafaring vessels add much in the way of credibility to his stories. In addition, fast-paced action, detailed description, and crisp dialogue serve to keep the reader actively interested in what is going to happen next. It is, after all, a good story that the reader of popular fiction is looking for; the main failure of books in the genre of popular fiction comes from the reader's fading desire to want to know what happens next, for there is generally insufficient character development, or logical cause and effect plot—which causes character development and growth—on which to rely in the event of lapses in the story.

When Riefe finds himself in danger of being uninteresting because the reader has become confident of the story's outcome, he uses coincidences and surprises—i.e., information which is known only to him—to cause a reversal or modification in the situation which heightens the reader's interest. Riefe also uses several subplots which are related to, and ultimately merge with, the main plot. These subplots are usually the various adventures of the separated loved ones. Rapid alternations between one plot and another (usually occurring in different geographical locations) serve to maintain and rekindle the reader's interest. (In one instance—in *This Ravaged Heart*—because of the use of witchcraft, the separation is made not only geographical but also temporal.) Should either of these methods fail, there are often graphic sexual interludes to add excitement.

Characterization and character development in these novels are often weak, as is generally the case in popular fiction, and many of the characters remain flat and undeveloped since they are, after all, merely vehicles for the action. Understandably, the character of the heroine is most clearly defined (although it doesn't often develop further in the course of the novel). The heroine exhibits 'true, undying love' and the expected moral character necessary to being a good wife. In addition to female beauty and alluring female charms, the traits of solid judgement, intelligence, great mental and emotional strength, and superhuman stamina reveal themselves when she is separated from her husband and allow her to outwit her adversaries and overcome apparently insurmountable situations, ultimately resulting in the rescue of the loved one. These heroines do not bear up under close scrutiny, for they are almost superhuman figures, the good aspects of several men and women rolled into one, but their dialogue when well contrived convinces the reader—momentarily, at least—that it is otherwise. The reader is quite willing to overlook the flaw in the interest of entertainment. Riefe departs from the typical damsel-in-distress romance heroine, and makes his heroines much more products of his century, than of the previous century where he places them in time.

All in all, when Riefe balances the elements which he uses in his novels, he is capable of producing a well-wrought, gripping bit of entertainment that rivals that of many of his competitors. This is especially evident in the first volume of the 'Dandridge Trilogy', *This Ravaged Heart*, perhaps the best of his romance novels. The second book, *Far Beyond Desire*, is also quite solid entertainment, although there is a prevalence of sexual interludes. The last book, *Fire and Flesh*, becomes a bit tedious because the reader must wade through a great deal of predictable exposition before arriving at the expected ending.

—Michael Held

RINEHART, Mary Roberts.
Nationality: American. **Born:** Pittsburgh, Pennsylvania, 12 August 1876. **Education:** elementary and high schools in Pittsburgh; Pittsburgh Training School for Nurses, graduated 1896. **Relations:** married Stanley Marshall Rinehart in 1896 (died 1932); three sons. **Career:** full-time writer from 1903; correspondent, *Saturday Evening Post*, Philadelphia, during World War I; reported presidential nominating conventions. Lived in Pittsburgh until 1920, in Washington, DC, 1920–32, and in New York from 1932. **Recipient:** Mystery Writers of America Special award, 1953. D.Litt.: George Washington University, Washington, DC, 1923. **Died:** 22 September 1958.

ROMANCE AND HISTORICAL PUBLICATIONS

Novels (series: Nurse Hilda Adams, 'Miss Pinkerton')

The Circular Staircase. Indianapolis, Bobbs Merrill, 1908; London, Cassell, 1909.
When a Man Marries. Indianapolis, Bobbs Merrill, 1909; London, Hodder and Stoughton, 1920.
The Man in Lower Ten. Indianapolis, Bobbs Merrill, and London, Cassell, 1909.
The Window at the White Cat. Indianapolis, Bobbs Merrill, 1910; London, Nash, 1911.
Where There's a Will. Indianapolis, Bobbs Merrill, 1912.
The Case of Jennie Brice. Indianapolis, Bobbs Merrill, 1913; London, Hodder and Stoughton, 1919.
The After House. Boston, Houghton Mifflin, 1914; London, Simpkin Marshall, 1915.
The Street of Seven Stars. Boston, Houghton Mifflin, 1914; London, Cassell, 1915.
K. Boston, Houghton Mifflin, and London, Smith Elder, 1915.
Bab, A Sub-Deb. New York, Doran, 1917; London, Hodder and Stoughton, 1920.
Long Live the King! Boston, Houghton Mifflin, and London, Murray, 1917.
Twenty-Three and a Half Hours' Leave. New York, Doran, 1918.
The Amazing Interlude. New York, Doran, and London, Murray, 1918.
Dangerous Days. New York, Doran, and London, Hodder and Stoughton, 1919.

The Truce of God. New York, Doran, 1920.

A Poor Wise Man. New York, Doran, and London, Hodder and Stoughton, 1920.

Sight Unseen, and The Confession. New York, Doran, and London, Hodder and Stoughton, 1921.

The Breaking Point. New York, Doran, and London, Hodder and Stoughton, 1922.

The Out Trail. New York, Doran, 1923.

The Red Lamp. New York, Doran, 1925; as *The Mystery Lamp*, London, Hodder and Stoughton, 1925.

The Bat (novelization of play), with Avery Hopwood. New York, Doran, and London, Cassell, 1926.

Lost Ecstasy. New York, Doran, and London, Hodder and Stoughton, 1927; as *I Take This Woman*, New York, Grosset and Dunlap, 1927.

Two Flights Up. New York, Doubleday, and London, Hodder and Stoughton, 1928.

This Strange Adventure. New York, Doubleday, and London, Hodder and Stoughton, 1929.

The Door. New York, Farrar and Rinehart, and London, Hodder and Stoughton, 1930.

Miss Pinkerton. New York, Farrar and Rinehart, 1932; as *The Double Alibi*, London, Cassell, 1932.

Mary Roberts Rinehart's Crime Book (Adams; 2 novellas). New York, Farrar and Rinehart, 1933; London, Cassell, 1958.

The Album. New York, Farrar and Rinehart, and London, Cassell, 1933.

The State Versus Elinor Norton. New York, Farrar and Rinehart, 1934; as *The Case of Elinor Norton*, London, Cassell, 1934.

Mr Cohen Takes a Walk. New York, Farrar and Rinehart, 1934.

The Doctor. New York, Farrar and Rinehart, and London, Cassell, 1936.

The Wall. New York, Farrar and Rinehart, and London, Cassell, 1938.

The Great Mistake. New York, Farrar and Rinehart, 1940; London, Cassell, 1941.

Haunted Lady (Adams). New York, Farrar and Rinehart, and London, Cassell, 1942.

The Yellow Room. New York, Farrar and Rinehart, 1945; London, Cassell, 1949.

The Curve of the Catenary. New York, Royce, 1945.

A Light in the Window. New York, Rinehart, and London, Cassell, 1948.

Episode of the Wandering Knife: Three Mystery Tales. New York, Rinehart, 1950; as *The Wandering Knife*, London, Cassell, 1952.

The Swimming Pool. New York, Rinehart, 1952; as *The Pool*, London, Cassell, 1952.

Short Stories (series: Letitia 'Tish' Carberry)

The Amazing Adventures of Letitia Carberry. Indianapolis, Bobbs Merrill, 1911; London, Hodder and Stoughton, 1919.

Tish. Boston, Houghton Mifflin, 1916; London, Hodder and Stoughton, 1917.

Love Stories. New York, Doran, 1920.

Affinities and Other Stories. New York, Doran, and London, Hodder and Stoughton, 1920.

More Tish. New York, Doran, and London, Hodder and Stoughton, 1921.

Temperamental People. New York, Doran, and London, Hodder and Stoughton, 1924.

Tish Plays the Game. New York, Doran, 1926; London, Hodder and Stoughton, 1927.

Nomad's Land. New York, Doran, 1926.

The Romantics. New York, Farrar and Rinehart, 1929; London, Hodder and Stoughton, 1930.

Married People. New York, Farrar and Rinehart, and London, Cassell, 1937.

Tish Marches On. New York, Farrar and Rinehart, 1937; London, Cassell, 1938.

Familiar Faces: Stories of People You Know. New York, Farrar and Rinehart, 1941; London, Cassell, 1943.

Alibi for Isabel and Other Stories. New York, Farrar and Rinehart, 1944; London, Cassell, 1946.

The Frightened Wife and Other Murder Stories. New York, Rinehart, 1953; London, Cassell, 1954.

The Best of Tish. New York, Rinehart, 1955; London, Cassell, 1956.

OTHER PUBLICATIONS

Plays

Seven Days, with Avery Hopwood (produced Trenton and New York, 1909; Harrogate, 1913; London, 1915). New York, French, 1931.

Cheer Up (produced New York, 1912).

Spanish Love, with Avery Hopwood (produced New York, 1920).

The Bat, with Avery Hopwood, adaptation of the novel *The Circular Staircase* by Rinehart (produced New York, 1920; London, 1922). New York, French, 1931.

The Breaking Point (produced New York, 1923).

Screenplay: *Aflame in the Sky*, with Ewart Anderson, 1927.

Other

Kings, Queens, and Pawns: An American Woman at the Front. New York, Doran, 1915.

Through Glacier Park: Seeing America First with Howard Eaton. Boston, Houghton Mifflin, 1916.

The Altar of Freedom. Boston, Houghton Mifflin, 1917.

Tenting Tonight: A Chronicle of Sport and Adventure in Glacier Park and the Cascade Mountains. Boston, Houghton Mifflin, 1918.

Isn't That Just Like a Man! New York, Doran, 1920.

My Story (autobiography). New York, Farrar and Rinehart, 1931; London, Cassell, 1932; revised edition, New York, Rinehart, 1948.

Writing Is Work. Boston, The Writer, 1939.

*

Film Adaptations: *The Bat Whispers*, 1930, *The Bat*, 1939, both from the play *The Bat*; *I Take this Woman*, 1931, from the novel *Lost Ecstasy*.

Manuscript Collection: University of Pittsburgh Library.

Critical Study: *Improbable Fiction: The Life of Mary Roberts Rinehart* by Jan Cohn, Pittsburgh, University of Pittsburgh Press, 1980.

*   *   *

When Mary Roberts Rinehart turned her pen from mystery with romance to romance by itself, her 'world' was still dominated by large houses with servants. This versatile craftsman produced novels and stories of sentiment, humour, and happy endings. Taken together, they offer a limited social history of the USA from the late-19th century to the late-1940s.

Early romances foreshadow. *When a Man Marries* is farce; its complications include a two-hour substitute 'wife' for the visit of an aunt who doles an allowance, an ex-wife, and a butler with small-pox. Vienna is the setting for *The Street of Seven Stars*, the romance of young Americans, the girl studying music, the man, medicine. They take care of a dying young boy. In *K*, 'K', a surgeon, is a steadying influence on an idealist nurse.

World War I is a backdrop for several works. *The Amazing Interlude* concerns an American girl who dispensed soup, cigarettes, and pure love to wounded soldiers behind the front lines and returned to wait for Henri, her Belgian true-love. *Dangerous Days* centers on a wealthy and patriotic munitions manufacturer, his plant, and his stale marriage. Only the Armistice finally offers a bright future. Hilarity in *Twenty-Three and a Half Hours' Leave* results from a quartermaster's attempt to deal with the problem of no uniforms for a troop about to sail. *Bab, a Sub-Deb* is also very amusing as 17-year-old Barbara Putnam Thatcher records her Experiences, some 'sickning'. 'For is not Romanse itself but breif, the thing of an hour, at least to the Other Sex?' During World War I, she helps to capture a spy.

The war is part of the ambitious scope of *This Strange Adventure* (life), a narrative of the Colfax family, mainly of the enduring Missy, from the 1880s to the war, and of *The Doctor* which chronicles the overlapping professional and love lives of Dr Arden from 1910 to 1927. In *A Light in the Window* the light is placed by the mother of Ricky for a son off to World War I and by Ricky herself for her son and daughter off to World War II. Lives and loves of two generations of a family unfold.

Other romances vary. *Long Live the King!* has a charming ten-year-old hero, European Prince Otto. *A Poor Wise Man* is an ill-advised attempt to delve into labour problems after World War I, and *The Truce of God* documents a change of heart on Christmas day in mediaeval times. Through the marriage of a cowboy and an Eastern girl, *Lost Ecstasy* contrasts the hardships of life in the West and the easy, sometimes superficial, life in the affluent East. Slight is the parable of *Mr Cohen Takes a Walk;* wealthy and elderly, he returns refreshed by good deeds.

Titles of the collections of short stories, except those of Tish, reveal diversified love stories. For 30 years, Tish (Letitia Carberry) led Lizzie, the narrator, and Aggie, the long-suffering, into the wild and woolly adventures of the M.A.T. (Middle-Aged Trio). Laugh-provoking, the stories are full of spirit, including that of Charlie Sand, nephew, and of the medicinal blackberry cordial.

In a long career, Rinehart proved an able storyteller, her plots more complex than can be noted here. For readers today, a weakness is the assumption that the best place for women, in spite of talent or intelligence, is in the home. Her humour cannot be faulted.

—Jane Gottschalk

RIPLEY, Alexandra.
Nationality: American. **Born:** Charleston, South Carolina, 8 January 1934. **Education:** Vassar College, Poughkeepsie, New York, A.B. 1955. **Relations:** two daughters. **Career:** full-time writer. Lives in Charlottesville, Virginia. **Agent:** William Morris Agency, 1350 Avenue of the Americas, New York 10019, USA.

ROMANCE AND HISTORICAL PUBLICATIONS

Novels (series: Tradd Family)

Charleston (Tradd Family). New York, Doubleday, 1981.
On Leaving Charleston (Tradd Family). New York, Doubleday, 1984.
The Time Returns. New York, Doubleday, 1985.

New Orleans Legacy. New York, Macmillan, 1987; London, Warner, 1988.
Scarlett. London, Macmillan, and New York, Warner, 1991.

OTHER PUBLICATIONS

Novel

Who's That Sleeping in the President's Bed? New York, Dodd Mead, 1972.

*   *   *

An historical saga set in both post-civil war America, and Ireland, with a handsome, dashing hero, and a beautiful, resilient heroine would be enough to hold the interest of any avid romantic-fiction fan. Identify the heroine as the infamous Scarlett O'Hara, and the hero as Rhett Butler, certainly among the most recognized characters of historical fiction, and one surely has the ingredients for an extremely successful book. There can be no doubt that Alexandra Ripley's novel, *Scarlett*, has brought the author much publicity and financial success. The question—how successful is *Scarlett* as the sequel to *Gone with the Wind*?—might however, meet a different answer. Kathryn Falk wrote in the *Romantic Times*, 'congratulations are in order to Ellen Herrick, director of publicity at Warner, and the enterprising president, Larry Kirshbaum, for pulling off the literary coup of the decade. To think they could get so many people excited about a sequel! . . . But what about the story?'.

Ripley's Scarlett is a very different character from the one who appears in Margaret Mitchell's *Gone with the Wind*. Gone is the wilful, spoilt woman who saves her beloved Tara, despises the delicate Melanie, and is fatefully in love with the dreamy Ashley Wilkes; gone is the woman who argues with Rhett Butler, and resents his attraction for her. Instead we find a Scarlett who mourns the death of her *friend*, Melanie, and who relentlessly pursues Rhett Butler—a man who in this book, runs away from Scarlett, and ends up marrying a school teacher whom he compromises. (What happened to the Rhett who offended Charleston by refusing to marry a woman whom he apparently ruined?). Rhett also has a mother and sister whom he cares deeply about: yet his family are curiously absent from the original book. Similarly, Scarlett finds her father's more Irish than the Irish family, the O'Haras. Despite being used to aristocratic company, she so empathizes with her working class relatives, particularly with the Irish priest Colum, that she leaves America to go to Ireland.

This decision is made partly from a desire to see the land her father revered, and partly because, as a result of a brief encounter with Rhett, she finds herself pregnant. Having profited financially from her husband, Scarlett decides to stay in Ireland, and contemplate the error of her ways. She buys back the lost O'Hara lands, and begins to restore them to their former glory (shades of post-civil war Tara). She does this so successfully that she becomes known as 'The O'Hara'. Mrs Fitzpatrick, Scarlett's housekeeper, and a secret Fenian, explains the title as originating 'in the Days of the High Kings, [when] each family had a leader, representative, champion. Today that designation has been reborn in you'.

Having fitted into Ireland successfully, Scarlett gives birth, very bloodily (and graphically) to a baby girl. To make matters a little more interesting, the birth is made possible by the local wise woman —and the baby is known locally as the witch child. Scarlett bonds immediately with her child, a fact which leads her to comment 'Hey, little baby', on its arrival—this shows that she has changed linguistically as well as emotionally. After becoming a woman of the earth, Scarlett reverts back to type, and becomes part of the leading social set in Ireland. She is taken up by a professional party organizer, and, inevitably becomes the hit of the season. In doing this she bumps into the now remarried Rhett, who has come to Ireland to buy some horses. It is interesting given the historical period and the level of development in transportation, that the protagonists seem to pop across the Atlantic, as if using Concorde rather than the steaming boats, and sail ships of the day.

Scarlett takes up with the handsome Earl of Fenton, who reminds her of Rhett. She accepts his cold proposal, although her decision to marry him makes her unpopular with the locals. The book ends with Scarlett's life in Ireland in tatters. Her house has been burned, but Rhett, in true hero fashion, turns up and saves her, and, of course, declares his undying love for her. This gives Scarlett the opportunity to tell him about his child. Scarlett and Rhett decide to return to Charleston briefly, although Rhett comments that '. . . the world is where we belong, all of it . . . we're adventurers . . . we can go anywhere, and as long as we're together it [the world] will belong to us'. This is a variation on the ' . . . tomorrow is another day' ending of *Gone with the Wind*. It also leaves the way open for *Gone with the Wind III*.

To be fair to Ripley, had this book been a normal historical saga, it would have been a good riveting read. However, in its capacity as the sequel to Mitchell's formidable novel, it fails to meet its brief. The characterization is inconsistent with the first book—both Scarlett and Rhett have changed almost beyond recognition. Similarly, gone is the authentic dialogue, and long descriptive passages which made *Gone with the Wind* an outstanding historical novel, and more than just a run-of-the-mill romance. The task of writing the sequel to probably the most famous historical novel written this century must have been a daunting one, and despite its faults, *Scarlett* is an entertaining book. It must also be remembered that Ripley has written some other very good historical works—*Charleston* and *The Time Returns* among them.

—P. Campbell

RITCHIE, Claire.
Pseudonym: Sharon Heath. **Nationality:** British. **Died:** 1979.

ROMANCE AND HISTORICAL PUBLICATIONS

Novels

The Sheltered Flame. London, Hodder and Stoughton, 1949.
Love Builds a House. London, Hodder and Stoughton, 1950.
Bright Meadows. London, Hodder and Stoughton, 1951.
Durable Fire. London, Hodder and Stoughton, 1951.
Lighted Windows. London, Hodder and Stoughton, 1952.
The Green Bough. London, Hodder and Stoughton, 1953.
The Heart Turns Homeward. London, Hodder and Stoughton, 1953.
The Gentle Wind. London, Hodder and Stoughton, 1954.
Sun on the Sea. London, Hodder and Stoughton, 1954.
Gift of the Heart. London, Hale, 1955.
Mending Flower. London, Hale, 1955.
The White Violet. London, Hale, 1956.
Dreaming River. London, Hale, 1957.
Love Will Lend Wings. London, Hale, 1957.
Date with an Angel. London, Hale, 1958.
The Sunflower's Look. London, Hale, 1958.
The Tempest and the Song. London, Hale, 1959.
Vagrant Dream. London, Hale, 1959.
Hatful of Cowslips. London, Hale, 1960.
Shadowed Paradise. London, Hale, 1960.
Sweet Bloom. London, Hale, 1961.

The Fair Adventure. London, Hale, 1961.
Doctor's Joy. London, Hale, 1962.
Heartsease Grows Here. London, Hale, 1962.
Summer at Silverwood. London, Hale, 1962.
You'll Love Me Yet. London, Hale, 1963.
Circle of Gold. London, Hale, 1964.
Ride on Singing. London, Hale, 1964.
For a Dream's Sake. London, Hale, 1965.
The Love That Follows. London, Hale, 1966.
To Greet the Morning. London, Hale, 1966.
Hope Is My Pillow. London, Hale, 1967.
As Waits the Sky. London, Hale, 1969.
This Summer's Rose. London, Hale, 1970.
Give All to Love. London, Hale, 1971.
Dream in the Heart. London, Hale, 1972.
Rainbow Romance. London, Hale, 1974.
Castle Perilous. London, Hale, 1979.
Season for Singing. London, Hale, 1979.
Lodestone for Love. London, Hale, 1980.

Novels as Sharon Heath

A Vacation for Nurse Dean. New York, Ace, 1966.
Nurse at Moorcroft Manor. New York, Ace, 1967.
Nurse on Castle Island. New York, Ace, 1968; as *Master of Trelona* (as Claire Ritchie), London, Hale, 1977.
Nurse at Shadow Manor. New York, Ace, 1973.
Nurse Elaine and the Sapphire Star. New York, Ace, 1973; as *Starshine for Sweethearts* (as Claire Ritchie), London, Hale, 1976.

OTHER PUBLICATIONS

Poetry

The White Garden and Other Poems. Crayke, Yorkshire, Guild Press, 1957.
The Mirror and Other Poems. Walton on Thames, Surrey, Outposts, 1970.

Other

Writing the Romantic Novel. London, Bond Street, 1962.

*   *   *

Claire Ritchie wrote romantic novels in the modern idiom: novels which are light and readable by young but mature adults.

The heroines in Ritchie's novels are up-to-date young ladies of their respective generations, as in *Bright Meadows* or *Castle Perilous*. The girls are not beautiful but pretty and attractive. They are generally rather ordinary, and, though somewhat experienced in love, still at a formative age. The experiences in the novels help them to mature, to develop a competence in life through a testing experience. Ritchie sets her later novels in holiday or seaside locations with some added glamour; the plots become more complex and action-filled, with an element of mystery and skulduggery which sometimes appears contrived and unrealistic, as in *Castle Perilous*.

These are moral lessons, but Ritchie learned to put them across in a more subtle way than the 'Loyalty is a rare quality nowadays' type of remark in *Bright Meadows*. The experiences of the main characters instil in them a wisdom.

The incidental details such as descriptions of women and the men who love them and the minor aspects of relationships are well handled. The novels are easy to read, having comparatively little dialogue and simple sentences. The main criticism that can be made is that the books are too chaste by modern standards. There is little passion in, for instance, *This Summer's Rose* where the hero makes do with confessing to himself that he is in love. The romantic climax of this novel is, in fact, an offer to share the middle years.

—P.R. Meldrum

RIVERS, Francine.

Nationality: American. **Born:** Berkeley, California, 12 May 1947. **Education:** University of Nevada, Reno, B.A.; California State University, Hayward. **Relations:** married Richard Rivers in 1969; two sons and one daughter. **Career:** former airline stewardess; teacher, Oakland, California. **Recipient:** Romance Writers of America golden medallion, 1985; Silver Pen award, 1986, 1987. **Agent:** Jane Jordan Browne, Multimedia Product Development Inc, 410 South Michigan Avenue, Suite 724, Chicago, Illinois 60605-1465, USA. **Address:** 364 Summer Rain Drive, Windsor, California 95493, USA.

ROMANCE AND HISTORICAL PUBLICATIONS

Novels

Kathleen. New York, Berkley, 1979.
Sycamore Hill. New York, Pinnacle, 1981.
Rebel in His Arms. New York, Ace, 1981.
This Golden Valley. New York, Berkley, 1983.
Sarina. New York, Berkley, 1983.
Hearts Divided. New York, Berkley, 1983.
Heart in Hiding. New York, Berkley, 1984.
Not So Wild a Dream. New York, Berkley, 1985.
Pagan Heart. New York, Berkley, 1985.
Outlaw's Embrace. New York, Berkley, 1986.
A Fire in the Heart. New York, Berkley, 1987.
Redeeming Love. New York, Bantam, 1991.
A Voice in the Wind. New York, Tindale, 1993.

*   *   *

Setting most of her novels in 19th-century California, Francine Rivers shows real talent in her descriptions of time and place. The reader feels the heat and dust of a California summer, sees the Sierras, and experiences some of the hardships of frontier life. *Kathleen, Sycamore Hill*, and *Rebel in His Arms* all are written in the first person, which lends a certain immediacy to the narrative, but her other novels also are fast-paced, with well-developed characters.

Frequently Rivers's heroines are young eastern girls compelled by circumstances to try their fortunes in a land alien to their experiences. Kathleen O'Reilly (*Kathleen*), raised as an orphan, discovers she is really the illegitimate child of an actress and a wealthy, married man. Her past shattered, she takes a job as governess to a rancher's niece and nephew. In *Sycamore Hill* Abby McFarland learns she has been cheated of her inheritance by her greedy guardians and must take a job as a schoolteacher in a small western town. Moira Cavendish in *This Golden Valley*, follows her brothers, the last of her family, to California, where they are caught by 'gold fever'. Amnesty Brown (*A Fire in the Heart*) is exiled after scandalizing Boston society with her radical views. Rivers's other heroines are born westerners but of widely varying classes. Kathryn Durham's family in *Rebel in His Arms* are homesteaders, while Sarina Azevedo Cahill's ancestors were among the first Spanish settlers (*Sarina*). Tempest McClaren, heroine of *Not So Wild a Dream*,

is the daughter of an Indian and a trapper, and Beth Tyrell in *Outlaw's Embrace* is a small town sheriff's daughter. No matter their background, however, all of these women demonstrate courage and fortitude when tested.

The men who match these women run the gamut of western heroes and include ranchers, sailors, a gunslinger, and a gambler. All are hard, tough men, who are changed by the gentling influence of a woman.

As might be expected, the characters face many dangers. Rivers manages to inject some new twists to these plots, although some might stretch the reader's credulity. Both Kathleen and Kathryn Durham are pursued by deranged killers from the past, who use such methods as shooting, poison, and rattlesnakes in their efforts to kill the heroines. Moira and her lover, Random Hawthorne, are almost killed by claim jumpers before they are 'rescued' by an enormous grizzly bear, the almost supernatural guardian of a huge gold deposit. Sarina, drugged with an hallucinogen, almost dies in childbirth and with her husband, Lang, survives a violent earthquake. Rivers even hints at the truly supernatural in *Sycamore Hill*. Someone terrorizes Abby McFarland by 'haunting' the schoolhouse where she lives. The ghost is supposed to be that of the previous teacher who committed suicide. After several minor accidents, Abby confronts the real villain, who confesses killing the teacher and tries to kill Abby. She is saved when the ghost attacks the killer. As a plot device, this is somewhat jarring, but a doubt remains as to whether there really was a ghost or if it is all in the heroine's imagination.

Rivers has proven herself adept at creating interesting characters, intriguing stories with more than a hint of mystery to keep the reader guessing, and spicing it all with a satisfying romance. She has not been a prolific author, but her books are all solid offerings.

—Barbara E. Kemp

ROBBINS, Kay. See HOOPER, Kay.

ROBERT, Adrian. See ST JOHN, Nicola.

ROBERTS, Elizabeth Madox

Nationality: American. **Born:** Perryville, Kentucky, 30 October 1881. Moved to Springfield, Kentucky, 1887. **Education:** Covington Institute, Springfield, Kentucky; Covington High School, Kentucky, 1896–1900; State College of Kentucky (now University of Kentucky), 1900, forced to leave due to ill-health; University of Chicago, 1917–21, Ph.B. in English, 1921 (Phi Beta Kappa); Riggs Foundation, Stockbridge, Massachusetts, 1923. **Relations:** close friends with James Cotton Noe, and associated with writers Glenway Wescott, Yvor Winters, Monroe Weeler, and the poet, Carl Sandburg. **Career:** teacher in private and public schools, Springfield, 1900–10 (went to Colorado to recover from tuberculosis). **Recipient:** McLaughlin prize for essay writing; Fiske prize, 1921, for poetry; The Poet Society's Caroline Sinkler memorial prize, 1931; O. Henry award, 1932, for 'The Sacrifice of the Maidens'. L.H.D.: Russell Sage College, Kentucky, 1933. **Died:** 13 March 1941.

ROMANCE AND HISTORICAL PUBLICATIONS

Novel

The Great Meadow. New York, Viking, and London, Cape, 1930.

OTHER PUBLICATIONS

Novels

The Time of Man. New York, Viking, 1926; London, Cape, 1927.
My Heart and My Flesh. New York, Viking, 1927; London, Cape, 1928.
Jingling in the Wind. New York, Viking, 1928; London, Cape, 1929.
A Buried Treasure. New York, Viking, 1931; London, Cape, 1932.
He Sent Forth a Raven. New York, Viking, and London, Cape, 1935.
Black Is My Truelove's Hair. New York, Viking, 1938; London, Hale, 1939.

Short Stories

The Haunted Mirror. New York, Viking, 1932; London, Cape, 1933.
Not by Strange Gods. New York, Viking, 1941.

Poetry

In the Great Steep's Garden. Colorado Springs, Gowdy-Simmons, 1915.
Under the Tree. New York, Huebsch, 1922; London, Cape, 1928; revised edition, New York, Viking, 1930.
Song in the Meadow. New York, Viking, 1940.

*

Manuscript Collection: Library of Congress, Washington, DC.

Critical Studies: *Elizabeth Madox Roberts: American Novelist* by Harry Modean Campbell and Ruel E. Foster, Norman, University of Oklahoma Press, 1956; *Herald to Chaos: The Novels of Elizabeth Madox Roberts* by Earl H. Rovit, Lexington, University of Kentucky Press, 1960; *Elizabeth Madox Roberts* by Frederick P.W. McDowell, New York, Twayne, 1963; *Fifty Southern Writers After 1900* edited by Joseph M. Flora and Robert Bain, New York, Greenwood Press, 1987; *American Novelists, 1910–1945* edited by James J. Martine, Detroit, Book Tower, 1981.

*   *   *

The works of Elizabeth Madox Roberts possess a great deal of thematic unity among themselves, and in addition, reflect a good deal of the author's own personal philosophy. Roberts's entrance into the literary world as a poet did much to influence her stylistic choices as a novelist. She blended one form into the other, trying, as she said, 'to achieve a balance where the uses of poetry and prose were identical', and focusing much of her narratives on 'the points where poetry touches life'. This lyrical approach to writing laid the foundation for a series of novels the pages of which are rich with myth and symbol, and with characters who make epic Odyssean journeys in search of themselves, discovering ultimately that the mystery of their vision of themselves evolves constantly with their shifting picture of the world around them.

Much as poetry and prose are blended together, so also are the physical and mental worlds in which her characters move closely allied. The inner and outer experiences are welded together, and her characters think not with their minds but with their whole beings, an end which comes as a direct result of Roberts's desire to 'bring the physical world close to the mind so the mind rushes out to the edge of sense' in her novels. Thus, the travels her heroines take are as much in their minds as with their bodies, as each struggles with a need to discover herself and create a harmony between herself and the earth that surrounds her. The mythical, sensual journey to ultimate spiritual rebirth can be best seen in one of Roberts's two best-known, most widely acclaimed novels, *The Great Meadow*, which is also her most historical novel.

In *The Great Meadow*, the story of pioneer woman Diony Hall's physical trek from relatively civilized Colonial Virginia to the unsettled wilds of the Kentucky territory, the spiritual development of Diony provides the backbone of the novel. The very first page has her calling out her own name, 'I, Diony Hall', as she 'subtract[s] herself from the diffused life of the house that closed about her'. Diony is clearly established from the opening paragraph as a woman searching for her own identity. After Diony marries, she travels westward with her husband, Berk Jarvis. Likewise, she travels into herself. With every step forward, she gains a greater sense of herself, and the past and the present begin to merge in her consciousness. Diony hears the bells on the horses and comes to know 'herself as the daughter of many, going back through ... England'. She becomes allied with this past, seeing a parallel between those who came before her and those who will follow after: Diony has become a pioneer, establishing her culture in a new land. She travels the symbolic road to self-discovery as she rides the trails to Kentucky.

Diony's maturation and self discovery are chronicled in a number of subtle ways which pay tribute to Roberts's skill as an author. Threads of ideas reappear throughout the novel. Long before Diony Hall became Diony Jarvis, she dreamed of rivers: 'Oh, to create rivers by knowing rivers, to move outward through the extended plain until it assumed roundness'. Here, it is interesting to note, Roberts reveals a bit of her own fascination with the thoughts of George Berkeley, an 18th-century philosopher. Berkeley argued that matter does not exist independent of one's perception of it, evident here as Diony describes 'creating rivers' by 'knowing them'. When coping with the reality of frontier life within a fort surrounded by hostile Indians, Diony reconsiders this desire for rivers, deciding that her 'pleasure of a river could wait. She knew herself to be the beginning of a new world'. Although the river is but a fleeting image in *The Great Meadow*, it clearly symbolizes Diony's growth from child to adult.

In addition to the harsh realities of life in a frontier fort, Diony Jarvis must overcome a series of other obstacles before realizing her goal of self-actualization at the conclusion of the novel. Surviving an Indian attack which killed Berk's mother, Diony faces the loss of her husband as well when Berk sets out to avenge the attack and fails to return for more than three years. In the time he is gone, Diony must again travel a path, one that necessitates her marrying again without ever having received definitive news of Berk's death. When Berk returns to the fort and finds Diony remarried and having given birth to a son by her new husband, she faces one of her most difficult challenges as she is forced to choose between the two men she loves. With the wisdom of her mythical namesake, Diony realizes that she must find 'harmony which men are able to make with one another or with a few kinds'. She has completed her journey; she recognizes the intricate web of spiritual strength which binds man to man and man to nature.

Diony's ascension to the plane of self-knowledge and her eventual ability to recognize the balance which exists between an individual and his surroundings is a theme typical of Roberts. Harry Modean Campbell and Ruel E. Foster argue, in *Elizabeth Madox Roberts: American Novelist*, that hers is 'a world constructed of two entities—external nature and the spirit of man—whose harmonious relationship is indispensable to human welfare and happiness'. Campbell and Foster also contend that Roberts's attempt to display this relationship provides the foundation for her work. Truly, the heroines of her novels discover the importance of the human spirit in overcoming the physical and emotional obstacles they face. In doing so, they fulfil one of Roberts's personal goals: she wrote of her desire to 'order ... the apparent chaos that is myself'.

Consistently throughout her novels, Roberts's characters experience a coupling of physical senses to mental processes. Events are not merely seen and comprehended. They are felt, tasted, smelled until the entire being experiences them. Roberts's mastery of diction and subtle employment of literary devices such as consonance, assonance, and onomatopoeia bring about this unity of experience, drawing the reader's senses into the experience as well. Her prose expresses the mind of her heroines with its 'poetic realism'. The reality is enhanced and heightened by the poetry of the language, rather than being glossed over or sentimentalized. The characters remain convincing. Roberts herself wrote of her belief that 'there is a connection between the world of the mind and the outer order—it is the secret of the contact that we are after, the point, the moment of union'. This is the connection for which her characters search. This is the purpose for their quest. After all, to Roberts, 'life is [driven] from within'.

—Elizabeth P. Boykin

ROBERTS, I. M. See **ROBERTS, Irene.**

ROBERTS, Irene.
Pseudonyms: Roberta Carr; Elizabeth Harle; I.M. Roberts; Ivor Roberts; Iris Rowland; Irene Shaw. **Nationality:** British. **Born:** Irene Williamson, London, 27 September 1925. **Education:** left school at age 13. **Military Service:** Women's Land Army during World War II. **Relations:** married Terence Granville Leonard Roberts in 1947; two sons and one daughter. **Career:** shop assistant, typist, and saleswoman, then journalist and writer; woman's page editor, *South Hams Review*, 1977–79, and weekly book reviewer in provincial newspapers. Since 1978, tutor in creative writing, Kingsbridge Community College, Devon. **Address:** Alpha House, Higher Town, Marlborough, Kingsbridge, South Devon TQ7 3RL, England.

ROMANCE AND HISTORICAL PUBLICATIONS

Novels (series: Ancient Egypt)

Love Song of the Sea. London, Fleetway, 1960.
Squirrel Walk. London, Gresham, 1961.
Only to Part. London, Fleetway, 1961.
Wind of Fate. London, Gresham, 1961.
Beloved Rascals. London, Gresham, 1962.
The Shrine of Marigolds. London, Gresham, 1962.
Come Back Beloved. London, Gresham, 1962.
The Dark Night. London, Fleetway, 1962.
Sweet Sorrel. London, Gresham, 1963.
Tangle of Gold Lace. London, Gresham, 1963.
Cry of the Gulls. London, Fleetway, 1963.
The Whisper of Sea-Bells. London, Hale, 1964.
Echo of Flutes. London, Hale, 1965.
The Mountain Sang. London, Hale, 1965.
Where Flamingoes Fly. London, Hale, 1966.
A Handful of Stars. London, Hale, 1967.
Shadows on the Moon. London, Hale, 1968.
Jungle Nurse. London, Hale, 1968.
Love Comes to Larkswood. London, Hale, 1968.
Alpine Nurse. London, Hale, 1968.
Nurse in the Hills. London, Hale, 1969.
The Lion and the Sun. London, Hale, 1969.

Thunder Heights. London, Hale, 1969.
Surgeon in Tibet. London, Hale, 1970.
Birds Without Bars. London, Hale, 1970.
The Shrine of Fire. London, Hale, 1970.
Gull Haven. London, Hale, 1971.
Sister at Sea. London, Hale, 1971.
Moon over the Temple. London, Hale, 1972.
The Golden Pagoda. London, Hale, 1972.
Desert Nurse. London, Hale, 1976.
Nurse in Nepal. London, Hale, 1976.
Stars above Raffael. London, Hale, 1977.
Hawks Barton. London, Hale, 1979.
Symphony of Bells. London, Hale, 1980.
Nurse Moonlight. London, Hale, 1980.
Weave Me a Moonbeam. London, Hale, 1982.
Jasmine for a Nurse. London, Hale, 1982.
Sister on Leave. London, Hale, 1982.
Nurse in the Wilderness. London, Hale, 1983.
Kingdom of the Sun (Ancient Egypt). London, Mills and Boon, 1987.
Sea Jade. London, Mills and Boon, 1987.
Song of the Nile (Ancient Egypt). London, Mills and Boon, 1987.

Novels as Iris Rowland

The Tangled Web. London, Gresham, 1962.
Island in the Mist. London, Gresham, 1962.
The Morning Star. London, Gresham, 1963.
With Fire and Flowers. London, Gresham, 1963.
Golden Flower! London, Gresham, 1964.
A Fountain of Roses. London, Gresham, 1966.
Valley of Bells. London, Gresham, 1967.
Blue Feathers. London, Gresham, 1967.
A Veil of Rushes. London, Gresham, 1967.
To Be Beloved. London, Gresham, 1968.
Rose Island. London, Gresham, 1969.
Cherries and Candlelight. London, Gresham, 1969.
Nurse at Kama Hall. London, Gresham, 1969.
Moon over Moncrieff. London, Gresham, 1969; New York, Lenox Hill Press, 1974.
The Knave of Hearts. London, Hale, 1970.
Star-Drift. London, Gresham, 1970.
Rainbow River. London, Gresham, 1970.
The Wild Summer. London, Gresham, 1970.
Orange Blossom for Tara. London, Gresham, 1971.
Blossoms in the Snow. London, Gresham, 1971.
Sister Julia. London, Hale, 1972.
To Lisa with Love. London, Hale, 1975.
Golden Bubbles. London, Hale, 1976.
Hunter's Dawn. London, Hale, 1977.
Forgotten Dreams. London, Hale, 1978.
Golden Triangle. London, Hale, 1978.
Dance Ballerina Dance. London, Hale, 1980.
The Romantic Lady. London, Hale, 1981.
Weave Me a Moonbeam. London, Hale, 1982.
Temptation. London, Hale, 1983.
Theresa. London, Hale, 1985.

Novels as Roberta Carr

Red Runs the Sunset. London, Gresham, 1963.
Sea Maiden. London, Gresham, 1965.
Fire Dragon. London, Gresham, 1967.
Golden Interlude. London, Gresham, 1970.

Novels as Elizabeth Harle

Golden Rain. London, Gresham, 1964; (as Irene Roberts) New York, Belmont, 1966.
Gay Rowan. London, Gresham, 1965.
Sandy. London, Gresham, 1967.
Spray of Red Roses. London, Gresham, 1971.
The Silver Summer. London, Hale, 1971.
Buy Me a Dream. London, Hale, 1972.
The Burning Flame. London, Hale, 1979.
Come to Me Darling. London, Hale, 1983.
Amber in Love. London, Hale, 1984.

Novels as Irene Shaw

The House of Lydia. London, Wright and Brown, 1967.
Moonstone Manor. London, Wright and Brown, 1968; as *Murder's Mansion*, New York, Doubleday, 1976.
The Olive Branch. London, Wright and Brown, 1968.

Novels as I.M. Roberts (series: Ancient Egypt; China)

The Throne Pharaohs (Ancient Egypt). London, Hale, 1974.
Hatshepsut, Queen of the Nile (Ancient Egypt). London, Hale, 1976.
Monsoon. London, Hale, 1983.
Moonpearl (China). London, Hale, 1983; revised edition (as Irene Roberts), London, Mills and Boon, 1986.
Time of the Seventh Moon (China). London, Hale, 1984.
Hour of the Tiger (China). London, Hale, 1985.

OTHER PUBLICATIONS

Novels as Ivor Roberts

Jump into Hell! London, Brown Watson, 1960.
Trial by Water. London, Micron, 1961.
Green Hell. London, Micron, 1961.

Other (for children)

Laughing Is Fun. London, Micron, 1963.
Holidays for Hanbury. London, Micron, 1964.

*

Irene Roberts comments:

To me writing is as natural as breathing. It is something that I had to do. To this end it was necessary to educate myself and learn to type and spell. Writing is, I find, as exciting as the first real spring day after a bad winter. I choose my characters and their situations from a great imaginary mixing-bowl of words that I keep in my head. I knead and shape these words into colourful beads that I love to string together in an interesting, meaningful way. While I am writing I am at one with my characters. I laugh with them and I feel their pain—that is why nine out of ten times I give them happy endings. My great interests are Ancient Egypt and China from the Opium War, Taiping and Boxer Rebellions.

*   *   *

Irene Roberts is a well-respected author, prolific as Roberta Carr, Elizabeth Harle, I.M. Roberts, Ivor Roberts, Iris Rowland, and Irene Shaw.

Her novels are set in exotic locations—India, Egypt, China, Vietnam—and contain long detailed descriptive passages which paint the background vividly for her readers. Roberts's heroines are generally young, vulnerable women, who have often experienced a bereavement. Tangy, in *Come Back Beloved*, is so traumatized by the death of her beloved father that she is driven into an almost comatose state; similarly, Kim Sunderland leaves India after her doctor father's death, only to work in harsh conditions in the Vietnamese jungle. These woman are usually extremely resilient, and given that Roberts's twisted plots throw a good deal into their paths, fundamentally they are survivors who earn the love and respect of their heroes.

The heroine often has two men who are in love with her. One is strong, and dependable (Roy Hamilton in *Echo of the Flutes*, Chris Bryant in *Birds Without Bars*, and Neil Grantham in *Jungle Nurse*), and is set up in opposition to the more frivolous, fun-loving man (Michael Lawrence in *Theresa*, and Paul, the pilot, in *Jungle Nurse*). The heroine normally chooses the more stable, strong man at the end of the book.

Roberts's novels are rescued from being run-of-the-mill romances by the introduction of a murder, mystery, or suspicious character who spices the plot up, and confuses the love story of the main characters. In *Echo of the Flutes* Myra is torn between her love for strong, sensible (and rich) Roy, and the seemingly mad Justin, who holds an unshakeable, and often indefinable attraction for her. Justin pursues Myra from London to India, having promised that he will follow her to the ends of the earth and destroy her. In a rather complicated plot twist, the reader discovers that Justin's elder brother, deranged with grief, believes that Myra killed his son in a hit and run accident, and is trying to seek his revenge by murdering her—Justin ends up saving Myra but dies in the process. Myra's dilemma of having to choose between Justin and Roy is thus solved in one easy stroke. Similarly, Tangy, in *Come Back Beloved*, gets involved with a perverted and obsessed man who promises to help her contact her dead father—she is saved by her uncle, and the man who loves her.

Although Roberts's heroines are, for the most part, chaste, the author is not afraid to introduce sex or passion into her books. Justin and Myra have an extremely obsessive passionate relationship which culminates in violent clinches, while Kully Jeffries and his live-in lover, Marsha, are involved in a frank and loving relationship—Marsha becomes pregnant before the couple marry. In Roberts's historical romances, sex is dealt with much more explicitly; sometimes forced into marriage the heroines are subjected to violent, rough sex which is seen as part of their duty to their husbands.

Roberts is a versatile writer who creates exciting, action-packed plots, and although her characters' actions may sometimes seem a little dated, her books are always an enjoyable read.

—P. Campbell

ROBERTS, Ivor. See ROBERTS, Irene.

ROBERTS, Janet Louise. American. 1925–84. See 2nd edition, 1990.

ROBERTS, Kenneth (Lewis).
Nationality: American. **Born:** Kennebunk, Maine, 8 December 1885. **Education:** schools in Malden, Massachusetts; Stone's School, Boston; Cornell University, Ithaca, New York (editor, *Cornell Widow*), 1904–08, A.B. 1908. **Military Service:** United

States Army, in the intelligence section of the Siberian Expeditionary Force, 1918–19: captain. **Relations:** married Anna Seiberling Mosser in 1911. **Career:** worked in leather business in Boston, 1908–09; reporter and columnist, Boston *Post*, 1909–18, and editor of *Sunday Post* humor page, 1915–18; editorial staff member, *Life* magazine, New York, 1915–18; correspondent, in Washington, DC, and Europe, *Saturday Evening Post*, Philadelphia, 1919–28; thereafter a full-time writer; lived in Italy, 1928–37, then in Kennebunkport, Maine. **Recipient:** special Pulitzer prize, 1957. D.Litt.: Dartmouth College, Hanover, New Hampshire, 1934; Colby College, Waterville, Maine, 1935; Bowdoin College, Brunswick, Maine, 1937; Middlebury College, Vermont, 1938; Northwestern University, Evanston, Illinois, 1945. **Member:** American Academy. **Died:** 21 July 1957.

ROMANCE AND HISTORICAL PUBLICATIONS

Novels (series: Arundel)

Arundel. New York, Doubleday, 1930; London, Lane, 1936.
The Lively Lady (Arundel). New York, Doubleday, 1931; London, Lane, 1935.
Rabble in Arms (Arundel). New York, Doubleday, 1933; London, Collins, 1939.
Captain Caution: A Chronicle of Arundel. New York, Doubleday, 1934; London, Collins, 1949.
Northwest Passage. New York, Doubleday, 1937; London, Collins, 1938.
Oliver Wiswell. New York, Doubleday, 1940; London, Collins, 1943.
Lydia Bailey. New York, Doubleday, and London, Collins, 1947.
Boon Island. New York, Doubleday, and London, Collins, 1956.

OTHER PUBLICATIONS

Plays

Panatela: A Political Comic Opera, with Romeyn Berry, music by T.J. Lindorff, H.C. Schuyler, and H.E. Childs (produced Ithaca, New York, 1907). Ithaca, New York, Cornell Masque, 1907.
The Brotherhood of Man, with Robert Garland. New York, French, 1934.

Other

Europe's Morning After. New York, Harper, 1921.
Sun Hunting: Adventures and Observations among the Native and Migratory Tribes of Florida. Indianapolis, Bobbs Merrill, 1922.
Why Europe Leaves Home. Indianapolis, Bobbs Merrill, and London, Fisher Unwin, 1922.
The Collector's Whatnot, with Booth Tarkington and Hugh Kahler. Boston, Houghton Mifflin, 1923.
Black Magic. Indianapolis, Bobbs Merrill, 1924.
Concentrated New England: A Sketch of Calvin Coolidge. Indianapolis, Bobbs Merrill, 1924.
Florida Loafing. Indianapolis, Bobbs Merrill, 1925.
Florida. New York, Harper, 1926.
Antiquamania. New York, Doubleday, 1928.
For Authors Only and Other Gloomy Essays. New York, Doubleday, 1935.
It Must Be Your Tonsils. New York, Doubleday, 1936.
Trending into Maine. Boston, Little Brown, 1938; revised edition, New York, Doubleday, 1944.
The Kenneth Roberts Reader. New York, Doubleday, 1945.

I Wanted to Write. New York, Doubleday, 1949.
Don't Say That about Maine! Waterville, Maine, Colby College Press, 1951.
Henry Gross and His Dowsing Rod. New York, Doubleday, 1951.
The Seventh Sense. New York, Doubleday, 1953.
Cowpens: The Great Morale-Builder. N.p., Westholm, 1957; as *The Battle of Cowpens*, New York, Doubleday, 1958.
Water Unlimited. New York, Doubleday, 1957.

Editor, *March to Quebec: Journals of Members of Arnold's Expedition*. New York, Doubleday, 1938; revised edition, 1940, 1953.
Editor and Translator, with Anna M. Roberts, *Moreau de St Méry's American Journey (1793–1798)*. New York, Doubleday, 1947.

*

Film Adaptations: *Northwest Passage*, 1940, *Mission of Danger*, 1959, both from the novel *Northwest Passage*.

Bibliography: *Kenneth Roberts: A Bibliography* by P. Murphy, privately printed, 1975.

Critical Study: *A Century of American History in Fiction: Kenneth Roberts' Novels* by Janet Harris, New York, Gordon Press, 1976; *Kenneth Roberts: The Man and His Works* by Jack Bales, Metuchen, New Jersey, Scarecrow Press, 1989.

*   *   *

A prolific verse, short story and editorial writer during the early years of his career, Kenneth Roberts's most memorable and lasting works of literature are found in the historical fiction created in the latter years of his life. Few authors of historical fiction can be as closely identified with the military side of the American Revolution and the early national period. A meticulous researcher, Roberts went to contemporary accounts of the events of which he wrote. He even edited the journal of John Pierce, a member of the Benedict Arnold expedition and translated a Frenchman's account of a journey to the United States. Possessing a conservative philosophy, Roberts's works reflected that perspective of people and events.

With a single exception, all of Roberts's historical fiction has a first-person narrator. His earliest historical novel, *Arundel*, is a tale of Benedict Arnold's expedition throughout the wilderness of present day Maine in an attempt to attack the British stronghold at Quebec. Steven Nason, his narrator, vividly documents the hardships of the march, the intrigues, the heroism and the cowardly actions. In a sense, Roberts tries to rehabilitate the public image of Benedict Arnold whose military reputation had been marred by his later treason. *Rabble in Arms*, continued the story of Arnold and his army from 1776 through 1777 and kept up the support of Arnold's military and naval acumen. Another narrator, Peter Merrill, appears and we see Phoebe Nason's instrumental involvement in the construction of the Colonial fleet on Lake Champlain. Unlike the earlier *Arundel*, the novel was a commercial success and set Roberts on the road to popular acceptance. Both of these novels led the way to *Northwest Passage*, a biography of Major Robert Rogers and his struggles in the French and Indian War and the quest for a northwest passage. In addition, he vividly portrayed the bureaucratic bungling associated with the quest along with the heroics of Rogers and his men. The book became an immediate bestseller and marked the peak of his writing career. Reprinted 15 times in the first year of issue, the book also found a following in Western and Central Europe.

In keeping with his interest in the least popular images of the American Revolutionary era, Roberts next wrote *Oliver Wiswell*, a tale of that time from the perspective of a loyalist. While sympathetic to the American Revolution, Roberts's narrative spoke of the short-comings of General Washington and the meanspirited conduct of the rebels. He did not fail, however, to point out the errors in judgment by the British general staff.

Lydia Bailey, his penultimate historical novel, quit the North American continent and covered not only Toussaint L'Ouverture's uprising in Haiti but the fledgling United States war with Tripoli at the beginning of the 19th century. Though the novel met with popular acceptance, its plot ranged over half the globe, its heroine appeared weak, and its adventures seemed too unbelievable. *Cowpens: The Great Morale-Builder* came to be published post-humously and told the story of the January 1781 Revolutionary War battle and its critical importance to the colonists' cause. The American leader, Daniel Morgan, comes in for praise by Roberts, when it is remembered that Morgan accompanied Benedict Arnold on his Quebec expedition.

To many European readers, it is Roberts's perception of the American Revolutionary era experience which captures the imagination. While the recipient of a special Pulitzer prize for his contribution to an interest in American history, Roberts longest lasting contribution may be in the journals he edited, the court-martial he discovered and the translation of *Moreau de St Méry's American Journey 1793–1798*.

—Frank R. Levstick

ROBERTS, Nora.
A pseudonym. **Nationality:** American. **Born:** Washington, DC. **Education:** Montgomery Blair High School, Silver Spring, Maryland. **Relations:** married Ronald Aufdem-Brinke in 1968; 2) Bruce Wilder in 1985; two sons. **Career:** secretary, Wheeler and Jarpeck, 1968–70, and R & R Lighting, 1970–75, both Maryland. **Agent:** Amy Berpower, Writers House, 21 West 26th Street, New York, New York 10010, USA.

ROMANCE AND HISTORICAL PUBLICATIONS

Novels (series: Calhoun Women; Cordina; Donovan Legacy; Hornblower; MacGregor; O'Hurley; Those Wild Ukranians)

Irish Thoroughbred. New York, Silhouette, and London, Hodder and Stoughton, 1981.
Blithe Images. New York, Silhouette, 1982.
Song of the West. New York, Silhouette, 1982.
Search for Love. New York, Silhouette, 1982.
Island of Flowers. New York, Silhouette, 1982.
The Heart's Victory. New York, Silhouette, 1982.
From This Day. New York, Silhouette, and London, Hodder and Stoughton, 1983.
Her Mother's Keeper. New York, Silhouette, 1983.
Reflections. New York, Silhouette, 1983.
Once More with Feeling. New York, Silhouette, 1983.
Untamed. New York, Silhouette, 1983; London, Hodder and Stoughton, 1984.
Dance of Dreams. New York, Silhouette, 1983.
Tonight and Always. New York, Silhouette, 1983.
This Magic Moment. New York, Silhouette, 1983.
Endings and Beginnings. New York, Silhouette, 1984.
Storm Warning. New York, Silhouette, 1984.
Sullivan's Woman. New York, Silhouette, 1984.
Rules of the Game. New York, Silhouette, 1984.
Less of a Stranger. New York, Silhouette, 1984.
A Matter of Choice. New York, Silhouette, 1984.
The Law Is a Lady. New York, Silhouette, 1984.

First Impressions. New York, Silhouette, 1984.
Opposites Attract. New York, Silhouette, 1984.
Promise Me Tomorrow. New York, Silhouette, and London, Severn House, 1984.
Playing the Odds (MacGregor). New York, Silhouette, 1985.
Partners. New York, Silhouette, 1985.
The Right Path. New York, Silhouette, 1985.
Tempting Fate (MacGregor). New York, Silhouette, 1985.
Boundary Lines. New York, Silhouette, 1985.
All the Possibilities (MacGregor). New York, Silhouette, 1985.
One Man's Art (MacGregor). New York, Silhouette, 1985.
Summer Desserts. New York, Silhouette, 1985.
Night Moves. Toronto, Harlequin, 1985.
Dual Image. New York, Silhouette, 1985.
The Art of Deception. New York, Silhouette, 1986.
Affaire Royale (Cordina). New York, Silhouette, 1986.
One Summer. New York, Silhouette, 1986.
Treasures Lost, Treasures Found. New York, Silhouette, 1986.
Risky Business. New York, Silhouette, 1986.
Lessons Learned. New York, Silhouette, 1986.
Second Nature. New York, Silhouette, 1986.
A Will and a Way. New York, Silhouette, 1986.
Home for Christmas. New York, Silhouette, 1986.
For Now, Forever (MacGregor). New York, Silhouette, 1987.
Mind Over Matter. New York, Silhouette, 1987.
Command Performance (Cordina). New York, Silhouette, 1987.
Hot Ice. New York, Bantam, 1987.
Temptation. New York, Silhouette, 1987.
The Playboy Prince (Cordina). New York, Silhouette, 1987.
Sacred Sins. New York, Bantam, 1987.
Local Hero. New York, Silhouette, 1988.
Irish Rose. New York, Silhouette, 1988.
Brazen Virtue. New York, Bantam, 1988.
The Last Honest Woman (O'Hurley). New York, Silhouette, 1988.
Dance to the Piper (O'Hurley). New York, Silhouette, 1988.
Rebellion. Toronto, Harlequin, 1988.
Skin Deep (O'Hurley). New York, Silhouette, 1988.
Name of the Game. New York, Silhouette, 1988.
Sweet Revenge. New York, Bantam, 1989.
Loving Jack. New York, Silhouette, 1989.
Best Laid Plans. New York, Silhouette, 1989.
Gabriel's Angel. Toronto, Harlequin, 1989.
Lawless. Toronto, Harlequin, 1989.
Time Was (Hornblower). New York, Silhouette, 1989; London, Silhouette, 1993.
Times Change (Hornblower). New York, Silhouette, 1989; London, Silhouette, 1993.
Taming Natasha (Those Wild Ukranians). New York, Silhouette, 1990.
Sweet Revenge. Toronto, Worldwide, 1990.
Tonight and Always. New York, Silhouette, 1990.
Partners. New York, Silhouette, 1990.
Public Secrets. New York, Bantam, 1990.
Genuine Lies. New York, Bantam, 1991.
With this Ring. Toronto, Harlequin, 1991.
Carnal Innocence. New York, Bantam, 1991.
Night Shift. New York, Silhouette, 1991.
Without a Trace (O'Hurley). New York, Silhouette, 1991.
Dual Image. New York, Silhouette, 1991.
Calhoun Women:
  Courting Catherine. New York, Silhouette, 1991.
  A Man for Amanda. New York, Silhouette, 1991.
  For the Love of Lilah. New York, Silhouette, 1991.
  Suzanna's Surrender. New York, Silhouette, 1991.
Luring a Lady (Those Wild Ukranians). New York, Silhouette, 1992.

Divine Evil. New York, Silhouette, 1992.
Honest Illusions. New York, Putnam, 1992; London, Joseph, 1993.
Donovan Legacy:
    Captivated. New York, Silhouette, 1992.
    Entranced. New York, Silhouette, 1992.
    Charmed. New York, Silhouette, 1992.
Falling for Rachel (Those Wild Ukranians). New York, Silhouette, 1993.
Private Scandals. New York, Putnam, 1993.

*

Nora Roberts commented (1989)

Over the past 10 years, I have specialized in writing romance novels. I write relationship works because I'm fascinated by relationships and why certain men and women are drawn together. In writing, my first goal is to entertain the reader. I like to think it's the finest goal any novelist can strive for.

*   *   *

Winner of many awards for her romance fiction, Nora Roberts is another of the prolific authors who have successfully expanded from category romances to mainstream single-title works. She continues to publish many original category romances even while her mainstream titles appear in hardcover editions. Her popularity in both areas is strong, so that many of her early titles have been reissued in a special 'Language of Love' series.

Roberts has written several series for Silhouette, usually revolving around a family. *Affaire Royale*, *Command Performance*, and *The Playboy Prince* tell the stories of the royal family of Cordina, a Monaco-like Mediterranean country. The fascinating MacGregor family is introduced in *Playing the Odds*, *Tempting Fate*, *All the Possibilities*, *One Man's Art*, *For Now, Forever*. The 'Donovan Legacy' is a trilogy about three cousins with special powers (*Captivated*, *Charmed*, and *Entranced*). This series is especially interesting in that Roberts successfully makes the reader believe, at least for a little while, that witches, healers, and psychics really do exist in present-day California. Her characters are presented as real people, not fantasy figures. The 'Calhoun Women' and 'Those Wild Ukranians' are other family series. All of these series have proven to be very popular, perhaps because they allow readers to develop a closer relationship to the characters. Roberts develops them with such skill that there is a real sense of belonging and continuity, much as there is in a real family.

A favourite Roberts plot is to place the heroine in real physical danger, often because of the hero himself. Blaming himself for her risk of injury, he realizes also the depth of his love and regrets not making a stronger commitment before she has been placed in jeopardy. In *Playing the Odds*, Justin Blade has been stalked by the son of a man he had killed in self defense many years ago. He bitterly blames himself when his lover, Serena MacGregor, is kidnapped and held hostage by his deranged tormentor. He is anguished because although he is a man of action and strength, he is essentially powerless to help her. Alexander, the Crown Prince of Cordina, is faced with a similar situation. His entire family is threatened by a criminal seeking revenge. Both his sister and his brother face danger in the 'Cordina' series, but in *Command Performance*, Alex's love, Eve, is almost caught in an explosion set as a warning. Later she takes a bullet to save him. Like Justin, Alex blames himself for not protecting the person he loves most. In *Night Shadow* Roberts adds even more suspense to a story of stalking danger. The hero is a masked crime fighter called Nemesis, who is bent on justice in a crime-ridden city.

Roberts provides some entertaining fantasy with the stories of the Hornblower brothers, travellers from 300 years in the future. Caleb Hornblower decides to remain in the 20th century with Liberty Stone in *Time Was*. In *Time Changes* Jacob, Caleb's brother, returns to take him 'back to the future', but instead meets Caleb's sister-in-law, Sunny Stone. Jacob and Sunny eventually return to his time, the year 2254, but Roberts leaves them discussing a possible return to visit Sunny's family for the holidays.

In her longer novels of romance and suspense, Roberts effectively creates tension and a sense of danger by developing an uneasy atmosphere that at times almost seems to be a character itself. While the outcome is never really in doubt, uncertainty and danger surround the hero and heroine. Several themes and plots recur in these titles. Psychopathic killers menace the heroines in *Sacred Sins*, *Brazen Virtue*, and *Carnal Innocence*. Jewel thieves are featured in *Hot Ice*, *Sweet Revenge*, and *Honest Illusions*. Past crimes create the current danger in *Sweet Revenge*, *Honest Illusions*, and *Divine Evil*. Repressed childhood memories of the heroine who witnessed something terrible trigger violence in *Divine Evil* and *Public Secrets*. In spite of such similarities, however, Roberts's skill in setting the scene and developing her characters as individuals keeps her work from being formulaic. While the situations may be familiar, the characters are not interchangable. She effectively builds suspense and tension to a heartstopping climax. For example, in *Sacred Sins* Tess Court, a psychiatrist, is helping the police track a serial killer. The reader can feel the tension build as Roberts conveys the killer's mental disintegration. Along with Tess and Ben Paris, a homicide detective, the reader also comes to realize that Tess will be the next victim. The unmasking of the killer provides an unexpected twist that surprises everyone. In *Brazen Virtue* Ben's partner, Ed Jackson investigates the murder of a phone-sex operator. Grace McCabe, the victim's sister, begins to investigate the crime herself and essentially teams up with Ed. Eventually she becomes a target too. Again the killer's identity is unusual and his final confrontation with Grace and Ed is tense.

Roberts's well deserved reputation and following are based on her skill as a writer. Readers know that she will provide an interesting, often adventure-filled plot, colourful, well-researched settings, well-defined, believable characters, and a satisfying love story. Consistency and quality are hallmarks of her work.

—Barbara E. Kemp

ROBERTS, Paula.   See LORIN, Amii.

ROBERTS, Willo Davis.
Nationality: American. **Born:** Grand Rapids, Michigan, 29 May 1928. **Education:** high school in Pontiac, Michigan, graduated 1946. **Relations:** married David W. Roberts in 1949; two daughters and two sons. **Career:** worked in hospitals and doctors' offices, 1964–72; currently conducts a writers' workshop in Granite Falls, Washington. **Recipient:** Mark Twain award, 1980, and Winner Young Readers of California award, 1980, for *The Girl with the Silver Eyes*; Mark Twain award, 1985, for *Baby Sitting Is a Dangerous Job*; Mystery Writers of America Edgar Allan Poe award, 1989, for *Megan's Island*; Washington Governor's award, 1990. **Agent:** Curtis Brown, 10 Astor Place, New York, New York 10019, USA. **Address:** 12020 West Engebretsen Road, Granite Falls, Washington 98252, USA.

ROMANCE AND HISTORICAL PUBLICATIONS

Novels (series: The Black Pearl)

Murder at Grand Bay. New York, Arcadia House, 1955.

The Girl Who Wasn't There. New York, Arcadia House, 1957.
Murder Is So Easy. Fresno, California, Vega, 1961.
The Suspected Four. Fresno, California, Vega, 1962.
Nurse Kay's Conquest. New York, Ace, 1966.
Once a Nurse. New York, Ace, 1966.
Nurse at Mystery Villa. New York, Ace, 1967.
Return to Darkness. New York, Lancer, 1969.
Shroud of Fog. New York, Ace, 1970.
Devil Boy. New York, New American Library, 1970; London, New English Library, 1971.
The Waiting Darkness. New York, Lancer, 1970.
Shadow of a Past Love. New York, Lancer, 1970.
The House at Fern Canyon. New York, Lancer, 1970.
The Tarot Spell. New York, Lancer, 1970.
Invitation to Evil. New York, Lancer, 1970.
The Terror Trap. New York, Lancer, 1971.
King's Pawn. New York, Lancer, 1971.
The Gates of Montrain. New York, Lancer, 1971.
The Watchers. New York, Lancer, 1971.
The Ghosts of Harrel. New York, Lancer, 1971.
Inherit the Darkness. New York, Lancer, 1972.
Nurse in Danger. New York, Ace, 1972.
Becca's Child. New York, Lancer, 1972.
Sing a Dark Song. New York, Lancer, 1972.
The Nurses. New York, Ace, 1972; as *The Secret Lives of the Nurses*, London, Pan, 1975.
The Face of Danger. New York, Lancer, 1972.
Dangerous Legacy. New York, Lancer, 1972.
Sinister Gardens. New York, Lancer, 1972.
The MD. New York, Lancer, 1972.
The Evil Children. New York, Lancer, 1973.
The Gods in Green. New York, Lancer, 1973.
Nurse Robin. New York, Lenox Hill Press, 1973.
Didn't Anybody Know My Wife? New York, Putnam, 1974; London, Hale, 1978.
White Jade. New York, Doubleday, 1975.
Key Witness. New York, Putnam, 1975; London, Hale, 1978.
Expendable. New York, Doubleday, 1976; London, Hale, 1979.
The Jaubert Ring. New York, Doubleday, 1976.
The House of Imposters. New York, Popular Library, 1977.
Cape of Black Sands. New York, Popular Library, 1977.
Act of Fear. New York, Doubleday, 1977; London, Hale, 1978.
The Black Pearl series:
    The Dark Dowry. New York, Popular Library, 1978.
    The Cade Curse. New York, Popular Library, 1978.
    The Stuart Stain. New York, Popular Library, 1978.
    The Devil's Double. New York, Popular Library, 1979.
    The Radkin Revenge. New York, Popular Library, 1979.
    The Hellfire Heritage. New York, Popular Library, 1979.
    The Macomber Menace. New York, Popular Library, 1979.
    The Gresham Ghost. New York, Popular Library, 1980.
The Search for Willie. New York, Popular Library, 1980.
Destiny's Woman. New York, Popular Library, 1980.
The Face at the Window. Toronto, Harlequin, and New York, Raven Press, 1981; London, Hale, 1983.
A Long Time to Hate. New York, Avon, 1982.
The Gallant Spirit. New York, Popular Library, 1982.
Days of Valor. New York, Warner, 1983.
The Sniper. New York, Doubleday, 1984.
Keating's Landing. New York, Warner, 1984.
The Annalise Experiment. New York, Doubleday, 1985.
My Rebel, My Love. New York, Pocket Books, 1986.
To Share a Dream. Toronto, Worldwide, 1986.
Madawaska. Toronto, Worldwide, 1988.

OTHER PUBLICATIONS

Other (for children)

The View from the Cherry Tree. New York, Atheneum, 1975.
Don't Hurt Laurie! New York, Atheneum, 1977.
The Minden Curse. New York, Atheneum, 1978; London, Macmillan, 1990.
More Minden Curses. New York, Atheneum, 1980; London, Macmillan, 1990.
The Girl with the Silver Eyes. New York, Atheneum, 1980.
House of Fear. New York, Scholastic, 1983.
The Pet-Sitting Peril. New York, Atheneum, 1983; London, Macmillan, 1985.
No Monsters in the Closet. New York, Atheneum, 1983.
Eddie and the Fairy Godpuppy. New York, Atheneum, 1984.
Elizabeth. New York, Scholastic, 1984.
Caroline. New York Scholastic, 1984.
Baby Sitting Is a Dangerous Job. New York, Atheneum, 1985.
Victoria. New York, Scholastic, 1985.
The Magic Book. New York, Atheneum, 1986.
Sugar Isn't Everything. New York, Atheneum, 1987.
Megan's Island. New York, Atheneum, 1988; London, Macmillan, 1990.
What Could Go Wrong? New York, Atheneum, 1989.
Nightmare. New York, Atheneum, and London, Macmillan, 1989.
To Grandmother's House. New York, Atheneum, 1990.
Scared Stiff. New York, Atheneum, 1990.
Dark Secrets. New York, Fawcett, 1991.
Jo and the Bandit. New York, Atheneum, 1992.
What Are We Going to Do about David?. New York, Atheneum, 1993.

*

Manuscript Collections: Bowling Green University, Ohio; Central Missouri State University.

*   *   *

The first quality which one recognizes in Willo Davis Roberts's work is her inclusion and perceptive descriptions of accident 'victims' and/or health problems. The penchant and thoroughness of her depiction may be the result of her medical training. In any event this accuracy lends credibility to her facile, trim plots. The majority of her novels emphasize mystery-romance more than gothic. *Invitation to Evil, King's Pawn,* and *Shroud of Fog,* all deal with deadly danger, catenulate episodes leading up to the answer to 'who did it'. Many of her novels have New England settings, and Roberts appears well-versed in this topography, placing the novels in remote areas. The elements of mystery are straightforward and unruffled: a concubitant heroine meets a hero with more than an abundance of panache, usually a man of almost superhuman indestructibility. Physical suffering in proportions excelling what mere mortals could endure occurs during the plot development. Events that at first seem tangentially related become part of the not-too-complicated interplay.

The heroine in *King's Pawn* continually and desperately needs to be reassured, assuming a volitionless capacity and eagerness to believe in the hero after the crises she endures; kidnapping, a fall from the tower into the ocean, etc. This is a plausible response, therefore, and she never becomes the awe-inspiring blank found in the heroines of many other romance novelists' pages. Indeed, the pain which the heroine suffers is vividly described, forcing the reader to explore and experience the discomfort with the victim. The graphic detail enables the reader to excuse the air of the miraculous which surrounds her survival.

A problem encountered frequently in her novels is her too hastily drawn conclusions in which all the sources of tension are conveniently reconciled. The abrupt endings are particularly disturbing in light of the otherwise well-constructed exposition.

Although her conclusions are often a disappointment, the reader can none the less be caught up in Roberts's love of the mystery.

—W.M. von Zharen

ROBINS, Denise (Naomi).
Pseudonyms: Denise Chesterton; Ashley French; Harriet Gray; Hervey Hamilton; Julia Kane; Francesca Wright. **Nationality:** British. **Born:** Denise Naomi Klein, London, 1 February 1897. **Education:** schools in Staten Island, New York, and San Diego, and at The Convent, Upper Norwood, London. **Relations:** married 1) Arthur Robins in 1918 (divorced 1938), three daughters, including Claire Lorrimer, *q.v.*; 2) R. O'Neill Pearson in 1939. **Career:** journalist, Dundee *Courier*, Scotland, 1914–15, then freelance writer, broadcaster, and journalist. After 1945 editor of the advice column, *She* magazine, London. Founding member, 1960, and president, 1960–66, Romantic Novelists Association. **Died:** 1 May 1985.

ROMANCE AND HISTORICAL PUBLICATIONS

Novels

The Marriage Bond. London, Hodder and Stoughton, 1924.
Sealed Lips. London, Hodder and Stoughton, 1924.
The Forbidden Bride. London, Newnes, 1926.
The Man Between. London, Newnes, 1926.
The Passionate Awakening. London, Newnes, 1926.
Forbidden Love. London, Newnes, 1927.
The Inevitable End. London, Mills and Boon, 1927.
Jonquil. London, Mills and Boon, 1927.
The Triumph of the Rat. London, Philip Allan, 1927.
Desire Is Blind. London, Mills and Boon, 1928.
The Passionate Flame. London, Mills and Boon, 1928.
White Jade. London, Mills and Boon, 1928.
Women Who Seek. London, Mills and Boon, 1928.
The Dark Death. London, Mills and Boon, 1929.
The Enduring Flame. London, Mills and Boon, 1929; New York, Ballantine, 1975.
Heavy Clay. London, Mills and Boon, 1929.
Love Was a Jest. London, Mills and Boon, 1929.
And All Because. . . . London, Mills and Boon, 1930; as *Love's Victory*, New York, Watt, 1933.
It Wasn't Love. London, Mills and Boon, 1930.
Swing of Youth. London, Mills and Boon, 1930.
Heat Wave: The Story of the Play by Roland Pertwee. London, Mills and Boon, 1930.
Crowns, Pounds, and Guineas. London, Mills and Boon, 1931; as *The Wild Bird*, New York, Watt, 1932.
Fever of Love. London, Mills and Boon, 1931.
Lovers of Janine. London, Mills and Boon, 1931.
Second Best. London, Mills and Boon, 1931; New York, Watt, 1933.
Blaze of Love. London, Mills and Boon, 1932.
The Boundary Line. London, Mills and Boon, and New York, Watt, 1932.
The Secret Hour. London, Mills and Boon, 1932.
There Are Limits. London, Mills and Boon, 1932; as *No Sacrifice*, New York, Watt, 1934.
Gay Defeat. London, Mills and Boon, 1933.
Life's a Game. London, Mills and Boon, 1933.

Men Are Only Human. London, Mills and Boon, and New York, Macaulay, 1933.
Shatter the Sky. London, Mills and Boon, 1933.
Strange Rapture. London, Mills and Boon, 1933.
Brief Ecstasy. London, Mills and Boon, 1934; New York, Ballantine, 1976.
Never Give All. London, Mills and Boon, and New York, Macaulay, 1934.
Slave-Woman. London, Mills and Boon, 1934; New York, Macaulay, 1935.
Sweet Love. London, Mills and Boon, 1934.
All This for Love. London, Mills and Boon, 1935.
Climb to the Stars. London, Nicholson and Watson, 1935.
How Great the Price. London, Mills and Boon, 1935.
Life and Love. London, Nicholson and Watson, 1935; New York, Avon, 1978.
Murder in Mayfair (novelization of play). London, Mills and Boon, 1935.
Love Game. London, Nicholson and Watson, 1936.
Those Who Love. London, Nicholson and Watson, 1936.
Were I Thy Bride. London, Nicholson and Watson, 1936; New York, Pyramid, 1966; as *Betrayal*, London, Hodder and Stoughton, 1976.
Kiss of Youth. London, Nicholson and Watson, 1937; New York, Avon, 1975.
Set Me Free. London, Nicholson and Watson, 1937.
The Tiger in Men. London, Nicholson and Watson, 1937; New York, Avon, 1979.
The Woman's Side of It. London, Nicholson and Watson, 1937.
Family Holiday (as Hervey Hamilton). London, Nicholson and Watson, 1937.
Restless Heart. London, Nicholson and Watson, 1938; New York, Arcadia House, 1940.
Since We Love. London, Nicholson and Watson, 1938; New York, Arcadia House, 1941.
You Have Chosen. London, Nicholson and Watson, 1938; New York, Ballantine, 1975.
Dear Loyalty. London, Nicholson and Watson, 1939.
Gypsy Lover. London, Nicholson and Watson, 1939.
I, Too, Have Loved. London, Nicholson and Watson, 1939; New York, Avon, 1979.
Officer's Wife. London, Nicholson and Watson, 1939.
Island of Flowers. London, Nicholson and Watson, 1940; New York, Avon, 1977.
Little We Know. London, Hutchinson, 1940.
Sweet Sorrow. London, Nicholson and Watson, 1940; as *Forget That I Remember*, New York, Arcadia House, 1940.
To Love Is to Live. London, Hutchinson, 1940.
If This Be Destiny. London, Hutchinson, 1941.
Set the Stars Alight. London, Hutchinson, 1941; New York, Avon, 1979.
Winged Love. London, Hutchinson, 1941; New York, Avon, 1978.
Love Is Enough. London, Hutchinson, 1941; New York, Avon, 1975.
This One Night. London, Hutchinson, 1942; New York, Avon, 1975.
War Marriage. London, Hutchinson, 1942; as *Let Me Love*, London, Hodder and Stoughton, 1979.
What Matters Most. London, Hutchinson, 1942.
The Changing Years. London, Hutchinson, 1943; New York, Beagle, 1974.
Daughter Knows Best. London, Hutchinson, 1943.
Dust of Dreams. London, Hutchinson, 1943; New York, Avon, 1976.
Escape to Love. London, Hutchinson, 1943; New York, Avon, 1976.

This Spring of Love. London, Hutchinson, 1943.

War Changes Everything. London, Todd, 1943.

Give Me Back My Heart. London, Hutchinson, 1944; New York, Avon, 1976.

How to Forget. London, Hutchinson, 1944.

Never Look Back. London, Hutchinson, 1944.

Desert Rapture. London, Hutchinson, 1945; New York, Avon, 1979.

Love So Young. London, Hutchinson, 1945.

All for You. London, Hutchinson, 1946; New York, Ballantine, 1975.

Heart's Desire. London, Foster, 1946.

Greater Than All. London, Hutchinson, 1946.

Separation. London, Foster, 1946.

The Story of Veronica. London, Hutchinson, 1946.

Figs in Frost (as Hervey Hamilton). London, Macdonald, 1946.

Forgive Me, My Love. Hanley, Staffordshire, Docker, 1947.

More Than Love. London, Hutchinson, 1947.

Could I Forget. London, Hutchinson, 1948; New York, Avon, 1976.

Khamsin. London, Hutchinson, 1948; New York, Avon, 1978.

Love Me No More! London, Hutchinson, 1948.

The Hard Way. London, Hutchinson, 1949.

To Love Again. London, Hutchinson, 1949; Toronto, Harlequin, 1961.

The Uncertain Heart. London, Hutchinson, 1949; New York, Avon, 1977.

The Feast Is Finished. London, Hutchinson, 1950; New York, Avon, 1979.

Love Hath an Island. London, Hutchinson, 1950.

Heart of Paris. London, Hutchinson, 1951.

Infatuation. London, Hutchinson, 1951.

Only My Dreams. London, Hutchinson, 1951; New York, Avon, 1976.

Second Marriage. London, Hutchinson, 1951; New York, Avon, 1979.

Something to Love. London, Hutchinson, 1951.

The Other Love. London, Hutchinson, 1952.

Strange Meeting. London, Hutchinson, 1952.

The First Long Kiss. London, Hutchinson, 1953; New York, Avon, 1976.

My True Love. London, Hutchinson, 1953; New York, Avon, 1977.

The Loves of Lucrezia (as Francesca Wright). London, Rich and Cowan, 1953; New York, Popular Library, 1954.

The Long Shadow. London, Hutchinson, 1954; New York, Avon, 1979.

Venetian Rhapsody. London, Hutchinson, 1954; New York, Avon, 1979.

Bitter-Sweet. London, Hutchinson, 1955.

The Unshaken Loyalty. London, Hutchinson, 1955.

All That Matters. London, Hutchinson, 1956.

The Enchanted Island. London, Hutchinson, 1956; New York, Avon, 1974.

The Seagull's Cry. London, Hutchinson, 1957; New York, Avon, 1979.

The Noble One. London, Hodder and Stoughton, 1957.

Chateau of Flowers. London, Hodder and Stoughton, 1958.

Do Not Go, My Love. London, Hodder and Stoughton, 1959; New York, Ballantine, 1974.

We Two Together. London, Hodder and Stoughton, 1959.

The Unlit Fire. London, Hodder and Stoughton, 1960.

Arrow in the Heart. London, Hodder and Stoughton, 1960.

I Should Have Known. London, Hodder and Stoughton, 1961.

A Promise for Ever. London, Hodder and Stoughton, 1961.

Put Back the Clock. London, Hodder and Stoughton, 1962; New York, Pyramid, 1967.

Mad Is the Heart. London, Hodder and Stoughton, 1963.

Nightingale's Song. London, Hodder and Stoughton, 1963; New York, Pyramid, 1966.

Reputation. London, Hodder and Stoughton, 1963.

Meet Me in Monte Carlo. London, Arrow, 1964; New York, Avon, 1979.

Moment of Love. London, Hodder and Stoughton, 1964; New York, Pyramid, 1966.

Loving and Giving. London, Hodder and Stoughton, 1965; New York, Ballantine, 1975.

The Strong Heart. London, Hodder and Stoughton, 1965.

O Love! O Fire! London, Panther, 1966.

Lightning Strikes Twice. London, Hodder and Stoughton, 1966.

The Crash. London, Hodder and Stoughton, 1966.

Wait for Tomorrow. London, Hodder and Stoughton, 1967.

House of the Seventh Cross. London, Hodder and Stoughton, 1967; as *House by the Watch Tower*, New York, Arcadia House, 1968.

Laurence, My Love. London, Hodder and Stoughton, 1968.

Love and Desire and Hate. London, Hodder and Stoughton, 1969.

A Love Like Ours. London, Hodder and Stoughton, 1969; New York, Ballantine, 1976.

She-Devil: The Story of Jezebel (as Francesca Wright). London, Corgi, 1970; revised edition, as *Jezebel* (as Denise Robins), London, Hodder and Stoughton, 1977.

Sweet Cassandra. London, Hodder and Stoughton, 1970.

Forbidden. London, Hodder and Stoughton, 1971.

The Snow Must Return. London, Hodder and Stoughton, 1971.

The Other Side of Love. London, Hodder and Stoughton, 1973; New York, Ballantine, 1975.

Twice Have I Loved. London, Hodder and Stoughton, 1973; New York, Ballantine, 1975.

Dark Corridor. London, Hodder and Stoughton, 1974.

Come Back Yesterday. London, Hodder and Stoughton, 1976.

Fauna (omnibus). New York, Avon, 1978.

Novels as Ashley French

Once Is Enough. London, Hutchinson, 1953.

The Bitter Core. London, Hutchinson, 1954.

Breaking Point. London, Hutchinson, 1956; (as Denise Robins), New York, Bantam, 1975.

Novels as Harriet Gray

Gold for the Gay Masters. London, Rich and Cowan, 1954; New York, Avon, 1956.

Bride of Doom. London, Rich and Cowan, 1956; as *Bride of Violence*, New York, Avon, 1957.

The Flame and the Frost. London, Rich and Cowan, 1957; in *Fauna* (as Denise Robins), 1978.

Dance in the Dust. London, Hale, 1959; (as Denise Robins), New York, Avon, 1978.

My Lady Destiny. London, Hale, 1961; (as Denise Robins), New York, Avon, 1978.

Novels as Denise Chesterton

Two Loves. London, Merit, 1955; (as Denise Robins), New York, Bantam, 1975.

The Price of Folly. London, Merit, 1955.

When a Woman Loves. London, Merit, 1955.

Novels as Julia Kane

Dark Secret Love. London, Hodder and Stoughton, 1962.

The Sin Was Mine. London, Hodder and Stoughton, 1964.

Time Runs Out. London, Hodder and Stoughton, 1965.

Short Stories

One Night in Ceylon and Others. London, Mills and Boon, 1931.
Light the Candles. London, Hurst and Blackett, 1959.

OTHER PUBLICATIONS

Play

Light the Candles, with Michael Pertwee, adaptation of the story by
    Robins. London, English Theatre Guild, 1957.

Poetry

Love Poems and Others. London, Mills and Boon, 1930.

Other

Stranger Than Fiction: Denise Robins Tells Her Life Story. London,
    Hodder and Stoughton, 1965.

Editor, *The World of Romance* (anthology). London, New English
    Library, 1964.

                    *   *   *

Denise Robins is worth noting not just for her prolificacy in writing around 170 novels in over 50 years, but for the variety of subject
and character treatment she has produced within this genre. Most of
her books concentrate on the contemporary love story, and she has
exploited nearly every conceivable situation both inside and outside
marriage. Even in her early works, the often taboo subjects of
divorce and extra-marital relationships are handled with care and
sensitivity, as in the poignant *More Than Love*, in which a young
girl tells of her affair with a married man, and all the problems such a
relationship incurs. Both *Put Back the Clock* and *The Crash* concern
marriage on the rebound; *The Bitter Core* deals with the marriage of
a woman in her forties to a much younger man; *Give Me Back My
Heart* is about an arranged marriage and the girl's struggle to marry
the man of her choice; while *O Love! O Fire!* introduces the moral
dilemma facing Candy, who, after much heart-searching, sleeps
with her boyfriend, only to become pregnant and bear his child
while realizing gradually that her love was mere infatuation.
Another controversial topic, even today, that of a mother leaving her
children with their father, is the theme of both *Figs in Frost* and
Once Is Enough. The latter tells of a mother's attempts to see her
daughter against her estranged husband's will; her mental anguish,
the child's bewilderment at being the centre of the struggle, and the
subsequent, inevitable tragedy are all movingly described.
Occasionally the fast-moving plots sport equal measures of suspense and romance, as in the strong and passionate drama *Heat
Wave*, set in Malaya.
    The characters and settings are equally as varied as the themes.
The central protagonists range in age from 18 to the mid-forties, and
vary considerably in temperament and social background; they are
treated in reasonable depth, changed for good or bad by the physical
and emotional experiences they undergo. The settings of the novels
embrace the streets of London, fashionable Paris, the Swiss mountains, and more exotic places such as Egypt, Ceylon, and Morocco,
described with just enough authenticity to imbue the story with their
particular flavour; sometimes a place is set more firmly in the memory, like the Chateau de Lurmines in *The Snow Must Return*. The
character of each decade of the 20th century can also be seen over
the range of her novels, especially in fashion details, the intrusion of
World War II, the slowly changing attitudes towards divorce and infidelity, and the freedom of women in particular regarding careers

and financial and moral independence, and the author keeps up-to-
date with both social and political scenes in order to give each novel
a realistic touch.
    Robins has also produced five historical romances under the
pseudonym Harriet Gray. *Gold for the Gay Masters*, *Bride of Doom*,
and *The Flame and the Frost* make up a trilogy set in the late
Georgian and early Victorian periods, tracing the history of a beautiful quadroon slave and her descendants. The stories are well punctuated with dramatic climaxes, moving fast and furiously against a
rich backcloth of elaborately painted characters and settings. The
two fictional biographies about Lucrezia Borgia and Jezebel, written under the name Francesca Wright, are highly embellished accounts, but equally well filled with drama, romance, and excitement.
Of her two collections of short stories, *One Night in Ceylon and
Others* is by far the stronger work, with each tale a swift, vigorous
slice of life, often with a neat, unexpected twist at the end, as in 'Perfectly Acted', 'This Is Marriage', and the title story.
    Although with such a vast output some of her work is bound to be
slighter in form, lacking pace, less well worked-out, and with
weaker characterization, Robins writes with a smooth, firm confidence gained from years of consistent popularity; plot and sub-plot
move rapidly in a polished flow across the page, the various
entanglements neatly resolving to a happy climax, with the passions
of both young and old relayed with a sympathy born of experience
and observation.

                                                    —Tessa Rose Chester

                              _____

ROBINS, Gina.   See FINCH, Carol

                              _____

ROBINS, Patricia.   See LORRIMER, Claire.

                              _____

ROBY, Mary Linn.
Pseudonyms: Pamela D'Arcy; Georgina Grey; Elizabeth Welles;
Mary Wilson. **Nationality:** American. **Born:** Bangor, Maine, 31
March 1930. **Education:** University of Maine, Orono, B.A. 1951
(Phi Beta Kappa). **Relations:** married Kinley E. Roby in 1951; two
children. **Career:** History teacher at State College High School,
Pennsylvania, and Orono High School. Since 1972, English teacher,
Concord/Carlisle High School, Massachusetts. **Address:** c/o Dell,
666 Fifth Avenue, New York, New York 10103, USA.

ROMANCE AND HISTORICAL PUBLICATIONS

Novels

Still as the Grave. New York, Dodd Mead, 1964; London, Collins,
    1965.
Afraid of the Dark. New York, Dodd Mead, 1965.
Before I Die. London, Hale, 1966.
Cat and Mouse. London, Hale, 1967.
In the Dead of the Night. New York, New American Library, 1969.
Pennies on Her Eyes. New York, New American Library, 1969.
All Your Lovely Words Are Spoken. New York, Ace, 1970.
Some Die in Their Beds. New York, New American Library, 1970.
If She Should Die. New York, New American Library, 1970.
Lie Quiet in Your Grave. New York, New American Library, 1970.
That Fatal Touch. New York, New American Library, 1970.
Dig a Narrow Grave. New York, New American Library, 1971.

This Land Turns Evil Slowly. New York, New American Library, 1971.
Reap the Whirlwind. New York, New American Library, 1972.
And Die Remembering. New York, New American Library, 1972.
When the Witch Is Dead. New York, New American Library, 1972.
The White Peacock. New York, Hawthorn, 1972; as *The Cry of the Peacock*, Aylesbury, Buckinghamshire, Milton House, 1974.
Shadow over Grove House. New York, New American Library, 1973.
Speak No Evil of the Dead. New York, New American Library, 1973.
The House at Kilgallen. New York, New American Library, 1973.
The Broken Key. New York, Hawthorn, 1973; Aylesbury, Buckinghamshire, Milton House, 1974.
Marsh House. New York, Hawthorn, 1974; London, Milton House, 1975.
The Tower Room. New York, Hawthorn, 1974; London, Milton House, 1975.
The Silent Walls. New York, New American Library, 1974.
Christobel. New York, Berkley, 1976.
The Treasure Chest. New York, Berkley, 1976.
Seagull Crag (as Elizabeth Welles). New York, Pocket Books, 1977.
The Hidden Book. New York, Berkley, 1977.
Trapped. New York, Dell, 1977.
A Heritage of Strangers. New York, Dell, 1978.
Fortune's Smile. New York, Warner, 1979.
My Lady's Mask. New York, Warner, 1979.
Passing Fancy. New York, Dell, 1980.
Love's Wilful Call. New York, Warner, 1981.

Novels as Mary Wilson

The Changeling. New York, Dell, 1975.
Wind of Death. New York, Dell, 1976.

Novels as Georgina Grey

The Hesitant Heir. New York, Fawcett, 1978.
Turn of the Cards. New York, Fawcett, 1979.
Both Sides of the Coin. New York, Fawcett, 1980.
Fashion's Frown. New York, Fawcett, 1980.
Franklin's Folly. New York, Fawcett, 1980.
The Last Cotillion. New York, Fawcett, 1980.
The Bartered Bridegroom. New York, Fawcett, 1981.
The Queen's Quadrille. New York, Fawcett, 1981.
The Reluctant Rivals. New York, Fawcett, 1981.

Novels as Pamela D'Arcy

Angel in the House. New York, Berkley, 1980.
Heritage of the Heart. New York, Berkley, 1980.
Magic Moment. New York, Berkley, 1980.

*   *   *

Whether she is writing a contemporary gothic or a historical romance, Mary Linn Roby manages to produce a competent, if not exceptional, novel.

Her gothics have all the required ingredients: brooding manors, danger and murder, complicated personal relationships (at least one of which will obviously lead to love), and last minute denouements. *The Tower Room* is a good example of Roby's gothic formula. Family and acquaintances gather in an isolated cliffside castle. An autocratic old woman manipulates those around her, reviving old memories and reopening old wounds. Several murders take place

and the young heroine finds herself in danger. Everyone is under suspicion, although the reader obviously knows that the hero and heroine are innocent. The tangled plot is gradually unraveled, the true villain revealed, and justice quickly and efficiently served.

Like her gothics, Roby's Regency romances can be viewed as good representatives of the prevailing formula for the genre. Bright, independent heroines and steadfast heroes overcome numerous obstacles to find true love and happiness. Roby does show one common theme or motif in these romances: the stage or the roles and impersonations carried out by the characters. A major stumbling block to Jennifer's happiness in *Passing Fancy* is the deception practiced by the Earl of Watching when he poses as the less important Sir John Evans. In *Love's Wilful Call* Hannah struggles to follow her father's footsteps in the theatre, yet when she reaches her goal she realizes that she really yearns more for the love of Lord Derwent. Roby brings both themes together in *My Lady's Mask*. Caroline plays the role of a great society lady and becomes involved with several theatre people, most notably the playwright, Lord Troyan, to whom she loses her heart. In spite of many difficulties encountered by the characters, Roby manages to end all of these novels in a happy spate of engagements and weddings. In the category of happy endings, however, few novels can beat *Fortune's Smile*, in which Roby provides at least four engagements and hints at two more to come, all in the final two chapters. Everyone is provided with a satisfactory partner.

As an author of both gothic novels and historical romances, Roby knows the conventions. She includes all the right elements, and the results are enjoyable but lack that extra spark that puts an author's work in the first rank.

—Barbara E. Kemp

ROCKFERN, Danielle. See **NOLAN, Frederick.**

ROFFMAN, Jan. See **SUMMERTON, Margaret.**

ROGERS, Rosemary.
Nationality: American. **Born:** Rosemary Jansz, Panadura, Ceylon (now Sri Lanka), 7 December 1932. **Education:** University of Ceylon, Colombo, B.A. **Relations:** married 1) Summa Navaratnam (divorced), two daughters; 2) Leroy Rogers (divorced), two sons. **Career:** feature writer and information officer, Associated Newspapers of Ceylon, Colombo, 1959–62; secretary, Travis Air Force Base, California, 1964–69, and Solano County Parks Department, Fairfield, California, 1969–74. Formerly reporter, Fairfield *Daily Republic*. **Address:** c/o Ballantine Books Inc., 201 East 50th Street, New York, New York 10022, USA.

ROMANCE AND HISTORICAL PUBLICATIONS

Novels (series: Ginny Brandon and Steve Morgan)

Sweet Savage Love (Brandon and Morgan). New York, Avon, 1974; London, Futura, 1977.
The Wildest Heart. New York, Avon, 1974; London, Futura, 1978.
Dark Fires (Brandon and Morgan). New York, Avon, 1975; London, Futura, 1977.
Wicked Loving Lies. New York, Avon, 1976; London, Futura, 1977.
The Crowd Pleasers. New York, Avon, 1978; revised edition, 1980.

The Insiders. New York, Avon, and London, Futura, 1979.
Lost Love, Last Love (Brandon and Morgan). New York, Avon, 1980.
Love Play. New York, Avon, 1981; London, Sphere, 1982.
Surrender to Love. New York, Avon, 1982; London, Corgi, 1985.
The Wanton. New York, Avon, 1983; London, Corgi, 1985.
Bound by Desire (Brandon and Morgan). New York, Avon, and London, Century, 1988.

*

Rosemary Rogers comments:
I write the kind of books I would like to read, both historical and contemporary.

*   *   *

In 1974 Avon published Rosemary Rogers's first swashbuckling tale of passion, *Sweet Savage Love*, an historical novel whose title gave a name to an entire genre. In this novel and those that followed, the respective heroines are ravished by an assortment of men, and suffer slavery, torture (but nothing that mars their breathtaking beauty), and a host of other horrors that would devastate the normal human female. These ladies, however, always emerge triumphant with the man they have loved and hated for approximately 600 pages. The typical Rogers heroine is lovely and ardently desired by every man who meets her. She thinks of herself as wilful and independent but then develops a spine of jelly when forced into the arms of the hero.

The male protagonist in hot pursuit of the maiden (which she usually is for the first few pages) must be virile, handsome, well educated or at least highly intelligent, but most of all must have a certain savagery in his lovemaking. Inevitably the heroine's innocence is taken from her by this male animal, who releases in her body an unimaginable passion. Heights of fulfilment the average person may never experience are reached again and again whenever the sweet/savage lovers copulate. The passages depicting this sexual ecstasy leave little to the imagination, but the language, however explicit, is rarely coarse.

Rogers's early works, such as *Sweet Savage Love*, *The Wildest Heart* and *Wicked Loving Lies*, are typical of the novels known in the publishing trade as 'bodice busters'. Set in the 19th century, the hero and heroine fight and bed their way across Europe and the American West. From the descriptions of the countryside and its inhabitants, it is apparent that Rogers knows this era of European and American history. All this is convincing background to what one book jacket described as 'a tale of unquenched desire . . . united in a blaze of undying passion and infinite love'. This quite accurately captures the essence of a Rogers novel. In *Sweet Savage Love* Ginny Brandon and Steve Morgan, travelling through Texas and Mexico, leave a fiery trail of passion, hate, lust, and ultimately love. But this is only the beginning of their story. They must pursue and torment each other through two more novels—*Dark Fires* and *Lost Love, Last Love*. In all of these stories Ginny and Steve separate (because of some absurd misunderstanding) and again and again go through the hate-lust-love routine. Meanwhile, each has tried to find consolation in the arms of different lovers, but their desire for one another cannot be quenched.

Rogers has also written novels with contemporary settings, although the basic sweet/savage theme remains. In *The Crowd Pleasers* a young and aristocratic actress/model becomes reluctantly involved with Webb Carnahan, an earthy, dominant male with a hint of cruelty. *Love Play* has the virginal and very uptight British Sara agreeing to impersonate her younger, outrageously liberated American half-sister, Delight. This permits Sara to elope with her rich boyfriend and to escape the evil clutches of his older brother,

Marco. Sara and Marco quickly become antagonists, although their mutual lust often infringes upon their interminable arguing.

Though the novels with modern day settings sold well, it is Rogers's historical novels that have proven to be the more popular. *The Wanton* is the story of Trista, a young woman who disguises herself as a man in order to become a doctor, lives through the horrors of the Civil War, and is alternately loved and hated by the handsome Blaze Davenan. *Surrender to Love*, which begins in the exotic locale of Ceylon, tells the passionate adventures of Alexa and Nicolas. And recently, *Bound by Desire* continues the saga of Ginny and Steve through the adventures of their daughter, the ravishingly beautiful Laura, who finds fulfilment, sexual and otherwise, in the strong arms of Trent Challenger.

It is true that all of these novels follow a predictable pattern yet the plots are often intricate and imaginative, and are built on a foundation of vivid, often witty dialogue. Intrigue of some sort usually surrounds the protagonists, throwing them together, then flinging them apart. But incredible good fortune always brings the lovers together for a passionate and searing conclusion. Love stories with a sado-masochistic touch have made Rogers one of today's most popular romance writers.

—Patricia Altner

———

ROME, Margaret.   British. See 2nd edition, 1990.

———

ROTHMAN, Judith.   See **PETERS, Maureen.**

———

ROWLAND, Iris.   See **ROBERTS, Irene.**

———

ROWLANDS, Effie.   See **ALBANESI, Madame.**

———

ROY, Brandon.   See **BARCLAY, Florence L.**

———

ROYAL, Rosamond.   See **SHERWOOD, Valerie.**

———

RUCK, Berta.
Nationality: British. **Born:** Amy Roberta Ruck, Murree, India, 2 August 1878. **Education:** St Winifred's School, Bangor, Wales; Lambeth School of Art, and Slade School of Art, both London; Calorossi's, Paris. **Relations:** married the writer Oliver Onions, in 1909 (died 1961); two sons. **Died:** 11 August 1978.

ROMANCE AND HISTORICAL PUBLICATIONS

Novels

His Official Fiancée. London, Hutchinson, and New York, Dodd Mead, 1914.
The Courtship of Rosamond Fayre. London, Hutchinson, 1915; as *The Wooing of Rosamond Fayre*, New York, Dodd Mead, 1915.

The Lad with Wings. London, Hutchinson, 1915; as *The Boy with Wings*, New York, Dodd Mead, 1915.

Miss Million's Maid. New York, Dodd Mead, 1915; London, Hutchinson, 1916.

The Girls at His Billet. London, Hutchinson, and New York, Dodd Mead, 1916.

In Another Girl's Shoes. New York, Dodd Mead, 1916; London, Hodder and Stoughton, 1917.

The Bridge of Kisses. London, Hutchinson, 1917; New York, Dodd Mead, 1920.

Three of Hearts. New York, Dodd Mead, 1917; London, Hodder and Stoughton, 1918.

The Girl Who Proposed! London, Hodder and Stoughton, 1918.

The Years for Rachel. London, Hodder and Stoughton, and New York, Dodd Mead, 1918.

Arabella the Awful. London, Hodder and Stoughton, 1918.

The Disturbing Charm. London, Hodder and Stoughton, and New York, Dodd Mead, 1919.

The Land-Girl's Love Story. London, Hodder and Stoughton, and New York, Dodd Mead, 1919.

The Wrong Mr Right. London, Hodder and Stoughton, 1919; New York, Dodd Mead, 1922.

Sweethearts Unmet. New York, Dodd Mead, 1919; London, Hodder and Stoughton, 1922.

Sweet Stranger. London, Hodder and Stoughton, and New York, Dodd Mead, 1921.

The Arrant Rover. London, Hodder and Stoughton, and New York, Dodd Mead, 1921.

Under False Pretences. London, Hodder and Stoughton, 1922.

The Subconscious Courtship. London, Hodder and Stoughton, and New York, Dodd Mead, 1922.

The Bride Who Ran Away—Nurse Henderson. London, Hodder and Stoughton, 1922.

The Elopement of Eve and Prince Playfellow. London, Hodder and Stoughton, 1922.

Sir or Madam? London, Hutchinson, and New York, Dodd Mead, 1923.

The Dancing Star. London, Hodder and Stoughton, and New York, Dodd Mead, 1923.

The Clouded Pearl. London, Hodder and Stoughton, and New York, Dodd Mead, 1924.

The Leap Year Girl. New York, Dodd Mead, 1924.

Lucky in Love. London, Hodder and Stoughton, and New York, Dodd Mead, 1924.

Kneel to the Prettiest. London, Hodder and Stoughton, and New York, Dodd Mead, 1925.

The Immortal Girl. London, Hodder and Stoughton, and New York, Dodd Mead, 1925.

Her Pirate Partner. London, Hodder and Stoughton, 1926; New York, Dodd Mead, 1927.

The Pearl Thief. London, Hodder and Stoughton, and New York, Dodd Mead, 1926.

The Mind of a Minx. London, Hodder and Stoughton, and New York, Dodd Mead, 1927.

Money for One. London, Hodder and Stoughton, 1927; New York, Dodd Mead, 1928.

One of the Chorus. London, Hodder and Stoughton, 1928; as *Joy-Ride*, New York, Dodd Mead, 1929.

The Youngest Venus; or, The Love Story of a Plain Girl. London, Hodder and Stoughton, and New York, Dodd Mead, 1928.

The Unkissed Bride. London, Hodder and Stoughton, and New York, Dodd Mead, 1929.

To-day's Daughter. London, Hodder and Stoughton, 1929; New York, Dodd Mead, 1930.

Post-War Girl. London, Hutchinson, 1930.

Missing Girl. London, Cassell, 1930; as *The Love-Hater*, New York, Dodd Mead, 1930.

Offer of Marriage. London, Cassell, 1930; New York, Dodd Mead, 1931.

Forced Landing. London, Cassell, 1931.

Dance Partner. New York, Dodd Mead, 1931.

The Lap of Luxury. London, Cassell, 1931; New York, Dodd Mead, 1932.

This Year, Next Year, Sometime—. London, Cassell, and New York, Dodd Mead, 1932.

Sudden Sweetheart. London, Cassell, 1932; New York, Dodd Mead, 1933.

Understudy. London, Hodder and Stoughton, and New York, Dodd Mead, 1933.

Eleventh Hour Lover. London, Hutchinson, 1933.

Change Here for Happiness, Written Especially for Those Who Want Some Happy Hours—and a Change! London, Hodder and Stoughton, and New York, Dodd Mead, 1933.

The Best Time Ever. London, Hodder and Stoughton, and New York, Dodd Mead, 1934.

Sunburst. London, Hodder and Stoughton, and New York, Dodd Mead, 1934.

Sunshine-Stealer: The Story of a Cruise. London, Hodder and Stoughton, and New York, Dodd Mead, 1935.

A Star in Love. London, Hodder and Stoughton, and New York, Dodd Mead, 1935.

Spring Comes to Miss Lonely Heart. London, Hodder and Stoughton, 1936; as *Spring Comes*, New York, Dodd Mead, 1936.

Half-Past Kissing Time. London, Hodder and Stoughton, 1936; as *Sleeping Beauty*, New York, Dodd Mead, 1936.

Love on Second Thoughts. London, Hodder and Stoughton, 1936; New York, Dodd Mead, 1937.

Romance Royal. London, Hodder and Stoughton, and New York, Dodd Mead, 1937.

Love Comes Again Later. London, Hodder and Stoughton, and New York, Dodd Mead, 1938.

Handmaid to Fame. London, Hodder and Stoughton, 1938; New York, Dodd Mead, 1939.

Wedding March. London, Hodder and Stoughton, and New York, Dodd Mead, 1938.

Mock-Honeymoon. London, Mills and Boon, and New York, Dodd Mead, 1939.

Arabella Arrives. New York, Dodd Mead, 1939.

Out to Marry Money. London, Mills and Boon, 1940; as *It Was Left to Peter*, New York, Dodd Mead, 1940.

He Learnt about Women. London, Mills and Boon, 1940; as *He Learned about Women*, New York, Dodd Mead, 1940.

Pennies from Heaven. London, Mills and Boon, 1940; as *Money Isn't Everything*, New York, Dodd Mead, 1940; revised edition, as *Third Love Lucky*, London, Hurst and Blackett, 1958; as *Third Time Lucky*, Dodd Mead, 1958.

Fiancées Count as Relatives. London, Mills and Boon, 1941; as *Fiancées Are Relatives*, New York, Dodd Mead, 1941.

Jade Earrings. New York, Dodd Mead, 1941.

Waltz-Contest. London, Mills and Boon, and New York, Dodd Mead, 1941.

Spinster's Progress. London, Mills and Boon, and New York, Dodd Mead, 1942.

Quarrel and Kiss. London, Mills and Boon, 1942.

Footlight Fever. New York, Dodd Mead, 1942.

Bread-and-Grease-Paint. London, Hutchinson, 1943.

Shining Chance. London, Hutchinson, and New York, Dodd Mead, 1944.

Intruder Marriage. New York, Dodd Mead, 1944, and London, Hutchinson, 1945.

You Are the One. New York, Dodd Mead, 1945; London, Hutchinson, 1946.

Surprise Engagement. New York, Dodd Mead, 1946; London, Hutchinson, 1947.

Throw Away Yesterday. London, Hutchinson, and New York, Dodd Mead, 1946.

Tomboy in Lace. London, Hutchinson, and New York, Dodd Mead, 1947.

She Danced in the Ballet. New York, Dodd Mead, 1948; London, Hutchinson, 1949.

Love and Apron-Strings. London, Hutchinson, 1949; as *Gentle Tyrant*, New York, Dodd Mead, 1949.

Hopeful Journey. London, Hutchinson, 1950; as *Joyful Journey*, New York, Dodd Mead, 1950.

Love at a Festival. London, Hutchinson, and New York, Dodd Mead, 1951.

Song of the Lark. London, Hutchinson, 1951; as *The Rising of the Lark*, New York, Dodd Mead, 1951.

Spice of Life. London, Hutchinson, and New York, Dodd Mead, 1952.

Fantastic Holiday. London, Hutchinson, and New York, Dodd Mead, 1953.

Marriage Is a Blind Date. London, Hutchinson, 1953; as *Blind Date*, New York, Dodd Mead, 1953.

The Men in Her Life. London, Hutchinson, and New York, Dodd Mead, 1954.

We All Have Our Secrets. London, Hutchinson, and New York, Dodd Mead, 1955.

Romance in Two Keys. New York, Dodd Mead, 1955; as *Romance of a Film Star*, London, Hutchinson, 1956.

A Wish a Day. London, Hutchinson, and New York, Dodd Mead, 1956.

Admirer Unknown. New York, Dodd Mead, 1957.

Leap Year Love. London, Hurst and Blackett, 1957; as *Leap Year Romance*, New York, Dodd Mead, 1957.

Mystery Boy-Friend. London, Hutchinson, 1957.

Romantic Afterthought. London, Hurst and Blackett, and New York, Dodd Mead, 1959.

Love and a Rich Girl. London, Hurst and Blackett, and New York, Dodd Mead, 1960.

Sherry and the Ghosts. London, Hurst and Blackett, 1961; New York, Dodd Mead, 1962.

Diamond Engagement Ring. London, Hurst and Blackett, 1962.

Runaway Lovers. London, Hurst and Blackett, 1963.

Rendezvous in Zagarella. London, Hurst and Blackett, 1964.

Shopping for a Husband. London, Hurst and Blackett, 1967.

Short Stories

Khaki and Kisses. London, Hutchinson, 1915.

The Great Unmet. New York, Harper's Bazaar, 1918.

Rufus on the Rebound. New York, Harper's Bazaar, 1918.

The Dream Domesticated. New York, Harper's Bazaar, 1918.

The Girl Who Was Too Good-Looking. London, Hodder and Stoughton, 1920.

The Post-War Girl and Other Stories. London, Hutchinson, 1922.

Wanted on the Voyage. London, Cassell, 1930.

OTHER PUBLICATIONS

Other

American Snap-Shots. New York, Dodd Mead, 1920.

The Berta Ruck Birthday Book, with Quotations. London, Hodder and Stoughton, and New York, Dodd Mead, 1920.

A Story-Teller Tells the Truth: Reminiscences and Notes. London, Hutchinson, 1935.

A Smile for the Past (autobiography). London, Hutchinson, 1959.

A Trickle of Welsh Blood. London, Hutchinson, 1967.

An Asset to Wales. London, Hutchinson, 1970.

Ancestral Voices. London, Hutchinson, 1972.

*   *   *

The Edwardian era is seen by many as a Golden Age of Romance, a time of gaiety, extravagance, luxury, and flamboyant wealth. Berta Ruck, who published the first of her many novels in 1914, used this background for a number of her stories. 'The Edwardian dinner parties', she said recalling that time in a radio interview: 'I've been to those . . . when I was very young and I don't think such things again exist . . . those long tables full of guests, and being 'taken in' to dinner. And the long skirts—skirt after skirt after skirt with perhaps a champagne cork caught in the flounce, you'd occasionally see. Masses of flowers—an absolute jungle of pink sweet peas and white gypsophila'.

Ruck proved to be an adaptable writer, changing her background, and style according to the times in which she lived. *Arabella the Awful* is a simple, cheery little tale with some light-hearted satire on the aristocracy thrown in, and jokey references to the German's silliness, and the Englishman's bravery, and was clearly intended as a morale-raiser in time of war. In 1922 appeared a story with a nursing background, *The Bride Who Ran Away*. And, like so many romantic novelists, she too was lured by the desert: 'That was, of course, one of those never-to-be-forgotten nights. The moon, instead of being silver, made everything amber and gold—the sands of the desert, I suppose—and the camels. Everything was so ageless'. In the 1960s, she was up on the times as shown by *Shopping for a Husband*, a novel dedicated to Heather Jenner, a principal and founder of one of the country's largest marriage bureaux, and written about the seemingly unromantic topic of marriage bureau matches. Kate, on the shelf in her late-twenties, and desperate for a marriage, is finally driven, as the title suggests, to go shopping for a husband. After working through numerous men on the bureau's books, she falls for a staggeringly rich north-country steel magnate, and proves that the services of a bureau can be as legitimate and wonderful a way of discovering true love as any more chancey, flash-in-the-pan meeting. As Heather Jenner, the bureau principal, explained in a book about modern marriage: 'The whole social concept of marriage has changed, but a man still seeks a wife who fits in with his background and who comes of wholesome stock'. After 50 years of writing, the rather cloying, sickly-sweet flavour of the earliest stories had given way to a quasi-stream of consciousness style, jerky and chatty, which leaves out finite verbs, definite articles and pronouns, while making the fullest possible use of upper case letters, unorthodox punctuation, and italics, sometimes entire paragraphs being italicized.

Her attitude to her work was optimistic. When accused of leaving out the 'unpleasant realities' of life, she justified it like this:

I belong to the School of Thought (the Non-Thinking School, if you like) that considers 'compensating dream fiction', not as opiate, but as tonic, and prefers to leave the tale on a note definitely gay and hopeful. People condemn the story-teller's cheerfully tidied-up last chapters as the flight from reality. Personally I regard it as the entrance into the original real world.

To the people who ask me why I can't face facts, I would suggest that it takes all kinds of facts to make a world; why should I not describe those I prefer? Why, people ask, do I falsify Life? Why, I ask, do they? I think it is very wrong to give Youth the impression that it is unalterably doomed to disappointment. '*C'est en croyant aux roses*', says a French proverb, '*qu'on les fait éclore'*. It is by believing in roses that one brings them into bloom ...

It is my creed that the world was created to go merry as a marriage-bell and for the whole human race to be healthy, wealthy and wise enough to be happy on all cylinders.

—Rachel Anderson

———

RUNDLE, Anne.   See **MANNERS, Alexandra.**

———

RYAN, Rachel.   See **BROWN, Sandra.**

———

RYBOT, Doris.   See **PONSONBY, D.A.**

———

SABATINI, Rafael.

Nationality: British. **Born:** Jesi, Italy, 29 April 1875. **Education:** Ecole Cantonale, Zoug, Switzerland, and in Oporto, Portugal. **Military Service:** War Office Intelligence Department during World War I. **Relations:** married 1) Ruth Goad Dixon in 1905 (divorced); 2) Christine Dixon in 1935. Lived in Clifford, Herefordshire. **Died:** 13 February 1950.

ROMANCE AND HISTORICAL PUBLICATIONS

Novels (series: Captain Blood)

The Lovers of Yvonne. London, Pearson, 1902; as *The Suitors of Yvonne*, New York, Putnam, 1902.
The Tavern Knight. London, Richards, 1904; Boston, Houghton Mifflin, 1927.
Bardelys the Magnificent. London, Nash, 1906; Boston, Houghton Mifflin, 1923.
The Trampling of the Lilies. London, Hutchinson, 1906; Boston, Houghton Mifflin, 1924.
Love-at-Arms. London, Hutchinson, 1907; Boston, Houghton Mifflin, 1924.
The Shame of Molly. London, Hutchinson, 1908; Boston, Houghton Mifflin, 1924.
St Martin's Summer. London, Hutchinson, 1909; Boston, Houghton Mifflin, 1924.
Anthony Wilding. London, Hutchinson, 1910; as *Arms and the Maid; or, Anthony Wilding*, New York, Putnam, 1910.
The Lion's Skin. London, Stanley Paul, and Boston, Houghton Mifflin, 1911.
The Justice of the Duke. London, Stanley Paul, 1912.
The Strolling Saint. London, Stanley Paul, 1913; Boston, Houghton Mifflin, 1924.
The Gates of Doom. London, Stanley Paul, 1914; Boston, Houghton Mifflin, 1926.
The Sea-Hawk. London, Secker, and Philadelphia, Lippincott, 1915.
The Banner of the Bull: Three Episodes in the Career of Cesare Borgia. London, Secker, and Philadelphia, Lippincott, 1915; first episode published as *The Urbinian*, Boston, Houghton Mifflin, 1924.
The Snare. London, Secker, and Philadelphia, Lippincott, 1915.
Scaramouche: A Romance of the French Revolution. London, Hutchinson, and Boston, Houghton Mifflin, 1921.
Captain Blood, His Odyssey. London, Hutchinson, and Boston, Houghton Mifflin, 1922.

Fortune's Fool. London, Hutchinson, and Boston, Houghton Mifflin, 1923.
Mistress Wilding. Boston, Houghton Mifflin, 1924.
The Carolinian. London, Hutchinson, and Boston, Houghton Mifflin, 1925.
Bellarion the Fortunate. London, Hutchinson, and Boston, Houghton Mifflin, 1926.
The Nuptials of Corbal. London, Hutchinson, and Boston, Houghton Mifflin, 1927.
The Hounds of God. London, Hutchinson, and Boston, Houghton Mifflin, 1928.
The Romantic Prince. London, Hutchinson, and Boston, Houghton Mifflin, 1929.
The Reaping. London, Readers Library, 1929.
The Minion. London, Hutchinson, 1930; as *The King's Minion*, Boston, Houghton Mifflin, 1930.
Captain Blood Returns. Boston, Houghton Mifflin, 1931; as *The Chronicles of Captain Blood*, London, Hutchinson, 1932.
The Black Swan. London, Hutchinson, and Boston, Houghton Mifflin, 1932.
The Stalking Horse. London, Hutchinson, and Boston, Houghton Mifflin, 1933.
Venetian Masque. London, Hutchinson, and Boston, Houghton Mifflin, 1934.
Chivalry. London, Hutchinson, and Boston, Houghton Mifflin, 1935.
The Fortunes of Captain Blood. London, Hutchinson, and Boston, Houghton Mifflin, 1936.
The Lost King. London, Hutchinson, and Boston, Houghton Mifflin, 1937.
The Sword of Islam. London, Hutchinson, and Boston, Houghton Mifflin, 1939.
The Marquis of Carabas. London, Hutchinson, 1940; as *Master-at-Arms*, Boston, Houghton Mifflin, 1940.
Columbus. London, Hutchinson, and Boston, Houghton Mifflin, 1942.
King in Prussia. London, Hutchinson, 1944; as *The Birth of Mischief*, Boston, Houghton Mifflin, 1945.
The Gamester. London, Hutchinson, and Boston, Houghton Mifflin, 1949.
Saga of the Sea (omnibus). London, Hutchinson, 1953.
Sinner, Saint, and Jester (omnibus). London, Hutchinson, 1954.
In the Shadow of the Guillotine (omnibus). London, Hutchinson, 1955; Boston, Houghton Mifflin, 1956.

Short Stories

The Historical Nights' Entertainment, 1st–3rd series. Boston, Houghton Mifflin, 3 vols, 1917–38; London, Secker, 1 vol, 1918; London, Hutchinson, 2 vols, 1919–37.
Stories of Love, Intrigue, and Battle, Being Selected Works of Rafael Sabatini. Boston, Houghton Mifflin, 1931.
Turbulent Tales. London, Hutchinson, 1946.
The Fortunes of Casanova and Other Stories, edited by Jack Adrian. London, Oxford University Press, 1993.

OTHER PUBLICATIONS

Plays

Kuomi, The Jester, with Stephanie Baring (produced Luton, Bedfordshire, 1903).
Bardelys the Magnificent, with Henry Hamilton, adaptation of the novel by Sabatini (produced Birmingham, 1910; London, 1911).
Fugitives (produced London, 1911).

The Rattlesnake, with J.E. Harold Terry (produced New York, 1921; London, 1922).
Scaramouche, adaptation of his own novel (produced New York, 1923; Glasgow and London, 1927).
In the Snare, with Leon M. Lion, adaptation of the novel *The Snare* by Sabatini (produced London, 1924).
The Carolinian, with J.E. Harold Terry, adaptation of his novel (produced Detroit and New York, 1925).
The Tyrant: An Episode in the Life of Cesare Borgia (produced Birmingham and London, 1925; New York, 1930). London, Hutchinson, 1925.

Screenplays: *Bluff*, 1921; *The Recoil*, 1922; *The Scourge* (*Fortune's Fool*), 1922.

Other

The Life of Cesare Borgia of Grance. London, Stanley Paul, 1911; New York, Brentano's, 1912.
Torquemada and the Spanish Inquisition. London, Stanley Paul, and New York, Brentano's, 1913; revised edition, Stanley Paul, and Boston, Houghton Mifflin, 1924.
Heroic Lives. London, Hutchinson, and Boston, Houghton Mifflin, 1934.

Editor, *A Century of Sea Stories*. London, Hutchinson, 1934.
Editor, *A Century of Historical Stories*. London, Hutchinson, 1936.
Editor, *The Book of the Sea Trout*, by Hamish Stuart. London, Cape, 1952.

*

Film Adaptations: *Captain Blood*, 1935; *The Sea Hawk*, 1940; *The Black Swan*, 1942; *The Fortunes of Captain Blood*, 1950; *Scaramouche*, 1952; *Captain Pirate* (*Captain Blood, Fugitive*), 1952, from the novel *Captain Blood Returns*.

*   *   *

Rafael Sabatini was called the 'new Dumas' by his admirers and a sleight-of-hand artist with a 'bag of tricks' by sceptics, but his narratives are well crafted and often sparkle with crisp dialogue and rousing adventure. The settings of what he called his period novels ranged over several centuries in England, France, Italy, and in the Caribbean during the heyday of piracy, with a few more scattered around America, Spain, Venice, and elsewhere. In addition to his romantic novels Sabatini wrote fiction and accounts of historical incidents for his three volumes of *Historical Nights' Entertainment*, recreated episodes from the Spanish Inquisition, and wrote novelizations and sketches of the lives of such cultural heroes as Columbus, Saint Francis of Assisi, Joan of Arc, Lord Nelson, and Florence Nightingale. He seems to have read history with great voracity, but he had no more respect for historians than many of them had for his own versions of past events.

Sabatini had been writing historical fiction, biography, and romance for over 30 years when he summarized his views on the writer's responsibilities to his art. Historians, Sabatini argued, are not necessarily more faithful to their material than are period novelists, and they seldom write as well. Citing the accounts of William Tell, the Man in the Iron Mask, and incestual relations among the Borgias as legends which had crept into histories of Europe, Sabatini concluded that historical 'facts' were all too often based on repeated errors, sensationalism, and the biased reports of dubious witnesses. Good period fiction requires equally serious research, a faithfulness to historical personages and events, and shrewd analysis of the available evidence. According to Sabatini there are ba-

sically three kinds of period novels: those which are concerned entirely with historical characters and happenings, those involving imaginary characters set 'against a real background to which story and characters must bear some real and true relationship', and those which blend 'events that are reasonably and logically imagined, and characters that lived with characters that the author has invented'.

Sabatini's *The Minion* (US title: *The King's Minion*) for which he 'scarcely invented even a minor character', is an example of the first type. The novel is concerned with intrigues leading to the murder of Sir Thomas Overbury in the court of James I, and Sabatini finds 'as a result of close study and close reasoning' that there were initially two conspiracies which later became entangled. *Scaramouche*, which is subtitled 'A Romance', is the second type: the title character is imaginary, but the setting is faithful to the milieu of revolutionary France. The hero is 'the natural offspring of the circumstances and habits of mind of the time', which moulded his character and shaped his fortunes. *Scaramouche* is aptly titled a romance. After being banished from the estate of his foster father, André-Louis Moreau takes the name Scaramouche and joins a travelling band of players. The death of a friend at the hands of a vicious aristocrat leads Scaramouche to seek revenge, and in turn to become a notorious polemicist, a fencing master, and a Revolutionary hero. In seeking revenge, André clashes with the aristocrat over an actress he thinks he loves and the lady he has always loved. At the culmination of the Revolution André learns that the aristocrat is his father. This physiological drama is woven interestingly into the players' story where the troupe moves from hard times under feudal leadership to great success through André's skills as an early capitalist; he collects personnel, organizes bookings, writes advertising, composes plays based on the classics, and stars in performances.

Sabatini's third kind of novel, a combination of the period novel and the historical romance, is found in *Captain Blood*. Peter Blood is based on Henry Pitman, an English surgeon who was sold into slavery at Barbados after being sentenced to death by Jeffreys at the Bloody Assize for ministering to wounded rebels during Monmouth's Rebellion. Sabatini follows Pitman's biography up to the point of his escape, then follows John [or A.O.] Exquemelin's *History of the Bucaniers of America* and other accounts, including that of Henry Morgan, for models of buccaneer adventures and characters. The success of *Captain Blood* led to *The Chronicles of Captain Blood* (U.S. title: *Captain Blood Returns*) in 1931 and *The Fortunes of Captain Blood* in 1936. The sea is an ideal setting and piracy a useful mode for portraying the struggle for reasonable loyalties in a world of shifting alliances. Like those in *The Sea-Hawk* and *The Black Swan*, Captain Blood's adventures allow Sabatini to play on those grey areas surrounding allegiance to particular nations, religions, and ideals of personal integrity.

In *The Sea-Hawk* Sir Oliver Tressilan loses his estate and is enslaved by Moslems after his brother accuses him of a murder he himself had committed, but Tressilan makes himself invaluable to his master and becomes Sakr-el-Bahr the pirate. *The Black Swan* finds French ex-buccaneer Charles de Bernis drawn into alliance with the last of the renegade pirates, Tom Leach, in order to save his own life.

Sabatini's fiction is effective to the extent that he created an opposition between the picaresque milieu in which action takes place and the chivalric idealism of the protagonists. In a world of court intrigues, war, and such outlawry as piracy the hero's position is associated with or appears to be compromised by shadowy motives and actions. Despite his protestations, in the lady's eyes the gentleman is compromised, because his chivalrous manner is at odds with what she sees of his actions in the world. Since the hero's immersion in the picaresque life has usually resulted from a betrayal of some sort, he must extract himself by avenging wrongs while he attempts to gain or regain his fortune. While he is away the lady should have the 'womanliness to be guided by natural instincts in the selection of her mate', but an admirable woman is courted by many men and since she distrusts him she might, 'for position, riches, and a great title barter herself in marriage', or be less cautious with another suitor. The reader identifies the love match early and much of the tension of the novels results from suspension of the courtship during periods of vigorous action. Because the potential lovers are ignorant or distrustful of one another's feelings yet drawn together by an instinctively powerful attraction, meetings between them crackle with misunderstandings and disdainful wit.

Sabatini's period novels and romances have not lost their charm over time for those readers willing to suspend disbelief in their romantic premises. His most popular works inspired motion pictures and he turned some of them into successful stage productions. His popularity weathered the abuse of critics who would have had more realism and historians who demanded more footnotes. His bag of tricks, which included stock characters, a liberal use of 'Chance', predictably honorable heroes and heroines, unlikely misunderstandings and so on, seldom intrude into the magical moments of high action and grand verbal exchanges. Readers who made *Scaramouche*, *The Sea-Hawk*, *Mistress Wilding*, *The Carolinian*, and *Captain Blood* best sellers were responding not merely to the lure of romantic fiction, but to energy and courage inspired by one of its most capable spokesmen.

—Larry N. Landrum

ST CLAIRE, Erin. See **BROWN, Sandra.**

St JOHN, Mabel.
Pseudonym for Henry St John Cooper. **Born:** half-brother of the actress Gladys Cooper. **Career:** contributor to Lord Northcliffe's *Girls' Friend*, *Girls' Reader*, and *Girls' Home*. **Died.**

ROMANCE AND HISTORICAL PUBLICATIONS

Novels (series: Polly Green)

Most Cruelly Wronged. London, Amalgamated Press, 1907.
Only a Singing Girl. London, Amalgamated Press, 1907.
Rival Beauties. London, Amalgamated Press, 1907.
Under a Ban. London, Amalgamated Press, 1907.
Her Father's Sin. London, Amalgamated Press, 1908.
Polly Green: A School Story [*and Coosha, at Cambridge,— Engaged, in Society, at Twenty-One*]. London, Amalgamated Press, 6 vols, 1909–11.
Romany Ruth: A Gipsy Love Story. London, Amalgamated Press, 1909.
Just a Barmaid. London, Amalgamated Press, 1909.
A Daughter Scorned. London, Amalgamated Press, 1911.
Jane Em'ly. London, Amalgamated Press, 1911.
The Twins of Twineham. London, Amalgamated Press, 1911.
The Dear Old Home. London, Amalgamated Press, 1912.
The Best Woman in the World. London, Fleetway House, 1913.
Nell of the Camp; or, The Pride of the Prairie. London, Fleetway House, 1913.
The Outcasts of Crowthorpe College. London, Fleetway House, 1913.
The Schoolgirl Bride. London, Fleetway House, 1913.
Faults on Both Sides. London, Fleetway House, 1914.
Fine Feathers! or, The Wife Who Would Be Smart. London, Fleetway House, 1914.

From Mill to Mansion. London, Fleetway House, 1914.
Kiddy, The Coffee-Stall Girl. London, Fleetway House, 1914.
Little Miss Millions. London, Fleetway House, 1914.
Married to Her Master. London, Fleetway House, 1914.
My Lancashire Queen. London, Fleetway House, 1914.
Sally in Our Alley. London, Fleetway House, 1914.
The Ticket-of-Leave Girl. London, Fleetway House, 1914.
When a Girl's Pretty. London, Fleetway House, 1914.
John Jordan, Slave-Driver. London, Fleetway House, 1915.
Just Jane Ann. London, Fleetway House, 1915.
The Lass That Loved a Sailor. London, Fleetway House, 1915.
Maggie Darling. London, Fleetway House, 1915.
My Girl, Regan. London, Fleetway House, 1915.
The Post Office Girl. London, Fleetway House, 1915.
Shielded from the World. London, Fleetway House, 1915.
Too Wilful for Words! London, Fleetway House, 1915.
The Worst Wife in the World. London, Fleetway House, 1915.
Born in Prison: The Story of a Mill-Girl's Sacrifice. London, Fleetway House, 1916.
Cook at School. London, Fleetway House, 1916.
How the Money Goes! London, Fleetway House, 1916.
In Mother's Place. London, Fleetway House, 1916.
The Mistress of the Fifth Standard. London, Fleetway House, 1916.
The Soul of the Mill. London, Fleetway House, 1916.
The Best Girls Are Here. London, Fleetway House, 1917.
Daisy Earns Her Living. London, Fleetway House, 1917.
Daisy Peach Abroad. London, Fleetway House, 1917.
Liz o' Loomland. London, Fleetway House, 1917.
Married at School. London, Fleetway House, 1917.
Our Nell. London, Fleetway House, 1917.
The 'Sixpenny Ha'penny' Duchess. London, Fleetway House, 1917.
What a Woman Can Do! London, Fleetway House, 1917.
The Autograph Hunters. London, Fleetway House, 1918.
Dolly Daydreams! London, Fleetway House, 1918.
For Her Lover's Sake. London, Fleetway House, 1918.
His Sealed Lips! or, The Tale He Would Not Tell! London, Fleetway House, 1918.
Little and Good. London, Fleetway House, 1918.
Little Miss Innocence. London, Fleetway House, 1918.
Millgirl and Dreamer. London, Fleetway House, 1918.
Old Smith's Nurse. London, Fleetway House, 1918.
Pearl of the West. London, Fleetway House, 1918.
Her Stolen Baby. London, Fleetway House, 1919.
Apronstrings. London, Amalgamated Press, 1919.
Ashamed of the Shop; or, Miss High-and-Mighty. London, Amalgamated Press, 1919.
The Belle of the Works. London, Amalgamated Press, 1919.
The Favourite Wins! or, The Bookmaker's Bride. London, Amalgamated Press, 1919.
Good Gracious, Marian! London, Amalgamated Press, 1919.
The Little 'Gutter Girl'. London, Amalgamated Press, 1919.
Betty on the Stage. London, Amalgamated Press, 1920.
The Wife Who Dragged Him Down! London, Amalgamated Press, 1920.
A Boxer's Sweetheart. London, Amalgamated Press, 1920.
The Wife Who Would Be 'Master'! London, Amalgamated Press, 1920.
The Cinderella Girl. London, Amalgamated Press, 1920.
In the Shadows! London, Amalgamated Press, 1920.
Mary Ellen—Mill-Lass. London, Amalgamated Press, 1920.
Mill-Lass o' Mine! London, Amalgamated Press, 1920.
Wedded But Not Wooed; or, Marry Me—Or Go to Prison! London, Amalgamated Press, 1920.
From Pillar to Post; or, No Home of Her Own. London, Amalgamated Press, 1921.
Wife—or Housekeeper? London, Amalgamated Press, 1921.

A House, But Not a Home. London, Amalgamated Press, 1921.
The Husband, The Wife, and the Friend. London, Amalgamated Press, 1921.
A Jealous Wife's Revenge! London, Amalgamated Press, 1921.
Just Jane Em'ly. London, Amalgamated Press, 1921.
Little Miss Lancashire; or, Moll o' the Mill. London, Amalgamated Press, 1921.
Lonely Little Lucy. London, Amalgamated Press, 1921.
Mad for Dress! London, Amalgamated Press, 1921.
Sally All-Smiles. London, Amalgamated Press, 1921.
The School Against Her! London, Amalgamated Press, 1921.
Scorned by 'His' Mother. London, Amalgamated Press, 1921.
Ann All-Alone: The Story of a Girl's Great Self-Sacrifice. London, Amalgamated Press, 1922.
Wife or Maid? or, Scorned by Her Workmates. London, Amalgamated Press, 1922.
The Brute! London, Amalgamated Press, 1922.
We Want Our Mummy! London, Amalgamated Press, 1922.
Gipsy Born! London, Amalgamated Press, 1922.
Tattling Tongues. London, Amalgamated Press, 1922.
The Gipsy Schoolgirl. London, Amalgamated Press, 1922.
Girl of the Prairie. London, Amalgamated Press, 1922.
The Home Without a Father! London, Amalgamated Press, 1922.
Mother Knows Best! or, Uttered in Anger! London, Amalgamated Press, 1922.
Mr Leslie's School for Girls. London, Amalgamated Press, 1922.
Nobody's Girl. London, Amalgamated Press, 1922.
Rich Girl—Charity Girl! London, Amalgamated Press, 1922.
Blood Money! London, Amalgamated Press, 1923.
The Disappearance of Barbara. London, Amalgamated Press, 1923.
Such a Fine Fellow! London, Amalgamated Press, 1923.
The Gipsy Actress. London, Amalgamated Press, 1923.
The Girl Who Married the Wrong Man! London, Amalgamated Press, 1923.
He Couldn't Take Money! or, The 'Old Fool' of the Family! London, Amalgamated Press, 1923.
His Wife—or His Mother? or, No Home of Her Own. London, Amalgamated Press, 1923.
I'm Not a Common Girl! London, Amalgamated Press, 1923.
Jenny Luck of Brendon's Mills. London, Amalgamated Press, 1923.
The New Girl at Bellforth. London, Amalgamated Press, 1923.
The Second Husband. London, Amalgamated Press, 1923.
Secrets of the Shop! London, Amalgamated Press, 1923.
Too Old for Her Husband! London, Amalgamated Press, 1924.
Bringing Up Becky! London, Amalgamated Press, 1924.
She Was an Actress. London, Amalgamated Press, 1924.
Go Borrowing—Go Sorrowing. London, Amalgamated Press, 1924.
A Son to Be Proud Of! London, Amalgamated Press, 1924.
He Married a Mill-Lass. London, Amalgamated Press, 1924.
The Island Girl. London, Amalgamated Press, 1924.
Married to His Wife's Family. London, Amalgamated Press, 1924.
She Wrecked Their Home! or, A Son's a Son till He Takes Him a Wife. London, Amalgamated Press, 1924.
Midsummer Madness! London, Amalgamated Press, 1924.
The Mill-Girl's Bargain! London, Amalgamated Press, 1924.
My Man of the Mill! London, Amalgamated Press, 1924.
Poisoned Lives! London, Amalgamated Press, 1924.
The 'Sports' of Lyndale. London, Amalgamated Press, 1925.
As the World Judged. London, Amalgamated Press, 1925.
When There's Love at Home. London, Amalgamated Press, 1925.
A Girl's Good Name. London, Amalgamated Press, 1925.
Where Is My Child To-night? London, Amalgamated Press, 1925.
Just 'Liz-beth Ann. London, Amalgamated Press, 1925.
Longing for Love. London, Amalgamated Press, 1925.

Pride Parted Them! London, Amalgamated Press, 1925.
Shamed by Her Husband! London, Amalgamated Press, 1925.
She Posed as Their Friend! London, Amalgamated Press, 1925.
She Shall Never Call You Mother! London, Amalgamated Press, 1925.
And Still She Loved Him. London, Amalgamated Press, 1926.
The Daughter He Didn't Want! London, Amalgamated Press, 1926.
Some Mother's Child! London, Amalgamated Press, 1926.
It Is My Duty! London, Amalgamated Press, 1926.
The Life He Led Her! London, Amalgamated Press, 1926.
Love Needs Telling. London, Amalgamated Press, 1926.
Maggie of Marley's Mill. London, Amalgamated Press, 1926.
The Man Who Married Again. London, Amalgamated Press, 1926.
Rivals at School—Rivals Through Life! London, Amalgamated Press, 1926.
She Sold Her Child! London, Amalgamated Press, 1927.
He'll Never Marry You! London, Amalgamated Press, 1927.
Thou Shalt Love Thy Neighbour—. London, Amalgamated Press, 1927.
Lizbeth Rose. London, Amalgamated Press, 1927.
Tied to Her Apron Strings! London, Amalgamated Press, 1927.
The Long, Long Wooing. London, Amalgamated Press, 1927.
Loved for Her Money. London, Amalgamated Press, 1927.
The New Girl. London, Amalgamated Press, 1927.
She'll Never Marry My Son! London, Amalgamated Press, 1927.
Some Mother's Son! London, Amalgamated Press, 1928.
A Beggar at Her Husband's Door! London, Amalgamated Press, 1928.
Utterly Alone! London, Amalgamated Press, 1928.
His Wife or His Work? London, Amalgamated Press, 1928.
His Wife's Secret! London, Amalgamated Press, 1928.
Nobody Wants You! London, Amalgamated Press, 1928.
He Shall Not Marry a Mill-Lass! London, Amalgamated Press, 1929.
The Husband She Wanted. London, Amalgamated Press, 1930.
Jess o' Jordan's. London, Amalgamated Press, 1930.
Wedded—But Alone! London, Amalgamated Press, 1930.
Another Girl Won Him. London, Amalgamated Press, 1935.

Novels as Henry St John Cooper

The Master of the Mill. London, Amalgamated Press, 1910.
A Shop-Girl's Revenge. London, Fleetway House, 1914.
The Cotton King. London, Fleetway House, 1915.
The Lass He Left Behind Him! London, Fleetway House, 1915.
The Black Sheep; or, Who Is My Brother? London, Fleetway House, 1916.
Ready—Aye Ready! A Story of the Bull-Dogs of the Ocean. London, Fleetway House, 1916.
The Man with the Money. London, Fleetway House, 1917.
Hero or Scamp? London, Fleetway House, 1918.
Miss Bolo; or, A Spy in the Home. London, Fleetway House, 1918.
The Man of Her Dreams. London, Amalgamated Press, 1919.
The Mill Queen. London, Fleetway House, 1919.
Sunny Ducrow. London, Sampson Low, 1919.
There's Just One Girl. London, Amalgamated Press, 1919.
Vagabond Jess. London, Amalgamated Press, 1919.
'Wild-Fire' Nan. London, Amalgamated Press, 1919.
Fair and False; or, A Whited Sepulchre. London, Amalgamated Press, 1920.
Her Mother-in-Law. London, Amalgamated Press, 1920.
James Bevanwood, Baronet. London, Sampson Low, 1920.
Just a Cottage Maid. London, Amalgamated Press, 1920.
A Lodger in His Own Home. London, Amalgamated Press, 1920.
Married to a Miser. London, Amalgamated Press, 1920.
Men Were Deceivers Ever. London, Amalgamated Press, 1920.

Mountain Lovers. London, Amalgamated Press, 1920.

Two Men and a Maid. London, Amalgamated Press, 1920.

Elizabeth in Dreamland. London, Amalgamated Press, 1921.

The Garden of Memories. London, Sampson Low, 1921.

The Island of Eve. London, Amalgamated Press, 1921.

Love's Waif. London, Amalgamated Press, 1921.

Mabel St John's Schooldays. London, Amalgamated Press, 1921.

Madge o' the Mill. London, Amalgamated Press, 1921.

Prison-Stained! London, Amalgamated Press, 1921.

We're Not Wanted Now! London, Amalgamated Press, 1921.

Carniss and Company. London, Sampson Low, 1922.

Above Her Station. London, Amalgamated Press, 1922.

A Daughter of the Loom; or, Go and Marry Your Mill-Girl! London, Amalgamated Press, 1922.

Fairweather Friends! or, Fleeced by His Family! London, Amalgamated Press, 1922.

The Imaginary Marriage. London, Sampson Low, 1922.

Poverty's Daughter. London, Amalgamated Press, 1922.

A Snake in the Grass. London, Amalgamated Press, 1922.

The Vagabond's Daughter. London, Amalgamated Press, 1922.

Could She Forgive? London, Amalgamated Press, 1923.

Gipsy Love. London, Amalgamated Press, 1923.

The 'Head' of the Family; or, Despised by Them All! London, Amalgamated Press, 1923.

Hidden Hearts. London, Amalgamated Press, 1923.

Kidnapped. London, Amalgamated Press, 1923.

Mary Faithful. London, Amalgamated Press, 1923.

Son o' Mine! London, Amalgamated Press, 1923.

Too Common for Him! London, Amalgamated Press, 1923.

Two's Company . . . ; or, Young Folks Are Best Alone. London, Amalgamated Press, 1923.

Yield Not to Temptation! London, Amalgamated Press, 1923.

The Broken Barrier. London, Amalgamated Press, 1924.

His Wife from the Kitchen! London, Amalgamated Press, 1924.

Just Plain Jim! or, One of the Rank and File. London, Amalgamated Press, 1924.

A Lover in Rags. London, Amalgamated Press, 1924.

Redway Street. London, Amalgamated Press, 1924.

The Unwanted Heiress. London, Amalgamated Press, 1924.

The Fortunes of Sally Luck. London, Sampson Low, 1925.

Lose Money—Lose Friends! London, Amalgamated Press, 1925.

Nan of No Man's Land. London, Amalgamated Press, 1925.

The Cottar's Daughter. London, Amalgamated Press, 1926.

The Gallant Lover: A Queen Anne Story. London, Sampson Low, 1926.

The Golconda Necklace. London, Sampson Low, 1926.

Whoso Diggeth a Pit—. London, Amalgamated Press, 1926.

The Woman Who Parted Them! London, Amalgamated Press, 1926.

The Amazing Tramp. London, Amalgamated Press, 1927.

Morning Glory. London, Sampson Low, 1927.

Golden Bait. London, Sampson Low, 1928.

The Red Veil. London, Sampson Low, 1928.

As Fate Decrees. London, Sampson Low, 1929.

Compromise. London, Sampson Low, 1929.

Retribution. London, Sampson Low, 1930.

The Millionaire Tramp. London, Sampson Low, 1930.

When a Man Loves. London, Sampson Low, 1931.

The Forbidden Road. London, Sampson Low, 1931.

Love That Divided. London, Sampson Low, 1932.

The Splendid Love. London, Sampson Low, 1932.

When Love Compels. London, Sampson Low, 1933.

Dangerous Paths. London, Sampson Low, 1933.

As a Woman Wills. London, Sampson Low, 1934.

The Hush Marriage. London, Sampson Low, 1934.

Toils of Silence. London, Sampson Low, 1935.

A Woman's Way. London, Sampson Low, 1935.

At Grips with Fate. London, Sampson Low, 1936.

The Call of Love. London, Sampson Low, 1936.

OTHER PUBLICATIONS

Other

Bull-Dogs and Bull-Dog Breeding. London, Jarrolds, 1905.

Bulldogs and Bulldog Men. London, Jarrolds, 1908.

Bulldogs and All about Them. London, Jarrolds, 1914.

*   *   *

Henry St John Cooper was a prolific and wide-ranging author. He not only churned out thousands of words of women's fiction every week, but regularly wrote stories of tough, Borstal-like boarding-schools for several boys' papers.

As Mabel St John he was one of the most popular writers of Lord Northcliffe's *Girls' Friend, Girls' Reader,* and *Girls' Home.* Before World War I, these periodicals catered for hardworking and frequently exploited working-girl readers, whose education had begun and ended at elementary schools. St John's championship of the underdog and the sheer gusto of the stories combined to create an instant recipe for success. (A large number of these magazine serial romances were subsequently reissued in the form of inexpensive paperback books.) Millgirl and maid-of-all-work readers could easily identify with St John's heroines, who often occupied similar positions to their own (*Just a Barmaid, Liz o' Loomland,* etc.) The fictional 'slaveys' and factory workers, however, had the advantage of stumbling more easily on redemptive romance with the bosses' sons than their real-life counterparts were likely to do in the rigid class divisions of Edwardian society.

St John, who was half-brother to Gladys Cooper, the celebrated actress, used theatrical settings for many of his stories. *Sunny Ducrow* is an attractive account of stage ambitions in a working-class girl. However, his theatre novels owed more to the rumbustious good humour of the music-hall than to the serious drama at which his sister excelled. Until 'Mr Right' came along to provide a permanent escape from their poorly paid drudgery, several St John heroines abandoned 'skivvying' for a career 'on the halls', where they would achieve success through unusual enterprise and endeavour. (Em Hammond, for example, despite her much vaunted 'yellow hair', managed convincingly to play the part of an Arab girl and also—no mean achievement this—to whistle 'The Man Who Broke the Bank at Monte Carlo' through her yashmak!)

The apotheosis of romantic madcap appeal was achieved in Polly Green, whom St John starred in six of his books. Rather surprisingly, Polly is not a working-class girl but a college student at Cambridge, where she inspires wholesale adulation from male undergraduates. Later she had London society at her feet, and enters into a forced engagement with a horribly ruthless member of the ruling class, whom she sensibly throws over as soon as circumstances permit. Happily he then not only commits suicide but obligingly leaves Polly his fortune, thus smoothing her way to marriage with her besotted but impecunious true love (St John championing the underdog again!). A notable feature of the Polly Green stories is that Polly had a very long-standing friendship, on equal terms, with Coocha, an outspoken and extremely lively natured black girl. This was for its time a progressive step, but one that seemed immensely popular with Edwardian readers.

With their melodramatic plots and flashes of iconoclastic humour, the St John romantic novels are certainly not in the classic mould. Their earthy acuteness, however, makes them more memorable than many mainstream love stories.

—Mary Cadogan

St JOHN, Nicole.
Pseudonyms: Elizabeth Bolton; Catherine E. Chambers; Kate Chambers; Pamela Dryden; Lavinia Harris; Norma Johnston; Adrian Robert. **Nationality:** American. **Born:** Ridgewood, New Jersey. **Education:** public schools, in Ramsey, New Jersey; Montclair State College, New Jersey, B.A.; Professional Training Program, American Theatre Wing, New York. **Career:** actress, editor, teacher, youth counsellor, and fashion retailer; founder and director, Geneva Players Inc; president, Dryden Harris St John Inc. **Agent:** McIntosh and Otis Inc, 310 Madison Avenue, New York, New York 10017, USA; or A. M Heath, 79 St Martin's Lane, London WC2N 4AA, England. **Address:** Dryden Harris St John Inc, 103 Godwin Avenue, Midland Park, New Jersey 07432, USA.

ROMANCE AND HISTORICAL PUBLICATIONS

Novels

The Medici Ring. New York, Random House, 1975; London, Collins, 1976.
Wychwood. New York, Random House, 1976; London, Heinemann, 1978.
Guinever's Gift. New York, Random House, 1977; London, Heinemann, 1979.

OTHER PUBLICATIONS

Fiction (for children) as Norma Johnston

The Wishing Star. New York, Funk and Wagnalls, 1963.
The Wider Heart. New York, Funk and Wagnalls, 1964.
Ready or Not. New York, Funk and Wagnalls, 1965.
The Bridge Between. New York, Funk and Wagnalls, 1966.
The Keeping Days. New York, Atheneum, 1973.
Glory in the Flower. New York, Atheneum, 1974.
Of Time and of Seasons. New York, Atheneum, 1975.
Strangers Dark and Gold. New York, Atheneum, 1975.
A Striving after Wind. New York, Atheneum, 1976.
The Sanctuary Tree. New York, Atheneum, 1977.
A Mustard Seed of Magic. New York, Atheneum, 1977.
If You Love Me, Let Me Go. New York, Atheneum, 1978.
The Swallow's Song. New York, Atheneum, 1978.
Both Sides Now. New York, Atheneum, 1978.
The Crucible Year. New York, Atheneum, 1979.
Pride of Lions. New York, Atheneum, 1979.
A Nice Girl Like You. New York, Atheneum, 1980.
Myself and I. New York, Atheneum, 1981.
The Days of the Dragon's Seed. New York, Atheneum, 1982.
Timewarp Summer. New York, Atheneum, 1982.
Gabriel's Girl. New York, Atheneum, 1983.
Watcher in the Mist. New York, Bantam, 1986.
Carlisle's Hope. New York, Bantam, 1986.
To Jess, with Love and Memories. New York, Bantam, 1986.
Carlisle's All. New York, Bantam, 1986.
Shadow of a Unicorn. New York, Bantam, 1987.
Whisper of the Cat. New York, Bantam, 1988.
Return to Morocco. New York, Macmillan, 1988.

The Potter's Wheel. New York, Morrow, 1988.
Riding Home (as Pamela Dryden). New York, Bantam, 1988.
The Delphic Choice. New York, Macmillan, 1989.
The Time of the Cranes. New York, Macmillan, 1990.
The Dragon's Choice. New York, Macmillan, 1990.

Novels as Kate Chambers

The Secret of the Singing Strings. New York, New American Library, 1983.
Danger in the Old Fort. New York, New American Library, 1983.
The Case of the Dog-Lover's Legacy. New York, New American Library, 1983.
Secrets on Beacon Hill. New York, New American Library, 1984.
The Legacy of Lucian Van Vandt. New York, New American Library, 1984.
The Threat of the Pirate Ship. New York, New American Library, 1984.

Fiction (for children) as Catherine E. Chambers

California Gold Rush: Search for Treasure. New York, Troll, 1984.
Daniel Boon and the Wilderness Road. New York, Troll, 1984.
Flatboats on the Ohio: Westward Bound. New York, Troll, 1984.
Frontier Dream: Life on the Great Plains. New York, Troll, 1984.
Frontier Farmer: Kansas Adventure. New York, Troll, 1984.
Frontier Village: A Town Is Born. New York, Troll, 1984.
Indian Days: Life in a Frontier Town. New York, Troll, 1984.
Log-Cabin Home: Pioneers in the Wilderness. New York, Troll, 1984.
Texas Roundup: Life on the Range. New York, Troll, 1984.
Wagons West: Off to Oregon. New York, Troll, 1984.

Novels as Elizabeth Bolton

Ghost in the House. New York, Troll, 1985.
The Secret of the Ghost Piano. New York, Troll, 1985.
The Secret of the Magic Potion. New York, Troll, 1985.
The Tree House Detective Club. New York, Troll, 1985.

Novels as Adrian Robert

The Awful Mess Mystery. New York, Troll, 1985.
Ellen Ross, Private Detective. New York, Troll, 1985.
My Grandma, the Witch. New York, Troll, 1985.
The Secret of the Haunted Chimney. New York, Troll, 1985.
The Secret of the Old Barn. New York, Troll, 1985.

Novels as Lavinia Harris

The Great Rip-Off. New York, Scholastic, 1985.
Soaps in the Afternoon. New York, Scholastic, 1985.
A Touch of Madness. New York, Scholastic, 1985.
Cover-Up. New York, Scholastic, 1986.

Other

Louisa May: The World and Works of Louisa May Alcott (as Norma Johnston). New York, Macmillan, 1991.

*

Manuscript Collection: Rutgers University Library, New Brunswick, New Jersey.

*   *   *

'I draw my strength from England', says the American novelist

Nicole St John. Indeed, English history is the underlying theme—the *bas-relief*, if you will—of two of St John's novels. Hidden within *Wychwood* is the story of Catherine Parr, widow of Henry VIII, and her lover Thomas Seymour, as well as ancient Anglo-Saxon occult rituals. *Guinever's Gift* is a reenactment of the Arthurian legend, as the central characters investigate its historical validity. *The Medici Ring*, the author's first novel, reveals her appreciation of fine art and antiques. Further, St John's love of English literature is reflected in her frequent references to Sir Thomas Malory, Shakespeare, Tennyson.

These are novels in the classic gothic tradition. Heroines (who tell their own stories) are always young and pretty, bright, curious, spunky, and alone in the world (typically, Lavinia Stanton, of *The Medici Ring*, is a 'young, impecunious, overeducated orphan'). All heroes in St John's novels are older and wiser, dark and mysterious, with flashing eyes (in short, *Jane Eyre*'s Rochester). The standard settings are: a mansion—the Culhaine mansion, on Marlborough Street in Boston, in *The Medici Ring;* Avalon, an Arthurian-type country house, in *Guinever's Gift;* an English cottage (*Wychwood*); each with many rooms, staircases, and hallways, some of them, of course, secret. The time: the Victorian Age. The plots that unfold are captivating and suspenseful.

Impelled by instinct, interest, and her newly orphaned status, the heroine is directed to the mansion (or country home or cottage), and there meets the dark stranger who, when his veil of mystery drops, will be revealed as her hero. In *The Medici Ring* the orphan Lavinia Stanton suffers another loss when her guardian, 'Uncle' Eustace Robinson, dies, leaving her with only a 15th-century ruby ring and a knowledge of art and antiques. Lavinia is invited by Damaris Culhaine, an old school friend, to help catalogue the family's collection of Renaissance art. The Culhaine mansion contains not only paintings and sculpture and jewels, but many mysteries: the possible poisoning of Damaris; the Marchesa Marina Orsini, Damaris's aunt; the theft and forgery of some of the Culhaine's valuable art works; the untimely death (some years before) of Damaris's mother, Isabel; and Damaris's father, the 'emerald-eyed' Ross Culhaine. The figures in a hidden Renaissance tapestry unravel these mysteries for Lavinia.

Wychwood, named for the English country cottage to which the orphan sisters Camilla and Nell Jardin move when Nell is paralyzed by an accident at boarding school, likewise abounds in mysteries and apparitions, particularly the 'ghost of the Copper Maid'. Camilla risks her life and sanity to discover the riddle of her inheritance and the secrets behind the frightening events that occur at Wychwood. Aided by a mysterious neighbour, Jeremy Bushell, she uncovers the secret story of Catherine Parr and Thomas Seymour, and gains her own rightful inheritance.

In *Guinever's Gift* Lydian Wentworth, after the death of her father, travels to Avalon at the invitation of Lord Charles Ransome, a scholar of the Arthurian legend. Although paralyzed, Charles further invites Lydian to marry him. She accepts. Lydian, Charles, and Lawrence Stearns, Charles' young research assistant, seem fated to re-enact the lives of Guinever, Arthur, and Lancelot, until Lydian's courage, determination, and her own knowledge of Arthurian lore save them from the tragic triangle.

St John writes with an easy elegance and literary *connaissance* that make her a worthy successor to the Brontës.

—Marcia G. Welsh

———

SALISBURY, Carola.
Pseudonym for Michael Butterworth. **Other Pseudonyms:** William Dobson; Sarah Kemp; Michael Marlowe; also wrote as Michael Butterworth. **Nationality:** British. **Born:** 10 January 1924.

Military Service: Royal Naval Volunteer Reserve: lieutenant. **Relations:** married Jenny Spalding in 1957; one son and four daughters, and one daughter by previous marriage. **Career:** tutor in drawing, Nottingham College of Art, 1950–51; editor, art director, and managing editor, Fleetway Publications, London, 1952–63. Full-time writer from the mid-1960s. **Died:** October 1986.

ROMANCE AND HISTORICAL PUBLICATIONS

Novels

Mallion's Pride. London, Collins, 1975; as *The Pride of the Trevallions*, New York, Doubleday, 1975.
Dark Inheritance. New York, Doubleday, 1975; London, Collins, 1976.
The 'Dolphin' Summer. New York, Doubleday, 1976; London, Collins, 1977.
The Winter Bride. London, Collins, and New York, Doubleday, 1978.
The Shadowed Spring. London, Collins, and New York, Doubleday, 1980.
Count Vronsky's Daughter. London, Collins, and New York, Doubleday, 1981.
An Autumn in Araby. London, Century, and New York, Doubleday, 1983.
Daisy Friday. London, Century, 1984.
A Certain Splendour. London, Century, 1985.
The Woman in Grey. London, Century, 1987.

OTHER PUBLICATIONS

Novels as Michael Butterworth

The Soundless Scream. London, Long, and New York, Doubleday, 1967.
Walk Softly, In Fear. London, Long, 1968.
Vanishing Act. London, Collins, 1970; as *The Uneasy Sun*, New York, Doubleday, 1970.
Flowers for a Dead Witch. London, Collins, and New York, Doubleday, 1971.
The Black Look. London, Collins, and New York, Doubleday, 1972; (as Sarah Kemp) Bath, Chivers, 1985.
Villa on the Shore. London, Collins, 1973; New York, Doubleday, 1974; (as Sarah Kemp) Bath, Chivers, 1984.
The Man in the Sopwith Camel. London, Collins, 1974; New York, Doubleday, 1975.
Mind-Breaks of Space, with J. Jeff Jones. New York, Pocket Books, 1975; London, Wingate, 1978.
Remains to Be Seen. London, Collins, and New York, Doubleday, 1976.
Festival! London, Collins, 1976.
The Time of the Hawklords. Henley-on-Thames, Ellis, 1976.
Queens of Deliria. London, W.H. Allen, 1977.
Planets of Peril. New York, Warner, 1977.
X Marks the Spot. London, Collins, and New York, Doubleday, 1978.
The Man Who Broke the Bank at Monte Carlo. London, Collins, and New York, Doubleday, 1983.
A Virgin on the Rocks. London, Collins, and New York, Doubleday, 1985.
The Five Million Dollar Prince. London, Collins, and New York, Doubleday, 1986.

Novels as Sarah Kemp

Goodbye, Pussy. London, Collins, 1979; as *Over the Edge*, New York, Doubleday, 1979.
No Escape. New York, Doubleday, 1984; London, Century, 1985.
The Lure of Sweet Death. London, Century, and New York, Doubleday, 1986.
What Dread Hand? London, Century, and New York, Doubleday, 1987.

*　　*　　*

Michael Butterwoth, who wrote as Carola Salisbury, was an accomplished author of gothic romances. His experience as a mystery writer clearly showed as he developed the tension of a story, releasing it in exciting, unexpected endings. The sudden realization that Piers Trevallion is still alive (*Mallion's Pride*), the discovery that Melloney has faked her invalid state (*The 'Dolphin' Summer*), the final revelation that an entire diplomatic mission has been a red herring to protect the real emissary (*The Shadowed Spring*), and the unmasking of a murderer (*An Autumn in Araby*) all show Butterworth's ability to develop and sustain a feeling of true suspense.

While Butterworth carefully developed his plots, he paid equal attention to the development of his characters. He was particularly adept at the first-person narrative of the heroines. Feminine thoughts and feelings are expressed so naturally that it was difficult to remember that the author was in reality a man. Seen through a woman's eyes, the action is described with just the right mixture of curiosity and fear, without lapsing into the hysteria which sometimes passes for sensitivity in depictions of a gently bred woman confronted by the violence, mystery, and terror in a gothic novel. Butterworth also handled the Victorian-accented dialogue well, which adds to the atmosphere.

The theme of the past affecting the present and the future is prevalent in the Salisbury novels. Previous events and actions taken by others weave a complex web which draws the current characters into a situation that explodes into a resolution of the mystery. Often the secret lies buried in a great family's history, as described in *Mallion's Pride* and *Dark Inheritance*. Old crimes, real or perceived, are resurrected to haunt the present in *The 'Dolphin' Summer*, *The Winter Bride*, and *An Autumn in Araby*. Even a classic is used to provide a past for *Count Vronsky's Daughter*, in which Anna Karenina's daughter is the heroine.

The Salisbury novels are carefully plotted to provide above average suspense and intrigue, with many twists to the plots which keep the reader guessing to the very end. Insanity, or at the very least instability, lurks in the minds of the least likely characters. The stories are peopled by colourful, complex characters who engage a reader's imagination and interest. Distinguished by action, adventure, and excitement, these novels must rank high on any list of period gothics. As one critic remarked 'you don't have to believe it to enjoy it'. It is a mark of Butterworth's talent, however, that you do believe while you are reading.

—Barbara E. Kemp

SALLIS, Susan.
Pseudonym: Susan Meadmore. **Nationality:** British. **Born:** Gloucester, 7 November 1929. **Education:** Girls' High School, Gloucester; St Matthias College of Education, Bristol. **Relations:** married Brian Sallis in 1951 (died 1983); one daughter and two sons. **Career:** teacher, Department of Education and Science, Backwell, Somerset. **Agent:** Mary Irvine, 11 Upland Park Road, Oxford OX2 7RU, England. **Address:** 21 Kingston Avenue, Clevedon, Somerset BS21 6DS, England.

ROMANCE AND HISTORICAL PUBLICATIONS

Novels (series: Rising Family; Richmond)

Return to Listowel. London, Hale, 1975.
Troubled Waters. London, Hale, 1975.
Richmond Inheritance. London, Corgi, 1991.
　Richmond Heritage. London, Corgi, 1977.
　Four Weeks in Venice. London, Corgi, 1978.
A Time for Everything. New York, Harper and Row, 1979; as *Thunder in the Hills* (as Susan Meadmore), London, Hale, 1981.
Rising Family:
　A Scattering of Daisies. London, Corgi, 1984; as *April Rising*, New York, St Martin's Press, 1984.
　The Daffodils of Newent. London, Corgi, 1985.
　Bluebell Windows. London, Corgi, 1987.
　Rosemary for Remembrance. London, Corgi, 1987.
Summer Visitors. London, Corgi, 1988; New York, St Martin's Press, 1989.
By Sun and Candlelight. London, Corgi, 1989.
An Ordinary Woman. London, Bantam, 1991.
Daughters of the Moon. London, Bantam, 1992.
Sweeter than Sweet. London, Corgi, 1994.

Novels as Susan Meadmore

Behind the Mask. London, Hale, 1980.
Mary, Mary. London, Hale, 1982.

OTHER PUBLICATIONS

Fiction (for children)

An Open Mind. New York, Harper, 1978; London, Penguin, 1985.
Only Love. New York, Harper, 1980; as *Sweet Frannie*, London, Heinemann, 1981.
Secret Places of the Stairs. New York, Harper, 1984.

*

Manuscript Collection: de Grummond Collection, University of Southern Mississippi, Hattiesburg.

Susan Sallis comments:

My books can be divided into three categories: contemporary romance, teenage fiction, and family sagas. They all deal with love: married love, family love, and friendship. The teenage fiction deals with young people coming to terms with the adult world and coping with mental and physical handicaps.

*　　*　　*

The sure basis of Susan Sallis's fiction is a warm sense of the value and importance of everyday life and quite ordinary emotions. She writes of life not perhaps as most of her readers have experienced it, but the gap between reality and romance is generally not one that demands too great an effort of the imagination, though there is, of course, some heightening of everyday situations and of the characters' responses to them.

Sallis's most ambitious work is the saga of the Rising family which is told in four volumes. Against a background of the great events of the first half of the 20th century, including the two world wars, Sallis traces the lives of the three daughters—March, May, and April—of Florence Rising, the wife of a struggling tailor in Gloucester. Every detail of the setting is described carefully, whether it is a matter of costume, living conditions or manners generally, and Sallis has an acute sense of the way in which social class conditioned ordinary people's everyday lives at the time. The consequence of all this is that the characters acquire a solidity which is generally convincing. Despite the rather coyly pretty titles of the four novels and the obvious contrivance of the girls' names, the stories are quite tough and explicit. Love is one spur to action, and the desire to escape from a vicious circle of poverty is another. The ambition is entirely understandable, but the price is often high in terms of betrayal by men who take advantage of the girls' desires to break out in a period when, for the first time, women were beginning to have more freedom.

A Scattering of Daisies introduces the characters, showing the clash between economic realities and dreams for self-fulfilment which shape these people's lives. *The Daffodils of Newent* in set in the 1920s, a time when gay young things sometimes seemed to find everything going their way but when the war still cast its long shadow and the economic crisis was just around the corner. The personal problems resulting from unstable sexual relationships are further explored in *Bluebell Windows*. It is set during the 1930s, and that troubled decade is reflected in the turmoil in the lives of the three sisters. They have grown older, of course, and become mothers, but problems remain, especially with regard to illegitimacy. The horrors of the air raids of World War II add to the strains on the three sisters in *Rosemary for Remembrance*. There is a touch of melodrama in some of the responses to family secrets, but it was a time when the improbable was often possible and danger readily brought hidden emotions to the surface with unusual force.

The 'Rising Family' series is essentially a family saga narrated from a female point of view, but the historical framework serves to bring out the personal dilemmas of the three sisters while creating a persuasive period atmosphere which has an interest of its own.

—Christopher N. Smith

SALVERSON, Laura Goodman.
Nationality: Canadian. **Born:** Winnipeg, Manitoba, 9 December 1890. **Education:** United States. **Relations:** married George Salverson in 1913; one son. **Recipient:** Governor-General's award, 1937, 1939. **Died:** 1970.

ROMANCE AND HISTORICAL PUBLICATIONS

Novels

The Viking Heart. New York, Doran, 1923; London, Bretano's, 1926.
When Sparrows Fall. Toronto, T. Allen, 1925.
Lord of the Silver Dragon: A Romance of Leif the Lucky. Toronto, McClelland, 1927.
Johan Lind. Toronto, McClelland, 1928.
The Dove of El-Djezaire. Toronto, Ryerson Press, 1933; as *The Dove*, London, Skeffington, 1933.
The Dark Weaver. Toronto, Ryerson Press, and London, Sampson Low, 1937.
Black Lace. Toronto, Ryerson Press, and London, Hutchinson, 1938.
Immortal Rock: The Saga of the Kensington Stone. Toronto, Ryerson Press, 1954; London, Angus and Robertson, 1955.

OTHER PUBLICATIONS

Poetry

Wayside Gleams. Toronto, McClelland, 1925.

Other

Confessions of an Immigrant's Daughter (autobiography). Toronto, Ryerson Press, and London, Faber, 1939.

*   *   *

Laura Goodman Salverson's historical novels make extensive use of her family's background as Icelandic immigrants to North America. Her own part of this experience is recorded in her autobiography, *Confessions of an Immigrant's Daughter*. Although Salverson greatly admired the treatment of the immigrant experience in Frederick Philip Grove's novels, a closer model for the approach she took to her subject may be found in the work of the early Canadian feminist, Nellie McClung, whose novels specifically deal with women's experiences during the settlement of the Canadian west.

Salverson's first novel, *The Viking Heart*, is a compelling depiction of the Icelandic settlement near Winnipeg, Manitoba, and documents the hardships, despair, and endurance of a family over three generations. In its attention to historical detail, the novel is less concerned with the smoothly dramatic plotting characteristic of the historical romance, than with the episodic non-closure of a stark, overarching Darwinian naturalism. Grove's influence can be felt in this aspect of Salverson's writing, but ultimately it is mitigated by a sense of the optimism and strength associated with the women seen in McClung's work.

While poverty and struggle with the land are at the core of *The Viking Heart*, in a later novel, *The Dark Weaver*, the early prosperity of merchant settlers is presented in a narrative style more consistent with the realism of historical romance. Dealing with two generations of two families, *The Dark Weaver* explores various aspects of women's experience including arranged marriage, the victimization of native women by male settlers, the tension between the old and new world mores of the generations, and the possibilities available to women in the New World. Developing the naturalism of *The Viking Heart*, the later novel denies the reader a happy ending, and the tension created through the narrative is left tantalizingly unresolved.

Salverson refers to a more ancient Viking past in *Lord of the Silver Dragon* and *Immortal Rock*. The former novel deals with the voyages and reign of Leif the Lucky and explores the possibilities of early Norse settlements along the Atlantic shores of North America. *Immortal Rock* depicts the last 24 hours in the lives of a group of Norse explorers. Salverson bases her plot on the assumption that the Kensington Stone (which appears to prove that Norsemen may have reached the Canadian prairies via Hudson's Bay and its river system) is authentic. Tension is built to an excruciating pitch while the men prepare for a final battle with the surrounding Indians. Similarly the tension in *Lord of the Silver Dragon* is created through the constant deferral of Leif's final voyage to Vineland. Both novels explore documented ancient connections between North America and Iceland skilfully and imaginatively.

Salverson leaves the Norse world behind altogether in *Black Lace*, a historical romance set early in the reign of the French king Louis XIV. Taking Colbert's anti-piracy policies as a point of departure, Salverson evokes a sense of this period as a time of change between a generation which could recall the days before the Fronde and one moving towards the French Revolution and the emergence of modern France.

A lesser known aspect of Icelandic history forms the basis of *The Dove*, which recounts the story of a woman, Steffania, captured in a raid on her village and sold into slavery in Algiers. She became known as the 'Dove of El-Djezair'. This novel is Salverson's most conventional historical romance, but the author successfully evokes the exotic setting through a skilful use of imagery. The forceful characterization of the female Icelandic slaves both establishes a link with Salverson's other work and increases the novel's dramatic effect.

All of Salverson's novels have strong characters and plots as well as the keen sense of time and place necessary to create good historical fiction. The novels dealing with the connection between Iceland and North America are arguably her best work. *The Viking Heart* and *The Dark Weaver* in particular provide an insight into the thoughts and feelings of women immigrants, allowing a valuable contrast to the conventionally accepted male immigrant's viewpoint, which is seen as representative of the immigrant experience in canonized novels of the Canadian west.

—Heather Iris Jones

SANDYS, Oliver. See BARCYNSKA, Countess.

SANTMYER, Helen Hooven.
Nationality: American. **Born:** Cincinnati, Ohio, 25 November 1895. **Education:** Wellesley College, Massachusetts, B.A. 1918; Oxford University, B. Litt. 1927. **Career:** secretary, *Scribners* magazine, New York, 1919–21; English teacher, Xenia High School, Ohio, 1921–22; chair, English Department, and Dean of Women, Cedarville College, Ohio, 1936–53; library assistant, Dayton and Montgomery County Public Library, Dayton, Ohio, 1953–60. **Recipient:** D.Hum.: Wright State University, Fairborn, Ohio, 1984. **Died:** 21 February 1986.

Romance and Historical Publications

Novels

Herbs and Apples. Boston, Houghton Mifflin, 1925.
The Fierce Dispute. Boston, Houghton Mifflin, 1929.
. . . and Ladies of the Club. Columbus, Ohio State University Press, 1982; London, Pan, 1985.
Farewell Summer. New York, Harper, 1988.

Other Publications

Other

The Spirit of Sisterhood. New York, Young Women's Christian Association, 1915.
Ohio Town: A Portrait of Xenia. Columbus, Ohio State University Press, 1963.

*   *   *

While critics have found her writing overburdened by detail and not particularly sensitive to minority groups and issues, Helen Hooven Santmyer's historical fiction, nevertheless, evokes the small-town life of yesteryear in middle America. Given Santmyer's near century-long life span, her fiction contains significant elements of a semi-autobiographical nature. One cannot ignore her intellectual interests in history, literature, and the human condition or separate them from her community of Xenia, Ohio.

Herbs and Apples, Santmyer's first novel, has as its main character, Derrick Thornton, an aspiring young woman writer of the early decades of the 20th century. Thornton leaves the fictitious town of Tecumseh, Ohio, to attend college in the north-eastern United States. While at college, she strikes up a friendship with a group of

literary women. After graduation, they all go to New York City where Thornton obtains employment as a secretary to the editor of a literary magazine. Family obligation, however, intervenes and Thornton returns to Tecumseh to care for her father and younger siblings. Once back home, she forsakes her promising New York literary career to teach English at the local high school. Interspersed throughout the narrative are the rich details of small-town social, religious, and economic routine, all of which mirror Santmyer's own life experiences up to the date of the publication of the novel.

Her second novel, *The Fierce Dispute*, portrays a young Lucy Ann Baird, residing in a mansion on the outskirts of town with her mother and grandmother; their only contact with the outside world is through a servant. While suggestive of life in Xenia, Ohio (Santmyer's home) and certain aspects of her family background, the novel is the least historically interesting of her novels, although the inclusion of Civil War letters lends an historical aspect of the novel.

Ohio Town, a collection of 13 essays, concentrates on the lives and institutions of Xenia and Greene County, Ohio, which Santmyer knew well from her family background and personal recollection. While the essays are not strictly historical, they are based on historical sources. The portraits she creates are blatantly nostalgic in tone, yet, the essays do not reflect a desire for the past but are a statement that there are constants in ordinary small town life regardless of the time period. Most changes are only superficial alterations. *Ohio Town* can be seen as a microcosm of American small-town society at its best.

Santmyer's longest and most enduring novel *. . . and Ladies of the Club*, recounts life in a fictitious Ohio town (Waynesboro) from the end of the Civil War to the beginning of the Great Depression. Again, the novel draws upon the author's attention to the details and intricacies of small-town life. While criticized for the level of detail by some reviewers, it is detail that makes the novel come alive to portray the social fabric of the time period it encompasses. The Waynesboro Women's Club, patterned after Santmyer's own Xenia Women's Club, gives structure to the lives of Anne Alexander Gordon and Sally Cochran Rausch, its major characters, as well as to the novel itself. The narrative is anchored by chapter headings listing club membership and a brief quotation from the club minutes highlighting specific local events. This device helps to chronicle the changing middle-class lives of its characters with an emphasis on major local historical events and the evolution of society through a 64-year period. Despite the patronizing treatment and near exclusion of African-Americans, the novel does correctly reflect the attitudes of its time period and locale. Santmyer captures the social consciousness of small-town middle-class white America, particularly the area of Ohio where Republican Party adherency was prominent, and racial attitudes intolerant.

—Frank R. Levstik

SAUNDERS, Jean.
Pseudonyms: Sally Blake; Jean Innes; Rowena Summers. **Nationality:** British. **Born:** London, 8 February 1932. **Education:** Weston-super-Mare, Avon. **Relations:** married Geoffrey Saunders in 1952; one son and two daughters. **Career:** full-time writer. Since 1993, chair, Romantic Novelists Association. **Address:** The Hayes, 23 Hobbiton Road, Weston-super-Mare, Avon BS22 0HP, England.

Romance and Historical Publications

Novels

The Tender Trap. London, Woman's Weekly, 1978.

Lady of the Manor. London, Woman's Weekly, 1978.
Rainbow's End. London, Woman's Weekly, 1978.
Enchantment of Merrowporth. New York, Cameo, 1980.
The Kissing Time. New York, Silhouette, 1982; London, Severn House, 1990.
Love's Sweet Music. New York, Silhouette, 1983.
The Language of Love. New York, Silhouette, 1983; London, Hodder and Stoughton, 1983.
Taste the Wine. New York, Silhouette, 1983; London, Hodder and Stoughton, 1984.
Partners in Love. New York, Silhouette, 1984; London, Hodder and Stoughton, 1991.
Scarlet Rebel. New York, Ballantine, 1985; London, Severn House, 1990.
Golden Destiny. New York, Pocket Books, 1986; London, Severn House, 1990.
For Better for Worse. London, Book Incentives for Premier Brands, 1988.
The Man from Venice. London, Book Incentives for Premier Brands, 1988.
Nightingale Valley. London, Book Incentives for Premier Brands, 1988.
Portrait of Sarah. London, Book Incentives for Premier Brands, 1988.
All in the April Morning. London, W.H. Allen, 1989; New York, Zebra, 1993.
The Bannister Girls. London, Grafton, 1991.
To Love and Honour. London, Grafton, 1992.
With This Ring. London, Grafton, 1993.

Novels as Jean Innes

Ashton's Folly. London, Hale, 1975; New York, Bantam, 1981.
Sands of Lamanna. London, Hale, 1975.
The Golden God. London, Hale, 1975.
The Whispering Dark. London, Hale, 1976.
Boskelly's Bride. London, Hale, 1976.
White Blooms of Yarrow. London, Hale, 1976.
The Wishing Stone. London, Hale, 1976.
Cobden's Cottage. London, Hale, 1978; New York, Bantam, 1981.
The Dark Stranger. London, Hale, 1979.
Silver Lady. London, Hale, 1981; New York, Bantam, 1982.
Legacy of Love. London, Hale, 1982.
Scent of Jasmine. New York, Bantam, 1982; London, Century Hutchinson, 1983.
Enchanted Island. New York, Bantam, 1982; Leicester, Linford, 1987.
Seeker of Dreams. London, Hale, 1983.
Buccaneer's Bride. New York, Zebra, 1989.
Dream Lover. New York, Zebra, 1990.
Golden Captive. New York, Zebra, 1990.
Secret Touch. New York, Zebra, 1992.
Tropical Fire. New York, Zebra, 1992.

Novels as Sally Blake

The Devil's Kiss. London, Macdonald Futura, 1981.
Moonlight Mirage. London, Macdonald Futura, 1982.
Outback Woman. London, Mills and Boon, 1989.
Lady of Spain. London, Mills and Boon, 1990.
Far Distant Shores. London, Mills and Boon, 1991.
A Royal Summer. London, Mills and Boon, 1992.
House of Secrets. London, Mills and Boon, 1993.

Novels as Rowena Summers (series: Cornish Trilogy)

Blackmaddie. London, Hamlyn, 1980; (as Jean Innes) New York, Zebra, 1990.
The Savage Moon. London, Severn House, 1982.
The Sweet Red Earth. London, Severn House, 1983.
Willow Harvest. London, Severn House, 1985.
Cornish Trilogy:
   Killigrew Clay. London, Severn House, 1986.
   Clay Country. London, Severn House, 1987.
   Family Ties. London, Severn House, 1988.
Highland Heritage. London, Mills and Boon, 1991.
Velvet Dawn. London, Severn House, 1991.
Angel of the Evening. London, Severn House, 1991.
Ellis Island. London, Severn House, 1993.

OTHER PUBLICATIONS

Fiction (for children)

The Fugitives. London, Heinemann, 1974.
Only Yesterday. London, Heinemann, 1975; New York, Scholastic, 1977.
Nightmare. London, Heinemann, 1977.
Roses All the Way. London, Heinemann, 1978.
Anchor Man. London, Heinemann, 1980.

Other

The Craft of Writing Romance. London, Allison and Busby, 1986.
Writing Step By Step. London, Allison and Busby, 1988.
How to Create Fictional Characters. London, Allison and Busby, 1992.
How To Research Your Novel. London, Allison and Busby, 1993.

*

Jean Saunders comments:

The term compulsive writer is perhaps a euphemistic one, yet it describes precisely how I regard myself. I am never happier than when I am writing, and the urge to do so has never diminished. My first aim is to entertain my readers, while producing novels of depth and insight into character. I am very conscious of the way that circumstances can change and mould people, and I apply this maxim to my fictional characters by giving them an emotive background in which to grow and develop, such as my novels involving two World Wars, *All in The April Morning*, and the *The Bannister Girls*. Research plays a very large part in my life, whether for contemporary locations and occupations or historical facts that must always be accurate. My writing is sometimes described as earthy. I prefer to call it realistic. I pull no punches in writing about birth and death and everything between. My heroines are always strong, feminine, and survivors against all the odds. I defend romance fiction wholeheartedly. I believe that any novel in any genre is enhanced by a love relationship between the main characters, and I take pride in making my characters and plots as visually believable to the reader as possible.

*   *   *

As well as neatly weaving historical events into her novels, Jean Saunders has the ability to absorb the atmosphere of a period and the attitudes of the people living at that time, then transpose them into her fictional works.

Scarlet Rebel, set in Scotland at the time of the Jacobite rebellion, involved considerable research, and Saunders admits that she found discrepancies in her sources. When it was not possible to verify facts she had to choose what seemed the most likely occurrences. In this novel particularly, she succeeds in conveying the feel of the period while continually progressing the gripping story of an intensely emotional romance between the fictional couple who are supporting the Young Pretender in his bid for the English throne. The graphic battle scenes add an extra dimension to the romantic storyline.

Katrina, the coppery-haired beauty from *Scarlet Rebel* makes a fleeting appearance in a later novel, *Golden Destiny*, but only as part of a family legend. *Golden Destiny* takes place more than 100 years later, when a 17-year-old girl sails to India to join her diplomat father. She becomes involved with a dashing male descendant of Katrina's, and faces danger with him by her side during a native uprising.

The author's gothic novels, written as Jean Innes, owe much of their atmosphere to their settings. *Sands of Lamanna* takes place in 19th-century Cornwall and exploits the rugged country-side and the mysterious grey stone houses as well as the folklore and superstitions which were rife in that part of the country at the time. The characters are clear and distinct. An unforgettable gypsy girl named Wenna plays a leading part in this novel. Her father lays a curse on her and her lover, the main male character, who then considers himself doomed. Other characters are involved in the notorious Cornish shipwrecking activities. There are murder, a trial, imprisonment, but in true gothic tradition good prevails and evil gets its just reward.

The novels written as Rowena Summers have a more lusty flavour, and take their inspiration from both historical events and locations. Particularly strong in its atmosphere, *The Savage Moon* begins its story in the bleak English Fen country and features two brothers who have fled from the Irish potato famine. They are not welcome in their new surroundings and come into strong conflict with a local family. The attraction between the two Irish boys and the two girls in the family make the male members more determined than ever to chase them off. The story moves on to North America and the Civil War, but desire, rivalry, and love still contrive to tear the two families apart.

Willow Harvest is set in the Somerset Levels with a background of willow harvesting and basket weaving. The father of the heroine takes his baskets to show at the Great Exhibition of 1851, and the heroine becomes involved with a class of people she has not known before. Anyone who reads this novel will find it hard to forget the revolting and libidinous Cyrus Hale's lecherous pursuit of the luckless heroine.

The Devil's Kiss by Sally Blake takes its title from the name of a mysterious Siamese ruby with alleged magical powers. The story, which begins on a tea plantation in Ceylon, moves to the misty Yorkshire moorlands, peopled with traditionally morose and single-minded Yorkshire characters. The gem plays a major role in the story by its influence on the characters.

All in the April Morning begins in San Francisco on the day of the 1906 earthquake which orphans two Irish immigrant girls. Bridget, the older girl, becomes obsessed with a desire to return to Ireland but is unable to do so. Her younger sister dies, and Bridget is trapped into an unhappy marriage. Eventually, widowed but with a daughter and pregnant with a son, she realizes her dream, and goes back to Ireland where she is befriended by a wealthy Englishman. There is constant and painful conflict between Bridget and her daughter as the story progresses to World War II. Then the daughter falls in love with an airman whose home is in San Francisco, a place Bridget never wants to see again. Involvement in an air raid shocks Bridget's mind with memories of the earthquake but also brings mother and daughter closer together than ever. After the war, Bridget goes back to San Francisco with a new husband, to see her grandson.

This novel which among other things explores with convincing authority and particular sensitivity the complex and moving relationship between the heroine and her daughter, demonstrates how Saunders has gradually expanded and developed her talent and ability to deal successfully with stronger themes and more complex relationships.

The Bannister Girls, shortlisted for the Romantic Novelist Associations novel of the year award in 1991, is set during World War I. The lives of Sir Fred and Lady Bannister's three daughters are changed by the war. The conventional marriage of the eldest one fails, the second daughter becomes involved with the suffragette movement, and the youngest falls in love with a man whom she meets in the darkened London streets, loses him, and finds him again after ordeals in the French battlefields. The emotional trauma faced by each of the girls, contained within the authentic atmosphere and attitudes of the period, result in a suspenseful and passionate, page-turning and satisfying novel.

Moving forward to the period of the General Strike, and the early days of cinema, *To Love and Honour* is a 'rags to riches' story with a difference. Amy Moore climbs from downstairs maid to garage and cafe proprietor, but marries the wrong man, and nurses a bitter secret which seems to constantly threaten her future and her happiness.

Saunders has also written a number of *How to ...* books for creative writers which cover a wider field than romantic and historical writing, but which are none the less helpful to anyone aspiring to work in those genres.

—W.H. Bradley

SAUNDERS, Jeanne. See **MANNERS, Alexandra.**

SAVAGE, Alan. See **NICOLE, Christopher.**

SAVAGE, Elizabeth.
Nationality: American. **Born:** Elizabeth Fitzgerald in Hingham, Massachusetts, in 1918. **Education:** Colby College, Waterville, Maine, B.A. 1940. **Relations:** married Thomas Savage in 1939; two sons and one daughter. **Died:** 15 July 1989.

ROMANCE AND HISTORICAL PUBLICATIONS

Novels

Summer of Pride. Boston, Little Brown, 1961; London, Hodder and Stoughton, 1962.
But Not for Love. Boston, Little Brown, 1970.
A Fall of Angels. Boston, Little Brown, 1971.
Happy Ending. Boston, Little Brown, 1972.
The Last Night at the Ritz. Boston, Little Brown, 1973.
A Good Confession. Boston, Little Brown, 1975.
The Girls from the Five Great Valleys. Boston, Little Brown, and London, Prior, 1977.
Willowwood. Boston, Little Brown, 1978; London, Prior, 1979.
Toward the End. Boston, Little Brown, 1980.

*   *   *

Adept at characterization, Elizabeth Savage also evoked place with great skill: the American far west or New England (settings most frequently used in her novels), the Jamaica of *A Fall of Angels*, or Dante Gabriel Rossetti's 19th-century London. Almost always, the weather and seasonal changes are key symbols, humour an enlivening device.

Reflecting Savage's life-long interest, *Willowwood* blends fact and fiction in the story of Rossetti and his talented, capricious circle. In its deft portrayal of intricate relationships among complex characters, *Willowwood*, an atypical Savage novel, is nevertheless linked closely with others among her works.

Less singular but no less intriguing than the pre-Raphaelites are the extended families Savage examines. The organizing event of *Summer of Pride* is the Oliver family's annual picnic which memorializes their history and accomplishments. Matt Oliver, a naively autocratic Idaho rancher, oversees his family's interests despite their best efforts to prevent his interference, even to planning his younger brother's career; but Paul, a poet, intends to marry a stranger whom the family distrusts, move east, and teach. Meanwhile the survival of Matt's own marriage depends largely upon his wife's self-redefinition. Under the eye of Emily, the matriarch, the brothers sort out their obligations, each learning to compromise.

Though their relationships are marred by confusion, misjudgment, and deceit, the clannish Hollister family of *But Not for Love* maintains a haughty façade, but ultimately, Winifred Hollister, the self-abasing wife of Peter, begins to see her in-laws and even her husband as 'only people. Very like herself'. Like several other female characters, Winifred also discovers her own unsuspected strength. The irony of its title informs almost every relationship and situation of the plot which leaves a dozen questions unanswered but all central problems confronted, its relatively open ending being both satisfying and appropriate.

A Fall of Angels examines a crucial period in the lives of Helena St John and Luke Strider, thus addressing one of Savage's most frequent topics: a marriage threatened with redefinition or dissolution just when outsiders (and even, perhaps, one of the partners) might pronounce it secure, even enviable. Less successful than other works in the canon, this novel, like *Willowwood*, is nonetheless a solid achievement.

Two of Savage's New England novels also depict marriages in crisis. However, neither protagonist wastes much time pitying herself; both immediately confront other important challenges. During the deathbed vigil which bounds the action of *A Good Confession*, Meg Atherton sorts out her reactions to her husband's extra-marital affair, comes to terms with her reckless uncle, and learns important lessons about her attractive, available first love. In *Toward the End* an arduous winter is the central symbol for Jessie Thorne's development after separating from her husband. Happily devoid of pat phrases and cant diagnoses, each plot depicts its protagonist's increasing self-confidence and her growing awareness of the choice most suitable to her needs, her wishes, and her responsibilities. Incorporating a telling portrait of life during the Depression, *Happy Ending* compares love stories, one old, one new. During a long, idyllic Montana winter, the elderly Russells celebrate the joys of family life and watch the developing love between their very young housekeeper, Maryalyse Tyler, an unwed mother, and Bud Perrault, their cowhand. The bonds of affection among this created family are strong and true. Here, Savage's title is quietly, firmly realistic but not ironic; her protagonists learn to change what they can, to accept what they must, and to cherish the good moments. Like all Savage novels, these are love stories informed by honest sentiment and brought to just conclusions. Savage's romances are unfailingly realistic, astringent but never acerbic.

One of the strongest qualities of *Happy Ending* is its adroitly managed, shifting point of view which prompts the reader to identify with several characters. The first-person point of view in *The Last Night at the Ritz*, perhaps Savage's best novel, is equally persuasive. Here, the unnamed narrator, believing herself to be fatally ill, reviews her life—marked by excitement, extravagance, and lost loves—by comparing it with that of her closest friend, Gay, who has led a settled, family-centred existence until her husband's infidelity and her son's rebellion call all their values into question. Able to laugh at herself, markedly sensitive to the needs of others, the narrator persuades readers of her reliability despite her own disclaimers, no mean authorial feat. The women's abiding friendship (one bond is their shared passion for reading, an especially nice touch) and the protagonist's profound affection for her friend's child are beautifully rendered.

The narrator of *The Girls from the Five Great Valleys* conceals her identity until the last sentence; yet her revelation prompts one to realize that Savage has so accurately evoked her character's buoyant, affirming tone that one should have known her all along. Vigorous (but not enduring) early friendship is the motif unifying this examination of three families whose teenage daughters are friends. Comparing and contrasting various parents' capacity for nurture and love, Savage comments tellingly upon child abuse, notes that occasionally youngsters flourish despite neglect, and firmly reminds readers that some families nurture very effectively. Powerful portraits of a wide array of characters of varying ages inform this excellent novel.

An acute observer of American life, Savage consistently demonstrates her understanding of human strengths and weaknesses as well as her technical skill; she is a very good writer.

—Jane S. Bakerman

SAWLEY, Petra. See WOODWARD, Lilian.

SAXE, Isobel. See RAYNER, Claire.

SAXTON, Judith.
Pseudonyms: Judith Arden; Lydia Balmain; Jennie Felix; Judy Turner. **Nationality:** British. **Born:** Norwich, Norfolk, 5 March 1936. **Relations:** married; four children. **Agent:** Caroline Sheldon, 71 Hillgate Place, London W8 7SS, England.

ROMANCE AND HISTORICAL PUBLICATIONS

Novels

The Bright Day Is Done. London, Constable, 1974.
Princess in Waiting. London, Constable, 1976.
Winter Queen. London, Constable, 1977.
Golden Chains (as Judith Arden). London, Macdonald, 1980.
The Pride. London, Hamlyn, 1981.
Golden Promises (as Judith Arden). London, Macdonald, 1981.
Masquerade (as Jenny Felix). London, Hamlyn, 1982.
Prisoner in Peking (as Jenny Felix). London, Hamlyn, 1982.
The Glory. London, Hamlyn, 1982.
The Splendour. London, Hamlyn, 1983.
Overland Trail (as Jenny Felix). London, Hamlyn, 1983.
Full Circle. London, Hamlyn, 1984.
Family Feeling. London, Century, 1986; New York, St Martin's Press, 1987.
All My Fortunes. London, Century, 1987; New York, St Martin's Press, 1988.
A Family Affair. London, Grafton, 1989; New York, St Martin's Press, 1989.
This Royal Breed. London, Grafton, 1991.
Nobody's Children. London, Grafton, 1991.
First Love, Last Love. London, HarperCollins, 1992.

The Blue and Distant Hills. London, Mandarin, 1994.

Novels as Judy Turner

Cousin to the Queen. London, Constable, 1972; New York, St Martin's Press, 1974.
Raleigh's Fair Bess. London, Hale, 1972; New York, St Martin's Press, 1974.
Feather Light, Diamond Bright. London, Hale, 1974.
My Master Mariner. London, Hale, 1974.
The Queen's Corsair. London, Hale, 1976.
Child of Passion. London, Hale, 1978.
The Merry Jade. London, Hale, 1978.
A Gift for Pamela. London, Mills and Boon, 1981.
Triple Tangle. London, Mills and Boon, 1981.
Sherida. London, Mills and Boon, 1981.
Follow the Drum. London, Mills and Boon, 1982.
The Arcade. London, New English Library, 1991.
Harbour Hill. London, New English Library, 1991.

Novels as Lydia Balmain

Caribbean Nurse. London, Mills and Boon, 1981.
Ice Venture Nurse. London, Mills and Boon, 1983.
Italian Nurse. London, Mills and Boon, 1984.
No Doctors Please. London, Mills and Boon, 1984.
Surgeon in the Snow. London, Mills and Boon, 1985.
Theatre of Love. London, Mills and Boon, 1987.
Hometown Hospital. London, Mills and Boon, 1991.

OTHER PUBLICATIONS

Novels

Sophie. London, Century, 1985.
Jenny Alone. London, Joseph, 1987.
Chasing Rainbows. London, Joseph, 1988.
Summer in the Lakes. London, Corgi, 1988.
Crock of Gold. London, Corgi, 1990.

*   *   *

The core of Judith Saxton's novels is a concept of the family as the essential social unit. Far-flung it may be, and not every member sees eye to eye with every other one, but across time as well as across the world the bonds of kinship remain, exerting a force that remains powerful through every trial. As if to demonstrate the strengths of the family unit Saxton sometimes likes to disconcert her readers by sudden leaps in her narrative, from one situation to another, with hardly a word of explanation; but her readers are only puzzled for a moment and then they can pick up the threads again, just as happens in many a home when old relationships are renewed after a lapse of time when an uncle or grandson returns unexpectedly.

The novels range widely in location, from New Zealand to the United States, over a period of three quarters of a century, but they are anchored firmly in the place that Saxton knows best, the delightful and lively cathedral city of Norwich where she grew up. What she chronicles is essentially the history of her own forebears from the late Victorian period to the time of World War II. Her prefaces are testimony to the research she has undertaken, and there can be no doubt that her portrayal of characters owes some of its solidity to the care she has taken to model them on real life. They live and move, moreover, against a closely observed background, which, once again, makes for plausibility and vitality. Public events, such as the

Norwich celebrations of Queen Victoria's Diamond Jubilee, mark epochs in the on-going life of the family, and the two world wars leave a deep imprint on it in ways that parallel the experiences that many have shared. But smaller things are accorded their rightful importance too, and a future social historian may well be interested to see how the development of transport, for instance, is seen to play its part in the way ordinary people lived as the horse gave way to the early motor car and the aeroplane replaced the ship as the normal means of long-distance travel.

The portrayal of the domestic sphere is even more interesting, and Saxton is particularly skilled in showing the everyday life of middle-class people. A quite prosperous Jewish family settled in East Anglia is the foundation of the story, and though they mix freely with those around them its members always possess not only a strong sense of mutual loyalty, which always reasserts itself even if it is strained at times, but also a sense of otherness, which makes them confident of their own worth. Sometimes made to feel strangers even in their own home town, they are more welcoming to foreigners than the common run of Norwich people are generally reckoned to be. The Jewish element is brought out too not in orthodox religious observance, which is shown as gradually slipping away, but in the keeping of family festivals and a partiality for certain creature comforts that recall an earlier period, before the immigration into England. There also seems to be something very characteristic in the way in which the males assume airs of superiority and demand care and attention when it is soon made clear enough that the dominating and most forceful personalities are female.

As Saxton develops the ramifications of her family saga far from its beginnings with a Jewish household in a provincial city in the east of England, there are many surprises and violent changes of fortune. Some might think there are even rather too many, for there are times when it is tempting to think these characters are disaster-prone. Perhaps it is a matter of truth being a little too strange for fiction. This is, however, only a minor criticism to make of a saga with a strong sense of period in which vivid, convincing and highly-sexed characters capture the imagination in a great human web of connections which finally come full circle.

The Blue and Distant Hills, Saxton's most recent novel, is set in Shropshire just after World War II.

—Christopher N. Smith

SCHULZE, Dallas.
Nationality: American. **Relations:** married. **Career:** doll couturier; full-time writer. Lived in Colorado; now lives in California. **Address:** 2820 Honolulu Avenue, Suite 348, Verdugo City, California 91046, USA.

ROMANCE AND HISTORICAL PUBLICATIONS

Novels

Moment to Moment. Toronto, Harlequin, 1986; New York, Silhouette, 1989.
Mackenzie's Lady. New York, Silhouette, 1986; Toronto, Harlequin, 1987.
Stormwalker. Toronto, Harlequin, 1987.
Tell Me a Story. Toronto, Harlequin, and New York, Silhouette, 1988.
Lost and Found. Toronto, Harlequin, 1988; New York, Silhouette, 1989.
Donovan's Promise. Toronto, Harlequin, 1988; New York, Silhouette, 1989.

The Morning After. Toronto, Harlequin, 1989.
Together Always. Toronto, Harlequin, 1989; New York, Silhouette, 1990.
Of Dream's and Magic. Toronto, Harlequin, 1989; New York, Silhouette, 1990.
So Much Love. New York, Crown, 1989.
Saturday's Child. Toronto, Harlequin, 1990.
A Summer to Come Home. Toronto, Harlequin, 1990; New York, Silhouette, 1991.
The Vow. Toronto, Harlequin, 1990; New York, Silhouette, 1991.
Angel and the Bad Man. Toronto, Harlequin, 1990.
Rafferty's Choice. Toronto, Harlequin, and New York, Silhouette, 1991.
The Baby Bargain. Toronto, Harlequin, 1991; New York, Silhouette, 1992.
A Practical Marriage. Toronto, Harlequin, 1991; New York, Silhouette, 1992.
Charity's Angel. Toronto, Harlequin, and New York, Silhouette, 1992.
Everything but Marriage. New York, Silhouette, 1992.
A Christmas Marriage. Toronto, Harlequin, 1992.
Strong Arms of the Lion. Toronto, Harlequin, 1992.
Temptation's Price. Toronto, Harlequin, 1992.
Secondhand Husband. Toronto, Harlequin, and New York, Silhouette, 1993.
The Hell-Raiser. Toronto, Harlequin, 1993.

*   *   *

Dallas Schulze has proven herself as an author of emotion-packed contemporary romances. She creates real empathy for her characters, drawing readers into a new world in which they can experience not only anguish, pain, and confusion, but also joy, triumph, and love.

Many of Schulze's principal characters are wounded emotionally or physically. Physical problems sharpen feelings, eliminate extraneous problems, and help the characters focus on what really counts. Charity Williams and Gabriel London (*Charity's Angel*) are attracted to each other when he comes into the store where she works, but neither acts on the attraction. Everything changes in a heartbeat when Gabriel, a policeman, accidently wounds Charity while trying to stop a holdup in the store. She is paralyzed, and he is consumed by guilt. As he tries to make it up to her, and she tries to cope with what might be permanent paralysis, they each learn that their top priority should be their growing love.

Donovan and Elizabeth Sinclair (*Donovan's Promise*) had to get married when she became pregnant as a teenager, but they did love one another. Over the years, Donovan grew to think of his financial success as proof of his love, but this was not enough for Elizabeth. When she decides to leave him after almost 20 years of marriage, he begins to take a long, hard look at what has gone wrong. This reassessment is taken to another level, however, when Donovan has a motorcycle accident and is threatened with the loss of a leg. Although he has pushed for a reconciliation, he begins to withdraw from Elizabeth. Schulze very effectively conveys the anguish and confusion both Elizabeth and Donovan feel at their estrangement, and their struggles to come to grips with so many changes in their lives.

Sometimes Schulze's characters must deal with physical danger as well as complex emotional problems. In *Moment to Moment*, Chase Buchanon, an executive of an electronics firm, is released by kidnappers only to discover that he is suffering from amnesia. Danger from the kidnappers shadows his life and that of his wife, Gwenn, but she also has the burden of knowing about the death of their child, which Chase has forgotten. Again, Schulze very convin-

cingly explores the emotional wounds Chase and Gwenn must face along with the danger that continues to threaten.

Together Always is interesting from two standpoints. Told in two distinct parts, it tells the story of Trace Dushane and his commitment to Lily Roberts which begins when he first sees eight year old Lily, when he is 15. Trace feels an immediate bond with her and runs away with her to protect her from harm. Book One tells of their meeting and the hard life he accepts to shield her. Book Two picks up their story as he tries to ignore her as a woman and convince both of them that she no longer needs him. Perhaps even more interesting than the format of the book, is Schulze's decision to tell the story strictly from Trace's point of view. Although many romance authors share the heroine's spotlight with the hero in specific scenes or even create a joint focus for the entire book, few place the primary emphasis on the male character. Schulze handles the masculine struggle to cope with the risks of such an emotional bond with great sensitivity.

Schulze also seems to be willing to allow some ambiguity for her characters. In *So Much Love*, Faith Holden marries her boss, Max Walsh, to help him cope with instant fatherhood. One of his former lovers suddenly leaves an infant girl with him, saying that he is the father, and that he can now care for her. Faith and Max care for her and grow to love her. They marry to ensure that Max will get custody of the child. In the end, when the mother returns, she finally confesses that she really does not know if Max is the father but that he could be. Leaving such a basic question unresolved is a bit unusual in the genre where a clear-cut answer is more the norm. It is not so much a question of Max's morality or the child's parentage as it is a question of tying up all the loose ends.

Schulze is an author who concentrates on creating vividly drawn characters, imbuing them with intense, often painful emotions and placing them in situations guaranteed to create tension and heighten the emotional conflict. Her well-crafted stories are sensitively written so that the interest and emotions of her readers become fully engaged.

—Barbara E. Kemp

SCOTLAND, Jay. See **JAKES, John.**

SCOTT, Evelyn.
Pseudonym: Ernest Souza. **Nationality:** American. **Born:** Elsie Dunn in Clarksville, Tennessee, 17 January 1893. **Education:** privately; Newcomb Preparatory School, Sophie Newcomb College, and Newcomb School of Art, all New Orleans. **Relations:** married 1) the painter and writer Frederick Creighton Wellman (pseudonym: Cyril Kay Scott) in 1913 (divorced 1928), one son; 2) the writer John Metcalfe in 1930. **Career:** freelance writer. Lived in Brazil; travelled in Bermuda, France, North Africa, and England. **Recipient:** Guggenheim fellowship, 1932. **Died:** 3 August 1963.

ROMANCE AND HISTORICAL PUBLICATIONS

Novels

The Narrow House. New York, Boni and Liveright, and London, Duckworth, 1921.
Narcissus. New York, Harcourt, 1922; as *Bewilderment*, London, Duckworth, 1922.
The Golden Door. New York, Seltzer, 1925.
Migrations: An Arabesque in Histories. New York, Boni and Liveright, and London, Duckworth, 1927.

The Wave. New York, Cape and Smith, and London, Cape, 1929.
A Calendar of Sin: American Melodramas. New York, Cape and Smith, 2 vols, 1931.
Eva Gay. New York, Smith and Haas, 1933; London, Lovat Dickson, 1934.
Breathe Upon These Slain. New York, Smith and Haas, and London, Lovat Dickson, 1934.
Bread and a Sword. New York, Scribner, 1937.
The Shadow of the Hawk. New York, Scribner, 1941.

Short Stories

Ideals: A Book of Farce and Comedy. New York, Boni, 1927.

OTHER PUBLICATIONS

Play

Love (produced New York, 1921).

Poetry

Precipitations. New York, Brown, 1920.
The Winter Alone. New York, Cape and Smith, 1930.

Other

Escapade (autobiography). New York, Seltzer, 1923; London, Cape, 1930.
In the Endless Sands (for children), with Cyril Kay Scott. New York, Holt, 1925.
Witch Perkins: A Story of the Kentucky Hills (for children). New York, Holt, 1929.
On William Faulkner's The Sound and the Fury. New York, Cape and Smith, 1929.
Blue Rum (for children; as Ernest Souza). New York, Cape and Smith, and London, Cape, 1930.
Billy, The Maverick (for children). New York, Holt, 1934.
Background in Tennessee (autobiography). New York, McBride, 1937.

*

Manuscript Collection: Humanities Research Center, University of Texas, Austin.

Critical Studies: *Pretty Good for a Woman: The Enigmas of Evelyn Scott* by D. A. Callard, London, Cape, 1985; New York, Norton, 1986.

*   *   *

Evelyn Scott's reputation has waned sadly since the time between the two world wars when she was hailed as one of America's most significant novelists, and her historical fiction was praised for its evocative powers, its psychological insight, and its technical daring. Much of her work is a reflection of the tensions and pressures of her own experience as a woman emerging from a restrictive environment, and she added an important extra dimension with three major novels which, though they may be read as if independent of one another, constitute a panorama of America history across a period of nearly three quarters of a century.

Migrations is set in the time of the 1849 Gold Rush; *The Wave* takes the titanic upheaval of the Civil War as its background and is said to have revealed the vast potential of that period as a resource

for subsequent American fiction and the films that were based on it; and *A Calendar of Sin: American Melodramas*, in two volumes, takes the form of a superior family chronicle, covering the years from 1867 to 1914.

In general scope and in the abundant detail, the historical basis of Scott's fiction is sound. Though Scott was quite open in admitting that she invented a great deal in her historical novels she also pointed out that where she added to or departed from acknowledged fact, she did so only after informing herself fully about reality as it is recorded, and critics have generally agreed that she did not abuse the freedom she allowed herself. Her object, in any case, is not to provide in her fiction substitutes for history books. Rather she creates a pervasive and persuasive sense of period by the juxtaposition of events, scenes, and characters in order to convey impressions of the experiences which people underwent at the time in question. Characters teem, emotions crowd in, as they do in real life during troubled times, and the richness of an epoch in American history is evoked in all its limitless variety.

For Scott the past, however, was not a time when people were essentially different, and she developed her historical fiction as a means of exploring the fundamental dilemmas that haunted her personally and are also expressed in her novels of contemporary life. In her presentation of the problems of two families as they respond to changing situations and unresolved strains in American life there is much that corresponds to her efforts to make sense of what she perceived as conflicting tendencies in her own heredity. *Migrations* plays upon the paradox that the American dream of 'going west to fashion a new life' is, sadly, only a dream, because wherever we may go we remain ourselves. *The Wave* shows how in the Civil War individuals are swept along by the tide of events which they cannot control and which soon cease to be in any way the expression of human will. *A Calendar of Sin* takes as its theme the problems that American women have had in achieving balanced attitudes towards the physical and emotional aspects of love. It is a telling indictment of attitudes that in the title 'sin' stands for 'sex', and the word 'calendar' spotlights not just the idea that this is a narrative of events lived day by day but also has the connotations of a record of crime. By the same token, there is bruising irony in the subtitle 'American melodramas', and Scott is not afraid to invent a series of distressingly violent incidents to illustrate her theme in exemplary fashion.

Scott's trilogy of historical novels has great power, and, especially in the context of the current interest in women's writing, it is surprising it has not attracted more interest of late. Perhaps the explanation lies in the substantial length of the books and the deliberate fragmentation of the narrative manner which might be seen as demanding rather too much of her readers.

—Christopher N. Smith

SCOTT, Jane. See McELFRESH, Adeline.

SCOTT, Janey. See LINDSAY, Rachel.

SCOTT, Paul (Mark).
Nationality: British. **Born:** Southgate, London, 25 March 1920.
Education: Winchmore Hill Collegiate School, London. **Military Service:** British Army, 1940–43: captain; Indian Army, India and Malaya, 1943–46. **Relations:** married Nancy Edith Avery in 1941; two daughters. **Career:** company secretary, Falcon Press, and Grey Walls Press, 1946–50; director, Pearn Pollinger and Higham, later

David Higham Associates, literary agents, London, 1950–60; British Council lecturer, India, 1972; visiting lecturer, University of Tulsa, Oklahoma, 1976–77. **Recipient:** Eyre and Spottiswoode literary fellowship, 1952; Arts Council grant, 1969; Booker prize, 1977, for *Staying On*. Fellow, Royal Society of Literature, 1963. **Died:** 1 March 1978.

ROMANCE AND HISTORICAL PUBLICATIONS

Novels (series: The Raj Quartet)

Johnnie Sahib. London, Eyre and Spottiswoode, 1952.
The Alien Sky. London, Eyre and Spottiswoode, 1953; as *Six Days in Marapore*, New York, Doubleday, 1953.
A Male Child. London, Eyre and Spottiswoode, 1956; New York, Dutton, 1957.
The Mark of the Warrior. London, Eyre and Spottiswoode, and New York, Morrow, 1958.
The Chinese Love Pavilion. London, Eyre and Spottiswoode, 1960; as *The Love Pavilion*, New York, Morrow, 1960.
The Birds of Paradise. London, Eyre and Spottiswoode, 1962.
The Bender: Pictures from an Exhibition of Middle Class Portraits. London, Secker and Warburg, and New York, Morrow, 1963.
The Corrida at San Felíu. London, Secker and Warburg, and New York, Morrow, 1964.
The Raj Quartet. London, Heinemann, and New York, Morrow, 1976.
  The Jewel in the Crown. London, Heinemann, and New York, Morrow, 1966.
  The Day of the Scorpion. London, Heinemann, and New York, Morrow, 1968.
  The Towers of Silence. London, Heinemann, and New York, Morrow, 1971.
  A Division of the Spoils. London, Heinemann, and New York, Morrow, 1975.
Staying On. London, Heinemann, and New York, Morrow, 1977.

OTHER PUBLICATIONS

Novel

After the Funeral (unfinished). London, Whittington Press, 1979.

Plays

Pillars of Salt. In *Four Jewish Plays*, edited by H.F. Rubinstein, London, Victor Gollancz, 1948.

Radio Plays: *Lines of Communication*, from his own novel *Johnnie Sahib*, 1951; *The Alien Sky*, 1954; *Sahibs and Memsahibs*, 1958.

Television Plays: *The Mark of the Warrior*, from his own novel, 1959.

Poetry

I, Gerontius. London, Favil Press, 1941.

Other

My Appointment with the Muse: Essays 1961–1975, edited by Shelley Reece. London, Heinemann, 1986; as *On Writing and the Novel*, New York, Morrow, 1987.

*

Film Adaptations: *Staying On*, 1980; *Jewel in the Crown*, 1984, from the tetralogy *The Raj Quartet*.

Manuscript Collections: University of Tulsa, Oklahoma; University of Texas, Austin.

Critical Studies: *Scott: Images of India* by Patrick Swinden, London, Macmillan, 1980; *Scott* by K. Bhaskara Rao, Boston, Hall, 1980; *Introducing the Raj Quartet* by Janis Tedesco and Janet Popham, Lanham, University Press of America, 1985; *Paul Scott: His Art and Ideas* by Indira Kohli, Meerut, Vimul Prakashan, 1987; *Scott's Raj* by Robin Moore, London, Heinemann, 1990; *Paul Scott: A Life* by Hilary Spurling, London, Hutchinson, 1990.

*   *   *

Paul Scott's 13 novels reveal two obsessions: an obsession with the relationship between a man and the work he does, and an obsession with British India.

Falling in love with India's landscape and people was as great as Scott's disillusionment with the emergence of consumerism in postwar Britain. His twin obsessions of vocation and India are thus linked by the fact that the British Raj had claimed to embody an ethic of service which struck a chord in the non-materialistic Scott.

This is not to say that Scott looked at the Raj through rose-tinted spectacles—far from it—but as a former accountant he realized that to go to the opposite extreme and see everything in terms of cost-benefit analysis would dehumanize as much as it would demystify. Indeed, he regarded the eventual devaluation of the Indian Jewel in the Crown in this cold light as not only responsible for that betrayal of trust whereby the British left a divided country and a bloodbath but also as symptomatic of the mother country's deeper spiritual malaise.

With the exception of *The Mark of the Warrior*, which has an almost mythic quality, Scott's early novels are all seriously flawed, with elements of melodrama in *The Alien Sky*, figures offstage dominating the action in both *Johnnie Sahib* and *A Male Child*, and an overblown symbolism that bogs down *The Chinese Love Pavilion*—a fate from which *The Birds of Paradise* only escapes because the double-edged nature of its central symbol (representing both British and princely India) is not fully revealed until the end of the book.

If *The Birds of Paradise* anticipates *A Division of the Spoils*, *The Bender: Pictures from an Exhibition of Middle Class Portraits* anticipates *Staying On* in terms of its comic yet touching treatment of characters entrapped by the legacy of the past. However, *The Bender* might be characterized as one step forward but two steps back in so far as it contains contrived plot devices (revolving around a tape recorder), and uncharacteristically stilted dialogue (in the shape of the jive-talking Eurasian Anina).

The Corrida at San Felíu finds Scott in Hemingway territory, with his most ambitious book. Some regard this as Scott's masterpiece, and it is certainly difficult to think of a better exploration of the actual process of novel writing. However, the book, for all its carefully crafted fragmentation suffers from the same central paradox as Peter Ackroyd's *Testament of Oscar Wilde*, namely that it presents dazzling passages from a writer who is allegedly suffering from a drying-up of creative inspiration.

The four novels that were ultimately to comprise *The Raj Quartet* were not conceived as a tetralogy yet Scott triumphantly solved the problem of keeping each self-contained yet related to the 800,000-word whole by drawing on the extensive range of narrative techniques which he refined in *The Corrida at San Felíu*.

In basing *The Jewel in the Crown* around a rape Scott invited the very comparison between his own work and E.M. Forster's *Passage to India* which Scott's critics had predictably made in the past. However, in the *Jewel in the Crown,* and the succeeding volumes, Scott passes this self-imposed test with ease, not least because his India—the India of 1942–1947—is the multi-faceted product of personal experience, acute insight, almost inexhaustible compassion, and increasingly exhaustive scholarship.

For all but an unholy alliance of the most blinkered devotees of the Raj on the one hand and political correctness on the other, Scott is at the height of his powers and succeeds in anchoring the epic events from the 'Quit India' resolution to Independence, in the lives of a range of characters about whom one comes to care intensely.

As befits the disturbing events which provide its historical setting, the work is characterized by a disorientation, dislocation,and displacement of peoples and values which is compounded and complemented structurally by Scott's narrative techniques, which repeatedly and unpredictably shift the reader's point of focus. What ensures that this does not result in a dizzying alienation is Scott's success in acting on his long-held conviction that each person is rooted in their own past: the baggage of history which they carry with them like Barbie Batchelor's battered tin truck.

Like the length of lace with its netted butterflies (which Mabel gives to Barbie and which she passes on to Sarah) we are all imprisoned by the past but each individual nevertheless repays attention. The fact that such relatively minor 'The Raj Quartet' characters as Lucy and Tusker Smalley could blossom as they wither in the tragi-comic *Staying On* is a tribute to the way in which Scott succeeds in investing all his characters with a past which informs their present.

Despite, or, perhaps, because of, Scott's (belated) success in winning the Booker prize in 1977 for *Staying On* (when he was already dying of cancer) and the enormous posthumous success of Granada TV's 14-part *The Jewel in the Crown* (which attracted nine million viewers each week when first broadcast in 1984) Scott's literary status is sharply contested. Even those who shared his experiences of the twilight years of the Raj are divided in their estimation of his achievement.

Scott himself would not have been surprised by this phenomenon as one of his greatest gifts as an historical novelist was precisely the appreciation that there are as many versions of the past as it has witnesses.

—John Plowright

SEALE, Sara. Died 1978. See 2nd edition, 1990.

SEBASTIAN, Margaret.
Pseudonym for Arthur M. Gladstone. **Other Pseudonyms:** Maggie Gladstone; Lisabet Norcross; Cilla Whitmore. **Nationality:** American. **Born:** Brooklyn, New York, 22 September 1921. **Education:** New York University, B.A. (cum laude) 1942, M.S. 1947. **Military Service:** United States Army Air Force, 1942–46. **Relations:** married 1) Margaret Sebastian in 1949 (died 1973); 2) Helen Worth in 1980. **Career:** chemist, Pittsburg Coke and Chemical Company, 1948–53; chief chemist and product manager, Nopco Chemical Company, Newark, New Jersey, 1953–59; administrative assistant to the president, Anchor Serum Company, St Joseph, Missouri, 1959–61; proposals director, Hercules Inc, Cumberland, Maryland, 1961–67; financial planner, Affiliated Business Machines, Brooklyn, 1967–68; supervising chemist, Chemical Insecticide Corporation, Edison, New Jersey, 1967–69; bench chemist,

Hartz Mountain Pet Foods, Harrison, New Jersey, 1969–74. Since 1974 full-time writer. **Address:** c/o Fawcett, 201 East 50th Street, New York, New York 10022, USA.

ROMANCE AND HISTORICAL PUBLICATIONS

Novels (series: Bow Street)

The Honorable Miss Clarendon. New York, Pyramid, 1973.
Meg Miller. New York, Berkley, 1976.
Bow Street Brangle. New York, Popular Library, 1977.
Bow Street Gentleman. New York, Popular Library, 1977.
Lord Orlando's Protegée. New York, Berkley, 1977.
Miss Letty. New York, Popular Library, 1977.
My Lord Rakehell. New York, Popular Library, 1977.
The Young Lady from Alton-St Pancras. New York, Popular Library, 1977.
The Courtship of Colonel Crowne. New York, Popular Library, 1978.
The Poor Relation. New York, Popular Library, 1978.
That Savage Yankee Squire! New York, Popular Library, 1978.
Lord Dedringham's Divorce. New York, Popular Library, 1978.
Dilemma in Duet. New York, Fawcett, 1979.
Her Knight on a Barge. New York, Popular Library, 1979.
The Awakening of Lord Dalby. New York, Popular Library, 1979.
The Plight of Pamela Pollworth. New York, Fawcett, 1980.
Byway to Love. New York, Fawcett, 1980.
Miss Keating's Temptation. New York, Fawcett, 1981.

Novels as Maggie Gladstone (series: Ballerina; Lacebridge Ladies)

Lacebridge Ladies:
    The Fortunate Belle. New York, Playboy Press, 1978.
    The Love Duel. New York, Playboy Press, 1978.
    The Scandalous Lady. New York, Playboy Press, 1978.
    The Impudent Widow. New York, Playboy Press, 1979.
The Love Tangle. New York, Playboy Press, 1979.
The Reluctant Debutante (Ballerina). New York, Playboy Press, 1979.
The Lady's Masquerade. New York, Playboy Press, 1980.
The Reluctant Protegée (Ballerina). New York, Playboy Press, 1980.
A Lesson in Love. New York, Playboy Press, 1981.

Novels as Lisabet Norcross

Masquerade of Love. New York, Berkley, 1978.
Reluctant Heiress. New York, Berkley, 1978.
The Lady and the Rogue. New York, Berkley, 1978.
My Lady Scapegrace. New York, Berkley, 1979.

Novels as Cilla Whitmore

His Lordship's Landlady. New York, Dell, 1979.
Manner of a Lady. New York, Dell, 1979.
Mansion for a Lady. New York, Dell, 1980.

*   *   *

Arthur M. Gladstone, who writes as Margaret Sebastian, Maggie Gladstone, Cilla Whitmore, and Lisabett Norcross is something of an enigma. He either has an extremely cynical attitude about romance or he is totally amused with the genre, and is determined to have as much fun out of writing his novels as his readers have in reading them.

Readers know exactly what to expect in each of Gladstone's modern comedies of manners. Stock characters abound. Befuddled heroes, shrewish heroines, and villainous villains spice his pages as characters tumble from one farcical event to the next. Gladstone also makes full use of the Regency period as a background for his novels. It is such a nice, tidy little world he manipulates so deftly. A handful of well-known lords and ladies, a social outlook rigidly enforced on all who matter, and a brief historical time that bridged the 18th and 19th centuries make up this world. In some cases the setting is immaterial because any relationship between Gladstone's Regency days and the real historical period are completely accidental. Indeed, one senses that some of Gladstone's novels should have started with 'once upon a time ...'. The purist reader of Regency novels may not enjoy Gladstone's irreverent attitude, but others will sit cosily back and enjoy the frothy light-heartedness in his novels.

Novels written under the name Margaret Sebastian have at least one series which include *Dilemma in Duet* and *Byway to Love*. The central characters are a pair of female twins who delight in confusing everyone, including their boyfriends. The fast-paced dialogue is kept alive by constant misunderstandings, irrelevant asides, and character obtuseness. In *The Honorable Miss Clarendon* one finds a more skilful blend of plot and characters. It is only midway through the story that one begins to catch the unique element that makes up Gladstone's style. In this novel, Lady Cynthia Clarendon, now a penniless orphan, sets out by public coach to take a position as a companion. The wreck of the coach, a meeting with the Duke of Somervale (mistaken for a servant), and an eventual misunderstanding between Cynthia and the Duke, leads to a merry chase of a hero in love and a heroine too proud to accept it.

Writing as Maggie Gladstone, he launched two series of heroines. 'The Ballerina' stories and the 'Lacebridge Ladies'. The ballerinas are individual members of the Royal Italian Opera House's ballet corps. In *The Reluctant Protegée* Nancy Faulconer, the heroine, becomes a member of the corps and is one of the few to achieve 'enpointe' dancing. This is toe dancing, and a new and untried method of ballet dance. Surprisingly, Nancy and Lord Anthony Faile, the hero, do not resolve their love in a happy-ever-after ending. She refuses to become his mistress, preferring to 'remain her own mistress'. This is certainly an unexpected ending to a romance.

The 'Lacebridge Ladies' series involves the stories of five sisters and how each one is launched into society and eventually into matrimony. Plotting naturally involves husbands, friends, and other relatives. In a way, the series is one grand plot with subplots for each sister. Characters from one novel reappear in the next.

As Cilla Whitmore, Gladstone still maintains his own individual sense of the ridiculous. In *Manner of a Lady*, the heroine, Miranda Thorpe, takes on the task of helping her uncle in his architectural firm. Her help, however, centres on wanting to be an architect. The unsuspecting hero, Viscount Anthony Farnsworth, commissions her uncle to design a fitting place for his future intended. Miranda cunningly corrupts the building workers, re-draws her uncle's plans, and ultimately constructs her own dream house. Fortunately, by the end of the story, Miranda also finds her perfect love in the form of Anthony.

In all, Gladstone has produced numerous romances that are light, fluffy bits of confection that require little effort to understand. Period details are kept to a minimum, characters are rounded enough to be characters, but barely, and plot lines teasing enough to keep the reader going. The bottom line, however, is that they are enjoyable silly little things that one keeps coming back to when needing that extra spice of lightness.

—Arlene Moore

SEDGES, John.   See **BUCK, Pearl S.**

SEDLEY, Kate.   See **CLARKE, Brenda.**

SEGER, Maura.
Pseudonyms: Jenny Bates; Sara Jennings; Anne MacNeill; Laurel Winslow. **Nationality:** American. **Born:** New York City, 16 September 1951. **Education:** attended university; degree in history and economics. **Relations:** married Michael Seger in 1975. **Career:** worked in advertising department, McGraw-Hill, publishers, New York. **Address:** c/o Silhouette Books, 300 East 42nd Street, New York, New York 10017, USA.

ROMANCE AND HISTORICAL PUBLICATIONS

Novels (series: Calvert)

Legacy. New York, Silhouette, 1981.
Sea Gate. New York, Silhouette, 1981.
Defiant Love. New York, Pocket Books, 1982; London, Coronet, 1983.
Flame on the Sun. New York, Pocket Books, 1983; London, Coronet, 1984.
Forbidden Love. New York, Pocket Books, 1983; London, Coronet, 1984.
Rebellious Love. New York, Pocket Books, and London, Coronet, 1983.
A Mind of Her Own (as Anne MacNeill). New York, New American Library, 1983.
Gilded Spring (as Jenny Bates). New York, Berkley, 1983.
Gift Beyond Price. New York, Silhouette, 1983.
Empire of the Heart. New York, Pocket Books, 1984.
Shadows of the Heart. New York, Silhouette, 1984.
Silver Zephyr. New York, Silhouette, 1984.
Dazzled (as Jenny Bates). New York, Berkley, 1984.
Heartsongs (as Laurel Winslow). New York, Avon, 1984.
Captured Images (as Laurel Winslow). New York, Avon, 1984.
Eye of the Storm. Toronto, Worldwide, 1985.
Echo of Thunder. Toronto, Worldwide, 1985.
Spring Frost, Summer Fire. Toronto, Harlequin, 1985.
Golden Chimera. New York, Silhouette, 1985.
Comes a Stranger. New York, Silhouette, 1985.
Cajun Summer. New York, Silhouette, 1986.
Edge of Dawn. New York, Silhouette, 1986.
Undercover. London, Mills and Boon, 1986.
Treasure Hunt. New York, Silhouette, 1986.
Quest of the Eagle. New York, Silhouette, 1986.
Dark of the Moon. New York, Silhouette, 1986.
Happily Ever After. New York, Silhouette, 1987.
Sarah (Calvert). Toronto, Worldwide, 1987.
Elizabeth (Calvert). Toronto, Worldwide, 1987.
Catherine (Calvert). Toronto, Worldwide, 1988.
Conflict of Interest. New York, Silhouette, 1988.
Day and Night. New York, Silhouette, 1988.
Summer Heat. New York, Crown, 1988.
Unforgettable. New York, Silhouette, 1988.
Change of Plans. New York, Silhouette, 1989.
Before the Wind. New York, Warner, 1989.
Perchance to Dream. New York, Avon, 1989.
Fortune's Tide. New York, Avon, 1990.
Painted Lady. New York, Silhouette, 1990.
Princess McGee. New York, Silhouette, 1992.
The Taming of Amelia. Toronto, Harlequin, 1993.
The Seduction of Deanna. Toronto, Harlequin, 1993.
Tapestry. New York, Harper, 1993.

Novels as Sara Jennings

Game Plan. New York, Dell, 1984.
Love Not the Enemy. New York, Dell, 1984.
Reach for the Stars. New York, Dell, 1984.
Star-Crossed. New York, Dell, 1985.

*   *   *

Maura Seger has an impressive record for writing outstanding romance novels. In 1986–87, Seger was recognized in the annual Reviewer's Choice awards of *Romantic Times*. She was selected as one of the best all-around series authors and *Legacy* was nominated as the best Silhouette Intimate Moments novel of the year. In 1987–88, *Sea Gate* was nominated as one of the best novels in the same series. Writing awards do not come easily, especially when there are so many outstanding romance writers being published. The fact that Seger has been recognized for her creativity and originality certainly indicates that her place in romance writing is extremely well deserved.

Readers familiar with Seger's novels know that she is published consistently in the various Silhouette lines as well as in the Harlequin Super-romances and Temptations. They may not know that she has published under several pseudonyms. As Jenny Bates, she wrote *Dazzled*, a Regency novel for the Second Chance at Love series. She has also used Sara Jennings, Anne MacNeill, and Laurel Winslow as pen names. The MacNeill novel appeared as a Signet Regency romance, *A Mind of Her Own*. Her Winslow novels includes a Velvet Glove mystery, *Captured Images* and an Avon novel, *Heartsongs*.

It is easy to compile lists of titles and plots. It is much more difficult to choose those novels that best represent Seger as a writer, for she is an eclectic person who is genuinely creative in several different areas. Seger slips deftly from contemporary adventure/mystery to historical or fantasy novels. All her books contain well-rounded characters, complex and exciting plots, as well as that elusive thing called style.

In *A Mind of Her Own* young Courtney Marlowe marries Lord Nigel Davies. Both are typical products of their times, the Regency period. Events within the story awaken Courtney's awareness to contemporary social problems. She stumbles on the fact that very young girls are being kidnapped for the brothels of London. She sets out to publicize their existence and also becomes involved with a children's shelter in East London. Her fight against child kidnapping eventually results in her own kidnapping and auction in a brothel. Lord Nigel arrives just in time to save her. Slowly, he begins to give fuller support to his wife's efforts. Courtney and Lord Nigel later travel to Manchester. During their visit, Courtney is trapped in the crowd that has come to hear a famous speaker. The meeting culminates in the notorious Peterloo Massacre of 1819. The reform movement emerges from the ranks of the working class and idealistic reformers and into the hands of powerful Lords who are able to help bring about the changes so desperately needed.

From the opening scene of marital seduction to the final, moving speech that Nigel makes in the House of Lords, the reader is caught in the furious pace of events. Seger's characters grow from the light, narcissistic images that people most Regency novels into complex, caring individuals who are not afraid to take a stand. This is more than the typical Regency novel and shows Seger at her best.

Seger's contemporary novels are just as exciting. Certainly *Sea Gate* illustrates her originality and her very definite ability as a writer. *Sea Gate* is not a fantasy; it is not science fiction, it is more— What if? What is so delightful is the fact that she makes us believe that 'what if' is possible. Andrew Paxton is a scientist working on classified government research. He and his three-year-old son, Billy, live on a secluded island home in the Caribbean. One night,

Billy finds a beautiful woman washed ashore. According to Federal agents, beautiful women don't accidentally arrive at security cleared islands. The woman's name is Marina and in spite of all efforts by the Federal agents to identify her, they simply cannot do so. As Andrew becomes more involved with Marina and more curious about her, he realizes that the limits of scientific knowledge are about to be pushed another step further. No! Marina is not a space alien, nor is she from a country with recognized diplomatic ties. This is one of Seger's most intriguing novels.

There is no easy way to summarize Seger's writing. She is good! Her characters are solidly developed. Her plots are more than imaginative and she captures her reader's attention so completely that few manage to put a book aside without finishing it. With her skills so finely developed, she can only continue to write even better novels.

—Arlene Moore

SEIDEL, Kathleen Gilles.
Nationality: American. **Born:** Lawrence, Kansas. **Education:** University of Chicago; Johns Hopkins University, Baltimore, Maryland, M.A., Ph.D. in English. **Relations:** married, two children. **Career:** writer. Lives in Arlington, Virginia. **Address:** c/o Adele Leone Agency, 26 Nantucket Place, Scarsdale, New York 10583, USA.

ROMANCE AND HISTORICAL PUBLICATIONS

Novels

The Same Last Name. Toronto, Harlequin, 1983.
A Risk Worth Taking. Toronto, Harlequin, 1983.
Mirrors and Mistakes. Toronto, Harlequin, 1984.
When Love Isn't Enough. Toronto, Harlequin, 1984.
After All These Years. Toronto, Harlequin, 1984.
Don't Forget to Smile. Toronto, Worldwide, 1986.
Maybe this Time. New York, Pocket Books, 1990.
More Than You Dreamed. New York, Pocket Books, 1991.

*   *   *

Kathleen Gilles Seidel began writing and publishing fiction in the early 1980s, a period of intense competition in the market for romance fiction. Harlequin, the North American distributor for Mills and Boon, had been challenged successfully by American romance publishers, including Simon and Schuster's Silhouette, and Dell's Candlelight series, which had attracted some Harlequin authors, and a percentage of Harlequin's readers, to the new series. To win back portions of its American audience, Harlequin inaugurated a new series, Harlequin American Romances, featuring books with American settings, more modern situations, and longer and more complex plots. To support the new series, the company also actively sought out and encouraged new American authors. Seidel was one of the new line's earliest and best writers, and her work exemplifies several important aspects of the changing series romance.

Seidel's academic background and her doctorate in English literature contribute to her work, from the playful inversion of two characters partially modelled on Tom Sawyer and Huck Finn in *After All These Years* to the sophisticated and multi-faceted plot of *Don't Forget to Smile*. As a specialist in the British novel, she brings to her novels an ability to adapt formal literary structures to traditional romance conventions, such as the marriage of convenience plot. More than many of her contemporaries, whose work is frequently loose and episodic, Seidel structures plots built on complex models of development. Extended flashbacks, for example, are rare in series romances, since some editors believe they slow the action; but in *A Risk Worth Taking*, Seidel wrote a fully dramatized, 45 page flashback explaining the hero and heroine's relationship in rural Georgia long before the novel opened. The characters had married as teenagers to protect the heroine from sexual abuse by her stepfather; the flashback added important development to the characters and their motivations while also updating the marriage of convenience plot device.

Seidel's plots and characters grow out of clearly defined American settings that are integral to each novel. No matter where they live, her characters always carry with them the traits and values of their pasts; and those regional factors contribute to an understanding of their motivations and actions. Although the hero of *The Same Last Name* is a successful New York lawyer, he can only be understood in the context of his childhood among the Virginia gentry. The heroine of *A Risk Worth Taking* maintains the traditional values of her Georgia upbringing through several years as a country music star. The main characters in *Mirrors and Mistakes* are undemonstrative New Englanders whose sense of propriety inhibits their emotional maturity. The hero of *After All These Years* has fled the painful memories of his past, while the heroine remained in rural South Dakota where they had grown up together. In *Don't Forget to Smile*, the heroine has escaped her southern past as a semi-professional entrant in beauty pageants by opening a bar in a working-class logging town in rural Oregon, where the hero is a union representative. The conflict between the main characters grows from the vast cultural gulf in their backgrounds. In *Maybe This Time*, two characters from a small town in Illinois have drifted apart since high school and must reconcile their different choices before they can marry. The heroine of *More Than You Dreamed*, who grew up in Hollywood, returns to her father's boyhood home in Virginia's Shenandoah Valley to discover the truth about his past.

In several of her books—*A Risk Worth Taking, When Love Isn't Enough, Mirrors and Mistakes, The Same Last Name*—Seidel skilfully delineates the conflicts of urban professionals whose careers seem to require a sacrifice of home and family values. Several of these characters come from more traditional areas of the country. Although they are ambitious for professional success, like the heroine of *When Love Isn't Enough*, they frequently yearn for a more settled, rooted way of life. But unlike some more traditional romance writers, Seidel portrays couples who make mutual accommodations rather than expecting the heroine to give up her own commitments for love. In *Maybe This Time* the hero agrees to move from a small town to Chicago to be with the heroine.

Seidel's prose is spare and ironic, especially in comparison to the sometimes lush and descriptive styles of her contemporaries. She delineates her characters in apt, understated phrases. Even in moments of extreme emotion, her characters are rarely effusive, nor do they withdraw in the sort of injured silence that implausibly extends some romance plots. Instead, they express themselves bluntly so that the grounds of disagreement are open and clear. Because her characters are articulate and honest with themselves and each other, the stock romance misunderstandings are absent from her books.

Conflicts are far more likely to derive from psychological factors or sincere differences in values than from shallow misunderstandings, accidents, or misinterpretations. Seidel's first novels were published in a period when editors and readers expected writers to include details of sexual relationships and when the old strictures against premarital sexual activity in romances had virtually disappeared. Seidel's characters are contemporary in their sexual behaviour—in *The Same Last Name* and *Mirrors and Mistakes* the characters marry because the heroine is pregnant—but the portrayals of sexuality in her books serve to advance the plot and are understated rather than emphasized.

Seidel was one of several talented romance writers who emerged in the early 1980s to redefine the traditional formula. Her particular contributions to the genre derived from a sure sense of the American landscape as a place for romance and in her high standards of plot construction and prose style. She continues to write, but, instead of writing series romances she is now concentrating on longer novels with romance elements.

—Kay Mussell

SEIFERT, Elizabeth.
Pseudonym: Ellen Ashley. **Nationality:** American. **Born:** Washington, Missouri, 19 June 1897. **Education:** Washington University, St Louis, A.B. 1918. **Relations:** married John J. Gasparotti in 1920; three sons and one daughter. **Recipient:** *Redbook*-Dodd Mead award, 1938. **Died:** 17 June 1983.

ROMANCE AND HISTORICAL PUBLICATIONS

Novels

Young Doctor Galahad. New York, Dodd Mead, 1938; as *Young Doctor*, London, Collins, 1939.
A Great Day. New York, Dodd Mead, 1939; London, Collins, 1940.
Thus Doctor Mallory. New York, Dodd Mead, 1940; as *Doctor Mallory*, London, Collins, 1941.
Hillbilly Doctor. New York, Dodd Mead, 1940; as *Doctor Bill*, London, Collins, 1941.
Bright Scalpel. New York, Dodd Mead, 1941; as *Healing Hands*, London, Collins, 1942; as *The Doctor's Healing Hands*, London, Severn House, 1982.
Army Doctor. New York, Dodd Mead, 1942; London, Collins, 1943.
Surgeon in Charge. New York, Dodd Mead, 1942; London, Collins, 1945.
A Certain Doctor French. New York, Dodd Mead, 1943; London, Collins, 1944.
Bright Banners. New York, Dodd Mead, 1943.
Girl in Overalls: A Novel of Women in Defense Today (as Ellen Ashley). New York, Dodd Mead, 1943.
Girl Intern. New York, Dodd Mead, 1944; as *Doctor Chris*, London, Collins, 1946.
Dr Ellison's Ambition. New York, Dodd Mead, 1944.
Dr Woodward's Ambition. New York, Dodd Mead, 1945; London, Collins, 1946.
Orchard Hill. New York, Dodd Mead, 1945; London, Collins, 1947.
Old Doc. New York, Dodd Mead, 1946; London, Collins, 1948.
Dusty Spring. New York, Dodd Mead, 1946.
Take Three Doctors. New York, Dodd Mead, 1947; London, Collins, 1949.
So Young, So Fair. New York, Dodd Mead, 1947; London, Collins, 1948.
The Glass and the Trumpet. New York, Dodd Mead, 1948.
Hospital Zone. New York, Dodd Mead, 1948.
The Bright Coin. New York, Dodd Mead, 1949; as *The Doctor Dares*, London, Collins, 1950.
Homecoming. New York, Dodd Mead, 1950.
Pride of the South. London, Collins, 1950.
The Story of Andrea Fields. New York, Dodd Mead, 1950.
Miss Doctor. New York, Dodd Mead, 1951; as *Woman Doctor*, London, Collins, 1951.
Doctor of Mercy. New York, Dodd Mead, 1951; London, Collins, 1953.

The Strange Loyalty of Dr Carlisle. New York, Dodd Mead, 1952; as *The Case of Dr Carlisle*, London, Collins, 1953.
The Doctor Takes a Wife. New York, Dodd Mead, 1952; London, Collins, 1954.
Doctor Mollie. London, Collins, 1952.
The Doctor Disagrees. New York, Dodd Mead, 1953; London, Collins, 1954.
Lucinda Marries the Doctor. New York, Dodd Mead, 1953; London, Collins, 1955.
Doctor at the Crossroads. New York, Dodd Mead, 1954; London, Collins, 1955.
Marriage for Three. New York, Dodd Mead, 1954; London, Collins 1956.
A Doctor in the Family. New York, Dodd Mead, 1955; London, Collins, 1956.
Challenge for Doctor Mays. New York, Dodd Mead, 1955; as *Doctor Mays*, London, Collins, 1957.
A Doctor for Blue Jay Cove. New York, Dodd Mead, 1956; as *Doctor's Orders*, London, Collins, 1958.
A Call for Doctor Barton. New York, Dodd Mead, 1956; London, Collins, 1957.
Substitute Doctor. New York, Dodd Mead, 1957; London, Collins, 1958.
The Doctor's Husband. New York, Dodd Mead, 1957; London, Collins, 1959.
The New Doctor. New York, Dodd Mead, 1958; as *Doctor Jamie*, London, Collins, 1959.
Love Calls the Doctor. New York, Dodd Mead, 1958; London, Collins, 1960.
Home-Town Doctor. New York, Dodd Mead, 1959; London, Collins, 1960.
Doctor on Trial. London, Dodd Mead, 1959; London, Collins, 1961.
When Doctors Marry. New York, Dodd Mead, 1960; London, Collins, 1961.
Doctors on Parade (omnibus). New York, Dodd Mead, 1960.
The Doctor's Bride. New York, Dodd Mead, 1960; London, Collins, 1962.
The Doctor Makes a Choice. New York, Dodd Mead, 1961; London, Collins, 1962.
Dr Jeremy's Wife. New York, Dodd Mead, 1961; London, Collins, 1963.
The Honor of Dr Shelton. New York, Dodd Mead, 1962; London, Collins, 1963.
The Doctor's Strange Secret. New York, Dodd Mead, 1962; London, Collins, 1964.
Dr Scott, Surgeon on Call. New York, Dodd Mead, 1963; as *Surgeon on Call*, London, Collins, 1965.
Legacy for a Doctor. New York, Dodd Mead, 1963; London, Collins, 1964.
Katie's Young Doctor. New York, Dodd Mead, 1964; London, Collins, 1965.
A Doctor Comes to Bayard. New York, Dodd Mead, 1964; London, Collins, 1966.
Doctor Samaritan. New York, Dodd Mead, 1965; London, Collins, 1966.
Ordeal of Three Doctors. New York, Dodd Mead, 1965; London, Collins, 1967.
Hegerty, MD. New York, Dodd Mead, 1966; London, Collins, 1967.
Pay the Doctor. New York, Dodd Mead, 1966; London, Collins, 1968.
Doctor with a Mission. New York, Dodd Mead, 1967; London, Collins, 1969.
The Rival Doctors. New York, Dodd Mead, 1967; London, Collins, 1969.

The Doctor's Confession. New York, Dodd Mead, 1968; London, Collins, 1971.
To Wed a Doctor. New York, Dodd Mead, 1968; London, Collins, 1970.
Bachelor Doctor. New York, Dodd Mead, 1969; London, Collins, 1971.
For Love of a Doctor. New York, Dodd Mead, 1969; London, Collins, 1970.
Doctor's Kingdom. New York, Dodd Mead, 1970.
The Doctor's Two Lives. New York, Dodd Mead, 1970; London, Collins, 1972.
Doctor in Judgment. New York, Dodd Mead, 1971; London, Collins, 1972.
The Doctor's Second Love. New York, Dodd Mead, 1971; London, Collins, 1973.
Doctor's Destiny. New York, Dodd Mead, and London, Collins, 1972.
The Doctor's Reputation. New York, Dodd Mead, 1972; London, Collins, 1974.
The Doctor's Private Life. New York, Dodd Mead, and London, Collins, 1973.
The Two Faces of Dr Collier. New York, Dodd Mead, 1973; London, Collins, 1974.
The Doctor and Mathilda. New York, Dodd Mead, 1974; London, Collins, 1976.
Doctor in Love. New York, Dodd Mead, 1974; London, Collins, 1976.
The Doctor's Daughter. New York, Dodd Mead, 1974; London, Collins, 1975.
Four Doctors, Four Wives. New York, Dodd Mead, 1975; London, Collins, 1976.
The Doctor's Affair. New York, Dodd Mead, 1975; London, Collins, 1977.
Two Doctors and a Girl. New York, Dodd Mead, 1976; London, Collins, 1978.
The Doctor's Desperate Hour. New York, Dodd Mead, 1976; London, Collins, 1977.
Doctor Tuck. New York, Dodd Mead, 1977; London, Collins, 1979.
The Doctors of Eden Place. New York, Dodd Mead, 1977; London, Collins, 1978.
The Doctors Were Brothers. New York, Dodd Mead, 1978; London, Collins, 1980.
Rebel Doctor. New York, Dodd Mead, 1978; London, Collins, 1980.
The Doctor's Promise. New York, Dodd Mead, 1979; London, Collins, 1981.
The Problems of Doctor A. New York, Dodd Mead, 1979; London, Collins, 1981.
Two Doctors, Two Loves. New York, Dodd Mead, 1982; London, Collins, 1983.

*

Manuscript Collection: Boston University.

Elizabeth Seifert commented (1982):
I have written novels of current life, often in small towns of America, and with only a few exceptions the subject matter has been medical.

*   *   *

One is not likely to find Elizabeth Seifert citations on academic reading lists, nor mention of her in college library catalogues or critical reference works; but go to almost any public library in the USA and you will find book after book, or you would if so many weren't in circulation, of this prolific writer—who produced one or two novels a year from 1938 to 1979. Her popularity has surely stood the test of time, since most of her early work has been reprinted. Nearly all Seifert's books have also been published in England, and many have been published in 14 other countries as well. How can this phenomenon be explained? Is the general reading public so intrigued by the mystique of the medical profession that any title with 'doctor' in it, as nearly all Seifert's titles have, will be avidly sought after? There's much more to it than this.

Though Seifert's books have medical backgrounds and centre primarily on the professional, social, and ethical problems of doctors and their families, usually in an American midwestern setting, they cannot be defined as medical fiction. Her stories are about people who happen to be doctors. Her books are easy to read and consist almost entirely of brief descriptions and dialogue. The reader is not subjected to long paragraphs of exposition. We learn about the characters by how they look, what they wear, what they say, and the plots unfold through their words and actions. We know what their homes look like, how they are furnished, how they are landscaped. And we know these people—for they exist in every neighbourhood in the Western world. Though her characters belong to a glamorous profession, they do the same things readers do— bake pies, tell each other how to raise their children, help each other look for lost dogs, plan programmes for cub scouts, grapple with problems of middle age. Seifert's male characters are apt to be heroic and larger than life, but she is right on target with women, their strengths and weaknesses, their hopes and fears. She generally closes with happy endings; but often they are bittersweet, as with her first book, the $10,000 prize novel—*Young Doctor Galahad*, whose protagonist won a professional battle but slid gallantly into marriage with a woman he didn't love.

Though her first novel dealt well with a post-depression town and proselytized in favor of clinics and socialized medicine, much to the chagrin of many doctors then as now—indeed, though the theme of public health is prevalent in many of her novels—her stories do not reflect the changing influences and current events of half a century, nor do they keep up with the many technological advances. But human nature does not change with the times, so her early novels are as valid in their characterizations as the later ones. Many of them form the Bayard Books, named for a Missouri town, featuring the same characters, one time in major roles, and the next only incidentally. The Bayard Folk become our own families, and it's no wonder that we eagerly wish to learn what happens to them. Seifert was successful because she was plain, direct, and recognizable; and because she liked people.

—Marion Hanscom

SELLERS, Alexandra.
Nationality: Canadian and British. **Education:** Royal Academy of Dramatic Art, London, 1969–71; University of British Columbia, Vancouver, 1986–87. **Relations:** two stepsons, and one stepdaughter. **Career:** writer. Lives in London. **Agent:** P. Tornetta, Box 423, Croton-on-Hudson, New York 10521, USA.

ROMANCE AND HISTORICAL PUBLICATIONS

Novels

The Indifferent Heart. New York, Dell, 1980; London, Hale, 1981.
Captive of Desire. Toronto, Harlequin, 1981.
Fire in the Wind. Toronto, Harlequin, 1982.
Season of Storm. Toronto, Harlequin, and New York, Worldwide, 1983.

The Forever Kind. Toronto, Harlequin, 1984.
The Real Man. New York, Silhouette, 1984.
The Male Chauvinist. New York, Silhouette, 1985.
The Old Flame. New York, Silhouette, 1986.

*   *   *

Both the challenge and the fun of writing fiction lies in the search for metaphors to carry the message the author wants to convey to readers. The more subtle and complex the message, the more difficult it is to find the right characters and action that will at the same time entertain and excite the imagination of readers. That Alexandra Sellers succeeds in doing just that within the confines of the category (series) romance is a commentary on both the ability of this exceptional writer and also the socio-political climate of the time in which she is writing. There is no better illustration of the changing and evolving sensibilities of the time, in fact, than the three novels Sellers wrote for the Silhouette Intimate Moments line—*The Real Man*, *The Male Chauvinist*, and *The Old Flame*—which stand as a trilogy of sorts, with each one describing a different kind of man.

What Sellers is really writing about, however, are the socially constructed perceptions of sexuality and gender that serve to make men the enemies of women (and sometimes the reverse), and which often hide our real values, motives, and feelings even from ourselves. Sellers's metaphors become more forceful and her ideas more clearly defined as the trilogy progresses. Sellers's love scenes are both sexually explicit and powerful (at times even shockingly unexpected, as is the scene on the boat dock early in *The Old Flame*). They are also among her best metaphors, conveying as they do the capacity of her characters to feel deeply and passionately, especially about some of the injustices and misunderstandings that have plagued relations between males and females through most of human history.

The Male Chauvinist opens with the heroine swimming topless at a beach in Greece, which occasions some reflexive (internal) dialogue on the subject of the arbitrary social constrictions her own society places on women. 'No inner voice had ever told her that certain parts of her body were shameful . . . . So, if [covering those parts of her body] was not instinctive in women, what had caused the taboo in the first place? Or who? Well, monotheistic religion, for a start. Judaism, Christianity, and Islam all seemed to have gone a little rabid on the subject of female modesty. But of course all the great monotheistic religions had more in common than the One God: they were all also fiercely male-supremacist'. While researching an article she's writing about the hero's archaeological dig, the heroine comes to the full realization that 'most of the Western world's art, literature and artifacts reflected the masculine. And nearly anything in the modern world that reflected the feminine reflected it from the masculine point of view, and a degrading point of view at that; a point of view that allowed women to be nothing much more than sex objects'. This hero is anything but a chauvinist, as it turns out. He is, in fact, searching for new evidence of an ancient matriarchal society, a place and time when women were central to society and its symbols, and is even able to articulate his empathy for her personal struggle. 'It must be very difficult to live in a world where the battle for a sense of self-worth is so arduous . . . so much of women's imagination is being diverted to that battle, it is no wonder they no longer rule the world'.

The lawyer heroine in *The Old Flame* runs up against 'the male club' in both her professional and personal life, a social phenomenon so slippery that most reporters of the social scene and even feminists find it difficult to identify in terms of specific behaviour or events. 'This was something no woman could explain to any man—or none that she had ever known. Men were a club when the chips were down. A club where each member defended the other against outside attack without question'. Sellers uses the trial of a man charged with rape, and a defence lawyer who attacks the victim as her metaphor, and makes her point when the hero, also a lawyer, excuses it as 'Just legal tactics. Everybody does it'. She accuses, he excuses. A male may not like what he sees or hears in other males, he explains, but 'suddenly the choices yawn in front of him: he can be true to himself and be ostracized, or he can shut up, and be part of the male club. And once you make the choice, it just gets easier and easier to block [what you don't like] out, to stick a grin on your face and let it all go by'. But because he loves her he tries harder to see his own behavior (and that of her other male colleagues as well) from her point of view, and in the process comes to know himself as he never has before. It is Sellers's hero who learns, as philosopher Robert Solomon has pointed out, that 'loving another is essential to discovering one's own identity'.

—Carol Thurston

SETON, Anya.
Nationality: British. **Born:** New York City in 1904 (?); daughter of the writer Ernest Thompson Seton. **Education:** privately in England; at Oxford University. **Military Service:** nurse during World War I. **Relations:** married Hamilton M. Chase (second marriage), one child; two children from previous marriage. **Career:** nurse; former member of the editorial Board, *Writers Magazine*. **Died:** 8 November 1990.

ROMANCE AND HISTORICAL PUBLICATIONS

Novels

My Theodosia. Boston, Houghton Mifflin, 1941; London, Hodder and Stoughton, 1945.
Dragonwyck. Boston, Houghton Mifflin, 1944; London, Hodder and Stoughton, 1945.
The Turquoise. Boston, Houghton Mifflin, and London, Hodder and Stoughton, 1946.
The Hearth and the Eagle. Boston, Houghton Mifflin, and London, Hodder and Stoughton, 1948.
Foxfire. Boston, Houghton Mifflin, and London, Hodder and Stoughton, 1951.
Katherine. Boston, Houghton Mifflin, and London, Hodder and Stoughton, 1954.
The Winthrop Woman. Boston, Houghton Mifflin, and London, Hodder and Stoughton, 1958.
Devil Water. Boston, Houghton Mifflin, and London, Hodder and Stoughton, 1962.
Avalon. Boston, Houghton Mifflin, 1965; London, Hodder and Stoughton, 1966.
Green Darkness. Boston, Houghton Mifflin, and London, Hodder and Stoughton, 1972.

OTHER PUBLICATIONS

Other (for children)

The Mistletoe and Sword: A Story of Roman Britain. New York, Doubleday, 1955; Leicester, Brockhampton Press, 1956.
Washington Irving. Boston, Houghton Mifflin, 1960.
Smouldering Fires. New York, Doubleday, 1975; London, Hodder and Stoughton, 1976.

*

Film Adaptations: *Dragonwyck*, 1946; *Foxfire*, 1955.

*   *   *

As a writer of long, meticulously researched historical romances, Anya Seton may be the best of her generation. Her output was relatively small for a romance writer, but the quality is uniformly high. Unlike some of her contemporaries who choose a historical period and stay with it for book after book, Seton selected a different time and place for each novel. Often she uses actual men and women in history as the basis for her plots, and she makes their stories both interesting and compelling.

Seton's early novel *Dragonwyck* is a straight gothic romance set along the Hudson River among the descendants of Dutch settlers. *The Hearth and the Eagle* is a romance set in Marblehead, Massachusetts. Both these novels had interest, but it was in *My Theodosia* that Seton displayed what would become the hallmark of her work: fictional re-creations of the lives of actual historical women. *My Theodosia* is the story of Theodosia Burr, the daughter of the American scapegrace politician Aaron Burr. Seton considered historical controversies about the Burrs as well as the legends that grew up around the romantic Theodosia, including stories about her early romance with Meriwether Lewis and about her mysterious death.

Seton's classic novel is probably *Katherine*, a fictional treatment of the life of Katherine Swynford, mistress and later wife of John of Gaunt, Duke of Lancaster, in the 14th century. Katherine is significant to history because of a fluke—her descendants (born bastards but legitimized by Parliament) won the War of the Roses, making her a direct ancestress of the British Royal Family. Seton's research for *Katherine* was extensive and meticulous. She used original documents in Middle French and Middle English to supplement her Latin, and she addressed historical controversies about the character of John of Gaunt, a difficult task considering the nature of the sources for the period. She also created an engaging fictional portrait of Katherine's brother-in-law, Geoffrey Chaucer. The 'Author's Note' delineates her research methods and the way she approached her subjects before she began to write.

In *Katherine* and later novels—*Devil Water, Avalon, The Winthrop Woman*—Seton blends historical accuracy (in so far as she can) with legend to produce love stories appealing to modern sensibilities. She portrays women who rise above historical limitations and who exemplify contemporary values about love, marriage, and family. Although Katherine Swynford lived in an age that valued women for their family connections more than personal qualities and in which marriage was often more political alliance than love match, Seton's Katherine is a woman who transcends her time. She is portrayed as an excellent wife and mother, even in an early marriage of convenience. After her long illicit liaison with John of Gaunt she deserves her elevation to Duchess of Lancaster because she remained faithful to him and genuinely repented for her sins against morality. The political realities of 14th-century England may have denied her a place as his wife until late in their lives, but because her situation was not 'her fault', she could be redeemed from disgrace.

The Winthrop Woman, one of the all-time American best sellers, is about Elizabeth Winthrop, the scandalous niece of John Winthrop who was the first governor of the Massachusetts Bay Colony. Again, Seton plays out the love story against a background of historical limits on women's lives. Elizabeth's desire for true love was thwarted by a repressive Puritan society. *Devil Water*, set in 18th-century England and America, is about the life of a woman who may exist only in a family legend. Most of the characters, however, are real; and Seton mixes fact and legend convincingly. *Avalon*, set in 10th-century England, Cornwall, and Iceland, takes her even farther away from the known and factual as she delineates the Age of Faith against a background of vicious Viking raids. *Green Darkness* is about the Protestant Reformation, although in this book Seton dabbles in reincarnation and sets short sections in the modern world. Other books, including *The Turquoise* and *Foxfire*, are not based on fact.

In many of her books, Seton uses an author's note to inform readers of both her research methods and her formulations about historical truth. She acknowledges that the lives of women in history were of only passing interest to the historical record and that it is extraordinarily difficult to re-create personal lives and motivations after many centuries. She describes how she determines the most likely version of the truth. In her books, fact and fiction often work together effectively to produce lengthy and fascinating portraits of her characters. Unlike some other authors in her subfield of romance, she does not take shortcuts or distort the historical record; instead, she spins her tale within the limits of the known.

Seton has the ability to use history as the vehicle for a compelling love story. Her books move quickly, building a record of historical detail without letting research dominate her characters. Her descriptions of places are both evocative and accurate, so that even today many of the locations about which she writes can be found without recourse to a map.

Seton's historical romances have remained in print over many years; it is her ability to make history accessible to modern readers that makes her stand out among her competitors.

—Kay Mussell

SEVERN, Donald. See **NOLAN, Frederick.**

SHAW, Irene. See **ROBERTS, Irene.**

SHEARD, Virna.
Nationality: Canadian. **Born:** Virna Stanton, Cobourg in Ontario, in 1865. **Relations:** married Charles Sheard in 1885 (died 1929). **Died:** 22 February 1943.

ROMANCE AND HISTORICAL PUBLICATIONS

Novels

Trevelyan's Little Daughter. Toronto, Briggs, 1898.
A Maid of Many Moods. Toronto, Copp Clark, New York, Potts, and London, Bagster, 1902.
By the Queen's Grace. New York, Stokes, 1904; revised edition, as *Fortune Turns Her Wheel,* Toronto, McClelland and Stewart, 1929.
Below the Salt. Toronto, Ryerson Press, 1936; London, Sampson Low, 1937.
Leaves in the Wind. Toronto, Ryerson Press, 1938.

Short Stories

The Golden Apple Tree. Toronto, McClelland and Stewart, and New York, Coward McCann, 1920.

OTHER PUBLICATIONS

Novel

The Man at Lone Lake. London, Cassell, 1912.

Poetry

The Miracle and Other Poems. Toronto, Dent, 1913.
Carry On! Toronto, Warwick and Rutter, 1917.
Candle Flame and Other Poems. Toronto, McClelland and Stewart, 1926.
Fairy Dors. Toronto, McClelland and Stewart, 1926.

Other

The Ballad of the Quest. Toronto, McClelland and Stewart, and New York, McCann, 1922.

*　　　*　　　*

In her historical fiction Virna Sheard specialized in novels set in 16th-century London. To evoke a sense of period she uses archaic language and careful descriptions of cultural and social practices and locale. While Sheard's characters and romantic scenarios are strictly conventional, her plots tend to be surprising.

In *The Golden Apple Tree* Sheard updates the fairy-tale. Indeed the King, Queen, Prince, and Princess scenario is undermined consistently by Sheard's 20th-century democratic sensibilities even while she adeptly weaves her seven enchanting stories. Although not conventional historical fiction, these stories merit mention because they demonstrate a sense of the history of ideas about women and the central place of these ideas in the fairy-tale genre.

Using a contemporary Canadian setting, *The Man at Lone Lake* presents the Canadian north as populated by Cree Indians, Métis, a young English Lord, a woodswoman, nuns, and the Royal Canadian Mounted Police. At the end of this pastiche of clichés, the heroine, Nance McCullough, and the hero, soon to be Sir Richard Wynn and the man of the title, leave for Scotland and civilization as if life in the Canadian north were nothing but a bad dream. Canadian readers will note with interest the nostalgic treatment of the British connection which reverses the trend of emigration as the Canadian, Nance, returns to the land from which her grandfather came.

In quite a different vein, *A Maid of Many Moods* involves a player in Shakespeare's the King's Men, Darby Thornbury, who has been assigned the role of Juliet in the new play being rehearsed. Sheard uses Darby's profession as an opportunity to address the issue of the ban on women stage players and skilfully develops her plot to include a triumphant performance in *Romeo and Juliet* by her heroine, Darby's look-alike sister, Deborah. This issue provides the cornerstone of provocative interest in what is otherwise a brief novel with a conventional romantic plot.

By the Queen's Grace is one of Sheard's more complex novels in which the heroine, Joyce Davenport, pits her personal integrity and need for love against both her father's mercenary motives, and an arranged marriage. Set in 1580s and 1590s London, the two different worlds of London Bridge and the Elizabethan Court at Somerset Palace are evoked with skill, imagination, and a convincing attention to details of convention, character, and locale. This novel was republished in a lengthened version in 1929 as *Fortune Turns Her Wheel.*

Sheard's other Canadian novel, *Below the Salt,* is set in mid-19th-century Ontario and follows the complex plot lines formed by an Irish patriarch farmer's attempt to control the lives of his family. Sheard's novels are balanced between the Canadian present and the English past. The historical novels have more detailed narratives, yet they share the smooth prose style which characterizes all of her work.

—Heather Iris Jones

SHEARING, Joseph. See **BOWEN, Marjorie.**

SHELBOURNE, Cecily. See **GOODWIN, Suzanne.**

SHELLABARGER, Samuel.
Pseudonyms: John Esteven; Peter Loring. **Nationality:** American.
Born: Washington, DC, 18 May 1888. **Education:** private schools;
Princeton University, New Jersey, 1905–09, A.B. 1909; studied in
Munich, 1910–11; Harvard University, Cambridge, Massachusetts,
1911–14, Ph.D. 1917. **Military Service:** Ordnance and Military
Intelligence, and as assistant military attaché, USA Legation, Stockholm, 1918–19: captain. **Relations:** married Vivan Borg in 1915;
two sons and two daughters. **Career:** instructor, 1914–16, and
assistant professor of English, 1919–23, Princeton University; lived
in Europe, 1923–31; headmaster, Columbus School for Girls, Ohio,
1938–46; full-time writer. **Died:** 20 March 1954.

ROMANCE AND HISTORICAL PUBLICATIONS

Novels

The Black Gale. New York, Century, 1929.
Grief Before Night (as Peter Loring). Philadelphia, Macrae Smith,
1938; London, Hodder and Stoughton, 1939.
Miss Rolling Stone (as Peter Loring). Philadelphia, Macrae Smith,
1939; as *He Travels Alone*, London, Hodder and Stoughton,
1939.
Captain from Castile. Boston, Little Brown, 1945; London, Mac-
millan, 1947.
Prince of Foxes. Boston, Little Brown, 1947; London, Hamish
Hamilton, 1948.
The King's Cavalier. Boston, Little Brown, 1950; as *Blaise of
France*, London, Hamish Hamilton, 1950.
Lord Vanity. Boston, Little Brown, 1953; London, Collins, 1954.
Tolbecken. Boston, Little Brown, 1956; London, Bles, 1957.

Novels as John Esteven

The Door of Death. New York, Century, 1928; London, Methuen,
1929.
Voodoo. New York, Doubleday, and London, Hutchinson, 1930.
By Night at Dinsmore. New York, Doubleday, and London, Harrap,
1935.
While Murder Waits. London, Harrap, 1936; New York, Double-
day, 1937.
Graveyard Watch. New York, Modern Age, 1938.
Blind Man's Night. London, Hodder and Stoughton, 1938.
Assurance Double Sure. London, Hodder and Stoughton, 1939.

OTHER PUBLICATIONS

Other

The Chevalier Bayard: A Study in Fading Chivalry. New York,
Century, 1928.
Lord Chesterfield. New York and London, Macmillan, 1935.
Lord Chesterfield and Manners (lecture). Claremont, California,
Pomona College, 1938.
Lord Chesterfield and His World. Boston, Little Brown, 1951.
The Token (for children). Boston, Little Brown, 1955.

*

Film Adaptation: *Captain from Castile,* 1947; *Prince of Foxes,*
1949.

*   *   *

Samuel Shellabarger is one of those rare authors who made a financially successful transition from academic life to fiction. Though
his most famous novels are rousing adventures, he will be best
remembered for his meticulous attention to historical detail, particularly of 16th-century Spain, Italy, and France. In his major novels,
Captain from Castile, Prince of Foxes, The King's Cavalier, and
Lord Vanity, his mastery of genealogy, battles, customs, manners,
and folklore is impressive. His backgrounds create an authentic
surface realism that survives the sometimes overly melodramatic
plots and superficial characterization often found in the historical
romance. It is tempting to dismiss the literary aspects of
Shellabarger's fiction, which critics who have underestimated the
difficulty of the genre have sometimes done, yet moments of art are
found throughout his work.

Shellabarger's early Rae Norse mysteries carried the pen name
John Esteven. As Peter Loring he wrote *Miss Rolling Stone,* a
romance set in Baghdad, and *Grief Before Night,* a light novel of
tangled love which drew its background from Shellabarger's residence in Sweden prior to and during World War I. It was not until the
publication of *Captain from Castile* in 1945, however, that Shellabarger achieved widespread popular success. After the publication
of this book several of his novels would be adapted to the motion
pictures and for more than a decade he could be assured of a recept-
ive audience.

Since *Captain from Castile* represents the pinnacle of
Shellabarger's success, it is useful to delineate several of its major
themes. The story follows the youthful son of a Spanish Don, Pedro
de Vargas, from his infatuation with the aristocrat Duena Luisa
through his adventures with Cortes in Mexico and back to Spain.
Woven into the plot is the conflict in Pedro's mind between the traditional match with Luisa, representing the now decadent chivalric
ideal, and Pedro's 'natural' attraction to the tavern dancer, Catana,
who follows him from Spain to Mexico and back. The episodic adventures of the novel are provided by the conquest of Mexico and
the machinations of the arch villain de Silva, who betrays the innocent de Vargas family to the Inquisition, casually marries Luisa in
Pedro's absence, allows Pedro and several comrades to be captured
for humiliation and sacrifice by the Aztecs, and tries to have Pedro
executed for betraying the king. Shellabarger neatly parallels the
Spanish Inquisition with Aztec sacrificial rites and has a corrupt
Inquisitor burned by the Aztecs. Underlying the surface of the novel
are characteristic American ambivalences of the time towards success and race. In order to avoid having Pedro directly profit from the
slaughter of the Aztecs, Shellabarger has Pedro's own treasure
given to him by an Indian whom he had helped escape from brutal
servitude in Spain. The Aztecs and Indians are nevertheless inferior;
Montezuma's 'stone-age self could not cope with the thrust of
Cortes's personality', and though the Indians side with the Spanish
against the Aztecs, 'it was the white force that counted'.

Pedro is not the clever hero of picaresque Romance, he is more
akin to those of Horatio Alger, and the Aztecs might as well have
been lifted from a western. Pedro does change from a spirited youth
dominated by his father to a man tempered by his experiences, but as
a character he remains undistinguished. Shellabarger further mined
the 16th century in *Prince of Foxes,* set in the court of the Borgias in
Italy, and in *The King's Cavalier,* set in France during the reign of
Francis I, while he moved the action of *Lord Vanity* to 18th-century
England, Italy, and France. In these novels Shellabarger continued
his struggle to create believable characters and eliminate cumber-

some plots while developing competent and sometimes brilliant settings and backgrounds.

—Larry N. Landrum

———

SHERRILL, Suzanne. See **WOODS, Sherryl.**

———

SHERWOOD, Valerie.
Pseudonyms: Jeanne Hines; Rosamond Royal. **Nationality:** American. **Address:** c/o Severn House Publishers Inc, 475 Fifth Avenue, New York, New York 10017, USA.

ROMANCE AND HISTORICAL PUBLICATIONS

Novels (series: Imogene and Georgiana Quartet; Tales of the Silver Wench Trilogy)

This Loving Torment. New York, Warner, 1977.
These Golden Pleasures. New York, Warner, 1977.
This Towering Passion. New York, Warner, 1978.
Rapture (as Rosamond Royal). New York, Popular Library, 1979.
Her Shining Splendor. New York, Warner, 1980; as *Her Shining Splendour*, London, Severn House, 1993.
Imogene and Georgiana Quartet:
   Bold Breathless Love. New York, Warner, 1981; London, Macdonald, 1985.
   Rash Reckless Love. New York, Warner, 1981; London, Macdonald, 1985.
   Wild Willful Love. New York, Warner, 1982; London, Macdonald, 1985.
   Rich Radiant Love. New York, Warner, 1983; London, Macdonald, 1985.
Lovely Lying Lips. New York, Warner, 1983.
Born to Love. New York, Warner, 1984; London, Macdonald, 1985.
Tales of the Silver Wench Trilogy:
   Lovesong. New York, Pocket Books, 1985; London, Grafton, 1986; published in two parts as *The Beauty and the English Lord,* Boston, Massachusetts, Hall, 1986; London, Severn House, 1987; and *The Beauty and the Buccaneer,* Boston, Massachusetts, Hall, 1986; London, Severn House, 1987.
   Windsong. New York, Pocket Books, 1986; London, Grafton, 1987.
   Nightsong. New York, Pocket Books, 1986; London, Grafton, 1988.
To Love a Rogue. New York, New American Library, 1987.
Lisbon. New York, New American Library, 1989.
This Towering Passion: The Lovers. London, Severn House, 1991.
This Towering Passion: The Mistress. London, Severn House, 1991.

Novels as Jeanne Hines

The Slashed Portrait. New York, Dell, 1973.
Tidehawks. New York, Popular Library, 1974.
Talons of the Hawk. New York, Dell, 1975.
Bride of Terror. New York, Popular Library, 1976.
Scarecrow House. New York, Popular Library, 1976.
The Keys to Queenscourt. New York, Popular Library, 1976.
The Legend of Witchwynd. New York, Popular Library, 1976.
The Third Wife. New York, Popular Library, 1977.

*

Valerie Sherwood comments:

17th-century buccaneers have always fascinated me, and although I have been diverted at times by bold highwaymen (*Rapture*), tales of the Monmouth Rebellion (*Lovely Lying Lips, Born to Love*), Cromwellian England and its aftermath (*This Towering Passion, Her Shining Splendor*), or by events such as the Alaskan Gold Rush (*These Golden Pleasures*), Bacon's Rebellion (*To Love a Rogue*), or the destruction of Lisbon in its golden era by earthquake, fire, and tidal wave (*Lisbon*), eight of my novels have dealt with the lives of buccaneers. They were a gallant band, and history has not been kind to them. Indeed, in most people's minds buccaneers are scrambled together with pirates, those 'mad dogs' of the seas who attacked all shipping with equal fury. Not so! In the beginning buccaneers were men without a country, driven to seek refuge in the West Indies where Spain, who felt she 'owned' the Western seas, tried to annihilate them with the sword, and with its 'scorched earth' policy. Desperate, these men struck back, first slipping in with rowboats and piraguas beneath the Spanish guns to take small ships, later towering galleons until—in what must have been a golden moment—they took a Spanish treasure fleet, and eventually blockaded Spain itself. These intrepid 'privateers' carried the banners of the countries who chose to disown them. Across the centuries my heart goes out to those lonely outcasts who fought the leading sea power of their time—and won, carving a world for themselves in the wild West Indies.

*   *   *

In the author's note of her novel *Nightsong* Valerie Sherwood extols the virtues of the buccaneers who sailed the 17th-century seas, preying upon the ships of Spain and disposing of their booty in England and its colonies. It was in this swashbuckling era that she sets many of her tales. An era that brings to mind the elegantly handsome Errol Flynn on the foredeck of a tall-masted schooner, sword in hand, fighting, and conquering an evil foe. For readers enraptured by such scenes Sherwood's books will satisfy any craving for stories of this glorified past. There are beautiful, enticing heroines in distress, and strong virile men willing to extricate them from their plight.

The Sherwood heroine, usually a blonde, has the kind of irresistible beauty expected in a romantic tale of several hundred pages. The hero is typically tall, dark, handsome, and completely captivated by the heroine's stunning good looks. The attraction between the two is immediate, and within a very short space of time they consummate their love. 'Fueled by bursts of passion, they spun together toward the farther stars, whirled as one toward infinity. Locked together, panting in soul shattering ecstasy, they went over the brink together' (*Lovely Lying Lips*). There will be several times throughout the novel when the lovers will share such bliss. Do not expect scenes of rape or graphic violence. At times the heroine may be reluctant and need to be coaxed by the hero, but always there exists an element of tenderness between them.

Most Sherwood plots have a young beauty who finds her true love in the handsome hero only to lose him for a time. Often she thinks he has abandoned her for another woman, but this, of course, is a misunderstanding on the heroine's part, and a series of improbable coincidences brings them back together for a satisfying conclusion.

For example Carolina Lightfoot, the silver-haired heroine of the 'Tales of the Silver Wench Trilogy' (*Lovesong, Windsong,* and *Nightsong*) thought she had found everlasting love in the arms of Irish buccaneer Rye Evistock, known on the high seas as Captain Kells. Yet in *Nightsong* she is convinced he has left her for a Spanish beauty and briefly seeks consolation in the arms of another man.

Sometimes the innocent young lady gives herself first to someone undeserving as Lorraine London (*To Love a Rogue*) does with the cad Philip. Soon enough, however, she finds a worthy man in the renegade gunrunner Raile Cameron. Another example is Imogene, who conceives a daughter, Georgiana, by Steve, a charmer with two wives. But it is in the strong arms of buccaneer van Ryker that she finds true happiness. The love stories of this mother and daughter are told in a series of four books: *Bold Breathless Love*, *Rash Reckless Love*, *Wild Willful Love*, and *Rich Radiant Love*. In the novel *Lisbon*, Charlotte marries the much older Rowan Keynes who has tricked her into believing that the poor sailor she loves has been killed in a tragic accident. Not until her own daughters are grown is she reunited with this man, who fathered her oldest child, and who is now a wealthy, titled gentleman.

There is romance, adventure, and sumptuous living aplenty in all of Sherwood's books. Although the historical data is detailed and accurate, its main purpose is to serve as background for a sensuous love story. Readers who understand this can sit back, relax, and enjoy a few hours of romantic fantasy.

—Patricia Altner

SHOESMITH, Kathleen A(nne).
Nationality: British. **Born:** Keighley, Yorkshire, 17 July 1938. **Education:** Avery Hill Teachers' Training College, London, diploma 1956. **Career:** teacher since 1958; since 1973 at Lees County Primary School, Keighley. **Address:** 351 Fell Lane, Keighley, Yorkshire BD22 6DB, England.

ROMANCE AND HISTORICAL PUBLICATIONS

Novels

Cloud over Calderwood. London, Hale, 1969; New York, Ace, 1973.
Jack O'Lantern. London, Hale, 1969; New York, Ace, 1973.
The Tides of Tremannion. London, Hale, 1970; New York, Ace, 1973.
Mallory's Luck. London, Hale, 1971; New York, Ace, 1974.
Return of the Royalist. London, Hale, 1971.
The Reluctant Puritan. London, Hale, 1972; New York, Ace, 1973.
Belltower. London, Hale, 1973; New York, Ace, 1974.
The Highwayman's Daughter. London, Hale, 1973; New York, Ace, 1974.
The Black Domino. London, Hale, 1975.
Elusive Legacy. London, Hale, 1976.
The Miser's Ward. London, Hale, 1977.
Smuggler's Haunt. London, Hale, 1978.
Guardian at the Gate. London, Hale, 1979.
Brackenthorpe. London, Hale, 1980.
Autumn Escapade. London, Hale, 1981.
Rustic Vineyard. London, Hale, 1982.
A Minor Bequest. London, Hale, 1984.

OTHER PUBLICATIONS

(for children)

Easy to Read (*Helen and Her Hamster*, *Karen and Her Kitten*, *Ruth and Her Rabbit*, *Gordon and His Goldfish*, *Tony and His Tortoise*, *Barry and His Budgerigar*). London, Charles, 6 vols, 1967.
The Judy Stories (*Judy in the Garden* [*in the Wind*, *in the Snow*, *on the Sand*]). London, Charles, 4 vols, 1967.

Playtime Stories (*The Birthday Kitten*, *Jack and the Robin*, *The Bird and the Milk*, *John's Ship*, *The Lost Ball*, *The Christmas Tree*). Leeds, E.J. Arnold, 6 vols, 1967.
How do They Grow? (*Apples*, *Butterflies and Moths*, *Daffodils*, *Frogs*). London, Charles, 4 vols, 1967.
Do You Know About Claws? [*Feathers?*, *Tails?*, *Wings?*, *Ears?*, *Hair?*, *Shells?*, *Teeth?*, *Clocks?*, *Steps?*, *Wheels?*, *Windows?*, *Bridges?*, *Feet?*, *Mirrors?*, *Skin?*]. London, Burke, 16 vols, 1970–75.
Use Your Senses (*Listen and Hear*, *Look and See*, *Scent and Smell*, *Taste and Flavour*, *Touch and Feel*). London, Burke, 5 vols, 1973.

*   *   *

Romance is the primary element in the novels of Kathleen A. Shoesmith. Love of the spirited heroine for the aloof, yet attractive hero is at the core of all her works, whose precise historical settings are an integral, yet secondary part of the novels as a whole. More than most, Shoesmith's works fit neatly into the category of historical romance, and her books display the skills of one of the most competent exponents of the form.

Her style is already well established in early novels such as *Jack O'Lantern* and *The Tides of Tremannion*, in which the familiar gothic and romantic themes serve as a background plot to the central love story. Its continuation, virtually unaltered, in subsequent works, together with the remarkably consistent level of her writing, has ensured that Shoesmith's novels achieve a fairly standard relation one to another, with none of the peaks and troughs associated with the work of other writers. Her vision appears to fix itself on a few, selected periods of history notably the English Civil War (*The Reluctant Puritan*, *Return of the Royalist*), the 18th century (*The Highwayman's Daughter*, *Smuggler's Haunt*, *Guardian at the Gate*), the Napoleonic era (*Elusive Legacy*, *The Black Domino*), and the early Victorian period of the 1840s and 1850s (*Belltower*, *The Miser's Ward*, *A Minor Bequest*).

Shoesmith's novels invariably have English locations, with Yorkshire and Sussex the favoured counties, although the early part of *A Minor Bequest* is set in Venice. Into these accurate, precisely noted times and places—Shoesmith usually gives a specific year to each novel—the author plunges hero and heroine together, enmeshing both in the drama and violence of the adventure. Her writing ransacks the gothic novel for themes, which recur continually.

Shoesmith's heroines, through whose eyes the action is presented, are invariably daughters of gentry fallen on hard times, poverty-stricken and sometimes orphaned, yet proud and self-reliant. Employed as governesses or tutors in ancestral homes, they encounter ghostly apparitions, learn dark family secrets, and explore underground passages in search of hidden treasure. Inheritances figure largely in Shoesmith's novels—*Elusive Legacy* and *A Minor Bequest* are typical examples—and not infrequently the heroine is transformed from rags to riches by the end. Heroes tend to be stern and remote, forbidding almost, their severe personalities thawed at last by love. Villains are sinister, and often foreign—Marie-Elizabeth Delon in *The Black Domino* and André Durand of *Elusive Legacy* are two who spring immediately to mind. Smugglers and spies abound, with the occasional miser or highwayman, and generally much violence ensues before their dastardly plans are thwarted. Deaths occur in most of Shoesmith's novels, but these are rarely depicted in a sensational manner—the brutal murder of Matthew Herald in *The Miser's Ward* takes place 'offstage', for example, and in most other cases the violent scenes are presented swiftly and with understatement. For instance, the fall of the villainous Crosbic from the Sussex cliffs in *Smuggler's Haunt* and the flurry of demises at the end of *The Black Domino* are noted rather than dwelt upon, meriting the slightest of pauses before the action continues.

Love, rather than violence, remains the centre of Shoesmith's fiction, and in spite of the threats and horrors of her villains, the author's vision is one of hope. Shoesmith's ghosts are mostly benevolent, her formidable heroes are warmed to humanity by the fires of passion, and good overcomes evil in the end. The sense of kinship one feels for her courageous heroines—heightened by the immediacy of a first person narrative in many cases—combines well with the compelling atmosphere, lively dialogue, and exciting plot to engage the interest of the reader.

Some of Shoesmith's novels show more invention in their themes than others; *Guardian at the Gate*, which describes young Marcus Grant's appointment as legal guardian to a proud gentry family reduced to poverty, and the problems he encounters, is perhaps one of the most imaginative. Similarly, *A Minor Bequest* has a deft storyline where the tutor heroine inherits money only on condition that she brings up an orphan child. Adoption is a theme which occurs again in *The Black Domino*, which also features a restless ghost, smugglers, and spies.

Whether unusual or familiar in their choice of themes, Shoesmith's books are never less than interesting. Her writing uses gothic conventions and elements in an individual manner, matching them neatly with precise chronology and the perennial pain and fulfilment of love.

—Geoffrey Sadler

SHUTE, Nevil.
Nationality: British. **Born:** Nevil Shute Norway in Ealing, London, 17 January 1899. **Education:** Dragon School, Oxford; Shrewsbury School, Oxford; Royal Military Academy, Woolwich, London; Balliol College, Oxford, 1919–22, E.A. in engineering 1922. **Military Service:** private in the Suffolk Regiment, British Army, 1918; commissioned in the Royal Naval Volunteer Reserve, 1940: lieutenant commander; retired 1945. **Relations:** married Frances Mary Heaton in 1931; two daughters. **Career:** calculator, de Havilland Aircraft Company, 1923–24; chief calculator, 1924–28, and deputy chief engineer, 1928–30, on the construction of Rigid Airship R.100 for the Airship Guarantee Company: twice flew Atlantic in R.100, 1930; managing director, Yorkshire Aeroplane Club Ltd, 1927–30; founder and joint managing director, Airspeed Ltd, aeroplane constructors, 1931–38. Lived in Australia after 1950. **Recipient:** Fellow, Royal Aeronautical Society, 1934. **Died:** 12 January 1960.

ROMANCE AND HISTORICAL PUBLICATIONS

Novels

Marazan. London, Cassell, 1926.
Landfall: A Channel Story. London, Heinemann, and New York, Morrow, 1940.
An Old Captivity. London, Heinemann, and New York, Morrow, 1940.
Pastoral. London, Heinemann, and New York, Morrow, 1944.
A Town Like Alice. London, Heinemann, 1950; as *The Legacy*, New York, Morrow, 1950.
The Far Country. London, Heinemann, and New York, Morrow, 1952.
Requiem for a Wren. London, Heinemann, 1955; as *The Breaking Wave*, New York, Morrow, 1955.
Stephen Morris. London, Heinemann, and New York, Morrow, 1961.

OTHER PUBLICATIONS

Novels

So Disdained. London, Cassell, 1928; as *Mysterious Aviator*, Boston, Houghton Mifflin, 1928.
Lonely Road. London, Cassell, and New York, Morrow, 1932.
Ruined City. London, Cassell, 1938; as *Kindling*, New York, Morrow, 1938.
What Happened to the Corbetts. London, Heinemann, 1939; as *Ordeal*, New York, Morrow, 1939.
Pied Piper. New York, Morrow, 1941; London, Heinemann, 1942.
Most Secret. London, Heinemann, and New York, Morrow, 1945.
The Chequer Board. London, Heinemann, and New York, Morrow, 1947.
No Highway. London, Heinemann, and New York, Morrow, 1948.
Round the Bend. London, Heinemann, and New York, Morrow, 1951.
In the Wet. London, Heinemann, and New York, Morrow, 1953.
Beyond the Black Stump. London, Heinemann, and New York, Morrow, 1956.
On the Beach. London, Heinemann, and New York, Morrow, 1957.
Trustee from the Toolroom. London, Heinemann, and New York, Morrow, 1960.

Play

Vinland the Good (screenplay). London, Heinemann, and New York, Morrow, 1946.

Other

Slide Rule: The Autobiography of an Engineer. London, Heinemann, and New York, Morrow, 1954.

*

Film Adaptations: *The Pied Piper*, 1942, *Crossing to Freedom*, 1990, both from the novel *The Pied Piper*; *Landfall*, 1949; *No Highway*, 1951; *A Town Like Alice* (*The Rape of Malaya*), 1956, 1981; *On the Beach*, 1959.

Manuscript Collection: National Library of Australia, Canberra.

Critical Study: *Nevil Shute (Nevil Shute Norway)* by Julian Smith, Boston, Twayne, 1976.

*   *   *

Nevil Shute, a popular novelist of the 1940s and 1950s best known for his futuristic novel *On the Beach*, based the majority of his 22 novels on his experiences as an aeronautical engineer and aviator in both world wars, and set many in Australia, where he finally settled. A good storyteller, with a quiet, understated style, superb technical details, and highly plausible personalities, Shute always includes a romance, though one unconventional or subordinated to his fascination with machinery, entrepreneurship, and exploration.

An Old Captivity focuses on an archaeological aerial survey in Greenland. Oxford professor Lockwood and his daughter, Alix, engage Donald Ross, a seaplane pilot experienced in far north flying, to help photograph Viking ruins. The hazardous environment of ice floes and fog strains Ross's nerves, which, already weakened by an addiction to sleeping pills, begin to fray as he dreams of Erik the Red, Leif Erikson, and the latter's fabled trip to Cape Cod, the Norsemen's 'Vinland the Good'. Once recovered from his drifting dream state, Ross still feels his fantasies are more real than his present life, and that Alix is in fact a reincarnation of Hekja, a Celtic slave girl that Ross, named Haki loved and settled down with in the New World a thousand years earlier. Physical proof of Haki and Hekja's existence found by Ross and the Lockwoods' trip to the Massachusetts coast lend substance to these incredible illusions.

The dream vision technique allows Shute to build the novel on his strengths, his precise knowledge of aviation, and his sensitivity to a modern love story, while indulging his taste for distant history. The modern characters and the Viking vision combine neatly and credibly in the eerie empty setting of Greenland, a place of stark landscapes where normality seems suspended. A flashback technique used in other Shute works here ameliorates the fantastic with a realistic frame: a much older Ross recounting his dream experience to a psychiatrist on a stalled train.

Vinland the Good expands the story of Leif Erikson and his two Scottish slaves, Haki and Haekia, in a film script format. Beginning with a schoolteacher newly returned from World War II, lecturing a history class about the discovery of America, the action cuts back and forth from class to story, with the teacher's lecture as voiceover. Like his professorial hero, Shute is taken by the lack of 'grandiose . . . pomp and dignity' in this 'journey by the common man, a farmer, seeking to get a load of lumber to build cowhouses and discovering America on the side'. Using the academic lecture as a frame allows Shute to stress the historical truth of his story, while fleshing out the characters with romantic dialogue to appeal to the schoolboy 'audience'. For example, Erik the Red's banishment from Norway to Iceland and then to Greenland is ascribed to his violence but also to his weakness for other men's wives; his son Leif the Lucky's affair with a Hebridean princess is set up as a bittersweet idyll replete with 'beautiful' scenes. Thus Shute has the best of both worlds: a scholarly historian narrator gives his tale credibility while his rhetorical need to captivate his youthful listeners justifies Shute's popularizing. Besides working out his historical interests, the frame allows Shute slyly to satirize the teaching of history in British schools, as his teacher hero, after a brilliant but unconventional lecture which has clearly engaged his pupils, is advised by his stuffy headmaster to pursue a job selling electric razors.

Shute's romances include more details about aviation and business than about the emotional states of the amorous couple and, in the early works, the love interest seems secondary, though it becomes more organic in the later works. Basically they suggest domesticity as a powerful civilizing force, one that might well spur men to dreams and action. Shute's men are industrious, competent, and driven, while his women are supportive, and ultimately save men from shortsightedness or from personal limitations. In *Stephen Morris*, a young engineer's work for a struggling aircraft builder takes precedence over his proposing to the girl of his dreams, while in *Marazan* Shute's adventurous heroine mainly provides a motive for the protagonist's economic success. In *Landfall*, when everyone rejects a Navy pilot who destroyed a British submarine, thinking it German, the barmaid he strove to seduce pieces together clues indicating two subs sunk in the same area; she thereby saves the pilot's reputation and his conscience, and wins his love and his hand, despite their class differences. *Pastoral*, in turn, is an ironic idyll of a soldier on leave who strikes up a romance by offering to share a huge pike with a young woman. *The Far Country* tells of English girl, who, while visiting on a sheep station in Australia, meets and falls in love with a Czech refugee, helps him amputate the leg of a man trapped under a bulldozer and operate on the crushed skull of another, and goes on to find with him a vitality undreamed of back home in England. *A Town Like Alice* is in part a contrived romance, an English woman's romantic search for the Australian lorry-driver who stood up for her and others against the Japanese occupation forces in Malaya, and her finding a new life in rural Australia.

Requiem for a Wren is typical of Shute's major love stories. Spanning the better part of a decade and two continents, it tells how Alan Duncan, the son of a wealthy Australian sheep farmer, returns to the family station in 1953 to discover that his parents' parlourmaid had committed suicide just before he arrived. Alan learns that, unknown to his family, she was Janet Prentice, the English Wren once engaged to his brother Bill. After Bill was killed just before the invasion of Normandy, Alan, having fallen in love with Janet, had searched unsuccessfully for her. The bulk of the text is a series of flashbacks as Alan reads Janet's diaries and recalls his obsessive search. As in *A Town Like Alice*, an Australian seeks in an English girl in England who in turn seeks him in Australia, but in this case with less happy results.

This sadly ironic love story with its finely drawn characters is set against detailed description of navy life near the Isle of Wight just prior to D-Day, with specifics of the physical landscape, words from contemporary navy slang, and much recounting of everyday occurrences painting an utterly convincing picture of period and place. The nervous preparations and rehearsals for the 'day the balloon goes up' are, ironically, the high point in the young lives of the protagonists, who will never again feel as useful nor as fulfilled by their later civilian lives. The war years liberate young women and mix the British classes, yet the sad survivors of this tumultuous period find themselves going back to conventional and banal lives. Thus Shute writes a classic World War II love story, but reverses the usual emphasis: these were the best of times far more than the worst of times.

Shute's forte is to reduce the historical and the romantic to lifesized dimensions, to capture the excitement of the humdrum and the ordinariness of the historic, to pursue the effects of change on the common man—all in an artfully casual style. His works reflect an old-fashioned sense of goodness; they involve characters with a strong sense of purpose, of decency, of right, characters who enjoy being caught up in the unfolding of great enterprises. Major Callender sums up Shute's view of history when he tells his class in *Vinland the Good:* 'History is made by plain and simple people like ourselves, doing the best we can with each job as it comes along'. Shute himself sums up his reason for including romance: 'people in love are normally clean and brave and self-sacrificing, at their best'.

—Gina and Andrew Macdonald

SINCLAIR, James.   See STAPLES, Mary Jane.

SINCLAIR, Julian.   See SINCLAIR, May.

SINCLAIR, M.A. St C.   See SINCLAIR, May.

SINCLAIR, Mary.   See SINCLAIR, May.

SINCLAIR, May.
Pseudonyms: Julian Sinclair, M.A. St C. Sinclair, Mary Sinclair. **Nationality:** British. **Born**: Mary Amelia St Clair Sinclair, Rock Ferry, Higher Bebington, Cheshire, 24 August 1863. **Military Service:** Red Cross Ambulance Corps, Belgium, 1914. **Education**: privately, and at Cheltenham Ladies College, 1881–82. **Career:** from 1895, full-time writer; active in Women's Freedom League, and the Women Writers Suffrage League, 1908–10; worked with the Hoover Relief Commission. Lived in Devon, Sidmouth, and

London. Settled in Bierton, near Aylesbury, Buckinghamshire, 1936. **Recipient:** Fellow, Royal Society of Literature, 1916. **Died:** 14 November 1946.

ROMANCE AND HISTORICAL PUBLICATIONS

Novels

Audrey Craven. Edinburgh, Blackwood, 1897; New York, Holt, 1906.
Mr and Mrs Nevill Tyson. Edinburgh and London, Blackwood, 1898; as *The Tysons*, New York, Dodge, 1906.
The Divine Fire. London, Constable, and New York, Holt, 1904.
The Helpmate. London, Constable, and New York, Holt, 1907.
Kitty Tailleur. London, Constable, 1908; as *The Immortal Moment*, New York, Doubleday Page, 1908.
The Creators: A Comedy. London, Constable, and New York, Dutton, 1910.
The Flaw in the Crystal. New York, Dutton, 1912.
The Combined Maze. London, Hutchinson, and New York, Harper, 1913.
The Return of the Prodigal. New York, Macmillan, 1914.
The Three Sisters. London, Hutchinson, and New York, Macmillan, 1914.
Tasker Jevons: The Real Story. London, Hutchinson, 1916; as *The Belfry*, New York, Macmillan, 1916.
The Tree of Heaven. London, Cassell, and New York, Macmillan, 1917.
Mary Olivier: A Life. London, Cassell, and New York, Macmillan, 1919.
The Romantic. London, Collins, and New York, Macmillan, 1920.
Mr Waddington of Wyck. London, Cassell, and New York, Macmillan, 1921.
Life and Death of Harriett Frean. London, Collins, and New York, Macmillan, 1922.
Anne Severn and the Fieldings. London, Hutchinson, and New York, Macmillan, 1922.
A Cure of Souls. London, Hutchinson, 1923; New York, Macmillan, 1924.
Arnold Waterlow: A Life. London, Hutchinson, and New York, Macmillan, 1924.
The Rector of Wyck. London, Hutchinson, and New York, Macmillan, 1926.
Far End. London, Hutchinson, and New York, Macmillan, 1926.
The Allinghams. London, Hutchinson, and New York, Macmillan, 1927.
History of Anthony Waring. London, Hutchinson, and New York, Macmillan, 1927.

OTHER PUBLICATIONS

Short Stories

Two Sides of a Question (novellas). London, Constable, and New York, Holt, 1901.
The Judgement of Eve and Other Stories. London, and New York, Harper, 1907.
Uncanny Stories (includes *The Flaw in the Crystal*). London, Hutchinson, and New York, Macmillan, 1923.
Fame. London, Hutchinson, 1929.
Tales Told by Simpson. London, Hutchinson, and New York, Macmillan, 1930.
The Intercessor and Other Stories. London, Hutchinson, 1931; New York, Macmillan, 1931.

Poetry

Nakiketas and Other Poems (as Julian Sinclair). London, Kegan Paul, 1886.
The Dark Night: A Novel in Verse. London, Cape, and New York, Macmillan, 1924.

Other

Essays in Verse. London, Kegan Paul, Trench, Trubner, 1891.
Feminism. London, The Women Writers' Suffrage League, 1912.
The Three Brontës (biography). London, Hutchinson, and Boston, Houghton Mifflin, 1912.
A Journal of Impressions of Belgium. London, Hutchinson, and New York, Macmillan, 1915.
America's Part in the War. New York, Commission for Relief in Belgium, 1915.
A Defence of Idealism. London, and New York, Macmillan, 1917.
The New Idealism. London, and New York, Macmillan, 1922.

Translator, *Outlines of Church History*, by Rudolf Sohm. London, Macmillan, 1895; Boston, Beacon Press, 1958.
Translator, *England's Danger, The Future of British Army Reform*, by Theodore von Sosnosky. London, Chapman and Hall, 1901.

*

Manuscript Collections: University of Pennsylvannia Library.

Critical Studies: *Miss May Sinclair: Novelist*, by T.E.M. Boll. Rutherford, New Jersey, Fairleigh Dickinson University Press, 1973; *May Sinclair*, by H. Zegger. Boston, Hall, 1976.

*   *   *

May Sinclair's prolific output of novels, short stories, and nonfiction writing, exemplifies the transition in thought from late Victorian to modernist. The coiner of the term 'stream of consciousness' (in a review of one of Dorothy Richardson's novels), Sinclair was acutely aware of developments in psychology and philosophy, some of which are reflected in her three innovative novels, *The Three Sisters*, *Mary Olivier: A Life*, and *Life and Death of Harriett Frean*. However, before this experimental phase, she had written novels that are similar to the late fiction of Thomas Hardy and George Meredith in their concern with the struggles of individuals to reach self-fulfilment within social constraints. Sinclair takes the romance story beyond the marriage ending of the typical Victorian novel to anatomize the troubled relationships of husbands and wives. In *Mr and Mrs Nevill Tyson* and *The Helpmate*, for example, the married couples cannot reconcile their spiritual and their animal impulses. The wife, in particular, split between roles of idealized woman and sexual creature, is seen at the centre of this conflict.

Sinclair found early support in the work of Havelock Ellis for her belief that sexual energy cannot be suppressed. Later, the ideas of Freud and, to some extent Jung, and Pierre Janet, gave her insights into what happens when the sexual instinct is denied. Repression leading to neurosis is the outcome in *Life and Death of Harriett Frean*, a chilling, superbly economic, and simple account of a girl who 'behaves beautifully'; in sacrificing desire she destroys both herself and those around her. In the autobiographical *Mary Olivier: A Life*, sublimation in learning and art is the path taken by a woman whose subjectivity and self-determination is threatened by a mother of overpowering femininity. However, it is in *The Three Sisters* that a range of alternative responses is explored fully, and the romance story is most thoroughly scrutinized.

Sinclair had written a series of introductions to the novels of the Brontë sisters between 1907 and 1914, and a biography, *The Three*

Brontës, in 1912. *The Three Sisters* is a revision of the Brontë myth in that it explores the sexual psychology of three young women living with their clergyman father in a moorland village. At the same time, it re-writes the novels for which the Brontës are famous, embodying in its female characters the repression, sublimation, neurosis, and 'normal' femininity which the Brontë heroines variously display. It thus uses the Brontës' biography as a narrative framework, and their fiction as deliberate intertexts by which to investigate sexual motives and negotiations. The three sisters are 'waiting for something to happen' and this something is the coming of two men—a doctor, and a dalesman-farmer. The sisters hear the men's voices on the road, and 'life, secret and silent, stirred in their blood and nerves. It quivered like a hunting thing held on the leash'. The novel enacts a marriage game—'You were three women to one man, and Mary was the one without a scruple', says a bystander to one of the sisters—and in this respect it glances back ironically to Jane Austen's fiction. Yet, where Austen was aware of the economic bases of her courtship games, *The Three Sisters* is one of the first novels in English explicitly to expose the libidinous motivation underlying domestic behaviour, and also the extremities of hysterical illness, duplicity, and ruthlessness that respectable women will go to in order to find a mate. The novel's powerful symbolism, its short chapters, add a terse style heavily reliant on dialogue, including an effective use of dialect, also constitute a discomforting critique of Victorian sentimentality, not least in its construction of a romantic Brontë myth which had robbed the sisters of the integrity of their lives. Sinclair's *The Three Sisters* seeks to restore psychological complexity to the kind of family life the Howarth parsonage may have witnessed.

Sinclair's novels of the late 1920s, none of which are in print, continue the debate about the relationship between sexuality, family life, art, and the health of the individual. The psychological intensity of *The Three Sisters* is replaced, however, by philosophical breadth, as in *Far End* which reflects on the life, loves, and development of a psychological novelist whose writing career runs parallel to Sinclair's own. The novelist-hero of *Far End*, is on a romance quest but as a man his quest more easily encompasses spiritual and artistic as well as sexual goals. It is interesting that Sinclair chose to give a fictional summary of her life as a writer (*Far End* written towards the end of her writing career) through the character of a male novelist. Her large intellectual pre-occupations, her interest in aesthetics and her audacious attitude towards sexuality could better find expression in the life story of a man. A woman's exemplary life story was still, at this time, circumscribed by the demands of the romance story; even though Sinclair could subvert it, she could only escape it by the masquerade of a male protagonist.

—Marion Shaw

SINCLAIR, Olga.
Pseudonyms: Ellen Clare; Olga Daniels. **Nationality:** British. **Born:** Olga Ellen Waters, Watton, Norfolk, 23 January 1923. **Education:** Convent of the Sacred Heart, Swaffham, Norfolk. **Relations:** married Stanley G. Sinclair in 1945; three sons. **Career:** since 1966, Justice of the Peace for Norfolk. **Recipient:** Society of Authors Margaret Rhondda award, 1972. **Address:** Dove House Farm, Potter Heigham, Norfolk NR29 5LJ, England.

ROMANCE AND HISTORICAL PUBLICATIONS

Novels

Man at the Manor. London, Gresham, 1967; New York, Dell, 1972.

Man of the River. London, Hale, 1968.
Hearts by the Tower. London, Hale, 1968; as *Night of the Black Tower*, New York, Lancer, 1968.
Bitter Sweet Summer. London, Hale, 1970; New York, Simon and Schuster, 1972.
Wild Dream. London, Hale, 1973.
Tenant of Binningham Hall. London, Woman's Weekly Library, 1975.
Where the Cigale Sings. London, Woman's Weekly Library, 1976.
My Dear Fugitive. London, Hale, 1976.
Never Fall in Love. London, Hale, 1977.
Master of Melthorpe. London, Hale, 1979.
Gypsy Julie. London, Woman's Weekly Library, 1979.
Ripening Vine (as Ellen Clare). London, Mills and Boon, 1981.
Orchids from the Orient. London, Hale, 1986.

Novels as Olga Daniels

Lord of Leet Castle. London, Mills and Boon, 1984.
The Gretna Bride. London, Mills and Boon, 1986.
The Bride from Faraway. London, Mills and Boon, 1987.
The Untamed Bride. London, Mills and Boon, 1988.
The Arrogant Cavalier. London, Mills and Boon, 1989.

OTHER PUBLICATIONS

Other (for children)

Gypsies. Oxford, Blackwell, 1967.
Dancing in Britain. Oxford, Blackwell, 1970.
Children's Games. Oxford, Blackwell, 1972.
Toys and Toymaking. Oxford, Blackwell, 1975.
Gypsy Girl. London, Collins, 1981.

Other

When Wherries Sailed By. North Walsham, Norfolk, Poppyland, 1987.
Gretna Green: A Romantic History. London, Unwin Hyman, 1989.
Potter Heigham: The Heart of the Broadland. North Walsham, Norfolk, Poppyland, 1989.

*

Olga Sinclair comments:

I enjoy writing historical romance and take great care to incorporate realistic background details into my novels. For this reason *The Bride from Faraway* is very special to me because I drew on the personal reminiscences of Lithuanian immigrants to Scotland in the early years of this century, among whom were my husband's ancestors. I am currently writing a saga with this same fascinating background of Scotland, Lithuania, and Tsarist Russia.

The Arrogant Cavalier was inspired by research into the history of the old flint farmhouse which is my home. It dates from those troubled, restless times of the mid-17th century when there was a civil war in England, and brave emigrants settling in the wilderness of America. My story links the terrors and dangers of both the old world and the new, and the love which grows between a Puritan maiden and a Royalist nobleman.

Gretna Green: A Romantic History is non-fiction but carries the same theme. For nearly 250 years this small village, just over the border that separates Scotland from England, has captured the attention and imagination of journalists and romantics everywhere. It calls itself 'the village of runaway marriages' and abounds with stories of young couples racing to marry there, with an irate and outraged father in hot pursuit, while the world holds its breath. The eloping lovers come from all walks of life, and from all parts of Britain, Europe, and indeed the world. The 'marriage trade' produced outlandish local characters, charlatans, scoundrels, and bigamists, but nothing can obscure the true spirit of love and romance which has highlighted the village right through time and is still there in the present day.

*   *   *

Olga Sinclair has written romantic and historical fiction with fairly plain plots and characters. Her romantic fiction normally has a Norfolk setting, and she writes with familiarity of the attractive English countryside. However, Sinclair has used other settings such as a seaside town, in *Hearts by the Tower*, and Czechoslovakia, Austria, and Germany, in *Bitter Sweet Summer*. The background adds a lot to Sinclair's novels, the Czechoslovakia of 1968 adding both topical excitement to a rather pedestrian story line, and a contrast to the tranquillity of the Austrian countryside.

Sinclair is at home setting her books in Norfolk. The loneliness of the Norfolk broads in winter features in *Wild Dream*, and the broads also feature in *Master of Melthorpe* and *Man of the River*. Sinclair's world is the world of village life rather than town life, although her heroines have often lived some time in London.

The novels revolve around young women as heroines, and generally concern triangles of attraction towards two lovers, one of whom is much less charming and worthy of her love than the other. The Sinclair heroine comes to question her feelings towards her boyfriend/fiancé, as in *Man of the River*, and is gradually attracted towards another suitor. In *Master of Melthorpe* the heroine at first finds the Lord of the Manor too dominating and arrogant, but ends up realizing his real nature and consenting to marry him.

Suspense features strongly, and the heroine is often surprised by the sudden unmasking of an enigmatic young man (*Bitter Sweet Summer*). Other novels employ strange plots with interesting twists. The heroine in *Wild Dream* is in peril in a black magic context; her father has a mystery past and she an unknown half-sister in *Man of the River*. Mysterious circumstances surround the heroine's predecessor, as wife in *Hearts by the Tower*, or as fiancée in *Master of Melthorpe*. Plots can be rather contrived and depend heavily on the 'mystery' as a central feature.

Characters are sometimes rather shallow, as the father in *Never Fall in Love*, although the women are developed a good deal more particularly as regards their romantic feelings. Love is, however, very chaste, and a kiss or an offer of marriage can be the climax of a book.

—P.R. Meldrum

_____

SISSON, Rosemary Anne.
Nationality: British. **Born:** London, 13 October 1923. **Education:** Cheltenham Ladies' College; University College, London, B.A. (honours) in English 1946; Newnham College, Cambridge, M.Lit. 1948. **Military Service:** Royal Observer Corps, 1943–45. **Career:** lecturer in English, University of Wisconsin, Madison, 1949–50, University College, London, 1950–53, and University of Birmingham, 1954–57; drama critic, Stratford-on-Avon *Herald*, 1954–57. Co-chairperson, Writers Guild of Great Britain, 1979–80. **Agent:** Andrew Mann Ltd, 1 Old Compton Street, London W1V 5PH. **Address:** 167 New King's Road, London SW6 4SN, England.

ROMANCE AND HISTORICAL PUBLICATIONS

Novels

The Exciseman. London, Mayflower, 1972.
The Stratford Story. London, W.H. Allen, 1975; as *Will in Love*, New York, Morrow, 1976.
The Queen and the Welshman. London, W.H. Allen, 1979.
Bury Love Deep. London, Love Stories, 1985; New York, Medallion, 1986.
Beneath the Visiting Moon. London, Love Stories, 1986.

OTHER PUBLICATIONS

Novels

The Killer of Horseman's Flats. London, Hale, and New York, Doubleday, 1973.
The Manions of America (novelization of television series). New York, Dell, 1981; London, Penguin, 1982.
The Bretts (novelization of television series). London, Penguin, 1987.

Plays

The Queen and the Welshman (produced London, 1957). London, French, 1958.
Fear Came to Supper (produced Birmingham, 1958). London, French, 1959.
The Splendid Outcasts (produced Pitlochry, Perth, 1959; London, 1960). In *Plays of the Year 19*, edited by J.C. Trewin, London Elek, 1959.
The Royal Captivity (produced London, 1960).
Home and the Heart (produced Lincoln, 1961).
Bitter Sanctuary (produced Salisbury, 1963). London, French, 1964.
The Acrobats (produced Coventry, 1965). London, French, 1965.
The Man in the Case (for children), in *Eight Plays 2*, edited by Malcolm Stuart Fellows. London, Cassell, 1965.
I Married a Clever Girl (produced Windsor, 1967).
Catherine of Aragon (televised 1970). In *The Six Wives of Henry VIII*, edited by J.C. Trewin, London, Elek, 1972.
The Marriage Game (televised 1971). In *Elizabeth R*, edited by J.C. Trewin, London, Elek, 1972.
For Love of Love (televised 1972; produced Leamington, Warwickshire, 1975).
A Ghost on Tiptoe, with Robert Morley (produced Birmingham and London, 1974). London, French, 1975.
The Dark Horse (produced Guildford and London, 1978). London, French, 1979.

Screenplays: *Ride a Wild Pony*, 1976; *Escape from the Dark (The Littlest Horse Thieves)*, with Burt Kennedy, 1976; *Candleshoe*, with David Swift, 1978; *The Watcher in the Woods*, with Brian Clemens and Harry Spalding, 1982; *The Wind in the Willows*, 1983.

Radio Plays: *Trapped*, 1968; *Dear Aunt Jane*, 1972.

Television Plays: *The Vagrant Heart*, 1959; *The Man from Brooklyn*, 1960; *The Ordeal of Richard Feverel*, from the novel by George Meredith, 1964; *The Rescue of Pluffles*, from story by Kipling, 1964; *The Mill on the Floss*, from the novel by George Eliot, 1965; *Catherine of Aragon* (*The Six Wives of Henry VIII* series), 1970; *The Expert Witness*, 1970; *The Marriage Game* (*Elizabeth R* series), 1971; *For Love of Love*, 1972; *Finders Keepers*, 1973; *Beyond Our Means*, 1973; *Upstairs, Downstairs* series (12 episodes), 1973–84;

iling to Report, 1974; Let's Marry Liz (Seven Faces of Woman
ies), 1974; A Patriotic Offering, 1974; The Hero's Farewell,
74; Laugh a Little Louder Please, 1975; Will Ye No' Come Back
ain, 1975; Joke Over, 1975; The Truth Game, 1975; The New
an, 1976; Horse in the House, from story by William Corbin,
77; Tug of War, 1977; Together, 1980; A Town Like Alice, with
m Hegarty, from the novel by Nevil Shute, 1981; The Manions of
nerica series, 1981; The Irish R.M. series, with others, from sto-
s by Edith Somerville and Martin Ross, 1983–85; The Wind in the
illows, from the story by Kenneth Grahame, 1984; Mistral's
aughter, with Terence Feely, from the novel by Judith Krantz,
84; Seal Morning, from the book by Rowena Farr, 1986; The
retts series, with others, 1987; Joy to the World, 1988, 1989, 1991,
92; The Chronicles of Indiana Jones, with others, created by
eorge Lucas, 1992.

ther Scripts: Heart of a Nation (son et lumière script), London,
)83; Dawn to Dusk (Royal Tournament script), London, 1984.

ther (for children)

he Adventures of Ambrose. London, Harrap, 1951; New York,
    Dutton, 1952.
he Impractical Chimney Sweep. London, Macmillan, and New
    York, Watts, 1956.
Ir Nobody. London, Macmillan, 1957.
he Young Shakespeare. London, Parrish, and New York, Roy,
    1959.
he Isle of Dogs. London, Macmillan, and New York, St Martin's
    Press, 1959.
he Young Jane Austen. London, Parrish, 1962; New York, Roy,
    1963.
he Young Shaftesbury. London, Parrish, 1964.
scape from the Dark (novelization of screenplay). London, W.H.
    Allen, 1976; as The Littlest Horse Thieves, New York, Pocket
    Books, 1977.

*

Rosemary Anne Sisson comments:

I have written many stage plays, television plays and series, and
novels, equally divided between the historical and the contempor-
ry—but then I have never really made the distinction between the
wo. The truth is that I try to write interesting stories about people
ve can care about, either on the stage or on television or, in the case
of a novel, acted out in the mind and imagination of the reader.

*   *   *

Rosemary Anne Sisson is a prolific writer who tackles a wide
variety of forms: radio, stage, screen, and television dramas, and
books for children as well as adult novels. She has converted television scripts into novels, and dramatized many famous novels, and is
equally at home in historical and modern settings. Sisson says she
does not make any distinction between plays and novels, but simply
ries to write interesting stories, and many of her plays, such as The
Royal Captivity, contain tender love stories set against stirring political events.

The Bretts is a novelization of the television series. Set in London
during the late 1920s, the Bretts are at the heart of a frenetic whirl in
Hampstead. They are a theatrical family—Charles, the father who is
a larger than life actor/manager, Lydia Wheatley, the mother, is a
musical comedy star, and five children. There are crazy goings-on,
eccentric servants and demanding children placed in conventionally
funny situations, the stuff of successful television comedy. The

Manions of America is another novel based on a television series,
but quite different. It is set against the Irish famine of the 1840s, and
follows the fortunes of Ross, a peasant, and Rachael, the rich girl
who falls in love with him, when they go to America.

Adaptations always suffer by being compared with the originals.
Many people dislike films or plays based on books they have read,
since the dramatization invariably differs for practical reasons, from
the novel. Books based on plays face similar difficulties. Readers
who have seen the television plays may be disappointed that all they
recall is not included, or that the interpretation is not quite as they remember it, while readers who have not seen the plays often feel the
book is episodic, or superficial, believing there should be more than
they are getting.

Bury Love Deep and Beneath the Visiting Moon are more modern
novels. The first of these, produced on television as Finders, Keepers, is set at the end of World War II, and is a study of lost love, and
the problems which can arise after a long separation. Anne, a
WAAF, loves Tom, a married airforceman. There can be no future
for them but they plan to write just once a year to keep in touch. Tom
returns home, while Anne goes to Cambridge, and discovers she is
incapable of responding to other men. Several years later Tom's
wife Betty has a minor operation but dies. He goes to find Anne, but
she has moved away. However, Tom's daughter, Lucy, meets her,
and there is a very tentative renewal of acquaintance. He has become an office equipment sales director, she an educational publisher's editor, and there is no common ground between them. After
a few embarrassing meetings Tom tells Anne that she is afraid of
love. He bullies her into an early morning drive and takes her to a
spot where they once had a picnic. At last they begin to talk about
old times, and themselves. They agree to marry but the way is still
not smooth. First Tom's daughter is upset, but Anne persuades her
to accept the marriage, then Anne has last minute nerves, and Lucy
in her turn convinces her everything will be all right. The book is
episodic, but as one would expect from an experienced playwright
the dialogue is good.

Beneath the Visiting Moon is quite different in that it contains surprisingly little dialogue, and does not have a conventionally happy
ending. Although this is based on Sisson's early experiences of writing and publishing plays the book is not autobiographical. Margaret,
a prim secretary, goes with a dancer friend to a party for an
important actor. She meets Alan, who had a sudden acting success at
25, and is married to an actress. They become friends and Alan reveals that he wants to play Hamlet—they almost inevitably end up
having an affair. The book has some delightful characters, dreamy
Margaret, their neighbours and friends, and is evocative of London
in the 1950s. There is a big build up to the first night of Hamlet, and
Alan is adequate in a generally lifeless production. The reviews are
bad, but he is determined to succeed, and Margaret ends up leaving
him.

The Exciseman is an historical adventure, told from the man's
point of view, with perceptive characterization, a believable love
story, and centring around the doubts of a young man who has to
earn his living in an occupation he thinks is not entirely respectable.
This doubt is intensified when he becomes involved with the innkeeper's family, falling in love with one daughter, and having immense pity for the other blind sister. He is torn between his duty and
his love. The happy ending is a pleasant variation on the smuggling
theme.

Similarly, The Stratford Story is an historical novel, and tells the
story of young Shakespeare, showing his family life in Stratford, his
meeting and marriage with Anne Hathaway, and his success as a
dramatist. The romance between his sister Joanne and friend Rufus
Hart provides a witty and argumentative sub-plot, although the main
focus is on Shakespeare's dilemma as he struggles with the driving
necessity of genius, the clash between ambition, and his love for his
family. There is good characterization of the varied country people

and members of his family, as well as the players who entrance him. Sisson's romances are enjoyable and tackle interesting themes.

—Marina Oliver

SLAUGHTER, Frank G(ill).
Pseudonyms: G. Arnold Haygood; C.V. Terry. **Nationality:** American. **Born:** Washington, DC, 25 February 1908. **Education:** Oxford High School, North Carolina; Duke University, Durham, North Carolina, A.B. (magna cum laude) 1926; Johns Hopkins Medical School, Baltimore, MD. 1930. **Military Service:** United States Army Medical Corps, 1942–46: lieutenant colonel. **Relations:** married Jane Mundy in 1933; two sons. **Career:** intern and resident surgeon, Jefferson Hospital, Roanoke, Virginia, 1930–34; resident in thoracic surgery, Herman Kiefer Hospital, Detroit, 1934; staff surgeon, Riverside Hospital, Jacksonville, Florida, 1934–42; later full-time writer. Fellow, American College of Surgeons. **Recipient:** D.H.L.: Jacksonville University, Florida. **Agent:** Brandt and Brandt, 1501 Broadway, New York, New York 10036, USA. **Address:** Box 14, Ortega Station, Jacksonville, Florida 32210, USA.

ROMANCE AND HISTORICAL PUBLICATIONS

Novels

That None Should Die. New York, Doubleday, 1941; London, Jarrolds, 1942.
Spencer Brade, MD. New York, Doubleday, 1942; London, Jarrolds, 1943.
Air Surgeon. New York, Doubleday, 1943; London, Jarrolds, 1944.
Battle Surgeon. New York, Doubleday, 1944.
A Touch of Glory. New York, Doubleday, 1945; London, Jarrolds, 1946.
In a Dark Garden. New York, Doubleday, 1946; London, Jarrolds, 1952.
The Golden Isle. New York, Doubleday, 1947; London, Jarrolds, 1950.
Sangaree. New York, Doubleday, 1948; London, Jarrolds, 1950.
Divine Mistress. New York, Doubleday, 1949; London, Jarrolds, 1951.
The Stubborn Heart. New York, Doubleday, 1950; London, Jarrolds, 1953.
Fort Everglades. New York, Doubleday, and London, Jarrolds, 1951.
The Road to Bithynia: A Novel of Luke, The Beloved Physician. New York, Doubleday, 1951; London, Jarrolds, 1952.
East Side General. New York, Doubleday, 1952; London, Jarrolds, 1953.
Storm Haven. New York, Doubleday, 1953; London, Jarrolds, 1954.
The Galileans: A Novel of Mary Magdalene. New York, Doubleday, 1953; London, Jarrolds, 1954.
The Song of Ruth. New York, Doubleday, 1954; London, Jarrolds, 1955.
The Healer. New York, Doubleday, and London, Jarrolds, 1955.
Flight from Natchez. New York, Doubleday, 1955; London, Jarrolds, 1956.
The Scarlet Cord: A Novel of the Woman of Jericho. New York, Doubleday, and London, Jarrolds, 1956.
The Warrior. New York, Doubleday, 1956; as *The Flaming Frontier*, London, Jarrolds, 1957.

The Mapmaker: A Novel of the Days of Prince Henry, The Navigator. New York, Doubleday, 1957; London, Jarrolds, 1958.
Sword and Scalpel. New York, Doubleday, and London, Jarrolds, 1957.
Daybreak. New York, Doubleday, and London, Jarrolds, 1958.
Deep Is the Shadow (as G. Arnold Haygood). New York, Doubleday, 1959; London, Hutchinson, 1975; as *Shadow of Evil* (as Frank G. Slaughter), New York, Pocket Books, 1975.
The Crown and the Cross: The Life of Christ. Cleveland, World, and London, Jarrolds, 1959.
The Thorn of Arimathea. New York, Doubleday, and London, Jarrolds, 1959.
Lorena. New York, Doubleday, 1959; London, Hutchinson, 1960.
Pilgrims in Paradise. New York, Doubleday, 1960; as *Puritans in Paradise*, London, Hutchinson, 1960.
Epidemic! New York, Doubleday, and London, Hutchinson, 1961.
The Curse of Jezebel: A Novel of the Biblical Queen of Evil. New York, Doubleday, 1961; as *Queen of Evil*, London, Hutchinson, 1962.
Tomorrow's Miracle. New York, Doubleday, and London, Hutchinson, 1962.
Devil's Harvest. New York, Doubleday, and London, Hutchinson, 1963.
Upon This Rock: A Novel of Simon Peter, Prince of the Apostles. New York, Coward McCann, 1963; London, Hutchinson, 1964.
A Savage Place. New York, Doubleday, and London, Hutchinson, 1964.
Constantine: The Miracle of the Flaming Cross. New York, Doubleday, 1965; London, Hutchinson, 1966.
The Purple Quest: A Novel of Seafaring Adventure in the Ancient World. New York, Doubleday, and London, Hutchinson, 1965.
Surgeon, USA. New York, Doubleday, 1966; as *War Surgeon*, London, Hutchinson, 1967.
Doctors' Wives. New York, Doubleday, 1967; London, Hutchinson, 1971.
God's Warrior. New York, Doubleday, and London, Hutchinson, 1967.
The Sins of Herod: A Novel of Rome and the Early Church. New York, Doubleday, 1968; London, Hutchinson, 1969.
Surgeon's Choice: A Novel of Medicine Tomorrow. New York, Doubleday, and London, Hutchinson, 1969.
Countdown. New York, Doubleday, and London, Hutchinson, 1970.
Code Five. New York, Doubleday, 1971; London, Hutchinson, 1972.
Convention, MD.: A Novel of Medical In-Fighting. New York, Doubleday, 1972; London, Hutchinson, 1973.
Women in White. New York, Doubleday, 1974; as *Lifeblood*, London, Hutchinson, 1974.
Stonewall Brigade. New York, Doubleday, 1975; London, Hutchinson, 1976.
Plague Ship. New York, Doubleday, 1976; London, Hutchinson, 1977.
Devil's Gamble. New York, Doubleday, 1977; London, Hutchinson, 1978.
The Passionate Rebel. New York, Doubleday, and London, Hutchinson, 1979.
Gospel Fever: A Novel about America's Most Beloved TV Evangelist. New York, Doubleday, 1980.
Doctor's Daughters. New York, Doubleday, 1981; London, Hutchinson, 1982.
Doctors at Risk. New York, Doubleday, and London, Hutchinson, 1983.
No Greater Love. New York, Doubleday, and London, Hutchinson, 1985.
Transplant. London, Hutchinson, 1987.

Novels as C.V. Terry

Buccaneer Surgeon. New York, Hanover House, 1954; as *Buccaneer Doctor*, London, Jarrolds, 1955.
Darien Venture. New York, Hanover House, and London, Jarrolds, 1955.
The Golden Ones. New York, Hanover House, 1955; London, Jarrolds, 1958.
The Deadly Lady of Madagascar. New York, Doubleday, and London, Jarrolds, 1959.

OTHER PUBLICATIONS

Play

Screenplay: *Naked in the Sun*, with John Hugh, 1957.

Other

The New Science of Surgery. New York, Messner, 1946; London, Sampson Low, 1948; revised edition, as *Science and Surgery*, New York, Permabooks, 1956.
Medicine for Moderns: The New Science of Psychosomatic Medicine. New York, Messner, 1947; London, Jarrolds, 1953; as *The New Way to Mental and Physical Health*, New York, Grosset and Dunlap, 1949; as *Your Body and Your Mind*, New York, New American Library, 1953.
Immortal Magyar: Semmelweis, Conqueror of Childbed Fever. New York, Schuman, 1950; as *Semmelweis, Conqueror of Childbed Fever*, New York, Collier, 1961.
Apalachee Gold: The Fabulous Adventures of Cabeza de Vaca (for children). New York, Doubleday, 1954; London, Hutchinson, 1955.
The Land and the Promise: The Greatest Stories from the Bible. Cleveland, World, 1960; London, Hutchinson, 1961.
David, Warrior and King: A Biblical Biography. Cleveland, World, 1962; London, Hutchinson, 1963.

*

Film Adaptations: *Sangaree*, 1953; *Naked in the Sun*, 1957, from the novel *The Warrior*; *Doctor's Wives*, 1971; *Women in White*, 1979.

Manuscript Collections: Mugar Memorial Library, Boston University; Duke University, Durham, North Carolina.

Frank G. Slaughter comments:

I am primarily a storyteller who writes to entertain and also inform. As such, I am meticulous in my research and polish my writings through an average of ten revisions. Critics have dubbed me 'the undisputed master of medical fiction', an accolade I prize very much.

*   *   *

Though Frank G. Slaughter has been turning out novels at the rate of about one every ten months for more than 50 years, he has received very little critical comment in the last few decades. However, he doesn't need it. His books will sell anyway. He is still a master craftsman, a professional who is expert at moving a story along from one climax to the next. Novice writers need only study a few of Slaughter's novels to learn about structure and style. Slaughter must be a happy millionaire by now. Over 60 million copies of his books have been sold, in 21 countries.

Though his talent is clearly evident in his depiction of action, background, colour, and plot, Slaughter lacks the touch of genius that would make him a great writer. His characterizations fall short. His people are just not believable. They talk in long, long sentences, especially in the medical novels which comprise the largest segment of his work. On the positive side, the medical novels surely do keep up with the time as far as medical technology and current events are concerned—from exposing to the public eye the none too admirable practices of many physicians in *That None Should Die*, to big city summer gang wars and public housing development problems in *Epidemic!*, to the energy shortage, Haitian refugees, and Florida condominiums in *Doctor's Daughters*; from his physician protagonists in all kinds of situations and through all the wars that the USA has suffered to the very recent controversy surrounding the inordinate number of coronary by-pass operations being done that might better be treated medically. His empathy with people, however, fails to keep pace, especially his women who do not even begin to reflect the very real changes that women have undergone in the last half of the 20th century. In my review of *Women in White* (1974), I wrote, 'Lest anyone think this new medical novel promotes the women's cause, forget it. The nurses are fine women; the female doctors have reached their high standing through judicious use of their lovely bodies, not their intellect'. In *Doctor's Daughters* (1981) he made a stab at rectifying this by featuring three sisters, all of them successful doctors in their own right who earned their caducei by study and hard work. But the denouement of the tale is finding of a true love for each one, all in one short week. Slaughter's women are glossy counterfeits. A pattern has emerged in most of his novels, even some of the biblical ones. There is usually a crusading hero, most often a physician with a cause, and two women, one of them naughty; the other, good, wholesome, and eminently marriageable. When the subject of demonic possession was in vogue, Slaughter brought these two women together in one body in *Devil's Gamble*—a neat trick.

Slaughter's novels are of three types: historical, biblical, and medical, or frequently a combination of these. His historical novels are least pedantic. They neither preach nor present long treatises on surgical procedures. When he writes under the name of C.V. Terry he seems to have more fun. His language is expansive and adventuresome. He tends more to the ribald and is freer in his portrayals of sexual encounters. In all his work, the historical research is accurate if lacking depth. His descriptions of places and events are marvellous—there is an especially graphic scene of a sea battle in *The Purple Quest*—but the significance of the event is not his primary concern. In both the historical and biblical novels, Slaughter has commandeered excessive dramatic licence when dealing with those famed personages who actually walked this earth by putting his words into their mouths and by ascribing his feelings to their hearts and minds.

Readers of gothic and romance literature have much to thank Slaughter for. He has lifted them out of their armchairs to many lands in many times, and perhaps sent some scurrying to their encyclopaedias to learn more about the Phoenicians, the Spanish Inquisition, the Civil War. Many have turned to their bibles to read what the scriptures have to say about Ruth, Jezebel, and Christ. What's more, his fascinating descriptions of dazzling new medical equipment and sophisticated technology have reassured his fans that they can enjoy long and healthy lives. With all this magic, who really cares that his characters lack vitality!

—Marion Hanscom

SLOANE, Sara.   See **BLOOM, Ursula.**

SMALL, Bertrice.
Nationality: American. **Born:** New York City, 9 December 1937.
Education: St Mary's School, Peekskill, New York, 1950–55;
Western College for Women, Oxford, Ohio, 1955–58; Katherine
Gibbs Secretarial School, New York, 1959. **Relations:** married
George Summer Small IV in 1963; one son. **Career:** secretary,
Young and Rubicam Advertising, New York, 1959–60; sales assist-
ant, Weed Radio and Television Representatives, 1960–61, and
Edward J. Petrie and Co, 1961–63, both New York; owner, Fat Cat
gift shop, Southold, New York, 1976–81. **Agent:** Edward J. Acton,
Acton Agency, 928 Broadway, New York, New York 10010, USA.
Address: P.O. Box 765, Southold, New York, 11971, USA.

ROMANCE AND HISTORICAL PUBLICATIONS

Novels (series: O'Malley Saga)

The Kadin. New York, Avon, 1978; London, Severn House,
    1989.
Love Wild and Fair. New York, Avon, 1978; London, Fontana,
    1979.
Adora. New York, Ballantine, and London, Fontana, 1980.
Skye O'Malley. New York, Ballantine, 1980; London, Severn
    House, 1990.
Unconquered. New York, Ballantine, 1982.
Beloved. New York, Ballantine, 1983.
All the Sweet Tomorrows (O'Malley). New York, Ballantine,
    1984.
This Heart of Mine (O'Malley). New York, Ballantine, 1985.
A Love for All Time (O'Malley). New York, New American Library,
    1986.
Enchantress Mine. New York, New American Library, 1987.
Blaze Wyndham. New York, New American Library, 1988.
Lost Love Found (O'Malley). New York, Ballantine, 1989.
The Spitfire. New York, Ballantine, 1990.
A Moment in Time. New York, Ballantine, 1991.
Wild Jasmine (O'Malley). New York, Ballantine, 1992.
To Love Again. New York, Ballantine, 1993.

*

Bertrice Small comments:

I write commercial fiction in the historical romance genre. I think
of myself as an author turned out from the same mould that cast
authors like Taylor Caldwell, Jan Westcott, Jean Plaidy, Sergeanne
Golon, and my personal favourite, Anya Seton. I plot my fiction
around historical events, in past eras, bringing to life actual historical personages who co-habit quite comfortably on the pages of my
books with my own fictitious characters. It's fun for me, and both
entertaining and informative for the readers, many of whom have
not been taught history, but find themselves fascinated by it. Unlike
straight historical fiction I give just enough of the flavour of a period
to make that period come to life, although I never alter historical
events to fit my plot. Rather, I plot to fit historical event. I may, however, disagree with certain historical interpretations. Historians are,
after all, only human and as subject to their own prejudices and
opinions as other mortals. It is particularly difficult to research
famous women of distant eras because women are usually identified
as someone's daughter, wife, or mistress, and had to be considered
either saints or sinners to get mentioned for anything other than their
reproductive abilities, or dynastic pretensions. It didn't help either
to have the historians of past eras men, and in the A.D. eras, usually

churchmen. I am particularly fond of British history, and early to
mid-Ottoman history.

*   *   *

Bertrice Small's historical romances are descended from
Sergeanne Golon's nine-volume saga (the first of which was published in the United States in 1960) about a heroine named An-
gelique who, buffeted by the winds of political change after being
separated from her newly-wed husband, sets out on a long and arduous trek across the world. Along the way she encounters one lover
(sub-hero) after another, some of whom are antiheroes, until she is at
last reunited with her first and only true love. Though many variations on the theme have appeared since, Small's *Skye O'Malley* is
easily the best—'the romance that has everything', as one reader describes it—including incest, rape, the *droit du seigneur*, a woman of
independent means, and true love repeated again and again, not to
mention a political tug-of-war with the queen of England. It was An-
gelique and Skye, along with hundreds of their sisters who came in
between, who ripped the fabric of the conventional wisdom that romance is virtually the only adventure literature allows females. In
the process, they stirred the embers of a revolution in romance that
within the space of one decade wrought dramatic changes in both
the character and conventions of the genre.

In *The Kadin* Small transports her heroine to the Middle East,
where she paints a breathtaking picture of the intimate and sensual
fantasies associated with life in a harem while involving her in a political power play in which the stakes are life or death for both herself and her son. Reminiscent of what is presumed to have happened
to Aimée Dubucq de Rivery (cousin to Napoleon's Josephine,
captured while on her way to Martinique and given to the Sultan of
Turkey), this interweaving of political intrigue with explicitly described sexual adventures has become a Small trademark.

Skye O'Malley has several sexual partners during the course of
her story, and truly loves four different men—alliances that depict
the love of one woman for more than one kind of man, and four
different kinds of relationships. No one male is fully developed as
the hero, however, until near the end of the sequel, though each one
plays that role for a limited time. All but the last of her liaisons,
which the reader is brought to realize is the mature relationship she
has been moving toward the entire time, exit via a coffin, allowing
the indomitable Skye to move on to the next instalment of her life
with vigour and enthusiasm—in full control of herself, her children,
and the family shipping business that has given her economic
independence. Niall Burke is Skye's first love and we assume, in
what appears to be the closing of a circle at the end of *Skye O'Malley*, her last. But as *All the Sweet Tomorrows* opens we discover that
he, too, has gone the way of the flesh. 'Niall Burke was essentially a
weak man', Small explains. 'He couldn't have held a woman like
Skye for any length of time (so) I had to get rid of him'. In *Wild Jasmine*, billed as the conclusion to the O'Malley saga, Small combines
elements from *The Kadin*, *Love Wild and Fair*, and *Skye O'Malley*.
Jasmine is Skye's granddaughter, Yasaman Kama Begum, who
flees 17th-century India for England, where she is caught up in the
machinations of her new family and the court of King James—and
follows in her grandmother's footsteps, having a penchant for both
political adventure, and sensual pleasure (with numerous lovers and
husbands).

Though some titles lack the verve and originality of her early
work (*The Spitfire* features a political hostage who falls in love with
her captor, by now a very tired device in this genre), Small's
strength continues to lie in her portrayal of strong women bent on
self-determination. Her heroines generally operate at two levels in
their struggle for power and autonomy, the personal or domestic,
and the political or worldly. Nor do they hesitate to take on the highest and mightiest—whether behind the scenes (*The Kadin*) or centre
stage (*Skye O'Malley*) on the land or the sea, in 14th-century

Byzantium, or 17th-century England (*Wild Jasmine*). And when Small is at her spirited best, as in *Love Wild and Fair*, she is very good indeed.

—Carol Thurston

———

SMITH, Doris E(dna Elliott).
Nationality: Irish. **Born:** Dublin, 12 August 1919. **Education:** Alexandra College, Dublin. From 1938 worked for an insurance group, Dublin. **Recipient:** Romantic Novelists Association major award, 1969. **Died.**

ROMANCE AND HISTORICAL PUBLICATIONS

Novels

Star to My Barque. London, Ward Lock, 1964.
The Thornwood. London, Ward Lock, 1966.
Song from a Lemon Tree. London, Ward Lock, 1966.
The Deep Are Dumb. London, Ward Lock, 1967.
Comfort and Keep. London, Ward Lock, 1968.
Fire Is for Sharing. London, Mills and Boon, 1968; Toronto, Harlequin, 1969.
To Sing Me Home. London, Mills and Boon, 1969; Toronto, Harlequin, 1970.
Seven of Magpies. London, Mills and Boon, and Toronto, Harlequin, 1970.
Cup of Kindness. London, Mills and Boon, 1971.
The Young Green Corn. London, Mills and Boon, 1971.
Dear Deceiver. London, Mills and Boon, and Toronto, Harlequin, 1972.
The One and Only. London, Mills and Boon, and Toronto, Harlequin, 1973.
The Marrying Kind. London, Mills and Boon, 1974.
Green Apple Love. London, Mills and Boon, 1974.
Haste to the Wedding. London, Mills and Boon, 1974.
Cotswold Honey. Toronto, Harlequin, 1975; London, Mills and Boon, 1976.
Smuggled Love. London, Mills and Boon, and Toronto, Harlequin, 1976.
Wild Heart. London, Mills and Boon, 1976; Toronto, Harlequin, 1977.
My Love Came Back. London, Mills and Boon, 1978.
Mix Me a Man. London, Mills and Boon, 1978.
Back o' the Moon. London, Mills and Boon, 1981.
Catch a Kingfisher. London, Hale, 1981.
Marmalade Witch. London, Mills and Boon, 1982.
Noah's Daughter. London, Hale, 1982.

* * *

Doris E. Smith was born in Ireland and grew up near Dublin. Her childhood and teenage years were spent there just before World War II and were quite happy ones. They opened her mind and imagination to all sorts of influences which later emerged in her writing. Her natural facility with words edged her towards writing, but she was over 40 before she was published. Although not a prolific writer, she is yet a good one. Recognition for her ability came in 1969 when the Romantic Novelists Association awarded her their prize for the best romance of that year.

Her novels combine a very slight hint of Irish charm, and an obvious love of words and descriptions. She is, in fact, one of the 'happy' writers who loves a good romance and who couldn't refrain from producing one every so often.

Predictably she used an Irish background in some of her novels, *Smuggled Love*, for instance, or *Dear Deceiver*. In the latter, she uses that part of Ireland she is most familiar with, the Wicklow area near Dublin. She did not limited herself to this background, however, for several of her novels take place against the physical beauty of the Cotswolds and the low rolling hills of the border country between Scotland and England. Smith has a slow, yet captivating way of letting her stories unfold, for she blends dialogue, description, and action in just the right amount to entice her readers on.

Wild Heart is perhaps one of the best examples of her work and illustrates the care and planning that went into her work. Victoria Elliott inherits a cottage in the Selkirk area of Scotland from her great-aunt Elizabeth and she goes there planning to sell it. Her sister, Lorraine, also goes with her. Lorraine has just experienced a shock as her fiancé has had second thoughts about marriage just days before their wedding. In the course of the novel, Lorraine grows up and realizes that she herself contributed to his decision by her own weaknesses and immaturity. Victoria, on the other hand, is one of the 'fighters' of the world who tries to stand on her own feet just as her great-aunt had. The owner of the nearby castle is Dugald Douglas and, from their first meeting, Victoria is intrigued by him. Her efforts to redevelop her aunt's animal shelter and later to deny her growing love for Dugald are the major focus points in the novel. The counterpoint of Lorraine's problems plays a motivating force in the plot. Smith has her characters' personalities well in hand during the novel. She is able to show the underlying facets of each personality in such a way that one is instantly sympathetic towards them. For all of Victoria's considerable success in her own field, she is still the sensitive child that her great-aunt had befriended with the words 'welcome to my world'—a world of stray dogs and abandoned kittens.

Smith's obvious love of animals emerges frequently as she uses settings that incorporate them. Charlotte Lavender in *Cotswold Honey* is a veterinary nurse who leaves a practice to go into a rural one. Dugald Douglas in *Wild Heart* has a famous kennel and raises and trains hunting dogs.

Smith's novels are quiet ones in a way; emotional yes, even unhappy at times, but the reader is allowed to peek behind the scenes and understand that everything will right itself before the ending. Misunderstandings and mis-read hints or words are clarified so that the reader leaves Smith's novels with a sense of happy completion.

—Arlene Moore

———

SMITH, Lady Eleanor (Furneaux).
Nationality: British. **Born:** Birkenhead, Cheshire, in 1902. **Education:** Miss Douglas's School, London, and at a boarding school. **Career:** publicist for the Great Carmo Circus; columnist, and film critic for London *Dispatch*, *Sphere*, and *Bystander*. **Died:** 20 October 1945.

ROMANCE AND HISTORICAL PUBLICATIONS

Novels

Red Wagon: A Study of the Tober. London, Gollancz, and Indianapolis, Bobbs Merrill, 1930.
Flamenco. London, Gollancz, and Indianapolis, Bobbs Merrill, 1931.

Ballerina. London, Gollancz, and Indianapolis, Bobbs Merrill, 1932.

Tzigane. London, Hutchinson, 1935; as *Romany*, Indianapolis, Bobbs Merrill, 1935.

Portrait of a Lady. London, Hutchinson, 1936; New York, Doubleday, 1937.

The Spanish House. London, Hutchinson, and New York, Doubleday, 1938.

Lovers' Meeting. London, Hutchinson, and New York, Doubleday, 1940.

The Man in Grey: A Regency Romance. London, Hutchinson, 1941; New York, Doubleday, 1942.

A Dark and Splendid Passion. New York, Ace, 1941.

Caravan. London, Hutchinson, and New York, Doubleday, 1943.

Magic Lantern. London, Hutchinson, 1944; New York, Doubleday, 1945.

Short Stories

Satan's Circus and Other Stories. London, Gollancz, 1932; Indianapolis, Bobbs Merrill, 1934.

Christmas Tree. London, Gollancz, and Indianapolis, Bobbs Merrill, 1933; as *Seven Trees*, Bobbs Merrill, 1935 (?).

OTHER PUBLICATIONS

Other

Life's a Circus (autobiography). London, Longman, 1939; New York, Doubleday, 1940.

British Circus Life, edited by W.J. Turner. London, Harrap, 1948.

The Etiquette of Letter Writing. Hemel Hempstead, Hertfordshire, John Dickinson, 1950 (?).

*

Film Adaptations: *Red Wagon*, 1935; *Men in her Life*, 1941, from the novel *Ballerina*; *The Man in Grey*, 1943; *Caravan*, 1946.

Critical Study: *Lady Eleanor Smith: A Memoir* by Lord Birkenhead, London, Hutchinson, 1953.

*   *   *

In her autobiography, *Life's a Circus*, Lady Eleanor Smith recounts a seemingly unusual life for a former debutante, and daughter of a lord. Among other things the author claimed to have a gypsy grandmother—whether true or not, Smith had a fascination with gypsy life and history which is reflected in her writing and, indeed, in the path that her life took. Gypsies, ballet, Spain, and the supernatural are all important and recurrent themes in her books.

Her first novel, *Red Wagon*, arose out of a chance meeting with Frederick Martin, who worked for Paramount, at a lunch. Martin was putting together a circus show to travel around Ireland, and offered Smith the job as publicist to the Great Carmo Circus. *Red Wagon* is based on Smith's experiences while on tour. The book recounts the life of Joe Prince, owner of a circus, and his relationship with his half-gypsy daughter. A vivid and detailed book, it presents a realistic image of circus life. The descriptions of the English countryside in the book were applauded by a critic in *The Bookman* as being, ' ... better than anything Mr Priestley has given us'.

Caravan expands on the gypsy theme introduced, albeit briefly, in *Red Wagon*, dealing with the life of the reclusive writer James Darrell. It uses the framework of a young journalist who goes to interview the almost forgotten writer. At the beginning of the book

Darrell is shown as a taciturn, private old man, but by the end of the book, he is revealed as having led a passionate, exciting life. Precociously bright, with a penchant for languages, Darrell is a changeling who makes friends with the gypsies and learns Romani. As a young man he meets Oriana, the daughter of a local squire, and the couple fall in love. Although James asks Oriana to wait two years for him to become a successful writer, she marries her cousin before James can become famous. In a chance encounter with a rich Spaniard, James travels to Spain where he is ambushed and left for dead. Rescued by a flamenco dancer who falls passionately in love with him, he ends up leading a careless existence in Spain, until his dancer wife is killed while saving his life. This leads James to go to Morocco where he publishes *The Spanish Journey*, a brutally honest account of the 'real' Spain. Returning to England to much critical acclaim, James encounters Oriana again and they begin a passionate affair, which ends tragically when the latter is killed in a carriage accident. The book ends with James dying by Oriana's graveside. The theme of eternal love which defies death is introduced and recurs in later novels. Considering this book was published in 1931, and is set partly in Victorian England, it contains frank descriptions of both gypsy life, and the love and passion which exists between James and Oriana.

Harold Nicholson wrote in the *Daily Express* that *Flamenco* is 'an unforgettable book ... it pulsates with passion ... It rouses the emotions of pity and terror and solves them in a burst of lyrical beauty'. In fact this book bears a distant resemblance to *Wuthering Heights*. Set in the 19th century it follows the lives of a band of exiled gypsies who travel from Spain to America, via England. In Devon, where the latter half of the book takes place, they encounter Richard Lovell, a drunk, weak aristocrat who takes a liking to their smallest child, Camilla, and buys her from them. Camilla is brought up as a sister to Richard's two sons, and rejects her gypsy heritage. She falls in love with the beautiful Evelyn, but Richard becomes so besotted with her that he arranges for her to be kidnapped and raped by another gypsy. Later Camilla returns and marries Evelyn, but then realizes that she is really in love with his brother, the taciturn and Heathcliff-like Harry. Camilla spends one night with Harry, which results in a son, Robin, who is fascinated by both gypsies and Harry. When Robin runs off to be with some gypsies who might very well be Camilla's siblings, she finally admits her love for Harry. *Flamenco* is a very passionately written book that is a tribute to the author's gypsy grandmother, and the time that Smith spent in Spain.

Ballerina is also based on Smith's own experiences. Smith wrote in her autobiography that it was inspired by the ballerina Anna Pavlova. As part of Diaghilev's circle, Smith attended Pavlova's rehearsals. She wrote *Ballerina* based on 'the last sad impression of a tired woman and of a divine artist'. The book follows the life of a 19th-century dancer, Paulina Varley, who becomes a famous prima ballerina, but who begun her life travelling with a circus. She marries an ex-dancer who re-creates her past and trains her properly, and later falls in love with a young English aristocrat. Although they part he remains her one true love, and she has numerous other lovers but dies old and worn out, having dedicated her life to dancing.

Lover's Meeting, and *The Man in Grey*, both share the themes of the supernatural and historical cycles. In *Lover's Meeting* the lives of George Henry Charles, Viscount Barradale, and Martina Sholto echo those of 19th-century lovers Lady Harriet Fane and her tutor. George and Martina first meet in Venice when Martina is in her teens, but it is only years later that they meet again by chance and fall in love. George takes Martina to his family house, and by an accident of time involving an old clock, they find themselves back in 1812, living the lives of their 19th-century counterparts. George manages to get back to the 20th century but Martina is left behind. He has a nervous breakdown and is suspected of her murder. He also orders that the clock be stopped—not realizing that Martina has no way of returning from the past. *The Man in Grey* is slightly more sinister in tone. Following the life of a young bride who comes to live in her husband's family home, it also tells the story of one of her husband's ancestors, 'The Ghost', through a diary. The book involves the murder of 'The Ghost's' first wife by his mistress. The narrator's life becomes so intertwined with those of the past that she eventually commits suicide.

Writing in the 1920s and 1930s, Smith managed to create novels that were teeming with passionate, romantic characters who often lived on the edge of society. Her unusual and diverse choice of subject matter, and her ability to create concise and stylishly written novels have made her an influential figure in romance and historical literature this century.

—P. Campbell

SMITH, Helen Zenna.   See **PRICE, Evadne.**

SMITH, Joan.
Pseudonym: Jennie Gallant. **Nationality:** American. **Born:** 1938. **Address:** c/o Fawcett, 201 East 50th Street, New York, New York 10022, USA.

ROMANCE AND HISTORICAL PUBLICATIONS

Novels

An Affair of the Heart. New York, Fawcett, 1977.
Escapade. New York, Fawcett, 1977.
La Comtesse. New York, Fawcett, 1978.
Imprudent Lady. New York, Walker, 1978.
Dame Durden's Daughter. New York, Walker, 1978.
Aunt Sophie's Diamonds. New York, Fawcett, 1979.
Flowers of Eden. New York, Fawcett, 1979.
Sweet and Twenty. New York, Fawcett, 1979.
Talk of the Town. New York, Walker, 1979.
Aurora. New York, Walker, 1980.
Babe. New York, Fawcett, 1980; London, Prior, 1981.
Endure My Heart. New York, Fawcett, 1980.
Lace for Milady. New York, Walker, 1980; London, Prior, 1981.
Delsie. New York, Fawcett, 1981.
Lover's Vows. New York, Fawcett, 1981.
The Blue Diamond. New York, Fawcett, 1981.
Valerie. New York, Fawcett, 1981.
Perdita. New York, Fawcett, 1981.
Love's Way. New York, Fawcett, 1982.
Reluctant Bride. New York, Fawcett, 1982.
Reprise. New York, Fawcett, 1982.
Wiles of a Stranger. New York, Fawcett, 1982.
Prelude to Love. New York, Fawcett, 1983.
Chance of a Lifetime. New York, Silhouette, 1984.
Royal Revels. New York, Fawcett, 1985.
The Devious Duchess. New York, Fawcett, 1985.
Midnight Masquerade. New York, Fawcett, 1985.
Bath Belles. New York, Fawcett, 1986.
Strange Capers. New York, Fawcett, 1986.
True Lady. New York, Fawcett, 1986.
Country Flirt. New York, Fawcett, 1987.
A Country Wooing. New York, Fawcett, 1987.

Love's Harbinger. New York, Fawcett, 1987.
Larcenous Lady. New York, Fawcett, 1988.
Thrill of the Chase. New York, Silhouette, 1989.
Apollo's Child. Philadelphia, Macrae, 1989.
The Polka Dot Nude. New York, Jove, 1989.
A Masculine Ending. New York, Fawcett, 1989.
It Takes Two. New York, Silhouette, 1990.
Sealed with a Kiss. New York, Silhouette, 1990.
Follow That Blonde. New York, Jove, 1990.
Cousin Cecilia. New York, Fawcett, 1990.
The Merry Month of May. New York, Fawcett, 1990.
A Whisper on the Wind. New York, Dorchester, 1990.
Gather Ye Rosebuds. New York, Fawcett, 1993.
No Place for a Lady. New York, Fawcett, 1994.

*   *   *

Of all the Georgette Heyer imitators, Joan Smith has been the most successful in duplicating Heyer's wit. Her heroines and heroes are always intelligent, and their conversations always amusing. She also has Heyer's gift for depicting various kinds of entertaining fools and dolts as minor characters. As comedies of character, these romances have much more substance than most in the genre. Unfortunately, her best books are her earliest, and her more recent works are in some cases somewhat dull.

Her first book, *An Affair of the Heart*, is one of her wittiest. A girl who lacks beauty, in a family of beauties, wins the heart of a lord, but can't believe it, especially when the hero's foolish best friend keeps telling her about her predecessor, complicating both the relationship and the plot. In *Escapade* a young woman who writes a gossip column falls in love with the chief target of her column. Among the minor characters, the three young ladies competing for the attentions of the hero are outstandingly absurd and amusing. In *Aunt Sophie's Diamonds*, the diamonds, which are supposed to be buried with her, touch off an inspired comedy (resembling Heyer's *The Talisman Ring* in situation, rather than plot). The heroine is a 24-year-old woman, deprived all her life of adventure, romance, and even friendship, who enters wholeheartedly into the young people's plans to dig up the corpse; the happy result for her is adventure, friendship, and romance. *La Comtesse* is a conventional good-bad girl story, in which Lord Dashford investigates the possibility that 'la Comtesse' is a Napoleonic spy, and falls in love with her despite himself. The story is not up to Smith's usual standard. *Imprudent Lady* is similar to Heyer's *Venetia* and *Black Sheep* in that an unworldly maiden lady receives the confidences of a confirmed rake, who falls in love with her. As the hero and heroine are writers, we are given a glimpse of the Regency's literary figures as well. The hero and heroine are among Smith's wittiest characters, and the heroine's uncle is a memorable ass. *Aurora* is about a missing heir, an heiress who wants him to stay that way, and a girl who falls in love with the *soi-disant* heir. This is unusual among Smith's works in the presence of downright villainy.

Endure My Heart and *Lace for Milady* are both about smuggling. The heroine of *Endure My Heart* falls into the leadership of a band of smugglers, but falls in love with the man assigned to catch them. Smith actually makes this sound plausible, and it is one of her entertaining books. *Lace for Milady* doesn't work anywhere near so well. *Delsie* resembles Heyer's *The Reluctant Widow* in every way except that it is not as interesting. *Lover's Vows* again deals with a woman in her mid-twenties, surrounded by fools, and unappreciated except by the hero. It is not Smith at her best, but despite this the book is well-written.

Despite the derivative nature of her work, Smith is capable of considerable originality and imagination. Her attention to period detail is excellent, though she occasionally jars the reader with a glaring anachronism. Even though her later works are not up to the standard she herself set, there is always a good chance that her books will provide entertainment and pleasure.

—Marylaine Block

SOMMERFIELD, Sylvie.
Nationality: American. **Born:** Newcastle, Pennsylvania, 22 November 1931. **Relations:** married John Sommerfield in 1954; two children. **Recipient:** gold certificate, 1987; Silver Pen award, 1988. **Agent:** Evan Marshal Agency, 22 South Park Street, Suite 216 Montclair, New Jersey 0104, USA. **Address:** 2080 West State Street, Westgate Plaza, Suite 9, Newcastle, Pennsylvania 16101, USA.

ROMANCE AND HISTORICAL PUBLICATIONS

Novels

Erin's Ecstasy. New York, Zebra, 1980.
Tazia's Torment. New York, Zebra, 1980.
Rebel Pride. New York, Zebra, 1980.
Rapture's Angel. New York, Zebra, 1981.
Deanne's Desire. New York, Zebra, 1981.
Tamara's Ecstasy. New York, Zebra, 1982.
Savage Rapture. New York, Zebra, 1982.
Kristen's Passion. New York, Zebra, 1983.
Cherish Me, Embrace Me. New York, Zebra, 1983.
Tame My Wild Heart. New York, Zebra, 1984; London, Severn House, 1993.
Betray Not My Passion. New York, Zebra, 1984.
Savage Kiss. New York, Zebra, 1985.
Captive Embrace. New York, Zebra, 1985.
Catalina's Caress. New York, Zebra, 1986.
Wild Wyoming Heart. New York, Zebra, 1987.
Elusive Swan. New York, Zebra, 1988.
Moonlit Magic. New York, Zebra, 1989.
Nightstar. New York, Pinnacle, 1991.
Passion's Raging Storm. New York, Pinnacle, 1992.
Love's Stolen Promises. New York, Pinnacle, 1992.
Moon Touched Promises. New York, Pinnacle, 1993.

OTHER PUBLICATIONS

Novel

Bittersweet. London, Severn House, and New York, Warner, 1991.

*   *   *

A prolific author of primarily historical romantic fiction, Sylvie Sommerfield uses a rather melodramatic style of writing to convey a spirit of love and romance. She also uses elements of mystery to increase the sense of tension for her readers. Sommerfield has set her novels in several time periods and locations, but she favours 18th- and 19th-century America.

Nightstar, Captive Embrace, Tamara's Ecstasy, and *Deanne's Desire* are among Sommerfield's works set in the 1700s. *Savage Rapture*, and its sequel, *Savage Kiss*, take place in the American West in the 1800s. The latter titles also feature one of her recurrent themes, stories of full-, and half-blooded Native Americans.

Several of Sommerfield's works take place in post-Civil War America and follow southerners as they turn from defeat and enorm-

ous personal losses to build a new future in the American West or to forge a new South. *Cherish Me, Embrace Me, Rebel Pride, Love's Stolen Promises, Moonlit Magic*, and *Moon Touched Promises* are among the novels that fall into this category. They also illustrate Sommerfield's style. *Love's Stolen Promises* is the convoluted story of poor Mitchell Flannery and rich Whitney Clayborn, who are lovers in antebellum South Carolina. Separated first by her snobbish mother and then by the Civil War, they endure betrayal, poverty, danger, and misunderstandings galore before winning through to a bright future. Courted by wealthy, mysterious Trent Donnelley after the war, Whitney cannot deny her feelings for Mitch when he finally returns home. However, she is embittered by what she believes to be his betrayal, and she conspires to hide their son from him. Although Trent is obviously a scoundrel from the start, Sommerfield lets fall hints of a deeper evil, gradually revealing that he worked as a double agent during the war, betraying both sides. It is also revealed that he is responsible for the destruction of Whitney's home, which his men looted and burned in an attempt to find some incriminating letters sent by her brother. This whole plot is made even murkier by the presence of a mysterious stranger lurking in the area, who, as it turns out, is actually Whitney's brother, Keith. Sommerfield also introduces a secondary couple, Blake Randolph and Noel Anderson, whose problems loosely mirror those of Mitch and Whitney. *Moonlit Magic* offers the strikingly similar story of Trace Cord and Jenny Graham. When Trace returns home from the war, he finds his parents dead and his brother missing. He also discovers that he and his sister could lose everything they own to taxes. A fortuitous offer from a railroad magnate, Maxwell Starett, gives Trace the chance to earn the money to get his plantation back. In his capacity as troubleshooter for the railroad, Trace meets Jenny Graham and falls in love with her instantly. She, however, is fiercely protective of her Colorado home and distrusts everyone connected with the railroad. This distrust is fostered by Taylor Jessup, the wealthy town banker, who wants both Jenny and her land. He is in a plot with Maxwell Starett's niece to block the railroad for their own gain, but each betrays the other. There is a secondary couple and a mysterious stranger—this time the latter is Trace's brother, Michael, who skulks around, keeping his identity secret from everyone but the reader, while he works to bring Jessup down. Michael later gets his own story in *Moon Touched Promises*, in which he finally wins Hannah Marshall, whom he met in the earlier work.

In these stories, Sommerfield has the core of a good romance story yet her style tends to get in the way. She attempts to bring in too many plot threads with the result that events can be glossed over and characters poorly developed. As the action quickens toward the end of her books, Sommerfield also attempts to cut between separate actions by alternating short paragraphs. While this can pick up the pace and increase the tension, at times it is confusing and distracting.

Sommerfield's first contemporary romance, *Bittersweet*, is more successful both as a romance and as a suspense story. Homicide detective Carl Forrester is haunted by the past when his young wife was killed by some criminals he had once captured and who swore revenge on him. Although he killed her murderers, he left town since he was unsuccessful in dealing with the tragedy on a personal level. Returning to his home town to help a friend catch a psychotic killer, he begins to face both personal and professional demons. He becomes involved with Beth Raleigh, a librarian, who herself is recovering from a bad marriage. Sommerfield portrays the hesitancy of both Carl and Beth to venture into a new relationship convincingly. She is more successful in developing tension about the true identity of the murderer, although the hunt drags on a little and becomes repetitious. The action flows more smoothly than in her historical novels.

Sommerfield is obviously a popular author as measured by the number of titles she has sold. Her novels are pleasant, rather light reading, but she cannot be considered among the first rank of romance authors. Her contemporary novel, *Bittersweet*, shows a development in style and skill as a writer that, if continued and applied to her historical novels, would increase her stature in the field.

—Barbara E. Kemp

SONTAG, Susan.
Nationality: American. **Born:** New York City, 16 January 1933. **Education:** University of California, Berkeley, 1948–49; University of Chicago, 1949–51, B.A. 1951; Harvard University, Cambridge, Massachusetts, 1954–57, M.A. 1955; St Anne's College, Oxford, 1957; Sorbonne, Paris, 1957–58. **Relations:** married Philip Rieff, 1950 (divorced 1958); one son. **Career:** instructor in English, University of Connecticut, Storrs, 1953–54; teaching fellow in Philosophy, Harvard University, 1955–57; editor, *Commentary*, New York, 1959; lecturer in Philosophy, City College of New York, and Sarah Lawrence College, Bronxville, New York, 1959–60; instructor in Religion, Columbia University, New York, 1960–64; writer-in-residence, Rutgers University, New Brunswick, New Jersey, 1964–65. President, PEN American Center, 1987–89. Lives in New York City. **Recipient:** American Association of University of Women fellowship, 1957; Rockefeller fellowship, 1965, 1974; Guggenheim fellowship, 1966, 1975; American Academy award, 1976; Brandeis University Creative Arts award, 1976; Ingram Merrill Foundation award, 1976; National Book Critics circle award, 1977; Academy of Sciences and American Academy award, 1979; Elmer Holmes Bobst award, 1991; Officer, Ordre des arts et des lettres, 1984. **Address:** c/o Farrar Straus and Giroux, 19 Union Square West, New York, New York 10003, USA.

ROMANCE AND HISTORICAL PUBLICATIONS

Novel

The Volcano Lover. New York, Farrar Straus, and London, Cape, 1992.

OTHER PUBLICATIONS

Novels

The Benefactor: A Novel. New York, Farrar Straus, 1963; London, Eyre and Spottiswoode, 1964.
Death Kit. New York, Farrar Straus, 1967; London, Secker and Warburg, 1968.

Short Stories

I, etcetera. New York, Farrar Straus, 1978; London, Gollancz, 1979.
The Way We Live Now, illustrated by Howard Hodgkin. London, Cape, 1991.

Plays

Duet for Cannibals. New York, Farrar Straus, 1970; London, Allen Lane, 1974.
Brother Carl. New York, Farrar Straus, 1974.
Alice in Bed: A Play in Eight Scenes. New York, Farrar Straus, 1993.

Screenplays: *Duet for Cannibals*, 1969; *Brother Carl*, 1971.

Other

Against Interpretation and Other Essays. New York, Farrar Straus, 1966; London, Eyre and Spottiswoode, 1967.

Trip to Hanoi. New York, Farrar Straus, and London, Panther, 1969.
Styles of Radical Will (essays). New York, Farrar Straus, and London, Secker and Warburg, 1969.
On Photography. New York, Farrar Straus, 1977; London, Allen Lane, 1978.
Illness as Metaphor. New York, Farrar Straus, 1978; London, Allen Lane, 1979.
Under the Sign of Saturn (essays). New York, Farrar Straus, 1980; London, Writers and Readers, 1983.
A Susan Sontag Reader. New York, Farrar Straus, and London, Allen Lane, 1989.
Aids and Its Metaphors. New York, Farrar Straus, and London, Allen Lane, 1989.

Editor, *Selected Writings of Artaud*, translated by Helen Weaver. New York, Farrar Straus, 1976.
Editor, *A Barthes Reader*. New York, Hill and Wang, and London, Cape, 1982; as *Barthes: Selected Writings*, London, Fontana, 1983.

*

Critical Study: *Susan Sontag: The Elegiac Modernist* by Sohnya Sayres, New York, Routledge Chapman and Hall, 1989; London, Routledge, 1990.

Theatrical Activities:
Director: **Plays**—*As You Desire Me* by Pirandello, Turin and Italian tour, 1979–80; *Jacques and His Master* by Milan Kundera, Cambridge, Massachusetts, 1985; *Waiting for Godot* by Samuel Beckett, Bosnia, 1993. **Films**—*Duet for Cannibals*, 1969; *Brother Carl*, 1971; *Promised Lands* (documentary), 1974; *Unguided Tour*, 1983.

*   *   *

The pretext for Susan Sontag's monumental yet exquisitely compassionate historical romance, *The Volcano Lover*, is a re-telling of the lives of Sir William Hamilton, Emma Hamilton, and Lord Nelson, primarily as they were played out against the backdrop of revolution in the closing decade of the 18th century. The novel focuses upon the variegated desire of William Hamilton for Emma, moving on to the 'grand' and much-travestied passion of Emma and Nelson. Interwoven with this is an exploration of other types of love and desire, such as the socially circumscribed love of Catherine, Hamilton's first wife, for her dispassionate husband; Catherine's platonic 'romance' with William Beckford of Fonthill; the maternal love of Mrs Cadogan for Emma; and the desires which inform aesthetic pleasure and political idealism.

The first section of the novel reconstructs the reflective consciousness of Hamilton, 'the Cavaliere', Sontag's character being avowedly the 'double' of the historical figure who was the British envoy to the Neapolitan court. In the lapidary, aphoristic style which is familiar from her essays, Sontag plots the labyrinths of desire with consummate precision. Her realization of the transformations of the late 18th-century sensibility of the Cavaliere, the aspiring 'envoy of decorum and reason' who strives to maintain an equilibrium between depression and enthusiasm, melancholy and irony, enables Sontag to reconsider some of her recurrent themes, such as the nature of spirituality, and the relation between aesthetic pleasure, ethical discernment, and moral action. The novel traces one of the ruling passions of the Cavaliere: collecting antiquities. Collecting provides a structure for 'free-floating desire' and it enables a sense of self-definition through identification with the lovingly-chosen objects. Such self-possession, Sontag suggests, is always sustained against anticipated loss—as indeed the Cavaliere is to lose and mourn a large part of his collection during the revolutionary tumult.

Ostensibly rational and controlled as the desire to collect is, at its borders lie obsession, madness, and hellish excess, as the Cavaliere realizes when he visits the grotesque follies of a Sicilian prince and Fonthill.

Counterpoised against the Cavaliere's finely modulated desire to collect is his preoccupation with the volcano Vesuvius, which, presiding over Naples, provides the novel's central metaphor. Her evocation of the Cavaliere's fascination with the volcano enables Sontag to continue her investigation of perception, perspective, and representation. The Cavaliere's scientific and aesthetic observations alternate with the detached gaze of the witness of the spectacle of the eruptions, a gaze which later becomes the distanced implacability of Hamilton, as of Emma and Nelson, during the savage purges of the proponents of the Parthenopean or Vesuvian Republic. Plates depicting the volcano from Hamilton's collection frame the novel, creating an impression of historical authenticity—and indeed Sontag seems to be carefully rendering some of the 'truths' of the period. Yet in so far as the volcano is a metaphor of revolution, its referents are constantly shifting through 'moments of slippage', just as the age of revolution was variously perceived as representing violence, terror, destruction or liberty and survival. History, Sontag suggests, was and is a matter of interpretation.

It is into this frame of the Cavaliere's double passion for collecting beautiful objects and witnessing the unruly energy of the 'monstrous' volcano that Emma Hart is introduced. The young Emma's beauty has already been mythologized, as by Romney's 'Bacchante', and to the Cavaliere, connoisseur that he is, it is at first, like the Portland vase or his favoured 'Venus', an object to be exhibited. Pygmalion-like, he can create her according to his will, and indeed the classical 'Attitudes' which he helps her to stage seem to evince feminine sensibility; pliant, desirous to please, to become what the observer wishes to see. But just as the Cavaliere moves from desire to love, so Emma Hamilton becomes 'no longer a model, but a subject'. Always withholding judgment from a woman whom history has variously represented, Sontag traces Emma's passion for Nelson, the 'hero' elected by the Bourbon king to defend Naples against the advancing French army and the Jacobean sympathizers within Naples. Her friendship with Queen Maria-Carolina, sister of Marie Antoinette and instigator of some of the brutal counter-revolutionary activity in Naples, has been the subject of virulent caricature, but Sontag balances an implicit consideration of the ethics of these activities against an explicit commentary on the misrepresentation of women who have had access to power. Similarly, the desires which produced the excesses which made Emma 'monstrous', the grotesque figure of Gillray's caricatures, are refracted through Sontag's prismatic critical lens.

The last section of the novel is given to the articulations of some of the women who have been silenced by misrepresentation. Testimonies are offered by the posthumous voices of Catherine, Mrs Cadogan, Emma, who died a pauper after being left by Nelson as a 'bequest to the nation', and finally Eleonora de Fonseca Pimentel, Neapolitan aristocrat and poet who was executed for her revolutionary activities. These ventriloquized voices powerfully testify to the poignancy of female desire sustained within and against disempowering social and cultural frameworks.

—Joanna Price

SOUZA, Ernest.   See SCOTT, Evelyn.

SPELLMAN, Cathy Cash.
Nationality: American. **Born:** New Jersey. **Education:** Vassar College, Poughkeepsie, New York. **Relations:** married Joseph X.

Spellman in 1975; two daughters. **Career:** creative director, J.P. Stevens, New York, 1965–69, and Revlon, New York, 1969–74; vice-president, Bloomingdale's, New York, 1974–76; president, Cathy Cash Spellman Inc, 1976–83, New York. Lives in Westport, Connecticut. **Agent:** Morton L. Janklow, 598 Fifth Avenue, New York, New York 10022, USA.

ROMANCE AND HISTORICAL PUBLICATIONS

Novels

So Many Partings. New York, Delacorte Press, and London, Heinemann, 1983.
An Excess of Love. New York, Delacorte Press, and London, Collins, 1985.
Paint the Wind. New York, Delacorte Press, and London, HarperCollins, 1990.

OTHER PUBLICATIONS

Novel

Bless the Child. New York, Warner, 1993.

Other

Notes to My Daughter. New York, Crown, 1981.

*   *   *

Cathy Cash Spellman's first two family sagas deal with the lives of the Irish on both sides of the Atlantic during the late-19th and early-20th centuries. Her first novel, *So Many Partings*, concentrates on Tom Dalton, the illegitimate son of an Anglo-Irish nobleman, Michael Harrington, and an Irish servant, Mary Dalton. Although Michael remains true to Mary and treats his son kindly, the rest of his family despises the pair. After Michael's untimely death, Mary and Tom are forced from the estate, she to the United States and he to a Roman Catholic boarding school. In America Mary remarries to escape her life as a servant, but she conceals her past from her husband. Tom's arrival in the United States after he reaches adulthood compromises her respectable life. After participating in the union battles of the longshoremen of New York City, Tom eventually amasses a fortune through a combination of luck and hard work. In his personal relationships, however, he remains decidedly unlucky. His wife is murdered; his children turn against him. Only in his granddaughter, Megan, does he find a kindred spirit. At the novel's end, she journeys to Ireland to claim the family legacy.

Spellman's second novel, *An Excess of Love*, concerns the events surrounding the Easter Uprising of 1916. The three children of an Irish Protestant lord, Con, Beth, and Des FitzGibbon, all aid the Republican cause to some degree. Family and political struggles continue into the next generation as Ireland plunges into civil war.

Although Spellman includes lengthy digressions on Irish myth and history in both books, the only non-fictional character in *So Many Partings* is union organizer Andrew Furuseth. Tom Dalton's experiences are based to some degree on those of Spellman's own maternal grandfather.

An Excess of Love contains many historical figures from Ireland's struggle for independence, including W.B. Yeats, Maud Gonne, Padraic Pearse, Eamon de Valera, and Michael Collins. In fact, the strain of integrating the historical events of the Irish uprising bogs down the narrative, especially after the deaths of Con FitzGibbon and her poet husband Tierney O'Connor, the two most compelling characters in the novel. Their romantic devotion to Ireland's struggle for liberty and their consuming love for each other make the civil war and selfish manoeuvring of the lacklustre generation after them seem petty in comparison. In short, Spellman is a more compelling author of romance than history.

In *Paint the Wind*, Spellman investigates another time and place, the American West in the second half of the 19th century. The action centres on two brothers, Charles (Chance) and Hart McAllister, and the love of both, Françoise (Fancy) Deverell. Rescued by a former slave from her family's burning Louisiana mansion, Fancy escapes death at the hand of marauding soldiers. Fleeing to the West, with its promise of gold, Fancy dreams of wealth and security. Her path crosses that of the McAllisters, and much of the novel takes place in Colorado, where they all eventually strike it rich. However, the action ranges from Hart's life with Geronimo's Apache band in the southwest, where his paintings chronicle the demise of a noble people, to Fancy's Broadway success. Fancy marries Chance, whose recklessness and lust for wealth matches hers, but eventually the widowed Fancy learns to value Hart's devotion. One of the more unusual strains of the book is the portrayal of the spirit world and alternative healing possibilities. From Atticus, the former slave, to Magda, the gypsy, and various Native Americans, characters demonstrate the ability to understand and intervene with unseen spirits on behalf of those they love.

Spellman portrays most rich people in her first two novels as uncaring and unemotional oppressors of the lower class. Those who sympathize with the poor usually must embrace poverty themselves to find true love. For example, Con exchanges her family estate for a Dublin tenement to share her life with Tierney. Her sister Beth leaves a loveless marriage to an Irish nobleman to find happiness with a revolutionary leader. Deirdre Mulvaney gives up her chance to marry into New York society to join Tom Dalton's life of poverty. The attitude towards wealth is more complex in *Paint the Wind*. Riches first bring Chance and Fancy together but ultimately drive them apart. The richest man in the novel, Jason Madigan, is a consummate villain, who will stoop to despicable acts to get what he wants. Yet, Hart and Fancy ultimately combine wealth and contentment.

Ironically, Spellman's main characters usually end up rich themselves. Tom Dalton accumulates enough wealth to buy the Harrington family estates from which he and his mother had been evicted. Tahg O'Connor inherits the FitzGibbon lands and fortune from his childless uncle. Hart and Fancy use their fortune to restore her ancestral plantation.

The books' romantic relationships are marked by passionate and enduring sexual relationships. Indeed, in Spellman's fictional worlds sexual satisfaction is an automatic by product of true love. As Tom tells Deirdre in *So Many Partings*, 'This gift of the love between a man and a woman makes us able to bear with all the rest of it'. Nothing else is as important to an individual as such a relationship.

Spellman excels in creating interesting characters with whom readers can empathize. Although her style is straightforward narrative in *So Many Partings*, and *Paint the Wind*, in *An Excess of Love* she experiments a bit by juxtaposing third-person perspective with Beth FitzGibbon's first-person reminiscences.

—Kathy Piehl

SPENCER, LaVyrle.
Nationality: American. **Born:** Browerville, Minnesota, 17 August 1943. **Education:** high school, Staples, Minnesota. **Relations:** married Dan Spencer in 1962; two daughters. **Career:** seamstress,

1969–72; instructional aide, Osseo Junior High School, Osseo, Minnesota, 1974–8; writer. **Address:** 6701 79th Avenue, Brooklyn Park, Minnesota 55445, USA.

ROMANCE AND HISTORICAL PUBLICATIONS

Novels

The Fulfillment. New York, Avon, 1979; London, Grafton, 1992.
The Endearment. New York, Pocket Books, 1982; London, Severn House, 1991.
A Promise to Cherish. New York, Berkley, 1983; London, Piatkus, 1989.
Hummingbird. New York, Berkley, 1983.
Sweet Memories. Toronto, Harlequin, 1984; London, Severn House, 1989.
Loved. New York, Berkley, 1984; London, Piatkus, 1990.
The Hellion. Toronto, Harlequin, 1984; New York, Berkley, 1989.
Spring Fancy. Toronto, Harlequin, and London, Mills and Boon, 1984.
Separate Beds. New York, Berkley, 1985; London, Macdonald, 1986.
A Heart Speaks (includes *A Promise to Cherish* and *Forsaking All Others*). New York, Berkley, 1986.
Years. New York, Berkley, 1986; London, Macdonald, 1987.
The Gamble. New York, Berkley, 1987; London, Macdonald, 1988.
Vows. New York, Berkley, 1988.
Morning Glory. New York, Putnam, 1989; London, Grafton, 1990.
Bitter Sweet. New York, Putnam, 1990; London, Grafton, 1990.
Forgiving. New York, Putnam, and London, Grafton, 1991.
Bygones. New York, Putnam, 1992; London, HarperCollins 1993.
November of the Heart. New York, Putnam, 1993.

*

Film Adaptation: *The Fulfillment of Mary Gray*, 1989, from the novel *The Fulfillment*.

*   *   *

Following in the tradition of Anya Seton as opposed to Sergeanne Golon, LaVyrle Spencer's novels focus on the inner life of her characters to explore the turf of ordinary people and the many faces love can wear. That she has done so with a delightful touch of humour is an indication of the understanding and compassion that marks her best work. Inspired by Kathleen Woodiwiss, but determined to create something very different from the bodice rippers so popular at the time she started writing, Spencer did just that with *The Fulfillment*, the story of a sterile Minnesota farmer, his childless wife, and his brother, whom the husband asks to serve in his stead to give him a son. Set in the late 1800s, the plot is neither original nor unique; it is Spencer's sensitively developed characters that stand out. But novels like *Hummingbird* are her real forté, in which she sets up a confrontation between contrasting types: a strait-laced Victorian virgin and a mustachioed lothario she believes to be a train robber. Rejected by Avon (Spencer's original publisher) as too humorous and 'too narrow in scope'—almost every scene takes place inside one house—and because the first sexual encounter between the main characters was a failure for her heroine, *Hummingbird* eventually became Spencer's most popular paperback title.

The Endearment is an historical romance with a difference as well, since the hero who orders a bride by mail is clearly the protagonist; he is also a virgin, while the heroine is not. In *Loved* Spencer sets up another triangle, with the heroine married first to a Nantucket sailor who is presumed dead when his whaler is lost at sea, and then to a childhood friend. When her first husband reappears, she is torn between two men, both of whom she loves but in different ways and for different reasons. Each has a history with her from which she cannot escape, bringing home to the reader the agony of a dilemma in which there is no single good or right answer. In *Sweet Memories*, Spencer's talent for plumbing the internal life of her characters comes to the fore again in a protagonist with such large breasts that they have a withering effect on her self-image and social development. Spencer details the emerging relationship between her heroine and the first man who even tries to see the woman behind the breasts, so to speak—who ultimately is able to breach the emotional barriers she has erected to protect herself. Eventually she decides (despite opposition from her insensitive mother, and without consulting the man she loves) to risk the loss of both sensitivity and function in exchange for physical and emotional health by having the surgery that will correct what is more than simply a cosmetic problem.

In her later novels Spencer has moved away from paperback originals into hardcovers that often appear on bestseller lists for a few weeks. But these stories have a soap opera like predictability evident even in the titles—*Vows*, *Forgiving*, *Bygones*, and *November of the Heart*. Like champagne gone flat, they lack both substance and freshness. 'They're not so much a love story anymore', one disenchanted reader commented, 'and please don't preach at me!'. In *Bygones*, for example, Spencer reunites a divorced couple who have grown bored with each other. Discovering that their lives are equally lacking and disappointing after they split, they are brought together by their children when they are older and wiser, and finally come to the conclusion that they can be happier with each other than they thought—not to mention comfortable. *November of the Heart* is almost a caricature of the simpering romance stereotype, complete with endless passages of precious description:

> The table spread with Irish linen bearing the Barnett family crest, was set with Tiffany silver flatware and Wedgwood Queen's ware. Its centrepiece held precisely 50 Bourbon Madame Isaac Pereire roses from the cottage's own gardens, their overpowering scent scarcely diluted by the 9 p.m. breeze fluttering in the lakeside windows. The walls of the room were decked in William Morris paper, spreading grape clusters and acanthus leaves across a burgundy background. The woodwork, crafted of ruby-rich . . .

Such impoverished writing from the author of *Loved* and *Sweet Memories* leaves one wondering if Spencer, like so many other writers, has fallen victim to her own success—a publishing schedule that requires a new hardcover novel every 12 months, at which time her last title shows up on the mass market paperback racks.

—Carol Thurston

SPRIGGE, Elizabeth (Miriam Squire).
Nationality: British. **Born:** London, 10 June 1900; daughter of the writer and editor Sir Squire Sprigg. **Education:** St Paul's Girls' School, London; Havergal College, Toronto; Bedford College, London University. **Relations:** married Mark Napier in 1921 (divorced 1946); two daughters. **Career:** Swedish specialist, British Ministry for Information, London, 1941–44; co-founder and director, Watergate Theatre Club, 1949–52; lecturer and broadcaster on literature and theatre. Lived in Sweden, 1923–25. **Died:** 9 December 1974.

ROMANCE AND HISTORICAL PUBLICATIONS

Novels

Home Is the Hunter, with H.T. Munn. New York, Knopf, 1930.
Castle in Andalusia. New York, Macmillan, and London, Heinemann, 1935.
The Raven's Wing. London, Macmillan, 1940.

OTHER PUBLICATIONS

Novels

A Shadowy Third. New York, Knopf, 1927.
Faint Amorist. New York, Knopf, 1927.
The Old Man Dies. New York, Macmillan, and London, Heinemann, 1935.
The Son of the House. London, Collins, 1937.

Plays

Elizabeth of Austria, with Katriona Sprigge (produced London, 1938).
Mary Stuart in Scotland, adaptation of a play by Bjørnstjerne Bjørnson (produced Edinburgh, 1960).

Other

Children Alone (for children). London, Eyre and Spottiswoode, 1935.
Pony Tracks (for children). London, Eyre and Spottiswoode, and New York, Scribner, 1936.
Two Lost on Dartmoor (for children). London, Eyre and Spottiswoode, 1940.
The Strange Life of August Strindberg. London, Hamish Hamilton, and New York, Macmillan, 1949.
Gertrude Stein: Her Life and Work. London, Hamish Hamilton, and New York, Harper, 1957.
The Dolphin Bottle (for children), with Elizabeth Müntz. London, Gollancz, 1965.
Jean Cocteau: The Man and the Mirror, with Jean Jacques Kihm. London, Gollancz, and New York, Coward McCann, 1968.
Sybil Thorndike Casson (biography). London, Gollancz, 1971.
The Life of Ivy Compton-Burnett. London, Gollancz, 1973.

Translator, with Claude Napier, *Kings, Churchills and Statesmen: A Foreigner's View*, by Knut Hjalmar Hagberg. London, Lane, and New York, Dodd Mead, 1929.
Translator, with Claude Napier, *Personalities and Power*, by Knut Hjalmar Hagberg. London, Lane, 1930.
Translator, with Claude Napier, *Sinners in Summertime*, by Sigurd Hoel. New York, Coward McCann, 1930.
Translator, with Claude Napier, *Economic Progress and Economic Crisis*, by Johan Henrik Akerman. London, Macmillan, 1932.
Translator, with Claude Napier, *Impressions of England 1809–1810*, by Erik Gustaf Geijer. London, Anglo-Swedish Literary Foundation, 1932.
Translator, with Claude Napier, *An Eyewitness in Germany*, by Martin Fredrik Christofferson Böök. London, Lovat Dickson, 1933.
Translator, with Claude Napier, *The Marriage of Ebba Garland*, by Dagmar Edqvist. London, Lovat Dickson, 1933.
Translator, with Claude Napier, *Riddles of the Gobi Desert*, by Sven Anders Hedin. London, Routledge, and New York, Dutton, 1933.
Translator, with Claude Napier, *The Street of the Sandalmakers*, by Nis Johan Petersen. London, Lovat Dickson, and New York, Macmillan, 1933.

Translator, with Claude Napier, *The Eaglet*, by Harald Victorin. London, Lovat Dickson, 1933.

Translator, with Claude Napier, *Tents in Mongolia—Yabonak: Adventures and Experiences among the Nomads of Central Asia*, by Henning Haslund-Christensen. London, Kegan Paul, and New York, Dutton, 1934.

Translator, with Claude Napier, *Men and Gods in Mongolia—Zayagan*, by Henning Haslund-Christensen. London, Kegan Paul, and New York, Dutton, 1935.

Translator, with Claude Napier, *The Head of the Firm*, by Hjalmar Fredrik Elgerus Bergman. London, Allen and Unwin, 1936.

Translator, with Claude Napier, *The Morning of Life*, by Kristmann Gudmundsson. London, Heinemann, 1936.

Translator, with Anna Sturge, *The Brig Three Lilies*, by Olle Mattson. London, University of London Press, 1960.

Translator, with Anna Sturge, *Michel Seafarer*, by Olle Mattson. London, University of London Press, 1961.

Translator, *Twelve Plays of Strindberg*. London, Constable, 1963.

Translator, *The Difficulty of Being*, by Jean Cocteau. London, Owen, 1966.

Translator, *The Red Room: Scenes of Artistic and Literary Life*, by August Strindberg. London, Dent, and New York, Dutton, 1967.

*   *   *

Elizabeth Sprigge's wrote novels about American urban middle-class life between the two world wars. Sprigge's interest in the disintegration of traditional values and the subsequent changes in living conditions caused by World War I can be seen in *The Raven's Wing*, *Home Is the Hunter*, and *Castle in Andalusia*.

The Raven's Wing follows the life of Elizabeth of Austria from her young girlhood, her marriage to Franz Joseph, to her approaching death. Sprigge develops a detailed picture of the waning years of European royalty at a time when the conventional conflict between personal happiness and monarchical duty gains a special poignancy due to the increasing social and cultural obsolescence of the imperial position in the modern world. Sprigge's novel presents a nostalgic atmosphere in its admiration of the power and tradition behind the arranged marriages and royal court intrigue. Yet its modern context is revealed in Elizabeth's recognition of the inevitable disintegration of her world.

Home Is the Hunter develops Sprigge's interest in naturalism. The novel is set in the mid-19th century and opens in the whaling town of Dundee, Scotland. Sprigge uses dialect and description skilfully but the main interest in the novel is the theme of heredity which was central to the literary expression of naturalism. A whaler, Alan Cameron, has fathered a child who is described as half-Eskimo. The plot follows his son, Alan, as his hereditary destiny works itself out. A brilliant engineer, he 'often felt vaguely discontented and had an inexplicable longing for some wider, wilder life in which he could come more directly to grips with the terrible, fascinating forces of nature'. Alan travels to New York where he meets a 'half-breed' couple, who speak a French-Canadian dialect, and goes with them to the Canadian northwest, to Fort Garry near present-day Winnipeg. Moving still further north, Alan marries an 'Eskimo' wife and, eventually, meets his natural mother. Sprigge's argument blends nicely with the period and the Darwinism that dominated ideas of heredity and natural selection at this time. She maintains a breath-taking pace of plot throughout the novel and skilfully weaves two major story lines into a satisfying conclusion.

In *Castle in Andalusia* Sprigge writes of her own times. Nevertheless, the novel has historical interest because, as in *The Raven's Wing*, she uses the opening of the Spanish Civil War to examine the passing of the era of the Dons and royal court life. One reviewer remarked that 'her story has pace and colour, and a passionate humanity. She writes with fairness and candour, if with a touch of the old

English prejudice against the Catholicism of Spain'. The same reviewer expressed the regret that Sprigge was so obviously on the side of the Republicans. Her English heroine, Catharine, has married a Don but loves the rebel Pedro. Sprigge's politics are written into the dynamics of this three-sided relationship.

Sprigge's interest in her later writing turned to biographical research which focused on important figures of her own time. Her interest in the modernist work of many of these people is reflected in *The Old Man Dies*, which was hailed as a 'brilliant performance' by J.E.S. Arrowsmith in the *London Mercury*. In this book, Sprigge concentrated on the evocation of character psychology and left behind the intricate and finely-wrought plots of her earlier, historical novels.

—Heather Iris Jones

————

STANFORD, Sondra.
Nationality: American. **Born:** Texas. **Education:** University of Southwestern Louisiana, Lafayette. **Relations:** married Huey Stanford in 1961; two daughters. **Career:** founding member, Romance Writers of America, Houston, Texas, 1980. **Agent:** Anita Diamant, 310 Madison Avenue, New York, New York 10017, USA. **Address:** 4117 Birchwood Drive, Corpus Christi, Texas 78412, USA.

ROMANCE AND HISTORICAL PUBLICATIONS

Novels

A Stranger's Kiss. London, Mills and Boon, and Toronto, Harlequin, 1978.
Bellefleur. London, Mills and Boon, and Toronto, Harlequin, 1980.
Golden Tide. New York, Silhouette, 1980.
Shadow of Love. New York, Silhouette, 1980.
No Trespassing. New York, Silhouette, 1980.
Storm's End. New York, Silhouette, 1980.
Long Winter's Night. New York, Silhouette, 1981.
And Then Came Dawn. New York, Silhouette, 1981.
Whisper Wind. New York, Silhouette, 1981.
Yesterday's Shadow. New York, Silhouette, 1981.
Tarnished Vows. New York, Silhouette, 1982.
Silver Mist. New York, Silhouette, 1982.
Magnolia Moon. New York, Silhouette, 1982.
Sun Lover. New York, Silhouette, 1982.
Love's Gentle Chains. New York, Silhouette, 1983.
The Heart Knows Best. New York, Silhouette, 1984.
For All Time. New York, Silhouette, 1984.
A Corner of Heaven. New York, Silhouette, 1984.
Cupid's Task. New York, Silhouette, 1985.
Bird in Flight. New York, Silhouette, 1986.
Equal Shares. New York, Silhouette, 1986.
Stolen Trust. New York, Silhouette, 1987.
Heart of Gold. New York, Silhouette, 1988.
Through All Eternity. New York, Silhouette, 1988.
Proud Beloved. New York, Silhouette, 1989.
A Man with Secrets. New York, Silhouette, 1990.
Secret Marriages. New York, Silhouette, 1991.

*   *   *

A prolific author of series romances, Sondra Stanford has focused many of her efforts on stories about relationships which have been damaged or destroyed. Her couples are given a rare second chance to correct old mistakes and rebuild on a solid foundation.

The lovers, who may have been married, have been separated by circumstances that caused one partner to lose trust in the other. In the appropriately titled *Stolen Trust* Alan Daniels gains a second chance with Rose Bennington seven years after jilting her only days before their wedding. Rose still loves him but says, 'I'm terrified he'll leave me again someday no matter how many times he promises he won't'. Unless she understands his reasons for leaving the first time, she cannot trust him not to hurt her again. Sometimes trust is destroyed by unreasoning jealousy or unfounded belief that a betrayal has occurred. Both men and women can be guilty of destroying trust. Tony Nugent drives Lisa Knight (*For All Time*) away by accusing her of betraying him. As she says to a friend, 'Of course I can forgive him. And I do love him ... But I can't endure his constant assumptions that I'm some sort of horrible monster out to stab him in the back!' Jana Parrish twice assumes her husband Miles is unfaithful (*Tarnished Vows*). The second time he tells her they are through because 'Love involves trust, and that's something you never could give me'.

In *Bird in Flight*, Bill Sheridan is reluctant to remarry Andrea because she had rejected his love once and he cannot help being afraid she would do it again. Many times this loss of trust is related to pride and an inability or unwillingness to communicate. Rather than discussing the original problem, the partner who feels betrayed opts out of the relationship by pushing the other away or by leaving herself/himself.

Stanford's novels involve more bitterness than is usual in most series romances. She is skilful enough that this tone does not overwhelm the characters yet it is clearly apparent. She draws the reader into a world of pain in which it is easy to understand how one can love another, yet still distrust that person. She conveys the inner turmoil such an emotional division causes. This is not an easy task when working within the confines of series romance formulas, but Stanford succeeds remarkably well.

—Barbara E. Kemp

STAPLES, Mary Jane.
Pseudonyms: James Sinclair, Robert Tyler Stevens. **Nationality:** British. **Born:** Reginald Thomas Staples, London, 26 November 1911. **Education:** West Square Grammar, 1923–28. **Relations:** married Florence A. Hume in 1937; one child. **Military Service:** British Army, 1940–46: sergeant. **Career:** managing director, Staples and Hancock Ltd, Croydon, Worthing, 1953–1966; managing director, Fullerton and Lloyd Ltd, Croydon, Merstham, from 1954; director, H.D. Vincent (printer) Ltd, Worthing, 1958–1966. Since 1971, chairman, Vista Sports Ltd, Merstham. **Agent:** Sheila Watson, Watson Little Ltd, 12 Egbert Street, London NW1 8LJ, England. **Address:** 52 Dome Hill, Caterham, Surrey, CR3 6EB, England.

ROMANCE AND HISTORICAL PUBLICATIONS

Novels

Down Lambeth Way. London, Bantam Press, 1988.
Our Emily. London, Bantam Press, 1989.
King of Camberwell. London, Bantam Press, 1990.
Two for Three Farthings. London, Bantam Press, 1990.
The Lodger. London, Bantam Press, 1991.
Rising Summer. London, Bantam Press, 1991.
Pearly Queen. London, Bantam Press, 1992.
Sergeant Joe. London, Bantam Press, 1992.
On Mother Brown's Doorstep. London, Bantam Press, 1993.

Novels as Robert Tyler Stevens

The Summer Day Is Done. London, Souvenir Press, and New York, Doubleday, 1976.
Flight from Bucharest. London, Souvenir Press, and New York, Doubleday, 1977.
Appointment in Sarajevo. London, Souvenir Press, and New York, Doubleday, 1978.
Woman of Cordova. London, Souvenir Press, and New York, Doubleday, 1979.
Field of Yesterday. London, Severn House, 1983.
Shadows in the Afternoon. London, Severn House, 1983.
The Hostage. London, Severn House, 1985.
The Woman in Berlin. London, Severn House, 1986.
The Professional Gentleman. London, Severn House, 1988.

Novels as James Sinclair

Warrior Queen. London, Souvenir Press, and New York, St Martin's Press, 1977.
Canis the Warrior. London, Souvenir Press, and New York, St Martin's Press, 1979.

*

Manuscript Collection: Mugar Memorial Library, Boston University, Massachusetts.

Mary Jane Staples comments:
I made half a name for myself as a writer with the publication of my first novel *The Summer Day Is Done*. I followed this with other novels of the historical fiction genre, then went slightly mad with a story relating to all I remembered of life in Walworth during World War I. I called it *Down Lambeth Way* under my old mother's name, Mary Jane Staples, and that and subsequent cockney stories have put me among the bestsellers, much to my amazement.

*   *   *

Reginald Thomas Staples has written nine very successful and highly enjoyable novels under the pseudonym Mary Jane Staples. These books are predominantly set in Walworth, London, during World War I and the inter-war period.

Down Lambeth Way is the first book to feature the Adams family. Narrated by Boots, one of the four Adams children, the book recounts the lives of a Cockney family surviving in the period before, and during World War I. The narrator's voice is cheekily colloquial as he builds up an image of his world. Boots'ss family consists of highly colourful characters. His mother is called 'Chinese Lady' because she has almond shaped eyes, works as a charwoman, and takes in washing. She epitomizes the strong working-class woman—struggling to bring up four children alone, on just a widow's pension. The Adams also have a lodger, Mr Finch, a fastidious man, who appears in later books.

Down Lambeth Way contains everything from murder and suspense to romance. One of the Adams's neighbours, Miss Chivers, is accused of murdering her own mother. Boots, who by this stage of the book has joined the army, gets involved as a material witness. His evidence proves Miss Chivers's innocence. The truth, however, is revealed at the end of the book: Mr Finch is a German spy, and Miss Chivers is his mistress. Romance appears in the form of Emily, the best friend of Lizzy, Boots's sister. At the beginning of the book Emily is viewed as loud and slipshod; she even gives the family headlice. By the end of the book, Boots is in love with Emily. Returning from the war blind, Boots asks Emily to marry him. The book is extremely good in its social setting and attention to detail. Life in working-class London is evoked well.

Our Emily and *King of Camberwell* also follow the lives of the Adams family. In *Our Emily*, Emily, now Boots's wife, has to go out and become the breadwinner. Lizzy's husband has lost his leg in the war, and the book is full of traumatized survivors of the war, coming to terms with demobilization. The setting of this book is very much England recovering from the war, with its food shortages, poverty, high unemployment, and cholera and typhoid fears. Issues such as contraception are dealt with efficiently. In *King of Camberwell* 19-year-old Sammy Adams has his story told. Sammy is somewhat of an entrepreneur, and has several shops. Boots manages the Camberwell Green shop for him. Susie, the manageress of one of his other shops, is the romantic involvement in the book, and Sammy marries her. Love for the older characters in the book is dealt with when Chinese Lady, who has been in a sanatorium, marries Mr Finch, who appeared in *Our Emily*.

The Lodger has much more of a murder suspense feel to it. The book opens with a strangler on the loose, who has a penchant for blonde women. Maggie Wilson is a 33-year-old widow with three young children, who brings in a lodger to help her pay her bills (quite a common occurrence during this period). The police decide to examine any newcomers to the area, and constable Harry Bradshaw meets Maggie and her children when questioning them about their lodger; their romance forms part of the plot. Mrs Emma Carter, a 28-year-old blonde suffragette is asked by the police to help in their enquiries. Emma acts as bait and helps to catch the strangler. The characterization and dialogue in this book are excellent.

Many of the issues handled in Staples's books are serious ones. Horace, aged ten, and Effel, aged seven, are orphaned during an influenza epidemic that killed many people. They are taken in by Jim Cooper, newly returned from the trenches. Their story is told in *Two for Three Farthings*. Similarly, the issue of illegitimate children is handled in *Rising Summer* when Tim Hardy finds out that the aunt who brought him up is actually his mother. Tim becomes a gunner during the war and meets Walworth evacuee Minnie Beavers, whom he eventually marries.

All of Staples's books have a romantic theme to them, and the main protagonists all eventually find love. The characters are richly drawn, and are a lively bunch of people, from Chinese Lady to Dolly Smith, the female interest in *Sergeant Joe*. The women tend to be survivors—through necessity and not through choice. Most are widowed and have small children. They work, doing whatever menial jobs they can find. They are supported in their endeavours by women like themselves, family, and an extended kinship network that gives them a rich local culture.

The characters are survivors, and deal with whatever hardships life thrusts at them; thus Boots deals with his blindness in a very prosaic way, as does his wife Emily. Death is seen as an inevitability, especially after the war, and is not romanticized in the least. The characters enjoy what life is left to them with a lust which is surprising, but enviable, given the hard circumstances of life in post-war Britain.

Staples depicts life in working-class London at the beginning of the century with a liveliness and thoroughness that make his books highly readable. His evocation of Walworth life is both entertaining and educating and his attention to even the smallest detail of cockney life makes him a widely read author.

—P. Campbell

STEEL, Danielle.
Nationality: American. **Born:** Danielle Fernande Schüelein-Steel, New York City, 14 August 1947. **Education:** schools in Europe; New York University, 1963–67; Parsons School of Art, New York.

Relations: married four times; 1) in 1964 (divorced 1973), two children; 2) Bill Troth in 1977; 4) John A Traina in 1981, five children, and two stepchildren. **Career:** copywriter, San Francisco, 1973–74; journalist; helped start a public relations firm, SuperGirls Ltd, in New York. **Agent:** Morton Janklow, 598 Madison Avenue, New York, New York 10022, USA. **Address:** c/o Delacorte Press, 1 Dag Hammarskjold Plaza, 245 East 47th Street, New York, New York 10017, USA.

ROMANCE AND HISTORICAL PUBLICATIONS

Novels

Going Home. New York, Pocket Books, 1973; London, Sphere, 1980.
Passion's Promise. New York, Dell, 1977; as *Golden Moments*, London, Sphere, 1980.
Now and Forever. New York, Dell, 1978; London, Sphere, 1979.
The Promise (novelization of screenplay). New York, Dell, and London, Sphere, 1978.
Season of Passion. New York, Dell, and London, Sphere, 1979.
The Ring. New York, Delacorte Press, 1980; London, Sphere, 1982.
Loving. New York, Dell, 1980; Loughton, Essex, Piatkus, 1981.
To Love Again. New York, Dell, 1980.
Remembrance. New York, Delacorte Press, 1981; London, Hodder and Stoughton, 1982.
Palomino. New York, Dell, 1981; Loughton, Essex, Piatkus, 1982.
Summer's End. New York, Dell, 1981; London, Sphere, 1992.
A Perfect Stranger. New York, Dell, and Loughton, Essex, Piatkus, 1982.
Once in a Lifetime. New York, Dell, 1982; Loughton, Essex, Piatkus, 1983.
Crossings. New York, Delacorte Press, 1982; London, Hodder and Stoughton, 1983.
Thurston House. New York, Dell, and London, Sphere, 1983.
Changes. New York, Delacorte Press, and London, Hodder and Stoughton, 1983.
Full Circle. New York, Delacorte Press, and London, Hodder and Stoughton, 1984.
Family Album. New York, Delacorte Press, and London, Joseph, 1985.
Secrets. New York, Delacorte Press, and London, Joseph, 1985.
Wanderlust. New York, Delacorte Press, and London, Joseph, 1986.
Fine Things. New York, Delacorte Press, and London, Joseph, 1987.
Kaleidoscope. New York, Delacorte Press, and London, Joseph, 1987.
Zoya. New York, Delacorte Press, and London, Joseph, 1988.
Star. New York, Delacorte Press, and London, Joseph, 1989.
Daddy. New York, Delacorte Press, and London, Bantam, 1989.
Message from Nam. New York, Delacorte Press, and London, Bantam, 1990.
No Greater Love. New York, Delacorte Press, and London, Bantam, 1991.
Heartbeat. London, Bantam, 1991; New York, Dell, 1992.
Jewels. New York, Delacorte Press, and London, Bantam, 1992.
Mixed Blessings. New York, Delacorte Press, and London, Bantam, 1992.
Vanished. London, Bantam, 1993.

OTHER PUBLICATIONS

Poetry

Love. New York, Dell, 1981; revised edition, New York, Delacorte Press, 1984.

Three-in-One. London, Piatkus, 1992.

Fiction (for children)

Martha's Best Friend [*New Daddy, New School*]. New York, Delacorte Press, 3 vols, 1989.
Max's Daddy Goes to Hospital. New York, Delacorte Press, 1989.
Max and the Baby Sitter. New York, Delacorte Press, 1989.
Max's New Baby. New York, Delacorte Press, 1989.
Martha's New Puppy. New York, Doubleday, 1990.
Max Runs Away. New York, Doubleday, 1990.

Other

Having a Baby. New York, Dell, 1984.

*

Film Adaptations: *Now and Forever*, 1983; *Crossings*, 1986; *Kaleidoscope*, 1990; *Fine Things*, 1990; *Changes*, 1991; *Daddy*, 1991; *Palomino*, 1991.

*   *   *

Danielle Steel's prolific writing career has produced a collection of love stories that are as diverse in their settings and ages, as is Steel's experimentation with the concept of love. Adroitly blending the element of romance, and very often history, with the protagonists' own personal saga, she turns out riveting, albeit occasionally far fetched, tales of love that hover dangerously on the razor's edge between works of serious romance and a frivolous dalliance with sentimentality. While the ease with which she writes about Nazi Germany or the Manchuria of 1934, as well as contemporary America ruled by the dictates of the élite (this is probably her forte), is unmistakable, the inherent weaknesses in the superficial portrayal of characters and plots render her novels unconvincing. The direction and scope of her works depend excessively on the role of events: some are dramatic yet intense enough to give shape to the entire novel (*The Promise, Palomino*), some more plausible, and thereby more realistic (as in the mother who leaves her family in *Daddy*; or problems encountered when two people with children of their own decide to get married in *Changes*), and some conveniently culled from history and deftly adapted to accommodate her own characters (as in the *The Ring, Zoya, Wanderlust*).

In a typical Steel novel, the story is dominated by the presence of a single character, usually a heroine. Her descriptions of their glamorous looks, genteel breeding and enviable lifestyles tend to be repetitive. More often than not, they exude a 'poor little rich girl' pathos. These women have everything but are unfulfilled, their love affairs are essentially cathartic experiences that provoke deeper enquiry by the heroine into herself. The predictable outcome in each of their stories is the emergence of a more resolute and strengthened being. The union of lovers 'happily ever after' is rarely the objective of a relationship and Steel makes no attempt to end her novels on this note. In *Passion's Promise*, it takes a tragic love affair for Kezia St Martin to come to terms with the glittering world she was born into yet blossoms as the serious writer she always wanted to be. Jessica Clarke, in *Now and Forever*, faced with the imminent imprisonment of her husband, reaches within for resources to fight the fears of loss and loneliness haunting her from the past. A heart rending extramarital relationship, in *Summer's End*, fortifies Deanne Durcass with the courage to break out of a confining marriage and establish herself as an artist. The shortcoming of these characterizations is their glaring remoteness from reality. While one is drawn into their intriguing trials, the persons portrayed and situations described are simply beyond the readers' empathy.

More recently, however, there appears to be a discernible shift in Steel's focus of writing as she toys with more down-to-earth people, their realistic problems and more conventional notions of love. The dominance of the single character situation appears to be gradually replaced by simultaneous storylines and love ending on a happy note is no longer anathema. *Secrets*, for example, brings together several actors and actresses, each with their own painful past, on to the set of a television soap opera. For each of them the camaraderie derived from the cast members is an uplifting experience taking them from their tragedies to the hope of finding happiness again. Oliver Watson, in *Daddy*, is left to pick up the pieces after his wife walks out on 18 years of marriage. In this novel Steel presents the stories of three generations of men: (Oliver, his father, and his son), and their sheer determination that helps them cope in a world of new experience and responsibilities. *Heartbeat*, relates the simultaneous stories of Adrianne Townsend and William Thigpen. Rejected by her husband for keeping the child he did not want, Adrianne befriends Bill, still scarred from a failed marriage and the loss of the sons he loved. In the story of their new found relationship, Steel stresses the relevance of timeless values—love for children, family, and homes are the clear messages that permeate throughout. Love of an entirely different kind is described in *No Greater Love*, in which Edwina Winfield selflessly devotes her life to the upbringing of her siblings after their parents perish in the tragedy of the *Titanic*. These storylines are filled with intense human emotion, yet Steel fails to develop these themes adequately. In the end she produces characters who appear emotionally retarded, plots that are either mindlessly tragic or unbelievably happy, and a novel where poignancy appears contrived.

Yet, Steel is among the most popular romance writers of today. The success of her works lies partly in the easy pace, unfettered by needless descriptions. Also, her ability to re-create, through the eyes of her main characters, the ambience of the period she writes about without having to provide substantial factual information is remarkable. Unlike many romance writers, Steel has attempted to present to her readers a multi-dimensional nature of love. Be it the moonlight and roses affair of lovers, the unchanging affection of a father or the selfless devotion of a sister, to Steel these are just among the wide range of human emotions that deserve the distinction of sublimity.

—Rachel Kumar

———

STEELE, Jessica.
Pseudonym: Marcia Steele. **Nationality:** British. **Born:** Marcia Glennys Howell, Royal Leamington Spa, Warwickshire, 9 May 1933. **Education:** Clapham Terrace Secondary Modern, London. **Relations:** married twice, 2) Jesse Peter Steele in 1967. **Career:** bookkeeper, estate agent, Royal Leamington Spa; civil servant, Worcestershire, 1971–78. Since 1978, full-time writer. **Address:** Whitebeams, West Malvern, Worcestershire, England.

ROMANCE AND HISTORICAL PUBLICATIONS

Novels

The Icicle Heart. London, Mills and Boon, and Toronto, Harlequin, 1979.
Pride's Heart. London, Mills and Boon, and Toronto, Harlequin, 1979.
Spring Girl. London, Mills and Boon, and Toronto, Harlequin, 1979.
Hostile Engagement. London, Mills and Boon, and Toronto, Harlequin, 1979.

Intimate Enemies. London, Mills and Boon, and Toronto, Harlequin, 1979.

Hostage to Dishonour. London, Mills and Boon, 1979; Toronto, Harlequin, 1980.

Turbulent Covenant. London, Mills and Boon, and Toronto, Harlequin, 1980.

The Other Woman. London, Mills and Boon, and Toronto, Harlequin, 1980.

The Magic of His Kiss. London, Mills and Boon,1980; Toronto, Harlequin, 1981.

Price to Be Met. London, Mills and Boon, 1980; Toronto, Harlequin, 1983.

Devil in Disguise. London, Mills and Boon, 1980; Toronto, Harlequin, 1981.

Innocent Abroad. London, Mills and Boon, and Toronto, Harlequin, 1981.

Bachelor's Wife. London, Mills and Boon, and Toronto, Harlequin, 1981.

Gallant Antagonist. London, Mills and Boon, 1981; Toronto, Harlequin, 1984.

The Other Brother. London, Mills and Boon, 1981; Toronto, Harlequin, 1982.

Dishonest Women. London, Mills and Boon, and Toronto, Harlequin, 1982.

But Know Not Why. London, Mills and Boon, and Toronto, Harlequin, 1982.

Distrust Her Shadow. London, Mills and Boon, 1982; Toronto, Harlequin, 1983.

Tethered Liberty. London, Mills and Boon, and Toronto, Harlequin, 1983.

No Quiet Refuge. London, Mills and Boon, and Toronto, Harlequin, 1983.

Reluctant Relative. London, Mills and Boon, 1983; Toronto, Harlequin, 1984.

Tomorrow-Come Soon. London, Mills and Boon, 1983; Toronto, Harlequin, 1984.

Imprudent Challenge. London, Mills and Boon, 1984; Toronto, Harlequin, 1985.

Ruthless in All. London, Mills and Boon, 1984; Toronto, Harlequin, 1985.

Bond of Vengeance. London, Mills and Boon, 1984; Toronto, Harlequin, 1985.

Façade. London, Mills and Boon, 1984; Toronto, Harlequin, 1985.

No Holds Barred. London, Mills and Boon, 1984; Toronto, Harlequin, 1985.

No Honourable Compromise. London, Mills and Boon, 1984; Toronto, Harlequin, 1985.

A Promise to Dishonour. London, Mills and Boon, and Toronto, Harlequin, 1985.

So Near, So Far. London, Mills and Boon, and Toronto, Harlequin, 1986.

Misleading Encounter. London, Mills and Boon, and Toronto, Harlequin, 1986.

Beyond Her Control. London, Mills and Boon, and Toronto, Harlequin, 1986.

Relative Strangers. london, Mills and Boon, and Toronto, Harlequin, 1987.

Unfriendly Alliance. London, Mills and Boon, 1987; Toronto, Harlequin, 1988.

Fortunes of Love. London, Mills and Boon, and Toronto, Harlequin, 1988.

Without Love. London, Mills and Boon, 1988; Toronto, Harlequin, 1989.

When the Loving Stopped. London, Mills and Boon, 1988; Toronto, Harlequin, 1989.

To Stay Forever. London, Mills and Boon, and Toronto, Harlequin, 1989.

Farewell to Love. London, Mills and Boon, and Toronto, Harlequin, 1989.

Frozen Enchantment. London, Mills and Boon, 1989; Toronto, Harlequin, 1990.

Unfriendly Proposition. London, Mills and Boon, 1989; Toronto, Harlequin, 1990.

Passport to Happiness. London, Mills and Boon, and Toronto, Harlequin, 1990.

Hidden Heart. London, Mills and Boon, and Toronto, Harlequin, 1990.

A First Time for Everything. London, Mills and Boon, and Toronto, Harlequin, 1990.

Without Knowing Why. London, Mills and Boon, and Toronto, Harlequin, 1990.

Flight of Discovery. London, Mills and Boon, and Toronto, Harlequin, 1991.

Runaway from Love. London, Mills and Boon, 1991; Toronto, Harlequin, 1992.

His Woman. London, Mills and Boon, 1991; Toronto, Harlequin, 1992.

Bad Neighbours. London, Mills and Boon, 1991; Toronto, Harlequin, 1992.

Destined to Meet. London, Mills and Boon, 1991; Toronto, Harlequin, 1992.

Hungarian Rhapsody. London, Mills and Boon, 1992.

West of Bohemia. London, Mills and Boon, 1993.

Relative Values. London, Mills and Boon, 1993.

Italian Invader. London, Mills and Boon, 1993.

Novels as Marcia Steele

Engaging Loyalty. London, IPC Magazines Ltd, 1978.
Tangled Emotions. London, IPC Magazines Ltd, 1978.
That Special Person. London, IPC Magazines Ltd, 1978.
Equality of Love. London, IPC Magazines Ltd, 1979.

*

Jessica Steele comments:

I write about romantic love, and genuine depth of feeling. While sexual intimacy has an important place in romantic love, it is not the be-all and end-all. For instance, when a couple in love greet each other after an absence of some length they do not straight away attempt to eat each other, but alternately they hug and stand back with hearts thumping, joy overflowing, to look into their dear one's face. That is the kind of romantic love I like to write about; to bring my heroes and heroines through their various trials, tribulations, physical attraction, and often surface hatred of each other, to eventual acceptance that they love, to the declaration of that love, and to the heart stopping wonder that the all consuming feeling of love—is returned.

*   *   *

The romances published by Mills and Boon have become increasingly focused on the relationship between hero and heroine, which is a style difficult to maintain with both conviction and pace. Jessica Steele succeeds admirably with both, and she is also able to sustain the intense emotion necessary, while at the same time varying it during the course of the book. The introspection by the heroine about her own feelings is done with skill and care, never becoming maudlin or tedious.

Many of the settings are in exotic parts of the world—Egypt, Peru, Thailand, Athens, the Bahamas, and Russia, but while the feel of these places is conveyed carefully the books never turn into travelogues. The backgrounds are used sensitively to enhance the stories without intruding. Occasionally some aspect is used cleverly to create situations for physical contact, for example the snow and ice in *Frozen Enchantment* and the heroine's fear of snakes in *Runaway from Love*.

A number of the plots involve some unselfish action on another woman's behalf—giving help to a cousin in *To Stay Forever*, escaping from entanglement with her sister's lover in *Runaway from Love*, helping a friend meet her lover without her estranged husband finding out, as in *His Woman*, rescuing her sister in *Beyond her Control*, looking after a baby in *Unfriendly Alliance*, or going to another country to search for her stepsister as in *Without Knowing Why*.

Stepbrothers and sisters are frequently involved, in *Without Knowing Why*, *Fortunes of Love*, and even a wicked stepmother in *Destined to Meet*. With so many broken and second marriages today this 'step' relationship is becoming more common, and from the viewpoint of a novelist offers more situations to explore.

Sometimes the heroine in Steele's books is very young and inexperienced, but often she is an independent woman who finds herself either indebted to or in the power of the hero. Sometimes this is because of necessary help provided in strange countries, as in *Without Knowing Why*, when Domengo de Zarmoza helps Erith look for her vanished sister, or Boden McLaine rescues Delphi when she is alone in Bangkok, as in *Runaway from Love*. At other times the help is more domestic, as when Jarvis Devilliers helps Bevin by taking her into his own apartment in *Destined to Meet*, or Cale Quartermain helps Anstey look after her friend's baby in *Unfriendly Alliance*.

In some books the heroine works for the hero, a situation which can complicate the developing relationship. In *Frozen Enchantment*, for example, a young secretary speaks a little Russian and is asked to stand in for the boss's personal assistant and go with him and two engineers to Russia on a business trip. Misunderstandings occur because of incidents in the office with another would-be amorous man before they leave, and wrong conclusions about his relationship with the absent personal assistant. The protagonists travel to other parts of Russia including Siberia, thus creating occasions for them to be together, and for misunderstandings about the hero's intentions to arise. There are a lot of descriptions of Russian food, and the Siberian village houses, though disappointingly little about Moscow or St Petersburg. The trend in Mills and Boon books towards less detail about these foreign backgrounds is one I do not welcome.

Many romantic novels delay the resolution until the final page or so. Although the reader is used to the conventions and knows the hero and heroine are going to get together, there is still a satisfactory feeling of suspense. However, sometimes too abrupt a conclusion can be unsatisfying. In her later books Steele has adopted the technique of a recapitulation about the development of the love affair, which can be effective in a different way. Hero and heroine discuss the reasons for their actions which may have seemed contrary at the time, and recall the moments when, for them, they first knew they were beginning to love one another. This enables the reader to dwell on favourite moments too, and is part of the reason for Steele's great popularity.

—Marina Oliver

STEELE, Marcia. See **STEELE, Jessica.**

STEEN, Marguerite.

Pseudonyms: Lennox Dryden; Jane Nicholson. **Nationality:** British. **Born:** Marguerite Elena May Benson in Liverpool, Lancashire, 12 May 1894; took surname of foster parents. **Education:** privately, and at Moorhurst School, Lancashire, 5 years; Kendal High School; Froebel School, Sheffield, 3 years. **Career:** kindergarten teacher in Hertfordshire, 1914–18; taught dance and eurythmics, Halifax, 1919–22; toured with the Fred Terry-Julia Neilson theatrical company, 1923–26; teacher and writer after 1926; columnist, *Sunday Graphic*, London, 1940s. Close friends with the actress Ellen Terry, and the writer Hugh Walpole. **Recipient:** Fellow, Royal Society of Literature. **Died:** 4 August 1975.

ROMANCE AND HISTORICAL PUBLICATIONS

Novels (series: Flood Trilogy; Spanish Trilogy)

The Gilt Cage. London, Bles, 1926; New York, Doran, 1927.
Duel in the Dark. London, Bles, 1928; as *Dark Duel*, New York, Stokes, 1929.
The Reluctant Madonna. London, Cassell, 1929; New York, Stokes, 1930.
They That Go Down. London, Cassell, 1930; as *They That Go Down in Ships*, New York, Cosmopolitan, 1931.
Ancestors (as Lennox Dryden). London, Cassell, 1930.
When the Wind Blows. London, Cassell, 1931.
Unicorn. London, Gollancz, 1931; New York, Century, 1932.
The Wise and the Foolish Virgins. London, Gollancz, and Boston, Little Brown, 1932.
Spider. London, Gollancz, and Boston, Little Brown, 1933.
Stallion. London, Gollancz, and Boston, Little Brown, 1933.
Spanish Trilogy:
    Matador. London, Gollancz, and Boston, Little Brown, 1934.
    The One-Eyed Moon. London, Gollancz, and Boston, Little Brown, 1935.
    The Tavern. London, Gollancz, 1935; Indianapolis, Bobbs Merrill, 1936.
Return of a Heroine. London, Gollancz, and Indianapolis, Bobbs Merrill, 1936.
Who Would Have Daughters? London, Collins, 1937.
The Marriage Will Not Take Place. London, Collins, 1938.
Family Ties. London, Collins, 1939.
Flood Trilogy:
    The Sun Is My Undoing. London, Collins, and New York, Viking Press, 1941.
    Twilight on the Floods. London, Collins, and New York, Doubleday, 1949.
    Phoenix Rising. London, Collins, 1952; as *Jehovah Blues*, New York, Doubleday, 1952.
Shelter (as Jane Nicholson). London, Harrap, and New York, Viking Press, 1941.
Rose Timson. London, Collins, 1946; as *Bell Timson*, New York, Doubleday, 1946.
Granada Window. London, Falcon Press, 1949.
The Swan. London, Hart Davis, 1951; Boston, Houghton Mifflin, 1953.
Anna Fitzalan. London, Collins, and New York, Doubleday, 1953.
Bulls of Parral. London, Collins, and New York, Doubleday, 1954.
The Unquiet Spirit. London, Collins, 1955; New York, Doubleday, 1956.
The Tower. London, Collins, 1959; New York, Doubleday, 1960.
The Woman in the Back Seat. London, Collins, and New York, Doubleday, 1959.
A Candle in the Sun. London, Longman, and New York, Doubleday, 1964.

Short Stories

A Kind of Insolence and Other Stories. London, Collins, 1940.

OTHER PUBLICATIONS

Plays

Oakfields Plays, Including the Inglemere Christmas Play (for children). London, Nicholson and Watson, 1932.
Peepshow (for children). London, Nicholson and Watson, 1933.
Matador, with Matheson Lang, adaptation of the novel by Steen (produced Edinburgh, 1937).
French for Love, with Derek Patmore (produced London, 1939). London, Collins, 1940.
The Grand Manner (produced Manchester, 1942).

Screenplays: *The Man from Morocco*, with others, 1945; *Beware of Pity*, with W.P. Lipscomb and Elizabeth Baron, 1946.

Other

Hugh Walpole: A Study. London, Nicholson and Watson, and New York, Doubleday, 1933.
The Lost One: A Biography of Mary—Perdita—Robinson. London, Methuen, 1933.
William Nicholson. London, Collins, 1943.
Little White King (on cats). London, Joseph, and Cleveland, World, 1956.
A Pride of Terrys: A Family Saga. London, Longman, 1962; Westport, Connecticut, Greenwood Press, 1978.
Looking Glass: An Autobiography. London, Longman, 1966.
Pier Glass: More Autobiography. London, Longman, 1968.

*   *   *

Born in Liverpool in 1894, Marguerite Steen was persuaded to take up writing by her friends, among them the author Hugh Walpole and the famous actress Ellen Terry. Her novels reflect her extensive travelling, with Bristol, Spain, and the American deep south providing a focus for some of her finest work. Bristol is the setting of her first significant book, *They That Go Down*, which describes the adventures of the lively Jane Carradus and her press-ganged lover during the period of Trafalgar. The style is strong—if elaborate in description—and characters and period strikingly portrayed. Steen's early work tends to the gothic, fixing on fierce extremes of human nature in remote situations. The headstrong Sanchia Mullyon of *When the Wind Blows* is a typical example. So too is Jim Devoke, the womanizing 'hero' of *Stallion*, a more impressive novel where a sensual violence pervades the pages. Jim's infidelities—a parallel to the stud services of the prize shire stallion he leads from one farm to the next—lead him to the satanic Tamar, whose love takes a savage toll when he rejects her at last. The quiet rural setting and stable family background serve to throw the characters into sharper relief.

Steen's mature fiction shows a change of emphasis, as well as a heightening of perception. The style is more direct and forceful, shorn of the earlier description. There is too a greater reliance on contemporary themes. Without a doubt her most important work is to be found in the 'Spanish' novels, and the trilogy based on the fortunes of the Flood family of Bristol. In the former, her knowledge of Spain and identification with its tradition—embodied in the ritual of the bullfight—are used to great effect. *Matador*, with its story of the retired torero living vicariously through his sons, is memorable as a study of the Spanish character in action. The theme of the bullfight was subsequently pursued, with success, in *Bulls of Parral*. The

'Flood Trilogy' follows the family of Bristol slavers to success and opulence as legitimate traders and squires, and examines the conflict of ideals raised by their inextricable involvement with Africa and black Africans. *The Sun Is My Undoing*, a bestseller and Book Society Choice, remains the best known, but its sequel, *Twilight on the Floods*, is equally good, switching adroitly from Victorian Bristol to West Africa at the time of the Ashantie war. *Phoenix Rising*, the final volume of the trilogy, is less satisfying, perhaps due to its being heavily cut prior to publication. Nevertheless, the trilogy as a whole deserves to be ranked with Steen's finest achievements.

Though less significant than the Spanish and Flood trilogies, a number of the contemporary novels are well worth consideration. *Family Ties* is an excellent study of personal lives in crisis in the publishing world, and both *Anna Fitzalan* and *Rose Timson*—the latter of a story of a mother's obsessive love for her daughters—are outstanding analyses of female character. Though not highly regarded by the author, Steen's last novel, *A Candle in the Sun*, is a clear and effective presentation of marital breakdown and its effects on a growing child.

—Geoffrey Sadler

———

STEINBECK, John (Ernst).
Nationality: American. **Born:** Salinas, California, 27 February 1902. **Education:** Salinas High School, graduated 1919; Stanford University, California, intermittently 1919–25. **Relations:** married 1) Carol Henning in 1930 (divorced 1942); 2) Gwyn Conger (i.e. the actress Gwen Verdon) in 1943 (divorced 1948), two sons; 3) Elaine Scott in 1950. **Career:** worked at various jobs, including reporter for New York *American*, apprentice hodcarrier, apprentice painter, chemist, caretaker of an estate at Lake Tahoe, California, surveyor, and fruit picker, 1925–35; full-time writer from 1935; settled in Monterey, California, then New York City; special writer for the United States Army Air Force during World War II; correspondent in Europe, New York *Herald Tribune*, 1943. **Recipient:** New York Drama Critics circle award, 1938; Pulitzer prize, 1940; King Haakon Liberty Cross (Norway), 1946; O. Henry award, 1956; Nobel prize for literature, 1962; Presidential medal of freedom, 1964; United States medal of freedom, 1964. **Member:** American Academy, 1939. **Died:** 20 December 1968.

ROMANCE AND HISTORICAL PUBLICATIONS

Novels

Cup of Gold: A Life of Henry Morgan, Buccaneer, with Occasional Reference to History. New York, McBride, 1929; London, Heinemann, 1937.
The Acts of King Arthur and His Noble Knights, from the Winchester Manuscripts of Malory and Other Sources, edited by Chase Horton. New York, Farrar Straus, and London, Heinemann, 1976.

OTHER PUBLICATIONS

Novels

The Pastures of Heaven. New York, Brewer Warren and Putnam, 1932; London, Philip Allan, 1933.
To a God Unknown. New York, Ballou, 1933; London, Heinemann, 1935.
Tortilla Flat. New York, Corvici Friede, and London, Heinemann, 1935.

In Dubious Battle. New York, Covici Friede, and London, Heinemann, 1936.

Of Mice and Men. New York, Covici Friede, and London, Heinemann, 1937.

The Grapes of Wrath. New York, Viking Press, and London, Heinemann, 1939; edited by Peter Lisca, New York, Viking Press, 1972.

The Moon Is Down. New York, Viking Press, and London, Heinemann, 1942.

Cannery Row. New York, Viking Press, and London, Heinemann, 1945.

The Wayward Bus. New York, Viking Press, and London, Heinemann, 1947.

The Pearl. New York, Viking Press, 1947; London, Heinemann, 1948.

Burning Bright: A Play in Story Form. New York, Viking Press, 1950; London, Heinemann, 1951.

East of Eden. New York, Viking Press, and London, Heinemann, 1952.

Sweet Thursday. New York, Viking Press, and London, Heinemann, 1954.

The Short Reign of Pippin IV: A Fabrication. New York, Viking Press, and London, Heinemann, 1957.

The Winter of Our Discontent. New York, Viking Press, and London, Heinemann, 1961.

Short Stories

Saint Katy the Virgin. New York, Covici Friede, 1936.

The Red Pony. New York, Covici Friede, 1937; London, Heinemann, 1949.

The Long Valley. New York, Viking Press, 1938; London, Heinemann, 1939.

The Short Novels. New York, Viking Press, 1953; London, Heinemann, 1954.

Plays

Of Mice and Men: A Play in Three Acts, with George S. Kaufman, adaptation of Steinbeck's novel (produced San Francisco and New York, 1937). New York, Covici Friede, 1937.

The Forgotten Village (screenplay). New York, Viking Press, 1941.

The Moon Is Down: A Play in Two Parts, adaptation of Steinbeck's novel (produced New York, 1942; London, 1943). New York, Dramatists Play Service, 1942; London, English Theatre Guild, 1943.

A Medal for Benny, with Jack Wagner and Frank Butler, in *Best Film Plays 1945*, edited by John Gassner and Dudley Nichols. New York, Crown, 1946.

Burning Bright: A Play in Three Acts, adaptation of Steinbeck's novel (produced New York, 1950). New York, Dramatists Play Service, 1951.

Viva Zapata! The Original Screenplay, edited by Robert E. Morsberger. New York, Viking Press, 1975.

Screenplays: *The Forgotten Village* (documentary), 1941; *Lifeboat*, with Jo Swerling, 1944; *A Medal for Benny*, with Jack Wagner and Frank Butler, 1945; *La Perla (The Pearl)*, with Jack Wagner and Emilio Fernandez, 1946; *The Red Pony*, 1949; *Viva Zapata!*, 1952.

Other

Their Blood Is Strong. San Francisco, Lubin Society of California, 1938.

John Steinbeck Replies (letter). New York, Friends of Democracy, 1940.

Sea of Cortez: A Leisurely Journal of Travel and Research, with Edward F. Ricketts. New York, Viking Press, 1941.

Bombs Away: The Story of a Bomber Team. New York, Viking Press, 1942.

The Viking Portable Library Steinbeck, edited by Pascal Covici. New York, Viking Press, 1943; abridged edition, as *The Steinbeck Pocket Book*, New York, Pocket Books, 1943; revised edition, as *The Portable Steinbeck*, Viking Press, 1946, 1958; revised edition, edited by Pascal Covici, Jr, Viking Press, 1971; London, Penguin, 1976; 1946 edition published as *The Indispensable Steinbeck*, New York, Book Society, 1950, and as *The Steinbeck Omnibus*, London, Heinemann, 1951.

The First Watch (letter). Los Angeles, Ward Ritchie Press, 1947.

Vanderbilt Clinic. New York, Presbyterian Hospital, 1947.

A Russian Journal, photographs by Robert Capa. New York, Viking Press, 1948; London, Heinemann, 1949.

The Log from the Sea of Cortez. New York, Viking Press, 1951; London, Heinemann, 1958.

Once There Was a War. New York, Viking Press, 1958; London, Heinemann, 1959.

Travels with Charley: In Search of America. New York, Viking Press, and London, Heinemann, 1962.

Speech Accepting the Nobel Prize for Literature . . . . New York, Viking Press, 1962(?).

Letters to Alicia. New York, Viking Press, 1965.

America and Americans. New York, Viking Press, and London, Heinemann, 1966.

Journal of a Novel: The East of Eden Letters. New York, Viking Press, 1969; London, Heinemann, 1970.

Steinbeck: A Life in Letters, edited by Elaine Steinbeck and Robert Wallsten. New York, Viking Press, and London, Heinemann, 1975.

Letters to Elizabeth: A Selection of Letters from John Steinbeck to Elizabeth Otis, edited by Florian J. Shasky and Susan F. Riggs. San Fransisco, Book Club of California, 1978.

Conversations with John Steinbeck, edited by Thomas Fensch. Jackson, University Press of Mississippi, 1988.

Working Days: The Journals of The Grapes of Wrath, edited by Robert DeMott. New York, Viking, 1989.

*

Film Adaptations: *Of Mice and Men*, 1939, 1992; *Tortilla Flat*, 1942; *The Moon Is Down*, 1943; *The Pearl*, 1948; *The Red Pony*, 1949, 1973; *East of Eden*, 1954, 1980; *The Wayward Bus*, 1957; *Cannery Row*, 1982; *The Winter of Our Discontent*, 1983.

Bibliography: *A New Steinbeck Bibliography 1929–1971* and *1971–1981* by Tetsumaro Hayashi, Metuchen, New Jersey, Scarecrow Press, 2 vols, 1973–83; *John Steinbeck: A Bibliographical Catalogue of the Adrian H. Goldstone Collection* by Adrian H. Goldstone and John R. Payne, Austin, University of Texas Humanities Research Center, 1974; *Steinbeck Bibliographies: An Annotated Guide* by Robert B. Harmon, Metuchen, New Jersey, Scarecrow Press, 1987.

Critical Studies (selection): *The Novels of John Steinbeck: A First Critical Study* by Harry T. Moore, Chicago, Normandie House, 1939, as *John Steinbeck and His Novels*, London, Heinemann, 1939; *Steinbeck and His Critics: A Record of Twenty-Five Years* edited by E.W. Tedlock, Jr, and C.V. Wicker, Albuquerque, University of New Mexico Press, 1957; *The Wide World of John Steinbeck*, New Brunswick, New Jersey, Rutgers University Press, 1958, and *Steinbeck, Nature, and Myth*, New York, Crowell, 1978, both by Peter Lisca; *John Steinbeck* by Warren French, New York, Twayne,

1961, revised edition, 1975; *John Steinbeck* by F.W. Watt, New York, Grove Press, and Edinburgh, Oliver and Boyd, 1962; *John Steinbeck: An Introduction and Interpretation* by Joseph Fontenrose, New York, Barnes and Noble, 1964; Steinbeck Monograph series, Muncie, Indiana, Ball State University English Department, from 1972, and *A Study Guide to John Steinbeck: A Handbook to His Major Works*, Metuchen, New Jersey, Scarecrow Press, 2 vols, 1974–79, both edited by Tetsumaro Hayashi, and *John Steinbeck: The Years of Greatness 1936–39* by Hayashi, Tuscaloosa, University of Alabama Press, 1993; *Steinbeck: A Collection of Critical Essays* edited by Robert Murray Davis, Englewood Cliffs, New Jersey, Prentice Hall, 1972; *John Steinbeck and Edward F. Ricketts: The Shaping of a Novelist* by Richard Astro, Minneapolis, University of Minnesota Press, 1973; *The Novels of John Steinbeck: A Critical Study* by Howard Levant, Columbia, University of Missouri Press, 1974; *John Steinbeck: The Errant Knight: An Intimate Biography of His California Years* by Nelson Valjean, San Francisco, Chronicle Books, 1975; *Steinbeck's Literary Achievement* by Roy Simmonds, Muncie, Indiana, Bull State University Press, 1976; *The Intricate Music: A Biography of John Steinbeck* by Thomas Kiernan, Boston, Little Brown, 1979; *John Steinbeck* by Paul McCarthy, New York, Ungar, 1980; *The True Adventures of John Steinbeck, Writer: A Biography* by Jackson J. Benson, New York, Viking, and London, Heinemann, 1984; *John Steinbeck: The California Years* by Brian St Pierre, San Francisco, Chronicle Books, 1984; *John Steinbeck's Re-vision of America* by Louis Owens, Athens, University of Georgia Press, 1985; *John Steinbeck's Fiction: The Aesthetics of the Road Taken*, Norman, University of Oklahoma Press, 1986, and *The Dramatic Landscape of John Steinbeck's Short Stories*, Norman, University of Oklahoma Press, 1990, both by John H. Timmerman; *Beyond the Red Pony: A Reader's Companion to Steinbeck's Complete Short Stories* by R.S. Hughes, Metuchen, New Jersey, Scarecrow Press, 1987; *Of Mice and Men: Guide* by John Mahoney and Stewart Martin, London, Letts, 1987; *Staging Steinbeck: Dramatising The Grapes of Wrath* by Peter Whitebrook, London, Cassell, 1988; *Looking for Steinbeck's Ghosts* by Jackson J. Benson, Norman, University of Oklahoma, 1988; *The Harvest Gypsies: On the Road to the Grapes of Wrath*, edited by Robert De Mott, Berkeley, California, Heyday, 1988, London, Penguin, 1989; *New Essays on the Grapes of Wrath* edited by David Wyatt, New York, Cambridge University Press, 1990; *The Short Novels of John Steinbeck: Critical Essays* edited by Jackson J. Benson, Durham, North Carolina, Duke University Press, 1990; *John Steinbeck: A Biography* by Jay Parini, London, Heinemann, 1994.

*   *   *

John Steinbeck's chief claim to fame is as a writer of the realist school, and as a chronicler of the contemporary American scene of the 1920s and 1930s. He did, however, write two historical novels. These two works stand at the beginning and the end of a distinguished literary career: *Cup of Gold*, loosely based on the life of the 17th-century buccaneer Henry Morgan, was published in 1929, and *The Acts of King Arthur and His Noble Knights*, a modern version of Malory's *Le Morte D'Arthur*, was published posthumously in an unfinished state in 1976.

Cup of Gold is very much an apprentice work. Sub-titled *A Life of Henry Morgan, Buccaneer, with Occasional Reference to History*, it is a hybrid production which arguably not only fails in many respects as fictionalized history, but also fails as an excursion into the fabular genre. Steinbeck's lifelong fascination with Arthurian legend is early established in the book with the introduction of the old Welsh seer, Merlin, to whom the young Henry goes to seek advice before embarking on his adventures in the West Indies. The Arthurian theme is perpetuated when Morgan's unformulated longings finally channel themselves into a search for his own version of the Holy Grail. This takes the form of an obsessive ambition to capture the fabulous city of Panama (the 'Cup of Gold' of the book's title), and to possess the legendary beauty, La Santa Roja. Once having achieved his goal, the city of Panama conquered and pillaged, Morgan experiences the inevitable destruction of his dreams. He is coldly rejected and humiliated by La Santa Roja, and, although he is subsequently knighted by his King and created Governor of Jamaica, he lives out his last days a broken and disillusioned man. On his deathbed, he inquires after Merlin, and, as if in confirmation of the ethereal quality of his past ambitions and desires, he is told that the old seer is 'herding dreams' in Avalon. Despite its shortcomings—its structural imbalance and its somewhat cardboard characters—*Cup of Gold* contains some vivid writing, heavily influenced by Donn Byrne and James Branch Cabell, and some moments of pleasing dry humour. As a first novel, it is certainly better than most. Many of the themes which were to be developed in Steinbeck's later and more accomplished fiction are already evident here.

Although uncompleted at the time of his death, *The Acts of King Arthur and His Noble Knights* was not, in fact, the last piece of writing Steinbeck worked on. He began his translation of Malory's masterpiece in New York during the summer of 1958, after having devoted several years of research to the subject, and continued to work on it through most of the following year while living in a cottage in Bruton, Somerset, close by Cadbury Hill, Glastonbury and the Vale of Avalon. He abandoned the work when he returned home to New York at the end of 1959. By then, he had translated only three of the first four of Malory's romances, having omitted the third romance, 'The Tale of the Noble King Arthur That Was Emperor Himself Through Dignity of His Hands', from his manuscript. He had a typescript of something over 500 pages, but he had still four more of Malory's romances, comprising something like two-thirds of the total work, to translate. Although to the end of his life he continued to plan to finish the book, he was clearly and understandably deterred by the enormity of the task and by the pressing need to produce books of a more commercial nature. The first five sections of *The Acts of King Arthur* are written in a beautifully controlled, economic style which closely follows Malory's text. Beginning with the story of the Triple Quest, however, Steinbeck's imagination takes wing, and he proceeds to open up the sparse narrative to create a detailed and living tapestry of those ancient days. In the Sir Lancelot story, Steinbeck's creativity soars to even greater heights, and he introduces into the narrative the sights and the sounds of the West Country he had explored and come to love while living in Bruton. *The Acts of King Arthur* could surely have been Steinbeck's *magnum opus*, and even in its unfinished state (the published text is further truncated by the omission of Steinbeck's version of the fourth of Malory's romances, 'The Tale of Sir Gareth of Orkney') it is impressive in its impeccable fusion of prose style, narrative, and scholarship. It is a literary tragedy of major proportions that Steinbeck never did complete the project.

—Roy S. Simmonds

STERN, G(ladys) B(ronwyn).
Nationality: British. **Born:** 17 June 1890. **Education:** Notting Hill High School, London. **Relations:** married Geoffrey Lisle Holdsworth in 1919 (divorced). **Died:** 19 September 1973.

<small>ROMANCE AND HISTORICAL PUBLICATIONS</small>

Novels (series: Matriarch)

See-Saw. London, Hutchinson, 1914.

Two and Threes. London, Nisbet, 1916.
Grand-Chain. London, Nisbet, 1917.
A Marrying Man. London, Nisbet, 1918.
Children of No Man's Land. London, Duckworth, 1919; as *Debatable Ground*, New York, Knopf, 1921.
Larry Munro. London, Chapman and Hall, 1920; as *The China Shop*, New York, Knopf, 1921.
The Room. London, Chapman and Hall, and New York, Knopf, 1922.
The Back Seat. London, Chapman and Hall, and New York, Knopf, 1923.
Tents of Israel (Matriarch). London, Chapman and Hall, 1924; as *The Matriarch: A Chronicle*, New York, Knopf, 1925; revised edition, Knopf, 1936; London, Virago Press, 1987.
Thunderstorm. London, Chapman and Hall, and New York, Knopf, 1925.
A Deputy Was King (Matriarch). London, Chapman and Hall, and New York, Knopf, 1926.
The Dark Gentleman. London, Chapman and Hall, and New York, Knopf, 1927.
Debonair: The Story of Persephone. London, Chapman and Hall, and New York, Knopf, 1928.
Modesta. New York, Knopf, 1929.
Petruchia. London, Chapman and Hall, 1929.
Mosaic (Matriarch). London, Chapman and Hall, and New York, Knopf, 1930.
Pantomime. London, Hutchinson, 1931.
The Shortest Night. London, Heinemann, and New York, Knopf, 1931.
Long-Lost Father. London, Benn, 1932; New York, Knopf, 1933.
The Rakonitz Chronicles. London, Chapman and Hall, 1932.
Little Red Horses. London, Heinemann, 1932; as *The Rueful Mating*, New York, Knopf, 1933.
The Augs. London, Heinemann, 1933; as *Summer's Play: An Exaggeration*, New York, Knopf, 1934.
Shining and Free: A Day in the Life of a Matriarch (Matriarch). London, Heinemann, and New York, Knopf, 1935.
Oleander River. London, Cassell, and New York, Macmillan, 1937.
The Ugly Dachshund. London, Cassell, and New York, Macmillan, 1938.
The Woman in the Hall. London, Cassell, and New York, Macmillan, 1939.
A Lion in the Garden. London, Cassell, and New York, Knopf, 1940.
The Young Matriarch (Matriarch). London, Cassell, and New York, Macmillan, 1942.
Trumpet Voluntary. London, Cassell, and New York, Macmillan, 1944.
The Reasonable Shores. London, Cassell, and New York, Macmillan, 1946.
No Son of Mine. London, Cassell, and New York, Macmillan, 1948.
A Duck to Water. London, Cassell, and New York, Macmillan, 1949.
Ten Days of Christmas. London, Collins, 1950.
The Donkey Shoe. London, Collins, and New York, Macmillan, 1952.
Johnny Forsaken. London, Collins, and New York, Macmillan, 1954.
For All We Know. London, Collins, and New York, Macmillan, 1956.
Seventy Times Seven. London, Collins, and New York, Macmillan, 1957.
Unless I Marry. London, Collins, and New York, Macmillan, 1959.
Bernadette. Edinburgh, Nelson, 1960.
One Is Only Human. Chicago, Regnery, 1960.
Credit Title. Edinburgh, Nelson, 1961.

Dolphin Cottage. London, Collins, 1962.
Promise Not to Tell. London, Collins, 1964.

Short Stories

Smoke Rings. London, Chapman and Hall, 1923; New York, Knopf, 1924.
Jack O'Manory. London, Chapman and Hall, 1927.
The Slower Judas. New York, Knopf, 1929.
Pelican Walking. London, Heinemann, 1934.
Long Short Story. London, Cassell, 1939.
Dogs in an Omnibus. London, Cassell, 1942.

OTHER PUBLICATIONS

Plays

A Dance at Dawn (produced London, 1909).
For One Night Only (produced London, 1911).
For Husbands Only, with Mrs D.F.C. Harding (produced London, 1920).
The Happy Medler, with Geoffrey Holdsworth. London, Ward Lock, 1926.
The Matriarch, adaptation of her novel *Tents of Israel* (produced London, 1929; New York, 1930). London, French, 1931.
Debonair, with Frank Vosper, adaptation of the novel by Stern (produced London, 1930).
Gala Night at The Willows, with Rupert Croft-Cooke. London, Deane, 1950.
Raffle for a Bedspread. London, Methuen, 1953.

Other

Bouquet: Travels in the Wine-Producing Regions. London, Chapman and Hall, and New York, Knopf, 1927.
Monogram (memoirs). London, Chapman and Hall, and New York, Knopf, 1936.
Another Part of the Forest (autobiography). London, Cassell, and New York, Macmillan, 1941.
Talking of Jane Austen, with Sheila Kaye Smith. London, Cassell, 1943; as *Speaking of Jane Austen*, New York, Harper, 1944.
Benefits Forgot (memoirs). London, Cassell, and New York, Macmillan, 1949.
More about Jane Austen, with Sheila Kaye Smith. New York, Harper, 1949; as *More Talk of Jane Austen*, London, Cassell, 1950.
Robert Louis Stevenson (biography). London, Longman, 1952.
A Name to Conjure With (autobiography). London, Collins, and New York, Macmillan, 1953.
All in Good Time (autobiography). New York, Sheed and Ward, 1954.
He Wrote Treasure Island: The Story of Robert Louis Stevenson. London, Heinemann, 1954; as *Robert Louis Stevenson: The Man Who Wrote Treasure Island*, New York, Macmillan, 1954.
The Way It Worked Out (autobiography). New York, Sheed and Ward, 1956.
And Did He Stop to Speak to You? London, Coram, 1957; Chicago, Regnery, 1958.
The Patience of a Saint; or, Example Is Better than Precept. London, Coram, 1958.
The Personality of Jesus (for children). New York, Doubleday, 1961.

*

Film Adaptations: *Long Lost Father*, 1934; *The Woman in the Hall*, 1947; *The Ugly Dachshund*, 1965.

* * *

The Times obituary of G.B. Stern acknowledged her as 'fluent, animated and accomplished', but suggested that she was someone whose early talent for the serio-comic gave promise of an excellence which was sadly not realized. It is often the case that writers who have varied and lengthy careers (Stern wrote fiction, plays, poems, biography, and even travel books, and her publication span was 50 years) are damned with faint praise as if productivity is somehow incompatible with talent. It is refreshing to see a recent resurgence of interest in Stern's work and her subsequent reassessment as a feminist writer.

All writers draw upon their own experiences of life whether consciously or not. In G.B. Stern's novels it is hard to separate fact from fiction, so closely does she reproduce incidents which took place within her own circle of family and friends, often with little attempt at disguise. Nuggets from this goldmine are used over and over again. For example, the list of her mother's idiosyncratic and largely incomprehensible rules for daily health and safety detailed in her memoir *Another Part of the Forest* ('Never lean back in a railway carriage, because how are you to know', 'Never eat greensweets', 'Never eat water-cress, because, you see, there may be cows!') appears on several fictional occasions, most notably in *Debonair* which offers a very similar mother-daughter relationship. The Rakonitz clan, which provides the backbone for Stern's lengthy chronicle of cosmopolitan Jewish life, the 'Matriarch' series (*Tents of Israel*, *A Deputy Was King*, *Mosaic*, *Shining and Free*, *The Young Matriarch*), is based on her own family and their history and even shares their name. The Matriarch herself is a half-factual, half-fictional portrait of Stern's great-aunt, Anastasia Schwabacher.

It is hardly surprising that Stern was devoted to Jane Austen's work. They share something of the same talent for observing human nature and wryly noting its foibles. Stern was interested in ordinary people, but seemed to prefer oddballs who allowed her to exercise her sense of humour, for example, the engagingly eccentric uncles in *Tents of Israel*. She observed her subjects closely, but, as several reviewers have noticed, she did not examine motivation too deeply, offering 'hows' rather than 'whys'. She enjoyed working with a large cast of characters, most notably in the 'Matriarch' series which is her homage to John Galsworthy's *Forsyte Saga*. Unlike Galsworthy, however, she has some trouble with consistency over a series of books and characters undergo changes of relationship from one story to the next.

Stern's current reputation centres on her Matriarch books which have been hailed as feminist in tone, stressing as they do, the importance of strong women to hold a family together. Anastasia, Toni and Berthe are all women who make their way in life without men to help them and it is interesting to note how often in the Rakonitz chronicles that male characters turn out to be broken reeds, not to be depended upon. For example, in *Tents of Israel*, Toni vows to settle a family debt of six hundred pounds. The male members of the clan agree in principle, but are slightly amused by her insistence that honour demands the money must be paid; they leave her to get on with her task which she eventually achieves through her own efforts after ten years. Admittedly the final shortfall in her savings is made up by a male relative's windfall, but only after Toni has cleverly worked upon him to extract the cash. The attitude of Stern women towards their menfolk is one of slightly amused tolerance and, although a husband is acknowledged to be socially necessary, once acquired he doesn't play a large part in their lives. Stern's own brief and unsuccessful venture into matrimony may have contributed to her rather shadowy portrayal of male characters; they certainly lack the vitality and warmth of her women.

Stern's non-Rakonitz stories are fluent and readable, but lively and often comic in tone, which has led to accusations of lack of depth. In many cases they have not stood the test of time. Stern acknowledges that the whimsy of her first books (for example, *Grand-Chain*, *A Marrying Man*) owes something to W.J. Locke, an author she greatly admired. *Debonair* has a lightness of touch and humour, but the lifestyle it portrays—the expatriate community in Italy between the wars—is one long since vanished and difficult to identify as are the social taboos of London at the same period. The heroine, Loveday (Stern is fond of whimsical names for her heroines—*Little Red Horses* features Halcyon), depends on her escorts' generosity with taxi fares and money for the powder room in order to live (foreshadowing Capote's Holly Golightly). Her central relationship is not with Charles, the wealthy lawyer, who ends up marrying her, but with her widowed mother, known as Lamb-bird, whose main aim for her child is to see her safely settled. Dorothy Parker reviewed the story memorably ('"Debonair" may be her lover's word for her, but "God-awful" will ever be her nickname with me') and also identified a quality which runs through all of Stern's writing; her ability to write well about people she disliked, but her total lack of success in presenting characters whom she likes and wants her reader to like. It is revealing that Stern herself acknowledged that her greatest success, the Matriarch, was based on a person to whom she was not deeply attached because of her despotic nature.

An interesting later experiment in Stern's career is a different blending of fact and fiction in *No Son of Mine*, about a man who tries to cash in on his likeness to Robert Louis Stevenson by claiming to be his son.

Stern's books mirror particular whims. Her fondness for walking sticks, dogs, travel, wine, food, music, and good company shines through all her work. And in many ways this is Stern's most attractive quality for readers.

—Frances Whitehead

———

STERN, Stuart. See **STIRLING, Jessica.**

———

STEVENS, Blaine. See **HORNER, Lance, Kyle ONSTOTT, and Ashley CARTER.**

———

STEVENS, Robert Tyler. See **STAPLES, Mary Jane.**

———

STEVENS, Tricia. See **BLAKE, Stephanie**

———

STEVENSON, Anne.
Pseudonym for Felicity Avery. **Nationality:** American. **Address:** c/o Harold Ober Associates Ltd, 425 Madison Avenue, New York, New York 10017, USA.

ROMANCE AND HISTORICAL PUBLICATIONS

Novels

Ralph Dacre. New York, Walker, and London, Collins, 1967.
Flash of Splendour. London, Collins, 1968.
A Relative Stranger. New York, Putnam, and London, Collins, 1970.

A Game of Statues. New York, Putnam, and London, Collins, 1972.

The French Inheritance. New York, Putnam, and London, Collins, 1974.

Coil of Serpents. New York, Putnam, and London, Collins, 1977.

Mask of Treason. New York, Putnam, 1979; Loughton, Essex, Piatkus, 1981.

Turkish Rondo. New York, Morrow, and Loughton, Essex, Piatkus, 1981.

*   *   *

Anne Stevenson's special gift as a writer of romantic suspense is her ability to place ordinary people in extraordinary, even improbable situations and yet to retain a strong sense of reality. The heroines of her novels are neither so glamorous and sophisticated nor so young and beautiful that the average reader cannot sympathize or identify with them. At the same time these women, from shop assistant to operatic costume designer, are not insipid marionettes wandering heedlessly into dangerous situations. Instead each deals competently with the challenges that she faces without relinquishing control of her life to the men who appear to offer protection and love. In fact, the crises weathered by these women serve to strengthen them.

It is notable that one of Stevenson's novels, *The French Inheritance*, features a hero rather than a heroine, with two female characters competing for his affections. This is a very neat reversal of the usual gothic pattern. The hero is as believable and as deftly drawn as all of Stevenson's creations. If a weakness can be found in any of these works it might be the occasionally jarring note in characterization. As an example, Ben, the child in *A Game of Statues*, seems at times both younger and older than his stated age of eight. Some of the other less-central characters, like Mr Rizzio in *Coil of Serpents*, lean close to caricature. These faintly false notes are only jarring in retrospect, however, since all the characters in the novels are woven so firmly into compelling plots that the reader is carried along.

Stevenson has a brisk and straightforward prose style which avoids the florid descriptive passages that often mark this genre. She also has a remarkably accurate ear for dialogue that renders such description unnecessary.

The plots of these relatively long novels are reminiscent of the work of both Mary Stewart and Helen MacInnes, although they are in no way derivative. The resolutions of the plots are neither obvious nor entirely unexpected, although several of the books feature a clever last-minute twist at the moment that a less confident writer might conclude the tale. No loose end ever remains dangling; often a minor character or scene from an early chapter is pivotal.

The romance element is invariably handled with delicacy and restraint. Romance is, of course, integral to novels of this kind, but these stories stand on their own as adventures. As wellcrafted contemporary works on suspense these books are likely to appeal to readers of gothics and to those ordinarily put off by the gothic approach.

—Susan Quinn Berneis

———

STEVENSON, D(orothy) E(mily).
Nationality: British. **Born:** Edinburgh, Scotland, in 1892. **Education:** privately in England and France. **Relations:** married James Reid Peploe in 1916; two sons and one daughter. **Died:** 30 December 1973.

ROMANCE AND HISTORICAL PUBLICATIONS

Novels (series: Mrs Tim; Miss Buncle)

Peter West. London, Chambers, 1923.

Mrs Tim of the Regiment (published anonymously). London, Cape, 1932; as *Mrs Tim Christie*, New York, Holt Rinehart, 1973.

Miss Buncle's Book. London, Jenkins, 1934; New York, Farrar and Rinehart, 1937.

Golden Days. London, Jenkins, 1934.

Divorced from Reality. London, Jenkins, 1935; as *Miss Dean's Dilemma*, New York, Farrar and Rinehart, 1938; as *The Young Clementina*, London, Collins, and New York, Holt Rinehart, 1970.

Miss Buncle, Married. London, Jenkins, 1936; New York, Farrar and Rinehart, 1937.

Smouldering Fire. London, Jenkins, 1936; New York, Farrar and Rinehart, 1938.

The Empty World: A Romance of the Future. London, Jenkins, 1936; as *A World in Spell*, New York, Farrar and Rinehart, 1939.

The Story of Rosabelle Shaw. London, Chambers, 1937; New York, Farrar and Rinehart, 1939; as *Rosabelle Shaw*, London, Collins, 1967.

Miss Bun, The Baker's Daughter. London, Collins, 1938; as *The Baker's Daughter*, New York, Farrar and Rinehart, 1938.

Green Money. London, Collins, and New York, Farrar and Rinehart, 1939.

The English Air. London, Collins, and New York, Farrar and Rinehart, 1940.

Rochester's Wife. London, Collins, and New York, Farrar and Rinehart, 1940.

Spring Magic. New York, Farrar and Rinehart, 1941; London, Collins, 1942.

Mrs Tim Carries On. London, Collins, and New York, Farrar and Rinehart, 1941.

Mrs Tim (omnibus). London, Collins, 1941.

Crooked Adam. New York, Farrar and Rinehart, 1942; London, Collins, 1969.

Celia's House. London, Collins, and New York, Farrar and Rinehart, 1943.

The Two Mrs Abbotts. London, Collins, and New York, Farrar and Rinehart, 1943.

Listening Valley. London, Collins, and New York, Farrar and Rinehart, 1944.

The Four Graces. London, Collins, and New York, Rinehart, 1946.

Kate Hardy. London, Collins, and New York, Rinehart, 1947.

Mrs Tim Gets a Job. London, Collins, and New York, Rinehart, 1947.

Young Mrs Savage. London, Collins, 1948; New York, Rinehart, 1949.

Trilogy:

Vittoria Cottage. London, Collins, and New York, Rinehart, 1949.

Music in the Hills. London, Collins, and New York, Rinehart, 1950.

Winter and Rough Weather. London, Collins, 1951; as *Shoulder the Sky*, New York, Rinehart, 1951.

Mrs Tim Flies Home. London, Collins, and New York, Rinehart, 1952.

Five Windows. London, Collins, and New York, Rinehart, 1953.

Charlotte Fairlie. London, Collins, 1954; as *Blow the Wind Southerly*, New York, Rinehart, 1954.

Amberwell. London, Collins, and New York, Rinehart, 1955.

Summerhills. London, Collins, and New York, Rinehart, 1956.

The Tall Stranger. London, Collins, and New York, Rinehart, 1957.

Anna and Her Daughters. London, Collins, and New York, Rinehart, 1958.
Still Glides the Stream. London, Collins, and New York, Rinehart, 1959.
The Musgraves. London, Collins, and New York, Holt Rinehart, 1960.
Bel Lamington. London, Collins, and New York, Holt Rinehart, 1961.
Fletchers End. London, Collins, and New York, Holt Rinehart, 1962.
The Blue Sapphire. London, Collins, and New York, Holt Rinehart, 1963.
Miss Buncle (omnibus). New York, Holt Rinehart, 1964.
Katherine Wentworth. London, Collins, and New York, Holt Rinehart, 1964.
Katherine's Marriage. London, Collins, 1965; as *The Marriage of Katherine*, New York, Holt Rinehart, 1965.
The House on the Cliff. London, Collins, and New York, Holt Rinehart, 1966.
Sarah Morris Remembers. London, Collins, and New York, Holt Rinehart, 1967.
Sarah's Cottage. London, Collins, and New York, Holt Rinehart, 1968.
Gerald and Elizabeth. London, Collins, and New York, Holt Rinehart, 1969.
The House of the Deer. London, Collins, 1970; New York, Holt Rinehart, 1971.

OTHER PUBLICATIONS

Poetry

Meadow-Flowers. London, Macdonald, 1915.
The Starry Mantle: Poems. London, Stockwell, 1926.

Other (for children)

Alister and Co. New York, Farrar and Rinehart, 1940.
It's Nice to Be Me (verse). London, Methuen, 1943.

*   *   *

The author of innumerable romances and family chronicles, as well as the popular 'Mrs Tim' books, D.E. Stevenson is an excellent example of a romance writer who expands the possibilities of the genre while recognizing its limitations.

Her novels might best be classified as novels of manners, in the same way as Dorothy L. Sayers's works are so described in the detective genre. The interest lies always in the development and exploration of character, in both the individual and collective sense. Thus, the Mrs Tim novels, written in the epistolary mode, reveal not only Mrs Tim's own psychological development, but also the changing nature of English wartime society. Her other novels, while they can be read on their own, often allude to characters and locations in previous works. What emerges is a kind of *roman fleuve* of English life and culture of a particular kind, at a particular time. This effect strikes one as being essentially unselfconscious, though it is obviously the result of considerable skill.

There is very little element of the gothic in Stevenson's work; what there is exists mainly in an atmosphere which is always essential to plot or theme: Celia's ghost in *Celia's House* is not so much an agent of the supernatural as of the house itself (the real 'hero' of the novel). The house, Dunnian, goes through various changes during the novel, over the period of the two world wars, and thus is both a device for revealing social change and a symbol of continuity.

While primarily novels of character, Stevenson's works are noteworthy also for their effective realization of locale. The Scottish setting of *Sarah's Cottage* is vividly described, as are the English locations in the same book. Setting is effectively related to character, and vice-versa; indeed, the interconnection of character and setting might be said to be a recurring theme in the novels, particularly in those with an Anglo-Germanic interest (*Sarah's Cottage, The English Air*).

Though skilfully plotted, the novels lack a major element of mystery or suspense of a conventional kind. Even when a mystery precipitates the plot, as in *Green Money*, it is ultimately a mystery of character, a why-dunnit rather than a who-dunnit. In *The English Air* the wartime exploits of the hero, Franz, are presented not as elements of an espionage thriller, but in relation to the character and his romance with his English cousin. Nevertheless, the novels are utterly engrossing, and probably represent the pure English modern romance at its very best.

—Joanne Harack Hayne

———

STEVENSON, Florence.
Pseudonyms: Zandra Colt; Lucia Curzon; Zabrina Faire; Ellen Fitzgerald. **Nationality:** American. **Born:** Los Angeles, California. **Education:** Yale University, New Haven, Connecticut; University of Southern California, Los Angeles, B.A., M.A. **Career:** drama columnist, Los Angeles *Mirror*, 1949–50; editorial assistant, *Mademoiselle*, New York, 1956–57; press assistant, James D. Proctor, 1957–58; assistant editor, 1959–60, and contributing editor, 1960–70, *Opera News*, New York; columnist ('Opera Boutique'), *Metropolitan Opera Program*, New York, ten years; columnist ('Things of Beauty'), *Lincoln Center Program*, New York, ten years; associate editor, *FM Guide*, New York, 1964–65; contributing editor, *Weight Watchers*, 1968–75, and *New Ingenue*, 1974–75, both New York. **Agent:** Phyllis Westberg, 425 Madison Avenue, 40 East 49th Street, New York, New York 10017, USA. **Address:** 227 East 57th Street, New York, New York 10022, USA.

ROMANCE AND HISTORICAL PUBLICATIONS

Novels (series: Kitty Telefair)

Ophelia. New York, New American Library, 1968.
Feast of Eggshells. New York, New American Library, 1970.
The Curse of the Concullens. New York, World, 1970.
The Witching Hour (Telefair). New York, Award, 1971.
Where Satan Dwells (Telefair). New York, Award, 1971.
Bianca, with Patricia Hagan Murray. New York, New American Library, 1973.
Kilmeny in the Dark Wood. New York, New American Library, 1973.
Altar of Evil (Telefair). New York, Award, 1973.
The Mistress of Devil's Manor (Telefair). New York, Award, 1973.
The Sorcerer of the Castle (Telefair). New York, Award, 1974.
Dark Odyssey. New York, New American Library, 1974.
The Ides of November. New York, New American Library, 1975.
A Shadow on the House. New York, New American Library, 1975.
Witch's Crossing. New York, New American Library, 1975.
The Silent Watcher (Telefair). New York, Award, 1975.
A Darkness on the Stairs. New York, New American Library, 1976.
The House at Luxor. New York, New American Library, 1976.
Dark Encounter. New York, New American Library, 1977.
The Horror from the Tombs. New York, Award, 1977.
Julie. New York, New American Library, 1978.

The Golden Galatea. New York, Berkley, 1979.
The Moonlight Variations. New York, Berkley, 1981.
The Cactus Rose (as Zandra Colt). New York, Berkley, 1982.
Splendid Savage (as Zandra Colt). New York, Berkley, 1983.
Household. New York, Dorchester, 1989.
The Sisterhood. New York, Dorchester, 1989.

Novels as Zabrina Faire

Lady Blue. New York, Warner, 1979.
The Midnight Match. New York, Warner, 1979.
The Romany Rebel. New York, Warner, 1979.
Enchanting Jenny. New York, Warner, 1979.
Wicked Cousin. New York, Warner, 1980.
Athena's Airs. New York, Warner, 1980.
Bold Pursuit. New York, Warner, 1980.
Pretender to Love. New York, Warner, 1981.
Pretty Kitty. New York, Warner, 1981.
Tiffany's True Love. New York, Warner, 1981.

Novels as Lucia Curzon

The Chadbourne Luck. New York, Berkley, 1981.
Adverse Alliance. New York, Berkley, 1981.
The Mourning Bride. New York, Berkley, 1982.
Queen of Hearts. New York, Berkley, 1982.
The Dashing Guardian. New York, Berkley, 1983.

Novels as Ellen Fitzgerald

A Novel Alliance. New York, New American Library, 1984.
Lord Caliban. New York, New American Library, 1985.
The Irish Heiress. New York, New American Library, 1985.

OTHER PUBLICATIONS

Other

The Story of Aida, Based on the Opera by Giuseppe Verdi (for children). New York, Putnam, 1965.
Call Me Counselor, with Sara Halbert. Philadelphia, Lippincott, 1977.

*   *   *

It is hard not to like an author who can inject as much humour in her books as can Florence Stevenson. Lucinda Ayers, a governess in *The Curse of the Concullens*, must be one of the most indomitable gothic heroines ever created. A mere slip of a girl, she encounters and copes with just about every occult manifestation possible. She befriends both the local banshee and the family vampire and deals calmly with the fact that her two young charges are werewolves. Even an encounter with the Devil himself does not shake her. Dimitri O'Hagan is an appropriately mysterious and brooding hero, given to clandestine activities. In fact he is an Irish patriot working against the hated British. The intrepid Lucy solves all the mysteries and manages to bring a degree of happiness to a remarkably unfortunate family, at the same time finding true love for herself.

Stevenson's selection of a pseudonym for most of her Regency novels, Zabrina Faire, again reflects a sense of humour and mischief. *Lady Blue*, one of Zabrina Faire's early novels, has a predictably happy ending after a somewhat rocky romance, but Stevenson develops the plot along some rather unusual lines. Meriel, also a governess, is the victim of a malicious prank played by her young charge. He spills ink on her hair, turning it blue. Dismissed for slap-

ping him, Meriel is hired by Lord Farr to impersonate a ghostly blue lady. Later she is kidnapped and forced to perform in a circus sideshow as a blue mermaid. Lord Farr, who luckily is a proficient magician, uses his skills to rescue her and foil the villains.

Unfortunately for those who appreciate such humour, Stevenson's later Regencies, both by Faire and a later pseudonym, Lucia Curzon, are standard formula novels. All the conventions are followed quite competently. The results are enjoyable to read but not readily distinguishable from most similar books. It is Stevenson's occasional humorous novel, gently spoofing the genre, which sets her apart, adding real sparkle to her work and keeping readers hoping for more.

—Barbara E. Kemp

———

STEWART, Mary.
Nationality: British. **Born:** Mary Florence Elinor Rainbow, Sunderland, County Durham, 17 September 1916. **Education:** Eden Hall, Penrith, Cumberland; Skellfield School, Ripon, Yorkshire; St Hilda's College, University of Durham, B.A. (honours) 1938, M.A. 1941. **Military Service:** Royal Observer Corps during World War II. **Relations:** married Sir Frederick Henry Stewart in 1945. **Career:** lecturer in English, Durham University, 1941–45. Lives in Edinburgh. **Recipient:** Crime Writers Association Silver Dagger, 1961; Mystery Writers of America award, 1964; Frederick Niven award, 1971; Scottish Arts Council award, 1975; Fellow, Newnham College, Cambridge, 1986. **Address:** c/o Hodder and Stoughton Ltd, Mill Road, Dunton Green, Sevenoaks, Kent TN13 2YA, England.

ROMANCE AND HISTORICAL PUBLICATIONS

Novels (series: Merlin Trilogy)

Madam, Will You Talk? London, Hodder and Stoughton, 1955; New York, Mill, 1956.
Wildfire at Midnight. London, Hodder and Stoughton, and New York, Appleton Century Crofts, 1956.
Thunder on the Right. London, Hodder and Stoughton, 1957; New York, Mill, 1958.
Nine Coaches Waiting. London, Hodder and Stoughton, 1958; New York, Mill, 1959.
My Brother Michael. London, Hodder and Stoughton, and New York, Mill, 1960.
The Ivy Tree. London, Hodder and Stoughton, 1961; New York, Mill, 1962.
The Moon Spinners. London, Hodder and Stoughton, 1962; New York, Mill, 1963.
This Rough Magic. London, Hodder and Stoughton, and New York, Mill, 1964.
Airs Above the Ground. London, Hodder and Stoughton, and New York, Mill, 1965.
The Gabriel Hounds. London, Hodder and Stoughton, and New York, Mill, 1967.
The Wind Off the Small Isles. London, Hodder and Stoughton, 1968.
Merlin Trilogy. New York, Morrow, 1980.
  The Crystal Cave. London, Hodder and Stoughton, and New York, Morrow, 1970.
  The Hollow Hills. London, Hodder and Stoughton, and New York, Morrow, 1973.
  The Last Enchantment. London, Hodder and Stoughton, and New York, Morrow, 1979.
Touch Not the Cat. London, Hodder and Stoughton, and New York, Morrow, 1976.

The Wicked Day. London, Hodder and Stoughton, and New York, Morrow, 1983.
Thornyhold. London, Hodder and Stoughton, and New York, Morrow, 1988.
Stormy Petrel. London, Hodder and Stoughton, 1991.

OTHER PUBLICATIONS

Poetry

Frost on the Window and Other Poems. London, Hodder and Stoughton, 1990.

Plays

Radio Plays: *Lift from a Stranger, Call Me at Ten-Thirty, The Crime of Mr Merry*, and *The Lord of Langdale*, 1957–58.

Other (for children)

The Little Broomstick. Leicester, Brockhampton Press, 1971; New York, Morrow, 1972.
Ludo and the Star Horse. Leicester, Brockhampton Press, 1974; New York, Morrow, 1975.
A Walk in Wolf Wood. London, Hodder and Stoughton, and New York, Morrow, 1980.

*

Film Adaptation: *The Moon-Spinners*, 1964.

Manuscript Collection: National Library of Scotland, Edinburgh.

*   *   *

Mary Stewart's career as a romance and historical writer of uncommon ability and imagination spans nearly 50 years of sustained popularity and acclaim. Although she is frequently reviewed as a genre writer, her work is more original and varied than that of most formula authors. From 1955 through 1967, Stewart wrote novels of romantic suspense that, for convenience, were often reviewed as gothics. But, although her novels had similarities to those of Victoria Holt and Phyllis Whitney (her two most popular contemporaries), Stewart transcended their work and the formula romance of which these were the three most significant writers. After *The Gabriel Hounds*, Stewart turned to historical fiction, writing an acclaimed trilogy (*The Crystal Cave, The Hollow Hills*, and *The Last Enchantment*) about Merlin and Arthur. In 1983, she returned to the material of the trilogy with *The Wicked Day*. In the mid-1970s, she published *Touch Not the Cat*, a return to romantic suspense but with a plot that depended upon telepathy, a new ingredient for her fiction. In 1988, she published another romance, *Thornyhold*, which is about witchcraft. She has also written fantasies for children.

Of her romance writings, Stewart's most important work came during her earlier period, although the 'Merlin Trilogy' may be her most enduring literary contribution. From *Madam, Will You Talk?* to *The Gabriel Hounds*, her books were excellent and original romances that relied heavily upon her ability to evoke a place, to create complex characters, and to weave sophisticated and compelling stories. Her two best contemporary romances are *Nine Coaches Waiting* and *My Brother Michael*, set respectively in France and Greece.

Nine Coaches Waiting is her only 'governess gothic', a novel about an orphaned heroine who is employed to teach the heir to a vast French estate. When she discovers the child's life is in danger, the heroine protects him and earns the love of the boy's older cousin, who has not been—despite appearances—part of the conspiracy. Stewart's academic background in literature informs this novel as it does each of her others. The heroine consciously recalls her literary predecessors (especially Cinderella and Jane Eyre) as Stewart plays off the resonance of the literary history of romance against the modern heroine's sensibility and experience. *My Brother Michael* employs a background of ancient and recent Greek history, myth, and legend with thematic elements from John Donne. The heroine joins the hero's search for the truth about the fate of his brother, who died during World War II near Delphi. *Wildfire at Midnight*, set on the Isle of Skye, works against a background of ancient Celtic myth. *This Rough Magic*, on Corfu, finds its inspiration in Shakespeare's *The Tempest. The Gabriel Hounds* derives from the story of Lady Hester Stanhope. Other novels are set in the south of France, in Northumbria, and in Austria. In each, Stewart evokes the place in a rich and compelling manner.

The originality of her literary sensibility is most fully realised in the nature of her characters. Stewart's heroes and heroines are people of commitment, not just to each other as in many other romances, but especially to others and to abstract concepts of truth and justice. Their values may seem archaic in the modern world, but Stewart portrays them so sensitively that they remain believable. Without preaching or moralizing, she places her characters in situations of extreme danger where it would be acceptable for them to walk away from someone else's trouble. They do not, and her delineation of their motivation and personal growth is always crucial to understanding their stories.

Although each of Stewart's contemporary romances contains a love story as an integral part of the plot, she does not allow the vicissitudes of the lovers to dominate. Her characters are selfless, sometimes (as the heroine of *Nine Coaches Waiting*) making decisions that require the apparent sacrifice of the love affair in the cause of justice. But despite their 'stiff upper lip' morality, the heroines are attractive, lively, and admirable without being either stuffy or priggish. Stewart portrays the success of the love relationship as a product of the heroine's maturity, rather than as an end in itself.

Her historical novels about King Arthur are heavily researched from traditional sources and told in the first person by Merlin. In dramatizing the Arthurian legends, Stewart makes few concessions to a mass audience, although her skill as a writer of narrative keeps the story moving. The novels use Anglo-Saxon and Latin proper names for characters and places; and Stewart notes her scholarly sources and describes some of the choices she made when authorities disagree. The Merlin novels were widely praised by critics and attracted many readers, and they established Stewart's reputation as a writer with appeal to a broader audience.

Stewart is a fine stylist. Reviewers consistently praise the quality of her prose, especially her descriptions of food and place as well as the charm and good humour with which her heroines tell their tales. Without padding her stories with extraneous details, she describes her scenes vividly; she offers not a travelogue but a concrete sense of what it must be like to experience an exotic place fraught with dramatic and emotional events. Stewart defies categorization. Although her books may resemble those of other writers, she remains, even in her weaker books, a writer of uncommon originality and grace. She may work within a formula, but her scene is the larger setting of romance through centuries of literature, making her novels both rewarding and inimitable.

—Kay Mussell

STIRLING, Jessica.
Originally pseudonym for Peggie Coghlan and Hugh C. Rae; since 1984, for Hugh C. Rae alone. **COGHLAN, Peggie. Nationality:** British. **Born:** Glasgow, Scotland, 26 January 1920. **Education:** Notre Dame High School. **Relations:** married Eugene O. Coghlan; two daughters. **Address:** 249 Morningside Street, Edinburgh, Scotland. **RAE, Hugh C(rauford). Other Pseudonyms:** James Albany; Robert Crawford; Caroline Crosby; R.B. Houston; Stuart Stern. **Born:** Glasgow, Scotland, 22 November 1935. **Education:** Knightswood School, Glasgow, 1940–51. **Military Service:** Royal Air Force, 1954–56. **Relations:** married Elizabeth Dunn in 1960; one daughter. **Career:** assistant, John Smith and Son, antiquarian bookseller, Glasgow, 1952–65; then full-time writer. Lecturer in creative writing, University of Glasgow. Founding member, Association of Scottish Writers; president, Romantic Novelists Association, Scotland. **Address:** Drumore Farm Cottage, Balfron Station, Stirlingshire, Scotland.

ROMANCE AND HISTORICAL PUBLICATIONS

Novels (series: Beckman Trilogy; Glasgow; Patterson Trilogy; Stalker Trilogy)

Stalker Trilogy:
> *The Spoiled Earth*. London, Hodder and Stoughton, 1974; as *Strathmore*, New York, Delacorte Press, 1975.
> *The Hiring Fair*. London, Hodder and Stoughton, 1976; as *Call Home the Heart*, New York, St Martin's Press, 1977.
> *The Dark Pasture*. London, Hodder and Stoughton, 1977; New York, St Martin's Press, 1978.

The Dresden Finch. New York, Delacorte Press, 1976; as *Beloved Sinner*, London, Pan, 1980.

Beckman Trilogy:
> *The Deep Well at Noon*. London, Hodder and Stoughton, 1979; as *The Drums of Time*, New York, St Martin's Press, 1980.
> *The Blue Evening Gone*. London, Hodder and Stoughton, and New York, St Martin's Press, 1981.
> *The Gates of Midnight*. London, Hodder and Stoughton, and New York, St Martin's Press, 1983.

Patterson Trilogy:
> *Treasures on Earth*. London, Hodder and Stoughton, and New York, St Martin's Press, 1985.
> *Creature Comforts*. London, Hodder and Stoughton, and New York, St Martin's Press, 1986.
> *Hearts of Gold*. London, Hodder and Stoughton, and New York, St Martin's Press, 1987.

Glasgow:
> *The Good Provider*. London, Hodder and Stoughton, 1988; New York, St Martin's Press. 1989.
> *The Asking Price*. London, Hodder and Stoughton, 1989; New York, St Martin's Press, 1990.
> *The Wise Child*. London, Hodder and Stoughton, and New York, St Martin's Press, 1990.
> *The Welcome Light*. London, Hodder and Stoughton, and New York, St Martin's Press, 1991.

Lantern for the Dark. London, Hodder and Stoughton, and New York, St Martin's Press, 1992.
The Haldanes (as Caroline Crosby). London, Hodder and Stoughton, 1992.
Shadows on the Shore. London, Hodder and Stoughton, 1993.

OTHER PUBLICATIONS by Hugh C. Rae

Novels

Skinner. London, Blond, and New York, Viking Press, 1965.

Night Pillow. London, Blond, and New York, Viking Press, 1967.
A Few Small Bones. London, Blond, 1968; as *The House at Balnesmoor*, New York, Coward McCann, 1969.
The Interview. London, Blond, and New York, Coward McCann, 1969.
The Saturday Epic. London, Blond, and New York, Coward McCann, 1970.
The Marksman. London, Constable, and New York, Coward McCann, 1971.
The Shooting Gallery. London, Constable, and New York, Coward McCann, 1972.
Two for the Grave (as R.B. Houston). London, Hale, 1972.
The Rock Harvest. London, Constable, 1973.
The Rookery. London, Constable, 1974; New York, St Martin's Press, 1975.
Harkfast: The Making of a King. London, Constable, and New York, St Martin's Press, 1976.
The Minotaur Factor (as Stuart Stern). London, Futura, 1977; Chicago, Playboy Press, 1978.
The Poison Tree (as Stuart Stern). London, Futura, and Chicago, Playboy Press, 1978.
Sullivan. London, Constable, and Chicago, Playboy Press, 1978.
The Travelling Soul. New York, Avon, 1978.
The Haunting at Waverley Falls. London, Constable, 1980.
Privileged Strangers. London, Hodder and Stoughton, 1982.

Novels as Robert Crawford

The Shroud Society. London, Constable, and New York, Putnam, 1969.
Cockleburr. London, Constable, 1969; New York, Putnam, 1970; as *Pay as You Die*, New York, Berkley, 1971.
Kiss the Boss Goodbye. London, Constable, 1970; New York, Putnam, 1971.
The Badger's Daughter. London, Constable, 1971.
Whip Hand. London, Constable, 1972.

Novels as James Albany

Warrior Caste. London, Pan, 1982.
Mailed Fist. London, Pan, 1982.
Deacon's Dagger. London, Pan, 1982.
Close Combat. London, Pan, 1983.
Marching Fire. London, Pan, 1983.
Last Bastion. London, Pan, 1984.
Borneo Story. London, Pan, 1984.

Plays

The Freezer (broadcast 1972; produced Leicester, 1973).

Radio Play: *The Freezer*, 1972.

Television Plays: *The Dear Ones*, 1966; Swallowtale, 1969.

Other

Editor, with Philip Ziegler and James Allen Ford, *Scottish Short Stories 1977*. London, Collins, 1977.
Editor, *Scottish Short Stories 1978*. London, Collins, 1978.

*

Peggie Coghlan commented (1982):
     For many years my writing was slanted exclusively in the direction of the magazine field. It was my friend and mentor Hugh C. Rae

who suggested that I change direction and write a novel. The help and guidance I received from Mr Rae cannot be estimated, and it is no exaggeration to say that without him the books would not have been written.

Contemplating the first book, and being a member of a fairly large family, I suppose it was natural that I should decide to write a family story. For me, the work of a book is divided into two parts. First, the research, which I enjoy very much and tend to spin out far beyond what is required, and the actual writing which is hard and demanding work but is at the same time deeply satisfying when what appears on the printed page nearly approximated what, at the beginning, I planned in my head and felt in my heart.

A picture, it is said, is worth more than a thousand words, so equally, too, will not a thousand words evoke a memorable picture? That, to me, is what novel writing is all about.

Hugh C. Rae comments:

In 1984 my co-author, Peggie Coghlan, elected to retire from writing and generously suggested that I might care to tackle future Jessica Stirling novels on my own. Peggie Coghlan's contribution had always been considerable, but, with trepidation and not a few teething troubles, I assumed the female persona. To judge by Jessica's continued popularity I learned my lessons well from Mrs Coghlan in the area of plotting and characterization, and will always be grateful for her generosity.

*   *   *

The strong female protagonists of Jessica Stirling's novels are believable, attractive, and beleaguered by difficulties. They 'carry on' and show their mettle while remaining stable and appealingly feminine. Careful character development and settings which powerfully complement and justify these characters are distinctive features of Stirling's fiction.

The search for dignity, independence, and love by Mirrin Stalker of the 'Stalker Trilogy' is played out against the background of a coal-mining village in 19th-century Scotland. The feudal system in which she and her family seem trapped begins to show some cracks, and Mirrin is among the first to realize that coalmaster Houston Lamont is as human and touchable as she, and therefore as vulnerable. Mirrin and her proud family get caught up in the changes taking place. The proprieties and bleakness of this narrow society are intricately presented with the powerful characters gaining advantages only to lose them again.

Holly Beckman, in the 'Beckman Trilogy', must also contend with disadvantage while trying to find her place in the world. Her disreputable father and evil brother pose continuous threats to the position she works so hard to maintain. In the first novel Holly finds her niche in the antiques trade in London just after World War I. Her employer, a kindly mentor, provides her with a share of the business after his death, giving her the chance to make something of herself. The antiques business adds interest and validity to the novels and allows Holly to obtain respectability and eventual affluence. Her personal life is often in turmoil, however. In *The Blue Evening Gone* Holly's mid-thirties 'crisis' is portrayed beautifully in counterpoint to the turmoil in Europe in the years prior to World War II. Holly's life circles around in *The Gates of Midnight* set during the London Blitz after she has been widowed and her son has joined the RAF. David Aspinall, Chris's real father, returns from the Orient and with sensitivity and style becomes a part of Holly's life again, this time on her terms.

The 'Patterson Trilogy' is set in 19th-century Scotland. It is the story of Elspeth Patterson from her start as a foundling pried from the arms of her dead mother to her rightful place as mistress of Balnesmoor and owner of a prosperous weaving empire. *Treasures on Earth* is largely the story of Gaddy Patterson, the drover's wo-

man whose life is changed when she finds a baby who desperately needs her care. She scratches out a living in a community where she is not welcome. She prevails, marries a farmer, and has another daughter, Anna. In *Creature Comforts* and *Hearts of Gold*, Elspeth comes of age, and the melodrama continues as her sister steals her beau, and a flood ruins the homestead, all but killing Gaddy. These events lead Elspeth to the practical solution of marrying James Moodie, the older, ruthless, weaver. She had been troubled by their strange platonic relationship and sought comfort with a romantic young man she met on the moors, bearing his child. As a result, Moodie's terrible secret comes out: Moodie was Elspeth's father, wracked by guilt over his abandonment of her mother. Elspeth, in horror, runs away, taking her daughter with her, ending up with a coalminer's family. Elspeth prevails in spite of the horrors of this life. It takes tragedy in the mine to reveal the knowledge to her that Moodie has committed suicide in order for her to inherit his estate and regain her rightful home.

These trilogies are written with style and passion, and the characters tie in with one another in astounding yet believable ways, often reappearing to change the course of events. After being asked by a father where his lost son was now, Elspeth replies, 'I don't know. I doubt if we—any of us—will hear of him again, though it's odd how things come round sometimes'. Stirling is masterful at making 'things come round' in her novels for her admirable women characters.

Stirling has also created intriguing male characters. One doesn't easily forget the brilliant and haughty Drew Stalker who, in *The Dark Pasture*, mellows only enough to seem human at last. Nor does one pass lightly over the men in Holly Beckman's life, from the caddish David Aspinall, her first lover, to highly sensitive Christopher Deems, the husband who perishes; as well as steadfast Kennedy King, her second husband and business partner, and attractive, but callow Peter Freeman, the American dancer who almost spoils it all. The 'Patterson Trilogy' has many interesting men who help or hinder Elspeth's desire to make a decent life for herself and her daughter. The evil but troubled James Moodie and the single-minded Jock Bennet, the coalman who never gives in, are powerful forces with whom she has to come to terms. Misguided Matt Sinclair weaves in and out of her life causing unexpected difficulties for Elspeth and her sister and the other fascinating families whose lives are linked in this rich tale.

All of Stirling's stories are well crafted, believably plotted, with intriguing characters seemingly constructed around the belief that Drew Stalker expressed in an off-guard moment, 'You are, you can be, what you choose to be'.

—Allayne C. Heyduk

* * *

STONE, Irving.
Nationality: American. **Born:** Irving Tannenbaum in San Francisco, California, 14 July 1903; adopted in 1912. **Education:** Lowell High School, San Francisco; Manual Arts High School, Los Angeles; University of California, Berkeley, A.B. 1923, graduate study, 1924–26; University of Southern California, Los Angeles, M.A. 1924. **Relations:** married Jean Factor in 1934; one daughter and one son. **Career:** teaching Fellow in Economics, University of Southern California, 1923–24, and University of California, Berkeley, 1924–26. Visiting lecturer in creative writing, University of Indiana, Bloomington, 1948, and University of Washington, Seattle, 1961; lecturer on the writing of biography and the biographical novel, University of Southern California, 1966; lecturer, California State Colleges, 1966, and New York University and Johns Hopkins University, Baltimore, 1985. From 1984 Regents professor, University of California, Los Angeles. Art critic, Los An-

geles *Mirror-News*, 1959–60. United States Department of State cultural exchange specialist, in the Soviet Union, Poland, and Yugoslavia, 1962. President, California Writers Guild, 1960–61; founder, Academy of American Poets, 1962; founder, California State Colleges Committee for the Arts, 1967; trustee, Douglass House Foundation, Watts, Los Angeles, 1967–74; president, Dante Alighieri Society, Los Angeles, 1968–69. From 1955 founder and president, fellow for Schweitzer, southern California; from 1963 vice president, Eugene V. Debs Foundation, Terre Haute, Indiana, and member, Advisory Board, University of California Institute for the Creative Arts; from 1969 president, Affiliates of the Department of English, University of California, Los Angeles. 'Irving Stone Day' observed in Los Angeles, 1983. Co-founder, with his wife, Jean, of two annual awards for best historical, and biographical novels published. **Recipient:** Christopher award, 1957; Western Writers of America Spur award, 1957; McGovern award, 1988. D.L.: University of Southern California, 1965; D.Litt.: Coe College, Cedar Rapids, Iowa, 1967; California State Colleges, 1971; LLD: University of California, Berkeley, 1968; D.H.L.: Hebrew Union College, Cincinnati, 1978. Commendatore (Knight Commander), Republic of Italy, 1962; Grande Ufficiale (Italy), 1982; Commandant, Order of Arts and Letters (France), 1984. **Died:** 26 August 1989.

ROMANCE AND HISTORICAL PUBLICATIONS

Novels

Lust for Life. New York, Longman, and London, Lane, 1934.
Sailor on Horseback. Boston, Houghton Mifflin, and London, Collins, 1939; as *Jack London, Sailor on Horseback*, New York, Doubleday, 1947.
Immortal Wife. New York, Doubleday, 1944; London, Falcon Press, 1950.
Adversary in the House. New York, Doubleday, 1947; London, Falcon Press, 1950.
The Passionate Journey. New York, Doubleday, 1949; London, Falcon Press, 1950.
The President's Lady. New York, Doubleday, 1951; London, Lane, 1952.
Love Is Eternal. New York, Doubleday, 1954; London, Collins, 1955.
The Agony and the Ecstasy. New York, Doubleday, and London, Collins, 1961.
Those Who Love. New York, Doubleday, 1965; London, Cassell, 1966.
The Passions of the Mind. New York, Doubleday, and London, Cassell, 1971.
The Greek Treasure. New York, Doubleday, and London, Cassell, 1975.
The Origin. New York, Doubleday, 1980; London, Cassell, 1981.
Depths of Glory. New York, Doubleday, and London, Bodley Head, 1985.

OTHER PUBLICATIONS

Novels

Pageant of Youth. New York, King, 1933.
False Witness. New York, Doubleday, 1940.

Plays

The Dark Mirror (produced New York, 1928).

The White Life: A Play Based on the Life of Baruch Spinoza (produced Jersey City, New Jersey, 1929). New York, League of Jewish Community Associations, 1932.
Truly Valiant (produced New York, 1936).

Screenplay: *The Magnificent Doll*, 1946.

Other

Clarence Darrow for the Defense. New York, Doubleday, 1941; as *Darrow for the Defence*, London, Lane, 1950.
They Also Ran: The Story of the Men Who Were Defeated for the Presidency. New York, Doubleday, 1943; revised edition, 1945.
The Evolution of an Idea. Privately printed, 1945.
Earl Warren. New York, Prentice Hall, 1948.
Men to Match My Mountains: The Opening of the Far West 1840–1900. New York, Doubleday, 1956; London, Cassell, 1967.
Three Views of the Novel, with John O'Hara and MacKinlay Kantor. Washington, DC, Library of Congress, 1957.
The Irving Stone Reader. New York, Doubleday, 1963.
The Story of Michelangelo's Pietà. New York, Doubleday, 1964.
The Great Adventure of Michelangelo (for children). New York, Doubleday, 1965.
There Was Light: Autobiography of a University, Berkeley 1868–1968. New York, Doubleday, 1970.
Mary Todd Lincoln: A Final Judgement? Springfield, Illinois, Abraham Lincoln Association, 1973.

Editor, *Dear Theo: The Autobiography of Vincent van Gogh*. Boston, Houghton Mifflin, and London, Constable, 1937.
Editor, with Richard Kennedy, *We Speak for Ourselves: Self Portrait of America*. New York, Doubleday, 1950.
Editor, with Allan Nevins, *Lincoln: A Contemporary Portrait*. New York, Doubleday, 1962.
Editor, with Jean Stone, *I, Michelangelo, Sculptor: An Autobiography Through Letters*. New York, Doubleday, 1962; London, Collins, 1963.
Editor, *Irving Stone's Jack London*. New York, Doubleday, 1977.

*

Film Adaptations: *The President's Lady*, 1953, from the novel *Immortal Wife*; *Lust for Life*, 1956; *The Agony and the Ecstacy*, 1965.

Bibliography: *Irving Stone: A Bibliography* by Lewis F. Stieg, Los Angeles, Friends of the Libraries of the University of Southern California, 1973.

Manuscript Collection: Special Collections, University of California Library, Los Angeles.

Irving Stone commented (1982):
   The biographical novel is a true and documented story of one human being's journey across the face of the years, transmuted from the raw material into the delight and purity of an authentic art form. The research must be honest and far reaching, but the result must stand as a compelling novel.

*   *   *

   The historian in Irving Stone co-habited with the artist through a dozen or so novels, and although the public sanctioned the arrangement by purchasing and reading the offspring books, the union is neither literarily nor historically holy. The novels that come of it suffer congenital defects; for all their broad appeal, there are problems with historical novels that are inescapable. Stone was an astute novelist, in so far as he recognized a compelling story and could control the reader's attention for the most part, and he was a willing historian who researched his material copiously. But in the novels the historian tended to inhibit the inventive imagination, embalming the dialogue and losing the plot for long periods in thickets of detail, while the artist always opened the history to a doubt that the most impressive bibliographical lists cannot still. This is, of course, true of all historical novelists, to an extent, but paradoxically, the generic difficulty is more acute in the case of more serious ones, such as Stone, than in the case of writers, such as Frank G. Slaughter, whose concern is entertainment and not authenticity, and whose works may be consumed like popcorn.

The point may be illustrated by any of Stone's novels. *Love Is Eternal*, for example, which treats the relationship between Mary Todd and Abraham Lincoln to the time of Lincoln's assassination, demonstrates Stone's characteristic use of the most minute details to evoke a sense of historical place. But while the setting and circumstances in which the main characters play are without doubt essentially correct, there remains the question of whether or not the conception of the characters is accurate as well. Stone attempted to restore the reputation of Mary Todd Lincoln, who has been excoriated by history. He may have been right in his judgment of her, or his vindication of her may be simply an act of sentimental gallantry. There is no way to be certain; if the novel is an unfounded interpretation of her, Stone misrepresented his character, and if there was historical evidence for his view, she would have been far better served by a documented history.

Stone was apparently aware, consciously or unconsciously, of the dilemma created by writing fiction that purports to echo fact. In *The Passionate Journey*, a fictional biography of the American painter John Noble, he was usually better when his characters acted and reacted with each other according to the scenario provided by historical fact than when he sought to interpret motivation. Perhaps the use of detail to the point of tediousness was an attempt to bring the problem that was imposed by the genre under control—an attempt to overwhelm it. *Those Who Love*, for instance, a treatment of the life and times of John and Abigail Adams, is not only lumbered with wooden dialogue, but overburdened with historical minutiae. The Michelangelo study, *The Agony and the Ecstasy*, as if to counter the effect of a great deal of love interest that smacks of modern interpolation, contains endless description of stone cutting and of anatomy, in a way that is reminiscent of Melville's whaling chapters but is less easily justifiable.

But the biographical novel does exist, of course, and Stone was undeniably one of its ablest practitioners. The history he created is far more palatable and interesting than popcorn, and it is no wonder that an enormous public should devour it.

—Alan R. Shucard

———

STORM, Virginia.   See **CHANDOS, Fay.**

———

STORY, Josephine.   See **LORING, Emilie.**

———

STRATTON, Rebecca.
Pseudonym: Lucy Gillen. **Nationality:** British. **Military Service:** Women's Auxiliary Air Force and the Fire Service during World War II. **Career:** worked at many jobs before becoming a civil servant for the Coventry County Court, 1957–67; then a full-time writer. **Died:** 5 January 1982.

ROMANCE AND HISTORICAL PUBLICATIONS

Novels

The Golden Madonna. London, Mills and Boon, 1973; Toronto, Harlequin, 1974.
The Bride of Romano. London, Mills and Boon, 1973; Toronto, Harlequin, 1974.
Castles in Spain. London, Mills and Boon, 1973; Toronto, Harlequin, 1974.
The Yellow Moon. London, Mills and Boon, 1974; Toronto, Harlequin, 1975.
Island of Darkness. London, Mills and Boon, 1974; Toronto, Harlequin, 1975.
Autumn Concerto. London, Mills and Boon, 1974; Toronto, Harlequin, 1975.
The Flight of the Hawk. London, Mills and Boon, 1974; Toronto, Harlequin, 1975.
Run from the Wind. London, Mills and Boon, and Toronto, Harlequin, 1974.
Fairwinds. London, Mills and Boon, and Toronto, Harlequin, 1974.
The Warm Wind of Farik. London, Mills and Boon, and Toronto, Harlequin, 1975.
Firebird. London, Mills and Boon, and Toronto, Harlequin, 1975.
The Fire and the Fury. London, Mills and Boon, 1975; Toronto, Harlequin, 1976.
The Goddess of Mavisu. London, Mills and Boon, 1975; Toronto, Harlequin, 1976.
Isle of the Golden Drum. London, Mills and Boon, 1975; Toronto, Harlequin, 1976.
Moon Tide. London, Mills and Boon, 1975; Toronto, Harlequin, 1976.
The White Dolphin. London, Mills and Boon, 1976.
Proud Stranger. London, Mills and Boon, and Toronto, Harlequin, 1976.
The Road to Gafsa. London, Mills and Boon, 1976; Toronto, Harlequin, 1977.
Gemini Child. London, Mills and Boon, 1976; Toronto, Harlequin, 1977.
Chateau d'Armor. London, Mills and Boon, and Toronto, Harlequin, 1976.
Dream of Winter. London, Mills and Boon, 1977; Toronto, Harlequin, 1978.
Girl in a White Hat. London, Mills and Boon, and Toronto, Harlequin, 1977.
More Than a Dream. London, Mills and Boon, and Toronto, Harlequin, 1977.
Spindrift. London, Mills and Boon, 1977; Toronto, Harlequin, 1978.
Inherit the Sun. London, Mills and Boon, 1977; Toronto, Harlequin, 1978.
The Sign of the Ram. London, Mills and Boon, 1977; Toronto, Harlequin, 1978.
The Velvet Glove. London, Mills and Boon, 1977; Toronto, Harlequin, 1978.
Lost Heritage. London, Mills and Boon, 1978.
Image of Love. London, Mills and Boon, and Toronto, Harlequin, 1978.
Bargain for Paradise. London, Mills and Boon, and Toronto, Harlequin, 1978.
The Corsican Bandit. London, Mills and Boon, and Toronto, Harlequin, 1978.

The Eagle of the Vincella. London, Mills and Boon, 1978.
Close to the Heart. London, Mills and Boon, and Toronto, Harlequin, 1979.
Lark in an Alien Sky. London, Mills and Boon, and Toronto, Harlequin, 1979.
The Tears of Venus. London, Mills and Boon, 1979; Toronto, Harlequin, 1980.
Trader's Cay. London, Mills and Boon, 1980.
The Leo Man. London, Mills and Boon, 1980.
The Inherited Bride. London, Mills and Boon, 1980.
Apollo's Daughter. London, Mills and Boon, 1980.
The Black Invader. London, Mills and Boon, 1981.
Dark Enigma. London, Mills and Boon, 1981.
The Silken Cage. London, Mills and Boon, 1981.
Charade. London, Mills and Boon, and Toronto, Harlequin, 1982.
The Golden Spaniard. London, Mills and Boon, and Toronto, Harlequin, 1982.
The Man from Nowhere. London, Mills and Boon, 1982; Toronto, Harlequin, 1983.

Novels as Lucy Gillen

The Ross Inheritance. London, Mills and Boon, 1969.
Good Morning, Doctor Houston. London, Mills and Boon, 1969; Toronto, Harlequin, 1970.
The Silver Fishes. London, Mills and Boon, 1969; Toronto, Harlequin, 1970.
A Wife for Andrew. London, Mills and Boon, 1969; Toronto, Harlequin, 1970.
Heir to Glen Ghyll. London, Mills and Boon, and Toronto, Harlequin, 1970.
Nurse Helen. London, Mills and Boon, 1970; Toronto, Harlequin, 1971.
Doctor Toby. London, Mills and Boon, 1970; Toronto, Harlequin, 1972.
The Girl at Smuggler's Rest. London, Mills and Boon, 1970; Toronto, Harlequin, 1971.
My Beautiful Heathen. London, Mills and Boon, 1970; Toronto, Harlequin, 1972.
The Whispering Sea. London, Mills and Boon, 1971.
Winter at Cray. London, Mills and Boon, 1971; Toronto, Harlequin, 1972.
Dance of Fire. London, Mills and Boon, 1971.
Marriage by Request. London, Mills and Boon, and Toronto, Harlequin, 1971.
Summer Season. London, Mills and Boon, 1971; Toronto, Harlequin, 1975.
The Enchanted Ring. London, Mills and Boon, 1971; Toronto, Harlequin, 1973.
Sweet Kate. London, Mills and Boon, 1971; Toronto, Harlequin, 1973.
That Man Next Door. London, Mills and Boon, 1971; Toronto, Harlequin, 1972.
A Time Remembered. London, Mills and Boon, 1971; Toronto, Harlequin, 1973.
The Pretty Witch. London, Mills and Boon, 1971; Toronto, Harlequin, 1974.
Dangerous Stranger. London, Mills and Boon, 1972; Toronto, Harlequin, 1973.
Glen of Sighs. London, Mills and Boon, 1972; Toronto, Harlequin, 1975.
Means to an End. London, Mills and Boon, 1972; Toronto, Harlequin, 1975.
The Changing Years. London, Mills and Boon, 1972; Toronto, Harlequin, 1975.

Painted Wings. London, Mills and Boon, 1972; Toronto, Harlequin, 1974.
The Pengelly Jade. London, Mills and Boon, 1972; Toronto, Harlequin, 1974.
The Runaway Bride. London, Mills and Boon, 1972; Toronto, Harlequin, 1974.
An Echo of Spring. London, Mills and Boon, 1973.
Moment of Truth. London, Mills and Boon, 1973.
A Touch of Honey. London, Mills and Boon, 1973; Toronto, Harlequin, 1975.
Gentle Tyrant. London, Mills and Boon, 1973; Toronto, Harlequin, 1975.
A Handful of Stars. London, Mills and Boon, 1973; Toronto, Harlequin, 1976.
The Stairway to Enchantment. London, Mills and Boon, 1973; Toronto, Harlequin, 1975.
Come, Walk with Me. London, Mills and Boon, 1974.
Web of Silver. London, Mills and Boon, 1974; Toronto, Harlequin, 1975.
All the Summer Long. London, Mills and Boon, 1975; Toronto, Harlequin, 1976.
Return to Deepwater. London, Mills and Boon, 1975; Toronto, Harlequin, 1976.
The Hungry Tide. London, Mills and Boon, 1975; Toronto, Harlequin, 1976.
The House of Kingdom. London, Mills and Boon, and Toronto, Harlequin, 1976.
Mark of Tregarron. London, Mills and Boon, 1976.
Master of Ben Ross. London, Mills and Boon, and Toronto, Harlequin, 1977.
Heron's Point. London, Mills and Boon, 1977; Toronto, Harlequin, 1978.
Back of Beyond. London, Mills and Boon, and Toronto, Harlequin, 1978.
Hepburn's Quay. London, Mills and Boon, 1979.
The Storm Eagle. London, Mills and Boon, 1980.

*   *   *

Rebecca Stratton was an unexpected mixture of late blooming talent, a chequered working career, and an unusual ability to write romances. In all, she produced more than 80 novels from 1969 to her death in 1982, with roughly half of them published under her pseudonym, Lucy Gillen. There is a progressive development evident in her work as she moves from sweet simplicity to the more sophisticated involvement that modern readers are looking for. In fact, two of her later novels appeared in the Harlequin Presents series. Because of this development, her readers sometimes find it difficult to decide which type of romance they prefer.

Writing as Lucy Gillen, her novels are more traditional with the plot kept fairly simple. Conflict actually depends on the heroine's gradual awakening to love, but in a slow, puzzled way that finds her wondering what is happening even as the hero declares himself. That is the situation that Kim Anders is in in the novel *That Man Next Door*. Kim has come to stay with an aunt and uncle and hopes to get a job as a secretary to a writer who lives near them. She also meets James Fleming and the three small relatives for whom he is temporarily caring. Since he lives right next door, their continued meeting can't be avoided, much as she would like to, considering his dislike of and cruelty to the children. Because of his attitude, Kim finds herself becoming more and more involved with them and in spite of childish remarks soon learns that the children have exaggerated his attitude. Her job as secretary, the return of James's former girlfriend, and constant upsets with the children offer numerous chances for misunderstandings and reactions. Through the whole story, Kim's emotional reactions swing constantly from gradual liking to renewed dislike. Finally, when she hears that he is going to marry, she forces herself to accept the fact that she had mistaken her feelings and his seeming encouragement. 'You *will* marry me, won't you?' forces her to revise her thoughts as the final misunderstanding is reconciled. Generally, the tone is light, although Kim is aware of unfamiliar emotional turmoil. The sub-plots and minor incidents offer humour and at times satisfaction as Kim feels that she has managed to score a point against James's rather autocratic disregard of the children.

Lost Heritage (Rebecca Stratton) offers a different kind of romance, for ultimate happiness seems very dim to Charlotte Kennedy as she encounters Raoul Menais. Suspense is much more heightened, character conflict more frequent and more damaging as Charlotte takes a job as a secretary/companion to Lizette Menais. Charlotte learns that she was adopted as a baby and was given a bracelet with the name 'Menais' on it. With her adoptive parents dead, Charlotte sets out to learn about her real parents. As she travels to France to live with the family, she gradually learns the hidden secrets of the Menais family. Confrontation with Raoul Menais occurs as he becomes suspicious of her when she is slowly drawn into the family conflicts. Tension is high as 20-year-old events surface and Charlotte learns the truth about her family. Charlotte's constant need to remain in the background, yet her equally compelling need to protect her employer, Lizette, forces her to face repeated difficulties with Raoul and others in the family. The fact that she falls in love with Raoul is an added burden to her heart for she feels that nothing can ever come of it, especially if her birth is questionable. The end, of course, gives her her answers and her heart's desire.

Readers instantly react to the different styles that Stratton uses in her novels and certainly there are many readers who prefer her Lucy Gillen stories. However, since 1974 she gradually chose to write under her own name and in the more sophisticated style that is becoming more acceptable to modern readers. Perhaps young love and tender naivety are becoming less realistic, even unbelievable, in today's world. Certainly Stratton's novels tend to be more complex with hidden psychological situations and sharper character delineations.

—Arlene Moore

STUART, Alex.   See **STUART, Vivian.**

STUART, Clay.   See **HORNER, Lance, Kyle ONSTOTT, and Ashley CARTER.**

STUART, Eleanor.   See **PORTER, Eleanor H.**

STUART, V.A.   See **STUART, Vivian.**

STUART, Vivian.
Pseudonym for Violet Vivian Mann. **Other Pseudonyms:** Barbara Allen; Fiona Finlay; William Stuart Long; Alex Stuart; V.A. Stuart. **Nationality:** British. **Born:** Violet Vivian Finlay in Rangoon, Burma, 2 January 1914. **Education:** University of London; Balogh Institute of Pathology, Hungary, pathology qualification, 1938; Technical Institute, Newcastle, New South Wales, Australia, dip-

loma in industrial chemistry and laboratory technique 1942. **Military Service:** British Army, non-combatant duty with Australian forces, 1942–43; Women's Auxiliary Service in Burma, Sumatra, Java, Singapore, and Malaya, 1944–45: lieutenant colonel. **Relations:** married Cyril William Mann in 1958 (second marriage); five children. **Career:** co-founder and chair, Romantic Novelists Association, 1960–63; chair, Writers Summer School, London, 1964–67, 1969–71. **Died:** August 1986.

ROMANCE AND HISTORICAL PUBLICATIONS

Novels

Proud Heart. London, Jenkins, 1953.
Along Came Ann. London, Jenkins, 1953.
Eyes of the Night. London, Jenkins, 1954.
The Unlit Heart. London, Jenkins, 1954.
Pilgrim Heart. London, Jenkins, 1955.
Lover Betrayed. London, Jenkins, 1955.
No Single Star. London, Hale, 1956.
Moon over Madrid (as Fiona Finlay), London, Mills and Boon, 1957; Toronto, Harlequin, 1968.
Life Is the Destiny. London, Hale, 1958.
The Summer's Flower. London, Hale, 1961.
Like Victors and Lords. London, Hale, 1964; as *Victors and Lords* (as V.A. Stuart), New York, Pinnacle, 1972.
The Valiant Sailors. London, Hale, 1964; (as V.A. Stuart) New York, Pinnacle, 1972.
Black Sea Frigate. London, Hale, 1971; as *Hazard's Command* (as V.A. Stuart), New York, Pinnacle, 1972.

Novels as Alex Stuart

The Captain's Table. London, Mills and Boon, 1953.
Ship's Nurse. London, Mills and Boon, 1954.
Soldier's Daughter. London, Mills and Boon, 1954.
Island for Sale. London, Mills and Boon, 1955.
Gay Cavalier. London, Mills and Boon, 1955.
Huntsman's Folly. London, Mills and Boon, 1956.
A Cruise for Cinderella. London, Mills and Boon, 1956.
Bachelor of Medicine. London, Mills and Boon, 1956.
The Last of the Logans. London, Mills and Boon, 1957.
Queen's Counsel. London, Mills and Boon, 1957.
Master of Guise. London, Mills and Boon, 1957.
Garrison Hospital. London, Mills and Boon, 1957.
Arcadia House. London, Mills and Boon, 1958.
Daughters of the Governor. London, Mills and Boon, 1958.
Master of Surgery. London, Mills and Boon, 1958.
Castle in the Mist. London, Mills and Boon, 1959.
The Peacock Pagoda. London, Mills and Boon, 1959.
Star of Oudh. London, Mills and Boon, 1960; as *On Her Majesty's Orders*, 1977.
Spencer's Hospital. London, Mills and Boon, 1961.
Sister Margarita. London, Mills and Boon, 1961.
Doctor Mary Courage. London, Mills and Boon, 1961.
Doctor on Horseback. London, Mills and Boon, 1962.
The Dedicated. London, Mills and Boon, 1962.
The Piper of Laide. London, Mills and Boon, 1963.
Maiden Voyage. London, Mills and Boon, 1964.
Samaritan's Hospital. London, Mills and Boon, 1965.
There But for Fortune. London, Mills and Boon, 1966.
Strangers When We Meet. London, Mills and Boon, 1968.
Random Island. London, Mills and Boon, 1968.
Young Doctor Mason. London, Mills and Boon, 1970.
Research Fellow. London, Mills and Boon, 1971.

The Bikers. London, New English Library, 1971.
A Sunset Touch. London, Mills and Boon, 1972.
The Last Trip. London, New English Library, 1972.

Novels as Barbara Allen

Serenade on a Spanish Guitar. London, Mills and Boon, 1956.
Doctor Lucy. London, Mills and Boon, 1956.
Someone Else's Heart. London, Mills and Boon, 1958.
The Gay Gordons. London, Mills and Boon, 1961.
The Scottish Soldier. London, Mills and Boon, 1965.

Novels as V.A. Stuart (series: Philip Hazard; Alexander Sheridan)

Brave Captains (Sheridan). New York, Pinnacle, 1972.
Hazard of Huntress. New York, Pinnacle, and London, Hale, 1973.
Hazard in Circassia. New York, Pinnacle, and London, Hale, 1973.
Massacre at Cawnpore (Hazard). New York, Pinnacle, 1973; London, Hale, 1974.
Victory at Sebastopol (Hazard). New York, Pinnacle, and London, Hale, 1973.
The Sepoy Mutiny (Sheridan). New York, Pinnacle, 1973; as *Mutiny in Meerat*, London, Hale, 1973; as *Mutiny at Dawn*, London, Tandem, 1975.
Cannons of Lucknow (Sheridan). New York, Pinnacle, 1974.
Hazard to the Rescue. New York, Pinnacle, 1974.
The Heroic Garrison (Sheridan). New York, Pinnacle, and London, Hale, 1975.
Guns to the Far East (Hazard). New York, Pinnacle, 1975; as *Shannon's Brigade*, London, Hale, 1976.
Battle for Lucknow (Sheridan). London, Hale, 1975.

Novels as William Stuart Long (series: The Australians in all books)

The Exiles. New York, Dell, 1979; Henley-on-Thames, Oxfordshire, Ellis, 1980.
The Settlers. New York, Dell, 1980; London, Futura, 1981.
The Traitors. New York, Dell, 1981; London, Futura, 1982.
The Explorers. New York, Dell, and Henley-on-Thames, Oxfordshire, Ellis, 1983.
The Adventurers. New York, Dell, and Henley-on-Thames, Oxfordshire, Ellis, 1983.
The Colonists. New York, Dell, and Henley-on-Thames, Oxfordshire, Ellis, 1984.
The Gold Seekers. New York, Dell, and Henley-on-Thames, Oxfordshire, Ellis, 1985.
The Gallant. New York, Dell, 1986; as *The Patriots*, Henley-on-Thames, Oxfordshire, Ellis, 1986.
The Empire Builders. Henley-on-Thames, Oxfordshire, Ellis, 1987.

OTHER PUBLICATIONS

Other

The Beloved Little Admiral: The Life and Times of Admiral of the Fleet, The Honourable Sir Henry Keppel 1809–1904. London, Hale, 1967; New York, Pinnacle, 1968.
His Majesty's Sloop-of-War Diamond Rock, with George T. Eggleston. London, Hale, 1978.

*   *   *

Vivian Stuart was a surprisingly creative writer. She was also one who saw opportunities to develop her craft. Instead of resting on past successes, she accepted a challenge so unique that few writers could dare face it and hope to achieve the worldwide recognition that she did. This opportunity was the chance to write a fictionalized historical account of the settlement of Australia.

Stuart began her writing career in the romance and gothic fields. Some of her earlier novels could be described as typical Mills and Boon or Harlequin romances. She wrote as Alex Stuart, Fiona Finlay, Barbara Allen, V.A. Stuart, and, finally, William Stuart Long. These early stories depended on sensitive characterization more than typical plot complications, although these played an important part in her novels as well. *Queen's Counsel* is representative of the early part of Stuart's writing career.

Normal misunderstandings, overheard conversations, deathly illness, and critical operations all weave a suspenseful story of love and devotion. While slightly melodramatic, Stuart still managed to carry off such tales with believability and finesse.

In the 1960s and 1970s Stuart turned her attention to historical novels. During this time, she wrote two major series that explored the history of the British Empire on the seas and in India. In fact, it was many years before V.A. Stuart, the author of the Philip Hazard series, was revealed as a woman. Her expertise in naval history made her such an authority on the subject that novels dealing with this period were frequently referred to her, to be checked for historical accuracy.

Two of her novels of this period reflect her writing ability and hint at her future directions. *On Her Majesty's Orders* was originally published in 1960 as *Star of Oudh* (written by Alex Stuart). For this novel she received recognition from the Romantic Novelists Association for one of the best romances of that year. This novel traces the inevitable breakdown of British rule in India by the East India Company. Caught in the very early days just before the impending massacres are Emma Lindsay and Captain Hugh Richmond. Emma believes, as do most of the other British residents, that it is inconceivable for the Indian regiments to revolt, in spite of growing evidence to the contrary. Captain Richmond knows better, but he is hampered by the division of authority between military leaders and civilian commissioners. Both Emma and Captain Richmond face death and danger during the critical months of summer 1857 and only his courage and resourcefulness ensure that he and Emma are among the few who reach safety.

Stuart's research of the Indian Mutiny of the 1850s later reappeared in her Sheridan series. What also emerged was her keen knowledge of British military thought and character. In *On Her Majesty's Orders*, she uses the anticipated anniversary of the Siege of Jawan as a point of illustration. The British officers saw no contradiction in celebrating a major defeat of Indian forces by using Indian Sepoy regiments as part of that celebration. Stuart shows the appalling lack of sensitivity on the part of many of the British as well as their deliberate blindness to events occurring all around them during this period.

Guns to the Far East gives another viewpoint of the mutiny in 1857. In this novel, Commander Philip Hazard leaves China on sick leave after sustaining wounds during the capture of the Canton River. He sails on a ship bound for Calcutta with relief forces for the British garrisons in India. Philip's two sisters, Harriet and Lavinia, are in the midst of the mutiny. Lavinia, caught at Cawnpore, is lost during the massacre, while Harriet is able to find refuge at Lucknow until the relief forces free them. The Hazard novels trace the career of Philip Hazard from his early days at sea through each promotion as a naval officer. Newer and swifter steamships change the old navy of Nelson into a modern force, capable of vast destruction of enemy forces. At the same time, it could and did ensure numerous victories for the British forces. In all, Stuart wrote seven novels of the Hazard series in which she traced the British fleet in the Crimean War and five novels covering the Indian Mutiny with Alexander Sheridan as the hero. Her style of writing is swift-moving, concentrating on tightly developed action. Her characters avoid the 'larger than life' image, instead, being humanly blessed with normal virtues and vices. Her work during these years earned her the reputation of being an outstandingly creative writer.

Stuart not only looked at individual events and people, but also at the broader view, illustrating quite graphically, at times, the consequences of past actions and beliefs. It is in this context that one must view her final series, 'The Australians'. This series is composed of nine novels by Stuart (*The Empire Builders* was completed after her death), with subsequent volumes by other authors using her name; it traces the early days of Australia as a penal colony through to the mid-19th century. Each volume covers a significant group of people as they make their impact on the isolated settlement in New South Wales.

This is not a series one would normally sit down to enjoy, in the purest sense of the word. Some readers might be repulsed by the cruelty and insensitivity of those early settlers and jailers. Others will look for hope and optimism and find very little. Nor will readers be able to draw a parallel between the settlement of the American colonies and Australia. In reality, Australia proved to be a vastly different sort of colony. Settlement was kept under rigid control by the military and civilian authorities and remained that way for many years. Once a convict, always a convict was a firmly held belief. As a consequence social classes split between the Exclusives and the Emancipists. For a brief time the country faced a real threat of internal rebellion and unrest.

This series was a complete departure from Stuart's previous works. The conciseness of her earlier writing is lost as she writes with an eye for minute detail and effect. Characters appear in several novels and their earlier importance is lost as events are forgotten. Family relationships become confused as readers seek to relate events from one story to the next. In fact, if one does not start with the first volume and read onward, much remains somewhat confused and contradictory. Given the complex history of Australia's early years, and the nearly impossible task of condensing it into readable novels, Stuart's achievement is impressive. At this time it is too soon to judge whether or not these novels will be her most remembered works.

—Arlene Moore

STUBBS, Jean.
Nationality: British. **Born:** Denton, Lancashire, 23 October 1926. **Education:** Manchester High School for Girls, 1938–44; Manchester School of Art, 1944–47. **Relations:** married; one daughter and one son. **Career:** reviewer, *Books and Bookmen*, London, 1966–80; writer in residence for Avon, 1984. **Recipient:** Tom-Gallon Trust award, for short story, 1965. **Agent:** Jennifer Kavanagh, 39 Camden Park Road, London NW1 9AX, England. **Address:** Trewin, Nancegollan, near Helston, Cornwall TR13 0AJ, England.

ROMANCE AND HISTORICAL PUBLICATIONS

Novels (series: Howarth Chronicles)

The Rose-Grower. London, Macmillan, 1962; New York, St Martin's Press, 1963.
The Travellers. London, Macmillan, and New York, St Martin's Press, 1963.
Hanrahan's Colony. London, Macmillan, 1964.
The Straw Crown. London, Macmillan, 1966.
The Passing Star. London, Macmillan, 1970; as *Eleanora Duse*, New York, Stein and Day, 1970.
An Unknown Welshman. London, Macmillan, and New York, Stein and Day, 1972.

Kit's Hill (Howarth). London, Macmillan, 1978; as *By Our Beginnings*, New York, St Martin's Press, 1979.
The Ironmaster (Howarth). London, Macmillan, 1981; as *An Imperfect Joy*, New York, St Martin's Press, 1981.
The Vivian Inheritance (Howarth). London, Macmillan, and New York, St Martin's Press, 1982.
The Northern Correspondent (Howarth). London, Macmillan, and New York, St Martin's Press, 1984.
A Lasting Spring. London, Macmillan, and New York, St Martin's Press, 1987.
Like We Used to Be. London, Macmillan, 1989; New York, St Martin's Press, 1990.
Summer Secrets. London, Macmillan, 1990; New York, St Martin's Press, 1992.
Light in Summer. London, Macmillan, and New York, St Martin's Press, 1991.
Kelly Park. London, Macmillan, and New York, St Martin's Press, 1992.

OTHER PUBLICATIONS

Novels (crime)

My Grand Enemy. London, Macmillan, 1967; New York, Stein and Day, 1968.
The Case of Kitty Ogilvie. London, Macmillan, 1970; New York, Walker, 1971.
Dear Laura. London, Macmillan, and New York, Stein and Day, 1973.
The Painted Face: An Edwardian Mystery. London, Macmillan, and New York, Stein and Day, 1974.
The Golden Crucible. New York, Stein and Day, 1976; London, Macmillan, 1977.

Play

Television Play: *Family Christmas*, 1965.

Other

100 Years Around the Lizard. Bodmin, Cornwall, Bossiney, 1985.
Great Houses of Cornwall. Bodmin, Cornwall, Bossiney, 1987.

*   *   *

Jean Stubbs, a gifted and versatile writer, has had success in a variety of genres. She has written crime novels, three of them in the 'Inspector Lintott' series, a four-volume historical saga, 'The Howarth Chronicles', and more recently has returned to writing contemporary novels. She has also had innumerable short stories published in magazines and collections.

'The Howarth Chronicles' are set in a fictional area in Lancashire, the county in which Stubbs spent her early years. The series follows the fortunes and misfortunes of the Howarth family between 1760 and 1833. Based on meticulous research and an intimate knowledge of the area, the rich social history in the novels is strengthened and enlarged by the clarity and perception of the characterization. Indeed, in all her writings, the quality of Stubbs's characterization is outstanding. She has a special ability to get inside the skins of the characters she creates.

After writing 'The Howard Chronicles', Stubbs returned to contemporary novels, the genre in which she had first been published 25 years earlier. The first novel in this group, *A Lasting Spring*, was giving her problems until her editor persuaded her to try writing in the first person. The story is of a woman, waiting for her husband to come home after. While she waits, she tells the moving story of the previous 17 years of her life.

Clearly Stubbs now enjoys working in first person form which she uses effectively. *Summer Secrets*, which followed three years later, is also written in the first person. Marina, named after the princess of that name by a working-class mother who had aspirations for her daughter, goes to Cornwall with her son to recover from the tragic loss of the boy's twin sister, Sarah. Memories of the girl haunt them, and friendship with a family holidaying nearby, although providing brief distraction, produces more problems for Marina. She suffers another loss when her mother dies, makes a devastating discovery about her husband's private life, and has an unsatisfying love affair. Yet this is not a depressing story. In Marina, Stubbs has created a character with tenacity and courage whom the reader cannot help but admire. Her gradual adjustment to changing circumstances is portrayed convincingly, with clear perception and sensitivity. In this novel, Stubbs also makes subtle use of present tense where the content is particularly emotional and where the character is in a suitably reflective mood and situation. Because of the skilful way in which it is done, the tense change is hardly noticeable, but at the same time it adds to the immediacy and emotional depth of the work.

Kelly Park is also written in the first person. This is a sensitive and moving account of a woman who, having had two failed relationships with men, focuses her love, care and affection on a country house which has fallen into disrepair. Flavia Pollard, the central character, divorced from her husband and in close partnership with the shallow Jack Rice, has successfully run a small restaurant in London. A talented chef, she has been the main reason for its success. Then Jack finds yet another lady friend who shows signs of permanence. Flavia decides it is time to get out. An old family friend, Humphrey Jarvis, is the owner of a country manor in Cornwall. Flavia, already familiar with the house, asks if she can stay there for a holiday. Ideas of renovation, of turning the dilapidated building into a guest house and restaurant, begin to form in her mind. Humphrey, realizing this may be the only means by which he can retain his ancestral home, agrees to finance her. Her scheme progresses through a number of setbacks and difficulties, but seems doomed following a tragic event near the end of the novel. Interwoven into the story are Flavia's teenage sons, Patrick and Jeremy, her flighty and overbearing mother, Lily, a number of characters from the local village who feel allegiance to the Jarvis family, and an itinerant Cornishman, Tom Faull, who alternately irritates and attracts Flavia, but finally restores her faith in the male species.

Stubbs, as always, has researched the setting and background for her novel assiduously. Living in Cornwall gave her the opportunity to absorb the atmosphere and the characteristics of the local people. She has transposed these elements into her novel, handling the dialect skilfully and with clarity, more by use and positioning of words than by phonetics. This adds to the atmosphere and the quality of characterization.

Realistic culinary details, and of the work required to be done on the house and the problems encountered, all add to the conviction of the story. The author spent time with people who had actually transformed a Cornish manor house into an hotel and restaurant in order to provide authentic detail. The resultant story is so realistic that one can imagine visitors to Cornwall asking for directions to *Kelly Park*.

—W.H. Bradley

STUYVESANT, Alice. See **WILLIAMSON, C.N. and A.M.**

STYRON, William.
Nationality: American. **Born:** Newport News, Virginia, 11 June 1925. **Education:** Christchurch School, Virginia; Davidson College, North Carolina, 1942–43; Duke University, Durham, North Carolina, 1943–44, 1946–47, B.A. 1947 (Phi Beta Kappa). **Military Service:** United States Marine Corps, 1944–45, 1951: 1st Lieutenant. **Relations:** married Rose Burgunder in 1953; three daughters and one son. **Career:** associate editor, McGraw Hill, publishers, New York, 1947. Since 1952 advisory editor, *Paris Review*, Paris and New York; member of the editorial board, *American Scholar*, Washington, DC, 1970–76. Since 1964 Fellow, Silliman College, Yale University, New Haven, Connecticut; Honorary Consultant in American Letters, Library of Congress, Washington, DC. **Recipient:** American Academy Rome prize, 1952, and Howells Medal, 1970; Pulitzer prize, 1968; American Book award, 1980; Connecticut Arts award, 1984; Duke University Distinguished Alumni award, 1984; Connecticut arts award, 1984; Prix Mondial del Duca, 1985; Edward MacDowell medal for excellence in the arts, 1988; Elmer Bobst award, 1989, for fiction; National Magazine award, 1990; National medal of the arts, 1993. D.Litt.: Duke University, 1968; Davidson College, North Carolina, 1986. **Member:** American Academy, and American Academy of Arts and Sciences; Commander, Order of Arts and Letters (France); Commander, Legion d'honneur; honorary member, Académie Gancourt, France. **Address:** 12 Rucum Road, Roxbury, Connecticut 06783, USA.

ROMANCE AND HISTORICAL PUBLICATIONS

Novel

The Confessions of Nat Turner. New York, Random House, 1967; London, Cape, 1968.

OTHER PUBLICATIONS

Novels

Lie Down in Darkness. Indianapolis, Bobbs Merrill, 1951; London, Hamish Hamilton, 1952.
The Long March. New York, Random House, 1956; London, Hamish Hamilton, 1962.
Set This House on Fire. New York, Random House, 1960; London, Hamish Hamilton, 1961.
Sophie's Choice. New York, Random House, and London, Cape, 1979.

Short Stories

Shadrach. Los Angeles, Sylvester and Orphanos, 1979.
A Tidewater Morning. New York, Random House, and London, Cape, 1993.

Play

In the Clap Shack (produced New Haven, Connecticut, 1972). New York, Random House, 1973.

Other

The Four Seasons, illustrated by Harold Altman. University Park, Pennsylvania State University Press, 1965.
Admiral Robert Penn Warren and the Snows of Winter: A Tribute. Winston-Salem, North Carolina, Palaemon Press, 1978.
The Message of Auschwitz. Blacksburg, Virginia, Press de la Warr, 1979.

Against Fear. Winston-Salem, North Carolina, Palaemon Press, 1981.

As He Lay Dead, a Bitter Grief (on William Faulkner). New York, Albondocani Press, 1981.

This Quiet Dust and Other Writings. New York, Random House, 1982; London, Cape, 1983.

Conversations with William Styron (interviews), edited by James L. W. West III. Jackson, University Press of Mississippi, 1985.

Darkness Visible (autobiography). New York, Random House, 1990; London, Cape, 1991.

Editor, *Best Short Stories from the Paris Review*. New York, Dutton, 1959.

*

Bibliography: *William Styron: A Descriptive Bibliography* by James L. W. West III, Boston, Hall, 1977; *William Styron: A Reference Guide* by Jackson R. Bryer and Mary B. Hatem, Boston, Hall, 1978; *William Styron: An Annotated Bibliography of Criticism* by Philip W. Leon, Westport, Connecticut, Greenwood Press, 1978.

Manuscript Collections: Library of Congress, Washington, DC; Duke University, Durham, North Carolina.

Critical Studies: *William Styron* by Robert H. Fossum, Grand Rapids, Michigan, Eerdmans, 1968; *William Styron* by Cooper R. Mackin, Austin, Texas, Steck Vaughn, 1969; *William Styron* by Richard Pearce, Minneapolis, University of Minnesota Press, 1971; *William Styron* by Marc L. Ratner, New York, Twayne, 1972; *William Styron* by Melvin J. Friedman, Bowling Green, Ohio, Popular Press, 1974; *The Achievement of William Styron* edited by Irving Malin and Robert K. Morris, Athens, University of Georgia Press, 1975, revised edition, 1981; *Critical Essays on William Styron* edited by Arthur D. Casciato and James L. W. West III, Boston, Hall, 1982; *The Root of All Evil: The Thematic Unity of William Styron's Fiction* by John K. Crane, Columbia, University of South Carolina Press, 1985; *William Styron* by Judith Ruderman, New York, Ungar, 1987.

* * *

'Less an "historical novel" in conventional terms than a meditation on history'. This is how William Styron described his only piece of historical fiction, *The Confessions of Nat Turner*. Whether or not this rather nebulous statement hints at contemporary parallels, the novel was immediately absorbed into the high-temperature political debate surrounding racial unrest in the late 1960s. It describes, through the first-person vantage of its protagonist, the inspiration, preparation, and execution of the only substantial black slave revolt in United States history.

In August 1831 a slave called Nat Turner, self-created preacher and prophet, led a bloody uprising in rural Virginia. Around 50 people were killed, and the hundred or so slaves he commanded came very close to overrunning the county seat, capturing weapons, and thus being in a position to inspire a wider insurrection. Those, at least, are the bare 'historical facts' of the matter. Naturally, in the year of the novel's publication (the year of the Watts riots and widespread black unrest) it excited much comment from all sides. White reactionary opinion predictably branded the author a liberal, and left the label at that. More surprisingly, perhaps, black writers also condemned the book, saying that Styron had adjusted the historical facts to suit his own purpose. They pointed out that his main historical source, a pamphlet that claimed to be a verbatim confession by Nat Turner, was a discredited piece of slave-owning propaganda aimed at the suspiciously abolitionist north by the southern

oligarchy. The fact that the earlier source served as the inspiration to a wealth of southern racist fantasies (among them Poe's *Arthur Gordon Pym*) merely added to their alarm. Vilified by both extremes, Styron's novel was none the less awarded the respectability of a Pulitzer prize that same year.

In many respects the political objections are grounded on an almost wilful neglect of the book's ironic complexity. Styron's black slaves are presented as Uncle Tom caricatures; but the point is made that only as such caricatures could slaves survive the bizarre society of the pre-Civil War south. More seriously, it has been alleged, the rebel group contains sociopathic monsters who delight in the atrocities they commit. If this is so, it reflects the thoughts of Frederick Douglass, who as an ex-slave saw that the inherent cruelty of the system produced nothing but brutality from master downwards: 'Everybody, in the South, wants the privilege of whipping everybody else'. It is this closed, claustrophobic world of reciprocal injustice that Styron's blood-frenzied slaves represent.

The only 'liberal' in the novel is Nat's first master, and namesake, Samuel Turner. Like Jefferson, this man aspires to a vague scheme of ultimate liberation for the slaves; but it is his inability to accept the continuing, current obscenity of slavery that causes him to lose all his slaves to shrewder and more realistic men. Naturally, the sold slaves all are destined for the *ne plus ultra* of slave society, the nightmarish territory of the deep south. Revealed to be weak and ineffectual, his slaves all sold down the river, it is Samuel Turner's failure that inspires in Nat the rage he needs to plan and execute comprehensive revenge on the white race. Again, Douglass's words on the matter seem prescient: 'Give a slave a *bad* master, and he aspires to a *good* master; give him a good master and he wishes to be his *own* master'. Nat achieves mastery not only over himself, but over a gathering conspiracy to which only his fervour can give direction.

It is in the character of Nat himself that Styron's narrative powers are revealed. Despite the fact that the whole narrative is related in the first person, the reader is still left in some doubt as to the protagonist's underlying sanity. The prophetic visions which visit him are credible both as the products of famine and of fevered imagination, or as extensions of the surreal society; in this light it is all too easy to believe he has indeed received divine sanction for his programme of righteous revenge. One scene could serve as a model for this. Immediately following Nat's central vision or hallucination (in which he sees black and white angels fighting in the sky) he encounters, in the company of his master, a starving 'free' black man. The starving man reacts not with the usual deference, but with a string of obscene abuse; in response, the white man is rendered impotent. The horror of this scene is exact and everyday, and rendered more powerful than the apocalyptic visions of Nat Turner.

If *The Confessions of Nat Turner* disappointed both white and black extremes, it is perhaps because it suggests no programmatic response to the undeniable ugliness of the racial injustice it portrays in the past and reflects in the present. It is an uneasy book, filled with unpleasantly hard facts; but the apocalypse it portrays attains somehow, almost despite the reader's revulsion, an undeniably tragic scale.

—Alan Murphy

SUMMERS, Essie

Nationality: New Zealander. **Born:** Ethel Snelson Summers in Christchurch, 24 July 1912. **Education:** North Linwood Primary School; Christchurch Technical College. **Relations:** married Reverend William N. Flett in 1940 (died 1984); one son and one daughter. **Career:** prior to World War II, worked for Londontown Drapers, Christchurch, 7 years, at Millers Ltd, 4 years; costing clerk,

Miss Sparkes Fashion Centre, Christchurch, 1939–40; columnist ('Parish Meditations' as Tamsin), Timaru *Herald*, 6 years; freelance journalist. **Address:** 32-A Tom Parker Avenue, Napier, New Zealand.

ROMANCE AND HISTORICAL PUBLICATIONS

Novels

New Zealand Inheritance. London, Mills and Boon, 1957; as *Heatherleigh*, Toronto, Harlequin, 1963.
The Time and the Place. London, Mills and Boon, 1958; Toronto, Harlequin, 1964.
Bachelors Galore. London, Mills and Boon, 1958; Toronto, Harlequin, 1965.
The Lark in the Meadow. London, Mills and Boon, 1959; as *Nurse Abroad*, Toronto, Harlequin, 1961.
The Master of Tawhai. London, Mills and Boon, 1959; Toronto, Harlequin, 1965.
Moon over the Alps. London, Mills and Boon, 1960; Toronto, Harlequin, 1964.
Come Blossom-Time, My Love. London, Mills and Boon, 1961; Toronto, Harlequin, 1963.
No Roses in June. London, Mills and Boon, 1961; Toronto, Harlequin, 1962.
The House of the Shining Tide. London, Mills and Boon, 1962; Toronto, Harlequin, 1963.
South to Forget. London, Mills and Boon, 1963; as *Nurse Mary's Engagement*, Toronto, Harlequin, 1964.
Where No Roads Go. London, Mills and Boon, and Toronto, Harlequin, 1963.
Bride in Flight. London, Mills and Boon, 1964; Toronto, Harlequin, 1965.
The Smoke and the Fire. London, Mills and Boon, and Toronto, Harlequin, 1964.
No Legacy for Lindsay. London, Mills and Boon, and Toronto, Harlequin, 1965.
No Orchids by Request. London, Mills and Boon, 1965; Toronto, Harlequin, 1966.
Sweet Are the Ways. London, Mills and Boon, 1965; Toronto, Harlequin, 1966.
Heir to Windrush Hill. London, Mills and Boon, 1966; Toronto, Harlequin, 1966.
His Serene Miss Smith. London, Mills and Boon, 1966; Toronto, Harlequin, 1967.
Postscript to Yesterday. London, Mills and Boon, 1966; Toronto, Harlequin, 1967.
A Place Called Paradise. London, Mills and Boon, and Toronto, Harlequin, 1967.
Rosalind Comes Home. London, Mills and Boon, 1968; Toronto, Harlequin, 1969.
Meet on My Ground. London, Mills and Boon, 1968; Toronto, Harlequin, 1969.
The Kindled Fire. London, Mills and Boon, 1969; Toronto, Harlequin, 1970.
Revolt—and Virginia. London, Mills and Boon, and Toronto, Harlequin, 1969.
The Bay of the Nightingales. London, Mills and Boon, and Toronto, Harlequin, 1970.
Summer in December. London, Mills and Boon, and Toronto, Harlequin, 1970.
Return to Dragonshill. London, Mills and Boon, and Toronto, Harlequin, 1971.
The House on Gregor's Brae. London, Mills and Boon, and Toronto, Harlequin, 1971.

South Island Stowaway. London, Mills and Boon, 1971; Toronto, Harlequin, 1972.
The Forbidden Valley. London, Mills and Boon, and Toronto, Harlequin, 1973.
A Touch of Magic. London, Mills and Boon, and Toronto, Harlequin, 1973.
Through All the Years. London, Mills and Boon, 1974; Toronto, Harlequin, 1975.
The Gold of Noon. London, Mills and Boon, 1974; Toronto, Harlequin, 1975.
Anne of Strathallan. London, Mills and Boon, and Toronto, Harlequin, 1975.
Beyond the Foothills. London, Mills and Boon, and Toronto, Harlequin, 1976.
Not by Appointment. London, Mills and Boon, and Toronto, Harlequin, 1976.
Adair of Starlight Peaks. London, Mills and Boon, 1977; Toronto, Harlequin, 1978.
Goblin Hill. London, Mills and Boon, and Toronto, Harlequin, 1977.
The Lake of the Kingfisher. London, Mills and Boon, 1978; Toronto, Harlequin, 1979.
Spring in September. London, Mills and Boon, and Toronto, Harlequin, 1978.
My Lady of the Fuchsias. London, Mills and Boon, and Toronto, Harlequin, 1979.
One More River to Cross. London, Mills and Boon, 1979; Toronto, Harlequin, 1980.
The Tender Leaves. London, Mills and Boon, and Toronto, Harlequin, 1980.
Autumn in April. London, Mills and Boon, 1981; Toronto, Harlequin, 1986.
Daughter of the Misty Gorges. London, Mills and Boon, 1981; Toronto, Harlequin, 1983.
A Lamp for Jonathan. London, Mills and Boon, 1982; Toronto, Harlequin, 1984.
A Mountain for Luenda. London, Mills and Boon, and Toronto, Harlequin, 1983.
Season of Forgetfulness. London, Mills and Boon, 1983; Toronto, Harlequin, 1984.
MacBride of Tordarroch. London, Mills and Boon, 1984.
Winter in July. London, Mills and Boon, 1984; Toronto, Harlequin, 1985.
To Bring You Joy. London, Mills and Boon, 1985; Toronto, Harlequin, 1986.
High Country Governess. London, Mills and Boon, 1987; Toronto, Harlequin, 1988.

OTHER PUBLICATIONS

Other

The Essie Summers Story. London, Mills and Boon, 1974.

*　　　*　　　*

Essie Summers, a New Zealand writer with a strong English background, grew up with traditions that honour the poet and storyteller. Perhaps this background accounts for her unique qualities as a writer of romance fiction. One does not sit down to read a novel by her with the intent of passing a brief hour or so. Her books have to be approached with plenty of time on one's hands, and they have to be saved for that special time when one needs a real sense of recreation. For that is what Summers does: she re-creates whole families, generations even, that fill her novels with deep vibrant love, both for each other and for their country, New Zealand.

Pace in her novels lends a slow unfolding of the story and characters so that one is able to grasp the subtle elements of conflict and tension between the main characters of the story. While most of her novels show initial antagonism between the lead characters, Summers will occasionally have a situation where another character deliberately causes trouble for those in love. For the most part, however, Summers depends on her characters to move the story along and to show the developing plot to her readers.

Usually her novels take place in remote farming areas of the country, and this in itself gives an added dimension to her works, for action, motivation, and resolution take place against an almost panoramic background of harsh, rugged country and hard-working people. It is impossible not to gain an understanding of the earlier settlers of the country and those who still hold the land as she incorporates these struggles in her stories.

For instance, in *Return to Dragonshill*, the heroine, Henrietta, agrees to return to the high-country sheep ranch to act as governess to the children there. She also meets the man she had loved (and she thought lost) several years ago for he has returned as well. His reason for returning is to build a bridge over an impassable river, an undertaking that is going to open that part of the country up to all-weather travel for the first time. Within her cast of characters, Summers takes special pains to create the character of Madame who is 100 years old. She and her husband were the very first settlers in that part of the country. Reminiscences of early tragedies, of stark, primitive living conditions, are woven into the narrative in such a way that one feels and sees the hardships of these early settlers.

Touches of homey, sentimental events instil a mood of serenity as Madame brings out scrap books of those early days containing touches of poetry, mention of short stories and essays, as well as newspaper clippings. There is a sense of timelessness and security that touches the lives of the characters in the stories, but also the lives of her readers, for much of the faith and belief that shine through these little scraps reach out to them as well.

Over and over again Summers draws vivid pictures of their way of life. Her ability to re-create the mood and life of her country and to people it with strong, sensitive characters shows remarkable creativity. The slow unfolding of her stories draws her readers towards the characters and makes them want to know that they do find a much deserved happiness. In a way, her readers feel that they have sat down with a long cosy letter from home that tells the joys and sorrows of well-loved friends and relatives. Of all modern romance writers, Summers has taken this unique way of telling her stories and has made it her own.

—Arlene Moore

SUMMERS, Rowena.   See **SAUNDERS, Jean.**

SUMMERTON, Margaret.
Pseudonym: Jan Roffman. **Nationality:** British. **Born:** Birmingham, Warwickshire. **Education:** convent school and schools in Derbyshire and London. **Career:** worked for a publishing house in Paris; reporter, London *Daily Mail* in the Netherlands and Germany during and immediately after World War II; after the war worked on several magazines in London. **Died.**

ROMANCE AND HISTORICAL PUBLICATIONS

Novels

The Sunset Hour. London, Hodder and Stoughton, 1957.

The Red Pavilion. London, Hodder and Stoughton, 1958.
A Small Wilderness. London, Hodder and Stoughton, 1959.
The Sea House. London, Hodder and Stoughton, and New York, Holt Rinehart, 1961.
Theft in Kind. London, Hodder and Stoughton, 1962.
Nightingale at Noon. London, Hodder and Stoughton, and New York, Dutton, 1963.
Quin's Hide. London, Hodder and Stoughton, 1964; New York, Dutton, 1965.
Ring of Mischief. London, Hodder and Stoughton, and New York, Dutton, 1965.
A Memory of Darkness. London, Hodder and Stoughton, and New York, Dutton, 1967.
The Sand Rose. London, Collins, and New York, Doubleday, 1969.
Sweetcrab. London, Collins, and New York, Doubleday, 1971.
The Ghost Flowers. London, Collins, and New York, Doubleday, 1973.
The Saffron Summer. London, Collins, 1974; New York, Doubleday, 1975.
A Dark and Secret Place. London, Collins, and New York, Doubleday, 1977.

Novels as Jan Roffman

With Murder in Mind. New York, Doubleday, 1963.
Likely to Die. London, Bles, 1964.
Winter of the Fox. London, Bles, 1964; as *Death of a Fox*, New York, Doubleday, 1964; as *Reflection of Evil*, New York, Ace, 1967.
A Penny for the Guy. London, Bles, and New York, Doubleday, 1965; as *Mask of Words*, New York, Ace, 1973.
The Hanging Woman. London, Bles, 1965.
Ashes in an Urn. New York, Doubleday, 1966.
A Daze of Fears. New York, Doubleday, 1968.
Grave of Green Water. London, Long, and New York, Doubleday, 1968.
Seeds of Suspicion. London, Long, 1968.
A Walk in the Dark. London, Long, 1969; New York, Doubleday, 1970.
A Bad Conscience. New York, Doubleday, 1972.
A Dying in the Night. New York, Doubleday, 1974; London, Macdonald and Jane's, 1975.
Why Someone Had to Die. London, Macdonald and Jane's, and New York, Doubleday, 1976.
One Wreath with Love. New York, Doubleday, 1978; London, Hale, 1979.

*   *   *

Conflicts of interest, clashes of loyalties, the quest for a loving family ... these are the characteristics of Margaret Summerton's novels of romantic suspense. While the settings may vary from well-described remote estates in England to exotic locales abroad (*The Sand Rose* in Tunisia, *The Ghost Flowers* in Cyprus, for instance) the novels typically focus on a competent woman with career interests who is in love with a man who seems to be unavailable, or who is surprised by love when she least expects it. Sometimes nursing memories of a dead or lost lover, she may be wooed by another man as well as the romantic hero. While the heroine wins her true love in the end, what usually escapes her is the comfort of a secure family.

Typically, Lucy in *Quin's Hide* suspects her half-brother, her employer, and Hamer, the man she has always loved, of being involved in a sinister scheme that starts with theft and fraud and develops into murder. Although Hamer is cleared, and finally declares his long-hidden love for Lucy, she loses forever the love of her foster mother and half-sister when the brother is killed escaping from the police. The sudden malice of a supposedly kind-hearted woman toward a girl who had lived with her since childhood is apparently all that can be expected in this hard life. The feeling, so pervasive in this novel, that one cannot know where to place one's trust, that one is ultimately alone in an unsafe world, is typical of Summerton's books.

In *The Sand Rose* Rachel's sister-in-law, a beautiful but arid woman who is the sole focus of her husband's devotion, attempts to locate her brother, politically at odds with the Tunisian government. Her actions thrust Rachel and the filmmaker she comes to love into a swirl of intrigue in a colourful background; but the pivotal moment comes when Rachel's brother reveals that she is completely unimportant to him in balance with his wife's happiness.

Even Elizabeth in *A Dark and Secret Place*, lucky in having a loving mother of her own, realizes that her father had cared more for her adoptive sister Olivia. It is Elizabeth who must rescue the rich Olivia from her evil husband and his sinister cohorts in Italy, with the help of Olivia's first love, who becomes Elizabeth's wooer. Just as Elizabeth becomes aware of the true affection she feels for Olivia, buried as it has been under years of resentment and jealousy, she must estrange her by taking away from her the love Olivia perceives as hers.

As stories told from a woman's point of view, Summerton's novels tend to concentrate on intangibles of mood and character. The heroes combine conventional romantic features—good looks, interesting jobs, kind natures—and are differentiated more by the interests of the different heroines than by anything intrinsic to themselves. The hero of *The Ghost Flowers* is as well realized as most, although he is physically absent for much of the book.

A stronger portrayal of a male character is found in *Why Someone Had to Die*, more strictly speaking a crime novel. It is also distinguished for the portrait of Georgina Latham, a good woman—wife and mother—but as committed as any other Summerton heroine to a relationship with a man she cannot trust even after many years of marriage. Georgina, trying to respond to the need she senses in her young lodger, risks her own life when the young woman mysteriously disappears. But her other motive, which she tries to hide even from herself, is the fear that her hot-tempered, unfaithful husband has done something to the mysterious 'Helen Jones'. Georgina is willing to make any sacrifice to conceal from her husband her fears for, and about, him.

Despite a strong initial situation and the usual effective depiction of place and atmosphere, *Sweetcrab* is not as well plotted as Summerton's other novels. Christina returns to the village where her aunt raised her and encounters again the family of her fiancé Cary who had fled after killing his father. In *Sweetcrab*, as in *The Saffron Summer*, there is no villainous criminal genius, just a number of people caught by events and circumstances, and making decisions that turn out badly. When Claudine comes as an orphan to her grandmother's estate in *The Saffron Summer*, she is looking for memories of her long-dead father; she is horrified to find her relatives, including her bastard half-brother, convinced that she is after a share of the old woman's fortune. Also in a false position is Maggie in *Ring of Mischief*, whose imperious godmother hinted to her victims that Maggie is helping her in her blackmail plot.

When Summerton does include a villain, his evil tends to be so excessive that one wonders why the other characters do not recognize it sooner. Heller, the smuggler, and Kim, his weak accomplice, fool Maria in her quest for her vanished employer in *The Ghost Flowers* for longer than is quite credible. The television star who attacks Maggie in *Ring of Mischief* has fooled all those who know him, but he reveals his evil to her as soon as they meet.

Along with the fear of betrayal and the impossibility of happy families, Summerton's books are recognizable by their evocative at-

mosphere, combining weather, place, and a pervasive sense of encroachment from hard-to-understand human emotions.

—Susan Branch

SUN, Annalise. See **LOWELL, Elizabeth.**

SUTCLIFF, Rosemary.
Nationality: British. **Born:** West Clandon, Surrey, 14 December, 1920. **Education:** privately educated, and at Bideford School of Art, Devon, 1935–39. **Career:** since 1945, full-time writer. **Recipient:** Carne medal, 1959; Library Association Carnegie medal, 1960, for *The Lantern Bearers*; Lewis Carroll Shelf award, 1971, for *The Witch's Brat*; The Other award, 1978, for *Song for a Dark Queen*; Phoenix award, 1985, for *The Mark of the Horse Lord*. OBE (Officer, Order of the British Empire), 1975, for services to children's literature; CBE (Commander, Order of the British Empire), 1992. **Member:** PEN, National Book League, Society of Authors, Royal Society of Miniature Painters. Fellow, Royal Society of Literature, 1982. **Died:** 23 July 1992.

ROMANCE AND HISTORICAL PUBLICATIONS

Novels

Lady in Waiting. London, Hodder and Stoughton, 1956; New York, Coward McCann, 1957.
The Rider of the White Horse. London, Hodder and Stoughton, 1959; as *Rider on a White Horse*, New York, Coward McCann, 1960.
Sword at Sunset. London, Hodder and Stoughton, 1963; New York, Coward McCann, 1964.
The Flowers of Adonis. London, Hodder and Stoughton, 1969; New York, Coward, 1970.
Blood and Sand. London, Hodder and Stoughton, 1987.

OTHER PUBLICATIONS

Plays

Mary Bedell, produced in Chichester, 1986.

Screenplays: *Ghost Story*, 1975.

Other

Rudyard Kipling. London, Bodley Head, 1960.
Blue Remembered Hills: A Recollection (autobiography). London, Bodley Head, 1983; New York, Morrow, 1984.

PUBLICATIONS FOR CHILDREN

Fiction

The Armourer's House, illustrated by C. Walter Hodges. London, and New York, Oxford University Press, 1951.
Brother Dusty-Feet, illustrated by C. Walter Hodges. London, Oxford University Press, and New York, Walck, 1952.
Simon, illustrated by Richard Kennedy. London, Oxford University Press, and New York, Walck, 1953.

Three Legions: A Trilogy. London, Oxford University Press, 1980.
  The Eagle of the Ninth, illustrated by C. Walter Hodges. London, Oxford University Press, 1954; New York, Walck, 1955.
  The Silver Branch, illustrated by Charles Keeping. London, Oxford University Press, 1957; New York, Walck, 1959.
  The Lantern Bearers, illustrated by Charles Keeping. London, Oxford University Press, and New York, Walck, 1959.
Outcast, illustrated by Richard Kennedy. London, Oxford University Press, and New York, Walck, 1955.
The Shield Ring, illustrated by C. Walter Hodges. London, Oxford University Press, and New York, Walck, 1956.
Warrior Scarlet, illustrated by Charles Keeping. London, Oxford University Press, and New York, Walck, 1958.
The Bridge-Builders. Oxford, Blackwell, 1959.
Knight's Fee, illustrated by Charles Keeping. London, Oxford University Press, and New York, Walck, 1960.
Dawn Wind, illustrated by Charles Keeping. London, Oxford University Press, 1961; New York, Walck, 1962.
The Mark of the Horse Lord, illustrated by Charles Keeping. London, Oxford University Press, 1965.
The Chief's Daughter, illustrated by Victor Ambrus. London, Hamish Hamilton, 1967.
A Circlet of Old Leaves, illustrated by Victor Ambrus. London, Hamish Hamilton, 1968.
The Witch's Brat, illustrated by Robert Micklewright. London, Oxford University Press, and New York, Walck, 1970.
The Truce of the Games, illustrated by Victor Ambrus. London, Hamish Hamilton, 1971.
Heather, Oak and Olive: Three Stories, illustrated by Victor Ambrus. New York, Dutton, 1972.
The Capricorn Bracelet, illustrated by Charles Keeping. London, Oxford University Press, and New York, Walck, 1973.
The Changeling, illustrated by Victor Ambrus. London, Hamish Hamilton, 1974.
We Lived in Drumfyvie, with Margaret Lyford-Pike. London, Blackie, 1975.
Blood Feud, illustrated by Charles Keeping. London, Oxford University Press, and New York, Dutton, 1977.
Shifting Sands, illustrated by Laszlo Acs. London, Hamish Hamilton, 1977.
Sun Horse, Moon Horse, illustrated by Shirley Felts. London, Bodley Head, 1977; New York, Dutton, 1978.
Song for a Dark Queen. London, Pelham, 1978; New York, Crowell, 1979.
Frontier Wolf. London, Oxford University Press, 1980; New York, Dutton, 1981.
Eagle's Egg, illustrated by Victor Ambrus. London, Hamish Hamilton, 1981.
Bonnie Dundee. London, Bodley Head, 1983; New York, Dutton, 1984.
The Roundabout Horse, illustrated by Alan Marks. London, Hamish Hamilton, 1986.
Flame-Coloured Taffeta. London, Oxford University Press, and New York, Farrar Straus, 1986.
A Little Dog Like You, illustrated by June Johnson. London, Orchard, 1987; New York, Farrar Straus, 1990.
Little Hound Found, illustrated by Jo Davis. London, Hamish Hamilton, 1989.
The Shining Company. London, Bodley Head, and New York, Farrar Straus, 1990.

Other

The Chronicles of Robin Hood, illustrated by C. Walter Hodges, London, Oxford University Press, and New York, Oxford University Press, 1950.

The Queen Elizabeth Story, illustrated by C. Walter Hodges. London, Oxford University Press, and New York, Walck, 1950.
Houses and History, illustrated by William Stobbs. London, Batsford, 1960; New York, Putnam, 1965.
Beowulf, illustrated by Charles Keeping. London, Bodley Head, 1961; New York, Dutton, 1962; as *Dragon Slayer*, London, Penguin, 1966.
The Hound of Ulster (Cuchulain Saga), illustrated by Victor Ambrus. London, Bodley Head, and New York, Dutton, 1963.
A Saxon Settler, illustrated by John Lawrence. London, Oxford University Press, 1965.
Heroes and History, illustrated by Charles Keeping. London, Batsford and New York, Putnam, 1965.
The High Deeds of Finn Mac Cool, illustrated by Michael Charlton. London, Bodley Head, and New York, Dutton, 1967.
Tristan and Iseult, illustrated by Victor Ambrus. London, Bodley Head, and New York, Dutton, 1971.
Arthurian Knights Trilogy
  The Light Beyond the Forest: The Quest for the Holy Grail, illustrated by Shirley Felts. London, Bodley Head, 1979; New York, Dutton, 1980.
  The Sword and the Circle: King Arthur and the Knights of the Round Table, illustrated by Shirley Felts. London, Bodley Head, and New York, Dutton, 1981.
  The Road to Camlann: The Death of King Arthur, illustrated by Shirley Felts. London, Bodley Head, 1981; New York, Dutton, 1982.
Black Ships Before Troy, with Alan Ley Frances. London, Lincoln, 1990.

Editor, with Monica Dickens, *Is Anyone There?* (on the Samaritans). London, Penguin, 1978.

*

Manuscript Collection: Kerlan Collection, University of Minnesota, Minneapolis, USA.

Critical Study: *Rosemary Sutcliff* by Margaret Meek, London, Bodley Head, and New York, Walck, 1962.

*   *   *

Rosemary Sutcliff is well known as an author of historical novels for children, but when she felt that a theme was too sophisticated, a story too political, a character too complex to be accessible to a younger audience, she wrote for adults.

Her books always contain rich language. Sutcliff had the ability to make her reader see what she observed, although this occasionally tipped over into purple prose. She set her scenes beautifully with wonderful descriptions of the countryside, the alternating seasons, and the varying colour of the sky. Flowers are a constant motif in Sutcliff's books. In *The Rider of the White Horse* the chilly snowdrops that come early and the Provence roses of summer appear regularly; in *The Flowers of Adonis* the Britons choose flowers as their field signs and as a grace note; and Thomas, in *Blood and Sand*, pays extra rent so that his wife will be able to pick a rose a day.

Sutcliff excelled at depicting battle scenes, and was equally at home describing fights between the Britons and the Saxons, the Royalists and the Roundheads, or desert warfare in 19th-century Arabia. She had a fine understanding of tactics and of the importance of topography in battle. She understood the serviceman's mind, his loyalties, and the bonds of comradeship that often make relationships between men far stronger than those between men and women. In *Blood and Sand*, Thomas's loyalty to his blood brother

Tussun is stronger than his albeit tender love for his wife; similarly, Artos has an unhappy marriage to Guenhumara (the Guinever of legend), and favours his friend and companion Bedwyr; and Black Tom Fairfax's love for his cousin is envied by Anne Fairfax. Alkibiades, the engaging rogue and hero of *The Flowers of Adonis*, trusts only his pilot, Antiochus—after his death Alkibiades begins to see Timandra, a flute girl, who adores him but whom he treats only with rough kindness. Similarly, animals—horses, dogs, and even a kitten—appear as beloved companions to Sutcliff's characters.

Sutcliff declared that she felt most at home with the Roman occupation of Britain and the Dark Ages. *Sword at Sunset*, arguably her best book, describes a demythologized version of the Matter of Britain (the literary term used for this period in history). Arthur, the future king, becomes Artos the Bear, warrior leader of the Romano-Britons fighting desperately to hold the Saxon invaders at bay. *Sword at Sunset* is full of fascinating characters and wonderful scenes. Sutcliff dispenses entirely with the Merlin part of the Matter of Britain, but introduces plausible explanations for the events that grew by exaggeration into the magical elements of the heroic tale. Artos's unwitting incest with his sister, which results in a son who will bring about his destruction, is pivotal to the plot, and when Artos dies it is as much to atone for this sin as in his role as a king dying for his people.

The Flowers of Adonis is a less successful book. Set in Greece in the 5th century B.C., the politics are difficult to understand and the number of characters are bewildering. The life of Alkibiades is told in the first person by a variety of people, and although this succeeds in showing the different sides of Alkibiades's character, it also diffuses the story and distances the reader from the main thrust of the book. The battle scenes take place at sea, and are not as stirring as Sutcliff's land fights. Alkibiades is a charismatic leader but also shows himself to be an opportunist who changes sides whenever it suits him. The book ends with his assassination and leaves the reader feeling that his life was wasted. In Sutcliff's other books that end with the protagonist's death, the hero dies willingly—Artos gives his life for his people, and Thomas Keith dies for his blood brother.

Blood and Sand is based on the true story of Thomas Keith, a young Scottish soldier who is wounded and is left behind during Napoleon's invasion of Egypt. He is bought and trained as a cavalryman among the Bedouin. His subsequent rise through the Turkish Viceroy's army, his friendship with Tussun, the Viceroy's son, his conversion to Islam, and his final triumph in becoming Emir of Medina are described in glorious detail. Descriptions of the desert contrast with the hothouse intrigue of the Viceroy's court. Sutcliff includes graphic battle scenes and two amazing (and true) hand-to-hand fights (a duel after Thomas is insulted, and a heroic single-handed defence after ten men set upon him at night).

Sutcliff's books are a feast for lovers of scrupulously researched historical novels full of tiny details that bring events alive, that explore interesting characters and evoke them so well that one feels one would know them if one met them in the street, and that show panoramas of beautifully described scenery. Above all, Sutcliff's stories make one feel uplifted.

—Pamela Cleaver

SWAN, Annie S.

Pseudonym: David Lyall. **Nationality:** British. **Born:** Mountskip, Gorebridge, Scotland. **Education:** Queen Street Ladies' College, Edinburgh; and privately. **Relations:** married James Burnett Smith in 1883 (died 1927); one daughter and one son. **Career:** writer and journalist from the 1870s; editor, *Woman at Home* magazine,

London, 1893–1917, the *Annie S. Swan Penny Stories*, later *Penny Weekly*, 1898–99, and the *Annie S. Swan Annual* from 1924. **Died:** 17 June 1943.

ROMANCE AND HISTORICAL PUBLICATIONS

Novels (series: Elizabeth Glen)

Ups and Downs: A Family Chronicle. London, Charing Cross, 1878.
Shadowed Lives. Glasgow, Marr, 1880.
Bess: The Story of a Waif. Glasgow, Marr, 1880.
Grandmother's Child. London, Partridge, 1882; as *Grannie's Little Girl*, 1925.
Inside the Haven. London, Blackie, 1882.
Aldersyde: A Border Tale of Seventy Years Ago. Edinburgh, Oliphant, and New York, Carter, 1883.
The Better Part. London, Partridge, 1884.
Carlowrie; or, Among Lothian Folks. Edinburgh, Oliphant, 1884; Cincinnati, Jennings and Pye, n.d.
Dorothea Kirke; or Free to Serve. Edinburgh, Oliphant, and Cincinnati, Cranston and Stowe, 1884.
Mark Desborough's Vow. London, Partridge, 1884.
Ursula Vivian, The Sister-Mother. Edinburgh, Oliphant, 1884; Cincinnati, Cranston and Stowe, 1890.
Warner's Chase; or, The Gentle Heart. London, Blackie, 1884.
Adam Hepburn's Vow: A Tale of Kirk and Covenant. London, Cassell, 1885; New York, Cassell, 1888.
A Divided House: A Study from Life. Edinburgh, Oliphant, 1885.
Thankful Rest. London, Nelson, 1885.
Freedom's Sword: A Tale of the Days of Wallace and Bruce. London, Cassell, 1886.
The Gates of Eden: A Story of Endeavour. Edinburgh, Oliphant, 1886; Cincinnati, Cranston and Stowe, 1890.
Robert Martin's Lesson. Edinburgh, Oliphant, 1886; Cincinnati, Cranston and Stowe, 1890.
Sundered Hearts. Edinburgh, Oliphant, 1886.
Thomas Dryburgh's Dream: A Story of the Sick Children's Hospital. Edinburgh, Oliphant, 1886.
Briar and Palm: A Study of Circumstance and Influence. Edinburgh, Oliphant, 1887; Cincinnati, Cranston and Stowe, 1890.
Jack's Year of Trial. London, Nelson, 1887.
The Strait Gate. London, Partridge, 1887.
Doris Cheyne: The Study of a Noble Life. Edinburgh, Oliphant, 1888; Cincinnati, Cranston and Stowe, 1890.
Hazell & Sons, Brewers. Edinburgh, Oliphant, 1888; Cincinnati, Cranston and Stowe, 1891.
The Secret Panel. Edinburgh, Oliphant, 1888.
St Veda's; or, The Pearl of Orr's Haven. Edinburgh, Oliphant, 1889; Cincinnati, Cranston and Stowe, n.d.
Sheila. Edinburgh, Anderson and Ferrier, 1890; Cincinnati, Cranston and Stowe, 1891.
Across Her Path. Cincinnati, Cranston and Stowe, 1890; London, Leng, 1925.
Maitland of Laurieston: A Family History. Edinburgh, Oliphant, 1890; Cincinnati, Jennings and Pye, n.d.
A Vexed Inheritance. Edinburgh, Oliphant, 1890; Cincinnati, Cranston and Stowe, 1893.
The Ayres of Studleigh. Edinburgh, Oliphant, and New York, Hunt and Eaton, 1891.
Who Shall Serve? A Story for the Times. Edinburgh, Oliphant, 1891.
The Guinea Stamp: A Story of Modern Glasgow. Edinburgh, Oliphant, and Cincinnati, Cranston and Stowe, 1892.
A Bitter Debt: A Tale of the Black Country. London, Hutchinson, 1893.

Homespun: A Study of Simple Folk. London, Hutchinson, 1893; New York, Dutton, n.d.

The Answer to a Christmas Prayer. New York, Collier, 1894.

A Foolish Marriage: An Edinburgh Story of Student Life. London, Hutchinson, 1894.

A Lost Ideal. Edinburgh, Oliphant, 1894.

A Victory Won. London, Hutchinson, 1895.

Fettered Yet Free: A Study in Heredity. New York, Dodd Mead, 1895.

Elizabeth Glen, MB: The Experience of a Lady Doctor. London, Hutchinson, 1895.

Kinsfolk. London, Hutchinson, 1896.

A Stormy Voyager. London, Hutchinson, 1896.

The Curse of Cowden. London, Hutchinson, 1897.

Mrs Keith Hamilton, MB: More Experiences of Elizabeth Glen. London, Hutchinson, 1897.

The Ne'er-Do-Weel. London, Hutchinson, 1897.

Conscience Money (as David Lyall). London, Hodder and Stoughton, 1898.

Greater Love (as David Lyall). London, Hodder and Stoughton, 1898.

Not Yet: A Page from a Noble Life. London, Hutchinson, 1898.

Wyndham's Daughter: A Story of To-day. London, Hutchinson, 1898.

A Son of Erin. London, Hutchinson, 1899.

Twice Tried. Cincinnati, Cranston and Stowe, n.d.; London, Leng, 1928.

An American Wife. London, Hutchinson, 1900; as *An American Woman*, New York, Dutton, n.d.

The Burden-Bearers. London, Hutchinson, 1900.

Love Grown Cold. London, Methuen, 1902.

Mary Garth: A Clydeside Romance. London, Hodder and Stoughton, 1904.

Christian's Cross; or, Tested and True. London, Hodder and Stoughton, 1905.

Love, The Master Key. London, Hodder and Stoughton, 1905.

A Mask of Gold: The Mystery of the Meadows. London, Hodder and Stoughton, 1906.

Nancy Nicholson; or, Who Shall Be Heir? London, Hodder and Stoughton, 1906.

Love Unlocks the Door. London, Hodder and Stoughton, 1907.

Anne Hyde, Travelling Companion. London, Hodder and Stoughton, 1908.

The Broad Road. London, Hurst and Blackett, 1908.

Hester Lane. London, Hodder and Stoughton, 1908.

The Inheritance. London, Hodder and Stoughton, 1909.

The Old Moorings: A Story of Modern Life. London, Hodder and Stoughton, 1909.

Love's Barrier. London, Cassell, 1910.

Love's Miracle. London, Hodder and Stoughton, 1910.

Margaret Holroyd; or, The Pioneers. London, Hodder and Stoughton, 1910.

The Mystery of Barry Ingram. London, Cassell, 1910.

Rhona Keith. London, Hodder and Stoughton, 1910.

What Shall It Profit? or, Roden's Choice. London, Partridge, 1910.

The Last of Their Race. London, Hodder and Stoughton, 1911.

To Follow the Lead. London, Kelly, 1911.

The Bondage of Riches. London, Partridge, 1912.

A Favourite of Fortune. London, Cassell, 1912.

Woven of the Wind. London, Hodder and Stoughton, 1912.

The Bridge Builders. London, Hodder and Stoughton, 1913.

The Farrants: A Story of Struggle and Victory. London, Kelly, 1913.

The Fairweathers: A Story of the Old World and the New. London, Hodder and Stoughton, 1913.

Prairie Fires. London, Cassell, 1913.

Corroding Gold. London, Cassell, 1914.

Meg Hamilton: An Ayrshire Romance. London, Hodder and Stoughton, 1914.

Love Gives Itself: The Story of a Blood Feud. London, Hodder and Stoughton, 1915.

The Step-Mother. London, Hodder and Stoughton, 1915.

The Woman's Part. London, Hodder and Stoughton, 1916.

Young Blood. London, Hodder and Stoughton, 1917.

Hands Across the Sea. London, Oliphant, 1919.

The Ruling Passion. London, Leng, 1920.

The Ivory God. London, Hodder and Stoughton, 1923.

Macleod's Wife: A Highland Romance. London, Hodder and Stoughton, 1924.

A Maid of the Isles: A Romance of Skye. London, Hodder and Stoughton, 1924.

Wrongs Righted. London, Leng, 1924.

Elsie Thorburn. London, Leng, 1926; as *The World Well Lost*, 1935.

Closed Doors. London, Leng, 1926.

The Pendulum. London, Hodder and Stoughton, 1926; New York, Doran, 1927.

For Love of Betty. London, Leng, 1928.

Love the Prodigal. London, Leng, 1929.

Fiona Macrae. London, Leng, 1929; as *The Pride of Fiona Macrae*, 1934.

A Wild Harvest. London, Leng, 1929.

The Forerunners. London, Hodder and Stoughton, 1930.

The House on the Rock. London, Leng, 1930.

The Marching Feet. London, Hodder and Stoughton, 1931.

The Luck of the Livingstones. London, Leng, 1932.

The Maclure Mystery. London, Leng, 1932.

The Shore Beyond. London, Hodder and Stoughton, 1932.

Christine Against the World. London, Leng, 1933.

The Last of the Laidlaws: A Romance of the Border. London, Leng, 1933.

The Little Stranger. London, Leng, 1933.

A Winsome Witch. London, Leng, 1933.

The Purchase Price. London, Leng, 1934.

Between the Tides. London, Hodder and Stoughton, 1935.

A Homing Bird. London, Leng, 1935.

The Way of Escape. London, Leng, 1935.

A Breaker of Hearts. London, Leng, 1937.

A Portrait of Destiny. London, Leng, 1937.

The Road to Damascus. London, Hodder and Stoughton, 1937.

The Family Secret. London, Leng, 1938.

The Greater Freedom. London, Leng, 1938.

The Head of the House. London, Leng, 1938.

The White House of Marisaig; or, The Interloper. London, Leng, 1938.

The Witch in Pink. London, Leng, 1938.

Double Lives. London, Leng, 1939.

These Are Our Masters. London, Hodder and Stoughton, 1939.

A Trust Betrayed. London, Leng, 1939.

The Uninvited Guest. London, Leng, 1939.

Peggy Fordyce. London, Leng, 1940.

Proud Patricia. London, Leng, 1940.

Rebel Hearts. London, Leng, 1940.

The Secret of Skye. London, Leng, 1940.

The Third Generation. London, Leng, 1940.

Dreams Come True. London, Leng, 1941.

The Mischief-Makers. London, Leng, 1941.

The Younger Brother. London, Leng, 1941.

The Dark House. London, Leng, 1941.

The Family Name. London, Leng, 1942.

Who Are the Heathen? London, Hodder and Stoughton, 1942.

Short Stories

Climbing the Hill. London, Blackie, 1883.
For Lucy's Sake: A Homely Story. London, Partridge, 1883.
Katie's Christmas Lesson. Edinburgh, Oliphant, 1883.
Marion Forsyth; or, Unspotted from the World. Edinburgh, Oliphant, 1883; with *Mistaken*, Cincinnati, Cranston and Stowe, 1892.
Mistaken. Edinburgh, Oliphant, 1883; with *Marion Forsyth*, Cincinnati, Cranston and Stowe, 1892.
Tony's Memorable Christmas. Edinburgh, Oliphant, 1883.
A Year at Coverley. London, Blackie, 1883.
The Bonnie Jean. Glasgow, Scottish Temperance Society, 1884.
Holidays at Sunnycroft. London, Blackie, 1885.
Wilful Winnie. London, Nelson, 1886.
Miss Baxter's Bequest. Edinburgh, Oliphant, 1888.
Climbing the Hill and Other Stories. London, Blackie, 1891.
A Bachelor in Search of a Wife, and Roger Marcham's Ward. Edinburgh, Oliphant, 1892.
The Bonnie Jean and Other Stories. Edinburgh, Oliphant, 1895.
The Secret of Dunston Mere. London, Hodder and Stoughton, 1898.
For the Sake of the Family. London, Hodder and Stoughton, 1898.
An Elder Brother. London, Hodder and Stoughton, 1898.
A Runaway Daughter. London, Hodder and Stoughton, 1898.
The Lady Housekeeper. London, Hodder and Stoughton, 1898.
A Blessing in Disguise. London, Hodder and Stoughton, 1898.
Alone in Paris. London, Hodder and Stoughton, 1898.
The Wedding of Kitty Barton. London, Hodder and Stoughton, 1898.
In Haste to Be Rich. London, Hodder and Stoughton, 1898.
The Dream of Mary Muldoon. London, Hodder and Stoughton, 1898.
Jasper Dennison's Christmas. London, Hodder and Stoughton, 1898.
Seth Newcome's Wife. London, Hodder and Stoughton, 1898.
The False and the True. London, Hodder and Stoughton, 1898.
Stephen Glyn. London, Hodder and Stoughton, 1898.
Married in Haste. London, Hodder and Stoughton, 1898.
What She Could. London, Hodder and Stoughton, 1898.
Sir Roderick's Will: A Love Story. London, Hodder and Stoughton, 1898.
Two Friends. London, Hodder and Stoughton, 1898.
A Married Man. London, Hodder and Stoughton, 1898.
An Only Son. London, Hodder and Stoughton, 1898.
A New Woman. London, Hodder and Stoughton, 1898.
Aunt Anne's Money. London, Hodder and Stoughton, 1898.
After Many Years. London, Hodder and Stoughton, 1899.
A Truant Wife. London, Hodder and Stoughton, 1899.
Good Out of Evil. London, Hodder and Stoughton, 1899.
Gable Farm. London, Hodder and Stoughton, 1899.
A Blessing in Disguise and Other Stories. London, Hodder and Stoughton, 1902.
The False and the True and Other Stories. London, Hodder and Stoughton, 1902.
Good Out of Evil and Other Stories. London, Hodder and Stoughton, 1902.
An Only Son and Other Stories. London, Hodder and Stoughton, 1902.
The Secret of Dunston Mere and Other Stories. London, Hodder and Stoughton, 1902.
Stephen Glyn and Other Stories. London, Hodder and Stoughton, 1902.
The Homecoming of the Boys. Edinburgh, Clark, 1916.
For Lucy's Sake and Other Stories. London, Wright and Brown, 1935.
The Collected Stories of Annie S. Swan. London, Clarke, 1942.

OTHER PUBLICATIONS

Poetry

Songs of Memory and Hope. Edinburgh, Nimmo, and New York, Caldwell, 1911; as *Love's Crown*, Nimmo, 1913.

Other

Courtship and Marriage, and the Gentle Art of Home-Making. London, Hutchinson, 1893.
Memories of Margaret Grainger, Schoolmistress. London, Hutchinson, 1896.
From a Turret Window. London, Hodder and Stoughton, 1902.
The Outsiders, Being a Sketch of the Social Work of the Salvation Army. London, Salvation Army, 1905.
Letters to a War Bride. London, Hodder and Stoughton, 1915.
An Englishwoman's Home. New York, Doran, 1918.
As Others See Her. Boston, Houghton Mifflin, 1919; as *America at Home: Impressions of a Visit in War Time*, London, Oliphant, 1920.
My Life: An Autobiography. London, Nicholson and Watson, 1934.
We Travel Alone. London, Nicholson and Watson, 1935.
The Land I Love. London, Nicholson and Watson, 1936.
Seed Time and Harvest: The Story of the Hundred Years' Work of the Women's Foreign Mission of the Church of Scotland. London, Nelson, 1937.
The Enchanted Door: A Fireside Philosophy. London, Nicholson and Watson, 1938.
The Letters of Annie S. Swan, edited by Mildred Robertson Nicoll. London, Hodder and Stoughton, 1945.

*   *   *

Annie S. Swan was, in her day, in the league of superwriters of romance fiction, and is said to have written over 250 novels and stories. Her advice was even marketed in non-fiction form. Her works were reprinted as late as the 1950s but today are largely of antiquarian interest, being unreadable by modern standards.

Settings of some of her novels are firmly of their period, such as the family-run department store in *Love, The Master Key* (1905) or the suffragette movement in *Margaret Holroyd* (1910). Some of the backgrounds are historical settings: *A Mask of Gold* (1906), *The Forerunners* (1930), and *Woven of the Wind* (1912) all have early 19th-century Scottish settings. It is not the historical novels which appear so dated, however, but the turn-of-the-century life which is often effectively portrayed, such as the hard-heartedness of City of London financiers in *What Shall It Profit?* (1910), or the penny trams so many of her heroines take and the toques that so many of them wear.

The world that Swan sees is essentially the world seen through women's eyes. This world is often hard ('It's a hard thing to be a woman') on the unemancipated women who live and sometimes work in it. Downtrodden shop assistants and servants get much less out of life than the upper-class ladies who also populate this world, and live by a hard, but also a Christian, fatalism. Pride is fierce and reputation important, even among those who suffer a genteel poverty, as in *Love Unlocks the Door* (1907); this novel also stresses the tight bonds of 19th-century social order. There is much thwarted ambition, thwarted nature, and stifled love in Swan's novels.

Some of the webs of relationships rival in complexity those of the novels of George Eliot but do not contain her intellectual depth. Many of the plots are very contrived, containing secret marriages and runaway sons and daughters. There are sometimes, as in *Love Unlocks the Door* and *For Lucy's Sake* (1883), violent confrontations between two principal male characters over the love of a girl. As well as some melodrama, there is also plenty of maudlin sentimentality, as in the death of Lucy, the climax of *For Lucy's Sake*, and the use of her gravestone inscription as the last few lines of the story.

The location of many of her books is Scotland and northeast England and this sometimes serves to add an element of caricature to character portrayal of oppressed women. The picture of Edinburgh in which she portrays the carefully graded strata of Scottish society is particularly authentic. But the use of the dialect 'Scotch' language by many characters (sometimes only at unguarded moments) lessens their credibility and also makes the books difficult for the modern reader; the Geordie dialect transliteration is almost incomprehensible. In her later novels, Swan uses less dialogue (*The Pendulum*, 1926), but uses a rather more exaggerated style of description.

Swan had a keen ear for the social groundswell of the period she lived in, and keeps this sense of period updated in her later novels. The characters in the later books tend to be better dressed, higher in the social scale, and English. Swan's characterization is much improved in her later novels, but this is offset by open invocation of the Christian religion and almost mystical tendencies. Her love scenes are always very chaste.

—P.R. Meldrum

SWANSON, Neil H(arman).
Nationality: American. **Born:** Minneapolis, Minnesota, 30 June 1896. **Education:** University of Minnesota, Minneapolis. **Military Service:** United States Army in France, 1914–18. **Career:** editorial assistant and managing editor, Minneapolis *Journal*; managing editor, Pittsburgh *Press*, 1930–32; assistant editor, Baltimore *Evening Sun*, 1932–39. **Died:** 5 February 1983.

ROMANCE AND HISTORICAL PUBLICATIONS

Novels

The Judas Tree. New York, Putnam, 1933.
The Flag Is Still There. New York, Putnam, 1933.
The Phantom Emperor. New York, Putnam, 1934.
The First Rebel. New York, Farrar and Rinehart, 1937.
The Forbidden Ground. New York, Farrar and Rinehart, 1938.
The Silent Drum. New York, Farrar and Rinehart, 1940.
The Unconquered: A Novel of the Pontiac Conspiracy. New York, Doubleday, 1947.
The Star-Spangled Banner, with Anne S. Swanson. Philadelphia, Winston, 1958.

OTHER PUBLICATIONS

Other

The Perilous Flight. New York, Farrar and Rinehart, 1945.

*   *   *

Neil H. Swanson began his writing career as a newspaper writer and editor. He held positions on several newspapers, including the Baltimore *Evening Sun*. He was also the author of several non-fiction books dealing with the American colonial period and became well-known for his expertise on the War of 1812. Swanson's fiction evolved from a writing plan to re-create the life and history of four colonies, Maryland, Virginia, Delaware, and Pennsylvania, as well

as the Ohio territory. His goal was to complete 30 novels, each an independent work, that built on characters and events in the others. He hoped that this series would give a continuous narrative of the American frontier and its settling as far west as the Mississippi.

This grand design began in 1933 with the publication of *The Judas Tree*. As intended, some of the characters later appeared in *The Silent Drum* and in *The Unconquered*. Swanson apparently had several volumes planned for he indicated their titles in the preface of *The Unconquered*, but he never completed them. He did complete *The Silent Drum*, *The Forbidden Ground*, and *The First Rebel*.

Swanson explored two major beliefs about the early colonial period. First, he sought to identify the nebulous concept of the 'American character'. He felt that by 1763 the elements that made the American character were well ingrained in the minds and thoughts of the colonists. These beliefs were not limited to people born there; new arrivals seemed instinctively to accept the concepts. He noted, 'They were not always pleasant people . . . . They weren't easy to conquer—they believed too deeply that whatever they wanted was right and was theirs by right'.

Hardships were forgotten or ignored, distance meant nothing to these early settlers and they were bound by no limits, few laws, and almost no social barriers.

The second element Swanson noted was the refusal of the colonists to remain 'Tide-water' bound. Until the French and Indian wars, colonial settlements remained on the eastern sea coast and extended only to the eastern slope of the Alleghenys. Settlements were limited by British military forces and colonial land grants. Explorers, trappers, and traders were all aware of the western slopes and beyond, but it was the war itself that eventually provided the impetus and chances for the western movement.

Swanson found that the continued battle for the Fort Pitt area was the key to making the expansion possible. Time and again he returned to this theme when he used Fort Pitt and the Ohio territory as the battleground between colonists and Indians. He held a firm belief that 'men create their own disasters'. The resulting bloody battles fought over the Ohio valley more than illustrate his opinion.

The Unconquered is more than a fast-paced exciting tale of Indian attacks and atrocities. It is more than a love story between a condemned felon, Abigail Martha Hale, and Christopher Holden, surveyor and colonist. It is also the story of treachery, cunning, and deliberate murder that Martin Garth resorts to as he sets out to control the vast territory of the Ohio Valley. The plot is actually straightforward. Chris returns from London where he traced Garth's activities in buying guns and other weapons to trade to the Indians. Garth is also the husband of Guyasuta's daughter, Hannah. Guyasuta, himself, is one of the foremost Seneca chiefs and close to Chief Pontiac. By allying himself to these Indians, Garth hopes to obtain absolute title to the lands of the Ohio Valley once the settlers have been driven out. Abigail is basically a pawn between Chris and Garth. Generally she reacts to situations with courage and strength, if not a great deal of understanding. Abby grows to love Chris after he manages to save her from Garth and the Indians.

The major action of the novel centres on Chris's attempts to warn the settlers of a massive Indian uprising, an event known as Pontiac's conspiracy. Its uniqueness centres on the fact that numerous Indian tribes, even those who were enemies, banded together to defeat the white invasion. The method used by the Indians is to encourage the forts to surrender with the promise of safe conduct under a flag of truce. The Indians, instead, massacre the settlers after their surrender. However, many settlers manage to flee to Fort Pitt and they are eventually relieved by a British military force.

Characterization is well done. Although some of the characters tend to be stereotypical, they are believable. Swanson had a definite feel for the British character, showing their gallantry and military stubbornness during this period with fascinating results. For instance, Chris is sent with peace belts to various Indian villages. He is gone for two weeks and covers several hundred miles. Yet, when he returns to Fort Pitt, he is arrested for dereliction of duty. Swanson's writing is tight, compelling, stark at times, forcing his readers to feel the emotions of his characters. His novels are exciting, action packed, vivid with detail, and entertaining.

Swanson is one of the few writers who sought to tell the story of this early period of American history. His work is meticulous and his obvious commitment to truth adds an unsurpassed dimension to his writing. He was truly an outstanding writer of historical fiction.

—Arlene Moore

* * *

SWINDELLS, Madge.
Address: c/o Little, Brown and Company (UK) Ltd, 165 Great Dover Street, London SE1 4YA, England.

ROMANCE AND HISTORICAL PUBLICATIONS

Novels

Summer Harvest. London, Macdonald, 1983; New York, Doubleday, 1984.
Song of the Wind. London, Macdonald, and New York, Doubleday, 1985.
Shadows on the Snow. London, Macdonald, 1987.
The Corsican Woman. London, Macdonald, and New York, Warner, 1988.

* * *

Madge Swindells's first novel, *Summer Harvest*, appeared in 1983. Set in South Africa and spanning 30 years, 1938 to 1968, it follows the fortunes of Anna van Achtenburgh. Born the daughter of a wealthy landowner, she marries impoverished Simon Smit. She is disinherited and works to create her own fortune—only to face ruin through scandal before she can achieve true happiness. Compared critically with Colleen McCullough's *The Thornbirds*, it joined the ranks of *Dallas*-style sagas exemplified by such writers as Judith Krantz and Jackie Collins, and sets the pattern for Swindells's subsequent novels.

Swindells's world is that of the wealthy and powerful. Her novels deal almost exclusively with characters who move in such circles whether in London or a Corsican village. Wealth and power are the most important criteria for success. When, as often happens, one of the protagonists falls on hard times, the poverty is usually extreme but allows the business acumen of those involved to be exercised, leading to success. Wealth is rarely inherited—rather it is the reward for hard work (and frequently cunning manoeuvring) and therefore deserved. However without love it is seen as a barren reward.

The background to the books is international—often cosmopolitan—South Africa, the fashion world of London, Yugoslavia, Corsica. However it rarely intrudes upon the action. Place is not important in terms of adding depth to the novels; it adds local colour to a certain extent—the descriptions of the Namib Desert and the coast of South Africa, the Corsican landscape as a background to resistance against the Nazis. But not even in *Summer Harvest*, set in the farming community of the Cape of Good Hope country, nor in *The Corsican Woman*, where the action is completely localized, is there any specific atmosphere of place. The events might be occurring anywhere.

Of far more importance to Swindells are the characters whose careers are followed over several years often by means of a flashback technique. She employs a large cast. Characterization is therefore not deep, but her protagonists are dramatic. Nor are there clear-cut distinctions between heroes (or heroines) and villains. Rather the chief characters, for all their good points, are seen as having some fatal obsession which almost destroys them, while many of the apparent villains are redeemed in the end.

The women, especially the female protagonists, are selfwilled, independent, intelligent, assertive, and beautiful, and are seen as succeeding in male-dominated areas of endeavour. Often presented as hard and calculating (Anna in *Summer Harvest*, Marika in *Song of the Wind*, Eleanor in *Shadows on the Snow*) they are really totally feminine underneath: 'tough outside, a stern unbending virago to strangers but warm and compassionate to those she knew and trusted'. It is usually the absence or failure of love that has caused this facade and it is not until the denouement that it can be broken by the rediscovery of love so long denied or rejected. Their beauty is almost always dramatic and is constantly emphasized in fulsome terms, like Sybilia in *The Corsican Woman*: 'but even then she was lovely with a bruised sensuous beauty that incited male aggression and the rancour of unfulfilled desires'. Marika in *Song of the Wind* is 'a woman of incredible loveliness. Her skin was porcelain white and quite flawless, her unusual golden hair hung around her shoulders, her features were perfect, her figure tempting and voluptuous, her face was dominated by her enormous slanting amber-brown eyes'.

The men likewise are unfailingly good looking and usually 'arrogantly male'. This, however, is tempered in the heroes by an innate sensitivity and kindness, while the villains display harshness, even cruelty. This is particularly apparent in the scenes of sexual passion when are an important and recurring feature of all of the novels. Rape has its place as an ingredient in the crowded plots, as does loss of virginity. Love is seen very much in terms of its physical expression.

But almost more important than sex, which is obligatory in novels of this type, is the revenge motif. It is desire for revenge that directs Swindells's characters and determines their actions and reactions. It is the implacable and unrelenting pursuit of revenge that leads to the near downfall of these characters. So Anna achieves success to gain revenge on her husband only to have it all snatched from her; Marika pursues a vendetta against the Nazi she blames for her parent's death—again to her detriment; Sybilia shoots her father-in-law as an act of revenge. Finally, dramatic revelation, frequently in court, is used to restore equilibrium and allow the action to reach a traditional happy ending.

—Ferelith Hordon

* * *

TANNAHILL, Reay.
Nationality: British. **Born:** Glasgow, Scotland, 9 December 1929. **Education:** Shawlands Senior Secondary School, Glasgow; University of Glasgow, Scotland, M.A. 1951. **Relations:** married Michael Edwardes, 8 August 1958 (divorced 1983). **Career:** journalist, *Times Education Supplement*, 1952–56; advertising manager, Thames and Hudson, London, 1956–58; advertising consultant, Folio Society, 1958–62. Since 1962, writer. **Recipient:** Chianti Ruffino Antico Fattore award, 1988; Boots Romantic Novel of the Year, 1990, for *Passing Glory*. **Agent:** Gill Coleridge, RCW, 20 Powis Mews, London W11 1JN, England.

ROMANCE AND HISTORICAL PUBLICATIONS

Novels

A Dark and Distant Shore. London, Century, and New York, St Martin's Press, 1983.

The World, the Flesh and the Devil. London, Century, 1985; New York, Crown, 1987.
Passing Glory. London, Century, 1989; New York, Crown, 1990.
In Still and Stormy Waters. London, Orion, 1992.

OTHER PUBLICATIONS

Other

Regency England: The Great Age of the Colour Print. London, Folio Society, 1964.
Paris in the Revolution. London, Folio Society, 1966.
The Fine Art of Food. London, Folio Society, 1968.
Food in History. London, Eyre Methuen, and New York, Stein and Day, 1973; revised edition, London, Penguin, 1988.
Flesh and Blood: A History of the Cannibal Complex. London, Hamilton, and New York, Stein and Day, 1975.
Sex in History. London, Hamilton, and New York, Stein and Day, 1980.

*   *   *

Reay Tannahill's knowledge of social history seems to be encyclopaedic which is not surprising as she has written authoritative non-fiction books on various aspects of life in the past. The details she uses are well-chosen and skilfully integrated into her exciting historical novels, set mainly in Scotland.

She writes family sagas set in the 19th century or early part of the 20th century with large casts, often covering several generations. However, *The World, the Flesh and the Devil* is different, covering the years of the 15th century. Ninian Drummond has been bought up in sophisticated Avignon by her uncle, Archdeacon Crozier, and comes to a bleak castle in Scotland as a bride. She falls in love with Gavin Cameron, Bishop of Glasgow, and chancellor to James I. Besides her love being forbidden by the Church, Ninian's family are feuding with Cameron. This book has too much ecclesiastical history and not enough romance, however this cannot be said of Tannahill's other books.

A Dark and Distant Shore was a bestseller, reaching the top ten in hardback and paperback. It covers 90 years from the beginning of the 19th century, and depicts Vilia Cameron's struggle to regain her family home from which she is reft at the age of five and tells of her three marriages and the stories of her descendants.

For *Passing Glory*, Tannahill deservedly won the Romantic Novel of the Year award. This saga is set on Clydeside and Dorset. It contrasts the Jardines who work in the shipyard with the Brittons who own it. The story starts with Queen Victoria's funeral in 1901, and ends just after Elizabeth II's coronation in 1953. The hero, Matthew Britton, is easily the most, attractive man in any of her books, although Rainer Blake in *In Still and Stormy Waters*, runs a close second.

In Still and Stormy Waters is another saga set in Victorian Scotland and Hong Kong. It contrasts the stories of Rachel and Sophie Macmillan, cousins whose lives and personalities are very different but who both want to own Juran, the castle they consider their birthright. Their characters are based on those of Mary Queen of Scots and Elizabeth I but this is not obtrusive.

Tannahill's descriptions are evocative and all the books have a strong sense of place, houses featuring strongly. Vilia's love of Kinveil, a castle in the western Highlands, is possessive and passionate as in Rachel's of Juran, another castle in the same area, which is the bone of contention between her and Sophie. Vilia's ancestor, Gavin Cameron, comes from Kinveil and although *Passing Glory* is set in Glasgow and Dorset, towards the end of the book, one of the characters mentions he is planning to buy an old Scottish castle called Kinveil.

Although she has attractive heroes, Tannahill's heroines dominate the books. These are women who, although very much of their times, (Tannahill never lets us forget how circumscribed the lives of women were in the past), have strong ambitions and almost modern feminist feelings. Several of them show they are capable of holding their own in a man's world. Ninian Drummond, unlike most women of her time, believes women have as much right to think for themselves as men do. Vilia Cameron finds herself having to become an ironmaster in 19th-century Glasgow, Jenny Jardine knows more about running a Clydeside shipyard than many of the men in the family into which she is married, Rachel efficiently runs a sporting estate while her rival Sophie, although feather-headed to begin with, takes a small part in the running of an import/export business in Hong Kong.

Her heroines tend to have disastrous first marriages, Vilia is not in love with her husband and doesn't meet the love of her life until she has already borne two children; Jenny loves her first husband but he is killed at the Battle of Jutland within a fortnight of their wedding day; she is afraid of her second husband and the man with whom she is in love is her first husband's brother, a forbidden relationship in the early-20th century. Ninian's arranged marriage is loveless—she has no say in the choice of groom—her true love is forbidden because he is a cleric. Sophie's first husband is a brutal drug addict and it is only Rachel who has just one marriage which is happy, although she hankers after Rainer Blake, Sophie's second husband—another bone of contention between them.

These books are well written, richly textured, extremely readable and admirably researched; the characterization is excellent and to curl up with one of her sagas is both enjoyable and rewarding.

—Pamela Cleaver

TATE, (John Orley) Allen.
Nationality: American. **Born:** Winchester, Kentucky, 19 November 1899. **Education:** Georgetown Preparatory School, Washington, DC; Vanderbilt University, Nashville, Tennessee, 1918–22, B.A. 1923. **Relations:** married 1) the writer Caroline Gorden in 1924 (divorced and remarried, 1946; separated, 1955; divorced, 1959), one daughter; 2) the poet Isabella Stewart Gardner in 1959 (separated 1965; divorced 1966); 3) Helen Heinz in 1966, twin sons. **Career:** co-founder of *The Fugitive*, Nashville, 1922–25; high school teacher, Lumberport, West Virginia, 1924; assistant to the editor, *Telling Tales* magazine, New York, 1925; lived in Patterson, New York, 1926–27, Paris, 1928–29, Clarksville, Tennessee, 1930–31, and France, 1932–33; lecturer in English, Southwestern College, Memphis, Tennessee, 1934–36; professor of English, The Woman's College, Greensboro, North Carolina, 1938–39; poet-in-residence, Princeton University, New Jersey, 1939–42; consultant in Poetry, Library of Congress, Washington, DC, 1943–44; editor, *Sewanee Review*, Tennessee, 1944–46; editor, Belles Lettres series, Henry Holt (publisher), New York, 1946–48; lecturer in Humanities, New York University, 1948–51; from 1951, professor of English, University of Minnesota, Minneapolis: Regents' professor, 1966; professor emeritus, 1968. Visiting professor in humanities, University of Chicago, 1949; Fulbright lecturer, Oxford University, 1953; University of Rome, 1953–54, and Oxford and Leeds Universities, 1958–59; Department of State lecturer, universities of Liège and Louvain, 1954, Delhi and Bombay, 1956, the Sorbonne, Paris, 1956, Nottingham, 1956, Urbino and Florence, 1961; visiting professor of English, University of North Carolina, Greensboro, 1966, and Vanderbilt University, 1967. Fellow, 1948, and senior fellow, 1956, Kenyon School of English, Kenyon College, Gambier, Ohio (now Indiana University School of Letters, Bloomington). **Recipient:** Guggenheim fellowship, 1928, 1929; American

Academy grant, 1948; Bollingen prize, 1957; Brandeis University creative arts award, 1960; Dante Society gold medal (Florence), 1962; Academy of American poets fellowship, 1963; National medal for literature, 1976. D.Litt.: University of Louisville, Kentucky, 1948; Coe College, Cedar Rapids, Iowa, 1955; Colgate University, Hamilton, New York, 1956; University of Kentucky, Lexington, 1960; Carleton College, Northfield, Minnesota, 1963; University of the South, Sewanee, Tennessee, 1970. **Member:** American Academy, 1964; chancellor, Academy of American Poets, 1964; American Academy of Arts and Sciences, 1965; president, National Institute of Arts and Letters, 1968. **Died:** 9 February 1979.

ROMANCE AND HISTORICAL PUBLICATIONS

Novels

The Fathers. New York, Putnam, and London, Eyre and Spottiswoode, 1938; revised edition, Denver, Swallow, and London, Eyre and Spottiswoode, 1960.

The Fathers and Other Fiction. Baton Rouge, Louisiana State University Press, 1977.

OTHER PUBLICATIONS

Poetry

The Golden Mean and Other Poems, with Ridley Wills. Privately printed, 1923.

Mr Pope and Other Poems. New York, Minton Balch, 1928.

Ode to the Confederate Dead. Being the Revised and Final Version of a Poem Previously Published on Several Occasions: To Which Are Added Message from Abroad and The Cross. New York, Minton Balch, 1930.

Three Poems. New York, Minton Balch, 1930.

Poems 1928–1931. New York, and London, Scribner, 1932.

The Mediterranean and Other Poems. New York, Alcestis Press, 1936.

Selected Poems. New York, Scribner, 1937.

Sonnets at Christmas. Cummington, Massachusetts, Cummington Press, 1941.

The Winter Sea: A Book of Poems. Cummington, Massachusetts, Cummington Press, 1944.

Poems 1920–1945: A Selection. London, Eyre and Spottiswoode, 1947.

Fragment of a Meditation. Cummington, Massachusetts, Cummington Press, and London, Eyre and Spottiswoode, 1947.

Poems 1922–1947. New York, Scribner, and London, Eyre and Spottiswoode, 1948.

Two Conceits for the Eye to Sing, If Possible. Cummington, Massachusetts, Cummington Press, 1950.

Poems. New York, Scribner, 1960.

The Swimmers and Other Selected Poems. Oxford, Oxford University Press, 1970; New York, Scribner, 1971.

Collected Poems 1919–1976. New York, Farrar Straus, 1977.

Play

The Governess, with Anne Goodwin Winslow (produced 1962).

Other

Stonewall Jackson: The Good Soldier: A Narrative. New York, Minton Balch, and London, Cassell, 1928.

Jefferson Davies: His Rise and Fall: A Biographical Narrative. New York, Minton Balch, 1929.

I'll Take My Stand: The South and the Agrarian Tradition, with others. New York, Harper, 1930.

Reactionary Essays on Poetry and Ideas. New York, Scribner, 1936.

Reason in Madness: Critical Essays. New York, Putnam, 1941.

Invitation to Learning, with Huntington Cairns and Mark Van Doren. New York, Random House, 1941.

Recent American Poetry and Poetic Criticism: A Selected List of References. Washington, DC, Library of Congress, 1943.

Sixty American Poets 1896–1944: A Preliminary Check-list. New York, Morrow, and London, Swallow Press, 1945.

On the Limits of Poetry: Selected Essays, 1928–48. New York, Alan Swallow, 1948.

The Hovering Fly and Other Essays. Cummington, Massachusetts, Cummington Press, 1948.

The Forlorn Demon: Didactic and Critical Essays. Chicago, Regnery, 1953.

Man of Letters in the Modern World: Selected Essays 1928–1955. New York, Meridian Books, and London, Thames and Hudson, 1955.

Collected Essays. Denver, Allen Swallow, 1959; as *Essays of Four Decades*, Chicago, Swallow Press, 1968; Oxford, Oxford University Press, 1969.

Christ and the Unicorn: An Address. Cummington, Massachusetts, Cummington Press, 1966.

Mere Literature and the Lost Traveller. Chicago, Swallow Press, 1968; Oxford, Oxford University Press, 1970.

The Translation of Poetry. Washington, DC, Library of Congress, 1972.

The Literary Correspondence of Donald Davidson and Allen Tate, edited by John Tyree Fain and Thomas Daniel Young. Athens, University of Georgia Press, 1974.

Memoirs and Opinions 1926–1974. Chicago, Swallow Press, 1975; as *Memories and Essays: Old and New 1926–1974*, Manchester, Carcanet, 1976.

The Republic of Letters in America: The Correspondence of John Peale Bishop and Tate, edited by Thomas Daniel Young and John J. Hindle. Lexington, University Press of Kentucky, 1981.

The Poetry Reviews of Tate 1924–1944, edited by Ashley Brown and Frances Neel Cheney. Baton Rouge, Louisiana State University Press, 1983.

The Lytle/Tate Letters, with Allen Tate, edited by Thomas Daniel Young and Elizabeth Sarcone. Jackson, University Press of Mississippi, 1987.

Editor, with others, *Fugitives: An Anthology of Verse.* New York, Harcourt, Brace, 1928.

Editor, with Herbert Agar, *Who Owns America? A New Declaration of Independence.* Boston, Houghton Mifflin, 1936.

Editor, with A. Theodore Johnson, *America Through the Essay: An Anthology for English Courses.* New York, Oxford University Press, 1938.

Editor, *The Language of Poetry.* Princeton, New Jersey, Princeton University Press, 1942.

Editor, *Princeton Verse Between Two Wars: An Anthology.* Princeton, Princeton University Press, 1942.

Editor, with John Peale Bishop, *American Harvest: Twenty Years of Creative Writing in the United States.* New York, Garden City Publishing, 1942.

Editor, *A Southern Vanguard: The John Peale Bishop Memorial Volume.* New York, Prentice Hall, 1947.

Editor, *The Collected Poems of John Peale Bishop.* New York, Scribner, 1948.

Editor, with Caroline Gordon. *The House of Fiction: An Anthology of the Short Story.* New York, Scribner, 1950; revised edition, 1960.

Editor, with David Cell, *Modern Verse in English, 1900–1950*. London, Jarrold, 1958.

Editor, with John Berryman and Ralph Ross, *The Arts of Reading* (anthology). New York, Crowell, 1960.

Editor, *Selected Poems of John Peale Bishop*. New York, Scribner, 1960.

Editor, with Robert Penn Warren, *Selected Poems*, by Denis Devlin. New York, Holt, Rinehart, and Winston, 1963.

Editor, *T.S. Eliot: The Man and His Work*. New York, Delacorte Press, 1966; London, Chatto and Windus, 1967.

Editor, *The Complete Poems and Selected Criticism of Edgar Allan Poe*. New York, New American Library, 1968.

Editor, *Six American Poets: From Emily Dickinson to the Present: An Introduction*. Minneapolis, University of Minnesota, 1972.

Translator, *The Vigil of Venus/Pervigilium Veneris*. Cummington Massachusetts, Cummington Press, 1943.

*

Bibliography: *Tate: A Bibliography* by Marshall Fallwell, Jr, New York, David Lewis, 1969.

Critical Studies: *The Last Alternatives: A Study of the Works of Allen Tate* by R.K. Meiners, Denver, Swallow Press, 1962; *Allen Tate* by George Hemphill, Minneapolis, University of Minnesota, 1964; *Allen Tate* by Ferman Bishop, Boston, Twayne, 1967; *Rumors of Morality: An Introduction to Allen Tate* by M.E. Bradford, Dallas, Argus Academic Press, 1969; *Allen Tate: A Literary Biography* by Radcliffe Squires, New York, Bobbs-Merrill, 1971, and *Allen Tate and His Work: Critical Evaluations* edited by Squires, Minneapolis, University of Minnesota, 1972; *Allen Tate and the Augustinian Imagination: A Study of the Poetry* by Robert S. Dupree, Baton Rouge, Louisiana State University Press, 1983; *Tate and the Poetic* edited by J. Larry Allums, Baton Rouge, Louisiana State University Press, 1984; *Allen Tate: A Recollection* by Walter Allen, Baton Rouge, Louisiana State University Press, 1988; *Hart Crane and Allen Tate: Janus-Faced Modernism* by Langdon Hammer, Princeton, New Jersey, Princeton University Press, and Chichester, Wiley, 1993.

*   *   *

Allen Tate's most ambitious work is set in old Georgetown in the District of Columbia and in neighbouring Virginia at the time of Southern secession and the outbreak of the Civil War. His two short stories written some years before the novel, provide a frame around it. The one with the earlier setting, 'The Migrants', does not involve the same characters as 'The Immortal Woman' or *The Fathers*; but rather provides a general background for understanding the settlement of the old Southwest and the expansion of slavery after the American Revolution. It describes the restless westward movement of several families, from an already economically depressed tidewater Virginia to more promising Tennessee and then Missouri, in search of greater opportunities between 1770 and 1820 by a narrator looking backward from 1851. Tate regarded it as an experiment to convince himself that he could master the details of pioneer life and give it a hint of Defoe-like verisimilitude.

Allen had thought that the Elwin family from this 'chronicle', as he fittingly labelled it, might provide one of two main subjects for a subsequent novel; but he decided before beginning it that he would not write again about pioneers. The story provides, however, the leit motif for Allen's whole wistful saga when the narrator observes, 'In my time and generation, we were always saying good-bye'. This tale of the gradual, unspectacular withering away of family and community ties is written in the same elegiac tone as Tate's most

famous poem, 'Ode to the Confederate Dead', pondering the wearing away of the names on gravestones behind 'the shut gate and the decomposing wall'.

The Fathers is a far more complex, obscure, and violent tale of conflicting loyalties in the seldom fictionally exploited region of the national capital at the time the Civil War broke out and threw families and neighbours reluctantly into deadly opposition. The action begins on the day in 1860 of the death of the mother of the teenaged narrator, Lacy Buchan, whose whole family is assembled for the last time, and flashed back to the summer of 1858, when George Posey from Georgetown won both the laurel crown of Fairfax, (Virginia) tournament and the hand of Lacy's sister Susan from angry local contenders.

Through the next two sections 'The Crisis' and 'The Abyss', Virginia's secession from the Union and the early battles across from Washington are seen through the eyes of a family torn by conflicting loyalties as George Posey takes over, bit by bit, old Major Buchan's control of the estate. The Major remains an ardent Unionist, who despairs as he sees those close to him seized by the rebellion fever. Finally, as he is dispossessed from his burning mansion, Pleasant Hill, by the Union forces he has supported, he hangs himself. George Posey, however, frequently escapes death during the ambiguous and often mysterious course he follows of paying only lip service to either cause while taking money from both sides.

Tate briefly revised the ending of the novel in 1975 in order to give it 'two heroes: Major Buchan, the classical hero whose hubris destroys him: George Posey, who may have seemed to some readers a villain, is now clearly a modern romantic hero'. In an Introduction to Faulkner's *Sanctuary*, Tate described the Southern myth that Faulkner and other writers cultivated as presenting the view that 'The South, afflicted with the curse of slavery—a curse, like that of Original Sin, for which no single person is responsible—had to be destroyed, the good along with the evil'. Tate's fiction, however, portrays individuals as bearing greater burdens of individual guilt. Near the end of the novel, Major Buchan explains to Lacy that it was never George Posey's 'intention to do evil but he does evil because he has not the will to do good. The only experience that he shares with humanity is the pursuing grave'. Commenting for a 1979 reprinting of the novel with the stories, Tate notes that in slightly clarifying the end of the novel, he intended to suggest that George's lack of principle 'will permit Lacy to survive in a new world in which not all the old traditions, which Lacy partially represents, are dead'.

Tate's description of the unprincipled Posey as a 'modern romantic hero' reveals the ironic attitude of American 'New Critics' towards Romanticism, as does the vision underlying 'The Immortal Woman', the earlier of the two short stories and the one that led down a devious path to the plotting of *The Fathers*. Conceived as an experiment in telling a story through a Jamesean 'trapped narrator'—a World War I wounded veteran confined to a wheelchair—who annually observes an unknown old lady come to sit before a house across the street without entering it, the narrative consists of his 'scattered impressions', which the reader is left to sort out. Tate confides, however, that the old lady is George Posey's sister, in *The Fathers*, and that a gentleman who comes to take her away for the last time 'could be her own son or grandson . . . a vigorous and inferentially prosperous American'. We also learn from a rent collector that 'It won't be five more years till there's Niggers in all these houses', including George Posey's once fashionable but now deserted Georgetown mansion. Tate's venture into historical fiction ends on the persistent note in all his work that change means loss, deterioration, goodbye—but not necessarily apocalypse.

—Warren French

TATE, Ellalice. See **PLAIDY, Jean.**

TATTERSALL, Jill. British. 1931—. See 2nd edition, 1990.

TAYLOR, Janelle (Diane Williams).
Nationality: American. **Born:** Athens, Georgia, 28 June 1944.
Education: Athens High School, 1958–62; Augusta College,
Georgia, 1980–81. **Relations:** married Michael Howard Taylor in
1965; two daughters. **Career:** orthodontic nurse, Athens, 1962–65,
and Augusta, 1967–68 and 1973–74; research technologist, Medical
College of Georgia, Augusta, 1975–77; lecturer in writing,
1982–85. **Agent:** Adele Leone Agency, 26 Nantucket Place, Scars-
dale, New York 10583, USA. **Address:** 4366 Deerwood Lane,
Evans, Georgia 30809, USA.

ROMANCE AND HISTORICAL PUBLICATIONS

Novels (series: Princess Alysa; Moondust; Sioux Saga)

Savage Ecstasy (Sioux). New York, Zebra, 1981.
Defiant Ecstasy (Sioux). New York, Zebra, 1982.
Forbidden Ecstasy (Sioux). New York, Zebra, 1982.
Brazen Ecstasy (Sioux). New York, Zebra, 1983.
Love Me with Fury. New York, Zebra, 1983.
Tender Ecstasy (Sioux). New York, Zebra, 1983.
First Love, Wild Love. New York, Zebra, 1984; London, Sphere,
   1986.
Golden Torment. New York, Zebra, 1984.
Valley of Fire. New York, Silhouette, 1984; London, Severn House,
   1993.
Savage Conquest (Sioux). New York, Zebra, 1985; London,
   Sphere, 1987.
Stolen Ecstasy (Sioux). New York, Zebra, 1985.
Destiny's Temptress. New York, Zebra, 1986; London, Sphere,
   1987.
Moondust and Madness (Moondust). New York, Bantam, 1986;
   London, Sphere, 1988.
Sweet, Savage Heart. New York, Zebra, 1986.
Bittersweet Ecstasy (Sioux). New York, Zebra, 1987; London,
   Sphere, 1987.
Wild Is My Love (Alysa). New York, Bantam, 1987.
Fortune's Flames. New York, Zebra, 1988.
Passions Wild and Free. New York, Zebra, 1988.
Wild Sweet Promise (Alysa). New York, Bantam, 1989.
Kiss of the Night Wind. New York, Zebra, 1989.
Whispered Kisses. New York, Zebra, 1990.
Follow the Wind. New York, Zebra, 1990.
Forever Ecstasy. New York, Zebra, 1991.
Stardust and Shadows (Moondust). New York, Zebra, 1992.
Midnight Secrets. New York, Zebra, 1992.
Taking Chances. New York, Zebra, 1993.
Promise Me Forever. New York, Zebra, 1993.
Sweet Savage Heart. New York, Zebra, 1993.
The Last Viking Queen. New York, Zebra, 1994.

*

Manuscript Collection: University of Georgia Library, Athens.

Janelle Taylor comments:
   Most of my works are authentic, adventurous, romantic historical
fiction. To catch and retain a reader's interest, I make every attempt
to be fast-paced, suspenseful, and original. My characters are
created with love and great care to be realistic, memorable, and admirable. I write about strong, passionate, courageous characters
who are a blend of real and fictional people. I weave tales around
factual events, difficult and heroic times, and fascinating periods to
reveal the traits, dreams, turmoil, and tests of people who made—or
could have made—America great. I have used the settling of the old
west, the Alaska Gold Rush, the Civil War, Texas ranger exploits,
the war of 1812, and the Indian conflicts as backdrops for my novels.
Although my main love and interest lie in the rip-roaring west, I've
written about England, Vikings, pirates, and British East Africa. I
usually prefer to remain in America, between 1700 and 1900. I try to
find a unique angle and fresh approach to plots used many times.
Determined to be authentic and detailed, I am very careful with research, to the point of checking out the smallest fact. It is my aim to
enlighten and enrich while entertaining. I want my readers to enjoy
learning about olden days and people, so I strive to bring history to
life in a stimulating way. My books touch their emotions; help them
through bad times; and teach them about the many facets of life,
love, and commitment. When people read my works, I want them to
finish feeling happy and satisfied with a well-told tale. My dream is
that more women and men will look beyond the often stigmatized
genre of romance to discover what well-crafted novels these are so
they, too, can enjoy them.

*   *   *

   Janelle Taylor has made her reputation in the romance field by
writing passionate sagas set in the old American west. Four of these
novels centre on the love story of a beautiful white woman, Alisha,
and a handsome Sioux warrior, Gray Eagle. In the muscular arms of
this handsome brave she finds a fulfilment she never believed possible. There are problems and resentments caused by this mixed
marriage but by the end of the fourth novel, *Brazen Ecstasy*, most of
those barriers have been destroyed. Their descendants pursue
similar lives of romance and adventure. For example, in *Stolen Ecstasy* the heroine, Rebecca Kinny, can remember how miserable she
was when she lived among her own white people. Her capture by
Bright Arrow, son of Gray Eagle and Alisha, gave her a chance at
true happiness. However, their happiness is jeopardized when
Bright Arrow's tribe banishes him for marrying a white woman instead of taking her as his slave.
   Lots of adventure awaits the characters in Taylor's work and,
when they are not dodging bandits or other assorted outlaws, the
hero and heroine spend a great deal of time making love, and
discussing where their relationship is leading them. In *Forever
Ecstasy*, Morning Star, the granddaughter of Gray Eagle, falls in
love with a white man, Joseph Lawrence. She eventually returns
with him, as his wife, to his plantation home in Virginia. Their
daughter Miranda (*Savage Conquest*) returns to the West and falls in
love with the Sioux warrior Blazing Star.
   The old West provides the background to Taylor's best novels.
Since the author has an obvious love for that time and has researched
the period thoroughly, her novels have an air of authenticity. Her depiction of life among Native Americans although glamorized still
includes enough accurate detail to portray the dignity and courage of
this often maligned people.
   Many of her stories centre on the interaction between western and
native cultures. Rana Michaels of *Sweet, Savage Heart* was
captured by the Sioux as a child. Years later her grandfather, a
wealthy rancher, finds out that she is still alive and, with the help of
the hero, Travis, sets out to find her. Travis knows the problems of
mixing cultures as he grew up among the Sioux (his mother's
people), but he was forced to leave that life as a young man.
   Taylor also writes more traditional western romances such as
Passions Wild and Free, in which heroine Randee Hollis seeks a

gunman to help avenge the murder of her uncle's family by the notorious Epson gang. The handsome stranger whom she hires is Marsh Logan, a special government agent, who has his own reasons for wanting to capture the outlaws. In *First Love, Wild Love*, Calinda Braxton goes to Texas to look for a father she hasn't seen since she was a child. His last known location was the Cardone ranch where she meets and soon falls under the spell of the virile, secretive Lynx. *Follow the Wind* tells the story of Texas beauty Jessica Lane, who loves and is loved by two men, one a rancher and the other a cold-blooded gunslinger.

Taylor has broken out of the western mode with such novels as *Destiny's Temptress*, set during the Civil War, and *Wild Is My Love*, which takes place in 5th-century Britain. Savannah, Georgia in the year 1875 is the setting of *Promise Me Forever*. The heroine is thrice widowed Rachel who is suspected of causing her last husband's death.

Taylor has also tried her hand at a science fiction/romance novel, *Moondust and Madness*. Unfortunately the plot is so ludicrous that even the soaring passion of the hero and heroine can not save it.

Taylor does best when she follows the advice most often given to writers—'write what you know'. Her tales of the old American West have a special zest reflecting her fascination with the period. Almost all of her historical romances appeal to readers who enjoy blazing romance set in turbulent times.

—Patricia Altner

TAYLOR, Jayne. See **KRENTZ, Jayne Ann.**

TEMPEST, Jan. See **CHANDOS, Fay.**

TEMPEST, Sarah. See **PONSONBY, D.A.**

TERRY, C.V. See **SLAUGHTER, Frank G.**

THANE, Elswyth.
Nationality: American. **Born:** Burlington, Iowa, 16 May 1900. **Relations:** married the naturalist William Beebe in 1927 (died 1962). **Career:** journalist and film writer. **Died.**

ROMANCE AND HISTORICAL PUBLICATIONS

Novels (series: Williamsburg)

Riders of the Wind. New York, Stokes, 1926; London, Murray, 1928.
Echo Answers. New York, Stokes, and London, Murray, 1927.
His Elizabeth. New York, Stokes, and London, Murray, 1928.
Cloth of Gold. New York, Stokes, and London, Murray, 1929.
Bound to Happen. New York and London, Putnam, 1930.
Queen's Folly. New York, Harcourt Brace, and London, Constable, 1937.
Tryst. New York, Harcourt Brace, and London, Constable, 1939.
Remember Today: Leaves from a Guardian Angel's Notebook. New York, Duell, 1941; London, Hale, 1948.

From This Day Forward. New York, Duell, 1941; London, Hale, 1947.
Williamsburg:
    Dawn's Early Light. New York, Duell, 1943; London, Hale, 1945.
    Yankee Stranger. New York, Duell, 1944; London, Hale, 1947.
    Ever After. New York, Duell, 1945; London, Hale, 1948.
    The Light Heart. New York, Duell, 1947; London, Hale, 1950.
    Kissing Kin. New York, Duell, 1948; London, Hale, 1951.
    This Was Tomorrow. New York, Duell, 1951; London, Hale, 1952.
    Homing. New York, Duell, 1957; London, Hale, 1958.
Melody. New York, Duell, 1950; London, Hale, 1952.
The Lost General. New York, Duell, 1953; London, Hale, 1954.
Letter to a Stranger. New York, Duell, 1954; London, Hale, 1955.

OTHER PUBLICATIONS

Plays

The Tudor Wench (produced London, 1933). London, French, 1933.
Young Mr Disraeli (produced London, 1934; New York, 1937). London, French, 1935.
Bound to Happen (produced New York, 1939).

Other

The Tudor Wench. New York, Brewer Warren and Putnam, 1932; London, Hurst and Blackett, 1933.
Young Mr Disraeli. New York, Harcourt Brace, and London, Constable, 1936.
England Was an Island Once. New York, Harcourt Brace, 1940; London, Constable, 1941.
The Bird Who Made Good. New York, Duell, 1947.
Reluctant Farmer. New York, Duell, 1950; as *The Strength of the Hills*, New York, Christian Herald House, 1976.
The Family Quarrel: A Journey Through the Years of the Revolution. New York, Duell, 1959; London, Hale, 1960.
Washington's Lady. New York, Duell, 1960.
Potomac Squire. New York, Duell, 1963.
Mount Vernon Is Ours: The Story of Its Preservation. New York, Duell, 1966.
Mount Vernon Family (for children). New York, Macmillan, 1968.
The Virginia Colony (for children). New York, Macmillan, 1969.
Dolley Madison: Her Life and Times. New York, Macmillan, 1970.
The Fighting Quaker: Nathanael Greene. New York, Hawthorn, 1972.

*   *   *

Elswyth Thane was a prolific writer notable for the variety of her work. She wrote a number of contemporary romantic novels in addition to her well-known biographies, yet she achieved greatest success with her historical romances, especially the popular Williamsburg novels. Her early works, all set in England, are improbable romantic adventures, in which briefly sketched characters move through confusing plots. *Queen's Folly* was the first work to break out of this mould with some success, and also introduced a supernatural theme which was to recur in Thane's later work. The characters in *Queen's Folly* are rather less fanciful than their predecessors, but Thane's major breakthrough is in her use of historical settings. Her most successful and most popular works combine her love of England and her ability convincingly to depict the past in love stories which still charm modern readers.

The 'Williamsburg' novels follow the fortunes of the intertwined Day-Sprague-Campion families from just before the American

Revolution to the London Blitz in World War II. Her characters experience the Revolutionary War (*Dawn's Early Light*), the Civil War (*Yankee Stranger*), the Spanish-American War (*Ever After*), World War I (*The Light Heart*), the rise of the Nazis (*Kissing Kin* and *This Was Tomorrow*), and the early stages of World War II (*Homing*). The plots are organized around historical events which Thane takes pains to describe accurately. Her descriptions of Williamsburg, New York in the 1890s, and the Cotswolds are quite detailed, and provide depth to the novels. While there are no real villains (Prince Conrad in the *The Light Heart* and his son, Victor, in *This Was Tomorrow* come close, but are tragically flawed rather than utterly wicked), war and totalitarianism are the serious threats to her lovers' happiness. The 'Williamsburg' novels should be read as part of a series, although the first three can stand on their own.

For all Thane's characters, family is tremendously important, and her few orphans (Julian in *Dawn's Early Light*, Gwen and Dinah in *Ever After*) find not just mates, but roots and well-branched family trees. The men are brave in battle and crisis, and they are portrayed as level-headed fellows used to taking charge and coping with major and minor tragedies. Many are journalists (Julian Day is a writer, Cabot and Bracken Murray and Jeff Day are newsmen), a device which allows them to observe and comment on the historical events of their periods. Thane's women are occasionally independent (Phoebe Sprague in *The Light Heart* is a writer) but are happy to settle down in blissful domesticity after their romantic adventures. From that secure position they can occasionally aid the next generation in its respective romantic involvements. Thane's heroines are frequently in need of rescue—from a drunken father, Yankee soldiers, the wreck of the *Lusitania*, even the snares of a Nazi spy—by her capable and experienced heroes. The lovers feel passion, but consummate their love discreetly within marriage—these novels are not 'bodice-rippers'. In *Homing* the hero and heroine are reincarnations of Julian and Tibby, the main characters of the first 'Williamsburg' novel (*Dawn's Early Light*), and the rescue is mutual. Mab/Tibby saves Jeff/Julian from his depression while he in turn rescues her from her own fears.

Thane used her own experiences and her careful historical research to enrich her work, so that her historical novels are somewhat denser and more compelling than others of the genre. Her attractive and likeable characters are easy to care for, and Thane's readers are carried into a happy world where men are true and women are gentle, and where true love triumphs, despite the adversities of war and revolution. The modern reader may be occasionally jarred to encounter stereotypes like the happy loyal slaves of the Williamsburg novels, but Thane's intent is to entertain, not to expose the less attractive aspects of the past.

—Mary C. Lynn

THOMAS, Rosie.

A pseudonym. **Nationality:** British. **Education:** St Hilda's College, Oxford. **Relations:** married the literary agent Caradoc King (divorced). **Career:** worked for A. and C. Black Ltd, London. **Recipient:** Romantic Novelists Association major award, 1985, for *Sunrise*. **Address:** c/o Michael Joseph Ltd, 27 Wright's Lane, London W8 5TZ, England.

ROMANCE AND HISTORICAL PUBLICATIONS

Novels

Love's Choice. New York, Avon, 1982.
Celebration. Loughton, Essex, Piatkus, 1982.

Follies. Loughton, Essex, Piatkus, 1983.
Sunrise. London, Piatkus, 1984.
The White Dove. London, Collins, and New York, Viking, 1986.
Strangers. London, Collins, and New York, Simon and Schuster, 1987.
Bad Girls, Good Women. London, Joseph, 1988; New York, Bantam, 1989.
A Woman of Our Times. London, Joseph, and New York, Bantam, 1990.
All My Sins Remembered. London, Joseph, and New York, Bantam, 1990.
Other People's Marriages. London, Joseph, 1993.

*   *   *

Although it was with one of Rosie Thomas's earlier novels (*Sunrise*) that she won the Romantic Novelists Association major award, it is with her more recent books that she has shown herself to be a writer of some stature.

Follies, one of Thomas's earliest novels, is littered with stereotyped characters—the poor but studious heroine, the rich doomed aristocrat (very reminiscent of Evelyn Waugh's Sebastian Flyte), the solid dependable type (so low key that you just know he will marry the heroine). Even though the novel itself does develop some pace and does engage the reader's interest to some extent, the characters themselves never develop to the level of those in Thomas's later novels.

The White Dove is a gripping portrayal of a relationship which transcends the barriers of class and social standing. The honourable Amy Lovell, born in 1912, is the daughter of Lord Lovell and Adeline, his second wife, a rich American heiress. Brought up to a life of luxury and privilege, Amy acquires a social conscience and starts to associate with communist sympathizers, then takes up nursing and eventually goes to Spain to nurse in the Civil War. The chief character in the other thread to the story is Nick Penry, a fiery Welsh miner and political activist; married with a handicapped son, Nick is forced to compromise his principles in order to support his family. The scenes involving the mining industry and those set at political meetings or rallies are convincing in their portrayal of the tensions of the time; these scenes lend interest and depth to what might otherwise be a formulaic romance novel. By the end of the novel, a year before the outbreak of World War II, the relationship between Amy and Nick has, after an exceedingly rocky start (but what else do you expect in a self-respecting romance novel?), taken root, flourished, and reached its inevitable conclusion. The widely differing settings range from the Hotel du Palais, Biarritz, to a poverty-stricken miner's cottage in South Wales; from a political meeting in East London to a psychiatric nursing home in Chertsey. Both Amy and Nick are completely credible characters; she with her doubts and self-doubts, trying to reconcile her lifestyle with her newly awakened beliefs, he with his unshakeable convictions. Their love is inevitable and so is its conclusion.

In *Strangers* Thomas again brings two characters together in a situation in which a love affair is the only possible outcome, and the termination of this affair is the only possible conclusion. In contrast to *The White Dove*, however, it is with some relief that one realizes that the lovers are not going to stroll happily into the sunset, as the hero is one of the less sympathetic creations of romance fiction—in fact he is totally selfish, and far from heroic. The novel starts promisingly: Annie, a rather bored suburban housewife, and Steve, a successful advertising executive, are both trapped in the rubble when a bomb destroys a crowded department store just before Christmas. In the terrifying hours before they are rescued each lends strength to the other, and the seeds of a relationship are sown.

Unfortunately for the balance of the plot, Thomas heightens the tension to such a degree that there is an unavoidable anticlimax, and the story never quite recovers its momentum. It is inevitable that the relationship will continue, and because of Steve's serious flaws, the fact that the love affair ends and Annie goes back to her husband is in fact a happy ending. Had Steve been a totally sympathetic character, and given the fact that Martin (Annie's husband) is pleasant but unexceptional, either of the possible resolutions would have been in some part unsatisfactory.

It is one of Thomas's strengths as a writer that she can take a similar combination of relationships and give them a totally dissimilar yet equally satisfactory ending. In *Sunrise* Angharad, the heroine, ultimately rejects Jamie, the kind, loving, and totally sympathetic man who has cared for her and her child, and resumes her relationship with the father of the child. The latter man is a complex character who develops (although we do not see this development as it takes place outside the pages of the novel) from a spoilt arrogant adolescent to a mature man willing to sacrifice his own and the heroine's happiness to protect his unbalanced and too-loving sister. Although the reader feels that the resolution of the problems (i.e., the heroine will obviously live her life with the father of her child) is the correct one romantically, we have a real and abiding sympathy for Jamie—yet this in no way detracts from the feeling that the conclusion is satisfactory. It is a measure of Thomas's confidence in her own capabilities that she obviously felt able to reject all the clichés with which she could have ended the story.

In *Celebration* Thomas writes in lighter vein, this time using the basic format of a traditional romance novel; she adds a touch of humour, an interesting and well researched background, and the two heroes whom we are now beginning to see as obligatory. The story sets traditional against modern values and, as in the previous two novels, we are for a while kept guessing as to which will triumph. The emancipated heroine, Bel, is forced to choose between a rich count who is cool and reserved, with an underlying smouldering passion (unfortunately he is also married, and even more unfortunately a devout Roman Catholic), and a lively, amusing, philandering American millionaire. The plot is lightly controlled and builds well towards the climax, which is an unusual duel to the death on motorbikes. The style is lighter than in most of her other works, but this by no means detracts from an entertainingly romantic novel.

Bad Girls, Good Women is the story of two independent and strong-willed women, from their rebellious girlhood to their respective successful careers—Mattie as an actress, Julia as a fashionable businesswoman. Each has had a disturbed childhood (Mattie was abused by her father while Julia, brought up in a repressive home, was adopted, although she does not find this out until later), each encounters setbacks and even tragedy in her adult life. The first part of the novel is set in the 1960s, a period now much written about, and here rather glamorized. Thomas, despite incorporating a large cast of lesser personalities, manages to avoid stereotypes—yet all the characters are believable, albeit a little larger than life. Each has an individuality which holds the reader's attention throughout this densely packed novel.

In addition to her consummate plotting and her creation of complex and believable characters, Thomas possesses the ability (by no means common to all novelists) to depict in words the visual appearance of totally imaginary objects. In *A Woman of Our Times*, businesswoman Harriet Peacock markets a complicated board-game called 'Meizu', and Thomas accomplishes the difficult task of enabling the reader to visualize the game. (She achieves the same effect in *All My Sins Remembered*, when describing a portrait of the two main characters.) *A Woman of Our Times* deals with Harriet's rise to, and fall from power in the space of a few years; single-minded, even ruthless, Harriet always has the reader's interest and sympathy, but it is only at times when she is vulnerable (as in the guilt she feels over the mental and physical breakdown of the inventor of her board-game), that she actually becomes the sort of human being with whom one can identify.

By contrast, *All My Sins Remembered* covers over 100 years in a thoroughly gripping family saga. It is built around the lives of nine cousins, the children of twin sisters Blanche and Eleanor Holborough, and in particular those of cousins Grace Stretton and Clio Hirsh, who are, to use Clio's words, ' . . . weight and counterweight. Equal, but needing opposition to balance us'. Thomas's use of the somewhat overworked flashback device in leading up to the ultimate tragedy of their relationship is truly skilful.

There is no doubt that Thomas is continuing to develop as a writer, and *All My Sins Remembered* bears the trademarks of enthralling plots, characters made believable by virtue of their mix of sympathetic and unsympathetic personality-traits, and some very stylish writing.

—Judith Rhodes

THOMPSON, E(rnest) V(ictor).
Nationality: British. **Born:** London in 1931. **Career:** served in Royal Navy, nine years. Founder member of the Bristol Police Force vice squad; investigator, British Overseas Airways Corporation; worked with the Hong Kong Police Narcotics Bureau; chief security officer, Rhodesia Department of Civil Aviation. Also factory worker, hotel detective, and civil servant, Plymouth dockyard. Since 1977 full-time writer. **Address:** c/o Macmillan Publishers (UK) Ltd, 4 Little Essex Street, London WC2R 3LF, England.

ROMANCE AND HISTORICAL PUBLICATIONS

Novels (series: Nathan Jago; Retallick)

Chase the Wind (Retallick). London, Macmillan, 1977.
Harvest of the Sun (Retallick). London, Macmillan, 1978; New York, Coward McCann, 1979.
The Music Makers. London, Macmillan, 1979.
Ben Retallick. London, Macmillan, 1980; New York, St Martin's Press, 1981.
The Dream Traders. London, Macmillan, 1981.
Singing Spears (Retallick). London, Macmillan, 1982.
The Restless Sea (Jago). London, Macmillan, 1983.
Cry Once Alone. London, Macmillan, 1984; as *Republic,* New York, Watts, 1985.
Polrudden (Jago). London, Macmillan, 1985.
The Stricken Land (Retallick). London, Macmillan, 1986.
Becky. London, Macmillan, 1988.
God's Highlander. London, Macmillan, 1989.
Lottie Trago (Retallick). London, Macmillan, 1990.
Cassie. London, Macmillan, 1991.
Wychwood. London, Macmillan, 1992.
Blue Dress Girl. London, Headline, 1992.
Mistress of Polrudden. London, Headline, 1993.

OTHER PUBLICATIONS

Other

Discovering Bodmin Moor. Bodmin, Cornwall, Bossiney, 1980.
Discovering Cornwall's South Coast. Bodmin, Cornwall, Bossiney, 1982.
Sea Stories of Devon. Bodmin, Cornwall, Bossiney, 1984.
E.V. Thompson's West Country. Bodmin, Cornwall, Bossiney, 1986.

* * *

Adventure is a central element in the novels of E.V. Thompson, whose writing matches a powerful story-telling style with the use of varied and exotic locations. Thompson's 'Retallick' series follows several generations of his characters from their native Cornwall to Southern Africa, spanning a period between the Napoleonic era and the latter stages of the Boer War, while other novels explore events in China, Texas, and the famine-stricken Ireland of the 1840s. At their best, his books manage to accommodate a strong humanitarian message while losing none of their pace and impact on the reader. Thompson's anger at past injustices is evident, and his sympathies are made plain by his heroes and their actions. At the same time his writing suggests a distrust of official solutions and a dislike of revolutionary violence. There is a constant sense of man's helplessness in the face of history, of the inevitability of tragedy and loss. The humane act of a Thompson character is seen to be hedged with limitations; there is no way his heroes can turn back the relentless tide of events.

These themes are recurrent threads in the six Retallick novels, the largest single sequence of works that Thompson has yet produced. *Chase the Wind* concerns the adventures of the mining engineer Josh Retallick in the Bodmin region of Cornwall, and his sentencing to transportation after his unwitting involvement in a riot of his fellow-miners. *Harvest of the Sun* continues the story with the shipwreck of Josh, his mistress, and his son Daniel in southern Africa, and their new life as neighbours of the powerful Matabele nation. In *Singing Spears* Daniel grows to manhood, fathers sons of his own, and eventually meets his death at the hands of the Matabele, who are themselves destroyed by the new imperialism of Cecil Rhodes. *The Stricken Land*, gives a hardhitting account of the Boer War, in which Daniel's sons find themselves fighting on opposite sides. Each novel is fraught with tragedy and violence, whether the rapes committed on several Retallick heroines, or the downfall of entire nations. Thompson depicts the extermination of the Bushmen, the defeat of the Matabele, with a resigned sympathy, presenting them as doomed figures in the path of progress.

Lottie Trago, the most recent of the Retallick novels, returns to the original Cornish setting, and explores the fortunes of Josh Retallick and his family as owners of the Shaptor tin mine in a period of economic decline. The fiery passions of the characters are capably blended with a strong social background, Thompson providing a memorable picture of the doomed mining industry, its owners in conflict with the emergent trade unions and the rise of Primitive Methodism. *Lottie Trago* shows Thompson at his best, and is a worthy addition to the canon.

Ben Retallick does not follow the main chronology, going back to early 19th-century Cornwall with the story of a mining community and its struggle against the parliamentary corruption and privilege that bind its people to the will of the landed Vincent family. In a series of dramatic scenes Thompson recounts the tale of Ben Retallick's love for Jesse Henna, his unwilling involvement in the reform movement, and his eventual overthrow of Colman Vincent. Here, more than in any of the Retallick novels, the detailed research of the author is made evident. Thompson's vision of the prison hulks, the public hanging of Judy Lean, the horrors of Newgate prison, weds descriptive power to authenticity of detail. *Ben Retallick* is a strongly written adventure novel which attacks injustice through living characters, in a credibly re-created historical setting. To a lesser extent, the same is true of the entire 'Retallick' series.

For all the obvious virtues of the Retallick novels, it could be argued that Thompson's finest work has been produced outside the major sequence. Of the non-Retallick novels, *The Restless Sea* and *Polrudden* are perhaps the weakest. A kind of 'minisaga' featuring the prize-fighter and fisherman Nathan Jago, these books contain plenty in the way of action, but there is about them a lack of that depth and coherence one associates with Thompson's other works. More impressive are *Cry Once Alone* and *The Music Makers*, where strength of narrative is combined with a forceful presentation of

historical events, the former set in pioneer Texas, the latter in the Ireland of the Great Famine.

Thompson's eye for unusual settings and viewpoints is epitomized in *Cassie*, which describes the adventures of a pregnant farm girl who follows her errant husband, as an army wife, through the battles of the Peninsular war. Cassie's response to the horrors of conflict, and her close companionship with other army wives and mistresses involved with the 32nd Regiment, reveals the author's sensitive insight into his character, and presents a view of the Napoleonic war all too rarely seen. *God's Highlander* is also imaginative in setting and treatment, its minister hero fighting a lone battle to safeguard his Highland parishioners from being evicted by an absentee landlord to make way for the more lucrative pasturing of sheep. Dealing with an under-reported and disturbing episode in Scottish history, Thompson once more blends romance with deprivation and violence in a highly individual manner. *Wychwood*, set in a Cotswold village and featuring the tension between gypsies and country folk, lacks the depth of historical background, but remains a lively and entertaining read.

Arguably Thompson's finest novel is *The Dream Traders*, whose action takes place in China at the time of the Opium War. Viewing developments through the eyes of his trader hero Luke Trewarne, Thompson explores the economics of the opium business, the political intrigues of East and West, and the nature of love and friendship between individuals of different races. Once again, his wellmeaning characters are thwarted by the overwhelming force of history, lives lost and an evil trade reintroduced at gunpoint in order to secure British economic interests. In *The Dream Traders* Thompson contains history and adventure in perfect balance throughout, the message ably presented while at no time impeding the momentum of the story. Similar terrain is re-examined from a mainly female viewpoint in *Blue Dress Girl*, whose Chinese heroine survives a brief career as a prostitute and injury on the high seas before being rescued by a British Royal Marine officer, with whom she falls in love. The turbulent setting of 1850s China, the Taiping rebellion, and the warlike incursion of the European 'foreign devils' are strikingly depicted by Thompson in cursory but effective action scenes. The interracial romance between She-she and Kernow Keats is not so convincing, and some of the lesser characters lack the strength and interest of those in his other novels. The idealized nature of the 'happy ending' also detracts frm the work, which is good in parts, but fails to equal *The Dream Traders*, the latter remaining unsurpassed among the author's creations.

—Geoffrey Sadler

THORN, Bridget. See **OLIVER, Marina.**

THORNE, Nicola. See **ELLERBECK, Rosemary.**

THORPE, Kay.
Nationality: British. **Relations:** married; one son. **Address:** c/o Mills and Boon Ltd, Eton House, 18–24 Paradise Road, Richmond, Surrey TW9 1SR, England.

ROMANCE AND HISTORICAL PUBLICATIONS

Novels

Devon Interlude. London, Mills and Boon, 1968; Toronto, Harlequin, 1969.

The Last of the Mallorys. London, Mills and Boon, and Toronto, Harlequin, 1968.

Opportune Marriage. London, Mills and Boon, 1968; Toronto, Harlequin, 1975.

Rising Star. London, Mills and Boon, and Toronto, Harlequin, 1969.

Curtain Call. London, Mills and Boon, and Toronto, Harlequin, 1971.

Man in a Box. London, Mills and Boon, 1972.

Not Wanted on Voyage. London, Mills and Boon, and Toronto, Harlequin, 1972.

Olive Island. London, Mills and Boon, 1972; Toronto, Harlequin, 1973.

Sawdust Season. London, Mills and Boon, and Toronto, Harlequin, 1972.

An Apple in Eden. London, Mills and Boon, 1973; Toronto, Harlequin, 1974.

The Man at Kambala. London, Mills and Boon, 1973; Toronto, Harlequin, 1974.

Remember This Stranger. London, Mills and Boon, 1974.

The Iron Man. London, Mills and Boon, 1974; Toronto, Harlequin, 1975.

The Shifting Sands. London, Mills and Boon, and Toronto, Harlequin, 1975.

Sugar Cane Harvest. London, Mills and Boon, 1975; Toronto, Harlequin, 1976.

The Royal Affair. London, Mills and Boon, and Toronto, Harlequin, 1976.

Safari South. London, Mills and Boon, 1976; Toronto, Harlequin, 1977.

Caribbean Encounter. London, Mills and Boon, 1976; Toronto, Harlequin, 1978.

The River Lord. London, Mills and Boon, and Toronto, Harlequin, 1977.

Storm Passage. London, Mills and Boon, and Toronto, Harlequin, 1977.

Lord of La Pampa. London, Mills and Boon, 1977; Toronto, Harlequin, 1978.

Bitter Alliance. London, Mills and Boon, 1978.

Full Circle. London, Mills and Boon, 1978.

Timber Boss. London, Mills and Boon, and Toronto, Harlequin, 1978.

The Wilderness Trail. London, Mills and Boon, 1978; Toronto, Harlequin, 1979.

The Dividing Line. London, Mills and Boon, 1979; Toronto, Harlequin, 1980.

The Man from Tripoli. London, Mills and Boon, and Toronto, Harlequin, 1979.

This Side of Paradise. London, Mills and Boon, 1979; Toronto, Harlequin, 1980.

Chance Meeting. London, Mills and Boon, and Toronto, Harlequin, 1980.

No Passing Fancy. London, Mills and Boon, 1980.

Copper Lake. London, Mills and Boon, and Toronto, Harlequin, 1981.

Floodtide. London, Mills and Boon, and Toronto, Harlequin, 1981.

Temporary Marriage. London, Mills and Boon, and Toronto, Harlequin, 1981.

The New Owner. London, Mills and Boon, and Toronto, Harlequin, 1982.

A Man of Means. London, Mills and Boon, 1982; Toronto, Harlequin, 1983.

The Land of the Incas. London, Mills and Boon, and Toronto, Harlequin, 1983.

Master of Morley. London, Mills and Boon, and Toronto, Harlequin, 1983.

Never Trust a Stranger. London, Mills and Boon, and Toronto, Harlequin, 1983.

The Inheritance. London, Mills and Boon, and Toronto, Harlequin, 1984.

Dangerous Moonlight. London, Mills and Boon, and Toronto, Harlequin, 1985.

Double Deception. London, Mills and Boon, and Toronto, Harlequin, 1985.

South Seas Affair. London, Mills and Boon, and Toronto, Harlequin, 1985.

Jungle Island. London, Mills and Boon, 1986; Toronto, Harlequin, 1987.

Win or Lose. London, Mills and Boon, and Toronto, Harlequin, 1986.

Time Out of Mind. London, Mills and Boon, 1987; Toronto, Harlequin, 1988.

Tokyo Tryst. London, Mills and Boon, 1987; Toronto, Harlequin, 1989.

Land of Illusion. London, Mills and Boon, 1988; Toronto, Harlequin, 1989.

Skin Deep. London, Mills and Boon, 1989; Toronto, Harlequin, 1990.

No Gentle Persuasion. London, Mills and Boon, 1990.

Steel Tiger. London, Mills and Boon, 1990.

Night of Error. London, Mills and Boon, 1990.

Intimate Deception. London, Mills and Boon, 1990.

The Inheritance. London, Mills and Boon, 1990.

Against All Odds. London, Mills and Boon, 1990.

Trouble on Tour. London, Mills and Boon, 1991.

Lasting Legacy. London, Mills and Boon, 1991.

Past All Reason. London, Mills and Boon, 1992.

Left in Trust. London, Mills and Boon, 1992.

Wild Streak. London, Mills and Boon, 1992.

Spanish Connection. London, Mills and Boon, 1993.

*   *   *

Kay Thorpe's steady output of series romances since 1968 includes a number of carefully crafted formula stories. She is particularly adept at portraying heroines in interesting professions and at writing novels that hinge upon successive misunderstandings and misinterpretations between potential lovers. Her books move swiftly and maintain their suspense.

In some books, her heroines are 'spoiled brats', who are too immature to sustain adult relationships. Inevitably, they behave badly and alienate the heroes or they must learn to make up for mistaken impressions and hasty judgments. In others, she portrays women who are misinterpreted as 'gold diggers', who must somehow convince the heroes to trust them. Some of her heroines have special insight into psychological trauma and, through love, are able to nurture a child (*Skin Deep*) or a potential lover (*Land of Illusion*) back to emotional health. Thorpe sets her novels in exciting and interesting places: the theatre, the circus, a cruise ship, a department store, the jungles of Venezuela, or a newspaper office. Her women are usually competent in their career fields, even though they must be instructed in love by the heroes.

An unusual feature of Thorpe's romances is that she sometimes leaves the relationship with room to grow at the end of the book. Most other series romance writers describe a complete reconciliation by the final page, but Thorpe does not always wrap up the ends so neatly. In *Bitter Alliance* and *Floodtide* her heroes at the end have not learned the difference between 'wanting' and 'loving', a critical issue in most series romances, for without an acknowledgement of that distinction, no self-respecting heroine can submit sexually to the hero. Thorpe's heroines remain confident that the hero will change in time and so they agree to be patient.

Because Thorpe is less prolific than many of her colleagues, her novels are sometimes more complex than theirs. She has been prominent as a series writer because of the care with which she constructs her plots.

—Kay Mussell

THORPE, Sylvia.
Pseudonym for June Sylvia Thimblethorpe. **Nationality:** British. **Born:** London in 1926. **Education:** school in Brondesbury, Kilburn High School for Girls, Slade School of Fine Arts, and University College, all London. **Career:** secretary, 1949–52; school teacher, 1952–53. **Recipient:** Romantic Novelists Association historical award, 1971. **Address:** Hutchinson, 20 Vauxhall Bridge Road, London SW1V 2SA, England.

ROMANCE AND HISTORICAL PUBLICATIONS

Novels

The Scandalous Lady Robin. London, Hutchinson, 1950; New York, Fawcett, 1975.
The Sword and the Shadow. London, Hutchinson, 1951; New York, Fawcett, 1976.
Beggar on Horseback. London, Hutchinson, 1953; New York, Fawcett, 1977.
Smugglers' Moon. London, Rich and Cowan, 1955; as *Strangers on the Moor,* New York, Pyramid, 1966.
The Golden Panther. London, Rich and Cowan, 1956; New York, Fawcett, 1976.
Sword of Vengeance. London, Rich and Cowan, 1957; New York, Fawcett, 1977.
Rogues' Covenant. London, Hurst and Blackett, 1957; New York, Fawcett, 1976.
Captain Gallant. London, Hurst and Blackett, 1958; New York, Fawcett, 1978.
Beloved Rebel. London, Hurst and Blackett, 1959; New York, Fawcett, 1978.
Romantic Lady. London, Hurst and Blackett, 1960; New York, Fawcett, 1976.
The Devil's Bondsman. London, Hurst and Blackett, 1961; New York, Fawcett, 1980.
The Highwayman. London, Hurst and Blackett, 1962; New York, Fawcett, 1979.
The House at Bell Orchard. London, Hurst and Blackett, 1962; New York, Fawcett, 1979.
The Reluctant Adventuress. London, Hurst and Blackett, 1963; New York, Fawcett, 1974.
Fair Shine the Day. London, Hurst and Blackett, 1964; New York, Fawcett, 1977.
Spring Will Come Again. London, Hurst and Blackett, 1965; New York, Fawcett, 1974.
The Changing Tide. London, Hurst and Blackett, 1967; New York, Fawcett, 1978.
Dark Heritage. London, Hurst and Blackett, 1968; as *Tarrington Chase,* London, Corgi, 1977.
No More A-Roving. London, Hurst and Blackett, 1970; New York, Fawcett, 1979.
The Scarlet Domino. London, Hurst and Blackett, 1970; New York, Fawcett, 1975.
The Scapegrace. London, Hurst and Blackett, 1971; New York, Fawcett, 1978.
Dark Enchantress. London, Hurst and Blackett, 1973; New York, Fawcett, 1980.

The Silver Nightingale. London, Hurst and Blackett, and New York, Fawcett, 1974.
The Witches of Conyngton. London, Hurst and Blackett, 1976.
A Flash of Scarlet. New York, Fawcett, 1978.
The Varleigh Medallion. London, Hurst and Blackett, and New York, Fawcett, 1979.
The Avenhurst Inheritance. London, Hutchinson, 1981.
Mistress of Astington. London, Hutchinson, 1983.

* * *

June Sylvia Thimblethorpe, better known as Sylvia Thorpe, is a very prolific historical novelist. Her stories are marked by careful attention to historical detail and extremely well-drawn characters.

Her Regency romances are among the best written. Combining romance with adventure and intrigue, they are filled with believable, sympathetic people. *The Silver Nightingale* is both a mystery and a love story in which snowbound travellers are threatened by a killer. Justin, Lord Chayle, must flush out the murderer in order to protect his fiancée, Sarah. In *Romantic Lady* Caroline's impetuousness leads her into danger and involves Guy Ravenshaw in several rescues in spite of himself. Thorpe's ladies are spirited and courageous, and are suitable mates for their dashing partners.

Similar in nature to the Regencies are Thorpe's Georgian romances. The same mixture of romance and adventure is present, with slightly more emphasis on forceful action as befits an earlier age. The heroes tend to be more roguish in these novels. The hero of *Captain Gallant* is a daring highwayman. Geraint St Arvan (*The Scarlet Domino*) is taken from the Common Debtors' Ward in Newgate to marry Antonia. Philip Digby in *Rogues' Covenant* has a mysterious past that leads to violence. In spite of these flaws (which really make the characters more interesting), these men are reformed, or at least captured, by the love of their heroines.

Many of Thorpe's historical romances are set in even earlier times. The Commonwealth under Cromwell is not one of the most popular eras for historical novelists to use, but it provides extremely fertile ground for Thorpe's imagination. The exiles and wanderers created by the English Civil War provide excellent material for action-packed tales of rogues and pirates. Set against the lush tropical background of the Caribbean, bold love stories come alive in the true swashbuckling tradition. Using a place and time of violent men, Thorpe wisely puts more focus on the men in these stories, but does so without slighting the women or diluting the romance. Thorpe's talent can be seen in the fact that women can read these novels for the romance, while men can enjoy an escape to high adventure. *The Golden Panther, No More A-Roving, The Devil's Bondsman,* and *The Sword and the Shadow* are all examples of Thorpe's ability to portray some rousing action.

Thorpe is a consummate storyteller. Her craftsmanship is evident in each of her novels, raising them above standard formula stories. Many authors could learn a great deal about writing historical romances by reading her books.

—Barbara E. Kemp

THUM, Marcella.
Nationality: American. **Born:** St Louis, Missouri. **Education:** Washington University, St Louis, 1948; University of California, Berkeley, M.L.S. 1954; Webster University, St Louis, M.A. 1977. **Relations:** divorced. **Career:** civilian librarian and historical writer, United States Army bases in Okinawa, Germany, Korea, and Hawaii, 1949–61; high school librarian, Affton, Missouri, 1962–67; librarian, St Louis Community College, 1968–78, and Air Transport School, Scott Air Force Base, Illinois, 1979–85. **Recipient:**

Mystery Writers of America Edgar Allan Poe award, 1965, for children's book. **Agent:** Eleanor Wood, 432 Park Avenue South, New York, New York 10016, USA. **Address:** 6507 Gramond Drive, St Louis, Missouri 63123, USA.

ROMANCE AND HISTORICAL PUBLICATIONS

Novels

Fernwood. New York, Doubleday, 1973; as *The Haunting Cavalier*, Aylesbury, Buckinghamshire, Milton House, 1974.
Abbey Court. New York, Doubleday, 1976.
The White Rose. New York, Fawcett, 1980.
Blazing Star. New York, Fawcett, 1983.
Jasmine. New York, Fawcett, 1984.
Wild Laurel. New York, Fawcett, 1987.
Margarite. New York, Fawcett, 1987.
Mistress of Paradise. New York, Fawcett, 1988.
The Thorn Trees. New York, Fawcett, 1991.

OTHER PUBLICATIONS

Novels

Mystery at Crane's Landing. New York, Dodd Mead, 1964.
Treasure of Crazy Quilt Farm. New York, Watts, 1966.
Librarian with Wings. New York, Dodd Mead, 1967.
Secret of the Sunken Treasure. New York, Dodd Mead, 1969.

Other

Anne of the Sandwich Islands (for children). New York, Dodd Mead, 1967.
The Persuaders: Propaganda in War and Peace, with Gladys Thum. New York, Atheneum, 1972.
Exploring Black America. New York, Atheneum, 1975.
Exploring Literary America. New York, Atheneum, 1979.
Exploring Military America. New York, Atheneum, 1982.
Airlift: Story of the Military Airlift Command, with Gladys Thum. New York, Dodd Mead, 1986.
Hippocrene USA Guide to Black America. New York, Hippocrene, 1991.

*

Marcella Thum comments:

Almost all my books, both historical novels and non-fiction, have required a lot of historical research. The writing is hard work; the research is fun. Of course, having been a reference librarian helps! To me, plot and characterization in a novel are important but they are only two dimensional without a well-researched, interesting background against which to place them.

*   *   *

Marcella Thum's clutch of popular, super-sized romances are 'bodice rippers' of the first rank. That is to say, they promise—and deliver—steamy adventures starring a bevy of unbelievably beautiful and spirited young women whose various tangled romances with a matching number of handsome, muscular, adventurous men may never run smoothly, but do run with predictable regularity towards the triumphant nuptials.

These young women, Star, Jasmine, Lucinda, and the rest, always eager virgins as the stories begin, and never as they end, quite frequently suffer the sort of sexual violence and indignity never visited upon the governesses and ladies' companions of milder popular romances. In *Wild Laurel*, for example, the heroine, in flight from an unjust accusation of the murder of her wealthy cousin Sophia, is hunted down and raped by a bountyhunting, sadistic murderer.

It is indicative of Thum's ambivalent treatment of her heroines that Laurel responds physically, though entirely unwillingly, to the practised, cruel assailant, exactly as he intends she should, even though she fears and loathes him. The rape, a sickening and unpleasant event, is, however, not allowed to affect her later, happier relationship with the man she will one day marry, and with whom she will leave the ugly memories behind to make a new life in California.

Thum's historical settings are widely varied and quite unusual, including Hawaii in the great days of the whaling ships, and later during the disturbance and political unrest of the reign of Queen Liliuokalani, in *Jasmine*, and again in the story of Lani, Jasmine's granddaughter, the *Mistress of Paradise.*

The flight of the starving Irish peasantry from their hungry land to the promise of a new life in America is the starting point for *Wild Laurel*, a romance-murder mystery. *The White Rose*, set in the days of the American Civil War, is a story of espionage, in which the heroine, actress Lucinda Appleton, is a Union spy, who successfully disguises herself as a black maidservant, Sukey, to gain access to Confederate secrets. She, like Laurel, suffers a forced sexual encounter; and there is a most disagreeable implication that the rape means less than it might have done, because Lucinda/Sukey is apparently black.

The same deplorable double standard is evident in the course of events of *Jasmine*, in which the hero, whaling captain Morgan Tucker, overcomes the resistance of a young women he presumes to be a 'wahine', and therefore fair game in spite of all protests, and discovers to his (somewhat) dismayed surprise that the girl had been until that moment a virgin. He does, however, 'do the right thing' when the girl's angry (and influential) father confronts him. It was all a mistake, and she is, after all, a *lady*.

Mistress of Paradise follows the adventures of Jasmine's and Morgan's granddaughter, Lani Tucker, who believes herself to be sole mistress of the great Hawaiian ranch 'Palekaiko' or Paradise, blissfully unaware that her guardian has lost the title to her beloved home in a card game. The new owner, Adam, is the brother of the villainous object of Lani's girlish infatuation. In the depths of a black night, foolish Lani steals into the wrong bedroom, to encounter, again all unknowingly, *good* brother Adam who will become her husband. Will she continue to moon over the phantom lover with whom she believes she shared her first experience of passion?

Blazing Star, and later the story of Star's adopted stepson Patrick and his love, *Margarite*, are set in Mexico and Austria. The more interesting of the two has as its background the story of the ill-fated Maximilian, Emperor of Mexico, and his sad, neglected Empress Carlota, who sat so briefly upon the Cactus Throne. Margarite is sent to her unknown uncle in Mexico to serve the caprice of her stepmother in Austria. When Uncle Don Manuel's party is attacked and savaged by fierce guerrillas, a blow on the head leaves the young Austrian countess, sole survivor of the outrage, amnesiac. Rescued by half-Mexican adventurer Patrick O'Malley, she rides with him and his men dressed as a boy: and since her name is unknown even to herself, she becomes la Niña. Slowly memory returns; and mistakenly she comes to fear that Patrick, her rescuer, was a party to the murder of her uncle. And you know where *that* will lead . . . .

It's all rich, ripe, sensual stuff, soft, sweet, and fuzzy as peach flesh. The heroines tend to merge into one: the colour of hair and eyes may vary, but the reader well knows that under the multicoloured icing the cake will be sugar and spice.

Thum's works do not greatly resemble life as it is really lived: but, as her popularity demonstrates, they *do* portray life, steamy, searing life, as a good many people love to imagine it.

—Joan McGrath

TORDAY, Ursula.   See **BLACKSTOCK, Charity.**

TOWERS, Regina.   See **PYKARE, Nina.**

TRANTER, Nigel (Godwin).
Pseudonym: Nye Tredgold. **Nationality:** British. **Born:** Glasgow, Scotland, 23 November 1909. **Education:** St James's Episcopal School, Edinburgh, 3 years; George Heriot's School, Edinburgh, 9 years. **Military Service:** Royal Artillery during World War II: lieutenant. **Relations:** married May Jean Campbell Grieve in 1933 (died 1979); one daughter, and one son (deceased). **Career:** accountant and inspector in family insurance company, Edinburgh, 1929–39. Since 1946 full-time writer, broadcaster, and lecturer. Chair, Scottish Convention, Edinburgh, 1948–51; Scottish president, PEN, 1962–66; Scottish Chairman, Society of Authors, 1966–72, and National Book League, 1973–78. M.A.: Edinburgh University, 1971; D. Litt.: Strathclyde University, Glasgow, 1991. Knight Commander, Order of St Lazarus of Jerusalem, 1961; OBE (Officer, Order of the British Empire), 1983. **Address:** Quarry House, Aberlady, East Lothian EH32 0QB, Scotland.

ROMANCE AND HISTORICAL PUBLICATIONS

Novels (series: MacGregor; Montrose; Robert the Bruce Trilogy; Stuart Trilogy)

Trespass. Edinburgh, Moray Press, 1937.
Mammon's Daughter. London, Ward Lock, 1939.
Harsh Heritage. London, Ward Lock, 1939.
Eagles Feathers. London, Ward Lock, 1941.
Watershed. London, Ward Lock, 1941.
The Gilded Fleece. London, Ward Lock, 1942.
Delayed Action. London, Ward Lock, 1944.
Tinker's Pride. London, Ward Lock, 1945.
Man's Estate. London, Ward Lock, 1946.
Flight of Dutchmen. London, Ward Lock, 1947.
Island Twilight. London, Ward Lock, 1947.
Root and Branch. London, Ward Lock, 1948.
Colours Flying. London, Ward Lock, 1948.
The Chosen Course. London, Ward Lock, 1949.
Fair Game. London, Ward Lock, 1950.
High Spirits. London, Collins, 1950.
The Freebooters. London, Ward Lock, 1950.
Tidewrack. London, Ward Lock, 1951.
Fast and Loose. London, Ward Lock, 1951.
Bridal Path. London, Ward Lock, 1952.
Cheviot Chase. London, Ward Lock, 1952.
Ducks and Drakes. London, Ward Lock, 1953.
The Queen's Grace. London, Ward Lock, 1953.
Rum Week. London, Ward Lock, 1954.
The Night Riders. London, Ward Lock, 1954.
There Are Worse Jungles. London, Ward Lock, 1955.

Rio d'Oro. London, Ward Lock, 1955.
The Long Coffin. London, Ward Lock, 1956.
MacGregor's Gathering. London, Hodder and Stoughton, 1957.
The Enduring Flame. London, Hodder and Stoughton, 1957.
Balefire. London, Hodder and Stoughton, 1958.
The Stone. London, Hodder and Stoughton, 1958; New York, Putnam, 1959.
The Man Behind the Curtain. London, Hodder and Stoughton, 1959.
The Clansman (MacGregor). London, Hodder and Stoughton, 1959.
Spanish Galleon. London, Hodder and Stoughton, 1960.
The Flockmasters. London, Hodder and Stoughton, 1960.
Kettle of Fish. London, Hodder and Stoughton, 1961.
The Master of Gray. London, Hodder and Stoughton, 1961.
Drug on the Market. London, Hodder and Stoughton, 1962.
Gold for Prince Charlie. London, Hodder and Stoughton, 1962.
The Courtesan. London, Hodder and Stoughton, 1963.
Chain of Destiny. London, Hodder and Stoughton, 1964.
Past Master. London, Hodder and Stoughton, 1965.
A Stake in the Kingdom. London, Hodder and Stoughton, 1966.
Lion Let Loose. London, Hodder and Stoughton, 1967.
Cable from Kabul. London, Hodder and Stoughton, 1968.
Black Douglas. London, Hodder and Stoughton, 1968.
Robert the Bruce Trilogy. London, Hodder and Stoughton, 1985.
  The Steps to the Empty Throne. London, Hodder and Stoughton, 1969; New York, St Martin's Press, 1971.
  The Path of the Hero King. London, Hodder and Stoughton, 1970; New York, St Martin's Press, 1973.
  The Price of the King's Peace. London, Hodder and Stoughton, 1971; New York, St Martin's Press, 1973.
The Young Montrose. London, Hodder and Stoughton, 1972.
Montrose, The Captain-General. London, Hodder and Stoughton, 1973.
The Wisest Fool. London, Hodder and Stoughton, 1974.
The Wallace. London, Hodder and Stoughton, 1975.
Stuart Trilogy. London, Coronet, 1986.
  Lords of Misrule. London, Hodder and Stoughton, 1976.
  A Folly of Princes. London, Hodder and Stoughton, 1977.
  The Captive Crown. London, Hodder and Stoughton, 1977.
Macbeth the King. London, Hodder and Stoughton, 1978.
Margaret the Queen. London, Hodder and Stoughton, 1979.
David the Prince. London, Hodder and Stoughton, 1980.
True Thomas. London, Hodder and Stoughton, 1981.
The Patriot. London, Hodder and Stoughton, 1982.
Lord of the Isles. London, Hodder and Stoughton, 1983.
Unicorn Rampant. London, Hodder and Stoughton, and New York, Beaufort, 1984.
The Riven Realm. London, Hodder and Stoughton, 1984; New York, Beaufort, 1985.
James, By the Grace of God. London, Hodder and Stoughton, 1985; New York, Beaufort, 1986.
Rough Wooing. London, Hodder and Stoughton, 1986; New York, Beaufort, 1987.
Columba. London, Hodder and Stoughton, 1987.
Cache Down. London, Hodder and Stoughton, 1987.
Flowers of Chivalry. London, Hodder and Stoughton, 1988.
Mail Royal. London, Hodder and Stoughton, 1989.
Warden of the Queen's March. London, Hodder and Stoughton, 1989.
Kenneth. London, Hodder and Stoughton, 1990.
Crusade. London, Hodder and Stoughton, 1991.
Children of the Mist (MacGregor). London, Hodder and Stoughton, 1992.
Druid Sacrifice. London, Hodder and Stoughton, 1993.
Tapestry of the Boar. London, Hodder and Stoughton, 1993.

OTHER PUBLICATIONS

Novels as Nye Tredgold

Thirsty Range. London, Ward Lock, 1949.
Heartbreak Valley. London, Ward Lock, 1950.
The Big Corral. London, Ward Lock, 1952.
Trail Herd. London, Ward Lock, 1952.
Desert Doublecross. London, Ward Lock, 1953.
Cloven Hooves. London, Ward Lock, 1954.
Dynamite Trail. London, Ward Lock, 1955.
Rancher Renegade. London, Ward Lock, 1956.
Trailing Trouble. London, Ward Lock, 1957.
Dead Reckoning. London, Ward Lock, 1957.
Bloodstone Trail. London, Ward Lock, 1958.

Other (for children)

Spaniards' Isle. Leicester, Brockhampton Press, 1958.
Border Rising. Leicester, Brockhampton Press, 1959.
Nestor the Monster. Leicester, Brockhampton Press, 1960.
Birds of a Feather. Leicester, Brockhampton Press, 1961.
The Deer Poachers. London, Blackie, 1961.
Something Very Fishy. London, Collins, 1962.
Give a Dog a Bad Name. London, Collins, 1963; New York, Platt
   and Munk, 1964.
Silver Island. London, Nelson, 1964.
Smoke Across the Highlands. New York, Platt and Munk, 1964.
Pursuit. London, Collins, 1965.
Fire and High Water. London, Collins, 1967.
Tinker Tess. London, Dobson, 1967.
To the Rescue. London, Dobson, 1968.

Other

*The Fortalices and Early Mansions of Southern Scotland 1400–
   1650.* Edinburgh, Moray Press, 1935.
The Fortified House in Scotland. Edinburgh, Oliver and Boyd, 4
   vols, 1962–66; London, Chambers, 1 vol, 1970; Edinburgh, Mer-
   cat Press, 5 vols, 1986.
The Pegasus Book of Scotland. London, Dobson, 1964.
Outlaw of the Highlands: Rob Roy. London, Dobson, 1965.
Land of the Scots. London, Hodder and Stoughton, and New York,
   Weybright and Talley, 1968.
The Queen's Scotland. London, Hodder and Stoughton, 4 vols,
   1971–77.
Portrait of the Border Country. London, Hale, 1972.
Portrait of the Lothians. London, Hale, 1979; revised edition, as
   The Illustrated Portrait of the Border Country, London, Hale,
   1987.
Nigel Tranter's Scotland: A Very Personal View. Glasgow, Drew,
   1981.
Scottish Castles: Tales and Traditions. London, Macdonald, 1982.
The Travellers Guide to the Scotland of Robert the Bruce, with
   Michael Cyprien. London, Routledge, 1985.
The Story of Scotland. London, Routledge, 1987.
Editor, *No Tigers in the Hindu Kush,* by Philip Tranter. London,
   Hodder and Stoughton, 1968.

*

Film Adaptation: *Bridal Path,* 1959.

Manuscript Collection: National Library of Scotland, Edinburgh.

Nigel Tranter comments:

   I wrote ordinary novels of adventure and romance, usually set in
Scotland, from 1938 onwards, including four written in the army

during active service. In 1961 I wrote *The Master of Gray,* the first
of many long and carefully researched historical novels, since then I
have concentrated on these, in an attempt to cover most of the spectrum of Scotland's colourful and dramatic story, in a way which
would make it palatable for the ordinary reader who would seldom
open a 'straight' history book. I have endeavoured to stick closely to
fact as far as possible with the very minimum of invented characters.

*   *   *

   To read Nigel Tranter's prolific output of historical novels is to
take a painless course in that subject. He is a scrupulous and indefatigable researcher, setting great store by accuracy, and he lovingly
portrays Scottish scenery in a way that makes you feel he knows
every moor, hill, and burn. His recipe for his books is to add romantic fiction to historical fact and mix invented characters with real
people.
   In *Gold for Prince Charlie* Tranter combines the fact that in 1745
French gold arrived too late to help the Jacobite rebellion with the
fictional love story of Duncan MacGregor and Caroline Cameron.
He has written several books about the MacGregors—in *Children of
the Mist* he tells how they fell foul of the powerful Campbells and
were proscribed; *MacGregor's Gathering* describes Rob Roy's
attempt to get the proscription of the clan lifted, and in *The Clansman* he shows Rob Roy's strange behaviour in holding his clan back
from the battle at Sherrifmuir, and offers his own explanation for it.
   If Tranter has a weakness, it is characterization, his fictitious
characters are sometimes two-dimensional, and their romances tend
to be run-of-the-mill. He is better at re-creating the real people of
history whom he brings vividly to life. He gives us very engaging
portraits of some monarchs, especially the child Alexander III in
Crusader (one of his most attractive books), and there is a lively
vignette of James VI in *Children of the Mist.* In *Margaret the Queen,*
he shows the Saxon princess who became Malcolm Canmore's
queen as a warm human being although she is known to history as a
saint.
   David the Prince tells of Margaret and Malcolm's son in the 12th
century. *True Thomas* set in the 13th century takes up Alexander
III's story where *Crusade* leaves it—more is made of the legendary
Thomas the Rhymer, and a plausible explanation is given for
Thomas's alleged stay with the Queen of Elfland. Scotland's strife
with England under Edward I (a noble king in English history books
but a double-dyed villain to the Scots) is depicted in *The Wallace.*
Robert the Bruce's life is depicted in a trilogy—*The Steps to the
Empty Throne, The Path of the Hero King,* and *The Price of the
King's Peace.*
   Tranter is particularly good at battles. The sea fights with the
Vikings in *Kenneth* are vivid and exciting, and in this book he
blends the meagre amount of known history with legends to make an
engaging story of the life of Kenneth MacAlpin, the first man to
unite the Picts and the Scots, and the founder of the Scottish nation.
   The rise in the house of Stuart is covered in *Lords of Misrule, A
Folly of Princes,* and *The Captive Crown.* James I is the subject of
Lion Let Loose, and James IV is the subject of *Chain of Destiny.* The
emotive character Mary Queen of Scots is portrayed through the
eyes of Thomas Kerr in *Warden of the Queen's March* but it is a
slightly blurred portrait. His series featuring the Master of Gray contrasts the Tudor court of Elizabeth with the Scottish court. In *Mail
Royal* Gray's bastard son sets out to find the hidden Casket letters
which Gray used to blackmail King James.
   All Tranter's books are craftsman-like works and from them the
reader can learn much factual history although his social hisotry is
less vividly depicted. One seldom gets the feeling that he is standing
in the shoes of the characters, nor does he give the reader a strong
feeling that through the characters' eyes one is seeing the world of
an earlier age, its different customs and ideas. The dialogue is some-

times stilted and those looking for romantic love stories with an historical background will be disappointed. But if you like facts, battles, and magnificent beautifully described scenery, these books will please.

——Pamela Cleaver

TRASK, Betty.
Nationality: British. **Born:** Margaret Elizabeth Trask in 1895.
Career: writer; lived in Frome, Somerset. **Died:** January 1983.

ROMANCE AND HISTORICAL PUBLICATIONS

Novels

Cotton Glove Country. London, Hodder and Stoughton, 1928.
Flute, Far and Near. London, Hodder and Stoughton, 1929.
Beauty, Retire. London, Hutchinson, 1932.
How Change the Moons. London, Hutchinson, 1932.
Mannequin. London, Collins, 1933.
A Bus at the Ritz. London, Collins, 1935.
Only the Best. London, Collins, 1935.
Desire Me Not. London, Collins, 1935.
Rustle of Spring. London, Collins, 1936.
Enticement. London, Collins, 1936.
She Shall Be Queen. London, Collins, 1936.
I Tell My Heart. London, Collins, 1937.
Love with a Song. London, Collins, 1937.
Feather Your Nest. London, Collins, 1938.
Give Me My Youth. London, Collins, 1938.
Love Locked Out. London, Collins, 1938.
Love Has No Limits. London, Collins, 1939.
Love Has Wings. London, Collins, 1939.
The Sun Fades the Stars. London, Collins, 1940.
Ring of Roses. London, Collins, 1940.
From Here to a Star. London, Collins, 1941.
Change for a Farthing. London, Collins, 1942.
Promise. London, Collins, 1944.
Pride to the Winds. London, Hale, 1946.
I Will Be True. London, Hale, 1948.
Evergold. London, Hale, 1950.
Grand. London, Hale, 1951.
Thunder Rose. London, Hale, 1952.
And Confidential. London, Hale, 1953.
Just a Song at Sunrise. London, Hale, 1954.
Bitter Sweetbriar. London, Hale, 1955.
Irresistible. London, Hale, 1955.
The Merry Belles of Bath. London, Hale, 1957.

*   *   *

The works of Betty Trask had virtually been forgotten when in 1983 her estate bequeathed £400,000 to the Society of Authors to fund the Betty Trask award, then Britain's richest literary prize. Surprisingly, for a woman whose generous bequest continues to sponsor new writing in the romance genre, in most of her own work Trask merely flirts with the theme of romance. The eventual outcome of her novels is of love won at last—or tainted forever, yet the path to one or other ending is indistinct, a side issue almost. It is an expression, perhaps, of the virtuous posture of post-war little England in which couples met and married, apparently having the decency to know little about one another as they tied the knot. Trask's would-be lovers admire from a distance or have brief, rather meaningless encounters during which the flames of passion are somehow fanned.

Towards the end of *Irresistible*, Dr Meynell, 'the most handsome young man in Vidcomb', meets his love, Terry Roper, in a tea shop. Until this point, they have met infrequently, and only in the early stages of the novel is there any mention of an attraction between them. At first sight there is a deep sensuality when they are together, heightened by the fact that Terry Roper is married to the parson and therefore forbidden territory, but this tails off disappointingly. Between these points however, Trask weaves a complex tale around an indomitable European dancer who takes over the doctor's house. So powerful is this subplot that it eclipses the relationship between Terry Roper and Dr Meynell. When they eventually meet in the tea shop (Terry Roper now released from her husband by his sudden death) they converse drably and there seems little reason for the doctor's anger at her apparent indifference to him—he has been sidetracked too long, and so have we. Oddly enough, the European dancer then fades from the scene, and another strong subplot is killed off by a falling statue. Red herrings disposed of, the Roper/ Meynell story is revealed as the novel's *raison d'être* and Meynell decides suddenly to marry his love.

And Confidential has as its central character a middle-aged estate agent who, twice widowed, is now beyond any desire for romantic liaison. He is an observer and it is through his eyes that we experience the love affairs of the young. These involve a quartet of characters: his youngest daughter; a disinherited poetess; a moody eccentric poet; and an unspecified young man named Tony Hertford. Yet here again Trask creates an intricate story which is eventually left hanging. The only resolution is of who ends up with whom out of the four. However, this is the sole clue for love interest being the novel's main subject. Unfortunately, the middle-aged observer is kept out of the picture, the affairs of the young being no business of his. As he then has only few occasions to exercise his intuition and as this is largely unreliable, we are left rather confused as to how, or if, the lovers have been loving at all.

Trask's problem in these books is that they revolve around decent, middle-class characters who live in small, nosy communities. They are hidebound by etiquette and a tendency to bury their emotions from the gaze of the outside world. Trask sometimes manages to release her characters and her writing from these narrow constraints, by the introduction of less conventional characters. These are frequently the personalities who form the sub-plots and are largely responsible for the loss of interest in the duller lovers at the centre of the action. Mme Doré, for instance, is the dancer in *Irresistible*. She explodes onto the scene, invites herself into Dr Meynell's house, and makes an excellent job of running his life. She struts and orders in the truly irresistible style of a European matriarch with just a trace of broken English. She has a startling intuitive skill too. When walking into a deserted house with Dr Meynell, she says: 'I will tell you the trouble which I sense as if I smelt it. Wicked persons, and worse, weak ones, have had power here. And foolish ones plan to come but perhaps they will learn wisdom'. Mme Doré is such a tour de force that both Dr Meynell and the reader believe she will be proved right. All the more anticlimactic when Trask fails to investigate Mme Doré's suspicions further. The house stands empty and as the novel progresses, Mme Doré becomes increasingly, and inexplicably, 'cool, detached and monstrously polite'. Trask's story and writing miss her badly.

Other such characters appear in the novels, all notably irrelevant to the love interest. Malevolent servants abound. There is a Dickensian pair in *And Confidential;* one a 'round-shouldered gnome', the other sporting 'truncheon elbows' and a 'nasty mouth'. Meanwhile, poor Dr Meynell lives under the shadow of his Irish housekeeper who entered his service 'with the intention of doing exactly as she pleased, which was very little when it was a question of keeping the place tidy, but far too much when it came to interfering'. In *The*

Merry Belles of Bath, a simplified *Pride and Prejudice*, a fantastic opera singer is introduced. He makes his entrance, 'a vast pink carnation topping the profile of a huge masculine chest' and converses with an intermittent exclamation of 'do-do-mi-rée-boum!'. Eventually, he bursts into song in the middle of a chintzed drawing room. Sadly, he like the others makes a token appearance only, though one feels that were he to stay longer, the demands of sustaining such a strong character would eventually fail Trask, as happens with Mme Doré.

There is an exception in the novel *Just a Song at Sunrise*. Here, the central character, Fairlight Vivian, is not accepted by small-town society. She is one of the 'less conventional' characters usually reserved for a bit-part. Described as 'outlandish' by the local matron, she is free to display real passion and so is released from the everydayness of the other lovers. She shivers with delight when invited into 'the set', yet recognizes how 'stony and unforgiving' it can be. And, being 'x-ho-tick', she may kiss her lover before the end of the novel, waylaying him half way through. She is the one who 'presses her cheek against his breast' and whose 'lips start questing'. Fairlight Vivian is black and although the setting is not dissimilar from that in *Irresistible* or *And Confidential*, she is not bound by the etiquette of the other leading characters, even though she does strive to acquire it. The love interest here shares its motive with the rest of the novel. Fairlight at first assumes rejection, then challenges indifference and eventually knows that she will rise above it to become not just accepted, but a leader. The strength of this character is demonstrated by the fact that Trask does not entirely resolve the story. It has become unnecessary because the character has grown through the novel. In the weaker novels, all the nothingness must be explained, for without real motive having been established, it would be impossible to predict an outcome.

Just a Song at Sunrise is problematic in a modern context. In its attempt to accommodate and understand immigrant feeling in 1950s Britain it is naive and its liberal views mildly racist. Fairlight Vivian is a sympathetic character because she assimilates into an English country lifestyle. Her flamboyant mother and brother by comparison are endearing figures of fun, though Trask does seem to admire and perhaps even envy them. Some of her most sensuous writing pictures a scene in which the whole Vivian family breaks into song over dinner:

Mom started to croon, little Robbitt scrambled into her lap and blew into her breast as into a great grand trombone. Victor got up and turned on the wireless and whistled to it ... from the vast rosette of his pursed lips came long, irresistible mating calls ... Then Fairlight began to sing against, with and glorying over the whistling, the wireless, the crooning and Robbitt's musical bubble in and out of the maternal trombone.

Scenes like this recur throughout the book and it is a relief to discover that the flashes of inventive description and well-observed characterization seen in other Trask novels can permeate an entire story and create a satisfying whole. The romance is more exciting for being tinged with a little seediness as well as spice, while both main and sub-plots maintain their direction. They are drawn together by the actions and feelings of Fairlight Vivian.

If Trask's plots generally suffer from coyness and inconsistency, she was a writer who could be sensitive, amusing, and sensual when non-conformity burst into her books. It is a pity that *Just a Song at Sunrise* is one of the few examples which display Trask's real ability and which show her to be a more imaginative and truly romantic writer than she perhaps allowed.

—Pat Gordon-Smith

TREAHEARNE, Elizabeth.   See **BLAKE, Jennifer.**

TREDGOLD, Nye.   See **TRANTER, Nigel.**

TREECE, Henry.
Nationality: British. **Born:** Wednesbury, Staffordshire, 22 December 1911. **Education:** Wednesbury High School for Boys; Birmingham University, B.A. 1933, Dip. Ed. 1934. **Military Service:** Royal Air Force, 1941–46: flight lieutenant. **Relations:** married Mary Woodman in 1939; two sons and one daughter. **Career:** teacher, Leicestershire Home Office School, Shustoke, 1934; English master, The College, Cleobury Mortimer, Shropshire, 1934–35, and Tynemouth School for Boys, Northumberland, 1935–38; English master, 1938–41, and senior English master, 1946–59, Barton on Humber Grammar School, Lincolnshire. **Recipient:** Arts Council prize, for play, 1955. **Died:** 10 June 1966.

ROMANCE AND HISTORICAL PUBLICATIONS

Novels

The Dark Island. London, Gollancz, and New York, Random House, 1952; as *The Savage Warriors*, New York, Avon, 1959.
The Rebels. London, Gollancz, 1953.
The Golden Strangers. London, Lane, 1956; New York, Random House, 1957; as *The Invaders*, New York, Avon, 1960.
The Great Captains. London, Lane, and New York, Random House, 1956.
Red Queen, White Queen. London, Bodley Head, and New York, Random House, 1958; as *The Pagan Queen*, New York, Avon, 1959.
The Master of Badger's Hall. New York, Random House, 1959; as *A Fighting Man*, London, Bodley Head, 1960.
Jason. London, Bodley Head, and New York, Random House, 1961.
The Amber Princess. New York, Random House, 1962; as *Electra*, London, Bodley Head, 1963.
Oedipus. London, Bodley Head, 1964; as *The Eagle King*, New York, Random House, 1965.
The Green Man. London, Bodley Head, and New York, Putnam, 1966.

Short Stories

I Cannot Go Hunting Tomorrow. London, Grey Walls Press, 1946.

OTHER PUBLICATIONS

Plays

Carnival King (produced Nottingham, 1954). London, Faber, 1955.
Footsteps in the Sea (produced Nottingham, 1955).
Hounds of the King, with Two Radio Plays (for children; includes *Harold Godwinson* and *William, Duke of Normandy*). London, Longman, 1965.

Radio Plays: *Harold Godwinson*, 1954; *William, Duke of Normandy*, 1954.

Poetry

38 Poems. London, Fortune Press, 1940.

Towards a Personal Armageddon. Prairie City, Illinois, Press of James A. Decker, 1941.
Invitation and Warning. London, Faber, 1942.
The Black Seasons. London, Faber, 1945.
Collected Poems. New York, Knopf, 1946.
The Haunted Garden. London, Faber, 1947.
The Exiles. London, Faber, 1952.

Other (for children)

Legions of the Eagle. London, Lane, 1954.
The Eagles Have Flown. London, Lane, 1954.
Desperate Journey. London, Faber, 1954.
Ask for King Billy. London, Faber, 1955.
Viking's Dawn. London, Lane, 1955; New York, Criterion, 1956.
Hounds of the King. London, Lane, 1955.
Men of the Hills. London, Lane, 1957; New York, Criterion, 1958.
The Road to Miklagard. London, Lane, and New York, Criterion, 1957.
Hunter Hunted. London, Faber, 1957.
Don't Expect Any Mercy! London, Faber, 1958.
The Children's Crusade. London, Bodley Head, 1958; as *Perilous Pilgrimage*, New York, Criterion, 1959.
The Return of Robinson Crusoe. London, Hulton Press, 1958; as *The Further Adventures of Robinson Crusoe*, New York, Criterion, 1958.
The Bombard. London, Bodley Head, 1959; as *Ride to Danger*, New York, Criterion, 1959.
Wickham and the Armada. London, Hulton Press, 1959.
Castles and Kings. London, Batsford, 1959; New York, Criterion, 1960.
The True Book about Castles. London, Muller, 1960.
Viking's Sunset. London, Bodley Head, 1960; New York, Criterion, 1961.
Red Settlement. London, Bodley Head, 1960.
The Jet Beads. Leicester, Brockhampton Press, 1961.
The Golden One. London, Bodley Head, 1961; New York, Criterion, 1962.
Man with a Sword. London, Bodley Head, 1962; New York, Pantheon, 1964.
War Dog. Leicester, Brockhampton Press, 1962; New York, Criterion, 1963.
Horned Helmet. Leicester, Brockhampton Press, and New York, Criterion, 1963.
Know about the Crusades. London, Blackie, 1963; as *About the Crusades*, Chester Springs, Pennsylvania, Dufour, 1966.
Fighting Men: How Men Have Fought Through the Ages, with Ewart Oakeshott. Leicester, Brockhampton Press, 1963.
The Burning of Njal. London, Bodley Head, and New York, Criterion, 1964.
The Last of the Vikings. Leicester, Brockhampton Press, 1964; as *The Last Viking*, New York, Pantheon, 1966.
The Bronze Sword. London, Hamish Hamilton, 1965; augmented edition, as *The Centurion*, New York, Meredith Press, 1967.
Splintered 'Sword. Leicester, Brockhampton Press, 1965; New York, Duell, 1966.
Killer in Dark Glasses. London, Faber, 1965.
Bang, You're Dead! London, Faber, 1966.
The Queen's Brooch. London, Hamish Hamilton, 1966; New York, Putnam, 1967.
Swords from the North. London, Faber and New York, Pantheon, 1967.
The Windswept City. London, Hamish Hamilton, 1967; New York, Meredith Press, 1968.
Vinland the Good. London, Bodley Head, 1967; as *Westward to Vinland*, New York, Phillips, 1967.

The Dream-Time. Leicester, Brockhampton Press, 1967; New York, Meredith Press, 1968.
The Invaders: Three Stories. Leicester, Brockhampton Press, and New York, Crowell, 1972.

Other

How I See Apocalypse. London, Drummond, 1946.
Dylan Thomas: 'Dog among the Fairies'. London, Drummond, 1949; New York, de Graff, 1954; revised edition, London, Benn, and New York, de Graff, 1956.
The Crusades. London, Bodley Head, and New York, Random House, 1962.

Editor, with J.F. Hendry, *The New Apocalypse.* London, Fortune Press, 1939.
Editor, with J.F. Hendry, *The White Horseman: Prose and Verse of the New Apocalypse.* London, Routledge, 1941.
Editor, with Stefan Schimanski, *Wartime Harvest.* London, Bale and Staples, 1943.
Editor, with Stefan Schimanski, *Transformation.* London, Gollancz, 1943.
Editor, with Stefan Schimanski, *Transformation 2–4.* London, Drummond, 3 vols, 1944–47.
Editor, *Herbert Read: An Introduction.* London, Faber, 1944; Port Washington, New York, Kennikat Press, 1969.
Editor, with John Pudney, *Air Force Poetry.* London, Lane, 1944.
Editor, with Stefan Schimanski, *A Map of Hearts: A Collection of Short Stories.* London, Drummond, 1944.
Editor, with J.F. Hendry, *The Crown and the Sickle: An Anthology.* London, King and Staples, 1945.
Editor, with Stefan Schimanski, *Leaves in the Storm: A Book of Diaries.* London, Drummond, 1947.
Editor, *Selected Poems*, by Algernon Charles Swinburne. London, Grey Walls Press, 1948.
Editor, with Stefan Schimanski, *New Romantic Anthology.* London, Grey Walls Press, 1949.

*

Critical Study: *Henry Treece* by Margery Fisher (includes bibliography by Antony Kamm), in *Three Bodley Head Monographs*, London, Bodley Head, 1969.

*   *   *

Henry Treece depicts a universe in the throes of violent change. His characters move through overturning worlds, proud but lonely figures in the eye of the storm. Delving back through history for the roots of primal myth, Treece explores the nature of kingship, its attributes of godhead and sacrifice, presenting individuals in situations of fearful choice. At once heroic and tragic, his re-creation of past ages and leaders celebrates while at the same time foretelling the inevitable catastrophe. A chronicler of violence, he is also an advocate of peace, stressing the need for reconciliation between victor and vanquished.

A late convert to literature, Treece came to the novel last of all, following recognition as a poet and radio dramatist. The apprenticeship proved useful, adding to the broader view of the novelist a poetic concentration of utterance and a feeling for dramatic construction and dialogue. The New Apocalypse poetic movement of which he was a founding member championed individual expression and the need for a unifying myth representative of the age, both vital aspects of Treece's personal vision. His athletic abilities provided a further dimension, lending his novels a unique animal vigour. Treece's writings share a striking visual power, long-vanished cultures presented with a force so breath-taking they seem to be less read than encountered intuitively through the senses. Yet closer analysis reveals the strong, controlling intelligence behind them.

The early stories in *I Cannot Go Hunting Tomorrow* show a writer still seeking an individual voice, and are competent but derivative. An exception is 'The Visitor', in which a tense account of a youth held at knifepoint by a psychopathic killer convinces utterly, and prefigures later use of the life-and-death situation in Treece's fiction. The title story, set in Roman Britain, is less powerful, but its concept and characters foreshadow his first novel, *The Dark Island*. This novel marks the emergence of Treece as a mature stylist. In it he describes the overthrow of the Catuvellauni, the destruction of the fixed order of their world by the Roman legions, and the downfall of their leader Caradoc. In a charged poetic prose, Treece traces the inexorable decline, revealing the flaws in the nature of the Celts that render them vulnerable to defeat. A grim, mysterious, smoky work of fiction, *The Dark Island* impresses by its visual and narrative force, bringing to life a hostile world and its lurking tribal magic. Although it is Treece's earliest novel, it is one of his best.

The Rebels, set in Victorian Staffordshire, explores the same theme in personal terms, showing the secure, privileged world of the Fisher family at the moment of disintegration. Unusually ambitious, it moves backward through chronological time, the opening scene gradually explained by various family members. The book is not completely successful—there are imbalances between individual sections, and too much secondary detail—but is nevertheless a powerful, compelling work. *The Great Captains* and *The Golden Strangers* complete the early phase of Treece's writing and constitute an advance on previous work. The former, an inspired, realistic portrayal of Arthurian legend, is a tour de force. Artos, the Celtic chieftain, is presented as a complex figure, half-savage yet a champion of Romano-British civilization against the invading Saxons. His doomed, heroic stand against the inevitable barbarian triumph is superbly evoked, Treece's vision of a desolate, ruined Britain living on in the mind. *The Golden Strangers*, one of his finest novels, records the collapse of the Neolithic culture at the hands of the Celts. Both peoples are brilliantly brought alive on the page, Treece seeming instinctively to enter the minds of his creations and their binding laws of ritual and taboo. Garroch, tribal chief and sacrificial godking, is portrayed as the archetype of all mythic heroes. Following him through the ritual dances, hunts, and battles, Treece blasts the consciousness of the reader with the sight, sound and scent of a vanished age. His grasp of the preliterate sensibility, the complexity of a supposedly 'primitive' culture, is stunning in its conviction. A milestone of achievement, *The Golden Strangers* succeeds totally and remains unique. Later works equal, but do not surpass it.

Red Queen, White Queen and *A Fighting Man* are lesser novels, but possess virtues of their own. The first, set at the time of Boudicca's rebellion, is the nearest thing to an 'entertainment' its author ever wrote. Fast-paced and enjoyable, its tragic theme is offset by bawdy humour and a final, moving reconciliation. *A Fighting Man* pictures the downfall of a Regency prize-fighter, who as an aged pauper recounts his days of glory from the workhouse in the manner of Oedipus at Colonus. It suffers from an over-elaborate plot whose loose ends are abruptly tied, but remains an effective portrayal of an elegant but vicious age.

With his trilogy of Greek novels Treece embarked on the final phase of his search, pursuing classical myth to its prehistoric origins, his individual tragedies cast against the background of worlds in turmoil. In *Jason*, where themes of identity, godhead, and quest pulse behind the narrative, the Minoan-Hellene conflict endures in a struggle between kings and priestesses, typified by Jason's lover and nemesis, the sinister Medea. A dark, terrifying work, *Jason* is overlong and lacks the coherence of *Electra*, where related themes are explored more narrowly but with greater intensity. The most

perfectly balanced of the trilogy, *Electra* has a tighter construction that lends its message an added force. Here, as in *Jason*, Treece tears aside the veneer of civilization to reveal the grim, bestial urges beneath. Both novels reek with darkness and corruption, their revelations increasingly repellent. Each is a tribute to the author who brings them so horribly to life. *Oedipus*, last of the sequence, breaks fresh ground, Treece attempting a synthesis of myths as he follows the club-foot hero—a child-man seeking father and mother—through the murky, violent world of prehistoric Greece. God-king and sacrificial scapegoat, Oedipus serves as a focus for the flux of migrating nations that merges Aryans and Nilotic African herders, and battles for supremacy with the priestess-queen Jocasta. Less overtly violent than its predecessors, *Oedipus* exudes a sense of looming horror, and in two extended dream-sequences interweaves myths and gods alike as Oedipus metamorphoses into Christ, Krishna, Arthur, and Hamlet. Using a hard, pared style Treece explores the fascinating blend of cultures that constitutes the ancient Mediterranean. An accomplished work, *Oedipus* with its attempted intermeshing of myths looks forward to *The Green Man* and the culmination of Treece's achievement.

In *The Green Man*, exploring the Hamlet legend to its Dark Age origins, Treece re-creates a brutal age whose archetypal herofigures embody basic animal urges, and whose underlying theme is the continual cyclic process of growth and decay. The intricate plot takes in murder, incest, madness and parricide, and accommodates several distinct mythic heroes. In a honed, bardic style reminiscent of Scandinavian saga, Treece brings each man powerfully to life— Amleth, the murderous innocent and potent fertility symbol, reincarnated as the Green Man; Beowulf, vain, glorious and cunning, a formidable warrior terrified at the thought of his own identity; and Arthur, the bitter, crippled veteran to whom Amleth appears as son and rival. These and others follow the story to its fearsome conclusion. Treece's poetic and intuitive qualities are at their most inspired, his pared style complementing a stunning visual sense. *The Green Man* completes the author's search, the unifying myth superbly achieved in a narrative which blends separate mythic strands into a single impressive work of art.

Treece's writing for younger readers parallels his adult novels, advancing from simple adventure stories like *Desperate Journey* and *Ask for King Billy* to a more mature form of expression. His Romano-British novels, *Legions of the Eagle* and *The Eagles Have Flown*, combine exciting action with deeper portrayals of the nature of friendship and betrayal against the background of war. The same is true of his magnificent Viking trilogy—*Viking's Dawn*, *The Road to Miklagard*, *Viking's Sunset*—which memorably evokes that restless, violent age. Treece returned to the same era with retellings of saga (*The Burning of Njal*) and the lives of such heroes as Hereward and Harald Hardrada, gradually adopting a terse, laconic style shorn of nonessential elements. As adventure gave way to deeper perceptions, he reemphasized the necessity for peace and co-operation, a message enshrined in his masterpiece, *The Dream-Time*. Set in the prehistoric past, and spanning several evolutionary periods, *The Dream-Time* presents the creative power of art as a positive force against the negatives of war, distrust, and separation. Twilight, the craftsman hero, in his search for new artistic forms, his hatred of taboos, wars, and secret languages, strongly expresses the author's beliefs. Treece ends by affirming the strength of dreams in the most appealing of his works.

—Geoffrey Sadler

TREMAIN, Rose.
Nationality: British. **Born:** Rose Thomson, London, 2 August 1943. **Education:** Frances Holland School, London, 1949–54;

Crofton Grange School, London, 1954–60; the Sorbonne, Paris, 1960–61, diploma in literature, 1962; University of East Anglia, Norwich, 1964–67, B.A. (honours) in English, 1967. **Relations:** married 1) Jon Tremain in 1971 (divorced 1978), one daughter; 2) Jonathan Dudley in 1982. **Career:** teacher, Lynhurst School, London, 1968–70; assistant editor, British Printing Corporation, London, 1970–72; part-time research jobs, 1972–79; creative writing fellow, University of Essex, Wivenhoe, 1979–80; lecturer in creative writing, Vanderbilt University, Nashville, 1987. Since 1980, full-time writer and part-time lecturer in creative writing, University of East Anglia. **Recipient:** Dylan Thomas prize, 1984, for short story, for *The Colonel's Daughter*; Giles Cooper award for radio play, 1985, for *Temporary Shelter*; Angel literary award, 1985, for *The Swimming Pool Season*, 1989, for *Restoration*; *Sunday Express* Book of the Year award, 1989, for *Restoration*; James Tait Black memorial prize, 1993, for *Secret Country*. Fellow, Royal Society of Literature, 1983. **Agent:** Richard Scott Simon, 43 Doughty Street, London WC1N 2LF, England. **Address:** 2 High House, South Avenue, Thorpe St Andrew, Norwich NR7 0EZ, England.

ROMANCE AND HISTORICAL PUBLICATIONS

Novel

Restoration. London, Hamish Hamilton, 1989; New York, Viking, 1990.

OTHER PUBLICATIONS

Novels

Sadler's Birthday. London, Macdonald, 1976; New York, St Martin's Press, 1977.
Letter to Sister Benedicta. London, Macdonald, 1978; New York, St Martin's Press, 1979.
The Cupboard. London, Macdonald, 1981; New York, St Martin's Press, 1982.
The Swimming Pool Season. London, Hamish Hamilton, 1989; New York, Viking, 1990.
Sacred Country. London, Sinclair Stevenson, 1992; New York, Atheneum, 1993.

Short Stories

The Colonel's Daughter and Other Stories. London, Hamish Hamilton, and New York, Summit, 1984.
The Garden of the Villa Mollini and Other Stories. London, Hamish Hamilton, 1987.

Plays

Mother's Day (produced London, 1980).
Yoga Class (produced Liverpool, 1981).
Temporary Shelter (broadcast 1984). In *Best Radio Plays of 1984*, Methuen, 1985.

Radio Plays: *The Wisest Fool*, 1976; *Dark Green*, 1977; *Blossom*, 1977; *Don't be Cruel*, 1978; *Leavings*, 1978; *Down the Hill*, 1979; *Half Time*, 1980; *Hell and McLafferty*, 1982; *Temporary Shelter*, 1984; *The Birdcage*, 1984; *Will and Lou's Boy*, 1986; *The Kite Flyer*, 1987; *Music and Silence*, 1992.

Television Plays: *Halleluiah, Mary Plum*, 1978; *Findings on a Late Afternoon*, 1980; *A Room for the Winter*, 1981; *Moving on the Edge*, 1983; *Daylight Robbery*, 1986.

Other

The Fight for Freedom for Women. New York, Ballantine, 1973.
Stalin: An Illustrated Biography. New York, Ballantine, 1975.
Journey to the Volcano (for children). London, Hamish Hamilton, 1985.

*   *   *

'The present', Rose Tremain said in the *Times Higher Education Supplement* (1991), 'is both too painful to get to grips with and is also moving too quickly to pin down in a novel'. This philosophy runs through all of Tremain's writing, which repeatedly problematizes time and history, emphasizing the fallibility of representation and elusiveness of truth. Tremain's characters struggle to understand their histories by attempting, always imperfectly, to tell their stories. Personal stories, however, (mis)behave like larger historical narratives. Nowhere in Tremain's writing is the dubiousness of history more pressing than it is in *Restoration*.

As a love story set far in a past, which spans the plague and the Great Fire of London, *Restoration* is a blend of the historical and the romantic. Almost invariably, *Restoration* has been labelled an historical novel. Seldom has it been called a romance. Yet because of its simultaneous invocation and subversion of the conventions of both historical and romance writing, the book would be described more accurately as '*anti*-historical'—as well as '*anti*-romantic'.

Implicit within the conventions of historical writing is the assumption that history can be captured and reliably reported. *Restoration* reveals the spuriousness of this presupposition. Its narrator, Robert Merivel, is a character whose place in time as he tells his story is impossible to pinpoint. This timelessness is achieved by Tremain's transitions between the past and present tense: 'I entered London at seven o'clock . . . . See me, then . . . I have stopped at an inn . . . I feel extraordinarily hot'. 'Do you see me now?', Merivel asks the reader, who can only wonder, when is now? Merivel remarks upon the 'lies and fictions underlying all human discourse', metafictionally drawing attention to the constructedness and lack of authority of any version of history: 'I am also in the middle of a story which might have a variety of endings . . . or . . . beginnings'. The text self-reflexively emphasizes the subjectivity and unreliability which operate in any narrative.

Art—in the forms of painting, drawing, and music—is used as a metaphor for history through which Tremain demonstrates the impossibility of ever creating a faithful version of events. Merivel's attempt to draw 'an entire body and not bits and pieces of it' can only fail. Through art, Tremain symbolizes the deceptiveness of any historical record: 'The background . . . must flatter. More, it must lend permanence to the life of the sitter, no matter how brief his actual existence'. Even as Tremain stresses that every event is a floating signifier with multiple and unstable interpretations, she also articulates the hopelessness of ever escaping one's history. Merivel is a surgeon whose 'desire to forget my former profession' becomes a metaphor for the desire to escape one's past and one's self. It is a metaphor which Tremain employs to demonstrate both individual and socio/cultural impoverishments and dangers of forgetfulness—as well as the impracticability of remembering perfectly. The text exploits the numerous, and often hidden, forms that narratives can take. Merivel says of the nipple that has caused a woman to be accused of being a witch: 'it is *your* mark . . . you alone know when it first came there, and . . . of what kind, if any, is the fluid or matter that comes out of it'. Here, the body becomes discourse—another way of telling history that suggests Tremain's familiarity with *écriture féminine*. The recipe for a prophylactic against the plague is written by a character upon wax paper to which ink will not adhere. When Merivel places 'the paper *in front* of the light, the words [are] magically illuminated, having been scratched into the wax'. The paper becomes a metaphor for the notion that one must employ different strategies to locate and decode a story.

Restoration deconstructs and defies the conventions of romance. It is a seduction story in which the heroine's traditional resistance to the hero does not melt into passion. It is a love story in which love is only ever unrequited, and the hero is ugly and fat with repulsive table manners. Tremain mimics the discourse of the potboiler: 'I bring her head towards mine. I feel her breasts against my chest. My head is throbbing and my breath coming in short gasps . . . . And then she spat at me'. Yet Tremain simultaneously subverts this discourse by giving Merivel language and acts that are both 'masculine' and 'feminine'. The text operates by dissolving instead of polarizing this perennial binary opposition—unlike conventional romance novels (and like Tremain's most recent novel *Sacred Country*). Stereotypically gendered behaviour and sexual politics do not construct *Restoration*. Rather, the novel analyses and exposes such behaviour, as when Merivel comments on his desire to 'possess and abuse' the very 'sweetness' in a woman that makes his 'heart tender.' While conventional romance novels marginalize or idealize the physicality of the human body, *Restoration* calls attention to its unromantic smells and substances in a way that undermines the subject matter of romance writing. Farts, excrement, mucus, blood, foetid breath, oozing body sores, decaying flesh, tumours, visible hearts, and caesarian births are a mere sampling of those delights of the body which are detailed explicitly and plentifully.

Restoration invokes the romance conventions of fairy-tales, for example, when the hero is set a difficult task which, if performed correctly, will win for him great rewards: Merivel will be Court Physician if he cures the King's dog. Yet Tremain draws upon fairy-tale conventions only to overturn them. She seduces her reader into anticipating a fairy-tale transformation, but the transformation which occurs is not that of the frog into a prince, but of hedonistic greed into spiritual grace. Transformed Merivel is not rewarded with the gratification of his desire for a woman. He is not given love, but rather, gives it himself in the 'high white space' of his selfless love for his daughter.

—Tracy Brain

TREMAINE, Jennie. See **CHESNEY, Marion.**

TRESILLIAN, Richard.
Pseudonym: Raynard Devine. **Address:** Hutchinson, 20 Vauxhall Bridge Road, London SW1V 2SA, England.

ROMANCE AND HISTORICAL PUBLICATIONS

Novels (series: Bloodheart; Bondmaster)

The Bondmaster. London, Arlington, 1977.
Blood of the Bondmaster. New York, Warner, 1977; London, Arlington, 1978.
The Bondmaster Breed. London, Arlington, 1979.
Fleur. London, Arlington, 1979.
Bondmaster Fury. London, Arlington, 1982.
Bondmaster's Revenge. London, Arlington, 1983.
Bondmaster Buck. London, Arlington, 1984.
Bloodheart. London, Century, 1985.
Bloodheart Royal. London, Century, 1986.
Bloodheart Feud. London, Sphere, 1988.
Giselle. London, Century, 1988.

Novels as Raynard Devine (series: Flesh Traders, in all books)

Master of Black River. London, Futura, 1984.
Black River Affair. London, Futura, 1985.
Black River Breed. London, Futura, 1985.
Revenge at Black River. London, Futura, 1985.

*   *   *

There is always tension in the sultry, enervating air in Richard Tresillian's 'Bondmaster' saga, and lust, fear, and violence make an explosive mixture. The setting of the novels is the remote Roxborough Estate on the West Indian island of Dominica, a British colony then, and the period is the early decades of the 19th century when increasingly effective regulation of the slave trade made it essential to replace traditional methods of supplementing the workforce by importing fresh slaves with a programme of making the best use of existing resources by breeding from existing stock. All thought of humanity is forgotten; the black slaves are treated like animals, and the terminology employed—bucks, fillies, whelps and so on—is borrowed flagrantly from the stock yard. The only concern shown for the individuals lies in their masters' desire to control mating so that the young men shall not become exhausted by over-exertion and so that the characteristics of the various African tribes are blended to produce offspring particularly suited to the various tasks to which they will be put later on in life, when they are sold on to new owners.

The Todds, the masters of Roxborough, live far from other Europeans, though they visit them from time to time, even crossing the Atlantic on occasion. Most of the time, however, they spend alone on the estate, quaffing rum, though sugar production has ceased to be the major business that once it was, keeping up some pretence of genteel manners, trying to preserve some heritage for the next generation, and finding sexual gratification with the privileged slaves who tend them in their home. For the men—the gentlemen, as they prefer to regard themselves—there are satisfactions in maintaining grim discipline among the slaves, and when they are bored they will go to the town for a break. The white women have a harder lot; when, to relieve the tedium and enjoy some tenderness, they turn to the more handsome of the slaves, a harsh double standard operates. What is acceptable in their husbands—even commendable, since light-skinned slaves command high prices—is regarded as abhorrent in their womenfolk, and savage retribution swiftly follows. Roxborough represents a society in decline, with poverty always a prospect and with rebellion, either by the slaves on the estate or by others who have run away earlier and formed desperate bands up in the hills, a menace which can never be entirely ignored. As tensions mount, the novels present a steady escalation of horror until it seems that there is no imaginable inhumanity left to inflict. There is, it is plain, some historical warrant for the picture presented here, but the piling up of atrocities eventually becomes hard to swallow and some readers will judge that the novels are too sensational to be genuinely sensuous.

The narrative moves rapidly, and the saga is so constructed that any individual novel can be read separately, though it is best to master the family tree before beginning the text as it contains facts of which even those characters most concerned are sometimes unaware until it is too late. Tresillian uses a sober style for the white masters of Roxborough with just the occasional turn of phrase that reminds us of the period of the novels. What mainly characterizes their speech is an unremitting directness in their references to the bodies and breeding of the slaves; as Carlton Todd puts it in *The Bondmaster's Revenge*, 'false modesty don't belong in a slave breeder'. Into the mouths of the slaves Tressilian puts a creole dialect, a form of English with a much simplified grammar, which serves as a constant indicator of their inferior status, just as the occasional unfamiliar noun, derived from French or local patois, helps create the West Indian scene.

The geographical location is different in the four volumes of *The Fleshtraders*, set in Mauritius, and in the *Bloodheart* novels—which relate the introduction of West Indian slavers methods in Ceylon at the beginning of the 19th century—and in *Fleur*—which sees things rather more from a female viewpoint in the American south just before the Civil War. The major theme of different races in close proximity remains, however, much the same, as does its underpinning with historical fact and, equally important, a sense of period.

—Christopher N. Smith

TROLLOPE, Joanna.
Pseudonym: Caroline Harvey. **Nationality:** British. **Born:** Gloucestershire, 9 December 1943. **Education:** St Hugh's College, Oxford (Gamble scholar), 1962–65, M.A. in English 1972. **Relations:** married 1) David Potter in 1966, two daughters; 2) the playwright Ian Curteis in 1985. **Career:** esearch assistant, Foreign Office, London, 1965–67; teacher in preparatory schools and adult foreign student classes, 1968–78. **Recipient:** Romantic Novelists Association Major award, 1980. **Agent:** A.D. Peters, Fifth Floor, The Chambers, Chelsea Harbour, Lots Road, London SW10 0XF, England. **Address:** The Mill House, Coln St Aldwyns, Cirencester, Gloucestershire, England.

Romance and Historical Publications

Novels

Eliza Stanhope. London, Hutchinson, 1978; New York, Dutton, 1979.
Parson Harding's Daughter. London, Hutchinson, 1979; as *Mistaken Virtues*, New York, Dutton, 1980.
Leaves from the Valley. London, Hutchinson, 1980; New York, St Martin's Press, 1984.
The City of Gems. London, Hutchinson, 1981.
The Steps of the Sun. London, Hutchinson, 1983; New York, St Martin's Press, 1984.
The Taverners' Place. London, Hutchinson, 1986; New York, St Martin's Press, 1987.
A Passionate Man. London, Bloomsbury, 1990.
The Rector's Wife. London, Bloomsbury, 1991.
The Men and the Girls. London, Bloomsbury, 1992.
A Second Legacy. London, Corgi, 1992.
A Spanish Lover. London, Bloomsbury, 1993.

Novels as Caroline Harvey (series: Legacy of Love)

Legacy of Love. London, Octopus, 1983.
  Charlotte. London, Sundial, 1980.
  Alexandra. London, Sundial, 1980.
  Cara. London, Octopus, 1983.

Other Publications

Novels

The Choir. London, Hutchinson, 1988.
The Village Affair. London, Bloomsbury, and New York, HarperCollins, 1989.

Other

Britannia's Daughters: Women of the British Empire. London, Hutchinson, 1983.

Editor, *The Country Habit: An Anthology*. London, Bantam, 1993.

*

Joanna Trollope comments:
There are, certainly, love stories in my books, but they are only a part of the whole. The whole is my desire to bring history to life, not just to superimpose a 20th-century story on to a historical background. I want to give a sense of life as it was lived in the past, and to that end I do more than twice as much research as I need for each book so that I am, myself, thoroughly familiar with each period.

*   *   *

Joanna Trollope is equally at home writing in the past and the present. She began her career with historical novels, each centred on a heroine with a serious character flaw that had to be overcome before the happy ending. After writing seven of these, she turned to contemporary books focusing on a small community and a marriage that is unravelling.

Eliza Stanhope, eponymous heroine of Trollope's first novel, said that she 'did not like being like other women and she did like doing what was forbidden': most of the heroines of her historical novels are in this mould while her contemporary heroines are married women suffering from frustration and trying to find themselves.

Eliza's flaw is that she is wilful and arrogant; following her soldier husband to the wars she learns humility and gains maturity through assisting a surgeon on the battlefield of Waterloo. In 18th-century India Caroline, in *Parson Harding's Daughter*, is trapped in a loveless marriage and lacks self-confidence; she finds it almost impossible to accept gracefully what is offered her out of kindness, let alone out of love. Maria, in *The City of Gems*, is arrogant, selfish, and imperious. Against the background of the barbaric splendor of Mandalay in the 1880s, she finally learns a little graciousness, but it is almost too late. She certainly does not deserve the delightful hero, Archie Tennant, the only man who understands her.

All the characters in *The Steps of the Sun* are flawed, none of them act as they stated they would when put to the test by the Boer war.

The saga, *Legacy of Love*, (under her pseudonym Caroline Harvey) is an omnibus containing three books. The first, *Charlotte*, is by far the best. Charlotte, a vivid adventurous girl, marries Hugh to get away from her claustrophobic life in England, dragging her timid sister Emily (the narrator) in her wake. Charlotte finds her true love in Kabul where she, Hugh, Emily, and her lover are caught up in the doomed retreat of 1842. *Alexandra* is Charlotte's granddaughter. Her life in Edwardian Scotland is dull and empty until great-aunt Emily invites her to Cornwall where she makes appalling mistakes, and learns many lessons, before finding happiness. Spoiled, selfish *Cara* is Alexandra's daughter who behaves badly when war breaks out; she too is chastened by events and finally achieves happiness. Alexandra and Cara are pale characters in comparison with Charlotte, but then they do not live in such colourful times.

When Trollope turns her attention to contemporary fiction she uses richer, more complex plots and larger casts of characters to explore marriages in crisis. The affair depicted in *The Village Affair* is a delicately handled lesbian relationship which has the same effect on the quiet village of Pitcombe as a bomb would. In *The Choir* besides telling a tale of intrigue and rivalry in a cathedral close, she explores the theme that the lives of clergy wives are hard. She repeats this again in *The Rector's Wife*, adding to it her constant key figure of a woman trapped in a loveless marriage. Anna, in *The Rector's Wife*, fits into both categories.

A Passionate Man dissects a marriage which is perfectly happy until Archie, unable to cope with his father's death, finds himself coveting his father's new wife. Archie and his wife are, as so many of Trollope's characters seem to be, 'trapped in littleness' but eventually they achieve a compromise. *The Men and the Girls* takes place in a wonderful, raffish house in Oxford where the relationships of all the characters are at crisis point; they all learn something important before the story ends, with everyone compromising.

Trollope's style is deceptively simple and extremely readable; her characterization always rings true, her child characters are especially good, and her choice of details to illuminate a scene or paint a picture is unerring. Like Jane Austen, she has realized that 'three or four families in a country village is the very thing to work on' and in doing so she holds up a mirror to contemporary middle-class country life, uncovering attitudes that are usually hidden.

Devotees of her historical stories will be pleased to know that she has not entirely forsaken this genre: more Caroline Harvey books are on their way.

—Pamela Cleaver

TROY, Katherine. See **MAYBURY, Anne.**

TUCKER, Audrie Manley. See **MANLEY-TUCKER, Audrie.**

TURNER, Judy. See **SAXTON, Judith.**

VAIZEY, Mrs George de Horne.
Nationality: British. **Born:** Jessie Bell Mansergh in 1857.

ROMANCE AND HISTORICAL PUBLICATIONS

Novels (series: Pixie O'Shaughnessy; Peggy Saville)

A Rose-Coloured Thread. London, Bowden, 1898.
About Peggy Saville. London, Religious Tract Society, 1900; New York, Putnam, 1917.
Sisters Three. London and New York, Cassell, 1900.
Tom and Some Other Girls: A Public School Story. London and New York, Cassell, 1901.
More About Peggy. London, Religious Tract Society, 1901.
A Houseful of Girls. London, Religious Tract Society, 1902.
Pixie O'Shaughnessy. London, Religious Tract Society, 1903; Philadelphia, Jacobs, 1907.
More about Pixie. London, Religious Tract Society, 1903.
The Daughters of a Genius: Story of a Brave Endeavour. London, Chambers, and Philadelphia, Lippincott, 1903.
How Like the King. London, Bousfield, 1905.
The Heart of Una Sackville. London, Partridge, 1907.
The Fortunes of the Farrells. London, Religious Tract Society, 1907; Philadelphia, Jacobs, 1908.

Betty Trevor. London, Religious Tract Society, 1907; New York, Putnam, 1917.
Big Game: A Story for Girls. London, Religious Tract Society, 1908.
Flaming June. London, Cassell, 1908.
The Conquest of Chrystabel. London, Cassell, 1909.
A Question of Marriage. London, Hodder and Stoughton, 1910; New York, Putnam, 1911.
Etheldreda the Ready: A School Story. London and New York, Cassell, 1910.
Cynthia Charrington. London and New York, Cassell, 1911.
A Honeymoon in Hiding. London and New York, Cassell, 1911.
The Adventures of Billie Belshaw. London, Mills and Boon, 1912.
A College Girl. London, Religious Tract Society, 1913; New York, Putnam, 1916.
An Unknown Lover. London, Mills and Boon, and New York, Putnam, 1913.
Grizel Married. London, Mills and Boon, 1914; as *Lady Cassandra*, New York, Putnam, 1914.
The Love Affairs of Pixie. London, Religious Tract Society, 1914.
Salt of Life. London, Mills and Boon, 1915.
The Independence of Claire. London, Religious Tract Society, 1915.
The Lady of the Basement Flat. London, Religious Tract Society, 1917.
Harriet Mannering's Paying Guests. London, Mills and Boon, 1917.

Short Stories

Old Friends and New. London, Hodder and Stoughton, 1909.
What a Man Wills. London, Cassell, and New York, Putnam, 1915.
The Right Arm and Other Stories. London, Mills and Boon, 1918.

*   *   *

Most of Mrs de Horne Vaizey's novels dealt with 'the essence of femininity in the springtide of life', and several were originally serialized in the *Girl's Own Paper*. They cannot, however, be classified as children's fiction but are essentially light Edwardian romances designed to appeal both to teenage girls and adult women.

For their time, the stories were refreshingly vigorous. Vaizey sent a string of heroines to college or to embark upon careers, although she actually disapproved of women's suffrage, and considered that men should manage the country and the business world. Even the most lively of her girls would eventually be forced into the realization that a woman's place was firmly in 'the shelter of her lover's arms' and subsequently, of course, in acquiescent domesticity.

Her most perceptive and rewarding book is *The Independence of Claire*, which vividly highlights a 19-year-old high-school teacher's struggles against poverty and prejudice, from which romance happily provides the ultimate escape. However, her most loved character is without doubt Pixie O'Shaughnessy, 'the wild Irish tornado'. Pixie must have been one of the first of the irrepressible Irish heroines who were eventually to become stock figures in the English light fiction genre. She progresses from exuberant schoolgirl—'the joy and terror of the school', in fact—to elegant adult in the course of the three books that describe her exploits.

These and the Peggy Saville stories were the most popular of Vaizey's works, but the author preferred *Salt of Life*, which was based on the experiences of her own family and friends. This is a perceptive and witty story about two families of girls on the threshold of adult life and romance. The romantic threads in her family sagas are low key rather than lush, but nevertheless effective. And at least the male characters for whom her heroines abdicate all their career ambitions are three-dimensional people, and not simply the cyphers of simplistic (and boring) masculinity that are featured in more run-of-the-mill romantic novels.

—Mary Cadogan

---

van der ZEE, Karen.
A pseudonym. **Other Pseudonym:** Mona van Wieren. **Nationality:** Dutch. **Born:** Sneek, Friesland, Netherlands, 26 May 1947. **Education:** Netherlands. **Career:** married in 1969; three children. **Career:** writer; lived in Kenya, Ghana, and Indonesia. **Address:** c/o Mills and Boon Ltd, Eton House, 18–24 Paradise Road, Richmond, Surrey TW9 1SR, England.

ROMANCE AND HISTORICAL PUBLICATIONS

Novels

Sweet Not Always. London, Mills and Boon, 1979.
Love Beyond Reason. London, Mills and Boon, 1980.
A Secret Sorrow. London, Mills and Boon, 1981.
Going Underground. London, Mills and Boon, 1982.
Waiting. London, Mills and Boon, 1982.
One More Time. London, Mills and Boon, 1983.
Soul Ties. London, Mills and Boon, 1984.
Staying Close. London, Mills and Boon, 1984.
Pelangi Haven. London, Mills and Boon, 1985.
Fancy Free. London, Mills and Boon, 1986.
Time for Another Dream. London, Mills and Boon, 1986.
Shadows on Bali. London, Mills and Boon, 1988.
Hot Pursuit. London, Mills and Boon, 1988.
Rhapsody in Bloom (as Mona van Wieren). New York, Silhouette, 1989.
Brazilian Fire. London, Mills and Boon, 1989.
Java Nights. London, Mills and Boon, 1990.
The Imperfect Bride. London, Mills and Boon, 1991.
Something in Return. London, Mills and Boon, 1992; Toronto, Harlequin, 1994.
A Prince Among Men. New York, Silhouette, 1992.
Kept Woman. London, Mills and Boon, 1991.
Passionate Adventure. London, Mills and Boon, 1993.
Making Magic. London, Mills and Boon, 1993.
Love Untamed. London, Mills and Boon, 1994.

*

Karen van der Zee comments:

I love writing because I am free to use my imagination, to draw word pictures, to create people and feelings—to make something that other people can enjoy. I'd like to think that I can bring to my readers worlds they may have no chance to explore themselves, and show them something new and exciting. This is the reason I like to read myself—entertainment and discovery.

I started writing my first romance in Ghana. I had struggled for years trying to perfect *my* English, as it made no sense to keep writing in Dutch. I'd had a couple of small successes in Holland, and I knew that writing was what I really wanted to do. Needless to say, I was ecstatic when I sold my first novel.

I like being my own boss and having the freedom to decide my own work schedule. I think I'll just keep on writing.

*   *   *

Karen van der Zee's romances usually involve an explosive piece of information which the heroine has discovered either about herself or about someone close to her. This news, usually tragic in nature, becomes the focus around which the rest of the novel evolves and develops. Often the heroine's inability to come to terms with or express the problem she encounters prevents the otherwise seemingly perfect love relationship. Van der Zee's romances are different from conventional ones in their characterization. Her heroes are not always inscrutable, mysterious and hard; rather, they are virile and competent, yet tolerant and sensitive. They frequently declare their love or attraction for the heroine early on in the story. It is the woman who is burdened with a secret or difficulty which creates a psychological and emotional barrier between the lovers.

Normally van der Zee's heroines are American girls living in the United States. However, some travel to distant lands, such as Australia, Bali, Kenya, St Barlow, or Brazil. These exotic places, their local people, food, and culture, are described in loving detail and with care in the novels. The protagonists are more than just tourists in these lands, they often work to help improve conditions there. While van der Zee's heroines tend to be young, in their early to mid-twenties, they are educated, and have interesting careers or goals, ranging from technical writers, translators, art directors, physiotherapists, to antique dealers. They are all portrayed as strong, independent women who would rather not rely on men to rescue them from their predicament.

The fatal plights that van der Zee's heroines fall into sometimes verge on the melodramatic; nevertheless, they are realistically explained. The author seems to be able to pick out and make use of some of the most common fears women have today as the basis for the heroine's quandry in her romances. Two interesting plots involving pregnancy and childbirth occur in *A Secret Sorrow* and *Staying Close*. In *A Secret Sorrow* Faye Sherwood finds out that because of a recent car accident, she is unable to bear children. She falls in love with a man who wants to raise many children in a ranch house in Texas. Much of the novel's emotional power comes from the sensitive psychological exploration of the heroine's source of depression. With insight van der Zee describes the heroine's pain: 'She wanted to scream. Children. I'll never have children . . . I'll never waddle around with a big belly worrying if I'll ever get my shape back. I'll never be a mother, never nurse a baby'. With the hero's help, Faye learns to accept the inevitable, and stops looking at herself as a 'machine with a defect'. They raise a large family by adopting less fortunate chidren from all over the world.

In *Staying Close* Kristen, pregnant with another man's child, becomes involved with Paul who takes care of her during her financially and physically difficult days. Van der Zee's skill shows through when she is able to blend passion with some of the harsher realities of being unmarried at the last trimester of maternity. Not all her novels are related to pregnancy and babies, however. *Going Underground* deals with a very current and real concern for working women: the pressures resulting from fulfilling one's ambition in a career, and the desire to succeed in an ideal love relationship at the same time. In *Brazilian Fire* van der Zee depicts with sensitivity the feeling of being culturally displaced in society through Chantal who is half-French and half-American. The heroine remarks: 'It was strange. I never knew where I belonged. In the States I felt French, and in France I felt American . . . I always felt pulled between two worlds'. She shares her isolation with a man who feels similarly alienated as the son of a Brazilian and an American.

The plots of van der Zee's novels are carefully orchestrated so that one gets a sense of the emotional dilemma of the characters. *Shadows on Bali* and *The Imperfect Bride* both use the conventional plot of the reunion of past and thwarted lovers. What makes them different from other romances is their use of particulars, such as the mention of goats on the road, the shade of a breadfruit tree, turtle stew. The author sensually evokes both the richness and the poverty of daily life on these sun-drenched islands. More importantly, what keeps the heroine and hero apart are real and human feelings of inadequacy, regret, guilt, loss, and pain. Their sexual unions are not just shallow adventures into ecstasy, but are fraught with more profound implications of coming to terms with weakness, of the inevitability of change, and of the imperfections in life.

In some novels, the sentimentality is lightened with touches of humour. In *Hot Pursuit* the hero is first attracted to the heroine by her bumper sticker written in Frisian, an obscure language, which reads, 'Be a sunbeam, others need one'. He follows her in his car until she acknowledges him. In *Kept Woman*, the young orphan Daniella lets the hero Marc believe that she is the mistress of his wealthy father. Marc's attempts to buy her off with thousands of dollars are unsuccessful because she really 'loves' her adopted father, and not for the material reasons that the tabloid newspapers announced. The romance concludes not only with the romantic love between the hero and the heroine, but also with the powerful drama of family reunion—between the estranged son and his neglectful father helped in part, by Daniella. This small sample of the ever-increasing work of Karen van der Zee illustrates her dexterity in writing romances which creatively handle some pertinent issues facing women of the 1980s and the 1990s.

—Eleanor Ty

VANSITTART, Peter.
Nationality: British. **Born:** Bedford, 27 August 1920. **Education:** Marlborough House School; Haileybury College, Hertford; Worcester College, Oxford (major scholar in modern history). **Career:** director, Burgess School, London, 1947–59; formerly, publisher, Park Editions, London. **Recipient:** Society of Authors travelling scholarship, 1969; Arts Council bursary, 1981, 1984. Fellow, Royal Society of Literature, 1986. **Agent:** Sheil and Associates Ltd, 43 Doughty Street, London WC1N 2LF, England. **Address:** 9 Upper Park Road, London, N.W.3, England; or, Little Manor, Kersey, Ipswich, Suffolk, England.

ROMANCE AND HISTORICAL PUBLICATIONS

Novels

Lancelot. London, Owen, 1978.
The Death of Robin Hood. London, Owen, 1981.
Three Six Seven. London, Owen, 1983.
Parsifal, London, Owen, 1988; Chester Springs, Pennsylvania, Dufour, 1989.
The Wall. London, Owen, 1990.

OTHER PUBLICATIONS

Novels

I Am the World. London, Chatto and Windus, 1942.
Enemies. London, Chapman and Hall, 1947.
The Overseer. London, Chapman and Hall, 1949.
Broken Canes. London, Lane, 1950.
A Verdict of Treason. London, Lane, 1952.
A Little Madness. London, Lane, 1953.
The Game and the Ground. London, Reinhardt, 1956; New York, Abelard Schuman, 1957.
Orders of Chivalry. London, Bodley Head, 1958; New York, Abelard Schuman, 1959.
The Tournament. London, Bodley Head, 1959; New York, Walker, 1961.

A Sort of Forgetting. London, Bodley Head, 1960.
Carolina. London, New English Library, 1961.
Sources of Unrest. London, Bodley Head, 1962.
The Friends of God. London, Macmillan, 1963; as *The Siege*, New York, Walker, 1963.
The Lost Lands. London, Macmillan, and New York, Walker, 1964.
The Story Teller. London, Owen, 1968.
Pastimes of a Red Summer. London, Owen, 1969.
Landlord. London, Owen, 1970.
Quintet. London, Owen, 1976.
Harry. London, Park, 1981.
Aspects of Feeling. London, Owen, 1986.
A Choice of Murder. London, Owen, 1992.

Other

The Dark Tower: Tales from the Past (for children). London, Macdonald, 1965; New York, Crowell, 1969.
The Shadow Land: More Stories from the Past (for children). London, Macdonald, 1967.
Green Knights, Black Angels: The Mosaic of History (for children). London, Macmillan, 1969.
Vladivostok (essay). London, Covent Garden Press, 1972.
Dictators. London, Studio Vista, 1973.
Worlds and Underworlds: Anglo-European History Through the Centuries. London, Owen, 1974.
Flakes of History. London, Park, 1978.
The Ancient Mariner and the Old Sailor: Delights and Uses of Words. London, Centre for Policy Studies, 1985.
Paths from a White Horse: A Writer's Memoir. London, Quartet, 1985.
London: A Literary Companion. London, Murray, 1992.

Editor, *Voices from the Great War.* London, Cape, 1981; New York, Watts, 1984.
Editor, *Voices: 1870–1914.* London, Cape, 1984; New York, Watts, 1985.
Editor, *John Masefield's Letters from the Front 1915–1917.* London, Constable, 1984; New York, Watts, 1985.
Editor, *Happy and Glorious: An Anthology of Royalty.* London, Collins, 1988.
Editor, *Voices of the French Revolution.* London, Collins, 1989.

*

Peter Vansittart comments:

Though I have published non-fiction, novels alone excite my ambitions; not plays, short stories, poems, manifestos, sermons. My novels have been appreciated, if not always enjoyed, more by critics than the reading public, which shows no sign of enjoying them at all. This must be partly due to my obsession with language and speculation at the expense of narrative, however much I relish narrative in others. Today I take narrative more seriously, though still relying, perhaps over-relying, on descriptive colour, unexpected imagery, the bizarre and curious—no formula for popular success. *The Game and the Ground, The Tournament, Lancelot,* and *Quintet,* have succeeded the most in expressing initial vision and valid situation in fairly accessible terms. Others—*A Verdict of Treason, A Sort of Forgetting*—had interesting and provocative material, clumsily handled. *The Story Teller,* my own favourite, failed through excess of ambition. *A Little Madness* and *Sources of Unrest,* through too little.

My novels range in time from the 2nd millennium BC, to AD 1986. They share the effect of time, and the apparently forgotten or exterminated on the present, time transmuting, distorting, travestying, ridiculing facts and ideas, loves and hates, generous institutions and renowned reputations. I was long impressed by the woeful distinction between the historical Macbeth and Shakespeare's: by the swift transformation of E.M. Forster's very English Mrs Moore into an Indian goddess. Such phenomena relate very immediately to my own work, in which myth can be all too real, and the real degenerate into fantasy.

*   *   *

There is nothing cosy about Peter Vansittart's historical novels. In prose that is spare and chaste, using words with rare respect to create vivid and compelling images of the past with no blurring from fustian archaism, he looks hard at a panorama of crumbling civilizations and finds little to cheer him. The precise relevance to our present age is not pointed out, yet the reader can scarcely ignore the implications.

Three Six Seven, for instance, portrays the period of the decline of Roman power in Britain through the eyes of Drusus who is presented as 'a very important person' and who would never for a moment imagine there was the slightest tinge of irony in that characterization. To convey the sense of the crumbling of authority and the decline of civilization into hideous barbarism Vansittart deploys both historical documentation and novelistic imagination, for disaster in public affairs is reflected in the distorting mirror of personality. Drusus is experienced, cool-headed and able, as he imagines, to appraise situations and even to profit from them; in fact he cannot remain alien from the climate of his age, and we realize that he is a victim of the values he has inherited from a Rome which can itself no longer uphold them.

A similar pessimism pervades *Lancelot*. From before Malory until after Byrne-Jones its hero has been swathed in romanticism, but Vansittart will have none of it. Instead he employs the familiar figure for an exploration of the final phase of the decline of Roman Britain and the confusion that accompanied the Saxon invasions. There are violence and atrocity at every turn, weird rites are practised, and sexuality, far from being etherealised, is brutish and strange. *The Death of Robin Hood* is more demanding on the reader than the earlier novels, for it is not a life-history or a fragment of one, but rather an evocation of a myth of liberation which is embodied in the freedom supposed to be located in the greenwood of Nottinghamshire. The first section describes the forest; the second is set in the time of John's attempt to usurp the throne of Richard I; the third transports us to the Luddite revolts of 1812; and in the fourth Vansittart comes up to the 1930s. Recurrent figures, as well as repeated themes, link the sections, each of which are introduced by a series of epigraphs borrowed from a wide variety of sources which start chains of thought and suggestions which readers must control as best they can.

Parsifal is no less ambitious, taking Richard Wagner for the starting point of an adventure in scholarship and imagination back into the past and forward into the 20th century. The effect is kaleidoscopic and always potentially chaotic, as fact and fiction are fused to form myth which at times is only fleetingly conveyed. Yet it is hard to reject these odd creations. An historian by training, Vansittart possesses real and unusual erudition; his evocations of the past, even when they are deliberately fragmented, carry conviction, and his characters, however remote, have psychological traits which ring true, so that we follow their fortunes with attention and listen to their opinions with more than usual interest, especially as they always seem to know more than they reveal. Sinister forces always seem to pose real threats, which creates tension, and Vansittart constantly juxtaposes rationality to powers which may prove stronger still. The mind is always alert, seeing and sensing, but whether it is in command is another question.

Vansittart's historical novels have received a mixed reception, some reviewers blaming him for obscurity and others disliking his prose which is sometimes clipped almost to the point of breathlessness. There are, however, a number of critics who find Vansittart one of the most exciting historical novelists of the present generation with a style which is very much his own.

—Christopher N. Smith

———

VAN SLYKE, Helen.

Pseudonym: Sharon Ashton. **Nationality:** American. **Born:** Helen Lenore Vogt, Washington, DC, 9 July 1919. **Relations:** married William Woodward Van Slyke in 1946 (divorced 1952). **Career:** fashion editor, Washington *Evening Star*, 1938–43; beauty editor, 1945–55, and promotion director, 1955–60, *Glamour* magazine, New York; promotion and advertising director, Henri Bendel, New York, 1960–61; vice-president and creative director, Norman Craig and Kummel, advertising agency, New York, 1961–63; president, House of Fragrance (Genesco), New York, 1963–68; vice-president for Creative Activities, Helena Rubinstein, New York, 1968–72; then full-time writer and lecturer. **Died:** 1979.

ROMANCE AND HISTORICAL PUBLICATIONS

Novels

The Rich and the Righteous. New York, Doubleday, 1971; London, Cassell, 1972.
All Visitors Must Be Announced. New York, Doubleday, 1972; London, Cassell, 1973; as *The Best People*, New York, Popular Library, 1976.
The Heart Listens. New York, Doubleday, 1973; London, New English Library, 1974.
The Santa Ana Wind (as Sharon Ashton). New York, Doubleday, 1974; London, New English Library, 1975.
The Mixed Blessing. New York, Doubleday, 1975; London, New English Library, 1976.
The Best Place to Be. New York, Doubleday, and London, New English Library, 1976.
Always Is Not Forever. New York, Doubleday, 1977; London, New English Library, 1978.
Sisters and Strangers. New York, Doubleday, 1978; London, Heinemann, 1979.
A Necessary Woman. New York, Doubleday, and London, Heinemann, 1979.
No Love Lost. Philadelphia, Lippincott, and London, Heinemann, 1980.
Public Smiles, Private Tears, completed by James Elward. New York, Harper, and London, Heinemann, 1982.

*   *   *

Helen Van Slyke viewed her books pragmatically: 'perhaps what I write is romantic sentimental nonsense, but if two million or more people want to read it, that's important. If you're in a business, you should act as if you're in a business, with something to sell, and every now and then you must forget about artistic merit. I know I don't write literature, for heaven's sake . . .'.

What she did write and promote are phenomenally successful 'women's novels', which she referred to as 'soap operas between covers'. Only the first book has a man as its central character. In the rest, the main characters are women who are usually affluent and often middle-aged. They confront problems familiar to the contemporary reader. Sheila Callahan in *The Best Place to Be* faces widowhood. Alice Winters (*Sisters and Strangers*) is married to a wife beater. Charlene Jenkins (*The Heart Listens*) is married to a black man, and her daughter Toni (*The Mixed Blessing*) must resolve identity problems resulting from her interracial heritage. Mary Morgan, in *A Necessary Woman*, has to deal with her successful career, and her weak husband.

Like Mary, Van Slyke's women are generally stronger than their male counterparts. Some of them use their strength to help others. Elizabeth Quigly (*The Heart Listens* and *The Mixed Blessing*) works indefatigably for her family and friends. Others use their power to destroy people's lives. Mary Morgan's sister Pat seduces Mary's husband to hurt her sister.

Although Van Slyke's women enjoy sex, they are more likely to remain faithful to their marriage commitments than are their husbands, many of whom assume that extramarital liaisons are a male prerogative. In *No Love Lost* that attitude eventually drives Pauline Thresher to leave her husband—with her mother-in-law's support.

Van Slyke's women need and like men, but they also have strong relationships with other women. A letter from her daughter helps Sheila Callahan resolve a long-standing conflict with her own mother. Relationships between sisters are explored in *A Necessary Woman* and *Sisters and Strangers*. The importance of friendship between women is evident in *Always Is Not Forever*. Susan Langdon's former boss is honest enough to help Susan confront her drinking problem, marital difficulties, and need for an identity apart from her husband.

But the exploration of character never dominates Van Slyke's action-filled stories. Like the soap operas to which she compared her books, her plots include one crisis after another. Van Slyke believed in 'the power of storytelling' to reach her readers with a tale 'that is comprehensible within the realm of their own experience'. The popularity of her books bears witness to her success in meeting her goal.

—Kathy Piehl

---

van WIEREN, Mona.   See **van der Zee, Karen.**

VERYAN, Patricia.
Pseudonym for Patricia V. Bannister. **Other Pseudonym:** Gwyneth Moore. **Nationality:** British/American (dual citizenship). **Born:** London, England, 21 November 1923. **Education:** Mitcham Central Girls School, Surrey, 1934–37; Miss Lodge Secretarial School, London, 1937–38. **Relations:** married Allan Louis Berg in 1946 (died 1980); one daughter and one son. **Career:** secretary, Navy, Army, and Air Force Institutes, London, 1938–40, Columbia Pictures, London, 1940–42, United States Army, London, Paris, and Frankfurt, 1942–46, Pacific telephone, Sacramento, California, 1949, National Cash Register Company, Los Angeles, 1950, Southern Counties Gas Company, Los Angeles, 1951–52, and Humble Oil and Refining Company, Los Angeles, 1952–55; secretary for Graduate Affairs, University of California, Riverside, 1971–85. **Agent:** Florence Feiler Literary Agency, 1524 Sunset Plaza Drive, Los Angeles, California 90069, USA. **Address:** 10129 Main Street, Apartment 204, Bellevue, Washington 98004, USA.

ROMANCE AND HISTORICAL PUBLICATIONS

Novels (series: Golden Chronicles; Sanguinet Saga; Tales of the Jeweled Men)

The Lord and the Gypsy. New York, Walker, 1978; as *Debt of Honour*, London, Souvenir Press, 1980.

Love's Duet. New York, Walker, 1979; as *A Perfect Match*, London, Souvenir Press, 1981.
Mistress of Willowvale. New York, Walker, 1980.
Some Brief Folly. New York, St Martin's Press, 1981.
Sanguinet Saga:
   1. *Nanette*. New York, Walker, 1981.
   2. *Feather Castles*. New York, St Martin's Press, 1982.
   3. *Married Past Redemption*. New York, St Martin's Press, 1983.
   4. *The Noblest Frailty*. New York, St Martin's Press, 1983.
   5. *Sanguinet's Crown*. New York, St Martin's Press, 1985.
   6. *Give All to Love*. New York, St Martin's Press, 1987.
The Wagered Widow. New York, St Martin's Press, 1984.
Golden Chronicles:
   1. *Practice to Deceive*. New York, St Martin's Press, 1985.
   2. *Journey to Enchantment*. New York, St Martin's Press, 1986.
   3. *The Tyrant*. New York, St Martin's Press, 1987.
   4. *Love Alters Not*. New York, St Martin's Press, 1987.
   5. *Cherished Enemy*. New York, St Martin's Press, 1988.
   6. *The Dedicated Villain*. New York, St Martin's Press, 1989.
Logic of the Heart. New York, St Martin's Press, 1990.
Time's Fool (Tales of the Jeweled Man). New York, St Martin's Press, 1990.
Had We Never Loved (Tales of the Jeweled Man). New York, St Martin's Press, 1991.
Poor Splendid Wings. London, Severn House, 1992.

Novels as Gwyneth Moore

Men Were Deceivers Ever. Toronto, Harlequin, 1989.
The Dirty Frog. Toronto, Harlequin, 1990.
Love's Lady Lost. Toronto, Harlequin, 1991.

*

Patricia Veryan comments:
   Almost every period of history has its highlights, its subtle nuances of life at every level that would warrant much happy digging and delving into, so as to gain a fairly well-rounded picture of the time. Of them all, however, I am most fascinated by Britain's crowded past: the perilous days of the Stuarts, the Jacobite uprisings, and the Regency (1811–20). This latter time I find especially intriguing, for it was surely, as Sir Arthur Bryant dubbed it, 'The Age of Elegance'. Were one to cover the era fully, and from every side, there must be some very dark pages, of course; and some, perhaps darkest of all, shadowed by the shape of things to come. I am not a historian, however, although I attempt to hold true to historical detail. I do not write to moralize, or educate, but to entertain, and if I may thereby leave my reader with a little deeper appreciation of the period, why, so much the better.
   And what a period it was! The Napoleonic Wars, and the incredible heroism of the men who fought them on land and sea, whether French, English, or their Allies. The many-faceted Regent himself, later to become George IV, who, despite his numerous failings, encouraged a deeper interest in art, music, and architecture, and left us so rich a heritage of beauty. The preoccupation with manners, the niceties of fashion, and that rare and wonderful intangible, the Code of Honour. Regency gentlemen lived, and sometimes died, by this same Code that valued honour above all things, and next to honour, courage, loyalty, and gentleness. By its unwritten yet inviolate precepts, parents must be respected and obeyed; women revered; children, the weak, and the helpless protected. A man's character was judged by his adherence to his given word, and the crime unforgivable was cowardice. A religion rather? Perhaps. A religion seldom spoken of, but quietly lived. It was a time of contrasts we now find astounding; of sordid poverty and squalor, and great wealth; medical horrors, and the emergence of self-cleanliness; exquisitely

gowned ladies instructed from the cradle in the graces and attributes necessary to becoming a good wife, gallant gentlemen, and the savageries of child labour; oppression and tyranny, and yet withal a prosperity unrivalled in the Europe of that day, and a nationwide and innate courtesy and chivalry.

Against this rich canvas, my books are set. They may differ slightly from others of the genre, in that I perhaps insert a trifle more of action and adventure than is the usual fashion, for it was so much a period of action.

If I have, to any extent, achieved success, much of the credit must go to my superb teachers. These have been many, for from every author one gleans something. In my own field however, two were outstanding: the first of these was Jeffrey Farnol, who wrote with such gentleness, warmth, and charm, in the early years of this century; the second, Georgette Heyer, whose wit, masterful style, rich humour, and knowledge of her period, were so incomparable. Without these two great friends, whom I dearly loved, and from whom I learned so much, countless happy hours would have been lost to me. For this, besides what they taught me, I do most humbly, if posthumously, thank them.

To others I leave the task of painting the harsh realities of life; the bewilderments of today's world; the savageries of drugs and the pity of lost morality. Life is difficult enough to live, I do not choose to carry such harshness into my writing. I fashion my tales lightly, in the hope that my readers—especially those who may be wearied of the daily grind, or ill, or discouraged, or lonely (surely the cruellest of sorrows)—may perhaps find a smile, or a tug at the heartstrings, or a tingle of excitement within the pages of my books, and thus escape to the thunderous elegance of not so long ago.

*   *   *

Patricia Veryan is one of the most outstanding authors of historical romance writing today. She is adept at creating fascinating characters, and has written some of the most original and intriguing stories to be found in the genre. She researchs her periods (usually Georgian or Regency England) well, and writes convincingly of the manners of the time. Her Harlequin Regency Romances (*Men Were Deceivers Ever*, *The Dirty Frog*, *Love's Lady Lost*), written as Gwyneth Moore, show the same quality of research and character and plot development.

A basic theme of her work is the preservation of honour and integrity in the face of betrayal and almost indescribable suffering. Both men and women must bear the burden, sometimes with great loneliness. In *Mistress of Willowvale* Leonie braves public disgrace and the contempt of the man she loves to protect her nephew and the memory of her sister by allowing people to believe that the boy is her child out of wedlock. The Marquis of Damon, hero of *Love's Duet*, endures his father's scorn and the shame of a dishonourable reputation in order to bring the true villains to justice. Lucian St Clair in *The Lord and the Gypsy* endures great emotional and physical suffering as the ultimate atonement for past wrongs committed. Similarly, Anthony Farrar, branded a coward and a murderer in *Love Alters Not*, undergoes great hardship before his name is cleared.

Veryan's books are distinguished by well-developed central characters and many interesting minor personages. Often the primary focus is on the male characters although the female characters are not slighted. The men are blessed with extremely loyal friends, who might be unable to articulate their deep feelings for one another but are always ready to sacrifice a great deal to aid one of their own. Even those outside these friendships can gain admittance by performing heroic, selfless acts. There is great romantic involvement, but no explicit sexual details, much in the fashion of mediaeval chivalry. It is easy to imagine many of her Regency heroes as gallant and courageous knights.

Veryan reserves some of her longest, most detailed passages for carefully orchestrated mayhem, which forms an integral part of the suffering to be borne by the hero. Lucian St Clair participates in, and almost loses a brutal sword fight; Harry Redmond (*Nanette*) becomes a fugitive hunted throughout England and eventually is thrown into Newgate Prison; Mitchel Redmond, Harry's brother, battles his way across England to save the Prince Regent (*Sanguinet's Crown*); and Christopher Thorndyke (*Mistress of Willowvale*) is branded a traitor and narrowly avoids death in an all-out battle which takes place in a kitchen. Detailed as the descriptions of the action become, there is no gratuitous violence, and Veryan tempers all the serious themes and action with humour and a very satisfying love story.

An unusual aspect of Veryan's work has been the gradual forging of complete social worlds for her characters. Where other authors often rely heavily on real historical figures, such as the Prince Regent, to create the sense of aristocratic society in which their characters move, Veryan creates her own worlds by introducing her readers to new members of those societies in each book. Often the protagonist in one book played a minor role in an earlier work or appears in a later one. This sense of society is, perhaps, strongest in the Regency novels. These stories chronicle the struggles of a dedicated band of friends to combat the evil Sanguinet brothers, An enclosed social world also is apparent in the novels which make up the 'Golden Chronicles' series. While *Practice to Deceive* is the first volume named in the series, several characters (the Duke of Marbury, his rogue of a grandson, Roland Otton/Mathieson, and Trevelyan de Villars) appear in the earlier *Mistress of Willowvale* and *The Wagered Widow*. Similarly, the two series are linked through families and estates. Marbury's estate, Dominer, returns as the location of *Some Brief Folly*, in which the reader learns that Garret Hawkhurst is descended from the Thorndykes. Horatio, Viscount Glendenning, who figured in *Love Alters Not* ('The Golden Chronicles') returns in 'Tales of the Jeweled Men' a series about a nefarious plot to overthrow Hanoverian royalty and establish a dictatorial republic. A secondary character in the first volume, *Time's Fool*, he finally takes centre stage in the second volume, *Had We Never Loved*.

The intertwining of stories, even across time, creates a real sense of continuity. The appearances of recurring characters never seem contrived but are worked into the narrative quite naturally. Soon it is like receiving news of old and dear friends. Now a common plot device for many authors, Veryan was among the first to use it and remains one of the most adept. She is unparalleled when writing about her chosen periods of history and remains a model for all historical novelists to follow.

—Barbara E. Kemp

VIDAL, Gore (Eugene Luther Vidal, Jr).
Pseudonym: Edgar Box. **Nationality:** American. **Born:** West Point, New York, 3 October 1925. **Education:** Los Alamos School, New Mexico, 1939–40; Phillips Exeter Academy, Exeter, New Hampshire, 1940–43. **Military Service:** United States Army, 1943–46: warrant officer. **Career:** editor, E.P. Dutton, publishers, New York, 1946. Lived in Antigua, Guatemala, 1947–49, and Italy, from 1967. Member, Advisory Board, *Partisan Review*, New Brunswick, New Jersey, 1960–71; Democratic-Liberal candidate for Congress, New York, 1960; member, President's Advisory Committee on the Arts, 1961–63; co-chairman, New Party, 1968–71. **Recipient:** Mystery Writers of America Edgar Allan Poe award, 1954, for television play; National Book Critics Circle award, 1983, for criticism. **Address:** La Rondinaia, Ravello, 84010

Salerno, Italy; or c/o Random House Inc, 201 East 50th Street, New York, New York 10022, USA.

ROMANCE AND HISTORICAL PUBLICATIONS

Novels

A Search for the King: A Twelfth Century Legend. New York, Dutton, 1950; London, New English Library, 1967.
Messiah. New York, Dutton, 1954; London, Heinemann, 1955; revised edition, Boston, Little Brown, 1965; Heinemann, 1966.
Julian. Boston, Little Brown, and London, Heinemann, 1964.
Washington, DC. Boston, Little Brown, and London, Heinemann, 1967.
Burr. New York, Random House, 1973; London, Heinemann, 1974.
1876. New York, Random House, and London, Heinemann, 1976.
Creation. New York, Random House, and London, Heinemann, 1981.
Lincoln. New York, Random House, and London, Heinemann, 1984.
Empire. New York, Random House, and London, Deutsch, 1987.

OTHER PUBLICATIONS

Novels

Williwaw. New York, Dutton, 1946; London, Panther, 1965.
In a Yellow Wood. New York, Dutton, 1947; London, New English Library, 1967.
The City and the Pillar. New York, Dutton, 1948; London, Lehmann, 1949; revised edition, Dutton, and London, Heinemann, 1965.
The Season of Comfort. New York, Dutton, 1949.
Dark Green, Bright Red. New York, Dutton, and London, Lehmann, 1950.
The Judgment of Paris. New York, Dutton, 1952; London, Heinemann, 1953; revised edition, Boston, Little Brown, 1965; Heinemann, 1966.
Three: Williwaw, A Thirsty Evil, Julian the Apostate. New York, New American Library, 1962.
Myra Breckinridge. Boston, Little Brown, and London, Blond, 1968.
Two Sisters: A Memoir in the Form of a Novel. Boston, Little Brown, and London, Heinemann, 1970.
Myron. New York, Random House, 1974; London, Heinemann, 1975.
Kalki. New York, Random House, and London, Heinemann, 1978.
Duluth. New York, Random House, and London, Heinemann, 1983.
Hollywood. New York, Random House, and London, Deutsch, 1990.
Live from Golgotha. New York, Random House, 1991; London, Deutsch, 1992.

Novels as Edgar Box

Death in the Fifth Position. New York, Dutton, 1952; London, Heinemann, 1954.
Death Before Bedtime. New York, Dutton, 1953; London, Heinemann, 1954.
Death Likes It Hot. New York, Dutton, 1954; London, Heinemann, 1955.

Short Stories

A Thirsty Evil: Seven Short Stories. New York, Zero Press, 1956; London, Heinemann, 1958.

Plays

Visit to a Small Planet (televised 1955). In *Visit to a Small Planet and Other Television Plays.* 1956; revised version (produced New York, 1957; London, 1960), Boston, Little Brown, 1957; in *Three Plays*, 1962.
Honor (televised 1956). in *Television Plays for Writers: Eight Television Plays*, edited by A.S. Burack, Boston, The Writer, 1957; revised version, as *On the March to the Sea: A Southron Comedy* (produced Bonn, Germany, 1961), in *Three Plays*, 1962.
Visit to a Small Planet and Other Television Plays (includes *Barn Burning, Dark Possession, The Death of Billy the Kid, A Sense of Justice, Smoke, Summer Pavilion, The Turn of the Screw*). Boston, Little Brown, 1956.
The Best Man: A Play about Politics (produced New York, 1960). Boston, Little Brown, 1960; in *Three Plays*, 1962.
Three Plays. London, Heinemann, 1962.
Romulus: A New Comedy, adaptation of a play by Friedrich Dürrenmatt (produced New York, 1962). New York, Dramatists Play Service, 1962.
Weekend (produced New York, 1968). New York, Dramatists Play Service, 1968.
An Evening with Richard Nixon and ... (produced New York, 1972). New York, Random House, 1972.

Screenplays: *The Catered Affair*, 1956; *I Accuse*, 1958; *The Scapegoat*, with Robert Hamer, 1959; *Suddenly, Last Summer*, with Tennessee Williams, 1959; *The Best Man*, 1964; *Is Paris Burning?*, with Francis Ford Coppola, 1966; *Last of the Mobile Hot-Shots*, 1970; *The Sicilian*, 1970; *Gore Vidal's Billy the Kid*, 1989.

Television Plays: *Barn Burning*, from the story by Faulkner, 1954; *Dark Possession*, 1954; *Smoke*, from the story by Faulkner, 1954; *Visit to a Small Planet*, 1955; *The Death of Billy the Kid*, 1955; *A Sense of Justice*, 1955; *Summer Pavilion*, 1955; *The Turn of the Screw*, from the story by Henry James, 1955; *Honor*, 1956; *The Indestructible Mr. Gore*, 1960; *Vidal in Venice* (documentary), 1985; *Dress Gray*, from the novel by Lucian K. Truscott IV, 1986.

Other

Rocking the Boat (essays). Boston, Little Brown, 1962; London, Heinemann, 1963.
Sex, Death, and Money (essays). New York, Bantam, 1968.
Reflections upon a Sinking Ship (essays). Boston, Little Brown, and London, Heinemann, 1969.
Homage to Daniel Shays: Collected Essays 1952–1972. New York, Random House, 1972; as *Collected Essays 1952–1972*, London, Heinemann, 1974.
Matters of Fact and of Fiction: Essays 1973–1976. New York, Random House, and London, Heinemann, 1977.
Sex Is Politics and Vice Versa (essay). Los Angeles, Sylvester and Orphanos, 1979.
Views from a Window: Conversations with Gore Vidal, with Robert J. Stanton. Secaucus, New Jersey, Lyle Stuart, 1980.
The Second American Revolution and Other Essays 1976–1982. New York, Random House, 1982; as *Pink Triangle and Yellow Star and Other Essays*, London, Heinemann, 1982.
Vidal in Venice, edited by George Armstrong, photographs by Tore Gill. New York, Summit, and London, Weidenfeld and Nicolson, 1985.
Armageddon? Essays 1983–1987. London, Deutsch, 1987; as *At Home: Essays 1983–1987*, New York, Random House, 1988.
Who Owns the US. Berkeley, California, Odonian, 1990.
A View from the Diner's Club: Essays 1983–87. London, Deutsch, 1991.
Screening History. Washington, HUP, and London, Deutsch, 1992.

United States: Essays 1952–92. New York, Random House, and London, Deutsch, 1993.

Editor, *Best Television Plays.* New York, Ballantine, 1956.

*

Film Adaptations: *Visit to a Small Planet*, 1960; *The Best Man*, 1964; *Myra Breckenridge*, 1970; *Gore Vidal's Lincoln*, 1988, from the novel *Lincoln*.

Bibliography: *Gore Vidal: A Primary and Secondary Bibliography* by Robert J. Stanton, Boston, Hall, and London, Prior, 1978.

Manuscript Collection: University of Wisconsin, Madison.

Critical Studies: *Gore Vidal* by Ray Lewis White, New York, Twayne, 1968; *The Apostate Angel: A Critical Study of Gore Vidal* by Bernard F. Dick, New York, Random House, 1974; *Gore Vidal* by Robert F. Kiernan, New York, Ungar, 1982; *Gore Vidal: Writers Against the Grain* edited by Jay Parini, New York, Columbia University Press, 1992.

Theatrical Activities:
Actor: **Film**—*Roma* (*Fellini Roma*), 1972.

*   *   *

Gore Vidal has written five novels about United States history, which, taken together, provide a panorama of the growth of empire, an idea apparent in the title of his recent work, *Empire.* Even before the design of Vidal's fictional history was apparent, however, he revealed his intent in *Washington, DC*, the first of his ventures into the American past. 'Overnight', Vidal wrote in reference to the impact of World War II, 'everyone took it for granted that without design and by God's election, the American Empire existed to rule the world'. While the birth of empire may appear to have arrived unannounced, history, as Vidal shows in his novels, indicates otherwise.

In *Burr* Vidal covers the period from the American Revolution to the 1830s in which great and small minds fought for power. He looks in particular at Jeffersonian expansionism as it affected the Presidency, the growth of Continental America, and the transformation of political attitudes from Jefferson to Jacksonian Democracy. In *Lincoln* and *1876* he describes America's great internal crises (the Civil War and Reconstruction), the consolidation of power, the emergence of the mercantile mind, and the subsequent alterations in culture and the body politic.

Empire deals with the Spanish-American war years, expansionist America, and the internationalization of political perspectives in the United States; and *Washington, DC*, focuses on the 20-year period from the late 1930s to the early 1950s—the zenith, as Vidal cynically remarks, of America's empire. From Jefferson and Burr in *Burr* to James Burden Day and Clay Overbury the political leaders in *Washington, DC* the growth of empire contrasts sharply with a decline in political character, almost as if world domination were predicated on a corresponding decline in vision, integrity, and depth of character. Vidal's usual pattern, in fact, is to contrast men of integrity with those who seek merely power. Aaron Burr and Martin Van Buren, heroes in Vidal's eyes, give way to the power-seekers, Jefferson and Jackson; Lincoln and Tilden are replaced by Grant and Hayes; McKinley and Franklin D. Roosevelt are succeeded by Teddy Rossevelt and Clay Overbury, Vidal's version of the media personalities who typify contemporary politics. From this point of view, Vidal's historical novels are a public record of the rise and fall of political giants and the private observation on the whole of the American experience. The path that leads from the 18th to the 20th century, from *Burr* to *Washington, DC*, from Thomas Jefferson to

Clay Overbury is clear and tragic to Vidal. This path, moreover, is one not necessarily marked in textbooks or in the minds of American citizenry.

In this sense Vidal belongs to the new school of American historical novelists—the revisionists and debunkers of mythic history such as Thomas Berger, Thomas Flanagan, John Barth, and Robert Coover—all of whom question history as generally presented and who blur distinction between fact and fiction since history is itself nothing more than a fictive version of the past. In his gossipy novels, Vidal attempts to reconstruct the missing pages of history by enlarging the personal lives of public figures whose historical reputations are themselves a blend of history and fiction.

In addition, Vidal ties his novels together (and makes history credible) through the presence of an 'historical' family—the descendants of Aaron Burr, father to a nation. The protagonist and narrator of *Burr* is Charlie Schuyler, Burr's illegitimate son who, disenchanted with the course of the American experiment, leaves for an extended stay in Europe with his daughter. For much of his background information, Vidal turned to documents of the period including an 1861 novel, *Margaret Moncrieff: The First Love of Aaron Burr* by Charles Burdett, the actual illegitimate son of Burr and the model for Schuyler. Vidal's interest in Burdett provided him with a plot within a plot featuring the quasi-historical Schuylers who appear in subsequent novels.

Lincoln, for example, closes with a scene at the palace of the Tuileries where a reception is being held for the diplomatic corps. At the reception, John Hay, Lincoln's former secretary, meets 'the American historian' Charles Schermerhorn Schuyler and his daughter Emma, the princess d'Agrigente. Schuyler left New York in 'thirty-six, to be, like you', he tells Hay, 'a diplomat. Only I went to Italy, and never returned home'. In this scene, Charlie's role as an American expatriate, curious about his changing homeland, is clear enough. His questions about Lincoln, the Presidency, and politics allow Vidal one last chance for a melancholy glance at the Lincoln years. Schuyler hints that it might be time for him to return to America 'which plainly bears no resemblances to the one I left'. In *1876* Schuyler and his daughter have indeed returned home where he is hired to write a campaign tract for Tilden, a work which turns out to be the manuscript of *1876* a cynical comment on a country which has lost its tradition and direction.

A generation later in *Empire*, Charlie and Emma are distant but still powerful shadows. Emma is mysteriously remembered as the 'darkly beautiful Princess d'Agrigente' and Charlie is described by Henry James as one who 'believed in the necessity of living on this side of the Atlantic, some distance from our newspapered democracy'. The Schuyler connection is extended to the protagonists, Caroline, the daughter of Emma and her second husband, Colonel Sanford, and her stepbrother Blaise, both of whom own newspapers in a country seemingly run by William Randolph Hearst who claims, 'I just made up this country pretty much as it happens to be at the moment'. Vidal's disdain for Hearst's America (and for history) is illustrated late in the novel in a conversation between Hearst and Teddy Roosevelt. 'History invented me, not you!' Roosevelt claims, to which Hearst replies, 'I am history—or at least the creator of the record'.

Vidal ends his historical cycle where he began it—in *Washington, DC* with Peter Sanford, son of Blaise. At various times the novel calls upon the ghosts of the past. A portrait of Aaron Burr hangs in the Sanford house, and Lincoln's name is invoked as a standard which America has never quite met. Vidal's real interest, however, is in the new phase of empire. Franklin D. Roosevelt, we are told, has reassembled the fragments of broken empires into a new pattern. What is more, he is the 'proud creator of the new imperium'. Vidal, through his spokesman, Senator James Burden Day, says that the United States has abandoned the design of the Republic and that elections are now only periodic referendums to change the dictator.

History is in the hands of the Clay Overburys and a new set of values and system far removed from the times and the likes of Aaron Burr, a man who made history. In fact, Hearst's and Roosevelt's debate about history becomes a mocking comment on history in the novel. 'Must we have history?', Peter Sanford is asked at the end of it all. Sanford's reply serves as an epitaph for all the novels and, sadly, as a comment on the American empire. 'It passes the time', Sanford responds.

In his five novels about the American past, Vidal is irreverent, witty, daring, and incisive. His historical landscape is charged with satirical energy while his narrative strategy, especially his on-going affair with the mysteries of Aaron Burr, reveals the mind of the leading historical novelist of the day. Over the last 20 years he has turned most often to history for his satire and, in the process, has produced the most noteworthy sequence of historical novels of any 20th-century American writer.

—Thomas S. Gladsky

VINCENT, Claire.   See ALLEN, Charlotte Vale.

VITEK, Donna (Kinel).
Pseudonym: Donna Alexander. **Born:** in Winston-Salem, North Carolina, 10 November 1947. **Education:** Appalachian State University, 1967–68. **Relations:** married Richard John Vitek in 1969; one son and one daughter. **Career:** factory employee, RJ Reynolds Tobacco Company, Winston-Salem, 1967–68. Since 1979, full-time writer. **Agent:** Scott Meredith, Scott Meredith Literary Agency Inc, 845 Third Avenue, New York, New York 10022, USA. **Address:** c/o Dell, 666 Fifth Avenue, New York, New York 10103, USA.

ROMANCE AND HISTORICAL PUBLICATIONS

Novels

Red Roses, White Lilies (as Donna Alexander). New York, Macfadden, 1979.
No Turning Back (as Donna Alexander). New York, Macfadden, 1979.
In from the Storm (as Donna Alexander). New York, Macfadden, 1979.
A Different Dream. New York, Silhouette, 1980.
Promises from the Past. New York, Silhouette, 1981.
Showers of Sunlight. New York, Silhouette, 1981.
Veil of Gold. New York, Silhouette, 1981.
Where the Heart Is. New York, Silhouette, 1981.
Valaquez Bride. New York, Silhouette, and London, Hodder and Stoughton, 1982.
A Game of Chance. New York, Silhouette, 1982; London, Hodder and Stoughton, 1983.
Garden of the Moongate. New York, Silhouette, 1982.
Sweet Surrender. New York, Silhouette, 1982.
Morning Always Comes. New York, Silhouette, 1982.
Passion's Price. New York, Silhouette, 1983.
Blue Mist of Morning. New York, Dell, 1983.
Dangerous Embrace. New York, Dell, 1983.
No Promise Given. New York, Dell, 1983.
Warmed by the Fire. New York, Dell, 1983.
Never Look Back. New York, Dell, 1983.
An Unforgettable Caress. New York, Dell, 1984.

Breaking the Rules. New York, Dell, 1984.
Asking for Trouble. New York, Dell, 1984.
Thrill of the Chase. New York, Dell, 1985.
Deep in the Heart. New York, Dell, 1985.
Players in the Shadows. New York, Dell, 1985.
One Step Ahead. New York, Dell, 1985.
Best-Kept Secret. New York, Dell, 1985.
Dream Maker. New York, Dell, 1986.
Playing with Fire. New York, Dell, 1986.
Morning Glory. New York, Dell, 1986.
Laying Down the Law. New York, Dell, 1986.
First-Class Male. New York, Dell, 1987.
Adventure with a Stranger. New York, Dell, 1987.

*   *   *

Donna Vitek has written a number of consistently good novels. She develops solid characters that reflect all of the contradictions and ambiguities of real people. Her heroines are women, not young girls. They cope quite well with their lives and are self-confident enough to take on anything that comes their way.

Vitek's heroes are equally individualistic. Usually they are professional men or they hold some sort of job that reflects a broad education. They are often in dangerous situations but are usually well trained to handle such occurrences. On the other hand, some of her heroes are hesitant about establishing permanent relations with a woman or they are unconsciously afraid of long-term commitments. Their ambivalence frequently causes misunderstandings, but these are finally resolved in the arms of the heroine. Both the hero and the heroine realize that the thought of the future without each other is more terrifying than making the initial commitment.

Vitek's plots are also an added element in her favour. Despite following the standard romance/intrigue/suspense formula, they are skilfully developed. Events and scenes keep the pages turning as crises are piled one on top of the other. She balances the various elements of her plots adding enough complication to round the novels out, yet not enough to detract from the essential conflict. She is just as careful to show the romantic relationships evolving in a believable way, weaving love and danger into a satisfying conclusion. Finally, she has such a readable style that it is very difficult to put one of her novels down.

One Step Ahead is a case in point. Callie Simpson is on vacation at St Croix in the Bahamas. Her rental boat is suddenly commandeered by Jonathan Harper, a magazine reporter. To suggest that his story is bizarre would be an understatement, and it is also one that the heroine has difficulty in believing. Jonathan has been researching a far-right political group in the United States who plan to take control of the government by supposedly legal means (plus a few terror tactics). He has uncovered the group, knows someone with written evidence, and is in pursuit of it while fleeing the group's own hit men. The chase goes from the Caribbean, to Houston, to Mexico, to Europe, and back to the States with Callie keeping step right along with Jonathan. In fact, her fast thinking and courage save the day and their lives several times. Callie is the one who actually secures the evidence and gives it to Jonathan. In all, the title is very appropriate. They are just one step ahead of danger throughout the novel.

First-Class Male is another good example of Vitek's style. In this novel, her writing is balanced between the conflict of the plot and the development of believable characters and their personal conflicts. Michelle Vance is a psychologist specializing in battered women. She is approached by Jon Wyatt to testify as an expert witness in his defense of Doris Keaton. Doris has been accused of the attempted murder of her husband, Vincent Keaton. The conflict in the novel centres on the wife and on Jon's preparation for the trial. Related to this is the fact that Michelle begins to receive threats, has her home vandalized, and eventually has to have Jon move in with her for protection.

Michelle and Jon are two settled professionals who have their own life style. They find that they have many things in common and as the novel progresses, they fall in love, but not without the usual spate of misunderstandings. In this novel Vitek concentrates on showing the motivation and growth of her central characters. Michelle is reserved and rather defensive around men. Jon is not exactly looking for a permanent relationship, but will not avoid one should it evolve. The art of compromise is a lesson well learned by each of them before the end of the novel.

Altogether, Vitek is well on her way to becoming a major romance writer.

—Arlene Moore

WADDELL, Helen (Jane).

Nationality: Irish. **Born:** Tokyo, Japan, 31 May 1889. **Education:** Victoria College; Queen's University, Belfast, B.A. (honours) in English 1911, M.A. 1912. **Career:** freelance writer, 1912–19; lecturer in Latin, Somerville College, Oxford 1920–22; Cassell lecturer, St Hilda's College, Oxford, 1921; lecturer, Bedford College, University of London, 1922–23; literary adviser and reader, Constable, publishers, London; assistant editor, *Nineteenth Century*, London, 1938–45. **Recipient:** Susette Taylor travelling fellowship, 1923; A.C. Benson silver medal, 1927. D.Litt.: University of Durham, County Durham, 1932; Columbia University, New York, 1934; Queen's University, 1934. Fellow, Royal Society of Literature, 1927; member, Irish Academy of Letters, 1932. **Died:** 5 March 1965.

ROMANCE AND HISTORICAL PUBLICATIONS

Novel

Peter Abelard. London, Constable, and New York, Holt, 1933.

OTHER PUBLICATIONS

Plays

The Spoiled Buddha (produced Dublin, 1919). Dublin, Talbot, and London, Unwin, 1919.
The Abbé Prévost (produced Croydon, Surrey, 1935). Privately printed, 1931.

Poetry

Lyrics from the Chinese (from J. Legge's prose translation of the Shih Ching). London, Constable, and Boston, Houghton Mifflin, 1913.

Other

The Wandering Scholars. London, Constable, and Boston, Houghton Mifflin, 1927; revised edition, Constable, 1932.
New York City. Newtown, Montgomeryshire, Gregynog Press, 1935.
Poetry in the Dark Ages (lecture). Glasgow, Barnes and Noble, 1948.
Stories from Holy Writ (for children). London, Constable, 1949; New York, Macmillan, 1950.
The Fairy Ring (for children). Leeds, E.J. Arnold, 1921; as *The Princess Splendour and Other Stories*, London, Longman, 1969.

Editor, *A Book of Mediaeval Latin for Schools.* London, Constable, 1931.

Translator, *Mediaeval Latin Lyrics.* London, Constable, 1929; New York, Smith, 1930; revised edition, Constable, 1933.
Translator, *The History of the Chevalier Des Grieux and of Manon Lescaut*, by Abbé Prévost. London, Constable, 1931.
Translator, *The Hollow Field*, by Marcel Aymé. London, Constable, 1933.
Translator, *Beasts and Saints* (saints' lives). London, Constable, and New York, Holt, 1934.
Translator, *The Desert Fathers.* London, Constable, 1936; New York, Sheed and Ward, 1942.
Translator, *A French Soldier Speaks*, by Jacques (i.e. Guy Robin). London, Constable, 1941.
Translator, *Lament for Damon*, by John Milton. London, Constable, 1943.
Translator, *More Latin Lyrics: From Virgil to Milton*, edited by Felicitus Corrigan. London, Gollancz, 1976.

*

Manuscript Collections: Queen's University Library, Belfast; Stanbrook Abbey, Worcester.

Critical Studies: *The Mark of the Maker* by Monica Blackett, London, Constable, 1973; *Helen Waddell: A Biography* by Felicitus Corrigan, London, Gollancz, 1986.

*   *   *

Helen Waddell is known primarily for her translations of mediaeval Latin literature and scholarship on the Middle Ages. Her work includes plays, compilations of both Chinese and mediaeval Latin poetry, and the novel *Peter Abelard*, an account of the love affair between Abelard and Héloïse in 12th-century Paris.

Peter Abelard's problem is that at the age of 37 he suddenly discovers passion. Until then, his life has been fulfilled by his theological contemplations, and teaching at the schools of Notre Dame and Ste Genevieve. Héloïse, to whom he is introduced by his great friend (and self-confessed hedonist) Gilles de Vannes, is forbidden to him because of his religious vows. This causes both Abelard and Héloïse great confusion, as they struggle to reconcile their emotions with their faith.

Héloïse lives in great awe of Abelard and offers him lodgings in her house, an offer conveyed to Abelard by Gilles with great misgivings, because Gilles recognizes their mutual attraction.

Fulbert remains the only man in Paris unaware of the love affair between Abelard and his niece. Abelard, meanwhile, is a changed man—his work and reputation suffer, and his scholars are outraged at his actions. One fateful night Fulbert discovers their secret and from that day keeps the lovers apart. However, Héloïse falls pregnant, and Abelard sends her to Brittany to live with his family. After the birth of their son, Abelard decides he must marry Héloïse. Gilles is completely aghast at the idea, as is Héloïse who would prefer to live with her reputation in tatters rather than risk Abelard's career. Abelard persuades her to return to Paris with him and marry him against her better judgement.

In Paris, Fulbert reveals that Héloïse and Abelard are married. Héloïse denies this stating that she is only his mistress, and in order to deny the rumours pretends to take the veil at the convent at Argenteuil. She fears Fulbert's determination for revenge—with good reason as Abelard is violently attacked. This puts an end to their passionate love affair—but not to their love.

Following his attack, Abelard enters the monastery at St Denis and Héloïse continues to live in Argenteuil but as a nun in reality. In

Paris, Abelard's many enemies have decided that his work is heretical and there is an attempt to judge him as such—which fails—but he is sent to do penance. After his release he lives in Champagne as a hermit, his love for Héloïse still strong. He thinks that God has forsaken him but after much soul searching he begins to understand some of his past and by the end of the novel we hear that he has finally found God.

Waddell is concerned with depicting not only Abelard and Héloïse's love story, but some outline of Abelard's religious and philosophical thinking as well. Abelard (who actually lived, and upon whose life this novel is based) was more dialectician than theologian, according to Margaret Drabble, in the *Oxford Companion to English Literature*, and as such attempted to reconcile Reason with Faith. His great work *Sic et Non*, is credited with being the founding stone of scholasticism, the principle religious philosophy from the 12th- to 15th-centuries.

We are also given an insight into the politics of the church at this time. The attempt to find Abelard heretical in the novel is as much a cover for the anger felt at his romance and marriage as at his theological writings. As Gilles, ever the cynic, and ever ready to point out hypocrisy and pride among the clergy, comments, Abelard could not in all fairness be tried for having a mistress, as most of the clergy would be guilty.

The fiery, passionate love of the two central characters is richly described as something overwhelming and ineluctable. Love makes Abelard a different man. His work, which prior to meeting Héloïse has been his only concern becomes less important than his feelings for her and finally, when he has lost her, he suffers a crisis of faith. Héloïse is portrayed as a strong, independent, intuitive woman, educated and intelligent. She is prepared to live with gossip and rumours, being known as Abelard's whore, rather than jeopardize his career by marrying him. However, she is ultimately guided by Abelard and, following their disaster spends the rest of her life in a convent partly because, Abelard admits, he will not have another man so much as look at her.

Much of the authenticism of the novel comes from the realism of the description of 12th-century clerical life in Paris and especially of the warmth and beauty of the Breton and Champagne countrysides. In addition, Waddell uses quotes from Abelard's work and correspondence, as well as from popular songs of the day, to illustrate his thinking and enrich the background of the novel.

—Sara Corben de Romero

WALKER, Lucy.
Pseudonym for Dorothy Lucy Sanders. **Other Pseudonym:** Shelley Dean. **Nationality:** Australian. **Born:** Dorothy Lucy McClemans, Boulder Gold Fields, Western Australia, 4 May 1907. **Education:** Perth College, Western Australia, ten years; University of Western Australia, Nedlands, part-time study, 4 years; Claremont Teachers College, teachers certificate 1938. **Relations:** married Colsell S. Sanders in 1936; two sons and one daughter. **Career:** teacher in Western Australia, 1928–36, and in London, 1936–38. Former member of the State Advisory Board to the Australian Broadcasting Commission, and member of the State Library Board, Western Australia. **Address:** 20 Jukes Way, Wembley Gardens, Western Australia 6016, Australia.

Romance and Historical Publications

Novels

The One Who Kisses. London, Collins, 1954.

Sweet and Faraway. London, Collins, 1955; New York, Arcadia House, 1957.
Come Home, Dear! London, Collins, 1956; New York, Ballantine, 1975.
Heaven Is Here. London, Collins, and New York, Arcadia House, 1957.
Master of Ransome. London, Collins, and New York, Arcadia House, 1958.
Orchard Hill. New York, Arcadia House, 1958.
The Stranger from the North. London, Collins, 1959; New York, Ballantine, 1976.
Kingdom of the Heart. London, Collins, 1959; New York, Ballantine, 1971.
Love in a Cloud. London, Collins, 1960.
The Loving Heart. London, Collins, 1960.
The Moonshiner. London, Collins, 1961; as *Cupboard Love,* New York, Arcadia House, 1963.
Wife to Order. London, Collins, 1961; New York, Arcadia House, 1962.
The Distant Hills. London, Collins, 1962.
Down in the Forest. London, Collins, 1962.
The Call of the Pines. London, Collins, 1963; New York, Arcadia House, 1966.
Follow Your Star. London, Collins, 1963; New York, Ballantine, 1976.
The Man from Outback. London, Collins, 1964; New York, Ballantine, 1974.
A Man Called Masters. London, Collins, 1965; New York, Ballantine, 1976.
The Other Girl. London, Collins, 1965; New York, Arcadia House, 1967.
Reaching for the Stars. London, Collins, 1966; New York, Ballantine, 1976.
The Ranger in the Hills. London, Collins, 1966.
South Sea Island (as Shelley Dean). London, Mills and Boon, 1966.
Island in the South (as Shelley Dean). London, Mills and Boon, 1967.
The River Is Down. London, Collins, 1967; New York, Ballantine, 1972.
Home at Sundown. London, Collins, 1968; New York, Ballantine, 1976.
The Gone-Away Man. London, Collins, 1969; New York, Ballantine, 1974.
Joyday for Jodi. London, Collins, 1971; New York, Ballantine, 1976.
The Mountain That Went to the Sea. London, Collins, 1971; New York, Beagle, 1973.
Girl Alone. London, Collins, 1973; New York, Ballantine, 1976.
The Runaway Girl. London, Collins, and New York, Ballantine, 1975.
Gamma's Girl. London, Collins, 1977.
So Much Love. New York, Ballantine, 1977.

Novels as Dorothy Lucie Sanders (series: Pepper Tree)

Fairies on the Doorstep. Sydney, Australasian, 1948; as *Pool of Dreams* (as Lucy Walker), New York, Ballantine, 1973.
The Randy. Sydney, Australasian, 1948.
Pepper Tree series:
Six for Heaven. London, Hodder and Stoughton, 1952.
Shining River. London, Hodder and Stoughton, 1954.
Waterfall. London, Hodder and Stoughton, 1956; as *The Bell Branch* (as Lucy Walker), London, Collins, 1971; New York, Ballantine, 1972.
Ribbons in Her Hair. London, Hodder and Stoughton, 1957.

Pepper Tree Bay. London, Hodder and Stoughton, 1959.
Monday in Summer. London, Hodder and Stoughton, 1961.

*　　*　　*

Australia has produced several outstanding romance writers. Few, however, achieve quite the same originality as Lucy Walker for she does more than use Australia as a background for her books.

Woven intricately through her novels and adding in some cases a tremendous emotional quality are the nearly mystical elements of aboriginal beliefs and customs. These touches lend support to the romantic involvement and seem to heighten the sense of inevitability as two people find each other. Not only does she use these native elements in her writing, but she also uses situations and events that may be unique to Australia, given their land tenure and mining policies. Thus we find Katie James in *The Ranger in the Hills* involved with mining surveys and the race to see that a mining right is recognized first.

In *So Much Love* Nairee has such close empathy with the aboriginal people that she unconsciously carries out a simple, primitive ritual of creating her own 'spirit land' by making a circle of pretty stones and dotting larger ones in its middle. Symbolically the circle is the home of a person's spirit. Nairee is a young girl, brought up in the outback by an old woman. She is an orphan who yet has people interested in her future. Her return to The Patch in the Outback is the beginning of the story as she finally learns who she is and to whom she really belongs.

Lucy Walker's heroines are typically nice girls, a little strong minded, often naive and groping into adulthood. They are not aggressively women's lib candidates; however, they don't mind trying something new and illustrate a determined sense of independence in their actions and outlook. *Kingdom of the Heart,* for instance, is about a girl who inherits half a cattle farm in the Australian outback and proceeds to go to live there. Kimberly Wentworth in *Home at Sundown* joins a botanical expedition into the outback to find samples of rare plants for medical studies.

Typically Walker's heroes are older, more experienced men. Often they are wealthy 'station' owners who have developed a sixth sense in avoiding the matrimonial trap. They flirt, and they draw women to them unwittingly and unintentionally at times by their masculinity and their habit of superiority. Frequently they personify their surroundings as they take on the bleak harshness of their land.

Walker balances the force of her characters against the force of the physical background where the story takes place. Constantly the tremendous isolation of the people living in the outback shapes and moves her characters. This isolation of station life in turn brings out qualities in character that she skilfully exploits to the fullest. In *Down in the Forest* Kim Baxter is more than a station manager; he is also appointed to turn his part of the country, the Darjalup district, into an international show case for foreign visitors. A bush fire neatly sets him back to the beginning and the story progresses from the arrival of Jill Dawson to become his 'right-hand man' in this gigantic undertaking.

In *The Call of the Pines* a plane crash leaves four people stranded in the dense outback jungle. Cherry Landin is a young girl hired to help with the children of the station and she is one of those in the plane. Stephen Denton, the owner of the station, has to call on all his ability to lead them out of the jungle and along a cattle trail until they are rescued, all the while watching out for poisonous plants, dangerous animals, and still finding them food and water for the journey.

In all, Walker gives her readers an unusual glimpse into another world entirely. Given the nature of her country, she could not create her novels without building on its uniqueness, and over and over again this special feeling for Australia comes through. In a sense, one could not justifiably say she uses Australia as a background; it is too much a part of the story, too much of a character within it, to be merely considered background.

—Arlene Moore

———————

WALKER, Margaret (Abigail).
Nationality: American. **Born:** Birmingham, Alabama, 7 July 1915. **Education:** Northwestern University, Evanston, Illinois, B.A. 1935; University of Iowa, Iowa City, M.A. 1940, Ph.D. 1965; Yale University, New Haven, Connecticut (Ford fellow), 1954. **Relations:** married Firnist James Alexander in 1943; two sons and two daughters. **Career:** social worker, reporter, and magazine editor; teacher at Livingstone College, Salisbury, North Carolina, 1941–42, 1945–46, and West Virginia State College, Institute, 1942–43. Since 1949 Professor of English, and since 1968, director of the Institute for the Study of the History, Life and Culture of Black Peoples, Jackson State College, Mississippi. **Recipient:** Yale Series of Younger Poets award, 1942; Rosenwald fellowship, 1944; Houghton Mifflin fellowship, 1966; Fulbright fellowship, 1971; National Endowment for the Arts grant, 1972. D.Litt.: North-western University, 1974; Rust College, Holly Springs, Mississippi, 1974; D.F.A.: Denison University, Granville, Ohio, 1974; D.H.L.: Morgan State University, Baltimore, 1976. **Address:** 2205 Guynes Street, Jackson, Mississippi 39213, USA.

Romance and Historical Publications

Novel

Jubilee. Boston, Houghton Mifflin, 1966.

Other Publications

Novel

Come Down from Yonder Mountain. Toronto, Longman, 1962.

Poetry

For My People. New Haven, Connecticut, Yale University Press, 1942.
Ballad of the Free. Detroit, Broadside Press, 1966.
Prophets for a New Day. Detroit, Broadside Press, 1970.
October Journey. Detroit, Broadside Press, 1973.

Recording: *The Poetry of Margaret Walker,* Folkways, 1975.

Other

How I Wrote Jubilee. Chicago, Third World Press, 1972.
A Poetic Equation: Conversations Between Margaret Walker and Nikki Giovanni. Washington, DC, Howard University Press, 1974.
Black Women and Liberation Movements. Washington, DC, Howard University Press, 1981.
The Daemonic Genius of Richard Wright. Washington, DC, Howard University Press, 1982.
This is My Country. Athens, University of Georgia Press, 1989.

*　　*　　*

The novelist, poet, and essayist Margaret Walker first achieved critical acclaim in 1942, following the publication of her volume of poetry, *For My People*, which won the Yale University younger poets award.

Walker's first novel, *Jubilee*, received similar recognition, and was a landmark in African American historical writing. This meticulously researched work took 30 years to complete—as Walker told Claudia Tate in *Black Women Writers at Work*, 'Living with the book over a long period of time was agonizing. Despite all of that *Jubilee* is the product of a mature person'.

In 1944, Walker received the Rosenwald fellowship which helped her to carry out the initial research on *Jubilee*. She began to envisage the work as a folk novel, and began to incorporate stories told to her as a child by her grandmother. She traced her grandmother's family from Alabama to Georgia, drawing on birth records and other primary sources to make her depiction of the life of a slave family as accurate as possible. Consequently, *Jubilee* incorporates slave songs in its narrative, and the protagonist, Vyry Dutton, is modelled on Walker's own great-grandmother.

The novel is divided into three sections and deals with antebellum Georgia, the Civil War, and Reconstruction, as seen through the eyes of Vyry, who begins the book as a slave on John Dutton's plantation. She has two children by a free blacksmith, Randall Ware, leaves him, and tries to escape her life of slavery only to be caught and flogged instead. Vyry's life is hard and bleak, but she is a determined, proud woman who rises above the outrages forced upon her. She brings up her family through the destruction of the Civil War, and the uncertainty of Reconstruction. Initially displaced she finds a place for herself as a midwife in the emerging society. *Jubilee* was one of the first novels to present plantation/slave society from a Black point of view—and is important because of Walker's representation of free-thinking Black people who maintain their dignity, even under oppression.

Responses to the novel were mixed. A critic on the *Washington Post* praised *Jubilee* as 'the first historical Black American novel'—however Wilma Dykernan, in the *New York Book Review*, thought the book both 'ambitious' and 'uneven'.

Jubilee was the first of a flood of well-written, meticulously researched books about the history and experiences of African Americans from a Black point of view. It is an outstanding novel that has influenced many African American writers in recent years.

—Marion Hatchard

WALPOLE, (Sir) Hugh (Seymour).
Nationality: British. **Born:** Auckland, New Zealand, 13 March 1884, of English parents. **Education:** King's School, Canterbury, Kent, and Durham School; Emmanuel College, Cambridge, 1903–06, B.A. (honours) in history 1906. **Military Service:** Russian Red Cross in Galicia, 1914–16; director, Anglo-Russian Propaganda Bureau, Petrograd, 1916–17. **Career:** lay minister, Mersey Mission to Seamen, 1906; travelled in France and Germany, 1907; assistant master, Epsom College, Surrey, 1908; full-time writer, in London, from 1909; became a friend of Henry James and Arnold Bennett; gave lecture tours in the United States, from 1919; Rede lecturer, Cambridge University, 1925; first chair of the Selection Committee, Book Society, London, from 1929; first chair, Society of Bookmen (now National Book League). **Recipient:** James Tait Black memorial prize, 1919, 1920. Fellow, Royal Society of Literature. CBE (Commander, Order of the British Empire), 1918. Knighted, 1937. **Died:** 1 June 1941.

ROMANCE AND HISTORICAL PUBLICATIONS

Novels (series: Herries)

The Dark Forest. London, Secker, and New York, Doran, 1916.
The Secret City. London, Macmillan, and New York, Doran, 1919.
The Cathedral. London, Macmillan, and New York, Doran, 1922.
The Herries Chronicle:
   Rogue Herries. London, Macmillan, and New York, Doubleday, 1930.
   Judith Paris. London, Macmillan, and New York, Doubleday, 1931.
   The Fortress. London, Macmillan, and New York, Doubleday, 1932.
   Vanessa. London, Macmillan, and New York, Doubleday, 1933.
   The Bright Pavilions. London, Macmillan, and New York, Doubleday, 1940.
   Katherine Christian (unfinished). New York, Doubleday, 1943; London, Macmillan, 1944.

OTHER PUBLICATIONS

Novels

The Wooden Horse. London, Smith Elder, 1909; New York, Doran, 1915.
Maradick at Forty: A Transition. London, Smith Elder, 1910; New York, Duffield, 1911.
Mr Perrin and Mr Traill: A Tragi-Comedy. London, Mills and Boon, 1911; as *The Gods and Mr Perrin*, New York, Century, 1911.
The Prelude to Adventure. London, Mills and Boon, and New York, Century, 1912.
Fortitude, Being the True and Faithful Account of the Education of an Explorer. London, Secker, and New York, Doran, 1913.
The Duchess of Wrexe, Her Decline and Death: A Romantic Commentary. London, Secker, and New York, Doran, 1914.
The Green Mirror: A Quiet Story. New York, Doran, 1917; London, Macmillan, 1918.
Jeremy. London, Cassell, and New York, Doran, 1919.
The Captives. London, Macmillan, and New York, Doran, 1920.
The Young Enchanted: A Romantic Story. London, Macmillan, and New York, Doran, 1921.
Jeremy and Hamlet. London, Cassell, and New York, Doran, 1923.
The Old Ladies. London, Macmillan, and New York, Doran, 1924.
Portrait of a Man with Red Hair: A Romantic Macabre. London, Macmillan, and New York, Doran, 1925.
Harmer John: An Unworldly Story. London, Macmillan, and New York, Doran, 1926.
Jeremy at Crale. London, Cassell, and New York, Doran, 1927.
Wintersmoon. London, Macmillan, and New York, Doubleday, 1928.
Farthing Hall, with J. B. Priestley. London, Macmillan, and New York, Doubleday, 1929.
Hans Frost. London, Macmillan, and New York, Doubleday, 1929.
Above the Dark Circus. London, Macmillan, 1931; as *Above the Dark Tumult*, New York, Doubleday, 1931.
Captain Nicholas. London, Macmillan, and New York, Doubleday, 1934.
The Inquisitor. London, Macmillan, and New York, Doubleday, 1935.
A Prayer for My Son. London, Macmillan, and New York, Doubleday, 1936.
John Cornelius. London, Macmillan, and New York, Doubleday, 1937.

The Joyful Delaneys. London, Macmillan, and New York, Double-
day, 1938.
The Sea Tower: A Love Story. London, Macmillan, and New York,
Doubleday, 1939.
The Blind Man's House. London, Macmillan, and New York,
Doubleday, 1941.
The Killer and the Slain. London, Macmillan, and New York,
Doubleday, 1942.

Short Stories

The Golden Scarecrow. London, Cassell, and New York, Doran,
1915.
The Thirteen Travellers. London, Hutchinson, and New York,
Doran, 1921.
The Silver Thorn. London, Macmillan, and New York, Doubleday,
1928.
All Souls' Night. London, Macmillan, and New York, Doubleday,
1933.
Cathedral Carol Service. London, Faber, 1934.
Head in Green Bronze and Other Stories. London, Macmillan, and
New York, Doubleday, 1938.
Mr Huffam and Other Stories. London, Macmillan, 1948.

Plays

Robin's Father, with Rudolf Besier (produced Liverpool, 1918).
The Cathedral, adaptation of his own novel (produced London,
1932). London, Macmillan, 1937.
The Young Huntress (produced London, 1933).
The Haxtons (produced Liverpool, 1939). London, Deane, and Bos-
ton, Baker, 1939.

Screenplays: *David Copperfield*, with Howard Estabrook, 1934;
Vanessa: Her Love Story, 1935; *Little Lord Fauntleroy*, 1936.

Radio Serial: *Behind the Screen*, with others, 1930.

Other

Joseph Conrad. London, Nisbet, and New York, Holt, 1916; revised
edition, Nisbet, 1924.
The Art of James Branch Cabell. New York, McBride, 1920.
A Hugh Walpole Anthology. London, Dent, and New York, Dutton,
1921.
The Crystal Box. Privately printed, 1924.
The English Novel: Some Notes on Its Evolution (lecture). Cam-
bridge, University Press, 1925.
Reading: An Essay. London, Jarrolds, and New York, Harper, 1926.
A Stranger (for children), with *Red Pepper*, by Thomas Quayle.
Oxford, Blackwell, 1926.
Anthony Trollope. London and New York, Macmillan, 1928.
My Religious Experience. London, Benn, 1928.
The Apple Trees: Four Reminiscences. Waltham St Lawrence,
Berkshire, Golden Cockerell Press, 1932.
A Letter to a Modern Novelist. London, Hogarth Press, 1932.
Extracts from a Diary. Privately printed, 1934.
Works (Cumberland Edition). London, Macmillan, 30 vols,
1934–40.
Claude Houghton: Appreciations, with Clemence Dane. London,
Heinemann, 1935.
Roman Fountain (travel). London, Macmillan, and New York,
Doubleday, 1940.
A Note ... on the Origins of the Herries Chronicle. New York,
Doubleday, 1940.
The Freedom of Books. London, National Book Council, 1940.

Open Letter of an Optimist. London, Macmillan, 1941.
Women Are Motherly. London, Todd, 1943.

Editor, *The Waverley Pageant: The Best Passages from the Novels
of Sir Walter Scott*. London, Eyre and Spottiswoode, 1932.
Editor, *Essays and Studies 18*. London, English Association, 1933.
Editor, with Wilfred Partington, *Famous Stories of Five Centuries*.
New York, Farrar and Rinehart, 1934.
Editor, with others, *The Nonesuch Dickens*. London, Nonesuch
Press, 23 vols, 1937–38.
Editor, *A Second Century of Creepy Stories*. London, Hutchinson,
1937.

*

Film Adaptations: *Vanessa: Her Love Story*, 1935; *Mr Perrin and
Mr Traill*, 1948.

Manuscript Collections: Fitz Park Museum, Keswick, Cumberland;
King's School, Canterbury, Kent; British Library, London; Berg
Collection, New York Public Library; Library of Congress, Wash-
ington, DC.

Critical Studies: *Hugh Walpole: A Study* by Marguerite Steen, Lon-
don, Nicholson and Watson, and New York, Doubleday, 1933;
Hugh Walpole: A Biography by Rupert Hart-Davis, London and
New York, Macmillan, 1952; *Hugh Walpole* by Elizabeth Steel,
New York, Twayne, 1972.

*   *   *

Some 40 green chunky novels, gold-lettered and dignified, by
Hugh Walpole, made a familiar clutch on pre-war shelves. On both
sides of the Atlantic they sold in their thousands, several being made
into films. His children's books popularized the name Jeremy.
Today, perhaps a dozen books survive in print, and the young may
know nothing of him. Students may still notice F.R Leavis's dis-
missal of an 'utterly untalented manufacturer of Book Society Classics'. Of one section of his most ambitious work, 'The Herries
Chronicle', his friend Virginia Woolf, whose admiration he craved
and never received, wrote, 'True, it's competent enough, spare in
the wording—but words without roots, yes, that's it, all a trivial
litter of bright objects to be swept up'.

Readers thought otherwise, and the main volumes of the Herries
saga, spanning 1730 to 1932, *Rogue Herries, Judith Paris, The
Fortress*, and *Vanessa*, can be found in public libraries and in
paperbacks, all much read, though perhaps by veterans from a pre-
television era, which cherished leisurely, sprawling plots and a
teeming variety of interrelated characters, breeding sequels that
ended only with their author's life. Enriched by historical facts, sentimental, lush, occasionally tragic, the Herries clan rivalled the
Forsytes. They are, however, more vigorously committed to heroic
adventure, villainous intrigue and betrayal, griefs, loves and
domestic tyranny, set against national conflict and social change,
public triumphs and disasters, ancient houses, London, alternately
tempestuous and grave, and, where Walpole was most at home, the
English countryside, particularly Cumberland, always changing,
now sullen and mysterious, now open and radiant.

Walpole himself judged this 'lakeland epic' his masterpiece. 'My
view of the Herries is frankly a romantic one . . . not realistic, comic,
scientific, but a piece of gaily-tinted tapestry worked in English
colours'.

Walpole wanted to be ranked among the best, but at no time has
his formula been a guarantee of critical acclaim, and in a literature
dominated by Joyce and Lawrence, Woolf and Huxley, Hemingway
and Fitzgerald, the dons scorned Walpole and the public that

cherished him. His most high-flying work, the Herries books and the Polchester novels, were dismissed as facile, careless, sententious, and academic. This last is true enough, meaning not that the work lacked life or talent, but that it conformed too closely to that of his beloved predecessors: Scott, Trollope, James. Here he took the novel as he found it, rejoiced in it, cheerfully worked within its limitations. The truth is, however, that only when he trusted his own experiences, in the wartime Russian Red Cross and in the hell-pit of a minor public school common room, did he achieve a success that may better endure.

Scott is the prevailing genius behind the Herries books, though Walpole's lively invention is all his own. He was a natural story-teller, sometimes grotesque, sometimes lyrical, but always in love with his subject. In these books, as in his short psychological thrillers, he was skilled in depicting cruelty. A notoriously vulnerable man, he had early realized the perils lurking outside a bright nursery, within a quiet cathedral town, a school playground, a Cumberland landscape of daffodils and blue water Written with no great subtlety, in broad, uninhibited, sometimes melodramatic strokes, the 'grand impetuosity' praised by J.B. Priestley, the historical romances do fail at the highest level. But they can still offer pleasures to those who seek highly-charged narrative from a writer not much perturbed by literary and psychological schools, and anything that seemed to question individual reality. He believed in his heroes and heroines, writing for those to whom 'well-made' was not a term of abuse.

—Peter Vansittart

WALSH, Sheila.

Pseudonym: Sophie Leyton. **Nationality:** British. **Born:** Birmingham, Warwickshire, 10 October 1928. **Education:** Notre Dame Convent, Birkdale, Lancashire; Southport College of Art, Lancashire, 1945–48. **Relations:** married Desmond Walsh in 1950; two daughters. **Career:** secretary, 1983, chair, 1985–87, and since 1981, vice-president, Romantic Novelists Association, London. **Recipient:** Romantic Novelists Association Netta Muskett award, 1973, and major award, 1984. **Agent:** Mary Irvine, 11 Upland Park Road, Oxford OX2 7RU, England. **Address:** 35 Coudray Road, Southport, Merseyside PR9 9NL, England.

ROMANCE AND HISTORICAL PUBLICATIONS

Novels

The Golden Songbird. London, Hurst and Blackett, and New York, New American Library, 1975.
Madalena. London, Hurst and Blackett, 1976; New York, New American Library, 1977.
The Sergeant Major's Daughter. London, Hurst and Blackett, 1977; New York, New American Library, 1978.
A Fine Silk Purse. London, Hurst and Blackett, 1978; as *Lord Gilmore's Bride,* New York, New American Library, 1979.
The Incomparable Miss Brady. London, Hutchinson, and New York, New American Library, 1980.
Lady Cecily's Dilemma (as Sophie Leyton). London, Octopus, 1980; as *The Pink Parasol* (as Sheila Walsh), New York, New American Library, 1985; London, Mills and Boon, 1991.
The Rose Domino. New York, New American Library, 1981; London, Hutchinson, 1982.
A Highly Respectable Marriage. London, Hutchinson, 1983.
The Runaway Bride. London, Hutchinson, 1984.
Cousins of a Kind. London, Mills and Boon, 1985; as *The Diamond Waterfall,* New York, New American Library, 1985.

Improper Acquaintances. London, Mills and Boon, 1985; as *The Incorrigible Rake,* New York, New American Library, 1985.
The Wary Widow. New York, New American Library, 1985; as *An Insubstantial Pageant,* London, Century, 1986.
Bath Intrigue. New York, New American Library, 1986; London, Century, 1987.
Lady Aurelia's Bequest. New York, New American Library, 1987; London, Century, 1989.
Minerva's Marquis. London, Mills and Boon, and New York, New American Library, 1988.
The Nabob. London, Mills and Boon, and New York, New American Library, 1989.
Arrogant Lord Alastair. New York, New American Library, 1990.
A Woman of Little Importance. London, Mills and Boon, 1991.
Until Tomorrow. London, Century, 1992; New York, Random House, 1993.

*

Sheila Walsh comments:

All my books to date have been set in or around the Regency period, and are essentially light-hearted amusing stories in the Georgette Heyer tradition—an entertaining 'read', I hope, for anyone wanting to forget their problems for a little while.

In 1992 I was commissioned to write a family saga set in Liverpool in the 1930s and 1940s, the result was *Until Tomorrow* which gave me great pleasure to write.

*   *   *

Sheila Walsh must rank as one of the best Regency romance writers, along with Joan Smith, and Mary Balogh. She has published over 20 novels, identifiable by their witty plots, charismatic characters who capture the reader's attention, and humour.

The Golden Songbird, one of Walsh's best novels, illustrates her strengths as a writer of historical romances. The book opens with a drunk and lascivious man putting up his beautiful stepdaughter as a stake in a card-game. Hugo, Marquis of Mandersley, one of the most eligible men in England, wins Lucia, and is forced, much against his better judgement, to take her to his highly respectable society aunt. In a twist of the plot, Lucia is revealed as the granddaughter of one of Aunt Aurelia's oldest friends. Miraculously restored to the bosom of her family, Lucia manages to melt the heart of her taciturn grandfather, endear herself to everyone around her, and shoot a brutal and perverted admirer, Sir Gideon Benedict.

Walsh's heroes change in a very Heyeresque manner from cynical, world-weary creatures into warm-hearted men who will do anything for their loved ones. Hugo shows the depth of his feelings for Lucia when she discovers a physically abused five-year-old chimney sweep in a bedroom. Horrified by the young boy's injuries, and distressed that such an abuse of young children should occur in a supposedly civilized society, Lucia persuades the marquis to let the boy sleep in his room—much to the amusement of everyone around him. The introduction of the peripheral character of the boy has a dual purpose in revealing Hugo's caring side, and also in showing the brutality and reality of life outside the closed world of the London elite.

Similarly, the plot is put into a historical context by the introduction of war. Again this is very much a peripheral event which only intrudes to disturb the characters' lives when Hugo and Lucia's friend, Toby, returns from the Spanish wars a much changed man. The protagonists travel to Dover to collect him and find the wounded are kept in inhuman, unsanitary conditions with little medication or medical attention. Lucia's warmth and charm save Toby, and help him to recover from his experiences.

Walsh's heroines, in the Heyeresque tradition, are gently reared women, who find themselves, usually through family circumstances, forced to rely on their own wit, charm, and resilience. Thus Charity Wingate, the guardian of her late sister's children in *A Woman of Little Importance* finds herself forced to go to their bitter grandfather for help; and Lady Cecily Merton, in *Lady Cecily's Dilemma*, relies on her charm, beauty, and grace to help her win a rich husband when she discovers the extent of her father's gambling debts.

An exception to the gently reared female prototype is Pilar (*A Fine Silk Purse*) who is discovered dancing in a gypsy camp. Forced into marriage by a very drunk Theodore, 6th Earl of Gilmore, Pilar has to become a lady very quickly. She is taken in hand by Theo's eccentric grandmother, and emerges as a vivacious, beautiful woman who has to face the jealousy of a malicious mistress, the revenge of the bitter brother of her 'natural' father, and a riot. Pilar's real father is an aristocrat, and she shows the nobility of her nature by refusing to reveal her true identity and thus bring about her father's social and political disgrace.

Walsh has recently written a family saga set in 1930s and 1940s Britain called *Until Tomorrow*.

—Marion Hatchard

WARE, Monica.   See **WOODWARD, Lilian.**

WARNER, Rex (Ernest).
Nationality: British. **Born:** Birmingham, Warwickshire, 9 March 1905. **Education:** St George's School, Harpenden, Hertfordshire; Wadham College, Oxford (open classical scholar), B.A. (honours) in classics and English literature 1928. **Military Service:** Home Guard, London, 1942–45. **Relations:** married 1) Frances Chamier Grove in 1929, two sons and one daughter; 2) Barbara, Lady Rothschild in 1949, one daughter; 3) remarried Frances Chamier Grove in 1966. **Career:** schoolmaster in Egypt and England, 1928–45; worked for the Control Commission in Berlin, 1945, 1947; director, British Institute, Athens, 1945–47; Tallman professor, Bowdoin College, Brunswick, Maine, 1962–63; professor of English, University of Connecticut, Storrs, 1964–74. **Recipient:** James Tait Black memorial prize, 1961. D.Litt.: Rider College, Trenton, New Jersey, 1968. Honorary Fellow, Wadham College, 1973. Commander, Royal Order of the Phoenix, Greece, 1963. **Died:** 24 June 1986.

ROMANCE AND HISTORICAL PUBLICATIONS

Novels

The Young Caesar. London, Collins, and Boston, Little Brown, 1958.
Imperial Caesar. London, Collins, and Boston, Little Brown, 1960.
Pericles the Athenian. London, Collins, and Boston, Little Brown, 1963.
The Converts. London, Bodley Head, and Boston, Little Brown, 1967.

OTHER PUBLICATIONS

Novels

The Wild Goose Chase. London, Boriswood, and New York, Knopf, 1937.
The Professor. London, Boriswood, 1938; New York, Knopf, 1939.

The Aerodrome. London, Lane, 1941; Philadelphia, Lippincott, 1946.
Why Was I Killed? A Dramatic Dialogue. London, Lane, 1943; as *Return of the Traveller*, Philadelphia, Lippincott, 1944.
Men of Stones: A Melodrama. London, Lane, 1949; Philadelphia, Lippincott, 1950.
Escapade: A Tale of Average. London, Lane, 1953.

Plays

Screenplays (documentaries): *World with End*, 1953; *The Immortal Land*, 1958.

Poetry

Poems. London, Boriswood, 1937; New York, Knopf, 1938; revised edition, as *Poems and Contradictions*, London, Lane, 1945.

Other

The Kite (for children). Oxford, Blackwell, 1936; revised edition, London, Hamish Hamilton, 1963.
English Public Schools. London, Collins, 1945.
The Cult of Power: Essays. London, Lane, 1946; Philadelphia, Lippincott, 1947.
John Milton. London, Parrish, 1949; New York, Chanticleer Press, 1950.
Views of Attica and Its Surroundings. London, Lehmann, 1950.
E.M. Forster. London, Longman, 1950.
Men and Gods. London, MacGibbon and Kee, 1950; New York, Farrar Straus, 1951.
Ashes to Ashes: A Post-Mortem on the 1950–51 Tests, with Lyle Blair. London, MacGibbon and Kee, 1951.
Greeks and Trojans. London, MacGibbon and Kee, 1951.
Eternal Greece, photographs by Martin Hurlimann. London, Thames and Hudson, and New York, Viking Press, 1953.
The Vengeance of the Gods. London, MacGibbon and Kee, 1954.
Athens. London, Thames and Hudson, and New York, Studio, 1956.
The Greek Philosophers. New York, New American Library, 1958.
Look at Birds (for children). London, Hamish Hamilton, 1962.
The Stories of the Greeks. New York, Farrar Straus, 1967; London, Granada, 1979.
Athens at War: Retold from the History of the Peloponnesian War of Thucydides. London, Bodley Head, 1970; New York, Dutton, 1971.
Men of Athens: The Story of Fifth Century Athens. London, Bodley Head, and New York, Viking Press, 1972.

Editor, with Laurie Lee and Christopher Hassall, *New Poems 1954*. London, Joseph, 1954.
Editor, *Look Up at the Skies! Poems and Prose*, by Gerard Manley Hopkins. London, Bodley Head, 1972.

Translator, *The Medea of Euripides*. London, Lane, 1944; New York, Chanticleer Press, 1949.
Translator, *Prometheus Bound*, by Aeschylus. London, Lane, 1947; New York, Chanticleer Press, 1949.
Translator, *The Persian Expedition*, by Xenophon. London, Penguin, 1949.
Translator, *Hippolytus*, by Euripides. London, Lane, 1949; New York, Chanticleer Press, 1950.
Translator, *Helen*, by Euripides. London, Lane, 1951.
Translator, *The Peloponnesian War*, by Thucydides. London, Penguin, 1954.
Translator, *The Fall of the Roman Republic: Marius, Sulla, Crassus, Pompey, Caesar, Cicero: Six Lives*, by Plutarch. London, Penguin, 1958; revised edition, 1972.

Translator, *Three Great Plays of Euripides: Medea, Hippolytus, Helen*, by Euripides. New York, New American Library of World Literature, 1959.

Translator, *Poems of George Seferis*. London, Bodley Head, 1960; Boston, Godine, 1979.

Translator, *War Commentaries of Caesar*. New York, New American Library, 1960.

Translator, *Confessions of St Augustine*. New York, New American Library, 1963.

Translator, with Th. D. Frangopoulos, *On the Greek Style: Selected Essays in Poetry and Hellenism*, by George Seferis. Boston, Little Brown, 1966; London, Bodley Head, 1967.

Translator, *A History of My Times*, by Xenophon. London, Penguin, 1966.

Translator, *Moral Essays*, by Plutarch. London, Penguin, 1971.

*

Film Adaptation: *The Aerodrome*, 1983.

Manuscript Collection: University of Connecticut, Storrs.

Critical Studies: *Rex Warner, Writer* by A.L. McLeod, Sydney, Wentworth Press, 1960, and *The Achievement of Rex Warner* (includes bibliography) edited by McLeod, Wentworth Press, 1965; *The Novels of Rex Warner: An Introduction* by N.H. Reeve, London, Macmillan, 1990.

*   *   *

Rex Warner, classical scholar, poet, essayist, novelist, won a pre-war reputation primarily for three novels, allegorical, at times surrealistic, sometimes glibly compared to Kafka with their experiments in grotesquely heightened vision of contemporary life and objects. Actually, however, their fantasy, imagery, and humour, were very English, almost Dickensian, with strong anti-totalitarian insights. Thenceforward, feeling perhaps that he was at a dead end, he made a severe change of course with his fiction, notably his historical novels set in the classical world.

Warner's historical novels are conventional, in a form popularized by Robert Graves, Naomi Mitchison, and Peter Green; they are written in a style clear, precise, vivid, with the poet's feeling for words. Each centres on a celebrated historical figure: Julius Caesar, Pericles, Augustine of Hippo. The dangers of this are obvious, but on a level serious, though without genius, they succeed admirably. Warner had always been profoundly engrossed with power, its responsibilities and pitfalls, its opportunities for human betterment and for frantic self-indulgence, its philosophical implications in the realm of good and evil. This theme pervades the historical novels, where he is thoroughly at home in the intricacies of Roman and Athenian politics, the tortuous debates of early Christians and North African Manichees.

In *The Young Caesar* Warner speaks through Julius, elegant, sophisticated, and intelligent, the paradoxical saviour of society who, disdainful of violence, nevertheless storms 800 cities and subdues 300 peoples. A realist, Caesar is shocked by stupidity, conceit, inefficiency, and greed for its own sake, so conspicuous among the power-politicians crowding around him, and the corrupt and unproductive Roman populace so easily fooled by doles and operatics. He shows magnanimity, both civilized and calculating in his own pursuit of power, first for personal, then for national survival. His self-belief grows with disappointments at the follies of others, and his disillusion with Republican traditions and institutions.

In this and the later novels Warner writes as if from the hero's hindsight, coolly, smooth as a lawyer's brief, without much tension or unusual factual or stylistic invention; here is Caesar:

It is, as experience will show, not at all uncommon for middle-aged men to fall passionately in love, and Pompey now fell in love with my daughter Julia. Nothing, of course, could suit my interests better than to have Pompey as my son-in-law: moreover, I was beginning to like him and could see that he would almost certainly make my daughter happy; Julia too was attracted both by him personally and not unreasonably, by the prospect of becoming the wife of one who was still known as the greatest man in the world. Then I had the somewhat embarrassing task of persuading my old friend Servilia that it was necessary to break off what had amounted to an engagement between Julia and her own son, young Brutus. Here, as so often, Servilia showed herself extremely sensible. It was about this time, I think, that I bought for her a pearl, for which I paid more money than had ever been paid before in Rome for a single piece of jewellery.

For some of Warner's original admirers, this passage may represent a failure of nerve. The whole enterprise could be dismissed as pastiche, cut-price scholarship, the successful product of an ageing, very literate scholar, of substance but without verve, certainly not quaint or antiquarian, but following trails long charted by others. There is certainly no more experiment. But the four novels, *The Young Caesar*, *Imperial Caesar*, *Pericles the Athenian*, and *The Converts*, are not escapist romances. They aim to put flesh on events and people fairly familiar but always engrossing, facing problems of power, belief, and self-mastery that remain topical. None is a great novel with complexities elevated to myth or epic, but each provides glosses on tales over which intelligent people have absorbed themselves for nearly two millennia.

—Peter Vansittart

———————

WARNER, Sylvia Townsend.
Nationality: British. **Born:** Harrow, Middlesex, 6 December 1893. **Education:** privately. **Career:** worked in a munitions factory, 1916; member of the editorial board, *Tudor Church Music*, Oxford University Press, London, 1917–26; lived with the writer Valentine Ackland, 1930–69; joined Communist Party, 1935; Red Cross volunteer, Barcelona, 1935; contributor to the *New Yorker* from 1936. **Recipient:** Katherine Mansfield-Menton prize, 1968. Fellow, Royal Society of Literature, 1967; honorary member, American Academy, 1972. **Died:** 1 May 1978.

ROMANCE AND HISTORICAL PUBLICATIONS

Novels

Summer Will Show. London, Chatto and Windus, and New York, Viking Press, 1936.

After the Death of Don Juan. London, Chatto and Windus, 1938; New York, Viking Press, 1939.

The Corner That Held Them. London, Chatto and Windus, and New York, Viking Press, 1948.

The Flint Anchor. London, Chatto and Windus, and New York, Viking Press, 1954; as *The Barnards of Loseby*, New York, Popular Library, 1974.

OTHER PUBLICATIONS

Novels

Lolly Willowes; or, The Loving Huntsman. London, Chatto and Windus, and New York, Viking Press, 1926.

Mr Fortune's Maggot. London, Chatto and Windus, and New York, Viking Press, 1927.

The True Heart. London, Chatto and Windus, and New York, Viking Press, 1929.

Short Stories

The Maze: A Story to Be Read Aloud. London, The Fleuron, 1928.

Some World Far from Ours; and Stay, Corydon, Thou Swain. London, Mathews and Marrot, 1929.

Elinor Barley. London, Cresset Press, and Chicago, Argus, 1930.

A Moral Ending and Other Stories. London, Joiner and Steele, 1931.

The Salutation. London, Chatto and Windus, and New York, Viking Press, 1932.

More Joy in Heaven and Other Stories. London, Cresset Press, 1935.

24 Short Stories, with Graham Greene and James Laver. London, Cresset Press, 1939.

The Cat's Cradle-Book. New York, Viking Press, 1940; London, Chatto and Windus, 1960.

A Garland of Straw and Other Stories. London, Chatto and Windus, and New York, Viking Press, 1943.

The Museum of Cheats. London, Chatto and Windus, and New York, Viking Press, 1947.

Winter in the Air and Other Stories. London, Chatto and Windus, 1955; New York, Viking Press, 1956.

A Spirit Rises. London, Chatto and Windus, and New York, Viking Press, 1962.

A Stranger with a Bag and Other Stories. London, Chatto and Windus, 1966; as *Swans on an Autumn River,* New York, Viking Press, 1966.

The Innocent and the Guilty. London, Chatto and Windus, and New York, Viking Press, 1971.

Kingdoms of Elfin. London, Chatto and Windus, and New York, Viking Press, 1977.

Scenes of Childhood. London, Chatto and Windus, 1981; New York, Viking Press, 1982.

One Thing Leading to Another and Other Stories, edited by Susanna Pinney. London, Chatto and Windus, and New York, Viking, 1984.

Selected Stories, edited by Susanna Pinney and William Maxwell. London, Chatto and Windus, 1988.

Poetry

The Espalier. London, Chatto and Windus, and New York, Dial Press, 1925.

Time Importuned. London, Chatto and Windus, and New York, Viking Press, 1928.

Opus 7: A Poem. London, Chatto and Windus, and New York, Viking Press, 1931.

Rainbow. New York, Knopf, 1932.

Whether a Dove or a Seagull, with Valentine Ackland. New York, Viking Press, 1933; London, Chatto and Windus, 1934.

Two Poems. Privately printed, 1945.

Twenty-eight Poems, with Valentine Ackland. Privately printed, 1957.

Boxwood: Sixteen Engravings by Reynolds Stone Illustrated in Verse. Privately printed, 1957; revised edition, as *Boxwood: Twenty-one Engravings,* London, Chatto and Windus-Cape, 1960.

King Duffus and Other Poems. Privately printed, 1968.

Azrael and Other Poems. Privately printed, 1978; as *Twelve Poems,* London, Chatto and Windus, 1980.

Collected Poems, edited by Claire Harman. Manchester, Carcanet, and New York, Viking Press, 1982.

Selected Poems. Manchester, Carcanet, and New York, Viking, 1985.

Other

Somerset. London, Elek, 1949.

Jane Austen 1775–1817. London, Longman, 1951; revised edition, 1957.

Sketches from Nature (reminiscences). Privately printed, 1963.

T.H. White: A Biography. London, Cape-Chatto and Windus, 1967; New York, Viking Press, 1968.

Letters, edited by William Maxwell. London, Chatto and Windus, 1982; New York, Viking Press, 1983.

Editor, *The Week-end Dickens.* London, Maclehose, 1932; New York, Loring and Mussey, 1932(?).

Editor, *The Portrait of a Tortoise: Extracted from the Journals and Letters of Gilbert White.* London, Chatto and Windus, 1946.

Translator, *By Way of Saint-Beuve,* by Marcel Proust. London, Chatto and Windus, 1958; as *On Art and Literature 1896–1917,* New York, Meridian, 1958.

Translator, *A Place of Shipwreck,* by Jean René Huguenin. London, Chatto and Windus, 1963.

Published Music: *Alleluia: Anthem for Five Voices,* London, Oxford University Press, 1925.

*

Critical Studies: *This Narrow Place: Sylvia Townsend Warner and Valentine Ackland: Life, Letters and Politics 1930–1951* by Wendy Mulford, London, Pandora Press, 1988; *Sylvia Townsend Warner: A Biography* by Claire Harman, London, Chatto and Windus, 1989.

*   *   *

In her historical novels Sylvia Townsend Warner provides a hint of what Jane Austen might have accomplished, had she chosen to step outside her private, middle-class world, and treat the world at large. Warner shares Austen's middle-class origins as well as her predilection for irony; but, in *Summer Will Show* and *After the Death of Don Juan,* she leaves the comfortable world of *Lolly Willowes* to follow the path of revolution into France and Spain.

Jack Lindsay, of Fanfrolico Press fame, had great faith in the historical novel 'as a fighting weapon and a cultural instrument'; and, for a time, at least, Warner seems to have shared that faith. Her first unequivocally historical novel, *Summer Will Show,* takes us back to 1848, the Year of Revolution, but at least one perceptive reviewer in the *Literary Digest* realized that it was also 'in a sense a parable of our own troubled time'. Sophia Willoughby, an upper-middle-class wife and mother, had often dreamed of 'leading a wild romantic life', but it takes the death of her children from smallpox to get her out of Blandamer House, Dorset. No revolutionary at first, she journeys to Paris in the hope that her errant husband, Frederick, will take time off from his Bohemian mistress, Minna Lemuel, to father another child. Once in Paris, however, Sophia is inexorably drawn into the revolution by the woman who is ostensibly her rival; for Minna has already achieved a personal freedom of which Sophia has only dreamed. We are obviously intended to draw the parallel between the revolution in progress on the barricades and that being stirred within Sophia herself. In particular, we are meant to recognize the shared economic roots of both. When Frederick freezes her assets and cuts off her income, Ingelbrecht, the revolutionary theorist, characterizes Sophia as the victim of a lockout. And Martin, the communist leader, chides her for her political naivety: 'Really Ma-lame, for an Englishwoman, reared at the very hearth of political economy, you have been a little dense'. By the end of the novel Sophia is ready to die for the revolution she had once disdained. Ironically, she is spared because the officer in charge of the firing squad exclaims: 'I cannot consent to the death of a *lady*'. The novel ends with Sophia reading—'obdurately attentive and by degrees absorbed'—a tract which calls for a Communist Manifesto.

In spite of being frankly political, *Summer Will Show* succeeds as a novel because it harmonizes the external struggle with the internal so well, and effects a triumphant integration of the individual into revolutionary society. As important as Sophia's political radicalization is her sexual reorientation. Sophia Willoughby is, to some extent, of course, a projection of Sylvia Warner (and Willoughby is not far from Willowes). Liberated from marriage, Sophia is drawn to a movement in which the key figure, Minna, is a woman and a storyteller. Soon enough, Sophia has stolen the affections of her estranged husband's mistress. The moment when their love crystallizes is over four lines of a poem by Andrew Marvell discovered by the two women at a secondhand bookstall:

> My love is of a birth as rare
> As 'tis of object strange and high
> It was begotten by despair
> Upon impossibility

Warner's own long-time relationship with Valentine Ackland, recently made public, in fact began in 1930; so the novel can now be read as doubly revolutionary, and as rather more than a political statement.

Warner's growing political commitment in the 1930s (she joined the Communist Party) led her to make two long trips to Spain during the Spanish Civil War—first to Barcelona in 1935, and then to Madrid and Valencia for the Writers Congress in 1937. On her return, she dedicated herself, with characteristic energy, to writing about the Republican cause—poems, reviews, and essays, many of which appeared in *Left Review*. Inevitably this commitment extended to her fiction, now to be written beneath the banner of 'Art for Man's Sake'. So although *After the Death of Don Juan* is set in late 18th-century Spain, it is properly regarded as Warner's contribution to the literature of the Spanish Civil War. For in the novel she attempts, with commendable restraint, to weigh the future of Spain in terms of its past. In a letter to Nancy Cunard, she later called it 'a parable [that word again], if you like the word, or an allegory . . . of the political chemistry of the Spanish War, with the Don Juan . . . developing as the Fascist of the piece'. The action is centred in Tenorio Viejo, a village too small even to be marked on the maps. Into this 'array of lime-washed hovels', comes a society group from Seville, led by Dona Ana and Don Ottavio, to inform Don Saturno of the terrible fate of his son, Don Juan, reportedly dragged down to Hell by devils. Don Saturno, owner of the estate within which the village lies, has brought education to his people, though well aware of the possible cost: 'All progress . . . must rebound upon the bestower. In times to come, no doubt, my simple village will be a hive of revolutionaries'. The unexpected reappearance of Don Juan, whose past extravagance has frustrated all hopes of a long-promised and much-needed irrigation system, leads to open conflict between the peasants and the nobility in the castle. Without his father's consent, Don Juan sends for troops who begin, reluctantly but bloodily, to put down the rebellion. In the final scene, two of the ringleaders, Diego and Ramon Perez, the village 'man of reason', are trapped in the schoolhouse, and face imminent death: 'They looked at each other long and intently, as though they were pledged to meet again and would ensure a recognition'.

In her two post-war novels Warner continues her preoccupation with society rather than with the individual. But where the two novels of the 1930s address, at least in part, the very nature of soci-

ety itself, the later novels retreat to a world every bit as circumscribed as that of Jane Austen, and, in some ways, far more claustrophobic. The settings are now both English and resolutely domestic. In *The Corner That Held Them* the focus is upon a 14th-century Benedictine convent. The nuns of Oby have consciously cut themselves off from the world, hoping to keep at bay both the Black Death and the not-so-distant rumblings of social unrest. Yet they prove to be no less subject to sin than outsiders, and they must still grapple with such calamities as the collapse of the convent spire and the defection of one of their members. Moreover, they are demonstrably 'prisoners of darkness, and fettered with the bonds of a long night', to quote the *Wisdom of Solomon*, source of the novel's title. Significantly too, their patron is St Leonard, 'patron of the convent and of all prisoners'.

The Flint Anchor is a 19th-century family chronicle with the same pervasive claustrophobic atmosphere as *The Corner That Held Them*. At the centre of the novel is the stern patriarch John Barnard, who, for all his righteousness, 'had spread around him a desert of mendacity and discomfort'. Some members of the Barnard family actually escape from behind the 12-foot flint walls of Anchor House; but for Euphemia it is a dubious escape to a Moravian religious community, while Ellen's dreams merely hover round a cloister.

—J. Lawrence Mitchell

WARRE, Mary Douglas. See **GREIG, Maysie.**

WARREN, Mary Douglas. See **GREIG, Maysie.**

WARREN, Robert Penn.
Nationality: American. **Born:** Guthrie, Kentucky, 24 April 1905. **Education:** Guthrie High School; Vanderbilt University, Nashville, Tennessee, 1921–25, B.A. (summa cum laude) 1925; University of California, Berkeley, M.A. 1927; Yale University, New Haven, Connecticut, 1927–28; Oxford University (Rhodes scholar), B. Litt. 1930. **Relations:** married 1) Emma Brescia in 1930 (divorced 1950); 2) the writer Eleanor Clark in 1952, one son and one daughter. **Career:** assistant professor, Southwestern College, Memphis, Tennessee, 1930–31, and Vanderbilt University, 1931–34; assistant and associate professor, Louisiana State University, Baton Rouge, 1934–42; professor of English, University of Minnesota, Minneapolis, 1942–50. Professor of Playwriting, 1950–56, professor of English, 1962–73, and from 1973 professor emeritus, Yale University. Member of the Fugitive Group of poets: co-founding editor, the *Fugitive*, Nashville, 1923–25; founding editor, *Southern Review*, Baton Rouge, Louisiana, 1935–42; advisory editor, *Kenyon Review*, Gambier, Ohio, 1942–63. Consultant in Poetry, Library of Congress, Washington, DC, 1944–45; Jefferson Lecturer, National Endowment for the Humanities, 1974. **Recipient:** Caroline Sinkler award, 1936, 1937, 1938; Levinson prize, 1936, Union League Civic and Arts Foundation prize, 1953, and Harriet Monroe prize, 1976 (*Poetry*, Chicago); Houghton Mifflin fellowship, 1939; Guggenheim fellowship, 1939, 1947; Shelley memorial award, 1943; Pulitzer prize, for fiction, 1947, for poetry, 1958, 1979; Screenwriters Guild Meltzer award, 1949; Foreign Book prize (France), 1950; Sidney Hillman prize, 1957; Edna St Vincent Millay Memorial prize, 1958; National Book award, for poetry, 1958; New York *Herald-Tribune* Van Doren award, 1965; Bollingen prize, for poetry, 1967; National Endowment for the Arts grant, 1968, and lec-

tureship, 1974; Henry A. Bellaman prize, 1970; Van Wyck Brooks award, for poetry, 1970; National Medal for Literature, 1970; Emerson-Thoreau Medal, 1975; Copernicus award, 1976; Presidential Medal of Freedom, 1980; Common Wealth award, 1981; MacArthur fellowship, 1981; Brandeis University Creative Arts award, 1983. D.Litt.: University of Louisville, Kentucky, 1949; Kenyon College, Gambier, Ohio, 1952; Colby College, Waterville, Maine, 1956; University of Kentucky, Lexington, 1957; Swarthmore College, Pennsylvania, 1959; Yale University, 1960; Fairfield University, Connecticut, 1969; Wesleyan University, Middletown, Connecticut, 1970; Harvard University, Cambridge, Massachusetts, 1973; Southwestern College, 1974; University of the South, Sewanee, Tennessee, 1974; Monmouth College, Illinois, 1979; New York University, 1983; Oxford University, 1983; LL.D.: Bridgeport University, Connecticut, 1965; University of New Haven, Connecticut, 1974; Johns Hopkins University, Baltimore, 1977. Member, American Academy, and American Academy of Arts and Sciences; Chancellor, Academy of American Poets, 1972. Poet Laureate, 1986. **Died:** 15 September 1989.

ROMANCE AND HISTORICAL PUBLICATIONS

Novels

World Enough and Time: A Romantic Novel. New York, Random House, 1950; London, Eyre and Spottiswoode, 1951.
Band of Angels. New York, Random House, 1955; London, Eyre and Spottiswoode, 1956.
Wilderness: A Tale of the Civil War. New York, Random House, 1961; London, Eyre and Spottiswoode, 1962.

OTHER PUBLICATIONS

Novels

Night Rider. Boston, Houghton Mifflin, 1939; London, Eyre and Spottiswoode, 1940.
At Heaven's Gate. New York, Harcourt Brace, 1943; London, Eyre and Spottiswoode, 1946.
All the King's Men. New York, Harcourt Brace, 1946; London, Eyre and Spottiswoode, 1948.
The Cave. New York, Random House, and London, Eyre and Spottiswoode, 1959.
Flood: A Romance of Our Time. New York, Random House, and London, Collins, 1964.
Meet Me in the Green Glen. New York, Random House, 1971; London, Secker and Warburg, 1972.
A Place to Come To. New York, Random House, and London, Secker and Warburg, 1977.

Short Stories

Blackberry Winter. Cummington, Massachusetts, Cummington Press, 1946.
The Circus in the Attic and Other Stories. New York, Harcourt Brace, 1948; London, Eyre and Spottiswoode, 1952.

Plays

Proud Flesh (in verse, produced Minneapolis, 1947; revised [prose] version, produced New York, 1947).

All the King's Men, adaptation of his own novel (as *Willie Stark: His Rise and Fall*, produced Dallas, 1958; as *All the King's Men*, produced New York, 1959). New York, Random House, 1960.

Poetry

Thirty-Six Poems. New York, Alcestis Press, 1936.
Eleven Poems on the Same Theme. New York, New Directions, 1942.
Selected Poems 1923–1943. New York, Harcourt Brace, 1944; London, Fortune Press, 1952.
Brother to Dragons: A Tale in Verse and Voices. New York, Random House, 1953; London, Eyre and Spottiswoode, 1954; revised edition, Random House, 1979.
To a Little Girl, One Year Old, in a Ruined Fortress. Privately printed, 1956.
Promises: Poems 1954–1956. New York, Random House, 1957; London, Eyre and Spottiswoode, 1959.
You, Emperors, and Others: Poems 1957–1960. New York, Random House, 1960.
Selected Poems: New and Old 1923–1966. New York, Random House, 1966.
Incarnations: Poems 1966–1968. New York, Random House, 1968; London, W. H. Allen, 1970.
Audubon: A Vision. New York, Random House, 1969.
Or Else: Poem/Poems 1968–1974. New York, Random House, 1974.
Selected Poems 1923–1975. New York, Random House, and London, Secker and Warburg, 1977.
Now and Then: Poems 1976–1978. New York, Random House, 1978.
Two Poems. Winston-Salem, North Carolina, Palaemon Press, 1979.
Being Here: Poetry 1977–1980. New York, Random House, and London, Secker and Warburg, 1980.
Love. Winston-Salem, North Carolina, Palaemon Press, 1981.
Rumor Verified: Poems 1979–1980. New York, Random House, and London, Secker and Warburg, 1981.
Chief Joseph of the Nez Perce. New York, Random House, and London, Secker and Warburg, 1983.
New and Selected Poems 1923–1985. New York, Random House, 1985.

Recordings: *Robert Penn Warren Reads from His Own Works*, CMS, 1975; *Robert Penn Warren Reads Selected Poems*, Caedmon, 1980.

Other

John Brown: The Making of a Martyr. New York, Payson and Clarke, 1929.
I'll Take My Stand: The South and the Agrarian Tradition, with others. New York, Harper, 1930.
Understanding Poetry: An Anthology for College Students, with Cleanth Brooks. New York, Holt, 1938; revised edition, 1950, Holt Rinehart, 1960, 1976.
Understanding Fiction, with Cleanth Brooks. New York, Crofts, 1943; revised edition, Appleton Century Crofts, 1959; Englewood Cliffs, New Jersey, Prentice Hall, 1979; abridged edition, as *The Scope of Fiction*, 1960.
A Poem of Pure Imagination: An Experiment in Reading, in *The Rime of the Ancient Mariner*, by Samuel Taylor Coleridge. New York, Reynal, 1946.
Modern Rhetoric: With Readings, with Cleanth Brooks. New York, Harcourt Brace, 1949; revised edition, 1958, 1970, 1979.

Fundamentals of Good Writing: A Handbook of Modern Rhetoric, with Cleanth Brooks. New York, Harcourt Brace, 1950; London, Dobson, 1952.

Segregation: The Inner Conflict in the South. New York, Random House, 1956; London, Eyre and Spottiswoode, 1957.

Selected Essays. New York, Random House, 1958; London, Eyre and Spottiswoode, 1964.

Remember the Alamo! (for children). New York, Random House, 1958; as *How Texas Won Her Freedom*, San Jacinto, Texas, San Jacinto Museum of History, 1959.

The Gods of Mount Olympus (for children). New York, Random House, 1959; London, Muller, 1962.

The Legacy of the Civil War: Meditations on the Centennial. New York, Random House, 1961.

Who Speaks for the Negro? New York, Random House, 1965.

A Plea in Mitigation: Modern Poetry and the End of an Era (lecture). Macon, Georgia, Wesleyan College, 1966.

Homage to Theodore Dreiser. New York, Random House, 1971.

John Greenleaf Whittier's Poetry: An Appraisal and a Selection. Minneapolis, University of Minnesota Press, 1971.

A Conversation with Robert Penn Warren, edited by Frank Gado. Schenectady, New York, The Idol, 1972.

Democracy and Poetry (lecture). Cambridge, Massachusetts, Harvard University Press, 1975.

Robert Penn Warren Talking: Interviews 1950–1978, edited by Floyd C. Watkins and John T. Hiers. New York, Random House, 1980.

Jefferson Davis Gets His Citizenship Back. Lexington, University Press of Kentucky, 1980.

A Robert Penn Warren Reader. New York, Random House, 1987.

Portrait of a Father. Lexington, University Press of Kentucky, 1988.

New and Selected Essays. New York, Random House, 1989.

Talking with Robert Penn Warren, edited by Floyd C. Watkins, John T. Hiers, and Mary Louise Weaks. Athens, University of Georgia Press, 1990.

Editor, with Cleanth Brooks and John Thibaut Purser, *An Approach to Literature: A Collection of Prose and Verse with Analyses and Discussions.* Baton Rouge, Louisiana State University Press, 1936; revised edition, New York, Crofts, 1939, Appleton Century Crofts, 1952; Englewood Cliffs, New Jersey, Prentice Hall, 1975.

Editor, *A Southern Harvest: Short Stories by Southern Writers.* Boston, Houghton Mifflin, 1937.

Editor, with Cleanth Brooks, *An Anthology of Stories from the Southern Review.* Baton Rouge, Louisiana State University Press, 1953.

Editor, with Albert Erskine, *Short Story Masterpieces.* New York, Dell, 1954.

Editor, with Albert Erskine, *Six Centuries of Great Poetry.* New York, Dell, 1955.

Editor, with Albert Erskine, *A New Southern Harvest.* New York, Bantam, 1957.

Editor, with Allen Tate, *Selected Poems*, by Denis Devlin. New York, Holt Rinehart, 1963.

Editor, *Faulkner: A Collection of Critical Essays.* Englewood Cliffs, New Jersey, Prentice Hall, 1966.

Editor, with Robert Lowell and Peter Taylor, *Randall Jarrell 1914–1965.* New York, Farrar Straus, 1967.

Editor, *Selected Poems of Herman Melville.* New York, Random House, 1970.

Editor and part author, with Cleanth Brooks and R.W.B. Lewis, *American Literature: The Makers and the Making.* New York, St Martin's Press, 2 vols, 1973.

Editor, *Katherine Anne Porter: A Collection of Critical Essays.* Englewood Cliffs, New Jersey, Prentice Hall, 1979.

Editor, *The Essential Melville.* New York, Ecco Press, 1987.

*

Bibliography: *Robert Penn Warren: A Reference Guide* by Neil Nakadate, Boston, Hall, 1977; *Robert Penn Warren: A Descriptive Bibliography 1922–79* by James A. Grimshaw, Jr, Charlottesville, University Press of Virginia, 1981.

Manuscript Collection: Beinecke Library, Yale University, New Haven, Connecticut.

Critical Studies (selection): *Robert Penn Warren* (in German) by Klaus Poenicke, Heidelberg, Winter, 1959; *Robert Penn Warren: The Dark and Bloody Ground* by Leonard Casper, Seattle, University of Washington Press, 1960; *The Faraway Country* by Louis D. Rubin, Jr, Seattle, University of Washington Press, 1963; *The Hidden God* by Cleanth Brooks, New Haven, Connecticut, Yale University Press, 1963; *Robert Penn Warren* by Charles H. Bohner, New York, Twayne, 1964, revised edition, 1981; *Robert Penn Warren* by Paul West, Minneapolis, University of Minnesota Press, 1964, London, Oxford University Press, 1965; *Robert Penn Warren: A Collection of Critical Essays* edited by John Lewis Longley, Jr, New York, New York University Press, 1965; *The Burden of Time* by John Lincoln Stewart, Princeton, New Jersey, Princeton University Press, 1965; *Web of Being: The Novels of Robert Penn Warren* by Barnett Guttenberg, Nashville, Vanderbilt University Press, 1975; *Robert Penn Warren: A Vision Earned* by Marshall Walker, Edinburgh, Harris, and New York, Barnes and Noble, 1979; *Robert Penn Warren: A Collection of Critical Essays* edited by Richard Gray, Englewood Cliffs, New Jersey, Prentice Hall, 1980; *Critical Essays on Robert Penn Warren* edited by William B. Clark, Boston, Twayne, 1981; *Robert Penn Warren: Critical Perspectives* edited by Neil Nakadate, Lexington, University Press of Kentucky, 1981; *The Achievement of Robert Penn Warren* by James H. Justus, Baton Rouge, Louisiana State University Press, 1981; *Homage to Robert Penn Warren* edited by Frank Graziano, Durango, Colorado, Logbridge Rhodes, 1982; *Robert Penn Warren* by Katherine Snipes, New York, Ungar, 1983; *A Southern Renascence Man: Views of Robert Penn Warren* edited by Walter B. Edgar, Baton Rouge, Louisiana State University Press, 1984; *Robert Penn Warren and American Idealism* by John Burt, New Haven, Connecticut, Yale University Press, 1988.

*   *   *

Honoured as a major American poet and novelist, Robert Penn Warren was a versatile man of letters whose awards included two Pulitzer prizes for poetry and fiction respectively. The subject of his novels, and much of his poetry, is life in the south. A native Kentuckian, Warren displayed a rootedness in his subject and its values, a concern with moral issues, and a gift for dialogue and detailed historical background that lend distinctiveness to his three novels classifiable as historical romance: *World Enough and Time*, *Band of Angels*, and *Wilderness: A Tale of the Civil War*. As a writer of historical fiction Warren was not constricted by allegiance to verifiable fact but used history as a backdrop for illuminating characters and thematic issues that speak to contemporary time.

'The story of every soul', Warren once commented, 'is the story of its self-definition for good or evil, salvation or damnation'. This statement highlights a major theme in Warren's fiction: the search for self-knowledge. This theme is often interwined with corollary themes of alienation, regeneration, the acceptance or rejection of a father figure, and the complexities of guilt and love and evil. A characteristic plot pattern focuses on a protagonist's search for self-definition and concludes either with a violent destiny when self-realization is defeated, or with regeneration when it succeeds. During the quest a father figure is confronted who is accepted or repulsed. This overall pattern is evident in Warren's historical fiction.

World Enough and Time imaginatively recreates a Kentucky murder case of the early-19th century. A narrator recounts the journal of Jeremiah Beaumont, a young attorney who becomes enamoured of a woman of quality whom he comes to learn has been seduced and betrayed by a prominent politician, his fatherly benefactor in the past. Beaumont's marriage proposal wins acceptance with the obligation to kill the seducer. Driven to forge his identity in the frontier world around him, the romantically idealistic hero pursues his chivalrous revenge like a knight in search of the Grail even as his wife Rachel urgently retracts her obligation. Beaumont basely murders the politician-seducer and is arrested, convicted, and sentenced to hang. Helped to escape, he and Rachel are taken to an outlaw settlement where his remorseful wife kills herself and he, drained of pretension, is murdered for bounty. Although the narrative is overlong and its arrogant hero unsympathetic, the novel is handsomely filled with detailed historical background, exciting melodrama, rich language, and a perceptive examination of evil wrought by the pursuit of false values.

Demonstrating a penetrating historical imagination, Warren created in *Band of Angels* a panoramic tapestry of the American Civil War and the Reconstruction era within which to weave his characters and issues. A submissive victim of dependency all her life, the novel's mulatto heroine Amantha Starr ('Manty') chronicles her life beginning as a Kentucky plantation owner's motherless daughter who discovers upon her debt-ridden father's death that she is legally a slave and must be sold as property. She describes her ownership by a caring slavemaster; her freedom after the fall and occupation of New Orleans; her encounters with abolitionist men, including one she marries, and a self-freed Black demanding her allegiance to her race. The kindly white men in Manty's life intensify her tensions as they reveal themselves unable to consider her as an equal. She ultimately discovers that true freedom of soul can only be gained by liberating herself and discarding the trap of dependence. While the heroine seems overly slow in achieving self-knowledge, the novel is effective in its lively epic plot, environmental detail, and diversely interesting characters.

Differing in form from its predecessors in the simplicity of its direct narrative, *Wilderness* tells the story of Adam Rosenzweig, a revolutionary's son and Bavarian Jew who journeys to America to fight for freedom in its Civil War. In New York Adam is shocked to confront the savagely anti-Black draft riots. A deformed foot precluding army recruitment, he reaches Union lines as a sutler. There he witnesses the callous prejudice of Yankee soldiers undedicated to Black freedom, and finally, upon shooting a Confederate, Adam realizes he is no better than other men. Warren uses his ability with words and ideas to compose an affecting portrait of an idealist who is forced to test his vision of reality against the real world, and who, when he discovers the deficiencies in that world and in himself, gains self-knowledge without abandoning his idealism.

Warren's rich re-imagining of the past with meanings for the present enhances the fiction of historical romance. Both craftsman and thinker, Warren was a genuine and powerful American voice dedicated to observing and questioning the American experience.

—Christian H. Moe

WAY, Margaret.
Address: c/o Mills and Boon Ltd, Eton House, 18–24 Paradise Road, Richmond, Surrey TW9 1SR, England.

ROMANCE AND HISTORICAL PUBLICATIONS

Novels

Blaze of Silk. London, Mills and Boon, 1970; Toronto, Harlequin, 1971.
King Country. London, Mills and Boon, 1970; Toronto, Harlequin, 1971.
The Time of the Jacaranda. London, Mills and Boon, and Toronto, Harlequin, 1970.
Return to Belle Amber. London, Mills and Boon, 1971; Toronto, Harlequin 1974.
Summer Magic. London, Mills and Boon, 1971; Toronto, Harlequin, 1972.
Bauhinia Junction. London, Mills and Boon, 1971; Toronto, Harlequin, 1975.
The Man from Bahl Bahla. London, Mills and Boon, and Toronto, Harlequin, 1971.
Noonfire. London, Mills and Boon, 1972; Toronto, Harlequin, 1973.
Ring of Jade. London, Mills and Boon, and Toronto, Harlequin, 1972.
A Man Like Daintree. London, Mills and Boon, 1972; Toronto, Harlequin, 1975.
Copper Moon. London, Mills and Boon, 1972; Toronto, Harlequin, 1975.
The Rainbow Bird. London, Mills and Boon, 1972; Toronto, Harlequin, 1975.
Storm over Mandargi. London, Mills and Boon, 1973; Toronto, Harlequin, 1974.
Wind River. London, Mills and Boon, 1973; Toronto, Harlequin, 1974.
Sweet Sundown. London, Mills and Boon, 1974; Toronto, Harlequin, 1975.
The Love Theme. London, Mills and Boon, and Toronto, Harlequin, 1974.
McCabe's Kingdom. London, Mills and Boon, 1974; Toronto, Harlequin, 1975.
Reeds of Honey. London, Mills and Boon, and Toronto, Harlequin, 1975.
Storm Flower. London, Mills and Boon, 1975; Toronto, Harlequin, 1976.
A Lesson in Loving. London, Mills and Boon, 1975; Toronto, Harlequin, 1976.
Flight into Yesterday. London, Mills and Boon, and Toronto, Harlequin, 1976.
The Man on Half-Moon. London, Mills and Boon, 1976; Toronto, Harlequin, 1977.
Red Cliffs of Malpara. London, Mills and Boon, and Toronto, Harlequin, 1976.
Swans' Reach. London, Mills and Boon, 1976; Toronto, Harlequin, 1977.
One Way Ticket. London, Mills and Boon, and Toronto, Harlequin, 1977.
Portrait of Jaime. London, Mills and Boon, 1977; Toronto, Harlequin, 1978.
Mutiny in Paradise. London, Mills and Boon, 1977; Toronto, Harlequin, 1978.
Black Ingo. London, Mills and Boon, 1977; Toronto, Harlequin, 1978.
The Awakening Flame. London, Mills and Boon, and Toronto, Harlequin, 1978.
Wake the Sleeping Tiger. London, Mills and Boon, 1978.
The Wild Swan. London, Mills and Boon, and Toronto, Harlequin, 1978.
Ring of Fire. London, Mills and Boon, 1978; Toronto, Harlequin, 1979.

Blue Lotus. London, Mills and Boon, 1979; Toronto, Harlequin, 1980.

The Butterfly and the Baron. London, Mills and Boon, 1979; Toronto, Harlequin, 1980.

Valley of the Moon. London, Mills and Boon, 1979.

White Magnolia. London, Mills and Boon, 1979.

The Winds of Heaven. London, Mills and Boon, 1979.

The Golden Puma. London, Mills and Boon, 1980.

Flamingo Park. London, Mills and Boon, 1980; Toronto, Harlequin, 1981.

Lord of the High Valley. London, Mills and Boon, 1980; Toronto, Harlequin, 1981.

Temple of Fire. London, Mills and Boon, 1980; Toronto, Harlequin, 1981.

Shadow Dance. London, Mills and Boon, and Toronto, Harlequin, 1981.

A Season for Change. London, Mills and Boon, and Toronto, Harlequin, 1981.

Home to Morning Star. London, Mills and Boon, 1981; Toronto, Harlequin, 1982.

The McIvor Affair. London, Mills and Boon, 1981; Toronto, Harlequin, 1982.

North of Capricorn. London, Mills and Boon, 1981.

Broken Rhapsody. London, Mills and Boon, and Toronto, Harlequin, 1982.

Hunter's Moon. London, Mills and Boon, 1982; Toronto, Harlequin, 1983.

The Silver Veil. London, Mills and Boon, 1982; Toronto, Harlequin, 1984.

Spellbound. London, Mills and Boon, 1982; Toronto, Harlequin, 1983.

The Girl at Cobalt Creek. London, Mills and Boon, and Toronto, Harlequin, 1983.

House of Memories. London, Mills and Boon, 1983.

No Alternative. London, Mills and Boon, 1983.

A Place Called Rambula. London, Mills and Boon, 1984.

Almost a Stranger. London, Mills and Boon, 1984.

Fallen Idol. London, Mills and Boon, 1984.

Eagle's Ridge. London, Mills and Boon, 1985.

Diamond Valley. London, Mills and Boon, 1986.

Innocent in Eden. London, Mills and Boon, 1986.

Tiger's Cage. London, Mills and Boon, 1986.

Devil Moon. London, Mills and Boon, 1988.

Mowana Magic. London, Mills and Boon, 1988.

Rise of an Eagle. London, Mills and Boon, 1988; Toronto, Harlequin, Toronto, Harlequin, 1989.

Hungry Heart. London, Mills and Boon, 1988; Toronto, Harlequin, 1989.

*   *   *

Margaret Way's romances are full of passionate, slightly unstable heroines, and 'saturnine', Byronic heroes, who find peace and chaos in each other's arms.

Love is the ultimate achievement for the Way heroine. Usually young—in her late teens or early twenties—the Way woman is extraordinarily beautiful, feminine, and highly strung. The hero, in contrast, is cool, very arrogant, and very sure of what he wants, and how to get it. From the beginning, the reader is aware that the hero wants the heroine, and will, come hell or high water, get her.

'I hate men', announces Morgan, heroine of *Rise of an Eagle*. 'You don't', responds hero Ty. 'What you need desperately is the right man in your life. Someone who can bring you love, and understanding, and joy above all'. Of course, this man is Ty. Similarly, Julian Strasberg, in *Spellbound*, bullies injured ballerina Lucienne Gerald into dancing again. He takes over her life, and forces her to

face up to her responsibilities—and her love for him. Sholto McNaughton, in *The Silver Veil*, also helps Roslynn remember the traumatic events that brought her from England to Australia, and in the process bind her to him forever. Way's hero normally has a family connection, or assumes a father-figure/guardian role. The couple have either known each other as children (*Rise of an Eagle*), or the hero takes the heroine into his own household, and controls her life (*Spellbound*, *The Silver Veil*, *Red Cliffs of Malpara*, and *The Man on Half-Moon*).

The relationships depicted in Way's books are all-intensive, life or death ones, in which neither partner can live without the other. In this sense Way's books are old-fashioned as the female protagonist, in particular, does not exist outside of her male counterpart.

Most of Way's books are set in Australia, and contain long descriptive passages of beautiful landscapes, sunsets, or customs, and her respect and love for the country always shines through.

—Marion Hatchard

———

WAYA, Ai Gvhdi.   See **McKENNA, Lindsay.**

———

WEALE, Anne.
Pseudonym: Andrea Blake. **Nationality:** British. **Relations:** married Malcolm Blakeney; one son. **Career:** formerly, staff reporter, *Eastern Evening News*, Norwich, *Western Daily Press*, Bristol, and *Yorkshire Evening Press*, York. **Address:** Apartado 150, San Carlos de la Rápita, Tarragona, Spain.

ROMANCE AND HISTORICAL PUBLICATIONS

Novels (series: David Castle; Longwarden)

Winter Is Past. London, Mills and Boon, 1955; Toronto, Harlequin, 1961.

The Lonely Shore. London, Mills and Boon, 1956; Toronto, Harlequin, 1966.

The House of Seven Fountains. London, Mills and Boon, 1957; Toronto, Harlequin, 1960.

Never to Love. London, Mills and Boon, 1958; Toronto, Harlequin, 1962.

Sweet to Remember. London, Mills and Boon, 1958; Toronto, Harlequin, 1964.

Castle in Corsica. London, Mills and Boon, 1959; Toronto, Harlequin, 1960.

Hope for Tomorrow. London, Mills and Boon, 1959; Toronto, Harlequin, 1965.

A Call for Nurse Templar. London, Mills and Boon, 1960; as *Nurse Templar*, Toronto, Harlequin, 1961.

Until We Met. London, Mills and Boon, 1961; Toronto, Harlequin, 1964.

The Doctor's Daughters. London, Mills and Boon, 1962; Toronto, Harlequin, 1963.

The House on Flamingo Cay. London, Mills and Boon, 1962; Toronto, Harlequin, 1963.

If This Is Love. London, Mills and Boon, 1963; Toronto, Harlequin, 1964.

The Silver Dolphin. London, Mills and Boon, and Toronto, Harlequin, 1963.

All I Ask. London, Mills and Boon, and Toronto, Harlequin, 1964.

Islands of Summer. London, Mills and Boon, 1964; Toronto, Harlequin, 1965.

Three Weeks in Eden. London, Mills and Boon, 1964.
Doctor in Malaya. London, Mills and Boon, and Toronto, Harlequin, 1965.
Girl About Town. London, Mills and Boon, 1965.
The Feast of Sara. London, Mills and Boon, 1965; Toronto, Harlequin, 1966.
Christina Comes to Town. London, Mills and Boon, and Toronto, Harlequin, 1966.
Terrace in the Sun. London, Mills and Boon, and Toronto, Harlequin, 1966.
The Sea Waif. London, Mills and Boon, and Toronto, Harlequin, 1967.
South from Sounion. London, Mills and Boon, and Toronto, Harlequin, 1968.
The Man in Command. London, Mills and Boon, and Toronto, Harlequin, 1969.
Sullivan's Reef. London, Mills and Boon, and Toronto, Harlequin, 1970.
That Man Simon. London, Mills and Boon, and Toronto, Harlequin, 1971.
A Treasure for Life. London, Mills and Boon, and Toronto, Harlequin, 1972.
The Fields of Heaven. London, Mills and Boon, and Toronto, Harlequin, 1974.
Lord of the Sierras. London, Mills and Boon, and Toronto, Harlequin, 1975.
The Sun in Splendour. London, Mills and Boon, 1975.
Now or Never. London, Mills and Boon, and Toronto, Harlequin, 1978.
The River Room. London, Mills and Boon, 1978.
Separate Bedrooms. London, Mills and Boon, 1979.
Stowaway. London, Mills and Boon, 1979; Toronto, Harlequin, 1983.
The Girl from the Sea. London, Mills and Boon, 1979.
The First Officer. London, Mills and Boon, 1980.
The Last Night at Paradise. London, Mills and Boon, 1980.
Touch of the Devil. London, Mills and Boon, 1980; Toronto, Harlequin, 1982.
Blue Days at Sea. London, Mills and Boon, 1981.
Passage to Paxos. London, Mills and Boon, 1981.
Rain of Diamonds. London, Mills and Boon, 1981.
Bed of Roses. London, Mills and Boon, 1981; Toronto, Harlequin, 1982.
Antigua Kiss. Toronto, Worldwide, 1982.
Portrait of Bethany (David Castle). London, Mills and Boon, and Toronto, Harlequin, 1982.
Wedding of the Year. London, Mills and Boon, 1982.
All That Heaven Allows. London, Century, and Toronto, Harlequin, 1983.
Ecstasy. London, Mills and Boon, 1983; Toronto, Harlequin, 1984.
Flora. Toronto, Worldwide, 1983.
Yesterday's Island. London, Mills and Boon, and Toronto, Harlequin, 1983.
Summer's Awakening. London, Mills and Boon, 1984.
Frangipani. London, Mills and Boon, 1985.
Girl in a Golden Bed (David Castle). London, Mills and Boon, 1986.
All My Worldly Goods (Longwarden). London, Century, 1987.
Lost Lagoon. London, Century, 1987.
Night Train. London, Mills and Boon, 1987.
Neptune's Daughter. London, Mills and Boon, 1987.
Catalan Christmas. London, Mills and Boon, 1988.
Do You Remember Babylon? London, Mills and Boon, 1989; Toronto, Harlequin, 1990.
Time and Chance (Longwarden). London, Century, 1989; New York, St Martin's Press, 1990.

Foundation of Delight. New York, St Martin's Press, 1990.
Thai Silk. London, Mills and Boon, 1990.
Sea Fever. London, Mills and Boon, 1990.
Pink Champagne. London, Mills and Boon, 1991.
Footprints in the Sand. London, Mills and Boon, 1992.
The Singing Tree. London, Mills and Boon, 1992.

Novels as Andrea Blake

September in Paris. London, Mills and Boon, and Toronto, Harlequin, 1963.
Now and Always. London, Mills and Boon, and Toronto, Harlequin, 1964.
Whisper of Doubt. London, Mills and Boon, and Toronto, Harlequin, 1965.
Night of the Hurricane. London, Mills and Boon, and Toronto, Harlequin, 1965.

*   *   *

A grande dame of the romance industry, Anne Weale was one of the earliest writers of books published by Mills and Boon and Harlequin. A prolific author, she has produced over 60 novels for the series since 1955. Today she continues to write category romances but is also producing longer and more complex novels. These novels have thematic and stylistic connections with her earlier works. They reveal her strong sense of traditional values—of family and heritage, of hearth and home.

Having travelled extensively, Weale often makes use of exotic and historically-rich landscapes as background in her romances. These settings, ranging from Hawaii to Fiji, Thailand, Italy, Spain, Corsica, New England, as well as the English countryside, are described in great detail in her books. For example, in *Yesterday's Island* we are given an elaborate and concise tour of Nantucket island, along with a history of its whaling and fishing industry. Weale attempts to capture not only the geography but also the local customs and manners of the inhabitants. Her protagonists always have the luxury of being able to hire good cooks or to go to the best restaurants in town, and hence, inevitably enjoy superb cuisine in these foreign locations.

Weale's heroines are most often, though not exclusively, young and inexperienced virgins in their early twenties who discover love and are initiated into the pleasures of sex by their older, worldly-wise, and usually, rich and handsome heroes. While the author does follow this basic pattern, she is careful to change the locale, the occupation, or hobby of the main characters, the circumstances of their meeting, and the eventual admission of their love for each other so that each romance is slightly different from the other. While they are sexually naive, her heroines are usually sensible, intelligent, and well-read. In *Yesterday's Island*, for example, Caroline Murray reads *Moby Dick* and cites Emerson as one of her favourite authors. In *All That Heaven Allows* the heroine, who has had no formal education, quotes Cardinal Newman and enjoys reading informative travel books. In *Frangipani* Cassandra Vernon re-encounters the aloof Nick Carroll at the opera *Lucia di Lammermoor* in a park in Sydney. Weale is well-read, and often sprinkles her romances with poetic quotations from current and classic writers.

Unlike those of Anne Mather or Violet Winspear, Weale's romances do not depict sex scenes explicitly or in sensuous detail. Weale focuses on other particulars and technicalities. She spends an inordinate amount of time on her protagonists' appearance, especially on the heroines' designer clothes. Other key elements in her romances are ancestral homes, gardens, art, family heirlooms and jewellery, aristocracy and royalty. Marriages of convenience, featured in such novels as *All That Heaven Allows*, *All My Worldly*

Goods, and *The Singing Tree* are still a popular device in Weale's works. Usually the partner with wealth marries in order to save the other's large, historic home. There is an element of the fairytale in Weale's romances as her characters are often titled or enamoured of royalty. The Princess of Wales is mentioned in *Neptune's Daughter* and *All That Heaven Allows*. Prince Charles talks to the heroine of *All My Worldly Goods*. Sometimes Weale uses actual personages of the past to give her characters historical importance. In *Time and Chance* Sir John Vanbrugh, the architect, designed the hero's ancestral home, Longwarden. The home contains many treasures, including art works designed by Boucher, objects originally belonging to Madame de Pompadour.

This attention to things of the past gives Weale's novels a curiously timeless quality. Her characters could just as easily have come from the pages of a Victorian novel as they do from a contemporary one. Despite the fact that her characters all make use of modern conveniences—computers, electronic security gates, the Concorde—they often express anachronistic values. Weale tries to make her heroines interesting and independent, however, they usually end up giving up their jobs or their goals entirely to be the devoted wife of an already successful man. Her novels reinforce the 19th-century beliefs in the domestic sphere as the proper place for women. The hero of *Catalan Christmas* says that women who want to work outside the home 'shouldn't marry ... A wife's first duty is to her husband and children'. Weale dislikes feminists because they do not place enough value on women as mothers, wives, and homemakers. Writing at the end of the 20th century, she still tends to cling to the stereotypical image of the female as the angel of the house.

Weale's full-length novels are developed from her earlier ones. Instead of a one-heroine novel, there are three to four stories unravelling at the same time. In *All My Worldly Goods* and *Time and Chance* the women are linked through the setting of Longwarden which becomes the unifying centre of activity. There are minor subplots to create suspense—the threat of a break-in, arson—but the main focus is on the women who are engaged in their individual quests for love. They range in age from the very young and inexperienced 19-year-old Sarah Lomax to the middle-aged countess Penelope Carlyon. Weale explores a wider spectrum of people and problems in these works. Unlike the category romances which focus mainly on the middle and upper classes, in these novels Weale gives vignettes of the troubled lives of the working class. In these sections of the novel, Weale shows that she has a good ear and captures the speech of the lower classes well. She also attempts to deal with sensitive issues such as sexual frigidity, incest, criminal behaviour, prostitution, and suicide, though she does not probe very deeply into the social causes or solutions to these questions. Characters with problems and trouble makers are killed off to allow for the triumph of love and romance between a man and a woman.

Weale's strength lies in her ability to evoke the grandeur and splendour of a time when men were gentlemen, and women were treated like queens. The continued popularity of her romances shows that many readers yearn for the charm of this golden age. Weale successfully blends the glory and nostalgia of the past with some of the concerns of the present, weaving unchanging plots into a credible contemporary setting.

—Eleanor Ty

WEAVER, Ward. See **MASON, F. Van Wyck.**

WEBB, Jean Francis. American. 1910—. See 2nd edition, 1990.

WEBSTER, Jean (Alice Jane Chandler Webster).
Nationality: American. **Born:** Fredonia, New York, 24 July 1876; grandniece of the writer Mark Twain. **Education:** schools in Fredonia; Lady Jane Grey School, Binghamton, New York, graduated 1896; Vassar College, Poughkeepsie, New York, B.A. in English and economics 1901. **Relations:** married Glenn Ford McKinney in 1915; one daughter. **Died:** 11 June 1916.

ROMANCE AND HISTORICAL PUBLICATIONS

Novels

The Wheat Princess. New York, Century, 1905; London, Hodder and Stoughton, 1916.
Jerry, Junior. New York, Century, and London, Gay and Bird, 1907; as *Jerry*, London, Hodder and Stoughton, 1916.
The Four-Pools Mystery (published anonymously). New York, Century, 1908; (as Jean Webster) London, Hodder and Stoughton, 1916.
Much Ado about Peter. New York, Doubleday, 1909; London, Hodder and Stoughton, 1916.
Daddy-Long-Legs. New York, Century, 1912; London, Hodder and Stoughton, 1913.
Dear Enemy. New York, Century, and London, Hodder and Stoughton, 1915.

Short Stories (series: Patty)

When Patty Went to College. New York, Century, 1903; as *Patty and Priscilla*, London, Hodder and Stoughton, 1915.
Just Patty. New York, Century, 1911; London, Hodder and Stoughton, 1915.

OTHER PUBLICATIONS

Play

Daddy Long-Legs, adaptation of her own novel (produced New York, 1914; London, 1916). New York, French, 1922; London, French, 1927.

Poetry

Vitriol and Lilacs. Cleveland, Press of Flozari, 1943.

*

Film Adaptations: *Daddy Longlegs*, 1931, 1955.

*   *   *

Mark Twain was Jean Webster's 'Uncle Sam': her maternal grandmother was Jane Clemens, Twain's elder sister, and her father was Charles Webster, Twain's publisher and partner, whose imprint appears on both *Huckleberry Finn* and General Grant's memoirs. After the failure of Twain's finances with the Paige typesetter in the late 1890s, Twain used Charley Webster as his scapegoat ('not a man, but a hog', as he wrote to W.D. Howells). That Webster at Vassar did not admit to the relationship with Twain may partly be traced to family animosities; her brother, 50 years later in *Mark Twain, Businessman*, noted that their great-uncle 'never forgave anyone he had injured', and that though 'a joy to live with', he was 'a devil to do business with'. But Twain privately praised Webster's first book (the only one he lived to read): 'it is limpid, bright, sometimes brilliant; it is easy, flowing, effortless, and brimming with girlish spirits .... Its humour is genuine, and not often overstrained'.

With her southern mother and northern father, there is in Webster something of the same division that one sees in her great-uncle. She wrote one mystery novel, *The Four-Pools Mystery*, the only work she published anonymously, in which a post-war plantation system is seen approvingly, and comic darkies abound, but in which the lordly temper of the master is seen as more responsible for his murder than the black who actually kills him—whom he has beaten, and who is allowed to escape the penalty of the law.

Of all her sentimental contemporaries—Mrs Rice, Mrs Wiggin, Mrs Montgomery, the two Mrs Porters—she comes closest to combining romance effectively with realism—surely Twain's great strength, though with her the realism most often takes the form of social concern. Implicitly, her most famous work, *Daddy-Long-Legs*, is a criticism of the contemporary treatment of the orphan; it is no fortuity that it produced, at Vassar and elsewhere, a system of sponsorship of parentless children by wealthy undergraduates. Her own favourite of her novels, *The Wheat Princess*, has elements of a Jamesian international novel—set in Italy and peopled largely by Americans—but it is more informed by a sense of the wrong done by the heroine's father, a tycoon who has cornered the wheat market. His action produces a famine amongst the Italian peasantry, who in revenge besiege the villa occupied by his brother, a philanthropist; and the heroine too is endangered. 'Some day', the hero says at the end of the book, 'I will tell you that I'm proud to be an American. Don't ask me just yet'. Which sounds more like Pudd'nhead Wilson than Pollyanna.

As a critic in the *New York Times* in 1915 stated it is this 'combination of serious social modernity with the other modernity of gayety and humour' that marks Webster's best work, *Daddy-Long-Legs* and its sequel *Dear Enemy*. The heroines of both novels, especially Judy in the first, are resourceful, much less accepting of their lots than Rebecca, Anne, or even (a special case) Pollyanna. Judy has been played by Ruth Chatterton in Webster's own stage adaptation, and by Mary Pickford and Leslie Caron on screen; and these are happier visual equivalents than her later impersonators. Judy fits Pickford's image of contemporary American girlhood better than the more conventionally girlish Rebecca or Pollyanna do—Shirley Temple, who repeated these last two roles, would be impossible as Judy. Even Janet Gaynor and Leslie Caron, however, are sentimentalized versions of the original—further stages in the normal evolution of a best-selling character, blurring and domesticating what may be threatening or anti-social.

Judy is generally thought to be based on Webster's college mate and fellow writer Adelaide Crapsey; so too is her next most attractive character, the Patty of her first book, as well as of *Just Patty*. The stories in *When Patty Went to College*, published in the Vassar newspaper, find the enterprising girl in a variety of scrapes, from which she almost always emerges triumphant—whether applying her Social Studies to her Latin class and leading a 'Virgil strike', or enrolling a fictitious student in the German club; her speciality is 'local colour' ('Baron Münchhausen himself would have blushed at her creations'). Patty is a more elegant Judy, equipped with wealthy parents; and in her private schools she is free of the restrictions of the orphanage.

But all of these 'juvenile' works create enclosed women's worlds into which men intrude as schoolmasters, janitors, brothers, fathers, occasionally suitors. That in her most popular work the suitor is also the father, the 'daddy' long legs, may say something about Webster's own urge to tame and even rival the highly undomesticated, dominating father of the Clemens family (Charley Webster had died when Jean was 15). But it no doubt says a great deal more about the continued appeal of her books to adolescent girls—if there are still such—who want the marital palm without the dust.

—Barrie Hayne

WELLES, Elizabeth. See **ROBY, Mary Linn.**

———

WELLS, Hondo. See **HORNER, Lance, Kyle ONSTOTT, and Ashley CARTER.**

———

WELTY, Eudora (Alice).
Nationality: American. **Born:** Jackson, Mississippi, 13 April 1909. **Education:** Mississippi State College for Women, Columbus, 1925–27; University of Wisconsin, Madison, B.A. 1929; Columbia University Graduate School of Business, New York, 1930–31. **Career:** part-time journalist, 1931–32; publicity agent, Works Progress Administration (WPA), 1933–36; staff member, *New York Times Book Review*, during World War II. Honorary consultant in American Letters, Library of Congress, Washington, DC, 1958. **Recipient:** Bread Loaf Writers Conference fellowship, 1940; O. Henry award, 1942, 1943, 1968; Guggenheim fellowship, 1942, 1948; American Academy grant, 1944; Howells medal, 1955, for *The Ponder Heart*, and gold medal, 1972; Ford fellowship, for drama; Brandeis University Creative Arts award, 1965; Edward MacDowell medal, 1970; Pulitzer prize, 1973, for *The Optimist's Daughter*; National medal for literature, 1980; Presidential medal of freedom, 1980; American book award, 1981, for *The Collected Stories of Eudora Welty*, and 1984, for *One Writer's Beginnings*; Bobst award, 1984; Commonwealth award, 1984; Mystery Writers of America award, 1985; National Medal of Arts, 1987; National Endowment for the Arts award, 1989; National Book Foundation medal, 1991. Chevalier, Ordre des Arts et des Lettres, 1987. D.Litt.: Denison University, Granville, Ohio, 1971; Smith College, Northampton, Massachusetts; University of Wisconsin, Madison; University of the South, Sewanee, Tennessee; Washington and Lee University, Lexington, Virginia. **Member:** American Academy, 1971. **Address:** 1119 Pinehurst Street, Jackson, Mississippi 39202, USA.

ROMANCE AND HISTORICAL PUBLICATIONS

Novels

Delta Wedding. New York, Harcourt Brace, 1946; London, Lane, 1947.
The Ponder Heart. New York, Harcourt Brace, and London, Lane, 1954.
Losing Battles. New York, Random House, 1970; London, Virago Press, 1982.
The Optimist's Daughter. New York, Random House, 1972; London, Deutsch, 1973.

OTHER PUBLICATIONS

Short Stories

A Curtain of Green. New York, Doubleday, 1941; London, Lane, 1943; as *A Curtain of Green and Other Stories*, New York, Harcourt Brace, 1964.
The Robber Bridegroom (novella). New York, Doubleday, 1942; London, Lane, 1944.
The Wide Net and Other Stories. New York, Harcourt Brace, 1943; London, Lane, 1945,
Music from Spain. Greenville, Mississippi, Levee Press, 1948.

The Golden Apples. New York, Harcourt Brace, 1949; London, Lane, 1950.

Short Stories. New York, Harcourt Brace, 1949.

Selected Stories (includes *A Curtain of Green*, and *The Wide Net and Other Stories*). New York, Modern Library, 1954.

The Bride of the Innisfallen, and Other Stories. New York, Harcourt Brace, and London, Hamish Hamilton, 1955.

Thirteen Stories, edited by Ruth M. Yande Kieft. New York, Harcourt Brace, 1965.

The Collected Stories of Eudora Welty. New York, Harcourt Brace, 1980; London, Boyars, 1981.

Moon Lake and Other Stories. Franklin Center, Pennsylvania, Franklin Library, 1980.

Retreat. Jackson, Mississippi, Palaeman Press, 1981.

Morgana: Two Stories from 'The Golden Apples'. Jackson, University Press of Mississippi, 1989.

Poetry

A Flock of Guinea Hens Seen from a Car. New York, Albondocani Press, 1970.

Plays

The Ponder House (produced Broadway, 1956).
The Robber Bridegroom (produced Broadway, 1978).

Screenplay: 'The Hitch-hikers', 1986.

Other

Short Stories (essay). New York, Harcourt Brace, 1949.

Place in Fiction (lectures). New York, House of Books, 1957.

Three Papers on Fiction (addresses). Northampton, Massachusetts, Smith College, 1962.

The Shoe Bird (for children). New York, Harcourt Brace, 1964.

A Sweet Devouring (on children's literature). New York, Albondocani Press, 1969.

One Time, One Place: Mississippi in the Depression; A Snapshot Album, photographs by Welty. New York, Random House, 1971.

A Pageant of Birds. New York, Albondocani Press, 1975.

Fairy Tale of the Natchez Trace. Jackson, Mississippi Historical Society, 1975.

The Eye of the Story: Selected Essays and Reviews. New York, Random House, 1978; London, Virago Press, 1987.

Women! Make Turban in Your Home. Winston-Salem, North Carolina, Palaemon, 1979.

Ida M'Toy (a memoir). Urbana, University of Illinois Press, 1979.

Miracles of Perception: The Art of Willa Cather, with Alfred Knopf and Yehudi Menuhin. Charlottesville, Virginia, Alderman Library, 1980.

Conversations with Eudora Welty, edited by Peggy Whitman Prenshaw. Jackson, University Press of Mississippi, 1984.

One Writer's Beginnings. Cambridge, Massachusetts, Harvard University Press, 1984; London, Faber, 1985.

Photographs. Jackson, University Press of Mississippi, 1989.

*

Bibliography: by Noel Polk, in *Mississippi Quarterly* (Mississippi State), Fall 1973; *Eudora Welty: A Reference Guide* by Victor H. Thompson, Boston, Hall, 1973; *Eudora Welty: A Critical Bibliography 1936–1958* by Bethany C. Swearington, Jackson, University Press of Mississippi, 1984; *The Welty Collection: A Guide to the Eudora Welty Manuscripts and Documents at the Mississippi Department of Archives and History* by Suzanne Marrs, Jackson, University Press of Mississippi, 1988.

Manuscript Collection: Mississippi Department of Archives and History, Jackson.

Critical Studies (selection): *Eudora Welty* by Ruth M. Vande Keift, New York, Twayne, 1962, revised edition, 1986; *A Season of Dreams: The Fiction of Eudora Welty* by Alfred J. Appel, Baton Rouge, Louisiana State University Press, 1965; *Eudora Welty* by Joseph A Bryant, Jr, Minneapolis, University of Minnesota Press, 1968; *The Rhetoric of Eudora Welty's Short Stories* by Zelma Turner Howard, Jackson, University Press of Mississippi, 1973; *A Still Moment: Essays on the Art of Eudora Welty* edited by John F. Desmond, Metuchen, New Jersey, Scarecrow Press, 1978; *Eudora Welty: Critical Essays*, edited by Peggy Whitman Prenshaw, Jackson, University Press of Mississippi, 1979; *Eudora Welty: A Form of Thanks* edited by Ann J. Abadie and Louis D. Dollarhide, Jackson, University Press of Mississippi, 1979; *Eudora Welty's Achievement of Order* by Michael Kreyling, Baton Rouge, Louisiana State University Press, 1980; *Eudora Welty* by Elizabeth Evans, New York, Ungar, 1981; *A Tissue of Lies: Eudora Welty and the Southern Romance* by Jennifer L. Randisi, Boston, University Press of America, 1982; *Eudora Welty's Chronicle: A Story of Mississippi Life* by Albert J. Devlin, Jackson, University Press of Mississippi, 1983, and *Welty: A Life in Literature*, edited by Devlin, University Press of Mississippi, 1988; *With Ears Opening Like Morning Glories: Eudora Welty and the Love of Storytelling* by Carol Manning, Bowling Green, Connecticut, Greenwood Press, 1985; *Sacred Groves and Ravaged Gardens: The Fiction of Eudora Welty, Carson McCullers, and Flannery O'Connor* by Louise Westling, Athens, University of Georgia Press, 1985; *Eudora Welty* by Ruth M. Kieft, Boston, Hall, 1987; *Eudora Welty* by Louise Westling, London, Macmillan 1989; *Eudora Welty: Eye of the Storyteller* edited by Dawn Trouard, Kent, Ohio, Kent State University Press, 1989; *Eudora Welty: Seeing Black and White* by Robert MacNeil, Jackson, University Press of Mississippi, 1990; *The Heart of the Story: Eudora Welty's Short Fiction* by Peter Schmidt, Jackson, University Press of Mississippi, 1991.

*   *   *

During the years immediately before World War II, when Margaret Mitchell's *Gone with the Wind* sparked a revival of interest in the legendary ante-bellum South, both Eudora Welty and Allen Tate by curious coincidence wrote two short stories and a related novel that should stand beside Faulkner's 'Yoknapatawpha Saga' as the most memorable and profound contributions to the creation of a southern mythology. The time settings of the two groups of tales are different; and, as might be anticipated, the subtexts motivating them present almost diametrically opposed attitudes toward the development of the region.

Both begin in colonial days, but Welty's works are confined to the frontier period in the old Southwest along the Natchez Trace. They are also as different as imaginable in style from Tate's daguerrotype realism. All these fables, as they are best described, involve important historical characters, but these intermingle with imaginary creations in unlikely events that are insignificant only symbolically. The novel *The Robber Bridegroom*, populates realistic landscapes with talking heads, flying cows and witches drawn from the tall stories from which the region is famous in a spectacular effort to create a mythology for a culture that has transformed a wilderness. Each tale ends with a startling surprise that intimates Welty's sardonic attitudes towards 'civilization'.

The short story, 'First Love', poses problems for readers not steeped in the history of the Trace, especially the cautionary career of Aaron Burr, once vice President of the United States, who was later tried for treason when he plotted to create an independent Southwestern empire. Welty provides no information about these events, but introduces Burr in Natchez at the time of his trial in 1807, as he is seen through the eyes of a 12-year-old deaf boy who idolizes Burr's captivating manner. This boy is privy to secret meetings Burr continues to hold with fellow conspirators, but understands nothing of the conversations about Burr's rise, fall, and dreams. When Burr finally sneaks away into the dark, the desolate boy feels only that 'he would never know the true course or the true outcome of any dream'.

The other story, 'A Still Moment', is climaxed by an even more disenchanting epiphany. It depicts an unlikely meeting one twilight in a wilderness swamp of Lorenzo Dow, a militant preacher with a call to convert all outcasts; James Murrell, dreaded outlaw of the Trace who has taken many others' money and lives, and John James Audubon, the naturalist, on his pilgrimage to make a pictorial record of American birds. As they confront each other uneasily, a solitary snowy heron lands before them to feed. Dow sees it as God's love made visible, while Murrell has a dark vision of the failure of his planned 'Mystic Rebellion' of outcasts. It is the idealistic scholar Audobon, however, who shatters this 'still moment' by shooting the bird that he needs as a model. Welty comments, 'What each of them wanted was simply <u>all</u>'—to save or destroy all men or to make a record of all wildlife even if it meant the death of specimens. She concludes that if this meeting had occurred, the trio would have taken 'the pride out of one another'.

These narrowly focused accounts of imagined revelations provide the side panels for a triptych with *The Robber Bridegroom* as centrepiece, presenting a dreamlike panorama of the transition of the primitive wilderness into the doomed Cotton Kingdom. Welty relished telling about the origins of the novel. For jobs that she had held in the 1930s creating propaganda to promote Mississippi tourism, she 'had to do a lot of reading on the Natchez Trace'. While she wasn't a writer who depended on research, reading old accounts of frontier days fired her imagination 'with how fairy-tale like the experiences in the early days were. So I just sat down and wrote it in a great spurt of pleasure'.

The novel follows a winding path through the experiences of Clement Musgrove, a pioneer planter, and his encounter with 'robber bridegroom' Jamie Lockhard, who is both the leader of the notorious bandits that plague the Trace and an elegant gentleman pursuing Musgrove's daughter. Hilarious complications arise from his plot to preserve the secret of his dual identity, but such ruses become unnecessary when the development of a civilized commercial community enables him to reunite his divided faces and capture his bride. When Musgrove visits the Lockharts' luxurious establishment in New Orleans, he discovers that 'the outward transfer of bandit to merchant had been almost too easy to count it as a change at all, and he was enjoying the same success he ever had'. But Jamie now knows, too, that he is a hero with 'the power to look both ways to see things from all sides'. Musgrove is invited to remain in town; but he refuses, for he is 'an innocent of the wilderness', whose pastoral age is ending, just as had that of the nomadic indigenes that it supplanted. Now 'the time of cunning has come', and this is a world he 'will have no part of'.

Eudora Welty, with her own remarkable power 'to see things from all sides', suggests that one might as well accept things as they are, for although lifestyles change superficially, old patterns persist behind new faces. After writing these three stories, she regrettably abandoned turning history into myth to concentrate on delighting us with accounts of how the principles evoked by these early tales apply to our contemporary world.

—Warren French

WENTWORTH, Sally.

Pseudonym for Doreen Hornsblow. **Nationality:** British. **Born:** Watford, Hertfordshire. **Relations:** married Donald Alfred Hornsblow; one son. **Career:** accounts clerk, Associated Newspapers Ltd, London, and Consumers' Association, Hertford. Founder chair, 1985, and now life president, Hertford Association of National Trust Members. **Address:** Braughingbury, Braughing, Hertfordshire, England.

ROMANCE AND HISTORICAL PUBLICATIONS

Novels

Island Masquerade. London, Mills and Boon, 1977; New York, Silhouette, 1978.
King of the Castle. London, Mills and Boon, and New York, Silhouette, 1978.
Conflict in Paradise. London, Mills and Boon, and New York, Silhouette, 1978.
Rightful Possession. London, Mills and Boon, and New York, Silhouette, 1978.
Liberated Lady. London, Mills and Boon, and New York, Silhouette, 1979.
Shattered Dreams. London, Mills and Boon, 1979; New York, Silhouette, 1983.
The Ice Maiden. London, Mills and Boon, 1979; New York, Silhouette, 1980.
Candle in the Wind. London, Mills and Boon, 1979; New York, Silhouette, 1980
Garden of Thorns. London, Mills and Boon, and New York, Silhouette, 1980.
Set the Stars on Fire. London, Mills and Boon, and New York, Silhouette, 1980.
Betrayal in Bali. London, Mills and Boon, and New York, Silhouette, 1980.
Race Against Love. London, Mills and Boon, 1980; New York, Silhouette, 1981.
Summer Love. London, Mills and Boon, and New York, Silhouette, 1981.
Say Hello to Yesterday. London, Mills and Boon, and New York, Silhouette, 1981.
King of Culla. London, Mills and Boon, and New York, Silhouette, 1981.
The Judas Kiss. London, Mills and Boon, 1981; New York, Silhouette, 1982.
The Sea Master. London, Mills and Boon, 1981; New York, Silhouette, 1982.
Semi-Detached Marriage. London, Mills and Boon, and New York, Silhouette, 1982.
Man for Hire. London, Mills and Boon, and New York, Silhouette, 1982.
Flying High. London, Mills and Boon, 1982; New York, Silhouette, 1983.
Jilted. London, Mills and Boon, and New York, Silhouette, 1983.
The Lion Rock. London, Mills and Boon, 1983; New York, Silhouette, 1984.
Backfire. London, Mills and Boon, 1983; New York, Silhouette, 1984.
Dark Awakening. London, Mills and Boon, and New York, Silhouette, 1984.
Viking Invader. London, Mills and Boon, and New York, Silhouette, 1984.
The Wings of Love. London, Mills and Boon, and New York, Silhouette, 1985.
Fatal Deception. London, Mills and Boon, and New York, Silhouette, 1985.

The Hawk of Venice. London, Mills and Boon, 1985; New York, Silhouette, 1986.

The Kissing Game. London, Mills and Boon, and New York, Silhouette, 1986.

Cage of Ice. London, Mills and Boon, 1986; New York, Silhouette, 1987.

Tiger in His Lair. London, Mills and Boon, 1986; New York, Silhouette, 1987.

Passionate Revenge. London, Mills and Boon, 1987; New York, Silhouette, 1988.

Ultimatum. London, Mills and Boon, 1987; New York, Silhouette, 1988.

Dishonourable Intentions. London, Mills and Boon, 1987; New York, Silhouette, 1988.

Mistaken Wedding. London, Mills and Boon, and New York, Silhouette, 1988.

Satan's Island. London, Mills and Boon, 1988; New York, Silhouette, 1989.

Driving Force. London, Mills and Boon, 1988; New York, Silhouette, 1989.

The Devil's Shadow. London, Mills and Boon, 1988; New York, Silhouette, 1989.

Strange Encounter. London, Mills and Boon, 1989; New York, Silhouette, 1990.

Echoes from the Past. London, Mills and Boon, 1989; New York, Silhouette, 1990.

Wish on the Moon. London, Mills and Boon, 1989; New York, Silhouette, 1990.

Fire Island. London, Mills and Boon, 1989; New York, Silhouette, 1991.

Lord of Misrule. London, Mills and Boon, 1990; New York, Silhouette, 1991.

Taken on Trust. London, Mills and Boon, 1990; New York, Silhouette, 1991.

Illusions of Love. London, Mills and Boon, 1990; New York, Silhouette, 1992.

Broken Destiny. London, Mills and Boon, 1990; New York, Silhouette, 1992.

The Devil's Kiss. London, Mills and Boon, 1991; New York, Silhouette, 1992.

Twin Torment. London, Mills and Boon, and New York, Silhouette, 1991.

Ghost of the Past. London, Mills and Boon, and New York, Silhouette, 1991.

The Golden Greek. London, Mills and Boon, 1991; New York, Silhouette, 1993.

Stormy Voyage. London, Mills and Boon, 1992; New York, Silhouette, 1993.

Wayward Wife. London, Mills and Boon, and New York, Silhouette, 1992.

Yesterday's Affair. London, Mills and Boon, 1992; New York, Silhouette, 1993.

Mirrors of the Sea. London, Mills and Boon, and New York, Silhouette, 1993.

Practise to Deceive. London, Mills and Boon, and New York, Silhouette, 1993.

Sicilian Spring. London, Mills and Boon, and New York, Silhouette, 1993.

*

Sally Wentworth comments:

My aim is to write a book the readers enjoy reading and I enjoy writing.

*   *   *

One of the most popular writers of Mills and Boon contemporary romances, Sally Wentworth frequently injects topical concerns into her novels, dealing with serious problems, such as single parenthood and abortion, which her characters have to resolve. For example in *The Golden Greek* the heroine Laurel is working on a 'dig' when she sprains her wrist. Bored, unable to work, she calls a former student friend Niko. They become lovers and when Laurel discovers she is pregnant Niko promises to marry her. However, his father forbids the marriage, and Laurel, refusing to give up her baby, struggles to make a living until Niko's father summons them to Greece. Niko is dead, and Laurel's son is the only child.

Pregnancy and abortion are dealt with in *The Devil's Kiss*. Miranda is headhunting staff when she hears from her student sister Rosalind that she is about to have an abortion. Rosalind refuses to reveal who the father is, but the clinic fees have been paid by Warren Hunter, and when Miranda tracks him down she discovers he heads his own computer consultancy. For revenge she headhunts several of his employees and plans that they will all resign on the same day. Warren Hunter meets her, insists his credit card was stolen, and forces her to go to York to confront Rosalind who confirms he was not her baby's father. On the way home the car is driven into a ditch, they find shelter in a boat, and make love.

Perhaps the most controversial theme for a light romance is in *Broken Destiny*. Jancy is young and beautiful, engaged to Duncan who worships her perfect body. While Duncan is working abroad she is told she has breast cancer and must have a mastectomy. Duncan would be revolted but would be too honourable to admit it. Devastated, refusing to tell anyone, she writes to break off the engagement and flees to her Yorkshire cottage where a widowed neighbour helps her settle in. But Duncan comes after her, and in the end reassures her that he loves her for real, not just for her body. This book is very moving, touching, and immensely encouraging to women who face the same problem. It is a measure of Wentworth's skill that she can treat such a serious topic sensitively and in depth within the confines of a category romance.

Wentworth does not use as many foreign locations as other Mills and Boon authors, though the West Indies, the Bahamas, Israel, Austria and Lanzarote all feature in her books. An exotic setting with another contemporary concern is used in *Conflict in Paradise*, where Tansy is a doctor on a South Pacific island, working with her father. The island is being surveyed as a possible NATO refuelling base, and Tansy comes into confrontation with the soldier Blake. When their love is recognized, but before they can leave, her father announces he is planning to marry a widow with children and live in Australia. One of them must stay on the island, so Tansy prepares to sacrifice her future.

Lord of Misrule provides adventure, excitement, and mystery to a greater extent than most romances. The heroine Verity goes with her pregnant, widowed friend Paula to the family home Paula has never seen, where they meet Paula's husband's stepmother and stepbrother Sebastian, who would inherit but for Paula's child. There follows a series of accidents, which might be attempts on Paula's life. This threat of murder is made much more of than in most Mills and Boon books, where the relationship usually predominates at the expense of plot, and is a most enjoyable read.

Taken on Trust is more like the conventional Mills and Boon romance. The heroine Lyn is a rich, spoilt brat who has run away rather than accept her parents' divorce and father's remarriage. When Morgan forces her home she is initially furious, then falls in love with him. When they marry she wonders whether he was bought by her father, who denies her nothing. After a disastrous honeymoon Lyn returns home alone and tries to rebuild her life. This book contains more introspection and self-analysis than most of Wentworth's books, and allows an initially unsympathetic heroine to grow and develop more attractive characteristics.

A variation on the single romance is contained in the two books *Twin Torment* and *Ghost of the Past*. Instead of one heroine there are two. Identical twins Ginny and Venetia fall in love with the same man. As models they have tried to capitalize on their sameness, even swapping assignments as they used to mislead their teachers. This time it is different. Only one of them can have Alex, and they have been advised only one of them can succeed as a model. The first book ends as they settle their differences in the usual way and toss for it. Five years later the loser returns, her way clear to win the hero. This is a different approach, but the jealousy and open squabbling and cheating make the twins less attractive than most heroines should be, and does not succeed as well as the other books.

Most of her heroines are strong, independent women. They all discover a great deal about themselves as they come to terms with love. Wentworth can provide real, rounded characters, and believable dialogue. She uses second girls and confidantes to a greater extent, which adds to the variety and interest. In most of the novels the resolution is delayed until the final few pages, maintaining the suspense until the very end.

—Marina Oliver

WESLEY, Elizabeth. See **McELFRESH, Adeline.**

WESLEY, Mary.
Nationality: British. **Born:** Mary Farmar, Englefield Green, Berkshire, 24 June 1912. **Education:** Queen's College, London, 1928–39; London School of Economics, 1931–32. **Relations:** married 1) Lord Swinfen in 1937 (divorced 1944), two sons; 2) Eric Siepmann in 1951, one son. **Career:** staff member, War Office, London, 1939–41. **Address:** c/o Bantam Press, 61–63 Uxbridge Road, London W5 5SA, England.

ROMANCE AND HISTORICAL PUBLICATIONS

Novels

Jumping the Queue. London, Macmillan, 1983; New York, Penguin, 1988.
Haphazard House. London, Dent, 1983.
The Camomile Lawn. London, Macmillan, 1984; New York, Summit, 1985.
Harnessing Peacocks. London, Macmillan, 1985; New York, Scribner, 1986.
The Vacillations of Poppy Carew. London, Macmillan, 1986; New York, Penguin, 1988.
Not That Sort of Girl. London, Macmillan, 1987; New York, Viking, 1988.
Second Fiddle. London, Macmillan, 1988; New York, Viking, 1989.
A Sensible Life. London, Bantam Press, and New York, Viking, 1990.
A Dubious Legacy. London, Bantam Press, 1992.
An Imaginative Experience. London, Bantam Press, 1994.

OTHER PUBLICATIONS

Other

The Sixth Seal. London, Macdonald 1969; New York, Stein and Day, 1971.

Speaking Terms (for children). London, Faber, 1969; Boston, Gambit, 1971.

*   *   *

Mary Wesley constructs light novels, full of delicious jokes and bizarre situations containing shrewdly observed truths. The stories are witty and charming, the writing astringent, charged with her sharp intelligence. Her eye for detail gives the books almost palpable texture.

Her characterization is acute: the protagonists, often endearingly naive girls, are realistically handled, while the minor characters who surround them are usually outrageously over the top yet perfectly believable. A great deal of happy, exuberant sex is enjoyed by her characters. She loves to give the reader little frissons of shock but these are handled with such high spirits and lightness that the shocks are pleasurable.

In *The Camomile Lawn*, five cousins meet in their aunt's house in Cornwall, in the feverish days of August 1939, for a romp before the inevitable coming of war. Sophy is still a child, Calypso is an innocent, Polly is secretive, Walter is determined to join up and Oliver is randy. During the war, we see them and their friends and relations in war-time London: the brittle gaiety, the brave jokes, the couplings and partings, the joys and sorrows and the way war changes them are brilliantly evoked.

Not That Sort of Girl is the story of Rose who promised never to leave her conventional husband Ned and always to come when her lover, Mylo, summons her. Through 50 years of married life, she carefully balances her two promises, never letting either of them down.

Wesley is particularly good at creating children: she understands the longings suffered by Sophy, in *The Camomile Lawn*, and ten-year-old Flora's loneliness and despair at the beginning of *A Sensible Life*. When she is on holiday in Brittany, ignored by her selfish parents, Flora makes friends with other English visitors and falls in love with Cosmo, Hubert, and Felix. It takes years of occasional meetings and ephemeral affairs before she decides which of them she really loves and wants to marry.

Hebe, in *Harnessing Peacocks*, runs away from her cold family who want her to have an abortion and defiantly has her illegitimate child. She has alternate bouts of high-class cooking and selective prostitution to keep herself and her son, always managing to keep her two worlds apart until the disastrous day that two of her lovers turn up while she is cooking for their aunt. Hebe is delightful and totally matter of fact about selling sex. The elderly characters are sharply observed and the web of relationships that form Hebe's circle is almost as full of coincidences as a Dickens novel. The book is funny and charming and the resolution when she finds her son's father is quite delightful.

The Vacillations of Poppy Carew introduces a vulnerable girl whose suitors are marvellously bizarre. The account of her trip to North Africa with one of them where she finds herself in a half-finished, cockroach-infested hotel is like something out of an Evelyn Waugh novel: he would have revelled in Furnival's Fun Funerals, the firm Poppy engages for her father's burial. This a fast-moving romp, yet the love story is touching.

A Dubious Legacy weaves its way backwards and forwards in time: it is the story of Henry Tillitson and his strange, eccentric wife, Margaret, the legacy of the title. When she first arrives at his house, in 1944, she takes to her bed and refuses to leave it except for an occasional foray which always ends in trouble. Ten years on, Henry determines to re-create one of his parents' alfresco summer dinner parties. James and Matthew, two young men bring their girlfriends, intending to propose to them in this romantic setting, other guests assemble and all goes well until Margaret decides to join them, dances on the table and decapitates a cockatoo. The relationships among the characters become convoluted as time goes on, Henry secretly fathering James and Matthew's children. It is a strange haunting book with overtones of sadness mixed in with wry humour.

One of the minor pleasures in reading Wesley's books is the way characters one has met in one book appear in another. Calypso Grant, first met as a naive young girl in *The Camomile Lawn*, appears as a mature sophisticated women in several books—she is the great-aunt of one of Hebe's lovers and gives him an exquisite scarlet hat as a talking point when he decides to become a milliner; she is a guest at the fateful dinner party in *A Dubious Legacy*, and a confidante of Poppy Carew's lover. The incestuous twins, in *Not That Sort of Girl*, reappear as the heroine's parents in *Second Fiddle*. It adds greatly to the authenticity of Wesley's fantasy world.

All her novels are beautifully written, entertaining, and thought provoking. Anyone who has not read one of Wesley's books yet has a treat in store.

—Pamela Cleaver

WEST, (Mary) Jessamyn.
Nationality: American. **Born:** North Vernon, Indiana, 18 July 1902. **Education:** Union High School, Fullerton, California, graduated 1919; Whittier College, California, 1919, 1921–23, A.B. in English 1923; Fullerton Junior College, 1920–21; University of California, Berkeley, 1929–31. **Relations:** married Harry Maxwell McPherson in 1923; two foster daughters. **Career:** teacher and secretary, Hemet, California, 1924–29; teacher, Bread Loaf Writers Conference, Vermont, Indiana University, Bloomington, University of Notre Dame, Indiana, University of Utah, Salt Lake City, University of Washington, Seattle, Stanford University, California, and Wellesley College, Cambridge, Massachusetts. **Recipient:** Monsen award, 1958; Janet Kafka prize, 1976. Honorary degrees: Whittier College; Mills College, Oakland, California; Swarthmore College, Pennsylvania; Indiana University; Western College for Women, Oxford, Ohio. **Died:** 23 February 1984.

ROMANCE AND HISTORICAL PUBLICATIONS

Novel

The Massacre at Fall Creek. New York, Harcourt Brace, and London, Macmillan, 1975.

Short Stories

The Friendly Persuasion. New York, Harcourt Brace, 1945; London, Hodder and Stoughton, 1946.
Except for Me and Thee: A Companion to The Friendly Persuasion. New York, Harcourt Brace, and London, Macmillan, 1969.

OTHER PUBLICATIONS

Novels

The Witch Diggers. New York, Harcourt Brace, 1951; London, Heinemann, 1952.
Little Men, in *Star Short Novels*, edited by Frederik Pohl. New York, Ballantine, 1954; published separately, as *The Chile-kings*, 1967.
South of the Angels. New York, Harcourt Brace, 1960; London, Hodder and Stoughton, 1961.
A Matter of Time. New York, Harcourt Brace, 1966; London, Macmillan, 1967.

Leafy Rivers. New York, Harcourt Brace, 1967; London, Macmillan, 1968.
The Life I Really Lived. New York, Harcourt Brace, 1979.
The State of Stony Lonesome. New York, Harcourt Brace, 1984.

Short Stories

Cress Delahanty. New York, Harcourt Brace, 1953; London, Hodder and Stoughton, 1954.
Love, Death, and the Ladies' Drill Team. New York, Harcourt Brace, 1955; as *Learn to Say Goodbye*, London, Hodder and Stoughton, 1957.
Crimson Ramblers of the World, Farewell. New York, Harcourt Brace, 1970; London, Macmillan, 1971.
The Story of a Story and Three Stories. Berkeley, University of California, 1982.
Collected Stories of Jessamyn West. San Diego, Harcourt Brace, 1986.

Plays

A Mirror for the Sky, music by Gail Kubik (produced Eugene, Oregon, 1958). New York, Harcourt Brace, 1948.

Screenplays: *Friendly Persuasion* (uncredited), with Michael Wilson, 1956; *The Big Country*, with others, 1958; *The Stolen Hours*, 1963.

Poetry

The Secret Look. New York, Harcourt Brace, 1974.

Other

The Reading Public (address). New York, Harcourt Brace, 1952.
Friends and Violence. Philadelphia, Friends General Conference, n.d.
To See the Dream. New York, Harcourt Brace, 1957; London, Hodder and Stoughton, 1958.
Love Is Not What You Think. New York, Harcourt Brace, 1959; as *A Woman's Love*, London, Hodder and Stoughton, 1960.
Hide and Seek: A Continuing Journey. New York, Harcourt Brace, and London, Macmillan, 1973.
The Woman Said Yes: Encounters with Life and Death: Memoirs. New York, Harcourt Brace, 1976; as *Encounters with Death and Life*, London, Gollancz, 1977.
Double Discovery: A Journey. New York, Harcourt Brace, 1980.

Editor, *The Quaker Reader.* New York, Viking Press, 1962.

*

Film Adaptations: *Friendly Persuasion*, 1956, 1975.

Manuscript Collection: Whittier College, California.

Critical Studies: *Jessamyn West* by Alfred S. Shivers, New York, Twayne, 1972; *Jessamyn West* by Ann Dahlstrom Farmer, Boise, Idaho, Boise State University, 1982.

* * *

Jessamyn West's credentials for admission into the ranks of historical writers rest primarily on her two collections of related short stories on Indiana Quaker life, *The Friendly Persuasion* and *Except for Me and Thee*. She is, however, a writer who resists any narrow classification. Her work ranges from vivid fiction created out of fragments of history (*The Massacre at Fall Creek*) to tender and perceptive stories of coming of age (*Cress Delahanty*, *The State of Stony Lonesome*). Some of her best work takes the form of short stories or vignettes that meld together into a sort of novel-without-plot but with a strong central theme. Romance is hardly a feature of West's work, because romance is rooted in unreality. What distinguishes all of her work, short stories or novels, is their clear, unflinching reality.

Character is obviously what interests West the most. All of her work revolves around the ways that people's lives and personalities are shaped, how they respond to tragedy and what makes them laugh. Like life, West's tales swing back and forth from tragedy through serenity to real comedy. Her Quaker characters Jess and Eliza, for example, in the course of two books face the loss of a child, the testing of their peaceful principles by the Civil War, and the trials of a hard life on the frontier. At the same time, they find beauty in their surroundings, Jess in his orderly outdoor world and Eliza in her faith and her family. Their flaws are as realistically and compassionately drawn as their strengths, which makes them real people to the reader. None of these people is faced with larger-than-life situations, yet the books are replete with drama. The most narrow, bigoted, and wrong-headed of West's creations, like George Benson in *The Massacre at Fall Creek*, is still so human that the reader can feel sympathy for his bewilderment in the face of change. History has moved along faster than George can cope with it.

Love, not romance, is a continuing theme in West's work; sometimes it is the love between man and woman, or between parent and child, or between people and their community. West recognizes that love is rarely free from conflict, that people make unfounded assumptions about each other and have expectations and beliefs that are unreasonable. These problems and the inability or unwillingness of people to communicate with one another are what drive the plots along. 'Fitting in' is another motif that interconnects with love; these are people who crave belonging, who wish to have a place for themselves among people who love them. The realization that belonging comes from acceptance of difference as much or more than from recognition of sameness marks maturation and real participation in the community. West's characters are most content when they can maintain their individuality successfully in the framework of their larger society.

The land plays a large role in West's novels and short stories. Sometimes the love for the land is a rejoicing in its beauty and plenty; sometimes it is merely greed for possession. Whatever the feelings of the characters toward the landscape, West never fails to notice and record the details of the terrain, the effects of the changing seasons, the play of light at different times of day. Often, indeed, the episodic elements of a book are divided by seasons, as in *Cress Delahanty*. There is a strong feel for setting here, whether the land is Indiana or California, that acquaints the reader with the moods and disguises of the countryside. The features of the scenery might change with the passage of time and with the efforts of the people, but the land itself is unchanging, a symbol of stability even when the fabric of society is threatened by war or crime or intolerance. There is a feeling in West's writing that much of the emotional development in it comes directly from West's own experiences. The repetitive themes of maturation and change have about them an honesty and an immediacy that makes the reader know that they come from the heart.

—Susan Quinn Berneis

WESTCOTT, Jan.

Nationality: American. **Born:** Jan Vlachos, Philadelphia, Pennsylvania, 23 February 1912. **Education:** Swarthmore College, Pennsylvania, 1929–30. **Relations:** married Robert P. Barden in 1954; two sons. **Agent:** Harold Matson Company, 276 Fifth Avenue, New York, New York 10001, USA.

ROMANCE AND HISTORICAL PUBLICATIONS

Novels

The Border Lord. New York, Crown, 1946; London, Sampson Low, 1948.
Captain for Elizabeth. New York, Crown, 1948.
The Hepburn. New York, Crown, 1950; London, Hodder and Stoughton, 1951.
Captain Barney. New York, Crown, 1951.
The Walsingham Woman. New York, Crown, 1953; London, Hodder and Stoughton, 1954.
The Queen's Grace. New York, Crown, 1959.
Condottiere. New York, Random House, 1962; as *The Mercenary*, London, Redman, 1963.
The White Rose. New York, Putnam, 1969; as *The Lion's Share*, London, Hale, 1972.
Set Her on a Throne. Boston, Little Brown, 1972.
The Tower and the Dream. New York, Putnam, 1974.
A Woman of Quality. New York, Putnam, 1978; London, Hale, 1980.

*   *   *

Jan Westcott holds an unassailable position in the ranks of historical fiction writers. While she has written of other periods, Westcott is best noted for her outstanding novels about the Tudor-Stuart period of English history.

Her novels offer depth and breadth in characterization, setting, and plot development. Most important, however, is her ability to weave factual information and historical personalities into her stories. In fact, several could almost be considered biographical in nature, except for the fact that she creates a fictional setting for everyday events. The immediacy of the events, personal conflicts, and her ability to make the actions of her characters seem inevitable adds to the enjoyment of her writing.

Westcott's earlier novels showed promise of her later abilities. In *Captain Barney*, she uses the American Revolution as the background for the novel. Events take place in the Caribbean and along the eastern sea coast of the colonies. The hero is a fictional presentation of a real person, Captain Joshua Barney of the American Navy. The fictional character is Captain Benjamin Barney, a naval captain who makes a policy of capturing British ships. One such capture results in him obtaining the Royal Navy's code books which he later uses to defeat a British naval force. Lady Douglass Harris, a widow, is an unlikely heroine who takes up residence in the colonies. She is a titled lady without money, rigidly opposed to the war and to the American cause. She also presents a definite problem for the hero.

The action centres on sea encounters and Dutch held islands in the Caribbean which are used as 'neutral' trading areas by all countries. The British later attack the islands and seize all goods. Events culminate with the French intervention in the war which results in the surrender of General Cornwallis.

Characterization and plotting make this an extremely readable novel, but there are flaws. Motivation is contradictory and even lacking at times. The historical details are interesting but too sketchy to give the larger events their proper significance within the story. Reviews of this early work rated it as 'good adventure, good historical romance'.

It is within the Tudor-Stuart period that Westcott really makes herself at home. Several of her novels deal with historical people and are fictionalized accounts of their lives. The *Border Lord* is about the 5th Earl of Bothwell. *The White Rose* deals with Elizabeth Woodville, Edward IV, and their children. The children later became better known as the 'Princes in the Tower'.

The Queen's Grace covers the life of Katherine Parr, the last wife of Henry VIII. As noted earlier, characterization in many of Westcott's novels borders on the biographical, and *The Queen's Grace* illustrates this point. Beginning with Katherine's meeting with Thomas Seymour in 1529, the novel follows her life through four marriages. The first to Lord Borough, then to Lord Latimer, then Henry VIII, and finally to Thomas Seymour. She died at the age of 35 after giving birth to a little girl. The novel traces the most intimate details of her life. The information about daily life in the period is exceptionally well done, as is the book's analysis of women's place in the scheme of things. Katherine accurately reflects the realities of life in the 1500s. Her rise to being Queen of England is dramatically detailed and makes this novel a rich tapestry of intrigue, power, and love.

A word of caution is in order, however. It is obvious that Westcott carries out extensive research for her novels. It is also obvious that her skill in weaving history and fiction together might create difficulties for some readers: how to separate the fact from the fiction? For instance, did Thomas Seymour arrive in time to free Katherine from her son-in-law immediately after Lord Borough's death? Did Lady Katherine really kill her stepson, Thomas Borough? He apparently came searching for her husband, Lord Latimer, who was suspected of being involved in the rebellion that preceded the Pilgrimage of Grace.

Unless one is a serious student of this period, one simply cannot sort out all of the actual facts. Readers should only assume that names and general characteristics of historical persons, dates, and major historical events are true. Detailed characterization, subplots, settings, and motivation are pure Westcott. With this in mind readers can sit back and enjoy another world and another time presented by an unusually perceptive and creative writer.

—Arlene Moore

WESTMACOTT, Mary.
Pseudonym for Agatha Mary Clarissa Christie. Also wrote as Agatha Christie. **Nationality:** British. **Born:** Agatha Mary Clarissa Miller, Torquay, Devon, 15 September 1890. **Education:** privately at home; studied singing and piano in Paris, 1906. **Relations:** married 1) Colonel Archibald Christie in 1914 (divorced 1928), one daughter; 2) the archaeologist Max Mallowan in 1930. **Career:** served as a Voluntary Aid Detachment nurse in a Red Cross Hospital in Torquay during World War I, and worked in the dispensary of University College Hospital, London, during World War II; worked with Mallowan on excavations in Iraq and Syria and on Assyrian cities. President, Detection Club. **Recipient:** Mystery Writers of America Grand Master award, 1954; New York Drama Critics Circle award, 1955. D.Litt.: University of Exeter, Devon, 1961. Fellow, Royal Society of Literature, 1950. CBE (Commander, Order of the British Empire), 1956; DBE (Dame Commander, Order of the British Empire), 1971. **Died:** 12 January 1976.

ROMANCE AND HISTORICAL PUBLICATIONS

Novels

Giants' Bread. London, Collins, and New York, Doubleday, 1930.

Unfinished Portrait. London, Collins, and New York, Doubleday, 1934.
Absent in the Spring. London, Collins, and New York, Farrar and Rinehart, 1944.
The Rose and the Yew Tree. London, Heinemann, and New York, Rinehart, 1948.
A Daughter's a Daughter. London, Heinemann, 1952; New York, Dell, 1963.
The Burden. London, Heinemann, 1956; New York, Dell, 1963.

OTHER PUBLICATIONS

as Agatha Christie

Novels

The Mysterious Affair at Styles. London, Lane, 1920; New York, Dodd Mead, 1927.
The Secret Adversary. London, Lane, and New York, Dodd Mead, 1922.
The Murder on the Links. London, Lane, and New York, Dodd Mead, 1923.
The Man in the Brown Suit. London, Lane, and New York, Dodd Mead, 1924.
The Secret of Chimneys. London, Lane, and New York, Dodd Mead, 1925.
The Murder of Roger Ackroyd. London, Collins, and New York, Dodd Mead, 1926.
The Big Four. London, Collins, and New York, Dodd Mead, 1927.
The Mystery of the Blue Train. London, Collins, and New York, Dodd Mead, 1928.
The Seven Dials Mystery. London, Collins, and New York, Dodd Mead, 1929.
The Murder at the Vicarage. London, Collins, and New York, Dodd Mead, 1930.
The Floating Admiral, with others. London, Hodder and Stoughton, 1931; New York, Doubleday, 1932.
The Sittaford Mystery. London, Collins, 1931; as *The Murder at Hazelmoor,* New York, Dodd Mead, 1931.
Peril at End House. London, Collins, and New York, Dodd Mead, 1932.
Lord Edgware Dies. London, Collins, 1933; as *Thirteen at Dinner,* New York, Dodd Mead, 1933.
Why Didn't They Ask Evans? London, Collins, 1934; as *The Boomerang Clue,* New York, Dodd Mead, 1935.
Murder on the Orient Express. London, Collins, 1934; as *Murder in the Calais Coach,* New York, Dodd Mead, 1934.
Murder in Three Acts. New York, Dodd Mead, 1934; as *Three Act Tragedy,* London, Collins, 1935.
Death in the Clouds. London, Collins, 1935; as *Death in the Air,* New York, Dodd Mead, 1935.
The A.B.C. Murders. London, Collins, and New York, Dodd Mead, 1936; as *The Alphabet Murders,* New York, Pocket Books, 1966.
Cards on the Table. London, Collins, 1936; New York, Dodd Mead, 1937.
Murder in Mesopotamia. London, Collins, and New York, Dodd Mead, 1936.
Death on the Nile. London, Collins, 1937; New York, Dodd Mead, 1938.
Dumb Witness. London, Collins, 1937; as *Poirot Loses a Client,* New York, Dodd Mead, 1937.
Appointment with Death. London, Collins, and New York, Dodd Mead, 1938.
Hercule Poirot's Christmas. London, Collins, 1938; as *Murder for Christmas,* New York, Dodd Mead, 1939; as *A Holiday for Murder,* New York, Avon, 1947.

Murder Is Easy. London, Collins, 1939; as *Easy to Kill*, New York, Dodd Mead, 1939.

Ten Little Niggers. London, Collins, 1939; as *And Then There Were None*, New York, Dodd Mead, 1940; as *Ten Little Indians*, New York, Pocket Books, 1965.

One, Two, Buckle My Shoe. London, Collins, 1940; as *The Patriotic Murders*, New York, Dodd Mead, 1941; as *An Overdose of Death*, New York, Dell, 1953.

Sad Cypress. London, Collins, and New York, Dodd Mead, 1940.

Evil under the Sun. London, Collins, and New York, Dodd Mead, 1941.

N or M? London, Collins, and New York, Dodd Mead, 1941.

The Body in the Library. London, Collins, and New York, Dodd Mead, 1942.

The Moving Finger. New York, Dodd Mead, 1942; London, Collins, 1943.

Five Little Pigs. London, Collins, 1942; as *Murder in Retrospect*, New York, Dodd Mead, 1942.

Death Comes as the End. New York, Dodd Mead, 1944; London, Collins, 1945.

Towards Zero. London, Collins, and New York, Dodd Mead, 1944.

Sparkling Cyanide. London, Collins, 1945; as *Remembered Death*, New York, Dodd Mead, 1945.

The Hollow. London, Collins, and New York, Dodd Mead, 1946; as *Murder After Hours*, New York, Dell, 1954.

Taken at the Flood. London, Collins, 1948; as *There Is a Tide . . .*, New York, Dodd Mead, 1948.

Crooked House. London, Collins, and New York, Dodd Mead, 1949.

A Murder Is Announced. London, Collins, and New York, Dodd Mead, 1950.

They Came to Baghdad. London, Collins, and New York, Dodd Mead, 1951.

They Do It with Mirrors. London, Collins, 1952; as *Murder with Mirrors*, New York, Dodd Mead, 1952.

Mrs McGinty's Dead. London, Collins, and New York, Dodd Mead, 1952; as *Blood Will Tell*, New York, Detective Book Club, 1952.

After the Funeral. London, Collins, 1953; as *Funerals Are Fatal*, New York, Dodd Mead, 1953; as *Murder at the Gallop*, London, Fontana, 1963.

A Pocket Full of Rye. London, Collins, 1953; New York, Dodd Mead, 1954.

Destination Unknown. London, Collins, 1954; as *So Many Steps to Death*, New York, Dodd Mead, 1955.

Hickory, Dickory, Dock. London, Collins, 1955; as *Hickory, Dickory, Death*, New York, Dodd Mead, 1955.

Dead Man's Folly. London, Collins, and New York, Dodd Mead, 1956.

4:50 from Paddington. London, Collins, 1957; as *What Mrs McGillicuddy Saw!*, New York, Dodd Mead, 1957; as *Murder She Said*, New York, Pocket Books, 1961.

Ordeal by Innocence. London, Collins, 1958; New York, Dodd Mead, 1959.

Cat Among the Pigeons. London, Collins, 1959; New York, Dodd Mead, 1960.

The Pale Horse. London, Collins, 1961; New York, Dodd Mead, 1962.

The Mirror Crack'd from Side to Side. London, Collins, 1962; as *The Mirror Crack'd*, New York, Dodd Mead, 1963.

The Clocks. London, Collins, 1963; New York, Dodd Mead, 1964.

A Caribbean Mystery. London, Collins, 1964; New York, Dodd Mead, 1965.

At Bertram's Hotel. London, Collins, 1965; New York, Dodd Mead, 1966.

Third Girl. London, Collins, 1966; New York, Dodd Mead, 1967.

Endless Night. London, Collins, 1967; New York, Dodd Mead, 1968.

By the Pricking of My Thumbs. London, Collins, and New York, Dodd Mead, 1968.

Hallowe'en Party. London, Collins, and New York, Dodd Mead, 1969.

Passenger to Frankfurt. London, Collins, and New York, Dodd Mead, 1970.

Nemesis. London, Collins, and New York, Dodd Mead, 1971.

Elephants Can Remember. London, Collins, and New York, Dodd Mead, 1972.

Postern of Fate. London, Collins, and New York, Dodd Mead, 1973.

Curtain: Hercule Poirot's Last Case. London, Collins, and New York, Dodd Mead, 1975.

Sleeping Murder. London, Collins, and New York, Dodd Mead, 1976.

The Scoop, and Behind the Scenes, with others. London, Gollancz, 1983.

Short Stories

Poirot Investigates. London, Lane, 1924; New York, Dodd Mead, 1925.

Partners in Crime. London, Collins, and New York, Dodd Mead, 1929; reprinted in part as *The Sunningdale Mystery*, Collins 1933.

The Under Dog. London, Readers Library, 1929.

The Mysterious Mr Quin. London, Collins, and New York, Dodd Mead, 1930.

The Thirteen Problems. London, Collins, 1932; as *The Tuesday Club Murders*, New York, Dodd Mead, 1933; selection, as *The Mystery of the Blue Geranium and Other Tuesday Club Murders*, New York, Bantam, 1940.

The Hound of Death and Other Stories. London, Collins, 1933.

Parker Pyne Investigates. London, Collins, 1934; as *Mr Parker Pyne, Detective*, New York, Dodd Mead, 1934.

The Listerdale Mystery and Other Stories. London, Collins, 1934.

Murder in the Mews and Three Other Poirot Cases. London, Collins, 1937; as *Dead Man's Mirror and Other Stories*, New York, Dodd Mead, 1937.

The Regatta Mystery and Other Stories. New York, Dodd Mead, 1939.

The Mystery of the Baghdad Chest. Los Angeles, Bantam, 1943.

The Mystery of the Crime in Cabin 66. Los Angeles, Bantam, 1943.

Poirot and the Regatta Mystery. Los Angeles, Bantam, 1943.

Poirot on Holiday. London, Todd, 1943.

Problem at Pollensa Bay, and Christmas Adventure. London, Todd, 1943.

The Veiled Lady, and The Mystery of the Baghdad Chest. London, Todd, 1944.

Poirot Knows the Murderer. London, Todd, 1946.

Poirot Lends a Hand. London, Todd, 1946.

The Labours of Hercules. London, Collins, and New York, Dodd Mead, 1947.

The Witness for the Prosecution and Other Stories. New York, Dodd Mead, 1948.

The Mousetrap and Other Stories. New York, Dell, 1949; as *Three Blind Mice and Other Stories*, New York, Dodd Mead, 1950.

The Under Dog and Other Stories. New York, Dodd Mead, 1951.

The Adventure of the Christmas Pudding, and Selection of Entrées. London, Collins, 1960.

Double Sin and Other Stories. New York, Dodd Mead, 1961.

13 for Luck! A Selection of Mystery Stories for Young Readers. New York, Dodd Mead, 1961; London, Collins, 1966.

Surprise! Surprise! A Collection of Mystery Stories with Unexpected Endings, edited by Raymond T. Bond. New York, Dodd Mead, 1965.

Star over Bethlehem and Other Stories (as Agatha Christie Mallowan). London, Collins, and New York, Dodd Mead, 1965.

13 Clues for Miss Marple. New York, Dodd Mead, 1966.

The Golden Ball and Other Stories. New York, Dodd Mead, 1971.

Poirot's Early Cases. London, Collins, 1974; as *Hercule Poirot's Early Cases*, New York, Dodd Mead, 1974.

Miss Marple's Final Cases and Two Other Stories. London, Collins, 1979.

The Agatha Christie Hour. London, Collins, 1982.

Hercule Poirot's Casebook: Fifty Stories. New York, Dodd Mead, 1984.

Miss Marple: Complete Short Stories. New York, Dodd Mead, 1985.

Plays

Black Coffee (produced London, 1930). London, Ashley, and Boston, Baker, 1934.

Ten Little Niggers, adaptation of Christie's novel (produced Wimbledon and London, 1943). London, French, 1944; as *Ten Little Indians* (produced New York, 1944), New York, French, 1946.

Appointment with Death, adaptation of Christie's novel (produced Glasgow and London, 1945). London, French, 1956; in *The Mousetrap and Other Plays*, 1978.

Murder on the Nile, adaptation of her novel *Death on the Nile* (as *Little Horizon*, produced Wimbledon, 1945; as *Murder on the Nile* produced London and New York, 1946). London and New York, French, 1948.

The Hollow, adaptation of Christie's novel (produced Cambridge and London, 1951; Princeton, New Jersey, 1952; New York, 1978). London and New York, French, 1952.

The Mousetrap, adaptation of Christie's story 'Three Blind Mice' (broadcast 1952; produced Nottingham and London, 1952; New York, 1960). London and New York, French, 1954.

Witness for the Prosecution, adaptation of her own story (produced Nottingham and London, 1953; New York, 1954). London and New York, French, 1954.

Spider's Web (produced Nottingham and London, 1954; New York, 1974). London and New York, French, 1957.

Towards Zero, with Gerald Verner, adaptation of the novel by Christie (produced Nottingham and London, 1956). New York, Dramatists Play Service, 1957; London, French, 1958.

Verdict (produced Wolverhampton and London, 1958). London, French, 1958; in *The Mousetrap and Other Plays*, 1978.

The Unexpected Guest (produced Bristol and London, 1958). London, French, 1958; in *The Mousetrap and Other Plays*, 1978.

Go Back for Murder, adaptation of her novel *Five Little Pigs* (produced Edinburgh and London, 1960). London, French, 1960; in *The Mousetrap and Other Plays*, 1978.

Rule of Three: Afternoon at the Seaside, The Patient, The Rats (produced Aberdeen and London, 1962; *The Rats* produced New York, 1974; *The Patient* produced New York, 1978). London, French, 3 vols., 1963.

Fiddlers Three (produced Southsea, 1971; London, 1972).

Akhnaton (as *Akhnaton and Nefertiti*, produced New York, 1979; as *Akhnaton*, produced London, 1980). London, Collins, and New York, Dodd Mead, 1973.

The Mousetrap and Other Plays (includes *Witness for the Prosecution, Ten Little Indians, Appointment with Death, The Hollow, Towards Zero, Verdict, Go Back for Murder*). New York, Dodd Mead, 1978.

Radio Plays: *The Mousetrap*, 1952; *Personal Call*, 1960.

Poetry

The Road of Dreams. London, Bles, 1925.

Poems. London, Collins, and New York, Dodd Mead, 1973.

Other

Come, Tell Me How You Live (travel). London, Collins, and New York, Dodd Mead, 1946; revised edition, 1976.

An Autobiography. London, Collins, and New York, Dodd Mead, 1977.

*

Film Adaptations (from the novels by Agatha Christie): *Lord Edgware Dies*, 1934, 1985, from the novel, *Thirteen at Dinner*; *Ten Little Niggers*, 1945, from the novel *And Then There Were None*; *Witness for the Prosecution*, 1957, 1982; *The Spider's Web*, 1960, 1985; *Mrs McGinty's Dead*, 1964, from the novel *Murder Most Foul*; *Ten Little Niggers*, 1965, from the novel *Ten Little Indians*; *The ABC Murders*, 1966, from the novel *The Alphabet Murders*; *Endless Night*, 1971; *Murder on the Orient Express*, 1974; *Death on the Nile*, 1978; *Why Didn't They Ask Evans?*, 1980; *The Mirror Crack'd from Side to Side*, 1980, from the novel *The Mirror Crack'd*; *Evil Under the Sun*, 1982; *Murder is Easy*, 1982; *A Caribbean Mystery*, 1983; *Sparkling Cyanide*, 1983; *The Body in the Library*, 1984; *The Moving Finger*, 1984; *Ordeal by Innocence*, 1985; *They Do It With Mirrors*, 1985, from the novel *Murder with Mirrors*; *A Pocketful of Rye*, 1985; *A Murder is Announced*, 1985, 1987; *At Beatram's Hotel*, 1986; *Murder at the Vicarage*, 1986; *Murder in Three Acts*, 1986; *Nemesis*, 1986; *Dead Man's Folly*, 1986; *The Hound of Hell*, 1987, from the novel *The Last Seance*; *Appointment with Death*, 1989; *The Man in the Brown Suit*, 1989; *Mysterious Affair at Styles*, 1990; *Poirot: Peril at End House*, 1991.

Bibliography: by Louise Barnard, in *A Talent to Deceive: An Appreciation of Agatha Christie* by Robert Barnard, London, Collins, and New York, Dodd Mead, 1980.

Critical Studies: *The Life and Crimes of Agatha Christie* by Charles Osborne, London, Collins, 1982, New York, Holt Rinehart, 1983; *The Agatha Christie Companion* by Dennis Sanders and Len Lovallo, New York, Delacorte Press, 1984, London, W. H. Allen, 1985; *Agatha Christie: A Biography* by Janet Morgan, London, Cape, 1984, New York, Knopf, 1985; *An A to Z of the Novels an Short Stories of Agatha Christie* by Ben Morselt, Phoenix, Arizona, Phoenix, 1986.

*   *   *

Agatha Christie was a product of the English upper-middle class. That society with which she was so familiar became the setting for her plots during the more than 56 years of her writing life. Her dozens of mystery novels are known to readers around the world. Since her death in 1976, many writers of the genre have been billed as Christie's successors. And Christie fans are frustrated that the annual Christie mystery is no longer the event they eagerly awaited each year.

There was another side to Christie the writer. Even staunch Christie fans may be unaware that she wrote six romances under a pseudonym. Writing as Mary Westmacott was Christie's alternative to plotting mysteries as well as her escape from being First Lady or Queen of Mysteries. While she was a best seller in the mystery field, her six 'straight' novels never enjoyed the same success.

Christie was ingenious in outlining mysteries, and when she wrote her romance novels she put them together like detective novels with an element of mystery introduced into each. The Westmacott mystery factor, however, revolved around people's character or relationships among individuals. Christie was better able to introduce psychological elements into her Westmacott books than in her mysteries. Some read like psychological studies of the characters.

However, Christie was never able to become a great success as a romance or gothic writer. Indeed, if she had not also been Christie, Mary Westmacott might have disappeared from the literary world forever.

The Westmacott novels are simple in style. The plots are uncomplicated. They are all about women and their problems or their lifestyle. If one reads any of the Christie biographies or even her autobiography, another common trait becomes apparent: much that transpires in the novels resembles events in Christie's life.

In *Giants' Bread*, the first of the Westmacott romances, Christie utilized her love for music in the plot and emphasized making choices based on personal preference as well as society's expectations. This book appeared about the time of her remarriage, two years after her divorce from Archibald Christie. There is a typical Christie country house setting. Tragic deaths in the Boer War and World War I create twists in the plots and force the characters into unfamiliar life styles. It was while her first husband was serving in World War I that Christie began writing; her first mystery was finally accepted for publication in 1920. After her husband's return from the war, the marriage began to founder. Thus, while planning and writing *Giants' Bread*, Christie herself was undergoing drastic changes in her life.

Christie's own childhood had been fairly quiet. She had been tutored by her mother and then had studied music in Paris. In both *Giants' Bread* and *Unfinished Portrait* the nursery motif, complete with mauve iris wallpaper, is repeated. In both these novels there is a tragedy leading to reduced family circumstances. Divorce from a husband depicted as a philanderer is another parallel to Christie's own life. Some biographers have felt Miriam in *Unfinished Portrait* is based on Christie's mother.

It was ten years before *Absent in the Spring* was published. The chief character, a woman en route back to England after visiting one daughter, spends several days in an isolated desert region, and begins thinking how she has controlled her husband's life to meet her desires in life rather than his, and how she has stage managed both daughters' lives. The isolation of the area and the lack of companionship force her into long periods of reflection. She must face the knowledge that she hasn't been the perfect wife and mother. Whether this is a parallel to Christie's life we don't know, but she incorporated her Middle East experiences with her second husband into the plot. Christie, writing from first hand experience, effectively depicts the isolation of the desert.

One of the talents of Christie the mystery writer was her use of narrators to tell the story. In *The Rose and the Yew Tree* an invalid becomes the very observant narrator of village life. Making unpopular life choices is the theme; characters with questionable backgrounds are the participants.

The last two Westmacott novels were written in the 1950s. *A Daughter's a Daughter* reverses the theme of *Absent in the Spring* with the daughter trying to manage her mother's romantic life. The two women almost reach the destructive point in their relationship before they realize what is happening. In *The Burden* a sister is guilt ridden by her brother's death and her wish for her sister's death. She seeks refuge in working for good causes.

Characteristic of the Westmacott books are several factors: deaths, usually in a war, causing reduced financial circumstances; choices made that are based on what society expects; the difficulty of making decisions that will change one's life; punishment of self for misdeeds imagined or real. Several settings or parts of stories are carried from book to book.

Because of her use of events from her own life, the reader may wonder if the plotting and writing of these romance novels was a form of catharsis for her. Was Mary Westmacott the depicter of what Christie envisioned happening or wanted to happen? The Westmacott novels often end unresolved or with endings unsatisfactory to the characters. Is this how Christie expected life to be? These novels lack the spark and plotting of the Christie mysteries, but offer a glimpse into how Christie viewed life.

—Jennifer Cargill

———

WESTWOOD, Gwen. British. 1915—. See 2nd edition, 1990.

———

WEYMAN, Stanley (John).
Nationality: British. **Born:** Ludlow, Shropshire, 7 August 1855. **Education:** Shrewsbury School; Christ Church College, Oxford, B.A. in modern history. **Career:** history master, King's School, Chester, one year. Called to the Bar, Inner Temple, London, 1881; lawyer for six years. Imprisoned in France for suspected espionage, 1886. Lived in Plas Llanrhyd, Denbighshire. **Died:** 10 April 1928.

ROMANCE AND HISTORICAL PUBLICATIONS

Novels

The House of the Wolf. London, Longman, 1890.
The New Rector. London, Smith Elder, 2 vols, 1891.
The Story of Francis Cludde. London, Cassell, 1891; New York, Longman, 1898.
A Gentleman of France, Being the Memoirs of Gaston de Bonne, Sieur de Marsac. London, Longman, 3 vols, 1893.
The Man in Black. London, Cassell, and New York, Longman, 1894.
My Lady Rotha. London, Cassell, and New York, Longman, 1894.
Under the Red Robe. London, Methuen, 2 vols, and New York, Longman, 2 vols, 1894.
From the Memoirs of a Minister of France. London, Cassell, and New York, Longman, 1895.
The Red Cockade. London, Longman, 1895; New York, Harper, 1896.
The Castle Inn. London, Smith Elder, and New York, Longman, 1898.
Shrewsbury: A Romance. London, Longman, 1898.
Sophia. London, Longman, 1900.
Count Hannibal. London, Smith Elder, and New York, Longman, 1901.
The Long Night. London, Longman, and New York, McClure Phillips, 1903.
The Abbess of Vlaye. London, Longman, 1904.
Starvecrow Farm. London, Hutchinson, and New York, Longman, 1905.
Chippinge. London, Smith Elder, 1906; as *Chippinge Borough*, New York, McClure Phillips, 1906.
The Great House. London, Murray, and New York, Longman, 1919.
Ovington's Bank. London, Murray, and New York, Longman, 1922.
The Traveller in the Fur Coat. London, Hutchinson, and New York, Longman, 1924.
Queen's Folly. London, Murray, and New York, Longman, 1925.

Short Stories

The King's Stratagem and Other Stories. New York, Caldwell, 1891.
For the Cause. Chicago, Sergel, 1897.
In King's Byways. London, Smith Elder, and New York, Longman, 1902.
Laid Up in Lavender. London, Smith Elder, and New York, Longman, 1907.

OTHER PUBLICATIONS

Novels

A Little Wizard. New York, Fenno, 1895.
The Wild Geese. London, Hodder and Stoughton, 1908; New York, Doubleday, 1909.
The Lively Peggy. London, Murray, and New York, Longman, 1928.

*   *   *

Stanley Weyman's novels present a colourful panorama of different periods in English, German, Swiss, and French history, from the middle of the 16th century to the end of the 18th, with an occasional look at 19th-century England in such tales as *Ovington's Bank*. Despite this range, Weyman was most famous in his day and is best remembered now for his swashbuckling romances of France in the stirring times of the last of the Valois kings and the first of the Bourbons.

The general influence of the swashbuckling tradition begun with such engaging vigour during the Romantic period by Alexandre Dumas *père*, the author of *The Three Musketeers* and a host of similar romances, certainly should not be discounted The more direct source of inspiration when Weyman turned to writing historical fiction was, however, the six-volume *History of the Huguenots*, published between 1879 and 1895, in which the eminent American scholar H. M. Baird explored sympathetically the long struggle of the French Protestants from the time of the Reformation, through the grim period of the Wars of Religion which culminated in the triumph of the charismatic Henri of Navarre, who became king of France in 1589, and on to the reassertion of Catholic supremacy under Richelieu and the final rejection of compromise between warring religious factions with the revocation of the Edict of Nantes in 1688. In these well documented accounts of troubled times when passions ran high and great personalities emerged and asserted their individuality Weyman did not only find exciting tales of derring-do, with gentlemen of high principle galloping across hostile country to save their masters from treachery and generally being rewarded for their breath-taking, hair's-breadth escapes with the love of some innocent maiden whose loveliness they had once glimpsed from afar. He also discovered characters and attitudes that appealed directly to his rather narrow preferences, which were, it must be added, those of many of his readers. He was not enough of an historian to think that more sympathy for Catholicism would have been fitting when treating French history. He was less concerned with being dispassionate than in finding vivid characters in strong situations.

Historical events, such as the massacre of St Bartholomew's Eve in 1572 or the assassination of the Duke de Guise 16 years later, are the foundations of Weyman's romances, and he takes some care over accuracy both in events and background. Though historical characters, also introduced with some scruple for fact, determine the general pattern of the action and cross the scene from time to time, the main focus of attention is on heroes who are Weyman's invention, albeit that imagination is tempered with some concern for truth to type. They are witnesses to the affairs of state with whom the reader can readily identify, rather than the personages who determine the outcome of history. It has to be admitted that their psychology is generally only fairly rudimentary, even in *A Gentleman of France*, the novel that really made Weyman's reputation in 1893 and is couched in the form of a first-person memoir. Gaston de Bonne, Sieur de Marsac, tells a rattling good yarn, but most of the time he has little idea of what is actually going on and his reflections on his predicament, even with the benefits of hindsight, are generally superficial, not to say puerile. There is some love interest too, but it is handled in a gingerly fashion, with females making only brief appearances. Weyman's narrative manner is leisurely and well-ordered, and his language, in dialogue as well as descriptions, tends to be staid, with a certain amount of archaism and, worse still, some display of erudition.

Weyman's romances still possess a certain boyish charm, and as well as *A Gentleman of France*, *Under the Red Robe* (in the France of Richelieu), *The Long Night* (featuring the famous 'night escalade' of Geneva in 1602), and *The Red Cockade* (a tale of Royalists during the French Revolution) are all worth the effort they demand of the reader. The stories in the collection called *In King's Byways* will provide a somewhat less strenuous introduction to Weyman's style of historical fiction.

—Christopher N. Smith

_____

WHARTON, Edith.
Pseudonym: David Olivieri. **Nationality:** American. **Born:** Edith Newbold Jones, New York City, 24 January 1862. **Education:** privately. **Relations:** married Edward Wharton in 1885 (divorced, 1913). Close friend of Henry James. **Career:** travelled in Italy, Spain, and France as a child; lived in Newport, Rhode Island, and in Europe from 1907. Helped organize the American Hostel for Refugees, and the Children of Flanders Rescue Committee, during World War I. **Recipient:** Pulitzer prize, 1921; American Academy gold medal, 1924. D.Litt.: Yale University, New Haven, Connecticut, 1923. Chevalier, Légion d'honneur, 1916; Order of Leopold (Belgium), 1919. **Member:** American Academy, 1930. **Died:** 11 August 1937.

ROMANCE AND HISTORICAL PUBLICATIONS

Novels

The Touchstone. New York, Scribner, 1900; as *A Gift from the Grave*, London, Murray, 1900.
The Valley of Decision. London, Murray, and New York, Scribner, 1902.
Sanctuary. London, Macmillan, and New York, Scribner, 1903.
The House of Mirth. London, Macmillan, and New York, Scribner, 1905; edited by Elizabeth Ammons, New York, Norton, 1990.
Madame de Treymes. London, Macmillan, and New York, Scribner, 1907.
The Fruit of the Tree. London, Macmillan, and New York, Scribner, 1907.
Ethan Frome. London, Macmillan, and New York, Scribner, 1911; edited by Blake Nevius, 1968.
The Reef. London, Macmillan, and New York, Scribner, 1912.
The Custom of the Country. London, Macmillan, and New York, Scribner, 1913.
Summer. London, Macmillan, and New York, Appleton, 1917.
The Marne: A Tale of the War. London, Macmillan, and New York, Appleton, 1918.
The Age of Innocence. London, and New York, Appleton, 1920.

The Glimpses of the Moon. New York, Appleton, 1922; London, Macmillan, 1923.

A Son at the Front. London, Macmillan, and New York, Appleton, 1923.

Old New York: False Dawn (The 'forties), The Old Maid (The 'fifties), The Spark (The 'sixties), New Year's Day (The 'seventies). London, and New York, Appleton, 1924.

The Mother's Recompense. London, and New York, Appleton, 1925.

Twilight Sleep. London, and New York, Appleton, 1927.

The Children. New York, Appleton, 1928; as *The Marriage Playground*, New York, Grosset and Dunlap, 1930.

Hudson River Bracketed. London, and New York, Appleton, 1929.

The Gods Arrive. London, and New York, Appleton, 1932.

The Buccaneers (incomplete, published posthumously). London, and New York, Appleton, 1938; (completed by Marion Mainwaring) New York, Viking, 1993; with *Fast and Loose*, edited by Violet Hopkins Winner, Charlottesville, University Press of Virginia, 1993.

Short Stories

The Greater Inclination. London, Lane, and New York, Scribner, 1899.

Crucial Instances. London, Murray, and New York, Scribner, 1901.

The Descent of Man and Other Stories. London, Macmillan, and New York, Scribner, 1904.

The Hermit and the Wild Woman, and Other Stories. London, Macmillan, and New York, Scribner, 1908.

Xingu and Other Stories. London, Macmillan, and New York, Scribner, 1916.

Tales of Men and Ghosts. London, Macmillan, and New York, Scribner, 1920.

Here and Beyond. London, and New York, Appleton, 1926.

Certain People. London, and New York, Appleton, 1930.

Human Nature. London, and New York, Appleton, 1933.

The World Over. London, and New York, Appleton, 1936.

Ghosts. London, and New York, Appleton, 1937.

Fast and Loose: A Novelette (as David Olivieri), edited by Viola Hopkins Winner, Charlottesville, University Press of Virginia, 1977; with *The Buccaneers*, edited by Viola Hopkins Winner, Charlottesville, University Press of Virginia, 1993.

Collected Short Stories, edited by R.W.B. Lewis, New York, Scribner, 1968.

Plays

The Joy of Living, from a play by Hermann Sudermann (produced, 1902).

The House of Mirth, from the novel by Wharton, with Clyde Fitch (produced 1906).

Poetry

Verses. Newport, Rhode Island, published anonymously, 1878.

Artemis to Actaeon and Other Verse. London, Macmillan, and New York, Scribner, 1909.

Twelve Poems. London, Medici Society, 1926.

Other

The Decoration of Houses, with Ogden Codman, Jr. London, Batsford, 1897; New York, Scribner, 1898.

Italian Villas and Their Gardens. London, Bodley Head, and New York, Century, 1904.

Italian Backgrounds. London, Macmillan, and New York, Scribner, 1905.

A Motor-Flight Through France. London, Macmillan, and New York, Scribner, 1908.

Fighting France: From Dunkerque to Belfort. London, Macmillan, and New York, Scribner, 1915.

Wharton's War Charities in France. N.p., 1918.

L'Amérique en Guerre. Paris, n.p., 1918.

French Ways and Their Meaning. London, Macmillan, and New York, Macmillan, 1919.

In Morocco. London, Macmillan, and New York, Scribner, 1920.

The Writing of Fiction. New York, Scribner, 1925.

A Background Glance (autobiography). London, and New York, Appleton, 1934.

An Edith Wharton Treasury, edited by Arthur Hobson Quinn. New York, Appleton, 1950.

Letters of Edith Wharton, edited by R.W.B. Lewis and Nancy Lewis. London, Simon and Schuster, 1988.

Henry James and Edith Wharton Letters, 1900–15, edited by Lyall H. Powers. London, Weidenfeld and Nicholson, 1990.

Editor, *Le Livre des sans-foyer.* 1915; as *The Book of the Homeless: Original Articles in Verse and Prose*, London, Macmillan, 1916.

Editor, with Robert Norton, *Eternal Passion in English Poetry.* 1939.

Translator, *The Joy of Living* by Hermann Sudermann, New York, Scribner, 1902.

*

Film Adaptations: *The House of Mirth* (silent), 1905; *The Glimpses of the Moon* (silent), 1923; *The Age of Innocence*, (silent), 1924, (sound), 1934, 1993; *The Marriage Playground*, 1929, from the novel *The Children*; *The Old Maid*, 1939; *Ethan Frome*, 1993.

Bibliography: *A Bibliography of the Writings of Edith Wharton* by Lavina Davis, Portland, Maine, Southworth Press, 1933; *Wharton: A Bibliography* by Vito J. Brenni, Morgantown, West Virginia University Library, 1966; *Wharton and Kate Chopin: A Reference Guide* by Marlene Springer, Boston, Hall, 1976; *Edith Wharton: An Annotated Secondary Bibliography* by Kristin O. Lauer and M.P. Murray, New York, Garland, 1990; *Edith Wharton: A Descriptive Bibliography* by Steven Garrison, Pittsburgh, Pennsylvannia, University of Pittsburgh Press, 1990.

Critical Studies: *Wharton: A Study of Her Fiction* by Blake Nevius, Berkeley, University of California Press, 1953; *Wharton: Convention and Morality in the Work of a Novelist* by Marilyn Jones Lyde, Norman, Oklahoma, University of Oklahoma, 1959; *Wharton*, Minneapolis, University of Minnesota, 1961, and *Wharton: A Woman in Her Time*, Minneapolis, University of Minnesota, 1971, both by Louis Auchincloss; *Wharton: A Collection of Critical Essays* edited by Irving Howe, New York, Prentice-Hall, 1962; *Wharton and Henry James: The Story of Their Friendship* by Millicent Bell, New York, Braziller, 1965; *Wharton: A Critical Interpretation* by Geoffrey Walton, New York, Fairleigh Dickinson University Press, 1970, revised edition, 1982; *Wharton: A Biography* by R.W.B. Lewis, London, Constable, and New York, Harper and Row, 1975; *Wharton and the Novel of Manners* by Gary Lindberg, Charlottesville, University Press of Virginia, 1975; *Edith Wharton* by Margaret B. McDowell, Boston, Twayne, 1976; *Edith Wharton* by Richard H. Lawson, New York, Ungar, 1977; *The Feast of Words: The Triumph of Edith Wharton* by Cynthia Griffin Wolff, Oxford, Oxford University Press, 1977; *Wharton's Argument with America* by Elizabeth Ammons, Athens, University of Georgia Press, 1980; *Wharton: Orphancy and Survival* by Wendy Gimbel, New York, Praeger, 1984; *Edith Wharton's New York Quartet* by Catherine M. Rae, Lanham, Maryland, University Press of America, 1984; *After the Fall, the Demeter-Persephone Myth in Wharton, Cather, and Glasgow* by Josephine Donovan, University Park, London, Pennsylvannia State University Press, 1989; *Edith Wharton and the Art of Fiction* by Penelope Vita-Finzi, London, Pinter, 1990; *Edith Wharton, Traveller in the Land of Letters* by Janet Goodwyn, London, Macmillan, 1990; *Edith Wharton's Women Friends and Rivals* by Susan Goodman, Hanover, New Hampshire, University of New England, 1990; *Verging on the Abyss, the Social Fiction of Kate Chopin and Edith Wharton* by Mary E. Papke, New York, Greenwood Press, 1990; *The Sexual Education of Edith Wharton* by Gloria C. Erlich, Berkley, University of California Press, 1992; *Edith Wharton and the Unsatisfactory Man* by David Holbrook, London, Vision, 1992; *Edith Wharton* by Katherine Joslin, London, Macmillan, 1992; *Edith Wharton: The Contemporary Reviews* edited by James W. Tuttleton, Kristin O. Lauer, and Margaret P. Murray, Cambridge, Cambridge University Press, 1993.

*   *   *

Edith Wharton's relation to popular traditions has been both over- and under-played. On the one hand her reputation has suffered in the usual way of the woman writer from the identification of her work with the romantic novelette. Wharton pursued bestseller status, but at the same time was often in dispute with such organs as *Ladies' Home Journal* and *Pictorial Review* over their attempts to cut her work in the interests of popularization. John Bayley comments that her style 'steers very close to a woman's magazine but usually shaves past it'.

Certainly, on occasion it is a fairly close shave. On the other hand the recognition that popular forms may serve to express occluded female realities has illuminated Wharton's career. Elizabeth Ammons, one of Wharton's most perceptive critics, has highlighted her use of muckraking (*The Fruit of the Tree*), melodrama (*The Touchstone*), historical romance (*The Valley of Decision*) and society novel (*The House of Mirth*), noting that Wharton wrote against the tide of contemporary bestsellers. Where turn-of-the-century America popularized the adventure story in which the heroine rebelled successfully against the past, Wharton tended to portray her heroines in defeat and disillusion. The same revisionary intent is visible in each of her forays into popular forms. Something of her later attitude is foreshadowed in her first major literary venture, a 30000 word novel, *Fast and Loose*, written secretly at the age of 15. As its title suggests the novel launched Wharton on her favourite topic, ill-starred romance. Yet she also composed fictitious reviews, roundly condemning it. Similarly, *The Valley of Decision*, Wharton's only major historical novel, draws upon the popular convention while also undermining it. The scene is set in 1761, in an imaginary Italian kingdom, heavily freighted with historical and geographical detail, and very much in the mould of such contemporary bestsellers as *Ben Hur* or *The Prisoner of Zenda*. The hero, Odo, is a liberal intent on reforming the constitution of his native land, curtailing the power of the church in favour of the interests of the people. In this project he is inspired by his mistress, Fulvia (whom he rescues from incarceration in a convent) a learned radical and type of the 'New Woman' who has no sooner returned to Odo's side (incidentally collecting a doctorate of philosophy) when there is a popular uprising *against* reform, and she is shot dead. Astutely Wharton uses the popular historical form to undermine political populism. Odo's subjects resist the freedoms which he has thrust upon them, and the hero, embittered, returns to the conservative fold. It is now 1795, and in the denouement the triumph of Napoleon entails Odo's rejection by his former Liberal allies who force his abdication. The novel's opposition of progressivism and traditionalism is firmly weighted towards the latter, with the French Revolution invoked only as an index of the brutalities carried out in the name of liberty. Indeed the novel has been read persuasively (by

Cynthia Griffin Wolff) as consciously composed *contra* Stendhal, ending where *La Chartreuse de Parme (The Charterhouse of Parma)* begins, but in disillusionment. For all the novel's political interest, however, critical reaction has been varied. *The Valley of Decision* sold reasonably well, but it had been heavily researched and Wharton did not always carry her considerable learning lightly. The plot struggles to survive beneath incidental details. Odo, while one of her more sympathetic characters, exemplifies the meaning of the phrase 'woolly liberalism'. His relationship with Fulvia, though between intellectual equals, does not carry erotic conviction. (Though Wharton was, perhaps, more daring than the modern reader appreciates. Roosevelt ignored the political theme but took Wharton to task for her portrayal of an illicit love relationship.) Henry James was warm in the novel's praise but also suggested that she should choose American subjects in future.

Although Wharton followed James's advice, the process of simultaneously exploiting and undermining popular forms continued in her later career, particularly in relation to her major theme of romantic passion. Where New England had been sentimentalized by regionalists in 'local colour' novels, Wharton's *Ethan Frome* painted a chilling picture of a culturally bankrupt community. The novella ends, not with the deaths of the lovers (wilfully crashing their sledge into a tree) but with survival into a half-life, the hero shackled forever to his crippled lover, now indistinguishable in whining misery from his hypochondriac wife. *The Custom of the Country* models its characters and plot on George Sand's *Indiana*, but the norms of romance are reshaped to ironic ends, as one might expect from a writer influenced by Darwin, Nietzsche, and Herbert Spencer. In the heroine, Undine Spragg, Wharton creates the 'American Girl' without the innocence of a Daisy Miller (or Henry James?). Undine is scheming, grasping, social-climbing, and utterly without redeeming scruple, and she flourishes cheerfully at the expense of husbands and offspring. In contrast Undine's polar opposite, Lily Bart, in *The House of Mirth*, descends steadily down the rungs of the social ladder in a novel which lambasts romantic delusions and establishes marriage as a commercial transaction. Relentlessly economic in focus *The House of Mirth* sold 30,000 copies in three weeks; 'Wall Street' novels were in vogue. Wharton's other romantic fiction is similarly attentive to issues of social and sexual politics. *The Reef*, for example, swiftly establishes sexual relations as the reef that shipwrecks the society individual. In the nymphet-heroine of *The Children* Wharton anticipates Nabokov's understanding of the American desire for infantilized women. Even her ghost stories (almost a third of her published tales) make social points, introducing what has been termed 'Business Gothic' in which the concealed forms of greed produce the disturbing effects.

Wharton's historical and romantic interests came together only once with complete success. Modern readers may well be familiar with 'The Old Maid' from the screen version (memorably filmed starring Bette Davis) as a romantic melodrama in which the eponymous heroine's illegitimate child never *does* call her mother, and her own love affair is brutally terminated. The tale takes its full meaning, however, from its position in a sequence of four novellas ('False Dawn', 'The Old Maid', 'The Spark', 'New Year's Day') which provide a decade-by-decade chronology of New York, from the 1840s to the 1870s. Here sexual mores are firmly bound to social contexts, art (in the characters of Whitman and Ruskin) interrogated in relation to political and economic values, and romance firmly subordinated to historical understanding.

—Judie Newman

WHITBY, Sharon. See **PETERS, Maureen.**

WHITE, Harriet.   See **HORNER, Lance, Kyle ONSTOTT, and Ashley CARTER.**

WHITE, Patrick (Victor Martindale).
Nationality: Australian. **Born:** London, England, 28 May 1912. **Education:** Tudor House, Moss Vale, and other schools in Australia, 1919–25; Cheltenham College, England, 1925–29; King's College, Cambridge, 1932–35, B.A. in modern languages 1935. **Military Service:** Royal Air Force, in the Middle East, 1941–45: Intelligence Officer. **Career:** travelled in Europe and the United States, and lived in London, before World War II; returned to Australia in 1948. **Recipient:** Australian Literature Society gold medal, 1939, for *Happy Valley*; Miles Franklin award, 1958, 1962; W.H. Smith award, 1959; National Conference of Christians and Jews Brotherhood award, 1962; Nobel prize for literature, 1973. AC (Companion, Order of Australia), 1975 (returned 1976). **Died:** 30 September 1990.

ROMANCE AND HISTORICAL PUBLICATIONS

Novels

The Tree of Man. New York, Viking Press, 1955; London, Eyre and Spottiswoode, 1956.
Voss. New York, Viking Press, and London, Eyre and Spottiswoode, 1957.
A Fringe of Leaves. London, Cape, 1976; New York, Viking Press, 1977.

OTHER PUBLICATIONS

Novels

Happy Valley. London, Harrap, 1939; New York, Viking Press, 1940.
The Living and the Dead. London, Routledge, and New York, Viking Press, 1941.
The Aunt's Story. London, Routledge, and New York, Viking Press, 1948.
Riders in the Chariot. New York, Viking Press, and London, Eyre and Spottiswoode, 1961.
The Solid Mandala. New York, Viking Press, and London, Eyre and Spottiswoode, 1966.
The Vivisector. New York, Viking Press, and London, Cape, 1970.
The Eye of the Storm. London, Cape, 1973; New York, Viking Press, 1974.
The Twyborn Affair. London, Cape, 1979; New York, Viking Press, 1980.
Memoirs of Many in One. London, Cape, and New York, Viking Press, 1986.

Short Stories

The Burnt Ones. New York, Viking Press, and London, Eyre and Spottiswoode, 1964.
The Cockatoos: Shorter Novels and Stories. London, Cape, 1974; New York, Viking Press, 1975.
A Cheery Soul and Other Stories. Tokyo, Kenkyusha, 1983.
Three Uneasy Pieces. London, Cape, 1988.

Plays

Bread and Butter Women (produced Sydney, 1935).

The School for Friends (produced Sydney, 1935).
Return to Abyssinia (produced London, 1947).
The Ham Funeral (produced Adelaide, 1961; Crewe, Cheshire, 1969). In *Four Plays*, 1965.
The Season at Sarsaparilla (produced Adelaide, 1962). In *Four Plays*, 1965.
A Cheery Soul, adaptation of his own story (produced Melbourne, 1963). Included in *Four Plays*, 1965.
Night on Bald Mountain (produced Adelaide, 1964). In *Four Plays*, 1965.
Four Plays. London, Eyre and Spottiswoode, 1965; New York, Viking Press, 1966; as *Collected Plays I*, Sydney, Currency Press, 1985.
Big Toys (produced Sydney, 1977). Sydney, Currency Press, 1978.
The Night the Prowler (screenplay). Melbourne, Penguin, 1977.
Signal Driver: A Morality Play for the Times (produced Adelaide, 1982). Sydney, Currency Press, 1983.
Netherwood (produced Adelaide, 1983). Sydney, Currency Press, 1983.
Shepherd on the Rocks (produced Adelaide, 1983).

Screenplay: *The Night the Prowler*, 1979.

Poetry

Thirteen Poems. Privately printed, 1930(?).
The Ploughman and Other Poems. Sydney, Beacon Press, 1935.
Habitable Places: Poems New and Selected. Dunvegan, Ontario, Cormorant, 1988.

Other

Flaws in the Glass: A Self-Portrait. London, Cape, 1981; New York, Viking Press, 1982.
Patrick White Speaks. London, Cape, 1990.

*

Bibliography: *A Bibliography of Patrick White* by Janette Finch, Adelaide, Libraries Board of South Australia, 1966.

Critical Studies (selection): *Patrick White* by Geoffrey Dutton, Melbourne, Lansdowne Press, 1961, revised edition, Melbourne, London, and New York, Oxford University Press, 1971; *Patrick White* by Robert F. Brissenden, London, Longman, 1966; *Patrick White* by Barry Argyle, Edinburgh, Oliver and Boyd, 1967; *Ten Essays on Patrick White Selected from Southerly* edited by G. A. Wilkes, Sydney and London, Angus and Robertson, 1970; *The Mystery of Unity: Theme and Technique in the Novels of Patrick White* by Patricia A. Morley, Montreal, McGill-Queen's University Press, 1972; *Fossil and Psyche* by Wilson Harris, Austin, University of Texas, 1974; *Patrick White* by Alan Lawson, Melbourne and New York, Oxford University Press, 1974, London, Oxford University Press, 1975; *The Eye in the Mandala: Patrick White: A Vision of Man and God* by Peter Beatson, London, Elek, and New York, Barnes and Noble, 1976; *Patrick White: A General Introduction* by Ingmar Bjorksten, translated by Stanley Gerson, St Lucia, University of Queensland Press, and Atlantic Highlands, New Jersey, Humanities Press, 1976; *Patrick White's Fiction* by William Walsh, London, Allen and Unwin, and Totowa, New Jersey, Rowman and Littlefield, 1977; *Patrick White: A Critical Symposium* edited by Ron E. Shepherd and Kirpal Singh, Bedford Park, South Australia, Flinders University Centre for Research, and Washington, DC, Three Continents, 1978; *Patrick White* by Manly Johnson, New York, Ungar, 1980; *Patrick White* by Brian Kiernan, London, Macmillan, and New York, St Martin's Press, 1980; *A Tragic Vision: The Novels of*

Patrick White by A.M. McCulloch, St Lucia, University of Queensland Press, 1983; *Aspects of Time, Ageing and Old Age in the Novels of Patrick White 1939-1979* by Mari-Ann Berg, Gothenburg, Gothenburg Studies in English, 1983; *Laden Choirs: The Fiction of Patrick White* by Peter Wolfe, Lexington, University Press of Kentucky, 1983; *Patrick White* by John Colmer, London, Methuen, 1984; *Patrick White* by John A. Weigel, Boston, Twayne, 1984; *Patrick White's Fiction: The Paradox of Fortunate Failure* by Carolyn Bliss, London, Macmillan, 1986; *Patrick White: Fiction and the Unconscious* by David J. Tacey, Oxford, Oxford University Press, 1988; *Vision and Style in Patrick White: A Study of Five Novels* by Rodney Stenning Edgecombe, University, University of Alabama Press, 1989; *Patrick White: A Life* by David Marr, New York, Knopf, 1992.

*   *   *

Patrick White, the 1973 Nobel Laureate and the grand old man of Australian letters, spearheaded the astonishing Antipodean literary movement which has developed since the end of World War II. Although a third-generation Australian, White was born in England, and spent the majority of his formative years from the age of 13 onwards in both England and Europe. This distancing from his true native roots at such a time enabled him, in many of the novels and short stories that he wrote after his permanent return to Australia in 1948, to contrast with a detached, quasi-European eye and sensibility the vast emptiness of the Australian interior with the crowded and swiftly expanding middle-class urban communities on the coast.

The fundamental conflict between nature and civilization is one of the principal themes inherent in each of his three historical novels, *The Tree of Man*, *Voss*, and *A Fringe of Leaves*. *The Tree of Man*, the first book White published (perhaps significantly following a seven-year silence) after returning to Australia, can be viewed in retrospect as possibly the book he felt the need to write to dispel the vestigial influences of what he had come to regard as the sterile intellectualism of post-war England, and thus establish a fresh, uncluttered base on which to build his future work. In many respects, *The Tree of Man* is the most purely indigenous of all White's major novels. While White does not entirely succeed in making the lives of his ordinary and mainly inarticulate main characters consistently interesting, this long, dense narrative certainly never becomes turgid in the telling. It follows the fortunes of Stan and Amy Parker and their neighbours as they struggle against drought, fire, and flood to bring up their families, and attempt to tame and cultivate the wilderness around the tiny community they have founded a few miles from turn-of-the-century Sydney. The uneasy Eden these simple folk have created is, however, under constant threat, not only from the elements but from civilization itself. The city limits encroach nearer and nearer, until eventually the tiny community is overrun and becomes absorbed into the suburbs.

There is, on the other hand, nothing intrinsically 'ordinary' about the characters in *Voss*, considered by many to be White's masterpiece. Loosely based on historical fact—Ludwig Leichhardt's ill-fated expedition of 1848 to cross the Australian continent from east to west—*Voss* tells the saga of a similar fictional expedition in the 1840s, led by the German, Johann Ulrich Voss. A supreme egoist and a precursor of the Nietzsche superman figure, Voss is financed by a prosperous Sydney draper, Edmund Bonner, and embarks with six disparate companions on his ill-conceived and ill-prepared journey, unshakeably confident of ultimate success. Voss's ruthless egoism and manic obsession inevitably spark off a mutiny, instigated by the ex-convict, Judd. Judd deserts, taking two others of the party with him. The remaining four men, accompanied by an aborigine guide, Jackie, whom they acquired en route, press on into the unknown. One of the four meets his death at the hands of the

tribe of aborigines which has been shadowing the little band; another commits suicide; another dies of hunger and exhaustion. Finally, Voss, ill and in a delirium, alone in the terrible landscape of the outback and surrounded by the hostile aborigines, is put to death by Jackie, who stabs him and then messily decapitates him. In the true-life Leichhardt expedition, there were no survivors and no trace was ever found of its members. In *Voss*, however, the mutineer Judd does survive, and returns to civilization 20 years later to tell his distorted version of events. Superimposed upon the story of the expedition is the strange love of Voss and Bonner's niece, Laura Trevelyan. Their love for each other is born during the few occasions on which they meet prior to Voss's departure into the interior, and then is subsequently perpetuated not only by correspondence, most of which is, of course, never delivered, but more potently by a powerful telepathic contact. Laura suffers Voss's vicissitudes by proxy. When he is killed, she is smitten by a mysterious illness, and almost succumbs. This mystical unity between Voss and Laura gives a tremendous, unforgettable depth to the novel, and is, moreover, perhaps the most convincing depiction of pure love between a man and a woman in the whole of White's fiction.

A Fringe of Leaves is also based on historical fact. Set in the 1830s, it follows fairly closely the story of Mrs Elizabeth Fraser (see, for example, Michael Alexander's 1971 account, *Mrs Fraser on the Fatal Shore*). The novel relates how Ellen Roxburgh, a respectable member of Moreton Bay society, returning with her husband by sea from a visit to her brother-in-law in Van Diemen's Land, is shipwrecked off the coast of Queensland. Passengers and crew take to the longboat, and after several weeks—during which Ellen, the only female among the survivors, gives birth to a stillborn child—they land on an in-hospitable shore. They are captured by aborigines, and all the men are killed. Ellen is taken into captivity, stripped of her clothes, and treated as a slave. She is able to survive all these ordeals by drawing on the resilience acquired from her lower class origins in Cornwall. Eventually, she is rescued by an escaped convict, Jack Chance, and returned to civilization, but back in Moreton Bay experiences some difficulty in accepting again the mantle of middle-class respectability her marriage had given her. In *A Fringe of Leaves*, the conflict between nature (in this case, the uninhibited, ritual society of the aborigines) and civilization (the artificial elegance and etiquette of 19th-century colonial society) is portrayed in consummate fashion in its most basic terms.

White wrote in a highly individual and mannered prose style, a style that vividly conveys the vast emptiness and awful grandeur of the Australian landscape, and provides what is at times an almost unbearable insight into the human psyche. White is one of the most carnal of modern intellectual writers; his obvious distaste for the frailties (in all aspects) of human flesh become more pronounced in his later work, as did the bitter and savage satirical posture he so often adopted when describing the mores of middle-class society. White was a writer of genius, and indisputably the most considerable literary figure to have emerged from the Antipodes since World War II.

—Roy S. Simmonds

————

WHITE, T(erence) H(anbury).   British. 1906–64. See 2nd edition, 1990.

————

WHITMORE, Cilla.   See **SEBASTIAN, Margaret.**

————

WHITNEY, Hallam.   See **HORNER, Lance, Kyle ONSTOTT, and Ashley CARTER.**

———

WHITNEY, Phyllis A(yame).
Nationality: American. **Born:** Yokohama, Japan, 9 September 1903. **Education:** schools in Japan, China, the Philippines, California, and Texas; McKinley High School, Chicago, graduated 1924. **Relations:** married 1) George A. Garner in 1925 (divorced 1945), one daughter; 2) Lovell F. Jahnke in 1950 (died 1973). **Career:** dance instructor, San Antonio, Texas, one year; children's books editor, Chicago *Sun*, 1942–46, and Philadelphia *Inquirer*, 1947–48; instructor in children's fiction writing, Northwestern University, Evanston, Illinois, 1945, New York University, 1947–58, and University of Colorado, Denver, 1952, 1954, 1956. Member, Board of Directors, 1959–62, and president, 1975, Mystery Writers of America. Lives in Brookhaven, Long Island, New York. **Recipient:** Mystery Writers of America Edgar Allan Poe award, for children's book, 1961, 1964, and Grand Master award, 1984. **Agent:** c/o McIntosh and Otis Inc, 310 Madison Avenue, New York, New York 10017, USA.

ROMANCE AND HISTORICAL PUBLICATIONS

Novels

Red Is for Murder. Chicago, Ziff Davis, 1943; as *Red Carnelian*, New York, Paperback Library, 1968; London, Coronet, 1976.
The Quicksilver Pool. New York, Appleton Century Crofts, 1955; London, Coronet, 1973.
The Trembling Hills. New York, Appleton Century Crofts, 1956; London, Coronet, 1974.
Skye Cameron. New York, Appleton Century Crofts, 1957; London, Hurst and Blackett, 1959.
The Moonflower. New York, Appleton Century Crofts, 1958; as *The Mask and the Moonflower*, London, Hurst and Blackett, 1960.
Thunder Heights. New York, Appleton Century Crofts, 1960; London, Coronet, 1973.
Blue Fire. New York, Appleton Century Crofts, 1961; London, Hodder and Stoughton, 1962.
Window on the Square. New York, Appleton Century Crofts, 1962; London, Coronet, 1969.
Seven Tears for Apollo. New York, Appleton Century Crofts, 1963; London, Coronet, 1969.
Black Amber. New York, Appleton Century Crofts, 1964; London, Hale, 1965.
Sea Jade. New York, Appleton Century Crofts, 1965; London, Hale, 1966.
Columbella. New York, Doubleday, 1966; London, Hale, 1967.
Silverhill. New York, Doubleday, 1967; London, Heinemann, 1968.
Hunter's Green. New York, Doubleday, 1968; London, Heinemann, 1969.
The Winter People. New York, Doubleday, 1969; London, Heinemann, 1970.
Lost Island. New York, Doubleday, 1970; London, Heinemann, 1971.
Listen for the Whisperer. New York, Doubleday, and London, Heinemann, 1972.
Snowfire. New York, Doubleday, and London, Heinemann, 1973.
The Turquoise Mask. New York, Doubleday, 1974; London, Heinemann, 1975.
Spindrift. New York, Doubleday, and London, Heinemann, 1975.
The Golden Unicorn. New York, Doubleday, 1976; London, Heinemann, 1977.

The Stone Bull. New York, Doubleday, and London, Heinemann, 1977.
The Glass Flame. New York, Doubleday, 1978; London, Heinemann, 1979.
Domino. New York, Doubleday, 1979; London, Heinemann, 1980.
Poinciana. New York, Doubleday, 1980; London, Heinemann, 1981.
Vermilion. New York, Doubleday, 1981; London, Heinemann, 1982.
Emerald. New York, Doubleday, and London, Heinemann, 1983.
Rainsong. New York, Doubleday, and London, Heinemann, 1984.
Dream of Orchids. New York, Doubleday, and London, Hodder and Stoughton, 1985.
The Flaming Tree. New York, Doubleday, and London, Hodder and Stoughton, 1986.
Silversword. New York, Doubleday, and London, Hodder and Stoughton, 1987.
Feather on the Moon. New York, Doubleday, and London, Hodder and Stoughton, 1988.
Rainbow in the Mist. New York, Doubleday, and London, Hodder and Stoughton, 1989.
The Singing Stones. New York, Doubleday, and London, Hodder and Stoughton, 1990.
A Mystery of the Golden Horn. New York, Fawcett, 1990.
Woman Without a Past. New York, Doubleday, and London, Hodder and Stoughton, 1991.
The Ebony Swan. New York, Doubleday, 1992.
Star Flight. New York, Crown, 1993.

OTHER PUBLICATIONS

Fiction (for children)

A Place for Ann. Boston, Houghton Mifflin, 1941.
A Star for Ginny. Boston, Houghton Mifflin, 1942.
A Window for Julie. Boston, Houghton Mifflin, 1943.
The Silver Inkwell. Boston, Houghton Mifflin, 1945.
Window Hill. New York, Reynal, 1947.
Ever After. Boston, Houghton Mifflin, 1948.
Mystery of the Gulls. Philadelphia, Westminster Press, 1949.
Linda's Homecoming. Philadelphia, McKay, 1950.
The Island of Dark Woods. Philadelphia, Westminster Press, 1951; as *Mystery of the Strange Traveler*, 1967.
Love Me, Love Me Not. Boston, Houghton Mifflin, 1952.
Step to the Music. New York, Crowell, 1953.
Mystery of the Black Diamonds. Philadelphia, Westminster Press, 1954; as *Black Diamonds*, Leicester, Brockhampton Press, 1957.
A Long Time Coming. Philadelphia, McKay, 1954.
Mystery on the Isle of Skye. Philadelphia, Westminster Press, 1955.
The Fire and the Gold. New York, Crowell, 1956.
The Highest Dream. Philadelphia, McKay, 1956.
Mystery of the Green Cat. Philadelphia, Westminster Press, 1957.
Secret of the Samurai Sword. Philadelphia, Westminster Press, 1958.
Creole Holiday. Philadelphia, Westminster Press, 1959.
Mystery of the Haunted Pool. Philadelphia, Westminster Press, 1960.
Secret of the Tiger's Eye. Philadelphia, Westminster Press, 1961.
Mystery of the Golden Horn. Philadelphia, Westminster Press, 1962.
Mystery of the Hidden Hand. Philadelphia, Westminster Press, 1963.
Secret of the Emerald Star. Philadelphia, Westminster Press, 1964.
Mystery of the Angry Idol. Philadelphia, Westminster Press, 1965.
Secret of the Spotted Shell. Philadelphia, Westminster Press, 1967.

Secret of Goblin Glen. Philadelphia, Westminster Press, 1968.
The Mystery of the Crimson Ghost. Philadelphia, Westminster Press, 1969.
Secret of the Missing Footprint. Philadelphia, Westminster Press, 1969.
The Vanishing Scarecrow. Philadelphia, Westminster Press, 1971.
Nobody Likes Trina. Philadelphia, Westminster Press, 1972.
Mystery of the Scowling Boy. Philadelphia, Westminster Press, 1973.
Secret of Haunted Mesa. Philadelphia, Westminster Press, 1975.
Secret of the Stone Face. Philadelphia, Westminster Press, 1977.

Other

Writing Juvenile Fiction. Boston, The Writer, 1947; revised edition, 1960.
Writing Juvenile Stories and Novels: How to Write and Sell Fiction for Young People. Boston, The Writer, 1976.
Guide to Fiction Writing. Boston, The Writer, 1982; London, Poplar Press, 1984.

*

Manuscript Collection: Mugar Memorial Library, Boston University.

Phyllis A. Whitney comments:

Since I have lived in many different places, I have no 'roots'. Thus I must look for a fresh setting for each suspense novel I write. Once I have chosen my setting, I visit it to collect impressions and information firsthand. Then I do a great deal of research at home. Eventually, I develop a young woman character with a serious problem facing her, and in my imagination I set her down in the background I mean to use. Around her I place other characters who will bring conflict and further problems into her life. As these characters grow, both in my mind and on paper, my story begins to emerge a bit at a time, until the whole thing is clear before I write. The setting itself often becomes an important character in my novels.

*   *   *

When the hero of Phyllis A. Whitney's *Woman Without a Past* questions the value of romantic writing as a genre the heroine, a writer, replies, 'Romantic? Yes ... in its older definition, meaning something strange and exotic and mysteriously beautiful. Mystery without detectives'.

Whitney's novels were originally described as gothic. She decided this was a limited connotation and too confining. As she explains in *Writing the Romance Suspense Novel*, she wrote herself away from it by stating that she preferred 'romantic suspense' if she had to be catalogued.

The element of surprise is important in this type of fiction and Whitney does it well. She builds characters who seem obvious at first but then turn unpredictable and contrary. Even her worst character isn't totally bad just as her heroes and heroines are never totally without fault. Her villains are hard to recognize. Her plots often involve murder. Secrets are uncovered, some from the past, many ongoing, and all leading to surprise, building the tension, the anxiety, and fear. She paces this well—never too much too soon.

In her female characterizations she shows admiration for the young modern woman who fights her own battles as she strives to accomplish or discover something. The heroine's goal is made evident to the reader soon after the opening. In the process of winning through, she gains a true understanding of herself, discovers new depths of courage and realizes her life is changed forever. This is exemplified in *Spindrift* when the troubled heroine finally acknowledges her husband as the one she loves.

Whitney's heroines are complex creatures. They often have hang-ups, one trait warring against another. This leads the plot to unexpected confrontations and the characters to unanticipated action. These women are likeable; the reader is empathetic and knows they deserve to win because they earned it.

In *Woman Without a Past* the much put-upon heroine's only goal is to solve the mystery of her birth and her actions are forced upon her by others without the do-or-die scenario. In the end she solves the mystery and achieves relief from adversity. All Whitney heroines experience anxiety as they progress toward their goal. The author uses this fear to escalate the tension and direct the action. Fear takes many shapes in her novels and transforms and grows in different directions. Often the heroine doesn't know what it is she fears; it's a shadow behind her or a glimpse of something around the next corner.

Counterbalanced by such independent heroines, the heroes in her novels play an active and important role but develop slowly. They are interesting men, never stereotypical. And the author keeps us guessing throughout most of the story as to who is hero and who is villain. There's no doubt an unpredictable romance is more interesting than an obvious one!

In 'Springboard to Fiction' (*The Writer*, October 1976) Whitney wrote, 'My own springboard, from which I take off in the beginning, is usually a new setting. I have a strong feeling toward places.' Echoing the author, a character in *The Ebony Swan* who is also a writer, 'always sought first for the feeling of a place, his own reactions to it, before he looked for factual details'.

Plot and character work together. There is continual change. The author has her main character enter a new setting as an outsider, a stranger with a quest. This provides the reader with a newcomer's viewpoint, a newcomer's reactions and, most important, a newcomer's objectivity in explaining and describing her unfamiliar surroundings to the reader. Settings and descriptions are the author's forte. She builds tension by postponing answers—exposition before denouement—but, although everything's clear and never too obvious, her expositions sometimes seem overlong.

Whitney is noted for exhaustive study of subjects relating to her novels. Her research has covered such areas as the history of twins and their development, channelling, and cats (*Woman Without a Past*), blindness (*Secret of the Emerald Star*), orchid cultivation and scuba diving (*Dream of Orchids*), and deafness and deaf languages for *Feather on the Moon*. For *The Singing Stones* published in 1990 when she was 87 years old, Whitney went up in a hot air balloon so she could use the experience in her novel.

At her best the author is able to interweave settings, both interior and exterior, into plot and character development, and each new background has its own individual possibility. Among these: the Red Rock country of Arizona where tall rocks standing in a row haunt the heroine of *Vermilion* who sees faces in the wind-etched surfaces; an old deserted mansion on Long Island where the heroine of *Rainsong* hears the voice of her murdered husband; the Colorado Rockies in *Domino* where a small ghost town blowing away in the dust reflects the heroine's life. Past happenings often shape the future for her subjects.

Whitney writes to entertain and she likes to keep her readers guessing. Her endings are always unexpected and always upbeat. After reading the heroine's novel, the hero in *Woman Without a Past* tells her, 'You are a good storyteller' and she feels he couldn't have said anything to please her more. This was the author speaking through her character. Whitney tells good stories, 'mysteries without detectives'.

—Nancy P. Stevenson

WHITTINGTON, Harry.   See **HORNER, Lance, Kyle ONSTOTT, and Ashley CARTER.**

WIAT, Philippa.
Pseudonym for Philippa Ferridge. **Nationality:** British. **Born:** Philippa Wyatt, London. **Education:** Wimbledon County School, London. **Relations:** married Dennis Ferridge; three daughters. **Address:** 19 Normandale, Bexhill-on-Sea, East Sussex TN39 3LU England.

ROMANCE AND HISTORICAL PUBLICATIONS

Novels (series: Black Boar; Charlton Mead; Edward III; Grey Family; Howard; Wilmington; Wyatt)

Like as the Roaring Waves (Howard). London, Hale, 1972.
The Heir of Allington (Wyatt). London, Hale, 1973.
The Master of Blandeston Hall (Wyatt). London, Hale, 1973.
The Knight of Allington (Wyatt). London, Hale, 1974.
The Rebel of Allington (Wyatt). London, Hale, 1974.
Lord of the Black Boar. London, Hale, 1975.
Sword of Woden (Black Boar). London, Hale, 1975.
Lion Without Claws (Howard). London, Hale, 1976; New York, St Martin's Press, 1977.
The Queen's Fourth Husband (Howard). London, Hale, 1976.
Tree of Vortigern (Black Boar). London, Hale, 1976.
My Lute Be Still (Wyatt). London, Hale, 1977.
Sound Now the Passing-Bell (Wyatt). London, Hale, 1977.
The Atheling (Black Boar). London, Hale, 1977.
Maid of Gold (Howard). London, Hale, 1978.
Raven in the Wind (Black Boar). London, Hale, 1978.
Yet a Lion (Howard). London, Hale, 1978.
The Four-Poster (Wilmington). London, Hale, 1979.
The Golden Chariot. London, Hale, 1979.
Westerfalca (Black Boar). London, Hale, 1979.
Lord of the Wolf (Black Boar). London, Hale, 1980.
Shadow of Samain (Wilmington). London, Hale, 1980.
The King's Vengeance. London, Hale, 1981.
The Mistletoe Bough (Charlton Mead). London, Hale, 1981.
Bride in Darkness (Charlton Mead). London, Hale, 1982.
Wychwood (Charlton Mead). London, Hale, 1982.
Children of the Spring (Grey). London, Hale, 1983.
Five Gold Rings (Grey). London, Hale, 1983.
Cartismandua. London, Hale, 1984.
Prince of the White Rose. London, Hale, 1984.
Queen-Gold (Edward III). London, Hale, 1985.
Fair Rosamond. London, Hale, 1985.
The Grey Goose Wing (Edward III). London, Hale, 1986.
The Whyte Swan (Edward III). London, Hale, 1986.
Wear a Green Kirtle (Howard). London, Hale, 1987.
The Cloister and the Flame. London, Hale, 1988.
Phantasmagoria. London, Hale, 1988.
The Kingmaker's Daughter. London, Hale, 1989.
One Child Bride. London, Hale, 1990.
The Lady Editha. London, Hale, 1991.
The Hammer and the Sword: A Novel of Wat Tyler. London, Hale, 1992.
The Lovers. London, Hale, 1993.

*

Philippa Wiat comments:

As an historical novelist, I write first and foremost about people. History as one learns it at school—or as I myself learned it at school—can be pretty daunting. It is not so much the monarchs, battles, and treaties that make the past such fascinating reading, as the people who lived in those times—those who were part and parcel of the Magna Carta and the Battle of Crécy; those who experienced the Black Death or saw Richard III and Wat Tyler.

To bring such people to life, to make history live and work for us, to heed its warnings and take part in its debates, is the task of the historical novelist. The secret? One must see into the minds of one's characters; be on the inside looking out, sharing their thoughts, beliefs, fears, and aspirations. One must subjugate one's identity to theirs.

*   *   *

In just over 20 years Philippa Wiat has written nearly 40 historical novels, prompted initially to do so by her researches into her own family, that of the poet and courtier Sir Thomas Wyatt. Her novels cover a wide range of periods—from the 1st century AD to the 16th century—with varying degrees of success. There is no doubt that Wiat is happiest when writing of the 16th century, and it is in this era that the bulk of her novels are set. Her approach varies—in some novels actual historical personages form the pivot of the story, in others the characters are wholly fictional, and one trilogy, the Charlton Mead novels, is based on an old Oxfordshire legend.

Every historical novelist has a decision to make about the use of spoken language within the framework of the narrative—should it be readable (and this usually means modern and colloquial) or should it be faithful to the period? Choosing the latter often results in stilted and unnatural phraseology, and unfortunately in some of Wiat's books this is indeed what the reader gets. Ironically the language is least ornate in those of her novels in which courtly language would not be out of place (i.e. those of the 16th century), and it is in those set in the 1st century that the speech reaches the ultimate in improbability. Would Prasatagus (*The Golden Chariot*) really have said 'Boadicea, for all your dignity and queenliness, you are at heart a primitive person, although perchance only I, your lover, recognize it'—or even words to that effect? The few modern idioms which do creep in jar all the more, given the over-formality of the rest of the speech.

Characterization is often the factor upon which the success of an historical novel can depend. The individuals need to be believable not only in the context of the setting but also in their actions and decisions. Wiat imputes to particular individuals decisions and actions which are known to have happened, but often without giving us any more than very shallow character sketches. However, where she does allow the personalities to develop, the novels at once become more interesting and more believable—notably in *The Whyte Swan*, the third part of a trilogy about Edward III. This is certainly one of her better novels, perhaps because the characters have had time to evolve over the length of the trilogy and the author may thus have a greater sense of involvement. One particular scene in this book, between Edward and his mother Isabella the She-Wolf of France, is especially successful because the strength of the personalities, and the interplay between them, are allowed full rein.

It is all too easy for an historical novel to be merely a romance, adventure, or mystery which happens to be set in historical times, and with those of Wiat's novels not involving actual people this is indeed the case, as she often fails to paint a realistic background. On the other hand, she is not afraid to tackle controversial subjects and place them in an historical setting. For example in *Five Gold Rings* and again in *Lord of the Wolf* the subject of incest is introduced as an integral part of the plot. In *The Cloister and the Flame* a young girl who is forced against her will to become a nun has an affair with an equally reluctant priest and becomes pregnant. Although the plot develops into a phenomenally improbable tangle of relationships and identities, the basic scenario is unusual and interesting, and a few touches of humour are provided in some of the convent scenes.

The painting in of background facts is always a problem for the novelist. The device of exposition through thought or conversation (i.e. one character thinking the plot aloud or telling another character what he or she must obviously already know) is often used successfully in drama (Shakespeare did it all the time!) but needs to be handled carefully in the context of a novel. If skilfully done this technique can be very effective, but unfortunately in many of Wiat's novels it is rather less than successful.

In her better novels Wiat shows that she is capable of strong characterization, unusual plots, and interesting exposition of historical facts. It is a shame that not all her novels demonstrate these strengths.

—Judith Rhodes

WIEBE, Rudy (Henry).
Nationality: Canadian. **Born:** Fairholme, Saskatchewan, 4 October 1934. **Education:** Alberta Mennonite High School; University of Alberta, Edmonton, 1953–56, 1958–60 (International Nickel graduate fellow, 1958–59; Queen Elizabeth graduate fellow, 1959–60), B.A. 1956, M.A. 1960; University of Tübingen, Germany (Rotary fellow), 1957–58; University of Manitoba, Winnipeg, 1961; University of Iowa, Iowa City, 1964. **Relations:** married Tena F. Isaak in 1958; one daughter and two sons. **Career:** research officer, Glenbow Foundation, Calgary, 1956; foreign service officer, Ottawa, 1960; high school teacher, Selkirk, Manitoba, 1961; editor, Mennonite Brethren *Herald*, Winnipeg, 1962–63; assistant professor of English, Goshen College, Indiana, 1963–67. Assistant professor, 1967–70, associate professor, 1970–77, and since 1977 professor of English, University of Alberta. Member: Writer's Advisory Committee to Ministry of Culture, Alberta, 1980–82; Arts Panel, Canada Council, 1974–77; Federal Cultural Policy Panel, 1981–84; Alberta Foundation for Literary Arts, 1984–87; founding president, Writers Guild, Alberta, 1980; vice-chair, Writers Union, Canada, 1973, chair, 1986–89; president, Newest Press, 1989. **Recipient:** Canada Council arts scholarship, 1964, award, 1971, grant, 1977; Lorne Pierce medal, 1987. D.Litt.: University of Winnipeg, Manitoba, 1986. Member, Royal Society of Canada, 1987. **Address:** Department of English, University of Alberta, Edmonton, Alberta T6G 2EI, Canada.

ROMANCE AND HISTORICAL PUBLICATIONS

Novels

Peace Shall Destroy Many. Toronto, McClelland and Stewart, 1962; Grand Rapids, Michigan, Eerdmans, 1964.
The Blue Mountains of China. Toronto, McClelland and Stewart, and Grand Rapids, Michigan, Eerdmans, 1970.
The Temptations of Big Bear. Toronto, McClelland and Stewart, 1973.
The Scorched-Wood People. Toronto, McClelland and Stewart, 1977.
The Mad Trapper. Toronto, McClelland and Stewart, 1980.

Short Stories

Where Is the Voice Coming From? Toronto, McClelland and Stewart, 1974.
Personal Fictions, with others, edited by Michael Ondaatje. Toronto, Oxford University Press, 1977.
Alberta: A Celebration, edited by Tom Radford. Edmonton, Alberta, Hurtig, 1979.

The Angel of the Tar Sands and Other Stories. Toronto, McClelland and Stewart, 1982.

OTHER PUBLICATIONS

Novels

First and Vital Candle. Toronto, McClelland and Stewart, and Grand Rapids, Michigan, Eerdmans, 1966.
My Lovely Enemy. Toronto, McClelland and Stewart, 1983.

Play

Far as the Eye Can See, with Theatre Passe Muraille. Edmonton, Alberta, NeWest Press, 1977.

Other

A Voice in the Land: Essays by and about Rudy Wiebe, edited by W. J. Keith. Edmonton, Alberta, NeWest Press, 1981.
Playing Dead: A Contemplation Concerning the Arctic. Edmonton, Alberta, NeWest Press, 1989.
Silence: The Word and the Sacred (essays). Waterloo, Ontario, Wilfrid Laurier University Press, 1989.

Editor, *The Story-Makers: A Selection of Modern Short Stories.* Toronto, Macmillan, 1970.
Editor, *Stories from Western Canada: A Selection.* Toronto, Macmillan, 1972.
Editor, with Andreas Schroeder, *Stories from Pacific and Arctic Canada: A Selection.* Toronto, Macmillan, 1974.
Editor, *Double Vision: An Anthology of Twentieth-Century Stories in English.* Toronto, Macmillan, 1976.
Editor, *Getting Here: Stories.* Edmonton, Alberta, NeWest Press, 1977.
Editor, with Aritha van Herk, *More Stories from Western Canada.* Toronto, Macmillan, 1980.
Editor, with Aritha van Herk and Leah Flater, *West of Fiction.* Edmonton, Alberta, NeWest Press, 1982.
Editor, with Bob Beal, *War in the West: Voices of the 1885 Rebellion.* Toronto, McClelland and Stewart, 1985.

*

Manuscript Collection: University of Calgary Library, Alberta.

Critical Studies: *The Comedians: Hugh Hood and Rudy Wiebe* by Patricia A. Morley, Toronto, Clarke Irwin, 1977; *Epic Fiction: The Art of Rudy Wiebe* by W.J. Keith, Edmonton, University of Alberta Press, 1981; articles in *A Voice in the Land,* 1981, and *Journal of Commonwealth Literature* (Edinburgh), vol 19, no 1, 1984.

*   *   *

The vastness of the Canadian North; a native population beset by ruthless adversaries, hunger, and diminishing numbers, scattered over several thousand miles; a gentle people devoted to utopian principles, driven throughout four continents, faced with hostile environments, and cruel governments. The scope and themes of Rudy Wiebe's fiction surpass, in area and agony at least, the combined exploits and wanderings of Odysseus and Aeneas. But the epic magnitude notwithstanding, Wiebe has no intention of embarking on any heroic saga. Instead he chooses a mode one might term contemplative, or simply poetic. The approach yields some intriguing patterns as well some uncanny personal reflections generated by those who are experiencing soul-searing moments.

Though circumstances are frequently harsh and unrelenting, and the prognosis far from promising, Wiebe's method rarely yields a tragic perspective. In *The Blue Mountains of China* a young Mennonite girl shows not only resilience in the face of a ceaseless succession of plague, poverty, and enforced migration, but she develops a self-contained comic outlook that is unselfconscious and remarkably sane. In reference to the onslaught of funerals (some of which are for her own siblings), she discovers in the mannerisms of the minister a fascination which yields an amusement that is in fact deep enjoyment rather than an escape from the intolerable. The sombre setting, the earth-deriding hymns, and the solemn faces provide for her a spectacle well worth repeating. This response is tendered in a manner that is by no means ghoulish, not even irreverent or rebellious. It is, however, intensely personal and, more important, self sustaining. More significantly, it contains an awareness of her own unique place in happenings which might ordinarily prompt the self to surrender to futility. The horror and magnitude of the situation remains, but the human spirit emerges as an artist who finds intense satisfaction in crafting perspectives and in giving even the inexorable the stamp of individuality.

Liesel the Mennonite girl, crammed among the afflicted nomads in the ship's steerage, bravely fixes her skirt the best she can in order to promenade undetected by effecting the habit of the fine ladies in First Class. She successfully makes her way to the upper deck, notices in full detail a couple making love, and is amazed not at what to her group would be sinful conduct, but at the awkwardness of the woman. Even with an intensely religious upbringing she can withhold judgement while relishing an opportunity to weave the actions and postures of others into a fabric that is her own. Such an authorlike stance is common among Wiebe's characters, even the minor ones. The ship ceases for a while to be a vehicle of exile and becomes an instrument which allows the willing to mingle freely among humanity's infinite variety and to focus eyes and thoughts upon the intriguing patterns produced by their conduct. Liesel does not abandon her faith. She does not have to. She is in her own way an artist and as such has the leverage of perspective with her at all times.

The Blue Mountains of China contains a considerable amount of historical detail on the problems and peregrinations of the Mennonites. Similarly there is a great amount of detail in *The Temptations of Big Bear*, where divisions between the Indian leaders and the insidious conduct of the government provide the setting for much of the reflective meditation that is Wiebe's forte. The treachery and hardships cannot eclipse the ultimate human challenge, to arrive at a resolution of approach to crisis while remaining faithful both to the self and the cause. The much-told tale of Louis Riel benefits from this multiperspective in *The Scorched-Wood People*.

Even in his most straightforward narrative, *The Mad Trapper*, Wiebe's subject, the enigmatic and largely unknown Albert Johnson, is created principally out of the theories and partial glimpses of journalists, law enforcement agents, and other coinhabitants of the North. Johnson did in fact exist, but on his death in 1932, Johnson's life and character was a mystery. Wiebe finds in him a figure fit for the immense and imponderable landscape in which inhabitants do considerably more than survive. Johnson, this dot upon the frozen tundra who weaves deftly in and out of herds of caribou, and who can thrive in a tent through Arctic winters, is the stuff from which legends are made, a narrative of a landscape that triggers the most distinctively human of all acts—contemplation.

It is not surprising that Wiebe named his book on the Arctic *Playing Dead: A Contemplation Concerning the Arctic*. Like Liesel, seemingly a faceless figure among the similarly attired Mennonites, and Johnson, the man of unknown dimensions, the Arctic might appear dead and unvaried. In fact it is the moulding mind of observation and thought, which inevitably leads on to the telling of tales.

Wiebe is among those ready to embrace this energy in all its fullness.

—Leonard R. Mendelsohn

WIGG, T.I.G. See **McCUTCHAN, Philip.**

WILDER, Thornton (Niven).
Nationality: American. **Born:** Madison, Wisconsin, 17 April 1897. **Education:** Thacher School, Ojai, California, 1912–13; Berkeley High School, California, graduated 1915; Oberlin College, Ohio, 1915–17; Yale University, New Haven, Connecticut, 1917, 1919–20, A.B. 1920; American Academy in Rome, 1920–21; Princeton University, New Jersey, 1925–26, A.M. 1926. **Military Service:** United States Coast Artillery Corps, 1918; in the United States Army Air Intelligence, rising to the rank of Lieutenant-Colonel, 1942–45: honorary MBE (Member, Order of the British Empire), 1945. **Career:** French teacher, 1921–25, and house master, 1927–28, Lawrenceville School, New Jersey; first produced play, *The Trumpet Shall Sound*, staged 1926. Full-time writer from 1928. Part-time lecturer in comparative literature, University of Chicago, 1930–36; visiting professor, University of Hawaii, Honolulu, 1935; Charles Eliot Norton professor of poetry, Harvard University, Cambridge, Massachusetts, 1950–51. United States Delegate: Institut de Coopération Intellectuelle, Paris, 1937; International PEN Club Congress, England, 1941; Unesco Conference of the Arts, Venice, 1952. **Recipient:** Pulitzer prize, for fiction, 1928, for drama, 1938, 1943; American Academy gold medal, 1952; Freedom prize (Frankfurt), 1957; Brandeis University creative arts award, 1959; MacDowell medal, 1960; presidential medal of freedom, 1963; National medal for literature, 1965; National Book award, for fiction, 1968. D.Litt.: New York University, 1930; Yale University, 1947; Kenyon College, Gambier, Ohio, 1948; College of Wooster, Ohio, 1950; Northeastern University, Boston, 1951; Oberlin College, 1952; University of New Hampshire, Durham, 1953; Goethe University, Frankfurt, 1957; University of Zurich, 1961; LLD: Harvard University, 1951. Chevalier, Légion d'honneur (France), 1951; member, Order of Merit (Peru); Order of Merit (Germany), 1957; honorary member, Bavarian Academy of Fine Arts; Mainz Academy of Science and Literature. **Member:** American Academy. **Died:** 7 December 1975.

Romance and Historical Publications

Novels

The Bridge of San Luis Rey. New York, Boni, and London, Longman, 1927.
The Woman of Andros. New York, Boni, and London, Longman, 1930.
Heaven's My Destination. London, Longman, 1934; New York, Harper, 1935.
The Ides of March. New York, Harper, and London, Longman, 1948.
The Eighth Day. New York, Harper, and London, Longman, 1967.

Other Publications

Novels

The Cabala. New York, Boni, and London, Longman, 1926.

Theophilus North. New York, Harper, 1973; London, Allen Lane, 1974.

Plays

St Francis Lake. In *Oberlin Literary Magazine* (Oberlin, Ohio), December 1915.

Flamingo Red. In *Oberlin Literary Magazine* (Oberlin, Ohio), January 1916.

Brother Fire. In *Oberlin Literary Magazine* (Oberlin, Ohio), May 1916.

A Christmas Interlude. In *Oberlin Literary Magazine* (Oberlin, Ohio), December 1916.

The Walled City. In *Yale Literary Magazine* (New Haven, Connecticut), April 1918.

In Praise of Guynemer. In *Yale Literary Magazine* (New Haven, Connecticut), December 1918.

The Trumpet Shall Sound (produced New York, 1926). In *Yale Literary Magazine* (New Haven, Connecticut), October-December 1919, January 1920.

The Angel That Troubled the Waters and Other Plays (includes *Nascuntur Poetae, Proserpina and the Devil, Fanny Otcott, Brother Fire, The Penny That Beauty Spent, The Angel on the Ship, The Message and Jehanne, Childe Roland to the Dark Tower Came, Centaurs, Leviathan, And the Sea Shall Give Up Its Dead, Now Thy Servant's Name Was Malchus, Mozart and the Gray Steward, Hast Thou Considered My Servant Job?, The Flight into Egypt*). New York, Coward McCann, and London, Longman, 1928.

The Long Christmas Dinner (produced New Haven, Connecticut, 1931; Liverpool, 1932). In *'The Long Christmas Dinner' and Other Plays*, 1931; libretto for opera version, as *Das Lange Weihnachtsmal*, music by Paul Hindemith (produced Mannheim, Germany, 1961; New York, 1963), Mainz and New York, Schott, 1961.

The Happy Journey to Trenton and Camden (produced New Haven, Connecticut, 1931). In *'The Long Christmas Dinner' and Other Plays*, 1931; revised version, as *The Happy Journey* (produced New York, 1939), New York, French, 1934; London, French, 1947.

Such Things Only Happen in Books (produced New Haven, Connecticut, 1931). In *'The Long Christmas Dinner' and Other Plays*, 1931.

Love and How to Cure It (produced New Haven, Connecticut, 1931; Liverpool, 1932). In *'The Long Christmas Dinner' and Other Plays*, 1931.

'The Long Christmas Dinner' and Other Plays in One Act. New York and New Haven, Connecticut, Coward McCann-Yale University Press, and London, Longman, 1931.

Queens of France (produced Chicago, 1932; New York, 1949). In *'The Long Christmas Dinner' and Other Plays*, 1931.

Pullman Car Hiawatha (produced New York, 1962). In *'The Long Christmas Dinner' and Other Plays*, 1931.

Lucrèce, adaptation of a play by André Obey (produced New York, 1932). Boston, Houghton Mifflin, and London, Longman, 1933.

A Doll's House, adaptation of a play by Ibsen (produced Central City, Colorado, 1937).

Our Town (produced Princeton, New Jersey, and New York, 1938; London, 1946). New York, Coward McCann, 1938; London, Longman, 1956.

The Merchant of Yonkers, adaptation of a play by Johann Nestroy, based on *A Well-Spent Day* by John Oxenford (produced Boston and New York, 1938; London, 1951). New York, Harper, 1939; revised version, as *The Matchmaker* (produced Edinburgh and London, 1954; Philadelphia and New York, 1955), in *Three Plays*, 1957; published separately, London, Longman, 1958.

The Skin of Our Teeth (produced New Haven, Connecticut, and New York, 1942; London, 1945). New York, Harper, 1942.

Our Century (produced New York, 1947). New York, Century, 1947.

The Victors, adaptation of a play by Sartre (produced New York, 1949).

Die Alkestiade (as *A Life in the Sun*, produced Edinburgh, 1955; as *Die Alkestiade*, music by Louise Talma, produced Frankfurt, 1962). Frankfurt, Fischer, 1960; as *The Alcestiad; or, A Life in the Sun*, with *The Drunken Sisters: A Satyr Play*, New York, Harper, 1977.

Bernice, and The Wreck of the 5:25 (produced Berlin, 1957).

The Drunken Sisters (produced New York, 1970). New York, French, 1957.

Three Plays (includes *Our Town, The Skin of Our Teeth, The Matchmaker*). New York, Harper, 1957; London, Longman, 1958.

Plays for Bleecker Street (includes *Infancy, Childhood, Someone from Assisi*) (produced New York, 1962; *Infancy* and *Childhood* produced London, 1972). *Childhood* and *Infancy* published New York, French, 2 vols, 1960–61.

Screenplays: *We Live Again*, with others, 1934; *Our Town*, with Frank Craven and Harry Chandlee, 1940; *Shadow of a Doubt*, with others, 1943.

Other

The Intent of the Artist, with others. Princeton, New Jersey, Princeton University Press, 1941.

James Joyce 1882–1941. Aurora, New York, Wells College Press, 1944.

Kultur in einer Demokratie. Frankfurt, Fischer, 1957.

American Characteristics and Other Essays, edited by Donald Gallup. New York, Harper, 1979.

The Journals of Thornton Wilder 1939–1961 (includes unfinished play *The Emporium*), edited by Donald Gallup. New Haven, Connecticut, Yale University Press, 1985.

*

Film Adaptations: *Our Town*, 1940; *The Bridge of San Luis Rey*, 1944; *The Matchmaker*, 1958, *Hello Dolly*, 1969, both from the play *The Matchmaker*; *Skin of our Teeth*, 1959; *Mr North*, 1988, from the novel *Theophilus North*.

Bibliography: *Thornton Wilder: An Annotated Bibliography of Works by and About Thornton Wilder* by Richard H. Goldstone and Gary Anderson, New York, AMS Press, 1982.

Manuscript Collection: Beinecke Library, Yale University, New Haven, Connecticut.

Critical Studies: *Thornton Wilder* by Rex Burbank, New York, Twayne, 1961, revised edition, 1978; *Thornton Wilder* by Bernard Grebanier, Minneapolis, University of Minnesota Press, 1964; *The Art of Thornton Wilder* by Malcolm Goldstein, Lincoln, University of Nebraska Press, 1965; *Thornton Wilder* by Helmut Papajewski, New York, Ungar, 1968; *Thornton Wilder* by Hermann Stresau, New York, Ungar, 1971; *Thornton Wilder: The Bright and the Dark* by Mildred Christophe Kuner, New York, Crowell, 1972; *Thornton Wilder: An Intimate Portrait* by Richard H. Goldstone, New York, Saturday Review Press, 1975; *Thornton Wilder: His World* by Linda Simon, New York, Doubleday, 1979; *A Vast Landscape: Time in the Novels of Thornton Wilder* by Mary Ellen Williams, Pocatello, Idaho State University Press, 1979; *Thornton Wilder and His Public* by Amos Wilder, Philadelphia, Fortress Press, 1980; *The*

Enthusiast: A Life of Thornton Wilder by Gilbert A. Harrison, New Haven, Connecticut, Ticknor and Fields, 1983; 'Thornton Wilder: Broadway Production History', in *Theatre History Studies 5*, 1985; *Thornton Wilder* by David Castronovo, New York, Ungar, 1986; 'Wilder in Germany: The Political Story After 1945', by Hans J. Lang, in *Yearbook of Comparative and General Literature*, 36, 1987; 'The Influence of the Oriental on Wilder's Writing' by Joanna Narkiewicz-Jodko, in *Acta Universitatis Wratislaviensis*, 1161, 1991.

Theatrical Activities:
Actor **Plays**—Stage Manager in *Our Town*, New York, 1938, and on other occasions; Mr Antrobus in *The Skin of Our Teeth*, Cohasset, Massachusetts, 1946, and on other occasions.

*   *   *

The historical romances of Thornton Wilder cannot be compared with those of any other American writer except Eudora Welty, and his work in this myth-making vein is more extensive. Almost all of his novels are historical, yet they are likely to puzzle or annoy readers who seek adventurous escape into the past or carefully researched reconstructions of other eras (like those of James A. Michener). Wilder, who wrote in his most ambitious work, *The Eighth Day*, that all history is one 'enormous tapestry', is not interested in detailed re-creations of great events, but in making broad statements about the significance of the past. He believes that 'there are no Golden Ages and no Dark Ages', but only 'the ocean like monotony of the generations of men under the alterations of fair and foul weather' (*The Eighth Day*). All times and places, he feels, are much alike, usually tragically self-destructive, but occasionally magically rewarding.

Wilder's first novel, *The Cabala*, published in 1926 at the peak of the Age of Ballyhoo, introduces some historical figures like the poet John Keats, but the lack of a chronological time scheme frustrates readers seeking historical information from this obscurist fantasy about American expatriates being the heirs to the triumphs and undoings of the pagan gods of classical Rome.

However, only a year later Wilder scored his greatest success with his next novel, *The Bridge of San Luis Rey*, a stylized fable set in colonial Peru, where a famous rope bridge over a deep chasm collapses while five travellers, all of whom just seemed to be starting to make new lives for themselves after wasted years, fall to their deaths. A scholarly monk piously sets out to learn all he can of their histories in an effort to determine whether the fall can be attributed to divine design or accident, but for his trouble both he and his work are burned by the Inquisition.

Wilder's third novel, *The Woman of Andros*, provoked an uproar in New York literary circles. It was attacked by Michael Gold, proletarian author of the novel *Jews Without Money*, as the work of a 'Christian gentleman' that was irrelevant to the sufferings of the poor during the Depression. Genteel critics rushed to the defense of the world-weary work that portrayed through the circumspect tale of a wise courtesan and her ambitious young lover how the ancient Greek world had given way to a Christian society that 2000 years later seemed about to share the fate of its predecessor.

Although Wilder ignored the controversy, he was obviously affected by it for his next novel was a folksy account of the contemporary American midwest; and he devoted most of the 1930s to theatrical works. It is impossible to discuss his historical fiction, however, without mentioning his highly successful play *The Skin of Our Teeth* (1942), a fantasy that traced the history of the human race from the ice age to World War II.

After army service Wilder returned, in fiction, to the ancient Rome conjured up in his first novel for the seeming start of a new career with *The Ides of March*. This bewilderingly complex work presents four tellings of the same basic tale about the profanation of an ancient ritual, each longer and encompassing more events than the preceding one. Wilder's leisurely paced cautionary tale about ominous parallels between the days of Julius Caesar's triumphs and those following the American victory in World War II was too subtle and dependent upon classical allusion to appeal to restless modern readers.

Readers' indifference led Wilder to abandon fiction for theatrical work; but 20 years later in 1967 at the age of 70 he surprised the literary world with his most ambitious novel, *The Eighth Day*, another extremely complicated narrative that moves back and forth through the 20th century to recount the fate of a talented inventor and potential human benefactor accused of murder in a small Illinois town early in the century and hounded by human piranhas most of his life until his ironic, accidental death after his vindication. The cleverly contrived mystery story is only, however, the backdrop for Wilder's observation that 'The human race gets no better. Mankind is vicious, slothful, quarrelsome, and self-centred', except for those rare individuals who transcend themselves through creative work.

This hard-hitting statement of fashionable alienation was not, however, Wilder's last word. He ended a career full of surprises with another when his final novel, *Theophilus North*, proved a mellow account of a seeming history of nine stages in the growth of the fashionable resort of Newport, Rhode Island. Again, however, the setting serves only as a backdrop for the story of a sensitive young man's exploration of nine possible careers before he discovers that he can encompass all of them by becoming a writer.

One learns little textbook history from Wilder's romances, but one may learn much of how a sense of history's ironic repetitions can liberate the imaginative individual from their 'ocean-like monotony'.

—Warren French

WILLIAMS, Bronwyn.   See BROWNING, Dixie.

WILLIAMS, Claudette.
Nationality: American. **Address:** c/o Fawcett, 210 East 50th Street, New York, New York 10022, USA.

ROMANCE AND HISTORICAL PUBLICATIONS

Novels

Spring Gambit. New York, Fawcett, 1976.
Sassy. New York, Fawcett, 1977.
Sunday's Child. New York, Fawcett, 1977.
After the Storm. New York, Fawcett, 1977.
Blades of Passion. New York, Fawcett, 1978; London, Arrow, 1979.
Cotillion for Mandy. New York, Fawcett, 1978.
Myriah. New York, Fawcett, 1978.
Cassandra. New York, Fawcett, and London, Arrow, 1979.
Jewelene. New York, Fawcett, 1979.
Lacey. New York, Fawcett, 1979.
Mary, Sweet Mary. New York, Fawcett, 1980.
Naughty Lady Ness. New York, Fawcett, 1980.
Passion's Pride. New York, Fawcett, 1980.
Desert Rose, English Moon. New York, Fawcett, 1981.
Sweet Disorder. New York, Fawcett, 1981.
Lady Magic. New York, Fawcett, 1983.
Song of Silkie. New York, Fawcett, 1984.

Fire and Desire. New York, Fawcett, 1985.
Regency Star. New York, Fawcett, 1985.
Wild Dawn Fever. New York, Fawcett, 1986.
Lady Bell. New York, Fawcett, 1986.
Lady Madcap. New York, Fawcett, 1987.
Heart of Fancy. New York, Fawcett, 1990.

*   *   *

Claudette Williams seems to be an author with a split personality. Where most writers of historical romances stick with one style or formula, at least for each pseudonym, Williams produces two distinct types of books under one name.

Her largest output has been in the familiar Regency formula novel. *Spring Gambit*, *Sassy*, *Jewelene*, *Lacey* are only some examples of her work in this genre. Her virginal heroines and handsome, rakish heroes fit the common mold but are elevated by some engaging dialogue. The earlier novels in this vein (*After the Storm*, *Sassy*, *Sunday's Child*) allowed for more development of character and plot, but the more recent titles seem to be hurried and place greater reliance on the formula: a little bit of danger to the heroine, but rescue always in time. Rarely is there a hint of more than a kiss or, perhaps, a discreetly passionate embrace.

Readers accustomed to this fare were in for a shock when *Blades of Passion* appeared. Suddenly Williams joined the ranks of those authors producing steamy, explicit sex scenes. The rules of the game change in this formula. Here the heroine loses her virginity before marriage but remains true to the hero throughout. Rape becomes seduction as lust turns into tenderness. The books are longer and so there are more dangerous situations to encounter, but most of the plot revolves around the antagonism which exists between hero and heroine, and how long it will take them to recognize it as love. *Passion's Pride* and, to a lesser extent, *Cassandra*, follow this formula too. *Passion's Pride* is less successful than *Blades of Passion* because of an awkward attempt to develop two parallel stories which only occasionally touch on one another. *Desert Rose, English Moon* is Williams's only novel in a modern setting, but all the elements of *Blades of Passion* are present.

Williams is a good romantic novelist. She has the ability to create likeable characters, and while her stories may stretch the reader's credulity, they are no more far-fetched than many other historical romances.

—Barbara E. Kemp

———

WILLIAMSON, C(harles). N(orris). and A(lice). M(uriel).
WILLIAMSON, C(harles) N(orris). Pseudonym: Charles de Crespigny; **Nationality:** British. **Born:** Exeter, Devon, in 1859. **Education:** University College, London. **Relations:** married Alice Livingston in 1895. **Career:** journalist, *Graphic*, 1882–90; founding editor, *Black and White* magazine, 1891. **Died:** 3 October 1920.
WILLIAMSON, A(lice) M(uriel). Pseudonyms: M.P. Revere; Dona Teresa de Savallo; Alice Stuyvesant; Mrs Harcourt Williamson. **Nationality:** American. **Born:** Alice Muriel Livingstone, near Poughkeepsie, New York, in 1869. **Education:** privately. **Career:** writer. Lived in England after 1893. **Died:** 24 September 1933.

ROMANCE AND HISTORICAL PUBLICATIONS

Novels (series: Loveland)

The Lightning Conductor: The Strange Adventures of a Motor-Car. London, Methuen, 1902; New York, Holt, 1903.
The Princess Passes: A Romance of a Motor Car. London, Methuen, 1904; New York, Holt, 1905.

My Friend the Chauffeur. London, Methuen, and New York, McClure, 1905.
The Car of Destiny and Its Errand to Spain. London, Methuen, 1906; as *The Car of Destiny*, New York, McClure, 1906.
Lady Betty Across the Water. London, Methuen, and New York, McClure, 1906.
Rosemary in Search of a Father. London, Hodder and Stoughton, and New York, McClure, 1906; as *Rosemary: A Christmas Story*, New York, Burt, 1909.
The Botor Chaperon. London, Methuen, 1907; as *The Chauffeur and the Chaperon*, New York, McClure, 1908; as *The Chaperon*, New York, Burt, 1912.
The Powers and Maxine. New York, Empire, 1907.
The Marquis of Loveland. New York, McClure, 1908.
Love and the Spy. London, Leng, 1908.
The Motor Maid. London, Hodder and Stoughton, 1909; New York, Doubleday, 1910.
Set in Silver. London, Methuen, and New York, Doubleday, 1909.
The Golden Silence. London, Methuen, and New York, Doubleday, 1910.
Lord Loveland Discovers America. London, Methuen, and New York, Doubleday, 1910.
The Demon. London, Methuen, 1912.
The Heather Moon. London, Methuen, and New York, Doubleday, 1912.
The Guests of Hercules. London, Methuen, and New York, Doubleday, 1912; as *Mary at Monte Carlo*, Methuen, 1920.
Champion: The Story of a Motor Car. London, Cassell, 1913.
The Love Pirate. London, Methuen, 1913; as *The Port of Adventure*, New York, Doubleday, 1913.
The Wedding Day. London, Methuen, 1914.
A Soldier of the Legion. London, Methuen, and New York, Doubleday, 1914.
It Happened in Egypt. London, Methuen, and New York, Doubleday, 1914.
Secret History. London, Methuen, 1915; as *Secret History Revealed by Lady Peggy O'Malley*, New York, Doubleday, 1915.
The Shop-Girl. London, Methuen, and New York, Grosset and Dunlap, 1916; as *Winnie Childs, The Shop Girl*, Grosset and Dunlap, 1926.
The War Wedding. London, Methuen, 1916; as *Where the Path Breaks* (as Captain Charles de Crespigny), New York, Century, 1916.
The Lightning Conductress. London, Methuen, 1916; as *The Lightning Conductress Discovers America*, New York, Doubleday, 1916.
Angel Unawares: A Story of Christmas Eve. New York, Harper, 1916.
This Woman to This Man. London, Methuen, 1917.
The Cowboy Countess. London, Methuen, 1917.
Tiger Lily. London, Mills and Boon, 1917.
Lord John in New York. London, Methuen, 1918.
Crucifix Corner: A Story of Everyman's Land. London, Methuen, 1918; as *Everyman's Land*, New York, Doubleday Press, 1918.
Briar Rose. London, Odhams Press, 1919.
The Lion's Mouse. London, Methuen, and New York, Doubleday, 1919.
The Second Latchkey. New York, Doubleday, 1920.
The Dummy Hand. London, Hutchinson, 1920.
Alias Richard Power. London, Hodder and Stoughton, 1921.
The Great Pearl Secret. London, Methuen, and New York, Doubleday, 1921.
The House of Silence. London, Hodder and Stoughton, 1921.
The Night of the Wedding. London, Hodder and Stoughton, 1921; New York, Doran, 1923.
Vision House. New York, Doubleday, 1921.

The Brightener. New York, Doubleday, 1921; London, Hutchinson, 1922.

The Lady from the Air. London, Hodder and Stoughton, 1922; New York, Doubleday, 1923.

Novels by A.M. Williamson

The Barn Stormers, Being the Tragical Side of a Comedy. London, Hutchinson, 1897; (as Mrs Harcourt Williamson) New York, Stokes, 1897.

Fortune's Sport. London, Pearson, 1898.

A Woman in Grey. London and New York, Routledge, 1898.

Lady Mary of the Dark House. London, Bowden, 1898.

The House by the Lock. London, Bowden, 1899; New York, Dodge, 1906.

The Newspaper Girl. London, Pearson, 1899.

My Lady Cinderella. London, Routledge, 1900; New York, Dodge, 1906.

Ordered South. London, Routledge, 1900.

The Adventure of Princess Sylvie. London, Methuen, 1900; as *The Princess Virginia*, New York, McClure, 1909.

Queen Sweetheart. London, White, 1901.

A Bid for a Coronet. London, Routledge, 1901.

'Twixt Devil and Deep Sea. London, Pearson, 1901.

Papa. London, Methuen, 1902.

The Silent Battle. London, Hurst and Blackett, 1902; New York, Doubleday, 1909.

The Woman Who Dared. London, Methuen, 1903.

The Little White Nun. London, White, 1903.

The Sea Could Tell. London, Methuen, 1904.

The Turnstile of Night. London, Hurst and Blackett, 1904.

The Castle of Shadows. London, Methuen, 1905; New York, Hudson Press, 1909.

The Girl Who Had Nothing. London, Ward Lock, 1905.

The House of the Lost Court (as Dona Teresa de Savallo). New York, McClure, 1908.

The Underground Syndicate. London, Hodder and Stoughton, 1910.

The Vanity Box (as Alice Stuyvesant). New York, Doubleday, 1911; as A. M. Williamson, London, Hodder and Stoughton, 1913.

The Flower Forbidden. London, Hodder and Stoughton, 1911.

The Girl of the Passion Play. London, Hodder and Stoughton, 1911.

The Bride's Hero (as M.P. Revere). New York, Stokes, 1912.

To MLG; or, He Who Passes. New York, Stokes, 1912.

The Life Mask. New York, Stokes, 1913.

What I Found Out in the House of a German Prince, by an English Governess. London, Chapman and Hall, and New York, Stokes, 1915.

Name the Woman. London, Methuen, 1924.

The Million Dollar Doll. New York, Doran, 1924.

The Man Himself. London, Philpot, 1925.

Secret Gold. London, Methuen, and New York, Doubleday, 1925.

Publicity for Anne. London, Mills and Boon, 1926.

Cancelled Love. London, Methuen, 1926; as *Golden Butterfly*, New York, Doran, 1926.

Sheikh Bill. London, Mills and Boon, 1927; as *Bill—The Sheik*, New York, Doran, 1927.

Hollywood Love. London, Chapman and Hall, 1928.

Black Sleeves: It Happened in Hollywood. London, Chapman and Hall, 1928.

Children of the Zodiac. London, Chapman and Hall, 1929.

Frozen Slippers. London, Chapman and Hall, 1930.

The Golden Carpet. London, Chapman and Hall, 1931.

Honeymoon Hate. London, Chapman and Hall, 1931.

Bewitched. London, Chapman and Hall, and New York, Kinsey, 1932.

Last Year's Wife. London, Benn, 1932.

Keep This Door Shut. London, Benn, 1933.

The Lightning Conductor Comes Back. London, Chapman and Hall, 1933.

The Girl in the Secret. London, Wright and Brown, 1934.

Short Stories

Scarlet Runner. London, Methuen, 1908.

The Minx Goes to the Front. London, Mills and Boon, 1919.

Berry Goes to Monte Carlo. London, Mills and Boon, 1921.

The Fortune Hunters and Others. London, Mills and Boon, 1923.

The Indian Princess (by A.M. Williamson). London, Mills and Boon, 1924.

Told at Monte Carlo (by A.M. Williamson). London, Mills and Boon, 1926; as *Black Incense: Tales of Monte Carlo*, New York, Doran, 1926.

OTHER PUBLICATIONS by A.M. Williamson

Other

Memoirs of the Life and Writings of Thomas Carlyle, by C.N. Williamson and Richard Herne Shepherd. London, W. H. Allen, 1881.

Queen Alexandra, The Nation's Pride. London, Partridge, 1902.

Princess Mary's Locked Book (published anonymously). London, Cassell, 1912; New York, Cassell, 1913.

The Bride's Breviary (published anonymously). London, Hodder and Stoughton, 1912.

The Lure of Monte Carlo. London, Mills and Boon, 1924; New York, Doubleday, 1926.

Alice in Movieland. London, Philpot, 1927; New York, Appleton, 1928.

The Inky Way (autobiography). London, Chapman and Hall, and New York, Putnam, 1931.

*   *   *

Charles Norris Williamson of Exeter, England, had co-authored a book on Thomas Carlyle before he met Alice Muriel Livingston of Poughkeepsie, New York, and after their marriage (in 1895) they combined their literary talents to write books of a very different nature. These were mostly romantic novels with motoring and travel backgrounds. Charles's informed interest in science and engineering gave the stories a sense of technical modernity, while Alice seems to have injected them with robust romanticism.

There is an Edwardian charm even in the novels that appeared during the 1920s, and much of the Williamsons' best work was published between 1900 and 1910. The couple made their home at Cap Martin and gave many of their books a continental setting, though the main characters, expectedly, were often British or American. *The Lightning Conductor, The Princess Passes, The Car of Destiny*, and *My Friend the Chauffeur* are notable examples of the Williamsons' roaming-European-romances, which convey motoring and sight-seeing adventures with wit and whimsy. The stories are, for their time, fast moving, and only romantic clinches are allowed sometimes to slow down the crackling pace.

In *The Botor Chaperon* three pairs of lovers—assortedly Dutch, English, and American—take to the canals and waterways of Holland. Anglo-American themes are expectedly prominent in the novels. The hero is frequently an impeccable English milord whose opinions (at first) seem to the more questioning American heroine to have survived 'crusted and spider-webbed from the cellars of the

Stone Age' (*Lord John in New York* and *Lord Loveland Discovers America*). Nevertheless the Williamsons appear to have a very soft spot for upper-crust Englishmen (though less for their female counterparts). Their aristocratic male arrogance could of course eventually be loosened by American honesty and liveliness, as embodied by a string of attractive heroines.

Many of these leading girl characters pursue careers, though romance generally marks the end of job ambitions. *The Newspaper Girl*, which Mrs Williamson wrote on her own, is a briskly perceptive account of an American incognito-heiress trying to scrape a living in London as a 'penny-a-liner journalist', but ending up, with relief, as an English Lady-by-marriage. The Williamsons apparently relished the creation of witty vignettes of exotic continental or American women trying to make advances to restrained Englishmen, and nobody does this better in their novels than Maxine de Renzie, the Polish actress/spy operating in Paris in *Love and the Spy*. She is beautiful, cultivated, quick-witted, and far-seeing in the plots and counterplots of espionage—and, of course, of romance.

—Mary Cadogan

WILLIAMSON, Harcourt. See **WILLIAMSON, C.N.**

WILSON, Mary. See **ROBY, Mary Linn.**

WINCH, John. See **BOWEN, Marjorie.**

WINSLOW, Laurel. See **SEGER, Maura.**

WINSOR, Kathleen.
Nationality: American. **Born:** Olivia, Minnesota, 16 October 1919. **Education:** University of California, Berkeley, A.B. 1938. **Relations:** married 1) Robert Herwig in 1936 (divorced 1946); 2) the musician Artie Shaw in 1946; 3) Arnold Robert Krakower in 1949 (divorced 1953); 4) Paul A. Porter in 1956 (died 1975). **Agent:** Roslyn Targ Literary Agency Inc, 105 West 13th Street, New York, New York 10011, USA.

ROMANCE AND HISTORICAL PUBLICATIONS

Novels

Forever Amber. New York, Macmillan, 1944; London, Macdonald, 1945.
Star Money. New York, Appleton Century Crofts, and London, Macdonald, 1950.
The Lovers. New York, Appleton Century Crofts, and London, Macdonald, 1952.
America, With Love. New York, Putnam, 1957; London, Davies, 1958.
Wanderers Eastward, Wanderers West. New York, Random House, and London, Davies, 1965.
Calais. New York, Doubleday, 1979; London, Sidgwick and Jackson, 1980.

Jacintha. New York, Crown, 1983; London, Inner Circle, 1985.
Robert and Arabella. New York, Crown, 1986; London, Severn House, 1987.

*

Film Adaptation: *Forever Amber*, 1947.

* * *

Kathleen Winsor is known for her best-selling novel set in the time of England's Restoration, *Forever Amber*, which was later made into a motion picture. Some reviewers rather unfairly faulted the author for her creation of a shameless heroine and her frank depiction of a bawdy, lustful age. To her credit, the novel's title character and lustiness (tame by today's standards) enticed many readers to learn about the Restoration. Winsor's research is apparent, her plentiful historical detail validly convincing. The story centres on a beautiful, headstrong young heroine named Amber St Clare, who in ten years raises herself from village maid to duchess at the court of Charles II and becomes one of his favourite mistresses. Born the illegitimate daughter of nobility and raised by a yeoman family, Amber at 16 loses her heart and virtue to the visiting Lord Carlton and persuades him to take her to London without any promise of marriage. Carlton remains the love of Amber's life, but being a merchant ship owner with business interests in the New World, he sees Amber for periodic visits only. Amber, pregnant after Carlton's departure, survives a torrent of adventures. She escapes from Newgate debtor's prison to become the kept woman of, successively, three men, while also becoming an actress and acquiring four husbands (losing three). Aware of her attractiveness to men, she gains wealth upon the death of one husband, the favour of the King, and enters the intrigues and licentiousness of Charles II's court. Moreover, the strong-minded protagonist survives such significant events as the Restoration, the Plague, and the Great Fire of London. At last, Amber falls from royal favour and embarks for North America, still abortively pursuing Carlton, a conclusion promising a sequel not yet written.

Despite some implausible coincidences in the narrative, the novel has pace and lively action in its story of Amber's consciousless career. The gallery of fictional and historical characters from Charles II to Nell Gwyn are stridently alive. The colourful, bawdy, amoral world of the Restoration is richly detailed in *Forever Amber*, with its compelling protagonist who arguably serves as a fictional model for other romance novels of our time.

Winsor's subsequent works have not been as popularly or critically successful as *Forever Amber*. Many of them project an Amberlike, independent woman as heroine, either determined by or determining sexual desire, operating outside the conventionally imposed standards of womanly behaviour and at the story's end seldom regretting costly choices not accomplishing desired happiness.

Although disclaimed as being autobiographical, the heroine of *Star Money*, Shireen Delaney, does bear a resemblance to Windsor: Shireen, a beautiful authoress, has written during World War II her first best-selling historical novel about an ebullient 18th-century heroine that launches her into immediate literary prominence and a prosperous life while her husband is overseas. Selling the film rights of her book for a large sum, she embarks on publicity tours where she meets persons of the publishing world and New York society and, fearful of loneliness, undertakes several affairs with a variety of men. Her later attempts to be a wife to her returning husband fail. Winsor's theme intends to show the pernicious effects of success upon a tempestuous woman, but the latter elicits little sympathy or interest. *Calais*, reflects a similar Winsor heroine by focusing on the career of a successful actress who combines toughness and vulnerability. As her own woman, following her own instincts and indulging a taste for men, the heroine generates a plot connecting her love life with events occurring at film locations or play rehearsals. The events are mildly interesting, but the novel lacks vigour and its characters lack verve.

Winsor made one departure from the large novel with three uneven-in-quality novelettes collectively titled *The Lovers*, bizarre fantasies about women and men frustrated in love and obsessed by dreams. These novellas seem to be germinal to two short novels of the 1980s: *Jacintha*, and *Robert and Arabella*. Jacintha, a beautiful young adulteress shot by her husband, finds herself in a mountain-land ruled by the Devil, an erotically handsome and robust male by whom Jacintha is willingly seduced. There Jacintha encounters her mother, also an adulteress killed in her youth, who becomes her rival for the Devil's sensual attentions. *Roberta and Arabella* tells a fable about a forbidden, sensually passionately love affair of a 14th-century French princess with a blond gypsy. The lovers flee from the forces of the king, Arabella's father, but are caught by the king's knights and killed before escaping across the sea. The central characters of both novellas are sufficiently defined and the action sufficiently baroque for the world of the romance novel.

In a departure from previous work and in what is probably her second best work, Winsor drew on childhood in *America With Love*. Set in a western American small town during the 1930s, the novel focuses on a year in the Spangler family neighbourhood, with 12-year-old Cassie and her small brother Don. Cassie and her pals experience imaginary thrills of what being grown up will be, considering sex from childhood's standpoint of embarrassment over parents' affectionate interchanges; curiosity about teenage girl's illegitimate pregnancy; excitement over an older girl's bashing by her jealous returning sailor-boyfriend. Winsor displays a distinctive feeling for the world of the young child and an excellent ear for the latter's rhythm and cadence.

The 1965 novel *Wanderers Eastward, Wanderers Westward*, turns to the post-Civil War America's expansion period. The setting oscillates between boomtowns and mining camps of the Montana Territory and New York City as the narrative follows the amorous, often violent adventures of a western and eastern family against an authentic historical background with lively descriptions of frontier, city slum, and Wall Street. Although the novel's characters tend to be stereotypical, the well-researched detail is commendable.

Winsor's contribution of *Forever Amber*, with its brazen central character and its vivid historicity, stands as a significant achievement which influenced the shaping of the contemporary romance novel as a genre. It is her first novel that indicates her talent.

—Christian H. Moe

WINSPEAR, Violet.
Nationality: British. **Born:** London, 28 April 1928. **Career:** factory worker in London, 1942–63. **Died:** January 1989.

ROMANCE AND HISTORICAL PUBLICATIONS

Novels

Lucifer's Angel. London, Mills and Boon, and Toronto, Harlequin, 1961.
Wife Without Kisses. London, Mills and Boon, 1961; Toronto, Harlequin, 1973.
The Strange Waif. London, Mills and Boon, 1962; Toronto, Harlequin, 1974.
House of Strangers. London, Mills and Boon, 1963; Toronto, Harlequin, 1973.

Beloved Tyrant. London, Mills and Boon, 1964; Toronto, Harlequin, 1966.
Cap Flamingo. London, Mills and Boon, 1964; as *Nurse at Cap Flamingo*, Toronto, Harlequin, 1965.
Love's Prisoner. London, Mills and Boon, 1964; Toronto, Harlequin, 1974.
Bride's Dilemma. London, Mills and Boon, 1965; Toronto, Harlequin, 1966.
Desert Doctor. London, Mills and Boon, and Toronto, Harlequin, 1965.
The Tower of the Captive. London, Mills and Boon, 1966; Toronto, Harlequin, 1967.
The Viking Stranger. London, Mills and Boon, 1966; Toronto, Harlequin, 1967.
Tender Is the Tyrant. London, Mills and Boon, 1967; Toronto, Harlequin, 1968.
The Honey Is Bitter. London, Mills and Boon, 1967; Toronto, Harlequin, 1973.
Beloved Castaway. London, Mills and Boon, 1968; Toronto, Harlequin, 1971.
Court of the Veils. London, Mills and Boon, 1968; Toronto, Harlequin, 1969.
The Dangerous Delight. London, Mills and Boon, 1968; Toronto, Harlequin, 1969.
Pilgrim's Castle. London, Mills and Boon, 1969; Toronto, Harlequin, 1973.
The Unwilling Bride. London, Mills and Boon, 1969; Toronto, Harlequin, 1973.
Blue Jasmine. London, Mills and Boon, 1969; Toronto, Harlequin, 1970.
Dragon Bay. London, Mills and Boon, 1969; Toronto, Harlequin, 1973.
Palace of the Peacocks. London, Mills and Boon, and Toronto, Harlequin, 1969.
The Chateau of St Avrell. London, Mills and Boon, 1970; Toronto, Harlequin, 1974.
The Cazalet Bride. London, Mills and Boon, and Toronto, Harlequin, 1970.
Tawny Sands. London, Mills and Boon, 1970; Toronto, Harlequin, 1974.
Black Douglas. London, Mills and Boon, 1971; Toronto, Harlequin, 1972.
Dear Puritan. London, Mills and Boon, 1971; Toronto, Harlequin, 1973.
Bride to Lucifer. London, Mills and Boon, 1971; Toronto, Harlequin, 1973.
The Castle of the Seven Lilacs. London, Mills and Boon, and Toronto, Harlequin, 1971.
Raintree Valley. London, Mills and Boon, 1971; Toronto, Harlequin, 1972.
The Little Nobody. London, Mills and Boon, 1972; Toronto, Harlequin, 1973.
The Pagan Island. London, Mills and Boon, and Toronto, Harlequin, 1972.
Rapture of the Desert. London, Mills and Boon, 1972; Toronto, Harlequin, 1973.
The Silver Slave. London, Mills and Boon, and Toronto, Harlequin, 1972.
The Glass Castle. London, Mills and Boon, 1973; Toronto, Harlequin, 1974.
Devil in a Silver Room. London, Mills and Boon, and Toronto, Harlequin, 1973.
Forbidden Rapture. London, Mills and Boon, 1973; Toronto, Harlequin, 1974.
The Kisses and the Wine. London, Mills and Boon, and Toronto, Harlequin, 1973.

Palace of the Pomegranate. London, Mills and Boon, 1974; Toronto, Harlequin, 1975.

The Girl at Golden Hawk. London, Mills and Boon, 1974; Toronto, Harlequin, 1975.

The Noble Savage. London, Mills and Boon, 1974; Toronto, Harlequin, 1975.

Satan Took a Bride. London, Mills and Boon, 1975; Toronto, Harlequin, 1976.

Dearest Demon. London, Mills and Boon, 1975; Toronto, Harlequin, 1976.

The Devil's Darling. London, Mills and Boon, and Toronto, Harlequin, 1975.

Darling Infidel. London, Mills and Boon, and Toronto, Harlequin, 1976.

The Burning Sands. London, Mills and Boon, 1976; Toronto, Harlequin, 1977.

The Child of Judas. London, Mills and Boon, and Toronto, Harlequin, 1976.

The Sun Tower. London, Mills and Boon, 1976; Toronto, Harlequin, 1977.

The Sin of Cynara. London, Mills and Boon, and Toronto, Harlequin, 1976.

The Loved and the Feared. London, Mills and Boon, 1977; Toronto, Harlequin, 1978.

Love Battle. London, Mills and Boon, 1977; Toronto, Harlequin, 1978.

Love in a Stranger's Arms. London, Mills and Boon, and Toronto, Harlequin, 1977.

Passionate Sinner. London, Mills and Boon, 1977; Toronto, Harlequin, 1978.

Time of the Temptress. London, Mills and Boon, 1977; Toronto, Harlequin, 1978.

The Valdez Marriage. London, Mills and Boon, 1978; Toronto, Harlequin, 1979.

The Awakening of Alice. London, Mills and Boon, and Toronto, Harlequin, 1978.

Desire Has No Mercy. London, Mills and Boon, 1979.

The Sheik's Captive. London, Mills and Boon, 1979.

Love Is the Honey. London, Mills and Boon, and Toronto, Harlequin, 1980.

A Girl Possessed. London, Mills and Boon, 1980; Toronto, Harlequin, 1981.

Love's Agony. London, Mills and Boon, and Toronto, Harlequin, 1981.

No Man of Her Own. London, Mills and Boon, 1981.

The Man She Married. London, Mills and Boon, 1982; Toronto, Harlequin, 1983.

Bride's Lace. London, Mills and Boon, 1984.

By Love Bewitched. London, Mills and Boon, 1984.

Secret Fire. London, Mills and Boon, 1984.

Sun Lord's Woman. London, Mills and Boon, 1985.

House of Storms. Toronto, Worldwide, and London, Mills and Boon, 1985.

The Honeymoon. Toronto, Worldwide, and London, Mills and Boon, 1986.

A Silken Barbarity. London, Mills and Boon, 1988.

*   *   *

Violet Winspear said: 'I am a true spinster of romances, for in the old days the word spinster meant a woman who spun, and in the writing of a story one spins and weaves and forms a pattern that is hoped will prove pleasant and satisfactory' (*Thirty Years of Harlequin*, 1979). In fact, a distinctive pattern has been woven into Winspear's storytelling, a pattern that has fulfilled the hopes of readers for over 20 years. Realizing people's need for escape, Win-spear creates fast-paced, dramatic romances set in exotic lands inhabited by strange and wonderful peoples.

Winspear's romances feature immediate, intense conflict between the hero and the heroine which gives way to passionate unification by the end of the novel. As early as page ten, the hero and heroine are engaged in open warfare. Often their first words to each other are hostile; their first encounter may lead to physical violence between them. They are attracted to each other, but are initially repulsed by the strength of their feelings. Winspear uses extreme contrasts and emphasizes the attraction of opposites to build the tension between the hero and heroine: heaven and hell, pleasure and pain, devil and angel, love and hate, saint and sinner, fire and ice, hard and soft, dark and fair.

The hero in Winspear's novels is an impossibly strong, dominant man who is smoothly cultured but who, at the slightest provocation from the heroine, reverts to the type of his primitive ancestors. Be he Danish, Greek, Spanish, or Arabic, the hero is a pagan and a pirate. Book titles like *Bride to Lucifer*, *Dearest Demon*, and *Satan Took a Bride* make reference to the demonic qualities of the hero. The hero is the most compelling character in a Winspear romance because he is a man with a secret. Neither the heroine nor the reader initially knows why the hero is attractively scarred, why he is so bitter about women, why he is temporarily estranged from his family, or why he is evasive about his past. Gradually, the hero's misleading devilish reputation is stripped away to reveal the saint within. He is a man who puts others before himself and his business, who is capable of making noble sacrifices without any acknowledgement, and who is capable of controlling his powerful sexuality even when incredibly aroused.

The typical Winspear heroine undergoes the reverse process. In the beginning, she is the ice-cool angel with the modesty of a Madonna. She is like an 'ice bombe, bursting with chilled cream and the tang of bitter cherry'. However, contact with the hero melts that icy exterior and reveals the temperamental sensualist within. Thus, the conflict and its resolution not only lead to a marriage of opposites, but also allow both characters to express previously hidden aspects of their selves. The reader is willing to allow Winspear her excesses and exaggerations of character traits because this is such a satisfying conclusion.

Winspear's flamboyancy is also apparent in her writing style. She has a stock of romantic words which inevitably surface in her descriptions of characters, objects, or scenery. These are words like tawny, creamy, smoky, silken, taut, honey, and savage, the latter because ' ... there is generally a touch of savagery in anything truly romantic, as if it has to be tested by steel or fire'. Winspear is willing to invent new forms of words if they are evocative, for example, ' ... he brought her tigerishly close to him. . . '. She frequently hyphenates words for romantic effect as well (the hero's 'iron-hard jaw' or 'sun-dark skin', the 'honey-warm air').

Another characteristic of Winspear's writing is that she liberally sprinkled foreign names and expressions, particularly endearments, throughout the novel. She did not concentrate on any one country or locale. Rather she varied her settings by writing about the Caribbean, South America, the Middle East, Europe, and the United States. Interestingly, in a genre that has usually been purged of any overt political references, Winspear did mention the political turmoil found in some of the countries she wrote about, and she occasionally used it as part of the plot, although such references are generally kept vague. Winspear's heroes are always citizens of these exciting lands but the heroines are invariably English.

The sense of worldly sophistication created in the novels by the multi-lingualism is further heightened by Winspear's literary references to Dante, Byron, Chekhov, Balzac, Browning, etc. The hero and heroine are likely to recite bits of poetry and prose during the course of the story. Winspear also likes to use mythology as a motif in her romances. Thus the hero and heroine will be compared to mythological characters such as Apollo and Daphne or Proserpina and Aidoneus, or 'romantic' historical figures like the Sabine women and their captors. Winspear also borrows from other popular fiction. For instance, *Blue Jasmine* is very closely modelled after E.M. Hull's *The Sheik*.

When asked why she did not write about an ordinary Englishman, a 'Herbert Smith', or her childhood home in London's East End, Winspear replied: 'Quite frankly I do often write about Herbert Smith but I give him a more romantic name and disguise him in a tailored suit'. She added: 'I often write about the East End, for my Eastern bazaars are straight out of Petticoat Lane. My Greeks and Italians reside there, the aroma of exotic food has been breathed there . . . I have often plucked strands for my stories from that rich tapestry'. The results show that Winspear had the ability to transform her observations of everyday people, places, and events into glamorous romances.

—Margaret Jensen

———

WINSTON, Daoma.
Nationality: American. **Born:** Washington, DC, 3 November 1922. **Education:** George Washington University, Washington, DC, A.B. 1946 (Phi Beta Kappa). **Relations:** married Murray Strasberg in 1944. **Career:** writer. Lives in Washington, DC. **Agent:** Jay Garon-Brooke Associates, 101 West 55th Street, New York, New York 10019-5348, USA.

ROMANCE AND HISTORICAL PUBLICATIONS

Novels

The Secrets of Cromwell Crossing. New York, Lancer, 1965; London, Piatkus, 1984.
Sinister Stone. New York, Paperback Library, 1966; London, Piatkus, 1985.
The Mansion of Smiling Masks. New York, New American Library, 1967.
Shadow of an Unknown Woman. New York, Lancer, 1967; Loughton, Essex, Piatkus, 1979.
The Castle of Closing Doors. New York, Belmont, 1967; London, Piatkus, 1991.
The Carnaby Curse. New York, Belmont, 1967; London, Piatkus, 1991.
Shadow on Mercer Mountain. New York, Lancer, 1967; London, Piatkus, 1988.
Pity My Love. New York, Belmont, 1967; London, Severn House, 1988.
The Traficante Treasure. New York, Lancer, 1968; London, Severn House, 1990.
The Long and Living Shadow. New York, Belmont, 1968; London, Piatkus, 1993.
Dennison Hill. New York, Paperback Library, 1970.
House of Mirror Images. New York, Lancer, 1970; Loughton, Essex, Piatkus, 1981.
The Love of Lucifer. New York, Lancer, 1970; London, Piatkus, 1986.
The Vampire Curse. New York, Paperback Library, 1971.
Flight of a Fallen Angel. New York, Lancer, 1971; Loughton, Essex, Piatkus, 1982.
The Devil's Daughter. New York, Lancer, 1971; London, Piatkus, 1989.
The Devil's Princess. New York, Lancer, 1971; Loughton, Essex, Piatkus, 1980.

Seminar in Evil. New York, Lancer, 1972.
The Victim. New York, Popular Library, 1972; London, Piatkus, 1985.
The Return. New York, Avon, 1972.
The Inheritance. New York, Avon, 1972; London, Piatkus, 1987.
Kingdom's Castle. New York, Berkley, 1972; Loughton, Essex, Piatkus, 1981.
Skeleton Key. New York, Avon, 1972; Loughton, Essex, Piatkus, 1980; as *The Mayeroni Myth*, New York, Lancer, 1972.
Moorhaven. New York, Avon, 1973; London, Futura, 1976.
The Trap. New York, Popular Library, 1973; London, Piatkus, 1989.
The Unforgotten. New York, Berkley, 1973.
The Haversham Legacy. New York, Simon and Schuster, 1974; London, Futura, 1977.
Mills of the Gods. New York, Avon, 1974; London, Macdonald and Jane's, 1980.
Emerald Station. New York, Avon, 1974; London, Futura, 1977.
The Golden Valley. New York, Simon and Schuster, 1975; London, Futura, 1978.
Gallows Way. New York, Simon and Schuster, 1976; London, Macdonald and Jane's, 1978.
The Adventuress. New York, Simon and Schuster, 1978; London, Macdonald and Jane's, 1979.
The Hands of Death. Loughton, Essex, Piatkus, 1982.
Family of Strangers. Loughton, Essex, Piatkus, 1983.
The Fall River Line. New York, St Martin's Press, 1983; London, Century, 1984.
A Double Life. London, Severn House, 1991.
Hannah's Gate. London, Piatkus, 1992.
Curse of Hannah's Gate. London, Piatkus, 1993.

OTHER PUBLICATIONS

Novels

Tormented Lovers. Derby, Connecticut, Monarch, 1962.
Love Her, She's Yours. Derby, Connecticut, Monarch, 1963.
The Wakefield Witches. New York, Award, 1966; London, Piatkus, 1987.
The Moderns. New York, Pyramid, 1968; London, Severn House, 1988.
Bracken's World. New York, Paperback Library, 1969.
Mrs Berrigan's Dirty Book. New York, Lancer, 1970.
Beach Generation. New York, Lancer, 1970.
Wild Country. New York, Paperback Library, 1970.
Sound Stage. New York, Paperback Library, 1970.
Death Watch. New York, Ace, 1975; London, Piatkus, 1986.
A Visit After Dark. New York, Ace, 1975; Loughton, Essex, Piatkus, 1983.
Walk Around the Square. New York, Ace, 1975; London, Piatkus, 1984.
The Dream Killers. New York, Ace, 1976; London, Severn House, 1987.
The Lotteries. New York, Morrow, and London, Macdonald, 1980.
A Sweet Familiarity. New York, Arbor House, 1981; London, Macdonald, 1983.
Mira. New York, Arbor House, and London, Macdonald, 1982.
Maybe This Time. London, Century, 1988.

*   *   *

Daoma Winston has written many gothic novels and some science fiction, but she appears here as a writer of romance and historical novels with heavy emphasis on 'romance'. Her success as a published novelist began in the 1960s with short, paperback gothics; by the late 1970s she was using history as the background for her books, which were beginning to be published in hard cover by established trade houses. She neither delves nor probes into the political and philosophical aspects of the historical events that took place during the periods of her stories, but rather uses those times and events as 'set decoration' against which to place her characters. She is adept at painting detailed word pictures of the dress, homes, furnishings, possessions, and the demeanour of her men and women.

The Winston novels have many aspects in common, they are family oriented centring on one woman. This woman, though inclined to love unwisely the first time around, is ultimately strong in character. There is frequently another woman, jealous, sometimes even evil, in the family, making all kinds of mischief. Suicides, murder, and madness abound. Several of these stories take place near the Washington, DC area where Winston lives, and a sprinkling of historical characters appears in each.

Marietta Garvey is the protagonist of *Gallows Way*, which takes place at Galloway, a plantation in North Carolina, just before the Civil war. The title comes from the road to Galloway where four runaway slaves were caught and hanged. The story has the romantic elements of misguided love, madness, jealousy, and murder, but its historical focus on slavery and the underground railroad makes for provocative and exciting scenes of slave rescues.

The Haversham Legacy, is one of Winston's best-selling novels, but it falls far short in historical value. It begins in Washington on the night Lincoln was shot, shortly after the heroine, Miranda Jervis arrives in town to claim a place with the wealthy Haversham family, to whom she is distantly related. She succeeds and for a while enjoys the best of Washington society, but at a cost. Her Haversham relatives turn out to be addicted to either drugs, drink, gambling, or shady business dealings, and though she finally marries the introspective brother she yearns for, the union brings only tragedy.

The costumes are delightful; the ladies' ball gowns are exquisitely described; the impeachment trial of Andrew Johnson affords an amusing account of Washington senators, big and small, dressed in the neat fashion of the East or in the frontier clothes of the West; some bearded, others clean shaven, some with hair flowing over their collars, others with hair clipped straight at the ears. The men and women bear themselves proudly, secure in their finery, and the senators are pompous with the knowledge of their self-importance.

Loria Bayler, *The Adventuress*, is a very modern woman for 1896, she supports herself and is unashamedly involved with a married man—handsome, virile Jeffrey Warden. Although Jeff is the newly elected attorney general for the state of Maryland, he is bad news, and is not above murder in his pursuit of the governorship. To a recently widowed young woman like Loria, with no family, his attentions are welcome. The story takes place in Annapolis, and is beautifully described. Loria, unaware of her lover's dark side, becomes dangerously entangled in the political intrigue of state politics.

The Fall River Line, is the most ambitious Winston novel. It is another family saga, this time covering 90 years and four generations. For once, an actual organization, the shipping line itself, plays a major role in the story. The protagonist is Augusta Kincaid Wakefield, born in 1847 on the day that the Bay State, the first passenger ship of the Fall River Line sailed on its maiden voyage. Augusta's parents had wisely invested in this new enterprise. As the line expands and new ships are built we follow not only Augusta's life and family but also the lives of other characters, vital to the line—ships' officers, passengers, deckhands. We see rich and poor, well-born and immigrant, sons, daughters and their progeny, from the Civil War through World War I, from the rise of the railroads, through the Great Depression to the decline of the shipping lines. The jealous, manipulative woman is present in Augusta's sister who seduces her husband and bears his child.

Many historical personages ride the ships from Fall River to New York discussing the events of the day—Presidents U.S. Grant, Theodore Roosevelt, Grover Cleveland; business giants Morgan, Belmont, Vanderbilt. Even Jim Fisk is given a speaking role, and Carrie Nation harangues drinking passengers in the grand saloon. Augusta dies on the day the line is disbanded in the company of her great grandchildren. However, by this time it is difficult to keep track of all the characters. Several family trees to illustrate would be helpful.

Very few of Winston's novels have been reviewed outside of library journals, but many have been discovered in stores and on public library shelves by folks eager for a good, easy read. Some earlier books are still in print, and some have been reprinted in large-print editions. Hardly a year goes by without a new Winston novel. She is a speedy, prolific, unpretentious writer with a special talent for colourful and detailed description.

—Marion Hanscom

———

WINTERSON, Jeanette.
Nationality: British. **Born:** Lancashire, in 1959. **Education:** St Catherine's College, Oxford. **Career:** variety of jobs including ice-cream van driver, make-up artist in a funeral parlour, and domestic assistant in a mental hospital. **Recipient:** Whitbread prize, 1985, for *Oranges Are Not the Only Fruit*; John Llewellyn Rhys prize, 1987, for *The Passion*; E.M. Forster award, American Academy of Arts and Letters, 1989. **Address:** c/o Jonathan Cape, 20 Vauxhall Bridge Road, London WW1V 2SA, England.

Romance and Historical Publications

Novels

Oranges Are Not the Only Fruit. London, Pandora Press, 1985; New York, Atlantic Monthly Press, 1987; with *Great Moments in Aviation*, London, Vintage, 1994.
The Passion. London, Bloomsbury, 1987; New York, Atlantic Monthly Press, 1988.
Sexing the Cherry. London, Bloomsbury, 1989.

Other Publications

Novels

Boating for Beginners. London, Methuen, 1985.
Written on the Body. London, Cape, and New York, Knopf, 1992.

Plays

Great Moments in Aviation; Oranges Are Not the Only Fruit (screenplays). London, Vintage, 1994.

Television Play: *Oranges Are Not the Only Fruit*, from her own novel, 1990.

Other

Fit for the Future: The Guide for Women Who Want to Live Well. London, Pandora Press, 1986.

Editor, *Passion Fruit: Romantic Fiction with a Twist*. London, Pandora Press, 1986.

*

Film Adaptation: *Great Moments in Aviation*, 1994.

*   *   *

Although best known for her history of a fundamentalist childhood followed by a sentimental education in 'unnatural passions' (*Oranges Are Not the Only Fruit*), Jeanette Winterson is most widely acclaimed by contemporary critics for her playful historical fantasias, *The Passion*, and *Sexing the Cherry*. These novels are peculiarly modern (or, more accurately, post-modern) instances of the historical romance—the historical romance as magic realism. They are detailed fantastic narratives which engage with the romance of history. Both of them are historical in so far as they are set, for the most part, in a clearly specified historical period—the Napoleonic Wars and the English Civil War respectively. They are also about history as a process and a narrative, and they both employ and interrogate the conventional devices and structures of the romance plot.

Winterson's post-modern investigation of the relationships between stories and history begins in earnest in the short, dense chapter 'Deuteronomy' in *Oranges Are Not the Only Fruit*. According to 'Deuteronomy, The last book of the law', story is 'a way of explaining the universe while leaving the universe unexplained, it's a way of keeping it alive, not boxing it into time'. History, on the other hand is 'very often . . . a means of denying the past' and thus refusing 'to recognize its integrity'. History books 'squeeze this oozing world between two boards and typeset' and reduce the flexibility of the past to mere malleability: 'Once it [the past] could change its mind, now it can only undergo change'. Winterson's narrator prefers a more dynamic and playful version of history as 'a hammock for swinging and a game for playing, the way cats play. Claw it, chew it, rearrange it'.

The hammock of history is certainly set swinging within great vigour in *The Passion*, which interweaves the stories of Henri, a naive French peasant who is uprooted from his simple village life by the great political events of the early 19th-century and by his hero-worshipping passion for Napoleon, and Villanelle, an androgynous, cross-dressing girl, a quasi-mythical creature born with the webbed feet usually possessed only by the boy-children of her Venetian boating community.

The Passion is a story of a particular time and particular places. Napoleon's campaigns provide the phantasmagoric landscapes of the novel, but the main geography of the novel is a geography of the mind. Whether the theatre of his existence is the battlefields of Napoleon's Europe, or the island cell in which he ends his days, Henri's mind is equally unbounded. Similarly Villanelle's Venice is a place of boundless and fantastic possibilities; 'the city of disguises [where] what you are one day will not constrain you on the next'. It is a city of the mind in which metaphors are literalized, and to lose one's heart means precisely that. In this fantastic narrative Villanelle can perform heroic feats of rowing while her heart beats in a jar in the room of the aristocratic lady with whom she has fallen passionately in love. Later Henri, in the manner of Romance heroes, successfully performs the task he has been set of recapturing Villanelle's heart from its hiding place. '*Not possible*?' As the narrator constantly reiterates, 'I'm telling you stories. Trust me'.

Time proves equally resistant to pinning down in Winterson's post-modern historiography. After a storm in which 2000 men are drowned, a particularly graphic instance of the way in which ordinary men and women undergo history at the behest of (and on behalf of) the 'great men' who make it, Henri starts to keep a diary, 'so that I wouldn't forget . . . [and] I'd have something clear and sure to set against my memory tricks'. But, according to his comrade Domino, the contemporary record is no more reliable than memory. 'The way you see it now is no more real than the way you'll see it then . . .

every moment you steal from the present is a moment you have lost for ever. There's only now'.

The status of the here and now, and the relationship between 'now' and 'then', are also among the central preoccupations of *Sexing the Cherry*, which, like *The Passion*, raises profound questions about time and 'the reality of the world'. The Hopi Indians, as one of the novel's epigraphs informs us, have 'no tenses for past, present and future. The division does not exist. What does this say about time?'. One of the things it says is that 'now' and 'then' are cultural constructs with no fixed reference. As the sailor-speaker of the novel's final paragraph concludes: 'The future and the present and the past exist only in our minds, and from a distance the borders of each shrink and fade like the borders of hostile countries seen from a floating city in the sky'.

Like the journeys which they narrate Winterson's novels are a form of time travel in which past and present are fused and juxtaposed. In *Sexing the Cherry*, the two main characters, the 17th-century sailor Jordan and his adoptive mother, the gargantuan Dog Woman who lives with her numerous dogs in her self-built Thameside hut, mutate into a 20th-century schoolboy obsessed with wooden sailing boats (he later becomes a naval deserter), and a heroic Greenham Common type protestor, a 'female chemist' encamped beside the Thames protesting against industrial pollution of rivers.

Physical and moral pollution, and resistance to them are among the main themes of this fantastic narrative. The shape-changing and gender bending of the androgynous Villanelle is continued in the disrupting of gender stereotypes in the man-eating Dog Woman, in whose bulky form Winterson reworks Ben Jonson's Ursula, the pig woman in *Bartholomew Fair*. Jonson's lubricious procuress is rewritten as a curiously a-sexual earth-mother, who is bemused by the ludicrousness of male sexual appetites and behaviours, and who, misunderstanding a request for oral sex, bites off the male organ that is thrust into her cavernous mouth. Like Jonson's pig woman, Winterson's Dog Woman also becomes the scourge of the hypocritical puritans who prohibited the innocent pleasures of others while pursuing their own perverse pleasures in the brothel.

As in *The Passion*, the narrative loops and wheels on itself as history and fantasy become impossibly interwoven. The sailor Jordan not only travels on his ship to new continents (where he discovers the pineapple), but he also travels in his mind on a journey in which: 'Time has no meaning, space and place have no meaning'. On Jordan's journey, 'All times can be inhabited, all places visited . . . The journey is not linear, it is always back and forth, denying the calendar, the wrinkles and lines of the body'. On his 'non-linear' journeying Jordan visits the home of the 12 dancing princesses who tell him the story of how they didn't live happily ever after their marriages to the princes. Winterson's rewriting of the traditional fairytale (like Angela Carter's revisions of fairytales in *The Bloody Chamber*), exposes its coercive ideology, and replaces its normative fiction with the narrative and sexual variety which the heterosexual romance of fairy stories is designed to exclude.

'Time is a great deadener', as Winterson's Book of Deuteronomy observes (*Oranges Are Not the Only Fruit*), but Winterson's historical romances are great enliveners of time, knotting up the cat's cradle of history so that readers may admire its intricate patterning.

—Lyn Pykett

WOOD, Barbara.
Pseudonym: Kathryn Harvey. **Nationality:** American. **Born:** Barbara Lewandowski in England, 30 January 1947. **Education:** University of California, Santa Barbara, 1964–66. **Relations:** married George Wood in 1966. **Career:** surgical technician, Santa Monica Hospital, California, 1973–77; instructor, University of

California, Riverside. **Address:** c/o Random House, 210 East 50th Street, New York, New York 10022, USA.

ROMANCE AND HISTORICAL PUBLICATIONS

Novels

The Magdalene Scrolls. New York, Doubleday, and London, Methuen, 1978.
Hounds and Jackals. New York, Doubleday, 1978; London, Eyre Methuen, 1979.
Curse This House. New York, Dell, 1978; London, Magnum, 1979.
Night Trains, with Gareth Wootton. New York, Morrow, and London, Eyre Methuen, 1979.
Yesterday's Child. New York, Doubleday, 1979; London, Hamlyn, 1981.
The Watchgods. New York, Dell, 1980; London, New English Library, 1981.
Childsong. New York, Doubleday, 1981; Loughton, Essex, Piatkus, 1982.
Domina. New York, Doubleday, and Loughton, Essex, Piatkus, 1983.
Vital Signs. New York, Doubleday, and London, Piatkus, 1985.
Soul Flame. New York, Random House, and London, Piatkus, 1987.
Green City in the Sun. New York, Random House, and London, Macmillan, 1988.
Butterfly (as Kathryn Harvey). New York, Villard, 1988; London, Headline, 1989.
The Dreaming. New York, Macmillan, 1991.
Stars (as Kathryn Harvey). New York, Villard, and London, Headline, 1992.
Virgins of Paradise. New York, Random House, and London, Little Brown, 1993.

*   *   *

Barbara Wood does not write pure love stories. She combines overtly disparate elements, and produces a hybrid of the genre that incorporates romance, mystery, cultural diversity, gender struggle, and even the esoteric. A common denominator evident throughout her work is the accent on medicine and the medical profession. While Wood's own training in the field may have provided this appropriate background, the very choice is advantageous to the dominant theme that weaves through her novels. She places considerable emphasis on duty, and this theme, exploited under the medical banner, enhances the nobility of her characters.

Wood does not shy from using unusual time and place settings in her novels. Neither does she hesitate to employ uncustomary techniques to relay the authenticity of period or expand the scope of her stories. Thus, works like *Yesterday's Child*, *Soul Flame* and *Green City in the Sun*, reach out from this tangible physical realm into one which experiences visions, ghosts and powers from beyond. What may generally be dubbed fanciful, is rendered plausible within the convincing context. Wood's perception of history is seen largely from an individual standpoint or a family chronicle. A recurring plot is the principal character searching for the truth about her family and origins.

Soul Flame illustrates both the author's skills and shortcomings. Set in the opening years of the Anno Domini (AD), it tells the story of Selene, born of unknown parentage, and raised by a healer woman, who finds that she also possessess unusual healing powers. Following the path of her destiny, she travels to many lands, sometimes as a captive, mostly as a fugitive. Reunited with her lover after 17 years apart, she sets out to fulfil her destiny by building a 'hospice' for the

sick and handicapped—a plan thwarted by Queen Agrippina. The queen discovers that Selene is the granddaughter of Julius Cesar and that she too has accession rights to the throne of the Roman Empire—subsequently she tries to kill Selene. In the final pages of the book, Selene is again a fugitive, waiting for another new beginning. Wood maintains the suspense throughout, and the climax of the book is made effective by the open and uncertain ending. Her characterization is strong and convincing. Selene, like most of Wood's heroines, is cast in a role that has her struggle to survive—sometimes physically, mostly professionally—with the odds piled against her. Selene, makes a subtle statement (as do the heroines of *Vital Signs*, *Domina*, and *Virgins of Paradise*) against a culture that attempts to deprive their women of power and status.

Wood's main flaw lies in her ineffectual re-creation of settings. While her detailed descriptions of places, customs, and attire present a picturesque image of the era, she superimposes the concerns of one culture onto another, accepting that problems faced in two societies of varying periods are similar. The following statement taken from *Soul Flame*, would be more appropriate for a contemporary society than AD 1, 'Rome's unemployment rate was outrageously high, and the government handouts supported a large proportion of the population, creating a jobless, uneducated, and rebel class'. Moreover, her novels with several threads of stories and covert meanings, tend to become overloaded. Their convergence, hastily done at the culmination of the story, is awkward and unsatisfactory.

Nevertheless, her reader finds Wood's novels more than mere entertainment. Her descriptions of medical practices are both exhaustive and informative. Her portrayal of culture, regardless of the age, is not superficial. She views society as an agent that actively impinges on an individual's decision making powers and several of her characters are fashioned in response to this 'individual-society' interaction. This added dimension to her stories evokes the readers' opinions on the multitude of issues, enlarging the scope and function of contemporary writers of romance fiction.

—Rachel Kumar

WOOD, Sara.
Nationality: British. **Born:** brought up in Portsmouth. **Relations:** married; two sons. **Career:** various jobs including a typist, and a teacher. Full-time writer. Lives in Cornwall. **Address:** c/o Mills and Boon Ltd, Eton House, 18–24 Paradise Road, Richmond, TW9 2SR, England.

ROMANCE AND HISTORICAL PUBLICATIONS

Novels

Pure Temptation. London, Mills and Boon, 1987.
The Count's Vendetta. London, Mills and Boon, 1988.
No Gentle Loving. London, Mills and Boon, 1988.
Tender Persuasion. London, Mills and Boon, 1988.
Love not Dishonour. London, Mills and Boon, 1989.
Master of Cashel. London, Mills and Boon, 1989.
Nights of Destiny. London, Mills and Boon, 1990.
Threat of Possession. London, Mills and Boon, 1990.
Desert Hostage. London, Mills and Boon, 1990.
Sicilian Vengeance. London, Mills and Boon, 1990.
Cloak of Darkness. London, Mills and Boon, 1992.
Dark Forces. London, Mills and Boon, 1992.
Mask of Deception. London, Mills and Boon, 1993; Toronto, Harlequin, 1994.

Southern Passions. London, Mills and Boon, 1993.
Dark Edge of Love. London, Mills and Boon, 1994.

*   *   *

One of the strengths of Sara Wood's novels is her ability to sustain a witty, sizzling dialogue for several chapters. Another is her imaginative, varied, and intriguing openings that have the reader hooked within a few lines. A sense of fun pervades the novels, and helps persuade the reader to accept unlikely scenarios.

One fascinating opening is in *Cloak of Darkness* which begins 'It wasn't a deep canal, as canals went, but that wasn't much consolation to the man who stood in it.' For several pages Suzy contemplates the man, devises plans, gives assistance, and watches as he is almost run over by a police launch. Many intriguing hints are thrown out, that she has been tailing him, that he is a criminal, she is a private detective, and not everything is quite what it seems. In another novel, *Threat of Possession*, the executive heroine has a male secretary, an interesting reversal of role models appropriate to the modern career woman, much favoured in contemporary Mills and Boon novels.

Sicilian Vengeance, unusually, opens with a scene from the hero's viewpoint, but when the heroine is introduced she is in full vivacious flood regaling friends at a party with a story of how she fought off a huge hairy hand in her tent with her filofax, and 'crawled out starkers . . . to see everyone on the beach and my father absolutely riveted', and later 'I sold more property that week in Cannes than we actually possessed'.

Wood uses exotic settings, Morocco, Arabia, Italy, Ireland, as well as England, but not simply as somewhere different to put her characters. The features of the country or city or people are very cleverly used to highlight or illuminate the story. In Sicily, for instance, the smouldering volcanoes are reflected in the characters of the people, while the Mafia reputation is invoked for the vengeance aspect. In Venice, as the characters float under the Bridge of Sighs the heroine reflects on whether she is trapped too, and when they go along a one-way canal the wrong way she wonders whether she is also on the wrong path. The backgrounds are sketched in lightly, always there, recognizable and important, like the wildlife details discovered by a city-bred girl who begins to feel at home in the country, but they are delicately drawn, never overstated or obtrusive.

Dialogue can be fast, funny and furious:

'You didn't look rushed off your feet when I came in. They were up in the air, displaying the only sole you possess. Do you do all your business from a horizontal position?'
'About the same amount as you,' she answered drily.
'That much?' he marvelled.

And later:

'Mandy, get Security up here, would you? Three of their huskiest men will do.'
'Three husky men and me?' he asked in astonishment. 'That's going it, isn't it?'
'Four men,' Jolanda said to Mandy.

And:

'Let one hand stray, just one finger, and I'll eat it,' she threatened, too tired to fight.
'Now I know what a man-eater is'.

Other characters are in the books only so far as they are absolutely essential to the plot, which could make the situations appear contrived and false. Mills and Boon books need the hero and heroine to be together for most of the time. Wood manages better than most Mills and Boon writers to keep her main characters together in realistic circumstances. This is done partly by having the story take place over a very short period of time, and partly by relating the background through conversation between hero and heroine.

Her heroines are tough, lively, independent, and usually very likeable women. The heroes may appear too aggressive, too bent on having their own way, suspicious of the heroine's motives and unwilling in the beginning to explain their own. In *Threat of Possession* Ethan appears greedy with his determination to recover his lost inheritance, but there is always a compelling reason for these masculine failings, often an insecure or deprived childhood. The vulnerability of the heroes saves them from being unsympathetic, and works on the emotions of the heroines as well as those of the readers.

The plots of these books are often concerned with righting wrongs, but to a large extent these admirable intentions are played down, incidental to the developing relationship of hero and heroine as they discover more about one another and overcome misconceptions, always to discover a happy ending.

Wood is deservedly one of the most popular writers of Mills and Boon romances.

—Marina Oliver

WOODHOUSE, Emma.   See HARROD-EAGLES, Cynthia.

WOODHOUSE, Sarah.
Nationality: British. **Recipient:** Romantic Novelists Association major award, 1989, for *The Peacock's Feather*. **Address:** c/o Century, 20 Vauxhall Bridge Road, London SW1V 2SA, England.

ROMANCE AND HISTORICAL PUBLICATIONS

Novels

A Season of Mists. London, Century, and New York, St Martin's Press, 1984.
The Indian Widow. London, Century, 1985; New York, McGraw Hill, 1986.
Daughter of the Sea. London, Century, 1986.
The Peacock's Feather. London, Century, and New York, St Martin's Press, 1988.
The Native Air. London, Century, 1990; New York, St Martin's Press, 1991.
Enchanted Ground. London, Penguin, 1993.

*   *   *

Sarah Woodhouse's historical novels are romantic in the best sense of the word. This is not say that the picture she gives us of country life at the turn of the 18th century is idealized—far from it; its harshness is depicted, its boredoms and trivialities are shown, the hardships caused by the vagaries of the weather and the difficulties of travel on rough roads in primitive forms of transport are not minimized but the characters she creates and their love stories are quite delightful.

In *Daughter of the Sea*, (the only one of her novels set in Victorian times) the heroine Theo says, 'some places get a hold on us'. This is the key to all her heroines, they are in love with places. For Theo it is Jersey but for the others their special places are in East

Anglia. For Lally, in *The Indian Widow*, it is a windswept heath in Norfolk, for Ann Gerard, in *A Season of Mists*, it is Thorn, her beloved farm in Norfolk, and for Lizzie Rayner, in *The Peacock's Feather*, it is Ramilles, the house in Suffolk in which she was born.

A Season of Mists, *The Peacock's Feather*, and *The Native Air*, make up a trilogy running from 1799 to 1803, the first and last telling Ann's story of love found, love lost and another deeper love discovered where it is least expected, and although she only makes a fleeting appearance in the middle book, Ann Gerard's presence is felt all through it. But these are not books that centre solely on a heroine: all the people living around her have their stories told, especially Dr Alexander French, who frequently acts as *deus ex machina* or catalyst and is an irascible, unconventional hero. All the people in these books are vividly alive, lovable, and engaging characters.

The Indian Widow, is the story of Lally Fletcher who has had a miserable loveless marriage in India and returns to the part of Norfolk in which she grew up and loves with a fierce passion. She is proud and penniless, unconventional and difficult to know. Like Lizzie Rayner, there is something in her past that the gossips have embroidered into scandal. Lally has two endearing suitors, piratical John Glory Lovatt who is even more unconventional than she is, and Sam Ufford a solid but charming farmer who can give her comfort and stability. This story is as romantic as anyone could wish, a book to laugh over, cry over, and put down at last with a sigh. In my opinion this should have won the Romantic Novel of the Year rather than *The Peacock's Feather* which did.

Daughter of the Sea begins in Jersey in 1853. Theo, a girl brought up by her father to love the sea and be the son he never had, is looking for a purpose in her life, stifled by her selfish repressive mother. She is sent to London to stay with her wonderfully eccentric godmother, Millie Boswell, who brings Theo out of her shell. Theo makes a disastrous marriage and follows her soldier husband to the Crimea where she suffers dreadful privations, and witnesses atrocities, and where her husband dies. Unlike Theo the reader is allowed to see who she will choose for her second husband, a man who will help her fulfil her ambition to be a ship-owner as her father was.

Woodhouse has a way with bizarre characters, not only is Millie Boswell eccentric but every member of her household is unusual, from her elderly woman friend who is an expert on small reptiles and corresponds with learned scholars, but also her strange servants and her monkey. Clodie M'Cool, in *The Native Air*, is an eccentric Irish woman who refuses to receive callers but can sell any horse she wishes and wears huge diamonds that were presented by a king.

These books are written with wit, and a delicate touch, they move slowly using felicitous details, and probe deeply into the characters' emotions. This is not the world of Jane Austen nor that of Georgette Heyer but somewhere in between.

—Pamela Cleaver

WOODIWISS, Kathleen E(rin).
Nationality: American. **Born:** Kathleen Erin Hogg, in Alexandria, Louisiana, 3 June 1939. **Education:** schools in Alexandria. **Relations:** married Ross Woodiwiss in 1956; three sons. **Address:** c/o Avon Books, 105 Madison Avenue, New York, New York 10016, USA.

ROMANCE AND HISTORICAL PUBLICATIONS

Novels

The Flame and the Flower. New York, Avon, 1972; London, Futura, 1975.

The Wolf and the Dove. New York, Avon, 1974; London, Piatkus, 1986.
Shanna. New York, Avon, and London, Futura, 1977.
Ashes in the Wind. New York, Avon, 1979; London, Macdonald Futura, 1980.
A Rose in Winter. New York, Avon, and Loughton, Essex, Piatkus, 1983.
Come Love a Stranger. New York, Avon, 1984; London, Piatkus, 1985.
So Worthy My Love. New York, Avon, 1989; London, Piatkus, 1990.
Forever in Your Embrace. New York, Avon, 1992.

*   *   *

Kathleen E. Woodiwiss's impact on the genre, especially in the United States, has been substantial, if not revolutionary. When *The Flame and the Flower*, her first novel, arrived at Avon Books in 1972, the field of romance publishing was still dominated by the contemporary 'gothics' of writers such as Mary Stewart, Victoria Holt, and Phyllis Whitney. A good 300 pages longer than the gothics, *The Flame and the Flower* differs from them further in that it contains long, erotic passages describing the sexual encounters of heroine and hero in surprising detail. When Woodiwiss's novel met with immediate success, her publishers followed it with Rosemary Rogers's similar *Sweet Savage Love* and then created a new romantic subgenre that has since been dubbed 'the erotic historical' or, less reverently, 'the bodice-ripper'.

Woodiwiss's novels, which include, *The Flame and the Flower*, *The Wolf and the Dove*, *Shanna*, *Ashes in the Wind*, *A Rose in Winter*, *Come Love a Stranger*, and *Forever in Your Embrace*, do not deserve the latter epithet, as do those of some of her imitators. Although her heroines encounter male violence as Heather does in *The Flame and the Flower* when she is raped by her future husband because he thinks her a prostitute, Woodiwiss never multiplies such scenes or dwells on their brutal details simply to titillate her readers. Not only are such events rare in her books but they are also carefully integrated into complex plots which all focus on the *gradual* development of love between the two principal characters. Unlike many of the writers of this subgenre who keep the heroine and hero apart until the final pages of the novel, Woodiwiss brings them into contact early in the tale. Having established their initial attraction for each other, she then shows how love develops between two extraordinary individuals, emphasizes that the relationship must be cultivated carefully, and demonstrates that compromise, tenderness, and generosity are necessary to maintain it. The erotic scenes in all of Woodiwiss's novels are presented as integral parts of this deepening relationship and, as a consequence, she places most of her emphasis on the increasing tenderness with which the hero treats the heroine.

Woodiwiss's stories are further distinguished from those of her imitators by the fact that her characters exhibit somewhat more androgynous personalities than do those that typically populate the genre. Although all her heroines are unusually beautiful, sensitive, and particularly adept at nursing or caring for others, they are also asserted to be willful, forceful, intelligent, and capable of initiating action on their own. Interestingly enough, each Woodiwiss heroine is more independent and active than was her predecessor. Aislinn (*The Wolf and the Dove*) and Shanna (*Shanna*) both challenge their heroes in ways Heather (*The Flame and the Flower*) does not, just as they are portrayed as the intellectual equals of their men. This apparent emphasis on equality is carried even further in *Ashes in the Wind* when Alaina masquerades as a boy throughout the entire first half of the novel, saves the hero's life, and generally proves herself capable of fending for herself. The heroes, on the other hand, though typically Byronic, commanding, and spectacularly male, are also capable of reflection, sympathy, and tenderness. By the end of her novels, each Woodiwiss hero, like Brandon in *The Flame and the Flower*, confesses openly his dependence on the heroine and his love for her special qualities. It seems possible, then, that although she does not challenge the validity of the romance's essential message that female happiness can be secured most successfuly in the arms of a protective male, Woodiwiss has been influenced by the feminism of the 1970s to the extent that she unfailingly asserts verbally that her heroines are not mere children whose every whim and desire must be gratified by a man. Rather, she insists, they are independent women who desire a loving relationship that is also an equal partnership. Her extraordinary and sudden popularity may well have been a function of this ability to embody some of the ideas of the feminist movement in changed types without also upsetting the traditional structural relationship between the sexes.

—Janice Radway

WOODMAN, Richard.
Nationality: British. **Born:** Hampstead, London, 10 March 1944. **Education:** Westminster City School, London. **Relations:** married Christine Hite, in 1969; two children. **Career:** apprentice midshipman, 1960–64, qualified as a navigating officer, 1964, and extra third and third officer, 1964–66, Alfred Holt and Company; third officer, Ocean Weather Service, North Atlantic, 1966–67; second officer, 1967–73, Trinity House, Home Waters, first officer, 1973–80, commander, 1980–92. Since 1993, captain, Trinity House, shore-based, Harwich, Essex. Obtained Master's Certificate, 1969. **Recipient:** Marine Society's Barbara Harmer award, 1978. **Agent:** Barbara Levy, 16 Jeffreys Place, London NW1 9PP, England. **Address:** 73 Fronks Road, Dovercourt, Harwich, Essex, CO12 ERS, England.

ROMANCE AND HISTORICAL PUBLICATIONS

Novels (series: Nathaniel Drinkwater in all books except *Wager*, *The Darkening Sea*, and *Endangered Species*)

An Eye of the Fleet. London, Murray, 1981; New York, Pinnacle, 1983.
A King's Cutter. London, Murray, 1982; New York, Pinnacle, 1983.
A Brig of War. London, Murray, 1983; New York, Pinnacle, 1983.
The Bomb Vessel. London, Murray, 1984; New York, Walker Books, 1986.
The Corvette. London, Murray, 1985; as *Arctic Treachery*, New York, Walker Books, 1987.
1805. London, Murray, 1985; as *Decision at Trafalgar*, New York, Walker Books, 1987.
Baltic Mission. London, Murray, 1986; New York, Walker Books, 1988.
In Distant Waters. London, Murray, 1988; New York, St Martin's Press, 1989.
A Private Revenge. London, Murray, 1989; New York, St Martin's Press, 1990.
Voyage East. London, Murray, 1988.
Wager. London, Murray, 1990.
The Darkening Sea. London, Murray, 1991.
Under False Colours. London, Murray, 1991.
The Flying Squadron. London, Murray, 1992.
Endangered Species. London, Little Brown, 1992.

OTHER PUBLICATIONS

Other

Keepers of the Sea. Dalton, Lavenham, 1983.
View from the Sea. London, Century, 1985.

*

Richard Woodman comments:
My twin obsessions with the sea and history led me to write my first novel, *An Eye of the Fleet*, which was published in 1981. This began a series of historical novels centred on the life of Nathaniel Drinkwater, set in the American War of Independence and the Wars of the French Revolution and Empire. Although clearly genre fiction, I resent categorization, believing this unfair, since compared with other genres, in which I chiefly write is inhabited by comparatively few authors. I believe that historical fiction must possess an authentic integrity and an accurate basis; consequently my novels are carefully researched and crafted around obscure incidents which, I believe, permit the historical novelist 'a constrained freedom'. My fiction is, however, unconstrained in terms of character, and a conscious melding of research and experience (from over three decades at sea) compounded with the fact that most of my titles were actually written at sea produce, I hope, highly atmospheric fiction. My knowledge of my subject has generated other novels outside the purely naval genre. I have tackled the knotty problem of a woman at sea in *Wager*, set in 1869, and my own lamentation over the decline of Britain's mercantile fleet is to to be found in *Endangered Species*. The 'autobiographical' novel *Voyage East* received considerable acclaim as a retrospective study. My books have been translated into German, Dutch, and Japanese.

*   *   *

Nathaniel Drinkwater, the hero of Richard Woodman's main sequence of novels, is a British naval officer who begins his career as a midshipman on the frigate *Cyclops* during the American Revolution, rising through the ranks of the Royal Navy of His Britannic Majesty King George III to become lieutenant and captain in the longer conflicts of the French Revolutionary and Napoleonic Wars. The novels chart his service on a variety of vessels and missions, setting Drinkwater's adventures against the background of the historical events of the time.

Woodman's sense of history is good and he conveys it well. Without exception, the books are credibly and intelligently plotted, marrying a firm command of nautical detail with a wide knowledge of their period. They are also ambitious in their scope and coverage. Thus the second novel in the series, *A King's Cutter*, opens with secret operations in the English Channel before and after the outbreak of the revolutionary wars in 1793, climaxing in an account of the naval mutinies of 1797 and the battle of Camperdown between the British and Dutch fleets. These events are woven into the more personal aspects of Drinkwater's career: his recruitment to work for the Admiralty's Secret Intelligence Department, his struggle for promotion and preferment, and his duel of wits with the French agent, Edouard Santhonax. Characters and themes are introduced and are then skilfully developed and reworked in subsequent books.

Woodman is equally successful at recapturing the drama of the great naval campaigns such as the attack on the Danish fleet at Copenhagen in 1801 and Nelson's defeat of the Franco-Spanish squadrons at Trafalgar four years later. The Copenhagen campaign is seen from Drinkwater's perspective as lieutenant-in-command of the bomb vessel, *Virago*, and is enlivened by the inclusion of portrayals of actual historical figures, among them Admirals Hyde Parker and Nelson. Nelson, indeed, appears as a significant participant in a number of the early books, while in *1805* Woodman attempts the even more difficult task of explaining the motives of the French Admiral, Villeneuve. In *Baltic Mission*, set against the negotiation of the Tilsit agreement between France and Russia in 1807, the Emperor Napoleon and Tsar Alexander I are included in the cast. In all cases, the great personages—and other, more minor, historical characters—are believably located in the context of the plot and the feeling of verisimilitude is faultlessly maintained. Woodman shows a sound appreciation, too, of the strategic and high-political dimensions of the events he describes and in relation to which Drinkwater's exploits take place.

The character of Drinkwater develops convincingly as the series proceeds. Introduced as a naive but enthusiastic newcomer to the navy, he is hardened by his early experiences and by disappointment in his search for promotion. Unlike a number of his fictional contemporaries (Ramage, Bolitho, even the inimitable Hornblower, with whom he has most in common), his rise is not rapid, Drinkwater attaining the coveted post-rank only in his mid-thirties after a successful cruise to protect the Arctic whaling fleet (described in *The Corvette*). He nevertheless shows himself to be a resourceful and determined officer, demonstrating a talent for command and a growing aura of authority. Sometimes verging on the puritanical, a professional sailor impatient of privilege and with a sense of duty unaffected by social pretensions or political ambitions, he is sustained throughout by a happy, uneventful marriage and a stern belief in providence, as well as by a limited, but colourful, circle of friends and subordinates, notably the Admiralty spymaster, Lord Dungarth, the one-handed Lieutenant Quilhampton and the faithful Cornish seaman Tregembo, who serves as Drinkwater's coxswain. Even more colourful, and important in giving shape to Drinkwater's personal odyssey, are his frequent adversaries—the Frenchman Santhonax, his bewitchingly beautiful wife, Hortense, and the unspeakably evil Augustus Morris—who bring Drinkwater into greater danger than the accumulated broadsides of Napoleon's navies.

All the books are well-constructed and stylishly written, with an interesting range of supporting characters. Woodman has the ability to evoke place and period with enviable economy; he has a good, literary, command of language, yet his writing is clear and straightforward and the dialogue is authentically atmospheric. Moreover, while they are primarily stories of action and adventure, the novels are not without a subtler side. Drinkwater himself is an introspective character in the Hornblower mould, and he and his companions engage in occasional moral, philosophical, and political speculations which nicely reproduce the intellectual and spiritual turmoil of the revolutionary years. The social distinctions of naval life are deftly explored, throwing the spotlight on to the personal rivalries of officers and the problems encountered by those at sea for long periods. Nor are the harsher aspects of life on board a man-of-war glossed over. The cruelties of naval discipline, the discomforts and discontents of the lower deck and their relationship to the wider injustices of Georgian Britain are feelingly described and at times play a crucial part in the action. In short, Woodman provides a genuinely panoramic view of Drinkwater's navy and his series represents a considerable achievement in a genre where the quality of the rivals is already high.

In addition to the Drinkwater series, Woodman has produced other works of historical maritime fiction. *Wager* is an exciting and entertaining tale set in the last days of the China tea-clippers and is unusual in having a woman as its central character. Another recent novel, *The Darkening Sea*, is a more ambitious attempt to encompass the story of Britain's naval decline, from the battle of Jutland in 1916 to the mid-1980s, within the history of a single family employed in the Royal Navy and the Merchant marine. The story is kept afloat by a fast pace of action, some strong characterization and a measure of personal commitment on the part of the author, but inevitably (and perhaps intentionally) the overall effect is one of anti-

climax, as if the whole of the 20th century were little more than a footnote to the days of British naval supremacy in the age of sail. It may be a measure of Woodman's achievement elsewhere that the ghost of Nathaniel Drinkwater casts such a long shadow.

—David Powell

WOODS, Sherryl.
Pseudonyms: Alexandra Kirk; Suzanne Sherrill. **Nationality:** American. **Born:** Washington DC, 23 July 1944. **Education:** Ohio State University, Columbus, Ohio, 1962–66, B.A. in journalism. **Career:** journalist, 1966–69, and television and radio editor, 1970–74, *Columbus Citizen Journal*, Ohio, and journalist, *Today*, Cocoa, Florida, 1969; amusement editor, *Palm Beach Post*, 1969–70; television and radio editor, *Miami News*, Florida, 1974–80; assistant administrator, University of Miami, Jackson Memorial Medical Center, Miami, Florida, 1981–86. Since 1980, full time writer. **Agent:** Denise Marcil Literary Agency, 685 West End Avenue 9-C, New York, New York 10025. **Address:** PO Box 490326, Key Biscayne, Florida 33149, USA.

ROMANCE AND HISTORICAL PUBLICATIONS

Novels (series: Mollie DeWitt; Amanda Roberts; Vows)

Restoring Love (as Suzanne Sherrill). New York, Dell, 1982.
Sand Castles (as Alexandra Kirk). New York, Bantam, and London, Century, 1982.
Images of Love (as Alexandra Kirk). New York, Bantam, 1982.
Desirable Compromise (as Suzanne Sherrill). New York, Dell, 1984.
Thrown for a Loss. New York, New American Library, 1984.
Jamaican Midnight. New York, Avon, 1984.
Shadow on the Hill (as Alexandra Kirk). New York, Golden Apple, 1985.
A Kiss Away. New York, Berkley, 1986.
A Prince Among Men. New York, Berkley, 1986.
All for Love. New York, Berkley, 1986.
Not at Eight. New York, Silhouette, 1986.
Safe Harbor. New York, Silhouette, 1987.
Best Intentions. New York, Berkley, 1987.
Yesterday's Love. New York, Silhouette, 1987.
Come Fly with Me. New York, Silhouette, 1987.
A Gift of Love. New York, Silhouette, 1987.
Two's Company. New York, Berkley, 1987.
Never Let Go. New York, Silhouette, 1988.
Second Chance at Love. New York, Silhouette, 1988.
Edge of Forever. New York, Silhouette, 1988.
Prince Charming Replies. New York, Berkley, 1988.
Can't Say No. New York, Silhouette, 1988.
Heartland. New York, Silhouette, 1989.
In Too Deep. New York, Silhouette, 1989.
One Touch of Moondust. New York, Silhouette, 1989.
Reckless (Amanda Roberts). New York, Warner, 1989.
Body and Soul (Amanda Roberts). New York, Warner, 1989.
Stolen Moments (Amanda Roberts). New York, Warner, 1990.
Miss Liz's Passion. New York, Silhouette, 1990.
Tea and Destiny. New York, Silhouette, 1990.
Next Time . . . Forever. New York, Silhouette, 1990.
Joshua and the Cowgirl. New York, Silhouette, 1991.
Fever Pitch. New York, Silhouette, 1991.
My Dearest Cal. New York, Silhouette, 1991.
Ties That Bind (Amanda Roberts). New York, Silhouette, 1991.

Vows Trilogy:
  Love. New York, Silhouette, 1992.
  Honor. New York, Silhouette, 1992.
  Cherish. New York, Silhouette, 1992.
Dream Mender. New York, Silhouette, 1992.
Hot Property (Molly Dewitt). New York, Dell, 1992.
Hot Secret (Molly DeWitt). New York, Dell, 1992.
Hot Money (Molly DeWitt). New York, Dell, 1993.
Kate's Vow. New York, Silhouette, 1993.
A Daring Vow. New York, Silhouette, 1993.
Bank on It (Amanda Roberts). New York, Warner, 1993.
Hide and Seek (Amanda Roberts). New York, Warner, 1993.

*

Sherryl Woods comments:
    Whether in romances or mysteries, I am most interested in characters and relationships. I am fascinated by the powerful emotions of love and hate, and the effect they have on the lives of everyday people.

*   *   *

    Another of Silhouette's prolific contemporary authors, Sherryl Woods can be counted on to provide a good, solid love story with entertaining characters. In her best category romances, she goes beyond entertainment to provide more thought provoking, poignant stories.
    In *Dream Mender*, Woods tackled a sensitive subject not usually treated in romance novels. Jenny Michaels, an occupational therapist, gets master carpenter, Frank Chambers as a client. Used to having others rely on him, he has great difficulty adjusting to his helplessness when his hands are badly injured in a fire. Although he makes progress in his physical therapy, the magnitude of the scarring on his hands embitters him. Jenny, who has come to love him, helps him through this crisis by revealing her own deep-seated anguish and suffering. Having lost a breast to cancer, she was rejected by a man because of the unsightliness of her scar. Not only must she bear the pain of this rejection, but she also feels she must put her personal life on hold as she endures yearly examinations to check for recurrence of the disease. Woods very touchingly conveys Jenny's feelings and courage as she faces a painful past and an uncertain future.
    In her 'Vows' series for Silhouette, Woods uses three generations of a wealthy Boston family to illustrate problems encountered by many couples. *Love* is the story of Jason Halloran, a vice-president in his family's textile firm. Used to doing what is expected of him, his orderly life is shaken by Dana Roberts, a street-smart young woman. On her own since her adolescence, Dana is responsible for her teenage brother, who is verging on delinquency. Jason must fight against his own prejudices and those of his family to bring Dana into his life and keep her there. Jason's father and mother, Kevin and Lacey, are the subjects of *Honor*. Like Dana, Lacey was from a lower social class than her husband and was opposed by his father. They appear to have had a successful marriage, but as Woods shows, this is the surface image, not the reality. Over the years, Kevin has become more and more obsessed with his work, driven to acquire material things, while Lacey feels more and more left out of his life. With Jason grown and settled, Lacey feels more and more estranged and decides to leave Kevin. When he is stricken by a heart attack, she agrees to accompany him to their refuge on Cape Cod while he recuperates, although she is still ambivalent about their relationship. This enforced slow down in their lives enables them to closely examine what has gone wrong and to begin to repair the damage. The domineering, meddling patriarch of the clan, Brendon Halloran, is featured in *Cherish*. Finally beginning to accept the changes in his family, he has an unusual chance to rectify past mistakes and gain a second chance at happiness. Finding Elizabeth Forsyte, his first love from the 1940s, gives him a new perspective on his life and love, especially after learning that he has an adult daughter he never knew. Woods even has offered an addendum to the series with *Kate's Vow*. Divorce lawyer, Kate Newton, feels left out when her mother, Elizabeth Forsyte Newton, rediscovers her old love, Brendon Halloran and her sister, Ellen, is acknowledged as his daughter. Coming on top of the cynicism she has developed as a result of her profession, these revelations cause her to doubt that real love is possible. This view is reinforced by her newest client, a ten-year-old boy, Davey Winthrop, who wants to 'divorce' his father. His widowed father, David, has been overwhelmed by his own loss and neglected Davey's needs. In all of these stories, Woods takes realistic contemporary family situations and probes deeply into the ease with which people can drift apart and the problems caused by poor communication.
    Woods has also displayed a talent for suspense mixed with romance in two series of romantic mysteries, each featuring a spirited, independent heroine. *Reckless* introduces two transplanted New Yorkers, now living in Georgia. Amanda Roberts is an investigative reporter, and Joe Donelli is an ex-cop, who claims he just wants to be a farmer. They meet when both are involved in a murder investigation and they begin to vie for clues. In spite of their rivalry, a romance develops between the two. Woods nurtures the romance through later volumes in the series, including *Body and Soul*, *Stolen Moments*, *Ties That Bind*, and *Bank On It*. Amanda and Joe even are due to be married at the beginning of *Ties That Bind* but murder, an FBI sting and the Ku Klux Klan all intrude on the plans.
    Molly DeWitt is the second of Woods's romantic thriller heroines. A public relations specialist for the fictional Miami/Dade Film Commission, she seems to attract murder (*Hot Property*, *Hot Secret*). She also attracts a sexy, macho Latino homicide detective named Michael O'Hara. Like the relationship between Amanda and Joe, Woods is building a relationship for Molly and Michael with each book. They sound one another out, while admitting their growing attraction. Woods shows a real talent for creating funny, bright dialogue that brings these characters to life.
    After several years of providing reliable, enjoyable, and diverting love stories, Woods has begun to break away from the larger field of competent authors of romantic fiction. Her treatment of serious, emotional subjects combined with her ability to create romantic suspense filled with humour make her appealing to a wide range of readers of the genre.

—Barbara E. Kemp

———

WOODWARD, Lilian.
Pseudonym for John Marsh. **Other Pseudonyms:** Julia Davis; John Elton; John Harley; Harrington Hastings; Irene Lawrence; Joan Marsh; Grace Richmond; Petra Sawley; Monica Ware. **Nationality:** British. **Born:** 1907. **Address:** Chalfont, Rawson Avenue, Halifax HX3 0LN, Yorkshire, England.

Romance and Historical Publications

Novels

Nursing Assignment. London, Hale, 1959.
Cruise to Romance. London, Hale, 1960.
Nurse Frayne's Strange Quest. London, Hale, 1960.
The Hidden Past. London, Hale, 1961.
Nurse to the Maharajah. London, Hale, 1961.
Appointment with Love. London, Hale, 1962.

The Wrong Love. London, Hale, 1962.
Love Me—Love Me Not. London, Hale, 1966.
The House on the Moor. London, Hale, 1967.
Flight to Romance. London, Hale, 1969.
Prisoner of Love. London, Hale, 1971.
The Tuscan Chalice. London, Hale, 1972.
So Dear to Their Hearts. London, Hale, 1974.
North Sea Nurse. London, Hale, 1975.
Mill Town Nurse. London, Hale, 1976; South Yarmouth, Massachusetts, Curley, 1990.
A Very Special Love. London, Hale, 1976.
That Man in Her Life. London, Hale, 1977.
Dangerous Secret. London, Hale, 1978; South Yarmouth, Massachusetts, Curley, 1989.
The Doctors of Doncastle. London, Hale, 1978.
Flying Nurse. London, Hale, 1979.
Folly of Love. London, Hale, 1979.
Nurse to Princess Jasmine. London, Hale, 1979.
Agency Nurse. London, Hale, 1980.
The Barrier Between Them. London, Hale, 1980.
Design for Loving. London, Hale, 1980.
Flight to Sandaha. London, Hale, 1981.
Love's a Magician. London, Hale, 1981.
Give All to Love. London, Hale, 1982.
Out of the Past. London, Hale, 1982.
Reflections of Love. London, Hale, 1983.
Lover from Yesterday. London, Hale, 1984.
Mystery Lover. London, Hale, 1985.

Novels as Grace Richmond

She Followed Her Heart. London, Fiction House, 1944.
June Fairley—Air Hostess. London, Hale, 1959.
When There's Love at Home. London, Hale, 1959.
Too Young to Wed. London, Hale, 1960.
The Touch of Your Hand. London, Hale, 1960.
Marriage Is Like That. London, Hale, 1961.
The Greater Love. London, Hale, 1961.
The Doctor's Secret. London, Hale, 1962.
The Love Race. London, Hale, 1967.
Island of Secrets. London, Hale, 1968.
Waters of Conflict. London, Hale, 1969.
Passport to Romance. London, Hale, 1969.
Yesterday's Love. London, Hale, 1972.
Run Away from Love. London, Hale, 1974.
Legacy Without Love. London, Hale, 1976.
Nurse to Doctor James. London, Hale, 1976.
Testament of Love. London, Hale, 1977.
Two Doctor Greys. London, Hale, 1977.
Don't Cling to the Past. London, Hale, 1978.
At the Villa Mimosa. London, Hale, 1978.
Believe the Heart. London, Hale, 1979.
Fugitive from Love. London, Hale, 1980.
Haunted Love. London, Hale, 1980.
Vision of Love. London, Hale, 1980.
Air Ambulance Nurse. London, Hale, 1981.
Nurse Hanson's Strange Case. London, Hale, 1981.
That Villa in Spain. London, Hale, 1981.
Guardian of the Trees. London, Hale, 1982.
The Cottage in the Wood. London, Hale, 1983.
House of Strangers. London, Hale, 1983.
No Place for Lovers. London, Hale, 1983.
Reach Out for Happiness. London, Hale, 1984.

Novels as John Harley

The Four Doctors. London, Hale, 1960.

Doctor with Four Hands. London, Hale, 1962.
Doctor to the House of Jasmine. London, Gifford, 1967.
Doctor in Spain. London, Hale, 1968.
Doctor in Danger. London, Hale, 1970.

Novels as Petra Sawley

No Time for Love. London, Gresham, 1967.
No Place for Love. London, Gresham, 1967.
Love on Ice. London, Gresham, 1967.
Their Mysterious Patient. London, Gresham, 1970.
Love's Dark Shadow. London, Gresham, 1970.
That Strange Holiday. London, Hale, 1972.
Doctor with a Past. London, Hale, 1973.
Dream of Past Loves. London, Hale, 1975.

Novels as Joan Marsh

Love in Peril. London, Gresham, 1967.
Love Spins the Wheel. London, Gresham, 1967.
Love Takes the Helm. London, Gresham, 1967.
The Bride's House. London, Gresham, 1968.
Prince of Hearts. London, Gresham, 1970.
Conflict of the Heart. London, Gresham, 1971.
The Truth About Janice Henderson. London, Hale, 1972.
Victim of Love. London, Hale, 1973.
Lord of Imchay. London, Hale, 1975.

Novels as Irene Lawrence

World Without Love. London, Gresham, 1967.
Love Is Like That. London, Gresham, 1967.
Switch on to Love. London, Gresham, 1967.
Love Rides the Skies. London, Gresham, 1968.
Love Came Unaware. London, Gresham, 1970.
Love's Last Barrier. London, Gresham, 1971.
Nurse Farnley's Secret. London, Hale, 1972.
Hostage of Love. London, Hale, 1973.
No Escape from Love. London, Hale, 1974.

Novels as Monica Ware

Au Pair Girl. London, Gresham, 1967.
Make Way for Love. London, Gresham, 1967.
Stranger to Love. London, Gresham, 1967.
The Ties of Love. London, Gresham, 1968.
Love Knows No Frontier. London, Gresham, 1970.
The Love She Hid. London, Gresham, 1970.
Her Mystery Man. London, Gresham, 1971.
Love in Danger. London, Hale, 1972.
Disco in Spain. London, Hale, 1976.

Novels as Julia Davis

Love in the Lead. London, Gresham, 1967.
Holiday for Lovers. London, Gresham, 1967.
Her Unexpected Summer. London, Gresham, 1967.
That Affair in Spain. London, Gresham, 1969.
Sands of Desire. London, Gresham, 1970.
The Doctor's Favourite Nurse. London, Gresham, 1971.
Nurse in Arabia. London, Hale, 1972.
Fly High, My Heart. London, Hale, 1972.
Love's Treasure Trove. London, Hale, 1973.
Magic of the Desert. London, Hale, 1976.
African Interlude. Aylesbury, Buckinghamshire, Hunt Barnard, 1982.

OTHER PUBLICATIONS as John Marsh

Novels

Criminal Square (with Florence Shepherd, as Harrington Hastings). London, Hutchinson, 1929.
The War Dog Stirs (with Florence Shepherd, as Harrington Hastings). London, Hutchinson, 1930.
Maiden Armour. London, Stanley Paul, 1932.
Lonely Pathway. London, Stanley Paul, 1933.
Return They Must. London, Stanley Paul, 1933.
The Wrong That Was Done. London, Leng, 1935.
Body Made Alive. London, Stanley Smith, 1936.
A Glimpse of Paradise. London, Boardman, 1944.
Many Parts. London, Swan, 1946.
Two Mrs Farrells. London, Boardman, 1946.
Shipwrecked Schoolship. London, Swan, 1949.
By the World Condemned. London, Amalgamated Press, 1949.
The Secret of the Seven Sisters. London, Ward, 1950.
The Brain of Paul Menoloff. London, Robertson, 1953.
The Cruise of the Carefree. London, Ward, 1955.
The Green Plantations (as John Elton). London, Ward Lock, 1955.
House of Echoes. London, Gifford, 1956.
The Hidden Answer. London, Gifford, 1956.
Murderer's Maze. London, Gifford, 1957.
Operation Snatch. London, Gifford, 1958.
City of Fear. London, Gifford, 1958.
The Reluctant Executioner. London, Hale, 1959.
Small and Deadly. London, Hale, 1960.
Girl in a Net. London, Hale, 1962.
The Golden Teddybear. London, Boardman, 1965.
Not My Murder. London, Gifford, 1967.
Monk's Hollow. London, Gifford, 1968; New York, Ace, 1969.
Hate Thy Neighbour. London, Hale, 1969.
Master of High Beck. London, Hale, 1969.

Other

The Young Winston Churchill. London, Evans, 1955.
Clip a Bright Guinea: The Yorkshire Coiners of the Eighteenth Century. London, Hale, 1971.

* * *

There is a skill to writing love stories. The mere existence of the formula (man, woman, attraction, problems, reconciliation, and rosy sunset) does not guarantee automatic success in practice. No matter how many incompetent hands it passes through, however, the principle remains. Modifications are made to keep up with the times of course, for sex precedes marriage and men now know where the tea towels are kept and how to use them, but generally there are few real differences. Men are men; women are women, and thus the twain shall meet.

Because John Marsh has written over such a long time-span, under the names of Julia Davis, John Harley, Irene Lawrence, Joan Marsh, Grace Richmond, Petra Sawley, and Lilian Woodward, the inevitable shifts in attitude can easily be traced between his earlier and later work. In *She Followed Her Heart* (1944, as Grace Richmond) Eve, who is kind to little old ladies and compassionate to RAF widows and orphans, falls instantly in love with a blue uniform and a pair of silver wings. She is the stereotypical dress shop assistant heroine. By *Waters of Conflict* (1969) however, the same figure has evolved into a woman of the world caught in the middle of a dispute between Welsh nationalists and the British government.

Marsh's greatest skill lies in his ability to recognize and respond to the new demands of his audience. We would not be satisfied with a figure like the protagonist of *June Fairley—Air Hostess* (1959) who is hysterical, weepy, and easily duped, but we do feel somewhat closer to the capable and resourceful Janet of *Passport to Romance* (1969). Marsh's more recent heroines resemble the earlier models by working in the caring roles of nannies and nurses (*Nurse to Princess Jasmine, Agency Nurse*).

These figures are now acceptable to today's readership because the setting has kept apace with the changing times. Maggie and Jill in *Air Ambulance Nurse* are in a traditional female profession, but Jill becomes a jet-setting career woman—something unthinkable for her counterpart in a romantic novel 20 years ago. Marsh's constant use of a medical background is arguably repetitious and unimaginative, but within it he works hard to reflect social changes. It serves as a constant base from which he can explore new perceptions.

The heroes are rarely the classic specimens of rough manhood tameable in the right hands, nor are they seductive charmers favoured by other writers. Instead of condescending to awaken adult feelings in the neurotic female with a kiss, they are warm and caring, the epitome of the boy next door. Occasionally the rugged persona does appear, for example Ralph in *Master of High Beck* or Ben in *No Place for Lovers*, but since this is a façade on the part of the proud and vulnerable male ego, they remain in line with their counterparts in Marsh's other books—sensitive and human.

Marsh does not usually rely on fantasy and escapism for appeal, but on accessibility and identification. Domestic affairs are central to his plots, with such marital problems as suspected infidelity frequently the focus (this happens on a grand scale in *When There's Love at Home*). In these situations the woman is usually the figure of power with the final say, and Marsh carries off this reversal with conviction. The later novels may be more fanciful and exotic, but at heart they too support these values.

Marsh stands above the normal run of romance fiction writers mainly because he turns the established format in a new direction, and yet retains enough of the essentials to be considered a writer of traditional romances. He takes risks with a popular genre, making him unusual in a field that relies heavily on the familiar.

—L.M. Quinn

———

WOOLF, Victoria. See **LAMB, Charlotte.**

———

WORBOYS, Anne.
Pseudonyms: Annette Eyre; Vicky Maxwell; Anne Eyre Worboys. **Nationality:** British. **Born:** Annette Isobel Eyre in Auckland, New Zealand. **Military Service:** Royal New Zealand Air Force, 1942–45. **Career:** married Walter Worboys in 1946; two daughters. **Recipient:** Mary Elgin award, 1975; Romantic Novelists Association major award, 1977. **Agent:** David Higham Associates Ltd, 5–8 Lower John Street, London WIR 4HA, England. **Address:** The White House, Leigh, near Tonbridge, Kent, England.

ROMANCE AND HISTORICAL PUBLICATIONS

Novels

The Lion of Delos. New York, Delacorte Press, 1974; London, Hodder and Stoughton, 1975.
Every Man a King. London, Hodder and Stoughton, 1975; New York, Scribner, 1976; as *Rendezvous with Fear*, New York, Ace, 1977.

The Barrancourt Destiny. London, Hodder and Stoughton, 1977; New York, Scribner, 1978.

The Bhunda Jewels. London, Severn House, 1980; New York, Ace, 1981.

Run, Sara, Run. New York, Scribner, 1981; London, Severn House, 1982.

A Kingdom for the Bold. London, Century, 1986.

Aurora Rose. New York, Dutton, 1988; London, New English Library, 1989.

China Silk. New York, St Martin's Press, and London, Piatkus, 1991.

Alice. London, Severn House, 1992.

Novels as Anne Eyre Worboys

Dream of Petals Whim. London, Ward Lock, 1961.

Palm Rock and Paradise. London, Ward Lock, 1961.

Call for a Stranger. London, Ward Lock, 1962.

Novels as Annette Eyre

Three Strings to a Fortune. London, Hurst and Blackett, 1962.

Visit to Rata Creek. London, Hurst and Blackett, 1964.

The Valley of Yesterday. London, Hurst and Blackett, 1965.

A Net to Catch the Wind. London, Hurst and Blackett, 1966.

Return to Bellbird Country. London, Hurst and Blackett, 1966.

The House of Five Pines. London, Hurst and Blackett, 1967.

The River and Wilderness. London, Hurst and Blackett, 1967; as *Give Me Your Love,* New York, New American Library, 1975.

A Wind from the Hill. London, Hurst and Blackett, 1968.

Thorn-Apple. London, Hurst and Blackett, 1968.

Tread Softly in the Sun. London, Hurst and Blackett, 1969.

The Little Millstones. London, Hurst and Blackett, 1970.

Dolphin Bay. London, Hurst and Blackett, 1970.

Rainbow Child. London, Hurst and Blackett, 1971.

The Magnolia Room. London, Hurst and Blackett, 1972; New York, New American Library, 1975.

Venetian Inheritance. London, Hurst and Blackett, 1973; New York, New American Library, 1975.

Novels as Vicky Maxwell

Chosen Child. London, Collins, 1973; New York, Ace, 1980.

Flight to the Villa Mistra. London, Collins, 1973; New York, Ace, 1981.

The Way of the Tamarisk. London, Collins, 1974; (as Anne Worboys) New York, Delacorte Press, 1975.

High Hostage. London, Collins, 1976.

The Other Side of Summer. London, Collins, 1977; New York, Ace, 1979.

*   *   *

Anne Worboys's earlier novels are in the style of Mary Stewart's adventure-romances. Set in exotic locations—India, Greece, Spain—they contain mystery, romance, and sometimes even murder.

The Lion of Delos, Worboys's first novel is set in Greece on the island of Mykonos. It features the disappearance of a young girl, and the smuggling of antiquities out of Greece. Reminiscent of Stewart's *This Rough Magic* and *The Moon Spinners,* the story is told by Virginia Sanderson who goes to Mykonos to find her identical twin sister, Lee. Followed from Athens by a mysterious but attractive man, Nat Ross, Virginia discovers that he is an archaeologist working undercover to find out how antiquities are leaving Greece illegally. They combine forces to find out the true story behind Lee's disappearance, and discover who is behind the smuggling trade.

The Barrancourt Destiny (similar to Stewart's *Nine Coaches Waiting*) finds Victoria travelling to Kent in disguise to discover the truth about her past. She becomes embroiled in the affairs of the Barrancourt family, and meets the heir, Hugo, and his cousin, Louis (whom she falls in love with). Similarly, *The Bhunda Jewels* leads Ashley Bellamy to a small village in India to trace her missing brother. She finds herself enmeshed in a plot to steal the sacred Bhunda jewels, and finds romance in the arms of Dr Clive Retford. Like all of Worboys's books *The Bhunda Jewels* contains a lot of detail, including a description of a rope sacrifice carried out in the villages of Himachel Pradesh.

China Silk, one of Worboys's most recent novels, is a much larger, more involved story that involves the heroine's rape, abduction, and forced marriage before she is finally reunited with her true love in Malaysia. Most of the book is set in and around Hong Kong, and there is great attention to the countryside and customs of the time.

Worboys also writes romance novels as Annette Eyre, and mysteries as Vicky Maxwell.

—Marion Hatchard

———

WORBOYS, Anne Eyre.   See WORBOYS, Anne.

———

WREN, P(ercival) C(hristopher).
Nationality: British. **Born:** Devon in 1885. **Education:** Oxford University, M.A. **Relations:** married; one son. **Career:** schoolmaster, journalist, farm hand, explorer, hunter, soldier; trooper in a British cavalry regiment, and served in the French Foreign Legion; lived in India; assistant director of education, Bombay, ten years, and justice of the Peace; major in the Indian Forces in East Africa during World War I: invalided home. **Died:** 22 November 1941.

ROMANCE AND HISTORICAL PUBLICATIONS

Novels (series: Geste Family; Sinbad Dysart)

Father Gregory; or, Lures and Failures: A Tale of Hindostan. London, Longman, 1913; New York, Stokes, 1926.

Snake and Sword. London, Longman, 1914; as *The Snake and the Sword,* New York, Stokes, 1923.

The Wages of Virtue. London, Murray, 1916; New York, Stokes, 1917.

Driftwood Spars. London, Longman, 1916; New York, Stokes, 1927.

Cupid in Africa; or, The Baking of Bertram in Love and War—A Character Study. London, Cranton, 1920.

Beau Geste. London, Murray, 1924; New York, Stokes, 1925.

Beau Sabreur (Geste). London, Murray, and New York, Stokes, 1926.

Beau Ideal (Geste). London, Murray, and New York, Stokes, 1928.

Soldiers of Misfortune: The Story of Otho Belleme. London, Murray, and New York, Stokes, 1929.

Mysterious Waye: The Story of 'The Unsetting Sun'. London, Murray, and New York, Stokes, 1930.

The Mammon of Righteousness: The Story of Coxe and the Box. London, Murray, 1930; as *Mammon,* New York, Stokes, 1930.

Sowing Glory: The Memoirs of 'Mary Ambree', The English Woman—Legionary. London, Murray, and New York, Stokes, 1931.

Valiant Dust. London, Murray, and New York, Stokes, 1932.

Action and Passion (Sinbad). London, Murray, and New York, Stokes, 1933.

Beggars' Horses. London, Murray, 1934; as *The Dark Woman*, Philadelphia, Macrae Smith, 1943.

Sinbad the Soldier. London, Murray, and Boston, Houghton Mifflin, 1935.

Explosion. London, Murray, 1935.

Spanish Maine. London, Murray, 1935; as *The Desert Heritage*, Boston, Houghton Mifflin, 1935.

Fort in the Jungle: The Extraordinary Adventures of Sinbad Dysart in Tonkin. London, Murray, and Boston, Houghton Mifflin, 1936.

Bubble Reputation. London, Murray, 1936; as *The Courtenay Treasure*, Boston, Houghton Mifflin, 1936.

The Man of a Ghost. London, Murray, 1937; as *The Spur of Pride*, Boston, Houghton Mifflin, 1937.

Worth Wile. London, Murray, 1937; as *To the Hilt*, Boston, Houghton Mifflin, 1937.

Cardboard Castle. London, Murray, and Boston, Houghton Mifflin, 1938.

Paper Prison. London, Murray, 1939; as *The Man the Devil Didn't Want*, Philadelphia, Macrae Smith, 1940.

The Disappearance of General Jason. London, Murray, 1940.

Two Feet from Heaven. London, Murray, 1940; Philadelphia, Macrae Smith, 1941.

Stories of the Foreign Legion (omnibus). London, Murray, 1947.

Short Stories

Dew and Mildew: Semi-Detached Stories from Karabad, India. London, Longman, 1912; as *Dew and Mildew: A Loose-Knit Tale of Hindustan*, New York, Stokes, 1927.

Stepsons of France. London, Murray, and New York, Stokes, 1917.

The Young Stagers, Being Further Faites and Gestes of the Junior Curlton Club of Karabad, India.... London, Longman, 1917; New York, Stokes, 1926.

Good Gestes: Stories of Beau Geste, His Brothers, and Certain of Their Comrades in the French Foreign Legion. London, Murray, and New York, Stokes, 1929.

Flawed Blades: Tales from the Foreign Legion. London, Murray, and New York, Stokes, 1933.

Port o' Missing Men: Strange Tale of the Stranger Regiment. London, Murray, 1934; Philadelphia, Macrae Smith, 1943.

Rough Shooting: True Tales and Strange Stories. London, Murray, 1938; Philadelphia, Macrae Smith, 1944.

Odd—But Even So: Stories Stranger Than Fiction. London, Murray, 1941; Philadelphia, Macrae Smith, 1942.

The Hunting of Henri. London, Vallancey Press, 1944.

Dead Men's Boot and Other Tales from the Foreign Legion. London, Gryphon, 1949.

Other Publications

Other

The Indian Teacher's Guide to the Theory and Practice of Mental, Moral, and Physical Education. Bombay, Longman, 1910.

Indian School Organization, Management, Discipline, Tone, and Equipment, Being the Indian Headmaster's Guide. Bombay, Longman, 1911.

The 'Direct' Teaching of English in Indian Schools. Bombay, Longman, 1911.

Chemistry and First Aid for Standard VII, with H. E. H. Pratt. Bombay, Longman, 1913.

Physics and Mechanics, with N. B. Macmillan. Bombay, Longman, 1914.

With the Prince Through Canada, New Zealand, and Australia. Bombay, Athenaeum Press, 1922.

Work, Wealth, and Wages (for children), revision of a work by Ernest F. Row. Bombay, Cooper, 1950.

First Lessons in English Grammar. Bombay, Cooper, 1961.

Editor, *The World and India, Adapted for Use in Indian Schools*. Calcutta, Oxford University Press, 1905.

Editor, *Ivanhoe* (simplified), by Scott. London, Frowde, 1912.

Editor, *Longmans' Science Series for Indian High Schools*. Bombay, Longman, 11 vols, 1913–14.

Editor, *Gulliver's Travels* (simplified), by Swift. Calcutta, Oxford University Press, 1963.

*

Film Adaptations: *Beau Ideal*, 1931; *Beau Geste*, 1939, 1966, 1984.

*　　*　　*

P.C. Wren's works range from potboilers indistinguishable from the fulminations of pulp writers to novels that present an integrated world-view and fully developed characters; these latter efforts were bids for recognition as a serious artist—a recognition that his popularity seemed to preclude. Wren mixed melodrama with the lightest comic banter, exotic settings with the most brutal realism, and romantic idealism with an almost overwhelmingly cynical fatalism.

The melodrama in Wren most often grows out of basic conflicts; circumstances demand the characters choose a course of action that frustrates personal needs but satisfies the character's sense of honour. Wren was also not afraid of employing outdated superstitions—e.g., prenatal conditioning (*Snake and Sword*) or yogic telepathy (*Beggars' Horses*)—in order to underscore his basic interest in fiction: men in a state of struggle, in which the external conflict only works as a metaphor for the internal conflict. Wren's melodramatic (Dickensian?) use of coincidence also serves a purpose apparently unnoticed by his contemporaries: it represents an attachment to Oriental fatalism that is deeply rooted in his own Anglo-Saxon origins—the warrior in conflict with Wyrd, with only individual courage and the aid of kinsmen to stave off an inevitable death.

Beneath the melodrama is the humorous banter of English boys that changes little as the public-school heroes grow into men. In Wren, the inevitable and thankless manifest destiny of the British Empire to shape the remote corners of the world is often set forth in schoolboy exchanges that counterpoint a complex emotional and psychological framework reminiscent of Conrad, though without his allusive obscurity. His characters are usually joined in a metaphorical or actual fraternity, most commonly in a military unit in which family relationships are disguised (*Beau Geste*) or unknown (*Wages of Virtue*). This ironic, half-humorous approach shows events in multiple focus: the stiff-upper-lip narration often reveals, beneath the total belief in Great Britain, a tottering personal emotional security pivoting on a conflict of honour against survival. Though the values of British upbringing appear never to be questioned, circumstances ironically point to an emotionally empty or fateful universe that overwhelms the values of the individual. The bland assurances of organized religion ring hollow for Wren's characters. Only in death does the sense of purpose or significance of individual life seem vindicated.

The most successful of Wren's books was *Beau Geste*, which incorporates the most characteristic themes and values of Wren's world-view. This story of three brothers who join the Foreign Legion in order to preserve the family honour and fulfil their own boyhood military fantasies becomes an elaborately realized celebration of the theme of human brotherhood. The Gestes (the Anglo-French pun, as always in Wren, is intended) are orphans whose real family is unknown to us. Their rootlessness is paralleled by the international and anonymous make-up of the French Foreign Legion whose brotherhood the Gestes soon join. The existential overtones of the defence of Fort Zinderneuf are obvious today through hindsight, but it may be doubted that many of Wren's original readers caught the philosophical significance of the repeated ascents of the watchtower by men marked for death or the dead soldiers standing watch at the machicolations while Digby prepares Beau's 'Viking's funeral'. Death with honour is the ultimate seal of human commitments. These themes of the commitment to brotherhood and of disguised relationships recur in the two sequels to *Beau Geste: Beau Sabreur* and *Beau Ideal*. (*Good Gestes*, Wren's farewell to the characters that made him famous, is a set of excellent stories that add nothing to our knowledge of the Gestes and could have been about anybody. And an indirectly connected work, *Spanish Maine*, appeared in 1935.)

Other series characters appear in later works, though none so fully or satisfactorily drawn as the Gestes. Sinclair Noel Brody Dysart ('Sinbad') appears in *Action and Passion, Sinbad the Soldier*, and *The Fort in the Jungle*. Several figures involved in British intelligence in India recur in novels the most interesting of which is *Beggars' Horses*, an ironic *tour de force*. This novel examines the disastrous effects on a handful of skeptical inquirers into the alleged prophecies of a famous yogi when the angry yogi *grants* each of them their dearest wish. Another outstanding departure is the neglected masterpiece of psychological disintegration and sexual captivity, *The Mammon of Righteousness*, in which Wren's insights into the effects of repression result in one of his most agonizing and involving stories.

In the face of all this sardonic irony, with characters moving under the shadow of imminent death, there is still in Wren's best work the clear affirmation that life has meaning, despite the efforts of a universe apparently antipathetic to human hopes and wishes. That meaning lies in commitment to our essential brotherhood and to the values and traditions of the British Empire.

—Thomas R. Tietze

WRIGHT, Francesca.   See ROBINS, Denise.

WYLIE, Laura.   See MATTHEWS, Patricia.

WYNDHAM, Esther.
Pseudonym for Mary Lutyens. **Nationality:** British. **Born:** London, 31 July 1908; daughter of the architect Edwin Lutyens; sister of the composer Elisabeth Lutyens. **Education:** at home; Queen's College, London, 1919–23. **Relations:** married 1) Anthony Sewell in 1930, one daughter; 2) Joseph G. Links in 1945. **Career:** writer from 1930: columnist ('Mrs Marriott'), *Woman's Weekly*, for few months during World War II and for *Woman and Home* for several years after World War II. **Recipient:** Fellow, Royal Society of Literature, 1976. **Agent:** Jane Turnbull, 13 Wendell Road, London W12 9RS. **Address:** 8 Elizabeth Close, London W9 1BN, England.

ROMANCE AND HISTORICAL PUBLICATIONS

Novels

Come Back, Elizabeth. London, Nimmo Hay and Mitchell, 1948.
Black Charles. London, Mills and Boon, 1952; Toronto, Harlequin, 1962.

Man of Steel. London, Mills and Boon, 1952.
Mistress of Merryweather. London, Mills and Boon, 1953.
Master of the Manor. London, Mills and Boon, 1953.
Above the Clouds. London, Mills and Boon, 1954; Toronto, Harlequin, 1964.
Tiger Hall. London, Mills and Boon, 1954; Toronto, Harlequin, 1965.
Once You Have Found Him. London, Mills and Boon, 1954; Toronto, Harlequin, 1964.
The House of Discontent. London, Mills and Boon, 1955; Toronto, Harlequin, 1966.
The Blue Rose. London, Mills and Boon, 1957; Toronto, Harlequin, 1967.

OTHER PUBLICATIONS as Mary Lutyens

Novels

Perchance to Dream. London, Murray, 1935.
Rose and Thorn. London, Murray, 1936.
Spider's Silk. London, Joseph, 1939.
Family Colouring. London, Joseph, 1940.
A Path of Gold. London, Joseph, 1941.
Together and Alone. London, Joseph, 1942.
So Near to Heaven. London, Joseph, 1943.
And Now There Is You. London, Hale, 1953.
Week-End at Hurtmore. London, Hutchinson, 1954.
The Lucian Legend. London, Hutchinson, 1955.
Meeting in Venice. London, Hutchinson, 1956.
Cleo. London, Joseph, 1973; New York, Stein and Day, 1974.

Short Stories

Forthcoming Marriages. London, Murray, and New York, Dutton, 1933.

Other

Julie and the Narrow Valley (for children). London, Guildford Press, 1947.
To Be Young: Some Chapters of Autobiography. London, Hart Davis, 1959.
Millais and the Ruskins. London, Murray, 1967; New York, Vanguard Press, 1968.
The Ruskins and the Grays. London, Murray, 1972.
Krishnamurti: The Years of Awakening. London, Murray, and New York, Farrar Straus, 1975.
The Lyttons in India: An Account of Lord Lytton's Viceroyalty 1876–1880. London, Murray, 1979.
Edwin Lutyens. London, Murray, 1980.
Krishnamurti: The Years of Fulfilment. London, Murray, and New York, Farrar Straus, 1983.
Krishnamurti: The Open Door. London, Murray, and New York, Farrar Straus, 1988.
The Life and Death of Krishnamurti. London, Murray, 1990; as *Krishnamurti: His Life and Death*, New York, St Martin's Press, 1991.

Editor, *Lady Lytton's Court Diary*. London, Hart Davis, 1960.
Editor, *Effie in Venice*. London, Murray, 1965; as *Young Mrs Ruskin in Venice: Her Picture of Society and Life with John Ruskin 1849–1852*, New York, Vanguard Press, 1966.
Editor, *Freedom from the Known*, by Krishnamurti. London, Gollancz, 1968; New York, Harper, 1969.

Editor, *The Only Revolution*, by Krishnamurti. London, Gollancz, and New York, Harper, 1970.

Editor, *The Penguin Krishnamurti Reader*. London, Penguin, 2 vols, 1970–73.

Editor, *The Urgency of Change*, by Krishnamurti. London, Gollancz, 1971.

Editor, *Krishnamurti's Notebook*. London, Gollancz, and New York, Harper, 1976.

Editor, *Rainy Days at Brig O'Turk: The Highland Sketch Book of John Everett Millais*, with Malcolm Warner. Westerham, Kent, Dalrymple, 1983.

*

Manuscript Collection: Mugar Memorial Library, Boston University.

Esther Wyndham comments:

I first started writing romantic serials in the late 1930s under the pseudonym of Esther Wyndham to supplement the inadequate income I was making from the novels I *wanted* to write. Since the fees were high and the stories were afterwards published as books, this work was very rewarding financially. The ten serials I wrote came out either in *Woman's Weekly or Woman and Home*. I had a wonderful editor at the Amalgamated Press, Winifred Johnson, who had first approached me and who taught me this difficult craft which should never be underrated. For ten instalments the hero and heroine had to meet constantly, yet could not be brought together until the last instalment, and each instalment had to end with an emotional cliff-hanger.

The hero and heroine had to conform to Miss Johnson's romantic formula. Lady Diana Spencer would never have qualified as a Johnson Heroine, except that she was a virgin and loved children, for she was far too beautiful, too rich, and had had too easy a life. The Prince of Wales might just have squeezed through as a Johnson hero, for in spite of being a prince he worked hard, had had rumoured involvements with other girls, and had not declared himself until the last instalment; however, there was a quality of mystery lacking in him.

One never penetrated the hero's mind until the end of the story, whereas every nuance of the heroine's feelings was revealed. In some stories she started by hating the hero because of his supposed arrogance until about instalment three when she began to feel drawn to him in spite of her better judgement. His behaviour was always a mystery to her. Disappointment and chagrin quickly followed those rare occasions when she felt he *cared*. There must invariably be another girl or older woman to make mischief out of jealousy, for it was only through misunderstandings on both sides that the couple could be kept apart for 70,000 words. A foreign setting was always a help.

The hero had to be brave, strong, rich, and frantically busy. It was best if he was self-made; if an aristocrat with inherited wealth he must be a model landlord who laboured to improve his estate for the sake of his tenants. The spirited heroine must not only have a wonderful way with children and old people but some previous tragedy or hardship in her life. And, of course, she had to work hard for her living. It was her character rather than her looks that attracted; she became beautiful only at rare moments, preferably when the hero was looking at her without her knowing it. Naturally, she became permanently beautiful at the end when irradiated with requited love.

Miss Johnson would give me guide-lines: 'We want a heroine this time of about 28 who feels that life has passed her by', or, 'Let's have a young girl in your next who has never been in love before'. When writing in the war years it was easier to have a hero in a reserved occupation, hence Miss Johnson's plea to her authors after the war, '*Please*, no more farmers or doctors'. When once the char-

acters and story-line were more or less settled one wrote from the heart. To write down would have been fatal and I never felt any temptation to do so.

Miss J. only started publishing a serial when she had the complete story. This had not been the rule when she first entered the office as a junior. The great Ethel M. Dell had then been writing serials for the Amalgamated Press, and in a late instalment of one story it transpired to the horror of the editor that the unwed heroine was going to have a baby. She searched frantically through previous instalments to see when this could have happened and found that the heroine had come back one day from a walk with the hero with harebells in her hair. Thereafter the injunction ran through the office, 'No more harebells'.

I would write an instalment in three or four days and post it to Miss J. Next day her assistant would ring up either to say, 'Go ahead', or 'Miss Johnson would like to see you'. Dread words, for I knew that somehow I had gone off the rails and would have to re-write the instalment. There was no arguing with Miss J. because she was quite deaf. Since her magazines sold widely in Ireland there must not be the slightest hint of impropriety, let alone 'harebells'. In one story when my hero was in Washington with the heroine, his secretary, and I had allowed her to sleep in the sitting-room of his hotel suite because all the hotels were full (a situation helpful to romance), Miss J. sent me a telegram, for I had gone abroad between instalments: 'Please make another effort to find Elizabeth a room of her own'. And when I was writing my first story, almost every instalment of which had to be re-written, and I had made the hero say that he was feeling ill in order to get away from a party, she wrote indignantly, 'Who can have respect for a man who feels ill at a party?'. A great editor, but one who could hardly have functioned successfully today.

*   *   *

It was one of Mary Lutyens's stories in *Forthcoming Marriages* that led to her being invited by Winifred Johnson to contribute romantic serials to the Amalgamated Press's women's papers. The first half of this story ('Mr Raymond Skedley and Miss Katherine N. Robinson') conveyed the current of the heroine's thoughts on her wedding morning; the second half was concerned with emotional incidents leading up to and surrounding the ceremony later that day. Without perhaps realizing it, Lutyens had already arrived at a satisfying and atmospheric balance of inner and outer mood that was exactly appropriate to the romantic story, and, as Esther Wyndham, in her subsequent serial/novels she explored and exploited this to the full.

In the tradition of the genre, her heroines suffer the usual tremulous feelings of inadequacy that are sparked off by the challenge of relating to handsome but arrogant and enigmatic heroes. Wyndham's leading ladies, however, are spirited, capable of decisive action, and, occasionally, of going against the tide of public opinion. (Generally they are working girls who take their careers quite seriously—an advanced shorthand-typist in *Come Back, Elizabeth*, a dedicated bookseller's assistant in *Above the Clouds*, an antique dealer in *Black Charles*.)

Even when overwhelmed by masculine magnetism and the intensity of their own sexual/romantic feelings, these heroines resolutely cling to a few robust strands of inner resource and intellectual independence. Their honest and slightly rueful self awareness makes them interesting and extremely sympathetic to read about, and marks them as forerunners of the intelligent and highly individualized heroines who were two or three decades later to be at the centre of thriller romances by Mary Stewart in England, and Barbara Michaels in the USA.

The stories are tightly structured, and punctuated with humorous incident to counterbalance strong suspense. There is plenty of the latter, because the novels were originally written as serials with cliff hanger endings to each episode.

The author's vivid feeling for place gives the books a special intensity, but, though adept at evoking exotic foreign and romantic settings (Venice, for example, in *Above the Clouds*), Wyndham is at her best with the traditional English country house background (as in *Black Charles*). This is, expectedly, not gruesomely Gothic but graciously Lutyens-esque!

—Mary Cadogan

WYNNE, May.

Pseudonym for Mabel Winifred Knowles. **Other Pseudonym:** Lester Lurgan. **Nationality:** British. **Born:** Streatham, London, in January 1875. **Education:** at home. **Career:** worked in an East End Church of England mission. **Died:** 29 November 1949.

ROMANCE AND HISTORICAL PUBLICATIONS

Novels

For Faith and Navarre. London, Long, 1904.
Ronald Lindsay. London, Long, 1904.
A King's Tragedy. London, Digby Long, 1905.
The Temptation of Philip Carr. London, Sonnenschein, 1905.
Maid of Brittany. London, Greening, 1906.
The Goal. London, Digby Long, 1907.
When Terror Ruled. London, Greening, 1907.
Henry of Navarre: A Romance of August, 1572 (as Mabel W. Knowles). New York, Putnam, 1908; (as May Wynne) London, Greening, 1909.
Let Erin Remember. London, Greening, 1908.
The Tailor of Vitré. London, Gay and Hancock, 1908.
For Church and Chieftain. London, Mills and Boon, 1909.
For Charles the Rover. London, Greening, 1909; New York, Fenno, 1910.
The Gipsy Count. New York, McBride, 1909.
A Blot on the Scutcheon. London, Mills and Boon, 1910; New York, Fenno, 1912.
A King's Masquerade. London, Greening, 1910.
Mistress Cynthia. London, Greening, 1910.
The Gallant Graham. London, Greening, 1911.
Honour's Fetters. London, Stanley Paul, 1911.
The Master Wit. London, Greening, 1911.
The Claim That Won. London, Everett, 1912.
Hey for Cavaliers! London, Greening, 1912.
The Red Fleur-de-Lys. London, Stanley Paul, 1912.
The Brave Brigands. London, Stanley Paul, 1913.
The Destiny of Claude. London, Stanley Paul, 1913.
The Secret of the Zenana. London, Greening, 1913.
A Run for His Money. London, Aldine, 1913.
The Curse of Gold. London, Aldine, 1914.
Goring's Girl. London, Mascot, 1914.
The Hero of Urbino. London, Stanley Paul, 1914.
The Silent Captain. London, Stanley Paul, 1914.
The Regent's Gift. London, Chapman and Hall, 1915.
Foes of Freedom. London, Chapman and Hall, 1916.
Marcel of the 'Zephyrs'. London, Jarrolds, 1916.
The Gipsy King. London, Chapman and Hall, 1917.
The Lyons Mail. London, Jarrolds, 1917.
Penance. London, Mascot, 1917.
A Spy for Napoleon. London, Jarrolds, 1917.
The Taint of Tragedy. London, Mascot, 1917.

The 'Veiled Lady', with Draycot M. Dell. London, Jarrolds, 1918.
The King of a Day. London, Jarrolds, 1918.
Queen Jennie. London, Chapman and Hall, 1918.
The Red Whirlwind, with Draycot M. Dell. London, Jarrolds, 1919.
Robin the Prodigal. London, Jarrolds, 1919.
Love Finds a Way. London, Greening, 1920.
A Prince of Intrigue: A Romance of Mazeppa. London, Jarrolds, 1920.
A Gallant of Spain. London, Stanley Paul, 1920.
Janie's Great Mistake. London, Odhams Press, 1920.
The Spendthrift Duke. London, Holden and Hardingham, 1920.
The Ambitions of Jill. London, Long, 1920.
Mog Megone. London, Jarrolds, 1921.
My Lady's Honour. London, Lloyds, 1921.
The Red Rose of Lancaster. London, Holden and Hardingham, 1921.
A Trap for Navarre. London, Holden, 1922.
A King in the Lists. London, Stanley Paul, 1922.
The Witch-Finder. London, Jarrolds, 1923.
Jill the Hostage. London, Pearson, 1925.
Rachel Lee. London, Leng, 1925.
Theodore. London, Rivers, 1926.
Gwennola. London, Rivers, 1926.
The Fires of Youth. London, Rivers, 1927.
Plotted in Darkness. London, Stanley Paul, 1927.
King Mandrin's Challenge. London, Stanley Paul, 1927.
A Royal Traitor. London, Stanley Paul, 1927.
Love's Penalty. London, Stanley Paul, 1927.
The Terror of the Moor. London, Rivers, 1928.
Gipsy-Spelled. London, Rivers, 1929.
Red Fruit. London, Rivers, 1929.
Hamlet: A Romance from Shakespeare's Play. London, Rivers, 1930.
The Girl Upstairs. London, Thomson, 1932.
The Unseen Witness. London, Leng, 1932.
Stella Maris. London, Leng, 1932.
The Tempter's Power. London, Leng, 1932.
Tangled Fates. London, Mellifont Press, 1935.
Flower o' the Moor. London, Houghton and Scott-Snell, 1935.
The Choice of Mavis. London, Mellifont Press, 1935.
Temptation. London, Mellifont Press, 1937.
Whither? London, Heath Cranton, 1938.
Love Dismayed. London, Mellifont Press, 1942.
Echoed from the Past. London, Mellifont Press, 1944.
The Pursuing Shadow. London, Mellifont Press, 1944.
The Unsuspected Witness. London, Mellifont Press, 1945.
The Secret of the Caves. London, Mellifont Press, 1945.

Novels as Lester Lurgan

Bohemian Blood. London, Greening, 1910.
The Mill-Owner. London, Greening, 1910.
The League of the Triangle. London, Greening, 1911.
A Message from Mars. London, Greening, 1912.
The Ban. London, Stanley Paul, 1912.
The Wrestler on the Shore. London, Everett, 1913.

OTHER PUBLICATIONS

Fiction (for children)

Mollie's Adventures. London, Russell, 1903.
Jimmy: The Tales of a Little Black Bear. London, Partridge, 1910.
Phil's Cousins. London, Blackie, 1911.

Crackers: The Tale of a Mischievous Monkey. London, Partridge, 1911.
The Story of Heather. London, Nelson, 1912; New York, Sully, 1913.
Tony's Chums. London, Blackie, 1914.
Murray Finds a Chum. London, Stanley Paul, 1914.
When Auntie Lil Took Charge. London, Blackie, 1915.
An English Girl in Serbia. London, Collins, 1916.
Three's Company. London, Blackie, 1917.
Stranded in Belgium. London, Blackie, 1918.
A Cousin from Canada. London, Blackie, 1918.
The Honour of the School. London, Nisbet, 1918.
Dick. London, Religious Tract Society, 1919.
Phyllis in France. London, Blackie, 1919.
The Little Girl Beautiful. London, Religious Tract Society, 1919.
Nan and Ken. London, Nelson, 1919.
Nipper & Co. London, Stanley Paul, 1919.
Scouts for Serbia. London, Nelson, 1919.
Comrades from Canada. London, Blackie, 1919.
The Adventures of Dolly Dingle: A Fairy Story. London, Jarrolds, 1920.
Adventures of Two. London, Blackie, 1920.
The Heroine of Chelton School. London, Stanley Paul, 1920.
The Girls of Beechcroft School. London, Religious Tract Society, 1920.
Roseleen at School. London, Cassell, 1920.
Three Bears and Gwen. London, Blackie, 1920.
Little Ladyship. London, Religious Tract Society, 1921.
Lost in the Jungle. London, Stanley Paul, 1921.
Mervyn, Jock, or Joe. London, Blackie, 1921.
Peggy's First Term. London, Ward Lock, 1922.
Angela Goes to School. London, Jarrolds, 1922; Cleveland, World, 1929.
The Girls of the Veldt Farm. London, Pearson, 1922.
The Red Boy's Gratitude. Exeter, Wheaton, 1922.
Christmas at Holford. London, Blackie, 1922.
Two Girls in the Wild. London, Blackie, 1923; abridged edition, as *Sisters Out West*, 1930.
The Best of Chums. London, Ward Lock, 1923.
A Heather Holiday. London, Blackie, 1923; as *Wendy's Adventure in Scotland*, 1933; as *An Adventurous Holiday* (reader), 1933.
Blundering Bettina. London, Religious Tract Society, 1924.
The Girl Who Played the Game. London, Ward Lock, 1924.
Bertie, Bobby, and Belle. London, Blackie, 1924.
The Girls of Clanways Farm. London, Cassell, 1924.
Kits at Clynton Court School. London, Warne, 1924.
The Sunshine Children. London, Nelson, 1924.
Three and One Over. London, Cassell, 1924.
A Rebel at School. London, Jarrolds, 1924.
Two and a Chum. London, Pearson, 1924.
Hootie Toots of Hollow Tree. Philadelphia, Altemus, 1925.
The Girls of Old Grange School. London, Ward Lock, 1925.
Over the Hills and Far Away. London, Religious Tract Society, 1925.
Dare-All Jack and the Cousins. London, Religious Tract Society, 1925.
Hazel Asks Why. London, Ward Lock, 1926.
Carol of Hollydene School. London, Sampson Low, 1926.
The Secret of Carrock School. London, Jarrolds, 1926.
Diccon the Impossible. London, Religious Tract Society, 1926.
The Girl over the Wall. London, Religious Tract Society, 1926.
Jean Plays Her Part. London, Religious Tract Society, 1926.
Dinah's Secret. London, Religious Tract Society, 1927.
Jean of the Lumber Camp. London, Ward Lock, 1927.
Robin Hood to the Rescue. Exeter, Wheaton, 1927.
Terry the Black Sheep. London, Pearson, 1928.

The Girls of Mackland Court. London, Ward Lock, 1928.
Little Sally Mandy's Christmas Present. Philadelphia, Altemus, 1929.
The House of Whispers. London, Ward Lock, 1929.
The Guide's Honour. London, Warne, 1929.
A Term to Remember. London, Aldine, 1930.
Two Girls in the Hawk's Den. London, Pearson, 1930.
Bobbety the Brownie. London, Warne, 1930.
The Masked Rider. Chicago, Laidlaw, 1931.
Patient Pat Joins the Circus. Philadelphia, Altemus, 1931.
Peter Rabbit and the Big Black Crows. Philadelphia, Altemus, 1931.
Juliet of the Mill. London, Ward Lock, 1931.
Girls of the Pansy Patrol. London, Aldine, 1931.
Patsy from the Wilds. London, Warne, 1931.
Belle and Her Dragons. London, Jarrolds, 1931.
The Secret of Marigold Marnell. London, Religious Tract Society, 1931.
The Old Brigade. London, Religious Tract Society, 1932.
Who Was Wendy? London, Newnes, 1932.
The Heart of Glenayrt. London, Nelson, 1932.
The School Mystery. London, Readers' Library, 1933.
The Camping of the Marigolds. London, Marshall Morgan and Scott, 1933.
The Greater Covenant. London, Marshall Morgan and Scott, 1933.
Pixie's Mysterious Mission. London, Newnes, 1933.
Enter Jenny Wren. London, Ward Lock, 1933.
Comrades to Robin Hood. London, Religious Tract Society, 1934.
Malys Rockell. London, Ward Lock, 1934.
The Smugglers of Penreen. London, Religious Tract Society, 1934.
The Mysterious Island. London, Mellifont Press, 1935.
Their Girl Chum. London, Religious Tract Society, 1935.
Under Cap'n Drake. London, Religious Tract Society, 1935.
Up to Val. London, Newnes, 1935.
'Peter', The New Girl. London, Queensway Press, 1936.
The Daring of Star. London, Religious Tract Society, 1936.
Bunny and the Aunt. London, Religious Tract Society, 1936.
The Haunted Ranch. London, Dean, 1936.
Thirteen for Luck. London, Ward Lock, 1936.
Vivette on Trial. London, Queensway Press, 1936.
The Secret of Brick House. London, Ward Lock, 1937.
Two Maids of Rosemarkie. London, Epworth Press, 1937.
The Luck of Penrayne. London, Religious Tract Society, 1937.
Audrey on Approval. London, Ward Lock, 1937.
The Girl Sandy. London, Ward Lock, 1938.
The Lend-a-Hand Holiday. London, Epworth Press, 1938.
Heather the Second. London, Nelson, 1938.
The Term of Many Adventures. London, Nelson, 1939.
The Unexpected Adventure. London, Ward Lock, 1939.
The Coming of Verity. London, Ward Lock, 1940.
Sadie Comes to School. London, Epworth Press, 1942; as *Sally Comes to School*, London, Ward Lock, 1949.
Little Brown Tala. London, Mellifont Press, 1944.
Brown Tala Finds Little Tulsi. London, Mellifont Press, 1945.
Little Brown Tala Stories. London, Harrap, 1947.
Patch the Piebald. Croydon, Surrey, Blue Book, 1947.
Playing the Game. Croydon, Surrey, Blue Book, 1947.
Snow Fairies. London, Mellifont Press, 1947.
Ginger Ellen. London, Nelson, 1947.
The Great Adventure. London, Ward Lock, 1948.
The Furry Fairies. London, Mellifont Press, 1949.
Merion Plays the Game. London, Readers' Library, 1951.
Secrets of the Rockies. London, Ward Lock, 1954.

Other

Life's Object; or, Some Thoughts for Young Girls. London, Nisbet, 1899.
In the Shadows; or, Thoughts for Mourners. London, Marshall, 1900.
Sympathy. London, Skeffington, 1901.
The Life and Reign of Victoria the Good. London, Stanley Paul, 1913.
The Seven Champions of Christendom: A Legendary Chronicle (for children). London, Jarrolds, 1919.

*   *   *

May Wynne infused romantic elements into the children's stories at which she excelled in the form of exotic locations and charismatic personalities. Her love stories for adults also exploit glamorously foreign settings and colourful people like gipsies or intrepid adventurer-explorers. *The Gipsy King* includes characters of both these types. Bampfylde Carew, who starts off as something of a wastrel, leaves his vicarage home, attracted by 'the merry fiddling of the gipsies ... and the crackling of their wood fires', sounds that, apparently, 'echo louder, more enticing, more alluring than the sonorous music of his father's preaching ... '. Wynne thus sets the scene for a much-used theme in her romances: the conflict between duty, which she sees as synonymous with the acceptance of orthodox Christianity, and the attractions of the 'free' and socially untrammelled life. Generally she includes the finding of true love and its attendant pattern of committal to married domesticity as part and parcel of the hero or heroine's redemptive adoption of a religious faith. However, Bampfylde Carew has a long way to go (roaming with the gipsies, having lusty adventures on the high seas and in the Indian territories of America) before he is eventually brought back to the path of Christian virtue by loyal and loving Letty Gray, from his own village.

The Fires of Youth (1927) is concerned with similar issues, and particularly with the return to rustic roots (also equatable in Wynne's stories with the romantic and religious experience). For Tom Tarrock, illusions of freedom take the shape of making money in a big way—but like Bampfylde in *The Gipsy King*, and many other of this author's heroes, he has an innocent village girl (in this case Jessamy Windell, who becomes a Church Army Sister), waiting patiently to feel—eventually—his passionate but purified kiss on her 'firm, sweet lips'.

With her insistent linking of romantic and domestic love to Christian conversion, Wynne is harking back to the mood of many Victorian 'tales of home life'. Her love stories, however, have less of the retributive tone of their 19th-century forerunners, though they never achieve the liveliness of her children's stories.

—Mary Cadogan

————

YARBRO, Chelsea Quinn. American. 1942—. See 2nd edition, 1990.

————

YATES, Dornford. British. 1885–1960. See 2nd edition, 1990.

————

YERBY, Frank (Garvin).
Nationality: American. **Born:** Augusta, Georgia, 5 September 1916. **Education:** Paine College, Augusta, A.B. 1937; Fisk University, Nashville, Tennessee, M.A. 1938; University of Chicago,

1939. **Relations:** married 1) Flora Helen Claire Williams in 1941 (divorced), two sons and two daughters; 2) Blanca Calle Pérez in 1956. **Career:** instructor, Florida Agricultural and Mechanical College, Tallahassee, 1938–39, and Southern University and A. and M. College, Baton Rouge, Louisiana, 1939–41; laboratory technician, Ford Motor Company, Dearborn, Michigan, 1941–44; Magnaflux inspector, Ranger (Fairchild) Aircraft, Jamaica, New York, 1944–45; full-time writer from 1945; settled in Madrid, 1954. **Recipient:** O. Henry award, 1944. D.Litt.: Fisk University, 1976. **Died:** 29 November 1991.

ROMANCE AND HISTORICAL PUBLICATIONS

Novels

The Foxes of Harrow. New York, Dial Press, 1946; London, Heinemann 1947.
The Vixens. New York, Dial Press, 1947; London, Heinemann, 1948.
The Golden Hawk. New York, Dial Press, 1948; London, Heinemann, 1949.
Pride's Castle. New York, Dial Press, 1949; London, Heinemann, 1950.
Floodtide. New York, Dial Press, 1950; London, Heinemann, 1951.
A Woman Called Fancy. New York, Dial Press, 1951; London, Heinemann, 1952.
The Saracen Blade. New York, Dial Press, 1952; London, Heinemann, 1953.
The Devil's Laughter. New York, Dial Press, 1953; London, Heinemann, 1954.
Benton's Row. New York, Dial Press, 1954; London, Heinemann, 1955.
Bride of Liberty. New York, Dial Press, 1954; London, Heinemann, 1955.
The Treasure of Pleasant Valley. New York, Dial Press, 1955; London, Heinemann, 1956.
Captain Rebel. New York, Dial Press, 1956; London, Heinemann, 1957.
Fairoaks. New York, Dial Press, 1957; London, Heinemann, 1958.
The Serpent and the Staff. New York, Dial Press, 1958; London, Heinemann, 1959.
Jarrett's Jade. New York, Dial Press, 1959; London, Heinemann, 1960.
Gillian. New York, Dial Press, 1960; London, Heinemann, 1961.
The Garfield Honor. New York, Dial Press, 1961; London, Heinemann, 1962.
Griffin's Way. New York, Dial Press, 1962; London, Heinemann, 1963.
The Old Gods Laugh: A Modern Romance. New York, Dial Press, and London, Heinemann, 1964.
An Odor of Sanctity. New York, Dial Press, 1965; London, Heinemann, 1966.
Goat Song: A Novel of Ancient Greece. New York, Dial Press, 1967; London, Heinemann, 1968.
Judas, My Brother: The Story of the Thirteenth Disciple. New York, Dial Press, and London, Heinemann, 1969.
Speak Now. New York, Dial Press, 1969; London, Heinemann, 1970.
The Dahomean. New York, Dial Press, 1971; as *The Man from Dahomey*, London, Heinemann, 1971.
The Girl from Storyville: A Victorian Novel. New York, Dial Press, and London, Heinemann, 1972.
The Voyage Unplanned. New York, Dial Press, and London, Heinemann, 1974.
Tobias and the Angel. New York, Dial Press, and London, Heinemann, 1975.

A Rose for Ana Maria. New York, Dial Press, and London, Heinemann, 1976.

Hail the Conquering Hero. New York, Dial Press, 1977; London, Heinemann, 1978.

A Darkness at Ingraham's Crest. New York, Dial Press, 1979; London, Granada, 1981.

Western: A Saga of the Great Plains. New York, Dial Press, 1982; London, Granada, 1983.

Devilseed. New York, Doubleday, and London, Granada, 1984.

McKenzie's Hundred. New York, Doubleday, 1985; London, Grafton, 1986.

*

Film Adaptations: *The Foxes of Harrow*, 1947; *The Golden Hawk*, 1952; *The Saracen Blade*, 1954.

Manuscript Collection: Mugar Memorial Library, Boston University.

Critical Studies: *Behind the Magnolia Mask: Frank Yerby as Critic of the South* by William Werdna Hill, Jr, unpublished thesis, Auburn University, Alabama, 1968; 'The Guilt of the Victim: Racial Themes in Some Frank Yerby Novels' by Jack B. Moore, in *Journal of Popular Culture* (Bowling Green, Ohio), Spring 1975; *Anti-Heroic Perspectives in the Life and Works of Frank Yerby* by James Lee Hill, unpublished thesis, University of Iowa, 1976.

Frank Yerby commented (1990):
It seemed a rather pleasant way to make a living. And for a while, it *was*. Now I wish I'd taken up plumbing!

*   *   *

In writing more than 30 novels, most of which are historical, Frank Yerby became one of the most popularly successful black novelists to appear in the United States. His novels made him rich but brought him little critical acclaim; rather, his works sold in the millions while being dismissed by most critics as melodramatic potboilers aimed solely at the cash register. He was also consistently attacked for betraying his race by not continuing to write the social protest fiction, such as the often anthologized 'Health Card', with which he began his career. Over the years, in facing this charge, Yerby repeatedly used some variation of a single defence: 'The novelist hasn't any right to inflict on the public his private ideas on politics, religion or race'. This attitude was directly related to his view of the novel itself: 'a novel is not life, but a deliberate distortion of it, solely designed to give pleasure to a reader'; that is, Yerby considered his fiction romance and its purpose 'entertainment', his own word. Nevertheless, in such works as *Speak Now*, a modern novel of interracial love, and *The Dahomean*, as much treatise on African culture as novel, Yerby wrote seriously, if not always with full control, on racial injustice and the African American heritage.

His longest statement on his fiction appeared in 'How and Why I Write the Costume Novel' (*Harper's Magazine*, October 1959). Though he stated that he did extensive research, the notes always bulking larger than the finished novel, and though there are often notes and references (*The Saracen Blade* has 17 pages of notes as an appendix), as well as historical digressions, even lectures, Yerby preferred 'costume novel' to historical novel, for he said that his publishers rightly removed 'ninety-nine and ninety-nine one-hundredths' of the history so that the novels will entertain. Aside from the history, his principal elements are a picaresque protagonist, who must be a dominant male, emotionally immature, which Yerby defined as 'romantic', in his relationships with women; an even more emotionally immature beautiful heroine; understated sex; 'a strong, exteriorized conflict, personified in a continuing, antagonist or antagonists', and presented dramatically; and as a theme, 'something ennobling to life'. He stated that he had been most successful with the theme of 'the eternal warfare of the sexes', but the true underlying theme of most of his fiction, and frequently expressed by his protagonists, is one that he says he has held since the late 1930s: 'many, if not most, of life's problems cannot be solved at all'.

Yerby's usually long novels have complex, if episodic, plot lines, providing for the introduction (and then elimination) of numerous minor characters, as well as historical colour, whether sordid, exotic, or idyllic. In some ways Yerby was a direct descendant of Sir Walter Scott: in his use of a clash of cultures—masters and slaves, aristocrats and plebeians, Saracens or Moors and Christians, Guelfs and Ghibellines, etc.—as a plot-unifying principle, and in the young hero, always more modern in thought and feeling than his adversaries, thrown into a world different from what he has previously known to make his way amidst brutality and treachery. In a sense, though the romance plot (most often of lovers separated by social circumstances) plays a much larger part in Yerby's novels than in Scott's, it still serves as a thread upon which to hang the historical events and local colour and to demonstrate that clash of cultures.

Except for the few early short stories and the two novels *The Old Gods Laugh* and *Speak Now*, Yerby's work ranges widely in history. His first novel, *The Foxes of Harrow*, which is set in Louisiana, was a gigantic success, and it has been followed by a number of antebellum, Civil War, and Reconstruction novels, including, among others, *The Vixens*, *Floodtide*, *A Woman Called Fancy*, *Benton's Row*, *Griffin's Way*, and *A Darkness at Ingraham's Crest*. As a result, Yerby was associated with the romance of the old South, but it is hardly a 'moonlight and magnolias' South, though all of the paraphernalia of that tradition is present—white-columned mansions on huge plantations, crinolined ladies, extensive description of food, manners, etc. Instead, it is a world of parvenues, greedy entrepreneurs, racists, and blind chauvinists, where wealth and position are more important than humanity. When not writing about his native South, Yerby moved back in time from the French and American Revolutions (*The Devil's Laughter* and *Bride of Liberty*), through the 17th century (*The Golden Hawk*), the Middle Ages (*An Odor of Sanctity* and *The Saracen Blade*), the time of Christ (*Judas, My Brother*) to ancient Greece (*Goat Song*). Such works are written to the same formulas as those of the old South, being, however, usually more episodic and covering more territory through the hero's travels. Their antagonists are similar, if more powerful, and identical motives—greed, lust for power, rivalry in love—generate the conflict.

To explain the enormous popularity of Yerby's novels is ultimately impossible, for other writers have used the same plot formulas, the same perfervid prose, the same aura of eroticism, and the same strongly typed and contrasted characters, without coming near his sales or public fame. Perhaps the principal reason, despite his critical reputation, is that readers can sense an ethical underpinning to the exciting action and sexy romance. His heroes are nearly always idealists or sceptics, and often the idealists become sceptics, if not stoics, thus fulfilling the theme that most of man's problems have no solutions. This existential view, however bleak, pervades the novels and accounts for the frequent less-than-happy endings. Yerby has yet to be taken as seriously as he deserves by either literary or sociological critics, the fate of most extremely popular writers. Yet his historical fiction is firmly based upon mid-20th-century *angst*, and in the interplay between historical action and contemporary sensibility lies the nexus of his achievement.

—Earl F. Bargainnier

—————

YORK, Alison. See **NICOLE, Christopher.**

—————

YORK, Andrew.   See NICOLE, Christopher.

—————

YORKE, Katherine.   See ELLERBECK, Rosemary.

—————

YOUNG, Stark.
Nationality: American. **Born:** Como, Mississippi, 11 October 1881. **Education:** University of Mississippi, Oxford, 1897–1901, B.A. in English 1901 (Phi Beta Kappa); Columbia University, New York, M.A. 1902. **Career:** assistant in English, University of Mississippi, 1904–07; instructor, 1907–10, and professor of English, 1910–15, University of Texas, Austin; professor of English, Amherst College, Massachusetts, 1915–21; drama critic, *New Republic*, Washington, DC, 1922–47; associate editor, *Theatre Arts* magazine, New York, 1922–48; drama critic, *New York Times*, 1924–25. Artist: paintings exhibited in New York, 1943–46. **Died:** 6 January 1963.

ROMANCE AND HISTORICAL PUBLICATIONS

Novels

Heaven Trees. New York, Scribner, 1926.
So Red the Rose. New York, Scribner, 1934; London, Cassell, 1935.

OTHER PUBLICATIONS

Novels

The Torches Flare. New York, Scribner, 1928.
River House. New York, Scribner, 1929.

Short Stories

The Street of the Islands. New York, Scribner, 1930.
Feliciana. New York, Scribner, 1935.

Plays

Guenevere. New York, Grafton Press, 1906.
Addio, Madretta and Other Plays (includes *The Star in the Trees, The Twilight Saint, The Dead Poet, The Seven Kings and the Wind, The Queen of Sheba*). Chicago, Sergel, 1912.
At the Shrine. New York, Theatre Arts, 1919.
The Colonnade (produced London, 1920). New York, Theatre Arts, and London, Benn, 1924.
The Queen of Sheba. New York, Theatre Arts, 1922.
The Saint (produced London, 1924). New York, Boni and Liveright, 1925.
The Twilight Saint. New York, French, 1925.
Sweet Times and the Blue Policeman (for children). New York, Holt, 1925.
The Sea Gull, adaptation of a play by Chekhov (produced New York, 1928). New York, Scribner, 1929.
Artemise. Privately printed, 1942.

Poetry

The Blind Man at the Window and Other Poems. New York, Grafton Press, 1906.

Other

The Flower in Drama. New York, Scribner, 1923.

The Three Fountains (travel). New York, Scribner, 1924.
Glamour: Essays on the Art of the Theatre. New York, Scribner, 1925.
Encaustics. New York, New Republic, 1926.
Theatre Practice. New York, Scribner, 1926.
The Theatre. New York, Doran, 1927.
Maurice Sterne: A Retrospective Exhibition. New York, New Republic, 1933.
Immortal Shadows: A Book on Dramatic Criticism. New York, Scribner, 1948.
The Pavilion: Of People and Times Remembered, of Stories and Places (autobiography). New York, Scribner, 1951.
The Flower in Drama and Glamour: Theatre Essays and Criticism. New York, Scribner, 1955; revised edition, New York, Octagon, 1973.
Stark Young: A Life in the Arts: Letters 1900–1962, edited by John Pilkington, Baton Rouge, Louisiana State University Press, 2 vols, 1975.

Editor, with others, *The English Humorists of the Eighteenth Century*. Boston, Ginn, 1911.
Editor, *A Southern Treasury of Life and Literature*. New York, Scribner, 1937.

Translator, *The Sole Heir*, by Jean François Regnard. Austin, University of Texas Press, 1912.
Translator, *George Dandin*, by Molière. New York, Theatre Arts, 1925.
Translator, *Mandragola*, by Machiavelli. New York, Macaulay, 1927.
Translator, *The Three Sisters*, by Chekhov. New York, French, 1941.
Translator, *The Cherry Orchard*, by Chekhov. New York, French, 1947.
Translator, *Uncle Vanya*, by Chekhov. New York, French, 1956.

*

Film Adaptation: *So Red the Rose*, 1935.

Critical Studies: *New York Jew* by Alfred Kazin, New York, Knopf, and London, Secker and Warburg, 1978; *Stark Young* by John Pilkington, Boston, Twayne, 1985.

*   *   *

Inveterate southerner Stark Young took an agrarian stand throughout his best work: an intense love of his native land, tremendous emphasis upon the family as a nourishing and culturally cohesive structure, and a political and social contempt for new south capitalism and industry. Like his intellectual forebear Thomas Jefferson, Young seemed to posit that those close to the earth are enriched and made noble by it.

A seldom read novel, or, as some see it, a set of loosely connected stories, *Heaven Trees* suggests the philosophical attitude which gave birth to Young's masterpiece *So Red the Rose*.

Heaven Trees focuses on Mississippi life in the 1850s, the golden era of southern plantation life. Lacking the realism of his better work, *Heaven Trees* idealizes the family home, a symbol for a way of life now lost. Using the history of his birthplace, Como, Mississippi, Young creates Panola, Mississippi, without commerce or trade—a pristine, agrarian ideal. The Hugh Stark McGehee family in the novel becomes the paradigm of the southern family.

In one month alone *So Red the Rose* sold in excess of 400,000 copies, making it the most popular and best known of all southern historical novels before Margaret Mitchell's *Gone with the Wind*

(1936). As John Pilkington observed, it became a 'commentary on a civilization rather than a history'. Historically oriented, this quintessential Civil War novel contains three movements: 'the prelude to the war, the war, and its aftermath' from November 1860 to November 1865.

Characteristic of Young's agrarianism, the novel centres on family, chronicling in near epic fashion the relationship of the McGehees and Bedfords of Portobello and Montrose plantations. The family drama was, in large part, drawn by the novelist from his own personal history. The most dramatic scene in the novel, the burning of Montrose, for example, was inspired by the burning of Bowling Green in Young's own family.

Donald Davidson, himself a leading agrarian, early recognized the theme of the novel when he noted that it 'draws into focus the battle between tradition and anti-tradition that has been waged since the Renaissance'. Deceptively set in the past, the novel nonetheless spoke directly to issues of the 1920s and 1930s. The McGehees and the Bedfords become repositories of traditional southern virtue, exponents of agrarianism. Their unification as a family suggests the cultural cohesion of the south. General Sherman, on the other hand, is the enemy of cultural cohesion: he is industrial sterility, a divided personality. Sam Shaw, is a personification for the new South, a sorry replacement for the planter aristocracy.

So Red the Rose takes its place alongside many novels on the same subject by later writers like Clifford Dowdey, William Faulkner, Caroline Gordon, Andrew Lytle, and Allen Tate. It was, however, the most realistic at its time of publication, establishing, as one critic noted, in 'critical grace the Civil War genre which had for so long been bogged in the 'treacly sentimentality' of crinolines and trailing banners ... '.

—George C. Longest

ADVISERS AND CONTRIBUTORS

ALTNER, Patricia. Librarian, Department of Defense, Washington, DC. Reviewer of historical fiction for *Library Journal*. Since 1980, associate editor, *The Year's Scholarship in Science Fiction, Fantasy, and Horror Literature*. **Essays:** Pamela Bennetts; Rebecca Brandewyne; Mary Ann Gibbs; Rosemary Hawley Jarman; Velda Johnstone; Annette Motley; Edith Pargeter; Rona Randall; Rosemary Rogers; Valerie Sherwood; Janelle Taylor.

ANDERSON, Rachel. Freelance writer: children's book reviewer for *Good Housekeeping*. Author of *The Purple Heart Throbs: The Sub-Literature of Love*, 1974, *Dream Lovers* (autobiography), 1978, and fiction for adults and children including, most recently, *Little Angel, Bonjour!*, 1988; *Paper Faces*, 1991; *Jessy Runs Away*, 1993, and *Jessy and the Long-Short Dress*, 1993. **Essays:** Madame Albanesi; Ruby M. Ayres; Florence L. Barclay; G.B. Burgin; Hall Caine; Ethel M. Dell; Maud Diver; Maysie Greig; E.M. Hull; Netta Muskett; Margaret Pedler; Berta Ruck.

BAKERMAN, Jane S. Professor emerita, Indiana State University, Terre Haute. Author of numerous critical essays, interviews, and reviews; editor, *Adolescent Female Portraits in the American Novel* (with Mary Jean DeMarr), 1983, *And Then There Were Nine: More Women of Mystery*, 1984, and general editor, *Women and Popular Culture* series, Popular Press; contributor to *Clues, A Journal of Detection*, and other periodicals. **Essays:** Edna Ferber; Elizabeth Savage.

BARGAINNIER, Earl F. Formerly Fuller E. Callaway professor of English Language and Literature, Wesleyan College, Macon, Georgia; editor, *Studies in Popular Culture*. Author of *The Gentle Art of Murder: The Detective Fiction of Agatha Christie*, 1980. Editor, *Ten Women of Mystery*, 1981, *Twelve Englishmen of Mystery*, 1984, (with George N. Dove) *Cops and Constables, American and British Policemen*, 1986, and *Comic Crime*, 1987. **Essays:** Edison Marshall; Frank Yerby.

BERGMANN, Linda S. Assistant professor of English, Department of Humanities, Illinois Institute of Technology. Author of 'Woman Against a Background of White: The Representation of Self and Nature in Women's Arctic Narratives', in *American Studies*, forthcoming; articles in *Beyond the Two Cultures: Essays in Science, Technology, and Literature*, edited by Judith Lee and Joseph Slade, and in *Women's Studies Quarterly*. **Essay:** Jean M. Auel.

BERNEIS, Susan Quinn. Freelance writer. Former librarian. **Essays:** Laura Black; Gwen Bristow; Cecily Crowe; Inglis Fletcher; Elisabeth Ogilvie; Anne Stevenson; Jessamyn West.

BLEILER, E.F. Freelance writer. Former executive vice-president, Dover Publications; editorial consultant, Scribner's. Author of *The Checklist of Science-Fiction and Supernatural Fiction*, 1978. Editor of *A Treasury of Victorian Detective Stories*, *A Treasury of Victorian Ghost Stories*, and of works by Ernest Bramah, R. Austin Freeman, Emile Gaboriau, Robert H. van Gulik, and Roy Vickers, and anthologies of dime novelists and Victorian sensational novelists. **Essays:** D.K. Broster; Robert Hichens.

BLOCK, Marylaine. Assistant director, McMullen Library, Davenport, Iowa. Book reviewer for *Library Journal*. **Essays:** Rachel Lindsay; Joan Smith.

BOYKIN, Elizabeth P. Writer, Richmond, Virginia. **Essay:** Elizabeth Madox Roberts.

BRADLEY, W. H. Freelance writer and author of the romance novels, *Savage Desire*, *Heritage of Love*, and *The Yielding Time*.

Creative Writing tutor. **Essays:** Marie Joseph; Jean Saunders; Jean Stubbs.

BRAIN, Tracy. Lecturer in English, Bath College of Higher Education, Avon. Contributor to *Times Literary Supplement*, and *Times Higher Education Supplement*, both London. Critical studies of Sylvia Plath and Margaret Atwood, forthcoming. **Essay:** Rose Tremain.

BRANCH, Susan. Reference librarian, Worthington, Ohio. **Essays:** Joan Aiken; Valerie Anand; H.C. Bailey; John Buchan; Elizabeth Cadell; Barbara Corcoran; Clare Darcy; Jeffery Farnol; Suzanne Goodwin; Jane Aiken Hodge; Penny Jordan; Margaret Summerton.

BUCHANAN, Jean. Freelance writer. Former lexicographer on *A Supplement to the Oxford English Dictionary* and *The Pocket Oxford Dictionary*, 6th edition. Author of *The History of the English Faculty Library, Oxford*, 1979, a romance novel *(No Remedy for Love)*, short stories, and a television play for children *(The Princess and the Lute Player)*. **Essays:** Marion Collin; Mabel Barnes Grundy; Baroness von Hutten; Nora Lofts; Mrs Patrick MacGill; Lady Miles.

BULL, Angela. Children's writer and critic. Author of several books of children's fiction including, most recently, *Up the Attic Stairs*, 1989, *Pink Socks*, 1990, *The Jiggery-Pokery Cup*, 1990, *The Shadows of Owlshap*, 1992, and *Winter Phantoms*, 1993, and of biographies of Anne Frank, Florence Nightingale, Marie Curie, Elizabeth Fry, and Noel Streatfeild. **Essay:** Phyllis Bentley.

BUTTS, Dennis. Freelance writer and critic; editor, *Henty Society Bulletin*. Formerly principal lecturer in English, Bulmershe College of Higher Education, Reading, Berkshire. Author of *Living Words* (with John Merrick), 1966, and *R.L. Stevenson*, 1966. Editor of *Pergamon Poets 8*, 1970, *Good Writers for Young Readers: Critical Essays*, 1977, and *The Secret Garden*, by Frances Hodgson Burnett, 1987, *Henty Verse*, 1991, *Stories and Society, Children's Literature in its Social Context*, 1992. **Essay:** A.E.W. Mason.

CADOGAN, Mary. Editor, *Collector's Digest*; company secretary, Krishnamurti Foundation. Author of three books on popular literature with Patricia Craig—*You're a Brick, Angela!*, 1976, *Women and Children First*, 1978, *The Lady Investigates*, 1981— three volumes of *The Charles Hamilton Companion* (with John Wernham), 1976–82, and *The Charles Hamilton Schoolgirl's Album; The Morcove Companion*, 1981, *From Wharton Lodge to Linton Hall: The Charles Hamilton Christmas Companion* both with Tommy Keen, 1984, *Richmal Crompton: The Woman Behind William*, 1986, and *Frank Richards: The Chap Behind the Chums*, 1988, *Chin Up, Chest Out, Jemima!*, 1989, *The William Companion*, 1990, *Women With Wings, Female Flyers in Fact and Fiction*, 1992. **Essays:** Barbara Cartland; Theresa Chandos; Jilly Cooper; Frances Cowen; R.F. Delderfield; Valerie Fitzgerald; Cynthia Freeman; Margery Hilton; Patricia Matthews; L.M. Montgomery; Baroness Orczy; Elizabeth O. Peter; Evadne Price; Mabel St John; Mrs George de Horne Vaizey; C.N. and A.M. Williamson; Esther Wyndham; May Wynne.

CAMPBELL, Jane. Associate professor of English, Wilfrid Laurier University, Waterloo, Ontario. Author of *Practical Vision: Essays in English Literature in Honour of Flora Roy*, 1978; *The Retrospective Review (1820–28 and The Revival of Seventeenth-Century Poetry)*, 1972. Contributor to *Studies in Short Fiction, Contemporary Literature, Critique, Journal of Narrative Technique*, and *English Studies in Canada*. **Essay:** A.S. Byatt.

CAMPBELL, Margaret. Freelance writer. Author of *Lend a Hand: Social Work for the Young*, 1966, articles on Oxfordshire personalities for *Limited Edition*, and articles and reviews for *British Book News, Countryman*, and other journals. Editor of *The Countryman Book Series*, 3 vols, 1973–75. **Essays:** Neil Munro.

CAMPBELL, P. Television producer. Freelance writer. **Essays:** Patricia Ainsworth; Mary Balogh; Gloria Bevan; Sheila Bishop; Mary Borden; Nancy Buckingham; Donn Byrne; Judy Chard; Marian Cockrell; Sara Craven; Emma Darcy; Viña Delmar; Jane Donnelly; Anne Eliot; Rosemary Ellerbeck; Carol Finch; Shelby Foote; Ernest J. Gaines; Peter Green; Julia Hamilton; Elizabeth Harrison; Norah James; Christian Laffeaty; Marjorie Lewty; Edwin Mullins; D.L. Murray; Susan Napier; Rosamunde Pilcher; Erin Pizzey; Ivy Preston; Alexandra Ripley; Irene Roberts; Lady Eleanor Smith; Mary Jane Staples.

CARGILL, Jennifer. Associate university librarian, Rice University, Houston, Texas. **Essay:** Mary Westmacott.

CARTLAND, Barbara. See her own entry.

CAVALIERO, Glen. Member of faculty of English, University of Cambridge. Author of *John Cowper Powys: Novelist*, 1973, *The Rural Tradition in the English Novel 1900–1939*, 1977, *A Reading of E. M. Forster*, 1979, *Charles Williams: Poet of Theology*, 1983. **Essays:** Bryher; William Golding; Rose Macaulay; H.F.M. Prescott.

CHESTER, Tessa Rose. Curator, Renier Collection of Children's Books, Bethnal Green Museum of Childhood, London. **Essays:** Denise Robins.

CLEAVER, Pamela. Freelance writer; tutor, London School of Journalism, and Fenfarm Arts. Author of *The Sparrow Book of Record Breakers [Animal Records]*, 2 vols, 1981–82, *Union Discount Centenary Album*, 1985, and *The Reluctant Governess* (as Emma Payne), 1993 . **Essays:** Pamela Belle; Marjorie Bowen; Ann Bridge; Louis Bromfield; Hester W. Chapman; Dorothy Dunnett; Catherine Gavin; M.M. Kaye; Dinah Lampitt; Jane Lane; Margaret Pemberton; Madeleine A. Polland; Rosemary Sutcliff; Reay Tannahill; Nigel Tranter; Joanna Trollope; Mary Wesley; Sarah Woodhouse.

COLLINS, Irene. Formerly reader in Modern History, University of Liverpool. Ex-president of the Historical Association. Author of books and articles on British and European History (18th and 19th century). Editor of *Recent Historical Novels*, 1990, and *Jane Austen and the Clergy*, 1994.

COOMBS, Scott. Freelance writer. **Essay:** Harriette Arnow.

CUSICK, Edmund. Lecturer in Literary Studies, Liverpool John Moores University. Formerly, lecturer in English Literature, Univerity of Lampeter; assistant editor, Oxford English Dictionaries. Author of 'Macdonald and Jung', in *The Gold Thread*, 1990; contributor to *New Welsh Review*. **Essays:** James A. Michener; Robert Nye.

CYGANOWSKI, Carol Klimick. Associate professor of English, and director of the Women's Studies Program, DePaul University, Chicago, Illinois. Author of *Magazine Editors and Professional Authors in Nineteenth-Century America*, 1988; consulting editor, Women's Studies Encyclopaedia. **Essay:** Toni Morrison.

D'CRUZ, Doreen. Senior lecturer, Department of English, Massey University, Palmerston North, New Zealand. Editor (with C.K. Lingam), *Playworks: A Collection of Plays for Secondary Schools*, Volumes I–II, 1987. Author of essays on Barbara Anderson, and Shashi Deshpadide, among others. **Essay:** Rosamond Lehmann.

DESY, Peter. Member of the English Department, Ohio University, Lancaster. Author of fiction and poetry in many journals and anthologies. **Essay:** Walter D. Edmonds.

DOWNEY, Mike. Associate publisher and director, *Moving Pictures International* (film trade paper). Former lecturer in Theatre Studies, University of Paris X, Nanterre. Author of *The Self Managing Screen*, 1987. Contributor to *Variety, Chaplin, Cinema Papers, Vogue, Cosmopolitan, Sovietsky Ekran, Jornal do Video, Camera du Cinema*, among others. Formerly, bureau chief for Germany and Eastern Europe, *Screen International*. **Essay:** Ruth Prawer Jhabvhala.

FOWLER, Bridget. Lecturer in Sociology, University of Glasgow, Scotland. Author of *The Alienated Reader: Women and Popular Romantic Fiction in the Twentieth Century*, 1991.

FRENCH, Warren. Professor emeritus of English, Indiana University, Indianapolis; honorary professor of American studies, University of Wales, Swansea; member of the Editorial Board, *American Literature* and *Twentieth-Century Literature;* series editor for Twayne publishers. Author of *John Steinbeck*, 1961 (revised 1975), *Frank Norris*, 1962, *J.D. Salinger*, 1963 (revised 1976), *A Companion to 'The Grapes of Wrath'*, 1963, *The Social Novel at the End of an Era*, 1966, *A Season of Promise*, 1968, *The South in Film*, 1981, and *Jack Kerouac*, 1986, *J.D. Salinger Revisited*, 1988, *The San Francisco Literar Renaissance, 1955–60*, 1991, *John Steinbeck Revisited: The Fiction*, 1993. Editor of a series on American literature, *The Thirties*, 1967, *The Forties*, 1968, *The Fifties*, 1971, and *The Twenties*, 1975. **Essays:** Henry Bellamann; Warwick Deeping; Thomas Dixon; Frances Parkinson Keyes; F. Van Wyck Mason; Grace Metalious; Allen Tate; Eudora Welty; Thornton Wilder.

GIFFORD, Judith A. Librarian, Newport Library, Rhode Island. Reviewer for Library Journal. **Essays:** Barbara Taylor Bradford; Rosalind Laker.

GILLEN, Paul. Lecturer, University of Technology, Sydney. **Essays:** Ion L. Idriess; Jack Lindsay; Hal Porter.

GLADSKY, Thomas S. Associate professor of English, Central Missouri State University, Warrensburg. Author of articles on historical fiction and ethnic literature in *New England Quarterly, Studies in the Novel, Critique, Modern Age, Southern Studies*, and other periodicals. **Essay:** Gore Vidal.

GORDON-SMITH, Pat. Commissioning editor, Cassell (publishers). **Essay:** Betty Trask.

GOTTSCHALK, Jane. Professor of English, University of Wisconsin, Oshkosh. Author of articles on Afro-American literature for *Wisconsin Review, Phylon, Renascence*, and on themes and types of mystery fiction for *Armchair Detective*. Contributor to *Mystery, Detective, and Espionage Magazines*, 1983, and *Twentieth-Century Crime and Mystery Writers*, 1985. **Essay:** Mary Roberts Rinehart.

GOUGH, John. Lecturer in Mathematics and Computer Education, Deakin University, Victoria, Australia. Author of texts, monographs, and articles on mathematics education, games, evaluation, and remedial mathematics; also contributed essays on children's literature. Contributor to *Twentieth-Century Children's Writers*, and *Twentieth-Century Science Fiction Writers*. **Essays:** Esther Forbes; Elizabeth Goudge.

GREY, Elizabeth. Freelance writer and broadcaster. Author of numerous books, including biographies on Edith Clavell and Amy Johnson, *The Story of Journalism*, 1968, and *The Noise of Drums and Trumpets*, 1971. Romantic and historical fiction reviewer for *The Times*, *Good Book Guide*, and *Books and Bookmen*. **Essay:** Anna Gilbert.

GUERARD, Albert. Professor emeritus, Stanford University, California. Author of *Robert Bridges*, 1942, *Joseph Conrad*, 1947; *Thomas Hardy*, 1949; *André Gide*, 1951; *Conrad the Novelist*, 1958, *The Triumph of the Novel: Dickens, Dostoevsky, Faulkner*, 1976, *The Touch of Time: Myth, Memory, and the Self*, 1980, and seven novels including, most recently, *Christine/Annette*, 1985. Editor of *Mirror and Mirage*, 1980. **Essay:** Janet Lewis.

GUILEY, Rosemary. Author of *Love Lines: The Romance Reader's Guide to Printed Pleasures*, 1983, *Career Opportunities for Writers* (revised edition), 1992. Editor, *Encyclopaedia of Ghosts and Spirits*, 1992.

HAEDICKE, Janet V. Assistant professor of English, Northeast Louisiana University, Monroe. Author of essays on drama, and a chapter on Lilian Hellman in *American Playwrights 1880–1945*, forthcoming. **Essay:** Jean Rhys.

HANSCOM, Marion. Assistant director for Special Collections and Fine Arts, State University of New York, Binghamton. Reviewer for *Library Journal*, and editor of two manuscript collections held at her library. **Essays:** Ernest K. Gann; Cecilia Holland; Elizabeth Seifert; Frank G. Slaughter; Daoma Winston.

HATCHARD, Marion. Artist. Freelance writer and producer. **Essays:** Mary Howard; Mary Lide; Wynne May; Adeline McElfresh; Henry Handel Richardson; Sheila Walsh; Margaret Way; Anne Worboys.

HAYNE, Barrie. Professor of English, St Michael's College, Toronto. Author of numerous papers for the Popular Culture Association. **Essays:** Eleanor H. Porter; Jean Webster.

HAYNE, Joanne Harack. Teacher of courses on detective literature in continuing studies programs. Author of several papers on crime and detective writing for the Popular Culture Association. **Essays:** Susan Ertz; D.E. Stevenson.

HELD, Michael. Freelance writer. **Essay:** Barbara Riefe.

HEYDUK, Allayne C. School librarian and freelance writer. Reviewer for *Library Journal* and *Magill Book Reviews*. **Essays:** Phyllis Hastings; Jessica Stirling.

HIGDON, David Leon. Paul Whitfield Horn professor of English, Texas Tech University, Lubbock. Author of *Time and English Fiction*, 1977, and *Shadows of the Past in Contemporary British Fiction*, 1984. Editor, *Joseph Conrad's Almayer's Folly*, 1993. Since 1973, general editor, *Conradiana*. **Essays:** John Fowles; George MacDonald Fraser.

HINKEMEYER, Joan. Librarian, Denver Public Library; columnist, *Energy/Environment Newsletter*, Denver. Former English professor, assistant editor, *Colorado Libraries*, and reviewer for *Library Journal* and *Rocky Mountain News*. **Essays:** Sophia Cleugh.

HOPKINS, Chris. Lecturer in English, Sheffield Hallam University. Author of *John Clare—Natural Poet?*, 1990, and essays on

Shelley, and *David Jones*. **Essays:** Radclyffe Hall; Storm Jameson; Julia O'Faolain.

HOPKINS, Lisa. Lecturer in English, Sheffield Hallam University. Author of *Elizabeth I and Her Court*, 1990, *Women Who Would Be Kings: Female Rulers of the Sixteenth Century*, 1991. **Essay:** Margaret Irwin.

HORDON, Ferelith. Freelance writer. **Essays:** Kate Alexander; Lindsey Davis; Lloyd C. Douglas; Cynthia Harrod-Eagles; Lindsay McKenna; Carole Mortimer; Madge Swindells.

JAMES, Louis. Professor of English and American Literature, Keynes College, University of Kent, Canterbury. Author of *The Islands in Between*, 1968, *Fiction for the Working Man 1830–60*, 1974, *Jean Rhys*, 1978, and *Writers from the Caribbean*, 1990. Editor, *Print and the People, 1819–51*, 1976, and *Performance and Politics in Popular Drama: Aspects of Popular Entertainment in Theatre, Film and Television* (with others), 1980. **Essays:** Marie Corelli; Anthony Hope.

JENSEN, Margaret. Associate professor of Sociology, Hamline University, St Paul, Minnesota. Author of *Love's Sweet Return: The Harlequin Story*, 1984, and articles in *A Room of One's Own*, *Minnesota Women's Press*, and *St Paul Pioneer Press*. **Essays:** Mary Burchell; Susan Johnson; Emilie Loring; Violet Winspear.

JONES, Heather Iris. Graduate student; freelance writer. Author of 'Laura Secord, History, and Melodrama; or, The Unmaking of a Feminist Nation' in *Canadian Literature*. **Essays:** Grace Murray Atkin; Evelyn Eaton; Madge Macbeth; Isabel M. Paterson; Laura Goodman Salverson; Virna Sheard; Elizabeth Sprigge.

KELLY, Richard. Lindsay Young professor of English, University of Tennessee. Author of *Graham Greene*, 1984; *Daphne du Maurier*, 1987, *V.S. Naipaul*, 1989; *Lewis Carroll*, 1990, *Graham Greene: A Study of the Short Fiction*, 1992, *The Carolina Waterman: Bug Hunters and Boatbuilders*, 1993. **Essay:** Daphne du Maurier.

KEMP, Barbara E. Library applications specialist, PSS.Tapesty, Reston, Virginia. Author of numerous professional articles; contributor to *Twentieth-Century Romance and Gothic Writers*, 1982, and *Twentieth-Century Romance and Historical Writers*, 1990. **Essays:** Sandra Brown; Robyn Carr; Elaine Raco Chase; Catherine Coulter; Caroline Courtney; Barbara Delinsky; Roberta Gellis; Kay Hooper; Linda Howard; Iris Johansen; Jayne Ann Krentz; Alice Chetwynd Ley; Johanna Lindsey; Laura London; Amii Lorin; Elizabeth Lowell; Laurie McBain; Judith McNaught; Linda Lael Miller; Diana Palmer; Heather Graham Pozzessere; Fayrene Preston; Emilie Richards; Francine Rivers; Nora Roberts; Mary Linn Roby; Carola Salisbury; Dallis Schulze; Sylvie Sommerfield; Sondra Stanford; Florence Stevenson; Sylvia Thorpe; Patricia Veryan; Claudette Williams; Sherryl Woods.

KERRIDGE, Richard. Lecturer in English and Creative Studies, Bath College of Higher Education. Recipient of the BBC wildlife award for nature writing, 1990, 1991. **Essay:** Thomas Keneally.

KUMAR, Rachel. Research into women and development, social science faculty, Centre for Management and Development, Trivandrum, Kerala, India. **Essays:** Noel Barber; Julie Ellis; Margaret Mitchell; Danielle Steel; Barbara Wood.

LANDRUM, Larry N. Associate Professor of English, Michigan State University, East Lansing. Author of *American Popular*

Culture, 1982. Co-editor, *Dimensions of Detective Fiction*, 1976; contributed 'Guide to Detective Fiction' to *Handbook of American Popular Culture*, 1978. **Essays:** Rafael Sabatini; Samuel Shellabarger.

LEE, Linda. Freelance writer and writing instructor. Author of *How to Write and Sell Romance Novels*, 1988, and of romance novels (as Hope Goodwin), including, most recently, *Shadows over Paradise*, 1987, and *Yesterday's Promises*, 1987. **Essays:** Dixie Browning; Brooke Hastings.

LEETE-HODGE, Lornie. Freelance writer and editor. Author of many children's books including, most recently, Oscar Wilde's *The Happy Prince*, 1986, and *Sinbad the Sailor*, 1986, and books on Wiltshire and the Royal Family. **Essays:** Ursula Bloom; D.A. Ponsonby.

LEVSTICK, Frank R. Archives and records regional administrator, Kentucky Department for Libraries and Archives, Frankfort. Director of the US Newspaper History Project in Kentucky, and former state archivist, Ohio. Author of *A Directory of State Archives in the United States*, 1977, *Kentucky Historical Records Needs Assessment*, 1982, and of numerous articles on United States history; co-author of *Union Bibliography of Ohio Printed State Documents*, 1974. **Essays:** Irving Bacheller; Kenneth Roberts; Helen Hooven Santmyer.

LEWIS, Barry. Lecturer, University of Newcastle. Contributor to *Contemporary Novelists*, 1990. Author of articles on Thomas Pynchon, Raymond Federman, Paul Auster; and Robert Coover. **Essay:** E.L. Doctorow.

LIGHT, Alison. Lecturer in English, Royal Holloway College, University of London. Author of *Forever England: Femininity Literature and Conservatism Between the Wars*, 1991. Member of editorial board of the *Feminist Review*.

LOCKHART, Marilyn. Freelance writer; former librarian. Reviewer for *Library Journal*. **Essay:** Frances Murray.

LONGEST, George C. Associate professor of English, Virginia Commonwealth University, Richmond. Author of *Three Virginia Writers: Mary Johnston, Thomas Nelson Page, and Amélie Rives Troubetzkoy: A Reference Guide*, 1978, and of many articles and reviews. **Essays:** Mary Johnston; Andrew Lytle; Stark Young.

LYNN, Mary C. Member of the American Studies Department, Skidmore College, Saratoga Springs, New York. **Essay:** Elswyth Thane.

MACDONALD, Andrew. Member of the English Department, Loyola University, New Orleans. Author of articles on Jonson, Shakespeare, English as a second language, science fiction, and popular culture. **Essays** (with Gina Macdonald): Anthony Burgess; Howard Fast; Nevil Shute.

MACDONALD, Gina. Assistant professor, Loyola University, New Orleons. Author of *The Foundations of Effective Writing*, 1994; and articles on southwestern writers, Shakespeare, Robert Greene, English as a second language, science fiction, and popular culture. **Essays:** Madelaine Brent; Anthony Burgess (with Andrew Macdonald); Brian Cleeve; Thomas B. Costain; Howard Fast (with Andrew Macdonald); Winston Graham; Susan Hufford; Barbara Ferry Johnson; Barbara Kevern; Marie Belloc Lowndes; Barbara Anne Pauley; Nevil Shute (with Andrew Macdonald).

MAY, Radmila. Freelance editor and indexer. Commissioning editor, Sweet and Maxwell (publishers). **Essay:** Lisa Appignanesi.

McFARLANE, Alan J. Postgraduate teaching assistant, Department of English, University of Aberdeen. **Essay:** Peter Ackroyd.

McGRATH, Joan. Library consultant, Toronto Board of Education; book review editor, *Reviewing Librarian*. Columnist for *In Review* and *Emergency Librarian*, and reviewer for Toronto *Star, Quill and Quire, Canadian Materials*, and *Canadian Book Review Annual*. Contributor to *Twentieth-Century Children's Writers, Growing with Books*, and *Writers on Writing*. **Essays:** Hervey Allen; Michael Arlen; Pearl S. Buck; Rachel Field; Gilbert Frankau; Rose Franken; Janice Holt Giles; W.G. Hardy; Fannie Hurst; Naomi Jacob; Margaret Kennedy; Doris Leslie; Rosamond Marshall; Frederick Niven; Charles Nordhoff and James Norman Hall; Gene Stratton Porter; Mary Renault; Marcella Thum.

McNALL, Sally Allen. Member of the English Department, University of Kansas, Lawrence. Author of *Who Is in the House? A Psychological Study of Two Centuries of Women's Fiction in America, 1795 to the Present*, 1981. **Essay:** Marilyn Harris.

MELDRUM, P.R. Freelance writer. Worked in the Public Record Office, London, 11 years. **Essays:** Mollie Chappell; Anne Duffield; Leila Mackinlay; Kate Norway; Claire Ritchie; Olga Sinclair; Annie S. Swan.

MENDELSOHN, Leonard R. Associate professor of English, Concordia University, Montreal. Former editor of *Children's Literature*. Author of 'The Survival of the Spirit in Holocaust Children's Literature' in *Triumph of the Spirit in Children's Literature* edited by Francelia Butler, 1986, and of articles on Aeschylus, Milton, Kafka, Renaissance drama, speed reading, toys, utopian writing, and other subjects in *Studies in English Literature, Comparative Drama, Studies in Short Fiction, Language Arts*, and other journals. **Essays:** James Boyd; Rudy Wiebe.

MITCHELL, J. Lawrence. Professor of English, University of Texas A & M University, College. Author of many articles in journals including *Powys Review, Planet, Scriptorium*, and *Canadian Journal of Linguistics*. Editor of *Computers in the Humanities*, 1974, and *Some Modern British Short Stories*, 1985. **Essay:** Sylvia Townsend Warner.

MOE, Christian H. Professor and chair, Department of Theatre, Southern Illinois University, Carbondale; member of the Advisory Board, Institute of Outdoor Drama; member of Dramatists Guild. Author of *Creating Historical Drama* (with George McCalmon), 1965, an essay on D.H. Lawrence as playwright, and, with Cameron Garbutt, several plays for children. Joint editor of *The William and Mary Theatre: A Chronicle*, 1968, 'Bibliography of Theatrical Craftsmanship' (published annually), 1971–80, and *Six New Plays for Children*, 1971; *Eight Plays for Youth: Varied Theatrical Experiences for Stage and Study*, 1992. **Essays:** Gary Jennings; Robert Penn Warren; Kathleen Winsor.

MOLDRICH, Charmaine. Freelance writer; radio journalist. Former administrative assistant, Australian Film Commission, London; advertising manager, Adelaide Fringe Festival, Australia. **Essays:** Charlotte Vale Allen; Lindsay Armstrong; Shirlee Busbee.

MOORE, Arlene. Reference and government documents librarian, Wichita State University, Kansas. Author of articles on popular culture and librarianship, and forthcoming works on anonymous literature of the 19th century, and on the author Bertha M. Clay. Co-editor, *The North American Union List of Victorian Periodicals*. **Essays:** Nan Asquith; Kathryn Blair; Charles Garvice; Elizabeth Hoy; Elizabeth Hunter; Flora Kidd; Laura Jean Libbey; Margaret

Pargeter; Dudley Pope; Nina Pykare; Margaret Sebastian; Maura Seger; Doris E. Smith; Rebecca Stratton; Vivian Stuart; Essie Summers; Neil H. Swanson; Donna Vitek; Lucy Walker; Jan Westcott.

MORRISEY, Thomas J. Professor and chair, English Department, State University of New York, Plattsburgh. Author of 'Flanagan's *The Year of the French* and the Language of Multiple Truth' in *Eire-Ireland*, 1984, and of articles on Donne, Synge, T.S. Eliot, and science fiction in journals including *Centennial Review*, *Notre Dame English Journal*, and *Science Fiction Studies*. **Essay:** Thomas Flanagan.

MOTTELER, Marilynn. Part-time lecturer, California Polytechnic State University, San Luis Obispo. **Essays:** Dorothy Eden; Anne Maybury.

MURPHY, Alan. Freelance writer and media monitor for a news agency. **Essays:** Thomas Berger; Robert Graves; John Masters; William Styron.

MUSSELL, Kay. Professor of Literature and American Studies; associate dean for undergraduate affairs, The American University, Washington, D.C. Author of *Women's Gothic and Romantic Fiction: A Reference Guide*, 1981, *Fantasy and Reconciliation: Contemporary Formulas of Women's Romance Fiction*, 1984. **Essays:** Mary Elgin; Charlotte Lamb; Anne Mather; Jean Plaidy; Kathleen Gilles Seidel; Anya Seton; Mary Stewart; Kay Thorpe.

NEUBURG, Victor. Former member of the School of Librarianship, Polytechnic of North London. Author of *Popular Literature: A History and Guide from the Beginning of Printing to the Year 1897*, 1977, *The Batsford Companion to Popular Literature*, 1982, and *A Guide to the Western Front: A Companion for Travellers*, 1988. Editor of *London Labour and the London Poor* by Henry Mayhew, 1985, and, with Neil Philip, of *A December Vision: His Social Journalism* by Charles Dickens, 1986.

NEWMAN, Judie. Reader in American and Post-Colonial Literature, University of Newcastle-upon-Tyne. Author of *Saul Bellow*, 1981, *John Updike*, 1988, *Nadine Gordimer*, 1988. Editor of *Harriet Beecher Stow, 'Dred'*, 1992. Associate editor, *British Association for American Studies Pamphlet Series*, 1900–96. Secretary, British Association for American Studies, 1993–96. Contributor to *Journal of Commonwealth Literature*, *Critique*, *WLWE*, *Journal of American Studies*, *Studies in the Literary Imagination*, and others. **Essay:** Edith Wharton.

O'LEARY, John. Freelance writer. **Essay:** Susan Hill.

OLIVER, Marina. See her own entry. **Essays:** Emma Blair; Anita Burgh; Marion Chesney; Rhona Martin; Diane Pearson; Elvi Rhodes; Rosemary Anne Sisson; Jessica Steele; Sally Wentworth; Sara Wood.

OLPIN, Larry. Professor of English, Central Missouri State University, Warrensburg. Author of *A New Classical Rhetoric* (with R.L. Kendreick and F.M. Paterson), 1980, and 'Hyperbole and Abstraction: The Comedy of Emily Dickinson' in *Dickinson Studies*, 1982. **Essays:** Willa Cather; Winston Churchill.

PAYNTER, Kim F. Freelance writer. **Essays:** Countess Barcynska; Clare Emsley; Jean S. MacLeod.

PIEHL, Kathy. Reference librarian, Mankato State University, Minnesota. Author of articles on children's writers, and Rumer Godden, E.L. Doctorow, and John Knowles; contributor to *Twen-*

tieth-Century Romance and Gothic Writers, 1982, *Twentieth-Century Romance and Historical Writers*, 1990, among others. Reviewer for *Library Journal*, and *School Library Journal*. **Essays:** Elizabeth Drummond; Judith Glover; Iris Gower; Sarah Neilan; Cathy Cash Spellman; Helen Van Slyke.

POGEL, Nancy H. Associate professor of American Thought and Language, Michigan State University, East Lansing. Author of *Woody Allen*, 1987, an article on Constance Mayfield Rourke in *American Woman Writers*, and sections in *Handbook of American Popular Culture*. **Essay:** George Barr McCutcheon.

PLOWRIGHT, John. Head of History, Repton School, Yorkshire. Author of 'Watching the Detectives', *Teaching History*, 1983; 'Political Economy and Christian Polity: The Influence of Henry George in England Reassessed', *Victorian Studies*, 1987, 'Revolution or Evolution', *British Army Review*, 1988. Contributor to *Recent Historical Novels*, edited by Irene Collins, 1990. Member of the editorial board, 'Conference and Common Room', 1990–91. **Essay:** Paul Scott.

POWELL, David. Senior lecturer in History, University College of Ripon & York St John. Author of various works on modern British political history, including *British Politics and the Labour Question, 1868–1900*, 1992, and articles and reviews on historical novels, military and naval fiction. Contributor to *Recent Historical Novels*, edited by Irene Collins, 1990. **Essays:** C. Northcote Parkinson; Richard Woodman.

PRICE, Joanna. Lecturer, Liverpool John Moores University. Former lecturer, King Alfred's College, Winchester, 1900–91. Author of 'Remembering Vietnam: Subjectivity and Mourning in American New Realist Writing', in *Journal of American Studies*, 1993. **Essay:** Susan Sontag.

PRINGLE, David. Editor, *Interzone* magazine. Editor, *Million: The Magazine about Popular Fiction*, 1990–93. Author of *Imaginary People: A Who's Who of Modern Fictional Characters*, 1987, among others.

PYKETT, Lyn. Senior lecturer in English, University of Wales, Aberystwyth. Author of *Emily Brontë*, 1989, *The Improper Feminine: The Women's Sensation Novel and the New Woman Writing*, 1992, *The Sensation Novel from 'The Woman in White' to 'The Moonstone'*, forthcoming. **Essay:** Jeanette Winterson.

QUIN, Naya. Freelance writer. Director, *Maya Travel Ltd.* Former nurse, St Bartholomew's Hospital, London. **Essays:** Lucilla Andrews; Betty Neels.

QUINN, L.M. Bookseller and freelance writer. **Essays:** C. Guy Clayton; Alice Harwood; Philip McCutchan; Lilian Woodward.

RADCLIFFE, Elsa J. Author of *Gothic Novels of the Twentieth Century: An Annotated Bibliography*, 1979.

RADFORD, Jean. Lecturer, Hatfield Polytechnic, Hertfordshire. Author of *Dorothy Richardson*, 1991. Editor of *The Progress of Romance: The Politics of Popular Fiction*, 1987.

RADWAY, Janice. Member of the American Civilization Department, University of Pennsylvania, Philadelphia. Author of *Reading the Romance: Women, Patriarchy, and Popular Literature*, 1984. **Essay:** Kathleen E. Woodiwiss.

REGAN, Nancy. Freelance writer. Author of 'A Home of One's Own: Women's Bodies in Recent Women's Fiction' in *Journal of*

Popular Culture, 1978, and *The Institute of Chartered Financial Analysts: A Twenty-Five Year History*, 1989. **Essays:** Faith Baldwin.

RHODES, Judith. Librarian, Leeds City Libraries, Yorkshire. Contributor to *Twentieth-Century Crime and Mystery Writers*, 1991. **Essays:** Tessa Barclay; Nancy Cato; Brenda Clarke; Catherine Cookson; Mazo de la Roche; Jude Deveraux; Christine Marion Fraser; Sarah Harrison; Audrey Howard; Eva Ibbotson; Brenda Jagger; Barbara Michaels; Sharon K. Penman; Rosie Thomas; Philippa Wiat.

ROBERTSON, Karen. Visiting assistant professor of English, Vassar College, Poughkeepsie, New York. Editor of *Sexuality and Renaissance Drama* (with Cardle Levin), and John Pikeryng's *Horestes* (with Jodi George). **Essay:** Doris Langley Moore.

de ROMERO, Sara Corben. Freelance writer. Lecturer; producer. **Essay:** Helen Waddell.

ROGERS, Lucy, and **Peggy YORK.** Lucy Rogers was a teacher and freelance writer. Deceased. Peggy York has worked in general nursing, then midwifery and district nursing; also a short story writer. **Essay:** Audrie Manley-Tucker.

ROWLAND, S.A. Researcher, University of Newcastle-upon-Tyne. **Essay:** Georgette Heyer.

ROWLAND, Sobhana. Solicitor. Freelance writer. **Essays:** Elisabeth Beresford; Catherine Fellows; Anne Hampson; John Jakes; Maureen Peters.

RUGGIERO, Josephine A., and **Louise C. WESTON.** Josephine Ruggiero is professor of Sociology, Providence College, Rhode Island. Louise Weston is President, Environmental Strategies Inc, Ridgefield, Connecticut. They have collaborated on several articles on women's issues. **Essay:** Susan Howatch.

SADLER, Geoffrey. Assistant librarian, Local Studies, Chesterfield, Derbyshire. Author of 19 western novels (as Jeff Sadler and Wes Calhoun), including *Matamoros Mission*, 1993, and *Sierra Trail* (as Wes Calhoun), 1993; as Geoff Sadler (with Antoni Snarski) *Journey to Freedom*, 1990, (with Ernest Roberts), *Shirebrook: Birth of a Colliery*, 1991, *Shirebrook in Old Picture Cards*, 1993. Editor, *Twentieth-Century Western Writers*, 1991. Since 1985, leader of the Shirebrook and District Writers Group. Chair, Shirebrook District Local History Group, 1990–91. **Essays:** Pat Barr; Bernard Cornwell; E.M. Delafield; Alfred Duggan; Alice Dwyer-Joyce; Catherine Gaskin; Constance Gluyas; Pamela Haines; Constance Heaven; MacKinlay Kantor; Claire Lorrimer; Eric Malpass; Naomi Mitchison; Christopher Nicole; Frederick Nolan; Pamela Oldfield; Kathleen Shoesmith; Marguerite Steen; E.V. Thompson; Henry Treece.

SAMBROOK, Hana. Freelance editor. Formerly assistant editor, Thomas Nelson and Sons (publisher); assistant librarian, Edinburgh University Library. Author of York Notes on *The Tenant of Wildfell Hall*, 1984, *Lark Rise to Candleford*, 1984, *My Family and Other Animals*, 1989, *Selected Works of Sylvia Plath*, 1990, *I'm the King of the Castle*, 1992. **Essays:** Maeve Binchy; Molly Keane; Hilary Mantel.

SAUNDERS, Jean. See her own entry.

SAWYER, Andy. Librarian/administrator, Science Fiction Foundation Collection, University of Liverpool Library; Former public librarian. Contributor to various magazines in the science fiction, fantasy, and popular fiction fields including *Million* magazine. Former editor 'Paperback Inferno' (review magazine of the British Science Fiction Association). **Essay:** Lance Horner, Kyle Onstott, and Ashley Carter.

SHAW, Marion. Professor, Department of English and Drama, Loughborough University. **Essays:** Winifred Holtby; May Sinclair.

SHIELDS, Anne M. Social worker. **Essays:** Charity Blackstock; Juliet Dymoke.

SHUCARD, Alan R. Professor and chair of English Department, University of Wisconsin-Parkside, Kenosha. Author of three books of poetry, a study of Countée Cullen, and *American Poetry: The Puritans Through Walt Whitman*, 1988, and *Modern American Poetry* (with Fred Moramarco and William Sullivan). General editor, Twayne Critical Poetry Series. **Essay:** Irving Stone.

SHUEY, Andrea Lee. Branch Manager, Dallas Public Library. Contributor to *Contemporary Literary Criticism;* editor of Dallas Country Library *Newsletter*, 1986–89; reviewer for *Library Journal*. **Essays:** Celeste de Blasis; Alexandra Manners.

SIMMONDS, Roy. Author of *Steinbeck's Literary Achievement*, 1976, *The Two Worlds of William March*, 1984, *William March: An Annotated Checklist*, 1988, and of articles on Steinbeck, March, Hemingway, and Edward O'Brien. **Essays:** John Steinbeck; Patrick White.

SMITH, Christopher N. Reader in French, School of Modern Languages and European History, University of East Anglia, Norwich; editor of *France et Grande Bretagne (1649–96)*, 1990, *Seventeenth-Century French Studies*, 1979–93, and *Aldeburgh and Around: Local Studies*. Author of *Alabaster, Bikinis, and Calvados: An A.B.C. of Toponymous Words*, 1985, and *Jean Anouilh: Life, Work and Criticism*, 1985. Editor of continental emblem books, and of works by Prévost, Betham-Edwards, and Balzac. **Essays:** Melvyn Bragg; H. Rider Haggard; Maurice Hewlett; Alexander Kent; Colin MacInnes; Carola Oman; Susan Sallis; Judith Saxton; Evelyn Scott; Richard Tresillian; Peter Vansittart; Stanley Weyman.

SMITHERS, David Waldron. Professor of Radiotherapy, University of London, retired. Author of *Dickens's Doctors*, 1979, *Castles in Kent*, 1980, *Jane Austen in Kent, Therefore Imagine: The Works of Clemence Dane*, 1988, *Not a Moment to Lose: Some Reminiscences*, 1989, *This Idle Trade: On Doctors Who Were Writers*, 1990, and numerous medical books. **Essays:** Clemence Dane; Arthur Conan Doyle.

STAPLES, Katherine. Head of the Technical Communications Department, Austin Community College, Texas. Contributor to *Twentieth-Century Crime and Mystery Writers*, 1980 (revised 1985), and *American Women Writers*, 1981. Translator of works by Rimbaud, Aragon, and Henri Rousseau. **Essays:** Taylor Caldwell; Elinor Glyn.

STEEL, Susannah. Editor, Dorland Kindersley; author of *Watercolour Colour*, 1993. **Essays:** Helen Forrester; Kate O'Brien.

STERNLICHT, Sanford. Adjunct professor of English, Syracuse University, New York. Author of *John Webster's Imagery and the Webster Canon*, 1972, *John Masefield*, 1977, *C.S. Forester*, 1981, *Padraic Colum*, 1985, *John Galsworthy*, 1987, and *R. F. Delderfield*, 1988; *Stephen Spender*, 1992. Editor, *In Search of Stevie Smith*, 1991. **Essays:** C.S. Forester.

STEVENSON, Nancy P. Freelance writer and editor. Former science editor, both for government and for Bioconsult (private company), 1988–93. Author of short stories; winner of the Canadian Broadcasting Corporation Children's Story Contest, 1991. **Essays:** Margaret Campbell Barnes; Phyllis A. Whitney.

STOPYRA, Jackie. Freelance writer. **Essay:** Marina Oliver.

SUMMERS, Judith. Freelance writer. Author of two novels—*Dear Sister*, 1985, and *I, Gloria Gold*, 1988—and of *Soho: A History of London's Most Colourful Neighborhood*, 1989. **Essays:** Maynah Lewis; Margaret Maddocks; Jean Marsh.

TAYLOR, Welford Dunaway. James A. Bostwick professor of English, University of Richmond. Author of *The Back Fever Papers*, 1971, *Amélie Rives (Princess Troubstzkey)*, 1973, *Sherwood Anderson*, 1977, *The Newsprint Mask*, 1991. Editor *Out American Cousin/The Play that Changed History*, 1990; former editor *The Winesberg Eagle*, 1975–87. **Essay:** Ellen Glasgow.

THOMAS, Marcia L. Director, Eureka Public Library District, Illinois. Member of the selection committe of *University Press Books for Secondary Schools and Public Libraries*, 1989–93. Contributor to *PLA Handbook for Writers of Public Library Policies*, 1993. **Essays:** Jacqueline Briskin; Belva Plain.

THOMPSON, Kate. Television producer; director, Merit Associates Ltd. Journalist, *Arts Review*, London; television critic. **Essays:** Elizabeth Buchan; Philippa Gregory; Claire Rayner.

THURSTON, Carol. Writer and market research consultant. Author of *The Romance Revolution: Erotic Novels for Women and the Quest for a New Sexual Identity*, 1987, two novels, and numerous articles in *Journal of Communication*, *Journal of Popular Culture*, *Journalism Quarterly*, and other periodicals. Co-author of *Case Studies in Institutional Licensee Management*, 1980. Former member of the Faculty of Journalism, University of Texas. **Essays:** Fern Michaels; Alexandra Sellers; Bertrice Small; LaVyrle Spencer.

TIETZE, Thomas R. Freelance writer. **Essay:** P.C. Wren.

TROTMAN, Felicity. Co-partner, Signpost Books, London. Formerly with the publishers Collins, Dent, Penguin, and Macmillan. Author of *The Travels of Marco Polo*, 1986, *The Sorcerer's Apprentice*, 1986, *Davy Crockett*, 1986, *William Tell*, 1987. Editor (with Treld Pelkley Bicknell), *How to Write and Illustrate Children's Books and Get Them Published!*, 1988. **Essays:** Rumer Godden; Patrick O'Brian.

TY, Eleanor. Assistant professor, English Department, Wilfrid Laurier University, Ontario, Canada. Author of *Unsex'd Revolutionaries: Five Women Novelists of the 1790s*, 1993; editor of *The Victim of Prejudice* by Mary Hays, 1993. Contributor to *Notes and Queries, Tulsa Studies in Women's Literature, Ariel, 1650–1850: Ideas, Aesthetics, and Inquiries in the Early Modern Era*. **Essays:** Timothy Findley; Karen van der Zee; Anne Weale.

VANSITTART, Peter. See his own entry. **Essays:** Hugh Walpole; Rex Warner.

WAKULENKO, Iris. Freelance writer and artist. Has worked in telvision, theatre, radio, and graphic arts. **Essays:** Josephine Cox; Ethel Edison Gordon.

WALSH, George. Publisher and freelance writer. **Essays:** Elizabeth von Arnim; Patricia Gallagher; Kathleen Norris.

WEARING, Catherine S. Freelance writer. Researcher on various projects for Pandora Press; contributor to *Encyclopaedia of British Women Writers*, 1988; co-author of a forthcoming book on women's work in the theatre and on television. **Essays:** J.G. Farrell; Ford Madox Ford.

WELSH, Marcia G. Assistant director, Guilford Free Library, Connecticut; reviewer for *Library Journal*. Contributor to *Twentieth-Century Children's Writers, Twentieth-Century Western Writers*. Reviewer for the *Library Journal*. Freelance writer and translator. **Essays:** Stephanie Blake; Lolah Burford; Pamela Hill; Natasha Peters; Nicole St John.

WESTON, Louise C. See the entry for Josephine A. Ruggiero above.

WHITE, Kerry. Freelance writer and bibliographer. Author of *Australian Children's Books, a Bibliography*, 1992, *Australian Children's Fiction, the Subject Guide*, 1993, numerous articles and reviews, and a forthcoming book on children's poetry collections. NSW judge for the Australian Children's Book Council awards, 1994, 1995. **Essays:** Eleanor Dark; Colleen McCullough.

WHITE, Ray Lewis. Professor of English, Illinois State University, Normal. Author of books on Sherwood Anderson, Gore Vidal, Heinrich Böll, Pär Lagerkvist, Günter Grass, and R.K. Narayan; his most recent books are *Gertrude Stein and Alice B. Toklas: A Reference Guide*, 1984, *Arnold Zweig in the USA*, 1986, *Index to Best American Short Stories and O. Henry Prize Stories*, 1988, *Sherwood Anderson: Early Writings*, 1989. **Essays:** John Barth; Ross Lockridge.

WHITEHEAD, Frances. Writer, speaker, and broadcaster on all aspects of mass-market fiction; editorial consultant. Co-author of *And then he kissed her ...*, an audio-cassette guide to writing romantic fiction, and *Behind the Hearts and Flowers*, a manual on how to prepare your book for publication. Former librarian, and former editorial director, Mills and Boon Ltd, London, 1986–94. **Essays:** Iris Bromige; Janet Dailey; Robyn Donald; O. Douglas; Audrey Erskine-Lindop; Lilian Peake; G.B. Stern.

WOOD, Dorothy. Co-partner, Signpost Books, London. Formerly with the publishers Allen and Unwin, Pantheon Books, Puffin Books, and Scholastic Publications. **Essays:** Lettice Cooper; Alexander Cordell.

WOODWARD, Margaret. Freelance writer. Formerly teacher. **Essays:** Evelyn Anthony; Jennifer Blake; Harry Bowling; James Clavell; Mollie Hardwick; Anne Melville.

YARDLEY, M. Jeanne. Lecturer in English, University of Waterloo, Ontario. Author of 'The Maple Leaf as Maple Leaf: Facing the Failure of the Search for Emblems in Canadian Literature' in *Studies in Canadian Literature*, 1987. Member of editorial board, *New Quarterly*, 1981–84. **Essay:** Philip Child.

YORK, Peggy. See the entry for Lucy Rogers above.

YOUNG, Alan R. Professor of English and head of department, Acadia University, Wolfville, Nova Scotia. Author of *Ernest Buckler*, 1976, *Henry Peacham*, 1979, *The English Prodigal Son Plays*, 1979, *Thomas Head Raddall: A Bibliography*, 1982, *Thomas Head Raddall*, 1983, *Tudor and Jacobean Tournaments*, 1987, and *The English Tournament Imprese*, 1988. **Essay:** Thomas Head Raddall.

ZHAREN, W.M. von. Freelance writer. **Essays:** Elizabeth Renier; Willo Davis Roberts.

READING
LIST

Abartis, Caesarea, 'The Ugly-Pretty, Dull-Bright, Weak-Strong Girl in the Gothic Mansion', in *Journal of Popular Culture* (Bowling Green, Ohio), Fall 1979.

Allen, Richard O., 'If You Have Tears: Sentimentalism as Soft Romanticism', in *Genre* (Plattsburgh, New York), June 1975.

Anderson, Rachel, *The Purple Heart Throbs: The Sub-Literature of Love*. London, Hodder and Stoughton, 1974.

Bailey, Margaret, 'The Women's Magazine Short-Story Heroine in 1957 and 1967', in *Journalism Quarterly* (Minneapolis), 1969.

Ballaster, Ros, *Seductive Forms, Women's Amatory Fiction from 1684–1740*. Oxford, Clarendon Press, 1992.

Bayer-Berenbaum, Linda, *The Gothic Imagination: Expansion in Gothic Literature and Art*. Rutherford, New Jersey, Fairleigh Dickinson University Press, 1982.

Beauman, Nicola, *A Very Great Profession: The Women's Novel 1914–1939*. London, Virago Press, 1983.

Berman, Phyllis, 'They Call Us Illegitimate', in *Forbes* (New York), 6 March 1978.

Blacker, Irving R., *The Old West in Fiction*. New York, Obolensky, 1961.

Britton, Anne, and Marion Collin, *Romantic Fiction*. London, Boardman, 1960.

Browne, Ray B., and Marshall W. Fishwick, editors, *The Hero in Transition*. Bowling Green, Ohio, Popular Press, 1983.

Buckley, J.A., and W.T. Williams, *A Guide to British Historical Fiction*. London, Harrap, 1912.

Budick, Emily Miller, *Fiction and Historical Consciousness, the American Romance Tradition*. New Haven, Yale University Press, 1989.

Buhle, Paul, editor, *Popular Culture in America*. Minneapolis, University of Minnesota Press, 1987.

Butterfield, Herbert, *The Historical Novel: An Essay*. Cambridge, Cambridge University Press, and New York, Macmillan, 1924.

Cahalan, James M., *Great Hatred, Little Room: The Irish Historical Novel*. New York, Syracuse University Press, 1983.

Cam, Helen, *Historical Novels*. London, Routledge, 1961.

Cantor, Norman P., and Michael S. Wertham, editors, *The History of Popular Culture*. New York, Macmillan, 1968.

Cawelti, John G., *Adventure, Mystery, and Romance: Formula Stories as Art and Popular Culture*. Chicago, University of Chicago Press, 1976.

Cecil, Mirabel, *Heroines in Love 1750–1974*. London, Joseph, 1974.

Cohn, Jan, *Romance and the Erotics of Property: Mass-Market Fiction for Women*. Durham, North Carolina, Duke University Press, 1988.

Collins, Irene, editor, *Recent Historical Novels*. London, Historical Association, 1991.

Cornillon, Susan Koppelman, editor, *Images of Women in Fiction: Feminist Perspectives*. Bowling Green, Ohio, Popular Press, 1972.

Cranny-Francis, Anne, *Feminist Fiction: Feminist Uses of Genre Fiction*. Oxford, Polity Press, 1989.

Dataller, Roger, *The Plain Man and the Novel*. London, Nelson, 1940.

Dawson, Graham, *Soldier Heroes*. London, Routledge, 1994.

Dekker, George, *The American Historical Romance*. Cambridge, Cambridge University Press, 1987.

Dickinson, A.T., Jr, *American Historical Fiction*. Metuchen, New Jersey, Scarecrow Press, 1958; revised edition, 1971.

Douglas, Ann, 'Soft-Porn Culture', in *New Republic* (Washington, DC), 30 August 1980.

Drake, Robert Y., Jr, 'Tara Twenty Years After', in *Georgia Review* (Athens), Summer 1958.

Duffy, Dennis, *Sounding the Iceberg: An Essay on Canadian Historical Novels*. Toronto, ECW Press, 1986.

Duggan, Alfred, *Historical Fiction*. London, Cambridge University Press, 1957.

Elliot, Thomas R., 'Genteel Violence: The Turn-of-the-Century American Historical Novel', in *Journal of Popular Culture* (Bowling Green, Ohio), Spring 1980.

Falk, Kathryn, *Love's Leading Ladies*. New York, Pinnacle, 1983.

Fallon, Eileen, *Words of Love: A Complete Guide to Romantic Fiction*. New York, Garland, 1983.

Ferris, Ina, *The Achievement of Literary Authority, Gender, and History, and the Waverley Novels*. New York, Cornell University Press, 1991.

Fishburn, Katherine, *Women in Popular Culture: A Reference Guide*. Westport, Connecticut, Greenwood Press, 1982.

Fisher, Margery, *The Bright Face of Danger*. London, Hodder and Stoughton, 1986.

Fleenor, Julian E., editor, *The Female Gothic*. Montreal, Eden Press, 1983.

Fowler, Bridget, *The Alienated Reader: Women and Popular Romantic Fiction in the Twentieth Century*. London, Harvester Wheatsheaf, 1991.

Franzwa, Helen, 'Female Roles in Women's Magazine Fiction 1940–1970', in *Woman: Dependent or Independent Variable?*, edited by Rhoda Kesler Unger and Florence L. Denmark. New York, Psychological Dimensions, 1975.

Frye, Northrop, *The Secular Scripture: A Study of the Structure of Romance*. Cambridge, Massachusetts, Harvard University Press, 1976.

Gaston, Edwin W., Jr, *The Early Novels of the Southwest*. Albuquerque, University of New Mexico Press, 1961.

Green, Martin, *Dreams of Adventure, Deeds of Empire*. London, Routledge, 1980.

Greenfeld, Beth, and Julian E. Fleenor, editors, *The Female Gothic*. St Albans, Vermont, Eden Press, 1982.

Guiley, Rosemary, *Love Lines: The Romance Reader's Guide to Printed Pleasures*. New York, Facts on File, 1983.

Hackett, Alice Payne, and James Henry Burke, *Eighty Years of Best Sellers 1895–1975*. New York, Bowker, 1977.

Harlequin 30th Anniversary 1949–1979: The First 30 Years of the World's Best Romance Fiction. Toronto, Harlequin, 1979.

Harrison, R., 'Women and Romantic Fiction: Subordination and Resistance', paper for BSA annual conference (Manchester), April 1982.

Hart, James D., *The Popular Book: A History of America's Literary Taste*. New York, Oxford University Press, 1950.

Harvey, Brett, 'Boy Crazy', in *Village Voice* (New York), 10 February 1982.

Hay, Valerie, 'The Necessity of Romance', in *Women's Studies Occasional Papers 30* (Canterbury), 1983.

Hazen, Helen, *Endless Rapture: Rape, Romance, and the Female Imagination*. New York, Scribner, 1983.

Higdon, David Leon, *Shadows of the Past in Contemporary British Fiction*. London, Macmillan, and Athens, University of Georgia Press, 1984.

Hoekstra, Ellen, 'The Pedestal Myth Reinforced: Women's Magazine Fiction 1900–1920', in *New Dimensions in Popular Culture*, edited by Russel B. Nye. Bowling Green, Ohio, Popular Press, 1972.

Hofstadter, Beatrice, 'Popular Culture and the Romantic Heroine', in *American Scholar* (Washington, DC), Winter 1960–61.

Hoggart, Richard, *The Uses of Literacy*, London, Chatto and Windus, 1957.

Honey, Maureen, 'New Roles for Women and the Feminine Mystique: Popular Fiction of the 1940's', in *American Studies* (Lawrence, Kansas), Spring 1983.

Hughes, Helen, *The Historical Romance*. London, Routledge, 1993.

Inge, M. Thomas, editor, *Handbook of American Popular Culture 1–2* (includes sections on gothic fiction and romantic fiction). Westport, Connecticut, Greenwood Press, 2 vols, 1979–80.

James, Louis, *Fiction for the Working Man 1830–1850*, London, Oxford University Press, 1963.

Jensen, Margaret, *Love's Sweet Return: The Harlequin Story*. Toronto, Women's Educational Press, 1984.

Karolides, Nicholas J., *The Pioneer in the American Novel 1900–1950*. Norman, University of Oklahoma Press, 1967.

Kay, Mary June, *The Romantic Spirit*. San Antonio, Texas, MJK Enterprises, 4 vols, 1982–88.

Kocmanporà, Jessie, 'Novel of Romance: Problems of Genre in Contemporary English Prose Fiction', in *Brno Studies in English* (Czechoslovakia), 1981.

Krentz, Jayne Ann, editor, *Dangerous Men and Adventurous Women*. Philadelphia, University of Pennsylvania Press, 1992.

Landrum, Larry N., *American Popular Culture*. Detroit, Gale, 1982.

Leavis, F.R., *Mass Civilisation and Minority Culture*. London, Cambridge University Press, 1930.

Leavis, Q.D., *Fiction and the Reading Public*. London, Chatto and Windus, 1932.

Lee, Linda, *How to Write and Sell Romance Novels: A Step-by-Step Guide*. Edmonds, Washington, Heartsong Press, 1988.

Leisy, Ernest F., *The American Historical Novel*. Norman, University of Oklahoma Press, 1950.

Levin, David, *In Defense of Historical Literature*. New York, Hill and Wang, 1967.

Light, Alison, 'Returning to Manderley—Romance Fiction, Female Sexuality, and Class', in *Feminist Review 16* (London), Summer 1984.

Light, Alison, *Forever England: Femininity, Literature and Conservatism Between the Wars*. London, Routledge, 1991.

Lively, Robert A., *Fiction Fights the Civil War*. Chapel Hill, University of North Carolina Press, 1957.

Lovell, Terry, *Consuming Fiction*. London, Verso, 1988.

Lyotard, Jean-François, *The Postmodern Condition: A Report on Knowledge*. Manchester, Manchester University Press, 1984.

Lytle, Andrew, 'The Image as Guide to Meaning in the Historical Novel', in *Sewanee Review* (Tennessee), 1953.

Madden, David, and Peggy Bach, editors, *Classics of Civil War Fiction*. Jackson, Mississippi, University of Mississippi Press, 1991.

Mann, Peter H., *The Romantic Novel: A Survey of Reading Habits, and A New Survey: The Facts about Romantic Fiction*. London, Mills and Boon, 2 vols, 1969–74.

Margolies, David, 'Mills and Boon: Guilt Without Sex', in *Red Letters 14* (London), 1982.

Martin, Rhona, *Writing Historical Fiction*. London, A. and C. Black, and New York, St Martin's Press, 1988.

McAleer, *Popular Reading and Publishing in Britain 1914–1950*, London, Oxford University Press, 1992.

McGarry, Daniel D., and Sarah Harriman White, *Historical Fiction Guide*. Metuchen, New Jersey, Scarecrow Press, 1963.

Meldrum, Barbara Howard, editor, *Under the Sun: Myth and Realism in Western American Literature*. Troy, New York, Whitston, 1985.

Menendez, Albert J., *Civil War Novels: An Annotated Bibliography*. New York, Garland, 1986.

Miner, Madonne M., *Insatiable Appetites: Twentieth-Century American Women's Bestsellers*. Westport, Connecticut, Greenwood Press, 1984.

Minundri, Regina, 'From Jane to Germaine, with Love', in *Library Journal* (New York), 15 February 1973.

Modleski, Tania, 'The Disappearing Act: A Study of Harlequin Romances', in *Signs 5* (Stanford, California), Autumn 1980.

Modleski, Tania, *Loving with Vengeance: Mass-Produced Fantasies for Women*. Hamden, Connecticut, Archon, 1982; London, Methuen, 1984.

Moers, Ellen, *Literary Women*. New York, Doubleday, 1976; London, W.H. Allen, 1977.

Montieth, Moira, editor, *Women's Writing: A Challenge to Theory*. Brighton, Harvester Press, 1986.

Mussell, Kay, 'Beautiful and Damned: The Sexual Woman in Modern Gothic Fiction', in *Journal of Popular Culture* (Bowling Green, Ohio), Summer 1975.

Mussell, Kay, *Women's Gothic and Romantic Fiction: A Reference Guide*. Westport, Connecticut, Greenwood Press, 1981.

Mussell, Kay, *Fantasy and Reconciliation: Contemporary Formulas of Women's Romance Fiction*. Westport, Connecticut, Greenwood Press, 1984.

Neild, Jonathan, *A Guide to the Best Historical Novels and Tales*. London, Mathews and Marrot, 1902; revised edition, 1902, 1904, 1911, 1929.

Neuburg, Victor, *The Batsford Companion to Popular Literature*, London, Batsford, 1982.

Nye, Russell B., editor, *New Dimensions in Popular Culture*. Bowling Green, Ohio, Popular Press, 1972.

Nye, Russel B., *The Unembarrassed Muse: The Popular Arts in America*. New York, Dial Press, 1970.

Orwell, George, 'Boys' Weelies', in *Selected Essays*. London, Penguin, 1957.

O'Toole, Patricia, 'Paperback Virgins', in *Human Behavior* (Los Angeles), February 1979.

Pawling, Christopher, editor, *Popular Fiction and Social Change*. London, Macmillan, 1984.

Pilkington, William T., editor, *Critical Essays on the Western American Novel*. Boston, Hall, 1980.

Pringle, David, *Imaginary People: A Who's Who of Modern Fictional Characters*, New York, Pharos Books, 1987.

Propp, V.Y., *Morphology of the Folk Tale*. Austin and London, 1968.

Pykett, Lyn, *The Improper Feminine: The Women's Sensation Novel and the New Woman Writing*. London, Routledge, 1992.

Rabine, Leslie W., 'Romance in the Age of Electronics: Harlequin Enterprises', in *Feminist Studies* (College Park, Maryland), 1985.

Rabine, Leslie W., *Reading the Romantic Heroine: Text, History, and Ideology*. Ann Arbor, University of Michigan Press, 1985.

Radcliffe, Elsa J., *Gothic Novels of the Twentieth Century: An Annotated Bibliography*. Metuchen, New Jersey, Scarecrow Press, 1979.

Radford, Jean, editor, *The Progress of Romance: The Politics of Popular Fiction*. London, Routledge, 1987.

Radstone, Susannah, editor, *Sweet Dreams: Sexuality, Gender and Popular Fiction*. London, Lawrence and Wishart, 1988.

Radway, Janice, 'The Utopian Impulse in Popular Literature: Gothic Romances and "Feminist' Protest"', in *American Quarterly* (Philadelphia), Summer 1981.

Radway, Janice, *Reading the Romance: Women, Patriarchy, and Popular Fiction*. Chapel Hill, University of North Carolina Press, 1987.

Randall, Rona, *Writing Popular Fiction*. London, A and C Black, 1992.

Regan, Nancy, 'A Home of One's Own: Women's Bodies in Recent Women's Fiction', in *Journal of Popular Culture* (Bowling Green, Ohio), Spring 1978.

Ritchie, Claire, *Writing the Romantic Novel*. London, Bond Street, 1962.

Robinson, Lillian S., 'On Reading Trash', in *Sex, Class, and Culture*. Bloomington, Indiana University Press, 1978.

Roe, Sue, editor, *Women Reading, Women's Writing*. Brighton, Harvester Press, 1987.

'Romance Fiction: A PW Special Report' edited by Daisy Maryles and Robert Dahlin, in *Publishers Weekly* (New York), 13 November 1981.

Rose, Suzanna, 'Is Romance Dysfunctional?' in *International Journal of Women's Studies* (Montreal), May-June 1985.

Rose, Willie Lee, *Race and Religion in American Historical Fiction: Four Episodes in Popular Culture*. Oxford, Clarendon Press, 1979.

Ruggiero, Josephine A., and Louise C. Weston, 'Pulp Feminists', in *Human Behavior* (Los Angeles), February 1978.

Ruggiero, Josephine A., and Louise C. Weston, 'Conflicting Images of Women in Romance Novels', in *International Journal of Women's Studies* (Montreal), January-February 1983.

Russ, Joanna, 'Somebody's Trying to Kill Me and I Think It's My Husband: The Modern Gothic', in *Journal of Popular Culture* (Bowling Green, Ohio), 1973.

Samuel, Raphael, *Theatres of Memory*. London, Verso, 1994.

Saunders, Jean, *The Craft of Writing Romance: A Practical Guide*. London, Allison and Busby, 1986.

Sheppard, Alfred T., *The Art and Practice of Historical Fiction*. London, Toulmin, 1930.

Smith, Herbert F., *The Popular American Novel 1865-1920*. Boston, Twayne, 1980.

Snitow, Ann Barr, 'Mass Market Romance: Pornography for Women Is Different' in *Desire: The Politics of Sensuality* edited by Snitow, Christine Stansell, and Sharon Thompson. London, Virago Press, 1984.

Starr, Nathan Comfort, *King Arthur Today: The Arthurian Legend in English and American Literature 1901–1953*. Gainesville, University of Florida Press, 1954.

Strout, Cushing, *The Veracious Imagination: Essays on American History, Literature, and Biography*. Middletown, Connecticut, Wesleyan University Press, 1981.

Sutherland, J.A., *Bestsellers: Popular Fiction of the 1970's*. London, Routledge, 1981.

Taylor, Helen, *Scarlett's Women: Gone with the Wind and Its Female Friends*. London, Virago Press, 1989.

Thomsen, Christen Kold, *Some Observations on Mass Market Fiction in America after 1945*. Odense, Denmark, Odense University, 1976.

Thurston, Carol, and Barbara Doscher, 'Supermarket Erotica: Bodice Busters Put Romantic Myths to Bed', in *Progressive* (New York), April 1982.

Thurston, Carol, 'Popular Historical Romances: Agent for Social Change? An Exploration of Methodologies', in *Journal of Popular Culture* (Bowling Green, Ohio), Summer 1985.

Thurston, Carol, *The Romance Revolution: Erotic Novels for Women and the Quest for a New Sexual Identity*. Urbana, University of Illinois Press, 1987.

Turner, Alice K., 'The Tempestuous, Turbulent, Torrid, and Terribly Profitable World of Paperback Passion', in *New York*, 1978.

Usborne, Richard, *Clubland Heroes: A Nostalgic Study of Some Recurrent Characters in the Romantic Fiction of Dornford Yates, John Buchan, and Sapper*. London, Constable, 1953; revised edition, London, Barrie and Jenkins, 1975.

Van Auken, Sheldon, 'The Southern Historical Novel in the Early Twentieth Century', in *Journal of Southern History* (Baton Rouge, Louisiana), 1948.

Walsh, Mary Roth, 'Images of Women Doctors in Popular Fiction', in *Journal of Popular Culture* (Bowling Green, Ohio), Summer 1978.

Wibberly, Mary, *To Writers with Love: On Writing Romantic Novels*. London, Buchan and Enright, 1985.

Welsh, Rebecca, 'The Tosh Horse', in *The Strange Necessity: Essays and Reviews*. London, Cape, 1928; reprinted, London, Virago, 1987.

Williams, Raymond, *Culture and Society 1780–1950*. London, Chatto and Windus, 1958.

Wilson, Edmund, *Patriotic Gore: Studies in the Literature of the American Civil War*. New York, Oxford University Press, and London, Deutsch, 1962.

Woodruff, Juliette, 'A Spate of Words, Full of Sound and Fury, Signifying Nothing; or, How to Read Harlequin', *Journal of Popular Culture* (Bowling Green, Ohio), 1985.

Zamora, Lois Parkinson, editor, *The Apocalyptic Vision in America*. Bowling Green, Ohio, Popular Press, 1982.

TITLE
INDEX

The following list includes the titles of all novels and short stories (designated 's') cited as romance and historical publications. The name in parenthesis is meant to direct the reader to the appropriate entry where fuller information is given.

Abandoned for Love (Courtney), 1982
Abba Abba (Burgess), 1977
Abbess of Vlaye (Weyman), 1904
Abbey Court (Thum), 1976
Abbeygate (Crowe), 1977
Abbie in Love (Corcoran), 1981
Abducted Heart (J. Blake, as Patrick), 1978
Abduction (Lamb), 1981
Abiding City (Bloom), 1958
Abigail (Corcoran), 1981
Abode of Love (Bowen, as Shearing), 1945
About Mrs Leslie (Delmar), 1950
Above All Things (Albanesi, as Rowlands), 1915
Above and Beyond (Brown, as St Claire), 1986
Above Her Station (M. St John, as St John Cooper), 1922
Above Rubies (Hampson), 1978
Above the Clouds (Wyndham), 1954
Above the Lattice (MacLeod), 1949
Abraham, Prince of Ur (Hardy), 1935
Absent in the Spring (Westmacott), 1944
Acapulco Moonlight (Lewty), 1985
Accident Call (E. Harrison), 1971
Accompanied by His Wife (Burchell), 1941
Ace of Cads (s Arlen), 1927
Aces High (Hooper), 1989
Achilles His Armour (Green), 1955
Across a Crowded Room (Peake), 1977
Across a Starlit Sea (Brandewyne), 1989
Across Her Path (Swan), 1890
Across the Counter (Burchell), 1960
Across the River of Yesterday (Johansen), 1987
Across the Years (Loring), 1939
Across the Years (s E. Porter), 1919
Act of Betrayal (Craven), 1985
Act of Darkness (P. Hastings), 1969
Act of Fear (W. Roberts), 1977
Act of God (Kennedy), 1955
Act of Love (B. Hastings), 1983
Act of Possession (Mather), 1985
Act of Will (Bradford), 1986
Acting Sister (Bloom, as Burns), 1968
Action and Passion (Wren), 1933
Action at Aquila (H. Allen), 1938
Action for Slander (Borden), 1936
Activities of Lavie Jutt (Barcynska, as Barclay), 1911
Acts of Kindness (C. Allen), 1979
Acts of King Arthur and His Noble Knights (Steinbeck), 1976
Adair of Starlight Peaks (Summers), 1977
Adam and Evelina (Blackstock, as Allardyce), 1956
Adam Hepburn's Vow (Swan), 1885
Adam of a New World (J. Lindsay), 1936
Adam Penfeather, Buccaneer (Farnol), 1940
Adam's Breed (Hall), 1926
Adam's Daughters (Bloom), 1947
Adam's Eden (Baldwin), 1977
Adam's Fall (Brown), 1988
Adams, Nurse Hilda series (Rinehart), from 1932
Adam's Rib (Blackstock, as Allardyce), 1963
Adam's Wife (MacLeod), 1972
Adelaide the Enchantress (Hooper), 1987
Admiral of the Ocean-Sea (M. Johnston), 1923
Admiral (Pope), 1982

Admiral's House (Asquith), 1969
Admiral's Lady (Gibbs), 1975
Admirer Unknown (Ruck), 1957
Adora (Small), 1980
Adorable Doctor (Bloom, as Essex), 1968
Adrien Leroy (Garvice), 1912
Adultress (Plaidy, as Carr), 1982
Advances (Burgh), 1992
Advantageous Marriage (Ley), 1977
Adventure in Love (Cartland), 1988
Adventure in Romance (Bloom, as Burns), 1955
Adventure of Princess Sylvie (Williamson, as A.M. Williamson), 1900
Adventure with a Stranger (Vitek), 1987
Adventurer (Cartland), 1977
Adventurer (Krentz), 1990
Adventurers (Hodge), 1965
Adventurers (Stuart, as Long), 1983
Adventures of Billie Belshaw (Vaizey), 1912
Adventures of Cuffy Mahony (s Richardson), 1979
Adventures of Gerard (s Doyle), 1903
Adventuress (Chesney), 1987
Adventuress (Winston), 1978
Adventurous Heart (Bloom, as Burns), 1940
Adversaries (Bennetts), 1969
Adversary in the House (Stone), 1947
Adverse Alliance (F. Stevenson, as Curzon), 1981
Affair in Tangier (K. Blair), 1962
Affair in Venice (R. Lindsay), 1975
Affair of Honor (Krentz, as James), 1983
Affair of Risk (Krentz, as Castle), 1982
Affair of the Heart (J. Smith), 1977
Affair to Forget (R. Lindsay), 1978
Affaire Royale (N. Roberts), 1986
Affairs of Love (Ellerbeck, as Thorne), 1983
Affairs of Men (Bowen), 1922
Affairs of the Heart (Pykare, as Powers), 1980
Affinities (s Rinehart), 1920
Afraid (Cartland), 1981
Afraid of the Dark (Roby), 1965
African Dream (Hoy), 1971
African Enchantment (Pemberton), 1982
African Interlude (Woodward, as Davis), 1982
African Mountain (Hunter, as Chace), 1960
After a Famous Victory (Andrews), 1984
After All These Years (Seidel), 1984
After-Glow (Ayres), 1936
After House (Rinehart), 1914
After Long Journeying (MacLeod), 1955
After Many Days (Albanesi, as Rowlands), 1910
After Many Years (s Swan), 1899
After Midnight (Palmer, as Kyle), 1993
After Noon (Ertz), 1926
After Office Hours (Burchell), 1939
After Rain (Muskett), 1931
After Sundown (Hampson), 1974
After the Death of Don Juan (S. Warner), 1938
After the Hurricane (MacLeod), 1987
After the Lady (Blackstock, as Allardyce), 1954
After the Loving (Mortimer), 1987
After the Music (Palmer), 1986
After the Night (Cartland), 1944

After the Storm (Dailey), 1975
After the Storm (Oldfield), 1981
After the Storm (Williams), 1977
After the Verdict (Hichens), 1924
After Tomorrow (Greig, as Ames), 1951
After Tomorrow (Hichens), 1895
Afterglow (Coulter), 1987
Afterglow (s Hichens), 1935
Afterglow and Nightfall (E. Pargeter), 1977
Afterlove (Briskin), 1973
Afternoon for Lizards (Eden), 1962
Afternoon of an Autocrat (Lofts), 1956
Afternoon Walk (Eden), 1971
Aftershocks (Coulter), 1985
Afterwards (s Lowndes), 1925
Again the Bugle (s Kantor), 1958
Again This Rapture (Cartland), 1947
Against All Gods (Carter), 1982
Against All Odds (K. Thorpe), 1990
Against the Rules (L. Howard), 1983
Against the Stream (Cartland), 1946
Against the World (Albanesi, as Rowlands), 1923
Age Cannot Wither (Bloom), 1942
Age of Innocence (Wharton), 1920
Agency Nurse (Woodward), 1980
Agony and the Ecstasy (Stone), 1961
Agrippa's Daughter (Fast), 1964
Air Ambulance (MacLeod), 1959
Air Ambulance Nurse (Woodward, as Richmond), 1981
Air Hostess in Love (Price), 1962
Air Liner (Bloom, as Burns), 1948
Air Ministry, Room 28 (Frankau), 1942
Air of Glory (Neilan), 1977
Air Surgeon (Slaughter), 1943
Airing in a Closed Carriage (Bowen, as Shearing), 1943
Airs Above the Ground (Stewart), 1965
Alaska (Michener), 1988
Alathea (Belle), 1985
Albany (Black), 1984
Albatross (Anthony), 1982
Albert the Beloved (Bloom, as Prole), 1974
Alberta (s Wiebe), 1979
Album Leaf (Bowen, as Shearing), 1933
Album (Rinehart), 1933
Alchemy (s Lytle), 1979
Aldersyde (Swan), 1883
Aleta's Terrible Secret (Libbey)
Alex and the Raynhams (Bromige), 1961
Alex Rayner, Dental Nurse (Lewty), 1965
Alexa (Melville), 1979
Alexa (Plaidy, as Burford), 1948
Alexander series (Renault), from 1969
Alexander's Bridge (Cather), 1912
Alexandra (Trollope, as Harvey), 1980
Alexandra's Story (F. Preston), 1989
Alianor (M. Peters), 1984
Alias Richard Power (Williamson), 1921
Alibi for Isabel (s Rinehart), 1944
Alice (Worboys), 1992
Alice, Where Are You? (Chandos, as Lance), 1940
Alice, Where Art Thou? (Cadell), 1959
Alicia series (Brown), from 1983
Alien Corn (Bloom), 1947
Alien Corn (R. Lindsay), 1954
Alien Sky (P. Scott), 1953
Alien There Is None (Forrester, as Rana), 1959

Alien Vengeance (Craven), 1985
Alien Wife (Mather), 1977
Alimony (Baldwin), 1928
Alinor (Gellis), 1978
All Consuming Passion (Mather), 1985
All Done by Kindness (Moore), 1951
All Earth to Love (P. Hastings), 1968
All Else Confusion (Neels), 1982
All Else Is Folly (Gaskin), 1951
All Enchantments Die (Maybury), 1941
All for Love (Gallagher), 1981
All for Love (Woods), 1986
All for Quinn (Hooper), 1993
All for the Love of a Fair Face (Libbey), 1889
All for You (Robins), 1946
All I Ask (Chandos), 1939
All I Ask (Weale), 1964
All in the April Morning (Saunders), 1989
All in the Family (Pozzessere), 1987
All Is Not Fair in Love (s Garvice), 1913
All Made of Wishes (Lewty), 1974
All Men Are Murderers (Blackstock, as L. Blackstock), 1958
All My Fortunes (Saxton), 1987
All My Sins Remembered (Thomas), 1990
All My Worldly Goods (Weale), 1987
All Over Again (Ayres), 1934
All over the Town (Delderfield), 1947
All Passion Spent (Chard), 1979
All She Can Be (F. Michaels), 1983
All That Glitters (Keyes), 1941
All That Glitters (L. Howard), 1982
All That Heaven Allows (Weale), 1983
All That Matters (Robins), 1956
All the Dear Faces (A. Howard), 1992
All the Fire (Mather), 1971
All the Hills Moved (Laffeaty), 1984
All the King's Sons (Clarke, as Honeyman), 1976
All the Possibilities (N. Roberts), 1985
All the Queen's Men (Anthony), 1960
All the Right Reasons (Richards), 1988
All the Rivers Run series (Cato), from 1958
All the Summer Long (Stratton, as Gillen), 1975
All the Sweet Tomorrows (Small), 1984
All the Trumpets Sounded (Hardy), 1942
All Their Kingdoms (Polland), 1981
All Things Come Round (Burgin), 1929
All This and Heaven Too (Field), 1938
All This for Love (Robins), 1935
All This I Gave (Chandos, as Tempest), 1937
All Those Years Ago (Richards), 1991
All Through the Day (Clarke), 1983
All Under Heaven (Buck), 1973
All Visitors Must Be Announced (Van Slyke), 1972
All Your Lovely Words Are Spoken (Roby), 1970
Allan and the Holy Flower (Haggard), 1915
Allan and the Ice-Gods (Haggard), 1927
Allan Quatermain (Haggard), 1887
Allandale's Daughters (Burgin), 1928
Allan's Wife and Other Tales (s Haggard), 1889
Allegra (C. Darcy), 1975
Alley-Cat (Muskett), 1937
Alley of Flashing Spears (s Byrne), 1933
Alley Urchin (Cox), 1990
Allinghams (M. Sinclair), 1927
All's Well with the World (Albanesi), 1932
Allure (F. Preston), 1987

Almond, Wild Almond (Broster), 1933
Almost a Stranger (Way), 1984
Almost Forever (L. Howard), 1986
Almost Heaven (McNaught), 1990
Aloha Always (Richards), 1987
Aloha Bride (E. Darcy), 1988
Alone and Afraid (Cartland), 1985
Alone in Paris (Cartland), 1978
Alone in Paris (s Swan), 1898
Along a Dark Path (V. Johnston), 1967
Along Came Ann (Stuart), 1953
Along Came Jones (Browning), 1988
Alphabet of Love (Libbey), 1892
Alpine Nurse (I. Roberts), 1968
Also the Hills (Keyes), 1943
Altar of Evil (F. Stevenson), 1973
Altar of Honour (Dell), 1929
Alternative (McCutcheon), 1909
Always (Johansen), 1986
Always a Rainbow (Bevan), 1975
Always and Forever (Finch, as Robins), 1992
Always and Forever (Freeman), 1990
Always Another Man (Chandos, as Tempest), 1941
Always in My Heart (Chandos, as Charles), 1985
Always Is Not Forever (Van Slyke), 1977
Always Love (E. Darcy), 1988
Always Tomorrow (Ayres), 1933
Always Yours (Burchell), 1941
Alyx (Burford), 1977
Amateur Gentleman (Farnol), 1913
Amateur Governess (Gibbs), 1964
Amazing Interlude (Rinehart), 1918
Amazing Tramp (M. St John, as St John Cooper), 1927
Amazon in an Apron (Neels), 1969
Ambassador's Women (Gaskin), 1985
Ambassadress (Keyes), 1938
Amber Cat (Gibbs, as Ford), 1976
Amber Enchantment (Delinsky, as Drake), 1982
Amber in Love (I. Roberts, as Harle), 1984
Amber Princess (Treece), 1962
Amberstone (Bennetts), 1980
Amberwell (D. Stevenson), 1955
Amberwood (Manners, as Rundle), 1972
Ambitions (A. Howard), 1986
Ambitions of Jill (Wynne), 1920
Ambulance Call (E. Harrison), 1972
Amelia (Palmer), 1993
America, With Love (Winsor), 1957
American (Fast), 1946
American Beauty (Ferber), 1931
American Bred (Franken, as Meloney), 1941
American Captain (E. Marshall), 1954
American Family (Baldwin), 1935
American Flaggs (Norris), 1936
American Heiress (Eden), 1980
American Wife (Swan), 1900
American Woman (Swan)
Americans (Jakes), 1980
Ames, Verity and Jonas Quarrel series (Krentz), from 1988
Ammie, Come Home (B. Michaels), 1968
Among Those Present (s Ferber), 1923
Amorous Bicycle (Bloom, as Essex), 1944
Amrita (Jhabvala), 1956
Amyot series (Nicole), from 1964
Ancestors (Steen, as Dryden), 1930
Ancient Allan (Haggard), 1920

Ancient Egypt series (I. Roberts, as I.M. Roberts), from 1974
Ancient Law (Glasgow), 1908
Ancient Sin (s Arlen), 1930
And All Because. . . (Robins), 1930
And Call It Accident (Lowndes), 1936
And Confidential (Trask), 1953
And Coosha, at Cambridge (M. St John), 1909
And Die Remembering (Roby), 1972
And Falsely Pledge My Love (Burchell), 1957
And Gold Was Ours (Brandewyne), 1984
And in the Morning (Drummond, as Darrell), 1986
. . . And Ladies of the Club (Santmyer), 1982
And New Stars Burn (Baldwin), 1941
And No Regrets (K. Blair, as Brett), 1948
And Now Tomorrow (Field), 1942
And One Rode West (Pozzessere, as Graham), 1992
And One Wore Gray (Pozzessere, as Graham), 1992
And Still She Loved Him (M. St John), 1926
And Still They Dream (Ayres), 1938
And the Desert Blooms (Johansen), 1986
And Then Came Dawn (Stanford), 1981
And Then Came Love (R. Lindsay, as Leigh), 1954
And Then Face to Face (s Ertz), 1927
And Then You Came (Bridge), 1948
And We in Dreams (MacLeod), 1947
Andalusian Affair (Laffeaty), 1985
Anderby Wold (Holtby), 1923
Anderson Line series (Nicole, as McKay), from 1984
Andersonville (Kantor), 1955
Andrew Leicester's Love (Albanesi, as Rowlands)
Angel (Bradford), 1993
Angel (Lindsey), 1992
Angel and the Bad Man (Schulze), 1990
Angel and the Saint (Richards), 1986
Angel Creek (L. Howard), 1991
Angel Fire (Finch, as Drake), 1987
Angel in Hell (Cartland), 1976
Angel in the House (Norris), 1933
Angel in the House (Roby, as D'Arcy), 1980
Angel of Evil (Albanesi, as Rowlands), 1905
Angel of Mercy (Pozzessere), 1988
Angel of the Evening (Saunders, as Summers), 1991
Angel of the Tar Sands (s Wiebe), 1982
Angel Runs Away (Cartland), 1986
Angel Unawares (Williamson), 1916
Angel Who Couldn't Sing (Cleugh), 1935
Angela's Lover (Garvice, as Hart)
Angelfire (Miller), 1989
Angell and Sons (P. Hill), 1992
Angels Cry Sometimes (Cox), 1988
Angel's Eyes (Barcynska), 1957
Angel's Kiss (Barcynska, as Sandys), 1937
Angel's Share (Pozzessere, as Graham), 1985
Angel's Wickedness (Corelli), 1900
Anger in the Sky (Ertz), 1943
Angevin King (Bennetts), 1972
Angry Tide 1798–1799 (Graham), 1977
Angry Wife (Buck, as Sedges), 1947
Animating Maria (Chesney), 1990
Anitra's Dance (Hurst), 1934
Ann All-Alone (M. St John), 1922
Ann and the Hoosier Doctor (McElfresh), 1955
Ann Foster, Lab Technician (McElfresh, as Wesley), 1956
Ann Kenyon, Surgeon (McElfresh), 1960
Ann of Cambray (Lide), 1984
Anna (Harrod-Eagles), 1990

Bad Neighbours (Steele), 1991
Badge of Glory (Kent, as Reeman), 1982
Bag of Saffron (Hutten), 1917
Bagatelle (s Bowen, as Preedy), 1930
Bailey, Bill series (Cookson), from 1986
Bait (Lide, as Lomer), 1961
Baker's Daughter (D. Stevenson), 1938
Baker's Dozen (s Norris), 1938
Balance Wheel (Caldwell), 1951
Balcony (Cowen), 1962
Balefire (Tranter), 1958
Ballad and the Source (Lehmann), 1944
Ballad-Maker of Paris (Blackstock, as Torday), 1935
Ballerina (E. Smith), 1932
Ballerina series (Sebastian, as Gladstone), from 1979
Baltic Mission (Woodman), 1986
Ban (Wynne, as Lurgan), 1912
Band of Angels (Warren), 1955
Bandersnatch (Hardwick), 1989
Bandit and the Priest (Erskine-Lindop), 1953
Bank on It (Woods), 1993
Bannaman Legacy (Cookson), 1985
Banner O'Brien (Miller), 1984
Banner of the Bull (Sabatini), 1915
Banners of Silk (Laker), 1981
Bannister Girls (Saunders), 1991
Banshee Tide (Dwyer-Joyce), 1977
Barabbas (Corelli), 1893
Barbara Owen, Girl Reporter (McElfresh, as Scott), 1956
Barbara Rebell (Lowndes), 1905
Barbara's Love Story (Albanesi, as Rowlands), 1911
Barbarian Lover (Pedler), 1923
Barbarian (Mitchison), 1961
Barbarian Stories (s Mitchison), 1929
Barbarians (F. Mason), 1954
Barbary Moon (K. Blair), 1954
Barbary Sheep (Hichens), 1907
Barbary Wharf series (Lamb), from 1992
Barberry Bush (Norris), 1927
Barbours and Bouchards series (Caldwell), from 1939
Barclay series (Nicole), from 1988
Bardelys the Magnificent (Sabatini), 1906
Barden, Julie series (Manley-Tucker), from 1968
Barforth series (Jagger), from 1980
Bargain Bride (Cartland), 1989
Bargain Bride (Kidd), 1976
Bargain for Paradise (Stratton), 1978
Bargain with the Devil (Krentz, as Castle), 1981
Barn Stormers (Williamson, as A.M. Williamson), 1897
Barnards of Loseby (S. Warner), 1974
Baron's Bride (Oliver), 1986
Barons of Runnymede (Bennetts), 1974
Barrancourt Destiny (Worboys), 1977
Barren Corn (Heyer), 1930
Barren Harvest (M. Lewis), 1981
Barren Metal (Jacob), 1936
Barrier Between Them (Woodward), 1980
Barrier Between Us (Maybury), 1940
Barriers Between (Garvice), 1910
Barringer House (Riefe), 1976
Barry Leroy (Bailey), 1919
Bars of Iron (Dell), 1916
Bartered Bride (MacGill), 1920
Bartered Bridegroom (Roby, as Grey), 1981
Bartholomew Fair (P. Hastings), 1974
Base Metal (Bloom), 1928

Bastard (Jakes), 1974
Bastard King (Plaidy), 1974
Bat (Rinehart), 1926
Bath Assembly (Bishop), 1977
Bath Belles (J. Smith), 1986
Bath Intrigue (Walsh), 1986
Bath Tangle (Heyer), 1955
Battle for Lucknow (Stuart, as V.A. Stuart), 1975
Battle for Possession (Lamb), 1992
Battle of Love (K. Blair), 1961
Battle of the Queens (Plaidy), 1978
Battle of the Villa Fiorita (Godden), 1963
Battle Prize (Krentz, as James), 1983
Battle Surgeon (Slaughter), 1944
Battle-Ground (Glasgow), 1902
Bauhinia Junction (Way), 1971
Bay of Stars (Donald), 1980
Bay of the Nightingales (Summers), 1970
Bayou Bride (J. Blake, as Patrick), 1979
Bayou Midnight (Richards), 1987
Bazalgettes (Delafield), 1935
Be An Angel (S. Harrison), 1993
Be Buried in the Rain (B. Michaels), 1985
Be More Than Dreams (Hoy), 1968
Be My Guest (Cadell), 1964
Be My Guest (Norway), 1966
Be Still, My Heart! (Chandos, as Tempest), 1936
Be Valiant Still (Lane), 1935
Beach of Sweet Returns (Hilton), 1975
Beads of Nemesis (Hunter), 1974
Bear Flag (Holland), 1990
Beat to Quarters (Forester), 1937
Beating the Odds (B. Hastings, as Gordon), 1990
Beatrice (Haggard), 1890
Beau and the Bluestocking (Ley), 1975
Beau Barron's Lady (Bennetts), 1981
Beau Brocade (Orczy), 1907
Beau Ideal (Wren), 1928
Beau Sabreur (Wren), 1926
Beau Wyndham (Heyer), 1941
Beaujeu (Bailey), 1905
Beaumaroy Home from the Wars (Hope), 1919
Beautiful Coquette (Libbey), 1892
Beautiful Ione's Lover (Libbey), 1892
Beautiful Is Vanished (Caldwell), 1951
Beauty (Baldwin), 1933
Beauty and the Beast (Norris), 1928
Beauty and the Buccaneer (Sherwood), 1986
Beauty and the English Lord (Sherwood), 1986
Beauty Beast (Kantor), 1968
Beauty of the Devil (Hamilton, as Fitzgerald), 1988
Beauty of the Season (Garvice), 1910
Beauty or Brains? (Cartland), 1990
Beauty, Retire (Trask), 1932
Beauty Surgeon (Bloom, as Burns), 1967
Beauty's Daughter (Hardwick), 1976
Beauty's Daughter (Norris), 1935
Beauty's Tears (Mackinlay), 1961
Beauvallet (Heyer), 1929
Because I Wear Your Ring (Chandos), 1947
Because My Love Is Come (Chandos, as Tempest), 1938
Because of Doctor Danville (Hoy), 1956
Because of These Things ... (Bowen), 1915
Because There Is Hope (Chandos, as Tempest), 1958
Becca's Child (W. Roberts), 1972
Beckman series (Stirling), from 1979

Beckoning Dream (Laffeaty), 1974
Beckoning Trails (Loring), 1947
Becky (Thompson), 1988
Becoming (C. Allen), 1977
Bed Disturbed (Plaidy, as Ford), 1952
Bed of Grass (Dailey), 1979
Bed of Roses (Weale), 1981
Bedford Row (Rayner), 1977
Bedford Village (H. Allen), 1944
Beds in the East (Burgess), 1959
Bedside Manner (Norway), 1971
Beechy (Hutten), 1909
Before I Die (Roby), 1966
Before I Kissed (M. Howard), 1955
Before I Make You Mine (Chandos), 1938
Before It's Too Late (Pykare, as N. Coombs), 1986
Before the Crossing (Jameson), 1947
Before the Storm (Lowndes), 1941
Before the Wind (Seger), 1989
Beggar at Her Husband's Door! (M. St John), 1928
Beggar Maid, Queen (M. Peters), 1980
Beggar Man (Ayres), 1920
Beggar on Horseback (S. Thorpe), 1953
Beggar Wished (Cartland), 1934
Beggars' Horses (Wren), 1934
Begin to Live (Plaidy, as Burford), 1956
Beginner's Luck (Browning), 1990
Beginning of the Affair (Lewty), 1992
Beginnings (McKenna, as Nauman), 1989
Behind a Closed Door (Donnelly), 1979
Behind the Cloud (Loring), 1958
Behind the Mask (Sallis, as Meadmore), 1980
Behold Your King (Mitchison), 1957
Bel Lamington (D. Stevenson), 1961
Belchamber Scandal (F. Murray), 1985
Belfry (M. Sinclair), 1916
Believe in To-morrow (Asquith), 1955
Believe Me, Beloved (Chandos, as Tempest), 1936
Believe the Heart (Plaidy, as Burford), 1950
Believe the Heart (Woodward, as Richmond), 1979
Believers (Giles), 1957
Believing in Giants (C. Allen, as Vincent), 1978
Bell Branch (L. Walker), 1971
Bell Timson (Steen), 1946
Bella (J. Cooper), 1976
Bella (Eden), 1964
Bella Donna (Hichens), 1909
Bellarion the Fortunate (Sabatini), 1926
Belle of Santiago (Burgin), 1911
Belle of the Works (M. St John), 1919
Bellefleur (Stanford), 1980
Belle-Mère (Norris), 1931
Bellerose Bargain (Carr), 1982
Belles of Vaudroy (Burgin), 1906
Bells along the Neva (Ponsonby), 1964
Bells of the City (Lamb, as Coates) , 1975
Bells Still Ring (Bloom, as Burns), 1976
Belltower (Shoesmith), 1973
Bellwood (Ogilvie), 1969
Belonging (Browning), 1987
Belonging to Taylor (Hooper, as Robbins), 1986
Beloved (Delmar), 1956
Beloved (Morrison), 1987
Beloved (Small), 1983
Beloved and Unforgettable (Bloom, as Burns), 1953
Beloved Ballerina (R. Lindsay, as Leigh), 1953

Beloved Betrayal (Finch), 1988
Beloved Burden (Barcynska), 1954
Beloved Captive (Gower), 1981
Beloved Castaway (Winspear), 1968
Beloved Creditor (Bloom), 1939
Beloved Deceiver (Kidd), 1987
Beloved Diana (Ley), 1977
Beloved Enemy (Albanesi), 1913
Beloved Enemy (Blackstock, as Allardyce), 1958
Beloved Enemy (Corcoran), 1981
Beloved Enemy (Duffield), 1950
Beloved Enemy (Maybury), 1957
Beloved Exile (Cordell), 1993
Beloved Knight (Greig, as Ames), 1958
Beloved Man (Bloom, as Burns), 1957
Beloved of the Gods (Orczy), 1905
Beloved Physician (Jacob), 1930
Beloved Rake (Hampson), 1972
Beloved Rascals (I. Roberts), 1962
Beloved Rebel (S. Thorpe), 1959
Beloved Scoundrel (Johansen), 1994
Beloved Sinner (Stirling), 1980
Beloved Stranger (Mather), 1966
Beloved Traitor (Gower), 1981
Beloved Tyrant (Winspear), 1964
Beloved Vagabond (Hampson), 1981
Beloved Woman (Norris), 1921
Below the Salt (Costain), 1957
Below the Salt (Sheard), 1936
Belshazzar (Haggard), 1930
Belt of Gold (Holland), 1984
Beltane the Smith (Farnol), 1915
Belvedere (Gibbs, as Ford), 1973
Bend in the River (Bromige), 1975
Bend Sinister (Dymoke), 1962
Bender (P. Scott), 1963
Bendish (Hewlett), 1913
Beneath a Spell (Albanesi, as Rowlands), 1900
Beneath the Magic (Hichens), 1950
Beneath the Moon (Lorrimer, as Robins), 1951
Beneath the Passion Flower (Bowen, as Preedy), 1932
Beneath the Visiting Moon (Sisson), 1986
Benefactress (Arnim), 1901
Bengal Tiger (E. Marshall, as Hunter), 1952
Benita (Haggard), 1906
Benjamin Blake (E. Marshall), 1941
Bennett's Welcome (Fletcher), 1950
Benton's Row (Yerby), 1954
Bernadette (Stern), 1960
Berry Goes to Monte Carlo (s Williamson), 1921
Bertrand of Brittany (Deeping), 1908
Beside a Norman Tower (de la Roche), 1934
Besieged (Lamb), 1992
Besieger of Cities (Duggan), 1963
Bess (Swan), 1880
Bess of the Woods (Deeping), 1906
Best Girls Are Here (M. St John), 1917
Best Intentions (Woods), 1987
Best Is Yet to Come (Palmer), 1991
Best Kept Secrets (Brown), 1989
Best-Kept Secret (Vitek), 1985
Best Laid Plans (Chase), 1984
Best Laid Plans (N. Roberts), 1989
Best Love of All (Maybury), 1932
Best Man for the Job (Browning), 1992
Best of His Family (Oman), 1933

Best of Kathleen Norris (Norris), 1955
Best People (Van Slyke), 1976
Best Place to Be (Van Slyke), 1976
Best Short Stories of Rider Haggard (s Haggard), 1981
Best Time Ever (Ruck), 1934
Best Way to Lose (Dailey), 1983
Best Woman in the World (M. St John), 1913
Beth Mason (Albanesi, as Rowlands), 1913
Betray Not My Passion (Sommerfield), 1984
Betrayal (Lamb), 1983
Betrayal (Robins), 1976
Betrayal in Bali (Wentworth), 1980
Betrayed (Chard), 1991
Betrayed (Mather), 1991
Betrayed by Love (Palmer), 1987
Better Love (Pedler), 1924
Better Part (Swan), 1884
Better Than Life (Garvice), 1910
Better to Forget (M. Pargeter), 1977
Better to Marry (Bloom), 1933
Better World Than This (Joseph), 1986
Betty (Baldwin), 1928
Betty on the Stage (M. St John), 1920
Betty Trevor (Vaizey), 1907
Between Friends (A. Howard), 1988
Between Pride and Passion (Kidd), 1982
Between Roc and a Hard Place (Pozzessere), 1993
Between the Lines (Krentz), 1986
Between the Tides (Swan), 1935
Between You and Me (Ayres), 1935
Beverly of Graustark (McCutcheon), 1904
Bevy of Maids (Duffield), 1941
Beware, Beware the Bight of Benin (McCutchan), 1974
Beware of the Banquet (Aiken), 1966
Beware of the Stranger (Dailey), 1978
Beware the Beast (Mather), 1976
Beware the Bight of Benin (McCutchan), 1975
Bewildered Heart (K. Blair), 1950
Bewildered Heart (James), 1973
Bewilderment (E. Scott), 1922
Bewitched (Cartland), 1975
Bewitched (Williamson, as A.M. Williamson), 1932
Bewitching Compulsion (Napier), 1989
Bewitching Grace (J. Blake, as Maxwell), 1974
Beyond All Frontiers (Drummond), 1983
Beyond Compare (Jordan), 1989
Beyond Control (Kidd), 1981
Beyond Ecstasy (Hamilton, as Fitzgerald), 1985
Beyond Eden (Coulter), 1992
Beyond Fantasy (Delinsky, as Douglass), 1983
Beyond Her Control (Steele), 1986
Beyond Reach (M. Pargeter), 1986
Beyond the Blue Mountains (Plaidy), 1947
Beyond the City (Doyle), 1893
Beyond the Foothills (Summers), 1976
Beyond the Lagoon (Lewty), 1981
Beyond the Mountain (Asquith), 1970
Beyond the Ranges (Bevan), 1970
Beyond the Reef (Kent), 1992
Beyond the Reef (MacLeod), 1984
Beyond the Rocks (Glyn), 1906
Beyond the Sound of Guns (Loring), 1945
Beyond the Starlit Forest (Brandewyne), 1991
Beyond the Sunrise (Balogh), 1992
Beyond the Sunset (Kidd), 1973
Beyond the Sweet Waters (Hampson), 1970

Beyond the Threshold (Miller), from 1992
Beyond the World (Clarke), 1991
Beyond This Limit (s Mitchison), 1986
Beyond Tomorrow (F. Michaels), 1981
Bhowani Junction (Masters), 1954
Bhunda Jewels (Worboys), 1980
Bianca (F. Stevenson), 1973
Bid for a Coronet (Williamson, as A.M. Williamson), 1901
Bid Me Live (Chappell), 1967
Big Barn (Edmonds), 1930
Big Ben (Ayres), 1939
Big Family (Delmar), 1961
Big Fellah (Ayres), 1931
Big Fisherman (L. Douglas), 1948
Big Frogs and Little Frogs (s Ertz), 1938
Big Game (Vaizey), 1908
Big Man (M. Howard), 1965
Big Sky Country (Dailey), 1978
Bikers (Stuart, as A. Stuart), 1971
Bill Bailey series (Cookson), from 1986
Bill—the Sheik (Williamson, as A.M. Williamson), 1927
Billy Bathgate (Doctorow), 1989
Bird in a Storm (Albanesi), 1924
Bird in Flight (Stanford), 1986
Bird in Hand (Browning), 1985
Bird in the Chimney (Eden), 1963
Bird in the Tree (Goudge), 1940
Bird of Passage (Ellerbeck, as Thorne), 1990
Birds (s du Maurier), 1968
Birds' Fountain (Hutten), 1915
Birds in a Gilded Cage (Glover), 1988
Birds of Paradise (P. Scott), 1962
Birds of Silence (Mackinlay), 1974
Birds Without Bars (I. Roberts), 1970
Birdwatcher (Gordon), 1974
Birth of Mischief (Sabatini), 1945
Birth of Roland (s Hewlett), 1911
Bishop of Hell (s Bowen), 1949
Bit of a Bounder (Gibbs), 1952
Bitter Alliance (K. Thorpe), 1978
Bitter Betrayal (Jordan), 1989
Bitter Bride-Bed (Manners, as Lamont), 1971
Bitter Conquest (Blackstock), 1959
Bitter Core (Robins, as French), 1954
Bitter Creek (Boyd), 1939
Bitter Debt (Swan), 1893
Bitter Harvest (Hampson), 1982
Bitter Heritage (Pedler), 1928
Bitter Homecoming (Donald), 1989
Bitter Lotus (s Bromfield), 1944
Bitter Loving (Peake), 1976
Bitter Masquerade (Hilton), 1970
Bitter Rapture (Duffield), 1937
Bitter Reason (Cowen), 1966
Bitter Revenge (Peake), 1982
Bitter Sweet (Albanesi, as Rowlands), 1910
Bitter Sweet (Spencer), 1990
Bitter Sweet Summer (O. Sinclair), 1970
Bitter Sweetbriar (Trask), 1955
Bitter Taste of Love (Peake), 1988
Bitter Winds (Cartland), 1938
Bitter Winds of Love, (Cartland), 1976
Bittersweet (Bloom), 1978
Bittersweet Ecstasy (Taylor), 1987
Bittersweet Honeymoon (Lewty), 1989
Bittersweet Rain (Brown, as St Claire), 1984

Bitter-Sweet (Robins), 1955
Bixby Girls (R. Marshall), 1957
Black Amber (Whitney), 1964
Black Bartlemy's Treasure (Farnol), 1920
Black Bethlehem (L. Cooper), 1947
Black Boar series (Wiat), from 1975
Black Cameron (MacLeod), 1964
Black Candle (Cookson), 1989
Black Charles (Wyndham), 1952
Black Dawn (Nicole), 1977
Black Domino (Shoesmith), 1975
Black Douglas (Tranter), 1968
Black Douglas (Winspear), 1971
Black Eagle (Hampson), 1973
Black Fire (Riefe), 1980
Black Flemings (Norris), 1926
Black Gale (Shellabarger), 1929
Black Gold (Gower), 1988
Black Harvest (Barcynska), 1960
Black Heart and White Heart (s Haggard), 1900
Black Hood (Dixon), 1924
Black Hunter (Donnelly), 1978
Black Incense (s Williamson), 1926
Black Ingo (Way), 1977
Black Invader (Stratton), 1981
Black Is White (McCutcheon), 1914
Black Knight (Dell), 1926
Black Knight (Kidd), 1976
Black Lace (Salverson), 1938
Black Laurel (Jameson), 1947
Black Lyon (Deveraux), 1980
Black Magic (Bowen), 1909
Black Majesty series (Nicole), from 1984
Black Man—White Maiden (Bowen, as Preedy), 1941
Black Milestone (Gavin), 1941
Black Moon (Graham), 1973
Black Moth (Heyer), 1921
Black Narcissus (Godden), 1939
Black Panther (Cartland), 1939
Black Pearl (Harrod-Eagles), 1982
Black Pearl series (W. Roberts), from 1978
Black Plantagenet (Bennetts), 1969
Black Rainbow (B. Michaels), 1982
Black River Affair (Tresillian, as Devine), 1985
Black River Breed (Tresillian, as Devine), 1985
Black Rose (Costain), 1945
Black Sand, White Sand (MacLeod), 1981
Black Sea Frigate (Stuart), 1971
Black Sheep (Ayres), 1917
Black Sheep (Heyer), 1966
Black Sheep (M. St John, as St John Cooper), 1916
Black Sleeves (Williamson, as A.M. Williamson), 1928
Black Spaniel (s Hichens), 1905
Black Sparta (s Mitchison), 1928
Black Sun (Horner), 1967
Black Swan (Plaidy, as Carr), 1991
Black Swan (Sabatini), 1932
Black Velvet Gown (Cookson), 1984
Black Virgin (Borden), 1937
Black Virgin of the Gold Mountain (P. Hastings), 1956
Blackberry Day (Pilcher), 1991
Blackberry Summer (P. Hastings), 1982
Blackbird's Tale (E. Blair), 1989
Blackground (Aiken), 1989
Blackmaddie (Saunders, as Summers), 1980
Blackmail (Jordan), 1982

Blackoaks series (Carter), from 1976
Black-Out Symphony (Barcynska), 1942
Blade of Justice (Renier), 1965
Blades (McCutcheon), 1928
Blades of Passion (Williams), 1978
Blair, Harriet series (S. Harrison), from 1985
Blaise of France (Shellabarger), 1950
Blaize (Melville), 1981
Blakeney Papers series (Clayton), from 1984
Blake's Reach (Gaskin), 1958
Blanche Fury (Bowen, as Shearing), 1939
Blanket of the Dark (J. Buchan), 1931
Blaze (S. Johnson), 1986
Blaze of Love (Robins), 1932
Blaze of Noon (Plaidy, as Burford), 1958
Blaze of Passion (S. Blake), 1978
Blaze of Silk (Way), 1970
Blaze of Sunlight (Baldwin), 1959
Blaze Wyndham (Small), 1988
Blazing Star (Thum), 1983
Bleak Heritage (MacLeod), 1942
Bledding Sorrow (Harris), 1976
Bless This House (Lofts), 1954
Blessing in Disguise (s Swan), 1898
Blessings (Plain), 1989
Blind Date (E. Darcy), 1986
Blind Date (Ruck), 1953
Blind Duty (Nolan), 1983
Blind Heart (Jameson), 1964
Blind Journey (MacLeod), 1942
Blind Loyalty (Pedler), 1940
Blind Man's Night (Shellabarger, as Esteven), 1938
Blind Man's Year (Deeping), 1937
Blind Miller (Cookson), 1963
Blind Mother (s Caine), 1892
Blind Passion (Mather), 1991
Blind Promises (Palmer, as Currie), 1984
Blind Raftery and His Wife Hilaria (Byrne), 1924
Blinkeyes (Barcynska, as Sandys), 1925
Bliss, Vicky series (B. Michaels, as Peters), from 1973
Blithe Images (N. Roberts), 1982
Blitz (Rayner), 1990
Blood and Sand (Sutcliff), 1987
Blood, Captain series (Sabatini), from 1922
Blood Kin (Pauley), 1972
Blood Money! (M. St John), 1923
Blood of the Martyrs (Mitchison), 1939
Blood Red, Sister Rose (Keneally), 1974
Blood Royal (Hardwick), 1988
Bloodheart series (Tresillian), from 1985
Bloodied Toga (Hardy), 1979
Bloodrose House (Crowe), 1985
Bloodstock (s Irwin), 1953
Bloody Field by Shrewsbury (E. Pargeter), 1972
Bloody Sunrise (Nicole), 1993
Blossom Like the Rose (Lofts), 1939
Blossoms in the Snow (I. Roberts, as Rowland), 1971
Blot on the Scutcheon (Wynne), 1910
Blow Hot, Blow Cold (Neels), 1969
Blow the Wind Southerly (D. Stevenson), 1954
Blue and Distant Hills (Saxton), 1994
Blue Bedroom (s Pilcher), 1985
Blue Camellia (Keyes), 1957
Blue Caribbean (K. Blair, as Conway), 1954
Blue Castle (Montgomery), 1926
Blue Cockade (Gibbs, as Ford), 1943

Blue Days at Sea (Weale), 1981
Blue Diamond (J. Smith), 1981
Blue Dress Girl (Thompson), 1992
Blue Evening Gone (Stirling), 1981
Blue Eyes and Grey (Orczy), 1928
Blue Falcon (Carr), 1981
Blue Feathers (I. Roberts, as Rowland), 1967
Blue Fire (Whitney), 1961
Blue Haze (Muskett), 1939
Blue Heather (Cartland, as McCorquodale), 1953
Blue Heaven, Black Night (Pozzessere, as Drake), 1986
Blue Hills of Sintra (Hampson), 1973
Blue Horizons (Baldwin), 1942
Blue Hurricane (F. Mason), 1954
Blue Jacaranda (Hoy), 1975
Blue Jasmine (Winspear), 1969
Blue Lenses (s du Maurier), 1970
Blue Lotus (Way), 1979
Blue Mist of Morning (Vitek), 1983
Blue Mountains of China (Wiebe), 1970
Blue Remembered Hills (I. Preston), 1965
Blue Rose (Wyndham), 1957
Blue Sapphire (D. Stevenson), 1963
Blue Scarab (Laffeaty), 1977
Blue Shutters (Mackinlay), 1947
Blue Skies and Shining Promises (Johansen), 1988
Blue Skies, Dark Waters (M. Pargeter), 1976
Blue Sky of Spring (Cadell), 1956
Blue Velvet (Johansen), 1985
Blue Water, Black Depths (Nicole, as Gray), 1990
Bluebell Windows (Sallis), 1987
Bluebird Winter (L. Howard), 1987
Blue-Eyed Witch (Cartland), 1976
Bluegrass King (Dailey), 1977
Blues in the Night (N. Peters), 1989
Bluewater (Deeping), 1939
Blunder of an Innocent (Albanesi), 1899
Body and Soul (Woods), 1989
Bodyguard (Krentz, as James), 1983
Bohemian Blood (Wynne, as Lurgan), 1910
Bolambo Affair (K. Blair, as Brett), 1961
Bold Breathless Love (Sherwood), 1981
Bold Pursuit (F. Stevenson, as Faire), 1980
Bolitho, Richard series (Kent), from 1968
Boma in the Bush (May), 1985
Bomb Vessel (Woodman), 1984
Bonaventure (Bailey), 1927
Bond of Blood (Gellis), 1965
Bond of the Flesh (R. Marshall), 1952
Bond of Vengeance (Steele), 1984
Bond Wife (M. Peters, as Black), 1983
Bondage of Riches (Swan), 1912
Bondmaid (Buck), 1949
Bondman (Caine), 1889
Bondmaster series (Tresillian), from 1977
Bonds of Matrimony (Hunter), 1975
Bonnie Jean (s Swan), 1884
Book of Daniel (Doctorow), 1971
Boomerang Bride (M. Pargeter), 1979
Boon Island (K. Roberts), 1956
Bordeaux Red (Clayton), 1986
Border Knight (Dymoke), 1987
Border Lord (Westcott), 1946
Bored Bridegroom (Cartland), 1974
Borgia Bull (Bennetts), 1968
Borgia, Lucretia series (Plaidy), from 1958

Borgia Prince (Bennetts), 1968
Born for Love (Bloom), 1978
Born for Victory (Dymoke), 1960
Born in Prison (M. St John), 1916
Born of the Wind (M. Pargeter), 1984
Born Out of Love (Mather), 1977
Born to Be King (Gluyas), 1974
Born to Love (Sherwood), 1984
Borodins series (Nicole, as Arlen), from 1980
Borrowed Angel (Pozzessere), 1992
Borrower of the Night (B. Michaels, as Peters), 1973
Boskelly's Bride (Saunders, as Innes), 1976
Boss Man from Ogallala (Dailey), 1975
Boss of Bali Creek (Hampson), 1973
Botany Bay (Nordhoff and Hall), 1941
Both Sides Now (B. Hastings), 1988
Both Sides of the Coin (Roby, as Grey), 1980
Botor Chaperon (Williamson), 1907
Bottle Party (Bailey), 1940
Bought with His Name (Jordan), 1982
Bound by a Promise (Palmer), 1979
Bound by Desire (Rogers), 1988
Bound to Happen (Thane), 1930
Boundary Line (Robins), 1932
Boundary Lines (N. Roberts), 1985
Boundless Water (Bowen), 1926
Bounty series (Nordhoff and Hall), from 1932
Boutique of the Singing Clocks (Bloom, as Prole), 1969
Bow Street series (Sebastian), from 1977
Bow to the Storm (M. Howard), 1950
Bow Window in Green Street (Ponsonby), 1949
Bowl of Stars (May), 1973
Boxer's Sweetheart (M. St John), 1920
Boy (Corelli), 1900
Boy for the Ages (Bacheller), 1937
Boy in the House (s de la Roche), 1952
Boy with Wings (Ruck), 1915
Boyds of Black River (Edmonds), 1953
Bracelet (Hichens), 1930
Brackenthorpe (Shoesmith), 1980
Braddock-Black series (S. Johnson), from 1986
Braeswood Tapestry (Carr), 1984
Braganza Pursuit (Neilan), 1976
Brand of Possession (Mortimer), 1980
Brandon, Ginny and Steve Morgan series (Rogers), from 1974
Brandy Kane (Gluyas), 1985
Brass Islands (Dwyer-Joyce), 1974
Brave Barbara (Albanesi), 1901
Brave Brigands (Wynne), 1913
Brave Captains (Stuart, as V.A. Stuart), 1972
Brave Employments (Bowen), 1931
Brave Heart (Albanesi, as Rowlands), 1911
Brave Heart (McKenna), 1993
Brave in Heart (Burchell), 1948
Brave Live On (Mackinlay), 1942
Brave Love (Albanesi, as Rowlands), 1926
Brave the Wild Wind (Lindsey), 1984
Brazen Ecstasy (Taylor), 1983
Brazen Virtue (N. Roberts), 1988
Brazenhead the Great (Hewlett), 1911
Brazilian Affair (R. Lindsay), 1978
Brazilian Fire (van der Zee), 1989
Bread and a Sword (E. Scott), 1937
Bread-and-Grease-Paint (Ruck), 1943
Bread into Roses (Norris), 1937
Bread of Deceit (s Lowndes), 1925

Bread of Tears (Burgin), 1899
Breadwinner (T. Barclay), 1982
Breadwinners (Bloom), 1932
Breaker of Hearts (Swan), 1937
Breakfast in Bed (Brown), 1983
Breakfast with the Nikolides (Godden), 1942
Breaking Away (Jordan), 1990
Breaking Point (E. Darcy), 1992
Breaking Point (s du Maurier), 1959
Breaking Point (Rinehart), 1922
Breaking Point (Robins, as French), 1956
Breaking the Rules (Vitek), 1984
Breaking Wave (Shute), 1955
Breath of Air (Godden), 1950
Breath of Life (Baldwin), 1942
Breath of Scandal (Brown), 1991
Breathe Upon These Slain (E. Scott), 1934
Breathless Summer (Hooper), 1982
Breathless Surrender (Hooper), 1982
Breeze from Camelot (Delmar), 1959
Breeze off the Ocean (Lorin), 1980
Brendan's Song (Richards), 1985
Breta's Double (Garvice)
Brethren (Haggard), 1904
Brewster's Millions (McCutcheon, as Greaves), 1903
Briar and Palm (Swan), 1887
Briar Patch (Blackstock), 1960
Briar Rose (Williamson), 1919
Bridal Array (Cadell), 1957
Bridal Lamp (Ainsworth), 1975
Bridal Path (Tranter), 1952
Bridal Sweet (Bloom, as Burns), 1942
Bridal Wreath (Mackinlay), 1971
Bride (Irwin), 1939
Bride Adorned (D. Murray), 1929
Bride Alone (Bloom, as Burns), 1943
Bride at Whangatapu (Donald), 1977
Bride by Candlelight (Eden), 1954
Bride for a Captain (Kidd), 1981
Bride for a Day (Libbey)
Bride for a Night (Hampson), 1979
Bride for King James (M. Peters), 1968
Bride from Faraway (O. Sinclair, as Daniels), 1987
Bride in Darkness (Wiat), 1982
Bride in Flight (Summers), 1964
Bride—Maybe (Bloom, as Burns), 1946
Bride of a Stranger (J. Blake, as Maxwell), 1974
Bride of Ae (P. Hill), 1983
Bride of Diamonds (E. Darcy), 1990
Bride of Doom (Robins, as Gray), 1956
Bride of Emersham (Chandos, as Lance), 1967
Bride of Liberty (Yerby), 1954
Bride of Mingalay (MacLeod), 1967
Bride of Moat House (Lofts, as Curtis), 1969
Bride of Pendorric (Plaidy, as Holt), 1963
Bride of Romano (Stratton), 1973
Bride of Tancred (Pearson), 1976
Bride of Terror (Sherwood, as Hines), 1976
Bride of the Delta Queen (Dailey), 1978
Bride of the Plains (Orczy), 1915
Bride of the Sun (Hunter), 1980
Bride of the Tiger (Pozzessere), 1987
Bride of the Wind (S. Blake), 1984
Bride of the Wind (Pozzessere, as Drake), 1992
Bride of Violence (Robins, as Gray), 1957
Bride Price (Hunter), 1974

Bride Said No (Lamb), 1985
Bride series (Coulter), from 1992
Bride to a Brigand (Cartland), 1984
Bride to Lucifer (Winspear), 1971
Bride to the King (Cartland), 1979
Bride Who Ran Away—Nurse Henderson (Ruck), 1922
Bride—Maybe (Bloom, as Burns), 1946
Bride's Dilemma (Winspear), 1965
Bride's Hero (Williamson, as Revere), 1912
Bride's House (Woodward, as Marsh), 1968
Bride's Lace (Winspear), 1984
Brides of Bellenmore (Maybury), 1964
Brides of Bunyon (Laffeaty), 1975
Bridge Builders (Swan), 1913
Bridge of a Hundred Dragons (Drummond), 1986
Bridge of Corvie (Pilcher, as Fraser), 1956
Bridge of Desire (Deeping), 1916
Bridge of Fear (Eden), 1966
Bridge of Kisses (Ruck), 1917
Bridge of Rainbows (Hamilton, as Fitzgerald), 1989
Bridge of San Luis Rey (Wilder), 1927
Bridge of Sighs (Lane), 1973
Bridge of Years (MacLeod), 1945
Bridge to the Moon (Maybury), 1960
Bridge to Yesterday (Gluyas), 1981
Bridges Over Time series (Anand), from 1990
Bridie Climbing (Ellerbeck, as Thorne), 1969
Brief Ecstasy (Robins), 1934
Brief Enchantment (MacLeod), 1979
Brief Fulfilment (MacLeod), 1945
Brief Gaudy Hour (Barnes), 1949
Brief Is the Glory (Gluyas), 1975
Brief Light (J. Lindsay), 1939
Brief Rapture (Duffield), 1938
Brief Springtime (Bloom), 1957
Brig of War (Woodman), 1983
Bright Banners (Seifert), 1943
Bright Cantonese (Cordell), 1967
Bright Coin (Seifert), 1949
Bright Day Is Done (Saxton), 1974
Bright Day Renewed (James), 1964
Bright Destiny (Ayres), 1952
Bright Flows the River (Caldwell), 1978
Bright Meadows (Ritchie), 1951
Bright Morning (Ellerbeck, as Thorne), 1986
Bright Morning (Randall), 1952
Bright Pavilions (Walpole), 1940
Bright Promise (Chappell), 1966
Bright Scalpel (Seifert), 1941
Bright Skies (Loring), 1946
Bright Son of York (Bennetts), 1971
Bright Tomorrow (Plaidy, as Burford), 1952
Bright Tomorrows (Alexander), 1985
Bright Winter (Chandos, as Lance), 1965
Bright Young Things (M. Howard, as Edgar), 1986
Brightener (Williamson), 1921
Brimstone Club (F. Mason), 1971
Brimstone in the Garden (Cadell), 1950
Bring Larks and Heroes (Keneally), 1967
Bringing Up Becky! (M. St John), 1924
Bristol Cousins (Ponsonby), 1951
Britannia All at Sea (Neels), 1978
Brittany Blue (Hunter, as Chace), 1967
Brittle Bondage (K. Blair, as Brett), 1951
Brittle Glass (Lofts), 1942
Brittle Glory (James), 1948

Brittle Shadow (Bloom), 1938
Broad Acres series (Jacob), from 1955
Broad Highway (Farnol), 1910
Broad Road (Swan), 1908
Broadway Interlude (Baldwin), 1929
Brocade (Muskett), 1953
Brocken (P. Hill), 1990
Broken (Ayres), 1928
Broken Armour (Mackinlay), 1963
Broken Barrier (M. St John, as St John Cooper), 1924
Broken Barriers (Cartland), 1938
Broken Bough (Bromige), 1973
Broken Destiny (Wentworth), 1990
Broken Gate (Chandos, as Tempest), 1940
Broken Halo (F. Barclay), 1913
Broken Journey (Laffeaty, as Fortina), 1969
Broken Key (Roby), 1973
Broken Rhapsody (Way), 1982
Broken Tapestry (Randall), 1969
Broken Threads (T. Barclay), 1989
Broken Wing (Burchell), 1966
Bronze Eagle (Orczy), 1915
Bronze Mystique (Delinsky), 1984
Bronzed Hawk (Johansen), 1983
Brooding Lake (Eden), 1966
Broome Stages (Dane), 1931
Brother Bedford (Clarke, as Honeyman), 1972
Brother of Gwynedd series (E. Pargeter), from 1974
Brother Saul (Byrne), 1927
Brothers and Enemies (Nicole), 1982
Brothers in Arms (Niven), 1942
Brown Eyes of Mary (Albanesi), 1905
Brown Fields (Pilcher, as Fraser), 1951
Brown Sugar (Ayres), 1921
Brown Sugar (Cato), 1974
Brumaire (Nicole, as Logan), 1978
Brute! (M. St John), 1922
Bubble over Thorn (Barcynska), 1951
Bubbling Springs (Duffield), 1940
Buccaneer (Pope), 1981
Buccaneer Doctor (Slaughter, as C.V. Terry), 1955
Buccaneer Surgeon (Slaughter, as C.V. Terry), 1954
Buccaneer's Bride (Saunders, as Innes), 1989
Buccaneers (Wharton), 1938
Builders (Glasgow), 1919
Bull from the Sea (Renault), 1962
Bulls of Parral (Steen), 1954
Bunch of Blue Ribbons (Albanesi, as Rowlands), 1926
Burden (Westmacott), 1956
Burden-Bearers (Swan), 1900
Burke, The Kingpin (F. Preston), 1986
Burn All Your Bridges (Drummond, as Drew), 1976
Burned Fingers (Norris), 1945
Burning Beacon (Chandos, as Charles), 1956
Burning Flame (I. Roberts, as Harle), 1979
Burning Glass (Bowen), 1918
Burning Inheritance (Mather), 1987
Burning Lamp (F. Murray), 1973
Burning Land (Drummond), 1979
Burning Memories (Lamb, as Hardy) , 1981
Burning Obsession (Mortimer), 1982
Burning Sands (Winspear), 1976
Burr (Vidal), 1973
Bury Love Deep (Sisson), 1985
Bury the Past (Greig, as Ames), 1939
Bus at the Ritz (Trask), 1935

Business Affair (R. Lindsay), 1960
Busmans Holiday (Andrews), 1977
But Know Not Why (Steele), 1982
But Never Free (Cartland), 1937
But Not for Love (Savage), 1970
But Not for Me (Burchell), 1938
But Still the Stream (Cato), 1962
But Yesterday— (Diver), 1927
Butter Market House (Gibbs, as Ford), 1958
Buttercup Joe (P. Hastings), 1980
Buttered Side Down (s Ferber), 1912
Butterflies (Barcynska, as Sandys), 1932
Butterflies in the Rain (Barcynska, as Sandys), 1958
Butterfly (Norris), 1923
Butterfly (B. Wood, as Harvey), 1988
Butterfly and the Baron (Way), 1979
Butterfly Man (McCutcheon), 1910
Butterfly Picnic (Aiken), 1972
Butterfly Plague (Findley), 1969
Buy Me a Dream (I. Roberts, as Harle), 1972
By a Side Wind (James), 1936
By Any Other Name (Browning), 1985
By Command of the Viceroy (McCutchan, as MacNeil), 1975
By Dangerous Ways (Garvice), 1909
By Firelight (E. Pargeter), 1948
By Fountains Wild (Hampson), 1970
By Love Bewitched (Winspear), 1984
By Night at Dinsmore (Shellabarger, as Esteven), 1935
By Order of the Company (M. Johnston), 1900
By Our Beginnings (Stubbs), 1979
By Request (Dell), 1927
By Right of Arms (Carr), 1986
By Sun and Candlelight (Laffeaty, as Carstens), 1976
By Sun and Candlelight (Renier), 1968
By Sun and Candlelight (Sallis), 1989
By the Gate of Pity (Ayres), 1927
By the Gods Beloved (Orczy), 1905
By the Green of the Spring (Masters), 1981
By the Light of the Moon (Heaven, as Fecher), 1985
By the Queen's Grace (Sheard), 1904
By the Silvery Moon (Corcoran), 1981
By the Sword Divided (Hardwick), 1983
By the World Forgot (Ayres), 1932
By This Strange Fire (E. Pargeter), 1948
Byeways (s Hichens), 1897
Bygones (Spencer), 1992
Byway to Love (Sebastian), 1980

C.J.'s Fate (Hooper), 1984
Cable from Kabul (Tranter), 1968
Cache Down (Tranter), 1987
Cactus and the Crown (Gavin), 1962
Cactus Has Courage (Bloom), 1961
Cactus Rose (F. Stevenson, as Colt), 1982
Cade Curse (W. Roberts), 1978
Cadence of Portugal (Hunter, as Chace), 1972
Caedmon (Harwood), 1937
Caesar Is Dead (J. Lindsay), 1934
Cage of Gold (R. Lindsay), 1973
Cage of Ice (Wentworth), 1986
Cage of Shadows (Mather), 1983
Caged Tiger (Jordan), 1982
Cajun Summer (Seger), 1986
Cake Without Icing (Greig), 1932
Calais (Winsor), 1979
Calculated Risk (Chase), 1983

Calder series (Dailey), from 1981
Calendar of Sin (E. Scott), 1931
Calf for Venus (Lofts), 1949
Calhoun (Palmer), 1988
Calhoun Women series (N. Roberts), from 1991
Calico Palace (Bristow), 1970
California Copper (Lorin, as Hohl), 1986
California Generation (Briskin), 1970
California Gold (Jakes), 1989
Call—And I'll Come (Burchell), 1937
Call Back Love (Franken, as Grant), 1937
Call Back the Past (MacLeod), 1988
Call Back Yesterday (Lamb), 1978
Call Back Yesterday (Leslie), 1975
Call for a Stranger (A.E. Worboys), 1962
Call for Doctor Barton (Seifert), 1956
Call for Nurse Templar (Weale), 1960
Call Home the Heart (Ogilvie), 1962
Call Home the Heart (Stirling), 1977
Call in the Night (Howatch), 1967
Call It Destiny (Krentz), 1984
Call of Fife and Drum (Fast), 1987
Call of Glengarron (Buckingham), 1968
Call of Love (M. St John, as St John Cooper), 1936
Call of the Blood (Hichens), 1906
Call of the Blood (Plaidy, as Kellow), 1956
Call of the Heart (Cartland), 1975
Call of the Heart (Corcoran), 1981
Call of the Heart (Garvice), 1914
Call of the Heathen (Hampson), 1980
Call of the Highlands (Cartland), 1982
Call of the Outback (Hampson), 1976
Call of the Pines (L. Walker), 1963
Call of the Veld (Hampson), 1977
Call of Trumpets (Lane), 1971
Call to Arms series (Nolan), from 1983
Call up the Storm (Donnelly), 1983
Callahans and the Murphys (Norris), 1924
Calling Dr Savage (Collin), 1970
Calm Waters (Barcynska, as Sandys), 1940
Calverley Inheritance (Lorrimer), 1990
Calvert series (Seger), from 1987
Came a Cavalier (Keyes), 1947
Came a Stranger (K. Blair, as Conway), 1960
Camelot Caper (B. Michaels, as Peters), 1969
Cameos (s Corelli), 1896
Cameron of Gare (MacLeod), 1952
Cameron's Crossing (McCutchan), 1993
Camomile Lawn (Wesley), 1984
Campaign for a Bride (Oliver), 1977
Campaign for Loving (Jordan), 1984
Campaigners (Harrod-Eagles), 1991
Can I Forget You? (Maybury), 1944
Canadian Affair (Kidd), 1979
Canadian Circus (Eaton), 1939
Canary Yellow (Cadell), 1965
Cancelled Love (Williamson, as A.M. Williamson), 1926
Candidate for Love (Greig), 1947
Candle for St Jude (Godden), 1948
Candle in Her Heart (Loring), 1964
Candle in the Sun (Muskett), 1943
Candle in the Sun (Steen), 1964
Candle in the Wilderness (Bacheller), 1930
Candle in the Wind (Wentworth), 1979
Candle Light (Ayres), 1924
Candle Rekindled (Ainsworth), 1969

Candleglow (Lorin), 1983
Candlemas Street (Manley-Tucker), 1963
Candlemass Road (G. Fraser), 1993
Candles in the Wind (Diver), 1909
Candles in the Wood (Manners), 1974
Candles of the Night (P. Hastings), 1977
Candleshades (Bloom), 1927
Candy (s Hutten), 1925
Candytuft—I Mean Veronica (Grundy), 1914
Canis the Warrior (Staples, as J. Sinclair), 1979
Cannons of Lucknow (Stuart, as V.A. Stuart), 1974
Canopy of Rose Leaves (Hunter, as Chace), 1976
Can't Say No (Woods), 1988
Cantrell, Roman and Nikki Holden series (Chase), from 1987
Cap Flamingo (Winspear), 1964
Cap of Youth (Albanesi), 1914
Cap of Youth (Jacob), 1941
Capable of Feeling (Jordan), 1986
Cape of Black Sands (W. Roberts), 1977
Capricious Caroline (Albanesi), 1904
Capricorn Stone (Brent), 1979
Capt. Desmond, V.C.(Diver), 1907
Captain Barney (Westcott), 1951
Captain Blood series (Sabatini), from 1922
Captain Caution (K. Roberts), 1934
Captain Dieppe (Hope), 1900
Captain for Elizabeth (Westcott), 1948
Captain from Castile (Shellabarger), 1945
Captain from Connecticut (Forester), 1941
Captain Gallant (S. Thorpe), 1958
Captain Ironhand (R. Marshall), 1957
Captain Judas (F. Mason), 1955
Captain Nemesis (F. Mason), 1931
Captain Rebel (Yerby), 1956
Captains and the Kings (Caldwell), 1972
Captain's Lady (Broster), 1947
Captain's Paradise (Hooper), 1988
Captain's Saga (E. Marshall), 1955
Captain's Table (Stuart, as A. Stuart), 1953
Captain's Wife (Jameson), 1939
Captain's Woman (Nicole, as Logan), 1977
Captivated (N. Roberts), 1992
Captive (Plaidy, as Holt), 1989
Captive Bride (Finch), 1987
Captive Bride (Lindsey), 1977
Captive Crown (Tranter), 1977
Captive Destiny (Mather), 1978
Captive Embrace (Sommerfield), 1985
Captive Enchantress (Finch, as Robins), 1989
Captive Freedom (Drummond), 1987
Captive Heart (Cartland), 1956
Captive Herd (Atkin), 1922
Captive Kisses (J. Blake, as Patrick), 1980
Captive Loving (Mortimer), 1983
Captive of Desire (Sellers), 1981
Captive of Fate (McKenna), 1983
Captive of Fate (M. Pargeter), 1985
Captive of Kensington Palace (Plaidy), 1972
Captive of Sahara (Hull), 1931
Captive Queen of Scots (Plaidy), 1963
Captive series (F. Michaels), from 1977
Captive Wife (Deeping), 1933
Captive Woman (Edmonds), 1962
Captives of the Past (Donald), 1986
Captivity (M. Pargeter), 1981
Capt'n Davy's Honeymoon (s Caine), 1892

Capture a Stranger (Peake), 1981
Capture the Rainbow (Johansen), 1984
Captured Images (Seger, as Winslow), 1984
Car of Destiny (Williamson), 1906
Cara (Trollope, as Harvey), 1983
Caradon's Castle (Laffeaty), 1982
Cara's Land (Rhodes), 1991
Caravan (E. Smith), 1943
Caravan of Chance (Bloom), 1971
Caravan to Xanadu (E. Marshall), 1954
Caravaners (Arnim), 1909
Carberry, Letitia 'Tish' series (s Rinehart), from 1911
Cardboard Castle (Wren), 1938
Cardigan Square, (Manners), 1977
Cardinal and the Queen (Anthony), 1968
Cardinal Rules (Delinsky), 1987
Career by Proxy (Baldwin), 1939
Career of David Noble (Keyes), 1921
Career of Katherine Bush (Glyn), 1916
Caretaker Within (Mackinlay), 1938
Carey, Come Back! (Chandos, as Tempest), 1937
Caribbean (Michener), 1989
Caribbean Encounter (K. Thorpe), 1976
Caribbean Gold (M. Pargeter), 1983
Caribbean Nurse (Saxton, as Balmain), 1981
Caribee (Nicole), 1974
Caring Kind (Lamb, as Holland), 1976
Carla (Albanesi, as Rowlands)
Carlowrie (Swan), 1884
Carlton's Wife (Albanesi, as Rowlands), 1911
Carnaby Curse (Winston), 1967
Carnal Innocence (N. Roberts), 1991
Carniss and Company (M. St John, as St John Cooper), 1922
Carnival at San Cristobal (Asquith), 1971
Carnival Coast (Lamb), 1973
Carnival of Florence (Bowen), 1915
Carolina series (Fletcher), from 1941
Caroline and Julia (C. Darcy), 1982
Caroline (Chappell), 1962
Caroline (Mather), 1965
Caroline and the Raider (Miller), 1992
Caroline Terrace (Deeping), 1955
Caroline, The Queen (Plaidy), 1968
Caroline's Waterloo (Neels), 1980
Carolinian (Sabatini), 1925
Carousel (Pilcher), 1982
Carpenter's Lady (Delinsky, as Douglass), 1983
Carr (Bentley), 1929
Carradine Affair (Blackstock, as Allardyce), 1976
Cartismandua (Wiat), 1984
Carver's Kingdom (Nolan), 1978
Casa Grande (Deveraux), 1982
Case of Dr Carlisle (Seifert), 1953
Case of Elinor Norton (Rinehart), 1934
Case of Jennie Brice (Rinehart), 1913
Case of the Confirmed Bachelor (Palmer), 1992
Case of the Mesmerising Boss (Palmer), 1992
Case of the Missing Secretary (Palmer), 1993
Cashelmara (Howatch), 1974
Cashmere (Ellerbeck, as Thorne), 1982
Cassandra (Williams), 1979
Cassandra by Chance (Neels), 1973
Cassie (Thompson), 1991
Cast the Spear (Muskett), 1950
Castaway (F. Murray), 1978
Castile for Isabella (Plaidy), 1960

Castle Barebane (Aiken), 1976
Castle Craneycrow (McCutcheon), 1902
Castle, David series (Weale), from 1982
Castle Dor (du Maurier), 1962
Castle in Andalusia (Sprigge), 1935
Castle in Corsica (Weale), 1959
Castle in Spain (Duffield), 1958
Castle in the Air (Greig), 1947
Castle in the Mist (Stuart, as A. Stuart), 1959
Castle in the Swamp (E. Marshall), 1948
Castle in the Trees (R. Lindsay), 1958
Castle Inn (Weyman), 1898
Castle Kelpiesloch (Chandos, as Charles), 1973
Castle Made for Love (Cartland), 1977
Castle of Closing Doors (Winston), 1967
Castle of Doves (Heaven), 1984
Castle of Eagles (Heaven), 1974
Castle of Fear (Cartland), 1974
Castle of Shadows (Williamson, as A.M. Williamson), 1905
Castle of Temptation (Kidd), 1978
Castle of the Enchantress (Hamilton, as Fitzgerald), 1987
Castle of the Seven Lilacs (Winspear), 1971
Castle on the Hill (Goudge), 1941
Castle Perilous (V. Johnston), 1971
Castle Perilous (Ritchie), 1979
Castle Raven (Black), 1978
Castles in Spain (Plaidy, as Burford), 1954
Castles in Spain (Stratton), 1973
Castles in the Air (Gallagher), 1976
Castles of Sand (Mather), 1981
Casualty Speaking (Norway), 1971
Casualty Ward (Bloom, as Burns), 1968
Cat among the Pigeons (Lane), 1959
Cat and Mouse (Roby), 1967
Cat-in-the-Manger (Bentley), 1923
Cat on a Broomstick (Manners, as Marshall), 1969
¡Catacrok! (s Graves), 1956
Catalan Christmas (Weale), 1988
Catalans (O'Brian), 1953
Catalina's Caress (Sommerfield), 1986
Catch a Falling Star (B. Hastings), 1988
Catch a Kingfisher (D. Smith), 1981
Catch at a Rainbow (Maybury), 1935
Catch of the Day (Collin), 1990
Catch the Gentle Dawn (Freeman), 1983
Catch Up to Love (Greig), 1960
Cathedral (Walpole), 1922
Catherine (Seger), 1988
Catherine Carmier (Gaines), 1964
Cat's Prey (Eden), 1952
Catspaw (Borden), 1950
Cattle Man (Burgin), 1898
Cattleman's Choice (Palmer), 1985
Caught by Love (Cartland), 1982
Cauldron of Desire (M. Peters, as Lloyd), 1981
Cautious Lover (Krentz, as James), 1985
Cavalier Courtship (Oliver), 1974
Cave of the White Rose (Kidd), 1972
Cazalet Bride (Winspear), 1970
Cease Firing (M. Johnston), 1912
Cecily (C. Darcy), 1972
Cedar Tree (Randall), 1957
Celebration (Thomas), 1982
Celeste (R. Marshall), 1949
Celestial City (Orczy), 1926
Celia Garth (Bristow), 1959

Celia's House (D. Stevenson), 1943
Centennial (Michener), 1974
Central Hospital series (E. Harrison), from 1966
Central Line (s Binchy), 1978
Ceremony of the Innocent (Caldwell), 1976
Certain Compass (L. Cooper), 1960
Certain Crossroad (Loring), 1925
Certain Doctor French (Seifert), 1943
Certain Magic (Balogh), 1991
Certain People (s Wharton), 1930
Certain People of Importance (Norris), 1922
Certain Smile (Lewty), 1979
Certain Splendour (Salisbury), 1985
Certain Spring (Asquith), 1956
Certified Bride (Barcynska), 1928
Chad Hanna (Edmonds), 1940
Chadbourne Luck (F. Stevenson, as Curzon), 1981
Chain Lightning (Lowell), 1988
Chain of Destiny (Neels), 1989
Chain of Destiny (Tranter), 1964
Chained Eagle (Maybury), 1939
Chains of Fate (Belle), 1984
Chains of Love (Melville, as Betteridge), 1965
Chains of Regret (M. Pargeter), 1983
Chaka series (Haggard), from 1912
Chalet in the Sun (MacLeod), 1948
Challenge for Doctor Mays (Seifert), 1955
Challenge of Love (Deeping), 1932
Challenge of Spring (Bromige), 1965
Challenge to Clarissa (Delafield), 1931
Challenge to Happiness (Greig), 1936
Challoner Bride (Krentz, as James), 1987
Champagne (Ellerbeck, as Thorne), 1989
Champagne Girl (Manley-Tucker), 1967
Champagne Girl (Palmer), 1986
Champagne Girls (T. Barclay), 1986
Champagne Gold (Ellerbeck, as Thorne), 1992
Champagne Kiss (Barcynska, as Sandys), 1929
Champagne Nights (Buckingham, as John), 1984
Champion (Williamson), 1913
Chance Encounter (Balogh), 1985
Chance for Love (Bromige), 1975
Chance Meeting (K. Thorpe), 1980
Chance of a Lifetime (J. Smith), 1984
Chance of a Lifetime (Krentz), 1987
Chance Romance (Bloom, as Burns), 1948
Chance the Winds of Fortune (McBain), 1980
Chance Tomorrow (Browning), 1981
Chances Are (Delinsky), 1985
Chandra (Coulter), 1984
Change for a Farthing (Trask), 1942
Change Here for Happiness (Ruck), 1933
Change of Air (Hope), 1893
Change of Heart (Albanesi, as Rowlands)
Change of Heart (Baldwin), 1944
Change of Heart (Bloom), 1979
Change of Plans (Seger), 1989
Change of Season (Goodwin), 1991
Changeling (s Byrne), 1924
Changeling (Plaidy, as Carr), 1989
Changeling (Roby, as Wilson), 1975
Changeling Queen (Hamilton), 1977
Changes (Steel), 1983
Changing Pilots (Ayres), 1932
Changing Tide (Bromige), 1987
Changing Tide (S. Thorpe), 1967

Changing Years (Robins), 1943
Changing Years (Stratton, as Gillen), 1972
Chant of Jimmie Blacksmith (Keneally), 1972
Chantal (Lorrimer), 1980
Chantemerle (Broster), 1911
Chaperon (Williamson), 1912
Chaperone (Gordon), 1973
Chappy—That's All (Barcynska, as Sandys), 1922
Charade (Stratton), 1982
Charge It (Bacheller), 1912
Charge Nurse (Norway, as Neal), 1965
Charge of Cowardice (McCutchan, as MacNeil), 1978
Charing Cross (Rayner), 1979
Charity Girl (Albanesi, as Rowlands), 1900
Charity Girl (Heyer), 1970
Charity's Angel (Schulze), 1992
Charity's Chosen (Ayres), 1926
Charles II series (Plaidy), from 1956
Charles Rex (Dell), 1922
Charles the King (Anthony), 1961
Charleston (Ripley), 1981
Charlie Come Home (Delderfield), 1976
Charlie Is My Darling (Hardwick), 1977
Charlotte (Lofts), 1972
Charlotte (Trollope, as Harvey), 1980
Charlotte Fairlie (D. Stevenson), 1954
Charlotte Wade (McElfresh), 1952
Charlotte's Hurricane (Mather), 1970
Charlton Mead series (Wiat), from 1981
Charmed (N. Roberts), 1992
Charmed Circle (Ertz), 1956
Charmed Circle (Gaskin), 1988
Charmian, Lady Vibart (Farnol), 1932
Charming Couple (Gibbs, as Ford), 1975
Charms of a Witch (Oliver), 1977
Chase a Green Shadow (Mather), 1973
Chase the Clouds (McKenna), 1983
Chase the Wind (Thompson), 1977
Chateau Bougy-Villars (Ellis, as Marvin), 1975
Chateau d'Armor (Stratton), 1976
Chateau in Provence (R. Lindsay), 1973
Chateau in the Palms (Hampson), 1979
Chateau in the Shadows (Ellis, as Marvin), 1969
Chateau of Flowers (Robins), 1958
Chateau of St Avrell (Winspear), 1970
Chateau Saxony (Ellis, as Richard), 1970
Chatelaine (Lorrimer), 1981
Chatterton (Ackroyd), 1985
Chauffeur and the Chaperon (Williamson), 1908
Cheap Day Return (Delderfield), 1967
Cheats (Bowen), 1920
Checkered Paths (s Pedler), 1935
Checkmate (Dunnett), 1975
Checkmate (Lofts), 1975
Cheerful, By Request (s Ferber), 1918
Chelsea Reach (Rayner), 1982
Chelynne (Carr), 1980
Chequered Pattern (Bromige), 1947
Cherish (Woods), 1992
Cherish Me, Embrace Me (Sommerfield), 1983
Cherish Tomorrow (Mortimer), 1985
Cherished Enemy (Veryan), 1988
Cherries and Candlelight (I. Roberts, as Rowland), 1969
Cherry (Barcynska, as Sandys), 1929
Cherry (Norris), 1958
Cherry-Blossom Clinic (Hunter), 1961

Cherry Blossom Love (Greig), 1961
Cherry Hat (s Bloom), 1904
Cherrystones (Barcynska, as Sandys), 1959
Chesapeake (Michener), 1978
Chesapeake Bay (Michener), 1990
Chess Players (Keyes), 1960
Cheval Glass (Bloom), 1973
Chevalier (Harrod-Eagles), 1984
Cheviot Chase (Tranter), 1952
Chian Wine (s O'Brian), 1974
Chianti Flask (Lowndes), 1934
Chicane (Barcynska, as Sandys), 1912
Chieftain (Dwyer-Joyce), 1980
Chieftain Without a Heart (Cartland), 1978
Child Called Freedom (M. Peters), 1976
Child from the Sea (Goudge), 1970
Child of Judas (Winspear), 1976
Child of Music (Burchell), 1970
Child of Passion (Saxton, as Turner), 1978
Child of Storm (Haggard), 1913
Child of the Flesh (M. Peters, as Darby), 1982
Child of the Revolution (Orczy), 1932
Child of the Sun (Horner), 1966
Child Royal (Broster), 1937
Children (Wharton), 1928
Children of Lucifer (P. Hill), 1984
Children of No Man's Land (Stern), 1919
Children of the Mist (Tranter), 1992
Children of the Rainbow (M. Peters, as Whitby), 1982
Children of the Spring (Wiat), 1983
Children of the Tempest (Munro), 1903
Children of the Wolf (Duggan), 1959
Children of the Zodiac (Williamson, as A.M. Williamson), 1929
Children's Nurse (K. Blair), 1961
Children's Ward (Rayner, as Brandon), 1964
Childsong (B. Wood), 1981
Chilling Deception (Krentz, as Castle), 1986
China Court (Godden), 1961
China Flight (Buck), 1945
China series (Nicole), from 1983
China series (I. Roberts, as I.M. Roberts), from 1983
China Shop (Stern), 1921
China Silk (Worboys), 1991
China Sky (Buck), 1942
Chinese Alice (Barr), 1981
Chinese Love Pavilion (P. Scott), 1960
Chinese Puzzle (Godden), 1936
Chink in the Armour (Lowndes), 1912
Chip and the Block (Delafield), 1925
Chippinge (Weyman), 1906
Chippinge Borough (Weyman), 1906
Chivalry (Sabatini), 1935
Choice of Mavis (Wynne), 1935
Choose the One You'll Marry (Burchell), 1960
Choose Which You Will (Burchell), 1949
Chosen Child (Worboys, as Maxwell), 1973
Chosen Course (Tranter), 1949
Christ series (Bloom, as Mann), from 1968
Christian (Caine), 1897
Christian Marlowe's Daughter (Keyes), 1934
Christian's Cross (Swan), 1905
Christina Comes to Town (Weale), 1966
Christina (Eliot, as Arnett), 1980
Christine Against the World (Swan), 1933
Christine (Arnim, as Cholmondeley), 1917
Christine Diamond (Lowndes), 1940

Christmas Affair (Mortimer), 1990
Christmas Beau (Balogh), 1991
Christmas Eve (Norris), 1949
Christmas in London (s Field), 1946
Christmas Marriage (Schulze), 1992
Christmas Promise (Balogh), 1992
Christmas Tree (s E. Smith), 1933
Christobel (Roby), 1976
Christopher and Columbus (Arnim), 1919
Christopher Strong (Frankau), 1932
Chronicles of Avonlea (s Montgomery), 1912
Chronicles of Count Antonio (Hope), 1895
Chronicles of the Imp (Farnol), 1915
Chronicles of Tingatel series (Brandewyne), from 1987
Cimarron (Ferber), 1930
Cinder Path (Cookson), 1978
Cinderella after Midnight (Burchell), 1945
Cinderella Girl (M. St John), 1920
Cinderella Had Two Sisters (Chandos, as Tempest), 1948
Cinderella in Mink (R. Lindsay, as Leigh), 1973
Cinders to Satin (F. Michaels), 1984
Cinnabar House (Lorrimer, as Robins), 1970
Circle in the Water (Bowen), 1939
Circle of Doubt (MacLeod), 1943
Circle of Evil (V. Johnston), 1972
Circle of Fate (Lamb), 1987
Circle of Friends (Binchy), 1990
Circle of Gold (Ritchie), 1964
Circle of Pearls (Laker), 1990
Circular Staircase (Rinehart), 1908
Circus for Love (Cartland), 1987
Cissy (Albanesi), 1913
Citizen Tom Paine (Fast), 1943
City in the Dawn (H. Allen), 1950
City Lies Foursquare (E. Pargeter), 1939
City of Bells (Goudge), 1936
City of Dreams (Hoy), 1959
City of Gems (Trollope), 1981
City of God (Holland), 1979
City of Libertines (Hardy), 1957
City of Masks (McCutcheon), 1918
Civil Conflict (Oliver), 1975
Civil Contract (Heyer), 1961
Civil War series (Kantor), from 1935
Civil War series (Pozzessere, as Graham), from 1992
Claim That Won (Wynne), 1912
Claire (Garvice), 1899
Claire and Circumstances (Albanesi), 1928
Clan of the Cave Bear (Auel), 1980
Clandara (Anthony), 1963
Clandestine Affair (Oliver, as James), 1980
Clandestine Betrothal (Ley), 1967
Clandestine Queen (Harwood), 1979
Clansman (Dixon), 1905
Clansman (Tranter), 1959
Clarissa (Eliot, as Arnett), 1976
Clarissa Oakes (O'Brian), 1992
Clarkton (Fast), 1947
Clash (Jameson), 1922
Classic Encounter (Richards), 1988
Classics of the Macabre (s du Maurier), 1987
Claudia (Eliot, as Arnett), 1978
Claudia series (Franken), from 1939
Claudine's Daughter (Laker), 1979
Claudius series (Graves), from 1934
Claw (Lofts), 1981

Crystal Cat (V. Johnston), 1985
Crystal Cave (Stewart), 1970
Crystal Clear (Cadell), 1953
Crystal Crow (Aiken), 1968
Crystal Crown (Harrod-Eagles), 1982
Crystal Flame (Krentz), 1986
Crystal Gull (Andrews), 1978
Crystal Villa (M. Howard), 1970
Crystal Window (Matthews, as Brisco), 1973
Csardas (Pearson), 1975
Cuba Libre (Kantor), 1940
Cuckoo at Candlemas (Manners, as Marshall), 1968
Cuckoo Cottage (Mackinlay), 1953
Cuckoo in Spring (Cadell), 1954
Cuckoo Never Weds (Bloom, as Burns), 1950
Cultured Handmaiden (Cookson), 1988
Cumbrian series (Bragg), from 1969
Cunning of the Dove (Duggan), 1960
Cunningham's Revenge (McCutchan, as MacNeil), 1980
Cup of Gold (Steinbeck), 1929
Cup of Kindness (D. Smith), 1971
Cup of Tea for Mr Thorgill (Jameson), 1957
Cupboard Love (R. Lindsay, as Leigh), 1976
Cupboard Love (L. Walker), 1963
Cupid in Africa (Wren), 1920
Cupid Rides Pillion (Cartland), 1952
Cupid's Task (Stanford), 1985
Curate's Egg (s Hutten), 1930
Cure for Love (Jordan), 1991
Cure of Souls (M. Sinclair), 1923
Curious Happenings (s Bowen), 1917
Curled Hands (Barcynska, as Sandys), 1926
Curse Not the King (Anthony), 1954
Curse of Cowden (Swan), 1897
Curse of Gold (Wynne), 1914
Curse of Halewood (Laker, as Paul), 1976
Curse of Hannah's Gate (Winston), 1993
Curse of Jezebel (Slaughter), 1961
Curse of the Clan (Cartland), 1977
Curse of the Clodaghs (Cowen), 1973
Curse of the Concullens (F. Stevenson), 1970
Curse of the Greys (M. Peters), 1974
Curse of the Kings (Plaidy, as Holt), 1973
Curse of the Pharaohs (B. Michaels, as Peters), 1981
Curse This House (B. Wood), 1978
Curtain Call (Randall), 1983
Curtain Call (K. Thorpe), 1971
Curtain Rises (Burchell), 1969
Curtain Will Go Up (Barcynska, as Sandys), 1936
Curve of the Catenary (Rinehart), 1945
Custom of the Country (Wharton), 1913
Cut and a Kiss (s Hope), 1899
Cutlass Empire (F. Mason), 1949
Cutting Edge (L. Howard), 1985
Cynthia Charrington (Vaizey), 1911
Cypresses Grow Dark (Bloom), 1932
Cyrilla Seeks Herself (Burgin), 1922

Daddy (Steel), 1989
Daddy-Long-Legs (Webster), 1912
Daffodil Anne (M. Peters, as Darby), 1991
Daffodils of Newent (Sallis), 1985
Dahomean (Yerby), 1971
Daisy Boy (Cleugh), 1931
Daisy Brooks (Libbey), 1889
Daisy Earns Her Living (M. St John), 1917

Daisy Friday (Salisbury), 1984
Daisy Gordon's Folly (Libbey), 1892
Daisy Peach Abroad (M. St John), 1917
Dakota Dreamin' (Dailey), 1981
Dale of Dreams (Burgin), 1927
Damaged Angel (Burchell), 1967
Damask Rose (Hunter, as Chace), 1968
Dame Durden's Daughter (J. Smith), 1978
Damsel and the Sage (Glyn), 1903
Damsel in Distress (Pozzessere, as Drake), 1992
Damsel in Green (Neels), 1970
Dance at the Four Corners (Burgin), 1894
Dance Ballerina Dance (I. Roberts, as Rowland), 1980
Dance Barefoot (Maddocks), 1966
Dance in the Dust (Robins, as Gray), 1959
Dance, Little Gentleman! (Frankau), 1929
Dance of Courtship (Kidd), 1976
Dance of Dreams (N. Roberts), 1983
Dance of Fire (Stratton, as Gillen), 1971
Dance of the Peacocks (Hunter, as de Guise), 1988
Dance on My Heart, (Cartland), 1977
Dance Partner (Ruck), 1931
Dance to My Tune (Peake), 1989
Dance to the Piper (N. Roberts), 1988
Dancer in Yellow (Ogilvie), 1979
Dancer of Dreams (Matthews), 1984
Dancer's Daughter (M. Howard, as Edgar), 1968
Dancers in the Dark (MacGill), 1929
Dancing Hill (Lamb, as Holland), 1978
Dancing in the Aisles (K. Blair), 1990
Dancing Master (Ayres), 1920
Dancing on a Rainbow (Cartland), 1987
Dancing on my Heart (T. Barclay, as Dell), 1974
Dancing Star (Ruck), 1923
Dancing with Clara (Balogh), 1994
Dandelion (Browning, as Williams), 1989
Dandelion Clock (Bloom), 1966
Dandridge series (Riefe), from 1977
Daneclere (P. Hill), 1978
Danger at Olduvai (McElfresh, as Blair), 1972
Danger by the Nile (Cartland, as McCorquodale), 1964
Danger in Eden (Greig, as Ames), 1950
Danger Wakes My Heart (Greig, as Ames), 1949
Dangerous (Krentz, as Quick), 1993
Dangerous (Lamb), 1981
Dangerous Assignments (McElfresh, as Blair), 1975
Dangerous Call (E. Harrison), 1976
Dangerous Child (Cowen), 1975
Dangerous Claim (Laffeaty), 1969
Dangerous Cruise (Greig), 1940
Dangerous Dandy (Cartland), 1974
Dangerous Days (Rinehart), 1919
Dangerous Deception (Peake), 1979
Dangerous Delight (Winspear), 1968
Dangerous Doctor (Bloom, as Essex), 1970
Dangerous Embrace (Vitek), 1983
Dangerous Enchantment (Mather), 1969
Dangerous Encounter (Kidd), 1983
Dangerous Engagement (Courtney), 1979
Dangerous Experiment (Cartland), 1936
Dangerous Flirtation (Libbey)
Dangerous Friendship (Hampson), 1976
Dangerous Holiday (Gibbs, as Ford), 1967
Dangerous Holiday (Greig, as Ames), 1939
Dangerous Husband (Bloom, as Prole), 1966
Dangerous Inheritance (M. Peters, as Black), 1969

Dangerous Interloper (Jordan), 1991
Dangerous Intruder (Pilcher, as Fraser), 1951
Dangerous Islands (Bridge), 1963
Dangerous Kind of Love (K. Blair), 1964
Dangerous Legacy (W. Roberts), 1972
Dangerous Living (Maybury), 1941
Dangerous Lover (Armstrong), 1992
Dangerous Loving (Burchell), 1963
Dangerous Magic (Krentz, as James), 1982
Dangerous Male (Lewty), 1983
Dangerous Masquerade (Dailey), 1976
Dangerous Moonlight (K. Thorpe), 1985
Dangerous Obsession (MacLeod), 1938
Dangerous Obsession (N. Peters), 1978
Dangerous Paths (M. St John, as St John Cooper), 1933
Dangerous Places (Chase), 1987
Dangerous Pretence (Kidd), 1977
Dangerous Rhapsody (Mather), 1969
Dangerous Secret (Woodward), 1978
Dangerous Stranger (Stratton, as Gillen), 1972
Dangerous Waters (K. Blair, as Brett), 1960
Dangerous Winter (Goodwin, as Ebel), 1965
Dangerous Woman (Albanesi, as Rowlands), 1910
Dangerous Years (Frankau), 1937
Dangerous Yesterday (Asquith), 1967
Daniel Airlie (Hichens), 1937
Danielle, My Darling (Bloom, as Essex), 1954
Daniel's Bride (Miller), 1992
Danny Boy (Dwyer-Joyce), 1979
Danse Macabre (Plaidy, as Kellow), 1952
Dante's Daughter (Pozzessere, as Graham), 1986
Danvers Touch (Lowell), 1983
Daphne (Chesney), 1984
Dare and Do (Albanesi, as Rowlands), 1911
Dare-Devil Doctor (Bloom, as Essex), 1965
Dare I Be Happy? (Burchell), 1943
Dare the Devil (Chase), 1986
Dare to Love (McKenna, as Nauman), 1985
Dare to Marry (Maybury), 1940
Darien Venture (Slaughter, as C.V. Terry), 1955
Daring Deception (Cartland), 1973
Daring Heart (Courtney), 1983
Daring Masquerade (Balogh), 1989
Daring Moves (Miller), 1990
Dark Abyss (Donald), 1981
Dark and Distant Shore (Tannahill), 1983
Dark and Secret Place (Summerton), 1977
Dark and Splendid Passion (E. Smith), 1941
Dark Ann (s Bowen), 1927
Dark Avenger (Hampson), 1972
Dark Awakening (Wentworth), 1984
Dark Before the Rising Sun (McBain), 1982
Dark Beneath the Moon (Laffeaty), 1968
Dark Beneath the Pines (Eliot), 1974
Dark Bondage (Manley-Tucker), 1961
Dark Captor (Armstrong), 1991
Dark Carnival (Greig), 1950
Dark Castle (Mather), 1975
Dark Changeling (Manners, as Lamont), 1970
Dark Conspiracy (Lane), 1952
Dark Corners (Chase), 1988
Dark Corridor (Robins), 1974
Dark Death (Robins), 1929
Dark Dominion (Lamb), 1979
Dark Dowry (W. Roberts), 1978
Dark Dream (Miles), 1929

Dark Duel (Steen), 1929
Dark Duet (B. Michaels), 1983
Dark Edge of Love (S. Wood), 1994
Dark Enchantress (S. Thorpe), 1973
Dark Encounter (F. Stevenson), 1977
Dark Enemy (Mather), 1971
Dark Enigma (Stratton), 1981
Dark Fantasy (Lamb, as Hardy) , 1983
Dark Farm (Bloom, as Essex), 1974
Dark Fire (Donald), 1994
Dark Fire (Lowell), 1988
Dark Fires (Rogers), 1975
Dark Forces (S. Wood), 1992
Dark Forest (Walpole), 1916
Dark Fortune (MacLeod), 1962
Dark Gemini (M. Peters, as Rothman), 1983
Dark Gentleman (Ayres), 1953
Dark Gentleman, Fair Lady (Bloom, as Essex), 1951
Dark Gentleman (Stern), 1927
Dark Heritage (E. Darcy), 1992
Dark Heritage (S. Thorpe), 1968
Dark Hills Rising (Hampson), 1971
Dark House (Deeping), 1941
Dark House (Swan), 1941
Dark Horse (Godden), 1981
Dark Horse, Dark Rider (Hoy), 1960
Dark Inheritance (R. Lindsay, as Leigh), 1952
Dark Inheritance (Salisbury), 1975
Dark Interval (Aiken), 1967
Dark Island (Treece), 1952
Dark Legacy (Chandos, as Charles), 1968
Dark Loch (Hoy), 1948
Dark Lover (Bloom, as Essex), 1957
Dark Masquerade (J. Blake, as Maxwell), 1974
Dark Master (Lamb), 1979
Dark Mile (Broster), 1929
Dark Moment (Bridge), 1951
Dark Moonless Night (Mather), 1974
Dark Morality (M. Howard), 1932
Dark Mosaic (Mather), 1989
Dark Music (Lamb), 1990
Dark Night (I. Roberts), 1962
Dark Noon (Nicole), 1963
Dark Oasis (M. Pargeter), 1980
Dark Odyssey (F. Stevenson), 1974
Dark of the Moon (Seger), 1986
Dark on the Other Side (B. Michaels), 1970
Dark Paradise (Craven), 1984
Dark Pasture (Stirling), 1977
Dark Pursuer (Donnelly), 1976
Dark Pursuer (Laffeaty), 1967
Dark Pursuit (Lamb), 1990
Dark Ransom (Craven), 1992
Dark Rosaleen (Bowen), 1932
Dark Rose (Harrod-Eagles), 1981
Dark Secret Love (Robins, as Kane), 1962
Dark Seduction (Kidd), 1983
Dark Shore (Howatch), 1965
Dark Side of Marriage (Hilton), 1978
Dark Star (Maybury), 1977
Dark Star Passing (P. Hill), 1990
Dark Stranger (Chandos, as Lance), 1946
Dark Stranger (Pozzessere), 1988
Dark Stranger (Saunders, as Innes), 1979
Dark Stream (Cartland), 1944
Dark Summer (Buckingham), 1968

Dark Summer Dawn (Craven), 1981
Dark Sun (Nicole), 1990
Dark Sunlight (Greig, as Ames), 1943
Dark Surrender (Palmer, as Blayne), 1983
Dark Surrender (M. Pargeter), 1980
Dark Surrender (M. Peters, as Lloyd), 1981
Dark Sweet Wanton (Lamb, as Lancaster) , 1979
Dark Tower (M. Howard, as Edgar), 1966
Dark Venetian (Mather, as Fleming), 1969
Dark Waters (Cockrell), 1944
Dark Weaver (Salverson), 1937
Dark Woman (Wren), 1943
Darkening Sea (Kent), 1993
Darkening Sea (Woodman), 1991
Darkening Skies (Chard), 1981
Darker Side of Desire (Jordan), 1984
Darker Side of Paradise (Donald), 1990
Dark-Eyed Queen (Bloom, as Prole), 1967
Dark-eyed Sister (Bloom, as Burns), 1968
Darkling Moon (Carter), 1985
Darkness and the Dawn (Costain), 1959
Darkness at Ingraham's Crest (Yerby), 1979
Darkness into Light (Mortimer), 1986
Darkness into Light (N. Peters), 1984
Darkness of the Heart (Lamb), 1983
Darkness on the Stairs (F. Stevenson), 1976
Darkwater (Eden), 1964
Darling Clementine (Eden), 1955
Darling Clementine (Greig), 1946
Darling District Nurse (Bloom, as Harvey), 1970
Darling Enemy (Palmer), 1983
Darling Infidel (Winspear), 1976
Darling Jenny (Dailey), 1978
Darling Radamanthas! (Hilton), 1966
Darrel of the Blessed Isles (Bacheller), 1903
Dashing Guardian (F. Stevenson, as Curzon), 1983
Date with a Doctor (Bloom, as Essex), 1962
Date with an Angel (Ritchie), 1958
Date with Danger (Greig), 1952
Date with Destiny (Laffeaty), 1983
Daughter (Blackstock), 1970
Daughter (Nicole, as Gray), 1992
Daughter He Didn't Want! (M. St John), 1926
Daughter Knows Best (Robins), 1943
Daughter of Anna (Plaidy, as Burford), 1941
Daughter of Aphrodite (Jagger), 1981
Daughter of Bugle Ann (Kantor), 1953
Daughter of Deceit (Plaidy, as Holt), 1991
Daughter of Destiny (S. Blake), 1977
Daughter of Hassan (Jordan), 1982
Daughter of Isis (M. Peters, as Grey), 1981
Daughter of Marignac (Heaven), 1983
Daughter of Midnight (P. Hill), 1979
Daughter of Satan (Plaidy), 1952
Daughter of the Devil (Bloom, as Prole), 1963
Daughter of the Gods (Hamilton, as Fitzgerald), 1986
Daughter of the Hawk (Forester), 1928
Daughter of the House (Gaskin), 1952
Daughter of the Land (G. Porter), 1918
Daughter of the Loom (M. St John, as St John Cooper), 1922
Daughter of the Medici (s Byrne), 1933
Daughter of the Misty Gorges (Summers), 1981
Daughter of the Northern Fields (Haines), 1987
Daughter of the Sea (Woodhouse), 1986
Daughter Scorned (M. St John), 1911

Daughter's a Daughter (Westmacott), 1952
Daughters (Goodwin), 1987
Daughters of a Genius (Vaizey), 1903
Daughters of a Granite Land series (Burgh), from 1989
Daughters of Ardmore Hall (Eden), 1968
Daughters of Babylon (Hichens), 1899
Daughters of England series (Plaidy, as Carr), from 1972
Daughters of Spain (Plaidy), 1961
Daughters of the Governor (Stuart, as A. Stuart), 1958
Daughters of the House (Ellerbeck, as Thorne), 1981
Daughters of the Moon (Sallis), 1992
Daughters of the Prince (Barber), 1989
Daughters of the Rectory (Bloom), 1955
Daughters of the Revolution (Clayton), 1984
Daughters of the Storm (E. Buchan), 1988
Daughter's Promise (Ellis), 1988
David Copperfield by Charles Dickens (Graves), 1934
David the Prince (Tranter), 1980
Dawn (Alexander, as Langley), 1980
Dawn (Bacheller), 1927
Dawn (Haggard), 1884
Dawn (E. Porter), 1919
Dawn Chorus (Plaidy, as Burford), 1959
Dawn Is Golden (Hampson), 1983
Dawn of Love (Cartland), 1979
Dawn of Splendour (Gavin), 1989
Dawn of Valor (McKenna), 1991
Dawn O'Hara, The Girl Who Laughed (Ferber), 1911
Dawn Song (Craven), 1993
Dawn Steals Softly (Hampson), 1980
Dawning of the Day (Ogilvie), 1954
Dawn's Desire (Finch), 1983
Dawn's Early Light (Thane), 1943
Dawson series (Nicole), from 1991
Day and Night (Seger), 1988
Day Comes Round (Ayres), 1949
Day Like Spring (Pilcher, as Fraser), 1953
Day of Possession (Peake), 1978
Day of Small Things (O. Douglas), 1930
Day of the Butterfly (Lofts), 1979
Day of the Dancing Sun (P. Hastings), 1971
Day of the Dog (McCutcheon), 1904
Day of the Scorpion (P. Scott), 1968
Day of the Storm (Gibbs, as Ford), 1971
Day of the Storm (Pilcher), 1975
Day Off (Jameson), 1933
Day Star (E. Pargeter), 1937
Day That the Rain Came Down (Hunter, as Chace), 1970
Day Will Come (A. Howard), 1992
Daybreak (Slaughter), 1958
Daylight Fear (Cowen), 1969
Days of Grace (Jagger), 1983
Days of Valor (W. Roberts), 1983
Days of Wine and Roses (Nicole), 1991
Days of Winter (Freeman), 1978
Daze of Fears (Summerton, as Roffman), 1968
Dazzle on the Sea (Kidd), 1971
Dazzled (Seger, as Bates), 1984
Dazzled Heart (Pykare), 1980
De Montfort Legacy (Bennetts), 1973
Dead Man in Deptford (Burgess), 1993
Dead March in Three Keys (Lofts, as Curtis), 1940
Dead Men's Bells (Niven), 1912
Dead Men's Boot (s Wren), 1949
Dead Reckoning (Parkinson), 1978
Dead Sea Cipher (B. Michaels, as Peters), 1970

Deadfall (Harrod-Eagles), 1982
Deadly Deceit (Buckingham, as Quest), 1992
Deadly Eurasian (Cordell), 1968
Deadly Lady of Madagascar (Slaughter, as C.V. Terry), 1959
Deadly Travellers (Eden), 1959
Deal of a Lifetime (Napier), 1991
Dealings of Captain Sharkey (s Doyle), 1925
Deanne's Desire (Sommerfield), 1981
Dean's Watch (Goudge), 1960
Dear Adversary (K. Blair), 1953
Dear and Glorious Physician (Caldwell), 1959
Dear Benefactor (Hampson), 1976
Dear Caliban (Donnelly), 1977
Dear Chance (Plaidy, as Burford), 1947
Dear Colleague (F. Murray), 1972
Dear Conquistador (Hilton), 1972
Dear Deceiver (D. Smith), 1972
Dear Delusion (Plaidy, as Burford), 1952
Dear Doctor Everett (MacLeod), 1954
Dear Enemy (Webster), 1915
Dear Fugitive (Hoy), 1960
Dear Kate (Goodwin, as Ebel), 1972
Dear Lost Love (Maybury), 1957
Dear Loyalty (Robins), 1939
Dear Mr Dean (Barcynska, as Sandys), 1957
Dear Old Home (M. St John), 1912
Dear Patience (Chandos, as Lance), 1983
Dear Plutocrat (Hampson), 1973
Dear Puritan (Winspear), 1971
Dear Sir (Burchell), 1958
Dear Stranger (Hampson), 1973
Dear Stranger (Hoy), 1946
Dear Tom (Pilcher, as Fraser), 1954
Dear Trustee (Burchell), 1958
Dearest Demon (Winspear), 1975
Dearest Doctor (Bloom, as Harvey), 1968
Dearest Enemy (K. Blair), 1951
Dearest Neighbour (Chappell), 1981
Dearest Tiger (Drummond, as Dawes), 1975
Dearly Beloved (Burchell), 1944
Dearly Beloved of Benjamin Cobb (Dane), 1927
Death among Friends (Cadell, as Ainsworth), 1964
Death Comes for the Archbishop (Cather), 1927
Death in the Castle (Buck), 1965
Death Is a Red Rose (Eden), 1956
Death, My Lover (Blackstock, as Allardyce), 1959
Death of a Fox (Summerton, as Roffman), 1964
Death of a Spartan King (s J. Lindsay), 1974
Death of Attila (Holland), 1973
Death of Love (Matthews), 1990
Death of Robin Hood (Vansittart), 1981
Death of the Red King (Bennetts), 1976
Death-Scented Flower (P. Hastings), 1977
Death to the French (Forester), 1932
Death Walk (Buckingham, as Quest), 1988
Debatable Ground (Stern), 1921
Debonair (Stern), 1928
Debt of Honor (Cartland), 1970
Debt of Honour (Veryan), 1980
Debutante in Uniform (Greig), 1938
Decade (Briskin), 1981
Decameron Cocktails (Barcynska), 1926
Deceit of a Pagan (Mortimer), 1980
Deceive Not My Heart (Busbee), 1984
Deceived (Balogh), 1993
Deceivers (Masters), 1952

December Love (Hichens), 1922
December Passion (Nicole, as Logan), 1979
Deception (Aiken), 1987
Deception (Krentz, as Quick), 1993
Deception (M. Pargeter), 1980
Deception's Sweet Kiss (Finch, as Robins), 1990
Decision at Trafalgar (Woodman), 1987
Deck with Flowers (Cadell), 1973
Decoy (Pope), 1983
Dedicated (Stuart, as A. Stuart), 1962
Dedicated Villain (Veryan), 1989
Dedication Jones (Norway), 1969
Dee, Dr series (McElfresh, as Wesley), from 1960
Deedee (Ellis, as A. Lord), 1969
Deeds of the Disturber (B. Michaels, as Peters), 1988
Deemster (Caine), 1887
Deep Are Dumb (D. Smith), 1967
Deep in the Heart (Vitek), 1985
Deep Is the Shadow (Slaughter, as Haygood), 1959
Deep Silence (Kent, as Reeman), 1967
Deep Summer (Bristow), 1937
Deep Water (Lewty), 1992
Deep Well at Noon (Stirling), 1979
Defector (Anthony), 1980
Defender of the Faith (Bowen), 1911
Defenders of the Faith (Plaidy, as Tate), 1956
Defiant Ecstasy (Taylor), 1982
Defiant Love (Seger), 1982
Definite Object (Farnol), 1917
Defy Not the Heart (Lindsey), 1989
Deirdre and Desire (Chesney), 1983
Delancey, Richard series (Parkinson), from 1973
Delaneys series (F. Preston), from 1987
Delaneys series (Hooper), from 1987
Delaneys series (Johansen), from 1987
Delayed Action (Tranter), 1944
Delayed Harvest (Randall), 1950
Delicate Balance (Gellis), 1993
Delicate Deceit (Hufford), 1976
Delicate Monster (Jameson), 1937
Delicia (Corelli), 1917
Delight (de la Roche), 1926
Delight of Angels (P. Hastings), 1981
Deliverance (Glasgow), 1904
Della's Handsome Lover (Libbey)
Delsie (J. Smith), 1981
Delta Blood (B. Johnson), 1977
Delta Ladies (F. Michaels), 1980
Delta Wedding (Welty), 1946
de'Medici, Catherine series (Plaidy), from 1951
Demelza (Graham), 1946
Demitrious Line (M. Pargeter), 1983
Demon (Williamson), 1912
Demon Lover (Plaidy, as Holt), 1982
Demon Rumm (Brown), 1987
Denim and Lace (Palmer, as Blayne), 1990
Dennison Hill (Winston), 1970
Dental Nurse at Denley's (Lewty), 1968
Depart in Peace (Eden), 1979
Departing Wings (Baldwin), 1927
Departures (s Fast), 1949
Depths of Glory (Stone), 1985
Deputy Pet (Barcynska, as Sandys), 1945
Deputy Was King (Stern), 1926
Descent of Man (s Wharton), 1904
Desert Barbarian (Lamb), 1978

Desert Castle (Hunter, as Chace), 1976
Desert Doctor (Winspear), 1965
Desert Fire (B. Hastings), 1980
Desert Flower (Randall), 1955
Desert Healer (Hull), 1923
Desert Heritage (Wren), 1935
Desert Hostage (S. Wood), 1990
Desert Moon (Duffield), 1939
Desert Nurse (I. Roberts), 1976
Desert Queen (Hamilton, as Fitzgerald), 1986
Desert Queen (Leslie), 1972
Desert Rapture (Robins), 1945
Desert Rose (May), 1993
Desert Rose, English Moon (Williams), 1981
Desert Sand (Pedler), 1932
Desert Shadows (Richards), 1991
Design for Love (Pykare, as Powers), 1980
Design for Loving (Burchell), 1972
Design for Loving (Mather), 1966
Design for Loving (Woodward), 1980
Design for Murder (Buckingham, as Quest), 1981
Design for Murder (R. Lindsay), 1964
Designing Woman (Chase), 1982
Desirable Compromise (Woods, as Sherrill), 1984
Desirable Residence (L. Cooper), 1980
Desire (Hampson), 1981
Desire (Lamb), 1981
Desire and Destiny (Miller), 1984
Desire for Revenge (Jordan), 1985
Desire Has No Mercy (Winspear), 1979
Desire in Disguise (Brandewyne), 1987
Desire Is Blind (Robins), 1928
Desire Is Not Dead (Bloom, as Burns), 1947
Desire Me Not (Trask), 1935
Desire Never Changes (Jordan), 1986
Desire of His Life (Dell), 1914
Desire of the Heart (Cartland), 1954
Desire's Captive (Jordan), 1982
Desmond's Daughter (Diver), 1916
Desolation and the Dream (Laffeaty), 1969
Desolation Island (O'Brian), 1978
Desperado (Brandewyne), 1992
Desperate Decision (Bishop), 1972
Desperate Defiance (Cartland), 1936
Desperate Desire (Kidd), 1984
Desperate Game (Krentz, as Castle), 1986
Desperate Holiday (Cowen), 1962
Desperate Measures (Craven), 1992
Desperate Remedies (Rayner, as Saxe), 1968
Desperation (Lamb), 1989
Despoiling Venus (J. Lindsay), 1935
Destined to Meet (Steele), 1991
Destinies (C. Allen), 1981
Destiny (Hampson), 1988
Destiny and Desire (Nicole, as Arlen), 1982
Destiny at Castle Rock (Marsh), 1985
Destiny Bay (s Byrne), 1928
Destiny of Claude (Wynne), 1913
Destiny's Duchess (Courtney), 1983
Destiny's Lady (M. Peters), 1973
Destiny's Temptress (Taylor), 1986
Destiny's Woman (W. Roberts), 1980
Destroyers (Kent, as Reeman), 1974
Details of Jeremy (Erskine-Lindop), 1955
Deveron Hall (V. Johnston), 1976
Devices and Desires (Ertz), 1972

Devil and Miss Hay (Lamb, as Holland), 1977
Devil at Archangel (Craven), 1978
Devil Boy (W. Roberts), 1970
Devil Defeated (Cartland), 1985
Devil in a Silver Room (Winspear), 1973
Devil in Clevely (Lofts), 1968
Devil in Disguise (Steele), 1980
Devil in Harbour (Gavin), 1968
Devil in Love (Cartland), 1975
Devil in My Arms (Hamilton, as Fitzgerald), 1989
Devil in My Heart (S. Blake), 1990
Devil in My Heart (M. Howard), 1941
Devil in Tartan (Ogilvie), 1980
Devil in Velvet (Mather), 1977
Devil Lover (Mortimer), 1981
Devil Moon (Way), 1988
Devil of a State (Burgess), 1961
Devil of Aske (P. Hill), 1972
Devil on Horseback (Plaidy, as Holt), 1977
Devil on Lammas Night (Howatch), 1970
Devil Snar'd (Bowen, as Preedy), 1932
Devil to Pay (Krentz, as James), 1984
Devil to Pay (Napier), 1991
Devil to Pay (Parkinson), 1973
Devil Water (Seton), 1962
Devilish Deception (Cartland), 1985
Devil-May-Care (B. Michaels, as Peters), 1977
Devil's Advocate (Caldwell), 1952
Devil's Arms (Lamb), 1978
Devil's Bondsman (S. Thorpe), 1961
Devil's Bride (M. Pargeter), 1979
Devil's Cub (Heyer), 1934
Devil's Darling (Winspear), 1975
Devil's Daughter (Coulter), 1985
Devil's Daughter (Winston), 1971
Devil's Desire (McBain), 1975
Devil's Double (W. Roberts), 1979
Devil's Due (Burgin), 1905
Devil's Embrace (Coulter), 1982
Devil's Emissary (Nicole, as Grange), 1968
Devil's Fire, Love's Revenge (Laker, as Paul), 1976
Devil's Flower (Donnelly), 1990
Devil's Gamble (Slaughter), 1977
Devil's Harvest (Slaughter), 1963
Devil's Hole (Ainsworth), 1971
Devil's Innocents (M. Howard, as Edgar), 1972
Devil's Jig (Bowen, as Paye), 1930
Devil's Kiss (Saunders, as Blake), 1981
Devil's Kiss (Wentworth), 1991
Devil's Lady (Manley-Tucker, as Howard), 1980
Devil's Laughter (Yerby), 1953
Devil's Mistress (Pozzessere, as Graham), 1986
Devil's Mode (s Burgess), 1989
Devil's Motor (Corelli), 1910
Devil's Mount (Mather), 1976
Devil's Own (Brown, as St Claire), 1987
Devil's Own (Lofts, as Curtis), 1960
Devil's Own (Nicole), 1975
Devil's Palace (Pemberton), 1983
Devil's Price (Mortimer), 1985
Devil's Princess (Winston), 1971
Devil's Shadow (Wentworth), 1988
Devil's Sonata (Hufford), 1976
Devil's Web (Balogh), 1990
Devilseed (Yerby), 1984
Devious Duchess (J. Smith), 1985

Devon Interlude (K. Thorpe), 1968
Devoted Ladies (Keane, as Farrell), 1934
Devotion (Hampson), 1983
Dew and Mildew (s Wren), 1912
Dewdrops (s Kennedy), 1928
Dewey Death (Blackstock), 1956
DeWitt, Mollie series (Woods), from 1992
Diamond Bay (L. Howard), 1987
Diamond Cage (Dwyer-Joyce), 1976
Diamond Cut Diamond (Donnelly), 1982
Diamond Engagement Ring (Ruck), 1962
Diamond Fire (Finch, as Robins), 1986
Diamond Fire (Mather), 1991
Diamond Girl (Palmer), 1984
Diamond Spur (Palmer, as Kyle), 1988
Diamond Valley (Way), 1986
Diamond Waterfall (Haines), 1984
Diamond Waterfall (Walsh), 1985
Diamonds and Daisies (May), 1989
Diamonds in the Dust (Laffeaty), 1984
Diana (Delderfield), 1960
Diana and Destiny (Garvice), 1906
Diana Comes Home (Bromige), 1955
Diana Falls in Love (Albanesi), 1919
Diana Goes to Tokyo (Greig, as Ames), 1961
Diana of Dreams (Burgin), 1910
Diana the Huntress (Chesney), 1985
Diana's Destiny (Garvice)
Diary of a Red-Haired Girl (Price), 1932
Diary of Isobelle (Lide), 1988
Dickie Dilver (Burgin), 1912
Dickon (Bowen), 1929
Did She? (Glyn), 1934
Didn't Anybody Know My Wife? (W. Roberts), 1974
Die For Love (B. Michaels, as Peters), 1984
Die She Must (Hutten), 1934
Died on a Rainy Sunday (Aiken), 1972
Different Dream (Vitek), 1980
Different Reality (Pykare, as Powers), 1985
Difficult Decision (Dailey), 1980
Difficult Man (Armstrong), 1993
Dig a Narrow Grave (Roby), 1971
Digby (P. Hill), 1987
Dilemma in Duet (Sebastian), 1979
Dilemma in Paradise (Donald), 1978
Dimbie and I—and Amelia (Grundy), 1907
DiMedici Bride (Pozzessere), 1986
Dina Cashman (Norris), 1942
Dinah (Gibbs), 1981
Dinah's Husband (Bloom), 1941
Dinner Along the Amazon (s Findley), 1984
Dinner at Antoine's (Keyes), 1948
Dinner of Herbs (Cookson), 1985
Diona and a Dalmation (Cartland), 1983
Diplomatic Honeymoon (Greig, as Ames), 1942
Director's Wife (Armstrong), 1991
D'Iri and I (Bacheller), 1901
Dirty Frog (Veryan, as Moore), 1990
Disappearance of Barbara (M. St John), 1923
Disappearance of General Jason (Wren), 1940
Disco in Spain (Woodward, as Ware), 1976
Disgraceful Duke (Cartland), 1976
Disheartened Doctor (Bloom, as Burns), 1961
Dishonest Women (Steele), 1982
Dishonourable Intentions (Wentworth), 1987
Dishonoured Wife (Price), 1951

Disorderly Knights (Dunnett), 1966
Disputed Crown (Anand), 1979
Disputed Passage (L. Douglas), 1939
Distant Choices (Jagger), 1986
Distant Dawn (Pedler), 1934
Distant Dream (Peake), 1976
Distant Drum (Chandos, as Charles), 1940
Distant Hills (L. Walker), 1962
Distant Island (Cato), 1988
Distant Paradise (MacLeod), 1984
Distant Song (Bromige), 1977
Distant Sound of Thunder (Mather), 1972
Distant Trap (Bevan), 1969
Distant Voices, A Fact or Fancy (Corelli), 1896
Distant Wood (Harrod-Eagles), 1981
Distinctions of Class (Burgh), 1987
District Nurse (Baldwin), 1932
Distrust Her Shadow (Steele), 1982
Disturbing Charm (Ruck), 1919
Disturbing Stranger (Lamb), 1978
Dive in the Sun (Kent, as Reeman), 1961
Divided Duty (Mackinlay), 1957
Divided Heart (Marsh), 1983
Divided House (Swan), 1885
Dividing Line (K. Thorpe), 1979
Divine Evil (N. Roberts), 1992
Divine Fire (M. Sinclair), 1904
Divine Folly (Orczy), 1937
Divine Mistress (Slaughter), 1949
Diviner (Harris), 1983
Division of the Spoils (P. Scott), 1975
Divorce? Of Course (Bloom, as Essex), 1945
Divorced from Reality (D. Stevenson), 1935
Do Not Go, My Love (Burchell), 1964
Do Not Go, My Love (Robins), 1959
Do Something Dangerous (Hoy), 1958
Do You Remember Babylon? (Weale), 1989
Doctor (Rinehart), 1936
Doctor and Lover (Bloom, as Essex), 1964
Doctor and Mathilda (Seifert), 1974
Doctor and the Dancer (Greig), 1965
Dr Artz (Hichens), 1929
Doctor at the Crossroads (Seifert), 1954
Doctor Barbara (McElfresh, as Wesley), 1958
Doctor Bill (Seifert), 1941
Doctor Brad's Nurse (Greig, as Ames), 1966
Doctor Called Caroline (E. Harrison), 1979
Doctor Called David (Bloom, as Burns), 1966
Doctor Called Harry (Bloom, as Harvey), 1971
Doctor Chaos (Bowen, as Preedy), 1933
Doctor Chris (Seifert), 1946
Doctor Comes to Bayard (Seifert), 1964
Doctor Dares (Seifert), 1950
Doctor Decides (Greig, as Warren), 1963
Doctor Dee (Ackroyd), 1993
Dr Dee series (McElfresh, as Wesley), from 1960
Doctor Delightful (Bloom, as Burns), 1964
Doctor Disagrees (Seifert), 1953
Doctor Divine (Bloom, as Burns), 1966
Dr Dorothy's Choice (McElfresh, as Wesley), 1944
Dr Ellison's Ambition (Seifert), 1944
Doctor Falls in Love (Randall), 1958
Doctor for Blue Jay Cove (Seifert), 1956
Doctor Gregory's Partner (Bloom, as Burns), 1960
Dr Guardian's Gate (Bloom, as Essex), 1962
Doctor Havelock's Wife (Randall), 1943

Dr Hudson's Secret Journal (L. Douglas), 1939
Doctor in Danger (Woodward, as Harley), 1970
Doctor in Exile (Greig), 1960
Doctor in Judgment (Seifert), 1971
Doctor in Love (Seifert), 1974
Doctor in Malaya (Weale), 1965
Doctor in Spain (Woodward, as Harley), 1968
Doctor in the Family (Seifert), 1955
Doctor in the Snow (Chandos, as Lance), 1980
Dr Irresistible, MD (Bloom, as Burns), 1962
Doctor Is a Lady (Greig), 1962
Doctor Is Engaged, (Asquith), 1962
Doctor Jamie (Seifert), 1959
Dr Jane series (McElfresh), from 1954
Dr Jeremy's Wife (Seifert), 1961
Doctor Lucy (Stuart, as Allen), 1956
Doctor Makes a Choice (Seifert), 1961
Doctor Mallory (Seifert), 1941
Doctor Mary Courage (Stuart, as A. Stuart), 1961
Doctor Mays (Seifert), 1957
Doctor Mollie (Seifert), 1952
Doctor of Mercy (Seifert), 1951
Doctor on Call (Bloom, as Essex), 1961
Doctor on Duty Bound (Bloom, as Essex), 1969
Doctor on Horseback (Stuart, as A. Stuart), 1962
Doctor on Trial (Seifert), 1959
Doctor on Wings (Greig), 1966
Doctor Overboard (MacLeod, as Airlie), 1966
Doctor Robert Comes Around, (Asquith), 1965
Doctor Rose (Rhodes), 1984
Doctor Samaritan (Seifert), 1965
Dr Scott, Surgeon on Call (Seifert), 1963
Doctor Takes a Holiday (Greig, as Ames), 1969
Doctor Takes a Wife (Randall), 1947
Doctor Takes a Wife (Seifert), 1952
Doctor Ted's Clinic (Greig, as Ames), 1967
Doctor Therne (Haggard), 1898
Doctor to the House of Jasmine (Woodward, as Harley), 1967
Doctor to the Rescue (Bloom, as Burns), 1961
Doctor Toby (Stratton, as Gillen), 1970
Doctor Tuck (Seifert), 1977
Doctor Westland (K. Blair), 1965
Doctor Who Fell in Love (Bloom, as Harvey), 1974
Doctor with a Mission (Seifert), 1967
Doctor with a Past (Woodward, as Sawley), 1973
Doctor with Four Hands (Woodward, as Harley), 1962
Dr Woodward's Ambition (Seifert), 1945
Doctor's Affair (Seifert), 1975
Doctors Are Different (Chandos), 1954
Doctor's Assistant, (K. Blair, as Conway), 1964
Doctors at Risk (Slaughter), 1983
Doctor's Bride (Seifert), 1960
Doctor's Confession (Seifert), 1968
Doctor's Daughter (Blackstock, as Allardyce), 1955
Doctor's Daughter (MacLeod), 1965
Doctor's Daughter (Seifert), 1974
Doctor's Daughters (Slaughter), 1981
Doctor's Daughters (Weale), 1962
Doctor's Delusion (Collin), 1967
Doctor's Desperate Hour (Seifert), 1976
Doctor's Destiny (Seifert), 1972
Doctor's Distress (Bloom, as Burns), 1964
Doctor's Favourite Nurse (Woodward, as Davis), 1971
Doctor's Healing Hands (Seifert), 1982
Doctor's Husband (Seifert), 1957
Doctor's Joy (Ritchie), 1962

Doctor's Kingdom (Seifert), 1970
Doctor's Love (Bloom, as Essex), 1974
Doctor's Marriage (James), 1972
Doctor's Nurse (Greig, as Ames), 1959
Doctors of Doncastle (Woodward), 1978
Doctors of Downlands (Rayner, as Brandon), 1968
Doctors of Eden Place (Seifert), 1977
Doctors on Parade (Seifert), 1960
Doctor's Orders (Seifert), 1958
Doctor's Private Life (Seifert), 1973
Doctor's Promise (Seifert), 1979
Doctor's Reputation (Seifert), 1972
Doctor's Second Love (Seifert), 1971
Doctor's Secret (Woodward, as Richmond), 1962
Doctor's Strange Secret (Seifert), 1962
Doctor's Sweetheart (s Montgomery), 1979
Doctors Three (Collin), 1964
Doctor's Two Lives (Seifert), 1970
Doctors Were Brothers (Seifert), 1978
Doctor's Wife (Greig), 1937
Doctors' Wives (Slaughter), 1967
Dog, a Horse, and a Heart (Cartland), 1993
Dogs in an Omnibus (s Stern), 1942
Dogs in Clover (Ponsonby), 1954
Dollars for the Duke (Cartland), 1981
Dollmaster (R. Marshall), 1954
Doll's House (Anthony), 1992
Dolly series (Dunnett, as Halliday), from 1968
Dolly Daydreams! (M. St John), 1918
Dolly Dialogues (Hope), 1894
Dolphin Bay (Bevan), 1976
Dolphin Bay (Worboys, as Eyre), 1970
Dolphin Cottage (Stern), 1962
'Dolphin' Summer (Salisbury), 1976
Domestic Blister (Bloom, as Essex), 1948
Domina (B. Wood), 1983
Domino (Whitney), 1979
Don Pedro's Captain (Bennetts), 1978
Dona Celestis (Dell), 1933
Donkey Shoe (Stern), 1952
Donovan Legacy series (N. Roberts), from 1992
Donovan's Promise (Schulze), 1988
Don't Ask Me Now (E. Darcy), 1986
Don't Cage Me Wild (Dwyer-Joyce), 1970
Don't Call it Love (Armstrong), 1984
Don't Cling to the Past (Woodward, as Richmond), 1978
Don't Cry Alone (Cox), 1992
Don't Forget to Smile (Seidel), 1986
Don't Give Your Heart Away (Chandos), 1966
Don't Look Now (s du Maurier), 1971
Don't Play Games (E. Darcy), 1985
Don't Walk Alone (Donnelly), 1969
Doom Castle (Munro), 1901
Doomsday (Deeping), 1927
Door (Rinehart), 1930
Door into the Rose Garden (Hoy), 1961
Door of Death (Shellabarger, as Esteven), 1928
Door Without a Key (Manley-Tucker), 1967
Dora Miller (Libbey), 1892
Dorinda's Lovers (Albanesi, as Rowlands), 1930
Doris (Garvice), 1911
Doris Cheyne (Swan), 1888
Dorothea Kirke (Swan), 1884
Dot on the Spot (Barcynska, as Sandys), 1949
Double Alibi (Rinehart), 1932
Double Dallilay (Bowen, as Preedy), 1933

Double Dealing (Krentz, as Castle), 1984
Double Deception (K. Thorpe), 1985
Double Deception (M. Peters, as Law), 1987
Double Entendre (Pozzessere), 1986
Double Harness (Hope), 1904
Double Heart (L. Cooper), 1962
Double Jeopardy (B. Hastings), 1986
Double Life (Winston), 1991
Double Lives (Swan), 1939
Double Occupancy (Chase), 1982
Double Rainbow (Goodwin, as Ebel), 1977
Double Shadow (Polland, as Adrian), 1977
Double Standards (McNaught), 1984
Double Take (James), 1967
Double Wager (Balogh), 1985
Doubtful Marriage (Neels), 1987
Doubting Heart (Mackinlay), 1937
Dove (Salverson), 1933
Dove in the Mulberry Tree (Bowen, as Preedy), 1939
Dove of El-Djezaire (Salverson), 1933
Dove's Nest (Hardwick), 1980
Down in the Forest (L. Walker), 1962
Down Lambeth Way (Staples), 1988
Dragon and the Pearl (Cartland), 1977
Dragon and the Rose (Gellis), 1977
Dragon and the Rose (M. Peters), 1982
Dragon at Noonday (E. Pargeter), 1975
Dragon Bay (Winspear), 1969
Dragon Blood (Nicole), 1989
Dragon for Edward (Bennetts), 1975
Dragonfly (Bloom), 1968
Dragonmede (Randall), 1974
Dragon's Cave (Hunter, as Chace), 1972
Dragon's Head (Leslie), 1973
Dragon's Lair (Craven), 1978
Dragon's Tail (Duffield), 1939
Dragon-Slayer (Loring), 1924
Dragonslayer (Richards), 1993
Dragonwyck (Seton), 1944
Drayton series (Randall), from 1985
Dream (Delinsky), 1990
Dream and the Destiny (Cordell), 1975
Dream and the Glory (Cartland), 1977
Dream Awhile (Bloom, as Burns), 1937
Dream Come True (Chase), 1982
Dream Come True (Neels), 1982
Dream Comes True (Delinsky), 1990
Dream Domesticated (s Ruck), 1918
Dream from the Night (Cartland), 1976
Dream in Spain (Cartland), 1986
Dream in the Heart (Ritchie), 1972
Dream Lover (Saunders, as Innes), 1990
Dream Maker (Vitek), 1986
Dream Master (Lamb, as Hardy) , 1982
Dream Mender (Woods), 1992
Dream of a Shadow (Laffeaty), 1970
Dream of Fair Serpents (M. Peters, as Darby), 1979
Dream of Mary Muldoon (s Swan), 1898
Dream of Orchids (Whitney), 1985
Dream of Past Loves (Woodward, as Sawley), 1975
Dream of Petals Whim (A.E. Worboys), 1961
Dream of the West (Pykare, as Powers), 1983
Dream of Winter (Stratton), 1977
Dream of Yesterday (Buckingham, as John), 1984
Dream on the Hill (Peake), 1974
Dream Prevails (Diver), 1938

Dream Towers (Blackstock), 1981
Dream Traders (Thompson), 1981
Dream Train (C. Allen), 1988
Dream Unfolds (Delinsky), 1990
Dream Within (Cartland), 1947
Dreamer in Portugal (Dixon), 1934
Dreamer Wakes (Ayres), 1945
Dreaming (Lamb), 1993
Dreaming (B. Wood), 1991
Dreaming Damozel (Hardwick), 1990
Dreaming In Color (C. Allen), 1993
Dreaming River (Ritchie), 1957
Dreaming Suburb (Delderfield), 1958
Dreaming Swimmer (Ogilvie), 1976
Dreaming Tower (Manners, as Marshall), 1969
Dreaming Tree (Matthews), 1989
Dreams Are Not Enough (Briskin), 1987
Dreams Come True (Swan), 1941
Dreams Do Come True (Cartland), 1981
Dream's End (Palmer), 1979
Dreams Get You Nowhere (Greig), 1937
Dreams of Fair Women (Cordell), 1993
Dreams 1–2 (Krentz), 1988
Dreamtime (Hampson), 1983
Drena and the Duke (Cartland), 1992
Dresden Finch (Stirling), 1976
Dreveilion Surprise (Mortimer), 1991
Driftwood Spars (Wren), 1916
Drink (Caine), 1906
Drinkwater, Nathaniel (Woodman), from 1981
Driving Force (Wentworth), 1988
Driving of Destiny (Bloom), 1925
Drop of the Dice (Plaidy, as Carr), 1981
Drug on the Market (Tranter), 1962
Druid Sacrifice (Tranter), 1993
Drum (Onstott), 1962
Drumbeat (Pope), 1968
Drummer of Corrae (MacLeod), 1966
Drums (Boyd), 1925
Drums Along the Khyber (McCutchan, as MacNeil), 1969
Drums Along the Mohawk (Edmonds), 1936
Drums of Love (Cartland), 1979
Drums of Mer (Idriess), 1933
Drums of Time (Stirling), 1980
Drury Randall (M. Johnston), 1934
Drusilla's Point of View (Albanesi), 1908
Dual Enchantment (Courtney), 1985
Dual Image (N. Roberts), 1985
Dubious Legacy (Wesley), 1992
Dublin 4 (s Binchy), 1982
Duchess (Deveraux), 1992
Duchess (M. Howard, as Edgar), 1976
Duchess Caine (P. Hill), 1983
Duchess Disappeared (Cartland), 1979
Duchess Hotspur (R. Marshall), 1946
Duchess in Disguise (Courtney), 1979
Duchess Intervenes (Lowndes), 1933
Duchess Laura series (Lowndes), from 1929
Duchess of Duke Street series (Hardwick), from 1977
Duck to Water (Stern), 1949
Ducks and Drakes (Tranter), 1953
Duel in the Dark (Steen), 1928
Duel of Desire (Lamb), 1978
Duel of Hearts (Cartland), 1949
Duel of Jewels (Cartland), 1993
Duel with Destiny (Cartland), 1977

Duelling Fire (Mather), 1981
Duke and the Preacher's Daughter (Cartland), 1979
Duke Comes Home (Cartland), 1984
Duke in Danger (Cartland), 1983
Duke Is Trapped (Cartland), 1993
Duke Street, Duchess of series (Hardwick), from 1977
Duke's Diamonds (Chesney), 1983
Duke's Stratagem (Burgin), 1931
Duke's Twins (Burgin), 1914
Dulcie (Garvice), 1910
Dummy Hand (Williamson), 1920
Duncan's Bride (L. Howard), 1991
Durable Fire (Bishop), 1958
Durable Fire (Clarke), 1993
Durable Fire (Donald), 1983
Durable Fire (Ritchie), 1951
Durrants (Muskett), 1948
Dust in the Sunlight (Gaskin), 1950
Dust Is My Pillow (P. Hastings), 1955
Dust of Dreams (Robins), 1943
Dusty Answer (Lehmann), 1927
Dusty Dawn (Duffield), 1949
Dusty Spring (Seifert), 1946
Dutch Uncle (Hilton), 1966
Dutiful Tradition (Norway), 1971
Dutiful Wife (Oldfield), 1989
Dweller on the Threshold (Hichens), 1911
Dwelling Place (Cookson), 1971
Dying in the Night (Summerton, as Roffman), 1974
Dynasty of Death (Caldwell), 1938
Dynasty of Love (Cartland), 1991
Dynasty series (Harrod-Eagles), from 1980
Dysart, Sinbad series (Wren), from 1933

Each Hour a Peril (MacGill), 1921
Each Time We Love (Busbee), 1993
Eager Search (Ayres), 1923
Eagle and the Raven (Michener), 1990
Eagle at the Gate (Randall), 1977
Eagle in the Sky (F. Mason), 1948
Eagle King (Treece), 1965
Eagle of the Vincella (Stratton), 1978
Eagle Swooped (Hampson), 1970
Eagles Feathers (Tranter), 1941
Eagles Gather (Caldwell), 1940
Eagle's Ridge (Way), 1985
Earl Escapes (Cartland), 1987
Earl (Holland), 1971
Earl Rings a Belle (Cartland), 1991
Earl's Daughter (Garvice), 1910
Earl's Heir (Garvice)
Early Autumn (Bromfield), 1926
Early Life of Stephen Hind (Jameson), 1964
Early Stories (s du Maurier), 1954
Earth Giant (E. Marshall), 1960
Earth Is the Lord's (Caldwell), 1941
Earth Queen, Sky King (Hamilton, as Fitzgerald), 1989
Earth's Children series (Auel), from 1980
East and West (s Buck), 1975
East of the Setting Sun (McCutcheon), 1924
East of Today (Browning), 1981
East Side General (Slaughter), 1952
East Wind (Ellis), 1983
East Wind: West Wind (Buck), 1930
Ebbing Tide (Ogilvie), 1947
Eben Holden series (Bacheller), from 1900

Ebony Swan (Whitney), 1992
Echo Answers (Thane), 1927
Echo of Applause (Mackinlay), 1948
Echo of Flutes (I. Roberts), 1965
Echo of Margaret (M. Peters, as Black), 1978
Echo of Passion (Lamb), 1988
Echo of Spring (Stratton, as Gillen), 1973
Echo of Thunder (Seger), 1985
Echoed from the Past (Wynne), 1944
Echoes (Binchy), 1985
Echoes and Embers (Gallagher), 1983
Echoes from the Hills (B. Johnson), 1983
Echoes from the Macabre (s du Maurier), 1976
Echoes from the Past (Wentworth), 1989
Echoes of Another Spring (Baldwin), 1965
Echoes of Love (Beresford), 1979
Echoing Green (Leslie), 1929
Echoing Yesterday (Manners), 1981
Ecstasy (Weale), 1983
Ecstasy's Embrace (Finch), 1985
Eddy and Edouard (Hutten), 1928
Eden (Ellis), 1975
Eden Burnings (Plain), 1982
Eden series (Harris), from 1977
Eden's Spell (Pozzessere, as Graham), 1986
Edge of Beyond (Hunter, as Chace), 1973
Edge of Dawn (Seger), 1986
Edge of Forever (Woods), 1988
Edge of Glass (Gaskin), 1967
Edge of Temptation (Mather), 1982
Edge of Terror (Cowen), 1970
Edge of Winter (Neels), 1976
Edinburgh Excursion (Andrews), 1970
Edna's Secret Marriage (Garvice), 1905
Education of Miss Paterson (Chesney), 1985
Edward, Edward (Burford), 1973
Edward III series (Wiat), from 1985
Edward Longshanks (Plaidy), 1979
Edward the Warrior (Clarke, as Honeyman), 1975
Edwardian Day-Dream (Bloom), 1972
Eight Banners (Nicole, as Savage), 1992
Eight Months on Ghazzah Street (Mantel), 1988
1805 (Woodman), 1985
1876 (Vidal), 1976
Eighth Champion of Christendom (E. Pargeter), 1945
Eighth Day (Wilder), 1967
Elaine (Garvice), 1911
Elder Brother (s Swan), 1898
Elder Sister (Greig, as Ames), 1938
Eldorado (Orczy), 1913
Eleanor Jowitt, Antiques (Bloom), 1950
Eleanor of Aquitaine (Lamb, as Holland), 1978
Eleanor the Queen (Lofts), 1955
Eleanora Duse (Stubbs), 1970
Electra (Treece), 1963
Electric Torch (Dell), 1934
Elephants and Castles (Duggan), 1963
Eleventh Hour Lover (Ruck), 1933
Elgin Marble (Hutten), 1937
Eliots of Damerosehay series (Goudge), from 1940
Elissa, and Black Heart and White Heart (s Haggard), 1900
Eliza (Blackstock, as Allardyce), 1975
Eliza for Common (O. Douglas), 1928
Eliza Stanhope (Trollope), 1978
Elizabeth and the Prince of Spain (Irwin), 1953
Elizabeth (Anthony), 1960

Elizabeth (Seger), 1987
Elizabeth Browne, Children's Nurse (K. Blair, as Brett), 1965
Elizabeth, Captive Princess (Irwin), 1948
Elizabeth I series (Irwin), from 1944
Elizabeth in Dreamland (M. St John, as St John Cooper), 1921
Elizabeth the Beloved (M. Peters), 1965
Elizabeth Visits America (Glyn), 1909
Elizabethan Lover (Cartland), 1953
Ellis Island (Saunders, as Summers), 1993
Elopement of Eve and Prince Playfellow (Ruck), 1922
Eloquent Silence (Brown, as Ryan), 1982
Elsie Brant's Romance (Albanesi, as Rowlands), 1913
Elsie Thorburn (Swan), 1926
Elusive as a Unicorn (Mortimer), 1986
Elusive as the Unicorn (Mortimer), 1990
Elusive Dawn (Hooper, as Robbins), 1983
Elusive Desire (Mather), 1983
Elusive Earl (Cartland), 1976
Elusive Harmony (Burchell), 1976
Elusive Legacy (Shoesmith), 1976
Elusive Lover (Cowen), 1981
Elusive Lover (Mortimer), 1982
Elusive Mistress (Armstrong), 1986
Elusive Obsession (Mortimer), 1992
Elusive Paradise (Peake), 1985
Elusive Quest (Cowen), 1965
Elusive Swan (Sommerfield), 1988
Elyza (C. Darcy), 1976
Embarrassment of Riches (Pemberton), 1992
Ember in the Ashes (Lane), 1960
Embers of Dawn (Matthews), 1982
Embrace and Conquer (J. Blake), 1981
Embrace the Wind (Carter), 1985
Embroidered Sunset (Aiken), 1970
Emerald (Bennetts), 1983
Emerald (Goodwin), 1980
Emerald (Whitney), 1983
Emerald Cave (Bevan), 1981
Emerald Station (Winston), 1974
Emerald Sunshine (F. Preston), 1988
Emergency Call (E. Harrison), 1970
Emergency in the Pyrenees (Bridge), 1965
Emily (Blackstock, as Allardyce), 1976
Emily (J. Cooper), 1975
Emily (Harrod-Eagles), 1992
Emily Goes to Exeter (Chesney), 1990
Emily series (Montgomery), from 1923
Emma and the Outlaw (Miller), 1991
Emma Hart (Bloom, as Prole), 1951
Emma McChesney & Co (s Ferber), 1915
Emma the Queen (Clarke, as Honeyman), 1978
Emma's Sparrow (Joseph), 1982
Emmett (Palmer), 1993
Emperor (Harrod-Eagles), 1988
Emperor's Candlesticks (Orczy), 1899
Emperor's Daughter (Hamilton), 1978
Empire (Matthews), 1982
Empire (Vidal), 1987
Empire Builders (Stuart, as Long), 1987
Empire of the Heart (Seger), 1984
Empress (Oman), 1932
Empty Heart (Gibbs, as Ford), 1957
Empty House (Pilcher), 1973
Empty Nest (Cadell), 1986
Empty World (D. Stevenson), 1936
Enamored (Palmer), 1988

Enchanted (Delmar), 1965
Enchanted (Hoy), 1952
Enchanted (Matthews), 1987
Enchanted April (Arnim), 1922
Enchanted Cup (Ainsworth), 1980
Enchanted Dawn (Hampson), 1972
Enchanted Eden (Randall), 1960
Enchanted Evening (I. Preston), 1966
Enchanted Garden (Bromige), 1956
Enchanted Grotto (M. Peters, as Black), 1972
Enchanted Ground (Woodhouse), 1993
Enchanted Island (Mather), 1969
Enchanted Island (Robins), 1956
Enchanted Island (Saunders, as Innes), 1982
Enchanted Isle (Harrod-Eagles), 1993
Enchanted Journey (Bloom), 1933
Enchanted Kingdom (Maybury), 1932
Enchanted Land (Deveraux), 1978
Enchanted Moment (Cartland), 1949
Enchanted Oasis (Baldwin), 1938
Enchanted Ring (Stratton, as Gillen), 1971
Enchanted Valley (Chandos, as Tempest), 1954
Enchanted Waltz (Cartland), 1955
Enchanted Wilderness (Hoy), 1940
Enchanter's Nightshade (Bridge), 1937
Enchanter's Nightshade (Maybury, as Troy), 1963
Enchanting Clementina (Cleugh), 1930
Enchanting Courtesan (Bloom, as Prole), 1955
Enchanting Evil (Cartland), 1968
Enchanting Island (K. Blair), 1952
Enchanting Jenny (F. Stevenson, as Faire), 1979
Enchanting Princess (Bloom, as Prole), 1970
Enchanting Samantha (Neels), 1973
Enchanting Witch (Keane, as Farrell), 1951
Enchantment (Chard), 1989
Enchantment (Duffield), 1937
Enchantment (Gibbs), 1952
Enchantment (Hampson), 1982
Enchantment at Hillcrest (I. Preston), 1984
Enchantment in Blue (Kidd), 1975
Enchantment of Merrowporth (Saunders), 1980
Enchantress Mine (Small), 1987
Enchantress series (Ellerbeck, as Yorke), from 1979
Encounter at Alpenrose (Bromige), 1970
Encounter (Blackstock), 1971
Encounter in Berlin (Chard), 1976
End Crowns All (Albanesi, as Rowlands), 1906
End of a Childhood (s Richardson), 1934
End of Cornwall (J. Lindsay, as Preston), 1937
End of Her Honeymoon (Lowndes), 1913
End of the Rainbow (Neels), 1974
End of the Summer (Pilcher), 1971
End of the World (Delmar), 1934
End of the World News (Burgess), 1982
End of Track (F. Mason, as Weaver), 1943
Endangered Species (Woodman), 1992
Endearing Young Charms (Chappell), 1957
Endearment (Spencer), 1982
Endings and Beginnings (N. Roberts), 1984
Endless Passion (Finch), 1983
Endure My Heart (J. Smith), 1980
Enduring Adventure (James), 1944
Enduring Flame (Robins), 1929
Enduring Flame (Tranter), 1957
Enduring Hills (Giles), 1950
Enemy from the Past (Peake), 1979

Enemy in Camp (Dailey), 1980
Enemy in Sight! (Kent), 1970
Enemy in the Blanket (Burgess), 1958
Enemy Within (Cordell), 1974
Enfant du Cirque (R. Marshall), 1930
Engaged to Jarrod Stone (Mortimer), 1980
Engaging Loyalty (Steele, as M. Steele), 1978
England for Sale (Lane), 1943
England's Mistress (M. Peters), 1991
English Air (D. Stevenson), 1940
English Daughter (Hunter, as Chace), 1972
English Family Robinson (D. Murray), 1933
English Paragon (Bowen), 1930
English Rose (Gibbs, as Ford), 1953
English Wife (Blackstock), 1964
Enlightening Delilah (Chesney), 1990
Entanglement (Fellows), 1979
Enter Mrs Belchamber (Cadell), 1951
Enter My Jungle (Armstrong), 1982
Enter Three Witches (D. Murray), 1942
Entertainment (s Delafield), 1927
Enticement (Trask), 1936
Enticers (N. Peters), 1981
Entranced (N. Roberts), 1992
Envious Eliza (Albanesi), 1909
Environment (Bentley), 1922
Envoy from Elizabeth (Bennetts), 1970
Epidemic! (Slaughter), 1961
Episode at Toledo (Bridge), 1966
Episode of Sparrows (Godden), 1955
Episode of the Wandering Knife (Rinehart), 1950
Epitaph for Three Women (Plaidy), 1981
Equal Chance (Clarke), 1989
Equal Opportunities (Jordan), 1989
Equal Shares (Stanford), 1986
Equality of Love (Steele, as M. Steele), 1979
Eric Brighteyes (Haggard), 1891
Erie Water (Edmonds), 1933
Erin's Ecstasy (Sommerfield), 1980
Ernestine Sophie (Cleugh), 1925
Escapade (Hodge), 1993
Escapade (Palmer, as Kyle), 1992
Escapade (J. Smith), 1977
Escape (Cartland), 1985
Escape at Midnight (s Buck), 1964
Escape from Cabiz (Miller), 1990
Escape from Desire (Jordan), 1982
Escape from Passion (Cartland), 1945
Escape from Santu (Kent, as Reeman), 1962
Escape Me Never (Craven), 1985
Escape to Happiness (Beresford), 1964
Escape to Love (Robins), 1943
Escape to Marriage (Price), 1952
Escape to Yesterday (s Frankau), 1942
Esmeralda (Neels), 1976
Esmond in India (Jhabvala), 1957
Establishment (Fast), 1979
Esther (Lofts), 1950
Eternal City (Caine), 1901
Eternal Justice (Burgin), 1932
Eternal Summer (Hampson), 1969
Eternal Tomorrow (Bloom), 1929
Eternity (Deveraux), 1992
Ethan (Palmer), 1990
Ethan Frome (Wharton), 1911
Etheldreda the Ready (Vaizey), 1910

Etruscan Smile (V. Johnston), 1977
Eugenia (C. Darcy), 1977
Eugénie (Bowen), 1971
Eugenie (Chapman), 1961
Eulalie (Ellis), 1976
Eva Gay (E. Scott), 1933
Eve and I (Chandos), 1943
Eve Didn't Care (Bloom, as Essex), 1941
Even Chance (Harrod-Eagles, as Bennett), 1984
Evening Star (Baldwin), 1966
Ever After (Thane), 1945
Ever Thine (Chapman), 1951
Evergold (Trask), 1950
Evergreen Gallant (Plaidy), 1965
Evergreen (Plain), 1978
Everlasting (Johansen), 1986
Everlasting Covenant (Carr), 1987
Everlasting Love (Mortimer), 1984
Every Day Is Mother's Day (Mantel), 1985
Every Goose a Swan (Manley-Tucker), 1972
Every Man a King (Worboys), 1975
Every Other Gift (Jacob), 1950
Every Soul Hath Its Song (s Hurst), 1916
Every Time I Love You (Pozzessere, as Graham), 1987
Every Woman's Doctor (Greig), 1964
Every Woman's Man (Greig), 1961
Everyman's Land (Williamson), 1918
Everything and More (Briskin), 1983
Everything but Marriage (Schulze), 1992
Everywoman (Frankau), 1933
Evil at Hillcrest (Ellis), 1971
Evil at Roger's Cross (Cookson, as Marchant), 1966
Evil Children (W. Roberts), 1973
Evil in the House (Plaidy, as Ford), 1954
Evil Island (McElfresh, as Blair), 1974
Except for Me and Thee (s West), 1969
Except My Love (Burchell), 1937
Excess of Love (Spellman), 1985
Exchange Royal (Bowen), 1940
Exciseman (Sisson), 1972
Exhibition Summer (Ponsonby), 1982
Exile (M. Johnston), 1927
Exiles (Deeping), 1930
Exiles (Stuart, as Long), 1979
Exit Renee (Barcynska), 1934
Exorcism (Blackstock), 1961
Exorcism (Jordan), 1985
Exotic Young Lady (Mackinlay), 1932
Expendable (W. Roberts), 1976
Experiments in Crime (s Frankau), 1937
Expert Teacher (Jordan), 1989
Expiation (Arnim), 1929
Exploits of Brigadier Gerard (s Doyle), 1896
Explorer (Keyes), 1964
Explorers (Stuart, as Long), 1983
Explorers of the Dawn (s de la Roche), 1922
Explosion (Wren), 1935
Explosion of Love (Cartland), 1979
Explosive Meeting (Lamb), 1985
Exposure (Anthony), 1993
Extraordinary Engagement (Lewty), 1972
Eye of the Beholder (Hooper, as Robbins), 1985
Eye of the Fleet (Woodman), 1981
Eye of the Storm (Seger), 1985
Eye of the Tiger (Palmer), 1986
Eye of the Wind (Hunter), 1984

Eyes of Doctor Karl (Bloom, as Burns), 1962
Eyes of Love (Deeping), 1933
Eyes of Love (Garvice)
Eyes of the Night (Stuart), 1954

Fabric of Dreams (MacLeod, as Airlie), 1951
Fabulous Beast (Krentz, as James), 1984
Fabulous Nell Gwynne (Bloom, as Prole), 1954
Facade (Bloom), 1948
Façade (Steele), 1984
Face at the Window (W. Roberts), 1981
Face in the Shadows (V. Johnston), 1971
Face of an Angel (Eden, as Paradise), 1961
Face of Danger (W. Roberts), 1972
Face of Evil (Nicole), 1971
Face of Innocence (Ogilvie), 1970
Face the Music—for Love (Chandos, as Tempest), 1938
Face the Tiger (Donnelly), 1983
Facets (Delinsky), 1991
Factor's Wife (Blackstock), 1964
Factory Nurse (Norway, as Neal), 1961
Facts of Love (R. Lindsay, as Leigh), 1978
Fade Out (Jacob), 1937
Failed Marriage (Mortimer), 1983
Faint Heart (Ayres), 1926
Faint Heart, Fair Lady (Greig), 1932
Faint with Pursuit (Bloom, as Burns), 1949
Fair Accuser (I. Preston), 1985
Fair Adventure (Ritchie), 1961
Fair and False (M. St John, as St John Cooper), 1920
Fair Company (Leslie), 1936
Fair Deal (Lorrimer, as Robins), 1952
Fair Game (Bishop), 1992
Fair Game (Tranter), 1950
Fair Horizon (K. Blair, as Brett), 1952
Fair Imposter (Garvice), 1909
Fair Invader (K. Blair), 1952
Fair Island (Hampson), 1972
Fair Kilmeny (M. Peters, as Black), 1972
Fair Maid of Kent (M. Peters), 1985
Fair Margaret (Haggard), 1907
Fair Prisoner (Bromige), 1960
Fair Rosamond (Wiat), 1985
Fair Shine the Day (S. Thorpe), 1964
Fair Shines the Day (Maddocks), 1952
Fair Stood the Wind (Oman, as Lenanton), 1930
Fair Tomorrow (Loring), 1931
Fair Wind of Love (Laker), 1974
Fair Young Phoenix (E. Pargeter), 1948
Fair Young Widow (Bowen, as Preedy), 1939
Fairer Than She (Chandos, as Charles), 1953
Fairest One of All (P. Hill), 1982
Fairies' Baby (s Goudge), 1919
Fairies on the Doorstep (L. Walker, as Sanders), 1948
Fairoaks (Yerby), 1957
Fairweather Friends! (M. St John, as St John Cooper), 1922
Fairweathers (Swan), 1913
Fairwinds (Stratton), 1974
Fairytales (Freeman), 1977
Faith, Hope, and Charity (Randall), 1954
Faithful Failure (Norway), 1968
Faithful Fool (Burgin), 1921
Faithful Traitor (Albanesi, as Rowlands), 1896
Faithful Type (E. Harrison), 1993
Faithless Dove (Bloom), 1945
Faithless One (Hoy), 1966

Falco, Marcus Didius series (Davis), from 1989
Falcon for a Queen (Gaskin), 1972
Falcon Gold (Ellerbeck, as Yorke), 1980
Falcon on the Hill (Lamb, as Holland), 1974
Falcon series (M. Peters, as Darby), from 1975
Falconhurst series (Horner, Onstott, Carter), from 1967
Falcon's Flight (Lorin, as Hohl), 1987
Falcon's Mistress (E. Darcy), 1988
Falcon's Prey (Jordan), 1981
Falcon's Shadow (Maybury, as Troy), 1964
Fall of a Nation (Dixon), 1911
Fall of Angels (Savage), 1971
Fall of Lucas Kendrick (Hooper), 1988
Fall of Midas (Lofts, as Astley), 1975
Fall River Line (Winston), 1983
Fallen Angel (Mather), 1978
Fallen Angels (Cornwell, as Kells), 1984
Fallen Idol (Way), 1984
Fallen Skies (Gregory), 1993
Fallen Woman (Hamilton, as Fitzgerald), 1981
Falling for Rachel (N. Roberts), 1993
Falling in Love (Lamb), 1993
Falling in Love Again (Lewty), 1988
Falling Star (Belle), 1990
Falling Stream (Chapman), 1954
Falls of Gard (Black), 1986
Falls the Shadow (Penman), 1988
False and the True (s Swan), 1898
False and True (Albanesi, as Rowlands)
False Colours (Heyer), 1963
False Faith (Albanesi, as Rowlands), 1911
False Morning (Norris), 1934
False Pretenses (Coulter), 1988
False Relations (Mackinlay), 1963
False Star (Duffield), 1939
Falstaff (Nye), 1976
Fame's Fetters (Mackinlay), 1931
Familiar Faces (s Rinehart), 1941
Familiar Stranger (Peake), 1973
Familiar Treatment (Peter), 1940
Families Are Such Fun (Chandos), 1952
Family (Ayres), 1928
Family (Glyn), 1919
Family! (Hurst), 1960
Family Affair (Lamb), 1974
Family Affair (Pilcher, as Fraser), 1958
Family Affair (Saxton), 1989
Family Affairs (Gaskin), 1980
Family Album (Steel), 1985
Family at Castle Trevissa (Marsh), 1979
Family at Redburn (Chappell), 1985
Family at the Farm (Chandos, as Lance), 1978
Family Chorus (Rayner), 1984
Family Favourites (Duggan), 1960
Family Feeling (Goodwin, as Ebel), 1973
Family Feeling (Saxton), 1986
Family Fortunes (Melville), 1984
Family Gathering (Cadell), 1979
Family Group (Bromige), 1958
Family Holiday (Robins, as Hamilton), 1937
Family Likeness (Gilbert), 1977
Family Man (Krentz), 1992
Family Name (Swan), 1942
Family of Jaspard (Ponsonby), 1950
Family of Strangers (Winston), 1983
Family Orchestra (M. Howard), 1945

Field of Honour (Nolan, as Rockfern), 1985
Field of Roses (P. Hastings), 1955
Field of the Forty Footsteps (P. Hastings), 1978
Field of Yesterday (Staples, as Stevens), 1983
Fielding's Folly (Keyes), 1940
Fields of Battle (Alexander), 1981
Fields of Heaven (Weale), 1974
Fierce Dispute (Santmyer), 1929
Fierce Eden (J. Blake), 1985
Fierce Encounter (Donnelly), 1983
Fiesta San Antonio (Dailey), 1977
Fifteen Streets (Cookson), 1952
Fifth Day of Christmas (Neels), 1971
Fifth Queen series (Ford), from 1906
Fight for Fight (Jordan), 1988
Fighting Man (Treece), 1960
Fighting Spirit (Albanesi, as Rowlands), 1930
Figs in Frost (Robins, as Hamilton), 1946
File on Devlin (Gaskin), 1965
Filigree of Fancy (May), 1990
Final Hour (Caldwell), 1944
Final Pattern (T. Barclay), 1990
Final Test (Burgin), 1928
Final Touch (Neels), 1991
Final Year (Rayner, as Brandon), 1962
Finch's Fortune (de la Roche), 1931
Find Another Eden (Chandos), 1953
Find Me a River (Giles), 1964
Find Out the Way (Burchell), 1946
Findernes' Flowers (Bowen, as Preedy), 1941
Finders Keepers (Browning), 1982
Fine Feathers (Albanesi, as Rowlands), 1928
Fine Feathers! (M. St John), 1914
Fine Silk Purse (Walsh), 1978
Fine Things (Steel), 1987
Finessing Clarissa (Chesney), 1989
Finger Prints (Delinsky), 1984
Finished (Haggard), 1917
Fiona (Gaskin), 1970
Fiona Macrae (Swan), 1929
Fire and Desire (Williams), 1985
Fire and Flesh (Riefe), 1978
Fire and Ice (Dailey), 1975
Fire and Ice (Palmer), 1983
Fire and Rain (Lowell), 1990
Fire and the Fury (Stratton), 1975
Fire and the Rope (Nicole, as York), 1979
Fire and the Rose (Bloom), 1977
Fire Brand (Palmer, as Kyle), 1989
Fire Down Below (Golding), 1989
Fire Down Below (Irwin), 1928
Fire Dragon (I. Roberts, as Carr), 1967
Fire from Heaven (Renault), 1969
Fire in the Ash (May), 1984
Fire in the Blood (Cartland), 1983
Fire in the Blood (Lamb), 1993
Fire in the Diamond (Lewty), 1976
Fire in the Heart (Rivers), 1987
Fire in the Rain (F. Preston), 1986
Fire in the Stubble (Orczy), 1912
Fire in the Wind (Sellers), 1982
Fire Is for Sharing (D. Smith), 1968
Fire Island (Wentworth), 1989
Fire Meets Fire (Hampson), 1976
Fire of Driftwood (s Broster), 1932
Fire of Love (Cartland), 1964

Fire of Spring (Lowell), 1986
Fire of Spring (Muskett), 1946
Fire of Youth (Pedler), 1930
Fire on the Snow (Cartland), 1975
Fire Opal (P. Hill), 1980
Fire over England (A. Mason), 1936
Fire People (Cordell), 1972
Fire Song (Gellis), 1984
Fire Still Burns (Heaven), 1989
Fire with Fire (Jordan), 1985
Fire Within (Pykare, as A. Coombs), 1978
Firebird (Hamilton, as Fitzgerald), 1983
Firebird (Stratton), 1975
Firedrake (Holland), 1966
Firefly Summer (Binchy), 1987
Fires in Smithfield (J. Lindsay), 1950
Fires in the Forest (Oliver, as Thorn), 1983
Fires of Brimstone (Gallagher), 1966
Fires of Eden (Lowell), 1986
Fires of Glenlochy (Heaven), 1976
Fires of the Heart (S. Blake), 1983
Fires of Winter (Gellis), 1987
Fires of Winter (Lindsey), 1980
Fires of Youth (Wynne), 1927
Fireship (Parkinson), 1975
First and Favourite Wife (Chandos), 1952
First and Last (Garvice), 1908
First, Best and Only (Delinsky), 1986
First Class (Nicole, as Gray), 1984
First Class, Lady? (Cartland), 1935
First-Class Male (Vitek), 1987
First Elizabeth (Bloom), 1953
First I Must Forget (Chandos, as Storm), 1951
First Impressions (N. Roberts), 1984
First Lady Brendon (Hichens), 1931
First Lady (Pizzey), 1986
First Long Kiss (Robins), 1953
First Love (Delafield), 1929
First Love—Last Love (Burchell), 1946
First Love, Last Love (Mortimer), 1981
First Love, Last Love (Saxton), 1992
First Love, Wild Love (Taylor), 1984
First Man In Rome (McCullough), 1990
First Night (Hodge), 1989
First Officer (Weale), 1980
First Rebel (Swanson), 1937
First Sir Percy (Orczy), 1920
First Snowdrop (Balogh), 1987
First the Blade (Dane), 1918
First, The Dream (Maybury), 1951
First Things First (Delinsky), 1985
First Things Last (Browning), 1984
First Time for Everything (Steele), 1990
First-Time of Asking (Chandos, as Tempest), 1954
First Wife (s Buck), 1933
First Year (Andrews), 1957
Fishy, Said the Admiral (Cadell), 1948
Fit for a King (Palmer), 1987
Five and Ten (Hurst), 1929
Five Farthings (Chappell), 1974
Five for Sorrow, Ten for Joy (Godden), 1979
Five Gold Rings (Wiat), 1983
Five-Hooded Cobra (Barcynska, as Sandys), 1932
Five Houses (Mackinlay), 1952
Five-Minute Marriage (Aiken), 1977
Five People (Bowen), 1925

Flowers from the Rock (Muskett), 1956
Flowers in Stony Places (Lewty), 1975
Flowers in the Grass (Hewlett), 1920
Flowers in the Rain (s Pilcher), 1991
Flowers in the Wind (K. Blair, as Conway), 1954
Flowers of Adonis (Sutcliff), 1969
Flowers of Chivalry (Tranter), 1988
Flowers of Eden (J. Smith), 1979
Flowers of Fire (S. Blake), 1977
Flowers of Fire (Burgin), 1908
Flowers of the Field (S. Harrison), 1980
Fludd (Mantel), 1989
Flute, Far and Near (Trask), 1929
Fly Beyond the Sunset (Hampson), 1978
Fly High, My Heart (Woodward, as Davis), 1972
Fly with My Love (Drummond, as Dawes), 1978
Flyers (McCutcheon), 1907
Flying Colours (Forester), 1938
Flying Dutchman (Arlen), 1939
Flying High (Wentworth), 1982
Flying Nurse (Bloom, as Burns), 1967
Flying Nurse (Woodward), 1979
Flying Squadron (Woodman), 1992
Flying Swans (Bloom), 1940
Flying Years (Niven), 1935
Flynn of the Inland (Idriess), 1932
Foes (M. Johnston), 1918
Foes of Freedom (Wynne), 1916
Fog (Gibbs, as Ford), 1933
Foggy, Foggy Dew (Blackstock), 1959
Follies (Thomas), 1983
Follies of the King (Plaidy), 1980
Follow a Shadow (Hampson), 1971
Follow a Shadow (Manners, as Marshall), 1974
Follow a Stranger (Lamb), 1973
Follow Me Down (Foote), 1950
Follow That Blonde (J. Smith), 1990
Follow the Drum (Saxton, as Turner), 1982
Follow the Shadow (Ayres), 1936
Follow the Wind (Taylor), 1990
Follow Your Dream (Greig, as Ames), 1957
Follow Your Heart (Loring), 1963
Follow Your Hearts (Maybury), 1955
Follow Your Love (Greig), 1959
Follow Your Star (L. Walker), 1963
Following of the Star (F. Barclay), 1911
Folly Bridge (D. Murray), 1945
Folly by Candlelight (Lamb, as Holland), 1978
Folly Island (Deeping), 1939
Folly of Eustace (s Hichens), 1896
Folly of Love (Woodward), 1979
Folly of Princes (Tranter), 1977
Folly's End (Leslie), 1944
Fond Adventures (s Hewlett), 1905
Fond Fancy (s Bowen), 1932
Food for Love (R. Lindsay), 1974
Food of Love (Mackinlay), 1960
Fool (Bailey), 1921
Fool and His Money (McCutcheon), 1913
Fool—Be Still (Hurst), 1964
Fool Beloved (Farnol), 1949
Fool Errant (Hewlett), 1905
Fool of the Family (Kennedy), 1930
Fool of Virtue (Mackinlay), 1964
Foolish Heart (Lorrimer, as Robins), 1956
Foolish Love (Marsh), 1982

Foolish Marriage (Ponsonby), 1952
Foolish Marriage (Swan), 1894
Foolish Virgin (Dixon), 1915
Foolish Virgin (Norris), 1928
Fool's Enchantment (Maddocks), 1968
Fool's Haven (M. Howard), 1954
Fools in Mortar (Leslie), 1928
Footfall in the Mist (M. Peters, as Black), 1971
Footlight Fever (Ruck), 1942
Footprints in the Sand (Weale), 1992
Footsteps in the Fog (Bennetts), 1979
Footsteps in the Park (Joseph), 1982
For a Dream's Sake (Chandos), 1949
For a Dream's Sake (Ritchie), 1965
For Adults Only (Lamb), 1984
For All Eternity (Cartland), 1981
For All Their Lives (F. Michaels), 1992
For All Time (Stanford), 1984
For All We Know (Stern), 1956
For All Your Life (Loring), 1952
For an Earldom (Garvice)
For Better, for Worse (Jordan), 1993
For Better for Worse (Saunders), 1988
For Bitter or Worse (Dailey), 1978
For Charles the Rover (Wynne), 1909
For Church and Chieftain (Wynne), 1909
For Ever and a Day (Albanesi, as Rowlands), 1911
For Ever and Ever (Burchell), 1956
For Ever True (Albanesi, as Rowlands), 1904
For Faith and Navarre (Wynne), 1904
For Her Lover's Sake (M. St John), 1918
For Her Only (Garvice), 1902
For Her to See (Bowen, as Shearing), 1947
For I Have Lived Today (Dwyer-Joyce), 1971
For Love (Ayres), 1918
For Love and Honor (Albanesi, as Rowlands)
For Love of a Doctor (Seifert), 1969
For Love of a Pagan (Hampson), 1978
For Love of Anne Lambert (Albanesi), 1910
For Love of Betty (Swan), 1928
For Love of Sigrid (Albanesi, as Rowlands), 1906
For Love of Speranza (Albanesi, as Rowlands), 1910
For Love of the King (Bloom, as Prole), 1960
For Love or Honor (Garvice, as Hart)
For Love or Lorenzo (Laffeaty), 1981
For Love's Sake Only (Chard), 1988
For Love's Sake Only (Hoy), 1951
For Lucy's Sake (s Swan), 1883
For Mike's Sake (Dailey), 1979
For My Great Folly (Costain), 1942
For My Sins (K. Blair, as Brett), 1966
For Now, Forever (N. Roberts), 1987
For One Night (Jordan), 1987
For One Sweet Grape (O'Brien), 1946
For the Cause (s Weyman), 1897
For the Love of a Stranger (Pizzey), 1993
For the Love of God (Dailey), 1981
For the Love of Lilah (N. Roberts), 1991
For the Love of Sami (F. Preston), 1984
For the Love of Sara (Mather), 1975
For the Record (Borden), 1950
For the Sake of the Family (s Swan), 1898
For Those in Love (Chandos, as Tempest), 1956
For What? (Cartland), 1930
Forbidden (Finch, as Robins), 1994
Forbidden (Lorrimer, as Robins), 1967

Forbidden (Lowell), 1993
Forbidden (Mather), 1976
Forbidden (Maybury), 1956
Forbidden (Robins), 1971
Forbidden Attraction (Peake), 1990
Forbidden Bride (Robins), 1926
Forbidden Ecstasy (Taylor), 1982
Forbidden Fiancé (Bloom, as Essex), 1957
Forbidden Fire (Lamb), 1979
Forbidden Fire (Pozzessere), 1991
Forbidden Flame (Mather), 1981
Forbidden Fruit (B. Hastings), 1987
Forbidden Fruit (Lamb), 1991
Forbidden Fruit (Pozzessere, as Graham), 1983
Forbidden Ground (Swanson), 1938
Forbidden Joy (Pykare, as N. Coombs), 1983
Forbidden Love (Courtney), 1980
Forbidden Love (R. Lindsay), 1977
Forbidden Love (Oliver, as Hunt), 1981
Forbidden Love (Robins), 1927
Forbidden Love (Seger), 1983
Forbidden Loving (Jordan), 1991
Forbidden Marriage (Libbey), 1888
Forbidden Music (s Deeping), 1929
Forbidden Music (s Frankau), 1929
Forbidden Rapture (MacLeod), 1941
Forbidden Rapture (Winspear), 1973
Forbidden Road (Albanesi), 1908
Forbidden Road (M. St John, as St John Cooper), 1931
Forbidden Surrender (Mortimer), 1982
Forbidden Valley (Summers), 1973
Force Field (Donnelly), 1987
Force of Feeling (Jordan), 1989
Forced Landing (Ruck), 1931
Forced to Marry (Cartland), 1987
Forefathers (Cato), 1982
Foreign Girl (Melville, as Betteridge), 1960
Foreign Parts (S. Harrison), 1992
Forerunners (Swan), 1930
Forest and the Fort (H. Allen), 1943
Forest Lovers (Hewlett), 1898
Forest Lure (Burgin), 1926
Forest of Fear (Manners, as Rundle), 1969
Forest of Stone (P. Hastings, as Mayfield), 1957
Forest of Terrible Things (Hull), 1939
Forest of the Night (Donnelly), 1978
Forests of the Night (S. Harrison), 1991
Forever (Lorrimer, as Robins), 1991
Forever (Pemberton), 1982
Forever Amber (Winsor), 1944
Forever and a Day (Loring), 1965
Forever Autumn (Bloom), 1979
Forever Dream (Johansen), 1985
Forever Ecstasy (Taylor), 1991
Forever in Your Embrace (Woodiwiss), 1992
Forever Instinct (Delinsky), 1985
Forever Kind (Sellers), 1984
Forever My Love (Brandewyne), 1982
Forever Spring (Lorin, as Hohl), 1988
Forever To-morrow (Duffield), 1946
Forge (Hall), 1924
Forget-Me-Not (Bowen, as Shearing), 1932
Forget Me Not (Lowell), 1984
Forget Not Ariadne (P. Hill), 1965
Forget That I Remember (Robins), 1940
Forget the Glory (Drummond), 1985

Forgive Me, My Love (Robins), 1947
Forgive Us Our Trespasses (L. Douglas), 1932
Forgiving (Spencer), 1991
Forgotten City (Cartland), 1936
Forgotten Dreams (I. Roberts, as Rowland), 1978
Forgotten Heir (Ponsonby), 1969
Forgotten Island (Hall, as Radclyffe-Hall), 1915
Forgotten Lover (Mortimer), 1982
Forgotten Marriage (R. Lindsay), 1978
Forgotten Passion (Jordan), 1983
Forgotten Smile (Kennedy), 1961
Forgotten Story (Graham), 1945
Form Line of Battle (Kent), 1969
Forsaking All Others (Loring), 1971
Forsaking All Others (Spencer), 1986
Fort (Jameson), 1942
Fort Everglades (Slaughter), 1951
Fort in the Jungle (Wren), 1936
Fortress (Gavin), 1964
Fortress (MacLeod), 1970
Fortress (Walpole), 1932
Fortress in the Forth (Lane), 1950
Fortunate Adventure (Ponsonby), 1971
Fortunate Belle (Sebastian, as Gladstone), 1978
Fortunate Mary (s E. Porter), 1928
Fortune at Stake (Oliver, as James), 1981
Fortune Hunter (Ayres), 1921
Fortune Hunters (Aiken), 1965
Fortune Hunters (s Williamson), 1923
Fortune in Romance (Greig), 1940
Fortune My Foe (Erskine-Lindop), 1947
Fortune of Bridget Malone (Lowndes), 1937
Fortune of War (O'Brian), 1979
Fortune Turns Her Wheel (Sheard), 1929
Fortune's Bride (Gellis), 1983
Fortune's Favourites (McCullough), 1993
Fortune's Flames (Taylor), 1988
Fortune's Fool (Sabatini), 1923
Fortune's Footballs (Burgin), 1897
Fortune's Knave (Lide, as Lomer), 1992
Fortune's Mistress (Napier), 1990
Fortunes of Casanova (s Sabatini), 1993
Fortunes of Garin (M. Johnston), 1915
Fortunes of Love (Courtney), 1980
Fortunes of Love (Steele), 1988
Fortunes of Richard Mahony series (Richardson), from 1917
Fortunes of Sally Luck (M. St John, as St John Cooper), 1925
Fortunes of the Farrells (Vaizey), 1907
Fortune's Slave (Mackinlay), 1975
Fortune's Smile (Roby), 1979
Fortune's Soldier (Lampitt), 1985
Fortune's Sport (Williamson, as A.M. Williamson), 1898
Fortune's Tide (Seger), 1990
Fortune's Whirlwind (Jakes), 1975
40 Acres and No Mule (Giles), 1952
Forty Is Beginning (Bloom, as Essex), 1952
Forward Pass (B. Hastings), 1986
Foul Matter (Aiken), 1983
Foundation of Delight (Weale), 1990
Founder of the House (Jacob), 1935
Founding Fathers (Duggan), 1959
Founding (Harrod-Eagles), 1980
Foundling (Heyer), 1948
Fountain of Roses (I. Roberts, as Rowland), 1966
Fountain of Youth (P. Hastings), 1959
Fountains of Paradise (Hunter), 1983

Four Days in June (Gibbs, as Ford), 1951
Four Doctors (Woodward, as Harley), 1960
Four Doctors, Four Wives (Seifert), 1975
Four Generations (Jacob), 1934
Four Graces (D. Stevenson), 1946
Four Swans 1795–1797 (Graham), 1976
Four Weeks in Venice (Sallis), 1978
Four Weeks in Winter (Donnelly), 1977
Four-Part Setting (Bridge), 1939
Four-Pools Mystery (Webster), 1908
Four-Poster (Wiat), 1979
1492 (M. Johnston), 1922
Fourteen Stories (s Buck), 1961
Fourteenth of October (Bryher), 1952
Fourth Cedar (Bloom), 1944
Fourth Chamber (Bowen, as Preedy), 1944
Fourth Mary (Cleeve), 1982
Fourth Queen (Paterson), 1926
Fox Farm (Deeping), 1911
Fox from His Lair (Cadell), 1965
Foxes of Harrow (Yerby), 1946
Foxfire (Seton), 1951
Foxfire Light (Dailey), 1982
Foxglove Country (Manley-Tucker, as Howard), 1977
Fractured Silence (Cowen), 1969
Fragile Years (Franken), 1952
Fragrant Flower (Cartland), 1976
Frail Sanctuary (Hilton), 1970
Frame of Dreams (Cartland), 1975
Frances Fights for Herself (Albanesi, as Rowlands), 1934
Frangipani (Weale), 1985
Franklin's Folly (Roby, as Grey), 1980
Fräulein Schmidt and Mr Anstruther (Arnim), 1907
Freckles (G. Porter), 1904
Freddy for Fun (Bloom, as Essex), 1943
Frederica (Heyer), 1965
Frederica in Fashion (Chesney), 1985
Free Fishers (J. Buchan), 1934
Free From Fear (Cartland), 1980
Free Spirit (Jordan), 1989
Free Spirit (F. Michaels), 1983
Free Traders (P. Hastings), 1984
Freebody Heiress (Gordon), 1974
Freebooters (Tranter), 1950
Freedom, Farewell! (Bentley), 1936
Freedom for Two (E. Pargeter, as Carr), 1939
Freedom Road (Fast), 1944
Freedom to Love (Mortimer), 1981
Freedom's Sword (Swan), 1886
Freer's Cove (Gordon), 1972
Freeways (Delmar), 1971
French Affair (Chesney), 1984
French Bride (Anthony), 1964
French Fortune (Gavin), 1991
French Girl in Love (Greig), 1963
French Husband (Gordon), 1977
French Inheritance (A. Stevenson), 1974
French Kiss (Nicole, as Logan), 1978
French Lieutenant's Woman (Fowles), 1969
French Revolution series (Dymoke), from 1979
French Silk (Brown), 1992
Frenchman (V. Johnston), 1976
Frenchman and the Lady (Cadell), 1952
Frenchman's Creek (du Maurier), 1941
Frenchwoman (Laker, as Paul), 1977
Frey and His Wife (Hewlett), 1916

Friday Spy (Nicole, as C R.Nicholson), 1980
Friday's Child (Heyer), 1944
Friedman, Belva series (Plain), from 1978
Friendly Air (Cadell), 1970
Friendly Persuasion (s West), 1945
Friends and Enemies (Alexander), 1981
Friends and Lovers (Palmer), 1983
Friendship Barrier (Jordan), 1984
Frightened Bride (Cartland), 1975
Frightened Heart (Greig, as Ames), 1952
Frightened Wife (s Rinehart), 1953
Fringe of Heaven (Bevan), 1978
Fringe of Leaves (White), 1976
Frivolous Cupid (s Hope), 1895
From a Distance (Richards), 1992
From Fairest Flowers (Chandos, as Charles), 1969
From Glowing Embers (Richards), 1987
From Hate to Love (Cartland), 1983
From Hell to Heaven (Cartland), 1981
From Here to a Star (Trask), 1941
From Mill to Mansion (M. St John), 1914
From Out the Vasty Deep (Lowndes), 1921
From Pillar to Post (M. St John), 1921
From Such a Seed (MacLeod, as Airlie), 1949
From the Housetops (McCutcheon), 1916
From the Memoirs of a Minister of France (Weyman), 1895
From the Snare of the Hunter (Lane), 1968
From the Vasty Deep (Lowndes), 1920
From This Day (N. Roberts), 1983
From This Day Forward (Ayres), 1934
From This Day Forward (Thane), 1941
From Want to Wealth (Garvice, as Hart)
From Worse Than Death (Garvice, as Hart)
Front Line (Andrews), 1990
Frontier (s Kantor), 1959
Frontier Passage (Bridge), 1942
Frost and the Fire (Bevan), 1973
Frost at Dawn (Mackinlay), 1968
Frost in the Sun (Lorrimer), 1986
Frost on the Rose (M. Peters), 1982
Frozen Enchantment (Steele), 1989
Frozen Fire (Lamb), 1980
Frozen Flame (O'Brian), 1953
Frozen Fountain (Maddocks), 1959
Frozen Heart (Donnelly), 1988
Frozen Jungle (Donnelly), 1981
Frozen Slippers (Williamson, as A.M. Williamson), 1930
Fruit of the Tree (Wharton), 1907
Fruit on the Bough (Bloom), 1931
Fruitful Vine (Hichens), 1911
Frustration (Lamb), 1979
Fugitive (Richards), 1990
Fugitive from Love (Cartland), 1978
Fugitive from Love (Chandos), 1950
Fugitive from Love (Woodward, as Richmond), 1980
Fugitive Romantic (Bloom, as Essex), 1960
Fugitive Wife (Craven), 1980
Fugue in Time (Godden), 1945
Fulfillment (Delinsky), 1988
Fulfillment (Spencer), 1979
Full Bloom (Krentz), 1988
Full Circle (K. Thorpe), 1978
Full Circle (Saxton), 1984
Full Circle (Steel), 1984
Full Flavour (Leslie), 1934
Full Fruit Flavour (Bloom, as Essex), 1949

Genevra (Alexander, as Langley), 1987
Gentian Hill (Goudge), 1949
Gentian series (Hamilton, as Watson), from 1986
Gentle Annie (Kantor), 1942
Gentle Awakening (Neels), 1987
Gentle Conquest (Balogh), 1987
Gentle Despot (Burgin), 1919
Gentle Feuding (Lindsey), 1984
Gentle Highwayman (Blackstock, as Allardyce), 1961
Gentle Obsession (Cowen), 1968
Gentle Pirates (Krentz, as Castle), 1980
Gentle Rogue (Lindsey), 1990
Gentle Sex (Blackstock, as Allardyce), 1974
Gentle Stranger (C. Allen), 1977
Gentle Tyrant (Ruck), 1949
Gentle Tyrant (Stratton, as Gillen), 1973
Gentle Wind (Ritchie), 1954
Gentleman (E. Marshall), 1956
Gentleman Adventurer (Bailey), 1914
Gentleman Anonymous (Lowndes), 1934
Gentleman Called James (Bloom, as Essex), 1951
Gentleman in Love (Cartland), 1979
Gentleman Insists (Lorin, as Hohl), 1989
Gentleman of Fortune (Bailey), 1907
Gentleman of France (Weyman), 1893
Gentleman Rogue (Blackstock, as Allardyce), 1975
Gentlemen Go By (Cadell), 1954
Gentlemen's Agreement (Hutten), 1936
Gentlewoman (James), 1940
Genuine Lies (N. Roberts), 1991
Georgian Rake (Ley), 1960
Georgian series (Plaidy), from 1967
Georgina (C. Darcy), 1971
Gerald and Elizabeth (D. Stevenson), 1969
Gerald Cranston's Lady (Frankau), 1924
Geste Family series (Wren), from 1926
Geste of Duke Jocelyn (Farnol), 1919
Get Ready for Battle (Jhabvala), 1962
Getting of Wisdom (Richardson), 1910
Ghost Flowers (Summerton), 1973
Ghost in Green Velvet (B. Michaels, as Peters), 1977
Ghost in Monte Carlo (Cartland), 1951
Ghost Kings (Haggard), 1908
Ghost of a Chance (Krentz), 1984
Ghost of Archie Gilroy (Blackstock, as Allardyce), 1970
Ghost of Fiddler's Hill (Bloom, as Essex), 1968
Ghost of June (Chandos, as Tempest), 1941
Ghost of Monsieur Scarron (J. Lewis), 1959
Ghost of the Past (Wentworth), 1991
Ghost Stories (s Arlen), 1927
Ghost That Haunted a King (Bloom, as Prole), 1963
Ghost Town (Blackstock), 1976
Ghost Who Fell in Love (Cartland), 1978
Ghosts (s Wharton), 1937
Ghosts of Fontenoy (Blackstock, as Keppel), 1981
Ghosts of Harrel (W. Roberts), 1971
Giant (Ferber), 1952
Giant in Chains (Bowen), 1938
Giant of Medabi (Dailey), 1978
Giants' Bread (Westmacott), 1930
Gibbet Fen (Dwyer-Joyce), 1984
Gideon's Fall (Browning, as Williams), 1991
Gift Beyond Price (Seger), 1983
Gift for a Lion (Craven), 1977
Gift for Pamela (Saxton, as Turner), 1981
Gift from the Grave (Wharton), 1900

Gift of Daisies (Balogh), 1989
Gift of Fire (Krentz), 1989
Gift of Gold (Krentz), 1988
Gift of Love (Woods), 1987
Gift of the Gods (Cartland), 1981
Gift of the Heart (Ritchie), 1955
Gifts of Love (C. Allen), 1978
Gifts of the Queen (Lide), 1985
Gigolo (s Ferber), 1922
Gilded Fleece (Tranter), 1942
Gilded Hoop (Muskett), 1941
Gilded Splendor (Laker), 1982
Gilded Spring (Seger, as Bates), 1983
Gilded Web (Balogh), 1989
Gildenford (Anand), 1977
Gilding the Lily (Richards), 1985
Gilian the Dreamer (Munro), 1899
Gillian (Yerby), 1960
Gilliane (Gellis), 1979
Gillyvors (Cookson), 1990
Gilt Cage (Steen), 1926
Gin and Bitters (Lane), 1945
Ginger Griffin (Bridge), 1934
Gingerbread House (Dwyer-Joyce), 1977
Ginger-Jar (Barcynska, as Sandys), 1926
Gingham Year (Norway), 1973
Ginny (Chesney, as Tremaine), 1980
Gipsy Actress (M. St John), 1923
Gipsy Born! (M. St John), 1922
Gipsy Count (Wynne), 1909
Gipsy Flower (Bloom), 1949
Gipsy King (Wynne), 1917
Gipsy Love (M. St John, as St John Cooper), 1923
Gipsy Lover (Bloom, as Harvey), 1973
Gipsy Schoolgirl (M. St John), 1922
Gipsy-Spelled (Wynne), 1929
Gipsy Vans Come Through (Bloom), 1936
Girl (Cookson), 1977
Girl About Town (Weale), 1965
Girl Alone (Peake), 1972
Girl Alone (L. Walker), 1973
Girl and Her Money (Greig), 1971
Girl at Cobalt Creek (Way), 1983
Girl at Golden Hawk (Winspear), 1974
Girl at Smuggler's Rest (Stratton, as Gillen), 1970
Girl at White Drift (K. Blair, as Brett), 1962
Girl Bewitched (Lewty), 1981
Girl by the Sea (Goodwin, as Ebel), 1974
Girl Called Ann (Randall), 1956
Girl Called Evelyn (Chandos, as Charles), 1959
Girl Crusoe (Hilton), 1969
Girl for a Millionaire (R. Lindsay, as Leigh), 1977
Girl for Sale (Grundy), 1920
Girl from Nowhere (Greig), 1936
Girl from Nowhere (Lamb), 1981
Girl from Paris (Aiken), 1982
Girl from Rome (Asquith), 1973
Girl from Storyville (Yerby), 1972
Girl from the Cotton Lane (Bowling), 1992
Girl from the Sea (Weale), 1979
Girl from the South (Garvice), 1910
Girl He Forsook (Libbey)
Girl in a Golden Bed (Weale), 1986
Girl in a White Hat (Stratton), 1977
Girl in Jeopardy (Greig), 1967
Girl in Love (Garvice), 1919

Girl in Love (Randall), 1961
Girl in Overalls (Seifert, as Ashley), 1943
Girl in the 'bacca Shop (s Garvice), 1920
Girl in the Blue Dress (Burchell), 1958
Girl in the Green Valley (Hoy), 1973
Girl in the Mauve Mini (Chandos, as Lance), 1979
Girl in the Secret (Williamson, as A.M. Williamson), 1934
Girl in White (Ellis), 1976
Girl Intern (Seifert), 1944
Girl Men Talked About (Greig), 1938
Girl Must Marry (Greig), 1931
Girl Named Rose (Neels), 1986
Girl Next Door (Ayres), 1919
Girl of His Choice (Mackinlay, as Grey), 1965
Girl of Spirit (Garvice), 1906
Girl of the Limberlost (G. Porter), 1909
Girl of the Passion Play (Williamson, as A.M. Williamson), 1911
Girl of the Prairie (M. St John), 1922
Girl on His Hands (Greig), 1939
Girl on the Beach (V. Johnston), 1987
Girl on the Make (Baldwin), 1932
Girl Outside (Melville, as Betteridge), 1971
Girl Possessed (Winspear), 1980
Girl to Love (Neels), 1982
Girl Upstairs (Wynne), 1932
Girl Who Got Out (Burgin), 1916
Girl Who Had Nothing (Williamson, as A.M. Williamson), 1905
Girl Who Loved Crippen (Bloom), 1955
Girl Who Married the Wrong Man! (M. St John), 1923
Girl Who Proposed! (Ruck), 1918
Girl Who Was Brave (Albanesi, as Rowlands), 1916
Girl Who Was Too Good-Looking (s Ruck), 1920
Girl Who Wasn't There (W. Roberts), 1957
Girl Who Wasn't Welcome (Greig), 1969
Girl with a Challenge (Burchell), 1965
Girl with a Heart (Albanesi, as Rowlands), 1911
Girl with a Million (Greig), 1945
Girl with Green Eyes (Neels), 1990
Girl with the Crystal Dove (Hardwick), 1985
Girl Without a Heart (s Garvice), 1912
Girl Without Credit (Greig), 1941
Girl Without Money (Greig), 1957
Girlie (s Bloom), 1904
Girls (Ellerbeck, as Thorne), 1967
Girls (Ferber), 1921
Girls at His Billet (Ruck), 1916
Girls from the Five Great Valleys (Savage), 1977
Girl's Good Name (M. St John), 1925
Girls in White (Randall), 1952
Girl's Kingdom (Albanesi, as Rowlands)
Giselle (Tresillian), 1988
Giuliano the Magnificent (J. Lindsay), 1940
Give All to Love (Lorrimer, as Robins), 1956
Give All to Love (Ritchie), 1971
Give All to Love (Veryan), 1987
Give All to Love (Woodward), 1982
Give Back Yesterday (Muskett), 1955
Give Her Gardenias (Chandos, as Tempest), 1953
Give Love the Air (Baldwin), 1947
Give Me Back My Dreams (Maybury), 1936
Give Me Back My Heart (Robins), 1944
Give Me My Youth (Trask), 1938
Give Me New Wings (Hoy), 1944
Give Me One Summer (Loring), 1936
Give Me the Daggers (Gavin), 1972
Give Me This Day (M. Lewis), 1964

Give Me Your Golden Hand (Eaton), 1951
Give Me Your Love (Worboys, as Eyre), 1975
Give Us This Day (Delderfield), 1973
Giving Him Up (Ayres), 1930
Glad Heart (Albanesi), 1910
Glad Summer (Farnol), 1951
Glade of Jewels (Hamilton, as Fitzgerald), 1989
Gladiola's Two Lovers (Libbey)
Glamorous Powers (Howatch), 1988
Glamour Girl (Price), 1937
Glasgow series (Stirling), from 1988
Glass and the Trumpet (Seifert), 1948
Glass-Blowers (du Maurier), 1963
Glass Castle (Winspear), 1973
Glass Flame (Whitney), 1978
Glass Heiress (Dwyer-Joyce), 1981
Glass Island (Clarke), 1978
Glass Palace (Gibbs), 1973
Glass Shoe (Hooper), 1989
Glass Slippers and Unicorns (Mortimer), 1986
Glass Virgin (Cookson), 1969
Gleam in the North (Broster), 1927
Gleam of Gold (T. Barclay), 1992
Glen, Elizabeth series (Swan), from 1895
Glen of Frost (M. Peters, as Grey), 1981
Glen of Sighs (Stratton, as Gillen), 1972
Glen o'Weeping (Bowen), 1907
Glendraco (Black), 1977
Glenrannoch (Randall), 1973
Glimpses of the Moon (Wharton), 1922
Glitter and the Gold (Chesney), 1993
Glitter-Dust (Dwyer-Joyce), 1978
Glittering Heights (Duffield), 1936
Glittering Images (Howatch), 1987
Glittering Lights (Cartland), 1974
Glorious Angel (Lindsey), 1982
Glorious Flames (Glyn), 1932
Glorious Morning (Ellis), 1982
Glory (Saxton), 1982
Glory and the Lightning (Caldwell), 1974
Glory Game (Dailey), 1985
Glory, Glory (Miller), 1990
Glory Road (Gavin), 1987
Glove Shop in Vienna (s Ibbotson), 1984
Go Ask the River (Eaton), 1969
Go Borrowing—Go Sorrowing (M. St John), 1924
Go In and Sink (Kent, as Reeman), 1973
Goal (Wynne), 1907
Goat Song (Yerby), 1967
Goblin Hill (Summers), 1977
God and Mr Aaronson (Barcynska), 1937
God and My Right (Duggan), 1955
God and the King (Bowen), 1911
God and the Wedding Dress (Bowen), 1938
God in the Car (Hope), 1894
God Is an Englishman (Delderfield), 1970
God Must Be Sad (Hurst), 1961
God of Clay (Bailey), 1908
God Within Him (Hichens), 1926
Goddess Abides (Buck), 1972
Goddess and the Gaiety Girl (Cartland), 1980
Goddess of Gray's Inn (Burgin), 1901
Goddess of Love (Cartland), 1987
Goddess of Mavisu (Stratton), 1975
Goddess of the Green Room (Plaidy), 1971
Gods Arrive (Wharton), 1932

Gods Forget (Cartland), 1939
God's Good Man (Corelli), 1904
God's Highlander (Thompson), 1989
Gods in Green (W. Roberts), 1973
God's Men (Buck), 1951
God's Playthings (s Bowen), 1912
God's Warrior (Slaughter), 1967
Godson (Dane), 1964
Going All the Way (Hufford), 1980
Going Home (Steel), 1973
Going Underground (van der Zee), 1982
Golconda Necklace (M. St John, as St John Cooper), 1926
Gold for Prince Charlie (Tranter), 1962
Gold for the Gay Masters (Robins, as Gray), 1954
Gold from Crete (s Forester), 1970
Gold in the Dust (Albanesi), 1929
Gold in the Gutter (Garvice), 1907
Gold Is the Sunrise (Hampson), 1971
Gold of Apollo (Lamb, as Holland), 1976
Gold of Noon (Summers), 1974
Gold Pennies (Franken), 1938
Gold Seekers (Stuart, as Long), 1985
Gold Slippers (Keyes), 1958
Golden Admiral (F. Mason), 1953
Golden Apollo (P. Hastings), 1958
Golden Apple Tree (s Sheard), 1920
Golden Bait (M. St John, as St John Cooper), 1928
Golden Barbarian (Johansen), 1992
Golden Bay (Bevan), 1987
Golden Bird (Mullins), 1987
Golden Bubbles (I. Roberts, as Rowland), 1976
Golden Butterfly (Burgh), 1990
Golden Butterfly (Williamson, as A.M. Williamson), 1926
Golden Cage (Bromige), 1950
Golden Cage (Cartland), 1986
Golden Captive (Saunders, as Innes), 1990
Golden Carpet (Williamson, as A.M. Williamson), 1931
Golden Chains (Saxton, as Arden), 1980
Golden Chance (Krentz), 1990
Golden Chariot (Wiat), 1979
Golden Chimera (Seger), 1985
Golden Chronicles series (Veryan), from 1985
Golden Collar (Cadell), 1969
Golden Cord (Deeping), 1935
Golden Cup (Plain), 1986
Golden Dawn (Albanesi, as Rowlands), 1912
Golden Days (D. Stevenson), 1934
Golden Destiny (Saunders), 1986
Golden Door (E. Scott), 1925
Golden Empire (Lowell, as A.E. Maxwell), 1979
Golden Fancy (J. Blake), 1979
Golden Fever (Mortimer), 1982
Golden Flame (Barcynska, as Sandys), 1961
Golden Flame (Bloom), 1941
Golden Flames (Hooper), 1988
Golden Fleece (Bailey), 1925
Golden Fleece (Graves), 1944
Golden Fleece (Lofts), 1944
Golden Flower! (I. Roberts, as Rowland), 1964
Golden Galatea (F. Stevenson), 1979
Golden Garden (Greig), 1968
Golden Girl (Nicole, as Gray), 1992
Golden Girls (Rhodes), 1988
Golden Goat (Byrne), 1930
Golden God (Saunders, as Innes), 1975
Golden Goddess (Krentz, as James), 1985

Golden Goddess (Nicole, as Grange), 1973
Golden Gondola (Cartland), 1958
Golden Greek (Wentworth), 1991
Golden Griffin (Clarke, as Honeyman), 1976
Golden Gypsy (Oliver, as James), 1978
Golden Harvest (Muskett), 1944
Golden Hawk (Yerby), 1948
Golden Horizons (Duffield), 1935
Golden Illusion (Cartland), 1976
Golden Interlude (I. Roberts, as Carr), 1970
Golden Isle (Slaughter), 1947
Golden Lasso (F. Michaels), 1980
Golden Lion (Haines), 1986
Golden Madonna (Stratton), 1973
Golden Mask (Donald), 1992
Golden Moments (Steel), 1980
Golden Mountain (Lowell, as Sun), 1990
Golden Ocean (O'Brian), 1956
Golden Ones (Slaughter, as C.V. Terry), 1955
Golden Pagoda (I. Roberts), 1972
Golden Panther (S. Thorpe), 1956
Golden Paradise (S. Johnson), 1990
Golden Parakeet (Marsh), 1986
Golden Penny (Burgin), 1937
Golden Promises (Saxton, as Arden), 1981
Golden Puma (Way), 1980
Golden Rain (I. Roberts, as Harle), 1964
Golden Road (Montgomery), 1913
Golden Roof (Bowen), 1928
Golden Rose (K. Blair), 1959
Golden Shoestring (Baldwin), 1949
Golden Silence (Williamson), 1910
Golden Skylark (s Goudge), 1941
Golden Snail (s Barcynska), 1927
Golden Songbird (Walsh), 1975
Golden Spaniard (Stratton), 1982
Golden Strangers (Treece), 1956
Golden Straw (Cookson), 1993
Golden Stud (Horner, Onstott), 1975
Golden Summer (Bromige), 1972
Golden Summer (Duffield), 1954
Golden Surrender (Pozzessere, as Graham), 1985
Golden Tally (Oldfield), 1985
Golden Threads (Hooper), 1989
Golden Tide (Stanford), 1980
Golden Torment (Taylor), 1984
Golden Touch (London, as James), 1982
Golden Triangle (I. Roberts, as Rowland), 1978
Golden Tulip (Laker), 1991
Golden Unicorn (Whitney), 1976
Golden Urchin (Brent), 1986
Golden Valkyrie (Johansen), 1984
Golden Valley (Winston), 1975
Golden Venture (Bloom), 1938
Golden Violet (Bowen, as Shearing), 1936
Golden Years (Hardwick), 1976
Goldhayes series (Belle), from 1983
Goldsmith's Row (Bishop), 1969
Goldsmith's Wife (Plaidy), 1950
Gollantz series (Jacob), from 1935
Gone (s Godden), 1968
Gone-Away Man (L. Walker), 1969
Gone Before Morning (Peake), 1973
Gone with the Wind (Mitchell), 1936
Good Behaviour (Keane), 1981
Good Confession (Savage), 1975

Good Duke Humphrey (Clarke, as Honeyman), 1973
Good Earth (Buck), 1931
Good Gestes (s Wren), 1929
Good Gracious, Marian! (M. St John), 1919
Good Ground (T. Barclay), 1984
Good Man's Love (Delafield), 1932
Good Morning, Doctor Houston (Stratton, as Gillen), 1969
Good Old Anna (Lowndes), 1915
Good Out of Evil (s Swan), 1899
Good Provider (Stirling), 1988
Good Sport (Greig, as Ames), 1934
Good Time Man (Richards), 1986
Good Venture (L. Cooper), 1928
Good Woman (Bromfield), 1927
Goodbye, Johnny (Norway), 1962
Goodbye, My Love (Maybury), 1952
Gooding Girl (Oldfield), 1985
Gorgeous Brute (Barcynska), 1949
Gorgeous Lover (s Bowen), 1929
Goring's Girl (Wynne), 1914
Gospel Fever (Slaughter), 1980
Goss Boys (Kantor), 1958
Gossamer Cord (Plaidy, as Carr), 1992
Gossamer Dream (Bloom), 1931
Gossip (Duffield), 1938
Gossip from the Forest (Keneally), 1975
Governess (P. Hill), 1985
Governor of England (Bowen), 1913
Governor's Lady (Raddall), 1960
Gower Street (Rayner), 1973
Grace Latouche and the Warringtons (s Bowen), 1931
Gracious Lady (Bloom), 1955
Gracious Lady (Mortimer), 1993
Grady, Emma series (Cox), from 1987
Grafton Girls (M. Howard), 1956
Graham, Davina series (Anthony), from 1981
Grain of Gold (May), 1971
Granada Window (Steen), 1949
Grand (Trask), 1951
Grand-Chain (Stern), 1917
Grand Duchess (Duffield), 1954
Grand Man (Cookson), 1954
Grand Passion (Krentz), 1994
Grand Relations (Greig), 1940
Grand Sophy (Heyer), 1950
Grandmère (Delmar), 1967
Grandmother and the Priests (Caldwell), 1963
Grandmother's Child (Swan), 1882
Granite Man (Lowell), 1991
Grannie's Little Girl (Swan), 1925
Grasp a Nettle (Neels), 1977
Grass Crown (McCullough), 1991
Graustark series (McCutcheon), from 1901
Grave of Green Water (Summerton, as Roffman), 1968
Grave of Truth (Anthony), 1980
Graveyard Watch (Shellabarger, as Esteven), 1938
Great Adventure (Giles), 1966
Great Alone (Dailey), 1986
Great Amulet (Diver), 1908
Great Beginning (Bloom), 1924
Great Black Oxen (Jacob), 1962
Great Boomerang (Idriess), 1941
Great Captains (Treece), 1956
Great Day (Seifert), 1939
Great Fright (Macbeth), 1929
Great House (Weyman), 1919

Great Husband Hunt (Grundy), 1922
Great Laughter (Hurst), 1936
Great Lion of God (Caldwell), 1970
Great Maria (Holland), 1974
Great Meadow (E. Roberts), 1930
Great Miss Driver (Hope), 1908
Great Mistake (Rinehart), 1940
Great Moment (Glyn), 1923
Great Moments in Aviation (Winterson), 1994
Great Oak (J. Lindsay), 1957
Great Pearl Secret (Williamson), 1921
Great Possessions (Alexander), 1989
Great Roxhythe (Heyer), 1922
Great Shadow (Doyle), 1892
Great Smith (E. Marshall), 1943
Great Son (Ferber), 1945
Great Tradition (Keyes), 1939
Great Unmet (s Ruck), 1918
Great Valley (M. Johnston), 1926
Greater Courage (Pedler), 1933
Greater Freedom (Swan), 1938
Greater Gain (Burgin), 1917
Greater Inclination (s Wharton), 1899
Greater Love (Swan, as Lyall), 1898
Greater Love (Woodward, as Richmond), 1961
Greater Than All (Robins), 1946
Greatest Enemy (Kent, as Reeman), 1970
Greatest Nurse of Them All (Bloom, as Prole), 1968
Greatheart (Dell), 1918
Grecian Rhapsody (Duffield), 1938
Greek Island Magic (Bevan), 1983
Greek Treasure (Stone), 1975
Greek Wedding (Hodge), 1970
Green Apple Burning (M. Peters), 1993
Green Apple Love (D. Smith), 1974
Green Bay Tree (Bromfield), 1924
Green Beetle (Gibbs, as Ford), 1972
Green Bough (Ritchie), 1953
Green Branch (E. Pargeter), 1962
Green Caravan (Barcynska, as Sandys), 1922
Green Carnation (Hichens), 1894
Green City in the Sun (B. Wood), 1988
Green Country (Albanesi), 1927
Green Darkness (Seton), 1972
Green Dolphin Country (Goudge), 1944
Green Dolphin Street (Goudge), 1944
Green Dragon, White Tiger (Motley), 1986
Green Empress (Cadell), 1958
Green Fancy (McCutcheon), 1917
Green Fire (Krentz, as James), 1986
Green Fire (Maybury), 1963
Green Gauntlet (Delderfield), 1968
Green Glass Moon (Manners, as Lamont), 1970
Green Grass (Maddocks), 1963
Green Grows the Vine (Cato), 1960
Green Harvest (Oldfield), 1983
Green Hat (Arlen), 1924
Green Judgment (Pedler), 1934
Green Leaves (K. Blair, as Brett), 1947
Green Light (L. Douglas), 1935
Green Light (Norway, as Norton), 1963
Green Lightning (Mather), 1983
Green Limelight (Mackinlay), 1943
Green Man (Jameson), 1952
Green Man (Treece), 1966
Green Money (D. Stevenson), 1939

Green Mountain Man (Dailey), 1978
Green Patch (Hutten), 1910
Green, Polly series (M. St John), from 1909
Green Rushes (MacLeod, as Airlie), 1953
Green Salamander (P. Hill), 1977
Green Valleys (Albanesi, as Rowlands), 1932
Green Vista (James), 1963
Greengage Summer (Godden), 1958
Greengirl (M. Peters, as Black), 1979
Greenwood, Alice series (Barr), from 1981
Greenwood Shady (Cadell), 1951
Gregg Barratt's Woman (Peake), 1981
Gresham Ghost (W. Roberts), 1980
Gretna Bride (O. Sinclair, as Daniels), 1986
Grey Beginning (B. Michaels), 1984
Grey Family series (Wiat), from 1983
Grey Ghyll (Manners, as Rundle), 1978
Grey Goose Wing (Wiat), 1986
Greygallows (B. Michaels), 1972
Greys series (M. Peters), from 1969
Grief Before Night (Shellabarger, as Loring), 1938
Griffin's Way (Yerby), 1962
Grizel Married (Vaizey), 1914
Groping (Jacob), 1933
Grotto of Jade (Hilton), 1967
Grove of Eagles (Graham), 1963
Grove of Olives (Goodwin, as Ebel), 1976
Grow Up, Little Lady! (Chandos, as Tempest), 1937
Growing Season (Lamb, as Holland) , 1975
Growth of a Man (de la Roche), 1938
Guarded Halo (Pedler), 1929
Guarded Heart (Donald), 1983
Guardian (Gibbs), 1958
Guardian at the Gate (Shoesmith), 1979
Guardian of the Heart (Courtney), 1979
Guardian of the Trees (Woodward, as Richmond), 1982
Gudrid the Fair (Hewlett), 1918
Guernsey Man (Parkinson), 1982
Guests of Hercules (Williamson), 1912
Guillotine (Nicole, as Logan), 1976
Guilt's Pavilions (Mackinlay), 1951
Guilty Love (Lamb), 1994
Guilty Secret (Pemberton), 1979
Guinea Stamp (Ley), 1961
Guinea Stamp (Swan), 1892
Guinever's Gift (N. St John), 1977
Guinevere's Lover (Glyn), 1913
Gull Haven (I. Roberts), 1971
Gun (Forester), 1933
Guns for Rebellion (F. Mason), 1977
Guns of Arrest (McCutchan), 1976
Guns to the Far East (Stuart, as V.A. Stuart), 1975
Gun-Toter (s Kantor), 1963
Gus and the Nice Lady (Browning), 1992
Guy Mervyn (F. Barclay, as Roy), 1891
Guyfford of Weare, (Farnol), 1928
Gwenda (Grundy), 1910
Gwendolen (C. Darcy), 1978
Gwennola (Wynne), 1926
Gyfford of Weare (Farnol), 1928
Gypsy (Mortimer), 1985
Gypsy Flame (Bloom), 1979
Gypsy, Gypsy (Godden), 1940
Gypsy Heiress (London), 1981
Gypsy Julie (O. Sinclair), 1979
Gypsy Lady (Busbee), 1977

Gypsy Lover (Robins), 1939
Gypsy Magic (Cartland), 1983
Gypsy Sixpence (E. Marshall), 1949

Habsburg series (Hamilton), from 1977
Had We Never Loved (Veryan), 1991
Hagar (M. Johnston), 1913
Hagen series (Hooper), from 1987
Haggard series (Nicole), from 1980
Hail! All Hail! (James), 1929
Hail the Conquering Hero (Yerby), 1977
Haircut for Samson (Bloom, as Essex), 1940
Halcyone (Glyn), 1912
Haldanes (Stirling, as Crosby), 1992
Half a Hero (Hope), 1893
Half a World Away (Bevan), 1980
Half-Enchanted (Goodwin, as Ebel), 1964
Half Moon (Ford), 1909
Half Open Door (Albanesi), 1934
Half Portions (s Ferber), 1920
Halfhyde, Lieutenant St Vincent series (McCutchan), from 1974
Half-Past Kissing Time (Ruck), 1936
Halfway House (Hewlett), 1908
Half-way to the Moon (Pilcher, as Fraser), 1949
Halfway to the Stars (Donnelly), 1971
Hallelujah (Hurst), 1944
Halliday Girls (Oldfield), 1991
Halo (Hutten), 1907
Halo for the Devil (Cartland), 1972
Hamilton series (Cookson), from 1983
Hamlet (Wynne), 1930
Hammer and the Sword (Wiat), 1992
Hammer for Princes (Holland), 1972
Hammer of the Scots (Plaidy), 1981
Hammersleigh (Ellerbeck), 1976
Hampton series (Ellis), from 1978
Hand of Fate (Albanesi, as Rowlands), 1914
Hand Painted (Barcynska), 1925
Handful of Dreams (Pozzessere, as Graham), 1986
Handful of Shells (MacLeod), 1993
Handful of Silver (Hunter, as Chace), 1968
Handful of Stars (I. Roberts), 1967
Handful of Stars (Stratton, as Gillen), 1973
Hand-Made Gentleman (Bacheller), 1909
Handmaid to Fame (Ruck), 1938
Hands Across the Sea (Swan), 1919
Hands of Death (Winston), 1982
Hands of Healing (D. Murray), 1961
Hands of Veronica (Hurst), 1947
Handsome Engineer's Flirtation (Libbey)
Handsome Road (Bristow), 1938
Hang My Wreath (F. Mason, as Weaver), 1941
Hanging Woman (Summerton, as Roffman), 1965
Hangman's Beach (Raddall), 1966
Hangman's House (Byrne), 1926
Hannah (Neels), 1980
Hannah Fowler (Giles), 1956
Hannah Massey (Cookson), 1964
Hannah's Gate (Winston), 1992
Hannibal Takes a Hand (J. Lindsay), 1941
Hanrahan's Colony (Stubbs), 1964
Haphazard House (Wesley), 1983
Happily Ever After (Seger), 1987
Happiness Stone (Barcynska, as Sandys), 1956
Happy Christmas (s du Maurier), 1940
Happy Day (Barcynska, as Sandys), 1934

Happy Ending (Savage), 1972
Happy Endings (s Ayres), 1935
Happy Fortress (Bromige), 1978
Happy-Go-Lucky Lotty (Libbey)
Happy Harvest (Farnol), 1939
Happy Hearts (Barcynska, as Sandys), 1962
Happy Highways (Jameson), 1920
Happy House (Hutten), 1919
Happy Is the Wooing (Chandos, as Tempest), 1952
Happy Island (Greig, as Ames), 1964
Happy Man (P. Hastings), 1958
Happy Meeting (Neels), 1992
Happy Mummers (Barcynska, as Sandys), 1937
Happy Now I Go (Chandos, as Charles), 1947
Happy Return (Forester), 1937
Happy To-Morrow (Muskett), 1938
Happy Valley (Nicole), 1989
Happy with Either (Chandos, as Tempest), 1946
Harbin's Ridge (Giles), 1951
Harbour Hill (Saxton, as Turner), 1991
Harbour Lights (Duffield), 1953
Harbour of Love (Hampson), 1977
Hard-Hearted Doctor (Bloom, as Essex), 1964
Hard Man (Jordan), 1985
Hard to Get (Mortimer), 1984
Hard to Handle (Appignanesi, as Ayre), 1983
Hard to Handle (B. Hastings), 1985
Hard Way (Robins), 1949
Hardie series (Melville), from 1987
Hark to Rover! (L. Cooper), 1933
Harlot (Pemberton), 1981
Harlot's Daughter (P. Hastings), 1967
Harness the Winds (Maybury), 1934
Harnessing Peacocks (Wesley), 1985
Harold (Cookson), 1985
Harold of the English (Clarke, as Honeyman), 1979
Harpoon in Eden (F. Mason), 1969
Harps in the Wind (Hichens), 1945
Harriet (J. Cooper), 1976
Harriet and the Piper (Norris), 1920
Harriet Mannering's Paying Guests (Vaizey), 1917
Harrogate Secret (Cookson), 1988
Harry the King (Clarke, as Honeyman), 1971
Harry's Last Love (Bloom, as Prole), 1958
Harsh Heritage (Tranter), 1939
Harte series (Bradford), from 1979
Harvest (Plain), 1990
Harvest-Home Come Sunday (Bloom), 1962
Harvest of a House (Bloom), 1935
Harvest of Hope (Baldwin), 1962
Harvest of the Sun (Thompson), 1978
Harvest of Thorns (T. Barclay), 1983
Harvester (G. Porter), 1911
Harvesting (Bacheller), 1934
Haste to the Wedding (D. Smith), 1974
Hasting Day (Chappell), 1970
Hasty Marriage (Neels), 1977
Hate Begins at Home (Aiken), 1967
Hate That Lasts (Burgin), 1925
Hatfield and McCoy (Pozzessere), 1993
Hatful of Cowslips (Ritchie), 1960
Hatshepsut, Queen of the Nile (I. Roberts, as I. R. Roberts), 1976
Haunted (Cartland), 1986
Haunted (Lamb), 1983
Haunted by the Past (Chard), 1982
Haunted Headsman (Bloom, as Prole), 1965

Haunted Heart (Cartland), 1990
Haunted House (Lofts), 1978
Haunted Lady (Rinehart), 1942
Haunted Landscape (Bromige), 1976
Haunted Life (Garvice, as Hart)
Haunted Light (Price), 1933
Haunted Love (Woodward, as Richmond), 1980
Haunted Sisters (Plaidy), 1966
Haunted Vintage (Bowen), 1921
Haunting Cavalier (Thum), 1974
Haunting Compulsion (Mather), 1981
Haunting Me (Blackstock, as Allardyce), 1978
Haunting of Gad's Hall (Lofts), 1979
Haunting of Helen Farley (Cowen), 1976
Haunting of Lamb House (Aiken), 1991
Haunting of Sara Lessingham (Bennetts, as James), 1978
Haunting Stranger (Laffeaty), 1985
Hauntings (s Lofts), 1975
Have Courage, My Heart (M. Howard), 1943
Haven of Fear (J. Blake, as Ponder), 1977
Haversham Legacy (Winston), 1974
Having Faith (Delinsky), 1990
Hawaii (Michener), 1959
Hawk and the Dove (Hampson), 1970
Hawk and the Honey (Browning), 1984
Hawk and the Lamb (Napier), 1993
Hawk in a Blue Sky (Lamb), 1977
Hawk of Venice (Wentworth), 1985
Hawk O'Toole's Hostage (Brown), 1988
Hawks Barton (I. Roberts), 1979
Hawk's Head (Chandos, as Lance), 1981
Hawks of Sedgemont (Lide), 1988
Hawk's Prey (Mortimer), 1987
Hawksmoor (Ackroyd), 1985
Haymaker (Cadell), 1972
Haymarket (Rayner), 1974
Hazard of Hearts (Cartland), 1949
Hazard, Philip series (Stuart, as V.A. Stuart), from 1973
Hazards of Belinda (Cleugh), 1933
Hazards of the Heart (Browning), 1993
Hazel of Heatherland (Grundy), 1906
Hazell & Sons, Brewers (Swan), 1888
He and Hecuba (Hutten), 1905
He Brings Great News (Dane), 1944
He Couldn't Take Money! (M. St John), 1923
He Is Mine (Lorrimer, as Robins), 1957
He Learned about Women (Ruck), 1940
He Loved but Was Lured Away (Libbey), 1891
He Loves Me, He Loves Me Not (Garvice), 1911
He Married a Doctor (Baldwin), 1944
He Married a Mill-Lass (M. St John), 1924
He Married His Parlourmaid (Barcynska), 1929
He Shall Not Marry a Mill-Lass! (M. St John), 1929
He Stooped to Conquer (Lane), 1943
He Travels Alone (Shellabarger), 1939
'Head' of the Family (M. St John, as St John Cooper), 1923
Head of the House (Swan), 1938
Headhunters of the Coral Sea (Idriess), 1941
Healer (Slaughter), 1955
Healing Hands (R. Lindsay), 1955
Healing Hands (Seifert), 1942
Healing Time (Andrews), 1969
Health unto His Majesty (Plaidy), 1956
Heart Appeal (Greig), 1934
Heart Cannot Forget (Burchell), 1953
Heart for Heart (Garvice)

Heart for Sale (Albanesi), 1929
Heart Has Wings (Baldwin), 1937
Heart, Have You No Wisdom? (Hoy), 1962
Heart in Darkness (Greig, as Ames), 1947
Heart in Hiding (Rivers), 1984
Heart in Pilgrimage (Eaton), 1948
Heart in the Sand (Ponsonby), 1970
Heart in the Sunlight (Peake), 1975
Heart Is Broken (Cartland), 1977
Heart Is Never Fair (Maybury), 1954
Heart Is Stolen (Cartland), 1980
Heart Knows Best (Stanford), 1984
Heart Line (Albanesi, as Rowlands), 1936
Heart Listens (Van Slyke), 1973
Heart Must Choose (Burchell), 1953
Heart Must Pause (Laffeaty), 1969
Heart of a Maid (Garvice), 1910
Heart of a Rose (R. Lindsay), 1961
Heart of a Stranger (Laffeaty), 1970
Heart of a Woman (Albanesi, as Rowlands), 1913
Heart of a Woman (Orczy), 1911
Heart of Angela Brent (Albanesi, as Rowlands), 1917
Heart of Fancy (Williams), 1990
Heart of Fire (L. Howard), 1993
Heart of Flame (M. Peters, as Darby), 1986
Heart of Gold (Stanford), 1988
Heart of Hetta (Albanesi, as Rowlands), 1900
Heart of His Heart (Albanesi), 1911
Heart of Honour (Courtney), 1980
Heart of Ice (Palmer), 1984
Heart of Little Shikara (s Marshall), 1922
Heart of Marble (Buckingham), 1967
Heart of Paris (Robins), 1951
Heart of Penelope (Lowndes), 1904
Heart of Princess Osra (s Hope), 1896
Heart of Rachael (Norris), 1916
Heart of Stone (Dailey), 1980
Heart of the Clan (Cartland), 1981
Heart of the Continent (Cato), 1989
Heart of the Eagle (McKenna), 1986
Heart of the Family (Goudge), 1953
Heart of the House (Jacob), 1951
Heart of the Lion (R. Lindsay, as Leigh), 1975
Heart of the Lion (Plaidy), 1977
Heart of the Matter (Armstrong), 1987
Heart of the Night (Delinsky), 1989
Heart of the Outback (E. Darcy), 1993
Heart of the Tiger (McKenna), 1988
Heart of the World (Haggard), 1895
Heart of Thunder (Lindsey), 1983
Heart of Una Sackville (Vaizey), 1907
Heart of War (Masters), 1980
Heart on Fire (Lamb), 1991
Heart Remembers (Baldwin), 1941
Heart Remembers (Hoy), 1946
Heart So Wild (Lindsey), 1986
Heart Speaks in Many Ways (Polland), 1982
Heart Speaks (Spencer), 1986
Heart Surgeon (Bloom, as Essex), 1971
Heart, Take Care! (Hoy), 1940
Heart Too Proud (London), 1978
Heart Triumphant (Cartland), 1976
Heart Turns Homeward (Ritchie), 1953
Heartbeat (Steel), 1991
Heartbreak for Two (Greig), 1942
Heartbreak Marriage (Ayres), 1929

Heartbreak Surgeon (Bloom, as Burns), 1963
Heartbreaker (L. Howard), 1987
Heartbreaker (Lamb), 1981
Heartbroken Melody (Norris), 1938
Hearth and the Eagle (Seton), 1948
Heartland (Brandewyne), 1990
Heartland (Woods), 1989
Heart's Afire (Plaidy, as Burford), 1954
Hearts Aflame (Lindsey), 1987
Hearts and Sweethearts (Albanesi), 1916
Hearts at Random (Hoy), 1942
Hearts at War (Albanesi, as Rowlands), 1913
Hearts by the Tower (O. Sinclair), 1968
Hearts Come Home (s Buck), 1962
Heart's Desire (Lorrimer, as Robins), 1953
Heart's Desire (Robins), 1946
Heart's Desires (C. Allen, as Marlowe), 1991
Hearts Divided (Rivers), 1983
Hearts Do Not Break (I. Preston), 1964
Hearts for Gold (Barcynska), 1938
Heart's Haven (Hoy), 1945
Hearts of Fire (Garvice, as Hart)
Hearts of Gold (Stirling), 1987
Hearts or Diamonds (Courtney), 1985
Heart's Triumph (Albanesi, as Rowlands), 1912
Heart's Victory (N. Roberts), 1982
Heartsease Grows Here (Ritchie), 1962
Heartsongs (Seger, as Winslow), 1984
Heat and Dust (Jhabvala), 1975
Heat of the Moment (Armstrong), 1988
Heat of the Night (Lamb), 1986
Heat Wave (Robins), 1930
Heather Blazing (O'Faolain), 1992
Heather Moon (Williamson), 1912
Heatherbloom (MacLeod), 1940
Heatherleigh (Summers), 1963
Heather's Song (Palmer), 1982
Heatherton Heritage (P. Hill), 1976
Heatwave (Delinsky), 1987
Heaven and Hell (Jakes), 1987
Heaven Here on Earth (Mortimer), 1983
Heaven in Hong Kong (Cartland), 1990
Heaven in Our Hearts (Lorrimer, as Robins), 1954
Heaven in Your Hand (s Lofts), 1958
Heaven Is Gentle (Neels), 1975
Heaven Is Here (L. Walker), 1957
Heaven Is High (Hampson), 1970
Heaven Isn't Here (Greig), 1941
Heaven Lies Ahead (Bloom, as Sloane), 1951
Heaven Round the Corner (Neels), 1981
Heaven Tree (E. Pargeter), 1960
Heaven Trees (Young), 1926
Heaven's My Destination (Wilder), 1934
Heaven's Price (Brown), 1983
Heavy Clay (Robins), 1929
Heel of Achilles (Delafield), 1921
Hegerty, M.D. (Seifert), 1966
Heir of Allington (Wiat), 1973
Heir of Vering (Garvice), 1902
Heir to Glen Ghyll (Stratton, as Gillen), 1970
Heir to Holtwood (Ponsonby), 1975
Heir to Rowanlea (Oliver, as James), 1981
Heir to Windrush Hill (Summers), 1966
Heiress (Anthony), 1964
Heiress (Dailey), 1987
Heiress of Cameron Hall (Libbey), 1889

Heiress of Frascati (Bowen, as Shearing), 1966
Heiress series (Gellis), from 1980
Heiress to the Isle (Chandos, as Lance), 1987
Heirs of Love (B. Johnson), 1980
Heirs of Polyrayne (Laffeaty), 1983
Heirs of Squire Harry (Lane), 1974
Helen (Heyer), 1928
Helena's Path (Hope), 1907
Helga in Hiding (Cartland), 1986
He'll Never Marry You! (M. St John), 1927
Hell or High Water (Mather), 1979
Hell! Said the Duchess (Arlen), 1934
Hell-Cat and the King (Cartland), 1977
Hellfire Heritage (W. Roberts), 1979
Hellion (Spencer), 1984
Hell-Raiser (Schulze), 1993
Help from the Heart (Cartland), 1984
Helping Hersey (s Hutten), 1914
Helpmate (M. Sinclair), 1907
Henrietta (Chesney, as Fairfax), 1979
Henrietta's Own Castle (Neels), 1975
Henry I series (Dymoke), from 1970
Henry of Navarre (Wynne, as Knowles), 1908
Henry of the High Rock (Dymoke), 1971
Henry the Ninth (Browning), 1987
Henry VIII and His Six Wives (M. Peters), 1972
Henry's Golden Queen (Bloom, as Prole), 1964
Hepburn (Westcott), 1950
Hepburn's Quay (Stratton, as Gillen), 1979
Her Brother's Keeper (Pedler), 1924
Her Dancing Partner (MacGill), 1926
Her Father's Daughter (G. Porter), 1921
Her Father's Sin (M. St John), 1908
Her Father's Sins (Cox), 1987
Her Father's Wish (Albanesi, as Rowlands), 1937
Her French Husband (P. Hastings), 1956
Her Golden Secret (Albanesi, as Rowlands)
Her Grace's Passion (Chesney), 1992
Her Heart's Desire (Garvice), 1900
Her Heart's Desire (Greig, as Ames), 1961
Her Heart's Longing (Albanesi, as Rowlands), 1910
Her Humble Lover (Garvice), 1904
Her Husband (Albanesi, as Rowlands), 1914
Her Husband and Her Love (Albanesi, as Rowlands), 1905
Her Kingdom (Albanesi, as Rowlands), 1910
Her Knight on a Barge (Sebastian), 1979
Her Love So True (Garvice)
Her Mad Month (Grundy), 1917
Her Mistake (Albanesi, as Rowlands), 1911
Her Mother-in-Law (M. St John, as St John Cooper), 1920
Her Mother's Keeper (N. Roberts), 1983
Her Mystery Man (Woodward, as Ware), 1971
Her Name Was Eve (Maybury), 1953
Her Pirate Partner (Ruck), 1926
Her Punishment (Albanesi, as Rowlands), 1910
Her Ransom (Garvice), 1903
Her Right to Love (Garvice, as Hart)
Her Shining Splendor (Sherwood), 1980
Her Sister's Children (Burchell), 1965
Her Stolen Baby (M. St John), 1919
Her Stolen Life (Price), 1954
Her Undying Past (MacGill), 1924
Her Unexpected Summer (Woodward, as Davis), 1967
Her Way and His (Ayres), 1921
Her Weight in Gold (s McCutcheon), 1911
Her Wild Voice Singing (Hoy), 1963

Her World of Men (Greig, as Ames), 1937
Herald of Joy (Belle), 1989
Herb for Happiness (Cartland), 1987
Herb of Grace (Goudge), 1948
Herb of Healing (Burgin), 1915
Herbs and Apples (Santmyer), 1925
Hercules, My Shipmate (Graves), 1945
Here and Beyond (s Wharton), 1926
Here and Then (Miller), 1992
Here Be Dragons (Penman), 1985
Here Be Dragons (M. Peters, as Whitby), 1980
Here Comes a Candle (Hodge), 1967
Here Comes the Candle (Jameson), 1938
Here Comes the Sun! (Loring), 1924
Here I Belong (Burchell), 1951
Here I Stay (B. Michaels), 1983
Here Lies Margot (P. Hill), 1957
Here Lies Our Sovereign Lord (Plaidy), 1957
Here Today and Gone Tomorrow (s Bromfield), 1934
Here Was a Man (Lofts), 1936
Heritage (Keyes), 1968
Heritage of Folly (Cookson, as Marchant), 1962
Heritage of Hate (Garvice), 1909
Heritage of Shadows (Brent), 1983
Heritage of Strangers (Roby), 1978
Heritage of the Heart (Pykare), 1982
Heritage of the Heart (Roby, as D'Arcy), 1980
Heritage Perilous (Farnol), 1946
Hermit and the Wild Woman (s Wharton), 1908
Hermit of Bonneville (Burgin), 1904
Hermit of Far End (Pedler), 1919
Hermits of Gray's Inn (Burgin), 1899
Hero for Love's Sake (Albanesi, as Rowlands)
Hero of Herat (Diver), 1912
Hero of Urbino (Wynne), 1914
Hero or Scamp? (M. St John, as St John Cooper), 1918
Heroes (Nicole), 1973
Heroes of Clone (Kennedy), 1957
Heroic Garrison (Stuart, as V.A. Stuart), 1975
Heroine's Sister (F. Murray), 1975
Heron series (Oldfield), from 1980
Heronbrook (Manners, as Rundle), 1974
Heron's Nest (Gibbs, as Ford), 1960
Heron's Point (Stratton, as Gillen), 1977
Herries series (Walpole), from 1930
Herring's Nest (Bloom, as Essex), 1949
Hesitant Heir (Roby, as Grey), 1978
Hessian (Fast), 1972
Hester (Cleeve), 1979
Hester Dark (E. Blair), 1984
Hester Lane (Swan), 1908
Hester Roon (Lofts), 1940
Hester Trefusis (Albanesi, as Rowlands), 1912
Heu-Heu (Haggard), 1924
Hey for Cavaliers! (Wynne), 1912
Heywood Inheritance (Fellows), 1975
Hibiscus House (Chandos), 1955
Hidden Beauty (T. Barclay), 1993
Hidden Book (Roby), 1977
Hidden by Love (Cartland), 1992
Hidden Evil (Cartland), 1963
Hidden Fires (Brown, as Jordan), 1982
Hidden Fires (MacGill), 1921
Hidden Flower (Buck), 1952
Hidden Gift (Albanesi), 1936
Hidden Heart (Cartland), 1946

Hidden Heart (Steele), 1990
Hidden Heart of Fire (Drummond, as Dawes), 1976
Hidden Hearts (M. St John, as St John Cooper), 1923
Hidden in the Flame (Mather), 1985
Hidden in the Wind (MacLeod, as Airlie), 1953
Hidden Love (Mortimer), 1982
Hidden Meanings (C. Allen), 1976
Hidden Past (Woodward), 1961
Hidden River (Jameson), 1955
Hidden Talent (Krentz), 1993
Hidden Terror (Garvice, as Hart), 1910
Hidden Years (Jordan), 1990
Hide and Seek (Lamb), 1987
Hide and Seek (Woods), 1993
Hiding (Cartland), 1992
High Adventure (Farnol), 1926
High Barbaree (T. Barclay, as Annandale), 1980
High Country (Nicole), 1988
High Country Governess (Summers), 1987
High-Country Wife (Bevan), 1974
High Fence (Muskett), 1959
High Heaven (Duffield), 1939
High Holiday (Norris), 1949
High Hostage (Worboys, as Maxwell), 1976
High Noon (Ayres), 1936
High of Heart (Loring), 1938
High Price to Pay (Craven), 1986
High Risk (E. Darcy), 1992
High Road (Baldwin), 1939
High Road (Greig, as Warren), 1954
High Spirits (Tranter), 1950
High Tide at Midnight (Craven), 1978
High Tide at Noon (Ogilvie), 1944
High Towers (Costain), 1949
High Valley (Mather), 1971
High Water (Kent, as Reeman), 1959
Highclyffe Hall series (Brandewyne), from 1988
Highest Bidder (Ayres), 1921
Highest Bidder (MacGill), 1921
Highest Peak (May), 1967
Highland Countess (Chesney), 1983
Highland Destiny (Oliver), 1979
Highland Heritage (Saunders, as Summers), 1991
Highland Interlude (Andrews), 1968
Highland Masquerade (Elgin), 1966
Highland Velvet (Deveraux), 1982
Highly Respectable Marriage (Walsh), 1983
Highwayman (Bailey), 1915
Highwayman (S. Thorpe), 1962
Highwayman's Daughter (Shoesmith), 1973
Highwayman's Hazard (Oliver), 1983
Hilary in His Heart (Chandos, as Tempest), 1938
Hilary on Her Own (Grundy), 1908
Hildegarde (Norris), 1926
Hill Country Nurse (McElfresh), 1959
Hillbilly Doctor (Seifert), 1940
Hills of Kalamata (Hampson), 1976
Hills of Maketu (Bevan), 1969
Hilltop Tryst (Neels), 1989
Hilltops Clear (Loring), 1933
Hilton and Warner series (Nicole), from 1974
Hindu (s Hichens), 1917
Hired Baby (s Corelli), 1891
Hired Man (Bragg), 1969
Hiring Fair (Stirling), 1976
His Dupe (MacGill), 1922

His Elizabeth (Thane), 1928
His Fight Is Ours (Lane), 1946
His Girl Friday (Palmer), 1989
His Guardian Angel (Garvice), 1911
His Hour (Glyn), 1910
His Lordship (s Burgin), 1893
His Lordship's Landlady (Sebastian, as Whitmore), 1979
His Love So True (Garvice), 1896
His Majesty's U-Boat (Kent, as Reeman), 1973
His Majesty's Well-Beloved (Orczy), 1919
His Majesty's Yankees (Raddall), 1942
His Official Fiancée (Ruck), 1914
His One Love (Albanesi, as Rowlands), 1912
His Perfect Trust (Garvice)
His Sealed Lips! (M. St John), 1918
His Serene Highness (Bailey), 1920
His Serene Miss Smith (Summers), 1966
His Ukelele Girl (MacGill), 1927
His Wife from the Kitchen! (M. St John, as St John Cooper), 1924
His Wife—or His Mother? (M. St John), 1923
His Wife or His Work? (M. St John), 1928
His Wife's Secret! (M. St John), 1928
His Woman (Steele), 1991
His Word of Honour (Ayres), 1921
Historical Nights' Entertainment (s Sabatini), 1917
History of Anthony Waring (M. Sinclair), 1927
HMS Saracen (Kent, as Reeman), 1965
HMS Surprise (O'Brian), 1973
Hold Back the Dark (Donnelly), 1993
Hold Back the Heart (Bloom, as Burns), 1951
Hold Close the Memory (Pozzessere, as Graham), 1985
Hold Fast 'Til Morning (McKenna, as Brookes), 1982
Hold Hard, My Heart (Bloom, as Burns), 1946
Hold Me Captive (M. Pargeter), 1976
Hold Me in Your Heart (Chard), 1983
Hold On to Your Heart (Baldwin), 1976
Hold the Dream (Bradford), 1985
Holiday (Oman, as Lenanton), 1928
Holiday Engagement (Gibbs, as Ford), 1963
Holiday for Lovers (Woodward, as Davis), 1967
Holiday with Violence (E. Pargeter), 1952
Holidays at Sunnycroft (s Swan), 1885
Hollanders series (Dymoke), from 1991
Hollow Hills (Stewart), 1973
Hollow Night (Harrod-Eagles), 1980
Hollow of Her Hand (McCutcheon), 1912
Hollywood Honeymoon (Barcynska, as Sandys), 1939
Hollywood Love (Williamson, as A.M. Williamson), 1928
Hollywood Madness (MacGill), 1936
Hollywood Star Dust (MacGill), 1936
Holy Flower (Haggard), 1915
Holy Orders (Corelli), 1908
Homage to a Rose (P. Hill), 1979
Home Again My Love (Browning, as Dozier), 1977
Home at Sundown (L. Walker), 1968
Home for Christmas (L. Douglas), 1937
Home for Christmas (N. Roberts), 1986
Home for Joy (Burchell), 1968
Home for the Wedding (Cadell), 1971
Home Is Goodbye (Hunter, as Chace), 1971
Home Is the Hero (Chandos), 1946
Home Is the Hunter (Sprigge), 1930
Home Is the Sailor (K. Blair), 1990
Home to Morning Star (Way), 1981
Home to My Country (M. Howard), 1971
Home To the Hills (MacLeod), 1992

Home Without a Father! (M. St John), 1922
Homecoming (Lide) 1992
Homecoming (Lofts), 1975
Homecoming (McElfresh), 1953
Homecoming (Seifert), 1950
Homecoming of the Boys (s Swan), 1916
Homeland (Jakes), 1993
Homeplace (Dailey), 1976
Homer's Daughter (Graves), 1955
Homesick for a Dream (Mackinlay), 1968
Homespun (Swan), 1893
Home-Town Doctor (Seifert), 1959
Hometown Hospital (Saxton, as Balmain), 1991
Homeward the Heart (Hoy), 1964
Homeward Winds the River (B. Johnson), 1979
Homing (Thane), 1957
Homing Bird (Swan), 1935
Honest Illusions (N. Roberts), 1992
Honey (Burchell), 1959
Honey for Tea (Cadell), 1961
Honey Is Bitter (Winspear), 1967
Honey Island (Asquith), 1957
Honey Pot series (Barcynska), from 1916
Honeyball Farm (Dell), 1937
Honeymoon (Ogilvie), 1947
Honeymoon (Winspear), 1986
Honeymoon Alone (Greig, as Ames), 1940
Honeymoon for One (Greig, as Ames), 1971
Honeymoon Hate (Williamson, as A.M. Williamson), 1931
Honeymoon Holiday (Hoy), 1967
Honeymoon in Hiding (Vaizey), 1911
Honeymoon in Manila (Greig, as Ames), 1962
Honeymoon Island (Bloom, as Burns), 1938
Honeymoon Island (Lewty), 1987
Honeymoons Arranged (Greig), 1938
Honey's Farm (Gower), 1993
Honor (Woods), 1992
Honor and Passion (Oliver, as Hathaway) 1992
Honor Bound (Baldwin), 1934
Honor Bound (Brown, as St Claire), 1986
Honor Bright (Keyes), 1936
Honor of Dr Shelton (Seifert), 1962
Honorable Miss Clarendon (Sebastian), 1973
Honorable Offer (Coulter), 1981
Honor's Price (Bloom), 1979
Honour Comes Back— (Jacob), 1935
Honour of Four Corners (Burgin), 1934
Honour this Day (Kent), 1987
Honourable Jim (Orczy), 1924
Honourable Mr Tawnish (Farnol), 1913
Honour's a Mistress (Jacob), 1947
Honour's Fetters (Wynne), 1911
Hoodman Blind (M. Peters, as Black), 1984
Hoodwinked (Palmer), 1989
Hope and Glory (Nicole, as Arlen), 1984
Hope for Tomorrow (Weale), 1959
Hope Is My Pillow (Ritchie), 1967
Hopeful Journey (Ruck), 1950
Horatia (Gibbs), 1961
Horizons of Love (Cartland), 1980
Hornblower, Horatio series (Forester), from 1937
Hornblower series (N. Roberts), from 1989
Horns of the Moon (Manners, as Lamont), 1979
Horror at Gull House (Matthews, as Brisco), 1970
Horror from the Tombs (F. Stevenson), 1977
Horseman Riding By (Delderfield), 1966

Hortensius, Friend of Nero (E. Pargeter), 1936
Hospital (James), 1932
Hospital Angles (James), 1966
Hospital Call (E. Harrison), 1975
Hospital Circles (Andrews), 1967
Hospital Corridors (Burchell), 1955
Hospital Heartbreaker (Oliver, as Thorn), 1988
Hospital Hill (McElfresh), 1961
Hospital of Fatima (Hunter, as Chace), 1963
Hospital of the Heart (Bloom, as Essex), 1966
Hospital on the Hill (I. Preston), 1967
Hospital Summer (Andrews), 1958
Hospital Zone (Seifert), 1948
Hostage (Staples, as Stevens), 1985
Hostage Bride (Dailey), 1981
Hostage Heart (McKenna, as Nauman), 1987
Hostage of Love (Woodward, as Lawrence), 1973
Hostage to Dishonour (Steele), 1979
Hostile Engagement (Steele), 1979
Hostile Shore (Gavin), 1940
Hostile Shore (Kent, as Reeman), 1962
Hosts of Rebecca (Cordell), 1960
Hot Breath (S. Harrison), 1985
Hot Day in High Summer (P. Hastings), 1962
Hot Ice (N. Roberts), 1987
Hot Money (Woods), 1993
Hot Property (Woods), 1992
Hot Pursuit (van der Zee), 1988
Hot Secret (Woods), 1992
Hotel De Luxe (Nicole, as Gray), 1985
Hotel De Luxe (Randall), 1961
Hotel Hostess (Baldwin), 1938
Hotel Mirador (K. Blair, as Brett), 1959
Hound of Ireland (s Byrne), 1934
Hounds and Jackals (B. Wood), 1978
Hounds of Carvello (Cowen), 1970
Hounds of God (Sabatini), 1928
Hounds of Sunset (E. Pargeter), 1976
Hour Before Midnight (V. Johnston), 1978
Hour Before Moonrise (Buckingham), 1967
Hour of the Siesta (M. Lewis), 1982
Hour of the Tiger (I. Roberts, as I. R. Roberts), 1985
Hours of Iris (Eaton), 1928
Hours to Cherish (Pozzessere, as Graham), 1984
House above Hollywood (V. Johnston), 1968
House above the Bay (I. Preston), 1976
House at Bell Orchard (S. Thorpe), 1962
House at Cupid's Cross (Plaidy, as Burford), 1949
House at Fern Canyon (W. Roberts), 1970
House at Kilgallen (Roby), 1973
House at Luxor (F. Stevenson), 1976
House at Old Vine (Lofts), 1961
House at Sunset (Lofts), 1962
House at Tegwani (K. Blair), 1950
House Behind the Judas Tree (s Deeping), 1929
House Behind the Judas Tree (s Frankau), 1929
House, But Not a Home (M. St John), 1921
House by the Lock (Williamson, as A.M. Williamson), 1899
House by the Sea (Lowndes), 1937
House by the Tree (James), 1938
House by the Watch Tower (Robins), 1968
House Called Edenhythe (Buckingham), 1970
House Divided (Buck), 1935
House for Sharing (Hunter, as Chace), 1964
House for Sister Mary (Andrews), 1966
House for the Season series (Chesney), from 1986

House in Candle Square (Bennetts), 1977
House in Lavender Grove (Laffeaty), 1979
House in the Dust (Leslie), 1942
House in the Woods (Chandos, as Lance), 1980
House of a Thousand Lanterns (Plaidy, as Holt), 1974
House of Adventure (Deeping), 1921
House of Bonneau (Rhodes), 1990
House of Candles (Matthews, as Brisco), 1973
House of Cards (Hooper), 1991
House of Conflict (Bromige), 1953
House of Conflict (Burchell), 1962
House of Cray (P. Hill), 1982
House of Discontent (Wyndham), 1955
House of Dreams (Collin), 1971
House of Dreams-Come-True (Pedler), 1919
House of Earth (Buck), 1935
House of Fand (Maybury, as Troy), 1966
House of Fiske (Burgin), 1927
House of Five Pines (Worboys, as Eyre), 1967
House of Granite (Renier), 1968
House of Happiness (s Dell), 1927
House of Hope (Alexander), 1992
House of Imposters (W. Roberts), 1977
House of Jackdaws (Dwyer-Joyce), 1980
House of Kingdom (Stratton, as Gillen), 1976
House of Larne (Cowen), 1980
House of Lies (M. Howard), 1960
House of Lorraine (R. Lindsay), 1959
House of Lydia (I. Roberts, as Shaw), 1967
House of Many Shadows (B. Michaels), 1974
House of Many Windows (Muskett), 1950
House of Memories (Way), 1983
House of Men (Cookson, as Marchant), 1963
House of Mirror Images (Winston), 1970
House of Mirth (Wharton), 1905
House of Moreys (Bentley), 1953
House of Nightingales (Goodwin, as Ebel), 1985
House of Oliver (MacLeod), 1947
House of Peril (Lowndes), 1935
House of Pines (Chandos, as Tempest), 1975
House of Ravensbourne (Gibbs), 1965
House of Scissors (Hunter, as Chace), 1972
House of Secrets (Saunders, as Blake), 1993
House of Seven Fountains (Weale), 1957
House of Silence (Williamson), 1921
House of Spies (Deeping), 1913
House of Storms (Winspear), 1985
House of Strange Music (Hilton), 1976
House of Strangers (Winspear), 1963
House of Strangers (Woodward, as Richmond), 1983
House of Sunshine (Albanesi, as Rowlands), 1912
House of the Amulet (Hilton), 1970
House of the Deer (D. Stevenson), 1970
House of the Lost Court (Williamson, as de Savallo), 1908
House of the Pines (Chandos, as Tempest), 1946
House of the Seventh Cross (Robins), 1967
House of the Shining Tide (Summers), 1962
House of the Three Ganders (Bacheller), 1928
House of the Twelve Caesars (P. Hastings), 1975
House of the Wolf (Weyman), 1890
House of Tomorrow (Lorrimer), 1987
House of Vandekar (Anthony), 1988
House of War (Gavin), 1970
House of Water (Renier), 1963
House of Whispers (Laffeaty, as Carstens), 1975
House of Women (Cookson), 1992

House of Women (Malpass), 1975
House on Bostwick Square (V. Johnston), 1987
House on Brinden Water (Asquith), 1958
House on Flamingo Cay (Weale), 1962
House on Gregor's Brae (Summers), 1971
House on Hay Hill (s Eden), 1976
House on Malador Street (P. Hastings), 1970
House on the Cliff (D. Stevenson), 1966
House on the Fens (Cookson, as Marchant), 1965
House on the Hill (Bloom), 1977
House on the Left Bank (V. Johnston), 1975
House on the Moor (Woodward), 1967
House on the Nile (Duffield), 1937
House on the Rock (Cleeve), 1980
House on the Rock (Swan), 1930
House on the Rocks (Chandos, as Charles), 1962
House on the Strand (du Maurier), 1969
House on Twyford Street (Gluyas), 1976
House Party (Delafield), 1931
House Possessed (Blackstock), 1962
House Surgeon at Luke's (Randall), 1962
House That Died Alone (Bloom), 1964
House That Hated People (M. Peters, as Black), 1974
House That Is Our Own (O. Douglas), 1940
House That Jane Built (Albanesi), 1921
House with the Myrtle Trees (Gibbs, as Ford), 1942
House with Two Faces (Bishop), 1960
House Without a Heart (Cowen), 1978
House Without Love (Bromige), 1964
Houseful of Girls (Vaizey), 1902
Household (F. Stevenson), 1989
Householder (Jhabvala), 1960
Houseless One (M. Peters, as Whitby), 1981
Houseman's Sister (Norway, as Neal), 1964
How Can I Forget? (Chandos, as Tempest), 1948
How Can the Heart Forget (Loring), 1960
How Change the Moons (Trask), 1932
How Dark, My Lady! (Bloom), 1951
How Dear Is My Delight! (Bloom, as Burns), 1955
How Far to Bethlehem? (Lofts), 1965
How Great the Price (Robins), 1935
How High the Moon (Mackinlay, as Grey), 1966
How Like the King (Vaizey), 1905
How Many Miles to Babylon? (Irwin), 1913
How Much You Mean to Me (Chandos, as Charles), 1966
How Rich Is Love? (Bloom, as Burns), 1957
How Sleep the Brave (Gavin), 1980
How the Money Goes! (M. St John), 1916
How to Forget (Robins), 1944
Howard series (Wiat), from 1972
Howards of Saxondale (Randall), 1946
Howarth series (Stubbs), from 1978
Howling in the Woods (V. Johnston), 1968
Hudson River Bracketed (Wharton), 1929
Human Nature (s Wharton), 1933
Human Symphony (MacLeod), 1937
Humbug (Delafield), 1921
Hummingbird (Spencer), 1983
Humoresque (s Hurst), 1919
Hundredth Chance (Dell), 1917
Hundredth Man (Burgin), 1927
Hungarian Rhapsody (Steele), 1992
Hungry for Love (Cartland), 1976
Hungry Heart (Way), 1988
Hungry Hill (du Maurier), 1943
Hungry Leopard (Borden), 1956

Hungry Tide (Stratton, as Gillen), 1975
Hunted Heart (James), 1941
Hunter (Palmer), 1991
Hunter of the East (Hampson), 1973
Hunter's Dawn (I. Roberts, as Rowland), 1977
Hunter's Green (Whitney), 1968
Hunter's Moon (Bloom), 1969
Hunter's Moon (Way), 1982
Hunting of Henri (s Wren), 1944
Hunting Shirt (M. Johnston), 1931
Hunting the Wolfe (Hooper), 1993
Huntsman's Folly (Stuart, as A. Stuart), 1956
Husband (Cookson), 1976
Husband and Foe (Albanesi, as Rowlands), 1900
Husband for Gail (Corcoran), 1981
Husband for Hire (Chandos), 1940
Husband Hunters (Cartland), 1976
Husband in Name (Mackinlay, as Grey), 1972
Husband She Wanted (M. St John), 1930
Husband, The Wife, and the Friend (M. St John), 1921
Husbands at Home (Chandos), 1955
Husbands of Edith (McCutcheon), 1908
Hush Marriage (M. St John, as St John Cooper), 1934
Hustler Joe (s E. Porter), 1924
Hut by the River (Burgin), 1916

I Am Gabriella! (Maybury), 1962
I Came to the Castle (V. Johnston), 1969
I Came to the Highlands (V. Johnston), 1974
I Cannot Go Hunting Tomorrow (s Treece), 1946
I Could Be Good to You (Blackstock, as Keppel), 1980
I Dare Not Dream (Maybury), 1937
I Dwelt in High Places (Bowen), 1933
I Hear Adventure Calling (Loring), 1948
I, Judas (Caldwell), 1977
I Know a Maiden (Albanesi), 1906
I Know My Love (Gaskin), 1962
I Live Again (Deeping), 1942
I Lost My Heart (Greig), 1935
I Love a Lass (Cadell), 1956
I Loved a Fairy (Barcynska), 1933
I Loved Her Yesterday (Greig), 1945
I Married a Doctor (Randall), 1947
I Married Mr Richardson (Greig, as Ames), 1945
I Met a Gypsy (s Lofts), 1935
I Met Him Again (Greig), 1948
I Met Murder on the Way (Blackstock), 1977
I Remember Love (Hardwick), 1982
I Return (Leslie), 1962
I Saw My Mortal Sight (Eaton), 1959
I Seek My Love (Greig, as Ames), 1936
I Should Have Known (Robins), 1961
I Start Counting (Erskine-Lindop), 1966
I Take This Man (Loring), 1954
I Take This Woman (Rinehart), 1927
I Tell My Heart (Trask), 1937
I Thank a Fool (Erskine-Lindop), 1958
I, The King (Keyes), 1966
I, The Maid (M. Peters), 1980
I, Too, Have Loved (Robins), 1939
I Was Shown Heaven (Barcynska), 1962
I Will Be Good (Chapman), 1945
I Will Be True (Trask), 1948
I Will Love You Still (Burchell), 1949
I Will Maintain (Bowen), 1910
I Will Repay (Orczy), 1906

Ibiza Surprise (Dunnett), 1991
Ice in His Veins (Mortimer), 1981
Ice into Fire (Peake), 1985
Ice Maiden (Wentworth), 1979
Ice Palace (Ferber), 1958
Ice Venture Nurse (Saxton, as Balmain), 1983
Iceberg (Donald), 1980
Iceberg in the Tropics (May), 1983
Icicle Heart (Steele), 1979
Ideal Wife (Balogh), 1991
Ideals (s E. Scott), 1927
Ides of March (Wilder), 1948
Ides of November (F. Stevenson), 1975
Idlers' Gate (Bowen, as Winch), 1932
If Dreams Came True (R. Lindsay, as Leigh), 1974
If Dreams Were Wild Horses (McElfresh), 1988
If Ever I Cease to Love (Keyes), 1943
If I Love Again (Chandos, as Tempest), 1937
If I Were You (Aiken), 1987
If Love Be Love (Kidd), 1972
If Love Were Wise (Hoy), 1954
If My Arms Could Hold (Ponsonby, as Doris Ponsonby), 1947
If Only (James), 1975
If She Should Die (Roby), 1970
If the South Had Won the Civil War (Kantor), 1961
If the Tree Is Saved (Cartland), 1929
If There Be Dragons (Hooper), 1984
If This Be Destiny (Robins), 1941
If This Be Love (Renier), 1971
If This Be Treason (Renier), 1965
If This Is Love (Weale), 1963
If This Were All (Burchell), 1949
If Tomorrow Ever Comes (Laffeaty), 1969
If We Will (Cartland), 1947
If Winter Comes (Palmer), 1979
If Wishes Were Horses (Barcynska), 1917
If You Believe the Soldiers (Cordell), 1973
If You Care (Burchell), 1948
If You'll Marry Me (Chandos, as Tempest), 1942
Ikon on the Wall (s Goudge), 1943
I'll Find You Again (Hoy), 1941
I'll Get over It (Greig), 1935
I'll Go With You (Burchell), 1940
I'll Never Be Young Again (du Maurier), 1932
I'll Ride Beside You (Chandos, as Lance), 1965
I'll Try Anything Once (Chandos, as Tempest), 1939
I'll Walk with My Love (Maybury), 1940
Illegal Possession (Hooper), 1985
Illicit Obsession (Laffeaty), 1987
Ills Men Do (Burgin), 1937
Illusion (Lamb), 1981
Illusions (C. Allen), 1987
Illusions of Love (Freeman), 1984
Illusions of Love (Wentworth), 1990
Illyrian Spring (Bridge), 1935
I'm Not a Common Girl! (M. St John), 1923
Image of a Lover (Ogilvie), 1974
Image of Love (Browning), 1984
Image of Love (Stratton), 1978
Image-Maker (P. Hastings), 1976
Images of Love (Mather), 1980
Images of Love (Woods, as Kirk), 1982
Images of Rose (Gilbert), 1974
Imaginary Marriage (M. St John, as St John Cooper), 1922
Imagination of the Heart (Glover), 1989
Imaginative Experience (Wesley), 1994

It Began in Vauxhall Gardens (Plaidy, as Kellow), 1955
It Had to Be You (Hoy), 1940
It Had to Happen (Bromfield), 1936
It Happened in Egypt (Williamson), 1914
It Happened in Paris (Hoy), 1970
It Happened One Flight (Greig), 1951
It Is My Duty! (M. St John), 1926
It Started in Hongkong (Greig, as Ames), 1961
It Takes a Thief (Hooper), 1989
It Takes All Kinds (s Bromfield), 1939
It Was Left to Peter (Ruck), 1940
It Was Like This (s H. Allen), 1940
It Was Romance (M. Howard), 1939
It Wasn't Love (Robins), 1930
Italian Invader (Steele), 1993
Italian Nurse (Saxton, as Balmain), 1984
Italian Woman (Plaidy), 1952
It's a Great World! (Loring), 1935
It's Rumoured in the Village (Burchell), 1946
It's Spring, My Heart! (Bloom, as Essex), 1958
It's Wise to Forget (Hoy), 1945
I've Always Loved You (Greig), 1943
Ivor Novello's King's Rhapsody (Chapman), 1950
Ivory Cane (Dailey), 1977
Ivory Child (Haggard), 1916
Ivory God (Swan), 1923
Ivy Tree (Stewart), 1961

Jacintha (Winsor), 1983
Jack Be Nimble (Barcynska, as Sandys), 1941
Jack London, Sailor on Horseback (Stone), 1947
Jack O'Lantern (Shoesmith), 1969
Jack O'Manory (s Stern), 1927
Jackal's Head (B. Michaels, as Peters), 1968
Jackie (Barcynska), 1921
Jackpot (Barcynska), 1957
Jack's Year of Trial (Swan), 1887
Jacob Ussher (Jacob), 1925
Jacobite series (Broster), from 1925
Jade (Barr), 1982
Jade Alliance (Drummond, as Darrell), 1979
Jade Dragon (Buckingham), 1974
Jade Earrings (Ruck), 1941
Jade Horse of Merle (Ponsonby), 1966
Jade Moon (Hamilton, as Fitzgerald), 1988
Jade of Destiny, (Farnol), 1931
Jade Pagoda (MacLeod), 1993
Jade Spider (Muskett), 1927
Jago, Nathan series (Thompson), from 1983
Jake Howard's Wife (Mather), 1973
Jamaica Inn (du Maurier), 1936
Jamaican Midnight (Woods), 1984
James Bevanwood, Baronet (M. St John, as St John Cooper), 1920
James, By the Grace of God (Tranter), 1985
James River series (Deveraux), from 1984
Jane (Corelli), 1897
Jane Cable (McCutcheon), 1906
Jane Em'ly (M. St John), 1911
Jane Fairfax (Aiken), 1990
Jane Hadden (R. Marshall), 1952
Jane of Lantern Hill (Montgomery), 1937
Jane Oglander (Lowndes), 1911
Jane—Our Stranger (Borden), 1923
Jane Ryan, Dietician (McElfresh, as Wesley), 1959
Jane's Parlour (O. Douglas), 1937
Janice (Greig), 1947

Janie's Great Mistake (Wynne), 1920
January Tale (Bryher), 1966
Janus Imperative (Anthony), 1980
Japan series (Nicole), from 1984
Japanese Doll (Ponsonby, as Rybot), 1961
Japanese Girl (s Graham), 1971
Japanese Lantern (Hunter, as Chace), 1960
Japanese Screen (Mather), 1974
Jarrett's Jade (Yerby), 1959
Jasmine (Thum), 1984
Jasmine Farm (Arnim), 1934
Jasmine for a Nurse (I. Roberts), 1982
Jasmine Sorcery (Delinsky), 1986
Jasmine—Take Care! (Greig), 1930
Jason (Treece), 1961
Jasper Dennison's Christmas (s Swan), 1898
Jasper Family series (Ponsonby), from 1951
Jassy (Lofts), 1944
Jaubert Ring (W. Roberts), 1976
Jaunty Jock (s Munro), 1918
Java Nights (van der Zee), 1990
Jazz (Morrison), 1992
Jealous Wife's Revenge! (M. St John), 1921
Jealousy (James), 1933
Jeanne (Garvice), 1902
Jeanne Margot (Cleugh), 1927
Jeannie Urquhart (P. Hill), 1988
Jeb (Ellis, as J. Lord), 1970
Jeff Benton, MD (McElfresh), 1962
Jehovah Blues (Steen), 1952
Jehovah's Day (Borden), 1928
Jennie series (Ogilvie), from 1984
Jennifer and Cage series (Brown, as St Claire), from 1985
Jenny Luck of Brendon's Mills (M. St John), 1923
Jenny Newstead (Lowndes), 1932
Jenny W.R.E.N. (Bloom, as Burns), 1945
Jeremy Poldark 1790–1791 (Graham), 1950
Jericho Sands (Borden), 1925
Jerry (Webster), 1916
Jerry, Junior (Webster), 1907
Jess (Haggard), 1887
Jess o' Jordan's (M. St John), 1930
Jessamy Court (Maybury), 1974
Jessica (Maybury), 1965
Jessica's Girl (Cox), 1993
Jessie Gray (E. Blair), 1986
Jest (Bowen), 1922
Jest of Fate (Garvice), 1904
Jewel in the Crown (P. Scott), 1966
Jewel of the Greys (M. Peters), 1972
Jeweled Dagger (Ellis), 1973
Jewelene (Williams), 1979
Jewelled Caftan (M. Pargeter), 1978
Jewelled Daughter (Maybury), 1976
Jewelled Path (Laker), 1983
Jewelled Serpent (Hamilton, as Fitzgerald), 1984
Jewelled Snuff Box (Ley), 1959
Jewels (Steel), 1992
Jewels of Helen (Donnelly), 1990
Jezebel (Robins), 1977
Jig-Saw (Cartland), 1925
Jill (Delafield), 1926
Jill the Hostage (Wynne), 1925
Jilted (Greig, as Ames), 1968
Jilted (Wentworth), 1983
Jilted Bridegroom (Mortimer), 1992

Jinks (Barcynska, as Sandys), 1931
Joan Haste (Haggard), 1895
Joan of the Lilies (M. Peters), 1969
Joan of the Tower (Deeping), 1911
Joanna (Gellis), 1978
Joanna at the Grange (Burchell), 1957
Job for Jenny (Baldwin), 1945
Johan Lind (Salverson), 1928
John Burnet of Barns (J. Buchan), 1898
John Galbraith's Wife (Albanesi, as Rowlands), 1910
John Helsby's Wife (Albanesi, as Rowlands), 1920
John Jordan, Slave-Driver (M. St John), 1915
John o' the Green (Farnol), 1935
John Splendid (Munro), 1898
Johnnie Sahib (P. Scott), 1952
Johnny Danger (Blackstock, as Allardyce), 1960
Johnny Forsaken (Stern), 1954
Johnny Osage (Giles), 1960
Johnny Tremain (Forbes), 1943
Johnson Johnson series (Dunnett, as Halliday), from 1968
Jolly Sally Pendleton (Libbey)
Jonquil (Robins), 1927
Jonty in Love (Hampson), 1975
Jordan County (Foote), 1954
Joshua and the Cowgirl (Woods), 1991
Joshua Tree (MacLeod), 1970
Josselyn's Wife (Norris), 1918
Journal of Mary Hervey Russell (Jameson), 1945
Journey (Michener), 1989
Journey from a Foreign Land (Melville, as Betteridge), 1972
Journey from Yesterday (Goodwin, as Ebel), 1963
Journey in the Dark (Greig, as Ames), 1945
Journey in the Dark (Norway), 1973
Journey in the Sun (MacLeod), 1957
Journey into Morning (Maybury), 1944
Journey into Spring (MacLeod), 1976
Journey into Stone (Erskine-Lindop), 1972
Journey to a Star (Cartland), 1984
Journey to Arcady (Randall), 1955
Journey to Enchantment (Veryan), 1986
Journey to Love (Randall), 1953
Journey to Paradise (Cartland), 1974
Journey to Quiet Waters (Browning), 1984
Journey Up (Hichens), 1938
Journeyer (Jennings), 1984
Journey's Eve (Cadell), 1953
Joy (Krentz), 1988
Joy Comes After (Barcynska), 1943
Joy of Life (Albanesi, as Rowlands), 1913
Joy Runs High (Alexander, as Armstrong), 1979
Joy Shop (Barcynska), 1931
Joy Street (Keyes), 1950
Joyday for Jodi (L. Walker), 1971
Joyful Journey (Ruck), 1950
Joyous Adventure (Orczy), 1932
Joy-Ride (Ruck), 1929
Jubilee (Rayner), 1987
Jubilee (M. Walker), 1966
Jubilee Hospital (Chandos, as Tempest), 1966
Jubilee Trail (Bristow), 1950
Judas Cloth (O'Faolain), 1992
Judas Figures (Erskine-Lindop), 1956
Judas Flowering (Hodge), 1976
Judas Iscariot—Traitor! (Bloom, as Prole), 1971
Judas Kiss (Plaidy, as Holt), 1981
Judas Kiss (Wentworth), 1981

Judas, My Brother (Yerby), 1969
Judas Trap (Mather), 1979
Judas Tree (Swanson), 1933
Judge of Jerusalem (Bloom), 1926
Judge of the Four Corners (Burgin), 1896
Judged by Fate (Albanesi, as Rowlands), 1913
Judgement of Love (Cartland), 1978
Judgement of the Sword (Diver), 1913
Judith (Cleeve), 1978
Judith (Neels), 1982
Judith Lammeter (Manners, as Rundle), 1976
Judith Paris (Walpole), 1931
Judy Bovenden (Bailey), 1928
Juice of the Pomegranate (Dell), 1938
Julia (P. Hill), 1967
Julia (Hutten), 1924
Julia (Riefe), 1982
Julia Ballantyne (Bowen, as Preedy), 1952
Julia in Ireland (Bridge), 1973
Julia Involved (Bridge), 1962
Julia Probyn series (Bridge), from 1956
Julia Roseingrave (Bowen, as Paye), 1933
Julian (Vidal), 1964
Julian Maze (P. Hastings), 1986
Julian Probert (Ertz), 1931
Julia's Sister (C. Allen), 1978
Julia's Sister (Goodwin, as Ebel), 1982
Julie (F. Stevenson), 1978
Jumping the Queue (Wesley), 1983
June Fairley—Air Hostess (Woodward, as Richmond), 1959
June for Enchantment (Hoy), 1949
June in Her Eyes (Chandos), 1949
Jungle (Blackstock), 1972
Jungle Captive (Hull), 1939
Jungle Island (K. Thorpe), 1986
Jungle Nurse (I. Roberts), 1968
Jungle of Desire (Kidd), 1977
Junie's Love Test (Libbey), 1886
Junior Pro (Norway), 1959
Juniper Bush (A. Howard), 1987
Juniper Tree (Baldwin), 1952
Just a Barmaid (M. St John), 1909
Just a Cottage Maid (M. St John, as St John Cooper), 1920
Just a Girl (Garvice), 1898
Just a Little Longer (Chandos), 1944
Just a Nice Girl (Burchell), 1941
Just a Song at Sunrise (Trask), 1954
Just Around the Corner (Gibbs, as Ford), 1952
Just Around the Corner (s Hurst), 1914
Just Before the Wedding (Chandos), 1954
Just David (E. Porter), 1916
Just Desserts (Browning), 1984
Just Fate (Cartland), 1992
Just for One Weekend (Chandos, as Charles), 1978
Just Jane Ann (M. St John), 1915
Just Jane Em'ly (M. St John), 1921
Just Kate (Miller), 1989
Just Lil (Barcynska, as Sandys), 1933
Just 'Liz-beth Ann (M. St John), 1925
Just Mother (s E. Porter), 1927
Just Off Piccadilly (Cartland), 1933
Just One Night (Mortimer), 1988
Just Plain Jim! (M. St John, as St John Cooper), 1924
Just Say Yes (Browning), 1991
Justice by Midnight (Farnol), 1956
Justice of the Duke (Sabatini), 1912

King's Favourite (Bowen), 1971
King's Fool (Barnes), 1959
King's General (du Maurier), 1946
King's Grey Mare (Jarman), 1973
Kings in Winter (Holland), 1968
King's Legacy (Heaven, as Fecher), 1967
King's Masquerade (Wynne), 1910
King's Minion (Sabatini), 1930
King's Minions (Clarke, as Honeyman), 1974
King's Mirror (Hope), 1899
King's Mistress (Hamilton, as Watson), 1970
King's Mistress (Plaidy), 1952
King's Pawn (W. Roberts), 1971
King's Plaything (Bloom, as Prole), 1962
King's Pleasure (Bloom, as Prole), 1954
King's Pleasure (Lofts), 1969
King's Pleasure (Plaidy), 1949
King's Ransom (Palmer), 1993
Kings Row (Bellamann), 1940
King's Secret Matter (Plaidy), 1962
King's series (C. Fraser), from 1986
King's Stratagem (s Weyman), 1891
King's Tale (Clarke, as Honeyman), 1977
King's Tragedy (Wynne), 1905
King's Traitor (Leslie), 1973
King's Vengeance (Wiat), 1981
King's Vixen (P. Hill), 1954
King's Wife (Bloom), 1950
King's Women (Lampitt), 1992
Kings-at-Arms (Bowen), 1918
Kingsmead (Hutten), 1909
Kinsfolk (Swan), 1896
Kinsman's Sin (Albanesi, as Rowlands)
Kirby, Jacqueline series (B. Michaels, as Peters), from 1972
Kirkby's Changeling (Brent), 1975
Kirkland Revels (Plaidy, as Holt), 1962
Kirov series (Harrod-Eagles), from 1990
Kiss (Burgin), 1924
Kiss and a Promise (Hampson), 1982
Kiss—and Forget (Chandos, as Tempest), 1936
Kiss Away (Woods), 1986
Kiss for the King (Cartland), 1975
Kiss from a Stranger (Cartland), 1990
Kiss from Aphrodite (Hamilton, as Fitzgerald), 1987
Kiss from Satan (Hampson), 1973
Kiss in Rome (Cartland), 1992
Kiss in Sunlight (Greig), 1956
Kiss is Still a Kiss (Lewty), 1989
Kiss Me Again, Stranger (s du Maurier), 1953
Kiss of a Tyrant (M. Pargeter), 1980
Kiss of Fire (Lamb), 1987
Kiss of Hot Sun (Buckingham), 1969
Kiss of Life (Cartland), 1981
Kiss of Paris (Cartland, as McCorquodale), 1956
Kiss of Promise (Greig), 1960
Kiss of Silk (Cartland, as McCorquodale), 1959
Kiss of the Devil (Cartland), 1955
Kiss of the Night Wind (Taylor), 1989
Kiss of the Rising Sun (Hunter), 1984
Kiss of Youth (Robins), 1937
Kiss Remembered (Brown, as St Claire), 1983
Kiss the Moon (Barcynska, as Sandys), 1951
Kiss the Moonlight (Cartland), 1977
Kissed by Magic (Hooper, as Robbins), 1983
Kisses and the Wine (Winspear), 1973
Kisses of Death (Plaidy), 1993

Kissing Game (Wentworth),1986
Kissing Gate (Haines), 1981
Kissing Kin (Thane), 1948
Kissing Time (Saunders), 1982
Kith and Kin (s Bentley), 1960
Kit's Hill (Stubbs), 1978
Kitty (Chesney, as Tremaine), 1980
Kitty (Deeping), 1927
Kitty (R. Marshall), 1943
Kitty Tailleur (M. Sinclair), 1908
Kleath (Macbeth), 1917
Knave of Diamonds (Dell), 1913
Knave of Hearts (Cartland), 1950
Knave of Hearts (Plaidy, as Carr), 1983
Knave of Hearts (I. Roberts, as Rowland), 1970
Kneel for Mercy (Cartland), 1982
Kneel to the Prettiest (Ruck), 1925
Knight at Arms (Bailey), 1924
Knight in Paris (Cartland), 1989
Knight in Shining Armor (Deveraux), 1989
Knight of Allington (Wiat), 1974
Knight of Fire (Pozzessere, as Drake), 1993
Knight of Spain (Bowen), 1913
Knight of the Cheerful Countenance (Keane, as Farrell), 1928
Knight with Armour (Duggan), 1950
Knightly Love (Delinsky, as Douglass), 1982
Knight's Acre (Lofts), 1975
Knight's Honor (Gellis), 1964
Knight's Keep (Randall), 1967
Knight's Possession (Mortimer), 1986
Knock at a Star (P. Hill), 1981
Knock at Midnight (Blackstock), 1966
Knock Four Times (Irwin), 1927
Knock on the Door (Hichens), 1909
Knot Garden (s Bowen, as Preedy), 1933
Kona Winds (Dailey), 1979
Königsmark (A. Mason), 1938
Kowhai Country (Bevan), 1979
Kristen's Passion (Sommerfield), 1983
Kuragin series (Heaven), from 1972
Kuzan series (S. Johnson), from 1979
Kyra's Fate (Garvice), 1908

Lab Nurse (Randall), 1962
Labor Dispute (Richards), 1990
Labour of Hercules (s Lowndes), 1943
Lace for Milady (J. Smith), 1980
Lacebridge Ladies series (Sebastian, as Gladstone), from 1978
Lacey (Williams), 1979
Lachlan's Woman (Dwyer-Joyce), 1979
Lackland's Bride (M. Peters), 1983
Lacquer Couch (Duffield), 1928
Lacy (Palmer), 1991
Lad with Wings (Ruck), 1915
Laddie (G. Porter), 1913
Ladies of Hanover Square (Randall), 1981
Ladies of Lark (Chappell), 1965
Ladies of Lyndon (Kennedy), 1923
Ladies of Missalonghi (McCullough), 1987
Ladies of the Manor (Burgin), 1903
Ladies Whose Bright Eyes (Ford), 1911
Lady and The Highwayman (Cartland), 1952
Lady and the Pirate (Blackstock, as Allardyce), 1957
Lady and the Rogue (Sebastian, as Norcross), 1978
Lady and the Unicorn (Godden), 1937
Lady and the Unicorn (Johansen), 1984

Lady Anne's Deception (Chesney, as Tremaine), 1986
Lady Aurelia's Bequest (Walsh), 1987
Lady Be Bad (Chase), 1984
Lady Bell (Williams), 1986
Lady Betty Across the Water (Williamson), 1906
Lady Blanche Farm (Keyes), 1931
Lady Blue (F. Stevenson, as Faire), 1979
Lady Cassandra (Vaizey), 1914
Lady Cecily's Dilemma (Walsh, as Leyton), 1980
Lady Chatterley's Daughter (Lorrimer, as Robins), 1961
Lady Editha (Wiat), 1991
Lady Fell in Love (M. Howard), 1956
Lady Fell in Love (Maybury), 1943
Lady Feo's Daughter (Albanesi, as Rowlands), 1926
Lady for a Chevalier (M. Peters), 1987
Lady for Ransom (Duggan), 1953
Lady from London (Ayres), 1944
Lady from the Air (Williamson), 1922
Lady Housekeeper (s Swan), 1898
Lady Ice (Lorin, as Hohl), 1987
Lady in a Veil (Bowen, as Preedy), 1943
Lady in Berkshire (Gibbs), 1970
Lady in the Mist (Chandos, as Charles), 1966
Lady in the Tower (Plaidy), 1986
Lady in Waiting (Sutcliff), 1956
Lady Incognita (Pykare), 1980
Lady, It Is Spring! (Maybury), 1938
Lady Living Alone (Lofts, as Curtis), 1945
Lady Lost in Time (Cato), 1985
Lady Love (Palmer), 1984
Lady Lucy's Lover (Chesney), 1992
Lady Madcap (Williams), 1987
Lady Magic (Williams), 1983
Lady Margery's Intrigues (Chesney), 1980
Lady Mary of the Dark House (Williamson, as A.M. Williamson), 1898
Lady Mary's Money (Burgin), 1918
Lady of Blossholme (Haggard), 1909
Lady of Darracourt (Garvice), 1902
Lady of Mallow (Eden), 1962
Lady of Quality (Heyer), 1972
Lady of Spain (Burgin), 1911
Lady of Spain (Saunders, as Blake), 1990
Lady of the Basement Flat (Vaizey), 1917
Lady of the Garter (Dymoke), 1979
Lady of the Heavens (Haggard), 1908
Lady of the House (Lane), 1953
Lady of the Lakes (Ellerbeck, as Yorke), 1981
Lady of the Manor (Saunders), 1978
Lady of the Masque (Bennetts), 1982
Lady of the Night (Richards), 1986
Lady of the Pool (Hope), 1894
Lady of the Torch (Mackinlay), 1944
Lady of the West (L. Howard), 1990
Lady of Wildersley (M. Howard, as Edgar), 1975
Lady on the Coin (Barnes), 1963
Lady Pamela (C. Darcy), 1975
Lady Patricia's Faith (Albanesi, as Rowlands), 1913
Lady Surrender (Mortimer), 1986
Lady Susan and Life (Jameson), 1924
Lady Thief (Hooper), 1981
Lady! This Is Love! (Bloom, as Burns), 1938
Lady Vixen (Busbee), 1980
Lady with a Black Umbrella (Balogh), 1989
Lady's Choice (Krentz), 1989
Lady's Masquerade (Sebastian, as Gladstone), 1980

Laid Up in Lavender (s Weyman), 1907
Laird of Glenfernie (M. Johnston), 1919
Laird of Locharrun (Hampson), 1980
Laird's Choice (R. Marshall), 1951
Lake in Kyoto (Lewty), 1985
Lake of Darkness (Cowen), 1971
Lake of Gold (J. Buchan), 1941
Lake of Silver (T. Barclay, as Dell), 1974
Lake of the Kingfisher (Summers), 1978
Lamb, Sergeant series (Graves), from 1940
Lamb to the Slaughter (Eden), 1953
Lambs (Norway), 1965
Lame Daddy (Barcynska, as Sandys), 1942
Lame Englishman (Deeping), 1910
Lament for a Lost Lover (Plaidy, as Carr), 1977
Lament for a Lover (MacLeod), 1967
Lamont of Ardgoyne (MacLeod), 1944
Lamorna (Laffeaty), 1977
Lamp for Jonathan (Summers), 1982
Lamp in the Desert (Dell), 1919
Lamp of Fate (Pedler), 1920
Lamp of Friendship (Albanesi, as Rowlands), 1936
Lamplight and the Stars (Malpass), 1985
Lancaster Men (Dailey), 1981
Lancelot (Vansittart), 1978
Land Beyond the Mountains (Giles), 1958
Land Called Deseret (Dailey), 1979
Land-Girl's Love Story (Ruck), 1919
Land of Afternoon (Macbeth, as Knox), 1925
Land of Enchantment (Dailey), 1975
Land of Green Ginger (Holtby), 1927
Land of Heart's Desire (MacLeod, as Airlie), 1957
Land of Illusion (K. Thorpe), 1988
Land of Living Waters (Laffeaty), 1983
Land of My Fathers (Cordell), 1983
Land of Silence (Burgin), 1904
Land of Spices (O'Brien), 1941
Land of the Incas (K. Thorpe), 1983
Land of the Lotus-Eaters (Hunter, as Chace), 1966
Landfall (Shute), 1940
Landowner Legacy (Plaidy, as Holt), 1984
Lands of the Sea (Mullins), 1988
Landscape of the Heart (Renier), 1978
Language of Love (Saunders), 1983
Language of the Heart (Cadell), 1962
Lantern for the Dark (Stirling), 1992
Lantern in the Night (Lamb, as Holland), 1973
Lantern Lane (Deeping), 1921
Lantern-Light (Duffield), 1933
Lap of Luxury (Ruck), 1931
Larcenous Lady (J. Smith), 1988
Larger than Life (Hooper), 1986
Lark Ascending (de la Roche), 1932
Lark in an Alien Sky (Stratton), 1979
Lark in the Meadow (Summers), 1959
Lark Shall Sing (Cadell), 1955
Larksbrook (Maddocks), 1962
Larksghyll (Heaven), 1986
Larry Munro (Stern), 1920
Larry Vincent (Keyes), 1952
Lass a King Loved (Bloom, as Prole), 1975
Lass He Left Behind Him! (M. St John, as St John Cooper), 1915
Lass of Silver, Lad of Gold (M. Peters, as Darby), 1982
Lass That Loved a Sailor (M. St John), 1915
Lasseter's Last Ride (Idriess), 1931
Last Act (Hodge), 1979

Last April Fair (Neels), 1980
Last Bannerman (Nicole, as Savage), 1993
Last Battle (Nicole), 1993
Last Bouquet (s Bowen), 1932
Last Bridge Home (Johansen), 1987
Last Camel Died at Noon (B. Michaels, as Peters), 1991
Last Cavalier (Pozzessere), 1993
Last Chance (Lorrimer, as Robins), 1961
Last Confession (s Caine), 1892
Last Cotillion (Roby, as Grey), 1980
Last Days with Cleopatra (J. Lindsay), 1935
Last Enchantment (Stewart), 1979
Last Farewell (McCutchan), 1991
Last Frontier (Fast), 1941
Last Galley (s Doyle), 1911
Last Gamble (Graham), 1955
Last Grand Passion (E. Darcy), 1993
Last Great Love (Harris), 1981
Last Heiress (T. Barclay), 1987
Last Honest Woman (N. Roberts), 1988
Last Love (Costain), 1963
Last Love of a King (Bloom, as Prole), 1974
Last Movement (Aiken), 1977
Last Night at Paradise (Weale), 1980
Last Night at the Ritz (Savage), 1973
Last of Summer (O'Brien), 1943
Last of the Greenwood (M. Peters, as Whitby), 1975
Last of the Kintyres (MacLeod, as Airlie), 1959
Last of the Laidlaws (Swan), 1933
Last of the Legions (s Doyle), 1925
Last of the Logans (Stuart, as A. Stuart), 1957
Last of the Mallorys (K. Thorpe), 1968
Last of the Stuarts (Plaidy), 1977
Last of the Tudors (Hamilton), 1971
Last of the Wine (Renault), 1956
Last of Their Race (Swan), 1911
Last Pool (s O'Brian), 1950
Last Princess (Freeman), 1988
Last Raider (Kent, as Reeman), 1963
Last Run (Harrod-Eagles, as Bennett), 1984
Last Seen Wearing (M. Peters, as Black), 1990
Last Straw for Harriet (Cadell), 1947
Last Supper (s Fast), 1955
Last Testament of Oscar Wilde (Ackroyd), 1983
Last Time (s Hichens), 1923
Last Trip (Stuart, as A. Stuart), 1972
Last Tsarina (Bloom, as Prole), 1970
Last Viking Queen (Taylor), 1994
Last Year's Nightingale (Lorrimer), 1984
Last Year's Roses (Chandos), 1945
Last Year's Wife (Williamson, as A.M. Williamson), 1932
Lasting Legacy (K. Thorpe), 1991
Lasting Lover (Bloom, as Burns), 1959
Lasting Spring (Stubbs), 1987
Latchkey Kid (Forrester, as Bhatia), 1971
Late and Soon (Delafield), 1943
Late Clare Beame (Caldwell), 1963
Late in the Afternoon (L. Cooper), 1971
Late Lark Singing (Jacob), 1952
Late Loving (Donald), 1987
Late Mrs Fonsell (V. Johnston), 1972
Late Mrs Lane (Randall), 1945
Late Rising Moon (Browning), 1984
Latitude of Love (R. Lindsay), 1971
Laugh on Friday (Lorrimer, as Robins), 1969
Laughing Cavalier (Greig), 1932

Laughing Cavalier (Orczy), 1914
Laughing Ghost (Eden), 1943
Laughing House (Deeping), 1946
Laughing Lady (Bloom), 1936
Laughing Stranger (Delmar), 1953
Laughter and Love Remain (Barcynska, as Sandys), 1962
Laughter in Cheyne Walk (Bloom), 1936
Laughter of Aphrodite (Green), 1965
Laughter of Life (Albanesi), 1908
Laura Sarelle (Bowen, as Shearing), 1940
Lauralee (Miller), 1987
Laurel of Stonystream (Baldwin), 1923
Laurell'd Captains (Bowen, as Preedy), 1935
Laurence, My Love (Robins), 1968
Laurian Vale (Bromige), 1952
Lavender's Love Story (Albanesi, as Rowlands), 1912
Law Is a Lady (N. Roberts), 1984
Law of Attraction (Jordan), 1992
Lawless (Jakes), 1978
Lawless (N. Roberts), 1989
Lawrence Clavering (A. Mason), 1897
Laying Down the Law (Vitek), 1986
Leading Lady (s du Maurier), 1945
Leading Lady (Hodge), 1990
Leading Lady (D. Murray), 1947
Leaf in the Storm (Hampson), 1978
Leaf in the Wind (Joseph), 1981
Leaf Turned Down (Albanesi), 1936
League of the Triangle (Wynne, as Lurgan), 1911
Leah's Story (F. Preston), 1989
Leap in the Dark (Randall), 1956
Leap Year Girl (Ruck), 1924
Leap Year Love (Ruck), 1957
Leap Year Romance (Ruck), 1957
Leaping Flame (Cartland), 1942
Learn to Laugh Again (Barcynska, as Sandys), 1947
Leatherface (Orczy), 1916
Leave It to Nancy (Chandos), 1953
Leave Love Alone (Armstrong), 1991
Leave Love to Itself (Garvice), 1908
Leave Me My Love (Plaidy, as Burford), 1953
Leave My Heart Alone (Lorrimer, as Robins), 1951
Leaves Before the Storm (Bloom), 1937
Leaves from the Valley (Trollope), 1980
Leaves in the Wind (Sheard), 1938
Leavetaking (Gilbert), 1979
Led Astray (Brown, as St Claire), 1985
Led by Love (Garvice), 1903
Left in Trust (K. Thorpe), 1992
Leftover Dreams (C. Allen), 1992
Leftover Love (Dailey), 1984
Legacy (Fast), 1981
Legacy (Krentz), 1985
Legacy (Lide), 1991
Legacy (Michener), 1987
Legacy (Seger), 1981
Legacy (Shute), 1950
Legacy for a Doctor (Seifert), 1963
Legacy of Doubt (MacLeod), 1989
Legacy of Love (Saunders, as Innes), 1982
Legacy of Love series (Trollope, as Harvey), from 1980
Legacy of Pride (Blackstock, as Allardyce), 1975
Legacy of the Past (Mather), 1975
Legacy of Tregaran (Lide), 1991
Legacy Without Love (Woodward, as Richmond), 1976
Legend (Anthony), 1969

Legend (Dane), 1919
Legend in Green Velvet (B. Michaels, as Peters), 1976
Legend of Baverstock Manor (Buckingham), 1968
Legend of Katmandu (Hunter, as Chace), 1969
Legend of Lexandros (Mather), 1969
Legend of the Seventh Virgin (Plaidy, as Holt), 1965
Legend of the Sun (Hunter), 1985
Legend of the Swans (Kidd), 1973
Legend of Witchwynd (Sherwood, as Hines), 1976
Leila Vane's Burden (Albanesi, as Rowlands), 1911
Lemmings (Blackstock), 1969
Lemon Tree (Forrester), 1990
Lenient God (Jacob), 1937
Leo Man (Stratton), 1980
Leola Dale's Fortune (Garvice), 1901
Leonie Locke (Libbey), 1889
Leonie (Manley-Tucker), 1958
Leonora (Fellows), 1972
Leopard and the Lily (Bowen), 1909
Leopard in the Snow (Mather), 1974
Leopards and Lilies (Duggan), 1954
Leopards and Spots (Jacob), 1942
Leopard's Lair (May), 1984
Leopard's Spots (Dixon), 1902
Lesley Forrest, MD (R. Lindsay), 1962
Leslie's Loyalty (Garvice), 1911
Less of a Stranger (N. Roberts), 1984
Lesson in Love (Sebastian, as Gladstone), 1981
Lesson in Loving (Chappell), 1961
Lesson in Loving (Way), 1975
Lesson to Learn (Jordan), 1992
Lessons in Love (Cartland), 1974
Lessons in Love (Chesney), 1987
Lessons Learned (N. Roberts), 1986
Let Erin Remember (Wynne), 1908
Let Loose the Tigers (Cox), 1987
Let Love Come Last (Caldwell), 1948
Let Me Love (Robins), 1979
Let the Storm Burst (Barcynska), 1941
Let's All Be Happy (Barcynska, as Sandys), 1952
Letter for Don (Burchell), 1950
Letter from Lydia (Chappell), 1974
Letter from Peking (Buck), 1957
Letter from Spain (Keyes), 1959
Letter of Marque (O'Brian), 1988
Letter to a Stranger (Thane), 1954
Letter to My Love (Cadell), 1963
Letter to My Love (Chandos), 1942
Letters for a Spy (Ley), 1970
Letters from Fleet Street (Barcynska, as Barclay), 1912
Letters to Sanchia (Hewlett), 1908
Letty (C. Darcy), 1980
Letty (Lofts), 1968
Letty and the Law (Baldwin), 1940
Letty Lynton (Lowndes), 1931
Levelling the Score (Jordan), 1988
Lewis Rand (M. Johnston), 1908
Liar's Moon (Pozzessere, as Graham), 1987
Liberated Lady (Wentworth), 1979
Libertine in Love (Courtney), 1982
Library Tree (Peake), 1972
Lie Down in Roses (Pozzessere, as Drake), 1988
Lie Quiet in Your Grave (Roby), 1970
Lies for Love (Cartland), 1983
Lieutenant of the Line (McCutchan, as MacNeil), 1970
Life and Death of Harriett Frean (M. Sinclair), 1922

Life and Death of My Lord Gilles de Rais (Nye), 1990
Life and Death of Richard Yea-and-Nay (Hewlett), 1900
Life—and Erica (Frankau), 1924
Life and Gabriella (Glasgow), 1916
Life and Love (Robins), 1935
Life and Times of Horatio Hornblower (Parkinson), 1970
Life Begins Tomorrow (Manley-Tucker), 1975
Life Everlasting (Corelli), 1911
Life for Two (MacLeod), 1936
Life He Led Her! (M. St John), 1926
Life Is the Destiny (Stuart), 1958
Life Line (Albanesi, as Rowlands), 1924
Life Mask (Williamson, as A.M. Williamson), 1913
Life Steps In (Ayres), 1928
Life Story (Bentley), 1948
Lifeblood (Slaughter), 1974
Lifelong Affair (Mortimer), 1983
Life's a Game (Robins), 1933
Life's Love (Albanesi, as Rowlands), 1911
Light a Penny Candle (Binchy), 1982
Light from One Star (Muskett), 1956
Light Heart (Hewlett), 1920
Light Heart (Thane), 1947
Light in Italy (J. Lindsay), 1941
Light in Summer (Stubbs), 1991
Light in the Clearing (Bacheller), 1917
Light in the Swamp (V. Johnston), 1970
Light in the Tower (MacLeod), 1971
Light in the Ward (Andrews), 1965
Light in the Window (Rinehart), 1948
Light of Love (Cartland), 1981
Light of the Gods (Cartland), 1984
Light of the Moon (Cartland), 1979
Light of the Moon (E. Buchan), 1991
Light on Lucrezia (Plaidy), 1958
Light That Lies (McCutcheon), 1916
Light the Candles (s Robins), 1959
Light to the Heart (Cartland, as McCorquodale), 1962
Light Woman (Gavin), 1986
Lighted Room (L. Cooper), 1925
Lighted Windows (Loring), 1930
Lighted Windows (Ritchie), 1952
Lighthearted Quest (Bridge), 1956
Lightly Like a Flower (Alexander, as Armstrong), 1978
Lightning Conductor (Williamson), 1902
Lightning Conductor Comes Back (Williamson, as A.M. Williamson), 1933
Lightning Conductress (Williamson), 1916
Lightning Lingers (London, as Curtis), 1986
Lightning Strike (Lewty), 1990
Lightning Strikes Twice (Robins), 1966
Lightning Tree (Aiken), 1980
Lights and Shadows (Albanesi, as Rowlands), 1928
Lights, Laughter and a Lady (Cartland), 1983
Lights of London (Andrews), 1985
Lights of Love (Cartland, as McCorquodale), 1958
Like as the Roaring Waves (Wiat), 1972
Like Us They Lived (Barnes), 1944
Like Victors and Lords (Stuart), 1964
Like We Used to Be (Stubbs), 1989
Likely to Die (Summerton, as Roffman), 1964
Likewise the Lyon (L. Cooper), 1928
Lil, The Dancing Queen (Garvice, as Hart)
Lilac Awakening (Delinsky, as Drake), 1982
Lilac Bus (s Binchy), 1984
Lilamani (Diver), 1911

Lilith (Plaidy, as Kellow), 1954
Lilla (Lowndes), 1916
Lilli Barr (Bromfield), 1926
Lillian Harley (Cockrell), 1943
Lillian's Vow (Garvice, as Hart)
Lily and the Leopards (Harwood), 1949
Lily and the Major (Miller), 1990
Lily Christine (Arlen), 1928
Lily Golightly (Oldfield), 1987
Lily Hand (s Pargeter), 1965
Lily-of-the-Valley (Bloom), 1938
Lime Street at Two (Forrester), 1985
Limelight for Jane (Gibbs, as Ford), 1970
Limited Engagement (Alexander, as Armstrong), 1980
Limmerston Hall (Chapman), 1972
Lincoln (Vidal), 1984
Lindy Lou (Cleugh), 1934
Lingering Shadows (Jordan), 1992
Linked by Fate (Garvice), 1905
Linnet Singing (Eden), 1972
Linnie (Garvice), 1908
Lion and the Sun (I. Roberts), 1969
Lion at the Door (P. Hastings), 1983
Lion Beat the Unicorn (James), 1935
Lion by the Mane (Drummond, as Dane), 1975
Lion in the Garden (Stern), 1940
Lion in the Valley (B. Michaels, as Peters), 1986
Lion in the Way (Cadell), 1982
Lion Let Loose (Tranter), 1967
Lion of Delos (Worboys), 1974
Lion of Justice (Plaidy), 1975
Lion of Languedoc (Pemberton), 1981
Lion of Mortimer (Dymoke), 1979
Lion of Trevarrock (Heaven, as Fecher), 1969
Lion Rock (Wentworth), 1983
Lion-Tamer (Hull), 1928
Lion Triumphant (Plaidy, as Carr), 1974
Lion Without Claws (Wiat), 1976
Lioness and the Lily (Cartland), 1981
Lionors (B. Johnson), 1975
Lion's Legacy (Dymoke), 1974
Lion's Mouse (Williamson), 1919
Lion's Shadow (Hunter), 1980
Lion's Share (Westcott), 1972
Lion's Skin (Sabatini), 1911
Lips for a Stranger (Greig, as Ames), 1949
Lisa Logan (Joseph), 1984
Lisbon (Sherwood), 1989
Listen for the Whisperer (Whitney), 1972
Listen to Danger (Eden), 1958
Listener (Caldwell), 1960
Listening Silence (Joseph), 1982
Listening Valley (D. Stevenson), 1944
Little Adventure (Cartland), 1973
Little and Good (Ayres), 1940
Little and Good (M. St John), 1918
Little Big Man (Berger), 1964
Little Bit of Luck (Melville, as Betteridge), 1967
Little Brown Girl (Chandos, as Tempest), 1940
Little Brown Mouse (Albanesi), 1906
Little Doctor (MacLeod), 1960
Little Dragon (Neels), 1977
Little Emperors (Duggan), 1951
Little 'Gutter Girl' (M. St John), 1919
Little Heiress (Cowen), 1961
Little Iliad (Hewlett), 1915

Little Impostor (Peake), 1976
Little Kit (Albanesi, as Rowlands), 1895
Little Lady (Albanesi), 1937
Little Lady Charles (Albanesi, as Rowlands), 1899
Little Lady in Lodgings (Ayres), 1922
Little Leafy (Libbey), 1891
Little Less Than Gods (Ford), 1928
Little Man (Ayres), 1931
Little Matron of the Cottage Hospital (Bloom, as Harvey), 1969
Little Millstones (Worboys, as Eyre), 1970
Little Miss Innocence (M. St John), 1918
Little Miss Lancashire (M. St John), 1921
Little Miss Millions (M. St John), 1914
Little Moonlight (Neels), 1991
Little Mountebank (Mackinlay), 1930
Little Nobody (Winspear), 1972
Little Novels of Italy (s Hewlett), 1899
Little Nurse (Bloom, as Essex), 1967
Little Pardner (s E. Porter), 1926
Little Pretender (Cartland), 1951
Little Princess (Garvice, as Hart)
Little Red Horses (Stern), 1932
Little Romp Edda (Libbey)
Little Rosebud's Lovers (Libbey), 1888
Little Ships (Norris), 1921
Little Sinner (Ayres), 1940
Little Sister (Burchell), 1939
Little Sisters Don't Count (Greig), 1932
Little Spot of Bother (Polland), 1967
Little Stranger (Swan), 1933
Little Tiger (Hope), 1925
Little Tongues of Fire (Cartland), 1988
Little Victoria (Bloom, as Prole), 1957
Little Wax Doll (Lofts, as Curtis), 1970
Little We Know (Robins), 1940
Little White Doves of Love (Cartland), 1980
Little White Lies (Lewty), 1992
Little White Nun (Williamson, as A.M. Williamson), 1903
Little Wig-Maker of Bread Street (Bloom, as Prole), 1959
Littl'st Lover (Ayres), 1917
Live Bait (s Dell), 1932
Live Happily—Love Song (Bloom, as Burns), 1952
Lively Lady (K. Roberts), 1931
Liverpool Basque (Forrester), 1993
Liverpool Daisy (Forrester, as Bhatia), 1979
Liverpool Family series (A. Howard), from 1984
Lives of a Woman (Hutten), 1935
Living Apart (Ayres), 1937
Living Phantom (Harwood), 1973
Living Reed (Buck), 1963
Living to Earn (Ponsonby), 1961
Living Together (Mortimer), 1981
Living with Adam (Mather), 1972
Living with Adam (Muskett), 1949
Liz o' Loomland (M. St John), 1917
Lizbeth Rose (M. St John), 1927
Lizzie Borden (Lowndes), 1939
Loaded Stick (Jacob), 1934
Loan of a Lover (Libbey)
Local Hero (N. Roberts), 1988
Lodestar (Belle), 1987
Lodestone for Love (Ritchie), 1980
Lodger (Lowndes), 1913
Lodger (Staples), 1991
Lodger in His Own Home (M. St John, as St John Cooper), 1920
Lofty Banners (Clarke), 1979

Log of a Naval Officer's Wife (Bloom), 1932
Logic of the Heart (Browning), 1982
Logic of the Heart (Veryan), 1990
London and Paris (s du Maurier), 1945
London Goes to Heaven (Lane), 1947
London, Here I Come (Greig), 1951
London Linnet (Alexander, as Langley), 1985
London Pride (Hunter), 1983
London Season (Bishop), 1975
London Transports (s Binchy), 1983
London Venture (Arlen), 1920
Londoners (Hichens), 1898
Lone Star Surrender (Finch), 1988
Lonely Bride (Duffield), 1947
Lonely Doctor (Baldwin), 1964
Lonely Farrow (MacLeod), 1940
Lonely Furrow (Diver), 1923
Lonely Furrow (Lofts), 1976
Lonely House (Lowndes), 1920
Lonely Little Lucy (M. St John), 1921
Lonely Man (Baldwin), 1964
Lonely Man (Frankau), 1932
Lonely One (Rayner, as Brandon), 1965
Lonely Parade (Hurst), 1942
Lonely Queen (Bailey), 1911
Lonely Quest (Lorrimer, as Robins), 1959
Lonely Road (Farnol), 1938
Lonely Road (Manley-Tucker), 1983
Lonely Season (Napier), 1986
Lonely Shore (Weale), 1956
Lonely Strangers (Blackstock), 1972
Lonesome Road (Chandos, as Tempest), 1966
Long Acre (Rayner), 1978
Long and Living Shadow (Winston), 1968
Long Barnaby (P. Hastings), 1961
Long Coffin (Tranter), 1956
Long Cold Winter (Jordan), 1982
Long Corridor (Cookson), 1965
Long Dance of Love (Melville, as Betteridge), 1963
Long Dark Night of the Soul (Ellis), 1978
Long Dark Summer (Oldfield), 1992
Long Day Wanes (Burgess), 1984
Long Division (Chapman), 1943
Long, Hot Days (M. Lewis), 1966
Long Hunt (Boyd), 1930
Long Journey (James), 1941
Long Journey Back (Donald), 1986
Long Lane to Happiness (Ayres), 1915
Long Live the King! (Rinehart), 1917
Long, Long Wooing (M. St John), 1927
Long-Lost Father (Stern), 1932
Long Masquerade (Brent), 1981
Long Night (Lytle), 1936
Long Night (Weyman), 1903
Long Remember (Kantor), 1934
Long Road (Muskett), 1951
Long Roll (M. Johnston), 1911
Long Shadow (Donnelly), 1973
Long Shadow (Gilbert), 1983
Long Shadow (Harrod-Eagles), 1983
Long Shadow (Robins), 1954
Long Shadows (Jacob), 1964
Long Short Story (s Stern), 1939
Long Summer Days (Delderfield), 1974
Long Summer Shadows (Bishop), 1978
Long Surrender (Lamb), 1978

Long Tall Texan series (Palmer), from 1988
Long Time Ago (Kennedy), 1932
Long Time Coming (Brown), 1989
Long Time to Hate (W. Roberts), 1982
Long Traverse (J. Buchan), 1941
Long Wait (Lorrimer, as Robins), 1962
Long Way from Home (Pilcher, as Fraser), 1963
Long Way Home (Chandos, as Tempest), 1943
Long Week-End (s Kennedy), 1927
Long Winter's Night (Stanford), 1981
Longest Pleasure (Mather), 1986
Longest Pleasure (Nicole), 1970
Longing for Love (M. St John), 1925
Longshadow (McElfresh, as Blair), 1976
Longwarden series (Weale), from 1987
Look, Listen, and Love (Cartland), 1977
Look of Innocence (Gilbert), 1975
Look Out for Liza (Baldwin), 1950
Look to the Spring (Ayres), 1932
Look to the Stars (Loring), 1957
Look with Love (Cartland), 1985
Lookalike Love (Buckingham, as John), 1986
Looking for Love (Cartland), 1982
Loom of Fate (Garvice), 1913
Loom of Love (M. Peters, as Grey), 1979
Loom of Tancred (Pearson), 1967
Loon Lake (Doctorow), 1980
Loose Ladies (s Delmar), 1929
Lord and the Gypsy (Veryan), 1978
Lord Caliban (F. Stevenson, as Fitzgerald), 1985
Lord Dedringham's Divorce (Sebastian), 1978
Lord Deverill's Heir (Coulter), 1980
Lord Fordington's Offer (Oliver, as James), 1982
Lord Geoffrey's Fancy (Duggan), 1962
Lord Gilmore's Bride (Walsh), 1979
Lord Harry's Folly (Coulter), 1980
Lord Hugo series (Oliver), from 1981
Lord John in New York (Williamson), 1918
Lord of Greenwich (Dymoke), 1980
Lord of Hawkfell Island (Coulter), 1993
Lord of Himself (Garvice), 1911
Lord of Imchay (Woodward, as Marsh), 1975
Lord of La Pampa (K. Thorpe), 1977
Lord of Leet Castle (O. Sinclair, as Daniels), 1984
Lord of Little Langton (Burgin), 1924
Lord of Misrule (Wentworth), 1990
Lord of Shadowhawk (McKenna), 1992
Lord of Sin (Nicole), 1980
Lord of the Far Island (Plaidy, as Holt), 1975
Lord of the Golden Fan (Nicole), 1973
Lord of the High Lonesome (Dailey), 1980
Lord of the High Valley (Way), 1980
Lord of the Isles (Tranter), 1983
Lord of the Sierras (Weale), 1975
Lord of the Silver Dragon (Salverson), 1927
Lord of the Wolf (Wiat), 1980
Lord of the Wolves (Pozzessere, as Graham), 1993
Lord of Zaracus (Mather), 1970
Lord Orlando's Protegée (Sebastian), 1977
Lord Ravenscar's Revenge (Cartland), 1978
Lord Sin (Gluyas), 1980
Lord Tony's Wife (Orczy), 1917
Lord Vanity (Shellabarger), 1953
Lords of Lancaster (Bennetts), 1973
Lords of Misrule (Tranter), 1976
Lords of Vaumartin (Holland), 1988

Love Forbidden (Cartland, as McCorquodale), 1957
Love, Forever More (Matthews), 1977
Love Game (Robins), 1936
Love Games (Lamb), 1984
Love Gives Itself (Swan), 1915
Love Goes South (Mackinlay), 1935
Love Grown Cold (Swan), 1902
Love Has His Way (Cartland), 1979
Love Has No Limits (Trask), 1939
Love Has No Resurrection (s Delafield), 1939
Love Has No Secrets (Bloom, as Harvey), 1972
Love Has Two Faces (M. Lewis), 1981
Love Has Wings (Trask), 1939
Love-Hater (Ruck), 1930
Love Hath an Island (Hampson), 1970
Love Hath an Island (Robins), 1950
Love Him or Leave Him (Burchell), 1950
Love Holds the Cards (Cartland), 1965
Love, Honour, and Obey (Greig), 1933
Love in a Cloud (L. Walker), 1960
Love in a Dry Season (Foote), 1951
Love in a Far Country (Greig, as Ames), 1960
Love-in-a-Mist (Albanesi), 1907
Love in a Mist (Lamb, as Holland), 1971
Love in a Rainy Country (Melville, as Betteridge), 1969
Love in a Snare (Garvice), 1912
Love in a Stranger's Arms (Winspear), 1977
Love in Amber (Muskett), 1942
Love in Apron Strings (Hoy), 1933
Love in Danger (Woodward, as Ware), 1972
Love in Disguise (R. Lindsay), 1975
Love in Disguise (Pykare), 1980
Love in Hazard (Marsh), 1989
Love in Hiding (Cartland), 1959
Love in Peril (Woodward, as Marsh), 1967
Love in Pity (Cartland), 1977
Love in Store (R. Lindsay, as Leigh), 1978
Love in the Clouds (Cartland), 1979
Love in the Dark (Cartland), 1979
Love in the Dark (Lamb), 1986
Love in the East (Greig, as Ames), 1960
Love in the Lead (Woodward, as Davis), 1967
Love in the Moon (Cartland), 1980
Love in the Moonlight (Peake), 1986
Love in the Valley (Napier), 1984
Love in Waiting (Courtney), 1984
Love in Winter (Jameson), 1935
Love Is a Dangerous Game (Lewty), 1980
Love Is a Flame (Lowndes), 1932
Love Is a Flower (Barcynska, as Sandys), 1938
Love Is a Frenzy (Lamb), 1979
Love Is a Gamble (Cartland), 1985
Love Is a Gamble (Greig, as Ames), 1954
Love Is a Lady (Barcynska), 1945
Love Is a Thief (Greig), 1959
Love Is an Eagle (Cartland), 1951
Love Is Contraband (Cartland), 1968
Love Is Dangerous (Cartland, as McCorquodale), 1963
Love Is Enough (Robins), 1941
Love Is Eternal (Stone), 1954
Love Is Everything (Bloom), 1933
Love Is Fire (Kidd), 1971
Love Is Heaven (Cartland), 1984
Love Is Innocent (Cartland), 1975
Love Is Invincible (Cartland), 1988
Love Is Like That (Woodward, as Lawrence), 1967

Love Is Mine (Cartland, as McCorquodale), 1952
Love Is My Reason (Burchell), 1957
Love Is Not Enough (Corcoran), 1981
Love Is So Blind (Ayres), 1933
Love Is the Enemy (Cartland), 1952
Love Is the Honey (Winspear), 1980
Love Is the Key (Cartland), 1990
Love Itself (Glyn), 1924
Love Joins the Clan (Cartland), 1986
Love Knot (M. Peters, as Darby), 1989
Love Knows No Frontier (Woodward, as Ware), 1970
Love Leaves at Midnight (Cartland), 1978
Love Letter (Norway, as Neal), 1963
Love Life (C. Allen), 1976
Love Lifts the Curse (Cartland), 1992
Love Like Ours (Robins), 1969
Love Locked In (Cartland), 1977
Love Locked Out (Trask), 1938
Love, Lords, and Lady-Birds (Cartland), 1978
Love Made the Choice (Burchell), 1942
Love Maggy (Barcynska), 1918
Love Match (Albanesi, as Rowlands), 1912
Love Match (Chesney), 1992
Love Match (Fellows), 1977
Love Match (R. Lindsay, as Leigh), 1980
Love Me (Greig), 1971
Love Me Before Dawn (McKenna), 1984
Love Me for Ever (Cartland), 1953
Love Me Forever, (Cartland), 1970
Love Me—Love Me Not (Woodward), 1966
Love Me No More! (Robins), 1948
Love Me Not (Armstrong), 1985
Love Me To-morrow (Bloom, as Burns), 1952
Love Me Tomorrow (Lorrimer, as Robins), 1966
Love Me with Fury (Taylor), 1983
Love Must Wait (Lorrimer, as Robins), 1958
Love Needs Telling (M. St John), 1926
Love Never Dies (Barcynska), 1943
Love Not Dishonour (S. Wood), 1989
Love Not the Enemy (Seger, as Jennings), 1984
Love of a Life Time (Garvice)
Love of His Life (Albanesi, as Rowlands), 1912
Love of Julie Borel (Norris), 1931
Love of Long Ago (s Corelli), 1920
Love of Lucifer (Winston), 1970
Love of My Life (Courtney), 1981
Love of Robert Dennison (Ayres), 1921
Love, Old and New (Bloom), 1933
Love on a Shoestring (Mackinlay), 1958
Love on Dark Wings (Greig, as Ames), 1957
Love on Ice (Woodward, as Sawley), 1967
Love on Second Thoughts (Ruck), 1936
Love on the Run (Cartland, as McCorquodale), 1965
Love on the Wind (Cartland), 1983
Love Only Once (Lindsey), 1985
Love Pavilion (P. Scott), 1960
Love Pirate (Cartland), 1977
Love Pirate (Williamson), 1913
Love Play (Rogers), 1981
Love Plays a Part (Pykare), 1981
Love Puzzle (Cartland), 1987
Love Race (Woodward, as Richmond), 1967
Love Remembered (Beresford), 1970
Love Rides the Skies (Woodward, as Lawrence), 1968
Love Rules (Cartland), 1982
Love She Hid (Woodward, as Ware), 1970

Love so Fearful (Pykare, as N. Coombs), 1983
Love So Rare (Hampson), 1983
Love So Young (Robins), 1945
Love Song for a Raven (Lowell), 1987
Love Song (Hamilton, as Watson), 1981
Love Song in Springtime (Manley-Tucker), 1960
Love Song of the Sea (I. Roberts), 1960
Love Spins the Wheel (Woodward, as Marsh), 1967
Love, Spread Your Wings (Manley-Tucker), 1967
Love Springs Eternal (Gallagher), 1985
Love Stories of India (s Marshall), 1950
Love Stories (s Rinehart), 1920
Love Storm (S. Johnson), 1981
Love-Story of Aliette Brunton (Frankau), 1922
Love Story of Duke (Bloom, as Essex), 1960
Love Story of Nurse Julie (Bloom, as Harvey), 1975
Love Strikes Satan (Cartland), 1991
Love Takes the Helm (Woodward, as Marsh), 1967
Love Talker (B. Michaels, as Peters), 1980
Love Tangle (Sebastian, as Gladstone), 1979
Love That Divided (M. St John, as St John Cooper), 1932
Love That Follows (Ritchie), 1966
Love That Is Stronger Than Life (Maybury), 1932
Love That Lasts (Burgin), 1913
Love That Lasts (Chandos, as Lance), 1974
Love That Lives (Albanesi), 1937
Love, The Adventurous (Garvice), 1917
Love, The Magician (Goodwin, as Ebel), 1956
Love, The Master Key (Swan), 1905
Love the Prodigal (Swan), 1929
Love, The Tyrant (Garvice), 1905
Love Theme (Way), 1974
Love Thing (Browning), 1984
Love This Enemy (K. Blair), 1958
Love This Stranger (K. Blair, as Brett), 1951
Love to the Rescue (Cartland), 1967
Love Token (Gellis, as Hamilton), 1979
Love Trap (Cartland), 1986
Love Trap (Delmar), 1949
Love Trap (Price), 1958
Love Triumphant (Courtney), 1980
Love Triumphant (Maybury), 1932
Love Undefeated (Laffeaty), 1986
Love under Fire (Cartland), 1960
Love Unlocks the Door (Swan), 1907
Love Unmasked (Courtney), 1979
Love Unspoken (Mortimer), 1983
Love Untamed (van der Zee), 1994
Love Was a Jest (Robins), 1929
Love While You Wait (Chandos, as Tempest), 1944
Love Wild and Fair (Small), 1978
Love Will Lend Wings (Ritchie), 1957
Love Will Win (Greig, as Ames), 1969
Love Wins (Albanesi, as Rowlands), 1912
Love Wins (Cartland), 1981
Love with a Song (Trask), 1937
Love with Honor (Loring), 1969
Love Without Wings (Ayres), 1953
Lovechild (Hamilton, as Watson), 1967
Loved (Spencer), 1984
Loved and the Cherished (Manley-Tucker), 1964
Loved and the Feared (Winspear), 1977
Loved for Her Money (M. St John), 1927
Loved for Himself (Cartland), 1992
Loveland series (Williamson), 1910
Loveless Marriage (Ayres), 1921

Lovely Clay (Greig), 1930
Lovely Destiny (Maybury), 1936
Lovely Liar (Cartland), 1988
Lovely Lying Lips (Sherwood), 1983
Lovely Shadow (Bloom), 1942
Lovely, Though Late (Chandos, as Tempest), 1946
Lovely Wanton (Heaven, as Fecher), 1977
Loveplay (Palmer), 1986
Lover (s du Maurier), 1961
Lover Betrayed (Stuart), 1955
Lover Dark, Lady Fair (M. Peters, as Black), 1983
Lover from the Sea (Delinsky, as Drake), 1983
Lover from Yesterday (Woodward), 1984
Lover in Pursuit (Krentz, as James), 1982
Lover in Rags (M. St John, as St John Cooper), 1924
Lover in the Rough (Lowell), 1984
Lover on Loan (MacGill), 1923
Lover Who Died (Ayres), 1922
Lovers (Ayres), 1929
Lovers (s Buck), 1977
Lovers (Goodwin), 1988
Lovers (Wiat), 1993
Lovers (Winsor), 1952
Lovers All Untrue (Lofts), 1970
Lovers and Outlaws (Nicole), 1982
Lover's Fate, and A Friend's Counsel (s Hope), 1894
Lovers in Lisbon (Cartland), 1987
Lovers in Paradise (Cartland), 1978
Lovers in the Afternoon (Mortimer), 1985
Lovers in the Dark (Greig, as Ames), 1946
Lovers' Knots (Bowen), 1912
Lovers Meeting (Hardwick), 1979
Lovers' Meeting (E. Smith), 1940
Lovers of Janine (Robins), 1931
Lovers of Yvonne (Sabatini), 1902
Lovers' Tale (Hewlett), 1915
Lovers' Touch (Jordan), 1988
Lovers under the Sun (Greig), 1954
Lover's Victory (Courtney), 1984
Lover's Vows (J. Smith), 1981
Love's a Magician (Woodward), 1981
Love's a Puzzle (Baldwin), 1933
Love's a Stage (London), 1980
Love's Agony (Winspear), 1981
Love's Avenging Heart (Matthews), 1977
Love's Barrier (Swan), 1910
Love's Blindness (Glyn), 1926
Love's Bold Journey (Matthews), 1980
Love's Bright Flame (Lamb, as Holland), 1978
Love's Choice (Thomas), 1982
Love's Choices (Jordan), 1988
Love's Cousin (Miles), 1927
Love's Cruel Whim (Albanesi, as Rowlands)
Love's Daring Dream (Matthews), 1978
Love's Dark Shadow (Woodward, as Sawley), 1970
Love's Defiance (MacGill), 1926
Love's Delusion (Pykare, as Pemberton), 1980
Love's Dilemma (Garvice), 1902
Love's Duel (Mortimer), 1982
Love's Duet (Veryan), 1979
Love's Encore (Brown, as Ryan), 1981
Love's Fire (Albanesi, as Rowlands), 1911
Love's Folly (Pykare), 1980
Love's Gentle Chains (Stanford), 1983
Love's Golden Destiny (Matthews), 1979
Love's Greatest Gift (Albanesi, as Rowlands), 1906

Love's Harbinger (J. Smith), 1987
Love's Harvest (Albanesi, as Rowlands), 1911
Love's Hidden Treasure (Finch), 1990
Love's Hour (Glyn), 1932
Love's Lady Lost (Veryan, as Moore), 1991
Love's Last Barrier (Woodward, as Lawrence), 1971
Love's Last Reward (Barcynska), 1920
Love's Logic (s Hope), 1908
Love's Magic Moment (Matthews), 1979
Love's Mask (Albanesi, as Rowlands), 1913
Love's Masquerade (Courtney), 1981
Love's Memory (Duffield), 1936
Love's Miracle (Swan), 1910
Loves of a Virgin Princess (Bloom, as Prole), 1968
Loves of an Actress (Hutten), 1929
Loves of Catrin (Gower), 1986
Loves of Ginerva (P. Hill), 1990
Loves of Lucrezia (Robins, as Wright), 1953
Love's Only Deception (Mortimer), 1983
Love's Pagan Heart (Matthews), 1978
Love's Penalty (Wynne), 1927
Love's Perilous Passage (Harrod-Eagles, as Woodhouse), 1978
Love's Playthings (Bloom), 1932
Love's Prisoner (Winspear), 1964
Love's Promise (Pykare), 1979
Love's Raging Tide (Matthews), 1980
Love's Reckless Rebel (Finch, as Robins), 1988
Love's Revenge (Lowndes), 1929
Love's Reward (Donald), 1989
Love's Rugged Path (Garvice, as Hart)
Love's Shadow (Heaven), 1994
Love's Stolen Promises (Sommerfield), 1992
Love's Sweet Agony (Matthews), 1980
Love's Sweet Music (Saunders), 1983
Love's Sweetest Secret (Finch, as Robins), 1991
Love's Treasure Trove (Woodward, as Davis), 1973
Love's Victory (Robins), 1933
Love's Waif (M. St John, as St John Cooper), 1921
Love's Way (J. Smith), 1982
Love's Wild Desire (J. Blake), 1977
Love's Wildest Promise (Matthews), 1977
Love's Wilful Call (Roby), 1981
Love's Young Dream (Albanesi, as Rowlands), 1914
Lovesong (Sherwood), 1986
Loving (Jordan), 1986
Loving (Steel), 1980
Loving and Giving (Keane), 1988
Loving and Giving (Robins), 1965
Loving Arrangement (Palmer, as Blayne), 1983
Loving Cup 1813–1815 (Graham), 1984
Loving Gamble (Kidd), 1988
Loving Gift (Mortimer), 1989
Loving Heart (Chappell), 1977
Loving Heart (L. Walker), 1960
Loving Heritage (Marsh), 1987
Loving Highwayman (Bennetts), 1983
Loving Is Giving (Burchell), 1956
Loving Jack (N. Roberts), 1989
Loving Meddler (R. Marshall), 1954
Loving Memory (Jameson), 1937
Loving Partnership (Marsh), 1978
Loving Relations (Hunter), 1984
Loving Rescue (Browning), 1982
Loving Sands, Deadly Sands (Blackstock, as Keppel), 1975
Loving Slave (M. Pargeter), 1981
Loving Spirit (du Maurier), 1931

Loving Without Tears (Keane, as Farrell), 1951
Low Country Liar (Dailey), 1979
Loyal Defence (Albanesi, as Rowlands), 1932
Loyal in All (Burchell), 1957
Loyal Lady (Cleugh), 1932
Loyal Man's Love (Albanesi, as Rowlands), 1910
Loyalties (Ellis), 1990
Loyalty (Albanesi), 1930
Lucasta (Bishop), 1978
Lucia in Love (Pozzessere), 1988
Lucifer and the Angel (Cartland), 1980
Lucifer's Angel (Winspear), 1961
Lucile Cléry (Bowen, as Shearing), 1932
Lucille (Garvice)
Lucinda (Hope), 1920
Lucinda Marries the Doctor (Seifert), 1953
Luck-Bride (M. Peters), 1987
Luck of the Livingstones (Swan), 1932
Luckiest Lady (Ayres), 1927
Lucky in Love (Cartland), 1982
Lucky in Love (Ruck), 1924
Lucky Lawrences (Norris), 1930
Lucky Number (Dell), 1920
Lucky One (Lewty), 1961
Lucretia (Riefe), 1982
Lucretia Lombard (Norris), 1922
Lucy (Chapman), 1965
Lucy (Chesney, as Tremaine), 1980
Lucy Carmichael (Kennedy), 1951
Lucy Gayheart (Cather), 1932
Lucy's Cottage (Bennetts), 1981
Lummox (Hurst), 1923
Lure of Eagles (Mather), 1979
Luring a Lady (N. Roberts), 1992
Lust for Life (Stone), 1934
Lute Player (Lofts), 1951
Luxury Husband (Greig), 1928
Luxury Ladies (Price, as Smith), 1933
Lydia (C. Darcy), 1973
Lydia Bailey (K. Roberts), 1947
Lydian Inheritance (Bromige), 1966
Lying in the Sun (s O'Brian), 1956
Lymond series (Dunnett), from 1969
Lyndall's Temptation (Libbey), 1892
Lyndley Waters (Bowen, as Preedy), 1942
Lynmara Legacy (Gaskin), 1975
Lyonhurst (Randall), 1977
Lyons Mail (Wynne), 1917
Lyon's Share (Dailey), 1977
Lyra, My Love (Chandos, as Tempest), 1969
Lysander (F. Mason), 1956
Lysbeth (Haggard), 1901

MD (W. Roberts), 1972
MF (Burgess), 1971
Mabel St John's Schooldays (M. St John, as St John Cooper), 1921
Macbeth, King of Scots (Clarke, as Honeyman), 1977
Macbeth the King (Tranter), 1978
MacBride of Tordarroch (Summers), 1984
MacGregor series (N. Roberts), from 1985
MacGregor series (Tranter), from 1957
Mackenzie's Lady (Schulze), 1986
Mackenzie's Mission (L. Howard), 1992
MacKenzie's Mountain (L. Howard), 1989
Mackinder series (Nicole), from 1988
Macleod's Wife (Swan), 1924

Maclure Mystery (Swan), 1932
MacLyon (Burford), 1974
Macomber Menace (W. Roberts), 1979
Mad Barbara (Deeping), 1908
Mad Betrothal (Libbey), 1890
Mad for Dress! (M. St John), 1921
Mad Is the Heart (Robins), 1963
Mad Puppetstown (Keane, as Farrell), 1931
Mad Trapper (Wiebe), 1980
Madalena (Walsh), 1976
Madam Claire (Ertz), 1923
Madam, Will You Talk? (Stewart), 1955
Madam, You Must Die (Blackstock, as Keppel), 1975
Madame Adastra (Barcynska, as Sandys), 1964
Madame Castel's Lodger (Keyes), 1962
Madame de Treymes (Wharton), 1907
Madame du Barry (Plaidy, as Tate), 1959
Madame Fears the Dark (s Irwin), 1935
Madame Geneva (Lane), 1946
Madame Juno (Mackinlay), 1931
Madame Serpent (Plaidy), 1951
Madame Tudor (Gluyas), 1979
Madawaska (W. Roberts), 1988
Maddalena (P. Hill), 1963
Madderleys Married (Chandos, as Tempest), 1963
Made to Marry (Chandos), 1944
Madeleine (Gavin), 1957
Madeleine (Rhodes), 1989
Mademoiselle Madelaine (Alexander, as Langley), 1981
Madensky Square (Ibbotson), 1988
Madge o' the Mill (M. St John, as St John Cooper), 1921
Madness of Love (Albanesi, as Rowlands), 1911
Madness of Love (Garvice, as Hart)
Madolin Rivers (Libbey), 1885
Madonna of the Seven Hills (Plaidy), 1958
Madselin (Lofts), 1969
Mag Pye (Hutten), 1917
Magdalene Scrolls (B. Wood), 1978
Maggie (Chesney, as Tremaine), 1984
Maggie Craig (Joseph), 1980
Maggie Darling (M. St John), 1915
Maggie, Her Marriage (Caldwell), 1953
Maggie Jordan (E. Blair), 1990
Maggie of Marley's Mill (M. St John), 1926
Maggie Rowan (Cookson), 1954
Maggot (Fowles), 1985
Magic and Mary Rose (Baldwin), 1924
Magic Flutes (Ibbotson), 1982
Magic for Marigold (Montgomery), 1929
Magic from the Heart (Cartland), 1991
Magic Garden (G. Porter), 1927
Magic in Maoriland (I. Preston), 1962
Magic in Vienna (Neels), 1985
Magic Lantern (E. Smith), 1944
Magic Moment (Roby, as D'Arcy), 1980
Magic of His Kiss (Steele), 1980
Magic of Living (Neels), 1974
Magic of Love (Cartland), 1977
Magic of Paris (Cartland), 1991
Magic of the Desert (Woodward, as Davis), 1976
Magic of You (Lindsey), 1993
Magic or Mirage? (Cartland), 1978
Magic Place (Bromige), 1971
Magic Scalpel of Dr Farrer (McElfresh), 1965
Magic series (Coulter), from 1987
Magnificent Affair (F. Preston), 1986

Magnificent Courtesan (Bloom, as Prole), 1950
Magnificent Folly (Johansen), 1987
Magnificent Marriage (Cartland), 1974
Magnificent Obsession (L. Douglas), 1929
Magnificent Rogue (Johansen), 1993
Magnolia Moon (Stanford), 1982
Magnolia Room (Worboys, as Eyre), 1972
Magnolias (Ellis), 1976
Mahatma and the Hare (Haggard), 1911
Mahdi (Caine), 1894
Mahound (Horner), 1969
Maid Called Wanton (M. Peters, as Lloyd), 1981
Maid of Brittany (Wynne), 1906
Maid of Buttermere (Bragg), 1987
Maid of Gold (Wiat), 1978
Maid of Judah (M. Peters), 1973
Maid of Many Moods (Sheard), 1902
Maid of Stonystream (Baldwin), 1924
Maid of the Isles (Swan), 1924
Maida (Garvice), 1901
Maiden (Deveraux), 1988
Maiden (Harrod-Eagles), 1985
Maiden Castle (Lamb, as Holland), 1978
Maiden of the Morning (Krentz, as Bentley), 1979
Maiden Voyage (Norris), 1934
Maiden Voyage (Stuart, as A. Stuart), 1964
Mail Order Bride (M. Peters, as Lloyd), 1981
Mail Royal (Tranter), 1989
Main Attraction (Krentz), 1987
Main d'Acier (R. Marshall), 1931
Mainwaring (Hewlett), 1920
Maisie's Romance (Albanesi), 1910
Maison Jennie (Ellis), 1984
Maitland of Laurieston (Swan), 1890
Maiwa's Revenge (Haggard), 1888
Major Grant (Oman), 1931
Make-Believe (Baldwin), 1930
Make-Believe Bride (Buckingham, as John), 1982
Make Believe Wife (Norris), 1947
Make the Man Notice You (Greig, as Ames), 1940
Make Way for Love (Woodward, as Ware), 1967
Make Way for Tomorrow (Bevan), 1971
Make Way for Tomorrow (M. Lewis), 1966
Makebelieve Marriage (Kidd), 1982
Makeshift Marriage (Lewty), 1982
Making Magic (van der Zee), 1993
Making of a Lover (Ayres), 1921
Making of a Man (Ayres), 1915
Malady in Madeira (Bridge), 1969
Malaspiga Exit (Anthony), 1974
Malayan series (Burgess), from 1956
Male Chauvinist (Sellers), 1985
Male Child (P. Scott), 1956
Malice Domestic (Hardwick), 1986
Malice of Men (Deeping), 1938
Mallen series (Cookson), from 1973
Mallion's Pride (Salisbury), 1975
Mallory's Luck (Shoesmith), 1971
Mallow Years (A. Howard), 1989
Maltese Angel (Cookson), 1992
Malvie Inheritance (P. Hill), 1973
Mammon (Wren), 1930
Mammon of Righteousness (Wren), 1930
Mammon's Daughter (Tranter), 1939
Mammoth Hunters (Auel), 1985
Mam'zelle Guillotine (Orczy), 1940

Man Always Pays (Mackinlay), 1940
Man and His Model (s Hope)
Man and Maid (Glyn), 1922
Man and Maid—Renaissance (Glyn), 1922
Man and the Moment (Glyn), 1914
Man—And Waif (Chandos, as Tempest), 1938
Man Apart (Donnelly), 1968
Man at Kambala (K. Thorpe), 1973
Man at Mulera (K. Blair), 1959
Man at the Gate (Albanesi, as Rowlands), 1911
Man at the Manor (O. Sinclair), 1967
Man at Windmere (V. Johnston), 1988
Man Behind (Burgin), 1923
Man Behind the Curtain (Tranter), 1959
Man Behind the Mask (Lorrimer, as Robins), 1967
Man Between (Robins), 1926
Man Called Cameron (M. Pargeter), 1978
Man Called Mallory (Donnelly), 1974
Man Called Masters (L. Walker), 1965
Man for Always (Buckingham, as John), 1981
Man for Amanda (N. Roberts), 1991
Man for Hire (Wentworth), 1982
Man for Margaret (Chandos), 1945
Man for Me (Chandos, as Charles), 1965
Man for the Ages (Bacheller), 1919
Man Friday (Ayres), 1943
Man from Bahl Bahla (Way), 1971
Man from Brodney's (McCutcheon), 1908
Man from Cannae (Jakes, as Scotland), 1977
Man from Ceylon (Ayres), 1950
Man from Dahomey (Yerby), 1971
Man from Half Moon Bay (Johansen), 1988
Man from Nowhere (Stratton), 1982
Man from Outback (L. Walker), 1964
Man from Singapore (M. Howard), 1946
Man from the Kimberleys (M. Pargeter), 1982
Man from the Mist (Elgin), 1965
Man from the West (Albanesi, as Rowlands), 1927
Man from Tripoli (K. Thorpe), 1979
Man from Turkey (Burgin), 1921
Man from Venice (Saunders), 1988
Man-Hater (Jordan), 1983
Man Himself (Williamson, as A.M. Williamson), 1925
Man Hunt (Lamb), 1985
Man in a Box (K. Thorpe), 1972
Man in a Million (R. Lindsay, as Leigh), 1975
Man in Authority (MacLeod), 1954
Man in Black (Weyman), 1894
Man in Chains (Deeping), 1953
Man in Charge (Peake), 1973
Man in Command (Weale), 1969
Man in Gray (Dixon), 1921
Man in Grey (E. Smith), 1941
Man in Her Life (Ayres), 1935
Man in Lower Ten (Rinehart), 1909
Man in the Corner (Burgin), 1939
Man in the Mirror (s Hichens), 1950
Man in the Next Room (Donnelly), 1971
Man in the Park (E. Darcy), 1986
Man in the Yellow Raft (s Forester), 1969
Man Is Always Right (Greig), 1940
Man Like Daintree (Way), 1972
Man-Made Miracle (Chandos, as Charles), 1949
Man of a Ghost (Wren), 1937
Man of Destiny (Laffeaty), 1969
Man of Granite (Peake), 1971

Man of Her Choosing (Pykare), 1980
Man of Her Dreams (M. St John, as St John Cooper), 1919
Man of His Time (Bentley), 1966
Man of His Word (Ayres), 1916
Man of Ice (R. Lindsay), 1980
Man of Kent (Hunter, as Chace), 1973
Man of Mark (Hope), 1890
Man of Means (K. Thorpe), 1982
Man of My Dreams (Chandos), 1937
Man of My Dreams (Lindsey), 1992
Man of Nazareth (Burgess), 1979
Man of Steel (Wyndham), 1952
Man of Stone (M. Howard), 1958
Man of the Family (Chandos, as Lance), 1952
Man of the Moment (Mackinlay), 1956
Man of the Outback (Hampson), 1980
Man of the People (Dixon), 1920
Man of the River (O. Sinclair), 1968
Man of Wrath (Blackstock, as Allardyce), 1956
Man on a Donkey (Prescott), 1952
Man on Half-Moon (Way), 1976
Man on the Island (Collin), 1968
Man on the Make (R. Lindsay, as Leigh), 1989
Man on the White Horse (Deeping), 1934
Man Out of Reach (Peake), 1972
Man Outside (Donnelly), 1975
Man Possessed (Jordan), 1986
Man She Bought (Greig), 1930
Man She Loved (Albanesi, as Rowlands), 1900
Man She Married (Albanesi, as Rowlands), 1910
Man She Married (Winspear), 1982
Man the Devil Didn't Want (Wren), 1940
Man the Women Loved (Ayres), 1925
Man to Be Feared (Hampson), 1976
Man to Follow (Chandos), 1943
Man to Protect You (Greig), 1939
Man to Tame (R. Lindsay), 1976
Man to Watch (Donnelly), 1979
Man-Trap (Lewty), 1990
Man Under Authority (Dell), 1925
Man Who Cried (Cookson), 1979
Man Who Died (Burgin), 1903
Man Who Found Himself (Jacob), 1929
Man Who Had Everything (Bromfield), 1935
Man Who Listens (Caldwell), 1961
Man Who Lived Alone (Ayres), 1950
Man Who Made Husbands Jealous (J. Cooper), 1993
Man Who Married Again (M. St John), 1926
Man Who Wasn't Mac (Chandos), 1939
Man Who Went Back (Deeping), 1940
Man with a Past (Krentz), 1985
Man with One Hand (Hurst), 1953
Man with Secrets (Stanford), 1990
Man with the Broken Nose (s Arlen), 1927
Man with the Money (M. St John, as St John Cooper), 1917
Man with the Scales (Bowen), 1954
Man Without a Heart (Ayres), 1923
Man Without a Heart (Hampson), 1981
Man Without a Heart (R. Lindsay, as Leigh), 1976
Man Without Honour (Hampson), 1982
Man Without Mercy (Hilton), 1971
Mandala (Buck), 1970
Mandingo Mansa (Carter), 1986
Mandingo (Onstott), 1957
Mandoa Mandoa! (Holtby), 1933
Manetta's Marriage (Burgin), 1922

Mango Walk (Martin), 1981
Manhattan Love Song (Norris), 1934
Manhattan Nights (Baldwin), 1937
Manhold (Bentley), 1941
Manila Galleon (F. Mason), 1961
Mannequin (Hurst), 1926
Mannequin (Trask), 1933
Manner of a Lady (Sebastian, as Whitmore), 1979
Mannion and Prentice Families (Dark), from 1941
Manor Farm (Greig, as Warren), 1951
Man's Estate (Tranter), 1946
Man's Mortality (Arlen), 1933
Man's Protection (Krentz, as Castle), 1982
Man's Way (Ayres), 1921
Man's World (Lamb), 1980
Mansfield Revisited (Aiken), 1984
Mansion for a Lady (Sebastian, as Whitmore), 1980
Mansion for My Love (Donald), 1982
Mansion of Smiling Masks (Winston), 1967
Mantle of Innocence (Mackinlay), 1957
Manxman (Caine), 1894
Many Ways (Pedler), 1931
Maplechester series (Gibbs, as Ford), from 1963
Mapmaker (Slaughter), 1957
Marazan (Shute), 1926
Marble City (Burgin), 1905
Marcaboth Women (Delmar), 1951
Marcel of the 'Zephyrs' (Wynne), 1916
March to Corunna (Dymoke), 1985
Marching Feet (Swan), 1931
Marching On (Boyd), 1927
Marchwood (Bromige), 1949
Marcia Drayton (Garvice), 1908
Margaret (Haggard), 1907
Margaret Dent (Albanesi, as Rowlands), 1913
Margaret Holroyd (Swan), 1910
Margaret Normanby (M. Howard, as Edgar), 1982
Margaret series (E. Porter), from 1907
Margaret the Queen (Tranter), 1979
Margaret Yorke (Norris), 1930
Margarite (Thum), 1987
Margery Daw (Albanesi), 1886
Margin of Error (Borden), 1952
Marguerite's Wonderful Year (Grundy), 1906
Maria (Hutten), 1914
Marian Sax (Albanesi), 1905
Marianna (Buckingham), 1981
Marie (Haggard), 1912
Mariette's Lovers (Burgin), 1925
Marigold (Cato), 1992
Marigold Field (Pearson), 1969
Mariner's Bride (Browning, as Williams), 1991
Marion Forsyth (s Swan), 1883
Marionette (Bennetts), 1979
Marivosa (Orczy), 1930
Marjorie of Scotland (P. Hill), 1956
Mark Desborough's Vow (Swan), 1884
Mark of the Warrior (P. Scott), 1958
Mark of Tregarron (Stratton, as Gillen), 1976
Marlborough's Unfair Lady (Bloom, as Prole), 1965
Marmalade Man (C. Allen), 1981
Marmalade Witch (D. Smith), 1982
Marne (Wharton), 1918
Marquess (Gibbs), 1982
Marquis and Miss Jones (Bennetts), 1981
Marquis (Garvice), 1896

Marquis of Carabas (Sabatini), 1940
Marquis of Loveland (Williamson), 1908
Marquis Takes a Bride (Chesney, as Crampton), 1982
Marquis Takes a Wife (R. Lindsay), 1976
Marquis Who Hated Women (Cartland), 1977
Marquis Wins (Cartland), 1990
Marr'd in Making (Hutten), 1901
Marriage Bond (Robins), 1924
Marriage-Broker (Lowndes), 1937
Marriage by Conquest (Deeping), 1915
Marriage by Request (Stratton, as Gillen), 1971
Marriage Chest (Eden), 1965
Marriage Deal (Craven), 1986
Marriage for Three (Seifert), 1954
Marriage Handicap (Ayres), 1925
Marriage Has Been Arranged (Blackstock, as Allardyce), 1959
Marriage Impossible (M. Pargeter), 1978
Marriage in Heaven (Bloom), 1943
Marriage in Mexico (Kidd), 1978
Marriage Is a Blind Date (Ruck), 1953
Marriage Is Like That (Woodward, as Richmond), 1961
Marriage Made in Heaven (Cartland), 1983
Marriage Made on Earth (Bishop), 1989
Marriage Masque (Fellows), 1974
Marriage of Barry Wicklow (Ayres), 1920
Marriage of Katherine (D. Stevenson), 1965
Marriage of Leonora (Bloom), 1953
Marriage of Margaret (Albanesi), 1909
Marriage of Martha Todd (Leslie), 1968
Marriage of Meggotta (E. Pargeter), 1979
Marriage of Pierrot (Bloom), 1936
Marriage Playground (Wharton), 1930
Marriage Racket (Delmar), 1933
Marriage Will Not Take Place (Steen), 1938
Marriage Without a Ring (Greig), 1972
Marriage Without Love (Jordan), 1981
Marriage-Broker (Lowndes), 1937
Married at School (M. St John), 1917
Married at Sight (Garvice), 1894
Married in Haste (Plaidy, as Burford), 1956
Married in Haste (s Swan), 1898
Married Lover (Plaidy, as Burford), 1942
Married Lovers (Kidd), 1987
Married Man (s Swan), 1898
Married or Unmarried (Hichens), 1941
Married Past Redemption (Veryan), 1983
Married People (s Rinehart), 1937
Married Quarters (Greig), 1964
Married to a Miser (M. St John, as St John Cooper), 1920
Married to Her Master (M. St John), 1914
Married to His Wife's Family (M. St John), 1924
Marry for Money (Baldwin), 1948
Marry in Haste (Greig), 1935
Marry in Haste (Hodge), 1969
Marry to Taste (Bloom, as Essex), 1942
Marryers (Bacheller), 1914
Marrying a Doctor (E. Harrison), 1984
Marrying Game (Armstrong), 1989
Marrying Harriet (Chesney), 1990
Marrying Kind (Cadell), 1980
Marrying Kind (D. Smith), 1974
Marrying Man (Stern), 1918
Marsh Blood (Andrews, as Marcus), 1980
Marsh House (Roby), 1974
Marshall Family (Burchell), 1967
Martie, The Unconquered (Norris), 1917

Martin Conisby's Vengeance (Farnol), 1921
Martin Make-Believe (Frankau), 1930
Martin Merriedew (Borden), 1952
Martin Valliant (Deeping), 1917
Martyrdom (s Deeping), 1929
Martyrdom (s Frankau), 1929
Martyred Love (Garvice), 1902
Mary Ann and Jane (Grundy), 1944
Mary Ann series (Cookson), from 1956
Mary Anne (du Maurier), 1954
Mary at Monte Carlo (Williamson), 1920
Mary Dunbar's Love (Albanesi, as Rowlands), 1921
Mary Ellen—Mill-Lass (M. St John), 1920
Mary Faithful (M. St John, as St John Cooper), 1923
Mary Garth (Swan), 1904
Mary Hallam (Ertz), 1947
Mary Lavelle (O'Brien), 1936
Mary Marie (E. Porter), 1920
Mary, Mary (Sallis, as Meadmore), 1982
Mary Midthorne (McCutcheon), 1911
Mary of Carisbrooke (Barnes), 1956
Mary of Delight (Jacob), 1949
Mary of Marion Isle (Haggard), 1929
Mary of Nazareth (Borden), 1933
Mary Olivier (M. Sinclair), 1919
Mary Pechell (Lowndes), 1912
Mary, Queen of France (Plaidy), 1964
Mary Queen of Scots series (Plaidy), from 1955
Mary Roberts Rinehart's Crime Book (Rinehart), 1933
Mary, Sweet Mary (Williams), 1980
Mary, The Infamous Queen (M. Peters), 1968
Mary Wakefield (de la Roche), 1949
Masculine Ending (J. Smith), 1989
Mask (Hichens), 1951
Mask and the Moonflower (Whitney), 1960
Mask of Apollo (Renault), 1966
Mask of Deception (S. Wood), 1993
Mask of Fortune (Oliver, as James), 1978
Mask of Gold (R. Lindsay), 1956
Mask of Gold (Swan), 1906
Mask of Love (Cartland), 1975
Mask of Passion (Hooper), 1982
Mask of Scars (Mather), 1973
Mask of the Enchantress (Plaidy, as Holt), 1980
Mask of Treason (A. Stevenson), 1979
Mask of Words (Summerton, as Roffman), 1973
Masked Deception (Balogh), 1985
Masque (Lamb, as Holland), 1979
Masque of Brontës (M. Peters), 1991
Masquerade (Dailey), 1990
Masquerade (Mather), 1966
Masquerade (Saxton, as Felix), 1982
Masquerade for the King (Oliver), 1978
Masquerade in Venice (V. Johnston), 1973
Masquerade Marriage (Kidd), 1987
Masquerade of Love (Sebastian, as Norcross), 1978
Masquerade of Vengeance (Ley), 1989
Masquerade with Music (Burchell), 1982
Masqueraders (Heyer), 1928
Masquerading Heart (Courtney), 1984
Masquers (N. Peters), 1979
Masques of Gold (Gellis), 1988
Massacre at Cawnpore (Stuart, as V.A. Stuart), 1973
Massacre at Fall Creek (West), 1975
Master (Bacheller), 1909
Master and Commander (O'Brian), 1969

Master and the Maiden (Ley), 1977
Master-at-Arms (Sabatini), 1940
Master-Christian (Corelli), 1900
Master Fiddler (Dailey), 1977
Master Man (Ayres), 1920
Master of Badger's Hall (Treece), 1959
Master of Ben Ross (Stratton, as Gillen), 1977
Master of Black River (Tresillian, as Devine), 1984
Master of Blacktower (B. Michaels), 1966
Master of Blandeston Hall (Wiat), 1973
Master of Cashel (S. Wood), 1989
Master of Chaos (Bacheller), 1932
Master of Comus (Lamb), 1977
Master of Falcon's Head (Mather), 1970
Master of Forrestmead (Hampson), 1978
Master of Glenkeith (MacLeod), 1955
Master of Gray (Bailey), 1903
Master of Gray (Tranter), 1961
Master of Guise (Stuart, as A. Stuart), 1957
Master of Heronsbridge (Bromige), 1969
Master of Jethart (Dwyer-Joyce), 1976
Master of Keills (MacLeod), 1967
Master of Liversedge (Ley), 1966
Master of Lynch Towers (Albanesi, as Rowlands), 1910
Master of Mahia (Bevan), 1981
Master of Malcarew (M. Peters, as Black), 1971
Master of Man (Caine), 1921
Master of Melthorpe (O. Sinclair), 1979
Master of Moonrock (Hampson), 1973
Master of Morley (K. Thorpe), 1983
Master of Penrose (Hodge), 1968
Master of Ransome (L. Walker), 1958
Master of Silence (Bacheller), 1892
Master of Stair (Bowen), 1907
Master of Surgery (Stuart, as A. Stuart), 1958
Master of Tawhai (Summers), 1959
Master of the House (Hall), 1932
Master of the House (Peake), 1974
Master of the Manor (Wyndham), 1953
Master of the Mill (M. St John, as St John Cooper), 1910
Master of Trelona (Ritchie), 1977
Master Painter (Mullins), 1989
Master Wit (Wynne), 1911
Master Workman's Oath (Libbey), 1892
Masters of Rome series (McCullough), from 1990
Masters of the Parachute Mail (E. Pargeter, as Carr), 1940
Masterson (Frankau), 1926
Matador (Steen), 1934
Match for a Murderer (Dunnett, as Halliday), 1971
Match Is Made (Chandos, as Tempest), 1950
Matchmakers (Dailey), 1978
Matchmaker's Moon (Browning), 1985
Matherson Marriage (Ayres), 1922
Matilda, Governess of the English (Cleugh), 1924
Matilda the Adventuress (Johansen), 1987
Mating Dance (Randall), 1979
Mating of Marcus (Grundy), 1923
Mating Season (Dailey), 1980
Matriarch series (Stern), from 1924
Matter for the Regiment (McCutchan, as MacNeil), 1982
Matter of Business (s Farnol), 1940
Matter of Chance (Neels), 1977
Matter of Choice (N. Roberts), 1984
Matter of Circumstance (Pozzessere), 1987
Matter of Honor (Pykare), 1982
Matter of Time (B. Hastings), 1982

Matter of Timing (Browning), 1987
Matter of Trust (Jordan), 1992
Matter of Will (Donald), 1989
Matters of the Heart (C. Allen), 1985
Matthew, Mark, Luke, and John (Bloom), 1954
Maulever Hall (Hodge), 1964
Maurice Durant (Garvice), 1875
Maurice Guest (Richardson), 1908
Mauritius Command (O'Brian), 1977
Maverick and the Lady (Pozzessere, as Graham), 1986
Maverton Heiress (Chandos, as Lance), 1975
Mavis of Green Hill (Baldwin), 1921
Mavreen (Lorrimer), 1976
Maximum Demolition (Nolan), 1991
May Fair (s Arlen), 1925
Maybe this Time (Seidel), 1990
Mayenga Farm (K. Blair), 1951
Mayeroni Myth (Winston), 1972
McAuslan in the Rough (s G. Fraser), 1974
McCabe's Kingdom (Way), 1974
McChesney, Emma series (s Ferber), from 1913
McIvor Affair (Way), 1981
McKeever (Delmar), 1976
McKenzie's Hundred (Yerby), 1985
Meadowsweet (Barcynska, as Sandys), 1942
Meadowsweet (Orczy), 1912
Means of Grace (E. Pargeter), 1956
Means to an End (Stratton, as Gillen), 1972
Meant for Each Other (Burchell), 1945
Meant to Meet (Chandos, as Tempest), 1967
Measure of Love (Chappell), 1961
Measure of Love (McKenna), 1987
Medical Center (Baldwin), 1940
Medici, Catherine de' series (Plaidy), from 1951
Medici Lover (Mather), 1977
Medici Mistress (Hamilton, as Watson), 1968
Medici Ring (N. St John), 1975
Mediterranean Madness (Bloom), 1934
Medusa Connection (Cowen), 1976
Meet Love on Holiday (Bloom, as Burns), 1940
Meet Me Again (Burchell), 1954
Meet Me by Moonlight (Chandos, as Tempest), 1953
Meet Me in Monte Carlo (Robins), 1964
Meet Me in Time (C. Allen), 1978
Meet on My Ground (Summers), 1968
Meeting at Midnight (Kidd), 1981
Meeting in Madrid (MacLeod), 1979
Meeting in the Spring (Gibbs, as Ford), 1954
Meg Hamilton (Swan), 1914
Meg Miller (Sebastian), 1976
Melbury Square (Eden), 1970
Melinda (Eliot, as Arnett), 1975
Melissa (Caldwell), 1948
Melody (Thane), 1950
Melody of Love (R. Lindsay, as Scott), 1960
Melody of Malice (Hufford), 1979
Melon in the Cornfield (Blackstock), 1969
Melt a Frozen Heart (Armstrong), 1983
Melting Fire (Mather), 1979
Mem (Hutten), 1934
Memoirs of Lord Byron (Nye), 1989
Memories (C. Allen), 1983
Memories of the Past (Mortimer), 1991
Memory and Desire (Appignanesi), 1991
Memory of Darkness (Summerton), 1967
Memory of Love (R. Lindsay, as Scott), 1959

Memory of Summer (Manley-Tucker), 1961
Memory's Embrace (Miller), 1986
Men Act That Way (Greig), 1933
Men Against the Sea (Nordhoff and Hall), 1933
Men and Angels (Cadell), 1952
Men and the Girls (Trollope), 1992
Men Are Dangerous (Lamb, as Hardy) , 1984
Men Are Only Human (Robins), 1933
Men Are Such Fools! (Baldwin), 1936
Men as Her Stepping Stones (Greig, as Barclay), 1937
Men Dislike Women (Arlen), 1931
Men in Her Life (Ruck), 1954
Men Made the Town (Ayres), 1931
Men, Maids, and Mustard-Pot (s Frankau), 1923
Men of Albemarle (Fletcher), 1942
Men of Forty-Eight (J. Lindsay), 1948
Men of Mysteries Past series (Hooper), from 1993
Men of the Frontier Force (Diver), 1930
Men on White Horses (Haines), 1978
Men on White Horses (Motley), 1988
Men Were Deceivers Ever (M. St John, as St John Cooper), 1920
Men Were Deceivers Ever (Veryan, as Moore), 1989
Menagerie (Cookson), 1958
Mending Flower (Ritchie), 1955
Menfreya (Plaidy, as Holt), 1966
Mercenary (Westcott), 1963
Mercenary series (Palmer), from 1985
Mercer (P. Hill), 1992
Merchant of the Ruby (Harwood), 1951
Merchant Prince (Bailey), 1926
Merchant's Daughter (Lamb, as Holland), 1980
Mercy in Your Hands (James), 1956
Mercy, Pity, Peace and Love (s Godden), 1989
Meridon (Gregory), 1990
Merivales (McCutcheon), 1929
Merlin (Nye), 1978
Merlin series (Stewart), from 1970
Merlin's Keep (Brent), 1977
Merlin's Keep (Norway), 1966
Merlyn's Magic (Mortimer), 1987
Merrily All the Way (Barcynska, as Sandys), 1943
Merry Andrews (Randall), 1954
Merry Belles of Bath (Trask), 1957
Merry Jade (Saxton, as Turner), 1978
Merry Maid (Hardwick), 1984
Merry Meeting (Ponsonby), 1948
Merry Month of May (J. Smith), 1990
Message from Mars (Wynne, as Lurgan), 1912
Message from Nam (Steel), 1990
Messalina of the Suburbs (Delafield), 1924
Messenger of Love (Cartland), 1961
Messer Marco Polo (Byrne), 1921
Messiah (Vidal), 1954
Micah Clarke (Doyle), 1889
Mice for Amusement (Hutten), 1933
Michael and All the Angels (Lofts), 1943
Michael Forth (M. Johnston), 1919
Michael O'Halloran (G. Porter), 1915
Michaelmas Tree (Bennetts), 1982
Michael's Wife (Frankau), 1948
Midas Touch (Kennedy), 1938
Middle Mist (Muskett), 1937
Middle Window (Goudge), 1935
Midnight Dancers (Maybury), 1973
Midnight Fires (Finch), 1984
Midnight Is Mine (Mackinlay), 1954

Midnight Jewels (Krentz), 1987
Midnight Lavender (Matthews), 1985
Midnight Lover (Lamb), 1982
Midnight Magic (M. Pargeter), 1978
Midnight Masquerade (Busbee), 1988
Midnight Masquerade (J. Smith), 1985
Midnight Match (F. Stevenson, as Faire), 1979
Midnight of Madness (Laffeaty), 1968
Midnight Rainbow series (L. Howard), from 1986
Midnight Sailing (Hufford), 1975
Midnight Secrets (Taylor), 1992
Midnight Sun's Magic (Neels), 1979
Midnight Walker (Randall), 1973
Midnight Waltz (J. Blake), 1985
Midnight Whispers (Matthews), 1981
Midsummer Madness! (M. St John), 1924
Midsummer Morning (Bennetts), 1984
Midsummer Star (Neels), 1983
Midsummer's Eve (Plaidy, as Carr), 1986
Midwinter (J. Buchan), 1923
Mighty Atom (Corelli), 1896
Mighty City (James), 1939
Mignonette (Bowen, as Shearing), 1948
Migrations (E. Scott), 1927
Milady Charlotte (Plaidy, as Kellow), 1959
Milady in Love (Chesney), 1987
Mill in the Meadow (Donnelly), 1972
Mill-Lass o' Mine! (M. St John), 1920
Mill-Owner (Wynne, as Lurgan), 1910
Mill Queen (M. St John, as St John Cooper), 1919
Mill Town Nurse (Woodward), 1976
Miller of Old Church (Glasgow), 1911
Miller's Dance 1812–1813 (Graham), 1982
Millgirl and Dreamer (M. St John), 1918
Mill-Girl's Bargain! (M. St John), 1924
Milliner's Shop (Gibbs), 1981
Million (Hichens), 1940
Million Dollar Doll (Williamson, as A.M. Williamson), 1924
Million Stars (Lewty), 1959
Millionaire Tramp (M. St John, as St John Cooper), 1930
Millionaire's Daughter (Eden), 1974
Mills of the Gods (Winston), 1974
Milly Comes to Town (Barcynska), 1928
Mind of a Minx (Ruck), 1927
Mind of Her Own (Seger, as MacNeill), 1983
Mind Over Matter (N. Roberts), 1987
Mind Tryst (Carr), 1991
Mine for a Day (Burchell), 1951
Mine Inheritance (Niven), 1940
Minerva (Chesney), 1982
Minerva Stone (Maybury), 1968
Minerva's Marquis (Walsh), 1988
Minion (Sabatini), 1930
Ministering Angel (Albanesi, as Rowlands), 1933
Mink Coat (Norris), 1946
Minor Bequest (Shoesmith), 1984
Minstrel for a Valois (M. Peters), 1989
Minstrel's Leap (M. Peters, as Black), 1973
Mint Walk (Barcynska), 1927
Minutes of a Murder (Polland), 1967
Minx Goes to the Front (s Williamson), 1919
Mirabelle (Glover), 1993
Miracle at Joe's (Norway, as Norton), 1965
Miracle at St Bruno's (Plaidy, as Carr), 1972
Miracle for a Madonna (Cartland), 1984
Miracle in Mexico (Cartland), 1990

Miracle in Music (Cartland), 1982
Miracle of Lac Blanche (M. Lewis), 1973
Miracle Stone of Wales (Barcynska, as Barclay), 1957
Miracles (Hufford), 1989
Mirage for Love (Hoy), 1939
Mirage of Love (Bloom), 1978
Mirage on the Horizon (Bloom), 1974
Miranda of the Island (Oliver, as James), 1977
Miranda's Marriage (Hilton), 1973
Miro, Donna and Lorna Doria series (Pozzessere, as Graham), from 1985
Mirror for Dreams (Muskett), 1931
Mirror Image (Brown), 1990
Mirror in Darkness series (Jameson), from 1935
Mirror of the Sun (Blackstock, as Torday), 1938
Mirrors (Matthews), 1988
Mirrors and Mistakes (Seidel), 1984
Mirrors of the Sea (Wentworth), 1993
Misadventure (Muskett), 1936
Misadventures of Bethany Price (Cockrell), 1979
Mischief-Makers (Swan), 1941
Miser of Mayfair (Chesney), 1986
Miser's Ward (Shoesmith), 1977
Misleading Encounter (Steele), 1986
Miss Barrett's Elopement (Oman, as Lenanton), 1929
Miss Baxter's Bequest (s Swan), 1888
Miss Bede Is Staying (Gilbert), 1982
Miss Billy series (E. Porter), from 1911
Miss Bolo (M. St John, as St John Cooper), 1918
Miss Bun, The Baker's Daughter (D. Stevenson), 1938
Miss Buncle series (D. Stevenson), from 1934
Miss Carmichael's Conscience (Hutten), 1900
Miss Charley (Blackstock), 1979
Miss Charlotte's Fancy (Lamb, as Holland) , 1980
Miss Columbine and Harley Quinn (Hilton), 1970
Miss Dean's Dilemma (D. Stevenson), 1938
Miss Delicia Allen (M. Johnston), 1933
Miss Doctor (Seifert), 1951
Miss Estcourt (Garvice), 1911
Miss Fenny (Blackstock), 1957
Miss Fiona's Fancy (Chesney), 1987
Miss Harriet Townshend (Norris), 1955
Miss Jonas's Boy (Blackstock, as Allardyce), 1972
Miss Keating's Temptation (Sebastian), 1981
Miss Letty (Sebastian), 1977
Miss Liz's Passion (Woods), 1990
Miss Martha Mary Crawford (Cookson, as Marchant), 1975
Miss Marvel (Forbes), 1935
Miss Mayhew and Ming Yun (Duffield), 1928
Miss Middleton's Lover (Libbey), 1888
Miss Million's Maid (Ruck), 1915
Miss Paraffin (Barcynska, as Sandys), 1944
Miss Philadelphia Smith (Blackstock, as Allardyce), 1977
Miss Pinkerton series (Rinehart), from 1932
Miss Rolling Stone (Shellabarger, as Loring), 1939
Miss Smith's Fortune (s Garvice), 1920
Miss Spring (Crowe), 1953
Miss Venus of Aberdovey (Barcynska), 1956
Miss Willie (Giles), 1951
Missing from Home (Burchell), 1968
Missing Girl (Ruck), 1930
Missing the Tide (Ayres), 1948
Mission to Argana (Marsh), 1988
Mission to Malaspiga (Anthony), 1974
Mission to Monte Carlo (Cartland), 1983
Mississippi Blues (F. Preston), 1985

Mississippi Mistress (Finch, as Robbins), 1990
Mist Across the Hills (MacLeod), 1938
Mist Across the Moors (Peake), 1972
Mist of Evil (Matthews, as Brisco), 1976
Mist on the Hills (M. Howard), 1950
Mist over Talla (Erskine-Lindop), 1957
Mistaken (s Swan), 1892
Mistaken Adversary (Jordan), 1992
Mistaken Virtues (Trollope), 1980
Mistaken Wedding (Wentworth), 1988
Mr American (G. Fraser), 1980
Mr and Mrs Nevill Tyson (M. Sinclair), 1898
Mr Anthony (Barcynska, as Sandys), 1925
Mr Bingle (McCutcheon), 1915
Mr Cardonnel (Bailey), 1931
Mr Christopoulos (Blackstock), 1963
Mr Cohen Takes a Walk (Rinehart), 1934
Mr Florian's Fortune (Ponsonby), 1971
Mr Gurney and Mr Slade (Deeping), 1944
Mr Leslie's School for Girls (M. St John), 1922
Mr Meeson's Will (Haggard), 1888
Mr Misfortunate (Bowen), 1919
Mr Rodriguez (M. Howard), 1979
Mr Rowl (Broster), 1924
Mr Scribbles (Barcynska, as Sandys), 1930
Mr Sermon (Delderfield), 1970
Mr Sister (Norway, as Neal), 1965
Mr Skeffington (Arnim), 1940
Mr Smith (Bromfield), 1951
Mr Tyler's Saints (Bowen), 1939
Mr Waddington of Wyck (M. Sinclair), 1921
Mister Washington (Bowen), 1915
Mr Witt's Widow (Hope), 1892
Mistletoe and Holly (Dailey), 1982
Mistletoe Bough (Wiat), 1981
Mrs Bridges' Story (Hardwick), 1975
Mistress Cynthia (Wynne), 1910
Mrs Daventry's Reputation (Pedler), 1924
Mrs de Winter (S. Hill), 1993
Mrs Drummond's Vocation (Hutten), 1913
Mistress for the Valois (Hamilton, as Watson), 1969
Mrs Harter (Delafield), 1924
Mrs Keith Hamilton, MB (Swan), 1897
Mrs Lancelot (Hewlett), 1912
Mrs Marden (Hichens), 1919
Mrs Maxon Protests (Hope), 1911
Mistress Nell Gwyn (Bowen), 1926
Mrs Newdigate's Window (Oman, as Lenanton), 1927
Mistress of Astington (S. Thorpe), 1983
Mistress of Castlemount (Chandos, as Tempest), 1961
Mistress of Court Regina (Garvice), 1909
Mistress of Darkness (Nicole), 1976
Mistress of Devil's Manor (F. Stevenson), 1973
Mistress of Fortune (Lamb, as Lancaster) , 1982
Mistress of Kingdoms (Borden, as Maclagan), 1912
Mistress of Magic (Pozzessere), 1992
Mistress of Martinscombe (Chandos, as Storm), 1973
Mistress of Mellyn (Plaidy, as Holt), 1960
Mistress of Merryweather (Wyndham), 1953
Mistress of Mooralee (Laffeaty), 1972
Mistress of Paradise (Thum), 1988
Mistress of Pillatoro (E. Darcy), 1987
Mistress of Polrudden (Thompson), 1993
Mistress of Rogues (R. Marshall), 1956
Mistress of Shenstone (F. Barclay), 1910
Mistress of Tanglewood (Marsh), 1981

Mistress of the Farm (Albanesi, as Rowlands), 1910
Mistress of the Fifth Standard (M. St John), 1916
Mistress of Willowvale (Veryan), 1980
Mrs Oliver Cromwell (s Irwin), 1940
Mrs Parkington (Bromfield), 1943
Mrs Shakespeare (Nye), 1993
Mrs Stoner and the Sea (s Buck), 1978
Mrs Tim series (D. Stevenson), from 1932
Mrs Westerby Changes Course (Cadell), 1924
Mistress Wilding (Sabatini), 1924
Mists of Memory (Cookson, as Marchant), 1965
Mists of the Moor (Mackinlay), 1967
Misty Angel (Barcynska, as Sandys), 1931
Mix Me a Man (D. Smith), 1978
Mixed Blessings (Cockrell), 1978
Mixed Blessings (Steel), 1992
Mixed Blessing (Van Slyke), 1975
Mixed Company (Cockrell), 1979
Mixed Emotions (C. Allen), 1977
Mixed Marriage (Cadell), 1963
Mixed Messages (Miller), 1990
Mixed Singles (Mackinlay, as Grey), 1971
Mock-Honeymoon (Ruck), 1939
Model Girl's Farm (Chandos), 1958
Model Murder (Buckingham, as Quest), 1991
Model of Deception (M. Pargeter), 1985
Modern Hero (Bromfield), 1932
Modern Juliet (Garvice), 1900
Modern Micawbers (Mackinlay, as Grey), 1933
Modern Tragedy (Bentley), 1934
Modern Witch (Albanesi, as Rowlands), 1912
Modesta (Stern), 1929
Mog Megone (Wynne), 1921
Moghul (Nicole, as Savage), 1991
Moll (Cordell), 1990
Moll Walbee (Cordell), 1989
Molly (Chesney, as Tremaine), 1980
Molly of the Lone Pine (MacGill), 1922
Molly's Flashings (Burgh, as Leith), 1991
Moment I Saw You (Chandos, as Tempest), 1941
Moment in Time (Small), 1991
Moment of Decision (MacLeod), 1972
Moment of Love (Robins), 1964
Moment of Truth (Jameson), 1949
Moment of Truth (Stratton, as Gillen), 1973
Moment Past Midnight (Krentz, as Bentley), 1979
Moment to Moment (Delinsky, as Drake), 1984
Moment to Moment (Schulze), 1986
Moments Harsh, Moments Gentle (Lorin, as Hohl), 1984
Moments of Glory series (McKenna), from 1992
Moments of Love (Cartland), 1982
Moments of Meaning (C. Allen), 1979
Monday in Summer (L. Walker, as Sanders), 1961
Monday Man (Norway, as Norton), 1963
Monday's Child (Hardwick), 1981
Money for One (Ruck), 1927
Money Isn't Everything (Ruck), 1940
Money, Love, and Kate (s E. Porter), 1923
Money, Magic, and Marriage (Cartland), 1980
Money Moon (Farnol), 1911
Money or Wife (Albanesi, as Rowlands), 1914
Moneylenders of Shahpur (Forrester), 1987
Moneyman (Costain), 1947
Monkey on a Chain (Blackstock), 1965
Monkey-Puzzle (Hutten), 1932
Monkey Tree in a Flower Pot (Bloom), 1958

Monkshood (Mather), 1972
Monsoon (I. Roberts, as I.R. Roberts), 1983
Montana Man (Delinsky), 1989
Montana Moonfire (Finch), 1990
Montezuma's Daughter (Haggard), 1893
Montgomery series (Deveraux), from 1983
Month Soon Goes (Jameson), 1963
Montrose series (Tranter), from 1973
Mooltiki and Poems of India (s Godden), 1957
Moon Dragon (Hampson), 1978
Moon Endureth (s J. Buchan), 1912
Moon in a Bucket (Gibbs), 1972
Moon in the Water (Ayres), 1939
Moon in the Water (Belle), 1983
Moon into Blood (Gavin), 1966
Moon Is Feminine (Dane), 1938
Moon Is Making (Jameson), 1937
Moon Is Square (Maddocks), 1975
Moon Lady (Donnelly), 1984
Moon Marriage (Manners, as Rundle), 1967
Moon of Aphrodite (Craven), 1980
Moon of Israel (Haggard), 1918
Moon of Laughing Flame (M. Peters, as Grey), 1980
Moon of Lavinia (Neels), 1976
Moon of Romance (Albanesi), 1932
Moon Out of Reach (Pedler), 1921
Moon over Eden (Cartland), 1976
Moon over Madrid (Stuart, as Finlay), 1957
Moon over Mombasa (May), 1991
Moon over Moncrieff (I. Roberts, as Rowland), 1969
Moon over Stamboul (Duffield), 1936
Moon over the Alps (Summers), 1960
Moon over the Temple (I. Roberts), 1972
Moon over the Water (Greig), 1956
Moon Returns (Randall), 1942
Moon series (M. Peters, as Darby), from 1977
Moon Song (Bloom), 1953
Moon Spinners (Stewart), 1962
Moon Through Glass (Albanesi), 1928
Moon Tide (Stratton), 1975
Moon Touched Promises (Sommerfield), 1993
Moon Witch (Mather), 1970
Moon Without Stars (Hampson), 1974
Moonbranches (Manners, as Rundle), 1986
Moondrift (Mather), 1984
Moondust series (Taylor), from 1986
Moonfire (Miller), 1988
Moonflete (M. Peters, as Black), 1972
Moonflower (MacLeod), 1967
Moonflower (Whitney), 1958
Moonflower Madness (Pemberton), 1993
Moongate Wish (Buckingham, as John), 1985
Moonlight and Magic (R. Lindsay), 1962
Moonlight Enchantress (Finch), 1992
Moonlight Lovers (s Balogh), 1993
Moonlight Mirage (Saunders, as Blake), 1982
Moonlight Mist (London), 1979
Moonlight on the Lake (I. Preston), 1976
Moonlight on the Sphinx (Cartland), 1984
Moonlight Rhapsody (Hooper, as Robbins), 1984
Moonlight Variations (F. Stevenson), 1981
Moonlighters (Blackstock, as Allardyce), 1966
Moonlit Door (Maybury), 1967
Moonlit Magic (Sommerfield), 1989
Moonlit Way (Dwyer-Joyce), 1974
Moonpearl (I. Roberts, as I. R. Roberts), 1983

Moonraker's Bride (Brent), 1973
Moonrise over the Mountains (Peake), 1975
Moon's Our Home (Baldwin), 1936
Moonshiner (L. Walker), 1961
Moonstone Manor (I. Roberts, as Shaw), 1968
Moonstruck Madness (McBain), 1977
Moorhaven (Winston), 1973
Mops (Barcynska, as Sandys), 1928
More about Pixie (Vaizey), 1903
More Tales of the West Riding (s Bentley), 1974
More Than a Dream (Stratton), 1977
More Than Friends (Delinsky), 1993
More Than Friendship (M. Howard), 1960
More Than Love (Robins), 1947
More Than You Dreamed (Seidel), 1991
Moreton's Kingdom (MacLeod), 1981
Morgan Wade's Woman (Lorin), 1981
Morgan's Merceneries series (McKenna), from 1993
Morgan's Woman (Gower), 1986
Morning After (Schulze), 1989
Morning Always Comes (Vitek), 1982
Morning Gift (Ibbotson), 1993
Morning Glory (M. St John, as St John Cooper), 1927
Morning Glory (Spencer), 1989
Morning Glory (Vitek), 1986
Morning Rose, Evening Savage (Lorin), 1980
Morning Star (Haggard), 1910
Morning Star (Norway), 1959
Morning Star (I. Roberts, as Rowland), 1963
Morning Tide (A. Howard), 1985
Morning Will Come (Jacob), 1953
Morningquest (Aiken), 1992
Morningstar (Pizzey), 1992
Moroccan Traffic (Dunnett), 1991
Mortimer Brice (Hichens), 1932
Mosaic (Stern), 1930
Moses, Prince of Egypt (Fast), 1958
Moses the Lawgiver (Keneally), 1975
Moss Rose (Bowen, as Shearing), 1934
Most Auspicious Star (Goodwin, as Ebel), 1968
Most Cruelly Wronged (M. St John), 1907
Most Determined Woman (E. Blair), 1988
Most Loving Mere Folly (E. Pargeter), 1953
Most Marvellous Summer (Neels), 1991
Most Precious Employee (Forrester, as Edwards), 1976
Most Romantic City (Gibbs), 1976
Most Sacred of All, (Farnol), 1948
Most Unsuitable Wife (R. Lindsay, as Leigh), 1990
Mostly Canallers (s Edmonds), 1934
Moth (Cookson), 1986
Moth to the Flame (Craven), 1979
Mother (Buck), 1934
Mother Knows Best! (M. St John), 1922
Mother Knows Best (s Ferber), 1927
Mother (Norris), 1911
Mother of the Bride (Mortimer), 1992
Mother's Recompense (Wharton), 1925
Mothers-in-Law (Hutten), 1922
Motionless Shadows (Norris), 1945
Motive (Lowndes), 1938
Motor Maid (Williamson), 1909
Motzart and the Wolf Gang (Burgess), 1991
Mountain Clinic (MacLeod), 1962
Mountain for Luenda (Summers), 1983
Mountain Laurel (Deveraux), 1990
Mountain Lovers (M. St John, as St John Cooper), 1920

Mountain Magic (I. Preston), 1979
Mountain of Fear (Randall), 1972
Mountain of Light (Gavin), 1944
Mountain of Stars (MacLeod, as Airlie), 1956
Mountain Sang (I. Roberts), 1965
Mountain That Went to the Sea (L. Walker), 1971
Mountford Show (Gibbs, as Ford), 1948
Mourning Bride (F. Stevenson, as Curzon), 1982
Mourning Trees (V. Johnston), 1972
Mouth of Truth (Hunter, as Chace), 1977
Moving Dream (Renier), 1977
Mowana Magic (Way), 1988
Much Ado about Peter (Webster), 1909
Much-Loved (Ayres), 1934
Much Needed Holiday (Lorin, as Hohl), 1986
Much Suspected of Me (M. Peters), 1990
Mud on My Stockings (Barcynska, as Sandys), 1938
Mullah from Kashmir (McCutchan, as MacNeil), 1976
Multitude of Sins (Pemberton), 1988
Mummy Case (B. Michaels, as Peters), 1985
Murder at Grand Bay (W. Roberts), 1955
Murder by Nail (Farnol), 1942
Murder for Charity (J. Blake, as Ponder), 1977
Murder in Focus (Dunnett, as Halliday), 1973
Murder in Mayfair (Robins), 1935
Murder in the Round (Dunnett, as Halliday), 1970
Murder in the Tower (Plaidy), 1964
Murder Is So Easy (W. Roberts), 1961
Murder Most Royal (Plaidy), 1949
Murder of Delicia (Corelli), 1896
Murder's Mansion (I. Roberts, as Shaw), 1976
Murders of Richard III (B. Michaels, as Peters), 1974
Murphy Goes A-Courtin' (McElfresh), 1990
Musgraves (D. Stevenson), 1960
Music at Midnight (MacLeod), 1952
Music from the Heart (Cartland), 1982
Music I Hear with You (Hoy), 1969
Music in the Hills (D. Stevenson), 1950
Music in Winter (Goodwin, as Ebel), 1975
Music Makers (Thompson), 1979
Music of Our House (Maybury), 1952
Music of the Heart (Burchell), 1972
Musk and Amber (A. Mason), 1942
Mustee (Horner), 1967
Mutiny! (Nordhoff and Hall), 1933
Mutiny at Dawn (Stuart, as V.A. Stuart), 1975
Mutiny in Meerat (Stuart, as V.A. Stuart), 1973
Mutiny in Paradise (Way), 1977
My Antonia (Cather), 1916
My Beautiful Heathen (Stratton, as Gillen), 1970
My Beloved Son (Cookson), 1991
My Best Girl (Norris), 1927
My Brother Michael (Stewart), 1960
My Caravaggio Style (Moore), 1959
My Catalina (M. Peters), 1988
My Cousin Rachel (du Maurier), 1951
My Darling Melissa (Miller), 1990
My Dear Aunt Flora (Cadell), 1946
My Dear Cousin (K. Blair, as Conway), 1959
My Dear Duchess (Chesney, as Fairfax), 1979
My Dear Fugitive (O. Sinclair), 1976
My Dear Innocent (Armstrong), 1981
My Dear Lover England (Bennetts), 1975
My Dear Miss Emma (Blackstock, as Allardyce), 1958
My Dearest Cal (Woods), 1991
My Dearest Elizabeth (Maybury), 1964

My Dearest Love (Loring), 1954
My Desert Friend (s Hichens), 1931
My Dream Is Yours (Asquith), 1954
My Enemy and I (Chandos, as Charles), 1941
My Enemy the Queen (Plaidy, as Holt), 1978
My Fellow Laborer (Haggard), 1888
My Four Uncles (P. Hastings), 1984
My Friend the Chauffeur (Williamson), 1905
My Friend the Professor (Andrews), 1960
My Girl, Regan (M. St John), 1915
My Glorious Brothers (Fast), 1948
My Head! My Head! (Graves), 1925
My Heart Has Wings (Hoy), 1957
My Heart Remembers (Kidd), 1971
My Heart's a Dancer (R. Lindsay, as Leigh), 1970
My Heart's Down Under (Greig), 1951
My Heart's in the Highlands (MacLeod), 1956
My Heart's Right There (F. Barclay), 1914
My Lady Benbrook (Gluyas), 1975
My Lady Caprice (Farnol), 1907
My Lady Cinderella (Williamson, as A.M. Williamson), 1900
My Lady Destiny (Robins, as Gray), 1961
My Lady Glamis (P. Hill), 1985
My Lady of Cleves (Barnes), 1946
My Lady of Dreadwood (Albanesi, as Rowlands), 1906
My Lady of Orange (Bailey), 1901
My Lady of Snow (Garvice), 1908
My Lady of the Fuchsias (Summers), 1979
My Lady Pride (Garvice), 1902
My Lady Rotha (Weyman), 1894
My Lady Scapegrace (Sebastian, as Norcross), 1979
My Lady Troubadour (M. Peters), 1983
My Lady's Crusade (Motley), 1977
My Lady's Honour (Wynne), 1921
My Lady's Mask (Roby), 1979
My Lancashire Queen (M. St John), 1914
My Life for My Sheep (Duggan), 1955
My 'Little Bit' (Corelli), 1919
My Lord Foxe (Gluyas), 1976
My Lord John (Heyer), 1975
My Lord of Wrybourne (Farnol), 1948
My Lord Rakehell (Sebastian), 1977
My Lords, Ladies, and Marjorie (Chesney), 1981
My Love (Loring), 1955
My Love Came Back (D. Smith), 1978
My Love Has a Secret (Maybury), 1958
My Love Kitty (Garvice), 1911
My Love! My Little Queen! (Bloom, as Prole), 1961
My Lute Be Still (Wiat), 1977
My Man of the Mill! (M. St John), 1924
My Master Mariner (Saxton, as Turner), 1974
My Mortal Enemy (Cather), 1926
My Name Is Clary Brown (Blackstock, as Keppel), 1976
My Name is Polly Winter (M. Peters, as Black), 1992
My Old Love Came (Ayres), 1930
My Old Love Came (Burchell), 1943
My Only Love (Chandos, as Charles), 1954
My Only Love (Chandos, as Tempest), 1939
My Only One (McKenna, as Nauman), 1991
My Philippa (M. Peters), 1984
My Pilgrim Love (M. Peters, as Black), 1982
My Pretty Sister (Price), 1952
My Rebel, My Love (W. Roberts), 1986
My Secret Love (Hoy), 1967
My Self, My Enemy (Plaidy), 1983
My Sister Celia (Burchell), 1961

My Sister Sophie (M. Howard, as Edgar), 1964
My Sister's Keeper (R. Lindsay), 1979
My Sweetheart Idabell (Libbey), 1890
My Tattered Loving (Bowen, as Preedy), 1937
My Theodosia (Seton), 1941
My True Love (Chandos, as Charles), 1971
My True Love (Robins), 1953
My Wanton Tudor Rose (Bloom, as Prole), 1956
My Wonderful Wife (Corelli), 1889
Myriah (Williams), 1978
Mystères de Chinatown (R. Marshall), 1934
Mystères de Londres (R. Marshall), 1935
Mysterious (F. Preston), 1986
Mysterious Maid-Servant (Cartland), 1977
Mysterious Waye (Wren), 1930
Mystery at Little Heaven (Delmar), 1933
Mystery Boy-Friend (Ruck), 1957
Mystery House (Norris), 1939
Mystery Lamp (Rinehart), 1925
Mystery Lover (Woodward), 1985
Mystery of Barry Ingram (Swan), 1910
Mystery of Pine Point (Norris), 1936
Mystery of Saligo Bay (Pemberton), 1976
Mystery of the Golden Horn (Whitney), 1990
Mystery on the Moors (B. Michaels), 1968
Mystic Rose (Gallagher), 1977
Mystical Paths (Howatch), 1992

Nabob (Walsh), 1989
Nada the Lily (Haggard), 1892
Naked Battle (Cartland), 1977
Naked Flame (Lamb), 1984
Naked Heart (Briskin), 1989
Naked Once More (B. Michaels, as Peters), 1989
Naked Runner (P. Hastings), 1987
Name for Evil (Lytle), 1947
Name in Lights (Goodwin, as Ebel), 1968
Name Is Mary (Hurst), 1951
Name of the Game (N. Roberts), 1988
Name the Woman (Williamson, as A.M. Williamson), 1924
Nameless Bess (Garvice, as Hart)
Nan—and the New Owner (Chandos), 1959
Nan of No Man's Land (M. St John, as St John Cooper), 1925
Nance (Garvice), 1900
Nancy Nicholson (Swan), 1906
Nanette (Veryan), 1981
Napoleon series (Gavin), from 1989
Napoleon Symphony (Burgess), 1974
Narcissus (E. Scott), 1922
Narrow House (E. Scott), 1921
National Provincial (L. Cooper), 1938
Native Air (Woodhouse), 1990
Nature of Passion (Jhabvala), 1956
Naughty Lady Ness (Williams), 1980
Necessary Woman (Van Slyke), 1979
Necklace of Love (Cartland), 1989
Nedra (McCutcheon), 1905
Ne'er-Do-Weel (Swan), 1897
Negotiated Surrender (Krentz, as Castle), 1982
Nell Gwyn (Bowen), 1926
Nell of Shorne Mills (Garvice), 1900
Nell of the Camp (M. St John), 1913
Nellie (Garvice), 1913
Nellie Wildchild (E. Blair), 1983
Nelson's Brand (Palmer), 1991
Nelson's Love (Bloom, as Prole), 1966

Neptune's Daughter (Weale), 1987
Nest of the Sparrowhawk (Orczy), 1909
Nesting Cats (Bloom, as Essex), 1941
Net to Catch the Wind (Worboys, as Eyre), 1966
Nethergate (Lofts), 1973
Nevada Silver (Lorin, as Hohl), 1987
'Never Again!' Said Nicola (Chandos, as Tempest), 1944
Never Another Love (Chandos, as Tempest), 1949
Never Call It Loving (Eden), 1966
Never Call It Loving (Lewty), 1958
Never Fall in Love (O. Sinclair), 1977
Never Forget Love (Cartland), 1986
Never Give All (Robins), 1934
Never Go Back (M. Pargeter), 1977
Never in a Lifetime (Peake), 1985
Never Laugh at Love (Cartland), 1976
Never Leave Me (Pemberton), 1986
Never Let Go (Woods), 1988
Never Look Back (Robins), 1944
Never Look Back (Vitek), 1983
Never Love a Stranger (Harrod-Eagles, as Woodhouse), 1978
Never Say Goodbye (Neels), 1983
Never Such Innocence (Ellerbeck, as Thorne), 1985
Never the Same (Greig), 1970
Never the Time and the Place (Neels), 1985
Never to Love (Weale), 1958
Never Too Late (Buckingham, as John), 1983
Never Too Late (Neels), 1983
Never Trust a Stranger (K. Thorpe), 1983
Never Turn Back (Donnelly), 1971
Never Victorious, Never Defeated (Caldwell), 1954
Never While the Grass Grows (Neels), 1978
New Americans series (Nicole), from 1982
New Canterbury Tales (s Hewlett), 1901
New Day (Barcynska, as Sandys), 1957
New Discovery (Appignanesi, as Ayre), 1984
New Doctor (Seifert), 1958
New Dominion (Jhabvala), 1972
New Girl (M. St John), 1927
New Girl at Bellforth (M. St John), 1923
New Girl in Town (Baldwin), 1975
New House (L. Cooper), 1936
New Life for Joanna (Bromige), 1957
New Lord Whinbridge (Chandos, as Lance), 1973
New Love for Cynthia (McElfresh, as Scott), 1958
New Moon Through a Window (Greig), 1937
New Orleans Lady (Delmar), 1949
New Orleans Legacy (Ripley), 1987
New Owner (Bromige), 1956
New Owner (K. Thorpe), 1982
New Rector (Weyman), 1891
New Road (Munro), 1914
New Sister Theatre (Andrews), 1964
New Way of Life (Hichens), 1942
New Woman (s Swan), 1898
New World (Atkin), 1921
New Year (Buck), 1968
New Zealand Inheritance (Summers), 1957
Newspaper Girl (Williamson, as A.M. Williamson), 1899
Next Time . . . Forever (Woods), 1990
Next Tuesday (Bloom), 1949
Niccolò series (Dunnett), from 1986
Nice Bloke (Cookson), 1969
Nice Girl Comes to Town (Greig), 1930
Nicola (Erskine-Lindop), 1959
Nicolette (Orczy), 1922

Nicolette (I. Preston), 1967
Night Bell (Mackinlay), 1936
Night Call (McElfresh), 1961
Night Child (De Blasis), 1975
Night Duty at Dukes (Norway, as Norton), 1960
Night Fever (Palmer, as Kyle), 1990
Night Flight (McKenna, as Nauman), 1990
Night Games (Harris), 1987
Night Heat (Mather), 1987
Night in Bombay (Bromfield), 1940
Night in Cold Harbour (Kennedy), 1960
Night Is Kind (Norway, as Norton), 1967
Night Is Thine (Lorrimer, as Robins), 1964
Night Magic (C. Allen), 1989
Night Moves (N. Roberts), 1985
Night Moves (Pozzessere), 1985
Night Music (Lamb), 1980
Night My Enemy (Maybury), 1962
Night of Carnival (Greig, as Ames), 1956
Night of Error (K. Thorpe), 1990
Night of Four Hundred Rabbits (B. Michaels, as Peters), 1971
Night of Gaiety (Cartland), 1981
Night of Love (Palmer), 1993
Night of Love (R. Lindsay, as Leigh), 1978
Night of Possession (Peake), 1983
Night of Stars (Plaidy, as Burford), 1960
Night of the Black Tower (O. Sinclair), 1968
Night of the Bulls (Mather), 1972
Night of the Candles (J. Blake, as Maxwell), 1978
Night of the Condor (Craven), 1987
Night of the Cotillion (Dailey), 1976
Night of the Enchantress (Maybury, as Troy), 1967
Night of the Hurricane (Weale, as Blake), 1965
Night of the Letter (Eden), 1967
Night of the Magician (Krentz, as James), 1984
Night of the Party (Bromige), 1974
Night of the Wedding (Williamson), 1921
Night of the Willow (M. Peters), 1981
Night of the Wolf (Heaven, as Fecher), 1972
Night of the Yellow Moon (Kidd), 1977
Night on the Mountain (Kidd), 1973
Night People (Norway), 1963
Night Riders (Tranter), 1954
Night, Sea and Stars (Pozzessere, as Graham), 1983
Night series (Coulter), from 1989
Night Shift (N. Roberts), 1991
Night Striker (Lorin), 1985
Night the Roof Blew Off (P. Hastings), 1962
Night Train (Weale), 1987
Night Trains (B. Wood), 1979
Night Visitor (Matthews, as Wylie), 1979
Night Way (Dailey), 1981
Night with a Stranger (Buckingham, as John), 1984
Nightbound (Hichens), 1951
Nightcap and Plume (Bowen, as Preedy), 1945
Nightfall (C. Allen, as Marlowe), 1993
Nightingale at Noon (Summerton), 1963
Nightingale Once Sang (Bloom, as Essex), 1958
Nightingale Sang (Cartland), 1979
Nightingale Touch (Norway), 1966
Nightingale Valley (Saunders), 1988
Nightingales (Burchell), 1980
Nightingale's Song (Robins), 1963
Nightmare (s Forester), 1954
Nightmare Ends (Cowen), 1970
Nightrunners of Bengal (Masters), 1951

Night's Dark Secret (Bowen, as Campbell), 1975
Night's Daughters (Norway, as Norton), 1966
Nights of Destiny (S. Wood), 1990
Nightshade at Morning (Bloom), 1944
Nightsong (Sherwood), 1986
Nightstar (F. Michaels), 1982
Nightstar (Sommerfield), 1991
Nightwalker (Krentz, as James), 1984
Nina (Ertz), 1924
Nine Coaches Waiting (Stewart), 1958
Nine Days a-Dying (M. Peters, as Whitby), 1982
Nine Lives (Bloom), 1951
Nine Moons Wasted (Manners, as Lamont), 1977
Ninth Earl (Farnol), 1950
Nitana (Burgin), 1928
No Adam in Eden (Metalious), 1963
No Alternative (Way), 1983
No Armour Against Fate (Pedler), 1938
No Barrier (Dark), 1953
No Bed of Roses (Baldwin), 1973
No Business to Love (R. Lindsay), 1966
No Country for Young Men (O'Faolain), 1980
No Darkness for Love (Cartland), 1974
No Disguise for Love (Cartland), 1992
No Doctors Please (Saxton, as Balmain), 1984
No Dowry for Jennifer (Greig), 1957
No Easier Road to Love (Chandos, as Charles), 1983
No Easy Way (Jacob), 1938
No Easy Way Out (Chase), 1983
No Enemy But Time (Anthony), 1987
No Escape from Love (Cartland), 1977
No Escape from Love (Chandos), 1937
No Escape from Love (Woodward, as Lawrence), 1974
No Evil Angel (Ogilvie), 1956
No Faint Heart (Barcynska, as Sandys), 1943
No Friend of Mine (Peake), 1972
No Gentle Love (Brandewyne), 1980
No Gentle Loving (S. Wood), 1988
No Gentle Persuasion (K. Thorpe), 1990
No Gentle Possession (Mather), 1975
No Gifts from Chance (Pedler), 1944
No Greater Love (Ellis), 1991
No Greater Love (Gallagher), 1979
No Greater Love (Orczy), 1938
No Greater Love (Slaughter), 1985
No Greater Love (Steel), 1991
No Guarantees (Donald), 1990
No Heart Is Free (Cartland), 1948
No Hearts to Break (Ertz), 1937
No Hero—This (Deeping), 1936
No Hint of Scandal, (Bishop) 1971
No Holds Barred (Steele), 1984
No Honourable Compromise (Steele), 1984
No Laggard in Love (Chandos, as Lance), 1971
No Legacy for Lindsay (Summers), 1965
No Limit to Love (Chandos), 1937
No Longer a Dream (Mortimer), 1986
No Love Lost (Van Slyke), 1980
No Man of Her Own (Winspear), 1981
No Man's Kisses (Pykare, as Powers), 1986
No Man's Mistress (R. Lindsay, as Leigh), 1989
No May in October (Muskett), 1951
No Mercy (Cox, as Brindle), 1992
No More A-Roving (S. Thorpe), 1970
No More Lonely Nights (Lamb), 1988
No More Loving (Lorrimer, as Robins), 1965

No Need to Say Goodbye (Neels), 1989
No One Hears But Him (Caldwell), 1966
No One Now Will Know (Delafield), 1941
No Orchids by Request (Summers), 1965
No Other Haven (K. Blair), 1950
No Other Man (Chandos, as Tempest), 1937
No Other Man (Peake), 1982
No Passing Fancy (K. Thorpe), 1980
No Peace for the Wicked (Blackstock, as Torday), 1937
No Place for a Lady (J. Smith), 1994
No Place for Love (M. Lewis), 1963
No Place for Love (Woodward, as Sawley), 1967
No Place for Lovers (Woodward, as Richmond), 1983
No Place to Run (Donnelly), 1987
No Place Too Far (Donald), 1990
No Price Too High (Polland), 1984
No Private Heaven (Baldwin), 1946
No Promise Given (Vitek), 1983
No Quarter Asked (Dailey), 1974
No Quarter Given (McKenna), 1991
No Question of Murder (Lofts, as Curtis), 1959
No Quiet Refuge (Steele), 1983
No Real Relation (Burchell), 1953
No Red Roses (Johansen), 1984
No Reprieve (Napier), 1990
No Retreat from Love (Greig), 1942
No Risk Affair (Mortimer), 1985
No Risks, No Prizes (E. Darcy), 1993
No Room at the Inn (s Ferber), 1941
No Room for Joanna (Gibbs, as Ford), 1964
No Room for Loneliness (Mackinlay), 1965
No Roses in June (Summers), 1961
No Sacrifice (Robins), 1934
No Second Parting (Peake), 1977
No Single Star (Stuart), 1956
No Smoke Without Fire (Harwood), 1964
No Son of Mine (Stern), 1948
No Song at Morningside (M. Peters, as Whitby), 1981
No Sooner Met (Hunter), 1965
No Stone Unturned (Lorrimer, as Robins), 1969
No Summer Beauty (Chandos, as Lance), 1967
No Surrender (McKenna), 1989
No Through Road (Chandos, as Charles), 1960
No Time for a Man (Chandos, as Tempest), 1942
No Time for Love (Cartland), 1976
No Time for Love (Loring), 1970
No Time for Love (Woodward, as Sawley), 1967
No Time for Marriage (R. Lindsay, as Leigh), 1985
No Time for Tears (Freeman), 1981
No Time Like the Present (Jameson), 1933
No Trespassers in Love (Bloom, as Burns), 1949
No Trespassing (Stanford), 1980
No Turning Back (Vitek, as Alexander), 1979
No Victory for the Soldier (Jameson), 1938
No Way Home (Bowen, as Preedy), 1947
No Way Out (Donnelly), 1980
Noah's Daughter (D. Smith), 1982
Noble House (Clavell), 1981
Noble in Reason (Bentley), 1955
Noble One (Robins), 1957
Noble Rogue (Orczy), 1912
Noble Savage (Winspear), 1974
Noblest Frailty (Veryan), 1983
Nobody Asked Me (Burchell), 1937
Nobody Else—Ever (Chandos, as Tempest), 1950
Nobody Wants You! (M. St John), 1928

Nobody's Child (MacLeod, as Airlie), 1954
Nobody's Children (Saxton), 1991
Nobody's Darling (Cox), 1993
Nobody's Girl (M. St John), 1922
Nobody's in Town (Ferber), 1938
Nobody's Lovers (Ayres), 1921
Nobody's Wife (Garvice, as Hart)
Nolan, Jill series (McElfresh), from 1962
Nomad's Land (s Rinehart), 1926
None Better Loved (Mackinlay), 1941
None But He (Lorrimer, as Robins), 1973
None Dare Call It Treason (Gavin), 1978
None So Blind (I. Preston), 1961
None So Pretty (Irwin), 1930
None Turn Back (Jameson), 1936
Nonesuch (Heyer), 1962
Noonday Queen (M. Peters), 1988
Noonfire (Way), 1972
Nor Any Dawn (Muskett), 1932
Nor Pride nor Pity (Laffeaty, as Carstens), 1972
Nora Meade, MD (McElfresh, as Wesley), 1955
Norah (P. Hill), 1976
Norah Stroyan (P. Hill), 1976
Norman Pretender (Anand), 1979
Norman series (Plaidy), from 1974
North and South series (Jakes), from 1982
North of Capricorn (Way), 1981
North Sea Nurse (Woodward), 1975
Northern Correspondent (Stubbs), 1984
Northern Magic (Dailey), 1982
Northern Sunset (Jordan), 1982
Northwater (Crowe), 1968
North-West by South (Cato), 1965
Northwest Passage (K. Roberts), 1937
Not a Marrying Man (Browning), 1992
Not a Marrying Man (R. Lindsay, as Leigh), 1978
Not after Midnight (s du Maurier), 1971
Not at Eight (Woods), 1986
Not at Home (Moore), 1948
Not by Appointment (Summers), 1976
Not Even for Love (Brown, as St Claire), 1982
Not Far Enough (M. Pargeter), 1982
Not Far from Heaven (Hampson), 1974
Not for This Alone (Chandos, as Tempest), 1945
Not Free to Love (Bloom, as Burns), 1950
Not Heaven Itself (Pedler), 1940
Not His Kind of Woman (R. Lindsay, as Leigh), 1992
Not in Our Stars (Plaidy, as Burford), 1945
Not in the Calendar (Kennedy), 1964
Not Love Alone (Cartland), 1933
Not Once but Twice (Neels), 1981
Not One of Us (Greig, as Ames), 1939
Not So Quiet (Price, as Smith), 1930
Not So Wild a Dream (Rivers), 1985
Not That Sort of Girl (Wesley), 1987
Not to Be Trusted (Appignanesi, as Ayre), 1981
Not Wanted on the Voyage (Findley), 1984
Not Wanted on Voyage (K. Thorpe), 1972
Not Without Love (R. Lindsay, as Leigh), 1989
Not Without You (Burchell), 1947
Not Yet (Swan), 1898
Notable Prisoner (F. Barclay), 1905
Note in Music (Lehmann), 1930
Nothing Hurts for Long, and Escort (s du Maurier), 1943
Nothing Is Safe (Delafield), 1937
Nothing Like the Sun (Burgess), 1964

Nothing Lovelier (Ayres), 1942
Nothing to Report (Oman), 1940
Notorious Angel (J. Blake, as Maxwell), 1977
Notorious Gentleman (Lamb, as Holland), 1980
Notorious Lady (Leslie), 1976
Notorious Mrs Gatacre (s Hutten), 1933
Notorious Rake (Balogh), 1992
Nourishing Life (Norway), 1967
Novel, A Novella and Four Stories (s Lytle), 1958
Novel Alliance (F. Stevenson, as Fitzgerald), 1984
November of the Heart (Spencer), 1993
November Tree (Maddocks), 1964
Now and Always (Chandos, as Tempest), 1950
Now and Always (Weale, as Blake), 1964
Now and Forever (Palmer), 1979
Now and Forever (Steel), 1978
Now Barabbas Was a Robber (Bloom, as Mann), 1968
Now East, Now West (Ertz), 1927
Now, God Be Thanked (Masters), 1979
Now I Can Forget (Chandos, as Lance), 1973
Now or Never (Weale), 1978
Now Rough—Now Smooth (Cartland), 1941
Now That April's Gone (Plaidy, as Burford), 1961
Now We Set Out (Ertz), 1934
No 2 Shovel Street (Borden), 1949
Numbered Account (Bridge), 1960
Nuptials of Corbal (Sabatini), 1927
Nurse Abroad (Summers), 1961
Nurse Adriane (James), 1933
Nurse Alice in Love (Chandos, as Charles), 1964
Nurse Alison's Trust (Burchell), 1964
Nurse at Barbazon, (K. Blair), 1964
Nurse at Cap Flamingo (Winspear), 1965
Nurse at Kama Hall (I. Roberts, as Rowland), 1969
Nurse at Moorcroft Manor (Ritchie, as Heath), 1967
Nurse at Mystery Villa (W. Roberts), 1967
Nurse at Rowanbank (Kidd), 1966
Nurse at Shadow Manor (Ritchie, as Heath), 1973
Nurse at St Catherine's (Greig), 1963
Nurse at the Top (Collin), 1964
Nurse Brookes (Norway), 1958
Nurse by Accident (Chandos, as Charles), 1974
Nurse Called Liza (Bloom, as Essex), 1973
Nurse Elaine and the Sapphire Star (Ritchie, as Heath), 1973
Nurse Elliot's Diary (Norway), 1960
Nurse Errant (Andrews), 1961
Nurse Farnley's Secret (Woodward, as Lawrence), 1972
Nurse for Mercy's Mission (McElfresh), 1976
Nurse for Rebels' Run (McElfresh, as Scott), 1960
Nurse Frayne's Strange Quest (Woodward), 1960
Nurse from Killarney (Bloom, as Essex), 1963
Nurse Hanson's Strange Case (Woodward, as Richmond), 1981
Nurse Harriet Goes to Holland (Neels), 1970
Nurse Helen (Stratton, as Gillen), 1970
Nurse in Arabia (Woodward, as Davis), 1972
Nurse in Confusion (I. Preston), 1983
Nurse in Danger (Greig), 1964
Nurse in Danger (W. Roberts), 1972
Nurse in Holland (Neels), 1970
Nurse in Nepal (I. Roberts), 1976
Nurse in Print (Norway), 1963
Nurse in the Dark (Collin), 1965
Nurse in the Hills (I. Roberts), 1969
Nurse in the Sun (Rayner, as Brandon), 1972
Nurse in the Wilderness (I. Roberts), 1983
Nurse in the Woods (Chandos, as Lance), 1969

Nurse Incognito (Chandos), 1964
Nurse Is Born (Norway, as Norton), 1962
Nurse Jane in Tenerife (MacLeod, as Airlie), 1967
Nurse Judy (McElfresh, as Wesley), 1958
Nurse Kathy (McElfresh), 1957
Nurse Kay's Conquest (W. Roberts), 1966
Nurse Lang (MacLeod), 1960
Nurse Laurie (K. Blair), 1962
Nurse Maria (Collin), 1963
Nurse Marika, Loyal in All (Burchell), 1963
Nurse Mary's Engagement (Summers), 1964
Nurse Meg's Decision (Norway, as Neal), 1966
Nurse Moonlight (I. Roberts), 1980
Nurse Nancy (McElfresh, as Scott), 1959
Nurse Off Camera (Norway, as Neal), 1964
Nurse on an Island (Collin), 1970
Nurse on Bodmin Moor (Bloom, as Harvey), 1970
Nurse on Castle Island (Ritchie, as Heath), 1968
Nurse on Holiday, (K. Blair, as Brett), 1963
Nurse Robin (W. Roberts), 1973
Nurse Stacey Comes Aboard (Randall), 1958
Nurse Templar (Weale), 1961
Nurse to Doctor James (Woodward, as Richmond), 1976
Nurse to Princess Jasmine (Woodward), 1979
Nurse to the Maharajah (Woodward), 1961
Nurse Verena in Weirwater (Chandos, as Lance), 1970
Nurse Who Fell in Love (Bloom, as Essex), 1972
Nurse Who Shocked the Matron (Bloom, as Burns), 1970
Nurse Willow's Ward (Chandos, as Tempest), 1965
Nursery Maid (Gibbs), 1975
Nurses (W. Roberts), 1972
Nurse's Holiday (Greig, as Ames), 1965
Nurses in the House (Collin), 1989
Nurse's Story (Greig, as Ames), 1965
Nursing Assignment (Woodward), 1959
Nutmeg of Consolation (O'Brian), 1991

O Genteel Lady! (Forbes), 1926
O Love! O Fire! (Robins), 1966
O Madcap Duchess (P. Hill), 1993
O Pioneers! (Cather), 1913
Oak Apple (Harrod-Eagles), 1982
Oasis (Matthews), 1988
Oath of Silence (Bentley), 1967
Obedient Bride (Balogh), 1989
Obedient Wife (O'Faolain), 1982
Obsession (Lamb), 1980
Obstacle Race (Dell), 1921
Occupying Power (Anthony), 1973
Octavia (Blackstock, as Allardyce), 1965
Octavia (J. Cooper), 1977
October Cabaret (Buckingham, as Quest), 1979
Odd—But Even So (s Wren), 1941
Odds (s Dell), 1922
Odds Against (M. Pargeter), 1984
Odds on Love (Greig), 1936
Odious Duke (Cartland), 1973
Odor of Sanctity (Yerby), 1965
Oedipus (Treece), 1964
Of Dream's and Magic (Schulze), 1989
Of Great Riches (Franken), 1937
Of Human Frailty (Malpass), 1987
Of Love and Dust (Gaines), 1967
Of No Fixed Abode (M. Lewis), 1968
Of the Ring of Earls (Dymoke), 1970
Off Limits (McKenna), 1992

Off White (Nicole), 1959
Off with the Old Love (Neels), 1987
Offer of Marriage (Ruck), 1930
Office Wife (Baldwin), 1930
Officer's Wife (Robins), 1939
Ogilvie, James series (McCutchan, as MacNeil), from 1969
Oh, Darling Joy! (Maybury), 1937
Oh, Money! Money! (E. Porter), 1918
O'Hurleys series (N. Roberts), from 1988
Ola and the Sea Wolf (Cartland), 1980
Old Adam (Bloom), 1967
Old Baxter Place (McElfresh), 1954
Old Captivity (Shute), 1940
Old Doc (Seifert), 1946
Old Dominion (M. Johnston), 1899
Old Elm Tree (Bloom), 1974
Old Enchantment (Neilan), 1990
Old-Fashioned Girl (Ayres), 1953
Old Fashioned Heart (Neels), 1993
Old Flame (Sellers), 1986
Old Fox (L. Cooper), 1927
Old Friends and New (s Vaizey), 1909
Old Glory (Duffield), 1942
Old Glory (Nicole), 1986
Old Gods Laugh (Yerby), 1964
Old Gray Homestead (Keyes), 1919
Old Hat (Barcynska, as Sandys), 1939
Old Love's Domain (Bromige), 1982
'Old Man's' Marriage (Burgin), 1897
Old Mischief (Deeping), 1950
Old Moorings (Swan), 1909
Old New York (Wharton), 1924
Old Passion (Donald), 1982
Old Patch's Medley (s Bowen), 1930
Old Pines (s Boyd), 1952
Old Priory (Lofts), 1981
Old Pybus (Deeping), 1928
Old Rectory (Bloom), 1973
Old Roses (Barcynska, as Sandys), 1923
Old Scarecrow (s Orczy), 1916
Old Smith's Nurse (M. St John), 1918
Old Wine and New (Deeping), 1932
Old World Dies (Deeping), 1954
Oleander River (Stern), 1937
Olive Branch (I. Roberts, as Shaw), 1968
Olive Grove (MacLeod), 1986
Olive Island (K. Thorpe), 1972
Oliver October (McCutcheon), 1923
Oliver Trenton, K.C (Frankau), 1951
Oliver Wiswell (K. Roberts), 1940
Olive's Courtship (Libbey), 1892
Olivia (Garvice), 1902
Olivia (Riefe), 1981
Olivia in India (O. Douglas), 1913
Olivia Mary (Albanesi), 1912
O'Malley of Shanganagh (Byrne), 1925
O'Malley series (Small), from 1984
On Call (E. Harrison), 1974
On Her Doorstep (Hooper, as Robbins), 1986
On Her Majesty's Orders (Stuart, as A. Stuart), 1977
On Leaving Charleston (Ripley), 1984
On Love's Altar (Garvice), 1892
On Mother Brown's Doorstep (Staples), 1993
On My Own (Pilcher), 1965
On the Air (Burchell), 1956
On the High Road (Albanesi, as Rowlands), 1914

On the Night of the Seventh Moon (Plaidy, as Holt), 1972
On the Screen (Hichens), 1929
On the Wings of Fate (Albanesi, as Rowlands), 1916
On the Wings of Magic (Hooper), 1983
On Wings of Dreams (Gallagher), 1985
On Wings of Love (Harrod-Eagles, as Woodhouse), 1978
On Wings of Passion (McKenna, as Brookes), 1983
On Wings of Song (Burchell), 1985
Once a Cheat (Donnelly), 1991
Once a Nurse (W. Roberts), 1966
Once a Princess (Lindsey), 1991
Once and Always (McNaught), 1987
Once Bitten, Twice Shy (Donald), 1992
Once for All Time (Neels), 1984
Once in a Life (Garvice), 1910
Once in a Lifetime (Steel), 1982
Once Is Enough (Robins, as French), 1953
Once More with Feeling (N. Roberts), 1983
Once They Were Rich (D. Murray), 1933
Once to Every Heart (MacLeod), 1951
Once upon a Christmas (s Buck), 1972
Once You Have Found Him (Wyndham), 1954
Ondine (Pozzessere, as Drake), 1988
One and Only (D. Smith), 1973
One Basket (s Ferber), 1947
One Between (Cowen), 1967
One Bright Day (James), 1945
One Broken Dream (I. Preston), 1979
One Chance at Love (Mortimer), 1988
One Child Bride (Wiat), 1990
One Dark Night (Bennetts), 1978
One Day, My Love (Bromige), 1980
One-Eyed Moon (Steen), 1935
One Fight More (Ertz), 1939
One Fine Day (Gibbs, as Ford), 1954
One Girl at a Time (R. Lindsay, as Leigh), 1990
One Girl in the World (Garvice), 1915
One Is Only Human (Stern), 1960
One Little Room (Chappell), 1960
One Love (MacLeod), 1945
One-Man Girl (Greig), 1931
One Man Woman (Appignanesi, as Ayre), 1982
One Man's Art (N. Roberts), 1985
One Man's Evil (Albanesi, as Rowlands), 1900
One Man's Heart (Burchell), 1940
One Man's War (McKenna), 1992
One Month at Sea (Ayres), 1929
One More Night (Armstrong), 1990
One More River to Cross (Summers), 1979
One More Time (Baldwin), 1972
One More Time (Hunter), 1982
One More Time (van der Zee), 1983
One Night in Ceylon (s Robins), 1931
One Night in London (Andrews), 1979
One of Ours (Cather), 1922
One of the Boys (Dailey), 1980
One of the Chorus (Ruck), 1928
One of the Crowd (Albanesi), 1913
One of the Family (Burchell), 1939
One of Those Ways (Lowndes), 1929
One Perfect Rose (Richards), 1992
One Room for His Highness (Greig), 1944
One Sees Stars (Ayres), 1952
One Step Ahead (Vitek), 1985
One Step from Heaven (Hoy), 1943
One Summer (Ayres), 1930

One Summer (N. Roberts), 1986
One Summer's Day (MacLeod, as Airlie), 1961
One that Got Away (E. Darcy), 1987
One Thing I Wanted (Chandos, as Tempest), 1944
One to Live With (Ayres), 1938
One Touch of Moondust (Woods), 1989
One Touch of Topaz (Johansen), 1988
One Tough Hombre (Lorin, as Hohl), 1987
One Traveller Returns (Burgin), 1931
One Ulysses Too Many (Jameson), 1958
One Unwanted (Ayres), 1921
One Way Out (Hutten), 1906
One Way Out (MacLeod), 1941
One Way Ticket (Way), 1977
One Way to Venice (Hodge), 1974
One Who Cares (Lorrimer, as Robins), 1954
One Who Counted (Albanesi), 1937
One Who Forgot (Ayres), 1919
One Who Kisses (Lewty), 1983
One Who Kisses (L. Walker), 1954
One Who Paid (Albanesi, as Rowlands), 1935
One Who Remembers (Chandos, as Charles), 1976
One Who Stood By (Ayres), 1923
One Woman (Dixon), 1903
One Woman (Albanesi, as Rowlands), 1911
One Woman Crusade (E. Darcy), 1990
One Woman Too Many (Ayres), 1952
One Woman's Freedom (Price, as Smith), 1932
One Wore Blue (Pozzessere, as Graham), 1992
One Wreath with Love (Summerton, as Roffman), 1978
Onesiphore, Our Neighbor (Macbeth), 1929
Onlooker (Bishop), 1970
Only a Dream (Cartland), 1988
Only a Girl's Love (Garvice), 1901
Only a Mechanic's Daughter (Libbey), 1892
Only a Singing Girl (M. St John), 1907
Only a Touch (Chandos), 1941
Only Forever (Miller), 1989
Only Her Husband (Mackinlay), 1939
Only His (Lowell), 1991
Only Love (Cartland), 1979
Only Lover (Mortimer), 1979
Only Love's Cross for Her (Libbey), 1908
Only Mine (Lowell), 1992
Only My Dreams (Robins), 1951
Only My Heart to Give (Asquith), 1955
Only One (Jordan), 1985
Only One Love (Garvice), 1910
Only Our Love (Bromige), 1968
Only Sin (Ellis), 1986
Only Son (s Swan), 1898
Only the Best (Trask), 1935
Only to Part (I. Roberts), 1961
Only Victor (Kent), 1990
Only World (Burgin), 1906
Only You (Lowell), 1992
Only You (M. Pargeter), 1979
Onyx (Briskin), 1982
Opal (Bennetts), 1986
Opal (Rhodes), 1984
Open Country (Hewlett), 1909
Open Day at the Manor (Gibbs, as Ford), 1977
Open Door (Maddocks), 1980
Open Marriage (Kidd), 1984
Open the Door to Love (Chandos, as Tempest), 1952
Open Window (Muskett), 1930

Open Wings (Cartland), 1942
Operation Nassau (Dunnett), 1993
Ophelia (F. Stevenson), 1968
Opportune Marriage (K. Thorpe), 1968
Opposites Attract (N. Roberts), 1984
Optimist (Delafield), 1922
Optimist's Daughter (Welty), 1972
Oracles (Kennedy), 1955
Orange Blossom for Sandra (Bloom), 1951
Orange Blossom for Tara (I. Roberts, as Rowland), 1971
Orange Blossom Shop (Chandos, as Tempest), 1946
Orange Blossoms (s Bowen, as Shearing), 1938
Orange Girl (Bloom, as Prole), 1972
Orange Sash (Dymoke), 1958
Orange Tree Plot (Harrod-Eagles), 1989
Oranges and Lemons (Hunter, as Chace), 1967
Oranges Are Not the Only Fruit (Winterson), 1985
Orchard Hill (Seifert), 1945
Orchard Hill (L. Walker), 1958
Orchards (Deeping), 1922
Orchid Girl (Chandos, as Lance), 1978
Orchids from the Orient (O. Sinclair), 1986
Ordeal of Elizabeth (Arnim), 1901
Ordeal of Three Doctors (Seifert), 1965
Ordered South (Williamson, as A.M. Williamson), 1900
Ordinary People (E. Pargeter), 1941
Ordinary Woman (Sallis), 1991
Origin (Stone), 1980
Original Miss Honeyford (Chesney), 1986
Orphan Train series (Miller), from 1990
Orphans (Ponsonby), 1962
Ortolans (Lorrimer), 1990
O'Shaughnessy, Pixie (Vaizey), 1903
Other Brother (Steele), 1981
Other Cathy (Buckingham), 1978
Other Girl (Garvice), 1911
Other Girl (L. Walker), 1965
Other Juliet (Maybury), 1955
Other Karen (V. Johnston), 1983
Other Linding Girl (Burchell), 1966
Other Lips Have Loved You (Burchell), 1938
Other Love (Robins), 1952
Other Lovers (Pizzey), 1989
Other Men's Arms (Greig, as Barclay), 1936
Other One (Chandos), 1953
Other People's Marriages (Thomas), 1993
Other Side (Jameson), 1946
Other Side of Love (Briskin), 1991
Other Side of Love (Robins), 1973
Other Side of Paradise (Barber), 1986
Other Side of Paradise (M. Lewis), 1975
Other Side of Paradise (M. Pargeter), 1985
Other Side of Sorrow (Chard), 1977
Other Side of Summer (Worboys, as Maxwell), 1977
Other Woman (Delmar), 1930
Other Woman (Garvice), 1905
Other Woman (Steele), 1980
Other Women's Beauty (Greig), 1938
Ottoman series (Nicole, as Savage), from 1990
Oubliette (Farnol), 1912
Our Admirable Betty (Farnol), 1918
Our Avenue (s Ayres), 1922
Our Dearest Emma (Bloom, as Prole), 1949
Our Emily (Staples), 1989
Our Lady of Marble (Bloom), 1926
Our Lady of the Beeches (Hutten), 1902

Our Living Stone Age (Idriess), 1963
Our Nell (M. St John), 1917
Our Valiant Few (F. Mason), 1956
Out of a Clear Sky (Albanesi, as Rowlands), 1925
Out of Control (Lamb), 1988
Out of Reach (Cartland), 1945
Out of the Ashes (Richards), 1989
Out of the Dark (Asquith), 1972
Out of the Dark (Lofts), 1972
Out of the House (Irwin), 1916
Out of the Nest (Cadell), 1987
Out of the Night (Jordan), 1990
Out of the Past (Garvice)
Out of the Past (Woodward), 1982
Out of the Rain (Cadell), 1987
Out of the Shadows (Chard), 1978
Out of the Shadows (Duffield), 1944
Out of the Swim (Burgin), 1930
Out of the War? (Lowndes), 1918
Out of the Whirlwind (Erskine-Lindop), 1951
Out of This Nettle (Lofts), 1938
Out to Marry Money (Ruck), 1940
Out Trail (Rinehart), 1923
Outback Nights (Richards), 1987
Outback Summer (Buckingham, as John), 1981
Outback Woman (Saunders, as Blake), 1989
Outcast (Cox), 1989
Outcast of the Family (Garvice), 1900
Outcasts of Crowthorpe College (M. St John), 1913
Outer Ring (Erskine-Lindop), 1955
Outlanders (Carter), 1983
Outlaw (Hewlett), 1919
Outlaw (Lowell), 1991
Outlaw Derek (Hooper), 1988
Outlaw Hearts (Brandewyne), 1986
Outlaw Love (Norris), 1928
Outlaw's Embrace (Rivers), 1986
Outrageous Fortune (Gibbs, as Ford), 1955
Outrageous Fortune (D. Murray), 1952
Outrageous Lady (Cartland), 1977
Outside Chance (Mackinlay), 1966
Outsider (Craven), 1987
Outsider (Delinsky), 1993
Over at the Crowleys' (s Norris), 1946
Over the Blue Mountains (Burchell), 1952
Over the Castle Wall (MacLeod), 1974
Over the Hills (Farnol), 1930
Over the Water (Oman), 1935
Over the Windmill (James), 1954
Overheard (Ayres), 1925
Overland Trail (Saxton, as Felix), 1983
Overlooker (P. Hastings), 1982
Overseas Nurse (Greig, as Ames), 1961
Overtures (Burgh), 1993
Ovington's Bank (Weyman), 1922
Owner Gone Abroad (Ayres), 1937
Oxen of the Sun (Bacheller), 1935

Pacific Paradise (Bevan), 1989
Pacific Street (Holland), 1992
Pack Mule (Bloom), 1931
Package to Spain (Polland), 1971
Paddington Green (Rayner), 1975
Pagan Adversary (Craven), 1983
Pagan Blossoms (Hamilton, as Fitzgerald), 1989
Pagan Enchantment (Mortimer), 1983

Pagan Encounter (Lamb), 1978
Pagan Heart (Rivers), 1985
Pagan Interlude (K. Blair, as Brett), 1947
Pagan Island (Winspear), 1972
Pagan King (E. Marshall), 1959
Pagan Lover (Hampson), 1980
Pagan Queen (Treece), 1959
Pagan Surrender (Donald), 1993
Pageant of Victory (Farnol), 1936
Pagoda (Bowen), 1927
Paid For! (Garvice), 1892
Paint Me Rainbows (F. Michaels), 1982
Paint the Wind (Spellman), 1990
Painted Angel (Bowen, as Preedy), 1938
Painted Butterflies (MacGill), 1931
Painted Heaven (Muskett), 1934
Painted Lady (Bloom), 1945
Painted Lady (Seger), 1990
Painted Lives (C. Allen), 1990
Painted Veil (Hunter), 1986
Painted Wings (Stratton, as Gillen), 1972
Pair Bond (Ellerbeck, as Yorke), 1984
Palace of the Peacocks (Winspear), 1969
Palace of the Pomegranate (Winspear), 1974
Pale Dawn, Dark Sunset (Mather), 1975
Pale Orchid (Mather), 1985
Palm Rock and Paradise (A.E. Worboys), 1961
Palomino (Steel), 1981
Paloverde (Briskin), 1978
Pam series (Hutten), from 1905
Panama (Carter), 1978
Pandora (Beresford), 1974
Pandora Lifts the Veil (Greig, as Ames), 1932
Panorama (s Bentley), 1952
Pantomime (Stern), 1931
Papa (Williamson, as A.M. Williamson), 1902
Paper Halo (Norway), 1970
Paper Marriage (Kidd), 1974
Paper Prison (Wren), 1939
Paper Roses (Ayres), 1916
Paradine Case (Hichens), 1933
Paradise (Duffield), 1936
Paradise (Forbes), 1937
Paradise (McNaught), 1991
Paradise (Neilan), 1981
Paradise for Two (Neels), 1988
Paradise Found (Cartland), 1986
Paradise in Penang (Cartland), 1989
Paradise Island (Beresford), 1963
Paradise Place (Deeping), 1949
Paradise Row (Blackstock, as Allardyce), 1976
Paradise Wild (Lindsey), 1981
Paragon Place (Bowling), 1990
Paragon Street (Leslie), 1965
Parasites (du Maurier), 1949
Parcel of Land (Gibbs), 1969
Parcel of Rogues (Lane), 1948
Parents Are a Problem (Greig), 1933
Pargeters (Lofts), 1984
Paris—And My Love (Burchell), 1960
Parris Mitchell of Kings Row (Bellamann), 1948
Parsifal (Vansittart), 1988
Parson Harding's Daughter (Trollope), 1979
Parson Kelly (A. Mason), 1900
Parson's Children (P. Hill), 1994
Parson's Daughter (Bishop), 1979

Parson's Daughter (Cookson), 1987
Parson's House (Cadell), 1977
Parson's Pleasure (Hardwick), 1987
Part of the Bargain (Miller), 1985
Parted by Fate (Libbey), 1890
Partners (N. Roberts), 1985
Partners Are a Problem (Chandos), 1957
Partners for Playtime (M. Howard), 1938
Partners in Love (Saunders), 1984
Partnership (Bentley), 1928
Parts Unknown (Keyes), 1938
Party in Dolly Creek (Blackstock), 1967
Party in Peking (Pemberton), 1989
Party of Baccarat (Byrne), 1930
Pasadoble (Hamilton, as Fitzgerald), 1986
Passage Perilous (Jacob), 1948
Passage to Mutiny (Kent), 1976
Passage to Paxos (Weale), 1981
Passage to Pontefract (Plaidy), 1981
Passerby (s Dell), 1925
Passing Fancy (Roby), 1980
Passing Glory (Tannahill), 1989
Passing Star (Stubbs), 1970
Passing Strangers (s Joseph), 1989
Passing Strangers (MacLeod, as Airlie), 1963
Passion (Winterson), 1987
Passion and Illusion (Delinsky, as Drake), 1983
Passion and the Flower (Cartland), 1978
Passion and the Glory (Nicole), 1989
Passion and the Pain (Laffeaty, as Carstens), 1970
Passion Flower (Bowen), 1932
Passion Flower (Garvice), 1910
Passion Flower (Norris), 1930
Passion Flower (Palmer), 1984
Passion for Treason (Nicole, as R. Nicholson), 1981
Passion from the Past (Mortimer), 1982
Passion Moon Rising (Brandewyne), 1988
Passionate Adventure (Beresford), 1983
Passionate Adventure (Bloom, as Burns), 1936
Passionate Adventure (van der Zee), 1993
Passionate Affair (Mather), 1982
Passionate Attainment (Cartland), 1935
Passionate Awakening (Robins), 1926
Passionate Brood (Barnes), 1945
Passionate Business (Krentz, as James), 1981
Passionate Choice (Kidd), 1986
Passionate Encounter (Kidd), 1979
Passionate Enemies (Plaidy), 1976
Passionate Exile (Oldfield), 1993
Passionate Flame (Robins), 1928
Passionate Heart (Bloom), 1930
Passionate Interlude (Duffield), 1931
Passionate Intruder (Peake), 1982
Passionate Involvement (Peake), 1977
Passionate Jade (Manners, as Bell), 1969
Passionate Journey (Stone), 1949
Passionate Lover (Mortimer), 1985
Passionate Man (Trollope), 1990
Passionate Pastoral (J. Lindsay), 1951
Passionate Pilgrim (Cartland, as McCorquodale), 1952
Passionate Princess (Cartland), 1988
Passionate Protection (Jordan), 1983
Passionate Puritan (M. Peters, as Grey), 1978
Passionate Pursuit (Kidd), 1984
Passionate Rebel (Slaughter), 1979
Passionate Relations (Jordan), 1987

Passionate Revenge (Wentworth), 1987
Passionate Savage (Gluyas), 1980
Passionate Sinner (Winspear), 1977
Passionate Springtime (Bloom, as Essex), 1956
Passionate Stranger (Kidd), 1981
Passionate Touch (Delinsky, as Drake), 1981
Passionate Winter (Mortimer), 1978
Passionate Witness (Plaidy, as Burford), 1941
Passion's Domain (Pykare, as N. Coombs), 1983
Passions in the Sand (Cartland), 1976
Passions of Chelsea Kane (Delinsky), 1992
Passions of the Mind (Stone), 1971
Passion's Price (Vitek), 1983
Passion's Pride (Williams), 1980
Passion's Promise (Steel), 1977
Passion's Raging Storm (Sommerfield), 1992
Passion's Vixen (Finch), 1984
Passions Wild and Free (Taylor), 1988
Passport for a Girl (Borden), 1939
Passport to Happiness (Greig), 1955
Passport to Happiness (Steele), 1990
Passport to Romance (Woodward, as Richmond), 1969
Past All Forgetting (Craven), 1978
Past All Reason (K. Thorpe), 1992
Past Master (Tranter), 1965
Past Passion (Jordan), 1992
Past Revenge (Mortimer), 1985
Past Tense of Love (Cadell), 1970
Pastel (Heyer), 1929
Pastoral (Bloom), 1934
Pastoral (Shute), 1944
Pastor's Wife (Arnim), 1914
Pat series (Montgomery), from 1933
Patchwork (M. Peters), 1989
Patchwork Quilt (Muskett), 1946
Path of the Hero King (Tranter), 1970
Path of the King (s J. Buchan), 1921
Path of the Storm (Kent, as Reeman), 1966
Paths of Peace (Alexander), 1984
Paths of Summer (Bromige), 1979
Pathway to Paradise (Greig), 1942
Patient in Love (Chandos, as Charles), 1963
Patricia and Life (Albanesi), 1920
Patricia Plays a Part (Grundy), 1913
Patrick Henry and the Frigate's Keel (s Fast), 1945
Patriot (Tranter), 1982
Patriots (Stuart, as Long), 1986
Patriot's Dream (B. Michaels), 1976
Pattern (Franken), 1925
Pattern of Deceit (E. Darcy), 1989
Patterson Limit (Macbeth), 1923
Patterson series (Stirling), from 1985
Patty series (s Webster), from 1903
Paul in Possession (Ayres), 1924
Pavilion (Bloom), 1951
Pavilion at Monkshood (Maybury), 1965
Pavilion of Honour (Bowen, as Preedy), 1932
Pavilion of Women (Buck), 1946
Pawn in Frankincense (Dunnett), 1969
Pay Me Tomorrow (Burchell), 1940
Pay the Doctor (Seifert), 1966
Pay the Piper (James), 1950
Paying Pests (Grundy), 1941
Payment Due (Jordan), 1991
Payment for the Piper (F. Murray), 1983
Payment in Full (Hampson), 1980

Payment in Kind (Jordan), 1990
Peabody, Amelia series (B. Michaels, as Peters), from 1975
Peace Shall Destroy Many (Wiebe), 1962
Peacock Bed (Manners, as Marshall), 1978
Peacock Hill (Mackinlay), 1948
Peacock in the Jungle (May), 1982
Peacock Pagoda (Stuart, as A. Stuart), 1959
Peacock Queen (M. Peters), 1972
Peacock Spring (Godden), 1975
Peacock's Feather (Woodhouse), 1988
Peak of the Furnace (May), 1986
Pearl (Bennetts), 1984
Pearl-Maiden (Haggard), 1903
Pearl of the Orient (Nicole), 1988
Pearl of the West (M. St John), 1918
Pearl Thief (Ruck), 1926
Pearls of Sharah series (F. Preston), from 1989
Pearly Queen (Staples), 1992
Pedigree of Honey (James), 1951
Pedlar's Pack (s Goudge), 1937
Pedlar's Row (Bowling), 1994
Peerless Jim (Cordell), 1984
Peggy by Request (Dell), 1928
Peggy Fordyce (Swan), 1940
Peggy of Beacon Hill (Greig), 1924
Peggy the Pilgrim (Burgin), 1907
Peking Picnic (Bridge), 1932
Pelangi Haven (van der Zee), 1985
Pelican Walking (s Stern), 1934
Pelicans (Delafield), 1918
Penalty for Living (MacLeod), 1942
Penance (Wynne), 1917
Pendulum (Swan), 1926
Penelope (Chesney, as Fairfax), 1982
Penelope Deveraux (Bishop), 1966
Pengelly Jade (Stratton, as Gillen), 1972
Penmarric (Howatch), 1971
Pennies from Heaven (Ruck), 1940
Pennies on Her Eyes (Roby), 1969
Penniless Heiress (Gibbs), 1975
Penniless Peer (Cartland), 1974
Penny Box (Dwyer-Joyce), 1980
Penny for the Guy (Summerton, as Roffman), 1965
Penny Plain (O. Douglas), 1920
Penny Trumpet (James), 1947
Peony (Buck), 1948
People from the Sea (V. Johnston), 1979
People in Glass Houses (Blackstock), 1975
People Like Ourselves (O. Douglas), 1938
People of My Own (E. Pargeter), 1942
People of the Mist (Haggard), 1894
People of This Parish (Ellerbeck, as Yorke), 1991
People on the Hill (V. Johnston), 1971
Pepper Tree Bay (L. Walker, as Sanders), 1959
Pepper's Way (Hooper), 1984
Perchance to Dream (Bloom), 1971
Perchance to Dream (Seger), 1989
Perchance to Marry (K. Blair, as Conway), 1961
Perdita (J. Smith), 1981
Perdita's Prince (Plaidy), 1969
Peregrine's Progress (Farnol), 1922
Perfect (McNaught), 1993
Perfect Fools (C. Allen), 1981
Perfect Gentleman (Chesney), 1988
Perfect Love (Gallagher), 1987
Perfect Match (Veryan), 1981

Perfect Partner (Mortimer), 1982
Perfect Partners (Krentz), 1992
Perfect Pearl (Cartland), 1989
Perfect Stranger (Goodwin, as Ebel), 1966
Perfect Stranger (Steel), 1982
Perfect Wife (Leslie), 1960
Perfect Wife and Mother (Ellerbeck, as Thorne), 1980
Perfecting Fiona (Chesney), 1990
Perfection of Love (Cartland), 1980
Performers series (Rayner), from 1973
Perfume of Paradise (J. Blake), 1987
Perfume of the Gods (Cartland), 1987
Perhaps Love (Armstrong), 1983
Pericles the Athenian (R. Warner), 1963
Peridot Flight (Leslie), 1956
Peril and the Prince (Cartland), 1984
Perilous Eden (Pozzessere), 1991
Perilous Quest (Greig, as Ames), 1960
Perish in July (Hardwick), 1989
Permission to Love (Jordan), 1985
Persian Boy (Renault), 1972
Persian Price (Anthony), 1975
Persian Ransom (Anthony), 1975
Person in the House (Burgin), 1900
Person Unknown (Chard), 1988
Personal Affair (Kidd), 1981
Personal Fictions, (s Wiebe), 1977
Personality Plus (s Ferber), 1914
Petals Drifting (Hampson), 1971
Petals in the Wind (I. Preston), 1972
Petenera's Daughter (Bellamann), 1926
Peter, A Parasite (Albanesi), 1901
Peter Abelard (Waddell), 1933
Peter Day-by-Day (Barcynska, as Barclay), 1916
Peter Jackson, Cigar Merchant (Frankau), 1920
Peter Jameson (Frankau), 1920
Peter West (D. Stevenson), 1923
Petronella's Waterloo (Oliver, as James), 1980
Petruchia (Stern), 1929
Petticoat Government (Orczy), 1910
Petticoat Rule (Orczy), 1910
Petworth series (Aiken), from 1978
Peyton Place series (Metalious), from 1957
Phantasmagoria (Wiat), 1988
Phantasy (Duffield), 1932
Phantom Cottage (V. Johnston), 1970
Phantom Emperor (Swanson), 1934
Phantom Garden (Bishop), 1974
Phantom Lover (Ayres), 1919
Phantom Marriage (Jordan), 1983
Phantom Pipes (MacLeod), 1975
Philippa (Muskett), 1954
Philomela's Miracle (Neels), 1978
Philosopher and the Sentimentalist (Corelli), 1911
Philosopher's Daughter (Ertz), 1976
Phoenix and the Laurel (Lane), 1954
Phoenix Rising (Steen), 1952
Phoenix Syndrome (Andrews), 1987
Photogenic Soprano (Dunnett, as Halliday), 1968
Phroso (Hope), 1897
Physicians (E. Harrison), 1966
Piccadilly (Rayner), 1985
Piccadilly Inn (Mackinlay), 1946
Pick Up and Smile (Barcynska), 1936
Pieces of Dreams (C. Allen), 1984

Poppy and the Rose (Barcynska, as Sandys), 1962
Poppy series (Rayner), from 1987
Port o' Missing Men (s Wren), 1934
Port of Adventure (Williamson), 1913
Portent (Harris), 1980
Portrait (Ford), 1910
Portrait in Gold (Ainsworth), 1971
Portrait of a Gentleman in Colours (Farnol), 1935
Portrait of a Lady (E. Smith), 1936
Portrait of a Marriage (Buck), 1945
Portrait of a Patient (James), 1959
Portrait of a Playboy (Deeping), 1947
Portrait of Bethany (Weale), 1982
Portrait of Destiny (Swan), 1937
Portrait of Jaime (Way), 1977
Portrait of Jenny (Dymoke), 1990
Portrait of Jill (Goodwin, as Ebel), 1972
Portrait of Love (Cartland), 1982
Portrait of Pierre (I. Preston), 1971
Portrait of Sarah (M. Peters, as Black), 1969
Portrait of Sarah (Saunders), 1988
Portrait of Susan (K. Blair, as Brett), 1956
Portraits (Freeman), 1979
Portuguese Affair (Melville, as Betteridge), 1966
Portuguese Escape (Bridge), 1958
Poseidon's Gold (Davis), 1993
Positive Approach (E. Darcy), 1987
Possession (Bromfield), 1925
Possession (Byatt), 1990
Possession (de la Roche), 1923
Possession (Lamb), 1979
Post Captain (O'Brian), 1972
Post of Honor (Delderfield), 1974
Post Office Girl (M. St John), 1915
Postscript to Yesterday (Summers), 1966
Post-War Girl (s Ruck), 1922
Pot Boils (Jameson), 1919
Potential Danger (Jordan), 1988
Potter's Niece (Randall), 1987
Pour the Dark Wine (Lampitt), 1989
Poverty's Daughter (M. St John, as St John Cooper), 1922
Powder and Patch (Heyer), 1930
Power (Jacob), 1927
Power and Seduction (Lorin), 1985
Power and the Glory (Bentley), 1940
Power and the Glory (Nicole), 1988
Power and The Passion (E. Darcy), 1989
Power and the Passion (Nicole, as C. Nicholson), 1977
Power and the Prince (Cartland), 1980
Power of Love (Albanesi, as Rowlands), 1911
Power of the Dog (Byrne), 1929
Power Play (Jordan), 1988
Power Play (Krentz, as Castle), 1982
Power to Kill (Hichens), 1934
Powers and Maxine (Williamson), 1907
Practical Dreamer (Browning), 1983
Practical Marriage (Schulze), 1991
Practice for Sale (Mackinlay), 1964
Practice to Deceive (Veryan), 1985
Practise to Deceive (Wentworth), 1993
Prairie Fires (Swan), 1913
Praise Singer (Renault), 1978
Pray for the Wanderer (O'Brien), 1938
Pray to the Earth (Eaton), 1938
Prayer for the Ship (Kent, as Reeman), 1958
Precious Jeopardy (L. Douglas), 1933

Precious Jewel (Balogh), 1993
Precious Waif (Hampson), 1969
Predestined (Duffield), 1929
Prelude to a Song (M. Pargeter), 1982
Prelude to Enchantment (Mather), 1972
Prelude to Freedom (Renier), 1967
Prelude to Kingship (Lane), 1936
Prelude to Louise (Maybury), 1954
Prelude to Love (Renier), 1972
Prelude to Love (J. Smith), 1983
Prelude to Yesterday (Bloom), 1961
Prescription for Love (R. Lindsay), 1977
Prescription for Melissa (Dwyer-Joyce), 1974
Presence and the Power (Bowen), 1924
Presence in an Empty Room (V. Johnston), 1980
President Is Born (Hurst), 1928
President's Lady (Stone), 1951
Pretence (R. Lindsay, as Leigh), 1956
Pretender to Love (F. Stevenson, as Faire), 1981
Pretenders (M. Howard), 1962
Prettiest Girl (Burchell), 1955
Pretty Dear (Barcynska), 1920
Pretty Freda's Lovers (Libbey), 1889
Pretty Horse-Breakers (Cartland), 1971
Pretty Kitty (F. Stevenson, as Faire), 1981
Pretty Madcap Dorothy (Libbey)
Pretty One (Greig), 1937
Pretty Ones (Eden), 1957
Pretty Penelope (Albanesi, as Rowlands), 1907
Pretty Penny (Alexander, as Langley), 1985
Pretty Polly (Chesney), 1989
Pretty Polly Pennington (Albanesi), 1908
Pretty Witch (Stratton, as Gillen), 1971
Pretty, Witty Nell! (Bloom, as Prole), 1953
Price Is Love (Cartland, as McCorquodale), 1960
Price of Folly (Robins, as Chesterton), 1955
Price of Honour (Garvice, as Gibson)
Price of Inheritance (Dwyer-Joyce), 1963
Price of Love (R. Lindsay), 1967
Price of Race (Orczy), 1942
Price of Surrender (Krentz, as James), 1983
Price of the King's Peace (Tranter), 1971
Price of Things (Glyn), 1919
Price Paid (Albanesi, as Rowlands), 1914
Price to Be Met (Steele), 1980
Priceless Love (E. Darcy), 1988
Pride (Saxton), 1981
Pride and Passion (F. Michaels), 1975
Pride and Power (Hampson), 1974
Pride and the Anguish (Kent, as Reeman), 1968
Pride and the Poor Princess (Cartland), 1980
Pride of Eve (Deeping), 1914
Pride of Fiona Macrae (Swan), 1934
Pride of Hannah Wade (Dailey), 1985
Pride of Her Life (Garvice)
Pride of Innocence (M. Lewis), 1971
Pride of Kings (Dymoke), 1978
Pride of Lions (Hunter, as Chace), 1972
Pride of Madeira (Hunter), 1977
Pride of Place (Ellerbeck, as Thorne), 1989
Pride of the Morning (Plaidy, as Burford), 1958
Pride of the Peacock (Plaidy, as Holt), 1974
Pride of the South (Seifert), 1950
Pride of the Trevallions (Salisbury), 1975
Pride of Vallon (Marsh), 1985
Pride Parted Them! (M. St John), 1925

Pride to the Winds (Trask), 1946
Pride's Castle (Yerby), 1949
Pride's Fancy (Raddall), 1946
Pride's Heart (Steele), 1979
Prime Minister's Wife (Leslie), 1961
Prime Time (Brown, as Ryan), 1983
Primrose Bride (K. Blair), 1961
Primula (Bowen, as Preedy), 1940
Primula and Hyacinth (Bloom, as Burns), 1950
Prince Among Men (van der Zee), 1992
Prince Among Men (Woods), 1986
Prince and Heretic (Bowen), 1914
Prince and the Pekingese (Cartland), 1979
Prince and the Quakeress (Plaidy), 1968
Prince Charming (Barcynska, as Sandys), 1937
Prince Charming Replies (Woods), 1988
Prince for Portia (Chandos, as Tempest), 1943
Prince for Sale (R. Lindsay), 1975
Prince of Darkness (B. Michaels), 1969
Prince of Darkness (Plaidy), 1978
Prince of Foxes (Shellabarger), 1947
Prince of Graustark (McCutcheon), 1914
Prince of Hearts (Woodward, as Marsh), 1970
Prince of Intrigue (Wynne), 1920
Prince of the White Rose (Wiat), 1984
Prince Philanderer (Bloom, as Prole), 1968
Princeling (Harrod-Eagles), 1981
Prince's Darling (Bowen, as Preedy), 1930
Prince's Story (Barcynska), 1959
Princess (Deveraux), 1988
Princess Alysa series (Taylor), from 1987
Princess Amelia (Oman), 1924
Princess and the Pagan (Hamilton, as Fitzgerald), 1983
Princess and the Pea (F. Preston), 1993
Princess Charming (Albanesi, as Rowlands), 1931
Princess in Distress (Cartland), 1978
Princess in Waiting (Saxton), 1976
Princess McGee (Seger), 1992
Princess of Celle (Plaidy), 1967
Princess of Desire (M. Peters), 1970
Princess of Fire (Pozzessere, as Drake), 1989
Princess of Poor Street (E. Blair), 1986
Princess Passes (Ayres), 1931
Princess Passes (Cowen, as Hyde), 1979
Princess Passes (Williamson), 1904
Princess Priscilla's Fortnight (Arnim), 1905
Princess Sophia (E. Marshall), 1958
Princess Virginia (Williamson, as A.M. Williamson), 1909
Princess's Game (Dell), 1920
Print Petticoat (Andrews), 1954
Priorsford (O. Douglas), 1932
Prison Wall (Dell), 1932
Prisoner in Paradise (Laffeaty), 1976
Prisoner in Paradise (Lewty), 1980
Prisoner in Peking (Saxton, as Felix), 1982
Prisoner of Desire (J. Blake), 1986
Prisoner of Fate (Laffeaty, as Fortina), 1969
Prisoner of Love (Cartland), 1979
Prisoner of Love (MacLeod), 1958
Prisoner of Love (Woodward), 1971
Prisoner of Passion (Courtney), 1985
Prisoner of the Heart (Lamb, as Holland) , 1972
Prisoner of Zenda (Hope), 1894
Prisoners of Hope (M. Johnston), 1898
Prison-Stained! (M. St John, as St John Cooper), 1921
Private Duty (Baldwin), 1936

Private Enterprise (L. Cooper), 1931
Private Hotel—Anywhere (Grundy), 1937
Private Lives (Mortimer), 1992
Private Revenge (Woodman), 1989
Private Scandals (N. Roberts), 1993
Private Wing (Rayner, as Brandon), 1971
Privy Seal (Ford), 1907
Probationer! (Price), 1934
Problems of Doctor A (Seifert), 1979
Problems of Love (Cartland), 1978
Procession (s Hurst), 1929
Prodigal Heart (Ertz), 1950
Prodigal Son (Caine), 1904
Prodigal Village (Bacheller), 1920
Professional Gentleman (Staples, as Stevens), 1988
Professional Hero (Greig), 1943
Professional Lover (Greig), 1933
Professional Secret (Norway), 1964
Professional Woman (T. Barclay), 1993
Professor's House (Cather), 1925
Progress of Julius (du Maurier), 1933
Prologue to Love (Caldwell), 1961
Promise (Steel), 1978
Promise (Trask), 1944
Promise at Midnight (Peake), 1980
Promise for Ever (Robins), 1961
Promise Kept (Browning, as Williams), 1992
Promise Me Forever (Taylor), 1993
Promise Me Moonlight (Finch), 1993
Promise Me Tomorrow (Pykare, as Powers), 1982
Promise Me Tomorrow (N. Roberts), 1984
Promise Not to Tell (Stern), 1964
Promise of Delight (M. Howard), 1952
Promise of Glory (Nolan), 1983
Promise of Happiness (Neels), 1979
Promise of Morning (Manley-Tucker), 1962
Promise of Paradise (Chandos, as Tempest), 1949
Promise of Spring (Balogh), 1990
Promise of the Unicorn (Craven), 1985
Promise to Cherish (Spencer), 1983
Promise to Dishonour (Steele), 1985
Promises (C. Allen), 1980
Promises (Gaskin), 1982
Promises from the Past (Vitek), 1981
Proper Place (O. Douglas), 1926
Property of a Gentleman (Gaskin), 1974
Prophet of Berkeley Square (Hichens), 1901
Prophetic Marriage (Deeping), 1920
Props (Jacob), 1932
Pro's Daughter (Mackinlay), 1934
Proselyte (Ertz), 1933
Proud and the Free (Fast), 1950
Proud Beloved (Stanford), 1989
Proud Bess (M. Peters), 1990
Proud Breed (De Blasis), 1978
Proud Citadel (Chandos, as Charles), 1967
Proud Citadel (Hoy), 1942
Proud Harvest (Mather), 1978
Proud Heart (Stuart), 1953
Proud Mary (Gower), 1984
Proud New Flags (F. Mason), 1951
Proud Patricia (Swan), 1940
Proud Princess (Cartland), 1976
Proud Servant (Irwin), 1934
Proud Stranger (Stratton), 1976
Proud Villeins (Anand), 1990

Provencal Summer (Goodwin, as Ebel), 1980
Provincial Lady series (Delafield), from 1930
Proxy Wedding (M. Peters, as Grey), 1982
Prude and the Prodigal (Cartland), 1980
Prudence (J. Cooper), 1978
Prudence Langford's Ordeal (Albanesi, as Rowlands), 1914
Psychiatrist's Wife (Gellis, as Jacobs), 1966
Public Secrets (N. Roberts), 1990
Public Smiles, Private Tears (Van Slyke), 1982
Publicity Baby (Barcynska), 1935
Publicity for Anne (Williamson, as A.M. Williamson), 1926
Puller of Strings (Burgin), 1917
Pullman (Dell), 1930
Pulse of Life (Lowndes), 1908
Punch and Judy (Albanesi), 1919
Punished with Love (Cartland), 1980
Punishment of a Vixen (Cartland), 1977
Puppets Parade (Leslie), 1932
Purchase Price (Swan), 1934
Pure and Untouched (Cartland), 1981
Pure as the Lily (Cookson), 1972
Pure Temptation (S. Wood), 1987
Puritan Strain (Baldwin), 1935
Puritans in Paradise (Slaughter), 1960
Purple Parasol (McCutcheon), 1905
Purple Quest (Slaughter), 1965
Pursuing Shadow (Wynne), 1944
Put Back the Clock (Robins), 1962
Pyramid (Hichens), 1936
Pyrates (G. Fraser), 1983

Quadrille (Chesney), 1981
Quaint Place (Barcynska, as Sandys), 1952
Quarrel and Kiss (Ruck), 1942
Quatermain, Allan series (Haggard), from 1885
Queen and Lord M (Plaidy), 1973
Queen and Mortimer (Clarke, as Honeyman), 1974
Queen and the Gypsy (Heaven), 1977
Queen and the Welshman (Sisson), 1979
Queen Anne's Lace (Keyes), 1930
Queen for England (Bloom, as Prole), 1957
Queen for the Regent (Bloom, as Prole), 1971
Queen from Provence (Plaidy), 1979
Queen-Gold (Wiat), 1985
Queen Guillotine (Bloom, as Prole), 1962
Queen in Waiting (Lofts), 1955
Queen in Waiting (Plaidy), 1967
Queen Jennie (Wynne), 1918
Queen Jezebel (Plaidy), 1953
Queen Kate (Garvice), 1909
Queen Lear (Keane), 1989
Queen of Diamonds (Plaidy, as Tate), 1958
Queen of Evil (Slaughter), 1962
Queen of Hearts (Cartland), 1992
Queen of Hearts (Krentz, as Castle), 1979
Queen of Hearts (Pozzessere, as Graham), 1985
Queen of Hearts (F. Stevenson, as Curzon), 1982
Queen of Lions (Nicole, as Savage), 1994
Queen of Paris (Nicole, as C. Nicholson), 1979
Queen of the Castle (Lane), 1958
Queen of the Dawn (Haggard), 1925
Queen of the Night (Nicole, as Savage), 1993
Queen of This Realm (Plaidy), 1984
Queen Saves the King (Cartland), 1992
Queen Sheba's Ring (Haggard), 1910
Queen Sweetheart (Williamson, as A.M. Williamson), 1901

Queen Truganini (Cato), 1976
Queen Who Never Was (M. Peters), 1972
Queen Who Was a Nun (Bloom, as Prole), 1967
Queenmaker (M. Peters), 1975
Queen's Affair (Bloom), 1979
Queen's Caprice (Bowen, as Preedy), 1934
Queen's Confession (Plaidy, as Holt), 1968
Queen's Corsair (Saxton, as Turner), 1976
Queen's Counsel (Stuart, as A. Stuart), 1957
Queen's Daughters (Bloom, as Prole), 1973
Queen's Delight (Heaven, as Fecher), 1966
Queen's Diamond (Dymoke), 1983
Queen's Favorite (Heaven, as Fecher), 1974
Queen's Favourites (Plaidy), 1966
Queen's Folly (Thane), 1937
Queen's Folly (Weyman), 1925
Queen's Fourth Husband (Wiat), 1976
Queen's Gift (Fletcher), 1952
Queen's Grace (Tranter), 1953
Queen's Grace (Westcott), 1959
Queen's Harbour (Gibbs, as Ford), 1944
Queen's Husband (Plaidy), 1973
Queen's Letter (Lamb, as Coates) , 1973
Queen's Messenger (Cartland), 1971
Queen's Midwife (Bloom, as Prole), 1961
Queens of England (Plaidy), from 1983
Queens' Play (Dunnett), 1964
Queen's Quadrille (Roby, as Grey), 1981
Queen's Quair (Hewlett), 1904
Queen's Secret (Plaidy), 1989
Quest (Asquith), 1964
Quest for Alexis (Buckingham), 1973
Quest for Love (Marsh), 1984
Quest of Glory (Bowen), 1912
Quest of the Eagle (Seger), 1986
Quest of Youth (Farnol), 1927
Questing Beast (Lane), 1970
Questing Trout (Bloom), 1934
Question of Honor (McKenna), 1989
Question of Honour (Drummond), 1991
Question of Love (Oliver, as Thorn), 1985
Question of Marriage (R. Lindsay), 1972
Question of Marriage (Vaizey), 1910
Question of Quality (Albanesi), 1909
Question of Temptation (s Orczy), 1925
Quick and the Dead (Bennetts), 1980
Quick Brown Fox (Bishop), 1972
Quickenberry Tree (Motley), 1983
Quicksilver Pool (Whitney), 1955
Quiet Gentleman (Heyer), 1951
Quiet Heart (Franken), 1954
Quiet Hills (Bromige), 1967
Quiet Holiday (K. Blair, as Brett), 1957
Quiet House (Maddocks), 1947
Quiet Island (Muskett), 1943
Quiet One (Norway, as Norton), 1959
Quiet Professor (Neels), 1993
Quiet Village (Bloom), 1965
Quiet Walks the Tiger (Pozzessere, as Graham), 1983
Quiet Wards (Andrews), 1956
Quietly My Captain Waits (Eaton), 1940
Quill's Window (McCutcheon), 1921
Quin's Hide (Summerton), 1964
Quisanté (Hope), 1900
Quorum (Bentley), 1950

Rabbits in the Hay (Lane), 1958
Rabble in Arms (K. Roberts), 1933
Race Against Love (Wentworth), 1980
Race for Love (Cartland), 1978
Race of Scorpions (Dunnett), 1989
Race of the Tiger (Cordell), 1963
Rachel Lee (Wynne), 1925
Rachel Trevellyan (Mather), 1974
Rachel's Confession (F. Preston), 1985
Radiance (Maybury), 1979
Radkin Revenge (W. Roberts), 1979
Rafe the Maverick (Hooper), 1986
Rafferty's Choice (Schulze), 1991
Rafferty's Wife (Hooper), 1987
Rag Nymph (Cookson), 1991
Ragamuffin (Greig), 1929
Rage and Desire (Nicole, as Arlen), 1982
Rage of Heaven (Laffeaty), 1977
Rage of Passion (Palmer), 1987
Ragged Rainbows (Miller), 1986
Raging Fire (Heaven), 1987
Raging Seas, Seering Skies (Nicole), 1988
Ragtime (Doctorow), 1975
Raider (Deveraux), 1987
Rain of Diamonds (Weale), 1981
Rain on the Wind (Hunter), 1984
Rainbird's Revenge (Chesney), 1988
Rainbow (Buck), 1974
Rainbow after Rain (Chandos, as Charles), 1977
Rainbow at Dusk (Loring), 1942
Rainbow Bird (Way), 1972
Rainbow Child (Worboys, as Eyre), 1971
Rainbow Days (MacLeod), 1973
Rainbow Fire (Richards), 1989
Rainbow Glass (Dwyer-Joyce), 1973
Rainbow in My Hand (Manley-Tucker), 1965
Rainbow in the Mist (Whitney), 1989
Rainbow Isle (MacLeod), 1939
Rainbow on the Road (Forbes), 1954
Rainbow River (I. Roberts, as Rowland), 1970
Rainbow Romance (Ritchie), 1974
Rainbow Summer (Harrod-Eagles, as Woodhouse), 1976
Rainbow Through the Rain (Rhodes), 1993
Rainbow to Heaven, (Cartland), 1976
Rainbow Valley (Montgomery), 1919
Rainbow's End (Brandewyne), 1992
Rainbow's End (Saunders), 1978
Raine's Story (F. Preston), 1989
Rains Came (Bromfield), 1937
Rainsong (Whitney), 1984
Raintree County (Lockridge), 1948
Raintree Valley (Winspear), 1971
Rainwood Family series (Bromige), from 1966
Raj series (P. Scott), from 1966
Rakehell (Manners, as Rundle), 1970
Rakes and Rogues (s Balogh), 1993
Rake's Companion (Pykare, as Towers), 1980
Rake's Progress (Bowen), 1912
Rake's Progress (Chesney), 1984
Rakonitz Chronicles (Stern), 1932
Rakóssy (Holland), 1967
Raleigh's Eden (Fletcher), 1940
Raleigh's Fair Bess (Saxton, as Turner), 1972
Ralph Carey (Miles), 1922
Ralph Dacre (A. Stevenson), 1967
Ramage, Lord Nicholas (Pope), from 1965

Rana Look (Brown), 1986
Rancher Needs a Wife (K. Blair, as Conway), 1962
Random Army (Polland), 1969
Random Island (Stuart, as A. Stuart), 1968
Random Winds (Plain), 1980
Randy (L. Walker, as Sanders), 1948
Ranger in the Hills (L. Walker), 1966
Raoul, Gentleman of Fortune (Bailey), 1907
Rape of the Fair Country (Cordell), 1959
Raptor (Jennings), 1992
Rapture (P. Hastings), 1966
Rapture (Sherwood, as Royal), 1979
Rapture in My Rags (P. Hastings), 1954
Rapture of the Desert (Winspear), 1972
Rapture's Angel (Sommerfield), 1981
Rapture's Dream (Finch), 1982
Rapture's Rogue (Coulter), 1986
Rascals' Heaven (F. Mason), 1965
Rash Reckless Love (Sherwood), 1981
Ratoon (Nicole), 1962
Ravelston Affair (E. Harrison), 1967
Raven in the Wind (Wiat), 1978
Raven on the Wing (Hooper), 1987
Ravenburn, (Black), 1978
Raven's Prey (Krentz, as James), 1984
Raven's Wing (Sprigge), 1940
Ravenscar (M. Peters), 1981
Ravenscrag (MacLeod), 1948
Ravenscroft (Eden), 1965
Ravensley series (Heaven), from 1978
Ravenstor (Renier), 1974
Ravished (Krentz, as Quick), 1992
Rawhide and Lace (Palmer), 1987
Rawhide Man (Palmer), 1984
Reach for the Shadows (Dwyer-Joyce), 1972
Reach for the Stars (Seger, as Jennings), 1984
Reach Out for Happiness (Woodward, as Richmond), 1984
Reach Out to Cherish (Browning), 1983
Reaching for the Stars (L. Walker), 1966
Ready—Aye Ready! (M. St John, as St John Cooper), 1916
Real David Copperfield (Graves), 1933
Real Gold (Albanesi, as Rowlands), 1924
Real Love or Fake? (Cartland), 1990
Real Man (Sellers), 1984
Real Thing (Delinsky), 1987
Real Thing (Peake), 1972
Realm of the Pagans (Hampson), 1982
Realms of Gold (Hunter), 1976
Reap the Whirlwind (Hampson), 1975
Reap the Whirlwind (Roby), 1972
Reap the Wind (Johansen), 1991
Reaping (Sabatini), 1929
Reason for Being (Jordan), 1989
Reason for Marriage (Jordan), 1986
Reason Why (Glyn), 1911
Reason Why (Lowndes), 1932
Reasonable Doubts (B. Hastings), 1984
Reasonable Shores (Stern), 1946
Reasons of the Heart (Napier), 1987
Rebecca (du Maurier), 1938
Rebel (Bailey), 1923
Rebel (Cornwell), 1993
Rebel Bride (Coulter), 1979
Rebel Bride (Hampson), 1971
Rebel Doctor (Seifert), 1978
Rebel Heart (Maybury), 1959

Rebel Heart (Oliver), 1986
Rebel Hearts (Swan), 1940
Rebel Heiress (Hodge), 1975
Rebel in His Arms (Rivers), 1981
Rebel in Love (Peake), 1978
Rebel Lover (Blackstock, as Allardyce), 1979
Rebel of Allington (Wiat), 1974
Rebel Pride (Sommerfield), 1980
Rebel Princess (Anthony), 1953
Rebel Princess (Cartland), 1985
Rebel Princess (Leslie), 1970
Rebel Waltz (Hooper), 1986
Rebel Wife (Randall), 1944
Rebellion (N. Roberts), 1988
Rebellious Love (Seger), 1983
Rebels (Jakes), 1975
Rebels (Treece), 1953
Reckless (Krentz, as Quick), 1992
Reckless (Woods), 1989
Reckless Angel (Lowndes), 1939
Reckless Love (Lowell), 1990
Reckless Passion (Krentz, as James), 1982
Reckless Pilgrim (MacLeod), 1941
Reckoning (Harrod-Eagles), 1992
Reckoning (Penman), 1991
Reconstruction series (Dixon), from 1902
Rector of Wyck (M. Sinclair), 1926
Rector's Daughter (Ellerbeck, as Thorne), 1992
Rector's Wife (Trollope), 1991
Red Ashes (Pedler), 1924
Red Bird (Manners), 1984
Red Carnelian (Whitney), 1968
Red Chalet (Norway, as Norton), 1960
Red Cherry Summer (Laker, as Óvstedal), 1973
Red Chief (Idriess), 1953
Red Cliffs of Malpara (Way), 1976
Red Cockade (Weyman), 1895
Red Cross Barge (Lowndes), 1916
Red Daniel (McCutchan, as MacNeil), 1973
Red Dawn (Nicole), 1985
Red Dust (Muskett), 1954
Red Eve (Haggard), 1911
Red Flame (Miles), 1921
Red Fleur-de-Lys (Wynne), 1912
Red for Danger! (Price), 1936
Red Fruit (Wynne), 1929
Red Hair (Glyn)
Red Is for Murder (Whitney), 1943
Red Lamp (Rinehart), 1925
Red Lotus (MacLeod, as Airlie), 1958
Red Midnight (Pozzessere, as Graham), 1984
Red Pavilion (Summerton), 1958
Red Queen, White Queen (M. Peters), 1982
Red Queen, White Queen (Treece), 1958
Red Rose (Balogh), 1986
Red Rose for Love (Mortimer), 1982
Red Rose of Anjou (Plaidy), 1982
Red Rose of Lancaster (Wynne), 1921
Red Roses for a Nurse (I. Preston), 1968
Red Roses, White Lilies (Vitek, as Alexander), 1979
Red Rowan Berry (F. Murray), 1976
Red Runs the Sunset (I. Roberts, as Carr), 1963
Red Saint (Deeping), 1909
Red Silence (Norris), 1929
Red Sky at Morning (Kennedy), 1927
Red Sky at Night (Hodge), 1977

Red Sky at Night (Plaidy, as Burford), 1959
Red Tail (McKenna), 1985
Red Veil (M. St John, as St John Cooper), 1928
Red Wagon (E. Smith), 1930
Red Whirlwind (Wynne), 1919
Red, White, and Grey (Miles), 1921
Redcoat (Cornwell), 1987
Redeemed by Love (Garvice, as Hart)
Redeeming Love (Rivers), 1991
Redway Street (M. St John, as St John Cooper), 1924
Redwood Empire (Lowell, as A.E. Maxwell), 1987
Reeds of Honey (Way), 1975
Reef (Wharton), 1912
Reef of Dreams (M. Howard), 1942
Refining Felicity (Chesney), 1988
Reflection of Evil (Summerton, as Roffman), 1967
Reflections (Hufford), 1981
Reflections (N. Roberts), 1983
Reflections in a Lake (Goodwin, as Ebel), 1988
Reflections of Ambrosine (Glyn), 1902
Reflections of Love (Woodward), 1983
Refugees (Doyle), 1893
Regency (Harrod-Eagles), 1990
Regency (D. Murray), 1936
Regency Buck (Heyer), 1935
Regency Gold (Chesney), 1980
Regency Morning (M. Peters, as Law), 1988
Regency Rogue (Bennetts), 1982
Regency Scandal (Ley), 1979
Regency Star (Williams), 1985
Regent's Daughter (Plaidy), 1971
Regent's Gift (Wynne), 1915
Regiment (Nicole), 1988
Regiment of Women (Dane), 1917
Regina (C. Darcy), 1976
Rehearsal for Love (Baldwin), 1940
Reilly's Woman (Dailey), 1978
Rekindled Flame (Marsh), 1982
Rekindled Passion (Jordan), 1989
Relative Betrayal (Mather), 1990
Relative Stranger (A. Stevenson), 1970
Relative Strangers (Steele), 1987
Relative Values (Steele), 1993
Release the Past (I. Preston), 1973
Relenting Fate (s Garvice), 1912
Relentless Adversary (Krentz, as Castle), 1982
Relentless Desire (Brown), 1983
Relentless Storm (Lorrimer), 1975
Relic (Anthony), 1991
Reluctant Adventuress (S. Thorpe), 1963
Reluctant Bride (Cartland), 1970
Reluctant Bride (Laffeaty), 1966
Reluctant Bride (Mackinlay), 1939
Reluctant Bride (J. Smith), 1982
Reluctant Cinderella (Greig, as Ames), 1952
Reluctant Debutante (Sebastian, as Gladstone), 1979
Reluctant Dreamer (Browning), 1986
Reluctant Father (Palmer), 1989
Reluctant Folly (MacLeod), 1942
Reluctant Governess (Mather), 1971
Reluctant Guest (K. Blair, as Brett), 1959
Reluctant Heiress (Sebastian, as Norcross), 1978
Reluctant Lark (Johansen), 1983
Reluctant Madonna (Steen), 1929
Reluctant Millionaire (Greig), 1944
Reluctant Mistress (B. Hastings), 1990

Reluctant Nightingale (Norway), 1970
Reluctant Odyssey (E. Pargeter), 1946
Reluctant Protegée (Sebastian, as Gladstone), 1980
Reluctant Puritan (Shoesmith), 1972
Reluctant Queen (Plaidy), 1990
Reluctant Relation (Burchell), 1961
Reluctant Relative (Steele), 1983
Reluctant Rivals (Roby, as Grey), 1981
Reluctant Widow (Heyer), 1946
Reluctant Wife (Armstrong), 1987
Remains to Be Seen (Cadell), 1983
Remedy for Love (Kidd), 1972
Remember (Bradford), 1992
Remember This Stranger (K. Thorpe), 1974
Remember Today (Thane), 1941
Remembered Kiss (Ayres), 1918
Remembered Serenade (Burchell), 1975
Remembered Spring (Maddocks), 1949
Remembering Louise (Gilbert), 1978
Remembrance (Steel), 1981
Renaissance Man (Krentz, as James), 1982
Renaissance series (Bowen), from 1928
Rendezvous (Anthony), 1967
Rendezvous (Buckingham, as John), 1985
Rendezvous (s du Maurier), 1980
Rendezvous (Franken), 1954
Rendezvous (Kent, as Reeman), 1972
Rendezvous (Krentz, as Quick), 1992
Rendezvous in Vienna (Ellis), 1976
Rendezvous in Zagarella (Ruck), 1964
Rendezvous with Danger (Pemberton), 1974
Rendezvous with Fear (Worboys), 1977
Rendezvous with Love (Chard), 1983
Renegade (Graham), 1951
Renegade Girl (Gibbs), 1981
Renegade Player (Browning), 1982
Renny's Daughter (de la Roche), 1951
Renshawe Inheritance (Renier), 1972
Rent a Wife (R. Lindsay, as Leigh), 1980
Repeating Pattern (M. Howard), 1968
Repent at Leisure (Duffield), 1945
Reprieve (Deeping), 1945
Reprise (J. Smith), 1982
Republic (Thompson), 1985
Reputation (Robins), 1963
Reputation Dies (Ley), 1984
Requiem for a Patriot (Cordell), 1988
Requiem for a Wren (Shute), 1955
Requiem for Idols (Lofts), 1938
Rescue Operation (Jordan), 1983
Research Fellow (Stuart, as A. Stuart), 1971
Research into Marriage (Jordan), 1987
Respectable Miss Parkington-Smith (Blackstock, as Allardyce), 1964
Response (Jordan), 1984
Rest Harrow (Hewlett), 1910
Rest Is Magic (Lewty), 1973
Rest of My Life with You (Baldwin), 1942
Restless Are the Sails (Eaton), 1941
Restless Beauty (Greig, as Ames), 1944
Restless Dream (Mackinlay), 1949
Restless Frontier (McCutchan, as MacNeil), 1979
Restless Heart (Beresford), 1982
Restless Heart (Robins), 1938
Restless Lady (s Keyes), 1963
Restless Passion (Delmar), 1947

Restless Sea (Thompson), 1983
Restless Years (MacLeod, as Airlie), 1950
Restoration (Tremain), 1989
Restoration Affair (Oliver), 1975
Restoring Love (Woods, as Sherrill), 1982
Resumptions (Nicole), 1992
Retallick series (Thompson), from 1977
Retreat from Love (Greig), 1937
Retribution (Lamb), 1981
Retribution (M. St John, as St John Cooper), 1930
Return (Anthony), 1978
Return (James), 1935
Return (Winston), 1972
Return Engagement (Hooper, as Robbins), 1982
Return Engagement (Mortimer), 1993
Return I Dare Not (Kennedy), 1931
Return Journey (Ayres), 1938
Return Journey (Delderfield), 1974
Return Match (Cadell), 1979
Return Match (Jordan), 1986
Return of a Hero (McKenna), 1989
Return of a Heroine (Steen), 1936
Return of Simon (K. Blair, as Conway), 1953
Return of the Cuckoo (Chandos, as Lance), 1976
Return of the Eagles (F. Mason), 1959
Return of the Gypsy (Plaidy, as Carr), 1985
Return of the Petticoat (Deeping), 1909
Return of the Prodigal (M. Sinclair), 1914
Return of the Royalist (Shoesmith), 1971
Return to Aylforth (Eliot), 1967
Return to Bellbird Country (Worboys, as Eyre), 1966
Return to Belle Amber (Way), 1971
Return to Darkness (W. Roberts), 1969
Return to Deepwater (Stratton, as Gillen), 1975
Return to Delphi (Melville, as Betteridge), 1964
Return to Dragonshill (Summers), 1971
Return to Glenshael (Elgin), 1965
Return to King's Mere (Chandos, as Lance), 1967
Return to Listowel (Sallis), 1975
Return to Love (M. Howard), 1946
Return to Love (Lorrimer, as Robins), 1968
Return to Love (Maybury), 1939
Return to Santa Flores (Johansen), 1984
Return to Sender (Manley-Tucker), 1968
Return to Spring (MacLeod), 1939
Return to Terror (Chandos, as Charles), 1966
Return to Tip Row (Gower), 1977
Return to Vienna (Buckingham), 1971
Return to Wuthering Heights (Ellerbeck, as L'Estrange), 1977
Return to Yesterday (Donald), 1983
Returned Empty (F. Barclay), 1920
Reuben (Garvice), 1912
Reunion in Reno (Greig, as Warren), 1941
Revealing Moment (Laffeaty), 1969
Revenge at Black River (Tresillian, as Devine), 1985
Revenge Is Sweet (Cartland), 1988
Revenge of the Heart (Cartland), 1984
Reverse of the Medal (O'Brian), 1986
Reversion to Type (Delafield), 1923
Revolt—and Virginia (Summers), 1969
Revolt of Sarah Perkins (Cockrell), 1965
Revolt of the Eaglets (Plaidy), 1977
Revolution of Love (Cartland), 1987
Revolution of Love (Cartland), 1988
Reward of Faith (s Goudge), 1950
Rhanna series (C. Fraser), from 1978

Rhapsody in Bloom (van der Zee, as van Wieren), 1989
Rhapsody of Love (Cartland), 1977
Rhiannon (Gellis), 1982
Rhona Keith (Swan), 1910
Rhythm of Flamenco (Hunter, as Chace), 1966
Rib of the Hawk (R. Marshall), 1956
Ribbons and Laces (Ayres), 1924
Ribbons in Her Hair (L. Walker, as Sanders), 1957
Ribs of Death (Aiken), 1967
Rice Dragon (Drummond), 1980
Rich and the Righteous (Van Slyke), 1971
Rich Are Different (Howatch), 1977
Rich Are Not Proud (Greig, as Warren), 1942
Rich as Sin (Mather), 1992
Rich Earth (Oldfield), 1980
Rich Friends (Briskin), 1976
Rich Girl—Charity Girl! (M. St John), 1922
Rich Girl, Poor Girl (Baldwin), 1938
Rich in Paradise (Hamilton, as Fitzgerald), 1992
Rich Is Best (Ellis), 1985
Rich Man, Poor Girl (Greig), 1935
Rich Man's Flowers (Polland), 1990
Rich Mrs Burgoyne (Norris), 1912
Rich Radiant Love (Sherwood), 1983
Rich Twin, Poor Twin (Greig), 1940
Richard and the Knights of God (Bennetts), 1970
Richard by Grace of God (Clarke, as Honeyman), 1968
Richard Carvel (Churchill), 1899
Richard Chatterton, V.C. (Ayres), 1915
Richard Temple (O'Brian), 1962
Richer Dust (Jameson), 1931
Riches of the Heart (Clarke), 1991
Richest Woman in Town (Bellamann), 1932
Richmond and Elizabeth (Clarke, as Honeyman), 1970
Richmond series (Sallis), from 1977
Riddle of a Lady (Mackinlay), 1955
Ride a Black Horse (M. Pargeter), 1975
Ride a White Dolphin (Maybury), 1971
Ride a Wild Horse (Donnelly), 1987
Ride on Singing (Ritchie), 1964
Ride Out the Storm (Donnelly), 1975
Ride the Blue Riband (Laker), 1977
Ride the Storm (E. Darcy), 1991
Ride the Thunder (Dailey), 1981
Ride the Tiger (McKenna), 1992
Ride to Glencoe (Dymoke), 1989
Ride with Me (Costain), 1944
Rider of the White Horse (Sutcliff), 1959
Rider on a White Horse (Sutcliff), 1960
Riders (J. Cooper), 1985
Riders of the Wind (Thane), 1926
Rides a Hero (Pozzessere, as Graham), 1989
Ridge of White Waters (Laffeaty, as Carstens), 1976
Ridin' High (Mackinlay), 1941
Riding to the Moon (Cartland), 1982
Riding to the Sky (Cartland), 1988
Rifleman Dodd (Forester), 1943
Right Arm (s Vaizey), 1918
Right Grand Girl (M. Howard), 1972
Right Line of Cedric (Duggan), 1961
Right of Possession (Krentz, as Castle), 1981
Right Path (N. Roberts), 1985
Right Touch (McKenna, as Nauman), 1986
Rightful Possession (Wentworth), 1978
Riley in the Morning (Brown), 1985
Rilla of Ingleside (Montgomery), 1921

Ring (Steel), 1980
Ring-a-Roses (Joseph), 1990
Ring for a Fortune (Peake), 1980
Ring for Nurse Raine (Chandos, as Charles), 1962
Ring in a Teacup (Neels), 1978
Ring in the New (Bentley), 1969
Ring o' Roses (Andrews), 1972
Ring of Crystal (Donnelly), 1985
Ring of Fire (Way), 1978
Ring of Hope (Mackinlay), 1965
Ring of Jade (Way), 1972
Ring of Mischief (Summerton), 1965
Ring of Roses (Trask), 1940
Ring on Her Finger (Burchell), 1953
Ring the Bell Softly (Bennetts), 1978
Ring Tree (Bloom), 1964
Ring Without Romance (Greig, as Ames), 1940
Ringed Castle (Dunnett), 1971
Rio d'Oro (Tranter), 1955
Ripening Vine (O. Sinclair, as Clare), 1981
Rise of an Eagle (Way), 1988
Rise of Henry Morcar (Bentley), 1946
Rising Family series (Sallis), from 1984
Rising of the Lark (Ruck), 1951
Rising Star (K. Thorpe), 1969
Rising Storm (Goodwin) 1992
Rising Summer (Staples), 1991
Rising Tide (Keane, as Farrell), 1937
Risk Worth Taking (Seidel), 1983
Risky Affair (Kidd), 1989
Risky Business (N. Roberts), 1986
Rites of Passage (Golding), 1980
Rites of Possession (Lamb), 1990
Rival Attractions (Jordan), 1990
Rival Beauties (M. St John), 1907
Rival Doctors (Seifert), 1967
Rival Heiresses (Garvice, as Hart)
Rival Potters (Randall), 1990
Rivals (J. Cooper), 1988
Rivals (Dailey), 1989
Rivals (Nicole, as McKay), 1985
Rivals at School—Rivals Through Life! (M. St John), 1926
River (Godden), 1946
Riven Realm (Tranter), 1984
River and Wilderness (Worboys, as Eyre), 1967
River Is Down (L. Walker), 1967
River Lady (Deveraux), 1985
River Lodge (Cadell), 1948
River Lord (K. Thorpe), 1977
River of Love (Cartland), 1981
River Road (Keyes), 1945
River Room (Weale), 1978
River Voices (Goodwin, as Ebel), 1976
Rivers of Damascus (s Byrne), 1931
Rivers of Glory (F. Mason), 1942
Riviera Romance (Lewty), 1984
Road (Deeping), 1931
Road from the Monument (Jameson), 1962
Road of the Gods (Paterson), 1930
Road Royal (Oman), 1924
Road That Bends (Ayres), 1916
Road to Bithynia (Slaughter), 1951
Road to Compiègne (Plaidy), 1959
Road to Damascus (Swan), 1937
Road to Destiny (Laffeaty), 1969
Road to Gafsa (Stratton), 1976

Road to Nowhere (Ogilvie), 1983
Road to Paradise Island (Plaidy, as Holt), 1985
Road to Revelation (Lofts), 1941
Road to Samarcand (O'Brian), 1954
Road to Understanding (E. Porter), 1917
Road to Yesterday (s Montgomery), 1974
Roads to Liberty (F. Mason), 1972
Roadway to the Past (MacLeod), 1951
Roanoke Hundred (Fletcher), 1948
Roast Beef, Medium (s Ferber), 1913
Robe (L. Douglas), 1942
Robe of Honor (Cordell), 1960
Robert and Arabella (Winsor), 1986
Robert Martin's Lesson (Swan), 1886
Robert of Normandy (Lide, as Lomer), 1991
Robert the Bruce series (Tranter), from 1985
Robert the Bruce Trilogy (Tranter), 1985
Roberts, Amanda series (Woods), from 1989
Robin and Her Merry People (F. Preston), 1987
Robin in a Cage (Bloom), 1943
Robin the Prodigal (Wynne), 1919
Rochester, The Mad Earl (Plaidy, as Kellow), 1957
Rochester's Wife (D. Stevenson), 1940
Rochford series (Lorrimer), from 1981
Rock (Masters), 1970
Rock and Sand (Jacob), 1926
Rock Pine (Muskett), 1952
Rocklitz (Bowen, as Preedy), 1930
Rocks of Valpré (Dell), 1913
Rocks Under Shining Water (Donnelly), 1973
Rococo (Bowen), 1921
Rodney Stone (Doyle), 1896
Roger Sudden (Raddall), 1944
Rogue (Dailey), 1980
Rogue (McKenna), 1993
Rogue and A Pirate (Mortimer), 1986
Rogue Cavalier (R. Marshall), 1955
Rogue Gentleman (E. Marshall), 1963
Rogue Herries (Walpole), 1930
Rogue Roman (Horner), 1965
Rogues' Covenant (S. Thorpe), 1957
Rogue's Harbor (Fletcher), 1964
Rogue's Lady (Blackstock, as Allardyce), 1979
Rogue's Lady (Carr), 1988
Rogue's March (Cordell), 1981
Rogue's Mistress (Gluyas), 1977
Rolande (C. Darcy), 1978
Roll River (Boyd), 1935
Roman Affair (R. Lindsay), 1976
Roman Cavalier (D. Murray), 1958
Roman Nights (Dunnett), 1991
Roman Republic series (J. Lindsay), from 1934
Roman series (Hardy), from 1957
Roman Wall (Bryher), 1954
Romance (Ford), 1903
Romance and Nurse Margaret (Bloom, as Burns), 1972
Romance at Hillyard House (Norris), 1948
Romance at Wrecker's End (Chandos, as Lance), 1976
Romance for Rose (Chandos, as Tempest), 1959
Romance for Sale (Greig, as Ames), 1934
Romance in Glenmore Street (I. Preston), 1974
Romance in Two Keys (Ruck), 1955
Romance Is Mine (Bloom, as Burns), 1941
Romance of a Film Star (Ruck), 1956
Romance of a Lifetime (Mortimer), 1991
Romance of a Plain Man (Glasgow), 1909

Romance of a Rogue (Ayres), 1923
Romance of Atlantis (Caldwell), 1975
Romance of Charles Dickens (Bloom), 1960
Romance of Dr Dinah (Bloom, as Essex), 1967
Romance of Enola (Libbey), 1893
Romance of Jenny W.R.E.N (Bloom, as Burns), 1944
Romance of Rosy Ridge (Kantor), 1937
Romance of Summer (Bloom, as Essex), 1959
Romance of Two Worlds (Corelli), 1886
Romance on a Cruise (Greig, as Ames), 1935
Romance on Ice (Chandos, as Tempest), 1942
Romance Royal (Ruck), 1937
Romantic (M. Sinclair), 1920
Romantic Afterthought (Ruck), 1959
Romantic Assignment (McElfresh), 1961
Romantic Cottage Hospital (Bloom, as Burns), 1967
Romantic Encounter (Neels), 1992
Romantic Frenchman (Gibbs), 1967
Romantic Fugitive (Bloom, as Burns), 1943
Romantic Intruder (Bloom, as Burns), 1952
Romantic Journey (Buckingham), 1968
Romantic Lady (s Arlen), 1921
Romantic Lady (Borden, as Maclagan), 1916
Romantic Lady (I. Roberts, as Rowland), 1981
Romantic Lady (S. Thorpe), 1960
Romantic Prince (Sabatini), 1929
Romantic Rivals (Courtney), 1980
Romantic Summer Sea (Bloom, as Burns), 1956
Romantic Theatre Sister (Bloom, as Essex), 1965
Romantic Touch (Chandos), 1957
Romantic Widow (Chappell), 1978
Romantics (s Rinehart), 1929
Romany (E. Smith), 1935
Romany Magic (Harrod-Eagles, as Woodhouse), 1977
Romany of the Marshes (Laffeaty, as Carstens), 1978
Romany Rebel (F. Stevenson, as Faire), 1979
Romany Ruth (M. St John), 1909
Romany Sister (Ponsonby, as Rybot), 1960
Rome for Sale (J. Lindsay), 1934
Rome Haul (Edmonds), 1929
Romeo in Moon Village (McCutcheon), 1925
Ronald Lindsay (Wynne), 1904
Room (Stern), 1922
Room with Dark Mirrors (V. Johnston), 1975
Room Without a Door (Manley-Tucker), 1970
Roomful of Roses (Palmer), 1984
Rooms at Mrs Oliver's (Plaidy, as Kellow), 1953
Rooney (Cookson), 1957
Root and Branch (Tranter), 1948
Rooted in Dishonour (Mather), 1978
Roots (Jacob), 1931
Roots of Evil (Dixon), 1911
Rope Dancer (Gellis), 1986
Roper's Row (Deeping), 1929
Rosa Mundi (s Dell), 1921
Rosabelle Shaw (D. Stevenson), 1967
Rosalba (Bishop), 1982
Rosalie's Career (Baldwin), 1928
Rosalind Comes Home (Summers), 1968
Rosary (F. Barclay), 1909
Rose and the Yew Tree (Westmacott), 1948
Rose-Coloured Thread (Vaizey), 1898
Rose Domino (Walsh), 1981
Rose for Ana Maria (Yerby), 1976
Rose for Virtue (Lofts), 1971
Rose from Lucifer (Hampson), 1979

Rose-Grower (Stubbs), 1962
Rose in Heather (Goodwin, as Ebel), 1978
Rose in May (Clarke), 1984
Rose in the Ring (McCutcheon), 1910
Rose in Winter (Woodiwiss), 1983
Rose Island (I. Roberts, as Rowland), 1969
Rose o' the Sea (Barcynska), 1920
Rose of Dawn (Dell), 1917
Rose of Glenconnel (MacGill), 1916
Rose of Hever (M. Peters), 1969
Rose of Life (Albanesi, as Rowlands), 1912
Rose of Rapture (Brandewyne), 1984
Rose of the World (Norris), 1924
Rose of Yesterday (Albanesi), 1908
Rose Princess (Chandos, as Lance), 1979
Rose, Rose, Where Are You? (Ellerbeck), 1978
Rose Sweetman (Bloom), 1933
Rose Timson (Steen), 1946
Roseanne (Albanesi), 1922
Rosebud and Stardust (Bloom, as Burns), 1951
Roseheath (Maybury, as Troy), 1969
Roselynde series (Gellis), from 1978
Rosemary (Williamson), 1909
Rosemary—For Forgetting (Ayres), 1941
Rosemary for Remembrance (I. Preston), 1962
Rosemary for Remembrance (Sallis), 1987
Rosemary in Search of a Father (Williamson), 1906
Rosemary Tree (Goudge), 1956
Roses and Champagne (Neels), 1983
Roses for Christmas (Neels), 1975
Roses Have Thorns (Neels), 1990
Roses in the Snow (Hoy), 1936
Roses round the Door (Beresford), 1965
Rosevean (Bromige), 1962
Rosewood Box (Burchell), 1970
Ross, Dr Esmond series (Dwyer-Joyce), from 1966
Ross Inheritance (Stratton, as Gillen), 1969
Rough Diamond (B. Hastings), 1982
Rough Diamond Lover (R. Lindsay), 1978
Rough Edges (Chase), 1994
Rough Seas to Sunrise (Greig, as Ames), 1956
Rough Shooting (s Wren), 1938
Rough Weather (Bromige), 1972
Rough Wooing (Tranter), 1986
Round Dozen (Cadell), 1978
Round Tower (Cookson), 1968
Rouseabout Girl (Bevan), 1983
Rowan Head (Ogilvie), 1949
Rowan series (M. Peters, as Darby), from 1982
Rowan Tree (MacLeod), 1943
Rowleston (Riefe), 1976
Royal Academy (D. Murray), 1950
Royal Affair (K. Thorpe), 1976
Royal Box (Keyes), 1954
Royal Dynasty (Gellis), from 1981
Royal Escape (Heyer), 1938
Royal Escape (M. Peters), 1972
Royal Flush (Irwin), 1932
Royal Griffin (Dymoke), 1978
Royal Intrigue (Anthony), 1954
Royal Jewel series (Bennetts), from 1983
Royal Passion (J. Blake), 1986
Royal Pledge (Cartland), 1970
Royal Punishment (Cartland), 1984
Royal Purple (Ponsonby), 1954
Royal Quest (Lide), 1987

Royal Regiment (Frankau), 1938
Royal Revels (J. Smith), 1985
Royal Road to Fotheringay (Plaidy), 1955
Royal Seduction (J. Blake), 1981
Royal Signet (Garvice)
Royal Slave (Hamilton, as Fitzgerald), 1978
Royal Summer (Saunders, as Blake), 1992
Royal Summons (Cadell), 1973
Royal Sword at Agincourt (Bennetts), 1971
Royal Traitor (Wynne), 1927
Royal William (Leslie), 1940
Ruaig Inheritance (MacLeod), 1978
Ruan (Bryher), 1960
Rubber Princess (Burgin), 1919
Ruby (Bennetts), 1984
Ruby (Delmar), 1953
Rueful Mating (Stern), 1933
Rufus on the Rebound (s Ruck), 1918
Rugged Path (Garvice), 1908
Ruinous Face (s Hewlett), 1909
Rule Britannia (du Maurier), 1972
Rules of Marriage (Bishop), 1978
Rules of the Game (Chase), 1980
Rules of the Game (Jordan), 1984
Rules of the Game (N. Roberts), 1984
Ruling Passion (Swan), 1920
Rum Affair (Dunnett), 1968
Rum Week (Tranter), 1954
Run Away from Love (MacLeod), 1939
Run Away from Love (Woodward, as Richmond), 1974
Run for His Money (Wynne), 1913
Run for Your Love (Peake), 1978
Run from the Wind (Stratton), 1974
Run, Sara, Run (Worboys), 1981
Runaway (Norris), 1939
Runaway Bride (Hodge), 1975
Runaway Bride (Hoy), 1939
Runaway Bride (Stratton, as Gillen), 1972
Runaway Bride (Walsh), 1984
Runaway Daughter (s Swan), 1898
Runaway from Love (Randall), 1956
Runaway from Love (Steele), 1991
Runaway Girl (L. Walker), 1975
Runaway Heart (Cartland, as McCorquodale), 1961
Runaway Lovers (Ruck), 1963
Runaway series (Richards), from 1990
Runaway Star (Cartland), 1978
Runaway Wife (Lamb), 1990
Runaways (Lorrimer, as Robins), 1962
Running Away (C. Allen), 1977
Running Free (s Barcynska), 1929
Running of the Tide (Forbes), 1948
Running Thursday (P. Hastings), 1980
Rupert of Hentzau (Hope), 1898
Russet Jacket (Barcynska), 1924
Rust of Rome (Deeping), 1910
Rustic Vineyard (Shoesmith), 1982
Rustle of Bamboo (K. Blair, as Conway), 1957
Rustle of Spring (Trask), 1936
Ruth Appleby (Rhodes), 1987
Rutherford, Justin and Anthea series (Ley), from 1984
Ruthless in All (Steele), 1984
Ruthless Rake (Cartland), 1974
Ruthless Yeoman (Anand), 1991
Ruth's Romance (Albanesi, as Rowlands), 1913

Sable for the Count (P. Hill), 1985
Sable Hunter (Manners), 1977
Sabre series (M. Peters, as Darby), from 1985
Sabrina (Polland), 1979
Sackcloth into Silk (Deeping), 1935
Sacked City (Bowen, as Preedy), 1949
Sacred Bullock (s de la Roche), 1939
Sacred Sins (N. Roberts), 1987
Sacrifice (James), 1934
Sacrifice (Melville, as Betteridge), 1973
Sacrifice to Art (Garvice), 1908
Sadhu on the Mountain Peak (McCutchan, as MacNeil), 1971
Safari for Seven (Muskett), 1952
Safari South (K. Thorpe), 1976
Safe at Last (Cartland), 1985
Safe Bridge (Keyes), 1934
Safe Harbor (McElfresh, as Blair), 1977
Safe Harbor (Woods), 1987
Safe in Paradise (Cartland), 1990
Safety-Curtain (s Dell), 1917
Saffron (Hamilton, as Watson), 1972
Saffron Sky (Hunter, as Chace), 1968
Saffron Summer (Summerton), 1974
Saffroned Bridesails (Jacob), 1928
Saga at Forty (Cartland), 1937
Saga of the Sea (Sabatini), 1953
Sail a Jeweled Ship (Laker), 1971
Sailor on Horseback (Stone), 1939
Sailor's Love (Bloom, as Essex), 1961
Saint and the Sinner (Cartland), 1977
St Julian's Day (Norway, as Norton), 1965
St Luke's Little Summer (Norway, as Norton), 1964
St Martha's Hospital series (Andrews), from 1979
St Martin's Summer (Sabatini), 1909
Saint or Satyr? (s Glyn), 1933
Saint or Sinner? (Plaidy, as Burford), 1951
St Thomas's Eve (Plaidy), 1954
St Veda's (Swan), 1889
Salamanca Drum (Eden), 1977
Salamander (Hamilton, as Fitzgerald), 1981
Sally (Chesney, as Tremaine), 1982
Sally All-Smiles (M. St John), 1921
Sally Gets Married (Albanesi), 1927
Sally in a Service Flat (Grundy), 1934
Sally in Her Alley (Albanesi), 1925
Sally in Our Alley (M. St John), 1914
Sally in the Sunshine (Hoy), 1937
Sally of Sloper's (Barcynska, as Sandys), 1930
Sally Scarth (Jacob), 1940
Sally Serene (Barcynska, as Sandys), 1924
Sally's Sweetheart (Burgin), 1923
Salt Harbor (Greig, as Warren), 1953
Salt of Life (Vaizey), 1915
Salt of the Earth (Ayres), 1946
Salute Me Darling (Greig), 1942
Salute to Adventurers (J. Buchan), 1915
Samantha (Eden), 1960
Samaritan's Hospital (Stuart, as A. Stuart), 1965
Same Last Name (Seidel), 1983
Sample of Prejudice (Garvice), 1908
Sanchez Tradition (Mather), 1971
Sanctuary (Wharton), 1903
Sanctuary for Louise (Marsh), 1983
Sand Against the Wind (Marsh), 1973
Sand Castles (Woods, as Kirk), 1982
Sand Rose (Summerton), 1969

Sandals for My Feet (P. Hastings), 1960
Sands of Desire (Woodward, as Davis), 1970
Sands of Lamanna (Saunders, as Innes), 1975
Sandstorm (Mather), 1980
Sandy (I. Roberts, as Harle), 1967
Sangaree (Slaughter), 1948
Sangor Hospital Story (Bloom, as Essex), 1963
Sangreal (M. Peters, as Darby), 1984
Sanguinet series (Veryan), from 1981
Sanguinet's Crown (Veryan), 1985
Sanity Jane (Barcynska), 1919
Santa Ana Wind (Van Slyke, as Ashton), 1974
Santiago Road (Horner), 1967
Sapphira and the Slave Girl (Cather), 1940
Sapphire (Bennetts), 1985
Sapphire (Matthews), 1989
Sapphire in the Sand (Lorrimer, as Robins), 1968
Sapphire Lightning (F. Preston), 1988
Sapphires in Siam (Cartland), 1987
Sara (Cleeve), 1976
Sara Dane (Gaskin), 1955
Sara Gay—Model Girl (R. Lindsay, as Scott), 1961
Saraband for Sara (M. Peters, as Grey), 1984
Saraband for Two Sisters (Plaidy, as Carr), 1976
Saracen Blade (Yerby), 1952
Sarah (Pearson), 1971
Sarah (Seger), 1987
Sarah Defiant (Borden), 1931
Sarah Gay (Borden), 1931
Sarah Morris Remembers (D. Stevenson), 1967
Sarah Whitman (Pearson), 1971
Sarah's Child series (L. Howard), from 1985
Sarah's Cottage (D. Stevenson), 1968
Sarah's Story (Hardwick), 1973
Saratoga Trunk (Ferber), 1941
Sargasso Sea (s Byrne), 1932
Sarina (Rivers), 1983
Sassy (Williams), 1977
Satan and the Nymph (Hampson), 1976
Satan Never Sleeps (Buck), 1952
Satan Took a Bride (Winspear), 1975
Satan's Circus (s E. Smith), 1932
Satan's Island (Wentworth), 1988
Satan's Master (Mortimer), 1981
Satan's Sunset (Hufford), 1977
Satin and Steele (F. Preston, as Conlee), 1982
Satin Ice (Johansen), 1988
Satin Straps (Greig), 1929
Satin Surrender (Finch), 1986
Saturday Life (Hall), 1925
Saturday's Child (Beresford), 1968
Saturday's Child (Neels), 1972
Saturday's Child (Norris), 1914
Saturday's Child (Schulze), 1990
Savage Adoration (Jordan), 1987
Savage Aristocrat (R. Lindsay, as Leigh), 1978
Savage Atonement (Jordan), 1983
Savage Beauty (Mather), 1973
Savage Conquest (Taylor), 1985
Savage Ecstasy (Taylor), 1981
Savage Eden (Gluyas), 1976
Savage Family series (Masters), from 1978
Savage Interlude (Mortimer), 1979
Savage Kiss (Sommerfield), 1985
Savage Land (Dailey), 1974
Savage Marquess (Chesney), 1988

Savage Moon (Saunders, as Summers), 1982
Savage Oaks (Ellis), 1977
Savage Place (Slaughter), 1964
Savage Possession (M. Pargeter), 1979
Savage Rapture (Sommerfield), 1982
Savage Sanctuary (Donnelly), 1979
Savage Sands (Nicole, as C. Nicholson), 1978
Savage Surrender (Lamb), 1980
Savage Surrender (N. Peters), 1977
Savage Thunder (Lindsey), 1989
Savage Warriors (Treece), 1959
Savage Web (M. Peters, as Whitby), 1982
Savanna (Giles), 1961
Savannah Purchase (Hodge), 1971
Saved by Love (Cartland), 1987
Saville, Peggy (Vaizey), from 1900
Saving Face (s Lofts), 1983
Saving Grace (Mortimer), 1993
Sawdust (Cartland), 1926
Sawdust and Dreams (Marsh), 1980
Sawdust and Spangles (Collin), 1972
Sawdust Season (K. Thorpe), 1972
Saxon's Lady (Krentz, as James), 1987
Saxton series (Coulter), from 1984
Say Hello to Yesterday (Wentworth), 1981
Say Yes, Samantha (Cartland), 1975
Say You're Sorry (Chandos, as Tempest), 1939
Scales of Gold (Dunnett), 1991
Scandal (Krentz, as Quick), 1991
Scandalous (Lamb), 1984
Scandalous Lady Robin (S. Thorpe), 1950
Scandalous Lady (Sebastian, as Gladstone), 1978
Scandalous Lady Wright (Chesney), 1990
Scandalous Risks (Howatch), 1990
Scandalous Season (Pykare), 1979
Scapegoat (Caine), 1891
Scapegoat (du Maurier), 1957
Scapegrace (S. Thorpe), 1971
Scar (Ayres), 1920
Scaramouche (Sabatini), 1921
Scarecrow House (Sherwood, as Hines), 1976
Scarecrow Lover (P. Hastings), 1960
Scarf of Flame (May), 1979
Scarlet (Cox, as Brindle), 1992
Scarlet Cloak (Plaidy, as Tate), 1957
Scarlet Cord (Slaughter), 1956
Scarlet Domino (S. Thorpe), 1970
Scarlet Heels (Muskett), 1940
Scarlet Kisses (S. Blake), 1981
Scarlet Mantle (Hardy), 1978
Scarlet Pimpernel series (Orczy), from 1905
Scarlet Princess (Nicole), 1984
Scarlet Rebel (Saunders), 1985
Scarlet Ribbons (E. Blair), 1992
Scarlet Runner (s Williamson), 1908
Scarlet Seed (E. Pargeter), 1963
Scarlet Shadows (Drummond), 1978
Scarlet Thread (Anthony), 1989
Scarlet Woman (Hamilton, as Fitzgerald), 1979
Scarlet Woman (M. Pargeter), 1986
Scarlet Women (Hamilton, as de Vere), 1969
Scarlett (Ripley), 1991
Scattering of Daisies (Sallis), 1984
Scent of Cloves (Lofts), 1957
Scent of Fear (Matthews), 1992
Scent of Jasmine (Saunders, as Innes), 1982

Scent of Juniper (MacLeod), 1971
Scent of Lilac (M. Peters, as Law), 1988
Scent of Lilacs (Lorin, as Hohl), 1986
Scent of Roses (Cartland), 1991
Scent of Water (Goudge), 1963
Scented Danger (Cowen), 1966
Scented Sword (Nicole, as York), 1980
Sceptre and the Rose (Leslie), 1967
School Against Her! (M. St John), 1921
School for Hearts (Albanesi, as Rowlands), 1934
School for Manners series (Chesney), from 1988
School in Belmont (Bishop), 1980
Schoolgirl Bride (M. St John), 1913
Schoolmaster's Daughters (Eden), 1948
Scorched-Wood People (Wiebe), 1977
Scorned by 'His' Mother (M. St John), 1921
Scorpion God (s Golding), 1971
Scorpions' Dance (Mather), 1978
Scots Never Forget (Cartland), 1984
Scotswoman (Fletcher), 1955
Scott Pelham's Princess (Loring), 1958
Scottish Soldier (Stuart, as Allen), 1965
Scoundrel (Cornwell), 1992
Scoundrel's Bride (Coulter), 1986
Screen Lover (Greig), 1969
Scribblers' Club (Garvice), 1909
Scudders (Bacheller), 1923
Sculptor's Wooing (Garvice)
Sea and the Sand (Nicole), 1986
Sea Ants (s Cato), 1964
Sea Beggars (Holland), 1982
Sea Captain (Bailey), 1913
Sea Change (MacLeod, as Airlie), 1965
Sea Could Tell (Williamson, as A.M. Williamson), 1904
Sea Fever (Weale), 1990
Sea Fret (Bloom), 1953
Sea Gate (Seger), 1981
Sea Gull (Norris), 1927
Sea-Grape Tree (Lehmann), 1976
Sea Gypsy (F. Michaels), 1980
Sea-Hawk (Sabatini), 1915
Sea House (Summerton), 1961
Sea Is So Wide (Eaton), 1943
Sea Jade (I. Roberts), 1987
Sea Jade (Whitney), 1965
Sea King's Daughter (B. Michaels), 1975
Sea Maiden (I. Roberts, as Carr), 1965
Sea Master (Wentworth), 1981
Sea series (Golding), from 1980
Sea-Song (Manners, as Marshall), 1973
Sea Urchins (Gibbs), 1968
Sea 'venture (F. Mason), 1961
Sea View (James), 1936
Sea Waif (Weale), 1967
Sea Without a Haven (Broster), 1941
Seacage (Burford), 1979
Seagull Crag (Roby, as Welles), 1977
Seagull's Cry (Robins), 1957
Sealed Knot (Lane), 1952
Sealed Lips (Robins), 1924
Sealed with a Kiss (J. Smith), 1990
Search for a Background (Jacob), 1960
Search for a New Dawn (Delinsky, as Douglass), 1982
Search for Love, (Cartland), 1937
Search for Love (N. Roberts), 1982
Search for the King (Vidal), 1950

Search for Willie (W. Roberts), 1980
Search for Yesterday (MacLeod), 1978
Search the Shadows (B. Michaels), 1987
Seas of Fortune (Nicole, as McKay), 1984
Season at Brighton (Ley), 1971
Season for Change (Way), 1981
Season for Love (Pozzessere, as Graham), 1983
Season for Singing (Ritchie), 1979
Season of Forgetfulness (Summers), 1983
Season of Mist (Mather), 1982
Season of Mists (Woodhouse), 1984
Season of Passion (Steel), 1979
Season of Storm (Sellers), 1983
Season of the Sun (Coulter), 1991
Seasons Hereafter (Ogilvie), 1966
Seasons of Miracles (Richards), 1986
Seasons of the Heart (Freeman), 1986
Seats of the Mighty (Harwood), 1956
Second Best (Robins), 1931
Second-Best Husband (Jordan), 1991
Second Chance at Love (Woods), 1988
Second Empire series (Gavin), from 1957
Second Fiddle (Wesley), 1988
Second Generation (Fast), 1978
Second Hand Wife (Norris), 1932
Second Harvest (Jacob), 1954
Second Honeymoon (Ayres), 1918
Second Honeymoon (Chandos, as Charles), 1970
Second Husband (Bishop), 1964
Second Husband (M. St John), 1923
Second Key (Lowndes), 1936
Second Latchkey (Williamson), 1920
Second Legacy (Trollope), 1992
Second Lesson (Miles), 1936
Second Love (Lorrimer, as Robins), 1964
Second Marriage (Burchell), 1971
Second Marriage (Robins), 1951
Second Mrs Rivers (Bromige), 1960
Second Nature (N. Roberts), 1986
Second String (Hope), 1910
Second Time (Dailey), 1982
Second Time Loving (Jordan), 1990
Second, to Death (Riefe), 1991
Second Tomorrow (Hampson), 1980
Second Wife (Krentz, as James), 1986
Second Winning (Maybury), 1933
Second World War series (Gavin), from 1976
Second Youth (Deeping), 1919
Secondhand Husband (Schulze), 1993
'Second-Sighter's' Daughter (Burgin), 1913
Secret Admirer (Napier), 1992
Secret Affair (Peake), 1980
Secret Armour (Andrews), 1955
Secret Chronicle (Lane), 1977
Secret City (Walpole), 1919
Secret Fear (Cartland), 1970
Secret Fire (Lindsey), 1987
Secret Fire (Winspear), 1984
Secret for a Nightingale (Plaidy, as Holt), 1986
Secret Gold (Williamson, as A.M. Williamson), 1925
Secret Harbour (Cartland), 1982
Secret Heart (Cartland), 1970
Secret History (Williamson), 1915
Secret History Revealed by Lady Peggy O'Malley (Williamson), 1915
Secret Hour (Robins), 1932

Secret in Her Life (Mackinlay), 1958
Secret Information (Hichens), 1938
Secret Intimacy (Lamb), 1983
Secret Island (Hodge), 1985
Secret Lives of the Nurses (W. Roberts), 1975
Secret Love (Buckingham, as John), 1986
Secret Love of Nurse Wilson (I. Preston), 1966
Secret Lover (Bloom), 1930
Secret Marriage (K. Blair, as Brett), 1947
Secret Marriage (Hunter, as Chace), 1966
Secret Marriage (Norris), 1936
Secret Marriages (Stanford), 1991
Secret Memoirs of Lord Byron (Nicole), 1978
Secret of Chateau Kendall (Ellis, as Richard), 1967
Secret of Chateau Laval (Ellis, as Marvin), 1973
Secret of Dunston Mere (s Swan), 1898
Secret of Mirror House (J. Blake, as Maxwell), 1970
Secret of Quarry House (Lorrimer), 1976
Secret of Skye (Swan), 1940
Secret of the Caves (Wynne), 1945
Secret of the Ghostly Shroud (Buckingham), 1969
Secret of the Glen (Cartland), 1976
Secret of the Marshbanks (Norris), 1940
Secret of the Mosque (Cartland), 1986
Secret of the Rose (Maybury), 1941
Secret of the Stone (Delinsky), 1985
Secret of the Tower (Hope), 1919
Secret of the Villa Como (Ellis, as Marvin), 1966
Secret of the Zenana (Wynne), 1913
Secret of Weir House (Cowen), 1975
Secret Panel (Swan), 1888
Secret Passion (Mortimer), 1988
Secret Pearl (Balogh), 1991
Secret Pleasure (Kidd), 1985
Secret Pool (Neels), 1986
Secret Power (Corelli), 1921
Secret Sanctuary (Deeping), 1923
Secret Services (s Frankau), 1934
Secret Sins (S. Blake), 1980
Secret Sorrow (van der Zee), 1981
Secret Splendor (Brown, as St Claire), 1983
Secret Splendor (Finch, as Robins), 1988
Secret to Tell (Pilcher), 1955
Secret Touch (Saunders, as Innes), 1992
Secret Valentine (Browning), 1983
Secret Woman (Plaidy, as Holt), 1970
Secretary Wife (R. Lindsay), 1976
Secrets (C. Allen, as Marlowe), 1992
Secrets (Cartland), 1985
Secrets (Steel), 1985
Secrets of Cromwell Crossing (Winston), 1965
Secrets of Hillyard House (Norris), 1947
Secrets of the Heart (Balogh), 1988
Secrets of the Heart (s Buck), 1976
Secrets of the Shop! (M. St John), 1923
Secrets to Keep (Lamb, as Holland) , 1980
Security Man (Browning), 1986
Sedgemont series (Lide), from 1984
Seduction (B. Hastings), 1991
Seduction (Krentz, as Quick), 1990
Seduction (Lamb), 1980
Seduction by Design (Brown, as St Claire), 1983
Seduction of Deanna (Seger), 1993
Seduction of Jason (F. Preston), 1983
Seduction of Keira (E. Darcy), 1992
Seduction Stakes (Armstrong), 1992

Shadow of Her Life (Garvice)
Shadow of Love (Stanford), 1980
Shadow of Murder (Blackstock), 1959
Shadow of My Loving (Maybury), 1938
Shadow of Palaces (P. Hill), 1955
Shadow of Polperro (Cowen), 1969
Shadow of Samain (Wiat), 1980
Shadow of Sin (Cartland), 1975
Shadow of Suspicion (Loring), 1955
Shadow of the Court (Collin), 1967
Shadow of the East (Hull), 1921
Shadow of the Hawk (Forester), 1928
Shadow of the Hawk (E. Scott), 1941
Shadow of the Hills (Hoy), 1938
Shadow of the Lynx (Plaidy, as Holt), 1971
Shadow of the Moon (Kaye), 1957
Shadow of the Past (Donald), 1979
Shadow of the Pines (Duffield), 1940
Shadow of the Pomegranate (Plaidy), 1962
Shadow of Theale (Cowen), 1974
Shadow of Yesterday (Browning), 1983
Shadow of Yesterday (Manley-Tucker), 1965
Shadow on Mercer Mountain (Winston), 1967
Shadow on Mockways (Bowen), 1932
Shadow on the Hill (Woods, as Kirk), 1985
Shadow on the Hills (MacLeod), 1989
Shadow on the House (F. Stevenson), 1975
Shadow on the Sun (MacLeod, as Airlie), 1960
Shadow over Grove House (Roby), 1973
Shadow over the Island (Greig, as Warren), 1955
Shadow Wife (Albanesi), 1925
Shadow Wife (Eden), 1968
Shadow Women (Price, as Smith), 1932
Shadowed Happiness (Albanesi, as Rowlands), 1906
Shadowed Lives (Swan), 1880
Shadowed Love (Blackstock, as Allardyce), 1977
Shadowed Paradise (Ritchie), 1960
Shadowed Spring (Salisbury), 1980
Shadowed Stranger (Mortimer), 1982
Shadows Across the Sun (Greig, as Ames), 1955
Shadows and Sunshine (Libbey), 1904
Shadows at Dawn (Lamb, as Holland), 1975
Shadows from the Sea (Donnelly), 1970
Shadows in Bronze (Davis), 1990
Shadows in the Afternoon (Staples, as Stevens), 1983
Shadows in the Fire (Drummond, as Dane), 1975
Shadows in the Jungle (Nicole), 1961
Shadows in the Moonlight (B. Michaels, as Peters), 1975
Shadows in the Sun (M. Howard), 1957
Shadow's Kiss (Lorin, as Hohl), 1994
Shadows of Passion (Gallagher), 1971
Shadows of the Heart (Seger), 1984
Shadows of Yesterday (s Bowen), 1916
Shadows on a Throne (Dymoke), 1976
Shadows on Bali (van der Zee), 1988
Shadows on the Moon (I. Roberts), 1968
Shadows on the Mountain (Harrod-Eagles), 1973
Shadows on the Rock (Cather), 1931
Shadows on the Sand (Hoy), 1974
Shadows on the Sand (Randall), 1949
Shadows on the Shore (Stirling), 1993
Shadows on the Snow (Swindells), 1987
Shadows on the Water (Cadell, as Ainsworth), 1958
Shadows Waiting (Eliot), 1969
Shadowy Third (Chandos, as Charles), 1968
Shady Grove (Giles), 1968

Shaft of Sunlight (Cartland), 1982
Shaftesbury Avenue (Rayner), 1983
Shakespeare Girl (Hardwick), 1983
Shakespeare series (Malpass), from 1973
Shall Love be Lost? (Bromige), 1974
Shallow Cup (Muskett), 1932
Shame of Molly (Sabatini), 1908
Shamed by Her Husband! (M. St John), 1925
Shamrock series (F. Preston), from 1986
Shamrock series (Hooper), from 1986
Shamrock series (Johansen), from 1986
Shanna (Woodiwiss), 1977
Shannon (Gallagher), 1967
Shannon's Brigade (Stuart, as V.A. Stuart), 1976
Shared Destiny (Hunter), 1983
Sharon James, Free-lance Photographer (McElfresh, as Wesley), 1956
Sharon Women (Maybury), 1950
Sharp Family series (Lorin, as Hohl), from 1986
Sharpe series (Cornwell), from 1981
Sharrow (Hutten), 1910
Shatter the Dream (James), 1930
Shatter the Rainbow (Hoy), 1946
Shatter the Sky (Robins), 1933
Shattered Dreams (Wentworth), 1979
Shattered Silk (B. Michaels), 1986
Shattered Summer (Polland), 1970
She and Allan (Haggard), 1921
She Danced in the Ballet (Ruck), 1948
She-Devil (Robins, as Wright), 1970
She Dwelt with Beauty (Lowndes), 1949
She Followed Her Heart (Woodward, as Richmond), 1944
She Goes to War (E. Pargeter), 1942
She Had to Be Queen (Harwood), 1948
She Had What It Takes (Bloom, as Essex), 1952
She Loved Him (Garvice), 1899
She Loved Not Wisely (Garvice, as Hart)
She Married Another (Mackinlay), 1953
She Moved to Music (Mackinlay), 1956
She Posed as Their Friend! (M. St John), 1925
She Saw Them Go By (Chapman), 1933
She series (Haggard), from 1886
She Shall Be Queen (Trask), 1936
She Shall Never Call You Mother! (M. St John), 1925
She Sold Her Child! (M. St John), 1927
She Walked into His Parlour (Greig), 1934
She Was an Actress (M. St John), 1924
She-Wolf (Bennetts), 1975
She Wrecked Their Home! (M. St John), 1924
Sheaf of Bluebells (Orczy), 1917
Sheep's-Head and Babylon (s Bowen), 1929
Sheik (Hull), 1919
Sheikh and the Dustbin (s G. Fraser), 1988
Sheikh Bill (Williamson, as A.M. Williamson), 1927
Sheik's Captive (Mortimer), 1993
Sheik's Captive (Winspear), 1979
Sheila (Swan), 1890
She'll Never Marry My Son! (M. St John), 1927
Shell Seekers (Pilcher), 1987
She'll Take the High Road (Greig, as Ames), 1948
Shelter (Steen, as Nicholson), 1941
Sheltered Flame (Ritchie), 1949
Sheltering Tree (Bromige), 1970
Sherida (Saxton, as Turner), 1981
Sheridan, Alexander series (Stuart, as V.A. Stuart), from 1972
Sheridan Family series (Drummond, as Darrell), from 1984

Sherrods (McCutcheon), 1903
Sherry (McCutcheon), 1919
Sherry and the Ghosts (Ruck), 1961
She's All the World to Me (Caine), 1885
Shetland Summer (Manley-Tucker), 1973
Shield of Love (Deeping), 1940
Shielded from the World (M. St John), 1915
Shield's Lady (Krentz, as Glass), 1989
Shifting Sands (K. Thorpe), 1975
Shifting Sands (MacGill), 1922
Shiloh (Foote), 1952
Shine My Wings (Barcynska, as Sandys), 1954
Shining and Free (Stern), 1935
Shining Chance (Ruck), 1944
Shining Cloud (Pedler), 1935
Shining Country (Alexander), 1991
Shining Failure (Barcynska, as Sandys), 1950
Shining River (L. Walker, as Sanders), 1954
Shining Threads (A. Howard), 1990
Shining Windows (Norris), 1935
Shining Years (Loring), 1972
Ship in a Bottle (Bloom), 1962
Ship Must Die (Kent, as Reeman), 1979
Ship of the Line (Forester), 1938
Ship of Truth (L. Cooper), 1930
Ship with No Name (Nicole), 1987
Ships Come Home (Barcynska), 1922
Ship's Doctor (Greig), 1966
Ships in the Bay! (Broster), 1931
Ships in the Night (Browning), 1990
Ship's Nurse (Stuart, as A. Stuart), 1954
Ships of Youth (Diver), 1931
Ship's Surgeon (K. Blair, as Conway), 1962
Shirt Front (Blackstock), 1977
Shiver Me a Story (M. Peters, as Whitby), 1982
Shivering Sands (Plaidy, as Holt), 1969
Shōgun (Clavell), 1975
Shoemaker's Daughter (Gower), 1991
Shoes of Fortune (Munro), 1901
Shooting Star (Melville, as Betteridge), 1968
Shop-Girl (Williamson), 1916
Shop-Girl's Revenge (M. St John, as St John Cooper), 1914
Shopping for a Husband (Ruck), 1967
Shore Beyond (Swan), 1932
Short-Cut to the Stars (Chandos, as Tempest), 1949
Short Engagement (Lewty), 1978
Short Stories of Warwick Deeping (s Deeping), 1930
Shortest Night (Stern), 1931
Shot with Crimson (McCutcheon), 1918
Shotgun Wedding (Lamb), 1991
Shoulder the Sky (D. Stevenson), 1951
Shout (s Graves), 1978
Show Boat (Ferber), 1926
Show Me (Dailey), 1976
Show Must Go On (Barcynska, as Sandys), 1936
Showers of Sunlight (Vitek), 1981
Shreds of Circumstance (Macbeth), 1947
Shrewsbury (Weyman), 1898
Shrine of Fire (I. Roberts), 1970
Shrine of Marigolds (I. Roberts), 1962
Shripney Lady (Laker), 1972
Shroud of Fog (W. Roberts), 1970
Shroud of Silence (Buckingham), 1970
Shrouded Tower (Chandos, as Charles), 1966
Shrouded Walls (Howatch), 1968
Shrouded Web (Mather), 1973

Sibylla and the Privateer (Oliver), 1976
Sicilian Spring (Wentworth), 1993
Sicilian Vengeance (S. Wood), 1990
Siege in the Sun (Eden), 1967
Siege of Krishnapur (Farrell), 1973
Siege Perilous (s Diver), 1924
Sight Unseen, and The Confession (Rinehart), 1921
Sight Unseen (Erskine-Lindop), 1969
Sign of Love (Cartland), 1977
Sign of the Ram (Stratton), 1977
Signal (Kent), 1974
Signa's Sweetheart (Garvice), 1910
Signpost Has Four Arms (P. Hastings), 1957
Signpost to Love (Cartland), 1980
Silas Strong (Bacheller), 1906
Silence of Herondale (Aiken), 1964
Silence of the Maharajah (Corelli), 1895
Silent Battle (Williamson, as A.M. Williamson), 1902
Silent Bondage (MacLeod), 1940
Silent Captain (Wynne), 1914
Silent Corridors (James), 1953
Silent Drum (Swanson), 1940
Silent Grow the Guns (s Kantor), 1958
Silent Lady (Dwyer-Joyce), 1964
Silent Ones (Ogilvie), 1981
Silent Pool (Cowen), 1977
Silent Song (Andrews), 1973
Silent Thunder (Randall), 1971
Silent Valley (MacLeod), 1953
Silent Walls (Roby), 1974
Silent Watcher (F. Stevenson), 1975
Silhouette in Scarlet (B. Michaels, as Peters), 1983
Silhouette Summer Sizzlers (s Palmer), 1991
Silk Vendetta (Plaidy, as Holt), 1987
Silken Barbarity (Winspear), 1988
Silken Bond (Kidd), 1980
Silken Bonds (Chesney), 1989
Silken Cage (Stratton), 1981
Silken Captive (Hamilton, as Fitzgerald), 1986
Silken Purse (Mackinlay), 1970
Silken Thunder (F. Preston), 1988
Silken Trap (Lamb), 1979
Silken Web (Brown, as Jordan), 1982
Silky (M. Peters, as Whitby), 1980
Silver (Jordan), 1989
Silver Angel (Lindsey), 1988
Silver Answer (Maddocks), 1965
Silver Bride (Dell), 1932
Silver Cage (Donnelly), 1976
Silver Castle (Buckingham, as Quest), 1978
Silver Chain (Beresford), 1980
Silver Chalice (Costain), 1952
Silver Cord (Randall), 1963
Silver Cross (M. Johnston), 1922
Silver Dolphin (V. Johnston), 1979
Silver Dolphin (Weale), 1963
Silver Dragon (MacLeod), 1961
Silver Falcon (Anthony), 1977
Silver Fishes (Stratton, as Gillen), 1969
Silver Flame (S. Johnson), 1988
Silver Flame (M. Pargeter), 1983
Silver Fox (Delinsky, as Drake), 1983
Silver Fruit upon Silver Trees (Mather), 1974
Silver-Gilt (Muskett), 1935
Silver Lady (Saunders, as Innes), 1981
Silver Leopard (F. Mason), 1955

Six Wax Candles (Mackinlay), 1950
Six White Horses (Dailey), 1977
Sixpence in Her Shoe (M. Howard), 1950
'Sixpenny Ha'penny' Duchess (M. St John), 1917
1649 (J. Lindsay), 1938
Sixth Beatitude (Hall), 1936
Sixth of October (Hichens), 1936
Sixth Wife (Plaidy), 1953
Sixties (Rayner), 1992
Skeleton Key (Winston), 1972
Skin Deep (Hufford), 1978
Skin Deep (N. Roberts), 1988
Skin Deep (K. Thorpe), 1989
Sky At Night (May), 1975
Skye Cameron (Whitney), 1957
Skye Harbour (McElfresh, as Blair), 1971
Skye O'Malley (Small), 1980
Skylark's Song (A. Howard), 1984
Skyscraper (Baldwin), 1931
Skyscraper Souls (Baldwin), 1932
Slade (Deeping), 1943
Slanderers (Deeping), 1905
Slashed Portrait (Sherwood, as Hines), 1973
Slave (Hichens), 1899
Slave Lady (Hamilton, as Fitzgerald), 1980
Slave Masters (Bennetts), 1983
Slave of the Lake (Garvice), 1908
Slave of the Wind (MacLeod), 1962
Slave Ship (M. Johnston), 1924
Slave-Woman (Robins), 1934
Slaves of Allah (Burgin), 1909
Slaves of Love (Cartland), 1976
Slaves of the Ring (Burgin), 1936
Sleep in Peace (Bentley), 1938
Sleep in the Woods (Eden), 1960
Sleeping Beauty (Baldwin), 1947
Sleeping Beauty (Ruck), 1936
Sleeping Bride (Eden), 1959
Sleeping Desire (Lamb), 1985
Sleeping Dogs (Grundy), 1924
Sleeping Partners (Lamb), 1991
Sleeping Princess (Cartland), 1991
Sleeping Sword (Jagger), 1982
Sleeping Swords (Cartland, as McCorquodale), 1942
Sleeping Tiger (Pilcher), 1967
Sleeveless Errand (James), 1929
Slender Thread (Bromige), 1985
Slinky Jane (Cookson), 1959
Slither of Silk (May), 1972
Sloop of War (Kent), 1972
Slow Awakening (Cookson, as Marchant), 1976
Slow Heat in Heaven (Brown), 1988
Slower Judas (s Stern), 1929
Small Hotel (James), 1965
Small Slice of Summer (Neels), 1975
Small Town Girl (Alexander, as Armstrong), 1984
Small Wilderness (Summerton), 1959
Smile in the Mirror (Barcynska), 1963
Smile of the Stranger (Aiken), 1978
Smith (Deeping), 1932
Smith and the Pharaohs (s Haggard), 1920
Smoke and Mirrors (B. Michaels), 1989
Smoke and the Fire (Summers), 1964
Smoke in the Wind (Donald), 1987
Smoke Rings (s Stern), 1923
Smoke Screen (Richards), 1988

Smokescreen (Mather), 1982
Smouldering Fire (D. Stevenson), 1936
Smouldering Flame (Mather), 1976
Smuggled Heart (Cartland), 1959
Smuggled Love (D. Smith), 1976
Smuggler's Bride (Laker), 1975
Smuggler's Haunt (Shoesmith), 1978
Smugglers' Moon (S. Thorpe), 1955
Snake and Sword (Wren), 1914
Snake-Bite (s Hichens), 1919
Snake in the Grass (M. St John, as St John Cooper), 1922
Snake, the Crocodile, and the Dog (B. Michaels, as Peters), 1992
Snapshots (s Melville), 1990
Snare (Sabatini), 1915
Snare of Serpents (Plaidy, as Holt), 1990
Snare the Wild Heart (Hoy), 1955
Sniper (W. Roberts), 1984
Snow and Roses (L. Cooper), 1976
Snow Angel (Balogh), 1991
Snow Blossom (M. Peters), 1980
Snow Bride (Hilton), 1979
Snow in April (Pilcher), 1972
Snow in Summer (Albanesi), 1932
Snow Kisses (Palmer), 1983
Snow Leopard of Shanghai (Pizzey), 1989
Snow Mountain (Gavin), 1973
Snow Must Return (Robins), 1971
Snow Queen (Hamilton), 1978
Snowbound Heart (J. Blake, as Patrick), 1979
Snowbound Weekend (Lorin), 1982
Snowfire (Pozzessere), 1993
Snowfire (Whitney), 1973
Snowflakes on the Sea (Miller), 1984
So Big (Ferber), 1924
So Bold a Choice (Ponsonby), 1960
So Close and No Closer (Jordan), 1989
So Dear to Their Hearts (Woodward), 1974
So Deep Suspicion (Gibbs, as Ford), 1950
So Evil My Love (Bowen, as Shearing), 1947
So Fair and Foul a Queen (M. Peters), 1974
So Fair, So False (Garvice), 1902
So Grand (Nicole, as Gray), 1985
So Like a Man (Albanesi, as Rowlands), 1905
So Long a Winter (Donnelly), 1981
So Loved and So Far (Hoy), 1954
So Many Miles (Ayres), 1932
So Many Partings (Spellman), 1983
So Many Tomorrows (Buckingham, as John), 1982
So Merciful a Queen, So Cruel a Woman (Harwood), 1939
So Much Good (Frankau), 1928
So Much Love (Schulze), 1989
So Much Love (L. Walker), 1977
So Near so Far (Parkinson), 1981
So Near, So Far (Steele), 1986
So Nearly Lost (Garvice), 1902
So Nearly Married (Chandos), 1956
So Red the Rose (Young), 1934
So Runs the River (James), 1952
So Speaks the Heart (Lindsey), 1983
So Sweet a Sin (B. Hastings), 1989
So the Dreams Depart (Plaidy, as Burford), 1944
So This Is Love (Lorrimer, as Robins), 1953
So Wicked My Desire (S. Blake), 1979
So Wicked the Heart (Riefe), 1980
So Wild a Heart (V. Johnston, as Jason), 1981
So Worthy My Love (Woodiwiss), 1989

So Young, So Fair (Seifert), 1947
Socialism series (Dixon), from 1903
Society Girl (Price), 1935
Soft Target (Nolan), 1992
Soft Velvet Night (Hampson), 1983
Soho Square (Rayner), 1976
Soldier at the Door (E. Pargeter), 1954
Soldier from Virginia (Bowen), 1912
Soldier of Fortune (Palmer), 1985
Soldier of the Legion (Williamson), 1914
Soldiers and Lovers (M. Howard), 1973
Soldier's Daughter (Stuart, as A. Stuart), 1954
Soldiers' Daughters Never Cry (Erskine-Lindop), 1948
Soldiers of Misfortune (Wren), 1929
Solita and the Spies (Cartland), 1989
Solitaire (Craven), 1979
Solitaire (McKenna), 1987
Solitary Horseman (Loring), 1927
Some Brief Folly (Veryan), 1981
Some Day (Ayres), 1935
Some Die in Their Beds (Roby), 1970
Some Far Elusive Dawn (Drummond), 1988
Some Kind of Madness (Donald), 1991
Some Men and Women (s Lowndes), 1925
Some Mother's Child! (M. St John), 1926
Some Mother's Son! (M. St John), 1928
Some Say Love (Armstrong), 1986
Somebody Else (Ayres), 1936
Someone Else's Heart (Stuart, as Allen), 1958
Someone in the House (B. Michaels), 1981
Someone New to Love (Chandos, as Tempest), 1936
Someone Waiting (Lorin, as Hohl), 1986
Someone Waiting (Maybury, as Troy), 1961
Someone Who Cares (Chandos, as Lance), 1982
Somersault (Goodwin, as Ebel), 1971
Something Between (Cockrell), 1946
Something Different (Hooper), 1984
Something Extra (Dailey), 1975
Something for Herself (Browning), 1985
Something in Return (van der Zee), 1992
Something so Right (Richards), 1986
Something Special (Baldwin), 1940
Something to Love (Robins), 1951
Something Wonderful (McNaught), 1988
Sometimes Spring Is Late (Ayres), 1941
Somewhere Out There (Richards), 1993
Somewhere to Lay My Head (Peake), 1977
Son at the Front (Wharton), 1923
Son o' Mine! (M. St John, as St John Cooper), 1923
Son of a Hundred Kings (Costain), 1950
Son of Dust (Prescott), 1932
Son of Erin (Swan), 1899
Son of Hagar (Caine), 1887
Son of Mammon (Burgin), 1901
Son of Summer (Mackinlay, as Grey), 1970
Son of the Morning (Frankau), 1949
Son of the People (Orczy), 1906
Son of York (Hamilton), 1973
Son to Be Proud Of! (M. St John), 1924
Song and the Sea (Hunter, as Chace), 1962
Song Begins (Burchell), 1965
Song Bird (Cleugh), 1930
Song Cycle (Burchell), 1974
Song for a Strolling Player (M. Peters), 1981
Song for Marguerite (M. Peters), 1984
Song for Two Voices (Corcoran), 1981

Song from a Lemon Tree (D. Smith), 1966
Song in My Heart (R. Lindsay), 1961
Song in the House (s Bridge), 1936
Song of a Wren (E. Darcy), 1985
Song of Life (s Hurst), 1927
Song of Love (Cartland), 1980
Song of Miriam (s Corelli), 1898
Song of Philomel (Bloom), 1950
Song of Promise (Deveraux), 1983
Song of Renny (Hewlett), 1911
Song of Ruth (Slaughter), 1954
Song of Salome (Bloom, as Mann), 1969
Song of Silkie (Williams), 1984
Song of Surrender (Hunter), 1984
Song of the Cardinal (G. Porter), 1903
Song of the Earth (Cordell), 1969
Song of the Lark (Cather), 1915
Song of the Lark (Ruck), 1951
Song of the Mocking Bird (Duffield), 1946
Song of the Nile (I. Roberts), 1987
Song of the Siren (Plaidy, as Carr), 1980
Song of the Waves (Hampson), 1976
Song of the West (N. Roberts), 1982
Song of the Wind (Swindells), 1985
Song series (Coulter), from 1985
Song Twice Over (Jagger), 1985
Songs of War (Alexander), 1987
Sonny's Girls (Richards)
Sonora Sundown (Dailey), 1978
Sons (Buck), 1932
Sons and the Daughters (Gallagher), 1961
Sons of the Sheik (Hull), 1925
Sons of the Wolf (B. Michaels), 1967
Sooner or Later (Glyn), 1933
Sophia (Lamb, as Holland), 1979
Sophia (Weyman), 1900
Sophy of Kravonia (Hope), 1906
Sophy Valentine (Ponsonby), 1946
Sorcerer of the Castle (F. Stevenson), 1974
Sorcerers (Barcynska, as Sandys), 1927
Sorrell and Son (Deeping), 1925
Sorrows of Satan (Corelli), 1895
S.O.S. Queenie (s Barcynska), 1928
Sot-Weed Factor (Barth), 1960
Soul Flame (B. Wood), 1987
Soul of Lilith (Corelli), 1892
Soul of Man in the Age of Leisure (Jameson), 1935
Soul of the Mill (M. St John), 1916
Soul Ties (van der Zee), 1984
Sound Now the Passing-Bell (Wiat), 1977
Sound of Thunder (Caldwell), 1957
Source (Michener), 1965
South African Quirt (Edmonds), 1985
South from Sounion (Weale), 1968
South Island Stowaway (Summers), 1971
South of Capricorn (Hampson), 1975
South of Mandraki (Hampson), 1971
South of the Moon (Hampson), 1979
South Riding (Holtby), 1936
South Sea Island (Walker, as Dean), 1966
South Seas Affair (K. Thorpe), 1985
South to Forget (Summers), 1963
Southarn Folly (Blackstock, as Allardyce), 1957
Southern Nights (Dailey), 1980
Southern Passions (S. Wood), 1993
Southern Rapture (J. Blake), 1987

Southern Star (Greig, as Warren), 1950
Southern Sunshine (Bevan), 1985
Southerner (Dixon), 1913
Souvenir from Sweden (Laker, as Óvstedal), 1974
Sovereign's Key (Laker), 1969
Sow the Seeds of Hemp (Jennings), 1976
Sow the Tempest (Lane), 1960
Sower Went Forth (T. Barclay), 1980
Sowing Glory (Wren), 1931
Sown among Thorns (Dell), 1939
Sown in the Wind (MacLeod), 1946
Spain for the Sovereigns (Plaidy), 1960
Spangle (Jennings), 1987
Spangles (Barcynska, as Sandys), 1934
Spaniard's Gift (Cookson), 1989
Spanish Bride (Heyer), 1940
Spanish Bridegroom (Plaidy), 1954
Spanish Connection (K. Thorpe), 1993
Spanish Doll (Renier), 1970
Spanish Galleon (Tranter), 1960
Spanish House (Buckingham, as John), 1981
Spanish House (E. Smith), 1938
Spanish Inheritance (Hunter), 1975
Spanish Jade (Hewlett), 1908
Spanish Lover (Trollope), 1993
Spanish Maine (Wren), 1935
Spanish Rose (Busbee), 1986
Spanish series (Steen), from 1934
Spanish Summer (M. Howard), 1977
Spares (Nicole, as Gray), 1993
Sparrow Falls (Collin), 1990
Spartacus (Fast), 1951
Speak No Evil of the Dead (Roby), 1973
Speak Now (Yerby), 1969
Speak to Me of Love (Eden), 1972
Speaking Likeness (Bishop), 1976
Special Breed (Giles), 1966
Special Delivery (Chase), 1985
Special Something (Delinsky), 1984
Special Treatment (Jordan), 1988
Spectral Bride (Bowen, as Shearing), 1942
Spell of the Enchanter (Hilton), 1972
Spell of the Island (Hampson), 1983
Spell of the Seven Stones (Donnelly), 1978
Spell of Ursula (Albanesi, as Rowlands), 1894
Spellbinder (Johansen), 1987
Spellbinding (Lamb), 1990
Spellbound (Krentz, as Castle), 1982
Spellbound (Way), 1982
Spencer Brade, M.D (Slaughter), 1942
Spencer's Hospital (Stuart, as A. Stuart), 1961
Spending of the Pile (Burgin), 1924
Spendthrift Duke (Wynne), 1920
Spice of Life (Ruck), 1952
Spiced with Cloves (Hunter), 1962
Spider (Steen), 1933
Spider and the Fly (Garvice)
Spider Dance (Mackinlay), 1950
Spider in the Cup (Bowen, as Shearing), 1934
Spider's Web (Hunter, as Chace), 1966
Spilled Salt (Bloom), 1927
Spin Me a Shadow (M. Peters, as Black), 1974
Spindrift (Manners, as Saunders), 1974
Spindrift (Stratton), 1977
Spindrift (Whitney), 1975
Spinner of the Years (Bentley), 1928

Spinner's Wharf (Gower), 1985
Spinning Wheel (Lorrimer), 1990
Spinster's Progress (Ruck), 1942
Spire (Golding), 1964
Spirit in Prison (Hichens), 1908
Spirit Lake (Kantor), 1961
Spirit of Atlantis (Mather), 1980
Spirit of Bambatse (Haggard), 1906
Spirit of the Season (Pozzessere, as Graham), 1993
Spirit of the Time (Hichens), 1921
Spitfire (Armstrong), 1981
Spitfire (Small), 1990
Splendid Destiny (Albanesi, as Rowlands), 1910
Splendid Friend (Albanesi, as Rowlands), 1917
Splendid Love (Albanesi, as Rowlands), 1911
Splendid Love (M. St John, as St John Cooper), 1932
Splendid Man (Albanesi, as Rowlands), 1905
Splendid Savage (F. Stevenson, as Colt), 1983
Splendour (Saxton), 1983
Split Code (Dunnett), 1991
Spoiled Earth (Stirling), 1974
Spoilt Music (Ayres), 1926
Sport Royal (s Hope), 1893
'Sports' of Lyndale (M. St John), 1925
Spotlight on Susan (Mackinlay), 1960
Spray of Red Roses (I. Roberts, as Harle), 1971
Spread Wings (Bloom), 1933
Spreading Sails (Chandos, as Lance), 1963
Sprig Muslin (Heyer), 1956
Spring (Cleugh), 1929
Spring Always Comes (Loring), 1966
Spring at the Villa (K. Blair, as Brett), 1961
Spring Comes (Ruck), 1936
Spring Comes to Miss Lonely Heart (Ruck), 1936
Spring Comes to the Crescent (Gibbs, as Ford), 1949
Spring Fancy (Spencer), 1984
Spring Frost, Summer Fire (Seger), 1985
Spring Gambit (Williams), 1976
Spring Girl (Steele), 1979
Spring Green (Cadell), 1953
Spring in Morocco (Melville, as Betteridge), 1962
Spring in September (Bloom), 1941
Spring in September (Summers), 1978
Spring in the Heart (Albanesi, as Rowlands), 1929
Spring Madness of Mr Sermon (Delderfield), 1963
Spring Magic (D. Stevenson), 1941
Spring of a Lion (Haggard), 1899
Spring of Granite Peaks (I. Preston), 1990
Spring of the Ram (Dunnett), 1987
Spring of the Tiger (Plaidy, as Holt), 1979
Spring Picture (s du Maurier), 1944
Spring Rainbow (Mackinlay), 1961
Spring-Time of Love (Garvice), 1910
Spring Will Come Again (S. Thorpe), 1965
Springtime (Bailey), 1907
Springtime for Sally (Chandos, as Lance), 1962
Springtime for Sophie (Chappell), 1983
Spun by the Moon (Chandos, as Lance), 1960
Spur of Pride (Wren), 1937
Spurned Proposal (Albanesi, as Rowlands)
Spy Concerto (Heaven, as Merlin), 1980
Spy for Napoleon (Wynne), 1917
Spy of Napoleon (Orczy), 1934
Squire (Barcynska, as Sandys), 1932
Squirrel Walk (I. Roberts), 1961
Stacy (R. Lindsay, as Leigh), 1958

Storm and the Splendor (J. Blake), 1979
Storm and Treasure (Bailey), 1910
Storm at Midnight (J. Blake, as Treahearne), 1973
Storm at Sea (J. Lindsay), 1935
Storm Bird (Bloom, as Burns), 1959
Storm Bluer Paradise (Donald), 1991
Storm Centre (Lamb), 1980
Storm Cycle (M. Pargeter), 1982
Storm Drift (Dell), 1930
Storm Eagle (Stratton, as Gillen), 1980
Storm Flower (Way), 1975
Storm Force (Craven), 1989
Storm Haven (Slaughter), 1953
Storm Heaven (Maybury), 1949
Storm House (Norris), 1929
Storm in a Rain Barrel (Mather), 1971
Storm in the Mountains (Buckingham), 1967
Storm in the Night (M. Pargeter), 1983
Storm of Time (Dark), 1945
Storm of Wrath (Dwyer-Joyce), 1977
Storm over Mandargi (Way), 1973
Storm over Roseheath (Maybury, as Troy), 1969
Storm over the Lake (Palmer), 1979
Storm Passage (K. Thorpe), 1977
Storm Tide (Ogilvie), 1945
Storm Warning (N. Roberts), 1984
Storm Winds (Johansen), 1991
Stormchild (Cornwell), 1991
Stormfire (Finch), 1989
Storm's End (Stanford), 1980
Storms of Love (Cartland), 1985
Stormspell (Mather), 1982
Stormswift (Brent), 1984
Stormwalker (Browning, as Williams), 1990
Stormwalker (Schulze), 1987
Stormwatch (Browning), 1984
Stormy Challenge (Krentz, as James), 1982
Stormy Haven (K. Blair, as Brett), 1952
Stormy Haven (Laffeaty), 1969
Stormy Masquerade (Hampson), 1980
Stormy Oasis (Laffeaty), 1968
Stormy Petrel (Stewart), 1991
Stormy Rapture (M. Pargeter), 1976
Stormy Springtime (Neels), 1987
Stormy the Way (Hampson), 1973
Stormy Vows (Johansen), 1983
Stormy Voyage (Wentworth), 1992
Stormy Voyager (Swan), 1896
Storrington Papers (Eden), 1978
Story Girl (Montgomery), 1911
Story of a Passion (Bacheller), 1899
Story of a Passion (Garvice), 1908
Story of Andrea Fields (Seifert), 1950
Story of Fish and Chips (Ayres), 1951
Story of Francis Cludde (Weyman), 1891
Story of Ivy (Lowndes), 1927
Story of John Willie (Ayres), 1948
Story of Julia Page (Norris), 1915
Story of Julian (Ertz), 1931
Story of Marco (E. Porter), 1911
Story of Marie Powell (Graves), 1943
Story of Rosabelle Shaw (D. Stevenson), 1937
Story of Veronica (Robins), 1946
Story Teller (s Kantor), 1967
Storyteller (s Binchy), 1990
Stowaway (Weale), 1979

Straight from the Heart (Delinsky), 1986
Strait Gate (Swan), 1887
Strand (Rayner), 1980
Strange Adventure (Craven), 1977
Strange as a Dream (Kidd), 1968
Strange Beauty (Greig), 1938
Strange Bedfellow (Dailey), 1979
Strange Beginning (Jacob), 1961
Strange Capers (J. Smith), 1986
Strange Case of Lucile Cléry (Bowen, as Shearing), 1941
Strange Case of Miss Annie Spragg (Bromfield), 1928
Strange Encounter (Wentworth), 1989
Strange Harvest (Onstott), 1986
Strange Involvement (Mackinlay), 1972
Strange Lady (Hichens), 1950
Strange Love Story (Albanesi, as Rowlands), 1919
Strange Loyalty of Dr Carlisle (Seifert), 1952
Strange Marriage (Garvice, as Hart)
Strange Meeting (Robins), 1952
Strange Paths (M. Howard), 1948
Strange Patient for Sister Smith (Bloom, as Essex), 1963
Strange Quest of Anne Weston (Burchell), 1964
Strange Quest of Nurse Anne (Burchell), 1965
Strange Rapture (Robins), 1933
Strange Recompense (MacLeod, as Airlie), 1952
Strange Roads (Diver), 1918
Strange Victory (Franken, as Meloney), 1939
Strange Visitation (Corelli), 1912
Strange Visitation of Josiah McNason (Corelli), 1904
Strange Waif (Winspear), 1962
Strange Week-end (Borden), 1938
Strange Yesterday (Fast), 1934
Strangeling (Harwood), 1954
Stranger Among the Stars (Laffeaty), 1975
Stranger at Pembroke (Eliot), 1971
Stranger at Plantation Inn (J. Blake, as Maxwell), 1971
Stranger at the Gate (M. Howard, as Edgar), 1973
Stranger at the Gates (Anthony), 1973
Stranger at Wildings (Brent), 1976
Stranger Came (Donnelly), 1972
Stranger from the North (L. Walker), 1959
Stranger from the Past (Jordan), 1992
Stranger from the Sea (I. Preston), 1987
Stranger from the Sea 1810–1811 (Graham), 1981
Stranger in Love (Chandos), 1966
Stranger in Love (M. Howard), 1939
Stranger in the Glen (Kidd), 1975
Stranger in the Mirror (Laffeaty), 1979
Stranger in the Night (Lamb), 1980
Stranger in Their Midst (MacLeod), 1953
Stranger on the Beach (Melville, as Betteridge), 1974
Stranger on the Beach (Peake), 1979
Stranger Passing By (Peake), 1992
Stranger Prince (Irwin), 1937
Stranger Sweetheart (Greig, as Ames), 1938
Stranger Than Truth (Albanesi, as Rowlands), 1913
Stranger to Love (Chandos, as Tempest), 1960
Stranger to Love (Woodward, as Ware), 1967
Strangers (Thomas), 1987
Strangers' Forest (P. Hill), 1978
Strangers in Company (Hodge), 1973
Strangers in Love (Delmar), 1951
Strangers in My House (Ponsonby), 1948
Strangers in Paradise (Pozzessere), 1988
Strangers into Lovers (Peake), 1981
Stranger's Kiss (Stanford), 1978

Strangers May Marry (Burchell), 1941
Strangers May Marry (Hampson), 1982
Strangers on the Moor (S. Thorpe), 1966
Strangers When We Meet (Stuart, as A. Stuart), 1968
Strap-Hangers (James), 1934
Strategy of Suzanne (Grundy), 1929
Stratford Affair (P. Hastings), 1978
Stratford Story (Sisson), 1975
Strathgallant (Black), 1981
Strathmore (Stirling), 1975
Stratton Story (Cadell), 1967
Straw Crown (Stubbs), 1966
Strawberries in the Sea (Ogilvie), 1973
Straws in Amber (Jacob), 1938
Street Below (Ayres), 1922
Street of Seven Stars (Rinehart), 1914
Street of the Five Moons (B. Michaels, as Peters), 1978
Street of the Singing Fountain (Randall), 1948
Street of the Sun (Horner), 1956
Street Song (E. Blair), 1986
Streets (s Hichens), 1928
Stricken Land (Thompson), 1986
Strife Beyond Tamar (Oliver), 1977
Strike at the Heart (E. Darcy), 1987
Strike from the Sea (Kent, as Reeman), 1978
Strike the Black Flag (Jakes, as Scotland), 1961
String of Silver Beads (Ainsworth), 1972
Strip (Ellis), 1970
Strip Girl (Price), 1934
Strolling Players (Dwyer-Joyce), 1975
Strolling Saint (Sabatini), 1913
Strong Arms of the Lion (Schulze), 1992
Strong City (Caldwell), 1942
Strong Hand (Deeping), 1912
Strong Heart (Robins), 1965
Strong, Hot Winds (Johansen), 1988
Strong Hours (Diver), 1919
Stronger Passion (Bloom, as Burns), 1941
Stronger than Yearning (Jordan), 1986
Strongest of All Things (Albanesi), 1907
Struggle for a Crown (M. Peters), 1970
Struggle for a Heart (Libbey), 1889
Stuart series (Tranter), from 1986
Stuart Sisters (Bloom, as Prole), 1958
Stuart Stain (W. Roberts), 1978
Stuarts series (Plaidy), from 1965
Stubborn Heart (Slaughter), 1950
Studies in Love and Terror (s Lowndes), 1913
Studies in Wives (s Lowndes), 1909
Subaltern's Choice (McCutchan, as MacNeil), 1974
Subconscious Courtship (Ruck), 1922
Substitute Bride (M. Pargeter), 1981
Substitute Doctor (Seifert), 1957
Substitute for Sherry (Chandos), 1940
Substitute Lover (Jordan), 1987
Subtle Revenge (Mortimer), 1983
Suburban Young Man (Delafield), 1928
Success Story (M. Howard), 1984
Success to the Brave (Kent), 1983
Such a Fine Fellow! (M. St John), 1923
Such Bitter Business (Plaidy, as Ford), 1953
Such Dark Magic (Donald), 1993
Such Is Love (Burchell), 1939
Such Men Are Dangerous (s Glyn), 1933
Such Mighty Rage (Clayton), 1985
Such Sweet Poison (Mather), 1991

Sudden Engagement (Jordan), 1983
Sudden Sweetheart (Ruck), 1932
Suddenly (Delinsky), 1993
Sue Verney (J. Lindsay), 1937
Suffer a Sea Change (De Blasis), 1976
Suffer to Sing (Barcynska, as Sandys), 1955
Suffolk series (Lofts), from 1959
Sugar Angel (Laffeaty), 1972
Sugar Candy Cottage (Cadell), 1958
Sugar Cane Harvest (K. Thorpe), 1975
Sugar in the Morning (Hunter, as Chace), 1969
Sugar Island (Duffield), 1951
Sugar Island (MacLeod), 1964
Sugar Mouse (Gibbs), 1965
Sugar Pavilion (Laker), 1993
Suitable Match (Neels), 1990
Suitors of Yvonne (Sabatini), 1902
Sullivan's Reef (Weale), 1970
Sullivan's Woman (N. Roberts), 1984
Summer (Wharton), 1917
Summer at Awakopu (Donald), 1978
Summer at Barbazon (K. Blair), 1960
Summer at San Milo (Asquith), 1965
Summer at Silverwood (Ritchie), 1962
Summer at Willowbank (I. Preston), 1980
Summer Change (Norway, as Norton), 1961
Summer Cypress (P. Hill, as Fiske), 1981
Summer Day Is Done (Staples, as Stevens), 1976
Summer Desserts (N. Roberts), 1985
Summer Dust (Eaton), 1936
Summer Games (Lowell), 1984
Summer Gone (Maddocks), 1957
Summer Harvest (Swindells), 1983
Summer Heat (Seger), 1988
Summer Idyll (Neels), 1984
Summer in December (Summers), 1970
Summer Island (MacLeod), 1968
Summer Love (Wentworth), 1981
Summer Magic (Way), 1971
Summer Mahogany (Dailey), 1978
Summer of Fear (Ellis, as Marvin), 1971
Summer of Pride (Savage), 1961
Summer of Sighs (Gallagher), 1971
Summer of the Barshinskeys (Pearson), 1984
Summer of the Dragon (B. Michaels, as Peters), 1979
Summer of the Osprey (Ogilvie), 1987
Summer of the Raven (Craven), 1981
Summer of the Spanish Woman (Gaskin), 1977
Summer of the Unicorn (Hooper), 1988
Summer People (Chandos, as Lance), 1969
Summer Promises (Rhodes), 1990
Summer Rain (MacLeod), 1938
Summer Rhapsody (Buckingham, as John), 1983
Summer Season (Stratton, as Gillen), 1971
Summer Secrets (Stubbs), 1990
Summer Smile (Johansen), 1985
Summer Song (Oldfield), 1984
Summer Stock Romance (McElfresh, as Wesley), 1961
Summer Storm (Donald), 1990
Summer Storm (James), 1953
Summer Storm (Lane), 1976
Summer Story (Chappell), 1972
Summer Sunday (Eden), 1946
Summer Tangle (Alexander, as Armstrong), 1983
Summer Thunder (Lowell), 1983
Summer to Come Home (Schulze), 1990

Summer Visitors (Sallis), 1988
Summer Wife (Kidd), 1976
Summer Will Show (S. Warner), 1936
Summerhills (D. Stevenson), 1956
Summer's Awakening (Weale), 1984
Summer's End (Steel), 1981
Summer's Flower (Stuart), 1961
Summer's Grace (Chandos, as Lance), 1961
Summer's Lease (Ertz), 1972
Summer's Play (Stern), 1934
Summer's Vintage (Bevan), 1992
Sun and Candlelight (Neels), 1979
Sun and the Dragon (Nicole), 1985
Sun and the Sea (Ayres), 1935
Sun Fades the Stars (Trask), 1940
Sun in Splendour (Dymoke), 1980
Sun in Splendour (Plaidy), 1982
Sun in Splendour (Weale), 1975
Sun in the Morning (Asquith), 1974
Sun Is My Undoing (Steen), 1941
Sun Lord's Woman (Winspear), 1985
Sun Lover (Stanford), 1982
Sun of Summer (Peake), 1975
Sun on Fire (Nicole), 1985
Sun on the Mountain (Collin), 1969
Sun on the Sea (Ritchie), 1954
Sun Rises (Nicole), 1984
Sun, Sea and Sand (May), 1970
Sun Spark (Pykare, as N. Coombs), 1984
Sun Tower (Winspear), 1976
Sun Virgin (Dixon), 1913
Sun Woman (McKenna), 1991
Sunburst (Ruck), 1934
Sunday Love (Bloom), 1978
Sunday's Child (Williams), 1977
Sundered Hearts (Swan), 1886
Sunflower's Look (Ritchie), 1958
Sunia (s Diver), 1913
Sunlight Beyond (Albanesi, as Rowlands), 1930
Sunlit Hills (Albanesi), 1914
Sunlit Seas (I. Preston), 1977
Sunne in Splendour (Penman), 1982
Sunny Chandler's Return (Brown), 1987
Sunny Ducrow (M. St John, as St John Cooper), 1919
Sunny Island (Greig, as Warren), 1952
Sunrise (Duffield), 1943
Sunrise (Thomas), 1984
Sunrise at Even (Cowen), 1982
Sunrise for Georgie (Ayres), 1941
Sunrise in the West (E. Pargeter), 1974
Sunset (Nicole), 1978
Sunset and Dawn (Albanesi, as Rowlands), 1915
Sunset Cloud (Hampson), 1976
Sunset Dream (Gavin), 1983
Sunset Embrace (Brown), 1984
Sunset Hour (Summerton), 1957
Sunset Is Dawn (Barcynska, as Barclay), 1953
Sunset Touch (Stuart, as A. Stuart), 1972
Sunshine and Shadow (London, as Curtis), 1986
Sunshine-Stealer (Ruck), 1935
Sup with the Devil (Craven), 1983
Surest Bond (Albanesi, as Rowlands), 1913
Surface with Daring (Kent, as Reeman), 1977
Surgeon at Sea (Bloom, as Burns), 1969
Surgeon at St Mark's (E. Harrison), 1986
Surgeon Called Amanda (E. Harrison), 1982

Surgeon from Holland (Neels), 1970
Surgeon in Charge (Seifert), 1942
Surgeon in the Snow (Saxton, as Balmain), 1985
Surgeon in Tibet (I. Roberts), 1970
Surgeon of Distinction (Burchell), 1959
Surgeon on Call (Seifert), 1965
Surgeon She Married (E. Harrison), 1988
Surgeon, USA (Slaughter), 1966
Surgeon's Affair (E. Harrison), 1985
Surgeon's Call (E. Harrison), 1973
Surgeon's Choice (Slaughter), 1969
Surgeon's Dilemma (M. Howard), 1961
Surgeon's Life (E. Harrison), 1983
Surgeon's Marriage (K. Blair), 1963
Surgeon's Mate (O'Brian), 1980
Surgeon's Reputation (Chandos, as Charles), 1979
Surgeon's Sweetheart (Bloom, as Burns), 1966
Surgeon's Sweetheart (Chandos, as Charles), 1981
Surprise Engagement (Ruck), 1946
Surrender (Krentz, as Quick), 1990
Surrender (Lamb), 1992
Surrender by Moonlight (Delinsky, as Drake), 1981
Surrender in Moonlight (J. Blake), 1984
Surrender to Desire (Coulter), 1986
Surrender to Love (Rogers), 1982
Susan Crowther (Jacob), 1945
Susannah and One Elder (Albanesi), 1903
Susannah and One Other (Albanesi), 1904
Susie (Chesney, as Tremaine), 1981
'Susies' Career (Hichens), 1935
Suspected Four (W. Roberts), 1962
Sussex series (Glover), from 1982
Sussex series (P. Hastings), from 1968
Sutburys (P. Hill), 1988
Sutton Place series (Lampitt), from 1983
Sutton's Way (Palmer), 1989
Suvla John (Deeping), 1924
Suzanna's Surrender (N. Roberts), 1991
Suzerain (Bennetts), 1968
Swallow (Haggard), 1899
Swan (Steen), 1951
Swan House (Hutten), 1930
Swan River Story (P. Hastings), 1968
Swan series (De Blasis), from 1984
Swann series (Delderfield), from 1970
Swans and Turtles (s Godden), 1968
Swans' Reach (Way), 1976
Swan Sea Place series (F. Preston), from 1990
Sweeping Tide (Duffield), 1940
Sweet Addiction (Lamb), 1992
Sweet Adventure (Burchell), 1952
Sweet Adventure (Cartland), 1957
Sweet and Faraway (L. Walker), 1955
Sweet and Lovely (Albanesi), 1933
Sweet and Twenty (J. Smith), 1979
Sweet Anger (Brown, as St Claire), 1985
Sweet Are the Ways (Summers), 1965
Sweet as a Rose (Garvice), 1910
Sweet as My Revenge (Napier), 1985
Sweet Bloom (Ritchie), 1961
Sweet Cassandra (Robins), 1970
Sweet Compulsion (Lamb, as Woolf), 1979
Sweet Cymbeline (Garvice), 1911
Sweet Danger (Greig), 1935
Sweet Deceiver (K. Blair), 1955
Sweet Disorder (Williams), 1981

Sweet Ember (Delinsky, as Drake), 1981
Sweet Enchantress (Cartland, as McCorquodale), 1958
Sweet Enemy (Palmer), 1979
Sweet Fortune (Krentz), 1991
Sweet Georgia Gal (Richards), 1985
Sweet Homecoming (Richards), 1987
Sweet Impulse (Bloom, as Burns), 1956
Sweet Is the Web (Hampson), 1977
Sweet Kate (Stratton, as Gillen), 1971
Sweet Kitty Clover (Libbey), 1898
Sweet Lass of Richmond Hill (Plaidy), 1970
Sweet Liar (Deveraux), 1993
Sweet Love (Robins), 1934
Sweet Love Remembered (Chard), 1982
Sweet Love, Survive (S. Johnson), 1985
Sweet Marie-Antoinette (Bloom, as Prole), 1969
Sweet Masquerade (Chesney), 1984
Sweet Meadows (Burchell), 1963
Sweet Memories (Spencer), 1984
Sweet Mockingbird's (Richards), 1986
Sweet Mountain Magic (Richards), 1986
Sweet Nell (Bloom, as Prole), 1965
Sweet Nightingale (Bishop), 1966
Sweet Not Always (van der Zee), 1979
Sweet Peril (Greig, as Ames), 1935
Sweet Piracy Fawcett (J. Blake, as Maxwell), 1978
Sweet Promise (Dailey), 1976
Sweet Punishment (Cartland), 1931
Sweet Red Earth (Saunders, as Summers), 1983
Sweet Revenge (Mather), 1970
Sweet Revenge (N. Roberts), 1989
Sweet Rocket (M. Johnston), 1920
Sweet Rosemary (Chandos), 1972
Sweet Sally Lunn (Oldfield), 1990
Sweet Sanctuary (Lamb), 1976
Sweet Savage Eden (Pozzessere, as Graham), 1989
Sweet, Savage Heart (Taylor), 1986
Sweet Savage Love (Rogers), 1974
Sweet Sea Spirit (Richards), 1986
Sweet Second Love (Hampson), 1984
Sweet Serenity (Delinsky, as Douglass), 1983
Sweet Sorrel (I. Roberts), 1963
Sweet Sorrow (Robins), 1940
Sweet Spring of April (Bloom), 1979
Sweet Starfire (Krentz), 1986
Sweet Stranger (Ruck), 1921
Sweet Sundown (Way), 1974
Sweet Surrender (Coulter), 1984
Sweet Surrender (Vitek), 1982
Sweet to Remember (Weale), 1958
Sweet Torment (Kidd), 1978
Sweet Vixen (Napier), 1983
Sweet Waters (K. Blair, as Brett), 1955
Sweet Will (Malpass), 1973
Sweet William (Albanesi), 1906
Sweet Wind of Morning (M. Peters, as Grey), 1979
Sweet Wind, Wild Wind (Lowell), 1987
Sweetbriar (Deveraux), 1983
Sweetbriar Lane (Barcynska), 1938
Sweetcrab (Summerton), 1971
Sweeter Music (C. Allen), 1976
Sweeter than Sweet (Sallis), 1994
Sweetest Thing (E. Blair), 1993
Sweetest Trap (Donald), 1988
Sweetheart Will You Be True? (Libbey), 1901
Sweethearts Unmet (Ruck), 1919

Swell Fellows (Barcynska, as Sandys), 1942
Sweyn's Eye series (Gower), from 1983
Swift Flows the River (Ellerbeck, as Yorke), 1988
Swift to Sever (James), 1949
Swift Water (Loring), 1929
Swiftest Eagle (Dwyer-Joyce), 1979
Swimming Pool (Rinehart), 1952
Swimming with Dolphins (Pizzey), 1990
Swindler (s Dell), 1914
Swing High, Swing Low (Greig, as Barclay), 1936
Swing of Youth (Robins), 1930
Switch on to Love (Woodward, as Lawrence), 1967
Sword and Scalpel (Slaughter), 1957
Sword and the Cross (Deeping), 1957
Sword and the Flame (P. Hill), 1991
Sword and the Shadow (S. Thorpe), 1951
Sword and the Swan (Gellis), 1977
Sword at Sunset (Sutcliff), 1963
Sword Decides! (Bowen), 1908
Sword in the Sun (Hoy), 1946
Sword of Islam (Sabatini), 1939
Sword of Mithras (Heaven, as Merlin), 1982
Sword of Pleasure (Green), 1957
Sword of the Golden Stud (Carter), 1977
Sword of Vengeance (S. Thorpe), 1957
Sword of Woden (Wiat), 1975
Sword series (Nicole, as Yorke), from 1990
Sword to the Heart (Cartland), 1974
Swordlight (Manners, as Rundle), 1968
Sybelle (Gellis), 1983
Sycamore Hill (Rivers), 1981
Sycamore Song (Hunter), 1975
Sydney (Garvice)
Sydney, The Temptress (F. Preston), 1987
Sylvester (Heyer), 1957
Sylvia Cary (Keyes), 1962
Sylvia Lyndon (Diver), 1940
Sylvia Sorelle (Hoy), 1944
Sympathetic Surgeon (Bloom, as Essex), 1968
Symphony for Two Players (M. Lewis), 1969
Symphony of Bells (I. Roberts), 1980

TLC (Delinsky), 1988
Tabitha in Moonlight (Neels), 1972
Table for Two (Greig), 1946
Tabloid News (s Bromfield), 1930
Taboo (Hamilton, as Fitzgerald), 1985
Taffy Came to Cairo (Duffield), 1944
Taggart's Woman (Mortimer), 1988
Tailor of Vitré (Wynne), 1908
Taint of Tragedy (Wynne), 1917
Tai-Pan (Clavell), 1966
Taj Mahal, Shrine of Desire (Bloom, as Prole), 1972
Take a Chance (Bloom, as Burns), 1937
Take a Chance (Chandos, as Lance), 1940
Take a Fax to the Kasbah (Dunnett), 1992
Take Courage (Bentley), 1940
Take Love Easy (Hoy), 1941
Take Me with You (Burchell), 1944
Take the Far Dream (Donnelly), 1970
Take This Man (Greig), 1947
Take This Woman (Cox), 1988
Take This Woman (Peake), 1988
Take Three Doctors (Seifert), 1947
Take Three Tenses (Godden), 1945
Take What You Want (Baldwin), 1970

Take What You Want (Mather), 1975
Take Your Choice, Lady (Greig, as Ames), 1946
Taken by Storm (Hooper, as Robbins), 1983
Taken by the Hand (O. Douglas), 1935
Taken on Trust (Wentworth), 1990
Taken Over (Jordan), 1985
Taking Chances (Keane, as Farrell), 1929
Taking Chances (Taylor), 1993
Tale of Three Cities (D. Murray), 1940
Tale of Three Lions, and On Going Back (Haggard), 1887
Tales from Sarson Magna series (Burgh, as Leith), from 1991
Tales from Tiger Bay (s Cordell), 1986
Tales of Grace and Favour (Leslie), 1956
Tales of Long Ago (s Doyle), 1922
Tales of Men and Ghosts (s Wharton), 1920
Tales of Pirates and Blue Water (s Doyle), 1922
Tales of the Jeweled Men (Veryan), from 1990
Tales of the Pacific (Richards), from 1987
Tales of the Silver Wench series (Sherwood), from 1985
Tales of Two People (Hope), 1907
Talisman (Crowe), 1979
Talisman Ring (Heyer), 1936
Talk of the Town (J. Smith), 1979
Tall Headlines (Erskine-Lindop), 1950
Tall Hunter (Fast), 1942
Tall Pines (K. Blair, as Conway), 1956
Tall Stranger (D. Stevenson), 1957
Talons of the Hawk (Sherwood, as Hines), 1975
Tamara (Norris), 1935
Tamara's Ecstasy (Sommerfield), 1982
Tamarind Seed (Anthony), 1971
Tamarisk (Lorrimer), 1978
Tamarisk (Muskett), 1935
Tamarisk Bay (K. Blair), 1956
Tamarisk in Bloom (I. Preston), 1963
Tamberlyn (Manley-Tucker), 1981
Tamboti Moon (May), 1969
Tame My Wild Heart (Sommerfield), 1984
Tame the Restless Heart (Matthews), 1986
Taming (Deveraux), 1989
Taming Charlotte (Miller), 1993
Taming Natasha (N. Roberts), 1990
Taming of Amelia (Seger), 1993
Taming of Annabelle (Chesney), 1983
Taming of Lady Lorinda (Cartland), 1977
Taming of Laura (R. Lindsay), 1959
Taming of Lisa (Kidd), 1972
Taming of Princess Olga (Garvice), 1908
Taming of the Tigress (Cartland), 1990
Tanamera (Barber), 1981
Tangle in Sunshine (K. Blair, as Brett), 1957
Tangle of Gold Lace (I. Roberts), 1963
Tangle of Torment (E. Darcy), 1983
Tangled Autumn (Neels), 1971
Tangled Destinies (Palmer, as Blayne), 1986
Tangled Destiny (James), 1961
Tangled Emotions (Steele, as M. Steele), 1978
Tangled Fates (Wynne), 1935
Tangled Hearts (Mortimer), 1987
Tangled Love (Norris), 1933
Tangled Roots (Bromige), 1948
Tangled Shadows (Kidd), 1979
Tangled Skein (Orczy), 1907
Tangled Tapestry (Mather), 1969
Tangled Thread (Harrod-Eagles), 1987
Tangled Threads (s E. Porter), 1919

Tangled Vines (Dailey), 1992
Tangled Web (Cartland), 1992
Tangled Web (I. Roberts, as Rowland), 1962
Tangled Web (Montgomery), 1931
Tangled Wood (Bromige), 1969
Tansy (M. Peters), 1975
Tapestry (Plain), 1988
Tapestry (Seger), 1993
Tapestry of Dreams (Gellis), 1985
Tapestry of Fear (Pemberton), 1979
Tapestry of the Boar (Tranter), 1993
Tara's Healing (Giles), 1951
Tara's Song (B. Johnson), 1978
Tarnish (Bloom), 1929
Tarnished Vows (Stanford), 1982
Tarot Spell (W. Roberts), 1970
Tarrington Chase (S. Thorpe), 1977
Tartan Touch (Hunter, as Chace), 1972
Tasker Jevons (M. Sinclair), 1916
Taste for Rich Things (Lorin, as Hohl), 1984
Taste the Wine (Saunders), 1983
Tattling Tongues (M. St John), 1922
Tattooed Road (Horner), 1960
Tavern (Steen), 1935
Tavern Knight (Sabatini), 1904
Taverners' Place (Trollope), 1986
Tawny Are the Leaves (May), 1968
Tawny Gold Man (Lorin), 1980
Tawny Sands (Winspear), 1970
Tazia's Torment (Sommerfield), 1980
Tea and Destiny (Woods), 1990
Tea at Gunter's (Haines), 1974
Tea Is So Intoxicating (Bloom, as Essex), 1950
Tea on Sunday (L. Cooper), 1973
Teach Me to Love (Chandos, as Tempest), 1947
Team (Norway, as Neal), 1965
Team-Up for Ann (McElfresh), 1959
Tears and Red Roses (Lamb, as Hardy), 1982
Tears of Gold (McBain), 1979
Tears of Love (Cartland), 1975
Tears of Peace (Barcynska), 1944
Tears of the Renegade (L. Howard), 1985
Tears of Venus (Stratton), 1979
Technique of Marriage (Borden), 1924
Telefair, Kitty series (F. Stevenson), from 1971
Tell Me a Story (Schulze), 1988
Tell Me My Fortune (Burchell), 1951
Tell Me My Heart (Baldwin), 1950
Tell Me No Lies (B. Hastings), 1984
Tell Me No Lies (Lowell), 1986
Telling of Lies (Findley), 1986
Temp (Melville, as Betteridge), 1976
Temperamental People (s Rinehart), 1924
Temperatures Rising (Brown), 1989
Tempest and the Song (Ritchie), 1959
Tempest at Sea (Johansen), 1983
Tempest in Eden (Brown), 1983
Tempestuous Affair (Courtney), 1983
Tempestuous Affair (Mortimer), 1985
Tempestuous April (Neels), 1975
Tempestuous Eden (Pozzessere, as Graham), 1983
Tempestuous Flame (Mortimer), 1979
Tempestuous Petticoat (Gibbs), 1977
Temple of Butterflies (Hamilton, as Fitzgerald), 1989
Temple of Dawn (Hampson), 1979
Temple of Fire (Way), 1980

Temple of Love (Cartland), 1988
Temple of the Moon (Craven), 1977
Temporal Power (Corelli), 1902
Temporary Address (Baldwin), 1941
Temporary Boy (P. Hastings), 1971
Temporary Marriage (K. Thorpe), 1981
Temporary Wife (R. Lindsay, as Leigh), 1975
Tempt me Not (Napier), 1991
Tempt Not This Flesh (Riefe), 1979
Temptation (Albanesi, as Rowlands), 1912
Temptation (Lamb), 1979
Temptation (I. Roberts, as Rowland), 1983
Temptation (N. Roberts), 1987
Temptation (Wynne), 1937
Temptation for a Teacher (Cartland), 1985
Temptation of Mary Barr (Albanesi, as Rowlands)
Temptation of Philip Carr (Wynne), 1905
Temptation of Torilla (Cartland), 1977
Temptation's Kiss (Brown), 1983
Temptations of Big Bear (Wiebe), 1973
Temptation's Price (Schulze), 1992
Tempted (Carr), 1987
Tempted by Desire (Mortimer), 1979
Tempted by Love (Albanesi, as Rowlands)
Tempted to Love (Cartland), 1983
Tempted to Love (Kidd), 1982
Tempter's Power (Wynne), 1932
Tempting Fate (N. Roberts), 1985
Temptress (Deveraux), 1980
Temptress (R. Marshall), 1952
Ten Cent Love (Greig), 1934
Ten Commandments (Deeping), 1931
Ten Days of Christmas (Stern), 1950
Tenant of Binningham Hall (O. Sinclair), 1975
Tenant of Chesdene Manor (Ley), 1974
Tenants of Time (Flanagan), 1988
Ten-Day Queen (Bloom, as Prole), 1972
Tender Barbarian (Browning), 1985
Tender Betrayal (J. Blake), 1979
Tender Deception (Pozzessere, as Graham), 1984
Tender Ecstasy (Taylor), 1983
Tender Glory (MacLeod), 1965
Tender Is the Storm (Lindsey), 1985
Tender Is the Tyrant (Winspear), 1967
Tender Leaves (Summers), 1980
Tender Night (Peake), 1975
Tender Persuasion (S. Wood), 1988
Tender Rebel (Lindsey), 1988
Tender Savage (Johansen), 1991
Tender Stranger (Palmer), 1985
Tender Taming (Pozzessere, as Graham), 1983
Tender Trap (Saunders), 1978
Tender Triumph (McNaught), 1983
Tender Victory (Caldwell), 1956
Tender Warrior (F. Michaels), 1983
Tender Yearnings (Chase), 1981
Tender Years (Hampson), 1982
Tension (Delafield), 1920
Tents of Israel (Stern), 1924
Terminus (Leslie), 1931
Terms of Surrender (Dailey), 1982
Terrace in the Sun (Weale), 1966
Terracotta Palace (Maybury), 1971
Terriford Mystery (Lowndes), 1924
Terror at Nelson Woods (Ellis, as Richard), 1973
Terror in the Sun (Cartland), 1979

Terror of the Moor (Wynne), 1928
Terror Trap (W. Roberts), 1971
Tesha, A Plaything of Destiny (Barcynska), 1923
Tessacott Tragedy (s Garvice), 1913
Test of Time (Krentz), 1987
Testament of Love (Woodward, as Richmond), 1977
Testament of Trust (Baldwin), 1960
Testimonies (O'Brian), 1952
Testimony (London, as Curtis), 1993
Testimony of Two Men (Caldwell), 1968
Tethered Liberty (Steele), 1983
Tetherstones (Dell), 1923
Texas (Michener), 1985
Texas Angel (Finch), 1987
Texas Bride (Coulter), 1986
Texas! Chase (Brown), 1990
Texas Fury (F. Michaels), 1989
Texas Gold (Lorin, as Hohl), 1986
Texas Heat (F. Michaels), 1986
Texas Lily (S. Blake), 1987
Texas! Lucky (Brown), 1990
Texas Rich (F. Michaels), 1985
Texas! Sage (Brown), 1992
Texas Spitfire (Coulter), 1986
Texas Sunrise (F. Michaels), 1993
Texas Temptation (Finch, as Robins), 1989
Texas Wildcat (McKenna), 1985
Thai Silk (Weale), 1990
Thames Camp (Grundy), 1902
Than This World Dreams Of (Ayres), 1934
Thank Heaven Fasting (Delafield), 1932
Thankful Rest (Swan), 1885
Thanks to Elizabeth (Burchell), 1944
That Affair in Spain (Woodward, as Davis), 1969
That Awful Scar (Garvice, as Hart)
That Boston Man (Dailey), 1979
That Carolina Summer (Dailey), 1981
That Enchantress (Leslie), 1950
That Fatal Touch (Roby), 1970
That Girl in Nice (Greig), 1954
That Girl, Jennifer! (Randall), 1946
That Island Summer (Hoy), 1973
That Lady (O'Brien), 1946
That Man in Her Life (Woodward), 1977
That Man Is Mine! (Baldwin), 1936
That Man Next Door (Stratton, as Gillen), 1971
That Man Simon (Weale), 1971
That Nice Nurse Nevin (Chandos, as Tempest), 1963
That Night at the Villa (Bishop), 1972
That None Should Die (Slaughter), 1941
That Old Feeling (F. Preston), 1983
That Pretty Young Girl (Libbey), 1889
That Savage Yankee Squire! (Sebastian), 1978
That Special Person (Steele, as M. Steele), 1978
That Strange Girl (Garvice), 1911
That Strange Holiday (Woodward, as Sawley), 1972
That Summer at Bacclesea (Gibbs, as Ford), 1956
That Sweet and Savage Land (Drummond), 1990
That Trouble Piece! (Barcynska), 1939
That Villa in Spain (Woodward, as Richmond), 1981
That Was Yesterday (Jameson), 1932
That Which Is Hidden (Hichens), 1939
That Which Is Passed (Atkin), 1923
That Wild Lie— (Jacob), 1930
Thawing of Mara (Dailey), 1980
The Good Deed of Asia, Past and Present (s Buck), 1969

The Woman Who Was Changed (s Buck), 1979
Thea (Maddocks), 1969
Theatre of Love (Cartland), 1991
Theatre of Love (Saxton, as Balmain), 1987
Theatre Sister in Love (Bloom, as Burns), 1963
Theft in Kind (Summerton), 1962
Theft of the Heart (Cartland, as McCorquodale), 1966
Their Flowers Were Always Black (P. Hastings), 1967
Their Mysterious Patient (Woodward, as Sawley), 1970
Their Was the Kingdom (Delderfield), 1971
Thelma (Corelli), 1887
Theme for Reason (Ogilvie), 1970
Theme Song (Mackinlay), 1938
Then Came the Test (Pedler), 1942
Then Come Kiss Me (Burchell), 1948
Then Shall We Hear Singing (Jameson), 1942
Theodora (Eliot, as Arnett), 1977
Theodore (Wynne), 1926
There and Now (Miller), 1992
There Are Limits (Robins), 1932
There Are Worse Jungles (Tranter), 1955
There But for Fortune (Stuart, as A. Stuart), 1966
There Came a Tyrant (Hampson), 1972
There Is a Season (Baldwin), 1966
There Is a Tide . . . (Chandos), 1950
There Is Always Love (Loring), 1940
There Is Always To-morrow (James), 1949
There Is But One (Lorrimer, as Robins), 1965
There Is No Parting (A. Howard), 1993
There is No Why (James), 1970
There May Be Heaven (Ogilvie), 1966
There Must Be Showers (Hampson), 1983
There Once Was a Lover (Browning), 1987
There Was a Fair Maid Dwelling (Delderfield), 1960
There Was a Time (Caldwell), 1947
There Was Another (Ayres), 1938
There Were Nine Castles (Hunter), 1967
There will be a Short Interval (Jameson), 1973
There Will I Follow (M. Howard), 1949
Therefore Must Be Loved (Chandos, as Charles), 1972
There's Just One Girl (M. St John, as St John Cooper), 1919
Theresa (I. Roberts, as Rowland), 1985
Theresa and a Tiger (Cartland), 1984
These Are Our Masters (Swan), 1939
These Changing Years (Barcynska), 1961
These Charming People (s Arlen), 1923
These Golden Pleasures (Sherwood), 1977
These Mortals (Irwin), 1925
These My Children (M. Lewis), 1977
These Old Shades (Heyer), 1926
These Roots Go Deep (Bloom), 1939
These White Hands (Deeping), 1937
Theseus series (Renault), from 1958
They Brought Their Women (s Ferber), 1933
They Came to Valeira (K. Blair, as Brett), 1950
They Dreamed Too Much (Maybury), 1938
They Hanged My Saintly Billy (Graves), 1957
They Knew Her When (Moore), 1938
They Laugh That Win (Albanesi, as Rowlands), 1899
They Left the Land (Jacob), 1940
They Lived with Me (Price, as Smith), 1934
They Met in Zanzibar (K. Blair), 1962
They That Go Down in Ships (Steen), 1931
They That Go Down (Steen), 1930
They Were Defeated (Macaulay), 1932
They Who Love (s Baldwin), 1948

Thicker than Water (Polland), 1965
Thicket (Gallagher), 1973
Thief of Love (Cartland, as McCorquodale), 1957
Thieving Magpie (Bloom), 1960
Thin Ice (Browning), 1989
Thine Is My Heart (Burchell), 1942
Third Boat (Mackinlay), 1967
Third Estate (Bowen), 1917
Third Eye (Glyn), 1940
Third Generation (Swan), 1940
Third George (Plaidy), 1969
Third Life (Nicole, as Gray), 1988
Third Love Lucky (Ruck), 1958
Third Miss Chance (Peter), 1933
Third Miss Wenderby (Grundy), 1911
Third Richard (Bennetts), 1972
Third Time Lucky (Ruck), 1958
Third Wife (Sherwood, as Hines), 1977
Thirteen Gun Salute (O'Brian), 1989
Thirteenth Girl (Greig), 1947
This Alien Heart (Duffield), 1942
This Brief Interlude (Pykare, as Powers), 1984
This Desirable Bachelor (Greig), 1941
This Dragon of Desire (Bloom, as Burns), 1958
This Errant Heart (Maybury), 1937
This Fearful Paradise (Greig), 1953
This Fierce Splendor (Johansen), 1988
This Flower (Miles), 1933
This for Caroline (Leslie), 1964
This Golden Valley (Rivers), 1983
This Heart of Mine (Small), 1985
This Heart So Wild (Laffeaty), 1968
This Is Marriage (Bloom), 1935
This Kind of Love (K. Blair), 1964
This Land Turns Evil Slowly (Roby), 1971
This Lovely Hour (Maybury), 1937
This Loving Torment (Sherwood), 1977
This Magic Moment (N. Roberts), 1983
This Man Her Enemy (Peake), 1976
This Man Is Not for Marrying (Bloom, as Essex), 1959
This Moment in Time (Peake), 1971
This Much to Give (MacLeod), 1945
This Must Be for Ever (Lewty), 1962
This One Night (Robins), 1942
This Other Eden (Gaskin), 1947
This Passion Called Love (Glyn), 1925
This Porcelain Clay (Jacob), 1939
This Proud and Savage Land (Cordell), 1987
This Proud Love (Riefe), 1985
This Ravaged Heart (Riefe), 1977
This Ravished Land (Oldfield), 1980
This Rough Beginning (P. Hill), 1981
This Rough Magic (E. Pargeter), 1953
This Rough Magic (Stewart), 1964
This Royal Breed (Saxton), 1991
This Shining Land (Laker), 1985
This Side of Glory (Bristow), 1940
This Side of Heaven (E. Blair), 1985
This Side of Innocence (Caldwell), 1946
This Side of Paradise (K. Thorpe), 1979
This Son of Adam (Burgin), 1910
This Splendid Folly (Pedler), 1918
This Spring of Love (Robins), 1943
This Strange Adventure (Rinehart), 1929
This Summer's Rose (Ritchie), 1970
This Sweet and Bitter Earth (Cordell), 1977

This Time It's Love, (Cartland), 1977
This Time It's Love (Chandos), 1951
This Towering Passion (Sherwood), 1978
This Was a Man (Plaidy, as Tate), 1961
This Was Tomorrow (Thane), 1951
This Way to Happiness (Greig), 1931
This Woman to This Man (Williamson), 1917
This Year, Next Year, Sometime— (Ruck), 1932
Thistle and the Rose (Plaidy), 1963
Thomas and Sarah (Hardwick), 1978
Thomas Dryburgh's Dream (Swan), 1886
Thorgils of Treadholt (Hewlett), 1917
Thorn-Apple (Worboys, as Eyre), 1968
Thorn of Arimathea (Slaughter), 1959
Thorn Trees (Thum), 1991
Thornbirds (McCullough), 1977
Thorne's Way (Lorin, as Hohl), 1982
Thornwood (D. Smith), 1966
Thornyhold (Stewart), 1988
Those Difficult Years (Baldwin), 1925
Those Dominant Hills (Barcynska), 1951
Those Endearing Young Charms (Chesney), 1986
Those Fragile Years (Franken), 1952
Those Who Love (Robins), 1936
Those Who Love (Stone), 1965
Thou Shalt Love Thy Neighbour (M. St John), 1927
Thou Shalt Not Kill (Lowndes), 1927
Though I Bid Farewell (Hoy), 1948
Though Worlds Apart (Burchell), 1967
Thought of Honour (Cordell), 1954
Thousandth Man (Ayres), 1939
Threads of Destiny (I. Preston), 1986
Threat of Love (Lamb), 1990
Threat of Possession (S. Wood), 1990
Threats and Promises (Delinsky), 1986
Three Bear Witness (O'Brian), 1952
Three Cedars (Bloom), 1937
Three Continents (Jhabvala), 1987
Three Crowns (Plaidy), 1965
Three Daughters of Madame Liang (Buck), 1969
Three Englishmen (Frankau), 1935
Three Faces of Love (Baldwin), 1957
Three for a Wedding (Neels), 1973
Three Harbours (F. Mason), 1938
Three Kingdoms (Jameson), 1926
Three Lives (L. Cooper), 1957
Three Loves (Lorrimer, as Robins), 1949
Three Marriages (s Delafield), 1939
Three Men and Diana (Norris), 1934
Three Men and Jennie (Jacob), 1960
Three of Hearts (Ruck), 1917
Three of Us (Chandos), 1970
Three Passionate Queens (Bloom, as Prole), 1964
Three People (Grundy), 1926
Three Pilgrims and a Tinker (Borden), 1924
Three Roads to Romance (Chandos), 1945
Three Rooms (Deeping), 1924
Three Sisters (M. Sinclair), 1914
Three Six Seven (Vansittart), 1983
Three Sons (Bloom), 1946
Three Stories of Romance (s Deeping), 1936
Three Stories of Romance (s Frankau), 1936
Three Strings to a Fortune (Worboys, as Eyre), 1962
Three Weeks (Glyn), 1907
Three Weeks in Eden (Weale), 1964
Three Wise Men of Gotham (s Corelli), 1896

Three Women (Baldwin), 1926
Three Women (K. Blair, as Conway), 1955
Three Women (Clarke), 1985
Three Women of Liverpool (Forrester), 1984
Three Years to Play (MacInnes), 1970
Three's Company (Duggan), 1958
Thresholds (Baldwin), 1925
Thrill of the Chase (J. Smith), 1989
Thrill of the Chase (Vitek), 1985
Thrill of Victory (Brown, as St Claire), 1989
Throne Pharaohs (I. Roberts, as I. R. Roberts), 1974
Through a Glass Darkly (Norris), 1957
Through All Eternity (Stanford), 1988
Through All the Years (Summers), 1974
Through Many Waters (Muskett), 1961
Through My Eyes (Delinsky), 1989
Through the Green Woods (Chard), 1974
Through the Mist (Albanesi), 1934
Through the Postern Gate (F. Barclay), 1912
Through Weal and Through Woe (Albanesi, as Rowlands), 1913
Throw Away Yesterday (Ruck), 1946
Throw-Back (Burgin), 1918
Throw Wide the Door (Loring), 1962
Throw Your Bouquet (Mackinlay, as Grey), 1967
Thrown for a Loss (Woods), 1984
Thunder and the Shouting (Nicole), 1969
Thunder Heights (I. Roberts), 1969
Thunder Heights (Whitney), 1960
Thunder in the Hills (Sallis, as Meadmore), 1981
Thunder of Her Heart (Beresford), 1978
Thunder of New Wings (de la Roche), 1932
Thunder on St Paul's Day (Lane), 1954
Thunder on the Right (Stewart), 1957
Thunder Rose (Trask), 1952
Thunder Underground (J. Lindsay), 1965
Thunder's Tender Touch (Finch), 1989
Thunderstorm (Stern), 1925
Thursday and the Lady (Matthews), 1987
Thursday's Child (Baldwin), 1976
Thursday's Child (Brown), 1985
Thursday's Child (Forrester), 1985
Thursday's Children (Godden), 1984
Thurston House (Steel), 1983
Thus Doctor Mallory (Seifert), 1940
Thy Bride Am I (Bloom, as Burns), 1942
Ticket of Destiny (I. Preston), 1969
Ticket-of-Leave Girl (M. St John), 1914
Tidal Wave (s Dell), 1919
Tidal Wave (MacLeod), 1991
Tide at Full (May), 1971
Tide of Life (Cookson), 1976
Tidehawks (Sherwood, as Hines), 1974
Tides of Love (Hunter), 1988
Tides of Love (Matthews), 1981
Tides of Spring Flow Fast (Bloom), 1956
Tides of Tremannion (Shoesmith), 1970
Tidewater Lover (Dailey), 1978
Tidewater Seduction (Mather), 1993
Tidewrack (Tranter), 1951
Tidings of Great Joy (Brown), 1987
Tie That Binds (s E. Porter), 1919
Tied to Her Apron Strings! (M. St John), 1927
Ties of Love (Woodward, as Ware), 1968
Ties That Bind (Krentz), 1986
Ties That Bind (Woods), 1991
Tiffany's True Love (F. Stevenson, as Faire), 1981

Tiger (s Bloom), 1903
Tiger and the Goat (Melville, as Betteridge), 1978
Tiger Hall (Wyndham), 1954
Tiger in His Lair (Wentworth),1986
Tiger in Men (Robins), 1937
Tiger Lilies (Glover), 1991
Tiger Lily (Busbee), 1985
Tiger Lily (Williamson), 1917
Tiger Man (Jordan), 1981
Tiger Prince (Brown, as St Claire), 1985
Tiger Prince (Johansen), 1993
Tiger's Cage (Way), 1986
Tiger's Claw (Burgin), 1900
Tiger's Heaven (P. Hastings), 1981
Tiger's Woman (De Blasis), 1981
Tight White Collar (Metalious), 1960
Tightening String (Bridge), 1962
'Til the End of Time (Johansen), 1987
Till the End of Time (Peake), 1973
Till Then, My Love (M. Lewis), 1968
Tilly (Chesney, as Tremaine), 1981
Tilly Trotter series (Cookson), from 1980
Tilly-Make-Haste (Barcynska, as Sandys), 1924
Tilsit Inheritance (Gaskin), 1963
Tilted Cross (H. Porter), 1961
Tilthammer (Lamb, as Lancaster) , 1980
Tim (McCullough), 1974
Timber Boss (K. Thorpe), 1978
Time after Time (Hooper), 1986
Time After Time (Keane), 1983
Time and Chance (Weale), 1989
Time and the Hour (Baldwin), 1974
Time and the Loving (Lewty), 1977
Time and the Place (Summers), 1958
Time and Tide (Browning), 1984
Time, Flow Softly (Cato), 1960
Time for a Tiger (Burgess), 1956
Time for Another Dream (van der Zee), 1986
Time for Everything (Sallis), 1979
Time for Happiness (Asquith), 1959
Time for Play (Muskett), 1943
Time for Pleasure (P. Hastings), 1957
Time for Rejoicing (Renier), 1973
Time for Silence (Plaidy, as Carr), 1991
Time for Titans (Delmar), 1974
Time for Trust (Jordan), 1990
Time Fuse (Jordan), 1985
Time Is Noon (Buck), 1967
Time May Change (Asquith), 1961
Time No Longer (Caldwell, as Reiner), 1941
Time of Curtain Fall (Hilton), 1976
Time of Dreaming (M. Howard, as Edgar), 1968
Time of Glory (Giles), 1966
Time of the Dragon (Eden), 1975
Time of the Hunter's Moon (Plaidy, as Holt), 1983
Time of the Jacaranda (Way), 1970
Time of the Seventh Moon (I. Roberts, as I. R. Roberts), 1984
Time of the Temptress (Winspear), 1977
Time of Their Lives (s Melville), 1974
Time on Her Hands (Mackinlay), 1942
Time Out of Mind (Field), 1935
Time Out of Mind (K. Thorpe), 1987
Time Piece (Jacob), 1936
Time Remembered (Stratton, as Gillen), 1971
Time Remembered, Time Lost (Randall), 1973
Time Returns (Ripley), 1985

Time Runs Out (Robins, as Kane), 1965
Time Stands Still (Pykare, as Powers), 1983
Time Suspended (MacLeod), 1974
Time to Dance (Bragg), 1990
Time to Dream (Jordan), 1991
Time to Heal (Deeping), 1952
Time to Love (Chard), 1987
Time to Love (Delinsky, as Douglass), 1982
Time to Love (R. Lindsay, as Scott), 1960
Time to Wed (Hunter), 1984
Time Was (N. Roberts), 1989
Timeless Land (Dark), 1941
Times Change (N. Roberts), 1989
Time's Fool (Veryan), 1990
Times of Triumph (C. Allen), 1979
Time/Steps (C. Allen), 1986
Timid Cleopatra (Greig, as Ames), 1962
Tinker's Pride (Tranter), 1945
Tinsel and the Gold (Barcynska, as Sandys), 1959
Tinsel Star (R. Lindsay), 1976
Tinted Dream (Greig, as Ames), 1936
Tiptoes (Barcynska, as Sandys), 1935
Tish series (s Rinehart), from 1911
Titans (Jakes), 1976
Titans (Nicole), 1992
Title Role (Harrod-Eagles, as Bennett), 1980
To an Unknown Shore (Jakes), 1975
To Be a Bride (Chandos, as Tempest), 1945
To Be a King (Chapman), 1934
To Be Beloved (I. Roberts, as Rowland), 1968
To Be So Loved (Chard), 1988
To Be the Best (Bradford), 1988
To Bed at Noon (Bowen, as Shearing), 1951
To Bring You Joy (Summers), 1985
To Buy a Bride (R. Lindsay, as Leigh), 1976
To Buy a Memory (Hampson), 1983
To Cage a Whirlwind (Donnelly), 1985
To Care Always (Norway), 1970
To Catch a Butterfly (Lewty), 1977
To Dance with Kings (Laker), 1988
To Dream Again (I. Preston), 1985
To Dream of Love (Chesney), 1986
To Each Her Dream (McElfresh), 1961
To Everything a Season (Freeman), 1991
To Everything a Season (Glover), 1986
To Follow the Lead (Swan), 1911
To Glory We Steer (Kent), 1968
To Greet the Morning (Ritchie), 1966
To Have and to Hold (M. Johnston), 1900
To Have and to Hold (Palmer), 1979
To Journey Together (Burchell), 1956
To Last a Lifetime (McElfresh, as Blair), 1977
To Lisa with Love (I. Roberts, as Rowland), 1975
To Live with Fear (Chard), 1985
To Look and Pass (Caldwell), 1974
To Love a Hero (Goodwin), 1989
To Love a Rogue (Sherwood), 1987
To Love a Stranger (Laker, as Paul), 1978
To Love Again (Mortimer), 1988
To Love Again (Robins), 1949
To Love Again (Small), 1993
To Love Again (Steel), 1980
To Love and Honour (Saunders), 1992
To Love and to Cherish (Albanesi, as Rowlands), 1912
To Love and to Cherish (Palmer), 1979
To Love and to Honor (Loring), 1950

To Love Is to Live (Robins), 1940
To Marry a Tiger (Hunter, as Chace), 1971
To Meet a Stranger (Plaidy, as Burford), 1957
To Mend a Heart (E. Harrison), 1977
To MLG (Williamson, as A.M. Williamson), 1912
To Mother with Love (s Richards), 1992
To Play with Fire (Kidd), 1977
To Reap a Bitter Harvest (Laffeaty), 1980
To Risks Unknown (Kent, as Reeman), 1969
To Save My Life (Chandos, as Charles), 1946
To See a Fine Lady (Lofts), 1946
To See Ourselves (Field), 1937
To See the Glory (Caldwell), 1963
To Seek a Star (Goodwin, as Ebel), 1973
To Serve Them All My Days (Delderfield), 1972
To Share a Dream (W. Roberts), 1986
To Sing Me Home (D. Smith), 1969
To Slay the Dreamer (Cordell), 1980
To Sleep No More (Lampitt), 1987
To Stay Forever (Steele), 1989
To Tame a Vixen (Hampson), 1978
To Tame a Wild Heart (E. Darcy), 1992
To Tame the Hunter (Krentz, as James), 1983
To Taste the Wine (F. Michaels), 1987
To Tell the Truth (Dailey), 1977
To the Ends of the Earth (Golding), 1991
To the Hilt (Wren), 1937
To the Stars (Lorrimer, as Robins), 1944
To the Valiant (James), 1930
To Trust Tomorrow (Buckingham, as John), 1981
To Wed a Doctor (Seifert), 1968
To Whom Be Glory (F. Mason), 1957
To Whom She Will (Jhabvala), 1955
To Win a Paradise (Hoy), 1947
Toast of the Town (Ley), 1969
Toast to Lady Mary (Leslie), 1954
Tobias and the Angel (Yerby), 1975
Today and Forever (s Buck), 1941
Today Is Mine (Bowen), 1941
To-Day Is Ours (Muskett), 1939
Today Is Yours (Loring), 1938
To-Day We Live (Maybury), 1942
To-day's Daughter (Ruck), 1929
Today's Virtue (Baldwin), 1931
Together (Diver), 1928
Together Again (Kidd), 1979
Together Always (Schulze), 1989
Together and Apart (Kennedy), 1936
Together They Ride (Plaidy), 1945
Toil of the Brave (Fletcher), 1946
Toils of Silence (M. St John, as St John Cooper), 1935
Tokens of Love (s Balogh), 1993
Tokyo Tryst (K. Thorpe), 1987
Tolbecken (Shellabarger), 1956
Told at Monte Carlo (s Williamson, as A.M. Williamson), 1926
Toll-Gate (Heyer), 1954
Tom and Some Other Girls (Vaizey), 1901
Tomalyn's Quest (Burgin), 1896
Tomboy in Lace (Ruck), 1947
Tomorrow-Come Soon (Steele), 1983
Tomorrow Comes the Sun (Renier), 1969
To-morrow for Apricots (Bloom), 1929
To-morrow Is Eternal (Bloom, as Burns), 1948
Tomorrow Is Forever (Bristow), 1943
Tomorrow Is Theirs (Duffield), 1952
Tomorrow the Glory (Pozzessere, as Drake), 1985

Tomorrow We Marry (Bloom, as Burns), 1953
To-morrow's Bargain (MacLeod), 1949
To-morrow's Hero (M. Howard), 1941
Tomorrow's Miracle (Slaughter), 1962
Tomorrow's Promise (Brown), 1983
Tomorrow's Sun (May), 1989
To-morrow's Tangle (Pedler), 1925
Tongues of Conscience (s Hichens), 1900
Tonight and Always (N. Roberts), 1983
To-night, Josephine! (Bloom, as Prole), 1954
Tontine (Costain), 1955
Tony's Memorable Christmas (s Swan), 1883
Tony's Wife (Albanesi), 1919
Too Bad to Be True (R. Lindsay, as Leigh), 1987
Too Close for Comfort (B. Hastings), 1987
Too Close for Comfort (Lamb), 1992
Too Common for Him! (M. St John, as St John Cooper), 1923
Too Few for Drums (Delderfield), 1964
Too Hot to Handle (Hampson), 1982
Too Hot to Handle (Lowell), 1986
Too Late for Tears (M. Lewis), 1972
Too Many Brides (Laffeaty), 1967
Too Many Women (Greig, as Ames), 1941
Too Much Alone (Greig, as Ames), 1950
Too Much Love of Living (Hichens), 1947
Too Much Together (Ayres), 1936
Too Much, Too Soon (Briskin), 1985
Too Near the Fire (McKenna), 1984
Too Old for Her Husband! (M. St John), 1924
Too Precious to Lose (Cartland), 1991
Too Short a Blessing (Jordan), 1987
Too Strong to Deny (E. Darcy), 1990
Too Wild to Wed (Krentz), 1991
Too Wilful for Words! (M. St John), 1915
Too Young for Love (R. Lindsay, as Leigh), 1977
Too Young to Marry (K. Blair, as Brett), 1958
Too Young to Wed (Woodward, as Richmond), 1960
Top of the Beanstalk (Chandos, as Tempest), 1940
Top of the Tree (Albanesi, as Rowlands), 1937
Top of the World (Dell), 1920
Topaz (Bennetts), 1987
Topaz Island (Lorrimer, as Robins), 1965
Tormentil (Chard, as Chase), 1984
Tormenting Flame (Buckingham, as John), 1981
Torpedo Run (Kent, as Reeman), 1981
Torquemada (Fast), 1966
Torrid Nights (McKenna, as Brookes), 1984
Tortoise (Borden), 1921
Total Surrender (M. Pargeter), 1985
Touch a Star (Cartland), 1982
Touch and Go (Parkinson), 1977
Touch Not the Cat (Stewart), 1976
Touch of Fire (L. Howard), 1992
Touch of Glory (Slaughter), 1945
Touch of Honey (Stratton, as Gillen), 1973
Touch of Love (Cartland), 1977
Touch of Magic (Hunter), 1981
Touch of Magic (Summers), 1973
Touch of Max (Hooper), 1993
Touch of Romance (Hampson), 1988
Touch of the Devil (Weale), 1980
Touch of Your Hand (Woodward, as Richmond), 1960
Touch the Horizon (Johansen), 1984
Touch the Wind (Dailey), 1979
Touched by Fire (Donnelly), 1978
Touching the Clouds (Greig), 1936

Touchstone (Muskett), 1962
Touchstone (Wharton), 1900
Tournament (Foote), 1949
Toward the End (Savage), 1980
Toward the Morning (H. Allen), 1948
Towards the Stars, (Cartland), 1971
Towards the Sun (K. Blair, as Brett), 1953
Tower (Steen), 1959
Tower and the Dream (Westcott), 1974
Tower of Kilraven (Crowe), 1965
Tower of Shadows (Craven), 1993
Tower of Strength (Hunter), 1983
Tower of the Captive (Winspear), 1966
Tower of the Winds (Hunter), 1973
Tower Room (Roby), 1974
Towers in the Mist (Goudge), 1938
Towers of Silence (P. Scott), 1971
Town House (Lofts), 1959
Town Like Alice (Shute), 1950
Town Nurse—Country Nurse (Lewty), 1970
Town That Nearly Died (M. Lewis), 1973
Townsman (Buck, as Sedges), 1945
Toy Sword (Cadell), 1962
Traceys (Bromige), 1946
Trackless Way (Bloom), 1931
Tradd Family series (Ripley), from 1981
Trade Wind (Kaye), 1963
Trader's Cay (Stratton), 1980
Trading Secrets (Krentz, as Castle), 1985
Tradition of Pride (Dailey), 1982
Tradition of Victory (Kent), 1981
Traficante Treasure (Winston), 1968
Trail of Conflict (Loring), 1922
Trailing Glory (Bloom), 1940
Train at Bundarbar (McCutchan, as MacNeil), 1981
Traitor (Dixon), 1907
Traitor (s Orczy), 1912
Traitors (Stuart, as Long), 1981
Traitors' Gate (Gavin), 1976
Traitors' Legion (Jakes, as Scotland), 1963
Traitor's Son (Heaven, as Fecher), 1967
Trampling of the Lilies (Sabatini), 1906
Tranquil Haven (MacLeod), 1946
Transformation of Philip Jettan (Heyer, as Martin), 1923
Transplant (Slaughter), 1987
Transplanted (Niven), 1944
Trap (Winston), 1973
Trap for Navarre (Wynne), 1922
Trapped (Roby), 1977
Travelers (Jhabvala), 1973
Traveling Man (Lowell), 1985
Traveller in the Fur Coat (Weyman), 1924
Travellers (Stubbs), 1963
Travelling Kind (Dailey), 1981
Travelling Man (Joseph), 1990
Travis series (McKenna), from 1985
Tread Softly (Miles), 1926
Tread Softly in the Sun (Worboys, as Eyre), 1969
Tread Softly, Nurse (Norway, as Neal), 1962
Tread Softly on Dreams (Mackinlay, as Grey), 1970
Treason in November (Dymoke), 1961
Treason's Gift (Belle), 1992
Treason's Harbour (O'Brian), 1983
Treasure (Norris), 1914
Treasure Chest (Roby), 1976
Treasure for Life (Weale), 1972

Treasure Hunt (Keane, as Farrell), 1952
Treasure Hunt (Seger), 1986
Treasure Is Love (Cartland), 1979
Treasure of Heaven (Corelli), 1906
Treasure of Pleasant Valley (Yerby), 1955
Treasure of the Lake (Haggard), 1926
Treasure Worth Seeking (Brown, as Ryan), 1982
Treasures Lost, Treasures Found (N. Roberts), 1986
Treasures (Nicole, as Gray), 1984
Treasures (Plain), 1992
Treasures on Earth (Stirling), 1985
Treasury of du Maurier Short Stories (s du Maurier), 1960
Tree Drops a Leaf (Ayres), 1938
Tree of Gold (Laker), 1986
Tree of Heaven (M. Sinclair), 1917
Tree of Idleness (Hunter), 1973
Tree of Man (White), 1955
Tree of Vortigern (Wiat), 1976
Treehaven (Norris), 1932
Trees Die at the Top) (Ferber), 1938
Tregaran (Lide), 1989
Tregaron's Daughter (Brent), 1971
Trelawney's Woman (Laffeaty), 1988
Trellised Walk (Manners, as Marshall), 1973
Trembling Hills (Whitney), 1956
Trespass (Tranter), 1937
Trespasser (Donnelly), 1992
Trespassing Hearts (Ellis), 1992
Trevelyan's Little Daughter (Sheard), 1898
Trevithick (P. Hill), 1989
Trial Marriage (Mather), 1977
Trial of Innocence (Hufford), 1978
Trial of Sören Qvist (J. Lewis), 1947
Trickster (Burgin), 1909
Tricolour (Nicole, as Logan), 1976
Trilby (Palmer), 1993
Trio (Bentley), 1930
Triple Tangle (Saxton, as Turner), 1981
Tristam of Blent (Hope), 1901
Triton Brig (Pope), 1969
Triumph (Gann), 1986
Triumph (Nicole), 1989
Triumph of Love (Albanesi, as Rowlands), 1911
Triumph of O'Rourke (Cleeve), 1972
Triumph of the Rat (Robins), 1927
Triumph of Time (Jameson), 1932
Triumph of Time series (Jameson), from 1927
Triumphant Beast (Bowen), 1934
Trojan Gold (B. Michaels, as Peters), 1987
Tropical Affair (Beresford), 1967
Tropical Affairs (Beresford), 1978
Tropical Fire (Saunders, as Innes), 1992
Tropical Issue (Dunnett), 1991
Tropical Tempest (Kidd), 1983
Troubadour's Romance (Carr), 1985
Trouble on Tour (K. Thorpe), 1991
Trouble with Andrew (Pozzessere), 1993
Trouble with Jared (Hooper), 1993
Trouble with Joe (Richards), 1994
Trouble with Product X (Aiken), 1966
Troubled Waters (Sallis), 1975
Troubles (Farrell), 1970
Troy Chimneys (Kennedy), 1952
Truant Happiness (Albanesi), 1918
Truant Wife (s Swan), 1899
Truce of God (Rinehart), 1920

Two Men and Gwenda (Grundy), 1910
Two Miss Speckles (Grundy), 1946
Two Mrs Abbotts (D. Stevenson), 1943
Two Names under the Shore (Ertz), 1947
Two of a Kind (Hampson), 1974
Two of Us (Greig, as Ames), 1964
Two Other People (Chandos), 1964
Two Paths (MacLeod), 1944
Two Pools in a Field (Bloom), 1967
Two Queen Annes (Bloom, as Prole), 1971
Two Ravens (Holland), 1977
Two Saplings (de la Roche), 1942
Two Selfish People (James), 1942
Two Studies (Richardson), 1931
Two Valleys (Fast), 1933
Two Waifs (Albanesi, as Rowlands), 1914
Two Walk Together (Mackinlay), 1945
Two Weeks to Remember (Neels), 1986
Two's Company . . . (M. St John, as St John Cooper), 1923
Two's Company (Woods), 1987
Tyler (Palmer), 1988
Tyrant (Veryan), 1987
Tysons (M. Sinclair), 1906
Tzigane (E. Smith), 1935

Ugly Dachshund (Stern), 1938
Ugly Head (Bloom), 1965
Ugly Prince (Chandos, as Storm), 1950
Ukelele Girl (MacGill), 1927
Ultima Thule (Richardson), 1929
Ultimate Choice (E. Darcy), 1989
Ultimate Prizes (Howatch), 1989
Ultimate Surrender (Chandos, as Charles), 1958
Ultimatum (Wentworth), 1987
Ulysses Too Many (Jameson), 1958
Unacceptable Offer (Balogh), 1988
Unbaited Trap (Cookson), 1966
Unbidden Dream (Marsh), 1981
Unbidden Melody (Burchell), 1973
Unborn Tomorrow (Frankau), 1953
Unbreakable Bond (Donald), 1986
Unbreakable Spell (Cartland), 1984
Unbroken Marriage (Jordan), 1982
Uncertain Destiny (Mortimer), 1988
Uncertain Heart (Chard), 1976
Uncertain Heart (Robins), 1949
Uncertain Joy (Lorrimer, as Robins), 1966
Uncertain Summer (Neels), 1972
Uncharted Romance (M. Howard), 1941
Uncharted Seas (Loring), 1932
Uncle Bernac (Doyle), 1897
Uncle Jeremy (Burgin), 1920
Uncle Patterley's Money (Burgin), 1936
Uncle Peel (Bacheller), 1933
Unconquered (Diver), 1917
Unconquered (Small), 1982
Unconquered (Swanson), 1947
Uncrowned King (Orczy), 1935
Uncrowned Queen (Harwood), 1983
Uncut Jade (Barr), 1983
Undarkening Green (Bloom), 1959
Undaunted (Lane), 1934
Undefended Gate (Ertz), 1953
Under a Ban (M. St John), 1907
Under Castle Walls (Bailey), 1906
Under False Colours (Woodman), 1991

Under False Pretences (Ruck), 1922
Under Fire (McKenna), 1991
Under Gemini (Pilcher), 1976
Under Heaven (Clarke), 1988
Under Joint Management (Burchell), 1947
Under Moonglow (Hampson), 1978
Under New Management (Jacob), 1941
Under the Big Top (Barcynska), 1933
Under the Red Robe (Weyman), 1894
Under the Sky (Lorrimer, as Robins), 1970
Under the Stars of Paris (Burchell), 1954
Under Which King (Niven), 1943
Undercover (Seger), 1986
Underground Stream (V. Johnston), 1992
Underground Syndicate (Williamson, as A.M. Williamson), 1910
Understudy (Ruck), 1933
Undertow (Norris), 1917
Undesirable Wife (Hunter, as Chace), 1978
Undressed Heroine (Grundy), 1916
Undying Love (Mortimer), 1983
Unearthly (Hichens), 1926
Uneaseful Death (Hardwick), 1988
Uneasy Alliance (Krentz), 1984
Uneasy Conquest (Mackinlay), 1959
Uneasy Eden (Laffeaty), 1970
Uneasy Lies the Head (Plaidy), 1982
Uneasy Summer (James), 1960
Uneducating Mary (Norris), 1923
Unfinished (Harrod-Eagles, as Bennett), 1983
Unfinished Portrait (Westmacott), 1934
Unforgettable Caress (Vitek), 1984
Unforgettable (Seger), 1988
Unforgiven (M. Lewis), 1974
Unforgiving Moment (Cowen), 1971
Unforgotten Face (M. Peters, as Whitby), 1975
Unforgotten (Winston), 1973
Unframed Portrait (Albanesi), 1935
Unfriendly Alliance (Steele), 1987
Unfriendly Proposition (Steele), 1989
Unfulfilled (Hardy), 1951
Ungrateful Governess (Balogh), 1988
Unguarded Hour (MacLeod, as Airlie), 1956
Unguarded Moment (Craven), 1982
Unhallowed House (Ponsonby), 1956
Unhappy Bargain (Albanesi, as Rowlands)
Unholy Desires (S. Blake), 1981
Unholy Woman (Plaidy), 1954
Unhurrying Chase (Prescott), 1925
Unicorn (Steen), 1931
Unicorn Hunt (Dunnett), 1993
Unicorn Rampant (Tranter), 1984
Unicorn Summer (Martin), 1984
Uninvited Guest (Chandos, as Tempest), 1939
Uninvited Guest (Swan), 1939
United States Navy series (Nicole), from 1986
Unjust Skies (Delderfield), 1962
Unkissed Bride (Ruck), 1929
Unknown Ajax (Heyer), 1959
Unknown Eros (Moore), 1935
Unknown Heart (Cartland), 1969
Unknown Joy (Chandos, as Tempest), 1941
Unknown Lover (Vaizey), 1913
Unknown Quantity (Dell), 1924
Unknown Shore (O'Brian), 1959
Unknown Welshman (Stubbs), 1972
Unless I Marry (Stern), 1959

Unless Two Be Agreed (Pedler), 1947
Unlikely Duchess (Balogh), 1990
Unlikely Lover (Palmer), 1986
Unlikely Romance (Neels), 1992
Unlit Fire (Robins), 1960
Unlit Heart (Stuart), 1954
Unlit Lamp (Hall), 1924
Unlived Year (MacLeod, as Airlie), 1962
Unmarried Couple (Greig), 1940
Unmasking (Richards), 1985
Unmasking Kelsey (Hooper), 1988
Unnamed Gentlewoman (Ponsonby), 1976
Unofficial Wife (Ayres), 1937
Unpredictable Bride (Cartland), 1964
Unpredictable Man (E. Darcy), 1986
Unquiet (Matthews), 1991
Unquiet Spirit (Steen), 1955
Unreasonable Summer (Browning), 1980
Unrest (Deeping), 1916
Unseen To-morrow (MacLeod), 1943
Unseen Witness (Wynne), 1932
Unshaken Loyalty (Robins), 1955
Unspoken Desire (Jordan), 1990
Unsuspected Witness (Wynne), 1945
Untamed (Lowell), 1993
Untamed (Mortimer), 1983
Untamed (N. Roberts), 1983
Untamed Bride (O. Sinclair, as Daniels), 1988
Untamed Desire (McKenna, as Brookes), 1983
Untamed Heart (M. Howard), 1940
Until I Find Her (Chandos, as Tempest), 1950
Until the Day Break (Bromfield), 1942
Until the Sun Falls (Holland), 1969
Until Tomorrow (Walsh), 1992
Until We Met (Weale), 1961
Untitled Story (Byrne), 1925
Unto Caesar (Orczy), 1914
Untouched Wife (R. Lindsay), 1981
Unusual Affair (Armstrong), 1992
Unusual Behaviour (L. Cooper), 1986
Unusual Tutor (Ponsonby), 1967
Unvanquished (Fast), 1942
Unwanted Bride (Hampson), 1982
Unwanted Heiress (M. St John, as St John Cooper), 1924
Unwanted Wedding (Cartland), 1984
Unwanted Wife (R. Lindsay), 1976
Unwary Heart (Hampson), 1969
Unwilling Bride (Winspear), 1969
Unwilling Bridegroom (R. Lindsay, as Leigh), 1976
Unwilling Desire (Mortimer), 1984
Unwinding Corner (Dwyer-Joyce), 1983
Unwise Wanderer (Mackinlay), 1952
Upas Tree (F. Barclay), 1912
Uphill Path (Mackinlay), 1979
Uphill Road (Ayres), 1921
Upon a Moon-Dark Moor (Brandewyne), 1988
Upon This Rock (Slaughter), 1963
Ups and Downs (Swan), 1878
Upstairs, Downstairs series (Hardwick), from 1973
Upstairs Lover (E. Darcy), 1993
Upstart (E. Marshall), 1945
Urbinian (Sabatini), 1924
Ursula Vivian, The Sister-Mother (Swan), 1884
Used-To-Be Lovers (Miller), 1988
Usurper (Garvice)
Uther and Igraine (Deeping), 1903

Utility Husband (Chandos, as Tempest), 1944
Utterly Alone! (M. St John), 1928
Uttermost Farthing (Lowndes), 1908

Vaaldorp Diamond (Drummond, as Dane), 1978
Vacant Possession (Mantel), 1986
Vacation for Nurse Dean (Ritchie, as Heath), 1966
Vacillations of Hazel (Grundy), 1905
Vacillations of Poppy Carew (Wesley), 1986
Vagabond Daughter (Mackinlay), 1955
Vagabond Harvest (Bloom), 1925
Vagabond Jess (M. St John, as St John Cooper), 1919
Vagabonds (Cox), 1990
Vagabond's Daughter (M. St John, as St John Cooper), 1922
Vagabond's Way (Leslie), 1962
Vagrant Dream (Ritchie), 1959
Vagrant Lover (Bloom, as Burns), 1945
Vail d'Alvery (Keyes), 1946
Vain Delights (Mackinlay), 1962
Vaisseau Fanôme (R. Marshall), 1933
Valaquez Bride (Vitek), 1982
Valdez Marriage (Winspear), 1978
Valentina (Anthony), 1966
Valentina (F. Michaels), 1978
Valentine's Night (Jordan), 1989
Valerie (J. Smith), 1981
Valiant Dust (Wren), 1932
Valiant Sailors (Stuart), 1964
Valley Deep, Mountain High (Mather), 1976
Valley Forge (Kantor), 1975
Valley Forge (F. Mason), 1950
Valley of Aloes (May), 1967
Valley of Bells (I. Roberts, as Rowland), 1967
Valley of Decision (Wharton), 1902
Valley of Desire (MacLeod, as Airlie), 1955
Valley of Fire (Taylor), 1984
Valley of Flowers (K. Blair), 1957
Valley of Heartache (Laffeaty), 1969
Valley of Horses (Auel), 1982
Valley of Lilacs (Chappell), 1972
Valley of Night (Farnol), 1942
Valley of Nightingales (Renier), 1966
Valley of Palms (MacLeod), 1950
Valley of Roses (Maybury), 1945
Valley of Secrets (Renier), 1970
Valley of Tall Chimneys (Manners, as Marshall), 1975
Valley of the Kings (Holland, as Carter), 1977
Valley of the Moon (Way), 1979
Valley of the Ravens (Buckingham), 1973
Valley of the Reindeer (Laker, as Óvstedal), 1973
Valley of the Snows (MacLeod), 1985
Valley of the Sun (Lowell), 1985
Valley of the Vapours (Dailey), 1976
Valley of Yesterday (Worboys, as Eyre), 1965
Valour (Deeping), 1918
Vampire Curse (Winston), 1971
Vanderlyn's Adventure (Lowndes), 1931
Vanessa (Fellows), 1978
Vanessa (Walpole), 1933
Vanish with the Rose (B. Michaels), 1992
Vanished (Steel), 1993
Vanity Box (Williamson, as Stuyvesant), 1911
Vanquished Heart (Hoy), 1949
Vanzant Family series (Lorin, as Hohl), from 1987
Variation on a Theme (Delinsky, as Douglass), 1985
Variations (s Lorrimer), 1991

Vital Signs (B. Wood), 1985
Vittoria Cottage (D. Stevenson), 1949
Vivian Inheritance (Stubbs), 1982
Vixen in Velvet (F. Michaels), 1976
Vixens (Yerby), 1947
Vixen's Revenge (Blackstock, as Allardyce), 1980
Voice in the Dark (Lorrimer), 1967
Voice in the Darkness (Bennetts), 1979
Voice in the Night (V. Johnston), 1984
Voice in the Thunder (Hunter), 1975
Voice in the Wind (Rivers), 1993
Voice of Bugle Ann (Kantor), 1935
Voice of the Dolls (Eden), 1950
Voice of the Heart (Bradford), 1983
Voice of the People (Glasgow), 1900
Voices from the Dust (s Farnol), 1932
Voices in a Haunted Room (Plaidy, as Carr), 1984
Voices in an Empty House (Aiken), 1975
Voices in Summer (Pilcher), 1984
Voices in the Night (Norway), 1973
Voices Long Hushed (Pauley), 1976
Voices of Summer (Pearson), 1992
Voices on the Wind (Anthony), 1985
Volcano Lover (Sontag), 1992
Vollands (P. Hill), 1990
Volunteer Nurse (Duffield), 1942
Voodoo (Shellabarger, as Esteven), 1930
Voss (White), 1957
Vote for Love (Cartland), 1977
Vow (Schulze), 1990
Vow of Chastity (M. Peters, as Black), 1991
Vow of Silence (M. Peters, as Black), 1991
Vow on the Heron (Plaidy), 1980
Vows (Spencer), 1988
Vows series (Woods), from 1993
Voyage East (Woodman), 1988
Voyage Home (Jameson), 1930
Voyage of Destiny (I. Preston), 1974
Voyage of the Destiny (Nye), 1982
Voyage to Santa Fe (Giles), 1962
Voyage Unplanned (Yerby), 1974

Wade Dynasty (Mortimer), 1986
Wager (Woodman), 1990
Wager for Love (Courtney), 1979
Wagered Weekend (Krentz, as Castle), 1981
Wagered Widow (Veryan), 1984
Wages of Virtue (Wren), 1916
Wagon to a Star (Greig), 1952
Waif of the River (Farnol), 1952
Waif's Wedding (Ayres), 1921
Wait for Night (Cowen), 1980
Wait for Tomorrow (Robins), 1967
Wait for What Will Come (B. Michaels), 1978
Waiting (van der Zee), 1982
Waiting at the Church (Blackstock, as Allardyce), 1968
Waiting Darkness (W. Roberts), 1970
Waiting for Willa (Eden), 1970
Waiting Game (Cadell), 1985
Waiting Game (Harrod-Eagles), 1972
Waiting Game (Krentz), 1985
Waiting Game (Palmer, as Blayne), 1982
Waiting Room (Norway, as Norton), 1961
Waiting Sands (Howatch), 1966
Waiting Wives (Pemberton, as Harland), 1991
Wake the Sleeping Tiger (Way), 1978

Wakefield's Course (de la Roche), 1941
Walk a Tightrope (Ellis), 1975
Walk in the Dark (Summerton, as Roffman), 1969
Walk in the Paradise Garden (Maybury), 1972
Walk in the Wood (Gilbert), 1989
Walk into Darkness (Ellis), 1973
Walk into My Parlour (Eden), 1947
Walk into My Parlour (Lofts), 1975
Walk into My Parlour (Randall), 1962
Walker (s O'Brian), 1955
Walker in Shadows (B. Michaels), 1979
Walking to Wonderland (Cartland), 1992
Wall (Rinehart), 1938
Wall (Vansittart), 1990
Wall of Partition (F. Barclay), 1914
Wallace (Tranter), 1975
Wallflower (Ayres), 1940
Walls of Gold (Norris), 1933
Walsingham Woman (Westcott), 1953
Waltz-Contest (Ruck), 1941
Waltz of Hearts (Cartland), 1980
Wanderers (s M. Johnston), 1917
Wanderers Eastward, Wanderers West (Winsor), 1965
Wanderer's Necklace (Haggard), 1914
Wandering Knife (Rinehart), 1952
Wandering Prince (Plaidy), 1956
Wandering Stars (Dane), 1924
Wanderings of Wenamen (J. Lindsay), 1936
Wanderlust (Steel), 1986
Wanted—a Wedding Ring (Cartland), 1987
Wanted—Girl Friday (Mackinlay), 1968
Wanted on the Voyage (s Ruck), 1930
Wanting (Jordan), 1984
Wanton (Rogers), 1983
Wanton Angel (Miller), 1987
Wanton Way (James), 1931
War and Passion (Nicole, as Arlen), 1981
War Changes Everything (Robins), 1943
War Marriage (Robins), 1942
War of the Roses series (Jarman), from 1971
War series (E. Pargeter), from 1945
War Surgeon (Slaughter), 1967
War to End Wars (Hardwick), 1975
War Wedding (Williamson), 1916
War-Workers (Delafield), 1918
Ward of Darkness (James), 1971
Ward of Lucifer (Burchell), 1947
Warden of the Queen's March (Tranter), 1989
Warfare Accomplished (E. Pargeter), 1947
Waring, Sir Robert series (Goodwin, as Ebel), from 1968
Warleggan 1792–1793 (Graham), 1953
Warm Side of the Island (Browning, as Dozier), 1977
Warm Wind of Farik (Stratton), 1975
Warmed by the Fire (Vitek), 1983
Warned by a Ghost (Cartland), 1991
Warner's Chase (Swan), 1884
Warrick (Harris), 1985
Warrior (Lowell), 1991
Warrior (Slaughter), 1956
Warrior King (Clarke, as Honeyman), 1972
Warrior King (Leslie), 1977
Warrior Queen (Staples, as J. Sinclair), 1977
Warriors (Jakes), 1977
Warrior's Woman (Lindsey), 1990
Wars (Findley), 1977
Wartime Beauty (s Bloom), 1943

Warwhoop (Kantor), 1952
Warwyck series (Laker), from 1979
Wary Widow (Walsh), 1985
Was She Sweetheart or Wife? (Libbey)
Washington, DC (Vidal), 1967
Washington, USA (Baldwin), 1943
Wasted Love (Garvice, as Hart)
Waster (Garvice), 1918
Watch the North Wind Rise (Graves), 1949
Watch the Wall, My Darling (Hodge), 1966
Watch the Wall My Darling (Hunter), 1963
Watchers (W. Roberts), 1971
Watchgods (B. Wood), 1980
Watchman's Stone (Randall), 1975
Water Meadows (E. Blair), 1993
Waterfall (L. Walker, as Sanders), 1956
Waterfalls of the Moon (Mather), 1973
Waterfront Hospital (Norway), 1961
Watermen (Michener), 1979
Waters of Conflict (Woodward, as Richmond), 1969
Waters on a Starry Night (Ogilvie), 1968
Watershed (Pizzey), 1983
Watershed (Tranter), 1941
Wave (E. Scott), 1929
Waves of Destiny (s Pedler), 1924
Waves of Fire (Hampson), 1971
Way Back Home (Richards), 1990
Way Beyond (Farnol), 1933
Way Home (Richardson), 1925
Way in the Dark (MacLeod), 1956
Way Men Love (Chandos, as Charles), 1967
Way of a Man (Hilton), 1981
Way of a Tyrant (Hampson), 1974
Way of Ambition (Hichens), 1913
Way of an Eagle (Dell), 1911
Way of Compassion (Maybury), 1933
Way of Escape (Swan), 1935
Way of Man (Dixon), 1919
Way of the Spirit (Haggard), 1906
Way of the Tamarisk (Worboys, as Maxwell), 1974
Way of Youth (Albanesi, as Rowlands), 1925
Way Out (Burgin), 1900
Way the Wind Blows (Asquith), 1963
Way Things Are (Delafield), 1927
Way Through the Valley (MacLeod), 1971
Way to the Lantern (Erskine-Lindop), 1961
Way Up (Hardwick), 1976
Way We Used to Be (Chandos, as Tempest), 1965
Ways of Love (MacLeod, as Airlie), 1955
Wayside Flower (May), 1982
Wayside Tavern (Lofts), 1980
Wayward as the Swallow (Chandos, as Charles), 1970
Wayward Heart (Marsh), 1989
Wayward Madonna (M. Peters, as Black), 1970
Wayward Wife (Wentworth), 1992
We All Have Our Secrets (Ruck), 1955
We Are for the Dark (Eden), 1944
We Are Ten (s Hurst), 1937
We Have Come to a Country (L. Cooper), 1935
We Lost Our Way (Barcynska), 1948
We Parted at the Altar (Libbey), 1892
We Ride the Gale! (Loring), 1934
We Speak No Treason (Jarman), 1971
We Two Together (Robins), 1959
We Want Our Mummy! (M. St John), 1922
We Women! (Barcynska), 1923

Wealth of the Islands (Hunter, as Chace), 1971
Wear a Green Kirtle (Wiat), 1987
Weathercock (Maddocks), 1971
Weave Me a Moonbeam (I. Roberts), 1982
Weave Me Some Wings (M. Howard), 1947
Web of Dreams (T. Barclay), 1988
Web of Love (Balogh), 1990
Web of Love (Hoy), 1952
Web of Passion (Buckingham, as John), 1982
Web of Silver (Stratton, as Gillen), 1974
Webs (Barcynska), 1922
Wed to Earth (James), 1955
Wedded—But Alone! (M. St John), 1930
Wedded But Not Wooed (M. St John), 1920
Wedding (E. Darcy), 1992
Wedding Bell Blues (Pozzessere), 1991
Wedding Bells for Willow (Chandos, as Tempest), 1956
Wedding Day (Williamson), 1914
Wedding Dress (Burchell), 1962
Wedding Guest (Gilbert), 1993
Wedding Journey (Edmonds), 1947
Wedding March (Ruck), 1938
Wedding of Kitty Barton (s Swan), 1898
Wedding of the Year (Weale), 1982
Week by the Sea (Gibbs, as Ford), 1962
Week-end Bride (Bloom, as Burns), 1939
Weekend in the Garden (Andrews), 1981
Week-End Marriage (Baldwin), 1932
Week-End Woman (Ayres), 1939
Weep and Know Why (Ogilvie), 1972
Weep Not for Dreams (Bloom, as Harvey), 1968
Weeping and the Laughter (Barber), 1988
Weeping and the Laughter (Chard), 1975
Weeping Ash (Aiken), 1980
Weir House (Muskett), 1962
Welcome Light (Stirling), 1991
Welcome to Hard Times (Doctorow), 1960
Well of Loneliness (Hall), 1928
Welles series (Coulter), from 1982
Wellington Wendy (Barcynska, as Sandys), 1941
Well-Matched Pair (Bishop), 1987
Well-Painted Passion (Harrod-Eagles, as Woodhouse), 1976
Wellspring (s Giles), 1975
Welsh series (Cordell), from 1959
Wendy Craig's Nanny (T. Barclay, as Bowden), 1981
Were I Thy Bride (Robins), 1936
We're Not Wanted Now! (M. St John, as St John Cooper), 1921
Wessex series (Anand), from 1977
West of Bohemia (Steele), 1993
West of Sunset (Anand), 1992
West Riding series (Bentley), from 1952
West Wind (Baldwin), 1962
West Wind Drift (McCutcheon), 1920
West with the Vikings (E. Marshall), 1961
Westerbury Inheritance (Chesney), 1982
Westerbury Sisters (Chesney), 1983
Westerfalca (Wiat), 1979
Western (Yerby), 1982
Western Man (Dailey), 1983
Western series (Lowell), from 1991
Westward to Laughter (MacInnes), 1969
Westward to My Love (Chandos, as Tempest), 1944
Wexford (Ellis), 1976
What a Man Wills (s Vaizey), 1915
What a Woman Can Do! (M. St John), 1917
What Became of Anna Bolton (Bromfield), 1944

What Dreams May Come (Hooper), 1991
What Emily Wants (F. Preston), 1993
What Happened Is This (Hutten), 1938
What I Found Out in the House of a German Prince (Williamson, as A.M. Williamson), 1915
What Is Love? (Delafield), 1928
What Matters Most (Robins), 1942
What of the Night? (s Lowndes), 1943
What Really Happened (Lowndes), 1926
What Shall It Profit? (Swan), 1910
What She Could (s Swan), 1898
What the Heart Keeps (Laker), 1984
What the Heart Says (Price), 1956
What Then Is Love (Loring), 1956
What Timmy Did (Lowndes), 1921
What We're Here For (Norway, as Norton), 1966
What You Made Me (Jordan), 1985
Whatagirl (Barcynska, as Sandys), 1939
What's-His-Name (McCutcheon), 1911
What's to Come (Jacob), 1958
Wheat Princess (Webster), 1905
Wheel of Fortune (Howatch), 1984
Wheel of Life (Glasgow), 1906
Wheels of Chance (MacLeod, as Airlie), 1964
Wheels of Fate (Burgin), 1933
Wheels of Time (F. Barclay), 1908
When a Girl's Pretty (M. St John), 1914
When a Man Loves (M. St John, as St John Cooper), 1931
When a Man Marries (Rinehart), 1909
When a Woman Doctor Loves (Bloom, as Essex), 1969
When a Woman Loves (Robins, as Chesterton), 1955
When All the World Is Young (Plaidy, as Burford), 1943
When Birds Do Sing (Kidd), 1970
When Clouds Part (Hampson), 1973
When Doctors Disagree (Franken, as Meloney), 1940
When Doctors Love (Bloom, as Burns), 1964
When Doctors Marry (Seifert), 1960
When Dreams Come True (E. Blair), 1987
When Dreams Come True (Burgin), 1932
When First I Loved . . . (Chandos, as Tempest), 1938
When Four Ways Meet (Chandos), 1961
When Hearts Are Light Again (Loring), 1943
When His Hour Came (Glyn), 1915
When His Love Grew Cold (Libbey), 1895
When I Say Goodbye, I'm Clary Brown (Blackstock, as Keppel), 1977
When Lightning Strikes (Donnelly), 1980
When Love Awaits (Lindsey), 1986
When Love Comes (Hampson), 1983
When Love Compels (M. St John, as St John Cooper), 1933
When Love Is Blind (Burchell), 1967
When Love Is Young (Garvice)
When Love Isn't Enough (Seidel), 1984
When Love Meets Love (Garvice), 1906
When Love Was Like That (s Joseph), 1991
When Lovely Maiden Stoops to Folly (Libbey), 1896
When Lovers Meet (Kidd), 1987
When Love's Beginning (Burchell), 1954
When May Follows (Neels), 1980
When Michael Came to Town (Albanesi), 1917
When Next We Love (Pozzessere, as Graham), 1983
When No Man Pursueth (Lowndes), 1910
When Other Hearts (Plaidy, as Burford), 1955
When Paris Fell (Bloom, as Prole), 1976
When Sparrows Fall (Salverson), 1925
When Terror Ruled (Wynne), 1907

When the Bough Breaks (Hampson), 1970
When the Bough Breaks (s Mitchison), 1924
When the Devil Drives (Craven), 1991
When the Dream Fades (Hoy), 1980
When the Gallows Is High (P. Hastings), 1971
When the Journey's Over (Chard), 1981
When the Loving Stopped (Steele), 1988
When the Music Stopped (Ogilvie), 1989
When the Night Grows Cold (Armstrong), 1987
When the Splendor Falls (McBain), 1985
When the Sun Goes Down (Blackstock), 1965
When the Wind Blows (Steen), 1931
When the Witch Is Dead (Roby), 1972
When the World Shook (Haggard), 1919
When There's Love at Home (M. St John), 1925
When There's Love at Home (Woodward, as Richmond), 1959
When Three Walk Together (Chandos), 1939
When Time Stands Still (Chandos), 1946
When Two Paths Meet (Neels), 1988
When We Are Married (Plaidy, as Burford), 1953
When We Two Parted (Chandos), 1940
When We're Alone (Donnelly), 1989
When Women Love (s Delafield), 1938
When You Have Found Me (Hoy), 1951
Where Are You Going? (Ayres), 1946
Where Beauty Dwells (Loring), 1941
Where Breezes Falter (May), 1970
Where Duty Lies (Lorrimer, as Robins), 1957
Where Eagles Nest (Hampson), 1980
Where Enchantment Lies (McKenna, as Brookes), 1986
Where Flamingoes Fly (I. Roberts), 1966
Where Is Holly Carleton? (Ellis, as Marvin), 1974
Where Is Love? (Cartland), 1971
Where Is My Child To-night? (M. St John), 1925
Where Is the Voice Coming From? (s Wiebe), 1974
Where Love Leads (Garvice), 1907
Where No Man Cries (E. Blair), 1982
Where No Roads Go (Summers), 1963
Where Ratas Twine (I. Preston), 1960
Where Satan Dwells (F. Stevenson), 1971
Where Shall I Wander? (Burchell), 1942
Where Stars May Lead (I. Preston), 1978
Where the Cigale Sings (O. Sinclair), 1976
Where the Dream Begins (Chard), 1982
Where the Heart Is (Chandos, as Tempest), 1955
Where the Heart Is (Vitek), 1981
Where the Hills Reply (Laffeaty), 1991
Where the Lost Aprils Are (Ogilvie), 1975
Where the Path Breaks (Williamson, as de Crespigny), 1916
Where the Rivers Meet (Ellerbeck, as Thorne), 1982
Where There Are Women (Barcynska, as Barclay), 1915
Where There's a Will (Rinehart), 1912
Where There's Smoke (Brown), 1993
Where Three Roads Meet (Dell), 1935
Which Woman? (Burgin), 1907
While Faith Endures (Albanesi, as Rowlands), 1929
While Murder Waits (Shellabarger, as Esteven), 1936
While Passion Sleeps (Busbee), 1983
While the Fire Rages (Lorin), 1984
While the Gentleman Go By (Laffeaty, as Carstens), 1977
While the Music Lasts (Goodwin), 1992
Whim of Fate (MacLeod), 1940
Whip (Cookson), 1983
Whirlpool of Passion (E. Darcy), 1987
Whirlwind (Clavell), 1986
Whirlwind (Lamb), 1987

Whirlwind Courtship (Krentz, as Taylor), 1979
Whisper in the Dark (Maybury, as Troy), 1961
Whisper My Name (F. Michaels), 1981
Whisper of Darkness (Mather), 1980
Whisper of Doubt (Weale, as Blake), 1965
Whisper of Sea-Bells (I. Roberts), 1964
Whisper on the Wind (J. Smith), 1990
Whisper to Me of Love (Busbee), 1992
Whisper Who Dares (M. Lewis), 1983
Whisper Wind (Stanford), 1981
Whispered Kisses (Taylor), 1990
Whispered Promise (Delinsky, as Drake), 1982
Whispering Dark (Saunders, as Innes), 1976
Whispering Grove (Hilton), 1971
Whispering Palms (K. Blair, as Brett), 1954
Whispering Sea (Stratton, as Gillen), 1971
Whispers (Plain), 1993
Whispers in the Sun (Greig), 1949
Whispers of Love (Finch, as Robins), 1991
Whistle and I'll Come (Kidd), 1966
Whistle for the Crows (Eden), 1962
Whistledown Woman (Cox), 1989
Whistling Thorn (Hunter, as Chace), 1977
White Abbey (Albanesi, as Rowlands), 1911
White Banners (L. Douglas), 1936
White Blooms of Yarrow (Saunders, as Innes), 1976
White Boy (Nicole), 1966
White Branches (Albanesi), 1933
White Christmas (Hurst), 1942
White Christmas in Saigon (Pemberton, as Harland), 1990
White Cockade (Dymoke), 1979
White Cockade (MacLeod), 1960
White-Collar Girl (Baldwin), 1933
White Company (Doyle), 1891
White Crow (Jameson), 1968
White Doctor (K. Blair, as Conway), 1961
White Dolphin (Stratton), 1976
White Dove (Thomas), 1986
White Flag (G. Porter), 1923
White Flame (Albanesi), 1930
White Gate (Deeping), 1913
White Guns (Kent, as Reeman), 1989
White Hell of Pity (Lofts), 1937
White House of Marisaig (Swan), 1938
White Hunter (Hoy), 1951
White in the Black (Albanesi), 1926
White Jacket (Norway), 1961
White Jade (W. Roberts), 1975
White Jade (Robins), 1928
White Ladies of Worcester (F. Barclay), 1917
White Lies (L. Howard), 1988
White Lilac (Cartland), 1984
White Magic (Baldwin), 1939
White Magnolia (Way), 1979
White Moths, (Manners), 1979
White Nights, Red Dawn (Nolan), 1980
White Oleander (K. Blair), 1953
White Pavilion (V. Johnston), 1973
White Peacock (Roby), 1972
White Prophet (Caine), 1909
White Rani (Nicole, as Gray), 1986
White Rose (Thum), 1980
White Rose (Westcott), 1969
White Rose of Winter (Mather), 1973
White Sand, Wild Sea (Palmer, as Blayne), 1983
White Satin (Johansen), 1985

White Violet (Ritchie), 1956
White Water (Oldfield), 1982
White Wings (s Goudge), 1952
White Witch (Browning, as Williams), 1988
White Witch (Goudge), 1958
White Wool (Jacob), 1944
Whiteoaks of Jalna series (de la Roche), from 1927
Whither? (Wynne), 1938
Whitney, My Love (McNaught), 1985
Whitton's Folly (P. Hill), 1975
Who Are the Heathen? (Swan), 1942
Who Can Deny Love? (Cartland), 1979
Who Knows Sammy Halliday? (M. Howard), 1974
Who Loses Pays (Burgin), 1935
Who Loves Believes (Hoy), 1955
Who Rides on a Tiger (Lowndes), 1935
Who Rides the Tiger (Mather), 1970
Who Shall Serve? A Story for the Times (Swan), 1891
Who Will Remember? (Irwin), 1924
Who Would Have Daughters? (Steen), 1937
Whole Armor (Baldwin), 1951
Whole New Light (Brown), 1989
Whole of the Short (s Bentley), 1935
Whom Love Hath Chosen (MacGill), 1919
Who's Been Sleeping in My Bed? (Lamb), 1985
Who's Calling (Plaidy, as Burford), 1962
Whoso Diggeth a Pit (M. St John, as St John Cooper), 1926
Why It Happened (Lowndes), 1938
Why Someone Had to Die (Summerton, as Roffman), 1976
Why They Married (s Lowndes), 1923
Why Wouldn't He Wait? (Chandos, as Tempest), 1940
Whyndham Legacy (Coulter), 1994
Whyte Swan (Wiat), 1986
Wicked Angel (Caldwell), 1965
Wicked Cousin (F. Stevenson, as Faire), 1980
Wicked Day (Stewart), 1983
Wicked Fire (Riefe), 1983
Wicked Godmother (Chesney), 1987
Wicked Is My Flesh (S. Blake), 1980
Wicked Jake Darcy (Johansen), 1990
Wicked Lady (Fletcher), 1962
Wicked Loving Lies (Rogers), 1976
Wicked Marquis (Cartland), 1973
Wicked Sir Dare (Garvice), 1938
Wicked Water (Kantor), 1949
Wide and Dark (Muskett), 1940
Wide House (Caldwell), 1945
Wide Is the Water (Hodge), 1981
Wide Pastures (K. Blair, as Conway), 1957
Wide Sargasso Sea (Rhys), 1966
Wideacre series (Gregory), from 1987
Widening Stream (R. Lindsay), 1952
Widow (Blackstock), 1967
Widow and the Wastrel (Dailey), 1977
Widow Jones (Chappell), 1956
Widow of Windsor (Plaidy), 1974
Widower's Wife (Chandos, as Charles), 1963
Widow's Daughters (Ponsonby), 1953
Wife after Work (Chandos, as Tempest), 1943
Wife by Arrangement (Burchell), 1946
Wife by Contract (Kidd), 1980
Wife for a Penny (Hampson), 1972
Wife for a Wager (Chandos), 1938
Wife for a Year (R. Lindsay, as Leigh), 1980
Wife for Andrew (Stratton, as Gillen), 1969
Wife for Sale (Norris), 1933

Wife for the Admiral (Gibbs), 1974
Wife in Exchange (Donald), 1978
Wife in Waiting (M. Peters), 1988
Wife of Martin Guerre (J. Lewis), 1941
Wife of the Red Haired Man (Andrews), 1959
Wife—or Housekeeper? (M. St John), 1921
Wife or Maid? (M. St John), 1922
Wife to Christopher (Burchell), 1936
Wife to Mr Milton (Graves), 1944
Wife to Order (L. Walker), 1961
Wife vs Secretary (s Baldwin), 1934
Wife Who Dragged Him Down! (M. St John), 1920
Wife Who Would Be 'Master'! (M. St John), 1920
Wife Without Kisses (Winspear), 1961
Wife's Triumph (Albanesi, as Rowlands), 1906
Wild About Harry (Miller), 1991
Wild Affair (Lamb), 1982
Wild and Wonderful (Dailey), 1980
Wild Apache Night (Finch), 1994
Wild Bells to the Wild Sky (McBain), 1983
Wild Bird (Diver), 1929
Wild Bird (Robins), 1932
Wild Boar Wood (Manners, as Marshall), 1972
Wild Cat (Black), 1979
Wild Concerto (Mather), 1983
Wild Country (Bromfield), 1948
Wild Crocus (K. Blair), 1956
Wild Cry of Love (Cartland), 1976
Wild Cry of Love (Laker, as Paul), 1978
Wild Daughter (Bloom, as Prole), 1963
Wild Dawn Fever (Williams), 1986
Wild Dream (O. Sinclair), 1973
Wild Drums Beat (F. Mason), 1954
Wild Enchantress (Mather), 1976
Wild Fire (Riefe), 1981
Wild Harvest (Nicole), 1985
Wild Harvest (Swan), 1929
Wild Heart (D. Smith), 1976
Wild Honey (F. Michaels), 1982
Wild Horizon (F. Mason), 1966
Wild Inheritance (M. Pargeter), 1977
Wild Is My Love (Taylor), 1987
Wild Is the River (Bromfield), 1941
Wild Jasmine (Small), 1992
Wild Justice (Chard), 1987
Wild Land (Hunter, as Chace), 1963
Wild Laurel (Thum), 1987
Wild Macraes (MacLeod, as Airlie), 1948
Wild Melody (Craven), 1977
Wild Memory (Duffield), 1935
Wild Mountain Honey (Finch), 1991
Wild Mountain Thyme (Pilcher), 1978
Wild Nights (N. Peters), 1986
Wild Rose (Albanesi, as Rowlands), 1911
Wild Rowan (M. Pargeter), 1978
Wild Silver (Johansen), 1988
Wild Streak (K. Thorpe), 1992
Wild Summer (I. Roberts, as Rowland), 1970
Wild Swan (Kennedy), 1957
Wild Swan (Way), 1978
Wild Sweet Promise (Taylor), 1989
Wild Texas Loving (Coulter), 1986
Wild Ukranians series (N. Roberts), from 1992
Wild, Unwilling Wife (Cartland), 1977
Wild Violets (Chandos), 1959
Wild Willful Love (Sherwood), 1982

Wild Wyoming Heart (Sommerfield), 1987
Wildcatter's Woman (Dailey), 1982
Wildcliffe Bird (Heaven), 1981
Wilderling (Lorrimer), 1982
Wilderness (Warren), 1961
Wilderness Passion (McKenna), 1984
Wilderness Trail (K. Thorpe), 1978
Wilderness Walk (Bishop), 1973
Wildest Dreams (J. Blake), 1993
Wildest Dreams (Krentz), 1993
Wildest Heart (Rogers), 1974
Wildfire at Midnight (Stewart), 1956
Wildfire (Finch), 1986
'Wild-Fire' Nan (M. St John, as St John Cooper), 1919
Wildford's Daughter (Manners), 1978
Wiles of a Siren (Albanesi, as Rowlands), 1906
Wiles of a Stranger (J. Smith), 1982
Wilful Maid (Garvice), 1911
Wilful Winnie (s Swan), 1886
Wilful Woman (Burgin), 1902
Will and a Way (N. Roberts), 1986
Will in Love (Sisson), 1976
. . . Will Not Now Take Place (Chandos, as Tempest), 1957
Will-o'-the-Wisp (Orczy), 1947
Willed to Wed (Mackinlay), 1933
Willful Gaynel (Libbey), 1890
William, By the Grace of God (Bowen), 1916
William III series (Bowen), from 1910
William's Wife (Plaidy), 1990
Williamsburg series (Thane), from 1943
Willing Surrender (Donald), 1986
Willow (Miller), 1984
Willow Harvest (Saunders, as Summers), 1985
Willow Herb (Randall), 1965
Willow Maid (M. Peters), 1974
Willowwood (Hardwick), 1980
Willowwood (Savage), 1978
Wilmington series (Wiat), from 1979
Win or Lose (K. Thorpe), 1986
Wind Bloweth (Byrne), 1922
Wind Brings Up the Rain (Malpass), 1978
Wind Dancer series (Johansen), from 1991
Wind from the Hill (Worboys, as Eyre), 1968
Wind from the Sea (Heaven), 1991
Wind in Summer (Ellerbeck, as Yorke), 1991
Wind in the Forest (Fletcher), 1957
Wind in the Green Trees (Chappell), 1969
Wind of Change (James), 1961
Wind of Complication (s Ertz), 1927
Wind of Death (Roby, as Wilson), 1976
Wind of Destiny (Nicole), 1987
Wind of Fate (I. Roberts), 1961
Wind Off the Small Isles (Stewart), 1968
Wind on the Heath (Jacob), 1956
Wind River (Way), 1973
Wind Sighing (MacLeod, as Airlie), 1954
Wind So Gay (Kidd), 1968
Wind Through the Heather (Lane), 1965
Wind Which Moved a Ship (Cleugh), 1936
Windflower (London), 1984
Windier Skies (M. Howard), 1930
Winding Stair (Hodge), 1968
Windleton Conspiracy (Laffeaty), 1978
Windmill of Love (Cartland), 1992
Windover (Hodge), 1992
Window at the White Cat (Rinehart), 1910

Window on the Square (Whitney), 1962
Window series (Lorin, as Hohl), from 1988
Window to Happiness (Buckingham, as John), 1983
Winds from the Sea (M. Pargeter), 1975
Winds in the Wilderness (K. Blair, as Brett), 1954
Winds of Chance, (Farnol), 1934
Winds of Enchantment (K. Blair, as Brett), 1949
Winds of Fear (Greig), 1956
Winds of Fortune (Farnol), 1934
Winds of Heaven (Way), 1979
Winds of Night (Maybury), 1967
Winds of Spring (Maybury), 1948
Winds of the World (Ayres), 1918
Windsong (Sherwood), 1986
Windward Crest (Hampson), 1973
Wine-Dark Sea (O'Brian), 1993
Wine Widow series (T. Barclay). from 1984
Wine, Women, and Waiters (s Frankau), 1932
Winged Escort (Kent, as Reeman), 1975
Winged Love (Robins), 1941
Winged Magic (Cartland), 1981
Winged Victory (Cartland), 1982
Wingless Bird (Cookson), 1990
Wings for Nurse Bennett (McElfresh), 1960
Wings in the Dust (Muskett), 1933
Wings in the West (Macbeth), 1937
Wings of Chance (Albanesi, as Rowlands), 1931
Wings of Ecstasy (Cartland), 1981
Wings of Love (Cartland), 1962
Wings of Love (Wentworth), 1985
Wings of the Falcon (B. Michaels), 1977
Wings of the Morning (Chard), 1985
Wings of the Night (Hampson), 1971
Wings on My Heart (Cartland, as McCorquodale), 1954
Winifred (s Bloom), 1903
Winner Take All (Ayres), 1937
Winner Take All (B. Hastings), 1981
Winnie Childs, The Shop Girl (Williamson), 1926
Winning Game (Macbeth), 1910
Winsome Witch (Swan), 1933
Winter and Rough Weather (D. Stevenson), 1951
Winter at Cray (Stratton, as Gillen), 1971
Winter Blossom (Browning), 1981
Winter Bride (Salisbury), 1978
Winter Harvest (Lofts), 1955
Winter in July (Summers), 1984
Winter Is Past (Weale), 1955
Winter Landscape (Clarke), 1986
Winter of Change (Neels), 1973
Winter of Discontent (Frankau), 1941
Winter of Dreams (Napier), 1992
Winter of Fear (Ponsonby, as Tempest), 1967
Winter of the Fox (Summerton, as Roffman), 1964
Winter of the Witch (Hamilton, as Watson), 1971
Winter People (Whitney), 1969
Winter Quarters (Duggan), 1956
Winter Queen (Saxton), 1977
Winter Sisters (Goodwin), 1980
Winter Song (Gellis), 1982
Winter Spring (Goodwin) 1978
Winter Wedding (Neels), 1979
Winter Woman (Browning), 1986
Wintercombe series (Belle), from 1988
Winter's Child (Jagger), 1984
Winter's Daughter (Dymoke), 1993
Winter's Day (Muskett), 1936

Winter's Passion (Moore), 1932
Wintersweet (Chappell), 1978
Winterwood (Eden), 1967
Winthrop Woman (Seton), 1958
Wire Blind (Muskett), 1944
Wisdom's Daughter (Haggard), 1923
Wise and the Foolish Virgins (Steen), 1932
Wise and the Steadfast (Barcynska, as Sandys), 1961
Wise Child (Stirling), 1990
Wise Forget (M. Howard), 1944
Wise Is the Heart (Duffield), 1947
Wise Woman (Gregory), 1992
Wisest Fool (Tranter), 1974
Wish a Day (Ruck), 1956
Wish Comes True (Cartland), 1991
Wish for Love (Cartland), 1983
Wish for the Moon (Mortimer), 1988
Wish on the Moon (Burchell), 1949
Wish on the Moon (Wentworth), 1989
Wish with the Candles (Neels), 1972
Wishes (Deveraux), 1989
Wishing Star (Greig), 1942
Wishing Stone (Saunders, as Innes), 1976
Witch (M. Johnston), 1914
Witch (B. Michaels), 1973
Witch Door (Ogilvie), 1959
Witch from the Sea (Plaidy, as Carr), 1975
Witch in Pink (Swan), 1938
Witch Queen (M. Peters), 1990
Witch Wood (J. Buchan), 1927
Witchchild (Mortimer), 1987
Witchcraft (Krentz), 1985
Witches (Lofts, as Curtis), 1966
Witches of Conyngton (S. Thorpe), 1976
Witches' Sabbath (Blackstock, as Allardyce), 1961
Witch-Finder (Wynne), 1923
Witching Hour (Craven), 1981
Witching Hour (F. Stevenson), 1971
Witching Hour (Randall), 1970
Witching Time (F. Preston), 1989
Witch's Crossing (F. Stevenson), 1975
Witch's Harvest (Craven), 1987
Witch's Head (Haggard), 1884
Witch's Spell (Cartland), 1984
Witchstone (Mather), 1974
With a Delicate Air (s Buck), 1962
With a Little Luck (Dailey), 1981
With All Dispatch (Kent), 1988
With All Her Heart (Garvice), 1910
With All My Heart (Asquith), 1954
With all My Heart (Barnes), 1951
With All My Love (Lorrimer, as Robins), 1963
With All My Worldly Goods (Burchell), 1938
With Banners (Loring), 1934
With Blood and Iron (Kent, as Reeman), 1964
With Every Year (Gaskin), 1949
With Fire and Flowers (I. Roberts, as Rowland), 1963
With Fondest Thoughts (Blackstock), 1980
With Heart so True (Albanesi, as Rowlands)
With Murder in Mind (M. Peters, as Rothman), 1975
With Murder in Mind (Summerton, as Roffman), 1963
With Somebody Else (Chandos, as Charles), 1981
With This Ring (Loring), 1959
With this Ring (N. Roberts), 1991
With This Ring (Saunders), 1993
Withering Fires (Bowen), 1931

Within a Year (Baldwin), 1934
Within Reach (Delinsky), 1986
Within the Bubble (Bowen, as Shearing), 1950
Within the Gates (Burgin), 1914
Within the Hollow Crown (Barnes), 1947
Without a Honeymoon (Chandos, as Tempest), 1952
Without a Trace (N. Roberts), 1991
Without Knowing Why (Steele), 1990
Without Love (Steele), 1988
Without My Cloak (O'Brien), 1931
Without Trust (Jordan), 1988
Without Warning (F. Michaels), 1981
Wizard (Haggard), 1896
Wizard (Krentz, as James), 1985
Wizard of Seattle (Hooper), 1993
Wizard's Daughter (B. Michaels), 1980
Wolf and the Dove (Woodiwiss), 1974
Wolf and the Unicorn (Hamilton, as Watson), 1971
Wolf in the Fold (McCutchan, as MacNeil), 1977
Wolf of Heimra (MacLeod), 1965
Wolfe Waiting (Lorin, as Hohl), 1994
Woman Against Her (Albanesi, as Rowlands)
Woman Against Woman (Albanesi, as Rowlands)
Woman Alive (Ertz), 1935
Woman at the Door (Deeping), 1937
Woman at the Wheel (Mackinlay), 1940
Woman Betrayed (Delinsky), 1992
Woman Called Fancy (Yerby), 1951
Woman Called Mary (Bloom, as Mann), 1960
Woman Decides (Garvice), 1908
Woman Despised (Ponsonby), 1988
Woman Doctor (Bloom), 1978
Woman Doctor (Seifert), 1951
Woman from the Sea (Renier), 1971
Woman Hater (Ayres), 1920
Woman Hater (Palmer), 1989
Woman in Berlin (Staples, as Stevens), 1986
Woman in Grey (Salisbury), 1987
Woman in Grey (Williamson, as A.M. Williamson), 1898
Woman in It (Garvice), 1911
Woman in Love (Norris), 1935
Woman in Love (Peake), 1984
Woman in the Back Seat (Steen), 1959
Woman in the Cloak (P. Hill), 1988
Woman in the Firelight (Barcynska, as Sandys), 1911
Woman in the Hall (Stern), 1939
Woman in the House (Hichens), 1945
Woman in the Wall (O'Faolain), 1975
Woman in the Woods (Blackstock, as L. Blackstock), 1958
Woman Like Us (Ellerbeck, as Thorne), 1979
Woman of Andros (Wilder), 1930
Woman of Cairo (Barber), 1984
Woman of Cordova (Staples, as Stevens), 1979
Woman of Dreams (Riefe), 1986
Woman of Experience (Barcynska), 1931
Woman of Fortune (Cleeve), 1993
Woman of Fury (Gluyas), 1978
Woman of Honour (E. Darcy), 1986
Woman of Iron (Lamb, as Holland), 1985
Woman of Knockaloe (Caine), 1923
Woman of Little Importance (Walsh), 1991
Woman of Our Times (Thomas), 1990
Woman of Property (M. Lewis), 1976
Woman of Quality (Westcott), 1978
Woman of Substance (Bradford), 1979
Woman of the Horizon (Frankau), 1917

Woman of the Shee (s Byrne), 1932
Woman of the West (Pykare, as Powers), 1989
Woman on Her Own (Baldwin), 1946
Woman Scorned (Albanesi, as Rowlands), 1899
Woman Thou Gavest Me (Caine), 1913
Woman Who Came Between (Albanesi, as Rowlands), 1895
Woman Who Dared (Williamson, as A.M. Williamson), 1903
Woman Who Fell from the Sky (Riefe), 1993
Woman Who Parted Them! (M. St John, as St John Cooper), 1926
Woman Who Was To-morrow (Bloom), 1940
Woman with White Eyes (Borden), 1930
Woman Without a Heart (Burgin), 1930
Woman Without a Past (Whitney), 1991
Woman Without Lies (Lowell), 1985
Woman Worth Winning (Albanesi, as Rowlands), 1911
Woman Wronged (Garvice, as Hart)
Woman's Estate (Gellis), 1984
Woman's Fault (Albanesi, as Rowlands), 1915
Woman's Heart (Albanesi, as Rowlands), 1911
Woman's Own (Carr), 1990
Woman's Part (Swan), 1916
Woman's Place (Ellerbeck, as Yorke), 1983
Woman's Side of It (Robins), 1937
Woman's Soul (Garvice), 1902
Woman's Touch (Krentz), 1989
Woman's War (Deeping), 1907
Woman's Way (Burgin), 1908
Woman's Way (Garvice), 1914
Woman's Way (M. St John, as St John Cooper), 1935
Woman's Wiles (Pykare, as Powers), 1985
Women Against Men series (Jameson), from 1933
Women Are Born to Listen (James), 1937
Women Are Like That (s Delafield), 1929
Women Are So Simple (Chandos), 1941
Women at Work (s Kennedy), 1966
Women Barbers of Drury Lane (P. Hastings), 1985
Women Have Hearts (Cartland), 1979
Women in His life (Bradford), 1990
Women in White (Slaughter), 1974
Women Live Too Long (Delmar), 1932
Women Money Buys (Greig), 1931
Women of Ashdon (Anand), 1992
Women of Glory series (McKenna), from 1991
Women of the Aftermath (Price, as Smith), 1931
Women Who Came Between (Garvice, as Hart)
Women Who Pass By (s Delmar), 1929
Women Who Seek (Robins), 1928
Women with the Fan (Hichens), 1904
Wonder Cruise (Bloom), 1933
Wonder of Love (Albanesi), 1911
Wonder of the World (Holland), 1970
Wonder Trip (Bloom, as Burns), 1939
Wonderful Dream (Cartland), 1993
Wondrous To-Morrow (Maybury), 1936
Wood and the Trees (Elgin), 1967
Wood Is My Pulpit (Barcynska), 1942
Wood Nymph (Balogh), 1987
Wooden Wives (Libbey), 1923
Woodville Wench (M. Peters), 1972
Wooing of Rosamond Fayre (Ruck), 1915
Wooing of Rose (Albanesi, as Rowlands), 1912
Words of Silk (Brown, as St Claire), 1984
Workaday Lady (Greig), 1936
Working Girl's Honor (Garvice, as Hart)
Works (Norris), 1920
World Apart (E. Darcy), 1983

World Apart (Joseph), 1988
World Ends (Jameson), 1937
World Enough and Time (Warren), 1950
World Full of Strangers (Freeman), 1975
World in Spell (D. Stevenson), 1939
World Is Like That (Norris), 1940
World Is Mine (S. Blake), 1988
World Keeps Turning (Hardwick), 1977
World of Dreams (Albanesi, as Rowlands), 1935
World Over (s Wharton), 1936
World, the Flesh and the Devil (Tannahill), 1985
World under Snow (Broster), 1935
World We Live In (s Bromfield), 1944
World Well Lost (Swan), 1935
World Without End (Frankau), 1943
World Without Love (Woodward, as Lawrence), 1967
World's a Stage (Plaidy, as Kellow), 1960
Worlds Apart (Chapman), 1946
World's Bane (s Bentley), 1918
World's Desire (Haggard), 1890
World's Fair (Doctorow), 1985
Wormwood (Corelli), 1890
Worst Wife in the World (M. St John), 1915
Worth Wile (Wren), 1937
Wounded Heart (Garvice), 1911
Wounded Name (Broster), 1922
Wounds of Passion (Lamb), 1993
Woven of the Wind (Swan), 1912
Woven on Fate's Loom, and The Snowdrift (Garvice), 1903
Wreath for Arabella (Leslie), 1948
Wreath of Holly (Chappell), 1959
Wreck of the Grey Cat (Graham), 1958
Wren of Paradise (Browning), 1981
Wrestler on the Shore (Wynne, as Lurgan), 1913
Write from the Heart (Greig, as Ames), 1972
Writing Man (Barcynska), 1939
Written in the Stars (Hunter), 1982
Wrong Love (Woodward), 1962
Wrong Mirror (E. Darcy), 1986
Wrong Mr Right (Ruck), 1919
Wrong Woman (Burgin), 1932
Wrongs Righted (Swan), 1924
Wyatt series (Wiat), from 1973
Wychwood (N. St John), 1976
Wychwood (Thompson), 1992
Wychwood (Wiat), 1982
Wyndham's Daughter (Swan), 1898
Wynne of Windwhistle (Ayres), 1926
Wyoming Ecstasy (Finch, as Robins), 1993

Xingu (s Wharton), 1916

Yankee Pasha (E. Marshall), 1948
Yankee Stranger (Thane), 1944
Yankee Wife (Miller), 1993
Year After (Ayres), 1916
Year at Coverley (s Swan), 1883
Year of the French (Flanagan), 1979
Year of the Pageant (Gibbs), 1971
Year of the Virgins (Cookson), 1993
Years Between (Bromige), 1991
Years for Rachel (Ruck), 1918
Year's Happy Ending (Neels), 1984
Years (Spencer), 1986
Years of Change (Hardwick), 1974
Yellow Brick Road (Cadell), 1960

Yellow God (Haggard), 1908
Yellow Is for Fear (s Eden), 1968
Yellow Joss (s Idriess), 1934
Yellow Moon (Stratton), 1974
Yellow Poppy (Broster), 1920
Yellow Room (Rinehart), 1945
Yellow Straw Hat (Chappell), 1983
Yes, Mama (Forrester), 1988
Yesterday Came Suddenly (M. Lewis), 1975
Yesterday Is Tomorrow (Barcynska, as Barclay), 1950
Yesterday's Affair (Wentworth), 1992
Yesterday's Child (B. Wood), 1979
Yesterday's Echoes (Jordan), 1993
Yesterday's Harvest (Pedler), 1926
Yesterday's Island (Weale), 1983
Yesterday's Love (Woods), 1987
Yesterday's Love (Woodward, as Richmond), 1972
Yesterday's Madness (Cockrell), 1943
Yesterday's Mischief (Renier), 1975
Yesterday's Promises (Ellerbeck, as Thorne), 1986
Yesterday's Shadow (Stanford), 1981
Yesterday's Tears (Mortimer), 1980
Yesterday's Tomorrow (Bloom), 1968
Yet a Lion (Wiat), 1978
Yet Love Remains (Burchell), 1938
Yet She Follows (Cartland), 1944
Yield Not to Temptation! (M. St John, as St John Cooper), 1923
Yolanda (Jacob), 1963
Yollop (McCutcheon), 1922
York the Renegade (Johansen), 1986
Yorke series (Pope), from 1979
You Are the One (Ruck), 1945
You Belong to Me (Hoy), 1938
You Can Love a Stranger (Lamb), 1988
You Can't Escape (Baldwin), 1943
You Can't Have Everything (Norris), 1937
You Can't Live Alone (Hoy), 1944
You Can't Lose Yesterday (Hoy), 1940
You Can't Run Away (Lane), 1940
You Have Chosen (Robins), 1938
You Owe Me (Jordan), 1985
You Should Have Warned Me (Chandos), 1940
You, The Jury (Borden), 1952
You Took My Heart (Hoy), 1939
You'll Love Me Yet (Ritchie), 1963
Young Ames (Edmonds), 1942
Young and Lonely King (Lane), 1969
Young Ann (Gibbs, as Ford), 1973
Young at Heart (Ayres), 1942
Young Bar (Pilcher, as Fraser), 1952
Young Bess (Irwin), 1944
Young Blood (Swan), 1917
Young Caesar (R. Warner), 1958
Young Clementina (D. Stevenson), 1970
Young Commissioner (Fletcher), 1951
Young Cosima (Richardson), 1939
Young Curmudgeon (Chandos, as Lance), 1964
Young Deloraine (Burgin), 1926
Young Diana (Corelli), 1918
Young Doctor (Seifert), 1939
Young Doctor Galahad (Seifert), 1938
Young Doctor Goddard (E. Harrison), 1978
Young Doctor Kenway (Randall), 1950
Young Doctor Kirkdene (Hoy), 1955
Young Doctor Mason (Stuart, as A. Stuart), 1970
Young Doctor Randall (McElfresh), 1957